TORT LAW: CASES, MATERIALS, PROBLEMS

THIRD EDITION
By

Jerry J. Phillips
*W.P. Toms Professor of Law and
Walter W. Bussart Distinguished
Professor of Tort Law
University of Tennessee*

Nicolas P. Terry
*Professor and Co-Director, Center
for Health Law Studies
Saint Louis University*

Frank L. Maraist
*Nolan J. Edwards and Holt B.
Harrison Professor of Law
Louisiana State University*

Frank McClellan
*Herman Stern Professor of Law
Temple University*

Thomas C. Galligan, Jr.
*Professor of Law and Dean
University of Tennessee*

Phoebe A. Haddon
*Professor of Law
Temple University*

Library of Congress Cataloging-in-Publication Data

Tort Law: Cases, Materials, Problems / Jerry J. Phillips. . .et al.—3rd. ed.
  Includes Bibliographical references and index.
    p. cm.–(Understanding series)
  ISBN 0-8205-5413-8
    1. Torts—United States. I. Phillips, Jerry J.,1935–
  KF1249.T65 2002
  346.7303—dc21   2002018649

This publication is designed to provide accurate and authoritative information in regard to the subject matter covered. It is sold with the understanding that the publisher is not engaged in rendering legal, accounting, or other professional services. If legal advice or other expert assistance is required, the services of a competent professional should be sought.

LexisNexis, the knowledge burst logo, and Michie are trademarks of Reed Elsevier Properties Inc, used under license. Matthew Bender is a registered trademark of Matthew Bender Properties Inc.

Copyright © 2002 Matthew Bender & Company, Inc., a member of the LexisNexis Group.
All Rights Reserved.

No copyright is claimed in the text of statutes, regulations, and excerpts from court opinions quoted within this work. Permission to copy material exceeding fair use, 17 U.S.C. § 107, may be licensed for a fee of 10¢ per page per copy from the Copyright Clearance Center, 222 Rosewood Drive, Danvers, Mass. 01923, telephone (978) 750-8400.

Editorial Offices
744 Broad Street, Newark, NJ 07102 (973) 820-2000
201 Mission St., San Francisco, CA 94105-1831 (415) 908-3200
701 East Water Street, Charlottesville, VA 22902-7587 (804) 972-7600
www.lexis.com

DEDICATION

FOR

Anne Phillips, Ellen Edwards, Catherine Maraist

Cara Leigh, a burgeoning scholar

Patrick, Sarah, Aisling, and Jennifer Galligan

PREFACE

Since the last edition there have been a number of changes in the field of tort law, and we have incorporated the major developments in this third edition. We have rearranged the order of chapters to make the book more logically sequential.

Omissions of text are indicated by ellipses, and citations are usually omitted without indication. Footnotes are also eliminated without indication. Supplementary and explanatory text is bracketed. We have compressed the text as much as possible without affecting the essential meaning of the material.

We are six different authors, with diverse backgrounds and views. We have made no attempt to homogenize those views in this book, since we believe that diversity of views is what good law school teaching is all about. However, we have tried to weave that diversity into one very useable fabric.

The law of torts is an effervescent subject. It is a primary example of the common law principle that legal stability is maintained through interstitial change to meet the evolving times. The student may initially despair at the broad-ranging scope of theory and practice that are encompassed in the law of torts. But eventually hopefully she will see that torts is but a microcosm of life. It is for you, the student, ultimately to judge the validity of tort law practice and policy, just as you do all other things in life, and to work as a lawyer to make things better.

Jerry J. Phillips	Frank M. McClellan
Nicolas P. Terry	Thomas C. Galligan, Jr.
Frank L. Maraist	Phoebe A. Haddon

ACKNOWLEDGMENTS

The authors gratefully acknowledge the permission of the American Law Institute to reprint the following sections and comments: RESTATEMENT (FIRST) OF TORTS § 520; (Copyright © 1938); RESTATEMENT (SECOND) OF TORTS §§ 25, 36, 76, 77, 84, 147, 197, 217, 218 and Comments *d, e,* and *f,* 222A, 242, 244, 262, 281, 283, 283B, 283C-Comment *d,* 284, 286, 295A-Comments *b* and *c,*; 299A-Comments *d* and *f,* 314 and Comment *c,* 315, 321, and Comment *a,* 322 and Comment *b,* 323, 324, 328E, 329, 335, 337-338, 342, 343-344, 390, 402A, 429, 431-Comment *a,* 432, 433, 433B(2), 433B(3), 483-Comments *c* and *d,* 504 and Comment *b,* 506 and Comment *b,* 507 and Comments *d* and *e,* 508 and Comment *a,* 511-513, 514 and Comment *a,* 516 and Comments *a* and *b,* 517 and Comment *d,* 519, 520 and Comment *f,* 520A, 551, 552-Comment *h,* 577A, 652B, 652D-Comment *a,* 653, 662, 870 and Comments *a* and *d,* 876, 886B(2), 892, 892A, 892C and Comment *c,* 895F, 909, 918 and Comment *a* (Copyright © 1965, 1977, 1979); UNIFORM CONTRIBUTION AMONG TORTFEASORS ACT § 1(c); RESTATEMENT OF CONTRACTS (SECOND) § 195 (Copyright © 1981); RESTATEMENT (THIRD) OF UNFAIR COMPETITION (1995) (Copyright © 1995); RESTATEMENT (SECOND) OF CONFLICT OF LAWS §§ 145-146 (Copyright © 1971). RESTATEMENT THIRD, TORTS: PRODUCTS LIABILITY (Copyright 1998), § 2, Comments *d* and *e* to § 2, §§ 3, 6, 9, 10, 11, 16; RESTATEMENT THIRD, TORTS: APPORTIONMENT (Copyright 2000), § 23.

The authors further acknowledge use of the following with permission of the authors and publishers:

Bovbjerg, Randall R., *Legislation on Medical Malpractice: Further Developments and a Preliminary Report Card,* 22 U.C. DAVIS L. REV. 499 (1989). Copyright © 1989 by the Regents of the University of California. Reprinted with permission.

Dilworth, TRIAL 19 (May 1996). Reprinted with the permission of the American Trial Lawyers Association.

Fleming, John G., THE AMERICAN TORT PROCESS, 18-19 (OXFORD 1988).

Harper, James & Gray, THE LAW OF TORTS (2d ed., Little Brown & Co.). Reprinted with permission of Aspen Law & Business, a division of Aspen Publishers, Inc.

Hursh, Robert D. & Bailey, Henry J., AMERICAN LAW OF PRODUCTS LIABILITY, §§ 52.14, 52.21, 52.22, Lawyers Co-Op (3d ed. 1987).

Krieger, Roy W., *On the line,* A.B.A.J. (Jan. 1994). Copyright © 1994 by the American Bar Association. Reprinted by permission of the ABA Journal.

Lind, E. Allan, et al. (RANDCORP.), The Institute for Civil Justice Ann. Reports, Apr. 1, 1990-March 31, 1991 at 18.

Macchiaorla, Frank J., *The Manville Personal Injury Settlement Trust: Lessons for the Future.* This article originally appeared in 7 CARDOZO L. REV.583 (1996). Reprinted with permission.

Miller, Richard S., *The Future of New Zealand's Accident Compensation Scheme,* 11 U. HAW. L. REV. 1, 7, *et. seq.* (1989).

Note (student article, unsigned), *The Manville bankruptcy: Treating Mass Tort Claims in Chapter 11 Proceedings,* 96 HARV. L. REV. 1122 (1983). Copyright © 1983 by the Harvard Law Review Association.

Phillips, *An Evaluation of the Federal Employers Liability Act,* 25 SAN DIEGO L. REV. 49, 52, 53, (1988). Copyright © 1985 San Diego Law Review Association. Reprinted with permission of the San Diego Law Review.

Post, *On the Popular Image of the Lawyer,* 75 CAL. L. REV. 386 (1987). Copyright © 1987 by the California Law Review, Inc. Reprinted from California Law Review. Vol. 75, 1987, pp. 379, 386 by permission.

Riskin, Leonard L., *Mediation and Lawyers.* Originally published in 43 OHIO ST. L. J. 29 (1982).

Smith, *Sequel to Workman's Compensation Acts,* 27 HARV. L. REV. 363, 367, 368 (1914). Copyright © 1914 by the Harvard Law Review Association.

Sugarman, *Doing Away With Tort Law,* 73 CAL. L. REV. 555, 587, 561 (1985). Copyright © 1985 by the California Law Review, Inc. Reprinted from the California law Review. Vol. 73, excerpt, by permission.

Terry, Nicholas P., *The Technical and Conceptual Flaws of Medical Malpractice Arbitration,* 30 ST. LOUIS U. L. J. 571, 631 (1986). Reprinted with permission by Saint Louis University Law Journal. 39 ATLA L. REP. 33 (Feb. 1995). Reprinted with permission of the American Trial Lawyers Association.

SUMMARY TABLE OF CONTENTS

	Page
Chapter 1 VALUES AND PROCESS INTRODUCTION	1
A. INTRODUCTION	1
B. STATING A CLAIM	1
C. LAW AND FACTS	9
Chapter 2 THEORIES OF LIABILITY	37
A. INTRODUCTION	37
B. INTENTIONAL OR ANTI-SOCIAL CONDUCT	37
C. REGULATING SOCIALLY DESIRABLE ACTIVITIES	50
Chapter 3 INTENTIONAL TORTS	99
A. INTRODUCTION	99
B. INTENT	99
C. BATTERY	102
D. ASSAULT	116
E. FALSE IMPRISONMENT AND FALSE ARREST	122
F. INTENTIONAL INFLICTION OF EMOTIONAL DISTRESS	135
G. MISUSE OF THE JUDICIAL PROCESS	148
H. TRESPASS TO PERSONALITY AND CONVERSION	158
I. TRESPASS TO REALTY, NUISANCE AND INTRUSION INTO SECLUSION	164
J. THE PRIMA FACIE OR INNOMINATE TORT	173
Chapter 4 DEFENSES TO INTENTIONAL TORTS	177
A. INTRODUCTION	177
B. CONSENT	177
C. SELF-DEFENSE AND DEFENSE OF OTHERS	191
D. DEFENSE OF PROPERTY	196
E. NECESSITY	202
F. JUSTIFICATION	211
G. PRIVILEGE	216
Chapter 5 THE STANDARD OF CARE IN NEGLIGENCE	221
A. INTRODUCTION	221
B. THE BASIC OBLIGATION	221
C. REASONABLE CARE AND PERSONAL CHARACTERISTICS	223
D. INDUSTRY AND PROFESSIONAL PRACTICES	255
E. RISKS AND UTILITIES	270
F. LEGISLATIVE STANDARDS	278
G. CIRCUMSTANTIAL EVIDENCE OF NEGLIGENCE	294
Chapter 6 CAUSE IN FACT	319

	Page
A. INTRODUCTION	319
B. BUT-FOR CAUSATION	320
C. THE SUBSTANTIAL FACTOR TEST	328
D. PROBABILITIES	332
E. MULTIPLE CAUSATION	350
F. TOXIC TORT CAUSATION ISSUES	362
G. MULTIPLE CAUSATION AND MULTIPLE TORTFEASORS	371

Chapter 7 DUTIES OF CARE AND LEGAL CAUSE ... 381

A. INTRODUCTION	381
B. DIRECT CAUSE OR FORESEEABILITY	382
C. BREACH, LEGAL CAUSE OR DUTY	395
D. THIRD PARTY CRIMINAL, INTENTIONAL OR NEGLIGENT ACTS	422
E. THIN SKULLS, SUBSEQUENT INJURY, RESCUERS, AND OTHER	
F. GOVERNMENTAL LIABILITY	436
G. RESPONSIBILITIES OF MEDIA, SUPPLIERS AND DISTRIBUTORS	441
H. THE DUTY TO ACT OR LACK THEREOF	468
I. SUICIDE AND OTHER DAMAGES	496
J. EMOTIONAL DISTRESS INJURIES	504
K. ECONOMIC LOSS	518
L. PRENATAL AND PRECONCEPTION INJURIES	528

Chapter 8 OWNERS AND OCCUPIERS OF LAND ... 555

A. INTRODUCTION	555
B. LIABILITY BASED ON CATEGORIZATION OF ENTRANT	555
C. LIMITING AND ABANDONING THE CATEGORIES	575
D. RECREATIONAL USE STATUTES	584
E. PROFESSIONAL RESCUERS	592

Chapter 9 PROCEDURE, PROOF AND DAMAGES ... 607

A. INTRODUCTION	607
B. PROBLEMS OF PROOF	607
C. EXPERT EVIDENCE	613
D. SPOLIATION AND OTHER MISCONDUCT	635
E. PERSONAL INJURY DAMAGES	640
F. MENTAL DISTRESS	655
G. DAMAGE TO PROPERTY AND ECONOMIC LOSS	677
H. DAMAGE TO RELATIONS	687
I. PUNITIVE DAMAGES	702

Chapter 10 AFFIRMATIVE DEFENSES: PLAINTIFF MISCONDUCT AND STATUTES OF LIMITATIONS ... 727

A. INTRODUCTION	727
B. CONTRIBUTORY NEGLIGENCE	728

C. COMPARATIVE FAULT 732
D. ASSUMPTION OF THE RISK 746
E. AVOIDABLE CONSEQUENCES 764
F. STATUTES OF LIMITATIONS AND REPOSE 769

Chapter 11 IMMUNITIES 781

A. INTRODUCTION 781
B. SOVEREIGN 784
C. INDIVIDUAL IMMUNITIES
D. CHARITABLE IMMUNITY 806
E. FAMILY IMMUNITIES 807

Chapter 12 JOINT AND SEVERAL LIABILITY, CONTRIBUTION, INDEMNITY, AND SETTLEMENTS 817

A. INTRODUCTION 817
B. JOINT AND SEVERAL LIABILITY 818
C. CONTRIBUTION AND INDEMNITY 828
D. SETTLEMENTS 839

Chapter 13 PROFESSIONAL MALPRACTICE 853

A. INTRODUCTION 853
B. THEORIES OF PROFESSIONAL LIABILITY 854
C. THE PROFESSIONAL STANDARD OF CARE 874
D. NON-CUSTOM BASED STANDARDS 882
E. CONSENT, INFORMATION AND AUTONOMY 900
F. EXTENDED PROFESSIONAL LIABILITY EXPOSURE 931

Chapter 14 VICARIOUS RESPONSIBILITY FOR THE CONDUCT OF OTHERS 959

A. INTRODUCTION 959
B. IMPUTED RESPONSIBILITY OF THE DEFENDANT 959
C. IMPUTED RESPONSIBILITY OF THE PLAINTIFF 993

Chapter 15 AN INTRODUCTION TO PRODUCTS LIABILITY 999

A. INTRODUCTION 999
B. THE NATURE OF MODERN PRODUCTS LIABILITY 1001
C. TYPES AND DEFINITIONS OF DEFECT 1015
D. THE LIMITS OF LIABILITY 1056

Chapter 16 STRICT LIABILITY FOR ABNORMALLY DANGEROUS ACTIVITIES 1085

A. INTRODUCTION 1085
B. STRICT LIABILITY FOR ANIMALS 1087
C. ABNORMALLY DANGEROUS ACTIVITIES 1095

Chapter 17 NUISANCE AND ENVIRONMENTAL TORTS 1121

Page

A. INTRODUCTION 1121
B. NUISANCE: ASSESSING REASONABLENESS OF LAND USE ..1122
C. NUISANCE AND RELATED ENVIRONMENTAL TORTS:
    IDENTIFYING COGNIZABLE HARM 1130
D. ASSESSING PROOF AND FASHIONING REMEDIES 1136

Chapter 18 DEFAMATION AND INVASION OF PRIVACY 1157

A. INTRODUCTION 1157
B. DEFAMATION 1158
C. INVASION OF PRIVACY 1223

Chapter 19 BUSINESS AND ECONOMIC TORTS 1267

A. INTRODUCTION 1267
B. MISREPRESENTATION 1267
C. APPROPRIATION OF INTANGIBLE PROPERTY IN
    GENERAL 1288
D. APPROPRIATION OF TRADE SECRETS 1308
E. WRONGFUL DISCHARGE 1328
F. WRONGFUL INTERFERENCE WITH CONTRACT OR BUSINESS
    RELATION 1340

Chapter 20 CONSTITUTIONAL AND STATUTORY TORTS 1351

A. INTRODUCTION 1351
B. CONSTITUTIONAL REMEDIES 1352
C. STATUTORY REMEDIES 1364

Chapter 21 INSURANCE 1399

A. INTRODUCTION 1399
B. TORT LAW AND THE INSURANCE INSTITUTION 1399
C. INSURANCE COVERAGE ISSUES 1411
D. INSURER DUTIES AND PENALTIES 1438
E. AUTOMOBILE INSURANCE 1450
F. INSURANCE AS AN ALTERNATIVE SYSTEM 1456

Chapter 22 TORT RETRENCHMENTS AND TORT
    ALTERNATIVES 1471

A. INTRODUCTION 1471
B. GUEST PASSENGER STATUTES 1471
C. THE IMPETUS FOR REFORM 1477
D. LIMITATIONS ON RECOVERY 1482
E. SUBSTANTIVE LAW REFORM 1486
F. JOINT AND SEVERAL LIABILITY 1490
G. ALTERNATIVE DISPUTE MECHANISMS: TRIAL-RELATED
    DEVICES 1492
H. ALTERNATIVE DISPUTE RESOLUTIONS: ARBITRATION AND
    MEDIATION ALTERNATIVES TO TRIAL 1501

  Page

I. ALTERNATIVES TO THE TORT SYSTEM 1509
J. OTHER LIMITED SCHEMES 1516
K. COMPARITIVE SYSTEMS 1517

TABLE OF CONTENTS

Page

Chapter. 1 VALUES AND PROCESS INTRODUCTION 1

A. INTRODUCTION 1
B. STATING A CLAIM 1
    Glick v. Olde Town Lancaster, Inc. 1
    Notes 6
    Problem 9
C. LAW AND FACTS 9
    Rorrer v. Cooke 9
    Notes 19
    Perez v. Wyeth Laboratories 20
    Notes 27
    Problem 30
    Nova Southeastern University, Inc. v. Gross 30
    Notes 34

Chapter. 2 THEORIES OF LIABILITY 37

A. INTRODUCTION 37
B. INTENTIONAL OR ANTI-SOCIAL CONDUCT 37
    Lucchesi v. Stimmell 37
    Notes 39
    Problem 39
    Jaworski v. Kiernan 40
    Notes 44
    Ghassemieh v. Schafer 45
    Notes 48
C. REGULATING SOCIALLY DESIRABLE ACTIVITIES 50
    Hardingham v. United Counseling Service 50
    Notes 54
    Restatement (Second) of Torts 54
    Notes 55
    Magrine v. Spector 57
    Notes 62
    Hammontree v. Jenner 62

	Page
Notes	64
Peterson v. Superior Court	65
Notes	73
Problem	74
Siegler v. Kuhlman	74
Notes	79
Problem	83
Crosby v. Cox Aircraft Co. of Washington	83
Notes	91
Helling v. Carey	91
Notes	94
Problem	96

Chapter. 3 INTENTIONAL TORTS 99

A. INTRODUCTION 99
B. INTENT 99
    Bazley v. Tortorich 99
    Notes 102
C. BATTERY 102
    Problem 102
    Brzoska v. Olson 102
    Notes 107
    McGuire v. Almy 110
    Notes 112
    Kiley v. Patterson 114
    Notes 115
    Problem 116
D. ASSAULT 116
    Castiglione v. Galpin 116
    Notes 117
    Holcombe v. Whitaker 117
    Notes 119
    Hall v. McBryde 120
    Notes 122
E. FALSE IMPRISONMENT AND FALSE ARREST 122

	Page
Comment	122
Dupler v. Seubert	122
Notes	125
Wright v. State	129
Notes	131

F. INTENTIONAL INFLICTION OF EMOTIONAL DISTRESS 135

White v. Monsanto Company	135
Notes	138
Gomez v. Hug	139
Notes	143

G. MISUSE OF THE JUDICIAL PROCESS 148

Dutt v. Kremp	148
Notes	152
Notes	156
Problem	158

H. TRESPASS TO PERSONALITY AND CONVERSION 158

Comment	158
Focal Point, Inc. v. U-Haul of Arizona, Inc.	158
Notes	160
Problem	163

I. TRESPASS TO REALTY, NUISANCE AND INTRUSION INTO SECLUSION 164

Comment	164
Cannon v. Dunn	164
Notes	167
Comment 169	
Dietemann v. Time, Inc.	169
Notes	172

J. THE PRIMA FACIE OR INNOMINATE TORT 173

Comment	173

Chapter. 4 DEFENSES TO INTENTIONAL TORTS 177

A. INTRODUCTION 177

B. CONSENT 177

	Page
Problem	177
Colby v. McClendon	178
Notes	180
Lee v. Nationwide Insurance Co.	181
Problem	184
Notes	184

C. SELF-DEFENSE AND DEFENSE OF OTHERS 191
    Bradley v. Hunter 191
    Notes 194

D. DEFENSE OF PROPERTY 196
    Problem 196
    Katko v. Briney 196
    Notes 200
    Problem 202

E. NECESSITY 202
    Harrison v. Wisdom 202
    Notes 204
    Vincent v. Lake Erie Transportation Co. 205
    Notes 208
    Problem 210

F. JUSTIFICATION 211
    Sindle v. New York City Transit Authority 211
    Notes 212

G. PRIVILEGE 216
    Samson Investment Co. v. Chevaillier 216
    Notes 219

Chapter. 5 THE STANDARD OF CARE IN NEGLIGENCE ... 221

A. INTRODUCTION 221
B. THE BASIC OBLIGATION 221
    Problem 221
    Notes 222
C. REASONABLE CARE AND PERSONAL CHARACTERISTICS ... 223

	Page
Robinson v. Lindsay	223
Notes	225
McCall v. Wilder	233
Notes	238
Creasy v. Rusk	240
Notes	246
Problem	247
Bodin v. City of Stanwood	248
Notes	254
Problem	255
D. INDUSTRY AND PROFESSIONAL PRACTICES	255
The T.J. Hooper	255
Notes	257
Ray v. American National Red Cross	259
Notes	263
Vuono v. New York Blood Center, Inc.	266
Notes	268
E. RISKS AND UTILITIES	270
United States v. Carroll Towing Co.	270
Notes	272
F. LEGISLATIVE STANDARDS	278
Ashwood v. Clark County	278
Notes	281
Crown v. Raymond	289
Notes	292
G. CIRCUMSTANTIAL EVIDENCE OF NEGLIGENCE	294
Kmart Corporation v. Bassett	294
Notes	299
Widmyer v. Southeast Skyways, Inc.	306
Notes	311
Problem	316

Chapter. 6 CAUSE IN FACT 319

A. INTRODUCTION 319
    Problem 319
B. BUT-FOR CAUSATION 320

	Page
Hill v. Lundin & Associates, Inc.	320
Notes	322
Dillon v. Twin State Gas & Electric Co.	322
Notes	324
Sharpe v. Peter Pan Bus Lines	324
Notes	326

C. THE SUBSTANTIAL FACTOR TEST 328
    Anderson v. Minneapolis, St. P. & S.S.M. Ry. 328
    Notes 329
    Problem 331

D. PROBABILITIES 332
    Perez v. Las Vegas Medical Center 332
    Notes 335
    Smith v. State Department of Health and Hospitals 339
    Notes 345
    Problem 350

E. MULTIPLE CAUSATION 350
    Black v. Abex Corp. 350
    Notes 355
    Problem 362

F. TOXIC TORT CAUSATION ISSUES 362
    Bockrath v. Aldrich Chemical Co., Inc. 362
    Notes 365
    Problem 370

G. MULTIPLE CAUSATION AND MULTIPLE TORTFEASORS ... 371
    Piner v. Superior Court 371
    Notes 378

Chapter. 7 DUTIES OF CARE AND LEGAL CAUSE **381**

A. INTRODUCTION 381
    Problem 381

B. DIRECT CAUSE OR FORESEEABILITY 382
    In re Polemis 382
    Notes 384
    Overseas Tankship (U.K.) Ltd. v. Morts Dock & Engineering Co. (The Wagon Mound) 385
    Notes 390

C. BREACH, LEGAL CAUSE OR DUTY 395

	Page
Palsgraf v. Long Island Railroad Co.	395
Notes	402
Bigbee v. Pacific Telephone & Telegraph Co.	404
Notes	407
Lodge v. Arett Sales Corp.	413
Notes	421

D. THIRD PARTY CRIMINAL, INTENTIONAL OR NEGLIGENT ACTS ... 422

    Posecai v. Wal-Mart Stores, Inc. ... 422
    Notes ... 426
    Problem ... 432

E. THIN SKULLS, SUBSEQUENT INJURY, RESCUERS, AND OTHER

    ProblemS ... 432
    Anaya v. Superior Court ... 433
    Notes ... 435
    Problem ... 436

F. GOVERNMENTAL LIABILITY ... 436

    Day v. State ... 436
    Notes ... 439

G. RESPONSIBILITIES OF MEDIA, SUPPLIERS AND DISTRIBUTORS ... 441

    Davidson v. Time Warner, Inc. ... 441
    Notes ... 445
    Problem ... 449
    Schooley v. Pinch's Deli Market, Inc. ... 449
    Notes ... 454
    Problem ... 460
    Hamilton v. Beretta U.S.A. Corp. ... 461
    Notes ... 467
    Problem ... 468

H. THE DUTY TO ACT OR LACK THEREOF ... 468

    Farwell v. Keaton ... 468
    Notes ... 472
    Estate of Morgan v. Fairfield Family Counseling Center ... 479
    Notes ... 490

I. SUICIDE AND OTHER DAMAGES ... 496

    McPeake v. Cannon, Esq., P.C. ... 496
    Notes ... 499

J. EMOTIONAL DISTRESS INJURIES ... 504

	Page
Problem	504
Consolidated Rail Corp. v. Gotshall	504
Notes	513
Dunphy v. Gregor	514
Notes	517

K. ECONOMIC LOSS ... 518
- Problem ... 518
- *People Express Airlines v. Consolidated Rail Corp.* ... 519
- Notes ... 523

L. PRENATAL AND PRECONCEPTION INJURIES ... 528
- *Stallman v. Youngquist* ... 528
- Notes ... 531
- Problem ... 533
- *Bader v. Johnson* ... 534
- Notes ... 539
- Problem ... 543
- *University of Arizona Health Science Center v. Superior Court* ... 543
- Notes ... 549
- Problem ... 552

Chapter. 8 OWNERS AND OCCUPIERS OF LAND ... 555

A. INTRODUCTION ... 555

B. LIABILITY BASED ON CATEGORIZATION OF ENTRANT ... 555
- Problem ... 555
- *Mendoza v. City of Corpus Christi* ... 556
- Notes ... 559
- *Webster v. Culbertson* ... 565
- Notes ... 568
- *Moore v. Tucson Electric Power Co.* ... 570
- Notes ... 572

C. LIMITING AND ABANDONING THE CATEGORIES ... 575
- *Mallet v. Pickens* ... 575
- Notes ... 582

D. RECREATIONAL USE STATUTES ... 584
- *Tuder v. Kell* ... 584
- Notes ... 588

E. PROFESSIONAL RESCUERS ... 592

Melton v. Crane Rental Company	592
Notes	596
Problem	602
Notes	602
Problem	605

Chapter 9. PROCEDURE, PROOF AND DAMAGES ... 607

A. INTRODUCTION ... 607
B. PROBLEMS OF PROOF ... 607
Williams v. Brown ... 607
Notes ... 610

C. EXPERT EVIDENCE ... 613
Kumho Tire Company, Ltd. v. Carmichael ... 613
Notes ... 621

D. SPOLIATION AND OTHER MISCONDUCT ... 635
Problem ... 635
Holmes v. Amerex Rent-a-Car ... 635
Notes ... 638
Problem ... 640

E. PERSONAL INJURY DAMAGES ... 640
Walters v. Hitchcock ... 641
Notes ... 643
McDougald v. Garber ... 645
Notes ... 650

F. MENTAL DISTRESS ... 655
Problem ... 655
Potter v. Firestone Tire & Rubber Co. ... 656
Notes ... 671
Problem ... 677

G. DAMAGE TO PROPERTY AND ECONOMIC LOSS ... 677
Louisiana ex. rel. Guste v. M/V Testbank ... 677
Notes ... 683
Problem ... 686

H. DAMAGE TO RELATIONS ... 687

	Page
Wehner v. Weinstein	687
Notes	690
Hibpshman v. Prudhoe Bay Supply, Inc.	694
Notes	699
Problem	702

I. PUNITIVE DAMAGES ... 702
- *Grimshaw v. Ford Motor Co.* ... 702
- Notes ... 711
- *St. Luke Evangelical Lutheran Church v. Smith* ... 716
- Notes ... 722
- Problem ... 725

Chapter 10 AFFIRMATIVE DEFENSES: PLAINTIFF MISCONDUCT AND STATUTES OF LIMITATIONS ... 727

A. INTRODUCTION ... 727
B. CONTRIBUTORY NEGLIGENCE ... 728
- Problem ... 728
- *Butterfield v. Forrester* ... 728
- Notes ... 729

C. COMPARATIVE FAULT ... 732
- Problem ... 732
- *Li v. Yellow Cab Co.* ... 733
- Notes ... 739

D. ASSUMPTION OF THE RISK ... 746
- Problem ... 746
- *Schutkowski v. Carey* ... 746
- Notes ... 750
- Problem ... 753
- *Howell v. Clyde* 753
- Notes ... 759
- Problem ... 764

E. AVOIDABLE CONSEQUENCES ... 764
- *Tanberg v. Ackerman Investment Co.* ... 764
- Notes ... 767

F. STATUTES OF LIMITATIONS AND REPOSE ... 769

	Page
Problem	769
Apgar v. Lederle Laboratories	769
Notes	771
Dunlea v. Dappen	774
Notes	776

Chapter. 11 IMMUNITIES 781

A. INTRODUCTION 781
Problem 781

B. SOVEREIGN
Federal Tort Claims Act 781
- Notes 783
- *Stencel Aero Engineering Corp. v. United States* 784
- Notes 788
- *Lindgren v. United States* 788
- Notes 791
- *Hacking v. Town of Belmont* 792
- Notes 795

C. INDIVIDUAL IMMUNITIES
- *LLMD of Michigan, Inc. v. Jackson-Cross Co.* 798
- Notes 804
- Problem 806

D. CHARITABLE IMMUNITY 806

E. FAMILY IMMUNITIES 807
- *Cates v. Cates* 807
- Notes 813

Chapter. 12 JOINT AND SEVERAL LIABILITY, CONTRIBUTION, INDEMNITY, AND SETTLEMENTS 817

A. INTRODUCTION 817

B. JOINT AND SEVERAL LIABILITY 818
- Problem 818
- *Glomb v. Glomb* 819
- Notes 821
- Problem 822
- *McIntyre v. Balentine* 823
- Notes 824

	Page
Problem	827
C. CONTRIBUTION AND INDEMNITY	828
Comment	828
Promaulayko v. Johns Manville Sales Corp.	830
Notes	835
D. SETTLEMENTS	839
Comment	839
Becker v. Crounse Corp.	839
Notes	845
Hess v. St. Francis Regional Medical Center	848
Notes	850
Problem	852

Chapter. 13 PROFESSIONAL MALPRACTICE ... 853

A. INTRODUCTION	853
B. THEORIES OF PROFESSIONAL LIABILITY	854
Problem	854
Guerrero v. Copper Queen Hospital	854
Notes	856
Destafano v. Grabrian	862
Notes	867
Problem	873
C. THE PROFESSIONAL STANDARD OF CARE	874
Brune v. Belinkoff	874
Notes	876
D. NON-CUSTOM BASED STANDARDS	882
Bowman v. Doherty	882
Notes	885
Darling v. Charleston Community Memorial Hospital	886
Notes	887
Terry Cove North, Inc. v. Marr & Friedlander, P.C.	888
Notes	890
Mireles v. Brodericl	892
Notes	895
Problem	900
E. CONSENT, INFORMATION AND AUTONOMY	900

	Page
Notes	901
Problem	902
Largey v. Rothman	902
Notes	907
Problem	909
Truman v. Thomas	910
Notes	914
Johnson v. Kokemoor	915
Notes	929
F. EXTENDED PROFESSIONAL LIABILITY EXPOSURE	**931**
Toro Co. v. Krouse, Kern & Co.	931
Notes	934
Wickline v. State of California	937
Notes	942
Pegram v. Herdich	946
Notes	957

Chapter. 14 VICARIOUS RESPONSIBILITY FOR THE CONDUCT OF OTHERS ... 959

A. INTRODUCTION	**959**
B. IMPUTED RESPONSIBILITY OF THE DEFENDANT	**959**
Ira S. Bushley & Sons v. United States	959
Notes	963
Lundberg v. State	968
Notes	970
Sherard v. Smith	973
Notes	974
Rockwell v. Sun Harbor Budget Suites	985
Notes	992
Problem	992
C. IMPUTED RESPONSIBILITY OF THE PLAINTIFF	**993**
LaBier v. Pelletier	993
Notes	997
Problem	998

Chapter. 15 AN INTRODUCTION TO PRODUCTS LIABILITY ... 999

A. INTRODUCTION	**999**

TABLE OF CONTENTS

Page

B. THE NATURE OF MODERN PRODUCTS LIABILITY 1001
    Castro v. QVC Network, Inc. 1001
    Notes 1006
    Halphen v. Johns-Manville Sales Corporation 1009
    Notes 1014
    Problem 1014

C. TYPES AND DEFINITIONS OF DEFECT 1015
    [1] Mismanufacure 1015
        Fitzgerald Marine Sales v. LeUnes 1015
        Notes 1016
        Williams v. Smart Chevrolet Co. 1017
        Notes 1019
        Problem 1020
    [2] Design Defect 1020
        Potter v. Chicago Pneumatic Tool Co. 1020
        Notes 1034
        Problem 1044
    [3] Failure to Warn .1044
        Hood v. Ryobi America Corp. 1044
        Notes 1048
    [4] Misrepresentation 1053
        Baxter v. Ford Motor Co. 1053
        Notes 1054

D. THE LIMITS OF LIABILITY 1056
    Notes 1057
    *In re Norplant Contraceptive Products Liability
    Litigation* 1060
    Notes 1063
    Problem 1064
    *East River Steamship Corp. v. Transamerica Delaval,
    Inc.* 1069
    Notes 1076
    Problem 1077
    Royer v. Catholic Medical Center 1078
    Notes 1081

**Chapter. 16 STRICT LIABILITY FOR ABNORMALLY
DANGEROUS ACTIVITIES** 1085

A. INTRODUCTION 1085
B. STRICT LIABILITY FOR ANIMALS 1087

	Page
Isaacs v. Powell	1087
Notes	1089
Problem	1094

C. ABNORMALLY DANGEROUS ACTIVITIES 1095

 Fletcher v. Rylands 1095
 Rylands v. Fletcher 1097
 Notes 1099
 The Clark-Aiken Company v. Cromwell-Wright Company, Inc. 1104
 Notes 1104
 Laterra v. Treaster 1108
 Notes 1110
 Copier by and through Lindsey v. Smith & Wesson 1115
 Notes 1118
 Problem 1119

Chapter. 17 NUISANCE AND ENVIRONMENTAL TORTS 1121

A. INTRODUCTION 1121

B. NUISANCE: ASSESSING REASONABLENESS OF LAND USE .. 1122

 Hendricks v. Stalnaker 1122
 Notes 1125

C. NUISANCE AND RELATED ENVIRONMENTAL TORTS: IDENTIFYING COGNIZABLE HARM 1130

 Golen v. The Union Corp. 1130
 Westchester Associates, Inc. v. Boston Edison Company .. 1133

D. ASSESSING PROOF AND FASHIONING REMEDIES 1136

 Sharp v. 251st Street Landfill, Inc. 1136
 Notes 1142
 Langan v. Bellinger 1146
 Notes 1148
 Problem 1156

Chapter. 18 DEFAMATION AND INVASION OF PRIVACY ... 1157

A. INTRODUCTION 1157

B. DEFAMATION 1158

	Page
Problem	1158
Lent v. Huntoon	1158
Notes	1162
Problem	1163
Lewis v. Equitable Life Assur. Soc.	1163
Notes	1166
Problem	1168
New York Times Co. v. Sullivan	1169
Notes	1178
Gertz v. Robert Welch, Inc.	1180
Notes	1188
Dun & Bradstreet, Inc. v. Greenmoss Builders, Inc.	1190
Notes	1195
Lund v. Chicago and Northwestern Transportation Company	1197
Notes	1204
Hustler Magazine v. Falwell	1206
Notes	1211
Esposito-Hilder v. SFX Broadcasting, Inc.	1213
Notes	1216
Problem	1216
Arneja v. Gildar	1217
Notes	1219
C. INVASION OF PRIVACY	1223
PETA v. Bobby Berosini, LTD.	1223
Notes	1228
Veeder v. Kennedy	1229
Notes	1233
Roshto v. Hebert	1234
Notes	1237
Rasmussen v. South Florida Blood Service	1239
Notes	1243
Problem	1247
White v. Samsung Electronics America, Inc.	1247
Notes	1253
Diamond Shamrock Refining and Marketing Company v. Mendez	1255
Notes	1263

Chapter. 19 BUSINESS AND ECONOMIC TORTS 1267

A. INTRODUCTION 1267

TABLE OF CONTENTS

	Page
B. MISREPRESENTATION	1267
Obde v. Schlemeyer	1267
Notes	1270
Problem	1272
Idaho Bank & Trust Co. v. First Bancorp of Idaho	1273
Notes	1275
Problem	1276
Crocker v. Winthrop Laboratories	1277
Notes	1279
Davis v. Board of County Comm'rs	1281
Problem	1287
C. APPROPRIATION OF INTANGIBLE PROPERTY IN GENERAL	1288
Problem	1288
Midler v. Ford Motor Co.	1288
Notes	1291
Problem	1302
Tuttle v. Buck	1302
Notes	1306
Problem	1307
D. APPROPRIATION OF TRADE SECRETS	1308
Rockwell Graphic Systems, Inc. v. Dev Industries, Inc.	1308
Notes	1314
Bendinger v. Marshalltown Trowel Co.	1319
Notes	1325
Problem	1327
E. WRONGFUL DISCHARGE	1328
Rinehimer v. Luzerne County Community College	1328
Notes	1333
Problem	1339
F. WRONGFUL INTERFERENCE WITH CONTRACT OR BUSINESS RELATION	1340
Fred Siegel Co., L.P.A. v. Arte & Hadden	1340
Notes	1345

Chapter. 20 CONSTITUTIONAL AND STATUTORY TORTS . . 1351

A. INTRODUCTION	1351
B. CONSTITUTIONAL REMEDIES	1352

	Page
Monroe v. Pape	1352
Notes	1354
Problem	1359
Paul v. Watchtower Bible & Tract Society	1359
Notes	1362
Problem	1364

C. STATUTORY REMEDIES 1364

Sedima, S.P.R.L. v. Imrex Co.	1364
Notes	1370
Problem	1376
White v. Samsung Electronics, Inc.	1376
Problem	1379
Notes	1379
Staron v. McDonald's Corp.	1380
Notes	1384
Lytle v. Malady	1387
Notes	1390
Problem	1392
Harris v. Forklift Systems, Inc.	1392
Notes	1395

Chapter. 21 INSURANCE 1399

A. INTRODUCTION 1399

B. TORT LAW AND THE INSURANCE INSTITUTION 1399

Notes	1399
Myers v. Robertson	1401
Notes	1410

C. INSURANCE COVERAGE ISSUES 1411

Altena v. United Fire & Casualty Co.	1411
Notes	1417
Johnson & Johnson v. Aetna Casualty & Surety Co.	1420
Notes	1426
Problem	1437

D. INSURER DUTIES AND PENALTIES 1438

Gruenberg v. Aetna Insurance Co.	1439
Notes	1445
Problem	1449

E. AUTOMOBILE INSURANCE 1450

	Page
Notes	1450
Problem	1455
F. INSURANCE AS AN ALTERNATIVE SYSTEM	1456
Pinnnick v. Cleary	1457
Notes	1468

Chapter 22 TORT RETRENCHMENTS AND TORT ALTERNATIVES ... 1471

- A. INTRODUCTION ... 1471
- B. GUEST PASSENGER STATUTES ... 1471
  - Problem ... 1471
  - *Henry v. Bauder* ... 1472
  - Notes ... 1475
- C. THE IMPETUS FOR REFORM ... 1477
- D. LIMITATIONS ON RECOVERY ... 1482
  - *Sofie v. Fibreboard Corp.* ... 1482
  - Notes ... 1484
- E. SUBSTANTIVE LAW REFORM ... 1486
  - [1] Products Liability ... 1486
  - [2] Medical Malpractice ... 1488
- F. JOINT AND SEVERAL LIABILITY ... 1490
  - Notes ... 1490
- G. ALTERNATIVE DISPUTE MECHANISMS: TRIAL-RELATED DEVICES ... 1492
  - [1] Introduction ... 1492
  - [2] Summary Jury Trial ... 1493
  - [3] Mini-Trials ... 1494
  - [4] Court-Induced and Other Settlement Techniques ... 1495
  - [5] Responses to Asbestos Litigation ... 1496
  - [6] Litigant Satisfaction with Resolution Alternatives ... 1499
    - Notes ... 1500
- H. ALTERNATIVE DISPUTE RESOLUTIONS: ARBITRATION AND MEDIATION ALTERNATIVES TO TRIAL ... 1501

	Page
Problem	1501
[1] Pretrial Arbitration	1501
[2] Medical Malpractice Arbitration Provisions	1502
[3] Mandatory Arbitration As A Substitute For Litigation	1504
Notes	1504
Problem	1505
[4] Mediation	1505
Virginia Mediation Act	1505
Problem	1506
Notes	1507
I. ALTERNATIVES TO THE TORT SYSTEM	1509
Notes	1512
[1] Workers' Compensation	1512
[2] Automobile No-Fault	1514
J. OTHER LIMITED SCHEMES	1516
K. COMPARITIVE SYSTEMS	1517
Notes	1520

Chapter 1
VALUES AND PROCESS INTRODUCTION

A. INTRODUCTION

Tort law encompasses the doctrines, processes, procedures and precepts that are invoked when a person seeks legal redress for an injury caused by the conduct, property or product of another. While the circumstances under which the parties interacted may also support a criminal charge or a claim for breach of contract, the torts case focuses on rights and liabilities that arise although no one promised to pay for the damages and without regard to whether the government can or does prosecute the actor for a crime.

The study of tort law customarily is placed in the first year curriculum because it offers the beginning law student a unique opportunity to gain insights into the law going far beyond the comprehension of a set of legal rules that define the various torts. The new law student will gain an appreciation of the fundamental value conflicts faced by judges, legislators, administrators and juries who must resolve tort claims. The student also should reflect on the process by which the legal system attempts to resolve the disputes, and the ethical dilemmas that arise out of the litigation process. Finally, a true appreciation of the public policy implications of tort law requires reflection on the immediate and long-range impact of the tort system.

The cases presented in this introductory chapter highlight and promote reflection and discussion on some of the basic features of the law. As you read each case, consider: (1) the inherent value preferences that support the plaintiff's claim for legal redress, and the defendant's proffered defense; (2) the value preferences inherent in the court's decision; (3) the process used to determine the facts (the events that produced the injuries) and the law (the rules determining who should bear the loss); and (4) the ethical dilemmas that arise because of the tactics employed by the litigants, and the procedures and processes relied on by the court to reach and justify its decision.

B. STATING A CLAIM

GLICK v. OLDE TOWN LANCASTER, INC.
369 Pa. Super. 419, 535 A.2d 621 (1987), app. den.
519 Pa. 665, 548 A.2d 255 (1988)

HESTER, JUDGE.

This case presents the issue of the circumstances under which a landowner can be held liable to a member of the public for injuries resulting from a criminal attack occurring on the landowner's property. Appellants allege that a landowner promised to resecure a vacant building and that appellant was raped by an unknown criminal therein before the building was secured. We hold that the landowner cannot be held liable under these circumstances and that the complaint failed to state a cause of action upon which relief may be granted. We therefore affirm the order of the trial court which sustained appellee's demurrer to the complaint.

In considering preliminary objections in the nature of a demurrer, the following standards apply:

> [P]reliminary objections in the nature of a demurrer admit as true all well and clearly pleaded material, factual averments and all inferences fairly deducible therefrom. Conclusions of law and unjustified inferences are not admitted by the pleading. Starting from this point of reference the complaint must be examined to determine whether it sets forth a cause of action which, if proved, would entitle the party to the relief sought. If such is the case, the demurrer may not be sustained.

We therefore take as true the following facts alleged in appellants complaint:

. . .5. On or about September 2, 1977, defendant, Olde Town Lancaster, Inc., purchased numerous dwellings located in and around the Historic District of the City of Lancaster, including those dwellings located at 123-125 South Christian Street.

6. Defendant, Olde Town Lancaster, Inc., remained the owner of 123-125 South Christian Street for approximately 6 years until May 25, 1984.

7. During this period of ownership by defendant, Olde Town Lancaster, Inc., the dwellings remained uninhabitable.

8. Prior to March 25, 1984, the defendants knew, or should have known, that this location was being frequented by itinerants, and other individuals who used the premises in order to carry on illicit activities, which were, or could have been, dangerous to the public.

9. Prior to March 25, 1984, the defendants unsuccessfully attempted to secure the dwellings to prevent entrance into them by partially boarding up windows and doors with material which was inadequate to prevent entrance.

10. Prior to March 25, 1984, the defendants knew, or should have known, that its prior attempt(s) to secure the dwellings were unsuccessful and that the dwellings continued to be used by these individuals for illicit purposes, which were, or could have been, dangerous to the public.

11. On March 20, 1984, defendants were notified by the Bureau of License and Structural Inspections for the City of Lancaster that inspection of the dwellings revealed that they were not secured from entrance and evidence was found that itinerants had been in the dwellings.

12. Defendants assured the Bureau of License and Structural Inspectors for the City of Lancaster that defendants would undertake to correct this problem by resecuring the doors and windows. However, the defendants failed to do so.

13. On Sunday, March 25, 1984, at approximately 9:00 a.m., plaintiff, Mary Jean Glick, was accosted by a still unknown individual on the first block of East Vine Street while she was walking to church.

14. The aforesaid individual forced plaintiff, Mary Jean Glick, to proceed west on Vine Street then turn south on Christian Street, proceed down Christian Street to the aforesaid dwellings located at 123-125 South Christian Street. Plaintiff was then forced to enter the dwelling from the rear through an unsecured, open doorway. Thereafter, she was assaulted, battered, and raped for approximately a two-hour period of time.

. . .Appellants assert that the trial court erred in holding that their complaint failed to state a valid cause of action under Pennsylvania law. Appellants, relying on various sections of the Restatement (Second) of Torts (1965), allege that Olde Town is liable to them, as "third persons," for negligently failing to resecure the building following its promise to the City of Lancaster to do so. Section 324A provides:

> § 324 A. *Liability to Third Person for Negligent Performance of Undertaking*
>
> One who undertakes, gratuitously or for consideration, to render services to another which he should recognize as necessary for the protection of a third person or his things, is subject to liability to the third person for physical harm resulting from his failure to exercise reasonable care to protect his undertaking, if
>
> (a) his failure to exercise reasonable care increases the risk of such harm, or
>
> (b) he has undertaken to perform a duty owed by the other to the third person, or
>
> (c) the harm is suffered because of reliance of the other or the third person upon the undertaking.

Appellants argue that the Pennsylvania Supreme Court's analysis in *Feld v. Merriam*, 506 Pa. 383, 485 A.2d 742 (1984), requires the conclusion that their complaint states a valid cause of action under section 324A. *Feld* established the principle that the landlord of an apartment complex has no duty, in the absence of a promise, to protect a tenant from criminal activity on the landlord's property. The *Feld* court held, however, that a landlord may be liable if he makes a promise to provide security and then negligently performs that promise, citing section 323 of the Restatement.

> [A]lthough there is a general rule against holding a person liable for the criminal conduct of another absent a preexisting duty, there is also an exception to that rule, i.e., where a party assumes a duty, whether gratuitously or for consideration, and so negligently performs that duty that another suffers damage.
>
> . . . When a landlord by agreement or voluntarily offers a program to protect the premises, he must perform the task in a reasonable manner and where a harm follows a reasonable expectation of that harm, he is liable. The duty is one of reasonable care under the circumstances. It is not the duty of an insurer and a landlord is not liable unless his failure is the proximate cause of the harm.

Feld, 506 Pa. at 392–94, 485 A.2d at 746–47. *Feld* thus adopted the principle of section 323 to hold that a landlord who makes a promise to his tenants to provide security creates for himself the duty to exercise reasonable care in performing the undertaking. Appellants ask us to apply this principle under section 324A to establish a duty of a landowner toward members of the public.

We hold that section 324A is inapplicable to this case because appellants were not within the class of persons the provision was designed to protect. In order for section 324A to apply, it must be established that the service of resecuring the dwellings was necessary for the protection of persons such as appellants.

We do not view the harm suffered by appellant Glick as being the type of risk which Olde Town's promise to resecure the dwellings was intended to avert. Securing vacant dwellings is intended to protect members of the public who might otherwise be tempted to trespass therein and to protect neighboring property owners from risks such as fire and unsanitary conditions which might be created by trespassers. The practice of securing vacant dwellings is not designed to prevent the abduction of citizens blocks or miles away and their removal to the vacant building to be assaulted and raped. The unsecured dwelling was a wholly fortuitous factor in the crimes committed against appellant Glick. Glick's rapist would have accomplished his atrocity whether or not Olde Town's property remained unsecured. He would simply have transported her to a different location: another dwelling, basement, automobile, hedge, ditch, park or field. The relationship between Olde Town's failure to secure its vacant real estate and the vicious crimes against Glick is far too attenuated to support a cause of action under Restatement § 324A.

Even if we were to conclude that Olde Town's promise to resecure its property was intended to protect against the type of harm suffered by appellant Glick, section 324A still would not apply. The provision additionally requires that one of the subdivisions be satisfied:

(a) his failure to exercise reasonable care increases the risk of such harm, or

(b) he has undertaken to perform a duty owed by the other to the third person, or

(c) the harm is suffered because of reliance of the other or the third person upon the undertaking.

None of these additional conditions is present.

Subsection (a) does not apply, for Glick's rapist could have abducted her to an infinite number of locations, and Olde Town's unsecured vacant property did not increase the risk of harm to Glick, as we have discussed.

Subsection (b) does not apply, for the city owed no duty to Glick to secure the Olde Town property.

Subsection (c) is also inapplicable, as it requires the harm to be caused either by the city or by Glick's reliance on Olde Town's promise. It is obvious that Glick herself did not rely on the promise, for she had no way of knowing about it. It is equally obvious that if the city placed any reliance on the promise, that reliance did not cause the harm suffered by Glick. It would be absurd to postulate that if Olde Town had not made its promise to the bureau of inspections, the City of Lancaster would have prevented Glick's rape, either by taking legal action before Sunday morning or by some other means.

Our holding is consistent with recent guidance from the Supreme Court of Pennsylvania in the interpretation of Restatement § 324A. In *Cantwell v. Allegheny County*, 506 Pa. 35, 483 A.2d 1350 (1984), the court analyzed section 324A and refused to apply it in that case. The third person plaintiff in *Cantwell* was a man who had been arrested for committing a series of rapes. The defendant was a crime lab which was responsible for assisting the prosecuting police departments by scientifically analyzing evidence. In rendering that service, the crime lab had been negligent. It failed to test all clothing and hospital specimens submitted to it for blood-typing, both before and after the plaintiff's arrest; it incorrectly informed the police that it was too late to perform blood typing; and it failed to perform properly those tests which it undertook to perform. Subsequent scientific tests performed while the plaintiff's criminal trial was in progress proved that he could not have committed three of the rapes charged against him and resulted in the dismissal of all charges. The plaintiff alleged that his wrongful incarceration, indictment and trial were caused by the crime lab's negligence in performing its scientific services for the police.

The supreme court's analysis focused on the requirement of foreseeability, stating that section 324A did not alter the traditional requirement that foreseeable harm befall a foreseeable plaintiff. If a defendant has no reason to foresee that his undertaking is necessary for the protection of the third person plaintiff, section 324A does not apply. The supreme court unanimously held that the crime lab had no reason to foresee that the scientific analyses it undertook to perform for the police were necessary for the protection of a criminal suspect such as Cantwell.

Applying *Cantwell*'s interpretation of section 324A to this case, we hold that Olde Town, when it promised to resecure its dwellings, had absolutely no reason to foresee that the service was necessary for the protection of kidnap victims such as appellant Glick.

Finally, we hold that appellant's complaint does not satisfy Restatement § 324A in that its factual allegations are insufficient to support the necessary finding of negligence by Olde Town in the performance of its undertaking. The complaint alleges that on Tuesday, March 20, 1984, Olde Town was notified by Lancaster's bureau of inspections that Olde Town's buildings were unsecured, and further alleges that Olde Town assured the bureau that Olde Town would undertake to correct the problem. On Sunday, March 25, 1984, appellant was kidnaped, taken to Olde Town's dwelling, and raped. Noticeably absent from the complaint are allegations as to when Olde Town received the notice from the inspection bureau and when Olde Town promised to resecure the buildings. There is no indication of the extent of the repairs necessary to resecure the dwellings, except that Olde Town's initial attempts to secure the dwellings had apparently been thwarted by trespassers who removed the boards covering the doors and windows, so that extraordinary measures would be required to resecure the dwellings. The allegations of the complaint are insufficient to support a finding of negligence on the part of Olde Town for its failure to complete such repairs within days or hours of its promise.

We therefore hold that the facts alleged by appellants do not state a cause of action under the Restatement (Second) of Torts § 324A and affirm the order sustaining appellee's demurrer and dismissing the complaint.

NOTES

1. *Broad Categories. Olde Town* involved the commission of a crime in and around the defendant's premises, and an allegedly broken promise by that defendant. What features characterize plaintiff's claim as "tort," rather than criminal law, property or contract?

2. *An Introduction to Process.* The plaintiff in *Olde Town* did not get an opportunity to prove her claim because the defendant was able to persuade the judge that the court should dismiss the claim on the basis of defendant's preliminary objections to the complaint. A civil lawsuit is initiated by filing a pleading setting forth "a short and plain statement of the claim showing that the pleader is entitled to relief." FED. R. CIV. PROC. 8(a). The defendant may respond by filing an answer that admits or denies the plaintiff's allegations of fact and contentions of law.

Prior to, or in addition to, answering the plaintiff's complaint, the defendant may file preliminary objections. *See* FED. R. CIV. P. 12(b). Typical preliminary objections include the contention that the court in which the party has been sued lacks the power to resolve the controversy because it does not have authority to hear this type of claim, or lacks authority to compel the defendant to litigate the claim in the particular geographic or governmental arena. These issues of power over the controversy (subject matter jurisdiction) and power over the particular litigant (jurisdiction over the person) are studied in detail in the course in civil procedure.

However, the type of preliminary objection raised in *Olde Town* concedes jurisdiction to hear the claim, but asserts that, even if plaintiff's factual allegations are true, as a matter of law, he is not entitled to the relief he seeks, or any relief, in a court. This type of objection is referred to in the common law as a demurrer. Some American jurisdictions still use the term to refer to this type of preliminary objection. In many jurisdictions, the contention that plaintiff is not entitled to relief despite the truth of his allegations is urged by a motion to dismiss for "failure to state a claim upon which relief can be granted." FED. R. CIV. P. 12(b)(6).

3. *Falling at the First Hurdle.* If the court decides to grant the demurrer or motion to dismiss, the defendant is spared the expense of defending the case on its merits and plaintiff does not get the opportunity to prove the facts alleged in the complaint. In addition, the dispute is resolved by the court, as a matter of law, rather than by a jury. Do you think that the type of claim presented in *Olde Town* should be resolved by way of preliminary objection? What political, social and economic consequences result from a procedure that permits dismissal of the claim by preliminary objection instead of allowing the jury to decide the claim? Which approach do you support? Why?

4. *Precedent.* In reaching its decision that Olde Town was not liable, the court reviewed prior cases decided in the jurisdiction and explained its view of the relevance or irrelevance of those decisions. What case precedent did the plaintiff rely on to support her claim? How did the court distinguish the case relied on by plaintiff? Do you agree with the court's reasoning in distinguishing this case? Why is it *necessary* for the court to distinguish a prior decision?

5. *Restated Precedent.* The court considered a section of the RESTATEMENT (SECOND) OF TORTS on the question of the liability of a defendant for harm caused by a third person or by some source external to the defendant. The Restatement — a publication containing the views of a group of judges, attorneys and law professors as to the current status of the law — is influential but not controlling upon a state court that is deciding a case. In other words, a state court may decide to adopt or reject a section of the Restatement in whole or in part. Can you quantify the extent to which the Restatement provided the "answer" for the court, compared to other sources you can identify?

6. *General Rules and Exceptions.* RESTATEMENT (SECOND) OF TORTS § 314 (1965) recognizes a general rule that, "The fact that the actor realizes or should realize that action on his part is necessary for another's aid or protection does not of itself impose upon him a duty to take such action." *Olde Town* makes specific reference to the Restatement, § 324A. That section represents an exception from the general rule contained in § 314. Is the court's decision in *Olde Town* explicable on the basis that courts give a narrower reading to exceptions than to general rules?

7. *Foresight?* The court in *Glick* makes reference to the *Cantwell* court's view that "section 324A did not alter the traditional requirement that foreseeable harm befall a foreseeable plaintiff." Is such a view supported by § 324A? What does "foreseeable" mean?

8. *Values and Goals.* What did the plaintiff claim that Olde Town did or did not do that was wrong? How did she claim the wrongful conduct contributed to her injuries? Should Olde Town's conduct be considered a wrong in the eyes of the law? Did Olde Town's conduct contribute to plaintiff's injuries? What goals are promoted by insulating Olde Town from financial responsibility for the plaintiff's injuries? What goals would be promoted by making Olde Town bear all or some of the costs of plaintiff's injuries? Which result is preferable if the dominant goal of tort law is to reduce accidents or increase public safety? What if the dominant goal is to compensate victims of accidents? Or to satisfy the community's sense of justice?

7. *Foresight and Hindsight.* Would the *Olde Town* court reach the same decision if another person were assaulted in this same abandoned property two weeks later, and sued Olde Town? Should it? If not, what accounts for the difference? Should it matter whether the person who perpetrated the second assault knew (or was) the person who committed the first assault on the property? Would it make a difference if the second perpetrator were aware of the first assault on the property?

8. *The Complexities of "Right" and "Wrong" Answers.* A claim for compensation such as the plaintiff presented in *Olde Town* is based on a tort claim of negligence. *Olde Town* turns on the two issues of a *prima facie* case of negligence that prove most troublesome to attorneys and courts in terms of theory and concept. They are duty and causation. The duty and causation issues are examined in detail in later chapters.

9. *The Neophyte's Complaint.* Understandable reactions to these questions include, "How should I know, I am a beginning law student. I know enough

to recognize terms of art when I see them," and "How can I know the content of 'duty' or 'causation' ?" Should your outrage at, indifference to, or approval of the result in *Olde Town* depend upon the extent of your legal training?

10. *The Art of the Conclusory Statement.* Assume that your suspicions are correct, and that "duty," "causation," and other words found in *Olde Town* such as "reasonable" and "foreseeable," are terms of art. Are the meanings of those terms static and objective, or do their contents vary depending upon the identity of the user of the term? For example, imagine yourself as plaintiff's attorney in *Olde Town*; would you have treated "duty" or "causation" as empirically discoverable facts, or would you have infused them with your view as to how the case should have been decided? Is it likely that your opponent for the defense or the judge would act or think any differently?

11. *Value Preferences, Decision Makers and Algebra.* Do we not assume that a judge without personal values is a desirable decision maker? Equally, do we not accept that a judge is seldom, if ever, able to completely shed her personal values when deciding a case? The law attempts to minimize the impact of the judge's personal (including political and economic) values on the resolution of a particular conflict by developing and articulating general rules of law that must be applied consistently to similar claims and similar facts. A trial judge is bound by the prior decisions of the appellate courts in the particular jurisdiction, to the extent that the appellate court has considered a similar claim on similar facts. In the same vein, the appellate courts are bound by their own prior decisions to the extent that they have considered the same claims on similar facts in the past and announced a rule of law that governs the claims. The principle invoked to preclude courts from deciding each case anew in terms of the applicable facts and rule of law is *stare decisis*.

The problem with placing too heavy a reliance on the principle of *stare decisis* as a protective mechanism is that a court often will determine that it is not bound by a prior decision relied upon by one of the parties because it views an important fact or facts in the case before it as materially different from the facts of the prior decision. In other words, the arguably precedential case will be "distinguished." For now, it is sufficient to understand that the content of a decision is intimately linked to the identity, and hence the value preference, of the decision-maker. Alternatively, the highest court of the jurisdiction may be so disturbed by the application of the rule to the case before it that it declares the rule is not to be followed. That declaration is called "overruling" the prior decision. The reasons given for the actual "overruling" usually are that the decision was wrong when decided, or that times (societal values) have changed so that the rule is no longer appropriate. The important point is that the resolution of legal disputes does not involve the same process as the resolution of a math problem. The factors that influence the resolution of legal disputes are too variable to allow the student, professor, attorney or judge to adopt any mechanical problem-solving method such as "facts × rule of law = decision." For classic discussions of the judicial process of decision-making, *see* J. FRANK, COURTS ON TRIAL (1949); K. LLEWELLYN, THE COMMON LAW TRADITION: DECIDING APPEALS (1960); Laswell and McDougal, *The Relation of Law to Social process; Trends in Theories About Law*, 37 U. PITT. L. REV. 465 (1976).

12. *The Limits of Doctrine.* In the study of law, the student sometimes can explain satisfactorily why a court reached a particular decision by reciting an applicable rule of law and explaining the logic of applying the rule to the particular facts. This is referred to as identifying the applicable black letter law or "doctrine." However, some court decisions elude a simple explanation. The student or lawyer attempting to anticipate the next court decision in a similar case may have difficulty in identifying the factors that influenced the court's decision. Sometimes courts do a good job in explaining the true basis of their decisions and sometimes their opinions leave much to be desired. Moreover, some courts believe that the judicial function *is* limited to the application of black letter law, while others acknowledge that much judicial decision-making is influenced by policy-making for the community. Thus, you will find that some opinions mechanically articulate and apply black letter rules, while others wrestle with questions regarding the impact of the decision on the community's economic, political or social values.

PROBLEM

Plaintiff's deceased drowned in a natural swimming pool created by a water stream on private land. The drowning occurred when the water current in the pool suddenly quickened as a result of a rapid influx of water from torrential rains upstream. Such changes in the current of the pool were not uncommon. The pool was a popular swimming area, and Anystate, with the permission of the landowner, had constructed a public parking lot near the pool, had improved and maintained a trail to the pool, and had included the pool on several official maps and state-sponsored visitor information brochures. Anystate did not provide a warning as to the danger of sudden current changes in the pool.

Should Anystate be liable for the death of plaintiff's deceased? Should the landowner? Why?

C. LAW AND FACTS

RORRER v. COOKE
313 N.C. 338, 329 S.E.2d 355 (1985)

MARTIN, JUSTICE.

. . . Plaintiff's suit is predicated upon the theory that Cooke negligently represented her during prosecution of her suit against Dr. Sardi. This Court's most thorough discussion of an attorney's legal obligation to his client is set forth in *Hodges v. Carter,* 239 N.C. 517, 519–20, 80 S.E.2d 144, 145–46 (1954):

> Ordinarily when an attorney engages in the practice of the law and contracts to prosecute an action in behalf of his client, he impliedly represents that (1) he possesses the requisite degree of learning, skill, and ability necessary to the practice of his profession and which others similarly situated ordinarily possess; (2) he will exert his best judgment in the prosecution of the litigation entrusted to him; and (3) he

will exercise reasonable and ordinary care and diligence in the use of his skill and in the application of his knowledge to his client's cause.

[The trial court granted the defendant's motion for summary judgment, and the court of appeals reversed the trial court.]

Plaintiff does not contend that Cooke did not possess the requisite degree of learning, skill, and ability necessary to the practice of law and which others similarly situated ordinarily possess. Nor would the record support such finding. It is uncontested that Cooke was duly licensed to practice law in North Carolina and engaged in such practice from that time until his death during the pendency of the present litigation. Plaintiff made no challenge to the statements of several of defendant's affiants that Cooke's reputation in Greensboro for the application of his legal skills was excellent. Therefore, the first criterion established by *Hodges* is not at issue.

Plaintiff does claim, however, that the affidavits she submitted in opposition to defendant's motion for summary judgment establish that there is a material question of fact as to whether Cooke's conduct of the litigation of her suit was in accord with the other two criteria set forth in *Hodges*. To place these affidavits in context we first review the undisputed facts as to the course of events culminating in the jury verdict in favor of Dr. Sardi.

Plaintiff first met with Cooke regarding suit against Dr. Sardi on 22 March 1972. At this conference both plaintiff and her husband stated emphatically that Dr. Sardi had told them that the cause of Mrs. Rorrer's tongue paralysis was probably too much pressure exerted by the clamp used during the course of [a tonsillectomy performed by Dr. Sardi]. The Rorrers also told Cooke that plaintiff had been seen and examined by Dr. T. Boyce Cole at the Duke University Medical Center. Mr. Rorrer also stated that Dr. Cole told him that although he had never seen or heard of a paralysis resulting from a tonsillectomy, he felt that something had occurred in the course of the operation to cause the paralysis and that pressure on the tongue was a possible explanation. After the Rorrers left, Mr. Cooke conducted extensive research in various medical treatises and other written materials in order to understand the medical aspects of Mrs. Rorrer's injury.

Mr. Cooke then obtained a copy of a written report prepared on 6 December 1971 by Dr. Joseph W. Stiefel, a neurologist to whom plaintiff had been sent by Dr. Sardi. . . . In an affidavit filed with his motion for summary judgment Cooke stated that he . . . construed this report of Dr. Stiefel as being entirely consistent with what Mr. and Mrs. Rorrer said had been stated to them by Dr. Sardi and as ruling out any psychosomatic problem as a cause for the tongue paralysis.

Cooke then contacted Dr. Gray Hunter, a Greensboro surgeon, and asked him whether or not it would be possible for the hypoglossal nerve to be severed or cut during the course of a tonsillectomy. Dr. Hunter said that in his opinion it would be virtually impossible for this to occur. . . . Mr. Cooke then proceeded to obtain and study all medical records relating to Mrs. Rorrer from (1) the Moses H. Cone Memorial Hospital, (2) Dr. Sardi, [and] (3) Dr. Stiefel, as well as copies of the reports of Dr. Cole and Drs. Joseph C. Farmer and Ng Khye Weng, doctors who practice at the Duke University Medical Center.

In one report Dr. Farmer stated, "It is possible that she (Mrs. Rorrer) could have a tongue muscle injury secondary to the retraction of the tongue at the tonsillectomy; however, this is most unusual." By his affidavit Cooke states that he construed this statement by Dr. Farmer as further supporting the supposition that the paralysis of the tongue was an injury secondary to the retraction of the tongue during the tonsillectomy, and that this was caused by pressure exerted on the tongue by the clamp in such a manner as to damage the hypoglossal nerve.

In a report dated 2 February 1972 obtained by Cooke, Dr. Cole stated:

"No explanation has been found to date for the difficulty and Dr. Weng referred her to obtain a tongue biopsy. . . . Certainly the time element as far as a tonsillectomy is concerned would point to an injury at the time; however, it is impossible for me to see how a direct injury could have caused this and while doing a tonsillectomy. I have never seen or heard of a similar incidence."

. . . In the affidavit . . . Cooke states.

"I construed this information from Dr. Cole as ruling out any cause for paralysis of the tongue other than something that occurred during the tonsillectomy by Dr. Sardi. . . . Based upon the information furnished to me by Mr. and Mrs. Rorrer, by the several doctors and by all medical records, I was of the opinion that the best theory and only theory of injury to the tongue was the placing of too much pressure on the tongue by the clamp by Dr. Sardi. I was of the opinion that I needed to determine whether evidence of too much pressure on the tongue which could result in a paralysis would be in accordance with the accepted standards of practice in performing a tonsillectomy. I decided that Dr. Cole, Mrs. Rorrer's own doctor, who had first-hand personal knowledge of her condition, and the resources at the Duke Medical Center at his disposal, was the best source of information on this."

After waiting for some time to elapse (in hopes that plaintiff's condition would improve) Cooke met personally with Dr. Cole in 1973. Cooke's affidavit states that he discussed with Dr. Cole the theory which was suggested by what Dr. Sardi had stated to Mr. and Mrs. Rorrer, that is, that too much pressure from the clamp used by Dr. Sardi during the operation had impaired the flow of blood to the hypoglossal nerve and had caused a paralysis thereof. "Dr. Cole told me that he had never heard of a similar result following a tonsillectomy, but that there seemed to be no other explanation for Mrs. Rorrer's condition. Dr. Cole did not suggest any other possibility. This discussion with Dr. Cole caused me to believe that Dr. Cole would respond to appropriate hypothetical questions in such manner as to provide adequate and sufficient expert testimony for taking a case against Dr. Sardi to the jury. I therefore concluded that a suit on behalf of Mrs. Rorrer against Dr. Sardi should be undertaken."

Cooke filed suit against Dr. Sardi on 7 June 1974 and later took depositions of Dr. Sardi and Dr. Cole. Cooke took Cole's deposition on 28 August 1975. Cooke's affidavit explains that:

". . . One of the reasons for Mrs. Rorrer going to Duke was to attempt to ascertain the cause of her condition. Dr. Cole was Mrs. Rorrer's treating physician, and he had not been consulted as a 'paid expert' merely for the purpose of trying to make out a case against Dr. Sardi. It was my best judgment that it would be much better to use Dr. Cole as a witness than it would be to try to seek out a paid expert from some other state or some other doctor who was not personally acquainted with and who had not treated Mrs. Rorrer, and that Dr. Cole would make a stronger and more convincing witness than would some doctor called in merely to testify even if some unknown doctor could be located who would give testimony adverse to Dr. Sardi."

Cooke explains that Cole's deposition, which was received into evidence at trial,

"goes to show that he was fully qualified and experienced as an expert otolaryngologist; was an associate teaching professor at Duke Medical Center; was a practicing surgeon at Duke Hospital; was experienced in performing tonsillectomies, adenoidectomies, laryngectomies, statadectomies, and other operations; was usually in the operating room every day and performed three to five operations per day. At the time of his deposition he had been at the Duke Medical Center for six years, seeing patients from a wide area. As both a practicing and teaching otolaryngologist, and as one of Mrs. Rorrer's treating physicians, it was my judgment that Dr. Cole provided an adequate source of information, and that I did not need to seek consultations with other otolaryngologists. The testimony of Dr. Cole identified Dr. Weng as an expert neurologist and Dr. Farmer as an expert otolaryngologist and associate professor, both at Duke Medical Center. Both saw Mrs. Rorrer. Information from them is in the trial record in the form of their reports and through the testimony of Dr. Cole. Thereby I had the benefit of information from two otolaryngologists from Duke and two neurologists in the persons of Dr. Weng and Dr. Stiefel. None of these four doctors gave to me any indication of any cause of Mrs. Rorrer's problem other than the possible pressure from the clamp used by Dr. Sardi. Dr. Sardi did not come up with any other explanation, and Dr. Sardi was the third otolaryngologist involved with the case. A careful study of the medical records of all of these doctors, and the testimony of Dr. Cole, as well as what Dr. Cole stated to me off the record, caused me to be of the opinion in my best judgment that there was no explanation for the trouble that Mrs. Rorrer had with her tongue other than damage to the hypoglossal nerve from pressure exerted by the clamp used by Dr. Sardi, and further, that the best interest of Mrs. Rorrer in my prosecution of her case against Dr. Sardi would not be served by my seeking consultations with other otolaryngologists. It was my best judgment that Mrs. Rorrer's interest was best served by my proceeding with her case as I did through the use of Dr. Cole as the plaintiff's expert witness, and when I learned Dr. Cole would not be available for the trial I felt that it was best to introduce his testimony through his deposition rather than again delaying the trial in order to have him testify in person. In my judgment there was no need to seek out other otolaryngologists for consultation or as witnesses, based upon all the information that was available to me."

At the medical malpractice trial the Rorrers both testified that Dr. Sardi admitted to them that pressure from a tongue clamp used during surgery caused the injury to plaintiff's tongue. Sardi denied the admission. Plaintiff also presented testimony of Dr. Stiefel and the deposition of Dr. Cole. Dr. Stiefel testified that upon initially examining plaintiff he believed her paralysis was caused by some injury or involvement to the hypoglossal nerve, the nerve which controls the tongue's movement. On cross-examination, however, Dr. Stiefel stated that after examining a subsequent pathology report on a biopsy of plaintiff's tongue, he found this report to be inconsistent with injury to the nerve. Dr. Sardi's evidence included his own testimony, as well as that of Dr. William M. Satterwhite, Jr., a Winston-Salem otolaryngologist. Dr. Satterwhite was of the opinion that there was nothing Dr. Sardi did or did not do during the surgery which could have damaged plaintiff's tongue.

The jury returned a verdict for Dr. Sardi after deliberating for twenty minutes. On behalf of Mrs. Rorrer, Mr. Cooke moved that the verdict be set aside as being against the greater weight of the evidence, and the trial judge responded that he would like to postpone ruling on the motion because he was "a little surprised in the verdict." Ultimately the motion was denied. Although Cooke filed notice of appeal on behalf of Mrs. Rorrer, appeal was never perfected.

Mrs. Rorrer filed a complaint against Cooke on 26 August 1982 alleging:

> Defendant was negligent in his representation of Mary Carol Rorrer and failed to apply the high degree of attention and care which he had agreed to in the prosecution of Mary Carol Rorrer's claim in the following respects:
>
> a. he failed to obtain adequate expert consultations from physicians qualified to evaluate plaintiff's claim;
>
> b. he failed to properly investigate, assemble and present relevant evidence at the trial;
>
> c. he failed to properly cross-examine Dr. Sardi concerning his treatment and evaluation of his patient;
>
> d. he failed to present the existing neurological evidence concerning plaintiff's tongue paralysis;
>
> e. he failed to properly cross-examine Dr. Satterwhyte [sic], a defense witness;
>
> f. he failed to properly cross-examine Dr. Steifel [sic];
>
> g. he failed to locate, subpoena and present the testimony of Carol Taylor, another patient of Dr. Sardi who experienced the same type of tongue paralysis following the same type of tonsillectomy procedure;
>
> h. he failed to properly cross-examine Dr. Sardi concerning statements made by him to plaintiffs [sic] herein;
>
> i. he failed to offer into evidence conversations and office records of Dr. Rosen and failed to subpoena Dr. Rosen or any of his office records;
>
> j. he failed to perfect an appeal from the judgment entered on the verdict even though notice of appeal was given and there was no conversation held between plaintiff and defendant concerning an abandonment of any appeal. . . .

On 1 October 1982 defendant moved for summary judgment . . . . On his motion for summary judgment defendant had the initial burden of showing that an essential element of plaintiff's case did not exist as a matter of law or showing through discovery that plaintiff had not produced evidence to support an essential element of her claim. Plaintiff was then required to come forward with a forecast of evidence showing the existence of a genuine issue of material fact with respect to the issues raised by the movant. In support of his motion, Mr. Cooke placed into evidence facts showing that there was no actionable negligence with respect to any of the contentions in plaintiff's complaint, that each contested action on his part constituted the good faith exercise of attorney judgment, and that the essential aspect of proximate cause was absent. Mr. Cooke also placed into evidence the testimony of Dr. Cole that there was "no other explanation" for plaintiff's condition than the theory of causation which was presented to the jury.

. . . Plaintiff submitted the affidavits of Dr. T. Boyce Cole and attorney Tim L. Harris in opposition to Mr. Cooke's motion for summary judgment. Plaintiff contends that her two affidavits raise genuine issues of material fact with respect to whether Cooke breached the criteria enunciated in *Hodges v. Carter*, 239 N.C. 517, 80 S.E.2d 144, and that therefore the Court of Appeals properly reversed the trial court's entry of summary judgment in favor of defendant. Defendant argues, of course, that summary judgment was properly entered in Cooke's favor because no such issues are raised by plaintiff's affidavits. Dr. Cole's affidavit begins by reciting his involvement with the medical examination and diagnosis of Mary Rorrer's paralysis. It states that before his deposition was taken by Cooke, he and Cooke discussed Mr. Cooke's theory of whether the tongue retractor used during the tonsillectomy could have placed sufficient pressure on the tongue to impair blood flow and cause ischemic damage to the tongue. "At that time, I told Mr. Cooke that I did not know what caused Mrs. Rorrer's tongue damage without knowing the details of the tonsillectomy procedure and I further told him that I thought it unlikely that a tongue retractor could exert enough pressure to produce this result. Mr. Cooke explained the purpose of a hypothetical question to me and asked me to assume as a hypothetical fact, that sufficient pressure was, in fact, exerted to the tongue by the tongue retractor to impair blood flow. I explained to Mr. Cooke that, assuming an impaired blood flow from whatever cause, it could have produced the tongue damage. However, I reiterated to Mr. Cooke more than once that it was my opinion that a tongue retractor could not place sufficient pressure on the tongue to cause ischemic damage. This explains my deposition testimony as to why I thought the tongue retractor theory to be an unlikely candidate for the tongue paralysis. I attempted to explain to Mr. Cooke that I could not support such a medical theory when he visited my office before taking my deposition."

The second affidavit plaintiff submitted states the following. "My name is Tim L. Harris and I am an attorney licensed to practice law in the State of North Carolina. Part of my practice involves the specialty of preparing and trying medical malpractice cases and I have, in fact, tried these types of cases. In reading Mr. Cooke's deposition, I have become familiar with his background, training and experience with regard to medical malpractice cases and I am further familiar with the standards of practice of attorneys with similar background and experience in communities similar to Greensboro, North Carolina, in the trial of these types of cases in May, 1978. It is my opinion that the standards of practice for attorneys who handle medical malpractice cases in communities similar to Greensboro, North Carolina, are high since preparation and trial of these actions is difficult and requires a thoroughly competent and skilled legal practitioner.

". . . I conclude that Mr. Cooke sought and received two medical consultations concerning the cause of the tongue paralysis of Mrs. Rorrer and whether or not Dr. Sardi's care and treatment of her met medical standards of care. He first sought the opinion of Dr. Gray Hunter, a general surgeon in Greensboro who informed him that he had not ever heard of this result following a tonsillectomy before. As Mr. Cooke testified on page 19 of his deposition, he stated that Dr. Hunter told him that he could virtually rule out the possibility of severing or damaging the hypoglossal nerve with an instrument during the surgery. I note on page 20 of his deposition that he did not ask Dr. Hunter to consider the possibility of injuring the tongue with a tongue retractor during this surgery. I note on page 21 of Mr. Cooke's deposition that he testifies that he did not ask Dr. Hunter what could have caused the paralysis to Mrs. Rorrer's tongue. Specifically, and most importantly, I note that Dr. Hunter is a general surgeon, not an otolaryngologist, and that Mr. Cooke testifies on page 22 of his depositions that, 'actually I didn't finally come to rest as the theory on which I proceeded in this case until after I had talked to Dr. Cole at Duke.' In other words, Mr. Cooke relies greatly on the fact that Dr. Cole lent support to the tongue retractor theory as having caused the tongue damage. However, from a reading of Dr. Cole's medical records, and from his affidavit, it appears clear that Dr. Cole denies having lent any support to a theory that would place any blame on the tongue retractor during this surgery. Apparently, in my opinion, Mr. Cooke tried to convince Dr. Cole that sufficient pressure was placed by the tongue retractor to cause the damage and, apparently from the affidavit of Dr. Cole, Dr. Cole tried to explain to Mr. Cooke that he could not place the blame on the tongue retractor. Even if Mr. Cooke was surprised by the testimony of Dr. Cole during his deposition on August 28, 1975, there was a period of almost two and one-half years after the deposition testimony of Dr. Cole for Mr. Cooke to further investigate the cause and nature of Mrs. Rorrer's problem and to obtain further consultation as to whether or not the care given by Dr. Sardi complied with accepted medical standards. I also note that, despite Mr. Cooke's knowledge as to the weak nature of the testimony of Dr. Cole contained in his deposition, Mr. Cooke failed to subpoena or secure the testimony of the other attending physicians which she had at Duke Hospital, including neurologists who ran electromyographic studies on her tongue which is an objective basis of proving nerve damage in the tongue and other medical witnesses. Also, I note that Mr. Cooke failed to read or exhibit to the jurors any of the exhibits which were identified and attached to the deposition of Dr. Cole and it is also clear that some of the more favorable notes of Dr. Cole that would support the claim of Mrs. Rorrer were not identified or introduced into evidence.

"On balance, and after having carefully considered the matter and the time of the trial, it is my opinion that the failure of this case was due to the fact that no medical witness supported, in any convincing manner, the medical theory which Mr. Cooke advanced at the trial. This medical theory also hampered Mr. Cooke in the cross-examination of the defendant's expert witnesses. Being tied to a medical theory which was not accepted by any medical witness who gave testimony in the case was an overwhelming reason why the jury was not convinced of the merits of Mrs. Rorrer's claim. In my opinion, it is very important in the preparation and trial of a medical malpractice case to have at least one medical witness who enthusiastically and convincingly will support the plaintiff attorney's medical theory of negligence. In this regard, Mr. Cooke failed to obtain the consultation advice of an otolaryngologist disassociated with Mrs. Rorrer's care for the purpose of thoroughly reviewing her case to arrive at a medical theory of negligence. In 1978, there were available medical consulting agencies who could have reviewed Mrs. Rorrer's claim objectively and, if meritorious, supported her with testimony in court. Also, Dr. Cole and the other physicians at Duke may well have been more inclined to support an alternative medical theory rather than the one advanced by Mr. Cooke. Thus, it is my opinion that the representation given by Mr. Arthur O. Cooke to Mrs. Mary Carol Rorrer to and through her trial did not comply with the existing standard for the handling of medical malpractice claims in May of 1978 and communities similar to Greensboro, North Carolina. It is further my opinion that the departures from these standards of care contributed greatly to the loss of Mrs. Rorrer's claim when it was tried."

We hold that the Court of Appeals erred in reversing the trial judge's entry of summary judgment in favor of defendant. Summary judgment is appropriately entered if the movant establishes that an essential part or element of the opposing party's claim is nonexistent. In a professional malpractice case predicated upon a theory of an attorney's negligence, the plaintiff has the burden of proving by the greater weight of the evidence (1) that the attorney breached the duties owed to his client, as set forth by *Hodges,* 239 N.C. 517, 80 S.E.2d 144, and that this negligence (2) proximately caused (3) damage to the plaintiff. . . .

In the instant case, as we explain below, plaintiff's affidavits do not sufficiently forecast evidence that would prove that in his representation of plaintiff Cooke failed to conform to the criteria enunciated in *Hodges*. Further, plaintiff's affidavits fail to show that any such alleged negligence proximately caused her any damage.

The materials submitted by plaintiff do not raise any material issue of fact with respect to whether Mr. Cooke breached the general duties of care set forth in *Hodges*. In item eight of her complaint against Cooke, plaintiff lists ten acts which Cooke allegedly did not perform in the course of his representation of her. Three of these concern largely pretrial investigation; the remainder allege certain inactions after trial commenced. Neither these allegations nor the affidavits submitted in opposition to defendant's motion for summary judgment establish the existence of a factual question of whether Mr. Cooke negligently misrepresented Mrs. Rorrer in her suit against Dr. Sardi.

The third prong of *Hodges* requires an attorney to represent his client with such skill, prudence, and diligence as lawyers of ordinary skill and capacity commonly possess and exercise in the performance of the tasks which they undertake. The standard is that of members of the profession in the same or similar locality under similar circumstances. Expert testimony is helpful to establish what the standard of care as applied in the investigation and preparation of medical malpractice lawsuits requires and to establish whether the defendant-attorney's performance lived up to such a standard. In opposition to defendant's motion for summary judgment, plaintiff submitted her complaint, the affidavit of Dr. Cole, and the affidavit of one attorney, Tim Harris, who testified as an expert with respect to Cooke's preparation and trial of Mrs. Rorrer's claim. Because it fails to state what the standard of care to which Cooke was subject required him to do, we hold that the affidavit for Harris is insufficient to forecast proof that Mr. Cooke's preparation for and conduct of trial was such that Cooke breached his duty of due care and diligence to Mrs. Rorrer. The closest the Harris affidavit comes to setting forth a standard of care for the handling of a medical malpractice case is the statement that "the standards of practice . . . are high." Although the Harris affidavit does outline several things that Cooke did not do and that presumably Harris would have done had he tried Mrs. Rorrer's case against Dr. Sardi (and tried it with the benefit of hindsight gained by the instant suit), the affidavit nowhere states that Cooke's inaction violated a standard of care required of similarly situated attorneys. Harris's statement that "[i]n my opinion, it is very important in the preparation and trial of a medical malpractice case to have at least one medical witness who enthusiastically and convincingly will support the plaintiff's attorney's medical theory of negligence" is merely an opinion. The affidavit does not state that the standard of care in such cases required Cooke to obtain such a witness. The mere fact that one attorney-witness testifies that he would have acted contrarily to or differently from the action taken by defendant is not sufficient to establish a prima facie case of defendant's negligence. The law is not an exact science but is, rather, a profession which involves the exercise of individual judgment. Differences in opinion are consistent with the exercise of due care. Similarly, Harris's allegations that "[i]n 1978 there were available medical consulting agencies who could have reviewed Mrs. Rorrer's claim objectively and, if meritorious, supported her with testimony in court . . . [and] the . . . physicians at Duke may well have been more inclined to support an alternative medical theory rather than the one advanced by Mr. Cooke" do not aver that the standard of care by which Cooke's conduct is to be measured required him to pursue this line of investigation. All we are left with is a conclusory statement that "it is my opinion that the representation given by Mr. Arthur O. Cooke to Mrs. Mary Carol Rorrer to and through her trial did not comply with the existing standard for the handling of medical malpractice claims in May of 1978 and communities similar to Greensboro, North Carolina." Given that the Harris affidavit was the only item presented to the trial judge on behalf of plaintiff's contention that Cooke breached his duty of care to Mrs. Rorrer in (1) investigating her claim before trial and (2) conducting the trial itself, we hold that plaintiff failed to forecast any evidence that Mr. Cooke in fact breached his duty of reasonable care and diligence in the prosecution of Mrs. Rorrer's suit against Dr. Sardi.

We further hold that plaintiff's affidavits fail to establish material issues of fact with respect to the second prong of the *Hodges* test. . . . There is no evidence of record that Mr. Cooke failed to exercise his best judgment in good faith at every decision point arising in the preparation for and trial of Mrs. Rorrer's suit against Dr. Sardi. Good faith is an objective, not subjective, standard. Defendant's affidavits establish that before making each decision involved in the suit — such as whether to consult additional witnesses or to pursue further cross-examination of a given witness — Cooke was informed of the pertinent legal issues and strategies and made decisions based only on the welfare of his client and her suit. Absent any evidence of a standard of care with which Cooke failed to comply and absent a showing that Cooke failed to exercise his best, informed judgment, he is immune from any allegedly erroneous judgmental decisions made during the preparation and trial of Mrs. Rorrer's lawsuit against Dr. Sardi. As plaintiff has not come forward with any evidence that would support her claim that Cooke's representation of her was negligent, summary judgment was properly entered against her.

Even assuming *arguendo* that she had set forth materials showing the existence of issues of fact with respect to Cooke's alleged negligence, we hold that Mrs. Rorrer's affidavits do not forecast evidence that would show that Cooke's alleged negligence was a proximate cause of the loss of her suit against Sardi.

. . . Generally, the principles and proof of causation in a legal malpractice action do not differ from an ordinary negligence case. To establish that negligence is a proximate cause of the loss suffered, the plaintiff must establish that the loss would not have occurred but for the attorney's conduct. Where the plaintiff bringing suit for legal malpractice has lost another suit allegedly due to his attorney's negligence, to prove that but for the attorney's negligence plaintiff would not have suffered the loss, plaintiff must prove that

(1) The original claim was valid;

(2) It would have resulted in a judgment in his favor; and

(3) The judgment would have been collectible.

We agree with defendant that plaintiff's contention that Mr. Cooke should have done something more than he did in preparation for trial is without meaning or significance absent the establishing of (1) specific evidence that Cooke could have gathered and, under the prevailing standard, should have gathered and presented at trial, and (2) its impact on the outcome of the trial against Dr. Sardi. The materials produced by plaintiff in response to defendant's motion for summary judgment have failed to forecast any evidence showing that had Mr. Cooke done anything differently plaintiff would have been successful in her litigation against Dr. Sardi.

Plaintiff has failed to show: who should or could have been consulted; what any person consulted would have said; whether any person consulted would have supported the pressure theory; whether any other theory or explanation for plaintiff's injury has ever existed; whether any person consulted would have supported any other theory; or whether any person consulted would have been available to testify. We note that Dr. Cole's affidavit filed in opposition to defendant's motion for summary judgment fails to offer any alternative explanation for Mrs. Rorrer's injury. The Harris affidavit is insufficient in the same respect. Plaintiff has failed to show that there was any other or better theory or any additional admissible evidence other than what Mr. Cooke considered and used.

We further note that Harris's conclusory statement that the (alleged) departure from standards of care "contributed greatly to the loss of Mrs.

Rorrer's claim when it was tried" is deficient in several respects. Not only is it not based upon specific facts, but it does not aver that but for Cooke's negligence Mrs. Rorrer would have prevailed in her suit against Dr. Sardi. The affidavit offers no specific facts suggesting how Cooke's alleged departure from the (again unenunciated) standard of care in prosecuting medical malpractice suits could or might have caused a jury to decide against Mrs. Rorrer, or how further preparation and investigation by Cooke would have produced a different result. Therefore, no genuine issue of material fact existed with respect to the issue of whether the loss of Mrs. Rorrer's suit against Dr. Sardi was proximately caused by defendant's negligence.

Summary judgment was properly entered for defendant. The decision of the Court of Appeals is reversed.

NOTES

1. *Variations in Jury Control.* Unlike the plaintiff in *Olde Town, supra,* the plaintiff in *Rorrer* did not have her claim dismissed by way of a preliminary objection or general demurrer. However, she also was deprived of an opportunity to present her legal malpractice claim to a jury. The trial court in *Rorrer* relied on summary judgment, another procedural mechanism to resolve the dispute without a trial. The parties to a civil case are allowed to use the power of the court to discover all of the relevant facts bearing on the parties' claims and defenses. The discovery rules allow a party to obtain testimony under oath (depositions) or answers to written questions (interrogatories). The parties may request documents and inspect premises, if the information they seek may lead to facts relevant to the lawsuit. Thus, neither party should be surprised about relevant facts or legal theories when the case is called for trial.

If the discovery and other evidence properly before the court on the motion shows that there is no genuine dispute regarding the facts of the case, but merely disagreement as to the appropriate law to be applied to the facts, the court should grant a summary judgment to the party favored by the law and the undisputed facts. For a concise discussion of the civil trial process, *see* M. FRANKLIN, THE BIOGRAPHY OF A LEGAL DISPUTE (1968).

When the court rules in favor of one party by way of summary judgment in a civil case, it expresses the view that that party is entitled to judgment on that particular issue without the burden and expense of a trial.

What specific reasons did the *Rorrer* court offer for denying the client the opportunity to present her claim of legal malpractice to the jury? If the affidavits filed in connection with a motion for summary judgment are conflicting on an important fact, how can the judge resolve the issue? Would such a conflict not require him to determine the credibility of the affiants? Can he do so from their affidavits?

2. *Arguing from the Record.* When a party requests a summary judgment, the court must base its decision exclusively upon the evidence in the record. For this reason, if a party has evidence to support or refute the propriety of the court's entry of a summary judgment and that evidence has not been made a part of the court record, he must bring it to the attention of the court by way of discovery or affidavit. In the view of the appellate court, why did the

affidavit of the plaintiff's expert witness fall short of asserting facts that entitled the plaintiff to take her malpractice claim to the jury?

3. *The Professional Standard.* In claims of negligence against professionals such as lawyers, doctors, or architects, the plaintiff must usually present the testimony of an expert from the same profession expressing his opinion that the injury was a result of conduct which fell below the standard of care in the profession. To a large extent, this requirement allows a profession to set its own standard of appropriate conduct and deprives members of the community of their own views as to what is appropriate professional conduct. Do you think this is a good approach in a tort case involving a professional? What reasons underlie the rule? What approaches might meet these concerns without allowing the professions to determine the propriety of their own conduct?

4. *A Medical Maloccurrence.* In *Rorrer,* what were the plaintiff's allegations of negligence in the underlying medical malpractice case? What evidence did plaintiff have? What evidence did defendant have? Should the defendant have sought dismissal for failure to state a claim (general demurrer)? Should either plaintiff or defendant have succeeded with a motion for summary judgment?

5. *A Legal Maloccurrence.* What errors did the plaintiff believe her attorney made in prosecuting the medical malpractice case? What evidence did plaintiff have? What evidence did defendant have?

How satisfied are you with the conduct of plaintiff's legal malpractice claim? Do you have any suggestions for any different approaches that the plaintiff's attorney could have taken? Would you go beyond the making of suggestions, and allege malpractice as to the prosecution of the legal malpractice claim?

6. *Welcome to the Profession. Rorrer* represents a tort claim flowing out of an unsuccessful attempt to prosecute another tort claim. Do you agree that the defendant-attorney in *Rorrer* made a mistake in judgment? Do you think that professionals should pay for such mistakes in judgment, or is this a risk that the client should bear? How do you defend your position in terms of what you perceive to be widely shared values?

How important to you is the public perception of (tort) lawyers? *See* Post, *On the Popular Image of the Lawyer. Reflections in a Dark Glass,* 75 CALIF. L. REV. 379, 386 (1987):

"[Lawyers] are a constant irritating reminder that we are neither a peaceable kingdom of harmony and order, nor a land of undiluted individual autonomy, but somewhere disorientingly in between. Lawyers, in the very exercise of their profession, are the necessary bearers of that bleak winter's tale, and we hate them for it."

PEREZ v. WYETH LABORATORIES INC.,
161 N.J. 1, 734 A.2d 1245 (1999)

O'HERN, J.

Our medical-legal jurisprudence is based on images of health care that no longer exist. At an earlier time, medical advice was received in the doctor's office from a physician who most likely made house calls if needed. The patient usually paid a small sum of money to the doctor. Neighborhood pharmacists compounded prescribed medicines.

Pharmaceutical manufacturers never advertised their products to patients, but rather directed all sales efforts at physicians. In this comforting setting, the law created an exception to the traditional duty of manufacturers to warn consumers directly of risks associated with the product as long as they warned health-care providers of those risks.

For good or ill, that has all changed. Medical services are in large measure provided by managed care organizations. Medicines are purchased in the pharmacy department of supermarkets and often paid for by third-party providers. Drug manufacturers now directly advertise products to consumers on the radio, television, the Internet, billboards on public transportation, and in magazines. . . .

The question in this case, broadly stated, is whether our law should follow these changes in the marketplace or reflect the images of the past. We believe that when mass marketing of prescription drugs seeks to influence a patient's choice of a drug, a pharmaceutical manufacturer that makes direct claims to consumers for the efficacy of its product should not be unqualifiedly relieved of a duty to provide proper warnings of the dangers or side effects of the product.

This appeal concerns Norplant, a Food and Drug Administration (FDA)-approved, reversible contraceptive that prevents pregnancy for up to five years. The Norplant contraceptive employs six thin, flexible, closed capsules that contain a synthetic hormone, levonorgestrel. The capsules are implanted under the skin of a woman's upper arm during an in-office surgical procedure characterized by the manufacturer as minor. A low, continuous dosage of the hormone diffuses through the capsule walls and into the bloodstream. Although the capsules are not usually visible under the skin, the outline of the fan-like pattern can be felt under the skin. Removal occurs during an in-office procedure, similar to the insertion process.

. . . According to plaintiffs, Wyeth began a massive advertising campaign for Norplant in 1991, which it directed at women rather than at their doctors. Wyeth advertised on television and in women's magazines such as Glamour, Mademoiselle and Cosmopolitan. According to plaintiffs, none of the advertisements warned of any inherent danger posed by Norplant; rather, all praised its simplicity and convenience. None warned of side effects including pain and permanent scarring attendant to removal of the implants. Wyeth also sent a letter to physicians advising them that it was about to launch a national advertising program in magazines that the physicians' patients may read.

Plaintiffs cite several studies published in medical journals that have found Norplant removal to be difficult and painful. One study found that thirty-three percent of women had removal difficulty and forty percent experienced pain. Another study found that fifty-two percent of physicians reported complications during removal. Medical journals have catalogued the need for advanced medical technicians in addition to general surgeons for Norplant removal. Plaintiffs assert that none of this information was provided to consumers.

In 1995, plaintiffs began to file lawsuits in several New Jersey counties claiming injuries that resulted from their use of Norplant. Plaintiffs' principal claim alleged that Wyeth, distributors of Norplant in the United States, failed to warn adequately about side effects associated with the contraceptive. Side effects complained of by plaintiffs included weight gain, headaches, dizziness, nausea, diarrhea, acne, vomiting, fatigue, facial hair growth, numbness in the arms and legs, irregular menstruation, hair loss, leg cramps, anxiety and nervousness, vision problems, anemia, mood swings and depression, high blood pressure, and removal complications that resulted in scarring. . . .

After a case management conference, plaintiffs' counsel sought a determination of whether the learned intermediary doctrine applied. . . .

In New Jersey, as elsewhere, we accept the proposition that a pharmaceutical manufacturer generally discharges its duty to warn the ultimate user of prescription drugs by supplying physicians with information about the drug's dangerous propensities. This concept is known as the "learned intermediary" rule because the physician acts as the intermediary between the manufacturer and the consumer. . . .

It is paradoxical that so pedestrian a concern as male-pattern baldness should have signaled the beginning of direct-to-consumer marketing of prescription drugs. Upjohn Company became the first drug manufacturer to advertise directly to consumers when it advertised for Rogaine, a hair-loss treatment. The ad targeted male consumers by posing the question, "Can an emerging bald spot . . . damage your ability to get along with others, influence your chance of obtaining a job or date or even interfere with your job performance?" A related ad featured an attractive woman asserting suggestively, "I know that a man who can afford Rogaine is a man who can afford me."

Advertising for Rogaine was the tip of the iceberg. Since drug manufacturers began marketing directly to consumers for products such as prescription drugs in the 1980s, almost all pharmaceutical companies have engaged in this direct marketing practice.

. . . Among the most controversial of the new marketing techniques employed by pharmaceutical manufacturers is direct-to-consumer prescription advertising in a variety of formats and media. Pharmaceutical remedies for varied problems such as allergies, nail fungus, hypertension, hair loss, and depression are placed directly before the consumer in magazines, television, and via the Internet. The utilization of direct consumer marketing raises questions and issues addressing manufacturer liability for failure to adequately warn of risks possibly associated with pharmaceutical use.

The American Medical Association (AMA) has long maintained a policy in opposition to product-specific prescription ads aimed at consumers. A 1992 study by the Annals of Internal Medicine reports that a peer review of 109 prescription ads found 92 per cent of the advertisements lacking in some manner. . . .

The difficulties that accompany this [type of advertising] practice are manifest. "The marketing gimmick used by the drug manufacturer often provides the consumer with a diluted variation of the risks associated with the drug product." Even without such manipulation, "[t]elevision spots lasting 30 or 60 seconds are not conducive to 'fair balance' [in presentation of risks]."

Given such constraints, pharmaceutical ads often contain warnings of a general nature. However, "[r]esearch indicates that general warnings (for example, see your doctor) in [direct-to-consumer] advertisements do not give the consumer a sufficient understanding of the risks inherent in product use." Consumers often interpret such warnings as a "general reassurance" that their condition can be treated, rather than as a requirement that "specific vigilance" is needed to protect them from product risks.

. . . [T]he New Jersey Products Liability Act provides:

> An adequate product warning or instruction is one that a reasonably prudent person in the same or similar circumstances would have provided with respect to the danger and that communicates adequate information on the dangers and safe use of the product, taking into account the characteristics of, and the ordinary knowledge common to, the persons by whom the product is intended to be used, or in the case of prescription drugs, taking into account the characteristics of, and the ordinary knowledge common to, the prescribing physician. If the warning or instruction given in connection with a drug or device or food or food additive has been approved or prescribed by the federal Food and Drug Administration under the "Federal Food, Drug, and Cosmetic Act," 52 Stat. 1040, 21 U.S.C. § 301 et seq., . . . a rebuttable presumption shall arise that the warning or instruction is adequate. . . .

[N.J.S.A. 2A:58C-4.]

. . . Although the statute provides a physician-based standard for determining the adequacy of the warning due to a physician, the statute does not legislate the boundaries of the doctrine. . . . Rather, the statute governs the content of an "adequate product warning," when required. As noted, direct-to-consumer marketing of prescription drugs was in its beginning stages. . . .

Our dissenting member suggests that we should await legislative action before deciding that issue. . . . We are satisfied that our decision today is well within the competence of the judiciary. Defining the scope of tort liability has traditionally been accepted as the responsibility of the courts. If we decline to resolve the question, we are making the substantive determination that the learned intermediary doctrine applies to the direct marketing of drugs, an issue recently debated but left unanswered by the drafters of the Restatement. Either course, then, requires us to adopt a principle of law. The question is which is the better principle.

A more recent review summarized the theoretical bases for the doctrine as based on four considerations:

> First, courts do not wish to intrude upon the doctor-patient relationship. From this perspective, warnings that contradict information supplied by the physician will undermine the patient's trust in the physician's judgment. Second, physicians may be in a superior position to convey meaningful information to their patients, as they must do to satisfy their duty to secure informed consent. Third, drug manufacturers lack effective means to communicate directly with patients, making it necessary to rely on physicians to convey the relevant

information. Unlike [over the counter products], pharmacists usually dispense prescription drugs from bulk containers rather than as unit-of-use packages in which the manufacturer may have enclosed labeling. Finally, because of the complexity of risk information about prescription drugs, comprehension problems would complicate any effort by manufacturers to translate physician labeling for lay patients.

Lars Noah, Advertising Prescription Drugs to Consumers: Assessing the Regulatory and Liability Issues, 32 GA. L.REV. 141, 157–59 (1997). These premises: (1) reluctance to undermine the doctor patient-relationship; (2) absence in the era of "doctor knows best" of need for the patient's informed consent; (3) inability of drug manufacturer to communicate with patients; and (4) complexity of the subject, are all (with the possible exception of the last) absent in the direct-to-consumer advertising of prescription drugs.

First, with rare and wonderful exceptions, the "'Norman Rockwell' image of the family doctor no longer exists." Informed consent requires a patient-based decision rather than the paternalistic approach of the 1970s.

Second, because managed care has reduced the time allotted per patient, physicians have considerably less time to inform patients of the risks and benefits of a drug.

Third, having spent $1.3 billion on advertising in 1998, drug manufacturers can hardly be said to "lack effective means to communicate directly with patients," Noah, *supra*, 32 GA. L.REV. at 158, when their advertising campaigns can pay off in close to billions in dividends.

Consumer-directed advertising of pharmaceuticals thus belies each of the premises on which the learned intermediary doctrine rests:

> First, the fact that manufacturers are advertising their drugs and devices to consumers suggests that consumers are active participants in their health care decisions, invalidating the concept that it is the doctor, not the patient, who decides whether a drug or device should be used. Second, it is illogical that requiring manufacturers to provide direct warnings to a consumer will undermine the patient-physician relationship, when, by its very nature, consumer-directed advertising encroaches on that relationship by encouraging consumers to ask for advertised products by name. Finally, consumer-directed advertising rebuts the notion that prescription drugs and devices and their potential adverse effects are too complex to be effectively communicated to lay consumers. Because the FDA requires that prescription drug and device advertising carry warnings, the consumer may reasonably presume that the advertiser guarantees the adequacy of its warnings. Thus, the common law duty to warn the ultimate consumer should apply.

Susan A. Casey, Comment, *Laying an Old Doctrine to Rest: Challenging the Wisdom of the Learned Intermediary Doctrine*, 19 WM. MITCHELL L.REV. 931, 956 (1993).

When all of its premises are absent, as when direct warnings to consumers are mandatory, the learned intermediary doctrine, "itself an exception to the manufacturer's traditional duty to warn consumers directly of the risk associated with any product, simply drops out of the calculus, leaving the duty of the manufacturer to be determined in accordance with general principles of tort law." *Edwards v. Basel Pharms.*, 116 F.3d 1341, 1343 (10th Cir.1997) . . . .

Concerns regarding patients' communication with and access to physicians are magnified in the context of medicines and medical devices furnished to women for reproductive decisions. In *MacDonald Ortho Pharmaceutical Corp.*, 394 Mass. 131, 475 N.E.2d 65, cert. denied, 474 U.S. 920, 106 S.Ct. 250, 88 L.Ed.2d 258 (1985), the plaintiff's use of oral contraceptives allegedly resulted in a stroke. The Massachusetts Supreme Court explained several reasons why contraceptives differ from other prescription drugs and thus "warrant the imposition of a common law duty on the manufacturer to warn users directly of associated risks." For example, after the patient receives the prescription, she consults with the physician to receive a prescription annually, leaving her an infrequent opportunity to "explore her questions and concerns about the medication with the prescribing physician." Consequently, the limited participation of the physician leads to a real possibility that their communication during the annual checkup is insufficient. The court also explained that because oral contraceptives are drugs personally selected by the patient, a prescription is often not the result of a physician's skilled balancing of individual benefits and risks but originates, instead, as a product of patient choice. Thus, "the physician is relegated to a . . . passive role."

Patient choice is an increasingly important part of our medical-legal jurisprudence. New Jersey has long since abandoned the "professional standard" in favor of the objectively-prudent-patient rule, recognizing the informed role of the patient in health-care decisions. When a patient is the target of direct marketing, one would think, at a minimum, that the law would require that the patient not be misinformed about the product. It is one thing not to inform a patient about the potential side effects of a product; it is another thing to misinform the patient by deliberately withholding potential side effects while marketing the product as an efficacious solution to a serious health problem. Further, when one considers that many of these "life-style" drugs or elective treatments cause significant side effects without any curative effect, increased consumer protection becomes imperative, because these drugs are, by definition, not medically necessary.

. . . Obviously, the learned intermediary doctrine applies when its predicates are present. "In New Jersey, as elsewhere, we accept the proposition that a pharmaceutical manufacturer generally discharges its duty to warn the ultimate users of prescription drugs by supplying physicians with information about the drug's dangerous propensities." *Niemiera v. Schneider*, 114 N.J. 550, 559 (1989). Had Wyeth done just that, simply supplied the physician with information about the product, and not advertised directly to the patients, plaintiffs would have no claim against Wyeth based on an independent duty to warn patients. The question is whether the absence of an independent duty to warn patients gives the manufacturer the right to misrepresent to the public the product's safety.

In reaching the conclusion that the learned intermediary doctrine does not apply to the direct marketing of drugs to consumers, we must necessarily consider that when prescription drugs are marketed and labeled in accordance with FDA specifications, the pharmaceutical manufacturers should not have to confront "state tort liability premised on theories of design defect or warning inadequacy.". . .

We believe that in the area of direct-to-consumer advertising of pharmaceuticals, the same rebuttable presumption should apply when a manufacturer complies with FDA advertising, labeling and warning requirements. That approach harmonizes the manufacturer's duty to doctors and to the public when it chooses to directly advertise its products, and simultaneously recognizes the public interest in informing patients about new pharmaceutical developments. Moreover, a rebuttable presumption that the duty to consumers is met by compliance with FDA regulations helps to ensure that manufacturers are not made guarantors against remotely possible, but not scientifically-verifiable, side-effects of prescription drugs, a result that could have a "significant anti-utilitarian effect."

We believe that this standard is fair and balanced. For all practical purposes, absent deliberate concealment or nondisclosure of after-acquired knowledge of harmful effects, compliance with FDA standards should be virtually dispositive of such claims. By definition, the advertising will have been "fairly balanced."

. . . On balance, we believe that the patient's interest in reliable information predominates over a policy interest that would insulate manufacturers.

. . . [T]he dramatic shift in pharmaceutical marketing to consumers is based in large part on significant changes in the health-care system from fee-for-service to managed care. Managed care companies negotiate directly with pharmaceutical companies and then inform prescribers which medications are covered by the respective plans. Because managed care has made it more difficult for pharmaceutical companies to communicate with prescribers the manufacturers have developed a different strategy, marketing to consumers. . . .

The direct marketing of drugs to consumers generates a corresponding duty requiring manufacturers to warn of defects in the product. The FDA has established a comprehensive regulatory scheme for direct-to-consumer marketing of pharmaceutical products. Given the presumptive defense that is afforded to pharmaceutical manufacturers that comply with FDA requirements, we believe that it is fair to reinforce the regulatory scheme by allowing, in the case of direct-to-consumer marketing of drugs, patients deprived of reliable medical information to establish that the misinformation was a substantial factor contributing to their use of a defective pharmaceutical product.

[The court notes that because of the procedural posture of the case, Wyeth has not had a chance to offer evidence in defense of Norplant and thus the product may be presently cast in an unfair light.]

Finally, we return briefly to the main theme of the dissent, that our decision is inconsistent with legislative mandate. We are certain that legislative codification of the learned intermediary doctrine—which generally relieves a pharmaceutical manufacturer of an independent duty to warn the ultimate user of prescription drugs, as long as it has supplied the physician with information about a drug's dangerous propensities—does not confer on pharmaceutical manufacturers a license to mislead or deceive consumers when those manufacturers elect to exercise their right to advertise their product directly to such consumers.

The judgment of the Appellate Division is reversed and the matter is remanded to the Law Division for further proceedings.

POLLOCK, J., dissenting.

With disarming understatement, the majority opinion raises profound questions about the purpose of judicial opinions, the role of courts, and the separation of powers. . . .

Judges, although they may disagree with a legislative policy, are bound to respect it. In adapting the common law to society's needs, this Court may not have favored manufacturers, including pharmaceutical companies, as enthusiastically as has the Legislature. The issue, however, is not whether the Court shares the Legislature's enthusiasm or even whether the majority would prefer to amend the common-law learned intermediary doctrine. Because of the enactment of the NJPLA, the issue is whether the majority should respect the learned intermediary doctrine as declared by the Legislature. . . .

NOTES

1. *Judicial and Legislative Roles.* Assume that there was no statute relevant to the issue of whether a drug company could be liable to a consumer for failing to directly warn the consumer about the dangers of its product. Would it be proper for the court to decide the issue in the first instance and create a precedent? Once the precedent has been set, would the court lack the power to change it? If it is proper for a court to create a precedent for liability, is it nevertheless proper for the state legislature to change the rules set by the court for allocating the risks? *Cf. Ives v. South Buffalo Railway Co.*, 201 N.Y. 271, 94 N.E. 431 (1911) (holding that the state legislature violated the due process rights of employers when it enacted a Worker's Compensation statute making employers in certain industries liable for workers injured on the job, regardless of fault); and *New York Central. R. Co. v. White,* 243 U.S. 188 (1917) (declaring that no man has a vested interest in the common law, and holding that it was not a violation of due process for the state to provide for employer liability without fault.) What is the distinction between a court's role and the legislature's role in creating new systems and standards for resolving tort disputes? What limitations exist, or ought to exist, in the American legal system on the power of the state legislature to adopt new approaches to compensating persons who are victims of accidents?

2. *Times Have Changed.* The majority in *Perez* explains the decision to adopt a new rule extending liability to drug companies to consumers, notwithstanding the "learned intermediary" rule, on the basis that methods of practicing medicine and selling prescription drugs have changed dramatically since the learned intermediary rule was adopted. Does the court have the power, and should it exercise the power, to change a tort rule if the legislature has enacted a new law on the same subject in recent years? Is the reasoning of the majority

in *Perez* persuasive on the question of whether the recently enacted New Jersey statute should govern the result in this case? For broad discussion of the impact of modern technologies and business models on tort rules, see Nicolas P. Terry, *Cyber-Malpractice: Legal Exposure for Cybermedicine*, 25 AM. J. LAW & MED. 327–66 (1999); *Structural and Legal Implications of e-Health*, 33(4) J. HEALTH L. 606 (2000).

3. *Value Preferences and Class Conflicts*. While the resolution of a dispute in a tort case immediately affects only the parties to the lawsuit, in the long run the rules adopted and applied will affect other persons with similar disputes and, sometimes, identifiable classes of persons. Decision-makers are influenced not only by the values at stake in the controversy but also by the value they place on the class of people who will benefit from or be hurt by a particular law. What classes are most affected by the controversy in *Perez?*

4. *Strict Liability vs. Negligence*: A dominant controversy in modern tort law has been whether it is just and economically efficient to hold persons responsible for injuries caused as a result of the production and sale of products or the carrying on of other useful activities. The *Perez* court reviews some of the major cases that explore whether the seller of prescription drugs may be held liable to the consumer on the basis of negligence or strict liability. Prescription drugs have been particularly troublesome and challenging to the courts and commentators. The predominant approach views prescription drugs as "unavoidably unsafe" but exceptionally useful products, and for those reasons the seller has not been held subject to strict liability. In contrast, the manufacturers of other injury-producing defective products have been subject to strict liability. The issues are quite complex, however, and will be explored in detail in Chapter 2 (Theories of Liability) and Chapter 15 (An Introduction to Products Liability).

5. *Class, Race and Gender*. America aspires to a system of law that treats all parties the same, regardless of race, class or gender. The ideal is not yet fully realized. If evidence shows that a product such as Norplant has a disproportionately damaging impact on individuals of a particular class, race or gender, should the court or jury consider take class, race, or gender issues into conscious consideration in a tort action brought against the seller of the product? What are the dangers of consciously considering or ignoring such issues? With respect to the Norplant controversy, one author who studied in great detail the marketing of the birth control device observes:

"At a time when legislatures nationwide are slashing social programs for the poor, public aid for Norplant became a popular budget item. Without financial assistance, the cost of Norplant would be prohibitive. The capsules cost $365 and the implantation procedure can run from $150 to $500. Removal costs another $150 to $500, or more if there are complications. The government sprang into action. Every state and the District of Columbia almost immediately made Norplant available to poor women through Medicaid. Tennessee passed a law in 1993 requiring that anyone who receives AFDD or other forms of public assistance be notified in writing about the state's offer of free Norplant. Women in Washington State who receive maternity care assistance also get information about Norplant.

"By 1994, states had already spent $34 million on Norplant-related benefits. As a result, at least half of the women in the United State who have used Norplant are Medicaid recipients." DOROTHY ROBERTS, KILLING THE BLACK BODY 108 (1997).

Professor Roberts sees a link between the actions of the states and race:

> Although we should not underestimate this class dimension of programs that regulate welfare mothers, it is crucial to see that race equally determines the programs' features and popularity. Because class distinctions are racialized, race and class are inextricably linked in the development of welfare policy. When Americans debate welfare reform, most have single Black mothers in mind.

Id. 110.

Is it relevant that only women use the product? For an introduction to feminist legal theory and methodology, *see* Katharine Bartlett, *Cracking Foundations as Feminist Method*, 8 AM. U. J. GENDER SOC. POL'Y & L. 31 (1999); Lorena Fries and Veronica Matus, *Why Does the Method Matter?* 7 AM. U.J. GENDER SOC. POL'Y & L. 291 (1999). For a discussion of gender issues in the specific context of tort law, *see* Leslie Bender, *A Primer on Feminist Tort Theory*, 36 J. LEG. ED. 3 (1998); D. WEISBERG, FEMINIST LEGAL THEORY (1993).

Would it be relevant if most of the women using the product were poor and women of color? In recent years some scholars have argued that assessing issues from a feminist perspective must be refined in some contexts to acknowledge differences in the experiences of women due to race and class. One author observes:

> The notion that there is a monolithic "women's experience" that can be descried independent of other facets of experience like race, class, and sexual orientation I refer to in this essay as "gender essentialism.". . . The result of essentialism is to reduce the lives of people who experience multiple forms of oppression to addition problems: "racism + sexism = straight black women's experience," or "racism + sexism + homophobia = black lesbian experience." Thus, in an essentialist world, black women's experience will always be forcibly fragmented before being subjected to analysis, as those who are "only interested in race" and those who are "only interested in gender" take their separate slices of our lives.

Angela P. Harris, *Race and Essentialism in Feminist Legal Theory*, 42 STAN. L. REV. 581 (1990) [reprinted in CRITICAL RACE THEORY: THE CUTTING EDGE 255 (Delgado ed.1995)].

Should attorneys representing the plaintiffs attempt to marshal that type of evidence and bring it to the court's attention? For different perspectives on these questions, *see* Martha Chamallas, *Questioning the Use of Race-Specific and Gender Specific Economic Data in Tort Litigation: A Constitutional Argument*, 63 FORDHAM L. REV. 73 (1994); Frank McClellan, *The Dark Side of Tort Reform: Searching for Racial Justice*, 48 RUTGERS L. REV. 761 (1996); Jody D. Armour, *Negrophobia and Reasonable Racism* (1997). For an in-depth exploration of the ramifications of addressing or ignoring race and gender issues in the development and application of the law, *see* generally J. PEREA, R, DELGADO, A. HARRIS AND S. WILDMAN, RACE AND RACES (2000). For articles exploring the relevance of race, gender and culture to the teaching of torts, *see* Taunya L. Banks, *Teaching Laws With Flaws: Adopting a Pluralist Approach to Torts,* 57 MO. L. REV. 443 (1992); Lucinda M. Finley, *A Break in the Silence: Including Women's Issues in a Torts Course*, 1 YALE J. L. & FEMINISM 41 (1992).

6. *Goals.* What values or goals dominate the *Perez* court's holding that the manufacturer of a prescription drug who directly advertises to consumers is subject to tort liability for failure to warn the consumer? Do you agree that these values ought to be given priority over other competing values that you can identify? When important community values such as these are in conflict, should a judge, jury or legislature decide which values should have priority?

PROBLEM

Southern Anystate School of Law (SAS) is a private law school located in downtown Anytown. The neighborhood surrounding the school includes restaurants, bars and small retail establishments. Few are open late at night. The law school leases space in several nearby parking garages that it then resells to its students. However, most students avoid the high-priced garages and park on the street closer to the law school. One night in the middle of the semester following a late night law review meeting Billy "Mad Dog" Elliott left the law school to walk to his car parked on the street six blocks from the law school. Half a block from the school an unknown assailant hit Billy over the head before stealing his notebook computer that contained all his class notes. Mad Dog sued the law school alleging that they knew that criminal activity had occurred in the immediate area, yet had failed to warn Billy of the dangerous conditions, provide adequate security forces or lighting or otherwise safeguard law school students from criminal acts. Billy's complaint also alleged that SAS had been heavily criticized for poor security during a recent accreditation process conducted by the American Bar Association (ABA) and that the law school Dean had sent a letter to the ABA agreeing to correct these problems immediately.

Who should be responsible for Billy's injuries? Does it matter whether or not the criminal assailant is captured? Why should anyone but Billy or the assailant be responsible? Given that the attack was by a criminal and happened on property near the law school that was contractually providing legal education to Billy, why would Billy bring an action in tort?

NOVA SOUTHEASTERN UNIVERSITY, INC. v. GROSS
760 So. 2d 86 (Fla. 2000)

QUINCE, J.

We have for review a decision on the following question certified by the Fourth District Court of Appeal in *Gross v. Family Services Agency, Inc.*, 716 So.2d 337 (Fla. 4th DCA 1998), to be of great public importance:

C. LAW AND FACTS

WHETHER A UNIVERSITY MAY BE FOUND LIABLE IN TORT WHERE IT ASSIGNS A STUDENT TO AN INTERNSHIP SITE WHICH IT KNOWS TO BE UNREASONABLY DANGEROUS BUT GIVES NO WARNING, OR INADEQUATE WARNING, TO THE STUDENT, AND THE STUDENT IS SUBSEQUENTLY INJURED WHILE PARTICIPATING IN THE INTERNSHIP?

. . . Bethany Jill Gross, a twenty-three year old graduate student attending Nova Southeastern University, was criminally assaulted while leaving an off-campus internship site. Gross filed a negligence action against Nova based on Nova's alleged negligence in assigning her to perform an internship at a facility which Nova knew was unreasonably dangerous and presented an unreasonable risk of harm. The trial court granted summary judgment for Nova, finding that there was no duty. . . .

The facts, as alleged in the sworn affidavits and other record evidence, and presented in the light most favorable to [Gross], the non-moving party, are briefly summarized as follows. [Gross] moved to Fort Lauderdale from North Carolina to study at Nova Southeastern University in the doctorate psychology program. As part of the curriculum, she was required to complete an eleven-month internship, called a "practicum." Nova provides each student with a listing of the approved practicum sites, complete with a description of the type of experience offered at each site. Each student selects six internships from the list and is placed, by Nova, at one of the selected sites. [Gross] submitted her six selections and was assigned, by Nova, to Family Services Agency, Inc. ("FSA").

FSA is located about fifteen minutes away from Nova. One evening, when leaving FSA, [Gross] was accosted by a man in the parking lot. She had just started her car when he tapped on her window with a gun. Pointing the weapon at her head, the assailant had [Gross] roll down the window. [She] was subsequently abducted from the parking lot, robbed and sexually assaulted. There was evidence that, prior to [Gross's] attack, Nova had been made aware of a number of other criminal incidents which had occurred at or near the FSA parking lot.[1]

The Fourth District reversed the trial court's summary judgment in favor of Nova, stating:

This case involves an adult student injured during an off-campus, but school related, activity, i.e., a university-mandated internship program at a site specifically approved and suggested by the university. The relationship between Nova and Gross can be characterized in various ways, but it is essentially the relationship between an adult who pays a fee for services, the student, and the provider of those services, the private university. The service rendered is the provision of an educational experience designed to lead to a college degree. A student can certainly be said to be within the foreseeable zone of known risks engendered by the university when assigning such student to one of its mandatory and approved internship programs. We need not go so far as to impose a general duty of supervision, as is common in the school-minor student context, to find that Nova had a duty, in this limited context, to use

---

[1] Gross settled her claim against Family Services Agency, Inc. for $900,000.

ordinary care in providing educational services and programs to one of its adult students. The "special relationship" analysis is necessary in this case only because the injury was caused by the allegedly "foreseeable" acts of a third party.

Nova seeks discretionary review based on the question certified by the district court, and Gross seeks review of a portion of the district court's opinion which she interprets to mean that Nova's sole duty to her was a duty to warn. Nova argues the certified question should be answered in the negative. In addition Nova opines the trial court's summary judgment was proper for three reasons: (1) Nova did not owe Gross any duty because she was an adult and Nova did not have control over her actions; (2) Nova did not owe Gross a duty to warn her of the dangers because Gross had equivalent or superior knowledge of the dangers; and (3) even if Nova owed Gross a duty to warn her of the dangers associated with the parking lot at Family Services Agency, Inc. (FSA), the failure to warn did not cause her injury because FSA had already warned her. In her cross-petition, Gross argues the Fourth District defined the duty owed by Nova too narrowly. She opines the Fourth District's opinion may be narrowly interpreted as only requiring Nova to warn students, but that the proper duty owed by a university in this situation is a duty to protect or to make students safe from foreseeable, unreasonable dangers.

Nova argues it did not owe Gross a duty because she was an adult student, and therefore not within the ambit of a special relationship between a school and a minor student. The special relationship doctrine creates a duty between parties, which would not exist but for their relationship. Nova points out that in *Rupp v. Bryant*, 417 So.2d 658 (Fla.1982), the Court stated:

"The genesis of this supervisory duty is based on the school employee standing partially in place of the student's parents. Mandatory schooling has forced parents into relying on teachers to protect children during school activity. But our problem is complicated by the fact that the injury did not occur during the school day or on school premises. As such, we must define the scope of the school's and employee's duty to supervise."

Thus, Nova argues it is inappropriate for the Fourth District to find there is a special relationship between a university, where attendance is not mandatory, and an adult student because the university is not standing *in loco parentis* to an adult student. While the Fourth District discussed the special relationship doctrine, the court did not base Nova's duty to Gross on the type of relationship that exists between a minor child and public school officials.

Although Nova is correct that the school-minor student special relationship evolved from the *in loco parentis* doctrine, the district court recognized that any duty owed by Nova to Gross was not the same duty a school and its employees owe to a minor student. The district court further recognized a different relationship existed between the university and its adult students, a relationship which does not necessarily preclude the university from owing a duty to students assigned to mandatory and approved internship programs. In *Rupp*, we said the extent of the duty a school owes to its students should be limited by the amount of control the school has over the student's conduct. Here, the practicums were a mandatory part of the curriculum that the students were required to complete in order to graduate. Nova also had the final say in assigning students to the locations where they were to do their practicums.

As Nova had control over the students' conduct by requiring them to do the practicum and by assigning them to a specific location, it also assumed the . . . correlative duty of acting reasonably in making those assignments. In a case such as this one, where the university had knowledge that the internship location was unreasonably dangerous, it should be up to the jury to determine whether the university acted reasonably in assigning students to do internships at that location.

Moreover, the Fourth District's analysis is supported by fundamental principles of tort law. In *Union Park Memorial Chapel v. Hutt*, 670 So.2d 64, 66–67 (Fla.1996), we stated:

"It is clearly established that one who undertakes to act, even when under no obligation to do so, thereby becomes obligated to act with reasonable care." See *Slemp v. City of North Miami*, 545 So.2d 256 (Fla.1989) (holding that even if city had no general duty to protect property owners from flooding due to natural causes, once city has undertaken to provide such protection, it assumes the responsibility to do so with reasonable care); *Banfield v. Addington*, 104 Fla. 661, 667, 140 So. 893, 896 (1932) (holding that one who undertakes to act is under an implied legal duty to act with reasonable care to ensure that the person or property of others will not be injured as a result of the undertaking); *Kowkabany v. Home Depot, Inc.*, 606 So.2d 716, 721 (Fla. 1st DCA 1992) (holding that by undertaking to safely load landscaping timbers into vehicle, defendant owed duty of reasonable care to bicyclist who was struck by timbers protruding from vehicle window); *Garrison Retirement Home v. Hancock*, 484 So.2d 1257, 1262 (Fla. 4th DCA 1985) (holding that retirement home that assumed and undertook care and supervision of retirement home resident owed duty to third party to exercise reasonable care in supervision of resident's activities). As this Court recognized over sixty years ago in *Banfield v. Addington*, "[i]n every situation where a man undertakes to act. . . he is under an implied legal obligation or duty to act with reasonable care, to the end that the person or property of others may not be injured." See also *Pate v. Threlkel*, 661 So.2d 278, 280 (Fla.1995) ("A duty is thus established when the acts of a defendant in a particular case create a foreseeable zone of risk."). We find this fundamental principle of tort law is equally applicable in this case. There is no reason why a university may act without regard to the consequences of its actions while every other legal entity is charged with acting as a reasonably prudent person would in like or similar circumstances.

Nova also argues it did not owe Gross a duty because she knew FSA was in a dangerous location, and Nova's knowledge of the dangerous location was not superior to Gross's knowledge. While this is a correct statement of the law with regard to negligence actions based upon premises liability, this is not a premises liability case. Gross is suing Nova under a common law negligence theory based upon Nova assigning her to do her mandatory practicum at an unreasonably dangerous location. Issues of Gross's knowledge should be considered when determining the issues of breach of duty and proximate cause of her injury and in attributing proportional fault. However, it does not eliminate the university's duty to use reasonable care in assigning students to practicum locations.

Lastly, Nova argues even if it had a duty to warn Gross, the failure to warn her did not cause her injury. This argument is one that this Court need not reach but is better left to the trier of fact. In this case, the motion for summary judgment was based solely upon Nova's lack of duty. Therefore, this Court will not consider whether Nova's failure to warn Gross caused her injuries.

Gross cross-petitions for review claiming the Fourth District's emphasis on Nova's failure to warn implies Nova only had a duty to warn. We do not read the Fourth District's opinion so narrowly. The court stated, "We need not go so far as to impose a general duty of supervision, as is common in the school-minor student context, to find that Nova had a duty, in this limited context, to use ordinary care in providing educational services and programs to one of its adult students." *Gross*, 716 So.2d at 339. We read this statement broadly as an indication that the duty, one of ordinary care under the circumstances, could include but is not necessarily limited to warning of the known dangers at this particular practicum site.

We do not make any specific findings as to what duty Nova owed Gross, other than to hold a jury should determine whether Nova acted reasonably in light of all of the circumstances surrounding the case. As the court said in *Silvers v. Associated Technical Institute, Inc.*, No. 93-4253, 1994 WL 879600 at 3 (Mass.Super.Ct. Oct. 12, 1994), "students . . . could reasonably expect that the school's placement office would make some effort to avoid placing [students] with an employer likely to harm them." This is the type of duty owed under the circumstances of this case.

Accordingly, we answer the certified question in the affirmative and approve the decision of the Fourth District.

NOTES

1. *Reconciling and Distinguishing Cases.* The persistent challenge of the common law to lawyers and courts is to reconcile or distinguish precedent. Are the decisions in *Glick* and *Nova* in harmony or in conflict?

2. *The Goal of Accident Cost Avoidance.* In a book that has had considerable influence on the trends of modern tort law, Guido Calabresi described the goals of tort law as including deterrence, cost spreading, and justice. G. CALABRESI, THE COSTS OF ACCIDENTS. A LEGAL AND ECONOMIC ANALYSIS (1970). He explores in depth the meaning and application of each of these goals except "justice." While acknowledging that justice is an important goal, he doubts whether one can say much about it independent of the other goals, except to acknowledge that it exists as an ultimate goal. Can you provide a definition of justice that does not refer to the other goals? Employing Calabresi's listing of goals, which goal should dominate the resolution of the controversy in *Perez*, and why? Is it possible to adopt an approach that would promote all of these goals in this fact situation?

3. *A General No-Fault System?* Today no-fault workers' compensation laws are widely applied and upheld. A number of states have extended no-fault

first-party insurance coverage to automobile accidents. Some persons contend that a no-fault compensation scheme should be adopted to cover virtually all accidents, as has been done in New Zealand. Do you agree?

4. *Overview.* For a good review of the basic elements of tort law and the public policies supporting that law, *see* Frank L. Maraist, *Of Envelopes and Legends: Reflections on Tort Law*, 61 La. L. REV 153 (2000).

Chapter 2
THEORIES OF LIABILITY

A. INTRODUCTION

In *Brown v. Kendall*, 60 Mass. 292, 295–96 (1850), Chief Justice Shaw ushered in the pre-modern era of tort law when he stated that "the plaintiff must come prepared with evidence to show either that the *intention* was unlawful, or that the defendant was *in fault*." Such a comment invites at least three questions pertaining to modern tort law. First, what is the relationship between intent (discussed in Chapters 3 and 4) and fault-based torts (discussion beginning in Chapter 5)? Second are there "degrees" of intent? Of fault? Third, how accurate a statement is it today that a plaintiff must always show "fault" to recover from a defendant engaged in conduct that, in general, is socially desirable, or are there fact patterns that attract strict or absolute liability? Such questions will recur, in varying formulations, throughout this book; this chapter provides an overview of some structures and approaches utilized in answering them.

B. INTENTIONAL OR ANTI-SOCIAL CONDUCT

LUCCHESI v. STIMMELL
149 Ariz. 76, 716 P.2d 1013 (1986)

HAYS, JUSTICE.

On November 22, 1979 (Thanksgiving Day), Mrs. Lucchesi went into premature labor with her first child. Upon arriving at Desert Samaritan Hospital, Mrs. Lucchesi was examined by her obstetrician, Dr. Shill. As a result of that examination, Dr. Shill determined that Mrs. Lucchesi's cervix was well dilated with bulging membranes.

Around 5:00 that morning, Dr. Shill spoke by telephone to Dr. Frederic N. Stimmell. Dr. Stimmell was the physician on call for the Arizona Perinatal [high risk birth] Project at Good Samaritan Hospital. During this conversation, Dr. Shill described Mrs. Lucchesi's condition and informedCed Dr. Stimmell that delivery was inevitable. The doctors discussed the fact that there was a fetal heartbeat and that the fetus' chance of survival, even though minimal, would be increased by transporting Mrs. Lucchesi to the perinatal program at Good Samaritan Hospital. It was also agreed that this plan would be better for the mother, psychologically, because it would reassure her that everything possible was being done. Dr. Stimmell advised Dr. Shill that, as the physician on call for the Arizona Perinatal Project, it would be his responsibility to assume Mrs. Lucchesi's care. Subsequent to this conversation, Dr. Shill informed Mrs. Lucchesi that Dr. Stimmell would be waiting for her at Good Samaritan Hospital and that his experience and expertise in this area were important.

Dr. Scott Partridge, a first-year intern, examined Mrs. Lucchesi shortly after she arrived at Good Samaritan Hospital. He found that she was completely dilated, fully effaced, had an abnormal presentation, and was contracting very actively. Following this examination, Dr. Partridge called Dr. Stimmell to report what he had found, including the abnormal presentation — which Dr. Partridge believed to be a breech or transverse presentation. Upon being told that delivery was likely inevitable, Dr. Stimmell instructed Dr. Partridge and Dr. Mac Whitford, a third-year resident, to rupture the membranes and deliver the infant.

The Lucchesis' baby was delivered stillborn at approximately 6:25 a.m. Upon beginning delivery, it was determined that the infant was in a "double-footing" breech position — a presentation which involves a much greater hazard to the fetus than other breech positions. Neither Dr. Partridge nor Dr. Whitford had delivered a child under such circumstances. During the delivery itself, the child was decapitated — apparently due to tugging on the child's hip area after the mother's cervix had contracted. The child's head was extracted shortly thereafter.

Following the delivery, the fetal remains were examined by the Pathology Department at Good Samaritan Hospital and found to have had a gestational age of 21–22 weeks. A neonatologist who received the hospital and pathology reports was of the opinion that the fetus was pre-viable and had no possibility of surviving even a normal delivery.

Dr. Stimmell arrived at Good Samaritan Hospital between 8:00 and 9:00 that morning. He talked with Mrs. Lucchesi, stating that the delivery had been traumatic, but he did not reveal that the baby had been decapitated. He again talked with Mrs. Lucchesi during her hospitalization, but did not mention the decapitation on that occasion either.

Several months later, Mrs. Lucchesi tried to discover the reason she had not received a Rhogam injection after the delivery. Following repeated requests, her hospital records were sent to Dr. Shill. It was Dr. Shill who then informed the Lucchesis of the full circumstances surrounding the birth of their baby.

It is the Lucchesis' position that Dr. Stimmell's failure to attend the delivery, and his decision not to inform the Lucchesis of the full details surrounding their child's birth, created a factual issue as to whether the conduct was so extreme and outrageous as to support a claim for intentional or reckless infliction of emotional distress. We agree.

. . . In the present case, a practicing obstetrician, Dr. Shill, determined that Mrs. Lucchesi's premature delivery constituted a particularly complex medical situation requiring the expertise of a specialist. Dr. Stimmell, a specialist in high-risk deliveries, agreed that if there was any hope of saving the baby, the mother must be transported to a hospital where special facilities were available. The specialist further agreed that transporting the mother would benefit her psychologically by alleviating some of the stress and emotional upset the situation was causing her. Then, after stating that he would assume responsibility for the mother's care, Dr. Stimmell made no effort to meet the mother at the hospital. Instead, Mrs. Lucchesi was left to be attended during a traumatic delivery by a first-year intern and a third-year resident — neither of whom had any experience with the type of breech delivery taking place (and who, presumably, had less experience than the obstetrician who originally indicated that the situation was too complex for his medical skills). The delivery was finally accomplished when the resident, tugging on the baby in an effort to extricate it from the birth canal, decapitated the child.

In explaining his decision not to leave home and await Mrs. Lucchesi's arrival at Good Samaritan Hospital, Dr. Stimmell testified at his deposition that it was normal practice for obstetricians to wait at home until the labor and delivery room staff called regarding the patient's condition. He further testified that had he left for Good Samaritan Hospital when he first learned of the urgency of Mrs. Lucchesi's condition from Dr. Shill, it would have taken only 25 minutes to leave his house, arrive at the hospital, scrub and prepare for delivery. We therefore believe that given the facts of this case, reasonable minds could differ as to whether Dr. Stimmell's decision to follow the "normal practice" in this case constituted an extreme and outrageous course of conduct.

. . . After carefully reviewing the record in this case, we believe the evidence concerning Dr. Stimmell's conduct before, during and after the birth of the Lucchesis' child created a factual issue so that a jury should have had an opportunity to decide whether defendant's conduct was outrageous and whether plaintiff suffered severe emotional distress. We are not declaring, as a matter of fact or law, that the circumstances in this case are to be equated with a tort of outrage. Rather, we merely hold that the conduct in this matter provided a jury question. . . . Accordingly, we find the trial court erred in granting summary judgment.

NOTES

1. *A Scale of "Wrongness" — Intent, Recklessness and Negligence.* Is it possible to establish a continuum of bad, wrongful or "tortious" behavior? If so, where would you place the defendant's conduct in *Lucchesi*? What criteria did you apply in making your decision? What was outrageous in *Lucchesi*, the result of the surgical procedure or the conduct of the defendant? *Compare Ross v. Patterson*, 817 S.W.2d 418 (Ark. 1991) (physician absence from a delivery due to treatment for alcohol and drug abuse did not constitute outrage).

2. *Function over Form (1) — Sending Messages.* In making their decisions as to the categorization of the "wrongness" displayed in *Lucchesi* and the cases that follow, do you think that the judges follow any particular agenda? Take the facts in *Lucchesi*. If a judge categorizes the defendant-physician's conduct as negligent, rather than intentional, what message is she sending to medical professionals or to their patients?

PROBLEM

The Caterham Classic is a regional tennis competition held every April in Caterham County. It attracts almost exclusively local amateur players, together with a few club "professionals" from around the region. By winning combinations of "round-robin" and single-elimination matches players can qualify for prizes such as rackets, tennis clothing and a few small cash amounts.

This year's final is well attended; the knowledgeable tennis crowd numbered several hundred. The final match is played between Caterham professional John Tantrum and Billy Speed, a relative newcomer to competitive tennis who was playing in his first final. During the first set tiebreaker Speed disputes a baseline call. Enraged, Tantrum hits a ball hard into the playing surface. Unexpectedly the ball hits the side of the umpire's chair and ricochets into the crowd where it hits Max Spectator in the eye. The umpire delays the game while paramedics treat Max and Tantrum is assessed a penalty point. When play resumes Tantrum leaps high for a lob and smashes the ball into the court. It bounces and then hits the umpire. Surprised, Tantrum loosens the grip on his racket, which flies over the net, hitting Speed. How should the court proceed in allocating the risks among the various parties?

JAWORSKI v. KIERNAN
241 Conn. 399, 696 A.2d 332 (1997)

CALLAHAN, C. J.

. . . The South Windsor recreation department sponsors an outdoor adult coed soccer league. On May 16, 1993, during a game, the defendant made contact with the plaintiff while she was shielding the soccer ball from the opposition so that the goalie on her team could retrieve the ball. As a result of this incident, the plaintiff suffered an injury to her left anterior cruciate ligament, which caused a 15 percent permanent partial disability of her left knee.

The plaintiff brought this action against the defendant in two counts. In the first count, she alleged that the defendant failed to exercise due care and that his conduct was negligent and careless in that he "hit" and "tripped" her from behind and that he challenged a female player, both in violation of league rules.[1] The plaintiff further alleged that the defendant's negligent conduct caused her injury. In the second count, the plaintiff alleged that the defendant's conduct was wanton and reckless, citing the same violations of league rules, and claiming that his conduct caused identical harm. The defendant moved to strike the plaintiff's negligence count, claiming that a participant in an athletic contest is, as a matter of law, not liable to a coparticipant for injuries sustained as a result of simple negligence during the playing of the game. The defendant's motion was denied. The defendant then filed a special defense to the plaintiff's action, alleging that the plaintiff's own conduct was negligent, and that the plaintiff's negligence exceeded his alleged negligence. The jury returned a verdict for the plaintiff on the first count of her complaint, the negligence count, and found no comparative negligence attributable to the plaintiff. The jury found for the defendant on the second count of the plaintiff's complaint wherein she had alleged reckless conduct. The jury awarded the

---

[1] One rule in effect for league games was the "challenge rule," which provides: "No male player may challenge a female player, however, he may 'post up' if more than six feet away at the time of possession. In the event of an infraction, the female player will be awarded a direct free kick (the exception is [the] goalie in the penalty area).

"Any male player who is called for challenging a female player twice during the course of a game may be charged with unsportsmanlike conduct (at discretion of referee) and awarded a yellow card." South Windsor Recreation Dept., Adult Coed Soccer Program Rules and Regs. (1992).

plaintiff damages in the amount of $ 20,910.33, the exact amount of her medical bills.

. . .The defendant moved to set aside the verdict and for judgment notwithstanding the verdict as to the negligence count, claiming, again, that an "action for personal injuries sustained in an athletic competition must be predicated on recklessness and not mere negligence."

. . .The plaintiff, in support of the trial court's conclusion that negligence is the proper standard of care to apply to team athletic competition, argues that the theory of negligence is flexible enough to fix a person's standard of care for any set of circumstances. In addition, the plaintiff cites *Walsh* v. *Machlin*, 128 Conn. 412, 23 A.2d 156 (1941), wherein the plaintiff was injured when struck by a golf ball, for the proposition that we have already determined that negligence is the appropriate standard to apply to conduct that occurs during an athletic contest. In particular, the plaintiff points to our statement in *Walsh* that "it is undisputed that the duty to the plaintiff which rested upon the defendant while playing this game was the usual one of reasonable care under the circumstances." Id., 414. . . .

The defendant, on the other hand, summarizes cases from foreign jurisdictions, the vast majority of which has adopted an intentional or reckless conduct standard of care for athletic contests. He also presents two public policy arguments, which he contends support that conclusion: (1) promoting vigorous competition and participation; and (2) avoiding a flood of litigation. . . .

Having concluded that the plaintiff's injury was a foreseeable consequence of the defendant's actions, we need to determine as a matter of policy the extent of the legal duty to be imposed upon the defendant. In order to determine the extent of the defendant's responsibility, we consider: (1) the normal expectations of participants in the sport in which the plaintiff and the defendant were engaged; (2) the public policy of encouraging continued vigorous participation in recreational sporting activities while weighing the safety of the participants; (3) the avoidance of increased litigation; and (4) the decisions of other jurisdictions. . . .

In athletic competitions, the object obviously is to win. In games, particularly those played by teams and involving some degree of physical contact, it is reasonable to assume that the competitive spirit of the participants will result in some rules violations and injuries. That is why there are penalty boxes, foul shots, free kicks, and yellow cards. Indeed, the specific rules applicable to *this game* demonstrate that rules violations were expected in the normal course of the game. Some injuries may result from such violations, but such violations are nonetheless an accepted part of any competition. Simply put, when competitive sports are played, we expect that a participant's main objective is to be a winner, and we expect that the players will pursue that objective enthusiastically. We also anticipate that players in their enthusiasm will commit inadvertent rules violations from which injuries may result. The normal expectations of participants in contact team sports include the potential for injuries resulting from conduct that violates the rules of the sport. These expectations, in turn, inform the question of the extent of the duty owed by one participant to another. We conclude that the normal expectations of participants in contact team sports counsel the adoption of a reckless or intentional conduct duty of care standard for those participants.

A proper balance of the relevant public policy considerations surrounding sports injuries arising from team contact sports also supports limiting the defendant's responsibility for injuries to other participants to injuries resulting from reckless or intentional conduct. The Appellate Court of Illinois, in *Nabozny* v. *Barnhill*, 31 Ill. App. 3d 212, 334 N.E.2d 258 (1975), was the first appellate court, of which we are aware, to address the issue that is before us today. In *Nabozny*, the court described the tension between two relevant public policy considerations as follows: "This court believes that the law should not place unreasonable burdens on the free and vigorous participation in sports by our youth. However, we also believe that organized, athletic competition does not exist in a vacuum. Rather, some of the restraints of civilization must accompany every athlete on to the playing field." Id., 215. The court thereafter concluded that a player was liable only for deliberate, willful or reckless conduct.

We too appreciate the tension between promoting vigorous athletic competition on the one hand and protecting those who participate on the other. As have most jurisdictions, we conclude that this balance is best achieved by allowing a participant in an athletic contest to maintain an action against a coparticipant only for reckless or intentional conduct and not for merely negligent conduct. We believe that participants in recreational sports will not alter their enthusiasm for competition or their participation in recreational activities for fear of liability for injuring someone because of their reckless or intentional conduct. We are convinced, however, that liability for simple negligence would have an opposite effect. We also are convinced that a recklessness standard will sufficiently protect participants in athletic contests by affording them a right of action against those who cause injuries not inherent in the particular game in which the participants are engaged. In other words, we believe that the reckless or intentional conduct standard of care will maintain civility and relative safety in team sports without dampening the competitive spirit of the participants.

A final public policy concern that influences our decision is our desire to stem the possible flood of litigation that might result from adopting simple negligence as the standard of care to be utilized in athletic contests. If simple negligence were adopted as the standard of care, every punter with whom contact is made, every midfielder high sticked, every basketball player fouled, every batter struck by a pitch, and every hockey player tripped would have the ingredients for a lawsuit if injury resulted. When the number of athletic events taking place in Connecticut over the course of a year is considered, there exists the potential for a surfeit of lawsuits when it becomes known that simple negligence, based on an inadvertent violation of a contest rule, will suffice as a ground for recovery for an athletic injury. This should not be encouraged.

The majority of jurisdictions addressing this issue have chosen to adopt either a reckless or an intentional conduct standard of care when determining liability for injuries that occur during an athletic contest. *Nabozny* v. *Barnhill*, supra, 31 Ill. App. 3d 212, also involved an injury received during a soccer game. The plaintiff was a goalie on one team and had fielded the ball within the penalty area surrounding his goal. The ball had been passed to the plaintiff by a teammate who was closely pursued by the defendant, an opponent. The defendant did not turn away after the plaintiff had fielded the ball, but continued to run toward him and subsequently kicked the plaintiff, causing injury. The court concluded that "a player is liable for injury in a tort action if his conduct is such that it is either deliberate, wilful or with a reckless disregard for the safety of the other player so as to cause injury to that player, the same being a question of fact to be decided by a jury." Id., 215.

In *Crawn* v. *Campo*, 136 N.J. 494, 496, 643 A.2d 600 (1994), the "plaintiff was playing catcher in a pickup softball game and was injured when [the] defendant, attempting to score from second base, either slid or ran into him at home plate." In rejecting the negligence standard, the court concluded: "One might well conclude that something is terribly wrong with a society in which the most commonly-accepted aspects of play — a traditional source of a community's conviviality and cohesion — spurs litigation. The heightened recklessness standard recognizes a commonsense distinction between excessively harmful conduct and the more routine rough-and-tumble of sports that should occur freely on the playing fields and should not be second-guessed in courtrooms." Id., 508.

Finally, we address the plaintiff's contention that in *Walsh* v. *Machlin*, supra, 128 Conn. 412, we imposed the negligence standard as the appropriate standard to be used for injuries occurring during athletic contests. *Walsh* is, however, distinguishable.

In *Walsh*, both the plaintiff's and the defendant's golf balls were roughly one hundred feet from the green. "Standing by the defendant's ball, the plaintiff and [the] defendant discussed the club the defendant should use and the defendant selected his mashie niblick.² The plaintiff, seeing the defendant about to prepare to take his shot, said, 'Now put it on the green,' and walked away at almost right angles to the direct and intended line of flight from the ball to the green. Without calling 'Fore,' the defendant swung at his ball, shanked it so that it was deflected at almost a ninety degree angle to the right and hit the plaintiff in the eye as he turned to look back over his left shoulder just as he had reached his ball, causing him serious injury." Id., 413.

Our conclusion herein does not conflict with *Walsh* because, initially, we decide the standard to be applied to only those injuries occurring during team athletic contests involving contact as part of the game. Golf, generally, is neither a team sport in the true sense nor a sport where contact with other participants is a part of the game. Further, the normal expectations of participants in a golf match are far different from those inherent in soccer, and therefore a different standard of care may be appropriate. We, therefore, leave the question of what standard of care might be applicable in other factual circumstances for another day.

Applying the foregoing considerations to the facts before us, we conclude that, as a matter of policy, it is appropriate to adopt a standard of care

---

² Mashie niblick: "An iron golf club with a loft between those of a mashie and a niblick — called also number six iron." Webster's Third New International Dictionary.

imposing on the defendant, a participant in a team contact sport, a legal duty to refrain from reckless or intentional conduct. Proof of mere negligence is insufficient to create liability.

The judgment is reversed in part and the case is remanded with direction to strike the first count of the plaintiff's complaint.

NOTES

1. *Doctrinal Options.* What would be the implications of the various doctrinal options for deciding sports cases, e.g., recklessness or intent to do harm, negligence, or, whatever the theory, in permitting compliance with the rules of the sport to operate as a defense?

2. *Non-contact sports?* In *Schick v. Ferolito*, 327 N.J. Super. 530, 744 A.2d 219 (2000), cert. granted, plaintiff hit his tee shot and then watched as defendant sliced his ball off the tee but not out of bounds. Plaintiff moved in front of the tee, but defendant unexpectedly took a "mulligan," that hooked and hit plaintiff in the face. In discussing the appropriate standard the court stated:

> [T]he standard among sports participants has generally been raised from that of "negligence" to "recklessness or intent to do harm" but only as to anticipated risks which are "an inherent or integral part of the game." This standard would apply to the risk of an errant golf ball straying from its intended course, the unintentional hitting of a "slice" or "hook", or the "shanking" of a golf ball. However, we conclude that hitting an unannounced and unexpected mulligan from the tee after all members of the foursome have teed off creates such an unanticipated risk to the other members of the foursome, from which they cannot protect themselves, that it cannot be considered an "inherent or integral part of the game." It should, therefore, be measured by an ordinary negligence standard.

744 A.2d at 221–22.

3. *Function over Form — The Allocation Decision.* If a court adopts an intentional, rather than negligence, tort categorization of a particular fact pattern, how will that affect the number of accidents of that type which will be redistributed from plaintiff class to defendant class? Does one categorization contain definite advantages for plaintiffs or defendants? If so, which categorization? Why? *See* Nicolas P. Terry, *Collapsing Torts*, 25 CONN. L. REV. 717 (1993).

4. *Structural and Other Explanations.* In *Trogun v. Fruchtman,* 58 Wis. 2d 596, 207 N.W.2d 297, 312 (1973), the Wisconsin Supreme Court, dealing with a situation in which plaintiff had alleged that he had not been informed of the potential side effects of drugs prescribed by the defendant, stated:

> Several reasons exist for the inadequacy of the assault and battery theory of liability in situations such as the instant case where the alleged misconduct on the part of the physician amounts to a failure to disclose the ramifications of a pending course of treatment, therapy, or surgery rather than the removal of an organ other than that

consented to. First, the act complained of in these cases simply does not fit comfortably within the traditional concepts of battery — the intent to unlawfully touch the person of another. In cases such as the instant one, physicians are invariably acting in good faith and for the benefit of the patient. While the result may not be that desired, the act complained of is surely not of an antisocial nature usually associated with the tort of assault and battery or battery. While the unauthorized removal of an organ yet fits the concept of battery, the failure to adequately advise of potential negative ramifications of a treatment does not. Second, and related to the first, the failure to inform a patient is probably not, in the usual case, an intentional act and hence not within the traditional concept of intentional torts. Third, the act complained of in informed consent cases is not within the traditional idea of "contact" or "touching." In the typical situation, as here, the physician impeccably performs the surgery or other treatment. Complained of are the personal reactions to such treatment which are unanticipated by the patient. Thus, for example, the instant drug therapy is not alleged to be an unpermitted touching but rather, the plaintiff alleges he ought to have been advised of the possibility of hepatitis which occurs without fault on anyone's part. Fourth, a valid question exists with respect to whether a physician's malpractice insurance covers liability for an arguably "criminal" act — battery. If not, it may be asked why a physician should be required to pay out of his own pocket for what is essentially an act of negligence — failing to inform a patient of the risks indigenous to the treatment? Fifth, these essentially negligence cases do not fit the traditional mold of situations wherein punitive damages can be awarded. For these reasons, we conclude it is preferable to affirmatively recognize a legal duty, bottomed upon a negligence theory of liability, in cases wherein it is alleged the patient-plaintiff was not informed adequately of the ramifications of a course of treatment.

Which of these reasons do you find the most persuasive? Do you think your clients would find them understandable?

GHASSEMIEH v. SCHAFER
52 Md. App. 31, 447 A.2d 84 (1982)

MOORE, JUDGE.

The appellant, Karen B. Ghassemieh, age 29 on February 24, 1977, was a teacher of art with the Baltimore County Schools, assigned to Old Court Junior High. On that date, she was teaching an 8th grade class of "above average" students, including the appellee, Elaine Schafer, then 13. While the teacher was about to sit down to assist another student, Elaine pulled the chair away.

At trial the teacher described what happened:

> I got to Terrie's seat and because I am very tall it is my practice either to kneel down next to the children or to sit down. Terrie got up very quickly and I went to sit in her seat. As I went to sit down,

I tucked the chair underneath me as I usually do. As I relaxed to sit down, the chair was gone. It was pulled out and I fell to the floor hurting my back.

Elaine Schafer testified that she pulled the chair away "as a joke."

She further testified on direct examination:

Q. When you pulled the chair, was there any doubt in your mind that she would miss the chair and fall to the floor?

A. I knew she was going to fall to the floor.

Q. Was that your intent?

A. Yes.

On cross-examination she repeated that, "I did it as a joke." She also said that she did not intend any injury. Thus:

Q. You mean you did not intend to have any harm done to her, is that right?

A. I intended for her to fall to the floor, not for her to be injured.

. . . At the close of the evidence, each side moved for a directed verdict. The appellee's (defendant's) motion was predicated on a claim that the evidence established a battery, an intentional tort, and not negligence, as alleged.

Both motions were denied. With respect to the defendant's motion, the court ruled:

> As to the motion of the defendant, the Court will deny that motion, but I will include in the instructions the definition of a battery and let the jury make the determination whether this in fact was, if it was a negligent act on the part of the defendant or if in fact it was a battery, which would certainly not be encompassed in the action brought by the plaintiff in this case, but I would allow that to go to the jury by way of instruction.
>
> . . . [The court instructed the jury as follows:]
>
> The case before you is an action based on a claim of negligence. . . . The Court has indicated that this is an action in negligence. A battery is an intentional touching which is harmful or offensive. Touching includes the intentional putting into motion of anything which touches another person or the intentional putting into motion of anything which touches something that is connected with or in contact with another person. A touching is harmful if it causes physical pain, injury or illness. A touching is offensive if it offends a person's reasonable sense of personal dignity.
>
> If you find that the defendant acted with the intent to cause a harmful or offensive touching of the plaintiff and that that offensive touching directly or indirectly resulted, then this constitutes a battery and your verdict must be for the defendant, as this suit has been brought in negligence and is not an action in battery.

The gravamen of the plaintiff's appeal [from defendant's verdict] is that the trial court erred in giving . . . the instruction on battery quoted above.

. . . In support of this principal contention, appellants maintain that:

(1) The mere fact that the evidence adduced may have established that the defendant acted intentionally in pulling the chair out from under the appellant, Karen B. Ghassemieh, does not preclude recovery of damages for a cause of action in negligence. . . .

[Holding that plaintiff had failed to adequately preserve the issue on appeal, nevertheless the court remarked:]

> [W]e observe that the case was not tried within the familiar framework of negligence: duty, breach, causation, and injury. The plaintiffs failed to develop evidence showing that Elaine Schafer had a duty to refrain from any act which a reasonable person should recognize as involving an unreasonable risk of harm to another. Duty requires the actor to conform to a certain standard of conduct for the protection of others against unreasonable risks. . . .

The defendant here stated several times that she did not mean to harm her teacher, that she meant it as a joke. The defendant was asked: "You knew it was wrong to do this, didn't you?" and "What did you think would happen when she did fall?" But the pivotal question was not asked: "Were you aware that a tall adult like Mrs. Ghassemieh could have been severely injured by your conduct?" An affirmative answer would have established her knowledge of the risk involved. A negative answer would have raised a jury question as to whether a reasonable 13-year-old should have known that such a prank constituted an unreasonable risk of harm to another, and thus, she had a duty to refrain from such conduct.

While it is true that ". . . the absence of intent is essential to the legal conception of negligence," *Adams v. Carey,* 172 Md. 173, 186, 190 A. 815 (1937), the presence of an intent to do an act does not preclude negligence. The concepts of negligence and battery are not mutually exclusive.

In understanding the overlap, Prof. Prosser's explication of the distinction between intended and unintended acts is helpful:

> In negligence, the actor does not desire to bring about the consequences which follow, nor does he know that they are substantially certain to occur, or believe that they will. There is merely a risk of such consequences, sufficiently great to lead a reasonable man in his position to anticipate them, and to guard against them. *If an automobile driver runs down a man in the street before him, with the desire to hit him, or with the belief that he is certain to do so, it is an intentional battery; but if he has no such desire or belief, but merely acts unreasonably in failing to guard against a risk which he should appreciate, it is negligence.* As the probability of injury to another, apparent from the facts within his knowledge, becomes greater, his conduct takes on more of the attributes of intent, until it reaches that substantial certainty of harm which juries, and sometimes courts, may find inseparable from intent itself. Such intermediate mental states, based upon a recognizable great probability of harm, may still properly be classed as "negligence," but are commonly called "reckless," "wanton," or even "wilful." They are dealt with, in many respects, as if the harm were intended, so that they become in effect a hybrid between

intent and negligence, occupying a sort of penumbra between the two. (Emphasis added.)

Prosser, § 31 at 145.

We see no reason why an intentional act that produces unintended consequences cannot be a foundation for a negligence action. Here, an intentional act — the pulling away of the chair — had two possible consequences: the intended one of embarrassment and the unintended one of injury. The battery — an indirect offensive touching, a technical invasion of the plaintiff's personal integrity, was proved. However, a specific instruction on negligence — namely, that the defendant had a duty to refrain from conduct exposing the plaintiff to unreasonable risk of injury and breached that duty, resulting in her injury was not requested. Nor was any exception made to the general negligence instruction that was given. Nor did the plaintiff at trial take the unequivocal position that she was proceeding on a theory of negligence, notwithstanding the co-existence of an intentional act, *i.e.*, a battery. In sum, appellants are asserting now the arguments they should have made at trial. Such hindsight can avail them nothing.

NOTES

1. *The Classic Intentional Tort.* As in *Garratt v. Dailey,* discussed in Chapter 3, *infra,* the issue in *Ghassemieh* revolved around the consequences, but not the harm, intended by the defendant. Is an intended offensive contact the same as an intended embarrassment here? What species of activity is the court attempting to deter with this narrow focus? What could have been the plaintiff's motivation in bringing her case in negligence?

2. *The Greedy Tort of Negligence.* As a rule of thumb, actionable negligence may be thought of as *the unreasonable running of a foreseeable risk.* Does it involve the same species of activity as that which concerns intentional tort law? Was *Ghassemieh* correctly decided? What criteria are you utilizing to make that judgment?

3. *The Specter of Insurance (1)* — *"Intent" or "Intentional?"* In *Pachucki v. Republic Ins. Co.,* 89 Wis. 2d 703, 278 N.W.2d 898 (1979), plaintiff was injured at his workplace by co-employees shooting bobby pin-like objects from rubber bands in a so-called "greening pin war." One of the pins injured the plaintiff's cornea. The aggressors in the "war" were insureds under homeowners policies which contained exclusions for "bodily injury . . . which is either expected or intended from the standpoint of the insured." The trial court granted judgment in favor of the insurance companies, finding that the defendants were shooting greening pins with the intention of hitting the plaintiff, but they had no intent to hit the plaintiff in the eye or cause the specific injury which occurred. However, the court was of the opinion that, "it was a substantial certainty that the plaintiff would sustain some kind of damage." The Supreme Court of Wisconsin stated:

> *Home Ins. Co. v. Nielsen,* 165 Ind. App. 448, 332 N.E.2d 240 (1975), outlines three general rules that have emerged with respect to the construction of an intentional tort exclusion:

(1) The minority view follows the classic tort doctrine of looking to the natural and probable consequences of the insured's act;

(2) The majority view is that the insured must have intended the act and to cause some kind of bodily injury;

(3) A third view is that the insured must have had the specific intent to cause the type of injury suffered. . . .

The majority position is summarized in the following: (1) it is necessary that the insured intend both the act as well as intending to cause bodily injury in order for the exclusion to apply; (2) intent may be actual or may be inferred by the nature of the act and the accompanying reasonable foreseeability of harm; (3) once it is found that harm was intended, it is immaterial that the actual harm caused is of a different character or magnitude than that intended. . . .

Some courts might characterize the defendants' conduct in this case as "horseplay" as there was no specific intent to do harm. However, the boys' actual knowledge based upon prior experience that a greening pin will cause harm when it strikes, especially when fired at the close range of six feet, distinguishes this appeal from the classic "horseplay" case of *Morrill v. Gallagher,* 370 Mich. 578, 122 N.W.2d 687 (1963). In *Morrill* the defendant Gallagher threw a cherry bomb into the plaintiff's office attempting to scare him but the result was a serious hearing impairment. The insurer, in its defense of the case, relied in part upon the intentional tort exclusion. The court rejected the defense position and stated: "There is nothing in this case to justify the conclusion that (the insured) intended to cause any physical harm to the plaintiff." In *Morrill* the remote possibility of harm cannot be equated with the substantial certainty that harm would result under the facts of this case.

The present case is properly similar to *Butler v. Behaeghe,* 37 Colo. App. 282, 548 P.2d 934 (1976), wherein the defendant's insurer refused to defend based on an identical exclusionary clause. The plaintiff and the insured got into an argument after an altercation between their two teen-aged sons. The insured ordered the plaintiff off his property and when the plaintiff refused to leave, the insured procured a steel pipe. Although he intended to strike the plaintiff in the stomach, he hit the plaintiff on the head and an injury ensued. Finding that the insured's conduct fell within the exclusionary provision, the court concluded:

> Where coverage is excluded if bodily injury is "intended or expected" by the insured, such exclusion is inapplicable if and only if the insured acts without any intent or any expectation of causing any injury, however slight. And conversely, such exclusion is applicable if the insured acts with the intent or expectation that bodily injury will result even though the bodily injury that does result is different either in character or magnitude from the injury that was intended.

Thus, we hold the applicable case law supports the trial court's findings that the facts and circumstances of this case bar recovery pursuant to the language contained in the intentional tort exclusionary sections in the respective policies. We affirm the trial court's finding that the defendants' intent to inflict injury to the plaintiff can be inferred from the evidence and circumstances in this case.

Compare Ambassador Ins. Co. v. Montes, 76 N.J. 477, 388 A.2d 603 (1978), in which a property owner set fire to two wooden tenement buildings, killing four occupants. The property owner was convicted of arson and murder. Plaintiff brought an action on behalf of a child killed in the fire, but the property owner's insurer denied liability under the policy. The court concluded, "When the insurance company has contracted to pay an innocent person monetary damages due to any liability of the insured, such payment when ascribable to a criminal event should be made so long as the benefit thereof does not enure to the insured."

What are the goals of the tort and insurance systems in cases such as these? Are these goals competing or even conflicting ones, or may they be harmonized?

4. *The Specter of Insurance (2) — Negligence or Intent?* The court in *Big Town Nursing Home, Inc. v. Newman,* 461 S.W.2d 195 (Tex. Civ. App. 1970), described the "treatment" meted out to a nursing home resident as in "utter disregard" of his legal rights and affirmed his verdict of damages for false imprisonment. Subsequently, the nursing home sought indemnity under its liability policy. Its insurer contended that the nursing home's conduct fell outside the insuring language of "malpractice, error or mistake." However, the Court of Appeals for the Fifth Circuit held that the conduct was covered, on the basis that the facility's conduct was "the exercise of a trained nursing judgment in obedience to an established medical policy." *Big Town Nursing Homes, Inc. v. Reserve Ins. Co.,* 492 F.2d 523 (5th Cir. 1974). What could be the basis for such different characterizations placed on the same conduct?

C. REGULATING SOCIALLY DESIRABLE ACTIVITIES

HARDINGHAM v. UNITED COUNSELING SERVICE
164 Vt. 478; 672 A.2d 480 (1995)

GIBSON, J.

. . . In November 1987, defendant United Counseling Service (UCS), a private, nonprofit organization providing counseling and psychiatric treatment to persons with mental illness, mental retardation, or substance-abuse problems, employed plaintiff, a known recovering alcoholic, as an emergency services counselor. On February 3, 1988, defendant John Halpin, United Counseling Service's executive director, became aware that plaintiff was drinking again. After failing to persuade plaintiff to seek psychological and medical attention, Halpin asked defendant Larry Gordon, UCS's coordinator of emergency services, to visit plaintiff. Gordon went to plaintiff's apartment on February 4 and found him in an inebriated condition. When plaintiff refused to seek treatment, Gordon called plaintiff's estranged wife, the emergency room at Southwestern Vermont Medical Center (SVMC), the police, and the Bennington Rescue Squad, but nobody was willing to take any action without plaintiff's cooperation. Gordon left plaintiff's apartment and took all the alcohol he could find. During a telephone conversation the next day, plaintiff told defendant David O'Brien, UCS's director of outpatient services, that he would enter a treatment program.

On February 11, Halpin went to plaintiff's apartment and discovered plaintiff in an inebriated, semi-conscious state. Halpin returned to UCS and explained plaintiff's condition to Gordon, O'Brien, and defendant Donald Kowalski, a psychiatrist and UCS's medical director. The three men went to plaintiff's apartment and found it in disarray. While the men were at the apartment, plaintiff got up, went to a sink, and began to drink from an apparently full container of windshield wiper fluid. O'Brien and Kowalski immediately took the container away from plaintiff, and Gordon called the police. Notwithstanding plaintiff's vehement protests, the three men took him outside and helped police place him in the back of a patrol car. The police took plaintiff to the SVMC emergency room. Kowalski rode with plaintiff in the patrol car, but did not go into the hospital; instead, Gordon and O'Brien accompanied plaintiff to the emergency room.

At the emergency room, plaintiff refused to take a blood test despite Gordon's request that he do so. When plaintiff would not agree to go to a residential treatment program, Gordon signed an incapacitation order, and plaintiff was taken to the Rutland Regional Correctional Center. At no time did any of the three men inform police, emergency room personnel, or corrections employees that plaintiff had ingested, or had attempted to ingest, a bluish liquid that may have been windshield wiper fluid. The following morning, plaintiff was admitted to the Rutland Medical Center and placed in the intensive care unit. Tests revealed the presence of methyl alcohol in plaintiff's blood in sufficient concentration to present a threat to his life. As a result of the methanol overdose, plaintiff suffered severe health problems, including blindness.

In his complaint, plaintiff alleged that defendants were negligent in failing to inform medical authorities that he had ingested windshield wiper fluid. Defendants sought summary judgment. The superior court granted their motions based on its conclusion that, as a matter of law given the facts of the case, (1) Vermont's Duty to Aid the Endangered Act, 12 V.S.A. § 519, immunized defendants from civil liability for acts of ordinary negligence, and (2) defendants' actions were not grossly negligent. On reargument, plaintiff contends that the superior court usurped the role of the jury by concluding, as a matter of law, that defendants' actions did not constitute gross negligence.

The concept of gross negligence has been defined by this Court in the context of our repealed guest-passenger statute. Deyo v. Kinley, 152 Vt. 196, 207–08, 565 A.2d 1286, 1293 (1989). In that context, we stated that gross negligence is " 'more than an error of judgment, momentary inattention, or loss of presence of mind' "; rather, " 'it amounts to a failure to exercise even a slight degree of care' " and an " 'indifference to the duty owed [to another].' " Rivard v. Roy, 124 Vt. 32, 35, 196 A 2d 497, 500 (1963) (quoting Emery v. Small, 117 Vt. 138, 140, 86 A.2d 542, 543 (1952)); see Shaw, Adm'r v. Moore, 104 Vt. 529, 531, 162 A. 373, 374 (1932) ("Gross negligence is substantially and appreciably higher in magnitude and more culpable than ordinary negligence. . . . It is a heedless and palpable violation of legal duty respecting the

Although the presence or absence of gross negligence turns on each particular set of circumstances and therefore is "generally a question for the jury," the trial court may decide the question as a matter of law "where the minds of reasonable persons cannot differ." Rivard, 124 Vt. at 35, 196 A.2d at 500. Several courts in other jurisdictions have granted summary judgment to rescuers on the ground that, as a matter of law, the plaintiffs had failed to show that the rescuers were grossly negligent in providing assistance, as required by the jurisdictions' Good Samaritan statutes.

When the facts do not present triable issues, courts must be especially vigilant in protecting rescuers from protracted litigation, particularly in view of the fact that the Legislature created partial immunity under 12 V.S.A. § 519 largely to allay the litigation fears of medical professionals and other would-be rescuers. The purpose of the Duty to Aid the Endangered Act is to encourage rescuers to assist others in danger by penalizing them for not acting while at the same time shielding them from civil liability for acts of ordinary negligence committed during the rescue. If rescuers were forced to go through an expensive trial any time there was the slightest evidence of ordinary negligence, even if it were clear that gross negligence was not present, the purpose of the statute would be thwarted.

Here, plaintiff neither demonstrated nor pled gross negligence against defendants. It is undisputed that the individual defendants visited plaintiff at his apartment, became alarmed at his condition, summoned the authorities, took the container of windshield wiper fluid away from him as he attempted to drink from it, physically removed him from his apartment so that he could be transported to the hospital, accompanied him to the hospital, and tried to get him to accept appropriate medical treatment. As the trial court noted, defendants' actions probably saved plaintiff's life. Given these facts, no reasonable person could conclude that defendants showed indifference to plaintiff or failed to exercise even a slight degree of care. We agree with the trial court that defendants' failure to tell medical personnel, during the course of an emergency room visit with a highly intoxicated and belligerent person, that plaintiff may have consumed a toxic substance demonstrates, at most, an error of judgment or a loss of presence of mind that could be viewed as negligent, but not grossly negligent. Accordingly, defendants cannot be liable in civil damages, and summary judgment in favor of defendants was proper.

DOOLEY, J., dissenting.

I disagree with the court's conclusion that there was insufficient evidence for a jury to find that defendants were grossly negligent.

I do not believe that the general language we have used to describe gross negligence is very helpful when viewed apart from the decisions that have applied the language. Thus, the majority fixes on our description of gross negligence as involving absence of "even a slight degree of care." We have, however, applied that language to allow a jury to find gross negligence where a motorist, traveling 10 miles per hour under the speed limit, lost control of her vehicle when she abruptly applied her brakes after hearing the sound of small stones hitting her fender. We also applied it to a motorist who, while driving 40 to 45 miles per hour on a highway, failed to negotiate a curve and left the road. Our decisions make clear that we have not adopted a wooden and narrow application of the definition of gross negligence.

As strongly as I disagree with the majority's analysis of the facts in light of the standard for summary judgment, my real differences are in the policy perspectives from which we approach this case. The majority approaches the Duty to Aid the Endangered Act as an immunity statute so we "must be especially vigilant in protecting rescuers from protracted litigation." I disagree with this analysis and approach. The main effect of the statute, unlike other Good Samaritan statutes adopted in this country, was to expand the limited common-law duty to rescue a person "exposed to grave physical harm" when the rescue can be achieved without danger or peril to the rescuer and without interference with important duties owed to others. This expanded duty was accompanied by a higher threshold of culpability before the rescuer could be found liable, but I think it is a mischaracterization to call this an immunity statute.

On this point, it is important to distinguish the Good Samaritan statutes that have been passed in other states. Many, modeled after the California statute, give the "good samaritan" immunity from any suit as long as the rescue action was taken in good faith. See Cal. Bus. & Prof. Code § 2395 (West 1990). Others allow suits against the rescuer only if based on willful or wanton misconduct, which typically requires actual or implied intent to injure. If the Vermont Legislature had passed one of these variations, the majority's decision here would have been fully supported, and I would agree with its policy rationale. The majority, however, reads too much into the statute that the Legislature actually passed.

Unfortunately, this is a lesson we once learned the hard way, and I fear history is repeating itself. In 1929, the Vermont Legislature, following the lead in other states, passed a statute providing that a guest-passenger who is injured in an automobile accident could sue the operator only for gross or willful negligence. In the forty years the statute was in effect until repealed in 1969, it spawned a flood of appeals to this Court, and decision after decision attempted to find the line between gross and ordinary negligence. In retrospect and in light of that experience, we found the terminology of the guest statute to be "ineffective as a definition of duty," Green v. Sherburne Corp., 137 Vt. 310, 313, 403 A.2d 278, 280 (1979), and we characterized our experience with the gross negligence test for liability as "unsatisfactory." Howard v. Spafford, 132 Vt. 434, 435, 321 A.2d 74, 75 (1974). In these assessments, we were echoing those of many courts and commentators who found the line-drawing required by the gross negligence standard difficult, if not impossible, to perform in a principled fashion.

Like many other courts, we found that the only reasonable course of action was to leave the decision of whether gross negligence was present to the jury except in the most extreme cases.

While I doubt that the Duty to Aid the Endangered Act will generate the flood of appeals the guest statute produced, I can't avoid the disquieting feeling that the real reason plaintiff will not be able to present his case to the jury is that this is the first case we have considered under the Act.

NOTES

1. To what extent are the distinctions between neglect and intent that are drawn by the courts abstract and objective in nature or contextual and functional?

2. *The Ghosts of Guest Statutes. Shea v. Olson,* 185 Wash. 143, 53 P.2d 615 (1936), concerned a group of revellers who had been out drinking and dancing for the evening. During their return to town, the defendant was driving at high speed. The other occupants of the car protested this speed, but the defendant declined to slow down. An accident occurred when the defendant failed to make a sharp turn in the road while attempting to overtake the vehicle of some fellow revellers. One of the guest-occupants was injured. At that time Washington had a "guest statute," which denied tort recovery to nonpaying passengers "unless such accident shall have been intentional on the part of said owner or operator." The plaintiff-guest included an intentional tort count in her complaint. The court disposed of the issue as follows:

> . . . [T]here was no evidence in this case warranting the jury in finding that the accident, that is the wreck and consequent injury, was intentional. The parties were friends, they were on pleasure bent, their object was a dance [in town], and [defendant's] immediate purpose was to overtake the other car, not to wreck his own. There was no evidence of any intention on the part of appellant to commit suicide, homicide, or mayhem, or to destroy property.

At what point does bad driving become intentional or willful or reckless? At 70 miles per hour? (No — *Goodnight v. Richardson,* 286 Ark. 38, 688 S.W.2d 941 (1985).) At 85–100 miles per hour? (Yes — *Cooper v. Chapman,* 226 Ark. 331, 289 S.W.2d 686 (1956).) Why?

RESTATEMENT (SECOND) OF TORTS (1977)

§ 519. General Principle

(1) One who carries on an abnormally dangerous activity is subject to liability for harm to the person, land or chattels of another resulting from the activity, although he has exercised the utmost care to prevent the harm.

(2) This strict liability is limited to the kind of harm, the possibility of which makes the activity abnormally dangerous.

§ 520. Abnormally Dangerous Activities

In determining whether an activity is abnormally dangerous, the following factors are to be considered:

(a) existence of a high degree of risk of some harm to the person, land or chattels of others;

(b) likelihood that the harm that results from it will be great;

(c) inability to eliminate the risk by the exercise of reasonable care;

(d) extent to which the activity is not a matter of common usage;

(e) inappropriateness of the activity to the place where it is carried on; and

(f) extent to which its value to the community is outweighed by its dangerous attributes.

NOTES

1. *Fundamental and Historical Criteria.* In *Fletcher v. Rylands,* [1866] L.R. 1 Exch. 265 (Exch. Ch.), *aff'd sub nom. Rylands v. Fletcher,* [1868] L.R. 3, 19 L.T. 220 (H.L.), the defendant was held liable without proof of personal fault when water from his reservoir worked its way through some disused coalworkings and flooded his neighbor's coal mine. In the words of Blackburn, J:

> We think that the true rule of law is, that the person who for his own purposes brings on his lands and collects and keeps there anything likely to do mischief if it escapes, must keep it in at his peril, and, if he does not do so, is prima facie answerable for all the damages which is the natural consequence of its escape.

Rylands has long been considered the "grandfather" of strict or absolute liability cases, and is discussed extensively, *infra Chapter 16.* However, the case itself is somewhat short on theoretical or conceptual justification for holding someone responsible "at his peril." Nevertheless, Blackburn, J., did make the following reference:

> . . . [I]t was further said [in the court below] that when damage is done to personal property, or even to the person, by collision, either upon land or at sea, there must be negligence in the party doing the damage to render him legally responsible; and this is no doubt true, and as was pointed out by [counsel] during his argument before us, this is not confined to cases of collision, for there are many cases in which proof of negligence is essential, as for instance, where an unruly horse gets on the footpath of a public street and kills a passenger; or where a person in a dock is struck by the falling of a bale of cotton which the defendant's servants are lowering, and many other similar cases may be found. But we think these cases distinguishable from the present. Traffic on the highways, whether by land or sea, cannot be conducted without exposing those whose persons or property are near it to some inevitable risk; and that being so, those who go on the highway, or have their property adjacent to it, may well be held to do so subject to their taking upon themselves the risk of injury from that inevitable danger; and persons who by the licence of the owner pass near to warehouses where goods are being raised or lowered, certainly do so subject to the inevitable risk of accident. In neither case, therefore, can they recover without proof of want of care or skill occasioning the accident. . . .

To what types of activities would you be more inclined to apply strict liability, those with high social utility but high risk, those with high social utility but low risk, or those with low social utility but with high (or low) risk? Why?

For Blackburn, J., what was the vital criterion that led him to justify strict liability in this situation but not in the case of a collision? Is the criterion valid? Of general applicability? Were Judge Blackburn's comments as to the risks attendant upon collisions *factual* or *normative*?

2. *Rylands Restated?* Do §§ 519–20 differ from *Rylands v. Fletcher*? How? What is the distinction between "strict" and "absolute" liability?

3. *Market-Approximating Considerations.* Should the likelihood that a member of a potential plaintiff group and a member of a defendant group will have been involved in pre-accident, face-to-face negotiations affect the choice of allocative rule?

4. *Seeking Ground Zero.* If we lived in a perfect world without transaction costs, where potential injurers and victims possessed "perfect information," then it is at least arguable that the market would guarantee the most efficient reduction of accidents and their costs. This reduction, it is said, would occur regardless of whether tort law allocated accident responsibility to defendants (by generally holding them liable for a particular activity's accident costs) or to plaintiffs (by generally *not* holding defendants liable). See Coase, *The Problem of Social Cost,* 3 J.L. & ECON. 1 (1960). Because of transaction costs and other reasons, such a world does not exist. See Kelman, *Consumption Theory, Production Theory, and Ideology in the Coase Theorem,* 52 S. CAL. L. REV. 669 (1979). As a result, it *does* matter where the initial accident avoidance responsibility (liability) rule is placed. As a result, much legal scholarship has concentrated on whether tort liability *historically* was fault-based (primary accident avoidance responsibility on plaintiffs) or strict liability-based (on defendants). *See, e.g.,* Malone, *Ruminations on the Role of Fault in the History of the Common Law of Torts,* 31 LA. L. REV. 1 (1970). *Cf.* Rabin, *The Historical Development of the Fault Principle: A Reinterpretation,* 15 GA. L. REV. 925 (1981) (critiquing that "historical search" approach). Where should we turn in the absence of any historical allocation of initial responsibility? According to Calabresi, *Optimal Deterrence and Accidents,* 84 YALE L.J. 656 (1975), the correct approach is to ask, "Who is best suited to make the cost-benefit analysis between accident costs and accident avoidance costs? In other words, one would ask who should bear the incentive *to decide correctly,* rather than what is the correct decision." *Id.* at 666. *See also* Fletcher, *Fairness and Utility in Tort Theory,* 85 HARV. L. REV. 537 (1972).

5. *Questionable Analogies.* The dissent in *Magrine,* below, makes reference to the imposition of strict liability by statute, in the case of "industrial accidents," "damage by airplanes" and "dog bites." In *Rylands v. Fletcher,* Blackburn, J., placed considerable emphasis on what he seemed to consider as the analogous strict liability tort of cattle trespass. What (if anything) do any or all of these fact patterns have in common?

C. REGULATING SOCIALLY DESIRABLE ACTIVITIES

MAGRINE v. SPECTOR
100 N.J. Super. 223, 241 A.2d 637 (App. Div. 1968),
aff'd 53 N.J. 259, 250 A.2d 129 (1969)

PER CURIAM.

. . . The sole issue presented here is whether a dentist is strictly liable to a patient injured by a defective instrument used in the course of treatment. In our opinion, the imposition of liability on the defendant-dentist cannot be justified on the basis of any of the accepted policies which underlie the doctrine of strict liability as it is presently understood. Nor are we persuaded that that doctrine should be extended under the circumstances of this case so as to render the defendant-dentist liable without fault for a defect in a needle which he merely purchased and used.

The judgment appealed from is therefore affirmed.

BOTTER, J.S.C., dissenting.

Plaintiff, Frances Magrine, was injured by a hypodermic needle which defendant, a dentist, had injected into her gum. In the course of the injection the needle broke. Defendant believes "there must have been some sort of a defect in the needle." At oral argument we were told that an operation was required to extract the broken portion of the needle. Plaintiff does not charge defendant with negligence, but asserts strict liability in tort . . . .

The trial court denied recovery. Strict liability was refused because the dentist was engaged in a profession, not a large-scale business; he was not a manufacturer or supplier of the needle, but a user of it; he could not discover a latent defect in the needle; and precedent in this state has not yet applied the doctrine beyond manufacturers, retailers, suppliers such as rental companies, and mass producers of homes. The majority of this court affirms.

. . . The issue posed is as old as jurisprudence: when an innocent person is injured through the inadvertent conduct of another, who should bear the loss? The answer has varied with the epoch and environment. From ancient times until the 19th century the answer given generally was in favor of strict liability. Thereafter, with some exceptions, the basic rule has been to deny recovery against a defendant who is free of negligence. In the 20th century no liability without fault has been the basic premise, but it has been replaced through legislation by strict liability for industrial accidents (workmen's compensation) and for other specific activities such as ground damage by airplanes and dog bites. In addition, the courts have restored strict liability in a broad area where a defective product or device has caused injury.

We may ask ourselves what objectives did the law seek in fashioning these rules of liability? In primitive cultures vengeance against the offending thing or person, not compensation, was a primary objective. If a man fell from a tree and died, the tree was delivered to his relatives or was chopped to pieces. Liability was visited upon the offending source, animate or inanimate, as well as persons connected with it, as if evil inhered in the instrument of harm. The reason may have been revenge or superstition or fear of an instrument of evil. . . .

This sweeping rule caught all harm-doers; but the difference between intentional and accidental harm was recognized at an early age in criminal law for the purpose of punishment and in civil wrongs for the purpose of mitigating damages. If a man's ox was killed by an ox whose owner was ignorant of its propensity "to push in time past," then "They shall sell the live ox, and divide the money of it; and the dead ox also they shall divide." Exodus 21:35, 36. This is one solution where both parties are blameless: have them share the loss. This approach has some parallel to workmen's compensation laws of the 1900's and to various suggestions made since the 1920's to compensate victims of motor vehicle accidents by a strict liability plan.

In the 19th century fault — the failure to act as an ordinary prudent man — became the central condition of liability for unintentional harm. The purpose that was championed was the right of individuals and corporations to act freely and unburdened unless harm is done through their negligence. Some areas of strict liability continued at common law, but the spirit of laissez faire and the momentum of the industrial revolution prevailed. "We must have factories, machinery, dams, canals and railroads," the court said in *Losee v. Buchanan,* 51 N.Y. 476, 484–85 (1873), denying recovery without proof of negligence for damage to property caused by an exploding boiler. "By becoming a member of civilized society," the court said, "natural rights" must be surrendered, but a benefit is gained through the surrender by others of the same rights. "I hold my property subject to the risk that it may be unavoidably or accidentally injured by those who live near me; and as I move about upon the public highways and in all places where other persons may lawfully be, I take the risk of being accidentally injured in my person by them without fault on their part." In 1881 Holmes shared these views; however, he also suggested that deterrence of harmful behavior was a product of the rule that makes fault a condition of liability. [Holmes, The Common Law, 95–96 (1881).]

In those days the problem was considered "on the assumption that plaintiff and defendant were alone involved and that what happened between them was the real issue — that tort liability was paid for out of the defendant's own pocketbook." 2 Harper & James, The Law of Torts, 762. The irony is that the fault rule, which was partly inspired by the desire to protect the growth of industry, was undone by the results of that very growth, namely, an increase in the harmful capacity of mechanized facilities, the inevitability of accidents in their use and the consequent toll of human life and losses.[3] The expansion of the economy, the broadening of distribution of goods and services and the new pervasiveness of liability insurance are all part of the environment for the tort law of the 20th century. In this environment new views have taken shape about the objectives of the law. What has become dominant in our time is the need to compensate victims of normal conditions of daily life.

There is a tendency to revive the idea of liability without fault not only in the frame of wide responsibility for agencies employed, but in placing upon an enterprise the burden of repairing injuries, without fault of him

---

[3] In World War II 313,000 soldiers were killed, but 386,000 people were killed in accidents during the same period. 2 Harper & James, *supra,* p. 729, n. 1. In 1966[,] 113,000 people were killed and 50,851,000 were injured in accidents of all kinds; of these, 53,000 were killed and 3,712,000 were injured in motor vehicle accidents alone. National Safety Council, Accident Facts, p. 2–3 (1967). Total payments for personal injury tort claims and workmen's compensation exceed three billion dollars per year. Conard, Morgan, Pratt, Voltz & Bombaugh, Automobile Accident Costs and Payments — Studies in the Economics of Injury Reparation, p. 45 (1964).

who conducts it, which are an incident to the undertaking. . . . There is a strong and growing tendency, where there is no blame on either side, to ask in view of the exigencies of social justice, who can best bear the loss. Pound, The Spirit of the Common Law, pp. 188-189 (1921).

Assuring compensation for victims of accidents is a matter of public policy which legislatures have promoted in various ways. Very recently the courts have come to serve this purpose by expanding liability without proof of negligence in the area of "product liability." This result followed naturally the change in economic and social organization. So long as direct sales brought goods from a manufacturer to a consumer the law had little difficulty in affording relief in contract or in tort. When the process of manufacturing and distribution became extended and diversified, determining liability seemed more complicated. . . .

The trial court agreed with defendant's contention that strict liability should not apply to one who is not a manufacturer or large-scale supplier of goods but who merely uses instruments acquired from others. Obviously we cannot determine the rule of liability on the basis of the size or resources of one of the parties. Strict liability applies to all manufacturers, big and small, and in most states where the doctrine prevails it applies to retailers as well, big and small. . . . [I]n this situation the dentist is not a "consumer" of the hypodermic needle. The patient must be viewed as the "ultimate consumer." The dentist purchased the needle for use on his patients; it is they who are exposed to the risk of the instrument.

The injured patient should have the option of suing the dentist directly. It is the dentist with whom plaintiff has dealt and in whose hands and confidence the patient has put herself. It may be more difficult to sue a manufacturer or supplier located in a distant state or a foreign country. The dentist chose the instrument. The dentist is in a better position to know and prove the identity of the manufacturer or distributor. If he cannot, the patient should not be denied recovery on that account. The dentist should also know the quality of the instrument and the reliability of his source of supply. This rule may encourage greater caution in purchasing equipment and examining for defects.

If an alleged manufacturer were sued other issues may arise. Here the needle was used eight times in a three week period. The dentist, not the patient, knows its history. The manufacturer may deny the existence of a latent defect and may assert that the instrument was used or cared for negligently. The parties best suited to litigate this issue are the dentist and the supplier. Often the real dispute will be between the insurance company for the dentist and the insurance company for the manufacturer, particularly where the source is in doubt or negligence in use is asserted.

The benefit that a patient receives in damages is not offset by an unfair burden placed on the dentist. The dentist does have a claim over against the supplier and manufacturer of the defective needle. He should know who they are in most cases. If strict liability would create higher insurance costs these costs may be mitigated through the claim over. Even without the claim over the loss may be distributed through fees for dental services or by insurance, the cost of which may be reflected in such fees.

Shifting the loss from A to B may not produce a net gain for society as a whole, but distribution of the loss does. Liability insurance is recognized as a means of distributing losses among the group involved in risk-producing activity. But the trial judge agreed with Dean Prosser's view that insurance cannot and should not be used "to determine whether the group shall bear them (losses) in the first instance — and whether, for example, consumers shall be compelled to accept substantial price increases on everything they buy in order to compensate others for their misfortunes." Prosser, "The Assault Upon the Citadel (Strict Liability to the Consumer)," 69 Yale L.J. 1099, 1121 (1960).[4] The argument is unrealistic and unpersuasive. Prof. James has replied that, "Today practically everybody worth suing is insured." James, "An Evaluation of the Fault Concept," 32 Tenn. L. Rev. 394, 397 (1965). Conard[5] shows that 98.8% of all payments for motor vehicle injury claims are received from insured sources. It is pointless to say that those who purchase goods should not be compelled to pay an item of cost for insurance to protect others. The protection is for the whole group. No one knows which consumer will be injured. The cost paid by each consumer assures his own satisfaction of a judgment if he gets one. The fact is that through the cost of goods and services consumers today do pay indirectly for insurance covering losses caused by the negligent activities of their suppliers. If this is just, granting consumer protection against defective products cannot be unjust.

The total compensation awarded for accidental loss by reason of tort liability and workmen's compensation is $3,178,000,000 annually. These losses would be devastating without loss distribution. Corporations (such as some public utilities) which are large enough to insure themselves distribute the loss to the public through the price of goods and services. Businessmen, professionals and individuals, who have sufficient assets to protect, are likely to carry insurance under existing law. It must be remembered that even with strict liability the exposure to liability for negligence continues as before. The extension of strict liability for defective goods and utensils merely expands the concept of tort liability. It has been called "negligence without fault." Those who do not carry insurance and are judgment-proof will probably be unaffected by this rule of law.

Insurance plays another role in the formulation of a desirable rule. It interferes with the achievement of the objectives sought by the fault principle. An injuror has to pay damages because he was negligent. With insurance, however, the negligent man pays no damages, although he pays for his insurance. The loss is shared by all who insure with the same company, or by its stockholders or by those who are participants in the activity. It was also believed that the threat of liability for negligence would encourage

---

[4] Similarly, in 1881, Holmes said it was no more justifiable for a man to indemnify a neighbor against injury from his faultless acts than it would be to require him to insure his neighbor against lightning. Holmes, *op. cit. supra*, p. 96. Holmes derided the idea that the state might insure its citizens against accidents and distribute the burden amongst all citizens as well as provide "a pension for paralytics, and state aid for those who suffered in person or estate from tempest or wild beasts." But the state has come to do these very things in the form of Medicare, disaster aid and unsatisfied judgment funds.

[5] Editor's Note. Conard, Morgan, Pratt, Voltz & Bombaugh, Automobile Accident Costs and Payments — Studies in the Economics of Injury Reparation, at pp. 45–50, note 54 (1964).

prudent conduct. The existence of insurance diminishes this threat. Moreover, the strict liability rule does not discourage prudence but may actually encourage examination for defects which are not obvious. Workmen's compensation laws have spurred safety consciousness by employers whose insurance rates depend upon loss experience. Insurance companies themselves have applied some of their resources to safety goals. In any case, the threat of liability for fault continues where strict liability applies. Lastly, the fear that lawful activities and growing industry would be unduly burdened by liability without fault is minimized by the loss-spreading effect of insurance.

Occasionally we are told that it violates a natural sense of justice to require a defendant to pay damages when he is not at fault. In my view our sense of justice is better served by the principle that holds a dentist accountable for injuries caused by a defective instrument which he has selected and used. The risk of harm to which an innocent patient is exposed by a defective instrument far exceeds the risk or burden which the dentist is asked to bear. The point may be made by reference to the automobile. Rollins, in "A Proposal to Extend the Compensation Principle to Accidents in the Streets," 4 Mass. L.Q. 392, 294 (1919), observed that in an impact between an automobile and a pedestrian the automobile can injure the pedestrian but the pedestrian cannot injure the automobile. The chances, he said, were all one way; and it is the automobile that gets the pleasure or profit but suffers none of the disadvantages. In such a case, he asks, who would say that it is unjust to have the motorist indemnify the pedestrian where both are blameless? It seems more unjust to leave the loss with the victim of an accident caused by a defective instrumentality which has the potential for harm. It does not offend our sense of justice to place the loss on the one responsible for the instrument. The law has done this very thing throughout its history. Justice requires only that we apply the rule in appropriate cases. A retailer who sells a can of beans containing a latent defect is no more culpable than a dentist who uses an instrument with a latent defect. The patient probably places more reliance upon the dentist than he does on the retailer. Yet in the case of a sale the legislature has expressed the public policy of our state to compensate the victim by holding the seller to a warranty of fitness for use despite his blamelessness. It is not unjust to hold a dentist to the same responsibility.

. . . Defendant's brief states that there is a "lack of scholarly comment" supporting the cause of action. It is true that few writers have focused on the specific area of service transactions as distinguished from sales, leases and bailments. However, I know of no academic comment opposing the application of strict liability to this type of case. Significantly, however, most current scholarly comment urges the total abolition of the negligence-fault principle in accidental injury cases. The scholars, therefore, go far beyond the needs of this case.

The law of torts should seek to compensate the injured, to encourage safety practices and to distribute losses justly. These objectives may be taken to express the needs of justice. In my view these objectives are advanced by granting plaintiff an award in this case. Dentistry as an enterprise should pay its own way. Denying compensation is to require an injured person who bears the loss alone to subsidize the risk-creating activities by which others profit.

For the foregoing reasons strict liability in tort should apply to a dentist who injures his patient by a latently defective instrument.

NOTES

1. *Social Utility*. Why wouldn't the dentist's conduct be "processed" by the intentional torts? Surely, he *intended* to place the hypodermic needle into the plaintiff's gum. Do the criteria discussed in *Trogun v. Fruchtman* following *Lucchesi*, provide a satisfactory answer?

2. *A Scale of Redistribution*. When a court applies strict liability, rather than negligence, to a particular allegation by plaintiff, what is the effect on a specific plaintiff's case? On cases brought by that class of plaintiffs in that type of fact pattern? Should the judge determine whether strict liability applies as a matter of law? Or is it a mixed question of law and fact, within the jury's prerogative where reasonable minds could differ? What difference does it make? *See* Nicolas P. Terry, *Collapsing Torts*, 25 CONN. L. REV. 717 (1993).

HAMMONTREE v. JENNER
20 Cal. App. 3d 528, 97 Cal. Rptr. 739 (1971)

LILLIE, ASSOCIATE JUSTICE.

The evidence shows that on the afternoon of April 25, 1967, defendant was driving his 1959 Chevrolet home from work; at the same time plaintiff Maxine Hammontree was working in a bicycle shop owned and operated by her and her husband; without warning defendant's car crashed through the wall of the shop, struck Maxine and caused personal injuries and damage to the shop.

Defendant claimed he became unconscious during an epileptic seizure, losing control of his car. He did not recall the accident but his last recollection before it, was leaving a stop light after his last stop, and his first recollection after the accident was being taken out of his car in plaintiffs' shop. Defendant testified he has a medical history of epilepsy and knows of no other reason for his loss of consciousness except an epileptic seizure; prior to 1952 he had been examined by several neurologists whose conclusion was that the condition could be controlled and who placed him on medication; in 1952 he suffered a seizure while fishing; several days later he went to Dr. Benson Hyatt who diagnosed his condition as petit mal seizure and kept him on the same medication; thereafter he saw Dr. Hyatt every six months and then on a yearly basis several years prior to 1967; in 1953 he had another seizure, was told he was an epileptic and continued his medication; in 1954 Dr. Kershner prescribed dilantin and in 1955 Dr. Hyatt prescribed phelantin; from 1955 until the accident occurred (1967) defendant had used phelantin on a regular basis which controlled his condition; defendant has continued to take medication as prescribed by his physician and has done everything his doctors told him to do to avoid a seizure; he had no inkling or warning that he was about to have a seizure prior to the occurrence of the accident.

In 1955 or 1956 the Department of Motor Vehicles was advised that defendant was an epileptic and placed him on probation under which every six months he had to report to the doctor who was required to advise it in writing of defendant's condition. In 1960 his probation was changed to a once-a-year report.

Dr. Hyatt testified that during the times he saw defendant, and according to his history, defendant "was doing normally" and that he continued to take phelantin; that "[the] purpose of the [phelantin] would be to react on the nervous system in such a way that where, without the medication, I would say to raise the threshold so that he would not be as subject to these episodes without the medication, so as not to have the seizures. He would not be having the seizures with the medication as he would without the medication compared to taking medication"; in a seizure it would be impossible for a person to drive and control an automobile; he believed it was safe for defendant to drive.

Appellants' contentions that the trial court erred in refusing to grant their motion for summary judgment on the issue of liability and their motion for directed verdict on the pleadings and counsel's opening argument are answered by the disposition of their third claim that the trial court committed prejudicial error in refusing to give their jury instruction on absolute liability.[6]

. . . [C]ases generally hold that liability of a driver, suddenly stricken by an illness rendering him unconscious, for injury resulting from an accident occurring during that time rests on principles of negligence. However, herein during the trial plaintiffs withdrew their claim of negligence and, after both parties rested and before jury argument, objected to the giving of any instructions on negligence electing to stand solely on the theory of absolute liability. The objection was overruled and the court refused plaintiffs' requested instruction after which plaintiffs waived both opening and closing jury arguments. Defendant argued the cause to the jury after which the judge read a series of negligence instructions. . . .

Appellants seek to have this court override the established law of this state which is dispositive of the issue before us as outmoded in today's social and economic structure, particularly in the light of the now recognized principles imposing liability upon the manufacturer, retailer and all distributive and vending elements and activities which bring a product to the consumer to his injury, on the basis of strict liability in tort. . . . Drawing a parallel with these products liability cases, appellants argue, with some degree of logic, that only that driver affected by a physical condition which could suddenly render him unconscious and who is aware of that condition can anticipate the hazards and foresee the dangers involved in his operation of a motor vehicle, and that the liability of those who by reason of seizure or heart failure or some other physical condition lose the ability to safely operate and control a motor vehicle resulting in injury to an innocent person should be predicated on strict liability.

---

[6] When the evidence shows that a driver of a motor vehicle on a public street or highway loses his ability to safely operate and control such vehicle because of some seizure or health failure, that driver is nevertheless legally liable for all injuries and property damage which an innocent person may suffer as a proximate result of the defendant's inability to so control or operate his motor vehicle.

This is true even if you find the defendant driver had no warning of any such impending seizure or health failure.

We decline to superimpose the absolute liability of products liability cases upon drivers under the circumstances here. The theory on which those cases are predicated is that manufacturers, retailers and distributors of products are engaged in the business of distributing goods to the public and are an integral part of the over-all producing and marketing enterprise that should bear the cost of injuries from defective parts. This policy hardly applies here and it is not enough to simply say, as do appellants, that the insurance carriers should be the ones to bear the cost of injuries to innocent victims on a strict liability basis. In *Maloney v. Rath,* 69 Cal. 2d 442, 71 Cal. Rptr. 897, 445 P.2d 513 (1968), appellant urged that defendant's violation of a safety provision (defective brakes) of the Vehicle Code makes the violator strictly liable for damages caused by the violation. While reversing the judgment for defendant upon another ground, the California Supreme Court refused to apply the doctrine of strict liability to automobile drivers. The situation involved two users of the highway but the problems of fixing responsibility under a system of strict liability are as complicated in the instant case as those in *Maloney v. Rath,* and could only create uncertainty in the area of its concern. As stated in *Maloney*:

> To invoke a rule of strict liability on users of the streets and highways, however, without also establishing in substantial detail how the new rule should operate would only contribute confusion to the automobile accident problem. Settlement and claims adjustment procedures would become chaotic until the new rules were worked out on a case-by-case basis, and the hardships of delayed compensation would be seriously intensified. Only the Legislature, if it deems it wise to do so, can avoid such difficulties by enacting a comprehensive plan for the compensation of automobile accident victims in place of or in addition to the law of negligence.

The instruction tendered by appellants was properly refused for still another reason. Even assuming the merit of appellants' position under the facts of this case in which defendant knew he had a history of epilepsy, previously had suffered seizures and at the time of the accident was attempting to control the condition by medication, the instruction does not except from its ambit the driver who suddenly is stricken by an illness or physical condition which he had no reason whatever to anticipate and of which he had no prior knowledge.

NOTES

1. *A Matter of Strategy.* Why did the plaintiffs in *Hammontree* withdraw their negligence claims? Did the plaintiffs have any choice but to attempt to persuade the court to re-categorize the fact pattern?

2. *Theoretical Consistency.* To what extent is the reasoning of the court in *Hammontree* in accord with the views on the applicability of strict liability discussed in note 3, following *Magrine, supra*? To what extent do drivers and pedestrians share the same risks in the paradigm automobile case? Did the court in *Hammontree* give the impression that they were dealing with anything other than a "driver-driver" fact pattern?

C.   REGULATING SOCIALLY DESIRABLE ACTIVITIES   65

3. *More Strategy.* What was the basis for the secondary objection to the strict liability instruction that was raised by the court? How would you rephrase the contended-for instruction to avoid that objectionable characteristic?

4. *First-party, or "Victim" Insurance.* In *Hammontree,* who was in the best position to insure against the injuries sustained by the plaintiff? Plaintiff? Defendant? Defendant's physician? The state?

5. *No-fault Automobile Insurance.* If you were to underwrite insurance for members of the plaintiff class in *Hammontree,* whom would you make purchase the coverage, and what risks would the policy insure against?

PETERSON v. SUPERIOR COURT
10 Cal. 4th 1185, 899 P.2d 905, 43 Cal. Rptr. 2d 836 (1995)

GEORGE, J.

Nadine L. Peterson alleged that, while a guest at the Palm Springs Marquis Hotel, she slipped and fell in the bathtub while taking a shower, sustaining serious head injuries. Plaintiff alleged that the bottom surface of the bathtub was "extremely slick and slippery" and that the bathtub had no "safety measures" such as "anti-skid surfaces, grab rails, rubber mats, or the like." Plaintiff named as defendants, among others, the owners of the hotel, Banque Paribas and Palm Springs Marquis, Inc.; the operator of the hotel, Harbaugh Hotel Management Corporation; and the manufacturer of the bathtub, the Kohler Company. In addition to a cause of action for negligence, plaintiff brought a cause of action for "strict liability in tort," asserting the bathtub was a "defective product" because the bathtub "was so smooth, slippery, and slick as to have provided no friction or slip resistance whatsoever"

The sole issue in the case before us is whether the trial court erred in granting defendants' *in limine* motion to preclude plaintiff from arguing that, pursuant to our decision in *Becker v. IRM Corp.,* 38 Cal. 3d 454 (1985), the proprietor of a hotel is strictly liable under the doctrine of products liability for injuries to hotel guests caused by defects in the premises. For the reasons that follow, we conclude, upon reconsideration, that the decision in *Becker* constitutes an unwarranted extension of the doctrine of products liability and should be overruled. As we explain, the circumstance that landlords and hotel proprietors lease residential dwellings and rent hotel rooms to the public does not bring them within the class of persons who properly may be held strictly liable under the doctrine of products liability.

The plaintiff in *Becker* was injured when he fell against a shower door in the apartment he rented from the defendant. The door, which was made of untempered glass, broke and severely lacerated the plaintiff's arm.

Relying upon the rule announced in *Greenman v. Yuba Power Products, Inc.,* 59 Cal. 2d 57, 27 Cal. Rptr. 697, 377 P.2d 897 (1963), and its progeny, which imposed strict liability for personal injury caused by a defective product placed into the stream of commerce, this court observed that "a lease for a dwelling contains an implied warranty of habitability" and concluded that, in renting a dwelling, a landlord makes an "implied assurance of safety." (*Becker, supra,* 38 Cal. 3d at pp. 462, 465.) Accordingly, this court held "that a landlord engaged in the business of leasing dwellings is strictly liable in tort for injuries resulting from a latent defect in the premises when the defect existed at the time the premises were let to the tenant. [Fn. omitted.]" (*Id.* at p. 464.)

The defendant in *Becker* argued that a landlord that purchases an existing building is not part of the manufacturing and marketing enterprise and, therefore, should not be held strictly liable in tort for injuries caused by defects in the premises. The defendant in that case argued that the reasons enumerated in *Vandermark v. Ford Motor Co.* (1964) 61 Cal. 2d 256, 262–263 [37 Cal. Rptr. 896, 391 P.2d 168] for imposing strict liability upon the retailer of a defective product do not apply to landlords: "Strict liability on the manufacturer and retailer alike affords maximum protection to the injured plaintiff and works no injustice to defendants, for they can adjust the costs of such protection between them in the course of their continuing business relationship." The defendant observed that a subsequent purchaser of a rental property never was in a business relationship with the builder and does not have a continuing business relationship with the builder that would permit adjustment of the cost of protecting tenants. The defendant also likened the landlord that purchases a building that is not new, to a seller of used machinery—such a seller not being strictly liable in tort. (*Becker, supra*, 38 Cal. 3d 454, 465.)

We rejected these arguments in *Becker*, concluding that "a continuing business relationship is not essential to imposition of strict liability." (*Becker, supra*, 38 Cal. 3d at p. 466.) The court stated: "The paramount policy of the strict products liability rule remains the spreading throughout society of the cost of compensating otherwise defenseless victims of manufacturing defects. [Citations.]" (*Ibid.*) Strict liability was imposed, therefore, because the court concluded "[t]he cost of protecting tenants is an appropriate cost of the enterprise." (*Ibid.*)

The decision in *Becker*, judicially engrafting products liability principles onto the law governing landlord liability and holding landlords strictly liable for injuries caused by defects in leased premises, represents a minority view that does not appear to be gaining acceptance. . . .

New Jersey expressly has rejected the imposition of strict liability upon landlords. In *Dwyer v. Skyline Apartments, Inc.* (1973) 123 N.J.Super. 48 [301 A.2d 463], a tenant who had occupied an apartment in a multi-unit building for 15 years was burned when she turned on the hot water faucet in the bathtub in her apartment and the entire fixture came out of the wall, causing scalding water to gush from the pipe. The plaintiff described the faucet as "very corroded" but stated she had no idea of its condition prior to the accident, because the corrosion had been hidden inside the wall. The trial court found for the plaintiff, despite the absence of actual or constructive notice to the landlord of the defect, holding the landlord strictly liable based upon an implied warranty of habitability. The intermediate appellate court reversed the judgment, stating: "Since his duty is not to insure the safety of tenants but only to exercise reasonable care, a landlord is liable only for injurious consequences to a tenant by reason of defects 'of which he has knowledge or of defects which have existed for so long a time that . . . he had both an opportunity to discover and to remedy.' [Citations.]" (301 A.2d at p. 465.) The

C. REGULATING SOCIALLY DESIRABLE ACTIVITIES 67

court rejected the argument that the landlord could be held strictly liable on a products liability theory: "The underlying reasons for the enforcement of strict liability against the manufacturer, seller or lessor of products or the mass builder-vendor of homes do not apply to the ordinary landlord of a multiple family dwelling. [P] Such a landlord is not engaged in mass production whereby he places his product—the apartment—in a stream of commerce exposing it to a large number of consumers. He has not created the product with a defect which is preventable by greater care at the time of manufacture or assembly. He does not have the expertise to know and correct the condition, so as to be saddled with responsibility for a defect regardless of negligence. . . ." (*Id.* at p. 467.)

. . .The effect of imposing upon landlords liability without fault is to compel them to insure the safety of their tenants in situations in which injury is caused by a defect of which the landlord neither knew nor should have known. . . .

Justifying its significant and unprecedented expansion of a landlord's liability for injuries to tenants by applying the law of products liability to the relationship between landlord and tenant, *Becker* reasoned that an apartment itself should be considered a "product" that a landlord places into the stream of commerce. *Becker*'s reasoning in reaching that conclusion, however, is flawed in several respects.

As noted in *Becker*, this court held in *Greenman v. Yuba Power Products, Inc.*, *supra*, 59 Cal. 2d 57, 62, that "[a] manufacturer is strictly liable in tort when an article he places on the market, knowing that it is to be used without inspection for defects, proves to have a defect that causes injury to a human being." In *Vandermark v. Ford Motor Co.*, *supra*, 61 Cal. 2d 256, 262–263, we held that a retailer of manufactured goods also is strictly liable in tort: "Retailers like manufacturers are engaged in the business of distributing goods to the public. They are an integral part of the overall producing and marketing enterprise that should bear the cost of injuries resulting from defective products. [Citation.] In some cases the retailer may be the only member of that enterprise reasonably available to the injured plaintiff. In other cases the retailer himself may play a substantial part in insuring that the product is safe or may be in a position to exert pressure on the manufacturer to that end; the retailer's strict liability thus serves as an added incentive to safety. Strict liability on the manufacturer and retailer alike affords maximum protection to the injured plaintiff and works no injustice to the defendants, for they can adjust the costs of such protection between them in the course of their continuing business relationship."

Most of the preceding reasons for imposing strict liability upon a retailer of a defective product do not apply to landlords or hotel proprietors who rent residential premises. A landlord or hotel owner, unlike a retailer, often cannot exert pressure upon the manufacturer to make the product safe and cannot share with the manufacturer the costs of insuring the safety of the tenant, because a landlord or hotel owner generally has no "continuing business relationship" with the manufacturer of the defective product. As one commentator has observed: "If the objective of the application of the stream of commerce approach is to distribute the risk of providing a product to society by allowing an injured plaintiff to find a remedy for injury along the chain of distribution, it will probably fail in the landlord/tenant situation. The cost of insuring risk will not be distributed along the chain of commerce but will probably be absorbed by tenants who will pay increased rents. One could argue that this was not the effect sought by the court in earlier cases which anticipated that the cost of risk would be distributed vertically in the stream of commerce." (Note, *Becker v. IRM Corporation: Strict Liability in Tort for Residential Landlords, supra*, 16 Golden Gate L.Rev. 349, 360.)

In the present case, for example, plaintiff's products liability claim is premised upon the assertion that the bathtub in her hotel room was defective because its surface was too slippery. But a hotel owner is not a part of the chain of distribution of a bathtub that is installed in a hotel room, just as a restaurant owner is not the equivalent of a retailer of toilets simply because the restaurant provides restroom facilities to its patrons, and just as an owner of a business is not the equivalent of a retailer of ceiling fans simply because one is installed on the premises to promote the comfort of customers of the business. In such circumstances, the bathtub, toilets, and ceiling fans left the stream of commerce when they were purchased and installed in the premises of the various businesses. The mere circumstance that it was contemplated customers of these businesses would use the products in question or be benefited by them does not transform the owners of the businesses into the equivalent of retailers of the products.

We need not, and do not, decide whether different considerations would apply in the event the landlord or hotel owner had participated in the construction of the building But in such circumstances strict liability would attach, if at all, based upon the landlord's status as a builder who is engaged in the business of constructing (i.e. manufacturing) rental properties.

The record before us in the present case does not disclose whether defendants constructed the hotel. Plaintiff did not argue in the courts below, or in the briefs filed in this court, that strict liability applies because defendants had constructed the hotel. Accordingly, neither the trial court nor the Court of Appeal ruled upon this issue. Thus, we express no opinion regarding whether, or under what circumstances, strict liability might be imposed upon a landlord or hotel proprietor who participated in the construction of the building or otherwise created the defective product that caused the injury. On remand, plaintiff may seek leave from the superior court to raise such issues.

The conclusion that a landlord or hotel proprietor, unlike a retailer, is not strictly liable in tort is supported by those cases holding that a seller of used machinery is not strictly liable in tort, unless the seller rebuilds or reconditions the product and thus assumes a role analogous to that of a manufacturer.

Tauber-Arons Auctioneers Co. v. Superior Court (1980) 101 Cal. App. 3d 268, 274 [161 Cal. Rptr. 789] held that an auctioneer is not strictly liable in tort for injuries caused by defects in used machinery sold at auction. (Accord, *Brejcha v. Wilson Machinery, Inc.* (1984) 160 Cal. App. 3d 630, 639–640 [206 Cal. Rptr. 688].) The decision states: "[T]he marketing enterprise, participation in which would justify imposition of strict liability for a defect created by the manufacturer, is the enterprise by which *initial* distribution of the particular manufacturer's products to the consuming public is effected." (101

Cal. App. 3d at p. 277, italics added.) Adopting the reasoning of the Oregon Supreme Court in *Tillman v. Vance Equipment Co.* (1979) 286 Ore. 747 [596 P.2d 1299], the court in *Tauber-Arons* identified three justifications for the imposition of strict liability for defective products—loss spreading, implied representation of safety, and impetus to manufacture a safer product. (101 Cal. App. 3d at p. 280.)

Regarding the final factor, the decision in *Tauber-Arons* quotes at length from the decision in *Tillman*: " 'As to the risk-reduction aspect of strict products liability, the position of the used-goods dealer is normally entirely outside the original chain of distribution of the product. As a consequence, we conclude, any risk reduction which would be accomplished by imposing strict liability on the dealer in used goods would not be significant enough to justify our taking that step. The dealer in used goods generally has no direct relationship with either manufacturers or distributors. Thus, there is no ready channel of communication by which the dealer and the manufacturer can exchange information about possible dangerous defects in particular product lines or about actual and potential liability claims.' " (*Tauber-Arons Auctioneers Co. v. Superior Court, supra*, 101 Cal. App. 3d 268, 281&ndash

This reasoning applies with even greater force to a landlord or hotel owner who purchases an apartment building or hotel. Defects in such a structure may have been created by the builder, a subcontractor, a manufacturer of building supplies or fixtures, a previous owner of the building, or a previous tenant of the apartment or guest of the hotel. Because the landlord or hotel owner generally has no continuing business relationship, or other ready channel of communication, with any of these persons or entities, only in rare cases would the imposition of strict liability upon the landlord or hotel owner create an impetus to manufacture safer products. As one commentator has recognized: "Unlike other suppliers . . ., landlords' ability to improve their products' safety is rather limited. Landlords cannot redesign the products or switch manufacturers; they can only repair the defects they know about. While imposing strict landlord liability will encourage landlords to make such repairs, it provides no greater safety incentive than imposing negligence liability." (Comment, *California's Approach to Landlord Liability for Tenant Injuries: Strict Liability Reexamined, supra*, 26 U.C. Davis L. Rev. 367, 405, fns. omitted.)

As to the second justification for the imposition of strict liability—an implied representation of safety—the decision in *Tauber-Arons* again quotes the decision in *Tillman*: " '[T]he sale of a used product, without more, may not be found to generate the kind of expectations of safety that the courts have held are justifiably created by the introduction of a new product into the stream of commerce.' " (*Tauber-Arons Auctioneers Co. v. Superior Court, supra*, 101 Cal. App. 3d 268,

This court in *Becker* held, to the contrary, that a tenant renting a dwelling has an expectation of safety similar to that of a consumer purchasing a new product, even if the building is not new. This conclusion was based upon the implied warranty of habitability contained in a residential lease, recognized in *Green v. Superior Court* (1974) 10 Cal. 3d 616 [111 Cal. Rptr. 704, 517 P.2d 1168]—a warranty that the court in *Becker* viewed as constituting an "implied assurance of safety made by the landlord." (*Becker, supra,* 38 Cal. 3d at p. 465.) The conclusion reached in *Becker,* however, overstates the effect of the implied warranty recognized in *Green.*

The reasoning in *Becker* is flawed because recognition of the implied warranty of habitability does not lead to the conclusion that a landlord is strictly liable for injuries to tenants caused by defects in the premises. Although, as noted above, nearly all states have recognized an implied warranty of habitability in residential leases, only California (by judicial decision) and Louisiana (by statute) hold landlords strictly liable for injuries to tenants caused by defects in the premises. One commentator has explained this trend as follows: "Gradually, . . . courts are realizing that the implied warranty is actually a covenant rather than a warranty, which means that breaches need not give rise to excessive tort liability. The landlord's repair covenant is (or at least should be) breached only if the landlord fails to fix a problem within a reasonable period after notice. It is the landlord's inaction —the landlord's negligence—that gives rise to liability." (Freyfogle, *The Installment Land Contract as Lease: Habitability Protections and the Low-income Purchaser, supra,* 62 N. Y. U. L.Rev. 293, 302, fns. omitted.) One advantage to the approach of viewing the implied warranty as a covenant is that it applies equally to all landlords, whether or not they are "in the business of leasing dwellings." (*Becker, supra,* 38 Cal. 3d at p. 464; *Vaerst v. Tanzman, supra,* 222 Cal. App. 3d at p. 1540 [a landlord "who leased his own family residence to the tenants on a temporary basis . . . is not within the purview of *Becker* . . . ."].)

The implied warranty of habitability recognized in *Green* gives a tenant a reasonable expectation that the landlord has inspected the rental dwelling and corrected any defects disclosed by that inspection that would render the dwelling uninhabitable. The tenant further reasonably can expect that the landlord will maintain the property in a habitable condition by repairing promptly any conditions, of which the landlord has actual or constructive notice, that arise during the tenancy and render the dwelling uninhabitable. A tenant injured by a defect in the premises, therefore, may bring a negligence action if the landlord breached its duty to exercise reasonable care. But a tenant cannot reasonably expect that the landlord will have eliminated defects in a rented dwelling of which the landlord was unaware and which would not have been disclosed by a reasonable inspection. The implied warranty of habitability, therefore, does not support an action for strict liability.

Even before the advent of the implied warranty of habitability applicable to residential leases, it was recognized that hotel proprietors have a special relationship with their guests that gives rise to a duty similar to that owed by common carriers "to protect them against unreasonable risk of physical harm." (Rest.2d Torts, § 314A.) "The duty in each case is only one to exercise reasonable care under the circumstances. The defendant is not liable where he neither knows nor should know of the unreasonable risk . . . ." (*Id.,* com. e, at p. 120.) We have recognized that an innkeeper, like a common carrier, is not an insurer of the safety of its guests. (*Lopez v. Southern Cal. Rapid Transit Dist.* (1985) 40 Cal. 3d 780, 785, 788 [221 Cal. Rptr. 840, 710 P.2d 907]; *Nash v. Fifth Amendment* (1991) 228 Cal. App. 3d 1106, 1111 [279 Cal. Rptr. 465].)

A hotel guest reasonably can expect that the hotel owner diligently will inspect the hotel room for defects and will correct any defects discovered. But the guest cannot reasonably expect that the owner will correct defects of which the owner is unaware and that cannot be discerned by a reasonable inspection. The duty of an innkeeper, therefore, like the duty of a landlord, does not support an action for strict liability.

The remaining justification for the imposition of strict liability discussed in *Tauber-Arons* is loss spreading. *Becker* relied upon this factor almost exclusively in distinguishing the rule, announced in *Tauber-Arons* and its progeny, that strict liability should not be imposed upon sellers of used merchandise: "The paramount policy of the strict products liability rule remains the spreading throughout society of the cost of compensating otherwise defenseless victims of manufacturing defects. [Citations.]" (*Becker, supra,* 38 Cal. 3d at p. 466.) But the court in *Tauber-Arons,* quoting a similar statement from this court's decision in *Price v. Shell Oil Co., supra,* 2 Cal. 3d 245, 251, that loss spreading was a "paramount policy" of products liability law, correctly observed that this court in *Price* "did not, however, abandon all other considerations." (*Tauber-Arons Auctioneers Co. v. Superior Court, supra,* 101 Cal. App. 3d 268, 283.) Instead, the decision in *Price* states: "In *Vandermark* we again emphasized the necessity for a continuous course of business as a condition to application of the rule," observing that, under such circumstances, the imposition of strict liability "works no injustice to the defendants." (*Price v. Shell Oil Co., supra,* 2 Cal. 3d 245, 253–254.)

In many instances, it would be unjust to hold a landlord strictly liable for an injury to a tenant caused by a defect of which the landlord had no knowledge and which would not have been disclosed by a reasonable inspection. One commentator posed a hypothetical situation in which a tenant was injured by a construction defect, the landlord was held strictly liable, and the resulting judgment exceeded the limits of the landlord's insurance coverage. Noting the "potential for harsh results" inherent in *Becker*'s rule of strict liability, the commentator observed: "When latent defects injure tenants, both landlords and tenants are innocent of any wrongdoing. The primary justification for shifting accident costs from innocent tenants to equally innocent landlords is 'loss-spreading.' The landlord has access to liability insurance, and thus, in theory, can spread the costs of injuries that would financially devastate an individual. In reality, however, insurance policies have limits, and, as in the hypothetical, holding landlords strictly liable sometimes substitutes one innocent victim for another." (Comment, *California's Approach to Landlord Liability for Tenant Injuries: Strict Liability Reexamined, supra,* 26 U.C. Davis L.Rev. 367, 371.)

For the same reasons, it often would be unjust to hold a hotel proprietor strictly liable for an injury to a hotel guest caused by a defect in the premises, of which the hotel proprietor was unaware, and which would not have been disclosed by a reasonable inspection. The economic consequences could be particularly onerous for the operators of small establishments, such as small motels or bed and breakfast inns, who, through no fault of their own, could be rendered financially insolvent if a grievous injury to a guest caused by an unknown defect in the premises resulted in a judgment that exceeded available insurance coverage.

Subsequent to the decision in *Becker*, this court reaffirmed in *Brown v. Superior Court*, (1988) 44 Cal. 3d 1049 [245 Cal. Rptr. 412, 751 P.2d 470], that loss spreading is not the sole consideration in determining whether to impose strict liability for injuries resulting from a defective product. The plaintiffs in *Brown* allegedly were injured in utero when their mothers, in order to prevent miscarriage, ingested the drug "DES" during pregnancy. In considering whether the manufacturers of this drug should be held strictly liable in tort, we noted that "the fundamental reasons underlying the imposition of strict liability are to deter manufacturers from marketing products that are unsafe, and to spread the cost of injury from the plaintiff to the consuming public." (*Id.* at p. 1062.) We recognized that "[t]hese reasons could justify application of the doctrine to the manufacturer of prescription drugs. It is indisputable . . . that the risk of injury from such drugs is unavoidable, that a consumer may be helpless to protect himself from serious harm caused by them, and that, like other products, the cost of insuring against strict liability can be passed on by the producer to the consumer who buys the item." (*Id.* at p. 1063.) Nevertheless, for reasons of public policy inapplicable to the present case, we held that the manufacturers of prescription drugs should not be held strictly liable in tort, even if the drug was defectively designed. . . .

Another problem with relying exclusively upon the doctrine of loss spreading to justify the imposition of liability without fault is that the same reasoning could be used to impose strict liability in *any* situation in which the defendant is in a superior position economically to bear or distribute the loss suffered by the plaintiff. As one commentator has observed: "Spreading the cost of injury throughout society amounts to no more than a judicially imposed insurance system. To use this rationale for imposing strict liability in isolation of other rationales is to write a judicial ticket to impose strict liability in any area of law where there are injured plaintiffs who may not be compensated." (Note, *A Bird in the Hand: California Imposes Strict Liability on Landlords in Becker v. IRM Corp.*, 20 Loyola L.A. L.Rev. 323, 370.)

As the foregoing discussion demonstrates, the reasons for not applying the doctrine of strict products liability to sellers of used goods support, as well, the conclusion that landlords and hotel owners should not be held strictly liable in tort for injuries to tenants and hotel guests caused by defects in the premises. A landlord or hotel owner who rents dwellings or hotel rooms differs significantly from a manufacturer or retailer of a product. Manufacturers and retailers can be expected to possess expert knowledge concerning the product being produced or sold, but the same is not necessarily true of a landlord or hotel owner. . . .

For all of the foregoing reasons, we conclude that the decision in *Becker* was incorrect in holding that a landlord is strictly liable on the basis of products liability for injuries to a tenant caused by a defect in a leased dwelling. To the extent it so holds, the decision in *Becker* is overruled. For these same reasons, we further hold that the proprietor of a hotel should not be held strictly liable on the basis of products liability for injuries to a guest caused by a defect in the premises.

As we noted at the outset of this opinion, the conclusion we reach by no means absolves hotel proprietors or landlords of all potential responsibility for such injuries; on the contrary, hotel proprietors and landlords still may be held liable under general tort principles for injuries resulting from defects in their premises if they have breached the applicable standard of care. Neither is the injured tenant or guest deprived of any strict products liability cause of action that may lie against the manufacturer, distributor, or retailer of a defective product that causes the injury. In the present case, for example, plaintiff named as a defendant the manufacturer of the bathtub and has entered into a settlement with the manufacturer for the sum of $ 600,000. Upon remand, plaintiff may proceed against the remaining defendants on her cause of action for negligence.

NOTES

1. *Analogizing to Products Liability.* The leading case of *Greenman v. Yuba Power Prods., Inc.*, 59 Cal. 2d 57, 27 Cal. Rptr. 697, 377 P.2d 897 (1963), articulated the rationale for the imposition of a strict liability system as follows:

> The purpose of such liability is to insure that the costs of injuries resulting from defective products are borne by the manufacturers that put such products on the market rather than by the injured persons who are powerless to protect themselves. Sales warranties serve this purpose fitfully at best. In the present case, for example, plaintiff was able to plead and prove an express warranty only because he read and relied on the representations of the [product's] ruggedness contained in the manufacturer's brochure. Implicit in the [product's] presence on the market, however, was a representation that it would safely do the jobs for which it was built. Under these circumstances, it should not be controlling whether plaintiff selected the machine because of the statements in the brochure, or because of the machine's own appearance of excellence that belied the defect lurking beneath the surface, or because he merely assumed that it would safely do the jobs it was built to do. It should not be controlling whether the details of the sales from manufacturer to retailer and from retailer to plaintiff's wife were such that one or more of the implied warranties of the sales act arose.

The leading doctrinal statement of this type of liability is to be found in RESTATEMENT (SECOND) OF TORTS (1965) § 402A. It reads as follows:

> (1) One who sells any product in a defective condition unreasonably dangerous to the user or consumer or to his property is subject to liability for physical harm thereby caused to the ultimate user or consumer, or to his property, if
>
> (a) the seller is engaged in the business of selling such a product, and
>
> (b) it is expected to and does reach the user or consumer without substantial change in the condition in which it is sold.
>
> (2) The rule stated in Subsection (1) applies although

(a) the seller has exercised all possible care in the preparation and sale of his product, and

(b) the user or consumer has not bought the product from or entered into any contractual relation with the seller.

Why and how is § 402A an example of strict liability? Was it a good analogy for the plaintiff in *Hammontree* to utilize?

Consider further this early reaction to the notion of strict products liability,

> The grand simplicity of the new doctrine — its sweeping aside of the concept of liability through fault — is its most dangerous aspect. The all-inclusive ring of "strict liability," will cause an overextension . . . of what is conceived by its progenitors to be a limited concept. Unlike its predecessor-doctrine of liability through "fault," which in the very statement of the principle suggests that the shifting of loss is to be the exception rather than the rule, the innuendos of the new verbiage are pervasive.

Bailey v. Montgomery Ward & Co., 431 P.2d 108, 119 (Ariz. 1967) (*per* Molloy, J.).

Assume that the court in *Hammontree* had granted plaintiff's contended-for instruction. What evidence must plaintiff have adduced? How could the defendant have responded?

2. In addition to the products liability doctrine, plaintiffs frequently have analogized their case, in which they were seeking a strict liability categorization, to the innkeeper-guest fact pattern, early considered an example of strict liability in risk-allocation. However, consider *Nova Stylings, Inc. v. Red Roof Inns, Inc.*, 242 Kan. 318, 747 P.2d 107 (1987), in which the plaintiff's jewelry samples case was stolen after she left it with a motel desk clerk. The court noted that most modern innkeepers' liability limitation statutes immunized innkeepers from *both* strict and negligence-based claims.

PROBLEM

Rocky, a quarry worker, became annoyed when Ivy, his girlfriend, moved 100 miles across state to attend college. Despite Rocky's pleas, Ivy refused to come home or even discuss their relationship. Rocky stole 50 pounds of dynamite from the quarry and used it to construct a bomb. He visited Ivy and told her that he would blow himself up if she didn't return home. Ivy called the campus police who tried to calm Rocky. However, he became distraught, set off the bomb and injured Francis, one of the officers. Francis brings an action against the rock quarry. What theories will Francis pursue? With what results?

SIEGLER v. KUHLMAN
81 Wash. 2d 448, 502 P.2d 1181 (1972)

HALE, ASSOCIATE JUSTICE.

. . . Aaron L. Kuhlman had been a truck driver for nearly 11 years after he completed the 10th grade in high school and after he had worked at other

C. REGULATING SOCIALLY DESIRABLE ACTIVITIES

jobs for a few years. He had been driving for Pacific Intermountain Express for about 4 months, usually the night shift out of the Texaco bulk plant in Tumwater. That evening of November 22nd, he was scheduled to drive a gasoline truck and trailer unit, fully loaded with gasoline, from Tumwater to Port Angeles. Before leaving the Texaco plant, he inspected the trailer, checking the lights, hitch, air hoses and tires. Finding nothing wrong, he then set out, driving the fully loaded truck tank and trailer tank, stopping briefly at the Trail's End Cafe for a cup of coffee. It was just a few minutes after 6 p.m., and dark, but the roads were dry when he started the drive to deliver his cargo — 3,800 gallons of gasoline in the truck tank and 4,800 gallons of gasoline in the trailer tank. With all vehicle and trailer running lights on, he drove the truck and trailer onto Interstate Highway 5, proceeded north on that freeway at about 50 miles per hour, he said, and took the offramp about 1 mile later to enter Highway 101 at the Capitol Lake interchange. Running downgrade on the offramp, he felt a jerk, looked into his left-hand mirror and then his right-hand mirror to see that the trailer lights were not in place. The trailer was still moving but leaning over hard, he observed, onto its right side. The trailer then came loose. Realizing that the tank trailer had disengaged from his tank truck, he stopped the truck without skidding its tires. He got out and ran back to see that the tank trailer had crashed through a chain-link highway fence and had come to rest upside down on Capitol Lake Drive below. He heard a sound, he said, "like somebody kicking an empty fifty-gallon drum and that is when the fire started." The fire spread, he thought, about 100 feet down the road.

The trailer was owned by defendant Pacific Intermountain Express. It had traveled about 329,000 miles prior to November 22, 1967, and had been driven by Mr. Kuhlman without incident down the particular underpass above Capitol Lake Drive about 50 times. When the trailer landed upside down on Capitol Lake Drive, its lights were out, and it was unilluminated when Carol House's car in one way or another ignited the spilled gasoline.

Carol House was burned to death in the flames. There was no evidence of impact on the vehicle she had driven, Kuhlman said, except that the left front headlight was broken.

Why the tank trailer disengaged and catapulted off the freeway down through a chain-link fence to land upside down on Capitol Lake Drive below remains a mystery. What caused it to separate from the truck towing it, despite many theories offered in explanation, is still an enigma.

. . . The jury apparently found that defendants had met and overcome the charges of negligence. Defendants presented proof that both the truck, manufactured by Peterbilt, a division of Pacific Car and Foundry Company, and the tank and trailer, built by Fruehauf Company, had been constructed by experienced companies, and that the fifth wheel, connecting the two units and built by Silver Eagle Company, was the type of connecting unit used by 95 percent of the truck-trailer units. Defendants presented evidence that a most careful inspection would not have revealed the defects or fatigue in the metal connections between truck and trailer; that the trailer would not collapse unless both main springs failed; there was evidence that, when fully loaded, the tank could not touch the wheels of the tank trailer without breaking the springs because the maximum flexion of the springs was less than 1 inch. Defendants presented evidence that the drawbar was secure and firmly attached; that the tanks were built of aluminum to prevent sparks; and that, when fully loaded with 4,800 gallons of cargo, there would be 2 or 3 inches of space between the cargo and top of the tank; that two safety cables connected the two units; that the truck and trailer were regularly serviced and repaired, and records of this preserved and put in evidence; that the unit had been subject to Interstate Commerce Commission spot checks and conformed to ICC standards; and that, at the time of the accident, the unit had traveled less than one-third of the average service life of that kind of unit. There was evidence obtained at the site of the fire that both of the mainsprings above the tank trailer's front wheels had broken as a result of stress, not fatigue — from a kind of stress that could not be predicted by inspection — and finally that there was no negligence on the driver's part.

. . . [T]here exists here an even more impelling basis for liability in this case than its derivation by allowable inference of fact . . . and that is the proposition of strict liability arising as a matter of law from all of the circumstances of the event.

Strict liability is not a novel concept; it is at least as old as *Fletcher v. Rylands* [discussed *supra* note 3 following *Magrine*]. In that famous case, where water impounded in a reservoir on defendant's property escaped and damaged neighboring coal mines, the landowner who had impounded the water was held liable without proof of fault or negligence. Acknowledging a distinction between the natural and nonnatural use of land, and holding the maintenance of a reservoir to be a nonnatural use, the Court of Exchequer Chamber imposed a rule of strict liability on the landowner. The ratio decidendi included adoption of what is now called strict liability, and . . . announced, we think, principles which should be applied in the instant case:

> [The] person who for his own purposes brings on his lands and collects and keeps there anything likely to do mischief if it escapes, must keep it in at his peril, and, if he does not do so, is prima facie answerable for all the damage which is the natural consequence of its escape.

. . . In many respects, hauling gasoline as freight is no more unusual, but more dangerous, than collecting water. When gasoline is carried as cargo — as distinguished from fuel for the carrier vehicle — it takes on uniquely hazardous characteristics, as does water impounded in large quantities. Dangerous in itself, gasoline develops even greater potential for harm when carried as freight — extraordinary dangers deriving from sheer quantity, bulk and weight, which enormously multiply its hazardous properties. And the very hazards inhering from the size of the load, its bulk or quantity and its movement along the highways presents another reason for application of the *Fletcher v. Rylands* rule not present in the impounding of large quantities of water — the likely destruction of cogent evidence from which negligence or want of it may be proved or disproved. It is quite probable that the most important ingredients of proof will be lost in a gasoline explosion and fire. Gasoline is always dangerous whether kept in large or small quantities because of its volatility, inflammability and explosiveness. But when several

C. REGULATING SOCIALLY DESIRABLE ACTIVITIES

thousand gallons of it are allowed to spill across a public highway — that is, if, while in transit as freight, it is not kept impounded — the hazards to third persons are so great as to be almost beyond calculation. As a consequence of its escape from impoundment and subsequent explosion and ignition, the evidence in a very high percentage of instances will be destroyed, and the reasons for and causes contributing to its escape will quite likely be lost in the searing flames and explosions.

. . . The rule of strict liability rests not only upon the ultimate idea of rectifying a wrong and putting the burden where it should belong as a matter of abstract justice, that is, upon the one of the two innocent parties whose acts instigated or made the harm possible, but it also rests on problems of proof:

> One of these common features is that the person harmed would encounter a difficult problem of proof if some other standard of liability were applied. For example, the disasters caused by those who engage in abnormally dangerous or extra-hazardous activities frequently destroy all evidence of what in fact occurred, other than that the activity was being carried on. Certainly this is true with explosions of dynamite, large quantities of gasoline, or other explosives. It frequently is the case with falling aircraft. Tracing the course followed by gases or other poisons used by exterminators may be difficult if not impossible. The explosion of an atomic reactor may leave little evidence of the circumstances which caused it. Moreover, application of such a standard of liability to activities which are not matters of common experience is well-adapted to a jury's limited ability to judge whether proper precautions were observed with such activities.
>
> Problems of proof which might otherwise have been faced by shippers, bailors, or guests at hotels and inns certainly played a significant role in shaping the strict liabilities of carriers, bailees, and innkeepers. Problems of proof in suits against manufacturers for harm done by defective products became more severe as the composition and design of products and the techniques of manufacture became less and less matters of common experience; this was certainly a factor bringing about adoption of a strict liability standard.

Peck, Negligence and Liability Without Fault in Tort Law, 46 Wash. L. Rev. 225, 240 (1971).

. . . Thus, the reasons for applying a rule of strict liability obtain in this case. We have a situation where a highly flammable, volatile and explosive substance is being carried at a comparatively high rate of speed, in great and dangerous quantities as cargo upon the public highways, subject to all of the hazards of high-speed traffic, multiplied by the great dangers inherent in the volatile and explosive nature of the substance, and multiplied again by the quantity and size of the load. Then we have the added dangers of ignition and explosion generated when a load of this size, that is, about 5,000 gallons of gasoline, breaks its container and, cascading from it, spreads over the highway so as to release an invisible but highly volatile and explosive vapor above it.

Danger from great quantities of gasoline spilled upon the public highway is extreme and extraordinary, for any spark, flame or appreciable heat is likely to ignite it. The incandescent filaments from a broken automobile headlight, a spark from the heat of a tailpipe, a lighted cigarette in the hands of a driver or passenger, the hot coals from a smoker's pipe or cigar, and the many hot and sparking spots and units of an automobile motor from exhaust to generator could readily ignite the vapor cloud gathered above a highway from 5,000 gallons of spilled gasoline. Any automobile passing through the vapors could readily have produced the flames and explosions which killed the young woman in this case and without the provable intervening negligence of those who loaded and serviced the carrier and the driver who operated it. Even the most prudent and careful motorist, coming unexpectedly and without warning upon this gasoline pool and vapor, could have driven into it and ignited a holocaust without knowledge of the danger and without leaving a trace of what happened to set off the explosion and light the searing flames.

Stored in commercial quantities, gasoline has been recognized to be a substance of such dangerous characteristics that it invites a rule of strict liability — even where the hazard is contamination to underground water supply and not its more dangerous properties such as its explosiveness and flammability. It is even more appropriate, therefore, to apply this principle to the more highly hazardous act of transporting it as freight upon the freeways and public thoroughfares.

Recently this court, while declining to apply strict liability in a particular case, did acknowledge the suitability of the rule in a proper case. In *Pacific Northwest Bell Tel. Co. v. Port of Seattle,* 80 Wash. 2d 59, 491 P.2d 1037 (1971), we observed that strict liability had its beginning in *Fletcher v. Rylands* but said that it ought not be applied in a situation where a bursting water main, installed and maintained by the defendant Port of Seattle, damaged plaintiff telephone company's underground wires. There the court divided — not on the basic justice of a rule of strict liability in some cases but in its application in a particular case to what on its face was a situation of comparatively minor hazards. Both majority and dissenting justices held, however, that the strict liability principles of *Fletcher v. Rylands* should be given effect in some cases; but the court divided on the question of whether underground water mains there constituted such a case.

. . . [W]e rejected the application of strict liability in *Pacific Northwest Bell Tel. Co. v. Port of Seattle* solely because the installation of underground water mains by a municipality was not, under the circumstances shown, an abnormally dangerous activity. Had the activity been found abnormally dangerous, this court would have applied in that case the rule of strict liability.

Contrast, however, the quiet, relatively safe, routine procedure of installing and maintaining and using underground water mains as described in *Pacific Northwest Bell Tel. Co. v. Port of Seattle* with the activity of carrying gasoline as freight in quantities of thousands of gallons at freeway speeds along the public highway and even at lawful lesser speeds through cities and towns and on secondary roads in rural districts. In comparing the quiescence and the passive job of maintaining underground water mains with the extremely heightened activity of carrying nearly 5,000 gallons of gasoline by truck, one cannot escape the conclusion that hauling gasoline as cargo is undeniably an abnormally dangerous activity and on its face possesses all of the factors necessary for imposition of strict liability as set forth in the Restatement . . . .

Transporting gasoline as freight by truck along the public highways and streets is obviously an activity involving a high degree of risk; it is a risk of great harm and injury; it creates dangers that cannot be eliminated by the exercise of reasonable care. That gasoline cannot be practically transported except upon the public highway does not decrease the abnormally high risk arising from the transportation. Nor will the exercise of due and reasonable care assure protection to the public from the disastrous consequences of concealed or latent mechanical or metallurgical defects in the carrier's equipment, from the negligence of third parties, from latent defects in the highways and streets, and from all of the other hazards not generally disclosed or guarded against by reasonable care, prudence and foresight. Hauling gasoline in great quantities as freight, we think, is an activity that calls for the application of principles of strict liability.

ROSELLINI, ASSOCIATE JUSTICE, concurring.

. . . I think the opinion should make clear, however, that the owner of the vehicle will be held strictly liable only for damages caused when the flammable or explosive substance is allowed to escape without the apparent intervention of any outside force beyond the control of the manufacturer, the owner, or the operator of the vehicle hauling it. I do not think the majority means to suggest that if another vehicle, negligently driven, collided with the truck in question, the truck owner would be held liable for the damage. But where, as here, there was no outside force which caused the trailer to become detached from the truck, the rule of strict liability should apply.

NOTES

1. *Whither Strict Liability?* Various criteria for the imposition of strict liability in the abstract are mentioned in *Siegler*. Do all of these criteria seem to carry the same weight?

2. *Doctrinal Basis.* Does the *Siegler* court base its decision primarily upon *Rylands v. Fletcher,* discussed *supra*, or RESTATEMENT (SECOND) OF TORTS §§ 519–520, *supra*? Are there any important differences between them? Applying the criteria in § 520 to the facts of *Siegler,* which would seem to favor plaintiff? Defendant?

3. *A Strange Detour.* In *Louisville Ry. Co. v. Sweeney,* 157 Ky. 620, 163 S.W. 739 (1914), a streetcar jumped its track on a steep grade at a curve, continued for some 150 feet and knocked over a telephone pole. The pole fell against the gate to plaintiff's lot, propelling the gate into the plaintiff. The defendant appealed from plaintiff's jury verdict complaining of the charge to the jury which, in essence, had tied defendant's liability to a showing of causation. The court affirmed the verdict, stating:

> The entry of the defendant upon [plaintiff's property] either by its street car or by the pole which it set in motion was a trespass. One who trespasses upon another and inflicts an injury is liable for the injury unless caused by the act of God or produced by causes beyond his control.

On what basis could defendant be found liable: trespass, negligence, *Rylands v. Fletcher,* ultrahazardous activity? None of the above?

4. *There Is Gas; and Then There Is Gas. New Meadows Holding Co. v. Washington Water Power Co.,* 102 Wash. 2d 495, 687 P.2d 212 (1984), concerned a fire and explosion which was caused by a natural gas leak several blocks away. The leak allegedly originated in some damage done to the gas line by a telephone company. Unable to permeate the frozen ground, the escaping gas entered the plaintiff's premises through a drain field. The Washington Supreme Court stated:

> Some degree of risk of natural gas pipeline leaks will always be present. This does not mean, however, that the "high degree of risk" with which section 520 is concerned cannot be eliminated by the use of reasonable care with regard to the dangerous character of the commodity. Gas companies are subject to strict federal and state safety regulations. Programs for corrosion control, pipeline testing, gas leak investigation, and awareness of construction work near gas company facilities must be maintained. Odorizers are placed in the gas itself to increase the likelihood of detection in those rare instances when natural gas does escape. In light of all this, we believe the high degree of risk involved in the transmission of natural gas through underground lines can be eliminated by the use of reasonable care and legislative safeguards.
>
> . . . The underground transmission of natural gas presents a significant contrast to the activity at issue in *Siegler*. Natural gas flows through a small (2-inch) pipe which is buried underground, away from the dangers of the surface world. There are no careless drivers, faulty brakes, or slippery roads with which to contend. The heightened danger resulting from the storage of a highly volatile substance in large commercial quantities, rolling at high speed on a well traveled highway, is also absent.
>
> . . . Here, the gas leak was allegedly caused when a contractor laying underground telephone cable for Pacific Northwest Bell damaged a 2-inch gas transmission line owned by defendant. Neither in its facts nor in its law does *Siegler* apply to this case.

Dissenting, Rosellini, J., stated:

> The transmission of natural gas is analogous to the transportation of gasoline. Natural gas, like gasoline, remains relatively safe if contained in its proper place, *i.e.*, gas lines, storage tanks or even automobiles. Once natural gas or gasoline escapes, however, the exercise of ordinary or even extraordinary care frequently is incapable of averting an explosion.
>
> . . . The majority ignores this similarity by observing that the transport of natural gas involves no negligent drivers, slippery roads or faulty brakes. This distinction neglects the risks that may occur, such as negligent excavators, faulty digging equipment or vandals who may remove or damage warning signs.
>
> . . . [P]rinciples of risk allocation support the premise that between two innocent parties, the one benefiting from an activity should bear

C. REGULATING SOCIALLY DESIRABLE ACTIVITIES 81

the risk of loss. Having received a benefit, that party is then in a position to spread the risk of loss to consumers of the products.

Furthermore, where the abnormally dangerous activity involves high risk of explosions, the one engaged in that activity has a better opportunity to determine the cause of the incident and can therefore seek indemnification. The injured plaintiff can prove negligence as to a third party only with great difficulty.

Finally, the imposition of strict liability here will spur the natural gas companies to greater safety precautions, such as periodic inspections and supervision of excavating activities within the vicinity of their lines.

Accord, Mahowald v. Minnesota Gas Co., 344 N.W.2d 856, 862 (Minn. 1984), "finding no compelling equitable reason for imposition of strict liability." *Williams v. Amoco Prod. Co.*, 241 Kan. 102, 734 P.2d 1113 (1987), "[A]pplying the Restatement (Second) of Torts test, we hold the drilling and operation of natural gas wells is not an abnormally dangerous activity in relation to the type of harm sustained by appellees. Further, such activity does not constitute a non-natural use of the land."

Ultimately, consumers would bear the higher costs associated with expanded liability for either gasoline or natural gas suppliers. Does the distinction lie in how utility rates are set?

5. *"Stricter" Liability? Yukon Equip., Inc. v. Fireman's Fund Ins. Co.*, 585 P.2d 1206 (Alaska 1978), concerned a munitions storage explosion set off by thieves to cover up a theft. The magazine contained 80,000 pounds of explosives. Dwellings and other buildings within a two-mile radius were damaged, and the ground concussion caused by the explosion registered 1.8 on the Richter scale 30 miles away. The defendants contended that this storage of munitions was not abnormally dangerous, in part because the magazine was situated on lands set aside by the federal government for that purpose, and that "the storage served a legitimate community need for an accessible source of explosives for various purposes." The Supreme Court of Alaska stated:

> [W]e do not believe that the Restatement (Second) approach should be used in cases involving the use or storage of explosives. Instead, we adhere to the rule of *Exner v. Sherman Power Constr. Co.* and its progeny imposing absolute liability in such cases. The Restatement (Second) approach requires an analysis of degrees of risk and harm, difficulty of eliminating risk, and appropriateness of place, before absolute liability may be imposed. Such factors suggest a negligence standard. The six factor analysis may well be necessary where damage is caused by unique hazards and the question is whether the general rule of absolute liability applies, but in cases involving the storage and use of explosives we take that question to have been resolved by more than a century of judicial decisions.
>
> The reasons for imposing absolute liability on those who have created a grave risk of harm to others by storing or using explosives are largely independent of considerations of locational appropriateness. We see no reason for making a distinction between the right of a

homesteader to recover when his property has been damaged by a blast set off in a remote corner of the state, and the right to compensation of an urban resident whose home is destroyed by an explosion originating in a settled area. In each case, the loss is properly to be regarded as a cost of the business of storing or using explosives. Every incentive remains to conduct such activities in locations which are as safe as possible, because there the damages resulting from an accident will be kept to a minimum. [The court further concluded that the intentional conduct of the thieves was not so "highly extraordinary" as to operate as a superseding cause.]

6. *Strict Liability and Negligence Revisited.* In *Harper v. Regency Dev. Co.,* 399 So. 2d 248 (Ala. 1981), a case involving blasting damage, the Supreme Court of Alabama purported to adopt §§ 519–520 RESTATEMENT (SECOND) OF TORTS (1977) but stated:

> The fault concept is preserved simply by transposing the basis for testing culpability from the degree of care exercised in the manner in which the blasting operation is conducted to the conduct of the blaster in carrying on an abnormally dangerous activity which subjects innocent parties to an unreasonable risk of harm. To treat the discharge of an abnormally dangerous substance under ultrahazardous conditions as wrongful conduct is not violative of the duty/breach of duty principle of tort law. The use of the explosives under abnormally dangerous conditions is negligence, and thus actionable if such conduct proximately causes damage to another.
>
> Our holding today is strikingly similar, both in kind and degree, to the Alabama extended manufacturer's liability doctrine. There, we lessened the consumer's burden of proof, but retained the fault concept, by transposing the basis for testing culpability from the degree of care exercised in the manufacturing process to the product's defective condition at the time of sale. Here, we simply shift the culpability test from the degree of care exercised in the discharge of the explosives to the carrying on of an abnormally dangerous activity. . . .
>
> While our law no longer permits, as a defense, proof of the degree of care with which a defective product was made and sold to the public, neither will it permit the blaster to defend on the ground that he carefully prepared and detonated the explosive. In either case, to carefully injure another is no longer an acceptable exercise of one's legal duty of due care.
>
> In neither case, however, is the claimant exempt from definitive standards of proof both as to culpability and as to proximate cause. Just as the plaintiff must prove the defective condition of the product and an injury or damage proximately resulting therefrom, one claiming blasting damage can establish liability of the blaster only by proving that such damage is the proximate result of an abnormally dangerous activity.

Is this an accurate reflection of the line between negligence and strict liability?

C.   REGULATING SOCIALLY DESIRABLE ACTIVITIES   83

PROBLEM

Tom specializes in the transportation and disposal of nontoxic and generally harmless chemicals. He owns a tractor-trailer for this purpose. One night the tractor, fully laden, is speeding along, westbound on Highway 127, a narrow two-lane blacktop. Highway 127 is elevated as it snakes through the small township of Typical. A small plastics factory is located on the north side of the highway, and a residential subdivision containing fifteen single-family homes is located on the south side. Traveling eastbound on Highway 127 is a large truck owned and driven by Ronnie. The two trucks reach the Typical intersection at precisely the same time as Thug, a resident of Typical, who is waiting in the middle of the highway to make a turn into the town. Thug's car is hit simultaneously by the truck and the tractor-trailer. Before the police arrive to close the highway, Turkey, a little wild from drink and angered by the destruction being wrought close to his hometown, accelerates his car to 70 miles per hour and drives it into the wrecked trucks. His vehicle flies off the highway and lands near the Panicky family's house. Guy Panicky immediately suffers a nervous collapse. The collision has caused some chemicals to leak from the tractor-trailer. A small stream of chemicals drips down from the north side of the highway, mixes with some plastic waste stored outside the factory and causes a huge explosion, sending into the air a ball of fire which descends on the other side of the highway and burns down three Typical houses.

How would you characterize the conduct of each potential defendant in terms both of culpability and responsibility? Can you find "intent?" "Fault?"

CROSBY v. COX AIRCRAFT CO. OF WASHINGTON
109 Wash. 2d 581, 746 P.2d 1198 (1987)

CALLOW, JUSTICE.

The case involves a claim for property damage caused when a plane owned by Cox Aircraft Co. and piloted by Hal Joines (the pilot) crash-landed onto Douglas Crosby's property. The plane was a DeHavilland DHC-3 Otter aircraft. Its engine had recently been converted from piston-driven to turbine and the conversion had been undertaken in strict conformity with Federal Aviation Administration (FAA) requirements. FAA certification of the plane's fuel system was still pending at the time of the accident.

On December 19, 1984, the pilot flew the airplane over the Olympic Peninsula and then turned back to Seattle, intending to land at Boeing Field. However, the engine ran out of fuel in mid-flight, and the pilot was forced to crash land the plane at Alki Point in West Seattle. The plane landed on the roof of Crosby's garage, causing $3,199.89 in damages.

Crosby sued both the pilot and Cox Aircraft. His complaint raised the following alternative allegations: (1) that the pilot was negligent in his operation of the plane; (2) that Cox Aircraft was negligent in its maintenance of the plane; (3) that Cox Aircraft, the alleged employer of the pilot, should be held vicariously liable for all negligence of the pilot under the doctrine of respondeat superior; and (4) that both the pilot and Cox Aircraft should be held strictly liable for all damages caused by the crash landing. The pilot and Cox Aircraft denied liability and filed a third-party complaint against Parker Hannifin Corporation alleging that Parker had equipped the plane with a defective fuel system control valve which failed to operate properly, thus causing the plane's engine to run out of fuel and forcing the pilot to make the crash landing.

The trial court granted partial summary judgment for Crosby, holding that both the pilot and Cox Aircraft were strictly liable for all damage done to Crosby's property. The court did not address Crosby's negligence claims, nor the third-party complaint against Parker. The pilot and Cox Aircraft appealed. We accepted certification.

. . . The defendants urge us to reject Restatement § 520A. They contend that aviation can no longer be designated an "abnormally dangerous activity" requiring special rules of liability. We agree.

. . . In 1922 the Commission on Uniform State Laws proposed a new Uniform Aeronautics Act which, *inter alia,* made owners of aircraft strictly liable for all ground damage caused by the "ascent, descent or flight of the aircraft." Twenty-three states originally adopted this act by statute. By 1943, however, the Commissioners recognized that the act had become "obsolete," and it was removed from the list of uniform laws.

The number of states imposing strict liability has diminished significantly. At present, only six states retain the rule, and even these states apply it only to the owner of the aircraft. The aircraft operator remains liable only for damages caused by his own negligence.

The modern trend followed by a majority of states is to impose liability only upon a showing of negligence by either the aircraft owner or operator. Several states have legislated this rule by providing that ordinary tort law (or the law applicable to torts on land) applies to aviation accidents. Other jurisdictions have case law to this effect. Moreover, a number of courts have expressly disavowed the notion that aviation is an "ultrahazardous activity" requiring special rules of liability. As observed in *Boyd v. White,* 128 Cal. App. 2d 641, 651, 276 P.2d 92 (1954):

> The courts and the law formerly looked upon aviation with the viewpoint still expressed in the American Law Institute, Restatement, Torts, Vol. 3, § 520, holding that aviation is an ultra-hazardous activity, similar to the operation of automobiles in the early days of the horseless carriage, and requiring those who take part in it to observe the highest degree of care. The Uniform Aeronautic Act, adopted in time by twenty-three states, imposed absolute liability on the owner, as well as the operator or lessee, of every aircraft for any damage to person or property caused by its operation provided there was no contributory negligence on the part of him who was thus harmed. With the passage of time, however, this view came to be modified, and the trend of decisions established it to be the general rule that, properly handled by a competent pilot exercising reasonable care, an airplane is not an inherently dangerous instrument, so that in the absence of statute the ordinary rules of negligence control, and the

owner (or operator) of an airship is only liable for injury inflicted upon another when such damage is caused by a defect in the plane or its negligent operation. By 1945, coincident with the opening of the postwar civilian aviation period, the number of states retaining the portions of the Uniform Aeronautic Act dealing with an owner's liability had dropped to eighteen.

We have discovered no cases relying on Restatement (Second) of Torts § 520A. That section is said to be a "special application" of § 519 and § 520 (a–f), which impose strict liability on persons engaging in abnormally dangerous activities. An analysis of the individual factors listed in § 520 further persuades us that strict liability is inappropriate here.

Factor (a) of § 520 requires that the activity in question contain a "high degree of risk of some harm to the person, land or chattels of others." No such showing has been made. Indeed, statistics indicate that air transportation is far safer than automobile transportation. Factor (b) speaks to the gravity of the harm — that is, in the unlikely event that an airplane accident occurs, whether there is a "likelihood that the [resulting harm] will be great." It is apparent that this possibility is present. However, this must be further evaluated in light of factor (c), which speaks of the "inability to eliminate the risk by the exercise of reasonable care." Given the extensive governmental regulation of aviation and the continuing technological improvements in aircraft manufacture, maintenance and operation, we conclude that the overall risk of serious injury from ground damage can be sufficiently reduced by the exercise of due care. Finally, factors (d), (e), and (f) do not favor the imposition of strict liability. Aviation is an activity of "common usage," it is appropriately conducted over populated areas, and its value to the community outweighs its dangerous attributes. Indeed, aviation is an integral part of modern society.

The causes of aircraft accidents are legion and can come from a myriad of sources. Every aircraft that flies is at risk from every bird, projectile and other aircraft. Accidents may be caused by improper placement of wires or buildings or from failure to properly mark and light such obstructions. The injury to the ground dweller may have been caused by faulty engineering, construction, repair, maintenance, metal fatigue, operation or ground control. Lightning, wind shear and other acts of God may have brought about a crash. Any listing of the causes of such accidents undoubtedly would fall short of the possibilities. In such circumstances the imposition of liability should be upon the blameworthy party who can be shown to be at fault.

. . . We are not persuaded that we should create a special rule of liability governing only ground damage caused by aircraft accidents. We note, for example, that passengers of airplanes involved in accidents must prove negligence to recover damages. . . .

This is true even though the likelihood of serious injury to a passenger is at least as great as is the case with persons or property on the ground.

We also emphasize that, although the plaintiff's recovery will depend on a showing of negligence, the plaintiff may of course employ the doctrine of *res ipsa loquitur,* if appropriate, to establish his negligence claim. *Res ipsa* is now frequently used in aviation crash cases and is widely recognized as an acceptable means of proving negligence.

Finally, the plaintiff raises an alternative argument that we apply the rule of strict liability to ground damages arising out of "test flights" of aircraft. We decline to do so. Plaintiff has cited no authority to support his claim that test flights of aircraft qualify as "abnormally dangerous" under Restatement (Second) of Torts § 519–20. The question is not whether test flights are more dangerous than routine aviation flights, but rather, whether they are so inherently dangerous that a "high degree of risk of harm" cannot be eliminated by the exercise of reasonable care. § 520(a), (c). In light of the extensive government regulation regarding the design, development, and testing of new and modified aircraft we conclude that test flights are not abnormally dangerous.

BRACHTENBACH, JUSTICE, dissenting.

What a peculiar, aberrant twist of tort law is created by the majority. Almost a decade ago we held that when a wine glass shatters in the hands of a wine drinker, the seller of the wine, who merely supplied the glass, is strictly liable. The law demanded and gave compensation without proof of fault. Today the majority tells the wholly innocent, inactive homeowner into whose home an airplane suddenly crashes "you must prove by a preponderance of the evidence that someone was at fault; never mind that you had no part in this damage, go forth and prove negligence and if you cannot, the loss is all yours." How can that be? The majority's answer is that it cannot fit these facts into a magic phrase — abnormally dangerous — which started in an 1868 case from England, *Rylands v. Fletcher* [discussed *supra* note 3 following *Magrine*].

In fact and theory, it is a policy question whether to impose liability upon the pilot and owner of an airplane which crashes into the person or property of a wholly innocent person on the ground.

Compelling, persuasive policy reasons exist to impose such strict liability. Those reasons should be explored and evaluated rather than simply accepting the pigeonhole conclusion that aviation is not abnormally dangerous as defined by the black letter rule of the Restatement (Second) of Torts, therefore, ipso facto, strict liability cannot be imposed. If the Restatement (Second) of Torts, is to be followed, as the majority proposes, strict liability should result as discussed hereafter.

. . . If we assume that the aircraft operator is without legal fault, *i.e.*, is not negligent, the policy issue is then clear. Which of two persons should bear the loss? In this case we have a totally innocent, nonacting homeowner whose property is suddenly invaded and damaged by an airplane — operated by the person who voluntarily chose to fly that airplane, for his own purpose and benefit. The result of the majority is that the wholly innocent, nonactive, nonbenefited, but damaged person must shoulder the burden of proving that the person who set in motion the forces which caused the damage was negligent.

It is apparent that fairness and common sense suggest that the loss should not be allocated to the innocent bystander. Much of the rationale for adopting strict product liability is applicable here and will be discussed hereafter.

. . . The majority ignores [the] underlying policy question [of who is best able to bear the loss] by noting that (1) air transportation is far safer than automobile transportation; (2) extensive governmental regulation and technological improvements reduce the overall risk of serious injury on the ground; (3) aviation is an integral part of society; and (4) the causes of aircraft accidents are legion. Those reasons are rather like consoling the widow by telling her that *statistically* her husband should have lived another 20 years.

One writer employs an appealing analysis which dictates strict liability. Professor Vold examines the benefits and creation of risks from a particular activity. If there is mutuality in the receipt of benefits and the creation of risks to others, the standard of liability is negligence. Thus where each user of a highway receives the direct benefit of such use but whose presence and conduct increases the risk of harm to the other, the law of negligence applies. But one-sidedness in the receipt of benefits and creation of risks should lead to strict liability. Vold, *Strict Liability for Aircraft Crashes and Forced Landings on Ground Victims Outside of Established Landing Areas*, 5 Hastings L.J. 1 (1953). This analysis is logical and satisfies the demands of justice. Its application here leads to strict liability.

Another factor favoring strict liability is the reality that the plaintiff in an aviation accident case faces difficult and potentially expensive burdens of proof. "Running through aviation cases, and frequently explaining their unusual results, is the frequently overwhelming difficulty and expense of investigation and preparation, and inherent problems and limitations of proof." 1 L. Kreindler, Aviation Accident Law § 1.03[1], at 1–12 (1986).

It is widely recognized that difficulties of proof may justify imposition of strict liability. Indeed, such fact is described as a common feature of strict liability cases.

The majority's holding is an extreme example of the unfairness of its conclusion and the denial of the realities of litigation. The plaintiff's only claim is for property damage of $3,199.89. The defendant aircraft owner denies negligence in maintenance or operation of the airplane. The defendant denies strict liability application. The defendant joined the manufacturer/distributor of a part used in the fuel system, alleging defective design or manufacture. The defendant joined six other property owners who may have been damaged. The hapless plaintiff, seeking a maximum of $3,199.89 is now, under the majority's holding, faced with the formidable task of proving negligence and is in the midst of a third-party fight over the very cause of the crash, plus an anticipated battle of experts over design and manufacture of an integral part of a fuel system in a plane being test flown for FAA certification. It takes no great insight to recognize that the expense of litigation amounts to a denial of plaintiff's right to damages.

. . . Another policy reason favoring strict liability is the ability of the offending activity to spread the financial risk through its enterprise or through liability insurance. Again, this is a judicially accepted rationale.

. . . To justify its rejection of the clear rule of § 520A, the majority holds that § 520A can have validity only if aviation can be denominated an abnormally dangerous activity. The majority then analyzes the factors set forth in § 520 to conclude that this particular activity did not meet the criteria of § 520, therefore § 520A does not apply. It relies upon comment a to § 520A: "This Section is a special application of the rule stated in § 519, together with that stated in § 520."

This result ignores the very scheme of these interrelated sections. Section 519 declares the general principle of liability; § 520 lists the factors to be considered in determining whether an activity is abnormally dangerous. Section 520A declares a special rule to ground damage. What the majority overlooks is that the authors of the Restatement (Second) of Torts in 1977 expressly intended that § 520A stand on its own, *i.e.*, that it in fact was a special rule, quite distinct from § 520 requirements.

The majority, instead, rejects the very judgment and conclusion which led to the insertion of § 520A. This is proved by comment a to § 519 which states that it must be read together with various sections, *including § 520A*.

. . . It is crystal clear that § 520A was not intended to be dependent upon a separate analysis under § 520 as the majority holds.

. . . The majority attempts to buttress its result by an analysis of each factor listed in § 520, finding most to be lacking. Such analysis is irrelevant in light of the language in the comments and of the history of § 520A. Nonetheless I will review the majority's conclusions. First, it is not necessary that each of the factors in § 520 be present to meet the test. Comment f states that ordinarily several of the six elements will be required for strict liability, but that it is not necessary that each of them be present, especially if others weigh heavily.

The heart of § 520 is contained in this language: "The essential question is whether the risk created is so unusual, either because of its magnitude or because of the circumstances surrounding it, as to justify the imposition of strict liability for the harm that results from it, even though it is carried on with all reasonable care." Restatement (Second) of Torts § 520, comment f (1977).

The first factor in § 520(a) is a high degree of risk of harm. The majority asserts that no such showing has been made, relying on statistics cited in several footnotes. This conclusion misses the point. The question is not whether it is statistically more safe to fly in an airplane than ride in a car, which is all the majority states. The question rather is whether there is a high degree of risk of some harm when an airplane lands on someone's house. Comment g makes it perfectly clear that if the potential harm is sufficiently great, the likelihood that it will take place may be comparatively slight and yet the activity be regarded as abnormally dangerous.

This comment is perfectly logical. The actor cannot hide behind relative statistics; if serious potential harm exists, that is enough. The harm need not occur in 51 percent of the activities. Any other interpretation, such as the majority's, would allow the defendant to escape by proving "while our dynamite leveled 3 square city blocks, it doesn't happen very often."

The majority acknowledges that the likelihood of great harm exists, factor (b). Factor (c) speaks of the inability to eliminate the risk by the exercise of reasonable care. The majority concludes that because of extensive governmental regulation and continuing technological improvements in aircraft manufacture, maintenance, and operation the overall risk of serious injury from ground damage can be "sufficiently reduced by the exercise of due care." Where the majority gets its technical information escapes me, although I know for certain that it is not from the record.

The comment makes clear that what is referred to is the unavoidable risk remaining even though the actor has taken reasonable care. It is interesting to note that after asserting that due care "sufficiently" (whatever that means) reduces the risk of serious injuries, the majority immediately states that the causes of aircraft accidents are legion, and can come from a myriad of sources including lightning, wind shear and acts of God. Indeed the majority speculates that any listing of accident causes undoubtedly would fall short of the possibilities.

Thus the majority's reasoning is that regulation and technology prove that aircraft can be operated with minimal risk, but the causes of accidents, including acts of God, are so legion that the possibilities cannot be listed.

The majority manipulates its own statistics about aviation safety by including statistics for regularly scheduled commercial airlines. To the extent that it is relevant, it is significant to note that the accident rate for general aviation is more than 6 ½ times greater than for scheduled commercial airlines. National Transportation Safety Board, Annual Report app. A (1985). Further casting doubt upon the validity of the majority's conclusory statements that regulation and improved technology has "sufficiently reduced" the risk of harm are the actual statistics. The accident rate per 100,000 hours for general aviation in 1980 was 9.86 whereas in 1984 it had only reduced to 9.56. National Transportation Safety Board, Annual Report app. G (1985). In any event, such statistics are of little consolation to this losing plaintiff.

The majority in five lines concludes that factors (d), (e), and (f) do not favor imposition of strict liability. Factor (d) is the extent to which the activity is not a matter of common usage. The majority simply says it is a matter of common usage. Once again the majority ignores the expressed thrust of the Restatement. Comment i indicates that an activity is a matter of common usage if it is customarily carried on by the great mass of mankind or by many people in the community. The majority likewise ignores the reasoning of our holding in *Langan v. Valicopters, Inc.,* 88 Wash. 2d 855, 864, 567 P.2d 218 (1977), where we recognized that crop dusting is prevalent and done in large portions of the Yakima Valley, but was not of common usage when carried on by 287 aircraft. An analogy makes clear the faulty premise in the majority's reasoning. Elevators are in common usage and are used by many. That does not make the operation of elevators a matter of common usage.

While there are relatively significant numbers of private pilots, such flying is hardly customarily carried on by the great mass of mankind or by many people in the community. "Many people in the community" is necessarily a relative term. How many people in the community carry on the activity in relation to the size of the community? Using the very statistics cited by the majority (Comment, *Aviation Law: Owner-Lessor Liability — The Need for Uniformity,* 36 Me. L. Rev. 93 1984) the percentage of private pilots in the

United States is.0003 percent of the population. When three people out of 10,000 are private pilots it is readily apparent that flying of private aircraft is not carried on by "many people in the community." To a certainty, private flying of a plane to test a noncertified fuel system is not of common usage, the majority's contrary bald assertion notwithstanding. I agree, as a general proposition, that flying over populated areas is not an inappropriate activity, factor (e). However, attempting to land in a populated area where there is no airport is not appropriate. The locale of the particular incident is what is important, *e.g.*, oil drilling in a residential area is not an appropriate activity. *Green v. General Petroleum Corp.*, 205 Cal. 328, 270 P. 952 (1928).

The last factor, (f), value to the community is marginally relevant and does not outweigh those factors which favor strict liability.

The drafters of the Restatement (Second) of Torts rejected the very points relied upon by the majority. They recognized the great improvement in safety, but found that the risk of harm to anyone on the ground is obvious, that it cannot be said that danger of ground damage has been so eliminated or reduced that ordinary rules of negligence would apply, and that the gravity of the harm is still a factor even though there may be relatively few cases where it occurs. Further, there was the obvious fact that those on the ground are quite helpless to select any locality in which they will not be exposed to the risk, however minimized it may be. Finally they note that while thousands participate in aviation, those who actually carry on the activity itself are relatively few. Restatement (Second) of Torts, at 1 (Tent. Draft No. 12, 1966).

Thus, if this court feels bound to meet some of the factors set forth in § 520 before applying the clear principle of § 520A, it can do so by the above analysis.

In 1969 this court did not hesitate to adopt Restatement (Second) of Torts § 402A (1965) to impose strict liability upon product manufacturers. . . . We have held that pile driving and crop dusting necessitate application of strict liability. We have forcefully recognized that policy may require the defendant to bear the cost of injury rather than the innocent plaintiff.

Now in this case the majority casts aside the principles and rationale of these enlightened decisions and places upon the innocent plaintiff a burden of proof which as a practical matter closes the courthouse door to this plaintiff.

Comment c to Restatement (Second) of Torts § 402A sets forth the justification for strict product liability. The seller of the product, by marketing it, has assumed a special responsibility to any member of the consuming public who may be injured by it. Should not a pilot, especially on a test flight, have a similar responsibility to innocent persons on the ground? The public has a right to expect that sellers will stand behind their goods. Persons on the ground expect aircraft to not crash into their homes. Public policy demands that the burden of accidental injuries caused by products be placed upon those who market them. Is it not equally logical that such burden be placed on persons who fly airplanes? The cost to sellers can be treated as a cost of production and insured against. Consumers are entitled to maximum protection at the hands of someone and the proper persons to afford it are those who market the products. Similarly, innocent persons on the ground are

C. REGULATING SOCIALLY DESIRABLE ACTIVITIES

entitled to protection. Who better to provide it than the enterprise for whose purpose and benefit the danger was created.

I suggest that were it not for the historical development of the concept of abnormally dangerous activity, there would be no reason or justification for denying strict liability for aircraft damage to persons or property on the ground. The philosophy which led to strict product liability should be and is equally relevant to aircraft liability.

NOTES

1. *A Doctrinal Aberration?* How, when and why did aircraft operation attract a strict liability categorization? Reference *Rochester Gas & Elec. Corp. v. Dunlop,* 148 Misc. 849, 266 N.Y.S. 469 (1933) discussed, *infra.*

2. *The "Special Application" of §§ 519–520.* RESTATEMENT (SECOND) OF TORTS (1977) § 520A provides:

> If physical harm to land or to persons or chattels on the ground is caused by the ascent, descent or flight of aircraft, or by the dropping or falling of an object from the aircraft,
>
> (a) the operator of the aircraft is subject to liability for the harm, even though he has exercised the utmost care to prevent it, and
>
> (b) the owner of the aircraft is subject to similar liability if he has authorized or permitted the operation.

Does § 520A constitute an example of strict or absolute liability?

HELLING v. CAREY
83 Wash. 2d 514, 519 P.2d 981 (1974)

HUNTER, ASSOCIATE JUSTICE.

The plaintiff suffers from primary open angle glaucoma. Primary open angle glaucoma is essentially a condition of the eye in which there is an interference in the ease with which the nourishing fluids can flow out of the eye. Such a condition results in pressure gradually rising above the normal level to such an extent that damage is produced to the optic nerve and its fibers with resultant loss in vision. The first loss usually occurs in the periphery of the field of vision. The disease usually has few symptoms and, in the absence of a pressure test, is often undetected until the damage has become extensive and irreversible.

The defendants . . . are partners who practice the medical specialty of ophthalmology. Ophthalmology involves the diagnosis and treatment of defects and diseases of the eye.

The plaintiff first consulted the defendants for myopia, nearsightedness, in 1959. At that time she was fitted with contact lenses. She next consulted the defendants in September 1963, concerning irritation caused by the contact lenses. Additional consultations occurred in October 1963; February 1967; September 1967; October 1967; May 1968; July 1968; August 1968; September 1968; and October 1968. Until the October 1968 consultation, the defendants considered the plaintiff's visual problems to be related solely to complications associated with her contact lenses. On that occasion, the defendant, Dr. Carey, tested the plaintiff's eye pressure and field of vision for the first time. This test indicated that the plaintiff had glaucoma. The plaintiff, who was then 32 years of age, had essentially lost her peripheral vision and her central vision was reduced to approximately 5 degrees vertical by 10 degrees horizontal.

Thereafter, in August of 1969, after consulting other physicians, the plaintiff filed a complaint against the defendants alleging, among other things, that she sustained severe and permanent damage to her eyes as a proximate result of the defendants' negligence. During trial, the testimony of the medical experts for both the plaintiff and the defendants established that the standards of the profession for that specialty in the same or similar circumstances do not require routine pressure tests for glaucoma upon patients under 40 years of age. The reason the pressure test for glaucoma is not given as a regular practice to patients under the age of 40 is that the disease rarely occurs in this age group. Testimony indicated, however, that the standards of the profession do require pressure tests if the patient's complaints and symptoms reveal to the physician that glaucoma should be suspected.

. . . In her petition for review [of defendants' jury verdict], the plaintiff's primary contention is that under the facts of this case the trial judge erred in giving certain instructions to the jury and refusing her proposed instructions defining the standard of care which the law imposes upon an ophthalmologist. As a result, the plaintiff contends, in effect, that she was unable to argue her theory of the case to the jury that the standard of care for the specialty of ophthalmology was inadequate to protect the plaintiff from the incidence of glaucoma, and that the defendants, by reason of their special ability, knowledge and information, were negligent in failing to give the pressure test to the plaintiff at an earlier point in time which, if given, would have detected her condition and enabled the defendants to have averted the resulting substantial loss in her vision.

We find this to be a unique case. The testimony of the medical experts is undisputed concerning the standards of the profession for the specialty of ophthalmology. . . . The issue is whether the defendants' compliance with the standard of the profession of ophthalmology, which does not require the giving of a routine pressure test to persons under 40 years of age, should insulate them from liability under the facts in this case where the plaintiff has lost a substantial amount of her vision due to the failure of the defendants to timely give the pressure test to the plaintiff.

The defendants argue that the standard of the profession, which does not require the giving of a routine pressure test to persons under the age of 40, is adequate to insulate the defendants from liability for negligence because the risk of glaucoma is so rare in this age group. . . .

. . . The incidence of glaucoma in one out of 25,000 persons under the age of 40 may appear quite minimal. However, that one person, the plaintiff in this instance, is entitled to the same protection, as afforded persons over 40, essential for timely detection of the evidence of glaucoma where it can be arrested to avoid the grave and devastating result of this disease. The test is a simple pressure test, relatively inexpensive. There is no judgment factor involved, and there is no doubt that by giving the test the evidence of glaucoma can be detected. The giving of the test is harmless if the physical condition of the eye permits. The testimony indicates that although the condition of the plaintiff's eyes might have at times prevented the defendants from administering the pressure test, there is an absence of evidence in the record that the test could not have been timely given.

Justice Holmes stated in *Texas & P. Ry. v. Behymer,* 189 U.S. 468, 470, 47 L. Ed. 905, 23 S. Ct. 622 (1903):

> What usually is done may be evidence of what ought to be done, but what ought to be done is fixed by a standard of reasonable prudence, whether it usually is complied with or not.

In *The T.J. Hooper,* 60 F.2d 737, 740 (2d Cir. 1932), Justice Hand stated . . . .

> [In] most cases reasonable prudence is in fact common prudence; but strictly it is never its measure; a whole calling may have unduly lagged in the adoption of new and available devices. It never may set its own tests, however persuasive be its usages. Courts must in the end say what is required; there are precautions so imperative that even their universal disregard will not excuse their omission.

Under the facts of this case reasonable prudence required the timely giving of the pressure test to this plaintiff. The precaution of giving this test to detect the incidence of glaucoma to patients under 40 years of age is so imperative that irrespective of its disregard by the standards of the ophthalmology profession, it is the duty of the courts to say what is required to protect patients under 40 from the damaging results of glaucoma.

We therefore hold, as a matter of law, that the reasonable standard that should have been followed under the undisputed facts of this case was the timely giving of this simple, harmless pressure test to this plaintiff and that, in failing to do so, the defendants were negligent, which proximately resulted in the blindness sustained by the plaintiff for which the defendants are liable.

UTTER, ASSOCIATE JUSTICE, concurring.

. . . The difficulty with [the majority] approach is that we as judges, by using a negligence analysis, seem to be imposing a stigma of moral blame upon the doctors who, in this case, used all the precautions commonly prescribed by their profession in diagnosis and treatment. Lacking their training in this highly sophisticated profession, it seems illogical for this court to say they failed to exercise a reasonable standard of care. It seems to me we are, in reality, imposing liability, because, in choosing between an innocent plaintiff and a doctor, who acted reasonably according to his specialty but who could have prevented the full effects of this disease by administering a simple, harmless test and treatment, the plaintiff should not have to bear the risk of loss. As such, imposition of liability approaches that of strict liability.

. . . Tort law has continually been in a state of flux. It is "not always neat and orderly. But this is not to say it is illogical. Its central logic is the logic that moves from premises — its objectives — that are only partly consistent, to conclusions — its rules — that serve each objective as well as may be while serving others too. It is the logic of maximizing service and minimizing disservice to multiple objectives." Keeton, *Is There a Place for Negligence in Modern Tort Law?*, 53 Va. L. Rev. 886, 897 (1967).

When types of problems rather than numbers of cases are examined, strict liability is applied more often than negligence as a principle which determines liability. Peck, *Negligence and Liability Without Fault in Tort Law,* 46 Wash. L. Rev. 225, 239 (1971). There are many similarities in this case to other cases of strict liability. Problems of proof have been a common feature in situations where strict liability is applied. Where events are not matters of common experience, a juror's ability to comprehend whether reasonable care has been followed diminishes. There are few areas as difficult for jurors to intelligently comprehend as the intricate questions of proof and standards in medical malpractice cases.

In applying strict liability there are many situations where it is imposed for conduct which can be defined with sufficient precision to insure that application of a strict liability principle will not produce miscarriages of justice in a substantial number of cases. If the activity involved is one which can be defined with sufficient precision, that definition can serve as an accounting unit to which the costs of the activity may be allocated with some certainty and precision. With this possible, strict liability serves a compensatory function in situations where the defendant is, through the use of insurance, the financially more responsible person. Peck, *Negligence and Liability Without Fault in Tort Law, supra* at 240–41.

If the standard of a reasonably prudent specialist is, in fact, inadequate to offer reasonable protection to the plaintiff, then liability can be imposed without fault. To do so under the narrow facts of this case does not offend my sense of justice. The pressure test to measure intraocular pressure with the Schiotz tonometer and the Goldman applanometer takes a short time, involves no damage to the patient, and consists of placing the instrument against the eyeball. An abnormally high pressure requires other tests which would either confirm or deny the existence of glaucoma. It is generally believed that from 5 to 10 years of detectable increased pressure must exist before there is permanent damage to the optic nerves.

Although the incidence of glaucoma in the age range of the plaintiff is approximately one in 25,000, this alone should not be enough to deny her a claim. Where its presence can be detected by a simple, well-known harmless test, where the results of the test are definitive, where the disease can be successfully arrested by early detection and where its effects are irreversible if undetected over a substantial period of time, liability should be imposed upon defendants even though they did not violate the standard existing within the profession of ophthalmology. . . .

NOTES

1. *The Majority Opinion; Doctrinal Sub-Categorization.* What was unreasonable about the defendant's conduct? His profession's conduct? What was the rule contended for by the plaintiff? Would the instruction which plaintiff sought have redistributed more ophthalmological risks? Why?

2. *Characterization Possibilities.* In *Hector v. Cedars-Sinai Med. Center,* 180 Cal. App. 3d 493, 225 Cal. Rptr. 595, 599 (1986), the court refused to impose strict liability upon a hospital which supplied and implanted a defective heart pacemaker, concluding that the hospital was not a seller of pacemakers, but a provider of medical services. The court stated:

> The hospital does not order pacemakers for itself, but may fill out the purchase requisitions for surgeons who order the devices. The hospital does not stock or recommend pacemakers or provide them to the general public, dealing with pacemakers only in the context of the courses of treatment for particular patients. Even then, it is the surgeon who chooses or recommends the particular device to be implanted; the hospital merely provides administrative services in connection with the order and support services in connection with the implantation.
>
> The essence of the relationship between hospital and patient is the provision of professional medical services necessary to effect the implantation of the pacemaker — the patient does not enter the hospital merely to purchase a pacemaker but to obtain a course of treatment which includes implantation of a pacemaker. As a provider of services rather than a seller of a product, the hospital is not subject to strict liability for a defective product provided to the patient during the course of his or her treatment.

See also *Cafazzo v. Central Medical Health Servs.,* 542 Pa. 526, 668 A.2d 521, 532 (1995), involving the implantation of a defective mandibular prosthesis, noting "The thrust of the inquiry is thus not on whether a separate consideration is charged for the physical material used in the exercise of medical skill, but what service is performed to restore or maintain the patient's health. The determinative question becomes not what is being charged, but what is being done."

Compare *Thomas v. St. Joseph Hosp.,* 618 S.W.2d 791 (Tex. Civ. App. 1981), which involved a patient who was severely burned, and subsequently died, when he dropped a match onto his hospital gown. The Texas appellate court stated:

> In our case the hospital furnished the gown to Mr. Thomas, and the cost of the gowns is considered in determining the overhead which must be recouped; some overhead costs are reflected in the room bill, but the director of materials management didn't know which overhead was in the room rate. The concept of strict liability generally does not apply to defective services, as opposed to defective products but the sales/service hybrid situation is less clear.
>
> . . . The appellee relies on a line of cases in this jurisdiction and others in which courts have declined to impose strict liability for injuries caused by defective products that were intimately and inseparably connected with the professional services rendered. The rationale supporting these holdings is that a hospital is not ordinarily engaged in the business of selling the products or equipment used in the course of its primary function of providing medical services. Strict liability

has not been found where there was no complaint that the product, *per se*, was defective, apart from the professional services connected with its use or . . . when the professional services could not have been rendered without using the product.

The appellant argues that our case is distinguishable because she specifically complains of a defective gown, not professional services, and because the supplying of the gown is not necessarily involved in or related to the professional services rendered by the hospital. She points out that no public policy supports extension of immunity to a hospital that supplies a defective product not integrally related to the professional services it renders. It is true that the essence of the relationship between a physician and his patient relates to the professional services and skill he offers and the patient purchases. Where, as here, a hospital apparently supplies a product unrelated to the essential professional relationship, we hold that it cannot be said that as a matter of law the hospital did not introduce the harmful product into the stream of commerce.

Is *Thomas* inconsistent with a service-product distinction, or does it make a further distinction between professional and merely administrative services? Even under *Hector v. Cedars-Sinai,* would the hospital escape the clutches of strict products liability if it sold a patient tainted candy from its gift shop?

PROBLEM

John Tweed resides in Youngstown, Anystate. Tweed, who had been drinking beer on a social basis for some 20 years, considered himself to be a moderate drinker, although he has admitted to being intoxicated on a few occasions. He enjoyed most brands of beer, but recently had become particularly enamored of the Sam Stoned Brewery's Extra Premium Ale, a new brand with a uniquely high alcohol content.

On the day in question, Tweed had been bar-hopping through some of his favorite taverns in Youngstown. He consumed two beers of unknown brands at other bars before settling down for an evening of bowling at the Youngstown Lanes. Between bowling frames, Tweed drank a few glasses of Sam Stoned, purchased at Youngstown Lanes. He later stated that he became intoxicated almost immediately after he started to consume the Sam Stoned. However, he also stated that he did not recollect consuming any alcohol after his first beer at the Youngstown Lanes, and that he did not remember driving home or the accident that occurred.

Deposition testimony from Youngstown Lanes personnel established that Tweed left the bowling alley at 11 p.m., in an obviously intoxicated state. It appeared to witnesses that Tweed had pushed the accelerator of his car to the floor and roared out of the Lanes' parking lot. As he attempted to merge into the traffic outside the bowling alley, he collided with a car driven by Vincent Victim. Vincent and Tweed were seriously injured. During his period of hospitalization, Tweed was diagnosed as suffering from a rare and recently discovered blood disorder which dramatically increased his susceptibility to alcohol dependence. No criminal charges were filed against Tweed following the accident.

The incident occurred at a particularly bad time for Sam Stoned. The brewery had suffered a declining market share over a two-year period. It was hoping to stage a recovery with its high-alcohol "niche" product, and had tripled its advertising budget in the Youngstown area. John Tweed fell within the demographic group targeted in Sam Stoned's television commercials.

Vincent Victim has filed negligence and strict liability claims against Tweed, Sam Stoned Brewery and Youngstown Lanes. Defendants have filed motions for partial summary judgment on the basis that plaintiff may not recover under Anystate law on any strict liability theory which could be advanced. The parties have agreed that Anystate's statutory immunity from negligence actions for retail vendors of alcohol would apply to Youngstown Lanes.

What should be Victim's specific theories of recovery? What arguments will the defendants make?

Chapter 3
INTENTIONAL TORTS

A. INTRODUCTION

This chapter presents many of the traditional intentional torts. These torts — battery, assault, false imprisonment, intentional infliction of emotional distress and the like — provide the student with an opportunity to develop analytical skills and with a benchmark to which negligence and strict and absolute liability can be compared. Other intentional torts, such as communicative torts, business torts, and constitutional and statutory torts, are more appropriately considered in connection with other materials, and appear elsewhere in this book. Recovery for emotional distress is more fully considered in the chapter on damages.

The "intentional torts" seem fairly straightforward. They are a collection of discrete, narrow, and descriptively entitled (or "nominate") causes of action. Compared to more "open-textured" torts such as negligence, the intentional torts appear simple, inflexible and unsophisticated. Sometimes, appearances can be deceptive.

The development of nominate intentional torts, as compared with the generic torts of negligence and strict liability, was primarily an historical accident—the result of the early development of tort law in England. (*See, e.g.,* Dobbs, *The Law of Torts*, 1999 (pp. 25–27); Prosser & Keeton on *Torts*, West, 1984 (5th Ed., p. 28–31). However, the historical accident has endured and has successfully resisted efforts to eliminate it. (*See* Subsection I, post).

B. INTENT

BAZLEY v. TORTORICH
397 So.2d 475 (La. 1981)

DENNIS, JUSTICE

(Generally, a worker injured in the course and scope of his employment may not maintain a tort action against his employer, but is relegated to statutorily fixed worker compensation benefits, which include medical expenses and a percentage of the worker's pre injury wages during the period of any disability caused by the accident. In 1976, the Louisiana Legislature amended the state worker compensation act to provide that the exclusiveness of the worker compensation remedy did not extend to "the liability of the employer. . .resulting from an intentional act. . . .").

* * *

Plaintiff, Sidney Bazley, a . . . garbage worker, filed suit against an unidentified co-employee truck driver, the co-employee's insurer, Sardo

Tortorich and Tortorich's insurer as result of work-related injuries Bazley received when he was struck by Tortorich's car while he was mounting the back of a parish garbage truck. In his petition, as supplemented and amended, Bazley alleged that the accident was caused by his co-employee's intentional acts in operating a garbage truck without a working horn, disregarding mechanical and electrical maintenance standards, failing to keep a lookout, failing to stop in a safe place and failing to warn plaintiff of danger. Bazley did not allege, however, that the co-employee desired the consequences of his acts or believed that they were substantially certain to follow his acts.

The trial court sustained an exception of no cause of action to Bazley's suit against the garbage truck driver on the ground that it constituted a negligence action against a co-employee based on a work-related injury in contravention of the exclusive remedy rule of the Compensation Act. . . .

* * *

We are called upon to decide. . .whether La.R.S. 23:1032, as amended, prevents an injured employee from seeking recovery in tort for a work-related injury negligently caused by his co-employee. . . .

* * *

In drawing a line between intentional and unintentional acts we believe the legislative aim was to make use of the well established division between intentional torts and negligence in common law. *See* W. Prosser, *Law of Torts*, § 7, et seq. (4th ed. 1971). . . . Universally, harmful conduct is considered more reprehensible if intentional. As Holmes said, "Even a dog distinguishes between being stumbled over and being kicked." Holmes, *The Common Law* 3 (1881). There is a definite tendency to impose greater responsibility upon a defendant whose conduct has been intended to do harm, or morally wrong. W. Prosser, *Law of Torts*, § 7 (4th ed. 1971). Bauer, *The Degree of Moral Fault as Affecting Defendant's Liability*, 1933, 81 U.Pa.L. Rev. 586; Note, 1962, 14 Stan. L. Rev. 362.

* * *

Plaintiff ingeniously has proposed. . .that the concept "intentional act" should be equated with "voluntary act." He interprets "intentional" to mean merely that before the actor acted he directed his mind on his own physical movement and not on the consequences of his act. Under his interpretation an injured employee may sue in tort on any voluntary act setting in motion events leading to his injury regardless of whether the harm appeared likely or was even apparent at all to the actor. For example, in the present case, plaintiff contends he alleged an intentional act triggering his escape from the compensation system when he averred that the defendant garbage truck driver intentionally did not blow his horn to warn plaintiff of an oncoming motorist, although plaintiff concedes that the driver did not intend for harm to come to him. Plaintiff's interpretation is incongruous, not only because it departs from the almost universal practice of differentiating between intentional and unintentional harms, prevalent in most workers' compensation

programs, but also because it ignores the accepted usage of the statutory terms in this state and generally, and his construction would thwart the legislative purpose.

Although the theorists have not always agreed, the words "act" and "intent" now have generally accepted meanings in the fields of tort and criminal law. The word act is used to denote an external manifestation of the actor's will which produces consequences. There cannot be an act subjecting a person to civil or criminal liability without volition. Therefore, a contraction of a person's muscles which is purely a reaction to some outside force, such as a knee jerk or the blinking of the eyelids in defense against an approaching missile, or the convulsive movements of an epileptic, are not acts of that person. *Restatement (Second) of Torts*, American Law Institute § 2 (1965). . . . *See also,* Prosser, *supra,* § 8; LaFave and Scott, *Criminal Law,* § 25 (1972). The meaning of "intent" is that the person who acts either (1) consciously desires the physical result of his act, whatever the likelihood of that result happening from his conduct; or (2) knows that that result is substantially certain to follow from his conduct, whatever his desire Torts, *supra,* § 8; LaFave and Scott, *Criminal Law,* § 28 (1972); *see also,* Prosser, *supra,* § 8.

* * *

Our jurisprudence likewise reflects approval of the general notions of act and intent. This Court as early as 1936, approvingly recited the following: "It seems clear that, in the absence of language expressing a contrary meaning, an 'act' involves an exercise of the will. It signifies something done voluntarily." *Heiman v. Pan American Life Ins. Co.,* 183 La. 1045, 165 So.195 (1936). Only where the actor entertained a desire to bring about the consequences that followed or where the actor believed that the result was substantially certain to follow has an act been characterized as intentional. *See Freeman v. Bell,* 366 So.2d 197 (La.App. 2d Cir. 1978), *writ denied*), 369 So. 23 151 (1979); *Monk v. Veillon,* 312 So.2d 377 (La. App. 3d Cir. 1975). *See also, Langlois v. Eschet,* 378 So.2d 189, 190 (La. App. 4th Cir. 1979) (word "intended" synonymous with having in mind as an end or aim, implying mind is directed to some definite end); *von Dameck v. St. Paul Fire & Marine Ins. Co.,* 361 So.2d 283 (La. App. 1st Cir.), *writ denied* 362 So.2d 94, 802 (1978) (if person has such a lack of reason, memory, and intelligence that prevents him from comprehending the nature and consequences of his acts, he cannot intentionally inflict injury).

Plaintiff's suggested interpretation of "intentional act," equates the term with "voluntary act" and robs it of any reference to the actor's state of mind concerning the consequences of his act. It is most unlikely the legislature intended the words as plaintiff suggests, rather than in their most usual signification and in the sense in which the lawmakers have used them in other legislation.

* * *

For these reasons, we construe the legislation under review as providing that the exclusive remedy rule shall be inapplicable to intentional torts or offenses. The meaning of intent in this context is that the defendant either desired to bring about the physical results of his act or believed they were substantially certain to follow from what he did. Several courts of appeal have stated the two prongs of the definition in the conjunctive, thus requiring a plaintiff to prove, in order to recover, that the defendant desired the physical results of his act in every case.

* * *

Intent is not, however, limited to consequences which are desired. If the actor knows that the consequences are certain, or substantially certain, to result from his act, and still goes ahead, he is treated by the law as if had in fact desired to produce the result. *Restatement (Second) of Torts*, § 8A, Comment; Prosser, *supra*, § 8.

NOTES

1. Negligence is defined as the failure to use reasonable care to avoid an unreasonable risk of harm. How does the mental attitude for negligence differ from that required for intentional torts, as described in *Bazley*. Could the truck driver in *Bazley* have been negligent?

C. BATTERY

PROBLEM

Wife (W) developed a slight sore throat while at work. During the course of the day she kissed Friend (F), hoping that she would not contaminate him thereby.

At the end of the day, W's sore throat was much worse. On arriving home she kissed Husband (H), hoping thereby to give him whatever illness she herself had.

After having several alcoholic drinks that evening, she put her Child (C) to bed and kissed him as she tucked him in, hoping thereby to immunize the child from any cold-related disease. Unknown to W, she then had a cut in her mouth which caused her to bleed slightly. F and H developed influenza, and C contracted hepatitis, as the result of kissing W. Does F, H or C have a valid battery action against W?

BRZOSKA v. OLSON
668 A.2d 1355 (Del. 1995)

WALSH, JUSTICE.

In this appeal from the Superior Court, we confront the question of whether a patient may recover damages for treatment by a health care provider afflicted with Acquired Immunodeficiency Syndrome ("AIDS") absent a showing of a resultant physical injury or exposure to disease. The appellants, plaintiffs below, are 38 former patients of Dr. Raymond P. Owens, a Wilmington dentist who died of AIDS on March 1, 1991. In an action brought against

C. BATTERY

Edward P. Olson, the administrator of Dr. Owens' estate, the plaintiffs sought recovery under theories of negligence, battery, and misrepresentation. After limited discovery, the Superior Court granted summary judgment in favor of Dr. Owens' estate, ruling that, in the absence of a showing of physical harm, plaintiffs were not entitled to recover under any theory advanced. Plaintiffs have appealed only the rulings disallowing recovery on the claims of battery and misrepresentation.

* * *

Prior to his death, Dr. Owens had been engaged in the general practice of dentistry in the Wilmington area for almost 30 years. Although plaintiffs have alleged that Dr. Owens was aware that he had AIDS for at least ten years, it is clear from the record that it was in March, 1989, that Dr. Owens was advised by his physician that he was HIV-positive.[1] Dr. Owens continued to practice, but his condition had deteriorated by the summer of 1990. Toward the end of 1990, he exhibited open lesions, weakness, and memory loss. In February, 1991, his physician recommended that Dr. Owens discontinue his practice because of deteriorating health. Shortly thereafter, on February 23, Dr. Owens was hospitalized. He remained hospitalized until his death on March 1, 1991.

Shortly after Dr. Owens' death, the Delaware Division of Public Health (the "Division") undertook an evaluation of Dr. Owens' practice and records, in part to determine if his patients had been placed at risk through exposure to HIV. The Division determined that Dr. Owens' equipment, sterilization procedures and precautionary methods were better than average and that he had ceased

---

[1] We take judicial notice of the following facts as derived from reputable scientific journals and well-accepted knowledge in the scientific community. AIDS is a viral disease that weakens or destroys the body's immune system. It is caused by Human Immunodeficiency Virus ("HIV"). HIV attacks the body's T-Lymphocyte cells, a critical part of the body's immune system. At least presently, AIDS is invariably fatal. The virus can survive only in the habitat of bodily fluids. Although HIV is present in every bodily fluid of those who are infected, the only fluids which can transmit the virus are blood, semen, vaginal fluids and breast milk. . . .

* * *

The virus is transmitted primarily by direct blood-to-blood contact or by the exchange of other bodily fluids with an infected individual. Generally, for transmission to occur, the infected fluid of the carrier must pass through some channel of infection and reach the bloodstream of the transferee. The normal modes of HIV transmission are sexual contact, the sharing of HIV contaminated intravenous needles and syringes, transfusions of tainted blood or its components, and from mother to infant during pregnancy or birth. . . .

* * *

Since intact skin is an absolute barrier to the virus, casual contact, social contact and skin-to-skin contact do not pose a risk of HIV transmission. . . .

* * *

For HIV to be transmitted from an infected dentist to a patient in a dental setting, therefore, the dentist's infected blood must come into contact with either the blood or a mucous membrane of the patient. . . .

doing surgery since being diagnosed as HIV-positive in 1989. Although the Division determined that the risk of patient exposure was "very small," it notified all patients treated by Dr. Owens from the time of his 1989 diagnosis until his death that their dentist had died from AIDS and that there was a possibility that they were exposed to HIV. The Division also advised the former patients that they could participate in a free program of HIV testing and counseling. Some patients availed themselves of the Division's testing while others secured independent testing. Of the 630 former patients of Dr. Owens who have been tested, none have tested positive for HIV.

* * *

In their Superior Court action, the plaintiffs alleged that each of them had been patients of Dr. Owens in 1990 or 1991. Each claimed to have received treatment, including teeth extraction, reconstruction and cleaning, during which their gums bled. The plaintiffs alleged that Dr. Owens was HIV-positive and that he exhibited open lesions and memory loss at the time of such treatment. The plaintiffs did not allege the contraction of any physical ailment or injury as a result of their treatment, but claimed to have suffered "mental anguish" from past and future fear of contracting AIDS. They also alleged embarrassment in going for medical testing to a State clinic which they found to be "an uncomfortable environment." Plaintiffs sought compensation and punitive damages for mental anguish, the cost of medical testing and monitoring, and reimbursement for monies paid to Dr. Owens for dental treatment.

* * *

After brief discovery, the Owens defendants ("Owens") moved for summary judgment. . . .(T)he Superior Court ruled that plaintiffs had no basis for recovery for "fear of AIDS" in the absence of an underlying physical injury. Accordingly, the court dismissed all counts of the complaint. Plaintiffs have appealed only the Superior Court ruling with regard to the battery and misrepresentation claims.

* * *

Under the Restatement (Second) of Torts, "[a]n actor is subject to liability to another for battery if (a) he acts intending to cause a harmful or offensive contact with the person. . . and (b) a harmful contact with the person of the other directly or indirectly results." Restatement (Second) of Torts § 18 (1965); see also W. Page Keeton, et. al., Prosser and Keeton on Torts, § 9 at 39 (5th ed. 1984) (hereafter "Prosser and Keeton") ("A harmful or offensive contact with a person, resulting from an act intended to cause the plaintiff or third person to suffer such a contact, or apprehension that such contact is imminent, is a battery.") This Court has recognized that, under appropriate factual circumstances, a patient may have a cause of action against a medical practitioner for the tort of battery for acts arising from the practitioner's professional conduct. . . .

In essence, the tort of battery is the intentional, unpermitted contact upon the person of another which is harmful or offensive. Lack of consent is thus an essential element of battery. . . . The intent necessary for battery is the intent to make contact with the person, not the intent to cause harm. . . . In addition, the contact need not be harmful, it is sufficient if the contact offends the person's integrity. . . . "Proof of the technical invasion of the integrity of the plaintiff's person by even an entirely harmless, yet offensive, contact entitles the plaintiff to vindication of the legal right by the award of nominal damages." Id. The fact that a person does not discover the offensive nature of the contact until after the event does not, ipso facto, preclude recovery. See *Restatement (Second) of Torts* § 18 cmt. D (1965).

Although a battery may consist of any unauthorized touching of the person which causes offense or alarm, the test for whether a contact is "offensive" is not wholly subjective. The law does not permit recovery for the extremely sensitive who become offended at the slightest contact. Rather, for a bodily contact to be offensive, it must offend a reasonable sense of personal dignity. *Restatement (Second) of Torts* § 19 (1965).

In order for a contact to be offensive to a reasonable sense of personal dignity, it must be one which would offend the ordinary person and as such one not unduly sensitive as to his personal dignity. It must, therefore, be a contact which is unwarranted by the social usages prevalent at the time and place at which it is inflicted. *Restatement (Second) of Torts* § 19 cmt. A (1965); Prosser and Keeton, § 9, at 42. The propriety of the contact is therefore assessed by an objective "reasonableness" standard.

Plaintiffs contend that the "touching" implicit in the dental procedures performed by Dr. Owens was offensive because he was HIV-positive. We must therefore determine whether the performance of dental procedures by an HIV-infected dentist, standing alone, may constitute offensive bodily contact for purposes of battery, i.e., would such touching offend a reasonable sense of personal dignity?

As noted, HIV is transmitted primarily through direct blood-to-blood contact or by the exchange of bodily fluids with an infected individual. In a dental setting, the most probable means of transmission is through the exchange of bodily fluids between the dentist and patient by percutaneous (through the skin) contact, by way of an open wound, non-intact skin or mucous membrane, with infected blood or blood-contaminated bodily fluids. During invasive dental procedures, such as teeth extraction, root canal and periodontal treatments, there is a risk that the dentist may suffer a percutaneous injury to the hands, such as a puncture wound caused by a sharp instrument or object during treatment, and expose the dentist and patient to an exchange of blood or other fluids. . . .Although the use of gloves as a protective barrier during invasive dental procedures reduces the risk of exposure of HIV, their use cannot prevent piercing injuries to the hands caused by needles, sharp instruments or patient biting. . . .

The risk of HIV transmission from a health care worker to a patient during an invasive medical procedure is very remote. In fact, even a person who is exposed to HIV holds a slim chance of infection. The CDC has estimated that the theoretical risk of HIV transmission from an HIV-infected health care worker to patient following actual percutaneous exposure to HIV-infected blood is, by any measure, less than one percent.

* * *

Although this is the first "fear of AIDS" case in Delaware based on the intentional tort of battery, this Court, in a negligence setting, has addressed the issue of whether one can recover for mental distress in the absence of an underlying physical injury. In *Mergenthaler*, this Court held that:

> In any claim for mental anguish, whether it arises from witnessing the ailments of another or from the claimant's apprehension, an essential element of the claim is that the claimant have a present physical injury. . . .

480 A.2d at 650 (citations omitted).

Here, plaintiffs have alleged no injuries which stem from their exposure to HIV. Instead, plaintiff's alleged "injuries" arise solely out of their fear that they have been exposed to HIV. In essence, they claim mental anguish damages for their "fear of AIDS." As noted in *Mergenthaler*, however, damages for claims of emotional distress or mental anguish (which would include fear of contracting a disease) are recoverable only if the underlying physical injury is shown. Id., 480 A.2d at 651. In this case, plaintiffs have sustained no physical injury, and therefore, they could not recover under a negligence theory. Id. We recognize, however, that where an intentional tort is the basis for a claim of emotional distress an accompanying physical injury is not required "if such conduct is viewed as outrageous." *Cummings v. Pinder, Del.Supr.*, 574 a.2d 843, 845 (1990).

As earlier noted, the offensive character of a contact in a battery case is assessed by a "reasonableness" standard. In a "fear of AIDS" case in which battery is alleged, therefore, we examine the overall reasonableness of the plaintiffs' fear in contracting the disease to determine whether the contact or touching was offensive. Since HIV causes AIDS, any assessment of the fear of contracting AIDS must, ipso facto, relate to the exposure to HIV. Moreover, because HIV is transmitted only through fluid-to-fluid contact or exposure, the reasonableness of a plaintiff's fear of AIDS should be measured by whether or not there was a channel of infection or actual exposure of the plaintiff to the virus.

* * *

It is unreasonable for a person to fear infection when that person has not been exposed to a disease. In the case of AIDS, actual exposure to HIV may escalate the threat of infection from a theoretical, remote risk to a real and grave possibility if the person exposed is motivated by speculation unrelated to the objective setting. Such fear is based on uninformed apprehension, not reality. In such circumstances, the fear of contracting AIDS is per se unreasonable without proof of actual exposure to HIV. In our view, the mere fear of contracting AIDS, in the absence of actual exposure to HIV, is not sufficient to impose liability on a health care provider. AIDS phobia, standing alone, cannot form the basis for recovery of damages, even under a battery theory because the underlying causation/harm nexus is not medically supportable.

AIDS is a disease that spawns widespread public misperception based upon the dearth of knowledge concerning HIV transmission. Indeed, plaintiffs rely upon the degree of public misconception about AIDS to support their claim that their fear was reasonable. To accept this argument is to contribute to the phobia. Were we to recognize a claim for the fear of contracting AIDS based upon a mere allegation that one may have been exposed to HIV, totally unsupported by any medical evidence or factual proof, we would open a Pandora's Box of "AIDS-phobia" claims by individuals whose ignorance, unreasonable suspicion or general paranoia cause them apprehension over the slightest of contact with HIV-infected individuals or objects. Such plaintiffs would recover for their fear of AIDS, no matter how irrational. See James C. Maroulis, Can HIV-Negative Plaintiffs Recover Emotional Distress Damages for Their Fear of AIDS? 62 FORDHAM L. REV. 225, 261 (1993) ("Allowing juries to decide whether the plaintiff's fear is reasonable even where there is no evidence of exposure invites jury speculation and may allow recovery based on ignorance or unreasonable fear of the disease."). We believe the better approach is to assess the reasonableness of a plaintiff's fear of AIDS according to the plaintiff's actual—not potential—exposure to HIV.

* * *

In sum, we find that without actual exposure to HIV, the risk of its transmission is so minute that any fear of contracting AIDS is per se unreasonable. We therefore hold, as a matter of law, that the incidental touching of a patient by an HIV-infected dentist while performing ordinary, consented-to dental procedure is insufficient to sustain a battery claim in the absence of a channel for HIV infection. In other words, such contact is "offensive" only if it results in actual exposure to the HIV virus. We therefore adopt an "actual exposure" test, which requires a plaintiff to show "actual exposure" to a disease-causing agent as a prerequisite to prevail on a claim based upon fear of contracting disease. Attenuated and speculative allegations of exposure to HIV do not give rise to a legally cognizable claim in Delaware.

* * *

NOTES

1. *Inferring Intent.* An actor is subject to liability to another for battery if she acts "intending to cause a harmful or offensive contact with the person of the other or a third person, or an imminent apprehension of such a contact," and a harmful or offensive contact with the person of the other directly or indirectly results. RESTATEMENT (SECOND) OF TORTS §§ 13, 18. The necessary intent can be inferred if the act is done "with knowledge on the part of the actor that such contact or apprehension is substantially certain to be produced." *See Garratt v. Dailey,* 46 Wash. 2d 197, 279 P.2d 1091 (1955), in which the defendant, five years and nine months old, committed battery by pulling a chair out from under the plaintiff, an "arthritic woman," when he knew that she had "begun the slow process of being seated" on the chair. According to RESTATEMENT (SECOND) OF TORTS § 8A, "The word 'intent' is used . . . to denote that the actor desires to cause consequences of his act, or that he believes that the consequences are substantially certain to result from it."

2. In *White v. University of Idaho,* 115 Idaho 564, 768 P.2d 827 (1989), the defendant touched the plaintiff's back without her consent while she was playing the piano, and she suffered injury as a result. The court, in holding that a claim for battery was stated, defined the necessary mental state of the defendant as the intent to make bodily contact that is harmful or offensive. Does this "intent" differ from that required in *Brzoska*? How?

3. *Of Lawful and License.* In *Vosburg v. Putney,* 80 Wis. 523, 50 N.W. 403 (1891), the defendant, slightly less than 12 years old, playfully kicked the 14-year-old plaintiff during class. Because of the plaintiff's sensitive condition, of which defendant was unaware, the kick resulted in severe injury. The court found that an action in battery would lie if the intention was either "unlawful" or if the defendant was "in fault":

> Hence, as applied to this case, if the kicking of the plaintiff by the defendant was an unlawful act, the intention of defendant to kick him was also unlawful. Had the parties been upon the play-grounds of the school, engaged in the usual boyish sports, the defendant being free from malice, wantonness, or negligence, and intending no harm to plaintiff in what he did, we should hesitate to hold the act of the defendant unlawful, or that he could be held liable in this action. Some consideration is due to the implied license of the play-grounds. But it appears that the injury was inflicted in the school, after it had been called to order by the teacher, and after the regular exercises of the school had commenced. Under these circumstances, no implied license to do the act complained of existed, and such act was a violation of the order and decorum of the school, and necessarily unlawful. Hence we are of the opinion that, under the evidence and verdict, the action may be sustained. . . .

Compare *Barouh v. Haberman*, 26 Cal App. 4th 40, 31 Cal Rptr. 2d 259 (1994), holding that it was error to charge a jury that a battery was "any intentional, unlawful and harmful contact." The court observed that

> Although it is not incorrect to say that battery is an unlawful touching (6 Am. Jur.2d, Assault and Battery, § 5), it is redundant to use "unlawful" in defining battery in a jury instruction, and may be misleading to do so without informing the jury what would make the conduct unlawful.

What is the "implied license" referred to in the *Vosburg* case? Compare *Neal v. Neal,* 873 P.2d 871 (Idaho 1994), where the court said that a fact question was presented as to whether the defendant husband committed a battery on his plaintiff wife by having sexual intercourse with her when he had been contemporaneously engaging in adultery with another woman. The wife contended she would not have consented to sexual intercourse if she had known of the adulterous relation. "Consent obtained by fraud or misrepresentation," the court said, "vitiates the consent and can render the offending party liable for battery." *See also Crawn v. Campo,* post.

4. *The Mistaken Battery.* In *Seigel v. Long,* 169 Ala. 79, 53 So. 753 (1910), the defendant mistakenly believed the plaintiff was the person who had frightened his team of horses the day before. He angrily accosted the plaintiff,

pushing back the plaintiff's hat in order to get a better look at his face. This touching was held to be a battery:

> It is true that defendant's testimony tended to show that defendant made a mistake as to the identity of the party whom he assaulted, and he told plaintiff that, if he was not the person who frightened his team, he owed him an apology; but this did not prevent what he did from being an assault and battery. It was an assault and battery, with or without mistaken identity.

In *Ranson v. Kitner*, 31 Ill. App. 241 (1889), the plaintiff sued defendants for the value of his dog, which defendants killed. "The defense was that [defendants] were hunting for wolves, that [plaintiff's] dog had a striking resemblance to a wolf, that they in good faith believed it to be one, and killed it as such." The court affirmed a jury finding of liability. Defendants, the court said, "are clearly liable for the damages caused by their mistake, notwithstanding they were acting in good faith." Compare the materials on conversion, Subsection H, post.

5. *Battery in the Air.* In *Pechan v. Dynapro, Inc.*, 251 Ill. App. 3d 1072, 622 N.E.2d 108 (1993), the plaintiff failed to state a claim for battery from secondhand workplace smoke. "As of this day and time, smoking remains a permitted activity in our society, although its glory days are waning," the court said. "Smoking is a legal activity and not an act of battery because, generally, smokers do not smoke cigarettes with the intent to touch nonsmokers with secondhand smoke." Compare *Leichtman v. WLW Jacor Commun., Inc.*, 92 Ohio App. 3d 232, 634 N.E. 2d 697 (1993), holding that a radio talk show antismoking guest stated a claim for battery against another guest who intentionally and repeatedly blew cigar smoke on her throughout the program.

6. *The Insult.* Battery fact patterns may involve only insult rather than physical injury. The least touching of "anything connected" with the plaintiff's person may be sufficient to constitute a battery "when done in an offensive manner." Thus in *Fisher v. Carrousel Motor Hotel, Inc.*, 424 S.W.2d 627 (Tex. 1967), plaintiff, an African-American, stated a valid claim for assault and battery when he proved that while standing in line for lunch with others at defendant's motor lodge, he was approached by one of defendant's employees, who snatched the plate from his hand, and shouted that no Negro could be served in the club. Plaintiff was not actually touched, and was in no apprehension of physical injury, but he was highly embarrassed and hurt by the conduct in the presence of his associates. In allowing recovery, the court observed: "Personal indignity is the essence of an action for battery; and consequently the defendant is liable not only for contacts which do actual physical harm, but also for those which are offensive and insulting." Would the touching of something in one's hand be the touching of the person for battery purposes? How far could this be extended? How about beating on a car in which a person is sitting? Could there be some other reason why the court in *Fisher* was willing to call this a battery?

7. *Transferred Intent.* The doctrine of "transferred intent" applies when A attempts to commit a trespassory tort on B and inadvertently commits such a tort on C instead. Thus if A shoots to frighten B but instead hits C, A has committed a battery on C. *Brown v. Martinez*, 68 N.M. 271, 361 P.2d 152

(1961). Or if A shoots at a dog and hits C, then A is liable to C for battery. *Corn v. Sheppard,* 179 Minn. 490, 229 N.W. 869 (1930). The transferred intent doctrine may apply only when the torts involved are one or more of the following: battery, assault, false imprisonment, trespass to land, or trespass to chattel. Prosser, *Transferred Intent,* 45 TEX. L. REV. 650 (1967). Is there any reason for such a limitation?

Reconsider *Ranson v. Kitner,* note 4, *supra.* Is that a transferred-intent case?

McGUIRE v. ALMY
297 Mass. 323, 8 N.E.2d 760 (1937)

QUA, J.

This is an action of tort for assault and battery. The only question of law reported is whether the judge should have directed a verdict for the defendant.

The following facts are established by the plaintiff's own evidence: In August, 1930, the plaintiff was employed to take care of the defendant. The plaintiff was a registered nurse and was a graduate of a training school for nurses. The defendant was an insane person. Before the plaintiff was hired she learned that the defendant was a "mental case and was in good physical condition," and that for some time two nurses had been taking care of her. The plaintiff was on "twenty-four hour duty." The plaintiff slept in the room next to the defendant's room. Except when the plaintiff was with the defendant, the plaintiff kept the defendant locked in the defendant's room. There was a wire grating over the outside of the window of that room. During the period of "fourteen months or so" while the plaintiff cared for the defendant, the defendant "had a few odd spells," when she showed some hostility to the plaintiff and said that "she would like to try and do something to her." The defendant had been violent at times and had broken dishes "and things like that," and on one or two occasions the plaintiff had to have help to subdue the defendant.

On April 19, 1932, the defendant, while locked in her room, had a violent attack. The plaintiff heard a crashing of furniture and then knew that the defendant was ugly, violent and dangerous. The defendant told the plaintiff and a Miss Maroney, "the maid," who was with the plaintiff in the adjoining room, that if they came into the defendant's room, she would kill them. The plaintiff and Miss Maroney looked into the defendant's room, "saw what the defendant had done," and "thought it best to take the broken stuff away before she did any harm to herself with it." They sent for one Emerton, the defendant's brother-in-law. When he arrived the defendant was in the middle of her room about ten feet from the door, holding upraised the leg of a lowboy as if she were going to strike. The plaintiff stepped into the room and walked toward the defendant, while Emerton and Miss Maroney remained in the doorway. As the plaintiff approached the defendant and tried to take hold of the defendant's hand which held the leg, the defendant struck the plaintiff's head with it, causing the injuries for which the action was brought.

The extent to which an insane person is liable for torts has not been fully defined in this Commonwealth.... In *Morain v. Devlin,* 132 Mass. 87, this court said, through Chief Justice Gray, "By the common law, as generally stated in the books, a lunatic is civilly liable to make compensation in damages to persons injured by his acts, although, being incapable of criminal intent, he is not liable to indictment and punishment," citing numerous cases (page 88). But the actual decision went no further than to hold the lunatic, as a landowner receiving the benefits of ownership, liable for the defective condition of his premises. . . .

Turning to authorities elsewhere, we find that courts in this country almost invariably say in the broadest terms that an insane person is liable for his torts. As a rule no distinction is made between those torts which would ordinarily be classed as negligent, nor do the courts discuss the effect of different kinds of insanity or of varying degrees of capacity as bearing upon the ability of the defendant to understand the particular act in question or to make a reasoned decision with respect to it, although it is sometimes said that an insane person is not liable for torts requiring malice of which he is incapable. Defamation and malicious prosecution are the torts more commonly mentioned in this connection. . . . These decisions are rested more upon grounds of public policy and upon what might be called a popular view of the requirements of essential justice than upon any attempt to apply logically the underlying principles of civil liability to the special instance of the mentally deranged. Thus it is said that a rule imposing liability tends to make more watchful those persons who have charge of the defendant and who may be supposed to have some interest in preserving his property; that as an insane person must pay for his support, if he is financially able, so he ought also to pay for the damage which he does; that an insane person with abundant wealth ought not to continue in unimpaired enjoyment of the comfort which it brings while his victim bears the burden unaided; and there is also a suggestion that courts are loath to introduce into the great body of civil litigation the difficulties in determining mental capacity which it has been found impossible to avoid in the criminal field.

The rule established in these cases has been criticized severely by certain eminent text writers both in this country and in England, principally on the ground that it is an archaic survival of the rigid and formal medieval conception of liability for acts done, without regard to fault, as opposed to what is said to be the general modern theory that liability in tort should rest upon fault. Notwithstanding these criticisms, we think that as a practical matter there is strong force in the reasons underlying these decisions. They are consistent with the general statements found in the cases dealing with the liability of infants for torts, including a few cases in which the child was so young as to render his capacity for fault comparable to that of many insane persons. Fault is by no means at the present day a universal prerequisite to liability, and the theory that it should be such has been obliged very recently to yield at several points to what have been thought to be paramount considerations of public good. Finally, it would be difficult not to recognize the persuasive weight of so much authority so widely extended.

But the present occasion does not require us either to accept or to reject the prevailing doctrine in its entirety. For this case it is enough to say that where an insane person by his act does intentional damage to the person or property of another he is liable for that damage in the same circumstances in which a normal person would be liable. This means that insofar as a particular intent would be necessary in order to render a normal person liable, the insane person, in order to be liable, must have been capable of entertaining that same intent and must have entertained it in fact. But the law will not inquire further into his peculiar mental condition with a view to excusing him if it should appear that delusion or other consequence of his affliction has caused him to entertain that intent or that a normal person would not have entertained it.

We do not suggest that this is necessarily a logical stopping point. If public policy demands that a mentally affected person be subjected to the external standard for intentional wrongs, it may well be that public policy also demands that he should be subjected to the external standard for wrongs which are commonly classified as negligent, in accordance with what now seems to be the prevailing view. We stop here for the present, because we are not required to go further in order to decide this case, because of deference to the difficulty of the subject, because full and adequate discussion is lacking in most of the cases decided up to the present time, and because by far the greater number of those cases, however broad their statement of the principle, are in fact cases of intentional rather than of negligent injury.

Coming now to the application of the rule to the facts of this case, it is apparent that the jury could find that the defendant was capable of entertaining and that she did entertain an intent to strike and to injure the plaintiff and that she acted upon that intent. We think this was enough.

NOTES

1. *Particular Intent.* What does the result in *McGuire v. Almy* disclose as to the form *and* function of a simple intentional tort such as battery? In contrast, what is the "particular intent" which, according to *McGuire v. Almy,* is required in some other intentional torts?

2. *The Wild Baby.* In *Fromenthal v. Clark,* 442 So. 2d 608 (La. App. 1983), *cert. denied,* 444 So. 2d 1242 (La. 1984), plaintiff, a two-week-old infant, was severely bitten by the defendant Clark, age two, while plaintiff was sleeping on a bed. The trial court held that "the child, Shawn Clark, was below the age of discernment and reason and, therefore, cannot be held liable for his delictual acts, negligent or intentional, because he lacks the ability to be legally at fault."

Why would a two-year-old bite the infant plaintiff? Could this motive be shown by circumstantial evidence? If so, would it make a difference?

3. *Parental Liability for the Delinquent Child.* In *Fromenthal,* note 2, *supra,* the court held that under Louisiana law the two-year old's father, who was also a defendant, could be held liable for the "delictual conduct" of his minor child. What sense does it make to hold the father liable, but not the child?

In most states, parents not personally at fault usually are not held liable for injuries caused by their children, except that a number of states provide by statute that a parent is vicariously liable in limited amounts for willful acts of their children, such as acts of vandalism. *See, e.g.,* TENN. CODE ANN. 37-10-101 ($10,000 maximum liability of parent or guardian for willful or malicious acts of minors under 18 living with such parent or guardian). A parent also may be liable in negligence for failure to control a child with a dangerous propensity of which the parent has reason to know. The dangerous propensity "must be of a very specific kind, however. There is no 'general responsibility for the rearing of incorrigible children.'" F. HARPER, F. JAMES & O. GRAY, 3 THE LAW OF TORTS § 18.7, at 738 (2d ed. 1986). In other words, a parent cannot be held responsible for his or her child's general incorrigibility.

4. *Intent Redux.* In *Janelsins v. Button,* 102 Md. App. 30, 648 A.2d 1039 (1994), plaintiff Button, a bar employee, was injured while attempting to escort defendant Janelsins, a drunk bar patron, to the latter's car:

> Although Janelsins admittedly had no memory of the events, it is apparent that he did not want anyone to force him into his car. Nor did he want anyone to drive it for him. When Button and the customers tried to push Janelsins into the back seat of his car, Janelsins resisted, shouting obscenities and threats. As Button attempted to put Janelsins's legs in the car, Janelsins kicked Button in the face. As a result, Button lost a tooth, and suit followed. The court rejected defendant's argument that there was insufficient evidence to support a battery claim:

> A battery is the "unpermitted application of trauma by one person upon the body of another person." *McGuiggan v. Boy Scouts of America,* 73 Md. App. 705, 714, 536 A.2d 137 (1988). Accidental or inadvertent contact does not constitute battery. Rather, the tort of battery requires *intent* by the actor "to bring about a harmful or offensive contact. . . . [It is] confined to intentional invasions of the interests in freedom from harmful or offensive contact." *Fowler v. Harper, et al.,* 1 *The Law of Torts* § 3.3, at 272–73, 276 (2d ed. 1986).

> Janelsins's insufficiency of the evidence argument must fail. The evidence, including Janelsins's threats and his flailing about, adequately supports a finding that he intended to strike Button. Although Janelsins apparently was inebriated at the time of the incident, his voluntary intoxication does not vitiate the intent element of battery.

> In *McEachern v. Muldovan,* 505 S.E. 2d 495 (Ga. 1998), decedent was killed as he and a minor friend, both of whom were under the influence of alcohol, took turns pointing a handgun at each other and pulling the trigger. The court observed that:

For more than a century, Georgia has followed the rule that one who becomes voluntarily intoxicated is held thereafter to the same standard as if he were a sober person.

* * *

That school of jurists who consider torts as akin to crimes apply to the case of a drunk man, as to his capacity both for negligence and for contributory negligence, the ancient maxim that drunkenness is no excuse for crime. The other school, although they do not base their theories of tort on the criminal law, just as uniformly hold the drunk man responsible for his conduct under a given state of circumstances as if he were sober. Irrespective of the various reasons given, all courts now hold that the drunk man, so far as his own conduct is concerned, is to be considered, in all matters of volition, judgment, caution, and general mental state, just as if he were sober. The state of mind produced by intoxication will be disregarded in viewing his actions, and he will be judged as if he possessed his normal capacities.

KILEY v. PATTERSON
760 A.2d 1253 (R. I. 2000)

FLANDERS, JUSTICE.

Playing second base during a recreational, coed-softball-league game, the plaintiff, Lori Kiley (Kiley) injured her knee when a male base runner, the defendant, Steven Patterson (Patterson), aggressively slid into her. He did so while attempting to advance from first to second base on a batted ground ball fielded by the third baseman. Presumably, he sought to break up a possible double play and force out at second base. In throwing himself into a slide, however, Patterson raised at least one of his feet high enough off the ground to cause it to collide with Kiley's knee as he slid into second base. Kiley's amended complaint sought to recover damages for the injuries she suffered as a result of the ensuing collision.

Can the injured second-sacker sue the runner for "negligently, recklessly or wantonly" colliding with her and causing her injuries? Not for mere negligence, we hold. But if she can prove the runner slid into her knee deliberately or in reckless disregard of creating an unreasonable risk of injury to her, then she can seek to hold him liable for allegedly executing a so-called forbidden "take-out slide." In baseball and softball parlance, this is a maneuver in which the base runner attempts to take the infielder out of the play by sliding "into a fielder attempting to off-balance that player and prevent his [or her] making a play." Although this softball league permitted sliding, some evidence available to the motion justice indicated that takeout slides were against the rules. Still other evidence suggested that Patterson may have acted willfully or recklessly when he slid into Kiley's knee. Finally, no evidence showed that Kiley knowingly and subjectively assumed the risk that she might be on the receiving end of a deliberate or reckless take-out slide when playing this sport. Thus, for the reasons batted around below, we reverse the Superior Court's summary judgment and remand this case for trial. . . .

This Court has not previously addressed whether the standard of care for determining liability for co-participants in an athletic event is either a heightened recklessness or deliberate misconduct standard or one of ordinary negligence. Most other courts that have considered this issue, however, have found that:

> "[T]he duty of care owed by participants in team athletic events to each other is measured not by ordinary negligence standards, but by willfulness or recklessness standards because of considerations of the participants' assumption of risk or their consenting to an invasion of personal interests or rights by taking part in the subject contest."

Stanley L. Grazis, Annotation, *Liability of Participant in Team Athletic Competition for Injury to or Death of Another Participant*, 55 A.L.R. 5th 529, 537 (1998). . . .

Kiley offered evidence to support her claim that when Patterson slid into her knee with his raised foot, he either willfully intended to strike her knee or else he acted recklessly in doing so. Significantly, the softball league's commissioner, John Leistritz, testified at his deposition that a specific rule prohibited this kind of "take-out slide" and the rule itself stated that a player may be warned or ejected from a game by an umpire for executing a "take-out slide" or for using unnecessary roughness on the base paths. As the motion justice recognized, the mere act of sliding in a softball game was not against the rules of this league. But she apparently overlooked the league rule allowing umpires to warn or eject players for executing "take-out slides" or indulging in unnecessary roughness on the base paths. . . .

To be sure, Kiley was a veteran softball player. Hence, she was well aware of the risks inherent in playing this game, including the common knowledge that players may slide into one another in the course of avoiding a force out at second base. She had played in numerous softball games and was experienced at playing this particular position. As a result, she must be deemed to have assumed the normal risks of contact inherent in playing softball, including the risk that other players might negligently injure her while sliding into second base. But it cannot be concluded as a matter of law that she assumed the risk of sustaining injuries as a result of deliberate or reckless misconduct on the part of opposing players acting in violation of league rules. A boxer may assume the risk of a negligent low blow, but a deliberate punch to his groin would still be actionable. . . .

We sustain Kiley's appeal, vacate the Superior Court's judgment, and remand this case for trial.

NOTES

1. *Unorganized Sports.* In *Marchetti v. Kalish*, 559 N.E. 2d 699 (Ohio, 1990), plaintiff was injured in a "kick the can" game. The court, finding that the kicking child was not liable, applied the same standard of liability to children's sports activities as to those of adults, and held that the kicker was liable only if he acted recklessly or with intent to injure, even though he was violating the "rules" of the game.

Why not say that one assumes the risk of (and therefore cannot recover for) injuries sustained in playing sports? What risks should be included? Is a courtroom the proper place to make such a determination? Would making such a determination in a courtroom "chill" athletic competition? Does the solution the court reaches in *Kiley* adequately balance the competing societal policies?

2. *Paddling.* The 12-year-old plaintiff in *Rinehart v. Board of Educ.*, 87 Ohio App. 3d 214, 621 N.E.2d 1365 (1993), was paddled for calling his teacher a "dickhead." The teacher followed the procedures set out by the school board, administering three strokes in the presence of two faculty witnesses. The court held the plaintiff failed to state a claim for battery on these facts.

Compare Miller v. Tony & Susan Alamo Found., 748 F. Supp. 695 (W.D. Ark. 1990), *aff'd* 924 F.2d 143 (8th Cir. 1991), where the minor plaintiff recovered $50,000 compensatory and $500,000 punitive damages for emotional distress arising out of a paddling inflicted by the leader of a religious organization. The plaintiff was struck 140 times while being held by four adults. The punishment was administered in public. The paddling was so severe that it caused bleeding to the plaintiff's buttocks.

Can you think of a reason why a paddling teacher would not be held liable and a paddling religious leader would?

PROBLEM

Wife sees standing in a crowd a man who she in good faith believes is her husband. She walks up behind him and playfully pats him on the derrière. In fact the man is a stranger, who suffers a heart attack as a result of the unexpected physical contact. What claims might the stranger have against wife? Would it be different if this occurred in their home, and the beneficiary of the "pat" was a late-arriving overnight guest about whose presence in the home the wife was unaware?

D. ASSAULT

CASTIGLIONE v. GALPIN
325 So. 2d 725 (La. App. 1976)

GULOTTA, JUDGE.

This is a suit for damages resulting from an alleged assault based on plaintiffs', Sewerage & Water Board employees, claims that they were placed in reasonable apprehension of receiving a battery when defendant pointed a shotgun at them. This incident occurred after plaintiffs informed defendant that the water would be turned off because of defendant's nonpayment of a water bill. The trial judge rendered judgment in favor of each plaintiff in the sum of $750.00. Defendant appeals. We affirm.

According to plaintiffs' versions of the incident, upon arrival at defendant's residence and after informing him that they were under instructions to turn the water off if the bill was not paid, Galpin stated, "I'll get a gun and shoot you if you dare to close that water." Whereupon, after reiterating the threat, defendant obtained a shotgun from inside the premises and returned to the front porch, where he pointed the gun at plaintiffs while they were preparing to turn the water off at the water main located in the front yard.

Defendant's version of the incident is that he objected to plaintiffs' stated intention to turn off the water and obtained a shotgun. However, he denied that he at any time pointed the weapon at plaintiffs. According to his version, he merely laid the gun across his knee while in a squatting position.

In the absence of trial court reasons, we are unable to ascertain whether the judge made a factual determination that the gun was either in defendant's lap, or pointed at plaintiffs. Nevertheless, we are convinced from the circumstances surrounding the incident that defendant's action (whether the gun remained on the defendant's lap or was pointed at plaintiffs) resulted in plaintiffs being placed in reasonable apprehension of receiving a battery and was sufficient to constitute an assault.

Words alone may not be sufficient to constitute an assault; however, threats coupled with the present ability to carry out the threats are sufficient when one is placed in reasonable apprehension of receiving an injury. It is clear that defendant threatened plaintiffs with bodily harm in the event they turned the water off and that defendant did possess the ability to carry out those threats. Under the circumstances, it is plausible that plaintiffs were in reasonable apprehension of receiving a battery. Accordingly, we find no error on the part of the trial judge finding defendant liable. . . .

NOTES

1. *Assault Doctrine.* According to RESTATEMENT (SECOND) OF TORTS § 21:

(1) An actor is subject to liability to another for assault if

(a) he acts intending to cause a harmful or offensive contact with the person of the other or a third person, or an imminent apprehension of such a contact, and

(b) the other is thereby put in such imminent apprehension.

(2) An action which is not done with the intention stated in Subsection (1)(a) does not make the actor liable to the other for an apprehension caused thereby although the act involves an unreasonable risk of causing it and, therefore, would be negligent or reckless if the risk threatened bodily harm.

2. *Impossibility.* Suppose that in *Castiglione* the defendant had unloaded the gun before the incident? The plaintiff nevertheless would be in apprehension, but would the defendant have the necessary intent? Suppose the plaintiff knows the gun is unloaded, but the defendant thinks it is loaded? The defendant would have the necessary intent, but would plaintiff be put in apprehension of a harmful contact? An offensive contact?

HOLCOMBE v. WHITAKER
294 Ala. 430, 318 So. 2d 289 (1975)

SHORES, JUSTICE.

This is an appeal from a judgment which was rendered on a jury verdict in favor of the plaintiff in the amount of $35,000. . . .

The plaintiff, Joan Whitaker, met the defendant, M. C. Holcombe, Jr., a medical doctor, in March or April 1970. Shortly thereafter the two began seeing each other socially; and about a month later the defendant moved into the plaintiff's apartment, where they lived together for some time. It was the plaintiff's testimony that the defendant told her he was a divorced man. Sometime after the defendant moved into the plaintiff's apartment, he invited her to accompany him to a medical convention in San Francisco. She did so, and testified that she was asked by the defendant to pose as Mrs. Holcombe at that meeting. Following the convention, the two flew to Las Vegas, Nevada, and were married there. They left Las Vegas and went to New Orleans for a "honeymoon" and finally returned to Birmingham, where they lived together as husband and wife for approximately a month. At about that time, Dr. Holcombe began seeing a woman he had been dating prior to his marriage to the plaintiff. He had previously told Miss Whitaker that he wanted to tell this woman personally about his having married. When the plaintiff objected to his resuming his relationship with this woman, he then told her that he was still married to his first wife. She then asked him to either have the marriage with her annulled or get a divorce from his first wife and marry her legally. Her testimony was that the defendant said "he wasn't going to do either one."

To say the least, the relationship between Miss Whitaker and Dr. Holcombe began to disintegrate from this point forward. He moved out of the apartment, but came back from time to time, staying for as long as a week on at least one occasion. The plaintiff continued to ask him to get an annulment or to get a divorce from his wife and legally marry her. She went to the apartment occupied by the woman the defendant was then seeing again and found him there. Again, she had a conversation with him about getting an annulment. On that occasion he said, "If you take me to court, I will kill you."

From that point on, the plaintiff testified that she began receiving telephone calls from Dr. Holcombe and from his lady friend at all hours of the night. She also received anonymous calls.

There was other evidence to the effect that, after Dr. Holcombe threatened the plaintiff the first time, she moved to another apartment and got an unlisted telephone number. For a period of time the calls from Dr. Holcombe and his friend stopped. Then her apartment was broken into and some of her clothes were soaked with what later appeared to be iodine. Thereafter, the calls resumed. After the break-in, she had new locks put on the door and the windows were nailed closed. She also had friends spend the night with her thereafter.

. . . The plaintiff claimed that the defendant committed an assault when in June of 1971, she went to see him and tried to get him to get an annulment and he said, "If you take me to court, I will kill you;" and again in October, 1971, after she had filed the instant suit on September 29, 1971, when he went to her apartment and beat on the door, tried to pry it open, and said again, "If you take me to court, I will kill you." The defendant claims this in no way can constitute an assault, because it was merely a conditional threat of violence and because no overt act was involved. In order to safeguard freedom from apprehension of harm or offensive conduct, the law provides an individual with a remedy at law.

An assault consists of "an intentional, unlawful offer to touch the person of another in a rude or angry manner under such circumstances as to create in the mind of the party alleging the assault a well-founded fear of an imminent battery, coupled with the apparent present ability to effectuate the attempt, if not prevented." *Western Union Telegraph Co. v. Hill,* 25 Ala. App. 540, 542, 150 So. 709, 710 (1933).

While words standing alone cannot constitute an assault, they may give meaning to an act and both, taken together, may constitute an assault. In addition, words may negative an act in a manner that apprehension in such a case would be unreasonable. "On the other hand, a show of force accompanied by an unlawful or unjustifiable demand, compliance with which will avert the threatened battery, is an assault." 1 Harper & James, The Law of Torts, page 223 (1956). "[T]he defendant is not free to compel the plaintiff to buy his safety by compliance with a condition which there is no legal right to impose." Prosser, Law of Torts, 40 (4th ed. 1971). It is obvious that the defendant in the instant case had no right to impose the condition he did on the plaintiff; and we cannot say that this condition explained away his threat to harm her.

The defendant says his conduct cannot constitute an assault because there was no overt action taken by him. The evidence from the plaintiff was that the defendant was pounding on her door making every effort to get into the apartment, and threatening to kill her if she persisted in "taking him to court." We cannot say, as a matter of law, that this was not sufficient to arouse an apprehension of harm or offensive conduct. We think it was a jury question, as was the question of whether the defendant had the apparent ability to effectuate the threatened act. . . .

NOTES

1. *Present Apprehension.* Recall that RESTATEMENT (SECOND) OF TORTS § 21 states that the apprehension must be of an "imminent" harmful or offensive contact. Thus, a threat to harm in the future is not an assault. *Tuberville v. Savage,* [1669] 86 Eng. Rep. 684 (defendant, arguing with plaintiff, put his hand on his sword and said, "If it were not assize-time, I would not take such language from you;" no assault, since it *was* assize-time). Was that apprehension present in *Holcombe*? What was plaintiff's evidence on the issue? *See, also,* RESTATEMENT (SECOND) OF TORTS § 30:

Conditional Threat

If the actor intentionally puts another in apprehension of an imminent and harmful or offensive contact, he is subject to liability for an assault although he gives to the other the option to escape the contact by obedience to a command given by the actor, unless the command is one which the actor is privileged to enforce by the infliction of the threatened contact or by a threat to inflict it.

Similarly, there is no assault if the plaintiff learns of the threatened contact after the peril has ended. RESTATEMENT (SECOND) OF TORTS § 22, comment b. illus. 1 (no assault where A learns of B's threat to shoot him only after the threat has passed). Why these restrictions?

2. *The Physical Act.* It frequently is stated that there is no assault unless the defendant makes some gesture or movement, indicating an intent to carry out the threat, *i.e.,* "mere words do not make an assault." Should that be a doctrinal element, or merely good evidence of intent or imminent apprehension? What if the heavyweight champion, whom you know to be such, tells you, as the elevator in which the two of you are riding begins a 50-story descent, that he is going to "beat you up now." Mere words? Substantially

certain to place you in apprehension of an immediate offensive touching? RESTATEMENT (SECOND) OF TORTS § 31 provides that "Words do not make the actor liable for assault unless together with other acts or circumstances they put the other in reasonable apprehension of an imminent harmful or offensive contact with his person."

3. *Faint Hearts.* RESTATEMENT (SECOND) OF TORTS § 27 provides that "if an act is intended to put another in apprehension of an immediate bodily contact and succeeds in so doing, the actor is subject to liability for an assault although his act would not have put a person of ordinary courage in such apprehension.

HALL v. McBRYDE
919 P.2d 910 (Colo. App.1996)

HUME, JUDGE.

Plaintiff, Eric Hall, appeals from a judgment entered in favor of defendant, Marcus McBryde (Marcus), on a claim of battery, and in favor of Marcus' parents, defendants, James McBryde and Kathleen McBryde, on claims of negligent maintenance of a weapon and negligent supervision. We affirm in part, reverse in part, and remand with directions.

On January 14, 1993, Marcus was at his parents' home with another youth after school. Although Marcus was, pursuant to his parents' wishes, actually living in a different neighborhood with a relative and attending a different high school in the hope of avoiding gang-related problems, he had sought and received permission from his father to come to the McBryde house that day to retrieve some clothing. Prior to that date, Marcus had discovered a loaded gun hidden under the mattress of his parents' bed. James McBryde had purchased the gun sometime earlier.

Soon after midday, Marcus noticed some other youths in a car approaching the McBryde house, and he retrieved the gun from its hiding place. After one of the other youths began shooting towards the McBryde house, Marcus fired four shots toward the car containing the other youths.

During the exchange of gunfire one bullet struck plaintiff, who lived next to the McBryde residence, causing an injury to his abdomen that required extensive medical treatment. Although plaintiff testified that it was Marcus who shot him, the trial court made no finding as to whether plaintiff was struck by a bullet fired by Marcus.

* * *

Plaintiff. . .contends that the trial court erred in entering judgment for James and Kathleen McBryde on the claim of negligent supervision. Again, we disagree.

A parent is not liable for the torts committed by his or her child merely because of the parent-child relationship. However, when a child has a known propensity to commit a potentially harmful act, the parent has a duty to use reasonable care to prevent the child from causing such harm if the parent knows or should know of the propensity and has the ability and opportunity to control the child. . . .

Here, the trial court found no evidence that Marcus had been a member of a gang, that he had ever been arrested prior to the shooting incident, or that he otherwise had any history of violent or improper behavior. The trial court also determined that allowing Marcus to return to the McBryde home unsupervised during the afternoon of the shooting to pickup clothing "was not a breach of [the parents'] duty of supervision that any reasonable person would recognize."

Once again, because more than one inference or conclusion may be drawn from the facts and because the trial court's determination is supported by evidence in the record, it will not be disturbed. . . .

Finally, plaintiff contends that the trial court erred in entering judgment for Marcus on the claim of battery. We agree.

An actor is subject to liability to another for battery if he or she acts intending to cause a harmful or offensive contact with the person of the other or a third person, or an imminent apprehension of such a contact, and a harmful or offensive contact with the person of the other directly or indirectly results. *Restatement (Second) of Torts §§ 13,18* (1965); W. Keeton, D. Dobbs, R. Keeton, D. Owen, Prosser & Keeton on the Law of Torts § 9 (5th ed. 1985). . . .

Here, the trial court found that there was no evidence indicating that Marcus intended to shoot at plaintiff. Furthermore, based upon statements by Marcus that he was not purposely trying to hit the other youths but, instead, was shooting at their car, the trial court also determined that plaintiff had failed to prove Marcus intended to make contact with any person other than plaintiff. Based upon this second finding. . .the trial court concluded that, in reaching its determination that no battery occurred, the trial court did not properly analyze the intent required for battery or the transferability of such intent.

As set forth above, the intent element for battery is satisfied if the actor either intends to cause a harmful or offensive contact or if the actor intends to cause an imminent apprehension of such contact. Moreover, with respect to the level of intent necessary for a battery and the transferability of such intent, *Restatement (Second) of Torts* § 16 (1965) provides as follows:

> (1) If an act is done with the intention of inflicting upon another an offensive but not a harmful bodily contact, or of putting another in apprehension of either a harmful or offensive bodily contact, and such act causes a bodily contact to the other, the actor is liable to the other for a battery although the act was not done with the intention of bringing about the resulting bodily harm.
>
> (2) If an act is done with the intention of affecting a third person in the manner stated in Subsection (1), but causes a harmful bodily contact to another, the actor is liable to such other as fully as though he intended so to affect him. (emphasis added)

See also Restatement (Second) of Torts § 20 (1965); *Alteiri v. Colasso*, 168 Conn. 329, 362 A.2d 798 (1975) (when one intends an assault, then, if bodily injury results to someone other than the person whom the actor intended to put in apprehension of harm, it is a battery actionable by the injured person); *Brown v. Martinez*, 68 N.M. 271, 361 P.2d 152 (1961).

Here, the trial court considered only whether Marcus intended to inflict a contact upon the other youths. It did not consider whether Marcus intended to put the other youths in apprehension of a harmful or offensive bodily contact.

However, we conclude, as a matter of law, that by aiming and firing a loaded weapon at the automobile for the stated purpose of protecting his house, Marcus did intend to put the youths who occupied the vehicle in apprehension of a harmful or offensive bodily contact. Hence, pursuant to the rule set forth in *Restatement (Second) of Torts* § 16(2) (1965), Marcus' intent to place other persons in apprehension of a harmful or offensive contact was sufficient to satisfy the intent requirement for battery against plaintiff.

NOTES

1. *Defenses.* Was there any justification for Marcus' conduct? If so, should it bar plaintiff's claim? Reconsider this when you reach self defense and defense of property.

E. FALSE IMPRISONMENT AND FALSE ARREST

COMMENT

The tort of false imprisonment occurs when the actor does an act which is substantially certain to confine another within fixed boundaries for an appreciable period of time. When the attempted confinement is pursuant to legal authority (a law officer or a person attempting a citizen's arrest), the tort may be termed "false arrest." Generally, the elements are the same. One important difference is that the actor who uses force upon the person of the victim in attempting the imprisonment may thereby commit a battery. A police officer however, is privileged to use reasonable force to effect an arrest.

DUPLER v. SEUBERT
69 Wis. 2d 373, 230 N.W.2d 626 (1975)

WILKIE, C.J.

This is a false imprisonment action. On April 23, 1971, plaintiff-appellant Ethel M. Dupler was fired from her job with the defendant-respondent Wisconsin Telephone Company. She was informed of her discharge during an hour-and-a-half session with her two superiors, defendants-respondents Keith Peterson and Helen Seubert, who, Dupler claims, falsely imprisoned her during a portion of this time period. A jury found that Peterson and Seubert did falsely imprison Dupler. [Plaintiff appealed an order of the trial court reducing the amount of the jury verdict. That order was affirmed.]

Dupler had worked for the telephone company as a customer service representative since 1960. At approximately 4:30 on April 23rd, Seubert asked

Dupler to come to Peterson's office. When all three were inside, sitting down, with the door closed, Seubert told Dupler the telephone company would no longer employ her and that she could choose either to resign or be fired. Dupler testified that she refused to resign and that in the conversation that followed, Peterson discussed several alternatives short of dismissal, all of which had been considered but rejected.

At approximately 5 o'clock, Dupler testified, she began to feel sick to her stomach and said "You have already fired me. Why don't you just let me go?" She made a motion to get up but Peterson told her to sit down in "a very loud harsh voice." Then, Dupler testified, she began to feel violently ill and stated "I got to go. I can't take this any more. I'm sick to my stomach. I know I'm going to throw up." She got up and started for the door but Seubert also arose and stood in front of the door. After Dupler repeated that she was sick, Seubert allowed her to exit, but followed her to the men's washroom, where Dupler did throw up. Following this, at approximately 5:25, Seubert asked Dupler to return to Peterson's office where she had left her purse to discuss the situation further. Dupler testified that she went back to the office and reached for her purse; Seubert again closed the door and Peterson said "[in] a loud voice 'Sit down. I'm still your boss. I'm not through with you.'" At approximately 5:40 Dupler told Peterson her husband was waiting for her outside in a car and Peterson told her to go outside and ask her husband to come inside. Dupler then went outside and explained the situation to her husband who said, "You get back in there and get your coat and if you aren't right out I'll call the police." Dupler returned to Peterson's office and was again told in a loud tone of voice to sit down. She said Seubert and Peterson were trying to convince her to resign rather than be fired and again reviewed the alternatives that had been considered. Dupler then said: "What's the sense of all this? Why keep torturing me? Let me go. Let me go." She stated that Peterson replied "No, we still aren't finished. We have a lot of things to discuss, your retirement pay, your vacation, other things." Finally, at approximately 6 o'clock Peterson told Dupler they could talk further on the phone or at her house, and Dupler left. When asked why she had stayed in Peterson's office for such a long time, Dupler replied:

> Well, for one thing, Helen, Mrs. Seubert, had blocked the door, and tempers had been raised with all the shouting and screaming, I was just plain scared to make an effort. There were two against one.

Peterson and Seubert did not dispute that Dupler had been fired on April 23rd, or that the conference lasted from 4:30 to 6 p.m., or that Dupler became very upset and sick to her stomach and had to leave to throw up. Peterson admitted that Dupler had asked to leave and that he requested that she stay and continue talking so she could indicate whether she wished to resign or be fired. Seubert said Dupler did not so indicate until "within three minutes of her leaving." Both denied that any loud or threatening language had been used, or that Dupler was detained against her will. Peterson said neither he nor Seubert even raised their voices. He said the session was so lengthy because Dupler continued to plead for another chance, and to request reasons for the dismissal.

. . . The essence of false imprisonment is the intentional, unlawful, and unconsented restraint by one person of the physical liberty of another. In

Maniaci v. Marquette University, 50 Wis. 2d 287, 184 N.W.2d 168 (1971), the court adopted the definition of false imprisonment contained in sec. 35 of the Restatement of Torts 2d, which provides in part:

False Imprisonment

(1) An actor is subject to liability to another for false imprisonment if

(a) he acts intending to confine the other or a third person within boundaries fixed by the actor, and

(b) his act directly or indirectly results in such a confinement of the other, and

(c) the other is conscious of the confinement or is harmed by it.

Sections 39 and 40 provide that the confinement may be caused by physical force or the threat of physical force, and the comment to sec. 40 indicates the threat may either be express, or inferred from the person's conduct. As Prosser comments:

The restraint may be by means of physical barriers, or by threats of force which intimidate the plaintiff into compliance with orders. It is sufficient that he submits to an apprehension of force reasonably to be understood from the conduct of the defendant, although no force is used or even expressly threatened. . . . This gives rise, in borderline cases, to questions of fact, turning upon the details of the testimony, as to what was reasonably to be understood and implied from the defendant's conduct, tone of voice and the like, which seldom can be reflected accurately in an appellate record, and normally are for the jury.

This is precisely such a case and we conclude that the record contains sufficient evidence from which the jury could have concluded that Mrs. Dupler was intentionally confined, against her will, by an implied threat of actual physical restraint. She testified that defendant Peterson ordered her in a loud voice to remain seated several times, after she expressed the desire to leave. She reported being "berated, screamed and hollered at," and said the reason she did not just walk out of the room was that "Mrs. Seubert had blocked the door, and tempers had been raised with all the shouting and screaming, I was just plain scared to make an effort. There were two against one." The jury obviously believed Mrs. Dupler's rather than the defendants' account of what transpired, as it had the right to do, and we conclude her testimony was sufficient to support the jury's verdict.

Defendants rely upon the 1926 case of *Weiler v. Herzfeld-Phillipson Co.* [208 N.W. 599], where this court held that an employer, who had detained an employee in his office for several hours upon suspicion of theft and then discharged her, was not liable for false imprisonment. This case is distinguishable, however, principally upon the ground that in *Weiler* the court emphasized several times that during the entire session the plaintiff was still employed by defendant and "was compensated for every minute of the time spent by her in the office." In the instant case, Dupler was compensated only through 5 p.m., and according to her testimony, she was not ordered to remain in the office, after she requested to leave, until after 5 p.m.

We conclude that *Weiler* is not controlling here and that the jury could properly find that defendants falsely imprisoned Dupler by compelling her to remain in Peterson's office against her will after 5 p.m. We conclude the imprisonment ceased when Dupler left the building to visit her husband, but resumed when she re-entered Peterson's office to get her coat in order to leave, but was commanded to stay. . . .

NOTES

1. *Employee Status.* Dupler implies that detention of an employee during working hours for questioning does not constitute false imprisonment. Compare *Fermino v. Fedco,* 7 Cal. 4th 701, 30 Cal. Rptr. 2d 18, 872 P.2d 559 (1994). There an employee was questioned by her employer during working hours about an alleged appropriation of $4.95 from the sale of a ring to a customer. Defendant falsely stated that the customer and a co-employee were outside the interrogation room ready to confirm the appropriation. Plaintiff was repeatedly asked to confess and prevented from leaving the room, profanities were "hurled" at her, and she was retained until she became "hysterical, and broke down into tears."

The court said that although an employer has a right to investigate alleged employee theft, the investigation must be for a reasonable time and in a reasonable manner. Here a jury could find that the investigation was unreasonable. The court rejected defendant's contention that there was "no false imprisonment . . . because the employee had received her normal compensation for the time during which she was held in interrogation." The right of an employer to require an employee to follow directions, the court said, does "not authorize the employer to forcibly detain the person of an employee for the purpose of compelling a confession of a theft."

2. *Psychological Restraint.* RESTATEMENT (SECOND) OF TORTS § 40A states: "The confinement may be by submission to duress other than threats of physical force, where such duress is sufficient to make the consent given ineffective to bar the action." Comment *a* continues:

> Under the rule stated in § 40, the confinement may be by submission to duress in the form of threats of physical force. Under this Section it may be by submission to other forms of duress, whenever the duress is sufficient to make ineffective the consent which would otherwise be involved in the submission. Thus there may be confinement by submission to a threat to inflict harm upon a member of the other's immediate family, or his property.

In *Fischer v. Famous-Barr Co.,* 646 S.W.2d 819 (Mo. App. 1982), a 74-year-old woman purchased two pantsuits from defendant's store. However, the salesperson failed to remove the security wafers attached to the clothing. Defendant's employee was alerted by a security alarm, and followed plaintiff. She tapped plaintiff on the shoulder as she descended an escalator and said, "You have something in that bag that don't belong to you." She continued, "Give me that, I will have to have your bag." She took the bag, saw the security wafers still attached to the clothing and the receipt for the purchase. She told plaintiff that she would "have to come back up on the fourth floor" with her. Plaintiff did not go willingly or voluntarily with the employee. Plaintiff testified, "I had to go." After the security wafers were removed, the employee, in a "harsh, rough and determined" voice, told plaintiff, "you may go." The court concluded:

> . . . In the instant case, the evidence on record shows that plaintiff was on her way down the escalator when she was stopped by defendant's employee and ordered to return to the fourth floor sales desk. Plaintiff did not go voluntarily or willingly with defendant's employee. Although no actual force was used other than a tap on the shoulder, it may be inferred that the harsh words of defendant's employee, her possession of the bag containing plaintiff's purchases, and plaintiff's belief that she must return to the fourth floor were sufficient to operate on plaintiff's will and to restrain her personal liberty. Accordingly, plaintiff made a submissible case of false imprisonment. . . .

From the moment when the employee found the receipt for the purchase, what was her "intent"?

3. In *Faniel v. Chesapeake & Potomac Tel. Co.*, 404 A.2d 147 (D.C. App. 1979), the plaintiff was accused of unauthorized use of her employer's equipment. She "was told that a trip to her home would be necessary to recover the equipment." Plaintiff claimed that she accompanied the employer's investigators to her home because she was afraid that if she did not, "I would lose my job." The court said this did not constitute false imprisonment:

> Submission to the mere verbal direction of another, unaccompanied by force or threats of any character, does not constitute false imprisonment. Similarly, fears of losing one's job, although a powerful incentive, does not render involuntary the behavior induced.

4. *Shoplifting Statutes.* Some states have enacted statutes granting shopkeepers the right to retain a suspected shoplifter for a reasonable time to permit a reasonable investigation. The terms of these statutes vary from jurisdiction to jurisdiction. They affect such matters as the amount of force that can be used, what constitutes probable cause, and whether the privilege extends beyond the premises. The right to detain a suspected shoplifter usually is asserted as an affirmative defense to a false arrest/imprisonment claim against the shopkeeper.

5. *Restraint Through Property.* In *Marcano v. Northwestern Chrysler-Plymouth Sales, Inc.*, 550 F. Supp. 595 (N.D. Ill. 1982), defendant sold a car to plaintiff Marcano. Some months thereafter, while plaintiff and her friend, also a plaintiff, were renegotiating the overdue payments on the car at defendant's place of business, defendant's employee Greene asked Marcano for the keys to the car, allegedly so that he could inspect it for damage. Plaintiff acquiesced, but on receiving the keys, Greene promptly locked the car and kept the keys. The contents of the car included the plaintiff's purse, house keys and medicine for her child. The plaintiffs remained at the dealership from 2:30 P.M. to 7:30 P.M., at which time a Northwestern employee drove them to their homes. The court commented as follows:

While it is clear that the modern concept of false imprisonment does not require that the confinement be by iron bars and stone walls, Prosser, Handbook of the Law of Torts § 11 at 42 (4th ed. 1971), it does require the "unlawful restraint of individual liberty of freedom of locomotion against a person's will." *Marcus v. Liebman,* 59 Ill. App. 3d 337, 339, 16 Ill. Dec. 613, 375 N.E.2d 486 (1978). In order for a false imprisonment to be present, there must be an actual or legal intent to restrain. Additionally, while actual force is not a requisite to an action for false imprisonment, *Marcus v. Liebman,* as Prosser notes, not every inducement to remain can rise to the level of false imprisonment.

In the view of this Court, the tort of false imprisonment contemplates an actual or perceived restraint on the freedom of the individual allegedly confined. Such a confinement must be "involuntary." *Fort v. Smith,* 85 Ill. App. 3d 479, 40 Ill. Dec. 886, 407 N.E.2d 117 (1980). While the facts as alleged in the instant case appear to show that plaintiff Marcano may have been justified in choosing to remain with the automobile and the personal belongings allegedly contained therein, such a choice does not raise the conduct of defendant to the level of a false imprisonment. Indeed, when plaintiffs Marcano and Provencio chose to leave the premises, they were clearly allowed to do so without interference.

Furthermore, the element of intent required to constitute a false imprisonment appears to be lacking from the instant case. While plaintiff's amended complaint reaches the conclusion that defendant's actions were taken "with the intent of restraining plaintiffs," the allegation is without basis in fact. No assertion of fact as to such an allegation is made nor is any allegation made as to the rationale or motivation behind such an asserted intent. The facts as alleged appear to reveal that defendant's intent was not to confine plaintiff personally, but only the automobile and its contents. . . .

Compare Marcano with Griffin v. Clark, 55 Idaho 364, 42 P.2d 297 (1935), where defendant, in an attempt to compel plaintiff to ride to another town in his automobile, removed her purse from the train in which she was sitting. The maneuver was successful, and plaintiff subsequently suffered injuries in an accident on the ensuing car trip. The court found that the defendant's conduct constituted false imprisonment.

Which defendant's conduct do you find more egregious? Is there another adequate remedy for the plaintiff in the *Marcano* case? Should that influence the outcome of her claim for false imprisonment? In *Griffin,* what was plaintiff really complaining about, her "imprisonment" or her automobile collision injuries?

6. *Religious Restraint.* The plaintiffs in *Molko v. Holy Spirit Ass'n,* 46 Cal. 2d 1092, 252 Cal. Rptr. 122, 762 P.2d 46 (1988), brought an action for fraud and deceit, intentional infliction of emotional distress and false imprisonment against the Holy Spirit Association for the Unification of World Christianity, headed by the Rev. Sun Myung Moon. Plaintiffs claimed they were fraudulently induced to join the association, then "brainwashed" and forced to remain

in the association by psychological pressures. They "escaped" only after they were kidnaped by relatives and "deprogrammed." RESTATEMENT (SECOND) OF TORTS § 40A, provides that "(t)he confinement may be by submission to duress other than threats of physical force, where such duress is sufficient to make the consent given ineffective to bar the action."

The court found that plaintiffs stated a claim for fraud and deceit because they were induced to join the association by misrepresentations as to its true nature. They also stated a claim for intentional infliction of emotional distress based on enforced fasting, poverty, silence, cloistered living, and long hours of work. This claim, however, could not rest on alleged threats of divine retribution, since these threats "were protected religious speech." For the same reason the claim of false imprisonment, arising from psychological coercion based on divine threats of retribution, would not lie.

7. *A Contractual Restraint?* In *Robinson v. Balmain New Ferry Co.*, [1910] A.C. 295 (P.C.), plaintiff appealed from a decision of the Australian High Court nonsuiting his verdict of £100 against the defendants for false imprisonment. Defendants, who maintained a ferry between Sydney and Balmain, charged a penny for entrance to the ferry wharf at Sydney, and another penny for exit from the wharf. No other charge was made for the use of the ferry, either to or from Balmain. A plainly visible notice advised prospective passengers of the defendants' "rules." Plaintiff, intending to cross to Balmain, entered the Sydney ferry wharf, but changed his mind and attempted to leave the wharf. He met resistance from defendants' employees when he attempted to exit without paying the additional penny:

> . . . The plaintiff was merely called upon to leave the wharf in the way in which he contracted to leave it. There is no law requiring the defendants to make the exit from their premises gratuitous to people who come there upon a definite contract which involves their leaving the wharf by another way; and the defendants were entitled to resist a forcible passage through their turnstile. The question whether the notice which was affixed to these premises was brought home to the knowledge of the plaintiff is immaterial, because the notice itself is immaterial.
>
> When the plaintiff entered the defendants' premises there was nothing agreed as to the terms on which he might go back, because neither party contemplated his going back. When he desired to do so the defendants were entitled to impose a reasonable condition before allowing him to pass through their turnstile from a place to which he had gone of his own free will. The payment of a penny was a quite fair condition, and if he did not choose to comply with it the defendants were not bound to let him through. He could proceed on the journey he had contracted for.
>
> Under these circumstances their Lordships consider that, when the defendants at the end of the case submitted that there ought to be a nonsuit, the learned judge ought to have nonsuited the plaintiff. . . .

E. FALSE IMPRISONMENT

WRIGHT v. STATE
231 Mont. 324, 752 P.2d 748 (1988)

HUNT, JUSTICE.

. . . On January 20, 1984, plaintiff John Wright was arrested for . . . disorderly conduct, and . . . criminal trespass, while attempting to renew his expired Montana driver's license at the Licensing Bureau offices in Bozeman. Wright entered the Bureau offices in midmorning with the intention of renewing his expired license. He was first waited upon by examiner Rena Knapp, who informed him that because his license was past 90 days expired, he was required to pass a complete driving examination before being issued a new license. Wright took and successfully passed the written exam and then was required by Knapp to fill out the standard application form called a DL-40. The form he filled out contained a clause that required the disclosure of his Social Security number. Although Montana law no longer mandates the use of a Social Security number, many of the old forms are still being used. Either Knapp or examiner Ray Houghton asked him what his number was. He indicated he did not wish to disclose his Social Security number and there is testimony that he replied by saying, "Hell, no." Additional testimony indicates he was given a random number.

At this point, examiner Houghton took over the application of Wright. After apparently completing the rest of the form, Wright left the office and returned with the vehicle he wished to use for the driving portion of the exam. Before he left he was advised by Houghton to be sure to bring back adequate proof of insurance.

Wright returned but with what Houghton thought to be inadequate proof of insurance, and he refused to allow Wright to finish the exam because an examiner is prohibited from getting into a vehicle without adequate proof of insurance. A loud argument ensued and ended when Wright called Houghton a "horse's ass." Houghton then told Wright not to come back that day as he would not be waited upon further. Wright left, attempting to slam the office door as he went. Wright did return later that day and tried to use an office phone restricted to office business only. Having several customers and not wanting a disturbance, Houghton called the police and Wright was arrested after refusing the police officer's request to leave. He was taken to the detention center, booked, and released on bail. The next Monday, Wright returned to the Bureau office, showed adequate proof of insurance and was given the driving portion of the exam by Houghton. He passed and was given a new driver's license. All charges were later dismissed. It should be noted that Wright's renewed license does not contain his Social Security number.

Wright brought suit for false arrest and other claims against the State of Montana, Houghton, City of Bozeman and the arresting officer, Ed Malone. All defendants filed a motion for summary judgment which was granted July 29, 1987. In its order, the District Court noted the lack of any evidence submitted in opposition to the motion and found no material issue of fact existed. Plaintiff appeals. . . .

The relevant depositions in the District Court file are all consistent on the point of Wright's Social Security number. Both Knapp and Houghton testified that Wright was not required to use his Social Security number and was in fact assigned a random number. There is no opposing evidence that shows he was forced to use his Social Security number. That number is not on his driver's license. Knapp's, Houghton's and Malone's depositions are consistent in showing that the conflict arose over Wright's lack of proof of insurance. Even if Wright's deposition showed an inconsistency it was not before the court and cannot be considered. The appellant failed to carry his burden and the District Court made its decision accordingly.

Appellant also argues that whether officer **Malone had** probable cause to arrest Wright is a question of fact which the appellant is entitled to present to a jury. The general rule is that where the facts are undisputed the question of whether an arrest was legal or illegal becomes a question of law for the court. Since no material fact exists the respondents were entitled to summary judgment as a matter of law. We therefore affirm the District Court's order for summary judgment.

SHEEHY, JUSTICE, dissenting.

In Hamlet's soliloquy, one of the "whips and scorns" which led the great Dane to consider whether death was better than life was "the insolence of office." In those few words, the Bard managed to express the aggravations and futilities pressed on any of us when public officials vent their sour stomachs in performing their duties. The authority to wear a badge or to wield a pen in power over others seems to fuel in us a sense of mastery, and not of service. It is a common failing, and all of us public servants succumb to it at some point.

. . . This Court assumes without question that the version of incidents propounded by the public officers in this case is the only version. It ignores the opposite version posed by the plaintiff, that he went to a public building to renew his driver's license; that his Social Security number was demanded; that he later produced proof of insurance but that the examiner refused to issue him a license that day, and told him to return on the following Monday; and that the examiner called the police and had him arrested; that the charges against him were disorderly conduct and criminal trespass; and that both of these charges were later dismissed. In short, he went to a public building for a driver's license and wound up handcuffed and led off to the police station.

The real question in this case is whether there was probable cause for Wright's arrest. If his arrest was groundless, he has a cause of action against the perpetrators. Neither the District Court nor this Court addresses that question. The deposition testimony of Rena Knapp is strong evidence that his arrest was groundless. She describes how the examiner (without any authority to do so) told Wright not to return for his license that day.

When Wright returned, with his proof of insurance, the examiner immediately, without exchanging a word with Wright, telephoned for the police. Rena Knapp describes the interval until the policeman came as no shouting and no threatening by Wright. When the policeman came and asked what the problem was, the examiner said that Wright had been asked to leave, and would not, and that the examiner wanted Wright out of the office; "that he would no longer be helped that day." There appears no justification for refusal to help Wright on that day, since he had paid for his license, successfully taken the written exam, and had insurance papers which entitled him to a test drive. For reasons of his own, it appears the patrolman was punishing Wright. Without any struggle or tumult, Wright was handcuffed and taken out of a public building where he had a right to be, and groundlessly charged with crimes. . . .

NOTES

1. *More "Whips and Scorns:" A Dissent Vindicated?* Contrast *Wright* with *Enright v. Groves,* 39 Colo. App. 39, 560 P.2d 851 (1977), in which plaintiff *did* recover for false arrest:

> The evidence at trial disclosed that on August 25, 1974, Officer Groves, while on duty as a uniformed police officer of the City of Fort Collins, observed a dog running loose in violation of the city's "dog leash" ordinance. He observed the animal approaching what was later identified as the residence of Mrs. Enright, the plaintiff. As Groves approached the house, he encountered Mrs. Enright's eleven-year-old son, and asked him if the dog belonged to him. The boy replied that it was his dog, and told Groves that his mother was sitting in the car parked at the curb by the house. Groves then ordered the boy to put the dog inside the house, and turned and started walking toward the Enright vehicle.
>
> Groves testified that he was met by Mrs. Enright with whom he was not acquainted. She asked if she could help him. Groves responded by demanding her driver's license. She replied by giving him her name and address. He again demanded her driver's license, which she declined to produce. Groves thereupon advised her that she could either produce her driver's license or go to jail. Mrs. Enright responded by asking, "Isn't this ridiculous?" Groves thereupon grabbed one of her arms, stating, "Let's go!"
>
> One eyewitness testified that Mrs. Enright cried out that Groves was hurting her. Her son who was just a few feet away at the time of the incident testified that his mother also screamed and tried to explain that her arm dislocated easily. Groves refused to release her arm, and Mrs. Enright struck him in the stomach with her free hand. Groves then seized both arms and threw her to the ground. With her lying on her stomach, he brought one of her arms behind her in order to handcuff her. She continued to scream in pain and asked him to stop hurting her. Groves pulled her up and propelled her to his patrol car where, for the first time, he advised her that she was under arrest.
>
> She was taken to the police station where a complaint was signed charging her with violation of the "dog leash" ordinance and bail was set. Mrs. Enright was released only after a friend posted bail. She was later convicted of the ordinance violation.
>
> . . . Appellants contend that Groves had probable cause to arrest Mrs. Enright, and that she was in fact arrested for and convicted

of violation of the dog-at-large ordinance. They assert, therefore, that her claim for false imprisonment or false arrest cannot lie, and that Groves' use of force in arresting Mrs. Enright was permissible. We disagree.

False arrest arises when one is taken into custody by a person who claims but does not have proper legal authority. Accordingly, a claim for false arrest will not lie if an officer has a valid warrant or probable cause to believe that an offense has been committed and that the person who was arrested committed it. Conviction of the crime for which one is specifically arrested is a complete defense to a subsequent claim of false arrest.

Here, however, the evidence is clear that Groves arrested Mrs. Enright, not for violation of the dog leash ordinance, but rather for refusing to produce her driver's license. This basis for arrest is exemplified by the fact that he specifically advised her that she would either produce the license or go to jail. We find no statute or case law in this jurisdiction which requires a citizen to show her driver's license upon demand, unless, for example, she is a driver of an automobile and such demand is made in that connection. . . . In *Stone* [174 Colo. 504, 485 P.2d 495] the precise issue was whether a narcotics agent violated the defendant's Fourth Amendment rights by stopping him and asking to examine his driver's license after he had been observed driving a vehicle. Whether an agent could affirmatively demand a driver's license was not specifically at issue, because the facts in *Stone* indicate that after the agent had asked for defendant's license, but before there could be any response thereto, the agent noticed fresh needle marks on his arm. Defendant was then put under arrest. The court emphasized that it did not intend by its decision to "grant free license to law enforcement officers to stop an individual to obtain identification or address."

Here, there was no testimony that Groves ever attempted to explain why he was demanding plaintiff's driver's license, and it is clear that she had already volunteered her name and address. Groves admitted that he did not ask Mrs. Enright if she had any means of identification on her person, but instead he simply demanded that she give him her driver's license.

We conclude that Groves' demand for Mrs. Enright's driver's license was not a lawful order and that refusal to comply therewith was not therefore an offense in and of itself. Groves was not therefore entitled to use force in arresting Mrs. Enright. Thus Groves' defense based upon an arrest for and conviction of a specific offense must, as a matter of law, fail.

2. *False Arrest and Probable Cause.* If probable cause, and especially actual guilt, is a defense to false arrest, there may nevertheless be some other tort committed when the method of arrest is unreasonable. *See Buckel v. Nunn* above, and recall the Rodney King incident. If probable cause is not a defense, for example, to false imprisonment, battery, or a civil rights violation, then why should it be a defense to false arrest? *See* RESTATEMENT (SECOND) OF

TORTS § 119, providing that a private person can lawfully arrest a misdemeanant for breach of the peace only if the breach is, or is about to be, committed in her presence. An arrest is not privileged if excessive force is used. *Id.* § 131. In *City of Miami v. Sanders*, 672 So. 2d 46 (Fla. 1996), the court observed that

> Traditionally, a presumption of good faith attaches to an officers's use of force in making a lawful arrest and an officer is liable for damages only where the force used is clearly excessive. . . . RESTATEMENT (SECOND) OF TORTS § 132 cmt. A (1965). If excessive force is used in an arrest, the ordinarily protected use of force by a police officer is transformed into a battery. . .
>
> A battery claim for excessive force is analyzed by focusing upon whether the amount of force used was reasonable under the circumstances. . . Law enforcement officers are provided a complete defense to an excessive use of force claim where an officer "reasonably believes [the force] to be necessary to defend himself or another from bodily harm while making the arrest."

In *Signorino v. National Super Mkts.*, 782 S.W.2d 100 (Mo. App. 1989), a customer recovered on a false arrest claim against a supermarket. The court said that proof of probable cause, as well as reasonableness of time and manner of restraint, constituted an affirmative defense, with the burden of proof on the defendant. Placing the burden on the defendant will mean that in all but the clearest cases the probable cause issue will be decided by the jury.

3. *Imprisonment by Exclusion?* In *Bird v. Jones*, 115 Eng. Rep. 668 (1845), plaintiff was prohibited from traversing a portion of the highway which was enclosed for spectators of a boat race. The court, finding no false imprisonment, observed that "the plaintiff was at liberty to move his person and go in any other direction, at his free will and pleasure." Thus "there was no imprisonment. To call it so appears to confound partial obstruction and disturbance with total obstruction and detention."

There can be false imprisonment in an entire city. *Allen v. Fromme*, 141 A.D. 362, 126 N.Y.S. 520 (1910). If so, could there not also be false imprisonment in an entire state, or in a country?

If all the world except the United States were totalitarian, and a totalitarian person was unlawfully barred from entering the United States, would that person be falsely imprisoned in the totalitarian portion of the world?

What is the reason for the rule of *Bird v. Jones*? Was the plaintiff in that case falsely arrested? RESTATEMENT (SECOND) OF TORTS § 112 defines an arrest as "the taking of another into the custody of the actor for the actual or purported purpose of bringing the other before a court, or of otherwise securing the administration of the law."

In *Morris v. Faulkner*, 361 N.E.2d 112 (Ill. App. 1977), the court said that "cases have stated that false imprisonment consists of any unlawful exercise or show of force by which a person is compelled to remain where he does not wish to remain or to go where he does not wish to go, or is prevented from doing what he desires." The court found the plaintiffs did not state a claim for false imprisonment based on exclusion from a tavern, since the tavern owner had the right to exclude them. The court also said, "it would be absurd to consider plaintiffs as having been confined to all the world but the tavern." Why absurd?

4. *Threat of Future Harm Revisited.* It generally is held that a threat of future injury does not constitute an assault, because the tort requires that the actor "put the other in apprehension of an *imminent* contact." *Dickens v. Puryear,* 302 N.C. 437, 276 S.E.2d 325 (1981).

However, intentional infliction of emotional distress can result from a threat of future harm. *See Wilson v. Wilkins,* 181 Ark. 137, 25 S.W.2d 428 (1930) (actionable claim stated where defendants threatened to harm plaintiff if he were not out of town by nightfall). A false imprisonment can also presumably occur from a threat of future harm. (*E.g.*, A says to B by long distance telephone call: "If you leave your room today, I will kill you the next time we meet." B would be falsely imprisoned if she remains in her room because of A's threat.) Why should a threat of present harm be necessary for assault, but not for intentional infliction of emotional distress or false imprisonment, since all three torts may be characterized as involving the infliction of emotional distress?

5. *Present Awareness Revisited.* The general rule is that an assault does not occur unless the victim is aware of the threat before it terminates. RESTATEMENT (SECOND) OF TORTS § 22. The Restatement gives the following illustration to demonstrate this principle:

> A, standing behind B, points a pistol at him. C overpowers A before he can shoot. B, hearing the noise turns around and for the first time realizes the danger to which he has been subjected. A is not liable to B.

This illustration presumably would apply no matter how severe the shock suffered by B, and even if the shock resulted in substantial physical injury, *e.g.*, a heart attack.

There is nothing to indicate, however, that a battery could not occur even though the victim is not aware of the harmful or offensive contact until after it has terminated. So, as one authority states, "It is a battery to strike a sleeping person, although the person struck does not discover it until afterward. . . ." PROSSER AND KEETON ON TORTS § 10, at 46 (5th ed. 1984). The result should be the same even if the contact were only offensive, *e.g.*, a stranger kissing a sleeping person, since a battery is defined as an act "intending to cause a harmful or offensive contact," RESTATEMENT (SECOND) OF TORTS § 18(1)(a).

In *Parvi v. Kingston,* 41 N.Y.2d 553, 362 N.E.2d 960, 394 N.Y.S.2d 161 (1977), the court noted "respected authorities have divided on whether awareness of confinement by one who has been falsely imprisoned should be a *sine qua non* for making out a case. . ." The court observed that the RESTATEMENT (SECOND) OF TORTS § 42 takes the position that knowledge of or harm by confinement is a necessary condition to liability. The *Parvi* court found that the issue of confinement was a jury question although the plaintiff

F.　　　　INTENTIONAL INFLICTION OF EMOTIONAL DISTRESS　　　　135

was drunk at the time of confinement and could not remember any events relating to the confinement.

Why should contemporaneous knowledge of the tort be necessary to prove assault, or false imprisonment, but not battery? Is such knowledge necessary to recover for infliction of emotional distress?

F. INTENTIONAL INFLICTION OF EMOTIONAL DISTRESS

WHITE v. MONSANTO COMPANY
585 So.2d 1205 (La. 1991)

HALL, JUSTICE.

Writs were granted in this case to review a judgment of the court of appeal affirming an award of $60,000 damages to an employee against her employer and a supervisory co-employee for intentional infliction of emotional distress occasioned by the supervisor's profane outburst while dressing down the employee and two other employees for not working as he thought they should. Finding that the supervisor's conduct, although crude and uncalled for, was not of such an extreme or outrageous nature as to give rise to a cause of action for an intentional tort, we reverse and render judgment for the defendants.

Plaintiff, Irma White, a church-going woman in her late forties with grown children, was employed in the labor pool at Monsanto Company's refinery for several years. In the spring of 1986, she had been assigned to work in the canning department for several weeks. Defendant, Gary McDermott, a long-time Monsanto employee, was industrial foreman of that department. On the date of the incident in question, plaintiff and three other employees were assigned at the beginning of the work day to transfer a certain chemical from a large container into smaller containers. When they arrived at their work station and noticed that the container was marked "hazardous-corrosive," they requested rubber gloves and goggles before starting their assigned task. A supervisor sent for the safety equipment. Shop rules required that employees busy themselves while waiting for equipment. One of the employees went to another area to do some work. Plaintiff started doing some clean-up or pick-up work around the area. The other two employees were apparently sitting around waiting for the equipment. Someone reported to McDermott that the group was idle, causing McDermott to become angry. He went to the work station and launched a profane tirade at the three workers present, including plaintiff, referring to them as "mother fuckers," accusing them of sitting on their "fucking asses," and threatening to "show them to the gate." The tirade lasted for about a minute, and then McDermott left the area.

Plaintiff was upset and began to experience pain in her chest, pounding in her head, and had difficulty breathing. She went to McDermott's office to discuss the incident. He said he apologized to her; she said he did not. She went to the company nurse, who suggested that plaintiff see a doctor. Plaintiff's family physician met her at the hospital, at which time plaintiff had chest pains, shortness of breath, and cold clammy hands. Fearing that she was having a heart attack, the doctor admitted her to the hospital.

Plaintiff spent two days in the coronary care unit and another day in a regular room, during which time she had intravenous fluids, had blood drawn, and had an EKG and other tests done. A heart attack was ruled out and the doctor's diagnosis was acute anxiety reaction, a panic attack. Plaintiff was released from the hospital after three days without restriction, but with medication to take if she had further trouble.

Ms. White returned to work within a week. She was paid her regular pay while off from work, and her medical bills, totaling about $3,200, were paid by the company's medical benefits program. Plaintiff has continued to work at Monsanto, later transferring to McDermott's department at her own request. She occasionally becomes upset thinking about or dreaming about the incident, and has occasionally taken the prescribed medicine, but is not one to take medication.

Ms. White sued Monsanto and McDermott, alleging that McDermott's conduct amounted to the intentional infliction of mental anguish and emotional distress upon plaintiff for which she was entitled to recover damages. After trial, the jury awarded her $60,000. Defendants appealed to the court of appeal, which affirmed, with one judge dissenting in part as to the amount of damages. . . .

* * *

Most states now recognize intentional infliction of emotional distress as an independent tort, not "parasitic" to a physical injury or a traditional tort such as assault, battery, false imprisonment or the like. See Annotation, Modern Status of Intentional Tort; "Outrage", 38 A.L.R. 4th 998 (1985), and cases cited therein. Discussed in the late 1930's by commentators who synthesized earlier cases, the tort was included in the 1948 supplement to the American Law Institute's *Restatement (Second) of Torts* § 46.[3]

* * *

(W)e affirm the viability in Louisiana of a cause of action for intentional infliction of emotional distress, generally in accord with the legal precepts set forth in the Restatement text and comments.

One who by extreme and outrageous conduct intentionally causes severe emotional distress to another is subject to liability for such emotional distress, and if bodily harm to the other results from it, for such bodily harm.[4]

Thus, in order to recover for intentional infliction of emotional distress, a plaintiff must establish (1) that the conduct of the defendant was extreme and outrageous; (2) that the emotional distress suffered by the plaintiff was severe;

---

[3] Restatement (Second) of Torts, § 46(1) provides:

"Outrageous Conduct Causing Severe Emotional Distress (1) One who by extreme and outrageous conduct intentionally or recklessly causes severe emotional distress to another is subject to liability for such emotional distress, and if bodily harm to the other results from it, for such bodily harm."

[4] Since the viability of plaintiff's claim in this case depends on the existence of an intentional act as distinguished from a reckless act, we do not deal with the Restatement's reference to "recklessly" causing severe emotional distress.

and (3) that the defendant desired to inflict severe emotional distress or knew that severe emotional distress would be certain or substantially certain to result from his conduct.

The conduct must be so outrageous in character, and so extreme in degree, as to go beyond all possible bounds of decency, and to be regarded as atrocious and utterly intolerable in a civilized community. Liability does not extend to mere insults, indignities, threats, annoyances, petty oppressions, or other trivialities. Persons must necessarily be expected to be hardened to a certain amount of rough language, and to occasional acts that are definitely inconsiderate and unkind. Not every verbal encounter may be converted into a tort; on the contrary, "some safety valve must be left for irascible tempers." Restatement, supra, comment d, § 46; Prosser and Keaton, The Law of Torts, § 12, p. 59 (5th ed. 1984).

The extreme and outrageous character of the conduct may arise from an abuse by the actor of a position, or a relation with the other, which gives him actual or apparent authority over the other, or power to affect his interests. Restatement, supra, comment e, § 46. Thus, many of the cases have involved circumstances arising in the workplace. See Annotation, Liability of Employer, Supervisor, or Manager for Intentionally or Recklessly Causing Employee Emotional Distress, 52 A.L.R. 4th 853 (1987). . . . A plaintiff's status as an employee may entitle him to a greater degree of protection from insult and outrage by a supervisor with authority over him than if he were a stranger. . . .

On the other hand, conduct which may otherwise be extreme and outrageous, may be privileged under the circumstances. Liability does not attach where the actor has done no more than to insist upon his legal rights in a permissible way, even though he is aware that such insistence is certain to cause emotional stress. Restatement, supra, comment g, § 46. Thus, disciplinary action and conflict in a pressure-packed workplace environment, although calculated to cause some degree of mental anguish, is not ordinarily actionable. Recognition of a cause of action for intentional infliction of emotional distress in a workplace environment has usually been limited to cases involving a pattern of deliberate, repeated harassment over a period of time. . . .

The distress suffered must be such that no reasonable person could be expected to endure it. Liability arises only where the mental suffering or anguish is extreme. Restatement, supra, comment j, § 46. . . .

The defendant's knowledge that plaintiff is particularly susceptible to emotional distress is a factor to be considered. But the mere fact that the actor knows that the other will regard the conduct as insulting, or will have his feelings hurt, is not enough. Restatement, supra, comment f, § 46. It follow that unless the actor has knowledge of the other's particular susceptibility to emotional distress, the actor's conduct should be judged in the light of the effect such conduct would ordinarily have on a person of ordinary sensibilities.

Liability can arise only where the actor desires to inflict severe emotional distress or where he knows that such distress is certain or substantially certain to result from his conduct. Restatement, supra, comment i, § 46. The conduct must be intended or calculated to cause severe emotional distress and not just some lesser degree of fright, humiliation, embarrassment, worry, or the like.

Applying these precepts of law to the facts of the instant case, we find that plaintiff has failed to recover from the defendants for an intentional tort.

The one-minute outburst of profanity directed at three employees by a supervisor in the course of dressing them down for not working as he thought they should does not amount to such extreme and outrageous conduct as to give rise to recovery for intentional infliction of emotional distress. The vile language used was not so extreme or outrageous as to go beyond all possible bounds of decency and to be regarded as utterly intolerable in a civilized community. Such conduct, although crude, rough and uncalled for, was not tortious, that is, did not give rise to a cause of action for damages under general tort law. . . . The brief, isolated instance of improper behavior by the supervisor who lost his temper was the kind of unpleasant experience persons must expect to endure from time to time. The conduct was not more than a person of ordinary sensibilities can be expected to endure. The tirade was directed to all three employees and not just to plaintiff specifically. Although the evidence certainly supports a finding that plaintiff was a decent person and a diligent employee who would not condone the use of vulgar language and who would be upset at being unjustifiably called down at her place of work, there was no evidence that she was particularly susceptible to emotional distress, or that McDermott had knowledge of any such susceptibility. It was obviously his intention to cause some degree of distress on the part of the employees, but there is no indication that his spontaneous, brief, intemperate outburst was intended to cause emotional distress of a severe nature.

The duty here was to not engage in extreme or outrageous conduct intended or calculated to cause severe emotional distress. The duty was not breached because the conduct was not extreme or outrageous to a degree calculated to cause severe emotional distress to a person of ordinary sensibilities and the supervisor did not intend to inflict emotional distress of a severe nature, nor did he believe such a result was substantially certain to follow from his conduct.

NOTES

1. *Assault or Outrage?* Suppose A says to B, "Watch out for that mad dog behind you!" There is no mad dog, but B reasonably believes there is and suffers a heart attack as a result. Arguably, A has not assaulted B, because of the conventional wisdom that "mere words do not make an assault," and A was not in a position to carry out his threat. However, the statement would give rise to an action for intentional infliction of emotional distress.

Section 25 of the RESTATEMENT (SECOND) OF TORTS provides: "To make the actor liable for an assault the actor need not have put the other in apprehension that the actor will himself inflict a bodily contact upon him." An illustration to this section states:

> A comes up behind B in the desert and sounds a buzzer which is an excellent imitation of a rattlesnake. B, believing that he is about

F. INTENTIONAL INFLICTION OF EMOTIONAL DISTRESS

to be bitten, is frightened, but suffers no bodily harm. A is subject to liability to B for an assault.

What is the distinction between this illustration and the first hypothetical in this problem? That there is an actual buzzer in the illustration, but only an imaginary dog in the hypothetical? But is this a distinction without a difference, since surely it could not matter to B whether the dog was imaginary or real? Compare *Allen v. Hannaford,* 138 Wash. 423, 244 P. 700 (1926), where appellant was held to have committed an assault by threatening respondent with an unloaded gun: "So far as the respondent is concerned the appellant had the apparent ability to make her threat good." On the other hand, if the conduct in the hypothetical constitutes an assault, does not the hypothetical eliminate the difference between assault and intentional infliction of emotional distress? What about present awareness and apprehension?

2. *In Search of a Rationale.* Why have the courts traditionally favored recovery for physical injury as opposed to psychic injury? Do any of the reasons withstand scrutiny today?

GOMEZ v. HUG
7 Kan. App. 2d 603, 645 P.2d 916 (1982)

WAHL, DISTRICT JUDGE.

. . . On April 21, 1978, Silvino Gomez was employed as a supervisor at the Shawnee County fairgrounds. His immediate supervisor was the fairgrounds administrator, Robert Kanatzer. During the evening hours of April 21, 1978, Gomez and Kanatzer were engaged in preparing an area of the fairgrounds for a horse show. They learned of a waterline break and, after determining the problem, proceeded to the administrator's office to phone a piping contractor.

Appellee Roland Hug, a member of the Board of County Commissioners of Shawnee County, and a companion, Robert Corbett, were in Kanatzer's office when Gomez and Kanatzer arrived. As they entered the office, Hug asked Kanatzer, "What is that fucking spic doing in the office?" Hug then repeated the question, again referring to Gomez as a "fucking spic." Hug then ordered Gomez over to where he was, again referring to Gomez as a "fucking spic." Gomez complied with Hug's order to approach him and inquired of Hug as to what he meant by that name. Gomez testified in his deposition that the following exchange took place between him and Hug:

> "A. . . . 'Commissioner, you have repeatedly stated that remark throughout the day and in the past day or two. Can you give me your interpretation of a fucking spic?' He said, 'You are a fucking spic.' I said, 'What does it mean?' He said, 'A fucking Mexican greaser like you, that is all you are. You are nothing but a fucking Mexican greaser, nothing but a pile of shit.' And he repeated it over and over and he raised his fist and he said, 'Now what are you going to do about it?' He got that close to me (indicating) and said, 'What are you going to do about it?' He kept hollering it out and hollering it out. He said, 'Go ahead and do something about it, you fucking Mexican greaser. I have told you what you are. You are nothing but a fucking spic.' And he

repeated it over and he kept shaking his fists in front of my eyes and pounding on the desk and he would come up to me and say, 'Are you going to do something, you coward, you greaser, you fucking spic? What are you going to do? Don't stand there like a damn fool because that is all you are is a pile of shit.'

". . . He kept threatening me. What was I going to do about it? He kept putting his fist in front of my face and pounding on that table, 'What are you going to do about it?' and repeating it over and over that I was nothing but a fucking spic. 'Now, you said you know what the definition of a spic is. You are nothing but a fucking spic and a Mexican greaser,' and he kept repeating it over and over, and he kept shaking his fist in front of me. I was froze because I was afraid of the man. For the first time in my life, I was terrified of one man calling me that. I was afraid for my job. I was afraid for my family."

It is variously estimated that this tirade lasted from five to fifteen minutes. After the exchange between Gomez and Hug, Kanatzer escorted Gomez out of the office and took him home. Gomez appeared to be upset.

Gomez began having serious medical problems. He sought medical advice and treatment from Dr. D. J. Weber, his family physician, Dr. Vinod Patel, a neurologist, and Dr. James N. Nelson, a psychiatrist. Both Dr. Nelson and Dr. Patel stated in their reports that Gomez' medical problems were related to the complained-of incident. Gomez was hospitalized from July 5, 1978, through July 18, 1978. He was unable to work due to his health-related problems and finally resigned his job with the county in November, 1979.

Appellees moved for summary judgment and the motion was sustained and judgment entered for the appellees. Gomez appealed. . . .

. . . The Kansas Supreme Court considered a comparable wrong in *Whitsel v. Watts,* 98 Kan. 508, 159 P. 401 (1916). There, the plaintiff suffered a miscarriage after being frightened when the defendant jumped from his buggy, ran towards the plaintiff in an angry, threatening manner, swearing, shaking his fist and saying, "You are fooling with the wrong person this time." The Court . . . held:

> Defendant insists that he inflicted no bodily injury upon her, that no physical injury was in fact threatened, that there was no assault upon her and that proof of a mere fright furnishes no basis for a recovery. It has long been the rule here that there can be no recovery for fright or mental anguish unless it results in or is accompanied by physical injury to the person. The plaintiff, however, is not asking a recovery for fright alone, but for the personal injuries directly resulting from fright caused by the willful tort of the defendant. It is argued that as the acts of the defendant did not amount to an assault she had no right to recover; but the defendant's liability does not depend upon whether his wrongful onset constituted an assault.

In *Dawson v. Associates Financial Services Co.,* 215 Kan. 814, 529 P.2d 104 (1974), the plaintiff, a former employee of Associates, was delinquent on a car loan from Associates due to having lost her job when she developed multiple sclerosis. She received four phone calls from Associates about the account

F. INTENTIONAL INFLICTION OF EMOTIONAL DISTRESS

similar in content to calls she had had to make to delinquent debtors when she worked there. She referred them to her insurance carrier on the first call. On the second call Associates threatened to repossess the car, sell it and hold her responsible for any deficiency. On the third call plaintiff was told when the car would be repossessed, that it would ruin her credit rating, and would somehow involve her parents' business. On the fourth call, plaintiff got emotional and told Associates to call her attorney. After receiving these calls, plaintiff suffered physical distress and had to go under a doctor's care.

In *Dawson,* the Court adopted the rule from *Restatement (Second) of Torts* § 46(1) (1965), which provides:

> One who by extreme and outrageous conduct intentionally or recklessly causes severe emotional distress to another is subject to liability for such emotional distress, and if bodily harm to the other results from it, for such bodily harm.

The Court further held:

> [T]hat it is for the court to determine, in the first instance, whether the defendant's conduct may reasonably be regarded as so extreme and outrageous as to permit recovery, or whether it is necessarily so, and where reasonable men may differ, the question is for the jury to determine. 215 Kan. at 824, 529 P.2d 104.

In *Dawson,* the trial court excluded evidence of telephone calls by Associates to plaintiff's parents about the delinquency of plaintiff's loan as being irrelevant. The Supreme Court held the evidence should have been admitted. . . .

The Supreme Court . . . concluded:

> Certainly creditors must be permitted to pursue reasonable methods of collecting debts, and debtors are protected only from extreme and outrageous conduct. Nonetheless, methods of collecting debts which might be reasonable in some circumstances, might also be regarded as outrageous in others where it is known that the debtor is particularly susceptible to emotional distress due to a disease such as multiple sclerosis. Here the appellant made claim for payments on an insurance policy which Associates had sold her.
>
> While only the substance of the evidence excluded by the trial court was proffered, the proffer discloses Associates said to the appellant's mother "they were going to ruin [appellant's] credit"; and that when the calls from Associates became more threatening the appellant's mother talked to the appellant about them. When the details of the evidence excluded are presented in open court, the appellant's evidence may be sufficiently strengthened to make a submissible case for the jury. 215 Kan. at 825, 529 P.2d 104.

[In] *Dotson v. McLaughlin,* 216 Kan. 201, 210, 531 P.2d 1 (1975), [t]he Court quoted comment d from § 46 of *Restatement (Second) of Torts*:

> The cases thus far decided have found liability only where the defendant's conduct has been extreme and outrageous. . . . Liability

has been found only where the conduct has been so outrageous in character, and so extreme in degree, as to go beyond all possible bounds of decency, and to be regarded as atrocious, and utterly intolerable in a civilized community. Generally, the case is one in which the recitation of the facts to an average member of the community would arouse his resentment against the actor, and lead him to exclaim "outrageous!"

The liability clearly does not extend to mere insults, indignities, threats, annoyances, petty oppressions, or other trivialities. The rough edges of our society are still in need of a good deal of filing down, and in the meantime plaintiffs must necessarily be expected and required to be hardened to a certain amount of rough language, and to occasional acts that are definitely inconsiderate and unkind. There is no occasion for the law to intervene in every case where someone's feelings are hurt. There must still be freedom to express an unflattering opinion, and some safety valve must be left through which irascible tempers may blow off relatively harmless steam. . . . (p. 73.)

No abusive language was employed. The mere fact of frequent phone calls from Dotson to McLaughlin to state that SBA loans would be foreclosed if McLaughlin did not cooperate was not sufficiently extreme or outrageous to give rise to liability.

Bradshaw v. Swagerty, 1 Kan. App. 2d 213, 563 P.2d 511 (1977), was an action for slander and outrage. The epithets in question were "nigger," "bastard" and possibly "knot-headed boy." Plaintiff's legitimacy was conceded. The trial court granted summary judgment to the defendant on both counts. The appellate court agreed that these words were " 'mere insults' of the kind which must be tolerated in our rough-edged society." 1 Kan. App. 2d at 216, 563 P.2d 511. . . .

The relative positions of Gomez and Hug are important here. Hug was the employer. Gomez was the employee. Hug spoke from the position of a county commissioner. These remarks had been made to Gomez by Hug over a period of several days. The tirade unleashed upon Gomez on April 21, 1978, was terrifying to him. He was afraid of Hug, afraid for his job, afraid for his family. Each party argues a different meaning from these statements of Gomez' fear. It is an issue for the trier of fact.

Contreras v. Crown Zellerbach Corp., 88 Wash. 2d 735, 565 P.2d 1173 (1977), concerned the allegations of a Mexican-American that he had been the object of racial insults, humiliation and embarrassment during the course of his employment. The Washington Court found that liability for infliction of mental distress could attach under the facts alleged. The Court held, 88 Wash. 2d at 741, 565 P.2d 1173:

When one in a position of authority, actual or apparent, over another has allegedly made racial slurs and jokes and comments, this abusive conduct gives added impetus to the claim of outrageous behavior. *Restatement (Second) of Torts* § 46 comment e. The relationship between the parties is a significant factor in determining whether liability should be imposed.

We can agree with the comment from Restatement of Torts quoted above. We cannot agree that it was for the trial court to rule that what was said to Gomez was a mere insult, a petty oppression or other triviality. This was a matter for the jury. Certainly there is no occasion for the law to intervene in every case where someone's feelings are hurt. Certainly the rough edges of our society still need smoothing down and there must still be freedom to blow off harmless steam. But this vituperation was well beyond the bounds of freedom to blow off harmless steam. It is not a burden of American citizenship in the State of Kansas that such vitriolic bullying as was turned by Hug against Gomez, and its emotional and physical consequences, must be accepted without possibility of redress and accepted as often as it amuses the speaker to utter it. Kansas courts are not so impotent. At the very least the victim of such an attack has the right to have his grievance heard by a jury of average members of the community to know whether they would exclaim, "Outrageous!"

It cannot be said that reasonable persons could reach but one conclusion from the evidence in this case. The trial court erred in sustaining the motion for summary judgment as to the allegation of intentional infliction of emotional distress by the defendant Hug. . .

NOTES

1. *Extreme and Outrageous Conduct.* In *Samms v. Eccles,* 11 Utah 2d 289, 358 P.2d 344 (1961), the court held that plaintiff stated a claim for emotional distress based on the following allegations:

> Plaintiff alleged that she is a respectable married woman; that she has never encouraged the defendant's attentions in any way but has repulsed them; that all during the time from May to December, 1957, the defendant repeatedly and persistently called her by phone at various hours including late at night, soliciting her to have illicit sexual relations with him; and that on one occasion came to her residence in connection with such a solicitation and made an indecent exposure of his person. She charges that she regarded his proposals as insulting, indecent and obscene; that her feelings were deeply wounded; and that as a result thereof she suffered great anxiety and fear for her personal safety and severe emotional distress for which she asks $1,500 as actual, and a like amount as punitive, damages.

Would the result be the same if he only asked her once? If he did not know she was married? Why?

In *Croft v. Wicker,* 737 P.2d 789, 793 (Alaska 1987), the plaintiffs brought an action for intentional infliction of emotional distress, alleging that the defendant, while a guest at his plaintiff-supervisor's home, sexually molested the supervisor's 14-year-old daughter. The trial court dismissed the action. Reversing, the supreme court stated, "[defendant's] alleged intentional behavior was not a simple annoyance or insult. It did not result in mere insult or indignity. It was, rather, the very brand of behavior which our society labels 'outrageous.'"

2. *Insults.* As noted in *Gomez,* RESTATEMENT OF TORTS (SECOND) § 46(1), comment *d* states, "liability clearly does not extend to mere insults, indignities, threats, annoyances, petty oppressions, or other trivialities."

In *Slocum v. Food Fair Stores of Fla., Inc.,* 100 So. 2d 396 (Fla. 1958), the court affirmed dismissal of a claim for intentional infliction of emotional distress in the absence of any allegation that the defendant's words were calculated to cause severe emotional distress — even though plaintiff alleged she suffered a heart attack as a result. Plaintiff, a customer in defendant's store, asked an employee of defendant the price of an item. In reply, the employee allegedly said: "If you want to know the price, you'll have to find out the best way you can. . . . You stink to me." In denying recovery, the court said: "There is no inclination to include all instances of mere vulgarities, obviously intended as meaningless abusive expressions." The court further noted:

> A broader rule has been developed in a particular class of cases, usually treated as a distinct and separate area of liability originally applied to common carriers. RESTATEMENT OF TORTS, § 48. The courts have from an early date granted relief for offense reasonably suffered by a patron from insult by a servant or employee of a carrier, hotel, theater, and most recently, a telegraph office. The existence of a special relationship, arising either from contract or from the inherent nature of a non-competitive public utility, supports a right and correlative duty of courtesy beyond that legally required in general mercantile or personal relationships.

However, the court found "no impelling reason" to extend the rule of such cases to "the area of business invitees generally."

3. *In the Presence of Outrageousness.* In *Croft v. Wicker,* note 1, *supra,* the plaintiff's daughter had not been molested in their presence. However, as the court noted:

> In *Richardson v. Fairbanks North Star Borough,* 705 P.2d 454 (Alaska 1985), this court denied recovery under [§ 46(1)] to plaintiffs who sought damages against the borough for emotional distress they sustained when their dog was killed by an employee of the borough animal shelter in violation of the shelter's policy. Today we extend this doctrine and hold that a third person who is foreseeably harmed by extreme and outrageous conduct may state a cause of action for intentional infliction of emotional distress. Applying this rule to the instant case, we find that the Crofts have stated such a claim.
>
> In *Richardson,* recovery was denied not because we do not recognize that the loss of a pet can be especially distressing under egregious circumstances, but rather because in that case the plaintiffs' offer of proof as to the severity of their emotional distress was, as a threshold matter, insufficient.
>
> We regard the facts of the instant case as being more egregious than those in *Richardson* . . . . Wicker's alleged conduct was the intentional sexual abuse of a minor child while a guest at her parents' home, with full knowledge that they were in close proximity of the incident.

737 P.2d at 792.

A number of courts require the plaintiff to be physically present in order to recover for "bystander" emotional distress, that is, for emotional distress suffered from witnessing injury to another. But no such restriction is imposed if the plaintiff is considered a "direct" victim of the defendant's tortious conduct. *See, e.g., R.D. v. W.H.,* 875 P.2d 26 (Wyo. 1994) (intentional inflicting of emotional distress claim allowed by survivors of woman who committed suicide allegedly due to defendant's wrongdoing).

It is tempting to conclude that victims of intentional infliction of emotional distress are direct victims, but that those who suffer negligently inflicted emotional distress are indirect victims. That distinction is not always made, however. Compare *Burgess v. Superior Ct.,* 2 Cal. 4th 1064, 9 Cal. Rptr. 615, 831 P.2d 1197 (1992) (mother may recover for negligent infliction of emotional distress in birth of baby even though she did not see the injury), with *Asaro v. Cardinal Glennon Mem. Hosp.,* 799 S.W.2d 595 (Mo. 1990) (no recovery by mother who did not witness injury to her five-year-old son). Conversely, a victim of intentional infliction of emotional distress may be unable to recover for "groundless" fears. *See Neal v. Neal,* 873 P. 2d 881 (Idaho App. 1993) (wife could not recover from unfaithful husband for fear of contracting venereal disease).

4. *Public Figures.* In *Falwell v. Flynt,* 797 F.2d 1270 (4th Cir. 1986), the Reverend Jerry Falwell brought an action for intentional infliction of emotional distress against *Hustler* magazine and its publisher, Larry Flynt. As the court noted,

> The "ad parody" which gives rise to the instant litigation attempts to satirize an advertising campaign for Campari Liqueur. In the real Campari advertisement celebrities talk about their "first time." They mean, their first encounter with Campari Liqueur, but there is double entendre with a sexual connotation. In the Hustler parody, Falwell is the celebrity in the advertisement. It contains his photograph and the text of an interview which is attributed to him. In this interview Falwell allegedly details an incestuous rendezvous with his mother in an outhouse in Lynchburg, Virginia. Falwell's mother is portrayed as a drunken and immoral woman and Falwell appears as a hypocrite and habitual drunkard. At the bottom of the page is a disclaimer which states "ad parody — not to be taken seriously." The parody is listed in the table of contents as "Fiction; Ad and Personality Parody."

In affirming a verdict of $100,000 compensatory damages and $50,000 each in punitive damages against the defendants, the Court of Appeals found that Falwell's distress was severe and that it was proximately caused by defendant's publication of the parody. Thus the court felt that there was sufficient evidence to sustain a jury verdict against the defendants for intentional infliction of emotional distress.

The U.S. Supreme Court reversed and dismissed the complaint on the grounds that this parody of plaintiff, a "public figure," was protected by the First Amendment of the United States Constitution. "Were we to hold otherwise," said the Court, "there can be little doubt that political cartoonists and satirists would be subjected to damages awards without any showing that their work falsely defamed its subject." The Court further noted:

> If it were possible by laying down a principled standard to separate [satire from tortious infliction of emotional distress], public discourse would probably suffer little or no harm. But we doubt that there is any such standard, and we are quite sure that the pejorative description "outrageous" does not supply one. "Outrageousness" in the area of political and social discourse has an inherent subjectiveness about it which would allow a jury to impose liability on the basis of the jurors' tastes or views, or perhaps on the basis of their dislike of a particular expression. An "outrageousness" standard thus runs afoul of our long-standing refusal to allow damages to be awarded because the speech in question may have an adverse emotional impact on the audience.

Hustler Magazine, Inc. v. Falwell, 485 U.S. 46, 108 S.Ct. 876 (1988).

If, as the Court suggests, "outrageousness" in the area of social discourse allows a jury to impose liability on the basis of the jurors' tastes, does this mean that (a) "outrageousness" is not a proper standard, or (b) "outrageousness" should be a question of law, or (c) the tort of intentional infliction of emotional distress depends upon one's luck and skill in selecting jurors? If "outrageousness" is a question of law, does not that subject the tort to a particular judge's tastes or views?

If the tort of intentional infliction of emotional distress (sometimes called the tort of outrage) cannot be brought by public figures, why should private figures be able to bring such a claim? Or does the Constitution bar such a claim if the outrage remotely resembles satire or parody?

5. *Intentional Versus Negligent Infliction.* There may be overlap between actions for intentional infliction and negligent infliction of emotional distress. Early cases required some physical manifestation of injury in order to recover for intentional infliction of emotional distress, *e.g., Harned v. E-Z Finance Co.,* 151 Tex. 641, 254 S.W.2d 81 (1953), and some courts still retain that requirement for negligent infliction of emotional distress, *see Reilly v. United States,* 547 A.2d 894 (R.I. 1988). This distinction is not consistently made today, however. *See Capital Holding Corp. v. Bailey,* 873 S.W.2d 187 (Ky. 1994) (contractor's employee subjected to asbestos exposure can recover from building owner for intentional infliction of emotional distress without physical manifestation of injury), and *In re Moorenovitch,* 634 F. Supp. 634 (D. Me. 1986) (same rule for negligence tort). Courts are particularly likely to allow an action for the tort of outrage when dead bodies are mishandled. Thus in *Johnson v. Woman's Hosp.,* 527 S.W.2d 133 (Tenn. Ct. App. 1975), plaintiff had a miscarriage while in defendant's hospital when she was pregnant with a 6 ½-month-old infant. When she returned to the hospital for a checkup six weeks later, she read a pathologist's report which indicated that the infant's body had not been buried or otherwise decently disposed of. Her inquiries led her to a hospital employee who said that she had the infant's body and that the body had been preserved. The employee then took from a refrigerator and handed to plaintiff a jar of formaldehyde containing the floating, shriveled body of her infant. Plaintiff subsequently suffered nightmares, insomnia and depression when around children. She also suffered from pseudo-pregnancy

which caused pelvic pain and nausea and led to exploratory surgery and psychiatric treatment. The court held that the plaintiff had a cause of action for intentional or reckless infliction of emotional distress; the facts "could be considered to cause the exclamation of 'outrage' from the general community."

In *Strachan v. John F. Kennedy Mem. Hosp.,* 109 N.J. 523, 538 A.2d 346 (1988), plaintiff parents stated a cause of action against defendant hospital which refused their request that the hospital promptly withdraw the life support system from their brain-dead son. "The failure of defendants to honor the family members' request posed a plain affront to their dignity and autonomy and exposed them to unnecessary distress at a time of profound grief." Would this be professional malpractice? What if the district or prosecuting attorney deemed withdrawal from a life support system a killing?

The plaintiff in *Browning v. Norton-Children's Hosp.,* 504 S.W.2d 713 (Ky. 1974), was denied recovery for mental anguish suffered when his leg, amputated during an emergency operation, was disposed of by cremation. However, in *Corso v. Crawford Dog & Cat Hosp.,* 97 Misc. 2d 530, 415 N.Y.S.2d 182 (1979), plaintiff was allowed actions for intentional and negligent infliction of emotional distress suffered when defendant animal hospital erroneously sent plaintiff the remains of a cat for burial, instead of the remains of plaintiff's pet dog. Are these cases distinguishable because distaste for cremation is not widely shared, but deep attachment to pets is?

6. *Outrage and Invasion of Privacy.* In *Kelley v. Schlumberger,* 849 F.2d 41 (1st Cir. 1988), an employee who was discharged after he twice tested positive in drug urinalysis sought damages from his former employer. The gravamen of his complaint was that defendant, seeking to ensure against adulteration or substitution of the sample, had a representative watch as the plaintiff provided the sample. "Direct observation of employees urinating was also at the core of the plaintiff's complaint." During the trial he described himself as being "disgusted by the whole idea of someone being paid to look at [his] penis while [he] urinated." Plaintiff recovered $125,000.

See, also, Cohen v. Smith, 648 N.E. 2d 329 (Ill App. 1995), holding that a patient stated a claim for intentional infliction of emotional distress where she informed the hospital of her religious beliefs against being seen unclothed by a male, and a male nurse, aware of that fact, was present during her cesarean delivery and touched patient's naked body.

7. Early tort law recognized the torts of alienation of affections (robbing a spouse of the conjugal society inherent in a normal marital relationship, such as by wooing the spouse into an illicit relationship), criminal conversation (sexual intercourse by a third person with a husband or wife), and seduction (a man's enticement of a woman to have unlawful intercourse with him by means of persuasion, solicitation or promises). These torts generally fell from favor in the earlier part of the Twentieth Century, and were abolished by legislation or by judicial decree. Can such actions be revived through the tort of intentional infliction of emotional distress? Should they be?

G. MISUSE OF THE JUDICIAL PROCESS

DUTT v. KREMP
111 Nev. 567, 894 P.2d 354 (1995)

SHEARING, JUSTICE:

This appeal arises from a jury verdict and judgment against attorney Virgil Dutt ("Dutt") in favor of respondent physicians in an action for malicious prosecution and abuse of process. Dutt had filed a malpractice action against the physicians on behalf of Jack Rentnelli ("Rentnelli"), which Rentnelli later voluntarily dismissed. This dismissed malpractice action formed the basis of the physicians' allegations of malicious prosecution and abuse of process against both Dutt and Rentnelli. At trial, at the close of the physicians' case, the district court dismissed the action against Rentnelli and awarded him costs. The case against Dutt was submitted to a jury, which returned a verdict against Dutt. Dutt appeals the judgment against him. The physicians cross-appeal on the issue of costs. The issues on appeal are whether the court rather than the jury should have decided certain issues, and whether there was sufficient evidence to support a verdict of malicious prosecution or abuse of process against Dutt.

In February and March, 1985, respondent physicians treated Rentnelli at a local hospital for an ailment that was eventually diagnosed as tuberculous meningitis and hydrocephalus. Rentnelli was given medication, and after approximately two weeks was discharged from the hospital. Rentnelli's son ("John"), testified that after treatment Rentnelli's condition continued to deteriorate, that John tried to reach one of the physicians by telephone, but was only allowed to speak with the staff and not with the doctor. Rentnelli's condition deteriorated to the point that after ten days John decided to seek new physicians and flew Rentnelli to a Santa Barbara hospital where a new doctor surgically implanted a shunt to relieve pressure on his brain. Immediately after this treatment, Rentnelli improved markedly. The Santa Barbara doctor told Rentnelli's son that if he had not brought Rentnelli in when he did, Rentnelli might not have lived.

Based on this series of events, Rentnelli and his family believed that he had not received proper care by respondent physicians and consulted Rentnelli's attorney, Virgil Dutt. Dutt interviewed Rentnelli and John, and obtained the medical records from the physicians in Reno and Santa Barbara. Dutt reviewed the records and researched both medical literature on meningitis and hydrocephalus and legal authorities regarding malpractice actions. Based on this review and research, Dutt filed a malpractice action against the physicians on December 30, 1985. After the action was filed, Dutt continued his factual investigation and research. Upon learning of the Medical Quality Foundation in Virginia, Dutt agreed with one of physicians' counsel that he would submit the Rentnelli records to that foundation for evaluation; if the Foundation supported his claims, he would continue to prosecute the action, if not, Dutt would dismiss it. The Medical Quality Foundation concluded that given Rentnelli's condition, the one month between Rentnelli's initial admission in Reno and the eventual shunt placement in Santa Barbara "would not produce significant brain damage," and that there was no provable negligence apparent from the records. On January 30, 1987, Dutt dismissed the malpractice action.

On December 29, 1987, the physicians filed their complaint for malicious prosecution and abuse of process against Rentnelli and Dutt. The court granted Rentnelli's motion for a directed verdict at the close of the physicians' case. The case against Dutt was tried before a jury which returned a verdict in the total amount of $40,000 in favor of the physicians against Dutt.

The questions presented in this appeal are: (1) whether the issue of probable cause should have been determined by the court rather than submitted to the jury, and (2) whether there was sufficient evidence to support the jury's verdict that Dutt was guilty of malicious prosecution or abuse of process.

The court instructed the jury on both malicious prosecution and abuse of process but the jury did not specify on which cause of action it based its verdict. This court has held that the difference between the two torts is that the action for abuse of process hinges on the misuse of regularly issued process, in contrast to malicious prosecution, which rests upon the wrongful issuance of process. Malice and want of probable cause are necessary elements for recovering in an action for malicious prosecution, but they are not essential to recovery for abuse of process. The fundamental elements of abuse of process are an ulterior purpose and a willful act in the use of process not proper in the regular conduct of the proceeding. Because the jury did not specify which it found, both causes of action will be discussed.

The elements that must be proved in a malicious prosecution action in addition to the filing of a prior action against the plaintiffs are: (1) a lack of probable cause to commence the prior action; (2) malice; (3) favorable termination of the prior action; and (4) damages. The first question presented in this appeal is whether, as appellant contends, the trial court erred by refusing to rule on the issue of probable cause.

When there is no dispute concerning the facts upon which an attorney acted in filing the prior action, the question of whether there was probable cause to institute the prior action is purely a legal question to be answered by the court. *Bonamy v. Zenoff*, 77 Nev. 250, 252, 362 P.2d 445, 447 (1961). Here, the trial court submitted the question of probable cause to the jury. We hold that this was error, because the facts upon which Dutt relied in filing the malpractice action are essentially undisputed. The existence of probable cause was a legal question which, under *Bonamy*, the district court should have decided. . . .

There is a division of authority as to whether the existence of probable cause in a malicious prosecution action should be judged by a strictly objective standard or by a combination of an objective and a subjective standard. . . .

We conclude that the objective test . . . is more appropriate. Under this test, the court must determine whether, on the basis of the facts known to the attorney, a reasonable attorney would have believed that the institution of the prior action was legally tenable. The standard is objective rather than subjective. The degree of expertise and the belief of the attorney are not relevant.

This court may determine whether Dutt had probable cause for filing the malpractice action in this case since the material facts were fully developed at trial and are essentially undisputed.

Dutt had information from Rentnelli's medical records, the description of events by Rentnelli and his son, John, and medical literature on meningitis and hydrocephalus. Judging Dutt's filing of the malpractice action under the objective standard, we conclude that a reasonable attorney would have believed that the action against the Reno doctors was legally tenable. The very fact that Rentnelli's condition continued to deteriorate after treatment by the Reno doctors but immediately improved after the Santa Barbara doctors' treatment would lead a reasonable person to believe that the first doctors did not adequately treat Rentnelli's ailments. A Santa Barbara doctor even told John that Rentnelli would have died if he had not brought Rentnelli in to them when he did. Dutt had no reason to believe that any of this information was unreliable. In fact, the medical records corroborated his client's statement of events.

There is no absolute requirement that an attorney obtain an expert medical opinion before filing a malpractice lawsuit. Whether enough information exists for a reasonable attorney to file a malpractice suit remains discretionary. In some situations the facts related by the patient may provide a sufficient basis to file suit, such as where a doctor amputates the wrong leg. In other situations, where the medical situation is more complex, more extensive research may be required, including consultation with medical experts. In the instant case, we hold that a reasonable attorney would have believed that he or she had sufficient information to justify filing a malpractice action.

It has never been the law that every piece of evidence necessary to prevail at trial must be available to the attorney before suit is filed. That is one of the functions of discovery.

The objectively reasonable standard set out above already applies in a malpractice suit against a physician. Physicians routinely make diagnoses and provide treatment based on the initial information given by the patient, even while planning further tests. When the doctor obtains additional information a different treatment may be indicated, but no one would suggest that taking preliminary action on the basis of the initial examination and history constitutes malpractice. Each professional may take objectively reasonable actions on the basis of information available at the time.

Just as an action for malicious prosecution will lie where a person commences an action without an objectively reasonable basis, an action will also lie where a person wrongfully continues a civil proceeding without probable cause. This theory was presented to the jury below, and respondents contend that the jury's verdict can be sustained on this basis. We disagree. The evidence adduced below does not support a finding against Dutt on this theory. Dutt received the Medical Quality Foundation's report on September 16, 1986, and he prepared a stipulation for dismissal the very next day. Moreover, after receiving the report, Dutt neither initiated further proceedings in the case nor conveyed any formal settlement demands to respondents. In our view, this evidence conclusively shows that Dutt discontinued the proceedings once he learned that a medical expert concluded that the delay in treatment did not cause significant damage, and that there was no probable negligence apparent from the medical records.

Since we have determined that Dutt had probable cause to file a complaint, no further inquiry is required as to the other elements of an action for malicious prosecution.

At the close of trial, Dutt moved for a directed verdict and for judgment notwithstanding the verdict or, in the alternative, for a new trial on the grounds that there was no evidence to support a verdict in favor of the physicians on their abuse of process claim. The trial court denied these motions, and Dutt contends that this was error. We agree.

An abuse of process claim consists of two elements: (1) an ulterior purpose other than resolving a legal dispute, and (2) a willful act in the use of process not proper in the regular conduct of the proceeding. An "ulterior purpose" includes any "improper motive" underlying the issuance of legal process. At trial, the physicians assigned two improper motives to appellant Dutt.

The physicians first argued that Dutt and Rentnelli filed the malpractice action in an effort to avoid paying the bill for medical services provided by respondents. Even if Rentnelli was motivated by a desire not to pay respondents, Dutt clearly was not. Nothing in the record supports such a claim where Dutt is concerned.

Second, the physicians asserted that Dutt filed the malpractice action to coerce a nuisance settlement. According to the physicians, this improper motive was demonstrated by Dutt's attempt to negotiate a settlement with the lawyer for one of the respondents after he had obtained the Medical Quality Foundation's report. The record does not support a finding of such improper motive. While the physicians attempted to analogize to *Bull v. McCuskey*, 96 Nev. 706, 615 P.2d 957 (1980), this case is readily distinguishable. In *Bull*, a jury award for a doctor in an abuse of process suit was supported by substantial evidence that the attorney filed a medical malpractice suit for the ulterior purpose of coercing a nuisance settlement. The attorney examined no medical records, conferred with no one, and then offered to settle the case for $750. This court held that this evidence was sufficient to sustain the verdict for abuse of process against the attorney. Unlike the defendant attorney in *Bull*, Dutt examined all the medical records, consulted medical and legal authorities, made no formal demand for settlement, and dismissed the complaint shortly after receiving the Medical Quality Foundation's report. Thus, we conclude that there is insufficient evidence to support a finding that appellant filed the malpractice action to coerce a nuisance settlement.

There is no evidence that appellant Dutt harbored an ulterior motive; because he was apparently merely attempting to resolve Rentnelli's apparent malpractice dispute with respondents, we need not consider the second element of an abuse of process claim, namely, whether appellant engaged in a willful act in the use of process not proper in the regular conduct of the proceeding.

For the reasons set forth above, we reverse the judgment entered below, and we remand this case to the district court for entry of judgment in favor of the appellant. Our decision renders the physicians' cross-appeal moot.

NOTES

1. *Malicious Prosecution and Probable Cause.* According to RESTATEMENT (SECOND) OF TORTS § 653, a private citizen is subject to a claim for malicious persecution if "(a) he initiates or procures the proceedings without probable cause and primarily for a purpose other than that of bringing an offender to justice, and (b) the proceedings have terminated in favor of the accused." For this purpose probable cause is defined as a correct or reasonable belief:

(a) that the person whom he accuses has acted or failed to act in a particular manner, and

(b) that those acts or omissions constitute the offense that he charges against the accused, and

(c) that he is sufficiently informed as to the law and facts to justify him in initiating or continuing the prosecution.

RESTATEMENT (SECOND) OF TORTS § 662.

2. *Inadequate Investigation to Determine Probable Cause.* Reversing the trial court's grant of summary judgment for the defendant, and the affirmance of that judgment by the court of appeals, the state supreme court in *Roberts v. Federal Express Corp.*, 842 S.W.2d 246 (Tenn. 1992), held that a jury question was presented as to whether the defendant employer had probable cause to institute criminal proceedings against the plaintiff, defendant's employee:

> Plaintiff Richard Roberts worked for Defendant Federal Express Corporation for nine years, compiling an exemplary job record. As a maintenance mechanic, his duties included working on Defendant's concealed security cameras.
>
> Defendant's sorting process sometimes results in contents being spilled from mutilated packages. Plaintiff had often picked up spilled contents and turned them in, although not necessarily on the same day. On one occasion he turned in a box of 13 diamond rings. Defendant has also experienced problems with employee theft. Plaintiff had, in the past, helped Defendant uncover employee dishonesty.
>
> On February 1, 1988, while at work, Plaintiff was taking medication for severe back pain. Although fellow employees urged him to go home, he continued to work. At some point while on the job, Plaintiff discovered a gold ring, an aerosol can, a videotape, silver spoon, chocolate candy, and a dildo on Defendant's premises. He placed the videotape in a sleeve, and the other articles in the pockets of his jacket. Sometime later that day, apparently affected by the medication, Plaintiff had a fellow employee take him to a break area. On the way there, Plaintiff told this employee of the items in his jacket and that he needed to turn them in. Upon reaching the break area, Plaintiff slept for the remainder of his shift.
>
> At approximately 5:00 p.m. at the end of his shift, Plaintiff was awakened by another employee. Plaintiff, still drowsy, was then driven to an employee exit that contained an electronic screening device. Plaintiff went to this exit despite holding special permission to leave the premises via locations not equipped with surveillance devices.

As Plaintiff was passing through one of these screening devices the alarm sounded. Plaintiff backed up and removed a set of keys and returned through the device. The alarm sounded a second time. Plaintiff then removed his jacket and a knife he had in his possession and passed back through the screening device. The alarm did not sound. Allegedly, that's when Plaintiff realized that he had left certain items that he had picked up from mutilated packages in his pockets. Plaintiff contends that he was disoriented and forgot the items were in his jacket due to medication he had been taking. Plaintiff appeared drowsy to the security guard.

Plaintiff explained to the security officers that he had found the items and forgot to turn them in and had no intention of stealing them. Plaintiff was retained for approximately four hours and questioned for about 30 to 45 minutes. The officers took Plaintiff's statement concerning the incident during this period. In addition, they discussed the valium tablets and Plaintiff took two security officers over to the location where he found the items. Thereafter, Plaintiff was released and given a suspension.

On February 10, 1988, Defendant caused an arrest warrant to be issued charging Plaintiff with grand larceny. A Shelby County Grand Jury later returned a no true bill.

In a footnote the court noted that prior to February 1, 1988 plaintiff had been given a set of plans by the defendant indicating its intent to use electronic screening devices for entering and exiting employees. Plaintiff knew these devices would be operable beginning February 1, 1988.

The Court continued:

A malicious prosecution is one brought in the absence of probable cause, and with malice. These two elements are distinct. Whereas malice concerns the subjective mental state of the prosecutor, appraisal of probable cause necessitates an objective determination of the reasonableness of the prosecutor's conduct in light of the surrounding facts and circumstances.

Properly defined, probable cause requires only the existence of such facts and circumstances sufficient to excite in a reasonable mind the belief that the accused is guilty of the crime charged. While a mind "beclouded by prejudice, passion, hate and malice" is not "reasonable," see *Poster v. Andrews*, 183 Tenn. 544, 554, 194 S.W. 2d 337, 341 (1946), the question whether a particular prosecutor is so motivated goes only to the element of malice. Probable cause is to be determined solely from an objective examination of the surrounding facts and circumstances. . . .

Under the facts presented, reasonable minds could differ as to whether probable cause existed for bringing charges against Plaintiff. The trial court, in line with existing procedural precedent, resolved the issue against Plaintiff and granted summary judgment for Defendant. The Court of Appeals affirmed. Because we now hold that where reasonable minds can differ as to the existence of probable cause a jury is to decide the issue, the judgments of the lower courts must be reversed.

Two final points must be addressed. First, Plaintiff asserts that a reasonable preprosecution investigation would have revealed certain exculpatory facts. Where such an allegation is made and there is evidence to support it, the jury is to determine the facts a reasonable investigation would have disclosed, and then base its probable cause determination considering those facts.

Second, Plaintiff asserts that the grand jury's refusal to indict creates a presumption that the prosecution was initiated without probable cause. We disagree. Termination of the prior proceeding in Plaintiff's favor has no bearing on whether probable cause existed at the time prosecution was initiated, and, where relevant, the jury shall be specifically so instructed.

3. *Probable Cause and Prior Conviction.* While an acquittal of a criminal charge does not establish lack of probable cause, as the *Roberts* court says, a conviction is often treated as conclusive proof of probable cause thus barring a later suit for malicious prosecution. In *Hanson v. City of Snohomish,* 121 Wash. 2d 552, 852 P.2d 295 (1993), the plaintiff Hanson was convicted in 1985 for "assault in the first degree." The conviction was based on identification testimony of the victim. The plaintiff appealed, alleging that (1) "the admission into evidence at the trial of fiction written by Hanson" was irrelevant and prejudicial, and (2) the identification evidence was based on procedures used by the police that were "so unreliable or suggestive as to give rise to a substantial likelihood of misidentification." The appeals court agreed with him on (1), but not on (2). The case was then remanded for a new trial, and Hanson was acquitted. He then brought the present suit against the City of Snohomish, alleging malicious prosecution. In dismissing the case, the court said probable cause was conclusively established by the original conviction, even though it was reversed on appeal and Hanson was acquitted on retrial. Moreover, said the court, on the facts of this case Hanson was collaterally estopped from relitigating the propriety of the identification procedures used by the police.

On the probable cause issue, the court said:

> If probable cause is established, the action fails, for probable cause is a complete defense to an action for malicious prosecution.

> A majority of courts hold that probable cause is established by the prior conviction of the malicious prosecution plaintiff, even where that conviction has been overturned. This also is the Restatement view. The RESTATEMENT (SECOND) OF TORTS § 667(1) (1977) provides:

> "The conviction of the accused by a magistrate or trial court, although reversed by an appellate tribunal, conclusively establishes the existence of probable cause, unless the conviction was obtained by fraud, perjury or other corrupt means."

> The comment to this subsection explains that the rule applies both when the proceedings are abandoned after the conviction has been set aside by the appellate court and when after a conviction has been set

aside, the accused is acquitted upon a second trial. Unless the conviction was obtained by fraud, perjury or other corrupt means, the opinion of the trier of fact expressed by its verdict under the rule that the guilt of the accused must be established beyond a reasonable doubt, is regarded as conclusive evidence that the person who initiated the proceedings had reasonable grounds for so doing. RESTATEMENT (SECOND) OF TORTS § 667, comment b, at 437 (1977). . . .

There is a distinction between a finding of probable cause and a finding of guilt. The issue here is not whether Hanson is guilty or innocent, it is whether the police and the City of Snohomish had probable cause to prosecute. The fact that a jury found Hanson guilty beyond a reasonable doubt established the existence of probable cause.

We now expressly hold that a conviction, although later reversed, is conclusive evidence of probable cause, unless that conviction was obtained by fraud, perjury or other corrupt means, or, of course, unless the ground for reversal was absence of probable cause.

Subsection 2 of the Restatement section involved here, states that the converse of the above rule is not the law, that is that an acquittal is not evidence of lack of probable cause. This court has not followed this rule and *Peasley* [13 Wash. 2d at 498, 125 P.2d at 681] held that a prima facie case of want of probable cause is established by proof of acquittal. Whether we would continue to adhere to the rule as stated in *Peasley* or would adopt the majority view set forth in the RESTATEMENT (SECOND) OF TORTS § 667(2) (1977) is not before us in the present case and we do not reach that issue.

Two justices, dissenting, argued:

Today, the majority endorses a draconian new limitation on the law of malicious prosecution which unfairly cuts off relief for persons who may have been injured by unlawful law enforcement action. Essentially, the majority holds that police and prosecutorial authorities may illegally arrest an individual without probable cause, prosecute that individual, and then create a shield for their actions by obtaining a conviction, even if that conviction is itself illegal. Furthermore, the majority adopts this new rule even though its application to this case was never raised by the parties. . . .

The majority has adopted the rule that a conviction, even if reversed, is conclusive evidence of probable cause, unless that conviction was obtained by perjury, fraud, or other corrupt means. Under the circumstances of this case, the court should not have reached the issue of the effect of Hanson's previous, reversed conviction because it was not raised by any of the parties. Even if the court reaches the question of the effect of the previous, reversed conviction, it should not adopt this particular rule. In its place, this court should apply the rule that a previous conviction, when reversed, is only prima facie evidence of probable cause, rather than conclusive evidence. Under this rule, plaintiffs would have the obligation to overcome that prima facie evidence of probable cause, rather than conclusive evidence. Under this rule, plaintiffs would have the obligation to overcome that prima facie evidence with competent and convincing evidence of a lack of probable cause.

NOTES

1. *Damages in Malicious Civil Prosecution.* Where a malicious prosecution action is based upon the prior institution of a civil — as opposed to a criminal — action, some courts have required that the plaintiff in the malicious prosecution suit show "special damages" resulting from the prior civil prosecution. *Nagy v. McBurney,* 392 A.2d 365 (R.I. 1978). Special damages may exist if the prior civil proceeding results in arrest or deprivation of property, involves allegations of insanity or insolvency, or repetitious civil proceedings. *See* RESTATEMENT (SECOND) OF TORTS §§ 677–679 (1977). The Restatement and some courts do not require proof of special damages in this context. RESTATEMENT (SECOND) OF TORTS § 674, comment a to § 679 (1977); *Shaffer v. Stewart,* 326 Pa. Super. 135, 473 A.2d 1017 (1984). Many courts refer to an action for malicious prosecution based upon a prior civil proceeding as a "wrongful civil proceeding."

2. *Whither Malice?* It is widely held that malice can be inferred in a malicious prosecution suit from the absence of probable cause. F. HARPER, F. JAMES & O. GRAY, 1 THE LAW OF TORTS § 4.6 at 446–47 (2d ed. 1986). Some courts permit an inference of malice to be made without regard to the issue of probable cause. *See* PROSSER AND KEETON ON TORTS 884 (5th ed. 1984). What purpose, then, does the malice requirement serve in a malicious prosecution suit?

3. *Hard-Ball Tactics as Abuse of Process? Board of Educ. v. Farmingdale Classroom Teachers Ass'n,* 38 N.Y.2d 397, 380 N.Y.S.2d 635, 343 N.E.2d 278 (1975), concerned a bitter dispute between a teachers' association and a school board, during which the association was charged with violating the civil service law. A hearing was scheduled beginning on October 5, 1972. The attorney for the association then subpoenaed 87 teachers to appear on that day. As a result the school board was forced to hire 77 substitute teachers to keep its schools open. The court held that a cause of action for abuse of process had been stated against the association:

> While it is true that public policy mandates free access to the courts for redress of wrongs and our adversarial system cannot function without zealous advocacy, it is also true that legal procedure must be utilized in a manner consonant with the purpose for which that procedure was designed. Where process is manipulated to achieve some collateral advantage, whether it be denominated extortion, blackmail or retribution, the tort of abuse of process will be available to the injured party.
>
> The appellants raise several arguments against the sufficiency of this complaint. The most troublesome contention raised is that it is standard, appropriate and proper practice to subpoena all witnesses for the first day of any judicial proceeding. While we acknowledge this as appropriate procedure and in no way intend this decision to proscribe it, we are obligated to determine appeals in the context in

which they are presented. Here we consider solely whether the complaint states a valid cause of action. If the proof at trial establishes that defendants attempted to reach a reasonable accommodation at a time when the accommodation would have been effectual, the cause of action will be defeated. However, on its face an allegation that defendants subpoenaed 87 persons with full knowledge that they all could not and would not testify and that this was done maliciously with the intent to injure and to harass plaintiff spells out an abuse of process. Another factor to be weighed at trial is whether the testimony of so many witnesses was material and necessary. As this complaint is framed, it may be inferred that defendants were effecting a not too subtle threat which should be actionable. . . .

4. Rule 11 of the Federal Rules of Civil Procedure provides that every pleading, written notice or other paper shall be signed by an attorney, or by an unrepresented party. By presenting such a signed paper to the court, the signer certifies that to the best of her knowledge, information or belief after reasonable inquiry:

(1) it is not being presented for any improper purpose, such as to harass or to cause unnecessary delay or needless increase in the cost of litigation;

(2) the claims, defenses, and other legal contentions therein are warranted by existing law or by a nonfrivolous argument for the extension, modification, or reversal of existing law or the establishment of new law;

(3) the allegations and other factual contentions have evidentiary support or, if specifically so identified, are likely to have evidentiary support after a reasonable opportunity for further investigation or discovery; and

(4) the denials of factual contentions are warranted on the evidence or, if specifically so identified, are reasonably based on a lack of information or belief.

The court may impose "an appropriate sanction" for violation of the Rule. Does this Rule provide an adequate remedy for malicious civil prosecution?

Federal Rule of Civil Procedure 26(g)(2) provides that "[e]very request, discovery response or objection . . . shall be signed. The signature . . . constitutes a certification that to the best of the signer's knowledge, information, and belief, formed after a reasonable inquiry," the request, response or objection is:

(A) consistent with these rules and warranted by existing law or a good faith argument for the extension, modification, or reversal of existing law;

(B) not interposed for any improper purpose, such as to harass or to cause unnecessary delay or needless increase in the cost of litigation; and

(C) not unreasonable or unduly burdensome or expensive, given the needs of the case, the discovery already had in the case, the amount in controversy, and the importance of the issues at stake in litigation.

Violation of the provision can result in sanctions which include payment of the opponent's costs and attorney's fees, and disbarment of other sanctions against an offending attorney. Do these rules provide an adequate remedy for abuse of process in discovery?

PROBLEM

Client came to Attorney complaining about what Client believed was medical malpractice committed on her by her Doctor. Attorney did not have any information about what occurred other than Client's statement, but since the statute of limitations would run on the claim the same day that Client came to see Attorney, Attorney hastily filed a claim against Doctor on that day.

The following day Doctor's Lawyer called Attorney stating that Client's claim was groundless. Attorney said he was authorized to settle the claim for $10,000, but Lawyer refused to settle the claim.

Assuming the evidence shows that the claim is meritless, discuss Doctor's claims against Attorney.

H. TRESPASS TO PERSONALITY AND CONVERSION

COMMENT

The law divides property into two general categories—real and personal. Real property generally consists of land and some buildings and improvements on it. All other tangible property is treated as personal (sometimes called chattels), and may consist of some intangible assets, such as debts. The law protects both kinds of property from tortious interference, but in different manners. Can you imagine why the law may provide more protection from minor disturbances to real property? Why the law may permit greater self-help in protecting personal property than real property? In the next two sections, we discuss the extent to which the law protects against intentional invasion of property interests.

FOCAL POINT, INC. v. U-HAUL OF ARIZONA, INC.
746 P.2d 488 (Ariz. App. 1986)

JACOBSON, JUDGE.

The issue in this appeal is whether the obtaining of possession of a chattel through mistake and the exercise of control over that chattel to ascertain its true owner is sufficient to subject the possessor to liability for conversion of the chattel.

This is an appeal from a summary judgment entered in favor of appellee, U-Haul Company of Arizona (U-Haul), and against appellant, Focal Point, Inc. (Focal Point). The issue on appeal is whether U-Haul converted a truck containing stored artwork which it had rented to Focal Point.

The facts are basically undisputed. On July 8, 1982, James W. Creason, an agent of Focal Point, leased a truck from U-Haul. The truck rental contract provided that the lease was to run from July 8 to July 15. The contract listed the lessee's address as 4215 North 63rd Drive, Phoenix, and the lessee's name as James W. Creason. Focal Point was not mentioned in the lease and no phone number was listed. After the truck was leased, it was loaded with artwork from Focal Point's inventory and parked unlocked in a vacant lot at 3820 N. 4th Street. On July 14, 1982, an employee of U-Haul, acting on a tip, removed the truck from the vacant lot, in the mistaken belief that the truck had been abandoned. The truck was taken to the North Central U-Haul Center where its contents were inventoried and examined by U-Haul. The truck was then placed in a secure, locked parking lot. Both the cab and the box of the truck were locked as well.

Focal Point noticed that the truck was missing on July 14. Initially Focal Point was unable to determine the truck's whereabouts, but subsequently contacted U-Haul was unable to provide Focal Point with the location of the truck, but suggested that Focal Point contact it again the following day.

On July 15, Focal Point re-contacted U-Haul. U-Haul admitted that it was in possession of the truck. Focal Point demanded that U-Haul return the truck to the vacant lot from which it had been removed. U-Haul requested that Focal Point come to the U-Haul lot to verify that the truck was indeed leased to Focal Point, at which time U-Haul would agree to release the truck. Focal Point responded by renewing its demand that U-Haul return the truck to the lot. This suit was filed the next day, July 16, 1982.

Based upon these undisputed facts, the trial court made the following relevant findings of fact and conclusions of law: (1) U-Haul did not exercise nor intend to exercise domain over Focal Point's property; (2) U-Haul never refused to relinquish the property to Focal Point; (3) U-Haul was not guilty of conversion; and (4) Focal Point was still the owner of the property in question. Accordingly, summary judgment was entered in favor of U-Haul on Focal Point's claim of conversion, which sought $62,000 in damages for the value of the art work. However, the trial court did determine, after a trial, that U-Haul was guilty of damaging Focal Point's property (under a bailment theory) and assessed damages in the sum of $10,000.00. This appeal followed.

Arizona law on the tort of conversion stems from the seminal case of *Shartzer v. Ulmer*, 85 Ariz. 179, 333 P.2d 1084 (1959), which defined conversion as "any act of dominion wrongfully exerted over another's personal property in denial of or inconsistent with his rights therein." Id. at 184, 333 P.2d at 1088.

From this definition, Focal Point argues that the taking of the truck and its load of art work during the term of the lease was a trespass, and that U-Haul's placing of the truck behind a fence with locked gates, and refusing to return the truck upon demand, both constituted acts of dominion inconsistent with Focal Point's possessory interest in its art work.

However, more recently, Division 2 (of this court) expanded the *Shartzer* definition by adopting the position enunciated in the *Restatement (Second) of Torts* § 222(A)(1) (1965). *Mobile Discount Corp. v. Schumacher*, 139 Ariz. 15, 676 P.2d 649 (App. 1984). Section 222(A)(1) defines conversion as:

> An international exercise of dominion or control over a chattel which so seriously interferes with the right of another to control it that the

actor may justly be required to pay the other the full value of the chattel (emphasis added).

As can be seen, the Restatement definition of conversion adds the element of serious interference to the simpler definition set forth in the prior case law. In our opinion, the adoption by Division 2 of the Restatement definition of conversion is a correct summation of Arizona law on the subject. . . .

Historically, tort law has drawn a distinction between mere interference with the chattel, and the "exercise of defendant's hostile control over it." *Restatement (Second) of Torts* § 222(A), Comment a, (1965), citing *Foulds v. Willoughby*, 8 M. & W. 540, 515 Eng.Rep. 1153 (1841). The basis for this distinction lies in the recognition that there are degrees of interference with property. This is reflected in the measure of damages assessed as a result of the interference. To determine the seriousness of the interference we take the following factors into account: (1) the extent and duration of U-Haul's alleged exercise of dominion or control; (2) U-Haul's alleged intent to assert a right in fact inconsistent with Focal Point's right of control; (3) the extent and duration of the resulting interference with Focal Point's right of control; (4) damage done to the truck and its contents; and (5) the inconvenience and expense caused to Focal Point. *Restatement (Second) of Torts* § 222(A)(2) (1965).[3]

Applying these factors to the instant case, we hold that no conversion of Focal Point's property occurred on either July 14 or July 15. Focal Point had only to travel the two miles to U-Haul's storage center, show right to possession and reclaim control over the truck and artwork. Focal Point had the opportunity to reclaim the property within a day of having been dispossessed of it. The inconvenience and expense were minimal. The artwork was placed into the truck for storage. There was no evidence to indicate that Focal Point was precluded from enjoyment of its property beyond the knowledge that such property was "safely" stored in an unlocked truck parked in a vacant lot. Also, it would have been far more efficacious for Focal Point to simply reclaim its property, than to seek a forced judicial sale of the artwork. Finally, the evidence supports the finding that U-Haul did not intend to assert a right which was in fact inconsistent with Focal Point's right of control. While U-Haul did possess the truck and artwork, it did not intend to hold the truck and artwork against Focal Point's ownership interest. Rather, it only attempted to verify that interest.

NOTES

1. *Trespass to Chattel and Conversion Compared.* RESTATEMENT (SECOND) OF TORTS § 217 states that a trespass to chattel may be committed "by intentionally (a) dispossessing another of the chattel, or (b) using or intermeddling with a chattel in the possession of another." Where dispossession is shown, "the action will lie although there has been no impairment of the condition,

---

[3] The court declines to adopt § 222(A)(2) in its entirety. Section 222(A)(2)(c) includes good faith as a factor determinative of the seriousness of the interference. Good faith belief or intention is no defense to a conversion action in Arizona. *Patton v. First Federal Savings and Loan Ass'n of Phoenix*, 118 Ariz. 473, 578 P.2d 152 (1976); *Jabczenski v. Souther Pacific Memorial Hospital*, 119 Ariz. 15, 579 P.2d 53 (1978).

quality, or value of the chattel, and no other harm to any interest of the possessor." Thus a police officer by writ of execution levies on a car, by notifying the owner that the car has been taken into possession of the law, "but does not remove it or otherwise interfere with it." An hour later the officer discovers that she has levied on the wrong person's car, and promptly so informs the owner. The officer is liable to the owner "for at least nominal damages." RESTATEMENT (SECOND) OF TORTS § 218, comment d, illus. 1.

If the trespass constitutes a mere use of or intermeddling with the chattel, however, as opposed to a dispossession, then the trespasser is liable only if "the chattel is impaired as to its condition, quality, or value," the possessor is "deprived of the use of the chattel for a substantial time," or harm is caused to the possessor or to some person or thing in which the possessor has a legally protected interest. RESTATEMENT (SECOND) OF TORTS § 218 and comment e thereto. Thus if a child climbs onto the back of a person's dog and pulls the dog's ears, but does not hurt the dog, there is no trespass. If A moves B's car four feet doing no harm to it, there is no trespass; but if A moves the car around the corner so that B on looking for the car is unable to find it for an hour, there is a trespass. § 218, illus. 2 to comment e, and illus. 3 & 4 to comment i.

Comment c to § 217 states that the intent necessary to make one liable for trespass to chattel "is similar to that necessary to make one liable for an invasion of another's interest in bodily security, in freedom from an offensive contact, or confinement." It is unclear whether there can be a trespass to intangible rights, within the terms of the Restatement.

A conversion is defined by § 222A of the RESTATEMENT (SECOND) OF TORTS:

> (1) Conversion is an intentional exercise of dominion or control over a chattel which so seriously interferes with the right of another to control it that the actor may justly be required to pay the other the full value of the chattel.
>
> (2) In determining the seriousness of the interference and the justice of requiring the actor to pay the full value, the following factors are important:
>
>> (a) the extent and duration of the actor's exercise of dominion or control;
>>
>> (b) the actor's intent to assert a right in fact inconsistent with the other's right of control;
>>
>> (c) the actor's good faith;
>>
>> (d) the extent and duration of the resulting interference with the other's right of control;
>>
>> (e) the harm done to the chattel;
>>
>> (f) the inconvenience and expense caused to the other.

Comment d to this section states: "No one factor is always predominant in determining the seriousness of the interference, or the justice of requiring the forced purchase at full value."

Section 244 of the RESTATEMENT (SECOND) OF TORTS states that an actor is not relieved from liability to another for trespass to chattel or for conversion "because of a mistake of law or fact not induced by the other" regarding the actor's right of possession of the goods, or of the existence of consent or other privilege to use the goods.

2. *Property, Promises or Mere Paper?* According to one commentator, the "traditional common law rule" was that "intangible properties such as paper which merely represented a right to get gold or silver" were not subject to conversion. D. DOBBS, TORTS AND COMPENSATION 59 (1985). The Restatement declares, however, that there can be conversion of "a document in which intangible rights are merged," and that one who "effectively prevents the exercise" of the rights in those documents is also guilty of conversion. RESTATEMENT (SECOND) OF TORTS § 242. Section 242 applies to "promissory notes, bonds, bills of exchange, share certificates, and warehouse receipts, whether negotiable or non-negotiable." *Id.*, comment b. Comment f to this section notes that the process of extension of liability for conversion of intangible property "has not, however, necessarily terminated," and the Restatement takes no position on whether other kinds of intangible rights should be subject to conversion.

3. *The Requisite Intent.* In *Mountain States Tel. & Tel. Co. v. Horn Tower Constr. Co.,* 147 Colo. 166, 363 P.2d 175 (1961), the trial court dismissed the trespass claim against a construction company which severed a buried cable while grading a street and installing a curb. The court concluded:

> The doctrine . . . has been universally accepted and applied and has been the basis for the fundamental principle of the law of negligence and its corollary, the law of wantonness, that fault of the actor is an essential ingredient of liability. The Restatement of the Law of Torts, § 218, has specifically recognized this. It declares that one who uses or otherwise intentionally intermeddles with a chattel in the possession of another is liable in trespass under conditions there set forth. Comment (b) to this section lays down the requirement that the intermeddling shall have been intentional. *See also* 1 Harper and James, The Law of Torts, 109, 110, wherein the authors in discussing this, say:
>
> > Under the principle of law that allows recovery for a trespass to chattels, it is necessary that the defendant have acted for the purpose of interfering with the chattel, or, what is almost the same thing, that he have acted with knowledge that such would be the result of his conduct. In other words, he must have intended the intermeddling. If he does not intend thus to meddle, he is not liable today as a trespasser; but if his conduct is negligent, he is liable under the principles of the law of negligence. . . . If he intends the interference with the plaintiff's goods, since the intent is the factor which makes the conduct tortious, liability is said to be for trespass.
>
> . . . While a trespass to chattels requires an intention to intermeddle with the goods, it does not require a guilty or culpable intention. All that is necessary is an intention physically to interfere with the goods themselves.

Is this an intentional tort, or is it liability without fault?

4. *Stolen Goods.* The general rule is that one cannot take good title to stolen goods, regardless of the acquirer's good faith. RESTATEMENT (SECOND) OF TORTS § 229. But one can acquire good title from another who has obtained the goods by fraud or deceit, if the acquirer acquires the goods in good faith for value. UCC § 2-403.

A bailee is typically not strictly liable for conversion merely for holding or transporting the goods of another. But he can be strictly liable if he takes or transfers title to the goods of another, or if he misdelivers goods. RESTATEMENT (SECOND) OF TORTS §§ 230–231, 233–234.

5. *Stolen Ideas and Such.* Can one "convert" an idea? As the court wrote in *Pearson v. Dodd*, 410 F. 2d 701 (D.C. Cir. 1969):

> the general rule has been that ideas or information are not subject to legal protection, but the law has developed exceptions to this rule.
>
> Where information is gathered and arranged at some cost and sold as a commodity on the market, it is properly protected as property. Where ideas are formulated with labor and inventive genius, as in the case of literary works or scientific researches, they are protected. Where they constitute instruments of fair and effective commercial competition, those who develop them may gather their fruits under the protection of law.

See, also, Schaefer v. Spence, 813 S.W. 2d 92 (Mo. App. 1991), where the court observed that:

> (T)here can be a conversion where there is a wrongful withholding by a broker of stock certificates. . .a diversion of funds paid to another for a specific purpose. . . .and the use of a trade name by one who by contract relinquished his right to use the name in the grocery business in the St. Louis area. . . . However, conversion does not lie for the appropriation of an idea. . . .
>
> Despite the relatively recent expansion of the types of property that are subject to conversion, limits remain. Schaefer contends the Spences converted the spice blend formula. He overlooks the limits on the types of property that can be converted. . . . Schaefer cites to us no Missouri appellate court opinion that expands conversion to embrace the appropriation of a formula, and we find no such authority. The status of conversion in Missouri appears aptly summarized by the following passage from Prosser and Keeton:
>
> "The American economy has experienced an increasing use of tangible ideas. It has been urged that conversion should expand to redress interference with all properties—tangible or intangible. But it would seem preferable to fashion other remedies, such as unfair competition, to protect people from having intangible values used and appropriated in unfair ways. . . ."

PROBLEM

Phil Philately, an errand boy for the Department of Commerce, was sent by his supervisor to the Post Office to buy a page of one hundred 34-cent stamps. The supervisor gave Phil $34 cash to make the purchase. At the time, Phil had no available money of his own.

On purchasing the page of stamps Phil, whose hobby was studying and collecting stamps, realized immediately that the page was worth a great deal of money because of an accidental, although not readily observable, imperfection in the design of this particular page. So, instead of taking the stamps to his supervisor, he took them to a nearby stamp collector who bought the page for $34,000. The collector realized when he purchased the stamps that they were worth at least four times what he paid for them. With the money obtained from the sale of the stamps, Phil returned to the Post Office and bought another, ordinary page of one hundred 34-cent stamps which he delivered to his employer. The stamps purchased by the collector from Phil were shortly thereafter accidentally destroyed by fire.

On learning of the above events, Phil's employer sued Phil and the collector, and Phil sued the collector, for trespass to chattel and for conversion. Do any of these claims have any validity?

I. TRESPASS TO REALTY, NUISANCE AND INTRUSION INTO SECLUSION

COMMENT

Three separate torts—trespass, nuisance and invasion of privacy—protect from intentional invasion by others a person's interest in the enjoyment of real property. These torts are loosely related but enjoy some similarities. They are discussed together in this chapter.

CANNON v. DUNN
145 Ariz. 115, 700 P.2d 502 (Ariz. App. 1985)

HOWARD, JUDGE.

This case involves the liability of an adjoining landowner for roots from a eucalyptus tree which invaded the subsurface of his neighbor's land. The trial court, sitting without a jury, and on the basis of conflicting evidence, found that the roots had caused actual damage. It denied an award of any damages and refused to grant injunctive relief by ordering the appellee to remove the offending roots and tree. Appellant contends the trial court erred in not granting the injunctive relief. We do not agree and we affirm.

Appellant urges us to adopt the view found in *Restatement (Second) of Torts* § 158 (1965), which states:

"One is subject to liability to another for trespass, irrespective of whether he thereby causes harm to any legally protected interest of the other, if he intentionally

(a) enters land in the possession of the other, or causes a thing or third person to do so, or

(b) remains on the land, or

(c) fails to remove from the land a thing which he is under a duty to remove."

Under the foregoing section a defendant would be liable irrespective of whether any actual harm was done to the plaintiff's land. Citing the case of *Waddell v. White*, 56 Ariz. 525, 109 P.2d 843 (1941), appellant contends that since Arizona has no applicable case law on the subject we must follow *Restatement (Second) of Torts* § 158 and reverse the decision of the trial court. We do not agree. It is true that our supreme court has stated on numerous occasions that in the absence of prior decisions to the contrary, this state will follow the Restatement whenever applicable. . . . However, it is also true that we do not follow the Restatement rule blindly. . . .

One of the reasons, if not the main reason that we follow the Restatement in the absence of prior Arizona decisions, is that the Restatement is supposed to represent the general law on the subject in the United States. If § 158 is applicable to our fact situation here, and we have grave doubts whether it is, it certainly does not represent the general law on liability of the adjoining landowner for roots of trees spreading into the subsurface of his neighbor's land. Our doubts about the applicability of § 158 to the situation here arise from the language in § 158(c) which talks about failing to remove from the land something which appellee is under a duty to remove. It seems obvious that one must first determine whether there is a duty to remove the object and that in this case § 158(c) really begs the question.

More on point is the *Restatement (Second) of Torts* § 840 (1979). This section deals with nuisances and the failure to abate a harmful natural condition of the land. It provides that a possessor of land is not liable to his adjoining landowner for a nuisance resulting solely from a natural condition of the land. Illustration 4 is especially appropriate to the facts of this case:

> "4. A purchases and takes possession of land on which have been planted a number of eucalyptus trees near the boundary line of B's land. The roots of the eucalyptus trees grow into B's land, with the result that walnut trees growing thereon are stunted and otherwise damaged. Although A knows of this, he does not cut down the eucalyptus trees. A is subject to the rule stated in § 839 [he is subject to liability for a nuisance], since the eucalyptus trees are not a natural condition." Restatement (Second) of Torts § 840(1), Comment a, illustration 4 (1979).

We note that in Illustration 4 the eucalyptus roots were actually causing damage to the neighbor's land.

A landowner who sustains injury by the branches or roots of a tree or plant on adjoining land intruding into his domain, regardless of their non-poisonous character may, without notice, cut off the offending branches or roots at his property line. . . .

When some actual and sensible or substantial damage has been sustained, the injured landowner may maintain an action for the abatement of the nuisance. . . . However, where no injury has been sustained, no action may be had for the abatement of the nuisance. . . . Nor may an action be had for damages in the absence of any injury. . . .

In *Smith v. Holt*, 174 Va. 213, 5 S.E. 2d 492 (1939), the court stated:

". . .[W]hen it appears that a sensible injury has been inflicted by the protrusion of roots from a noxious tree or plant under the land of another, he has, after notice, a right of action at law for the trespass committed.

But when it appears that the roots and branches of privet hedge, which is not noxious in its nature, protrude on adjoining land, and that no 'sensible injury' has been inflicted, it is our opinion that the complainant is not entitled to pursue his remedy in a court of equity, but is bound by the rule prevailing at common law and must bear the burden of protecting himself from protruding roots which emanate from a hedge growing upon the land of an adjoining owner." 5 S.E. 2d at 495.

We agree with the Virginia court in *Smith v. Holt, supra*. However, we hold that not only does the landowner upon whom a sensible injury has been inflicted by the protrusion of the roots of a noxious tree or plant have the right to an action at law in trespass, but he also can bring an action for injunctive relief to abate the nuisance.

Consider *Burt v. Beautiful Savior Lutheran Church of Broomfield*, 809 P. 2d 1064 (Colo. App. 1990), where the court wrote that

the concept of trespass developed much earlier than the concept of negligence. *Publix Cab Co. v. Colorado National Bank*, 139 Colo. 205, 338 P.2d 702 (1959). *See* C. Gregory, Trespass to Negligence to Absolute Liability, 37 W.Va. L. Rev. 359 (1951).

In early English law, the writ of "trespass" had a basic criminal character and provided a cause of action for all direct and immediate injuries to person or property. "Trespass on the case," a separate writ which developed later, originally allowed remedies for all indirect injuries. It was from this latter writ that negligence emerged as a separate cause of action. Later, the original writ of "trespass" also evolved into separate torts. W. Prosser & W. Keeton, The Law of Torts § 6 (5th Ed. 1984).

In defining the modern tort of trespass to property, some jurisdictions still make a distinction between direct and indirect injuries, labeling the former an intentional or "simple" trespass and the latter, negligent trespass. These jurisdictions apply the defense of contributory or comparative negligence to the tort of negligent trespass. . .

In Colorado, however, the present tort of trespass to property has no reference to the nature or immediacy of the harm, nor do we recognize the tort of "negligent trespass.". . .Consequently, the fact that, as defendant alleges here, the trespass in this case may have been caused by a negligent act is irrelevant. In Colorado, liability for trespass requires only an intent to do the act that itself constitutes, or inevitably causes, the intrusion. . . .Specifically, trespass is the physical intrusion upon property of another without the permission of the person lawfully entitled to the possession of the real estate. . . . "One is subject to liability to another for trespass, irrespective of whether he thereby causes harm to any legally protected interest of the other, if he intentionally . . . enters land in the possession of the other, or causes a thing or a third person to do so. . . ."

NOTES

1. *Trespass and Nuisance.* A trespass is a tangible invasion of the land of another. There also may be intangible invasions, such as noise, or other use of one's land which unreasonably interferes with a neighbor's enjoyment of his or her land. Trespass and nuisance may arise out of the same act, as where a neighbor's actions cause a flood on adjoining land. There are two kinds of nuisances, public and private. A public nuisance is an act or omission which interferes with the exercise of rights common to all citizens. A private nuisance is defined as "a nontrespassory invasion of another's interest in the private use and enjoyment of land." RESTATEMENT (2D) OF TORTS, SEC. 821D. A private nuisance may result from an intentional or negligent act, or a person may be strictly or absolutely liable for a nuisance. Trespass, however, is classified as an intentional tort, although, where the entry on the lands of another is the result of a reasonable mistake, *see also,* RESTATEMENT (2D) TORTS, Sec. 164, one may argue that the law is imposing absolute liability. However, the entry must be deliberate. *See, e.g.,* RESTATEMENT 2(D) OF TORTS, Section 166 (non-liability for accidental intrusion).

2. *Trespass to Airspace. Rochester Gas & Elec. Corp. v. Dunlop,* 148 Misc. 849, 266 N.Y.S. 469 (Cnty. Ct. 1933), concerned the nighttime crash of defendant's aeroplane into plaintiff's fifty foot steel tower, after the aeroplane's engine had stopped without warning. Plaintiff claimed that he should have been granted his motion for directed verdict with regard to his allegation of trespass. The appellate court observed that:

> . . . What then, should the court have decided on the subject of trespass? This involves the broader question, What is, or is to be, the law regarding the ancient maxim, "Cujus est solum ejus est usque ad coelum?" Not to go beyond the necessities of this case, it may be confidently stated that, if that maxim ever meant that the owner of land owned the space above the land to an indefinite height, it is no longer the law. As said by the United States Circuit Court of Appeals, in *Swetland v. Curtiss Airports Corporation,* 55 F.2d 201, 203, 83 A.L.R. 319, 325 (6th Cir. 1932): "In every case in which it (the maxim referred to) is to be found it was used in connection with occurrences common to the era, such as overhanging branches or eaves. These decisions are relied upon to define the rights of the new and rapidly growing business of aviation. This cannot be done consistently with the traditional policy of the courts to adapt the law to the economic and social needs of the times. . . . We cannot hold that in every case it is a trespass against the owner of the soil to fly an aeroplane through the airspace overlying the surface."
>
> It is plain, however, that, outside of the sovereign police power, no rule has been or will be made, which abridges the exclusive right of the owner of lands to the space above it, to such height as he may build a structure upon the land; therefore, for the purpose of this case,

it may be assumed that, when the aeroplane came in contact with the top of this tower, the rights and responsibilities of the respective parties were exactly the same as they would have been had the aeroplane come in contact with the earth below. . . .

. . . "It is common knowledge that airplanes fall in a great many instances from causes over which the pilot has absolutely no control. Time and again we read in the newspapers where a complete inspection of the plane is made before starting and that for some unknown reason the engine stops requiring a forced landing which often results in a crash." [Respondent's brief.] The correctness of that statement we believe cannot be questioned, at least in the present state of aircraft development. When, therefore, a man takes over another man's land a machine which he knows is liable to crash upon and do injury to that land and the structures upon it, can it be said that he is an accidental trespasser within the meaning of those decisions which have exempted the trespasser from liability? . . . It must be kept in mind that, when damage occurs in such a case, one or the other party has to stand it, and no reason readily suggests itself why it should not be the one who has brought about the chance occurrence. As was said by Chief Judge Rugg, of the Supreme Judicial Court of Massachusetts, in the case of *Smith v. New England Aircraft Co.,* 270 Mass. 511, 528, 170 N.E. 385 (1930): "Aerial navigation, important as it may be, has no inherent superiority over the landowner where their rights and claims are in actual conflict." And again, "Air navigation, important as it is, cannot rightly levy toll upon the legal rights of others for its successful prosecution." 270 Mass. 511, 530, 170 N.E. 385. To hold that the defendant here is absolved from liability, because he was himself free from negligence, is to hazard all the chimneys in the land, as well as live stock on the farms, and even the people in their homes. The other alternative seems by far the more reasonable, namely: Such chance as there may be that a properly equipped and well-handled aeroplane may still crash upon and injure private property shall be borne by him who takes the machine aloft.

How well do you think this opinion has stood the test of time? *See, e.g.* RESTATEMENT (SECOND) OF TORTS, § 159, providing that:

(1) Except as stated in Subsection (2), a trespass may be committed on, beneath, or, above the surface of the earth.

(2) Flight by aircraft in the air space above the land of another is a trespass if, but only if,

(a) it enters into the immediate reaches of the air space next to the land, and

(b) it interferes substantially with the other's use and enjoyment of his land.

The federal government can establish minimum altitudes for air flight, and flights above these altitudes are not trespasses. *United States v. Causby,* 328 U.S. 256, 66 S. Ct. 106 (1946). Cases have held that even flights below these altitudes are not trespasses unless they interfere with the actual, as opposed

I. TRESPASS TO REALTY

to the potential, use of land. *See* RESTATEMENT (SECOND) OF TORTS § 159, comment k.

3. *Liability To Whom, and For What?* Although trespass may be a form of absolute liability, the damages may be limited. RESTATEMENT (SECOND) OF TORTS § 162 provides that:

> A trespass on land subjects the trespasser to liability for physical harm to the possessor of the land at the time of the trespass, or to the land or to his things, or to members of his household or to their things, caused by any act done, activity carried on, or condition created by the trespasser, irrespective of whether his conduct is such as would subject him to liability were he not a trespasser.

Section 165 provides that "(o)ne who recklessly or negligently, or as a result or an abnormally dangerous activity, enters land in the possession of another or causes a thing or third person so to enter is subject to liability to the possessor if, but only if, his presence or the presence of the thing or the third person upon the land causes harm to the land, to the possessor, or to a thing or a third person in whose security the possessor has a legally protected interest.

4. *Overstaying One's Welcome.* A trespass may result from the failure to remove oneself or one's property from the land of another after a permission to enter or remain ends. *See, e.g.*, RESTATEMENT (SECOND) OF TORTS, § 160, providing that "(a) trespass may be committed by the continued presence on the land of a structure, chattel, or other thing which the actor or his predecessor in legal interest has placed on the land (a) with the consent of the person then in possession of the land, if the actor fails to remove it after the consent has been effectively terminated, or (b) pursuant to a privilege conferred on the actor irrespective of the possessor's consent, if the actor fails to remove it after the privilege has been terminated, by the accomplishment of its purpose or otherwise.

COMMENT

The tort of invasion of privacy consists of four separate wrongs: (1) appropriation of a person's name and likeness, (2) unreasonable intrusion into solitude, (3) placing a person in a false light in the public eye, and (4) public disclosure of private facts. *See, e.g., Jaubert v. Crowley Post-Signal, Inc.*, 375 So.2d 1386 (La. 1979). The first is a kind of "business tort" and is discussed in Chapter 18. The third and fourth kinds of invasions of privacy are "communicative" torts and are discussed in Chapter 18. The tort of unreasonable intrusion into solitude is much akin to trespass and nuisance and is discussed in the following case and materials.

DIETEMANN v. TIME, INC.
449 F.2d 245 (9th Cir. 1971)

HUFSTEDLER, CIRCUIT JUDGE.

. . . The facts, as narrated by the district court, are these:

"Plaintiff, a disabled veteran with little education, was engaged in the practice of healing with clay, minerals, and herbs — as practiced, simple quackery.

"Defendant, Time, Incorporated, a New York corporation, publishes Life Magazine. Its November 1, 1963 edition carried an article entitled 'Crackdown on Quackery.' The article depicted plaintiff as a quack and included two pictures of him. One picture was taken at plaintiff's home on September 20, 1963, previous to his arrest on a charge of practicing medicine without a license, and the other taken at the time of his arrest.

"Life Magazine entered into an arrangement with the District Attorney's Office of Los Angeles County whereby Life's employees would visit plaintiff and obtain facts and pictures concerning his activities. Two employees of Life, Mrs. Jackie Metcalf and Mr. William Ray, went to plaintiff's home on September 20, 1963. When they arrived at a locked gate, they rang a bell and plaintiff came out of his house and was told by Mrs. Metcalf and Ray that they had been sent there by a friend, a Mr. Johnson. The use of Johnson's name was a ruse to gain entrance. Plaintiff admitted them and all three went into the house and into plaintiff's den.

"The plaintiff had some equipment which could at best be described as gadgets, not equipment which had anything to do with the practice of medicine. Plaintiff, while examining Mrs. Metcalf, was photographed by Ray with a hidden camera without the consent of plaintiff. One of the pictures taken by him appeared in Life Magazine showing plaintiff with his hand on the upper portion of Mrs. Metcalf's breast while he was looking at some gadgets and holding what appeared to be a wand in his right hand. Mrs. Metcalf had told plaintiff that she had a lump in her breast. Plaintiff concluded that she had eaten some rancid butter 11 years, 9 months, and 7 days prior to that time. Other persons were seated in the room during this time.

"The conversation between Mrs. Metcalf and plaintiff was transmitted by radio transmitter hidden in Mrs. Metcalf's purse to a tape recorder in a parked automobile occupied by Joseph Bride, Life employee, John Miner of the District Attorney's Office, and Grant Leake, an investigator of the State Department of Public Health. While the recorded conversation was not quoted in the article in Life, it was mentioned that Life correspondent Bride was making notes of what was being received via the radio transmitter, and such information was at least referred to in the article.

"The foregoing events were photographed and recorded by an arrangement among Miner of the District Attorney's Office, Leake of the State Department of Public Health, and Bride, a representative of Life. It had been agreed that Life would obtain pictures and information for use as evidence, and later could be used by Life for publication.

"Prior to the occurrences of September 20, 1963, on two occasions the officials had obtained recordings of conversations in plaintiff's home; however, no pictures had been secured. Life employees had not participated in obtaining the recordings on these occasions.

"On October 15, 1963, plaintiff was arrested at his home on a charge of practicing medicine without a license in violation of Section 26280, California Health and Safety Code. At the time of his arrest, many pictures were made by Life of plaintiff at his home. Plaintiff testified that he did not agree to pose for the pictures but allowed pictures because he thought the officers could require it. Also present were newspaper men who had also been invited by the officials to be present at the time of arrest.

"Defendant contends that plaintiff posed for pictures at the time of his arrest and thus permission was given to take those pictures. As hereinafter pointed out, it is unnecessary to decide whether or not permission was given to take pictures at the time of his arrest.

"Plaintiff, although a journeyman plumber, claims to be a scientist. Plaintiff had no listings and his home had no sign of any kind. He did not advertise, nor did he have a telephone. He made no charges when he attempted to diagnose or to prescribe herbs and minerals. He did accept contributions.

"Life's article concerning plaintiff was not published until after plaintiff was arrested but before his plea on June 1, 1964 of nolo contendere for violations of Section 2141 of the California Business and Professions Code and Section 26280 of the California Health and Safety Code (misdemeanors).

. . . "Defendant's claim that the plaintiff's house was open to the public is not sustained by the evidence. The plaintiff was administering his so-called treatments to people who visited him. He was not a medical man of any type. He did not advertise. He did not have a phone. He did have a lock on his gate. To obtain entrance it was necessary to ring a bell. He conducted his activities in a building which was his home. The employees of defendant gained entrance by a subterfuge."

The district court concluded: "The publication in Life Magazine on November 1, 1963 of plaintiff's picture taken without his consent in his home on September 20, 1963 was an invasion of his privacy under California law for which he is entitled to damages. The acts of defendant also constituted an invasion of plaintiff's right of privacy guaranteed by the Constitution of the United States which would entitle him to relief under Section 1983, Title 42, United States Code." The court awarded $1,000 general damages "for injury to [Dietemann's] feelings and peace of mind." Time appeals from that decision. . . .

Plaintiff's den was a sphere from which he could reasonably expect to exclude eavesdropping newsmen. He invited two of defendant's employees to the den. One who invites another to his home or office takes a risk that the visitor may not be what he seems, and that the visitor may repeat all he hears and observes when he leaves. But he does not and should not be required to take the risk that what is heard and seen will be transmitted by photograph or recording, or in our modern world, in full living color and hi-fi to the public at large or to any of it that the visitor may select. A different rule could have a most pernicious effect upon the dignity of man and it would surely lead to guarded conversations and conduct where candor is most valued, *e.g.*, in the case of doctors and lawyers.

The defendant claims that the First Amendment immunizes it from liability for invading plaintiff's den with a hidden camera and its concealed electronic instruments because its employees were gathering news and its instrumentalities "are indispensable tools of investigative reporting." We agree that news gathering is an integral part of news dissemination. We strongly disagree, however, that the hidden mechanical contrivances are "indispensable tools" of news gathering. Investigative reporting is an ancient art; its successful practice long antecedes the invention of miniature cameras and electronic devices. The First Amendment has never been construed to accord newsmen immunity from torts or crimes committed during the course of news gathering. The First Amendment is not a license to trespass, to steal, or to intrude by electronic means into the precincts of another's home or office.[4]

It does not become such a license simply because the person subjected to the intrusion is reasonably suspected of committing a crime. . . .

No interest protected by the First Amendment is adversely affected by permitting damages for intrusion to be enhanced by the fact of later publication of the information that the publisher improperly acquired. Assessing damages for the additional emotional distress suffered by a plaintiff when the wrongfully acquired data are purveyed to the multitude chills intrusive acts. It does not chill freedom of expression guaranteed by the First Amendment. A rule forbidding the use of publication as an ingredient of damages would deny to the injured plaintiff recovery for real harm done to him without any countervailing benefit to the legitimate interest of the public in being informed. The same rule would encourage conduct by news media that grossly offends ordinary men.

[Affirmed.]

NOTES

1. *Privacy in a Public Place; An Offensive Presence.* In *Knight v. Penobscot Bay Med. Center,* 420 A.2d 915 (Me. 1980), plaintiffs appealed from a finding of no invasion of privacy. Defendant Robie was the husband of nurse Robie. He came to the hospital to pick up his wife, but she was unable to leave because a severe snowstorm had delayed the arrival of her replacement.

When he learned that she would be detained, he decided to stay at the hospital until she finished her work. To give her husband something interesting to do while he was waiting for her, Nurse Robie asked Dr. Lantinen for permission to have her husband witness a birth. He was permitted by the defendant hospital and doctors to witness plaintiff Knight as she gave birth to her baby.

Mr. Robie stood behind a viewing window in the surgical corridor, approximately twelve feet from the delivery table. From where he stood, Mr. Robie had a side view of Mrs. Knight's body, and her body was entirely covered by draping, except for her face and hands. Hence, Mr. Robie did not witness the actual process of delivering; what he saw was the baby being lifted up and then being placed on the mother's abdomen.

Plaintiff objected to the trial court's failure to instruct the jury as follows:

---

[4] In this respect the facts of this case are different from those in *Pearson v. Dodd,* 410 F.2d 701 (D.C. Cir. 1969). In *Pearson,* the defendant received documents knowing that they had been removed by the donor without the plaintiff's consent. But the donor was not the defendant's agent, and the defendant did not participate in purloining the documents.

The occasion of the birth of a child is one of the most sacred in our society and no one has the right to intrude unless invited or because of some real and pressing necessity. There is no pretense that such a necessity existed in this case. Mrs. Knight had a legal right to the privacy of the delivery room at such a time and the law secured this to her and to her husband after he joined her and the law requires others to observe it and to abstain from its violation.

This instruction was based on an 1881 case, *De May v. Roberts,* 46 Mich. 160, 9 N.W. 146 (1881), where the defendant doctor asked a lay person to assist in a childbirth. The plaintiff thought the lay person was a medical assistant. She was permitted to recover.

The court found that the *DeMay* instruction was erroneous:

First, it failed to refer to the essential element that the defendant must intend as the result of his conduct that there be an intrusion upon another's solitude or seclusion.

Second, in reference to whether Mr. Robie's presence in the delivery area was "unnecessary" to serve the functional purpose involved, requested instruction #8 was couched in the language of a case decided almost a century ago. It erroneously stated that Mr. Robie's "unnecessary" presence in the delivery area was sufficient, without more, to establish as a matter of law that Mr. Robie had unlawfully intruded upon the plaintiffs' interest in seclusion.

The trial court had correctly instructed the jury by quoting RESTATEMENT (SECOND) OF TORTS § 652B:

One who intentionally intrudes, physically or otherwise, upon the solitude or seclusion of another or his private . . . concerns, is subject to liability to the other for invasion of his privacy, if the intrusion would be highly offensive to a reasonable person.

2. *Stalking.* The court in *Rumbauskas v. Cantor,* 138 N.J. 173, 649 A.2d 853 (1994), held that stalking and threats of violence constituted an intrusion into seclusion. The action, the court said, was governed by the two-year statute of limitations for "injury to the person."

Could stalking also constitute an intentional infliction of emotional distress? Assault?

J. THE PRIMA FACIE OR INNOMINATE TORT

COMMENT

Intentional torts developed as separate types of specific torts by historical accident. *See, e.g., Prosser & Keeton On Torts,* Fifth Ed., Sec. 6 (1984). Similarly, the defenses to intentional torts became nominate specific defenses, such as self-defense and consent, although the essence of each is that the actor reasonably but mistakenly believed that his or her conduct would not be harmful or offensive to the person at whom it was directed or was justified by the circumstances. From time to time "reformers" have attempted to eliminate the "categories" of intentional torts and designate one innominate intentional tort: "an act which is substantially certain to affect a protected interest." The most notable effort has been RESTATEMENT (SECOND) OF TORTS, § 870 (1977), which provides that:

> "One who intentionally causes injury to another is subject to liability to the other for that injury, if his conduct is generally culpable and not justifiable under the circumstances. This liability may be imposed although the actor's conduct does not come within a traditional category of tort liability."

In comment a to § 870 the Restaters say:

> This Section is intended to supply a generalization for tortious conduct involving harm intentionally inflicted. Generalizations have long existed for negligence liability, involving conduct producing unreasonable risk of harm to others (*see* §§ 282, 291–294), and for strict liability, involving the carrying on of an activity that is abnormally dangerous. (*See* §§ 519–520). As for conduct intentionally causing harm, however, it has traditionally been assumed that the several established intentional torts developed separately and independently and not in accordance with any unifying principle. This Section purports to supply that unifying principle and to explain the basis for the development of the more recently created intentional torts. More than that, it is intended to serve as a guide for determining when liability should be imposed for harm that was intentionally inflicted, even though the conduct does not come within the requirements of one of the well established and named intentional torts.

The comment points out that in New York the principle stated in this section "has been given the appellation 'prima facie tort' and efforts have been made to set forth its requirements with more rigidity." As Prof. Vandevelde notes, New York has added to the requirements of an intentional infliction of injury without justification "three additional elements: disinterested malevolence as the defendant's sole motivation; conduct not actionable under another tort; and special damages." Kenneth J. Vandevelde, *Prima Facie Tort,* 19 HOFSTRA L. REV. 447, 494 (1990). Other courts have taken a more open-ended approach to the tort, which as the Restaters say in comment *a* "is sometimes called an innominate form of the action of trespass on the case."

In comment d the Restaters say:

> In many situations in which liability has been imposed under the principle stated in this Section, newly recognized categories of intentional tort have been developed or are still in the process of development. A prime example of a tort presently not fully developed is intentional infliction of emotional distress; its contours are not yet fully clear. (*See* §§ 46–48.) Other categories of fairly recent development include injurious falsehood, interference with contractual relations and interference with prospective economic advantage. The more mature the stage of development the more definite the contours of the tort and of the privileges that may be defenses to it.

In describing the form of the innominate tort, the Restaters say in comment j:

The new tort may be closely related to an established tort and thus allow tort recovery when a restrictive rule of the traditional tort would not permit it. For example, the tort of assault has traditionally required the creation of apprehension of an imminent battery. Some cases have permitted recovery when the threat is not imminent but still is a very real one of a serious battery, to take place in the near future. Again, the tort of false imprisonment requires the setting of boundaries confining the plaintiff. It has been held that an innominate action of case may permit recovery for restraining a person from going into a place where he has a right to go. In determining whether a new tort can appropriately eliminate a restrictive feature of a traditional tort it is important to give careful consideration to the nature of the restriction. If it came about as a historical accident or for reasons that no longer have real significance, the new tort without it may serve a useful purpose. If the restriction expresses an important policy of the law against liability, however, the significance of that policy should continue regardless of the name of the tort involved or the date of its origin.

The prima facie or innominate tort has not received wide acceptance, *see Beavers v. Johnson Controls World Services,* 859 P.2d 497 (N.M. 1993), and its application has been largely restricted to business tort actions, *see* Vandevelde *supra.* It has the potential for widespread development however. As Professor Vandevelde asserts:

> Its capacity to expand and to contain liability allowed the prima facie tort doctrine to further the ends of judges with sharply opposed political convictions. . . . [T]he rise of the prima facie tort was both an important doctrinal innovation and an exemplar of the general transformation in legal thought which accompanied the collapse of formalism.

19 HOFSTRA L. REV. at 496–97.

Chapter 4
DEFENSES TO INTENTIONAL TORTS

A. INTRODUCTION

This chapter covers defenses that typically are raised in connection with intentional torts. The list is not exhaustive. There can of course be other defenses as well, *e.g.,* statute of limitations, immunity, lack of jurisdiction, etc. nor are the defenses considered here necessarily limited to intentional tort claims. They may also apply in suits involving negligence and strict liability.

The reason for treating separately the defenses considered here is that they raise fundamental questions about the nature of intentional tort liability and, for that matter, about the nature of tort liability in general: When should a person be permitted to harm others with impunity? What are the policy reasons for allowing such harmful conduct to go unpunished? Defense of self and of others appeals to primordial instincts, but it is not always easy to tell what constitutes a sufficient threat to justify such a defense. What is the relationship between self-defense and necessity? Should mistake be a defense? Should one be permitted to consent to the commission of a tort? The latter question implicates the defenses of contributory negligence and assumption of the risk, considered in connection with defenses to negligence.

B. CONSENT

PROBLEM

Plaintiff consulted defendant, an ear specialist, about trouble she was having with her right ear. On examining the ear the defendant discovered a diseased condition, and plaintiff consented to defendant's operating on the ear. During the operation on the sedated plaintiff, defendant discovered a more serious condition in the left ear. Because the condition with the left ear would soon require surgery, defendant proceeded to operate on it also. Does the operation on the left ear constitute a battery? Did the defendant have the plaintiff's implied consent to operate? Should this depend on how serious the condition in the left ear was? On whether the condition in the left ear was related to that in the right ear? On whether there were relatives of the plaintiff close at hand whom the defendant could consult? On whether the operation was a success, or had untoward consequences?

COLBY v. McCLENDON
85 Okla. 293, 206 P. 207 (1922)

MCNEILL, JUSTICE.

This is an action commenced in the district court of McClain county by Ann McClendon, surviving widow of T.L. McClendon, against J. H. Colby and Wade Stovall, to recover damages for the wrongful and intentional killing of her husband on August 16, 1911. From a judgment in favor of the plaintiff and against the defendants, the defendants have appealed.

The plaintiffs in error brief but two questions. The first is stated as follows:

"Where two persons voluntarily engage in a mutual combat, resulting in the death of one at the hands of the other, the latter is not civilly liable in damages therefor."

Plaintiffs in error allege this controversy grew out of a controversy over a schoolhouse site between the school authorities of school district No. 47 and defendant Colby. The facts are stated about as follows: Mrs. Yoder, a Choctaw Indian, was allotted 40 acres of land in what is now McClain county. In July 1905, she and her husband executed a mortgage payable in five years. After the execution of the mortgage she permitted the school authorities to build a schoolhouse on an acre of said land. There was no conveyance made of the school site to the school district, but school was regularly carried on and conducted in the schoolhouse for years. After statehood Mrs. Yoder conveyed the land, subject to the mortgage to Mr. Glasco, who went into possession thereof. Glasco built a residence on the school site near the schoolhouse, which was used and occupied by a tenant. The school authorities had no recorded title to the acre of land, and Glasco refused to recognize their rights to the land. The building of the residence on the school site interfered with the running of the school, so the school district brought suit against Glasco for the purpose of quieting title to the school site and to compel the removal of the dwelling from the school site. Judgment was rendered in favor of the school district and against Glasco, directing him within 90 days to remove the residence from the school site.

In this suit it is alleged that defendant Colby and Glasco entered into a conspiracy to secure possession of said school site. Colby was not a party to the suit between the school district and Glasco, although he testified in that case. A few months prior to maturity of the mortgage executed by Mrs. Yoder on this land, Colby purchased the same, and after the mortgage matured he had the land sold by advertising, as provided under the Arkansas law. Colby bought in the property. After Colby secured the certificate of purchase, being entitled to possession, he went into possession through a tenant named Vincent. This possession was taken after the judgment in the case of *School District v. Glasco* and prior to the 90 days which Glasco had to remove the premises. Colby proceeded to build a wire fence around the schoolhouse and keep the school authorities out. The directors protested. Colby secured the services of Stovall, a supposed gunman. He introduced Stovall to people in that vicinity as Prof. Wade, and stated that Prof. Wade was going to open up school the next day, and notified the people to come, stating that "Stovall would not teach with schoolbooks, but with shotguns and shells." Colby and

Stovall went to the residence located on the school site, and both were armed with Winchesters, and the next day proceeded to build the fence. The school trustees and patrons, about 12 in number, assembled, and all or a portion of them with firearms, started toward the schoolhouse site to prevent the building of the fence.

It is admitted the evidence is conflicting about what occurred. Colby contends that he and Stovall saw the parties assemble, and when the parties started to where he was, he and Stovall started to the house where their guns were, and before reaching the house shots were fired at them. After reaching the house, the battle ensued between Colby, and Stovall, and the trustees and patrons. Colby was shot and injured, and [the] deceased [McClendon] and another party were killed. The evidence upon behalf of defendant in error was to the effect that the trustees called to Colby to stop, as the directors wanted to talk to him; but he and Stovall proceeded to the house and secured their guns and immediately opened fire upon the directors and patrons.

The plaintiffs in error contended that, under this state of facts, this amounted to a mutual combat voluntarily entered into between the parties, and that, the deceased having voluntarily entered into the combat, Colby would not be liable for damages. The plaintiffs in error requested instructions to this effect, which were refused by the court, and the court instructed the jury, if the parties entered into a mutual combat voluntarily, this would not relieve the party in an action for damages. Plaintiffs in error admit that there is a conflict in the decisions upon this question, and admit that the majority of the Courts hold contrary to that contention.

The rule prevailing in the majority of the states may be stated as follows:

> "Where the parties engage in mutual combat in anger, each is civilly liable to the other for any physical injury inflicted by him during the fight. The fact that the parties voluntarily engaged in the combat is no defense to an action by either of them to recover damages for personal injuries inflicted upon him by the other."

. . . The minority rule is stated as follows:

> "Where parties engage in a mutual combat in anger, the act of each is unlawful, and relief will be denied them in a civil action; at least, in the absence of a showing of excessive force or malicious intent to do serious injury upon the part of the defendant."

. . . [Cases supporting both positions are] well annotated in 6 A.L.R. 394, and the annotator, in comparing the rules, stated as follows.

> "A comparison of the results reached in the cases that sustain the respective rules suggests that those results have been somewhat less affected by the difference in the rules than might have been expected; since in many, at least, of the cases that declare the majority rule, the facts show that the defendant used excessive and disproportionate force, and so might have been held liable even under the minority rule. However, the possibility of a serious injury to one combatant at the hands of another, who does not use what, in the circumstances, amounts to excessive or disproportionate force, affords some scope for difference in the respective rules."

This court has never passed upon the question, but it seems that the majority rule is supported by the best reasoning. We think it should be followed in a case where the parties enter into a mutual combat with deadly weapons. The minority rule is announced in cases where the injury resulted from fist fights, although the case of *Lykins v. Hamrick,* 144 Ky. 80, 137 S.W. 852 (1911), was where parties were engaged in a cutting scrape. We think it would be against public policy to apply the minority rule in a case where persons enter into a mutual combat with deadly weapons. . . .

For the reasons stated, the judgment of the court is affirmed.

NOTES

1. *Consent.* As defined by the Restatement, consent is "willingness in fact for conduct to occur." RESTATEMENT (SECOND) OF TORTS § 892. The general rule is that "One who effectively consents to conduct of another intended to invade his interests cannot recover in an action of tort . . ." *Id.,* § 892A.

2. *Consent to Unlawful Acts.* Assume that the goals of the tort system are to deter accident-causing conduct, and to compensate those injured by such conduct. If the majority rule prevails, which goal is approximated? If the minority rule prevails?

In *Hudson v. Craft,* 33 Cal. 2d 654, 204 P.2d 1 (1949), the plaintiff, a loser in a prizefight, sued his victorious opponent. If the majority rule applies, who wins? If the minority rule applies, who wins?

In fact, Hudson's opponent was doubly quick on his feet, and escaped service of process. However, Hudson proceeded against the promoter of the fight on a battery theory, as the "aider and abettor" of his opponent. Under that theory, the promoter's liability would be dependent upon Hudson establishing the liability of the opponent. The court approved of the minority rule as to the liability of the combatants *inter se,* but added the following gloss:

> In view of the public policy of this state as expressed by initiative, legislation, the rules of the Athletic Commission, and the Constitution, the promoter must be held liable as a principal [for violation of such regulations] regardless of what the rule may be as between the combatants.

204 P.2d at 3. How would you analyze this result in terms of the goals discussed above?

3. *Support for the Minority Rule?* ALASKA STAT. § 09.17.030 (Michie Supp. 1989) provides that:

> A person who suffers personal injury or death may not recover damages for the personal injury or death if the injuries or death occurred while the person was engaged in the commission of a felony, the person has been convicted of the felony, including conviction based on a guilty plea or plea of nolo contendere, and the felony substantially contributed to the injury or death. . . .

Compare RESTATEMENT (SECOND) OF TORTS § 892C(1): "[C]onsent is effective to bar recovery in a tort action although the conduct consented to is a crime," and § 889: "One is not barred from recovery . . . merely because at the time of the [defendant's interference] he was committing a tort or a crime. . . ."

How do these positions differ? Suppose that the criminal conduct complained of exceeds the consent granted by the victim? Consider § 892C comment c, illustration 5:

> After an altercation, A and B agree to a fight with fists. In the course of the fight A draws a knife and stabs B. B's consent does not bar his recovery for the knife wound.

Is the issue in these cases really the narrow one of whether "consent" bars recovery, or is it a broader determination that tort consequences should not follow certain types of conduct? *See, e.g., Bowlan v. Lunsford,* 176 Okla. 115, 54 P.2d 666 (1936) (adult woman precluded on public policy grounds from pursuing battery action against sexual partner for inducing her to have pregnancy terminated). How does the minority rule differ from the defense of self-defense, considered *infra*?

4. *Colby and the Restatement.* The RESTATEMENT (SECOND) OF TORTS, §§ 892–892C, replaces the *Colby* rules with a general rule of consent barring recovery. It is unclear whether *Colby*, or the Restatement, would be followed today.

LEE v. NATIONWIDE INSURANCE CO.
497 S.E. 2d 328 (Va. 1998)

LACY, JUSTICE.

In this case we consider whether the trial court erred in holding as a matter of law that the defense of illegality barred the claim for damages of a 13-year-old boy rather than submitting to the jury the issue of the boy's consent to the illegal act.

Late in the evening of November 1, 1993, 13-year-old Roy James Lee locked his bedroom door and left his house, apparently through his bedroom window. His parents did not know he was gone. Lee went to the home of his friend, William Randall Slate, a high school freshman who was 16 years old. Around 11:00 p.m., Lee called his girlfriend, 12-year-old Jessica Lee Fisher, and told her to take the keys to her mother's car from the coffee table and meet Lee and Slate at the basement door of her house. Fisher's mother had already gone to bed.

Fisher changed her clothes, got the keys, and met the boys as planned. She gave the keys to Lee who, in turn, gave them to Slate. When the group walked to Mrs. Fisher's car, they heard the motor running on a neighbor's car parked nearby. They decided not to take Mrs. Fisher's car at that time because they feared being discovered. Instead, Lee and Slate unsuccessfully tried to take a motorized bicycle parked nearby. The group then walked to Slate's house where they stayed for about an hour.

When the three youths returned to Fisher's house, the motor of the neighbor's car was no longer running. Fisher got into the back seat of her mother's car and Slate got in the driver's seat. To avoid the possibility that Mrs. Fisher might hear the engine start, Lee pushed the car some distance away from its parking place. Lee then got into the front passenger's seat. For the next hour and a half, Slate drove the group around the area in Mrs. Fisher's car. Both Fisher and Lee knew that Slate had only a learner's driving permit.

At some point, Fisher asked Slate to return to her home, and he agreed to do so. Around 2:00 a.m. on the return trip, Fisher noticed that Slate was driving at a speed of between 40 and 45 m.p.h. and asked him to slow down. She also observed a "loose gravel" sign.

About one hour later, at 3:10 a.m., Virginia State Trooper Gene E. Ayers received a call to investigate an accident on a portion of Route 605 that was under construction. The road at the accident location was an unmarked gravel surface 15 feet wide with ditches on both sides. When Trooper Ayers reached the accident scene, he found 270 feet of wavy tire marks in the gravel leading to one of the ditches. Mrs. Fisher's car was approximately 30 feet off the road. Trooper Ayers found Fisher "in and out of consciousness" in the back seat of the car. Lee was outside the car, halfway between the car and the road. The temperature was below freezing and some of the blood on both Lee and Fisher had begun to freeze. Slate was not at the scene of the accident when Ayers arrived.

Lee suffered severe head injuries in the accident resulting in catastrophic, permanent brain damage, and permanent disability.

Lee's mother, Debra S. Lee, filed a motion for judgment against Slate on her own behalf and on behalf of Lee as his next friend. Since Slate was an uninsured motorist, Nationwide Mutual Insurance Company (Nationwide), Debra Lee's uninsured motorist insurance carrier, defended the action. Nationwide filed an answer and a special plea asserting the defense of illegality. At trial, on motion by Nationwide, the court struck Lee's evidence and held that, as a matter of law, Lee freely and voluntarily, without coercion or duress, consented to participation in the illegal act that resulted in his injuries. The trial court entered judgment in favor of Nationwide. Lee appeals, claiming the trial court erred in its application of the illegality defense.

The illegality defense is based on the principle that a party who consents to and participates in an illegal act may not recover from other participants for the consequences of that act. The defense will be applied to bar recovery if the evidence shows that the plaintiff freely and voluntarily consented to participation in the illegal act, without duress or coercion. As with other defenses, the party raising the defense has the burden to establish it.

While none of our prior cases has involved the application of the defense of illegality to acts of a person younger than 14 years of age, Lee does not contend that the defense is unavailable in such cases. Nor does Lee dispute that taking Mrs. Fisher's car without permission was an illegal act. Rather, Lee asserts that the evidence presented conflicting factual issues as to whether Lee freely and voluntarily, without duress or coercion, consented to participation in the illegal act, and, therefore, that the trial court should have submitted resolution of these issues to the jury rather than deciding them as a matter of law. In support of his position, Lee argues that the trial court's error was based on both its failure to apply a rebuttable evidentiary presumption that a person between the ages of 7 and 14 is incapable of consenting to an illegal act and its failure to consider the evidence in the light most favorable to Lee. However, Lee's position is not supported by either the record in this case or the law of this Commonwealth.

Lee argues that minors between the ages of 7 and 14 are afforded the protection of certain rebuttable presumptions of incapacity when charged with criminal culpability, citing *Law v. Commonwealth*, 75 Va. 885, 889 (1881), or contributory negligence, citing *Doe v. Dewhirst*, 240 Va. 266, 268, 396 S.E. 2d 840, 842 (1990). The trial court, according to Lee, either should have applied those presumptions here or created and applied an ad hoc rebuttable presumption based on the circumstances of this case. We disagree.

Neither of the above standards is applicable to a determination of whether a person has engaged in an illegal act, for purposes of the illegality defense. That determination is an objective inquiry. However, whether the defense will be applied requires more than a simple showing that the plaintiff committed the illegal act. As we have said, the defendant must also prove that the plaintiff consented to the commission of the illegal act and engaged in it, freely and voluntarily, without duress or coercion. This evidentiary burden necessarily includes consideration of the maturity, intelligence, and mental capacity of the plaintiff, regardless of age. Given this burden of proof, the rebuttable presumption suggested by Lee would serve no additional purpose and would provide no additional protection to the minor plaintiff. Thus, there is no legal basis or persuasive rationale for imposing the type of presumption suggested by Lee, and the trial court correctly declined to do so.

We now turn to Lee's assertion that the evidence of voluntary consent, duress, and coercion was in conflict, and therefore, the trial court should have submitted the issue to the jury. Viewing the evidence in the light most favorable to Lee, as we must when reviewing a motion to strike, *Austin v. Shoney's, Inc.*, 254 Va. 134, 135, 486 S.E. 2d 285, 285 (1997); *Meador v. Lawson*, 214 Va. 759, 761, 204 S.E. 2d 285, 287 (1974), we conclude that the trial court did not err in holding that reasonable persons could not disagree that Lee freely and voluntarily, without duress or coercion, consented to his participation in an illegal act.

The record shows that Lee was capable of understanding the nature of his acts and had the ability to make choices about his behavior. At the time of the illegal act, Lee was almost 14 years old. He performed at an average level in school and was capable of better performance. His behavior at school was average, and he played on organized sports teams. He complied with his parents' directions not to ride a motorized bicycle under certain circumstances. While described as a "follower" in his relationship with Slate, there is no evidence to support a finding that Lee was incapable of withholding consent or making other choices regarding his behavior.

With regard to the incident in question, the record shows that, outside the presence of Slate, Lee actively planned to take Mrs. Fisher's car and referred to the plan as "steal[ing]" the car when talking to Fisher. He told Fisher to take the keys, locked his bedroom window. He turned the keys over to Slate. Lee pushed the car away from Fisher's house to avoid detection and, according to Fisher's testimony, during the ride in Mrs. Fisher's car, never tried to stop Slate, alter the way Slate was driving, or get out of the car.

Lee argues that his actions were taken, not freely and voluntarily, but under duress and coercion by Slate. Lee relies on Fisher's testimony that Slate was the "leader" and Lee the "follower," that Lee wanted to impress Slate, that Lee would not get into trouble unless Slate was present, and that Lee would "act differently" when Slate was around. Lee also relies on Fisher's testimony that when Lee called her to plan the taking of her mother's car, she heard Slate in the background directing Lee to "tell me if we didn't take mom's car, then they were going to bust out the windshield."

This evidence suggests that when Lee was with Slate he engaged in activity which he might not have undertaken by himself or with others. This evidence does not, however, support a conclusion that the change in Lee's demeanor or his actions were the result of coercion or duress by Slate, or that Lee had no control over his actions when he was with Slate. Rather, the evidence suggests that Lee engaged in actions which he believed would impress Slate and keep Slate as his friend. No expert evidence was presented that Slate's relationship with or influence on Lee in some way deprived Lee of his ability to make choices about his actions either on the night in question or at any other time. Therefore, we conclude that, based on the record, the trial court was correct when it decided that reasonable persons could not disagree that Lee consented to his participation in an illegal act and that the illegality defense barred his recovery for injuries sustained as a result of that illegal act.

Accordingly, the judgment of the trial court will be affirmed.

PROBLEM

A 14-year-old boy, aided by another youngster, tilted a soft-drink machine forward at night outside a business establishment, in order to dislodge cans of drink which they could then steal. They were unable to steady the machine and it fell forward, killing the boy. The boy's estate sued the machine manufacturer for wrongful death, alleging the machine was defectively designed because it had no anti-theft device to prevent cans from falling out when the machine was tipped forward, and because there were no brackets to anchor the machine to the ground.

Is a jury question presented? Suppose the defendant was aware of other such accidents that had occurred as a result of similar theft attempts?

NOTES

1. *Consent, But to What?* In *Hellriegel v. Tholl*, 69 Wash. 2d 97, 417 P.2d 362 (1966), a teenager named Dicka was injured when three of his friends attempted to throw him into a lake "during an afternoon spent in water-skiing, sunbathing, and engaging in horseplay." Accepting the defendants' plea of consent, the court concluded:

> [W]e have Dicka's own statement that he had joined in the pillow throwing and the grass throwing. Dicka also stated that he and the boy who fell on him . . . were used to wrestling together prior to this accident. Dicka was very athletic and this activity was regarded by

all of the boys as "fun." Under the circumstances shown by the evidence, it would be a strained and unreasonable interpretation of Dicka's statement [Oh, you couldn't throw me in even if you tried] to the boys to construe it as a warning not to try to throw him into the lake, because he did not want to be thrown in, even in fun, and that he would resist such an attempt.

Appellant's counsel argues in his brief that, even if Dicka gave any consent, it was consent to being thrown into the lake, and not a consent to have his neck broken, i.e., that the scope of the consent did not include this battery. Of course, Dicka did not consent to having his neck broken. As we pointed out above, Dicka did not even consent to being thrown into the lake — he consented only to having his three friends try to throw him into the lake, while he resisted their attempt. In other words, he consented to rough and tumble horseplay.

RESTATEMENT (SECOND) OF TORTS § 892A treats the issue in this manner:

(1) One who effectively consents to conduct of another intended to invade his interests cannot recover in an action of tort for the conduct or for harm resulting from it.

(2) To be effective, consent must be

(a) by the one who has the capacity to consent or by a person empowered to consent for him, and

(b) to the particular conduct, or to substantially the same conduct.

(3) Conditional consent or consent restricted as to time, area or in other respects is effective only within the limits of the condition or restriction.

(4) If the actor exceeds the consent, it is not effective for the excess.

(5) Upon termination of consent its effectiveness is terminated, except as it may have become irrevocable by contract or otherwise, or except as its terms may include, expressly or by implication, a privilege to continue to act.

If the *Hellriegel* court applied the Restatement, would the outcome be different? Why?

In *Doe v. High-Tech Institute, Inc.*, 972 P.2d 1060 (Colo. App. 1998), the plaintiff, a student in defendant's medical assistant training program, consented to a blood test by the defendant to test for rubella. Without plaintiff's knowledge, the defendant also tested the blood for HIV and found that plaintiff was HIV positive. The plaintiff sued the defendant alleging invasion of privacy, and the court held the plaintiff stated a cause of action. The plaintiff "gave only limited consent to the testing of his blood," and any testing beyond that consent was tortious.

2. *Marking*. The court in *Smith v. Calvary Christian Church*, 614 N.W. 2d 590 (Mich. 2000), said the plaintiff had no cause of action against the defendant church for invasion of privacy or for intentional infliction of emotional distress. The minister of the church revealed to the congregation that plaintiff had previously frequented prostitutes. Plaintiff had withdrawn

his church membership before the revelation occurred, but remained involved in the church's activities. By so remaining involved, the court said, the plaintiff consented to the "marking," or public censure, given by the minister pursuant to the Bible, Matt. 18:15–17.

3. *Sports Injuries.* Reconsider *Kiley v. Patterson,* given in Chp. 3.

4. *Vitiated Consent.* Consent obtained through the defendant's misrepresentation does not constitute a defense; the fraud "vitiates" the consent. RESTATEMENT (SECOND) OF TORTS § 892B provides that if "the person consenting . . . is induced to consent by a substantial mistake concerning the nature of the invasion of his interests or the extent of the harm to be expected from it and the mistake is known to the other or is induced by the other's misrepresentation, the consent is not effective for the unexpected invasion or harm." The same section also provides that consent given under duress is not effective.

The classic example of vitiated consent is supplied by § 892B comment d, illus. 7:

> A, believing B to be a physician, removes her clothing and permits B to lay hands on her person for the purpose of a medical examination. B is not a physician and knows that A believes him to be one. B is subject to liability to A for battery.

Compare Micari v. Mann, 126 Misc. 2d 422, 481 N.Y.S.2d 967 (1984), in which the plaintiffs, in their early 20s, alleged that the defendant, their acting teacher, caused them to perform various sexual acts with him, or in his presence. The plaintiffs did not allege that the defendant had employed physical force or threats. According to the court, "They asserted, however, that defendant individually told them that this sexual activity was intended to release their inhibitions and thus improve their acting skills. They indicated that, in light of defendant's outstanding reputation as an acting teacher who had taught many famous members of the profession, they trusted him, although they each professed doing so with a certain amount of trepidation." The court, in a decision primarily dealing with the question of damages, indicated that § 892B applied to bar recovery. Why? Did the students understand what they were doing? Given the abusive conduct by the defendant, and the existence of the teacher-student relationship, would reliance on the tort of intentional infliction of emotional harm be more sound?

5. *Consent to Medical Treatment.* RESTATEMENT (SECOND) OF TORTS § 892B is concerned with misrepresentation and duress. But what if consent is obtained through "nonrepresentation," *i.e.,* the actor knows about a risk of harm and knows or should know that the consenting party is not aware of the severity of the risk or harm, and fails to warn him in advance? The most frequent case is the physician who obtains consent to surgery without disclosing to the patient the risks of harm and the alternatives available about which the patient is unaware. Initially, the ensuing operation was treated as a battery. The matter now is treated as a branch of malpractice, *i.e.,* the physician breached his duty to obtain informed consent.

In *Moser v. Stallings,* 387 N.W.2d 599 (Iowa 1986), plaintiff elected to undergo a facial, eyelid and forehead plasty, a chin implant and a dermabrasion of the upper lip. During the surgery, defendant plastic surgeon decided not to perform the chin implant. Plaintiff alleged that because of the surgery her appearance had been worsened due to "large and disfiguring scars, a substantially displaced hairline, and an unsatisfactory rearrangement of her face, scalp and neck areas." The trial court directed a verdict for defendant on plaintiff's allegation of battery, concluding that:

> A medical battery claim is appropriate only in circumstances when a doctor performs an operation to which the patient has not consented. The requisite elements of battery are met by showing the wrongdoer intended to inflict a harmful or offensive contact upon the body of the plaintiff. A battery occurs when the patient consents to one type of treatment and the doctor intentionally deviates from the consent and performs a substantially different treatment. . . .
>
> Plaintiff asserts that her battery claim is premised on the deviation by defendant from plaintiff's consent to surgery. She concedes that she signed a consent form, but points out that part of the treatment was for a chin implant which was not performed. She notes that defendant testified he purposely did not do a chin implant but instead rearranged her chin muscles in "what is called in plastic surgery circles canal platysma plasty." Defendant further testified he elected not to perform the chin implant because he thought "we got a great result achieved with her own tissue without having to do the chin implant."
>
> We believe the evidence clearly shows there was no deviation by the defendant from plaintiff's consent to surgery. There is no material evidence that defendant performed a substantially different treatment. Rather, the evidence shows defendant believed that by performing the extensive face lift, including his work under plaintiff's chin, the need for the implant was obviated. The face lift was clearly authorized. Plaintiff's signed consent form authorized the defendant "to perform such surgical procedures as Dr. Stallings deems necessary for the purpose of attempting to improve my appearance with respect to the following conditions. . . . facial . . . chin deformity." In her testimony plaintiff admitted that she considered the surgery under her chin to be part of the face lift. Defendant's failure to provide the chin implant may serve as a legitimate complaint in challenging the amount of the fee or in a contract action. The omission does not, however, constitute battery. The trial court correctly removed the issue of battery from jury consideration. . . .

6. *Substituted Consent.* The law generally protects a person's right to do what she wishes with her own body. Where the choice will impose a heavy burden upon society, should the right to choose be withdrawn? When the person is unable to make the choice, and the lack of a choice may impose a heavy burden upon society, whose choice should be substituted? Is there an institution which represents the "state" which is in a better position to make the choice than the family of the person?

The elderly hospital patient in *In re Westchester County Med. Center on Behalf of O'Connor,* 72 N.Y.2d 517, 531 N.E.2d 607, 534 N.Y.S.2d 886 (1988), was mentally incompetent and unable to obtain food or drink without medical assistance. Her daughters objected to the insertion of a nasogastric tube to provide her with sustenance. The court stated that:

> It has long been the common-law rule in this State that a person has the right to decline medical treatment, even lifesaving treatment, absent an overriding State interest. In 1981, we held, in two companion cases, that a hospital or medical facility must respect this right even when a patient becomes incompetent, if while competent, the patient stated that he or she did not want certain procedures to be employed under specified circumstances (*In re Storar and In re Eichner, in* 52 N.Y.2d 363, 438 N.Y.S.2d 266, 420 N.E.2d 64 (1981), *cert. denied,* 454 U.S. 858, 70 L. Ed. 2d 153, 102 S.Ct. 309 (1981)). In *Storar,* involving a retarded adult suffering from terminal cancer, who needed blood transfusions to keep him from bleeding to death, we declined to direct termination of the treatment because it was impossible to determine what his wish would have been were he competent and it would be improper for a court to substitute its judgment for the unascertainable wish of the patient. Commenting on this latter principle in a subsequent case we noted that the right to decline treatment is personal and, under existing law in this State, could not be exercised by a third party when the patient is unable to do so.
>
> In contrast to the patient in *Storar,* the patient in *Eichner* had been competent and capable of expressing his will before he was silenced by illness. In those circumstances, we concluded that it would be appropriate for the court to intervene and direct the termination of artificial life supports, in accordance with the patient's wishes, because it was established by "clear and convincing evidence" that the patient would have so directed if he were competent and able to communicate. We selected the "clear and convincing evidence" standard in *Eichner* because it " 'impress[es] the factfinder with the importance of the decision' . . . and it 'forbids relief whenever the evidence is loose, equivocal or contradictory' " (*Matter of Storar, supra,* at 379). Nothing less than unequivocal proof will suffice when the decision to terminate life supports is at
>
> In *Eichner,* we had no difficulty finding "clear and convincing" evidence of the patient's wishes. Brother Fox, the patient in *Eichner*, was a member of a religious order who had conscientiously discussed his moral and personal views concerning the use of a respirator on persons in a vegetative state. The conclusion that "he carefully reflected on the subject . . . [was] supported by his religious beliefs and [was] not inconsistent with his life of unselfish religious devotion." Further, his expressions were "solemn pronouncements and not casual remarks made at some social gathering, nor c[ould] it be said that he was too young to realize or feel the consequences of his statements." Indeed, because the facts in Brother Fox's case were so clear, we had no need to elaborate upon the kind of showing necessary to satisfy the "clear and convincing" standard.

The facts in this case present a much closer question and require us to explore in more detail the application of that standard in this context. . . .

At the outset . . . our focus must always be on what the patient would say if asked today whether the treatment in issue should be terminated. However, we can never be completely certain of the answer to our question, since the inquiry assumes that the patient is no longer able to express his or her wishes. Most often, therefore, the inquiry turns on interpretation of statements on the subject made by the patient in the past. This exercise presents inherent problems.

For example, there always exists the possibility that, despite his or her clear expressions in the past, the patient has since changed his or her mind. . . . Thus, almost inevitably, the medical circumstances in the mind of the patient at the time the statements were made will not coincide perfectly with those which give rise to the need for the inquiry. In addition, there exists the danger that the statements were made without the reflection and resolve that would be brought to bear on the issue if the patient were presently capable of making the decision.

But the existence of these problems does not lead inevitably to the conclusion that we should abandon the inquiry entirely and adopt as guideposts the objective factors used in the so-called "substituted judgment" approach. That approach remains unacceptable because it is inconsistent with our fundamental commitment to the notion that no person or court should substitute its judgment as to what would be an acceptable quality of life for another. Consequently, we adhere to the view that, despite its pitfalls and inevitable uncertainties, the inquiry must always be narrowed to the patient's expressed intent, with every effort made to minimize the opportunity for error. . . .

The ideal situation is one in which the patient's wishes were expressed in some form of a writing, perhaps a "living will," while he or she was still competent. The existence of a writing suggests the author's seriousness of purpose and ensures that the court is not being asked to make a life-or-death decision based upon casual remarks. Further, a person who has troubled to set forth his or her wishes in a writing is more likely than one who has not to make sure that any subsequent changes of heart are adequately expressed, either in a new writing or through clear statements to relatives and friends. In contrast, a person whose expressions of intention were limited to oral statements may not as fully appreciate the need to "rescind" those statements after a change of heart.

Although Mrs. O'Connor's statements about her desire to decline life-saving treatments were repeated over a number of years, there is nothing, other than speculation, to persuade the fact finder that her expressions were more than immediate reactions to the unsettling experience of seeing or hearing of another's unnecessarily prolonged death. Her comments — that she would never want to lose her dignity before she passed away, that nature should be permitted to take its course, that it is "monstrous" to use life-support machinery — are, in fact, no different than those that many of us might make after witnessing an agonizing death. Similarly, her statements to the effect that she would not want to be a burden to anyone are the type of statements that older people frequently, almost invariably make. If such statements were routinely held to be clear and convincing proof of a general intent to decline all medical treatment once incompetency sets in, few nursing home patients would ever receive life-sustaining medical treatment in the future. The aged and infirm would be placed at grave risk if the law uniformly but unrealistically treated the expression of such sentiments as a calm and deliberate resolve to decline all life-sustaining medical assistance once the speaker is silenced by mental disability. . . .

We do not mean to suggest that, to be effective, a patient's expressed desire to decline treatment must specify a precise condition and a particular treatment. . . . Nevertheless, it is relevant to the fundamental question — the patient's desires — to consider whether the infirmities she was concerned with and the procedures she eschewed are qualitatively different than those now presented. Not that the exact nature of her condition would be dispositive in this analysis — it is but another element to be considered in the context of determining whether her pronouncement made on some previous occasion bears relevance to her present condition.

[Mrs. O'Connor's] statements with respect to declining artificial means of life support were generally prompted by her experience with persons suffering terminal illnesses, particularly cancer. However, Mrs. O'Connor does not have a terminal illness, except in the sense that she is aged and infirm. Neither is she in a coma nor vegetative state. She is awake and conscious; she can feel pain, responds to simple commands, can carry on limited conversations, and is not experiencing any pain. She is simply an elderly person who as a result of several strokes suffers certain disabilities, including an inability to feed herself or eat in a normal manner. She is in a stable condition and if properly nourished will remain in that condition unless some other medical problem arises. Because of her age and general physical condition, her life expectancy is not great. But that is true of many nursing home patients. The key thing that sets her apart — though there are likely thousands like her — is her inability to eat or obtain nourishment without medical assistance.

It is true, of course, that in her present condition she cannot care for herself or survive without medical assistance and that she has stated that she never wanted to be a burden and would not want to live, or be kept alive "artificially" if she could not care for herself. But no one contends, and it should not be assumed, that she contemplated declining medical assistance when her prognosis was uncertain. Here both medical experts agreed that she will never regain sufficient mental ability to care for herself, but it is not clear from the record that the loss of her gag reflex is permanent and that she will never be able to obtain food and drink without medical assistance.

C. SELF-DEFENSE AND DEFENSE OF OTHERS

... In sum, on this record it cannot be said that Mrs. O'Connor elected to die under circumstances such as these. Even her daughters, who undoubtedly know her wishes better than anyone, are earnestly trying to carry them out, and whose motives we believe to be of the highest and most loving kind, candidly admit that they do not know what she would do, or what she would want done under these circumstances.

Who is responsible for the future medical expenses of such a patient? Suppose she suffers further complications, and dies after a painful illness? Can the hospital be found liable for this pain and suffering? Can Mrs. O'Connor's children take her home from the hospital? If they do so and then withhold the medical treatment applied for here, with the resulting death of their mother, could they be held liable for her wrongful death?

See also Cruzan v. Director, Missouri Dep't of Health, 497 U.S. 261, 111 L. Ed. 2d 224, 110 S. Ct. 2841 (1990) (state could require "clear and convincing" evidence of incompetent's wishes as to whether to terminate life-sustaining treatment).

Compare *Curran v. Bosze,* 141 Ill. 2d 473, 566 N.E. 2d 1319 (1990), where the Court found it not in the best interest of 3½-year-old twins to require them to donate bone marrow to their 12-year-old half brother, who was suffering from bone cancer. The twins' mother objected, their natural father (and father of the twins' half brother) did not have custody of the twins, and the chances of successful treatment of the half brother were small. The danger to the twins from general anesthesia required for the operation was small, but grave.

C. SELF-DEFENSE AND DEFENSE OF OTHERS

BRADLEY v. HUNTER
413 So. 2d 674 (La. Ct. App. 1982)

CUTRER, JUDGE.

The shooting death of J.W. Bradley (J.W.) took place at approximately 9.00 P.M., on May 14, 1980, in Campti, Louisiana. J. W. was shot by defendant, Aurila F. Hunter (Aurila), in front of the "Honeydripper Cafe" which is operated by Aurila and her mother, Ora Edwards (Ora), also named as a defendant in this suit.

Plaintiff, Susie Mae Bradley, "wife"[1] of decedent, filed this suit on her own behalf and that of her four children seeking damages for the death of her "husband," and the loss of the children's father. J.W. is survived by four children, the last of which was born posthumously. . . . Aurila testified that J. W., a twenty-eight-year-old man, came into the "Honeydripper" around 9:00 to 9:30 P.M., May 14, 1980, wanting to purchase a soft drink ("coke"). Aurila is sixty-five years old, not in particularly good health, unmarried and lives

---

[1] Susie Mae Bradley was not legally married to J.W. Bradley during their relationship which was one of concubinage. However, all children born of that relationship are the natural children of J.W. Bradley and Susie Mae Darby (Bradley).

with her eighty-two-year-old mother, Ora, who owns the cafe. Ora,[2] a widow, also in poor health and under a doctor's care, works in the cafe with Aurila. No one else is employed in the restaurant. The cafe sells food, a little beer and no hard liquor.

Aurila testified at trial that she has had trouble with J. W. on at least two prior occasions and told him not to come into the cafe. That night J. W. entered wanting his "coke" but Aurila refused to serve him. Ora offered J.W. the "coke" but he refused. J. W. began to threaten and curse Aurila who restrained herself despite his cursing the two old women. She told him to go home. He did not leave until he had finished cursing and threatening Aurila.

A Smith & Wesson Model 10.38 caliber revolver was kept under the counter near the cash register. While J. W. remained in the store Aurila did not pick up the gun but she did so after he had left. J. W. walked out of the cafe cursing and threatening the women. After he had left, Ora went outside to see if J. W. had gone. Aurila went out onto the porch to see about her mother. As she stood on the porch, Aurila saw J.W. coming toward her, walking rapidly, as she said he had a tendency to do, with his arms flailing away, fists clenched, and cursing and threatening her. She then pulled the gun from her blouse pocket and told J.W. not to come to the cafe. She fired one warning shot (probably two, as three shots were fired but only one hit J.W.), and fired again whenever J. W. kept coming, walking fast, cursing and threatening Aurila. She fired from about thirty feet away; the bullet struck J.W. in the head, killing him.

Aurila testified that J. W. had threatened her two weeks before the incident in question, after she had refused to sell him some beer. She stated that he threatened to "get her" should she go outside to the mailbox. From that time until the incident in question, Aurila stated that she did not go to the mailbox for fear of J. W. She stated that she had known J. W. since he was a small child and knew of his reputation in the community. Aurila stated that she knew J. W. had previously shot a man in the back with a shotgun. Also, she saw him strike another person across the back with a crutch for refusing him a drink of wine. J. W.'s "wife" and aunt both stated that he had spent considerable periods of time in jail. Plaintiff stated that since they began living together in 1972 or 1973, he had spent over one-half of the time in prison. Deputy Dowden, an investigating officer, stated that he had known the decedent due to having received calls about him and his prior arrests. He further testified that J. W. was very belligerent toward the law enforcement officers; he had made threats to them and felt he was capable of carrying them out.

. . . As can be gleaned from the testimony presented by plaintiff, J. W. was considered to be less than a model citizen. He was known to have a quick temper and violent propensities. He was a young man of twenty-eight who had threatened, cursed and intimidated two old women aged sixty-five and eighty-two. At the time of the shooting J. W. was walking rapidly toward the two women, who were standing on their porch. He was cursing and throwing his arms about in a threatening manner. A warning both verbally and by a

---

[2] Ora did not testify at trial due to bad health.

C. SELF-DEFENSE AND DEFENSE OF OTHERS

discharge of the gun failed to dissuade J.W. from his continued harassment of Aurila and Ora. Aurila fired again in fear of her and her mother's safety, killing J.W. Aurila stated that she was really fearful for her and her mother's safety at the time of the incident.

. . . The law applicable to a case of this kind is clear and well settled. In the case of *Roberts v. American Employers Ins. Co.*, 221 So. 2d 550 (La. Ct. App. 1969), this court stated as follows:

> The privilege of self-defense in tort actions is now well recognized by our jurisprudence. Where a person reasonably believes he is threatened with bodily harm, he may use whatever force appears to be reasonably necessary to protect against the threatened injury. . . . Of course, each case depends on its own facts, such as, for instance, the relative size, age and strength of the parties, their reputations for violence, who was the aggressor, the degree of physical harm reasonably feared and the presence or absence of weapons.

In summary, the trial judge found decedent, J.W. Bradley, to be a man "*of a pugnacious and aggressive nature, with a long record, ever since he had been an adult, and perhaps even before, a long record of violence, which brought him into contact with the law.*" The trial judge pointed out that J.W. had spent about four of the last nine years in prison. J.W. had been warned on prior occasions to stay out of the "Honeydripper Cafe," yet he refused; he entered the cafe that fateful night cursing and threatening the two elderly women who operated it. He refused to leave, despite their request, until he had sufficiently cursed them. Aurila took the gun with her when she went onto the porch to see about her mother who had gone out to see if J.W. had left:

> "Then, with the passage of some period of time, here he comes back again, rushing at her with his fists balled up and walking at her and threatening her, while she stood on her own porch. She warned him. Her testimony was that she told him, 'Go away.' She fired a warning shot. Even Mr. Kirkendoll, who was cold sober, according to his testimony, testified that the first shot did not hit Bradley. And his testimony was that Bradley was not hit and said something to her, or something of that nature. But, this didn't slow him down. He kept on coming at her. The evidence, as a whole, indicates to me that the decedent made Mrs. Hunter shoot him. And the finding of the Court is that this was a case of justifiable self-defense and the motion for the directed verdict is granted in favor of the defendant. The case is dismissed."

From our perusal of the record, we conclude that the trial court was correct in finding that Aurila acted in self-defense.

Plaintiff cites the case of *Brasseaux v. Girouard*, 269 So. 2d 590 (La. Ct. App. 1972), *writ denied*, 271 So. 2d 262 (La. 1973), as a basis for the contention that Aurila did not shoot in self-defense. We disagree. In *Brasseaux*, self-defense was disallowed. It is, however, clearly distinguishable from the case at hand.

In *Brasseaux*, the plaintiff and defendant were involved in a boundary dispute. On the day in question, during daylight hours, plaintiff and defendant each drove their vehicles to an open pasture. A fence separated the parties. Accompanying defendant in his pickup truck were four men: defendant's brother-in-law, a son-in-law and two nephews. Brasseaux was accompanied by one person who remained in the vehicle during the incident. Defendant got out of his truck with a shotgun and stood behind his truck as Brasseaux walked from his vehicle toward the fence. When Brasseaux was near the fence, defendant shot him while he was thirty-five feet away and had made no effort to cross the fence. The court observed as follows:

> ". . . Girouard's position behind the truck near four relatives and armed with an automatic shotgun was ample protection from Brasseaux who was at least 35 feet away, alone and not making an attempt to cross the fence. To the argument that Girouard feared that Brasseaux's hidden hand concealed a weapon, we state that Girouard had the drop on Brasseaux and could have readily ascertained that Brasseaux was unarmed. . . ."

The court concluded that:

> ". . . We do not feel that under the circumstances presented here a reasonable person would or could have believed in good faith that it was necessary for him to shoot plaintiff in self defense."

In the case at hand, Aurila and her mother did not have the protection of four men, the fence or truck. Under the circumstances of this case, Aurila, as a reasonable person, could have believed in good faith that it was necessary for her to shoot J.W. to prevent bodily harm to her and/or her mother.

[Affirmed.]

NOTES

1. *Defense Against "Ordinary" Harm.* In *Boston v. Muncy,* 204 Okla. 603, 233 P.2d 300 (1951), plaintiff and defendant argued over a commercial matter. Defendant contended that "plaintiff called him a liar and hit him with his fist," and that defendant "then struck plaintiff in self-defense." The court held it was error for the trial court to refuse to instruct "that one who is assaulted or interfered with by another without provocation may use sufficient force to repel the attack without being guilty of assault even though he may not believe himself to be in danger of great bodily harm."

2. *Limitations on the Right of Self-Defense.* The privilege to use force to defend one's self is narrowly circumscribed. When the assault or battery is no longer threatened, the privilege ends. One may use only reasonable force, *i.e.,* the force that reasonably appears necessary to protect against the threatened harm. A person may not use force likely to cause death or great bodily harm unless he has a reasonable apprehension of suffering the same kind of harm from the threatened conduct.

In *Courvoisier v. Raymond,* 23 Colo. 113, 47 P. 284 (1896), the defendant repelled some rioters, who broke into his house at night, by firing a pistol at them. The firing attracted the plaintiff, a police officer, whom the defendant shot as the plaintiff was proceeding toward him, the defendant mistaking the plaintiff for one of the rioters.

The trial judge instructed the jury. "[I]f you believe, from the evidence, that, at the time the defendant shot the plaintiff, the plaintiff was not assaulting the defendant, then your verdict should be for the plaintiff." The appellate court held this instruction was erroneous. The court found that a "riot was in progress, and the defendant swears he was attacked with missiles, hit with stones, brickbats, etc." Defendant testified:

> "I saw a man come away from the bunch of men, and come up towards me, and as I looked around I saw this man put his hand to his hip pocket. I didn't think I had time to jump aside, and therefore turned around and fired at him. I had no doubts but it was somebody that had come to rob me, because some weeks before, Mr. Wilson's store was robbed. It is next door to mine."

The court held that self-defense was indicated as the evidence for the defendant was "such as to lead a reasonable man to believe that his life was in danger, or that he was in danger of receiving great bodily harm at the hands of the plaintiff, and the defendant testified that he did so believe." *Accord* RESTATEMENT (SECOND) OF TORTS § 75.

Assume that defendant did make a reasonable mistake as to the identity of the assailant, but then opened fire from his premises with a semi-automatic weapon, spraying the crowd outside. What issues arise in the actions brought by those injured?

3. *Defense of Others.* RESTATEMENT (SECOND) OF TORTS § 76 provides:

> The actor is privileged to defend a third person from a harmful or offensive contact or other invasion of his interests of personality under the same conditions and by the same means as those under and by which he is privileged to defend himself if the actor correctly or reasonably believes that:
>
> > (a) the circumstances are such as to give the third person a privilege of self-defense, and
> >
> > (b) his intervention is necessary for the protection of the third person.

The Restatement represents the majority rule. Under the minority rule, the actor takes the risk of whether the person on whose behalf he interferes is actually privileged to defend himself.

The court in *Wardlaw v. Pickett,* 1 F.3d 1297 (D.C. Cir.1993), held that justifiable defense of another was a defense to a tort action brought against the intervening defender, but that the defender could not use the justified intervention as a basis for suing the attacker for injuries received in the intervention. This holding is contrary to cases that allow justified intervention as a basis for the intervenor to sue in tort for resulting injuries. See *Dixon v. Richer,* 922 F.2d 1456 (10th Cir. 1991); *Gortarez v. Smitty's Super Valu, Inc.,* 680 P. 2d 807 (Ariz. 1984).

4. *Mistake.* Suppose a person mistakenly trespasses on A's land, and then mistakenly undertakes to defend herself against A— both mistakes being reasonably made? *See* RESTATEMENT (SECOND) OF TORTS § 72. (An actor is not privileged to defend against force which another is privileged to use, unless

the other's privilege is based on a reasonable mistake of fact not caused by the actors fault).

D. DEFENSE OF PROPERTY

PROBLEM

Eric Pitfall owns a convenience store at the corner of Regent and Oxford. Recently, there have been several robberies at night at the store. Particularly popular amongst the criminal fraternity has been the cash left in the vending machines located in the entrance to the store. Eric, determined to abort this local crime wave, removed all the candy bars from one of the vending machines, and replaced them with several sticks of dynamite, wired to explode if the lock was forced. Seven-year-old Nigel, who was trying burglary for the first time, broke into the convenience store and was severely maimed when the machine exploded. Would Eric succeed with a plea of defense of property?

Assume in the alternative that Eric was a frail 90-year-old who had been severely beaten by 24-year-old Thug during a robbery at the convenience store the previous week. Eric has set a remote control trigger for the vending machine booby-trap. Eric triggers the trap when he sees Saul, Thug's twin brother, break into the convenience store late at night. Could Eric successfully urge defense of property?

KATKO v. BRINEY
183 N.W.2d 657 (Iowa 1971)

MOORE, CHIEF JUSTICE.

The primary issue presented here is whether an owner may protect personal property in an unoccupied boarded-up farm house against trespassers and thieves by a spring gun capable of inflicting death or serious injury.

We are not here concerned with a man's right to protect his home and members of his family. Defendants' home was several miles from the scene of the incident to which we refer *infra*.

Plaintiff's action is for damages resulting from serious injury caused by a shot from a 20-gauge spring shotgun set by defendants in a bedroom of an old farm house which had been uninhabited for several years. Plaintiff and his companion, Marvin McDonough, had broken into and entered the house to find and steal old bottles and dated fruit jars which they considered antiques.

At defendants' request plaintiff's action was tried to a jury consisting of residents of the community where defendants' property was located. The jury returned a verdict for plaintiff and against defendants for $20,000 actual and $10,000 punitive damages.

After careful consideration of defendants' motions for judgment notwithstanding the verdict and for new trial, the experienced and capable trial judge overruled them and entered judgment on the verdict. Thus we have this appeal by defendants.

D. DEFENSE OF PROPERTY

. . . Most of the facts are not disputed. In 1957 defendant Bertha L. Briney inherited her parents' farm land in Mahaska and Monroe Counties. Included was an 80-acre tract in southwest Mahaska County where her grandparents and parents had lived. No one occupied the house thereafter. Her husband, Edward, attempted to care for the land. He kept no farm machinery thereon. The outbuildings became dilapidated.

For about 10 years, 1957 to 1967, there occurred a series of trespassing and housebreaking events with loss of some household items, the breaking of windows and "messing up of the property in general." The latest occurred June 8, 1967, prior to the event on July 16, 1967 herein involved.

Defendants through the years boarded up the windows and doors in an attempt to stop the intrusions. They had posted "no trespass" signs on the land several years before 1967. The nearest one was 35 feet from the house. On June 11, 1967 defendants set "a shotgun trap" in the north bedroom. After Mr. Briney cleaned and oiled his 20-gauge shotgun, the power of which he was well aware, defendants took it to the old house where they secured it to an iron bed with the barrel pointed at the bedroom door. It was rigged with wire from the doorknob to the gun's trigger so it would fire when the door was opened. Briney first pointed the gun so an intruder would be hit in the stomach but at Mrs. Briney's suggestion it was lowered to hit the legs. He admitted he did so "because I was mad and tired of being tormented" but "he did not intend to injure anyone." He gave no explanation of why he used a loaded shell and set it to hit a person already in the house. Tin was nailed over the bedroom window. The spring gun could not be seen from the outside. No warning of its presence was posted.

. . . Prior to July 16, 1967 plaintiff and McDonough had been to the premises and found several old bottles and fruit jars which they took and added to their collection of antiques. On the latter date about 9.30 p.m. they made a second trip to the Briney property. They entered the old house by removing a board from a porch window which was without glass. While McDonough was looking around the kitchen area plaintiff went to another part of the house. As he started to open the north bedroom door the shotgun went off striking him in the right leg above the ankle bone. Much of his leg, including part of the tibia, was blown away. Only by McDonough's assistance was plaintiff able to get out of the house and after crawling some distance was put in his vehicle and rushed to a doctor and then to a hospital. He remained in the hospital 40 days.

. . . There was undenied medical testimony plaintiff had a permanent deformity, a loss of tissue, and a shortening of the leg.

. . . Plaintiff testified he knew he had no right to break into and enter the house with intent to steal bottles and fruit jars therefrom. He further testified he had entered a plea of guilty to larceny in the nighttime of property of less than $20 value from a private building. He stated he had been fined $50 and costs and paroled during good behavior from a 60-day jail sentence. Other than minor traffic charges, this was plaintiff's first brush with the law. . . . The main thrust of defendants' defense in the trial court and on this appeal is that "the law permits use of a spring gun in a dwelling or warehouse for the purpose of preventing the unlawful entry of a burglar or thief. . . ."

In the statement of issues the trial court stated plaintiff and his companion committed a felony when they broke into and entered defendants' house. In instruction 2 the court referred to the early case history of the use of spring guns and stated under the law their use was prohibited except to prevent the commission of felonies of violence and where human life is in danger. The instruction included a statement that breaking and entering is not a felony of violence.

Instruction 5 stated: "You are hereby instructed that one may use reasonable force in the protection of his property, but such right is subject to the qualification that one may not use such means of force as will take human life or inflict great bodily injury. Such is the rule even though the injured party is a trespasser and is in violation of the law himself."

Instruction 6 stated: "An owner of premises is prohibited from willfully or intentionally injuring a trespasser by means of force that either takes life or inflicts great bodily injury; and therefore a person owning a premise is prohibited from setting out 'spring guns' and like dangerous devices which will likely take life or inflict great bodily injury, for the purpose of harming trespassers. The fact that the trespasser may be acting in violation of the law does not change the rule. The only time when such conduct of setting a 'spring gun' or a like dangerous device is justified would be when the trespasser was committing a felony of violence or a felony punishable by death, or where the trespasser was endangering human life by his act."

Instruction 7, to which defendants made no objection or exception, stated: "To entitle the plaintiff to recover for compensatory damages, the burden of proof is upon him to establish by a preponderance of the evidence each and all of the following propositions:

"1. That defendants erected a shotgun trap in a vacant house on land owned by defendant, Bertha L. Briney, on or about June 11, 1967, which fact was known only by them, to protect household goods from trespassers and thieves.

"2. That the force used by defendants was in excess of that force reasonably necessary and which persons are entitled to use in the protection of their property.

"3. That plaintiff was injured and damaged and the amount thereof.

"4. That plaintiff's injuries and damages resulted directly from the discharge of the shotgun trap which was set and used by defendants."

The overwhelming weight of authority, both textbook and case law, supports the trial court's statement of the applicable principles of law.

Prosser on Torts, Third Edition, pages 116-118, states:

". . . the law has always placed a higher value upon human safety than upon mere rights in property, it is the accepted rule that there is no privilege to use any force calculated to cause death or serious bodily injury to repel the threat to land or chattels, unless there is also such a threat to the defendant's personal safety as to justify self-defense. . . . [S]pring guns and other man-killing devices are not justifiable against a mere trespasser, or even a petty thief. They are privileged only upon those whom the landowner, if he were present in person would be free to inflict injury of the same kind."

Restatement of Torts, section 85, page 180, states: "The value of human life and limb, not only to the individual concerned but also to society, so outweighs the interest of a possessor of land in excluding from it those whom he is not willing to admit thereto that a possessor of land has, as is stated in § 79, no privilege to use force intended or likely to cause death or serious harm against another whom the possessor sees about to enter his premises or meddle with his chattel, unless the intrusion threatens death or serious bodily harm to the occupiers or users of the premises. . . . A possessor of land cannot do indirectly and by a mechanical device that which, were he present, he could not do immediately and in person. Therefore, he cannot gain a privilege to install, for the purpose of protecting his land from intrusions harmless to the lives and limbs of the occupiers or users of it, a mechanical device whose only purpose is to inflict death or serious harm upon such as may intrude, by giving notice of his intention to inflict, by mechanical means and indirectly, harm which he could not, even after request, inflict directly were he present."

In Volume 2, Harper and James, The Law of Torts, section 27.3, pages 1440, 1441, this is found: "The possessor of land may not arrange his premises intentionally so as to cause death or serious bodily harm to a trespasser. The possessor may of course take some steps to repel a trespass. If he is present he may use force to do so, but only that amount which is reasonably necessary to effect the repulse. Moreover if the trespass threatens harm to property only — even a theft of property — the possessor would not be privileged to use deadly force, he may not arrange his premises so that such force will be inflicted by mechanical means. If he does, he will be liable even to a thief who is injured by such device."

. . . The facts in *Allison v. Fiscus,* 156 Ohio St. 120, 100 N.E.2d 237, decided in 1951, are very similar to the case at bar. There plaintiff's right to damages was recognized for injuries received when he feloniously broke a door latch and started to enter defendant's warehouse with intent to steal. As he entered a trap of two sticks of dynamite buried under the doorway by defendant owner was set off and plaintiff [was] seriously injured. The court held the question whether a particular trap was justified as a use of reasonable and necessary force against a trespasser engaged in the commission of a felony should have been submitted to the jury. The Ohio Supreme Court recognized plaintiff's right to recover punitive or exemplary damages in addition to compensatory damages.

. . . In addition to civil liability many jurisdictions hold a landowner criminally liable for serious injuries or homicide caused by spring guns or other set devices. . . .

The legal principles stated by the trial court in instructions 2, 5 and 6 are well established and supported by the authorities cited and quoted *supra.* There is no merit in defendants' objections and exceptions thereto. Defendants' various motions based on the same reasons stated in exceptions to instructions were properly overruled. . . .

This opinion is not to be taken or construed as authority that the allowance of punitive damages is or is not proper under circumstances such as exist here. We hold only that question of law not having been properly raised cannot in this case be resolved. . . .

NOTES

1. *Sequels.* Subsequent to the decision in *Katko v. Briney,* the Nebraska legislature passed a law providing in part that "no person . . . shall be placed in jeopardy. . . for protecting, by any means necessary, himself, his family, or his real or personal property." However, the statute was held unconstitutional in *State v. Goodseal,* 186 Neb. 359, 183 N.W.2d 258, *cert. denied,* 404 U.S. 845, 92 S. Ct. 146, 30 L. Ed. 2d 82 (1971). The court held the statute unconstitutionally delegated to the defender the power to determine the amount and extent of force to be used in self-defense, this power being placed exclusively in the legislature by the state constitution. For a fascinating commentary on *Katko v. Briney,* see Palmer, *The Iowa Spring Gun Case. A Study in American Gothic,* 56 IOWA L. REV. 1219 (1971).

Assume that a landlord boarded up her disused property and set spring guns because she was concerned that criminals might use the property to commit violent crimes. Recall *Glick v. Olde Town Lancaster, Inc.,* 369 Pa. Super. 419, 535 A.2d 621 (1987), *app. denied,* 519 Pa. 665, 548 A.2d 255 (1988), discussed in Chapter 1, *supra.*

Does the existence of a criminal penalty provide a sufficient deterrence in cases such as this? *See People v. Ceballos,* 12 Cal. 3d 470, 116 Cal. Rptr. 233, 526 P.2d 241 (1974) (assault with deadly weapon conviction appropriate against property owner who set trap gun to prevent burglarizing of garage where he sometimes slept but was not so sleeping when his victim attempted to burglarize premises; the "if he were present" exception was inappropriate for criminal law, the court said, and there was no threat of death or serious bodily harm).

How would a case such as *Katko v. Briney* be decided in a state with a statute such as the Alaska provision discussed in the notes following *Colby v. McClendon,* given above?

2. *Defense of Real Property Cum Defense of Person.* Recall that in *Courvoisier v. Raymond,* 23 Colo. 113, 47 P. 284 (1896), discussed in the notes following *Bradley v. Hunter, supra,* the defendant opened fire from his premises upon someone he thought was a trespasser. Why was he permitted to use such deadly force?

3. *Less-Threatening Mechanical Devices.* The result in *Katko v. Briney* is endorsed by RESTATEMENT (SECOND) OF TORTS § 85. Note, however, RESTATEMENT (SECOND) OF TORTS § 84:

> The actor is so far privileged to employ, for the purpose of protecting his possession of land or chattels from intrusion, a device not intended or likely to cause death or serious bodily harm that he is not liable for bodily harm done thereby to a deliberate intruder, if
>
> (a) the use of such a device is reasonably necessary to protect the land or chattels from intrusion, and
>
> (b) the use of the particular device is reasonable under the circumstances, and
>
> (c) the device is one customarily used for such a purpose, or reasonable care is taken to make its use known to probable intruders.

D.   DEFENSE OF PROPERTY   201

What mechanical devices are contemplated by this provision? What criteria will you apply to determine reasonableness in subsections (a)–(c)? What judicial value preferences may be reflected in the application of "reasonable" in this situation? Should a "balancing" approach such as that used in § 84 be extended to the classic spring gun case? *See generally* Posner, *Killing or Wounding to Protect a Property Interest,* 14 J.L. & Econ. 201, 214-17 (1971).

4. *Repelling Trespassers.* According to RESTATEMENT (SECOND) OF TORTS § 77,

> An actor is privileged to use reasonable force, not intended or likely to cause death or serious bodily harm, to prevent or terminate another's intrusion upon the actor's land or chattels, if
>
> (a) the intrusion is not privileged or the other intentionally or negligently causes the actor to believe that it is not privileged, and
>
> (b) the actor reasonably believes that the intrusion can be prevented or terminated only by the force used, and
>
> (c) the actor has first requested the other to desist and the other has disregarded the request, or the actor reasonably believes that a request will be useless or that substantial harm will be done before it can be made.

Subsection (c) is related to the old common law plea of *molliter manus imposuit* ("he gently laid hands upon"), which well conveys the sense of how this kinder, gentler model of dispossession may be used as a defense in the trespasser's subsequent battery action. *See also* RESTATEMENT (SECOND) OF TORTS § 90 (necessity of demand to precede re-entry upon land).

5. *Defense of Personal Property.* The retaking of previously dispossessed chattels ("recaption") is governed by RESTATEMENT (SECOND) OF TORTS §§ 101–106. The defense is dependent upon tortious taking of the chattel by the plaintiff, typically without "claim of right," RESTATEMENT (SECOND) OF TORTS § 101, the immediate right to possession of the chattel by the defendant, § 102, and the defendant's attempted retaking occurring promptly after the dispossession, § 103. Consistent with other "self-help" activities associated with the protection of property, the Restatement encourages a pre-action demand, § 104, and prohibits force likely to cause death or serious injury, § 106. For example, in *Godwin v. Stanely,* 331 S.W.2d 341, 342 (Tex. Civ. App. 1959), an altercation began when defendant sought to "repossess" an accordion he had sold to plaintiffs. In affirming plaintiffs' judgment based upon battery, the court wrote that:

> We think this record clearly shows that the appellant [defendant] went to the home of appellees [plaintiff] with the idea of taking the accordion regardless of any protests on the part of the appellees. . . . [W]hen [defendant] insisted on looking for the accordion, and Mrs. Stanley ordered him from her home, he refused to leave, but started into the bedroom and then she stepped into the door and refused to permit him to proceed — this is what provoked the difficulty. We think she had this right. . . . If appellees were delinquent in their payments the appellant had a legal remedy to get possession of the accordion.

The taking of such possession, however, must be by legal action or must be effected peaceably; that is, the exercise of force or violence will not be permitted.

Is RESTATEMENT (SECOND) OF TORTS § 77, *given in the preceding note,* relevant? Did Mrs. Stanley comply with its terms?

PROBLEM

Defendant owns a field that is fenced. Plaintiff, because of a grudge he held against Defendant, enters the field and begins to systematically pull down Defendant's fence. Defendant observes this conduct for a few minutes and then shoots and wounds Plaintiff.

At trial Plaintiff argues that Defendant should have requested him to leave before shooting him. Defendant argues that Plaintiff was a violent trespasser to whom a warning need not have been given. Is either correct?

E. NECESSITY

HARRISON v. WISDOM
54 Tenn. 99 (1872)

SNEED, JUSTICE.

The defendants were, on the 17th of February, 1862, citizens of the city of Clarksville, and were present and participated in the proceedings of a public meeting of the citizens of said city, convened at the Mayor's office on that day. The meeting was called to concert measures for the protection of the people of said city in anticipation of an immediate invasion by the Federal forces, to whom Fort Donelson, which seems to have been regarded as the military key to Clarksville, had surrendered on the day preceding. The city of Clarksville was about thirty miles distant from Fort Donelson, and the occupation of the city was expected as the immediate result of the capitulation of the fort. There was at the time in the hands of merchants and dealers in the city a large quantity of whiskey and other spirituous liquors, which it was supposed would imperil the lives and property of the inhabitants if it should fall into the hands of the Federal soldiery, then flushed with victory and inflamed with the evil passions of civil war. It was therefore resolved by the citizens, convened as aforesaid, to destroy said spirituous liquors, as a measure of safety, and to recommend to the common council of said city, and to the county authorities, to levy a special tax upon the people in order to raise a fund for the reimbursement of those whose property should be thus destroyed. To this end agents were appointed to advise the owners of the resolution aforesaid, to invoke their acquiescence and to carry out the objects of the meeting. The plaintiff was the owner of a considerable quantity of whiskey, brandy, and wine stored in said city, and he was called upon by one of the agents, who advised him of the action of the meeting, and he thereupon delivered his key to his salesman, with instructions to deliver the liquors to the agent, by whom it was destroyed.

This action was brought by the plaintiff . . . to recover of defendants, who were among the citizens composing said meeting, the value of the liquors so destroyed. The cause was submitted to a jury on the general issue and the defendants' special plea of public necessity, and resulted in a verdict and judgment for the defendants, from which the plaintiff has appealed in error. . . .

We come now to consider the last and most important question involved in this case, and that is, whether the law of the case was correctly expounded to the jury. The defendants insist that at the time of the alleged trespass upon the plaintiff's property there existed an absolute public necessity for its destruction. The right of defense and self-preservation is a right inherent in communities as well as individuals. Whether an imminent and absolute necessity exists to destroy private property for the common good, is a question to be determined by a jury upon the facts of each particular case. An individual may take life to preserve his own, if he be in danger of death or great bodily harm, or think himself so upon reasonable grounds. But the grounds of his apprehension must be founded upon such facts as will acquit him of acting upon a mere fancied peril or with reckless incaution. The law is jealous in the protection it throws around human life and property, and the right to take either as a measure of self-preservation is to be exercised in a moment of extraordinary exigency when the private or public necessity absolutely demands it. The right to destroy property in cases of extreme emergency, as to prevent the spread of a conflagration, or as in the case now under consideration, is not the exercise of the right of eminent domain, nor the taking of property for public use, but a right existing at common law, founded on necessity, and it may be exercised by individuals in any proper case, free from all liability for the value of the property destroyed. . . . [F]amiliar examples are cited in the English books, as where the plaintiff's dog was killed in the act of pursuing the defendant's deer in his park, or rabbits in his warren, or poultry within his own grounds, this will justify the killing without the proof of any higher necessity. 2 Greenl. Ev., s. 630; 3 Lev., 28; Cro. Jac., 45; 1 Campb., 41; 11 East, 568. We have cited these general principles in the language of the books, to illustrate as nearly as possible the nature and character of that necessity which will justify the destruction of private property in like cases. It is difficult to define it except in general terms and each case must depend upon its own facts. An unsubstantial panic is not such a necessity, but such a state of facts must be shown as to leave no doubt of an impending and imminent peril, or that a reasonable ground existed for the apprehension of such a peril, to justify the act; or in the language of Mr. Greenleaf already cited, if the defendant justifies the destruction of the plaintiff's property by the defense of his own he must show he could not otherwise preserve his own property. 2 Greenl. Ev., 630. The advance of the hostile army is cited as among the exigencies when such a necessity might exist to justify the destruction of private property. But what kind of private property may be thus destroyed would depend much upon the character of the warfare waged at the time, and upon the circumstances existing in the community. Thus the destruction of a bridge or a boat, to check the advance of an army, or the explosion of a magazine of powder, or the destruction of munitions of war or military supplies, or any articles contraband or war, would be but the exercise of a recognized belligerent right, and the rapid advance of a hostile army known to be undisciplined and licentious, and whose occupation of captured places in the line of march was known to be accompanied by acts of besotted vandalism, imperiling the lives and property of the people, would upon the ground of public necessity justify the destruction of such property as is calculated to increase the public peril. But all these facts must enter into the consideration of the question whether the public peril did exist, or whether there were reasonable and substantial grounds to believe so. Necessity, says Lord Coke, makes that lawful which would be otherwise unlawful. 8 Coke, 69. It is the law of a particular time and place. Hale P.C., 54. It overcomes the law. Hob., 144; and it defends what it compels. Hale P.C., 54. In these brief maxims is written the whole reason of the law that justifies the destruction of private property for the public good. We are unable to discover wherein his honor the Circuit Judge has made any material departure from the principles herein announced, either in his general or supplemental charge. But, for the errors in his rulings upon questions of evidence, the judgment will be reversed and a new trial awarded.

NOTES

1. *Public Necessity.* According to RESTATEMENT (SECOND) OF TORTS § 262:

> One is privileged to commit an act which would otherwise be a trespass to a chattel or a conversion if the act is or is reasonably believed to be necessary for the purpose of avoiding a public disaster.

A similar rule applies in the case of trespass to land. One is privileged to enter land in the possession of another if it is, or if the actor reasonably believes it to be, "necessary for the purpose of averting an imminent public disaster." RESTATEMENT (SECOND) OF TORTS § 196.

The court stated in *Customer Co. v. City of Sacramento*, 10 Cal. 4th 368, 41 Cal. Rptr. 2d 658, 895 P.2d 900 (1995):

> A felony suspect, reputed to be armed and dangerous, took refuge in a store and refused to surrender. In the course of apprehending the suspect, the police fired tear gas into the store, causing extensive property damage. The issue we address is whether the owner of the store may bring an action for inverse condemnation against the public entities that employed the law enforcement officers, on the theory that the damage caused by the officers constituted a taking or damaging of private property for public use within the meaning of the "just compensation" clause of the California Constitution. (Ca. Const., art. I, § 19.)

Although the court noted a division of authority on the issue, it applied the majority rule, "the so-called emergency exception to the just compensation requirement," and held that the City was not liable under the takings provision of the Constitution:

> In the present case an action for inverse condemnation does not lie, because the efforts of the law enforcement officers to apprehend a felony suspect cannot be likened to an exercise of the power of eminent

domain. This is not a case in which law enforcement officers commandeered a citizen's automobile to chase a fleeing suspect, or appropriated ammunition from a private gun shop to replenish an inadequate supply. Conceivably, such unusual actions might constitute an exercise of eminent domain, because private property would be taken for public use.

Suppose an employee of the store had been physically injured by the tear gas. Would the City be liable to the employee?

2. *Necessity of War.* In *United States v. Caltex (Philippines), Inc.,* 344 U.S. 149, 73 S. Ct. 200, 97 L. Ed. 157 (1952), *reh. denied,* 344 U.S. 919, 73 S. Ct. 345, 97 L. Ed. 708 (1953), the Court held that the U.S. Army was justified in destroying plaintiff's petroleum dump to prevent its capture by the advancing enemy. This was not a compensable taking under the United States Constitution. But in *Burmah Oil Co. v. Lord Advocate,* [1964] 2 All E.R. 348, the court held the Crown was required to provide compensation under similar circumstances. Note that the Restatement is neutral on the issue of any liability for harm in public necessity cases. RESTATEMENT (SECOND) OF TORTS § 196, comment h.

VINCENT v. LAKE ERIE TRANSPORTATION CO.
109 Minn. 456, 124 N.W. 221 (1910)

O'BRIEN, JUSTICE.

The steamship Reynolds, owned by the defendant, was for the purpose of discharging her cargo on November 27, 1905, moored to plaintiffs' dock in Duluth. While the unloading of the boat was taking place a storm from the northeast developed, which at about ten o'clock p.m., when the unloading was completed, had so grown in violence that the wind was then moving at fifty miles per hour and continued to increase during the night. There is some evidence that one, and perhaps two, boats were able to enter the harbor that night, but it is plain that navigation was practically suspended from the hour mentioned until the morning of the twenty ninth, when the storm abated, and during that time no master would have been justified in attempting to navigate his vessel, if he could avoid doing so. After the discharge of the cargo the Reynolds signaled for a tug to tow her from the dock, but none could be obtained because of the severity of the storm. If the lines holding the ship to the dock had been cast off, she would doubtless have drifted away; but, instead, the lines were kept fast, and as soon as one parted or chafed it was replaced, sometimes with a larger one. The vessel lay upon the outside of the dock, her bow to the east, the wind and waves striking her starboard quarter with such force that she was constantly being lifted and thrown against the dock, resulting in its damage, as found by the jury, to the amount of $500.

We are satisfied that the character of the storm was such that it would have been highly imprudent for the master of the Reynolds to have attempted to leave the dock or to have permitted his vessel to drift away from it. One witness testified upon the trial that the vessel could have been warped into a slip, and that, if the attempt to bring the ship into the slip had failed, the worst that could have happened would be that the vessel would have been blown ashore upon a soft and muddy bank. The witness was not present in Duluth at the time of the storm, and, while he may have been right in his conclusions, those in charge of the dock and the vessel at the time of the storm were not required to use the highest human intelligence, nor were they required to resort to every possible experiment which could be suggested for the preservation of their property. Nothing more was demanded of them than ordinary prudence and care, and the record in this case fully sustains the contention of the appellant that, in holding the vessel fast to the dock, those in charge of her exercised good judgment and prudent seamanship.

It is claimed by the respondent that it was negligence to moor the boat at an exposed part of the wharf, and to continue in that position after it became apparent that the storm was to be more than usually severe. We do not agree with this position. The part of the wharf where the vessel was moored appears to have been commonly used for that purpose. It was situated within the harbor at Duluth, and must, we think, be considered a proper and safe place, and would undoubtedly have been such during what would be considered a very severe storm. The storm which made it unsafe was one which surpassed in violence any which might have reasonably been anticipated.

The appellant contends . . . that, because its conduct during the storm was rendered necessary by prudence and good seamanship under conditions over which it had no control, it cannot be held liable for any injury resulting to the property of others, and claims that the jury should have been so instructed. An analysis of the charge given by the trial court is not necessary, as in our opinion the only question for the jury was the amount of damages which the plaintiffs were entitled to recover, and no complaint is made upon that score.

The situation was one in which the ordinary rules regulating property rights were suspended by forces beyond human control, and if, without the direct intervention of some act by the one sought to be held liable, the property of another was injured, such injury must be attributed to the act of God, and not to the wrongful act of the person sought to be charged. If during the storm the Reynolds had entered the harbor, and while there had become disabled and been thrown against the plaintiffs' dock, the plaintiffs could not have recovered. Again, if while attempting to hold fast to the dock the lines had parted, without any negligence, and the vessel carried against some other boat or dock in the harbor, there would be no liability upon her owner. But here those in charge of the vessel deliberately and by their direct efforts held her in such a position that the damage to the dock resulted, and, having thus preserved the ship at the expense of the dock, it seems to us that her owners are responsible to the dock owners to the extent of the injury inflicted.

In *Depue v. Flateau,* 100 Minn. 299, 111 N.W. 1 (1907), this court held that where the plaintiff, while lawfully in the defendants' house, became so ill that he was incapable of traveling with safety, the defendants were responsible to him in damages for compelling him to leave the premises. If, however, the owner of the premises had furnished the traveler with proper accommodations and medical attendance, would he have been able to defeat an action brought against him for their reasonable worth?

In *Ploof v. Putnam,* 81 Vt. 471, 71 A. 188 (1908), the supreme court of Vermont held that where, under stress of weather, a vessel was without permission moored to a private dock at an island in Lake Champlain owned by the defendant, the plaintiff was not guilty of trespass, and that the defendant was responsible in damages because his representative upon the island unmoored the vessel, permitting it to drift upon the shore, with resultant injuries to it. If, in that case, the vessel had been permitted to remain, and the dock had suffered an injury, we believe the shipowner would have been held liable for the injury done.

Theologians hold that a starving man may, without moral guilt, take what is necessary to sustain life; but it could hardly be said that the obligation would not be upon such person to pay the value of the property so taken when he became able to do so. And so public necessity, in times of war or peace, may require the taking of private property for public purposes; but under our system of jurisprudence compensation must be made.

Let us imagine in this case that for the better mooring of the vessel those in charge of her had appropriated a valuable cable lying upon the dock. No matter how justifiable such appropriation might have been, it would not be claimed that, because of the overwhelming necessity of the situation, the owner of the cable could not recover its value.

This is not a case where life or property was menaced by any object or thing belonging to the plaintiffs, the destruction of which became necessary to prevent the threatened disaster. Nor is it a case where, because of the act of God, or unavoidable accident, the infliction of the injury was beyond the control of the defendant, but is one where the defendant prudently and advisedly availed itself of the plaintiffs' property for the purpose of preserving its own more valuable property, and the plaintiffs are entitled to compensation for the injury done.

LEWIS, JUSTICE, dissenting.

I dissent. It was assumed on the trial before the lower court that appellant's liability depended on whether the master of the ship might, in the exercise of reasonable care, have sought a place of safety before the storm made it impossible to leave the dock. The majority opinion assumes that the evidence is conclusive that appellant moored its boat at respondents' dock pursuant to contract, and that the vessel was lawfully in position at the time the additional cables were fastened to the dock, and the reasoning of the opinion is that, because appellant made use of the stronger cables to hold the boat in position, it became liable under the rule that it had voluntarily made use of the property of another for the purpose of saving its own.

In my judgment, if the boat was lawfully in position at the time the storm broke, and the master could not, in the exercise of due care, have left that position without subjecting his vessel to the hazards of the storm, then the damage to the dock, caused by the pounding of the boat, was the result of an inevitable accident. If the master was in the exercise of due care, he was not at fault. The reasoning of the opinion admits that if the ropes, or cables, first attached to the dock had not parted, or if, in the first instance, the master had used the stronger cables, there would be no liability. If the master could not, in the exercise of reasonable care, have anticipated the severity of the storm and sought a place of safety before it became impossible, why should he be required to anticipate the severity of the storm, and, in the first instance, use the stronger cables?

I am of the opinion that one who constructs a dock to the navigable line of waters, and enters into contractual relations with the owner of a vessel to moor the same, takes the risk of damage to his dock by a boat caught there by a storm, which event could not have been avoided in the exercise of due care, and further, that the legal status of the parties in such a case is not changed by renewal of cables to keep the boat from being cast adrift at the mercy of the tempest.

NOTES

1. *Private Necessity*. The defense of private necessity is endorsed by RESTATEMENT (SECOND) OF TORTS § 197:

(1) One is privileged to enter or remain on land in the possession of another if it is or reasonably appears to be necessary to prevent serious harm to

(a) the actor, or his land or chattels, or

(b) the other or a third person, or the land or chattels of either, unless the actor knows or has reason to know that the one for whose benefit he enters is unwilling that he shall take such action.

(2) Where the entry is for the benefit of the actor or a third person, [the entrant] is subject to liability for any harm done in the exercise of the privilege stated in Subsection (1) to any legally protected interest of the possessor in the land or connected with it, except where the threat of harm to avert which the entry is made is caused by the tortious conduct or contributory negligence of the possessor.

A similar rule applies to interference with chattels, RESTATEMENT (SECOND) OF TORTS § 263.

2. *Necessity, Fault and Scope of the Risk*. The privilege of necessity does not apply if the peril which the actor seeks to avoid is one caused by his own fault. It then may be said that the damage he sought to avoid, and resulting damage to the plaintiff's property, were within the scope of the risk of his original faulty conduct. Thus, in *Southport Corp. v. Esso Petrol. Co.,* [1954] 2 Q.B. 182 (C.A.), *rev'd in part,* [1953] 3 All E.R. 864 (H.L.), defendants' tanker developed a steering fault and stranded on a revetment wall. To save the vessel and crew from grave danger, the master jettisoned 400 tons of oil which damaged plaintiff's shore. The court held defendants liable to plaintiffs for this damage because it was caused by defendants' fault:

> The defendants seek to justify themselves by saying that it was necessary for them to discharge the oil because their ship was in danger. She had been driven by rough seas on to the revetment wall, and it was necessary to discharge the oil in order to get her off. If she had not got off, lives might have been lost. This is, no doubt, true at that stage in the story, but the question is: How came she to get on the wall? If it was her own fault, then her justification fails, because no one can avail himself of a necessity produced by his own default.

See also Protectus Alpha Navigation Co. v. North Pacific Grain Growers, Inc., 767 F.2d 1379 (9th Cir. 1985) (grain terminal owner, who cast off from dock a burning vessel on which firefighters had gathered, held liable on negligence *per se* theory for breach of criminal statute prohibiting interference with operations of Fire Department).

3. *Bodily Safety.* In *Eilers v. Coy,* 582 F. Supp. 1093 (D.C. Minn. 1984), the plaintiff was a member of a religious group, "Disciples of the Lord Jesus Christ." There was "ample evidence" that the group was "directed with an iron hand" by its leader, and that plaintiff's "personality, and to some extent his appearance, changed substantially after he became a member of the group." Fearing for the plaintiff's health, his parents hired defendants to kidnap the plaintiff and to subject him to a deprogramming regimen. This they did:

> While leaving the Winona Clinic on August 16, 1982, the plaintiff, who was on crutches at the time due to an earlier fall, was grabbed from behind by two or more security men, forced into a waiting van, and driven to the Tau Center in Winona, Minnesota. Forcibly resisting, he was carried by four men to a room on the top floor of the dormitory-style building. The windows of this room were boarded over with plywood, as were the windows in his bathroom and in the hallway of the floor. The telephone in the hallway had been dismantled.
>
> The plaintiff was held at the Tau Center for five and one-half days and subjected to the defendants' attempts to deprogram him. Shortly after his arrival at the Tau Center, and after a violent struggle with his captors, the plaintiff was handcuffed to a bed. He remained handcuffed to the bed for at least the first two days of his confinement. During this initial period, he was allowed out of the room only to use the bathroom, and was heavily guarded during those times.

Plaintiff brought an action for false imprisonment, and moved for a directed verdict on liability which the court granted:

> As justification for their actions, the defendants rely on the defense of necessity. They claim that the confinement and attempted deprogramming of the plaintiff was necessary to prevent him from committing suicide or from otherwise harming himself or others.
>
> The defense of necessity has three elements. The first element is that the defendants must have acted under the reasonable belief that there was a danger of imminent physical injury to the plaintiff or to others.

Although the evidence was in dispute, the court assumed for purposes of the motion that the plaintiff was in imminent danger of causing physical injury to himself or others:

> The second and third elements of the necessity defense are intertwined. The second element is that the right to confine a person in order to prevent harm to that person lasts only as long as is necessary to get the person to the proper lawful authorities. The third element is that the actor must use the least restrictive means of preventing the apprehended harm.

In this case, the defendants' conduct wholly fails to satisfy either of these elements of the necessity defense. Once having gained control of the plaintiff, the defendants had several legal options available to them. They could have:

1) turned the plaintiff over to the police;

2) sought to initiate civil commitment proceedings against the plaintiff pursuant to [state statute];

3) sought professional psychiatric or psychological help for the plaintiff with the possibility of emergency hospitalization if necessary pursuant to [state statute].

At no time did the defendants attempt, or even consider attempting, any of these lawful alternatives during the five and one-half days they held the plaintiff, the first five of which were business days. Instead, they took the plaintiff to a secluded location with boarded-up windows, held him incommunicado, and proceeded to inflict their own crude methods of "therapy" upon him — methods which even the defendants' own expert witness has condemned. Well aware that the police were searching for the plaintiff, the defendants deliberately concealed the plaintiff's location from the police. . . .

The Court has assumed for the purposes of this motion that the defendants were justified in initially restraining the plaintiff based upon their belief that he was in imminent danger of harming himself or others. But even under those circumstances, the defense of necessity eventually dissipates as a matter of law. No specific time limit can be set, because the period during which an actor is acting out of necessity will vary depending on the circumstances of each case. In this particular case, however, where the defendants held the plaintiff, a 24-year-old adult, for five and one-half days with no attempt to resort to lawful alternatives available to them, the Court could not sustain a jury verdict in the defendants' favor on the issue of false imprisonment. Accordingly, the Court rules as a matter of law that the plaintiff was falsely imprisoned without justification.

The court recognized that this "will not be a popular decision." Expressing "substantial sympathy for the feelings and reactions" of the plaintiff's parents, the court nevertheless felt that it was bound by law to hold for the plaintiff.

How would you characterize "deprogramming?" As a process designed to provide a church or cult member with "an opportunity in a neutral setting to sleep, to eat, to evaluate the manner in which he wishes to live his life and then, well-rested and well-fed, to make an independent decision about whether to remain involved in the group?" Or as "a process involving kidnaping and forcing an individual to renounce his religious beliefs?" *See Colombrito v. Kelly,* 764 F.2d 122, 125 (2d Cir. 1985).

PROBLEM

Defendant was driving a bus containing 20 elderly persons down a steep narrow mountain road, en route to a senior citizens' function, when the bus brakes suddenly gave way. The bus quickly reached a high rate of speed. There was no safe place to pull off the road; on one side was a steep rock wall, and on the other, a deep canyon.

Ahead of the bus was the entrance to a private subdivision, which provided the driver with the only chance to save the lives of her passengers and herself. Five school children were awaiting a school van pickup at the entrance to the subdivision, and the driver could not enter it without hitting the children. The driver's horn failed to function when she attempted to use it. Prior to the accident, the driver had no reason to know that the brakes or horn on the bus would fail.

If the driver hits the children, will she be liable in tort to them? If she does not attempt to use the subdivision entrance, will she be liable in tort to her passengers? Is she liable for entry into, or any damage to the subdivision?

F. JUSTIFICATION

SINDLE v. NEW YORK CITY TRANSIT AUTHORITY
33 N.Y.2d 293, 307 N.E.2d 245, 352 N.Y.S.2d 183 (1973)

JASEN, JUSTICE.

At about noon on June 20, 1967, the plaintiff, then 14 years of age, boarded a school bus owned by the defendant, New York City Transit Authority, and driven by its employee, the defendant Mooney. It was the last day of the term at the Elias Bernstein Junior High School in Staten Island and the 65 to 70 students on board the bus were in a boisterous and exuberant mood. Some of this spirit expressed itself in vandalism, a number of students breaking dome lights, windows, ceiling panels and advertising poster frames. There is no evidence that the plaintiff partook in this destruction.

The bus made several stops at appointed stations. On at least one occasion, the driver admonished the students about excessive noise and damage to the bus. When he reached the Annadale station, the driver discharged several more passengers, went to the rear of the bus, inspected the damage and advised the students that he was taking them to the St. George police station.

The driver closed the doors of the bus and proceeded, bypassing several normal stops. As the bus slowed to turn on to Woodrow Road, several students jumped without apparent injury from a side window at the rear of the bus. Several more followed, again without apparent harm, when the bus turned onto Arden Avenue.

At the corner of Arden Avenue and Arthur Kill Road, departing from its normal route, the bus turned right in the general direction of the St. George police station. The plaintiff, intending to jump from the bus, had positioned himself in a window on the right-rear side. Grasping the bottom of the window sill with his hands, the plaintiff extended his legs (to mid-thigh), head and shoulders out of the window. As the bus turned right, the right rear wheels hit the curb and the plaintiff either jumped or fell to the street. The right rear wheels then rolled over the midsection of his body, causing serious personal injuries.

The plaintiff, joined with his father, then commenced an action to recover damages for negligence and false imprisonment. At the outset of the trial, the negligence cause was waived and plaintiffs proceeded on the theory of false imprisonment. At the close of the plaintiffs' case, the court denied defendants' motion to amend their answers to plead the defense of justification. The court also excluded all evidence bearing on the justification issue.

We believe that it was an abuse of discretion for the trial court to deny the motion to amend and to exclude the evidence of justification. It was the defendants' burden to prove justification — a defense that a plaintiff in an action for false imprisonment should be prepared to meet — and the plaintiffs could not have been prejudiced by the granting of the motion to amend. The trial court's rulings precluded the defendants from introducing any evidence in this regard and were manifestly unfair. Accordingly, the order of the Appellate Division must be reversed and a new trial granted.

In view of our determination, it would be well to outline some of the considerations relevant to the issue of justification. In this regard, we note that, generally, restraint or detention, reasonable under the circumstances and in time and manner, imposed for the purpose of preventing another from inflicting personal injuries or interfering with or damaging real or personal property in one's lawful possession or custody is not unlawful. (Cf. Penal Law, §§ 35.20, 35.25; see, also, General Business Law, § 218, which affords a retail merchant a defense to an action for false arrest and false imprisonment where a suspected shoplifter is reasonably detained for investigation or questioning.) Also, a parent, guardian or teacher entrusted with the care or supervision of a child may use physical force reasonably necessary to maintain discipline or promote the welfare of the child.

Similarly, a bus driver, entrusted with the care of his student-passengers and the custody of public property, has the duty to take reasonable measures for the safety and protection of both — the passengers and the property. In this regard, the reasonableness of his actions — as bearing on the defense of justification — is to be determined from a consideration of all the circumstances. At a minimum, this would seem to import a consideration of the need to protect the persons and property in his charge, the duty to aid the investigation and apprehension of those inflicting damage, the manner and place of the occurrence, and the feasibility and practicality of other alternative courses of action.

NOTES

1. *Justification.* Does the defense of justification apply in any case in which the defendant intentionally harms the plaintiff or his property, and the societal value of the defendant's conduct outweighs society's interest in protecting the invasion of the plaintiff's interests? If so, why not a generic defense of "justification" which would encompass consent, self-defense and all of the "pigeonhole" defenses which have been considered in this chapter? Why not a "generic" intentional tort, *i.e.*, if one does an act which is substantially certain to cause harm to a protected interest, he has committed an intentional tort? Apart from history, is there any justification for the "pigeonholing" that

2. *The Privilege of Discipline.* According to RESTATEMENT (SECOND) OF TORTS § 147,

> (1) A parent is privileged to apply such reasonable force or to impose such reasonable confinement upon his child as he reasonably believes to be necessary for its proper control, training or education.
>
> (2) One other than a parent who has been given by law or has voluntarily assumed in whole or in part the function of controlling, training, or educating a child, is privileged to apply such reasonable force or to impose such reasonable confinement as he reasonably believes to be necessary for its proper control, training, or education except in so far as the parent has restricted the privilege of one to whom he has entrusted the child.

How do you determine what is "reasonable" force? In *Thomas v. Bedford*, 389 So. 2d 405 (La. App. 1980), Goff, a 14-year-old school student, struck Bedford, a teacher, a light blow in the back with his hand. Instead of going to his class, as instructed by Bedford, Goff then picked up a rubber band and from a distance of about two feet propelled it into Bedford's face. Goff then turned and ran into his classroom, chased by Bedford who threw a two-foot-long, 1-inch by 2-inch board at the youngster, but missed him. Bedford went to his classroom where he remained for ten or fifteen minutes. He then returned to Goff's classroom and pulled the youngster into an adjoining vacant "project" room where he struck him three or four times on the body with his fist. According to the court:

> . . . [A] minor's school teacher, while the youngster is attending school, stands in the place of the parent for the purpose of enforcing discipline and, in connection therewith, may use a reasonable degree of corporal punishment. The factual question presented by each individual case is whether the punishment was unreasonable or excessive under the circumstances.
>
> . . . [T]he trial judge concluded that "although the teacher's action *greatly exceeded reasonable force* (emphasis added), nevertheless, there is sufficient provocation by plaintiff for Mr. Bedford to have lost his temper in rendering corporal punishment on Joseph Goff." In a previous portion of that opinion the minor had been characterized as the "aggressor."
>
> The "aggressor doctrine" contemplates an altercation provoked by the aggressor against a party who defends himself. Even if, under the facts of this case, Goff's striking Bedford in the back and hitting him with a rubber band rendered him an aggressor, it is obvious that the subsequent altercation in the "project" room, some 10 or 15 minutes later after Bedford had admittedly calmed down, was in fact a separate incident and not a spontaneous reaction to the original provocation. Therefore, the "aggressor doctrine" is inapplicable. The pivotal issue here is whether the corporal punishment meted out by Bedford was unreasonable. The trial judge explicitly answered that question in the

affirmative. Since this is a factual question and our review of the record does not show that the trial judge was clearly wrong in his conclusion, we must accept that ruling. Consequently, under our jurisprudence Bedford, his employer and the latter's insurance carrier are liable for Goff's injuries.

Legitimate concern for disciplinary problems in our schools, ably articulated by the conscientious trial judge, does not permit us to disregard our responsibility to accord due deference to the rights of all those participants in the educational process, students as well as teachers and administrators. Needless to say, our law does not by any means render the latter impotent in the face of rule infractions. Where appropriate, corporal punishment may be administered in a reasonable manner as a measured, rational response to serious acts of misconduct.

Some courts have held that the physical discipline by a teacher is actionable only where it is maliciously motivated or willfully and wantonly inflicted. *See, e.g., Gordon v. Oak Park School Dist.*, 24 Ill. App. 3d 131, 320 N.E.2d 389 (1974), *Baikie v. Luther High School South*, 51 Ill. App. 3d 405, 9 Ill. Dec. 285, 366 N.E.2d 542 (1977). How would such an approach affect the result in *Thomas v. Bedford*? Note also that some state statutes specifically permit teachers to administer corporal punishment, as long as it is not "excessive or unduly severe." *See, e.g., Maddox v. Boutwell*, 176 Ga. App. 492, 336 S.E.2d 599 (1985).

3. *Corporal Punishment and the Constitution.* In *Ingraham v. Wright*, 430 U.S. 651, 97 S. Ct. 1401, 51 L. Ed. 2d 711 (1977), the U.S. Supreme Court, in a 5-4 decision, held that corporal punishment in the public schools does not violate the 8th or 14th amendments, even where the punishment was alleged to be "severe" and "exceptionally harsh." The Court said 8th amendment protection against cruel and unusual punishment applies only to criminal proceedings. The requirement of procedural due process under the 14th amendment could be satisfied by "the traditional common-law remedies" in tort for the excessive use of force. A "universal constitutional requirement" of a hearing, even an informal hearing, would "significantly burden the use of corporal punishment as a disciplinary measure:"

> Elimination or curtailment of corporal punishment would be welcomed by many as a societal advance. But when such a policy choice may result from this Court's determination of an asserted right to due process, rather than from the normal processes of community debate and legislative action, the societal costs cannot be dismissed as insubstantial. We are reviewing here a legislative judgment, rooted in history and reaffirmed in the laws of many States, that corporal punishment serves important educational interests. This judgment must be viewed in light of the disciplinary problems commonplace in the schools. As noted in *Goss v. Lopez*, 419 U.S. 565, 95 S. Ct. 729, 42 L. Ed. 2d 725 (1975): "Events calling for discipline are frequent occurrences and sometimes require immediate, effective action." Assessment of the need for, and the appropriate means of maintaining, school discipline is committed generally to the discretion of school

authorities subject to state law. "[T]he Court has repeatedly emphasized the need for affirming the comprehensive authority of the States and of school officials, consistent with fundamental constitutional safeguards, to prescribe and control conduct in the schools."

4. *Justification Through Mistake.* In *Ranson v. Kitner*, 31 Ill. App. 241 (1889), the court said the defendant hunters had no defense of good faith mistake in shooting plaintiff's dog, which they believed to be a wolf. They were liable to the plaintiff for the value of the dog.

Suppose the defendants in *Kitner* mistakenly but in good faith believed the dog was about to attack them when they shot it. Could the owner recover for the value of the dog?

Suppose the defendants reasonably believed that plaintiff's dog was about to attack and kill their dog. Could they kill plaintiff's dog with impunity in order to protect their dog? REST. 2d TORTS § 260, comm. *c*, illus. 5, indicates that the relative value of the dogs and the ability to rescue their dog by other means "are factors to be considered" in determining the defendant's liability.

Compare Maryland Cas. Ins. Co. v. Welchel, 257 Ga. 259, 356 S.E.2d 877 (1987), *on remand,* 184 Ga. App. 105, 361 S.E.2d 285 (1987). The plaintiff subrogee insurer sought recovery against the defendant towing company for conversion of a truck belonging to plaintiff's insured. The insured requested the defendant to tow a truck having transmission problems to a transmission repair shop. However, the driver dispatched by the defendant "mistakenly, but in good faith, went to the wrong location" and towed another truck of the insured to the repair shop, where the truck was stolen. In a 4-3 decision, the court held that "the plaintiff may not . . . hold the defendant strictly liable for the loss [where] the theft was not reasonably foreseeable by the defendant." The dissent thought "the converter should be held absolutely liable for loan of the property," and "[q]uestions of negligence and foreseeability should not affect the outcome."

This case is not in accord with Illustration 3 of comment d of RESTATEMENT (SECOND) OF TORTS § 222A. In that Illustration, A on leaving a restaurant "by mistake takes B's hat from the rack, believing it to be his own." On reaching the sidewalk, as A puts on the hat "a sudden gust of wind blows it from his head, and it goes down an open manhole and is lost. This is a conversion."

In *Crabtree v. Dawson,* 119 Ky. 148, 83 S.W. 557 (1904), the court held that defendant was entitled to strike the plaintiff, whom the defendant reasonably mistook to be an assailant. Accord *Courvoisier v. Raymond,* following *Bradley v. Hunter, given above.* If the belief was reasonable, then what is the need for the defense of mistake? Is there any discrete nominate *defense* of "mistake," or merely cases where defendant lacked the necessary intent?

G. PRIVILEGE

SAMSON INVESTMENT CO. V. CHEVAILLIER
988 P.2d 327 (Okla. 1999)

SUMMERS, C.J..

We granted the motion to retain this appeal in order to address the issue of whether an attorney's circulation of a draft petition in a probable lawsuit to a prospective client can be the basis of a defamation lawsuit. We hold that the attorneys' actions were protected under the litigation privilege as recognized in our case of *Kirschstein v. Haynes*, 788 P.2d 941 (Okla. 1990). The trial court correctly granted judgment for the attorneys.

The defendants in this case are individual attorneys and the law firms with which they are associated. The attorneys caused a draft of a petition for a lawsuit to be prepared, and circulated it to at least one prospective client, Russell Caston. The petition alleged that the defendants named therein (being the Samson entities and Continental Drilling Company, the plaintiffs in this case now before us, hereinafter referred to as Samson) had defrauded investors in transactions involving oil and gas limited partnerships. The draft petition did not contain a plaintiff's name or the name of a court. The prospective client, along with others, ultimately hired the defendants, and a class action lawsuit was filed in Oklahoma County.

Samson brought this lawsuit in Tulsa County, alleging that the petition contained false material which was defamatory and which induced the prospective client to file suit. Chevaillier, Federman and the law firms with which they are associated filed motions to dismiss. Conant and Harris, along with their law firm, filed a motion for summary judgment. These pleadings essentially made the same argument: that the information contained in the draft petition was privileged, as it was made preliminary to a judicial proceeding. Because it was privileged, it cannot be the subject of a defamation lawsuit. Samson countered by urging that because there was no attorney-client relationship between Caston and any of the attorneys at the time of the petition's circulation, the asserted privilege did not prevent a defamation lawsuit. Samson urged that it was irrelevant that Caston eventually hired defendants, and pursued a judicial remedy. The trial court granted the motions to dismiss and the motion for summary judgment. Samson appealed and we retained the case.

At the heart of this case is the privilege, sometimes termed the litigation privilege, which accords attorneys, parties, jurors and witnesses immunity for comments or writings made during the course of or preliminary to judicial or quasi-judicial proceedings. . . . A large number of jurisdictions have adopted this privilege, either by statue or by case law. All agree that the question of whether a communication is privileged is a question of law to determined by the court.

In *Kirschstein*, a client hired an attorney to obtain a delayed birth certificate. During this process the attorney drafted an affidavit, and sent it to the physician who was present at the birth of the client. The affidavit, signed by the physician, stated that plaintiff was the client's mother, a fact that turned out to be false. The affidavit was used by an attorney to obtain a birth certificate. The plaintiff brought suit for defamation. The attorney raised the litigation privilege as a defense.

We quoted with approval from the Restatement on Torts (Second), Sections 586, 587 and 588, which explained this privilege. Section 586, provides as follows:

> An attorney at law is absolutely privileged to publish defamatory matter concerning another in *communications preliminary to a proposed judicial proceeding*, or in the institution of, or during the course and as a part of, a judicial proceeding in which he participates as counsel, if it has some relation to the proceeding. (Emphasis added.)

Sections 587 and 588 contain substantially the same language in regard to publications made by parties and witnesses, respectively. Comment *a* to § 586 provides in pertinent part as follows:

> The privilege stated in this section is based upon a public policy of securing to attorneys as officers of the court the utmost freedom in their efforts to secure justice for their clients. Therefore the privilege is absolute. *It protects the attorney from liability in an action for defamation irrespective of his purpose in publishing the defamatory matter, his belief in its truth, or even his knowledge of its falsity.... The publication of defamatory matter by an attorney is protected not only when made in the institution of the proceedings or in the conduct of litigation before a judicial tribunal, but in conferences and other communications preliminary to the proceeding.* The institution of a judicial proceeding includes all pleadings and affidavits necessary to set the judicial machinery in motion....

Id. at 947 (emphasis in original).

We agreed that the litigation privilege should apply to communications preliminary to judicial or quasi-judicial proceedings if the "communication has some relation to a proceeding that is contemplated in good faith and under serious consideration." *Id.* at 948 quoting Restatement (Second), Section 586, comment e. We explained that the privilege does not give free reign to attorneys to defame; rather the litigation privilege applies only when the communication is (1) relevant or has some relation to a proposed proceeding and (2) circumstances surrounding the communication have some relation to the proposed proceeding. *Id.* at 951. We noted that the privilege applies "regardless of whether they [the communications] are true or false." *Id.* at 950.

Relying on *Russell v. Clark*, 620 S.W. 2d 865, 868 (Tex. Civ. App. 1981), we explained the public policy behind the privilege:

> Public policy demands that attorneys be granted the utmost freedom in the efforts to represent their clients. To grant immunity short of absolute privilege to communications relating to pending or proposed litigation, and thus subject an attorney to liability for defamation, might tend to lessen an attorney's efforts on behalf of his client. The conduct of litigation requires more than in-court procedures. An attorney must seek discovery of evidence, interrogate potential witnesses, and often resort to ingenious methods to obtain evidence; thus,

he must not be hobbled by the fear of reprisal by actions for defamation. Yet this absolute privilege must not be extended to an attorney carte blanche. The act to which the privilege applies must bear some relationship to a judicial proceeding in which the attorney is employed, and must be in furtherance of that representation.

Id. at 951.

In *Russell*, 620 S.W. 2d at 869, the Texas court noted that the privilege had been extended to cover communications to a prospective defendant. See *Sriberg v. Raymond*, 370 Mass. 105, 345 N.E. 2d 882 (1976). In *Sriberg* an attorney sent a letter threatening a lawsuit. This letter became the subject of a defamation action. The court held that it was privileged, being related to a probable judicial proceeding. In *Chard v. Galton*, 277 Or. 109, 559 P.2d 1280 (1977), the Oregon Supreme Court held that the litigation privilege extended to communications preliminary to a lawsuit, since the preliminary communication in the form of a letter had some relation to the impending lawsuit. . . .

Samson urges that the privilege does not apply in this instance, even thought the petition was clearly a communication related to probable lawsuit, because the communication was a solicitation by an attorney to gain clients. As such, Samson claims that the absence of an attorney-client relationship prevents the application of the litigation privilege. This issue was addressed in *Kittler v. Eckberg, Lammers, Briggs, Wolff & Vierling* [535 N.W. 2d 653 (MN. APP. 1995)]. There, corporate officers and directors brought a defamation suit against a law firm. The basis of the suit was the law firm's circulation of a letter which stated that the firm, at the request of some former shareholders, was considering the filing of a law suit against the corporation. The letter stated the firm's fee before undertaking such a suit. It was sent to fifty-six former shareholders. The court held that this communication was privileged as a matter of law. Citing the Restatement, § 586, the court noted that this was clearly a communication preliminary to a probable judicial proceeding. The court continued by explaining that "attorneys' letters of solicitation are protected as commercial free speech." *Id.* at 655. The court reasoned that "we can imagine few communicative acts more clearly within the scope of the privilege than those alleged in the amended complaint. . ." *Id., quoting Rubin v. Green*, 4 Cal. 4th 1187, 17 Cal. Rptr. 2d 828, 847 P.2d 1044 (1993). Likewise, the North Carolina appellate court held that the contents of an unfiled complaint were privileged. *Harris v. NCNB National Bank for North Carolina*, 85 N.C. App. 669, 355 S.E. 2d 838 (1987).

No case is cited by Samson, and our research has revealed none, to support its argument that the litigation privilege only applies after the client has retained an attorney. The Restatement does not support this position, as it only requires that the communication be relevant to the probable proceeding. *Kirschstein* does not support the argument, because it clearly states that preliminary communications are privileged as long as they are relevant to the proceeding and the circumstances surrounding the communication are relevant to the proceeding. The purpose behind the litigation privilege of permitting open communication to facilitate "the right of access to judicial and quasi-judicial proceedings," *Hawkins*, at 289 would be thwarted if Samson's argument was adopted.

However, we again reiterate that the litigation privilege is not a license to defame. *Kirschstein* sets limits on this privilege in the form of the aforementioned requirements. We must determine if this communication meets these requirements. First, we hold that the proposed petition meets the requirement of being relevant to a judicial proceeding. Obviously, the petition is the first building block of any law suit, and is essential to the commencement of a judicial proceeding. As for the second requirement, the circumstances surrounding the petition's distribution to the prospective client Caston were also related to the proposed judicial action. The petition communicated to Caston the allegations to be made during the course of the law suit. He was a potential client, and a potential plaintiff. His viewing of the petition was a necessary step toward filing the class action suit. The case was filed in Oklahoma county District Court. This communication met both requirements of *Kirschstein*.

As a matter of law the plaintiffs cannot prevail in this action. The summary judgment and the order of dismissal for failure to state a claim were both proper. The judgment of the District Court of Tulsa County is affirmed.

NOTES

1. *More Litigation Privilege.* Attorney Mary Lou Godbe represented Robert DeBry in a divorce proceeding between him and his wife, Janice DeBry. During the course of the lawsuit an unknown caller said an anonymous threat, in which "Ms. DeBry was somehow involved," had been made on the life of Mr. DeBry. This call was reported to the court.

After the close of the evidence and while the judge had the case under advisement, Ms. Godbe's home telephone line was cut and a glass panel to the sliding door in her kitchen was broken by some sort of missile. She reported these incidents to the police and to the judge, and implied in her reports that she thought Ms. DeBry "was probably" the cause of the incidents.

Ms. DeBry sued Ms. Godbe claiming defamation and intentional infliction of emotional distress caused by these reports. The court struck the claims, holding the reports were protected by the "judicial proceeding privilege." This privilege, the court said, applied to statements "made by one acting in his or her capacity as judge, juror, witness, litigant, or counsel," if the statements had "some relationship to the cause or subject matter involved." The privilege applied to "all claims" arising from the "statements," including the claims for defamation and emotional distress.

Ms. DeBry claimed the privilege was abused, or lost, because Ms. Godbe "excessively published" the statement, that is, she made the statement "to more persons than the scope of the privilege required to effectuate it purpose." There was no abuse, the court said, in Ms. Godbe sending the statement to her attorney and to the parties and attorneys involved in the divorce proceeding. Ms. Godbe also attempted to send the statement by fax to the person she was speaking with on the phone when her window was broken, but the fax never reached that person and therefore was not an excessive publication. *DeBry v. Godbe*, 992 P.2d 979 (Utah 1999).

Was the statement of Ms. Godbe to the police privileged?

2. *Public Prosecutors.* The Court in *Buckley v. Fitzsimmons,* 113 S.Ct. 2606 (1993), held that public prosecutors are entitled to an absolute immunity for conduct "intimately associated with the judicial phase of the criminal process," but only a qualified immunity for investigatory and administrative acts in connection with a prosecution. Alleged manufacturing of evidence before there was probable cause to arrest, and false statements to the press, were only qualifiedly immune. The qualified immunity will be abused if the prosecutor is not acting in good faith.

3. *The Adverse Attorney.* The plaintiff Mitchell, in *Mitchell v. Chapman*, 10 S.W. 3d 810 (Tx. App. 2000), sued the defendant Chapman, a lawyer, alleging that Chapman had "willfully or negligently" denied the existence of documents that were important to plaintiff in prior litigation between the plaintiff and a defendant, for whom Chapman had been the attorney. The court said Mitchell had no cause of action against Chapman because "Mitchell's interests" were "outweighed by the public's interest in loyal, faithful, and aggressive representation by attorneys employed as advocates. If Chapman's conduct violated his professional responsibility, the remedy is public rather than private."

4. *Comparative Fault Anticipated.* As we will see in a later chapter on affirmative defenses, contributory fault of the plaintiff is widely used as a basis for reducing the plaintiff's recovery by the percentage of fault attributable to the plaintiff. But the court in *McLain v. Training and Development Corp.,* 572 A.2d 494 (Me. 1990), refused to apply comparative fault "as a defense to the intentional tort of assault and battery." What policies would support such a rule as that adopted by the *McLain* court?

Chapter 5
THE STANDARD OF CARE IN NEGLIGENCE

A. INTRODUCTION

The standard of care in negligence law is variously referred to as reasonable, prudent or due care and, for many, it is the defining concept of the tort of negligence. The issues presented in the determination of the appropriate standard of care represent something of a microcosm of modern accident law. Thus, this chapter reflects the tensions inherent in the torts system as a whole: To what extent should standards be objective rather than subjective? Are our rules of liability driven by compensation rather than culpability concerns? To what extent should we attempt to tailor liability to particular fact patterns rather than apply broad rules? What is the appropriate degree of control that the judiciary should exercise over the jury in the determination of fault?

This chapter canvasses the primary tools used by the courts to set the standard of care in the tort of negligence—reasonable care, customary practices, risk-utility analysis and statutory standards. The chapter concludes with an examination of some of the issues involved in proving such negligence, including an examination of the doctrine of res ipsa loquitur.

B. THE BASIC OBLIGATION

PROBLEM

Bill is a local farmer who is widely liked and respected for his good farming judgment in the neighborhood. After he successfully brought in his harvest, he built a large haystack close to the boundary of his farm. Unfortunately, the method of construction he chose for the haystack created the danger of spontaneous combustion of the hay. Pat, his neighbor, watched the construction of the haystack, and repeatedly warned Bill about the danger involved. On one such occasion, Bill informed Pat "he would chance it." Subsequently, Bill's haystack ignited and caused damage to Pat's farmhouse.

Questions:

1. Should Pat bring his action in negligence rather than intentional tort or strict liability? Why?

2. Does Pat have anything to gain by attempting to prove that Bill acted recklessly?

3. In a negligence action by Pat, would his attorney seek a subjective or an objective jury instruction on the standard of care? What jury instruction would the defendant seek? How would such formulations differ?

4. What is the most compelling evidence of Bill's negligence?

RESTATEMENT OF TORTS § 281 (1965) states:

> The actor is liable for an invasion of an interest of another, if:
>
> (a) the interest invaded is protected against unintentional invasion, and
>
> (b) the conduct of the actor is negligent with respect to the other, or a class of persons within which he is included, and
>
> (c) the actor's conduct is a legal cause of the invasion, and
>
> (d) the other has not so conducted himself as to disable himself from bringing an action for such invasion.

NOTES

1. *The Unreasonable Running of a Foreseeable Risk.* Blyth v. Birmingham Water Works Co., 11 Exch. 781, 156 Eng. Rep. 1047, 1049 (1856), concerned property damage suffered by the plaintiff when water escaped from the defendant's water pipes during an extremely cold winter. The trial judge permitted the jury to consider whether the defendant had acted negligently in failing to remove ice from its fireplugs, which should have served as safety valves. In reversing plaintiff's jury verdict, Alderson, B., remarked:

> Negligence is the omission to do something which a reasonable man, guided upon those considerations which ordinarily regulate the conduct of human affairs, would do, or doing something which a prudent and reasonable person would not do. . . . A reasonable man would act with reference to the average circumstances of the temperature in ordinary years. The defendants had provided against such frosts as experience would have led men, acting prudently, to provide against; and they are not guilty of negligence, because their precautions proved insufficient against the effects of the extreme severity of the frost of 1855, which penetrated to a greater depth than any which ordinarily occurs south of the polar regions. Such a state of circumstances constitutes a contingency against which no reasonable man can provide. The result was an accident, for which the defendants cannot be held liable.

Consider also RESTATEMENT (SECOND) OF TORTS (1965) § 284, which defines negligent misfeasance as "an act which the actor as a reasonable [person] should recognize as involving an unreasonable risk of causing an invasion of an interest of another."

2. *An Anthropomorphic Concept of Justice?* Lord Radcliffe said in *Davis Contractors v. Fareham U.D.C.,* [1956] 2 All E.R. 145, 160 (H.L.), "the spokesman of the fair and reasonable man, who represents after all no more than the anthropomorphic conception of justice, is, and must be, the court itself." Who really does embody the reasonable person: judge or jury? Why would a court ever require expert testimony as to what is reasonable?

3. *Negligence and Juries?* In *Ford v. London & South Western Ry. Co.,* 2 F. & F. 730, 732–33, 175 Eng. Rep. 1260, 1261 (1862), a claim of negligence was brought against a railway company after one of its trains was derailed. Earle, C.J., instructed the jury as follows:

Negligence is not to be defined, because it involves some inquiry as to the degree of care required and that is the degree which the jury think is reasonably to be required from the parties, considering all the circumstances. The railway company is bound to take reasonable care; to use the best precautions in known practical use, for securing the safety and convenience of their passengers. If they have done so they have done their duty, and are not guilty of negligence; if they have failed in their duty, and their negligence has caused the injury, then they are liable in the action. You are to consider what is reasonable care, and whether they have used the proper precautions. They are entrusted with most important interests, with human lives, and a jury may reasonably require an amount of care proportioned to those interests. At the same time a jury would not be entitled to expect the utmost care that could possibly be conceived, or the highest possible degree of skill. It is to be borne in mind that railways themselves are of recent introduction, and that their management is a matter of experience and of practical knowledge which increases day by day. It is not to be expected that the directors shall at once have in use every invention or discovery of science. It is sufficient if they use every precaution in known practical use, for the safety and convenience of the passengers. Both objects must be looked to. It is easy to conceive a precaution, for example, a slower rate of speed, which would add a very small degree of security, while it would entail a very great degree of inconvenience. And a company ought not to be found guilty merely because they possibly might have done something more for safety, at a far greater sacrifice of convenience.

Should the jury be given guidance as to what conduct falls below the standard of reasonable care? Why? If they are not given guidance, what are jurors likely to equate to reasonable care? Are there specific classes of cases where the jury should not be given as much leeway?

C. REASONABLE CARE AND PERSONAL CHARACTERISTICS

ROBINSON v. LINDSAY
92 Wash.2d 410, 598 P.2d 392 (1979)

UTTER, C.J.

An action seeking damages for personal injuries was brought on behalf of Kelly Robinson who lost full use of a thumb in a snowmobile accident when she was 11 years of age. The petitioner, Billy Anderson, 13 years of age at the time of the accident, was the driver of the snowmobile. After a jury verdict in favor of Anderson, the trial court ordered a new trial.

The single issue on appeal is whether a minor operating a snowmobile is to be held to an adult standard of care. The trial court failed to instruct the jury as to that standard and ordered a new trial because it believed the jury should have been so instructed. We agree and affirm the order granting a new trial.

The trial court instructed the jury under WPI 10.05 that:

> In considering the claimed negligence of a child, you are instructed that it is the duty of a child to exercise the same care that a reasonably careful child of the same age, intelligence, maturity, training and experience would exercise under the same or similar circumstances.

Respondent properly excepted to the giving of this instruction and to the court's failure to give an adult standard of care.

The question of what standard of care should apply to acts of children has a long historical background. Traditionally, a flexible standard of care has been used to determine if children's actions were negligent. Under some circumstances, however, courts have developed a rationale for applying an adult standard.

In the courts' search for a uniform standard of behavior to use in determining whether or not a person's conduct has fallen below minimal acceptable standards, the law has developed a fictitious person, the "reasonable man of ordinary prudence." That term was first used in *Vaughan v. Menlove*, 132 Eng. Rep. 490 (1837).

Exceptions to the reasonable person standard developed when the individual whose conduct was alleged to have been negligent suffered from some physical impairment, such as blindness, deafness, or lameness. Courts also found it necessary, as a practical matter, to depart considerably from the objective standard when dealing with children's behavior. Children are traditionally encouraged to pursue childhood activities without the same burdens and responsibilities with which adults must contend As a result, courts evolved a special standard of care to measure a child's negligence in a particular situation.

. . .The current law in this state is fairly reflected in WPI 10.05, given in this case. In the past we have always compared a child's conduct to that expected of a reasonably careful child of the same age, intelligence, maturity, training and experience. This case is the first to consider the question of a child's liability for injuries sustained as a result of his or her operation of a motorized vehicle or participation in an inherently dangerous activity.

Courts in other jurisdictions have created an exception to the special child standard because of the apparent injustice that would occur if a child who caused injury while engaged in certain dangerous activities were permitted to defend himself by saying that other children similarly situated would not have exercised a degree of care higher than his, and he is, therefore, not liable for his tort. Some courts have couched the exception in terms of children engaging in an activity which is normally one for adults only. *See, e.g., Dellwo v. Pearson*, 259 Minn. 452, 107 N.W.2d 859, 97 A.L.R.2d 866 (1961) (operation of a motorboat). We believe a better rationale is that when the activity a child engages in is inherently dangerous, as is the operation of powerful mechanized vehicles, the child should be held to an adult standard of care.

Such a rule protects the need of children to be children but at the same time discourages immature individuals from engaging in inherently dangerous activities. Children will still be free to enjoy traditional childhood activities without being held to an adult standard of care. Although accidents sometimes

C. REASONABLE CARE AND PERSONAL CHARACTERISTICS

occur as the result of such activities, they are not activities generally considered capable of resulting in "grave danger to others and to the minor himself if the care used in the course of the activity drops below that care which the reasonable and prudent adult would use. . . ." *Daniels v. Evans*, 107 N.H. 407, 408, 224 A.2d 63 (1966).

Other courts adopting the adult standard of care for children engaged in adult activities have emphasized the hazards to the public if the rule is otherwise. We agree with the Minnesota Supreme Court's language in its decision in *Dellwo v. Pearson, supra* at 457–58:

> Certainly in the circumstances of modern life, where vehicles moved by powerful motors are readily available and frequently operated by immature individuals, we should be skeptical of a rule that would allow motor vehicles to be operated to the hazard of the public with less than the normal minimum degree of care and competence.

Dellwo applied the adult standard to a 12-year-old defendant operating a motorboat. Other jurisdictions have applied the adult standard to minors engaged in analogous activities. *Goodfellow v. Coggburn*, 98 Idaho 202, 203–04, 560 P.2d 873 (1977) (minor operating tractor); *Williams v. Esaw*, 214 Kan. 658, 668, 522 P.2d 950 (1974) (minor operating motorcycle); *Perricone v. DiBartolo*, 14 Ill. App. 3d 514, 520, 302 N.E.2d 637 (1973) (minor operating gasoline-powered minibike); *Krahn v. LaMeres*, 483 P.2d 522, 525–26 (Wyo. 1971) (minor operating automobile). The holding of minors to an adult standard of care when they operate motorized vehicles is gaining approval from an increasing number of courts and commentators.

The operation of a snowmobile likewise requires adult care and competence. Currently 2.2 million snowmobiles are in operation in the United States. 9 BNA Envir. Rptr. 876 [1978 Current Developments]. Studies show that collisions and other snowmobile accidents claim hundreds of casualties each year and that the incidence of accidents is particularly high among inexperienced operators.

At the time of the accident, the 13-year-old petitioner had operated snowmobiles for about 2 years. When the injury occurred, petitioner was operating a 30-horsepower snowmobile at speeds of 10 to 20 miles per hour. The record indicates that the machine itself was capable of 65 miles per hour. Because petitioner was operating a powerful motorized vehicle, he should be held to the standard of care and conduct expected of an adult.

The order granting a new trial is affirmed.

NOTES

1. *A General Standard of Care.* RESTATEMENT (SECOND) OF TORTS (1965) § 283 provides: "Unless the actor is a child, the standard of conduct to which he must conform to avoid being negligent is that of a reasonable [person] under like circumstances." Is this general standard "subjective" or "objective"? Are some aspects of the general standard contained in § 283 less objective than others? What are the practical advantages and disadvantages of using either a subjective or an objective standard? To what extent does the standard chosen reveal certain judicial value preferences?

2. *An External Rationale.* In *Daniels v. Evans,* 107 N.H. 407, 224 A.2d 63, 64, 66 (1966), the court, relying upon the absence of any distinction between adults and children in state licensing and driving statutes, observed:

> We agree that minors are entitled to be judged by standards commensurate with their age, experience, and wisdom when engaged in activities appropriate to their age, experience, and wisdom. Hence when children are walking, running, playing with toys, throwing balls, operating bicycles, sliding or engaging in other childhood activities their conduct should be judged by the rule of what is reasonable conduct under the circumstances among which are age, experience, and stage of mental development of the minor involved.
>
> However, the question raised by the defendant in this case is whether the standard of care applied to minors in such cases should prevail when the minor is engaged in activities normally undertaken by adults. In other words, when a minor undertakes an adult activity which can result in grave danger to others and to the minor himself if the care used in the course of the activity drops below that care which the reasonable and prudent adult would use, the defendant maintains that the minor's conduct in that instance should meet the same standards as that of an adult.
>
> . . . [I]n the circumstances of today's modern life, where vehicles moved by powerful motors are readily available and used by many minors, we question the propriety of a rule which would allow such vehicles to be operated to the hazard of the public, and to the driver himself, with less than the degree of care required of an adult.
>
> . . . We hold therefore that a minor operating a motor vehicle, whether an automobile or a motorcycle, must be judged by the same standard of care as an adult.

3. *Variations in Doctrinal Subcategories.* There are a considerable variety of judicial approaches in the categorization of cases like *Robinson.* Some courts apply the adult standard to children using "dangerous instrumentalities." Others apply the adult standard to "adult activities" or "adult *and* dangerous activities." Still others are specific as to the activities covered, *e.g.,* driving an automobile. What considerations underlie such different formulations? Can one expect that different jurisdictions will reach differing conclusions on what activities are appropriate for adults? Why?

4. *Victim-Incurred Information Costs.* Should imposition of an "adult duty" upon a child depend upon who is the best accident avoider? *See, e.g., Dellwo v. Pearson,* 259 Minn. 452, 107 N.W.2d 859, 863–64 (1961), where the issue was the negligence of a 12-year-old driver of a powerboat. The court concluded:

> While minors are entitled to be judged by standards commensurate with age, experience, and wisdom when engaged in activities appropriate to their age, experience, and wisdom, it would be unfair to the public to permit a minor in the operation of a motor vehicle to observe any other standards of care and conduct than those expected of all others. A person observing children at play with toys, throwing balls, operating tricycles or velocipedes, or engaged in other childhood

activities may anticipate conduct that does not reach an adult standard of care or prudence. However, one cannot know whether the operator of an approaching automobile, airplane, or powerboat is a minor or an adult, and usually cannot protect himself against youthful imprudence even if warned. Accordingly, we hold that in the operation of an automobile, airplane, or powerboat, a minor is to be held to the same standard of care as an adult.

In *Adams v. Lopez,* 75 N.M. 503, 407 P.2d 50 (1965), the court stated:

> It is our view that when the minor assumed the responsibility of operating a motor scooter upon the public streets and highways, he assumed the responsibilities of an adult for that activity, and should not be allowed to hold others responsible for his own injuries occasioned by his departure from the standards expected of persons of mature years. This is necessarily true. Neither drivers nor pedestrians have any way of ascertaining whether the driver of any other vehicle is a child or an adult, nor can such driver be expected to guard against the operation of such a dangerous instrumentality merely because it is operated by a minor.

Are these views consistent with a statement that the age of a potential child victim may impose upon the adult actor a "higher standard of care?" *See Kilpack v. Wignall,* 604 P.2d 462 (Utah 1979); *Buckley v. Exxon Corp.,* 390 So. 2d 512 (La. 1980) (motorist who sees a child on or near the road is under a high degree of care and must anticipate that the child, possessed of limited judgment, might be unable to appreciate impending danger, is likely to be inattentive, and might suddenly place himself in a position of peril). Compare *Vitale v. Belmont Springs,* 916 P.2d 359 (Utah App. 1996) (standard of care required by a defendant to a plaintiff over the age of 14 is the same as that required for an adult).

5. *Factoring in Judgmental Capacity.* What are we measuring (or purporting to measure) in these child standard cases, physical characteristics or intelligence? How do (or should) we measure the latter? See Goss v. Allen, 70 N.J. 442, 360 A.2d 388 (1976), in which the court held, "[w]e think it judicially noticeable that skiing as a recreational sport, save for limited hazardous skiing activities, is engaged in by persons of all ages. Defendant's attempt to negotiate the lower end of the beginners' slope certainly cannot be characterized as a skiing activity that as a matter of law was hazardous to others and required that he be held to an adult standard of conduct." Schreiber, J., dissenting, noted:

> The standard of care now made generally applicable to minors does not square with reality, nor does its purported application justify the charge given.
>
> . . . [The trial court's final instruction] simply stated that Allen had to exercise the same care as someone of the same age, experience and background. This charge does not equate with the standard adopted today by the majority, namely that Allen must act in accordance with the conduct of a reasonable person of the same age, intelligence and experience under the same circumstances.

The significance of the omission of intelligence in the charge becomes apparent when one recognizes the importance of that factor in fixing the required standard of care. Intelligence in this context relates to mental and judgmental capacity but not the exercise of that capacity. The distinction between exercise of mental or judgmental capacity and the capacity itself points to the objective-subjective elements in the test. The defendant's conduct is to be measured against the conduct of the average or usual 17-year-old having the same judgmental capacity.

The crucial element in determining the standard of care to be established for infants centers about the judgmental capacity factor to comprehend, understand and perceive risk and danger. Age, experience, education, social background and intellectual capability have their respective places in the formation of judgmental capability. Whether the infant should or should not have acted or reacted in a certain manner depends on whether the theoretical average infant having the same capacity would have acted or reacted in the same fashion.

. . . The RESTATEMENT (SECOND) OF TORTS, § 283A, advocates that a child's acts or omissions be compared to that of a reasonable person of the same age, experience, and intelligence. The majority has apparently adopted this rule. Although the RESTATEMENT does not on its face view age, experience, and intelligence as simply some elements to determine judgmental capacity, in its discussion under Comment *b*, it recognizes that the fact finder must analyze those factors to determine judgmental capacity. The RESTATEMENT asks whether that hypothetical person with the same judgmental capacity would have acted or reacted in the same manner. The trial court's supplemental charge omitted any reference to the defendant's intellectual capacity and failed to clearly instruct the jury to measure the defendant's judgment against that of the average 17-year-old with the same intellectual capacity. The jury could not possibly have understood the subjective-objective test which the Court is adopting this day. So even assuming the correctness of the principle adopted by the majority, in view of the several conflicting instructions given to the jury, a new trial is warranted.

. . .Under the norm adopted this day where the negligence or contributory negligence of an infant between ages 7 and 18 is in issue, his activity or inactivity is to be measured by a reasonable person of the same age, intelligence and experience under similar circumstances unless the activities "are so potentially hazardous as to require that the minor be held to an adult standard of care." There are several inherent difficulties in and inequitable consequences of this rule.

What criteria are to be employed by the jury to ascertain whether an activity is "potentially hazardous"? If a "potentially hazardous" activity is one which results in serious or permanent injury, then almost any activity might fall within that category. The injured person who has lost the sight of an eye resulting from a carelessly thrown dart, or stone, or firecracker, the death caused by a bicycle, or an individual seriously maimed due to an errant skier all are indisputable proof of "potentially hazardous" activity. The majority prescribes no guideline except to imply that whenever licensing is required, the "potentially hazardous" test is met. But the State does not impose a licensing requirement on all "potentially hazardous" activities and whether one has a license or not is often not relevant in measuring conduct of a reasonably prudent person. Whether the driver of a automobile is licensed, for example, is not relevant in adjudicating if the automobile was being driven in a reasonable prudent manner. . . .

To the injured party, his loss is the same irrespective of the wrongdoer's date of birth and it is inequitable and unjust that a minor should not be expected to exercise the same degree of care as the mythical reasonable and prudent person, at least when engaged in adult activities. The majority's proposition unnecessarily sanctions the imposition of the burden of young people's hazards on innocent victims. Whenever an infant participates in activities in which adults normally engage, the infant should be held to the adult standard of care. . . .

Inherent in these approaches, either on the basis of activities or on age well below legal adulthood, is recognition of the realism and justness in applying the adult objective standard. In some measure this is probably due to the expansion of experiences and activity of minors, as well as the protection afforded all members of the family by comprehensive liability insurance policies. Functionally, skiing is as much a sport for people over 18, as under 18. It is no different than golf or cycling. And the hazards to the public whether operating a motor vehicle, power boat, motor scooter, bicycle, tractor or hitting a golf ball, or skiing are self-evident. Third persons may be exposed to serious injury because of the dangers which occur when the activity is not being performed in a reasonably prudent manner by a reasonably prudent person and no sound reason exists for not holding the child defendant to the standard of the reasonably prudent adult.

. . . The 18-year demarcation line ignores the earlier mental development of young people. . . . Selection of the 16th year is a more reasonable age at which to draw the line for the individual to be held to an adult standard of care irrespective of the activity.

I would adopt a rule that an infant 16 years or over would be held to an adult standard of care and that an infant between ages 7 and 16 would be rebuttably presumed to have the duty to act, while engaged in an adult activity, that is, one in which adults normally or usually engage, as a reasonably prudent person, but that, upon a showing that adult judgmental capacity for that type of activity is not warranted, the subjective-objective criteria of the Restatement and adopted by the majority be applied. Application of this rule recognizes the difference between negligence and contributory negligence since the required judgmental capacity in foreseeing and avoiding the hazards created by others may be substantially greater than that to be comprehended by one's own acts. If the infant between ages 7 and 16 is found not to have been occupied in an adult activity, the RESTATEMENT rule adopted by the majority would be applicable. As to those 16 or over I would apply the adult standard.

6. *Judge and Jury.* Should the court or the jury make the determination as to whether an activity is "potentially hazardous" or "adult" in nature? What are the effects of your decision on this issue?

7. *Risk-Shifting.* How do children shift the risk of their alleged negligence? Are they worth suing? Do your answers affect the choice of the responsibility rule for which you would argue?

8. *Children of "Tender Years".* A few courts have grappled with the question as to whether some children simply are too immature to be responsible in negligence. For example, in *DeLuca v Bowden,* 42 Ohio St. 2d 392, 71 Ohio Ops. 2d 375, 329 N.E.2d 109, 111 (1975), the court held a seven-year-old child was incapable of negligence, remarking that:

> The basic dilemma of all these cases is that a child of tender years has only some dim and imponderable responsibility for his acts—and yet those acts, as those of an adult, may cause injury to others. It is probably inevitable as a part of growing up that in rare cases a child will cause severe injuries to others. Yet it is most difficult to attach blame to a child of tender years for those injuries in any sense comparable to the blame attachable to an adult, whom we hold responsible for his acts. Our laws and our moral concepts assume actors capable of legal and moral choices, of which a young child is incapable. For that reason, a child under seven years of age was at common law considered incapable of criminal responsibility. For the same reason, we cannot accept those rules which hold a child strictly liable, or which permit a jury to find liability, in cases of intentional tort. Our choice is between rules which permit the imposition of a legal judgment upon a young child for his intentional acts, and a rule which holds that members of society must accept the damage done by very young children to be no more subject to legal action than some force of nature or act of God. Our choice is the latter rule.

Consider also *Christian v. Goodwin,* 188 Cal. App. 2d 650, 10 Cal. Rptr 507 (1961) (child under age of five incapable of contributory negligence); *Gladney v. Cutrer,* 440 So. 2d 938 (La. Ct. App. 1983), *cert. denied,* 443 So. 2d 596 (La. 1983), (nine-year-old child capable of negligence and contributory negligence); *Barrett v. Carter,* 248 Ga. 389, 283 S.E.2d 609 (1981) (statute providing child under the age of 13 is immune from tort suit); *Mastland, Inc. v. Evans Furniture, Inc.,* 498 N.W.2d 682 (Iowa 1993) (child three years of age incapable as a matter of law of contributory negligence by playing with lighter); *Fromenthal v. Clark,* 442 So. 2d 608 (La. Ct. App. 1983), *cert. denied,* 444 So. 2d 1242 (La. 1983) (two-year-old not responsible for battery [biting] of two-week-old baby). *Compare Camerlinck v. Thomas,* 209 Neb. 843, 312 N.W.2d 260 (1981) (minor's responsibility was not to be subject to arbitrary line drawing, but should be determined on a case-by-case basis).

In *Dunn v. Teti,* 280 Pa. Super. 399, 421 A.2d 782 (1980), the court took a different approach, recognizing:

The application of this (child of like age, experience, capacity and development) standard is clarified by the use of several presumptions delineating convenient points to aid in drawing the uncertain line between capacity to appreciate and guard against danger and incapacity: (1) minors under the age of seven years are conclusively presumed incapable of negligence; (2) minors between the ages of seven and fourteen years are presumed incapable of negligence, but the presumption is a rebuttable one that weakens as the fourteenth year is approached; (3) minors over the age of fourteen years are presumptively capable of negligence, with the burden placed on the minor to prove incapacity.

How do the *DeLuca, Dunn* and *Camerlinck* approaches differ in practical terms and in their distributional effects?

9. *Children of Tender Years Engaged in Adult Activities.* In *Smedley v. Piazzolla,* 59 A.D.2d 940, 399 N.Y.S.2d 460 (1977), the court held that the adult standard rule for driving did not apply to a four-year-old suspected of having released the emergency brake of an automobile.

10. *The Unreasonably Mature Child.* Assume that a three-year-old does not benefit from any "tender years" immunity, and allegedly has acted negligently in the course of a non-adult activity. Could any *rational* jury find the child liable?

In *Deliso v. Cangialosi,* 117 Misc. 2d 105, 457 N.Y.S.2d 396, 398 (1982), in which a set of keys struck a car during a game of "Monkey-in-the-Middle," the court held that "an eleven-year-old has the capacity to appreciate the inherent risk and danger of throwing a small metal object on to a public walkway or street."

11. *Intentional Tort Revisited.* Recall *Brown v. Dellinger,* 355 S.W.2d 742 (Tex. Civ. App. 1962), discussed in Chapter 3 *supra.* Contrast *Horton v. Reaves,* 186 Colo. 149, 526 P.2d 304, 307 (1974), where the court noted that:

> [O]ften as a matter of policy, other jurisdictions hold infants liable for their intentional torts, so as to avoid inflicting financial loss upon an innocent victim. It is our view, however, that the requisite intent required must include some awareness of the natural consequences of intentional acts. Though the extent of the resulting harm need not be intended, nor even foreseen, the infant must appreciate the offensiveness or wrongfulness of his act before liability inures.

12. *Case-by-Case Determination of the Appropriate Standard of Care.* In *Jackson v. McCuiston,* 247 Ark. 862, 448 S.W.2d 33, 35 (1969), where the issue was the negligence of a 14-year-old tractor operator, the court stated:

> We find it unnecessary in this case to adopt a rule in such broad form as [the adult activity categorization]. For the present we think it wiser to solve the problem as it is presented in the setting of a given case. In the case before us the adult defendants trained the minor defendant in the operation of a dangerous machine—dangerous particularly to third persons who found themselves in close proximity during operation. Young McCuiston regularly operated all different types of

farm tractors since he was twelve years of age. Unquestionably he was performing a job normally expected to be done by adults. Since he had been made proficient in the operation of the equipment it was his responsibility, and that of his masters, to see that he was apprised of those safeguards for others which would be possessed by an adult operator. If he is negligent in that important aspect of the operation then neither the minor operator nor his master should be permitted to invoke the aid of his minority. We therefore hold that in the ambit of this case, the defendant operator should be held to the standard of care of a reasonably careful adult.

What are the implications of this approach to the issue?

13. *Negligence Once Removed.* In *Ardinger v. Hummell*, 982 P.2d 727 (Alaska 1999), a 15-year-old driver was killed when he lost control of the car and collided with a utility pole. His passenger was the 14-year-old daughter of the car's owner. She had taken her mother's car keys without her mother's knowledge or permission. The driver's mother sued the passenger and her mother for negligent entrustment. The court instructed the jury to decide whether the daughter used the reasonable care "ordinarily used by children of the same age, intelligence, knowledge, and experience in circumstances similar to those shown by the evidence." After a jury verdict for the defendant the plaintiff contended that an adult standard should have been used. The court concluded:

> . . .Under Alaska law, exercising physical control of a motor vehicle on a roadway is an adult activity requiring a driver's license. Alaska law recognizes that operating a motor vehicle includes exercising dominion over or physical control of a motor vehicle just as it includes driving a motor vehicle. Children who physically control vehicles must, for public safety reasons, be held to an adult standard of care.
>
> In this case it is undisputed that Normandy had physical possession and control of the car when she allegedly allowed Joshua to drive. She took the keys from her mother; she drove the car to Joshua's house, where, assuming entrustment, she transferred physical control of the vehicle to Joshua. From the moment she assumed control of the car, any decisions she made as to the exercise and relinquishment of that control should be evaluated under an adult standard.
>
> We therefore conclude that Normandy engaged in adult conduct by taking control of the car. Her ability to entrust the car to Joshua necessarily stemmed from her exertion of actual possession and control over the vehicle. Thus, the jury should have been instructed that if Normandy entrusted the vehicle to Joshua, her actions should be evaluated under an adult standard of care. Failure to instruct the jury in this manner was reversible error.

14. *The Double-Standard Debate.* Does it matter whether it is the plaintiff (facing an affirmative defense of contributory or comparative fault), or the defendant, who is the child attracting an adult standard? What if both plaintiff and defendant are minors?

In *Goss v. Allen, supra,* the court opined, "Most of the cases which apply this standard have been concerned with the minor's contributory negligence

C. REASONABLE CARE AND PERSONAL CHARACTERISTICS 233

and not primary negligence. It has been suggested that a different standard might well apply where the minor's conduct causes injury to others. While this Court has not previously had occasion to consider this question, the Appellate Division has held that the principles enunciated by this Court regarding the contributory negligence of a child would also apply to a case where the primary negligence of a child is involved. We think that a rational basis exists for applying the same standard whether the issue involves a question of contributory negligence of a child, or primary negligence. Moreover, to hold otherwise would further complicate an already difficult area of tort law. The practicalities of the situation weigh heavily in favor of a single standard."

In *Daniels v. Evans*, 107 N.H. 407, 408, 224 A.2d 63, 66 (1966), the court stated, "[W]hen a minor is operating a motor vehicle there is no reason for making a distinction based on whether he is charged with primary negligence, [or] contributory negligence."

However, in *Dellwo v. Pearson*, 259 Minn. 452, 107 N.W.2d 859, 863 (1961), the court stated,

> [T]his court has previously recognized that there may be a difference between the standard of care that is required of a child in protecting himself against hazards and the standard that may be applicable when these activities expose others to hazards.

What are the reasons for this "double standard" debate? What tensions in the system does it highlight? How should the debate be resolved?

McCALL v. WILDER
913 S.W.2d 150 (Tenn. 1995)

WHITE, J.

. . .Plaintiff sued defendant in the Blount County General Sessions Court alleging that defendant's decedent hit plaintiffs vehicle head-on damaging the vehicle and injuring plaintiff. . . .. The basis for defendant's motion [for summary judgment] was that the accident was an unavoidable consequence of a sudden emergency created when the decedent suffered a seizure while driving. Defendant's motion was supported by the affidavit of a board certified physician practicing in the field of neurosurgery who treated decedent from the day of the accident until his death approximately three months later. According to the affidavit, a CT scan performed on the decedent after the accident revealed evidence of a brain tumor. Further evaluation and testing revealed that the tumor was located in a "very highly epileptogenic region of [the] brain." Surgery confirmed the presence of the brain tumor. The doctor opined that the tumor was present in decedent's brain on the day of the accident and that it made him susceptible to seizures. Therefore, the doctor concluded, within a reasonable degree of medical certainty, "that it is very likely that [decedent] suffered a seizure while driving his vehicle. . . which in turn caused the motor vehicle accident of December 12, 1990."

In response to defendant's motion for summary judgment, plaintiff filed the affidavit of a board certified physician concentrating in the fields of pathology and laboratory medicine. The affidavit reflected the parties" stipulations that decedent had experienced seizures prior to the day of the accident and that decedent knew he had a seizure disorder which caused loss of consciousness. The affidavit concluded, based upon independent research, including a review of decedent's medical records, consultation with a neurologist, a neuropathologist, and a family practitioner, that decedent "took an unreasonable risk by driving his vehicle knowing he suffered from a seizure disorder which caused a loss of consciousness. It was certainly foreseeable that an accident might occur if [decedent] experienced a seizure while driving his vehicle."

The trial court granted defendant's motion for summary judgment. In a divided decision, the Court of Appeals affirmed. The majority of the court reasoned that the case fell within the "established principles in this state that an automobile accident resulting from an unavoidable sudden emergency, such as an epileptic seizure, negates negligence.". . .

We granted plaintiffs application for permission to appeal to address the question of whether, and under what circumstances, liability may be imposed upon the driver of a car who suddenly loses control because the driver is rendered physically incapacitated by a medical disorder known to the driver. . . ..

. . .Perhaps surprisingly, this Court has not previously dealt with the liability of one who suddenly loses consciousness or control from a known medical disorder while driving. The Court of Appeals has faced the issue, but in only a limited number of cases, many of which are unpublished. In the earliest case, *Wishone v. Yellow Cab Co.*, 20 Tenn. App. 229, 97 S.W.2d 452 (Tenn. App.), cert. denied, (Tenn. 1936), a passenger in a taxicab was injured when the driver suddenly, and without warning, suffered an epileptic seizure. The driver had been experiencing such attacks, which caused unconsciousness, for several years prior to the accident. With little analysis, the Court of Appeals merely concluded that "there was no negligence immediately connected with the accident." Id.

In the only other relevant reported Tennessee decision, *Robinson v. Moore*, 512 S.W.2d 573 (Tenn. App.), cert. denied, (Tenn. 1974), a bus driver, who had slipped into a diabetic coma, ran a red light and caused an accident, The Court of Appeals found in favor of the employer and noted that the driver had been driving the bus for twenty-one years, had received numerous driving safety awards, and had never experienced a sudden blackout, although he knew he had diabetes and was receiving treatment for it. Additionally, the court focused on the absence of medical proof finding that plaintiff "adduced no medical testimony to the effect that the physical diseased condition of [defendant] rendered [defendant] incompetent [to drive.]" *Id.* at 578.

The unreported cases focus similarly on the substance of the medical evidence. In one, a driver experienced an epileptic seizure while driving. Though he knew he had epilepsy, the driver was under a physician's care, faithfully took his medication, had not had a seizure in the last two and one-half years, and had been advised by his physician that there was no reason to refrain from driving. A finding of no liability was affirmed.

In another case involving an accident caused by an epileptic seizure, the injured plaintiff relied on the fact that defendant had not taken her prescribed medication and had not asked her physician what the effect might be. Nonetheless, the judgment for plaintiff was reversed because plaintiff had not established that defendant's failure to take her medication had caused plaintiffs damages or that defendant's driving with the epileptic condition was an unreasonable risk.

The court deemed the absence of medical testimony establishing a foreseeable risk of danger by driving as critical because of the impossibility of evaluating the reasonableness of the risk without a medical evaluation of the severity of the condition, the effectiveness of the medication, and the likelihood of seizures with or without medication.

Our case law, as reflected in these few opinions, is generally consistent with the approach of other jurisdictions faced with similar situations. The generally accepted approach is to accept as a defense the sudden loss of physical capacity or consciousness while driving provided that the loss of capacity or consciousness was unforeseeable. ...

The rule recognized by these cases has been succinctly summarized as follows:

> The operator of a motor vehicle is not ordinarily chargeable with negligence because he becomes suddenly stricken by a fainting spell or loses consciousness from an unforeseen cause, and is unable to control the vehicle. In other words, fainting or momentary loss of consciousness while driving is a complete defense to an action based on negligence if such loss of consciousness was not foreseeable. ...
>
> If the operator of a motor vehicle knows that he [or she] is subject to attacks in the course of which he [or she] is likely to lose consciousness, such a loss of consciousness does not constitute a defense in an action brought by a person injured as a result of the operator's conduct.

7A Am. Jur.2d Automobiles and Highway Traffic, § 773 (1980). See also Travers, Annotation, Liability for Automobile Accident Allegedly Caused By Driver's Blackout, Sudden Unconsciousness, or the Like, 93 A.L.R.3d 326 (1979) ("Cases decided under negligence theories have uniformly held that a sudden loss of consciousness while driving is a complete defense to an action based on negligence . . . if such loss of consciousness was not foreseeable."). The rule covers accidents caused by, among other incapacitating events, actual loss of consciousness, dizziness, temporary loss of vision, stroke, heart attack, or seizure.

The key to establishing the physical capacity or loss of consciousness defense is foreseeability. Consequently, the defense would be inappropriate if the driver was aware of facts sufficient to cause a reasonably prudent person to anticipate that his or her driving might likely lead to an accident. Courts differ, however, in the strictness of the approach. For example, some courts hold that any driver suffering from a medical disorder capable of producing a seizure or unconsciousness is liable, as a matter of law, for driving at all. Other courts recognize that such knowledge creates a question for the jury as to whether there was a breach of the standard of care. Still other courts hold that the mere knowledge of past incapacitating medical episodes or a history of an incapacitating medical condition is insufficient notice to warrant a finding of negligence. These courts often require symptoms on the day of or immediately before the accident.

Our careful consideration of the jurisprudence of other jurisdictions and our own leads us to adopt the following rule: A sudden loss of consciousness or physical capacity experienced while driving which is not reasonably foreseeable is a defense to a negligence action. To constitute a defense, defendant must establish that the sudden loss of consciousness or physical capacity to control the vehicle was not reasonably foreseeable to a prudent person. As a result, the defense is not available under circumstances in which defendant was not made aware of facts sufficient to lead a reasonably prudent person to anticipate that driving in that condition would likely result in an accident.

In determining whether the loss of capacity or consciousness was foreseeable, pertinent, nonexclusive considerations would include: the extent of the driver's awareness or knowledge of the condition that caused the sudden incapacity; whether the driver had sought medical advice or was under a physician's care for the condition when the accident occurred; whether the driver had been prescribed, and had taken, medication for the condition; whether a sudden incapacity had previously occurred while driving; the number, frequency, extent, and duration of incapacitating episodes prior to the accident while driving and otherwise; the temporal relationship of the prior incapacitating episodes to the accident; a physician's guidance or advice regarding driving to the driver, if any; and medical opinions regarding the nature of the driver's condition, adherence to treatment, foreseeability of the incapacitation, and potential advance warnings which the driver would have experienced immediately prior to the accident. These factors, and any other relevant ones under the circumstances, would tend to establish whether the duty to exercise reasonable care was breached.

We agree with the Court of Appeals" reluctance to adopt a rule that would exclude individuals who had once suffered an incapacitating episode from ever driving again. Nonetheless, we can envision without much difficulty situations in which driving at all might constitute negligence. One who is ill or incapacitated at times may be negligent in driving at all when he or she is aware that a sudden incapacitation could likely occur at any moment. Restatement (Second) of Torts, § 283C, comment c (1965).[2]

Here, plaintiff contends that disputed issues of material fact exist as to whether decedent took an unreasonable risk by driving knowing that he suffered from a seizure disorder which caused loss of consciousness, and whether it was reasonably foreseeable that an accident might occur in the event he experienced a seizure while driving. In addition to the affidavit filed by plaintiff, plaintiff relies on two stipulated facts. First, plaintiff relies on the fact that decedent suffered seizures prior to the date of the accident. Second, plaintiff relies on the fact that decedent was aware that he suffered seizure disorders that caused, at times, a loss of consciousness.

---

[2] "An automobile driver who suddenly and quite unexpectedly suffers a heart attack does not become negligent when [the driver] loses control of [the] car and drives it in a manner which would otherwise be unreasonable, but one who knows that he [or she] is subject to such attacks may be negligent in driving at all." Restatement of Torts, § 283C, comment c (1965).

Conversely, defendant contends that the fact that the accident was caused by a suddenly occurring disability negates liability as a matter of law. Specifically it is defendant's contention that the record contains no facts from which a reasonable juror could find negligence. There is no evidence that decedent was prescribed medication or that he failed to follow a physician's recommendations. Further, there is no evidence of decedent's history or frequency of incapacitation and whether any debilitating episodes had occurred while he was driving.

In light of the stipulated facts that decedent had suffered seizures prior to the accident and was aware of the medical condition causing unconsciousness, we have no difficulty concluding that a jury could find that an accident with resulting injury to others was reasonably foreseeable. Even without the stipulated facts, decedent, under the law of this state, would owe a duty to act reasonably in light of the inherent dangers associated with driving. Unquestionably, decedent owed plaintiff a duty to act as a reasonably prudent person would act in light of the inherent dangers associated with driving and exacerbated by his known incapacitating medical condition.

Our second inquiry is whether the duty of reasonable care was breached. We are persuaded that defendant's argument that liability is negated as a matter of law sweeps too broadly and is inconsistent with the weight of authority from other jurisdictions. Additionally, defendant's assertion that he is entitled to summary judgment because plaintiff did not establish facts from which the jury could find negligence is equally unpersuasive. To survive the summary judgment motion filed by defendant, plaintiff was obliged to demonstrate that reasonable persons might draw differing conclusions from the facts. Plaintiff was not required to prove her case by a preponderance of the evidence in order to successfully counter defendant's summary judgment motion. Viewing the evidence in a light most favorable to plaintiff, and drawing all reasonable inferences in her behalf, as we must, we conclude that reasonable jurors could reach different conclusions as to whether decedent was acting as a reasonably prudent person in driving at the time the accident occurred.

. . .Finally, defendant's reliance on the sudden emergency doctrine is misplaced. The sudden emergency doctrine, which has now been subsumed into Tennessee's comparative fault scheme, Eaton v. McLain, 891 S.W.2d 587, 592 (Tenn. 1995), recognizes that a person confronted with a sudden or unexpected emergency which calls for immediate action is not expected to exercise the same accuracy of judgment as one acting under normal circumstances who has time for reflection and thought before acting.

The doctrine no longer constitutes a defense as a matter of law but, if at issue, must be considered as a factor in the total comparative fault analysis. Accordingly, the doctrine of sudden emergency does not negate defendant's liability in the case before us as a matter of law.

Therefore, summary judgment was improper. For these reasons, the judgment of the Court below granting and affirming summary judgment for defendant is vacated. The case is remanded to the trial court for proceedings consistent with this opinion.

NOTES

1. *Subjective Objectivism.* Although objective in nature, the decision-making process continually exhibits subjective characteristics. Furthermore, despite the essentially objective nature of the applied standard, the ability to fine-tune it for a particular defendant is institutionalized in the commonly found tag to the jury charge, "in all the circumstances." The "in all the circumstances" tag found in the typical objective negligence instruction permits the consideration of specific, detailed factors, and thus derogates from a totally objective model. What does this apparent ambivalence in the instruction tell us about the competing goals of accident law, and the tension likely to be encountered? Which "circumstances" are relevant to the negligence inquiry? Which are, or should be, irrelevant? Theoretical and structural considerations notwithstanding, degrees of flexibility continue to manifest themselves in jury instructions. Of all the specific elements that have been recognized as having continued relevance in the determination of objectively tested negligence, none has been as perplexing as the actor's personal characteristics.

2. *Sudden Emergencies.* In *Myhaver v. Knutson*, 189 Ariz. 286; 942 P.2d 445 (1997), the defendant accelerated and swerved left, avoiding what he perceived to be an impending head-on collision with another driver. In doing this, he crossed the double-yellow line into oncoming traffic and collided with plaintiff's pickup. The trial judge ruled that the "sudden emergency" instruction was appropriate under the facts and instructed the jury as follows:

> In determining whether a person acted with reasonable care under the circumstances, you may consider whether such conduct was affected by an emergency. . . .. An "emergency" is defined as a sudden and unexpected encounter with a danger which is either real or reasonably seems to be real. If a person, without negligence on his or her part, encountered such an emergency and acted reasonably to avoid harm to self or others, you may find that the person was not negligent. This is so even though, in hindsight, you find that under normal conditions some other or better course of conduct could and should have been followed.

On appeal, the Arizona Supreme Court affirmed, noting:

> One of the more careful analyses of the subject was made in *McKee v. Evans*, 380 Pa. Super. 120, 551 A.2d 260 (1988). The Pennsylvania court found that the instruction had been improperly given in favor of a driver involved in a ten-mile pursuit. The court concluded that the instruction was not favored and should be given only in those cases in which evidence showed that (1) the party seeking the instruction had not been negligent prior to the emergency, (2) the emergency had come about suddenly and without warning, and (3) reaction to the emergency was spontaneous, without time for reflection. While these factors are certainly not all-inclusive, we believe they help describe the situations to which the instruction should be confined.

> Having noted that the instruction is but a factor to be considered in determining reasonable care, is subsumed within the general concept of negligence, is a matter of argument rather than a principle

of law and can single out and unduly emphasize one factor and thus mislead a jury, we join those courts that have discouraged use of the instruction and urge our trial judges to give it only in the rare case. The instruction should be confined to the case in which the emergency is not of the routine sort produced by the impending accident but arises from events the driver could not be expected to anticipate.

We do not, however, join those courts that absolutely forbid use of the instruction. There are cases in which the instruction may be useful or may help to explain the need to consider a sudden emergency and the consequent reflexive actions of a party when determining reasonable care. We believe, however, that in those few cases in which the instruction is given, it would be important to explain that the existence of a sudden emergency and reaction to it are only some of the factors to be considered in determining what is reasonable conduct under the circumstances. Even though a judge may exercise his discretion and give a sudden emergency instruction in a particular case, it will rarely, if ever, be error to refuse to give it.

Applying these principles to the case at bench, we conclude that the trial judge did not abuse his discretion in giving the instruction. This is a case in which there was no evidence of antecedent negligence by [the defendant], in whose favor the instruction was given. In light of the testimony of the various witnesses, there was no question about the existence of an emergency. [The defendant] was faced with a situation not ordinarily to be anticipated and one of imminent peril when [another driver] pulled out of the shopping center and suddenly turned toward him in the wrong lane of traffic. Finally, [defendant's] reaction—swerving across the center line into the path of [plaintiff's] oncoming vehicle—was probably both reflexive in nature and the type of conduct that absent a sudden emergency would almost automatically be found as negligence, if not negligence per se. Given these facts, the real and only issue was whether [defendant's] conduct was reasonable under the circumstances of the emergency. We believe, therefore, the trial judge had discretion to instruct on the sudden emergency as a factor in the determination of negligence.

Compare the views of the Alaska Supreme Court in *Lyons v. Midnight Sun Transportation Services, Inc.*, 928 P.2d 1202 (Alaska 1996),

We believe that the sudden emergency instruction is a generally useless appendage to the law of negligence. With or without an emergency, the standard of care a person must exercise is still that of a reasonable person under the circumstances. With or without the instruction, parties are still entitled to present evidence at trial which will establish what the circumstances were, and are also entitled to argue to the jury that they acted as a reasonable person would have in light of those circumstances. Thus, barring circumstances that we cannot at the moment hypothesize, a sudden emergency instruction serves no positive function. Further, the instruction may cause confusion by appearing to imply that one party is less blameworthy than the other. Therefore, we hold that it should not be used unless a court finds that the particular and peculiar facts of a case warrant more explanation of the standard of care than is generally required.

Consider also *Raimondo v. Harding,* 41 A.D.2d 62, 341 N.Y.S.2d 679 (1973), in which the 14-year-old plaintiff had been called a "punk" and threatened by some "fraternity guys." The plaintiff was running away when he was hit by defendant's vehicle. The court held that the jury should have been instructed on the so-called "emergency charge" when determining the issue of plaintiff's contributory negligence.

3. *Distracting Circumstances.* In *Harfield v. Tate,* 598 N.W.2d 840 (N.D. 1999), the court examined the related doctrines of "distracting circumstances" and "momentary forgetfulness," concluding:

> The "distracting circumstances" doctrine does not lower or minimize one's expected standard of care. Under such circumstances the person invoking the doctrine is required to exercise that degree of care which an ordinarily prudent person would exercise under similar circumstances. A person invoking the doctrine is not exonerated merely because of the presence of distracting circumstances. As we have stated with regard to the sudden emergency doctrine, "the doctrine is simply a principle of law to be utilized in determining the issue of negligence where the actor is suddenly confronted with [distracting circumstances] not of his own making or fault." *Gronneberg v. Hoffart,* 466 N.W.2d 809, 812 (N.D. 1991) 598 NW2d at 845.

4. *Physical Disabilities.* RESTATEMENT (SECOND) OF TORTS (1965) § 283C provides:

> If the actor is ill or otherwise physically disabled, the standard of conduct to which he must conform to avoid being negligent is that of a reasonable [person] under like disability.

What is a physical disability? Which disabilities should or should not be taken into account? Why should the court concern itself with any such personal determinant of liability? Does such a concern unjustifiably focus our attention on the wrongdoer at the expense of the victim? Suppose the defendant was an alcoholic. Would the court then permit an instruction phrased in terms of a reasonably prudent inebriate? How should that compare to the standard expected of a hyperglycemic diabetic?

CREASY v. RUSK
730 N.E.2d 659 (Ind. 2000)

SULLIVAN, JUSTICE.

. . .In July, 1992, Lloyd Rusk's wife admitted Rusk to the Brethren Healthcare Center ("BHC") because he suffered from memory loss and confusion and Rusk's wife was unable to care for him. Rusk's primary diagnosis was Alzheimer's disease. Over the course of three years at BHC, Rusk experienced periods of anxiousness, confusion, depression, disorientation, and agitation. Rusk often resisted when staff members attempted to remove him from prohibited areas of the facility. On several occasions, Rusk was belligerent with both staff and other residents. In particular, Rusk was often combative, agitated, and aggressive and would hit staff members when they tried to care for him.

BHC had employed Creasy as a certified nursing assistant for nearly 20 months when the incident at issue occurred. Creasy's responsibilities included caring for Rusk and other patients with Alzheimer's disease. Creasy did not have specialized training on how to care for people with Alzheimer's disease, but she did attend a short BHC presentation on the pathological effects of Alzheimer's. Residents with Alzheimer's had bruised Creasy during the course of her work for BHC, and Creasy knew that Rusk had Alzheimer's disease.

On May 16, 1995, Creasy and another certified nursing assistant, Linda Davis, were working through their routine of putting Rusk and other residents to bed. Creasy knew that Rusk had been "very agitated and combative that evening." By Creasy's account:

> [Davis] was helping me put Mr. Rusk to bed. She was holding his wrists to keep him from hitting us and I was trying to get his legs to put him to bed. He was hitting and kicking wildly. During this time, he kicked me several times in my left knee and hip area. My lower back popped and I yelled out with pain from my lower back and left knee.

Creasy filed a civil negligence suit against Rusk, seeking monetary damages for the injuries she suffered as a result of Rusk's conduct. Rusk moved for summary judgment and the trial court granted his motion. . . ..

In many, if not most, jurisdictions, the general duty of care imposed on adults with mental disabilities is the same as that for adults without mental disabilities. See Restatement (Second) of Torts § 283B (1965). Adults with mental disabilities are held to the same standard of care as that of a reasonable person under the same circumstances without regard to the alleged tortfeasor's capacity to control or understand the consequences of his or her actions.

. . .Judge Kirsch, writing for the Court of Appeals in this case, found that Indiana law does not follow the Restatement rule. The Court of Appeals held "that a person's mental capacity, whether that person is a child or an adult, must be factored [into] the determination of whether a legal duty exists." *Creasy v. Rusk*, 696 N.E.2d 442, 446 (Ind. Ct. App. 1998). We believe that the Court of Appeals accurately stated Indiana law but that the law is in need of revision.

With respect to children, Indiana has incorporated the essence of the Restatement standard for determining the liability of children for their alleged tortious acts. The Restatement standard of conduct for a child is "that of a reasonable person of like age, intelligence, and experience under like circumstances." Restatement (Second) of Torts § 283A (1965) (hereinafter, "Restatement rule"). Indiana reformulates the Restatement rule into a three-tiered analysis:

> Children under the age of 7 years are conclusively presumed to be incapable of being contributorily negligent, from 7 to 14 a rebuttable presumption exists they may be guilty thereof, and over 14, absent

special circumstances, they are chargeable with exercising the standard of care of an adult.

Bailey v. Martz, 488 N.E.2d 716, 721 (Ind. Ct. App. 1986). In the age seven to fourteen category, Indiana applies the Restatement standard and ascertains whether the child exercised the care under the circumstances of a child of like age, knowledge, judgment, and experience.

Consistent with recognizing a rule that holds a child to a standard of care proportionate to his or her capacity Judge Kirsch observed that Indiana has also indicated a willingness to consider the mental capacity of an adult with mental disabilities when determining negligence liability, *Creasy*, 696 N.E.2d at 445. . . . [T]he Court of Appeals held that the rule in Indiana is "that a person's mental capacity, whether that person is a child or an adult, must be factored [into] the determination of whether a legal duty exists." *Creasy*, 696 N.E.2d at 446.

. . . [T]he generally accepted rule in jurisdictions other than Indiana is that mental disability does not excuse a person from liability for "conduct which does not conform to the standard of a reasonable man under like circumstances." Restatement (Second) of Torts § 283B; accord Restatement (Third) of Torts § 9 (Discussion Draft Apr. 5, 1999) ("Unless the actor is a child, the actor's mental or emotional disability is not considered in determining whether conduct is negligent."). People with mental disabilities are commonly held liable for their intentional and negligent torts. No allowance is made for lack of intelligence, ignorance, excitability, or proneness to accident.

Legal scholars and authorities recognize that it is "impossible to ascribe either the volition implicit in an intentional tort, the departure from the standard of a 'reasonable' person which defines an act of ordinary negligence, or indeed any concept of 'fault' at all to one who . . . is by definition unable to control his [or her] own actions through any exercise of reason." *Anicet v. Gant*, 580 So. 2d 273, 275 (Fla. Dist. Ct. App. 1991) (citations omitted). Rather, the Restatement rule holding people with mental disabilities liable for their torts was founded upon public policy considerations.

The public policy reasons most often cited for holding individuals with mental disabilities to a standard of reasonable care in negligence claims include the following.

(1) Allocates losses between two innocent parties to the one who caused or occasioned the loss. *See, e.g., Gould v. American Family Mut. Ins.*, 198 Wis. 2d 450, 543 N.W.2d 282, 286 (Wis. 1996). Under this rationale, the one who experienced the loss or injury as a result of the conduct of a person with a mental disability is presumed not to have assumed risks or to have been contributorily negligent with respect to the cause of the injury. This policy is also intended to protect even negligent third parties from bearing excessive liabilities.

(2) Provides incentive to those responsible for people with disabilities and interested in their estates to prevent harm and "restrain" those who are potentially dangerous.

(3) Removes inducements for alleged tortfeasors to fake a mental disability in order to escape liability. The Restatement mentions the ease with which mental disability can be feigned as one possible basis for this policy concern.

C. REASONABLE CARE AND PERSONAL CHARACTERISTICS

(4) Avoids administrative problems involved in courts and juries attempting to identify and assess the significance of an actor's disability. As a practical matter, it is arguably too difficult to account for or draw any "satisfactory line between mental deficiency and those variations of temperament, intellect, and emotional balance."

(5) Forces persons with disabilities to pay for the damage they do if they "are to live in the world." The Restatement adds that it is better that the assets, if any, of the one with the mental deficiency be used "to compensate innocent victims than that [the assets] remain in their hands.". A discussion draft for the Restatement (Third) of Torts rephrases this policy rationale and concludes: "If a person is suffering from a mental disorder so serious as to make it likely that the person will engage in substandard conduct that threatens the safety of others, there can be doubts as to whether this person should be allowed to engage in the normal range of society's activities; given these doubts, there is nothing especially harsh in at least holding the person responsible for the harms the person may cause by substandard conduct."

To assist in deciding whether Indiana should adopt the generally accepted rule, we turn to an examination of contemporary public policy in Indiana as embodied in enactments of our state legislature.

Since the 1970s, Indiana law has strongly reflected policies to deinstitutionalize people with disabilities and integrate them into the least restrictive environment. National policy changes have led the way for some of Indiana's enactments in that several federal acts either guarantee the civil rights of people with disabilities or condition state aid upon state compliance with desegregation and integrationist practices. . ..

These legislative developments reflect policies consistent with those supporting the Restatement rule generally accepted outside Indiana in that they reflect a determination that people with disabilities should be treated in the same way as non-disabled persons.

We pause for a moment to consider in greater detail the [argument] that the Restatement rule may very well have been grounded in a policy determination that persons with mental disabilities should be institutionalized or otherwise confined rather than "live in the world." It is clear from our recitation of state and federal legislative and regulatory developments that contemporary public policy has rejected institutionalization and confinement for a "strong professional consensus in favor of . . . community treatment . . . and integration into the least restrictive . . . environment." Indeed, scholarly commentary has noted that "new statutes and case law . . . have transformed the areas of commitment, guardianship, confidentiality, consent to treatment, and institutional conditions." We observe that it is a matter of some irony that public policies favoring the opposite ends of institutionalization and confinement on the one hand and community treatment and integration into the least restrictive environment on the other should nevertheless yield the same common law rule: that the general duty of care imposed on adults with mental disabilities is the same as that for adults without mental disabilities.

In balancing the considerations presented in the foregoing analysis, we reject the Court of Appeals's approach and adopt the Restatement rule. We hold that a person with mental disabilities is generally held to the same standard of care as that of a reasonable person under the same circumstances without regard to the alleged tortfeasor's capacity to control or understand the consequences of his or her actions.

We turn now to the question of whether the circumstances of Rusk's case are such that the general duty of care imposed upon adults with mental disabilities should be found to run from him to Creasy.

In asking this question, we recognize that exceptions to the general rule will arise where the factual circumstances negate the factors supporting imposition of a duty particularly with respect to the nature of the parties' relationship and public policy considerations. For example, courts in jurisdictions that apply the reasonable person standard to individuals with mental disabilities have uniformly held that Alzheimer's patients who have no capacity to control their conduct do not owe a duty to their caregivers to refrain from violent conduct because the factual circumstances negate the policy rationales behind the presumption of liability. *See Colman v. Notre Dame Convalescent Home, Inc.*, 968 F. Supp. 809 (D. Conn. 1997) (holding that while an adult with mental disabilities is ordinarily responsible for injuries resulting from negligence, no duty arises between an institutionalized patient and his or her caregiver); *Gould v. American Family Mut. Ins. Co.*, 198 Wis. 2d 450, 543 N.W.2d 282 (Wis. 1996) (carving out an exception to the presumption of liability for institutionalized mentally disabled people who are unable to control or appreciate the consequences of their conduct when they injure paid caregivers and noting that these circumstances negate the rationale behind the presumption and that application of the presumption would place an unreasonable burden on people with mental disabilities who are institutionalized); *Herrle v. Estate of Marshall*, 45 Cal. App. 4th 1761, 53 Cal. Rptr. 2d 713 (Ct. App. 1996) (concluding that public policy precluded imposition of liability because the healthcare provider, not the patient, is in the best position to protect against risk of injury to the service provider where the risk is rooted in the reason for the treatment), review denied; *Mujica v. Turner*, 582 So. 2d 24 (Fla. Dist. Ct. App. 1991) (holding nursing home patient with Alzheimer's was not liable for injury to a physical therapist), review denied; *Anicet v. Gant*, 580 So. 2d 273 (Fla. Dist. Ct. App. 1991) (concluding that a person who has no capacity to control his or her conduct does not owe a duty to refrain from violent conduct toward a person who is specifically employed to treat or control the patient), review denied.

We find that the relationship between Rusk and Creasy and public policy concerns dictate that Rusk owed no duty of care to Creasy. . ..

Unlike the typical victim supporting the Restatement rationale, Creasy was not a member of the public at large, unable to anticipate or safeguard against the harm she encountered. Creasy knew of Rusk's violent history. She could have changed her course of action or requested additional assistance when she recognized Rusk's state of mind on the evening when she received the alleged injury. Rusk's inability to comprehend the circumstances of his relationship with Creasy and others was the very reason Creasy was employed to support Rusk. The nursing home and Creasy, through the nursing home, were "employed to encounter, and knowingly did encounter, just the dangers which injured" Creasy. In fact, caregivers and their employers under these circumstances are better positioned to prevent caregiver injury and to protect against risks faced as a result of job responsibilities. In Indiana, the workers' compensation system, not the tort system, exists to cover such employment-related losses. To the extent that the workers' compensation system is inadequate as Creasy asserts, the inadequacy reflects defects in the workers' compensation system and is not a ground for alternative recovery under tort law.

The first rationale behind the Restatement rule justifies imposing a duty on a defendant with a mental disability where it seems unfair to force a plaintiff who did not contribute to the cause of his or her injury to bear the cost of that injury. This policy concern overlaps with the relationship analysis set forth *supra*. The nature of Creasy and Rusk's relationship was such that Creasy cannot be "presumed not to have assumed risks . . . with respect to the cause of the injury." See Rationale (1), *supra*. Therefore, imposing a duty on Rusk in this circumstance is not justified by the first Restatement policy rationale.

The second Restatement policy rationale creates an inducement for those responsible for a person with a mental disability to prevent harm to others. By placing Rusk in a nursing home, we presume Rusk's wife made a difficult decision based on her desire to prevent Rusk from being violent and harming himself, herself, or others. Without endorsing the incentives for confinement arguably fostered by the Restatement rationale, we agree with the conclusion set forth by the Wisconsin Supreme Court in *Gould* that a family member who places a relative in a long-term care facility, institution, nursing home, or similarly restrictive environment is unlikely to need further inducement to restrain the one for whom they are responsible. *See Gould*, 543 N.W.2d at 287. Mrs. Rusk entrusted her husband's care, including prevention of the harm he might bring to others, to the nursing home staff and the nursing home. And as a business enterprise, the nursing home received compensation for its services.

With respect to the third policy rationale, "it is virtually impossible to imagine circumstances under which a person would feign the symptoms of mental disability and subject themselves to commitment to an institution in order to avoid some future civil liability." *Id. See also* Rationale (3), supra. To the extent that such circumstances exist, there is no evidence whatsoever that they are present under the facts in this case.

Finally, there are no administrative difficulties in this case with respect to determining the degree and existence of Rusk's mental disability.[3] Under the relationship analysis set forth above and the present policy analysis, it is unnecessary to determine the degree of Rusk's mental disability. We need only

---

[3] Many legal scholars have questioned the significance of the "administrative difficulties and judicial efficiency" policy rationale behind the Restatement rule. They argue that our legal system regularly entrusts judges and juries as fact-finders to make difficult determinations about mental competence for a range of legal issues (e.g., guardianship, contract and testamentary capacity, criminal proceedings, contributory negligence allocations in tort claims, and commitment hearings) because fact-finders are uniquely positioned to weigh evidence, judge credibility, assess witness testimony, and apply the law thereto.

conclude that Rusk had a mental disability which served as the reason for his presence in the nursing home and the foundation of his relationship with Creasy.

[T]here was no material question of fact as to the existence, let alone the advanced stage, of Rusk's Alzheimer's disease and his inability to appreciate or control his violent behavior. Rusk was admitted to the nursing home because he was confused and suffering from memory loss such that his wife could not care for him. By May 1995, when Creasy was injured by Rusk, Rusk had been a resident of the nursing home for three years and his condition had deteriorated. He regularly displayed behaviors characteristic of a person with advanced Alzheimer's disease such as aggression, belligerence, and violence. As evidence of Rusk's state of mind, Rusk presented an affidavit from Sharon Ayres [a licensed practical nurse employed by the nursing home] stating that Rusk was in the advanced stage of Alzheimer's and was therefore unable to appreciate the consequences of his actions. . ..

In addition to the public policy concerns behind the Restatement rule, we find that it would be contrary to public policy to hold Rusk to a duty to Creasy when it would place "too great a burden on him because his disorientation and potential for violence is the very reason he was institutionalized and needed the aid of employed caretakers." *Gould*, 543 N.W.2d at 286.

Rusk was entitled to summary judgment because public policy and the nature of the relationship between Rusk, Creasy, and the nursing home preclude holding that Rusk owed a duty of care to Creasy under these factual circumstances.

. . .[W]e now affirm the trial court, finding that Rusk did not owe a duty to Creasy, and grant Rusk's motion for summary judgment.

NOTES

1. *Psychological Characteristics.* RESTATEMENT (SECOND) OF TORTS (1965) § 283B provides:

> Unless the actor is a child, his insanity or other mental deficiency does not relieve the actor from liability for conduct which does not conform to the standard of a reasonable man under like circumstances.

Why should physical, but not mental, characteristics be taken into account?

Contrast Hammontree v. Jenner, 20 Cal. App. 3d 528, 97 Cal. Rptr. 739 (1971), discussed in Chapter 2, *supra. Compare* the fireman's rule, discussed in Chapter 8, *infra*.

Which is the more *efficient* approach: *Creasy,* or that followed in the Restatement? Does the RESTATEMENT contemplate liability only in the case of a more or less permanent mental disability, as opposed to a sudden seizure? Why should any such distinction be drawn?

In *Goff v. Taylor,* 708 S.W.2d 113 (Ky. App. 1986), involving an unprovoked killing by a defendant who was apparently mentally unstable, the court made these comments about the criticisms of the RESTATEMENT approach:

That [a] subjective standard would afford fairer treatment of a defendant afflicted with a mental disability cannot be disputed. The question the commentators do not attempt to reach is the fairness to the victim of the wrongful conduct. Is a victim any less entitled to compensation for his loss because of the mental deficiencies of his tortfeasor? We believe that the answer is no, and the tort law as it stands has long served to accommodate that principle. This view does not penalize the mentally incompetent, it merely places them on a par with the rest of society in terms of responsibility for their wrongful acts. The mentally deficient are insulated from punitive damages, reinforcing our belief that tort law has kept faith with its duty to balance the protection of society at large with compassion for those unable to conform their conduct to the expected standard.

Contrast *McGuire v. Almy,* 297 Mass. 323, 8 N.E.2d 760 (1937), discussed in Chapter 3, *supra.* Does *Goff* stop at placing such a defendant "on a par with the rest of society," or is the risk of the mentally ill defendant's conduct being shifted elsewhere?

2. *Voluntary and Involuntary Intoxication.* RESTATEMENT (SECOND) OF TORTS (1965) § 283C, comment *d*, provides in part:

> The rule [of nonliability] stated in this Section applies to involuntary intoxication, as in the highly unusual case in which one who believes he is drinking tea is plied with liquor, and so becomes disabled. . . . Where, however, the intoxication is voluntary, or where it results from deliberate drinking with knowledge of what is being consumed, so that the result is deliberately risked, the policy of the law has refused to make any allowance for the resulting disability, and the rule stated in this Section is not applied.

What standard of care is expected of a voluntarily intoxicated pedestrian? Of a voluntarily intoxicated automobile driver?

PROBLEM

Dana Derby was driving through downtown Filly, heading south. While Dana was stopped at an intersection for a red light, two strangers walked toward Dana's car with rags and window cleaner in hand. Dana, who lived in the suburbs, was frightened and stepped on the accelerator, speeding into the intersection just as Bo Burt's car was entering the intersection from the west. In the ensuing collision, Bo's car was damaged, and Bo sued Dana.

The speed limit for driving in the city was 35 miles per hour. Both parties stipulated that Bo entered the intersection at approximately 45 miles per hour.

1. Should the judge merely instruct the jury that Dana's conduct must be evaluated in light of what the ordinary prudent person would do in similar circumstances? What instruction should Dana's attorney request to evaluate whether Dana's conduct was negligent?

2. Should the judge permit evidence that people customarily drove at 45 miles per hour at the intersection?

BODIN v. CITY OF STANWOOD
130 Wn.2d 726, 927 P.2d 240 (1996)

MADSEN, J.

In November 1990, flood waters twice overflowed the Stillaguamish River and overtopped dikes surrounding the City of Stanwood's sewage treatment lagoon, resulting in floodwaters and sewage flowing out of the lagoon and onto adjacent property owned or rented by plaintiffs. . ..

Since 1962, the City has operated a 40-acre sewage treatment facility and oxidation lagoon on a floodplain near the Stillaguamish River. Sewage pumped from the City is treated and then discharged into the river. Lagoon dikes surround the facility. . ..

Periodic flooding has occurred in the City and surrounding area as a result of high tides and high Stillaguamish river flows. The City knew that high floods could result in flooding of the lagoon. In the late 1970's an engineering firm recommended that the City raise the dikes surrounding the lagoon to 12 feet because floodwaters had nearly breached the dikes during floods. In 1982, a private engineer providing engineering services to the City estimated that the dikes could be raised at a cost of about $50,000.00. An application for funding was submitted to the Department of Ecology, which turned down the application. During the early and mid-1980's, the City considered plans for flood control. Following a flood in 1986, engineers prepared a report recommending that during a five-year period ending in 1992 the City raise the level of the dikes and make other improvements to handle floodwaters, including building a dam across a nearby slough and placing floodgates on the Stillaguamish River. In 1987, an application for a federal Housing and Urban Development (HUD) block grant was submitted in connection with a proposed flood improvement control plan, which included raising the lagoon dikes. HUD agreed to provide funds beginning in 1989. Prior to, and following this agreement, permitting, land acquisition, and design were undertaken by the City and its engineer.

In November of 1990, before the lagoon dikes were raised, heavy rains and warm temperatures caused severe flooding along rivers throughout western Washington, including the Stillaguamish. Twice, floodwater flowed over the top of the lagoon dikes into the lagoon, and then out, spilling sewer effluent and floodwaters across plaintiffs' properties. The November 10, 1990, flood peaked at 10.51 feet, and the November 24, 1990, flood peaked at 10.63 feet. Early in 1991 the City raised the height of the dikes to 12 feet.

Plaintiffs sued the City of Stanwood, alleging their properties were damaged as a result of the floods. They claimed the City was negligent in designing, constructing, and maintaining the sewage treatment lagoon and facility. . ..

Plaintiffs then moved in limine to preclude the City from presenting evidence that it had insufficient funds to make repairs or changes in the dikes to prevent floodwaters from overtopping the dikes. The City's counsel argued that evidence of efforts to obtain grant funds and the lengthy process involved were relevant to the reasonableness of the City's response to the perceived need to raise the dikes. She explained that the City did not intend to claim that it lacked funds to raise the dikes. The trial court denied the motion, stating that the question of reasonable efforts was for the jury. Later, the court reaffirmed this ruling, but stated that if the City presented evidence of its efforts to obtain grant funds, plaintiffs' would be permitted to show that the City had sufficient funds of its own to raise the dikes. At trial, the City presented evidence of its efforts to obtain grant funds, and the process involved in the HUD funding. Plaintiffs presented uncontroverted evidence that the City had sufficient funds to raise the level of the dikes before the HUD grant application process, and well before the 1990 floods.

The jury was instructed on the City's duty, in connection with the sewer lagoon and treatment facility, to adjacent property holders. Plaintiffs proposed additional instructions on the City's duty, which the trial court refused to give. The trial court also refused to give plaintiffs' proposed instructions directing the jury that it could not consider the evidence of the City's efforts to obtain grant funds.

The jury returned a verdict in favor of the City. . .

The defendant has a duty to exercise ordinary care in connection with the construction, design, maintenance and repair of its sewer lagoon and tide gate and pump station and to keep, construct, and maintain them in a manner and condition that is reasonably safe for adjacent property owners. This instruction is virtually the same as an instruction proposed by plaintiffs.

. . .The trial court . . . correctly rejected plaintiffs' proposed instruction that the City was liable for its tortious conduct to the same extent as if it were a private person and that a lack of funds or the City's desire to use federal, state or county funds is not a defense to the failure to raise the lagoon dikes. As this opinion will explain, the City did not assert a "defense" based upon lack of funds or the desire to use grant money. Instead, its attempts to obtain grant funds constitute admissible evidence on whether the City acted reasonably under the circumstances. The proposed instruction was therefore misleading and, under the circumstances of this case, a misstatement of the law. Other instructions correctly stated the law with regard to the City's liability for its negligence, if any.

Plaintiffs' chief complaint is that the trial court erred in ruling that evidence of the City's efforts to procure grant funds to raise the level of the dikes surrounding the sewage lagoon was admissible. The City claims that the evidence was admissible on the question whether the City complied with its duty to use reasonable care.

For conduct to be negligent, it must be unreasonable in light of a recognizable danger. W. Page Keeton et al., Prosser and Keeton on Torts sec. 31, at 170 (5th ed. 1984). The "ordinary" or "reasonable" care which a municipality must exercise is "that care which an ordinarily reasonable person would exercise under the same or similar circumstances." *Berglund v. Spokane County*, 4 Wash. 2d 309, 315, 103 P.2d 355 (1940). In assessing the standard of reasonable care, a risk-benefit analysis is usually part of the determination. The analysis involves balancing the risk of harm, "in the light of the social value of the interest threatened, and the probability and extent of the harm, against the value of the interest which the actor is seeking to protect, and the expedience of the course pursued." Keeton et al. sec. 31, at 173. Among other things, consideration must be given to alternative courses open to the actor. Id. at 172. Further, "while mere inconvenience or cost are often insufficient in themselves to justify proceeding in the face of danger, they will justify taking some risks which are not too extreme." *Id*.

Thus, as in the case of a private defendant charged with negligence, the determination whether a municipality has exercised reasonable care "must in each case necessarily depend upon the surrounding circumstances." *Berglund*, 4 Wash. 2d at 316. In *Berglund*, the court observed that factors relevant to the determination whether the county there complied with its duty to use reasonable care in keeping its public ways in a reasonably safe condition included "the financial burden, technical considerations, and other factual considerations . . . ." *Id*. at 319.

Plaintiffs' urge that allowing the City to submit evidence of the efforts to obtain grant money amounted to allowing the City to present a so-called "poverty" or "hardship" defense, rather than evidence on the reasonableness of the City's conduct. However, the City did not claim that it lacked funds to raise the level of the dikes, and indeed evidence was presented to the jury that the City had sufficient funds in its sewer construction account to raise the level of the dikes well before the 1990 floods. In denying the plaintiffs' motion for a new trial, the trial court recognized the distinction between a poverty defense and evidence going to the reasonableness of the City's conduct, stating that there was no allowing in this case of the City to argue—and the City did not argue—that it didn't have the money to undertake these improvements. In fact, I think there is undisputed testimony that the money was there to do the improvements, but that the City did not perceive the risk to be such that they needed to act any more promptly than they did. Factually, there is no merit to plaintiffs' claim that a "poverty" defense was allowed.

Plaintiffs also maintain that the City was allowed to use the evidence to "excuse" its inaction and to "exonerate" itself of negligence. These claims also misapprehend the purpose for which the evidence was admitted and the principles by which negligence is determined. Plaintiffs maintained that by failing to raise the lagoon dikes, the City was negligent. The City then sought to show that rather than the inaction plaintiffs claimed, the City was in fact taking steps to improve the lagoon dikes as part of overall flood control measures while at the same time relying upon flood fighting efforts, including sandbagging and controlled breaches of dikes to direct floodwaters, efforts which had been effective in prior floods. The evidence of the engineering studies and designs, planning, grant applications, compliance with grant conditions, permitting and land acquisition was evidence of the City's response to the perceived danger, as was the evidence of its flood fighting efforts which had previously been successful. Although there was evidence of seepage into the lagoon during flooding before November 1990, the 1990 floods were the first to overtop the lagoon dikes.

Notably, the City's response to the risk cannot be assessed independently of the risk itself. The probability and extent of the harm must be considered in the balance. Disputed evidence was presented both as to the height of a 100-year flood, and the height of the lagoon dikes, with the City presenting evidence that the dikes were sufficient to withstand 100-year floods, and evidence that the November 1990 floods exceeded 100-year flood levels and were nearly unprecedented in terms of the cubic feet per second of water which flooded the lagoon and surrounding area in a very short time.

Whether one charged with negligence has exercised reasonable care is ordinarily a question of fact for the trier of fact. The question for the jury was what a reasonable person would do "under the same or similar circumstances.'" Keeton et al. sec. 32, at 175 (quoting Restatement (Second) of Torts sec. 283). The reasonable person standard "must make proper allowance for the risk apparent to the actor . . . ." Id. at 174. As noted, the alternative courses of action available and the expedience of the course chosen must be considered. Contrary to plaintiffs' claim that the City did nothing during the time between the time it allegedly had notice of a dangerous condition and the November 1990 floods, the City embarked upon one of at least three alternative courses open to it, i.e., inaction, immediately raising the level of the dikes, and the course it chose, protecting against harm by its flood fighting efforts, including sandbagging, while conducting studies and looking to a long term solution involving an overall flood control program funded at least in part through grant money, with raising of the lagoon dikes being a component of that program. Given the conflicting evidence on the questions of what constituted a 100-year flood and the height of the dikes, the degree of risk posed by the lagoon could be perceived by the jury as great or not, depending upon the evidence the jury believed. It was, however, for the jury to decide whether the City's assessment of the risk and its decision, in light of that risk, to delay raising the dike and rely upon its flood fighting efforts in the interim was reasonable. Without the evidence of attempts to obtain grant money and the lengthy process entailed, the City could not adequately explain how it was responding to the risk of harm, and the reasonableness of its selection among various alternative courses of action could not be adequately assessed.

. . .Plaintiffs contend, though, that the evidence showed the City's particular financial circumstances and fiscal strategy, and maintain such evidence is not relevant to the reasonableness of the City's conduct, nor would it be evidence which a private person would be entitled to have admitted. While the precise issue in this case has not previously been addressed, Washington cases support our conclusion that the trial court did not abuse its discretion in ruling the evidence admissible. First, we have recognized, for example, that municipalities may present evidence of practicality, cost or otherwise, of guardrails and barriers on roads and bridges. As noted above, "the financial burden, technical considerations, and other factual circumstances" are all relevant factors to consider in whether a municipality has exercised reasonable care. *Berglund v. Spokane County*, 4 Wash. 2d 309, 319, 103 P.2d 355 (1940).
. . .Washington cases thus demonstrate that financial considerations may be relevant to the issue of the reasonableness of a municipality's conduct. The City here chose not to use money in its sewer construction fund, which it explains was viewed as a reserve for unanticipated expenditures for the total sewer system, but instead chose to seek outside funds.

Plaintiffs claim, though, that this case is like *Savage v. State*, 72 Wash. App. 483, 864 P.2d 1009 (1994), aff'd in part and reversed in part, 127 Wash. 2d 434, 899 P.2d 1270 (1995), and argue the evidence was inadmissible under the holding there that the trial court did not abuse its discretion in refusing to give an instruction that the availability of funding to the State could be considered in deciding whether parole officers' actions in supervising parolees were reasonable. The court reasoned that no authority was cited for the proposition that a private person or a corporation would be entitled to such an instruction. Initially we note that refusal to give the instruction was upheld by this court on the basis that the State presented no evidence of its available resources or its resource allocation policy and there was accordingly insufficient evidence to justify the instruction. Moreover, unlike Savage, the *City* here did not seek a specific instruction regarding its financial resources or its resource allocation policy, and none was given.

Further, this case is unlike *Cramer v. Van Parys*, 7 Wash. App. 584, 500 P.2d 1255 (1972), which plaintiffs rely upon for the proposition that a private party would not be entitled to present the evidence of attempts to obtain grant money. In that case, which involved alleged negligence for failure to remove snow and negligence per se for failing to comply with a stair rail ordinance at an apartment building, the court held that a landlord was not entitled to present evidence of his monthly income from the building to show that he could not afford someone to manage his apartments. The court said that "evidence of the financial circumstances of the parties to an action is ordinarily immaterial and irrelevant[,]" and that "the purpose for which the evidence was offered does not convince us of its materiality here. Financial hardship cannot be an excuse for failing to perform a duty undertaken for economic benefit." *Cramer*, 7 Wash. App. at 593–94. Here, the City never claimed that it could not afford to raise the dikes and has not claimed financial hardship, nor is a municipality's operation of a sewage treatment facility undertaken for economic benefit. Further, as *Cramer* implicitly recognizes, evidence of financial circumstances may be material depending upon the situation. In this case, the evidence was material, considering all the facts and circumstances, including the conflicting evidence on the degree of risk and probability of harm, and the evidence that the City could meet that risk by continuing its flood fighting efforts while obtaining grant money to raise the dikes as part of an overall flood control strategy. While hindsight shows the City's course of action did not prevent the harm from being realized, a waiver of sovereign immunity does not render the governmental entity liable for every harm flowing from government action or inaction, but only that harm resulting from tortious misconduct. . . .

Plaintiffs maintain, though, that a private person whose automobile has unsafe brakes would not be able to introduce evidence of attempts to obtain a loan to repair the vehicle in order to establish it acted reasonably in driving the automobile without repairing it. The analogy fails, for the same reason that plaintiffs' other arguments ultimately fail: it simply does not take into account that the reasonableness of defendant's conduct must be assessed in light of the circumstances under which the defendant acted or failed to act. In the situation involving unsafe brakes, the probability of harm is exceedingly high, with the alternatives to prevent that harm including refusal to drive the vehicle in such an unsafe condition or making the necessary repairs to eliminate any unreasonable risk. Delaying repairs for whatever reason while continuing to drive the vehicle quite simply poses an unreasonable risk of

C. REASONABLE CARE AND PERSONAL CHARACTERISTICS

harm, and evidence of attempting to procure loan money for repairs is not relevant evidence tending to show the reasonableness of defendant's conduct in driving the vehicle with unsafe brakes. In this case, there was a dispute about the degree of risk involved in delaying raising the height of the dike lagoons and the probability that harm would occur if the City continued its flood control and flood fighting programs. . ..

Because we hold that the evidence of the City's attempts to obtain grant money was admissible on the question of the reasonableness of its conduct, it follows that the trial court did not abuse its discretion by refusing to give two proposed instructions offered by plaintiffs which would have directed the jury that it could not consider the evidence.

The judgment in favor of the City of Stanwood is affirmed.

JOHNSON, J., dissenting

This case presents the relatively straightforward question of whether evidence of the City's efforts to obtain grant money to raise lagoon dikes was relevant to the issue of negligence. However, the majority confuses the basic test regarding the admissibility of relevant evidence in a negligence action. The majority concludes the City's evidence of efforts to obtain federal and state grant funds was admissible to prove it acted reasonably. I disagree. The proper inquiry in this case is whether failure to raise the level of the surrounding dikes breached the duty to the landowners. Evidence of reasons or excuses for failure or delay in action is not relevant to the basic issues of duty and breach. For this reason, I dissent. To admit this evidence in this case allowed the City, in essence, to mount a poverty defense. Such a defense is not allowed in negligence actions because the duty of care owed to another does not change according to a party's financial situation.

The basis of any negligence action is the failure to exercise reasonable care when one has a duty to exercise such care. Restatement (Second) of Torts sec. 282 (1965). Here, if the City had a duty to use reasonable care in the operation of the sewer lagoon and to maintain the lagoon in a manner reasonably safe for adjacent property owners, evidence of financial inability to comply with that duty is not a defense. . .. Therefore, if lack of funds is not a defense, evidence of such is not relevant to the issue of duty.

The trial record in this case shows the City acknowledged it had enough money to cover the cost of raising the dikes. The City did not present a "poverty defense" in the sense of asking for a jury instruction stating the City had no duty to the Plaintiffs because of a lack of funds. To the contrary, the City acknowledged it had a duty to the adjacent property owners to use reasonable care in the operation of the sewage lagoon. However, neither the City nor the majority explains what use the jury could have made of the evidence of efforts to obtain grant funds other than to infer it was reasonable for the City to delay raising the dikes because of its financial strategy and constraints. In other words, the majority appears to allow this evidence to imply a defense. But if the height of the dikes surrounding the lagoon presented an unreasonable risk of harm, the City had a duty to remedy the problem notwithstanding the availability of grant funds.

. . .The majority states that our cases demonstrate financial considerations may be relevant to the issue of the reasonableness of a municipality's conduct.

However, in none of the cited cases has this court allowed a defendant to go beyond the introduction of costs, practicalities, or available resources to allow evidence of the timing chosen to incur costs as part of a budgetary consideration or overall financial strategy.

. . . .This case lost proper focus when the jury was allowed to consider monetary matters beyond "cost evidence." Just as a duty of care does not change because of financial strategy, cost evidence should not vary from defendant to defendant. If it is allowed to vary, the jury can apply these varying financial strategies or situations to the standard of care (duty) and, therefore, to the ultimate issue of liability. . . .

NOTES

1. *The Poverty Defense.* The court's attitude to poverty (or wealth) in negligence cases can be traced back at least as far as *Denver & R.G.R. Co. v. Peterson*, 30 Colo. 77, 69 P. 578 (1902), in which the plaintiff had argued that a fire which burned the defendant's freight depot was caused by the defendant's negligence. In setting the stage for a retrial the court noted: "The care required of a warehouseman is the same whether he be rich or poor. For, if the fact that he is rich requires of him greater care than if he possessed only moderate means or is poor, then, if he were extremely poor, the care required might be such as practically to amount to nothing; and no one would claim that such an uncertain and sliding rule should be the measure of his liability." Should the poverty defense apply where, as the court suggested in *Bodin*, the defendant has no practical option but to continue the activity — here, the operation of sewage treatment facilities?

2. *Evidence of insurance.* If wealth or poverty is not relevant, how should a court rule on the question of a party's liability insurance coverage? The general rule is stated as follows:

> [I]n a personal injury or death action evidence is inadmissible which informs the jury that the defendant is insured against liability. Such evidence is not only inadmissible because it ordinarily is irrelevant as to any of the issues in the case, but because it tends not only to influence jurors to bring in verdicts against defendants on insufficient evidence, but to bring in verdicts for more than they would if they believed that the defendants themselves would be required to pay them.

Annot. Admissibility Of Evidence, And Propriety And Effect Of Questions, Statements, Comments, Etc., Tending To Show That Defendant In Personal Injury Or Death Action Carries Liability Insurance, 4 A.L.R.2d 761, 765 (1949). By parity of reasoning, should evidence of lack of insurance also be inadmissible?

3. *Discretionary Immunity.* Most state entities, including municipalities, are permitted to assert a statutory defense of the exercise of discretion. That defense takes into account the availability and allocation of funds. The defense is permitted even when the discretion is abused — or exercised negligently. *See* Chapter 11 *infra*. The city in *Bodin* cross-appealed the trial court's denial of summary judgment based on the defense of discretionary immunity, but

the appellate court never reached the issue since the judgment below for the defendant was affirmed.

PROBLEM

The Old Ferry Creek bed in northern Anystate has become the regular Saturday afternoon haunt of the Suzonda All-Terrain Vehicle Club. The club, which is run by Fred, has a membership of approximately 20 children, all of whom are less than eighteen years of age. The club rents the powerful all-terrain vehicles (ATVs) from local motorcycle dealers and provides them to the children as a community service. One Saturday, Fred was supervising a group of riders, including Jason, his 15-year-old son, and six-year-old Chris.

The session progressed well, albeit noisily, until Chris and Jason decided upon an impromptu race and left the other riders. Attempting to turn at high speed, both riders lost control of their machines. Chris headed back toward the main group at high speed. Fred saw him coming and rushed to head him off, but succeeded only in colliding with Chris. Fred suffered serious injuries in the collision.

Meanwhile, Jason exited the creek bed at high speed and proceeded onto the street. He was beginning to regain control of his machine when he swerved onto the sidewalk. There, he struck Timmy, who had been skateboarding down the sidewalk at high speed. Timmy and Jason were seriously injured.

Timmy and Jason were in the same grade at school and had been involved in numerous scuffles. A primary cause of the scuffles was Jason's jealousy over Timmy's victory in the state skateboarding championship.

After the accident, Fred was found to have a minute quantity of alcohol in his blood system. In Anystate, the minimum age for an operator's permit for a motorcycle is 15 years. It is illegal for any person to operate an ATV on a public road. Fred brings an action in negligence against Chris, and Timmy brings an action in negligence against Jason. Both Chris and Jason counter with allegations of contributory negligence.

1. Assume that the cases go to trial. What jury instructions will be sought by Chris, Jason, Fred and Timmy? What arguments will they employ, and how should the court resolve the issues?

2. Should Timmy consider bringing anything other than a negligence action against Jason?

3. Should Fred or Timmy consider joining any other parties as defendants? What allegations could they make, and what difficulties would they face?

D. INDUSTRY AND PROFESSIONAL PRACTICES

THE T.J. HOOPER
60 F.2d 737 (2d Cir. 1932)

L. HAND, CIRCUIT JUDGE.

The barges No. 17 and No. 30, belonging to the Northern Barge Company, had lifted cargoes of coal at Norfolk, Virginia, for New York in March, 1928.

They were towed by two tugs of the petitioner, the *Montrose* and the *Hooper*, and were lost off the Jersey Coast on March tenth, in an easterly gale. The cargo owners sued the barges under the contracts of carriage; the owner of the barges sued the tugs under the towing contract, both for its own loss and as bailee of the cargoes; the owner of the tug filed a petition to limit its liability. All the suits were joined and heard together, and the judge found that all the vessels were unseaworthy; the tugs, because they did not carry radio receiving sets by which they could have seasonably got warnings of a change in the weather which should have caused them to seek shelter in the Delaware Breakwater en route. . . .

The weather bureau at Arlington broadcasts two predictions daily, at ten in the morning and ten in the evening. Apparently there are other reports floating about, which come at uncertain hours but which can also be picked up. The Arlington report of the morning read as follows: "Moderate north, shifting to east and southeast winds, increasing Friday, fair weather tonight." The substance of this, apparently from another source, reached a tow bound north to New York about noon, and, coupled with a falling glass, decided the master to put in to the Delaware Breakwater in the afternoon. The glass had not indeed fallen much and perhaps the tug was over cautious; nevertheless, although the appearances were all fair, he thought discretion the better part of valor. Three other tows followed him, the masters of two of which testified. Their decision was in part determined by example; but they too had received the Arlington report or its equivalent, and though it is doubtful whether alone it would have turned the scale, it is plain that it left them in an indecision which needed little to be resolved on the side of prudence; they preferred to take no chances, and chances they believed there were. Courts have not often such evidence of the opinion of impartial experts, formed in the very circumstances and confirmed by their own conduct at the time.

Moreover, the *Montrose* and the *Hooper* would have had the benefit of the evening report from Arlington had they had proper receiving sets. This predicted worse weather; it read: "Increasing east and southeast winds, becoming fresh to strong, Friday night and increasing cloudiness followed by rain Friday." The bare "increase" of the morning had become "fresh to strong." To be sure this scarcely foretold a gale of from forty to fifty miles for five hours or more, rising at one time to fifty-six; but if the four tows thought the first report enough, the second ought to have laid any doubts. The master of the *Montrose* himself, when asked what he would have done had he received a substantially similar report, said that he would certainly have put in. The master of the *Hooper* was also asked for his opinion, and said that he would have turned back also, but this admission is somewhat vitiated by the incorporation in the question of the statement that it was a "storm warning," which the witness seized upon in his answer. All this seems to us to support the conclusion of the judge that prudent masters, who had received the second warning, would have found the risk more than the exigency warranted; they would have been amply vindicated by what followed. To be sure the barges would, as we have said, probably have withstood the gale, had they been well found; but a master is not justified in putting his tow to every test which she will survive, if she be fit. There is a zone in which proper caution will avoid putting her capacity to the proof; a coefficient of prudence that he should not disregard. Taking the situation as a whole, it seems to us that these masters would have taken undue chances, had they got the broadcasts.

They did not, because their private radio receiving sets, which were on board, were not in working order. These belonged to them personally, and were partly a toy, partly a part of the equipment, but neither furnished by the owner, nor supervised by it. It is not fair to say that there was a general custom among coastwise carriers so as to equip their tugs. One line alone did it; as for the rest, they relied upon their crews, so far as they can be said to have relied at all. An adequate receiving set suitable for a coastwise tug can now be got at small cost and is reasonably reliable if kept up; obviously it is a source of great protection to their tows. Twice every day they can receive these predictions, based upon the widest possible information, available to every vessel within two or three hundred miles and more. Such a set is the ears of the tug to catch the spoken word, just as the master's binoculars are her eyes to see a storm signal ashore. Whatever may be said as to other vessels, tugs towing heavy coal-laden barges, strung out for half a mile, have little power to maneuver, and do not, as this case proves, expose themselves to weather which would not turn back stauncher craft. They can have at hand protection against dangers of which they can learn in no other way.

Is it then a final answer that the business had not yet generally adopted receiving sets? There are yet, no doubt, cases where courts seem to make the general practice of the calling the standard of proper diligence; we have indeed given some currency to the notion ourselves. Indeed in most cases reasonable prudence is in fact common prudence; but strictly it is never its measure; a whole calling may have unduly lagged in the adoption of new and available devices. It may never set its own tests, however persuasive be its usages. Courts must in the end say what is required; there are precautions so imperative that even their universal disregard will not excuse their omission. But here there was no custom at all as to receiving sets; some had them, some did not; the most that can be urged is that they had not yet become general. Certainly in such a case we need not pause; when some have thought a device necessary, at least we may say that they were right, and the others too slack. The statute does not bear on this situation at all. It prescribes not a receiving, but a transmitting set, and for a very different purpose; to call for help, not to get news. We hold the tugs therefore because had they been properly equipped, they would have got the Arlington reports. The injury was a direct consequence of this unseaworthiness.

NOTES

1. *A Reasonable Minority; An Unreasonable Majority.* The court in *T.J. Hooper* concluded that

> [H]ere there was no custom at all as to receiving sets; some had them, some did not; the most that can be urged is that they had not yet become general. Certainly in such a case we need not pause; when some have thought a device necessary, at least we may say that they were right, and the others too slack.

On what doctrinal basis, therefore, did the court find negligence? Is the reasonable person standard inapplicable in such a case?

2. *Custom Curtailed.* RESTATEMENT (SECOND) OF TORTS § 295A (1965) comments *b* and *c* provide:

> *b. Relevance of custom.* Any such custom of the community in general, or of other persons under like circumstances, is always a factor to be taken into account in determining whether the actor has been negligent. Evidence of the custom is admissible, and is relevant, as indicating a composite judgment as to the risks of the situation and the precautions required to meet them, as well as the feasibility of such precautions, the difficulty of any change in accepted methods, the actor's opportunity to learn what is called for, and the justifiable expectation of others that he will do what is usual, as well as the justifiable expectation of the actor that others will do the same. If the actor does what others do under like circumstances, there is at least a possible inference that he is conforming to the community standard of reasonable conduct; and if he does not do what others do, there is a possible inference that he is not so conforming. In particular instances, where there is nothing in the situation or in common experience to lead to the contrary conclusion, this inference may be so strong as to call for a directed verdict, one way or the other, on the issue of negligence. Thus, even in the absence of any applicable traffic statute, one who drives on the right side of a [road] is under ordinary circumstances clearly not negligent in doing so, and one who drives on the left side is under ordinary circumstances clearly negligent.
>
> On the same basis, evidence of the practices of the parties to the action in dealing with each other is admissible, and relevant, as indicating an understood standard of conduct, or the reasonable expectation of each party as to what the other will do.
>
> *c. When custom not controlling.* Any such custom is, however, not necessarily conclusive as to whether the actor, by conforming to it, has exercised the care of a reasonable man under the circumstances, or by departing from it has failed to exercise such care. Customs which are entirely reasonable under the ordinary circumstances which give rise to them may become quite unreasonable in the light of a single fact in the particular case. It may be negligence to drive on the right side of the road, and it may not be negligence to drive on the left side when the right side is blocked by a dangerous ditch. Beyond this, customs and usages themselves are many and various. Some of them are the result of careful thought and decision, while others arise from the kind of inadvertence, neglect, or deliberate disregard of a known risk which is associated with negligence. No group of individuals and no industry or trade can be permitted, by adopting careless and slipshod methods to save time, effort, or money, to set its own uncontrolled standard at the expense of the rest of the community. If the only test is to be what has always been done, no one will ever have any great incentive to make any progress in the direction of

safety. It follows, therefore, that whenever the particular circumstances, the risk, or other elements in the case are such that a reasonable man would not conform to the custom, the actor may be found negligent in conforming to it; and whenever a reasonable man would depart from the custom, the actor may be found not to be negligent in so departing.

3. *A Step in the Dark?* The court believed that judicial regulation was indicated when the precautions to be taken were "so imperative." How do we know when that level of risk has been reached? Suppose there was evidence that radio forecasts were needed by tugs only once or twice a year, and traditional methods of forecasting were otherwise perfectly safe. Suppose further that, at this stage of the development of the telecommunications industry, the amortized installed cost of suitable equipment would be approximately one-third to one-half of the net annual profit generated by a tug.

4. *Jury Competence and the Search for Relevant Judgmental Standards.* How will a defendant with expertise in an obscure specialty react to a charge to the jury to apply a reasonable person standard? What evidence should the plaintiff introduce to allay the fears of the court in such a case? Recall *Helling v. Carey,* 83 Wash.2d 514, 519 P.2d 981 (1974).

5. *Specific Regulation.* As the court in *T.J. Hooper* noted, a federal statute did cover some aspects of the compulsory outfitting of tugs with radios. On the basis of that evidence, what arguments would you have made on behalf of plaintiff? Defendant?

6. *The Hidden Costs of Judicial Regulation.* With his famous words, "courts must in the end say what is required," Judge Learned Hand ushered in a period of explicit judicial regulation that has remained more or less in fashion to the present time.

In addition to the general costs associated with litigation which *T.J. Hooper* imposes, does the opinion allocate to industry the information costs for future judicial decision-making? Contrast the opportunity for consultation provided by traditional governmental regulatory agencies prior to the promulgation of safety regulations.

According to one torts scholar, "There are many competitors for this questionable honor, but Hand's famous bon mot is perhaps the most influential, and mischievous, sentence in the history of the law of torts." Richard A. Epstein, The Path to the T.J. Hooper: The Theory and History of Custom in the Law of Torts, 21 J LEGAL STUD. 1, 38 (1992). Does T.J. Hooper mark the beginning of the so-called "torts crisis?"

RAY v. AMERICAN NATIONAL RED CROSS
696 A.2d 399 (D. C. App. 1996)

RUIZ, ASSOCIATE JUDGE.

Roland Ray contracted the human immunodeficiency virus (HIV), the virus that causes acquired immune deficiency syndrome (AIDS), through a blood transfusion. The blood was collected in July 1984 by the American National Red Cross. Roland Ray and Janet Ray, who are married, commenced this action to recover damages, alleging that the Red Cross was negligent in failing to take adequate measures to ensure that persons at risk of HIV infection were prevented from donating blood, and that donated blood likely to contain HIV was not used for human transfusion. The jury returned a verdict for the Red Cross, finding that it had not been negligent. The trial court entered judgment on the verdict.

. . .In August 1984, Mr. Ray was shot during a robbery of his convenience store. He was infected with HIV during treatment of the wound as the result of a transfusion of a blood product supplied by the Red Cross. The infected blood was traced to a unit donated in July 1984 by a bisexual man at a blood drive that the Red Cross conducted at his workplace. The evidence showed that Mrs. Ray had not, as of the time of trial, contracted the virus.

At trial, the Rays sought to show that had the Red Cross screened prospective donors by taking greater care to inform them of the groups at risk for HIV infection, confidentially inquiring regarding their sexual history, and providing them with a more confidential method of self-deferral, the donor of the unit of blood that infected Mr. Ray would have deferred and his blood would not have entered the blood supply from which Mr. Ray was transfused. The Rays also attempted to show that, although no test for detecting HIV had yet been developed in 1984, HIV infection was known and had the Red Cross used one or more available "surrogate tests" for other infections or conditions that often accompany HIV infection, the unit of blood that eventually infected Mr. Ray would not have been used for human transfusion. The Rays' evidence consisted of expert opinion testimony that, based on the knowledge concerning HIV available in July 1984 and the degree of risk posed by the possibility of HIV-infected blood being used for transfusion, a reasonably prudent blood collector would have employed such donor screening and blood testing procedures. The Rays also presented the testimony of the blood donor, who testified that he was semi-illiterate and did not know that he was in a high-risk group. The donor also testified that if he had been informed of the risk and given the opportunity to defer confidentially, he would not have donated blood.

In its defense, the Red Cross established that in July 1984, the vast majority of blood collectors, including the Red Cross, did not use the kind of screening and testing procedures the Rays contended a reasonable blood collector would employ. Furthermore, the Red Cross presented evidence tending to show that its procedures conformed to those recommended by government agencies. The Red Cross also presented testimony that in July 1984, it was thought that implementation of more thorough donor screening procedures would have strenuously been objected to by high risk donors and, consequently, that implementation of more stringent screening procedures would have resulted in lowered blood donations by high risk donors and perhaps even in purposeful contamination of the blood supply by donors offended by the screening procedures.

The Rays contend that the Red Cross was obliged to act as a reasonable blood bank, that possessed the knowledge and skill of the Red Cross, would have acted under the circumstances; the Red Cross contends that it had only to act as any ordinary blood bank reasonably would have acted under the circumstances. To support their respective contentions concerning the nature and source of the standard of care applicable in this case, the parties have quoted phrases from numerous medical malpractice cases from this jurisdiction. . ..

The various verbal formulations of the standards that were employed in those cases, without dispute and express judicial consideration, do not alter the fundamental proposition that in our law of negligence there is but one "'uniform standard of conduct: that of reasonable care under the circumstances.'" *Sinai v. Polinger Co.*, 498 A.2d 520, 529 (D.C. 1985) (quoting *Morrison*, 407 A.2d at 560). We have previously rejected the proposition that a defendant's conformity to ordinary custom and practice is an absolute defense to a claim premised on negligence. In *Beard v. Goodyear Tire & Rubber Co.*, 587 A.2d 195 (D.C. 1991), several merchants had extended credit to a person who fraudulently assumed the identity of the plaintiff. The plaintiff, seeking compensation for the resulting damage to his credit rating, sued the merchants, contending that they negligently failed to verify the information in the fraudulent credit applications. The merchants sought and obtained summary judgment, supporting their motion with affidavits to the effect that their handling of the applications was consistent with the practice in the industry. We held that although the conduct of people possessing or charged with skills and knowledge similar to the defendant's under similar circumstances is *evidence* relevant to establishing how a reasonable and prudent person would act under the circumstances, it is not dispositive on the issue; the fact that some or most persons who are in a position similar to the defendant fail to act reasonably and prudently does not absolve the defendant of liability.

Although we rejected the merchants' defense of custom and practice, we nevertheless affirmed summary judgment in their favor. The act in question in *Beard*—processing of credit applications—was a matter beyond the ken of the common juror. Hence, the plaintiff was required to present testimony by experts with special skill or training in the area of credit application processing. The purpose of the expert testimony is to assist the jury in deciding what would be reasonable under the circumstances. We described the sort of expert evidence required of the plaintiff in these terms:

> To determine whether a procedure is reasonable, it would be helpful to secure an informed assessment of its benefits, and also of its cost, which is likely to be passed on to the consumer. We do not think a lay person can be expected to know what kinds of measures would have the potential for detecting applications filed by unauthorized individuals, or how much it would cost the merchant or, ultimately, the merchant's customers to adopt and utilize such measures, or whether any additional detection which more exacting requirements might achieve would be worth the additional costs. There may be other considerations, besides a cost-benefit assessment, which would be pertinent to this analysis; the ordinary citizen may not even know what questions to ask. These are technical subjects on which jurors need expert advice.

Id. at 201.

Because the plaintiff in *Beard* had not supplied any such expert evidence, or rebutted the merchants' evidence regarding custom and practice, we affirmed the grant of summary judgment in favor of the merchants. We expressly rejected as being tantamount to strict liability the plaintiff's assertion that the merchants should not be permitted to save the expense of thorough verification of credit applications without also being liable to those third parties, like the plaintiff, who are harmed as the result of fraudulent applications. Although we did not explain in *Beard* why we rejected a rule of strict liability for the consequences of each person's acts, the reason is the one articulated by Oliver Wendell Holmes over a century ago:

> A man need not, it is true, do this or that act, — the term *act* implies a choice, — but he must act somehow. Furthermore, the public generally profits by individual activity. As action cannot be avoided, and tends to the public good, there is obviously no policy in throwing the hazard of what is at once desirable and inevitable upon the actor.
>
> . . .The state does [not enforce an insurance regime], and the prevailing view is that [government's] cumbrous and expensive machinery ought not to be set in motion unless some clear benefit is to be derived from disturbing the *status quo*. State interference is an evil, where it cannot be shown to be a good. Universal insurance, if desired, can be better and more cheaply accomplished by private enterprise. The undertaking to redistribute losses simply on the ground that they resulted from the defendant's act would not only be open to these objections, but . . . to the still graver one of offending the sense of justice. Unless my act is of a nature to threaten others, unless under the circumstances a prudent man would have foreseen the possibility of harm, it is no more justifiable to make me indemnify my neighbor against the consequences, than to make me do the same thing if I had fallen upon him in a fit, or to compel me to insure him against lightning.

OLIVER W. HOLMES, THE COMMON LAW 95–96 (1881).

Thus, our modern rule of negligence liability proceeds from a balance struck between an actor's freedom of choice and another's security in person and property: that one whose act unintentionally causes injury to another is generally liable to compensate the other only if the act was not reasonable under the circumstances—that is, only if the act created a foreseeable risk that could have been mitigated at a cost not disproportionate in light of the gravity and probability of the foreseeable harm. As Holmes suggested, the rule is the result of a balance among many conflicting policies, including those favoring private activity, compensation of persons injured through no fault of their own, and conservation of the government and private resources that must be expended in proceedings to shift losses among individuals. Those considerations and others, however, and therefore the balance struck, may vary with the context of the claim.

The Red Cross contends that the context of the Rays' claim is different from that considered in *Beard* because this case involves "professionals." The Red Cross does not offer any definition delimiting the scope of the term, "professional." As a basis for its objection to a standard of care measured by reasonableness instead of the accepted practice of the profession, however, the Red Cross attacks the lay after-the-fact "second-guessing of medical judgments made by the entire medical, scientific and public health communities" that it says would result from allowing in the present case the type of proof we said in *Beard* was permissible. Thus, it appears that for the purpose of the Red Cross's proposed distinction, a professional is one who exercises skill or learning not possessed by persons who do not belong to the same profession.

The Red Cross's objection is ill-founded. *Beard* did in fact concern actions taken by persons with special skill and learning. In *Beard,* we held that the means of preventing jury speculation was not to limit proof of negligence to professional custom and practice, but instead to require the plaintiff to present expert evidence concerning the factors relevant to the setting of the standard of care: those facts and considerations that would be considered by a reasonable person under similar circumstances in deciding upon a course of conduct. In *Beard,* we considered and rejected the notion that to prevent jury speculation we must preclude the jury from making any decision concerning the proper course of professional conduct, even when the plaintiff provides evidence to inform the jury's determination. Consistent with Beard, the jury, informed by expert testimony where appropriate, determines what the applicable standard of care is in a particular case. That standard is measured by "the course of action that a reasonably prudent [professional] with the defendant's specialty would have taken under the same or similar circumstances." *Meek v. Shepard,* 484 A.2d 579, 581 (D.C. 1984); *see Morrison v. MacNamara,* 407 A.2d 555, 560 (D.C. 1979)("The duty of reasonable care requires that those with special training and experience adhere to a standard of conduct commensurate with such attributes. It is this notion of specialized knowledge and skill which animates the law of professional negligence."). . . .

[Reversed and remanded because of deficient instructions.]

NOTES

1. *Evidentiary Issues; Offensive Versus Defensive Custom.* Assume that the defendant in *Ray* had been the only blood center *not* to utilize a particular safety procedure. Would that warrant summary judgment in favor of plaintiff?

2. *Customary Standards and Professionals.* In *Osborn v. Irwin Memorial Blood Bank,* 5 Cal. App. 4th 234, 7 Cal. Rptr. 2d 101 (1992), the question arose whether a blood bank could be held liable for failing to run anti-HBc tests for AIDS in early 1983, a time when there had been some discussion of such testing but that no such testing was being used. The court stated:

> Plaintiffs contend that custom and practice are relevant, but not conclusive, on the standard of care. This is the general rule in cases of ordinary negligence. . . ..
>
> This is a case of professional negligence, however, and we must assess the role of custom and practice in that context. The question presented here is whether California law permits an expert to second-guess an entire profession. We have found no definitive precedent on this issue and it is not one that is likely to arise.

Custom and practice are not controlling in cases, unlike ours, where a layperson can infer negligence by a professional without any expert testimony. In *Leonard v. Watsonville Community Hosp.* (1956) 47 Cal.2d 509 [305 P.2d 36], for example, where a clamp was left in the plaintiff's body after surgery, the lack of an " 'established practice' " of counting clamps did not preclude a finding of negligence: "Defendants seek to avoid liability on the theory that they were required to exercise only that degree of skill employed by other hospitals and nurses in the community. It is a matter of common knowledge, however, that no special skill is required in counting instruments. Although *under such circumstances* proof of practice or custom is some evidence of what should be done and may assist in the determination of what constitutes due care, it does not conclusively establish the standard of care." (*Id.*, at p. 519 [italics added].)

On the other hand, in cases like ours where experts are needed to show negligence, their testimony sets the standard of care and is said to be "conclusive." . . . Qualified expert opinion will thus generally preclude a directed verdict in a professional negligence case.

This case, however, is distinguishable. Experts' testimony ordinarily cannot be "disregarded" because it cannot be said that their opinions about what should have been done do not reflect the custom and practice of the profession. When an expert describes the "standard technique" for a knee operation, or what a reasonable attorney would do to settle a wrongful death action, or how long an architect should take to approve change orders on a construction, it is impossible to say that no surgeon, lawyer or architect was doing what the expert said was required. Here it is undisputed that no blood bank in the country was doing what the plaintiffs' experts' standard of care would require of Irwin, and we have an unusual situation where we are called upon to address the significance of a universal practice.

. . .While it may be true that "an increasing number of courts are rejecting the customary practice standard in favor of a reasonable care or reasonably prudent doctor standard" (Prosser & Keeton, The Law of Torts (5th ed., 1988 pocket supp., p. 30, fn. 53), numerous commentaries have noted that custom generally sets the standard of care. . ..

Most commentators have urged that a customary or accepted practice standard is preferable to one that allows for the disregard of professional judgment. Indeed, the more recent commentaries are not concerned with whether customary practices should be the maximum expected of medical practitioners, but rather with whether those practices should continue to set a minimum standard in a time of increasing economic constraints.

The basic reason why professionals are usually held only to a standard of custom and practice is that their informed approach to matters outside common knowledge should not be "evaluated by the ad hoc judgments of a lay judge or lay jurors aided by hindsight."

. . .It follows that Irwin cannot be found negligent for failing to perform tests that no other blood bank in the nation was using.

Judgment notwithstanding the verdict was properly granted to Irwin on the issue of anti-HBc testing because there was no substantial evidence that failure to conduct the tests was not accepted *practice* for blood banks in January and February of 1983.

7 Cal. Rptr. 2d at 128.

3. *The Unkindest Cut of All.* Assume that the defendant in *Ray* had failed to follow its own internal safety guidelines, but that those guidelines exceeded industry custom *and* "reasonable person" standards. Should the defendant be held liable? Does a re-examination of the goals of the negligence system assist in answering that question?

4. *Custom and Common Prudence. Ray* agreed with the court's remark in *The T.J. Hooper,* that "in most cases reasonable prudence is in fact common prudence." Is that observation more or less honored with regard to allegations of personal, professional or corporate negligence?

5. *Evidentiary Issues.* If custom is not controlling what other evidence will the parties rely upon?

6. *The Rejection of Customary Standards and the Abrogation of Efficiency.* Can it be argued that the use of a custom standard is a good approximation of the most efficient method of accident avoidance in a given fact pattern? According to W.M. LANDES & R.A. POSNER, THE ECONOMIC STRUCTURE OF TORT LAW, 131 (1987), "(t)he adoption of a safety practice by most members of the industry shows that its cost is less than its expected benefit in accident avoidance; there is no reason for the industry to adopt the practice otherwise."

7. *Inadmissible Expertise?* Are there situations where expert testimony should be held *inadmissible*? See, e.g., *Board of Supervisors v. Lake Services, Inc.*, 247 Va. 293, 297, 440 S.E.2d 600, 602 (1994):

> Expert testimony is inadmissible regarding "matters of common knowledge" or subjects "such that [persons] of ordinary intelligence are capable of comprehending them, forming an intelligent opinion about them, and drawing their own conclusions therefrom." Thus, when the question presented can be resolved by determining what precautions a reasonably prudent person would have taken under like circumstances, no expert testimony is required or permitted.
>
> Further, expert testimony is admissible only when specialized skill and knowledge are required to evaluate the merits of a claim. Issues of this type generally arise in cases involving the practice of professions requiring advanced, specialized education, such as engineering, medicine, and law, or those involving trades that focus upon scientific matters, such as electricity and blasting, which a jury cannot understand without expert assistance.

VUONO v. NEW YORK BLOOD CENTER, INC.
696 F. Supp. 743 (D. Mass. 1988)

YOUNG, DISTRICT JUDGE.

. . . On May 16, 1983, the plaintiff Frank Vuono, a Rhode Island resident, was hospitalized at the Deaconess in order to undergo coronary bypass surgery. During the evening of May 22 and the morning of May 23, Mr. Vuono received an infusion of serum albumin which is a fractionated blood plasma derivative. One vial of the serum albumin administered to Mr. Vuono was contaminated at the time of infusion and, as a result, he became ill, suffered septic shock and Herpes Simplex, and subsequently was prevented from undergoing open heart surgery. The contaminated vial was processed by defendant Blood Center, a New York corporation, which is a federally-licensed blood fractionation facility.

"Fractionation" at the blood processing facility involves separating the serum albumin from the blood plasma, dispensing the serum albumin into glass vials, sealing the vials with rubber stoppers, covering the vials with protective aluminum foil, and packaging the vials in a series of cardboard containers. This process also included filtering out any bacteria in the blood plasma and subjecting the serum albumin to a heat bath for the purpose of killing any contaminants which elude the filtration procedure. The vials of serum albumin were processed in "lots," which were assigned particular identifying numbers. The vial which is the subject of the present lawsuit was part of the Blood Center's lot number 5D33A, and was processed in August, 1982.

Although there is no evidence that the Blood Center failed to follow its standard procedures for processing the serum albumin in this case, there is evidence that the particular glass vial contained a flaw. Specifically, there was a narrow fold in the glass surface, known as a "line over." This "line over" extended across the top of the finish and down the inside of the vial past the sealing contact areas of the rubber stopper. Evidence also exists that this flaw is visually identifiable and that the glass fold in the vial is sufficient to catch a fingernail.

Further, there is evidence that this defect interfered with the integrity of the sealed vial, and thus permitted contamination from ambient sources. An April 12, 1985 memorandum by an employee of the glass manufacturer Wheaton reports on post-incident testing by Wheaton of the particular vial at issue here. The report states that the test data "indicated the complete lack of seal caused by the 'line over' condition on the glass finish. Zero vacuum readings were found in less than 4 hours storage on the complaint bottle."

On May 9, 1986, the Vuonos brought this action against defendants Blood Center, Red Cross, Wheaton, the Deaconess and unnamed doctors and nurses, alleging various causes of action under Massachusetts law . . . . On May 6, 1988, the Court . . . granted summary judgment for Blood Center on the [strict liability] claims . . . and *res ipsa loquitur*.

With respect to the Blood Center's motion for summary judgment, the issue remaining before this Court is whether the Vuonos have raised a genuine issue of material fact concerning the negligence claim asserted against the Blood

D. INDUSTRY AND PROFESSIONAL PRACTICES

Center; specifically, whether there is a genuine issue of material fact concerning the Blood Center's duty to test and inspect the glass vials containing the serum albumin.

In the law of torts, negligence is commonly recognized as the omission to do something which a reasonable person, guided by those considerations which ordinarily regulate the conduct of human affairs, would do, or the doing of something which a prudent and reasonable person would not do. In other words, the standard of conduct in determining the existence of negligence is whether the actor exercised the duty of care which an ordinarily prudent person would exercise under the same or similar circumstances. There is, however, no absolute liability for all harmful conduct; an actor is not an insurer for all her acts.

Applying this negligence standard often requires that the actor's conduct be tested against a background of ordinary usage and custom. The customs of the community, however, although both admissible and relevant on the issue of negligence, are not conclusive, especially where such customs are clearly dangerous and careless. . . .

In this respect, the negligent standard of the ordinarily prudent person may be a higher standard of care than that standard which is followed by a particular community or industry. Under Massachusetts law, the fact that a certain device or practice is in common use is evidence that its use is not negligent, but such a fact is not conclusive evidence of due care because a large number of persons may fail to exercise due care in their usual practices. The plaintiff may still try to show that the practice of the entire industry is unreasonable, that the community custom lacks "ordinary care."[1]

In the present case, Blood Center argues that the plaintiffs' negligence claims cannot survive on the grounds that the Vuonos fail to set forth any facts demonstrating that the Blood Center breached the prevailing standard of care applicable to blood products manufacturers. Specifically, the Blood Center contends that the standard of care which the Blood Center owed to Mr. Vuono is that standard established by the blood products manufacturing industry and the applicable FDA regulations. Moreover, the quality control procedures used in testing lot #5D33A, the batch which contained the vial of serum albumin administered to Mr. Vuono, equaled or exceeded both the standard of care of the industry and the FDA regulations . . . .

As previously discussed, however, conformity with the customs and standards of the industry does not establish conclusively the absence of negligence. Rather, the Court must evaluate any evidence that either the industry custom

---

[1] There are, however, certain circumstances where "[i]f one does what others do in like circumstances, the inference that he is conforming to the community standard of reasonable conduct may be so strong . . . as to establish that the individual was not negligent." *Breault v. Ford Motor Co.*, 364 Mass. 352, 356, 305 N.E.2d 824 (1973) (noting that most courts have held that an individual injured in a car accident was not negligent when, like most people, she did not wear a seatbelt where "the beneficial effect of seat belts [was] not [generally] assumed and no special circumstances existed calling for" their use). If there is undisputed evidence that the defendant acted in accordance with the uniform custom of persons engaged in a similar business, in the absence of showing that such custom is in fact negligent, then the defendant did not act negligently. In this context, however, there must be a lack of evidence showing that the custom itself is negligent.

or the Blood Center's conduct was unreasonable under the circumstances. Given all of the facts presented by the Vuonos, the Court rules that a genuine issue of material fact exists concerning the Blood Center's duty to inspect and test the glass vials containing the serum albumin.

This Court's opinion is founded on two sources: A) the deposition of Dr. Martin Stryker, and B) the report on the defective vial. First, Dr. Stryker testified that: 1) "when it's time to fill the vials, the person who loads the vials onto the conveyor belt going into the vial washing and sterilization equipment is instructed to look at the vials," 2) the defect in the glass vial which contained the serum albumin administered to Mr. Vuono existed at the time of the visual inspection, 3) the defect in the vial is "fairly apparent if you look at it closely," 4) the Blood Center had experienced problems with the quality of the Wheaton glass vials, problems which initially occurred in 1980 and resurfaced in April, 1983, and 5) Blood Center ceased purchasing the Wheaton 250 milliliter vials for the packaging of serum albumin in late 1983. Second, the Wheaton report on the glass vial stated, "The bottle . . . did have a 'line over' which is a narrow fold in the glass surface. The 'line over' extended across the top of the finish and down the inside past the sealing contact areas of the rubber stopper . . . . Depth of the glass fold was sufficient to catch a fingernail *which is the factory guideline for rejection of this defect*." Exhibit D at 1 (emphasis supplied).

Since the attendant dangers of manufacturing and packaging serum albumin may constitute a hazard to human life the standard of care required of the Blood Center in this case is extremely high. In this context, the Blood Center's duty of care may be viewed as a matter of the following variables: 1) the probability that a defective vial will be used in packaging the serum albumin; 2) the resulting injuries if such a vial is used; and 3) the burden of adequate precautions. Given the facts that 1) in late 1980, the Blood Center was dissatisfied with the quality of the Wheaton vials; 2) an unsterile product caused by a defective vial may constitute a hazard to human life; 3) the person who loads the vials onto the conveyor is instructed to look at the vials; and 4) the defect in this vial is allegedly "fairly apparent if you look at it closely," this Court cannot rule, as matter of law, that Blood Center was not negligent in testing and inspecting the glass vials which contain the serum albumin.

NOTES

1. *Majoritarian Conduct.* For the custom standard to apply, must it be established that "the defendant acted in accordance with the uniform custom of persons engaged in a similar business?" *Vuono, supra.* Is a custom instruction invariably contraindicated when there is evidence that a "respectable" minority use a different approach to accident avoidance?

2. *Negligent and Nonnegligent Customs.* The *Vuono* court distinguished the *Breault* seatbelt case apparently on the basis that there was a lack of evidence showing that the customary absence of seatbelt use was itself negligent. What evidence of negligence was tendered in *Vuono*? On whom does the court place the burden of persuasion?

Is a close-knit industry more or less likely than an individual to obtain a custom instruction? Why?

3. *Custom Supplanted.* If custom did not constitute the decisional tool utilized in *Vuono*, with what was it replaced?

4. *Custom and Rules of the Game. Condon v. Basi,* [1985] 2 All E.R. 453, [1985] 1 W.L.R. 866 (C.A.), involved injuries suffered in a local league soccer match. The referee's report concluded, "The slide tackle came late, and was made in a reckless and dangerous manner, by lunging with his boot studs showing about a foot—18 inches from the ground." In affirming the plaintiff's verdict, the Court of Appeal approved of the following passage from *Rootes v. Shelton,* [1968] AUSTL. L.R. 33, 37, *per* KITTO, J.:

> [I]n a case such as the present, it must always be a question of fact, what exoneration from a duty of care otherwise incumbent upon the defendant was implied by the act of the plaintiff joining in the activity. Unless the activity partakes of the nature of a war or of something else in which all is notoriously fair, the conclusion to be reached must necessarily depend, according to the concepts of the common law, upon the reasonableness, in relation to the special circumstances, of the conduct which caused the plaintiff's injury. That does not necessarily mean the compliance of that conduct with the rules, conventions or customs (if there are any) by which the correctness of conduct for the purposes of the carrying on of the activity as an organized affair is judged, for the tribunal of fact may think that in the situation in which the plaintiff's injury was caused a participant might do what the defendant did and still not be acting unreasonably even though he infringed the "rules of the game." Non-compliance with such rules, conventions or customs (where they exist) is necessarily one consideration to be attended to upon the question of reasonableness but it is only one, and it may be of much or little or even no weight in the circumstances.

Finally, the court rejected defendant's additional argument:

> [I]t was submitted by counsel on behalf of the defendant that the standard of care was subjective to the defendant and not objective, and if he was a wholly incompetent football player, he could do things without risk of liability which a competent football player could not do. For my part I reject that submission. The standard is objective, but objective in a different set of circumstances. Thus there will of course be a higher degree of care required of a player in a First Division football match than of a player in a local league football match. But none of these sophistications arise in this case, as is at once apparent when one looks at the facts.

Courts differ as to whether an intentional, reckless, or negligent standard should be used in determining liability for sports-related injuries. See *Lestina v. West Bend Mut. Ins. Co.,* 176 Wis.2d 901, 501 N.W.2d 28 (1993). Would custom be relevant in determining whether each of these three standards was breached?

E. RISKS AND UTILITIES

UNITED STATES V. CARROLL TOWING CO.
159 F.2d 169 (2d Cir. 1947)

. . . On June 20, 1943, the Conners Company chartered the barge, "Anna C.," to the Pennsylvania Railroad Company at a stated hire per diem, by a charter of the kind usual in the Harbor, which included the services of a bargee, apparently limited to the hours 8 A.M. to 4 P.M. On January 2, 1944, the barge, which had lifted the cargo of flour, was made fast off the end of Pier 58 on the Manhattan side of the North River, whence she was later shifted to Pier 52. At some time not disclosed, five other barges were moored outside her, extending into the river; her lines to the pier were not then strengthened. At the end of the next pier north (called the Public Pier), lay four barges; and a line had been made fast from the outermost of these to the fourth barge of the tier hanging to Pier 52. The purpose of this line is not entirely apparent, and in any event it obstructed entrance into the slip between the two piers of barges. The Grace Line, which had chartered the tug, "Carroll," sent her down to the locus in quo to "drill" out one of the barges which lay at the end of the Public Pier; and in order to do so it was necessary to throw off the line between the two tiers. On board the "Carroll" at the time were not only her master, but a "harbormaster" employed by the Grace Line. Before throwing off the line between the two tiers, the "Carroll" nosed up against the outer barge of the tier lying off Pier 52, ran a line from her own stem to the middle bit of that barge, and kept working her engines "slow ahead" against the ebb tide which was making at that time. The captain of the "Carroll" put a deckhand and the "harbormaster" on the barges, told them to throw off the line which barred the entrance to the slip; but, before doing so, to make sure that the tier on Pier 52 was safely moored, as there was a strong northerly wind blowing down the river. The "harbormaster" and the deckhand went aboard the barges and readjusted all the fasts to their satisfaction, including those from the "Anna C." to the pier.

After doing so, they threw off the line between the two tiers and again boarded the "Carroll," which backed away from the outside barge, preparatory to "drilling" out the barge she was after in the tier off the Public Pier. She had only got about seventy-five feet away when the tier off Pier 52 broke adrift because the fasts from the "Anna C," either rendered, or carried away. The tide and wind carried down the six barges, still holding together, until the "Anna C" fetched up against a tanker, lying on the north side of the pier below — Pier 51— whose propeller broke a hole in her at or near her bottom. Shortly thereafter: *i.e.*, at about 2:15 P.M., she careened, dumped her cargo of flour and sank. The tug, "Grace," owned by the Grace Line, and the "Carroll," came to the help of the flotilla after it broke loose; and, as both had siphon pumps on board, they could have kept the "Anna C" afloat, had they learned of her condition; but the bargee had left her on the evening before, and nobody was on board to observe that she was leaking. The Grace Line wishes to exonerate itself from all liability because the "harbormaster" was not authorized to pass on the sufficiency of the fasts of the "Anna C" which held the tier to Pier 52; the Carroll Company wishes to charge the Grace Line with the entire liability because the "harbormaster" was given an over-all authority. Both wish to charge the "Anna C" with a share of all her damages, or at least with so much as resulted from her sinking. The Pennsylvania Railroad Company also wishes to hold the barge liable. The Conners Company wishes the decrees to be affirmed.

The first question is whether the Grace Line should be held liable at all for any part of the damages. The answer depends first upon how far the "harbormaster's" authority went, for concededly he was an employee of some sort. [There was evidence that] the master of the "Carroll" deputed the deckhand and the "harbormaster," jointly to pass upon the sufficiency of the "Anna C's" fasts to the pier. . . .. The fact that the deckhand shared in this decision, did not exonerate [the harbormaster], and there is no reason why both should not be held equally liable, as the judge held them.

We cannot, however, excuse the Conners Company for the bargee's failure to care for the barge, and we think that this prevents full recovery. . . .. [I]f the bargee had been on board, and had done his duty to his employer, he would have gone below at once, examined the injury, and called for help from the "Carroll" and the Grace Line tug. Moreover, it is clear that these tugs could have kept the barge afloat, until they had safely beached her, and saved her cargo. This would have avoided what we shall call the "sinking damages." Thus, if it was a failure in the Conner Company's proper care of its own barge, for the bargee to be absent, the company can recover only one third of the "sinking" damages from the Carroll Company and one third from the Grace Line. For this reason the question arises whether a barge owner is slack in the care of his barge if the bargee is absent.

. . .It appears from the foregoing review that there is no general rule to determine when the absence of a bargee or other attendant will make the owner of the barge liable for injuries to other vessels if she breaks away from her moorings. However, in any cases where he would be so liable for injuries to others obviously he must reduce his damages proportionately, if the injury is to his own barge. It becomes apparent why there can be no such general rule, when we consider the grounds for such a liability. Since there are occasions when every vessel will break from her moorings, and since, if she does, she becomes a menace to those about her; the owner's duty, as in other similar situations, to provide against resulting injuries is a function of three variables: (1) The probability that she will break away; (2) the gravity of the resulting injury, if she does; (3) the burden of adequate precautions. Possibly it serves to bring this notion into relief to state it in algebraic terms: if the probability be called P; the injury, L; and the burden, B; liability depends upon whether B is less than L multiplied by P: i.e., whether B less than PL. Applied to the situation at bar, the likelihood that a barge will break from her fasts and the damage she will do, vary with the place and time; for example, if a storm threatens, the danger is greater; so it is, if she is in a crowded harbor where moored barges are constantly being shifted about. On the other hand, the barge must not be the bargee's prison, even though he lives aboard; he must go ashore at times. We need not say whether, even in such crowded waters as New York Harbor, a bargee must be aboard at night at all; it may be that the custom is otherwise, as Ward, J., supposed in "The Kathryn B.

Guinan," 176 F.2d 301, and that, if so, the situation is one where custom should control. We leave that question open; but we hold that it is not in all cases a sufficient answer to a bargee's absence without excuse, during working hours, that he has properly made fast his barge to a pier, when he leaves her. In the case at bar the bargee left at five o'clock in the afternoon of January 3rd, and the flotilla broke away at about two o'clock in the afternoon of the following day, twenty-one hours afterwards. The bargee had been away all the time, and we hold that his fabricated story was affirmative evidence that he had no excuse for his absence. At the locus in quo — especially during the short January days and in the full tide of war activity — barges were being constantly 'drilled' in and out. Certainly it was not beyond reasonable expectation that, with the inevitable haste and bustle, the work might not be done with adequate care. In such circumstances we hold—and it is all that we do hold—that it was a fair requirement that the Conners Company should have a bargee aboard (unless he had some excuse for his absence), during the working hours of daylight. . ... [Reversed and remanded.]

NOTES

1. *Economic Analysis.* Judge Hand's formula was destined to become part of torts lore, and is the underpinning of much of today's economic analysis of the torts system. The challenges thrown down by this mathematical approach to accident redistribution are as fresh today as they were in 1947.

2. *Restated Doctrine.* RESTATEMENT (SECOND) OF TORTS § 291 provides:

> Where an act is one which a reasonable man would recognize as involving a risk of harm to another, the risk is unreasonable and the act is negligent if the risk is of such magnitude as to outweigh what the law regards as the utility of the act or of the particular manner in which it is done.

The Restatement then supplies detail as follows:

> § 292. FACTORS CONSIDERED IN DETERMINING UTILITY OF ACTOR'S CONDUCT
>
> In determining what the law regards as the utility of the actor's conduct for the purpose of determining whether the actor is negligent, the following factors are important:
>
> (a) the social value which the law attaches to the interest which is to be advanced or protected by the conduct;
>
> (b) the extent of the chance that this interest will be advanced or protected by the particular course of conduct;
>
> (c) the extent of the chance that such interest can be adequately advanced or protected by another and less dangerous course of conduct.
>
> § 293. FACTORS CONSIDERED IN DETERMINING MAGNITUDE OF RISK
>
> In determining the magnitude of the risk for the purpose of determining whether the actor is negligent, the following factors are important:

(a) the social value which the law attaches to the interests which are imperiled;

(b) the extent of the chance that the actor's conduct will cause an invasion of any interest of the other or of one of a class of which the other is a member;

(c) the extent of the harm likely to be caused to the interests imperiled;

(d) the number of persons whose interests are likely to be invaded if the risk takes effect in harm.

3. *Between a Rock and a Hard Place.* Consider *Cooley v. Public Serv. Co.,* 90 N.H. 460, 10 A.2d 373, 676–77 (1940). There, a storm caused the defendant power company's cable to fall onto a telephone line, injuring the plaintiff telephone user's ear with a loud noise. Plaintiff argued that the power cable should have been insulated. Evidence suggested, however, that this could produce the result that the cable would not ground if it fell. The court noted,

> In the case before us, there was danger of electrocution in the street. As long as the Telephone Company's safety devices are properly installed and maintained, there is no danger of electrocution in the house. The only foreseeable danger to the telephone subscriber is from noise —fright and neurosis. Balancing the two, the danger to those such as the plaintiff is remote, that to those on the ground near the broken wire is obvious and immediate. The balance would not be improved by taking a chance to avoid traumatic neurosis of the plaintiff at the expense of greater risk to the lives of others. To the extent that the duty to use care depends upon relationship, the defendant's duty of care towards the plaintiff is obviously weaker than that towards the man in the street.
>
> The defendant's duty cannot, in the circumstances, be to both. If that were so, performance of one duty would mean nonperformance of the other. . . . The law could tolerate no such theory of "be liable if you do and liable if you don't . . . ."

4. *Practical Utility.* Does the "Hand formula" operate at a decisional level, or only at a theoretical one? Can the formula operate on an individual decisional basis, or only with regard to broad categories of fact patterns, *e.g.,* is it more useful when resolving "standard of care" or "duty" issues? Does this type of analysis operate so as to determine the issue of negligence or nonnegligence in a given case, or is this style of analysis better suited, not to mention more efficiently executed, in a more abstract determination of redistribution in general types of fact patterns? *See, e.g., Union Oil Co. v. Oppen,* 501 F.2d 558 (9th Cir. 1974). *See generally* Fletcher, *Fairness and Utility in Tort Theory,* 85 HARV. L. REV. 537 (1972).

In *Johnson v. Thompson,* 111 Ga. App. 654, 143 S.E.2d 51 (1965) the plaintiff was injured in defendant's drive-in theatre as he walked between parked automobiles to the snack bar. The defendant did not provide a safe walk way to the snack bar from the parking rows behind the snack bar, where the plaintiff was parked, and, as the plaintiff raised the wire leading from a post between parked cars to the speaker box placed in one of the cars, to pass under the wire, a person seated in the car opened the door and the door struck the plaintiff in his left eye and caused him to be seriously injured.

In view of the uses for which the defendant invited patrons to the premises, reasonable men could disagree and it is a question of fact whether the risk of a patron walking to the snack bar being struck by a car door, was foreseeable. The next question is more difficult. If the risk was foreseeable, was it an unreasonable risk—was it a risk of such magnitude as to outweigh what the law regards as the utility of the defendant's alleged negligent conduct (not providing a walkway to the snack bar where this risk would not be present)? American Law Institute, Restatement, Torts 785 et seq., §§ 291–293. This standard is complex but affords an opportunity for reaching substantial justice. The magnitude of a risk involves the social value of the interests imperiled (in this case the plaintiff's interest in bodily safety), the probability of harm to those to whom a duty is owed, and the extent of harm likely to be caused to them by exposure to the risk. Id. 791, § 293. Factors relating to the utility of particular conduct are the social usefulness of the enterprise (in this case the drive-in theatre), the value to the defendant of the particular way of conducting the enterprise (the alleged acts and omissions of negligence), and the extent to which the defendant's interest can be adequately advanced by another and less dangerous course of conduct (such as providing a special walk way to the snack bar). Id., 788, § 292. We again believe that reasonable men could disagree whether, if the risk to the plaintiff was foreseeable, it was reasonable or unreasonable, considering the magnitude of the risk and the utility of the defendant's alleged negligent conduct.

143 S.E.2d at 54.

5. *The Hand Formula as the Criteria for the Negligence Determination.* According to Professor now Judge Posner,

> Hand was adumbrating, perhaps unwittingly, an economic meaning of negligence. Discounting (multiplying) the cost of an accident if it occurs by the probability of occurrence yields a measure of the economic benefit to be anticipated from incurring the costs necessary to prevent the accident.

Posner, *A Theory Of Negligence,* 1 J. LEG. STUD. 29, 32 (1972). *See also* R.A. POSNER, ECONOMIC ANALYSIS OF LAW, 147–51 (3d ed. 1986); G. CALABRESI, THE COST OF ACCIDENTS: A LEGAL AND ECONOMIC ANALYSIS (1970); Vandall, *Judge Posner's Negligence-Efficiency Theory: A Critique,* 35 EMORY L.J. 383 (1986); England, *The System Builders: A Critical Appraisal of Modern American Tort Theory,* 9 J. LEG. STUD. 27 (1980); Weinrib, *Toward a Moral Theory of Negligence Law,* 2 LAW & PHIL. 37 (1983).

In *McCarty v. Pheasant Run, Inc.,* 826 F.2d 1554, 1556–57 (7th Cir. 1987), a case involving innkeeper liability under Illinois law, Judge Posner remarked:

> There are various ways in which courts formulate the negligence standard. The analytically (not necessarily the operationally) most precise is that it involves determining whether the burden of precaution is less than the magnitude of the accident, if it occurs, multiplied by the probability of occurrence. (The product of this multiplication,

or "discounting," is what economists call an expected accident cost.) If the burden is less, the precaution should be taken. This is the famous "Hand Formula"....

We are not authorized to change the common law of Illinois, however, and Illinois courts do not cite the Hand Formula but instead define negligence as failure to use reasonable care, a term left undefined. But as this is a distinction without a substantive difference, we have not hesitated to use the Hand Formula in cases governed by Illinois law. The formula translates into economic terms the conventional legal test for negligence. This can be seen by considering the factors that the Illinois courts take into account in negligence cases: the same factors, and in the same relation, as in the Hand Formula. Unreasonable conduct is merely the failure to take precautions that would generate greater benefits in avoiding accidents than the precautions would cost.

Do you agree that the distinction between "reasonable care" and the Hand formula is one "without a substantive difference?"

6. *Life, Death, and Dollars(1)*. Can B, P, and L satisfactorily be quantified? In *McCarty v. Pheasant Run, Inc., supra,* Judge Posner observed,

Ordinarily . . . the parties do not give the jury the information required to quantify the variables that the Hand Formula picks out as relevant. That is why the formula has greater analytic than operation significance. Conceptual as well as practical difficulties in monetizing personal injuries may continue to frustrate efforts to measure expected accident costs with the precision that is possible, in principle at least, in measuring the other side of the equation—the cost of burden of precaution. For many years to come juries may be forced to make rough judgments of reasonableness, intuiting rather than measuring the factors in the Hand Formula. . . .

826 F.2d at 1557.

Recall that in *Cooley v. Public Serv. Co.,* 90 N.H. 460, 10 A.2d 673 (1940) one of the costs associated with the safety device suggested by plaintiff was an increased risk of electrocution to a different class of potential plaintiffs.

7. *Life, Death, and Dollars (2)*. After a series of injuries and deaths allegedly caused by Ford Pinto and Mercury Bobcat fuel tanks rupturing in rear-end collisions, it was reported that the manufacturer had known of a defect but, on the basis of the following cost-benefit analysis, decided not to remedy the defect by installing $11 rubber bladders in the fuel tanks. *See generally* Dowie, *Pinto Madness,* MOTHER JONES, Sept./Oct. 1977, 18 at 24:

Benefits and Costs Relating to Fuel Leakage Associated with the Static Rollover Test Portion of FMVSS 208:

Benefits

Savings: 180 burn deaths, 180 serious burn injuries, 2,100 burned vehicles.

Unit Cost: $200,000 per death, $67,000 per injury, $700 per vehicle.

Total Benefit: 180 s ($200,000) + 180 s ($67,000) + 2,100 s ($700) = **$49.5 million.**

Costs

Sales: 11 million cars, 1.5 million light trucks.

Unit Cost: $11 per car, $11 per truck.

Total Cost: 11,000,000 s ($11) + 1,500,000 s ($11) = **$137 million.**

This excerpt, dealing with rollover damages, allegedly from an internal Ford memorandum entitled *Fatalities Associated with Crash-Induced Fuel Leakage and Fires,* and known as the "Grush-Saunby Report," was excluded from the most famous Ford Pinto trial. See *Grimshaw v. Ford Motor Co.,* 119 Cal. App. 3d 757, 174 Cal. Rptr. 348, 376 (1981), dealing with damages from a rear-end collision. See Gary Schwartz, *The Ford Pinto Case*, 43 RUTGERS L. REV. 1013 (1991).

In a Pinto rollover case involving a fire from fuel leakage, would you accept any of the following conclusions?

(1) In a situation such as this, where B > PL, it would be a misallocation of resources to redistribute accident costs through the torts system.

(2) Whatever the merits of the Hand formula as a judicial tool, its strategic use by potential defendants will not be tolerated.

(3) If the automobile market had operated properly (*e.g.,* if consumers had known of the contents of the memorandum), the manufacturer would have been forced to correct the defect and governmental or judicial intervention would have been unnecessary.

(4) The whole point of the torts system is to intervene and deter when the market creates intolerable results.

(5) The memorandum involves retrofit costs and does not provide the data necessary for the application of the Hand formula.

(6) The automobile manufacturer should have been prosecuted for reckless homicide.

8. *The Maritime History of the Hand Formula.* Federal courts, and particularly those dealing with maritime issues, have shown the greatest interest in the literal application of the Hand formula. For example, in *United States Fidelity & Guaranty Co. v. Jadranska Slobodna*, 683 F.2d 1022 (7th Cir. 1982), Judge Posner noted:

> Though mathematical in form, the Hand formula does not yield mathematically precise results in practice; that would require that B, P, and L all be quantified, which so far as we know has never been done in an actual lawsuit. Nevertheless, the formula is a valuable aid to clear thinking about the factors that are relevant to a judgment of negligence and about the relationship among those factors. It gives federal district courts in maritime cases, where the liability standard is a matter of federal rather than state law, a useful framework for evaluating proposed jury instructions, for deciding motions for directed verdict and for judgment notwithstanding the verdict. . . . We do not want to force the district courts into a straitjacket, so we do not hold that they must use the Hand formula in all maritime negligence cases. We merely commend it to them as a useful tool—one we have found helpful in this case in evaluating the plaintiff's challenge to the jury instructions and its contention that negligence was shown as a matter of law.

9. *The "Market" Placed in Evidence.* What is the relationship between custom and risk-utility analysis? In *Jadranska Slobodna* Judge Posner stated:

> The fact that the practice of leaving the hatches open in darkened holds was customary (or so the jury could find) and not just an idiosyncrasy of this Yugoslavian ship or ship owner has additional relevance to this case. Although custom is not a defense to a charge of negligence, *The T. J. Hooper,* 60 F.2d 737, 740 (2d Cir. 1932), it is a material consideration in evaluating the charge, especially where the victim and the alleged tortfeasor are linked, even if indirectly, in a voluntary relationship, as they were here. If a ship owner were to follow a practice that flunked the Hand formula—that in other words was not cost-justified, because the expected accident costs associated with the practice exceeded the costs of abandoning the practice and so preventing any accident from happening—then he would have to pay his stevedores higher rates, to compensate them for the additional risk to their employees, the longshoremen, whom the stevedores must compensate under 33 U.S.C. § 904, regardless of fault, for any injury the longshoremen sustain in the course of their employment. And since by hypothesis the cost to the stevedores of the additional compensation—the expected accident cost, in other words—would exceed the cost of abandoning the practice (for otherwise the practice would be cost-justified), it would pay the ship owner to abandon it. Hence if the ship owner persists in a dangerous practice —if the whole trade persists in the practice—that is some evidence, though not conclusive, that the practice is cost-justified, and not negligent.

F. LEGISLATIVE STANDARDS

ASHWOOD v. CLARK COUNTY
113 Nev. 80, 930 P.2d 740 (1997)

SPRINGER, J.

. . .On September 1, 1990, Ashwood and her family attended a horseshow at Horseman's Park in Las Vegas. The park is owned by defendant/respondent Clark County. On the date in question, the park was leased to defendant/respondent Nevada State Horseman's Association (NSHA), the sponsor of the event.

The park includes a barn area surrounded by a chain-link fence. There are several gateways through the fence, although on the night in question only the main gateway to the south remained unlocked. Ashwood was assigned a stall in Barn "C" near the western fence line. While in the barn area, she heard the sounds of a runaway horse and cries for help. She observed a rider lying on the ground in an open area to the west of the barn area and on the other side of the fence.

Ashwood, who is trained in CPR, believed that the fallen rider needed immediate assistance and ran toward the nearest gate in the barn area fence to assist the injured rider. The nearest gate was the west gate, which was locked. Concerned that the fallen rider might be unconscious and not breathing, Ashwood attempted to climb over the chain-link fence, rather than run through the open main gate approximately 150 feet away. Unfortunately, Ashwood fell in the process and sustained a severe injury to her knee.

Ashwood brought suit against Clark County, the NSHA, and the manager of the barn area, Dixie Bennett (referred to collectively as "Respondents"). Ashwood claims that Respondents are liable in negligence for failing to keep the west gate unlocked. After substantial discovery, Respondents moved for summary judgment. Ashwood filed a response to Respondents' motion and filed a cross-motion for partial summary judgment on the issue of duty.

In support of her motion for summary judgment, Ashwood presented the district court with the affidavit of Dan Cashdan (Cashdan), a registered civil engineer employed by the State of Nevada. Cashdan is thoroughly familiar with the Uniform Building Code ("U.B.C.") in effect in Clark County at the time of the incident, and his duties include reviewing building plans for compliance with the Building Code. Cashdan testified that the Building Code required the west gate be operable from inside the barn area. According to Cashdan, the padlocked west gate was a "clear violation" of the Building Code and a danger to public safety.

Ashwood also supported her motion with the affidavit of Drusilla E. Malavase (Malavase), an expert in equestrian training and safety for the past forty years and an organizer of horseshows. Malavase testified that Respondents' conduct was below the national standard of care, which "mandates that gates shall not be locked during the show and while the public is present.". . .

Ashwood also presented the district court with the lease agreement between NSHA and Clark County, under which NSHA was obligated to comply with all laws and ordinances of the State of Nevada and Clark County. . . . Finally, Ashwood presented evidence that, at past horseshows, people had climbed over fences to rescue fallen riders.

. . .Ashwood contends that the district court erred in granting summary judgment because there are material facts remaining to be tried and that, therefore, respondents were not entitled to judgment as a matter of law.

. . .It is the courts and not juries that have the ultimate responsibility of defining duty in relation to particular circumstances and to define the legal standard of reasonable conduct "in the light of the apparent risk.'" *Merluzzi v. Larson*, 96 Nev. 409, 412–13, 610 P.2d 739, 742 (1990) (quoting W. Prosser, Law of Torts, § 53 at 324 (4th ed. 1971). . . .. By defining the scope of duty in negligence cases that come before them, the courts are making a vital "expression of the aggregate of those policy considerations which cause the law to conclude that protection is owed." *Merluzzi*, 96 Nev. at 409, 610 P.2d at 742.

Ashwood presents two arguments on the duty question. First, she argues that there was a specific duty to keep the west gate unlocked because it was foreseeable that in an emergency she would need to use the padlocked gate to exit the barn area. Ashwood also argues that the respondents should have foreseen that during an emergency people would attempt to exit the barn area by climbing the fence if the gate were locked.

Foreseeability of harm is, of course, a predicate to establishing the element of duty, and respondents contend that a fallen rider in another part of the park is not the kind of foreseeable emergency that would give rise to a duty, enforceable by Ashwood, to keep the west gate unlocked. Respondents emphasize the unquestioned fact that there was an alternate safe means for Ashwood to carry out the intended rescue, namely, by going through the other, unlocked main gate that was less than 150 feet away. Respondents argue that there was no duty to provide the shortest or quickest route to any area of the horseshow grounds.

Ashwood has presented no evidence to suggest that the main gate, located 150 feet away from the locked gate, would have been inadequate to effect the intended rescue. Ashwood did not contend that she was physically incapable of traversing the additional distance nor that going to the open gate would have put her in personal danger or unacceptably delayed her attempted rescue. The exigent circumstances presented by the fallen rider did not constitute the kind of emergency alluded to by Ashwood's own experts—such as a fire, panic, or stampede—where an alternative means of egress may not have been reasonably available and where the immediacy of the danger combined with the inability to use the locked gate might have necessitated an attempt to scale the fence rather than to proceed to the unlocked gate. Under the circumstances, we agree with Respondents that this case really boils down to whether there existed a duty to provide Ashwood the shortest or quickest route from one area of the park to another. We conclude that there was no such duty. . . ..

In light of the particular risk present in this case, Respondents' common law duty of reasonable care did not give rise to a specific duty to keep the west gate unlocked.

Ashwood also contends that a duty to keep the west gate unlocked arose under the Clark County Building Code (the Code).[4] In response, Respondents first argue that the sections of the Code cited by Ashwood are not applicable either to the barn area or to the area surrounding the fence. Second, Respondents argue that, even if Respondents did violate the Code, the violations do not amount to negligence per se.

A violation of statute establishes the duty and breach elements of negligence only if the injured party belongs to the class of persons that the statute was intended to protect, and the injury is of the type against which the statute was intended to protect.

Ashwood contends that the Code prohibits Respondents from padlocking the west gate while the public is present. Ashwood's contention depends upon the barn area being a "Group A Occupancy" under U.B.C. section 601 and the west gate being a required "exit." Exit doors in a Group A Occupancy are not to be latched or locked except with "panic hardware," a latching device that allows egress from the structure in an emergency. See U.B.C. § 3317(d). We are not convinced that the Horseman's Park barn area is a "Group A Occupancy," nor are we convinced that the west gate is a required exit; we need not decide this issue, however, because even if locking the west gate was a violation of section 3317(d), the violation would not be negligence per se in this case.

Ashwood argues that the Code is a "safety enactment." As discussed above, however, Ashwood herself was never in any danger; she was simply in a hurry to get from one part of horseman's park to another and chose, unwisely it turns out, to climb the fence rather than exiting through the open south gate. Clearly, the Code was not intended to ensure good samaritans the shortest route from one part of a public facility to another. Under the circumstances, we conclude as a matter of law that Ashwood is not a member of the class of persons the "panic hardware" provision of the building code was meant to protect. Accordingly, even if the Code was violated, the violation was not negligence per se and did not establish a duty owed to Ashwood to keep the west gate unlocked.

Neither the common law, Clark County ordinances, nor the Horseman's Park lease agreement imposed upon Respondents a duty owing to Ashwood to keep the west gate unlocked; we conclude, therefore, that Respondents have negated an essential element of Ashwood's case. We hold, accordingly, that the district court did not err in entering summary judgment against Ashwood.

ROSE, J., with whom SHEARING, J., joins, dissenting:

. . .In rejecting the Ashwoods' negligence per se [argument], the majority concludes that Ms. Ashwood was not a member of the class of persons meant to be protected by U.B.C. § 3317(d). . . . I conclude that whether or not the building code provision [was] meant to protect Ms. Ashwood were clearly questions of fact that should have been submitted to the jury. . ..

---

[4] Clark County has, with certain express exceptions, adopted the U.B.C. by the International Conference of Building Officials (1994 edition) as the building code of Clark County. See Clark County Ordinance § 22.04.010. Accordingly, where applicable, citations are to the U.B.C.

F.   LEGISLATIVE STANDARDS   281

NOTES

1. *Negligence Per Se or Strict Liability for Negligence?* Is there any difference between negligence *per se* and strict liability?

2. *The Orthodox Position Restated.* RESTATEMENT (SECOND) OF TORTS (1965) § 286 provides:

> The court may adopt as the standard of conduct of a reasonable man the requirements of a legislative enactment or an administrative regulation whose purpose is found to be exclusively or in part
>
> (a) to protect a class of persons which includes the one whose interest is invaded, and
>
> (b) to protect the particular interest which is invaded, and
>
> (c) to protect that interest against the kind of harm which has resulted, and
>
> (d) to protect that interest against the particular hazard from which the harm results.

Sec. 288A states that unless a statute or administrative regulation "is construed not to permit such excuse," a violator of the statute or regulation may be excused, *inter alia*, if he shows that "he neither knows or should know of the occasion for compliance, or that he is "unable after reasonable diligence or care to comply." Thus the effect of proof of negligence *per se* in most situations is to shift the burden of proof to the defendant to prove due care on her part. How could the defendant have carried this burden in *Smith v. Owen, infra*? Will the issue normally be one of fact, no matter what proof the defendant offers?

3. *Judge or Jury?* Do you agree with the dissenting judge in *Ashwood* that the applicability or inapplicability of the building code was a matter for the jury? In a *per se* case, exactly what is the role of the jury?

4. *Rowdy Behavior.* In *Newport v. Moran*, 80 Or. App. 71, 721 P.2d 465 (1985), a stray dog wandering the neighborhood was taken in by plaintiff and her husband. They tried to find a home for the dog, because they could not keep it confined. They offered it to their neighbors, the defendants, who first declined but later accepted it. One day when plaintiff left her house to get her mail Rowdy was roaming unattended in the yard. Plaintiff tried to "shoo" him home, but he responded by sitting down at the street end of plaintiff's driveway. Subsequently the plaintiff heard a noise, turned around, and was struck on her right knee by Rowdy's shoulder, causing her to fall and suffer a broken leg. She relied, inter alia, on a claimed violation of County Code § 5.255(1), which provides:

> (1) No dog owner shall permit a dog to be at large.
>
> (2) A dog owner, whose dog runs at large, commits a Class B infraction.

The Lane County ordinance defines a dog being at large as,

> (5) A dog off the premises of the owner and not under the owner's immediate control.

The court held that:

> Violation of an ordinance may be negligence *per se* if the violation is the cause of the injury, the plaintiff is within the class of persons intended to be protected by the legislation and the injury is within the area of risk intended to be avoided by the ordinance.

The Lane County ordinance is substantively equivalent to the Washington County ordinance considered in *Kathren v. Olenik, supra,* which involved a dog bite. We held that the Washington County ordinance operated against a dog's owners only if they knew or should have known that the dog had a propensity to bite, saying:

> This evinces concurrence with the general knowledge that dogs as a class of animal do not normally attack human beings. Because it is not reasonably foreseeable that dogs will attack persons, injury from dog bites is not within the area of risk the running at large provision was designed to avoid.

46 Or. App. at 724, 613 P.2d 69. The trial judge ruled that, although *Kathren* held that dog bites were not within the area of risk that the dog-at-large ordinance was designed to avoid, that decision did not explain what risks were contemplated by the ordinance. Therefore, the trial judge submitted the issue to the jury on the basis that dogs knocking people down could be one of the anticipated risks covered by the statute.

. . .Plaintiff claimed that Rowdy charged her with his shoulder in an unprovoked assault. That kind of animal behavior is less likely than biting and, correspondingly, even less likely to be the kind of harm that is within the area of risk contemplated by the ordinance. Therefore, we conclude that the evidence did not warrant submission of the case to the jury on the theory of negligence *per se* for violation of the dog control ordinance.

Judge Newman, dissenting, stated,

> Even if dog bites are not within the area of risk contemplated by the ordinance, *Kathren v. Olenik*, 46 Or. App. 713, 724, 613 P.2d 69 (1980), I do not believe that it necessarily follows that dog knock-downs are similarly outside the scope of the ordinance. Although, as we stated in *Kathren*, dogs as a class are not vicious and do not attack people, they do tend to roam at large along streets and in yards and get under foot. The ordinance was intended to protect the public from harm caused by this type of dog behavior.

Why didn't the plaintiff in *Newport* rely upon a theory of strict animal liability?

5. *Defective Electrical Wiring.* The plaintiff tenants, parents and child, sued the defendant landlord in *Smith v. Owen*, 841 S.W.2d 828 (Tenn. App. 1992), for electrical shock received by the child while playing near a clothes dryer. The shock occurred because the back of the dryer was energized owing to faulty wiring which had been done before the defendant acquired the premises. At the time the plaintiffs leased the premises an applicable city ordinance

required that every owner or lessor of a dwelling shall install and maintain the electrical outlets therein in good and safe working condition. The appellate court said:

> The trial court found that the defendant's violation of the ordinance was the proximate cause of the injury. As we have stated, the ordinance imposed a duty on defendant to inspect the wiring before turning the premises over to plaintiffs. In the instant case, the electrician discovered the faulty wiring using a meter with which any electrician would be familiar. The trial court specifically found that "an inspection of the premises prior to the lease would have revealed the defective condition." The preponderance of the evidence supports the trial court's finding of proximate cause.

A dissent argued:

> The record reflects that the defective wiring was installed without the knowledge or consent of the defendant-landlord before the enactment of the city code which, according to the majority, made the landlord an insurer of the safety of the premises. This is contrary to the long established law of landlord and tenant in this State.

6. *Risk Identification.* In *Larrimore v. American Nat'l Ins. Co.*, 184 Okla. 614, 89 P.2d 340 (1939), the plaintiff, a coffee shop employee, was injured in an explosion while attempting to light the burner on a steam table. Her match ignited a can of "Rat Doom" under the table. She sued the lessor of the premises who had provided the rat poison to her employer. She relied on a statute providing, "Whoever shall, except in a safe place on his own premises, lay out strychnine or other poison, is guilty of a misdemeanor." The court concluded:

> It is clear enough that the substance laid out was poison. It may further be said that if the owner had not furnished the lessee with the rat poison the plaintiff would not have been injured; and still it does not follow that the statute makes defendant liable for plaintiff's injury. It is clear that the purpose of the above statute is to protect persons and animals from injury by being poisoned. The injury here was not the class of injury intended to be prevented by the statute. There was no connection between the poisonous nature of the substance and plaintiff's injury.

> It is not enough for a plaintiff to show that the defendant neglected a duty imposed by statute. He must go further and show that his injury was caused by his exposure to a hazard from which it was the purpose of the statute to protect him. Negligence is a breach of duty. Those only to whom that duty is due and who have sustained injuries of the character its discharge was designed to prevent can maintain actions for its breach.

> The rule in this jurisdiction is that one who does an unlawful act is not thereby placed outside of the protection of the law, but that to have this effect the unlawful act must have some causal connection with the injury complained of. Plaintiff having in no way become poisoned by the "Rat Doom" furnished by defendant, the above section

of our statute does not, of itself, render the defendant negligent as to plaintiff's injury.

It may be observed that there is still another reason why our conclusion in this respect is correct. The statute forbids the laying out of strychnine or other poison "except in a safe place." The "safe place" contemplated by the statute obviously means that place which would be safe in regard to the substance's character as poison. What would be a safe place for poison might not be a safe place for gasoline, and vice versa. The evidence reveals that the can was placed by Mrs. Schultz on the floor, under the lower metal shelf of the steam table, which shelf was about six inches above the floor, and said poison was pushed back under the shelf some eight or ten inches. It might also be said that it was hidden. At any rate, it could not correctly be said that the can was placed other than in a safe place for poison, in view of the particular circumstances of the case. . . .

Was *Larrimore* concerned with legal or factual causation? Was not the defendant in *Larrimore* put on notice of the danger of explosion by the label which referred to the phosphorous content of the poison, although not the percentage of that content, as follows: "Rat Doom, Poison, This phosphorus paste is guaranteed to rid any premise of rats and mice. In case of poisoning take an emetic to cause vomiting, after which take a stimulant and consult a physician at once."

Would the plaintiff have been more likely to recover had there been no statutory provision?

7. *Sanitation Versus Safety.* In *Gorris v. Scott,* [1874] 9 Ex. 125, defendant violated a statute requiring transporters of animals by water to provide separate pens for the animals while being transported. Because the sheep were not separated, they were washed overboard during a storm. The court found the statutory violation did not provide the plaintiff with a cause of action, since the statute was intended as a sanitation rather than a safety measure. Suppose, because of the absence of pens, the sheep became diseased, and then washed overboard during a storm because of their weakness from the disease?

8. *Keys-in-Cars.* In *Ross v. Hartman,* 139 F.2d 14 (D.C. Cir. 1943), plaintiff was struck by defendant's stolen truck. Defendant had left his keys in the truck. A traffic ordinance provided:

> Locks on Motor Vehicles. Every motor vehicle shall be equipped with a lock suitable to lock the starting lever, throttle, or switch, or gearshift lever, by which the vehicle is set in motion, and no person shall allow any motor vehicle operated by him to stand or remain unattended on any street or in any public place without first having locked the lever, throttle, or switch by which said motor vehicle may be set in motion.

Noting authority suggesting that there would be no liability at common law, the court continued:

> But the existence of an ordinance changes the situation. If a driver causes an accident by exceeding the speed limit, for example, we do

not inquire whether his prohibited conduct was unreasonably dangerous. It is enough that it was prohibited. Violation of an ordinance intended to promote safety is negligence. If by creating the hazard which the ordinance was intended to avoid it brings about the harm which the ordinance was intended to prevent, it is a legal cause of the harm. This comes only to saying that in such circumstances the law has no reason to ignore and does not ignore the causal relation which obviously exists in fact. The law has excellent reason to recognize it, since it is the very relation which the makers of the ordinance anticipated. This court has applied these principles to speed limits and other regulations of the manner of driving.

The same principles govern this case. The particular ordinance involved here is one of a series which require, among other things, that motor vehicles be equipped with horns and lamps. Ordinary bicycles are required to have bells and lamps, but they are not required to be locked. The evident purpose of requiring motor vehicles to be locked is not to prevent theft for the sake of owners or the police, but to promote the safety of the public in the streets. An unlocked motor vehicle creates little more risk of theft than an unlocked bicycle, or for that matter an unlocked house, but it creates much more risk that meddling by children, thieves, or others will result in injuries to the public. The ordinance is intended to prevent such consequences. Since it is a safety measure, its violation was negligence. This negligence created the hazard and thereby brought about the harm which the ordinance was intended to prevent. It was therefore a legal or "proximate" cause of the harm. Both negligence and causation are too clear in this case, we think, for submission to a jury.

The car in *McClenahan v. Cooley*, 806 S.W.2d 767 (Tenn. 1991), was stolen from private property—a public parking area in a shopping center. The trial court denied the plaintiff's cause of action, construing Tennessee precedent as not applying the state's key-in-the-ignition statute to cars left on private property. While seeing "little justification to foster the distinction [between public and private property] currently entrenched in precedent," the state supreme court sidestepped the issue by holding that the plaintiff stated a common law cause of action. In deference to legislative intention, should a common law remedy be established if the statute does not apply?

The key-in-the ignition statutes typically prohibit leaving a car "unattended" with the key in the ignition. The court in *Mackey v. Dorsey*, 104 Md. App. 273, 655 A.2d 1345 (1995), held that that state's statute did not apply in a suit by Mackey against Dorsey. The court stated the facts as follows:

> Mr. Mackey is employed as a bus driver for the Washington Metropolitan Area Transit Authority in the District of Columbia. On the morning of June 9, 1988, he was stopped at a bus terminal at the intersection of Thirteenth Street and Pennsylvania Avenue in downtown D.C. While Mackey was waiting for passengers to board his bus, appellee, Michael R. Dorsey, parked his vehicle across the street in the median behind a police car. Dorsey exited his car in order to ask the officer for assistance with his passenger, Audrey Cooper. Dorsey

had picked up Cooper when he found her wandering on the highway on his way to work. She had indicated to him that she was lost and was looking for her mother. According to Dorsey, when he exited his vehicle he took his car keys with him. The officer informed him that he should take Cooper directly to D.C. General Hospital. When Dorsey returned to his vehicle, it did not start. Dorsey alleges that he then exited the car again in order to look under the hood. The policy officer assisted him as he checked some wiring and the car's battery. He then reentered the car, successfully started the engine, "and exited again only long enough to shut the hood of the car." "At that time," Cooper slid over to the driver's seat and locked the door. Despite efforts by Dorsey and the police officer to stop her, Cooper pulled away from the median and collided with the bus driven by Mr. Mackey. Cooper was subsequently placed under arrest for unauthorized use of a motor vehicle.

Mr. Mackey's version of what transpired after Dorsey parked in the median in somewhat different. He contends Dorsey exited his vehicle on only one occasion, never left the car with his keys, and never unlatched the hood of the car to check underneath it.

Said the court:

> Thus, there is no requirement in section 21-1101 that when a driver leaves his or her vehicle with the keys in the ignition, the occupant who remains in the vehicle must be competent to drive a motor vehicle. In order for the vehicle to be "unattended," the person need only be incapable of preventing a thief or other unauthorized person from taking the car. The facts of the present case, however, are unique. Here, Ms. Cooper was not only the lone occupant of the car when Dorsey exited it, she also became the "unauthorized person" or thief against whom the statute was designed to protect. Appellants make much of the fact that Cooper was allegedly intoxicated or under the influence of drugs. Even assuming that this was relevant to determining whether Cooper was capable of preventing a third party from taking the car, there is nothing in the record before us to support appellants' allegations. She very well could have been capable of preventing a third party from stealing the car.

Even assuming arguendo that defendant violated the statute, the court concluded:

> When Dorsey exited his vehicle and left the keys still in the ignition, he significantly increased the chances of an unauthorized person, including a passenger in his own vehicle, taking the car without his permission. While there was no evidence that Ms. Cooper was intoxicated, under the influence of drugs, or otherwise incompetent to drive, apparently she may have been disoriented. While we do not believe that, under the unique circumstances of the present case, it was foreseeable that Ms. Cooper would attempt to slide under the wheel and drive the car away, even if we were to assume otherwise, the negligent manner in which she drove the car clearly was not foreseeable. Her negligence was an independent intervening event that broke

the chain of causation initiated by Dorsey. Dorsey's act of leaving his keys in the ignition, although potentially a violation of the unattended motor vehicle statute and perhaps negligent itself, was not, as a matter of law, the proximate cause of appellants' injuries.

9. *Dram Shop Liability.* *Vesely v. Sager,* 5 Cal. 3d 153, 95 Cal. Rptr. 623, 486 P.2d 151, 159 (1971), illustrates the classic use of the *per se* doctrine. There, a motorist was injured in an automobile accident with an allegedly drunk tavern patron. Holding the tavern owner potentially liable on the basis of selling liquor to an intoxicated person in violation of the state's dram shop act, the court noted that:

> A duty of care, and the attendant standard of conduct required of a reasonable man, may of course be found in a legislative enactment which does not provide for civil liability. In this state a presumption of negligence arises from the violation of a statute which was enacted to protect a class of persons of which the plaintiff is a member against the type of harm which the plaintiff suffered as a result of the violation of the statute. The Legislature has recently codified this presumption with the adoption of Evidence Code section 669: "The failure of a person to exercise due care is presumed if: (1) He violated a statute, ordinance, or regulation of a public entity; (2) The violation proximately caused death or injury to person or property; (3) The death or injury resulted from an occurrence of the nature which the statute, ordinance, or regulation was designed to prevent; and (4) The person suffering the death or the injury to his person or property was one of the class of persons for whose protection the statute, ordinance, or regulation was adopted."
>
> In the instant case a duty of care is imposed upon defendant [by the dram shop act] which provides: "Every person who sells, furnishes, gives, or causes to be sold, furnished, or given away, any alcoholic beverage to any habitual or common drunkard or to any obviously intoxicated person is guilty of a misdemeanor." This provision . . . was adopted for the purpose of protecting members of the general public from injuries to person and damage to property resulting from the excessive use of intoxicating liquor.
>
> Our conclusion concerning the legislative purpose . . . is compelled by Business and Professions Code . . . which states that one of the purposes of the Alcoholic Beverage Control Act is to protect the safety of the people of this state. Moreover, our interpretation . . . finds support in the decisions of those jurisdictions in which similar statutes, and statutes prohibiting the sale of alcoholic beverages to minors, have been found to have been enacted for the purpose of protecting members of the general public against injuries resulting from intoxication.

10. *The Class to be Protected.* Statutes in Oklahoma prohibited selling or giving alcoholic beverages to anyone under 21, and prohibited anyone under 21 from consuming such beverages. In *Busby v. Quail Creek Golf & Country Club,* 885 P.2d 1326 (Okla. 1994), the court held the defendant could be liable for injuries received by a minor as a result of consuming alcoholic beverages

furnished to her by the defendant. "Following the reasoning of the majority of states," the court had previously "refused to extend the duty of the tavern owner to the adult customer who voluntarily consumed intoxicants and injured himself." But this case was different:

> We agree with jurisdictions which allow a cause of action against a commercial vendor on behalf of a minor who voluntarily drinks to the point of intoxication and is thereby injured, regardless of whether the minor violated statutes in attempting to purchase or to consume beer. The Legislature, recognizing the foreseeable danger to both third parties and to minors who injure themselves, has taken specific steps to treat minors differently from adults by preventing minors from consuming and possessing alcohol. We believe that 37 O.S. 1991 § 241, which prohibits selling beer to a minor, and 37 O.S. 1991 § 246, which prohibits minors from consuming and possessing beer, constitute legislative recognition of the foreseeable danger to both third parties and to minors who injure themselves. As a matter of public policy, minors as a class are incompetent by reason of their youth and inexperience to deal responsibly with the effects of alcohol.

11. *The Merger of Negligence and Negligence Per Se.* A regulation in *C.T. v. Martinez*, 845 P.2d 246 (Utah 1992), required the Department of Social Services (DSS) to deny a day-care license if any person living in the home of the licensee "has a criminal record". But a rule construing this regulation stated:

> If there is any evidence or reason to believe that the care giver or any person working or living in the facility would be harmful to children, the person's criminal record, as well as the Central Register for Child Abuse, may be reviewed and clearance required before licensure. An individual may be asked to obtain a letter of certification indicating they have no criminal record.

The licensee's husband sexually abused the plaintiff's minor child. The husband had been previously convicted of sexual crimes against children. The Department was not liable, however, for failure to investigate, the court said:

> This provision does not require DSS to investigate the criminal record of a member of a care giver's household unless DSS has some "reason to believe" that person might be harmful to children. Indeed, rather than mandating the investigation of each household member's criminal record, this rule only authorizes the investigation of a household member's criminal record when there is a reasonable basis for doing so. In this case, plaintiff has not alleged that DSS suspected or had any reason to believe that Mr. Martinez posed a risk of harm to children. Hence, Plaintiff's claim falls outside the statutorily based duty owed by DSS.

In view of this holding, the court said it need not reach the "difficult decisions regarding sovereign immunity issues." UTAH CODE ANN. § 63-30-10(1)(c) provided:

> (1) Immunity from suit of all governmental entities is waived for injury proximately caused by a negligent act or omission of an employee

committed within the scope of employment except if the injury arises out of:

. . .(c) the issuance, denial, suspension, or revocation of, or by the failure or refusal to issue, deny, suspend, or revoke, any permit, license, certificate, approval, order, or similar authorization.

CROWN v. RAYMOND
159 Ariz. 87, 764 P.2d 1146 (1988)

FERNANDEZ, JUDGE.

Appellants Jack and Claudia Crown appeal from a summary judgment entered against them in their wrongful death suit against appellees Claude Raymond and his wife. We find that a material fact issue exists which precluded entry of summary judgment.

The Crowns' daughter Janet was born July 21, 1967. On October 31, 1984, when she was 17 years old, she telephoned Raymond at his gun shop, C&J Arms. She told him, "I would like to know what the laws are for purchasing a gun in Arizona." Raymond informed her she had to have proof that she was at least 21 and that an Arizona driver's license would be sufficient for that proof. Janet then inquired about the price range of handguns. Approximately two hours later, Janet arrived at Raymond's store and told him she was the one who had called earlier. Janet stood five feet one-half inch tall and weighed 95 pounds. She was wearing "double colored" dark glasses and had on a large black hat and high heels.

Janet told Raymond she wanted a gun for target shooting, and he recommended a Smith & Wesson .22. Janet decided she did not want the gun after she learned it cost over $300. She then selected a .380 caliber Iver Johnson handgun. Raymond told her that gun was not considered a target gun and that the cost of ammunition for it made it expensive to shoot. Janet replied that she was small and the gun fit her. She then purchased the gun for $262.15 and bought a box of ammunition for $16, paying cash in $20 bills. For identification, Janet showed Raymond her Arizona driver's license, and he copied the number on it to the federal form required for gun sales.

The transaction took place about 1:30 p.m. on October 31. At 6:00 a.m. on November 1, Janet Crown used the gun to kill herself. The police officer who found Janet's body also found her Arizona driver's license at the scene. Raymond told the officer it was the same license Janet had showed him. The year of birth on the license had very obviously been altered and looked somewhat as though "63" was the year of birth, but the three was very smudged and appeared to have been written either in pencil or in an ink color different than that of the rest of the writing. The picture indicates that Janet was very young in appearance. Raymond told the police officer, "I can't read the numbers. I'm half blind." Raymond has a cataract in his right eye and his vision in that eye is very blurred. In addition, he has a double astigmatism in his left eye. Although he correctly copied the driver's license number on to the federal firearms form, and although he later commented to Janet that they were both born in the same month, he told the police officer he had not noticed that the last digit of the year of birth had been obliterated.

Janet's parents sued Raymond for wrongful death. Both parties moved for summary judgment, and the trial court granted Raymond's motion, finding that there were "no facts upon which the Court can find that the event in question was reasonably foreseeable."

The Crowns contend on appeal that the trial court erred in granting Raymond's motion. They contend that they are entitled to summary judgment on the issue of Raymond's liability and that the case should be remanded for trial on the issues of the amount of damages and the defenses of contributory negligence and assumption of the risk only. That contention is based on their claim that the pertinent statute in this case is an "exceptional statute" which imposes strict liability on Raymond.

. . . A.R.S. § 13-3109(A) provides as follows:

> A person who sells or gives to a minor, without written consent of the minor's parent or legal guardian, a firearm, ammunition or toy pistol by which dangerous and explosive substances may be discharged, is guilty of a class 2 misdemeanor.

The federal statute, 18 U.S.C. § 922(b), provides as follows:

> It shall be unlawful for any licensed importer, licensed manufacturer, licensed dealer, or licensed collector to sell or deliver—

> (1) any firearm or ammunition to any individual who the licensee knows or has reasonable cause to believe is less than eighteen years of age, and, if the firearm or ammunition is other than a shotgun or rifle, or ammunition for a shotgun or rifle, to any individual who the licensee knows or has reasonable cause to believe is less than twenty-one years of age.

The Crowns argue that those statutes constitute "exceptional statutes" under the reasoning of *Del E. Webb Corp. v. Superior Court of Arizona,* 151 Ariz. 164, 726 P.2d 580 (1986). The supreme court discussed exceptional statutes at length in that case.

> Included in the class of statutes that impose a standard of conduct of the kind which creates civil liability is a narrow subclass called "exceptional statutes." The violation of an exceptional statute not only gives the injured party a private cause of action and establishes defendant's negligence *per se*, but, in addition, denies the defendant the affirmative defenses of contributory negligence and assumption of the risk. This is a form of absolute liability for breach of statutory duty. . . .

> Statutes intended to protect people from the consequences of their own conduct primarily are those applicable to specific groups deemed incapable of protecting themselves such as the mentally deficient and children. Children, for instance, will not be barred from recovery by their own conduct if their injury was the result of a violation of a statute expressly aimed at protecting them from a particular harm.

151 Ariz. at 167, 726 P.2d at 583. The court held in that case that statutes which prohibit the sale of liquor to minors are intended primarily to protect the general public and therefore are not exceptional statutes, the violation

of which results in absolute liability. We find sufficient similarities between the statute prohibiting the sale of liquor to minors and the statutes prohibiting the sale of firearms to minors to conclude that the latter do not constitute exceptional statutes under the reasoning of *Del E. Webb* so as to warrant the imposition of absolute liability upon Raymond.

The evidence shows that Raymond violated either the Arizona or the federal statute prohibiting the sale of firearms to minors when he sold the handgun to 17-year-old Janet. The Crowns contend that the trial court erred in granting Raymond's summary judgment motion, arguing that the violations constituted negligence *per se* and that the issue should have been submitted to the jury.

"It is the prevailing rule, recognized in Arizona, that a breach of a statute intended as a safety regulation is not merely evidence of negligence but is negligence *per se*." *Brannigan v. Raybuck*, 136 Ariz. 513, 517, 667 P.2d 213, 217 (1983). In that case, the supreme court ruled that the statute which prohibits the furnishing of liquor to a person under 19, together with the statute which requires a liquor licensee to demand identification from persons seeking to purchase liquor, "constitutes legislative recognition of the foreseeable danger to both the patron and third parties, and an effort to meet that danger by enactment of laws designed to regulate the industry, to protect third persons, and to protect those who are underage from themselves." *Id*. We see no less a legislative recognition of the danger to minors and to third persons in a statute which prohibits the sale or gift of a firearm or ammunition to a minor without written parental consent. That statute is part of a chapter which prohibits various types of misconduct involving weapons and explosives.

In *Brannigan*, the supreme court reversed two summary judgments which had been entered in favor of a tavern owner and remanded the cases for trial. The plaintiffs there were the parents of three minors who had purchased a number of drinks at the defendants' establishment where no identification had been required and who had been killed shortly after they left the tavern while riding in a pickup truck driven by one of the minors. The court found that defendants owed a duty to all three minors.

Raymond contends that violation of the statutes does not constitute negligence *per se* because the harm suffered by Janet is not the harm the statutes were designed to protect against. . . . Raymond concedes that, as a minor, Janet comes within the class of persons the statute was intended to protect. He argues, however, that the statute was intended to protect against negligent handling of guns by children, not intentional handling. We find no such distinction in the statute.

The Arizona statute prohibits the furnishing of a firearm to a minor without the child's parents' consent. We read the statute as evidence of the legislature's concern about children having possession of or the opportunity to use firearms without their parents' knowledge and consent. Such a blanket prohibition against the possession of firearms by children acknowledges the possibility that minors may use firearms either negligently or intentionally, thereby causing harm either to themselves or to others. We believe the proper analysis of the facts of this case is not whether the harm suffered falls outside the protection of the statute, but whether the nature of the harm suffered precludes the Crowns from recovering under the defense of contributory negligence. That analysis is consistent with the holding in *Brannigan, supra,* in which the supreme court held that both the statutory and the common-law duty applied not only to the two minor passengers but also to the minor who drove the truck, although the driver had not only intentionally consumed the alcohol but had also intentionally driven the vehicle while he was intoxicated. We hold that Raymond's violation of the statute constituted negligence *per se.* Under *Brannigan,* Raymond is entitled to attempt to show an excusable violation to the jury.

As Raymond has pointed out, even though negligence *per se* has been shown, in order for the Crowns to recover, they must show that Raymond's violation of the statute was the proximate cause of Janet's death. Raymond contends that the Crowns are unable to show proximate cause in this instance because Janet's suicide was not foreseeable to Raymond. In support of his argument, Raymond cites his affidavit in which he stated that Janet appeared cheerful when she purchased the gun from him, that he noticed no unusual behavior on her part, and that he had no indication that she was depressed. Raymond's argument would be persuasive if this were a case involving an adult purchaser of a handgun. Because Janet was a minor, however, the focus of the foreseeability determination is different.

If Janet had been 22 when she purchased the gun from Raymond, we would require that she have exhibited some type of conduct which would have triggered a warning in Raymond's mind about her intended use of the gun. Because Janet was only 17, however, she comes within the ambit of the statute, which is a statement of concern by the legislature about children possessing guns without the knowledge and consent of their parents. The existence of the statute itself expresses an awareness by the legislature that children in possession of guns are at risk of injuring either themselves or others, either negligently or intentionally. . . . Thus, in enacting the statute, the legislature declared that injury to themselves or others is foreseeable when guns are sold to minors without their parents' knowledge or consent.

We conclude that the trial court erred in granting summary judgment for Raymond. It was error for the trial court to determine as a matter of law that Janet's use of the gun to commit suicide was not reasonably foreseeable.

The judgment is reversed and the case is remanded for trial.

NOTES

1. *Crime and Punishment.* Courts may impose a variety of civil consequences for the violation of a criminal statute. Of course, the statute may be inapplicable because it was not designed to promote safety or to protect against a particular harm or hazard. Where the statute is relevant, however, it may either meet plaintiff's burden of producing evidence (make out a prima facie case), create a rebuttable presumption of negligence (shifting either the burden of producing evidence or the burden of persuasion, or both), or it may give rise to absolute liability under the guise of an irrebuttable presumption of negligence. Another consequence is that the plaintiff's substandard conduct will not defeat or diminish recovery (the "exceptional statute" theory).

2. *"Exceptional Statutes"*. RESTATEMENT (SECOND) OF TORTS § 483, comment c (1965), provides:

> There are . . . exceptional statutes which are intended to place the entire responsibility for the harm which has occurred upon the defendant. A statute may be found to have that purpose particularly where it is enacted in order to protect a certain class of persons against their own inability to protect themselves.

In *Del E. Webb Corp. v. Superior Court of Arizona*, 151 Ariz. 164, 726 P.2d 580, 583 (1986), plaintiff brought a dram shop action against a resort after the drowning death of her intoxicated husband. Defendant raised traditional defenses of contributory negligence and assumption of risk. Plaintiff argued that such defenses were inapplicable. The court disagreed:

> . . . Assertion of the traditional defenses is precluded because permitting plaintiff's fault to be raised as a bar to his recovery would defeat the fundamental purpose of a statute specifically enacted to protect the plaintiff against his inability to protect himself.
>
> In general, courts will bar these defenses only when they find a clear legislative purpose to impose absolute liability for statutory violation. Thus, an initial distinction must be drawn between statutes intended for the protection of the general public and those "exceptional" in the sense that they were intended to protect a particular class of plaintiffs against their own acts. The former are unlikely to qualify as exceptional statutes. Thus, general safety statutes merely establish a duty of ordinary care for the protection of the public against an unreasonable risk; the plaintiff's own negligent conduct may bar his recovery, just as with a breach of a common law duty.
>
> Statutes intended to protect people from the consequences of their own conduct primarily are those applicable to specific groups deemed incapable of protecting themselves such as the mentally deficient and children. Children, for instance, will not be barred from recovery by their own conduct if their injury was the result of a violation of a statute expressly aimed at protecting them from a particular harm. Child labor laws are a typical example of statutes intended to place all responsibility on the employer.

3. *The Adult Standard of Care*. The *Crown* court indicated that the statutes there involved, as in *Del E. Webb Corp.*, were not exceptional statutes. Therefore, the affirmative defenses of contributory negligence and assumption of the risk would be available.

Would Janet Crown be held to an adult standard of care because she was engaged in an adult activity? Would her mental instability, if any, be no defense?

4. *Negligence or Causation*. In *Martin v. Herzog*, 228 N.Y. 164, 126 N.E. 814, 816 (1920), the court, in the context of an alleged statutory violation, stated: "We must be on our guard, however, against confusing the question of negligence with that of the causal connection between the negligence and the injury." However, in *Ross v. Hartman*, 139 F.2d 14, 15 (D.C. Cir. 1943),

the court referred to the defendant's conduct as follows: "This negligence created the hazard and thereby brought about the harm which the ordinance was intended to prevent. It was therefore a legal or 'proximate' cause of the harm." Wherein lies the distinction?

Contrast *Peak v. Barlow,* 765 S.W.2d 577 (Ky. App. 1988). A passenger in a pickup truck was killed when the pickup truck collided with another vehicle which turned immediately in front of the truck and into a service entrance off U.S. 62. The defendant owners of the premises involved did not have a permit allowing them to maintain the service entrance, as required by statute. All parties were familiar with the existence of the service road and the view of oncoming traffic at that point. Both drivers testified their view of the highway and oncoming traffic was clear and unobstructed. The court affirmed summary judgment for the defendant, stating:

> Failure to comply with the terms of a statute is negligence *per se.* However, in an action for damages, the violation of the statute must be the proximate cause of the injury to permit recovery.
>
> [T]he statute violated by [defendant] deals with the establishment of a condition, an entrance across and to property owned by the Commonwealth.
>
> A prior and remote cause creating a condition for an incident to occur in does not in and of itself create liability.
>
> We find the creation of the service entrance by [defendant], while in violation of [the statute], a condition too remote to be a proximate cause of Peak's death. When the original negligence is remote and only furnishes the occasion of the injury, it is not the proximate cause thereof.

5. *Different Types of Negligence Per Se.* The Arizona statue in *Crown* prohibited the sale or gift of a firearm or ammunition to a minor. The federal statute contained a similar prohibition if "the licensee knows or has reasonable cause to believe" the recipient is minor. How, if at all, does the federal statute change the common law?

G. CIRCUMSTANTIAL EVIDENCE OF NEGLIGENCE

KMART CORPORATION v. BASSETT
769 So. 2d 282 (Ala. 2000)

SEE, JUSTICE.

In January 1995, Christine Bassett, an 83-year-old woman who walked with the aid of a cane, went to a Kmart store in Montgomery. Bassett stepped on a rubber mat outside the store to open the automatic doors. The doors swung open, and she began walking into the store. When she was about one-third of the way onto the rubber safety mat inside the store, the doors began to close. Bassett alleges that one of the doors struck her left hip and caused her to fall. In the fall, Bassett suffered a broken hip. After the accident, the store manager examined the doors. They worked properly and did not need to be repaired.

G. CIRCUMSTANTIAL EVIDENCE

In January 1996, Bassett sued Kmart, alleging negligent or wanton maintenance or repair. . . .. The jury returned a verdict in favor of Bassett, awarding her $289,000 in damages. Kmart moved for a judgment as a matter of law or, alternatively, for a new trial or a remittitur. The motion was denied. . . and Kmart appealed.

. . .[I]n order to defeat Kmart's motion for a judgment as a matter of law on her negligence claim, Bassett had to present substantial evidence indicating that Kmart had failed to use reasonable care to maintain its automatic doors in a reasonably safe condition and that Kmart's failure proximately caused the doors to malfunction in such a way as to injure her. Bassett, however, did not produce any evidence at trial to indicate what caused the automatic doors to malfunction as she entered the store.

Kmart argues that Bassett failed to make out a prima facie case of negligence because, it argues, she failed to produce substantial evidence indicating that Kmart breached its duty of care to her. She argues that she produced substantial circumstantial evidence indicating that Kmart had negligently maintained the automatic doors. Specifically, she argues that she presented evidence indicating that the company that installed the doors sold maintenance contracts as part of its business; that Kmart had no maintenance contract for the doors; that Kmart had a policy of waiting until the doors needed repair or maintenance before calling someone to work on them; that the Kmart store manager, Doug Stanley, knew that the doors occasionally malfunctioned by failing to work at all; and that without preventive maintenance, automatic doors will malfunction or stop working properly.

However, Bassett's evidence is insufficient to prove a breach of duty, an element of her negligence cause of action. She did not produce substantial evidence indicating that Kmart failed to maintain the automatic doors in a reasonably safe condition or that the maintenance Kmart provided was unreasonable. Bassett impliedly argues that Kmart's failure to have a preventive-maintenance contract was a breach of duty. However, Bassett's own expert, Jack Cherry, the owner of the door company that had installed the automatic doors, testified that he did not try to sell such a contract to Kmart because he did not think Kmart needed one. Cherry also testified that if the doors had been inspected six months before the date of Bassett's fall, that would have been reasonable maintenance on Kmart's part. Bassett's fall occurred slightly less than seven months after the most recent inspection. However, Cherry did not testify that a failure to inspect the doors for a period exceeding six months would have been unreasonable. Hence, Kmart's policy of not contracting with the door company for its preventive-maintenance program, but, instead, waiting until a door needed repair or maintenance and then calling for repairs, standing alone, is not substantial evidence of negligence.[5]

Bassett also argues that she produced evidence that, under the doctrine of *res ipsa loquitur*, permitted the jury to infer that Kmart had negligently

---

[5] This case would be quite different if Cherry had been asked about, and had described, a point beyond which Kmart's failure to inspect the doors would have been unreasonable maintenance and if that period had elapsed before Bassett's accident occurred; however, that case is not before us.

maintained the automatic doors. Specifically, she argues that evidence that the automatic doors closed while she was still standing on the inside mat is sufficient to allow the jury to infer that Kmart was negligent. The trial court agreed with Bassett; it denied Kmart's motions for a judgment as a matter of law and instructed the jury on the doctrine of *res ipsa loquitur*. Kmart argues that the trial court erred in submitting Bassett's case to the jury under the *res ipsa loquitur* doctrine because, it argues, Bassett did not satisfy the requirements for applying the doctrine of *res ipsa loquitur*. Specifically, Kmart argues that Bassett failed to satisfy the second requirement for applying that doctrine—that she did not "foreclose the possibility that [the company that installed the door or another company that sometimes serviced the door] was negligent, that the safety mat itself was inherently defective, or . . . that the alleged malfunction could have occurred even in the absence of any negligence." We agree.

The *res ipsa loquitur* doctrine allows "an inference of negligence where there is no direct evidence of negligence." *Ex parte Crabtree Industrial Waste, Inc.*, 728 So. 2d 155, 156 (Ala. 1998). For the doctrine to apply, a plaintiff must show that:

> (1) the defendant . . . had full management and control of the instrumentality which caused the injury; (2) the circumstances [are] such that according to common knowledge and the experience of mankind the accident could not have happened if those having control of the [instrumentality] had not been negligent; [and] (3) the plaintiff's injury . . . resulted from the accident.

Crabtree Industrial Waste, 728 So. 2d at 156. However, "if one can reasonably conclude that the accident could have happened without any negligence on the part of the defendant[], then the res ipsa loquitur presumption does not apply." *Crabtree Industrial Waste*, 728 So. 2d at 158.

Thus, the issue is whether the malfunctioning of Kmart's automatic doors is something that "according to common knowledge and the experience of mankind . . . could not have happened if those having control of [the doors] had not been negligent." A court may take judicial notice of certain facts that are within the common knowledge. Whether a fact is a matter of common knowledge is an issue to be determined by the court.

Bassett argues, relying on *Rose v. Port of New York Authority*, 61 N.J. 129, 137, 293 A.2d 371, 375 (1972), that it is common knowledge and the experience of the community that the malfunctioning of an automatic door is "unusual." In *Rose*, the New Jersey court held that evidence indicating that an automatic door malfunctioned is sufficient to allow the trier of fact to infer, under the doctrine of res ipsa loquitur, that the premises owner was negligent. The New Jersey court reasoned that because "what happened to the plaintiff [was] . . . unusual and not commonplace[,] it strongly suggested a malfunction which in turn suggested neglect." 61 N.J. at 136–37, 293 A.2d at 375.

We find the New Jersey court's reasoning unpersuasive. The New Jersey court inferred negligence on the part of the premises owner from the inference of the door's malfunction. Such reasoning violates Alabama's rule against deriving an inference from another inference. "An inference cannot be derived from another inference.' An inference must be based on a known or proved fact." *Khirieh v. State Farm Mut. Auto. Ins. Co.*, 594 So. 2d 1220, 1224 (quoting *Malone Freight Lines, Inc. v. McCardle*, 277 Ala. 100, 167 So. 2d 274 (1964)). Even if the door's malfunction were proved by direct evidence (and, thus, was not an inference), a mere malfunction would be insufficient to invoke the doctrine of res ipsa loquitur under Alabama law, because "one can reasonably conclude that the accident could have happened without any negligence on the part of the defendant[]." *Crabtree Industrial Waste*, 728 So. 2d at 158.

For example, the malfunction could have occurred because the doors were defective or because the company that serviced the doors had been negligent. Also, "mechanical devices, such as [the automatic doors] here involved, get out of working order, and sometimes become dangerous and cause injury without negligence on the part of anyone." *Darlington Corp. v. Finch*, 113 Ga. App. 825, 827 149 S.E.2d 861, 862 (1966) (holding that the doctrine of res ipsa loquitur did not apply to allow, from the fact that automatic elevator doors closed on an invitee, the inference that the building owner was negligent). Therefore, we do not consider it to be common knowledge that automatic doors cannot malfunction unless the premises owner is negligent in maintaining the doors. *See Roberts Constr. Co. v. Henry, supra*, 265 Ala. 608, 93 So. 2d 498.

The doctrine of *res ipsa loquitur* can still be applied if expert testimony is presented. See W. Page Keeton et al., Prosser and Keeton on the Law of Torts, § 39, at 247 (5th ed. 1984) (stating that "even where such a basis of common knowledge is lacking, . . . expert testimony may provide a sufficient foundation" for the inference of negligence). Therefore, we must consider whether Bassett produced sufficient expert testimony indicating that Kmart's automatic doors could not have malfunctioned unless Kmart had failed to use reasonable care to keep its automatic doors in a safe condition.

Jack Cherry testified by deposition that, "without preventive maintenance, eventually the doors are going to malfunction or stop working properly." That is the extent of Cherry's testimony as to the circumstances in which automatic doors malfunction. That testimony is insufficient to show that automatic doors cannot malfunction unless the premises owner fails to use reasonable care to keep them in a safe condition. Therefore, Bassett did not satisfy the second requirement for applying the doctrine of res ipsa loquitur, because she did not show that "according to common knowledge and the experience of mankind [or according to expert testimony] the accident could not have happened" absent Kmart's failure to "use reasonable care in maintaining its premises in a reasonably safe manner." *Hose*, 658 So. 2d at 404.

We conclude that the doctrine of res ipsa loquitur does not apply to the facts of this case. Because Bassett did not produce substantial evidence indicating that Kmart breached its duty to her, the trial court erred in denying Kmart's motion for a judgment as a matter of law.

HOOPER, CHIEF JUSTICE (dissenting).

I must respectfully dissent. I believe the doctrine of *res ipsa loquitur* applies in this case. I also believe Ms. Bassett produced sufficient evidence of Kmart's negligence to support the jury's finding. The majority of jurisdictions faced with cases like this one have decided that the doctrine of res ipsa loquitur applies to automatic-door malfunctions. However, this Court has chosen to follow the reasoning of the minority of courts holding that the doctrine does not apply. I believe today's holding departs from the traditional view of res ipsa loquitur and runs counter to the rationale behind the development of that doctrine. . . ..

The Restatement (Second) of Torts, § 328 D, Cmt. e (1965), suggests: "The plaintiff need not . . . conclusively exclude all other possible explanations . . . . It is enough that the facts proved reasonably permit the conclusion that negligence is the more probable explanation . . . ." Members of the public routinely use automatic doors without sustaining injury. Ms. Bassett should not have to prove that automatic doors cannot malfunction in the absence of negligence; she should have only to present facts that would permit the jury to conclude that negligence was the more probable explanation. In this case, the jury could reasonably conclude that the closing of the automatic door on Ms. Bassett was the kind of sudden, unusual malfunction that would not normally occur in the absence of negligence.

In addition, Ms. Bassett should not be required to disprove all other possible reasons for the malfunction, as the majority suggests. I agree with the rationale of the Supreme Court of Nebraska:

> The plaintiff is not required to eliminate with certainty all other possible causes or inferences, which would mean that the plaintiff must prove a civil case beyond a reasonable doubt. All that is needed is evidence from which reasonable persons can say that on the whole it is more likely that there was negligence associated with the cause of the event than that there was not. It is enough that the court cannot say that the jury could not reasonably come to that conclusion.

Brown v. Scrivner, Inc., 241 Neb. 286, 289, 488 N.W.2d 17, 19 (1992) (*quoting Anderson v. Service Merchandise Co.*, 240 Neb. 873, 880, 485 N.W.2d 170, 176 (1992)).

Kmart admitted that it was responsible for the maintenance and operation of the doors. It is common knowledge that automatic doors do not normally close on people; this common knowledge suggests negligence on the part of the entity in control of the doors, Kmart. Ms. Bassett's injury resulted from the accident. Therefore, the question whether the doctrine of res ipsa loquitur was to be applied was properly submitted to the jury.

. . .Mr. Cherry stated on cross-examination that he did not think Kmart needed a maintenance contract, because, he said, the doors of the Kmart store would not deteriorate as fast as the doors at a grocery store would. Again, I believe I am a fair-minded person, and I disagree with Mr. Cherry's opinion. This accident took place shortly after the Christmas shopping season, and it is reasonable to expect that during that time of the year automatic doors would undergo a significant amount of deterioration. Mr. Cherry did not base his opinion (that Kmart did not need a maintenance contract) on an actual examination of Kmart's automatic doors.

Furthermore, the jury is not bound by Mr. Cherry's testimony and is free to conclude for itself whether it was reasonable for Kmart not to have regular maintenance performed on its automatic doors. "Opinion testimony of an expert witness is binding upon a jury only when it concerns a subject exclusively within the knowledge of experts and the testimony is uncontroverted." *Allen v. Turpin*, 533 So. 2d 515, 517 (Ala. 1988). Whether Kmart was negligent is precisely the issue the jury was to determine; therefore, that issue obviously did not concern a subject exclusively within the knowledge of experts. The uncontroverted evidence indicating that Kmart never had a maintenance contract for its automatic doors and never serviced the doors until they malfunctioned is sufficient for a reasonable person to conclude that Kmart was negligent in maintaining its automatic doors. Therefore, Kmart was not entitled to a judgment as a matter of law. . ..

Cook, Justice (dissenting).

. . .In this case, Kmart was the only entity in control of the instrument. It did not even have a maintenance contract with anyone to service its doors. If a plaintiff cannot use the doctrine of res ipsa loquitur in such cases as suggested in Rose, supra, a premises owner has no incentive to maintain doors so as to prevent a malfunction and injury to the public. . ..

NOTES

1. *Circumstantial Evidence.* To an extent *res ipsa* is a common sense application of the rules governing the strength of circumstantial evidence. If (1) the accident ordinarily would not occur unless the person in control of an instrumentality at a certain time was negligent, and (2) defendant was in control of the instrumentality at the relevant time, reasonable minds could conclude that more probably than not defendant was negligent. Adding a Latin title and giving the evidence stronger weight (such as requiring an inference of negligence unless the defendant provides rebuttal evidence) have given *res ipsa* a life of its own. However, not every circumstantial evidence case involves res ipsa.

Negri v. Stop & Shop, Inc., 65 N.Y.2d 625, 491 N.Y.S.2d 151, 480 N.E.2d 740 (1985), concerned a negligence action against a supermarket by a shopper who allegedly slipped and fell on some broken jars of baby food. There was evidence that the baby food was "dirty and messy" and a witness had not heard any jars falling from the shelves prior to the accident. There was further evidence that the aisle had not been inspected for about an hour. The court concluded:

> Viewing the evidence in a light most favorable to the plaintiffs and according plaintiffs the benefit of every reasonable inference, it cannot be said, as a matter of law, that the circumstantial evidence was insufficient to permit the jury to draw the necessary inference that a slippery condition was created by jars of baby food which had fallen and broken a sufficient length of time prior to the accident to permit defendant's employees to discover and remedy the condition.

How does this differ from a *res ipsa* case?

See also Brewster v. United States, 542 N.W.2d 524 (Iowa 1996), in which the plaintiff was injured when the automatic doors of the defendant's hospital closed on her while she was walking through them. The court concluded that res ipsa loquitur precluded summary judgment for the defendant when the only facts are the occurrence and the injury. Discussing the relationship between circumstantial evidence and res ipsa loquitur, the court noted:

> Negligence must be proved, and "the mere fact that an accident . . . has occurred, with nothing more, is not evidence. . . ." W. Page Keeton et al., *Prosser & Keeton on the Law of Torts* § 39, at 242 (5th ed. 1984) [hereinafter Prosser]. To establish negligence, the plaintiff must produce "evidence from which reasonable persons may conclude that, upon the whole, it is more likely that the event was caused by negligence than that it was not." *Id.*
>
> Negligence, however, is a fact and "like any other fact, may be proved by circumstantial evidence." Id. Circumstantial evidence is the proof "of one fact, or of a set of facts, from which the existence of the fact to be determined may reasonably be inferred." *Id.* Circumstantial evidence involves two things: (1) "the assertion of witnesses as to what they have observed," and (2) "a process of reasoning, or inference, by which a conclusion is drawn." *Id.* Circumstantial evidence "must be based upon the evidence given, together with a sufficient background of human experience to justify the conclusion." *Id.* at 243.
>
> When the plaintiff uses circumstantial evidence to establish negligence, the inference drawn "must cover all of the necessary elements of negligence, and must point to a breach of the defendant's duty.". . . Res ipsa loquitur (Latin phrase for "the thing speaks for itself") is one type of circumstantial evidence.
>
> . . .The second requirement—the accident is one such as in the ordinary course of things does not happen in the absence of negligence—is another way of stating a principle of circumstantial evidence. That principle requires that the event must be such that in the light of ordinary experience the event gives rise to an inference of negligence on someone's part. Based on this principle, courts have applied res ipsa loquitur to a wide range of events: objects falling from defendant's premises, falling elevators, collapsing buildings, and boiler explosions. As Prosser notes, "there is an element of drama, and of the freakish and improbable in a good many of these cases." *Id.* at 245. On the other hand, even common place events can call for the application of res ipsa loquitur. *Id.* at 246.
>
> The purpose of the "under the management of defendant" requirement is "to link the defendant with the probability, already established, that the accident was negligently caused." *Id.* at 248. Failure to connect the defendant with the negligent event defeats the application of res ipsa loquitur.
>
> . . .As we said, res ipsa loquitur is no more than one form of circumstantial evidence. If "there is no direct evidence to show cause of injury, and the circumstantial evidence indicates that the negligence of the defendant is the most plausible explanation for the injury," res ipsa loquitur applies. Prosser at 257. . . .
>
> Procedurally, if the plaintiff produces substantial evidence as to both prongs of res ipsa loquitur the plaintiff overcomes a motion for

directed verdict. At this point the plaintiff simply has the right to have the case submitted to the jury on plaintiff's general negligence theory.

The burden of persuasion, however, remains with the plaintiff. The defendant has no burden to introduce any evidence. However, if the defendant fails to do so, the defendant runs the risk of the jury finding for the plaintiff. . . .

All this is another way of saying that res ipsa loquitur permits the jury to infer negligence from the facts, but the jury is not required to draw this inference. The jury simply weighs the circumstantial evidence but in the end may or may not accept it as sufficient as to negligence or causation.

If the defendant chooses to offer rebutting evidence, then the jury must balance any inference of negligence to be drawn from the circumstances of the case, which the jury may choose to draw or reject, and which has weight only so long as reasonable persons may still draw it from the facts in evidence.

. . .The defendant's rebutting evidence must be so strong that the court can say as a matter of law that res ipsa loquitur does not apply.

. . .Our rule is that "the res ipsa [loquitur] inference of negligence [can] not be relied on unless within the common experience of lay persons the occurrence [is] such that in the ordinary course of things it would not have happened if reasonable care had been used." *Id.* As we said, this common experience requirement is "another way of stating an obvious principle of circumstantial evidence: that the event must be such that in the light of ordinary experience [the event] gives rise to an inference that someone must have been negligent." Prosser at 244. This ordinary experience is one common to the whole community, upon which the jury is simply permitted to rely. *Id.* at 247. "This common experience may include the common experience of experts." *Reilly*, 282 N.W.2d at 694; see also Prosser at 247.

Because res ipsa loquitur applies to civil cases only, a plaintiff is not required to eliminate with certainty all other possible causes or inferences. The plaintiff need only produce evidence from which a reasonable person could say that on the whole it is more likely than not that there was negligence associated with the cause of the event. If the court is unable to say that the jury could not come to this conclusion, res ipsa loquitur applies. Prosser at 248. This is another way of saying there is substantial evidence to support the common experience prong of res ipsa loquitur.

. . .Here the magistrate concluded as a matter of law that the automatic doors were under the exclusive control of VAMC at the time of the accident. This is the first prong of the res ipsa loquitur doctrine and is conceded for the purpose of the summary judgment motions. The fighting issue is whether there is a genuine issue of material fact as to the second prong of the doctrine: whether the premature closing of the automatic doors is such as in the ordinary course of things would not happen if reasonable care had been used.

> . . .We agree with the majority of courts that have concluded an automatic door malfunction does not occur in the absence of negligence. We think it is within the common experience of lay people to come to this conclusion. In other words, reasonable people could conclude that it is more likely than not that there is negligence associated with the automatic door's malfunction.
>
> We also think it is not incumbent upon a plaintiff to come forward with proof as to the precise nature of the probable malfunction. It is precisely because facts proving causation in personal injury cases are generally within the exclusive dominion and control of the defendant that the res ipsa loquitur doctrine developed. The doctrine in effect "levels the playing field" for the injured plaintiff. In fact, proving the precise cause could—under Iowa law—deprive the plaintiff of the doctrine's benefit.

542 N.W.2d at 532.

2. *Genesis of Res Ipsa Loquitur.* The doctrine of *res ipsa loquitur* had its origin in *Byrne v. Boadle,* [1863] 2 H. & C. 722, 159 Eng. Rep. 299. The plaintiff there was struck on the head by a barrel of flour that rolled out of a window of defendant's warehouse. Plaintiff could not prove how the barrel escaped; however, holding for plaintiff, Baron Pollock remarked: "There are certain cases of which it may be said *res ipsa loquitur,* and this seems one of them."

3. *Characterizing the Conduct.* The core of the inference of negligence, via the *res ipsa* principle, is the characterization of the occurrence as one that ordinarily does not happen absent negligence.

In *Ebanks v. New York City Transit Auth.,* 118 A.D.2d 363, 504 N.Y.S.2d 640 (1986), the plaintiff's foot was caught in a gap between the step and a side of defendant's escalator. The majority concluded:

> [T]o permit the existence of such a dangerous gap on a public conveyance used by densely packed crowds of commuters is an event of "a kind which ordinarily does not occur in the absence of someone's negligence," and therefore to fault plaintiff for offering no evidence on this score is simply to misapprehend that the res ipsa rule is precisely designed to relieve plaintiff of that burden by invoking such rebuttable presumption based on circumstantial evidence. There was further proof by plaintiff's expert that the gap would have necessarily exceeded 3/8 inches, and defendant's sole witness conceded that this was probably accurate based upon his inspection immediately after the accident. It was virtually conceded that a gap in excess of 3/8 inches is violative of both the Building Code and industry standards.

Dissenting, ASCH, J., remarked,

> The inference of negligence on the part of defendant was not the only one which could fairly and reasonably be drawn from the evidence, and the trial court, therefore, improperly charged *res ipsa loquitur.* The jury reasonably could have found, based upon testimony of both plaintiff and his expert, that the accident happened because plaintiff put his foot, covered with a soft, rubber overshoe, dangerously close to the side of the escalator, where it became caught.

In addition, although plaintiff asserts that the space or gap existed because of defendant's improper maintenance and failure to properly inspect the escalator, plaintiff offered no proof as to defendant's inspection and maintenance procedures. Testimony by an employee of defendant was to the effect that a gap could have been caused by vandalism rather than by improper maintenance. Defendant supported its view by furnishing verification evidence that the escalator was maintained and inspected on three occasions in the week before the accident.

In *Coury v. Safe Auto Sales, Inc.,* 32 N.Y.2d 162, 297 N.E.2d 88, 344 N.Y.S.2d 347 (1973), the trial court had charged the jury that they could not infer negligent driving solely from the fact that the defendant had crossed the center line into opposing traffic. The appellate court reversed and remanded, stating:

"The jury should have been instructed that the crossing over was a circumstance for their consideration in determining whether the driver had exercised reasonable care in the operation of his vehicle, even though that fact, standing alone, did not necessarily require a finding that he was negligent. "

In *Pinecrest Stables, Inc. v. Hill,* 487 So.2d 82 (Fla. Dist. App. 1986), the owner of a horse claimed that it had suffered a rib injury while at defendant's stables. The injury had not been noticed until the owner had removed the horse from the stables. The owner admitted that horses may be injured during transport and during training, by running into other horses, fences or trees. The court held that a *res ipsa* instruction was inappropriate. The injury was one which could have occurred other than from negligence. Furthermore, the horse was in the exclusive control of its owner, not the stables, during transportation when the injury could have occurred.

4. *An Exculpatory or Explanatory Burden?* The general rule is that <u>res ipsa creates an explanatory burden for the defendant</u>. If defendant subsequently fails to "explain," then a *prima facie* case of negligence is made out. See *American Elevator Co. v. Briscoe,* 93 Nev. 665, 572 P.2d 534, 537 (1977). In other words, the raising of the inference, and thus the explanatory burden, protects plaintiff from a directed verdict in favor of defendant. *See, e.g., Sullivan v. Snyder,* 374 A.2d 866 (D.C. App. 1977). A subsequent failure by the defendant to meet that explanatory burden is sufficient to support a jury verdict in *plaintiff's* favor.

However, some jurisdictions give greater weight to the establishment of the foundational facts for *res ipsa*. *Newing v. Cheatham,* 15 Cal. 3d 351, 540 P.2d 33, 124 Cal. Rptr. 193, 202–03 (1975), involved a light airplane crash not unlike that in *Widmyer,* infra. The craft took off in good weather and there was no evidence that weather conditions contributed in any way to the crash or that the plane had collided with another aircraft. There was circumstantial evidence suggesting that the pilot had run out of fuel. The court concluded:

> The evidence presented in the trial court, therefore, was such as to satisfy all three conditions for the applicability of *res ipsa loquitur* as a matter of law. Since the facts giving rise to the doctrine were undisputed, the inference of negligence arose as a matter of law; to

put it another way, the conclusion is compelled that there is a balance of probabilities pointing to the decedent's negligence. This gave rise to a presumption affecting the burden of producing evidence. . . . It then became defendant's obligation to introduce sufficient evidence to sustain a finding either that the accident resulted from some cause other than [defendant's decedent's] negligence, or, else, that [defendant's decedent] exercised due care in all possible respects wherein he might have been negligent. Defendant introduced no such evidence. He has at most argued that the crash could have resulted from causes other than the negligence of his decedent. Mere speculation of this sort is insufficient to discharge defendant's burden of explanation. Consequently, the trial court was correct in concluding that *res ipsa loquitur* established [defendant's decedent's] negligence as a matter of law.

Does the foregoing passage merely suggest that, in appropriate circumstances, a *res ipsa* inference can support a directed verdict for plaintiff, or does it suggest that the *res ipsa* inference allocates an exculpatory burden to the defendant?

5. *Res Ipsa and Expert Testimony.* In *Morgan v. Children's Hosp.*, 18 Ohio St. 3d 185, 480 N.E. 2d 464 (1985), the court held that the doctrine of *res ipsa* applied to a medical malpractice action, even though expert testimony was required to establish the cause of the injury. "Much as the courts have implemented the malpractice standard of care through expert testimony, the court can adapt *res ipsa loquitur* to malpractice by requiring expert testimony that the injury bespeaks negligence." See also Scott v. James, 731 A.2d 399 (D.C. 1999), in which the plaintiff was alleging negligence by a hair stylist in the application of a hair relaxer. The trial court had directed a verdict in favor of the defendant because the plaintiff had failed to present expert testimony to show the standard of care in applying the hair relaxer. The court concluded:

> Ms. Scott insists that application or administration of a hair relaxer is a matter of common knowledge and therefore expert testimony was unnecessary. We disagree.
>
> For analytical purposes, we have identified three categories of earlier hair treatment cases: (1) permanent hair wave with the use of devices such as electrically heated curlers or rods and heat-generated machines; (2) permanent hair wave with the use of machineless processes—usually conditioners or chemical solutions; and (3) permanent hair wave with the use of rods or curlers and a permanent wave compound or solution. These categories enable us to determine better how courts approached the first prong of the *res ipsa loquitur* doctrine whose satisfaction is dependent upon common knowledge or expert testimony: whether "[the occurrence is] of the kind which ordinarily does not occur in the absence of someone's negligence."
>
> Cases falling into our first category—permanent hair wave with the use of devices such as electrically heated curlers or rods and heat-generated machines—involve less complicated processes used with familiar and historic heat-induced or electrical devices such as curling irons, rather than the more recently manufactured, less well known

and structurally complex chemical hair relaxers. Lay persons historically have had common knowledge regarding the effects of heat generated by electrical devices and wood or coal heated equipment, but little or no common knowledge concerning the effects of chemical substances applied to the hair or scalp. Through the centuries and years, children have learned at an early age that heated devices may burn and cause damage to the body if touched in the wrong way. This knowledge has carried over into adulthood for eons. Thus, in the early 1930s and 1940s permanent wave cases involving heated devices and machines, the appellants focused mainly on showing actual damages in the form of burns and blisters because of "a widespread consensus of a common understanding" that improper application of heat devices and machines to the body may produce burns.

The later permanent wave cases in our second and third categories which involved the use of chemical solutions and compounds and which arose in the decades of the fifties, sixties and seventies, required a greater evidentiary foundation before courts accepted the *res ipsa loquitur* doctrine as an aid to proving negligence. Undoubtedly this greater evidentiary foundation was required because children and adults, even today, do not generally expect liquid solutions or creams contained in a jar to burn when applied to the body. Unlike the cases pertaining to the use of electrical or other heat-induced devices and machines, lay persons do not have common knowledge about the effects of chemical solutions, including hair relaxers. Therefore, the appellants in our second and third categories of permanent wave cases did not resort solely to a "common knowledge" argument with respect to the application of the *res ipsa loquitur* doctrine. Rather. . . they introduced expert opinion to show that their injuries ordinarily would not occur in the absence of negligence.

. . .Ms. Scott contends, in essence, that lay persons have common knowledge concerning the application of chemical hair relaxers. That contention has no support either in the record on appeal or in the permanent wave cases where chemical solutions and compounds were used. A machineless chemical hair relaxer was used on Ms. Scott. The purpose of a hair relaxer is to "break chemical bonds in the hair and alter the structure," thereby producing a "straightening effect which usually lasts until new hair grows out." Michael R. Flaherty, Annotation, *Products Liability: Hair Straighteners and Relaxants*, 84 A.L.R. 4th 1090, 1093 (1993). Hair relaxers "generally contain one of the following active ingredients: sodium hydroxide, ammonium or sodium bisulfite, or thioglycolate." *Id*. Lay persons simply do not have common knowledge either of hair relaxers or the chemical content of such products. Certainly there is no "widespread consensus of a common understanding" that hair damage does not "ordinarily occur [after the use of hair relaxers] without negligence." No "expert testimony [was] presented [in this case demonstrating] that such accidents do not occur in the absence of negligence." *Id*. Moreover, in Ms. Scott's case, neither the judge nor the jurors had any hint as to the chemical composition of the relaxer, the actual process used to apply the chemical relaxer or the proper procedure for putting the relaxer onto Ms. Scott's hair or scalp. As the trial court properly ruled, it was incumbent upon Ms. Scott to present expert evidence as to the standard of care and process for application of the hair relaxer used on her scalp or hair.

The mere fact that Ms. Scott may have experienced dry hair that broke off after her treatment is insufficient in and of itself to invoke the *res ipsa loquitur* doctrine. . . .

In short, in this case, Ms. Scott produced no expert cosmetology testimony as to the nature and chemical content of the relaxer used or its exact method of application; nor did she present medical testimony as to the type of injury she sustained during her treatment. In fact, she admitted during cross-examination that she did not seek medical attention until some two years after her 1992 treatment. The doctor whom she saw in 1994, Dr. Eileen Blum, prescribed medication for a dry skin condition which Ms. Scott applied to her hands. Although Ms. Scott saw another cosmetologist, Ms. Diane Broadus, no testimony from her was presented at trial. In addition to testimony by Ms. Scott, the only other witness in her behalf was her then roommate who stated, without explanation, that Ms. Scott's hair was "a mess" when she returned from her hair relaxer treatment. This testimony from Ms. Scott and her witness falls far short of the evidentiary foundation discussed above in which courts allowed the *res ipsa loquitur* presumption to be invoked. Had this case gone to the jury, jurors would have been left to speculate concerning key factual elements of the case, and to pile inference upon inference. Thus. . . we are constrained to conclude that Ms. Scott has not satisfied the first prong of the *res ipsa loquitur* doctrine. . . and thus, this case is not appropriate for the application of the *res ipsa loquitur* doctrine.

731 A.2d at 407.

Does the application of the *res ipsa* doctrine turn on the occurrence of an accident which "ordinarily" does not happen in the absence of negligence? If so, in cases where the ordinariness of an event must be determined by expert testimony, does the doctrine lose its moorings?

WIDMYER v. SOUTHEAST SKYWAYS, INC.
584 P.2d 1 (Alaska 1978)

BOOCHEVER, CHIEF JUSTICE.

On November 15, 1974, a DeHavilland Beaver airplane, owned by Southeast Skyways, Inc., and piloted by Richard Norvell, crashed in the waters of False Bay, Chichagof Island, Alaska. The pilot and three passengers . . . were killed in the crash. . . . [P]ersonal representatives of the estates of the deceased passengers brought this action for wrongful death against appellees, Southeast Skyways, Inc., and James Norvell, personal representative of the estate of Richard Norvell.

A jury returned a verdict for Skyways. Numerous issues have been raised on this appeal including the refusal of the trial court to instruct regarding . . . the doctrine of *res ipsa loquitur*. . . .

G. CIRCUMSTANTIAL EVIDENCE

The airplane left Juneau on November 15, 1974 bound for Tenakee Springs. William Bernhardt, who piloted another plane from Juneau on the 15th bound for Basket Bay, testified that the weather at Juneau International Airport was generally "good" on that day. Both planes proceeded toward their destinations and, in so doing, traveled in a southerly direction down Chatham Strait which separates Admiralty and Chichagof Islands. Bernhardt observed Skyways' airplane in a parallel flight pattern near Hawk Inlet on Admiralty Island. A heavy snow squall was encountered by both airplanes. Bernhardt overtook Skyways' craft near Point Marsden on Admiralty Island; and, at that time, both airplanes were flying at an altitude of 50 to 100 feet. Bernhardt lost sight of the Skyways' craft when it executed a turn to the right, away from the Admiralty Island beach, and disappeared from view.

The Skyways' craft was next sighted on the Chichagof side of the Chatham Strait by Charles and Esther Kaze. The airplane was flying at low altitude near their cabin, and it crashed a few seconds after they observed it. There was no change in the audible pitch of the motor prior to impact. It was snowing very hard, and visibility was poor. They found the craft wreckage in a vertical, nosedown position in rough tidal water; there were no survivors.

James Nielson, a witness for the plaintiffs and an expert on accident reconstruction, testified that, in his opinion, the crash was due to a "stall/spin" that he attributed to pilot error. He stated that the pilot also was in violation of Visual Flight Rules (VFR) of the Federal Aviation Administration.

William Bernhardt, who had observed the craft on the Admiralty side of the Strait, testified to his opinion that the pilot had crossed the Chatham Strait, looking for the Chichagof beach, which was not visible from Point Marsden; and that when he encountered the trees, he was forced to pull up and make a sharp turn, which stalled the aircraft.

Skyways' evidence focused on inclement weather as a cause of the accident. Harold Searby, a defense witness and an expert in meteorology, testified that the weather in Southeast Alaska on the day of the crash was unstable; and that, in his opinion, strong and severe turbulence existed in False Bay at the time of the crash.

Ray Renshaw, a defense witness and an expert on aviation in Southeast Alaska, testified to his opinion that Richard Norvell, whom he had supervised and trained, was an experienced pilot with approximately 3,000 hours of flight. He then testified to his opinion that, after completing his turn from the Admiralty side of the Chatham Strait, Norvell was in clear air; that he crossed the Strait and proceeded down a corridor on the Chichagof side in clear air; that he encountered a snow squall and attempted to land in False Bay when the craft was struck by an unexpected gust of wind; and that the crash was not due to pilot error.

Renshaw further stated that one of his assumptions was that Norvell did not commit pilot error. Plaintiffs' objections to expert testimony based on such an assumption were overruled.

. . . Plaintiffs allege error in the superior court's denial of their proposed instruction on the doctrine of *res ipsa loquitur*.

The doctrine of *res ipsa loquitur,* meaning "the thing or transaction speaks for itself," permits a finding of negligence from the circumstances surrounding the injury. It does not allow negligence to be established from the mere fact of injury itself. The doctrine, where applicable, is a bridge, dispensing with the requirement that a plaintiff specifically prove breach of duty, once that duty and proximate cause have been established.[6]

Plaintiffs requested an instruction stating in part:

> From the happening of the accident involved in this case, you may draw an inference that a proximate cause of the occurrence was some negligent conduct on the part of the defendant.
>
> However, you shall not find that a proximate cause of the occurrence was some negligent conduct on the part of the defendant unless you believe, after weighing all the evidence in the case and drawing such inferences therefrom as you believe are warranted, that it is more probable than not that the occurrence was caused by some negligent conduct on the part of the defendant. . . .

The instruction was rejected, and the following instruction was given:

> The mere fact that an accident happened, standing alone, does not permit the jury to draw the inference that the accident was caused by anyone's negligence.

The doctrine of *res ipsa loquitur* is recognized law in Alaska and in nearly all jurisdictions in the United States. Traditionally, the doctrine has been applied when the following requirements are met:

> 1) the accident is one which ordinarily does not occur in the absence of someone's negligence;
>
> 2) the agency or instrumentality is within the exclusive control of the defendant;

---

[6] Sec. 328 D of the RESTATEMENT OF TORTS (SECOND) (1965) provides:

(1) It may be inferred that harm suffered by the plaintiff is caused by negligence of the defendant when;

(a) the event is of a kind which ordinarily does not occur in the absence of negligence;

(b) other responsible causes, including the conduct of the plaintiff and third persons, are sufficiently eliminated by the evidence; and

(c) the indicated negligence is within the scope of the defendant's duty to the plaintiff.

(2) It is the function of the court to determine whether the inference may reasonably be drawn by the jury, or whether it must necessarily be drawn.

(3) It is the function of the jury to determine whether the inference is to be drawn in any case where different conclusions may reasonably be reached.

The RESTATEMENT comment pertaining to § 328 D(1)(b) reads:

Eliminating other responsible causes. It is never enough for the plaintiff to prove that he was injured by the negligence of some person unidentified. It is still necessary to make the negligence point to the defendant. On this too the plaintiff has the burden of proof by a preponderance of the evidence; and in any case where there is no doubt that it is at least equally probable that the negligence was that of a third person, the court must direct the jury that the plaintiff has not proved his case. Again, however, the plaintiff is not required to exclude all other possible conclusions beyond a reasonable doubt, and it is enough that he makes out a case from which the jury may reasonably conclude that the negligence was, more probably than not, that of the defendant. *Id.* at 160.

G. CIRCUMSTANTIAL EVIDENCE 309

3) the injurious condition or occurrence was not due to any voluntary action or contribution on the part of the plaintiff.

Before these requirements are examined, however, two preliminary issues will be discussed.

The first concerns the applicability of *res ipsa loquitur* when specific acts of negligence are alleged. Although there is a split of authority on whether the doctrine is applicable to cases in which the plaintiff introduces specific evidence of negligence, Alaska does not preclude use of the doctrine unless the specific acts furnish a "complete explanation" of the accident. We have declined to apply *res ipsa loquitur* in an air crash case when the injured plaintiff, the only passenger, testified to specific acts of the pilot prior to the crash. We stated:

> . . . if the evidence discloses the circumstances of the accident to the extent that there is nothing left to infer, then the doctrine of *res ipsa loquitur*, which is founded upon inference, is no longer needed.

Crawford v. Rogers, 406 P.2d 189, 193 (Alaska 1965).

Skyways argues that plaintiffs proffered a "complete explanation" here:

> . . . plaintiffs' evidence, if believed, was that Norvell flew blindly into a snow squall at low altitude, stalled his aircraft in an attempt to avoid some trees, and crashed. . . . There was accordingly nothing left to infer.

We do not agree. It would follow from Skyways' argument that, whenever an expert gives an opinion as to the cause of a crash and is corroborated in part by witnesses, no *res ipsa loquitur* instruction is permitted. Of note is the fact that in the Alaska cases which have applied this "complete explanation" standard regarding evidence of specific acts of negligence, there has been direct, rather than circumstantial evidence: in each case, a witness directly involved at the time of the occurrence had been available to testify.

We have previously referred to the applicability of *res ipsa loquitur* only in cases with "incomplete factual descriptions." We do not find that in the present case in which heavy reliance was placed by both parties on inferences of expert witnesses, that a complete factual explanation was offered. There were matters of considerable uncertainty, including the exact path of the plane from the Admiralty to the Chichagof side of the Chatham Strait and the precise sequence of events which occurred immediately prior to the crash. In an accident in which there are not survivors to testify and no other direct evidence of the cause, we do not believe that plaintiffs should be precluded from utilizing the doctrine of *res ipsa loquitur* because they have offered a possible explanation to the jury.

The second preliminary issue involves the question of superior knowledge. The superior court specifically noted Skyways' lack of superior knowledge as to the cause of the crash in denying a *res ipsa loquitur* instruction. In this case, neither party possessed superior knowledge: both were equally ignorant of the facts which occurred immediately prior to the crash.

. . . Skyways cites no Alaska case specifically requiring superior knowledge on a defendant's part as to the immediate cause of a crash before *res ipsa loquitur* may be invoked. There are no compelling reasons to apply such a rule to an aircraft accident in which there are no survivors and in which the parties place heavy reliance upon expert testimony. Moreover, while the carrier may not have superior knowledge as to the specific circumstances at the time of the crash, it has superior knowledge as to the characteristics of the particular airplane involved, its maintenance, the training and instruction of its pilots and its general operating procedure under varying conditions.

We now return to analysis of the three traditional prerequisites to the applicability of *res ipsa loquitur:* an accident that normally does not happen without negligence; exclusive control of the instrumentality by the defendant; and absence of voluntary action or contribution by the plaintiff.

The requirements are, in essence, "foundation facts," which must be established before invoking the doctrine.

. . . Skyways relies primarily on the weather conditions incident to the crash to refute plaintiffs' argument that the requirements have been met. Weather conditions, however, are not material to the issue of plaintiff contribution. Accordingly, we shall first address this prerequisite.

Plaintiff contribution is not the equivalent of contributory negligence. Instead, the former term refers to the question of control: the doctrine of *res ipsa loquitur* will not apply if the plaintiff had control of the instrumentality. Skyways argues that plaintiffs have not established lack of plaintiff contribution, since the passengers could have interfered with the controls. Reliance is placed on *Crawford v. Rogers,* 406 P.2d 189 (Alaska 1965), a case in which there was evidence of passenger interference before the court. Here, however, there was no evidence regarding passenger interference presented by any of the parties.

If the requirement of no plaintiff contribution is strictly applied, no *res ipsa loquitur* instruction could be given where the plaintiff lacks sufficient evidence, or any evidence, upon which to prove a negative. . . . We believe that there must be some evidence upon which a jury could find plaintiff contribution before a *res ipsa loquitur* instruction can be denied for this reason. In the face of a silent record, the conclusion that a passenger did not interfere with the operation of an aircraft is much more compelling than the conclusion that he did interfere.

While it is clear that *res ipsa loquitur* is applicable in general to aviation cases, it is not necessarily applicable to every such case since the specific circumstances will vary. Weather may impinge upon the first prerequisite for *res ipsa loquitur* in that it may contribute to a set of circumstances in which it is not more likely than not that the crash was caused by the defendant's negligence. Again, the totality of the circumstances must be considered in each factual setting.

Cases involving in-flight injuries to passengers as a result of bumps, lurches or jerks of an aircraft in turbulence do not give rise to the application of the doctrine. In cases involving crashes, some courts, in applying *res ipsa loquitur,* have specifically noted the absence of evidence of weather as a causative factor.

To require a plaintiff to show that a crash was not caused by weather, as a prerequisite to the application of *res ipsa loquitur,* presents the problems inherent in proving a negative. Again, a strict application of this requirement would have disallowed the *res ipsa loquitur* instruction in *Haasman,* [100 F. Supp. 1 (D. Alaska 1951)], where the plane disappeared without a trace. We will not require a plaintiff to negate the possibility of weather as a cause of an airplane crash in order to obtain the benefit of a *res ipsa loquitur* instruction.

The general safety record of air travel and the present state of air technology compel us to conclude that air crashes do not normally occur absent negligence, even in inclement weather. In *Alaska Airlines, Inc. v. Sweat,* 568 P.2d 916, 925 (Alaska 1977), we stated:

> [Air] travel may no longer be regarded as inherently dangerous and . . . flights aboard certified carriers do not involve an unreasonable risk of harm.

Thus, under the circumstances of this case, we find no reason to preclude the applicability of the doctrine of *res ipsa loquitur.* We find the lack of an instruction on the doctrine to be error.

NOTES

1. *Identifying the Risk-Taker (1); Exclusive Control by Defendant.* The *res ipsa* doctrine is premised both upon circumstantial evidence of negligence and evidence, circumstantial or direct, linking that conduct to the defendant. In *American Elevator Co. v. Briscoe,* 93 Nev. 665, 572 P.2d 534, 537 (1977), the defendant held the maintenance contract on an elevator for several years. The plaintiff was injured during a "speeding" episode. There was evidence of other anomalies in the elevator's operation, and there was no evidence of maintenance by others, or of design defects. The court concluded:

> To require a plaintiff to establish exclusive control in the defendant with respect to *any possible cause* of the accident before permitting the application of *res ipsa loquitur* would emasculate the doctrine. He was required, *as was done,* only to produce sufficient evidence from which it could be said that it was more likely than not that it was negligence on the part of his adversary. There was a reasonable showing by respondent of variances from the recognized standards of maintenance and that the same could have possibly proximately caused his injuries.
>
> Had appellants established a possible design defect, a contrary verdict may have been rendered. However, there was no evidence of design defect, and the jury found that appellants failed to discharge their burden of explanation. Once the *prima facie res ipsa* case had been established, the burden shifted to the appellants to exculpate themselves by showing that the negligence of another was an equally plausible cause or that no failure of duty on their parts was a cause. On this record, the jury was not constrained to find that appellants had satisfied the burden that had shifted to them.

Suppose the evidence suggested that the accident in question may have been the result of concurrent causes. Should *res ipsa* be permitted? Consider *Tompkins v. Northwestern Union Trust Co.*, 198 Mont. 170, 645 P.2d 402 (1982) (doctrine applicable when pilot error may have combined with equipment failure caused by negligent maintenance of a third party, resulting in airplane crash).

2. *Identifying the Risk-Taker (2); Defendant No Longer in Exclusive Control.* Courts have not been dogmatic over the timing of defendant's exclusive control. Thus, in *Zentz v. Coca Cola Bottling Co. of Fresno*, 39 Cal. 2d 436, 247 P.2d 344, 348 (1952), the plaintiff who had been injured by an exploding bottle was permitted to utilize the *res ipsa* doctrine even though her injuries were suffered about one hour after the defendant's servant had delivered cases of the beverage to a restaurant. The court noted the plaintiff's ability to "fill the gap" with direct evidence and preserve the applicability of *res ipsa*:

> The requirement of control is not an absolute one. Although, as we have seen, the doctrine will not ordinarily apply if it is equally probable that the negligence was that of someone other than the defendant, the plaintiff need not exclude all other persons who might possibly have been responsible where the defendant's negligence appears to be the more probable explanation of the accident.
>
> Further, it is settled that the fact that the accident occurs some time after the defendant relinquishes control of the instrumentality which causes the accident does not preclude application of the doctrine provided there is evidence that the instrumentality had not been improperly handled by the plaintiff or some third person, or its condition otherwise changed, after control was relinquished by the defendant.

However, in *Dermatossian v. New York City Transit Auth.*, 67 N.Y.2d 219, 501 N.Y.S.2d 784, 492 N.E.2d 1200 (1986), a case in which plaintiff was injured when he struck his head on a defective grab handle in defendant's bus, the court concluded:

> [P]laintiff did not establish control of the grab handle by defendant of sufficient exclusivity to fairly rule out the chance that the defect in the handle was caused by some agency other than defendant's negligence. The proof did not adequately exclude the chance that the handle had been damaged by one or more of defendant's passengers who were invited to use it.

3. *Identifying the Risk-Taker (3); Exclusive Control, But of What?* In *Victory Park Apts., Inc. v. Axelson*, 367 N.W.2d 155 (N.D. 1985), plaintiff brought an action against one of its tenants following a fire in her apartment. Plaintiff's theory was that a smoked cigarette had been negligently dropped between the cushions of the couch. Plaintiff requested a *res ipsa* instruction on the basis that the defendant had exclusive control of the couch and the apartment. The court disagreed because it characterized the instrumentality in question as the cigarette, and there was insufficient evidence that the tenant, rather than other smokers who had been in the apartment earlier, had exclusive control of the cigarette. *Cf. Olswanger v. Funk*, 63 Tenn. App. 201, 470 S.W.2d 13 (1970) (only tenants had been in the apartment shortly before fire).

G. CIRCUMSTANTIAL EVIDENCE 313

4. *Identifying the Risk-Taker (4); Eliminating the Plaintiff.* In the aircraft crash case of *Newing v. Cheatham,* 15 Cal. 3d 351, 540 P.2d 33, 124 Cal. Rptr. 193, 201 (1975), the court noted:

> The purpose of [the innocence of the plaintiff] requirement, like that of control by the defendant is to establish that the defendant is the one probably responsible for the accident. The plaintiff need not show that he was entirely inactive at the time of the accident in order to satisfy this requirement, so long as the evidence is such as to eliminate his conduct as a factor contributing to the occurrence.

The court concluded that the foundational fact was established in part because

> the body of plaintiffs' decedent was found by the rescue party in one of the rear seats of the four-seater aircraft. From that position, it is difficult to imagine how he could have interfered physically with the operation of the aircraft in any way.

124 Cal. Rptr. at 202.

5. *Res Ipsa Loquitur and Comparative Fault.* Most jurisdictions that have considered the issue have held that when the contributory negligence bar has been replaced with comparative negligence, the third foundational fact (eliminating the plaintiff's contribution) in the *res ipsa* doctrine no longer is required. *See, e.g., Montgomery Elevator Co. v. Gordon,* 619 P.2d 66 (Colo. 1980). Why? Consider this scenario: defendant's car leaves the street, jumps the curb and strikes plaintiff, who, intoxicated, is lying on the sidewalk. Should res ipsa apply, although plaintiff plainly is contributorily negligent? Why?

6. *Res Ipsa and Information Costs.* To what extent is the *res ipsa* doctrine designed to identify the party who must expend the cheapest information costs in order to identify the risk-taker? Is that requirement of disparate information *all* that the traditional doctrinal elements are seeking to approximate? Consider the following statement by the Supreme Court of Alabama:

> The function of the doctrine is to supply a fact which must have existed in the causal chain stretching from the act or omission of the defendant to the injury suffered by the plaintiff, but which the plaintiff, because of circumstances surrounding the causal chain, cannot know and cannot prove to have actually existed. The missing fact is that the defendant was negligent. The rationale of the theory, in part, is that [the] defendant in charge of the instrumentality which caused the injury is possessed of superior knowledge and by reason thereof is better advantaged than plaintiff to know the true cause and therefore, negligence is presumed and the burden is upon the defendant to adduce proof to overcome the presumption.

Alabama Power Co. v. Berry, 254 Ala. 228, 236, 48 So. 2d 231, 238 (1950).

The majority of cases, however, hold that application of *res ipsa* does not turn on superior knowledge of the defendant. *See, e.g., Johnson v. Foster,* 202 So. 2d 520 (Miss. 1967) (car unaccountably leaves highway—driver and passenger both dead). If the doctrine does not depend on superior knowledge, then what is the basis for its application?

7. *Direct Evidence of Negligence.* Should direct evidence of negligence preclude the application of the *res ipsa loquitur* doctrine? A Colorado appellate court observed that:

> *Res ipsa loquitur* is a rule which presumes evidence which applies when it is judicially determined that a particular unexplained occurrence creates a prima facie case of negligence without proof of specific misfeasance. . . . A corollary requirement is that no direct evidence exists establishing that a specific act of negligence was the only likely cause for the harm. . . . The mere introduction of evidence as to how an accident could have occurred and its *possible* causes does not necessarily preclude application of *res ipsa loquitur* so long as that evidence does not clearly resolve the issue of culpability.

Kitto v. Gilbert, 39 Colo. App. 374, 379, 570 P.2d 544, 548 (1977). *See, also, Swann v. Prudential Insurance Company of America*, 620 A.2d 989 (Md. App. 1993) ("the majority of American jurisdictions . . . hold that 'an unsuccessful attempt to prove specific negligence on the defendant's part, or the introduction of evidence of specific negligence not clearly establishing the precise cause of injury, will not deprive the plaintiff of the benefits otherwise available under the doctrine. . . .'")

8. *Allocational Ramifications.* In *Widmyer,* the court noted the inapplicability of the *res ipsa* doctrine to cases involving passengers' in-flight injuries caused by turbulence. Why?

9. *Identifying the Risk-Taker (5); Multiple Defendants. King v. Searle Pharmaceuticals, Inc.*, 832 P.2d 858 (Utah 1992), concerned an intrauterine contraceptive device (IUD) known as the Cu-7 that was manufactured by one defendant and had been implanted by another, plaintiff's doctor. The court addressed how res ipsa applies to such situations as follows:

> An unexplained and unexpected injury can be the basis for requiring multiple defendants collectively in control of the circumstances to explain how the injury occurred. The doctrine of shared control is, however, an exception to the general rule that "the plaintiff does not make out a preponderant case against either of two defendants by showing merely that the plaintiff has been injured by the negligence of one or the other." W. PAGE KEETON ET AL., PROSSER & KEETON ON THE LAW OF TORTS § 39, at 251 (5th ed. 1984) (footnote omitted). The general rule applies in *res ipsa loquitur* cases.
>
> In *Ballow v. Monroe*, 699 P.2d 719, 723 (Utah 1985), we reiterated that *res ipsa loquitur* does not establish a presumption of negligence, either rebuttable or irrebuttable, and does not shift the burden of producing evidence. The burden of proof principle stated by Professor Keeton and the *Ballow* court, that the plaintiff generally has the burden of producing evidence against multiple defendants, was applied in *Talbot v. Dr. W.H. Groves' Latter-Day Saints Hospital, Inc.*, 21 Utah 2d 73, 440 P.2d 872 (1968). There, the plaintiff suffered an injury to an arm because of a lack of blood supply to the nerves after back surgery. The Court refused to apply *res ipsa loquitur* against a number of defendants who had successive management, control, or partial

control of the plaintiff during and after the surgery, because the injury could have been caused by an act or omission of any one of the defendants outside the observation of the others.

We have, however, narrowed and carved out exceptions to this general rule. In *Dalley v. Utah Valley Regional Medical Center*, 791 P.2d 193, 200 (Utah 1990), the plaintiff suffered a burn on her leg during a caesarean operation. The evidence showed that the burn occurred while the plaintiff was unconscious in the operating room, but did not show who or what caused the burn. The evidence was clear that the operating staff was responsible for all probable causes of the injury. Application of *res ipsa loquitur* in that case was based on the inference, logically based on the common experience and knowledge of lay persons, that a patient does not suffer that kind of injury during a caesarean operation absent negligence on the part of the medical staff. We modified the rule in *Talbot* by holding that "all defendants who are charged with the safety of a helpless patient may be held liable where the only possible instrumentalities that could cause injury were within the defined area of an operating room under the control of all defendants. . . ." *Id*. at 200. Thus, *Dalley* stands for the proposition that when the second element of the res ipsa foundation rests on the defendants' exclusive management or control of all possible causation factors, the burden of producing evidence does change.

The case now before this Court, however, is different from *Dalley*. Here, plaintiff has sued two defendants, a doctor and a medical device manufacturer. The liability of each, if any, is separate and independent from the other. Plaintiff has not established exclusive management or control by defendants of the possible causative factors that would justify shifting the burden of producing evidence in this case.

Shifting the burden in *Dalley* was justified because the inference was strong that the injury had occurred while the plaintiff was within the observation and control of all the defendants. Here, Searle had no knowledge of the care with which Dr. Porter inserted the Cu-7 and certainly no control over the process. Dr. Porter had no knowledge of Searle's research and manufacturing process and no control over Searle. Plaintiff therefore is not entitled to rely on the shared control exception.

Compare Ybarra v. Spangard, 25 Cal. 2d 486, 154 P.2d 687 (1944), where *res ipsa* was applied to health care providers that attended the plaintiff during an appendectomy, and also to those that attended him afterwards in the recovery room. *See also Anderson v. Somberg*, 67 N.J. 291, 338 A.2d 1 (1975), where *res ipsa* was applied to a doctor, a hospital and a manufacturer for injuries received when a rongeur broke in plaintiff's spinal column during a laminectomy operation.

10. *Judge or Jury?* Some jurisdictions utilize a variant of the doctrine entitled *conditional res ipsa,* which involves making the existence of the foundational facts a jury question. What are the ramifications of such an

approach? For a further discussion of conditional *res ipsa,* see *Clark v. Gibbons,* 66 Cal. 2d 399, 58 Cal. Rptr. 125, 426 P.2d 525 (1967).

PROBLEM

Sammy was enrolled as an undergraduate student at Anystate College in Anystate Springs. A number of incidents including thefts and assaults had occurred on the campus. Sammy had not been a victim herself, although she had been outraged by the College's apparent failure to tighten up security. Sammy had written to the school newspaper complaining that the attacks had led many students to confine themselves to their dorms. The letter threatened to sue the college for conspiracy and sexual harassment unless conditions were improved. In partial response the University President issued a press release stating that the College's current financial condition made it impossible to hire more security personnel. Sammy's mood worsened further after she was seriously frightened one evening when Geordie, one of her classmates in "Intro to Medieval Philosophy," pretended to be a mugger and jumped out at her from some shrubbery near her dorm.

Finally responding to pressure from the student newspaper, Anystate College arranged a self-defense class at a nearby gym. The college employed Barry to conduct the classes. For five years Barry had been an Anystate Springs police officer. However, he had suffered a back injury in a high-speed chase of a fleeing felon, and had been forced to retire. Barry frequently has disturbing flashbacks to the chase and the accident. During the first class the students worked in pairs. After having received instruction from Barry, they practiced on one another. Sammy's partner was Geordie. The first exercise was a hip throw. The person executing the hip throw grasps the partner by the shoulders and turns quickly. By throwing the person grasped over the hip it causes her (or him) to lose balance. Sammy threw the 200-pound Geordie six feet down the mat. Geordie landed where two of the gym's floor mats had come apart. Sammy was heard by other students to have muttered, "That'll teach him!"

Barry decided to carry the seriously injured Geordie to the college's Emergency Health Center (EMC) located near the University's main administrative building in the middle of the campus. Barry soon found Geordie to be something of a "dead weight." He saw Sammy's Honda outside the gym with the keys left in it; he quickly put Geordie on the back seat and drove the car towards the EMC. Unfortunately, the tension caused Barry to temporarily black out and lose his way. By the time he recovered and reached the administrative building he was so flustered that he rammed the University president's illegally parked Mercedes. Both the Mercedes and the Honda were badly damaged.

Before Barry left the gym he asked Daisy, one of the more advanced students to "take the mat," and substitute for him for the rest of the class. Daisy was a "first-degree black belt," a rank or status certifying to and requiring weekly school attendance, knowledge as to lower ranks, understanding of judo training and instructional methods, and qualifying as able to conduct classes with the approval of the ranking "yudansha" or black belt instructor. Daisy had assisted in instructing judo classes at the local YMCA and she scrupulously followed the training conventions used there.

Daisy now asked Sammy to assist her in demonstrating the next move. This move was the "osotogari," a leg throw in which one leg is used to sweep the opponent's leg out from under her. Sammy fell on her arm, breaking it.

Following an emergency call, an ambulance rushed Sammy to the EMC. She arrived just after Barry came in with the unconscious Geordie. Unfortunately, the EMC was unable to locate an emergency care physician. In the interim Sammy and Geordie were wheeled into a treatment room. In serious pain and concerned that her treatment would be further delayed, Sammy reached over to Geordie's gurney and switched charts with him. As soon as the doctor arrived, Sammy was the first patient to be treated. Medical reports suggested that if Geordie had been treated earlier he would have been less likely to suffer from the permanent disability with which he is now afflicted.

What issues of tort law arise? How are they likely to be resolved?

Chapter 6
CAUSE IN FACT

A. INTRODUCTION

Courts have divided the issue of *"causation"* into *cause in fact* and *legal (or proximate) cause*. According to orthodox tort theory, cause in fact is concerned with whether A's conduct caused B's injury. It is an inquiry into the legal response to factual, scientific or forensic evidence that relates to the relationship between the defendant's conduct and the plaintiff's damage (literally, *did X cause Y?*). Supposedly, cause in fact is a factual question.

Legal cause is a normative issue. Given that A has caused B's injury in a factual sense (cause in fact), should A be liable for B's damages (legal cause)? Legal cause, like "Duty," raises a more explicit normative question—*should A be liable, as a matter of policy, for B's injuries?* Another way to ask the question might be, should A, who has caused B's injuries in a factual sense, nonetheless be relieved of liability for policy reasons? One key question, which we will begin to address in the next chapter, is: what policies are relevant to this determination and who should apply those policies to the particular case-judge or jury? In essence, then, legal cause has little to do with causation in any factual or scientific sense.

While, cause in fact is supposedly a factual issue and legal cause a policy issue, predictably, courts have experienced difficulty in distinguishing between the issues involved in this chapter and those dealing with proximate or legal cause. This is just one of the problems you will face as you work through the next few very important chapters.

PROBLEM

Mary Martin's 10-year-old son was injured in a "hit and run" accident in which the negligent driver was speeding through a school zone. The next week, Mary observed Jim Jones driving through the same school zone at a speed far in excess of the speed limit. She reported this observation to the local police, who monitored the scene for the next week with radar guns and caught 50 people, including Jim Jones, speeding through the zone. Each person caught speeding was subjected to a monetary fine that was collected by the state. Should they also have to pay for all or part of the injuries sustained by Mary or her son?

Suppose the evidence shows that Jim Jones was in fact the person who hit Mary's son and that, at the time of the accident, Jim was driving 30 mph in a 15 mph zone. However, the accident occurred when Mary's son unexpectedly ran into the path of the car after running from the sidewalk between two parked cars. Should Jim be required to pay for any or all of the damages sustained by Mary or her son?

B. BUT-FOR CAUSATION

HILL v. LUNDIN & ASSOCIATES, INC.
260 La. 542, 256 So.2d 620 (1972)

BARHAM, JUSTICE.

This is an action [in tort] for damages for injuries the plaintiff received when she tripped and fell over a metal ladder lying on the ground. The plaintiff, Celeste Hill, was working as a maid and babysitter for one of the defendants, Mrs. Rosemary Delouise, when the accident happened, and the ladder over which she tripped had been left on the Delouise premises by the other defendant, Lundin & Associates, Inc., a home repair contractor. Mrs. Delouise had employed Lundin to repair damage to her house caused by Hurricane Betsy. Because of the unusual number of repair jobs necessitated by hurricane damage, the urgency of making repairs immediately so that further damage would not result, and the shortage of equipment and men, Lundin organized his contracts for maximum speed and efficiency. The materials and equipment were delivered to the various job sites by truck, the repairmen for a particular job came at the first opportunity in automobiles, and after completion of a job a company truck returned when possible to pick up the equipment and any materials left over.

After the repairs to the Delouise house had been finished, among Lundin's property remaining on the premises was a metal ladder left standing in an upright position against the side of the house. At some time before the accident, which occurred a few days after completion, someone (not an employee of the defendant Lundin) moved the ladder and laid it in the yard. The plaintiff was well aware of the position of the ladder on the ground. On the day of the accident she was caring for the youngest Delouise child, who was two or three years old, and doing the family wash. She left the house through the back door to hang the wash on the clothesline in the yard. Going from the back door to the clothesline, the plaintiff had to walk past the ladder, which she observed lying on the ground. As she was hanging up the wash, she heard the door of the house slam, and turned and saw the young child running to her, directly toward the ladder. Hurrying in his direction to stop him from falling over the ladder, she tripped on the ladder, fell, and was hurt. . .

. . .[T]he sole issue before us is the question of Lundin's liability to the plaintiff. We are of the opinion that the plaintiff has failed to establish actionable negligence on Lundin's part, and we reverse.

The accident in this case occurred because the plaintiff fell over a ladder lying on the ground. We first inquire whether any causal relationship existed between the harm to the plaintiff and the defendant's allegedly negligent conduct. If the defendant had not left the ladder on the premises, it could not have later been placed on the ground in the yard. To this extent it may be said that the defendant's act had something to do with the harm. . .

. . . It is only that conduct which creates an appreciable range of risk for causing harm that is prohibited. Leaving a ladder unattended under certain conditions may create an unreasonable risk of harm to others which would impose a reciprocal duty upon the actor. If we assume that the defendant was under a duty not to leave the ladder leaning against the house because of an unreasonable risk of harm, the breach of that duty does not necessarily give rise to liability in this case. Although the defendant would owe a duty to protect certain persons under certain circumstances from this risk, it is not an insurer against every risk of harm which is encountered in connection with the ladder.

Here a third party had moved the ladder to the ground, and the plaintiff was injured as she sought to prevent the child from tripping on the ladder. The basic question, then, is whether the risk of injury from a ladder lying on the ground, produced by a combination of defendant's act and that of a third party, is within the scope of protection of a rule of law which would prohibit leaving a ladder leaning against the house?

Foreseeability is not always a reliable guide, and certainly it is not the only criterion for determining whether there is a duty-risk relationship. Just because a risk may foreseeably arise by reason of conduct, it is not necessarily within the scope of the duty owed because of that conduct. . . . Neither are all risks excluded from the scope of duty simply because they are unforeseeable. . . . The ease of association of the injury with the rule relied upon, however, is always a proper inquiry. . . .

Where the rule of law upon which a plaintiff relies for imposing a duty is based upon a statute, the court attempts to interpret legislative intent as to the risk contemplated by the legal duty, which is often a resort to the court's own judgment of the scope of protection intended by the Legislature. *Dixie Drive It Yourself System v. American Beverage Co.*, 242 La. 471, 137 So.2d 298; *Pierre v. Allstate Ins. Co., supra*. Where the rule of law is jurisprudential and the court is without the aid of legislative intent, the process of determining the risk encompassed within the rule of law is nevertheless similar. Malone, Ruminations on Dixie Drive It Yourself, 30 La.L.Rev. 363 (1970); McDonald, Proximate Cause in Louisiana, 16 La.L.Rev. 391 (1956). The same policy considerations which would motivate a legislative body to impose duties to protect from certain risks are applied by the court in making its determination. "All rules of conduct, irrespective of whether they are the product of a legislature or are a part of the fabric of the court-made law of negligence, exist for purposes. They are designed to protect some persons under some circumstances against some risks. Seldom does a rule protect every victim against every risk that may befall him, merely because it is shown that the violation of the rule played a part in producing the injury. The task of defining the proper reach or thrust of a rule in its policy aspects is one that must be undertaken by the court in each case as it arises. How appropriate is the rule to the facts of this controversy? This is a question that the court cannot escape." Malone, Ruminations on Cause-In-Fact, 9 Stanford L.Rev. 60, 73 (1956).

This defendant's alleged misconduct, its alleged breach of duty, was in leaving the ladder leaning against the house unattended. The risk encountered by the plaintiff which caused her harm was the ladder lying on the ground where it was placed by another, over which she tripped as she moved to protect the child. The record is devoid of any evidence tending to establish that the defendant could have reasonably anticipated that a third person would move the ladder and put it in the position which created this risk, or that such a "naked possibility" was an unreasonable risk of harm. . . .

A rule of law which would impose a duty upon one not to leave a ladder standing against a house does not encompass the risk here encountered. We are of the opinion that the defendant was under no duty to protect this plaintiff from the risk which gave rise to her injuries. The plaintiff has failed to establish legal and actionable negligence on the part of the defendant.

The judgment of the Court of Appeal is reversed, and plaintiff's suit is dismissed at her costs.

NOTES

1. *The "But For" Test.* The court applies a but for test for cause in fact. Can one say that but for the defendant's negligence the plaintiff's injuries would not have occurred? What is the particular alleged act of negligence in *Hill*? What are the plaintiff's injuries? Is the "but for" test effective in establishing cause in fact? Can you point to the relevant part of the opinion in which the court determines cause in fact? In the rest of its opinion the court makes a determination about responsibility, not about cause *per se*. We will consider the implications of that determination about responsibility in the next chapter.

2. *Some Examples.* Suppose A makes a left hand turn without signaling and runs over a pedestrian who is blind. Is the failure to signal a cause in fact of the pedestrian's injuries?

What if A drives off a canyon road and his car falls two hundred feet before bursting into flames. A is killed. Even though the passenger section of the car is severely burned as is A's body, an expert establishes that the car's air bag did not open. Do you think that the failure of the air bag to open is a cause in fact of A's death under the but for test?

Note how the but for test sets up a counterfactual inquiry. It asks the factfinder to decide if what happened would have happened anyway if the defendant had not done whatever it is that the plaintiff said defendant did wrong. Counterfactual inquiries can be troublesome because they ask us to make decisions about a world that did not come to pass.

3. *Careful and Precise Analysis and Articulation.* Before applying the but for test, it is critical to carefully and precisely identify the particular alleged act of negligence and the particular injuries allegedly caused by the alleged negligent act. *See generally*, Robertson, *The Common Sense of Cause-In-Fact*, 75 Tex. L. Rev. 1765 (1997).

DILLON v. TWIN STATE GAS & ELECTRIC CO.
85 N.H. 449, 163 A. 111 (1932)

The defendant maintained wires to carry electric current over a public bridge in Berlin. In the construction of the bridge there were two spans of girders on each side between the roadway and footway. In each span the girders at each end sloped upwards towards each other from the floor of the bridge until connected by horizontal girders about nineteen feet above the floor.

The wires were carried above the framework of the bridge between the two rows of girders. To light the footway of the bridge at its center a lamp was hung from a bracket just outside of one of the horizontal girders and crossing over the end of the girder near its connection with a sloping girder. Wires ran from a post obliquely downward to the lamp and crossed the horizontal girder a foot or more above it. The construction of the wire lines over and upon the bridge is termed aerial. The wires were insulated for weather protection but not against contact.

The [14-year-old] decedent and other boys had been accustomed for a number of years to play on the bridge in the daytime, habitually climbing the sloping girders to the horizontal ones, on which they walked and sat and from which they sometimes dived into the river. No current passed through the wires in the daytime except by chance.

The decedent, while sitting on a horizontal girder at a point where the wires from the post to the lamp were in front of him or at his side, and while facing outwards from the side of the bridge, leaned over, lost his balance, instinctively threw out his arm, and took hold of one of the wires with his right hand to save himself from falling. The wires happened to be charged with a high voltage current at the time and he was electrocuted. [Defendant's motion for a directed verdict was refused.]

ALLEN, JUSTICE.

The bridge was in the compact part of the city. It was in evidence that at one time the defendant's construction foreman had complained to the city marshal about its use by boys as a playground, and in his complaint had referred to the defendant's wires. The only wires were those over the bridge superstructure. From this evidence and that relating to the extent of the practice for boys to climb up to and upon the horizontal girders an inference that the defendant had notice of the practice was reasonable. The occasion for the complaint might be found due to apprehension of danger from proximity to the wires. This only came about from climbing upon the upper framework of the bridge. There was no suggestion of danger in any use of the bridge confined to the floor level.

The use of the girders brought the wires leading to the lamp close to those making the use, and as to them it was in effect the same as though the wires were near the floor of the bridge. While the current in the wires over the bridge was mechanically shut off during the daytime, other wires carried a commercial current, and there was a risk from many causes of the energizing of the bridge wires at any time. It is claimed that these causes could not be overcome or prevented. If they could not, their consequences might be. Having notice of the use made of the girders, and knowing the chance of the wires becoming charged at any time, the defendant may not say that it was not called upon to take action until the chance happened. Due care demanded reasonable measures to forestall the consequences of a chance current if the chance was too likely to occur to be ignored. . . .

The circumstances of the decedent's death give rise to an unusual issue of its cause. In leaning over from the girder and losing his balance he was entitled to no protection from the defendant to keep from falling. Its only liability was in exposing him to the danger of charged wires. If but for the current in the wires he would have fallen down on the floor of the bridge or into the river, he would without doubt have been either killed or seriously injured. Although he died from electrocution, yet, if by reason of his preceding loss of balance he was bound to fall except for the intervention of the current, he either did not have long to live or was to be maimed. In such an outcome of his loss of balance, the defendant deprived him, not of a life of normal expectancy, but of one too short to be given pecuniary allowance, in one alternative, and not of normal, but of limited, earning capacity, in the other.

If it were found that he would have thus fallen with death probably resulting, the defendant would not be liable, unless for conscious suffering found to have been sustained from the shock. In that situation his life or earning capacity had no value. To constitute actionable negligence there must be damage, and damage is limited to those elements the statute prescribes.

If it should be found that but for the current he would have fallen with serious injury, then the loss of life or earning capacity resulting from the electrocution would be measured by its value in such injured condition. Evidence that he would be crippled would be taken into account in the same manner as though he had already been crippled.

His probable future but for the current thus bears on liability as well as damages. Whether the shock from the current threw him back on the girder or whether he would have recovered his balance, with or without the aid of the wire he took hold of, if it had not been charged, are issues of fact, as to which the evidence as it stands may lead to different conclusions.

NOTES

1. *Practicing But-For.* Sharpen your understanding of the but-for test with the facts in *Dillon*. What injuries did the defendant's negligence cause? What facts does your answer depend upon?

2. *Safety Net.* The court said the decedent "was entitled to no protection from the defendant to keep from falling." Why not?

SHARPE v. PETER PAN BUS LINES
401 Mass. 788, 519 N.E.2d 1341 (1988)

WILKINS, JUSTICE.

On Sunday morning, February 22, 1981, Sharon Lee Glynn, a sixteen-year-old who had purchased a bus ticket to go home after visiting a friend in Westfield, was waiting in the Springfield bus terminal to board a Peter Pan bus. Without warning and without provocation, one Patrick Werner, a stranger to Sharon, walked up behind her while she was talking with two young friends seated with her in the terminal, and stabbed her three times in the back, killing her. The circumstances of the crime and Werner's appeal from his conviction of murder in the second degree appear in *Commonwealth v. Werner*, 16 Mass. App. Ct. 686, 454 N.E.2d 919 (1983).

B. BUT-FOR CAUSATION

In this action the jury found by a special verdict that each defendant was negligent and that its negligence was a proximate cause of Sharon's death. They awarded damages for wrongful death and for conscious suffering. We transferred the appeals of the defendant bus company (Peter Pan) and the defendant bus terminal (Springfield) to this court. We affirm the judgment.

. . . We turn then to the issue whether the evidence presented a case for the jury. Our inquiry first concerns the question whether either defendant failed to act reasonably in the circumstances to provide the utmost care and diligence to protect patrons of the terminal. The second issue, by far the harder question of the two to answer, is whether any breach of duty may have been a reasonably foreseeable cause of the attack on Sharon.

We have little hesitancy in ruling that the evidence warranted a finding that each defendant failed to fulfil its high duty of care concerning security in the terminal. The jury would have been warranted in finding that the terminal was in a rundown section of the city. Homeless people and drunks frequented the area. The terminal was in an active area for crimes against the person, one characterized by a Springfield police captain as an area of high criminal activity. There had been robberies in the terminal's restrooms and assaults in the terminal. Evidence concerning the neighborhood of a bus terminal and the people who frequent it is relevant to a case of this type. The terminal management called the police every week because of a security or other problem. The terminal had no uniformed security person working for it. The defendants were aware of a need to have security present in some form but had no security plan. Because of security problems, the management of the terminal had asked the local police to make periodic patrols. Sunday morning was a time of substantial activity in the terminal; as many as fifteen buses would arrive at or leave the terminal each hour.

There was evidence warranting a finding that the stabbing of Sharon was within the reasonably foreseeable risks created by each defendant's breach of duty. The jury could have reasonably found that the defendants were negligent in failing to provide a uniformed security force in the terminal. It is likely that a uniformed security officer in the terminal could not have prevented Werner's attack on Sharon. The fact that a physical attack could not have been prevented, once a person had decided to undertake it, however, does not fully answer the causation question.

The presence of uniformed police or security personnel provides a deterrent effect. Lay people would have a sense that this is true. In this case, an expert on security procedures testified that uniformed police or security officers are the best deterrent to crime that one could have and that a security officer could have been placed effectively in the terminal. The jury could reasonably have concluded that as a deterrent to crime the defendants had a duty to provide uniformed security personnel in the terminal at the time of the attack.

The question, of course, is not simply whether crime in general might have been deterred by a police presence, but whether the jury would have been warranted in finding that it was more probable than not that sudden, unprovoked attacks, such as Werner's attack on Sharon, could have been prevented. The jury could have found that Werner was concerned about not being caught. He fled the scene, hid the knife, tried to elude the police, and was found hiding in the vicinity. The evidence warranted a finding that Werner probably would have been deterred from attacking Sharon if a uniformed security guard had been present. The plaintiff's expert answered responsively to a question on cross-examination that, if a uniformed security guard had been there, the attack probably could have been prevented. On the evidence, it was within the jury's province to reach the same conclusion, as they did. . . .

LYNCH, JUSTICE, dissenting. . . .

Moreover, the negligent act of failing to provide *uniformed* security personnel did not create the opportunity for the criminal act inflicted upon the plaintiff's decedent. The attack on Sharon occurred in broad daylight in a terminal full of people. Sharon sat with two friends, one of whom was a two-hundred-pound, six-foot-tall young man. In such circumstances, the presence or absence of a uniformed security guard could have had little effect on whether the attack would or would not have occurred. One could speculate over such a question. Perhaps a security guard would have intervened successfully in the attack, or perhaps he would have been at the other end of the waiting room. Possibly a uniformed security guard would have deterred the killer from entering the station. In all likelihood, since the killer was an ordinary traveler on his way through Massachusetts from Colorado, the presence of a security guard would have had no effect at all. The jury are entitled to draw reasonable inferences from the evidence. They are not entitled to base a verdict on conjecture. The question whether the defendants' failure to employ a uniformed guard was the proximate cause of Sharon's death may be resolved only through the exercise of conjecture. Therefore, it is a question not properly for the jury. . . .

NOTES

1. *Proving a Causal Positive.* The distinction between misfeasance and nonfeasance is frequently accorded more importance than it warrants. Nevertheless, it raises some interesting issues in the case of factual causation. The paradigm cause in fact issue concerns a jury inquiry into whether X's negligent *act* caused Y's injuries. Theoretically at least, and notwithstanding the standard of proof required in any particular jurisdiction, it should be *possible* to answer that question with scientific certainty. However, can the same be said with regard to the question whether X's failure to provide a safety device or procedure *caused* injuries suffered by Y from a non-X source? The prevalent view ignores any such distinction. For example, in *Jackson v. Ray Kruse Constr. Co.,* 708 S.W.2d 664, 667–68 (Mo. 1986), the court affirmed a jury verdict in favor of a 4-year-old against the owner of the apartment complex where she lived, following injuries she suffered when she was struck by a speeding bicycle rider in the parking lot. Her theory of liability was that the bicycle would not have been traveling so fast if there had been "speed bumps" installed in the parking lot. The court concluded:

> The defendants argue vigorously . . . that the plaintiff has not established the element of causation. The accident was precipitated, of course, by the bicycle rider, who no doubt could be faulted for excessive speed and inattention. There may, however, be more than one

proximate cause of an accident. . . . [T]he subject of causation has been the subject of much discussion among legal scholars, often because of bizarre hypotheticals such as the one in which two persons fire at a third at the same time, with each inflicting a wound which would have been fatal without regard to the other shot. Another favorite has a person furnishing to another a car with brakes he knows to be defective, with the driver making no effort to apply the brakes. A recent article summarizing the views of the several distinguished commentators is that of Professor Richard W. Wright, *Causation in Tort Law*, 73 CAL. L. REV. 1737 (1985).

This case would be characterized by Professor Wright as one of "doubtful" causation, akin to a case involving a public swimming pool in which a child drowns while the lifeguard is absent. It is extremely difficult to prove that the drowning would not have occurred if the lifeguard had been present, but it would certainly be reasonable for a jury to conclude that the presence of a lifeguard would make the chances of rescue "more likely than not." Professor Wright argues that no more should be required and his view has substantial support. There are obvious difficulties in this case in setting up a counterfactual situation which definitively projects the sequence of events under the assumption that a safety bump had been in place. Striving for certainty is a *tour de force*. The jury must deal in terms of probabilities.

. . . [T]he jury could have believed a speed bump at the place [the plaintiff's expert] suggested could have greatly reduced the chance of an accident, either by slowing down the bicycle or shifting its direction. No more should be required. The law deals with probabilities. . . .

Would it help to analyze the question in *Jackson* as one of duty? How did the court in *Peter Pan* characterize the issue? Did the dissent characterize it differently?

2. *Clearer Cases?* In *Ford v. Trident Fisheries Co.*, 232 Mass. 400, 122 N.E. 389 (1919), a seaman on defendant's steam trawler fell overboard while climbing a flight of four steps when the ship suddenly rolled. The seaman disappeared immediately. The steps did not have a rail. The lifeboat was lashed to the deck and only had one oar. The fact that defendant negligently maintained its lifeboat was held immaterial. Similarly, in *McWilliams v. Sir William Arrol & Co.*, [1962] W.L.R. 295 (H.L.), plaintiff alleged the defendant was at fault in failing to provide a safety belt to a steel erector who plunged 70 feet to his death. The court affirmed a verdict for the defendant because the facts established an "irresistible inference" that the decedent would not have worn a safety belt if it had been provided.

3. *In Case of Doubt.* Where the evidence is doubtful, as in *Jackson*, who should have the burden of proof? According to RESTATEMENT (SECOND) OF TORTS § 433B(1), "the burden of proof that the tortious conduct of the defendant has caused the harm to the plaintiff is upon the plaintiff."

4. *Statutory Violations.* In *Haft v. Lone Palm Hotel*, 3 Cal. 3d 756, 478 P.2d 465, 91 Cal. Rptr. 745 (1970), defendant motel violated a statutory obligation to provide a lifeguard, or suitable warning that no lifeguard was present, at

its swimming pool. Plaintiff's father and son drowned in the pool. The court presumed causation (drowning because of lack of lifeguard *or* warning). To hold otherwise would allow the defendant to evade liability through its own misconduct, *i.e.,* defendant's misconduct made proof of causation unavailable. Contrast *Stachniewicz v. Mar-Cam Corp.,* 259 Or. 583, 488 P.2d 436 (1971), which indicates that plaintiff has the burden of proving causation even where negligence *per se* is involved.

In *Stachniewicz,* the defendant, a bar owner, violated a statute by serving alcohol to and failing to remove a visibly intoxicated patron who thereafter assaulted the plaintiff. The defendant argued that plaintiff did not prove causation because he did not show that plaintiff's injury was the result of the defendant's (1) service of alcohol to a visibly intoxicated person, or (2) failure to remove that person from the bar. The court held that the jury had sufficient evidence to infer that the second, but not the first, statutory violation of the bar owner caused the plaintiff's injury. Should the plaintiff have argued that the bar owner's service of the intoxicated patron made unavailable proof as to whether the assault would have occurred in the absence of such service?

5. *When But-For Cause is an Unsatisfactory Test.* The but for test will provide the answer to the cause in fact question in the great bulk of cases, but not always. The rest of this chapter is concerned with cases where the but for test does not provide a clear answer to the cause in fact question. When that is true, is the court just deciding a factual question or is it making a decision based on policy? If it is making a policy decision then is it deciding cause in fact or is it also deciding legal cause?

C. THE SUBSTANTIAL FACTOR TEST

ANDERSON v. MINNEAPOLIS, ST. P. & S.S.M. RY.
146 Minn. 430, 179 N.W. 45 (1920)

LEES, C.

[This] appeal is from an order denying [defendant's] motion in the alternative for judgment notwithstanding the verdict or for a new trial.

The complaint alleged, that early in August, 1918, sparks from one of defendant's locomotive engines set a fire on or near the right of way, and that this fire spread until it finally reached plaintiff's land, where it destroyed some of his property. The answer was a general denial followed by an allegation that, if plaintiff was damaged by fire, the fire was not due to any act of defendant, was of unknown origin, and, by reason of extraordinary weather conditions, became a huge conflagration. The reply put these allegations in issue.

Plaintiff's case in chief was directed to proving that in August, 1918, one of defendant's engines started a fire in a bog near the west side of plaintiff's land; that it smoldered there until October 12, 1918, when it flared up and burned his property, shortly before it was reached by one of the great fires which swept through Northeastern Minnesota at the close of that day. Defendant introduced evidence to show that on and prior to October 12th fires were burning west and northwest of, and were swept by the wind towards, plaintiff's premises. It did not show how such fires originated, neither did it clearly and certainly trace the destruction of plaintiff's property to them. By cross-examination of defendant's witnesses and by his rebuttal evidence, plaintiff made a showing which would have justified the jury in finding that the fires proved by defendant were started by its locomotive on or near its right of way in the vicinity of Kettle river. . . .

The following proposition is stated in defendant's brief and relied on for a reversal:

> "If plaintiff's property was damaged by a number of fires combining, one being the fire pleaded, the others being of no responsible origin, but of such sufficient or such superior force that they would have produced the damage to plaintiff's property regardless of the fire pleaded, then defendant was not liable."

This proposition is based upon *Cook v. Minneapolis, S. P. & S.S.M. R. Co.*, 98 Wis. 624, 74 N.W. 561 (1898). In *Farrell v. Minneapolis & R.R. Ry.*, 121 Minn. 357, 141 N.W. 491 (1913), this court considered the case, but refrained from expressing approval or disapproval of its doctrine. The Supreme Court of Michigan has referred to it as good law. The Supreme Court of Idaho says the opinion is logical and well reasoned, but the discussion is in a large measure theoretical and academic. Judge Thompson in his work on Negligence (Vol. 1, § 739), says that the conclusion reached is so clearly wrong as not to deserve discussion. If the Cook Case merely decides that one who negligently sets a fire is not liable if another's property is damaged, unless it is made to appear that the fire was a material element in the destruction of the property, there can be no question about the soundness of the decision. But if it decides that if such fire combines with another of no responsible origin, and after the union of the two fires they destroy the property, and either fire independently of the other would have destroyed it, then, irrespective of whether the first fire was or was not a material factor in the destruction of the property, there is no liability, we are not prepared to adopt the doctrine as the law of this state. If a fire set by the engine of one railroad company unites with a fire set by the engine of another company, there is joint and several liability, even though either fire would have destroyed plaintiff's property. . . . We, therefore, hold that the trial court did not err in refusing to instruct the jury in accordance with the rule laid down in the Cook Case. In the foregoing discussion we have assumed, although it is doubtful, that the evidence was such that a foundation was laid for the application of the rule if it was otherwise applicable.

. . . We find no error requiring a reversal, and hence the order appealed from is affirmed.

NOTES

1. *"But For" in Anderson.* Do you see why the "but for" test posed a problem for the plaintiff in its claim against the railroad? What test does the court apply instead?

2. *"Substantial Factor."* RESTATEMENT (SECOND) OF TORTS § 430 states that an actor is not liable for his negligent conduct unless that conduct is a "legal cause" of another's harm. Legal cause is defined as conduct which is a "substantial factor" in bringing about the harm, § 431. Section 433 states:

> The following considerations are in themselves or in combination with one another important in determining whether the actor's conduct is a substantial factor in bringing about harm to another:
>
> (a) the number of other factors which contribute in producing the harm and the extent of the effect which they have in producing it;
>
> (b) whether the actor's conduct has created a force or series of forces which are in continuous and active operation up to the time of the harm, or has created a situation harmless unless acted upon by other forces for which the actor is not responsible;
>
> (c) lapse of time.

RESTATEMENT (SECOND) OF TORTS § 431, comment *a* recognizes that "substantial cause" is not content-neutral, stating,

> The word "substantial" is used to denote the fact the defendant's conduct has such an effect in producing the harm as to lead reasonable men to regard it as a cause, using that word in the popular sense, in which there always lurks the idea of responsibility, rather than in the so-called "philosophic sense," which includes every one of the great number of events without which any happening would not have occurred.

Is the "substantial factor" test intended to be used in conjunction with or instead of the "but for" test? If the considerations described in § 433 of the RESTATEMENT are applied, is there any purpose served in applying the "but for" test? If the "but for" test is applied, is there any reason to apply the "substantial factor" test? Is "substantial factor" a substitute for "but for" or the starting point for a legal cause analysis?

See Daugert v. Pappas, 104 Wash. 2d 254, 704 P.2d 600, 605–06 (1985) (refusal to apply substantial factor test to legal malpractice case):

> Such a change in the test for cause in fact is normally justified only when a plaintiff is unable to show that one event alone was the cause of the injury. As noted by Dean Prosser, the substantial factor test aids in the disposition of three types of cases. First, the test is used where either one of two causes would have produced the identical harm, thus making it impossible for plaintiff to prove the but for test. In such cases, it is quite clear that each cause has played so important a part in producing the result that responsibility should be imposed on it. Second, the test is used where a similar, but not identical, result would have followed without the defendant's act. Third, the test is used where one defendant has made a clearly proven but quite insignificant contribution to the result, as where he throws a lighted match into a forest fire. W. PROSSER & W. KEETON, TORTS § 41 (5th ed. 1984).

C. THE SUBSTANTIAL FACTOR TEST

See also In re Bendectin Litigation, 857 F.2d 290, 311 (6th Cir. 1988):

> The substantial factor standard applies only to initial negligent actors in determining their liability in the face of action by a subsequent actor, or in determining causation between simultaneous actors, both of whose acts could have been "but for" causes of plaintiffs' injuries.

3. *Two Forces Actively Operating.* RESTATEMENT (SECOND) OF TORTS § 432 provides that:

> (1) Except as stated in Subsection (2), the actor's negligent conduct is not a substantial factor in bringing about harm to another if the harm would have been sustained even if the actor had not been negligent.
>
> (2) If two forces are actively operating, one because of the actor's negligence, the other not because of any misconduct on his part, and each of itself is sufficient to bring about harm to another, the actor's negligence may be found to be a substantial factor in bringing it about.

As an example of this proposition, the RESTATEMENT gives the "two-fires" situation of *Anderson.*

Why are not the various forces brought to bear in *Dillon* "actively operating?"

4. *Reciprocity of Cause and the Philosophy of Causation.* The discussion in *Anderson* poses such questions as, did fire A or fire B cause the damage to the plaintiff's property? Was the fire or the weather that helped the fires spread responsible for the damage? However, was not the presence of the plaintiff's property near the railroad as much a cause of the damage? For an economist, the only question is which distribution of responsibility will promote the most efficient allocation of resources. Thus, causation has no meaningful role, other than to signify a conclusion as to the most efficient allocation (that is, the wealth maximizer). *See, e.g.,* Coase, *The Problem of Social Cost,* 3 J. LAW & ECON. 1 (1960); W.M. LANDES & R.A. POSNER, THE ECONOMIC STRUCTURE OF TORT LAW, 228–30 (1987). As a result, those holding such views have attracted the label "causal minimalists," although "causal nihilists" might be more appropriate. *See generally* Howarth, *"O Madness of Discourse, That Cause Sets Up With and Against Itself!",* 96 YALE L.J. 1389, 1392 (1987) (an excellent primer). Hart & Honoré disagree not only with the causal nihilists, but also those who (more appropriately) attract the title of causal minimalists—those who relegate the causal question to "but for," and proceed to label all other "causal" issue as normative, and thus matters of duty, legal cause or the like. H.L.A. HART & T. HONORÉ, CAUSATION IN THE LAW (2d ed. 1985). For Hart & Honoré, such a minimalist approach robs causation of much of its "common sense" or "ordinary usage." *See* Howarth, *supra,* at 1394–98. Do you have such a usage or sense of causation? Do you share it with others? *See* Howarth, *supra,* 96 YALE L.J. at 1402–05.

PROBLEM

A state statute requires that any house constructed after 1985 must be built to withstand winds up to 100 mph. Defendant built and sold to plaintiff in

1989 a new house that was capable of withstanding winds only up to 75 mph. Two months after plaintiff moved into the house an extraordinary wind of 125 mph raged through the town, blowing the roof off plaintiff's house and causing other severe damage. Assuming that defendant was negligent in constructing the house in a manner that failed to meet the requirements of the statute and plaintiff was unaware of this negligence when he purchased the house, was the defendant's negligence the cause in fact of the plaintiff's damages?

D. PROBABILITIES

PEREZ v. LAS VEGAS MEDICAL CENTER
805 P.2d 589 (Nev. 1991)

ROSE, JUSTICE:

This is an appeal from a summary judgment entered against the appellant (hereinafter, Ms. Perez) in a wrongful death action. The district court held that Ms. Perez could not prove that the alleged negligence of the health care provider was the legal cause of the death, because the decedent probably would have died anyway due to his serious preexisting medical condition. We adopt the "loss of chance" doctrine for medical malpractice cases, and under that doctrine Ms. Perez raised genuine issues of material fact to the district court. Accordingly, we reverse the grant of summary judgment and remand this case for further proceedings.

The pertinent facts submitted by the parties in connection with respondents' motion for summary judgment are as follows. On April 15, 1985, Marco Lopez, a prisoner at the Clark County Detention Center, died of a massive brain hemorrhage, due apparently to an aneurism or a congenital defect in an artery.

Lopez had been detained and incarcerated on April 3, 1985. Two days later, after he complained that he was ill, Lopez was taken to the Las Vegas Medical Center, which was under contract to treat prisoners from the detention center. From April 5–9, Lopez was confined in the medical ward. During this time physicians made no attempt to diagnose the persistent headaches of which Lopez was complaining. Lopez was returned to jail. On April 15, Lopez was discovered in his cell by a nurse who thought Lopez was having seizures. Although the duty physician, Dr. Gregory, was notified by telephone of the seizures, no examination or treatment other than administration of Valium and phenobarbital was given Mr. Lopez. A few hours later, Mr. Lopez was found dead in his cell. Based on this death, Ms. Perez brought the present lawsuit, alleging wrongful death due to negligence on the part of the responsible medical providers. Dr. Tiholiz, a general practitioner from Los Angeles, testified in a deposition on behalf of Ms. Perez. Dr. Tiholiz stated that Lopez would have had a "reasonable chance" of surviving the hemorrhage if he had been given prompt and proper medical care. Dr. Tiholiz admitted, however, that Lopez probably did not have a greater than fifty percent chance of surviving the hemorrhage, even given proper medical care. Additionally, Carolyn Sabo, a professor of nursing at the University of Nevada Las Vegas, testified in a deposition that, if given proper medical care and diagnosis, Lopez "might" have lived. An expert on behalf of the respondents, however, suggested that Mr. Lopez' chances of surviving such a hemorrhage would be very slight. Respondents moved for summary judgment against Ms. Perez on the ground that any negligence by health care providers could not have been the legal cause of Lopez' death, since Lopez probably would have died anyway due to his serious preexisting condition. Based on the evidence stated above, the district court entered summary judgment in favor of respondents. Ms. Perez appeals the order granting summary judgment.

The issue disputed on this appeal is whether Ms. Perez failed, as a matter of law, to establish the existence of actual causation, i.e., that the alleged medical malpractice actually caused the harm complained of. As a general rule in medical malpractice cases, the plaintiff must prove that the alleged negligence more probably than not caused the ultimate injury (rule of proving causation by a preponderance of evidence). Respondents argue that the evidence shows that Mr. Lopez probably would have died anyway due to his serious preexisting physical condition. Therefore, respondents contend, only the preexisting medical ailment, and not the alleged medical malpractice, can be considered the probable, or preponderant, cause of Lopez' death. In short, respondents contend that Ms. Perez cannot, as a matter of law, establish the element of actual causation according to the traditional preponderance requirement.

The issue of first impression presented by respondents' argument is whether the preponderance requirement for proof of causation operates to bar recovery in medical malpractice cases where there is a fifty percent or greater chance that the patient's underlying ailment caused the death (i.e., where the plaintiff has a fifty-fifty or lower chance of survival due to a serious preexisting medical problem). There are many cases coming down on both sides of this question. Applying the traditional preponderance requirement strictly, some courts have held that plaintiffs with fifty-fifty or lower chances of survival due to their original ailment cannot demonstrate that medical malpractice was the actual cause of the death. Several other courts have relaxed the traditional preponderance requirement for causation to allow limited recovery under these circumstances.

We conclude that the large line of cases which permits recovery under these circumstances represents the better view. There are many good arguments against applying the preponderance rule of causation strictly to bar recovery in cases such as this. Of the various arguments against the position urged by respondents, the following is most fundamental: the respondents' position would bar any recovery in tort on behalf of the survivors of many potentially terminal patients, no matter how blatant the health care provider's negligence. Through negligence, a physician or other health care provider could reduce a patient's chances of survival from as high as fifty percent to, for example, ten percent, and yet remain unanswerable in the law of tort. This position is simply untenable. As the *McKellips* court explains:

> Health care providers should not be given the benefit of the uncertainty created by their own negligent conduct. To hold otherwise would in effect allow care providers to evade liability for their negligent

actions or inactions in situations in which patients would not necessarily have survived or recovered, but still would have a significant chance of survival or recovery.

McKellips, 741 P.2d at 474. The disadvantages of the position urged by respondents are both more certain and more severe than any disadvantages of the position we adopt today. Additionally, it is important to recall that no cause of action will lie absent some instance of negligence by the health care provider.

As discussed in *McKellips*, courts have adopted various rationales in order to avoid the harsh and unjustified result just discussed. We conclude that the best rationale supporting recovery in these circumstances is the "loss of chance" doctrine. Under this doctrine, the injury to be redressed by the law is not defined as the death itself, but, rather, as the decreased chance of survival caused by the medical malpractice. Of course, the plaintiff or injured person cannot recover merely on the basis of a decreased chance of survival or of avoiding a debilitating illness or injury; the plaintiff must in fact suffer death or debilitating injury before there can be an award of damages. Additionally, the damages are to be discounted to the extent that a preexisting condition likely contributed to the death or serious debilitation. Specifically, "[t]he amount of damages recoverable is equal to the percent of chance [of survival] lost [due to negligence] multiplied by the total amount of damages which are ordinarily allowed in a wrongful death action." *McKellips*, 741 P.2d at 476.

By defining the injury as the loss of chance of survival, the traditional rule of preponderance is fully satisfied. In cases in which the plaintiff prevails, it can be said that the medical malpractice more probably than not decreased a substantial chance of survival and that the injured person ultimately died or was severely debilitated. Specifically, in order to create a question of fact regarding causation in these cases, the plaintiff must present evidence tending to show, to a reasonable medical probability, that some negligent act or omission by health care providers reduced a substantial chance of survival given appropriate medical care. In accord with other courts adopting this view, we need not now state exactly how high the chances of survival must be in order to be "substantial." We will address this in the future on a case by case basis. There are limits, however, and we doubt that a ten percent chance of survival as referred to in the example in the dissenting opinion would be actionable. Survivors of a person who had a truly negligible chance of survival should not be allowed to bring a case fully through trial. Perhaps more importantly, in cases where the chances of survival were modest, plaintiffs will have little monetary incentive to bring a case to trial because damages would be drastically reduced to account for the preexisting condition.

Having addressed the applicable legal standards, we turn now to the question of whether Ms. Perez presented sufficient proof in connection with the motion for summary judgment to create a question of fact on the issue of causation. We conclude that she did. As in *McKellips*, we do not require that the expert testimony specifically quantify the percentage chance of survival in order to create a question of fact on causation; specific percentages are necessary only at later stages in determining the precise measure of damages.

McKellips, 741 P.2d at 475. In the present case, Dr. Tiholiz testified that Mr. Lopez had a reasonable chance of survival given proper medical attention. We recognize that Mr. Lopez' preexisting condition appears to have been grave indeed and that Dr. Tiholiz's opinion is not particularly strong or specific. Nevertheless, under the summary judgment standards stated above, we must accept this statement as true and, moreover, we must draw all inferences from this statement in a manner which is favorable to the party opposing summary judgment. Interpreted in a manner most favorable to Ms. Perez, Dr. Tiholiz's statement and other deposition testimony fairly imply that, through prompt and proper decompression and other treatment, Mr. Lopez would have had a substantial chance of survival. Because more than a slight doubt remains as to Lopez' chances of survival, Ms. Perez was entitled to bring the issue of causation to trial. Therefore, Ms. Perez succeeded in raising a genuine issue of material fact on the issue of causation pursuant to the loss of chance doctrine and the motion for summary judgment was improvidently granted.

The nature and quality of Mr. Perez' survival is not an issue with which we must concern ourselves at this time. It was not fully explored below and not the basis for the district court's decision. Further, Dr. Tiholiz, the plaintiff's expert, used the term survival without qualification. Giving every reasonable inference to the appellant against whom summary judgment was granted, we conclude that Dr. Tiholiz's unqualified use of the word survival meant survival with a reasonable quality of life. If the respondents felt it was important to explore what Dr. Tiholiz meant by survival, they could have examined further on this point.

The dissent expresses fears that the floodgates of litigation will be opened by this opinion. Nothing of the sort will occur. Rather, the rule will give deserved redress in infrequent situations similar to this case. And by adopting the "loss of chance" doctrine, a health care provider will not be able to avoid responsibility for negligent conduct simply by saying that the patient would have died anyway, when that patient had a reasonable chance to live. For the reasons stated above in this opinion, the order granting respondents' motion for summary judgment is reversed and the case remanded for further proceedings consistent herewith.

NOTES

1. *Sharpening Your Skills*. Why doesn't but-for work to establish cause in fact? Is it because statistically the decedent would have died anyway? But doesn't that assume that the injury is death? If the injury is redefined as loss of a chance of survival then doesn't the but for test work? If it does, then is the case more about cause in fact or is it about legal cause, duty, or damages, i.e., the recognition of a new cause of action?

2. *No Loss of Chance Recovery*. The court in *Kilpatrick v. Bryant*, 868 S.W.2d 594 (Tenn. 1993), considered the loss of a chance theory of causation:

> In this medical malpractice case, the Plaintiffs, Sandra and William Kilpatrick, have appealed from a decision of the Court of Appeals affirming the grant of summary judgment in favor of Dr. James W. Bryant, Defendant-Appellee. We granted the Plaintiffs' Rule 11 application to decide whether a cause of action for "loss of chance" is

cognizable in Tennessee. For the reasons discussed below, we decline to recognize such a cause of action and hold that there can be no liability in a medical malpractice case for negligent diagnosis or treatment that decreases a patient's chances of avoiding death or other adverse medical condition where the death or adverse medical condition would probably have occurred anyway.

The Plaintiffs alleged in their complaint that on May 18, 1987, Dr. Bryant examined Sandra Kilpatrick at which time a lump was detected in her right breast. Dr. Bryant ordered a mammogram which was performed on May 21, 1987, by Dr. Thipavan Boone. Dr. Boone interpreted the xeromammography films and stated that no definite outline of a mass or indication of malignancy was seen. Mrs. Kilpatrick avers that Dr. Bryant informed her that the mammogram results were negative. Approximately four months later, in September, Mrs. Kilpatrick was examined by another physician who did a biopsy. Cancer was detected and Mrs. Kilpatrick underwent a right radical mastectomy a month later for removal of the cancer of the right breast.

The Plaintiffs sued Dr. Bryant and the radiologists who performed the mammogram, although the radiologists were later voluntarily dismissed from the case. The Plaintiffs claim that Dr. Bryant was negligent in the treatment of Mrs. Kilpatrick in relying upon the findings of the radiologists and in failing to inform her of the need to seek follow-up care. Specifically, their complaint alleges that

> [t]he Defendant, James W. Bryant, was negligent and careless in the treatment of the Plaintiff, Sandra K. Kilpatrick, inasmuch as he should not have relied totally upon the findings of the radiologists, and that further he failed to even suggest the need for follow-up examination or further consultation; that likewise, as a direct and proximate result of his negligence, Plaintiff, Sandra K. Kilpatrick, suffered more serious complications and a general worsening of her cancerous condition as a result of her cancer going undetected for approximately four months.

> It is further claimed by the Plaintiffs that Dr. Bryant's negligence required Mrs. Kilpatrick to seek additional medical treatment, suffer loss of earning capacity and enjoyment of life, experience pain and disablement, and has made her medical condition worse than it would otherwise be. Mr. Kilpatrick seeks recovery for loss of consortium. . . .

We decline to relax traditional cause in fact requirements and recognize a new cause of action for loss of chance. Accordingly, the Plaintiffs in this case are not entitled to recover damages for the impaired opportunity for obtaining a more favorable medical result, the increase in the risk of harm, or the loss of a better chance of recovery or survival. Plaintiffs also seek damages for additional medical treatment, pain and suffering, loss of earning capacity, etc., directly attributable to the negligence of the Defendant. We conclude that these items of damages are recoverable because the Plaintiffs have shown that such damages would not have been incurred but for the Defendant's negligence. Thus, the grant of summary judgment to the Defendant is sustained to the extent that it relates to the loss of chance or the increase in the risk of harm. Summary judgment as to the Plaintiffs' claims for the other items of damages noted above is reversed.

Justice Daughtrey, concurring and dissenting, stated in part:

> The courts in the 30 or more jurisdictions that have recognized the "loss of chance" doctrine or permitted recovery for "increased risk of harm" certainly cannot be accused of doing so with the intent to dismantle the law of proximate cause in medical malpractice cases. They have, instead, recognized the reality of medical practice and the difficulty of predicting with any scientific certainty which patients with a life-threatening disease will survive and which will not. Without a crystal ball to guide them, medical experts must fall back on statistics, on percentages, and on five-year and ten-year survival rates.

Reconsider *Dillon*: didn't the electric wire deprive young Dillon of a chance of regaining his balance?

3. *Burden of Proof Revisited.* In *Kramer Serv., Inc. v. Wilkins,* 186 So. 625, 184 Miss. 483 (1939), plaintiff was hit in the forehead by a piece of glass that fell from a broken transom as he opened a door in defendant's hotel. Plaintiff established negligence by showing that the transom had been in a broken condition long enough to charge defendant with notice of it. The forehead wound did not heal, and two years after the injury a skin specialist found that skin cancer had developed at the point of the wound. Plaintiff could not recover from defendant for this skin cancer, however, since the medical testimony was that there was no causal connection between the injury and the cancer, and that while such a connection was possible, the chances of causation were only one out of a hundred.

If there had been no medical testimony of any kind about causation, could plaintiff then recover for the cancer? Would it make a difference if plaintiff sued in *res ipsa loquitur*? Compare *Goldstein v. Levy,* 74 Misc. 463, 132 N.Y.S. 373 (1911), where a shade from a chandelier in defendant's music hall inexplicably broke and fell, injuring plaintiff. The negligent cause of the accident was presumed to be attributable to the defendant. Had unexplained skin cancer developed, would this *res ipsa* plaintiff recover—or is the presumed cause only of the instrumentality, and not damages? If *res ipsa* includes a presumption of damages, why should the *res ipsa* plaintiff be favored in this regard over one who proves actual fault on the part of the defendant?

4. *Expert Testimony as to Medical Causation.* Causation may be established without expert medical testimony if the alleged consequential disability arises coincidentally with the negligence of the defendant. See *Robbins v. Jewish Hosp. of St. Louis,* 663 S.W.2d 341 (Mo. App. 1983). Consider this language:

> In a personal injury suit, the plaintiff bears the burden of proving a causal relationship between the accident and the injuries complained of. The test is whether the plaintiff has shown through medical

testimony that more probably than not the subsequent medical treatment was necessitated by trauma suffered in the accident. When symptoms of an injury appear shortly after a traumatic incident that are consistent with that incident and continuously worsen, a defendant who contests the cause-in-fact relationship must show some other particular incident could have caused the injury in question to overcome plaintiff's case.

See also Housley v. Cerise, 579 S.2d 973 (La. 1991) ("The trial court found that plaintiffs proved causation, but the court of appeal reversed. After reviewing the record in its entirety, we find the record supports the factual finding of the trial court, and hold that the court of appeal erred in reversing. When the medical testimony is considered in light of the temporal relationship between Mrs. Housley's fall and the bursting of her water bag, the trial court's conclusion that plaintiffs proved causation by a preponderance of the evidence was not manifestly erroneous.").

5. *Common Knowledge or Expert Testimony?* In *Bushman v. Halm*, 798 F.2d 651, 659–60 (3d Cir. 1986), the plaintiff had been injured in an automobile accident in a no-fault state, a jurisdiction which denied recovery for tort damages unless the victim sustained "permanent injuries". The defendant's motion for summary judgment in tort was premised on the plaintiff's failure to establish a causal nexus between the accident and his allegedly "permanent injuries." In opposition to the defendant's motion, the plaintiff proffered an affidavit setting forth his description of the accident and an account of the pain he suffered following the accident. The plaintiff also submitted a letter from his treating orthopaedic surgeon which confirmed that plaintiff had complained of pain. The summary judgment was vacated, the court noting:

> If the question of causal relation is so esoteric that lay minds cannot form any intelligent judgment about it without expert aid, an opinion from an expert may be required. Such a theory is a rational outgrowth of the legal premise that inferred factual conclusions may be drawn from basic facts only to the extent that logic and human experience indicate a probability that certain consequences can and do follow from the basic facts. On the other hand, circumstantial evidence or common knowledge may provide a sound basis from which a causal sequence may be inferred.
>
> Harper and James, in their treatise on the law of torts, specifically refer to an example of a medical condition easily identifiable by lay persons as causally related to an accident: a broken leg sustained in an automobile accident. HARPER & JAMES, THE LAW OF TORTS, § 20.2, at 1118. Thus, as a matter of ordinary experience, a particular act or omission might be expected under the circumstances to produce a particular result. If that result has indeed followed, it may be permissible to conclude that a causal relation exists. On the other hand, the correlation between certain conditions such as psychiatric illness and injury may be beyond lay knowledge. Therefore, expert medical testimony should be used to aid their comprehension that a particular condition may arise out of a specific injury. *Id.*

... [A] treating or examining physician may be an expert on causation in a particular case. The ... cases cited by the trial court neither discuss nor require special experts whose only function is to testify on probability theories. At a minimum, a plaintiff should not be expected to defend against a ... motion [for summary judgment] by appending the sworn affidavit of an expert in the field of probability. Rather, a physician's report setting forth a qualitative and quantitative description of a common injury is sufficient to pass judicial scrutiny on summary judgment. The cases cited by the district court ... involve plaintiffs who have alleged conditions such as psychiatric illnesses which cannot be said to be clearly related to the type of injury originally claimed to have been sustained. In the instant case, there is no alleged injury or condition which would not logically flow from the motor vehicle accident. We conclude that the district court erred in holding that expert testimony was required in this case to prove causation as an element of the tort of negligence.

SMITH v. STATE DEPARTMENT OF HEALTH AND HOSPITALS
676 So.2d 543 (La. 1997)

LEMMON, JUSTICE.

...In August 1987, Benjamin Smith went to E.A. Conway Memorial Hospital, complaining of a sore on top of his right foot. The attending physician diagnosed cellulitis with lymphangitis, and Smith underwent minor surgery to drain the fluid from his foot.

Smith's five-day hospitalization included a routine chest x-ray which the staff radiologist reported as showing "a mediastinal mass projected to the right of the trachea." The doctor stated that "lymphoma must be considered in the differential diagnosis" and recommended a CT scan of the thoracic area. The hospital staff failed to inform Smith or his family of the x-ray results or to recommend further testing. Smith was simply discharged from the hospital without any information about the mass in his chest.

Almost fifteen months later, Smith returned to E.A. Conway, complaining of a three-week history of "left pleuritic chest pain, fever, and chills." A second chest x-ray on October 31, 1988, compared with the August 1987 x-ray, revealed that the mass had doubled in size. Smith and his family then learned for the first time of the August 1987 x-ray report.

Further testing confirmed the diagnosis of small cell carcinoma of the lungs, a fast-acting and lethal cancer. By this time, Smith's cancer had progressed to the "extensive" stage, in that the cancer was present in both lungs and was non-operable.[1] Despite aggressive drug treatment and chemotherapy, Smith died on March 16, 1989, nineteen months after the initial x-ray. He was forty-five years old at his death.

...At trial, the parties presented evidence by several doctors relating to the percentage chance of survival for certain periods of time after discovery

---

[1] The experts contrasted "extensive" stage with "limited" stage, in which the cancer is limited to one side of the thorax or treatable by one radiation point. Smith apparently was in the "limited" stage at the time of the first x-ray.

of small cell carcinoma of the lung at various stages of progression of the disease. The trial court ruled that plaintiffs had not met their burden of proving that the fifteen-month delay in treatment resulting from the State's admitted negligence had caused Smith to die or to lose a chance of survival. . . .

The court of appeal reversed, concluding that the trial court was plainly wrong in failing to find the loss of a chance of survival. . . .

As to the method of measuring those damages, the intermediate court rejected plaintiffs' contention that they were entitled to full damages for the death, noting that plaintiffs failed to prove, more probably than not, that Smith would have survived but for the Department's malpractice. Drawing heavily on Joseph H. King, Jr., *Causation, Valuation and Chance in Personal Injury Torts Involving Preexisting Conditions and Future Consequences*, 90 YALE L.J. 1353 (1981), the court reasoned that granting recovery upon lesser proof than the more-probable-than-not rule should be balanced by a concomitant reduction of the potential damages for a case where the tort victim's death probably would not have occurred but for the defendant's fault. However, the court pointed out that the plaintiff in a loss of a chance of survival case still retains the burden of proving by a preponderance of the evidence that the defendant's negligence caused the loss of a chance.

Accordingly, the court held that "the percentage probability of loss, if less than 50%, is the proper measure of the plaintiff's damages in a case of wrongful death due to medical malpractice. . . ." Referring to expert evidence that recurrence of cancer after five years is rare, the court then reviewed other expert testimony as to the chance of survival for five years. Four doctors testified that the chance of survival, at the stage of the disease when the initial x-ray was taken, was one to twelve percent, ten to fifteen percent, five percent, and seven to twenty-five percent respectively.[3] The experts further agreed that Smith's chance of survival at the time of the October 1988 x-ray was less than one percent. Analyzing this evidence de novo, the court concluded that the evidence preponderated to show that the Department's negligence was a substantial factor in depriving Smith of a ten percent chance of surviving for five years. Fixing the total damages at $764,347,[4] the court reduced this amount proportionate to the lost ten percent chance of survival and awarded a total of $76,434 to Mrs. Smith and her two minor children.

. . .The issues in loss of a chance of survival cases are whether the tort victim lost any chance of survival because of the defendant's negligence[5] and

---

[3] From this testimony, the court concluded that a range of seven to twelve percent encompasses most of the experts' estimates.

[4] The court fixed the total damages as follows:

Wrongful death damages (one-third each)	$ 450,000
Funeral expenses	4,004
Future lost earnings and value of household services	250,343
Survival action damages	60,000
	$ 764,347

[5] The pre-existing condition causes the conceptual problem. The jury should focus on the damages that the defendant caused—the loss of a chance of avoiding a death that might not have occurred if the health care provider had performed properly. The court should instruct the jury to determine the amount of damages for this specific loss on the basis of all the evidence.

the value of that loss. The question of degree may be pertinent to the issue of whether the defendant's negligence caused or contributed to the loss, but such a tort-caused loss in any degree is compensable in damages.

Allowing recovery for the loss of a chance of survival is not, as the court of appeal suggested, a change or a relaxation of the usual burden of proof by a preponderance of the evidence. Rather, allowing such recovery is a recognition of the loss of a chance of survival as a distinct compensable injury caused by the defendant's negligence, to be distinguished from the loss of life in wrongful death cases, and there is no variance from the usual burden in proving that distinct loss.

Thus, in a medical malpractice case seeking damages for the loss of a less-than-even chance of survival because of negligent treatment of a pre-existing condition, the plaintiff must prove by a preponderance of the evidence that the tort victim had a chance of survival at the time of the professional negligence and that the tortfeasor's action or inaction deprived the victim of all or part of that chance, and must further prove the value of the lost chance, which is the only item of damages at issue in such a case.

All experts testified that Smith had some chance of survival if he had been treated immediately after the August 1987 x-ray, and that he had virtually no chance of survival in October 1988 after he went almost fifteen months without treatment because of the Department's negligence. Smith's chance of survival in August 1987, though not better than even, was still a chance that was denied him as a result of the Department's failure to meet its standard of care. That chance had some value when viewed from the standpoint of the tort victim and his heirs, and that value is the appropriate focus of the analysis in this case.

Courts and commentators have recognized three possible methods of valuation of the loss of a chance of survival in professional malpractice cases.

The first, and the method we adopt today in this decision, is for the fact-finder—judge or jury—to focus on the chance of survival lost on account of malpractice as a distinct compensable injury and to value the lost chance as a lump sum award based on all the evidence in the record, as is done for any other item of general damages.

The second method, as advocated by plaintiffs, is to allow full survival and wrongful death damages for the loss of life partially caused by malpractice, without regard to the chance of survival. We reject this argument, agreeing with the court of appeal that full recovery is not available for deprivation of a chance of survival of less than fifty percent. To allow full recovery would ignore the claimants' inability to prove by a preponderance of the evidence that the malpractice victim would have survived but for the malpractice, which is a requirement for full recovery.

The third method, and the method adopted by the court of appeal in this case, is to compute the compensable chance as "the percentage probability by which the defendant's tortious conduct diminished the likelihood of achieving some more favorable outcome." Joseph H. King, Jr., *Causation, Valuation and Chance in Personal Injury Torts Involving Preexisting Conditions and Future Consequences*, 90 YALE L.J. 1353, 1382 (1981). Professor King's percentage-probability-of-loss theory estimates "the compensable value of the victim's life if he survived" and reduces that estimate according to the percentage chance of survival at the time of the malpractice. *Id.* This method has gained acceptance by the courts and commentators because of its pragmatic appeal, providing concrete guidelines for calculating damages and alleviating the perceived "pulling out of the hat problem" allegedly associated with the method that we adopt today.

Our point of disagreement with the court of appeal's method of computing damages for the loss of a chance of survival is its rigid use of a precise mathematical formula, based on imprecise percentage chance estimates applied to estimates of general damages that never occurred, to arrive at a figure for an item of general damages that this court has long recognized cannot be calculated with mathematical precision. When these total hypothetical damages are reduced by a numerical factor determined from evidence of percentage rates of survival for certain periods after discovery of the disease at various stages of the disease, the uncertainty progresses geometrically.

The starting point of our analysis is to recognize that the loss of a less-than-even chance of survival is a distinct injury compensable as general damages which cannot be calculated with mathematical certainty. Next, we recognize that the factfinder should make a subjective determination of the value of that loss, fixing the amount of money that would adequately compensate the claimants for that particular cognizable loss. On the other hand, the approach of the court of appeal requires the factfinder first to make a hypothetical determination of the value of survival and wrongful death claims that are not really at issue and then to discount that value mathematically. This mathematical discounting of the subjective valuation of inapplicable claims does not magically make that approach more precise or more accurate than simply allowing the factfinder to value directly the loss of a chance of survival that is the sole item of damages at issue in the case.

The lost chance of survival in professional malpractice cases has a value in and of itself that is different from the value of a wrongful death or survival claim.[9] The jury can calculate the lost chance of survival without going through the illusory exercise of setting a value for the wrongful death or survival claims and then mechanically reducing that amount by some consensus of the expert estimates of the percentage chance of survival. The methodology for fixing damages attributable to the loss of a chance of survival should not be so mechanistic as to require the jury merely to fill in the blanks on

---

[9] Valuation of the loss of a chance of survival in this medical malpractice case is similar to the valuation of the loss of a chance of recovery by judgment or settlement in a legal malpractice action in which a lawyer lets a case prescribe and the tort victim sues the lawyer for malpractice. In the early cases, a plaintiff could only recover by trying a "case-within-a-case"—that is, by proving that he or she would have prevailed on the underlying cause of action. If not, the plaintiff could not recover. (The parallel in the medical malpractice area is the jurisprudence that rejects entirely the loss of a chance of survival doctrine.) Recognizing the unfairness to tort victims who had a chance of recovery and lost it because of legal malpractice, the courts, including this one, modified the case-within-a-case doctrine somewhat by shifting the burden of proof to the negligent attorney. Even under this approach, however, the jury must engage in a pretend exercise of measuring damages based on events that never in reality occurred or can occur. The preferable approach in legal malpractice cases (although not yet adopted by a holding of this court) is to let the jury value the lost chance of recovery based on the value of the claim before prescription [i.e., time-bar]. . . .

a verdict sheet with a consensus number for the percentage chance of survival and the total amount of damages, and then have the judge perform the multiplication task.

The calculation of damages for the loss of a chance of survival is not like the calculation of comparative fault damages. In the comparative fault context, the jury determines the entire amount of general and special damages actually sustained by the tort victim, which is an amount that would be awarded in the absence of contributory negligence. The percentage reduction merely implements the law of comparative fault in fixing the tortfeasor's total obligation. But in the loss of a chance of survival context, the award of damages for this particular loss is the "bottom line" figure. Any theoretical figure representing the amount the claimants would have been awarded if they had been successful in proving the defendant's fault more probably than not caused the loss of the tort victim's life is not a concrete figure that can properly be subjected to a reduction because of plaintiffs' failure of proof. Rather, the jury in a loss of a chance of survival case merely considers the same evidence considered by a jury in a survival and wrongful death action, and the loss-of-chance jury then reaches its general damages award for that loss on that evidence as well as other relevant evidence in the record.[10]

This approach for valuation of the loss of a chance of survival is more appropriate than the method used by the court of appeal in that it allows the jury to render a verdict in the lump sum amount of damages attributable only to the lost chance of survival. This is a valuation of the only damages at issue—the lost chance—which is based on all of the relevant evidence in the record, as is done for any other measurement of general damages. Allowing the jury to consider all the evidence, including expert medical testimony regarding the percentage chances of survival, and to value directly the lost chance is more logical than requiring the jury to calculate damages for wrongful death when the physician's negligence was not the more probable cause of the death. The method we adopt today will not leave the jury without any guidance or any factors to consider. The jury will be allowed to consider an abundance of evidence and factors, including evidence of percentages of chance of survival along with evidence such as loss of support and loss of love and affection, and any other evidence bearing on the value of the lost chance. The jury's verdict of a lump sum amount of damages can be tested on appeal for support in the record by reviewing the percentage chances and the losses incurred by the tort victim and his or her heirs, and any other relevant evidence, thus providing assurance against speculative verdicts.

. . .For these reasons, the judgment of the court of appeal is set aside, and the case is remanded to the district court for further proceedings in accordance with this opinion.

---

[10] Evidence of loss of support, loss of love and affection and other wrongful death damages is relevant, but not mathematically determinative, in loss of a chance of survival cases, as is evidence of the percentage chance of survival at the time of the malpractice. The plaintiff may also present evidence of, and argue, other factors to the jury, such as that a ten percent chance of survival may be more significant when reduced from ten percent to zero than when reduced from forty to thirty percent. The jury may also consider such factors as that the victim, although not likely to survive, would have lived longer but for the malpractice.

VICTORY, JUSTICE, dissenting.

. . .My disagreement with the Court's adoption of the lost chance of survival doctrine is both pragmatic and theoretical. From a pragmatic standpoint, the doctrine yields unfair results. How the doctrine of lost chance results in erroneous and inequitable outcomes is illustrated by the Court of Appeals of Maryland:

> Because loss of chance of recovery is based on statistical probabilities, it might be appropriate to examine the statistical probabilities of achieving a "just" result with loss of chance damages . . . To compare the two rules, assume a hypothetical group of 99 cancer patients, each of whom would have had a 33 1/3 % chance of survival. Each received negligent medical care, and all 99 die. Traditional tort law would deny recovery in all 99 cases because each patient had less than a 50% chance of recovery and the probable cause of death was the preexisting cancer not the negligence. Statistically, had all 99 received proper treatment, 33 would have lived and 66 would have died; so the traditional rule would have statistically produced 33 errors by denying recovery to all 99. The lost chance rule would allow all 99 patients to recover, but each would recover 33 1/3 % of the normal value of the case. Again, with proper care 33 patients would have survived. Thus, the 33 patients who statistically would have survived with proper care would receive only one-third of the appropriate recovery, while the 66 patients who dies as a result of the preexisting condition, not the negligence, would be overcompensated by one-third. The loss of chance rule would have produced errors in all 99 cases.

Fennell v. Southern Maryland Hospital, 320 Md. 776, 580 A.2d 206, 212–13 (1990) (declining to adopt the doctrine of loss of chance of survival [in Maryland]). . . .

. . . The majority's approach ignores this trend and allows the jury to simply arrive at a damage figure without properly explaining the basis of the figure. This "rabbit-out-of-the-hat" approach will be virtually impossible to review on appeal under the manifest error standard. The reviewing court will have little idea of what chance of survival the jury determined was lost, thus little basis to determine if the jury was manifestly erroneous.

The "percentage probability test" proposed by Professor King is a much fairer and much more precise test than that adopted by the majority. . . . Under this test, damages in lost chance of survival cases are measured according to the "percentage probability by which defendant's tortious conduct diminished the likelihood of achieving some more favorable result." King, *supra* at 1382. To illustrate, Professor King states:

> [C]onsider a patient who suffers a heart attack and dies as a result. Assume that the defendant-physician negligently misdiagnosed the patient's condition, but that the patient would have had only a 40% chance of survival even with a timely diagnosis and proper care. Regardless of whether it could be said that the defendant caused the decedent's death, he caused the loss of a chance, and that chance-interest should be completely redressed in its own right. Under the

proposed rule, the plaintiff's compensation for the loss of the victim's chance of surviving the heart attack would be 40% of the compensable value of the victim's life had he survived (including what his earning capacity would otherwise have been in the years following death). The value placed on the patient's life would reflect such factors as his age, health, and earning potential, including the fact that he had suffered the heart attack and the assumption that he survived it. The 40% computation would be applied to that base figure.

King, *supra* at 1382.

This approach is much more sensible and fair than that proposed by the majority because it insures that the damages awarded redress the actual injury, which is the decreased chance of survival or recovery, not the actual death. A majority of our sister states have adopted the "percentage probability test." I would follow the lead of these states and utilize this formula for calculating damages in lost chance of survival cases: Lost Chance of Survival Damages = (the percent of chance of survival lost due to negligence) multiplied by (the total amount of damages which are ordinarily allowed in wrongful death actions). . . .

NOTES

1. *The Percentage Loss of Recovery.* If one recovers, *e.g.*, 10% of one's damages for loss of a 10% chance of survival, then why not recover only 60% of one's damages in a situation of the loss of a 60% chance of survival?

2. *The Non-Medical Loss of Chance.* In a footnote, the *Smith* court limited its holding to medical malpractice cases, leaving to "another day" the application of that doctrine "against other types of tortfeasors," citing *Hardy v. SW. Bell Tel. Co.*, 910 P.2d 1024 (Okla. 1996).

In *Hardy* the court held that "an action for loss of chance of survival may not be expanded to apply in an ordinary negligence action brought against one other than a medical practitioner or a hospital." The court stated the facts in *Hardy* as follows:

> Plaintiff, Dr. Homer Hardy, brought this action for wrongful death against Southwestern Bell Telephone Company alleging that its negligence caused a failure of the 911 emergency system which resulted in his wife's death from a heart attack she suffered in their Tulsa home the morning of July 18, 1992, because plaintiff was unable to promptly summon emergency assistance and an ambulance for her.

Plaintiff claimed that the unsuccessful attempt to summon the emergency service was due to a "system lock-up" owing to telephone overload.

Although the court had adopted the loss of chance doctrine in medical malpractice case of *McKellips v. St. Francis Hosp.*, 741 P.2d 467 (Okla. 1987), it refused to apply that doctrine here:

> The public policy concerns of medical practice which have been held to justify a reduced burden of causation in lost chance cases do not transfer over to ordinary negligence cases. Public policy is not served

by extending the causation exception to the "but for" rule to other tortfeasors. Under the decisions discussed and other "loss of chance" medical provider opinions, the physician had the opportunity to perform properly under the terms of the physician-patient special relationship but was alleged to have failed to do so.

The essence of the doctrine is the special relationship of the physician and the patient. In these cases the duty is clear, the negligence is unquestioned and the resulting harm, the destruction of a chance for a better outcome, has obvious value and is not so speculative as to be beyond being reasonably considered a result of defendant's negligence.

In *Daugert v. Pappas*, 104 Wash. 2d 254, 704 P.2d 600 (1985), the Supreme Court of Washington rejected an attempt to apply principles of loss of chance to an action for legal malpractice based on failure to file an appeal. The court found that while the loss of chance to recover from misdiagnosis of cancer such as was present in *Herskovits v. Group Health Coop of Puget Sound*, 99 Wash. 2d 609, 664 P.2d 474 (1983), resulted in a very real injury with definite value which would require compensation, there is no commensurate harm, no lost chance, in a legal malpractice case as the matter may eventually be reviewed. Neither, held the court, is there in a legal malpractice action a separate and distinguishable harm, a diminished chance.

Plaintiff presents no convincing arguments regarding application of the loss of chance doctrine to this situation. In *Coker v. Southwestern Bell Telephone Co.*, 580 P.2d 151 (Okla. 1978), we held that plaintiff did not state a cause of action against the telephone company for damages sustained when fire destroyed his place of business with the theory that the defective telephone prevented him from summoning emergency assistance to extinguish the fire. We held that the petition did not assert the requisite causal connection between alleged negligence of the defendant and the resulting damages. We observed that it would be "necessary to heap conclusion upon conclusion as to the course events would have taken had the telephone operated properly" in order to establish the causal connection between the defective telephone and the ultimate destruction of appellant's business. Addressing the issue of causation we found the failure of phone service was too remote from plaintiff's loss to establish grounds for recovery and stated "that the number and character of the random elements which must come together in precisely the correct sequence at exactly the right time in order for it to be established that failure of telephone service was an efficient cause of appellant's loss so far removes appellee's act of negligence from the ultimate consequences as to break any asserted causal connection." *Id.*, at 154.

We relied in large part on a Washington decision, *Foss v. Pacific Telephone and Telegraph Co.*, 26 Wash. 2d 92, 173 P.2d 144, 149 (1946), which we noted had ruled on facts virtually identical to *Coker*. In *Foss* the Supreme Court of Washington had collected and analyzed many decisions addressing the very points we considered regarding causation and we set forth the following instructive discussion of causation from that decision:

> "Appellant's claim of causation rests on pure speculation. Surely we could not hold that anyone could ever say that if respondent's operator had promptly answered appellant's call and made connection of his telephone with the fire department in Kent that the fire department would have immediately answered the telephone; would have promptly left the house where the fire department equipment is kept; would have proceeded rapidly to the scene of the fire without mishap; would have quickly arranged its equipment to fight the fire with only minor damage to the building."

> The trier of fact in the instant case would likewise be forced to heap conclusion upon conclusion as to the course events would have taken if the 911 system had worked properly and have no more than mere conjecture as to what damages plaintiff suffered by reason of defendant's action. Plaintiff's claim of causation is far too speculative and too remote to be sustained here. Plaintiff presents us with no convincing argument as to why a loss of chance relaxed standard of causation limited by the Court to medical malpractice actions should be applied here to reduce his burden.

> We would be remiss in our duty if we failed to observe here that the application of the lost chance of survival doctrine to these facts as urged by plaintiff would cause a fundamental redefinition of the meaning of causation in tort law. While the majority of the Court were persuaded in *McKellips* that the particular facts and circumstances of that case required creating an exception to the "more likely than not" requirement of traditional causation, we refuse to effect a total restructuring of tort law by applying the lost chance doctrine beyond the established boundary of medical malpractice to ordinary negligence actions.

Would it be more accurate to read the *Hardy* court holding not as saying that loss of chance is inapplicable outside medical malpractice, but that the plaintiff in *Hardy* failed to prove that loss by a preponderance of the evidence? The court in *Smith* said the lower court was "correct in holding that plaintiff proved by a preponderance of the evidence" that defendant deprived Smith of a less-than-50% chance of survival.

In a legal malpractice action arising out of mishandled litigation, the plaintiff traditionally had to prove not only that the defendant lawyer committed malpractice but that the malpractice prevented the plaintiff from winning the earlier suit. Predictably malpracticing attorneys would be happy to tell the court in the malpractice case that the first suit was a loser! Even if the plaintiff had less than a fifty percent chance of prevailing in the earlier suit, didn't the attorney's malpractice deprive the plaintiff of a chance of prevailing? Alternatively, wouldn't the settlement value of the earlier suit be an appropriate measure of damages? Surely expert testimony could establish a range of settlement values.

3. *Breach of Contract and the Loss of a Chance.* The plaintiff in *Wachtel v. Nat. Alfalfa Jour. Co.*, 176 N.W. 801 (Iowa 1920), entered a contest established by the defendant:

The defendant, the National Alfalfa Journal Company, is a corporation having a place of business at Sioux Falls, S.D. Some time prior to April 2, 1917, defendant offered prizes to persons residing in 42 counties of this state who would engage in a contest for subscriptions to the Alfalfa Journal. The territory was divided into four districts and 49 prizes were to be awarded to contestants receiving the largest number of votes in each district, based upon the number of subscriptions obtained, and also a Hudson Super-Six seven passenger touring car valued at $1,650, a grand prize to the contestant receiving the largest number of votes in the 42 counties, making 50 prizes in all. A capital prize, together with a large number of minor prizes, was offered to each of the 49 successful contestants in each district as follows:

To the one securing the largest number an upright; "likewise in each district a $150 phonograph will be awarded to the candidate who secures the third largest number of votes; a $100 diamond ring to the candidate who secures the fourth largest number of votes; a $75 diamond ring to the fifth; a $25 jewelry set to the sixth, seventh, eighth, ninth, tenth, and eleventh; a $20 gold watch to the twelfth, thirteenth, fourteenth, fifteenth and sixteenth; a Carola phonograph to the seventeenth, eighteenth, nineteenth, twentieth, twenty-first, twenty-second, twenty-third, twenty-fourth, twenty-fifth, and twenty-sixth; a 'Paragon' 34-piece silver set to the twenty-seventh, twenty-eighth, twenty-ninth, thirtieth, and thirty-first; an Eastman [K]odak to the thirty-second, thirty-third, thirty-fourth, thirty-fifth, thirty-sixth, thirty-seventh, thirty-eighth, thirty-ninth, fortieth, and forty-first; and a 26-piece set of Roger's silverware to the forty-second, forty-third, forty-fourth, forty-fifth, forty-sixth, forty-seventh, forty-eighth, forty-ninth, and fiftieth."

The voting power of each subscription decreased as the end of the contest, which was to open April 2d and close June 16th, approached. From April 2d to May 12th each subscription obtained for one year entitled the contestant to 3,000 votes, for three years, 6,000, and for five years 15,000; from May 14th to June 2d for one year 2,000 votes, three years 4,000, five years 10,000; and from June 2d to June 16th for one year 1,000, three years 2,000, and five years 5,000.

Plaintiff accepted defendant's offer, entered the contest, and continued to work for subscriptions until April 28th, when defendant advised her by letter that the management had decided to abandon the contest in districts 3 and 4. Plaintiff resided in the latter district, but each contestant had the right to secure subscriptions anywhere without as well as within the district. At the time the contest was closed in district No. 4, on April 28th, plaintiff stood first in the number of subscriptions obtained and was entitled to more votes than any of her competitors. Each contestant failing to obtain one of the prizes was to secure a commission of 10 per cent. upon the amount turned in on subscriptions. Plaintiff alleged in her petition that on account of the termination and abandonment of the contest in district No. 4, she was deprived of a right to participate therein and win one of the prizes offered, and asks damages in the sum of $850.

Defendant in its answer admitted that a contest was begun as alleged, that plaintiff obtained subscriptions and forwarded $17 in cash to defendant, and that she was prevented by the discontinuance of the contest from further participation therein, but denied that she is entitled in any event to recover more than nominal damages. The court awarded her nominal damages, together with 10 per cent. of the amount received on subscriptions procured by her.

Reversing the trial court, the state supreme court held "that the question of damages was for the jury, and that the court erred in awarding nominal damages only." The court said:

> . . . If the situation thus shown continued to the end of the campaign, plaintiff was absolutely sure to win a prize, and, if she finished fifth, it would have been a $75 diamond ring. She had a chance, however, to win either the seven-passenger or $850 automobile. Was there, therefore, such uncertainty in the probabilities of plaintiff's winning a valuable prize as to limit her recovery, as a matter of law, to nominal damages?
>
> As already indicated, the defendant ostensibly terminated the contract because the participants in the contest showed a lack of interest, but doubtless primarily because it had become apparent that a continuance thereof was sure to result in financial loss. Had plaintiff finished first in the district contest, she would have earned an automobile worth $850. The right under the contract to do this was of some value, and, under the facts disclosed, she was practically certain to win one of the five best minor prizes. It should be further remembered that 50 valuable prizes in all were offered to the successful contestants. . . .
>
> Recoverable damages are often incapable of exact determination; i.e., damages for pain and suffering; permanent injuries, loss of profits. The measure of plaintiff's damages was the value of the contract, the value of the right to compete for one of the prizes offered. In estimating damages to be allowed, the jury would have a right to take into consideration the number, character, and value of the prizes offered, the number of contestants, the extent of territory covered by the contract, the standing of plaintiff at its termination, her reasonable probability, if shown, of winning some one of the prizes, and such other facts and circumstances as might reasonably bear thereon. There is, of necessity, much uncertainty as to what might have been the outcome of the contest, but the probabilities of plaintiff's winning a prize under the facts disclosed were not so uncertain, indefinite, and contingent as to limit her right of recovery, as a matter of law, to nominal damages only. The measure of her damages, as already indicated, was not the value of any one of the 50 prizes offered, because the jury would have no means of ascertaining which prize she would have won, if any. Apparently there was little probability, however, that she would have failed to win something. The contest was well along

toward its close at the time it was terminated, and the voting power of subscriptions decreased as it progressed.

PROBLEM

Farmer Brown owns a prize bull that stands a fair chance of winning the first, second, or third prize in the annual state fair competition. The first prize carries a $100,000 cash award, the second $75,000, and the third $50,000. In addition, the first-place winner stands to win a lot of commercial publicity that will redound to his owner's benefit. Counting Brown's bull, there are 20 bulls slated to enter the contest.

Brown contracts with Railroad to transport his bull to the state fair. Owing to negligent maintenance, Railroad's train is disabled en route to the fair and Brown's bull misses the competition as a result.

Can Brown recover for loss of a chance? How would he go about proving his damages?

E. MULTIPLE CAUSATION

BLACK v. ABEX CORP.
693 N.W.2d 182 (N.D. 1999)

KAPSNER, JUSTICE.

Rochelle Black appeals from a summary judgment dismissing her wrongful death and survival claims premised upon market share or alternative liability against numerous asbestos manufacturers. Concluding Black has failed to raise a genuine issue of material fact which would preclude summary judgment, we affirm.

Rochelle Black's husband, Markus, served in the Air Force as an auto mechanic from 1971 to 1986. He died of lung cancer in 1991. Black sued forty-eight asbestos manufacturers, alleging her husband's death had been caused by his occupational exposure to asbestos-containing products. Included in her complaint were claims based upon market share and alternative liability.

The defendants moved for partial summary judgment requesting dismissal of the market share and alternative liability claims. The court granted the motion for partial summary judgment and dismissed those claims in its Pretrial Order dated August 29, 1995.

Subsequently, all remaining claims against the defendants were either settled or voluntarily dismissed prior to the scheduled trial. On February 25, 1999, the court entered a "Concluding Order" covering this and several other consolidated asbestos cases, indicating all of the cases had been "fully and finally disposed of and the time for all appeals of this Court's orders and judgments in those cases has run." Black filed a notice of appeal from the Concluding Order and from the 1995 Pretrial Order granting the motion for summary judgment. . . .

Black asserts the district court erred in dismissing her claims based upon market share liability. She argues market share liability is a viable tort theory under North Dakota law and its application is appropriate under the facts of this case.

The genesis of market share liability lies in the California Supreme Court's decision in *Sindell v. Abbott Laboratories*, 26 Cal.3d 588, 163 Cal. Rptr. 132, 607 P.2d 924 (1980). In *Sindell*, the court held that women who suffered injuries resulting from their mothers' ingestion of the drug DES during pregnancy could sue DES manufacturers, even though the plaintiffs could not identify the specific manufacturer of the DES each of their respective mothers had taken. The court fashioned a new form of liability which relaxed traditional causation requirements, allowing a plaintiff to recover upon showing that she could not identify the specific manufacturer of the DES which caused her injury, that the defendants produced DES from an identical formula, and that the defendants manufactured a "substantial share" of the DES the plaintiff's mother might have taken. The court held each defendant would be liable for a proportionate share of the judgment based upon its share of the relevant market, unless it demonstrated it could not have made the product which caused the plaintiff's injury.

The essential elements of market share liability are summarized in W. Page Keeton et al., Prosser and Keeton on the Law of Torts, § 103, at 714 (5th ed.1984):

> The requirements for market-share liability seem to be: (1) injury or illness occasioned by a fungible product (identical-type product) made by all of the defendants joined in the lawsuit; (2) injury or illness due to a design hazard, with each having been found to have sold the same type product in a manner that made it unreasonably dangerous; (3) inability to identify the specific manufacturer of the product or products that brought about the plaintiff's injury or illness; and (4) joinder of enough of the manufacturers of the fungible or identical product to represent a substantial share of the market.

The overwhelming majority of courts which have addressed the issue have held market share liability is inappropriate in cases alleging injury from exposure to asbestos. . . . The most oft-cited rationale is that asbestos is not a fungible product, as evidenced by the wide variety of asbestos-containing products, the varying types and amounts of asbestos in those products, and the varying degrees of risk posed by those products. . . . The leading treatise recognizes:

> [I]t can reasonably be argued that it would not be appropriate to apply this fungible product concept to asbestos-containing products because they are by no means identical since they contain widely varying amounts of asbestos.

Prosser, supra, § 103, at 714.

Black essentially concedes market share liability is inappropriate in a "shotgun" asbestos case, where the plaintiff is alleging injury from exposure to many different types of asbestos products. Black asserts, however, market share liability may be appropriate when the plaintiff seeks to hold liable only manufacturers of one type of asbestos-containing product. Relying upon *Wheeler v. Raybestos-Manhattan*, 8 Cal. App.4th 1152, 11 Cal. Rptr.2d 109

(1992), Black asserts she should be allowed to proceed in her market share claims against the manufacturers of asbestos-containing "friction products," including brake and clutch products. In *Wheeler*, the California Court of Appeal held a plaintiff could proceed on a market share theory against manufacturers of asbestos-containing brake pads. The court overturned the trial court's order granting a nonsuit in favor of the manufacturers, concluding the plaintiff's offer of proof sufficiently alleged that the brake pads, although not identical, were "fungible" because they contained percentages of asbestos within a "restricted range" of between forty and sixty percent and posed nearly equivalent risks of harm.

Black requests that we recognize market share liability as a viable tort theory under North Dakota law. Black further requests that we follow *Wheeler* and hold that automotive "friction products," including asbestos-containing brake and clutch products, are sufficiently fungible to support a market share claim.

This Court has never addressed whether market share liability is recognized under North Dakota tort law. Other courts faced with the question have reached varying conclusions on the general availability of this novel remedy. See 1 Louis R. Frumer & Melvin I. Friedman, Products Liability § 3.06 [5] (1999); Richard E. Kaye, Annotation, "Concert of Activity," "Alternate Liability," "Enterprise Liability," or Similar Theory as Basis for Imposing Liability Upon One or More Manufacturers of Defective Uniform Product, in Absence of Identification of Manufacturer or Precise Unit or Batch Causing Injury, 63 A.L.R.5th 195 at § 4 (1998), and cases collected therein. We find it unnecessary to resolve this general issue because we conclude, assuming market share liability were recognized in this state, summary judgment was still appropriate based upon the record in this case.

The dispositive question presented is whether Black has raised a genuine issue of material fact on the issue of fungibility. Market share liability is premised upon the fact that the defendants have produced identical (or virtually identical) defective products which carry equivalent risks of harm. Accordingly, under the market share theory, it is considered equitable to apportion liability based upon the percentage of products each defendant contributed to the entire relevant market.

This reasoning hinges, however, upon each defendant's product carrying an equal degree of risk. As the Supreme Court of Oklahoma explained in *Case*, 743 P.2d at 1066:

> In the *Sindell* case, and those following it, it was determined that public policy considerations supporting recovery in favor of an innocent plaintiff against negligent defendants would allow the application of a theory of liability which shifted the burden of proof of causation from plaintiff to defendants. However, as previously stated, that theory was crafted in a situation where each potential defendant shared responsibility for producing a product which carried with it a singular risk factor. The theory further provided that each potential defendant's liability would be proportional to that defendant's contribution of risk to the market in which the plaintiff was injured. This situation thus provided a balance between the rights of the defendants and the

rights of the plaintiffs. A balance being achieved, public policy considerations were sufficient to justify the application of the market share theory of liability.

Similar reasoning was employed by the Supreme Court of Ohio in *Goldman*, 514 N.E.2d at 701.

Crucial to the *Sindell* court's reasoning was this fact: there was no difference between the risks associated with the drug as marketed by one company or another, and as all DES sold presented the same risk of harm, there was no inherent unfairness in holding the companies accountable based on their share of the DES market.

Numerous other courts have stressed the importance of a singular risk factor in market share cases. . . .

Unless the plaintiff can demonstrate that the defendants' products created a "singular risk factor," the balance between the rights of plaintiffs and defendants evaporates and it is no longer fair or equitable to base liability upon each defendant's share of the relevant market. The rationale underlying market share liability, as developed in *Sindell*, is that it did not matter which manufacturer's product the plaintiff's mother actually ingested; because all DES was chemically identical, the same harm would have occurred. Thus, any individual manufacturer's product would have caused the identical injury, and it was through mere fortuity that any one manufacturer did not produce the actual product ingested. Under these circumstances, viewing the overall DES market and all injuries caused thereby, it may be presumed each manufacturer's products will produce a percentage of those injuries roughly equivalent to its percentage of the total DES market. As the *Sindell* court recognized, "[u]nder this approach, each manufacturer's liability would approximate its responsibility for the injuries caused by its own products." 163 Cal. Rptr. 132, 607 P.2d at 937.

In order to prevail on its market share claims, Black would therefore have to demonstrate that the asbestos-containing "friction products" her husband was exposed to carried equivalent degrees of risk. Black asserts this problem has been "disposed of" by the holding in *Wheeler*. Although *Wheeler* recognized that non-identical products may give rise to market share liability if they contain roughly equivalent quantities of a single type of asbestos fiber, the court did not hold that all asbestos-containing friction brake products in all cases will be considered fungible. In fact, the court in *Wheeler* indicated that such products must carry a nearly equivalent risk of harm to support market share liability. 11 Cal. Rptr.2d at 111–12. Furthermore, *Wheeler* was a reversal of a nonsuit based upon an offer of proof made by the plaintiff. The court stressed its holding was narrow: the plaintiffs had not proven the elements of a market share case, but were merely being afforded the opportunity to prove it. Clearly, *Wheeler* does not serve as evidence of fungibility and equivalent risks of harm of the products in this case.

Black points to uncontroverted evidence in this record that the four remaining defendants produced friction products which contained between seven and seventy-five percent asbestos fibers. This is a far greater range than the forty to sixty percent the *Wheeler* court considered "roughly comparable" for purposes of fungibility under *Sindell*.³ *Wheeler*, 11 Cal. Rptr.2d at 111. It is closer to the fifteen to one-hundred percent range which the Supreme Court of Ohio held precluded market share liability as a matter of law. . . . It seems obvious that a product which contains seventy-five percent asbestos would create a greater risk of harm than one which contains only seven percent. . . . Absent introduction of expert evidence demonstrating that in spite of the differences the products would produce equivalent risks of harm, application of market share liability would be inappropriate.

Black failed to present competent, admissible evidence from which a fact finder could determine the "friction products" her husband was exposed to carried equivalent risks of harm and were fungible under *Sindell*. Accordingly, summary judgment was appropriate.

Black asserts the district court erred in dismissing her claims based upon alternative liability.

Alternative liability was first recognized by the Supreme Court of California in *Summers v. Tice*, 33 Cal.2d 80, 199 P.2d 1 (1948). In *Summers*, the plaintiff was struck by a shot fired by one of the defendants, who had simultaneously fired at a quail near the plaintiff. When the plaintiff could not prove which of the two negligently fired shots had struck him, the court shifted the burden of proving causation to the defendants. *Id.* at 3–4; see also W. Page Keeton et al., Prosser and Keeton on the Law of Torts, § 41 (5th ed.1984). The rule of *Summers* has been adopted in the Restatement (Second) of Torts § 433B(3):

> Where the conduct of two or more actors is tortious, and it is proved that harm has been caused to the plaintiff by only one of them, but there is uncertainty as to which one has caused it, the burden is upon each such actor to prove that he has not caused the harm.

This Court has not previously addressed whether alternative liability, as embodied in *Summers* and Section 433B(3), is recognized under North Dakota law. Courts addressing the issue have reached varying results. See Richard E. Kaye, Annotation, "Concert of Activity," "Alternate Liability," "Enterprise Liability," or Similar Theory as Basis for Imposing Liability Upon One or More Manufacturers of Defective Uniform Product, In Absence of Identification of Manufacturer of Precise Unit or Batch Causing Injury, 63 A.L.R.5th 195 at § 3 (1998), and cases collected therein. We find it unnecessary to resolve this general issue because we conclude, assuming alternative liability were recognized in this state, summary judgment was appropriate under the facts of this case.

As recognized by the Supreme Court of Texas in *Gaulding v. Celotex Corp.*, 772 S.W.2d 66, 69 (Tex.1989), "[a] crucial element to alternative liability is that all possible wrongdoers must be brought before the court." Thus, most courts addressing the issue have rejected application of alternative liability in asbestos cases. . . . As the court explained in *Lineaweaver v. Plant*

---

³ We also note the holding in *Wheeler* was limited to asbestos-containing brake pads. Black seeks to include a broader range of products—brake and clutch "friction products"—in her market share claims. Black has not drawn our attention to any evidence in this record demonstrating how, or if, the different nature and function of brake and clutch products affect their relative degree of risk.

Insulation Co., 31 Cal. App.4th 1409, 37 Cal. Rptr.2d 902, 907 (1995) (quoted in *Rutherford*, 67 Cal. Rptr.2d 16, 941 P.2d at 1220–21):

> Unlike *Summers*, there are hundreds of possible tortfeasors among the multitude of asbestos suppliers. As our Supreme Court has recognized, the probability that any one defendant is responsible for plaintiff's injury decreases with an increase in the number of possible tortfeasors. When there are hundreds of suppliers of an injury-producing product, the probability that any of a handful of joined defendants is responsible for plaintiff's injury becomes so remote that it is unfair to require defendants to exonerate themselves. The probability that an individual asbestos supplier is responsible for plaintiff's injury may also be decreased by the nature of the particular product. Asbestos products have widely divergent toxicities. Unlike the negligent hunters of *Summers*, all asbestos suppliers did not fire the same shot. Yet, under a burden shifting rule, all suppliers would be treated as if they subjected plaintiff to a hazard identical to that posed by other asbestos products.

Black does not assert she has included as defendants all possible manufacturers of the asbestos-containing brake and clutch "friction products" which her husband was exposed to during his lengthy career as a mechanic. Accordingly, alternative liability is inapplicable in this case.

The summary judgment dismissal of Black's market share and alternative liability claims is affirmed.

NOTES

1. *Identifying the Responsible Defendant.* How do the issues discussed in *Black*—alternative liability and market share liability—differ from those discussed in other cases in this chapter, specifically from *Anderson v. Minneapolis, St. P. & S.S.M. Ry. (supra)*, and *Piner v. Superior Court (infra)*?

2. *Unapportionable Fault and Alternative Liability.* In *Martin v. Owens-Corning Fiberglass Corp.*, 528 A.2d 947 (Pa. 1987), the court refused to apportion damages between defendant's asbestos product and plaintiff's smoking, because the evidence did not support such an apportionment. But such an apportionment was made in *Davler v. Raymark Indus., Inc.*, 611 A.2d 136 (N.J. App. Div. 1992), *aff'd* 622 A.2d 1305 (N.J. 1993):

> We conclude that there was ample basis in the record of this trial to submit the issue of apportionment to the jury. The extant legal precedent supports rational efforts to apportion responsibility in such circumstances rather than require one party to absorb the entire burden. The jury obviously accepted the epidemiological testimony based on relative risk factors, the smoking history over 45 years, and the substantial occupational exposure over six years. The synergistically resultant disease, lung cancer, was produced by a relative risk factor of 10:1 contributed by plaintiff and 5:1 contributed by defendant. The jury probably shaded the apportionment slightly in defendant's favor, 70% instead of two-thirds, because of the strong emphasis on

cigarette smoking as the greatly predominant overall cause of lung cancer in the country.

Would the result in *Summers* be the same in a jurisdiction that had abandoned joint and several liability in favor of several liability?

3. *Concert of Activity.* It is widely held that defendants are jointly liable if they act in concert. Why isn't *Black* a concert of activity case? Should it make a difference as to how many tortfeasors are acting in concert? How would you define concert of activity? *See* RESTATEMENT (SECOND) OF TORTS § 876. In one frequently cited, if not followed, early products liability case, *Hall v. E.I. Du Pont de Nemours & Co., Inc.,* 345 F.Supp. 353 (E.D. N.Y. 1972), the plaintiffs were 13 children who had been injured by explosion of blasting caps. The injuries had occurred in 12 different incidents in 10 different states. The defendants were six United states blasting cap manufacturers and their trade association. While the defendants represented virtually the entire domestic industry, there were also some Canadian manufacturers. The plaintiffs alleged that the defendants failed to provide a warning on individual blasting caps and did not otherwise take reasonable safety measures to prevent the plaintiffs' injuries. There was also evidence that the defendants adhered to an industry wide standard regarding certain safety aspects of their caps and had delegated certain safety functions, such as labeling, to the trade association. Under those circumstances, the court held that if the plaintiffs could prove that the injuring caps were manufactured by one of the defendants then the burden of proving (or disproving) causation would shift to the defendants who jointly controlled the risk.

Why doesn't *Summers* or *Hall* apply in a case like *Black*?

4. *The Market Share Theory.* As noted in *Black,* the seminal case on the defendant identification issue in products liability cases is *Sindell v. Abbott Labs.,* 26 Cal. 3d 588, 607 P.2d 924, 163 Cal. Rptr. 132 (1980), *cert. denied,* 449 U.S. 912 (1980). Exactly how does market share liability differ from alternative liability? Conceptually and operationally?

5. *The Mechanics of Market Share Liability.* In *Zafft v. Eli Lilly & Co.,* 676 S.W.2d 241 (Mo. 1984), Judge Gunn, in dissent, addressed not only some of the objections to the market share approach, but also some of the practical issues involved:

> The majority opinion notes the danger that if less than all of the manufacturers whose products may have been purchased by a plaintiff's mother are named as defendants, the responsible manufacturer may not be held liable and those who are named may pay more than their fair share. Nevertheless, the ability of manufacturers to interplead other manufacturers whose product accounted for a significant portion of the market reduces this risk, although certainly does not eliminate it. The "substantial share of the appropriate market" threshold in *Sindell* does no more than shift to defendants the hazard that certain manufacturers may be defunct or otherwise not amenable to suit.
>
> Furthermore, it is not clear whether the *Sindell* court intended to apportion plaintiff's damages based on a defendant's share of the

market relative to the other named defendants or a defendant's share of the market relative to all other manufacturers of DES. This latter approach would be more consistent with probability and more consistent with a theory of "apportionment of causation" as opposed to apportionment of fault. Such a scaling of liability in accordance with probability would vitiate the danger of proceeding against less than all of the manufacturers who may have manufactured the product which caused the harm and would render the "substantial share" threshold unnecessary.

The majority expresses concern that the *Sindell* court did not define the "relevant market" concept. It would seem that there are actually two different concepts of "relevant market" applicable to this situation. The first is a component of the threshold requirement that the named defendants together account for a substantial share of the relevant market, i.e., a substantial likelihood that their products were actually purchased and consumed by the DES mother. Since this threshold need not be a stringent one to meet, this likelihood could be demonstrated by fairly general proof regarding defendants' shares of the total amount of DES marketed. No great degree of specificity should be required of plaintiffs prior to discovery.

The second "relevant market" concept comes into being once plaintiff has survived a motion to dismiss. At that point the precise issue becomes the relative likelihood that the plaintiff's mother actually purchased the product manufactured by the individual defendant. The relevant market is the area of her residence, her drugstore, her pharmacist. While proof of this issue may be fraught with difficulty, it is a difficulty which is more appropriately borne by the manufacturers than by the plaintiffs—a legitimate concept in products liability. In either sense of the term, the "relevant market" is defined by the DES mother herself, the only real distinction being the means of proof used to describe that market.

The *Sindell* approach, applied in the context of modern apportionment of fault and third-party practice, affords a high degree of correlation between the individual manufacturer's share of the risk and its liability for damages. Quite apart from the evident policy concerns, this correlation (expressed in terms of probability) provides the justification for the presumption embodied in the shifting burden of proof.

6. *Insubstantial Shares.* In *Murphy v. E.R. Squibb & Sons,* 40 Cal. 3d 672, 221 Cal. Rptr. 447, 710 P.2d 247 (1985), the California Supreme Court affirmed a trial court ruling that 10 percent of the national market for DES was not a "substantial percentage" under *Sindell.* The court noted:

> Plaintiff, relying on general definitions of the word "substantial," asserts that the term must be defined in the context of a particular case, and since Squibb was alleged to be the second largest seller of DES in the country, its 10 percent market share must be deemed substantial in the framework of DES litigation.

We reject this contention because it is contrary to the theoretical justification underlying the market share doctrine. . . . We declined to apply an unmodified *Summers* rationale to the facts in *Sindell,* because only five of the two hundred manufacturers of the DES which could have harmed plaintiff were before the court, and therefore there was "no rational basis upon which to infer that any defendant in this action caused plaintiff's injuries, nor even a reasonable possibility that they were responsible." Instead, we concluded that the likelihood that one of the defendants supplied the DES should be determined not by the number of manufacturers joined in the action but by the percentage which the DES sold by each to prevent miscarriage bore to the entire production of the drug sold for that purpose. We held that if the plaintiff joined in the action the manufacturers of a substantial share of the DES which her mother might have taken, the injustice of shifting the burden of proof to defendants to exonerate themselves would be significantly diminished. We declined to declare a specific percentage of the market which would satisfy application of the doctrine, but stated only that it must be substantial.

Since Squibb had only a 10 percent share of the DES market, there is only a 10 percent chance that it produced the drug causing plaintiff's injuries, and a 90 percent chance that another manufacturer was the producer. In this circumstance, it must be concluded that she failed to meet the threshold requirement for the application of the market share doctrine.

7. *Sharing the National Market.* In *Hymowitz v. Eli Lilly & Co.,* 73 N.Y.2d 487, 541 N.Y.S.2d 941, 539 N.E.2d 1069 (1989), the court concluded:

. . . Turning to the structure to be adopted in New York, we heed both the lessons learned through experience in other jurisdictions and the realities of the mass litigation of DES claims in this State. Balancing these considerations, we are led to the conclusion that a market share theory, based upon a national market, provides the best solution. As California discovered, the reliable determination of any market smaller than the national one likely is not practicable. Moreover, even if it were possible, of the hundreds of cases in the New York courts, without a doubt there are many in which the DES that allegedly caused injury was ingested in another State. Among the thorny issues this could present, perhaps the most daunting is the specter that the particular case could require the establishment of a separate market share matrix. We feel that this is an unfair, and perhaps impossible burden to routinely place upon the litigants in individual cases.

. . . We are aware that the adoption of a national market will likely result in a disproportion between the liability of individual manufacturers and the actual injuries each manufacturer caused in this State. Thus our market share theory cannot be founded upon the belief that, over the run of cases, liability will approximate causation in this State. Nor does the use of a national market provide a reasonable link between liability and the risk created by a defendant to a particular plaintiff. Instead, we choose to apportion liability so as to correspond to the overall culpability of each defendant, measured by the amount of risk of injury each defendant created to the public at large. Use of a national market is a fair method, we believe, of apportioning defendants' liabilities according to their total culpability in marketing DES for use during pregnancy. Under the circumstances, this is an equitable way to provide plaintiffs with the relief they deserve, while also rationally distributing the responsibility for plaintiffs' injuries among defendants.

In *Enright v. Eli Lilly & Co.*, 568 N.Y.S.2d 550, 570 N.E.2d 198 (1991), the court held that a grandchild could not recover for injuries resulting from her grandmother's ingestion of DES. The line must be drawn somewhere, the court said. *Enright* was followed in *Grover v. Eli Lilly & Co.*, 591 N.E.2d 696 (Ohio 1992).

8. *Market Share Liability Beyond DES.* In *Hamilton v. Beretta U.S.A. Corp.*, 96 N.Y.2d 222, 750 N.E.2d 1055 (2001), plaintiffs, relatives of people killed by handguns, sued handgun manufacturers in Federal court. Eventually, seven plaintiffs went to trial against 25 of the manufacturers alleging negligent marketing (discussed in the next chapter). Only one of the guns was recovered and plaintiffs were permitted over defense objections to proceed on a market share theory of liability against all the manufacturers, asserting that they were severally liable for failing to implement safe marketing and distribution procedures, and that this failure sent a high volume of guns into the underground market. Responding to a certified question from the Court of Appeals for the Second Circuit the court stated:

> Market share liability provides an exception to the general rule that in common-law negligence actions, a plaintiff must prove that the defendant's conduct was a cause-in-fact of the injury. This Court first examined and adopted the market share theory of liability in Hymowitz v Eli Lilly & Co. (73 N.Y.2d 487, 541 N.Y.S.2d 941, 539 N.E.2d 1069, supra). In Hymowitz, we held that plaintiffs injured by the drug DES were not required to prove which defendant manufactured the drug that injured them but instead, every manufacturer would be held responsible for every plaintiff's injury based on its share of the DES market. Market share liability was necessary in Hymowitz because DES was a fungible product and identification of the actual manufacturer that caused the injury to a particular plaintiff was impossible. The Court carefully noted that the DES situation was unique. Key to our decision were the facts that (1) the manufacturers acted in a parallel manner to produce an identical, generically marketed product; (2) the manifestations of injury were far removed from the time of ingestion of the product; and (3) the Legislature made a clear policy decision to revive these time-barred DES claims (see, id., at 508).
>
> Circumstances here are markedly different. Unlike DES, guns are not identical, fungible products. Significantly, it is often possible to identify the caliber and manufacturer of the handgun that caused injury to a particular plaintiff. Even more importantly — given the negligent marketing theory on which plaintiffs tried this case —

plaintiffs have never asserted that the manufacturers' marketing techniques were uniform. Each manufacturer engaged in different marketing activities that allegedly contributed to the illegal handgun market in different ways and to different extents. Plaintiffs made no attempt to establish the relative fault of each manufacturer, but instead sought to hold them all liable based simply on market share.

In Hymowitz, each manufacturer engaged in tortious conduct parallel to that of all other manufacturers, creating the same risk to the public at large by manufacturing the same defective product. Market share was an accurate reflection of the risk they posed. Here, the distribution and sale of every gun is not equally negligent, nor does it involve a defective product. Defendants engaged in widely-varied conduct creating varied risks. Thus, a manufacturer's share of the national handgun market does not necessarily correspond to the amount of risk created by its alleged tortious conduct. No case has applied the market share theory of liability to such varied conduct and wisely so.

We recognize the difficulty in proving precisely which manufacturer caused any particular plaintiff's injuries since crime guns are often not recovered. Inability to locate evidence, however, does not alone justify the extraordinary step of applying market share liability (see Healey v Firestone Tire & Rubber Co., 87 N.Y.2d 596, 601, 640 N.Y.S.2d 860, 663 N.E.2d 901 [loss of an allegedly defective multi-piece truck tire rim which caused the plaintiff's injuries did not obviate the requirement that the plaintiff identify its exact manufacturer]; see also Matter of New York State Silicone Breast Implant Litigation, 166 Misc 2d 85, 90, 631 N.Y.S.2d 491 [refusal to apply market share liability to silicone breast implants; "(t)he reality of a plaintiff's plight when product identification cannot be made is like any other plaintiff who claims injury from a product that has been lost or destroyed"], affd for reasons stated 234 A.D.2d 28. Rather, a more compelling policy reason — as was shown in the DES cases — is required for the imposition of market share liability.

Notably, courts in New York and other jurisdictions have refused to extend the market share theory where products were not fungible and differing degrees of risk were created (see, e.g., Brenner v American Cyanamid Co., 263 A.D.2d 165, 699 N.Y.S.2d 848 [lead pigment used in paint]; Matter of New York State Silicone Breast Implant Litigation, supra [silicone breast implants]; DaSilva v American Tobacco Co.. 175 Misc 2d 424, 667 N.Y.S.2d 653 [cigarettes]; see also Sanderson v International Flavors & Fragrances, Inc., 950 F. Supp. 981 [CD Cal 1996] [perfumes containing different aldehydes]; Doe v Cutter Biological, 852 F. Supp. 909 [D. Idaho 1994] [blood clotting agent]; 210 East 86th Street Corp. v Combustion Eng'g. Inc., 821 F. Supp. 125 [SDNY 1993] [asbestos]; Skipworth v Lead Indus. Ass'n, Inc., 547 Pa. 224, 690 A.2d 169 [Pa 1997] [lead paint pigments]). Similarly, plaintiffs here have not shown a set of compelling circumstances akin to those in Hymowitz justifying a departure from traditional common-law principles of causation. . . .

9. *Joint and Several Liability.* In *Brown v. Superior Court,* 44 Cal. 3d 1049, 245 Cal. Rptr. 412, 751 P.2d 470 (1988), the Supreme Court of California examined whether joint and several liability applied in a market share case:

> If such defendants are jointly and severally liable, a plaintiff may recover the entire amount of the judgment from any of the defendants joined in the action. Since the plaintiff is required under *Sindell* to join the manufacturers of only a substantial share of the appropriate market for DES, it follows that if joint liability were the rule, a defendant could be held responsible for a portion of the judgment that may greatly exceed the percentage of its market share. Under several liability, in contrast, because each defendant's liability for the judgment would be confined to the percentage of its share of the market, a plaintiff would not recover the entire amount of the judgment (except in the unlikely event that all manufacturers were joined in the action) but only the percentage of the sum awarded that is equal to the market shares of the defendants joined in the action. In the one case, it would be the plaintiff who would bear the loss resulting from the fact that some producers of DES that might have been found liable under the market share theory were not joined in the action (or if a defendant became insolvent), whereas in the other such losses would fall on the defendants. Since, as we pointed out in *Sindell,* there is little likelihood that all manufacturers of DES in the appropriate market would be amenable to suit, the adoption of one or the other basis for liability could significantly affect the amount of a plaintiff's recovery and, concomitantly, a defendant's liability.
>
> . . . It is apparent that the imposition of joint liability on defendants in a market share action would be inconsistent with [the *Sindell*] rationale. Any defendant could be held responsible for the entire judgment even though its market share may have been comparatively insignificant. Liability would in the first instance be measured not by the likelihood of responsibility for the plaintiff's injuries but by the financial ability of a defendant to undertake payment of the entire judgment or a large portion of it. A defendant that paid a larger percentage of the judgment than warranted by its market share would have the burden of seeking indemnity from other defendants, and it would bear the loss if producers of DES that might have been held liable in the action were not amenable to suit, or if a codefendant was bankrupt. In short, the imposition of joint liability among defendant manufacturers in a market share action would frustrate *Sindell*'s goal of achieving a balance between the interests of DES plaintiffs and manufacturers of the drug.
>
> [Plaintiff] suggests that if we conclude that joint liability is not appropriate, each defendant's liability should be 'inflated' in proportion to its market share in an amount sufficient to assure that plaintiff would recover the entire amount of the judgment. While this ingenious approach would not be as unjust to defendants as joint liability, we decline to adopt the proposal because it would nonetheless represent a retreat from *Sindell*'s attempt to achieve as close an approximation

as possible between a DES manufacturer's liability for damages and its individual responsibility for the injuries caused by the products it manufactured.

10. *Other Approaches to Market Share Liability.* The Wisconsin Supreme Court, in *Collins v. Eli Lilly Co.,* 116 Wis.2d 166, 342 N.M.2d 37 (1984), tied liability not to market share but held that each defendant would be liable in proportion to the amount of risk that it created. Washington, in *Martin v. Abbott Labs*, 102 Wash.2d 581, 689 P.2d 368 (1984), adopted a complex version of market share liability in which defendants were allowed to exculpate themselves form liability but unexculpated defendants were presumed to have equal market shares, totaling 100%. Thereafter, unexculpated defendants could rebut the presumption that their market shares were equal. *See also George v. Parke-Davis*, 107 Wash.2d 584, 733 P.2d 507 (1987).

PROBLEM

A and B, manufacturers, both discharge acidic gases into the air. C's property is damaged by acidic gases similar to those discharged by A and B. Does subsection (2) or (3) of RESTATEMENT (SECOND) OF TORTS § 433B apply? Does it make a difference which applies? Are more facts needed to determine whether either subsection applies?

F. TOXIC TORT CAUSATION ISSUES

BOCKRATH v. ALDRICH CHEMICAL CO., INC.,
21 Cal.4th 71, 980 P.2d 398, 86 Cal. Rptr.2d 846 (1999)

MOSK, ACTING C.J.

. . . Plaintiff, now deceased, contracted multiple myeloma, a form of cancer, while working at Hughes Aircraft Company from January 1973 to March 1994. His suit named at least 55 defendants, including the manufacturers of common products such as WD-40 and rubber cement, and he alleged that the disease arose through his exposure to harmful substances in their products. His second amended complaint, at issue here, contained causes of action for negligence, strict liability for failure to warn and for design defect, ultra hazardous activity, fraudulent concealment, breach of warranty, and battery.

In his complaint, which is long, rambling, and detailed, plaintiff alleged that he believed he and his immediate coworkers used "most, and perhaps all, of the . . . products." Through his and his immediate coworkers' use, he believed he inhaled and had direct skin contact with "most and perhaps all" of them. As for the others, plaintiff alleged he believed that because "all" of the products were used or improperly stored somewhere at the Hughes plant and circulated by its ventilation system, the environment contained "all" of them, and he inhaled or had skin contact with "all" of them. He further alleged that "the foregoing chemicals and chemical ingredients . . . [produce] carcinogenic effects."

Plaintiff continued: "Upon reaching the internal organs of Plaintiff's body, including but not limited to the liver and spleen, the foregoing chemicals and

F. TOXIC TORT CAUSATION ISSUES

chemical products were transformed by metabolic processes, resulting in the formation of toxic metabolites, free radicals, and residual unmetabolized products, by various complex biological mechanisms. . . . Upon being so metabolized, residual unreacted products, toxic metabolites, free radicals and other chemicals resulting from metabolic processes migrated to the bone marrow, where such products, by products, and toxic metabolites caused hemotoxic, hematotoxic, immunotoxic, genotoxic and carcinogenic injuries to the blood and blood-forming organs within Plaintiff's bones, thereby initiating and/or promoting the development of Plaintiff's multiple myeloma and other related and consequential injuries, which will be further established and clarified according to proof at the time of trial."

In discussing the first amended complaint, which was also prolix, the trial court stated: "This complaint is extremely vague, very broad and very global. You have to be very specific as to each defendant and as to each chemical and causation issue. It is not here. It is a global claim. Everybody is responsible for your client's medical problem, but we don't know which defendant and we don't know which chemical it is. We have no idea in terms of causation." The trial court rejected plaintiff's argument that "[w]e have alleged [that] every one of these defendants and every one of these defendants' products caused the disease. That is all we have to do on demurrer. We don't have to prove the case in the demurrer hearing. The case law is quite clear . . . . that causation may be generally pled[,] meaning [that] to adequately plead a cause of action the element of causation simply needs to state that the defendants caused the injury."

Certain defendants demurred to the second amended complaint, and the court renewed its criticism, decided that plaintiff had stated as strong a case as he could, and sustained the demurrers of two defendants without leave to amend. It took the others' demurrers off calendar, ruling that they were moot following its order. Later it entered judgment in all defendants' favor. The Court of Appeal affirmed.

In the ordinary personal injury lawsuit, in which the complaint's factual recitations show plainly the connection between cause and effect, it suffices to plead causation succinctly and generally. . . . The pleading requirements in such a case are unlike those of certain suits in which pleading with particularity is required, such as suits claiming fraud . . . or, as a rule, asserting statutory causes of action . . . .

But when, by contrast, " 'the pleaded facts of negligence and injury do not naturally give rise to an inference of causation[,] the plaintiff must plead specific facts affording an inference the one caused the other.' " (*Christensen v. Superior Court*, (1991) 54 Cal.3d 868, 900–901, 2 Cal. Rptr.2d 79, 820 P.2d 181.) That is, the plaintiff must allege facts, albeit as succinctly as possible, explaining how the conduct caused or contributed to the injury. . .

Defendants may be understood to contend that plaintiff has failed to satisfy *Christensen's* requirement.

. . .Though we regard the complaint as poorly drafted, and it appears to be internally inconsistent in places, we understand plaintiff to be attempting to allege that defendants' products cause cancer, he was exposed to them, and they migrated to his internal organs and caused his multiple myeloma. In sum, each defendant manufactured a chemical product that, as used or foreseeably misused, caused injury.

In light of *Rutherford v. Owens-Illinois, Inc.* (1997) 16 Cal.4th 953, 67 Cal. Rptr.2d 16, 941 P.2d 1203, the foregoing allegations were insufficient. But that is understandable, given that the parties disputed the complaint's sufficiency more than a year before we filed *Rutherford*. We will remand the cause to give plaintiff an opportunity to allege, if he can properly do so (*see post*, 86 Cal. Rptr.2d at pp. 405–406, 980 P.2d at pp. 853–854), that each defendant's product was a substantial factor, as that term is defined in *Rutherford*, in causing his multiple myeloma. Specifically:

(1) Plaintiff must allege that he was exposed to each of the toxic materials claimed to have caused a specific illness. An allegation that he was exposed to "most and perhaps all" of the substances listed is inadequate.

(2) He must identify each product that allegedly caused the injury. It is insufficient to allege that the toxins in defendants' products caused it.

(3) He must allege that as a result of the exposure, the toxins entered his body.

(4) He must allege that he suffers from a specific illness, and that each toxin that entered his body was a substantial factor in bringing about, prolonging, or aggravating that illness.

(5) Finally, except in a case (unlike this one) governed by the principle of liability based on market share for a uniform product that we outlined in *Sindell v. Abbott Laboratories* (1980) 26 Cal.3d 588, 612, 163 Cal. Rptr. 132, 607 P.2d 924, he must allege that each toxin he absorbed was manufactured or supplied by a named defendant.

. . . Plaintiffs who know more should, of course, allege additional facts that are important in apprising the defendant of the basis for the claim. The complaint quoted in *Haun v. Tally* (1919) 40 Cal. App. 585, 181 P. 81, is an example. In *Haun* the plaintiff alleged personal injury because a negligently installed overhead fan fell on him. He alleged the additional fact that a form of pressure caused the fan to dislodge. (*Id.* at pp. 586–587, 181 P. 81.) But he "did not attempt to particularize what the defects in the fan were" (*id.* at p. 588, 181 P. 81) that permitted the pressure to separate it from its motor. Again, plaintiffs should allege any additional facts succinctly. . . .

That brings us to the Court of Appeal's conclusion that the demurrer must also be sustained without leave to amend because plaintiff admitted in discovery that he was unable to identify which products had caused his injury. It is true, as the Court of Appeal observed, that a complaint's allegations may be disregarded when they conflict with judicially noticed discovery responses. (*Del E. Webb Corp. v. Structural Materials Co.* (1981) 123 Cal. App.3d 593, 604, 176 Cal. Rptr. 824.)

Justice Godoy Perez disagreed with this portion of the Court of Appeal's analysis. She explained, regarding one defendant: "[Plaintiff's] interrogatory responses . . . contended that exposure to benzene in Sanford's rubber cement was a cause of his myeloma. Read in this context, and considering that expert medical and scientific evidence would be required to prove [his] case, his lack of personal knowledge regarding the precise mechanism by which this occurred should not be viewed as an admission that he cannot identify which specific products caused his injuries."

We agree with Justice Godoy Perez's conclusion. Five defendants asked plaintiff, in interrogatories, to provide a "verified, legally sufficient response[]" to this question: "For each . . . product which you contend caused your multiple myeloma, identify the mechanism" by which it occurred. Each interrogatory defined mechanism as "the physical or chemical process [by] which a certain effect is obtained."

To each defendant, plaintiff answered that he did not personally know how its product caused his illness. He also told defendant American Cyanamid Company that he was "unaware of the identities of any persons who have such knowledge," defendant Cytec Industries, Inc., that he had no "training as a physician or toxicologist" and could not explain the etiology of his illness, and defendants Ciba-Geigy Corporation, Mallinckrodt Chemical, Inc., and J.T. Baker, Inc., that the "only information possibly available . . . which would be responsive to this interrogatory would be the medical and scientific research undertaken by [his] attorneys, which information is privileged. . . ." The record shows that he answered other defendants' questions in the same or similar language.

Plaintiff's admissions may be read only to acknowledge that he did not personally know the precise mechanism that caused his cancer and that he did not personally know the identity of those who would know. As his counsel explains in his brief to this court, plaintiff was a physicist, "not a medical toxicologist, and therefore lacked personal knowledge how [defendants'] chemical products caused his cancer." "That [he] lacked [this] personal knowledge . . . in no way constituted an admission that expert medical testimony could not be provided to establish causation at trial." In sum, the answers are irrelevant with regard to the objective mechanisms that allegedly caused his illness, and invoking them against the complaint cannot succeed.

Defendants also rely on *Setliff v. E.I. Du Pont de Nemours & Co.* (1995), 32 Cal. App.4th 1525, 38 Cal. Rptr.2d 763. *Setliff*, however, is unhelpful to them. In that case, a paint store employee sued 40 makers of paint, glue, strippers, and solvents, for injuring him. Setliff judicially admitted that he could not identify which of the products injured him, and the Court of Appeal concluded that his inability to do so left him unable to allege causation. (*Id.* at pp. 1533–1534, 38 Cal. Rptr.2d 763.) In this case, as distinguished from *Setliff*, plaintiff did identify the products that allegedly injured him. He only admitted that he could not state the precise mechanism by which they caused his illness.

The judgment of the Court of Appeal is reversed and the cause is remanded to that court with directions to remand the matter to the trial court for further proceedings consistent with this opinion.

NOTES

1. *Toxic Torts*. As a shorthand, cases in which the plaintiffs allege her exposure to some substance has caused injury or disease may be referred to as toxic torts.

2. *Causation in Toxic Tort Cases. Bockrath* and *Black* point out some of the causation issues that arise in toxic tort cases. Traditional tort law was not well equipped to deal with these problems. Has tort law adequately adjusted its rules as to causation?

3. *Toxic Tort Claims.* In addition to claims for medical expenses, lost wages or earning capacity, pain and suffering, mental anguish, and loss of enjoyment of life, plaintiffs in toxic tort cases may seek other types of damages or make other claims, including fear of developing a disease in the future, increased risk of developing some adverse health condition, and medical monitoring.

4. *Fear of Developing a Disease.* Should a person be allowed to recover for their fear of developing a disease in the future because of an exposure to a substance that has already occurred. We will consider this issue in Chapter 9.

5. *Increased Risk.* What if, as a result of exposure to a toxic substance, the plaintiff has a 20% chance of developing a disease in the future? Should that increased risk be compensable? If it is and the plaintiff subsequently develops the disease, should the later claim be barred by the earlier recovery? Would the later claim be time barred under the statute of limitations?

What if the plaintiff did develop the disease but the evidence establishes that 1 in 10 people get the disease without exposure to the substance? 3 in 10? What if the plaintiff was a smoker and the evidence is that 5 in 10 smokers develop the disease but that 8 in 10 smokers who are exposed to the toxic substance to which plaintiff was exposed develop the disease?

6. *Medical Monitoring.* Many plaintiffs who are exposed to a toxic substance that might cause some future adverse health consequences seek to recover medical monitoring damages-the costs of medical testing and monitoring to determine if the disease has developed. The purpose of medical monitoring is to encourage early detection of the relevant disease, treatment, and minimization of the health risks associated with the disease. Several courts have recognized the claim. *See, e.g., Ayers v. Township of Jackson*, 106 N.J. 557, 525 A.2d 287 (1987). There the court said:

> . . . The claim for medical surveillance expenses stands on a different footing from the claim based on enhanced risk. It seeks to recover the cost of periodic medical examinations intended to monitor plaintiffs' health and facilitate early diagnosis and treatment of disease caused by plaintiffs' exposure to toxic chemicals. At trial, competent medical testimony was offered to prove that a program of regular medical testing and evaluation was reasonably necessary and consistent with contemporary scientific principles applied by physicians experienced in the diagnosis and treatment of chemically-induced injuries.
>
> . . . Recognition of pre-symptom claims for medical surveillance serves other important public interests. The difficulty of proving causation, where the disease is manifested years after exposure, has caused many commentators to suggest that tort law has no capacity to deter polluters, because the costs of proper disposal are often viewed by polluters as exceeding the risk of tort liability. However, permitting

recovery for reasonable pre-symptom, medical-surveillance expenses subjects polluters to significant liability when proof of the causal connection between the tortious conduct and the plaintiffs' exposure to chemicals is likely to be most readily available. The availability of a substantial remedy before the consequences of the plaintiffs' exposure are manifest may also have the beneficial effect of preventing or mitigating serious future illnesses and thus reduce the overall costs to the responsible parties.

Other considerations compel recognition of a pre-symptom medical surveillance claim. It is inequitable for an individual, wrongfully exposed to dangerous toxic chemicals but unable to prove that disease is likely, to have to pay his own expenses when medical intervention is clearly reasonable and necessary. In other contexts, we have intervened to provide compensation for medical expenses even where the underlying disease was not compensable. In *Procanik v. Cillo,* 97 N.J. 339, 478 A.2d 755 (1984), an action for "wrongful birth," we allowed compensation for medical expenses but disallowed the claims for pain and suffering and for a diminished childhood attributable to birth defects. In *Schroeder v. Perkel,* 87 N.J. 53, 432 A.2d 834 (1981), we upheld the claim of parents for incremental medical costs associated with raising a child who suffered from cystic fibrosis, without recognizing a "wrongful birth" cause of action based on that condition.

. . . In our view, the use of a court-supervised fund to administer medical-surveillance payments in mass exposure cases, particularly for claims under the Tort Claims Act, is a highly appropriate exercise of the Court's equitable powers. *Cf. In re "Agent Orange" Prod. Liab. Litig.,* 611 F. Supp. 1396 (E.D. N.Y. 1985) at 1402–03 (since "implementation of any distribution plan based on traditional tort principles is impossible because of a virtual absence of proof of causation," it was appropriate to consider "alternate methods of distributing [the] settlement fund [that] may be premised on a rationale similar to the cy pres doctrine of testamentary interpretation.") Such a mechanism offers significant advantages over a lump-sum verdict. . . . For Tort Claims Act cases, it provides a method for offsetting a defendant's liability by payments from collateral sources. Although the parties in this case sharply dispute the availability of insurance coverage for surveillance-type costs, a fund could provide a convenient method for establishing credits in the event insurance benefits were available for some, if not all, of the plaintiffs.

In addition, a fund would serve to limit the liability of defendants to the amount of expenses actually incurred. A lump-sum verdict attempts to estimate future expenses, but cannot predict the amounts that actually will be expended for medical purposes. Although conventional damage awards do not restrict plaintiffs in the use of money paid as compensatory damages, mass-exposure toxic-tort cases involve public interests not present in conventional tort litigation. The public health interest is served by a fund mechanism that encourages regular medical monitoring for victims of toxic exposure. Where public entities are defendants, a limitation of liability to amounts actually expended for medical surveillance tends to reduce insurance costs and taxes, objectives consistent with the legislature's admonition to avoid recognition of novel causes of action.

. . . However, we decline to upset the jury verdict awarding medical-surveillance damages in this case. Such a result would be unfair to these plaintiffs, since the medical-surveillance issue was tried conventionally, and neither party requested the trial court to withhold from the jury the power to return a lump-sum verdict for each plaintiff in order that relief by way of a fund could be provided. Moreover, the jury verdict for medical-surveillance damages was based, as was the verdict for plaintiffs' other claims, on various factors distinguishing the individual plaintiffs, including age, and duration and extent of exposure to toxic chemicals. Accordingly, the verdict for medical-surveillance damages was in a specific amount for each of the plaintiffs, thereby limiting in this case the applicability of the fund concept, which contemplates an aggregate lump-sum award available to reimburse the medical-surveillance expenses of any plaintiff, without the constraint of individually-allocated limitations. We also recognize that the fund mechanism that we now endorse in toxic-tort cases is novel and represents a sharp break with our prevailing practice. In such circumstances, we have previously recognized the wisdom of limiting the application of a new rule of law or confining its application only to matters that arise after the rule has been announced. Under the circumstances, we think it would be inappropriate to impose this effective but novel procedure on these litigants at this late stage in litigation that has already been protracted and extensive. Accordingly, the judgment of the Appellate Division setting aside the jury verdict for medical surveillance damages is reversed and the jury verdict is reinstated. [The court denied recovery for emotional distress as not recoverable under the N.J. Tort Claims Act, but allowed recovery for deterioration of the quality of life as in the nature of damages for nuisance.]

In *Metro-North Commuter Railroad Company, Inc. v. Buckley*, 521 U.S. 424 (1997), the United States Supreme Court reversed a lump sum award for medical monitoring where the lower court had given no consideration to relevant available insurance.

In *Bourgeois v. A.P. Green Industries, Inc.*, 716 So.2d 355 (La. 1998), the Louisiana Supreme Court in a carefully analyzed and worded decision recognized a claim for medical monitoring. It said, in relevant part.

After consideration of the law in both Louisiana and other states, we are persuaded that the reasonable cost of medical monitoring is a compensable item of damage under Civil Code article 2315, provided that a plaintiff satisfies the following criteria: . . .

(1) Significant exposure to a proven hazardous substance. Exposure, as used in this factor, means ingestion, inhalation, injection or absorption into the body by some other means. . . .. Such exposure must be significant in intensity and/or duration, meaning that a plaintiff must

prove exposure greater than normal background levels. . . . In addition, the substance to which a plaintiff is exposed must have been proven hazardous to human health.

(2) As a proximate result of this exposure, plaintiff suffers a significantly increased risk of contracting a serious latent disease. No particular level of quantification is necessary to satisfy the requirement of increased risk. . . . The injury in question is plaintiff's demonstrated need for medical monitoring and the costs which correspond to such care. Hence, plaintiff need not prove a certain probability of actually suffering physical harm because of his or her exposure. It is sufficient that plaintiff show a significant degree of increased risk. . . . In addition, plaintiff must prove that the illness, the risk of which has been increased by exposure, is both serious and latent. By this we mean an illness that is dormant and that, in its ordinary course, may result in significant impairment or death. . . .

(3) Plaintiff's risk of contracting a serious latent disease is greater than (a) the risk of contracting the same disease had he or she not been exposed and (b) the chances of members of the public at large of developing the disease. This factor serves to ensure that plaintiff's need for medical monitoring is a result of his or her exposure to the particular hazardous substance at issue. It further serves to ensure that exposures suffered by the public at large, which increase the entire population's risk of disease, do not form the basis of medical monitoring claims.

(4) A monitoring procedure exists that makes the early detection of the disease possible. If no such test exists, then periodic monitoring is of no assistance and the cost of such monitoring is not recoverable. If a test is later developed that will detect the disease, plaintiff would retain the right to demonstrate the effectiveness of the test and be compensated for utilizing it, assuming plaintiff can satisfy the other elements of the damage proof. . . .

(5) The monitoring procedure has been prescribed by a qualified physician and is reasonably necessary according to contemporary scientific principles. Plaintiff must show that administration of the diagnostic test is medically advisable for him or her specifically. . . . This factor conforms with the fact that the injury being remedied is the plaintiff's incurrence of medical monitoring expenses. Absent the advisability of monitoring for a specific individual, the associated costs should not be recoverable. . . . In addition, plaintiff must show that the testing is of a type that a reasonable physician in the area of specialty would order for a similarly situated patient. . . . This dual requirement prevents recovery for costs of treatment not generally accepted by the medical community.

(6) The prescribed monitoring regime is different from that normally recommended in the absence of exposure. Plaintiff must demonstrate that his or her increased risk of disease warrants medical monitoring beyond that which an individual should pursue as a matter of general

good sense and foresight. Thus, there can be no recovery for preventative medical care and checkups to which members of the public at large should prudently submit.

(7) There is some demonstrated clinical value in the early detection and diagnosis of the disease. In order to fully establish medical monitoring expenses as a cognizable damage under Article 2315, plaintiff must show that there is some medical benefit to be gained through early detection of the disease. In other words, plaintiff must show that an existing treatment, administered before the illness becomes apparent to a layperson, is effective in curing or ameliorating the consequences of the illness. . . . Unless such a treatment is available, then there is nothing for plaintiff to gain from a hastened diagnosis and the cost of such testing is not recoverable.

Finally, to ensure that only meritorious claims are compensated, plaintiff's recovery of medical monitoring costs must be both reasonable and limited in duration to the maximum latency period (if known) of the diseases for which there is an increased risk.

The legislature acted quickly to overrule *Bourgeois*. La. Civ. Code Article 2315, the source of all tort liability in Louisiana's civil code, now provides, in part:

Damages do not include costs for future medical treatment, services, surveillance, or procedures of any kind unless such treatment, services, surveillance, or procedures are directly related to a manifest physical or mental injury or disease.

Presumably if the plaintiff develops the disease the cost of monitoring would then be recoverable. What if the plaintiff developed the disease and sued for damages arising as a result of the disease and the defendant argues that the failure to seek medical monitoring made the condition worse than it would otherwise have been? How does the Code article affect the resolution of that argument?

Is the medical monitoring issue a cause-in-fact question at all?

PROBLEM

XYZ, Inc. is in the business of residential and commercial weed control. XYZ bought almost identical chemical formulations of a certain herbicide from various manufacturers. XYZ mixed the herbicides in large vats and then distributed the mixture to its employees who applied it at XYZ's customers' homes and places of business.

Various XYZ employees and customers have now filed suit against all American herbicide manufacturers alleging that as a result of their exposure to herbicide they have developed lung cancer, colon cancer, fear of developing cancer, increased risk of developing cancer, and the need to seek medical monitoring. What issues arise?

G. MULTIPLE CAUSATION AND MULTIPLE TORTFEASORS

PINER v. SUPERIOR COURT
192 Ariz. 182, 962 P.2d 909 (1999)

FELDMAN, JUSTICE.

On his way to work on Friday, October 12, 1990, William Piner stopped his truck to let a pedestrian cross the street. While he was stopped, a car driven by Billy Jones hit Piner's truck from behind. Police were called to investigate the incident. Piner waited for the police to finish their investigation before calling his physician to complain of pain in his neck, upper back, left arm, and head. The doctor's staff told Piner that the doctor was unavailable but would call him back later that day. Piner then fixed the broken tail lights on his truck and went to work.

Later that day, Piner was driving to lunch when the car ahead of him stopped to let some pedestrians cross the street. Piner stopped and was again hit from the rear, this time by a vehicle driven by Cynthia Richardson. Feeling similar pain symptoms after this accident, Piner called his doctor's office and was again told that the doctor was occupied and would contact him later.

Piner was unable to see his physician until Monday. After examination, the doctor concluded that Piner suffered a number of injuries as a result of the collisions. Due to the nature of the injuries, however, neither she nor any other physician has been able to attribute any particular part of Piner's total injuries to one accident or the other.

Piner filed an action against Jones and Richardson (together "Defendants") alleging indivisible injuries resulting from the successive impacts. Neither defendant has asserted that he or she could apportion the particular physical harm Piner suffered between the separate accidents. Apparently, all parties agree that both collisions contributed to Piner's total physical injuries.

Piner moved for partial summary judgment, arguing that because his injuries are indivisible, Defendants should be held jointly and severally liable. See Holtz v. Holder, 101 Ariz. 247, 418 P.2d 584 (1966). According to Piner, in a successive accident, indivisible injury case, defendants have the burden of proving apportionment; if neither defendant can demonstrate what portion of the total damage he or she caused, they should be held jointly and severally liable for the entire amount.

Richardson responded that A.R.S. § 12-2506 abolished the system of joint and several liability, leaving only two exceptions in which the doctrine can still be invoked. See A.R.S. § 12-2506(D) and (F). Richardson concluded that because neither exception applied to Piner's claim, "the trier of fact must be directed to either apportion, or deny damages in this case." After hearing oral argument on the motion, the trial judge, in a June 4, 1996 order, denied Piner's motion for "the reasons stated [by] Defendant Richardson. . . ."

When the parties met later for a pretrial conference with the newly assigned trial judge, the main issue in contention was what effect should be given the prior ruling denying Piner's motion for partial summary judgment on the issue of apportionment. Judge Hilliard stated that the previous ruling bound her to instruct the jury that Piner had the burden of proving apportionment of damages between the two collisions and that if he did not meet this burden, Piner could not recover. Recognizing the potentially devastating effect on Piner's case, the judge granted a continuance to allow Piner to file a special action in the nature of mandamus or prohibition to determine the propriety of the earlier ruling on apportionment. . . .The court of appeals declined jurisdiction of Piner's special action. We granted review to determine which rule of liability applies to cases in which successive acts of negligence combine to produce separate but indivisible injuries.

Black-letter tort law tells us that as an essential element of the action, the plaintiff must provide evidence that the defendant's conduct caused plaintiff's damage. W. PAGE KEETON ET AL., PROSSER & KEETON ON THE LAW OF TORTS § 41, at 263 (5th ed.1984). A plaintiff's case failed if that plaintiff was unable to establish the damage attributable to a defendant's conduct. *See id.* The law eventually recognized an exception for multiple, culpable actors if the plaintiff, through no fault of his own, was unable to apportion causation for a single injury. In such instances, many courts placed the "burden of proof on the issue of causation [apportionment] upon the . . . defendants. . . . [This] seems a very desirable solution where negligence on the part of both defendants is clear, and it is only the issue of causation which is in doubt, so that the choice must be made between letting a loss due to failure of proof fall upon the innocent plaintiff or the culpable defendants." *Id.* at 271.

The present case involves a somewhat different problem. Instead of producing a single injurious event, Defendants' successive acts of negligence resulted in two injuries yielding an indivisible result. The question nevertheless is causation, a concept that presents a "series of distinct problems, more or less unrelated" but includes "apportionment of damages among causes." *Id.* § 42, at 279.

Differentiating between doctrines involving joint tortfeasors acting in concert and joinder of defendants, Prosser's treatise approaches apportionment of damages as a separate topic. *See id.* §§ 46 and 47, at 322–30. The apportionment question arises not only in successive injury cases but every time the total damage results from multiple causes:

> Once it is determined that defendant's conduct has been a cause of some damage suffered by the plaintiff, a further question may arise as to the portion of the total damage sustained which may properly be assigned to the defendant, as distinguished from other causes. The question is primarily not one of the fact of causation, but of the feasibility and practical convenience of splitting up the total harm into separate parts which may be attributed to each of two or more causes. Where a factual basis can be found for some rough practical apportionment, which limits the defendant's liability to that part of the harm of which that defendant's conduct has been a cause in fact, it is likely that the apportionment will be made. Where no such basis can be found, the courts generally hold the defendant for the entire loss, notwithstanding the fact that other causes have contributed to it.

G. MULTIPLE CAUSATION

The distinction is one between injuries which are reasonably capable of being separated and injuries which are not.

Id. § 52, at 345; *see also Summers v. Tice*, 33 Cal.2d 80, 199 P.2d 1, 3–4 (1948) (defendants jointly and severally liable for entire damage resulting from independent acts, even though plaintiff could not prove which defendant caused the injury).

The evolution of Arizona law on the subject reflects these common-law principles. In 1928, Arizona recognized joint and several liability as a well-settled rule but one that applied only in cases involving tortious injury brought about by concerted action of two or more tortfeasors. *See White v. Arizona Eastern R. Co.*, 26 Ariz. 590, 594, 229 P. 101, 102 (1924), overruled in part by *Holtz*, 101 Ariz. 247, 418 P.2d 584. *Salt River Valley Water Users' Ass'n v. Cornum* further limited the definition of joint tortfeasors, holding only those tortfeasors who pursued a "community of purpose" jointly and severally liable to the plaintiff. 49 Ariz. 1, 8, 63 P.2d 639, 643 (1937).

In *Cornum*, the negligent conduct of the two defendants was neither concerted nor related in character or time. Thus, the court held that the defendants could not be joined in one action,[1] they were not jointly liable, and the verdict for the plaintiff against one of the defendants for the entire amount of damages was reversed. *Id.* at 9–10, 63 P.2d at 643–44. However, if proximate cause had been established, the plaintiff would have been "given the option of deciding against which defendant he would proceed." *Id.* at 10, 63 P.2d at 644. The effect was to require the plaintiff, on pain of dismissal, to apportion damages caused by separate and independent acts of negligence, even when those acts caused an indivisible injury. The same rule was applied in a successive accident case, *Sweet Milk Co. v. Stanfield*, 353 F.2d 811, 813 (9th Cir.1965) (applying Arizona law).

White and *Cornum* recognized one exception: when the negligence of different tortfeasors "coincided in time, place, and character," such as "cases involving the negligent operation of colliding instrumentalities," joint and several liability could be applied even though the defendants' actions were not concerted. *Cornum*, 49 Ariz. at 9, 63 P.2d at 643. When the plaintiff's case fell outside the exception, the plaintiff would have to apportion damage by causation or prove that one of the tortfeasors was the proximate cause of the entire injury. *Id.* at 11, 63 P.2d at 644. If the plaintiff was unable to do so, the case failed. *Id.*

In 1966, *Holtz* recognized another circumstance in which a plaintiff could be excused from apportioning damages. The facts in Holtz are similar to those in both *Sweet Milk* and the present case. Holtz, like Piner, suffered an indivisible injury from separate accidents. We held that the tortfeasors were jointly and severally liable for Holtz's entire damage. 101 Ariz. at 251, 418 P.2d at 588. Such a result was "desirable as a matter of policy" even though it extended the exception recognized in *White* and *Cornum* to include incidents of successive injury. *Id.*

To reach this result, *Holtz* actually applied two different rules. First, when the injury was indivisible, even though caused by successive accidents, the

---

[1] This problem was cured by modern rules of pleading. See Rules 18–20, Ariz. R. Civ. P.

plaintiff could assert a claim against all wrongdoers without having the burden of "proving the extent of damage or injury caused by each. . . ." *Id.* at 250, 418 P.2d at 587. We described this as the "'single indivisible injury' rule." *Id. Holtz* shifted the burden of apportionment to the defendants and gave them incentive to apportion cause by holding each liable for the entire amount of unapportioned damages. Successive tortfeasors are responsible for the entire amount of damages if "their acts occur closely in time and place" and the plaintiff receives successive injuries that "the trier of fact determines to be unapportionable between or among the several tortfeasors." *Id.* at 251, 418 P.2d at 588; *see also Dietz v. General Elec. Co.*, 169 Ariz. 505, 508, 821 P.2d 166, 169 (1991). Thus, as in *Summers*, if the plaintiff could not apportion fault between negligent, potential tortfeasors, the burden of apportionment shifted to the tortfeasors.[2]

Holtz's rule on indivisibility of damages necessarily incorporated another: damages were not to be apportioned on the basis of fault. Thus, all defendants were jointly and severally liable for the whole amount of damage. At common law, degrees of fault were never assigned to the parties involved and were unnecessary because they were unrelated to the damages assessed. This rule applied to both contributory negligence and apportionment between tortfeasors. See KEETON ET AL., *supra* § 67, at 470, 475–77. This, of course, was the common law in Arizona—each tortious actor was jointly and severally liable for all of the damage caused by his conduct, even if one was much more at fault than another. *See, e.g., Gehres v. City of Phoenix*, 156 Ariz. 484, 487, 753 P.2d 174, 177 (App.1987).

Defendants claim the Uniform Contribution Among Tortfeasors Act (UCATA) (§§ 12-2501 to 12-2509) effectively overruled *Holtz* and its progeny, thus requiring the factfinder to apportion damages between multiple actors and making each tortfeasor severally liable only for the portion of damages caused by his conduct. If the plaintiff is unable to provide enough evidence to form a basis for apportionment of damages, then, Defendants argue, the claim must be dismissed. We disagree with this view because UCATA does not require limiting liability by apportioning damages but by apportioning fault.

The Arizona Legislature enacted its first version of UCATA in 1984. . . . These provisions replaced contributory negligence with comparative fault and abolished the rule forbidding contribution between joint tortfeasors. Under this new regime, the factfinder allocated a percentage of fault to each culpable actor. Even though the culpable defendants were still jointly and severally liable for all damages, the legislature established a right of contribution that

---

[2] When two or more persons by their acts are possibly the sole cause of a harm, or when two or more acts of the same person are possibly the sole cause, and the plaintiff has introduced evidence that the one of the two persons, or the one of the same person's two acts, is culpable, then the defendant has the burden of proving that the other person, or his other act, was the sole cause of the harm. . . . The real reason for the rule that each joint tortfeasor is responsible for the whole damage is the practical unfairness of denying the injured person redress simply because he cannot prove how much damage each did, when it is certain that between them they did all; let them be the ones to apportion it among themselves. Since, then, the difficulty of proof is the reason, the rule should apply whenever the harm has plural causes, and not merely when they acted in conscious concert. *Summers v. Tice*, 199 P.2d 1 (1948).

allowed a defendant held liable for more than his share of fault to recover from the other tortfeasors in proportion to their several contributions of fault. . . . This change was intended to bring about a system in which each tortfeasor would eventually contribute only a portion of damage equal to the percentage of fault attributed to that tortfeasor by the factfinder. *See Dietz*, 169 Ariz. at 508, 510, 821 P.2d at 171, 173. But Arizona's negligence law still produced harsh results when one defendant was insolvent, thus leaving the others unable to obtain contribution. *See, e.g., Gehres*, 156 Ariz. 484, 753 P.2d 174 (defendants assigned five percent of fault held jointly and severally liable for one hundred percent of damages).

In response, the Arizona Legislature amended UCATA, abolishing joint liability and replacing it with a system that requires the court to allocate responsibility among all parties who caused the injury, whether or not they are present in the action. . . . Under the present version of UCATA, "the liability of each defendant is several only and not joint." § 12-2506(D). Taken in isolation, this wording tends to support Defendants' argument, but several factors militate against such an interpretation. First, the legislative intent was to cure the *Gehres* "deep pocket" problem of a defendant only minimally at fault yet liable for the full amount of damages. . . .

A second factor is that the old rule conditioned the plaintiff's recovery on the impossible: if unable to divide the indivisible, the plaintiff was denied relief and the culpable parties were relieved of all responsibility. The injustice inherent in this policy has been repeatedly recognized by our courts. *See, e.g., Holtz*, 101 Ariz. 247, 418 P.2d 584; *Czarnecki v. Volkswagen of America*, 172 Ariz. 408, 413, 837 P.2d 1143, 1148 (App.1991) (applying the indivisible injury rule to a second impact, crash worthiness case); *see also* Michael A. Beale, *Torts—Liability— Independent Tortfeasors Jointly and Severally Liable for Separate Acts of Negligence Where Harm is Indivisible Holtz v. Holder* (Ariz.1966), 9 ARIZ. L. REV. 129, 134 (1967). We do not believe that when the legislature attempted to eliminate the injustice it perceived in the deep pocket problem, it also intended to reestablish an unfair regime under which an innocent victim is denied any relief because the damages caused by independent wrongdoers result in an indivisible, unapportionable injury.

Most important, the clear text of UCATA does not require that a defendant's liability be limited by apportioning damages, but only by apportioning fault:

> A. In an action for personal injury, property damage or wrongful death, the liability of each defendant for damages is several only and is not joint. . . . Each defendant is liable only for the amount of damages allocated to that defendant in direct proportion to that defendant's percentage of fault. . . . [T]he trier of fact shall multiply the total amount of damages recoverable by the plaintiff by the percentage of each defendant's fault, and that amount is the maximum recoverable against the defendant. . . .
>
> B. In assessing percentages of fault the trier of fact shall consider the fault of all persons who contributed to the alleged injury. . . .
>
> F. (2) "Fault" means an actionable breach of legal duty, act or omission proximately causing or contributing to injury or damages sustained

by a person seeking recovery, including negligence in all of its degrees, contributory negligence, assumption of risk, strict liability, breach of express or implied warranty of a product, products liability and misuse, modification or abuse of a product.

§ 12-2506(A), (B), & (F)(2).

Thus, while UCATA requires the plaintiff to prove that a defendant's conduct was a cause of injury, it does not instruct us to limit liability by apportioning damages. Instead, each tortfeasor whose conduct caused injury is severally liable only for a percentage of the total damages recoverable by the plaintiff, the percentage based on each actor's allocated share of fault. § 12-2506(B) & (F)(2).

We conclude, therefore, that the present version of UCATA has left intact the rule of indivisible injury, relieving the plaintiff of apportioning damage according to causal contribution. When the tortious conduct of more than one defendant contributes to one indivisible injury, the entire amount of damage resulting from all contributing causes is the total amount "of damages recoverable by the plaintiff," as that term is used in § 12-2506(A). The second part of the *Holtz* rule, however, was abrogated by § 12-2506(A). Contrary to the common law and cases such as *Gehres*, the fault of all actors is compared and each defendant is severally liable for damages allocated "in direct proportion to that defendant's percentage of fault." § 12-2506(A). To determine each defendant's liability "the trier of fact shall multiply the total amount of damages recoverable by the plaintiff by the percentage of each defendant's fault, and that amount is the maximum recoverable against the defendant." *Id.*

Thus in an indivisible injury case, the factfinder is to compute the total amount of damage sustained by the plaintiff and the percentage of fault of each tortfeasor. Multiplying the first figure by the second gives the maximum recoverable against each tortfeasor. This result conforms not only with the intent of the legislature and the text of the statute but also with common sense. When damages cannot be apportioned between multiple tortfeasors, there is no reason why those whose conduct produced successive but indivisible injuries should be treated differently from those whose independent conduct caused injury in a single accident. Like our predecessors in *Holtz*, we see no reason to employ a different rule if the injuries occur at once, five minutes apart or, as in the present case, several hours apart. The operative fact is simply that the conduct of each defendant was a cause and the result is indivisible damage.

The interpretation we give the statute also accords with the principles of fairness espoused by modern common law. The Restatement (Second) of Torts, for example, requires damages for harm to be apportioned among the various actors whose conduct contributed to the result if the harm is "distinct" or if "there is a reasonable basis for determining the contribution of each cause to a single harm." Restatement (Second) of Torts § 433A; *see also Potts v. Litt*, 171 Ariz. 98, 100, 828 P.2d 1239, 1241 (App.1991). The Restatement goes on to provide that the plaintiff has the burden of proving that the conduct of each defendant was a cause of the injury, but when a defendant "seeks to limit his liability on the ground that the harm is capable of apportionment . . . . the burden of proof as to the apportionment is upon each such actor." Id. § 433B.

Finally, as in *Holtz*, the Restatement provides that it is the court's function to determine "questions of causation and apportionment, in any case in which the jury may not reasonably differ." But the jury's function is "to determine, in any case in which it may reasonably differ on the issue, . . . the apportionment of the harm to two or more causes." *Id.* § 434(b); see also *Holtz*, 101 Ariz. at 249–51, 418 P.2d at 586–88.

In the present case, the trial judge erred in placing the burden of proof on apportionment on Piner. Assuming Piner proves that the conduct of both Jones and Richardson contributed to the final result, the burden of proof on apportionment is on them. If the judge concludes there is no evidence that would permit apportionment, then the case should be treated as one involving indivisible injuries. If the judge further concludes there is no evidence on which to base a jury finding of inability to apportion, then the jurors must be instructed to apportion. If the evidence on the question of apportionment is conflicting, the jurors should be instructed that if they are able to apportion damages, they should do so, allocating fault and damages for each accident separately. They should also be instructed that if they are unable to apportion damages, then they are to determine Piner's total damages resulting from both accidents. In such case, the indivisible injury rule will apply. In all cases in which the indivisible injury rule applies as either a matter of law or on a jury finding of inability to apportion, the plaintiff's recovery will be the total damage sustained. But in all such indivisible injury cases, the jurors must be instructed to allocate fault in accordance with § 12-2506. The judge is then to multiply each tortfeasor's percentage of fault by the amount recoverable by the plaintiff. Each tortfeasor in an indivisible injury case is then severally liable for the product of that calculation.

We are aware that the factfinder in an indivisible injury case will be required to allocate a percentage of fault to each of several defendants and possible non-parties involved in more than one accident. This will perhaps be more difficult than the already difficult task of allocating percentages of fault in cases in which there has been a chain of cause and effect that produces injury in a single accident. *See, e.g., Hutcherson v. City of Phoenix*, 1998 WL 351098 (Ariz.1998); *Zuern v. Ford Motor Co.*, 188 Ariz. 486, 937 P.2d 676 (App.1996) (causation of injury is a condition precedent to but different from allocation of fault for the accident; once causation of injury is determined, the factfinder must apportion fault between all parties and non-parties pursuant to § 12-2506(C)). We address that problem in an effort to assist trial courts in implementing the substantive rule of indivisible injury.

Zuern cites several authorities that shed some light on the problem, including VICTOR E. SCHWARTZ, COMPARATIVE NEGLIGENCE § 17-1(A), at 352 (3d ed. 1994) ("The process is not allocation of physical causation, which could be scientifically apportioned, but rather of allocating fault, which cannot be scientifically measured."); *Day v. General Motors Corp.*, 345 N.W.2d 349 (N.D.1984) (allocation of fault encompasses both fault that produced the accident and fault that enhanced the injury). We believe the appropriate method is to have the jurors apportion one hundred percent of the fault for each accident separately. The trial judge would then combine the findings and divide by the number of accidents. Using a case involving two accidents as an example, suppose for the first accident the jurors apportion twenty percent fault to the plaintiff, forty percent to non-party # 1, and forty percent to defendant X; for the second accident the jurors apportion fifteen percent fault to the plaintiff, ten percent to non-party # 2, seventy percent to defendant Y, and five percent to defendant Z. In calculating the amount for which each party is responsible, the trial judge would simply divide each allocation by two and multiply the figure so obtained by the total, indivisible damage sustained by the plaintiff.

In the hypothetical given, therefore, the plaintiff would be allocated seventeen and one-half percent fault for the two accidents combined, non-party # 1 twenty percent, defendant X twenty percent, defendant Y thirty-five percent, non-party # 2 five percent, and defendant Z two and one-half percent. Each percentage would then be multiplied by the total of the indivisible damage sustained by plaintiff to produce the amount for which each defendant was liable under § 12-2506(A).[3]

The method of allocation we have described would, we believe, comply with the statutory requirement of § 12-2506(B) that the factfinder "shall consider the fault of all persons who contributed to the alleged injury" in making allocations of fault. It would also comply with the holding in *Zuern*:

> [C]ommon sense in the fair application of [a] pure comparative negligence system mandates that the negligence of all parties [and non-parties], including original tortfeasors and crash worthiness tortfeasors, which proximately causes enhanced injuries . . . must be compared.

Zuern, 188 Ariz. at 491, 937 P.2d at 681 (quoting *Cleveland v. Piper Aircraft Corp.*, 890 F.2d 1540, 1550 (10th Cir.1989)).

The trial court's June 4, 1996 order denying Piner's motion for partial summary judgment and July 31, 1996 ruling regarding jury instruction content are vacated. The trial court may proceed in accordance with this opinion.

NOTES

1. *Unapportionable Cause.* According to RESTATEMENT (SECOND) OF TORTS § 433B(2):

---

[3] Expressed in numbers, the computation would look like this:

ACCIDENT	PLAINTIFF	DEFENDANT X	DEFENDANT Y	DEFENDANT Z	NON-PARTY # 1 & # 2	TOTAL
First	20.0	40.0	NA	NA	40.0	100.0
Second	15.0	NA	70.0	5.0	10.0	100.0
Totals for both accidents	35.0	40.0	70.0	5.0	50.0	200.0
Percentage allocation per accident	17.5	20.00	35.0	2.5	25.0	100.0

Thus, if plaintiff's total damages were found to be $10,000, defendant X would be liable for $2,000, defendant Y for $3,500, and defendant Z for $250.

Where the tortious conduct of two or more actors has combined to bring about harm to the plaintiff, and one or more of the actors seeks to limit his liability on the ground that the harm is capable of apportionment among them, the burden of apportionment is upon each such actor.

Are the principal case and RESTATEMENT (SECOND) section 433B(2) different from the two fires at issue in *Anderson*? One difference is that we know who the two tortfeasors are in *Piner*. Is that the only difference? If *Anderson* had identified the parties responsible for both fires and sued both, would the case be essentially the same as *Piner*?

RESTATEMENT (SECOND) OF TORTS § 433B(3) provides that where the conduct of two or more actors is tortious, "and it is proved that harm has been caused to the plaintiff by only one of them, but there is uncertainty as to which caused it, the burden is upon each such actor to prove that he has not caused the harm."

2. *Divisible Injuries, Indivisible Injuries, and Joint and Several Liability.* If the cause of the injury is divisible, the plaintiff may recover from each wrongdoer the damages which that wrongdoer caused. For instance if B caused A to suffer a broken leg and C caused A to suffer a broken arm, B would be liable for the leg and C would be liable for the arm. The injuries would be divisible. Unfortunately, as the principal case illustrates, life is not always that simple. What if the jury had found that the second accident had caused no injury at all, i.e., no new injury and no aggravation of an earlier injury? Then, the second tortfeasor would not be liable at all. Alternatively, what if the jury concludes that the second tortfeasor did cause some injury but it cannot apportion the injury between the first tortfeasor and the second tortfeasor. Then, it is said that the injury is indivisible.

If the injury is indivisible, application of the general rule (plaintiff must prove, more probably than not, the damages which he sustained was caused by the particular defendant's wrongful conduct) would have the effect of denying plaintiff recovery from any of the wrongdoers.

Shifting the burden of proving cause in fact from the plaintiff to each defendant has the effect of making each defendant liable for all of the plaintiff's damages. It has the effect of making the defendants jointly and severally liable which means that the plaintiff can recover 100% of her damages. For example, if B and C negligently cause A to suffer a broken back, an indivisible injury, B and C might be jointly and severally liable. A could recover 100% of his damages from B or C (or part from one and the rest from the other).

Let's take the hypothetical a step further, to a jurisdiction that allocates fault between tortfeasors. Assume A is blameless, B is 60% at fault and C is 40% at fault (note that the allocated fault must add up to 100%). Further assume that A has suffered $100,000 in damages. If the jurisdiction still holds joint tortfeasors jointly and severally liable, A could recover $100,000 from either B or C. If A chose to recover $100,000 from C, most jurisdictions would give C a right of contribution against B to recover the amount C paid over his allocated share. Here C would be able to recover 60% or $60,000 from B. If B is insolvent, C is left holding the liability bag.

In a jurisdiction that has eliminated joint and several liability, like Arizona, B would be liable for $60,000 and C would be liable for $40,000. If B was insolvent, A would recover $40,000 from C and A would be left without full compensation.

The *Piner* case also raises the difficulties inherent in allocating fault where there is more than one accident involved. *See* footnote 3 of the opinion.

Is responsibility apportioned between two causal agents on the basis of both causation and fault? If apportionment is made separately for cause and fault, which apportionment comes first—the one based on cause, or the one based on fault? *See Whitehead v. Toyota Motor Corp.*, 897 S.W.2d 684 (Tenn. 1995).

3. *Crashworthiness and Second Collisions.* In the so called second-collision, or crashworthiness, cases, where one agent causes an accident but a second agent—the defendant's defective product—exacerbates the injury, some courts require the plaintiff to apportion damages between the first and second agent while others shift the burden of proof of apportionment to the defendant. *See Polston v. Boomershine Pontiac-GMC Truck, Inc.*, 262 Ga. 616, 423 S.E.2d 659 (1992). These cases frequently arise in the automobile collision context, but they may arise in other contexts as well. *See, e.g., Cartell Capital Corp. V. Fireco of New Jersey*, 81 N.J. 548, 410 A.2d 674 (1980) (defective fire extinguisher).

If one agent is viewed as exacerbating an injury caused by a prior agent, the prior agent may be liable for the subsequent exacerbation if that exacerbation is proximately caused by the prior agent. *See Futch v. Commercial Union Ins. Co.*, 64 So.2d 766 (La. App. 1995) ("the duty to refrain from negligent automobile operation encompasses the risk that an accident victim's medical treatment may cause him further damage"). So, if B negligently causes A to suffer a back injury in an automobile accident and Dr. C, in the course of treating A, commits malpractice that aggravates the injury, traditional legal cause rules held B responsible for Dr. C's malpractice, unless it was unforeseeably reckless.

In a several-liability jurisdiction, what would be the result today? Does it matter if the injury is divisible or indivisible?

Chapter 7
DUTIES OF CARE AND LEGAL CAUSE

A. INTRODUCTION

A defendant may have engaged in conduct that falls beneath the requisite standard of care. That conduct may have been a cause-in-fact of the plaintiff's damage. However, in tort law (and particularly in the case of the tort of negligence) there is much more to be considered.

Should the defendant be liable to the particular plaintiff for the particular injury which occurred in the particular manner in which the injury occurred? This is a critical question Its answer may involve questions of general policy and the application of general policy to particular factual circumstances. It may involve difficult decisions about the closeness of connection between what the defendant did and the injury suffered. Third party actors may have intervened in some manner and their effect upon the defendant's liability may be critical.

Additionally, making matters even more complex, the legal issue may be phrased in terms of whether the defendant owed the particular plaintiff a duty to guard against the particular risk or it may be phrased in terms of the scope of the defendant's duty. Or, the issue may be characterized as whether the plaintiff's injuries or type of injuries were foreseeable. Or, in even more traditional parlance, it may be phrased in terms of whether the defendant proximately or legally caused the plaintiff's injuries.

This area of the law calls upon all the lawyer's skills. One might persuasively claim that the crux of tort law revolves around the key question: should this defendant be liable to this plaintiff for these injuries which occurred in this manner? It is the heart of the matter.

This chapter collects cases dealing with foreseeable risk, duty and legal (or proximate) cause.

Several broad themes are at play. First, what test should a judge or jury use in deciding the scope of liability? Second, what is in part at stake is who gets to decide what—i.e., judge or jury? If a court makes a decision based on the existence or absence of a duty, it is making a decision as a matter of law. Alternatively, proximate or legal cause is usually a question for the jury. Third, there are some generally recurring patterns in which something close to rules can be said to exist although it may be more honest to call these so-called rules nothing more than guidelines or rules of thumb.

PROBLEM

Nitro, Inc. owns a gasoline storage facility in which it stores 30-gallon containers of gasoline. Adjacent to the gasoline storage yard is an office building owned by Petro, Inc., a wholly owned subsidiary of Nitro. On the other side of Petro's office building is a retail store owned by Thrifty, Inc.

One evening there is a large fire on the premises of Nitro, Inc. A resulting explosion flings a gasoline container out of the storage area. The container explodes when it makes contact with the Petro building, which is destroyed in the resulting fire. The fire then spreads to Thrifty's premises and from there destroys a neighboring home owned by Sam.

Thrifty and Sam file suit in negligence against Nitro. Nitro's only real argument is that plaintiffs' damages are "too remote."

What result, and which, if any, of the following is the correct characterization of the issue?

(1) A question of duty or no duty, or whether there was a breach of any duty?

(2) A question of duty (or no duty), and thus resolution is dependent upon whether this (or this general type of) damage was foreseeable.

(3) A question of duty or no duty, and thus resolution is dependent upon whether this (or this general type of) plaintiff was foreseeable.

(4) A matter of reasonableness or unreasonableness of Nitro's storage practices, and thus whether the risks to the surrounding property owners were foreseeable.

(5) If Nitro had stored the gasoline in a manner contrary to a municipal fire regulation, the question might be phrased in terms of whether this type of risk was one that the statute was designed to protect against.

(6) A question as to whether, as a matter of law, Nitro's negligence was a substantial factor in the injuries suffered by the plaintiffs.

(7) Whether the loss suffered by the plaintiffs was a direct consequence of the defendant's negligence.

(8) Whether the loss suffered by the plaintiffs was a foreseeable consequence of the defendant's negligence.

Is it important how the issue is framed (or characterized)? In each case would the issue be for the judge (*e.g.*, dismissal, summary judgment for plaintiff or summary judgment for defendant) or for the jury?

B. DIRECT CAUSE OR FORESEEABILITY

IN RE POLEMIS
[1921] 3 K.B. 560, 90 L.J.K.B. 1353, 126 L.T. 154 (C.A.)

Appeal from the judgment of Sankey J. on an award in the form of a special case.

The owners of the Greek steamship *Thrasyvoulos* claimed to recover damages for the total loss of the steamship by fire.

By a charter party dated February 21, 1917, Messrs. Polemis and Boyazides, the owners of the Greek steamship *Thrasyvoulos* (hereinafter called the owners), chartered the steamship to Furness, Withy & Co., Ltd. (hereinafter called the charterers), for the period of the duration of the war and at charterers' option up to six months afterwards. . . .

The vessel by the directions of the charterers or their agents in or about the months of June and July, 1917, loaded at Nantes a part cargo of cement and general cargo for Casablanca, Morocco. She then proceeded to Lisbon and was loaded with further cargo, consisting of cases of benzine and/or petrol and iron for Casablanca and other ports on the Morocco coast. She arrived at Casablanca on July 17, and there discharged a portion of her cargo. . . . The cargo in No. 1 hold included a considerable quantity of cases of benzine or petrol which had suffered somewhat by handling and/or by rough weather on the voyage, so that there had been some leakage from the tins in the cases into the hold. On July 21 it had become necessary to shift from No. 1 lower hold a number of cases of benzine which were required to be taken on by the ship to Safi, and for this purpose the . . . stevedores had placed heavy planks across the forward end of the hatchway in the 'tween decks, using it as a platform in the process of transferring the cases from the lower hold to the 'tween decks. There were four or five of the . . . shore laborers in the lower hold filling the slings which, when filled, were hove up by means of the winch situated on the upper deck to the 'tween decks level of the platform on which some [men]. . .were working. In consequence of the breakage of the case there was a considerable amount of petrol vapor in the hold. In the course of heaving a sling of the cases from the hold the rope by which the sling was being raised or the sling itself came into contact with the boards placed across the forward end of the hatch, causing one of the boards to fall into the lower hold, and the fall was instantaneously followed by a rush of flames from the lower hold, and this resulted eventually in the total destruction of the ship.

The owners contended (so far as material) that the charterers were liable for the loss of the ship; that fire caused by negligence was not an excepted peril; and that the ship was in fact lost by the negligence of the stevedores, who were the charterers' servants, in letting the sling strike the board, knocking it into the hold, and thereby causing a spark which set fire to the petrol vapor and destroyed the ship.

The charterers contended . . . that the danger and/or damage were too remote—i.e., no reasonable man would have foreseen danger and/or damage of this kind resulting from the fall of the board.

The three arbitrators made the following findings of fact . . .

> (d) That the fall of the board was caused by the negligence of [those] (other than the winchman) engaged in the work of discharging. . . .
>
> (f) That the causing of the spark could not reasonably have been anticipated from the falling of the board, though some damage to the ship might reasonably have been anticipated. . . .

Subject to the opinion of the Court on any questions of law arising the arbitrators awarded that the owners were entitled to recover from the charterers the before-mentioned sum [of £ 196,165].

If the Court should be of opinion that the above award was wrong, then the arbitrators awarded that the owners should recover nothing from the charterers . . . .

BANKS, L.J.

. . . In the present case the arbitrators have found as a fact that the falling of the plank was due to the negligence of the defendants' servants. The fire appears to me to have been directly caused by the falling of the plank. Under these circumstances I consider that it is immaterial that the causing of the spark by the falling of the plank could not have been reasonably anticipated. The appellant's junior counsel sought to draw a distinction between the anticipation of the extent of damage resulting from a negligent act, and the anticipation of the type of damage resulting from such an act. He admitted that it could not lie in the mouth of a person whose negligent act had caused damage to say that he could not reasonably have foreseen the extent of the damage, but he contended that the negligent person was entitled to rely upon the fact that he could not reasonably have anticipated the type of damage which resulted from his negligent act. I do not think that the distinction can be admitted. Given the breach of duty which constitutes the negligence, and given the damage as a direct result of that negligence, the anticipations of the person whose negligent act has produced the damage appear to me to be irrelevant. I consider that the damages claimed are not too remote . . . .

For these reasons I think that the appeal fails, and must be dismissed with costs.

NOTES

1. *Closeness of connection.* What is Lord Justice Banks' test for determining whether the defendant is liable to the plaintiff for the fire?

2. *Directness.* How does one tell if the defendant directly caused the plaintiff's injuries? Is it directness in terms of time? Space? The absence of any, some, or many intervening causes? Note that Banks says, "the claimed damages are not too remote . . . ." Remote damages are the opposite of direct damages. Thus direct cause means liability; remote means no liability. But direct and remote are merely conclusions, aren't they? Do those words help you decide what is direct and what isn't?

3. *Directness vs. Foreseeability.* Does some risk have to be foreseeable? Isn't that foreseeable risk what makes the defendant negligent? The *Polemis* court apparently imposes liability even though the risk that the plank would fall and cause a spark and resulting fire was not foreseeable. Does foreseeability matter at all?

Does *Polemis* stand for the proposition that once there is some foreseeable risk of harm that the defendant fails to exercise reasonable care to avoid, then the defendant is liable for any risk or injury that directly results, even though those risks are not foreseeable? Is that good policy? Is it fair to make someone liable for injuries she could not foresee? Will it cause people to be too careful? On the other hand, is it fair for an injured plaintiff not to be able to recover from a defendant whose negligence was a cause-in-fact of their injuries?

4. *Arguendo.* As the *Polemis* court noted: "The appellant's junior counsel sought to draw a distinction between the anticipation of the extent of damage resulting from a negligent act, and the anticipation of the type of damage

resulting from such an act." Try to think of an example of the point counsel was trying to make.

5. *Legal Cause.* There have been many attempts to explain the intricacies of legal cause. Some approaches have only served to render the subject more opaque. Thus, according to one court:

> The area within which liability is imposed is that which is within the circle of reasonable foreseeability using the original point at which the negligent act was committed or became operative, and hence looking in every direction as the semidiameter of the circle, and those injuries which from this point could or should have been reasonably foreseen as something likely to happen, are within the field of liability, while those which, although foreseeable, were foreseeable only as remote possibilities, those only slightly probable, are beyond and not within the circle — in all of which time, place and circumstance play their respective and important parts.
>
> The difficulty is not in the rule, but in applying the facts of a particular case, and in determining whether the facts bring the case within the circle which limits the rule, or whether they fall beyond it. . . .

Mauney v. Gulf Ref. Co., 9 So. 2d 780, 781 (Miss. 1942).

A notably more successful approach was taken by Professor (now Judge) Robert E. Keeton, in his book LEGAL CAUSE IN THE LAW OF TORTS (1963). His thesis is that "[a] negligent actor is legally responsible for that harm, and only that harm, of which the negligent aspect of his conduct is a cause in fact." R. Keeton, *Id.* at 9. Thus, if one carelessly stores an unlabeled can of poison near a hot stove in a restaurant, the risk is that someone will be poisoned, but not that someone will be injured by an explosion of the can. *Id.* at 3. If the defendant negligently transports dynamite in an unmarked truck, the risk here is one of injury by explosion on collision, but not of injury on impact with someone who suddenly darts in front of the truck. *Id.* at 21. To hold the store liable for injury by explosion in the first instance, and the trucker liable for personal injury in the second, would be "unfair" because these injuries were not within the scope of the respective risks created by the actors' negligent conduct. Do you agree? Why does the question of fairness even enter into the picture, for the negligent or careless defendant who probably has not thought about the risk she is creating in the first place? Alternatively, if she has thought about the risk and has consciously decided to expose others to it, what is unfair about holding such a callous risk-creator liable for risks that she did not foresee?

OVERSEAS TANKSHIP (U.K.) LTD. v. MORTS DOCK & ENGINEERING CO. (THE WAGON MOUND)
[1961] A.C. 388, 1 All E.R. 404, 2 W.L.R. 126 (P.C)

. . . The respondents at the relevant time carried on the business of ship-building, ship-repairing and general engineering at Morts Bay, Balmain, in the Port of Sydney. They owned and used for their business the Sheerlegs

Wharf, a timber wharf about four hundred feet in length and forty feet wide, where there was a quantity of tools and equipment. In October and November, 1951, a vessel known as the *Corrimal* was moored alongside the wharf and was being refitted by the respondents. Her mast was lying on the wharf and a number of the respondents' employees were working both on it and on the vessel itself, using for this purpose electric and oxy-acetylene welding equipment.

At the same time, the appellants were charterers by demise of *The S.S. Wagon Mound,* an oil-burning vessel which was moored at the Caltex Wharf on the northern shore of the harbour at a distance of about six hundred feet from the Sheerlegs Wharf. She was there from about 9 a.m. on Oct. 29, until 11 a.m. on Oct. 30, 1951, for the purpose of discharging gasoline products and taking in bunkering oil.

During the early hours of Oct. 30, 1951, a large quantity of bunkering oil was, through the carelessness of the appellants' servants, allowed to spill into the bay, and, by 10:30 on the morning of that day, it had spread over a considerable part of the bay, being thickly concentrated in some places and particularly along the foreshore near the respondents' property. The appellants made no attempt to disperse the oil. The *Wagon Mound* unberthed and set sail very shortly after.

When the respondents' works manager became aware of the condition of things in the vicinity of the wharf, he instructed their workmen that no welding or burning was to be carried on until further orders. He inquired of the manager of the Caltex Oil Co., at whose wharf the *Wagon Mound* was then still berthed, whether they could safely continue their operations on the wharf or on the *Corrimal*. The results of this inquiry, coupled with his own belief as to the inflammability of furnace oil in the open, led him to think that the respondents could safely carry on their operations. He gave instructions accordingly, but directed that all safety precautions should be taken to prevent inflammable material falling off the wharf into the oil.

For the remainder of Oct. 30 and until about 2 p.m. on Nov. 1, work was carried on as usual, the condition and congestion of the oil remaining substantially unaltered. But at about that time the oil under or near the wharf was ignited and a fire, fed initially by the oil, spread rapidly and burned with great intensity. The wharf and the *Corrimal* caught fire and considerable damage was done to the wharf and the equipment on it.

The outbreak of fire was due, as the learned judge found, to the fact that there was floating in the oil underneath the wharf a piece of debris on which lay some smoldering cotton waste or rag which had been set on fire by molten metal falling from the wharf; that the cotton waste or rag burst into flames; that the flames from the cotton waste set the floating oil afire either directly or by first setting fire to a wooden pile coated with oil and that, after the floating oil became ignited, the flames spread rapidly over the surface of the oil and quickly developed into a conflagration which severely damaged the wharf. . . .

VISCOUNT SIMONDS.

. . . The trial judge also made the all-important finding, which must be set out in his own words: "The raison d'etre of furnace oil is, of course, that it shall burn, but I find the [appellants] did not know and could not reasonably be expected to have known that it was capable of being set afire when spread on water." This finding was reached after a wealth of evidence which included that of a distinguished scientist, Professor Hunter. . . .

One other finding must be mentioned. The judge held that, apart from damage by fire, the respondents had suffered some damage from the spillage of oil in that it had got on their slipways and congealed on them and interfered with their use of the slips. He said: "The evidence of this damage is slight and no claim for compensation is made in respect of it. Nevertheless it does establish some damage, which may be insignificant in comparison with the magnitude of the damage by fire, but which nevertheless is damage which beyond question was a direct result of the escape of the oil." It is on this footing that their Lordships will consider the question whether the appellants are liable for the fire damage. . . .

It is inevitable that first consideration should be given to the case of *In Re Polemis and Furness, Withy & Co., Ltd.* which will henceforward be referred to as *Polemis*. For it was avowedly in deference to that decision and to decisions of the Court of Appeal that followed it that the full court was constrained to decide the present case in favor of the respondents. In doing so, MANNING, J., after a full examination of that case, said:

> To say that the problems, doubts and difficulties which I have expressed above render it difficult for me to apply the decision *In Re Polemis* with any degree of confidence to a particular set of facts would be a grave understatement. I can only express the hope that, if not in this case, then in some other case in the near future, the subject will be pronounced upon by the House of Lords or the Privy Council in terms which, even if beyond my capacity fully to understand, will facilitate for those placed as I am, its everyday application to current problems.

This *cri de coeur* would, in any case, be irresistible, but in the years that have passed since its decision, *Polemis* has been so much discussed and qualified that it cannot claim, as counsel for the respondents urged for it, the status of a decision of such long standing that it should not be reviewed.

 . . . There can be no doubt that the decision of the Court of Appeal in *Polemis* plainly asserts that, if the defendant is guilty of negligence, he is responsible for all the consequences, whether reasonably foreseeable or not. The generality of the proposition is, perhaps, qualified by the fact that each of the lords justices refers to the outbreak of fire as the direct result of the negligent act. There is thus introduced the conception that the negligent actor is not responsible for consequences which are not "direct," whatever that may mean. It has to be asked, then, why this conclusion should have been reached. The answer appears to be that it was reached on a consideration of certain authorities, comparatively few in number, that were cited to the court.

 . . . The impression that may well be left on the reader of the scores of cases in which liability for negligence has been discussed is that the courts were feeling their way to a coherent body of doctrine, and were at times in grave danger of being led astray by scholastic theories of causation and their ugly and barely intelligible jargon. . . .

Enough has been said to show that the authority of *Polemis* has been severely shaken, though lip-service has from time to time been paid to it. In their Lordships' opinion, it should no longer be regarded as good law. It is not probable that many cases will for that reason have a different result, though it is hoped that the law will be thereby simplified, and that, in some cases at least, palpable injustice will be avoided. For it does not seem consonant with current ideas of justice or morality that, for an act of negligence, however slight or venial, which results in some trivial foreseeable damage, the actor should be liable for all consequences, however unforeseeable and however grave, so long as they can be said to be "direct." It is a principle of civil liability, subject only to qualifications which have no present relevance, that a man must be considered to be responsible for the probable consequences of his act. To demand more of him is too harsh a rule, to demand less is to ignore that civilized order requires the observance of a minimum standard of behavior.

This concept, applied to the slowly developing law of negligence has led to a great variety of expressions which can, as it appears to their Lordships, be harmonized with little difficulty with the single exception of the so-called rule in *Polemis*. For, if it is asked why a man should be responsible for the natural or necessary or probable consequences of his act (or any other similar description of them), the answer is that it is not because they are natural or necessary or probable, but because, since they have this quality, it is judged, by the standard of the reasonable man, that he ought to have foreseen them. Thus it is that, over and over again, it has happened that, in different judgments in the same case and sometimes in a single judgment, liability for a consequence has been imposed on the ground that it was reasonably foreseeable, or alternatively on the ground that it was natural or necessary or probable. The two grounds have been treated as conterminous, and so they largely are. But, where they are not, the question arises to which the wrong answer was given in *Polemis*. For, if some limitation must be imposed on the consequences for which the negligent actor is to be held responsible—and all are agreed that some limitation there must be—why should that test (reasonable foreseeability) be rejected which, since he is judged by what the reasonable man ought to foresee, corresponds with the common conscience of mankind, and a test (the "direct" consequence) be substituted which leads to nowhere but the never ending and insoluble problems of causation. "The lawyer," said Sir Frederick Pollock, "cannot afford to adventure himself with philosophers in the logical and metaphysical controversies that beset the idea of cause." Yet this is just what he has most unfortunately done and must continue to do if the rule in *Polemis* is to prevail. A conspicuous example occurs when the actor seeks to escape liability on the ground that the "chain of causation" is broken by a "nova causa" or "novus actus interveniens. . . ."

In the same connection may be mentioned the conclusion to which the full court finally came in the present case. Applying the rule in *Polemis* and holding, therefore, that the unforeseeability of the damage by fire afforded no defence, they went on to consider the remaining question. Was it a "direct" consequence? On this, MANNING, J., said:

> Notwithstanding that, if regard is had separately to each individual occurrence in the chain of events that led to this fire, each occurrence

was improbable and, in one sense, improbability was heaped upon improbability, I cannot escape from the conclusion that if the ordinary man in the street had been asked, as a matter of common sense, without any detailed analysis of the circumstances, to state the cause of the fire at Morts Dock, he would unhesitatingly have assigned such cause to spillage of oil by the appellants' employees.

Perhaps he would, and probably he would have added, "I never should have thought it possible." But, with great respect to the full court, this is surely irrelevant, or, if it is relevant, only serves to show that the *Polemis* rule works in a very strange way. After the event even a fool is wise. Yet it is not the hindsight of a fool, but it is the foresight of the reasonable man which alone can determine responsibility. The *Polemis* rule, by substituting "direct" for "reasonably foreseeable" consequence, leads to a conclusion equally illogical and unjust.

. . . It is, no doubt, proper when considering tortious liability for negligence to analyze its elements and to say that the plaintiff must prove a duty owed to him by the defendant, a breach of that duty by the defendant, and consequent damage. But there can be no liability until the damage has been done. It is not the act but the consequences on which tortious liability is founded. Just as (as it has been said) there is no such thing as negligence in the air, so there is no such thing as liability in the air. Suppose an action brought by A for damage caused by the carelessness (a neutral word) of B, for example a fire caused by the careless spillage of oil. It may, of course, become relevant to know what duty B owed to A, but the only liability that is in question is the liability for damage by fire. It is vain to isolate the liability from its context and to say that B is or is not liable, and then to ask for what damage he is liable. For his liability is in respect of that damage and no other. If, as admittedly it is, B's liability (culpability) depends on the reasonable foreseeability of the consequent damage, how is that to be determined except by the foreseeability of the damage which in fact happened—the damage in suit? And, if that damage is unforeseeable so as to displace liability at large, how can the liability be restored so as to make compensation payable?

But, it is said, a different position arises if B's careless act has been shown to be negligent and has caused some foreseeable damage to A. Their Lordships have already observed that to hold B liable for consequences, however unforeseeable, of a careless act, if, but only if, he is at the same time liable for some other damage, however trivial, appears to be neither logical nor just. This becomes more clear if it is supposed that similar unforeseeable damage is suffered by A and C, but other foreseeable damage, for which B is liable, by A only. A system of law which would hold B liable to A but not to C for the similar damage *suffered by each* of them could not easily be defended. Fortunately, the attempt is not necessary. For the same fallacy is at the root of the proposition. It is irrelevant to the question whether B is liable for unforeseeable damage that he is liable for foreseeable damage, as irrelevant as would the fact that he had trespassed on Whiteacre be to the question whether he had trespassed on Blackacre. Again, suppose a claim by A for damage by fire by the careless act of B. Of what relevance is it to that claim that he has another claim arising out of the same careless act? It would surely not prejudice his claim if that other claim failed; it cannot assist it if it succeeds. Each of them rests on its own bottom and will fail if it can be established that the damage could not reasonably be foreseen. . . .

Their Lordships conclude this part of the case with some general observations. They have been concerned primarily to displace the proposition that unforeseeability is irrelevant if damage is "direct." In doing so, they have inevitably insisted that the essential factor in determining liability is whether the damage is of such a kind as the reasonable man should have foreseen. This accords with the general view thus stated by Lord Atkin in *Donoghue v. Stevenson:* "The liability for negligence, whether you style it such or treat it as in other systems as a species of 'culpa,' is no doubt based upon a general public sentiment of moral wrongdoing for which the offender must pay." [1932] A.C. 562, 580. It is a departure from this sovereign principle if liability is made to depend solely on the damage being the "direct" or "natural" consequence of the precedent act. Who knows or can be assumed to know all the processes of nature? But if it would be wrong that a man should be held liable for damage unpredictable by a reasonable man because it was "direct" or "natural," equally it would be wrong that he should escape liability, however "indirect" the damage, if he foresaw or could reasonably foresee the intervening events which led to its being done.

NOTES

1. *Closeness Redux.* What is the court's test for liability or proximate cause?

2. *Directness Discounted?* Does the *Polemis* "direct cause" test play any role at all? If not, is the concept of the intervening cause irrelevant? Note that even though the *Wagon Mound (No. 1)* court purports to overrule *Polemis*, the direct cause test retains its vitality in many jurisdictions and you should keep it in mind as an analytical tool.

3. *Breach and Remoteness of Damage.* RESTATEMENT (SECOND) OF TORTS § 284 (1965) defines negligent conduct as "an act which the actor as a reasonable [person] should recognize as involving an unreasonable risk of causing an invasion of an interest of another." What is the relationship between the doctrinal requirement of an unreasonable risk and the *Wagon Mound's* approach to limiting the potential exposure of a defendant?

4. *Foresight and Hindsight.* How does one tell if a risk is foreseeable or not? After the fact, even a fool is wise. Does that fact mean that the decision-maker has to decide what is foreseeable by putting itself in the reasonable person's shoes before the injury, i.e., at the time the defendant did whatever it was that the plaintiff alleges was negligent? How might that inquiry relate to the Learned Hand formula for negligence? Does the *Wagon Mound* court hold that the defendant was not negligent at all? It does not seem to so hold; recall that spilling the oil posed the risk of and caused greasy spillways on plaintiff's dock. Does the court hold defendant was not negligent vis-a-vis the risk of fire? In saying that the defendant was not the proximate cause of the fire, isn't it essentially saying that in relation to fire, the defendant was not negligent? That's a breach issue, isn't it?

5. *Decision Maker?* Who decides whether the injuries are direct or remote or foreseeable or unforeseeable? Is that allocation of decision-making power at issue in *Polemis?* In *Wagon Mound?* Proximate cause is traditionally viewed as a decision for the jury when a case is being tried to a jury.

6. *The Importance of Facts and of Strategy.* In a later case, *Overseas Tankship (U.K.) Ltd. v. Miller S.S. Co. Pty., The Wagon Mound (No. 2),* [1967] A.C. 617, [1966] 2 All E.R. 709, [1966] 3 W.L.R. 498 (P.C.), involving the same accident, the plaintiffs, owners of neighboring wharves damaged by the fire, *were* permitted to recover. The trial judge made the finding that reasonable persons in the position of the officers of the *Wagon Mound* "would regard furnace oil as very difficult to ignite on water," but that if they had "given attention to the risk of fire from the spillage, they would have regarded it as a possibility, but one which could become an actuality only in very exceptional circumstances."

The court held that the trial judge was in error in finding on these facts that the fire was not reasonably foreseeable. "In *Wagon Mound (No.1)* the [court was] not concerned with degrees of foreseeability because the finding was that the fire was not foreseeable at all." Here, concluded the court, the risk was small, but there was no counterbalancing utility in taking the risk:

> In the present case there was no justification whatever for discharging the oil into Sydney Harbour. Not only was it an offence to do so, but also it involved considerable loss financially. If the ship's engineer had thought about the matter there could have been no question of balancing the advantages and disadvantages. From every point of view it was both his duty and his interest to stop the discharge immediately.

Why do you suppose the plaintiff in *Wagon Mound (No. 1)* failed to adduce evidence of risk? Bad case preparation? Strategy? (After all, the plaintiff in the first *Wagon Mound* case was the one who was using the fire-producing welder.) *See generally* Dias, *Trouble on Oiled Waters: Problems of The Wagon Mound (No. 2),* [1967] CAMBRIDGE. L.J. 62. In the first case, if the plaintiff had emphasized foreseeability, mightn't the fact finder have found that the plaintiff was guilty of contributory negligence?

7. *Time and Place.* In *Lamb v. Camden London Borough Council,* [1981] Q.B. 625, 643, 2 All E.R. 408, 2 W.L.R. 1038, (C.A.), plaintiff's rental dwelling was severely damaged when the defendant's servants broke a water main outside the property. The escaping water undermined the building's foundations, the walls cracked, and the tenant moved out. A year later squatters invaded the house causing further damage. The court concluded that this latter damage was too remote. Oliver, L.J., remarked:

> I confess that I find it inconceivable that the reasonable man wielding his pick in the road in 1973 could be said reasonably to foresee that his puncturing of a water main would fill the plaintiff's house with uninvited guests in 1974.

And, according to Watkins, L.J.:

> It seems to me that if the sole and exclusive test of remoteness is whether the fresh damage has arisen from an event or act which is

reasonably foreseeable, or reasonably foreseeable as a possibility, or likely or quite likely to occur, absurd, even bizarre, results might ensue in actions for damages for negligence. . . .

I do not think that words such as, among others, "possible," "likely" or "quite likely" assist in the application of the test of reasonable foreseeability. If the crisply stated test which emanates from the *Wagon Mound* (No. 2) is to be festooned with additional words supposedly there for the purpose of amplification or qualification, an understandable application of it will become impossible. In my view, the *Wagon Mound* test should always be applied without any of the gloss which is from time to time being applied to it.

But when so applied it cannot in all circumstances in which it arises conclude consideration of the question of remoteness, although in the vast majority of cases it will be adequate for this purpose. In other cases, the present one being an example of these in my opinion, further consideration is necessary, always providing, of course, a plaintiff survives the test of reasonable foreseeability.

This is because the very features of an event or act for which damages are claimed themselves suggest that the event or act is not on any practical view of it remotely in any way connected with the original act of negligence. These features will include such matters as the nature of the event or act, the time it occurred, the place where it occurred, the identity of the perpetrator and his intentions, and responsibility, if any, for taking measures to avoid the occurrence and matters of public policy.

A robust and sensible approach to this very important area of the study of remoteness will more often than not produce, I think, an instinctive feeling that the event or act being weighed in the balance is too remote to sound in damages for the plaintiff. I do not pretend that in all cases the answer will come easily to the inquirer. But that the question must be asked and answered in all these cases I have no doubt.

While it is clear that the court denies recovery and the language about the factors to consider might be viewed as helpful, what is the point of the word remoteness? Is it helpful at all? Is it more helpful than saying the injuries were not foreseeable?

8. *Characterizing the Risk and the Harm.* Among other things, *In re Polemis* and *The Wagon Mound (No. 1)* differ over the question of whether all damages from an accident are recoverable as long as some damage is foreseeable. In *Petition of Kinsman Transit Co. (No. 1),* 338 F.2d 708 (2d Cir. 1964), a concatenation of events led to plaintiffs' injuries:

The Buffalo River flows through Buffalo from east to west, with many turns and bends, until it empties into Lake Erie. Its navigable western portion is lined with docks, grain elevators, and industrial installations; during the winter, lake vessels tie up there pending resumption of navigation on the Great Lakes, without power and with only a shipkeeper aboard. About a mile from the mouth, the City of

Buffalo maintains a lift bridge at Michigan Avenue. Thaws and rain frequently cause freshets to develop in the upper part of the river and its tributary, Cazenovia Creek; currents then range up to fifteen miles an hour and propel broken ice down the river, which sometimes overflows its banks.

On January 21, 1959, rain and thaw followed a period of freezing weather. The United States Weather Bureau issued appropriate warnings which were published and broadcast. Around 6 P.M. an ice jam that had formed in Cazenovia Creek disintegrated. Another ice jam formed just west of the junction of the creek and the river; it broke loose around 9 P.M.

The MacGilvray Shiras, owned by The Kinsman Transit Company, was moored at the dock of the Concrete Elevator, operated by Continental Grain Company, on the south side of the river about three miles upstream of the Michigan Avenue Bridge. She was loaded with grain owned by Continental. The berth, east of the main portion of the dock, was exposed in the sense that about 150 feet of the Shiras' forward end, pointing upstream, and 70 feet of her stern—a total of over half her length—projected beyond the dock. This left between her stem and the bank a space of water seventy-five feet wide where the ice and other debris could float in and accumulate. The position was the more hazardous in that the berth was just below a bend in the river, and the Shiras was on the inner bank. None of her anchors had been put out. From about 10 P.M. large chunks of ice and debris began to pile up between the Shiras' starboard bow and the bank; the pressure exerted by this mass on her starboard bow was augmented by the force of the current and of floating ice against her port quarter. The mooring lines began to part, and a "deadman," to which the No. 1 mooring cable had been attached, pulled out of the ground—the judge finding that it had not been properly constructed or inspected. About 10:40 P.M. the stern lines parted, and the Shiras drifted into the current. During the previous forty minutes, the shipkeeper took no action to ready the anchors by releasing the devil's claws; when he sought to drop them after the Shiras broke loose, he released the compressors with the claws still hooked in the chain so that the anchors jammed and could no longer be dropped. The trial judge reasonably found that if the anchors had dropped at that time, the Shiras would probably have fetched up at the hairpin bend just below the Concrete Elevator, and that in any case they would considerably have slowed her progress, the significance of which will shortly appear.

Careening stern first down the S-shaped river, the Shiras, at about 11 P.M., struck the bow of the Michael K. Tewksbury, owned by Midland Steamship Line, Inc. The Tewksbury was moored in a relatively protected area flush against the face of a dock on the outer bank just below a hairpin bend so that no opportunity was afforded for ice to build up between her port bow and the dock. Her shipkeeper had left around 5 P.M. and spent the evening watching television with a girlfriend and her family. The collision caused the Tewksbury's mooring lines to part; she too drifted stern first down the river, followed by the Shiras. The collision caused damage to the Steamer Druckenmiller which was moored opposite the Tewksbury.

A timely call was made to the Michigan Avenue bridge to raise the bridge so the unmoored ships careening down the river would clear the bridge. The bridge crew did not act in a timely manner.

The bridge crew consisted of an operator and two tenders; a change of shift was scheduled for 11 P.M., The inference is rather strong, despite contrary testimony, that the operator on the earlier shift had not yet returned from a tavern when the telephone call from the fire station was received; that the operator on the second shift did not arrive until shortly before the call from the elevator where the Tewksbury had been moored; and that in consequence the bridge was not raised until too late.

The first crash was followed by a second, when the south tower of the bridge fell. The Tewksbury grounded and stopped in the wreckage with her forward end resting against the stern of the Steamer Farr, which was moored on the south side of the river just above the bridge. The Shiras ended her journey with her stern against the Tewksbury and her bow against the north side of the river. So wedged, the two vessels substantially dammed the flow, causing water and ice to back up and flood installations on the banks with consequent damage as far as the Concrete Elevator, nearly three miles upstream. Two of the bridge crew suffered injuries. Later the north tower of the bridge collapsed, damaging adjacent property.

The court held that the owner of the Shiras, the grain company where it was moored, and the city (the bridge owner) were liable in negligence for the physical damage done by the breakaway ships. The failure of the city to act in a timely fashion was held not to be a superseding cause.

In a later case involving the same accident, *Petition of Kinsman Transit Co. (No. 2),* 388 F.2d 821 (2d Cir. 1968), the court denied recovery for economic losses suffered by cargo carriers who were unable to use the river for a period of about two months because of the accident.

Numerous principles have been suggested to determine the point at which a defendant should no longer be held legally responsible for damage caused "in fact" by his negligence. Such limiting principles must exist in any system of jurisprudence for cause and effect succeed one another with the same certainty that night follows day and the consequences of the simplest act may be traced over an ever-widening canvas with the passage of time. In Anglo-American law, as Edgerton has noted, "[except] only the defendant's intention to produce a given result, no other consideration so affects our feeling that it is or is not just to hold him for the result so much as its foreseeability." *Legal Cause,* 72 U. PA. L. REV. 211, 352 (1924). . ..

In the final analysis, the circumlocution whether posed in terms of "foreseeability," "duty," "proximate cause," "remoteness," etc. seems unavoidable. As we have previously noted, we return to Judge Andrews' frequently quoted statement in *Palsgraf v. Long Island R.R. Co.*, 248 N.Y. 339, 354–355, 162 N.E. 99, 104, 59 A.L.R. 1253 (1928) (dissenting opinion): "It is all a question of expediency . . . of fair judgment, always keeping in mind the fact that we endeavor to make a rule in each case that will be practical and in keeping with the general understanding of mankind."

Suppose a plaintiff in *Kinsman (No. 1)* also was a plaintiff in *Kinsman (No. 2)*. Assume, for example, that the backed-up water flooded the ground floor of the plaintiff's grain elevator, causing physical damage; and, because of the blocked-up bridge, the plaintiff lost profits on grain shipments stored in the elevator. Could the plaintiff recover for both types of damage? Would it make a difference if the loss of profits was caused by the ground-floor flooding, which prevented the grain from being removed from the elevator for shipment (either upstream or by railroad) to market?

C. BREACH, LEGAL CAUSE OR DUTY

PALSGRAF v. LONG ISLAND RAILROAD CO.
248 N.Y. 339, 162 N.E. 99 (1928)

CARDOZO, C.J.

Plaintiff was standing on a platform of defendant's railroad after buying a ticket to go to Rockaway Beach. A train stopped at the station, bound for another place. Two men ran forward to catch it. One of the men reached the platform of the car without mishap, though the train was already moving. The other man, carrying a package, jumped aboard the car, but seemed unsteady as if about to fall. A guard on the car, who had held the door open, reached forward to help him in, and another guard on the platform pushed him from behind. In this act, the package was dislodged, and fell upon the rails. It was a package of small size, about fifteen inches long, and was covered by a newspaper. In fact it contained fireworks, but there was nothing in its appearance to give notice of its contents. The fireworks when they fell exploded. The shock of the explosion threw down some scales at the other end of the platform, many feet away. The scales struck the plaintiff, causing injuries for which she sues.

The conduct of the defendant's guard, if a wrong in its relation to the holder of the package, was not a wrong in its relation to the plaintiff, standing far away. Relative to her it was not negligence at all. Nothing in the situation gave notice that the falling package had in it the potency of peril to persons thus removed. Negligence is not actionable unless it involves the invasion of a legally protected interest, the violation of a right. "Proof of negligence in the air, so to speak, will not do. . . ." The plaintiff as she stood upon the platform of the station might claim to be protected against intentional invasion of her bodily security. Such invasion is not charged. She might claim to be protected against unintentional invasion by conduct involving in the thought of reasonable men an unreasonable hazard that such invasion would ensue. These, from the point of view of the law, were the bounds of her immunity, with perhaps some rare exceptions, survivals for the most part of ancient forms of liability, where conduct is held to be at the peril of the actor. If no hazard was apparent to the eye of ordinary vigilance, an act innocent and harmless, at least to outward seeming, with reference to her, did not take to itself the quality of a tort because it happened to be a wrong, though apparently not one involving the risk of bodily insecurity, with reference to someone else. "In every instance, before negligence can be predicated on a given act, back of the act must be sought and found a duty to the individual complaining, the observance of which would have averted or avoided the injury. . . ." The plaintiff sues in her own right for a wrong personal to her, and not as the vicarious beneficiary of a breach of duty to another.

A different conclusion will involve us, and swiftly too, in a maze of contradictions. A guard stumbles over a package which has been left upon a platform. It seems to be a bundle of newspapers. It turns out to be a can of dynamite. To the eye of ordinary vigilance, the bundle is abandoned waste, which may be kicked or trod on with impunity. Is a passenger at the other end of the platform protected by the law against the unsuspected hazard concealed beneath the waste? If not, is the result to be any different, so far as the distant passenger is concerned, when the guard stumbles over a valise which a truckman or a porter has left upon the walk? The passenger far away, if the victim of a wrong at all, has a cause of action, not derivative, but original and primary. His claim to be protected against invasion of his bodily security is neither greater nor less because the act resulting in the invasion is a wrong to another far removed. In this case, the rights that are said to have been violated, the interests said to have been invaded, are not even of the same order. The man was not injured in his person nor even put in danger. The purpose of the act, as well as its effect, was to make his person safe. If there was a wrong to him at all, which may very well be doubted, it was a wrong to a property interest only, the safety of his package. Out of this wrong to property, which threatened injury to nothing else, there has passed, we are told, to the plaintiff by derivation or succession a right of action for the invasion of an interest of another order, the right to bodily security. The diversity of interests emphasizes the futility of the effort to build the plaintiff's right upon the basis of a wrong to some one else. The gain is one of emphasis, for a like result would follow if the interests were the same. Even then, the orbit of the danger as disclosed to the eye of reasonable vigilance would be the orbit of the duty. One who jostles one's neighbor in a crowd does not invade the rights of others standing at the outer fringe when the unintended contact casts a bomb upon the ground. The wrongdoer as to them is the man who carries the bomb, not the one who explodes it without suspicion of the danger. Life will have to be made over, and human nature transformed, before prevision so extravagant can be accepted as the norm of conduct, the customary standard to which behavior must conform.

The argument for the plaintiff is built upon the shifting meanings of such words as "wrong" and "wrongful," and shares their instability. What the plaintiff must show is "a wrong" to herself, *i.e.*, a violation of her own right, and not merely a wrong to some one else, nor conduct "wrongful" because unsocial, but not "a wrong" to any one. We are told that one who drives at reckless speed through a crowded city street is guilty of a negligent act and, therefore, of a wrongful one irrespective of the consequences. Negligent the act is, and wrongful in the sense that it is unsocial, but wrongful and unsocial in relation to other travelers, only because the eye of vigilance perceives the risk of damage. If the same act were to be committed on a speedway or a race course, it would lose its wrongful quality. The risk reasonably to be perceived defines the duty to be obeyed, and risk imports relation; it is risk to another or to others within the range of apprehension. This does not mean, of course, that one who launches a destructive force is always relieved of liability if the force, though known to be destructive, pursues an unexpected path. "It was not necessary that the defendant should have had notice of the particular method in which an accident would occur, if the possibility of an accident was clear to the ordinarily prudent eye. . . ." Some acts, such as shooting, are so imminently dangerous to any one who may come within reach of the missile, however unexpectedly, as to impose a duty of prevision not far from that of an insurer. Even to-day, and much oftener in earlier stages of the law, one acts sometimes at one's peril. Under this head, it may be, fall certain cases of what is known as transferred intent, an act willfully dangerous to A resulting by misadventure in injury to B. These cases aside, wrong is defined in terms of the natural or probable, at least when unintentional. The range of reasonable apprehension is at times a question for the court, and at times, if varying inferences are possible, a question for the jury. Here, by concession, there was nothing in the situation to suggest to the most cautious mind that the parcel wrapped in newspaper would spread wreckage through the station. If the guard had thrown it down knowingly and willfully, he would not have threatened the plaintiff's safety, so far as appearances could warn him. His conduct would not have involved, even then, an unreasonable probability of invasion of her bodily security. Liability can be no greater where the act is inadvertent.

Negligence, like risk, is thus a term of relation. Negligence in the abstract, apart from things related, is surely not a tort, if indeed it is understandable at all. Negligence is not a tort unless it results in the commission of a wrong, and the commission of a wrong imports the violation of a right, in this case, we are told, the right to be protected against interference with one's bodily security. But bodily security is protected, not against all forms of interference or aggression, but only against some. One who seeks redress at law does not make out a cause of action by showing without more that there has been damage to his person. If the harm was not willful, he must show that the act as to him had possibilities of danger so many and apparent as to entitle him to be protected against the doing of it though the harm was unintended. Affront to personality is still the keynote of the wrong. . . .

The law of causation, remote or proximate, is thus foreign to the case before us. The question of liability is always anterior to the question of the measure of the consequences that go with liability. If there is no tort to be redressed, there is no occasion to consider what damage might be recovered if there were a finding of a tort. We may assume, without deciding, that negligence, not at large or in the abstract, but in relation to the plaintiff, would entail liability for any and all consequences, however novel or extraordinary. There is room for argument that a distinction is to be drawn according to the diversity of interests invaded by the act, as where conduct negligent in that it threatens an insignificant invasion of an interest in property results in an unforeseeable invasion of an interest of another order, as, *e.g.*, one of bodily security. Perhaps other distinctions may be necessary. We do not go into the question now. The consequences to be followed must first be rooted in a wrong.

The judgment of the Appellate Division and that of the Trial Term should be reversed, and the complaint dismissed, with costs in all courts.

ANDREWS, JUSTICE, dissenting.

Assisting a passenger to board a train, the defendant's servant negligently knocked a package from his arms. It fell between the platform and the cars. Of its contents the servant knew and could know nothing. A violent explosion followed. The concussion broke some scales standing a considerable distance away. In falling they injured the plaintiff, an intending passenger.

Upon these facts may she recover the damages she has suffered in an action brought against the master? The result we shall reach depends upon our theory as to the nature of negligence. Is it a relative concept — the breach of some duty owing to a particular person or to particular persons? Or where there is an act which unreasonably threatens the safety of others, is the doer liable for all its proximate consequences, even where they result in injury to one who would generally be thought to be outside the radius of danger? This is not a mere dispute as to words. We might not believe that to the average mind the dropping of the bundle would seem to involve the probability of harm to the plaintiff standing many feet away whatever might be the case as to the owner or to one so near as to be likely to be struck by its fall. If, however, we adopt the second hypothesis we have to inquire only as to the relation between cause and effect. We deal in terms of proximate cause, not of negligence.

Negligence may be defined roughly as an act or omission which unreasonably does or may affect the rights of others, or which unreasonably fails to protect oneself from the dangers resulting from such acts. Here I confine myself to the first branch of the definition. Nor do I comment on the word "unreasonable." For present purposes it sufficiently describes that average of conduct that society requires of its members.

There must be both the act or the omission, and the right. . . .

But we are told that "there is no negligence unless there is in the particular case a legal duty to take care, and this duty must be one which is owed to the plaintiff himself and not merely to others." (SALMOND, TORTS [6th ed.], 24.) This, I think is too narrow a conception. Where there is the unreasonable act, and some right that may be affected there is negligence whether damage does or does not result. That is immaterial. Should we drive down Broadway at a reckless speed, we are negligent whether we strike an approaching car or miss it by an inch. The act itself is wrongful. It is a wrong not only to those who happen to be within the radius of danger but to all who might have been there — a wrong to the public at large. Such is the language of the street. Such the language of the courts when speaking of contributory negligence. Such again and again their language in speaking of the duty of some defendant and discussing proximate cause in cases where such a discussion is wholly irrelevant on any other theory. As was said by Mr. Justice Holmes many years

C. BREACH, LEGAL CAUSE OR DUTY 399

ago, "[T]he measure of the defendant's duty in determining whether a wrong has been committed is one thing, the measure of liability when a wrong has been committed is another." (*Spade v. Lynn & B. R.R. Co.,* 52 N.E. 747, 172 Mass. 488 (1899).) Due care is a duty imposed on each one of us to protect society from unnecessary danger, not to protect A, B or C alone. It may well be that there is no such thing as negligence in the abstract. "Proof of negligence in the air, so to speak, will not do." In an empty world negligence would not exist. It does involve a relationship between man and his fellows. But not merely a relationship between man and those whom he might reasonably expect his act would injure. Rather, a relationship between him and those whom he does in fact injure. If his act has a tendency to harm some one, it harms him a mile away as surely as it does those on the scene. We now permit children to recover for the negligent killing of the father. It was never prevented on the theory that no duty was owing to them. A husband may be compensated for the loss of his wife's services. To say that the wrongdoer was negligent as to the husband as well as to the wife is merely an attempt to fit facts to theory. An insurance company paying a fire loss recovers its payment of the negligent incendiary. We speak of subrogation — of suing in the right of the insured. Behind the cloud of words is the fact they hide, that the act, wrongful as to the insured, has also injured the company. Even if it be true that the fault of father, wife or insured will prevent recovery, it is because we consider the original negligence not the proximate cause of the injury.

In the well-known *Polemis* case [1921] 3 K.B. 560, SCRUTTON, L. J., said that the dropping of a plank was negligent for it might injure "workman or cargo or ship." Because of this possibility the owner of the vessel was to be made good for his loss. The act being wrongful the doer was liable for its proximate results. Criticized and explained as this statement may have been, I think it states the law as it should be and as it is.

The proposition is this. Every one owes to the world at large the duty of refraining from those acts that may unreasonably threaten the safety of others. Such an act occurs. Not only is he wronged to whom harm might reasonably be expected to result, but he also who is in fact injured, even if he be outside what would generally be thought the danger zone. There needs be duty due the one complaining but this is not a duty to a particular individual because as to him harm might be expected. Harm to some one being the natural result of the act, not only that one alone, but all those in fact injured may complain. We have never, I think, held otherwise. . . . Unreasonable risk being taken, its consequences are not confined to those who might probably be hurt.

If this be so, we do not have a plaintiff suing by "derivation or succession." Her action is original and primary. Her claim is for a breach of duty to herself — not that she is subrogated to any right of action of the owner of the parcel or of a passenger standing at the scene of the explosion.

The right to recover damages rests on additional considerations. The plaintiff's rights must be injured, and this injury must be caused by the negligence. We build a dam, but are negligent as to its foundations. Breaking, it injures property downstream. We are not liable if all this happened because of some reason other than the insecure foundation. But when injuries do result from our unlawful act we are liable for the consequences. It does not matter that they are unusual, unexpected, unforeseen and unforeseeable. But there is one limitation. The damages must be so connected with the negligence that the latter may be said to be the proximate cause of the former.

These two words have never been given an inclusive definition. What is a cause in a legal sense, still more what is a proximate cause, depends in each case upon many considerations, as does the existence of negligence itself. Any philosophical doctrine of causation does not help us. A boy throws a stone into a pond. The ripples spread. The water level rises. The history of that pond is altered to all eternity. It will be altered by other causes also. Yet it will be forever the resultant of all causes combined. Each one will have an influence. How great only omniscience can say. You may speak of a chain, or if you please, a net. An analogy is of little aid. Each cause brings about future events. Without each the future would not be the same. Each is proximate in the sense it is essential. But that is not what we mean by the word. Nor on the other hand do we mean sole cause. There is no such thing.

Should analogy be thought helpful, however, I prefer that of a stream. The spring, starting on its journey, is joined by tributary after tributary. The river, reaching the ocean, comes from a hundred sources. No man may say whence any drop of water is derived. Yet for a time distinction may be possible. Into the clear creek, brown swamp water flows from the left. Later, from the right comes water stained by its clay bed. The three may remain for a space, sharply divided. But at last, inevitably no trace of separation remains. They are so commingled that all distinction is lost.

As we have said, we cannot trace the effect of an act to the end, if end there is. Again, however, we may trace it part of the way. A murder at Sarajevo may be the necessary antecedent to an assassination in London twenty years hence. An overturned lantern may burn all Chicago. We may follow the fire from the shed to the last building. We rightly say the fire started by the lantern caused its destruction.

A cause, but not the proximate cause. What we do mean by the word "proximate" is, that because of convenience, of public policy, of a rough sense of justice, the law arbitrarily declines to trace a series of events beyond a certain point. This is not logic. It is practical politics. Take our rule as to fires. Sparks from my burning haystack set on fire my house and my neighbor's. I may recover from a negligent railroad. He may not. Yet the wrongful act as directly harmed the one as the other. We may regret that the line was drawn just where it was, but drawn somewhere it had to be. We said the act of the railroad was not the proximate cause of our neighbor's fire. Cause it surely was. The words we used were simply indicative of our notions of public policy. Other courts think differently. But somewhere they reach the point where they cannot say the stream comes from any one source.

Take the illustration given in an unpublished manuscript by a distinguished and helpful writer on the law of torts. A chauffeur negligently collides with another car which is filled with dynamite, although he could not know it. An explosion follows. A, walking on the sidewalk nearby, is killed. B, sitting in a window of a building opposite, is cut by flying glass. C, likewise sitting in

C. BREACH, LEGAL CAUSE OR DUTY 401

a window a block away, is similarly injured. And a further illustration. A nursemaid, ten blocks away, startled by the noise, involuntarily drops a baby from her arms to the walk. We are told that C may not recover while A may. As to B it is a question for court or jury. We will all agree that the baby might not. Because, we are again told, the chauffeur had no reason to believe his conduct involved any risk of injuring either C or the baby. As to them he was not negligent.

But the chauffeur, being negligent in risking the collision, his belief that the scope of the harm he might do would be limited is immaterial. His act unreasonably jeopardized the safety of any one who might be affected by it. C's injury and that of the baby were directly traceable to the collision. Without that, the injury would not have happened. C had the right to sit in his office, secure from such dangers. The baby was entitled to use the sidewalk with reasonable safety.

The true theory is, it seems to me, that the injury to C, if in truth he is to be denied recovery, and the injury to the baby is that their several injuries were not the proximate result of the negligence. And here not what the chauffeur had reason to believe would be the result of his conduct, but what the prudent would foresee, may have a bearing. May have some bearing, for the problem of proximate cause is not to be solved by any one consideration. It is all a question of expediency. There are no fixed rules to govern our judgment. There are simply matters of which we may take account. We have in a somewhat different connection spoken of "the stream of events." We have asked whether that stream was deflected — whether it was forced into new and unexpected channels. This is rather rhetoric than law. There is in truth little to guide us other than common sense.

There are some hints that may help us. The proximate cause, involved as it may be with many other causes, must be, at the least, something without which the event would not happen. The court must ask itself whether there was a natural and continuous sequence between cause and effect. Was the one a substantial factor in producing the other? Was there a direct connection between them, without too many intervening causes? Is the effect of cause on result not too attenuated? Is the cause likely, in the usual judgment of mankind, to produce the result? Or by the exercise of prudent foresight could the result be foreseen? Is the result too remote from the cause, and here we consider remoteness in time and space. Clearly we must so consider, for the greater the distance either in time or space, the more surely do other causes intervene to affect the result. When a lantern is overturned the firing of a shed is a fairly direct consequence. Many things contribute to the spread of the conflagration — the force of the wind, the direction and width of streets, the character of intervening structures, other factors. We draw an uncertain and wavering line, but draw it we must as best we can.

Once again, it is all a question of fair judgment, always keeping in mind the fact that we endeavor to make a rule in each case that will be practical and in keeping with the general understanding of mankind.

Here another question must be answered. In the case supposed it is said, and said correctly, that the chauffeur is liable for the direct effect of the explosion although he had no reason to suppose it would follow a collision.

"The fact that the injury occurred in a different manner than that which might have been expected does not prevent the chauffeur's negligence from being in law the cause of the injury." But the natural results of a negligent act — the results which a prudent man would or should foresee — do have a bearing upon the decision as to proximate cause. We have said so repeatedly. What should be foreseen? No human foresight would suggest that a collision itself might injure one a block away. On the contrary, given an explosion, such a possibility might be reasonably expected. I think the direct connection, the foresight of which the courts speak, assumes prevision of the explosion, for the immediate results of which, at least, the chauffeur is responsible.

It may be said this is unjust. Why? In fairness he should make good every injury flowing from his negligence. Not because of tenderness toward him we say he need not answer for all that follows his wrong. We look back to the catastrophe, the fire kindled by the spark, or the explosion. We trace the consequences — not indefinitely, but to a certain point. And to aid us in fixing that point we ask what might ordinarily be expected to follow the fire or the explosion.

This last suggestion is the factor which must determine the case before us. The act upon which defendant's liability rests is knocking an apparently harmless package onto the platform. The act was negligent. For its proximate consequences the defendant is liable. If its contents were broken, to the owner; if it fell upon and crushed a passenger's foot, then to him. If it exploded and injured one in the immediate vicinity, to him also as to A in the illustration. Mrs. Palsgraf was standing some distance away. How far cannot be told from the record — apparently twenty-five or thirty feet. Perhaps less. Except for the explosion, she would not have been injured. We are told by the appellant in his brief "it cannot be denied that the explosion was the direct cause of the plaintiff's injuries." So it was a substantial factor in producing the result — there was here a natural and continuous sequence — direct connection. The only intervening cause was that instead of blowing her to the ground the concussion smashed the weighing machine which in turn fell upon her. There was no remoteness in time, little in space. And surely, given such an explosion as here it needed no great foresight to predict that the natural result would be to injure one on the platform at no greater distance from its scene than was the plaintiff. Just how no one might be able to predict. Whether by flying fragments, by broken glass, by wreckage of machines or structures no one could say. But injury in some form was most probable.

Under these circumstances I cannot say as a matter of law that the plaintiff's injuries were not the proximate result of the negligence. That is all we have before us. The court refused to so charge. No request was made to submit the matter to the jury as a question of fact, even would that have been proper upon the record before us.

The judgment appealed from should be affirmed, with costs.

NOTES

1. *Duty or Proximate Cause?* How did Justice Cardozo decide the *Palsgraf* case? Did he decide that the railroad was not the proximate cause of Mrs.

Palsgraf's injuries? He didn't, did he? He decided that the defendant railroad did not owe a duty to Mrs. Palsgraf to protect her from the risk which caused her injuries, didn't he? Why did he decide on the issue of duty? If the case had been decided on grounds of proximate cause, a la *In re Polemis*, [1921] 3 K.B. 569, which the dissent says was the controlling rule in New York at that time, what result? What result if the case had been decided on the basis of foreseeability, see *The Wagon Mound*, [1961] A.C. 388, 1 All E.R. 404? Justice Andrews thought the critical element was proximate cause, not duty. What was Justice Andrews' test for duty?

What difference does it make? More basically, who cares? One important thing turns on whether the legal responsibility issue is one of duty or proximate cause. The judge decides duty as a matter of law and traditionally, at least, the jury decides proximate cause. What guidelines does Cardozo provide us about when the judge should decide the case as a matter of duty and when the jury should decide it?

2. *Cardozo's Opinion.* What is Cardozo's test for determining whether the railroad is responsible for Mrs. Palsgraf's injuries? What must be foreseeable? The plaintiff? The risk? The plaintiff and the risk? The plaintiff and some risk to the plaintiff? If some risk must be foreseeable to the plaintiff, then would Cardozo hold the defendant liable or responsible for all the injuries suffered? If so, how different is his approach from *Polemis*? Alternatively, must the particular risk which causes the injury be foreseeable? If so, how different is Cardozo's approach from *Wagon Mound (No. 1)*? Can you answer these questions from his opinion? Or, can you answer them all "yes" from his opinion? What language do you rely upon?

3. *How Close Is Near?* Cardozo's majority opinion in *Palsgraf* suggests that a factor in denying recovery was that the plaintiff was a significant distance from the explosion. On petition for rehearing, counsel pointed out that Mrs. Palsgraf was much closer to the explosion than the majority opinion appeared to indicate. In denying the petition, the court said:

> If we assume that the plaintiff was nearer the scene of the explosion than the prevailing opinion would suggest, she was not so near that the injury from a falling package, not known to contain explosives, would be within the range of reasonable prevision.

249 N.Y. at 511. She was "not so near" as to permit recovery. Could she have recovered, under the majority opinion, if she had been standing next to the person carrying the fireworks and had been injured by the explosion?

4. *Andrew's Opinion.* What is Justice Andrew's test for responsibility? Or, would it be better to say, what are his *tests* for responsibility? Is his a kitchen sink approach, i.e., throw all the tests in the kitchen sink and make a decision based on "practical politics," not "logic." In particular, focus on his application of the foreseeable risk test. Is it the same as the foreseeable risk test in *Wagon Mound (No.1)*? Is it the same "foreseeable risk" test Cardozo applies? Is Justice Andrews' "foreseeable risk" test a foresight inquiry? Or is it a hindsight test?

5. *Foreseeable Risk / Unforeseeable Manner.* Even to courts applying the *Wagon Mound (No.1)* foreseeable risk test, there is respectable authority that if a foreseeable risk arises in an unforeseeable manner, there will be liability. For

instance, in *Hughes v. Lord Advocate,* [1963] A.C. 837, 845, 1 All E.R. 705, 2 W.L.R. 779 (H.L.), workers left a hole in the street unguarded, but covered with a tent and surrounded by paraffin-burning lights. An 8-year-old boy entered the tent and knocked over one of the lamps, which fell into the hole causing a freak, violent explosion. The court held that the damage was foreseeable on the basis that there *was* a foreseeable risk of fire, albeit one from contact with a lamp, rather than a fiery explosion. Lord Reid commented that "[A defendant] is liable, although the damage may be a good deal greater in extent than was foreseeable. He can only escape liability if the damage can be regarded as differing in kind from what was foreseeable."

6. *A Rose by Another Name?* Andrew J. McClurg wrote a spoof on *Palsgraf* in the ABAJ 16 (Jan. 2001). Among other things, he suggests the opinion did not correctly reflect the facts. Quoting Prosser, he says the "event could not possibly have happened" as described in the opinion, because the unfortunate passenger was carrying "ordinary fireworks which fell onto the tracks below a sturdy platform. No one testified to seeing a scale fall. Mrs. [Palsgraf's] first complaint alleged that stampeding passengers knocked the scale over." Assuming Prosser, or McClurg, has the facts right, should the different facts make a difference in the outcome of the case?

BIGBEE v. PACIFIC TELEPHONE & TELEGRAPH CO.
34 Cal. 3d 49, 192 Cal. Rptr. 857, 665 P.2d 947 (1983)

BIRD, CHIEF JUSTICE.

On November 2, 1974 . . . at approximately 12:20 a.m., plaintiff was standing in a public telephone booth located in the parking lot of a liquor store on Century Boulevard in Inglewood, California. Roberts, who was intoxicated, was driving east along Century Boulevard. She lost control of her car and veered off the street into the parking lot, crashing into the booth in which plaintiff was standing.

Plaintiff saw Roberts' car coming toward him and realized that it would hit the telephone booth. He attempted to flee but was unable to do so. According to the allegations of the complaint, the telephone booth was so defective in design and/or manufacture, or so negligently installed or maintained that the door to the booth "jammed and stuck, trapping" plaintiff inside. Had the door operated freely, [plaintiff] averred, he would have been able to escape and would not have suffered injury.

Additionally, plaintiff alleged that the telephone booth was negligently located in that it was placed too close to Century Boulevard, where "traffic . . . traveling easterly, generally and habitually speeded in excess of the posted speed limit," thereby creating an unreasonable risk of harm to anyone who used the telephone booth.

. . . [D]efendants argued that they had no duty to protect phone booth users from the risk encountered by plaintiff — a car veering off the street and crashing into the phone booth — since that risk was unforeseeable as a matter of law. For the same reason, they maintained that Roberts' intervening negligent driving constituted a "superseding cause" of plaintiff's injuries.

Therefore, no act or omission of [defendants] could be found to be a proximate cause of those injuries.

[Defendants established that] the phone booth in which plaintiff was standing when injured was one of two booths located in the parking lot of the Fortune Liquor Store. The booths were situated close to the front wall of the store, between the front door and the sidewalk bordering Century Boulevard, near an entrance to the parking lot. Plaintiff occupied the booth nearest the street, 15 feet to the south of the curb line of Century Boulevard, . . . [and also] Roberts may have been speeding when she lost control of her car. In the opinion of defendants' expert witness, her car was traveling at a speed of 30 to 35 miles per hour when it struck the phone booth. . . .

. . . [P]laintiff introduced declarations which established that this accident was not the first one involving a phone booth at this particular location. On February 13, 1973, some 20 months prior to plaintiff's accident, another car struck a phone booth in this same location. Following this previous accident, defendants placed three steel "bumper posts" between the phone booths and the parking lot. No such posts were placed between the booths and Century Boulevard.

In addition, plaintiff introduced a telephone company manual which states that telephone booth doors, when operating normally, "should open with a slight pull on the handle. . . ."

At the hearing on the motion [to dismiss] . . . the court granted the motion and entered a judgment of dismissal. This appeal by the plaintiff followed.

Defendants contend that their duty to use due care in the location, installation, and maintenance of telephone booths does not extend to the risk encountered by plaintiff and that neither their alleged negligence in carrying out these activities nor any defect in the booth was a proximate cause of plaintiff's injuries. These contentions present the same issue in different guises. Each involves this question — was the risk that a car might crash into the phone booth and injure plaintiff reasonably foreseeable in this case? . . .

Ordinarily, foreseeability is a question of fact for the jury. (*Weirum v. RKO General, Inc.,* 15 Cal. 3d 40, 46, 123 Cal. Rptr. 468, 539 P.2d 36 (1975)).

. . . Turning to the merits of this case, the question presented is a relatively simple one. Is there room for a reasonable difference of opinion as to whether the risk that a car might crash into the phone booth and injure an individual inside was reasonably foreseeable under the circumstances set forth above?

In pursuing this inquiry, it is well to remember that "foreseeability is not to be measured by what is more probable than not, but includes whatever is likely enough in the setting of modern life that a reasonably thoughtful (person) would take account of it in guiding practical conduct." . . . One may be held accountable for creating even "the risk of a slight possibility of injury if a reasonably prudent (person) would not do so." . . . Moreover, it is settled that what is required to be foreseeable is the general character of the event or harm — *e.g.*, being struck by a car while standing in a phone booth — not its precise nature or manner of occurrence.

Here, defendants placed a telephone booth, which was difficult to exit, in a parking lot 15 feet from the side of a major thoroughfare and near a driveway. Under these circumstances, this court cannot conclude as a matter of law that it was unforeseeable that the booth might be struck by a car and cause serious injury to a person trapped within. A jury could reasonably conclude that this risk was foreseeable. . . . This is particularly true where, as here, there is evidence that a booth at this same location had previously been struck.

Indeed, in light of the circumstances of modern life, it seems evident that a jury could reasonably find that defendants should have foreseen the possibility of the very accident which actually occurred here. Swift traffic on a major thoroughfare late at night is to be expected. Regrettably, so too are intoxicated drivers. . . . Moreover, it is not uncommon for speeding and/or intoxicated drivers to lose control of their cars and crash into poles, buildings or whatever else may be standing alongside the road they travel — no matter how straight and level that road may be.

Where a telephone booth, which is difficult to exit, is placed 15 feet from such a thoroughfare, the risk that it might be struck by a car veering off the street, thereby causing injury to a person trapped within, cannot be said to be unforeseeable as a matter of law.

It is of no consequence that the harm to plaintiff came about through the negligent or reckless acts of Roberts. "If the likelihood that a third person may act in a particular manner is the hazard or one of the hazards which makes the actor negligent, such an act whether innocent, negligent, intentionally tortious, or criminal does not prevent the actor from being liable for harm caused thereby." (Restatement (Second) of Torts, § 449.) Here, the risk that a car might hit the telephone booth could be found to constitute one of the hazards to which plaintiff was exposed.

. . . Considering the case law and the circumstances of this case, this court cannot conclude as a matter of law that injury to plaintiff, inflicted by negligent or reckless third party drivers, was unforeseeable. . . .

This is not to say, of course, that defendants are liable for plaintiff's injury. This court decides only that this question is one that should be reserved for a jury.

Reversed and remanded.

KRONINGER, Justice, concurring in part and dissenting in part.

. . .Whether a duty of care is owed in any particular instance is a question of law and "is the court's 'expression of the sum total of those considerations of policy which lead the law to say that the particular plaintiff is entitled to protection.' " (*Weirum v. RKO General, Inc.* 15 Cal.3d 40, 46, 123 Cal.Rptr. 468, 539 P.2d 36 (1975)) There are a number of such considerations; "the major ones are the foreseeability of harm to plaintiff, the degree of certainty that the plaintiff suffered injury, the closeness of the connection between the defendant's conduct and the injury suffered, the moral blame attached to the defendant's conduct, the policy of preventing future harm, the extent of the burden to the defendant and consequences to the community of imposing a duty to exercise care with resulting liability for breach, and the availability, cost, and prevalence of insurance for the risk involved." (*Rowland v. Christian* 69 Cal.2d 108, 113, 70 Cal.Rptr. 97, 443 P.2d 89 (1968)) Thus, foreseeability is but one of many considerations in weighing the question of whether a duty should be found to exist.. . .

The location of the telephone booth here, 15 feet from the curb, beside a straight and level roadway, and adjacent to a building, provided, if anything, more protection from the risk of curb-jumping automobiles than the adjacent sidewalk itself. To hold that defendants could be found liable for locating the booth where they did is tantamount to holding that one may be found negligent whenever he conducts everyday activities on or adjacent to the public sidewalk. It will go far toward making all roadside businesses insurers of safety from wayward travelers.

There is no suggestion of anything defendants might reasonably have done differently with respect to siting except simply not to maintain a telephone booth in the vicinity at all. Public telephones have, in fact, long been maintained adjacent to streets and highways for the convenience of the public, despite the obvious but remote risks. But "virtually every act involves some conceivable danger. Liability is imposed only if the risk of harm resulting from the act is deemed unreasonable — *i.e.*, if the gravity and likelihood of the danger outweigh the utility of the conduct involved." (*Weirum v. RKO General, Inc., supra*, at 47). Balancing the gravity and likelihood of danger against the usefulness of conveniently located public telephones, and applying each of the other "considerations" enumerated in *Rowland, supra*, I would opt for encouraging their continued maintenance adjacent to streets and highways, and would hold that on the present facts there arose no duty which could impose liability based on location of the booth.

. . . It does not follow, however, that defendants might not be found liable for injury resulting from defective maintenance. The sticky door, if it existed, increased plaintiff's danger by frustrating effective use of his own self-protective faculties. Needlessly to increase the usual risks could be found negligent by the jury. The risk of a sidewalk-jumping car is a risk a pedestrian might seek to avoid by getting out of the way. Such an occurrence could be deemed not to supersede but to concur with negligently impeding plaintiff's freedom to take protective action. The judgment is properly reversed on that question.

NOTES

1. *Issue Spotting*. What was the issue in *Bigbee*? Negligence? Duty or Legal Cause? What was the test for duty? Who should be the arbiter of duty?

2. *Duty Lore*. Most California and many other courts favor the *Weirum-Rowland* factor analysis. See *McCall v. Wilder*, 913 S.W.2d 150 (Tenn. 1995), wherein the court opined:

> A claim of negligence requires proof of the following elements: (1) a duty of care owed by defendant to plaintiff; (2) conduct below the applicable standard of care that amounts to a breach of that duty; (3) an injury or loss; (4) cause in fact; and (5) proximate, or legal, cause.

Although the concept of duty was not part of the early English common law of torts, it has since become an essential element in all negligence cases. Properly defined, duty is the legal obligation owed by defendant to plaintiff to conform to a reasonable person standard of care for the protection against unreasonable risks of harm. A risk is unreasonable and gives rise to a duty to act with due care if the foreseeable probability and gravity of harm posed by defendant's conduct outweigh the burden upon defendant to engage in alternative conduct that would have prevented the harm. Restatement (Second) of Torts, § 291 (1964) ("Where an act is one which a reasonable [person] would recognize as involving a risk of harm to another, the risk is unreasonable and the act is negligent if the risk is of such magnitude as to outweigh what the law regards as the utility of the act or of the particular manner in which it is done.").

Several factors must be considered in determining whether a risk is an unreasonable one. Those factors include the foreseeable probability of the harm or injury occurring; the possible magnitude of the potential harm or injury; the importance or social value of the activity engaged in by defendant; the usefulness of the conduct to defendant; the feasibility of alternative, safer conduct and the relative costs and burdens associated with that conduct; the relative usefulness of the safer conduct; and the relative safety of alternative conduct. Stated succinctly, a duty of reasonable care exists if defendant's conduct poses an unreasonable and foreseeable risk of harm to persons or property.

Once it is determined that defendant owed plaintiff a legal obligation to conform to a reasonable person standard of conduct, i.e., a duty — the question becomes whether defendant failed to exercise reasonable care under the circumstances, i.e., whether defendant breached the duty. "What the defendant must do, or must not do, is a question of the standard of conduct required to satisfy the duty." Prosser and Keeton on the Law of Torts, *supra*, at § 356.

Is the court's test for duty helpful? Does it authorize a trial court to make a factually specific determination about the existence of a duty in every case? What is the jury's role in all of this? Note that some of the factors are very similar to the Learned Hand negligence formula. Is that formula a test for the existence of a duty? Breach? Both?

3. *Duty (Over) Simplified?* In *Webb v. Jarvis*, 575 N.E.2d 992, 995 (Ind. 1991), the court stated: "Whether the law recognizes any obligation on the part of a particular defendant to conform his conduct to a certain standard for the benefit of the plaintiff is a question of law. [T]hree factors must be balanced, *viz.* (1) the relationship between the parties, (2) the reasonable foreseeability of harm to the person injured, and (3) public policy concerns." Does the court tell you anything you did not know? Does it tell you how to apply those three factors? Does it tell you the relative weight of the three factors? Does it tell you the relationship between the duty determination and proximate cause?

4. *Duty and Foreseeability*. One of the most confusing aspects of the duty issue involves its apparent reliance on foreseeability as a vital ingredient. In

the proximate cause area, foresight is used primarily as a limitation on recoverable damages. However, in the duty context foreseeability is a manipulable cover for a legion of different judicial concerns, including many of the same ones that are at issue in proximate cause and in the determination of breach. *See generally* P. CANE, ATIYAH'S ACCIDENTS, COMPENSATION AND THE LAW, 60-93 (4th ed. 1987); Green, *The Duty Problem in Negligence Cases,* 28 COLUM. L. REV. 1014 (1928); Thode, *Tort Analysis: Duty-Risk v. Proximate Cause and the Rational Allocation of Functions Between Judge and Jury,* 1977 UTAH L. REV. 1.

The carefully chosen words of one court may present a useful starting point:

> [A] court's task in determining "duty" is not to decide whether a particular plaintiff's injury was reasonably foreseeable in light of a particular defendant's conduct, but rather to evaluate more generally whether the category of negligent conduct at issue is sufficiently likely to result in the kind of harm experienced that liability may appropriately be imposed on the negligent party.
>
> The jury, by contrast, considers "foreseeability" in two more focused, fact-specific settings. First, the jury may consider the likelihood or foreseeability of injury in determining whether, in fact, the particular defendant's conduct was negligent in the first place. Second, foreseeability may be relevant to the jury's determination of whether the defendant's negligence was a proximate or legal cause of the plaintiff's injury."

Ballard v. Uribe, 41 Cal. 3d 564, 573 n.6, 224 Cal. Rptr. 664, 715 P.2d 624 (1986). So, foreseeability for duty is a more general inquiry than it is when the jury decides proximate cause? Is that consistent with Cardozo's analysis in *Palsgraf*? In the light of *Ballard* how would you characterize the approaches taken by the majority and minority opinions in *Bigbee*?

5. *Duty Function.* "[L]egal duties are not discoverable facts of nature, but merely conclusory expressions that, in cases of a particular type, liability should be imposed for damage done." *Tarasoff v. Regents of University of Cal.,* 17 Cal. 3d 425, 131 Cal. Rptr. 14, 551 P.2d 334, 342 (1976).

The function of the duty concept is to provide a basic filtering device at an early stage in the litigation process. The "duty-no duty" determination arguably applies to whole classes of cases. As such, it should be the least fact-sensitive aspect of the tort of negligence. But that is not true of Justice Cardozo's opinion in *Palsgraf*, is it? His "no duty" determination is rather fact specific. And, doesn't the Tennessee Supreme Court's duty "test" in *McCall* leave open the possibility of case-specific duty determinations by judges?

6. *Generalized "No Duty" Determinations.* The "no-duty" argument may be invoked for a variety of reasons, some of which are internal to the torts system, others of which are not. The most famous example of a systemic concern is the so-called "floodgates" argument, perhaps best expressed in the words of Justice Cardozo that we should be sensitive to exposing defendants to "liability in an indeterminate amount for an indeterminate time to an indeterminate class." *Ultramares Corp. v. Touche, Niven & Co.,* 255 N.Y. 170, 179, 174 N.E. 441, 444 (1931).

Other courts have utilized the limited duty concept for allocational reasons in an almost legislative vein. For example, in *Wilson v. Kuenzi*, 751 S.W.2d 741, 746 (Mo. 1988) (*per* Welliver, J.), the Supreme Court of Missouri stated:

> A finding by this court today that we will not create and will not recognize either a new tort for wrongful life or for wrongful birth is in our opinion totally compatible with the policy considerations expressed by our legislature in attempting to limit the statute of limitations for malpractice actions, attempting to place a cap or limit on malpractice recoveries, and attempting legislative tort reform in general.

Note how these determinations are not case specific. They are not determinations based on the particular facts of the case. Rather they are determinations based on policies applicable to a broad type or group of cases.

7. *Judge or Jury, Again?* In *Kentucky Fried Chicken of California, Inc. v. Superior Court*, 14 Cal. 4th 814, 927 P.2d 1260, 59 Cal. Rptr. 2d 756 (1997), Kennard, J., remarked:

> The focus of the duty analysis should not be on the details of a defendant's conduct. The pertinent inquiry is whether a defendant must take steps to avoid causing a given type of harm to the victim. *What* steps a defendant must take to avoid the harm is a question of whether the defendant has met the standard of care by acting reasonably under the circumstances; also, it is a question that arises only after a duty has been found to exist.
>
> It is always possible to recast any question of whether the standard of care has been breached as a question of "duty," as the majority does here. Thus, instead of asking whether an automobile driver who failed to stop in time used the care of a reasonable driver under like circumstances, we could ask whether the driver had a "duty" to begin braking sooner; instead of asking whether a doctor treated a feverish patient with the care of a reasonable physician we could ask whether the doctor had a "duty" to administer penicillin. If a court does so, however, it abandons the flexibility inherent in the application of the reasonable person standard and instead dictates a rigid, inflexible rule of conduct that applies not only to the defendant in the case before it but also to all defendants in future cases who are confronted by a risk of the same type of harm to another, regardless of differences in the surrounding circumstances. For good reason, most courts have rejected this course.
>
> When courts impose a duty on a defendant, they generally do so without imposing a rigid, specific, and inflexible course of conduct. "In most cases, courts have fixed no standard of care for tort liability more precise than that of a reasonably prudent person under like circumstances."
>
> There are at least three good reasons why negligence law has allocated the judgment of the reasonableness of a defendant's conduct to the jury as a matter for case-by-case determination, rather than having courts, under the rubric of "duty," establish as a matter of law

fixed and unvarying rules of conduct for various categories of human activity. The first reason arises from the irreducible variety of circumstances which may surround an event that causes harm to someone. Because of this variety, an individualized rather than categorical determination of what constitutes reasonable care to avoid a particular type of harm usually will provide a more precise measure of what conduct is reasonable under the circumstances.

If the term "negligence" signified an absolute quantity or thing to be measured in all cases in accordance with some precise standard, much of the difficulty which besets courts in the solution of this class of cases would be at once dissipated. But, unfortunately, it does not. Negligence is not absolute, but is a thing which is always relative to the particular circumstances of which it is sought to be predicated. For this reason it is very rare that a set of circumstances is presented which enables a court to say as matter of law that negligence has been shown.

The greater accuracy that results from determining the propriety of the defendant's conduct by application of the reasonable person standard of care advances the economic function of tort law. The reasonable person standard of negligence liability, by asking whether a reasonable person would have taken additional precautions under the circumstances, examines how the risk of harm from the defendant's activity and the benefits of conducting the activity vary depending upon the precautions taken to avoid the harm. In economic terms, it encourages the optimal level of care on the part of both victims and injurers, optimal being defined as the point at which the cost of any additional precautions will be greater than the benefit of avoiding additional injury. An individualized determination of reasonableness increases efficiency because it allows for the optimal level of care to be determined under the circumstances of each case; it asks not whether in general the cost of additional precautions would be greater than the cost of additional injuries but whether, under the specific circumstances of the case at hand, additional precautions would have been cost effective. It asks this question, of course, not formally but intuitively by asking whether a reasonable person would have taken additional precautions to avoid the accident. To fix the conduct required to avoid a given harm as an absolute standard that does not vary with the accompanying circumstances . . . . inevitably means that in numerous cases the law will require something other than optimal care.

There is a second reason why it is preferable to leave the question of what conduct is required under the circumstances to the jury for an individualized determination, rather than attempting to mandate detailed rules of conduct categorically. Doing so allows successive juries to reassess what precautions are reasonable as social, economic, and technological conditions change over time. Accordingly, the reasonable person standard of care, because it does not dictate a fixed course of conduct to avoid the harm in question, encourages innovations that reduce the cost of precautions and substitutions of less costly preventative measures that are equally or more effective in avoiding the harm. By contrast, locking defendants forever into a straitjacket of prescribed conduct removes the incentive for them to lower the cost and increase the level of precautions they provide.

The third reason for allocating the determination of the reasonableness of defendant's care to the jury in a negligence case is that the jury, in addition to providing an individualized judgment of defendant's conduct, also has the potential to bring a wider array of practical experience and knowledge to that task than could a single individual such as a judge. The jury is a repository of collective wisdom and understanding concerning the conditions and circumstances of everyday life that it can bring to bear on the determination of what conduct is reasonable. As the conscience of the community, the jury plays an essential role in the application of the reasonable person standard of care.

The court makes an eloquent argument for the proposition that juries should decide breach, not judges. Is the argument as applicable to proximate cause? What would Cardozo say in response? Should courts have the power to decide cases at the duty stage to avoid putting society through the costs of expensive trials? Would directed verdicts on breach or legal (proximate) cause be as effective?

Are duty, cause or breach labels or the determination of the identity of the decision-maker allocationally neutral? Which will defendant favor?

8. *Within the Risk and Revisiting Confusion?* It should be apparent to you by now that whoever decides the legal responsibility issue—judge or jury—one key analytical factor or tool is whether the injury was within the foreseeable risks posed by defendant's conduct. Consider the following two cases.

Defendant doctor negligently misdiagnosed patient's condition, informing patient that the latter was in good health. Relying on this diagnosis, the patient canceled his life insurance policy which named his wife as beneficiary. Shortly thereafter the patient died of cancer. The court said the wife had no claim against the doctor:

> Here, taking the facts of the complaint as true, decedent decided to cancel his life insurance policy upon being erroneously informed by the physician that he was in good health. Furthermore, he would not have done so had he been correctly diagnosed as having cancer. However, the law does not impose upon a physician the burden of knowing every use to which his diagnoses may be put by his patients. The cancellation of insurance is an act not reasonably foreseeable to a physician as a probable consequence of a diagnosis of a patient's condition. Hence, we hold that defendant's duty of care to decedent did not extend to plaintiff as the beneficiary of the life insurance policy unforeseeably canceled by decedent.

Estate of Blacher v. Garlett, 857 P.2d 566 (Colo. Ct. App. 1993). The court decides that a patient's canceling an insurance policy is not within the group of foreseeable risks that would make the failure to diagnose cancer negligent. But is the court deciding there is no duty as a matter of law? That's what it seems to say. What if plaintiff had told the doctor about his decision to cancel his life insurance policy if the doctor gave him a clean bill of health? Would that mean there was a duty owed? Who would decide?

Plaintiff's deceased was struck by lightning and killed while playing on defendant's golf course, in *Hames v. State*, 808 S.W.2d 41 (Tenn. 1991). The court said the defendant had no duty to provide lightning-proof weather shelters on the course:

> With regard to conduct falling below the applicable standard of care, and on a more fundamental level than proximate cause, is the realization that lightning is such a highly unpredictable occurrence of nature, that it is not reasonable to require one to anticipate when and where it will strike. Stated another way, the risk to be guarded against is too remote to impose legal liability. We also think the risks and dangers associated with playing golf in a lightning storm are rather obvious to most adults. It would have taken less than two minutes for the decedent and his companions to reach the relative safety of the clubhouse. It is reasonable to infer that a reasonably prudent adult can recognize the approach of a severe thunderstorm and know that it is time to pack up the clubs and leave before the storm begins to wreak havoc.

Does the court's language sound like duty language or legal cause language?

9. *Legal Cause Reconsidered.* Given the duty recognized by the majority opinion in *Bigbee* what happened to the defendant's legal (or intervening) cause argument?

LODGE v. ARETT SALES CORP.
246 Conn. 563, 717 A.2d 215 (1998)

CALIHAN, CHIEF JUSTICE

The dispositive issue in these appeals is whether the defendants, who negligently caused the transmission of a false fire alarm, are liable to firefighters injured during an accident precipitated by the negligent maintenance and failure of the brakes on the responding fire engine. The plaintiffs are two Waterbury firefighters, the representatives of the estates of two Waterbury firefighters, and three of the firefighters' spouses. They brought this action against three defendants—Baker Protective Services, Inc., Wells Fargo Alarm Services Division (Wells Fargo), Arett Sales Corporation (Arett), and Advanced Automatic Sprinkler Protection Systems, Inc. (Advanced). The plaintiffs alleged that the defendants negligently caused the transmission of a false fire alarm to which the plaintiffs responded. They allege further that, while they were responding to the false alarm, the brakes of their fire engine failed, causing the engine to strike a tree. As a result of the collision, two firefighters died and the surviving plaintiffs suffered serious injuries. The jury returned a verdict against the defendants in favor of the plaintiffs in excess of $4.4 million. The defendants appealed from the judgment of the trial court to the Appellate Court, and we transferred the appeal to this court. . .

Wells Fargo installed a burglar and fire alarm system at premises owned by Arett in Waterbury. After Wells Fargo began monitoring the system, but prior to the time the system became fully operational, Wells Fargo contracted with Advanced to perform certain services on the system. Although Advanced asked both Wells Fargo and Arett whether the system was operational and monitored, both responded that it was not. On the morning of May 10, 1990, Advanced proceeded to perform the necessary services without first testing whether the system was operational and without taking steps to shut the system down. At no time during the course of the services being performed by Advanced was the alarm monitoring station or the local fire dispatch center notified that service was being performed on the Arett system. The failure to give such notice was contrary to both the internal policies of Wells Fargo and the standards of the National Fire Protection Association. It is likely that proper notification would have prevented a response to the false alarm that resulted from the performance of services on Arett's alarm system.

Additionally, on the morning on which Advanced was working on the system, the Wells Fargo monitoring station received two supervisory signals, which are indicative of a problem with the system. Although proper procedures mandated that the monitoring station contact the client to determine the nature of the problem, the monitoring station never contacted Arett. Had the station followed proper procedure, it would have learned that service was being performed on the system and could have made the necessary notation to avoid reporting the subsequent false alarm. Two minutes after the second supervisory signal was received at the monitoring station, an alarm was received indicating the existence of a fire at Arett. When a system transmits a fire alarm soon after a supervisory signal, it often indicates that the system is being serviced and that the alarm is false. Nonetheless, the monitoring station erroneously notified the Waterbury fire department at approximately 11:20 a.m. that a fire was in progress at Arett's business location. Waterbury Fire Engine Company 11 (Engine Company 11) was dispatched to respond to the alarm. Engine Company 11 was operating Engine Number 9 (engine), a spare vehicle provided to them while their primary vehicle was undergoing repairs. A fire engine carries water and hoses, as opposed to a fire truck, which provides aerial ladders.

Prior to receiving the alarm concerning Arett, James Morotto, the driver for Engine Company 11, had been advised by the previous driver that the engine's brakes were not functioning properly. When Morotto tested the brakes, however, they appeared to be adequate. When the engine crew attended a training session that morning, however, Morotto observed while in transit that the engine's brakes were not operating correctly. After the training session, therefore, Morotto brought the engine to the city garage for repair. The mechanic on duty noted that the engine's brakes needed minor adjustments, but informed the crew that he was unable to perform the service until after lunch.

The alarm from Arett was received soon after Engine Company 11 returned to its base and before the engine's brakes were repaired. The engine crew responded to the alarm, which they believed to be legitimate. Because of wet road conditions, Morotto flipped a switch to eliminate power to the engine's front brakes because, although this reduces braking power by approximately 50 percent, it is usually safer to operate without front brakes on wet roads.

After having gone approximately three blocks, the engine began to descend a hill. It was traveling at approximately fifteen miles per hour when Morotto realized that the engine's brakes had failed. Attempts to use the engine's auxiliary brake were unsuccessful. Because cars were stopped at the bottom of the hill, Morotto attempted to veer into a parking lot, the entrance to which was partially blocked by a car. While attempting to swerve around the car, Morotto struck an embankment, which caused him to lose control of the vehicle and strike a tree.

The engine's brake failure was caused by a leak in a water hose. The city had been aware of the leak for some time, and the engine's crew had made repeated requests to repair the hose. Several requests to repair the brakes also had been made. The leaking water had caused the engine's braking mechanism to rust, creating the braking problem.

The plaintiffs, as employees of the city of Waterbury, were subject to workers' compensation law and received benefits pursuant to the Workers' Compensation Act. . . . Consequently, they have no cause of action against the city for negligence for allowing the brakes to fail. . . . The plaintiffs brought this action against Arett, Advanced and Wells Fargo seeking to hold them liable for the full extent of the plaintiffs' harm owing to the negligent transmission of the false alarm to which the plaintiffs were responding when they were killed or injured.

It cannot be disputed that there was adequate evidence from which the jury could have found that the defendants acted negligently in causing and reporting the false alarm, and the defendants concede that if they owed a duty to the plaintiffs, a breach of that duty could have been found. As a threshold matter, therefore, it is necessary to determine whether, as a matter of law, the defendants owed the plaintiffs a duty of care to protect them from the harm that occurred while they were responding to the false alarm. The defendants argue that they cannot be held to have owed a duty to the plaintiffs because the failure of the engine's brakes, which precipitated the collision, is beyond the scope of the reasonably foreseeable risks created by their negligent conduct. The plaintiffs contend, however, that any collision of a fire engine with any object, for any reason, is a foreseeable risk whenever an engine is responding to an emergency, and, therefore, a duty toward them must be imposed on the defendants.. . .

"Our first step in an analysis of whether a duty exists and the extent of the defendant[s'] duty, therefore, is to determine the foreseeability of the plaintiff[s'] injury. . . ." *Jaworski v. Kiernan*, 241 Conn. at 406, 696 A.2d 332. Both the plaintiffs and the defendants agree that to meet the test of foreseeability, the exact nature of the harm suffered need not have been foreseeable, only the "general nature" of the harm. They diverge, however, with respect to the proper interpretation of the permissible level of generality of the harm. The plaintiffs assert that the general nature of the harm at issue is the possibility of a collision of a fire engine occurring while it is responding to an alarm. They would have us conclude that the brake failure is essentially irrelevant to the determination of foreseeability and should be viewed as no more than one of many possible contributing factors.

The defendants, on the other hand, assert that the general nature of the harm is a collision precipitated by the brake failure of the fire engine owing to negligent maintenance by the city of Waterbury. The defendants argue that by employing a foreseeability test that incorporates such a high level of generality to the harm in this case, the plaintiffs have essentially created a strict liability standard. That is, under the plaintiffs' argument, any accident involving a fire engine responding to a negligently transmitted false alarm would be a basis for imposing liability on the initiator of the alarm, irrespective of the direct cause of the accident. Although the defendants concede that there are certain foreseeable risks of accidents that stem from a fire engine responding to a false alarm, they contend that the failure of the engine's brakes introduced a risk not merely of a different degree, but of a different kind for which they reasonably cannot be held liable. The defendants maintain that the brake failure and the resulting collision were not foreseeable consequences of their negligent conduct.

We agree with the defendants that the analysis of foreseeability logically cannot be extended so far that the term "general harm" incorporates any accident involving a fire engine responding to a false alarm with no consideration given to the direct cause of the accident. It is impractical, if not impossible, to separate the question of duty from an analysis of the cause of the harm when the duty is asserted against one who is not the direct cause of the harm.[2] In defining the limits of duty, we have recognized that "[w]hat is relevant . . . is the . . . attenuation between [the defendant's] conduct, on the one hand, and the consequences to and the identity of the plaintiff, on the other hand." RK Constructors, Inc. v. Fusco Corp., supra, 231 Conn. at 387–88, 650 A.2d 153. Articulated another way, the attenuation between the plaintiffs' harm and the defendants' conduct is nothing more than a determination of whether the harm was a reasonably foreseeable consequence of the defendants' conduct.[3] It is a well established tenet of our tort jurisprudence

---

[2] We noted in RK Constructors, Inc., quoting from the leading treatise on the law of torts, that the duty inquiry relating to the attenuation between the plaintiff's harm and the defendant's negligent conduct is "quite similar to the analysis that we engage in with respect to the third element of negligence, proximate causation. Indeed, as Professors Prosser and Keeton have noted, '[t]he question whether there is a duty has most often seemed helpful in cases where the only issue is in reality whether the defendant stands in any such relation to the plaintiff as to create any legally recognized obligation of conduct for the plaintiff's benefit. Or, reverting again to the starting point, whether the interests of the plaintiff are entitled to legal protection at the defendant's hands against the invasion which has in fact occurred. Or, again reverting, whether the conduct is the "proximate cause" of the result. The circumlocution is unavoidable, since all of these questions are, in reality, one and the same.' W. Prosser & W. Keeton, [Torts (5th Ed.1984)] § 42, p. 274. . . ."

[3] With respect to the question of a defendant's liability for the unforeseeable consequences of its negligent conduct, Professors Prosser and Keeton have noted that "[a]t the risk of becoming wearisome, it must be repeated that the question is primarily not one of causation and never arises until causation has been established. It is rather one of the fundamental policy of the law, as to whether the defendant's responsibility should extend to such results. In so far as the defendant is held liable for consequences which do not lie within the original risk which the defendant has created, a strict liability without fault is superimposed upon the liability that is logically to be attributed to the negligence itself. It is simpler, and no doubt more accurate, to state the problem in terms of legal responsibility: is the defendant legally responsible to protect the plaintiff against such unforeseeable consequences of the defendant's own negligent acts?" W. Prosser & W. Keeton, Torts (5th Ed.1984) § 43, pp. 280–81. Although the parties have briefed

that "[d]ue care does not require that one guard against eventualities which at best are too remote to be reasonably foreseeable. *See Palsgraf v. Long Island R. Co.*, 248 N.Y. 339, 345, 162 N.E. 99 [1928]. . . .[A] defendant [is] not required to take precautions against hazards [that are] too remote to be reasonably foreseeable. Due care is always predicated on the existing circumstances." *Roy v. Friedman Equipment Co.*, 147 Conn. 121, 124, 157 A.2d 599 (1960).

Inasmuch as virtually all harms, in hindsight, are "literally 'foreseeable'", *RK Constructors, Inc. v. Fusco Corp.*, 231 Conn. at 386, 650 A.2d 153, we might conclude that the engine's brake failure technically was foreseeable. It is for this reason that the law has rejected a literal "foreseeability" test as the fulcrum of duty. . . . "[T]he conclusion that a particular injury to a particular plaintiff or class of plaintiffs possibly is foreseeable does not, in itself, create a duty of care. As we . . . stated in *RK Constructors, Inc. v. Fusco Corp.*, 650 A.2d 153: 'Many harms are quite literally "foreseeable," yet for pragmatic reasons, no recovery is allowed. . . . A further inquiry must be made, for we recognize that duty is not sacrosanct in itself, but is only an expression of the sum total of those considerations of policy which lead the law to say that the plaintiff is entitled to protection. . . . While it may seem that there should be a remedy for every wrong, this is an ideal limited perforce by the realities of this world. Every injury has ramifying consequences, like the rippling of the waters, without end. The problem for the law is to limit the legal consequences of wrongs to a controllable degree.'" *Waters v. Autuori*, 676 A.2d 357.

We recognize, as we have in the past, that the issue of foreseeability cannot be neatly compartmentalized and considered wholly separate from the policy issues that are central to our legal determination of duty. . . . We focus our decision, therefore, equally on the policy implications of this case rather than strictly upon the foreseeability of the plaintiffs' harm. For the reasons subsequently discussed, we conclude that the defendants owed no duty to the plaintiffs in these circumstances because: (1) the harm was not reasonably foreseeable; and (2) "the fundamental policy of the law, as to whether the defendant[s'] responsibility should extend to such results", *Jaworski v. Kiernan*, 696 A.2d 332, weighs in favor of concluding that there should be no legal responsibility of the defendants to the plaintiffs under the circumstances.

Notwithstanding the retrospective foreseeability of the possibility of the engine's brake failure, we agree with the defendants that the harm suffered by the plaintiffs qualifies under the category of an unforeseeable consequence. Liability may not be imposed merely because it might have been foreseeable that some accident could have occurred; rather, liability attaches only for reasonably foreseeable consequences. . . . We conclude that the brake failure of a negligently maintained fire engine is beyond the scope of the reasonably foreseeable risks created by the transmission of a false alarm and that legal responsibility for the resulting accident should not extend to these defendants.

---

and argued the issue of foreseeability as an independent causation issue, we believe that this issue relates more directly to a determination of whether liability should be imposed for unforeseeable consequences of a defendant's negligent conduct and is more appropriately resolved as a question of duty.

Negligent transmission of a false alarm, by unnecessarily causing an emergency response, does increase the usual road hazards attendant on the operation of an emergency vehicle on the public roadways. Such increased road hazards might include the danger that the driver of the fire engine or the operators of other vehicles might cause accidents as a result of high rates of speed and congested streets. It might be reasonable in some such circumstances to impose liability on the initiator of the false alarm. It cannot reasonably be said, however, that liability for negligently causing a false alarm should include the risk that the emergency vehicle will be negligently maintained and utilized, causing it to experience brake failure. Imposing liability on these defendants for a harm that they reasonably could not be expected to anticipate and over which they had no control would serve no legitimate objective of the law. . . .

In every case in which a defendant's negligent conduct may be remotely related to a plaintiff's harm, the courts must draw a line, beyond which the law will not impose legal liability. Although that line is often amorphous and difficult to discern, we conclude that it has been crossed in this case. The possibility that a city would so negligently maintain its vehicles and that firefighters would operate a fire engine, the mechanical soundness of which was clearly in doubt, is sufficiently remote that a reasonable person should not be expected to anticipate such an event. "To hold otherwise would be to convert the imperfect vision of reasonable foreseeability into the perfect vision of hindsight." *Burns v. Gleason Plant Security, Inc.*, 10 Conn.App. 480, 486, 523 A.2d 940 (1987). Consequently, we conclude that the defendants owed the plaintiffs no duty to prevent the harm suffered because that harm was not reasonably foreseeable.

In addition, we are persuaded that liability should not attach because of those policy considerations relating to the underlying purposes of tort recovery. "[T]he fundamental policy purposes of the tort compensation system [are] compensation of innocent parties, shifting the loss to responsible parties or distributing it among appropriate entities, and deterrence of wrongful conduct. . . ." *Mendillo v. Board of Education*, 717 A.2d 1177 (1998). "It is sometimes said that compensation for losses is the primary function of tort law . . . [but it] is perhaps more accurate to describe the primary function as one of determining when compensation [is] required." W. Prosser & W. Keeton, *Torts* (5th Ed.1984) § 4, p. 20. An equally compelling function of the tort system is the "'prophylactic' factor of preventing future harm. . . . The courts are concerned not only with compensation of the victim, but with admonition of the wrongdoer." Id., p. 25. "[I]mposing liability for consequential damages often creates significant risks of affecting conduct in ways that are undesirable as a matter of policy. Before imposing such liability, it is incumbent upon us to consider those risks." *Mendillo v. Board of Education*, 717 A.2d 1177 (1998). Under the factual circumstances of this case, we conclude that the benefits to be derived from requiring these defendants to compensate the plaintiffs are outweighed by the costs associated with that compensation.

The potential benefit achieved from the imposition of liability in this case is limited to providing recovery for the plaintiffs from one other than the principal tortfeasor. The plaintiffs have already been compensated for their injuries by the city of Waterbury, as their employer, for injuries sustained in the course of their employment. The fact that the plaintiffs' recovery against the defendants would exceed that which would be available as workers' compensation benefits cannot justify the imposition of liability for an accident that was not a reasonably foreseeable consequence of the defendants' negligent conduct. We have concluded that "the public [rather than individual defendants] should compensate its safety officers both in pay that reflects the hazard of their work and in workers' compensation benefits for injuries suffered when the risks inherent in the occupation materialize." *Furstein v. Hill*, 218 Conn. 610, 619, 590 A.2d 939 (1991). Because firefighters knowingly engage in a dangerous occupation, we have concluded that they are owed only the limited duty owed to licensees by landowners upon whose property they sustain injury in the course of performing their duty. . . . The policies supporting the application of a narrow scope of duty owed by individual landowners to firefighters counsels us to conclude that it would be inappropriate to establish a broad scope of duty owed by these defendants to guard against unforeseen consequences. It would be irrational to conclude that firefighters are owed a greater duty by individual members of the public while they are en route to the scene of an emergency than when they arrive at the scene. The plaintiffs have been compensated for their risk by society as a whole by way of workers' compensation as well as other statutory benefits provided to injured firefighters.. . . To impose additional liability on the defendants under these circumstances would impose an undue burden on individual members of the public. .].

The plaintiffs assert that the imposition of liability on the defendants is necessary to achieve a stated purpose of tort law, namely, to encourage alarm companies to use due care in the installation and servicing of their products. We are unpersuaded. The nature of remote monitoring virtually guarantees that some false alarms will occur, regardless of the level of care exercised to avoid such events. Alarm companies already have adequate incentives to avoid negligent conduct that causes false alarms in that they may be held liable for the reasonably foreseeable consequences of their negligent conduct. As noted previously, those consequences may include those accidents that normally and naturally occur as a result of a fire engine's operation under emergency conditions. Consequently, alarm companies already have significant incentives to avoid generating false alarms. Imposing liability for unforeseen consequences would not increase their impetus to act with due care.

Moreover, fire departments regularly receive false alarms, and every emergency response entails a substantial risk that harm may result from the emergency conditions that prevail in answering any alarm. It is an unfortunate aspect of the dangerous nature of a firefighter's duty that he or she is subject to a risk of injury in responding to alarms, whether false or legitimate. The imposition of liability under the circumstances presented here would not appreciably reduce that risk given the absence of a direct causal connection between the negligent conduct of generating a false alarm, and the accident owing to the brake failure of a negligently maintained fire engine. The fact that the alarm was false, in itself, did not contribute to the cause of this accident. Had the alarm been legitimate, the brake failure still would have occurred. No degree of care on the part of the defendants could have prevented the brake failure. Admittedly, but for the alarm, the fire engine probably would not have been on the road at the time of the accident. Although actual causation has always been a prerequisite to liability, it has never been sufficient, in and of itself, to justify the imposition of liability. . . .

We conclude, therefore, that imposing liability on the defendants would achieve little in preventing the type of harm suffered by the plaintiffs. Indeed, it is likely that the opposite result would occur. Imposing liability on these defendants would have the deleterious effect of exempting the party that is primarily responsible for the plaintiffs' harm from all liability. Pursuant to General Statutes § 31-293(a), . . . the city normally would be entitled to recover the full costs of workers' compensation benefits paid to the plaintiffs from any judgment against these defendants. Such exemption would reward the city for the conduct that directly caused this accident by shifting the entire burden of liability to the shoulders of the defendants for their tangential role in initiating the sequence of events that led to the plaintiffs' injuries. The city is in the best position to ensure the safety of the mechanical equipment used by its firefighters. We decline to interpret the defendants' applicable duty so broadly that the city would be insulated from liability for its failure to do so.

Counterbalancing the limited benefit of providing these plaintiffs with greater compensation than is available through workers' compensation and other statutory disability and survivor benefits are the significant costs that would derive from imposing liability under the facts presented. We frequently have concluded that when the social costs associated with liability are too high to justify its imposition, no duty will be found. . . . If one who initiates a false alarm may be liable for those consequences that are not reasonably foreseeable, but, rather, are significantly attenuated from the original negligent conduct, that liability will impose an unreasonable burden on the public. The costs stemming from this undue burden may include a substantial chilling of the willingness to report an emergency prior to investigating further to determine whether it is legitimate. Such delay may cost precious time, possibly leading to the unnecessary loss of life and property. It also may reduce the willingness of property owners to install alarms for fear of liability. Furthermore, imposing liability for such remote consequences undoubtedly will increase the cost of installing and monitoring alarms. Although those social costs may not be sufficient to prompt us to conclude that public policy dictates that there should be no duty in a case where the harm and the negligence are less attenuated or where the benefits of imposing liability are more substantial, under the circumstances of this case, we find them compelling.

Finally, we note that by concluding that the defendants did not owe a duty of care to these plaintiffs under the factual circumstances presented, we do not create immunity for alarm companies, their clients or subcontractors. Under most circumstances, alarm companies, and their associates, will owe the same duty of care that is expected of any enterprise for those harms that are reasonably foreseeable and within the scope of the risk created by their negligent conduct. We conclude only that, on the facts presented, the defendants cannot be held liable to the plaintiffs for the harm suffered as a result

C. BREACH, LEGAL CAUSE OR DUTY 421

of the brake failure of the city's fire engine simply because the defendants negligently caused the transmission of a false alarm to which the engine was responding. Such unforeseeable consequences are not within the scope of the risk created, and the law cannot countenance the extension of legal responsibility to such an attenuated and unexpected result.

The judgment is reversed and the case is remanded to the trial court with direction to render judgment for the defendants Wells Fargo and Advanced on the plaintiffs' complaints.

NOTES

1. *Jargon and Approach.* Does the court ever use the phrase superseding cause? (i.e., a cause that destroys proximate cause). How does the court resolve the case? Had the decision been based on the lack of proximate cause because of a superseding cause, what would the superseding cause have been? Is the court's two-pronged approach to duty—foreseeability and policy—appealing? Is a case-specific policy discussion persuasive? Have we seen as well developed a discussion of policy in this chapter? But why is a court better at making that case-specific policy analysis than a jury?

2. *Intervening Third Parties.* The oft-cited case of *Weirum v. RKO Gen., Inc.*, 15 Cal. 3d 40, 123 Cal. Rptr. 468, 539 P.2d 36 (1975), arose out of a promotional campaign by a Los Angeles radio station. As a part of the contest, one of the station's disc jockeys, known as "the Real Don Steele," rode in a conspicuous red automobile throughout the Los Angeles metropolitan area. His whereabouts and destination were broadcast and the first person to locate him could win a cash prize. Two teenagers who were unsuccessful in winning at one location followed Steele to his next location, often at high speed. At one point in the "chase," another vehicle was forced off the road, killing an occupant. In a wrongful death action against the radio station, the Supreme Court of California stated:

> [T]he record amply supports the finding of foreseeability. These tragic events unfolded in the middle of a Los Angeles summer, a time when young people were free from the constraints of school and responsive to relief from vacation tedium. Seeking to attract new listeners, KHJ devised an "exciting" promotion. Money and a small measure of momentary notoriety awaited the swiftest response. It was foreseeable that defendant's youthful listeners, finding the prize had eluded them at one location, would race to arrive first at the next site and in their haste would disregard the demands of highway safety.
>
> Indeed, "The Real Don Steele" testified that he had in the past noticed vehicles following him from location to location. He was further aware that the same contestants sometimes appeared at consecutive stops. This knowledge is not rendered irrelevant, as defendant suggests, by the absence of any prior injury. Such an argument confuses foreseeability with hindsight, and amounts to a contention that the injuries of the first victim are not compensable. . . .
>
> It is of no consequence that the harm to decedent was inflicted by third parties acting negligently. Defendant invokes the maxim that

an actor is entitled to assume that others will not act negligently. This concept is valid, however, only to the extent the intervening conduct was not to be anticipated. . . . Here, reckless conduct by youthful contestants, stimulated by defendant's broadcast, constituted the hazard to which decedent was exposed.

. . . We need not belabor the grave danger inherent in the contest broadcast by defendant. The risk of a high speed automobile chase is the risk of death or serious injury. Obviously, neither the entertainment afforded by the contest nor its commercial rewards can justify the creation of such a grave risk. Defendant could have accomplished its objectives of entertaining its listeners and increasing advertising revenues by adopting a contest format which would have avoided danger to the motoring public.

. . . Defendant is fearful that entrepreneurs will henceforth be burdened with an avalanche of obligations: an athletic department will owe a duty to an ardent sports fan injured while hastening to purchase one of a limited number of tickets; a department store will be liable to injuries incurred in response to a "while-they-last" sale. This argument, however, suffers from a myopic view of the facts presented here. The giveaway contest was no commonplace invitation to an attraction available on a limited basis. It was a competitive scramble in which the thrill of the chase to be the one and only victor was intensified by the live broadcasts which accompanied the pursuit. In the assertedly analogous situations described by defendant, any haste involved in the purchase of the commodity is an incidental and unavoidable result of the scarcity of the commodity itself. In such situations there is no attempt, as here, to generate a competitive pursuit on public streets, accelerated by repeated importuning by radio to be the very first to arrive at a particular destination. Manifestly the "spectacular" bears little resemblance to daily commercial activities.

D. THIRD PARTY CRIMINAL, INTENTIONAL OR NEGLIGENT ACTS

POSECAI v. WAL-MART STORES, INC.
752 So. 2d 762 (La. 1999)

MARCUS, JUSTICE.

Shirley Posecai brought suit against Sam's Wholesale Club ("Sam's") in Kenner after she was robbed at gunpoint in the store's parking lot. On July 20, 1995, Mrs. Posecai went to Sam's to make an exchange and to do some shopping. She exited the store and returned to her parked car at approximately 7:20 p.m. It was not dark at the time. As Mrs. Posecai was placing her purchases in the trunk, a man who was hiding under her car grabbed her ankle and pointed a gun at her. The unknown assailant instructed her to hand over her jewelry and her wallet. While begging the robber to spare her life, she gave him her purse and all her jewelry. Mrs. Posecai was wearing her most valuable jewelry at the time of the robbery because she had attended a downtown luncheon earlier in the day. She lost a two and a half carat diamond ring given to her by her husband for their twenty fifth wedding anniversary, a diamond and ruby bracelet and a diamond and gold watch, all valued at close to $19,000.

When the robber released Mrs. Posecai, she ran back to the store for help. The Kenner Police Department was called and two officers came out to investigate the incident. The perpetrator was never apprehended and Mrs. Posecai never recovered her jewelry despite searching several pawn shops.

At the time of this armed robbery, a security guard was stationed inside the store to protect the cash office from 5:00 p.m. until the store closed at 8:00 p.m. He could not see outside and Sam's did not have security guards patrolling the parking lot. At trial, the security guard on duty, Kenner Police Officer Emile Sanchez, testified that he had worked security detail at Sam's since 1986 and was not aware of any similar criminal incidents occurring in Sam's parking lot during the nine years prior to the robbery of Mrs. Posecai. He further testified that he did not consider Sam's parking lot to be a high crime area, but admitted that he had not conducted a study on the issue.

The plaintiff presented the testimony of two other Kenner police officers. Officer Russell Moran testified that he had patrolled the area around Sam's from 1993 to 1995. He stated that the subdivision behind Sam's, Lincoln Manor, is generally known as a high crime area, but that the Kenner Police were rarely called out to Sam's. Officer George Ansardi, the investigating officer, similarly testified that Lincoln Manor is a high crime area but explained that Sam's is not considered a high crime location. He further stated that to his knowledge none of the other businesses in the area employed security guards at the time of this robbery.

An expert on crime risk assessment and premises security, David Kent, was qualified and testified on behalf of the plaintiff. It was his opinion that the robbery of Mrs. Posecai could have been prevented by an exterior security presence. He presented crime data from the Kenner Police Department indicating that between 1989 and June of 1995 there were three robberies or "predatory offenses" on Sam's premises, and provided details from the police reports on each of these crimes. The first offense occurred at 12:45 a.m. on March 20, 1989, when a delivery man sleeping in his truck parked in back of the store was robbed. In May of 1992, a person was mugged in the store's parking lot. Finally, on February 7, 1994, an employee of the store was the victim of a purse snatching, but she indicated to the police that the crime was related to a domestic dispute.

In order to broaden the geographic scope of his crime data analysis, Mr. Kent looked at the crime statistics at thirteen businesses on the same block as Sam's, all of which were either fast food restaurants, convenience stores or gas stations. He found a total of eighty-three predatory offenses in the six and a half years before Mrs. Posecai was robbed. Mr. Kent concluded that the area around Sam's was "heavily crime impacted," although he did not compare the crime statistics he found around Sam's to any other area in Kenner or the New Orleans metro area.

Mrs. Posecai contends that Sam's was negligent in failing to provide adequate security in the parking lot considering the high level of crime in the surrounding area. Seeking to recover for mental anguish as well as for her property loss, she alleged that after this incident she had trouble sleeping and was afraid to go out by herself at night. After a bench trial, the trial judge held that Sam's owed a duty to provide security in the parking lot because the robbery of the plaintiff was foreseeable and could have been prevented by the use of security. A judgment was rendered in favor of Mrs. Posecai, awarding $18,968 for her lost jewelry and $10,000 in general damages for her mental anguish.. . .

The sole issue presented for our review is whether Sam's owed a duty to protect Mrs. Posecai from the criminal acts of third parties under the facts and circumstances of this case.

This court has adopted a duty-risk analysis to determine whether liability exists under the particular facts presented. Under this analysis the plaintiff must prove that the conduct in question was the cause in fact of the resulting harm, the defendant owed a duty of care to the plaintiff, the requisite duty was breached by the defendant and the risk of harm was within the scope of protection afforded by the duty breached. Under the duty-risk analysis, all four inquiries must be affirmatively answered for plaintiff to recover.. . .

We now join other states in adopting the rule that although business owners are not the insurers of their patrons' safety, they do have a duty to implement reasonable measures to protect their patrons from criminal acts when those acts are foreseeable. We emphasize, however, that there is generally no duty to protect others from the criminal activities of third persons. This duty only arises under limited circumstances, when the criminal act in question was reasonably foreseeable to the owner of the business. Determining when a crime is foreseeable is therefore a critical inquiry.

Other jurisdictions have resolved the foreseeability issue in a variety of ways, but four basic approaches have emerged. The first approach, although somewhat outdated, is known as the specific harm rule. According to this rule, a landowner does not owe a duty to protect patrons from the violent acts of third parties unless he is aware of specific, imminent harm about to befall them. Courts have generally agreed that this rule is too restrictive in limiting the duty of protection that business owners owe their invitees.

More recently, some courts have adopted a prior similar incidents test. Under this test, foreseeability is established by evidence of previous crimes on or near the premises. The idea is that a past history of criminal conduct will put the landowner on notice of a future risk. Therefore, courts consider the nature and extent of the previous crimes, as well as their recency, frequency, and similarity to the crime in question. This approach can lead to arbitrary results because it is applied with different standards regarding the number of previous crimes and the degree of similarity required to give rise to a duty.

The third and most common approach used in other jurisdictions is known as the totality of the circumstances test. This test takes additional factors into account, such as the nature, condition, and location of the land, as well as any other relevant factual circumstances bearing on foreseeability. As the Indiana Supreme Court explained, "[a] substantial factor in the determination of duty is the number, nature, and location of prior similar incidents, but the lack of prior similar incidents will not preclude a claim where the landowner knew or should have known that the criminal act was foreseeable." Delta Tau Delta, 712 N.E.2d at 973. The application of this test often focuses on the level of crime in the surrounding area and courts that apply this test are more willing to see property crimes or minor offenses as precursors to more violent crimes. In general, the totality of the circumstances test tends to place a greater duty on business owners to foresee the risk of criminal attacks on their property and has been criticized "as being too broad a standard, effectively imposing an unqualified duty to protect customers in areas experiencing any significant level of criminal activity." McClung, 937 S.W.2d at 900.

The final standard that has been used to determine foreseeability is a balancing test, an approach which has been adopted in California and Tennessee.. . . The Tennessee Supreme Court formulated the test as follows: "In determining the duty that exists, the foreseeability of harm and the gravity of harm must be balanced against the commensurate burden imposed on the business to protect against that harm. In cases in which there is a high degree of foreseeability of harm and the probable harm is great, the burden imposed upon defendant may be substantial. Alternatively, in cases in which a lesser degree of foreseeability is present or the potential harm is slight, less onerous burdens may be imposed." McClung, 937 S.W.2d at 902. Under this test, the high degree of foreseeability necessary to impose a duty to provide security, will rarely, if ever, be proven in the absence of prior similar incidents of crime on the property.

We agree that a balancing test is the best method for determining when business owners owe a duty to provide security for their patrons. The economic and social impact of requiring businesses to provide security on their premises is an important factor. Security is a significant monetary expense for any business and further increases the cost of doing business in high crime areas that are already economically depressed. Moreover, businesses are generally not responsible for the endemic crime that plagues our communities, a societal problem that even our law enforcement and other government agencies have been unable to solve. At the same time, business owners are in the best position to appreciate the crime risks that are posed on their premises and to take reasonable precautions to counteract those risks.

With the foregoing considerations in mind, we adopt the following balancing test to be used in deciding whether a business owes a duty of care to protect its customers from the criminal acts of third parties. The foreseeability of the crime risk on the defendant's property and the gravity of the risk determine the existence and the extent of the defendant's duty. The greater the foreseeability and gravity of the harm, the greater the duty of care that will be imposed on the business. A very high degree of foreseeability is required to give rise to a duty to post security guards, but a lower degree of foreseeability may support a duty to implement lesser security measures such as using surveillance cameras, installing improved lighting or fencing, or trimming shrubbery. The plaintiff has the burden of establishing the duty the defendant owed under the circumstances.

The foreseeability and gravity of the harm are to be determined by the facts and circumstances of the case. The most important factor to be considered is the existence, frequency and similarity of prior incidents of crime on the premises, but the location, nature and condition of the property should also be taken into account. It is highly unlikely that a crime risk will be sufficiently foreseeable for the imposition of a duty to provide security guards if there have not been previous instances of crime on the business' premises.

In the instant case, there were only three predatory offenses on Sam's premises in the six and a half years prior to the robbery of Mrs. Posecai. The first of these offenses occurred well after store hours, at almost one o'clock in the morning, and involved the robbery of a delivery man who was caught unaware as he slept near Sam's loading dock behind the store. In 1992, a person was mugged while walking through the parking lot. Two years later, an employee of the store was attacked in the parking lot and her purse was taken, apparently by her husband. A careful consideration of the previous incidents of predatory offenses on the property reveals that there was only one other crime in Sam's parking lot, the mugging in 1992, that was perpetrated against a Sam's customer and that bears any similarity to the crime that occurred in this case. Given the large number of customers that used Sam's parking lot, the previous robbery of only one customer in all those years indicates a very low crime risk. It is also relevant that Sam's only operates during daylight hours and must provide an accessible parking lot to the multitude of customers that shop at its store each year. Although the neighborhood bordering Sam's is considered a high crime area by local law enforcement, the foreseeability and gravity of harm in Sam's parking lot remained slight.

We conclude that Sam's did not possess the requisite degree of foreseeability for the imposition of a duty to provide security patrols in its parking lot. Nor was the degree of foreseeability sufficient to support a duty to implement lesser security measures. Accordingly, Sam's owed no duty to protect Mrs. Posecai from the criminal acts of third parties under the facts and circumstances of this case. Having found that no duty was owed, we do not reach the other elements of the duty-risk analysis that must be proven in establishing a negligence claim.

For the reasons assigned, the judgment of the court of appeal is reversed. It is ordered that judgment be rendered in favor of Wal Mart Stores, Inc. d/b/a Sam's Wholesale Club and against Shirley Posecai, dismissing plaintiff's suit at her cost.

NOTES

1. *Duelling Tests. Seibert v. Vic Regnier Bldrs., Inc.*, 856 P.2d 1332 (Kan. 1993). The plaintiff was shot in the head in defendant mall owner's underground parking lot, in the course of an armed robbery by an unknown assailant. Her proof of prior criminal acts in the mall was scanty, but she stressed the dim and inadequate lighting and the lack of security protection in the subterranean garage. Reversing a summary judgment for the defendant, the court held the liability of the defendant should be determined under the "totality of the circumstances."

Rejecting a "totality of the circumstances" approach in favor of a "prior similar incidents" rule, the court in *Ann M. v. Pacific Plaza Shopping Center*,

6 Cal. 4th 666, 863 P.2d 207, 25 Cal. Rptr. 2d 137 (1993), refused to hold a shopping center liable for a rape to a store employee of one of the shopping center tenants:

> . . . While a landowner's duty includes the duty to exercise reasonable care to discover that criminal acts are being or are likely to be committed on its land, Pacific Plaza presented uncontroverted evidence that it had implemented "a standard practice . . . to note or record instances of violent crime" and that Pacific Plaza's records contain no reference to violent criminal acts prior to Ann M.'s rape. Moreover, even assuming that Pacific Plaza had notice of these incidents, Ann M. concedes that they were not similar in nature to the violent assault that she suffered. Similarly, none of the remaining evidence presented by Ann M. is sufficiently compelling to establish the high degree of foreseeability necessary to impose upon Pacific Plaza a duty to provide security guards in the common areas. Neither the evidence regarding the presence of transients nor the evidence of the statistical crime rate of the surrounding area is of a type sufficient to satisfy this burden.

Finding an absence of "prior similar incidents," the court in *Sharon P. v. Arman, Ltd.*, 989 P.2d 121 (Cal. 1999), refused to hold a business premises owner liable for a sexual assault occurring to plaintiff in defendants' underground parking garage. The court rejected plaintiff's claim that liability should be imposed because such a parking area was "inherently dangerous."

Compare Sharp v. W. H. Moore, Inc., 118 Idaho 297, 796 P.2d 506 (1990) (suit against company following attack on plaintiff by unidentified party, court said the "solid and growing national trend has been toward the rejection of the 'prior similar incidents' rule").

2. *How Safe Is Your Law School?* In *Donnell v. California Western Sch. of Law*, 200 Cal. App. 3d 715, 246 Cal. Rptr. 199, 206–08 (1988), plaintiff, a law student, left defendant law school's library at approximately 10 p.m. While walking along the adjacent city street the plaintiff was stabbed by an unknown assailant. Plaintiff alleged that the law school was negligent in failing to provide adequate lighting and security around the law school, despite knowledge of previous criminal activity in the area. In affirming defendant's summary judgment, the court held that the school did not have sufficient control over the adjoining city sidewalk to serve as a basis for liability. Dissenting, Justice Weiner stated:

> . . . The policy of preventing future harm would be served by imposing liability on Cal Western. The economic burden of installing exterior lighting on the Third Avenue side of the law school building was minimal; testimony also indicated video monitors could be installed at a modest price. There is little question insurance is commonly available for the type of injury suffered by Donnell. With respect to the question of moral blame, it is perhaps an indictment of our litigation-minded society that a law school repeatedly rejected its employees' and students' requests for increased lighting and other security measures in the face of known risk of criminal assault because of nominal

expense and the danger the school would be assuming liability if lights were installed.

Control is only one part — a small part — of the duty analysis required in the determination of premises liability. Obviously control can play a more significant role in cases where implicit in the absence of control is the notion that people cannot be expected to take action where they are, in fact, powerless. In other words, we could not expect Cal Western to fix the sidewalk adjacent to buildings two blocks away from the law school entrance even though students routinely use those sidewalks. "Control" in that situation is nothing more than a conclusionary way of saying that we do not impose impossible burdens on people. Here Cal Western makes no claim it is powerless to improve the lighting. It did, in fact, install the requested lighting shortly after the assault on Donnell.

Lack of control may also be relevant to the duty analysis in those cases in which the costs associated with making the premises tort-proof are prohibitive. If the only way to improve the safety of students here was to install an expensive radar device complete with electronic sensors, the cost might well outweigh the benefits to be served by such a device and the extension of tort liability might involve an increase in the cost of legal education with its resultant effect on society. However, Cal Western does not say exterior lighting was too expensive. At most a finding of no control eliminates one of several factors to be considered in establishing duty in the first place.

. . . The majority opinion also ignores the facts of this case. Here Cal Western not only controlled the means of installing lighting over the approaches to the law school by virtue of its ownership of the building, but had, in fact, exercised control over the approaches through lighting and other means in the past. The law school is situated in a large building which occupies an entire city block. The building is bordered on three sides by the city sidewalks along Third Avenue on the west, Fourth Avenue on the east, and Cedar Street on the south. The north side of the building abuts a freeway right-of-way. Cal Western illuminated the law school entrance with small floodlights attached to the building. There were also two gas lamp poles on the Cedar Street sidewalk in front of the school which the business manager testified were owned and maintained by Cal Western. The back of the building was sealed off with security gates to discourage transients. The west side where Donnell was attacked was the darkest side of the building. . . . Cal Western exercised its limited right of control over that portion of the approach to the law school by installing lighting shortly after the January 1984 attack "to increase visibility out there at night."

Cal Western also exercised its limited right of control over the sidewalks approaching the law school by instructing security personnel as early as 1978 to escort persons to their cars after dark on request because of the nature of the neighborhood. "If it was a student that had a parking place, then they would go to the parking lot. If it was a student that had parked on the street, then they would have to go to the car." Dean Avery observed the security personnel kept the front door of the law school in view when providing the escort service. The guard stayed on the Cedar Street sidewalk "watching the woman go out to her car and get in and drive away and then coming back to the building." The majority assertion Cal Western did not assume responsibility for or exercise at least limited control over the approaches to the law school building, including the city-owned sidewalk where Donnell was injured, is factually incorrect.

How does *Donnell* differ from Nova Southeastern University, Inc., v. Gross, 760 So. 2d 86 (Fla. 2000), discussed in Chapter 1?

3. *Non-Compliant Victims*. In Kentucky Fried Chicken of California, Inc. v. Superior Court, 14 Cal. 4th 814, 927 P.2d 1260, 59 Cal. Rptr. 2d 756 (1997), the plaintiff was the sole customer in the defendant's restaurant when she was seized by a robber. The complaint alleged that because an employee did not comply promptly with the robber's demands, the latter became extremely agitated, shoved his gun harder into plaintiff's back, and told the employee he would shoot plaintiff if the employee did not "quit playing games." The court summed up the generally accepted position as follows:

> [N]o state has held that the law imposes a duty to comply with a robber's demands. While some hold that a shopkeeper may actively resist the robbery attempt only if the resistance is reasonable in light of the threat to third persons, none hold that the duty to avoid harm to patrons or others on the premises is breached if the shopkeeper simply refuses to surrender property. Although there was no active resistance to the robber in this case, decisions in which the shopkeeper or employee did resist are instructive. None of those which hold that resistance may be unreasonable in some circumstances suggest that a shopkeeper who does not actively resist or intentionally engage in other provocative conduct has breached a duty to a patron, and the majority of courts which have considered the question hold that active resistance is permitted.

Dissenting, KENNARD, J., argued,

> The majority errs by mistakenly framing the issue before us as an issue of duty to be decided by the court as a matter of law rather than as an issue of reasonable care for the jury. For the majority, the issue is whether a business proprietor always (or never) has a "duty" to comply with the demands of a robber who threatens a customer with harm; the majority concludes that a business proprietor need never protect its customers by doing so.

> The issue before us, however, is properly a question of whether defendant's cashier, in initially refusing to comply with the robber's demand, breached the reasonable person standard of care, not whether defendant was under a "duty" to follow a prescribed course of conduct. By framing the issue as a question of duty, the majority usurps the jury's historic function in a negligence case to determine the reasonableness of defendant's conduct under the surrounding circumstances.

4. *The Unique Crime.* Lopez v. McDonald's, 193 Cal. App. 3d 495, 238 Cal. Rptr. 436 (1987), concerned a mass killing at a fast food restaurant. The assailant, armed with a 9 mm. semi-automatic rifle, a semi-automatic 9 mm. pistol and a .12 gauge shotgun, indiscriminately slaughtered 21 patrons and employees before he was killed by a police sharpshooter. He showed no intent to rob the restaurant; as the court put it, "[h]is single apparent purpose was to kill as many people as possible before he himself was slain." Plaintiffs alleged McDonald's failed to provide adequate safety devices or security personnel to protect customers from dangerous and known risks. In approving of the trial court's grant of a defense motion for summary judgment the court stated:

> [W]e conclude as a matter of law the unforeseeability of the unique, horrific San Ysidro event require negligence liability to be restricted here. First, as to the foreseeability of harm to plaintiffs, the theft-related and property crimes of the type shown by the history of its operations, or the general assaultive-type activity which had occurred in the vicinity bear no relationship to purposeful homicide or assassination. In other words, under all the circumstances presented, the risk of a maniacal, mass murderous assault is not a hazard the likelihood of which makes McDonald's conduct unreasonably dangerous. Rather, the likelihood of this unprecedented murderous assault was so remote and unexpected that, as a matter of law, the general character of McDonald's nonfeasance did not facilitate its happening. Huberty's deranged and motiveless attack, apparently the worst mass killing by a single assailant in recent American history, is so unlikely to occur within the setting of modern life that a reasonably prudent business enterprise would not consider its occurrence in attempting to satisfy its general obligation to protect business invitees from reasonably foreseeable criminal conduct.
>
> Plaintiff's reliance on the evidence of mostly theft-related crimes on and nearby the San Ysidro premises and the crime rate in the surrounding area, to show the event here was reasonably foreseeable, is misplaced. We recognize foreseeability of third-party criminal conduct does not require prior identical or even similar incidents. However, here the proffered evidence does not portend disasters of this type. As McDonald's argues: "To the extent it can be foreseen at all, such an attack, like a meteor falling from the sky, can occur in any neighborhood regardless of the crime rate." Rather, the predominantly theft-related character of the crimes is simply probative of the foreseeability of such crimes, more precisely defining its duty to provide protective measures designed to deter theft-related and ordinary criminal conduct (*i.e.*, vandalism). In comparison, not only was Huberty's crime not theft-related, but the narrow focus on slaughter and Huberty's obvious suicidal motive are unrelated to the area's general crime rate as a matter of law. . . .
>
> A review of the surrounding circumstances emphasized by plaintiffs does not render the occurrence of a mass murderous assault any more foreseeable. First, Holley's deposition relating his bid to sell security

to McDonald's simply proves it knew of the high crime area and the availability of uniformed, licensed security officers at $5.75 per hour. Unlike the parking structures and the all-night convenience stores . . . a fast-food restaurant does not create "an especial temptation and opportunity for criminal misconduct" of this nature. In other words, McDonald's facilities, even considering the alleged construction defects of the tinted windows and the restaurant's elevation above the other buildings in the surrounding area, did not present a particular risk for this type of criminal attack.

. . . [N]egligence liability should be restricted here. Preliminarily, under these circumstances, it would be difficult for a trier of fact to discern a causal nexus between McDonald's nonfeasance and the resulting injuries where reasonable precautions would not likely deter a suicide-bent murderer or protect his random victims from harm. Moreover, within the context of the third-party criminal conduct involved here, no moral blame attaches to defendant's nonfeasance. Further, although the policy of preventing future harm is great, the extent of the burden to the defendant and the consequences to the community of imposing a duty to protect against heavily-armed, suicidal murderers is onerous. As already explained, where the burden of preventing future harm is great a high degree of foreseeability is required. Absent such a high degree of foreseeability, the courts have declined to declare a duty where its imposition "would place an extremely onerous burden on both the defendant and the community, and where the defendant is not morally culpable, and where the proposed duty and the measures to be applied in discharge of the duty defy exact delineation and suffer from inherent vagueness. . . ." *Cohen v. Southland Corp.,* 157 Cal. App. 3d 130, 142, 203 Cal. Rptr. 572 (1984). Finally, without infringing upon the issue of causation, what protective measures should be pursued to protect against a mass murderous assault truly defy exact delineation, because how can one know which measures will be effective against a degenerate, a psychopath or a psychotic? Where minimal precautionary measures providing a "vital first line of defense" could have had an appreciable effect in preventing the lesser crimes they addressed, none apparently exist here as neither party has suggested such a measure.

. . . On this record, we conclude plaintiffs have failed to establish any triable issue that there was a causal nexus between McDonald's nonfeasance, if any, and the resulting injuries. Any reasonable protective measure such as security cameras, alarms and unarmed security guards might have deterred ordinary criminal conduct because of the potential of identification and capture, but could not reasonably be expected to deter or hinder a maniacal, suicidal assailant unconcerned with his own safety, bent on committing mass murder.

5. *Leaving the Key in the Ignition.* There is a recurring fact pattern involving an intervening act that has vexed courts. Defendant (usually in violation of some statute) leaves his or her keys in the car. A thief steals the car and injures plaintiff while driving the car. Should the defendant car owner be

liable or not? *See Hill v. Yaskin*, 75 N.J. 139, 380 A.2d 1107 (1977). In *McClenahan v. Cooley*, 806 S.W.2d 767 (Tenn. 1991), the court said that the car owner would be liable where the accident occurred "during the flight of the thief relatively close thereto in time and distance." Both *Hill* and *McClenahan* involved the imposition of a common law duty, not negligence per se.

PROBLEM

It is a warm and sunny spring day on the University of Allstate campus. Dirk, the president of the law school's Student Bar Association, has completed his final accounts for the year. Realizing that the S.B.A. coffers are full, primarily because he has organized no events during the school year, Dirk decides to hold one giant festive event to celebrate the end of the semester. Since his social consciousness has been raised after being offered the post of assistant public defender, Dirk decides to make it a charitable affair, and advertises a day-long happy hour entitled "S.B.A. Pig-Out for Famine Relief."

The event is extremely well attended; hardly surprising, since pitchers of beer cost only 25 cents apiece. By 7 p.m., most of the students in attendance are quite drunk. Dirk begins to worry that the event is getting out of hand, so he calls the campus police for assistance. Worried that he might get drawn into any further problems, Dirk tells his bartenders to keep on serving beer and then quietly slips away.

One hour later the campus police arrive and close down the festivities. One of the third-year students, Ferd, strenuously protests their actions. He becomes so obstreperous that the campus police briefly handcuff him until one of the other students, Hans, assures them he will get Ferd home safely. The campus police release Ferd, and Hans leads him away. As they get into Ferd's car and Ferd drives off, Ferd shouts at the campus police, "Somebody's gonna pay for this!" As soon as the campus police car is out of sight, Ferd pulls up and tells Hans that he will have to find his own way home because he "has something he's got to do." Hans knows better than to argue with a drunk law student and goes off to get his own car.

Ferd drives back to the student dorms. Unchallenged, he walks up to the third floor to Dirk's room and proceeds to beat the S.B.A. president senseless. Meanwhile, Hans has made his way to the student parking lot. As he unlocks his car, an unknown assailant slips out of the darkness and mugs him. Ferd, having dealt with Dirk, returns to his car and, as he speeds away from the dorms, he strikes a pedestrian, Gunner, a first-year law student who has just left the dwindling party crowd.

Gunner, Dirk and Hans want to bring suit against Allstate University. What theories of liability could they use? What issues would be raised? How would you resolve them?

E. THIN SKULLS, SUBSEQUENT INJURY, RESCUERS, AND OTHER PROBLEMS

The law has long recognized that if a defendant whose negligent act causes a plaintiff to suffer more serious injuries than a normal person would suffer because of some peculiar or unique condition, the defendant is liable. This is known as the thin skull rule. Often, it is restated in the economic phrase: the defendant takes his plaintiff as he finds him. Of course, the defendant must be negligent in the first place; if defendant's conduct does not pose an unreasonable risk of harm, there is no liability. But, once negligent, defendant is liable for all plaintiff's injuries. Should the rule apply to emotional damages as well? Some courts say that it does. *See, e.g., Bartolone v. Jeckovich*, 103 A.D.2d 632, 481 N.Y.S.2d 545 (1984).

ANAYA v. SUPERIOR COURT
78 Cal.App.4th 971, 93 Cal.Rptr.2d 228 (2000)

. . . Anaya and Vides allege that their 11-year-old daughter, Norma Vides, was with them when their car collided with a Los Angeles City trash truck that was stopped in the number two lane of a road. Injured in the crash, Norma was airlifted by City helicopter; the helicopter crashed and Norma died. Anaya and Vides sued City of Los Angeles and the individual drivers of the trash truck, Ralph Diaz and Gabriel Lara, for, inter alia, wrongful death. They also named Robert Everton, but the complaint does not set forth any facts as to Everton.[1]

City and individual defendants Diaz, Lara, and Everton demurred. Respondent court overruled City's demurrer, but sustained the demurrer of the individual defendants on the basis that Norma's death was not foreseeable.

An actor may be liable if the actor's negligence is a substantial factor in causing an injury, and the actor is not relieved of liability because of the intervening act of a third person if such act was reasonably foreseeable at the time of the original negligent conduct. . . . "The foreseeability required is of the risk of harm, not of the particular intervening act." (*Torres v. Xomox Corp.* (1996) 49 Cal.App.4th 1, 18, 56 Cal.Rptr.2d 455.)

To determine that " 'a negligent actor [is] liable for another's harm, it is necessary not only that the actor's conduct be negligent toward the other, but also that the negligence of the actor be a legal cause of the other's harm.' 'Legal cause' exists if the actor's conduct is a 'substantial factor' in bringing about the harm and there is no rule of law relieving the actor from liability." (*Nola M. v. University of Southern California* (1993) 16 Cal.App.4th 421, 427, 20 Cal.Rptr.2d 97.)

It has long been the rule that a tortfeasor responsible for the original accident is also liable for injuries or death occurring during the course of medical treatment to treat injuries suffered in that accident. In *Ash v. Mortensen* (1944) 24 Cal.2d 654, 150 P.2d 876, the Supreme Court stated: "It is settled that where one who has suffered personal injuries by reason of the tortious act of another exercises due care in securing the services of a doctor and his injuries are aggravated by the negligence of such doctor, the law regards the

---

[1] The points and authorities in support of the demurrer does not clearly lay out the sequence of events, but it appears that Everton had stopped his trash truck to collect garbage on his route when another vehicle collided with his truck. Diaz and Lara, in a different truck, saw that his truck was disabled and stopped their truck to assist. Blinded by the setting sun, the driver of the Vides car collided with Diaz and Lara's truck.

act of the original wrongdoer as a proximate cause of the damages flowing from the subsequent negligent medical treatment and holds him liable therefor."

In *Hastie v. Handeland* (1969) 274 Cal.App.2d 599, 79 Cal.Rptr. 268, a case involving a vehicular collision and subsequent death of the victim following medical care, Division One of the Fourth District determined that the original tortfeasor was liable for the subsequent injury suffered during medical treatment. "If death resulted from a risk inherent in the medical treatment reasonably required to cure the injuries caused by the accident, respondents [original tortfeasors] would be liable irrespective of whether such treatment was rendered in a proper or a negligent manner. The question is one of causation, and where the additional harm results either from the negligence of doctors or hospitals who furnish necessary medical care, or from the materialization of a risk inherent to necessary medical care, the chain of causation set in motion by the original tort remains unbroken.". . . .

Obviously, if the original tortfeasor is liable for injuries or death suffered during the course of the treatment of injuries suffered in the accident, the original tortfeasor is liable for injuries or death suffered during transportation of the victim to a medical facility for treatment of the injuries resulting from the accident.

In *Pridham v. Cash & Carry Building Center, Inc.* (1976), 116 N.H. 292 [359 A.2d 193], Herbert Pridham was injured in an accident that occurred on Cash & Carry's premises and died when the ambulance transporting him to a hospital crashed. The New Hampshire Supreme Court determined that the jury should have been instructed that Cash & Carry was liable for Pridham's death. The New Hampshire Supreme Court explained the principle: "[I]f a tortfeasor's negligence causes harm to another which requires the victim to receive medical, surgical or hospital services and additional bodily harm results from a normal effort of persons rendering such services, whether done in a proper or negligent manner, the original tortfeasor's negligence is a legal cause of the injuries received because of the injured party's involuntary submission to such services." The New Hampshire Supreme Court continued: "Medical services necessitated by the negligence of a tortfeasor are in most cases administered in a hospital. The conveyance of [plaintiff] Pridham by ambulance to a hospital was a necessary step in securing medical services required by the accident at Cash & Carry [the original tortfeasor]. Therefore, the rule holding the original tortfeasor liable for additional harm from medical care rendered because of the original injury should be extended to, and include, injuries sustained while being transported to a hospital where medical services can be obtained."

The allegation that the helicopter was negligently maintained does not establish a superseding cause. " '[T]he fact that an intervening act of a third person is done in a negligent manner does not make it a superseding cause if . . . the act is a normal response to a situation created by the defendant's conduct and the manner in which the intervening act is done is not extraordinarily negligent.' " (*Martinez v. Vintage Petroleum, Inc.* (1998) 68 Cal.App.4th 695, 701, 80 Cal.Rptr.2d 449.)

The allegations that the helicopter malfunctioned and that the manufacturer is strictly liable for the helicopter's malfunction do not establish the manufacturer as a superseding actor. . . .

The demurrer of individual defendants Diaz, Lara, and Everton should have been overruled, because it is foreseeable that, after a traffic collision, the victim's injuries suffered in the collision would require the victim to be transported for medical care to a medical facility (whether by automobile or helicopter). The tortfeasors liable for the original accident that necessitated transportation of the victim of that accident by ambulance are liable in damages for any injuries (or death) suffered by the victim on the way to the hospital. It follows that, on the facts as alleged in the complaint, Diaz, Lara, and Everton are liable for Norma's death, which occurred while she was being transported to a medical facility for treatment of injuries suffered in an accident caused by Diaz, Lara, and Everton. Those that built and maintained the helicopter did not become superseding actors. . . ..

NOTES

1. *Several Liability*. What result if the applicable jurisdiction no longer recognizes joint and several liability but a tortfeasor is only liable for its share of the fault? *See e.g., Gray v. Ford Motor Co.*, 914 S. W. 2d 464 (Tenn. 1996) (initial tortfeasor and subsequent medical tortfeasor are severally liable). How does one allocate fault between the initial tortfeasor and the negligent second injurer? If the allocation is accurate would it mean that the rule of the principal case would be abrogated?

2. *Danger Inviting Rescue*. In *Saltsman v. Corazo*, 317 N.J. Super. 237, 721 A.2d 1000 (1998), the plaintiff was an invitee at an outdoor entertainment complex. The complex's manager, an acquaintance of the plaintiff, became involved in (and arguably caused) a dispute with another customer that led to the manager being attacked by several customers. The plaintiff went to the manager's aid, but himself became the victim of an attack by one of combatants armed with a golf club. Reversing a summary judgment for the complex the court stated:

> As Justice Cardozo stated long ago, "danger invites rescue." *Wagner v. International Ry. Co.*, 232 N.Y. 176, 133 N.E. 437, 437 (Ct. App. N.Y. 1921). Originally, the rescue doctrine was created to prevent a plaintiff from being found contributorily negligent as a matter of law when he voluntarily placed himself in danger so as to save another from peril. The doctrine, in its traditional form, also created a duty of care on the part of a person who through his own negligence placed a third party in a situation of imminent peril that invited the plaintiff rescuer to intervene. In such cases, the victim is blameless, and suit is brought by the plaintiff rescuer against the party who created the peril. Defendants contend in their brief that the rescue doctrine is limited to that factual scenario, and thus, plaintiff could only bring suit against [the dispute instigating customer] under the rescue doctrine, not [the manager]. We disagree.
>
> The doctrine has been expanded to circumstances where a person is injured in undertaking a rescue and seeks recovery for injuries from

the victim whose own negligence helped create the situation necessitating the rescue. In that context, the rescue doctrine establishes not only the victim defendant's duty to the plaintiff, but also that the victim defendant's negligence in creating the rescue-inducing peril was a legal cause of the injury for which recovery is sought, although it may not have been the cause in fact of such injury.

. . .[W]e find no impediment to the application of the rescue doctrine. . . to situations where the rescuer plaintiff sues the rescued victim who is either completely, or partially, at fault for creating the peril that invited the rescue. Therefore, we remand the matter for a jury determination as to whether [the manager] negligently instigated the altercation with [the customer] by either insulting his female companions, throwing the first punch, or both. If the jury finds [the manager] blameworthy in this respect, it must then determine whether [the manager] could have reasonably anticipated that plaintiff, a social acquaintance and business invitee, might intervene to rescue him from the assault which his negligence at least partially created. In such circumstances, because the intervention itself cannot be deemed to be negligent, plaintiff's recovery is discounted only if the jury determines that he acted unreasonably during his rescue effort.

721 A.2d 1005–07.

PROBLEM

Nicolai was eighty-five years old and suffered from multiple sclerosis; he was severely disabled and bedridden. Romanova, an employee of Nurse-by-Day, Inc., was his home-care nurse. Romanova worked from 8 am to 4 pm, Monday through Friday. In the evenings and on weekends Nicolai was looked after by his niece, Maria, an EMS technician. On the weekday in question Romanova left Nicolai's apartment at 2:30 pm. A fire broke out in the apartment sometime after 3 pm, its cause unknown. Maria arrived home at 3:45 pm to see smoke billowing out of her uncle's apartment. Maria rushed into the apartment but both she and her uncle died in the fire. Discuss the potential liability of Nurse-by-Day, Inc.

F. GOVERNMENTAL LIABILITY

DAY v. STATE
1999 Utah 46, 980 P.2d 1171 (1999)

STEWART, JUSTICE:

On March 18, 1991, at approximately 5:45 p.m., Officer Colyar was parked just off Interstate 15 near Santaquin, Utah, to monitor traffic. With a radar gun he clocked a northbound black 1982 Buick at 75 miles per hour, ten miles per hour over the posted speed limit. Intending only to stop the vehicle and issue a citation for speeding, Officer Colyar pulled onto I-15 and drove up behind the vehicle. Floyd, the driver of the vehicle, increased his speed and exited I-15 at Santaquin. Ignoring a stop sign, he turned onto a two-lane highway and proceeded, at times in heavy traffic and at speeds of up to 120 miles per hour, through the towns of Springville, Payson, Salem, and Spanish Fork, Utah. Officer Colyar followed in close pursuit. At least two other local law enforcement officers joined the chase through several populated areas in the towns and villages at speeds far in excess of posted limits. Floyd and Officer Colyar wove in and out between cars in heavy traffic in both the southbound and northbound lanes, passing cars on both the left and the right and forcing several cars off the road. Local police officers Brad James and Ed Asay unsuccessfully attempted to block Floyd's way and later joined in the pursuit.

At one point, Floyd drove onto a freeway entrance ramp with Officer Colyar close behind and collided with a semi-trailer truck. Floyd's vehicle spun almost 240 degrees around and temporarily came to a stop. Officer Colyar also stopped, but he neither drew his gun nor attempted to disable Floyd's vehicle; however, he was close enough to read the vehicle's license plate. Floyd eluded Officer Colyar and again entered the freeway with Officer Colyar in pursuit through heavy traffic and at speeds in excess of 100 miles per hour. Floyd entered an off-ramp at high speed, ran a red light while driving at approximately 60 miles per hour, and collided with the Day vehicle and three other vehicles.

Mr. Day died immediately, and Mrs. Day suffered numerous serious injuries. She was diagnosed with acute respiratory failure, fractures in her ankle, hip, and ribs, various abrasions, and trauma. She lay in a coma for several hours. The impact of the collision also aggravated previously existing medical conditions, including cancer and osteoporosis. Mrs. Day brought this suit against the State of Utah.

The trial court entered summary judgment against plaintiff and in favor of all defendants.

The public duty doctrine provides that although a government entity owes a general duty to all members of the public, that duty does not impose a specific duty of due care on the government with respect to individuals who may be harmed by governmental action or inaction, unless there is some specific connection between the government agency and the individuals that makes it reasonable to impose a duty.

At least four circumstances may give rise to a special relationship between the government and specific individuals. A special relationship can be established (1) by a statute intended to protect a specific class of persons of which the plaintiff is a member from a particular type of harm; (2) when a government agent undertakes specific action to protect a person or property; (3) by governmental actions that reasonably induce detrimental reliance by a member of the public; and (4) under certain circumstances, when the agency has actual custody of the plaintiff or of a third person who causes harm to the plaintiff.

The first exception applies in this case. Officer Colyar had a statutory duty to exercise reasonable care in using his patrol car to pursue Floyd. The Motor Vehicle Code in effect at the time of the accident, Utah Code Ann. § 41-6-14 (1988), imposed a duty on operators of emergency vehicles such as police cars to act with due regard for the safety of other persons on the road. . .

Whether the State might be liable in the instant case raises an issue of proximate cause as to whether it was reasonably foreseeable that Colyar's continuing the chase might result in Floyd's car colliding with another. In similar instances, we have held that such an issue is for the jury. The issue of whether police officers owe a duty of care to third parties who are injured by fleeing suspects is an issue that a number of other states have decided. The majority of recent cases holds that an action will lie in such circumstances. The New Jersey Supreme Court, in *Tice v. Cramer*, 133 N.J. 347, 627 A.2d 1090, 1103–04 (N.J. 1993), stated: "The majority of recent cases, however, hold that a police officer or a governmental employer may be held liable for third-party injuries when the police officer is negligent in continuing a vehicular chase."

Several of these cases are closely on point. The Washington Supreme Court, in *Mason v. Bitton*, 85 Wash. 2d 321, 534 P.2d 1360 (Wash. 1975), construing an emergency vehicle statute with nearly identical provisions to Utah Code Ann. § 41-6-14, rejected the argument that the State advances in the instant case. The court concluded that the Washington Legislature, by enacting the statute, intended to protect "persons and property from all consequences resulting from negligent behavior of the enforcement officers," including injury to third parties caused by fleeing suspects.

The Michigan Supreme Court in *Fiser v. City of Ann Arbor*, 417 Mich. 461, 339 N.W.2d 413 (Mich. 1983), also construed a statute similar to Utah's and held that a police officer owes a duty to other drivers on the road who may be injured as a proximate result of his negligence. As in the instant case, Fiser involved a motorist whose vehicle was struck by a fleeing suspect. The court stated that the legislative intent behind the statute was clear: "Emergency vehicles must be driven with due regard for the safety of others," 339 N.W.2d at 417, and the jury, in deciding whether a police officer breached this duty, should consider, among other things, the speed and location of the chase, the presence of pedestrians and other vehicles, and the reason for initiating the pursuit.

The State argues that a pursuing officer owes no duty of care to protect other persons on the highway from a negligent or reckless fleeing suspect. Specifically, the State asserts that because Officer Colyar could not directly control Floyd's actions, Floyd alone was responsible for Mrs. Day's injuries and her husband's death. However, the cases discussed above and Utah Code Ann. § 41-6-14(3)(a) support the proposition that Officer Colyar had a duty of care to other users of the highways and streets. Those cases also support the proposition that his conduct could be found to be a proximate cause of the Days' injuries if they were reasonably foreseeable. This Court has held that one may be liable for the reckless or negligent acts of another if they are reasonably foreseeable. According to the State, Officer Colyar owed only a generalized duty to the public at large to enforce the law; therefore, the State cannot be held liable for Floyd's conduct.

[The cases relied upon by the State] are clearly distinguishable. First, none of them dealt with facts similar to those in the instant case. Second, in none of the cases was there a statute that imposed a duty of care on the government employee with respect to others in the particular circumstances. Third, the defendants in those cases were not, as here, acting in a continuous manner that created a direct, obvious, and imminent hazard to third persons that could have been obviated by the officer's ceasing the conduct creating the risk. Clearly, those cases in which injuries are caused by persons who have been chased or have escaped from custody stand for different principles than those applicable to this case.

The nature of Officer Colyar's pursuit of Floyd created an immediate, obvious, and significant threat of serious harm to other users of the highway that would no doubt have ended had he terminated his pursuit. Although law enforcement officers have a general duty to apprehend those who break the law, that duty is not absolute, especially where the violation is only a misdemeanor or an infraction—such as driving ten miles per hour over the speed limit—and the attempt to apprehend the person creates a serious risk of death or injury to third persons or the fugitive. It has been held that, in apprehending someone, a law enforcement officer must act reasonably and may not use all available means to apprehend a fleeing suspect to arrest him for a misdemeanor. The threat of injury to the safety of the person fleeing and to the safety of bystanders is significant enough, and the magnitude of the possible harm so momentous, to dictate that the fleeing person be allowed to escape rather than imperiling his safety or the safety of others.

In conclusion, while police officers and drivers of other emergency vehicles are not bound by all traffic laws and do not necessarily violate a duty of due care when they exceed the speed limit or do not comply with certain other safety regulations, a police officer in pursuing another on a public highway or street nevertheless does owe a duty of reasonable care under the circumstances to other motorists on the road. We certainly do not suggest that police officers are never justified in engaging in high-speed pursuits. The need to apprehend a person who is a danger to others because of the serious and violent nature of the crime for which he or she is sought or because his or her presence on the highway presents a threat to public safety may well outweigh the risks that a high-speed pursuit poses to innocent third parties.

The test is whether the driver of the emergency vehicle acted reasonably and with appropriate care for the safety of others in light of all the circumstances. Among the factors that should be considered in deciding whether an officer acts with reasonable care for the safety of others using the highways and streets are the density of traffic and population of the area in which the pursuit occurs; whether the area is rural or urban; the nature of the street, e.g., whether freeway or city streets with stop signs and semaphores; the presence of pedestrians and school zones; the weather and visibility; and, of course, the urgency of apprehending the fleeing person and whether allowing that person to escape may itself pose a serious threat to the safety of others.

Reversed and remanded to the district court for trial.

NOTES

1. *Midnight Mass.* The plaintiffs were injured in *Ferreira v. Strack*, 636 A.2d 682 (R.I. 1994), after attending midnight mass at defendant's church:

On December 24, 1986, Amelia, Frank, and Florinda drove to the church to attend Midnight Mass. As was the practice of many parishioners, they parked their car in a small parking lot, which was owned by a third party, across the street from the church. The parking lot is separated from the church by Broadway, which is a public highway in the city of Newport.

After Mass ended, Amelia, Frank, and Florinda left the church and proceeded to cross Broadway to reach their car in the parking lot. While in the crosswalk, Amelia and Florinda were struck by a vehicle driven by William Strack, Jr. (Strack), who was later determined to be legally intoxicated. Florinda died within hours of the accident, and Amelia suffered severe and permanent injuries.

On prior occasions the church had contacted the Newport police department (police) and requested that a traffic officer be dispatched to control traffic on Broadway after various Masses. The police had dispatched traffic officers pursuant to the church's request on a so-called as-available basis. At no time did the church have a contract with the police to provide traffic officers. No representative of the church had contacted the police to request traffic control for Midnight Mass on December 24, 1986.

. . .The plaintiffs proffered two theories for imposing liability upon the church. First, plaintiffs contend that the church owed them a duty to control traffic on Broadway, a public highway, because the church knew that a substantial number of parishioners would cross Broadway to reach the parking lot late at night after Mass ended. Second, plaintiffs argue in the alternative that even if no duty existed, the church voluntarily assumed a duty to patrol traffic by its past conduct of occasionally contacting the police and requesting the assignment of traffic officers to Broadway. Under this line of reasoning, plaintiffs argue, parishioners relied upon the church's gratuitous assumption of a duty and the presence of such officers on Broadway. Therefore, the church had a duty to warn parishioners when a traffic officer was not present. . . .

The plaintiffs implicitly recognize that the church lacks control over Broadway by asserting that the church "could have" requested that local authorities assign an officer to control traffic on Broadway that evening. The fact that a landowner may request public traffic control on a public street does not vest in that landowner the personal right or obligation to control such a public way. Consequently the church's request for public traffic control would not confer on the church any authority or obligation to control a public highway such as Broadway. . . .

The same principles that militate against the duty to control traffic on public highways would also preclude the gratuitous assumption of such a duty. Indeed our statutory framework and our cases strongly indicate that any attempt on the part of a private person gratuitously to assume control of a public highway would be contra to public policy. Consequently, whether or not the church had followed a practice of requesting aid from the police, however sporadically or frequently, no such duty could be assumed by an abutting landowner.

The court affirmed a summary judgment in favor of the defendant.

Compare Mulvaney v. Auletto's Catering, 680 A.2d 793 (N. J. Super. 1996), where the court held that liability could be imposed on the defendant on facts similar to those of *Ferreira*.

See also *Hoff v. Vacaville Unified School District*, 19 Cal. 4th 925, 968 P.2d 522, 80 Cal. Rptr. 2d 311 (1998), in which plaintiff was injured when a student exiting a high school parking lot in his car "floored the accelerator," peeled out" with the wheels "screeching," "fishtailed," and jumped the curb striking the plaintiff who was on the sidewalk across the street. Plaintiff argued that the school district breached its duty to supervise the student. Denying the plaintiff a cause of action the court stated:

> Under this rule, any common law duty of [School] District employees to supervise students did not run to Hoff. According to Hoff's opening statement, the accident occurred "off-campus," on the sidewalk across the street from the school's overflow parking lot. School personnel considered Lozano a "[g]ood kid" who was "[r]esponsible" and "never disobeyed them." Thus, they neither knew nor had reason to know that Lozano had a propensity to operate his car recklessly (if, in fact, he did). Accordingly, they owed Hoff no duty

2. *More Time and Place.* A jailer negligently permits an inmate to escape. The inmate injures a third person running out of the jailhouse. What if he rapes or mugs a victim the next day, 10 miles away? The next year, a thousand miles away? What is the very risk that makes the jailer's conduct negligent? How is the line to be drawn? Why must it be drawn? *Compare Brown v. American Druggists' Ins. Co.*, 476 So. 2d 881 (La. App. 1985) (liability where injury inflicted a few hours after escape and a few miles from the jail), *with Nelson v. Washington Parish*, 805 F.2d 1236 (5th Cir. 1986) (applying Louisiana law, the court held that there was no liability for rape and murder by convicted rapist-escapee where crime occurred 13 days after the escape and 750 miles from the jail).

G. RESPONSIBILITIES OF MEDIA, SUPPLIERS AND DISTRIBUTORS

DAVIDSON v. TIME WARNER, INC.
1997 U.S. Dist. LEXIS 21559 (S. D. Tex. 1997)

RAINEY, J.

In April of 1992, Ronald Howard ("Howard") was driving a stolen automobile through Jackson County, Texas. Officer Bill Davidson, a state trooper, stopped Howard for a possible traffic violation unrelated to the theft of the vehicle. During the traffic stop, Howard fatally shot Officer Davidson with a nine millimeter Glock handgun. At the time of the shooting, Howard was listening to an audio cassette of *2Pacalypse Now*, a recording performed by Defendant Tupac Amaru Shakur that was produced, manufactured and distributed by

Defendants Interscope Records and Atlantic Records.[6] In an attempt to avoid the death penalty, Howard claimed that listening to *2Pacalypse Now* caused him to shoot Officer Davidson.[7] The jury apparently did not believe this explanation, because it sentenced Howard to death.

The Davidsons then brought this civil action, echoing several of the arguments made by Howard during his criminal trial. First, the Davidsons claim that the album *2Pacalypse Now* does not merit First Amendment protection because it: (1) is obscene, (2) contains "fighting words," (3) defames peace officers like Officer Davidson, and (4) tends to incite imminent illegal conduct on the part of individuals like Howard. Because the recording lacks constitutional protection, the Davidsons argue that Defendants are liable for producing violent music that proximately caused the death of Officer Davidson.

Texas courts employ a risk-utility balancing test to determine the existence of a legal duty:

> In determining whether to impose a duty we are to consider the risk, foreseeability, and likelihood of injury weighed against the social utility of the actor's conduct, the magnitude of the burden of guarding against the injury and the consequences of placing that burden on the actor.

Venetoulias v. O'Brien, 909 S.W.2d 236, 241 (Tex. App., Houston 1995, writ dism'd).

Foreseeability is the most significant factor when using the risk-utility test. After reviewing the facts of this case and drawing all inferences in the Davidsons' favor, the Court must conclude that Defendants had no duty to prevent the distribution of *2Pacalypse Now..*

Research by the parties and the Court unveils few cases interpreting Texas law that address foreseeability when a widely distributed publication (such as a recording or magazine) causes injuries to another. Unfortunately for the Davidsons, none of these cases imposed a duty upon a publisher to refrain from distributing a published work. Because of these cases and the policies that support them, the Court predicts that Texas Courts would rule in favor of Defendants on their motion for summary judgment.

In *Eimann v. Soldier of Fortune Magazine,* 880 F.2d 830 (5th Cir. 1989), *cert. denied,* 493 U.S. 1024, 110 S. Ct. 729, 107 L. Ed. 2d 748 (1990), Plaintiff sued *Soldier of Fortune* for negligence and gross negligence for publishing a personal services classified advertisement through which the victim's husband hired an assassin. *Id.* at 831. Plaintiff presented evidence of some three dozen classified ads from *Soldier of Fortune* that offered services as a "Mercenary for Hire," or "bounty hunter." Other ads promised to perform "dirty work" or to "do anything, anywhere at the right price." *Id.* at 832. Plaintiff presented evidence that at least seven of these advertisements were linked to criminal

---

[6] Actually, Howard was listening to a pirated copy of *2Pacalypse Now,* not a cassette distributed by Defendants. However, this distinction does not affect the Court's analysis.

[7] The Davidsons do not allege which song Howard was listening to at the time he brutally murdered Officer Davidson. As described later, the songs of *2Pacalypse Now* vary in their content and message. However, at least one song on the recording describes the commission of violence against police officers.

activity. Perhaps most importantly, law enforcement officials contacted the magazine's staff during investigations of two crimes linked to *Soldier of Fortune* classifieds. Thus, the editors of *Soldier of Fortune* were aware that certain classified advertisements were connected to criminal activity.

Despite this evidence, the Fifth Circuit held that the magazine "owed no duty to refrain from publishing a facially innocuous classified advertisement when the ad's context — at most — made its message ambiguous." *Id.* at 834. To reach this result, the Fifth Circuit employed Texas law and its risk-utility balancing test. The Fifth Circuit determined that the probability and gravity of the threatened harm was high because of evidence that several classified ads in the magazine had been linked to criminal activity. "The prospect of ad-inspired crime represents a threat of serious harm." *Id.* at 835.

However, the Fifth Circuit recognized that the burden of preventing the harm also was high, given the ambiguous nature of the advertisement at issue and the pervasiveness of advertising in society. Although the ad in question expressed the desire for " 'high risk assignments' . . . its bare terms reveal no identifiable offer to commit crimes." *Id.* at 836. "The ambiguity persists even if we assume that *[Soldier of Fortune]* knew other ads had been tied to criminal plots. No evidence linked the other ads and crimes to Hearn [the hired assassin]." *Id.*

Finally, although the Fifth Circuit decided not to reach *Soldier of Fortune's* First Amendment arguments, the Court noted "the Supreme Court's recognition of limited first amendment protection for commercial speech . . . highlights the important role of such communication for purposes of risk-benefit analysis." *Id.* at 836. Although the plaintiff noted that the advertising of illegal activity is not protected by the First Amendment, the Fifth Circuit countered that "the possibility of illegal results does not necessarily strip an ad of its commercial speech protection." *Id.* At 837.

Although in this case the variables of the risk-utility equation differ from *Eimann,* the calculation yields the same result, There is no question that *2Pacalypse Now* depicts violence, and a reasonable jury could find that the recording entreats others to act on Shakur's violent message. However, playing a musical recording (even tasteless, violent music like *2Pacalypse Now)* is fundamentally different from placing a classified advertisement seeking employment as a mercenary. The probability that a listener of *2Pacalypse Now* would act on Shakur's message is substantially less than the chance that a person responding to a *Soldier of Fortune* advertisement would hire a "hit man" for illegal activity. The evidence illustrates this common-sense difference. In *Eimann,* the plaintiff presented evidence that at least seven of the magazine's classified ads were tied to criminal activity. By contrast, the Davidsons present no evidence that *2Pacalypse Now* has been the source of "music-inspired crime"; after more than 400,000 sales of *2Pacalypse Now,* the case at bar is the only one alleging violence after listening to Shakur's virulent music. Thus, the probability of harm is very low.

In addition, the burden of preventing the harm is very high, both to Defendants and to society at large. To create a duty requiring Defendants to police their recordings would be enormously expensive and would result in the sale of only the most bland, least controversial music. *See McCollum v.*

Columbia Broadcasting Sys., Inc., 202 Cal. App. 3d 989, 1005–1006, 249 Cal. Rptr. 187, 197 (1988). ("it is simply not acceptable to a free and democratic society to impose a duty upon performing artists to limit and restrict their creativity in order to avoid the dissemination of ideas in artistic speech which may adversely affect emotionally troubled individuals. Such a burden would quickly have the effect of reducing and limiting artistic expression to only the broadest standard of taste and acceptance and the lowest level of offense, provocation and controversy. No case has ever gone so far. We find no basis in law or public policy for doing so here."). Further, the *Eimann* Court recognized that First Amendment considerations impact the risk-benefit analysis. Unlike *Eimann,* which addressed commercial speech receiving limited First Amendment protection, *2Pacalypse Now,* as music, receives full First Amendment protection.

Further, at least one Texas court has found media-related injuries to be unforeseeable. In *Way v. Boy Scouts of America,* 856 S.W.2d 230 (Tex. App., Dallas 1993, writ denied), a twelve-year-old boy was shot and killed after he read a shooting supplement in *Boy's Life.* The youngster, curious about guns after reading the supplement, located an old rifle. The rifle discharged, killing the child. The parents subsequently sued, claiming that *Boy's Life* was negligent in printing the shooting supplement. The Texas Court of Appeals affirmed the trial court's grant of summary judgment, employing the state's risk-utility balancing test.

Although experimentation with firearms obviously poses serious risks to children, to merely focus on that risk would be to ignore the context in which the supplement presented the use of firearms. . . . Of greatest significance, the record does not support a conclusion that Rocky's experimentation with the rifle and cartridge was a reasonably foreseeable consequence of the publication. *Way,* 856 S.W.2d at 236. The court noted that the supplement emphasized supervision when using firearms. "Similarly, features present the use of firearms not as an experiment, but as a supervised and safety-conscious activity. A number of manufacturer advertisements in the supplement also depict a child's use of firearms as a supervised activity." *Id.* By contrast, the deadly experiment in which the child engaged was unsupervised. The court concluded, "encouragement of safe and responsible use of firearms by minors in conjunction with Boy Scout and other supervised activities is of significant social utility." *Id.*

The record indicates that Defendants could not reasonably foresee that distributing *2Pacalypse Now* would lead to violence. To be sure, Shakur's music is violent and socially offensive. This fact, by itself, does not make violence a foreseeable result of listening to *2Pacalypse Now.* The killing of Officer Davidson was not a random act of violence against a peace officer; it was an attempt to elude justice by an adult gang member driving a stolen automobile.[8] Other courts have found foreseeability lacking in similar

---

[8] Plaintiff's expert on musicology, Dr. Clarence Joseph Stuessey, Jr., supports this point. *See,* Dkt. # 54, Ex. A at 4. Dr. Stuessey suggests that rap music may become "almost hypnotic" in its effect to the listener, but concludes that Howard reacted violently because rap music was played in a context that Defendants could not have possibly controlled: "Howard's environment, background, experience and attitudes and because Howard was driving a stolen car." Further, the expert presents no evidence of other people who have been entranced by rap music in general or by *2Pacalypse Now* in particular.

situations. *Sakon v. Pepsico., Inc.*, 553 So. 2d 163, 166 (Fla. 1989) (no legal liability when child duplicated stunt in commercial); *McCollum v. CBS, Inc.*, 202 Cal. App. 3d at 1005, 249 Cal. Rptr. at 196. (no liability after juvenile committed suicide after hearing Ozzy Osbourne song, "Suicide Solution").

. . . [In omitted portions the court held that the plaintiffs did not have a strict products liability action and that the First Amendment protected Shakur from liability.]

For these reasons, summary judgment should be GRANTED as to the Davidsons' negligence claim.

NOTES

1. *Foreseeability and the First Amendment.* McCollum v. CBS, Inc., 202 Cal. App. 3d 989, 249 Cal. Rptr. 187 (1988), concerned the suicide of a 19-year-old who had been listening incessantly to two albums of music recorded by Ozzy Osbourne, "Blizzard of Oz" and "Diary of a Madman." Plaintiffs alleged that Osbourne conveyed the message that life is filled with nothing but despair and hopelessness and suicide is not only acceptable, but desirable. One of the songs the plaintiff's decedent had been listening to, "Suicide Solution," included a 28-second instrumental break with some hidden lyrics:

Ah know people
You really know where it's at
You got it
Why try, why try
Get the gun and try it
Shoot, shoot, shoot.

The court noted:

> . . . [T]o justify a claim that speech should be restrained or punished because it is (or was) an incitement to lawless action, the court must be satisfied that the speech (1) was directed or intended toward the goal of producing imminent lawless conduct *and* (2) was likely to produce such imminent conduct. Speech directed to action at some indefinite time in the future will not satisfy this test.
>
> In the context of this case we must conclude, in order to find a culpable incitement, (1) that Osbourne's music was *directed and intended* toward the goal of bringing about the imminent suicide of listeners *and* (2) that it was *likely* to produce such a result. It is not enough that John's suicide may have been the result of an unreasonable reaction to the music; it must have been a specifically intended consequence.
>
> We can find no such intent or likelihood here. Apart from the "unintelligible" lyrics quoted above from "Suicide Solution," to which John admittedly was not even listening at the time of his death, there is nothing in any of Osbourne's songs which could be characterized as a command to an immediate suicidal act. None of the lyrics relied upon by plaintiffs, even accepting their literal interpretation of the words, purport to order or command anyone to any concrete action at

any specific time, much less immediately. Moreover, as defendants point out, the lyrics of the song on which plaintiffs focus their primary objection can as easily be viewed as a poetic device, such as a play on words, to convey meanings entirely contrary to those asserted by plaintiffs. We note this here not to suggest a reliance upon a construction which is contrary to plaintiffs' allegations, but to illuminate the very serious problems which can arise when litigants seek to cast judges in the role of censor. [W]e conclude that, as a matter of law, they fail to meet the *Brandenburg v. Ohio,* 395 U.S. 444, 89 S. Ct. 1827, 23 L. Ed. 2d 430 (1969), standard for incitement and that therefore Osbourne's music is speech protected by the First Amendment.

. . . The threshold and, in this case, dispositive question with respect to the assertion of a claim for negligence is whether any duty was owed to the plaintiffs.

Foreseeability is one of several factors to be weighed in determining whether a duty is owed in a particular case. "In this balancing process, foreseeability is an elastic factor. The degree of foreseeability necessary to warrant the finding of a duty will thus vary from case to case. For example, in cases where the burden of preventing future harm is great, a high degree of foreseeability may be required. On the other hand, in cases where there are strong policy reasons for preventing the harm, or the harm can be prevented by simple means, a lesser degree of foreseeability may be required." Here, a very high degree of foreseeability would be required because of the great burden on society of preventing the kind of "harm" of which plaintiffs complain by restraining or punishing artistic expression. The "countervailing policies" which arise out of the First Amendment "have a substantial bearing upon the issue whether there should be imposed upon [defendants] the exposure to liability of the kind for which plaintiffs contend." (*Bill v. Superior Court, supra.*)

Plaintiffs rely on *Weirum* [*v. RKO*, given above] for the proposition that harm to John from listening to Osbourne's music was foreseeable. . . . In our view, plaintiffs' reliance on *Weirum* is not justified. As the court there noted, the issue was "civil accountability for the foreseeable results of a broadcast which created an undue risk of harm to decedent. The First Amendment does not sanction the infliction of physical injury merely because achieved by word, rather than act." Indeed, it would not be inappropriate to view the reckless importuning in *Weirum* as a specie of incitement to imminent lawless conduct for which no First Amendment protection is justified. What the conduct in *Weirum* and culpable incitement have in common, when viewed from the perspective of a duty analysis, is a very high degree of foreseeability of undue risk of harm to others. Under such circumstances, imposition of negligence liability does not offend the First Amendment.

The court, in *Olivia II, supra,* placed *Weirum* in its proper perspective when it stated, in language equally applicable here, "[a]lthough the language utilized by the Supreme Court was broad, it must be understood in light of the particular facts of that case. The radio station's broadcast was designed to encourage its youthful listeners to be the first to arrive at a particular location in order to win a prize and gain momentary glory. The *Weirum* broadcasts actively and repeatedly encouraged listeners to speed to announced locations. Liability was imposed on the broadcaster for urging listeners to act in an inherently dangerous manner." (*Id.*, at p. 496, 178 Cal. Rptr. 888.) That they were very likely to do so was clearly foreseeable. Not so here. Osbourne's music and lyrics had been recorded and produced years before. There was not a "real time" urging of listeners to act in a particular manner. There was no dynamic interaction with, or live importuning of, particular listeners.

Plaintiffs' case is not aided by an examination of the other factors which are a part of the duty analysis. It can not be said that there was a close connection between John's death and defendants' composition, performance, production and distribution years earlier of recorded artistic musical expressions. Likewise, no moral blame for that tragedy may be laid at defendants' door. John's suicide, an admittedly irrational response to Osbourne's music, was not something which any of the defendants intended, planned or had any reason to anticipate. Finally, and perhaps most significantly, it is simply not acceptable to a free and democratic society to impose a duty upon performing artists to limit and restrict their creativity in order to avoid the dissemination of ideas in artistic speech which may adversely affect emotionally troubled individuals. Such a burden would quickly have the effect of reducing and limiting artistic expression to only the broadest standard of taste and acceptance and the lowest level of offense, provocation and controversy. No case has ever gone so far. We find no basis in law or public policy for doing so here.

Are you satisfied with the line drawn between *McCollum* and *Weirum*? For example in *Weirum,* 123 Cal. Rptr. at 472, the court had stated:

> Defendant's contention that the giveaway contest must be afforded the deference due society's interest in the First Amendment is clearly without merit. The issue here is civil accountability for the foreseeable results of a broadcast which created an undue risk of harm to decedent. The First Amendment does not sanction the infliction of physical injury merely because achieved by word, rather than act.

Suppose that plaintiff's decedent had committed suicide while attending a live performance of the material discussed in *McCollum*? During a dramatized music video broadcast on cable television?

See also Watters v. TSR Inc., 904 F.2d 378 (6th Cir. 1990) (manufacturer of "Dungeons & Dragons" video game entitled to summary judgment in action brought by mother of teenage suicide; judgment affirmed on First Amendment and causation grounds).

3. *Heavy Metal on the Defensive.* Consider *Judas Priest v. Second Judicial Court,* 760 P.2d 137 (Nev. 1988) (British band members subject to personal

jurisdiction, concerning allegations pertaining to the Judas Priest album "Stained Class," following a teenage suicide pact). Apparently, plaintiffs had avoided dismissal because the trial judge refused to extend First Amendment protection to "subliminals." *See* Billard, *Heavy Metal Goes on Trial,* ROLLING STONE, July 12, 1990, at 83, 84. However, after a 17-day trial, the judge ruled that although a subliminal message ("do it") existed, its presence was unintentional. L.A. TIMES, Aug. 25, 1990, at F1, col. 2. *See generally* Brown & Hendee, *Adolescents and Their Music; Insights Into the Health of Adolescents,* 262 J.A.M.A. 1659 (1989).

4. *Hit Man.* In *Rice v. Paladin Enterprises,* 128 F.3d 233 (4th Cir. 1997), several murders were committed by a hired killer. In soliciting, preparing for, and committing these murders, the killer followed closely the publisher defendant's book "Hit Man" that contained 130 pages of detailed factual instructions on how to murder and to become a professional killer. The court concluded:

> Here, it is alleged, and a jury could reasonably find. . .that Paladin aided and abetted the murders at issue through the quintessential speech act of providing step-by-step instructions for murder (replete with photographs, diagrams, and narration) so comprehensive and detailed that it is as if the instructor were literally present with the would-be murderer not only in the preparation and planning, but in the actual commission of, and follow-up to, the murder; there is not even a hint that the aid was provided in the form of speech that might constitute abstract advocacy. As the district court itself concluded, Hit Man "merely teaches what must be done to implement a professional hit." Moreover, although we do not believe such would be necessary, we are satisfied a jury could readily find that the provided instructions not only have no, or virtually no, noninstructional communicative value, but also that their only instructional communicative "value" is the indisputably illegitimate one of training persons how to murder and to engage in the business of murder for hire. . . Aid and assistance in the form of this kind of speech bears no resemblance to the "theoretical advocacy,". . . Indeed, this detailed, focused instructional assistance to those contemplating or in the throes of planning murder is the antithesis of speech protected under *Brandenburg*. It is the teaching of the "techniques" of violence, *Scales,* 367 U.S. at 233, the "advocacy and teaching of concrete action. . ." the "preparation . . . for violent action and [the] steeling . . . to such action," It is the instruction in the methods of terror of which Justice Douglas spoke in *Dennis v. United States,* when he said, "If this were a case where those who claimed protection under the First Amendment were teaching the techniques of sabotage . . . I would have no doubts. The freedom to speak is not absolute; the teaching of methods of terror . . . should be beyond the pale . . ." 341 U.S. 494, 581, 71 S. Ct. 857, 95 L. Ed. 1137 (1951). . . As such, the murder instructions in Hit Man are, collectively, a textbook example of the type of speech that the Supreme Court has quite purposely left unprotected, and the prosecution of which, criminally or civilly, has historically been thought subject to few, if any, First Amendment constraints. Accordingly, we

hold that the First Amendment does not pose a bar to the plaintiffs' civil aiding and abetting cause of action against Paladin Press. If, as precedent uniformly confirms, the states have the power to regulate speech that aids and abets crime, then certainly they have the power to regulate the speech at issue here.

The court was impressed by the fact that defendant admitted it designed "Hit Man," among other purposes, "to aid and abet persons in committing murder."

PROBLEM

Dastardly Dee operates a pornographic web site. Customers can connect to the site and see graphic descriptions of well-known celebrities participating in numerous bestial acts.

Five-year-old Jason was molested by 10-year-old Albert. Jason brings an action against Dee alleging that Albert was a frequent visitor of her web site, and that Albert's exposure to the graphic descriptions caused the attack. Dee moves for dismissal on the basis of First Amendment protection and failure to state a cause of action. What result?

SCHOOLEY v. PINCH'S DELI MARKET, INC.
134 Wn.2d 468, 951 P.2d 749 (1998)

MADSEN, J.

On August 25, 1989, Russell Bowser invited five of his friends, all of whom were under 21, over for a party while his parents were out of town. Everyone at the party wanted beer so Bowser, then 19, Lori Schooley, then 18, and the others decided to pool their money and purchase beer. They drove to Pinch's Deli and Bowser and two others entered the store to buy beer. Schooley and the others remained in the car. Bowser purchased four cases of beer. He was not asked to produce identification when purchasing the beer.

After purchasing the beer, Bowser, Schooley, and the others returned to Bowser's house. Schooley drank two or three beers and then consumed an unknown quantity while playing a drinking game with the others. Later, Bowser and one of the other boys carried Schooley to the pool to throw her in. She asked them if she could strip down to her swimsuit, which she had on underneath her clothes, before they threw her in. The boys let her down and she took off her clothes. However, before they could throw her in she dove into the water. The pool was only two feet deep where Schooley dove and consequently she fractured her spinal cord and is now quadriplegic.

Schooley sued Pinch's Deli for damages for negligently selling alcohol to minors. The trial court granted Pinch's motion for summary judgment.

After Congress repealed Prohibition in 1933, the Washington Legislature passed the Washington alcoholic beverage control (WABC) act. In part, this Act prohibits selling alcohol to any minor, or giving or otherwise supplying liquor to any minor.

The issue presented in this case is one of first impression in the State of Washington. To date, we have found that an injured intoxicated minor purchaser and third persons injured by the intoxicated minor purchaser both have a cause of action in negligence against the vendor who sold alcohol to the minor. In this case, however, a somewhat different scenario has occurred; a third person minor who obtained alcohol from a minor purchaser was injured. Thus, the issue here is whether a vendor who sells alcohol to a minor who subsequently furnishes the alcohol to another minor can be held liable for foreseeable alcohol-related injuries arising from the initial sale of alcohol.

We turn first to the contention that Schooley is not within the class of persons protected by the statute.

The WABC Act explicitly prohibits commercial vendors from "selling any intoxicating liquor to any minor." RCW 66.44.320; see also RCW 66.44.270(1) ("it is unlawful for any person to sell . . . liquor to any person under the age of twenty-one years. . .").

Petitioner argues that the statute protects only the immediate minor purchaser, and not other third person minors who may receive the liquor from the minor purchaser. While the legislation focuses primarily on the minor purchaser, the notion that the prohibition against selling liquor to minors imposes a duty toward persons other than the minor purchaser is not a new concept. In *Purchase*, we found that third persons injured by a minor purchaser have a cause of action against the liquor vendor stating the vendor's duty extends not only to the minor purchaser but "to members of the general public as well." *Purchase*, 108 Wash. 2d at 228. To conclude that the commercial vendor's duty extends to third persons whom the minor purchaser injures but not minors with whom the alcohol was shared would be an arbitrary distinction not supported by the recognized purpose of the statute.

We have repeatedly emphasized that "persons under 21 years of age are neither physically nor mentally equipped to handle the consumption of intoxicating liquor." The recognized purpose of legislation prohibiting the sale of alcohol to minors is to protect minors' health and safety interests from their "own inability to drink responsibly" and to protect against the particular hazard of "alcohol in the hands of minors." Because minors who drink commonly do so with other minors, protecting all those injured as a result of the illegal sale of alcohol to minors is the best way to serve the purpose for which the legislation was created, to prevent minors from drinking. Thus, we find that Schooley is part of the protected class.

Petitioner next contends that, although underage, Schooley does not need the protection of the statute. Petitioner cites no authority for this proposition, arguing only that Schooley's history of alcohol consumption supports the conclusion that unlike other minors who are neither physically nor mentally equipped to handle the consumption of alcohol, she had been intoxicated before and was well aware of the effects of alcohol. This argument is without merit. The statute does not provide for such an exception, and, moreover, it is illogical to assume the Legislature would implicitly intend to carve out an exception and allow vendors of alcohol to sell intoxicating liquor to minors who are "experienced" drinkers. Such a conclusion is in direct contradiction to the policy behind the statute that minors as a class are not physically or mentally equipped to handle the consumption of alcohol.

As we found, Schooley is within the protected class and foreseeability serves to define the scope of the duty owed. Where harm to a person protected by a statute is a foreseeable result of the statute's violation, liability may be imposed. Foreseeability is used to limit the scope of the duty owed because actors are responsible only for the foreseeable consequences of their acts. Foreseeability is normally an issue for the trier of fact and will be decided as a matter of law only where reasonable minds cannot differ.

Pinch's Deli argues that, as a matter of law, its conduct did not create a foreseeable risk to Schooley because it did not sell alcohol directly to her. We disagree and find that reasonable minds could conclude that a minor purchasing substantial amounts of alcohol would share that alcohol with friends. Thus, it is a question for the jury as to whether under these facts it was foreseeable that the alcohol would be shared with others. Factors that may be considered include, but are not limited to, the amount and character of the beverages purchased, the time of day, the presence of other minors on the premises or in a vehicle, and statements made by the purchaser.

Additionally, the trier of fact must determine whether the harm sustained in this case, diving into the shallow end of a pool, was foreseeable. "The harm sustained must be reasonably perceived as being within the general field of danger covered by the specific duty owed by the defendant." In *Hansen v. Friend*, 118 Wash.2d 476, 824 P.2d 483 (1992), the defendant argued that the duty owed to the plaintiff should be limited only to those minors who drive while intoxicated and not to minors who drown as a result of intoxication. We found that many minors do not drive; thus, it was for the trier of fact to determine whether drowning as result of the intoxication was foreseeable. Likewise, it is for the trier of fact to determine if Schooley's injuries were foreseeable.

Thus, we find Schooley is part of the protected class and the jury must determine whether her injuries were a foreseeable result of Pinch's illegal sale of alcohol.

Petitioner argues that even if it owed a legal duty to Schooley, it was not the legal cause of her injuries. Proximate causation is divided into two elements: cause in fact and legal causation. "Cause in fact" refers to the actual, "but for," cause of the injury, i.e., "but for" the defendant's actions the plaintiff would not be injured. Establishing cause in fact involves a determination of what actually occurred and is generally left to the jury. Unlike factual causation, which is based on a physical connection between an act and an injury, legal cause is grounded in policy determinations as to how far the consequences of a defendant's acts should extend. Thus, where the facts are not in dispute, legal causation is for the court to decide as a matter of law.

The focus in the legal causation analysis is whether, as a matter of policy, the connection between the ultimate result and the act of the defendant is too remote or insubstantial to impose liability.

The Court of Appeals indicates the analysis involved [in whether a duty is owed to the plaintiff and whether the defendant's actions were the legal cause of the injuries to the plaintiff] is identical. The Court of Appeals goes so far in this case as to state that if a duty of care is owed to the plaintiff then legal causation is automatically satisfied.

This court has recognized that the issues regarding whether duty and legal causation exist are intertwined. This is so because some of the policy considerations analyzed in answering the question whether a duty is owed to the plaintiff are also analyzed when determining whether the breach of the duty was the legal cause of the injury in question. However, a court should not conclude that the existence of a duty automatically satisfies the requirement of legal causation. This would nullify the legal causation element and along with it decades of tort law. Legal causation is, among other things, a concept that permits a court for sound policy reasons to limit liability where duty and foreseeability concepts alone indicate liability can arise.

[I]t is apparent that in some cases the policy considerations involved in determining whether a duty is owed to the plaintiff will be revisited in deciding whether legal causation is established. However, this does not mean that once a court finds a duty exists it need not analyze legal causation or that the result will automatically be the same. Thus, legal causation should not be assumed to exist every time a duty of care has been established.

Turning to the present case, Washington's policy regarding minors and alcohol is clear. It is illegal to sell minors alcohol and if a vendor breaches this duty it will be responsible for the foreseeable injuries which result. Legislation prohibiting the sale of alcohol to minors was enacted to protect minors' health and safety interests against the effects of alcohol.

Petitioner's main argument as to why it was not the legal cause of Schooley's injuries is that her injuries are too remote and that the legal consequences of the sale of alcohol to the first minor should not extend to minors who share the alcohol with the minor purchaser. The only policy reason given by Petitioner is the fear of unlimited liability, arguing once a vendor has sold the alcohol it has no control over ensuing events.

The alcohol vendor, however, has full control at the point of sale. The duty is not onerous. All the vendor has to do is ask the purchaser for valid identification in order to verify that he or she is of legal age to purchase alcohol. Moreover, the alcohol vendor has within its own control the power to immunize itself from liability for a minor's alcohol-related conduct. If, after a purchaser presents identification, the vendor still has doubts about the purchaser's age the vendor can fill out and have the purchaser sign a certification card complying with RCW 66.20.190. If the vendor completes these simple steps, but, nevertheless, the minor purchases alcohol, the vendor is immune from any criminal or civil liability regarding the sale of alcohol to the minor.

Additionally, even if an alcohol vendor sells alcohol to a minor in violation of the law, other legal concepts exist to prevent Petitioner's fear of unlimited liability. First, foreseeability serves to limit liability by only holding persons liable for the foreseeable consequences of their actions. Thus, an alcohol vendor will be responsible only for the foreseeable consequences of its negligent sale of alcohol.

Second, a minor who purchases, possesses, or consumes alcohol is also in violation of the law and may be found to be contributorily negligent. Moreover, if the minor's intoxication results in that person being more than 50 percent at fault for his or her own injuries then no recovery is allowed.

Finally, the doctrine of superseding cause serves as a significant limitation on a commercial vendor's liability. A defendant's negligence is a proximate cause of the plaintiff's injury only if such negligence, unbroken by any new independent cause, produces the injury complained of. When an independent intervening act of a third person is one which was not reasonably foreseeable then there is a break in the causal connection between the defendant's negligence and the plaintiff's injury. Thus, it is evident that if a commercial vendor negligently sells alcohol the resulting liability will not be endless.

Next Petitioner argues as a matter of policy that Pinch's should not be held liable for Schooley's irresponsible conduct. In *Kelly v. Falin*, 127 Was.2d 31, 896 P.2d 1245 (1995), we found that RCW 66.44.200, which prohibits selling alcohol to an obviously intoxicated adult, was not intended to shield the drunk driver from responsibility for his or her own actions. Thus, the injured intoxicated adult had no cause of action against the vendor who sold him alcohol. Petitioner in this case argues that, although a minor, she was over the age of 18 and therefore an adult who, like the individual in *Kelly*, should be held responsible for her own actions.

Using this analysis to preclude liability would, however, lead to an illogical and insupportable result whereby alcohol vendors would be absolved of liability when they sell alcohol to persons between the ages of 18 and 21. The Legislature has not created such an exception for those 18 and older. In fact, in Kelly, this court emphasized the distinction between minors and adults in the context of commercial vendor liability.

> While commercial vendors have a duty to minors and innocent bystanders, no duty arises when intoxicated adults harm themselves. The distinction between intoxicated adults and intoxicated minors is simple. The Legislature has determined that, unlike adults, "persons under 21 years of age are neither physically nor mentally equipped to handle the consumption of intoxicating liquor."

Kelly, 127 Wash. 2d at 40 (quoting *Young*, 99 Wash. 2d at 660).

Petitioner's concern is better addressed as an argument that Schooley was contributorily negligent. As previously noted, the purchase and consumption of alcohol by a person under the age of 21 is illegal and a minor's violation of the statute may be introduced as evidence of that minor's contributory negligence. The issue of contributory negligence is a question for the jury. Finding Petitioner's arguments unpersuasive we conclude that legal cause is satisfied in this case. The injury suffered is not so remote as to preclude liability and the policy considerations behind the legislation are best served by holding vendors liable for the foreseeable consequences of the illegal sale of alcohol to minors. The policy behind the prohibition was not intended to protect only the one minor who purchases the alcohol. Minors often share alcohol with others and this prohibition was intended to also protect those minors which share in the fruits of the illegal sale. We find that summary judgment should not have been granted in this case and affirm the decision of the Court of Appeals.

NOTES

1. *"Social" Engineering. Reynolds v. Hicks*, 134 Wash.2d 491, 951 P.2d 761 (Wash. 1998), was a companion case to *Schooley*. There a minor driver who allegedly became intoxicated at a wedding reception injured the plaintiff. The plaintiff sued the bride and groom. The Washington court held that a social host who furnishes alcohol to a minor does not owe a duty of care to an injured third person. The court noted:

> Because of the inherent differences between social hosts and commercial vendors, we have indicated our reluctance to allow a cause of action against a social host to the same extent that we have recognized commercial vendor liability. We have explained:
>
> "There is good reason to withhold common law liability for social hosts even though such liability already exists for commercial and quasi-commercial hosts. Social hosts are not as capable of handling the responsibilities of monitoring their guests' alcohol consumption as are their commercial and quasi-commercial counterparts. . . .
>
> "The commercial proprietor has a proprietary interest and profit motive, and should be expected to exercise greater supervision than in the (non-commercial) social setting. Moreover, a person in the business of selling and serving alcohol is usually better organized to control patrons, and has the financial wherewithal to do so. . . .
>
> "Additionally, the implications of social host liability are much more wide-sweeping and unpredictable in nature than are the implications of commercial host liability. While liability for commercial providers affects only a narrow slice of our population, social host liability would touch most adults in the state on a frequent basis. Because social hosts are generally unaccustomed to the pressures involved in taking responsibility for the intoxication of their guests, we cannot predict how well social hosts would respond when the scope of their duties would be so ill defined." Burkhart v. Harrod, 110 Wash. 2d 381, 386–87, 755 P.2d 759 (1988).
>
> Because of these important concerns, this court does not recognize a cause of action in negligence for a third person injured by an intoxicated adult against the social host that served the person while in an obviously intoxicated state but does recognize a cause of action against a commercial vendor in the same situation. This case dramatically highlights the concerns expressed above. To expect Jamie and Anna Hicks, on their wedding day, to monitor their minor guests' alcohol consumption in the same manner as we expect of an alcohol vendor is unrealistic and has far-reaching social implications.
>
> Recognizing an expanded duty to protect third persons raises problematic questions for social hosts in all contexts. Is the host required to card persons at social and family gatherings? Must the host hire a bartender to control and monitor the alcohol in the home so that a minor cannot obtain alcohol at a party? Must the host assure that a minor has not brought outside alcohol to the gathering? Must the host obtain a breathalyzer to check all minor guests before they

leave the premises? The differences between the ability of commercial vendors and social hosts in regulating the consumption of alcohol along with the far reaching implications of social host liability are persuasive reasons for not expanding liability in this case.

Compare *Kelly v. Gwinnell,* 96 N.J. 538, 476 A.2d 1219 (1984), where the court held that:

> . . . a host who serves liquor to an adult social guest, knowing that the guest is intoxicated and will thereafter be operating a motor vehicle, is liable for injuries inflicted on a third party as a result of the negligent operation of a motor vehicle by the adult guest when such negligence is caused by the intoxication. . . . While we recognize the concern that our ruling will interfere with accepted standards of social behavior; will intrude on and somewhat diminish the enjoyment, relaxation, and camaraderie that accompany social gatherings at which alcohol is served; and that such gatherings and social relationships are not simply tangential benefits of a civilized society but are regarded by many as important; we believe that the added assurance of just compensation to the victims of drunken driving as well as the added deterrent effect of the rule on such driving outweigh the importance of those other values. Indeed, we believe that given society's extreme concern about drunken driving, any change in social behavior resulting from the rule will be regarded ultimately as neutral at the very least, and not as a change for the worse; but that in any event if there be a loss, it is well worth the gain.

2. *Statutory Modifications.* There has been considerable legislative action in this area. For example, CAL. CIV. CODE ANN. § 1714 (2001) provides:

> (b) . . . [T]he furnishing of alcoholic beverages is not the proximate cause of injuries resulting from intoxication, but rather the consumption of alcoholic beverages is the proximate cause of injuries inflicted upon another by an intoxicated person.
>
> (c) No social host who furnishes alcoholic beverages to any person shall be held legally accountable for damages suffered by such person, or for injury to the person or property of, or death of, any third person, resulting from the consumption of such beverages.

OR. REV. STAT. § 30.950 (1987) provides:

> No licensee, permittee or social host is liable for damages incurred or caused by intoxicated patrons or guests off the licensee, permittee or social host's premises unless:
>
> (1) The licensee, permittee or social host has served or provided alcoholic beverages to the patron or guest, while the patron or guest was visibly intoxicated; and
>
> (2) The plaintiff proves by clear and convincing evidence that the patron or guest was served alcoholic beverages while visibly intoxicated.

MO. REV. STAT. § 537.053 (1987) abrogates dram shop liability, except in the case of certain persons previously convicted of selling liquor to a minor or to an "obviously intoxicated person."

3. *Minor to Minor.* In *Kapres v. Heller*, 536 Pa. 551, 640 A.2d 888 (1994), the court refused to hold minor social hosts liable for injuries to another minor resulting from the hosts serving alcoholic beverages to the other minor:

> In the present case the Plaintiff argues that we should hold the minor defendants to the standard required of adults, while providing to him the protections specially afforded minors under the same principle. The illogic of this argument is apparent on its face. Both the plaintiff and the defendant are considered under the law incompetent to handle alcohol. Both the plaintiff and the defendant would be responsible under the law for their own actions in furnishing or consuming alcohol. Thus, it is more logical and consistent with the prevailing view on social host liability in this Commonwealth to find that one minor does not owe a duty to another minor regarding the furnishing or consumption of alcohol.

Should the result in *Kapres* be the same if the plaintiff were a third party injured by the other minor as a result of the latter's intoxication?

4. *Self-Inflicted Wounds.* The court in *Kelly v. Falin*, 896 P.2d 1245 (Wash. 1995), held that a commercial vendor was not liable for serving alcohol to obviously intoxicated adult patrons who later injured themselves as a result of the intoxication:

> . . . As a matter of public policy, we have premised the duty of commercial vendors on the need to protect *innocent bystanders* from intoxicated patrons. . . .
>
> A rule that allows an intoxicated adult to hold a commercial vendor liable fosters irresponsibility and rewards drunk driving. Rather than deterring drunk driving, excessive drinking, and the callow and imprudent behavior of intoxicated adults, such a rule would actually compensate patrons who drink beyond obvious intoxication.

Compare Jarrett v. Woodward Bros., Inc., 751 A.2d 972, 981 (D.C. 2000). An intoxicated underage patron wandered onto a highway and was struck by a car. The court permitted a wrongful death action against the restaurant-bar that served him liquor, noting: "We recognize that a voluntarily-intoxicated underage patron is not as appealing a claimant as innocent third parties, but we conclude that to exclude intoxicated underage patrons from the zone of the statute's protection would be contrary to legislative intent."

In *Gattman v. Favro,* 306 Or. 11, 757 P.2d 402 (1988), the Supreme Court of Oregon limited the state's dram shop statutes and cases solely to automobile injuries. The court left open the question whether the plaintiff, who had been stabbed, had a common law cause of action against the restaurant which had served alcohol to his attacker. *See also Di Ossi v. Maroney,* 548 A.2d 1361 (Del. 1988), where it was held that a social host at a party that included a large number of minors owed a duty of care to their parking valet because they should have anticipated that the minors would consume alcohol and then attempt to operate motor vehicles, injuring the valet.

5. *Complicitous Hosts.* In *Aanenson v. Bastien,* 438 N.W.2d 151 (N.D. 1989), the question presented was whether the plaintiff's purchase of drinks for the

primary tortfeasor (the inebriated driver) constituted "complicity" and thus a defense that could be raised by the secondary tortfeasor (the tavern-owner).

> Although the writer of this opinion cannot speak from great personal experience, it is believed that it is the accepted practice of those who find sociability in taverns, bars, nightclubs, and restaurants that serve alcoholic beverages, to take turns purchasing those drinks. That being the likely and customary practice it would seem to defeat the objective of the Dram Shop Act, which is to prevent sales to intoxicated persons and the attendant disastrous consequences of such sales, if sales under such accepted customary practices were exempt from the provisions of the Act. Presumably, the dram shop merchant is refraining from imbibing alcohol while engaging in the business of selling and dispensing alcoholic beverages and thus is in a much better position to know when the imbibers have become intoxicated than the imbibers themselves.

Contrast *Martin v. Heddinger*, 373 N.W.2d 486 (Iowa 1985) (complicity instruction should have included condition of voluntary participation to a material and substantial extent). And in *Pollard v. Village of Ovid*, 180 Mich. App. 1, 446 N.W.2d 574 (1989), plaintiff was precluded from bringing a wrongful death action against social hosts for furnishing alcohol to a minor because plaintiff's decedent admittedly participated in the minor's intoxication.

6. *Negligent Entrustment.* RESTATEMENT (SECOND) OF TORTS § 390 (1965) provides:

> One who supplies directly or through a third person a chattel for the use of another whom the supplier knows or has reason to know to be likely because of his youth, inexperience, or otherwise, to use it in a manner involving unreasonable risk of physical harm to himself and others whom the supplier should expect to share in or be endangered by its use, is subject to liability for physical harm resulting to them.

Consider *Osborn v. Hertz Corp.*, 205 Cal. App. 3d 703, 252 Cal. Rptr. 613 (1988), holding that a car rental company was not liable on a negligent entrustment theory where it failed to inquire of a sober driver whether he had a record of drunk driving or had his license suspended or revoked. Compare *O'Toole v. Carlsbad Shell Serv. Station*, 202 Cal. App. 3d 151, 247 Cal. Rptr. 663 (1988), where employees of a gas station sold gasoline to an obviously intoxicated driver in violation of company policy. The employees talked to the driver for one and one-half hours, made her drink four or five cups of coffee, gave her money to call her mother and generally discouraged her from driving. On her way home she struck a motorcycle, killing the driver and the passenger. Defendants relied on a statutory provision severely curtailing liability for furnishing alcohol to intoxicated persons. However, the court imposed liability on a negligent entrustment theory; not entrustment, as is often the case, of the motor vehicle itself, but of its motive power, the gasoline.

7. *An Employer's Responsibility.* In *Meany v. Newell*, 367 N.W.2d 472 (Minn. 1985), an intoxicated employee left an office Christmas party and was involved

in an automobile accident. The court felt compelled by statute to hold that the employer, not being a commercial vendor, was not subject to dram shop liability. The court considered the possible application of RESTATEMENT (SECOND) OF TORTS § 317.* However, the court concluded,

> "Section 317 has typically been used when the employee is acting negligently on the work premises, albeit during off-duty hours, such that the employer could control the employee's action. The difficulty in discerning when the employer's duty to control ends, leads us to reject extending that duty to off-premises actions. Since [this employee] was neither on the premises nor using the employer's chattels, we reject the applicability of the Restatement to this case."

8. *A Defendant Once Removed.* In *Andres v. Alpha Kappa Lambda Fraternity*, 730 S.W.2d 547 (Mo. 1987), a negligence *per se* action was brought against a fraternity and its local chapter after a fraternity house resident died of acute alcohol poisoning during a fraternity "mixer." The court held that the local chapter could not be liable because Missouri did not permit dram shop actions against social hosts. In the claim against the national chapter, the court concluded:

> We now turn to the respondents' argument that the National was negligent through its failure to adopt a policy which prohibited the furnishing of alcoholic beverages by local chapters to those individuals who are under the lawful age for consumption. The National contends that it did not owe a duty to decedent to promulgate a policy which forbad the serving of alcoholic beverages by local chapters to those members under the age permitted by law.
>
> It would be anomalous to impose a duty on the National to establish a policy *forbidding the furnishing of alcoholic beverages* by local chapters to members under the lawful age for consumption while the Local which *actually furnished alcoholic beverages* to those under twenty-one years in this cause had no civil duty at law to refrain from such practice. The National did not participate in the day-to-day management of its chapters and thus was more remote than the Local from the events surrounding the death of respondents' son. Having found no civil liability on the part of the Local, we must similarly find that the National, an entity even further removed than the Local from the

---

* RESTATEMENT (SECOND) OF TORTS § 317 (1965) states:

A master is under a duty to exercise reasonable care so to control his servant while acting outside the scope of his employment as to prevent him from intentionally harming others or from so conducting himself as to create an unreasonable risk of bodily harm to them, if

  (a) the servant

    (i) is upon the premises in possession of the master or upon which the servant is privileged to enter only as his servant, or

    (ii) is using a chattel of the master, and

  (b) the master

    (i) knows or has reason to know that he has the ability to control his servant, and

    (ii) knows or should know of the necessity and opportunity for exercising such control.

said events leading to this tragedy, is not civilly liable for failing to establish a policy prohibiting the service of alcoholic beverages by local chapters to those under the age permitted by law.

Assume that social host liability had been recognized in the jurisdiction. Would the court's answer with regard to the national chapter have changed?

9. *Duty or Proximate Cause?* In a 4-3 decision, the Colorado Supreme Court held that a tavern keeper who served a "visibly intoxicated" patron could be liable, under negligence and negligence *per se* theories, for the subsequent wrongful death of the patron in an automobile accident caused by the intoxication. *Lyons v. Nasby,* 770 P.2d 1250 (Colo. 1989). The court said:

> Those courts that have refused to recognize an inebriate's right to pursue a negligence claim have typically done so on one of two grounds: the lack of a tavern owner's duty, as a matter of public policy, to one who is voluntarily drunk; or the lack of a proximate cause between the serving of alcohol and the injury producing event. We have rejected both of these arguments in the context of third-party claims.

The court found duty and proximate cause. As to the duty issue, the court remarked:

> A person has a duty to act or refrain from acting when it is reasonably foreseeable that the failure to act or refrain will create an unreasonable risk of harm to another. The existence of a duty is a question of law to be determined by the court. In determining whether the law should impose a duty the court must consider several factors, including the extent, foreseeability and likelihood of injury, the social utility of the defendant's conduct, the magnitude of the burden placed on the defendant to guard against injury, and the consequences of placing that burden on the defendant.

On the issue of proximate cause, the court stated:

> A defendant proximately causes an injury when his or her wrongful conduct is a substantial factor in bringing about the plaintiff's injury. Whether proximate cause exists is a question for the jury and only in the clearest of cases, where reasonable minds can draw but one inference from the evidence, does the question become one of law to be determined by the court. . . . While the chain of causation in some cases may be so attenuated that no proximate cause exists as a matter of law, such is not the case here.

In response to the defendant's claim that allowing the suit would open a floodgate of litigation, the court noted that after the case arose, the Colorado legislature passed a statute providing that no civil action may be brought by a person to whom alcoholic beverage or alcoholic beverages have been sold or served, or by his estate or representative. The court stated that Colorado's comparative fault statute, barring recovery if plaintiff is 50% or more at fault, applied to this suit.

The dissent contended that recognizing a duty of a provider of alcoholic beverages "to protect a consumer from his own intoxication denigrates the concept of individual responsibility, encourages overindulgence, and contravenes public policy." It noted that a seller "already has a statutory duty not to serve intoxicants to one who is visibly intoxicated. If he breaches this duty, he risks both criminal penalties and civil suits brought by injured third parties."

10. *Alcohol Purveyors and a Duty Rationale.* Early case law, since superseded by statute, tended to resolve the issue of the liability of alcohol purveyors through proximate cause. Liability was dependent upon whether the court considered the tavern owner's serving of the alcohol or the intoxicated patron's driving the proximate cause of the accident. *See, e.g., Rappaport v. Nichols,* 31 N.J. 188, 156 A.2d 1 (1959). However, in *Vesely v. Sager,* 5 Cal. 3d 153, 95 Cal. Rptr. 623, 486 P.2d 151, 159 (1971), the Supreme Court of California succinctly re-characterized the issue as "not one of proximate cause, but rather one of duty."

However, some statutory pronouncements on this issue continue to make ill-advised use of proximate cause language. *See, e.g.,* Mo. Rev. Stat. § 537.053.2 (1987) ("The legislature, hereby declares . . . the consumption of alcoholic beverages, rather than the furnishing of alcoholic beverages, to be the proximate cause of injuries inflicted upon another by an intoxicated person.").

11. *Bar Brawl.* The plaintiffs in *Zueger v. Carlson,* 542 N.W.2d 92 (N.D. 1996), were injured in a bar fight in defendant's bar. The court held plaintiffs stated a cause of action against defendant for failure to prevent or stop the fight:

> On October 29, 1993, Zueger and Kudrna were injured in a fight at Boomers, a bar in Mandan, North Dakota. According to the complaint, Mark Carlson, an off-duty bouncer at Boomers, violently and without provocation attacked Zueger and Kudrna, causing serious and permanent injuries. Zueger and Kudrna assert Boomers failed to provide adequate security, and Boomers' employees and security personnel failed to come to their aid during the attack. Zueger and Kudrna further assert the assault was stopped only when other patrons finally restrained Carlson. . . .
>
> In this case, Zueger asserts Boomers knew fights had occurred on the premises in the past, Carlson was a violent person, and Carlson himself had been involved in prior altercations at Boomers. This raises material issues of fact on the foreseeability of the assault. If the assault was foreseeable, Boomers had a duty to use reasonable care to protect its patrons from injury. Even if the specific attack was not foreseeable, Boomers had a duty once the attack began to exercise reasonable care to stop the attack.

PROBLEM

Mother-to-be, who seldom drank alcoholic beverages before, began drinking heavily to relieve discomfort and distress during her first trimester of pregnancy. Because of her heavy consumption of alcohol during pregnancy, she gave birth to a child with severe birth defects caused by Fetal Alcohol Syndrome.

Can she recover on behalf of herself or the child from the manufacturers of the alcohol she consumed during her pregnancy for failure to warn her of the risk of Fetal Alcohol Syndrome associated with drinking during pregnancy?

Would the result be different if Mother was an alcoholic, and drank during her pregnancy?

What if federal law required such a warning to be included on the label of each bottle of alcoholic beverage sold, but no such warning was included on the bottles of alcohol purchased by Mother?

HAMILTON v. BERETTA U.S.A. CORP.
96 N.Y.2d 222, 750 N.E.2d 1055, 727 N.Y.S.2d 7 (2001)

WESLEY, J.

In January 1995 plaintiffs—relatives of people killed by handguns—sued 49 handgun manufacturers in Federal court alleging negligent marketing, design defect, ultra-hazardous activity and fraud. A number of defendants jointly moved for summary judgment. The United States District Court for the Eastern District of New York (Weinstein, J.), dismissed the product liability and fraud causes of action, but retained plaintiffs' negligent marketing claim (see Hamilton v Accu-Tek, 935 F. Supp. 1307, 1315). Other parties intervened, including plaintiff Stephen Fox, who was shot by a friend and permanently disabled. The gun was never found; the shooter had no recollection of how he obtained it. Other evidence, however, indicated that he had purchased the gun out of the trunk of a car from a seller who said it came from the "south." Eventually, seven plaintiffs went to trial against 25 of the manufacturers.

Plaintiffs asserted that defendants distributed their products negligently so as to create and bolster an illegal, underground market in handguns, one that furnished weapons to minors and criminals involved in the shootings that precipitated this lawsuit.. . .

After a four-week trial, the jury returned a special verdict finding 15 of the 25 defendants failed to use reasonable care in the distribution of their guns.. . .

Defendants unsuccessfully moved for judgment as a matter of law.. . . On appeal, the Second Circuit certified the following [question] to us:

". . .Whether the defendants owed plaintiffs a duty to exercise reasonable care in the marketing and distribution of the handguns they manufacture?"

. . .Plaintiffs argue that defendant-manufacturers have a duty to exercise reasonable care in the marketing and distribution of their guns based upon four factors: (1) defendants' ability to exercise control over the marketing and distribution of their guns, (2) defendants' general knowledge that large numbers of their guns enter the illegal market and are used in crime, (3) New York's policy of strict regulation of firearms and (4) the uniquely lethal nature of defendants' products.

According to plaintiffs, handguns move into the underground market in New York through several well-known and documented means including straw purchases (a friend, relative or accomplice acts as purchaser of the weapon for another), sales at gun shows, misuse of Federal firearms licenses and sales by non-stocking dealers (i.e., those operating informal businesses without a retail storefront). Plaintiffs further assert that gun manufacturers have oversaturated markets in states with weak gun control laws (primarily in the Southeast), knowing those "excess guns" will make their way into the hands of criminals in states with stricter laws such as New York, thus "profiting" from indiscriminate sales in weak gun states. Plaintiffs contend that defendants control their distributors' conduct with respect to pricing, advertising and display, yet refuse to institute practices such as requiring distribution contracts that limit sales to stocking gun dealers, training salespeople in safe sales practices (including how to recognize straw purchasers), establishing electronic monitoring of their products, limiting the number of distributors, limiting multiple purchases and franchising their retail outlets.

Defendants counter that they do not owe a duty to members of the public to protect them from the criminal acquisition and misuse of their handguns. Defendants assert that such a duty — potentially exposing them to limitless liability — should not be imposed on them for acts and omissions of numerous and remote third parties over which they have no control. Further, they contend that, in light of the comprehensive statutory and regulatory scheme governing the distribution and sale of firearms, any fundamental changes in the industry should be left to the appropriate legislative and regulatory bodies.

The threshold question in any negligence action is: does defendant owe a legally recognized duty of care to plaintiff? Courts traditionally "fix the duty point by balancing factors, including the reasonable expectations of parties and society generally, the proliferation of claims, the likelihood of unlimited or insurer-like liability, disproportionate risk and reparation allocation, and public policies affecting the expansion or limitation of new channels of liability" (Palka v Servicemaster Mgt. Servs. Corp., 83 N.Y.2d 579, 586, 611 N.Y.S.2d 817, 634 N.E.2d 189; see also, Strauss v Belle Realty Co., 65 N.Y.2d 399, 402–403, 492 N.Y.S.2d 555, 482 N.E.2d 34). Thus, in determining whether a duty exists, "courts must be mindful of the precedential, and consequential, future effects of their rulings, and 'limit the legal consequences of wrongs to a controllable degree'" (Lauer v City of New York, 95 N.Y.2d 95, 100, 711 N.Y.S.2d 112, 733 N.E.2d 184 [quoting Tobin v Grossman, 24 N.Y.2d 609, 619, 301 N.Y.S.2d 554, 249 N.E.2d 419]).

Foreseeability, alone, does not define duty — it merely determines the scope of the duty once it is determined to exist (see, Pulka v Edelman, 40 N.Y.2d 781, 785, 390 N.Y.S.2d 393, 358 N.E.2d 1019, rearg denied 41 N.Y.2d 901; see also, Eiseman v State of New York, 70 N.Y.2d 175, 187, 518 N.Y.S.2d 608, 511 N.E.2d 1128). The injured party must show that a defendant owed not merely a general duty to society but a specific duty to him or her, for "without a duty running directly to the injured person there can be no liability in damages, however careless the conduct or foreseeable the harm" (Lauer, supra, at 100). That is required in order to avoid subjecting an actor "to limitless liability to an indeterminate class of persons conceivably injured by any negligence in that act" (Eiseman, supra, at 188). Moreover, any extension of the scope of duty must be tailored to reflect accurately the extent that its social benefits outweigh its costs (see, Waters v New York City Hous. Auth., 69 N.Y.2d 225, 230, 513 N.Y.S.2d 356, 505 N.E.2d 922).

The District Court imposed a duty on gun manufacturers "to take reasonable steps available at the point of. . . sale to primary distributors to reduce the possibility that these instruments will fall into the hands of those likely to misuse them" (Hamilton v Accu-Tek, supra, 62 F. Supp. 2d, at 825). We have been cautious, however, in extending liability to defendants for their failure to control the conduct of others. "A defendant generally has no duty to control the conduct of third persons so as to prevent them from harming others, even where as a practical matter defendant can exercise such control" (D'Amico v Christie, 71 N.Y.2d 76, 88, 524 N.Y.S.2d 1, 518 N.E.2d 896). This judicial resistance to the expansion of duty grows out of practical concerns both about potentially limitless liability and about the unfairness of imposing liability for the acts of another.

A duty may arise, however, where there is a relationship either between defendant and a third-person tortfeasor that encompasses defendant's actual control of the third person's actions, or between defendant and plaintiff that requires defendant to protect plaintiff from the conduct of others. Examples of these relationships include master and servant, parent and child, and common carriers and their passengers.

The key in each is that the defendant's relationship with either the tortfeasor or the plaintiff places the defendant in the best position to protect against the risk of harm. In addition, the specter of limitless liability is not present because the class of potential plaintiffs to whom the duty is owed is circumscribed by the relationship. We have, for instance, recognized that landowners have a duty to protect tenants, patrons or invitees from foreseeable harm caused by the criminal conduct of others while they are on the premises. However, this duty does not extend beyond that limited class of plaintiffs to members of the community at large (see Waters v New York City Hous. Auth., supra, 69 NY2d, at 228–231). In Waters, for example, we held that the owner of a housing project who failed to keep the building's door locks in good repair did not owe a duty to a passerby to protect her from being dragged off the street into the building and assaulted. The Court concluded that imposing such a duty on landowners would do little to minimize crime, and the social benefits to be gained did "not warrant the extension of the landowner's duty to maintain secure premises to the millions of individuals who use the sidewalks of New York City each day and are thereby exposed to the dangers of street crime" (id., at 230).

A similar rationale is relevant here. The pool of possible plaintiffs is very large — potentially, any of the thousands of victims of gun violence. Further, the connection between defendants, the criminal wrongdoers and plaintiffs is remote, running through several links in a chain consisting of at least the manufacturer, the federally licensed distributor or wholesaler, and the first retailer. The chain most often includes numerous subsequent legal purchasers or even a thief. Such broad liability, potentially encompassing all gunshot crime victims, should not be imposed without a more tangible showing that the defendants were a direct link in the causal chain that resulted in the plaintiffs' injuries, and that the defendants were realistically in a position to prevent the wrongs. Giving plaintiffs' evidence the benefit of every favorable inference, they have not shown that the gun used to harm plaintiff Fox came from a source amenable to the exercise of any duty of care that plaintiffs would impose upon defendant manufacturers.

Plaintiffs make two alternative arguments in support of a duty determination here. The first arises from a manufacturer's "special ability to detect and guard against the risks associated with [its] products [and] warrants placing all manufacturers, including these defendants, in a *protective relationship with those foreseeably and potentially put in harm's way by their products*" (Hamilton v Accu-Tek, supra, 62 F. Supp. 2d, at 821 [emphasis added]). Plaintiffs predicate the existence of this protective duty — particularly when lethal or hazardous products are involved — on foreseeability of harm and our products liability cases such as MacPherson v Buick Motor Co. (217 NY 382, 111 N.E. 1050).

As we noted earlier, a duty and the corresponding liability it imposes do not rise from mere foreseeability of the harm. Moreover, none of plaintiffs' proof demonstrated that a change in marketing techniques would likely have prevented their injuries. Indeed, plaintiffs did not present any evidence tending to show to what degree their risk of injury was enhanced by the presence of negligently marketed and distributed guns, as opposed to the risk presented by all guns in society.

The cases involving the distribution or handling of hazardous materials, relied upon by plaintiffs, do not support the imposition of a duty of care in marketing handguns. The manufacturer's duty in each case was based either on a products liability theory — that is, the product was defective because of the failure to include a safety feature — or on a failure to warn (see, e.g., Hunnings v Texaco, Inc., 29 F.3d 1480 [11th Cir 1994] [defectively packaged hazardous substance accompanied by lack of adequate warnings]; Blueflame Gas, Inc. v Van Hoose, 679 P.2d 579 [Colo 1984] [insufficiently odorized propane gas]; Flint Explosive Co. v Edwards, 84 Ga. App. 376, 66 S.E.2d 368 [Ga App 1951] [defective dynamite]). Certainly too, a manufacturer may be held liable for complicity in dangerous or illegal activity (see, e.g., Suchomajcz v Hummel Chem. Co., 524 F.2d 19 [3d Cir 1975] [manufacturer sold chemicals to retailer with knowledge that retailer intended to use them in making and selling illegal firecracker assembly kits]). Here, defendants' products are concededly not defective — if anything, the problem is that they work too well. Nor have plaintiffs asserted a defective warnings claim or presented sufficient evidence to demonstrate that defendants could have taken reasonable steps that would have prevented their injuries. Likewise, this case can hardly be analogized to those in which a duty has been imposed upon owners or possessors of hazardous substances to safeguard against unsupervised access by children (see, Kush v City of Buffalo, 59 N.Y.2d 26, 31, 462 N.Y.S.2d 831, 449 N.E.2d 725; Kingsland v Erie County Agric. Socy., 291 NY 409, 426).

Plaintiffs also assert that a general duty of care arises out of the gun manufacturers' ability to reduce the risk of illegal gun trafficking through control of the marketing and distribution of their products. The District Court accepted this proposition and posited a series of structural changes in defendants' marketing and distribution regimes that might "reduce the risk of criminal misuse by insuring that the first sale was by a responsible merchant to a responsible buyer" (Hamilton v Accu-Tek, supra, 62 F. Supp. 2D, at 820). Those changes, and others proposed by plaintiffs that a jury might reasonably find subsumed in a gun manufacturer's duty of care,[10] would have the unavoidable effect of eliminating a significant number of lawful sales to "responsible" buyers by "responsible" Federal firearms licensees (FFLs) who would be cut out of the distribution chain under the suggested "reforms." Plaintiffs, however, presented no evidence, either through the testimony of experts or the submission of authoritative reports, showing any statistically significant relationship between particular classes of dealers and crime guns. To impose a general duty of care upon the makers of firearms under these circumstances because of their purported ability to control marketing and distribution of their products would conflict with the principle that any judicial recognition of a duty of care must be based upon an assessment of its efficacy in promoting a social benefit as against its costs and burdens. Here, imposing such a general duty of care would create not only an indeterminate class of plaintiffs but also an indeterminate class of defendants whose liability might have little relationship to the benefits of controlling illegal guns.

Finally, plaintiffs and the District Court identify an alternative basis for imposing a duty of care here under the negligent entrustment doctrine, arising out of the firearms manufacturers' authority over "downstream distributors and retailers" to whom their products are delivered. The owner or possessor of a dangerous instrument is under a duty to entrust it to a responsible person whose use does not create an unreasonable risk of harm to others (see Rios v Smith, 95 N.Y.2d 647, 722 N.Y.S.2d 220, 744 N.E.2d 1156; Splawnik v DiCaprio, 146 A.D.2d 333, 335, Restatement [Second] of Torts § 390). The duty may extend through successive, reasonably anticipated entrustees. There are, however, fatal impediments to imposing a general duty of care here under a negligent entrustment theory.

The tort of negligent entrustment is based on the degree of knowledge the supplier of a chattel has or should have concerning the entrustee's propensity to use the chattel in an improper or dangerous fashion. Gun sales have subjected suppliers to liability under this theory (see Splawnik, supra; see also Cullum & Boren-McCain Mall, Inc. v Peacock, 267 Ark. 479, 592 S.W.2d 442 [Ark 1980]; Semeniuk v Chentis, 1 Ill. App. 2d 508, 117 N.E.2d 883 [Ill App Ct 1954]). Of course, without the requisite knowledge, the tort of negligent entrustment does not lie (see Earsing v Nelson, 212 A.D.2d 66, 629 N.Y.S.2d 563 [dismissing a negligent entrustment claim against the manufacturer of a BB gun because a dealer's knowledge of the individual's ability to use the gun safely could not be imputed to the manufacturer]).

The negligent entrustment doctrine might well support the extension of a duty to manufacturers to avoid selling to certain distributors in circumstances where the manufacturer knows or has reason to know those distributors are

---

[10] For example, limiting the volume of sales in states with weak gun controls to insure against circulation of the oversupply to strong gun control states such as New York; restricting distribution entirely to established retail stores carrying stocks of guns; franchising of retail outlets; and barring distribution to dealers who sell at unregulated gun shows (see Hamilton v Accu-Tek, 62 F. Supp. 2d 802, at 826, 829–832).

engaging in substantial sales of guns into the gun-trafficking market on a consistent basis.[11] Here, however, plaintiffs did not present such evidence. Instead, they claimed that manufacturers should not engage in certain broad categories of sales. Once again, plaintiffs' duty calculation comes up short. General statements about an industry are not the stuff by which a common-law court fixes the duty point. Without a showing that specific groups of dealers play a disproportionate role in supplying the illegal gun market, the sweep of plaintiffs' duty theory is far wider than the danger it seeks to avert.

At trial, plaintiffs' experts did surmise that since manufacturers receive crime gun trace requests conducted by the Bureau of Alcohol, Tobacco and Firearms (BATF), they could analyze those requests to locate retailers who disproportionately served as crime gun sources, and cut off distributors who do business with them. In essence, plaintiffs argue that defendants had an affirmative duty to investigate and identify corrupt dealers. This is neither feasible nor appropriate for the manufacturers.

Plaintiffs' experts explained that a crime gun trace is the means by which the BATF reconstructs the distribution history of a gun used in a crime or recovered by the police.[12] While manufacturers may be generally aware of traces for which they are contacted, they are not told the purpose of the trace, nor are they informed of the results. The BATF does not disclose any subsequently acquired retailer or purchaser information to the manufacturer. Moreover, manufacturers are not in a position to acquire such information on their own. Indeed, plaintiffs' law enforcement experts agreed that manufacturers should not make any attempt to investigate illegal gun trafficking on their own since such attempts could disrupt pending criminal investigations and endanger the lives of undercover officers.

Federal law already has implemented a statutory and regulatory scheme to ensure seller "responsibility" through licensing requirements and buyer "responsibility" through background checks. While common-law principles can supplement a manufacturer's statutory duties, we should be cautious in imposing novel theories of tort liability while the difficult problem of illegal gun sales in the United States remains the focus of a national policy debate (see Lytton, Tort Claims Against Gun Manufacturers, supra, 65 Mo L Rev, at 52–54 [analyzing courts' capacities and limitations in analyzing complex statistical data]).

In sum, analysis of this State's longstanding precedents demonstrates that defendants — given the evidence presented here — did not owe plaintiffs the

---

[11] An analysis of Bureau of Alcohol, Tobacco and Firearms (BATF) data for 1998 reveals that a very small number of FFLs do account for a significant portion of guns used in crimes.. . . Because of BATF's continued pursuit in identifying how handguns enter the illegal market, it may well be that a core group of corrupt FFLs will emerge at some future time. This might alter the duty equation.

[12] Tracing involves the process of tracking a recovered crime gun's history from its source through the chain of distribution to its first retail purchaser. If the BATF is unable to trace the gun from its own records, it contacts the manufacturer and asks for the identity of the Federally-licensed distributor to whom the gun was sold. The BATF then follows up with the named distributor and the subsequently named retailer to determine the identity of the first purchaser (see, Commerce in Firearms in the United States, BATF Document, February 2000, at 19–20; Youth Crime Gun Interdiction Initiative, BATF Document, February 1999, at 5).

duty they claim; we therefore answer the . . .certified question in the negative.. . .

This case challenges us to rethink traditional notions of duty, liability and causation. Tort law is ever changing; it is a reflection of the complexity and vitality of daily life. Although plaintiffs have presented us with a novel theory — negligent marketing of a potentially lethal yet legal product, based upon the acts not of one manufacturer, but of an industry — we are unconvinced that, on the record before us, the duty plaintiffs wish to impose is either reasonable or circumscribed. Nor does the market share theory of liability accurately measure defendants' conduct. Whether, in a different case, a duty may arise remains a question for the future.

NOTES

1. *Municipal Suits.* How will the outcome of *Hamilton* affect the claims of municipalities against gun manufacturers for costs incurred by the cities because of firearm-related injuries?

2. *A Basis of Liability.* Sec. 389 of the REST. 2D OF TORTS provides:

> One who supplies directly or through a third person a chattel for another's use, knowing or having reason to know that the chattel is unlikely to be made reasonably safe before being put to a use which the supplier should expect it to be put, is subject to liability for physical harm caused by such use to those whom the supplier should expect to use the chattel or to be endangered by its probable use, and who are ignorant of the dangerous character of the chattel or whose knowledge thereof does not make them contributorily negligent, although the supplier has informed the other for whose use the chattel is supplied of its dangerous character.

To what products besides guns might sec. 389 apply?

3. *To Protect.* . . The District Court had discussed the type of relationship that could give rise to a protective duty as follows:

> Unpersuasive is defendants' contention that the absence of a "special relationship" between themselves and the plaintiffs relieved them of any duty to anticipate the conduct of the shooters in these cases. Two types of relationships giving rise to liability for the acts of third parties under New York law exist here.
>
> First, the special ability to detect and guard against the risks associated with their products warrants placing all manufacturers, including these defendants, in a protective relationship with those foreseeably and potentially put in harm's way by their products.. . .
>
> Second, a duty is created by virtue of a manufacturer's relationship with downstream distributors and retailers, giving it "sufficient authority and ability to control," the latter's conduct for the protection of prospective victims. Purdy, 72 N.Y.2d 1, 8, 526 N.E.2d 4, 7, 530 N.Y.S.2d 513, 516 (1988). Such a duty is analogous to that owed to persons foreseeably endangered by the negligent entrustment of a

chattel. . ... Placing restrictions on sales by cutting off distributors who sell disproportionate numbers of crime guns or who sell through dubious channels is possible and may be found by a jury to be appropriate.

A third basis for finding duty may be found in the concept described by Professor Rabin as "enhancement of risk." Robert L. Rabin, Enabling Torts, 49 DePaul L. Rev. (1999). Professor Rabin characterizes plaintiffs' negligent marketing claim as an example of an "enabling tort" in which liability is predicated on defendants' affirmative enhancement of risk.. . .

Hamilton v Accu-Tek, 62 F. Supp. 2d, at 820. Does the Court of Appeals opinion adequately rebut these arguments?

PROBLEM

AnyCity, once a peaceful Midwestern industrial town, recently has leapt to No.3 on the FBI's list of cities with high crime rates. AnyCity's problems have been fueled in large part by drug trafficking. However, the city also seems to be in the throes of a gun "epidemic;" 45% of AnyCity crimes now involve the use of firearms. In addition to gun-related crimes and crimes involving guns, there has been an increase in teenage suicides by shooting and accidental deaths and injuries involving children and the elderly. In the last two years legal gun sales have increased by 400% and, according to law enforcement estimates, illegal gun sales by 800%. Rather than targeting damage done by, say, a particular gun, lawyers for cities are beginning to ask questions about what the industry has done to protect the public safety, and to market its product responsibly, as other manufacturers of other products (beer, for example) do.

You are the attorney for AnyCity in AnyState. You are considering bringing tort claims against representative manufacturers, retailers, pawnshops, homeowners from whom guns later used in crimes have been stolen, and the National Rifle Association (NRA).

What tort claims could you bring on behalf of the city and against whom? Identify the claims that likely will be most successful.

H. THE DUTY TO ACT OR LACK THEREOF

FARWELL v. KEATON
396 Mich. 281, 240 N.W.2d 217 (1976)

LEVIN, JUSTICE.

[Wrongful death action brought on behalf of beneficiaries of Farwell estate.]

On the evening of August 26, 1966, Siegrist and Farwell drove to a trailer rental lot to return an automobile which Siegrist had borrowed from a friend who worked there. While waiting for the friend to finish work, Siegrist and Farwell consumed some beer.

Two girls walked by the entrance to the lot. Siegrist and Farwell attempted to engage them in conversation; they left Farwell's car and followed the girls to a drive-in restaurant down the street.

The girls complained to their friends in the restaurant that they were being followed. Six boys chased Siegrist and Farwell back to the lot. Siegrist escaped unharmed, but Farwell was severely beaten. Siegrist found Farwell underneath his automobile in the lot. Ice was applied to Farwell's head. Siegrist then drove Farwell around for approximately two hours, stopping at a number of drive-in restaurants. Farwell went to sleep in the back seat of his car. Around midnight Siegrist drove the car to the home of Farwell's grandparents, parked it in the driveway, unsuccessfully attempted to rouse Farwell, and left. Farwell's grandparents discovered him in the car the next morning and took him to the hospital. He died three days later of an epidural hematoma.

At trial, plaintiff contended that had Siegrist taken Farwell to the hospital, or had he notified someone of Farwell's condition and whereabouts, Farwell would not have died. A neurosurgeon testified that if a person in Farwell's condition is taken to a doctor before, or within half an hour after, consciousness is lost, there is an 85 to 88 percent chance of survival. Plaintiff testified that Siegrist told him that he knew Farwell was badly injured and that he should have done something.

The jury returned a verdict for plaintiff and awarded $15,000 in damages. The Court of Appeals reversed, finding that Siegrist had not assumed the duty of obtaining aid for Farwell and that he neither knew nor should have known of the need for medical treatment.

Two separate, but interrelated questions are presented:

> A. Whether the existence of a duty in a particular case is always a matter of law to be determined solely by the Court?
>
> B. Whether, on the facts of this case, the trial judge should have ruled, as a matter of law, that Siegrist owed no duty to Farwell?

. . . The existence of a duty is ordinarily a question of law. However, there are factual circumstances which give rise to a duty. The existence of those facts must be determined by a jury. In *Bonin v. Gralewicz,* 378 Mich. 521, 526–527, 146 N.W.2d 647, 649 (1966), this Court reversed a directed verdict of no cause of action where the trial court had determined as a matter of law that the proofs were insufficient to establish a duty of care.

Usually, in negligence cases, whether a duty is owed by the defendant to the plaintiff does not require resolution of fact issues. However, in some cases, as in this one, fact issues arise. When they do, they must be submitted to the jury, our traditional finders of fact, for ultimate resolution, and they must be accompanied by an appropriate conditional instruction regarding defendant's duty, conditioned upon the jury's resolution of the fact dispute.

. . . Without regard to whether there is a general duty to aid a person in distress, there is a clearly recognized legal duty of every person to avoid any affirmative acts which may make a situation worse. . . .

In a case such as the one at bar, the jury must determine, after considering all the evidence, whether the defendant attempted to aid the victim. If he did, a duty arose which required defendant to act as a reasonable person:

Professor Green argues that it is impossible in the nature of things for the duty problem to be decided by the jury, for if the court sends the issue to the jury this "necessarily operates as a ruling that there is a duty or else he would never have submitted the case to the jury at all." But that is not so. As in the case of any other issue, the judge will leave the question to the jury if it is a debatable one, but the jury may decide that (for example) plaintiff was beyond the apparent scope of danger from defendant's conduct, and so beyond the scope of the duty to perform it carefully, even where they are quite ready to find defendant's conduct clearly below the standard of reasonable care. 2 Harper & James, The Law of Torts, p. 1060.

There was ample evidence to show that Siegrist breached a legal duty owed Farwell. Siegrist knew that Farwell had been in a fight, and he attempted to relieve Farwell's pain by applying an ice pack to his head. While Farwell and Siegrist were riding around, Farwell crawled into the back seat and lay down. The testimony showed that Siegrist attempted to rouse Farwell after driving him home but was unable to do so.

In addition, Farwell's father testified that admissions made to him by Siegrist:

> Q. Witness, just before the jury was excused, I asked whether you had any conversation with Mr. Siegrist after this event occurred. You answered, "Yes, the day after in the living room of Mrs. Grenier's [the deceased's mother's] home." Then, the jury was excused, and we made a special record, and now I would like to ask you some questions that I asked and that you answered out of the presence of the jury.
>
> A. Yes.
>
> Q. What did Mr. Siegrist say, how did the conversation go?
>
> A. I asked him why he left Ricky [the deceased] in the driveway of his grandfather's home.
>
> Q. What did he say?
>
> A. He said, "*Ricky was hurt bad, I was scared.*" I said, "*Why didn't you tell somebody, tell his grandparents?*" He said, "*I know I should have, I don't know*" (emphasis added).

The question at trial came down to whether Siegrist acted reasonably under all the circumstances. . . .

The jury in this case found that Siegrist did not act reasonably, and that his negligence was the proximate cause of Farwell's death. . . .

Siegrist contends that he is not liable for failure to obtain medical assistance for Farwell because he had no duty to do so.

Courts have been slow to recognize a duty to render aid to a person in peril. Where such a duty has been found, it has been predicated upon the existence of a special relationship between the parties; in such a case, if defendant knew or should have known of the other person's peril, he is required to render reasonable care under all the circumstances.

In *Depue v. Flateau,* 100 Minn. 299, 111 N.W. 1 (1907), the Supreme Court of Minnesota reversed an order of the trial court dismissing the cause of action and said that if the defendants knew their dinner guest was ill, it was for the jury to decide whether they were negligent in refusing his request to spend the night and, propping him on his wagon with the reins thrown over his shoulder, sending him toward home.

The Sixth Circuit Court of Appeals, in *Hutchinson v. Dickie,* 162 F.2d 103, 106 (6th Cir. 1947), said that a host had an affirmative duty to attempt to rescue a guest who had fallen off his yacht. The host controlled the only instrumentality of rescue. The Court declared that to ask of the host anything less than that he attempt to rescue his guest would be "so shocking to humanitarian considerations and the commonly accepted code of social conduct that the courts in similar situations have had no difficulty in pronouncing it to be a legal obligation."

Farwell and Siegrist were companions on a social venture. Implicit in such a common undertaking is the understanding that one will render assistance to the other when he is in peril if he can do so without endangering himself. Siegrist knew or should have known when he left Farwell, who was badly beaten and unconscious, in the back seat of his car that no one would find him before morning. Under these circumstances, to say that Siegrist had no duty to obtain medical assistance or at least to notify someone of Farwell's condition and whereabouts would be "shocking to humanitarian considerations" and fly in the face of "the commonly accepted code of social conduct." . . .

Farwell and Siegrist were companions engaged in a common undertaking; there was a special relationship between the parties. Because Siegrist knew or should have know of the peril Farwell was in and could render assistance without endangering himself he had an affirmative duty to come to Farwell's aid.

The Court of Appeals is reversed and the verdict of the jury reinstated.

FITZGERALD, JUSTICE (dissenting).

. . . Plaintiff argues that once having voluntarily undertaken the duty of caring for decedent, defendant could not discontinue such assistance if, in so doing, he left the decedent in a worse position than when such duty was assumed. Defendant's knowledge of the seriousness of decedent's injury and the failure to advise decedent's grandparents, the close personal relationship that existed between defendant and the decedent, and the supposition that the decedent relied upon defendant for assistance leads plaintiff to conclude that defendant did not act "with the reasonable prudence and care of a reasonable man in the same or like circumstances." Defendant's position is that there was no volunteered assumption of duty to care for the safety of the decedent. He argues that the facts within his knowledge on the evening of August 26, 1966, and the evidence introduced at trial failed to establish that defendant should have seen that Richard Farwell had suffered a potentially fatal injury requiring immediate attention.

Defendant did not voluntarily assume the duty of caring for the decedent's safety. Nor did the circumstances which existed on the evening of August 26, 1966, impose such a duty. Testimony revealed that only a qualified physician would have reason to suspect that Farwell had suffered an injury which required immediate medical attention. The decedent never complained of pain and, in fact, had expressed a desire to retaliate against his attackers. Defendant's inability to arouse the decedent upon arriving at his grandparent's home does not permit us to infer, as does plaintiff, that defendant knew or should have known that the deceased was seriously injured. While it might have been more prudent for the defendant to insure that the decedent was safely in the house prior to leaving, we cannot say that defendant acted unreasonably in permitting Farwell to spend the night asleep in the back seat of his car.

The close relationship between defendant and the decedent is said to establish a legal duty upon defendant to obtain assistance for the decedent. No authority is cited for this proposition other than the public policy observation that the interest of society would be benefited if its members were required to assist one another. This is not the appropriate case to establish a standard of conduct requiring one to legally assume the duty of insuring the safety of another. Recognizing that legal commentaries have expressed moral outrage at those decisions which permit one to refuse aid to another whose life may be in peril, we cannot say that, considering the relationship between these two parties and the existing circumstances, defendant acted in an unreasonable manner.

Plaintiff believes that a legal duty to aid others should exist where such assistance greatly benefits society and only a reasonable burden is imposed upon those in a position to help. He contends further that the determination of the existence of a duty must rest with the jury where questions of foreseeability and the relationship of the parties are primary considerations.

It is clear that defendant's nonfeasance, or the "passive inaction or a failure to take steps to protect [the decedent] from harm" is urged as being the proximate cause of Farwell's death. We must reject plaintiff's proposition which elevates a moral obligation to the level of a legal duty, where, as here, the facts within defendant's knowledge in no way indicated that immediate medical attention was necessary and the relationship between the parties imposes no affirmative duty to render assistance. The posture of this case does not permit us to create a legal duty upon one to render assistance to another injured or imperiled party where the initial injury was not caused by the person upon whom the duty is sought to be imposed.

NOTES

1. *The General Rule.* RESTATEMENT (SECOND) OF TORTS § 314 (1965), Duty to Act for Protection of Others:

> The fact that the actor realizes or should realize that action on his part is necessary for another's aid or protection does not of itself impose upon him a duty to take such action.

Comment c to this section states:

The rule stated in this section is applicable irrespective of the gravity of the danger to which the other is subjected. . . .

The RESTATEMENT (SECOND) articulates the traditional rule that there is no duty to act to help another. But is it true that a reasonable person would never help another? If a reasonable person would, in fact, act to help another, why does the law refuse to recognize a duty? *See generally,* Thomas C. Galligan, Jr., *Aiding and Altruism: A Mythopsycholegal Analysis,* 27 U. MICH. J. OF L. REF. 439 (1994). Predictably, such a harsh rule is loaded with exceptions.

2. *Outdated Individualism.* In *Dorset Yacht Co. v. Home Office,* [1970] A.C. 1004, 1060, 2 W.L.R. 1140, 2 All E.R. 294 (H.L.) (*per* Lord Diplock), it was stated:

> The very parable of the good Samaritan (Luke 10, v 30) . . . illustrates, in the conduct of the priest and of the Levite who passed by on the other side, an omission which was likely to have as its reasonable and probable consequence damage to the health of the victim of the thieves, but for which the priest and Levite would have incurred no civil liability in English law.

According to Bohlen, *The Moral Duty to Aid Others as a Basis of Tort Liability,* 56 U. PA. L. REV. 217, 219–20 (1908),

> [t]here is no distinction more deeply rooted in the common law and more fundamental than that between misfeasance and non-feasance, between active misconduct working positive injury to others and passive inaction, a failure to take positive steps to benefit others, or to protect them from harm not created by any wrongful act of the defendant. This distinction is founded on that attitude of extreme individualism so typical of Anglo-Saxon legal thought.

What rationales, whether related to allocational or process concerns, may be cited in support of the traditional distinction between misfeasance and nonfeasance? Is the act-omission dichotomy maintainable in a real world composed of people who *omit* to apply their brakes or steer around other road users in time to avoid an accident?

In *Stansbie v. Troman,* [1948] 2 K.B. 48, 1 All E.R. 599, a contractor working in the plaintiff's home left the property for a short time, leaving the door unlocked. A thief entered and took some of the plaintiff's property. The court permitted recovery against the contractor. In *Yania v. Bigan,* 397 Pa. 316, 155 A.2d 343, 346 (1959), the defendant enticed a business invitee to jump into a strip-mining trench filled with water. The defendant made no attempt to rescue the invitee, who drowned. The court denied liability, stating that "[t]he mere fact that [defendant] saw [decedent] in a position of peril in the water imposed upon him no legal, although a moral, obligation or duty to go to his rescue, unless [defendant] was legally responsible, in whole or in part, for placing [decedent] in the perilous position." On what basis can *Stansbie* be distinguished from *Yania?*

3. *Extravagant Collectivism. See Griffith v. Southland Corp.,* 94 Md. App. 242, 617 A.2d 598 (1992), where an off-duty police officer became the victim of a savage beating while attempting to restore order on the premises of a store owned by the defendant. Defendant's employee was asked to summon aid, refused, and the officer was severely injured. The court stated that the "suggested duty, i.e., to call 911 when there is no imminent risk of danger to the caller, does no violence to the doctrine of stare decisis; there is no break from precedent because there is no precedent which permits a bystander to

refuse to call 911 when not exposed to imminent danger. Even if there were such an uncivilized and shocking principle, blind allegiance would invite disdain and disrespect for the courts." 617 A2d at 606.

See also *Soldano v. O'Daniels,* 141 Cal. App. 3d 443, 190 Cal. Rptr. 310 (1983), where liability was imposed on a bar owner who allegedly refused to allow use of his telephone to call police prior to the shooting death of plaintiff's decedent at an eating establishment across the street. *Compare Stangle v. Fireman's Fund Ins. Co.,* 190 Cal. App. 3d 971, 244 Cal. Rptr. 103 (1988), in which plaintiff's ring was stolen while it was on the premises of the defendant. Plaintiff discovered the theft immediately after it occurred and sought to use defendant's telephone to call the police, but defendant's receptionist refused access to her telephone, saying it was "for building use only." The court stated that *Soldano* was limited to cases of clear communication to a bystander of imminent danger of physical harm.

4. *A Duty to Provide an Employment Reference?* The plaintiffs' decedent was severely beaten and murdered by a co-worker. His estate sued the co-worker's former employer, alleging that the latter was negligent in failing to give a job reference stating the co-worker's known violent propensities. The defendant said it had not been asked for a reference, but even if it had it would have provided no information other than dates of employment. The defendant had a policy of not providing any further information, apparently out of fear of being sued for defamation. In dismissing the claim, the court held as a matter of law that an employer had no duty to disclose a former employee's "dangerous proclivities to an inquiring prospective employer." *Moore v. St. Joseph Nursing Home, Inc.*, 184 Mich. App. 766, 459 N.W.2d 100 (1990).

5. *Special Relationships Between the Defendant Non-Actor and the Victim.* Innkeepers and common carriers are duty-bound to protect their charges against "unreasonable risk of physical harm," and to provide succor if "they are ill or injured, and to care for them until they can be cared for by others." RESTATEMENT (SECOND) OF TORTS § 314A(1)(2) (1965). For example, in *Lopez v. Southern Cal. Rapid Transit Dist.,* 40 Cal. 3d 780, 221 Cal. Rptr. 840, 710 P.2d 907 (1985), a bus company was held to owe a duty of care to passengers injured in a fight after a group of juveniles began harassing passengers. Employers are under a similar duty to protect their servants whom they know to be in peril or hurt and helpless. RESTATEMENT (SECOND) OF TORTS § 314B (1965).

More broadly put, where there is a special relationship between the defendant non-actor and the victim the court will impose a duty to exercise reasonable care to act. The relationship between common carrier and passenger, between innkeeper and guest, and between employer and employee have been held to be duty-triggering special relationships. What about parent and child? Teacher and student?

In *Farwell*, the court seems to say that the defendant and decedent had a duty-triggering special relationship because they were on a joint social adventure. Is that just a fancy way to say they were friends? Should friends have a legal duty to help one another? At least where help or rescue is "easy?" If so, is the no-duty-to-act rule as important as it might at first appear?

6. *The Duty to Act: Negligent and Innocent Injurers.* RESTATEMENT (SECOND) OF TORTS § 321 (1965) (Duty to Act When Prior Conduct Is Found to Be Dangerous) provides:

> (1) If the actor does an act, and subsequently realizes or should realize that it has created an unreasonable risk of causing physical harm to another, he is under a duty to exercise reasonable care to prevent the risk from taking effect.
>
> (2) The rule stated in Subsection (1) applies even though at the time of the act the actor has no reason to believe that it will involve such a risk.

Further, comment *a* states:

> The rule stated in Subsection (1) applies whenever the actor realizes or should realize that his act has created a condition which involves an unreasonable risk of harm to another, or is leading to consequences which involve such a risk. The rule applies whether the original act is tortious or innocent. If the act is negligent, the actor's responsibility continues in the form of a duty to exercise reasonable care to avert the consequences which he recognizes or should recognize as likely to follow. But even where he has had no reason to believe, at the time of the act, that it would involve any unreasonable risk of physical harm to another, he is under a duty to exercise reasonable care when, because of a change of circumstances, or further knowledge of the situation which he has acquired, he realizes or should realize that he has created such a risk.

RESTATEMENT (SECOND) OF TORTS § 322 (1965) (Duty to Aid Another Harmed by Actor's Conduct) provides:

> If the actor knows or has reason to know that by his conduct, whether tortious or innocent, he has caused such bodily harm to another as to make him helpless and in danger of further harm, the actor is under a duty to exercise reasonable care to prevent such further harm.

Comment *a*:

> The rule stated in this Section applies not only where the actor's original conduct is tortious, but also where it is entirely innocent. If his act, or an instrumentality within his control, has inflicted upon another such harm that the other is helpless and in danger, and a reasonable man would recognize the necessity of aiding or protecting him to avert further harm, the actor is under a duty to take such action even though he may not have been originally at fault. This is true even though the contributory negligence of the person injured would disable him from maintaining any action for the original harm resulting from the actor's original conduct.

Comment *b*:

> The words "further harm" include not only an entirely new harm due to the dangerous position in which the other has been placed by

the actor's tortious act, but also any increase in the original harm caused by the failure to give assistance, and any protraction of the harm which prompt attention would have prevented.

Put differently, it might be said that an injurer, whether tortious or innocent, has a duty to help those whom it has injured.

7. *A Statutory Duty to Aid*. The State of Vermont has enacted a Duty to Aid the Endangered Act, VT. STAT. ANN. tit. 12, § 519. The Act provides:

> (a) A person who knows that another is exposed to grave physical harm shall, to the extent that the same can be rendered without danger or peril to himself or without interference with important duties owed to others, give reasonable assistance to the exposed person unless that assistance or care is being provided by others.
>
> (b) A person who provides reasonable assistance in compliance with subsection (a) of this section shall not be liable in civil damages unless his acts constitute gross negligence or unless he will receive or expects to receive remuneration. Nothing contained in this subsection shall alter existing law with respect to tort liability of a practitioner of the healing arts for acts committed in the ordinary course of his practice.
>
> (c) A person who willfully violates subsection (a) of this section shall be fined not more than $100.00.

Other states have also enacted statutes imposing limited duties and/or criminalizing the failure to act in certain situations.

8. *Assuming a Duty: Half-Hearted Rescuers*. *Farwell* may be viewed as a special relationship case; it may also be viewed as an application of the principles recognized in RESTATEMENT (SECOND) OF TORTS § 324 (1965), providing that:

> One who, being under no duty to do so, takes charge of another who is helpless adequately to aid or protect himself is subject to liability to the other for any bodily harm caused to him by
>
> (a) the failure of the actor to exercise reasonable care to secure the safety of the other while within the actor's charge, or
>
> (b) the actor's discontinuing his aid or protection, if by so doing he leaves the other in a worse position than when the actor took charge of him.

Do either of the scenarios envisaged in § 324 support plaintiff's position in *Farwell*?

9. *Contract or Tort?* RESTATEMENT (SECOND) OF TORTS § 323 (1965) provides:

> One who undertakes, gratuitously or for consideration, to render services to another which he should recognize as necessary for the protection of the other's person or things, is subject to liability to the other for physical harm resulting from his failure to exercise reasonable care to perform his undertaking, if
>
> (a) his failure to exercise such care increases the risk of such harm, or

(b) the harm is suffered because of the other's reliance upon the undertaking.

See also § 324A providing:

One who undertakes, gratuitously or for consideration, to render services to another which he should recognize as necessary for the protection of a third person or his things, is subject to liability to the third person for physical harm resulting from his failure to exercise reasonable care to perform his undertaking, if

(a) his failure to exercise reasonable care increases the risk of such harm, or

(b) he has undertaken to perform a duty owed by the other to the third person, or

(c) the harm is suffered because of reliance of the other or the third person upon the undertaking."

Taken together these sections may be said to provide a third exception to the no-duty-to-act rule. A person who assumes a duty to help another must exercise reasonable care in providing that help.

In *Paz v. State*, 22 Cal. 4th 550, 994 P.2d 975, 93 Cal. Rptr. 2d 703 (2000), the plaintiff was injured in a traffic accident at a dangerous intersection allegedly because some contractors had failed to obtain the permits necessary to complete new traffic signals. The court concluded as follows:

In this case, none of these three conditions for section 324A liability is present. The evidence fails to support an inference that defendants' conduct increased the risk of physical harm to plaintiff beyond that which allegedly existed at the intersection. Plaintiff alleged that the intersection was dangerous because of restricted sight lines. However, nothing in the record suggests that defendants did anything that increased the risk to motorists that allegedly existed because of these sight lines. Instead, defendants simply did not succeed in completing—before plaintiff's collision—a project that might have reduced the preexisting hazard at the intersection. In this instance, where the record shows that nothing changed but the passage of time, a failure to alleviate a risk cannot be regarded as tantamount to increasing that risk.

Neither the record nor the law shows any basis for satisfying the second alternative condition required for section 324A liability. In agreeing to the traffic signal installation condition, Stoneman (and by extension KOA) did not undertake to perform a duty that the City owed to plaintiff. As our cases and statutes establish, cities generally have no affirmative duty to install traffic control signals. Nothing in this record suggests any reason for departing from that rule.

Finally, plaintiff did not submit, and the record does not contain, any evidence that he was harmed because either he or the City relied on defendants' timely installation of traffic control signals. The only reasonable inferences available from the record are to the contrary. The City and Stoneman did not make a contract to install the traffic signals. Instead, the City only made the signals a condition of Stoneman's condominium development project. If Stoneman had abandoned the development project—a decision that real property developers may face if financing becomes uncertain or if litigation entangles a project—Stoneman would not have been obliged to install the traffic signals at all. Thus, imposing the traffic signal installation as a condition of development did not give the City a basis for relying on the installation's being completed at any time before the condominium project's completion.

The fact that the City was not relying on defendants to complete the traffic signal installation within any particular time is further demonstrated by the City's own conduct in the matter. The uncontradicted evidence showed that the City's disagreements with Caltrans over traffic striping issues delayed issuance of KOA's encroachment permit. Furthermore, the City did not apply for its own encroachment permit, necessary to operate and maintain the signals, for more than two months after Caltrans stopped KOA's work on the project just days before it would have been completed.

In sum, none of the three alternative conditions to liability under section 324A is satisfied here. As a result, the considerations and policy interests that are embodied in the negligent undertaking theory of section 324A preclude defendants' liability. In performing their undertaking with the City, defendants did not increase the hazards to which motorists were exposed as a result of the preexisting conditions at the intersection. The defendants did not undertake a duty the City owed to motorists such as plaintiff. Nor is there any evidence that any reliance by the City, much less by the plaintiff, resulted in plaintiff's injury. Consequently, under the established principles of our common law of negligence as reflected in section 324A, the trial court properly granted summary judgment for [defendants].

Would a mere promise ever be a sufficient undertaking to impose a duty in tort? Should it?

10. *Good Samaritans as an Endangered Species.* In *McCorkle v. City,* 70 Cal. 2d 252, 74 Cal. Rptr. 389, 449 P.2d 453 (1969), a police officer, investigating an accident, directed the plaintiff to accompany him to the middle of the intersection where the accident had occurred; when he did so, plaintiff was struck by another vehicle. The police officer was held liable for plaintiff's injuries.

However, in *Williams v. State of California,* 34 Cal. 3d 18, 192 Cal. Rptr. 233, 664 P.2d 137, 143 (1983), the allegations against the investigating officers were that they failed to properly investigate the cause of the underlying accident or secure identification of witnesses so as to facilitate plaintiff's potential civil action. The court found no duty of care and stated that,

[t]he officers did not create the peril in which plaintiff found herself; they took no affirmative action which contributed to, increased, or changed the risk which would have otherwise existed; there is no indication that they voluntarily assumed any responsibility to protect

plaintiff's prospects for recovery by civil litigation; and there are no allegations of the requisite factors to a finding of special relationship. . . .

ESTATES OF MORGAN v. FAIRFIELD FAMILY COUNSELING CENTER
77 Ohio St. 3d 284, 673 N.E.2d 1311 (1997)

On the evening of July 25, 1991, Matt Morgan was playing cards with his parents, Jerry and Marlene Morgan, and sister, Marla Morgan. Matt excused himself from the table, went upstairs, and obtained a gun. He came back downstairs and shot and killed his parents and seriously injured his sister. During the previous year, Matt had been examined by or received counseling from various mental health professionals who were either employed by or served as consultants to appellee, the Fairfield Family Counseling Center ("FFCC"). This case involves the liability of those mental health professionals and FFCC for the injuries and deaths resulting from the tragic events of July 25, 1991.. . .

The trial court entered summary judgment in favor of Dr. Brown, FFCC, and its employees.. . .

ALICE ROBIE RESNICK, J.

In *Littleton v. Good Samaritan Hosp. & Health Ctr.* (1988), 39 Ohio St. 3d 86, 529 N.E.2d 449, this court determined that under certain circumstances a psychiatrist can be held liable for the violent acts of a voluntarily hospitalized patient following the patient's release from the hospital. The question left open in *Littleton*, however, was "whether a psychiatrist's duty to protect a person from the violent propensities of the psychiatrist's patient extends to the outpatient setting. See, generally, *Tarasoff v. Regents of the University of California* (1976), 17 Cal. 3d 425, 131 Cal. Rptr. 14, 551 P.2d 334." *Littleton*, 39 Ohio St. 3d at 92, 529 N.E.2d at 455, fn. 3. This is the issue we must decide today.

. . .[F]oreseeability alone is not always sufficient to establish the existence of a duty. This court has followed the common-law rule, as set forth at 2 Restatement of the Law 2d, Torts (1965) 116–130, Sections 314 to 319, that there is no duty to act affirmatively for another's aid or protection absent some "special relation" which justifies the imposition of a duty.

Restatement Section 314 states the general rule that there is no duty to act affirmatively for another's aid or protection. Section 315 "is a special application of the general rule stated in § 314." 2 Restatement of Torts, *supra*, at 122, Section 315, Comment a. It provides that there is no duty to control the conduct of a third person to prevent him from causing physical harm to another unless a "special relation" exists between the defendant and the third person or between the defendant and the other. Sections 316 to 319 set forth the relations between the defendant and the third person which require the defendant to control the third person's conduct. In *Littleton, supra*, 39 Ohio St. 3d at 92–93, 529 N.E.2d at 455, we relied on Section 319 of the Restatement in finding that a special relation exists between a psychiatrist and his patient in the hospital setting. Section 319 states that:

"One who takes charge of a third person whom he knows or should know to be likely to cause bodily harm to others if not controlled is under a duty to exercise reasonable care to control the third person to prevent him from doing such harm."

The issue, therefore, becomes whether the relationship between a psychotherapist and the outpatient constitutes a "special relation" which imposes a duty upon the psychotherapist to protect others against and/or control the patient's violent conduct.

In *Tarasoff, supra*, 17 Cal. 3d 425, 131 Cal. Rptr. 14, 551 P.2d 334, the Supreme Court of California found that the psychotherapist-outpatient relationship constitutes such a special relation. In so finding, the court did not engage in a traditional Restatement analysis. Under a traditional Restatement analysis, Section 319 would take center stage. In *Tarasoff*, the court treated Section 315 *et seq.* as reflective of an overall principle that affirmative duties to control should be imposed whenever the nature of the relationship warrants social recognition as a special relation. In this way, the court subjected Section 315 to an expansive reading. Thus, the court noted that "courts have increased the number of instances in which affirmative duties are imposed not by direct rejection of the common law rule [of nonliability for nonfeasance], but by expanding the list of special relationships which will justify departure from that rule." *Id.* at fn. 5.

The court then engaged in a two-part analysis. First, the court drew an analogy to cases which have imposed a duty upon physicians to diagnose and warn about their patient's contagious disease, and concluded that "'by entering into a doctor-patient relationship the therapist becomes sufficiently involved to assume some responsibility for the safety, not only of the patient himself, but also of any third person whom the doctor knows to be threatened by the patient.'

Second, the court weighed various public policy concerns, concluding that the public interest in safety from violent assaults outweighs the countervailing interests of safeguarding the confidential character of psychotherapeutic communications and the difficulty inherent in forecasting dangerousness.

The court held, therefore, that:

"When a therapist determines, or pursuant to the standards of his profession should determine, that his patient presents a serious danger of violence to another, he incurs an obligation to use reasonable care to protect the intended victim against such danger. The discharge of this duty may require the therapist to take one or more of various steps, depending upon the nature of the case. Thus it may call for him to warn the intended victim or others likely to apprise the victim of the danger, to notify the police, or to take whatever other steps are reasonably necessary under the circumstances."

Since *Tarasoff*, a majority of courts that have considered the issue have concluded that the relationship between the psychotherapist and the outpatient constitutes a special relation which imposes upon the psychotherapist an affirmative duty to protect against or control the patient's violent propensities. Recognizing that the duty is imposed by virtue of the relationship, these courts acknowledge that the duty can be imposed not only upon psychiatrists, but also on psychologists, social workers, mental health clinics and other mental health professionals who know, or should have known, of their patient's violent propensities. The courts do not impose any single formulation as to what steps must be taken to alleviate the danger. Depending upon the facts and the allegations of the case, the particular psychotherapist-defendant may or may not be required to perform any number of acts, including prescribing medication, fashioning a program for treatment, using whatever ability he or she has to control access to weapons or to persuade the patient to voluntarily enter a hospital, issuing warnings or notifying the authorities and, if appropriate, initiating involuntary commitment proceedings.

Most of the courts engage in a *Tarasoff*-type analysis by which Section 315 is subjected to an expansive reading. Others find a duty to exist under the rule stated in Section 319. Collectively, they recognize that there are various levels of being in "control" pursuant to Section 315, or being in "charge" pursuant to Section 319, with corresponding degrees of responsibility for the patient's violent actions. Thus, although the psychotherapist may have less ability to control the patient in the outpatient setting than in the hospital setting, this lesser degree of control is not held to justify a blanket negation of the duty to control.

Generally, the courts focus their attention on balancing the countervailing public interests that were weighed in *Tarasoff*, including the additional concern that patients be placed in the least restrictive environment and that nonviolent patients not be subjected to hospitalization against their will in an effort to avoid liability. These courts conclude that the interests of society to be protected against the violent acts of mental patients outweigh the concerns of confidentiality, overcommitment, and difficulty of predicting violent acts.

In addition, a number of courts have relied on *Tarasoff* in finding that a psychotherapist can be held liable for the violent acts of a patient following the patient's release from the hospital.

The parties do not dispute that the psychotherapist-outpatient relationship justifies the imposition of a common-law duty upon the psychotherapist to control the violent propensities of the patient. In fact, Dr. Brown readily admits that "in *Tarasoff, supra,* the Supreme Court of California set then-novel but reasonable parameters on a psychotherapist's liability for violent acts of outpatients." However, our research discloses that *Tarasoff* does not enjoy universal acceptance. Some courts have concluded that the typical psychotherapist-outpatient relationship lacks sufficient elements of control necessary to satisfy Sections 315 and/or 319. These courts reason that the duty to control is corollary to the right, power, or ability to control, and criticize *Tarasoff* for not specifically addressing the issue of a psychotherapist's control over the outpatient. In addition, some of these courts find that public policy militates against the imposition of a duty in the outpatient setting.

In light of the opposing views on the subject, we deem it necessary to resolve the issue of duty in the outpatient setting by balancing the various factors which are the focus of judicial attention on both sides of the issue. These factors consist of the following: (1) the psychotherapist's ability to control the outpatient; (2) the public's interest in safety from violent assault; (3) the difficulty inherent in attempting to forecast whether a patient represents a substantial risk of physical harm to others; (4) the goal of placing the mental patient in the least restrictive environment and safeguarding the patient's right to be free from unnecessary confinement; and (5) the social importance of maintaining the confidential nature of psychotherapeutic communications.

. . .[T]here is no more magic inherent in the conclusory term "special relation" than there is in the term "duty." Both are part and parcel of the same inquiry into whether and how the law should regulate the activities and dealings that people have with each other. As society changes, as our sciences develop and our activities become more interdependent, so our relations to one another change, and the law must adjust accordingly. "Duty" is not a rigid formalistic concept forever embedded in the standards of a simplistic yester-year. Relations perhaps regarded as tenuous in a bygone era may now be of such importance in our modern complicated society as to require certain assurances that risks associated therewith be contained. These principles do not shed their inherent flexibility when applied in the context of a defendant's duty to control the violent conduct of a third person.

There is indeed a current running through the relevant Restatement sections that in order for a special relation to exist between the defendant and the third person, the defendant must have the ability to control the third person's conduct. Moreover, the cases from which these sections derive indicate that the ability to control is not the fictitious control which provides the basis for vicarious liability. Instead, "control" is "used in a very real sense." Further, it would be tantamount to imposing strict liability to require the defendant to control a third person's conduct where he lacks the ability to do so.

However, those courts which find the ability to control to be lacking in the outpatient setting tend to take a rather myopic view of the level or degree of control needed to impose the duty. They appear to assume that in order to satisfy Section 315 in general, or Section 319 in particular, there must be actual constraint or confinement, whereby the third person's physical liberty is taken away or restricted. In viewing the issue in this way, these courts fail to recognize that the duty to control the conduct of a third person is commensurate with such ability to control as the defendant actually has at the time. In other words, it is within the contemplation of the Restatement that there will be diverse levels of control which give rise to corresponding degrees of responsibility.

. . .Dr. Brown testified that neuroleptic medication controls symptoms of schizophrenia in approximately seventy percent of schizophrenics. Lambert acknowledged that the symptoms of schizophrenia can be controlled with antipsychotic medication such as Navane, and that one of the possible risks associated with taking a medication-controlled schizophrenic off his medication is that he can become dangerous to himself or others. Until Dr. Brown weaned Matt off his medication, Matt was a medication-controlled and treatment-compliant patient. Drs. Goff and Tanay were both of the opinion that Matt would have remained compliant with his treatment and medication had Dr. Brown not weaned him off the Navane, and that had Matt remained on medication, he would not have had the overt psychotic symptoms that led him to kill his parents and injure his sister.

In addition, Drs. Goff and Tanay testified that at various points in time after October 11, 1990, the last time Dr. Brown saw Matt, a number of other steps could have been taken by Dr. Brown, FFCC and its employees to prevent Matt's dangerous proclivities from manifesting. According to their testimony, Dr. Brown should have closely monitored Matt's condition for at least six months after withdrawing his medication. If this had been done, Dr. Brown could have reinstated Matt's medication upon the reappearance of symptoms. Since this was not accomplished, Matt's condition eventually deteriorated to the point of noncompliance while under the care of FFCC. At this point, Drs. Goff and Tanay opined, FFCC should have taken aggressive action to persuade Matt to continue treatment and have his medication reinstated by Dr. Brown. Such action should have included, among other things, strong family involvement, making Matt's participation in vocational therapy contingent upon continued treatment, and telling Matt that he faced involuntary hospitalization unless he resumed taking his medication. If such measures had proved to be ineffective, and Matt nevertheless continued to deteriorate as he did, he would need to be involuntarily hospitalized, which, Drs. Goff and Tanay opined, should have taken place in May or June 1991.

Thus, we conclude that the psychotherapist-outpatient relationship embodies sufficient elements of control to warrant a corresponding duty to control.

Society has a strong interest in protecting itself from those mentally ill patients who pose a substantial risk of harm.. . .

One goal of modern psychiatry is to place patients in the least restrictive environment. Mental hospitals are not dumping grounds for all persons whose behavior might prove to be inconvenient or offensive to society.. . .

These are important interests, not to be lightly infringed upon. Accordingly, there is some trepidation concerning the imposition of a duty because of the fear that therapists will attempt to protect themselves from liability by involuntarily hospitalizing nonviolent mental patients.

This fear, however, has no reliable statistical support. Instead, the statistical evidence that is available indicates that "*Tarasoff* has not discouraged therapists from treating dangerous patients, nor has it led to an increased use of involuntary commitment of patients perceived as dangerous."

. . .As to the importance of safeguarding the confidentiality of psychotherapeutic communications, this interest comes into play primarily when the psychotherapist is required to warn a potential victim of a patient's propensity for violence. However, as we noted in *Littleton,* "an exception [to confidentiality] exists for disclosures necessary to protect individual or public welfare.

The American Medical Association has long allowed breaches of confidence when "it becomes necessary in order to protect the welfare of the individual or of the community." Principles of Medical Ethics of the American Medical Association (1957), Section 9.

. . .We conclude that the relationship between the psychotherapist and the patient in the outpatient setting constitutes a special relation justifying the imposition of a duty upon the psychotherapist to protect against and/or control the patient's violent propensities. The outpatient setting embodies sufficient elements of control to warrant the imposition of such a duty, and such a duty would serve the public's interest in protection from the violently inclined mental patient in a manner that is consistent with Ohio law. On the other hand, the imposition of such a duty would not impose undue burdens upon the therapist or result in overcommitment, nor would it significantly affect the confidential character of psychotherapeutic communications.

In *Littleton,* 39 Ohio St. 3d 86, 529 N.E.2d 449, we balanced the various policy considerations in determining the appropriate standard of care to be applied to psychiatric decisions releasing voluntarily hospitalized mental patients from the hospital. The court concluded that the malpractice standard of ordinary care should not be applied, but that a "professional judgment standard" should be applied similar to the "business judgment rule." Accordingly, the holding of *Littleton* describes an application of the professional judgment standard to three different situations in the voluntary hospitalization setting.

We explained in part as follows:

"Under such a 'psychotherapist judgment rule,' the court would not allow liability to be imposed on therapists for simple errors in judgment. Instead, the court would examine the 'good faith, independence and thoroughness' of a psychotherapist's decision not to commit a patient. . . Factors in reviewing such good faith include the competence and training of the reviewing psychotherapists, whether the relevant documents and evidence were adequately, promptly and independently reviewed, whether the advice or opinion of another therapist was obtained, whether the evaluation was made in light of the proper legal standards for commitment, and whether other evidence of good faith exists."

Plaintiffs-appellants argue that the good faith judgment rule applies only to decisions on "whether hospitalization of the patient is required," and only in "those cases in which a standard of care cannot be determined by the expert witnesses." We disagree.

The nature of the duty imposed requires the therapist to determine the interrelated questions of whether a patient poses a risk of harm to others and how to prevent such harm from coming to fruition. It does not necessarily require in all cases that the therapist hospitalize or medicate the patient, warn others, or take any single specific step to avert the danger. What is required, if anything is required, depends upon the facts and allegations of each case. Thus, when courts indiscriminately refer to the "duty to warn" or the "duty to hospitalize," they are merely describing how particular therapists, under particular circumstances, failed to fulfill their overall duty. We reject the notion that divergent standards of care should be applied to what is essentially a single duty.

The psychotherapist judgment rule is a compromise between "declining to recognize a duty at all, or recognizing a duty and liability under a traditional negligence theory." The overriding concern is to protect the public from assault by the violent mentally ill. Fundamentally, the duty is imposed because the therapist is the best, if not the only, line of defense society has against the danger posed by the violent mental patient. Because of their special training, skill and contact with the patient, psychotherapists are especially equipped to thwart the danger.

However, the public interest would not be served by a standard of care which intrudes upon the integrity of the psychotherapeutic relationship. To maintain its efficacy, the psychotherapeutic relationship must instill confidence in the patient and afford a certain degree of autonomy for the therapist in rendering decisions. Although the concerns over predictability, overcommitment, and confidentiality are overstated, they appear nevertheless to cause some trepidation on the part of the patient and therapist alike which can affect the viability of the relationship. Without good medical care, society would stand unprotected from mental patients with violent propensities.

Thus, the professional judgment rule adopted in *Littleton* seeks to strike an appropriate balance by not allowing the psychotherapist to act in careless disregard of the harm presented to others by violently inclined patients, yet preserving the confidence, autonomy, and flexibility necessary to the psychotherapeutic relationship. There is nothing in the analysis itself that would suggest a different result in the outpatient setting.

Accordingly, we hold that when a psychotherapist knows or should know that his or her outpatient represents a substantial risk of harm to others, the therapist is under a duty to exercise his or her best professional judgment to prevent such harm from occurring.

Dr. Brown urges the court to adopt the "specific threats to specific victims" rule articulated in *Brady v. Hopper*, 751 F.2d 329, 331(10th Cir. 1984), and *Thompson v. Alameda Cty.* (1980), 27 Cal. 3d 741, 167 Cal. Rptr. 70, 614 P.2d 728. Under this rule, "absent allegations in a complaint that a psychiatrist is aware of his patient's specific threats to specific victims, there exists no legal duty or obligation on the part of the psychiatrist for harm done by the patient."

The rule, at least as articulated in *Brady*, encompasses three elements as a precondition to liability: (A) that the therapist is actually aware that the patient represents a threat of harm to others, (B) that the threat of harm be specific, and (C) that the target of such threats be precisely and specifically identified. Although these elements tend to overlap and meld together in application, for purposes of analysis we will consider them separately.

In Ohio, a cause of action for professional negligence is not dependent upon actual awareness of the potential for harm. Instead, the duty to protect others is imposed when the medical professional knows *or should know* that the patient is likely to cause harm to others. Moreover, as the court in *Bardoni v. Kim*, 151 Mich. App. 169, 390 N.W.2d 218, 223–224 (1986), aptly explained:

"If a duty to take reasonable steps to protect a third person is limited only to those victims which are actually known to the psychiatrist, . . . an extremely negligent psychiatrist may not ascertain that the patient is even dangerous or that the patient is dangerous to anyone in particular. For example: a psychiatric hospital's records of a patient indicate that the patient has violently focused his aggression on a named or particular person, . . . but the treating psychiatrist fails to read the records and is not apprised of this fact. Thus the target of the violence is identified or readily identifiable, but the defendant psychiatrist is not even aware that there exists a particular target of his patient's aggression. The relevant determination then becomes whether the psychiatrist should have ascertained, by acting in accordance with the standards of his profession, *e.g.*, by reading the hospital records, that there existed a target of his patient's aggression and the identity of the target. Thus, whether the treating psychiatrist actually knows of a target and whether that target is actually identified or readily identifiable by the psychiatrist is not always the appropriate focus in determining the extent of a psychiatrist's duty to persons endangered by his patient."

. . .[I]n Ohio evidence of specific threats is not necessarily required in order to hospitalize a mentally ill patient against his will. A mentally ill patient is also subject to involuntary commitment when his dangerous proclivities are found to be imminent by virtue of "evidence of . . . other violent behavior . . . or other evidence of present dangerousness." It would indeed be curious to apply a stricter standard as a precondition to the psychotherapist's common-law duty to control, especially since that duty, in its most confining aspect, would require the therapist to institute those very commitment proceedings. Moreover, there are obviously circumstances where, despite the lack of a specific threat, it can nevertheless be ascertained that the patient presents a danger to others and who the likely victims will be.

The advent of *Thompson* and *Brady* has compelled courts to confront the question of whether and when the "readily identifiable victim" rule is applicable and, if applicable, what degree of specificity is needed. The parties in the case *sub judice* tend to categorize the various cases which have addressed this issue according to whether they adopt the readily identifiable victim rule or reject it in favor of a more encompassing standard of foreseeability. Having drawn this line of demarcation, the parties would have us choose between what they perceive to be opposing options. However, we find the query as to which is the better option to be a misdirected question in this case. The views seen by the parties as being divergent are for the most part separate standards applied in different contexts.

The "readily identifiable victim" rule has its genesis in *Thompson*, where it was applied only to allegations concerning the failure to warn, as the allegations concerning the defendants' failure to otherwise control the patient's violent conduct were disposed of on other grounds. The court in *Thompson* summarized its holding by explaining that "within this context and for policy reasons the duty to warn depends upon and arises from the existence of a prior threat to a specific identifiable victim." The court reasoned that requiring warnings to the public at large would be "unwieldy and of little practical value," producing "a cacophony of warnings that by reason of their sheer volume would add little to the effective protection of the public."

After *Thompson*, cases that have limited the duty of care to identifiable victims have focused on the failure to warn. Within this context, they have also restricted the application of the rule, allowing a psychotherapist to be held liable to others in close relationship or close proximity to the victim, or finding that certain circumstances fall between the extremes of requiring warnings to be issued to the public at large and limiting it to a specifically named victim. On the other hand, cases that have rejected the rule have focused on a myriad of other alternative precautions alleged to have been reasonably necessary to control the patient. These cases vary in the standards of foreseeability that they impose, ranging from limiting the scope of the duty to those within the "zone of danger" to expanding it to cover the general public or all the world.

At first blush, the cases may lead one to believe that a choice must be made between adopting or rejecting the readily identifiable victim rule across the board. This is because many of the cases involve allegations concerning the psychotherapist's failure to take a number of steps to control the patient or protect the potential victim in addition to the giving of warnings. Upon closer scrutiny, however, it becomes apparent that the "readily identifiable victim" rule is applied only in the context of failure to warn. On the other hand, when the propriety of other steps alleged to have been required are examined, the focus shifts away from the special policy considerations and practical difficulties which have been said to justify limiting the scope of the duty in failure-to-warn cases. Thus, the "readily identifiable victim" rule is born, lives, and grows in failure-to-warn cases.

The appropriate question, therefore, is not which approach should be chosen, but whether it is wise to extend the readily identifiable victim rule beyond the failure-to-warn case.. . .

We need not determine at this time whether and to what extent the readily identifiable victim rule should attach in a failure-to-warn case. The case *sub judice* does not involve any allegation that Dr. Brown or FFCC was negligent in failing to warn Matt's family. The policy considerations and practical difficulties leading to a limitation on the duty in failure-to-warn cases are not present here. Accordingly, we reject such a limitation in this case.. . .

Dr. Brown also argues that he owed no duty to plaintiffs-appellants as a matter of law because the shootings took place over nine months after the last time he treated Matt. Thus, he contends, it cannot be found that the necessary element of control was present during those nine months, especially since FFCC took over Matt's care.

This argument commingles two distinct issues, that of duty and proximate cause. The control portion of the argument goes to the issue of duty. In this regard, the argument may be reduced to a proposition that there can be no duty unless the patient was under the care of the therapist at the time the harm was inflicted. Dr. Brown cites no authority for this position. Moreover, such a proposition runs counter to negligence principles. Viewing the facts most favorably to plaintiffs-appellants, the gravamen of Dr. Brown's alleged negligence in this case is the very act of withdrawing medication and relinquishing care of Matt. It is clearly unsound to absolve a negligent defendant because of the very act which made his conduct negligent.

The issue of remoteness in time—a question of proximate cause—cannot be resolved as a matter of law.. . .

Thus, no fixed rule can be established as to how quickly the harm must occur in order to hold the defendant liable. Some courts have found periods ranging between three and a half months to two years and five months to be too remote, while other courts have found periods ranging from five and one-half months to three years not to be too remote.

Physical or temporal remoteness, therefore, may be an important consideration in whether negligent conduct is a substantial factor in producing harm; but the mere lapse of time, in the absence of intervening causes, is not of itself sufficient to prevent the defendant's negligence from being the legal cause, regardless of how much time has passed.

In light of the testimony of Drs. Goff and Tanay that part of Dr. Brown's negligence lay in the relinquishment of Matt's care to FFCC and that Dr. Brown's negligence did contribute to the events of July 25, 1991, it cannot be found as a matter of law that FFCC's actions constitute an intervening cause. Accordingly, there remains a genuine issue of material fact as to whether Dr. Brown's alleged negligence in treating Matt was a substantial factor in producing the injuries and deaths occurring on July 25, 1991.

Viewing the evidence most favorably to plaintiffs-appellants, we find that reasonable minds could conclude that Dr. Brown failed to exercise his best professional judgment in diagnosing and controlling Matt's propensity for violence. When Dr. Brown first saw Matt on July 19, 1990, he noted that Matt was "recently discharged from a mental health unit of some sort in Philadelphia, Pennsylvania, on Elavil and Navane," and sought to obtain the C.A.T.C.H. records which he received sometime prior to Matt's next scheduled appointment on August 16, 1990. According to Drs. Goff and Tanay, those records revealed that Matt was a medication-controlled schizophrenic who, without medication, would more likely than not have a relapse of his psychosis, placing him at substantial risk for conflict with his parents and potential violence.

However, instead of reading the C.A.T.C.H. records or contacting Dr. Ladenheim, Dr. Brown noted on October 11, 1990, the date of his last appointment with Matt, that he had "no further insight as to just what happened to get him [Matt] into the mental hospital in Philadelphia or why they may have prescribed neuroleptic [medication] for him." Thus, he diagnosed Matt in part as a malingerer intent on gaining Social Security disability benefits, and weaned him off his medication.

. . .[W]e find that reasonable jurors could conclude that Dr. Brown's failure to review the C.A.T.C.H. records or contact Dr. Ladenheim to obtain a thorough and accurate history on Matt amounted to something less than the exercise of professional judgment. Thus, summary judgment was entered improperly in favor of Dr. Brown, and the decision of the court of appeals is affirmed as to this issue.

We find further that summary judgment in favor of FFCC was inappropriate for several reasons. First, the testimony of Drs. Goff and Tanay, if believed, reveals that FFCC and its employees conducted a meaningless evaluation into whether Matt was subject to involuntary hospitalization in May or July 1991. Dr. Goff testified that Matt was committable by June 14, 1991, and "that a vocational therapist has no business making decisions about what is appropriate and what's not appropriate in terms of involuntary hospitalization." Dr. Tanay testified that Matt was likely committable in May 1991, and that Lambert and Reid "had no business doing what they were doing. And [FFCC] had no business assigning them that role. This was a responsibility absolutely beyond their competence." Instead, he opined, at least one psychiatrist or psychologist well-trained in the area of dealing with psychotic individuals is required for a meaningful evaluation of whether a patient is subject to involuntary hospitalization.

. . . The second reason why summary judgment in favor of FFCC was inappropriate is that there is sufficient testimony which, if believed, establishes that FFCC was ill-equipped to deal with psychotic individuals such as Matt. Dr. Tanay testified that FFCC "was not equipped to deal with psychotics. It had neither the resources, and I would even believe not even the interest, in providing care for psychotics. [Instead] psychotics were used, exploited to get funds, but they were provided virtually no meaningful care. . . ."

Third, although disputed, social worker Barbara Sharp testified that FFCC had an unwritten policy that it would not initiate involuntary hospitalization proceedings, but would become involved only after such were initiated by the patient's family. The court of appeals found that "there is no evidence that this unwritten policy guided the counseling center in this case." We find, however, that there is sufficient evidence which allows for an inference that FFCC acted in accordance with such a policy.

FFCC received repeated notices of Matt's deteriorating condition. It was informed of Matt's violent outbursts and of his deposit on the purchase of a gun. Mrs. Morgan specifically stated her concern that Matt may become violent, and repeatedly begged FFCC to do something before violence erupted. Instead of taking her seriously, Lambert believed that she was exaggerating and emergency assessments were performed by what Drs. Goff and Tanay described as untrained personnel. Under these circumstances, a reasonable juror could infer that FFCC's unwritten policy guided their actions.

In light of the foregoing, we find that a genuine issue of material fact remains as to whether FFCC exercised professional judgment in evaluating and treating Matt. Accordingly, we hold that summary judgment was inappropriate in favor of FFCC and its employees, and reverse the court of appeals as to this issue.

COOK, J., dissenting.

I respectfully dissent. The law recognizes the fundamental unfairness of blaming one person for the acts of another. Thus, the Restatement favors the general rule that there is no duty to act for the protection of others, with four explicit exceptions. 2 Restatement of the Law 2d, Torts (1965), Section 315. The exceptions set forth in the Restatement are a parent's duty to control his child, a master's duty to control his servant, a land possessor's duty to control his licensees, and the duty of one who "takes charge" of another person who he knows or should know is likely to harm another to control that person. 2 Restatement of Torts, *supra*, Sections 316 to 319. The common factor among these four exceptions is that due to a "special relation" there exists the inherent *ability* or *right* to control another's conduct.. . .

In this case, Dr. Brown did not have the requisite "special relation" with Matt when Matt killed his parents and injured his sister because Dr. Brown lacked both the right and the ability to control Matt. Dr. Brown had not met with Matt for over nine months. Dr. Brown stated that he did not monitor

Matt's progress after October 1990 because he relied on the fact that an experienced psychologist, a vocational rehabilitation person, and a case manager were working with Matt, "all looking for, aware of, and knowing the signs of relapse." The individuals at Fairfield Family Counseling Center ("FFCC") caring for Matt after October 1990 knew to return him to Dr. Brown upon signs of illness and did, in fact, schedule an appointment for Matt with Dr. Brown for May 23, 1991, which Matt canceled.

Similarly, Dr. Brown had no ability to control Matt through medication because he could not force Matt to take his medication. When Matt first presented to Dr. Brown, he apparently had not been taking his medication regularly or in the amounts prescribed. Even during the time that Matt was meeting with Dr. Brown, Matt had independently decided to reduce his medication to only half the prescribed dosage.

In reaching its decision, the majority relies on *Tarasoff*. However, *Tarasoff* did not consider the issue of whether the psychiatrist had sufficient *ability* to control the patient but simply opined that "such a relationship may support affirmative duties for the benefit of third persons." *Tarasoff* addressed only the duty of a psychotherapist to warn and only in those situations when the patient has confided to the therapist his specific intention to kill a specific individual. In *Thompson* the Supreme Court of California seemingly limited the scope of *Tarasoff* in finding that "public entities and employees have no affirmative duty to warn of the release of an inmate with a violent history who has made *nonspecific threats of harm directed at nonspecific victims*."

. . .Today, this court appears to hold that, as a matter of law, any psychotherapist-patient relationship constitutes a special relation justifying the imposition of liability upon the psychotherapist for violent acts of the patient. It finds this duty even where the psychiatrist met with the patient only three times in an outpatient setting, where the patient communicated to the psychiatrist no specific threats to specific individuals, and where, upon the patient's mental health deteriorating, other mental health professionals scheduled an appointment with the psychiatrist which the patient failed to keep.

If the majority has found a special relation between Dr. Brown and Matt and between FFCC and Matt under the tenuous facts of this case, are all persons employed in the psychotherapy field now strictly liable for the acts of their patients? When does a "special relation" begin in the psychotherapist-outpatient setting and when, if ever, does it terminate? Is the special relation formed during the first consultation? After three consultations? How many appointments must the outpatient cancel before the outpatient can be said to have terminated the special relation?. . .

NOTES

1. *Special Relationships Between the Defendant Non-Actor and the Perpetrator of the Wrong: Positive Duties to Control.* RESTATEMENT (SECOND) OF TORTS § 315 (1965) provides:

There is no duty so to control the conduct of a third person as to prevent him from causing physical harm to another unless

(a) a special relation exists between the actor and the third person which imposes a duty upon the actor to control the third person's conduct, or

(b) a special relation exists between the actor and the other which gives to the other a right to protection.

Is the "no duty to control" principle even more firmly entrenched than the "no duty to rescue" rule? Why?

2. *Children.* One of the few well-established exceptions to the "no duty to control" rule concerns parental liability for children with violent proclivities. RESTATEMENT (SECOND) OF TORTS § 316 (1965) provides:

A parent is under a duty to exercise reasonable care so to control his minor child as to prevent it from intentionally harming others or from so conducting itself as to create an unreasonable risk of bodily harm to them, if the parent

(a) knows or has reason to know that he has the ability to control his child, and

(b) knows or should know of the necessity and opportunity for exercising such control.

See, e.g., Ellis v. D'Angelo, 116 Cal. App. 2d 310, 253 P.2d 675 (1953) (a first-time baby-sitter was held to state a cause of action against the parents of her four-year-old charge who attacked her).

In *Eldredge v. Kamp Kachess Youth Serv., Inc.,* 90 Wash. 2d 402, 583 P.2d 626 (1978), a similar duty was imposed on the operators of a camp for delinquents when three residents escaped, stole the plaintiff's vehicle and wrecked it. An analogous duty is imposed by RESTATEMENT (SECOND) OF TORTS § 319 (1965) ("Duty of Those in Charge of Person Having Dangerous Propensities") although, by its terms, liability is limited to cases of "bodily harm."

A similar duty is imposed on employers to control their employees. *See* RESTATEMENT (SECOND) OF TORTS § 317 (1965).

3. *Genesis of the Duty to Control Patients. Tarasoff v. Regents of Univ. of Cal.,* 17 Cal. 3d 425, 131 Cal. Rptr. 14, 551 P.2d 334, 347 (1976), arose out of the events that preceded the killing of Tatiana Tarasoff by one Poddar. Plaintiffs alleged that Poddar had confided his intentions to kill Tatiana to a psychologist employed by the defendant university. Although the campus police investigated Poddar, no one warned Tatiana or her parents. Writing for the majority, Justice Tobriner concluded:

Our current crowded and computerized society compels the interdependence of its members. In this risk-infested society we can hardly tolerate the further exposure to danger that would result from a concealed knowledge of the therapist that his patient was lethal. If the exercise of reasonable care to protect the threatened victim requires the therapist to warn the endangered party or those who can reasonably be expected to notify him, we see no sufficient societal interest that would protect and justify concealment.

In *Schuster v. Altenberg,* 144 Wis. 2d 223, 424 N.W.2d 159, 168 (1988), the court noted that "the duty which was recognized in *Tarasoff* was not limited to a duty to warn but extended to 'whatever other steps are reasonably necessary under the circumstances.' While the decision is principally noted for its holding, establishing a duty to warn third parties, the duty recognized in *Tarasoff* was significantly broader."

4. *A Scarlet Letter?* If the information costs imposed on potential victims most concern us, perhaps we should make parolees and others post large signs on their homes stating, for example, DANGEROUS PSYCHOPATH: KEEP YOUR DISTANCE. Would such a condition of probation or parole violate constitutional protection against cruel and unusual punishment, or first amendment guarantees against "forced" speech?

The most famous state reaction to such issues is the New Jersey Registration and Community Notification Law, N.J.S.A. 2C:7-1 *et seq.* (known as "Megan's Law" in memory of seven-year-old Megan Kanka). Other states have passed similar registration laws. More stringent measures are likely following the U.S. Supreme Court's upholding of Kansas' Sexually Violent Predator Act, which establishes procedures for the civil commitment of persons who, due to a "mental abnormality" or a "personality disorder," are likely to engage in "predatory acts of sexual violence." KAN. STAT. ANN. §§ 59-29a01 *et seq.* (1994). *See Kansas v. Hendricks*, 521 U.S. 346 (1997).

5. *Type of Treatment as a Determinant. Perreira v. State,* 768 P.2d 1198, 1209–14 (Colo. 1989), concerned the fatal shooting of a police officer by an acute paranoid psychotic with a long history of involuntary evaluations and treatments at a state mental health facility. The patient had a history of being extremely delusional about the police. The trial judge refused the facility's and physicians' motions for dismissal, and the supreme court affirmed. The court fashioned a novel analysis of the case law:

> Cases addressing the existence and scope of a psychiatrist's duty to protect others from the violent acts of a mentally ill patient have applied these general principles of duty in varying degrees. These cases range over a continuum that reflects diverse levels of control over the patient's treatment with corresponding degrees of responsibility for the patient's actions.
>
> At one end of the continuum are cases involving the treatment of a mentally ill person who voluntarily seeks treatment as an outpatient. . . .
>
> Because in these cases the therapist is treating the mentally disturbed person as a voluntary outpatient and has limited opportunity to observe and determine the patient's violent propensities, with even less opportunity to control the patient's behavior, some courts have limited the duty to take protective action to those instances in which the patient makes a specific threat against a readily identifiable victim. Other courts have not so limited the psychiatrist's duty, but instead have imposed a duty of reasonable care to protect potential victims against the voluntary patient's acts of violence whenever the psychiatrist has reason to foresee, in accordance with accepted psychiatric standards of practice, that the patient presents an unreasonable risk of serious bodily harm to others. . . .

At midpoint in the continuum are cases involving a mentally ill person who voluntarily seeks psychiatric treatment in a hospital as an inpatient. Here again, there are divergent views on the issue of duty. In *Hasenei v. United States,* 541 F. Supp. 999 (D. Md. 1982), although dealing with a situation involving a voluntary outpatient being treated at a Veterans Administration outpatient clinic for schizophrenia and alcoholism, the court concluded that the typical relationship between a psychiatrist and a voluntary patient was such that the relationship lacked sufficient elements of control to give rise to a legal duty to protect third parties from violent acts by the patient. . . .

Other courts have held that when a treating psychiatrist knows or has reason to know that the patient, if released, will present a risk of serious bodily harm to others, the psychiatrist has a duty to take reasonable precautions — including, if necessary, the temporary detention of the patient until an involuntary commitment can be accomplished — in order to protect potential victims from the patient's violent propensities.

At the end of the continuum are those cases dealing with a mentally ill person who has been involuntarily committed to a mental hospital by order of court. . . .

6. *Absence of Preexisting Relationship.* In *Mann v. State,* 70 Cal. App. 3d 773, 780, 139 Cal. Rptr. 82, 86 (1977), a police officer stopped to aid two stranded motorists. He parked behind them, turned on his emergency lighting, and called a tow truck. As soon as the tow truck arrived, the officer left without putting out flares or informing the motorists that they were no longer protected from the rear of their vehicle. A few minutes later, another vehicle crashed into the stationary vehicles. The court stated,

> While no special relationship may exist between members of the California Highway Patrol and the motoring public generally, or between the Patrol and stranded motorists generally, once a state traffic officer has chosen to investigate the plight of specific persons on a freeway and informed himself of the foreseeable danger to them from passing traffic, a special relationship requiring him to protect them . . . arises.

Compare Ezell v. Cockrell, 902 S.W.2d 394 (Tenn. 1995), involving the issue of whether a police officer had a duty to make an arrest. The court stated the facts as follows:

> On March 1, 1991, James Hillis and Donna Blankenship were drinking at the Boondocks' Saloon in the City of Elkton in Giles County, Tennessee. At approximately 8:45 p.m., Blankenship left the bar and entered her automobile in the parking lot of the Boondocks' Saloon. She was approached by Chief William Adams of the Elkton Police Department, who asked her to step out of the car. When Blankenship stepped out of the car, Chief Adams concluded that she was too intoxicated to drive. At that point, Hillis came out of the bar and volunteered to drive Blankenship home in her car. According to

the plaintiff's complaint, Chief Adams allowed Hillis to drive away in the car when he knew, or should have known, that Hillis was also intoxicated.

Approximately one hour later, Hillis, while driving Blankenship's black Chevrolet Cavalier on the wrong side of the road with the headlights off, collided head-on with a pick-up truck on U.S. Highway 31. As a result of the collision, one passenger in the truck, the plaintiff, Kimberly Ezell, was seriously injured, and another passenger, her husband, Tarrence Ezell, was killed. Hillis was also killed in the collision.

The court held that under the public duty doctrine, the officer had no duty to arrest the apparently drunken driver:

> Having decided that the public duty doctrine is viable, we consider it both desirable and necessary to retain, and further refine, the "special duty" exception. After considering the various formulations of the doctrine, we conclude that a special duty of care exists when 1) officials, by their actions, affirmatively undertake to protect the plaintiff, and the plaintiff relies upon the undertaking; 2) a statute specifically provides for a cause of action against an official or municipality for injuries resulting to a particular class of individuals, of which the plaintiff is a member, from failure to enforce certain laws; or 3) the plaintiff alleges a cause of action involving intent, malice, or reckless misconduct. Applying that analysis to the facts presumed to be true in this case, we conclude that the Court of Appeals correctly affirmed the trial court's dismissal of the complaint.

7. *A Medical Duty to Third Parties.* In *Bradshaw v. Daniel*, 854 S.W.2d 865 (Tenn. 1993), the husband of the plaintiff's deceased was treated for Rocky Mountain Spotted Fever by defendant doctor. The husband died from the disease, which is caused by tick bites. Although the defendant communicated with the wife during the husband's illness, he never told her of the risk of the disease. Subsequently she contracted and died from the disease, and the plaintiff brought this wrongful death action against the doctor, alleging that the doctor owed her a duty to warn of the danger of contracting the disease.

Reversing the dismissal of plaintiff's case, the court said the defendant had a legal duty to warn plaintiff's deceased:

> In determining the existence of a duty, courts have distinguished between action and inaction. Professor Prosser has commented that "the reason for the distinction may be said to lie in the fact that by 'misfeasance' he has at least made his situation no worse, and has merely failed to benefit him by interfering in his affairs."
>
> Because of this reluctance to countenance nonfeasance as a basis of liability, as a general rule, under the common law, one person owed no affirmative duty to warn those endangered by the conduct of another.
>
> To mitigate the harshness of this rule, courts have carved out exceptions for cases in which the defendant stands in some special

relationship to either the person who is the source of the danger, or to the person who is foreseeably at risk from the danger.

One of the most widely known cases applying that principle is *Tarasoff*, in which the California Supreme Court held that when a psychotherapist determines or, pursuant to the standards of his profession, should determine that his patient presents a serious danger of violence to another, the therapist has an affirmative duty to use reasonable care to protect the intended victim against such danger, and the duty may require the physician to warn the intended victim of the danger. The special relationship of the patient to his psychotherapist supported imposition of the affirmative duty to act for the benefit of third persons.

Decisions of other jurisdictions have employed the same analysis and have held that the relationship of a physician to his patient is sufficient to support the duty to exercise reasonable care to protect third persons against foreseeable risks emanating from a patient's physical illness. Specifically, other courts have recognized that physicians may be liable to persons infected by a patient, if the physician negligently fails to diagnose a contagious disease, or having diagnosed the illness, fails to warn family members or others who are foreseeably at risk from exposure to the disease.

8. *Nonprofessionals.* In *Rozycki v. Peley,* 199 N.J. Super. 571, 489 A.2d 1272 (1984), the wife of a pedophiliac was held to owe no duty to warn the parents of neighborhood children of her husband's proclivities because she was a lay person, not a medical health professional. *Cf. Pamela L. v. Farmer,* 112 Cal. App. 3d 206, 169 Cal. Rptr. 282 (1980), positing liability on a special relationship created by the wife in inviting minor children into her home (knowing her husband was a child molester).

9. *Intimate Relationships. B.N. v. K.K.,* 312 Md. 135, 538 A.2d 1175 (Md. 1988), arose out of an intimate sexual relationship between a physician and a nurse. The physician had active genital herpes but never disclosed this to the nurse. The nurse contracted the disease. The court concluded, "She was a clearly identified potential victim. . . . As a consequence, Dr. K. had a duty either to refrain from sexual contact with Ms. N. or to warn her of his condition." What is the standard of care in a case such as this? For example, when would a nonphysician be held to have sufficient knowledge of his own status as a carrier? In such a case, would you recommend that defendant argue plaintiff's contributory negligence?

Does the considerable publicity given to AIDS suggest that there is as much a duty to inquire as to the health of a sexual partner as there is to warn? Does a doctor who has tested HIV positive have a duty to warn his patients? If he informs his health care facility, should it revoke or limit his privileges?

10. *Attenuated Relationships.* In *Olson v. Children's Home Soc'y,* 204 Cal. App. 3d 1362, 252 Cal. Rptr. 11 (1988), a single woman placed her child for adoption through the defendant agency. Later, she married and her second child was born thirteen years after her first. Plaintiff alleged that the agency knew, or should have known, that her first child subsequently was diagnosed

as suffering from a genetically transmitted disease. She argued that if the adoption agency had informed her of these facts she would not have conceived her second child or would have been able to obtain timely medical treatment for him. Her second child died of the same disease at the age of six months. The court held that there was no special relationship between the woman and the adoption agency. Specifically, the court distinguished *Tarasoff* on the basis that in that case there had existed "a nexus between the impending peril and the specific duties undertaken by the [defendant]." What was that "nexus"?

Consider further *Andrews v. Wells,* 204 Cal. App. 3d 533, 251 Cal. Rptr. 344 (1988), in which a bar was held not to owe a duty of care to an intoxicated customer who had asked the bartender to arrange a ride home for him. The bartender was busy at the time of the request and shortly afterwards the customer left the bar. Not long thereafter the customer was struck and killed by a nonnegligent driver. The court held that no triable issue existed on whether there was a special relationship between the bartender and the customer. Why not?

I. SUICIDE AND OTHER DAMAGES

McPEAKE v. CANNON, ESQ., P.C.
381 Pa. Super. 227, 553 A.2d 439 (1989)

HOFFMAN, JUDGE.

This appeal arises from the order of August 26, 1987, granting appellee's preliminary objections and dismissing appellants' complaint with prejudice. Appellants contend that the trial court erred in granting appellee's preliminary objections because the complaint set forth a valid claim of legal malpractice. For the reasons that follow, we affirm the order below.

On January 11, 1985, appellants' decedent was arrested for burglary, rape, indecent assault, corrupting the morals of a minor, and possession of an instrument of crime. Decedent retained the legal services of appellee to represent him on the above-mentioned charges. On August 18, 1986, after a jury found decedent guilty on all counts, he suddenly jumped from a closed fifth floor window of the courtroom and killed himself. Appellants filed a legal malpractice, wrongful death and survivors' action against appellee, alleging that appellee's negligent representation of decedent caused his fatal leap from the courtroom window after the jury found him guilty of rape. Appellants averred in their complaint eighteen instances of alleged negligent conduct on the part of appellee which led to decedent's conviction. Appellee filed preliminary objections in the nature of a demurrer. The court granted appellee's preliminary objections and the complaint was dismissed with prejudice. This timely appeal followed. . . .

. . . The gravamen of appellants' complaint is that appellee's negligent representation during trial amounted to legal malpractice, and caused decedent to commit suicide. Generally, suicide has not been recognized as a legitimate basis for recovery in wrongful death cases. This is so because suicide constitutes an independent intervening act so extraordinary as not to have been reasonably foreseeable by the original tortfeasor. There are, however, limited exceptions to this rule. For example, Pennsylvania has recognized suicide as a legitimate basis for wrongful death claims involving hospitals, mental health institutions and mental health professionals, where there is a custodial relationship and the defendant has a recognized duty of care towards the decedent. In other cases, where the defendant was not associated with a hospital or mental health institution, courts have required both a clear showing of a duty to prevent the decedent's suicide and a direct causal connection between the alleged negligence and the suicide. A third line of cases which have recognized suicide as a basis for recovery involve suits brought under the worker's compensation statute. Under this statute, compensation will be granted if a suicide was caused by pain, depression or despair resulting from a work-related injury so severe as to override rational judgment.

On review, the issue presented for us is whether an attorney may be held liable for his client's suicide that has allegedly resulted from the attorney's negligent representation. More specifically, the question is whether an attorney's duty of representation extends to protecting a client from his own suicidal tendencies. The issue is one of first impression in Pennsylvania.

Appellants proceed under a theory of legal malpractice. As a general matter, the plaintiff in a legal malpractice action must be prepared to show:

1. the employment of the attorney or other basis for duty;
2. the failure of the attorney to exercise ordinary skill and knowledge;
3. that such negligence was the proximate cause of the plaintiff's injuries.

These elements must be proven by a preponderance of the evidence. An attorney will be found to have been negligent if he or she has failed to use that ordinary skill, knowledge, and care which would normally be possessed and exercised under the circumstances by members of the legal profession. Once the plaintiff has established that a duty of care is breached, the plaintiff must still establish a causal connection between the defendant's negligent conduct and the plaintiff's injuries.

"Proximate" or "legal" causation in turn is defined as "[t]hat which, in a natural and continuous sequence, unbroken by any sufficient intervening cause, produces injury, and without which the result would not have occurred." *Wisniewski v. Great Atlantic and Pacific Tea Co.*, 226 Pa. Super. 574, 582, 323 A.2d 744, 748 (1974). Moreover, Prosser has noted that the question of "proximate" causation "becomes essentially a question of whether the policy of the law will extend the responsibility for the conduct to the consequences which have in fact occurred. Quite often this has been stated, and properly so, as an issue of whether the defendant is under any duty to the plaintiff, or whether his duty includes protection against such consequences." W. Prosser, § 42, at 244.

Thus, a defendant will not be found to have had a duty to prevent a harm that was not a reasonably foreseeable result of the prior negligent conduct. The rationale behind this rule is that it would be unfair to impose a duty upon persons to prevent a harm that they could not foresee or avoid.

Here, appellants assert that as a result of appellee's negligent representation decedent committed suicide. More specifically, appellants claim that decedent committed suicide while possessed by an uncontrollable insane frenzy brought on by the jury's verdict of guilty. Appellants further allege that appellee knew of decedent's emotional problems because they were manifested by the uncontrollable twitching of his limbs and his prior expressed intention to take his own life. Appellants therefore argue that decedent's suicide was foreseeable, and that appellee's negligent legal representation was the direct cause. The trial court, in sustaining appellee's preliminary objections, stated that:

> The court concludes as a matter of law, assuming the malpractice or negligence of [appellee] is true as alleged, that jumping out of a window is not foreseeable and therefore the alleged actions or omissions of [appellee] are not the proximate or legal cause of [decedent's] injuries. The court will not elaborate further as this issue is a matter of common sense.

Our research has revealed only one reported case which deals directly with suicide as the alleged result of legal malpractice. In *McLaughlin v. Sullivan,* 123 N.H. 335, 461 A.2d 123 (1983), the New Hampshire Supreme Court rejected a wrongful death claim brought against an attorney based upon his client's suicide following the client's conviction in a criminal case. The issue presented in *McLaughlin,* as here, was whether, as a matter of law, legal malpractice could be a legal or proximate cause of suicide. The Court held that a lawyer's duty of representation does not extend to protecting a client from his suicidal tendencies, and thus, proximate causation could not be established as a matter of law. We agree with the *McLaughlin* Court and adopt its holding as a matter of Pennsylvania law.

The duty of an attorney in a criminal case is to provide competent legal representation to his client. If an attorney does not provide adequate representation, he has breached his duty and is liable to his client for the resulting injuries. An attorney, however, is responsible only for the loss proximately caused his client by his negligence. Suicide has been recognized as an act that is so extraordinary as not to be reasonably foreseeable and thus courts have held that it is not the type of harm that can proximately result from ordinary negligence.[13]

The exceptions to this rule usually involve defendants with some special knowledge or duty, such as institutions, hospitals, and mental health professionals. An attorney, unlike a hospital or mental health professionals, has no special expertise or professional training, that would enable him either to foresee that a client is likely to commit suicide, or, if he could make that determination, to adopt a response to the threat. The *McLaughlin* Court's reasoning in this regard is instructive:

> [W]e do not believe that lawyers generally have either the expertise or training necessary to judge or foresee that a client will commit

---

[13] We note that the allegations in appellants' complaint are limited to ordinary negligence. Because appellants' proceeded solely under this theory, we need not address the question whether liability may be premised upon a suicide caused by alleged intentional misconduct

suicide, or to fashion appropriate responses to a risk. It follows that such a risk should not be found to be a hazard against which a lawyer can fairly be said to have the duty to guard. We find the connection between negligence in the practice of law, and the harm which befell the decedent in the case to be simply too attenuated to impose legal liability on the part of the defendant. *Id.* at 342, 461 A.2d at 127–28.

Because an attorney does not possess the ability either to perceive that a client is likely to commit suicide, or to prevent the suicide, we will not impose liability upon him for failing to prevent a harm that is not a foreseeable result of prior negligent conduct.[14]

Moreover, we agree with the *McLaughlin* Court that, as a matter of policy, it would be inappropriate to impose liability upon an attorney for a suicide that allegedly resulted from his negligence. To impose liability based on a client's suicide

> would undoubtedly open the floodgates of unexpected and inequitable liability on the part of attorneys. Neither are we unmindful of the fact that attorneys, if exposed to such liability, would naturally be discouraged from representing what may be a sizeable number of depressed or unstable criminal defendants, in the fear that it would later be alleged that one such client committed suicide out of despondence over a "wrongful" conviction based on inadequate representation. *Id.* at 342–47, 461 A.2d at 127–28.

In light of the foregoing, we find, as a matter of law, that the alleged negligence of appellee could not be the proximate cause of decedent's injuries, and thus we hold that an attorney's duty to provide adequate representation does not encompass the duty to foresee and protect a client from his own possible suicidal tendencies. Thus, even assuming that appellee negligently represented the decedent, he cannot be held liable for decedent's subsequent suicide. We therefore conclude that the trial court properly granted appellee's preliminary objections and that appellants' negligence action seeking damages for decedent's suicide was properly dismissed. Accordingly, we affirm the order below.

NOTES

1. *Suicide — Deliberating the Act.* Contrast *Fuller v. Preis,* 35 N.Y.2d 425, 322 N.E.2d 263, 363 N.Y.S.2d 568 (1974), in which the court held that the plaintiff could recover in a wrongful death action for the suicide of plaintiff's deceased, committed some seven months after the deceased was severely injured in an automobile accident negligently caused by the defendant. Recovery was conditioned on a showing by the plaintiff that the deceased committed suicide as the result of an "irresistible impulse" arising from his automobile accident injuries. In a similar case, *Grant v. F.P. Lathrop Constr.*

---

[14] We note that other jurisdictions have recognized that liability should not be imposed upon an attorney for failing to prevent an unforeseeable harm. *See Gautam v. De Luca,* 215 N.J. Super. 388, 521 A.2d 1343 (1987) (claim for negligent infliction of emotional distress rejected in malpractice setting since it is not ordinarily situation in which it is foreseeable that failure to provide effective representation may cause serious mental distress).

Co., 81 Cal. App. 3d 790, 146 Cal. Rptr. 45 (1978), the court held the plaintiff could recover if he showed the deceased committed suicide as the result of an "uncontrollable impulse." Why require proof of "irresistible" or "uncontrollable" impulse?

In *Pigney v. Pointers Transp. Serv.,* [1957] All E.R. 807, plaintiff's deceased committed suicide as a result of anxiety, neurosis and depression from an accident negligently caused by the defendant. Relying on *Polemis,* the court held that the deceased's surviving spouse could recover, although the evidence indicated that the deceased was sane when he took his life. The court held that while it would be against public policy for the deceased to benefit from his own wrong, nevertheless his surviving spouse could recover because she was "prosecuting a statutory cause of action under the Fatal Accidents Act of 1846, which does not benefit the estate of her deceased husband." How would the case be decided under *The Wagon Mound*?

See also *Stafford v. Neurological Med., Inc.,* 811 F.2d 470 (8th Cir. 1987), in which a successfully recovering cancer patient received a CAT scan to determine whether the cancer had spread to her brain. The scan was correctly interpreted by the defendant as revealing no cancer. The defendant then submitted its bill for this diagnosis to the regional fiscal Medicare intermediary. Because of some previous problems with the intermediary, the defendant entered "brain tumor" rather than "R/O [rule out] brain tumor" in the box on the form requiring diagnosis. The patient eventually received a copy of the form, and, shortly thereafter, committed suicide. The federal court applied Missouri law and held that the plaintiff's expert testimony and circumstantial evidence had created a jury issue on the question of proximate cause. Why proximate cause? Why not duty? Another judicial sleight of hand?

2. *The Agitated Client.* The court stated the facts in *Wellons v. Grayson,* 583 So. 2d 1166 (La. App. 1991), as follows:

> On May 13, 1987, plaintiff, an attorney whose office was located at 1160 Florida Street, in Baton Rouge, Louisiana, was standing on the front porch of his office discussing a case with his law partner, when defendant Scott, whose office was immediately adjacent to that of plaintiff's, at 1150 Florida Street, came out to the front porch of his office with his former client, Eddie Lee Grayson. Both plaintiff and defendants separately leased their respective premises; the porches of the two buildings are approximately eight feet apart.
>
> Scott had previously represented Grayson in a criminal proceeding as part of his duties as Assistant Public Defender in City Court in Baton Rouge, and Grayson had later retained Scott to represent him in a civil matter. Grayson discharged Scott and retained new counsel some six months before the incident at issue in this lawsuit, and a dispute had arisen between Scott and Grayson concerning the return of a retainer fee of $75.00 which Grayson had paid to Scott. Grayson had telephoned Scott's office and had visited, unannounced, on several occasions, demanding the return of his money. Scott had learned during his earlier representation of Grayson that he had been hospitalized in mental institutions and was mentally unstable.

I. SUICIDE AND OTHER DAMAGES 501

On May 13, 1987, Grayson had arrived at Scott's office and once again demanded the return of the retainer fee. Because he had a client waiting to see him when he came downstairs and saw Grayson, Scott asked Grayson to step outside on the porch with him. The two men were talking, and Grayson demanded the return of $75.00. Scott refused, and Grayson, saying "I'll get my money," went into his waistband with his right hand and pulled out a gun wrapped in a white handkerchief. Grayson shot once, and he and Scott began wrestling on the porch; they fell, and while the two were fighting on the ground, Grayson shot an additional three times. Scott, realizing he could not get the gun away from Grayson, jumped back on the porch and ran into the office building; one more shot was fired at that point by Grayson. A constable from City Court, located down the street from Scott's office, heard the shots, saw Grayson running down the street, and apprehended him. Grayson was charged with attempted murder, but was found mentally incompetent to stand trial.

In the meantime, plaintiff and his law partner witnessed the entire episode. Plaintiff testified in his deposition, as did his law partner, Gail McKay, that Scott was "intimidating" Grayson and hollering, screaming, and "talking all kind of crazy talk" to him. Scott was physically larger than Grayson. Scott testified he spoke calmly to Grayson.

When Grayson shot at Scott the first time, McKay ran for the door of their office; plaintiff turned and ran away from the direction of the gunshots. While running, he fell off the porch, sustaining serious injuries to his leg. He heard five more shots. Convinced that McKay and Scott, who were both unarmed, were dead, he crawled under the side of his porch on his uninjured leg to hide from Grayson. An ambulance arrived about fifteen minutes later and extricated plaintiff from under the porch. Plaintiff was hospitalized for three weeks after his accident; his injuries included a shattered kneecap and several broken bones in his leg.

In holding that defendant Scott and his partnership were not liable to plaintiff Wellons for his injuries, the court said:

No facts whatsoever in the record establish that Grayson's action in shooting Scott was in any way foreseeable by him. Although Scott was aware of Grayson's past mental problems and criminal record, plaintiff presented no further evidence to indicate that defendants knew Grayson was armed, or that he would attempt to shoot Scott. Defendants' secretary testified that she believed Grayson was mentally deficient, but not that he was capable of violence. Obviously Scott, had he been aware of Grayson's propensity for violence, would have taken the precaution of arming himself against him, or of evicting Grayson from his premises.

3. *Impolite Driving.* The plaintiff, Bansasine, brought suit against defendant Rajsavong for the wrongful death of her father, a passenger in defendant's car:

Rajsavong was driving northbound on Interstate 15 with plaintiff's father when Lucas Bodell drove up close behind them, blinding Rajsavong with his lights. Rajsavong changed lanes, letting Bodell pass. Angered at being blinded, Rajsavong got behind Bodell and flipped on his high beams. He then sped up, passed Bodell, and changed back into the lane in which Bodell was driving. In response, Bodell drove up parallel to Rajsavong on the passenger side. Rajsavong then sped up to seventy-five miles per hour only to have Bodell follow suit. As Bodell caught up with Rajsavong, plaintiff's father made an obscene gesture at Bodell. Bodell pulled out a gun and displayed it in his palm. Rajsavong sped up in an effort to get away from Bodell. As Bodell drove by in his truck, Rajsavong heard a "bang," and plaintiff's father told Rajsavong that he had been shot. Rajsavong took plaintiff's father to a hospital, where he later died. . . .

We conclude the trial court was correct in determining that a reasonable juror could not have found that defendant's driving was the proximate cause of the death of plaintiff's father. We agree that a reasonable juror could not find that defendant should foresee that another driver on the road would fire a gun into his car simply because he shined his high beams on that person, passed him, then sped up as the driver tried to approach. If such a response were so common as to make it foreseeable, the streets and highways of this country would be empty.

Plaintiff next claims that it is enough to prove only that defendant could have foreseen the general risk of harm that occurred. Specifically, plaintiff argues that defendant could reasonably foresee that aggressive behavior of some kind might be a response to his rude driving, which is exactly what occurred although the specific action was different from what might reasonably be expected, *i.e.*, a car accident or running the defendant off the road. While we agree that "only the general nature of the injury need be foreseeable," *Steffensen v. Smith's Management Corp.*, 862 P.2d 1342, 1346 (Utah 1993), plaintiff goes too far in defining what "general nature" means. As the RESTATEMENT (SECOND) OF TORTS § 442B (1965) states:

> Where the negligent conduct of the actor creates or increases the risk of a particular harm and is a substantial factor in causing that harm the fact that the harm is brought about through the intervention of another force does not relieve the actor of liability, except where the harm is intentionally caused by a third person and *is not within the scope of the risk created by the actor's conduct*. (Emphasis added.) Although we recognize that many aspects of today's society are becoming more violent and confrontational, we cannot conclude that a gunshot is within the scope of the risk created by defendant's rude and reckless driving.

Finally, plaintiff argues that defendant only needed to be able to foresee the injury that occurred, i.e., death, and not the specific means that caused that injury. In particular, plaintiff claims that because death was a foreseeable outcome of reckless driving—such as through a collision or being run off the road—it does not matter that the death resulted from a gunshot. Plaintiff misperceives the law. While plaintiff again correctly states that only the "general nature of the injury need be foreseeable," *Steffensen*, 862 P.2d at 1346, plaintiff misunderstands its meaning. In this case, the general nature of the injury is not death. Rather, death is the result of the injury; the injury was a gunshot wound. Thus, as above, for plaintiff to prevail, defendant must have been able to foresee that his reckless driving might lead to a shooting. As previously stated, defendant could not have foreseen this result, and thus, his reckless driving could not have been the proximate cause of plaintiff's injuries.

Bansasine v. Bodell, 927 P.2d 675 (Utah Ct. App. 1996). Does this case leave the general-specific "principle" of foreseeability-proximate cause in shambles?

4. *The Unforeseeable Divorce.* The defendant doctor iN *Chizmar v. Mackie*, 896 P.2d 196 (Alaska 1995), erroneously reported to plaintiff patient and her husband that she had tested positive for human immunodeficiency virus (HIV). It was later determined that the test was a false positive.

Plaintiff sued for emotional distress. She also sought damages for economic loss resulting from her divorce, which she claimed was brought about by defendant Mackie's negligent testing and by his wrongfully advising her husband of the test results. Denying the claim for economic loss resulting from the divorce, the court said:

> As Dr. Mackie argues in his brief, divorce is never the direct result of actions by a third-party tortfeasor. It is the character of the spouses, and the character of the marriage itself, which determines whether a divorce will occur. Clearly, a variety of outcomes may result from a diagnosis of AIDS, ranging from bringing the married couple closer together to driving them apart. To hold a third-party responsible for economic losses resulting from a divorce in such a case would extend potential liability too far.

5. *"Pre-Accident" or "Accident" Injury?* The foregoing discussion of the extent of the defendant's responsibility for the plaintiff's injuries is premised on the ability to discriminate between those items of plaintiff's damages existing prior to and following the accident. However, consider *La Moureaux v. Totem Ocean Trailer Express, Inc.*, 632 P.2d 539 (Alaska 1981), *on reh.* 651 P.2d 839 (Alaska 1982). Plaintiff suffered from a preexisting condition (injury "A"), which was aggravated by the accident caused by the tortfeasor (injury "B"). In addition, plaintiff suffered other injuries related solely to the accident (injury "C"). Clearly, defendant is responsible for "C" and, because of the thin-skull rule, for "B." Equally clearly, the defendant is not responsible for "A." The question, however, is who has the burden of distinguishing between "A" and "B?" In *La Moureaux,* the plaintiff had requested an instruction that if the jury could not distinguish between "A" and "B," then the defendant was responsible for both "A" and "B," effectively shifting the burden of proof on the issue. The appellate court upheld the trial court's refusal to give that instruction. Since both the pre-existing condition and the post-accident injuries were the plaintiff's, it was *the plaintiff* who was in the best position

to come forward with discriminating evidence. *But see Tolan v. ERA Helicopters, Inc.,* 699 P.2d 1265, 1272 (Alaska 1985) ("A statement to the jury as to the plaintiff's burden, without qualification as to the relaxed requirement of proof on this issue, may be inappropriate"). A shift in the burden of proof was, however, approved in *Bigley v. Craven,* 769 P.2d 892, 898 (Wyo. 1989), as follows:

> [If] the record contains conflicting evidence on whether or not apportionment can be made, then a question of fact is presented which the jury as fact finder must resolve under proper instructions. Part of those instructions must include the charge that if the jury is unable to apportion the plaintiff's disability between preexisting and accident-caused conditions, then the defendant is liable for the entire disability.

J. EMOTIONAL DISTRESS INJURIES

PROBLEM

Husband and Friend recklessly engage in a motorcycle race, and Husband is seriously injured as a result. Can Husband's Wife recover from Husband or from Friend for infliction of emotional distress or for loss of consortium?

CONSOLIDATED RAIL CORP. v. GOTSHALL
512 U. S. 532 (1994)

JUSTICE THOMAS delivered the opinion of the Court.

These cases require us to determine the proper standard for evaluating claims for negligent infliction of emotional distress that are brought under the Federal Employers' Liability Act. Because the standard adopted by the Court of Appeals is inconsistent with the principles embodied in the statute and with relevant common-law doctrine, we reverse the judgments below.

Respondents James Gottshall and Alan Carlisle each brought suit under the Federal Employers' Liability Act (FELA), 45 U.S.C. §§ 51–60, against their former employer, petitioner Consolidated Rail Corporation (Conrail). We set forth the facts of each case in turn.

Gottshall was a member of a Conrail work crew assigned to replace a stretch of defective track on an extremely hot and humid day. The crew was under time pressure, and so the men were discouraged from taking scheduled breaks. They were, however, allowed to obtain water as needed. Two and one-half hours into the job, a worker named Richard Johns, a longtime friend of Gottshall, collapsed. Gottshall and several others rushed to help Johns, who was pale and sweating profusely. They were able to revive him by administering a cold compress. Michael Norvick, the crew supervisor, then ordered the men to stop assisting Johns and to return to work. Five minutes later, Gottshall again went to Johns' aid after seeing his friend stand up and collapse. Realizing that Johns was having a heart attack, Gottshall began cardiopulmonary resuscitation. He continued the process for 40 minutes.

Meanwhile, Norvick attempted to summon assistance, but found that his radio was inoperative; unbeknownst to him, Conrail had temporarily taken the nearest base station off the air for repairs. Norvick drove off to get help, but by the time he returned with paramedics, Johns had died. The paramedics covered the body with a sheet, ordered that it remain undisturbed until the coroner could examine it, and directed the crew not to leave until the coroner had arrived. Norvick ordered the men back to work, within sight of Johns' covered body. The coroner, who arrived several hours later, reported that Johns had died from a heart attack brought on by the combined factors of heat, humidity, and heavy exertion.

The entire experience left Gottshall extremely agitated and distraught. Over the next several days, during which he continued to work in hot and humid weather conditions, Gottshall began to feel ill. He became preoccupied with the events surrounding Johns' death, and worried that he would die under similar circumstances. Shortly after Johns' funeral, Gottshall was admitted to a psychiatric institution, where he was diagnosed as suffering from major depression and post-traumatic stress disorder. During the three weeks he spent at the institution, Gottshall experienced nausea, insomnia, cold sweats, and repetitive nightmares concerning Johns' death. He lost a great deal of weight and suffered from suicidal preoccupations and anxiety. Gottshall has continued to receive psychological treatment since his discharge from the hospital.

Gottshall sued Conrail under FELA for negligent infliction of emotional distress. He alleged that Conrail's negligence had created the circumstances under which he had been forced to observe and participate in the events surrounding Johns' death. The District Court granted Conrail's motion for summary judgment, holding that FELA did not provide a remedy for Gottshall's emotional injuries.

A divided panel of the United States Court of Appeals for the Third Circuit reversed and remanded for trial. *Gottshall v. Consolidated Rail Corp.*, 988 F.2d 355 (1993). The court observed that most States recognize a common-law cause of action for negligent infliction of emotional distress, but limit recovery to certain classes of plaintiffs or categories of claims through the application of one or more tests. Id., at 361 (discussing "physical impact," "zone of danger," and "relative bystander" tests). The Third Circuit suggested that because "an emotional injury is easier to fake" than a physical injury, these tests have been "judicially developed to screen causes of action and send only the meritorious ones to juries." Ibid.

The court below identified what it considered to be a fundamental tension between the restrictive attitude of the common law toward claims for negligent infliction of emotional distress on the one hand, and the general policy underlying FELA on the other. According to the Third Circuit, the common law places harsh and arbitrary limits on recovery for emotional injury, while FELA has consistently been interpreted to accord liberal relief to railroad workers injured through the negligence of their employers.

In the Third Circuit's view, the only way to reconcile the apparent tension was to give preference to the liberal recovery policy embodied in FELA over the common law: "[D]octrinal common law distinctions are to be discarded when they bar recovery on meritorious FELA claims." Id., at 369. Determining that judges could weed out fraudulent emotional injury claims through careful scrutiny of the facts, the court held that the facts alleged in support of a claim under FELA for negligent infliction of emotional distress must "provide a threshold assurance that there is a likelihood of genuine and serious emotional injury." Id., at 371. The Third Circuit suggested that a court's factual inquiry might include consideration of the plaintiff's claim in light of the present state of the common law.

After reviewing the facts of Gottshall's case, the Third Circuit concluded that Gottshall had made a sufficient showing that his injuries were genuine and severe. Because his claim had met the court's threshold "genuineness" test, the court next considered whether the claim adequately alleged the usual FELA elements of breach of a duty of care (that is, conduct unreasonable in the face of a foreseeable risk of harm), injury, and causation. The panel majority concluded that there were genuine issues of material fact concerning whether Gottshall's injuries were foreseeable by Conrail, whether Conrail had acted unreasonably, and whether Conrail's conduct had caused cognizable injury to Gottshall. The court therefore remanded for trial.

Judge Roth dissented in part because she believed that there was no triable issue regarding breach of duty. She reasoned that "outside of the interruption of the communications link, the allegedly negligent conditions created by Conrail at the time of Johns' collapse consisted in fact of the members of the work gang performing the negotiated duties of their jobs under conditions which may indeed have been difficult but which had occurred in the past and will probably occur again in the future." Id., at 385. In her view, these negotiated duties could not support a finding of negligence. Judge Roth concluded that "Conrail could not reasonably have foreseen that its negligence in interrupting the work gang's communication[s] link might cause James Gottshall's severe emotional reaction to the death of Richard Johns." Id., at 386.

Respondent Carlisle began working as a train dispatcher for Conrail in 1976. In this position, he was responsible for ensuring the safe and timely movement of passengers and cargo. Aging railstock and outdated equipment made Carlisle's job difficult. Reductions in Conrail's work force required Carlisle to take on additional duties and to work long hours. Carlisle and his fellow dispatchers frequently complained about safety concerns, the high level of stress in their jobs, and poor working conditions. In 1988, Carlisle became trainmaster in the South Philadelphia yards. With this promotion came added responsibilities that forced him to work erratic hours. Carlisle began to experience insomnia, headaches, depression, and weight loss. After an extended period during which he was required to work 12-to 15-hour shifts for weeks at a time, Carlisle suffered a nervous breakdown.

Carlisle sued Conrail under FELA for negligent infliction of emotional distress. He alleged that Conrail had breached its duty to provide him with a safe workplace by forcing him to work under unreasonably stressful conditions, and that this breach had resulted in foreseeable stress-related health problems. At trial, Carlisle called medical experts who testified that his breakdown and ensuing severe depression were caused at least in part by the strain of his job. The jury awarded Carlisle $386,500 in damages.

The Third Circuit affirmed, "uphold[ing] for the first time a claim under the FELA for negligent infliction of emotional distress arising from work-related stress." *Carlisle v. Consolidated Rail Corp.*, 990 F.2d 90, 97–98 (1993). In rejecting Conrail's argument that Carlisle had failed to make out a claim under FELA because he had not alleged any accident or physical injury or impact, the court noted that in *Gottshall* (decided the month before), it had "upheld recovery under the FELA for negligent infliction of emotional distress without proof of any physical impact." 990 F.2d, at 96. Restating its holding in *Gottshall*, the court advised that, when evaluating a claim under FELA for negligently inflicted emotional distress, district courts within the Third Circuit "should engage in an initial review of the factual indicia of the genuineness of a claim, taking into account broadly used common law standards, then should apply the traditional negligence elements of duty, foreseeability, breach, and causation in weighing the merits of that claim." 990 F.2d, at 98.

In the case before it, however, the court did not examine Carlisle's suit in light of any of the various common-law tests for dealing with negligent infliction of emotional distress claims. Instead, it shifted its primary emphasis to the foreseeability of the alleged injury and held that "when it is reasonably foreseeable that extended exposure to dangerous and stressful working conditions will cause injury to the worker, the employer may be held to be liable under the FELA for the employee's resulting injuries." Id., at 97. The Third Circuit held that Carlisle had produced sufficient evidence that his injury had been foreseeable to Conrail. The court also found sufficient evidence that Conrail had breached its duty to provide Carlisle with a safe workplace by making his employment too demanding, and that this breach had caused Carlisle's injury.

Pursuant to this Court's Rule 12.2, Conrail petitioned for review of the Third Circuit's decisions in Gottshall and Carlisle. We granted certiorari to resolve a conflict among the Courts of Appeals concerning the threshold standard that must be met by plaintiffs bringing claims for negligent infliction of emotional distress under FELA.

In these cases, we address questions left unanswered in *Atchison, T. & S.F.R. Co. v. Buell*, 480 U.S. 557, 107 S.Ct. 1410, 94 L.Ed.2d 563 (1987). . . . Today, we must resolve one of the questions reserved in *Buell*: whether recovery for negligent infliction of emotional distress is available under FELA.[2] If we conclude that it is, we must consider the proper scope of that availability. Our FELA jurisprudence outlines the analysis we must undertake when deciding whether, and to what extent, this new category of claims should be cognizable under the statute.

First, as in other cases involving the scope of the statute, we must look to FELA itself, its purposes and background, and the construction we have given it over the years. . . .

We turn first to the statute. Section 1 of FELA provides that "[e]very common carrier by railroad . . . shall be liable in damages to any person suffering injury while he is employed by such carrier . . . for such injury or death resulting in whole or in part from the negligence of any of the officers, agents, or employees of such carrier." 45 U.S.C. § 51. Our task today is determining under what circumstances emotional distress may constitute "injury" resulting from "negligence" for purposes of the statute. . . . Cognizant of the

---

[2] We are not concerned here with the separate tort of intentional infliction of emotional distress.

physical dangers of railroading that resulted in the death or maiming of thousands of workers every year, Congress crafted a federal remedy that shifted part of the " 'human overhead' " of doing business from employees to their employers. *Tiller v. Atlantic Coast Line R. Co.*, 318 U.S. 54, 58, 63 S.Ct. 444, 446–447, 87 L.Ed. 610 (1943). *See also Wilkerson v. McCarthy*, 336 U.S. 53, 68, 69 S.Ct. 413, 420, 93 L.Ed. 497 (1949) (Douglas, J., concurring) (FELA "was designed to put on the railroad industry some of the cost for the legs, eyes, arms, and lives which it consumed in its operations"). In order to further FELA's humanitarian purposes, Congress did away with several common-law tort defenses that had effectively barred recovery by injured workers. Specifically, the statute abolished the fellow servant rule, rejected the doctrine of contributory negligence in favor of that of comparative negligence, and prohibited employers from exempting themselves from FELA through contract; a 1939 amendment abolished the assumption of risk defense. See 45 U.S.C. §§ 51, 53–55.

We have liberally construed FELA to further Congress' remedial goal. For example, we held in *Rogers v. Missouri Pacific R. Co.*, 352 U.S. 500, 77 S.Ct. 443, 1 L.Ed.2d 493 (1957), that a relaxed standard of causation applies under FELA. We stated that "[u]nder this statute the test of a jury case is simply whether the proofs justify with reason the conclusion that employer negligence played any part, even the slightest, in producing the injury or death for which damages are sought." Id., at 506, 77 S.Ct., at 448. In *Kernan*, we extended the reach of the principle of negligence per se to cover injuries suffered by employees as a result of their employers' statutory violations, even if the injuries sustained were not of a type that the relevant statute sought to prevent. 355 U.S., at 432–436, 78 S.Ct., at 398–400. And in *Urie*, we held that occupational diseases such as silicosis constitute compensable physical injuries under FELA, thereby rejecting the argument that the statute covered only injuries and deaths caused by accidents. 337 U.S., at 181, 69 S.Ct., at 1030.

That FELA is to be liberally construed, however, does not mean that it is a workers' compensation statute. We have insisted that FELA "does not make the employer the insurer of the safety of his employees while they are on duty. The basis of his liability is his negligence, not the fact that injuries occur." *Ellis v. Union Pacific R. Co.*, 329 U.S. 649, 653, 67 S.Ct. 598, 600, 91 L.Ed. 572 (1947). . . . Because FELA is silent on the issue of negligent infliction of emotional distress, common-law principles must play a significant role in our decision.

We turn, therefore, to consider the right of recovery pursued by respondents in light of the common law. The term "negligent infliction of emotional distress" is largely self-explanatory, but a definitional point should be clarified at the outset. The injury we contemplate when considering negligent infliction of emotional distress is mental or emotional injury, apart from the tort law concepts of pain and suffering. Although pain and suffering technically are mental harms, these terms traditionally "have been used to describe sensations stemming directly from a physical injury or condition." Pearson, Liability to Bystanders for Negligently Inflicted Emotional Harm—A Comment on the Nature of Arbitrary Rules, 34 U.Fla.L.Rev. 477, 485, n. 45 (1982). The injury we deal with here is mental or emotional harm (such as fright or anxiety) that is caused by the negligence of another and that is not directly brought about by a physical injury, but that may manifest itself in physical symptoms.

Nearly all of the States have recognized a right to recover for negligent infliction of emotional distress, as we have defined it. No jurisdiction, however, allows recovery for all emotional harms, no matter how intangible or trivial, that might be causally linked to the negligence of another. Indeed, significant limitations, taking the form of "tests" or "rules," are placed by the common law on the right to recover for negligently inflicted emotional distress, and have been since the right was first recognized late in the last century.

Behind these limitations lie a variety of policy considerations, many of them based on the fundamental differences between emotional and physical injuries. "Because the etiology of emotional disturbance is usually not as readily apparent as that of a broken bone following an automobile accident, courts have been concerned . . . that recognition of a cause of action for [emotional] injury when not related to any physical trauma may inundate judicial resources with a flood of relatively trivial claims, many of which may be imagined or falsified, and that liability may be imposed for highly remote consequences of a negligent act." *Maloney v. Conroy*, 208 Conn. 392, 397–398, 545 A.2d 1059, 1061 (1988). The last concern has been particularly significant. Emotional injuries may occur far removed in time and space from the negligent conduct that triggered them. Moreover, in contrast to the situation with physical injury, there are no necessary finite limits on the number of persons who might suffer emotional injury as a result of a given negligent act. The incidence and severity of emotional injuries are also more difficult to predict than those of typical physical injuries because they depend on psychological factors that ordinarily are not apparent to potential tortfeasors.

For all of these reasons, courts have realized that recognition of a cause of action for negligent infliction of emotional distress holds out the very real possibility of nearly infinite and unpredictable liability for defendants. Courts therefore have placed substantial limitations on the class of plaintiffs that may recover for emotional injuries and on the injuries that may be compensable. *See, e.g., Thing v. La Chusa*, 48 Cal.3d 644, 654, 257 Cal.Rptr. 865, 870, 771 P.2d 814, 819 (1989) ("[P]olicy considerations mandat[e] that infinite liability be avoided by restrictions that . . . narrow the class of potential plaintiffs"); *Tobin v. Grossman*, 24 N.Y.2d 609, 616, 301 N.Y.S.2d 554, 559, 249 N.E.2d 419, 423 (1969). Some courts phrase the limitations in terms of proximate causation; that is, only certain plaintiffs or injuries are reasonably foreseeable. Other courts speak of the limitations in terms of duty; the defendant owes only a certain class of plaintiffs a duty to avoid inflicting emotional harm. These formulations are functionally equivalent. We shall refer to the common-law limitations as outlining the duty of defendants with regard to negligent infliction of emotional distress.

Three major limiting tests for evaluating claims alleging negligent infliction of emotional distress have developed in the common law. The first of these has come to be known as the "physical impact" test. It originated a century ago in some of the first cases recognizing recovery for negligently inflicted emotional distress. At the time Congress enacted FELA in 1908, most of the major industrial States had embraced this test. Under the physical impact test, a plaintiff seeking damages for emotional injury stemming from a negligent act must have contemporaneously sustained a physical impact (no matter how slight) or injury due to the defendant's conduct. Most jurisdictions have abandoned this test, but at least five States continue to adhere to it.

The second test has come to be referred to as the "zone of danger" test. It came into use at roughly the same time as the physical impact test, and had been adopted by several jurisdictions at the time FELA was enacted. Perhaps based on the realization that "a near miss may be as frightening as a direct hit," Pearson, 34 U.Fla.L.Rev., at 488, the zone of danger test limits recovery for emotional injury to those plaintiffs who sustain a physical impact as a result of a defendant's negligent conduct, or who are placed in immediate risk of physical harm by that conduct. That is, "those within the zone of danger of physical impact can recover for fright, and those outside of it cannot." Id., at 489. The zone of danger test currently is followed in 14 jurisdictions.

The third prominent limiting test is the "relative bystander" test, which was first enunciated in *Dillon v. Legg*, 68 Cal.2d 728, 69 Cal.Rptr. 72, 441 P.2d 912 (1968). In *Dillon*, the California Supreme Court rejected the zone of danger test and suggested that the availability of recovery should turn, for the most part, on whether the defendant could reasonably have foreseen the emotional injury to the plaintiff. The court offered three factors to be considered as bearing on the question of reasonable foreseeability:

> "(1) Whether plaintiff was located near the scene of the accident as contrasted with one who was a distance away from it. (2) Whether the shock resulted from a direct emotional impact upon plaintiff from the sensory and contemporaneous observance of the accident, as contrasted with learning of the accident from others after its occurrence. (3) Whether plaintiff and the victim were closely related, as contrasted with an absence of any relationship or the presence of only a distant relationship." Id., at 740–741, 69 Cal.Rptr., at 80, 441 P.2d, at 920.

The courts of nearly half the States now allow bystanders outside of the zone of danger to obtain recovery in certain circumstances for emotional distress brought on by witnessing the injury or death of a third party (who typically must be a close relative of the bystander) that is caused by the defendant's negligence. Most of these jurisdictions have adopted the *Dillon* factors either verbatim or with variations and additions, and have held some or all of these factors to be substantive limitations on recovery.[11]

Having laid out the relevant legal framework, we turn to the questions presented. As an initial matter, we agree with the Third Circuit that claims for damages for negligent infliction of emotional distress are cognizable under FELA. A combination of many of the factors discussed above makes this conclusion an easy one. A right to recover for negligently inflicted emotional distress was recognized in some form by many American jurisdictions at the time FELA was enacted, and this right is nearly universally recognized among

---

[11] Many jurisdictions that follow the zone of danger or relative bystander tests also require that a plaintiff demonstrate a "physical manifestation" of an alleged emotional injury, that is, a physical injury or effect that is the direct result of the emotional injury, in order to recover. *See, e.g., Garvis v. Employers Mut. Casualty Co.*, 497 N.W.2d 254 (Minn.1993).

the States today. Moreover, we have accorded broad scope to the statutory term "injury" in the past in light of FELA's remedial purposes. . . .

When setting out its view of the proper scope of recovery for negligently inflicted emotional distress under FELA, the Third Circuit explicitly refused to adopt any of the common-law tests described above; indeed, the court in *Gottshall* went so far as to state that "doctrinal common law distinctions are to be discarded when they bar recovery on meritorious FELA claims." 988 F.2d, at 369. Instead, the court developed its own test, under which "[t]he issue is whether the factual circumstances . . . provide a threshold assurance that there is a likelihood of genuine and serious emotional injury." Id., at 371. If this threshold test is satisfied, the claim should be evaluated in light of traditional tort concepts such as breach of duty, injury, and causation, with the focus resting on the foreseeability of the plaintiff's injury. In Gottshall, the Third Circuit did at least consider the plaintiff's claim in light of the common law of negligent infliction of emotional distress as part of its factual "genuineness" inquiry. By the time the court next applied the *Gottshall* genuineness test, however, the common-law aspect of its analysis had completely disappeared; *Carlisle's* stress-related claim was not evaluated under any of the common-law tests. In *Carlisle*, the Third Circuit refined its test to two questions—whether there was convincing evidence of the genuineness of the emotional injury claim (with "genuine" meaning authentic and serious), and if there was, whether the injury was foreseeable. If these questions could be answered affirmatively by the court, there was "no bar to recovery under the FELA." 990 F.2d, at 98.

The Third Circuit's standard is fatally flawed in a number of respects. First, as discussed above, because negligent infliction of emotional distress is not explicitly addressed in the statute, the common-law background of this right of recovery must play a vital role in giving content to the scope of an employer's duty under FELA to avoid inflicting emotional injury. . . .

Perhaps the court below believed that its focus on the perceived genuineness of the claimed emotional injury adequately addressed the concerns of the common-law courts in dealing with emotional injury claims. But the potential for fraudulent and trivial claims—the concern identified by the Third Circuit—is only one of the difficulties created by allowing actions for negligently inflicted emotional distress. A more significant problem is the prospect that allowing such suits can lead to unpredictable and nearly infinite liability for defendants. The common law consistently has sought to place limits on this potential liability by restricting the class of plaintiffs who may recover and the types of harm for which plaintiffs may recover. This concern underlying the common-law tests has nothing to do with the potential for fraudulent claims; on the contrary, it is based upon the recognized possibility of genuine claims from the essentially infinite number of persons, in an infinite variety of situations, who might suffer real emotional harm as a result of a single instance of negligent conduct.

Second, we question the viability of the genuineness test on its own terms. The Third Circuit recognized that "there must be some finite limit to the railway's potential liability" for emotional injury claims under FELA, and suggested that liability could be restricted through application of the genuineness test. *Gottshall*, supra, at 379. But as just explained, testing for the "genuineness" of an injury alone cannot appreciably diminish the possibility of infinite liability. Such a fact-specific test, moreover, would be bound to lead to haphazard results. Judges would be forced to make highly subjective determinations concerning the authenticity of claims for emotional injury, which are far less susceptible to objective medical proof than are their physical counterparts. To the extent the genuineness test could limit potential liability, it could do so only inconsistently. Employers such as Conrail would be given no standard against which to regulate their conduct under such an ad hoc approach. In the context of claims for intangible harms brought under a negligence statute, we find such an arbitrary result unacceptable. Cf. Stadler v. Cross, 295 N.W.2d 552, 554 (Minn.1980).

Third, to the extent the Third Circuit relied on the concept of foreseeability as a meaningful limitation on liability, we believe that reliance to be misplaced. If one takes a broad enough view, all consequences of a negligent act, no matter how far removed in time or space, may be foreseen. Conditioning liability on foreseeability, therefore, is hardly a condition at all. "Every injury has ramifying consequences, like the ripplings of the waters, without end. The problem for the law is to limit the legal consequences of wrongs to a controllable degree." *Tobin*, 24 N.Y.2d, at 619, 301 N.Y.S.2d, at 560, 249 N.E.2d, at 424. See also Thing, 48 Cal.3d, at 668, 257 Cal.Rptr., at 881, 771 P.2d, at 830 ("[T]here are clear judicial days on which a court can foresee forever and thus determine liability but none on which that foresight alone provides a socially and judicially acceptable limit on recovery").

This is true as a practical matter in the FELA context as well, even though the statute limits recovery to railroad workers. If emotional injury to Gottshall was foreseeable to Conrail, such injury to the other seven members of his work crew was also foreseeable. Because one need not witness an accident to suffer emotional injury therefrom, however, the potential liability would not necessarily have to end there; any Conrail employees who heard or read about the events surrounding Johns' death could also foreseeably have suffered emotional injury as a result. Of course, not all of these workers would have been as traumatized by the tragedy as was Gottshall, but many could have been. Under the Third Circuit's standard, Conrail thus could face the potential of unpredictable liability to a large number of employees far removed from the scene of the allegedly negligent conduct that led to Johns' death.

Finally, the Third Circuit in *Carlisle* erred in upholding "a claim under the FELA for negligent infliction of emotional distress arising from work-related stress." 990 F.2d, at 97–98. We find no support in the common law for this unprecedented holding, which would impose a duty to avoid creating a stressful work environment, and thereby dramatically expand employers' FELA liability to cover the stresses and strains of everyday employment. Indeed, the Third Circuit's ruling would tend to make railroads the insurers of the emotional well-being and mental health of their employees. We have made clear, however, that FELA is not an insurance statute. For the foregoing reasons, we reject the Third Circuit's approach.

Conrail suggests that we adopt the common-law zone of danger test as delimiting the proper scope of an employer's duty under FELA to avoid subjecting its employees to negligently inflicted emotional injury. We agree that the zone of danger test best reconciles the concerns of the common law with the principles underlying our FELA jurisprudence. . . .

SOUTER, J. concurred. GINSBURG, BLACKMUN, and STEVENS, JJ., dissented.

NOTES

1. *The Three Tests.* Justice Thomas indicates there are three major tests for recovering for negligent infliction of emotional distress, and suggests that a jurisdiction follows one of the three. But *Doe v. Philad. Community Health*, 745 A.2d 25 (Pa. Super. 2000), recognizes that a plaintiff can sue for such distress based on the impact, zone-of-danger, and close-family bystander tests, whichever the facts will support. Isn't *Doe* more in line with the general tort rule that a plaintiff can sue on as many theories as the facts will support? See also *Metro-North Commuter RR. Co. v. Buckley, infra*.

2. *Fear of AIDS.* Plaintiffs, airline baggage handlers, were exposed to HIV-contaminated blood that leaked from a bag as they were unloading it. Plaintiffs asserted that, at the time of the incident, each of them was suffering from open wounds on their hands. They subsequently tested negative for HIV. They sued FHP, shipper of the blood, for "serious mental distress" which they allegedly suffered between the time of exposure and their discovery that they had not contracted HIV. The court said they could recover, *Roes v. FHP, Inc.*, 985 P.2d 661 (Haw. 1999), without proof of physical injury, as long as their mental distress was of the sort that "a reasonable man, normally constituted, would be unable to cope with."

Why the "reasonable person" standard? Whatever happened to the thin-skull doctrine?

In *Williamson v. Waldman*, 696 A.2d 14 (N. J. 1997), the plaintiff trash collector was stuck by medical needles that had been disposed of negligently. The court said the plaintiff could recover for fear of HIV even though he had not actually been exposed to the virus.

3. *Fear of Future Injury.* The Court in *Metro-North Commuter RR. Co. v. Buckley*, 117 S. Ct. 2113 (1997), applied a physical impact analysis to an FELA claim for negligent infliction of emotional distress. There the plaintiff, a pipefitter employed by the defendant railroad, was exposed to asbestos products in the course of his employment. Although he never contracted any discernible asbestos-related disease, he was afraid that he would do so and sued to recover for that fear.

In denying his claim, the Court said the impact required under the physical impact test was more than just physical exposure to a substance. The test required some sort of "immediate traumatic harm." The purpose of this rule was to prevent the threat of "unlimited and unpredictable liability" and the "potential for a flood" of comparatively unimportant and "trivial" claims.

How is the type of fear suffered in *Buckley* different from that suffered by the plaintiffs in *Roes v. FHP, Inc.*?

DUNPHY v. GREGOR
642 A.2d 372 (N.J. 1994)

HANDLER, J.

Many states, including our own, recognize the tort commonly referred to as "bystander" liability. Bystander liability allows recovery for the emotional injury suffered by a person, who, as a bystander, witnesses the wrongful death or serious physical injury of another person with whom the bystander had a close, substantial, and enduring relationship. In this case, the central inquiry focuses on the nature of that relationship. The specific issue presented is whether bystander liability allows recovery by a person who was not legally married to a deceased victim but who cohabitated with and was engaged to marry the decedent.

The issue is sharpened by the conflicting opinions of the lower courts. The trial court ruled that an action for negligent infliction of emotional distress was not available to a claimant who was neither married to nor involved in an intimate familial relationship with the decedent. The Appellate Division ruled that a jury should be allowed to determine whether the relationship of cohabitants engaged to be married was the functional equivalent of an intimate familial relationship. A dissent in the Appellate Division expressed the view that only persons legally married would be entitled to such a cause of action.

The appeal is before this Court as a matter of right because of the dissenting opinion.

Eileen Dunphy and Michael T. Burwell became engaged to marry in April 1988 and began cohabitating two months later. The couple set a date of February 29, 1992, for their wedding. On September 29, 1990, the couple responded to a friend's telephone call for assistance in changing a tire on Route 80 in Mount Arlington. As Michael changed the left rear tire of the friend's car on the shoulder of the roadway, he was struck by a car driven by defendant, James Gregor. After being struck by the vehicle, his body was either dragged or propelled 240 feet. Eileen, who had been standing approximately five feet from Michael, witnessed the impact, and ran to him immediately. Realizing that he was still alive, she cleared pebbles and blood from his mouth to ease his breathing. She attempted to subdue his hands and feet as they thrashed about, all the while talking to him in an effort to comfort him. The following day, after a night-long vigil at Dover General Hospital, Eileen was told that Michael Burwell had died as a result of his injuries. Since the accident, Eileen has undergone psychiatric and psychological treatment for depression and anxiety. She instituted an action seeking to recover damages for the "mental anguish, pain and suffering" experienced as a result of witnessing the events that led to the death of her fiancé.

Eileen testified at her deposition that both she and Michael had taken out life-insurance policies making each other beneficiaries. They had maintained a joint checking account from which they had paid their bills, and also they had jointly purchased an automobile. In addition, Michael had asked her several times to elope with him, and he had introduced her in public as his wife. . . .

Although a foreseeable risk is the indispensable cornerstone of any formulation of a duty of care, not all foreseeable risks give rise to duties. The imposition of a duty is the conclusion of a rather complex analysis that considers the relationship of the parties, the nature of the risk — that is, its foreseeability and severity — and the impact the imposition of a duty would have on public policy. Ultimately, whether a duty exists is a matter of fairness. We have recognized, in numerous settings, that traditional principles of tort liability can be adapted to address areas in which recognition of a cause of action and the imposition of a duty of care are both novel and controversial. E.g., *Hopkins v. Fox and Lazo*, 132 N.J. 426, 625 A.2d 1110 (1993) (imposing duty of care on real-estate brokers with respect to safety of visitors to "open-houses"); *Weinberg v. Dinger*, 106 N.J. 469, 524 A.2d 366 (1987) (imposing duty of care on water companies to ensure adequacy of water-pressure for fire safety); *People Express Airlines, Inc.*, 100 N.J. 246, 495 A.2d 107 (imposing duty of care to protect against foreseeable economic losses of victim of negligence); *Kelly*, 96 N.J. 538, 476 A.2d 1219 (imposing duty of care on social hosts who serve alcohol to visibly intoxicated guests who are later involved in automobile accidents).

Although novel, applying the standard of an intimate familial relationship to an unmarried cohabitant such as Eileen Dunphy and affording her the protections of bystander liability is hardly unfair. She represents an eminently foreseeable but clearly discrete class of potential plaintiffs. Moreover, the other elements of the bystander cause of action — contemporaneous observation, death or serious injury to the victim, and severe emotional injury to the plaintiff — structure the kind of "particularized foreseeability" that ensures that the class is winnowed even further and that limitless liability is avoided.

One can reasonably foresee that people who enjoy an intimate familial relationship with one another will be especially vulnerable to emotional injury resulting from a tragedy befalling one of them. Foreseeability based on that standard, as recognized by the Appellate Division majority, preserves the distinction that must be made between ordinary emotional injuries that would be experienced by friends and relatives in general and those "indelibly stunning" emotional injuries suffered by one whose relationship with the victim "at the time of the injury, is deep, lasting, and genuinely intimate." 261 N.J. Super. at 123, 617 A.2d 1248. Persons engaged to be married and living together may foreseeably fall into that category of relationship. "[G]iven the widespread reality and acceptance of unmarried cohabitation, a reasonable person would not find the plaintiff's emotional trauma to be 'remote and unexpected.'" *Elden*, 250 Cal. Rptr. at 263, 758 P.2d at 591 (Broussard, J., dissenting).

Nor can we discern any additional, unfair burden that would be placed on potential wrongdoers in general, or, as in this case, negligent drivers. The identical acts of reasonable care that would have prevented the fatal accident that claimed the life of Michael Burwell would have preserved the emotional security of Eileen Dunphy. Certainly the extension of such a duty of care to an engaged cohabitant as a foreseeable and protectable person does not increase the burden of care or extend it beyond what is ordinarily expected and appropriate for reasonable drivers. . . .

Our courts have shown that the sound assessment of the quality of interpersonal relationships is not beyond a jury's ken and that courts are capable of dealing with the realities, not simply the legalities, of relationships to assure that resulting emotional injury is genuine and deserving of compensation. Thus, "to achieve substantial justice in other cases, we have adjusted the rights and duties of parties in light of the realities of their relationship." *Crowe v. De Gioia*, 90 N.J. 126, 135, 447 A.2d 173 (1982).

The task of exploring and evaluating an interpersonal relationship when necessary to adjudicate claims arising from that relationship poses no special obstacles in the context of bystander liability. As noted by the Appellate Division:

> Irrespective of the label placed upon a particular relationship, it is a jury question whether the inter-personal bonds upon which the cause of action is based actually exist. A defendant should always have the right, even in the case of a parent and child or a husband and wife, to test the operative facts upon which the claim is based irrespective of the *de jure* relationship.

[261 N.J. Super. at 122, 617 A.2d 1248.]

We acknowledge that this critical determination must be guided as much as possible by a standard that focuses on those factors that identify and define the intimacy and familial nature of such a relationship. That standard must take into account the duration of the relationship, the degree of mutual dependence, the extent of common contributions to a life together, the extent and quality of shared experience, and, as expressed by the Appellate Division, "whether the plaintiff and the injured person were members of the same household, their emotional reliance on each other, the particulars of their day to day relationship, and the manner in which they related to each other in attending to life's mundane requirements." *Id.* at 123, 617 A.2d 1248. . . .

. . . The State's interest in marriage would not be harmed if unmarried cohabitants are permitted to prove on a case-by-case basis that they enjoy a steadfast relationship that is equivalent to a legal marriage and thus equally deserves legal protection. Marriage will still maintain its preferential status under the law. Allowing tort recovery in circumstances such as these — for persons who have developed an emotional security from a sound and strong relationship — will not discourage marriage as a worthwhile and desirable relationship or erode society's commitment to the institution of marriage. *Crowe*, 90 N.J. 126, 447 A.2d 173; *Kozlowski*, 80 N.J. 378, 403 A.2d 902 (recognizing enforceability of support agreements made between cohabitants to extent not based on relationship proscribed by law or promise to marry).

Nor are we persuaded that allowing engaged cohabitants to recover will have a significant adverse effect on automobile insurance premiums sufficient to undermine any considerations of public policy, as argued by defendant. *Frame*, 115 N.J. at 650, 560 A.2d 675 (concluding that "any added cost to the medical profession from the recognition of such a claim [for emotional distress based on bystander liability] is outweighed by the suffering of severe emotional distress from the shock of observing a misdiagnosis that results in immediate injury to a loved one"). No empirical evidence supports such a claim.

Finally, we have no sense that the application of bystander liability to an engaged cohabitant constitutes an elusive expansion of tort liability. The recognition of the justness and fairness of such a cause of action is shared by other jurisdictions. Some courts prefer to require a strict blood relationship between the plaintiff and the victim for the plaintiff to maintain a cause of action. Other states, however, focus on the nature and integrity of the relationship and have held that a blood tie between the plaintiff and the victim need not exist for bystander recovery. That latter view comports with our own. . . .

The judgment of the Appellate Division is affirmed.

NOTES

1. *Zone of Danger.* Many courts permitted bystander recovery for emotional distress if the bystander was in the zone of danger, *i.e.*, in danger of being injured herself by the defendant's conduct that injures the victim. Indeed, the zone of danger rule was the one in effect in California before the decision in *Dillon v. Legg.* Why was the zone of danger rule not applied in *Dunphy v. Gregor*?

In *Hansen v. Sea Ray Boats, Inc.*, 830 P.2d 236 (Utah 1992), boat passengers brought suit to recover for negligent infliction of emotional distress as the result of their witnessing other passengers receive electrical shock while in the water. Applying the zone of danger rule, the court said that one of the plaintiffs who was in the boat could not recover because she was objectively not within the zone of danger, even though she may have subjectively thought she was.

2. *The Impact Rule.* Some courts hold that if the plaintiff suffers a physical impact, however slight, from the defendant's tortious conduct she can recover for negligent infliction of emotional distress. *See, e.g., Laxton v. Orkin Exterm. Co.*, 639 S.W.2d 431 (Tenn. 1982).

In *Tomikel v. Commonwealth of Pa.*, 658 A.2d 861 (Pa. Commw. 1995), the driver of a vehicle was negligently struck by a state excavator at a construction site. She suffered emotional distress from the impact, and also from fear for the safety of her son who was in the back seat of the vehicle. The court said she could recover for fear of her son's safety, even though in fact he was not injured, because "she suffered physical impact during the collision" so that "all consequent psychological emotional pain and suffering" were compensable.

3. *Contemporaneous Observance of the Injury.* Most courts applying the bystander rule of *Dillon* and *Dunphy* require that the plaintiff observe the injury to the victim as it happens, not afterwards, in order to recover for negligent infliction of emotional distress. So in *Gendrek v. Poblete*, 139 N.J. 291, 654 A.2d 970 (1995), parents were not permitted to recover for negligent infliction of emotional distress caused by the alleged malpractice of the defendants in treating their newborn son, since they did not witness the malpractice. Similarly, in *Asaro v. Cardinal Glennon Mem. Hosp.*, 799 S.W.2d 595 (Mo. 1990), a plaintiff mother could not recover for the same reason, where the defendant allegedly committed medical malpractice in the treatment of

plaintiff's 5-year-old son. In both cases the plaintiffs witnessed their child's suffering shortly after the alleged malpractice had occurred.

4. *The Direct Victim.* If the plaintiff suffers emotional distress as a "direct" victim of the defendant's negligence, then none of the bystander rules apply. Thus, in *Molien v. Kaiser Found. Hosps.*, 27 Cal. 3d 916, 167 Cal. Rptr. 831, 616 P.2d 813 (1980), where the defendant doctor negligently diagnosed a woman as having a venereal disease and advised her that her husband should be examined, the husband could recover as a direct victim for his emotional distress resulting from the misdiagnosis. The mother of a child who was sexually abused by a psychotherapist could recover for emotional distress from the psychotherapist as a direct victim. *Marlene F. v. Affiliated Psych. Med. Clinic*, 48 Cal. 3d 583, 257 Cal. Rptr. 98, 770 P.2d 278 (1989). A mother whose child was negligently injured during childbirth could recover for her emotional distress as a direct victim of the defendant obstetrician's negligence even though she did not observe the injury to her child. *Burgess v. Superior Ct.*, 2 Cal. 4th 1064, 9 Cal. Rptr. 2d 615, 831 P.2d 1197 (1992).

Why was Carlisle not a direct victim, in *Consol. R. Corp. v. Gotshall?*

Why was the mother in *Burgess* any more of a direct victim than the parents in *Gendrek* and *Asaro*? Perhaps the direct-indirect distinction should be done away with in negligent-infliction cases. *See Doe v. Cuomo*, 43 Conn. Super. 222, 649 A.2d 266 (1994) (rape of plaintiff's child).

5. *Intentional Infliction.* The victim of intentional infliction of emotional distress is treated as a direct victim. *See R.D. v. W.H.*, 875 P.2d 26 (Wyo. 1994) (intentional infliction claim on behalf of survivors of woman who committed suicide allegedly due to defendant's intentional wrongdoing). Presumably the same result would obtain in the case of reckless misconduct. *See* RESTATEMENT (SECOND) OF TORTS § 46, comment *i*, illus. 15–16.

The intent to inflict emotional distress may be inferred from wilful or reckless misconduct. *Blakeley v. Shortal's Estate*, 20 N.W. 2d 28 (Iowa 1945) (estate of house guest who killed himself by slitting his own throat was liable to hostess who suffered emotional distress when she returned home and discovered the guest's body).

Intentional and negligent infliction of emotional distress may overlap. The parents in *Croft v. Wickes*, 737 P.2d 789 (Alaska 1987), stated a claim for both types of distress against a house guest whom they observed sexually assault their 14-year-old daughter.

K. ECONOMIC LOSS

PROBLEM

Through a gas company's negligence, a fire broke out on its premises. The fire created combustible conditions in the area that lasted for a week after the fire was extinguished. The owner of a nearby plant decided to hire a special fire prevention squad and to close down for the week, rather than run the risk of explosion or fire. The owner of the plant then sues the gas company for the cost of those fire prevention measures. Employees of the same plant file suit, seeking recovery for their lost wages. Neighborhood restaurants sue to recover for their lost luncheon business during the period when the plant is closed. Local residents sue for the emotional harm they have suffered because of the likelihood of a fire or explosion. Which claims should the gas company fight rather than settle?

PEOPLE EXPRESS AIRLINES v. CONSOLIDATED RAIL CORP.
100 N.J. 246, 495 A.2d 107 (1985)

HANDLER, J.

On July 22, 1981, a fire began in the Port Newark freight yard of defendant Consolidated Rail Corporation (Conrail) when ethylene oxide . . . escaped from a tank car, punctured during a "coupling" operation with another rail car, and ignited. . . .

The plaintiff asserted at oral argument that at least some of the defendants were aware from prior experiences that ethylene oxide is a highly volatile substance; further, that emergency response plans in case of an accident had been prepared. When the fire occurred that gave rise to this lawsuit, some of the defendants' consultants helped determine how much of the surrounding area to evacuate. The municipal authorities then evacuated the area within a one-mile radius surrounding the fire to lessen the risk to persons within the area should the burning tank car explode. The evacuation area included the adjacent North Terminal building of Newark International Airport, where plaintiff People Express Airlines' (People Express) business operations are based. Although the feared explosion never occurred, People Express employees were prohibited from using the North Terminal for twelve hours.

The plaintiff contends that it suffered business-interruption losses as a result of the evacuation. These losses consist of canceled scheduled flights and lost reservations because employees were unable to answer the telephones to accept bookings; also, certain fixed operating expenses allocable to the evacuation time period were incurred and paid despite the fact that plaintiff's offices were closed. No physical damage to airline property and no personal injury occurred as a result of the fire.

. . . The trial court granted Conrail's summary judgment motion on the ground that absent property damage or personal injury economic loss was not recoverable in tort. . . .

. . . The single characteristic that distinguishes parties in negligence suits whose claims for economic losses have been regularly denied by American and English courts from those who have recovered economic losses is, with respect to the successful claimants, the fortuitous occurrence of physical harm or property damage, however slight. It is well-accepted that a defendant who negligently injures a plaintiff or his property may be liable for all proximately caused harm, including economic losses. Nevertheless, a virtually *per se* rule barring recovery for economic loss unless the negligent conduct also caused physical harm has evolved throughout this century. . . .

The reasons that have been advanced to explain the divergent results for litigants seeking economic losses are varied. Some courts have viewed the general rule against recovery as necessary to limit damages to reasonably foreseeable consequences of negligent conduct. This concern in a given case is often manifested as an issue of causation and has led to the requirement of physical harm as an element of proximate cause. In this context, the physical harm requirement functions as part of the definition of the causal relationship between the defendant's negligent act and the plaintiff's economic damages; it acts as a convenient clamp on otherwise boundless liability. The physical harm rule also reflects certain deep-seated concerns that underlie courts' denial of recovery for purely economic losses occasioned by a defendant's negligence. These concerns include the fear of fraudulent claims, mass litigation, and limitless liability, or liability out of proportion to the defendant's fault.

The assertion of unbounded liability is not unique to cases involving negligently caused economic loss without physical harm. Even in negligence suits in which plaintiffs have sustained physical harm, the courts have recognized that a tort-feasor is not necessarily liable for all consequences of his conduct. While a lone act can cause a finite amount of physical harm, that harm may be great and very remote in its final consequences. A single overturned lantern may burn Chicago. Some limitation is required; that limitation is the rule that a tort-feasor is liable only for that harm that he proximately caused. Proximate or legal cause has traditionally functioned to limit liability for negligent conduct. Duty has also been narrowly defined to limit liability. Thus, we proceed from the premise that principles of duty and proximate cause are instrumental in limiting the amount of litigation and extent of liability in cases in which no physical harm occurs just as they are in cases involving physical injury.

Countervailing considerations of fairness and public policy have led courts to discard the requirement of physical harm as an element in defining proximate cause to overcome the problem of fraudulent or indefinite claims. In this context . . . we have subordinated the threat of potential baseless claims to the right of an aggrieved individual to pursue a just and fair claim for redress attributable to the wrongdoing of another. The asserted inability to define damages in cases arising under the cause of action for negligent infliction of emotional distress absent impact or near-impact has not hindered adjudication of those claims. Nor is there any indication that unfair awards have resulted.

The troublesome concern reflected in cases denying recovery for negligently-caused economic loss is the alleged potential for infinite liability, or liability out of all proportion to the defendant's fault. This objection is also not confined to negligently-caused economic injury. The same objection has been asserted and, ultimately, rejected by this Court and others in allowing recovery for other forms of negligent torts and in the creation of the doctrine of strict liability for defective products, and ultrahazardous activities. The answer to the allegation of unchecked liability is not the judicial obstruction of a fairly grounded claim for redress. Rather, it must be a more sedulous application of traditional concepts of duty and proximate causation to the facts of each case.

It is understandable that courts, fearing that if even one deserving plaintiff suffering purely economic loss were allowed to recover, all such plaintiffs could recover, have anchored their rulings to the physical harm requirement. While the rationale is understandable, it supports only a limitation on, not a denial of, liability. The physical harm requirement capriciously showers compensation along the path of physical destruction, regardless of the status or circumstances of individual claimants. Purely economic losses are borne by innocent victims, who may not be able to absorb their losses. In the end, the challenge is to fashion a rule that limits liability but permits adjudication of meritorious claims. The asserted inability to fix crystalline formulae for recovery on the differing facts of future cases simply does not justify the wholesale rejection of recovery in all cases.

Further, judicial reluctance to allow recovery for purely economic losses is discordant with contemporary tort doctrine. The torts process, like the law itself, is a human institution designed to accomplish certain social objectives. One objective is to ensure that innocent victims have avenues of legal redress, absent a contrary, overriding public policy. This reflects the overarching purpose of tort law: that wronged persons should be compensated for their injuries and that those responsible for the wrong should bear the cost of their tortious conduct . . . .

One group of exceptions is based on the "special relationship" between the tort-feasor and the individual or business deprived of economic expectations. Many of these cases are recognized as involving the tort of negligent misrepresentation, resulting in liability for specially foreseeable economic losses. Importantly, the cases do not involve a breach of contract claim between parties in privity; rather, they involve tort claims by innocent third parties who suffered purely economic losses at the hands of negligent defendants with whom no direct relationship existed. Courts have justified their finding of liability in these negligence cases based on notions of a special relationship between the negligent tortfeasors and the foreseeable plaintiffs who relied on the quality of defendants' work or services, to their detriment. The special relationship, in reality, is an expression of the courts' satisfaction that a duty of care existed because the plaintiffs were particularly foreseeable and the injury was proximately caused by the defendant's negligence.

The special relationship exception has been extended to auditors, surveyors, termite inspectors, engineers, attorneys, notaries public, architects, weighers, and telegraph companies.

A related exception in which courts have allowed recovery for purely economic losses has been extended to plaintiffs belonging to a particularly foreseeable group, such as sailors and seamen, for whom the law has traditionally shown great solicitude.

Courts have found it fair and just in all of these exceptional cases to impose liability on defendants who, by virtue of their special activities, professional training or other unique preparation for their work, had particular knowledge or reason to know that others, such as the intended beneficiaries of wills or the purchasers of stock who were expected to rely on the company's financial statement in the prospectus would be economically harmed by negligent conduct. In this group of cases, even though the particular plaintiff was not always foreseeable, the particular class of plaintiffs was foreseeable as was the particular type of injury.

A very solid exception allowing recovery for economic losses has also been created in cases akin to private actions for public nuisance. Where a plaintiff's business is based in part upon the exercise of a public right, the plaintiff has been able to recover purely economic losses caused by a defendant's negligence. *See, e.g., Union Oil Co. v. Oppen,* 501 F.2d 558 (9th Cir. 1974) (fishermen making known commercial use of public waters may recover economic losses due to defendant's oil spill). . . . The theory running throughout these cases, in which the plaintiffs depend on the exercise of the public or riparian right to clean water as a natural resource, is that the pecuniary losses suffered by those who make direct use of the resource are particularly foreseeable because they are so closely linked, through the resource, to the defendants' behavior.

Particular knowledge of the economic consequences has sufficed to establish duty and proximate cause in contexts other than those already considered. In *Clay v. Jersey City,* 74 N.J. Super. 490, 181 A.2d 545 (1962), *aff'd,* 84 N.J. Super. 9, 200 A.2d 787 (1964), for example, a lessee-manufacturer had to vacate the building in which its business was located because of the defendant city's negligent failure to maintain its sewer line while the line was repaired. While there was some property damage, the court treated the tenant's and owner's claims separately; the tenant's claims were purely economic, stemming from the loss of use of its property right, as in the instant case. Further, the city had had notice of the leak since 1957 and should have known about it even earlier. Duty, breach and proximate cause were found to exist; the plaintiff-tenant recovered lost profits and expenses incurred during the shut-down.

These exceptions expose the hopeless artificiality of the *per se* rule against recovery for purely economic losses. When the plaintiffs are reasonably foreseeable, the injury is directly and proximately caused by defendant's negligence, and liability can be limited fairly, courts have endeavored to create exceptions to allow recovery. The scope and number of exceptions, while independently justified on various grounds, have nonetheless created lasting doubt as to the wisdom of the *per se* rule of nonrecovery for purely economic losses. Indeed, it has been fashionable for commentators to state that the rule has been giving way for nearly fifty years, although the cases have not always kept pace with the hypothesis. . . .

We hold therefore that a defendant owes a duty of care to take reasonable measures to avoid the risk of causing economic damages, aside from physical injury, to particular plaintiffs or plaintiffs comprising an identifiable class with respect to whom defendant knows or has reason to know are likely to suffer such damages from its conduct. A defendant failing to adhere to this duty of care may be found liable for such economic damages proximately caused by its breach of duty.

We stress that an identifiable class of plaintiffs is not simply a foreseeable class of plaintiffs. For example, members of the general public, or invitees such as sales and service persons at a particular plaintiff's business premises, or persons traveling on a highway near the scene of a negligently-caused accident, such as the one at bar, who are delayed in the conduct of their affairs and suffer varied economic losses, are certainly a foreseeable class of plaintiffs.

Yet their presence within the area would be fortuitous, and the particular type of economic injury that could be suffered by such persons would be hopelessly unpredictable and not realistically foreseeable. Thus, the class itself would not be sufficiently ascertainable. An identifiable class of plaintiffs must be particularly foreseeable in terms of the type of persons or entities comprising the class, the certainty or predictability of their presence, the approximate numbers of those in the class, as well as the type of economic expectations disrupted.

We recognize that some cases will present circumstances that defy the categorization here devised to circumscribe a defendant's orbit of duty, limit otherwise boundless liability and define an identifiable class of plaintiffs that may recover. In these cases, the courts will be required to draw upon notions of fairness, common sense and morality to fix the line limiting liability as a matter of public policy, rather than an uncritical application of the principle of particular foreseeability. . . .

We are satisfied that our holding today is fully applicable to the facts that we have considered on this appeal. Plaintiff has set forth a cause of action under our decision, and it is entitled to have the matter proceed to a plenary trial. Among the facts that persuade us that a cause of action has been established is the close proximity of the North Terminal and People Express Airlines to the Conrail freight yard; the obvious nature of the plaintiff's operations and particular foreseeability of economic losses resulting from an accident and evacuation; the defendants' actual or constructive knowledge of the volatile properties of ethylene oxide; and the existence of an emergency response plan prepared by some of the defendants (alluded to in the course of oral argument), which apparently called for the nearby area to be evacuated to avoid the risk of harm in case of an explosion. We do not mean to suggest by our recitation of these facts that actual knowledge of the eventual economic losses is necessary to the cause of action; rather, particular foreseeability will suffice. The plaintiff still faces a difficult task in proving damages, particularly lost profits, to the degree of certainty required in other negligence cases. The trial court's examination of these proofs must be exacting to ensure that damages recovered are those reasonably to have been anticipated in view of the defendants' capacity to have foreseen that this particular plaintiff was within the risk created by their negligence.

NOTES

1. *Economic Loss and the Risk of Danger*. The Supreme Court of Canada in *Winnipeg Condominium Corp. No. 36 v. Bird Constr. Co.*, 1 S.C.R. 85, 121 D.L.R.4th 193 (1995), held that a purchaser from the original owner of an apartment building could recover against the contractors who constructed the building, for the repair costs of making the building safe. The exterior cladding of the building was allegedly negligently installed, and created a danger from falling off. Some of the cladding had in fact fallen off, although no one had been injured. The court said:

> . . . If a contractor can be held liable in tort where he or she constructs a building negligently and, as a result of that negligence,

the building causes damage to persons or property, it follows that the contractor should also be held liable in cases where the dangerous defect is discovered and the owner of the building wishes to mitigate the danger by fixing the defect and putting the building back into a non-dangerous state. In both cases, the duty in tort serves to protect the bodily integrity and property interests of the inhabitants of the building.

2. *Identifiable, Particularly Foreseeable Plaintiffs.* In *George Mattingly v. Sheldon Jackson College,* 743 P.2d 356 (Alaska 1987), the plaintiff was hired by the defendant college to clean an underground drain. The defendant's employees dug a trench to provide access. While three of the plaintiff's employees, including his son, were working on the drain, the trench collapsed on them. Plaintiff claimed temporary and permanent economic losses. Following *People Express,* the court held that the plaintiff was "foreseeable and particularized." Would a mere passerby who stopped to look at the college but fell into the trench be able to recover against the college? Suppose a student at the college fell into the trench and, because of her injuries, was unable to take her final exams, graduate, or accept her lucrative investment banking position?

3. *Lost Wages.* In *Robinson v. Gonzalez,* 213 N.J. Super. 364, 517 A.2d 479 (1986), the plaintiff suffered personal injuries in a commonplace traffic accident. However, in addition to her claim for wages lost during the time of her physical disability, plaintiff alleged that her employer had followed his policy of discharging employees who missed more than five days of work per year. As a result, plaintiff made an additional claim for $26,000 for her period of unemployment. The court stated:

> It is . . . clear that the type of claim involved, loss of wages, foreseeably results from automobile accidents. We further think that while defendant obviously had no reason to be aware of plaintiff's employer's policy before the accident, it is foreseeable that a party injured in an automobile accident might miss enough work so as to cause her employer to discharge her.
>
> [W]e hold that the court should have considered whether defendant could have reasonably foreseen that a person injured in an automobile accident could as a result of the injuries become unemployed. We think it clear that that question must be answered affirmatively.
>
> We are, however, concerned that our opinion may be read too broadly. We emphasize that the loss for which plaintiff seeks a recovery, a wage loss, is a traditional damage claim. There are less conventional claims that might factually be attributed to an automobile accident but nevertheless as a matter of law cannot be regarded as proximately caused by a driver's negligence. . . .
>
> We also point out that there are other limitations on our decision. While we deal with a sparse record that does not reveal exactly how long plaintiff was unemployed, in view of her substantial claim it must have been for a lengthy period. It is not our intention to encourage persons who have been injured but who recover and are able to return

to work to remain unemployed at the expense of defendants or their insurance carriers. Thus we emphasize that plaintiff has the burden to establish that defendant's negligence was the proximate cause of her unemployment and wage loss. She might not be able to establish this at all to the satisfaction of the jury or she might be able to establish it only as to a portion of her period of unemployment.

Suppose the plaintiff in *Robinson* had not suffered any personal injury, but had missed work to have her car fixed or to answer police inquiries about the accident?

4. *An Economic Analysis?* In *Union Oil Co. v. Oppen*, 501 F.2d 558 (9th Cir. 1974), commercial fishermen sought damages they sustained because of a major oil spill in the Santa Barbara channel. Defendants contended that no cause of action lies for preventing a plaintiff from obtaining a prospective pecuniary advantage. The court noted:

> Their argument has strength. It rests upon the proposition that a contrary rule, which would allow compensation for all losses of economic advantages caused by defendant's negligence, would subject the defendant to claims based upon remote and speculative injuries which he could not foresee in any practical sense of the term. Accordingly, in some cases it has been stated as the general rule that the negligent defendant owes no duty to plaintiffs seeking compensation for such injuries. In other of the cases, the courts have invoked the doctrine of proximate cause to reach the same result; and in yet a third class of cases the "remoteness" of the economic loss is relied upon directly to deny recovery. The consequence of these cases is that a defendant is normally relieved of the burden to defend against such claims, and the courts of a class of cases the resolution of which is particularly difficult.
>
> The general rule has been applied in a wide variety of situations. Thus, the negligent destruction of a bridge connecting the mainland with an island, which caused a loss of business to the plaintiff who was a merchant on the island, has been held not to be actionable. A plaintiff engaged in commercial printing has been held unable to recover against a negligent contractor who, while engaged in excavation pursuant to a contract with a third party, cut the power line upon which the plaintiff's presses depended.
>
> . . . [W]e cannot escape the conclusion that under California law the presence of a duty on the part of the defendants in this case would turn substantially on foreseeability. That being the crucial determinant, the question must be asked whether the defendants could reasonably have foreseen that negligently conducted drilling operations might diminish aquatic life and thus injure the business of commercial fishermen. We believe the answer is yes. The dangers of pollution were and are known even by school children. The defendants understood the risks of their business and should reasonably have foreseen the scope of their responsibilities. To assert that the defendants were unable to foresee that negligent conduct resulting in a substantial oil spill could diminish aquatic life and thus injure the

plaintiffs is to suppose a degree of general ignorance of the effects of oil pollution not in accord with good sense. . . .

Calabresi's final guideline [Guido Calabresi, The Cost of Accidents (1973)] unmistakably points to the defendants as the best cost-avoider. Under this guideline, the loss should be allocated to that party who can best correct any error in allocation, if such there be, by acquiring the activity to which the party has been made liable. CALABRESI at 150–52. The capacity "to buy out" the plaintiffs if the burden is too great is, in essence, the real focus of Calabresi's approach. On this basis there is no contest — the defendants' capacity is superior.

. . . Finally, it must be understood that our holding in this case does not open the door to claims that may be asserted by those, other than commercial fishermen, whose economic of personal affairs were discommoded by the oil spill of January 28, 1969. The general rule urged upon us by defendants has a legitimate sphere within which to operate. Nothing said in this opinion is intended to suggest, for example, that every decline in the general commercial activity of every business in the Santa Barbara area following the occurrences of 1969 constitutes a legally cognizable injury for which the defendants may be responsible. The plaintiffs in the present action lawfully and directly make use of a resource of the sea, viz., its fish, in the ordinary course of their business. This type of use is entitled to protection from negligent conduct by the defendants in their drilling operations. Both the plaintiffs and defendants conduct their business operations away from land and in, on and under the sea. Both must carry on their commercial enterprises in a reasonably prudent manner. Neither should be permitted negligently to inflict commercial injury on the other. We decide no more than this.

5. *Attorney Negligence*. Client Stone sued attorney Savitz and his law firm for legal malpractice, in *Stone v. Chicago Title Ins. Co.*, 330 Md. 329, 624 A.2d 496 (1993):

In September of 1989, Marc Stone, the appellant, purchased a home in Washington, D.C. for $285,000. James E. Savitz and his law firm, Gimmel, Weiman, Savitz and Kronthal, P.A., were employed by Stone to handle the settlement of that purchase, including the examination of the title of the property for marketability, document preparation, the release of any liens encumbering the property, and obtaining a title insurance policy. At settlement on September 15, 1989, a title insurance policy was issued by Chicago Title Insurance Company of Maryland. In June, 1990, Stone applied to Maryland National Bank for a home equity loan in the amount of $50,000 to purchase "stock puts" to protect his financial position in the stock market in response to anticipated margin calls on certain stocks he had purchased on credit. The loan was to be secured by a second mortgage on his home. The loan was provisionally approved on July 2; however, in mid-July, the bank notified Stone that a deed of trust which encumbered his title had not been released of record. Between July 18 and August 2, Stone and representatives of Maryland National Bank and its title company made numerous attempts to contact Savitz or someone else at his law firm to get the deed of trust which was recorded against his home released. Meanwhile, on August 1, 1990, Stone's broker called his margin account loans with an August 9, 1990 pay-off date. Without the home equity loan funds, Stone was forced to sell stock at a substantial loss to meet his broker's demand.

In addition to these facts, in his amended complaint, Stone alleged that Savitz was not reached until early August when he proceeded to clear up the matter. The release of the outstanding lien was recorded on August 6, 1990. The loan funds from Maryland National were released on August 15, 1990. Stone alleges that as a result of Savitz's failure to record a release of the outstanding lien, he was unable to close on the home equity loan in a timely fashion and, as a result, was forced to sell stock at a substantial loss to raise the money to meet the margin call. There was no allegation in the amended complaint that either Savitz, his firm, or Chicago Title had knowledge at any time that Stone was speculating on credit in the stock market and that the Maryland National home equity loan was the only source of funds available to him in case of financial emergency. . . .

In the instant case, Stone would have us hold that his loss arising from the August, 1990 collapse in the market in certain stocks in which he was speculating was proximately caused by his sale of those stocks, which was caused by his lack of funds to pay off other loans, which was caused by his inability to secure a second mortgage before August 6, 1990, which in turn was caused by Savitz's failure to record timely the release of the extinguished lien on his home. He argues that but for Savitz's negligence he would have secured a home equity loan and used the proceeds to meet his broker's margin call, thus avoiding the sale of stock to raise capital in a falling market. We disagree. We believe that Stone's stock market damages were a highly extraordinary result of Savitz's failure to timely record the release. We hold that there was no acceptable nexus between Savitz's negligent conduct and the stock market losses suffered by Stone and, consequently, that Savitz's negligence was not the proximate cause of the ensuing harm which befell Stone.

There was no allegation in the amended complaint that Savitz or his firm had knowledge at any time that Stone was buying stock on margin. No reasonable person would have foreseen that almost a year after the settlement which Savitz conducted Stone would have an emergency need for cash, would attempt to borrow against his home to satisfy that need, and unable to do so would have to sell stock in a depressed market to raise it. Furthermore, there is no allegation that Savitz was notified of Stone's financial crisis at the time the problem was brought to his attention. The result might be different if Stone had informed Savitz at the settlement, or when notifying Savitz of the outstanding lien against his home, that he was an active player in the stock market, that he had purchased stock on margin, and that one of the purposes for purchasing the house was to have a ready source of collateral should he have to raise cash to meet a margin call to avoid the need to sell stock in a weak market.

What was the foreseeable risk of the defendant attorney's negligent failure to release the deed of trust on plaintiff's land?

L. PRENATAL AND PRECONCEPTION INJURIES

STALLMAN v. YOUNGQUIST
125 Ill. 2d 267, 126 Ill. Dec. 60, 531 N.E.2d 355 (1988)

JUSTICE CUNNINGHAM delivered the opinion of the court.

Plaintiff, Lindsay Stallman, brought suit by her father and next friend, Mark Stallman, against defendant Bari Stallman and codefendant Clarence Youngquist (not a party to this appeal) for prenatal injuries allegedly sustained by plaintiff during an automobile collision between Bari Stallman's automobile and the automobile driven by Clarence Youngquist. Defendant Bari Stallman is the mother of plaintiff. Defendant was approximately five months pregnant with plaintiff and was on her way to a restaurant when the collision occurred.

. . . Count II of plaintiff's second amended complaint, the subject matter of this appeal, charged defendant with negligence, the direct and proximate result of which caused the fetus (the unborn plaintiff) to be thrown about in the womb of her mother (defendant) resulting in serious and permanent injury to plaintiff.

. . . The issue whether a cause of action exists by or on behalf of a fetus, subsequently born alive, against its mother for the unintentional infliction of prenatal injuries is an issue of first impression in this court. We begin with a review of the area of tort liability for prenatal negligence as it has developed in regards to third persons.

It was not until 1884, in *Dietrich v. Northampton*, 138 Mass. 14 (1884), that such a case came before a court in the United States alleging a cause of action for prenatal injuries. In *Dietrich*, Judge Oliver Wendell Holmes held that the common law did not recognize a cause of action in tort for prenatal injuries to a fetus. Judge Holmes denied that such an action may lie primarily because the fetus "was a part of the mother at the time of the injury, [and] any damage to it which was not too remote to be recovered for at all was recoverable by her." (138 Mass. at 17.) After *Dietrich* and until 1946 [*Bonbrest v. Kotz*, 65 F. Supp. 138 (D.C. 1946)], all courts in the United States which considered the question agreed: no action would lie for injuries sustained by a fetus which became apparent on its birth.

This court was one of the first to consider the question of the liability of third persons for prenatal negligence after the *Dietrich* case. In *Allaire v. St. Luke's Hospital*, 184 Ill. 359, 56 N.E. 638 (1900), it was held that no action would lie for injuries to a fetus, only days away from birth, due to the negligence of the defendant hospital where the mother of the plaintiff was a patient awaiting the delivery of the plaintiff. . . .

Allaire is primarily remembered today for the dissent of Mr. Justice Boggs, who asked the question:

> Should compensation for his injuries be denied on a mere theory, known to be false, that the injury was not to his [or her] person but to the person of the mother? 184 Ill. at 374 (Boggs, J., dissenting).

The rule recognizing the right to bring an action for injuries inflicted on a fetus by a person not its mother is as pervasive and established now as was the contrary rule before 1946. This court overruled *Allaire* in *Amann v. Faidy*, 415 Ill. 422, 114 N.E.2d 412 (1953), and recognized a cause of action under the wrongful death statute for the death of an infant who, while in a viable condition, sustained a prenatal injury due to the negligence of a third person. Later, in *Rodriquez v. Patti*, 415 Ill. 496, 114 N.E.2d 721 (1953), this court recognized a common law right of action for personal injuries to an infant, a viable fetus, when wrongfully injured due to the negligence of third persons. Much later, in *Chrisafogeorgis v. Brandenberg*, 55 Ill.2d 368, 304 N.E.2d 88 (1973), this court held that a wrongful death action could be maintained on behalf of a stillborn child who sustained injuries due to the negligence of third persons while a viable fetus.

The early reliance by courts on viability as a point at which with certainty it could be said that the fetus and the woman who is the mother of the fetus are two separate entities proved to be troublesome. Most courts have since abandoned viability as a requirement for a child to bring an action for prenatal injuries inflicted by third persons. . . .

In *Renslow v. Mennonite Hospital*, 67 Ill.2d 348, 10 Ill. Dec. 484, 367 N.E.2d 1250 (1977), this court rejected viability as a requirement in a cause of action for prenatal injuries suffered by a fetus due to the negligence of third persons. According to the plurality, *Renslow* involved the issue of whether "a child, not conceived at the time negligent acts were committed against its mother, [has] a cause of action against the tortfeasors for its injuries resulting from their conduct." (67 Ill. 2d at 349). . . .

The above case law has grown out of circumstances in which the defendant was a third person and not the mother of the plaintiff. Plaintiff in the instant case asserts that she should be able to bring a cause of action for prenatal injuries against her mother just as she would be able to bring a cause of action for prenatal injuries against a third person. . . . In *Grodin v. Grodin*, 102 Mich. App. 396, 301 N.W.2d 869 (1980), a child brought suit against his mother for prenatal negligence. The plaintiff in *Grodin* had developed brown and discolored teeth because the defendant mother had taken tetracycline during the time when she was pregnant with the plaintiff. The suit alleged failure on the part of the mother to request from a doctor a pregnancy test, failure to seek proper prenatal care, and failure to report to a doctor that the mother was taking tetracycline.

The *Grodin* court failed to understand that the question of the application of Michigan's partial abrogation of the parental immunity doctrine was a separate question from that of recognizing a cause of action by a fetus, subsequently born alive, against its mother for the unintentional infliction of prenatal injuries. The *Grodin* court would have the law treat a pregnant woman as a stranger to her developing fetus for purposes of tort liability. The *Grodin* court failed to address any of the profound implications which would result from such a legal fiction and is, for that reason, unpersuasive. . . .

This court has never been asked to decide if, by becoming pregnant, a woman exposes herself to a future lawsuit by or on behalf of the fetus which will become her child. At one time a fetus was seen as only a part of the woman who was the mother of the child. When someone tortiously injured a pregnant woman and her fetus sustained injury as a result, no legal protection would have been extended to the subsequently born child. Today, when the tortious acts of another towards a woman who is or may become pregnant harm a fetus, there is a legally cognizable cause of action for the injury to both the woman and the subsequently born child.

In the path which some courts have taken on the road which has recognized recovery for a child for injuries inflicted on it as a fetus, there has been an articulation of a "legal right to begin life with a sound mind and body" [citations]. The articulation of this right to recover against third-person tortfeasors has served to emphasize that it is not just the pregnant woman alone who may be harmed by the tortious act of another but also the fetus, whose injuries become apparent at its birth.

It is clear that the recognition of a legal right to begin life with a sound mind and body on the part of a fetus which is assertable after birth against its mother would have serious ramifications for all women and their families, and for the way in which society views women and women's reproductive abilities. The recognition of such a right by a fetus would necessitate the recognition of a legal duty on the part of the woman who is the mother; a legal duty, as opposed to a moral duty, to effectuate the best prenatal environment possible. The recognition of such a legal duty would create a new tort: a cause of action assertable by a fetus, subsequently born alive, against its mother for the unintentional infliction of prenatal injuries.

It is the firmly held belief of some that a woman should subordinate her right to control her life when she decides to become pregnant or does become pregnant: anything which might possibly harm the developing fetus should be prohibited and all things which might positively affect the developing fetus should be mandated under penalty of law, be it criminal or civil. Since anything which a pregnant woman does or does not do may have an impact, either positive or negative, on her developing fetus, any act or omission on her part could render her liable to her subsequently born child. While such a view is consistent with the recognition of a fetus having rights which are superior to those of its mother, such is not and cannot be the law of this State.

A legal right of a fetus to begin life with a sound mind and body assertable against a mother would make a pregnant woman the guarantor of the mind and body of her child at birth. A legal duty to guarantee the mental and physical health of another has never before been recognized in law. Any action which negatively impacted on fetal development would be a breach of the pregnant woman's duty to her developing fetus. Mother and child would be legal adversaries from the moment of conception until birth.

The error that a fetus cannot be harmed in a legally cognizable way when the woman who is its mother is injured has been corrected; the law will no longer treat the fetus as only a part of its mother. The law will not now make an error of a different sort, one with enormous implications for all women who have been, are, may be, or might become pregnant: the law will not treat a fetus as an entity which is entirely separate from its mother.

. . . If a legally cognizable duty on the part of mothers were recognized, then a judicially defined standard of conduct would have to be met. It must be asked, By what judicially defined standard would a mother have her every act or omission while pregnant subjected to State scrutiny? By what objective standard could a jury be guided in determining whether a pregnant woman did all that was necessary in order not to breach a legal duty to not interfere with her fetus' separate and independent right to be born whole? In what way would prejudicial and stereotypical beliefs about the reproductive abilities of women be kept from interfering with a jury's determination of whether a particular woman was negligent at any point during her pregnancy?

Holding a third person liable for prenatal injuries furthers the interests of both the mother and the subsequently born child and does not interfere with the defendant's right to control his or her own life. Holding a mother liable for the unintentional infliction of prenatal injuries subjects to State scrutiny all the decisions a woman must make in attempting to carry a pregnancy to term, and infringes on her right to privacy and bodily autonomy. . . . Logic does not demand that a pregnant woman be treated in a court of law as a stranger to her developing fetus.

It would be a legal fiction to treat the fetus as a separate legal person with rights hostile to and assertable against its mother. The relationship between a pregnant woman and her fetus is unlike the relationship between any other plaintiff and defendant. No other plaintiff depends exclusively on any other defendant for everything necessary for life itself. No other defendant must go through biological changes of the most profound type, possibly at the risk of her own life, in order to bring forth an adversary into the world. It is, after all, the whole life of the pregnant woman which impacts on the development of the fetus. As opposed to the third-party defendant, it is the mother's every waking and sleeping moment which, for better or worse, shapes the prenatal environment which forms the world for the developing fetus. That this is so is not a pregnant woman's fault: it is a fact of life. . . .

NOTES

1. *To Be Or Not To Be?* In *Bonte v. Bonte*, 136 N.H. 286, 289, 616 A.2d 464 (1992), the court held:

> Because our cases hold that a child born alive may maintain a cause of action against another for injuries sustained while *in utero*, and a child may sue his or her mother in tort for the mother's negligence, it follows that a child born alive has a cause of action against his or her mother for the mother's negligence that caused injury to the child when *in utero*.

A dissent countered:

> Such after-the-fact judicial scrutiny of the subtle and complicated factors affecting a woman's pregnancy may make life for women who

are pregnant or who are merely contemplating pregnancy intolerable. For these reasons, we are convinced that the best course is to allow the duty of a mother to her fetus to remain a moral obligation which, for the vast majority of women, is already freely recognized and respected without compulsion by law.

136 N.H. at 293.

2. *Preconception Contrasted with Prenatal Actions.* In *Bergstreser v. Mitchell*, 577 F.2d 22 (8th Cir. 1978), the court relied in part upon a prior Missouri case permitting a prenatal cause of action as a predictor of Missouri's approach to preconception injuries, and held that a child stated a cause of action against medical care providers for injuries allegedly sustained as the result of a negligently performed Caesarean section upon the child's mother several years prior to the child's birth. What different arguments arise in the preconception rather than the prenatal type of case?

3. *Preconception Actions Against Third Parties.* In *Monusko v. Postle*, 175 Mich. App. 269, 437 N.W.2d 367 (1989), a child born with rubella syndrome brought an action against medical care providers who allegedly had failed to test her mother for, or immunize her against, rubella prior to the child's conception. The court noted:

> Defendants rely heavily on a New York case prohibiting recovery for an alleged preconception tort. In that case the plaintiff was born with brain damage allegedly the result of a perforated uterus the plaintiff's mother received during an abortion several years prior to the plaintiff's birth. *Albala v. New York,* 54 N.Y.2d 269, 429 N.E.2d 786 (1981). The court rejected the plaintiff's claim, principally on the basis of policy. Concluding that "foreseeability alone is not the hallmark of legal duty," the court ruled that it would require an extension of traditional tort concepts beyond manageable bounds to allow the plaintiff to go forward.
>
> We cannot agree with that reasoning in the instant case. Here, plaintiffs have alleged that the failure of defendants to test Jill Rose Monusko for her rubella status and to immunize her against rubella prior to conception resulted in Andrea's injuries. The tests and immunization, relatively simple and straight-forward to administer, are designed specifically to alleviate the sort of injuries we have in this case. It is readily foreseeable that someone not immunized may catch rubella and, if pregnant, bear a child suffering from rubella syndrome. We conclude that plaintiffs have stated a cause of action in alleging that defendants' failure to administer the test and immunization specifically designed to prevent rubella syndrome resulted in Andrea's being born with rubella syndrome. We hold that defendants owed a duty to Andrea, even though she was not conceived at the time of the alleged wrongful act.

4. *Fetal Wrongful Death Actions.* In *Aka v. Jefferson Hospital Assn.* 42 S.W.3d 508 (Ark. 2001), the Supreme Court of Arkansas reversed its prior position and held that a viable fetus was a "person" for the purposes of the state's wrongful death statute. In so doing the court noted:

Thirty-two jurisdictions permit a wrongful-death action on behalf of a viable fetus. (Of those thirty-two jurisdictions, four permit an action for an unviable fetus (Connecticut, Missouri, South Dakota, and West Virginia)). Four jurisdictions permit an action, even for unviable fetuses, but have a live birth or stillbirth requirement (Louisiana, Maryland, Oklahoma, and Pennsylvania). One jurisdiction permits an alternative remedy by allowing an action for damages resulting in stillbirth caused by negligence (Florida). One jurisdiction noted in dicta that a wrongful-death action might be permitted but declined to reach the merits on procedural grounds (Utah). Three jurisdictions prohibit an action for an unborn nonviable fetus but have not reached the issue of whether a viable fetus may maintain an action (Alaska, Oregon, and Rhode Island). Four jurisdictions have no case law on the issue (Colorado, Guam, Puerto Rico, and Wyoming). Only nine jurisdictions, including Arkansas, reject a wrongful-death action for a viable fetus.

Compare Milton v. Cary Med. Center, 538 A.2d 252 (Me. 1988), holding that "person" in the context of the Maine Wrongful Death statute did not include a fetus, and attracting the dissenting words of Wathen, J.:

> [W]e are now left with the result that prenatal injury is actionable while prenatal death is not. The absurdity of such a result is usually illustrated by the hypothetical of twins suffering simultaneous prenatal injuries, with one dying moments before birth and the other dying moments after birth." 538 A.2d at 258.

See also Giardina v. Bennett, 111 N.J. 412, 545 A.2d 139 (1988), holding that a fetus was not a "person" for the purposes of the New Jersey Wrongful Death Act, but permitting the parents to bring an emotional distress action against the physician for damages associated with the prebirth death.

5. *Fetal Wrongful Death Actions and Voluntary Terminations.* In *Light v. Proctor Community Hosp.,* 182 Ill. App. 3d 563, 538 N.E.2d 828 (1989), plaintiff brought a wrongful death claim on behalf of her unborn fetus, alleging that defendants were negligent in failing to determine if she was pregnant prior to performing a thyroid scan. Because of the possibility of damage to the fetus by the scanning, plaintiff terminated her pregnancy. The court denied her cause of action because the Illinois wrongful death statute included the following provision: "There shall be no cause of action against a physician or a medical institution for the wrongful death of a fetus caused by an abortion where the abortion was permitted by law and the requisite consent was lawfully given."

PROBLEM

For socio-economic reasons, Husband underwent a vasectomy operation which was negligently performed by Doctor. There was no indication of any medical risk in Husband and Wife having children. Doctor instructed Husband to return to Doctor's office three weeks after the operation "to validate the operation," but Husband failed to make this return visit. Approximately ten months after the operation, Wife gave birth to a child afflicted with Down's

Syndrome. Is there any liability on the part of the Doctor? Would it make any difference if the child were born healthy, but subsequently suffered severe brain damage on being inoculated as an infant with the DPT (diphtheria-pertussis-tetanus) vaccine?

BADER v. JOHNSON
732 N. E. 2d 1212 (Ind. 2000)

RUCKER, JUSTICE.

The facts most favorable to the Johnsons as nonmoving parties show they gave birth to their first child in 1979. Born with hydrocephalus and severe mental and motor retardation, the child required extensive medical care until her death at four months of age. When Connie became pregnant again in 1982, the Johnsons were fearful of bearing another child with congenital defects so they sought consultation with Dr. Bader. Testing showed the pregnancy was normal. Apparently the birth proceeded without complication. The Johnsons again sought counseling with Dr. Bader when Connie became pregnant in 1991. An amniocentesis performed at 19 1/2 weeks gestation revealed no abnormalities. However, Dr. Bader performed an ultrasound test the same day that revealed a fetus with a larger than expected cavity within the brain and an unusual head shape. Dr. Bader requested her staff to schedule Connie for follow-up testing. Due to an office error however Connie was not scheduled and the ultrasound report was not forwarded to Connie's treating physician.

At 33 weeks gestation Connie's treating physician performed his own ultrasound test and discovered that the unborn child had hydrocephalus. It was too late to terminate the pregnancy and Connie gave birth on September 4, 1991. In addition to hydrocephalus, the child had multiple birth defects and died as a result four months later. The Johnsons alleged negligence in Healthcare Providers' failure to inform the Johnsons of the result of the ultrasound test conducted at 19 1/2 weeks gestation. Healthcare Providers responded with a motion for summary judgment contending Indiana does not recognize a claim for wrongful birth, and even if it does recognize such a claim, the trial court needed to determine what if any damages were recoverable.

Although not disputing the operative facts in this case, Healthcare Providers contend the trial court erred in denying its motion for summary judgment because as a matter of law Indiana does not recognize a claim in tort for wrongful birth. Although a popular characterization among some commentators and a number of jurisdictions the term "wrongful birth" seems to have its genesis as a play upon the statutory tort of "wrongful death." However, as the Nevada Supreme Court observed, "we see no reason for compounding or complicating our medical malpractice jurisprudence by according this particular form of professional negligence action some special status apart from presently recognized medical malpractice or by giving it the new name of 'wrongful birth.'" *Greco v. United States*, 111 Nev. 405, 893 P.2d 345, 348 (Nev. 1995). We agree. It is unnecessary to characterize the cause of action here as "wrongful birth" because the facts alleged in the Johnsons' complaint either state a claim for medical malpractice or they do not. Labeling the Johnsons' cause of action as "wrongful birth" adds nothing to the analysis, inspires confusion, and implies the court has adopted a new tort.

This jurisdiction has long recognized a physician's duty to disclose to her patient material facts relevant to the patient's decision about treatment. *Boruff v. Jesseph*, 576 N.E.2d 1297, 1299 (Ind. Ct. App. 1991). Although a discussion of this duty has generally arisen in cases involving informed consent and the doctrine of fraudulent concealment, neither of which is alleged here, the underlying premise is still the same. In order for a patient to make an informed decision about her health, she must have the relevant facts at her disposal. If the physician has possession of those facts, then the physician has a duty to disclose them. "This duty arises from the relationship between the doctor and patient, and is imposed as a matter of law as are most legal duties." *Culbertson v. Mernitz*, 602 N.E.2d 98, 101 (Ind. 1992). In this case, the Johnsons allege they consulted Healthcare Providers to obtain information having a direct bearing on Connie's health, namely: a decision to terminate the pregnancy. According to the Johnsons the ultrasound test conducted by Healthcare Providers, revealing pre-natal abnormalities, was precisely the kind of information the couple needed to make an informed decision. For purposes of this summary judgment action we accept the Johnsons' assertions as true. As a matter of law Healthcare Providers owed a duty to the Johnsons to disclose the result of the test.

Assuming duty and breach of duty, we next address the third element of a medical malpractice cause of action: compensable injury proximately caused by the breach. According to the Johnsons, as a result of Healthcare Providers' conduct they were not informed of the fetus' condition until it was too late to terminate the pregnancy, resulting in Connie carrying to term and giving birth to a severely deformed child. An indispensable element of a negligence claim is that the act complained of must be the proximate cause of the plaintiff's injuries. A negligent act is the proximate cause of an injury if the injury is a natural and probable consequence, which in the light of the circumstances, should have been foreseen or anticipated.

On the question of causation, Healthcare Providers make two claims: (1) there is an insufficient nexus between the Johnsons' claimed injury and the alleged act of negligence, and (2) Healthcare Providers did not "cause" the Johnsons' injury. At a minimum, proximate cause requires that the injury would not have occurred but for the defendant's conduct. The "but for" test presupposes that absent the defendant's conduct, a plaintiff would have been spared suffering the claimed injury. The Johnsons' claimed injury is that but for Healthcare Providers' failure to provide them with the result of the ultrasound test, the pregnancy would have been terminated. Whether the Johnsons can carry their burden of proof on this point at trial remains to be seen. However, at this stage of the proceedings the question is whether the Johnsons' carrying to term and giving birth to a severely deformed child can be the natural and probable consequence of Healthcare Providers' breach of duty, which Healthcare Providers should have foreseen or anticipated. This question must be answered affirmatively. Again, for purposes of this summary judgment action only, we accept as true the allegations contained in the Johnsons' complaint and the reasonable inferences to be drawn therefrom. The record shows the Johnsons consulted Healthcare Providers in 1982 when Connie was pregnant with her second child and again in 1991 when she became pregnant with her third child. The consultations were inspired by experiences the Johnsons encountered with their first child who was born with severe defects. The facts most favorable to the Johnsons suggest that Healthcare Providers knew or reasonably should have known that depending on the results of the ultrasound test, the Johnsons would not carry the pregnancy to term. We conclude, therefore that the Johnsons have made a *prima facie* claim of legal causation.

Advancing several public policy arguments, Healthcare Providers contend that even assuming duty, breach, and proximate cause the Johnsons still should not be allowed to pursue their claim. Chief among its arguments is that the court is being called upon "to weigh life (however imperfect) against the non-existence of life as that directly impacts the parents of the child." Brief of Appellant at 20. Characterizing the Johnsons' injury as the birth of a child with congenital defects, Healthcare Providers argue "life, even life with severe defects, cannot be an injury in the legal sense." Brief of Appellant at 24 (quoting *Cowe*, 575 N.E.2d at 635).

We first observe that the injury claimed in this case is not the child's defects themselves. The Johnsons do not claim that the negligence of Healthcare Providers "caused" their child's defects. Instead, they contend that Healthcare Providers' negligence caused them to lose the ability to terminate the pregnancy and thereby avoid the costs associated with carrying and giving birth to a child with severe defects. In the context of this medical malpractice action, the distinction between causing the Johnsons to forego termination of the troubled pregnancy and causing a defective birth is significant. The former is a matter of causation while the latter goes to the question of damages, which we discuss in more detail in the next section of this opinion. This distinction was amplified in *Cowe* where we were confronted with a claim by a child born to a mentally retarded mother. While in the custody of a nursing home the mother was raped, resulting in the child's birth. The child sued the nursing home contending, among other things, that because of the nursing home's negligence in failing to protect the mother from rape, the child was wrongly born "into a world in which there was no natural parent capable of caring for and supporting him." 575 N.E.2d at 632. We rejected the child's claim on two interrelated grounds: (1) "a general conceptual unwillingness to recognize any cognizable damages for a child born with a genetic impairment as opposed to not being born at all", and (2) "the impossibility of calculating compensatory damages to restore a birth defective child to the position he would have occupied were it not for the defendant's negligence." *Cowe*, 575 N.E.2d at 634. Both interrelated grounds go to the issue of damages. It was in that context we declared "life, even life with severe defects, cannot be an injury in the legal sense." *Cowe*, 575 N.E.2d at 635.

Thus, in *Cowe*, the injury was life itself. And as with numerous other jurisdictions we were unwilling to allow a child plaintiff to proceed with this cause of action, in part because it involved "a calculation of damages dependant upon the relevant benefits of an impaired life as opposed to no life at all . . . a comparison the law is not equipped to make." *Cowe*, 575 N.E.2d at 634. Here, however, the injury is the lost opportunity and ability to terminate the pregnancy. Failure to allow the Johnsons to proceed with their claim would "immunize those in the medical field from liability for their performance in one particular area of medical practice." *Garrison v. Foy*, 486 N.E.2d 5, 8 (Ind. Ct. App. 1985) (recognizing the existence of a cause of action for wrongful pregnancy). We decline to carve out an exception in this case, and see no reason to prohibit the Johnsons from pursuing their claim.

It is a well-established principle that damages are awarded to fairly and adequately compensate an injured party for her loss, and the proper measure of damages must be flexible enough to fit the circumstances. In tort actions generally, all damages directly related to the wrong and arising without an intervening agency are recoverable. In negligence actions specifically, the injured party is entitled to damages proximately caused by the tortfeasor's breach of duty. In order for a negligent act to be a proximate cause of injury, the injury need only be a natural and probable result thereof; and the consequence be one which in light of the circumstances should reasonably have been foreseen or anticipated.

Viewing this case as asserting a tort of "wrongful birth" the trial court determined that the Johnsons could recover the following damages: (1) the extraordinary costs necessary to treat the birth defect, (2) any additional medical or educational costs attributable to the birth defect during the child's minority, (3) medical and hospital expenses incurred as a result of the physician's negligence, (4) the physical pain suffered by the mother, (5) loss of consortium, and (6) the mental and emotional anguish suffered by the parents. The Court of Appeals also viewed this case as one for "wrongful birth." Thus, following the lead from other jurisdictions, with the exception of mental and emotional distress, the Court of Appeals agreed the Johnsons were entitled to recover the foregoing damages. However, we have determined that this case should be treated no differently than any other medical malpractice case. Consequently, we need not evaluate the type of damages that may be allowed in a claimed "wrongful birth" action. Rather, we look at the damages the Johnsons contend they suffered and determine whether, if proven, they be can said to have been proximately caused by Healthcare Providers' breach of duty.

Consolidated and rephrased the Johnsons' complaint essentially sets forth the following damages: (1) hospital and related medical expenses associated with the pregnancy and delivery, (2) costs associated with providing the infant with care and treatment, (3) lost income, (4) emotional distress, and (5) loss of consortium. Indiana subscribes to the general principle of tort law that all damages directly attributable to the wrong done are recoverable. As we have indicated, the Johnsons' claimed injury in this case is the lost opportunity and ability to terminate the pregnancy. In turn, the loss can be measured by the medical and other costs directly attributable to Connie carrying the child to term. In addition to emotional distress damages, which we discuss below, the damages the Johnsons seek are consistent with those naturally flowing from Healthcare Providers' breach of duty.

In *Shuamber v. Henderson*, 579 N.E.2d 452 (Ind. 1991), a mother and daughter sought recovery for the emotional distress they suffered when their son/brother was killed. The death occurred when the car in which the three were traveling was struck by a drunk driver. Indiana's traditional "impact rule" precluded mother and daughter from obtaining relief. The rule required that damages for mental distress or emotional trauma could be recovered only where the distress was accompanied by and resulted from a physical injury caused by an impact to the person seeking recovery. Mother and daughter could not recover because their emotional trauma was not triggered by their own injuries, but rather by witnessing the injuries of their son/brother. Although not abolishing the rule, this court modified it as follows:

> When, as here, a plaintiff sustains a direct impact by the negligence of another and, by virtue of that direct involvement sustains an emotional trauma which is serious in nature and of a kind and extent normally expected to occur in a reasonable person, . . . such plaintiff is entitled to maintain an action to recover for that emotional trauma without regard to whether the emotional trauma arises out of or accompanies any physical injury to the plaintiff.

Shuamber, 579 N.E.2d at 456.

The underlying rationale for Indiana's traditional impact rule was that "absent physical injury, mental anguish is speculative, subject to exaggeration, likely to lead to fictitious claims, and often so unforeseeable that there is no rational basis for awarding damages." *Cullison v. Medley*, 570 N.E.2d 27, 29 (Ind. 1991). As modified, the rule still requires physical impact as distinguished from physical injury. However, the rationale for requiring some type of physical impact is still the same. Stated somewhat differently, as the United States Supreme Court observed "because the etiology of emotional disturbance is usually not as readily apparent as that of a broken bone following an automobile accident, courts have been concerned . . . that recognition of a cause of action for [emotional] injury when not related to any physical trauma may inundate judicial resources with a flood of relatively trivial claims, many of which may be imagined or falsified, and that liability may be imposed for highly remote consequences of a negligent act." *Consolidated Rail Corporation v. Gottshall*, 512 U.S. 532, 545, 114 S. Ct. 2396, 129 L. Ed. 2d 427 (1994).

Indiana's physical impact requirement embraces these concerns. Thus, when the courts have been satisfied that the facts of a particular case are such that the alleged mental anguish was not likely speculative, exaggerated, fictitious, or unforeseeable, then the claimant has been allowed to proceed with an emotional distress claim for damages even though the physical impact was slight, or the evidence of physical impact seemed to have been rather tenuous.

In this case we find that Connie's continued pregnancy and the physical transformation her body underwent as a result, satisfy the direct impact requirement of our modified impact rule. Provided she can prevail on her negligence claim, we see no reason why Connie should not be able to claim damages for emotional distress. By contrast, Ronald did not suffer a direct impact as a result of Healthcare Provider's alleged negligence. We disagree with his argument to the contrary. Rather, at most Ronald is a relative bystander, a classification of potential victims this court has recently adopted in *Groves v. Taylor*, 729 N.E.2d 569, 572–73 (Ind. 2000). Whether Ronald can prevail on his claim for emotional distress damages depends on the evidence adduced at trial.

DICKSON, JUSTICE, dissenting

Actions for "wrongful life" and "wrongful birth" are different from other kinds of negligence actions. In *Cowe*, we held that "damages for wrongful life are not cognizable under Indiana law," id. at 635, for two principal reasons: (1) "[a] general conceptual unwillingness to recognize any cognizable damages for a child born with a genetic impairment as opposed to not being born at all," and (2) the impossibility of calculating compensatory damages to restore a child born with a birth defect to the position he would have occupied were it not for the defendant's negligence, *id.* at 634. But it was primarily the former concern upon which we focused, concluding that " 'life, even life with severe defects, cannot be an injury in the legal sense.' " *Id.* at 635. Although this case presents a claim for wrongful birth, the same concerns permeate it as

The majority opinion, treating the claim as a routine negligence claim, establishes troubling precedent, particularly as to the nature and extent of damages. If such claimants may recover all damages naturally flowing from a medical provider's breach of duty, would this not also include the costs of raising and educating such "unwanted" children? Will the birth of a child with even slight congenital anomalies entitle the parents to claim medical malpractice damages, contending that "if they had only known" their child would have a birth defect, they would have terminated the pregnancy? Will our courts face actions by parents seeking child-rearing costs because the gender of their child was not as expected, when they had sought genetic counseling for the purpose of terminating the pregnancy in the event that the child was of the "wrong" gender? Will defendant health-care providers be entitled to claim a reduction in damages by presenting evidence and arguing that, if the plaintiff-parents had elected to terminate the pregnancy, they would likely have suffered substantial and continuing psychological trauma? Will the process of jury selection (and resulting appeals) become a new battleground for intense disagreements regarding the issue of abortion? These are but a few of the troubling, foreseeable consequences of the majority opinion.

I believe that, because of the resulting complex philosophical, moral, and political implications, this Court should not expand Indiana common law to permit parents to seek damages resulting from the loss of an opportunity to terminate a pregnancy. As we noted in *Cowe*, this involves "a calculation of damages dependent upon the relative benefits of an impaired life as opposed to no life at all." *Cowe*, 575 N.E.2d at 634. Courts are ill-equipped to provide fair, reasonable, and intelligent resolutions to these questions.

I therefore dissent and believe that summary judgment should be entered in favor of the defendants.

NOTES

1. *A Causal Solution?* In *Wilson v. Kuenzi*, 751 S.W.2d 741, 744–45 (Mo. 1988), defendant doctor allegedly failed to advise parents in their mid-thirties of the availability of the amniocentesis test for Down's Syndrome. In denying the parents' claim the court stated:

> A reading of all of the cases persuades us that the real underlying problem in these cases stems from the fact that the courts have either

closed their eyes to traditional tort causation, or have leaped over causation. Most courts have tried to cover the leap over causation by blending some causation language into their discussion of damages or into their discussions of public policy considerations. . . . The heart of the problem in these cases is that the physician cannot be said to have caused the defect. The disorder is genetic and not the result of any injury negligently inflicted by the doctor. In addition it is incurable and was incurable from the moment of conception. Thus the doctor's alleged negligent failure to detect it during prenatal examination cannot be considered a cause of the condition by analogy to those cases in which the doctor has failed to make a timely diagnosis of a curable disease. The child's handicap is an inexorable result of conception and birth.

[B]y holding the doctor responsible for the birth of a genetically handicapped child, and thus obligated to pay most, if not all, of the costs of lifetime care and support, the court has created a kind of medical paternity suit. . . . The limits of this new liability cannot be predicted. But if it is to be limited at all it would appear that it can only be confined by drawing arbitrary and artificial boundaries which a majority of the court consider popular or desirable. This alone should be sufficient to indicate that these cases pose a problem which can only be properly resolved by a legislative body, and not by courts of law. *Becker v. Schwartz,* 46 N.Y.2d 401, 417–22, 386 N.E.2d 807, 816–19, 413 N.Y.S.2d 895, 904–07 (1978), (Wachtler, J. concurring in part and dissenting in part).

We find no case which has directly and effectively dealt with the problems of causation raised by Judge Wachtler. All, in our opinion, have either closed their eyes to the requirements of causation; or, have blended causation into social policy reasons for permitting recovery; or have blended causation into the discussion of the types of damage permitted to be recovered.

Those who have practiced family law during the past two decades have with some frequency become painfully aware of the difficulty of satisfactorily determining and knowing the real reason why a given woman may or may not choose to have an abortion. In the wrongful birth action, the right to recovery is based solely on the woman testifying, long after the fact and when it is in her financial interest to do so, that she would have chosen to abort if the physician had but told her of the amniocentesis test. The percentage of women who under pressure refuse to consider abortion, whether for reasons of religious belief, strong motherly instincts, or for other reasons, is sometimes astounding. It would seem that testimony either more verifiable based upon experience or more verifiable by some objective standard should be required as the basis for any action for substantial damages.

Contrast Lininger v. Eisenbaum, 764 P.2d 1202 (Colo. 1988), wherein the court stated:

We disagree . . . because we do not find that the injury to the parents is simply that their child is impaired. Rather . . . the parents are injured to the extent they choose, based on the physicians alleged misrepresentation, to conceive and deliver an impaired child therefore incurring extraordinary medical expenses.

Quaere: How do courts deal with causation issues in informed consent cases and "loss of a chance" cases? How do wrongful birth and impaired life cases differ from informed consent and lost chance cases on the issues of consent and causation?

2. *Turpin v. Sortini*, 31 Cal. 3d 220, 182 Cal. Rptr. 337, 643 P.2d 954 (1982), is one of the few cases in which a genetically harmed child has been held to state a claim for damages. In *Turpin* the plaintiff's sibling was misdiagnosed. The plaintiff, Joy, was conceived subsequently, her parents alleging that they would not have conceived the second child if they had known of the risk of hereditary deafness:

> [D]efendants' basic position — supported by the numerous out-of-state authorities — is that Joy has suffered no legally cognizable injury or rationally ascertainable damages as a result of their alleged negligence. Although the issues of "legally cognizable injury" and "damages" are intimately related and in some sense inseparable, past cases have generally treated the two as distinct matters and, for purposes of analysis, it seems useful to follow that approach.
>
> While it thus seems doubtful that a child's claim for general damages should properly be denied on the rationale that the value of impaired life, as a matter of law, always exceeds the value of nonlife, we believe that the out-of-state decisions are on sounder grounds in holding that — with respect to the child's claim for pain and suffering or other general damages — recovery should be denied because (1) it is simply impossible to determine in any rational or reasoned fashion whether the plaintiff has in fact suffered an injury in being born impaired rather than not being born, and (2) even if it were possible to overcome the first hurdle, it would be impossible to assess general damages in any fair, nonspeculative manner.
>
> We believe, however, that there is profound qualitative difference between the difficulties faced by a jury in assessing general damages in a normal personal injury or wrongful death action, and the task before a jury in assessing general damages, in a wrongful life case. In the first place, the problem is not simply the fixing of damages for a conceded injury, but the threshold question of determining whether the plaintiff has in fact suffered an injury by being born with an ailment as opposed to not being born at all. . . .
>
> Furthermore, the practical problems are exacerbated when it comes to the matter of arriving at an appropriate award of damages. As already discussed, in fixing damages in a tort case the jury generally compares the condition plaintiff would have been in but for the tort, with the position the plaintiff is in now, compensating the plaintiff for what has been lost as a result of the wrong. Although the valuation of pain and suffering or emotional distress in terms of dollars and cents is unquestionably difficult in an ordinary personal injury action,

jurors at least have some frame of reference in their own general experience to appreciate what the plaintiff has lost — normal life without pain and suffering. In a wrongful life action, that simply is not the case, for what the plaintiff has "lost" is not life without pain and suffering but rather the unknowable status of never having been born. In this context, a rational, nonspeculative determination of a specific monetary award in accordance with normal tort principles appears to be outside the realm of human competence.

. . . Although we have determined that the trial court properly rejected plaintiff's claim for general damages, we conclude that her claim for the "extraordinary expenses for specialized teaching, training and hearing equipment" that she will incur during her lifetime because of her deafness stands on a different footing.

. . . Although the parents and child cannot, of course, both recover for the same medical expenses, we believe it would be illogical and anomalous to permit only parents, and not the child, to recover for the cost of the child's own medical care. If such a distinction were established, the afflicted child's receipt of necessary medical expenses might well depend on the wholly fortuitous circumstances of whether the parents are available to sue and recover such damages or whether the medical expenses are incurred at a time when the parents remain legally responsible for providing such care.

3. *Agency for Life or Death.* Turpin, *supra,* suggests that the parents of the fetus act as its agents for the receipt of information as to its genetic health so that "when a defendant negligently fails to diagnose an hereditary ailment, he harms the potential child as well as the parents by depriving the parents of information which may be necessary to determine whether it is in the child's own interest to be born with defects or not to be born at all." This approach supplies the most cogent theoretical basis for the impaired life cause of action, in that it seems analogous to an informed consent action. *See, e.g., Shack v. Holland,* 89 Misc. 2d 78, 389 N.Y.S.2d 988 (1976), holding that a child may bring a post-natal wrongful life action for breach of the duty to obtain informed consent when adequate information had not been conveyed pre-natally to his mother. Ironically, this theoretical basis for the impaired life cause of action does not provide a rational basis for the general damages — special damages distinction also adopted in *Turpin.*

4. *Parental Emotional Distress.* A child's poorly received wrongful life claim for *general* damages is essentially one of damages for pain and suffering. Recovery of such damages could be approximated to a remarkable extent if the court would permit the *parents* to bring a claim for *their* emotional harm. Courts considering this "back-door" approach generally have been unsympathetic. *See, e.g., Becker v. Schwartz,* 46 N.Y.2d 401, 413 N.Y.S.2d 895, 386 N.E.2d 807, 813–14 (1978). *Compare Berman v. Allan,* 80 N.J. 421, 404 A.2d 8, 14 (1979):

> In failing to inform [plaintiff] of the availability of amniocentesis, defendants directly deprived her . . . of the option to accept or reject a parental relationship with the child and thus caused [plaintiffs] to experience mental and emotional anguish upon their realization that

they had given birth to a child afflicted with Down's Syndrome. We feel that the monetary equivalent of this distress is an appropriate measure of the harm suffered by the parents deriving from [plaintiff's] loss of her right to abort the fetus.

Are pain and suffering damages awarded to approximate the contingent attorney's fees which plaintiff must pay from her total recovery? If so, what messages are the courts sending in denying such damages?

5. *The Purpose of Limited Recovery.* Part of the *Turpin* rationale is that the child should not be further burdened because her parents fail to make the claim. Thus, the child should be able to recover through her impaired life action the damages that the parents should have been able to recover in a wrongful birth action. This begs the question as to what the parents should be able to recover: costs for the whole of the child's life expectancy, or costs until their obligation of support terminates? *See, e.g., Haymon v. Wilkerson,* 535 A.2d 880, 885–86 (D.C. App. 1987); *Viccaro v. Milunsky,* 406 Mass. 777, 551 N.E.2d 8 (1990).

6. *Child Versus Parent.* How should a court respond to an action brought by a child suffering from a hereditary defect against her mother for failing to terminate the pregnancy after being informed of the adverse results of her amniocentesis?

PROBLEM

Mr. and Ms. Beethoven live in Anyville. Distressed at the thought of how their careers and Danish furniture might suffer, they decided not to have a family. In 1983, Ms. Beethoven suspected that she was pregnant. She purchased a pregnancy testing kit which rendered a negative result. Two months later Ms. Beethoven realized that she was pregnant. She went to Dr. Chain, her Ob-Gyn, and told him that her husband's family had a history of genetic disorders. However, Dr. Chain did not perform any genetic tests. When Mr. and Ms. Beethoven's son, Ludwig, is born, he suffers from a hereditary hearing defect that will require routine medical care and special equipment to even partially alleviate such a serious impairment to the enjoyment of his life. Notwithstanding, by the time he is two years old, it has become obvious that young Ludwig has prodigious musical talents. As a result, Mr. and Ms. Beethoven have resigned from their jobs and now accompany Ludwig on the concert and talk-show circuits. At his most recent routine check-up, Ludwig's physician informed him that when he is fully grown he will be considerably shorter than average. The physician ascribed this to the fact that Mrs. Beethoven smoked cigarettes while she was pregnant. What (if any) damages will members of the Beethoven family recover? From whom? And why?

UNIVERSITY OF ARIZONA HEALTH SCIENCE CENTER v. SUPERIOR COURT
136 Ariz. 579, 667 P.2d 1294 (1983)

FELDMAN, JUSTICE

The real parties in interest are Patrick Heimann and Jeanne Heimann. . . . The Heimanns claimed that one of the hospital's employees, a doctor, had negligently performed a vasectomy operation upon Patrick Heimann, that as a result Jeanne Heimann became pregnant and on October 4, 1981 gave birth to a baby girl. The Heimanns alleged in the underlying tort action that the vasectomy had been obtained because "already having three children, [they] decided . . . that they desired to have no more children. As a result of this decision they further decided that a vasectomy was the best means of contraception for them." The baby girl is normal and healthy, but the Heimanns argue that they are financially unable to provide for themselves, their other three children and the newest child whose birth was neither planned nor desired. Accordingly, they seek damages from the doctor and his employer.

. . . The first question is whether parents of a child who was neither desired nor planned for but who was, fortunately, normal and healthy, have been damaged at all by the birth of that child. An overview of the authorities indicates rather clearly that the law will recognize at least some types of damage which result from unwanted procreation caused by the negligence of another. The real controversy centers around the nature of the damages which may be recovered. On this issue there are three distinct views.

The first line of authority limits damages by holding that the parents may recover only those damages which occur as the result of pregnancy and birth, and may not recover the cost of rearing the child.

A second view could be characterized as the "full damage" rule and allows the parents to recover all damages and expenses, including the cost of the unsuccessful sterilization procedure, the economic loss from pregnancy, and the economic, physical and emotional cost attendant to birth and rearing the child. These cases appear to be a distinct minority.

A substantial number of cases have adopted a third rule which allows the recovery of all damages which flow from the wrongful act but requires consideration of the offset of benefits. *See* Restatement (Second) of Torts § 920 (1977).[9] Under this view, the trier of fact is permitted to determine and award all past and future expenses and damages incurred by the parent, including the cost of rearing the child, but is also instructed that it should make a deduction for the benefits that the parents will receive by virtue of having a normal, healthy child. . . .

. . . The hospital claims that the trial court was bound by law to adopt the first view, that the cost of rearing and educating the child are not compensable elements of damage. The Heimanns claim, on the other hand, that the proper rule is the second view, which permits the recovery of all damage and does not permit the jury to consider and offset benefits. We disagree with both positions.

We consider first the strict rule urged by the hospital. Various reasons are given by the courts which adopt the view that damages for rearing and educating the child cannot be recovered. Some cases base their decision on

---

[9] Restatement (Second) of Torts § 920 states: When the defendant's tortious conduct has caused harm to the plaintiff or to his property and in so doing has conferred a special benefit to the interest of the plaintiff that was harmed, the value of the benefit conferred is considered in mitigation of damages, to the extent that this is equitable.

the speculative nature of the necessity to assess "such matters as the emotional effect of a birth on siblings as well as parents, and the emotional as well as pecuniary costs of raising an unplanned and, perhaps, an unwanted child in varying family environments." *Coleman v. Garrison,* 327 A.2d 757, 761 (Del. Super. Ct. 1974), *aff'd,* 349 A.2d 8 (1975). We think, however, that juries in tort cases are often required to assess just such intangible factors, both emotional and pecuniary, and see no reason why a new rule should be adopted for wrongful pregnancy cases. Another reason given for the strict view is the argument that the benefits which the parents will receive from having a normal, healthy child outweigh any loss which the parents might incur in rearing and educating the child. No doubt this is true in many cases, but we think it unrealistic to assume that it is true in all cases. We can envision many situations in which for either financial or emotional reasons, or both, the parents are simply unable to handle another child and where it would be obvious that from either an economic or emotional perspective — or both — substantial damage has occurred.

A third basis for the strict rule is the argument that the "injury is out of proportion to the culpability of the [wrongdoer]; and that the allowance of recovery would place an unreasonable burden upon the [wrongdoer], since it would likely open the way for fraudulent claims. . . ." *Beardsley v. Wierdsma,* 650 P.2d 288, 292 (Wyo. 1982). This, of course, is the hue and cry in many tort cases and in essence is no more than the fear that some cases will be decided badly. Undoubtedly, the system will not decide each case correctly in this field, just as it does not in any field, but here, as in other areas of tort law, we think it better to adopt a rule which will enable courts to strive for justice in all cases rather than to rely upon one which will ensure injustice in many.

The final basis for the strict rule is the one which gives this court greater pause than any of the others. It is well put by the Illinois Supreme Court in *Cockrum v. Baumgartner,* 95 Ill. 2d 193, 198–201, 69 Ill. Dec. 168, 171–72, 447 N.E.2d 385, 388–89 (1983). The court used the following words to justify the denial of recovery of damages for the rearing and educating of the unplanned child:

> A parent cannot be said to have been damaged by the birth and rearing of a normal, healthy child. . . . [I]t is a matter of universally-shared emotion and sentiment that the intangible but all important, incalculable but invaluable "benefits" of parenthood far outweigh any of the mere monetary burdens involved. Speaking legally, this may be deemed conclusively presumed by the fact that a prospective parent does not abort or subsequently place the "unwanted" child for adoption. On a more practical level, the validity of the principle may be tested simply by asking any parent the purchase price for that particular youngster. Since this is the rule of experience, it should be, and we therefore hold that it is, the appropriate rule of law.
>
> . . . One can, of course, in mechanical logic reach a different conclusion, but only on the ground that human life and the state of parenthood are compensable losses. In a proper hierarchy of values,

the benefit of life should not be outweighed by the expense of supporting it. Respect for life and the rights proceeding from it are the heart of our legal system and, broader still, our civilization.

These sentiments evoke a response from this court. In most cases we could join in the "universally shared emotion and sentiment" expressed by the majority of the Illinois court, but we do not believe we hold office to impose our views of morality by deciding cases on the basis of personal emotion and sentiment, though we realize we cannot and should not escape the effect of human characteristics shared by all mankind. However, we believe our function is to leave the emotion and sentiment to others and attempt to examine the problem with logic and by application of the relevant principles of law. In this case, we believe that the strict rule is based upon an emotional premise and ignores logical considerations. While we recognize that in most cases a family can and will adjust to the birth of the child, even though they had not desired to have it, we must recognize also that there are cases where the birth of an unplanned child can cause serious emotional or economic problems to the parents. We therefore reject the hospital's claim that the cost of rearing and educating the child can never be compensable elements of damage.

We consider next the "full damage" rule urged by the Heimanns. . . . The courts applying this rule have relied on traditional tort principles and determined that the cost of rearing the child is a foreseeable consequence of the physician's negligence and therefore compensable. We agree that these damages are compensable; however, we believe that rule which does not allow for an offset for the benefits of the parent-child relationship prevents the trier of fact from considering the basic values inherent in the relationship and the dignity and sanctity of human life. We believe that these "sentiments," if they may be called such, are proper considerations for the fact finder in tort cases, whether they be used to mitigate or enhance damages. No doubt ascertaining and assigning a monetary value to such intangibles will be a difficult task, but we do not believe it more difficult than the task of ascertaining the pecuniary and non-pecuniary damages that the parents will experience after the birth of the child. Therefore, we agree with the Illinois Supreme Court that the "full damage" approach is an exercise in mechanical logic and we reject it.

In our view, the preferable rule is that followed by the courts which, although permitting the trier of fact to consider both pecuniary and non-pecuniary elements of damage which pertain to the rearing and education of the child, also require it to consider the question of offsetting the pecuniary and non-pecuniary benefits which the parents will receive from the parental relationship with the child. Some may fear that adoption of such a rule will permit juries to recognize elements of damage which, because of our private philosophy or views of ethics, we, as judges, believe should not be recognized. We feel, however, that the consensus of a cross-section of the community on such important issues is better and more accurately obtained from the verdict of a jury than from the decision of any particular group of that community. A jury verdict based on knowledge of all relevant circumstances is a better reflection of whether real damage exists in each case than can be obtained from use of any abstract, iron-clad rule which some courts would adopt and apply regardless of the circumstances of the particular case.

There may be those who fear that the rule which we adopt will permit the award of damages where no real injury exists. We feel this danger is minimized by giving weight and consideration in each case to the plaintiff's reason for submitting to sterilization procedures. Such evidence is perhaps the most relevant information on the question of whether the subsequent birth of a child actually constitutes damage to the parents. The parents' preconception calculation of the reasons for preventing procreation is untainted by bitterness, greed or sense of duty to the child and is perhaps the most telling evidence of whether or to what extent the birth of the child actually injured the parents. For example, where the parent sought sterilization in order to avoid the danger of genetic defect, the jury could easily find that the uneventful birth of a healthy, non-defective child was a blessing rather than a "damage." Such evidence should be admissible, and the rule which we adopt will allow the jury to learn all the factors relevant to the determination of whether there has been any real damage and, if so, how much. We are confident that the inherent good sense of the jury is the best safeguard to "runaway" verdicts and unfounded speculation in the award of damages, provided that the jury is allowed to consider the issues in realistic terms.

It may be argued also that the rule which we adopt will have the unhappy effect of creating situations in which parents will testify to their feeling or opinion that the child is "not worth" the burden of having the rearing. Such testimony could be harmful if or when the child learns of it. "We are not convinced that the effect on the child will be significantly detrimental in every case, or even in most cases; . . . we think the parents, not the courts, are the ones who must weigh the risk."

. . . We see no reason why ordinary damage rules, applicable to all other tort cases, should not be applicable to this situation. By allowing the jury to consider the future costs, both pecuniary and non-pecuniary, of rearing and educating the child, we permit it to consider all the elements of damage on which the parents may present evidence. By permitting the jury to consider the reason for the procedure and to assess and offset the pecuniary and non-pecuniary benefits which will inure to the parents by reason of their relationship to the child, we allow the jury to discount those damages, thus reducing speculation and permitting the verdict to be based upon the facts as they actually exist in each of the unforeseeable variety of situations which may come before the court. We think this by far the better rule. The blindfold on the figure of justice is a shield from partiality, not from reality.

GORDON, VICE CHIEF JUSTICE (concurring in part and dissenting in part).

The rule of damages established by the majority in this case may indeed be logical and legally scientific. Logic and science may, however, lead to results at variance with public policy. Although I have a very high degree of respect for our country's system of civil justice, and readily admit that our common law concepts of tort liability have caused products manufactured in the United States to be among the safest in the world, I feel that there are some human misfortunes that do not lend themselves to solution by combat in the courtroom. Wrongful pregnancy, in my opinion, is one of those. I believe the rule allowing damages recovery beyond the costs of birth in cases such as these would violate what I consider the public policy of our state in several ways.

As is pointed out in the majority opinion, the prosecution of this type of action requires parents to deny the worth of the child, thus placing the values of the parents over those of the child. Under the "benefits rule," a judgment for the parents is a conclusion by the court that a child is not worth what it takes to raise him or her. This problem has been recognized by several authors who refer to such a child as an "emotional bastard" when attempting to describe the stigma that will attach to the child when he learns the true circumstances of his upbringing. . . .

The decision in this matter will likely impinge upon the availability and costs of sterilization surgery in Arizona. It is conceivable that hereafter many health care providers will either refuse to perform these procedures, or they will become so expensive that only the wealthy will be able to afford them. If the intended result of the majority is to lessen the number of unwanted pregnancies by requiring more skill and caution in the performance of sterilization procedures, I believe that this case will be self-defeating. There will probably be an increase in the number of unwanted pregnancies due to the increased cost and relative unavailability of surgical sterilization.

Finally, it is well known that our courts are already overcrowded with cases. The majority has by this decision created a new and expansive concept which will generate new and protracted litigation. . . .

A further non-policy criticism that I have of the majority opinion is that it is not entirely consistent. If the Court is to allow some of the logical principles of tort law to apply in this very sensitive area, then I feel that all of them should apply. The majority, however, fails to do so in at least two instances. First, in the usual lawsuit if a plaintiff has failed to mitigate his or her damages this fact is allowed as an offset against recovery. In this case the Court, although eschewing emotions and sentiment, has for unexplained reasons decided that the parents' failure to choose abortion or adoption should not be considered in mitigation. The majority has apparently decided that these methods of mitigating damages are unreasonable as a matter of law. The question of the reasonableness of a method of mitigating damages, however, is generally a question of fact to be decided by the trier of fact. In some cases abortion or adoption will not be reasonable, while in others it will be reasonable. If we are going to open the door, logically, we should open it all the way. If the plaintiff parents — who have endeavored not to have a child, pleaded his or her birth as an injury to them, and claimed substantial damages — chose not to take advantage of abortion or adoption, the defendant should be permitted to establish that by so doing the parents unreasonably failed to mitigate their damages.

Second, the majority misapplies Restatement (Second) of Torts § 920 (1977). Section 920 specifically states that for a benefit to be considered in mitigation of damages it must be "a special benefit to the interest of the plaintiff that was harmed. . . ." Furthermore, a comment to § 920 explains how the "same interest" requirement operates:

> *Limitation to same interest.* Damages resulting from an invasion of one interest are not diminished by showing that another interest has been benefited. Thus one who has harmed another's reputation by defamatory statements cannot show in mitigation of damages that the

other has been financially benefited from their publication . . . unless damages are claimed for harm to pecuniary interests. . . . Damages for pain and suffering are not diminished by showing that the earning capacity of the plaintiff has been increased by the defendant's act. . . . Damages to a husband for loss of consortium are not diminished by the fact that the husband is no longer under the expense of supporting the wife.

Restatement, *supra,* § 920 comment *b.* A proper application of the "same interest" requirement in a wrongful pregnancy case would require that pecuniary harm of raising the child be offset only by corresponding pecuniary benefit, and emotional benefits of the parent-child relationship be applied as an offset only to corresponding emotional harm.

. . . I am convinced that the proper balance between strict tort law principles and sound public policy would be struck by precluding recovery of the future costs of raising and educating the child.

NOTES

1. *Protected Interests.* In *Lovelace Medical Center v. Mendez,* 111 N.M. 336, 805 P.2d 603 (1991), the court analyzed the parents' claims as follows:

[W]e believe the couple suffered at least two forms of harm. First, as indicated previously, Mrs. Mendez remained fertile despite her desire to be infertile. From the standpoint of the couple, their desire to limit the size of their family — to procreate no further — was frustrated.

Second, their interest in financial security — in the economic stability of their family — was impaired. The undesired costs of raising another child to adulthood — costs which they had striven to avoid and had engaged Lovelace to help them avert — were suddenly thrust upon them. This was a detriment to their pecuniary advantage — i.e., harm. Was it legally compensable — i.e., an injury, an invasion of a legally protected interest?

The interest in one's economic stability is clearly an example of an interest that receives legal protection in a wide variety of contexts. In the context of a negligently performed, unsuccessful sterilization operation, the Supreme Court of Wisconsin has recently held that the costs of raising the child to majority may be recovered because, among other things:

Individuals often seek sterilization precisely because the burdens of raising a child are substantial and they are not in a position to incur them. . . .

. . . The love, affection, and emotional support they [the parents] are prepared to give do not bring with them the economic means that are also necessary to feed, clothe, educate and otherwise raise the child. That is what this suit is about. . . . Relieving the family of the economic costs of raising the child may well add to the emotional well-being of the entire family, including this child, rather than bring damage to it.

Marciniak v. Lundborg, 153 Wis. 2d 59, 67, 450 N.W.2d 243, 246 (1990).

We hold, therefore, that the Mendezes' interest in the financial security of their family was a legally protected interest which was invaded by Lovelace's negligent failure properly to perform Maria's sterilization operation (if proved at trial), and that this invasion was an injury entitling them to recover damages in the form of the reasonable expenses to raise Joseph to majority.

Like the interest in financial security, the interest in family planning has in recent years received extensive — indeed, constitutional — protection in the courts.

We have no hesitancy in concluding that in addition to the injury inflicted on them by the invasion of their interest in financial security, Mr. and Mrs. Mendez suffered an injury through the invasion of their legally protected interest in limiting the size of their family.

However, we admit to far less certainty as to the measure of the damages that flow from such an injury, if and to the extent that such damages differ from (exceed) the damages flowing from their economic injury. We have said that Mrs. Mendez is entitled to damages for the pain and suffering, if any, that were associated with her pregnancy and Joseph's birth. What other elements of damage should be awarded to her and her husband for invasion of their interest in family planning? Put another way, what kind of harms, in addition to economic loss, are compensable for an injury of this type?

All of these nonpecuniary harms resulting from interference with the parents' interests in limiting the size of their family would, we think, properly be subject to mitigation or offset under Restatement (Second) of Torts 920 (1979).

[T]his "offsetting benefits" principle applies only to reduction of damages for invasion of the same interest as the one that has been harmed. It thus, in theory, would permit proof of emotional and psychological benefits to the parents from the birth of the additional child to offset the same kind of detriments, but not to offset detriments flowing from invasion of a different interest, such as the interest in financial security. A trial over such issues, however, could result in the unseemly spectacle of the parents' attempting to prove how slight or nonexistent was the psychological benefit they derived from their additional child in order to minimize the offset to their nonpecuniary interests. We hold that permitting such a dispute to be litigated would be contrary to public policy. We therefore agree with the court of appeals that the emotional distress, if any, caused by an additional child is not compensable. We also agree, applying Section 920 of the Restatement, that the emotional benefits from having an additional (healthy) child do not mitigate the economic costs of rearing the child.

2. *Mitigation and Reproductive Autonomy.* To what extent would a common law rule providing for mitigation of damages through, for example, abortion or adoption run counter to the privacy guarantees espoused in *Griswold v. Connecticut,* 381 U.S. 479, 85 S. Ct. 1678, 14 L. Ed. 2d 510 (1965) and *Roe v. Wade,* 410 U.S. 113, 93 S. Ct. 705, 35 L. Ed. 2d 147 (1973)?

3. *Life Outside of Yuppiedom.* In *Cockrum v. Baumgartner,* 95 Ill. 2d 193, 69 Ill. Dec. 168, 447 N.E.2d 385, 394 (1983), Clark J., dissenting, noted:

> A couple privileged to be bringing home the combined income of a dual professional household may well be able to sustain and cherish an unexpected child. But I am not sure the child's smile would be the most memorable characteristic to an indigent couple, where the husband underwent a vasectomy or the wife underwent a sterilization procedure, not because they did not desire a child, but rather because they faced the stark realization that they could not afford to feed an additional person, much less clothe, educate and support a child when that couple had trouble supporting one another. The choice is not always giving up personal amenities in order to buy a gift for the baby; the choice may only be to stretch necessities beyond the breaking point to provide for a child that the couple had purposely set out to avoid having.

4. *Quantification.* In *Jones v. Malinowski,* 299 Md. 257, 473 A.2d 429, 436 (1984), the Court of Appeals of Maryland remarked:

> The child rearing costs here in issue are neither too unquantifiable nor too speculative to deny their recovery under settled rules applied by the cases. The computation of such costs requires a routine calculation of reasonably foreseeable expenses that will be incurred by the parents to maintain, support and educate the child to majority age. Such calculations are based on well-recognized economic factors regularly made by actuaries for estate planners and insurance companies; indeed, the expenses associated with raising a child are well appreciated by the average citizen through first hand experience.

See also Zehr v. Haugen, 318 Or. 647, 871 P.2d 1006 (1994), where the court held plaintiffs could recover the costs of raising a healthy child who was born as a result of a negligent tubal ligation.

5. *Termination Expenses.* Suppose the victim of a wrongful pregnancy chose abortion over birth; should the defendant be liable for the costs of termination — including the emotional "costs?"

Consider also *Lynch v. Bay Ridge Obstetrical & Gynecological Assocs.,* 72 N.Y.2d 632, 532 N.E.2d 1239 (1988), holding patient stated a claim against her gynecologist, who failed to diagnose her pregnancy and prescribed medication which could cause birth defects, thus forcing the patient to choose between abortion and a potentially defective child.

6. *Status Complaints.* From the earliest decision in *Zepeda v. Zepeda,* 41 Ill. App. 2d 240, 190 N.E.2d 849 (1963), *cert. denied,* 379 U.S. 945, children born without physical impairments have been denied claims based upon, for example, their illegitimacy or poverty. *See Beardsley v. Wierdsma,* 650 P.2d

288, 290 (Wyo. 1982). However, given the reasoning of *Turpin* in permitting a limited action by the child to recover those items of damages which her parents could have recovered, should not the same consideration be given the child whose parents' action has been negated by, for example, a statute of limitations? *Cf. Miller v. Duhart,* 637 S.W.2d 183 (Mo. App. 1982).

7. *Wrongful Adoption Actions.* In *Burr v. Board of County Comm'rs,* 23 Ohio St. 3d 69, 491 N.E.2d 1101 (1986), adoptive parents brought an action in fraud against the county adoption division. The 17-month-old boy they adopted had been represented as the son of a young unmarried mother who was leaving the state. In fact, the child's mother was actually a 31-year-old mental patient at the state hospital. The child was born at the institution, and it was presumed that his father also was a mental patient. The child shared many of the same mental impediments as his mother and was diagnosed as suffering from Huntington's Disease, a genetically inherited disease which destroys the central nervous system. The court found that the evidence supported plaintiffs' verdict.

Meracle v. Children's Serv. Soc'y of Wis., 149 Wis. 2d 19, 437 N.W.2d 532, 537 (1989), concerned an action against a private adoption agency which had allegedly told the adoptive parents that although the child's grandmother had died of Huntington's Disease, her father had tested negative, and thus the child was no more at risk than any other child. In fact, there was no reliable test as to inheritance of the disease, and a good chance that the child would inherit it. Five years later the child was diagnosed as suffering from the disease. The court refused the adoptive parents' claim for emotional damages because of an absence of physical manifestation of injury. However, the court permitted the cause of action for extraordinary medical expenses. Distinguishing California authority, which denied a cause of action to parents who had been told that the child was healthy (*P. v. Vista Del Mar Child Care Serv.,* 106 Cal. App. 3d 860, 165 Cal. Rptr. 370 (1980)), the court noted:

> This is not a case in which an adoption agency placed a child without discovering and informing the prospective parents about the child's health problems. Therefore we need not and do not address the question of whether adoption agencies have a duty to discover and disclose health information about children they place for adoption. In this case, accepting the alleged facts as true for purposes of this summary judgment motion, [defendant] affirmatively misrepresented [the child's] risk of developing Huntington's Disease. The agency assumed the duty of informing the [plaintiffs] about Huntington's Disease and about [the child's] chances of developing the disease. Having voluntarily assumed this duty, the complaint alleges, [defendant] negligently breached it.

PROBLEM

Husband and Wife sought sterilization of Husband by doctor because they feared the risk of the birth of a child with the kind of mental defects from which Husband suffered. Doctor allegedly negligently performed a vasectomy on Husband, and Wife subsequently became pregnant and gave birth to a mentally defective child. Owing to the mental defect, Child as a juvenile shot and killed Wife (his mother).

What claims, if any, do Husband, Child, and Wife's estate have against Doctor?

Chapter 8
OWNERS AND OCCUPIERS OF LAND

A. INTRODUCTION

The fact pattern with which this chapter deals is injuries suffered by those who enter the premises of another when such injuries are related to some condition of the premises. For years, the duty that the occupier of the land owed was based upon the status of the injured person. Courts slowly responded, moving towards a broader reasonable care standard. But old rules die slowly. Moreover, there has been some legislative action in the changing landscape of landowner law, especially in the recreational land area. One may find it hard to contain the boundaries of this chapter. Since so many torts arise out of the use and occupation of land you may find yourself wondering whether a case you are reading in another section does not involve some of the issues discussed in this chapter. Welcome, once again, to the uncertain world of the common law and torts in particular.

B. LIABILITY BASED ON CATEGORIZATION OF ENTRANT

PROBLEM

Ian, Leonard, Paul and Ted are riding home together from work. They detour and stop en route so that Ian can collect his completed tax forms from his accountant's office, which the accountant maintains in her home. As they arrive, the accountant's husband sees Ian and signals him to come into the house. Subsequently, Ian's accountant sees Leonard, an old college pal, sitting outside in the car. She asks Leonard to come in for a drink. Ted becomes bored with waiting for Ian and Leonard and wanders around to the back of the house. Paul declines an invitation by the accountant to leave the car, which is parked on the public street. The accountant's 12-year-old child, working with his science project in the garage, causes a massive explosion. Ian, Leonard, Paul and Ted are seriously injured as a result of the explosion.

In determining the claims of Ian, Leonard, Paul and Ted, what basic decisions will the court make? Is there any additional information which the court will require? How can you justify the categorization decisions that you predict? Is the accountant, her husband, or their son liable?

MENDOZA v. CITY OF CORPUS CHRISTI
700 S.W.2d 652 (Tex. App. 1985)

NYE, CHIEF JUSTICE.

This is an appeal from a judgment non obstante veredicto granted [defendant] by the trial court in a wrongful death and survival action. . . .

At the time of his death, Hector Mendoza was working for Lanphier Construction Company, removing debris from Lanphier's land which adjoined Lake Corpus Christi. On August 31, 1982, Mendoza told a co-worker he was going swimming. His co-workers later became concerned when he failed to return to work after a lunch break. His body was found about ten yards off Lanphier's pier in about two and a half feet of water. His neck was broken and the cause of death was drowning.

Appellants' theory of the case was that Mendoza met his death when he dove off the pier into the shallow water below. They alleged that the City of Corpus Christi was negligent in its failure to post warning signs that the water at the end of this pier was shallow. The jury found that the City had knowledge of the shallow water condition of the area where Mendoza dove; that the City in the exercise of ordinary care should have discovered this condition; that the City failed to give adequate warning of the dangerous condition; all of which constituted negligence and the proximate cause of Mendoza's injuries. They found that Mendoza was contributorily negligent to the extent of forty-nine percent. After the jury verdict, the trial court granted the City's motion to disregard the jury's answer to the special issue which inquired into the City's actual notice of a dangerous condition.

. . . The City's duty to Mendoza in this instance is directly related to his status at the time of the accident. Was he a trespasser, a licensee or an invitee in this situation? A trespasser is one who enters upon the property of another without any right, lawful authority, or express or implied invitation, permission, or license, not in performance of any duties to the owner, but merely for his own purpose, pleasure or convenience. The legal duty the landowner owes a trespasser is only not to injure him willfully, wantonly or through gross negligence. A licensee's presence on the premises is for his own convenience or on business for someone other than the owner. The duty owed a licensee is not to injure willfully, wantonly, or through gross negligence and to warn of or make safe dangerous conditions actually known. The standard of conduct required of a premises occupier toward his invitees is the ordinary care that a reasonably prudent person would exercise under all pertinent circumstances. The test to determine if an individual is upon the land as an invitee is whether the injured person has business relations with the owner at the time of the injury which would render his presence of mutual aid to both. Liability depends on whether the owner acted reasonably in light of what he knew or should have known about the risks accompanying a premises condition.

The evidence in this case shows that Hector Mendoza was on Lanphier's property for the purpose of removing trash and debris. After eating lunch he decided to go swimming. He did not have permission from the landowner, his supervisor, or the City to swim or dive off the pier. He left the area around

B. LIABLITY BASED ON CATEGORIZATION OF ENTRANT 557

which he had been conducting business for Mr. Lanphier and proceeded on a venture of his own choosing.

The permit that was issued by the City to construct the pier was limited to fishing or loading purposes only. It was not a diving or swimming pier, nor was it open to the public for any purpose. Mendoza had no business relationship with the City, and there was nothing about his venture off the pier that was for the mutual benefit or aid to both himself and the City. It is clear from the undisputed evidence, therefore, that Mendoza was not an invitee. He was never given permission by the City to swim or dive into the waters at Lanphier's pier.

It is apparent that Mendoza was either a trespasser or, at most, a licensee. Actually, it is unnecessary for us to determine in this instance which status he carried because, under either theory, the evidence does not bear out the jury's finding that the City had actual notice of the shallow condition of the water in the particular area where Mendoza dove. There is no contention by the appellants, nor was there any evidence presented, that the City's conduct was willful, wanton or constituted gross negligence. Appellants did not plead nor did they prove any grossly negligent conduct on the City's part. If, indeed, Mendoza was a trespasser as to the City, which unquestionably he was, it is clear that the City was not liable because they committed no grossly negligent acts or omissions toward Mendoza.

In order for the City to be held liable under the best possible status (the licensee theory), Mendoza's survivors were required to prove that: 1) the City had actual knowledge that the Lake waters were shallow at Lanphier Pier; 2) they knew that Mendoza or someone of the same status would dive off the Lanphier pier; and 3) the City failed to warn Mendoza and/or make safe this allegedly dangerous condition.

Appellants' main argument is that the City's on-site representative visited the pier on several occasions prior to the accident, and was aware of the dangerous condition that the pier would present to divers because of his actual knowledge of the falling lake level. They also contend that the on-site representative conducted continuous inspections to monitor lake levels, but supplied such information to the public only by newspaper. They further allege the City had notice of numerous other drowning deaths at the lake prior to Hector Mendoza's death.

The evidence in the record, however, shows that the City's representative visited the pier in question only four times. The representative went to the site where the accident happened approximately one week after the accident took place (early September of 1982). The representative testified that he visited this same site two times in March of 1983 and on one other occasion (no time or date shown in the record). There is no evidence to show that this other occasion was any time prior to the accident. There is no evidence to show that anyone from the City visited the site prior to the accident. There was evidence, however, that the City had a representative who, on a part-time basis only, drove around the lake and its environs on occasion. These inspections covered an area of more than 200 miles of shoreline and more than 1,200 private piers. These inspections were not for safety purposes.

Riley, the City representative, testified that the City measured the level of the lake above sea level, but not its depth. He testified that the only means to actually determine the depth at any particular location would be to measure the distance from the lake bottom to the water's surface. It is clear that the City knew that the lake level was falling, but this knowledge did not serve as evidence to show that the City knew that the water at the end of the private Lanphier Pier was too shallow for Mendoza or someone such as him to dive into or that this constituted a dangerous condition for which the City had a duty to warn Mendoza.

Appellants also argued that the City was aware of other drowning accidents on the lake. They contend that this knowledge imputed knowledge on the part of the City of a dangerous condition at Lanphier Pier. Appellants refer us to a portion of the record in which the City representative testified that he did not know of a diving accident which had occurred at Sunrise Beach in 1977. They also refer us to an exhibit and accompanying testimony which listed all drowning accidents on the lake since 1960. There was no evidence that any of these deaths were diving accidents; nor was there any evidence that these accidents occurred anywhere near the Lanphier Pier. We find no evidence that the City had actual knowledge of a dangerous condition in the lake where Hector Mendoza was injured. We also find no evidence of any conduct on the part of the City which was willful, wanton or grossly negligent. Therefore, whether Mendoza was a trespasser or a licensee, the evidence does not support the jury's finding that the City had actual notice of a dangerous condition at the Lanphier pier. [Affirmed.]

DORSEY, JUSTICE, dissenting.

. . . The lake into which Mr. Mendoza dove is a municipal reservoir owned and operated by the City of Corpus Christi and used by members of the public for recreational purposes. . . . [T]here were neither signs nor ordinances prohibiting diving and swimming where the incident occurred. I disagree with the majority's characterization of Mr. Mendoza as a trespasser in a publicly owned and operated lake under the circumstances.

. . . In the instant case, I believe there was some evidence to support the jury's findings. The City had a representative at the lake who took readings twice daily of the lake level. Those readings reflected that the lake had fallen 1.5 feet in the 60 days prior to the accident; that the City's agent would routinely drive or boat around the lake to check the piers located, as was Lanphier's, around the perimeter of the lake, and that at the time of the accident one half of Lanphier's pier (40 feet) was over dry land, whereas prior to the lake level falling, the entire 80 feet was over water. I do not think it necessary that there be direct evidence that prior to the accident the City knew the precise depth of the water off Lanphier's pier and that as such it constituted a dangerous condition in order for the jury to affirmatively answer the question of the City's actual knowledge. It is not necessary for a citizen to abandon his common sense and reasoning when he takes the oath as a juror. The jury could well have reasoned that because the City knew that, as the level of the lake fell, the water receded from the shoreline, and the water under piers attached to the shoreline became shallower all around the lake, then the City would know that water underneath Lanphier's pier was shallow also, and as such constituted a dangerous condition.

NOTES

1. *A Duty Owed by Possessors of Land.* In *Leichter v. Eastern Realty Co.,* 358 Pa. Super. 189, 516 A.2d 1247 (1986) *app. denied,* 515 Pa. 581, 527 A.2d 542 (1987), the decedent was abducted from a shopping center parking lot owned by the defendant, and suffered a fatal myocardial infarction. Fourteen stores in the shopping center were the tenants of the defendant. One of those fourteen, the supermarket co-defendant, possessed an easement for ingress and egress with a privilege to park in the lot. The abduction occurred when decedent was returning from shopping in the supermarket. RESTATEMENT (SECOND) OF TORTS § 328E (1965) provides:

> A possessor of land is
>
> (a) a person who is in occupation of the land with intent to control it, or
>
> (b) a person who has been in occupation of land with intent to control it, if no other person has subsequently occupied it with intent to control it, or
>
> (c) a person who is entitled to immediate occupation of the land, if no other person is in possession under clauses (a) or (b).

The court held that the question as to whether the supermarket was a possessor of land was properly for the jury. We deal with the problem of third party criminal acts elsewhere but the status of the victim may be relevant in a jurisdiction that still relies upon the status of the plaintiff to determine the defendant's duty.

To what extent should property law classifications be relevant and/or conclusive? Should the extent of a landowner's responsibility depend on whether the plaintiff is or is not on the premises? *See, e.g., Salevan v. Wilmington Park, Inc.,* 45 Del. 290, 72 A.2d 239 (1950) (pedestrian hit by ball while walking on a street outside baseball park; owner of park was held liable in negligence).

2. *Restatement Classifications.* RESTATEMENT (SECOND) OF TORTS § 329 (1965) states:

> A trespasser is a person who enters or remains upon land in the possession of another without a privilege to do so created by the possessor's consent or otherwise.

§ 330 defines a licensee as "a person who is privileged to enter or remain on land only by virtue of the possessor's consent."

And, according to § 332,

> (1) An invitee is either a public invitee or a business visitor.
>
> (2) A public invitee is a person who is invited to enter or remain on land as a member of the public for a purpose for which the land is held open to the public.
>
> (3) A business visitor is a person who is invited to enter or remain on land for a purpose directly or indirectly connected with business dealings with the possessor of the land.

Did plaintiff's decedent in *Mendoza* fall into any of these categories?

3. *Trespasser or Licensee?* In *Coleman v. United Fence Co.,* 282 Ark. 344, 668 S.W.2d 536 (1984), the plaintiff parked his car on defendant's land without permission. Subsequently, the defendant contracted with a fence company to dig post holes on the defendant's property. The fence company requested that plaintiff remove his car. When plaintiff went to retrieve his car he stepped into a post hole and suffered injuries. The court concluded that plaintiff was a trespasser, on the basis that his failure to remove the car resulted in a continuing trespass.

Stone v. Taffe, [1974] 3 All E.R. 1016 (C.A.), concerned the aftermath of a private party held in a "pub" by a local lodge of the Royal and Antediluvian Order of Buffaloes. The plaintiff's decedent fell down an unlighted staircase at 1 a.m. The permitted hours for serving alcohol had expired at 10:30 p.m. Both the decedent and the manager of the pub were "Buffs," and members of the lodge met regularly at the pub. The court held that despite the expiration of the lawful time for the serving of alcohol, the decedent had not ceased to be a lawful visitor.

4. *The Social Guest; Licensee or Invitee?* In *Younce v. Ferguson,* 106 Wash. 2d 658, 724 P.2d 991, 996–97 (1986), the plaintiff, who had been a social guest at a "kegger" party for a high school graduation, challenged the trial court's classification of her status as that of a licensee:

> [Plaintiff] contends that she was a member of the public on the land for a purpose for which the land is held open and therefore is an invitee. We disagree. The facts of this case do not parallel the facts of other cases where the plaintiff was found to be a public invitee. In *McKinnon v. Washington Fed. Sav. & Loan Ass'n,* 68 Wash. 2d 644, 414 P.2d 773 (1966), a federal savings and loan association posted a sign saying it had meeting rooms available for public use. The plaintiff in *McKinnon* was part of a Girl Scout group using the room for Scout meetings. In *Fosbre v. State,* 70 Wash. 2d 578, 424 P.2d 901 (1967), the plaintiff was injured at a recreational area on a National Guard fort. The area had been improved and maintained for use by National Guard families of which plaintiff was a member. In these "invitee" cases, "the occupier, *by his arrangement of the premises or other conduct,* has led the entrant to believe that the premises were intended to be used by visitors, as members of the public, for the purpose which the entrant was pursuing, and *that reasonable care was taken to make the place safe for those who enter for that purpose.*" *McKinnon,* at 649.

This implied assurance helps to distinguish between invitees and social guests, who are considered licensees. As explained in comment h(3) to RESTATEMENT (SECOND) OF TORTS, § 330 (1965):

> The explanation usually given by the courts for the classification of social guests as licensees is that there is a common understanding that the guest is expected to take the premises as the possessor himself uses them, and does not expect and is not entitled to expect that they will be prepared for his reception, or that precautions will be taken for his safety, in any manner in which the possessor does

not prepare or take precautions for his own safety, or that of the members of his family.

Under the facts of this case, it is hard to imagine how the [defendants] could have prepared or could have been expected to prepare a dairy farm for a kegger party.

The trial court correctly identified [plaintiff] as a licensee. She was privileged to enter or remain on the land only by virtue of the owner's consent.

5. *Moving Between Categories.* In *Eden v. Conrail,* 87 N.J. 467, 435 A.2d 556, 561 (1981), the plaintiff fell onto defendant's railroad tracks while suffering from a grand mal epileptic seizure. Schreiber, J., concurring, noted:

> An inadvertent involuntary deviation from the area of invitation does not necessarily destroy the status as an invitee. It has been held that some intrusions upon the lands of others do not transform the individual into a trespasser. For example, a pedestrian on a public highway may detour onto adjoining land to avoid an obstruction; or an inadvertent slip into adjoining land does not affect invitee status.
>
> . . . The plaintiff was a business invitee on the common carrier's platform, a place to which the public was invited, and involuntarily fell upon the tracks due to an unexpected grand mal seizure. . . . I would hold that the plaintiff continued to be an invitee and was in a position comparable to the user of a public highway who inadvertently fell into an adjacent area.

6. *The "Slip and Fall" Case.* In a typical "slip and fall" claim, the plaintiff must prove either that the occupant or its employees created the condition, or that the condition existed for such a period of time that the occupant should have discovered and remedied it in the exercise of reasonable care. *See, e.g., Fuller v. First National Supermarkets, Inc.*, 38 Conn. App. 299, 661 A.2d 110 (1995).

If, however, the dangerous condition is a common occurrence, defendant's knowledge of the condition may be implied. Thus in *Beske v. Opryland USA, Inc.,* 923 S.W. 2d 544 (Tenn. App. 1996), plaintiff was injured when she slipped and fell on a wet pavement while entering defendant's train at a turnstile:

> Passengers were not permitted to carry liquid refreshment aboard the train, hence refreshments were discarded before entering the train. Some refreshments were not placed in receptacles but were simply thrown on the ground or walkway. Management was aware that spilled beverages were a common occurrence at the entrance to the turnstiles. The surface where plaintiff fell was of poured concrete which could be slick when wet. Some of the spilled beverages were "cleaned up" by spreading with a broom to accelerate drying. If nearby employees were too busy they did not clean up the spill. As plaintiff passed through the turnstile, it was crowded, she did see water on the pavement, but she fell at that point, and felt ice cold water on the pavement as she lay on the pavement after her fall.

Although "no evidence was presented to show that defendant created or had actual knowledge of the hazard," defendant's knowledge of the dangerous condition could be inferred, the court said, from "evidence of the recurrent problem of discarded beverages in the area and of the failure of defendant to reasonably monitor this recurrent dangerous condition."

7. *Open and Obvious Dangers.* RESTATEMENT (SECOND) OF TORTS § 343A (1965) states that a possessor of land is not liable to invitees for a condition on the land "whose danger is known or obvious," unless the possessor should anticipate harm despite such obviousness. In *Harrison v. Taylor,* 115 Idaho 588, 768 P.2d 1321 (1989), the Supreme Court of Idaho abolished obviousness as a bar to recovery because the bar was inconsistent with the state's comparative negligence rule. *See also Ward v. K Mart Corporation,* 136 Ill. 2d 132, 554 N.E.2d 223 (1990), where the court held that an occupant's duty of reasonable care encompassed the risk that a customer, while carrying a large bulky item, would walk into the occupant's store. The court observed that:

> . . . In the present case defendant was clearly aware of the post which it maintained just outside the customer entrance door, and . . . it was reasonably foreseeable that a customer might be injured by colliding with the post.
>
> We find it clear that injury of the type suffered by plaintiff is a likely result of collision with a concrete post. We further find that the magnitude of the burden on defendant to exercise reasonable care to protect its customers from the risk of colliding with the post is slight, as noted above. A simple warning may well serve to remove the unreasonableness of the danger posed by the post.

Compare *Eaton v. McLain,* 891 S.W. 2d 587 (Tenn. 1994), where the court held a landowner had no duty to guard against an overnight guest falling down an unlighted basement stairway, when she got up in the dark to go to the bathroom and opened the wrong door. Defendants had no duty to leave a light on in the hall or to lock the basement door. Plaintiff's failure to turn on a light was not reasonably foreseeable, the court said.

8. *A Duty Owed to Business Invitees Regarding Off-Premises Dangers.* In *Mostert v. CBL & Assocs.,* 741 P.2d 1090 (Wyo. 1987), the court deviated from the general rule in concluding that a movie theatre operator had an affirmative duty to advise its patrons of severe weather conditions existing outside of its premises. However, in *Fuhrer v. Gearhart by the Sea, Inc.,* 306 Or. 434, 760 P.2d 874 (1988), the court affirmed the dismissal of the claim of plaintiff, whose decedent, a hotel guest, drowned while attempting to save some children trapped in an undertow in the adjoining ocean.

In *Cyr v. Adamar Associates Limited Partnership*, 752 A.2d 603 (Me. 2000), a hotel guest left an on-premises lounge and never returned. Her dead body was found in an adjacent field and before her death the guest had been raped. Before she left, her murderer had been in the lounge and had been staring at her. The court found that there was no liability because, even though the hotel had a duty to exercise reasonable care, "no evidence exists to support a conclusion that the Ramada proximately caused Williams' death. Although it would not be unreasonable to assume that Millet [the killer] abducted Williams from the Ramada premises, the evidence does not reveal whether

Williams voluntarily left the Ramada property with Millet or whether he abducted her. The lack of such evidence and the discovery of Williams' body on property not owned by the Ramada manifest that the relation between the Ramada's security measures and Williams' death is too uncertain and tenuous to hold [defendant] liable."

Id. at 604.

9. *Licensees, Traps and Active Negligence.* In *Keller v. Holiday Inns, Inc.,* 105 Idaho 649, 652, 671 P.2d 1112, 1115 (App. 1983), *vacated on other grounds,* 107 Idaho 593, 691 P.2d 1208 (1984), the court summarized the general rule as follows: "A person who enters the property of another with passive permission or as a mere social guest traditionally has been held to understand that he must take the land as the possessor uses it." Thus, according to RESTATEMENT (SECOND) OF TORTS § 342 (1965):

> A possessor of land is subject to liability for physical harm caused to licensees by a condition on the land if, but only if,
>
> (a) the possessor knows or has reason to know of the condition and should realize that it involves an unreasonable risk of harm to such licensees, and should expect that they will not discover or realize the danger, and
>
> (b) he fails to exercise reasonable care to make the condition safe, or to warn the licensees of the condition and the risk involved, and
>
> (c) the licensees do not know or have reason to know of the condition and the risk involved.

In *Le Poidevin v. Wilson,* 111 Wis. 2d 116, 330 N.W.2d 555, 558–59 (1983), the 17-year-old plaintiff conceded she was a licensee who had been given permission to swim at a lake. She alleged that the defendant property owner was vicariously liable for the negligence of his son-in-law who was acting as the owner's agent in the capacity of chaperon. According to the plaintiff's complaint, the property owner's son and son-in-law ridiculed, taunted and challenged the plaintiff to enter the water for some twenty minutes. Subsequently, the son-in-law grabbed plaintiff's towel from behind, and "surprised, startled, frightened, distracted, and greatly embarrassed," plaintiff dove into the water, unaware that the water was only three feet deep. The court noted that "[a] landowner or occupier might be liable for injuries to a licensee in two situations — when the injury was caused by a "trap" on the premises concealed from the licensee but known to the landowner or when the injury was caused by the active negligence of the landowner." Continuing, the court stated:

> In landowner-licensee cases "active negligence" is to be distinguished from a condition of the premises. Although a landowner does not owe a duty of ordinary care to a licensee as to the condition of the premises, a landowner who carries on an affirmative act, an active operation or activity, does have an obligation to exercise ordinary care for the protection of a licensee.

The court concluded that the taunting and other conduct constituted "active negligence," changing the issue to whether there had been a breach of the duty of ordinary care. In that regard, the court ruled that there was a jury issue as to whether the defendants should have foreseen that their conduct would have endangered the plaintiff.

In *Shannon v. Butler Homes Inc.,* 102 Ariz. 312, 428 P.2d 990 (1967), a nine-year-old social guest (and hence, according to the court, a licensee) was injured when she collided with and broke a glass door. The plaintiff alleged that the glass door's "deceptive illusion," together with prevailing lighting conditions and the absence of markings or warnings, constituted a trap. Held, summary judgment was improper since a peril could be "hidden" to a child because of the child's lack of appreciation of the risk.

10. *The Limited Duty to Trespassers and the Occupier's Immunity.* According to the RESTATEMENT (SECOND) OF TORTS §§ 333–338 (1965), a possessor of land is not liable to trespassers for any failure to exercise reasonable care except in a few cases involving highly dangerous activities or artificial conditions, and in the case of constant or known trespassers. Why are trespassers so scorned by the torts system? Is it because their presence is unanticipated? Because *they* are the wrongdoers? Because historically the common law has protected property over the person? Because a trespasser's randomized presence places excessively high information costs on the occupier of the premises, who thus ceases to be an efficient cost avoider? Would any of these rationales support occupier immunity from intentional or wilful conduct directed at a trespasser?

11. *An Anthropopathic Classification System?* In *Tutton v. A.D. Walter Ltd.,* [1986] 1 Q.B. 61, [1985] 3 All E.R. 757, [1985] 3 W.L.R. 797, defendant farmer, attempting to repel seed weevils, sprayed his fields of brightly colored oil seed rape with an insecticide which was particularly harmful to bees. The colonies of the adjoining beekeepers were decimated. The defendant contended that the bees were merely trespassers, to which the court replied:

> I must say, for my part, I find great difficulty . . . in accepting the concept that bees may be invitees, licensees or trespassers. In my opinion it is unreal to divide bees into those categories and attempt to force on to them the subtleties of the common law when dealing with human beings who either had or had not permission to enter on to the land on which they were injured.
>
> My reasons are as follows: trespassers in the eyes of the law are wrongdoers. It is unreal to look at bees in this light. Bees are useful insects; their use to the neighbourhood in which they forage is universal and not peculiar to certain neighbourhoods. True, that utility is limited or latent in the case of a neighbouring landowner whose crop for that year is self-pollinating, but the bees' utility to the neighbourhood remains. I am invited to make a distinction, dividing bees' foraging grounds for each season into areas where, on the one hand, they are currently useful and beneficial, improving the farmer's yield (for example, orchards) where they should be treated as invitees and owed a duty of care; and those areas, on the other hand, where they are at best tolerated, where it is said that they are trespassers and their negligent destruction must be accepted as being within the law, provided it is not reckless.

I find this unreal, particularly as it is both beyond the power of their keepers to control where they go to forage, and beyond the practical power of the landowner to exclude them. Whether the landowner thinks he needs or wants bees to come on to his property, or whether he would rather be without them, he is bound, in the real world, to recognise that they will be wherever pollen and nectar are to be found, and in the case of a flowering field of oil seed rape this is not just a possibility but a certainty; their presence in such a field is simply an inevitable incident, or adjunct, to the use to which the owner has chosen to put that field. In all these circumstances it seems to me entirely appropriate that in their own neighbourhood bee keepers and bees should be protected by the common duty of care, judged by the "neighbour" criterion.

WEBSTER v. CULBERTSON
158 Ariz. 159, 761 P.2d 1063 (1988)

MOELLER, JUSTICE.

Plaintiff Joe Webster was severely injured in 1984 while riding his horse on the defendant-landowner's property. He ran into a fence of unmarked barbed wire which defendant had strung across the wash at her property line. Plaintiff sued for personal injuries, and the defendant defended on the ground that plaintiff was a trespasser to whom she owed only the duty of refraining from willful or wanton injury.

In the trial court, the defendant moved for summary judgment. In response, plaintiff claimed that there was sufficient evidence of willful or wanton injury to defeat the motion but that, in any event, § 335 of the Restatement (Second) of Torts (hereafter Restatement) entitled "Artificial Conditions Highly Dangerous to Constant Trespassers on Limited Area" applied. The trial court granted summary judgment, ruling that § 335 did not apply, and that the evidence was insufficient to support a finding of willful or wanton injury. On motion for rehearing, the trial court considered and rejected plaintiff's additional contention that § 337 of the Restatement entitled "Artificial Conditions Highly Dangerous to Known Trespassers" applied. . . .

Defendant's property is in Pima County, southwest of Tucson, in a semi-rural area consisting of desert with residences on parcels ranging from one and one-quarter to five acres in size.

Culbertson acquired the property in 1967 and decided to fence it in 1977. One of the reasons she decided to do so was to prevent people from riding dunebuggies and horses through the front part of the property. The wash is on the rear of the property, and, at deposition, she acknowledged that she assumed the same people who had been using the front portion of the property also used the wash for recreational use. In any event, the defendant constructed the fence and, except for the portion going across the wash, she used "field fence." However, where the fence crossed the wash, barbed wire, instead of field fence, was used, although defendant acknowledged that a person was more likely to be injured by contact with barbed wire than by contact with field fence. There were no fenceposts in the wash itself where they would have washed out. The posts on the river banks were obscured by trees and brush, and were virtually invisible to people approaching the fence from the wash. When the defendant first erected the fence she hung white cloth or aluminum foil from the barbed wire at the wash crossing to warn people of the fence. However, by the time of the accident in 1984, there were no cloth strips, foil, tapes, or warning signs of any type on the fence.

The wash was visible from Culbertson's house and she went to it approximately weekly for the purpose of dumping cat litter in the wash. Evidence from sources other than the defendant indicated that, at the time of the accident, the wash was used by pedestrians, children, motorcyclists, four-wheel drive vehicles, dunebuggies, and equestrians, and that tire tracks, footprints and hoofprints were visible in the wash. An equestrian trail crossed the wash less than fourteen yards from the spot where the wash enters defendant's property.

Plaintiff lived approximately one-half mile from the accident scene. On the evening of the accident in May, 1984, he and a riding companion entered the wash on horseback approximately one-quarter to one-half mile from the fence. He had not sought anyone's permission to enter or use the wash, and he saw no "private property" or "no trespassing" signs as he approached defendant's property. Neither he nor his riding companion had been to the scene before the accident. He approached the fence at approximately 7:30 p.m. Although it was still daylight, the sun was starting to go down. A photograph of the barbed wire taken shortly after the accident confirms its virtual invisibility. He first saw the fence when he and his horse were approximately ten feet from it, but he was unable to stop his horse in time. The barbed wire gouged a fist-sized chunk of muscle from his leg resulting in approximately fifty percent permanent muscle immobility in that leg.

. . . In the typical "trespasser" case, plaintiff may not recover unless the landowner has been guilty of some willful or wanton disregard for the plaintiff's safety. This is true because a property owner is not usually obliged to assume that others will trespass on his property. In other words, a landowner need not exercise reasonable care for the safety of a trespasser when there is no reason to anticipate a trespasser's presence.

However, § 337 of the Restatement recognizes an exception to, or modification of, this general rule. It provides:

Artificial Conditions Highly Dangerous to Known Trespassers.

A possessor of land who maintains on the land an artificial condition which involves a risk of death or serious bodily harm to persons coming in contact with it, is subject to liability for bodily harm caused to trespassers by his failure to exercise reasonable care to warn them of the condition if

(a) the possessor knows or has reason to know of their presence in dangerous proximity to the condition, and

(b) the condition is of such a nature that he has reason to believe that the trespasser will not discover it or realize the risk involved.

. . . Section 337 is a sound and sensible rule: When a landowner knows or has reason to know that trespassers come upon his property, he cannot, without liability, maintain a dangerous artificial condition on his property when he also has reason to believe that the trespasser will not discover the dangerous condition or realize its risk. We agree with the reasoning of the New Jersey Supreme Court:

> In the choice of competing considerations of societal policy, the need for protection against the reasonably foreseeable risk of death or severe personal injury outweighs the freedom of action that would otherwise characterize the relation of the possessor of land to a trespasser.

Imre v. Riegel Paper Corp., 24 N.J. 438, 443, 132 A.2d 505, 510 (1957).

Since no Arizona law conflicts with § 337, and since it represents a sound and fair policy, we will follow it.

. . . The court of appeals, in its analysis of the facts, concluded that § 337 was factually inapplicable. The court of appeals set forth three reasons for its conclusion:

> First, the lawful erection of a four-strand barbed wire fence does not charge one with knowledge that it is likely to cause death or serious bodily harm. Second, the use of barbed wire fences does not create highly dangerous artificial conditions. They exist throughout rural Arizona, in and across washes, and are commonly encountered by trespassers. Third, there is no evidence that Culbertson knew that horseback riders frequently ran their horses down the wash toward her fence.

Webster v. Culbertson, 158 Ariz. at 157–58, 761 P.2d at 1061–1062.

Taking the last point first, we must disagree with the court of appeals' analysis of the record. There is ample evidence in the record to support a jury finding that defendant Culbertson knew or had reason to know that trespassers, including equestrians, were sometimes dangerously close to the fence as required by subsection (a) of § 337.

Either of the first two statements by the court of appeals in support of its view of the non-applicability of § 337 are correct in the abstract. However, determination of whether § 337 applies in a given case is a highly fact-intensive determination. Given the particular circumstances of this case we believe a jury could find that each factual predicate of § 337 is present in this case. Plaintiff does not rely upon the mere act of putting up a barbed wire fence. Plaintiff contends that defendant erected and maintained a dangerously invisible fence with knowledge or reason to know that trespassers who would not perceive the risk would be present. We find the plaintiff's version of the evidence entirely plausible.

Lastly, the court of appeals concluded that § 337 was inapplicable unless the defendant had "actual knowledge" that a trespasser was about to come in contact with a highly dangerous artificial condition maintained on her property. . . .

The text of § 337 does not impose the condition of "actual knowledge" that the court of appeals imposed. Insofar as the landowner's knowledge concerning the trespasser's presence in proximity to the artificial condition, § 337 applies when the landowner "knows or has reason to know" of the presence of the trespassers. "Reason to know" is not equivalent to "actual knowledge."...

Comment (a) to § 337, relied upon by the court of appeals, states, in part:

> The rule stated in this Section relates only to the conditions under which a possessor of land is subject to liability to a trespasser whom he knows to be about to come in contact with a highly dangerous artificial condition maintained by him upon the land.

... [W]e nevertheless choose to follow the text of the Restatement itself. Under it, "reason to know" is a sufficient state of knowledge. We conclude that, taking the evidence in the light most favorable to the plaintiff, there are sufficient facts and inferences in the record which, if introduced at trial, would be sufficient to take the case to a jury on a § 337 theory.

... Based upon our examination of the record in this case, we agree with the court of appeals and with the trial court that there is insufficient evidence to support a finding that the defendant was guilty of "willful or wanton" conduct as those terms are used in assessing duties toward trespassers. Accordingly, we affirm the grant of summary judgment in favor of the defendant landowner on that theory. ...

NOTES

1. *The "Discovered" Trespasser Exception; Artificial or Dangerous Conditions.* In addition to § 337, discussed in *Webster,* RESTATEMENT (SECOND) OF TORTS § 336 (1965) provides:

> A possessor of land who knows or has reason to know of the presence of another who is trespassing on the land is subject to liability for physical harm thereafter caused to the trespasser by the possessor's failure to carry on his activities upon the land with reasonable care for the trespasser's safety.

Further, § 338 provides:

> A possessor of land who is in immediate control of a force, and knows or has reason to know of the presence of trespassers in dangerous proximity to it, is subject to liability for physical harm thereby caused to them by his failure to exercise reasonable care
>
> (a) so to control the force as to prevent it from doing harm to them, or
>
> (b) to give a warning which is reasonably adequate to enable them to protect themselves.

The term "reason to know" is defined in REST. 2D OF TORTS § 12(1) (1965) as "denot[ing] the fact that the actor has information from which a person of reasonable intelligence . . . would infer that the fact in question exists."

In *Lee v. Chicago Transit Authority*, 152 Ill. 2d 432, 605 N.E. 2d 493 (1992), cert. den. 113 S.Ct. 2337 (1993), the court upheld a jury verdict under REST. 2D OF TORTS § 337 (1965) where the plaintiff's deceased, in a drunken "stupor," was electrocuted when he urinated on defendant's allegedly inadequately guarded third rail which carried 600 volts of electricity at a street level crossing of defendant's trains. Although there were posted "Danger," "Keep Out" and "Electric Current" signs, the deceased (a Korean immigrant) was unable to read English. The $3 million plaintiff's verdict was reduced by 50% owing to the deceased's negligence.

2. *An Affirmative Duty?* In *Pridgen v. Boston Hous. Auth.*, 364 Mass. 696, 308 N.E.2d 467 (1974), an 11-year-old child climbed through the escape hatch of an elevator and onto the platform which formed the roof of the elevator. When his companion moved the elevator up and down, the child slipped from the roof and became trapped below the elevator, which moved down and struck him. The child's mother was told that the child was in the elevator. She went to the defendant's building and called to her son. She asked a man standing in the hall, who later was identified as defendant's janitor, for assistance. He replied that there was nothing he could do. He ignored her subsequent request to turn off "the lights." After emergency services arrived, but before the power could be turned off or the child rescued, the elevator moved down and severely injured him. In holding that the evidence was sufficient to support a verdict for plaintiff, the court remarked:

> [M]any courts in other jurisdictions have described this standard in terms of a duty of reasonable care to avoid injuring the trespassing plaintiff whose trapped position is known. The statement of the rule in terms of a duty to exercise reasonable care "to avoid injuring" a trapped trespasser is unfortunate, we think. It has caused numerous cases to be decided on the basis of the traditional common law distinction between acts of "misfeasance" and "nonfeasance," with resulting liability for acting negligently but not for failing or refusing to act at all, with reference to a person who is in peril and helpless. . . .
>
> In the context of the relationship between an owner or occupier of property and a trapped, imperiled and helpless trespasser thereon, we reject any rule which would exempt the owner from liability if he knowingly refrains from taking reasonable action which he is in a position to take and which would prevent injury or further injury to the trespasser. It should not be, it cannot be, and surely it is not now the law of this Commonwealth that the owner in such a situation is rewarded with immunity from liability as long as he ignores the plight of the trapped trespasser and takes no affirmative action to help him.

3. *The "Beaten Path" Exception; Artificial or Dangerous Conditions and Persistent Trespassers.* In addition to "known" trespassers, the occupier may or should know of habitual trespassing on some limited part of her property; typically this involves the "short cut" or "beaten path" scenario. REST. 2D OF TORTS § 335 (1965) provides:

> A possessor of land who knows, or from facts within his knowledge should know, that trespassers constantly intrude upon a limited area of the land, is subject to liability for bodily harm caused to them by an artificial condition on the land, if
>
> (a) the condition
>
> (i) is one which the possessor has created or maintains and

(ii) is, to his knowledge, likely to cause death or serious bodily harm to such trespassers and

(iii) is of such a nature that he has reason to believe that such trespassers will not discover it, and

(b) the possessor has failed to exercise reasonable care to warn such trespassers of the condition and the risk involved.

Rest. 2d of Torts § 334 (1965) provides a rule similar to § 335 for dangerous activities.

Are all these rules and subrules and exceptions worth the trouble? Should they be rules of law? Or, do all these rules unduly confuse judge, lawyer, law student, and law professor? Aren't a lot of rules evidence that there are some flaws with the primary rule?

MOORE v. TUCSON ELECTRIC POWER CO.
158 Ariz. 187, 761 P.2d 1091 (1988)

Howard, Presiding Judge.

This is an appeal from a defense verdict in a personal injury action.

The minor in this case, Brooke Burwell, was seriously injured when he received electrical burns after scaling one of defendant's power poles. At the time of the accident he was 14 years old. The pole, located in an alley where children play, was supported by two sets of guy wires of two wires each. These wires were attached at one end to the ground and at the other to portions of the pole near its top. Brooke was able to climb the guy wires, which nearly formed a 45-degree angle, by placing his feet on the lower set of wires and his hands on the higher set. This was not the first time he had done this. About one month earlier he had climbed another pole in the same manner. In fact, this was not Brooke's first adventurous climb. Prior to this accident he had undertaken numerous dangerous and unorthodox climbing activities, including the bell tower and television antennae at the University of Arizona.

After Brooke climbed the pole upon which he was injured, he sat on the crossarm and watched the sunset. Then he decided to traverse the power lines to the other pole. He put his hand out to reach for a transmission line and received a shock which rendered him unconscious. He then fell from the pole.

During Brooke's previous electrical pole climb, he had walked out across the line strung between two poles. These were uncovered metal wires. Brooke thought that he would not get "zapped" by touching uncovered metal wires. The wires on which he was injured looked just like the wires that he had walked on one month before without incident.

At the time of the accident, Brooke was a person of superior intelligence. He attended University High School, a school for intellectually gifted students. He excelled throughout his schooling in mathematics and science courses and was an intellectually curious person.

The appellant contends that the court erred in excluding certain evidence, in failing to give certain of its requested instructions, in giving certain instructions and in continuing what appellant contends is the outmoded distinction among trespassers, invitees and licensees. We affirm.

. . . Ordinarily the duty of a landowner to a trespasser is not to wilfully or wantonly injure him. Where children are concerned an exception to this rule has developed which is commonly known as the doctrine of attractive nuisance.

The Restatement (Second) of Torts § 339 (1965) recognizes that a possessor of land may be liable to a child trespasser if certain conditions are present:

> A possessor of land is subject to liability for physical harm to children trespassing thereon caused by an artificial condition upon the land if
>
> (a) the place where the condition exists is one upon which the possessor knows or has reason to know that children are likely to trespass, and
>
> (b) the condition is one of which the possessor knows or has reason to know and which he realizes or should realize will involve an unreasonable risk of death or serious bodily harm to such children, and
>
> (c) the children because of their youth do not discover the condition or realize the risk involved in intermeddling with it or in coming within the area made dangerous by it, and
>
> (d) the utility to the possessor of maintaining the condition and the burden of eliminating the danger are slight as compared with the risk to children involved, and
>
> (e) the possessor fails to exercise reasonable care to eliminate the danger or otherwise to protect children.

Although the jury was instructed on this doctrine, we do not believe that it was applicable here for two reasons. First, the owner or occupier of the premises must have reason to anticipate the presence of the child at the place of danger. If the power pole is easily climbable, then the owner has reason to anticipate that children will climb it, if it is located in an area where there are children. However, if it takes an unusual effort to reach the place of danger, in this case to climb the pole, the pole does not constitute an attractive nuisance. See *Ross v. Sequatchie Valley Elec. Co-op.*, 198 Tenn. 638, 281 S.W.2d 646 (1955) (no liability under doctrine of attractive nuisance where 12-year-old boy held onto top guy wire tied to electrical light pole on electrical co-op's right-of-way and was struck by high voltage electricity).

The second reason why, as a matter of law, the doctrine of attractive nuisance was not applicable to this case, was the age, experience and knowledge of Brooke. Brooke's testimony showed he knew the danger of wires on power poles. He knew he could get "zapped." His mistaken belief that the wires were not dangerous if they were uninsulated does not detract from his knowledge of the danger.

The doctrine of attractive nuisance did not apply, and therefore Brooke was a trespasser.

[Affirmed.]

NOTES

1. Recall the arguable, or at least apparent, rationales for the occupier's limited liability to trespassers. How does the age of plaintiff change the application of any or all of those rationales? *Cf.* PROSSER & KEETON ON TORTS (1984), § 59, "Almost from the beginning the new [attractive nuisance] rule met with vigorous opposition on the part of some of the courts, who denounced it . . . as a barefaced fiction and a piece of sentimental humanitarianism, founded on sympathy rather than law or logic."

2. *Attractive Nuisances.* The "attractive nuisance" doctrine arose in American law when the United States Supreme Court allowed recovery to a trespassing child injured while playing on a railroad turntable, *Sioux City & Pacific Railroad Co. v. Stout*, 84 U.S. 657 (1873), and is sometimes known as the "turntable doctrine." The policy which supports the doctrine is that the landowner, rather than the child or the child's parents, is often in the best position to avoid the harm to the child. The rule has been much criticized and generally is limited to artificial conditions on the landowner's premises. Thus in *Hall v. Edlefson*, 498 S.W.2d 514 (Tex. Civ. App. 1973), a Shetland pony from which plaintiff had fallen was held not to be an attractive nuisance as a matter of law. *Hampton v. Hammons*, 743 P.2d 1053, 1061 (Okla. 1987), concerned a five-year-old child who was mauled by his neighbor's pit bull as he was leaving the neighbor's property after rescuing his own puppy which had strayed into the neighbor's yard. The court noted:

> The dog . . . was neither [the plaintiff's] reason for crossing the fence nor is a dog an artificial condition. The majority rule is that ordinary domestic creatures cannot constitute attractive nuisances because they are too common to be considered inherently dangerous even to a child.

3. *Natural Conditions.* On what basis may the distinction between *artificial* and *natural* conditions be justified?

In *McIntyre v. McIntyre*, 558 S.W.2d 836 (Tenn. 1977), plaintiff motorcyclist's attractive nuisance argument was based on an allegation that defendant permitted minors to ride motorcycles on the rolling hills of his agricultural land where two cyclists collided. In holding that the attractive nuisance doctrine did not apply, the court stated:

> There is no allegation that defendant maintained upon his premises any condition, artificial or natural, that would constitute an unusual or hidden danger. . . . While we acknowledge the picturesque beauty of the rolling hills and majestic mountains of Tennessee and agree that they are attractive, the fortunate fact that God has strewn His splendor with such a lavish hand and blessed our state with great beauty, and has made it a veritable playground, hardly affords a reason to classify any normal topographical feature as an attractive nuisance. To so hold would subject every landowner in Tennessee to potential liability by virtue of the mere ownership of land.

For the *McIntyre* court, would a natural condition ever be included within the attractive nuisance doctrine?

4. *Attractive Nuisance; Active or Passive?* Must the nuisance "cause" the child to trespass? In *Hampton v. Hammons,* note 2 *supra,* the court denied liability under the attractive nuisance doctrine, partly "because [the plaintiff] did not enter the [defendant's] property because of any attraction to the animal." Early cases, typified by *United Zinc & Chem. Co. v. Britt,* 258 U.S. 268, 276–77, 42 S. Ct. 299, 66 L. Ed. 615 (1922), suggested a causative role for the allurement or attraction. For example, *Britt* involved a child's drowning in a poisonous pool. Justice Holmes opined, "[I]t is at least doubtful whether the water could be seen from any place where the children lawfully were and there is no evidence that it was what led them to enter the land. But that is necessary to start the supposed duty." Under the Restatement formulation in § 339, is there any requirement that the condition of the premises must have induced the child to trespass? What does that indicate about the goals of the Restatement? As a matter of doctrine, does attractive nuisance (or § 339, if different) affect the categorization of a particular child trespasser, or does it involve a more fundamental reassessment of landowner responsibility and liability?

Burk Royalty Co. v. Pace, 620 S.W.2d 882 (Tex. Civ. App. 1981), involved injuries suffered by a nine-year-old while playing on the "pitman arm" of an oil well pump. The well site was near a highway and a lightly populated residential area, and a beaten path led from the well site to the residential area. There were no natural or artificial barriers around the well site. The court found that there was sufficient evidence to satisfy the Restatement element that "the place where the condition exists is one upon which the possessor knows or has reason to know that children are likely to trespass." Further, the court noted, "It is now a time-honored precept in our jurisprudence that attraction or allurement is no longer an essential element of the doctrine except insofar as foreseeability is concerned. If the dangerous condition is in fact an attraction to children, that factor is only important 'insofar as it may mean the presence of children is to be anticipated. . . .'"

5. *Reasonable and Unreasonable Dangers.* In *Ochampaugh v. Seattle,* 91 Wash. 2d 514, 588 P.2d 1351, 1356 (1979), the court, declining to apply the doctrine to the drowning deaths of two young boys in a pond, remarked:

> The most significant factor, we believe, to be considered when it must be decided whether liability will be imposed upon the possessor for a condition existing upon the land, is the likelihood or probability of harm to others which it involves. As the undisputed testimony given by depositions and affidavits in this case demonstrates, the incidence of drownings in ponds such as that involved continues to be slight when compared with the extent of use that is made of such bodies of water for recreational purposes. The numerous ponds, lakes, rivers, creeks, and miles of shoreline in this state comprise one of its most cherished amenities, and to require that they be drained, filled, or surrounded by impregnable fences (which appear to be the only means of making them child proof) in order to escape liability for the occasional drowning which occurs, would not only impose an unreasonable burden on the owner but would also run counter to the public policy of this state.

Should one conclude that the application of the attractive nuisance doctrine depends upon a fact-sensitive cost-benefit analysis? Should the doctrine apply to a swimming pool? In *Mozier v. Parsons*, 256 Kan. 769, 887 P.2d 692 (1995), the court observed that "[w]hile we do not rule out the remote possibility that there could be a highly unusual and aggravated factual situation that might support consideration of the . . . doctrine, . . . generally, swimming pools, whether public or private, do not constitute an attractive nuisance. . . ."

6. *The Age of Majority?* According to RESTATEMENT OF TORTS § 339 (1934), the occupier's modified duty applied only to "young" children. RESTATEMENT (SECOND) OF TORTS § 339 (1965) eliminated the word "young" but the change has not quieted discussion of the issue. *Hughes v. Quarve & Anderson Co.*, 338 N.W.2d 422 (Minn. 1983), involved serious injuries suffered by a youth when he dove into a quarry pond. One issue was whether an attractive nuisance instruction was appropriate when the trespassing child was about 16 years of age:

> There is authority for the proposition that a trespassing boy of approximately 16, who injures himself by diving into an artificial body of water, is an adult trespasser as a matter of law. But that determination can be made only upon a review of the facts and circumstances of a particular case. We observe at the outset that the large number of cases involving teen-aged boys diving into shallow water indicates that mature judgment at age 16, at least as it regards personal safety, cannot be assumed to be the norm. Beyond that, there is evidence in the record through the testimony of [a] psychologist, that [plaintiff] was very immature and not even operating on the same level of maturity as other 16-year-olds. Under the facts of this case, we cannot say that the trial court erred in not holding [plaintiff] to be an adult trespasser as a matter of law.
>
> We have held that the question as to whether there is the required youth for application of the Restatement rule is one for determination by the jury. Courts should not set age limits for the applicability of section 339, which depends on the age and maturity of the child, the character of the danger and the child's ability to avoid the danger. . . .
>
> It would be inappropriate for the court to allow the jury to choose which rule of law to apply to the facts. The court, not the jury, determines the law of a case, and the jury decides the factual issues based on the law submitted to them. We have found no case with similar facts and issues in which the trial court submitted alternate theories of landowner liability, nor do we deem such submission appropriate here. If a plaintiff requests and obtains a section 339 instruction, he must prove, inter alia, that "(c) [he] because of [his] youth [does] not discover the condition or realize the risk involved in intermeddling with it or in coming within the area made dangerous by it." He risks complete denial of recovery if the jury believes him mature enough to appreciate the risk. If he passes the threshold of requirement (c), not having the requisite maturity, he must then proceed to establish the four remaining section 339 requirements [reason to know of child trespassers and of the danger, lack of

reasonable care by the land possessor, and a balancing of the risk against the utility of the danger]. If he does not pass that threshold, there can be no recovery against the landlord and no need to proceed to section 335 to determine landowner liability to an adult trespasser.

C. LIMITING AND ABANDONING THE CATEGORIES

MALLET v. PICKENS
206 W.Va. 145, 522 S.E.2d 436 (1999)

McGRAW, JUSTICE.

Appellants Patricia A. Mallett and Ernest R. Mallet appeal a grant of summary judgment entered against them in their tort action, in which they sought damages for an injury Mrs. Mallet sustained when visiting the home of their friends, Selbert Pickens and Anita Pickens. The lower court granted summary judgment on the basis that Mrs. Mallet, as a social guest, was merely a licensee upon the property of the Pickenses, and that the Pickenses had no duty to Mrs. Mallet, save to refrain from willfully or wantonly injuring her. The Mallets appeal, claiming that Mrs. Mallet should be considered an invitee, or, alternatively, that this Court should instead apply a duty of reasonable care upon landowners with respect to all non-trespassing entrants. Because we concur with the Mallets and choose to abolish the common law distinction between licensees and invitees, following the modern trend in the development of premises liability law, we must reverse the decision of the lower court.

On July 23, 1994, the appellants, Patricia and Ernest Mallet, decided to visit their good friends, the Pickens family. Mrs. Pickens had been injured some time before in an auto accident, and the Mallets wanted to wish her well in her recovery. Although the two families often visited one another, the Pickenses did not know that the Mallets were coming to visit that day.

The Pickenses were having work done to their home, so at the time of the visit, the only access to the front door of the house was by way of a set of temporary, wooden stairs, which did not have a railing or banister. Additionally, because of the construction, a masonry block had been left on the ground near the steps. When Mrs. Mallet exited the home after the visit, the stairs shifted under her weight and she fell, striking her head on the block. Mrs. Mallet suffered broken bones in her face that required surgery.

The Mallets' health insurance carrier originally denied Mrs. Mallet's claim, on the basis that a third party (the Pickenses) was at fault, and that the third party should pay the medical bills. The Pickenses submitted their friend's medical bills to their insurance carrier, which denied the claim. The Mallets filed suit, and the lower court granted summary judgment in favor of Mr. and Mrs. Pickens, ruling that Mrs. Mallet was a licensee, and the Pickenses did not breach their duty of care toward Mrs. Mallet, which was merely the duty not to willfully or wantonly injure her.

This Court's right to respond to changes in the law is also manifest. Though some have argued that it is not this Court's prerogative to alter the common law in any substantial way, and that our Constitution prohibits such amendments, we have held that, "Article VIII, Section 13 of the West Virginia Constitution and W. Va.Code, 2-1-1, were not intended to operate as a bar to this Court's evolution of common law principles, including its historic power to alter or amend the common law." *Morningstar v. Black and Decker Mfg. Co.*, 162 W.Va. 857, 253 S.E.2d 666 (1979). . . .

Today we make our own assessment of the reasonableness of the ancient common law distinction between licensees and invitees, and find that it does not comport with the present condition of our society.

West Virginia common law presently recognizes a difference regarding the duty owed to entrants of land. An entrant of land must fit into the licensee, invitee, or trespasser category and is owed a different duty of care from a landowner, depending upon that status. . . .[1]

From the outset we must bear in mind that the categories of licensee, invitee, and trespasser evolved in a much different time, and in a significantly different legal climate than exists today. Scholars studying the subject regard the English cases of *Parnaby v. Lancaster Canal Co.*, 11 Ad. & E. 223, 113 Eng. Rep. 400 (Ex. 1839), and *Southcote v. Stanley*, 1 H. & N. 247, 156 Eng. Rep. 1195 (Ex. 1856), as the progenitors of the licensee/invitee distinction, soon adopted by jurisdictions in this country. . .

The ancient precept of "sanctity of property," and the concept of "privity of contract," were the basic principles underpinning the employment of these categories. . . . One of the main "benefits," as seen through eyes of the time, of employing the licensee/invitee/trespasser trichotomy was the protection of property owners, who were a privileged minority, from the vagaries of juries, comprised mostly of land entrants and not landowners.

Inherent in such a scheme was the notion that a jury could not be trusted to enter a just verdict; however, we have long ago cast off such suspicion of the jury system:

Chesterton, the "prince of paradox," framing the experience of two millennia in TREMENDOUS TRIFLES: THE TWELVE MEN, said:

> "Our civilization has decided, and very justly decided, that determining the guilt or innocence of men [natural or artificial] is a thing too important to be trusted to trained men. It wishes for light upon that awful matter, it asks men who know no more law than I know, but who can feel the things that I felt in the jury box. When it wants a library catalogued, or the solar system discovered, or any trifle of that kind, it uses up its specialists. But when it wishes anything done which is really serious, it collects twelve of the ordinary men standing round. The same thing was done, if I remember right, by the Founder of Christianity." Gilbert K. Chesterton, TREMENDOUS TRIFLES: THE TWELVE MEN 86–87 (1922).

Delp v. Itmann Coal Co., 176 W.Va. 252, 256, 342 S.E.2d 219, 223 (1986) (McGraw, J., dissenting).[5] In the case before us, the important matter of

---

[1] We make no change today to our law and its treatment of trespassers, nor to the complex body of law dealing with exceptions to the normal standard of care with regard to trespassers.

[5] In fact, we have even gone so far as to hold that complex and confusing legal determinations

liability for Mrs. Mallet's injuries was never presented to the jury; the old scheme served its purpose in limiting juror discretion, effectively eliminating the jury entirely from the consideration of the case. This is the most pernicious side effect of the common law trichotomy, and it is no longer in step with the times.

We must examine the continuing relevance of the common law trichotomy by viewing it in the context of the time in which it was developed. We must not overlook the fact that some of the hoary and "well-established" principles that held sway at the time the common law categories were introduced in the mid-19th Century included, slavery, see *Dred Scott v. Sandford*, 60 U.S. (19 How.) 393, 15 L.Ed. 691 (1856), and a lack of women's suffrage, see *Minor v. Happersett*, 88 U.S. (21 Wall.) 162, 22 L.Ed. 627 (1874) (confining the right of suffrage to males did not deprive women of property without due process of law), both of which, had they not been abandoned, would, to say the least, have had a negative impact on the recent composition of this Court.

Justice Starcher, joined by Justice Workman, recognized in their concurrence in *Self v. Queen* that many "established" rules must give way as society progresses:

> When Justice Oliver Wendell Holmes spoke of "fixed and uniform standards of external conduct" in his 1881 lecture series (now found in THE COMMON LAW (1909)), we must keep in mind that Holmes was writing in a time when the harsh rules of contributory negligence, assumption of the risk, and the fellow-servant doctrine were taking root in the law. These rules, which were once new, shiny principles designed to immunize entrepreneurs and businesses from liability at a time of early industrialization, have since weathered and fallen in the face of time, reason, and a growing intolerance for human suffering that has accompanied the post-industrial era. See *Bradley v. Appalachian Power Co.*, 163 W.Va. 332, 256 S.E.2d 879 (1979) (abolishing contributory negligence rule and adopting modified comparative negligence principles); *King v. Kayak Mfg. Corp.*, 182 W.Va. 276, 387 S.E.2d 511 (1989) (abolishing assumption of risk and adopting comparative assumption of risk); W. Va.Code, 23-1-1, et seq. (abrogating fellow-servant doctrine by providing workers' compensation benefits to workers injured in the course of and as a result of their employment, including injuries by fellow employees).

199 W.Va. at 641, 487 S.E.2d at 299 (Starcher, J., concurring). The outmoded distinction between invitees is just the sort of principle which, though perhaps once an accurate reflection of society's values, no longer comports with our notions of fairness, and for that reason should be abandoned.

---

should always be submitted to a jury to ensure that a common-sense result may obtain. Although included in a discussion of jury nullification, which is not before us in this case, we have noted that, in some instances where old rules create unexpected consequences, it is better to let a jury consider the matter:

> Consequently, we would suggest that when a civil case involves law that is sufficiently obscure, tenuous and convoluted that a reasonable person could find it surprising, a court may submit the matter to a jury in order to guarantee that the judgment accords with the community's sense of moral probity. *State v. Morgan Stanley & Co., Inc.* 194 W.Va. 163, 174–175, 459 S.E.2d 906, 917–918 (1995).

Courts, in their efforts to distinguish between licensees and invitees, have felled whole forests and sacrificed them in an often vain attempt to explain the difference. These efforts have resulted in some opinions that strain the credulity of an honest observer. Courts on both sides of the Atlantic have pointed out the confusing complexities encountered when applying the common law classifications:

> "A canvasser who comes on your premises without your consent is a trespasser. Once he has your consent, he is a licensee. Not until you do business with him is he an invitee. Even when you have done business with him, it seems rather strange that your duty towards him should be different when he comes up to your door from what it is when he goes away. Does he change his colour in the middle of the conversation? What is the position when you discuss business with him and it comes to nothing? No confident answer can be given to these questions. Such is the morass into which the law has floundered in trying to distinguish between licensees and invitees."

Mariorenzi v. Joseph DiPonte, Inc., 114 R.I. 294, 306 n. 4, 333 A.2d 127, 133 n. 4 (1975) (abolishing distinctions between trespasser, licensee, and invitee) (quoting *Dunster v. Abbot*, 2 All E.R. 1572, 1574 (C.A.1953) (Eng.)).

Quite often, the facts of a particular premises liability case will require a departure from Aristotelian logic in its search for common sense realism. The Indiana Court of Appeals demonstrated the mental gymnastics sometimes necessary to hold onto the old distinction in *Markle v. Hacienda Mexican Restaurant*, 570 N.E.2d 969 (Ind.Ct.App.1991). In *Markle*, the plaintiff decided to eat at a restaurant, but upon driving into the strip mall parking lot where the restaurant was located, stopped when he saw a friend. He got out of his car to transfer an item to the friend's car, and was injured when he stepped into a pothole. Although the court decided that a jury question existed as to the duty the restaurant owed the plaintiff, they found necessary the following exercise in arcane logic:

> We would reach this same result if, for instance, Markle was discussing business with an associate while eating dinner at the restaurant and injured himself in the same parking lot by stepping into the same chuckhole when going out to his car for some papers to use in the discussion. One could say that Markle stepped out of his role as an invitee—although briefly—by leaving the restaurant to get the papers. However, it is also reasonable that the owners could anticipate patrons would meet to discuss business over dinner. Thus, the question of whether the patron who has left the restaurant to get some papers from his car has stepped out of his role as invitee is one properly left to the trier of fact. Likewise, the question of whether the Shopping Center could have anticipated that Markle—or any other customer—would transact business in the parking lot is one properly left to the trier of fact.

Markle, 570 N.E.2d at 975 n. 2. A search of other jurisdictions reveals case after case where a court, bound by the old, common law categories, is forced to ask the wrong question.

C. LIMITING AND ABANDONING THE CATEGORIES

The question in instances such as this should not be, "was the plaintiff emblazoned with the magic letters 'L' or 'I' at the moment of injury?," but rather "was the parking lot safe?" Or, alternatively, "did the landowner exercise reasonable care under the circumstances, to ensure that the parking lot was safe for a reasonably foreseeable event, namely, that somebody might walk across it?" Framing the question in this manner is important, because it recognizes that neither landowners nor entrants make decisions with these archaic distinctions in mind. . . .

If we wish for our law to be predictable, and we do, then we have a duty to shape it in such a way that it meshes with the general, reasonable assumptions that people make in their daily lives. Because the common law distinction between invitee and licensee does not meet that standard, it should be discarded.

A growing number of courts have taken Occam's Razor to this problem, in search for a simpler and more predictable rule. Nearly 40 years ago, the Supreme Court of the United States declined to apply the common law categories to admiralty law, and identified the conflict between a feudally-derived liability standard and modern tort theory:

> The distinctions which the common law draws between licensee and invitee were inherited from a culture deeply rooted to the land, a culture which traced many of its standards to a heritage of feudalism. In an effort to do justice in an industrialized urban society, with its complex economic and individual relationships, modern common-law courts have found it necessary to formulate increasingly subtle verbal refinements, to create subclassifications among traditional common-law categories, and to delineate fine gradations in the standards of care which the landowner owes to each. Yet even within a single jurisdiction, the classifications and subclassifications bred by the common law have produced confusion and conflict. As new distinctions have been spawned, older ones have become obscured. Through this semantic morass the common law has moved, unevenly and with hesitation, towards "imposing on owners and occupiers a single duty of reasonable care in all the circumstances."

Kermarec v. Compagnie Generale Transatlantique, 358 U.S. 625, 630–31, 79 S.Ct. 406, 410, 3 L.Ed.2d 550, 554–55 (1959) (footnotes omitted). Clearly the justices underestimated the degree of hesitation, but today we do our part by wading out of the "semantic morass. . . ."

Soon after the opinion in *Kermarec,* several states abandoned the old scheme, starting with California in *Rowland v. Christian,* 69 Cal.2d 108, 70 Cal.Rptr. 97, 443 P.2d 561 (1968). Over 30 years ago, the California court realized that the old classifications were outmoded:

> Complexity can be borne and confusion remedied where the underlying principles governing liability are based upon proper considerations. Whatever may have been the historical justifications for the common law distinctions, it is clear that those distinctions are not justified in the light of our modern society and that the complexity and confusion which have arisen is not due to difficulty in applying

the original common law rules—they are all to easy to apply in their original formulation—but is due to the attempts to apply just rules in our modern society within the ancient terminology.

Rowland, 69 Cal.2d at 117, 70 Cal.Rptr. at 103, 443 P.2d. at 567. The *Rowland* court could see that application of the old distinction in premises liability cases often yields a result that seems unjust by the standards of today, especially when viewed in light of the general principles of negligence that we employ in other tort cases.

Broad generalizations about the state of premises liability law in other jurisdictions are always subject to caveats and limitations. Several states have special rules for invited social guests; others limit landowner liability via recreational use statutes, or employ a distinction between "active" and "passive" negligence. Having said that, our research reveals that at least 25 jurisdictions have abolished or largely abandoned the licensee/invitee distinction. Among these 25 jurisdictions that have broken with past tradition, at least 17 have eliminated or fundamentally altered the distinction. Another eight of the 25 have eliminated even the trespasser distinction. And, of those retaining the old scheme, judges in at least five of those states have authored vigorous dissents or concurrences arguing for change.

A look at some of these cases provides an example of the logic that persuades us to join the modern trend. In a recent Nebraska case, a father visited his daughter, who worked at a hospital, and injured his back when he slipped on snow-covered stairs as he left the building. The lower court held that, because the father was visiting the daughter, he was a licensee and could not recover in a suit against the hospital. The Supreme Court of Nebraska recognized this absurd result:

> When he was injured, Heins was exiting a county hospital, using the main entrance to the hospital, over the lunch hour. If Heins had been on the hospital premises to visit a patient or purchase a soft drink from a vending machine, he could have been classified as an invitee. . . . However, he came to visit his daughter and was denied recovery as a matter of law.
>
> Thus Heins was denied the possibility of recovering under present law, merely because on this trip to the hospital he happened to be a licensee rather than an invitee. In the instant case, the hospital would undergo no additional burden in exercising reasonable care for a social visitor such as Heins, because it had the duty to exercise reasonable care for its invitees. A patient visitor could have used the same front entrance at which Heins fell and would have been able to maintain a negligence action; however, Heins has been denied the opportunity to recover merely because of his status at the time of the fall.

Heins v. Webster County, 250 Neb. 750, 759–60, 552 N.W.2d 51, 56 (1996). The *Heins* court perceived the obvious question, "did the hospital exercise reasonable care under the circumstances?" The court went on to abolish the common law categories: "We conclude that we should eliminate the distinction between licensees and invitees by requiring a standard of reasonable care for all lawful visitors." Id. at 761, 552 N.W.2d at 57.

C. LIMITING AND ABANDONING THE CATEGORIES 581

Another recent case in which a court abandoned the old scheme is *Nelson v. Freeland*, 349 N.C. 615, 507 S.E.2d 882 (1998). In *Nelson*, Mr. Freeland requested that his friend Mr. Nelson pick him up at his home for a business meeting the two were going to attend. In doing so, Mr. Nelson tripped over a stick Mr. Freeland had left lying on his porch. Mr. Freeland won summary judgment, which Mr. Nelson appealed. After a lengthy, exhaustive, and well-written analysis of the history of the common law trichotomy, the North Carolina Supreme Court abandoned the licensee/invitee distinction:

> Given the numerous advantages associated with abolishing the trichotomy, this Court concludes that we should eliminate the distinction between licensees and invitees by requiring a standard of reasonable care toward all lawful visitors. Adoptions of a true negligence standard eliminates the complex, confusing, and unpredictable state of premises-liability law and replaces it with a rule which forces the jury's attention upon the pertinent issue of whether the landowner acted as a reasonable person would under the circumstances.

Nelson, 349 N.C. at 631, 507 S.E.2d at 892.

Some would argue, and indeed this Court has stated in the past, that the strength of the old system is that it engenders predictability. We are no longer persuaded by this argument. As we noted above, the average person has no idea that such a rule exists. Indeed, in situations such as the case before us, homeowners would probably imagine that if anyone is entitled to protection on their property (and coverage under a homeowners policy), surely their friends and loved ones would qualify. In fact, it is counterintuitive to most lay persons, and many a law student, that those closest to us are not afforded the same protection the law provides to the meter reader or the paper boy. Complicating this confusion among property owners is the fact that an entrant can cascade chameleon-like through the various "colors" of entrant status, from trespasser to licensee to invitee and back, in the course of a single visit.

Today we hold that the common law distinction between licensees and invitees is hereby abolished; landowners or possessors now owe any non-trespassing entrant a duty of reasonable care under the circumstances. We retain our traditional rule with regard to a trespasser, that being that a landowner or possessor need only refrain from willful or wanton injury. Though our decision might seem a radical departure from past cases, in its basic philosophy it is not.

We have held since the 19th Century that: "Negligence is the violation of the duty of taking care under the given circumstances. It is not absolute, but is always relative to some circumstances of time, place, manner, or person." *Dicken v. Liverpool Salt & Coal Co.*, 41 W.Va. 511, 23 S.E. 582 (1895). Although before today we have allowed the old labels to limit a court's examination of a negligent act, we have recognized that the foreseeability of an injury is dispositive of the duty owed:

> The ultimate test of the existence of a duty to use care is found in the foreseeability that harm may result if it is not exercised. The test is, would the ordinary man in the defendant's position, knowing what he knew or should have known, anticipate that harm of the general nature of that suffered was likely to result?

Sewell v. Gregory, 179 W.Va. 585, 371 S.E.2d 82 (1988). In so holding in *Sewell*, we were in accord with Justice Cardozo's celebrated maxim: "The risk reasonably to be perceived defines the duty to be obeyed . . . ." *Palsgraf v. Long Island R. Co.*, 248 N.Y. 339, 344, 162 N.E. 99, 100 (1928).

We are quick to recognize, however, that foreseeability is not all that the trier of fact must consider when deciding if a given defendant owed a duty to a given plaintiff, even in the absence of the licensee/invitee distinction:

> While the existence of a duty is defined in terms of foreseeability, it also involves policy considerations including "the likelihood of injury, the magnitude of the burden of guarding against it, and the consequences of placing that burden on the defendant."

Harris v. R.A. Martin, Inc., 204 W.Va. 397, 401, 513 S.E.2d 170, 174 (1998) (per curiam) (quoting *Robertson v. LeMaster*, 171 W.Va. at 611, 301 S.E.2d at 567). Some factors that other jurisdictions have included in the analysis of whether a landowner or occupier has exercised reasonable care under the circumstances include the seriousness of an injury, the time, manner and circumstances under which the injured party entered the premises, and the normal use made of the premises.

We hold that, in determining whether a defendant in a premises liability case met his or her burden of reasonable care under the circumstances to all non-trespassing entrants, the trier of fact must consider (1) the foreseeability that an injury might occur; (2) the severity of injury; (3) the time, manner and circumstances under which the injured party entered the premises; (4) the normal or expected use made of the premises; and (5) the magnitude of the burden placed upon the defendant to guard against injury. . . .

We hold that the invitee/licensee distinction is abandoned. Our cases that rely upon it and their progeny, are overruled to the extent that they rely upon an invitee/licensee distinction. In light of these developments, Mr. and Mrs. Mallet should be afforded another attempt at recovery, and all similar claims, in the future, should be adjudicated under the new standards we have articulated. Accordingly, the lower court's grant of summary judgment is reversed and this case is remanded for proceedings consistent with this opinion.

Reversed and remanded.

NOTES

1. *Rowland's Reassessment of the Redistribution Rationale.* In the seminal case of *Rowland v. Christian,* 69 Cal. 2d 108, 70 Cal. Rptr. 97, 443 P.2d 561 (1968), the court stated:

> Without attempting to labor all of the rules relating to the possessor's liability, it is apparent that the classifications of trespasser, licensee, and invitee, the immunities from liability predicated upon those classifications, and the exceptions to those immunities, often do not reflect the major factors which should determine whether immunity should be conferred upon the possessor of land. Some of those factors, including the closeness of the connection between the injury

and the defendant's conduct, the moral blame attached to the defendant's conduct, the policy of preventing future harm, and the prevalence and availability of insurance, bear little, if any, relationship to the classifications of trespasser, licensee and invitee and the existing rules conferring immunity.

Although in general there may be a relationship between the remaining factors and the classifications of trespasser, licensee, and invitee, there are many cases in which no such relationship may exist. Thus, although the foreseeability of harm to an invitee would ordinarily seem greater than the foreseeability of harm to a trespasser, in a particular case the opposite may be true. The same may be said of the issue of certainty of injury. The burden to the defendant and consequences to the community of imposing a duty to exercise care with resulting liability for breach may often be greater with respect to trespassers than with respect to invitees, but it by no means follows that this is true in every case. In many situations, the burden will be the same, i.e., the conduct necessary upon the defendant's part to meet the burden of exercising due care as to invitees will also meet his burden with respect to licensees and trespassers. The last of the major factors, the cost of insurance, will, of course, vary depending upon the rules of liability adopted, but there is no persuasive evidence that applying ordinary principles of negligence law to the land occupier's liability will materially reduce the prevalence of insurance due to increased cost or even substantially increase the cost.

Why did the court in *Mallet* preserve the limited duty rule for trespassers?

2. *Application of the Unitary Doctrine.* In *Basso v. Miller,* 40 N.Y.2d 233, 386 N.Y.S.2d 564, 352 N.E.2d 868, 872 (1976), the court noted:

While the likelihood of a plaintiff's presence had been an implicit consideration in the determination of status and the duty commensurate therewith, it now becomes a primary independent factor in determining foreseeability and the duty of the owner or occupier will vary with the likelihood of plaintiff's presence at the particular time and place of the injury. While status is no longer determinative, considerations of who plaintiff is and what his purpose is upon the land are factors which, if known, may be included in arriving at what would be reasonable care under the circumstances.

Is this an accurate reflection of the application of the unitary approach, or an invitation to continue making traditional, arbitrary distinctions?

3. *A Trend in Retreat? Rowland's* rejection of categories has met with rejection in many jurisdictions. *See, e.g., Carter v. Kinney,* 896 S.W.29, 926 (Mo. 1995). In *Adams v. Fred's Dollar Store,* 497 So. 2d 1097, 1102 (Miss. 1986), the court observed: "To adopt such a position now would cause an upheaval of the common law and needlessly inject uncertainty into the realm of commercial and private legal relations. We here reaffirm our intention to follow the common law distinctions."

D. RECREATIONAL USE STATUTES

TUDER v. KELL
739 So.2d 1069 (Ala. 1999)

LYONS, JUSTICE.

The plaintiffs—Randy Tuders, James Tuders, Larry Nance, individually and as personal representative of the estate of Bobbi Jo Nance, deceased and Anita Hicks, individually and as mother of Amanda Hicks and Kyle Hicks, deceased minors—appeal from a summary judgment entered in favor of the defendant, Paul Kell, doing business as Kell Realty Company. We affirm.

On July 4, 1995, Randy Tuders and his son James Tuders; Larry Nance and his wife Bobbi Jo Nance; and Anita Hicks and her children Amanda and Kyle Hicks (all referred to as "the boaters"), were passengers in a boat on Neely Henry Lake when a severe thunderstorm developed suddenly. As the weather got worse and the boaters saw lightning in their vicinity, they decided to get off the water immediately. The nearest shelter from the lightning and rain was a pier and boathouse, still under construction, that belonged to Kell. They tied the boat to the pier and stood on the pier under an overhanging portion of the boathouse roof to wait out the storm. Approximately 15 minutes later the boathouse collapsed. Bobbi Jo Nance, Amanda Hicks, and Kyle Hicks died; the others were injured. At the time of the accident, Kyle Hicks, Amanda Hicks, and James Tuders were ages 4, 8, and 16, respectively.

Kell had drawn a sketch of the boathouse he wanted and then had hired someone to build it for him. The plaintiffs testified that it was apparent that the boathouse was under construction. It had a roof, but the outside walls were incomplete. Bracing had been used to stabilize the walls of the boathouse during its construction; however, the bracing had been removed from the north wall before the construction was complete and before the boaters took shelter there. The evidence does not indicate who removed the bracing from the boathouse.

Randy Tuders, James Tuders, Larry Nance, and Anita Hicks filed a wrongful-death and personal-injury complaint against Kell and others. They alleged that the defendants had negligently caused the deaths and personal injures incurred in the July 4, 1995, incident. The trial court entered a summary judgment in favor of Kell, holding that the boaters were trespassers on Kell's property; that the only duty Kell owed to the boaters was to refrain from wantonly or intentionally injuring them; that the plaintiffs did not present substantial evidence indicating that Kell had wantonly or intentionally injured them; and that §§ 35-15-1 to -5, Ala.Code 1975, shielded Kell from any liability in this case. The plaintiffs appealed. All defendants other than Kell have been dismissed.

We first address whether the Code sections governing the recreational use of land, §§ 35-15-1 to -5 ("the recreational-use statute"), apply to a situation like that presented in this case. If so, then a landowner like Kell is liable only for willfully or maliciously injuring those who enter the land for recreational purposes. Kell argues that the recreational-use statute applies to him and that it limits his liability for accidents occurring on his property that arise out of certain recreational uses, among them water sports and boating. The plaintiffs argue that in order for the recreational-use statute to apply, a landowner must have granted permission to the general public to use the land for recreational purposes. Kell disagrees, arguing that it is not necessary for the landowner to give permission to the general public to use the land, and that cases interpreting the recreational-use statute, such as *Clark v. Tennessee Valley Authority*, 606 F.Supp. 130 (N.D.Ala.1985), require that it be construed liberally in order to limit a landowner's liability.

Section 35-15-1 states:

> An owner, lessee or occupant of premises owes no duty of care to keep such premises safe for entry and use by others for hunting, fishing, trapping, camping, water sports, hiking, boating, sight-seeing, caving, climbing, rappelling or other recreational purposes or to give any warning of hazardous conditions, use of structures or activities on such premises to persons entering for the above-stated purposes, except as provided in section 35-15-3.

This section refers to the rights of "persons entering" for certain activities (hunting, fishing, etc.). Section 35-15-1 does not specify whether the legislature intended that the "persons entering" were doing so lawfully. Section 35-15-3, cross-referenced in § 35-15-1, deals with the activities in the context of permission given for such use. Section 35-15-2 also deals with the effect of permission given for such activities. The principles of statutory construction require that we construe statutes dealing with the same subject matter in pari materia. Furthermore, those principles call for us to refrain from using a strained or unnatural construction during the process of interpretation. We therefore hold that in § 35-15-1, the legislature, in speaking of "recreational purposes," was speaking of activities carried on or conducted by persons lawfully on the premises of the "owner, lessee or occupant."

This Court has previously given such a construction to the recreational-use statute. See *Wright v. Alabama Power Co.*, 355 So.2d 322 (Ala.1978), where this Court stated:

> "The [recreational-use statute] was intended to [ensure] that landowners were not to be held to a standard of due care toward persons upon their land with permission for hunting, fishing and recreational purposes. . . . The legislation [gives] persons upon the land with permission or invitation, but for purposes unrelated to the owner's business, . . . the status of licensees[,] with the [landowner's] duty being the duty owed to licensees."

355 So.2d at 324. Although the recreational-use statute does not require that, for the statute to apply, the landowner must have given the general public permission to use the land, it is necessary that the landowner have given permission to the person or persons using the land to use it for recreational purposes. It is undisputed that Kell had not given anyone permission to use his land, pier, or boathouse. Therefore, Kell is not entitled to the immunity provided by the recreational-use statute.

We note that § 35-15-3 provides that the recreational-use statute "does not limit the liability which otherwise exists for [willful] or malicious failure to guard or warn against a dangerous condition, use, structure or activity." As we discuss, Kell's conduct in regard to the incident of July 4, 1995, was neither willful nor malicious. Furthermore, the landowner's liability recognized by § 35-15-3 (liability "for [willful] or malicious failure to guard or warn") is premised upon someone's using real property after the "owner, lessee or occupant" has given permission to use the land for recreation—that circumstance is far removed from the situation presented in this case, where the plaintiffs claim they and the other boaters had permission implied by law pursuant to the "doctrine of necessity." The recreational-use statute applies to landowners who have given express permission for their land to be used for recreational purposes.

Having determined that the recreational-use statute does not apply, we now consider whether the boaters were trespassers or were licensees. "This Court looks to the status of the injured party in relation to the defendant's land or premises in deciding whether the defendant should be held liable for an injury to a visitor upon the land or premises." *Hambright v. First Baptist Church-Eastwood*, 638 So.2d 865, 868 (Ala.1994). If a person is on the landowner's property without the consent of the landowner, then that person is a trespasser. If a person is visiting the landowner's property with the landowner's consent or as the landowner's guest, but with no business purpose, then that person is a licensee.

The plaintiffs argue that one who seeks shelter on another's land because of an emergency should be considered an "implied licensee," rather than a trespasser, pursuant to the "doctrine of necessity." The plaintiffs argue that under the principles stated in Restatement (Second) of Torts § 330 (1965), a person who enters another's land because of an emergency or necessity may enter under an "implied license." Kell points out that Alabama courts have not adopted Restatement § 330. He argues that because he was not present when the boaters came onto his property, did not extend any invitation to them to come onto his pier or into his boathouse, and did not know they were present, they were trespassers.

A marine patrol officer who had been stationed on Neely Henry Lake for approximately 30 years testified that the storm that arose on July 4, 1995, was the worst storm he had ever seen on that lake. Clearly, the boaters could not have reached their destination before the storm overtook them, so they sought shelter on the nearest property. According to the testimony presented, it is not unusual for boaters on Neely Henry Lake to do that. Kell testified that he had sought shelter on a stranger's land during a storm, but said he had taken shelter only on the land, not on a pier or near a building.

Section 330, Restatement (Second) of Torts, states the principle that "[a] licensee is a person who is privileged to enter or remain on land only by virtue of the possessor's consent." The Restatement recommends, however, that courts recognize a license implied by custom:

> The well-established usages of a civilized and Christian community" entitle everyone to assume that a possessor of land is willing to permit him to enter for certain purposes until a particular possessor expresses unwillingness to admit him. Thus a traveler who is overtaken by a violent storm or who has lost his way, is entitled to assume that there

is no objection to his going to a neighboring house for shelter or direction. So too, if there is a local custom for possessors of land to permit others to enter it for particular purposes, residents in that locality and others knowing of the custom are justified in regarding a particular possessor as conversant with it and, therefore, in construing his neglect to express his desire not to receive them as a sufficient manifestation of a willingness to admit them.

Section 330, cmt. e.

We need not decide in this case whether to recognize a privilege implied by custom to enter another's land in a case of emergency or necessity. Even if we assume that the boaters were licensees and not trespassers, we must conclude that Kell did not breach any duty he would have owed them. It follows that he also did not breach any duty he would have owed the boaters as trespassers.[3]

If the boaters were licensees, then Kell, as the landowner, would have owed them the following duty:

> The duty owed by a landowner to a licensee is to abstain from willfully or wantonly injuring the licensee and to avoid negligently injuring the licensee after the landowner discovers a danger to the licensee. This duty is not an active one to safely maintain the premises; instead, the landowner has the duty not to set traps or pitfalls and not to willfully or wantonly injure the licensee.

Hambright, 638 So.2d at 868.

The plaintiffs argue that if this Court determines that the boaters were licensees, then Kell's removal of the bracing on the boathouse wall must be considered to have been "willful" and "wanton" because, they say, the bracing on the boathouse wall was a "safety device"—i.e., they say his removal of that "safety device" constituted wantonness. . . .

The plaintiffs acknowledge that the boaters recognized the boathouse to be in an incomplete state of construction when they chose to seek shelter under it during what apparently was the worst storm on Neely Henry Lake in 30 years. We are persuaded by the reasoning of *Helvich v. George A. Rutherford Co.*, 96 Ohio App. 367, 114 N.E.2d 514 (1953), regarding the circumstances presented by unfinished construction:

> When a property is under construction, there are, of necessity, hazards created as the work progresses which are only eliminated by its completion. Anybody who goes upon such property with knowledge that it is under construction must meet with and guard himself against such natural and necessarily created dangers. A contractor is not compelled, in the exercise of ordinary care, to guard against such natural dangers after the work day is over and the property is closed for ordinary purposes to business visitors, licensees or frequenters.

---

[3] If the boaters were trespassers, Kell would have owed them the duty "not to wantonly or intentionally injure [them] and to warn [them] of dangers known by [him] after [he] was aware of danger to [them]." *Copeland v. Pike Liberal Arts School*, 553 So.2d at 102.

96 Ohio App. at 381, 114 N.E.2d at 522. By the use of reasonable care, the boaters would have avoided resort to the shelter of an incomplete structure, in favor of the nearby shore. When reasonable care would lead one to avoid potential dangers, there is no trap. *Hambright*, 638 So.2d at 868.

We find no evidence in the record that remotely suggests Kell set a "trap" or a "pitfall" for the boaters or that he consciously removed the bracing from the boathouse with the knowledge that his doing so probably would result in injury. Indeed, Randy Tuders and Larry Nance both testified that they knew of no evidence indicating that Kell intentionally or maliciously caused the collapse of the boathouse. The plaintiffs argue, however, that if they were licensees and if Kell's actions were not wanton, then, still, he owed them a duty not to expose them to a "new hidden danger" that they say resulted from negligence on his part as a landowner; they argue that the removal of the bracing on the boathouse wall was an affirmative act that exposed them to a "new hidden danger," and they argue that they should be allowed to pursue a negligence claim against Kell. Kell argues, in response, that he did not know the boaters were on his property and therefore could not have discovered that they were in danger. . . .

. . . There is no dispute that Kell did not discover that the boaters had been present on his land, much less that they had been in any peril, until after the boathouse had already collapsed. Therefore, even assuming that the boaters were licensees, we conclude that the evidence does not indicate that Kell breached any duty he owed a licensee.

The Court has struggled with the difficult facts presented by this case. Certainly the events of July 4, 1995, were tragic for all concerned. Our function, however, is to apply the applicable law to the facts, even when those facts are difficult. Although we have concluded that the recreational-use statute did not apply to Kell and that it is unnecessary to decide whether the boaters were trespassers or were licensees, the trial court nevertheless correctly entered the summary judgment in favor of Kell. This Court will affirm a summary judgment properly entered, notwithstanding that it was entered on a rationale different from that on which we find it proper.

AFFIRMED.

NOTES

1. *Recreational Use For a Fee.* Most states have enacted recreational use statutes. Which category of visitor is most affected by the immunity afforded by the typical recreational use statute? What effect does such a statute have in a state which has abrogated the traditional categories? Does it make them applicable again, at least as to certain visitors?

The recreational use immunity generally does not apply when a fee is paid to enter the land. Thus, in *Jansen v. Howard,* 215 Cal. App. 3d 992, 263 Cal. Rptr. 776 (1989), it was held that a $6 horse race entry fee which went to the sponsor of the race, and not to the landowner, constituted entry "for a consideration" under the applicable statute.

In *Jacobsen v. City Of Rathdrum,* 115 Idaho 266, 766 P.2d 736 (1988), the court held that one effect of the Idaho recreational use statute was that a recreational user was to be legally treated as a trespasser.

2. *Willful and Wanton Conduct. Klepper v. Milford,* 825 F.2d 1440, 1447 (10th Cir. 1987), concerned a typical statutory provision and an equally typical fact pattern, a dive into shallow water. The statute did not provide immunity in cases of "willful or malicious failure to guard or warn against a dangerous condition, use, structure, or activity." The court concluded that, "[g]iven the . . . phrase 'willful failure to guard' and not 'wanton failure to guard,' Kansas law directs the conclusion that unless the defendants intended to injure the plaintiff or otherwise had a designed purpose or intent to do wrong, they were not guilty of willful failure to guard."

In *Mandel v. United States,* 719 F.2d 963 (8th Cir. 1983), the court dealt with an Arkansas provision excepting from immunity "wilful or malicious failure to guard or warn against a dangerous condition, use, structure, or activity." The court held that the trial judge's grant of summary judgment was erroneous when there was evidence that a warning, which had been recommended by a park ranger, was not posted at the swimming hole, and that park rangers had been aware of the dangers of submerged rocks throughout the river in question.

3. *Public Use.* In *Bauer v. Minidoka Sch. Dist. No. 331,* 116 Idaho 586, 778 P.2d 336 (1989), a high school student suffered a broken leg when he fell over some sprinkler pipes during a supervised football game prior to the commencement of morning classes. In holding that the state recreational use statute did not apply, the court stated:

> [Plaintiff] was not the type of recreational user contemplated in the recreational use statute. He was a public school student who came to school early before classes and began to play football with his classmates. If he had come to the school grounds to play a game of football that was not organized or sanctioned by the school on a day when school was not in session, we would have no trouble in applying the statute to limit the liability of the district. Nor would we have any difficulty in applying the statute, if he had come to the school grounds on a school day to play a game of football that was not organized or sanctioned by the school before the faculty and other students who were not involved in the game began arriving. The problem we have in applying the recreational use statute to these facts is that [plaintiff] arrived to play football at the very time that the school was beginning its operations for the day, although no classes had begun. He was not just a member of "the public" referred to in the recreational use statute. He was there as a student to begin the school day with a game of football. Some students may come early to talk to their teachers, some to visit with their classmates, some to study and others to participate in informal activities such as football. All of these are legitimate activities within the scope of a student's special relationship with the school.
>
> It would be entirely artificial to apply the recreational use statute to activities of students up to the moment the first bell rings and classes begin. No purpose would be served by drawing this line for application of the recreational use statute. When the principal is present, some faculty members are on duty and students have arrived,

the school day has begun and the recreational use statute has no application to a student who is injured on the school grounds.

4. *Residential, Urban Property and Social Guests.* Wymer v. Holmes, 429 Mich. 66, 412 N.W.2d 213 (1987), addressed the applicability of Michigan's recreational land use act (RUA) to social guests invited to the respective defendants-landowners' residential homes to engage in recreation. These guests subsequently were either injured or died while swimming at the property of the residential landowners. The statute then in force provided,

> No cause of action shall arise for injuries to any person who is on the lands of another without paying to such other person a valuable consideration for the purpose of fishing, hunting, trapping, camping, hiking, sightseeing, motorcycling, snowmobiling, or any other outdoor recreational use, with or without permission, against the owner, tenant, or lessee of said premises unless the injuries were caused by the gross negligence or wilful and wanton misconduct of the owner, tenant, or lessee.

The court concluded:

> The legislative history of the recreational land use statute and its two predecessor statutes, as well as other interpretative aids, also indicate that the Legislature intended the act to apply specifically to certain enumerated outdoor activities (fishing, hunting, trapping, camping, hiking, sightseeing, motorcycling, snowmobiling) which, ordinarily, can be accommodated only on tracts of land which are difficult to defend from trespassers and to make safe for invited persons engaged in recreational activities. The commonality among all these enumerated uses is that they generally require large tracts of open, vacant land in a relatively natural state. This fact and the legislative history of the RUA make clear to us that the statute was intended to apply to large tracts of undeveloped land suitable for outdoor recreational uses. Urban, suburban, and subdivided lands were not intended to be covered by the RUA. The intention of the Legislature to limit owner liability derives from the impracticability of keeping certain tracts of lands safe for public use. The same need to limit owner liability does not arise in the case of recreational facilities which, in contrast, are relatively easy to supervise and monitor for safety hazards.
>
> . . . As our analysis reveals, Michigan's recreational use statute redirected the focus of landowner liability from the status of the user of the property, making the purpose of going on the land and the character of land central to the determination of the owner's liability. Accordingly, we have determined the applicability of the statute in these cases with that same focus in mind, as opposed to the status-of-the-user focus applied by the lower courts when emphasizing the status of the plaintiffs as social guests.

Similarly, in *Loyer v. Buchholz*, 38 Ohio St. 3d 65, 526 N.E.2d 300, 302–03 (1988), the court stated:

> [This recreational use statute] was clearly not intended to confer immunity on owners of private residential swimming pools whose social guests are injured while swimming. Ordinarily, privately owned backyard pools are not kept open to the general public. Owners of such pools typically restrict the use thereof to family members, friends, neighbors and other acquaintances. It is seldom, if ever, expected that all members of the general population are welcome to enter the premises and utilize the swimming facilities.
>
> Since the purpose of the legislation conferring immunity is to encourage owners of premises suitable for recreational pursuits to open their lands for public use, it follows that where the land in question is not held open to the public, the immunity does not apply.

However, the court further remarked,

> Our refusal to apply [the recreational use statute] to immunize appellants is unrelated to the fact that the land on which the injury occurred is apparently suburban rather than rural.

5. *Recreational Use.* In *Miller v. Dayton,* 42 Ohio St. 3d 113, 537 N.E.2d 1294 (1989), plaintiff was injured while sliding into second base during a softball game played at a municipal field. In holding the state recreational use statute applicable, the court stated:

> In determining whether a person is a recreational user. . . the analysis should focus on the character of the property upon which the injury occurs and the type of activities for which the property is held open to the public.
>
> . . . [T]he presence of man-made improvements on a property does not remove the property from statutory protection. . . . To qualify for recreational-user immunity, property need not be completely natural, but its essential character should fit within the intent of the statute.
>
> Generally speaking, recreational premises include elements such as land, water, trees, grass, and other vegetation. But recreational premises will often have such features as walks, fences and other improvements. The significant query is whether such improvements change the character of the premises and put the property outside the protection of the recreational-user statute. To consider the question from a different perspective: Are the improvements and man-made structures consistent with the purpose envisioned by the legislature in its grant of immunity? In other words, are the premises (viewed as a whole) those which users enter upon ". . . to hunt, fish, trap, camp, hike, swim, or engage in other recreational pursuits"?

See also, Keelen v. State of Louisiana, 463 So.2d 1287 (La. 1985)(statute applies to "undeveloped, nonresidential rural or semi-rural land areas" and an "injury-causing condition or instrumentality. . . of the type normally encountered in the true outdoors.")

The immunity applies to the land occupant, *i.e.,* one who has the power to admit or deny entry onto the land. *See Ward v. State,* 890 P.2d 1144 (Ariz. 1995).

6. *Recreational Use and Attractive Nuisance.* In *Stanley v. Tilcon Maine, Inc.,* 541 A.2d 951 (Me. 1988), a 14-year-old was injured while tobogganing in a sandpit. In the face of plaintiff's contention that a minor's claim based on attractive nuisance was not barred by the recreational use statute, the court stated "there is nothing in the language of the statute or the legislative history to suggest that the Legislature intended to limit liability only with respect to claims by adults."

However, in *Paige v. North Oaks Partners,* 134 Cal. App. 3d 860, 184 Cal. Rptr. 867, 869 (1982), a child who was injured in a shopping center parking lot when he rode his bicycle into a trench in a construction area was not barred by the state recreational use statute. In the words of the court:

> Here, although plaintiff's purpose was undoubtedly recreational, the nature of the property in question shows that it is not within the intent of [the statute]. We find nothing in the legislative history to suggest that the Legislature intended to relieve all landowners of liability to trespassing children, whose activities usually are recreational.

7. *Purpose and Use Revisited.* In an especially harsh decision, the California Supreme Court applied that state's recreational use statute to an 8-year-old plaintiff, who accompanied others onto defendant's property and was injured by a dangerous condition of farm equipment on the land. In applying the statute, the court said "whether plaintiff entered the property to play on the equipment, or merely accompanied the other children at play, is immaterial." Nor need the property be "suitable" for recreational purposes in order for the statute to apply. "As the instant case indicates, the concept of 'suitability' is elusive and unpredictable." The court noted, however, that some courts had applied a suitability requirement to exclude "active construction sites" from the coverage of recreational use statutes. *Ornelas v. Randolph,* 847 P. 2d 560 (Cal. 1993).

E. PROFESSIONAL RESCUERS

MELTON v. CRANE RENTAL COMPANY
742 A.2d 875 (D.C. Ct. App. 1999)

WASHINGTON, ASSOCIATE JUDGE:

The primary issue on appeal is whether this jurisdiction will recognize an exception to the Professional Rescuer's Doctrine[1] (doctrine) for independent acts of negligence. Appellant, Isadore Melton, challenges the trial judge's grant of summary judgment in favor of Crane Rental Company (Crane). The trial judge ruled that the doctrine barred a tort action by Melton for injuries sustained in a traffic accident while Melton was acting within the scope of his employment as an emergency medical technician (EMT). Melton argues that the trial court erred in ruling that the doctrine applied because Crane

---

[1] "The doctrine bars those engaged in rescue work as part of their employment from recovering damages for injuries sustained on the job as the result of negligence of the person rescued." *Lee v. Luigi,* 696 A.2d 1371, 1373–74 (D.C.1997) (citing *Gillespie v. Washington,* 395 A.2d 18, 20 (D.C.1978)).

was a third party unrelated to the rescued victim and the negligent act was independent from the emergency to which Melton was responding. We agree, reverse the trial court's decision, and remand.

On June 2, 1996, Melton and another EMT, Hassan Umarani, responding to an emergency, were transporting a pregnant woman to the hospital. Melton was stationed in the rear of the ambulance attending to the rescued party, and Umarani was driving the ambulance. The ambulance was traveling south on Vermont Avenue, N.W. with its emergency lights and siren activated. Melton attests that the ambulance came to a complete stop at the intersection of Vermont Avenue and L Street, N.W. Melton further asserts that all vehicles stopped for the ambulance, except for a truck crane owned and operated by Crane. The truck crane struck the ambulance. Melton sustained permanent injuries from the accident. . . .

This court has addressed the scope and applicability of the doctrine previously in three cases, *Gillespie*,[2] supra note 1, *Young v. Sherwin-Williams, Inc.*,[3] 569 A.2d 1173 (D.C.1990); and *Lee*,[4] supra note 1. In those cases, this court developed and applied the test for determining under what circumstances the doctrine bars recovery by a professional rescuer for injuries sustained within the course of his/her employment. In *Gillespie*, we held that the proper test for determining whether the doctrine applies to bar recovery by a professional rescuer is "whether the hazard ultimately responsible for causing the injuries is inherently within the ambit of those dangers which are unique to and generally associated with the particular rescue activity." *Gillespie*, 395 A.2d at 20–21. In all three cases we recognized that the legal underpinning of the doctrine was to prevent the proliferation of suits in tort by rescuers in inherently dangerous jobs because they "have assumed the risks inherent in the profession for which they are compensated by the public." *Lee*, 696 A.2d at 1374.[5] However broad that underlying policy appears to be, this court in *Gillespie* also declared that "[professional rescuers] . . . do not assume the risk of all injury in the course of their duties." *Gillespie*, 395 A.2d at 20–21. In those cases, this court applied this narrower assumption of risk analysis and determined that the doctrine properly precluded recovery because there existed a definite connection between the negligent act which gave rise to the injury and the rescued person[6] and/or the situs[7] of the emergency; and thus

---

[2] Application of the doctrine prohibited recovery by a harbor patrol police officer, who was injured while attempting to upright a capsized boat, against the estate of the deceased owner who may have been drinking and speeding at the time the boat struck an abutment.

[3] Application of the doctrine prohibited recovery by a firefighter who was injured by his attempt to catch a truck driver as he fell fifty feet from a bridge. The suit against the employer, for negligently hiring a driver with a history of drinking, was barred under the doctrine.

[4] Application of the doctrine prohibited recovery by a police officer who was injured in a fall on the stairway of a restaurant while investigating a suspected burglary in response to an activated burglar alarm.

[5] Although not expressly documented in any of the three cases in this jurisdiction, it is also well recognized public policy that the doctrine seeks to prevent a chilling effect that may occur if citizens in need of help were not free to solicit the assistance of professional rescuers for fear of tort liability. See, e.g., *Lanza v. Polanin*, 581 So.2d 130, 132 (Fla.1991).

[6] In *Gillespie*, the harbor officer's injuries were sustained while attempting to save the party responsible for capsizing the boat.

In *Young*, it was asserted that because the suit was brought against a negligent third party

the injuries sustained were "uniquely associated" to the "particular emergency." Although there was discussion about a possible independent tort exception to the doctrine in both *Young* and *Lee*, this court reserved judgment on the issue because the exception was not applicable to the facts of either case. This case presents us with the first real opportunity to explore the limits of the doctrine with respect to injuries caused to professional rescuers by the independent negligence of unrelated third parties.[8] In this case, unlike in *Gillespie*, *Young*, and *Lee*, there is no nexus between the injuries suffered by the rescuer and the negligence of the rescued party either personally or at the site of the rescue.

Our neighboring jurisdictions, Maryland and Virginia, both recognize an exception to the doctrine based on independent acts. See *Tucker v. Rio Vista Plaza*, 354 Md. 413, 731 A.2d 884 (1999); *Benefiel v. Walker*, 244 Va. 488, 422 S.E.2d 773 (1992). In *Tucker*, the Maryland court rejected the notion that the doctrine should be understood under a transactional approach, that "[a]ny injury which occurred during the entire transaction of responding to the call must be within the scope of the fireman's rule." 731 A.2d at 888. This holding is particularly relevant to the facts of the present case because it demands that a negligent act have a significant connection to the emergency, something more than the fortuitous chance that the negligent act occurred during the scope of the rescuer's employment. Accordingly, the fact that the EMT was en route to the hospital when the accident transpired would be insufficient, alone, to invoke the doctrine.

The Supreme Court of Virginia, likewise, acknowledges an exception to the doctrine based on independent acts of a third party or subsequent negligent acts. The factual scenario in *Benefiel* is, for the most part, identical to the facts of the instant case, and the reasoning utilized in *Benefiel* is helpful in justifying the recognition of an exception based on independent acts of negligence in the District. In *Benefiel*, a fireman injured while riding on a fire truck that was struck by another motorist was not precluded from bringing an action in tort. . . .

Benefiel carefully distinguished "between those situations where the injury occurred from the very circumstance which gave rise to the emergency and those circumstances where the negligent act was subsequent to that giving rise to the emergency." *Irby v. Doe*, 46 Va. Cir. 323 (1998). Moreover, the court in *Benefiel* speaks directly to our conclusion in the present case, that some nexus is required between the negligence and the emergency via either a connection with the negligent person rescued or situs of the emergency. . . .

---

who was not the rescuee, then the exception to the doctrine was actuated. However, this court found that the third party's negligent hiring of a truck operator with a history of drinking was part of the same chain of events that lead to the creation of the risk. The association between the employer and the employee who caused the accident was akin to a theory of respondeat superior. Thus, the court found a relationship between the negligent act and the rescued party.

[7] In *Lee*, there was no relationship between the rescuer's injuries and the burglary to which the officer responded. However, this court did find that the injury was sustained on the premises of the restaurant, the scene of the emergency.

[8] It is important to note that the crane operator was a third party and was not associated with the emergency. There may very well be an instance in which a third party is affiliated with the emergency, and thus the negligence of that related third party may be protected under the doctrine.

Maryland and Virginia are not alone in adopting an independent tort exception to the doctrine. In fact, we know of no other jurisdiction that has failed to recognize such an exception to the doctrine, and Crane could not proffer an authority from any jurisdiction to the contrary.[10]

Although EMT's regularly ride in emergency vehicles as part of their employment obligations, the fact that the emergency vehicle might become involved in a traffic accident is not a risk associated with the reason for the rescuer's presence at the scene. "[Melton] may have exposed himself to the risk of [vehicular traffic], but he has not consented to relieve a [third party of] any future duty to act with reasonable care."[11] W. PAGE KEETON ET AL., § 68, at 485. Crane owed Melton a duty of reasonable care and any question as to the propriety of allowing recovery to an EMT in an emergency vehicle, authorized to travel against the normal dictates of traffic laws, is a question of contributory negligence and not assumption of risk.[12]

Nothing precludes Crane from arguing that the operation of the emergency vehicle was not reasonable under the circumstances and the jury finding Melton contributorily negligent.

It is precisely because a professional rescuer can not be held to assume all risks that the doctrine envisions some nexus between the rescuee, the specific rescue activity, and the negligent act causing injury. Therefore, the only activities that the doctrine seeks to immunize from liability are those negligent acts that occasioned the professional rescuer's presence at the scene. The

---

[10] Crane relies on *Rosa v. Dunkin' Donuts*, 122 N.J. 66, 583 A.2d 1129 (1991), as authority supporting the application of the doctrine in a circumstance of negligence unrelated to the emergency that necessitated the officer's presence on the scene. However, Crane gives too little note to the importance of the slip and fall occurring on the premises of the donut shop—the scene of the incident. Further, the decision in *Rosa* was later reversed by the New Jersey Legislature, indicating that fairness and public policy exact a more restricted interpretation of the doctrine.

Crane also proffers a Michigan Court of Appeals case, Harris-Fields v. Syze, 229 Mich.App. 195, 581 N.W.2d 737 (1998), as authority supporting the application of the doctrine to an independent negligent act by an unrelated third party. However, this decision was overruled, and the Supreme Court of Michigan held that "[t]he fireman's rule does not bar an action in a case such as this in which the alleged negligence of the defendant was unrelated to the events that brought the officer to the location where the injury occurred," without demanding more than a claim of ordinary negligence. *Harris-Fields v. Syze*, 461 Mich. at 189, 600 N.W.2d 611. Like New Jersey, the Michigan Legislature enacted a statute, MICH. COMP. LAWS § 600.2967 (1998), instructing that a firefighter or police officer may recover damages, in certain circumstances, for injuries sustained while acting in his or her official capacity. In particular, recovery is allowed if the injury was caused by a person's ordinary negligence, and the negligent person is not someone whose act resulted in the rescuer's presence at the emergency.

[11] "Knowledge of the general danger may not be enough." W. PAGE KEETON ET AL., PROSSER AND KEETON ON THE LAW OF TORTS § 68, at 489 (5th ed.1984). Assumption of risk requires knowledge and consent, that "an individual had knowledge of a danger and voluntarily acquiescence in it." Id.

[12] A pedestrian who walks down the street in the middle of a block, through a stream of traffic traveling at excessive speed, cannot by any stretch of the imagination be found to consent that the drivers shall not use care to watch for him and avoid running him down. On the contrary, he is insisting that they shall. This is contributory negligence pure and simple. It is not assumption of the risk. And if A leaves an automobile stopped at night on the travelled portion of the highway, and his passenger remains sitting in it, it can readily be found that there is consent to the prior negligence of A, . . . but not to the subsequent negligence of B, who thereafter runs into the car from the rear.

W. PAGE KEETON ET AL., supra note 11, § 68, at 485.

absence of such a nexus, in effect, would immunize all negligent and reckless conduct by third parties based solely on status distinctions. . . .

Reversed and remanded.

NOTES

1. *The Appropriate Rationale.* In *Flowers v. Rock Creek Terrace Ltd. Pt'ship*, 308 Md. 432, 520 A.2d 361 (1987), a volunteer fireman fell 12 stories in an apartment building elevator shaft. The defendant building owners, apartment security company and elevator manufacturer argued that they owed no duty of care to a fireman whose injuries arose out of the nature of his occupation. Agreeing with this position, the court examined the theoretical basis for the fireman's rule:

> The history of the fireman's rule in Maryland is like that in many other states. Earlier cases in this country involving firemen's attempts to recover for negligently caused injuries sustained while firefighting largely focused on the status of the firemen on the premises where the injuries occurred. These cases indicated that firemen came upon the premises under a privilege conferred by legal authority, and, not being invited by the landholder, took the property as they found it. Later cases, while still sounding in premises liability law, recognized that it is a fireman's job to fight fires, and as such he normally takes the risk of fire-related injuries which may be attributable to the landowner or occupier's negligence. Thus, whether purporting to apply premises liability law, or under a rationale based on the relationship between firemen and the public whom they serve, courts held that landowners and occupiers ordinarily owed firemen no duty of reasonable care.
>
> . . . [T]he use of a premises liability rationale would not seem to be entirely appropriate for resolving the issues in cases like this. A premises liability rationale does not encompass cases in which a fireman is injured by a fire caused by the negligence of someone other than the owner or occupier of the premises. In the present case, [the elevator manufacturer] and [security company] are not landowners or occupiers but have invoked the fireman's rule. In addition, other public employees, such as postmen and building inspectors, are generally held to be entitled to due care even though their counterparts in the fire and police departments are not. Nevertheless, postal workers and building inspectors, like firemen and policemen, often enter land pursuant to legal authority rather than express invitation. Nothing in traditional premises liability law, however, furnishes a ground for classifying some of these public employees as invitees and others as licensees. Moreover, although prior cases sounding in premises liability law had begun to define the extent to which firemen are deemed to anticipate certain occupational risks, the premises liability rationale itself does not provide a basis for delimiting the duties owed to firemen. Instead, it is an analysis of the relationship between firemen and the public whom they serve which best explains the fireman's rule.

... Many cases emphasize a public policy derived from the unique relationship between firefighters and the public. The courts reason that firemen cannot recover for negligence in starting fires because it is precisely their duty to take all reasonable measures to protect lives and property from fires.

In addition, some courts have pointed out that firemen receive compensation, such as salary, workers' compensation, and special injury compensation, to fight fires for the public, and that taxpayers should not have to pay such moneys for the firefighting service and then be subject to liability if they call upon the service.

We agree that the fireman's rule is best explained by public policy. . . . [I]t is the nature of the firefighting occupation that limits a fireman's ability to recover in tort for work-related injuries. Instead of continuing to use a rationale based on the law of premises liability, we hold that, as a matter of public policy, firemen and police officers generally cannot recover for injuries attributable to the negligence that requires their assistance. This public policy is based on a relationship between firemen and policemen and the public that calls on these safety officers specifically to confront certain hazards on behalf of the public. A fireman or police officer may not recover if injured by the negligently created risk that was the very reason for his presence on the scene in his occupational capacity. Someone who negligently creates the need for a public safety officer will not be liable to a fireman or policeman for injuries caused by this negligence.

We reiterate, however, that firemen and policemen are not barred from recovery for all improper conduct. Negligent acts not protected by the fireman's rule may include failure to warn the firemen of preexisting hidden dangers where there was knowledge of the danger and an opportunity to warn. They also may include acts which occur subsequent to the safety officer's arrival on the scene and which are outside of his anticipated occupational hazards. [T]he fireman's rule should not apply "when the fireman sustains injuries after the initial period of his anticipated occupational risk, or from perils not reasonably foreseeable as part of that risk." In these situations a fireman or policeman is owed a duty of due care. Moreover, the fireman's rule does not apply to suits against arsonists or those engaging in similar misconduct.

Thus courts have justified the rule based on premises liability classifications, assumption of the risk, and the fact that professional rescuers receive compensation in the form of worker compensation benefits when injured protecting the public. *See Roberts v. Vaughn*, 587 N.W.2d 249 (Mich. 1998). There, in the course of holding that a volunteer firefighter was not subject to the rule, the court said:

"As we have explained, the firefighter's rule is based on considerations of a public policy derived from the unique relationship between professional safety officers and the public. In accordance with that public policy, we concluded that no duty is owed for ordinary negligence because professional safety officers are presumably extensively trained and specially paid to confront dangerous situations in order to protect the public, and that, therefore, these safety officers undertake their profession with the knowledge that their personal safety is at risk. Because of the unique relationship between the public, the safety officer, and those third parties who require the services of the officer, the otherwise applicable duty of care toward the safety officer is replaced by the third party's contribution to tax-supported compensation for those services: when injury occurs, liberal compensation is provided."

However, the availability of worker's compensation benefits normally does not bar a worker's tort suit against a non-employer tortfeasor. Why here? Do you suppose that inconsistency is one of the reasons why courts frequently find the professional rescuer rule does not apply?

2. *A Risk-Shifting Rationale.* In his dissent in *Walters v. Sloan,* 20 Cal. 3d 199, 142 Cal. Rptr. 152, 571 P.2d 609, 619 (1977), Justice Tobriner noted:

> An additional argument that often is forcefully urged in support of the fireman's rule is that the rule serves the beneficial public policy of "spreading the risk" of a fireman's injuries to all taxpayers, and avoids imposing an unreasonable burden on a single negligent tortfeasor. To be sure, the policy of spreading the risk is a sound one, comporting with one of the central themes of modern tort law which attempts to ensure that an injured party does not bear a staggering cost as a result of an unfortunate injury. For several reasons, however, I cannot agree that this risk-spreading policy supports the preservation of the fireman's rule.
>
> In the first place, the suggestion that the retention of the fireman's rule spreads the risk of the fireman's injuries from the negligent tortfeasor to the taxpaying public cannot stand. In denying a fireman any recovery from a negligent tort-feasor, the fireman's rule does not simply require the fireman to recover his tort damages from the public at large, but instead totally precludes the fireman from recovering these damages at all. Although the fireman may, of course, recover worker's compensation benefits from the general public, all other injured workers are entitled to recover such compensation benefits and also to obtain their additional tort damages from a third party tortfeasor. Thus, instead of spreading the risk of fireman's injuries, the fireman's rule in reality requires the injured fireman personally to shoulder a loss which other employees are not required to bear.
>
> Moreover, although some courts have been apprehensive that the abolition of the fireman's rule will necessarily place an unreasonable burden on a single negligent tort-feasor, these decisions appear to ignore the significant role that insurance presently plays in spreading the risk of loss among policyholders. Many fires arise on business premises or as a result of commercial activities and such commercial ventures will normally carry liability insurance that would cover a fireman's tort action. In the case of such commercial enterprises I can perceive no justification for failing to treat the negligent injury of a fireman as much a "cost of doing business" as the negligent injury of

any other person in the course of the commercial operation. In addition, comprehensive "homeowners" policies available to the average homeowner or renter commonly contain personal liability coverage that would shield a negligent individual from the full brunt of the fireman's claim. Accordingly, the "spreading the risk" desideratum does not justify the retention of the fireman's rule.

3. *The Rule Rejected.* Some jurisdictions have abrogated both primary and secondary forms of implied assumption of risk. Re-examining the doctrinal basis for the "fireman's rule" in the light of such an abrogation, the court in *Christensen v. Murphy,* 296 Or. 610, 678 P.2d 1210, 1217 (1984), found that:

> [I]ts major theoretical underpinning is gone. Therefore, because the rule is not sustainable under implied assumption of risk analysis, we must determine if any other supportable theory under the general rubric of "policy" will provide the foundation for the rule. The most often cited policy considerations include: 1) To avoid placing too heavy a burden on premises owners to keep their premises safe from the unpredictable entrance of fire fighters; 2) To spread the risk of fire fighters' injuries to the public through workers' compensation, salary and fringe benefits; 3) To encourage the public to call for professional help and not rely on self-help in emergency situations; 4) To avoid increased litigation.
>
> Frequently, the so-called policy reasons are merely redraped arguments drawn from premises liability or implied assumption of risk, neither of which are now available as legal foundations in this state. For example, policy consideration "1" above focuses on the fire fighter as a class from whom the premises owner needs immunity (akin to a licensee or trespasser), not on the reasonableness of the activity of the premises owner in the circumstances. Thus, it can be seen that the unusual hazard or hidden danger exception to the "fireman's rule" (allowing the fire fighter to recover under the old premises liability or the new foreseeability tests), discloses not a governmental policy concerning conduct of a landowner but a veiled form of assumption of risk analysis.

4. *A Statutory Approach.* CAL. CIV. CODE § 1714.9 (West 1985) provides:

> (a) Notwithstanding statutory or decisional law to the contrary, any person is responsible not only for the results of that person's willful acts causing injury to a peace officer, firefighter, or any emergency medical personnel employed by a public entity, but also for any injury occasioned to that person by the want of ordinary care or skill in the management of the person's property or person, in any of the following situations:
>
> (1) Where the conduct causing the injury occurs after the person knows or should have known of the presence of the peace officer, firefighter, or emergency medical personnel.
>
> (2) Where the conduct causing the injury occurs after the person knows or should have known of the presence of the peace officer,

firefighter, or emergency medical personnel, violates a statute, ordinance, or regulation, and was the proximate cause of an injury which the statute, ordinance, or regulation was designed to prevent, and the statute, ordinance, or regulation was designed to protect the peace officer, firefighter, or emergency medical personnel. . . .

(3) Where the conduct causing the injury was intended to injure the peace officer, firefighter, or emergency medical personnel.

(4) Where the conduct causing the injury is arson. . .

As the principal case notes, New Jersey and Michigan have also passed legislation dealing with the professional rescuer's rule.

5. *Limiting the rule.* As noted, even in the jurisdictions that adhere to the rule, there are exceptions. Some limit the application of the rule to firefighters and the police. Thus, in *Lees v. Lobasco*, 265 N.J. Super. 95, 625 A.2d 573 (1993), the court held that the "firefighter's rule" did not apply to a suit brought by a municipally-employed emergency medical technician. Generally, the courts are divided on the expansion of the fireman's rule to other rescue personnel. *See, e.g.,* 89 A.L.R. 4th 1079 (1991).

Even if the rule is applicable to the plaintiff as professional rescuer, it might not apply to a risk independent of the risk to which the professional is responding, or to a risk that arises after the professional is summoned, *see, Gould v. Brox*, 623 A.2d 1325 (N.H. 1993), or to a risk that bears no nexus to the reason why the professional was summoned. For instance, in *Rivas v. Oxon Hill Joint Venture*, 744 A.2d 1076 (Md. App. 2000), a deputy sheriff slipped and fell on a patch of ice in landlord's parking lot while going to serve tenant with a summons. The court held that the professional rescuer's rule did not apply because:

> He was not in the process of serving the subpoena when he was injured and his injuries were not brought about by the activity of subpoena serving.

Id. at 1080. Had the activity of serving the subpoena not begun when Rivas slipped and fell? *See also, Tucker v. Shoemaker*, 731 A.2d 884 (Md. App. 1999)(professional rescuer rule did not apply when a police officer slipped and fell on an improperly seated manhole cover while at a trailer park to respond to a domestic violence call; slip and fall risk was independent of the cause of plaintiff's presence on the property).

Other exceptions may apply where the defendant property owner was wanton or reckless or where the injuring risk was not unique to the professional but one common to the general public. For instance, in *Southland Corp. v. Griffith*, 332 Md. 704, 633 A. 2d. 84 (1993), the court said the plaintiff, "an out of uniform off-duty police officer," stated a cause of action against the defendant store for failure to timely call for aid when plaintiff, identified as a policeman, was attacked by teenagers in defendant's parking lot. The plaintiff was a "business invitee" when he entered the store to purchase food, and defendant owed a duty of reasonable care "to keep the premises safe and to protect the invitee from injury."

Do all these exceptions lead you to question the wisdom of the rule? Some courts continue to adhere to the rule and refuse to recognize broad exceptions.

In *Young v. Sherwin-Williams Co.,* 569 A.2d 1173 (D.C. 1990), the driver of an 18-wheeler consumed enough vodka to register a blood-alcohol level three times the legal level, which may have had some causal relationship with his subsequent loss of control of the vehicle. When the vehicle crashed into a bridge guardrail, the door swung open and the driver was left hanging by the steering wheel some fifty feet above the ground. A fireman, who had been called to the scene of a small fire beneath the bridge, saw the driver's peril and caught him when he fell. Both the driver and the heroic firefighter survived but suffered injuries. The firefighter brought an action against the driver and the driver's employer. The court held that the firefighter's actions were barred by a "professional rescuer doctrine." The court declined to adopt any sub-rules excepting the operation of the immunity, either in cases where the rescuer was acting outside the scope of his professional duties, or the defendant was acting willfully or wantonly, or where the defendant had committed acts of neglect which were not the reason for the rescuer's presence.

6. *Products Liability and the Fireman's Rule.* The question has arisen as to whether the "fireman's rule" insulates manufacturers of defective products. In *Court v. Grzelinski,* 72 Ill. 2d 141, 19 Ill. Dec. 617, 379 N.E.2d 281, 284 (1978), a fireman was injured in an explosion while fighting a vehicle fire. In an action against the gas tank manufacturer and the used car dealer who had installed the tank, the court stated:

> The rule cannot be extended to a free-floating proposition that a fireman cannot recover for injuries resulting from risks inherently involved in fire fighting. In products liability actions such as this, assumption of risk is a bar to recovery only if the plaintiff is aware of the product defect and voluntarily proceeds in disregard to the known danger. In either case, assumption of risk is an affirmative defense interposed against a plaintiff who voluntarily exposes himself to a specific, known risk, not a preclusion of recovery against a plaintiff whose occupation inherently involves general risks of injury.

Contrast *Mignone v. Fieldcrest Mills,* 556 A.2d 35 (R.I. 1989), in which an injured firefighter brought an action against the manufacturer of the electric blanket allegedly responsible for the fire to which she was responding at the time. Recognizing that the firefighter's rule was no longer rooted in the limited duty owed a licensee, but rather in the doctrine of primary assumption of risk, the court affirmed the trial court's grant of summary judgment in favor of the defendant.

7. *A Simplified Model? Danger Invites Rescue. Ogwo v. Taylor,* [1988] 1 A.C. 431, [1987] 3 All E.R. 961, 3 W.L.R. 1145 (HL), involved injuries suffered by a fireman fighting a fire negligently started by the defendant homeowner in the course of burning paint off his house with a blow lamp. In denying the applicability of any special rule which would limit a fireman's recovery to cases of unusual or exceptional risks or dangers, Lord Bridge stated:

> I can see no basis of principle which would justify denying a remedy in damages against the tortfeasor responsible for starting a fire to a professional fireman doing no more and no less than his proper duty and acting with skill and efficiency in fighting an ordinary fire who

is injured by one of the risks to which the particular circumstances of the fire give rise. Fire out of control is inherently dangerous. If not brought under control, it may, in most urban situations, cause untold damage to property and possible danger to life. The duty of professional firemen is to use their best endeavours to extinguish fires and it is obvious that, even making full use of all their skills, training, and specialist equipment, they will sometimes be exposed to unavoidable risks of injury, whether the fire is described as "ordinary" or "exceptional." If they are not to be met by the doctrine of volenti, which would be utterly repugnant to our contemporary notions of justice, I can see no reason whatever why they should be held at a disadvantage as compared to the layman entitled to invoke the principle of the so-called "rescue" cases.

PROBLEM

The Cuyahoga Native American reservation is located in a mountainous area in the northern part of Anystate. The reservation is open for public access and recreational use during the summer months. There is a swimming hole in the middle of the reservation which is notable for its unpolluted, spring-fed water supply and the natural beauty of the spectacular rocky outcrops surrounding it. The Bureau of Indian Affairs runs a concession stand near the swimming hole, from which it rents bathing towels and sells a small guidebook describing the source of the spring water. The depth of water varies extensively during the summer, creating a considerable hazard for those diving into the water from the rocks. When the reservation was first opened to the public two years ago, a visitor was slightly injured in just such a circumstance.

At that time, the local administrator of the Bureau of Indian Affairs considered banning all swimming. However, he concluded that the water was so clear that it should be obvious when it was unsafe to dive into the water. He therefore determined that the most cost-effective response would be to ban diving or bathing by children, and he had signs to that effect erected. Rangers employed by the BIA frequently expelled children from the reservation for violating the ban.

On a recent summer day when the reservation was crowded with vacationers, sixteen-year-old Jason dove into the swimming hole and was knocked unconscious when his head made contact with the bottom of the swimming hole. Kathy, a State Highway Patrol officer who was visiting the reservation as part of a departmental awareness program, saw Jason's body in the water and dived in to rescue him. However, she struck a concealed tree stump at the bottom of the hole.

Both Jason and Kathy suffered severe injuries and wish to bring suit against the United States. What arguments will the defense make? Assume further that Anystate has a "recreational use" statute similar to that in *Tuders, supra*. How would that affect your answer?

NOTES

1. *Dwelling as Product.* In *Kaneko v. Hilo Coast Processing,* 65 Haw. 447, 654 P.2d 343 (1982), the court applied strict products liability principles to

a manufacturer of a prefabricated building. The court reasoned that such a characterization of a prefabricated dwelling as a product would maximize protection for injured persons, that the manufacturer was in the best position to distribute the risk of injury, and that imposition of liability would provide the manufacturer with an incentive to avoid further defects.

However, in *Dwyer v. Skyline Apts., Inc.,* 123 N.J. Super. 48, 50, 301 A.2d 463, *aff'd* 63 N.J. 577, 311 A.2d 1 (1973), the court said:

> [A] landlord is not engaged in mass production whereby he places his product — the apartment — in a stream of commerce exposing it to a large number of consumers. He has not created the product with a defect which is preventable by greater care at the time of manufacture or assembly. He does not have the expertise to know and correct the condition so as to be saddled with responsibility for a defect regardless of negligence.
>
> An apartment involves several rooms with many facilities constructed by many artisans with differing types of expertise, and subject to constant use and deterioration from many causes. It is a commodity wholly unlike a product which is expected to leave the manufacturer's hands in a safe condition with an implied representation upon which the consumer justifiably relies.

2. *Landlord-Tenant Liability in Negligence.* In *Jendralski v. Black,* 176 Cal. App. 3d 897, 222 Cal. Rptr. 396 (1986), plaintiff, who lived in a five-unit apartment complex, was invited into a neighbor's apartment, where she saw "hundreds of birds, parakeets and cockatoos, cockatiels, finches, lovebirds, a macaw, as well as squirrels and a monkey." She was attacked and injured by the monkey. The jury was instructed that plaintiff had the burden of establishing "the defendant [landlord] knew or in the exercise of reasonable care must have known that the tenant . . . was harboring wild animals." Noting the immunity traditionally enjoyed by landlords for dangerous conditions created by the tenant after taking possession unless the landlord knew about and had the ability to eliminate the condition, the court nevertheless concluded:

> [A] landlord may be held liable for a dangerous condition of which he knew or should have known even though they are created by a tenant after taking possession of leased premises. Here the monkey was presumed to be dangerous. Its presence for several weeks was an ultrahazardous activity conducted on the premises of a multiunit apartment complex threatening the health and safety of the other tenants. Moreover, such conduct violated the lease, permitting the landlord to take swift action to eliminate the dangerous condition. Under these circumstances, the standard to be applied is not just actual knowledge, but rather whether the landlord exercised reasonable care.

However, in *Chariton v. Day Island Marina, Inc.,* 46 Wash. App. 784, 732 P.2d 1008 (1987), plaintiffs' decedents were poisoned by exhaust fumes from a boat engine they were running in a boathouse leased from the defendant. The tenant had fitted a canvas cover which partially sealed the entrance to the boathouse. The court concluded:

As a landlord, [defendant] can be held liable only if the deaths were caused by obscure or latent defects of which it had actual knowledge.

. . . [T]he structural conditions in the instant case that allowed the exhaust gases to accumulate in the boathouse were entirely open and obvious. Thus, even assuming arguendo that the absence of ventilation features other than the two doors and other openings may be considered a defect, such a defect would not be latent or obscure, but obvious or patent and therefore not a basis for liability on the part of [defendant].

Morris v. Scottsdale Mall Partners, Ltd., 523 N.E.2d 457 (Ind. App. 1988), concerned a patron at a mall restaurant who slipped and fell on a common stairway. The court affirmed the grant of summary judgment in favor of the restaurant on the basis of the traditional rule that tenants are not responsible for common areas over which the landlord has retained control. Is "control" the most appropriate test? What about economic interest?

3. *Landlord Liability to Third Parties.* In *Bellikka v. Green,* 306 Or. 630, 762 P.2d 997 (1988), the plaintiff was injured when she fell into a concealed hole in the lawn of leased premises while accompanying her children "trick or treating" on Halloween. In the course of a wide-ranging analysis, the court observed:

The Restatement provision expressed in section 356 that a lessor of land is not liable to "others on the land" for physical harm caused by any dangerous condition which existed when the lessee took possession is based on a conveyance concept of property. . . .

. . .[I]n the early 1970s, some courts, having recognized the antecedents of the common-law rule stated in section 356 and finding that its raison d'etre was no longer valid, abolished the landlord immunity to third persons injured by reason of a dangerous condition of the premises. The leading case seems to be *Sargent v. Ross,* 113 N.H. 388, 308 A.2d 528 (1973). There, a child who was a guest of a tenant fell to her death on steep stairs in a residential building. The child's mother brought an action for damages. The mother contended that the landowner was negligent on two alternative theories. They appear to be those recognized as exceptions to the rule of section 356, namely, section 360 (parts of land retained in lessor's control) and section 362 (negligent repairs by lessor). The court believed that it could strain or broaden the limits of either exception to impose liability, but forthrightly chose to vitiate the rule of immunity: "[W]e today discard the rule of 'caveat lessee' and the doctrine of landlord nonliability in tort to which it gave birth. We thus bring up to date the other half [in addition to warranty of habitability] of landlord-tenant law. Henceforth, landlords as other persons must exercise reasonable care not to subject others to an unreasonable risk of harm. A landlord must act as a reasonable person under all of the circumstances including the likelihood of injury to others, the probable seriousness of such injuries, and the burden of reducing or avoiding the risk. We think this basic principle of responsibility for landlords as for others best expresses the principles of justice and reasonableness upon which our law of torts is founded. The questions of control, hidden defects and common or public use, which formerly had to be established as to a landlord, will now be relevant only inasmuch as they bear on the basic tort issues such as the foreseeability and unreasonableness of the particular risk of harm." 308 A.2d at 534.

The court in *Anderson v. Sammy Redd and Assoc.*, 278 N.J. Super. 50, 650 A. 2d 376 (1994), held that the landlord had a duty to provide reasonably safe window screens. The tenant's two-year-old fell to his death from a third floor window. Plaintiff's administratix alleged that "only two metal prongs at the top and bottom secured the window screen and the screen still did not properly fit to the frame." The court treated the deceased child of the tenant the same as a tenant.

4. *Louisiana—Civil Law?* While Louisiana probably continues to apply a form of strict liability in the landlord-tenant setting, La. Civ. Code art. 2695, it has legislatively overruled its former strict liability regime for injuries caused by unreasonably dangerous risks of harm posed by buildings or things.

PROBLEM

Fred, a guest in Bill's apartment, opened a skylight to get a better view of an approaching meteor shower. Because of a defect in the construction of the frame of the skylight, it collapsed on Fred. Fred sues Bill's landlord. What is the landlord's best argument in support of his motion for summary judgment?

Chapter 9
PROCEDURE, PROOF AND DAMAGES

A. INTRODUCTION

It goes without saying that the substantive law of torts is heavily affected by considerations of procedure, proof and remedy. In determining the validity of a tort claim a lawyer considers the applicable law and, equally importantly, how she can prove or defend against the claim. Even if a claim can be proven, it is of little value unless damages can also be shown.

One of the most litigated areas in American law — both civil and criminal — concerns the use and abuse of expert testimony. Many cases cannot be established without expert testimony. The United States Supreme Court has intervened on the issue of expert witness qualification. In still other cases, the use of an expert may be inappropriate because the witness adds little or nothing to lay testimony and may unduly prejudice the jury. The choice and preparation of expert witnesses is often the key to preparing a winning case or defense.

Every lawyer realizes the critical importance of pretrial discovery in civil cases. Recently, courts have become especially concerned about discovery abuse. In addition, courts have been concerned with other types of lawyer and client misconduct stemming from the adversarial system, and with the appropriate sanctions to be imposed in such cases. Cross-reference should be made in this regard to the materials on abuse of process in chapter 3.

The traditional and most common remedy for a tort victim is an award of money damages. However, other remedies may be available. For example, if there is a significant likelihood that the tortious conduct will be repeated, the victim may be entitled to injunctive relief, or if the tortfeasor has deprived the victim of property, restitution may lie. But in nearly all tort suits, the victim's sole or primary remedy is an award of money damages against the wrongdoer.

B. PROBLEMS OF PROOF

WILLIAMS v. BROWN
860 S.W.2d 854 (Tenn. 1993)

ANDERSON, JUSTICE.

In this wrongful death action, we are asked to decide a question of first impression — whether the defendant's payment, without contest, of a fine for a traffic offense is admissible in evidence in a separate civil case. The trial court held in this action that payment of a fine for improper passing was not admissible on the issue of negligence and sustained a motion for directed verdict in favor of the defendant, Samuel Brown. The Court of Appeals affirmed. For the reasons stated below, we affirm the Court of Appeals' holding that evidence of the defendant's payment of a traffic fine, without contest, was inadmissible; but we reverse and remand for a new trial because reasonable minds could differ as to whether the defendant was negligent based on the remaining evidence in the record. As a result, there is a jury question and the trial court should not have directed a verdict.

There was material evidence in the record to show the following:

That on February 1, 1989, Lance Williams was driving a 1980 Corvette north on Varnell Road in Bradley County, Tennessee. He was followed by Samuel Brown, who was driving a 1970 Chevrolet pick-up truck in the same direction. Brown attempted to pass Williams on a stretch of a two-lane rural road which approached an "S" curve.

As Brown passed, he saw the headlights of an oncoming vehicle and applied his brakes. Thereafter, both drivers lost control of their vehicles. Williams' car traveled some seven hundred feet, spun in the grass beside the road, struck the left guardrail, and then crashed into a tree on the left side of the road. The gas tank ruptured as a result of the collision; and the car exploded, killing Williams. Brown's truck hit the guardrail on the left side of the road and spun around until coming to rest safely in a ditch on the right side of the road and across from Williams' car.

The investigating Highway Patrolman testified at trial that the lanes were divided by a solid yellow line; that it was one-quarter mile through the "S" curve to the crest of the hill; but that the view from where the wreck occurred was obstructed by cedar trees. He testified that the Department of Safety had adopted rules of the road which defined solid yellow lines as restrictive in character. He said that "[w]e classify a solid yellow line as restrictive if it's in an area of a narrow roadway or a county road or something like that we figure it means . . . some of us figure it's the same as two (2) lines solid, no passing." The patrolman also said that Brown told him there was contact between the two vehicles on the roadway.

An accident reconstruction expert testified that the only tire skid marks on the road matched Brown's pick-up truck, and the photographic evidence showed the tire marks began in the northbound lane occupied by the Corvette.

The plaintiff's theory was that while Brown was in the process of passing Williams, he saw the headlights of an oncoming vehicle, applied his brakes and began to skid sideways. The skidding caused Brown's truck to slow down enough so that Williams' vehicle pulled slightly ahead. "Chased," in effect, by Brown's out-of-control vehicle, Williams veered toward the right shoulder of the road where he hit a depression between the road and the shoulder that caused his vehicle to cross the road and hit the guardrail. The impact from the collision with the guardrail sent Williams' vehicle into the fatal spin.

The defendant's theory was that Williams sped up when Brown attempted to pass and Brown continued to try to pass, but when Brown saw the headlights of the oncoming vehicle, he applied his brakes. Simultaneously, Williams' vehicle ran off the right shoulder of the road, returned to the road and hit Brown's truck, thereby causing both vehicles to lose control. Brown's truck then hit the guardrail and spun backwards into the ditch. Williams' car hit the guardrail, traveled backwards into the grass, hit the tree, and exploded into flames.

Brown was issued a traffic citation by the investigating Highway Patrolman for improper passing, which he paid without contest. Prior to trial, the trial court granted a motion in limine to exclude proof that Brown had paid the traffic fine.

At the conclusion of the plaintiff's proof, the trial court granted Brown's motion for a directed verdict. The plaintiff appealed upon the grounds that the trial court erred by granting the motion for a directed verdict and by excluding the evidence of the payment of the fine. The Court of Appeals affirmed the judgment of the trial court.

The first question we must decide is whether the fact that the defendant paid, without contest, a traffic fine for improper passing is admissible evidence in a later civil action concerning the underlying occurrence. The plaintiff asserts that payment of the fine was a plea of guilty which is admissible into evidence. The defendant argues that, unlike an appearance and guilty plea in open court, simply paying the fine is not an admission of guilt and is, therefore, not admissible as evidence. This is an issue of first impression in Tennessee.

Under Tennessee law, a person cited for a traffic offense "may elect not to contest the charge and may, in lieu of appearance in court, submit the fine and costs to the clerk of the court." Tenn.Code Ann. § 55-10-207(d) (1988). A jurisdiction which allows payment of a prescheduled amount is said to employ the "cafeteria" system. States employing the "cafeteria" system have, either by statute or case law, almost unanimously excluded from evidence payment of the traffic fine in a later action based on the same accident or occurrence that resulted in the traffic citation.[1]

We think that the payment of a traffic fine is very closely analogous to a plea of *nolo contendere* which, translated from Latin, means simply "I will not contest it." *Black's Law Dictionary* 1048 (6th ed. 1990. That conclusion is supported by the statute which characterizes the out-of-court payment of a traffic fine as an election "not to contest the charge." Tenn.Code Ann. § 55-10-207(d) (1988). Pleas of *nolo* contendere are not admissible in Tennessee. Tenn.R.Evid. 410.

We conclude that payment of a traffic fine in lieu of an appearance in court is neither a guilty plea nor an express acknowledgment of guilt. There are

---

[1] Many states do, however, admit evidence of a defendant's guilty plea to a traffic citation if it were entered in open court. *See e.g. Kelch v. Courson*, 103 Ariz. 576, 447 P.2d 550, 553 (1968) (evidence of the plea is admissible and the jury must determine its proper weight): *Ferguson v. Boyd*, 448 S.W.2d 901, 903 (Mo. 1970) (evidence of the guilty plea is admissible, but the defendant may explain the reason for the plea). Those decisions are inapposite here because there was no guilty plea entered in open court. We note, however, that some commentators have criticized the practice of admitting guilty pleas to misdemeanor offenses as admissions of a party-opponent because it tends to frustrate the policy of the hearsay exception for judgments of previous convictions, excluding misdemeanor convictions, because of their unreliability. N. Cohen, D. Paine, S. Sheppeard, *Tennessee Law of Evidence* § 803(1.2).2 (2d ed. 1990); M. Graham, *Handbook of Federal Evidence* 779 (3d ed. 1991); 4 Weinstein's Evidence P 803(22)(01) at 354–55 (1984).

many legitimate and plausible reasons for choosing to pay such a fine by mail or otherwise, without intending to concede guilt. "Common experience demonstrates that the payment of a traffic citation is simply a matter of expedience." *LePage v. Bumila*, 407 Mass. 163, 552 N.E.2d 80, 82 (Mass. 1990). The cost of defense compared with the amount of the fine and the inconvenience, as well as indirect economic losses of court appearances, are practical considerations which often motivate an individual cited for a traffic violation to simply pay the fine. We conclude, as did the Massachusetts Supreme Court, that if the payment of a traffic citation were construed to be an admission of guilt that could be used in subsequent civil or criminal actions, "the courts would be flooded with challenges to such citations" and "[t]he proverbial 'floodgates of litigation' would be opened, destroying the expedited, streamlined system now in place." *LePage*, 552 N.E.2d at 83.

Accordingly, we conclude that evidence of payment of a traffic fine without contest is not admissible in a later action based on the underlying event resulting in the traffic citation. We do not reach and expressly reserve the question of admissibility where the defendant personally appears in court and pleads guilty. The judgment of the Court of Appeals affirming the trial court's exclusion of the evidence is affirmed.

Based on our review of the record, we are of the opinion that the trial court erred in granting a directed verdict for the defendant. Taking the most legitimate view of all the evidence in favor of the plaintiff, and allowing all reasonable inferences therefrom, there is material evidence in the record to support the plaintiff's theory, and reasonable minds could differ as to whether, based on the conditions and circumstances, the defendant was negligent in attempting to pass at the time and place where the accident occurred. . . .

NOTES

1. *The Hearsay Exception*. Fed. R. Evid. 803 (22) provides:

> Evidence of a final judgment, entered after a trial or upon a plea of guilty (but not upon a plea of nolo contendere), adjudging a person guilty of a crime punishable by death or imprisonment in excess of one year, to prove any fact essential to sustain the judgment, but not including, when offered by the Government in a criminal prosecution for purposes other than impeachment, judgments against persons other than the accused. The pendency of an appeal may be shown but does not affect admissibility.

The comment to this provision states:

> Practical considerations require exclusion of convictions of minor offenses, not because the administration of justice in its lower echelons must be inferior, but because motivation to defend at this level is often minimal or nonexistent.

2. *A Combined Admission-Remedial Measure*. In *Rush v. Troutman Investment Co.*, 854 P.2d 968 (Or. App. 1993), the plaintiff was injured when she was looking at clothing on a table at a sidewalk sale outside defendant's store. Behind her were sweaters hanging on a "z-rack," which "is an upright

rectangle with a z-shaped base." She touched the sleeve of a sweater and resumed looking at the clothing on the table in front of her. A few minutes later, the rack fell onto the back of her head, bounced off her neck and shoulders and pinned her to the table. Before trial, the court granted defendant's motion to exclude evidence that defendant had removed the Z-rack from the sale area after the accident occurred. During the trial, plaintiff's attorney asked her about the incident:

> Q. [After the accident, did the store manager] eventually come out?
>
> A. Yes, he did come out.
>
> Q. What did he say?
>
> A. He asked if I was hurt, and I told him I wasn't sure yet. I was still dazed, and I was holding onto the table, trying to get my bearings, and I was kind of feeling around for [my] earring. *And he said, "Well, you don't look hurt to me." And he told the sales clerk to get the rack, to get the rack back in the store and put the clothes on tables, that it wasn't safe.* (Emphasis supplied.)

Defendant moved for a mistrial on the ground that plaintiff had "impermissibly testified about a subsequent remedial measure that the defendant had taken." The subsequent remedial measure rule is defined by the Oregon Rules of Evidence in part as "When, after an event, measures are taken which, if taken previously, would have made the event less likely to occur, evidence of the subsequent measures is not admissible to prove negligence or culpable conduct in connection with the event." The trial court denied the defendant's motion, and the appellate court affirmed:

> Plaintiff contends that she did not testify about a "subsequent remedial measure," because her testimony only described the manager's instructions to the sales clerk. The issue is whether the manager's instruction was a measure that, "if taken previously, would have made the event less likely to occur." It is reasonable to infer that, had the manager previously instructed the sales clerk to put the Z-rack in the store and place the clothing on tables, the clerk would likely have followed the manager's directions. If that had happened, then the rack would not have fallen on plaintiff. The manager's instructions, if given before the accident, would have made the accident less likely to occur. Instructions to take remedial measures are themselves remedial measures. Plaintiff's testimony about the manager's instructions to the clerk was not admissible as proof of defendant's negligence.
>
> The manager's instructions were, however, accompanied by his assessment "that [the Z-rack] wasn't safe." That conclusion was a relevant admission that was not excludable by any rule of evidence. In the light of the manager's contemporaneous admission that the rack was not safe, the admission of his instructions to the clerk was unlikely to have caused prejudice to defendant's case. The court did not abuse its discretion by denying defendant's first motion for a mistrial.

3. *A Day in the Life.* A worker's widow brought a product liability action against the defendant asbestos manufacturer in *Schiavo v. Owens-Corning*

Fiberglas Corp., 282 N.J. Super. 362, 660 A.2d 515 (1995), alleging that the worker died from mesothelioma as a result of exposure to defendant's asbestos product while working aboard ship. Appealing a verdict for the plaintiff, the defendant objected among other things to the admission in evidence of a "day in the life" videotape of the decedent. The jury was not told that the time of the taping was three weeks before decedent's death, although that date appeared on the screen:

> Defendant claims that the videotape was cumulative evidence that had no purpose but to inflame the jury and that it should have been excluded under Evid.R. 4 (N.J.R.E. 403). Defendant further argues that the videotape was misleading in two ways. First, it did not depict decedent's condition as it existed during most of his illness, but rather only as it existed in the terminal phase when his condition had greatly deteriorated. Second, defendant claims that the videotape had in effect been staged because it had been edited.
>
> Plaintiffs did not assert that the videotape depicted the entire period from June 1988 when the mesothelioma was first diagnosed through the death on August 21, 1990. Also, it was explained and in any event was self-evident that the tape did not depict an entire twenty-four hour period. The video camera obviously was turned off while decedent slept or when there was no activity. As much as there may have been testimonial explanations of decedent's condition, his suffering and the rigors imposed by his care were demonstrated by the videotape far more effectively than through mere testimony. If the videotape increased the compensatory awards, we cannot say that this augmentation was through any error, as opposed to the jurors' normal reaction to a graphic exposure to the effects of advanced mesothelioma.
>
> While there is no New Jersey case specifically authorizing a "day in the life" tape, such tapes have been permitted once the trial judge has examined the content to determine whether it is relevant and probative and is an accurate representation of the impact of the injuries upon the subject's day-to-day activities.
>
> There was no challenge to the authenticity of the videotape. And there certainly could be no claim that this videotape was staged to depict a condition that did not in fact exist. This is not a case where an injured victim could highlight the most difficult parts of his life and gloss over tasks that could easily be performed. Decedent, as testified by his wife, was unable to function. While the camera may have been turned off because no one was performing a service for him at the time, there was no doubt that decedent did not use these breaks to be free from the cancer that was killing him. The videotape was a relevant aid to the jury as it could "uniquely demonstrate the nature and extent of" decedent's injuries. *Jones v. City of Los Angeles*, 24 Cal. Rptr. 2d at 531.

C. EXPERT EVIDENCE

KUMHO TIRE COMPANY, LTD. v. CARMICHAEL
526 U.S. 137, 119 S. Ct. 1167, 143 L. Ed. 2d 238 (1999)

JUSTICE BREYER delivered the opinion of the Court.

. . .On July 6, 1993, the right rear tire of a minivan driven by Patrick Carmichael blew out. In the accident that followed, one of the passengers died, and others were severely injured. In October 1993, the Carmichaels brought this diversity suit against the tire's maker and its distributor, whom we refer to collectively as Kumho Tire, claiming that the tire was defective. The plaintiffs rested their case in significant part upon deposition testimony provided by an expert in tire failure analysis, Dennis Carlson, Jr., who intended to testify in support of their conclusion.

Carlson's depositions relied upon certain features of tire technology that are not in dispute. A steel-belted radial tire like the Carmichaels' is made up of a "carcass" containing many layers of flexible cords, called "plies," along which (between the cords and the outer tread) are laid steel strips called "belts." Steel wire loops, called "beads," hold the cords together at the plies' bottom edges. An outer layer, called the "tread," encases the carcass, and the entire tire is bound together in rubber, through the application of heat and various chemicals.

Carlson's testimony also accepted certain background facts about the tire in question. He assumed that before the blowout the tire had traveled far. (The tire was made in 1988 and had been installed some time before the Carmichaels bought the used minivan in March 1993; the Carmichaels had driven the van approximately 7,000 additional miles in the two months they had owned it.) Carlson noted that the tire's tread depth, which was 11/32 of an inch when new had been worn down to depths that ranged from 3/32 of an inch along some parts of the tire, to nothing at all along others. He conceded that the tire tread had at least two punctures which had been inadequately repaired.

Despite the tire's age and history, Carlson concluded that a defect in its manufacture or design caused the blow-out. He rested this conclusion in part upon three premises which, for present purposes, we must assume are not in dispute: First, a tire's carcass should stay bound to the inner side of the tread for a significant period of time after its tread depth has worn away. Second, the tread of the tire at issue had separated from its inner steel-belted carcass prior to the accident. Third, this "separation" caused the blowout.

Carlson's conclusion that a defect caused the separation, however, rested upon certain other propositions, several of which the defendants strongly dispute. First, Carlson said that if a separation is *not* caused by a certain kind of tire misuse called "overdeflection" (which consists of underinflating the tire or causing it to carry too much weight, thereby generating heat that can undo the chemical tread/carcass bond), then, ordinarily, its cause is a tire defect. Second, he said that if a tire has been subject to sufficient overdeflection to cause a separation, it should reveal certain physical symptoms. These symptoms include (a) tread wear on the tire's shoulder that is greater than the tread wear along the tire's center; (b) signs of a "bead groove," where the beads have been pushed too hard against the bead seat on the inside of the tire's rim; (c) sidewalls of the tire with physical signs of deterioration, such as discoloration; and/or (d) marks on the tire's rim flange. Third, Carlson said that where he does not find *at least two* of the four physical signs just mentioned (and presumably where there is no reason to suspect a less common cause of separation), he concludes that a manufacturing or design defect caused the separation.

Carlson added that he had inspected the tire in question. He conceded that the tire to a limited degree showed greater wear on the shoulder than in the center, some signs of "bead groove," some discoloration, a few marks on the rim flange, and inadequately filled puncture holes (which can also cause heat that might lead to separation). But, in each instance, he testified that the symptoms were not significant, and he explained why he believed that they did not reveal overdeflection. For example, the extra shoulder wear, he said, appeared primarily on one shoulder, whereas an overdeflected tire would reveal equally abnormal wear on both shoulders. Carlson concluded that the tire did not bear at least two of the four overdeflection symptoms, nor was there any less obvious cause of separation; and since neither overdeflection nor the punctures caused the blowout, a defect must have done so.

Kumho Tire moved the District Court to exclude Carlson's testimony on the ground that his methodology failed Rule 702's reliability requirement. The court agreed with Kumho that it should act as a *Daubert*-type (*Daubert* v. *Merrell Dow Pharmaceuticals, Inc.*, 509 U.S. 579, 125 L. Ed. 2d 469, 113 S. Ct. 2786 (1993)) reliability "gatekeeper," even though one might consider Carlson's testimony as "technical," rather than "scientific." The court then examined Carlson's methodology in light of the reliability-related factors that *Daubert* mentioned, such as a theory's testability, whether it "has been a subject of peer review or publication," the "known or potential rate of error," and the "degree of acceptance . . . within the relevant scientific community." 923 F. Supp. at 1520 (citing *Daubert*, 509 U.S. 579 at 592–594). The District Court found that all those factors argued against the reliability of Carlson's methods, and it granted the motion to exclude the testimony (as well as the defendants' accompanying motion for summary judgment).

The plaintiffs, arguing that the court's application of the *Daubert* factors was too "inflexible," asked for reconsideration. And the Court granted that motion. After reconsidering the matter, the court agreed with the plaintiffs that *Daubert* should be applied flexibly, that its four factors were simply illustrative, and that other factors could argue in favor of admissibility. It conceded that there may be widespread acceptance of a "visual-inspection method" for some relevant purposes. But the court found insufficient indications of the reliability of

> the component of Carlson's tire failure analysis which most concerned the Court, namely, the methodology employed by the expert in analyzing the data obtained in the visual inspection, and the scientific basis, if any, for such an analysis.

It consequently affirmed its earlier order declaring Carlson's testimony inadmissible and granting the defendants' motion for summary judgment.

The Eleventh Circuit reversed.... It noted that "the Supreme Court in *Daubert* explicitly limited its holding to cover only the 'scientific context,'" adding that "a *Daubert* analysis" applies only where an expert relies "on the application of scientific principles," rather than "on skill or experience-based observation." It concluded that Carlson's testimony, which it viewed as relying on experience, "falls outside the scope of *Daubert*," that "the district court erred as a matter of law by applying *Daubert* in this case," and that the case must be remanded for further (non-*Daubert*-type) consideration under Rule 702.

...We granted certiorari in light of uncertainty among the lower courts about whether, or how, *Daubert* applies to expert testimony that might be characterized as based not upon "scientific" knowledge, but rather upon "technical" or "other specialized" knowledge.

In *Daubert*, this Court held that Federal Rule of Evidence 702 imposes a special obligation upon a trial judge to "ensure that any and all scientific testimony . . . is not only relevant, but reliable." 509 U.S. at 589. The initial question before us is whether this basic gatekeeping obligation applies only to "scientific" testimony or to all expert testimony. We, like the parties, believe that it applies to all expert testimony.

For one thing, Rule 702 itself says:

> If scientific, technical, or other specialized knowledge will assist the trier of fact to understand the evidence or to determine a fact in issue, a witness qualified as an expert by knowledge, skill, experience, training, or education, may testify thereto in the form of an opinion or otherwise.

This language makes no relevant distinction between "scientific" knowledge and "technical" or "other specialized" knowledge. It makes clear that any such knowledge might become the subject of expert testimony. In *Daubert*, the Court specified that it is the Rule's word "knowledge," not the words (like "scientific") that modify that word, that "establishes a standard of evidentiary reliability." 509 U.S. at 589–590. Hence, as a matter of language, the Rule applies its reliability standard to all "scientific," "technical," or "other specialized" matters within its scope. We concede that the Court in *Daubert* referred only to "scientific" knowledge. But as the Court there said, it referred to "scientific" testimony "because that was the nature of the expertise" at issue.

Neither is the evidentiary rationale that underlay the Court's basic *Daubert* "gatekeeping" determination limited to "scientific" knowledge. *Daubert* pointed out that Federal Rules 702 and 703 grant expert witnesses testimonial latitude unavailable to other witnesses on the "assumption that the expert's opinion will have a reliable basis in the knowledge and experience of his discipline." Id. at 592 (pointing out that experts may testify to opinions, including those that are not based on firsthand knowledge or observation). The Rules grant that latitude to all experts, not just to "scientific" ones.

Finally, it would prove difficult, if not impossible, for judges to administer evidentiary rules under which a gatekeeping obligation depended upon a distinction between "scientific" knowledge and "technical" or "other specialized" knowledge. There is no clear line that divides the one from the others.

Disciplines such as engineering rest upon scientific knowledge. Pure scientific theory itself may depend for its development upon observation and properly engineered machinery. And conceptual efforts to distinguish the two are unlikely to produce clear legal lines capable of application in particular cases.

Neither is there a convincing need to make such distinctions. . . .The trial judge's effort to assure that the specialized testimony is reliable and relevant can help the jury evaluate that foreign experience, whether the testimony reflects scientific, technical, or other specialized knowledge.

We conclude that *Daubert*'s general principles apply to the expert matters described in Rule 702. The Rule, in respect to all such matters, "establishes a standard of evidentiary reliability." 509 U.S. at 590. It "requires a valid . . . connection to the pertinent inquiry as a precondition to admissibility." Id. at 592. And where such testimony's factual basis, data, principles, methods, or their application are called sufficiently into question, the trial judge must determine whether the testimony has "a reliable basis in the knowledge and experience of [the relevant] discipline." 509 U.S. at 592.

The petitioners ask more specifically whether a trial judge determining the "admissibility of an engineering expert's testimony" *may* consider several more specific factors that *Daubert* said might "bear on" a judge's gate-keeping determination. These factors include:

— Whether a "theory or technique . . . can be (and has been) tested";

— Whether it "has been subjected to peer review and publication";

— Whether, in respect to a particular technique, there is a high "known or potential rate of error" and whether there are "standards controlling the technique's operation"; and

— Whether the theory or technique enjoys "general acceptance" within a "relevant scientific community."

Emphasizing the word "may" in the question, we answer that question yes.

Engineering testimony rests upon scientific foundations, the reliability of which will be at issue in some cases. In other cases, the relevant reliability concerns may focus upon personal knowledge or experience. As the Solicitor General points out, there are many different kinds of experts, and many different kinds of expertise. Our emphasis on the word "may" thus reflects *Daubert*'s description of the Rule 702 inquiry as "a flexible one." 509 U.S. at 594. *Daubert* makes clear that the factors it mentions do *not* constitute a "definitive checklist or test." Id. at 593. And *Daubert* adds that the gatekeeping inquiry must be " 'tied to the facts' " of a particular "case." Id. at 591 (quoting *United States* v. *Downing*, 753 F.2d 1224, 1242 (CA3 1985)). We agree with the Solicitor General that "the factors identified in *Daubert* may or may not be pertinent in assessing reliability, depending on the nature of the issue, the expert's particular expertise, and the subject of his testimony." The conclusion, in our view, is that we can neither rule out, nor rule in, for all cases and for all time the applicability of the factors mentioned in *Daubert*, nor can we now do so for subsets of cases categorized by category of expert or by kind of evidence. Too much depends upon the particular circumstances of the particular case at

C. EXPERT EVIDENCE

Daubert itself is not to the contrary. It made clear that its list of factors was meant to be helpful, not definitive. Indeed, those factors do not all necessarily apply even in every instance in which the reliability of scientific testimony is challenged. It might not be surprising in a particular case, for example, that a claim made by a scientific witness has never been the subject of peer review, for the particular application at issue may never previously have interested any scientist. Nor, on the other hand, does the presence of *Daubert*'s general acceptance factor help show that an expert's testimony is reliable where the discipline itself lacks reliability, as, for example, do theories grounded in any so-called generally accepted principles of astrology or necromancy.

At the same time, and contrary to the Court of Appeals' view, some of *Daubert*'s questions can help to evaluate the reliability even of experience-based testimony. In certain cases, it will be appropriate for the trial judge to ask, for example, how often an engineering expert's experience-based methodology has produced erroneous results, or whether such a method is generally accepted in the relevant engineering community. Likewise, it will at times be useful to ask even of a witness whose expertise is based purely on experience, say, a perfume tester able to distinguish among 140 odors at a sniff, whether his preparation is of a kind that others in the field would recognize as acceptable.

We must therefore disagree with the Eleventh Circuit's holding that a trial judge may ask questions of the sort *Daubert* mentioned only where an expert "relies on the application of scientific principles," but not where an expert relies "on skill or experience-based observation." 131 F.3d at 1435. We do not believe that Rule 702 creates a schematism that segregates expertise by type while mapping certain kinds of questions to certain kinds of experts. Life and the legal cases that it generates are too complex to warrant so definitive a match.

To say this is not to deny the importance of *Daubert*'s gatekeeping requirement. The objective of that requirement is to ensure the reliability and relevancy of expert testimony. It is to make certain that an expert, whether basing testimony upon professional studies or personal experience, employs in the courtroom the same level of intellectual rigor that characterizes the practice of an expert in the relevant field. Nor do we deny that, as stated in *Daubert*, the particular questions that it mentioned will often be appropriate for use in determining the reliability of challenged expert testimony. Rather, we conclude that the trial judge must have considerable leeway in deciding in a particular case how to go about determining whether particular expert testimony is reliable. That is to say, a trial court should consider the specific factors identified in *Daubert* where they are reasonable measures of the reliability of expert testimony.

The trial court must have the same kind of latitude in deciding *how* to test an expert's reliability, and to decide whether or when special briefing or other proceedings are needed to investigate reliability, as it enjoys when it decides *whether* that expert's relevant testimony is reliable. Our opinion in *Joiner* makes clear that a court of appeals is to apply an abuse-of-discretion standard when it "reviews a trial court's decision to admit or exclude expert testimony."

522 U.S. at 138–139. That standard applies as much to the trial court's decisions about how to determine reliability as to its ultimate conclusion. Otherwise, the trial judge would lack the discretionary authority needed both to avoid unnecessary "reliability" proceedings in ordinary cases where the reliability of an expert's methods is properly taken for granted, and to require appropriate proceedings in the less usual or more complex cases where cause for questioning the expert's reliability arises. Indeed, the Rules seek to avoid "unjustifiable expense and delay" as part of their search for "truth" and the "just determination" of proceedings. Fed. Rule Evid. 102. Thus, whether *Daubert*'s specific factors are, or are not, reasonable measures of reliability in a particular case is a matter that the law grants the trial judge broad latitude to determine. See *Joiner, supra,* at 143. And the Eleventh Circuit erred insofar as it held to the contrary.

We further explain the way in which a trial judge "may" consider *Daubert*'s factors by applying these considerations to the case at hand, a matter that has been briefed exhaustively by the parties and their *amici*. The District Court did not doubt Carlson's qualifications, which included a masters degree in mechanical engineering, 10 years' work at Michelin America, Inc., and testimony as a tire failure consultant in other tort cases. Rather, it excluded the testimony because, despite those qualifications, it initially doubted, and then found unreliable, "the methodology employed by the expert in analyzing the data obtained in the visual inspection, and the scientific basis, if any, for such an analysis." After examining the transcript in "some detail," and after considering respondents' defense of Carlson's methodology, the District Court determined that Carlson's testimony was not reliable. It fell outside the range where experts might reasonably differ, and where the jury must decide among the conflicting views of different experts, even though the evidence is "shaky." *Daubert*, 509 U.S. at 596. In our view, the doubts that triggered the District Court's initial inquiry here were reasonable, as was the court's ultimate conclusion.

For one thing, and contrary to respondents' suggestion, the specific issue before the court was not the reasonableness *in general* of a tire expert's use of a visual and tactile inspection to determine whether overdeflection had caused the tire's tread to separate from its steel-belted carcass. Rather, it was the reasonableness of using such an approach, along with Carlson's particular method of analyzing the data thereby obtained, to draw a conclusion regarding *the particular matter to which the expert testimony was directly relevant*. That matter concerned the likelihood that a defect in the tire at issue caused its tread to separate from its carcass. The tire in question, the expert conceded, had traveled far enough so that some of the tread had been worn bald; it should have been taken out of service; it had been repaired (inadequately) for punctures; and it bore some of the very marks that the expert said indicated, not a defect, but abuse through overdeflection. The relevant issue was whether the expert could reliably determine the cause of *this* tire's separation. Nor was the basis for Carlson's conclusion simply the general theory that, in the absence of evidence of abuse, a defect will normally have caused a tire's separation. Rather, the expert employed a more specific theory to establish the existence (or absence) of such abuse. Carlson testified precisely that in the absence of *at least two* of four signs of abuse (proportionately greater tread wear on the shoulder; signs of grooves caused by the beads; discolored sidewalls; marks on the rim flange) he concludes that a defect caused the separation. And his analysis depended upon acceptance of a further implicit proposition, namely, that his visual and tactile inspection could determine that the tire before him had not been abused despite some evidence of the presence of the very signs for which he looked (and two punctures).

For another thing, the transcripts of Carlson's depositions support both the trial court's initial uncertainty and its final conclusion. Those transcripts cast considerable doubt upon the reliability of both the explicit theory (about the need for two signs of abuse) and the implicit proposition (about the significance of visual inspection in this case). Among other things, the expert could not say whether the tire had traveled more than 10, or 20, or 30, or 40, or 50 thousand miles, adding that 6,000 miles was "about how far" he could "say with any certainty." Id. at 265. The court could reasonably have wondered about the reliability of a method of visual and tactile inspection sufficiently precise to ascertain with some certainty the abuse-related significance of minute shoulder/center relative tread wear differences, but insufficiently precise to tell "with any certainty" from the tread wear whether a tire had traveled less than 10,000 or more than 50,000 miles. And these concerns might have been augmented by Carlson's repeated reliance on the "subjectiveness" of his mode of analysis in response to questions seeking specific information regarding how he could differentiate between a tire that actually had been overdeflected and a tire that merely looked as though it had been. They would have been further augmented by the fact that Carlson said he had inspected the tire itself for the first time the morning of his first deposition, and then only for a few hours. (His initial conclusions were based on photographs.).

Moreover, prior to his first deposition, Carlson had issued a signed report in which he concluded that the tire had "not been . . . overloaded or underinflated," not because of the absence of "two of four" signs of abuse, but simply because "the rim flange impressions . . . were normal." Id. at 335–336. That report also said that the "tread depth remaining was 3/32 inch," id. at 336, though the opposing expert's (apparently undisputed) measurements indicate that the tread depth taken at various positions around the tire actually ranged from .5/32 of an inch to 4/32 of an inch, with the tire apparently showing greater wear along *both* shoulders than along the center, id. at 432–433.

Further, in respect to one sign of abuse, bead grooving, the expert seemed to deny the sufficiency of his own simple visual-inspection methodology. He testified that most tires have some bead groove pattern, that where there is reason to suspect an abnormal bead groove he would ideally "look at a lot of [similar] tires" to know the grooving's significance, and that he had not looked at many tires similar to the one at issue. Id. at 212–213, 214, 217.

Finally, the court, after looking for a defense of Carlson's methodology as applied in these circumstances, found no convincing defense. Rather, it found (1) that "none" of the *Daubert* factors, including that of "general acceptance" in the relevant expert community, indicated that Carlson's testimony was reliable, 923 F. Supp. at 1521; (2) that its own analysis "revealed no countervailing factors operating in favor of admissibility which could outweigh those identified in *Daubert*," App. to Pet. for Cert. 4c; and (3) that the "parties identified no such factors in their briefs," *ibid.* For these three reasons *taken together,* it concluded that Carlson's testimony was unreliable.

Respondents now argue to us, as they did to the District Court, that a method of tire failure analysis that employs a visual/tactile inspection is a reliable method, and they point both to its use by other experts and to Carlson's long experience working for Michelin as sufficient indication that that is so. But no one denies that an expert might draw a conclusion from a set of observations based on extensive and specialized experience. Nor does anyone deny that, as a general matter, tire abuse may often be identified by qualified experts through visual or tactile inspection of the tire. As we said before, the question before the trial court was specific, not general. The trial court had to decide whether this particular expert had sufficient specialized knowledge to assist the jurors "in deciding the particular issues in the case."

The particular issue in this case concerned the use of Carlson's two-factor test and his related use of visual/tactile inspection to draw conclusions on the basis of what seemed small observational differences. We have found no indication in the record that other experts in the industry use Carlson's two-factor test or that tire experts such as Carlson normally make the very fine distinctions about, say, the symmetry of comparatively greater shoulder tread wear that were necessary, on Carlson's own theory, to support his conclusions. Nor, despite the prevalence of tire testing, does anyone refer to any articles or papers that validate Carlson's approach. . . .Indeed, no one has argued that Carlson himself, were he still working for Michelin, would have concluded in a report to his employer that a similar tire was similarly defective on grounds identical to those upon which he rested his conclusion here. Of course, Carlson himself claimed that his method was accurate, but, as we pointed out in *Joiner,* "nothing in either *Daubert* or the Federal Rules of Evidence requires a district court to admit opinion evidence that is connected to existing data only by the *ipse dixit* of the expert." 522 U.S. at 146.

Respondents additionally argue that the District Court too rigidly applied *Daubert*'s criteria. They read its opinion to hold that a failure to satisfy any one of those criteria automatically renders expert testimony inadmissible. The District Court's initial opinion might have been vulnerable to a form of this argument. There, the court, after rejecting respondents' claim that Carlson's testimony was "exempted from *Daubert*-style scrutiny" because it was "technical analysis" rather than "scientific evidence," simply added that "none of the four admissibility criteria outlined by the *Daubert* court are satisfied." 923 F. Supp. at 1522. Subsequently, however, the court granted respondents' motion for reconsideration. It then explicitly recognized that the relevant reliability inquiry "should be 'flexible,'" that its "'overarching subject [should be] . . . validity' and reliability," and that "*Daubert* was intended neither to be exhaustive nor to apply in every case." And the court ultimately based its decision upon Carlson's failure to satisfy either *Daubert*'s factors *or any other* set of reasonable reliability criteria. In light of the record as developed by the parties, that conclusion was within the District Court's lawful discretion.

In sum, Rule 702 grants the district judge the discretionary authority, reviewable for its abuse, to determine reliability in light of the particular facts and circumstances of the particular case. The District Court did not abuse its discretionary authority in this case. Hence, the judgment of the Court of Appeals is *Reversed*.

JUSTICE SCALIA, with whom JUSTICE O'CONNOR and JUSTICE THOMAS join, concurring.

I join the opinion of the Court, which makes clear that the discretion it endorses—trial-court discretion in choosing the manner of testing expert reliability—is not discretion to abandon the gatekeeping function. I think it worth adding that it is not discretion to perform the function inadequately. Rather, it is discretion to choose among *reasonable* means of excluding expertise that is *fausse* and science that is junky. Though, as the Court makes clear today, the *Daubert* factors are not holy writ, in a particular case the failure to apply one or another of them may be unreasonable, and hence an abuse of discretion.

NOTES

1. *Trial Court as Gatekeeper. Westberry v. Gislaved Gummi AB*, 178 F.3d 257 (4th Cir. 1999), involved a talc lubricant placed on rubber gaskets that allegedly caused aggravation of a sinus condition. The court discussed the trial court's role regarding proffered expert testimony as follows:

> Expert testimony is admissible under Rule 702 . . . if it concerns (1) scientific, technical, or other specialized knowledge that (2) will aid the jury or other trier of fact to understand or resolve a fact at issue. The first prong of this inquiry necessitates an examination of whether the reasoning or methodology underlying the expert's proffered opinion is reliable—that is, whether it is supported by adequate validation to render it trustworthy. The second prong of the inquiry requires an analysis of whether the opinion is relevant to the at issue. Thus, an expert's testimony is admissible under Rule 702 if it "rests on a reliable foundation and is relevant." *Kumho Tire Co.* at 1171 (1999)

> A district court considering the admissibility of expert testimony exercises a gatekeeping function to assess whether the proffered evidence is sufficiently reliable and relevant. The inquiry to be undertaken by the district court is "a flexible one" focusing on the "principles and methodology" employed by the expert, not on the conclusions reached. In making its initial determination of whether proffered testimony is sufficiently reliable, the court has broad latitude to consider whatever factors bearing on validity that the court finds to be useful; the particular factors will depend upon the unique circumstances of the expert testimony involved. The court, however, should be conscious of two guiding, and sometimes competing, principles. On the one hand, the court should be mindful that Rule 702 was intended to liberalize the introduction of relevant expert evidence. And, the court need not determine that the expert testimony a litigant seeks to offer into evidence is irrefutable or certainly correct. As with all other admissible evidence, expert testimony is subject to being tested by "vigorous cross-examination, presentation of contrary evidence, and careful instruction on the burden of proof." On the other

hand, the court must recognize that due to the difficulty of evaluating their testimony, expert witnesses have the potential to "be both powerful and quite misleading." And, given the potential persuasiveness of expert testimony, proffered evidence that has a greater potential to mislead than to enlighten should be excluded.

. . .[Defendant] argues that the district court erred in failing to undertake a determination of the reliability and relevance of the evidence as required by Rule 702 because it believed such an analysis was applicable only to novel scientific opinions. We agree. As the Supreme Court recently made clear, the obligation of a district court to determine whether expert testimony is reliable and relevant prior to admission applies to all expert testimony.

As to the specific issue in the case the defendant argued that the plaintiff's expert was not based on reliable methodology. In the absence of epidemiological studies, peer-reviewed published studies, animal studies, or laboratory data plaintiff's expert relied on "differential diagnosis—supported in part by the temporal relationship between Westberry's exposure to talc and the problems he experienced with his sinuses—in reaching the conclusion that Westberry's sinus problems were caused by his exposure to talc from [defendant's] gaskets." The court agreed stating: "Differential diagnosis, or differential etiology, is a standard scientific technique of identifying the cause of a medical problem by eliminating the likely causes until the most probable one is isolated. A reliable differential diagnosis typically, though not invariably, is performed after 'physical examinations, the taking of medical histories, and the review of clinical tests, including laboratory tests,' and generally is accomplished by determining the possible causes for the patient's symptoms and then eliminating each of these potential causes until reaching one that cannot be ruled out or determining which of those that cannot be excluded is the most likely. This technique has widespread acceptance in the medical community, has been subject to peer review, and does not frequently lead to incorrect results."

2. *Epidemiological Expert Evidence.* The plaintiffs in *Bloomquist v. Wapello County*, 500 N.W.2d 1 (Iowa 1993), brought a suit for damages sustained as the result of alleged exposure to toxic insecticide spray, primarily flea spray, in the Department of Human Services building where they worked. They established causation on the basis of the expert testimony of their treating doctors.

Defendants contended that traditional proof of causation was not sufficient in a toxic tort case, and that expert epidemiological evidence was required. The court disagreed:

> Epidemiology is an accepted scientific discipline dealing with the integrated use of statistics and biological/medical science to identify and establish the causes of human disease. Through epidemiology it is possible to assess a percentage of the risk of a disease that is properly attributable to a given factor such as exposure to an allegedly harmful substance. Through the use of epidemiologic standards courts are provided with a rational and consistent means for evaluating evidence of a causal relationship between exposure to a particular

factor and the incidence of a disease. B. Black & D. Lilienfeld, *Epidemiologic Proof in Toxic Tort Litigation*, 52 Fordham L.Rev. 732, 736 (1984).

An epidemiological study attempts to determine the incidence of certain problems with the exposure of the patient to certain alleged causes. Epidemiological studies do not provide direct evidence that a particular victim was injured by exposure to a substance. They have the potential, however, of generating circumstantial evidence of cause and effect. *DeLuca v. Merrell Dow Pharmaceuticals, Inc.*, 911 F.2d 941, 945 (3d Cir.1990). Epidemiological studies involve

> a process which "amounts to an attempt to falsify the null hypothesis and by exclusion accept the alternative." The null hypothesis is the hypothesis that there is no association between two studied variables; in this case the key null hypothesis would be that there is no association between [the suspected] exposure and [the alleged effects]. The important alternative hypothesis in this case is that [the suspected agent's] use is associated with [the plaintiff's problem]. *Id.* (citations omitted).

According to one authority, the most important generalized evidence of causation of illnesses whose cause is incompletely understood is epidemiology. Michael Dore, *A Commentary on the Use of Epidemiological Evidence in Demonstrating Cause-in-Fact*, 7 Harv.Envtl.L.Rev. 429, 430–31 (1983) [hereinafter Dore]. One example of such studies involve the effect of cigarette smoking in causing lung cancer. *Id.* However, as Dore notes, epidemiological evidence is often inaccurate. For example, if the normal incidence of leukemia of 107 per 100,000 population is doubled, by radiation on the job, to an additional 107 per 100,000 population, the question in a particular case would still be whether the plaintiff contracted leukemia from the radiation on the job or from some other source. Dore, at 4366–37. Another problem is that it tends to be too complex for juries to understand. *Id.* at 437.

This potential for confusing a jury is evident in this discussion of the complex study of epidemiology:

> Significance testing has a "P value" focus; the P value "indicates the probability, assuming the null hypothesis is true, that the observed data will depart from the absence of association to the extent that they actually do, or to a greater extent, by actual chance." If P is less than .05 (or 5%) a study's finding of a relationship supportive of the alternative hypothesis is considered statistically significant, if P is greater than 5% the relationship is rejected as insignificant. Accordingly, the results of a particular study are reported as simply "significant" or "not significant" or as P<.05 or P>.05.

DeLuca, 911 F.2d at 947 (citation omitted).

There is a risk that the difference between epidemiologist testimony and the testimony of treating doctors might be confused by the jury, Dore, at 437, and experts must make numerous subjective decisions in choosing the control population, evaluating the underlying data, and interpreting the results. The best that can be said for epidemiology is that it can prove the risk but cannot prove individual causation. Dore, at 440.

The *DeLuca* court discussed this problem in the context of Bendectin exposure. As it noted,

> a showing of increased risk for birth defects among women using Bendectin in a particular study does not automatically prove that Bendectin use creates a higher risk of having a child with birth defects because the discrepancy between the exposed and unexposed groups could be the product of chance resulting from the use of only a small sample of the relevant populations.

Id. at 946 (footnote omitted).

Another problem in epidemiological studies is that they require large numbers of patients whose backgrounds are similar in every respect except their exposure to the suspected substance. When studies are made of only a small sample of the relevant population, a so-called "sampling error," the validity of the epidemiological study is brought into question. *Id.* at 946–47.

To be effective, an epidemiological study requires a large number of cases. For example, in one epidemiological study involving Bendectin, 2218 "pairs" of women were studied. *Oxendine v. Merrell Dow Pharmaceuticals, Inc.*, 506 A.2d 1100, 1107 (D.C.App.1986). . . . We decline to apply a per se requirement of epidemiological evidence simply because of a lack of substantial numbers of cases. The lack of similar cases, of course, would affect the weight of the plaintiffs' evidence of proximate cause.

In our view, while epidemiological evidence is helpful, it should not be held to be an absolute requirement in establishing causation.

3. *Lay vs. Expert Testimony:* In *Cotilletta v. Tepedino*, 151 Misc. 2d 660, 573 N.Y.S.2d 396 (1995), plaintiff brought a medical malpractice action on behalf of plaintiff's decedent. Defendant moved to dismiss plaintiff's claim for pain and suffering on the ground that the decedent was unconscious after the alleged malpractice and in a coma until her death:

> In this medical malpractice action, decedent Josephine Cotilletta was admitted to defendant St. John's Queens Hospital on May 6, 1986 for a Caesarian section delivery of her second child. After delivery of a healthy baby boy and while skin closure was being performed, a Code 99 was called. Mrs. Cotilletta was resuscitated and transferred to ICU. Forty (40) days later on June 16, 1986, another Code 99 was called but this time, Mrs. Cotilletta could not be resuscitated. Defendants contend that no claim for conscious pain and suffering can be maintained since Mrs. Cotilletta was unconscious and in a coma from the time she was placed under anesthesia on May 6, 1986 until her death on June 16, 1986. In support of the motion, defendant Dr. Shin has attached two affidavits of Dr. Martin A. Green, a board certified neurologist, who upon reviewing the reports and hospital chart is of the opinion that decedent was in deep unconscious state and would

have been unable to suffer any conscious pain and suffering. Defendants claim that Dr. Green's opinion is supported by the examining physician and former defendant, Dr. Lopresti in his examination before trial. In addition, defendants assert that since plaintiff has not proffered any medical affidavit to rebut the expert's affidavits that the motion must be granted.

Plaintiff in opposition to the motion contends that the examination before trial testimony of decedent's husband, Mr. Cotilletta and her mother Paola Giacalone indicates that when they visited Mrs. Cotilletta, she exhibited awareness of her environment. In her examination before trial, Mrs. Giacalone testified as follows: "Q. As a layperson, in other words, as someone who is not a doctor was it your impression at any time from May 6, 1986 up until the date that your daughter passed away that she was ever awake, at any time that you saw her? A. She was never fully conscious, but when she would speak to her of the children tears would come out of her (daughter's) eyes." Mr. Cotilletta also indicated that his wife, on several occasions, appeared to resist having a needle inserted in her arm and ". . . showed some tears and — when I was talking to her . . ." Plaintiff maintains that these responses indicate that decedent had an awareness of her environment sufficient to establish consciousness—accounting for any movement or activity by the decedent as involuntary and automatic neurologic responses.

The court said there is "no dispute that pain and suffering is not compensable without conscious awareness," and "mere movement of head and limbs without manifestation of pain" is not sufficient to establish pain and suffering. The case, however, was inappropriate for summary judgment on behalf of the defendant. While the defendant made out a prima facie case for summary judgment with expert witness evidence, plaintiff met this evidence with lay testimony:

> There are many areas of evidence where ordinary persons are permitted to give an opinion as to the apparent physical condition of a person which is open to ordinary observation. In fact, in *Sachs v. Nassau County*, 151 A.D.2d 558, 559, 542 N.Y.S.2d 337, it was stated that the jury would be free to "use their 'common sense and good judgment' and draw on 'their common knowledge and general experience'" in determining whether a person experienced conscious pain and suffering . . . .

> While an expert's opinion may be given great weight by the trier of the facts, it is nevertheless assessed in the context of all of the evidence in a case, "expert or other" (see, PJI Instruction 1A:90). Mr. Cotilletta and Mrs. Giacalone, as lay witnesses, may testify to their observations and opinions as to consciousness based upon their day to day contact and experiences with the decedent. So, too, may defendants' experts, based upon the hospital charts and other criteria in evidence, give their medical opinions as to any lack of consciousness.

> It is thus apparent that the mere superiority of intellectual credentials does not require exclusion of lay evidence nor mandate a specific

finding of fact. Stated otherwise, lay opinions may compete with medical opinions where the issue relates to matters cognizable by either.

Plaintiff is only required to rebut expert opinion evidence by use of an expert where the matters are not within the ordinary experience and knowledge of laymen. As we have already determined, the issue at hand, despite being as to a material fact, is susceptible to lay opinion evidence.

In addition, implicit in the requirement that plaintiff come forward with a medical affidavit in these types of cases, is that the material fact relates to the medical malpractice. Here, however, the facts do not relate to malpractice but rather to the question of consciousness. This, as we have determined, may be established by lay opinion evidence. Therefore, it must be concluded that plaintiff need not present affidavits in order to prevail in these motions.

4. *No Expert Required.* In *Coll v. Johnson,* 636 A.2d 336 (Vt. 1993), the plaintiff brought an action against the defendant city and its policeman for the use of unreasonable and excessive force in making an arrest:

> At approximately 2:30 a.m. on September 21, 1988, Rene Coll and a companion robbed a convenience store in Rutland. Police responded to the call and spotted the fleeing suspects. Coll halted at the corner of a garage, his escape blocked by police officers. He refused to give up and told the police he had a gun, although he was armed only with a knife. Officer Johnson arrived with a police dog. He released the dog and it went for Coll, who held it off with his knife. Officer Johnson's testimony at the trial was that he was approximately twenty feet from Coll when Coll moved aggressively toward him and reached toward his belt for what Officer Johnson believed was a gun. Fearing for his life, Officer Johnson fired at Coll, wounding him in the abdomen. Coll's testimony was that he went into a crouch, holding the dog at bay with his knife, and never moved for fear that the dog would attack.

After the jury was unable to agree, the trial court directed a verdict for the defendants on the ground that the plaintiff "had failed to provide expert testimony to establish the standard of care for discharge of a weapon by a police officer in making an arrest." Reversing, the state supreme court said:

> Expert testimony is not generally required "where the alleged violation of the standard of care is so apparent that it may be understood by a lay trier of fact without the aid of an expert." *Larson v. Candlish,* 144 Vt. 449, 502, 480 A.2d 417, 418 (1984). In cases of professional misconduct or malpractice, expert testimony may be necessary to establish the prevailing standard of care. Even in medical malpractice cases, however, expert testimony is not required where the alleged violation is so apparent it may be understood by a lay person.
>
> Defendants contend that the conduct of officers in life-threatening situations involves special procedures and standards that are not within a lay person's common knowledge. Juries, defendants assert,

cannot determine the standard of care in these cases without expert guidance. We cannot agree. First, as we have already stated, it is for the court to instruct the jury on the standard of care to apply to the facts. In cases where plaintiffs allege excessive force, that standard will be whether the force used was objectively reasonable under the circumstances. *Graham*, 490 U.S. at 399, 109 S.Ct. at 1873.

Second, in excessive-force cases there is usually no causal obscurity requiring expert testimony for the jury to understand how an injury might have occurred. See *Houghton v. Leinwohl*, 135 Vt. 380, 384, 376 A.2d 733, 737 (1977) (no obscure causation where person felt bad strain immediately upon lifting heavy object and disability closely followed injury); cf. *Deyo*, 152 Vt. at 204, 565 A.2d at 1291 (in medical malpractice cases, "normally a complicated medical procedure, not easily evaluated by a lay person, is at issue"). Simply put, an arrest is not heart surgery. Once it is established that the force exerted by police caused the harm to a given plaintiff, the determination for the jury is whether that force was reasonable under the circumstances. This determination does not involve the "scientific, technical, or other specialized knowledge" contemplated by Rule 7702. V.R.E. 702; see *State v. Carpenter*, 155 Vt. 59, 63, 580 A.2d 497, 500 (1990) (expert medical testimony not necessary for jury to determine substantial risk of death for aggravated assault "when a person is choked to the point of passing out").

While *Graham* emphasized that the determination of excessive force should be judged from the point of view of a reasonable police officer on the scene, no cases have held that this determination requires expert testimony. Moreover, the cases cited by defendants where expert testimony was required to prove police negligence involve other and more specialized standards of care. In *District of Columbia v. White*, 442 A.2d 159 (D.C. 1982), the court held that "expert testimony is required when the subject presented is 'so distinctly related to some science, profession, business or occupation as to be beyond the ken of the average layman.'" The issue in *White*, however, was not whether the police officer had used excessive force, but whether the District of Columbia had been negligent in training the officer in the use of his weapon. That is an issue that could well require expert testimony inasmuch as the standard of care for the training of police officers is a technical subject not within the common knowledge of the average lay person. See *District of Columbia v. Peters*, 527, A.2d 1269, 1273 (D.C. 1987) (expert testimony necessary to establish standard of care necessary in training officers to deal with mentally disturbed persons or those under influence of drugs); see also *Cunningham v. District of Columbia*, No. Civ. A. 87-0095, 1988 WL 68863, at (D.D.C.1988) (expert testimony required to support allegation of negligent supervision and assignment of police officer). One other case cited by defendants, *Selkowitz v. County of Nassau*, 45 N.Y.2d 97, 408 N.Y.S.2d 10, 12, 379 N.E.2d 1140, 1143 (1978), is not pertinent, because it deals only with the admissibility, not the necessity, of a police officer's testimony as an expert on the safe handling of police cars in high-speed chases.

5. *Erroneous Consideration of Expert Evidence.* In *Washington State Physicians Insur. Exchange v. Fisons Corp.*, 858 P.2d 1054 (Wash. 1993), defendant drug company and its attorneys were accused of abuse of discovery rules in withholding documents in an underlying products liability action. The trial court found that "the conduct of the drug company and its counsel was consistent with the customary and accepted litigation practices of the bar of Snohomish County and of this state." Reversing, the state supreme court said it was error for the trial court to consider "the opinions of attorneys and others as to whether sanctions should be imposed. . . . Legal opinions on the ultimate *legal* issue before the court are not properly considered under the guise of expert testimony. . . . [I]ntent need not be shown before sanctions are mandated. . . . Conduct is to be measured against the spirit and purpose of the rules, not against the standard of practice of the local bar."

The plaintiff in *Adams v. Amore*, 895 P.2d 1016 (Ariz.App. 1994), brought a wrongful discharge action against the town and others, alleging that she was fired as a police dispatcher because she provided internal investigative reports to a discharged officer and his lawyer. She alleged that "the town violated public policy by discharging her for being a whistle-blower."

The town appealed a $250,000 verdict against it and the court of appeals reversed, holding that the trial court erroneously admitted testimony on behalf of the plaintiff:

> Donald Soeken testified for plaintiff as an expert on the behavioral characteristics of whistle-blowers. Soeken is a licensed clinical social worker with the Commission on Mental Health for the District of Columbia, who, in his spare time, studies people claiming to be whistle-blowers. The town objected that Soeken's testimony was wholly inadmissible both because it lacked any scientific basis and because the subject was one on which the jury required no expert. The trial court declined to exclude Soeken's testimony altogether. Instead, the court permitted Soeken to testify about the profile of whistle-blowers and to relate Adams's experience to that profile, but excluded testimony that Adams was a whistle-blower, that the town had retaliated against her, and that she had been damaged by her experience with the town.
>
> Soeken testified that he developed a whistle-blower profile by mailing a questionnaire to two hundred self-described whistle-blowers and analyzing the responses of the eighty-seven persons who chose to complete the profile and mail it back. He characterized a typical whistle-blower as someone suffering from post traumatic stress syndrome, "acting out of conscience," and doing "the right thing." Describing a retaliation phase of whistle-blowing, he stated that "[n]inety percent of the whistle-blowers lost their job or were demoted." Retaliation is typical, he stated, "even though [the] charges are proved true." Soeken testified that Adams had the characteristics of a whistle-blower and that she had experienced the kind of retaliation—harassment, transfer to a different position, and ultimate loss of

job—that whistle-blowers typically undergo. According to Soeken, the only characteristic that set Adams apart from the profile was that "[s]he's one of the . . . more mature whistle-blowers."

Trial courts have broad discretion in admitting expert testimony, *Lay v. Mesa*, 168 Ariz. 552, 554, 815 P.2d 921, 923 (App. 1991); "[h]owever, when the admissibility of expert opinion evidence is a question of 'law or logic', it is this court's responsibility to determine admissibility." *State v. Moran*, 151 Ariz. 378, 381,718 P.2d 248, 251 (1986). Here we find the introduction of Doeken's expert testimony inadmissible for two reasons.

First, plaintiffs failed to lay the foundation that Soeken based his opinions on facts or data "of a type reasonably relied upon by experts in [his] particular field." Ariz. R.Evid. 703. Specifically, they failed to establish the representative validity of Soeken's sampling, and there is considerable question whether they could have done so, as Soeken merely generalized a profile from the unverified reports of the eighty-seven respondents to his inquiry who chose to characterize themselves as whistle-blowers.

Second, even if plaintiffs had laid an adequate foundation for the validity of Soeken's methodology, his testimony would still have been improper, because this jury had no need for expert testimony. Expert testimony is inappropriate if "the jury is qualified without such testimony 'to determine intelligently and to the best possible degree the particular issue without enlightenment from those having a specialized understanding of the subject.'" *State v. Chapple*, 135 Ariz. 281, 293, 660 P.2d 1208, (1983) (quoting Fed.R.Evid. 702, advisory committee note). This was such a case.

In support of the admissibility of Soeken's whistle-blower profile, plaintiffs analogize to expert testimony concerning the behavioral characteristics of victims of sexual or child abuse. The analogy does not hold. The function of an expert witness is "to provide testimony on subjects that are beyond the common sense, experience and education of the average juror." *Lindsey*, 149 Ariz. at 475, 720 P.2d at 76. Arizona courts have permitted testimony concerning the behavioral characteristics of victims of sexual and child abuse because such characteristics are beyond the knowledge and experience of the average juror, *id.*, and because such evidence is relevant to give juries a context for evaluating the uncertain or conflicting recollections common to victims of sexual and child abuse. Courts have come to accept scientific documentation of a behavior pattern among such victims that explains testimonial uncertainty or inconsistency that would otherwise defeat their credibility.

No comparable need for testimonial context faced the jurors here; they could derive no specialized knowledge from reviewing the behavioral characteristics of whistle-blowers that would assist them in evaluating Adams's credibility or in resolving any other issue material to the case. Plaintiffs' roundabout purpose in introducing Soeken's testimony — accomplished by comparison of Adams to the profile —

was to inform the jury that Adams acted "out of conscience," sought to do "the right thing," experienced retaliation, and suffered emotional stress. This testimony was nothing but an opinion on how the jury ought to decide the case; it invaded the province of the jury, and the trial court should have ruled it out of bounds.

Distinguishing prior precedent, the state supreme court in *Angrand v. Key*, 657 So.2d 1146 (Fla.1995), held that the trial court could in its discretion have excluded the expert testimony of a "grief expert" in a medical malpractice wrongful death action. The expert testified as to the grief suffered by the surviving members of the deceased's family. The supreme court agreed with the court of appeals that the witness did not testify to anything that was "outside the common experience" of the jury, that his testimony "added nothing beyond which the survivors themselves, their minister, and other family members testified to" as to the close family relationship between the deceased and her husband and son, and that the "testimony was unfairly prejudicial because the jury, based on the fact that the testimony came from an expert, might have given it undue weight."

In *Logerquist v. McVey*, 1 P.3d 113 (Ariz. 2000), the court held a jury question was presented as to the reliability of expert witness testimony regarding plaintiff's repressed memory, in a suit by plaintiff against her psychiatrist for alleged childhood sexual abuse. The *Frye* test of general acceptance in the scientific community did not apply because the testimony did not involve scientific evidence. The court refused to apply the *Kumho* test to nonscientific expert testimony because that test would undermine the role of the jury.

6. *Junk Science*. Peter Huber has been a foremost critic of what he considers to be expert testimony based on "junk science." See PETER HUBER, GALILEO'S REVENGE: JUNK SCIENCE IN THE COURTHOUSE (1991). What do you suppose he means by the term "junk science"?

7. *Discovery—Blood Donor Identity*. Plaintiff underwent elective coronary artery bypass surgery and an aortic valve replacement in 1984, during the course of which he received a blood transfusion from which he allegedly contracted AIDS. He and his wife sued Bergen Community Blood Center (BCBC) for negligence in screening the donor of the blood, and in that connection sought discovery of the donor's records. The defendant resisted discovery in order to protect the donor's confidentiality. *Snyder v. Mekhjian*, 244 N.J. Super. 281, 582 A.2d 307 (1990).

In permitting discovery, the court said:

> To begin with, we note that BCBC has already supplied plaintiffs with the registration form of the donor of unit number 29F9784 with his name and any other identifying information redacted. This form consists of a series of questions relating to medical history, previous blood donation and vital signs at the time of the donation. BCBC asserts that this information is adequate for plaintiff's purposes. It also asserts that any further information either identifying the donor or in any other way permitting plaintiff to penetrate the donor's anonymity or privacy would breach BCBC's obligation of confidentiality imposed both by considerations of public policy and by the dictates of N.J.S.A. 26:5C-5 to -14 (confidentiality of records of AIDS patients).

We consider first plaintiff's need for further information. He claims that he requires it for several reasons. First, none of the defendants is now willing to admit that unit number 29F0784 was contaminated. While there is no question that the donor of that unit testes positive for HIV antibodies in 1986, defendants apparently insist on putting plaintiff to his proof that the donor had been infected as far back as August 1984. It is certainly inferential from the circumstances that he was then infected, particularly in view of the medical assurance referred to *supra* that plaintiff had no other risk factor. But defendants' refusal to concede the point entitles plaintiff to seek direct proof that the donor was HIV-positive in 1984.

In a footnote the court noted that more direct proof of causation "may be available by way of discovery, permitted by court order, of the medical records of other donors or components of the 29F9784 donation."

The court continued:

Beyond that causation issue, plaintiff cogently asserts a need in respect of the question of BCBC's negligence. Illustratively, it was known before August 1984 that early symptoms of AIDS infection include particular lymph-node swelling and skin disorders, and, in fact, by 1983 the commercial blood bankers were conducting routine physical examinations of donors to determine the presence of these symptoms. Did the donor here have those symptoms then? Was he asked about them? Was he physically examined in this respect? Was he given the appropriate high-risk group self-screening information? Was a reasonable effort made to determine if he was in a high-risk category? Were his responses to the medical history questions accurately recorded? Were the questions adequately explained to him? Would present screening requirements, short of laboratory testing have revealed his AIDS infection? Undoubtedly other relevant lines of interrogation would suggest themselves. All of this information is, in our view, highly pertinent to the issue of BCBC negligence and is, moreover, to a large extent not available from any source other than the donor himself.

The question then is how to balance plaintiff's need to gain relevant information against the donor's right to privacy and the public's need to maintain confidentiality, which is said to be a cornerstone of the nation's blood donation program. We start with N.J.S.A. 26:5C-5 to -14, which is intended to protect the confidentiality of individual AIDS records while assuring their limited availability for essential health, scientific and other legitimate purposes. The statute stipulates that unless disclosure is expressly provided for by N.J.S.A. 26:5C-8, it may be obtained only by court order for good cause shown. N.J.S.A. 26:5C-9(a). In assessing good cause, moreover, the court is required to "weigh the public interest and need for disclosure against the injury to the person who is the subject of the record, to the physician-patient relationship, and to the services offered by the program [of diagnosis and treatment of AIDS and conditions related to HIV infection]." Moreover, if good cause is found, the court is required to determine the extent to which disclosure is necessary and to impose appropriate safeguards.

We are convinced that confidentiality of blood bank AIDS records rest upon significant public and private considerations and is ordinarily essential to assure the continued effectiveness of the screening process, the willingness of donors to continue to participate in blood collection efforts, and the general integrity of the nation's blood programs. Nevertheless where, as here, a litigant's discovery need cannot otherwise be met and it is possible to accommodate that need with limited and controlled intrusion, some access under careful court supervision is appropriate and justifiable.

Plaintiff has not yet been able to determine if the donor is still alive. That is the first order of business for BCBC's disclosure. If he is not alive, the trial judge shall explore with counsel the possibility of obtaining information respecting the stage of his disease in 1984, his membership in a high-risk category, and any other relevant information from other sources. The donor's personal representative will, moreover, have to be noticed of these proceedings. If the donor is alive, the court shall determine procedures best calculated to provide plaintiff with the information he requires while giving maximum protection to the donor. For example, the donor's name need not be supplied if his "veiled" deposition is permitted. If such a deposition were to be permitted, the court could appropriately limit in advance the areas of questioning and impose such other conditions as would insure the donor's anonymity. If, on the other hand, only a deposition on written questions pursuant to *R.* 4:15 were permitted, the court could rule on the list of questions prior to their submission and permit an alias identification and oath. It may also be that the donor would have no objection to providing, openly and frankly, the information plaintiff requires or he may authorize his physician to do so. Thus it may also be prudent for the court itself initially to communicate with the donor. In addition, it is likely that the parties themselves will be able to suggest to the court further limitations on the substance of the inquiry and the technique by which it is to be pursued that will afford plaintiff a reasonable discovery opportunity at the least possible cost to the confidentiality interests here implicated.

The ultimate point of course is that plaintiff has suffered a most grievous harm which was apparently inflicted upon him by this donor, whether unwittingly or not. He does not seek redress from the donor but rather from those defendants whose responsibility it was to stand protectively between them. The degree of plaintiff's injury, his right to redress from those who may have negligently failed to protect him, and his need for information which only the donor can provide if redress is to be obtained, all justify the limited disclosure we here sanction without unduly prejudicing the interests of the public and the donor's privacy rights.

8. *Protective Order to Prevent Abuse of Discovery.* The parents in *Bucaretzky v. Swersky,* 151 Misc.2d 136, 572 N.Y.S.2d 285 (1991), brought a medical

malpractice action to recover damages arising out of the birth of a child with Down's Syndrome. The defendants moved for an order compelling the plaintiffs to disclose the identity of their religious advisors. In denying the motion the court said:

> This unusual request arises from the nature of the medical malpractice action. Mrs. Bucaretzky, a plaintiff, gave birth to a daughter in May 1990. The child was born with Down's Syndrome. The complaint alleges that the defendants failed to advise the plaintiffs of the possibility of giving birth to a child with this condition and failed to conduct the appropriate tests in order to rule out Down's Syndrome. The defendants contend that their advice was proper and that the plaintiff declined amniocentesis and chorionic villus sampling for religious reasons. A critical element of the defendants' defense is the assertion that Mrs. Bucaretzky would not have had an abortion even if she had been advised of the results of the genetic screening.
>
> The papers submitted by the plaintiffs' attorney, unfortunately, shed more heat than light on the issues raised on the motion. On its own initiative, this Court has the power to make a protective order to prevent the abuse of the disclosure process. CPLR 3103(a). Such an order may be designed to prevent unreasonable annoyance or embarrassment to a party. The Court balances the materiality and necessity of the demanded disclosure against the harm experienced by the party against whom such disclosure is demanded.
>
> The defendants argue that the disclosure of the plaintiffs' religious advisors would help them learn the "state of mind" of the plaintiffs during the pregnancy. In fact, such disclosure strikes at the heart of the plaintiffs' credibility, allowing the defendants to utilize any prior inconsistent statements for purposes of impeachment. Two issues may preclude such disclosure. Communications between a religious advisor and a congregant may be privileged pursuant to CPLR 4505, especially if such communication was elicited to provide aid, advice or comfort. Also, allowing non-party disclosure at this time may not only impinge upon a privilege. Granting the motion may result in the plaintiffs being exposed to embarrassment before their co-religionists. Mrs. Bucaretzky may be a member of a religious congregation with certain scruples regarding abortion. However, Mrs. Bucaretzky is also free not to act in conformity with those beliefs. To expose the plaintiffs to this disclosure may not only embarrass them, it may also have a chilling effect on the prosecution of the lawsuit. This form of disclosure is perfectly suited to the application of CPLR 3103.

9. *Pre-Discovery Disclosure.* Rule 26(a) of the Federal Rules of Civil Procedure, as amended in 1993, provides in part:

> **(1) *Initial Disclosures.*** Except to the extent otherwise stipulated or directed by order or local rule, a party shall, without awaiting a discovery request, provide to other parties:
>
> > **(A)** the name and, if known, the address and telephone number of each individual likely to have discoverable information relevant

to disputed facts alleged with particularity in the pleadings, identifying the subjects of the information;

(B) a copy of, or a description by category and location of, all documents, data compilations, and tangible things in the possession, custody, or control of the party that are relevant to disputed facts alleged with particularity in the pleadings;

(C) a computation of any category of damages claimed by the disclosing party, making available for inspection and copying as under Rule 34 the documents or other evidentiary material, not privileged or protected from disclosure, on which such computation is based, including materials bearing on the nature and extent of injuries suffered; and

(D) for inspection and copying as under Rule 34 any insurance agreement under which any person carrying on an insurance business may be liable to satisfy part or all of a judgment which may be entered in the action or to indemnify or reimburse for payments made to satisfy the judgment . . . .

A party shall make its initial disclosures based on the information then reasonably available to it and is not excused from making its disclosures because it has not fully completed its investigation of the case or because it challenges the sufficiency of another party's disclosures or because another party has not made its disclosures.

(2) *Disclosure of Expert Testimony*

(A) In addition to the disclosures required by paragraph (1), a party shall disclose to other parties the identity of any person who may be used at trial to present evidence under Rules 702, 703, or 705 of the Federal Rules of Evidence.

(B) Except as otherwise stipulated or directed by the court, this disclosure shall, with respect to a witness who is retained or specially employed to provide expert testimony in the case or whose duties as an employee of the party regularly involve giving expert testimony, be accompanied by a written report prepared and signed by the witness. The report shall contain a complete statement of all opinions to be expressed and the basis and reasons therefor; the data or other information considered by the witness in forming the opinions; any exhibits to be used as a summary of or support for the opinions; the qualifications of the witness, including a list of all publications authored by the witness within the preceding ten years; the compensation to be paid for the study and testimony; and a listing of any other cases in which the witness has testified as an expert at trial or by deposition within the preceding four years. . . .

(3) *Pretrial Disclosures.* In addition to the disclosures required in the preceding paragraphs, a party shall provide to other parties the following information regarding the evidence that it may present at trial other than solely for impeachment purposes:

(A) the name and, if not previously provided, the address and telephone number of each witness, separately identifying those whom the party expects to present and those whom the party may call if the need arises;

(B) the designation of those witnesses whose testimony is expected to be presented by means of a deposition and, if not taken stenographically, a transcript of the pertinent portions of the deposition testimony; and

(C) an appropriate identification of each document or other exhibit, including summaries of other evidence, separately identifying those which the party expects to offer and those which the party may offer if the need arises.

The Rule sets out various time sequences within which these disclosures must be made. Is this Rule likely to decrease, or increase, litigation?

10. *Expert Witness Malpractice.* Reviewing the cases, the court in *Murphy v. A. A. Matthews*, 841 S.W. 2d 671, 680 (Mo. 1998), held that witness immunity "should not apply to bar a suit for damages against a privately retained professional who negligently provides litigation support services." In Missouri, the court said, witness immunity "generally has been restricted to defamation, defamation-type, or retaliatory cases against adverse witnesses."

D. SPOLIATION AND OTHER MISCONDUCT

PROBLEM

An attorney had valuable data in her car pertaining to her client's case. There was no available copy of the data. While driving home, planning to review the data that night, the attorney was involved in an automobile accident that resulted in the destruction of the data. Discuss any claims client might have against attorney for loss of the data.

HOLMES v. AMEREX RENT-A-CAR
180 F.3d 294 (DC Cir. 1999)

GINSBURG, CIRCUIT JUDGE:

. . .The essential facts, as set forth in our prior opinion, are as follows. In November, 1988, while driving a car he had rented from Amerex Rent-a-Car, Ronnie Holmes was involved in an accident that left him seriously injured. He asked Amerex, which had taken possession of the wrecked car following the accident, to hold it so that he could have it inspected by an expert. Amerex agreed to leave the car undisturbed until June 15, 1989. On June 14, an Amerex claims representative agreed to sell the car to Holmes for $200. Unbeknownst to the claims representative, however, another Amerex employee had already sold the car to a salvage company, which had destroyed its engine. Without the engine, it was impossible to determine whether the car was defectively designed or manufactured or maintained in a way that might have caused the accident.

Holmes sued Chrysler (the manufacturer of the car) and Amerex in the District of Columbia Superior Court, alleging that Chrysler had negligently designed, and that Amerex had negligently maintained, the engine of the car. After Chrysler removed the case to federal court, Holmes filed an amended complaint naming Amerex as the sole defendant. The amended complaint asserts claims for negligent spoliation of evidence and tortious interference with Holmes's prospective civil action against Chrysler (again by spoliation of evidence). In support of these claims Holmes submitted an affidavit from an expert in biomechanics, crashworthiness, and accident reconstruction stating that "if the vehicle were available in the same condition that it was immediately following the accident, [Holmes] would have a substantial possibility of proving that the [car] at issue was defectively designed and/or manufactured and/or maintained." The district judge granted summary judgment to Amerex on this claim, concluding that Holmes had not met what it (erroneously) thought was the law of spoliation in the District of Columbia, namely, that a plaintiff must demonstrate that, were it not for the destruction of the evidence, it is more probable than not that he would prevail upon the underlying claim.

Holmes's amended complaint also included counts for breach of contract and promissory estoppel arising out of Amerex's sale of the car to the salvage company. The district court referred those claims to a magistrate judge. After a bench trial, the magistrate first found for Holmes on the contract claim but awarded him only nominal damages because his "purpose in seeking possession of the salvage was not for its intrinsic value but solely for its evidential value in a potential tort action against the manufacturer"; when the district court had granted summary judgment in favor of Amerex on the spoliation claims, it had "removed the basis for any damages [Holmes] could claim" arising out of Amerex's breach of contract. The magistrate then rejected Holmes's promissory estoppel claim, upon the ground that Holmes had been "less than diligent in protecting his own interests with respect to an inspection of the salvage of the vehicle." The district court adopted the magistrate's report and recommendation in full.

Holmes appeals the district court's grant of summary judgment for Amerex on the spoliation claims, the magistrate's failure to award him more than nominal damages for Amerex's breach of contract, and the magistrate's denial of his promissory estoppel claim.

In answer to our certification of questions of law, the District of Columbia Court of Appeals enumerated the elements of a cause of action for negligent or reckless spoliation of evidence, as follows:

> (1) existence of a potential civil action; (2) a legal or contractual duty to preserve evidence which is relevant to that action; (3) destruction of that evidence by the duty-bound defendant; (4) significant impairment in the ability to prove the potential civil action; (5) a proximate relationship between the impairment of the underlying suit and the unavailability of the destroyed evidence; (6) a significant possibility of success of the potential civil action if the evidence were available; and (7) damages adjusted for the estimated likelihood of success in the potential civil action.

710 A.2d at 854.

The evidence presented in this case, viewed in the light most favorable to Holmes, would allow a reasonable juror to conclude that (1) Holmes had a potential civil action arising out of the accident in which he was involved; (2) Amerex had a contractual obligation to preserve the car for Holmes; (3) Amerex negligently allowed the car to be sold and dismantled; (4) Holmes's ability to prove his case in the potential civil action was significantly impaired; (5) the impairment of the underlying suit was proximately related to the dismantling of the car and the attendant loss of evidence relating to the design, manufacturing, and maintenance of the car; (6) Holmes would have had a significant possibility of success in the potential civil action if the evidence were available; and (7) Holmes suffered damages.

In concluding that a reasonable juror could find that Holmes would have had a "significant possibility" of success in his underlying lawsuit if the evidence had not been lost, we are mindful that the District of Columbia has, unlike some states, rejected the requirement that a plaintiff demonstrate a "reasonable probability" of success.

> A "reasonable probability" of success still requires a showing that success was probable. In our view, this comes too close to requiring that the plaintiff show success by what amounts to "a preponderance of the evidence." . . . This standard is too high. Instead, we believe we should require that the plaintiff show that the underlying lawsuit enjoyed a significant possibility of success. We choose this term as it implies a showing higher than the already recognized standard of "significant evidence" but lower than the standard of "preponderance of the evidence." The plaintiff must demonstrate a substantial and realistic possibility of succeeding, but need not cross the threshold of demonstrating that such success was more likely than not, something that would be realistically impractical of proof.

710 A.2d at 852.

Holmes submitted the affidavit of an expert in accident reconstruction who, after reviewing photographs of the car taken after the accident, determined that the car appears to have lacked reasonable "crashworthiness." He therefore concluded that "if the vehicle were available in the same condition that it was immediately following the accident, [Holmes] would have a substantial possibility of proving that the [car] . . . was defectively designed and/or manufactured and/or maintained." We think a reasonable jury could find that the evidence that led Holmes's expert to conclude that he would have a "substantial possibility" of success gives rise to the "significant possibility" of success Holmes needs in order to recover for the negligent spoliation of his evidence. It follows that the district court erred in granting summary judgment in favor of Amerex on the negligent spoliation claim. It follows as well that the magistrate judges's decision to award Holmes only nominal damages on his breach of contract claim, upon the premise that his spoliation claim could not succeed, must be reconsidered in light of the ultimate resolution of the spoliation claim.

Turning to the promissory estoppel count, we affirm the judgment in favor of Amerex. The judge first found that Holmes unreasonably failed to inspect the car despite having had ample opportunity to do so. He then held that judgment for Amerex was appropriate because promissory estoppel "requires the promisee to have acted reasonably in justifiable reliance on the promise." Although Holmes urges us to reverse the judge's decision, he challenges neither step of this reasoning. Instead, he focuses upon evidence showing that he relied upon Amerex's representation that it would preserve the car and that he was injured when that representation proved false. That may be so, but it does nothing to undermine the magistrate's finding that he was unreasonably dilatory in inspecting the car. Therefore, we are constrained to approve the magistrate's denial of the claim based upon promissory estoppel.

In view of the answer given by the District of Columbia Court of Appeals to the questions of law we certified, we reverse the grant of summary judgment in favor of Amerex on the claim for negligent spoliation of evidence, vacate the award of nominal damages on the claim for breach of contract, and affirm the judgment of the district court on the claim based upon promissory estoppel. This matter is remanded to the district court for further proceedings consistent with this opinion.

NOTES

1. *Redundancy?* The court in *Goff v. Harold Ives Trucking Co., Inc.*, 27 S.W. 3d 387 (Ark. 2000), refused to recognize the tort of spoliation against the defendant motorist that was involved in an accident with the plaintiff, where the defendant lost or destroyed valuable information related to the accident:

> In declining to adopt an independent tort of spoliation, we further note that the recognition of the tort is not. . . . a "growing trend" in this country. The majority of jurisdictions which have considered it have either expressly rejected the cause of action or have declined to reach the question on the facts presented.
>
> . . .We join those jurisdictions that have expressly declined to recognize the tort of intentional spoliation of evidence. As discussed above, we believe that there are sufficient other avenues, short of creating a new cause of action, that serve to remedy the situation for a plaintiff. Most significant, an aggrieved party can request that a jury be instructed to draw a negative inference against the spoliator. Additionally. . . the plaintiff can ask for discovery sanctions or seek to have a criminal prosecution initiated against the party who destroyed relevant evidence. In short, we do not find it necessary to create a new tort out of whole cloth in order to provide a party with a remedy.

The court in *Smith v. Atkinson*, 771 So.2d 429 (Ala. 2000), said an action for negligent spoliation against a third party "can be stated under existing negligence law without creating a new tort." If the third party, with knowledge of pending or potential litigation by plaintiff against another, agrees to preserve evidence relating to that litigation but then loses or destroys the evidence, a rebuttable presumption arises "that but for the fact of the spoliation of evidence the plaintiff would have recovered in the pending or potential litigation; the [third party] must overcome that rebuttable presumption or else be liable for damages."

2. *More Spoliation.* In *Allstate Ins. Co. v. Sunbeam Corp.*, 53 F.3d 804 (7th Cir. 1995), the court held an insurer's subrogation claim was barred by spoliation of evidence. The insurer paid a claim for fire damage to the insured's house, and then brought a products liability claim against the manufacturer of a grill that allegedly caused the fire. The court dismissed the claim because of the insurer's disposal of parts of the grill that would have "shed light upon" whether there was "an alternative cause of the fire."

An employer may owe a duty to its employee to preserve evidence essential to the employee's claim against a third party. *Viviano v. CBS, Inc.*, 597 A.2d 543 (N.J. Super. 1991). *But see Wilson v. Beloit Corp.*, 921 F.2d 765 (8th Cir. 1990).

3. *Client Misconduct.* The court in *Adcock v. Brakegate, Ltd.*, 247 Ill.App.2d 824, 617 N.E.2d 885 (1993), held that a default judgment in favor of the plaintiff was not an excessive sanction where the defendant failed, on demand, to produce its former president and medical director as witnesses in asbestos litigation. Their testimony was sought to establish defendant's knowledge of the danger of the product. The court said the defendant's failure to produce the witnesses constituted a conspiracy to withhold information.

4. *Counsel Misconduct.* In *Chevron Chem. Co. v. Deloitte & Touche*, 501 N.W.2d 15 (Wis. 1993), the court entered a judgment notwithstanding the verdict in favor of a general creditor against an accounting firm on a claim of negligent misrepresentation. The judgment was entered as a sanction for continuing misconduct of the firm's counsel. The trial court had sanctioned the firm four times for discovery disputes. In addition, the firm had violated a sequestration order, had mischaracterized the content of exhibits, had misrepresented the availability of a witness, and had made improper comments in the presence of the jury. This conduct, the court said, violated the attorney's oath and court rules requiring candor toward the court and fairness to opposing counsel:

> There is a perception both inside and outside the legal community that civility, candor, and professionalism are on the decline in the legal profession and that unethical, win-at-all-costs, scorched-earth tactics are on the rise. The issue of the appropriateness of entry of judgment as a sanction after a jury has returned a verdict in an important one that is likely to recur. . . .
>
> A fine line may often divide proper advocacy from improper conduct. Yet, the conduct of Deloitte's counsel far exceeded the proper bounds of advocacy. True, this was a somewhat complex matter. However, Deloitte's counsel was not a novice making mistakes in good faith. Deloitte's counsel was an experienced litigator.
>
> Any of the incidents we have reviewed in and of themselves may not justify imposing judgment as a sanction. We find this holding professionally distasteful, yet necessary. We caution that attorneys should not view this holding as a sign to begin trying each other instead of their cases. Indeed, such conduct is itself improper if not justified by egregious circumstances such as those present in this case.

PROBLEM

Freddy underwent surgery to replace his ankle prosthesis. Freddy alleges that prior to the surgery he mentioned to the surgical team that there may have been a defect in the original prosthesis and that he was considering "seeing a lawyer about it." Following the operation hospital personnel destroyed the prosthesis. Subsequently, Freddy commenced a lawsuit against the manufacturer of the original prosthesis, but at trial his own expert witness testified that it was impossible to determine what caused the failure of the device without the original prosthesis and the court directed a verdict for the manufacturer. Plaintiff filed an action against the hospital where the prosthesis had been replaced seeking damages for the destruction of the device. Advise the hospital

E. PERSONAL INJURY DAMAGES

The kind of damages sustained sometimes dictates whether the victim has any remedy at all. A defamation victim may not have a legally enforceable claim against the defamer unless the victim has sustained actual damages. A victim who suffers mental anguish unaccompanied by physical injury or an "impact" may be deprived of a tort remedy against the inflicter of the anguish. The rule of law that precludes recovery of these kinds of damages may be phrased in terms of "limited duty," or no "legal" or "proximate" cause.

The amount of damages that may be recovered also has an enormous practical impact upon the process of tort law. If the victim has sustained little recoverable damages, it is unlikely that the claim will be pursued. Legal services are expensive, and lawyers ordinarily do not accept small-claim cases on a contingent fee basis. In such cases, the potential for dispute resolution offered by some non-traditional mechanisms should be examined.

There are three general categories of damages: nominal, compensatory and punitive. Nominal damages are a trivial amount ($1 is the sum frequently used) awarded when either the law recognizes a technical invasion of the plaintiff's rights but there is no economic harm, or plaintiff has sustained a real injury but the evidence fails to establish the amount. The role of nominal damages has declined, in some cases because the declaratory judgment has become a satisfactory substitute remedy. Compensatory damages are awarded to compensate the plaintiff for the harm he has sustained and established by the proof. The purpose of the award is to make the plaintiff "whole," *i.e.*, place him in the position he would have been in if he had not been the victim of the tort. Thus, when the tort causes personal injury, the victim may recover for his pain and suffering, his loss of earnings or earning capacity, and his medical expenses. (Of course he is not really made whole, since money can never be an adequate compensation for loss of sound body or health.) The growth of the third type of damages, punitive or exemplary, has contributed to the volatility of tort law in the second half of the twentieth century. The purpose of exemplary damages is to punish the wrongdoers and to deter them and others similarly situated from repetition of the proscribed conduct. However, the sheer size of some awards, the uncertainty of the criteria for their determination, the potential for repetitive recoveries in mass tort litigation, and the perceived impact of such awards upon American business, have generated many efforts to restrict or abolish punitive damages.

A particularly litigious area of damages today involves recovery for emotional distress. When emotional distress accompanies physical injury, it is part of the recovery for personal injury. Special problems arise, however, when the predominant or sole basis for recovery is for emotional distress.

WALTERS v. HITCHCOCK
237 Kan. 31, 697 P.2d 847 (1985)

McFarland, Justice.

This is a medical malpractice action wherein plaintiff Lillian K. Walters received a $2,000,000 damage award against defendant C. Thomas Hitchcock, M.D. The defendant physician appeals from the jury's verdict and certain pretrial and post-trial rulings of the district court.

The facts may be summarized as follows. In December 1979, a lump on the neck of Lillian Walters was discovered by her family physician. Mrs. Walters was, at the time, approximately 32 years of age, married, with four minor children. She was not employed outside the home. The family physician conducted a number of tests and advised her to consult with a surgeon. Mrs. Walters was seen by defendant Hitchcock, a surgeon, on January 7, 1980. As a result of the prior testing and his physical examination of her, Dr. Hitchcock recommended surgical removal of diseased areas of the thyroid gland. There were indications of a possibly malignant condition. Surgery was scheduled for January 22, 1980. Mrs. Walters was advised the operation was a relatively low risk procedure with an anticipated three-day hospital stay and a small residual scar.

The operation proceeded in what appeared at the time to be a routine manner. Specimens were sent to the pathology laboratory and no malignancy was detected. The patient was sutured and sent to the recovery room. One day later Mrs. Walters' condition rapidly deteriorated. Her head ballooned in size, she became blind and suffered extreme respiratory distress. She was taken to the intensive care unit where a breathing tube was inserted. Shortly thereafter, Dr. Hitchcock was advised by the hospital pathology department that a one inch by one and one-half inch piece of esophagus tissue was connected to the thyroid specimen sent to the laboratory during surgery. Mrs. Walters' wound was now badly infected. She was taken to surgery. Dr. Hitchcock reopened the wound and observed a significant hole in the left front portion of her esophagus. He concluded that repair was not possible and sewed the esophagus shut — thereby closing it permanently.

At this point feeding was possible only through a tube inserted directly into Mrs. Walters' stomach. She regained her vision. Numerous hospitalizations and surgical procedures followed. Ultimately, colon interposition surgery was performed which involved making a sort of bypass esophagus from a portion of Mrs. Walters' colon. Additional facts relative to Mrs. Walters' condition and the quality of her life will be set forth in the discussion of the issue relative to the amount of damages awarded herein.

Mrs. Walters brought this action against Dr. Hitchcock based upon negligence in cutting into the esophagus and in failing to make prompt repair thereof. She sought $4,000,000 in damages. Dr. Hitchcock denied negligence and blamed the injury to the esophagus on the abnormal physiology of Mrs. Walters. The jury awarded Mrs. Walters $2,000,000 in damages and Dr. Hitchcock appeals therefrom.

The first issue on appeal concerns alleged misconduct of plaintiff's counsel during closing argument. In his closing argument plaintiff's counsel stated: "Who would sell their esophagus for $4 million? I would not sell mine." Defendant contends this constitutes a prohibited "golden rule" argument. This term relates to arguments of counsel that jurors should place themselves in the position of the plaintiff. Such arguments are usually improper and may constitute reversible error.

Plaintiff argues the remarks were not asking the jurors to place themselves in plaintiff's shoes, and were merely hypothetical in nature.

The remarks actually span two categories. The comment commencing "Who would sell . . ." is, we believe, a fair argument relative to claimed damages and is not a "golden rule" argument. The comment that counsel would not sell his esophagus for that sum is testimonial in nature as it is a statement of counsel's personal opinion. This is an improper argument. Does this improper comment constitute reversible error? We believe not. To constitute reversible error there must be a likelihood that the improper remarks changed the result of the trial. We have examined the record and conclude that, in the totality of the circumstances, the improper comment constituted only harmless error.

Additionally, we note that counsel made a timely objection to the remarks and the objection was sustained. Counsel did not request a jury admonition and none was given. Further, the jury had been instructed:

> "The evidence you should consider consists only of the testimony of the witnesses and the exhibits which the Court has received.
>
> "Opening statements are made by the attorneys to acquaint you with the facts they expect to prove. Closing arguments, which you are about to hear, are made by the attorneys to discuss the facts and circumstances in this case, and should be confined to the evidence and to reasonable inferences to be drawn therefrom. *Neither opening statements nor closing arguments are evidence, and any statement or argument made by the attorneys which is not based on the evidence should be disregarded.*" (Emphasis supplied.)

We conclude this issue is without merit.

. . .For his final issue, defendant challenges the size of the verdict. In his brief defendant states:

> "In advancing this argument, the defendant is definitely aware of the long line of Kansas cases on the subject and the guidelines that have evolved in those cases. The defendant realizes that the trial court will not be reversed in an order denying new trial *unless* the amount of the verdict, in light of the evidence, shocks the conscience of the appellate court." (Citations omitted.)

Defendant, in support of his argument that the verdict was excessive, directs our attention to the following:

"1. Plaintiff's medical bills by the time of trial were approximately $59,000.

"2. There was no claim nor was the jury instructed with regard to lost wages or diminished future earning capacity as Mrs. Walters was not employed during the course of her 19-year marriage.

"3. The repair surgery and reconstruction by colon interposition were working properly at the time of trial, and no further surgery, with respect to the surgical complication that occurred during the thyroidectomy, was contemplated. . . . No further evidence was presented regarding future medical expenses."

The evidence herein bears out that medical science has done all that it can do to alleviate plaintiff's condition and no further surgery is contemplated, although the same is not ruled out. This does not mean the damage done to Mrs. Walters has been undone and that she has been restored to her previous condition. It simply means her condition cannot be helped by further surgery or treatment. The substitute esophagus fashioned from a part of Mrs. Walters' colon is, apparently, functioning as well as can be expected but that level of function is a source of permanent problems for Mrs. Walters. When she swallows, food does not automatically go to her stomach. It piles up in grotesque bulges in her throat and upper chest. It is necessary for her to manually massage the bulges downward to force the food to her stomach. The process is physically painful. As there is no valve to keep the contents of her stomach from traveling back up the makeshift esophagus, she cannot lie flat and must remain in a position where gravity will keep the contents of her stomach in place. Her condition is embarrassing, distasteful to persons around her, and a major obstacle to leading a normal life. She has serious ongoing digestive problems. At the time of trial her life expectancy was 41.9 years. The years between Mrs. Walters' injury and attainment of her present level of functioning were a nightmare of pain, disability, hospitalizations and surgical procedures. She has severe disfiguring scars on her neck and torso. Many activities, such as eating and sitting, continue to be painful.

After having reviewed the record, we conclude our collective consciences are not shocked by the size of the verdict herein.

[Affirmed.]

NOTES

1. *Pain and Suffering.* What is a "fair" award for pain and suffering caused by a broken arm? $100,000? $1,000,000? Can you fashion an objective standard? Should the jury be instructed to award the amount of money it would pay to avoid the pain and suffering? The amount it would accept to endure the same pain and suffering? Is that an objective standard? This "Golden Rule" argument usually is not permitted. *See, e.g.,* D. DOBBS, REMEDIES, § 8.1, at 545; *Henker v. Preybylowski,* 216 N.J. Super. 513, 524 A.2d 455 (**1987**). Should the lack of an objective standard operate to deny the plaintiff **any** recovery

for his pain and suffering? Are you really compensating the plaintiff for something he has lost because of the tort? Given the lack of an objective standard for determining such damages, why should we impose this burden upon the tortfeasor? According to Judge Posner:

> We disagree with those students of tort law who believe that pain and suffering are not real costs and should not be allowable items of damages in a tort suit. No one likes pain and suffering and most people would pay a good deal of money to be free from them. If they were not recoverable in damages, the cost of negligence would be less to the tort-feasor and there would be more negligence, more accidents, more pain and suffering, and hence higher social costs.

Kwasny v. United States, 823 F.2d 194, 197 (7th Cir. 1987).

2. *What Is Fair?* The victim who sustains personal injury is entitled to an award to fairly compensate him for his pain and suffering. As one court observed, "[t]here is no exact yardstick by which pain and suffering can be measured and the various factors involved are not capable of proof in dollars. For this reason, the only standard for evaluation is such amount as twelve reasonable persons estimate to be fair compensation when that amount appears to be in harmony with the evidence and arrived at without passion or prejudice." *Tucker v. Lower,* 200 Kan. 1, 434 P.2d 320, 327 (1967).

3. *Division of Damages.* Where the plaintiff seeks recovery for damages caused by multiple tortfeasors in successive accidents, the burden of apportioning damages between or among the defendants rests on the plaintiff, the court said in *Goodman v. Fairlawn Garden Ass'n., Inc.*, 601 A.2d 766 (N.J. Super. 1992). It is only when the defendants' negligence concurrently causes the plaintiff's injuries that the burden of apportionment shifts to the defendants, the court said.

But in *Smith v. Pulcinella,* 656 A.2d 494 (Pa. Super. 1995), the court said that the burden of apportionment rests on the defendants where successive injuries are involved. The plaintiff Smith's car was tortiously hit in the rear by a car driven by defendant Pulcinella, and about 15 minutes later plaintiff's car was tortiously struck by another driver, with whom plaintiff settled.

In a suit by Smith against Pulcinella, the defendant claimed that Smith had the burden of apportioning damages between the two tortfeasors. Plaintiff's treating physician testified that he could not differentiate between injuries to plaintiff's back caused by the first collision and those caused by the second collision. The trial court said Pulcinella could be found liable for plaintiff's entire damages. In affirming, the appellate court said:

> Viewing the evidence as we must, in the light most favorable to Smith as the verdict winner, we find that the facts support the trial court's determination that Smith's injuries were not capable of apportionment as between Pulcinella and the driver of the second vehicle. Here, the duty of care owed by Pulcinella and the second driver to the other motorist, Smith, was identical and both were negligent in an identical fashion and at almost the same time and place in failing to control their cars in the rainy weather conditions. Additionally, the harm caused to Smith as a result of the drivers' combined negligence

was single and indivisible, the plaintiff's medical expert having testified that he was unable to differentiate between the injuries Smith sustained in the first impact and those caused by the second impact. Finally, but for Pulcinella's negligence, Smith would not have been along the shoulder of the road in a location where she was susceptible to being struck a second time.

The court in *Lovely v. Allstate Ins. Co.*, 658 A.2d 1091 (Me. 1995), reached a similar result to that in *Smith v. Pulcinella*.

Is there any reason to treat concurrently and successively caused indivisible injuries differently? Should the result turn on the length of time between successive injuries?

Many jurisdictions have abolished joint liability, and require liability to be divided on the basis of fault. *See, e.g., McIntyre v. Balentine*, 833 S.W.2d 52 (Tenn. 1992). Presumably the burden of division here rests on the defendant. Should the factfinder make two divisions, one on the basis of cause and the other on fault? Assuming causation is indivisible, should a division by fault nevertheless be made?

McDOUGALD v. GARBER
73 N.Y.2d 246, 538 N.Y.S.2d 937, 536 N.E.2d 372 (1989)

WACHTLER, CHIEF JUDGE.

This appeal raises fundamental questions about the nature and role of nonpecuniary damages in personal injury litigation. By nonpecuniary damages, we mean those damages awarded to compensate an injured person for the physical and emotional consequences of the injury, such as pain and suffering and the loss of the ability to engage in certain activities. Pecuniary damages, on the other hand, compensate the victim for the economic consequences of the injury, such as medical expenses, lost earnings and the cost of custodial care.

The specific questions raised here deal with the assessment of nonpecuniary damages and are (1) whether some degree of cognitive awareness is a prerequisite to recovery for loss of enjoyment of life and (2) whether a jury should be instructed to consider and award damages for loss of enjoyment of life separately from damages for pain and suffering. We answer the first question in the affirmative and the second question in the negative.

On September 7, 1978, plaintiff Emma McDougald, then 31 years old, underwent a Caesarian section and tubal ligation at New York Infirmary. Defendant Garber performed the surgery; defendants Armengol and Kulkarni provided anesthesia. During the surgery, Mrs. McDougald suffered oxygen deprivation which resulted in severe brain damage and left her in a permanent comatose condition. This action was brought by Mrs. McDougald and her husband, suing derivatively, alleging that the injuries were caused by the defendants' acts of malpractice.

. . . At trial, defendants sought to show that Mrs. McDougald's injuries were so severe that she was incapable of either experiencing pain or appreciating her condition. Plaintiffs, on the other hand, introduced proof that Mrs.

McDougald responded to certain stimuli to a sufficient extent to indicate that she was aware of her circumstances. Thus, the extent of Mrs. McDougald's cognitive abilities, if any, was sharply disputed.

The parties and the trial court agreed that Mrs. McDougald could not recover for pain and suffering unless she were conscious of the pain. Defendants maintained that such consciousness was also required to support an award for loss of enjoyment of life. The court, however, accepted plaintiffs' view that loss of enjoyment of life was compensable without regard to whether the plaintiff was aware of the loss. Accordingly, because the level of Mrs. McDougald's cognitive abilities was in dispute, the court instructed the jury to consider loss of enjoyment of life as an element of nonpecuniary damages separate from pain and suffering.

. . . We conclude that the court erred, both in instructing the jury that Mrs. McDougald's awareness was irrelevant to their consideration of damages for loss of enjoyment of life and in directing the jury to consider that aspect of damages separately from pain and suffering.

We begin with the familiar proposition that an award of damages to a person injured by the negligence of another is to compensate the victim, not to punish the wrongdoer. To be sure, placing the burden of compensation on the negligent party also serves as a deterrent, but purely punitive damages — that is, those which have no compensatory purpose — are prohibited unless the harmful conduct is intentional, malicious, outrageous, or otherwise aggravated beyond mere negligence.

Damages for nonpecuniary losses are, of course, among those that can be awarded as compensation to the victim. This aspect of damages, however, stands on less certain ground than does an award for pecuniary damages. An economic loss can be compensated in kind by an economic gain; but recovery for noneconomic losses such as pain and suffering and loss of enjoyment of life rests on "the legal fiction that money damages can compensate for a victim's injury" (*Howard v. Lecher,* 42 N.Y.2d 109, 111, 397 N.Y.S.2d 363, 366 N.E.2d 64 (1977)). We accept this fiction, knowing that although money will neither ease the pain nor restore the victim's abilities, this device is as close as the law can come in its effort to right the wrong. We have no hope of evaluating what has been lost, but a monetary award may provide a measure of solace for the condition created.

Our willingness to indulge this fiction comes to an end, however, when it ceases to serve the compensatory goals of tort recovery. When that limit is met, further indulgence can only result in assessing damages that are punitive. The question posed by this case, then, is whether an award of damages for loss of enjoyment of life to a person whose injuries preclude any awareness of the loss serves a compensatory purpose. We conclude that it does not.

Simply put, an award of money damages in such circumstances has no meaning or utility to the injured person. An award for the loss of enjoyment of life "cannot provide [such a victim] with any consolation or ease any burden resting on him. . . . He cannot spend it upon necessities or pleasures. He cannot experience the pleasure of giving it away" (*Flannery v. United States,*

718 F.2d 108, 111 (1983), *cert. denied,* 467 U.S. 1226, 81 L. Ed. 2d 874, 1045 S. Ct. 2679 (1984)).

We recognize that, as the trial court noted, requiring some cognitive awareness as a prerequisite to recovery for loss of enjoyment of life will result in some cases "in the paradoxical situation that the greater the degree of brain injury inflicted by a negligent defendant, the smaller the award the plaintiff can recover in general damages" (*McDougald v. Garber,* 132 Misc. 2d 457, 460, 504 N.Y.S.2d 383 (1986)). The force of this argument, however — the temptation to achieve a balance between injury and damages — has nothing to do with meaningful compensation for the victim. Instead, the temptation is rooted in a desire to punish the defendant in proportion to the harm inflicted. However relevant such retributive symmetry may be in the criminal law, it has no place in the law of civil damages, at least in the absence of culpability beyond mere negligence.

Accordingly, we conclude that cognitive awareness is a prerequisite to recovery for loss of enjoyment of life. We do not go so far, however, as to require the fact finder to sort out varying degrees of cognition and determine at what level a particular deprivation can be fully appreciated. With respect to pain and suffering, the trial court charged simply that there must be "some level of awareness" in order for plaintiff to recover. We think that this is an appropriate standard for all aspects of nonpecuniary loss. No doubt the standard ignores analytically relevant levels of cognition, but we resist the desire for analytical purity in favor of simplicity. A more complex instruction might give the appearance of greater precision but, given the limits of our understanding of the human mind, it would in reality lead only to greater speculation.

We turn next to the question whether loss of enjoyment of life should be considered a category of damages separate from pain and suffering.

There is no dispute here that the fact finder may, in assessing nonpecuniary damages, consider the effect of the injuries on the plaintiff's capacity to lead a normal life. Traditionally, in this State and elsewhere, this aspect of suffering has not been treated as a separate category of damages; instead, the plaintiff's inability to enjoy life to its fullest has been considered one type of suffering to be factored into a general award for nonpecuniary damages, commonly known as pain and suffering.

Recently, however, there has been an attempt to segregate the suffering associated with physical pain from the mental anguish that stems from the inability to engage in certain activities, and to have juries provide a separate award for each.

Some courts have resisted the effort, primarily on the ground that duplicative and therefore excessive awards would result. Other courts have allowed separate awards, noting that the types of suffering involved are analytically distinguishable. Still other courts have questioned the propriety of the practice but held that, in the particular case, separate awards did not constitute reversible error.

. . . We do not dispute that distinctions can be found or created between the concepts of pain and suffering and loss of enjoyment of life. If the term "suffering" is limited to the emotional response to the sensation of pain, then the emotional response caused by the limitation of life's activities may be considered qualitatively different. But suffering need not be so limited — it can easily encompass the frustration and anguish caused by the inability to participate in activities that once brought pleasure. Traditionally, by treating loss of enjoyment of life as a permissible factor in assessing pain and suffering, courts have given the term this broad meaning. If we are to depart from this traditional approach and approve a separate award for loss of enjoyment of life, it must be on the basis that such an approach will yield a more accurate evaluation of the compensation due to the plaintiff. We have no doubt that, in general, the total award for nonpecuniary damages would increase if we adopted the rule. That separate awards are advocated by plaintiffs and resisted by defendants is sufficient evidence that larger awards are at stake here. But a larger award does not by itself indicate that the goal of compensation has been better served.

The advocates of separate awards contend that because pain and suffering and loss of enjoyment of life can be distinguished, they must be treated separately if the plaintiff is to be compensated fully for each distinct injury suffered. We disagree. Such an analytical approach may have its place when the subject is pecuniary damages, which can be calculated with some precision. But the estimation of nonpecuniary damages is not amenable to such analytical precision and may, in fact, suffer from its application. Translating human suffering into dollars and cents involves no mathematical formula; it rests, as we have said, on a legal fiction. The figure that emerges is unavoidably distorted by the translation. Application of this murky process to the component parts of nonpecuniary injuries (however analytically distinguishable they may be) cannot make it more accurate. If anything, the distortion will be amplified by repetition.

Thus, we are not persuaded that any salutary purpose would be served by having the jury make separate awards for pain and suffering and loss of enjoyment of life. We are confident, furthermore, that the trial advocate's art is a sufficient guarantee that none of the plaintiff's losses will be ignored by the jury.

The errors in the instructions given to the jury require a new trial on the issue of nonpecuniary damages to be awarded to plaintiff Emma McDougald. Defendants' remaining contentions are either without merit, beyond the scope of our review or are rendered academic by our disposition of the case.

Accordingly, the order of the Appellate Division, insofar as appealed from, should be modified, with costs to defendants, by granting a new trial on the issue of nonpecuniary damages of plaintiff Emma McDougald, and as so modified, affirmed.

TITONE, JUDGE, dissenting.

The majority's holding represents a compromise position that neither comports with the fundamental principles of tort compensation nor furnishes a satisfactory, logically consistent framework for compensating nonpecuniary loss. Because I conclude that loss of enjoyment of life is an objective damage item, conceptually distinct from conscious pain and suffering, I can find no fault with the trial court's instruction authorizing separate awards and permitting an award for "loss of enjoyment of life" even in the absence of any awareness of that loss on the part of the injured plaintiff. Accordingly, I dissent.

. . . The capacity to enjoy life — by watching one's children grow, participating in recreational activities, and drinking in the many other pleasures that life has to offer — is unquestionably an attribute of an ordinary healthy individual. The loss of that capacity as a result of another's negligent act is at least as serious an impairment as the permanent destruction of a physical function, which has always been treated as a compensable item under traditional tort principles. Indeed, I can imagine no physical loss that is more central to the quality of a tort victim's continuing life than the destruction of the capacity to enjoy that life to the fullest.

Unquestionably, recovery of a damage item such as "pain and suffering" requires a showing of some degree of cognitive capacity. Such a requirement exists for the simple reason that pain and suffering are wholly subjective concepts and cannot exist separate and apart from the human consciousness that experiences them. In contrast, the destruction of an individual's capacity to enjoy life as a result of a crippling injury is an objective fact that does not differ in principle from the permanent loss of an eye or limb. As in the case of a lost limb, an essential characteristic of a healthy human life has been wrongfully taken, and, consequently, the injured party is entitled to a monetary award as a substitute, if, as the majority asserts, the goal of tort compensation is "to restore the injured party, to the extent possible, to the position that would have been occupied had the wrong not occurred."

Significantly, this equation does not suggest a need to establish the injured's awareness of the loss. The victim's ability to comprehend the degree to which his or her life has been impaired is irrelevant, since, unlike "conscious pain and suffering," the impairment exists independent of the victim's ability to apprehend it. Indeed, the majority reaches the conclusion that a degree of awareness must be shown only after injecting a new element into the equation. Under the majority's formulation, the victim must be aware of the loss because, in addition to being compensatory, the award must have "meaning or utility to the injured person." This additional requirement, however, has no real foundation in law or logic. "Meaning" and "utility" are subjective value judgments that have no place in the law of tort recovery, where the primary goal is to find ways of quantifying, to the extent possible, the worth of various forms of human tragedy.

Moreover, the compensatory nature of a monetary award for loss of enjoyment of life is not altered or rendered punitive by the fact that the unaware injured plaintiff cannot experience the pleasure of having it. The fundamental distinction between punitive and compensatory damages is that the former exceed the amount necessary to replace what the plaintiff lost.

. . . Having concluded that the injured plaintiff's awareness should not be necessary precondition to recovery for loss of enjoyment of life, I also have no difficulty going on to conclude that loss of enjoyment of life is a distinct damage item which is recoverable separate and apart from the award for conscious pain and suffering. The majority has rejected separate recovery, in part because it apparently perceives some overlap between the two damage categories and in part because it believes that the goal of enhancing the precision of jury awards for nonpecuniary loss would not be advanced. However, the overlap the majority perceives exists only if one assumes, as the majority evidently has, that the "loss of enjoyment" category of damages is designed to compensate only for *"the emotional response* caused by the limitation of life's activities" and *"the frustration and anguish caused by* the inability to participate in activities that once brought pleasure" (emphasis added), both of which are highly *subjective* concepts.

In fact, while "pain and suffering compensates the victim for the physical and mental discomfort caused by the injury; . . . loss of enjoyment of life compensates the victim for the limitations on the person's life created by the injury," a distinctly objective loss (*Thompson v. National R.R. Passenger Corp.,* [621 F.2d 814, 824 (6th Cir.), *cert. denied,* 449 U.S. 1035, 101 S. Ct. 611, 66 L. Ed. 2d 497 (1980)]. In other words, while the victim's "emotional response" and "frustration and anguish" are elements of the award for pain and suffering, the "limitation of life's activities" and the "inability to participate in activities" that the majority identifies are recoverable under the "loss of enjoyment of life" rubric. Thus, there is no real overlap, and no real basis for concern about potentially duplicative awards where, as here, there is a properly instructed jury.

NOTES

1. *The Reformists' Bête Noire.* Recovery of damages for pain and suffering has been the subject of much criticism. *See, e.g.,* Seavey, *Torts and Atoms,* 46 CALIF. L. REV. 3 (1958); Plant, *Damages for Pain and Suffering,* 19 OHIO ST. L.J. 200 (1958); Peck, *Compensation for Pain: A Reappraisal in Light of New Medical Evidence,* 72 MICH. L. REV. 1355 (1974). The defenders of the pain and suffering award point out that it is a balm for the outrage which the victim suffers from the injury, and helps to compensate him for the attorney's fees he must expend and which he usually cannot recover from the defendant. Professor Jeffrey O'Connell has suggested a trade-off. *See* O'Connell, *A Proposal to Abolish Defendants' Payment for Pain and Suffering in Return for Payment of Claimants' Attorneys' Fees,* 1981 U. ILL. L. REV. 333 (1981).

2. *A Reasonable Tradeoff?* The threshold "No-Fault" insurance system bars recovery of damages for pain and suffering unless the victim's injury exceeds a "threshold," which may be determined by the type of injury or by the amount of medical or other special damages the victim sustains.

3. *Disfigurement, Pain and Suffering, and Loss of Enjoyment.* Tort victim, a beautiful woman or handsome man, is left with a disfiguring facial scar. Victim is entitled to an award of damages for the scar (disfigurement). *See* Annot., 88 A.L.R.3d 117 (1969). Undoubtedly, the victim will suffer mental anguish because of the scar. Is the victim entitled to separate awards for the disfigurement and for the mental anguish caused by the disfigurement? *See Arlan v. Cervini,* 478 A.2d 976 (R.I. 1984). Given society's preoccupation with physical good looks, is the victim likely also to suffer a reduction in social

opportunities? Is this "loss of enjoyment of life" a compensable item of damages, or is it part of the victim's mental pain and suffering? What practical difference does it make? Some courts permit loss of enjoyment of life as an element of damages separate from, and in addition to, mental pain and suffering, and others do not.

The court in *Overstreet v Shoney's, Inc.*, 4 S.W. 3d 694 (Tenn. App. 1999), allowed recovery for pain and suffering, disfigurement, and loss of enjoyment of life as separate items of damages.

4. *Hedonic Damages.* Some courts allow recovery for loss of enjoyment of life, under the name of hedonic damages, as a separate item of recovery. *Sena v. New Mexico State Police*, 892 P.2d 604 (N.M. App. 1995).According to THE NAT. L.J. A15 (9 Apr. 2001), loss of enjoyment, or hedonic, damages are recoverable in wrongful death suits only in Conn., Ga., N.M., and Minn., and in federal civil rights suits under 42 U.S.C. § 1983.

Some courts reject expert evidence regarding hedonic damages that are based on economic studies of what the average person would be willing to pay for the satisfaction or pleasure of living. *Montalvo v. Lapez*, 77 Haw. 282, 884 P.2d 345 (1994). As the court said in *Ayers v. Robinson*, 887 F. Supp. 1049 (N.D. Ill. 1995), in rejecting such evidence, "the willingness-to-pay model estimates the value of a statistical life — a nameless, faceless member of society," while the jury's task is to "value the life of a specific individual."

5. *A Statistical Approach to Lost Earning Capacity.* A statute may prescribe the use of certain work life or life expectancy tables. Courts usually take judicial notice of mortality tables in general use in the insurance industry. Annot., 50 A.L.R.2d 419 (1986). The parties may introduce evidence as to normal work life or life expectancy of the particular plaintiff in the particular industry, and may rebut with evidence that the plaintiff had a different life expectancy. *See, e.g., Christiansen v. Hollings*, 44 Cal. App. 2d 332, 112 P.2d 723 (1941).

6. *Discounting.* Damages for future loss of earnings are reduced to present value because the plaintiff is awarded in a lump sum at time of trial the earnings which he would have received later. Present value is determined by calculating how much money the plaintiff would need presently in order to enable her to invest at interest so as to recover her full value of expectable damages when they occur at a later date. The interest-rate discount is usually reduced to take account of expected inflation. *See Jones & Laughlin Steel Corp. v. Pfeifer*, 462 U.S. 523, 103 S. Ct. 2541, 76 L. Ed. 2d 768 (1983). Some treat the interest rate as being completely offset by inflation, so that no reduction to present value need be made. *See Kaczkouski v. Bolubasz*, 491 Pa. 561, 421 A.2d 1027 (1980).

Should damages for future pain and suffering be discounted to present value? What argument can you make that they should not? The courts are in disagreement on this issue. *Compare Metz v. United Technologies Corp.*, 754 F.2d 63 (2d Cir. 1985), and *Abbott v. Northwestern Bell Tel. Co.*, 197 Neb. 11, 246 N.W.2d 647 (1976), with *Taylor v. Denver & R.G.W.R. Co.*, 438 F.2d 351 (10th Cir. 1971). See Annot., 60 A.L.R.2d 1347 (1958).

7. *Loss of Earning Capacity but an Absence of Employment.* Because this award is for loss of earning capacity, the victim need not be employed at the

time of the accident. Thus, a child victim may be entitled to recover loss of earning capacity on the basis of the minimum wage. Greater recovery may be too speculative, although the jury may be given wide discretion. Should evidence of a child victim's intelligence, or skill, or future plans, be relevant? See Markel, *Children Take Their Lumps — The Sorry State of Children's Tort Recovery,* 12 U.C. DAVIS L. REV. 797 (1979); Trial, Feb. 1986, p. 37. *See also Lesniak v. County of Bergen,* 117 N.J. 12, 563 A.2d 795 (1989).

The homemaker victim presents a similar problem. Some courts may permit an award for loss of earning capacity. *Nelson v. Patrick,* 73 N.C. App. 1, 326 S.E.2d 45 (1985). If not, an award for value of the homemaker's household services would be appropriate. *See, e.g., De Long v. County of Erie,* 60 N.Y.2d 296, 469 N.Y.S.2d 611, 457 N.E.2d 717 (1983). *See also* Comment, *Tort Damages for the Injured Homemaker,* 50 U. COLO. L. REV. 59 (1978); Johnson, *Calculating the Economic Value of Lost Homemaker Services in Wrongful Death/Personal Injury Litigation,* 29 TRIAL LAW GUIDE 136 (1985).

8. *Lost Earnings and Expert Testimony.* In establishing the value of the lost earning capacity, the plaintiff ordinarily will present the testimony of an expert witness (usually an economist) who will give his opinion as to future inflation and interest rates, and also will make the calculations to assist the jury in reducing the award to present value. *See, e.g.,* Annot., 23 A.L.R.3d 1189 (1990 and current Supp.); Fisher, *Use of an Economist to Prove Future Economic Losses,* 18 S. TEX. L.J. 403 (1977).

9. *Tax and Damage Awards.* In *Norfolk & W.R.R. v. Liepelt,* 444 U.S. 490 (1980), the Court held that in a case arising under the Federal Employers' Liability Act, (1) evidence of the income taxes payable on the victim's past and estimated future earnings is relevant to a determination of such earnings, and (2) the judge should instruct the jury that an award of personal injury damages is not subject to income taxation. The majority of the state courts do not require the judge to instruct the jury that the award is not subject to federal income tax. *See, e.g., Griffin v. General Motors Corp.,* 380 Mass. 362, 403 N.E.2d 402 (1980); *Tennis v. General Motors Corp.,* 625 S.W.2d 218 (Mo. App. 1981). *Liepelt* has not caused a wholesale abandonment of that position. *Barnette v. Doyle,* 622 P.2d 1349 (Wyo. 1981); *Klawonn v. Mitchell,* 105 Ill. 2d 450, 475 N.E.2d 857, 86 Ill. Dec. 478 (1985).

The majority rule among the state courts is that income taxes should not be taken into consideration in making an award for loss of earning capacity. *See, e.g., Cates v. Brown,* 278 Ark. 242, 645 S.W.2d 658 (1983); *Dinger v. Department of Natural Resources,* 147 Mich. App. 164, 383 N.W.2d 606 (1985); *Pennsylvania Dep't of Transp. v. Phillips,* 488 A.2d 77 (Pa. 1985); *compare Smith v. Industrial Constrs., Inc.,* 783 F.2d 1249 (5th Cir. 1986).

10. *Future Medical Expenses.* The defendant in *Marchetti v. Ramirez,* 673 A.2d 567 (Conn. App. 1996), objected to submission of the issue of plaintiff's future medical expenses to the jury, in the absence of evidence that it was "reasonably probable" that such expenses would be incurred. In overruling the objection, the court said:

> It is not speculation or conjecture to calculate future medical expenses based upon the history of medical expenses that have

accrued as of the trial date, particularly when there is also a degree of medical certainty that future medical expenses will be necessary. . . . Future medical expenses do not require the same degree of certainty as past medical expenses. . . . Where the doctor testifies that the injured party *might* need future treatment and the injured party testifies he still suffers pain, that testimony is sufficient for consideration of the element of future medical expense. Here, there was testimony that the plaintiff might incur future medical expenses, and the plaintiff testified that he still suffers pain. Therefore, the jury could properly award future medical damages.

11. *Taxability of the Contingent Fee*. The IRS, Tax Court and Circuit Courts have tended to disagree over whether plaintiff's portion of a judgment or settlement that is payable to an attorney pursuant to a contingent fee is part of the plaintiff's gross income. In *Srivastava v. Commissioner*, 220 F.3d 353 (5th Cir. 2000), the court answered in the negative but not before commenting: "Were we ruling on a *tabula rasa*, we might be inclined to include contingent fees in gross income. Principles of tax neutrality, if nothing else, dictate that result, for when a taxpayer recovers from a favorable judgment or litigation settlement, and compensates his attorney on a non-contingent basis, the full amount of the recovery may be treated as gross income. . . . There is no apparent reason to treat contingent fees differently or to believe that Congress intended to subsidize contingent fee agreements in such a fashion."

12. *Reasonable Medical Expenses*. The personal injury victim may recover the reasonable value of any medical expenses incurred as a result of the injury. This usually includes physician, hospital and medical services (tests and x-rays) charges, but also may include travel expenses to obtain medical treatment, and any special equipment needed in connection with the treatment. A distinction must be made between past medical expenses (those incurred prior to trial) and future medical expenses. Courts require proof that past medical expenses were incurred and were reasonable. This may require expert medical testimony. Is this a wise rule, particularly where the medical expenses are minimal? Assume that a physician unnecessarily treats an accident victim. Upon whom should the risk fall? *See, e.g., Hillebrandt v. Holsum Bakeries, Inc.*, 267 So. 2d 608 (La. App. 1972); *Whitaker v. Kruse*, 495 N.E.2d 223 (Ind. App. 1986). Should a patient be permitted to recover that portion of a hospital bill which reflects the cost of meals? What arguments can you make in support of such recovery? The trier of fact may make an award for future medical expenses, if there is sufficient proof of the necessity and reasonable value of such expenses. An award for future medical expenses should be discounted to present value.

13. *Post-Accident Occurrences*. What if the victim dies or suffers a disabling injury from an unrelated source before the trial? Or the spouse of the wrongful death victim remarries? Should damages be calculated as of the date of the accident, without consideration of post-accident occurrences which might reduce recovery? Some courts permit the trier of fact to consider post-accident death from an unrelated source in determining damages. *Jurney v. Lubeznik*, 72 Ill. App. 2d 117, 218 N.E.2d 799 (1966); *Victorson v. Milwaukee & Suburban Transp. Co.*, 70 Wis. 2d 336, 234 N.W.2d 332 (1975). *Compare Buchalski v.*

Universal Marine Corp., 393 F. Supp. 246 (W.D. Wash. 1975) (plaintiff longshoreman's work disability claim not reduced by subsequent non-work-related heart attack that caused same disability). Most courts do not permit consideration of the surviving spouse's remarriage in a wrongful death claim. *See* Annot., 88 A.L.R.3d 926 (1978). Is this consistent with the rule permitting consideration of post-accident promotion possibilities? Of inflationary increases in future earnings?

14. *Medical Monitoring.* In *Hansen v. Mountain Fuel Supply Co.*, 858 P.2d 970 (Utah 1993), the plaintiff renovation workers sought recovery against the owner of an office building for future medical expenses expected to be incurred in monitoring their risk of contracting disease from exposure to asbestos while performing renovation work on the defendant's building. To recover such damages, the court said, a plaintiff must prove:

(1) exposure

(2) to a toxic substance,

(3) which exposure was caused by the defendant's negligence,

(4) resulting in an increased risk

(5) of a serious disease, illness, or injury

(6) for which a medical test for early detection exists

(7) and for which early detection is beneficial, meaning that a treatment exists that can alter the course of the illness,

(8) and which test has been prescribed by a qualified physician according to contemporary scientific principles.

The court discussed the policy reasons for allowing such recovery:

Allowing recovery for such expenses avoids the potential injustice of forcing an economically disadvantaged person to pay for expensive diagnostic examinations necessitated by another's negligence. Indeed, in many cases a person will not be able to afford such tests, and refusing to allow medical monitoring damages would in effect deny him or her access to potentially life-saving treatment. It also affords toxic-tort victims, for whom other sorts of recovery may prove difficult, immediate compensation for medical monitoring needed as a result of exposure. Additionally, it furthers the deterrent function of the tort system by compelling those who expose others to toxic substances to minimize risks and costs of exposure. Allowing such recovery is also in harmony with the important public health interest in fostering access to medical testing for individuals whose exposure to toxic chemicals creates an enhanced risk of disease.

Despite these policy arguments, some contend that medical monitoring should be allowed only for those able to show actual, present, physical injury. Because of the latent nature of most diseases resulting from exposure to toxic substances, however, most toxic-tort plaintiffs cannot establish an immediate physical injury of the type contemplated in traditional tort actions. Instead, the physical injury resulting from exposure to toxic substances usually manifests itself years after exposure. Although the physical manifestations of an injury may not appear for years, the reality is that many of those exposed have suffered some legal detriment; the exposure itself and the concomitant need for medical testing constitute the injury.

See also *Potter v. Firestone Tire & Rubber Co.*, 25 Cal. Rptr. 2d 550, 863 P.2d 795 (1993) (*Potter* is further discussed in the next section). Landowners who lived next to a landfill brought suit to recover, *inter alia*, for medical monitoring expenses from a tire manufacturer whose hazardous wastes were disposed of at the landfill. In determining the reasonableness and necessity of monitoring, the court said:

> The following factors are relevant: (1) the significance and extent of the plaintiff's exposure to chemicals; (2) the toxicity of the chemicals; (3) the relative increase in the chance of onset of disease in the exposed plaintiff as a result of the exposure, when compared to (a) the plaintiff's chances of developing the disease had he or she not been exposed, and (b) the chances of the members of the public at large developing the disease; (4) the seriousness of the disease for which the plaintiff is at risk; and (5) the clinical value of early detection and diagnosis. Under this holding, it is for the trier of fact to decide, on the basis of competent medical testimony, whether and to what extent the particular plaintiff's exposure to toxic chemicals in a given situation justifies future periodic medical monitoring.
>
> We are confident that our holding will not, as Firestone and *amici curiae* warn, open the floodgates of litigation. The five factors provide substantial evidentiary burdens for toxic exposure plaintiffs and do not, as Firestone insists, allow medical monitoring damages to be based solely upon a showing of an increased but unquantified risk resulting from exposure to toxic chemicals. Moreover, toxic exposure plaintiffs may recover only if the evidence establishes the necessity, as a direct consequence of the exposure in issue, for specific monitoring beyond that which an individual should pursue as a matter of general good sense and foresight. Thus there can be no recovery for preventative medical care and checkups to which members of the public at large should prudently submit. Finally, contrary to the protestations of Firestone and *amici curiae*, medical monitoring costs are not speculative because they are based upon the specific dollar costs of reasonable and necessary periodic examinations.

F. MENTAL DISTRESS

PROBLEM

Plaintiff ate seafood at defendant's restaurant and, as a result, became sick and vomited. After this experience she would no longer eat any kind of seafood, which had previously been her favorite type of food. What damages, if any, can she and her husband recover from the restaurant?

POTTER v. FIRESTONE TIRE & RUBBER CO.
6 Cal. 4th 965, 25 Cal. Rptr. 2d 550, 863 P.2d 795 (1993)

BAXTER, JUSTICE.

. . . This is a toxic exposure case brought by four landowners living adjacent to a landfill. As a result of defendant Firestone's practice of disposing of its toxic wastes at the landfill, the landowners were subjected to prolonged exposure to certain carcinogens. While none of the landowners currently suffers from any cancerous or precancerous condition, each faces an enhanced but unquantified risk of developing cancer in the future due to the exposure.. . .

From 1963 until 1980, Firestone operated a tire manufacturing plant near Salinas. In 1967, Firestone contracted with Salinas Disposal Service and Rural Disposal (hereafter SDS), two refuse collection companies operating the Crazy Horse landfill (hereafter Crazy Horse), for disposal of its industrial waste. Firestone agreed to deposit its waste in dumpsters provided by SDS located at the plant site. SDS agreed to haul the waste to Crazy Horse and deposit it there.

Crazy Horse, a class II sanitary landfill owned by the City of Salinas, covers approximately 125 acres suitable for the disposal of household and commercial solid waste. Unlike dump sites that are classified class I, class II landfills such as Crazy Horse prohibit toxic substances and liquids because of the danger that they will leach into the groundwater and cause contamination.

At the outset of their contractual relationship, SDS informed Firestone that no solvents, cleaning fluids, oils or liquids were permitted at Crazy Horse. Firestone provided assurances that these types of waste would not be sent to the landfill.

Notwithstanding its assurances, Firestone sent large quantities of liquid waste to Crazy Horse, including banbury drippings (a by-product of the tire manufacturing process) containing a combination of semiliquid toxic chemicals. Firestone also sent liquid waste oils, liquid tread end cements, and solvents to the landfill.

In May 1977, Firestone's plant engineer, who was in charge of all environmental matters, sent a memorandum to Firestone's plant managers and department heads. The memorandum, reflecting official plant policy, explained liquid waste disposal procedures and described the particular waste materials involved and the proper method of handling them.

In order to comply with this policy, Firestone initially made efforts to take the waste materials to a class I dump site. However, Firestone accumulated more waste than had been anticipated and disposing of the waste proved costly. When noncompliance with the policy became widespread, the plant engineer sent another memorandum to plant management complaining about the lack of compliance and pointing out that the policy was required by California law.

During this time, the Salinas plant operated under a production manager who had been sent from Firestone's company headquarters in Akron, Ohio for the purpose of "turning the plant around" and making it more profitable.

This manager became angered over the costs of the waste disposal program and decided to discontinue it. As a consequence, Firestone's hazardous waste materials were once again deposited at Crazy Horse.

Frank and Shirley Potter owned property and lived adjacent to Crazy Horse. Joe and Linda Plescia were their neighbors.

In 1984, the Potters and the Plescias (hereafter plaintiffs) discovered that toxic chemicals had contaminated their domestic water wells. The chemicals included: benzene; toluene; chloroform; 1,1-dichloroethene; methylene chloride; tetrachloroethane; 1,1,1-trichloroethane; trichloroethane; and vinyl chloride. Of these, both benzene and vinyl chloride are known to be human carcinogens. Many of the others are strongly suspected to be carcinogens.

In 1985, plaintiffs filed separate suits against Firestone for damages and declaratory relief. Their complaints against Firestone stated causes of action for, *inter alia*, negligence, negligent and intentional infliction of emotional distress, and strict liability/ultrahazardous activity. The two cases were tried together in a court trial. After considering all the evidence, the court found that Firestone was negligent; that negligent and intentional infliction of emotional distress were established; and that Firestone's conduct was an ultrahazardous activity that would subject Firestone to strict liability for resulting damages. Judgment was entered in favor of plaintiffs.

In its statement of decision, the trial court concluded that Firestone's waste disposal practices from 1967 until 1974 constituted actionable negligence. In particular, it determined that Firestone's dumping of liquid and semiliquid wastes at Crazy Horse, despite having been told that such dumping was prohibited, fell below the appropriate standard of care. In rejecting Firestone's argument that it was not negligent because the dangers posed by toxins were not widely known until the mid-1970's, the trial court concluded that: (1) Firestone had been informed by SDS that no solvents, cleaning fluids, oils or liquids were permitted at Crazy Horse; (2) it fell below the standard of care for a large, international corporation with scientific and legal experts in its employ, having been alerted to the impropriety of disposing of these wastes at the landfill, to violate these regulations without at least making reasonable inquiry into the reasons for the restrictions; and (3) if Firestone had made a minimal inquiry, it would have discovered, among other things, the dangers to groundwater from landfill leachates and the potential for contaminating domestic wells.

The trial court also concluded that Firestone was liable for intentional infliction of emotional distress. The court found that the 1977 memorandum detailing how liquid wastes should be disposed reflected Firestone's increased knowledge at that time about the dangers of toxic waste. Given the evidence regarding this memorandum and the fact that the memorandum represented Firestone's official waste disposal policy, the court concluded that Firestone's decision to dump its waste at Crazy Horse in violation of that policy in order to reduce costs was extreme and outrageous conduct.

Finally, the trial court determined that the dumping of large amounts of toxic wastes in a class II landfill constituted an ultrahazardous activity.

In finding liability, the trial court determined that the toxic chemicals in plaintiffs' drinking water were the same chemicals or "daughter" chemicals as those used at the Firestone plant. Firestone was the heaviest single contributor of waste at Crazy Horse and the only contributor with the identical "suite" of chemicals to those found in the water. The court also noted the expert testimony established that the chemicals that migrated off the Firestone plant site so closely resembled those in the water that the comparison constituted a virtual "fingerprint" identifying Firestone as the source of the contaminants.

The court did not attribute any item of damage to any one specific theory of recovery. After noting that plaintiffs' likelihood of harm due to their toxic exposure was the subject of conflicting medical opinions at trial, the court concluded there was convincing evidence that the prolonged nature of the exposure had "enhanced" plaintiffs' risk of developing cancer and other maladies, and that this enhanced susceptibility was a "presently existing physical condition." The court observed that although there was no way to quantify this risk, the risk was nevertheless very real. In its view, reliable scientific opinion and common sense both supported the conclusion that a prolonged period of exposure substantially increased the susceptibility to disease.

The court also stated that although plaintiffs testified to a constellation of physical symptoms which they attributed to the toxic chemicals, it was "not possible to demonstrate with sufficient certainty a causal connection between these symptoms and the well water contamination. Nevertheless, plaintiffs will always fear, and reasonably so, that physical impairments they experience are the result of the well water and are the precursors of life threatening disease. Their fears are not merely subjective but are corroborated by substantial medical and scientific opinion." Based on these findings, plaintiffs were awarded damages totaling $800,000 for their lifelong fear of cancer and resultant emotional distress.

The court further concluded that since plaintiffs now live with an increased vulnerability to serious disease, it was axiomatic that they should receive periodic medical monitoring to detect the onset of disease at the earliest possible time and that early diagnosis was unquestionably important to increase the chances of effective treatment. Accordingly, the court awarded damages totaling $142,975 as the present value of the costs of such monitoring, based on plaintiffs' life expectancies.

The court also awarded plaintiffs damages totaling $269,500 for psychiatric illness and the cost of treating such illness, as well as damages totaling $108,100 for the general disruption of their lives and the invasion of their privacy.[2] Finally, the court awarded punitive damages totaling $2.6 million based on Firestone's conscious disregard for the rights and safety of others in dumping its toxic wastes at the landfill after 1977.

Firestone appealed, arguing that the damage awards were not supported by any of the legal theories relied on by the trial court and that the evidence was insufficient to support the trial court's findings. It claimed that the award for "fear of cancer" in the absence of physical injury was an unwarranted extension of liability for negligent infliction of emotional distress, that if such

---

[2] This award reflected the necessity for plaintiffs to shower elsewhere, use bottled water, and submit to intrusions by numerous agencies involved in testing water and soil.

fear is compensable it should not be so where the plaintiff cannot establish that he or she has a "probability" of developing cancer, and that the amount of damages awarded each plaintiff was not based on proof of individualized injury. The award for "psychiatric injury" was challenged on the ground that the injury was indistinguishable from fear of cancer and was not supported by the evidence.

Firestone asserted a number of other errors in its appeal. It argued that intentional infliction of emotional distress had not been established because its conduct was not shown to be "extreme and outrageous," and the evidence did not support the finding that it was undertaken with the intent to cause or reckless disregard of the probability of causing such injury. Firestone further contended that the elements of a cause of action for strict liability for ultrahazardous activity had not been established, and that, in any event, if damages for fear of cancer could not be awarded on a negligence theory, it followed that they should not be awarded on a strict liability for ultrahazardous activity theory. . . .

The Court of Appeal reversed the awards for medical monitoring costs, as well as a postjudgment order directing Firestone to pay costs and interest, but otherwise affirmed the judgment. The court held that, given the circumstances in which plaintiffs ingested the carcinogens, it was unnecessary for them to establish a present physical injury in order to recover for their fear of cancer. It further held it was unnecessary for plaintiffs to prove they were likely to develop cancer, noting their fear was certain, definite and real, and not contingent on whether they in fact develop the disease. Plaintiffs had proven the elements of a negligence cause of action and had demonstrated, under an objective standard, that their emotional distress was serious. The court also held Firestone was properly found liable for intentional infliction of emotional distress. . . . The court affirmed the amount of the compensatory damages award and found the punitive damage award proper. . . .

"Fear of cancer" is a term generally used to describe a present anxiety over developing cancer in the future. Claims for fear of cancer have been increasingly asserted in toxic tort cases as more and more substances have been linked with cancer. Typically, a person's likelihood of developing cancer as a result of a toxic exposure is difficult to predict because many forms of cancer are characterized by long latency periods (anywhere from 20 to 30 years), and presentation is dependent upon the interrelation of myriad factors.

The availability of damages for fear of cancer as a result of exposure to carcinogens or other toxins in negligence actions is a relatively novel issue for California courts. Other jurisdictions, however, have considered such claims and the appropriate limits on recovery. Factors deemed important to the compensability of such fear have included proof of a discernible physical injury.

We must now consider whether, pursuant to California precedent, emotional distress engendered by the fear of developing cancer in the future as a result of a toxic exposure is a recoverable item of damages in a negligence action.

Because it initially appeared plaintiffs might have suffered damage to their immune systems, we solicited the views of the parties on whether such damage constitutes physical injury. We did so because it is settled in California that in ordinary negligence actions for physical injury, recovery for emotional distress caused by that injury is available as an item of parasitic damages. Where a plaintiff can demonstrate a physical injury caused by the defendant's negligence, anxiety specifically due to a reasonable fear of a future harm attributable to the injury may also constitute a proper element of damages.

Although the availability of parasitic damages for emotional distress engendered by a fear of developing cancer in the future appears to be an issue of first impression in California, other jurisdictions have concluded that such damages are recoverable when they are derivative of a claim for serious physical injuries. . . .

No California cases address whether impairment of the immune system response and cellular damage constitute "physical injury" sufficient to allow recovery for parasitic emotional distress damages. Courts in other jurisdictions that have considered this issue recently have come to differing conclusions.

Plaintiffs, citing several such cases, contend that immune system impairment and cellular damage is a physical injury for which parasitic damages for emotional distress are available. . . .

Conversely, Firestone contends that mere subcellular changes that are unaccompanied by clinically verifiable symptoms of illness or disease do not constitute a physical injury sufficient to support a claim for parasitic emotional distress damages. To support this contention, Firestone relies on a case in which workers' claims for fear of cancer from asbestos exposure were denied because they had failed to show that their fear was based on knowledge that their lungs were functionally impaired. (*In re Hawaii Federal Asbestos Cases* (D. Haw. 1990) 734 F. Supp. 1563, 1569–70.) There it was held that a physical injury was not established by the mere presence of asbestos fibers in the lungs or by evidence of physiological changes in the lungs such as pleural thickening and pleural plaques. Firestone also relies on cases holding that in the absence of some verifiable impairment, asbestos-related subcellular changes do not give rise to valid claims for physical injury. . . .

It is not clear from the record in this case, however, that these plaintiffs' emotional distress is parasitic to this type of supposed injury. The statement of decision by the trial court does not include an express finding that plaintiffs' exposure to the contaminated well water resulted in physical injury, cellular damage or immune system impairment. The court made no mention of plaintiffs' immune system response, cellular systems or cells, and made no specific determination of damage or impairment thereto. While the trial court concluded that plaintiffs do have an enhanced "susceptibility" or "risk" for developing cancer and other maladies, it characterized this as a "presently existing physical condition," not as a physical injury. We conclude, therefore, that we lack an appropriate factual record for resolving whether impairment to the immune response system or cellular damage constitutes a physical injury for which parasitic damages for emotional distress ought to be available. . . .

Amici curiae argue that no recovery for emotional distress arising from fear of cancer should be allowed in any case unless the plaintiff can establish a present physical injury such as a clinically verifiable cancerous or precancerous condition. *Amici curiae* advance several legal and policy arguments to support this position. None is persuasive.

Significantly, we recently reaffirmed the principle that in California, "damages for negligently inflicted emotional distress may be recovered in the absence of physical injury or impact. . . ." (*Burgess, supra*, 2 Cal. 4th at 1074, 9 Cal. Rptr. 2d 615, 831 P.2d 1197.) We held that "physical injury is not a prerequisite for recovering damages for *serious* emotional distress." . . .

Contrary to *amici curiae's* assertions, this principle has never been restricted to cases involving bystanders or preexisting relationships. Notably, *amici curiae* cite no authority even suggesting such a limitation. Nor is there any question but that Firestone had a duty to any person who might foreseeably come in contact with its hazardous waste to use care in the disposal of that material, care which includes compliance with all government regulations governing the location and manner of disposal. In this court Firestone has abandoned any claim that it was not negligent or that plaintiffs were not foreseeable victims of its negligence.

Amici curiae next contend that substantial policy reasons nevertheless support a physical injury requirement for recovery of fear of cancer damages where no preexisting relationship exists. They suggest that allowing recovery in the absence of a physical injury would create limitless liability and would result in a flood of litigation which thereby would impose onerous burdens on courts, corporations, insurers and society in general. Allowing such recovery would promote fraud and artful pleading, and would also encourage plaintiffs to seek damages based on a subjective fear of cancer. In *amici curiae's* view, a physical injury requirement is thus essential to provide meaningful limits on the class of potential plaintiffs and clear guidelines for resolving disputes over liability without the necessity for trial.

This argument overlooks the reasons for our decision to discard the requirement of physical injury. As we observed more than a decade ago, "[t]he primary justification for the requirement of physical injury appears to be that it serves as a screening device to minimize a presumed risk of feigned injuries and false claims." (*Molien v. Kaiser Foundation Hospitals* (1980) 27 Cal. 3d 916, 925-26, 167 Cal. Rptr. 831, 616 P.2d 813. Such harm was "believed to be susceptible of objective ascertainment and hence to corroborate the authenticity of the claim."

In *Molien*, we perceived two significant difficulties with the physical injury requirement. First, "the classification is both over inclusive and under inclusive when viewed in the light of its purported purpose of screening false claims." It is over inclusive in that it permits recovery whenever the suffering accompanies or results in physical injury, no matter how trivial, yet under inclusive in that it mechanically denies court access to potentially valid claims that could be proved if the plaintiffs were permitted to go to trial.

Second, we observed that the physical injury requirement "encourages extravagant pleading and distorted testimony." We concluded that the retention of the requirement ought to be reconsidered because of the tendency of victims to exaggerate sick headaches, nausea, insomnia and other symptoms in order to make out a technical basis of bodily injury upon which to predicate a parasitic recovery for the more grievous disturbance, consisting of the mental and emotional distress endured.

Therefore, rather than adhere to what we perceived as an artificial and often arbitrary means of guarding against fraudulent claims, we acknowledged that "[t]he essential question is one of proof." Thus, "[i]n cases other than where proof of mental distress is of a medically significant nature, the general standard of proof required to support a claim of mental distress is some guarantee of genuineness in the circumstances of the case."

Our reasons for discarding the physical injury requirement in *Molien* remain valid today and are equally applicable in a toxic exposure case. That is, the physical injury requirement is a hopelessly imprecise screening device — it would allow recovery for fear of cancer whenever such distress accompanies or results in any physical injury, no matter how trivial, yet would disallow recovery in all cases where the fear is both serious and genuine but no physical injury has yet manifested itself. While we agree with *amici curiae* that meaningful limits on the class of potential plaintiffs and clear guidelines for resolving disputes in advance of trial are necessary, imposing a physical injury requirement represents an inherently flawed and inferior means of attempting to achieve these goals.

We next consider whether recovery of damages for emotional distress caused by fear of cancer should depend upon a showing that the plaintiff's fears stem from a knowledge that there is a probable likelihood of developing cancer in the future due to the toxic exposure. This is a matter of hot debate among the parties and *amici curiae*. Firestone and numerous *amici curiae* argue that because fear of cancer claims are linked to a future harm which may or may not materialize, such claims raise concerns about speculation and uncertainty and therefore warrant a requirement that the plaintiff show the feared cancer is more likely than not to occur. Plaintiffs and other *amici curiae* respond that such a requirement is inappropriate in the context of a mental distress claim, and that there are viable methods, apart from requiring quantification of the cancer risk, to screen claims and determine the reasonableness and genuineness of a plaintiff's fears.

Plaintiffs favor the approach adopted by the Court of Appeal, which requires the following showing. The toxic exposure plaintiff must first prove the elements of a negligence cause of action. The plaintiff must then establish that his or her fear of cancer is serious, and that the seriousness meets an objective standard (*i.e.*, the distress must be reasonable under the circumstances). Although a plaintiff is not required to establish that the cancer is likely to occur, the finder of fact should consider evidence regarding the likelihood that cancer will occur (*i.e.*, evidence that the disease is only a remote possibility could lead a trier of fact to conclude that a plaintiff's fears were unreasonable). Finally, the finder of fact should test the genuineness of the plaintiff's fear under the factors discussed in *Molien*, including expert testimony, a juror's own experience, and the particular circumstances of the case.

In affirming the fear of cancer award, the Court of Appeal remarked that "the fact that [plaintiffs'] water supply was contaminated by carcinogens is, *by itself*, surely a circumstance which is likely to cause emotional distress in most reasonable persons." (Italics added.) In addition, although the Court of Appeal purported to call for a showing of the actual likelihood that the feared cancer will occur, the court indicated that the absence of such evidence is immaterial where, as here, the trier of fact finds a significantly increased risk of cancer.

We decline to adopt the Court of Appeal's approach. Although the court properly recognized that a toxic exposure plaintiff is required to establish the reasonableness of his or her fear of cancer, it erred in concluding that reasonableness is established by the mere fact of an exposure or a significant increase in the risk of cancer.

A carcinogenic or other toxic ingestion or exposure, without more, does not provide a basis for fearing future physical injury or illness which the law is prepared to recognize as reasonable. The fact that one is aware that he or she has ingested or been otherwise exposed to a carcinogen or other toxin, without any regard to the nature, magnitude and proportion of the exposure or its likely consequences, provides no meaningful basis upon which to evaluate the reasonableness of one's fear. For example, nearly everybody is exposed to carcinogens which appear naturally in all types of foods. Yet ordinary consumption of such foods is not substantially likely to result in cancer. (See Ames & Gold, *Too Many Rodent Carcinogens: Mitogenesis Increases Mutagenesis* (1990) 249 Science 970, 971, fn. 10 [observing that apples, celery, coffee, carrots, cauliflower, grapes, honey, orange juice, potatoes and many other common foods naturally produce carcinogenic pesticides that have been found to induce tumors when administered to rodents in large doses].) Nor is the knowledge of such consumption likely to result in a reasonable fear of cancer.

Moreover, permitting recovery for fear of cancer damages based solely upon a plaintiff's knowledge that his or her risk of cancer has been significantly increased by a toxic exposure, without requiring any further showing of the actual likelihood of the feared cancer due to the exposure, provides no protection against unreasonable claims based upon wholly speculative fears. For example, a plaintiff's risk of contracting cancer might be significantly increased by 100 or more percent due to a particular toxic exposure, yet the actual risk of the feared cancer might itself be insignificant and no more than a mere possibility. As even plaintiffs appear to concede, evidence of knowledge that cancer is only a remote possibility could lead a trier of fact to conclude that a claimed fear is objectively unreasonable. This concession only proves the point — the way to avoid damage awards for unreasonable fear, *i.e.*, in those cases where the feared cancer is at best only remotely possible, is to require a showing of the actual likelihood of the feared cancer to establish its significance.

Accordingly, we reject the Court of Appeal's approach because it attaches undue significance to the mere ingestion of a carcinogen, and because it focuses on the increased risk of cancer in isolation.

We turn now to Firestone's argument that fear of cancer should be compensable only where the fear is based upon knowledge that cancer is probable, *i.e.*, that it is more likely than not that cancer will develop. In evaluating this argument, we first consider whether it is reasonable for a person to genuinely and seriously fear a disease that is not probable, and if so, whether the emotional distress engendered by such fear warrants recognition as a compensable harm.

We cannot say that it would never be reasonable for a person who has ingested toxic substances to harbor a genuine and serious fear of cancer where reliable medical or scientific opinion indicates that such ingestion has significantly increased his or her risk of cancer, but not to a probable likelihood. Indeed, we would be very hard pressed to find that, as a matter of law, a plaintiff faced with a 20 percent or 30 percent chance of developing cancer cannot genuinely, seriously and reasonably fear the prospect of cancer. Nonetheless, we conclude, for the public policy reasons identified below, that emotional distress caused by the fear of a cancer that is not probable should generally not be compensable in a negligence action.

As a starting point in our analysis, we recognize the indisputable fact that all of us are exposed to carcinogens every day. . . .

Thus, all of us are potential fear of cancer plaintiffs, provided we are sufficiently aware of and worried about the possibility of developing cancer from exposure to or ingestion of a carcinogenic substance. The enormity of the class of potential plaintiffs cannot be overstated; indeed, a single class action may easily involve hundreds, if not thousands, of fear of cancer claims.

With this consideration in mind, we believe the tremendous societal cost of otherwise allowing emotional distress compensation to a potentially unrestricted plaintiff class demonstrates the necessity of imposing some limit on the class. Proliferation of fear of cancer claims in California in the absence of meaningful restrictions might compromise the availability and affordability of liability insurance for toxic liability risks. . . .

A second policy concern that weighs in favor of a more likely than not threshold is the unduly detrimental impact that unrestricted fear liability would have in the health care field. As *amicus curiae* California Medical Association points out, access to prescription drugs is likely to be impeded by allowing recovery of fear of cancer damages in negligence cases without the imposition of a heightened threshold. To wit, thousands of drugs having no known harmful effects are currently being prescribed and utilized. New data about potentially harmful effects may not develop for years. If and when negative data are discovered and made public, however, one can expect numerous lawsuits to be filed by patients who currently have no physical injury or illness but who nonetheless fear the risk of adverse effects from the drugs they used. Unless meaningful restrictions are placed on this potential plaintiff class, the threat of numerous large, adverse monetary awards, coupled with the added cost of insuring against such liability (assuming insurance would be available), could diminish the availability of new, beneficial prescription drugs or increase their price beyond the reach of those who need them most. . . .

Fear of cancer liability in the context of physicians prescribing drugs will surely exacerbate the medical malpractice crisis. Specifically, for every patient who might actually develop cancer because of a particular drug, there could be hundreds or thousands of patients who might allege they were negligently prescribed the drug. Not only will the additional expense of insuring against fear lawsuits and fear liability under these circumstances add to the cost of physician services, but physicians who would otherwise prescribe and administer new or innovative drugs might be discouraged from doing so for fear of potential liability. This would inhibit physicians in their ability to provide quality care to patients, as well as increase the practice of defensive medicine.

A third policy concern to consider is that allowing recovery to all victims who have a fear of cancer may work to the detriment of those who sustain actual physical injury and those who ultimately develop cancer as a result of toxic exposure. That is, to allow compensation to all plaintiffs with objectively reasonable cancer fears, even where the threatened cancer is not probable, raises the very significant concern that defendants and their insurers will be unable to ensure adequate compensation for those victims who actually develop cancer or other physical injuries. . . .

A fourth reason supporting the imposition of a more likely than not limitation is to establish a sufficiently definite and predictable threshold for recovery to permit consistent application from case to case. Indeed, without such a threshold, the likelihood of inconsistent results increases since juries may differ over the point at which a plaintiff's fear is a genuine and reasonable fear, *i.e.*, one jury might deem knowledge of a 2 or 5 percent likelihood of future illness or injury to be sufficient, while another jury might not. A more definite threshold will avoid inconsistent results and may contribute to early resolution or settlement of claims.

Plaintiffs and *amici curiae* advance several reasons why a more likely than not threshold for fear of cancer claims should be rejected. None is convincing.

First, plaintiffs argue that a more likely than not restriction is unworkable because the risk of contracting cancer from any one source is unquantifiable. In their view, adoption of such a rule would effectively preclude any emotional distress recovery.

We are unpersuaded by this argument because its factual premise appears highly suspect. Although the experts in this case asserted it was impossible to quantify the risk of cancer from any particular toxic exposure, experts in other cases do not share that view. . . .

Second, plaintiffs and *amici curiae* point out that while decisions from other jurisdictions have employed a more likely than not limitation for the so-called "increased risk" claim, they have thus far declined to do so in the context of a fear of cancer claim. Those decisions, it is asserted, allowed recovery for a plaintiff's fear of cancer in situations similar to those present here without proof that cancer was more likely than not to occur.

We remain unconvinced. Although it is true that the cited cases permitted fear of cancer recovery so long as the plaintiffs' fears were genuine and reasonable, many of them involved plaintiffs who, in addition to their emotional distress, sustained serious or permanent physical injury as a result of a particular toxic exposure. It is clear from passages in these cases that the respective courts were acutely aware of the plaintiffs' existing physical injuries and were deciding the appropriate basis for fear of cancer recovery in that context. Because these cases were decided within the context of a much narrower class of potential plaintiffs, they did not implicate or address the important public policy considerations at issue here.. . . .

We are satisfied that the more likely than not threshold for fear of cancer claims in negligence actions strikes the appropriate balance between the interests of toxic exposure litigants and the burdens on society and judicial administration.

To summarize, we hold with respect to negligent infliction of emotional distress claims arising out of exposure to carcinogens and/or other toxic substances: Unless an express exception to this general rule is recognized: in the absence of a present physical injury or illness, damages for fear of cancer may be recovered only if the plaintiff pleads and proves that (1) as a result of the defendant's negligent breach of a duty owed to the plaintiff, the plaintiff is exposed to a toxic substance which threatens cancer; and (2) the plaintiff's fear stems from a knowledge, corroborated by reliable medical or scientific opinion, that it is more likely than not that the plaintiff will develop the cancer in the future due to the toxic exposure. Under this rule, a plaintiff must do more than simply establish knowledge of a toxic ingestion or exposure and a significant increased risk of cancer. The plaintiff must further show that based upon reliable medical or scientific opinion, the plaintiff harbors a serious fear that the toxic ingestion or exposure was of such magnitude and proportion as to likely result in the feared cancer.

Plaintiffs argue that if damages for fear of cancer in the absence of physical injury are limited to cases in which the cancer will more likely than not occur, the court should distinguish intentional conduct. We agree that certain aggravated conduct may warrant different treatment. In this part, we recognize an exception to the general rule set out above.

Plaintiffs suggest that the more likely than not threshold should not be applied where a defendant intentionally violates a statute or regulation prohibiting the disposal of toxins. Plaintiffs are quick to point out that the policy concerns for limiting liability in ordinary negligence cases are not triggered in cases involving such defendants.

Although an exception to the general rule appears appropriate, we do not believe it should focus on intentional violators of the law. For one thing, while a defendant may be aware that its conduct is wrong and potentially dangerous, it may not have knowledge of a particular statute or regulation proscribing it. There may be times where a defendant does not specifically intend to violate the law, yet the defendant proceeds to act egregiously in conscious disregard of others.

With these considerations in mind, we conclude it preferable to recognize an exception that focuses on the totality of circumstances in evaluating a defendant's conduct. Accordingly, we hold that a toxic exposure plaintiff need not meet the more likely than not threshold for fear of cancer recovery in a negligence action if the plaintiff pleads and proves that the defendant's conduct in causing the exposure amounts to "oppression, fraud, or malice" as defined in Civil Code section 3294, which authorizes the imposition of punitive damages. Thus, for instance, fear of cancer damages may be recovered without demonstrating that cancer is probable where it is shown that the defendant is guilty of "despicable conduct which is carried on by the defendant with a willful and conscious disregard of the rights or safety of others." (Civ. Code, § 3294, subd. (c)(1) [defining one type of "malice"].) "A person acts with conscious disregard of the rights or safety of others when [he] [she] is aware of the probable dangerous consequences of [his] [her] conduct and willfully and deliberately fails to avoid those consequences." (BAJI No. 14.71 (7th ed. pocket part 1992 Rev.) [defining "malice"].)

When a defendant acts with oppression, fraud or malice, no reason, policy or otherwise, justifies application of the more likely than not threshold. Any burden or consequence to society from imposing liability is offset by the deterrent impact of holding morally blameworthy defendants fully responsible for the damages they cause, including damage in the form of emotional distress suffered by victims of the misconduct who reasonably fear future cancer.

Under such circumstances, the potential liability of a defendant is not disproportionate to culpability. While the imposition of liability for emotional distress resulting from negligent handling of toxic substances may result in costs out of proportion to the culpability of the negligent actor, this concern is diminished or nonexistent when the conduct is despicable and undertaken in conscious disregard of the danger to the health or interests of others. The significance of the size of the potential class of plaintiffs is similarly diminished and the moral blame heightened since the defendant is aware of the danger posed by its conduct and acts in conscious disregard of the known risk. For these reasons, the more likely than not threshold should not be available as a shield when the defendant acts with a sufficient degree of moral blameworthiness.

Once the plaintiff establishes that the defendant has acted with oppression, fraud or malice, the plaintiff must still demonstrate that his or her fear of cancer is reasonable, genuine and serious in order to recover damages. In determining what constitutes reasonable fear, we refer to our previous discussion in which we observed that it is not enough for a plaintiff to show simply an ingestion of a carcinogen or a significant increase in the risk of cancer. In addition, the plaintiff must show that his or her actual risk of cancer is significant before recovery will be allowed. Under this reasoning, a plaintiff's fear is not compensable when the risk of cancer is significantly increased, but remains a remote possibility.

. . . In our view, Firestone's conduct brings this case within the "oppression, fraud or malice" exception for recovery of fear of cancer damages. The trial court determined that in May of 1977, officials in key management positions at Firestone's Salinas plant had increased knowledge regarding the dangers involved with the careless disposal of hazardous wastes, and had a specific, written policy for hazardous waste disposal. However, these officials, while professing support for the policy in written distributions, in actuality largely ignored the policy. The court found especially reprehensible the fact that Firestone, through its plant production manager, actively discouraged compliance with its internal policies and California law solely for the sake of reducing corporate costs. Under these circumstances, we believe there are sufficient facts supporting the trial court's conclusion that such conduct displayed a conscious disregard of the rights and safety of others.[3]

The trial court ruled that after May 1977, Firestone's continued dumping of its hazardous wastes at Crazy Horse amounted to outrageous conduct: "The materials were known to be and specifically designated as hazardous. It was clear that there was a great probability of these materials infiltrating and contaminating neighboring wells. Defendant had to realize that the eventual discovery of such a condition by those drinking the contaminated water would almost certainly result in their suffering severe emotional distress. In fact, with the knowledge that the defendant had at this time there also would have come an understanding of the dangerous condition that had been created by the dumping that had taken place over previous years. Nevertheless, defendant went ahead with its illegal dumping. This not only displayed a reckless disregard of the probability of causing emotional distress but also amounted to a ratification of its past acts in this regard." The court then determined that plaintiffs suffered severe emotional distress as a direct result of Firestone's intentional acts.

The Court of Appeal agreed that Firestone's conduct after 1977 was sufficiently extreme and outrageous to support liability for intentional infliction of emotional distress. The court noted in particular Firestone's knowledge of the health hazards posed by its dumping and its deliberate disregard of these hazards in an effort to cut costs. . . .

After the Court of Appeal rendered its decision, we issued our opinion in *Christensen v. Superior Court*, 54 Cal. 3d 868, 2 Cal. Rptr. 2d 79, 820 P.2d 181, and asked the parties to address the impact of that opinion on the award of compensatory and punitive damages for intentional infliction of emotional distress in this case. As we will explain, it is questionable whether the record here supports a finding of intentional infliction of emotional distress by Firestone.

"The elements of the tort of intentional infliction of emotional distress are: " '(1) extreme and outrageous conduct by the defendant with the intention of causing, or reckless disregard of the probability of causing, emotional distress; (2) the plaintiff's suffering severe or extreme emotional distress; and (3) actual and proximate causation of the emotional distress by the defendant's outrageous conduct. . . .' " Conduct to be outrageous must be so extreme as to exceed all bounds of that usually tolerated in a civilized community.' The defendant must have engaged in 'conduct intended to inflict injury or engaged in with the realization that injury will result.'" (*Christensen*, 54 Cal. 3d at p. 903, 2 Cal. Rptr. 2d 79, 820 P.2d

In *Christensen*, we held that " '[t]he law limits claims of intentional infliction of emotional distress to egregious conduct *toward plaintiff* proximately caused by defendant.' The only exception to this rule is that recognized when the defendant is aware, but acts with reckless disregard, of the plaintiff and the probability that his or her conduct will cause severe emotional distress to that

---

[3] Although this case falls within the oppression, fraud or malice exception announced above, any award of fear of cancer damages will still depend on whether plaintiffs' fears are reasonable with reference to the actual likelihood of cancer due to the toxic exposure.

plaintiff. Where reckless disregard of the plaintiff's interests is the theory of recovery, the presence of the plaintiff at the time the outrageous conduct occurs is recognized as the element establishing a higher degree of culpability which, in turn, justifies recovery of greater damages by a broader group of plaintiffs than allowed on a negligent infliction of emotional distress theory." (*Christensen*, 54 Cal. 3d at pp. 905–906, 2 Cal. Rptr. 2d 79, 820 P.2d 181, italics in original, fn. omitted.)

Thus, "[i]t is not enough that the conduct be intentional and outrageous. It must be conduct *directed at the plaintiff*, or occur in the presence of a plaintiff of *whom the defendant is aware.*" (*Christensen*, 54 Cal. 3d at 903, 2 Cal. Rptr. 2d 79, 820 P.2d 181, italics added.) "The requirement that the defendant's conduct be directed primarily at the plaintiff is a factor which distinguishes intentional infliction of emotional distress from the negligent infliction of such injury." (*Id.*, at 904, 2 Cal. Rptr. 2d 79, 820 P.2d 181.)

In this case, it is ambiguous whether the lower courts determined that Firestone's conduct was directed at these particular plaintiffs in the sense intended by *Christensen*. Although the Court of Appeal correctly rejected Firestone's contention that Firestone was not liable because it did not know the particular names of any individual whose groundwater was contaminated by the hazardous waste, it is unclear whether it believed that Firestone was actually aware of the presence of these particular plaintiffs and their consumption and use of the water.

Furthermore, it is questionable whether the trial court made a finding that Firestone possessed the requisite knowledge, and if so, whether such a finding would be supported by substantial evidence.[4] Although the trial court concluded that Firestone "had to realize" that the eventual discovery of the toxic contamination "by those drinking the contaminated water would almost certainly result in their suffering severe emotional distress," this may be interpreted in one of two ways. First, this may have been a finding that Firestone actually knew of these particular plaintiffs and their consumption of the water, and nevertheless sent prohibited wastes to Crazy Horse despite a realization that plaintiffs would almost certainly suffer severe emotional distress upon their discovery of the facts. Alternatively, this may have been a finding that Firestone had to have realized that its misconduct was almost certain to cause severe emotional distress to any person who might foreseeably consume the water and subsequently discover the facts. Although the knowledge requirement is met under the first interpretation of the court's ruling, it is not satisfied under the second because knowledge of *these particular plaintiffs* is lacking.

This conclusion is consistent with the result reached in *Christensen*. There we held that, even though it was alleged that defendants' conduct in mishandling the remains of deceased persons was intentional and outrageous and

---

[4] Firestone asserts in its brief on the merits that there is no evidence in the record showing that it knew of anyone living near Crazy Horse or that it had any interaction with plaintiffs. Plaintiffs do not specifically contest these assertions. Rather, they point out that Firestone was informed that Crazy Horse was not equipped to prevent toxins from leaching into the groundwater, that Firestone agreed not to send any toxic materials to the landfill, and that despite its knowledge that the reason for the no toxic requirement was to protect "plaintiffs' water source," Firestone chose to return the toxins to Crazy Horse where they found their way into the water source.

was substantially certain to cause extreme emotional distress to relatives and close friends of the deceased, the plaintiffs' cause of action for intentional infliction of emotional distress was not sufficiently supported where there was no allegation that the defendants' misconduct was directed primarily at plaintiffs, or that it was calculated to cause them severe emotional distress, or that it was done with knowledge of their presence and with a substantial certainty that they would suffer severe emotional injury.

For guidance of the lower courts should the Court of Appeal determine that a retrial on this claim is appropriate, we hold that recovery of fear of cancer damages in actions for intentional infliction of emotional distress should not depend on a showing of a medically corroborated belief that it is more likely than not that the plaintiff will develop the feared cancer as a result of the toxic exposure.

The reasons for not applying the more likely than not threshold are obvious. First, the intentional infliction cause of action requires a showing of "extreme and outrageous conduct" which is directed at the plaintiff. Thus, a high degree of culpability is required which justifies recovery of greater damages by a broader group of plaintiffs than allowed in an ordinary negligence action. Moreover, where a defendant undertakes extreme and outrageous conduct toward the plaintiff, the concern that liability will be imposed out of proportion to fault is not present. Finally, the requirement of extreme and outrageous conduct directed at the plaintiff places adequate limitations on the class of potential plaintiffs who might sue for fear of cancer under this theory. Therefore, the public policy concerns supporting application of the heightened threshold are not implicated.

Of course, even though the heightened threshold is not applicable in intentional infliction actions, it must nevertheless be established that the plaintiff's fear of cancer is reasonable, that is, that the fear is based upon medically or scientifically corroborated knowledge that the defendant's conduct has significantly increased the plaintiff's risk of cancer and that the plaintiff's actual risk of the threatened cancer is significant. Reasonableness of the fear is required because in intentional infliction actions, recovery is allowed only for "severe or extreme emotional distress.". . .

As indicated, *ante*, we believe there is sufficient evidence to support the trial court's conclusion that Firestone acted reprehensibly in conscious disregard of the rights and safety of others. But because the trial court was of the view that Firestone's conduct constituted intentional infliction of emotional distress when it assessed punitive damages against Firestone, and might not have made the award or might have awarded a lesser sum had it not made that finding, that aspect of the judgment should also be reversed. It is not necessary therefore to consider Firestone's several challenges to the propriety of awarding punitive damages in this case. For guidance of the court should there be a retrial we note, however, that punitive damages sometimes may be assessed in unintentional tort actions under Civil Code section 3294, so long as "actual, substantial damages" have been awarded.

[The court held that plaintiffs were entitled to recover reasonable expenses for medical monitoring absent a showing of "present physical injury or . . . proof that injury is reasonably certain to occur in the future," provided there "is a significant but not necessarily likely risk of serious disease" as a result of the exposure.

[The court also said that plaintiffs' smoking could be used in an appropriate case to reduce plaintiffs' recovery under comparative fault principles, if "a portion of the plaintiff's fear of developing cancer is attributable to the smoking." But here, defendant "apparently introduced no evidence at trial suggesting that any portion of plaintiffs' fear was attributable to their own smoking." The court also observed that evidence of smoking can be relevant in determining whether a plaintiff's fear is "reasonable and genuine. Thus, if a plaintiff had smoked heavily for 20 years without fearing cancer, the trier of fact may consider that evidence in assessing the legitimacy of the plaintiff's fear of cancer claim."]

NOTES

1. *Delayed Diagnosis. Compare Boryla v. Pash*, 960 P.2d 123 (Colo. 1998), involving a physician's alleged failure to promptly diagnose a patient's breast cancer where the court noted:

> In our view, the more probable than not standard articulated in *Potter* is not appropriate in cases where the plaintiff's fear of cancer results from a delayed medical diagnosis. Contrary to toxic exposure cases, where the plaintiff has yet to experience the onset of cancer, fear of cancer cases in the medical setting usually involve a negligent misdiagnosis of a patient's existing cancer. In cases where the plaintiff demonstrates that her cancerous condition physically worsened as a result of the delayed diagnosis, the plaintiff has demonstrated a sufficient physical injury to permit the recovery of emotional distress damages. Thus, the usual reservations courts have concerning jury speculation and conjecture in cases involving plaintiffs seeking purely emotional damages are inapplicable in a case such as [this].
>
> Additionally, the sweeping policy rationales relevant in a toxic tort case are not present here because the class of potential plaintiffs in a medical malpractice case is "clearly limited" to the parties in dispute. Furthermore, the court of appeals correctly notes that as to the contention that failure to require a more probable than not standard will promote inconsistent jury verdicts, we note that any action submitted to a jury is susceptible to this criticism. Taken to its logical end, the criticism is of juries per se. For these reasons, traditional negligence principles which focus on proximate cause as well as the reasonableness of the plaintiff's fear are sufficient to evaluate fear of cancer claims in medical malpractice cases.

960 P.2d at 128–29.

2. *Intentional Infliction of Emotional Distress.* A contractor's employee who was subjected to asbestos exposure could sue the owner of the building containing the asbestos for intentional infliction of emotional distress, even though the employee suffered no physical injury, the court said in *Capital Holding Corp. v. Bailey*, 873 S.W.2d 187 (Ky. 1994).

Can a plaintiff recover for negligent and intentional infliction of emotional distress, based on the same conduct of the defendant?

3. *Negligence and Emotional Distress.* Recovery for negligently inflicted emotional distress was discussed above in the chapter on duty and proximate cause. How does that issue differ from the one discussed in *Potter*? From *Brzoska v. Olson*, 668 A.2d 1355 (1995)? Recovery for reasonable but unfounded fear is not limited to AIDS phobia, see *Marchica v. Long Island R. Co.*, 31 F.3d 1197 (2d Cir. 1994). For example, in *Jones v. Howard Univ.*, 589 A.2d 419 (D.C. App. 1991), the plaintiff stated a claim for emotional distress against her physicians and a hospital for failure to determine that she was pregnant when she was subjected to x-rays and surgery during the first trimester of her pregnancy, even though her pregnancy resulted in the birth of healthy twins.

4. *The Impact Doctrine.* Many courts have traditionally allowed recovery for emotional distress where the plaintiff suffers a physical impact, however slight, as the result of defendant's negligence. See *Laxton v. Orkin Exterm. Co.*, 639 S.W.2d 431 (Tenn. 1982); F. HARPER, F. JAMES & O. GRAY, THE LAW OF TORTS § 18.4 (2d ed. 1986). Why was this impact rule not applied in *Potter*?

5. *The Tell-Tale Heart.* The plaintiff in *Angus v. Shiley*, 989 F.2d 142 (3d Cir. 1993), sued for emotional distress resulting from her receipt of a heart valve which she later learned was of a design that had resulted in a number of fracture failures. The court denied recovery because the plaintiff failed to allege "that the valve implanted in her was defective, a prerequisite to liability in products liability."

6. *Land Values.* In *Criscuola v. Power Auth.*, 621 N.E.2d 1195 (N.Y. App. 1993), the court said that the plaintiff could recover for the decreased value of his land resulting from the public's fears of electromagnetic risks from defendant's nearby electrical power line. The plaintiff need not prove that these fears were reasonable, the court said.

But in *Adams v. Star Enters.*, 51 F.3d 417 (4th Cir. 1995), the court held that the plaintiffs could not recover for diminished property values caused by fear of health risks from defendant's discharge of oil extending under their properties. The court said that the oil spill was undetectable, and the law did not permit recovery for a private nuisance that was not visible or otherwise detectable.

7. *Death and Dead Bodies.* A doctor was held liable in *Strickland v. Madden*, 456 S.E.2d 414 (S.C. App. 1994), for mistakenly telling the plaintiff that her father was dead.

The plaintiffs in *Christensen v. Superior Ct.*, 54 Cal. 3d 868, 2 Cal. Rptr. 2d 79, 820 P.2d 181 (1991), close family members of the decedents, were permitted to recover from the mortuary and crematory defendants for negligent mishandling of their decedents' remains, where the plaintiffs were aware that funeral or crematory services were allegedly being performed for their decedents by the defendants.

In *Flores v. Baca*, 871 P.2d 962 (N.M. 1994), decedent's wife and children were allowed to recover for emotional distress from the defendant funeral director for the director's failure to completely embalm the decedent's body as required by the contract for funeral services. And in *Brown v. Matthews Mortuary, Inc.*, 801 P.2d 37 (Idaho 1990), the widow and son of the deceased were permitted to recover against the defendant mortuary and crematorium for negligence and breach of contract in losing the remains of the deceased.

But in *Millington v. Kuba*, 5 32 N.W.2d 787 (Iowa 1995), the adult children of the deceased were not permitted to recover against the defendant funeral home for negligent infliction of emotional distress in wrongfully cremating their father's remains. The plaintiffs, living in Michigan, were too far removed from the defendant's alleged misconduct in Iowa, the court said. They also could not recover for intentional infliction of emotional distress because they failed to present sufficient evidence "to generate a fact question as to severe or extreme emotional distress."

8. *Contractual Vagaries*. In *Erlich v. Menezes*, 21 Cal. 4th 543, 981 P.2d 978, 87 Cal. Rptr. 2d 886 (1999), the issue was whether emotional distress damages were recoverable for the negligent breach of a contract to construct a house. The court noted:

> "Contract damages are generally limited to those within the contemplation of the parties when the contract was entered into or at least reasonably foreseeable by them at that time; consequential damages beyond the expectation of the parties are not recoverable. This limitation on available damages serves to encourage contractual relations and commercial activity by enabling parties to estimate in advance the financial risks of their enterprise. . . . In contrast, tort damages are awarded to [fully] compensate the victim for [all] injury suffered." (*Applied Equipment Corp. v. Litton Saudi Arabia Ltd* 7 Cal. 4th 503, 515–16 (1994)).
>
> "'[T]he distinction between tort and contract is well grounded in common law, and divergent objectives underlie the remedies created in the two areas. Whereas contract actions are created to enforce the intentions of the parties to the agreement, tort law is primarily designed to vindicate 'social policy.'" (*Hunter v. Up-right, Inc.* (1993) 6 Cal. 4th 1174, quoting *Foley v. Interactive Data Corp.* (1988) 47 Cal. 3d 654, 683. While the purposes behind contract and tort law are distinct, the boundary line between them is not (*Freeman & Mills, Inc. v. Belcher Oil Co.* (1995) 11 Cal. 4th 85, 106, and the distinction between the remedies for each is not "'found ready made.'" (*Ibid.*, quoting Holmes, The Common Law (1881) p. 13.) These uncertain boundaries and the apparent breadth of the recovery available for tort actions create pressure to obliterate the distinction between contracts and torts—an expansion of tort law at the expense of contract principles which Grant Gilmore aptly dubbed "contorts". . . .
>
> Tort damages have been permitted in contract cases where a breach of duty directly causes physical injury (*Fuentes v. Perez* (1977) 66 Cal. App. 3d 163, 168, fn. 2); for breach of the covenant of good faith and fair dealing in insurance contracts (*Crisci v. Security Ins. Co.* (1967) 66 Cal. 2d 425, 433–434); for wrongful discharge in violation of fundamental public policy (*Tameny v. Atlantic Richfield Co.* (1980) 27 Cal. 3d 167, 175–176); or where the contract was fraudulently induced.

(*Las Palmas Associates v. Las Palmas Center Associates* (1991) 235 Cal. App. 3d 1220, 1238–1239.) In each of these cases, the duty that gives rise to tort liability is either completely independent of the contract or arises from conduct which is both intentional and intended to harm. . . .

The question thus remains: is the mere negligent breach of a contract sufficient? The answer is no. It may admittedly be difficult to categorize the cases, but to state the rule succinctly: "[C]ourts will generally enforce the breach of a contractual promise through contract law, except when the actions that constitute the breach violate a social policy that merits the imposition of tort remedies." (*Freeman & Mills*, supra, 11 Cal. 4th at p. 107 (conc. and dis. opn. of Mosk, J.).)

Cf. VW v. Dillard, 579 So. 2d 1301 (Ala. 1991) (emotional distress recovery for breach of warranty in failing to repair car).

See also *Gagliardi v. Denny's Restaurants, Inc.*, 815 P.2d 1362 (Wash. 1991), where the court refused to allow recovery of damages for emotional distress for an alleged breach of employment contract resulting in wrongful termination of employment. The court said that "under the traditional rule . . . the overwhelming majority of courts deny recovery for mental distress damages" arising out of breach of contract, even though such damages might be foreseeable within the rule stated in *Hadley v. Baxendale*, [1854] 9 Ex. 341, 156 Eng. Rep. 145:

> The impact of allowing emotional distress damages for breach of contract would indeed be enormous. It is easily predictable there would be a jury issue on emotional distress in nearly every employee discharge case and in fact nearly every breach of contract case. The contractual consensus of the parties will become secondary to an action in tort.

Similarly, in *Keltner v. Washington County*, 800 P.2d 752 (Or. 1990), the 14-year-old plaintiff, who disclosed a murderer's identity and location of the murder weapon on a police promise of anonymity, could not recover for emotional distress when the police breached this agreement. The court said that contract damages could not be awarded solely for mental suffering.

9. *Distressful Attorneys.* In *McPeake v. Cannon, Esq., P.C.*, 381 Pa. Super. 227, 553 A.2d 439 (1989), the court held that the plaintiffs could not recover for the suicide of their decedent caused by defendant's alleged legal malpractice that resulted in the decedent's criminal conviction. Plaintiffs alleged that the defendant knew of decedent's emotional problems since they were "manifested by the uncontrollable twitching of his limbs and his prior expressed intention to take his own life." Nevertheless, the court said, the defendant had "no special expertise or professional training that would enable him either to foresee that a client is likely to commit suicide, or, if he could make that determination, to adopt a response to the threat." The court said that "as a matter of policy" it would be inappropriate to impose liability, since "attorneys, if exposed to such liability, would naturally be discouraged from representing what may be a sizeable number of depressed or unstable criminal defendants, in the fear that it would later be alleged that one such client committed suicide

out of despondence over a 'wrongful' conviction based on inadequate representation."

A law firm was not liable for a distraught partner's suicide in *Cutler v. Klass, Whichler & Mishne*, 473 N.W.2d 178 (Iowa 1991). The claim was premised on a letter to the partner from the firm, stating that they were delaying a decision on whether to allow the partner to return to work following hospitalization for severe depression. The firm's conduct and the letter were not so "outrageous" as to support a claim for negligent or intentional infliction of emotional distress, the court said.

On the other hand, the plaintiff in *Beis v. Bowers*, 649 So. 2d 1094 (La. App. 1995), stated a claim for emotional distress resulting from her attorney's alleged malpractice in failing to timely pursue her medical malpractice claim. She could recover such damages without showing that she probably would have prevailed in the medical malpractice claim.

The plaintiffs in *Kohn v. Schiappa*, 281 N.J. Super. 235, 656 A.2d 1322 (1995), stated a claim for emotional distress against their attorney for negligently representing them in an adoption proceeding:

> Defendant's alleged malpractice arises from having served the adoption complaint on the birth parents, thereby erroneously disclosing to them privileged information, including the name and address of the adoptive parents and the adoptee. This breach of confidentiality, plaintiffs assert, has caused them to suffer severe emotional distress.

In a legal malpractice action, the court said, "damages are typically measured by that amount which the client would have recovered but for the attorney's negligence." But, said the court:

> Since no economic "claim" was impaired by counsel's alleged negligence, the "suit within a suit" framework, typically utilized in adjudicating legal malpractice actions, has no application. Consequently, without the ability to seek redress for emotional distress damages, negligent counsel would have virtual immunity for any malpractice committed when retained for non-economic purposes. The unfairness of such a result is quickly manifest given the wide variety of attorney-client relationships other than adoption proceedings, which are not predicated upon economic interests. Drafting a living will, contested child custody or visitation disputes, criminal defense work, as well as numerous pursuits in the general equity courts are but a few examples. In such instances one would be unable to quantify any economic loss. On the other hand, severe mental and emotional distress, resulting from the loss of custody or visitation rights, or wrongful incarceration, is readily foreseeable.

A plaintiff stated a claim for intentional infliction of emotional distress against defense counsel in *Falgoust v. Herbert, Mouledoux & Bland*, 655 So. 2d 337 (La. 1995). The plaintiff, a seaman, was injured at work and filed a Jones Act claim against his employer. His orthopedist recommended lumbar surgery, but delayed proceeding with the surgery when defendants, the employer's attorneys, wrote the doctor stating that they did not believe the surgery was necessary and would "recommend that our client take whatever action is necessary" if the surgery occurred. The firm had previously filed a claim against the doctor in another case for alleged unnecessary surgery.

In *Juday v. Rotunno & Rotunno*, 276 Cal. Rptr. 445 (Cal. App. 1990), the plaintiff client was awarded a $½ million judgment against her attorney for emotional distress arising out of the attorney's misappropriation of the client's funds.

Applying what it called "the general rule," the court in *Reed v. Mitchell & Timbanard, P.C.*, 903 P.2d 621 (Ariz. App. 1995), refused to allow the plaintiff to recover for emotional distress in a legal malpractice action against her attorney for negligently failing to adequately secure a note given to her by her former husband:

> We hold that simple legal malpractice resulting in pecuniary loss which in turn causes emotional upset, even with physical symptoms, will not support a claim for damages for emotional distress.
>
> One Arizona case, *Deno v. Transamerica Title Ins. Co.*, 126 Ariz. 527, 530, 617 P.2d 35, 38 (App. 1980), has held that in the absence of outrageous conduct or bad faith, a person who suffers pecuniary loss as the result of a negligently prepared title report, is not entitled to recover damages for emotional distress resulting from the loss. Most other jurisdictions which have considered this issue in the context of legal malpractice have held that "damages for emotional injuries are not recoverable where they are a consequence of other damages caused by the attorney's negligence." 1 Ronald E. Mallen & Jeffrey M. Smith, Legal Malpractice § 16.11 at 904 (3d ed. 1989 and Supp. 1993) (citing cases from numerous jurisdictions); *see also* D. Dusty Rhoades and Laura W. Morgan, Recovery for Emotional Distress Damages in Attorney Malpractice Cases, 45 S.C.L.R. 837, 839 (1994), in which the authors, in describing the holdings of some courts, say, "consequential damages for emotional distress are not recoverable when the client's direct damages are strictly economic or pecuniary."

10. *End Runs.* The tort of alienation of affection has been widely abolished. *Dupuis v. Hand*, 814 S.W.2d 340 (Tenn. 1991). So has the tort of criminal conversation. *Destefano v. Grabrian*, 763 P.2d 275 (Colo. 1988). A plaintiff cannot circumvent these restrictions by filing a claim for intentional infliction of emotional distress. *Koestler v. Pollard*, 471 N.W.2d 7 (Wis. 1991).

Similar issues apply in workers' compensation cases. See e.g., *Hebert v. International Paper Co.*, 638 A.2d 1161 (Me. 1994), where an employee who was made fun of at work while he was at home recovering from a back injury could sue his employer for negligent infliction of emotional distress, the court held. The court held that the workers' compensation exclusivity rule was no bar to this tort claim.

11. *Pain and Suffering Caps.* Statutory caps on the amount of recoverable damages for pain and suffering have been enacted in several states. These caps are subject to constitutional challenge. *Compare Murphy v. Edmonds*, 325 Md. 342, 601 A.2d 102 (1992) ($350,000 cap on noneconomic damages in personal injury action does not violate equal protection clause of Maryland constitution) *with Morris v. Savoy*, 61 Ohio St. 3d 684, 576 N.E.2d 765 (1991)

($200,000 cap on noneconomic damages violates due process clause of state constitution under rational basis test). *See* F. HARPER, F. JAMES & O. GRAY, THE LAW OF TORTS § 25.10 n.5, at 564 (1992 Cum. Supp. No. 2).

PROBLEM

Plaintiff heard a car crash at a point where she had seen her child playing moments before. Thinking that her child had been hit, she rushed to the scene of the crash where she found her child covered with pieces of bloody broken glass from the car. The blood was from the car driver, who was seriously injured. In removing the glass from the child's body, plaintiff accidentally cut herself with one of the bloody pieces. It turned out that her child was unharmed from the crash, except for a few minor scratches. On being hospitalized, the driver of the car was diagnosed as HIV positive. Discuss the plaintiff's possible claims for emotional distress against the car driver.

G. DAMAGE TO PROPERTY AND ECONOMIC LOSS

PROBLEM

A barge ruptures an underwater pipeline, causing an interruption of gas supply to an adjacent plant. The plant owner must purchase fuel from another supplier at a price less favorable than that obtained from the pipeline owner. Plant owner sues barge owner for the difference in cost of the fuel. What result? Would the answer be different if the plant were closed temporarily while the pipeline was being repaired, and the plant workers sued for their loss of income? What if the plant were unionized? Would the union contract, and the bargaining therefor, be relevant to your inquiry? Why?

LOUISIANA ex rel. GUSTE v. M/V TESTBANK
752 F.2d 1019 (5th Cir. 1985)

HIGGINBOTHAM, CIRCUIT JUDGE.

We are asked to abandon physical damage to a proprietary interest as a prerequisite to recovery for economic loss in cases of unintentional maritime tort. We decline the invitation.

In the early evening of July 22, 1980, the *M/V Sea Daniel*, an inbound bulk carrier, and the *M/V Testbank*, an outbound container ship, collided at approximately mile forty-one of the Mississippi River Gulf outlet. At impact, a white haze enveloped the ships until carried away by prevailing winds, and containers aboard *Testbank* were damaged and lost overboard. The white haze proved to be hydrobromic acid and the contents of the containers which went overboard proved to be approximately twelve tons of pentachlorophenol, PCP, assertedly the largest such spill in United States history. The United States Coast Guard closed the outlet to navigation until August 10, 1980 and all fishing, shrimping, and related activity was temporarily suspended in the outlet and four hundred square miles of surrounding marsh and waterways.

Forty-one lawsuits were filed and consolidated before the same judge in the Eastern District of Louisiana. These suits presented claims of shipping interests, marina and boat rental operators, wholesale and retail seafood enterprises not actually engaged in fishing, seafood restaurants, tackle and bait shops, and recreational fishermen.

Defendants moved for summary judgment as to all claims for economic loss unaccompanied by physical damage to property. The district court granted the requested summary judgment as to all such claims except those asserted by commercial oystermen, shrimpers, crabbers, and fishermen who had been making a commercial use of embargoed waters. The district court found these commercial fishing interests deserving of a special protection akin to that enjoyed by seamen.[5]

On appeal a panel of this court affirmed, concluding that claims for economic loss unaccompanied by physical damage to a proprietary interest were not recoverable in maritime tort. 728 F.2d 748 (5th Cir. 1984). The panel, as did the district court, pointed to the doctrine of *Robins Dry Dock & Repair Co. v. Flint*, 275 U.S. 303, 48 S. Ct. 134, 72 L. Ed. 290 (1927), and its development in this circuit. After extensive additional briefs and oral argument, we are unpersuaded that we ought to drop physical damage to a proprietary interest as a prerequisite to recovery for economic loss. To the contrary, our reexamination of the history and central purpose of this pragmatic restriction on the doctrine of foreseeability heightens our commitment to it. Ultimately we conclude that without this limitation foreseeability loses much of its ability to function as a rule of law.

The meaning of *Robins Dry Dock & Repair v. Flint*, 275 U.S. 303, 48 S. Ct. 134, 72 L. Ed. 290 (1927) (Holmes, J.), is the flag all litigants here seek to capture. We turn first to that case and its historical setting.

In *Robins,* the time charterer of a steamship sued for profits lost when the defendant dry dock negligently damaged the vessel's propeller. The propeller had to be replaced, thus extending by two weeks the time the vessel was laid up in dry dock, and it was for the loss of use of the vessel for that period that the charterer sued. The Supreme Court denied recovery to the charterer, noting:

> [N]o authority need be cited to show that, as a general rule, at least, a tort to the person or property of one man does not make the tortfeasor liable to another merely because the injured person was under a contract with that other unknown to the doer of the wrong (citation omitted). The law does not spread its protection so far.

275 U.S. at 309, 48 S. Ct. at 135.

The principle that there could be no recovery for economic loss absent physical injury to a proprietary interest was not only well established when *Robins Dry Dock* was decided, but was remarkably resilient as well. Its strength is demonstrated by the circumstance that *Robins Dry Dock* came ten

---

[5] Stated more generally, the summary judgment denied the claims asserted by shipping interests suffering losses from delays or rerouting, marina and boat operators, wholesale and retail seafood enterprises not actually engaged in fishing, shrimping, crabbing, or oystering in the area, seafood restaurants, tackle and bait shops, and recreational fishermen, oystermen, shrimpers and crabbers. The rights of commercial fishermen who survived summary judgment are not before us.

years after Judge Cardozo's shattering of privity in *MacPherson v. Buick Motor Co.*, 217 N.Y. 382, 111 N.E. 1050 (1916). Indeed this limit on liability stood against a sea of change in the tort law. Retention of this conspicuous bright-line rule in the face of the reforms brought by the increased influence of the school of legal realism is strong testament both to the rule's utility and to the absence of a more "conceptually pure" substitute. The push to delete the restrictions on recovery for economic loss lost its support and by the early 1940's had failed. In sum, it is an old sword that plaintiffs have here picked up.

Plaintiffs would confine *Robins* to losses suffered for inability to perform contracts between a plaintiff and others, categorizing the tort as a species of interference with contract. When seen in the historical context described above, however, it is apparent that *Robins Dry Dock* represents more than a limit on recovery for interference with contractual rights. Apart from what it represented and certainly apart from what it became, its literal holding was not so restricted. If a time charterer's relationship to its negligently injured vessel is too remote, other claimants without even the connection of a contract are even more remote.

In a sense, every claim of economic injury rests in some measure on an interference with contract or prospective advantage. It was only in this sense that profits were lost in *Byrd v. English* [43 S.E. 419 (Ga. 1903)] when the electrical power to plaintiffs printing plant was cut off. The printing company's contractual right to receive power was interfered with, and in turn, its ability to print for its customers was impinged. That the printing company had a contract with the power company did not make more remote the relationship between its loss of profits and the tortious acts. To the contrary, the contract reduced this remoteness by defining an orbit of predictable injury smaller than if there were no contract between the power company and the printer. When the loss is economic rather than physical, that the loss caused a breach of contract or denied an expectancy is of no moment. If a plaintiff connected to the damaged chattels by contract cannot recover, others more remotely situated are foreclosed *a fortiori*. Indisputably, the *Robins Dry Dock* principle is not as easily contained as plaintiff would have it.

Plaintiffs urge that the decisions in *Petition of Kinsman Transit Co.*, 388 F.2d 821 (2d Cir. 1968) (*Kinsman II*), and *Union Oil Co. v. Oppen*, 501 F.2d 558 (9th Cir. 1974), support their arguments that the *Robins Dry Dock* principle should be abandoned. We disagree. The policy considerations on which both those decisions are bottomed confirm our opinion that pragmatic limitations on the doctrine of foreseeability are both desirable and necessary.

In *Kinsman* "an unusual concatenation of events on the Buffalo River" resulted in a disaster which disrupted river traffic for several months.[6] Because

---

[6] *Kinsman II*, 388 F.2d at 822. Judge Kaufman briefly summarized the facts of *Kinsman* as follows:

> [A]s result of the negligence of the Kinsman Transit Company and the Continental Grain Company the S.S. MacGilvray Shiras broke loose from her moorings and careened stern first down the narrow, S-shaped river channel. She struck the S.S. *Michael K. Tewksbury*, which in turn broke loose from her moorings and drifted down-stream — followed by the *Shiras* — until she crashed into the Michigan Avenue Bridge. The bridge

of the disruption, the plaintiffs incurred extra expenses in fulfilling their contracts to supply and transport wheat and corn. In a previous panel decision arising out of the same facts, the court had rejected the defendants' arguments that recovery by such plaintiffs should be disallowed because their injuries were not foreseeable. Judge Friendly stated that while "[f]oreseeability of danger [was] necessary to render conduct negligent," it was not required that the defendants envision the precise harm resulting from their conduct before liability could be imposed. *Petition of Kinsman Transit Co.,* 338 F.2d 708, 724 (2d Cir. 1964), *cert. denied,* 380 U.S. 944, 13 L. Ed. 2d 963, 85 S. Ct. 1026 (1965) (*Kinsman I*).

In *Kinsman II* the defendants argued that the plaintiff's claims should be denied because there was no cause of action for negligent interference with a contractual right. The court dismissed the claims, but did so on the basis that the damages were too remote. Thus, plaintiffs argue, *Kinsman* supports using foreseeability to determine whether their claims are cognizable in maritime tort. We think the opinion itself answers that contention. While rejecting any bright line rule, the court recognized that foreseeability was not a panacea and that limits on the concept should be maintained.

> [I]t was a foreseeable consequence of the negligence . . . that the river would be dammed. . . . It may be that the specific manner was not foreseeable in which the damages to Cargill and Cargo Carriers would be incurred but such strict foreseeability . . . has not been required. [Yet] . . . somewhere a point will be reached when courts will agree that the link has become too tenuous . . . (citation omitted). We believe that this point has been reached with the Cargill and Cargo Carriers claim. . . .
>
> In the final analysis, the circumlocution whether posed in terms of "foreseeability," "duty," "proximate cause," "remoteness," etc. seems unavoidable. . . . [W]e return to Judge Andrews' frequently quoted statement in *Palsgraf* . . . . "It is all a question of expediency . . . of fair judgment, always keeping in mind the fact that we endeavor to make a rule in each case that will be practical and in keeping with the general understanding of mankind."

Kinsman II, 388 F.2d at 824–25.

As we explain in . . . this opinion, we disagree with a case-by-case approach because we think the value of a rule is significant in these maritime decisions. *Kinsman II*'s general analysis of the problem, however, recognizing as it does the need for the imposition of limitations on recovery for the foreseeable consequences of an act of negligence, is compatible with our own. In *Union Oil,* vast quantities of raw crude were released when the defendant oil company negligently caused an oil spill. The oil was carried by wind, wave, and tidal currents over large stretches of the California coast disrupting, among other things, commercial fishing operations. While conceding that ordinarily

---

collapsed and its wreckage, together with the *Tewksbury* and the *Shiras,* formed a dam which caused extensive flooding and an ice jam reaching almost 3 miles upstream. As a result of this disaster, transportation on the river was disrupted [for] a period of about 2 months.

G. DAMAGE TO PROPERTY AND ECONOMIC LOSS 681

there is no recovery for economic losses unaccompanied by physical damage, the court concluded that commercial fishermen were foreseeable plaintiffs whose interests the oil company had a duty to protect when conducting drilling operations. The opinion pointed out that the fishermen's losses were foreseeable and direct consequences of the spill, that fishermen have historically enjoyed a protected position under maritime law, and suggested that economic considerations also supported permitting recovery.

Yet *Union Oil's* holding was carefully limited to commercial fishermen, plaintiffs whose economic losses were characterized as "of a particular and special nature." *Union Oil*, 501 F.2d at 570. The *Union Oil* panel expressly declined to "open the door to claims that may be asserted by . . . other[s] . . . whose economic or personal affairs were discommoded by the oil spill" and noted that the general rule denying recovery for pure economic loss has "a legitimate sphere within which to operate." *Id.*

In sum, the decisions of courts in other circuits convince us that *Robins Dry Dock* is both a widely used and necessary limitation on recovery for economic losses. The holdings in *Kinsman and Union Oil* are not to the contrary. The courts in both those cases made plain that restrictions on the concept of foreseeability ought to be imposed where recovery is sought for pure economic losses.

Plaintiffs urge that the requirement of physical injury to a proprietary interest is arbitrary, unfair, and illogical, as it denies recovery for foreseeable injury caused by negligent acts. At its bottom the argument is that questions of remoteness ought to be left to the trier of fact. Ultimately the question becomes who ought to decide — judge or jury — and whether there will be a rule beyond the jacket of a given case. The plaintiffs contend that the "problem" need not be separately addressed, but instead should be handled by "traditional" principles of tort law. Putting the problem of which doctrine is the traditional one aside, their rhetorical questions are flawed in several respects.

Those who would delete the requirement of physical damage have no rule or principle to substitute. Their approach fails to recognize limits upon the adjudicating ability of courts. We do not mean just the ability to supply a judgment; prerequisite to this adjudicatory function are preexisting rules, whether the creature of courts or legislatures. Courts can decide cases without preexisting normative guidance but the result becomes less judicial and more the product of a managerial, legislative or negotiated function.[7]

Review of the foreseeable consequences of the collision of the *Sea Daniel* and *Testbank* demonstrates the wave upon wave of successive economic

---

[7] As Professor Henderson put it:

When asked, cajoled, and finally forced to try to solve unadjudicable problems, courts will inevitably respond in the only manner possible — they will begin exercising managerial authority and the discretion that goes with it. Attempts will be made to disguise the substitution, to preserve appearances, but the process which evolves should (and no doubt eventually will) be recognized for what it is — not adjudication, but an elaborate, expansive masquerade.

Henderson, *Expanding the Negligence Concept: Retreat From the Rule of Law,* 51 Ind. L.J. 467, 476–77 (1976).

consequences and the managerial role plaintiffs would have us assume. The vessel delayed in St. Louis may be unable to fulfill its obligation to haul from Memphis, to the injury of the shipper, to the injury of the buyers, to the injury of their customers. Plaintiffs concede, as do all who attack the requirement of physical damage, that a line would need to be drawn — somewhere on the other side, each plaintiff would say in turn, of its recovery. Plaintiffs advocate not only that the lines be drawn elsewhere but also that they be drawn on an ad hoc and discrete basis. The result would be that no determinable measure of the limit of foreseeability would precede the decision on liability. We are told that when the claim is too remote, or too tenuous, recovery will be denied. Presumably then, as among all plaintiffs suffering foreseeable economic loss, recovery will turn on a judge or jury's decision. There will be no rationale for the differing results save the "judgment" of the trier of fact. Concededly, it can "decide" all the claims presented, and with comparative if not absolute ease. The point is not that such a process cannot be administered but rather that its judgments would be much less the products of a determinable rule of law. In this important sense, the resulting decisions would be judicial products only in their draw upon judicial resources.

The bright line rule of damage to a proprietary interest, as most, has the virtue of predictability with the vice of creating results in cases at its edge that are said to be "unjust" or "unfair." Plaintiffs point to seemingly perverse results, where claims the rule allows and those it disallows are juxtaposed — such as vessels striking a dock, causing minor but recoverable damage, then lurching athwart a channel causing great but unrecoverable economic loss. The answer is that when lines are drawn sufficiently sharp in their definitional edges to be reasonable and predictable, such differing results are the inevitable result — indeed, decisions are the desired product. But there is more. The line drawing sought by plaintiffs is no less arbitrary because the line drawing appears only in the outcome — as one claimant is found too remote and another is allowed to recover. The true difference is that plaintiff's approach would mask the results. The present rule would be more candid, and in addition, by making results more predictable, serves a normative function. It operates as a rule of law and allows a court to adjudicate rather than manage.

That the rule is identifiable and will predict outcomes in advance of the ultimate decision about recovery enables it to play additional roles. Here we agree with plaintiffs that economic analysis, even at the rudimentary level of jurists, is helpful both in the identification of such roles and the essaying of how the roles play. Thus it is suggested that placing all the consequences of its error on the maritime industry will enhance its incentive for safety. While correct, as far as such analysis goes, such *in terrorem* benefits have an optimal level. Presumably, when the cost of an unsafe condition exceeds its utility there is an incentive to change. As the costs of an accident become increasing multiples of its utility, however, there is a point at which greater accident costs lose meaning, and the incentive curve flattens. When the accidents costs are added in large but unknowable amounts the value of the exercise is diminished.

With a disaster inflicting large and reverberating injuries through the economy, as here, we believe the more important economic inquiry is that of relative cost of administration, and in maritime matters administration quickly involves insurance. Those economic losses not recoverable under the present rule for lack of physical damage to a proprietary interest are the subject of first party or loss insurance. The rule change would work a shift to the more costly liability system of third party insurance. For the same reasons that courts have imposed limits on the concept of foreseeability, liability insurance might not be readily obtainable for the types of losses asserted here. As Professor James has noted, "[s]erious practical problems face insurers in handling insurance against potentially wide, open-ended liability. From an insurer's point of view it is not practical to cover, without limit, a liability that may reach catastrophic proportions, or to fix a reasonable premium on a risk that does not lend itself to actuarial measurement." [James, 25 VAND. L. REV. 43, 53]. By contrast, first party insurance is feasible for many of the economic losses claimed here. Each businessman who might be affected by a disruption of river traffic or by a halt in fishing activities can protect against that eventuality at a relatively low cost since his own potential losses are finite and readily discernible. Thus, to the extent that economic analysis informs our decision here, we think that it favors retention of the present rule.

WISDOM, CIRCUIT JUDGE, dissenting.

Robins is the Tar Baby of tort law in this circuit. And the brier-patch is far away. This Court's application of *Robins* is out of step with contemporary tort doctrine, works substantial injustice on innocent victims, and is unsupported by the considerations that justified the Supreme Court's 1927 decision.

Robins was a tort case grounded on a contract. Whatever the justification for the original holding, this Court's requirement of physical injury as a condition to recovery is an unwarranted step backwards in torts jurisprudence. The resulting bar for claims of economic loss unaccompanied by any physical damage conflicts with conventional tort principles of foreseeability and proximate cause. I would analyze the plaintiffs' claims under these principles, using the "particular damage" requirement of public nuisance law as an additional means of limiting claims. Although this approach requires a case-by-case analysis, it comports with the fundamental idea of fairness that innocent plaintiffs should receive compensation and negligent defendants should bear the cost of their tortious acts. Such a result is worth the additional costs of adjudicating these claims, and this rule of liability appears to be more economically efficient. Finally, this result would relieve courts of the necessity of manufacturing exceptions totally inconsistent with the expanded *Robins* rule of requiring physical injury as a prerequisite to recovery.

NOTES

1. *The Requirement of Physical Injury, and Severability of Damages.* In *Spartan Steel v. Martin & Co.* [1973], Q.B. 27, the defendant negligently caused a power shutoff to plaintiff's steel plant, resulting in a shutdown in production. Because of the shutdown, metal in process of production cooled and solidified, and the metal thus became commercially useless. In addition, plaintiff lost profits on metal product orders that had to be canceled as a result of the shutdown. The court held that the loss resulting from the metal

solidification was recoverable as property damage, but that the lost profits from canceled orders constituted economic loss not recoverable in tort.

In *Dutsch v. Sea Ray Boats, Inc.,* 845 P.2d 187 (Okla. 1992), the plaintiff recovered damages in products liability for personal injury and destruction of his boat. The damages resulted from a fire caused by a defect in the boat, which was manufactured by the defendant. The defendant contended that damage to the boat itself was economic loss, not recoverable in tort, but only in warranty. In affirming the plaintiff's verdict, the court said:

> Sea Ray asserts that the trial court erred in allowing recovery by Dutsch for the boat itself. Relying on *Waggoner v. Town & Country Mobile Homes,* 808 P.2d 649 (Okla. 1990), Sea Ray claims that a plaintiff may not recover for the product itself under a theory of manufacturer's products liability. The jury awarded damages for the boat in the amount of $115,000.00.
>
> In *Waggoner,* the plaintiff brought a manufacturer's products liability action to recover damage to the product in question, a mobile home. There were no other asserted damages to property or persons. We ruled that no action lies in manufacturer's products liability for purely economic injury to the product itself. In so holding we observed that the purpose of adopting the theory of manufacturer's product liability in tort cases was not to do away with contractual liability under the Uniform Commercial Code. When purely economic damages occur and there is no damage to person or other property, U.C.C. remedies are sufficient to protect the plaintiff.
>
> *Waggoner* was a narrow ruling dealing with the situation where there was damage only to the product itself:
>
>> We adopt this rationale and hold that in Oklahoma no action lies in manufacturer's products liability for injury only to the product itself resulting in purely economic loss. *Id.* at 653.
>
> *Waggoner* did not address the situation presented here, where there is personal injury as well as damage to the product. In this situation prior case law indicates that both types of damages are recoverable under a products liability theory.
>
> In fact, *Waggoner* specifically stated that manufacturer's products liability provides for the recovery of personal injury damages and damages to other property. *Id.* at 652. Recognizing that manufacturer's products liability and the U.C.C. provide "parallel remedies" in these instances, we simply pointed out that there was no need for the products liability theory to extend to the situation where the only damage was to the product itself.
>
> *Waggoner* does not require that plaintiff recover under two different theories if there is damage to the product in addition to other damages. The purpose of *Waggoner* — to preserve the remedies of the U.C.C. — is upheld by limiting a plaintiff seeking only recovery for the product itself to U.C.C. remedies. This policy would not be furthered by requiring a plaintiff to proceed under two different theories to recover two different types of damage if one type of damage claimed

is recoverable in manufacturer's products liability. Thus, we decline to extend *Waggoner* beyond those situations in which a plaintiff suffers damage only to the product itself. The trial court was correct in permitting recovery for the loss of the boat.

2. *Economic Harm to One Person for Damage to Another.* The court in *M/V Testbank* was concerned with the issue of economic harm to a victim because of damage to the property of a third person. When a victim sustains personal injury, he may recover the economic harm resulting therefrom, usually his loss of earning capacity. What if the claim is economic harm to the victim because of personal injury, or death, of a third person? The general rule is that there is no recovery. Exceptions have been created as for example for wrongful death or loss of consortium where the victim is a close family member. What if the victim is a key employee whose replacement is costly? *See* Annot., 4 A.L.R.4th 504 (1981). What if the victim is the sole shareholder of the corporation? Is the measure of damages the corporation's loss of profits, or the cost to replace the victim's services? *See, e.g., Baughman Surgical Assocs. v. Aetna Cas. & Sur. Co.,* 302 So. 2d 316 (La. App. 1974).

3. *Further Up the Food Chain.* Can a seafood processor or restaurateur protect himself against the kind of loss sustained by the plaintiffs in the principal case? How? Is he likely to do so?

Can a seaman or wage earner protect himself against the loss of wages in a similar situation? Is he likely to do so?

4. *Damage to Real Property.* If wrongful conduct causes damage to land or structures, the victim is entitled to an amount that will compensate him for the diminution in value of the property. There are two primary methods of determining this diminution: (a) the value of the property immediately before the loss, less the value immediately after, or (b) the cost of repair. Some types of loss dictate the method which should be used, such as where the damage is irreparable. *Mid-Continent Pipe Line Co. v. Eberwein,* 333 P.2d 561 (Okla. 1958) (permanent destruction of water supply), or where the cost of repairs exceeds the pre-accident value of the property. *Kirkbride v. Lisbon Contrs., Inc.,* 385 Pa. Super. 292, 560 A.2d 809 (1989). If the cost of repair method is used, it may be appropriate to reduce the award to reflect the fact that the repaired property will be more valuable than the damaged property. *See, e.g., Northwestern Mut. Fire Ass'n v. Allain,* 226 La. 788, 77 So. 2d 395 (1954).

Other items of damage which may be appropriate under the circumstances include (a) loss of use or loss of earnings (profits) from the damaged property, and (b) damages for invasion of the victim's proprietary interest in the property. This latter element, a purely dignitary one, may take the form of an award for inconvenience or mental anguish.

Punitive damages may be awarded for damage to or destruction of property, where the defendant's conduct is so egregious that it will support an award of exemplary damages under the appropriate state law. Some states have passed special statutes authorizing double or treble damages for trespass, particularly where timber is removed by the trespasser. *See, e.g.,* LA. REV. STAT. § 3:4278.1 (1989); CAL. CIV. CODE, § 3346 (1990). *See* Wiener, *Timber Trespass,* 47 OR. L. REV. 260 (1968).

5. *Damage to Chattels*: When chattel property is destroyed, the owner is entitled to recover from the tortfeasor the fair market value of the property at the time of destruction or, in the case of commodities of fluctuating value that are customarily traded on an exchange, the highest replacement value within a reasonable time during which replacement might have been made. RESTATEMENT (SECOND) OF TORTS § 927. Fair market value usually is defined as the price at which a willing buyer would buy and a willing seller would sell. The Restatement suggests that an award for loss of use "not otherwise compensated" would be appropriate, although many jurisdictions deny recovery for "loss of use" when the property is totally destroyed, sometimes on the theory that the victim should immediately purchase a replacement and avoid the loss of use. Is this practical? The Restatement also would award interest from the time at which the value is fixed. Would an award of interest on the cost of replacement and an award for loss of use constitute "double recovery"?

If the property is so special that "fair market value" cannot be determined, the court may award the owner the replacement cost, less depreciation. In some cases, the owner may not be able to establish fair market value (as when a family heirloom or memento is destroyed) or replacement cost (as when large, old trees are destroyed). In those cases, the tendency is to permit the trier of fact "wide latitude" to award "actual value," which must not include "fanciful or sentimental" value. *Nelson v. Coleman Co.*, 249 S.C. 652, 155 S.E.2d 917 (1967); *DeSpirito v. Bristol County Water Co.*, 227 A.2d 782 (R.I. 1967).

6. *Recovery for the Loss of a Contingent Fee Client.* Suppose an attorney leaves a firm taking with her a case involving a contingent fee client, and ultimately recovers in the case. What part of the recovery is the firm entitled to? It has been held that the firm is entitled to a *quantum meruit* recovery, plus expenses, and also to an amount sufficient to compensate the firm for the risk it assumed in taking the case. *La Mantia v. Durst*, 561 A.2d 276 (N.J. App. 1989); *In re L-Tryptophan Cases*, 518 N.W.2d 616 (Minn. App. 1994). How would this risk factor be valued?

7. *The Bivens Action and Attorneys' Fees.* If a federal employee tortiously violates a person's federal constitutional rights, the person can bring a constitutional tort claim against the employee under *Bivens v. Six Unknown Named Agents*, 403 U.S. 388, 91 S. Ct. 1999, 29 L. Ed. 2d 619 (1971). The Equal Access to Justice Act, 28 U.S.C. § 2412(d)(2)(C), provides for an award of attorneys' fees to the prevailing party in any civil suit against an "official of the United States acting in his or her official capacity." The court in *Kreines v. United States*, 33 F.3d 1105 (9th Cir. 1994), said that this statute did not provide for an award of attorneys' fees in a *Bivens*-type case, because "*Bivens* actions are against governmental employees in their individual capacities." Thus, the court found, an official acting in his individual capacity would not be acting in his official capacity within the meaning of the statute.

PROBLEM

Ann was involved in a one-car accident when she lost control of her car coming out of her ice-covered driveway, causing the car to run into a retaining wall. Her insurance company appraised the value of the automobile before the accident at $600. Because the lowest repair estimate Ann was able to obtain was $1,000, the company declared the automobile a total loss, paid her $500 and allowed her to keep the car, which had a salvage value of $100. Although the body of the car was severely damaged, it was still drivable. The day after Ann received payment from her insurance company, Jones ran into Ann's car from the rear as she was stopped at a red light. Cost of repairing the damage done by Jones is $2,000, making the total cost of repairing the car $3,000. Assuming that Jones is negligent, what does he owe Ann?

H. DAMAGE TO RELATIONS

WEHNER v. WEINSTEIN
191 W.Va. 149, 444 S.E.2d 27 (W. Va. 1994)

MILLER, JUSTICE.

These appeals are brought by the defendants in three civil actions that were consolidated for trial in the Circuit Court of Monongalia County. The plaintiffs are the administrator of the estate of Jennifer Wehner, who was killed when she was struck on a public sidewalk by a runaway pizza delivery car, and Nicole Fisher and Jessica Landau, who were injured in the same accident. The decedent and the two individual plaintiffs were students at West Virginia University. The jury returned verdicts against all the defendants and awarded $1,978,623 to the Wehner estate; $132,090.25 to Nicole Fisher; and $87,158.85 to Jessica Landau.

Brett Barry Weinstein, a defendant below and a member of the Sigma Phi Epsilon Fraternity (Fraternity), does not appeal the adverse jury verdict which found him to be 75 percent at fault. Shortly before the accident, Mr. Weinstein was at the Fraternity and was attempting to leave in his car, but was blocked by a pizza delivery car. In order to move the delivery car, Mr. Weinstein opened the car's door, released its hand brake, and placed the gear shift in neutral. He was assisted by the defendant Matthew Kiser, who was a pledge of the Fraternity. The jury found Mr. Kiser to be 5 percent at fault.

The delivery car was owned by Bossio Enterprises, Inc., dba Mario's Pizza, and was being driven by David Turner, who was delivering an order to an individual at the Fraternity. The jury found Mr. Turner was negligent in the manner he parked the vehicle, and it found Mario's Pizza, as the employer, to be 10 percent at fault.

The Fraternity was sued on the theory that it failed to supervise and control the actions of Mr. Weinstein and Mr. Kiser. The jury found Mr. Kiser to be negligent and also found him to be an agent of the Fraternity, thus making it vicariously liable. The Fraternity was found to be 5 percent at fault.

The Sigma Phi Epsilon Building Association, Inc. (Association), another defendant below, owns the real estate on which the Fraternity is located. The Association was sued on the basis that the premises were dangerous because of its location on a steep hill, that it failed to provide proper warnings for traffic entering and leaving the property, and that it did not supervise and control the actions of Mr. Weinstein and Mr. Kiser. The Association was found to be 5 percent at fault.

The defendants, except for Mr. Weinstein, each claim that as a matter of law, they should be found not liable. Each claim a common error as to the damages awarded in the wrongful death action. They assert that the damages should have been reduced by the reasonable value of the anticipated personal consumption expenses of the decedent throughout her normal life expectancy. We begin by discussing the liability of each defendant.

Mario's Pizza argues it was not reasonably foreseeable that after the car was parked with the brake on and the ignition key removed, that someone would enter the car, disengage the brake, put the car in neutral, and cause it to roll. . . .

We believe there was sufficient evidence of proximate cause. The delivery car driver, Mr. Turner, had delivered pizza to the fraternity house on other occasions, and was familiar with the topography. He was aware that there was a parking lot adjacent to the house and used it on other occasions. However, this time, rather than park in the lot, he parked his vehicle against the normal traffic flow and blocked the driveway to the house.

Mr. Turner also knew the area where he parked was immediately adjacent to the steep sloping driveway. The area below the driveway contained many student-housing facilities. If the car moved from where Mr. Turner parked it, it would roll down the hill injuring any one of the students who frequently used the streets and adjacent sidewalks below the fraternity.

Mr. Turner also acknowledged that a number of students lived in the fraternity house and used the driveway that he blocked. He also was aware that parked vehicles had been tampered with in this area. He knew that he would be going inside the house to deliver the order and that the car doors were not locked and access could be gained to the interior of the car. Moreover, he was aware that the car had a standard transmission which could be shifted by the clutch pedal without a key in the ignition.

With these facts in mind, we believe it was for the jury to determine whether it was reasonably foreseeable under the circumstances that some person would attempt to move the vehicle to gain access to the driveway. The jurors could realize from their common knowledge the impetuous nature of college students and their tendency to act without mature consideration. This situation is no more extreme than the employer we found to be liable under proximate cause principles in *Robertson v. LeMaster*, 171 W. Va. 607, 301 S.E.2d 563 (1983). There, an employee who made several requests to leave finally was permitted to do so after he had worked some twenty-seven hours. While driving home, he fell asleep and ran into another vehicle injuring the plaintiffs. Suit was brought against the employer. We held it was reasonably foreseeable that such an event could occur under all the circumstances. . . .

What Mario's Pizza actually is arguing is not so much a foreseeability issue, but a claim that the actions of Mr. Weinstein and Mr. Kiser in releasing the hand brake, placing the car in neutral, and attempting to move it were independent or intervening causes of the accident. Mario's Pizza does not assert it was without any negligence, and, indeed, on this record, it could not.

By utilizing what amounts to an intervening cause argument, it seeks to escape liability. . . .

. . . However, an intervening cause must operate independently of any other act. We do not believe in this case that this test can be met. The location of the delivery car blocking ingress and egress coupled with its close proximity to the steep driveway and the car's accessibility are all circumstances resulting from Mr. Turner's actions that contributed to cause the ultimate accident. It is the combination of negligent acts that is the hallmark of concurrent negligence.

[The court found the fraternity and the Association were not negligent. Failure to post signs "designating visitor, tenant and no parking areas" was "but a passive or static condition of the premises" and had nothing to do with the intervening acts of the other defendants." It also found that Mr. Kizer was not acting as an agent of the fraternity at the time of the accident.]

The defendants urge us to adopt a rule that in a wrongful death action where future loss of earnings is claimed, there be an offset for the decedent's personal living expenses. In this case, the trial court refused to accept this principle although urged to do so by the defendants. The parties recognize that in note 6 of *Harris v. Matherly Machinery, Inc.*, 187 W. Va. 234, 417 S.E.2d 925 (1992), we declined to address the issue. Consequently, this issue is a matter of first impression.

The Washington Supreme Court in *Hinzman v. Palmanteer*, 81 Wash. 2d 327, 332–33, 501 P.2d 1228, 1232 (1972), made this general summary of the law:

> "Three theories have been developed for measuring the lost earning capacity of a decedent. . . . (1) The probable worth of the decedent's future net earnings had he lived to his normal life expectancy. Personal expenses are deducted from gross earnings to reach the net. . . . (2) The present worth of decedent's probable future savings had he lived to a normal life expectancy. Probable personal and family expenditures are both subtracted from probable gross earnings. . . . (3) The present worth of decedent's future gross earnings. No expenses are deducted from the award computed."

The Washington court adopted the first theory by deducting the decedent's personal living expenses.

We recognize the defendants' claim that a majority of state courts that have considered the question allow a deduction for the decedent's personal consumption expenses. However, in reviewing these cases, we find that in most instances, the discussion in the cases of this issue is quite cursory. Often there is nothing more than a brief restatement of the rule without any analysis of its rationale or citation to other jurisdictions. In some jurisdictions the wrongful death statute relating to damages expressly provides a deduction for personal expenses, *see, e.g., Air Florida, Inc. v. Hobbs*, 477 So. 2d 40 (Fla. Dist. Ct. App. 1985); *Romano v. Duke*, 111 R.I. 459, 304 A.2d 47 (1973), or in the case of North Carolina use the term "[n]et income." In most jurisdictions, the wrongful death statute as to the amount of damages to be awarded is quite general often utilizing only a standard of fair and just compensation for the pecuniary loss. There is no statutory language that speaks to recovery of lost earnings in many of these statutes. As a consequence, the courts in those jurisdictions are accorded considerable flexibility in determining the elements of damages that may be recovered and any limitations by way of deductions.

On the other hand, our wrongful death statute is quite detailed as to the various categories of damages that may be awarded. See W. VA. CODE, 55-7-6(c) (1992).[8] In particular, it allows for "compensation for reasonably expected loss of (i) income of the decedent[.]" W. VA. CODE, 55-7-6(c)(1)(B)(i). We traditionally have stated that the elements of damages in a wrongful death action and their manner of distribution are governed by our statute. See *Arnold v. Turek*, 185 W. Va. 400, 407 S.E.2d 706 (1991); *Bond v. City of Huntington*, 166 W. Va. 581, 276 S.E.2d 539 (1981). In *Bond, supra*, we discussed our earlier cases that had added various damage components to our wrongful death statute. We determined that punitive damages could be recovered even though the statute did not specifically authorize them and came to this conclusion in Syllabus Point 1 of *Bond*:

> "Not only has the Legislature liberalized the wrongful death recovery statute through the years, but this Court has adopted a liberal construction of the statute from our earliest cases."

In the absence of any clear legislative language, we refuse to construe the phrase "reasonably expected loss of . . . income of the decedent," IN W. VA. CODE, 55-7-6(c)(1)(B)(i), to mean "net income." We, therefore, hold that the language of W. VA. CODE, 55-7-6(c)(1)(B)(i), that allows as part of the elements of damages in a wrongful death action compensation for reasonably expected loss of income of the decedent, does not require a deduction for estimated personal living expenses.

For the foregoing reasons, we affirm the judgment of the Circuit Court of Monongalia County against Matthew Kiser and Bossio Enterprises, Inc., dba Mario's Pizza, but we reverse the judgment against Sigma Phi Epsilon, a national fraternal organization and association, and Sigma Phi Epsilon Building Association, Inc., a corporation.

NOTES

1. *Wrongful Death Statutes.* Early English and American common law denied recovery when the victim or the tortfeasor died. The common law rule has been abrogated by statute in all 50 states. Massachusetts also has recognized a limited right of recovery at common law. See *Gaudette v. Webb*, 362 Mass. 60, 284 N.E.2d 222 (1972). However, recovery for wrongful death generally is governed by the language and judicial interpretation of the statute in the particular jurisdiction.

---

[8] The text of W. Va. Code, 55-7-6(c), states: "(1) The verdict of the jury shall include, but may not be limited to, damages for the following: (A) Sorrow, mental anguish, and solace which may include society, companionship, comfort, guidance, kindly offices and advice of the decedent; (B) compensation for reasonably expected loss of (i) income of the decedent, and (ii) services, protection, care and assistance provided by the decedent; (C) expenses for the care, treatment and hospitalization of the decedent incident to the injury resulting in death; and (D) reasonable funeral expenses."

The courts have been reluctant to create a common law cause of action for wrongful death. But the Supreme Court did just that in *Moragne v. State Marine Lines*, 398 U.S. 375, 90 S. Ct. 1772, 26 L. Ed. 2d 339 (1970), where neither federal nor state law provided a statutory cause of action for the death of a longshoreman killed while working aboard a vessel in navigable waters within the State of Florida. The Federal Death on the High Seas Act, 46 U.S.C. §§ 761–762, did not apply, and the Florida Wrongful Death Statute did not encompass unseaworthiness as a basis of liability. Overruling precedent, the Supreme Court recognized a federal common law maritime cause of action on behalf of the deceased.

Where there is an applicable wrongful death statute, the courts usually consider themselves reduced to interpreting the statute. Compare, however, the development of the common law warranty and strict tort causes of action that parallel the statutory warranty cause of action in products liability.

2. *Wrongful Death Benefits or Survival.* There are two general types of benefits available under the statutes — wrongful death benefits and survival benefits. A statute may be denominated by one name or both, *i.e.*, it may be titled a "Wrongful Death Statute" or a "Survival Statute" or a "Wrongful Death/Survival Statute." The terminology usually is not important. The major issues are what benefits are recoverable by which beneficiaries, and the effect of the victim's misconduct upon recovery. The wrongful death claim, properly speaking (as contrasted to the survival claim), establishes a new cause of action in favor of a designated beneficiary for the loss that beneficiary sustained as a result of the death of the victim. The elements of damage may include loss of support, loss of services, loss of society, and in the appropriate case, loss of other consortium with the victim. The survival statute traditionally allows recovery for the victim's conscious pain and suffering from injury to death, loss of earnings from injury to death, and medical expenses. Funeral expenses do not fit comfortably under either statute, and are variously recoverable under one or the other of these statutes.

There is a striking difference between survival and wrongful death claims. "In most states the recourse of creditors [of the deceased] is limited to proceeds of a survival action and does not extend to the proceeds of a wrongful death action (which is for the exclusive benefit of the designated survivors)." F. HARPER, F. JAMES & O. GRAY, THE LAW OF TORTS § 24.6 n.12 (2d ed. 1986).

3. *Non-Pecuniary Damages.* The first wrongful death/survival statutes, patterned after the Lord Campbell's Act described in *Moragne,* limited recovery to pecuniary damages, *i.e.*, loss of support and services. One motivation may have been to avoid the use of the loss of life as the measure of damages because that measurement was deemed both impossible and repugnant. "Arguably, no jury verdict could be excessive. The death of a family member, particularly a child, involves inconsolable grief for which no amount of money can compensate." *Roberts v. Stevens Clinic Hosp.,* 345 S.E.2d 791 (W. Va. 1986). Some states still limit recovery to pecuniary damages, although a majority will permit recovery of non-pecuniary damages. Some courts have been creative in defining pecuniary damages. *See, e.g., Haumersen v. Ford Motor Co.,* 257 N.W.2d 7 (Iowa 1977) (award of present value of estate which seven-year-old decedent would reasonably be expected to have accumulated

as a result of his own efforts from the date of majority through normal term of his life.)

4. *Hedonic Damages.* There is a division of authority regarding whether hedonic damages (loss of enjoyment of life) are recoverable in a wrongful death action. *Compare Romero v. Byers*, 117 N.M. 422, 872 P.2d 840 (1994) (allowing such damages), *with Spencer v. A-I Crane Serv.* 880 S.W.2d 938 (Tenn. 1994) (denying such damages). There is also a division of authority as to whether the victim must be aware of his condition in order to recover for loss of enjoyment of life. *Compare Flannery v. United States*, 171 W. Va. 27, 297 S.W.2d 433 (1983) (holding that "a plaintiff in a personal injury action who has been rendered permanently semi-comatose is entitled to recover for impairment of his capacity to enjoy life as a measure of the permanency of his injuries even though he may not be able to sense his loss of enjoyment of life"), *with Flannery v. United States*, 718 F.2d 108 (4th Cir. 1983) (damages for loss of enjoyment of life are not recoverable under the FTCA by a plaintiff who "is unaware of his loss," since he cannot use the money, he "cannot spend it upon necessities and pleasures," and he "cannot experience the pleasure of giving it away"). Reconsider *McDougald v. Garber*, given in Section B of this chapter.

Recovery of hedonic damages may be objectionable in any case, whether wrongful death or personal injury, where the evidence of such damages is based on expert testimony regarding willingness-to-pay economic studies. *See Montalvo v. Lapez*, 77 Haw. 282, 884 P.2d 345 (1994). As the court said in *Ayers v. Robinson*, 887 F. Supp. 1049 (N.D. Ill. 1995), economists' views concerning the accuracy of such studies vary widely, and the data values a statistical life rather than a particular person's life. Are these objections unique to hedonic damages evidence?

5. *Loss of Support.* The award for loss of support usually is determined by calculating the victim's loss of earnings (or earning capacity) during his projected lifetime and reducing that by the amount of those earnings that the victim would have spent on himself, *i.e.*, his personal consumption. Some courts also may reduce the award by the amount that the victim would have saved. In that case, the beneficiary may be entitled to an award for loss of his increased inheritance. *See, e.g., O'Toole v. United States*, 242 F.2d 308 (3d Cir. 1957).

In *Wehner v. Weinstein*, given above, the court held that a wrongful death recovery would not be reduced by the amount of projected living expenses of the deceased. Does this holding represent an application of the collateral source rule, or some other principle?

6. *Wrongful Death of a Minor Child.* If the wrongful death statute limits recovery to pecuniary benefits only, and the victim is a child, what is the measure of the parents' recovery? If the cost of rearing the child is offset against the support the parents probably would have received from the child, there arguably is no pecuniary loss. Early decisions sometimes denied the parents' recovery. Later cases permit recovery for loss of companionship and society. *See generally Siciliano v. Capitol City Shows, Inc.*, 124 N.H. 719, 475 A.2d 19 (1984); *Davis v. Elizabeth Gen. Med. Ctr.*, 228 N.J. Super. 17, 548 A.2d 528 (1988).

7. *The Death of a Fetus.* The cases divide on whether a fetus must be viable at the time of injury in order to support an action for prenatal tortious injuries. The majority of courts today have abandoned the viability requirement, *Stallman v. Youngquist*, 125 Ill. 2d 267, 531 N.E.2d 355 (1988), whether the action is brought for personal injuries, or for wrongful death as in *Washington v. Barnes Hosp.*, 897 S.W.2d 611 (Mo. 1995).

More difficult issues arise when the action is brought under a wrongful death statute. Typical is *Crosby v. Glasscock Trucking Co.*, 532 S.E.2d 856, 532 S.E.2d 896 (S.C. 2000), stating: "Consistent with our decision in *West v. McCoy*, 233 S.C. 369, 105 S.E.2d 88 (1958), the majority of courts have held a nonviable stillborn fetus cannot maintain an independent wrongful death action. Courts addressing this issue have invariably deferred to the legislature in rejecting a wrongful death action by a nonviable stillborn fetus. The dissent would have us join a minority of jurisdictions to judicially allow such an action, a minority that includes only West Virginia. Because a wrongful death action is a legislatively created one, we find deference to the legislature especially appropriate in this matter." See also Tenn. Code Ann. § 20-5-106(c) (1999) ("'person' includes a fetus which was viable at the time of injury. A fetus shall be considered viable if it had achieved a stage of development wherein it could reasonably be expected to be capable of living outside the uterus").

8. *The Transsexual Spouse.* In *Littleton v. Prange*, 9 S.W.3d 223 (Tex. App. 1999), *cert. denied* 2000 U.S. LEXIS 5855, Christie Cavazos married Jonathon Mark Littleton in Kentucky in 1989, and she lived with him until his death in 1996. Christie filed a medical malpractice suit under the Texas Wrongful Death and Survival Statute in her capacity as Jonathon's surviving spouse. The sued doctor filed a motion for summary judgment challenging her status as a proper wrongful death beneficiary. The court held:

> In our system of government it is for the legislature, should it choose to do so, to determine what guidelines should govern the recognition of marriages involving transsexuals. The need for legislative guidelines is particularly important in this case, where the claim being asserted is statutorily-based. The statute defines who may bring the cause of action: a surviving spouse, and if the legislature intends to recognize transsexuals as surviving spouses, the statute needs to address the guidelines by which such recognition is governed. When or whether the legislature will choose to address this issue is not within the judiciary's control.
>
> It would be intellectually possible for this court to write a protocol for when transsexuals would be recognized as having successfully changed their sex. Littleton has suggested we do so, perhaps using the surgical removal of the male genitalia as the test. As was pointed out by Littleton's counsel, "amputation is a pretty important step." Indeed it is. But this court has no authority to fashion a new law on transsexuals, or anything else. We cannot make law when no law exists: we can only interpret the written word of our sister branch of government, the legislature. Our responsibility in this case is to determine whether, in the absence of legislatively-established guidelines, a jury can be called upon to decide the legality of such marriages. We

hold they cannot. In the absence of any guidelines, it would be improper to launch a jury forth on these untested and unknown waters.. . .

We hold, as a matter of law, that Christie Littleton is a male. As a male, Christie cannot be married to another male. Her marriage to Jonathon was invalid, and she cannot bring a cause of action as his surviving spouse.

9 S.W.3d at 230–31.

9. *The Negligent Decedent.* The victim's contributory negligence or assumption of the risk bars or reduces recovery in the survival action, depending upon the effect given to those defenses in the particular jurisdiction. This result is logical, since the survival action merely continues the victim's cause of action beyond his death. However, many courts have reached the same conclusion in the wrongful death action. Because the latter action is a new claim on behalf of the beneficiary that arises upon the death of the victim, the application of the victim's fault to bar or reduce recovery is a form of imputed contributory fault.

HIBPSHMAN v. PRUDHOE BAY SUPPLY, INC.
734 P.2d 991 (Alaska 1987)

RABINOWITZ, CHIEF JUSTICE.

Thomas Hibpshman was severely injured while employed on the North Slope. He thereafter instituted suit against Prudhoe Bay Supply, Inc., and Alaska Explosives, Ltd. [hereinafter collectively referred to as "Prudhoe Bay"], for damages for personal injuries, alleging negligent breach of a duty to provide premises free from unreasonable defects and hazards. In this same complaint, his wife Rebecca Hibpshman asserted a claim for loss of spousal consortium.

The four minor children of Thomas and Rebecca subsequently asserted a claim against the same defendants for loss of parental consortium. Prudhoe Bay moved in the alternative to dismiss the children's complaint on the ground that it failed to state a claim upon which relief can be granted, or to consolidate the children's claim with those of their parents.

The superior court entered a final order dismissing the loss of parental consortium claim, and the Hibpshman children now appeal that order, requiring us to determine whether minor children have an independent cause of action for loss of parental consortium resulting from injuries tortiously inflicted on their parents by a third person.

Although a majority of the courts which have considered the issue have refused to recognize a child's cause of action based on loss of parental consortium resulting from negligent injury to a parent, legal commentators have criticized the majority rule, and six of the eleven state supreme courts which have considered the issue since the start of 1980 have endorsed the loss of parental consortium claim.

In the past we have not hesitated, where appropriate, to adopt novel common law theories concerning injuries to family members. For example, we rejected the doctrines of interspousal and parental immunity in the context of negligence-based claims, even though most jurisdictions espoused the immunity defenses at the time of our decisions. *See Cramer v. Cramer,* 379 P.2d 95, 96 (Alaska 1963) (interspousal immunity); *Hebel v. Hebel,* 435 P.2d 8, 9 (Alaska 1967) (parental immunity). Moreover, in *Schreiner v. Fruit,* 519 P.2d 462, 466 (Alaska 1974), we concluded that a wife or husband has a right to sue for loss of consortium caused by negligently inflicted injury to his or her spouse. In reaching this result, we reasoned:

> [I]t would be inappropriate for this court to wait for legislative action in order to give recognition to the wife's right to sue for loss of consortium. Although Fruit and Equitable argue that neither husband nor wife should have a claim for loss of consortium, we decline to adopt this position. A claim for loss of consortium provides a means of recovery for an injury not otherwise compensable. It should be recognized as "compensating the injured party's spouse for interference with the continuance of a healthy and happy marital life." The interest to be protected is personal to the wife, for she suffers a loss of her own when the care, comfort, companionship, and solace of her spouse is denied her. The basis for recovery is no longer the loss of services, but rather the injury to the conjugal relation. We therefore hold that the claim for loss of consortium, in both husband and wife, should be given recognition in Alaska.

Id. at 465–66 (footnotes omitted).

Of particular importance to the resolution of the issue presented in this appeal is the Alaska statute that expressly specifies that loss of consortium is an element of the damages recoverable in a wrongful death action. AS 09.55.580 provides in part:

> (a) When the death of a person is caused by the wrongful act or omission of another, the personal representatives of the former may maintain an action therefor against the latter, if the former might have maintained an action, had the person lived, against the latter for an injury done by the same act or omission. The amount recovered, if any, shall be exclusively for the benefit of the decedent's spouse and children when the decedent is survived by a spouse or children, or other dependents. . . .
>
> (c) In fixing the amount of damages to be awarded under this section, the court or jury shall consider all the facts and circumstances and from them fix the award at a sum which will fairly compensate for the injury resulting from the death. In determining the amount of the award, the court or jury shall consider but is not limited to the following:
>
> (4) loss of consortium. . . .

To a significant extent, our decision today to accord legal recognition to a minor child's claim for loss of parental consortium was foreshadowed by our decisions in *Fruit, Cramer, and Hebel,* as well as by subsection (c)(4) of our wrongful death statute. In reaching this result, we find the analysis of those decisions which have recognized the cause of action more persuasive than that of the decisions which have not. Our specific reasons for recognizing a claim for loss of parental consortium follow.

Prudhoe Bay does not dispute that children of injured parents do themselves suffer an actual injury. When a parent is seriously injured, his or her child suffers a loss of enjoyment, care, guidance, love and protection, and is also deprived of a role model. *Theama v. Kenosha*, 117 Wis. 2d 508, 344 N.W.2d 513, 516 (1984). Even courts that deny the parental consortium cause of action have acknowledged the reality of such emotional and psychological injury to the child, and the Alaska legislature has implicitly done so in allowing recovery by children for loss of consortium under Alaska's wrongful death statute.[9]

Precluding minor children from maintaining a cause of action for loss of parental consortium arising from their parent's injury would, in our view, be inconsistent with the legislature's authorization of such recovery when the parent dies, and with our prior holding in *Fruit* that a husband or wife may recover damages for loss of consortium when an injured spouse survives. The claim for loss of parental consortium presented in this case is not sufficiently distinguishable from either spousal consortium claims in injury cases or children's consortium claims in death cases to warrant non-recognition. By this holding we expressly reject the arguments against recognition of the parental consortium cause of action advanced by Prudhoe Bay. We will address each of these arguments in turn.

Prudhoe Bay asserts that permitting claims for parental consortium would augment rather than alleviate any injury to intrafamilial relationships because allowing independent recovery by the child — and thus guarding the child against the possibility that the parents may not spend their financial resources for the child's benefit — disrupts the normal course of parent-child relations in which the parents have full discretion regarding family expenditures. We find this argument meritless. In the circumstances at bar, the possibility of a threat to family harmony is no different from that which arises in other cases involving family litigation, including wrongful death actions. The Alaska legislature has specifically provided for independent recoveries by family members in wrongful death suits, and thus impliedly rejected family harmony as a significant threat. Moreover, we expressly rejected potential intrafamilial conflicts as a ground for denying relief when we abolished both interspousal immunity, and parental immunity with respect to the negligent injury of a child. As the Hibpshman children observe, these types of actions

---

[9] Prudhoe Bay insists that wrongful death actions differ from those in which the parent is merely injured because they constitute the only available means of securing compensation.

. . . We consider this argument an insufficient basis for denying the parental consortium cause of action. As the Washington Supreme Court in *Ueland v. Pengo Hydra-Pull Corp.*, 103 Wash. 2d 131, 691 P.2d 190, 192 (1984) observed:

> The state of the law in this area is anomalous in that a child may recover for loss of consortium if the parent dies as a result of another's negligence, but not if the severely injured parent remains alive but in a vegetative state. Surely the child's loss of the parent's love, care, companionship and guidance is nearly the same in both situations. Also, permitting a husband or wife but not children to recover for loss of consortium erroneously suggests that an adult is more likely to suffer emotional injury than a child.

This point is well taken even when the parent is not so severely injured as to be in a vegetative state; the amount of loss of consortium damages will reflect the degree of the child's loss.

H. DAMAGE TO RELATIONS

are surely more disruptive of family relationships than a suit involving consortium claims against a third person.

Prudhoe Bay additionally asserts that we should defer to the legislature on this issue because of the significant policy considerations involved. However, we faced a similar contention in *Fruit* in the context of expanding spousal consortium claims and explicitly refused to await legislative action. Moreover, loss of consortium has been repeatedly recognized as a cause of action created and developed by the courts. We have long recognized our responsibility to adapt the common law to the needs of society as justice requires where the legislature has not spoken.

The parties also dispute whether the difficulty of ascertaining the child's true damages should bar recognition of the parental consortium claim. Prudhoe Bay cites both the speculative nature of the child's intangible damages and the danger of double recovery — that is, for the loss to the parent for his or her inability to care for the children and for the children's loss from the parent's inability to care for them — as militating against recognition of the cause of action.

These arguments are hereby rejected. First, in regard to damage claims for loss of spousal consortium, we have indicated that concern about the purported speculative nature of such claims is overstated and "is inherent in the nature of a jury's assessment of the extent to which an injury may have affected a marital relationship and the somewhat ephemeral nature of the elements of this relational interest." *Rutherford v. State*, 605 P.2d 16, 26 (Alaska 1979). We see no reason to consider the calculation of damages for a child's loss of parental consortium any more speculative or difficult than that necessary in other consortium, wrongful death, emotional distress, or pain and suffering actions. Second, we think that the potential problem of double recovery can be eliminated by recognizing that pecuniary damages such as lost income which would have been used for the benefit of a child or the cost of substitute child care services are damages recoverable by the parent, not the child; the child's damages would thus be limited primarily to an emotional suffering award in most cases. *See Theama v. Kenosha*, 117 Wis. 2d 508, 344 N.W.2d 513, 521–22 (1984) ("The problem may be easily cured by limiting the injured parent's recovery to the child's loss of the parent's pecuniary ability to support the child. Similarly, the child's cause of action can be limited to the loss of the parent's society and companionship."). As the Washington Supreme Court stated in speaking to the double recovery issue:

> We are not persuaded by this argument since it asks us to recognize that juries do not follow the instructions of the trial court. The proper approach is to bring out in the open the children's damages and properly instruct the jury that they are separate and distinct from the parent's injury. This will prevent the double recovery feared by petitioners.

In *Berger v. Weber*, 411 Mich. 1, 17, 303 N.W.2d 424 (1981), the Michigan Supreme Court . . . stated:

> Rather than having juries make blind calculations of the child's loss in determining an award to the parent, a child's loss could be openly

argued in court and the jury could be instructed to consider the child's loss separately. The award would accrue directly to the child rather than be lumped in with that of the parent who may or may not spend it for the child's benefit.

(Citation omitted.)

By distinctly specifying the child's damages and properly instructing the jury, we believe the possibility of a double recovery will be prevented.

Prudhoe Bay further contends that recognition of the parental consortium cause of action will lead to increased litigation. We see no merit in this position. As noted by the Wisconsin Supreme Court, this argument "has been voiced in almost every instance where the courts have been asked to recognize a new cause of action." *Theama,* 344 N.W.2d at 521. Several other jurisdictions have flatly refused to deny recognition to parental consortium claims because of such contentions:

> No doubt there are genuine wrongs that courts are ill suited to set right, and others that do not merit the social costs of litigation. But if these courts costsare to be the reason for denying an otherwise meritorious cause of action, that is one judgment to be made by legislatures rather than by courts. . . . If existing procedures make it difficult to consolidate different claims for trial or to avoid overlapping recoveries for the same loss, the obvious answer is not to deny that there is a claim but to reform the procedures. Shortfalls in procedural reform do not justify shortchanging otherwise valid claims.

Norwest v. Presbyterian Intercommunity Hosp., 293 Or. 543, 652 P.2d 318, 323 (1982) (denying recognition on other grounds).

Advancing a related argument, Prudhoe Bay asserts that recognition of parental consortium should be withheld because the social costs, in particular increased insurance rates and a projected rise in the number uninsured tortfeasors, outweigh the benefit to the child. We are in agreement with those courts which have concluded that any burden to society is offset by the benefit to the child. In this regard, the Oregon Supreme Court accurately observed that:

> [a] person's liability in our law still remains the same whether or not he has liability insurance; properly, the provision and cost of such insurance varies with potential liability under the law, not the law with the cost of the insurance.

Norwest, 652 P.2d at 323.

Lastly, Prudhoe Bay argues that recognition of loss of parental consortium will increase the potential for future complex litigation arising from multiple claims which have not been instituted contemporaneously. Other jurisdictions have required joinder of a minor's consortium claim with the injured parent's claim. The instant case does not present the alleged problems since the claims in question were filed within Alaska's two-year tort statute of limitations, and all parties desire consolidation of the minor children's claims with the pending suit of their parents. Nevertheless, we conclude that a practical and fair solution to the problem is to require joinder of the minors' consortium claim with the injured parent's claim whenever feasible.

We hold that minor children have an independent cause of action for loss of parental consortium resulting from injuries tortiously inflicted on their parent by a third person. We further hold that this separate consortium claim must be joined with the injured parent's claim whenever feasible.

NOTES

1. *Loss of Consortium.* When an accident victim dies, her close relatives will suffer mental anguish and grief and a loss of support, services and society. Some or all of these elements are compensable under the wrongful death and/or survival statutes, as *Hibpshman* reflects. Close relatives may experience the same kinds of suffering and loss if the victim is injured, particularly if the injury is catastrophic. Courts have been hesitant to award damages for mental anguish caused by injury to another, basing denial of recovery upon the concepts of limited duty or proximate or legal cause. The common law's treatment of the remaining elements — loss of support, services and society — has been more liberal. At early common law the master whose servant was injured by tortious conduct could recover damages from the tortfeasor for the loss of the servant's services. Because the husband was entitled to his wife's services, he also was permitted to recover for loss of those services from the tortfeasor who injured the wife. Recovery was expanded to include loss of society with the injured wife. However, if the husband was injured, the wife could not recover for loss of society, because she was not entitled to the husband's services. Constitutional considerations of equal protection condemned this dual standard, and nearly every state has opted for permitting either spouse to recover for loss of consortium with the other injured spouse.

2. *The Relation of Loss of Consortium Claims for Injury and for Death.* In *Clark v. Hauck Mfg. Co.*, 910 S.W.2d 247 (Ky. 1995), the court said that a wife's loss of consortium claim for tortious injury to her husband lasted only to date of death and did not extend beyond her husband's death from the tort, since such an extension would result in a "double recovery for the surviving spouse beyond that which the wrongful death statute affords." But in *Hinde v. Butler*, 35 Conn. Super. 292, 408 A.2d 668 (1979), the court said that the surviving spouse could assert a claim for loss of consortium after her husband's death, where the wrongful death statute made no provision for recovery of damages for mental suffering by the surviving spouse. See also *Jordan v. Baptist Three Rivers Hosp.*, 984 S.W.2d 593, 596 (Tenn. 1999) ("Tennessee law previously permitted the anomalous result of allowing spousal consortium losses in personal injury cases but not in cases of wrongful death. Upon review of the modern trend of authority and careful scrutiny of our statutory scheme, we hold that loss of consortium claims should not be limited to personal injury suits. We hold that the pecuniary value of a deceased's life includes the element of damages commonly referred to as loss of consortium").

3. *A Self-Inflicted Tort?* Can a spouse recover for loss of consortium where the other spouse injures herself? A person cannot tortiously injure herself. But she can tortiously injure another, can she not? Does resolution of this imbroglio depend on whether the consortium claim is independent or derivative? *See General Motors Corp. v. Doupnik*, 1 F.3d 862 (9th Cir. 1993), indicating that one spouse has no claim against the other for loss of consortium.

4. *Consortium Claims by Children.* The law generally has not extended loss of consortium damages beyond spouses. A famous Wisconsin case permitted recovery by the parent for loss of consortium with the injured child. *Shockley v. Prier,* 66 Wis. 2d 394, 225 N.W.2d 495 (1975). It has been followed in several other states. *Howard Frank, M.D., P.C. v. Superior Ct. of Ariz.,* 150 Ariz. 228, 722 P.2d 955 (1986). Compare *Baxter v. Superior Ct. of Los Angeles Cty.,* 19 Cal. 3d 461, 138 Cal. Rptr. 315, 563 P.2d 871 (1977), denying recovery.

A Louisiana statute also permits recovery of loss of consortium by those persons who would be entitled to wrongful death benefits if the victim died. LA. CIV. CODE § 2315 (1986). Thus, a parent may recover loss of consortium for injury to the child, if the child has neither spouse nor children.

Louisiana's statute also permits a sibling to recover for loss of consortium with an injured sibling, if the trauma victim has no wife, child or living parent. *Id.* If you were a legislator, would you vote for such a measure? Why?

As reflected in *Hibpshman,* there now is substantial authority for recovery by a child for loss of consortium of an injured parent. *See, e.g., Berger v. Weber,* 411 Mich. 1, 303 N.W.2d 424 (1981). The majority of courts still deny recovery, however. *See, e.g., Norwest v. Presbyterian Intercommunity Hosp.,* 293 Or. 543, 652 P.2d 318 (1982); *Borer v. American Airlines,* 19 Cal. 3d 441, 138 Cal. Rptr. 302, 563 P.2d 858 (1977).

5. *Consortium Claims by Parents and Others.* In *Gates v. Richardson,* 719 P.2d 193 (Wyo. 1986), the court held that parents could not recover for loss of consortium of their injured child. Defendants maintained that "eighteen of twenty-three jurisdictions that have considered filial consortium have rejected it." Is there any reason for treating loss of child consortium differently from loss of parental consortium?

In *Fernandez v. Walgreen Hastings Co.,* 126 N.M. 263, 968 P.2d 774 (1998), the plaintiff claimed loss of consortium damages asserting that she was her granddaughter's guardian, caretaker, and provider of parental affection. Plaintiff had observed her twenty-two-month-old granddaughter suffocate and die after defendants negligently misfilled Margarita's prescription. The court concluded:

> . . . In New Mexico grandparents enjoy a special legal status in relation to their grandchildren. In our state, it is not uncommon for several generations of a family to live in the same home, as in this case. We hold that such foreseeability can exist where: (1) the victim was a minor; (2) the plaintiff was a familial care-taker, such as a parent or grandparent, who lived with and cared for the child for a significant period of time prior to the injury or death; (3) the child was seriously physically injured or killed; and (4) the plaintiff suffered emotional injury as a result of the loss of the child's companionship, society, comfort, aid, and protection. In recognizing such a duty to the spouse of the injured party, we noted that "our recognition of spousal consortium will not disrupt settled expectations" because this claim "'imposes no new obligation of conduct on potential defendants.'" *Romero,* 117 N.M. at 426, 872 P.2d at 844 (quoting *Ramirez,* 100 N.M. at 542, 673 P.2d at 826). The same is true

It is foreseeable that a negligent actor may cause harm or injury to a minor child's caretaker and provider of parental affection, as well as to the child. It is not unreasonable to compensate such a family care-giver for loss of consortium. Further, merely because the plaintiff is a grandparent of the child should not foreclose an award of damages if he or she is able to prove the elements identified above. On remand, Plaintiff shall be given the opportunity to prove, if she can, that she uniquely suffered a loss of her grandchild's consortium.

968 P.2d at 784. Cf. *Ford Motor Car v. Miles*, 967 S.W.2d 377 (Tex. 1998) (limiting loss of consortium to spouses and parents and children, rejecting sibling and stepparent loss of consortium).

6. *When Does the Deprivation Occur?* In *Angelini v. OMD Corp.*, 575 N.E. 2d 41 (Mass. 1991), the plaintiff child was a nonviable fetus at the time the child's mother was tortiously injured. The court held the child could maintain an action for loss of parental consortium if it were subsequently born alive and could establish a reasonable expectation of a dependant relationship with the injured parent.

7. *Marrying a Cause of Action?* Where the marriage takes place after the spouse has sustained the injury, courts generally refuse recovery. *See, e.g., Gunter v. Marine Offshore Catering Co.*, 617 F. Supp. 1018 (W.D. La. 1985), and cases cited therein.

8. *Overlapping Spousal Claims.* There is a danger of duplicative awards where both spouses are permitted to recover damages caused by the injury to one of them. Thus, a wife should not be entitled to loss of financial support as an element of consortium damages if the husband recovers for loss of earnings or earning capacity. Are the awards duplicative if the consortium claimant recovers for loss of services and the trauma claimant recovers for loss of enjoyment of life or diminished earning capacity?

9. *Decedent Misconduct and Consortium Claims.* The typical survival statute permits recovery of the damages which the victim could have recovered if he had lived. If the victim's recovery was barred by his contributory negligence or assumption of the risk, or by his compromise of his claim, or reduction of the claim to judgment, then he could not have made a recovery thereafter if he had lived, and the claim of his beneficiaries may be barred.

This same rationale has frequently been applied to consortium claims, resulting in the rule that the consortium plaintiff may not recover if the trauma victim cannot recover. To this extent, the consortium claim is said to be "derivative." The rule has been criticized, *see, e.g.,* Gregory, *The Contributory Negligence of Plaintiff's Wife or Child in an Action for Loss of Services*, 2 U. CHI. L. REV. 173 (1935), and its impact has been softened by the advent of comparative negligence. Some states permit the reduction of the consortium claimant's recovery by the fault chargeable to the trauma victim, *Scott v. Hospital Serv. Dist.*, 496 So. 2d 270 (La. 1986). Other states repudiate the "derivative" rule and do not permit any reduction for the trauma victim's fault. *Feltch v. General Rental Co.*, 383 Mass. 603, 421 N.E.2d 67 (1981). Consider what the result would be if the consortium claim is not reduced by the trauma victim's fault, the trauma victim is assessed with 90% of the fault, and there is joint and several liability among joint tortfeasors. Would the crucial issue be whether the joint tortfeasor is entitled to contribution or indemnity from the trauma victim? If he is not, does the result offend your sense of justice?

PROBLEM

Plaintiff and her husband enter defendant's supermarket and begin shopping, moving up and down the aisles. Plaintiff intends to purchase sugar, and turns into the aisle where the sugar is stocked. Her husband precedes her. In the aisle, ahead of them, lies a broken glass jar of cooking oil; the oil has spread across the aisle. Husband observes the oil, but manages to step across it. He says nothing to the plaintiff, who is looking at items on the shelves as she approaches the oil. She steps into the oil, and slips and falls.

As a result, the 42-year-old plaintiff suffers back and knee injuries, must undergo a back operation, is in constant pain during the year between the accident and the surgery, and after the surgery is left with a 15% disability of the knee and a 25% disability of the back. She is no longer able to do housework, to work in the family's bookstore, or to engage in most of her former hobbies and pastimes. Although she was working full-time in the family store, she did not draw a salary, and no one was hired to replace her. The injury affected the wife's personality and her relations with her husband, her 18-year-old college daughter, her six-year-old son, and her mother. Husband has performed most of the housework since the wife's injury.

Who may recover damages? For what losses?

I. PUNITIVE DAMAGES

GRIMSHAW v. FORD MOTOR CO.
119 Cal. App. 3d 757, 174 Cal. Rptr. 348 (1981)

TAMURA, ACTING PRESIDING JUSTICE.

A 1972 Ford Pinto hatchback automobile unexpectedly stalled on a freeway, erupting into flames when it was rear-ended by a car proceeding in the same direction. Mrs. Lilly Gray, the driver of the Pinto, suffered fatal burns and 13-year-old Richard Grimshaw, a passenger in the Pinto, suffered severe and permanently disfiguring burns on his face and entire body. Grimshaw and the heirs of Mrs. Gray (Grays) sued Ford Motor Company and others. Following a six-month jury trial, verdicts were returned in favor of plaintiffs against Ford Motor Company. Grimshaw was awarded $2,516,000 compensatory damages and $125 million punitive damages; the Grays were awarded $559,680 in compensatory damages. On Ford's motion for a new trial, Grimshaw was required to remit all but $3½ million of the punitive award as a condition of denial of the motion.

Ford appeals from the judgment and from an order denying its motion for a judgment notwithstanding the verdict as to punitive damages. Grimshaw appeals from the order granting a conditional new trial and from the amended judgment entered pursuant to the order. The Grays have cross-appealed from the judgment and from an order denying leave to amend their complaint to seek punitive damages.

In November 1971, the Grays purchased a new 1972 Pinto hatchback manufactured by Ford in October 1971. The Grays had trouble with the car from the outset. During the first few months of ownership, they had to return the car to the dealer for repairs a number of times. Their car problems included excessive gas and oil consumption, down shifting of the automatic transmission, lack of power, and occasional stalling. It was later learned that the stalling and excessive fuel consumption were caused by a heavy carburetor float.

On May 28, 1972, Mrs. Gray, accompanied by 13-year-old Richard Grimshaw, set out in the Pinto from Anaheim for Barstow to meet Mr. Gray. The Pinto was then 6 months old and had been driven approximately 3,000 miles. Mrs. Gray stopped in San Bernardino for gasoline, got back onto the freeway (Interstate 15) and proceeded toward her destination at 60–65 miles per hour. As she approached the Route 30 off-ramp where traffic was congested, she moved from the outer fast lane to the middle lane of the freeway. Shortly after this lane change, the Pinto suddenly stalled and coasted to a halt in the middle lane. It was later established that the carburetor float had become so saturated with gasoline that it suddenly sank, opening the float chamber and causing the engine to flood and stall. A car traveling immediately behind the Pinto was able to swerve and pass it but the driver of a 1962 Ford Galaxie was unable to avoid colliding with the Pinto. The Galaxie had been traveling from 50 to 55 miles per hour but before the impact had been braked to a speed of from 28 to 37 miles per hour.

At the moment of impact, the Pinto caught fire and its interior was engulfed in flames. According to plaintiffs' expert, the impact of the Galaxie had driven the Pinto's gas tank forward and caused it to be punctured by the flange or one of the bolts on the differential housing so that fuel sprayed from the punctured tank and entered the passenger compartment through gaps resulting from the separation of the rear wheel well sections from the floor pan. By the time the Pinto came to rest after the collision, both occupants had sustained serious burns. When they emerged from the vehicle, their clothing was almost completely burned off. Mrs. Gray died a few days later of congestive heart failure as a result of the burns. Grimshaw managed to survive but only through heroic medical measures. He had undergone numerous and extensive surgeries and skin grafts and must undergo additional surgeries over the next 10 years. He lost portions of several fingers on his left hand and portions of his left ear, while his face required many skin grafts from various portions of his body. Because Ford does not contest the amount of compensatory damages awarded to Grimshaw and the Grays, no purpose would be served by further description of the injuries suffered by Grimshaw or the damages sustained by the Grays.

In 1968, Ford began designing a new subcompact automobile which ultimately became the Pinto. Mr. Iacocca, then a Ford vice president, conceived the project and was its moving force. Ford's objective was to build a carat or below 2,000 pounds to sell for no more than $2,000.

Ordinarily marketing surveys and preliminary engineering studies precede the styling of a new automobile line. Pinto, however, was a rush project, so that styling preceded engineering and dictated engineering design to a greater degree than usual. Among the engineering decisions dictated by styling was the placement of the fuel tank. It was then the preferred practice in Europe and Japan to locate the gas tank over the rear axle in subcompacts because a small vehicle has less "crush space" between the rear axle and the bumper than larger cars. The Pinto's styling, however, required the tank to be placed behind the rear axle leaving only 9 or 10 inches of "crush space" — far less than in any other American automobile or Ford overseas subcompact. In addition, the Pinto was designed so that its bumper was little more than a chrome strip, less substantial than the bumper of any other American car produced then or later. The Pinto's rear structure also lacked reinforcing members known as "hat sections" (two longitudinal side members) and horizontal crossmembers running between them such as were found in cars of larger unitized construction and in all automobiles produced by Ford's overseas operations. The absence of the reinforcing members rendered the Pinto less crush resistant than other vehicles. Finally, the differential housing selected for the Pinto had an exposed flange and a line of exposed bolt heads. These protrusions were sufficient to puncture a gas tank driven forward against the differential upon rear impact.

During the development of the Pinto, prototypes were built and tested. Some were "mechanical prototypes" which duplicated mechanical features of the design but not its appearance while others, referred to as "engineering prototypes," were true duplicates of the design car. These prototypes as well as two production Pintos were crash-tested by Ford to determine, among other things, the integrity of the fuel system in rear-end accidents. Ford also conducted the tests to see if the Pinto as designed would meet a proposed federal regulation requiring all automobiles manufactured in 1972 to be able to withstand a 20-mile-per-hour fixed barrier impact without significant fuel spillage and all automobiles manufactured after January 1, 1973, to withstand a 30-mile-per-hour fixed barrier impact without significant fuel spillage.

The crash tests revealed that the Pinto's fuel system as designed could not meet the 20-mile-per-hour proposed standard. Mechanical prototypes struck from the rear with a moving barrier at 21 miles per hour caused the fuel tank to be driven forward and to be punctured, causing fuel leakage in excess of the standard prescribed by the proposed regulation. A production Pinto crash-tested at 21 miles per hour into a fixed barrier caused the fuel neck to be torn from the gas tank and the tank to be punctured by a bolt head on the differential housing. In at least one test, spilled fuel entered the driver's compartment through gaps resulting from the separation of the seams joining the rear wheel wells to the floor pan. The seam separation was occasioned by the lack of reinforcement in the rear structure and insufficient welds of the wheel wells to the floor pan.

Tests conducted by Ford on other vehicles, including modified or reinforced mechanical Pinto prototypes, proved safe at speeds at which the Pinto failed. Where rubber bladders had been installed in the tank, crash tests into fixed barriers at 21 miles per hour withstood leakage from punctures in the gas tank. Vehicles with fuel tanks installed above rather than behind the rear axle passed the fuel system integrity test at 31-miles-per-hour fixed barrier. A Pinto with two longitudinal hat sections added to firm up the rear structure passed a 20-mile per hour rear impact fixed barrier test with no fuel leakage.

When a prototype failed the fuel system integrity test, the standard of care for engineers in the industry was to redesign and retest it. The vulnerability of the production Pinto's fuel tank at speeds of 20-and 30-miles-per-hour fixed barrier tests could have been remedied by inexpensive "fixes," but Ford produced and sold the Pinto to the public without doing anything to remedy the defects. Design changes that would have enhanced the integrity of the fuel tank system at relatively little cost per car included the following: Longitudinal side members and cross members at $2.40 and $1.80, respectively; a single shock absorbent "flak suit" to protect the tank at $4; a tank within a tank and placement of the tank over the axle at $5.08 to $5.79; a nylon bladder within the tank at $5.25 to $8; placement of the tank over the axle surrounded with a protective barrier at a cost of $9.95 per car; substitution of a rear axle with a smooth differential housing at a cost of $2.10; imposition of a protective shield between the differential housing and the tank at $2.35; improvement and reinforcement of the bumper at $2.60; addition of eight inches of crush space a cost of $6.40. Equipping the car with a reinforced rear structure, smooth axle, improved bumper and additional crush space at a total cost of $15.30 would have made the fuel tank safe in a 34-to 38-mile-per-hour rear-end collision by a vehicle the size of the Ford Galaxie. If, in addition to the foregoing, a bladder or tank within a tank were used or if the tank were protected with a shield, it would have been safe in a 40-to 45-mile-per-hour rear impact. If the tank had been located over the rear axle, it would have been safe in a rear impact at 50 miles per hour or more.

The idea for the Pinto, as has been noted, was conceived by Mr. Iacocca, then executive vice-president of Ford. As the project approached actual production, the engineers responsible for the components of the project "signed off" to their immediate supervisors who in turn "signed off" to their superiors and so on up the chain of command until the entire project was approved for public release by Vice Presidents Alexander and MacDonald and ultimately by Mr. Iacocca. The Pinto crash tests results had been forwarded up the chain of command to the ultimate decision-makers and were known to the Ford officials who decided to go forward with production.

Harley Copp, a former Ford engineer and executive in charge of the crash testing program, testified that the highest level of Ford's management made the decision to go forward with the production of the Pinto, knowing that the gas tank was vulnerable to puncture and rupture at low rear impact speeds, creating a significant risk of death or injury from fire, and knowing that "fixes" were feasible at nominal cost. He testified that management's decision was based on the cost savings which would inure from omitting or delaying the "fixes."

Mr. Copp's testimony concerning management's awareness of the crash tests results and the vulnerability of the Pinto fuel system was corroborated by other evidence.

Ford contends that it was entitled to a judgment notwithstanding the verdict on the issue of punitive damages on two grounds: First, punitive damages are statutorily and constitutionally impermissible in a design defect case; second, there was no evidentiary support for a finding of malice or of corporate responsibility for malice. In any event, Ford maintains that the punitive damage award must be reversed because of erroneous instructions and excessiveness of the award.

The concept of punitive damages is rooted in the English common law and is a settled principle of the common law of this country. The doctrine was a part of the common law of this long before the Civil Code was adopted. When our laws were codified in 1872, the doctrine was incorporated in Civil Code section 3294, which at the time of trial read: "In an action for the breach of an obligation not arising from contract, where the defendant has been guilty of oppression, fraud, or malice, express or implied, the plaintiff, in addition to the actual damages, may recover damages for the sake of example and by way of punishing the defendant."[10]

Ford argues that "malice" as used in section 3294 and as interpreted by our Supreme Court requires *animus malus* or evil motive — an intention to injure the person harmed — and that the term is therefore conceptually incompatible with an unintentional tort such as the manufacture and marketing of a defectively designed product. This contention runs counter to our decisional law. As this court recently noted, numerous California cases have interpreted the term "malice" as used in section 3294 to include not only a malicious intention to injure the specific person harmed, but conduct evincing "a conscious disregard of the probability that the actor's conduct will result in injury to others."

In *Taylor v. Superior Court of Los Angeles County,* 24 Cal. 3d 890, 157 Cal. Rptr. 693, 598 P.2d 854 (1979), our high court's most recent pronouncement on the subject of punitive damages, the court observed that the availability of punitive damages has not been limited to cases in which there is an actual intent to harm plaintiff or others. (*Id.,* at p. 895.) The court concurred with the *Searle* (*G.D. Searle & Co. v. Superior Court of Sacramento County*, 49 Cal. App. 3d 22, 122 Cal. Rptr. 218 (1975)) court's suggestion that conscious disregard of the safety of others is an appropriate description of the *animus malus* required by Civil Code section 3294, adding: "In order to justify an award of punitive damages on this basis, the plaintiff must establish that the defendant was aware of the probable dangerous consequences of his conduct, and that he wilfully and deliberately failed to avoid those consequences." (*Id.*, at pp. 895–896.)

The interpretation of the word "malice" as used in section 3294 to encompass conduct evincing callous and conscious disregard of public safety by those who manufacture and market mass produced articles is consonant with, and furthers the objectives of, punitive damages. The primary purposes of punitive damages are punishment and deterrence of like conduct by the wrongdoer and

---

[10] Section 3294 was amended in 1980 (Stats. 1980, ch. 1242, § 1, p. 4217, eff. Jan. 1, 1981) to read: "(a) In an action for the breach of an obligation not arising from contract, where the defendant has been guilty of oppression, fraud, or malice, the plaintiff, in addition to the actual damages, may recover damages for the sake of example and by way of punishing the defendant."

others. In the traditional noncommercial intentional tort, compensatory damages alone may serve as an effective deterrent against future wrongful conduct but in commerce-related torts, the manufacturer may find it more profitable to treat compensatory damages as a part of the cost of doing business rather than to remedy the defect. Deterrence of such "objectionable corporate policies" serves one of the principal purposes of Civil Code Section 3294. Governmental safety standards and the criminal law have failed to provide adequate consumer protection against the manufacture and distribution of defective products. Punitive damages thus remain as the most effective remedy for consumer protection against defectively designed mass produced articles. They provide a motive for private individuals to enforce rules of law and enable them to recoup the expenses of doing so which can be considerable and not otherwise recoverable.

Ford's contention that the statute is unconstitutional has been repeatedly rejected. Ford's argument that its due process rights were violated because it did not have "fair warning" that its conduct would render it liable for punitive damages under Civil Code Section 3294 ignores the long line of decisions in this state beginning with *Donnelly v. Southern Pacific Co.,* 18 Cal. 2d 863, 869–870, 118 P.2d 465 (1941), holding that punitive damages are recoverable in a nondeliberate or unintentional tort where the defendant's conduct constitutes a conscious disregard of the probability of injury to others. The related contention that application of Civil Code Section 3294 to the instant case would violate the ex post facto prohibition of the federal Constitution because at the time it designed the 1972 Pinto Ford had no warning that its conduct could be punished under Civil Code Section 3294 is equally without merit. This constitutional prohibition extends to criminal statutes and penalties, not to civil statutes. Moreover, at the very least since *Toole v. Richardson-Merrell, Inc.,* 251 Cal. App. 2d 689, 60 Cal. Rptr. 398 (1967), it should have been clear that a manufacturer of a dangerous, defective product might be liable for punitive damages if it knowingly exposed others to the hazard.

Equally without merit is the argument that the statute permits an unlawful delegation of legislative power because it fails to provide sufficient guidance to the judge and jury. As we have explained, the doctrine of punitive damages and its application are governed by common law principles. Judicial development of common law legal principles does not constitute an unlawful usurpation of legislative power; it is a proper exercise of a power traditionally exercised by the judiciary. The precise contention now advanced has been previously rejected.

The related contention that the potential liability for punitive damages in other cases for the same design defect renders the imposition of such damages violative of Ford's due process rights also lacks merit. Followed to its logical conclusion, it would mean that punitive damages could never be assessed against a manufacturer of a mass produced article. No authorities are cited for such a proposition; indeed, as we have seen, the cases are to the contrary. We recognize the fact that multiplicity of awards may present a problem, but the mere possibility of a future award in a different case is not a ground for setting aside the award in this case, particularly as reduced by the trial judge. If Ford should be confronted with the possibility of an award in another case for the same conduct, it may raise the issue in that case. We add, moreover, that there is no necessary unfairness should the plaintiff in this case be rewarded to a greater extent than later plaintiffs. As Professor Owen has said in response to such a charge of unfairness: "This conception ignores the enormous diligence, imagination, and financial outlay required of initial plaintiffs to uncover and to prove the flagrant misconduct of a product manufacturer. In fact, subsequent plaintiffs will often ride to favorable verdicts and settlements on the coattails of the first comers." (Owen, *Punitive Damages in Products Liability Litigation*, 74 Mich. L. Rev. 1258, 1325 (1976), fn. omitted.) That observation fits the instant case.

Ford contends that its motion for judgment notwithstanding the verdict should have been granted because the evidence was insufficient to support a finding of malice or corporate responsibility for such malice. The record fails to support the contention.

Through the results of the crash tests Ford knew that the Pinto's fuel tank and rear structure would expose consumers to serious injury or death in a 20-to 30-miles-per-hour collision. There was evidence that Ford could have corrected the hazardous design defects at minimal cost but decided to defer correction of the shortcomings by engaging in a cost-benefit analysis balancing human lives and limbs against corporate profits. Ford's institutional mentality was shown to be one of callous indifference to public safety. There was substantial evidence that Ford's conduct constituted "conscious disregard" of the probability of injury to members of the consuming public.

Ford's argument that there can be no liability for punitive damages because there was no evidence of corporate ratification of malicious misconduct is equally without merit.

California follows the Restatement rule that punitive damages can be awarded against a principal because of an action of an agent if, but only if, " '(a) the principal authorized the doing and the manner of the act, or (b) the agent was unfit and the principal was reckless in employing him, or (c) the agent was employed in a managerial capacity and was acting in the scope of employment, or (d) the principal or a managerial agent of the principal ratified or approved the act." (Restatement (Second) of Torts (Tent. Draft No. 19, 1973) § 909.)" (*Egan v. Mutual of Omaha Ins. Co.*, 24 Cal. 3d 809, 822, 169 Cal. Rptr. 691, 620 P.2d 141 (1979), *cert. denied and app. dism'd*, 445 U.S. 912, 63 L. Ed. 2d 597, 100 S. Ct. 1271 (1980); *Merlo v. Standard Life & Acc. Ins. Co.*, 59 Cal. App. 3d 5, 18, 130 Cal. Rptr. 416 (1976)). The present case comes within one or both of the categories described in subdivisions (c) and (d).

There is substantial evidence that management was aware of the crash tests showing the vulnerability of the Pinto's fuel tank to rupture at low speed rear impacts with consequent significant risk of injury or death of the occupants by fire. There was testimony from several sources that the test results were forwarded up the chain of command; Vice President Robert Alexander admitted to Mr. Copp that he was aware of the test results; Vice President Harold MacDonald, who chaired the product review meetings, was present at one of those meetings at which a report on the crash tests was considered and a decision was made to defer corrective action; and it may be inferred that Mr.

Alexander, a regular attender of the product review meetings, was also present at that meeting. McDonald and Alexander were manifestly managerial employees possessing the discretion to make "decisions that will ultimately determine corporate policy." (*Egan v. Mutual of Omaha Ins. Co., supra,* 24 Cal. 3d 809, 823.) There was also evidence that Harold Johnson, an assistant chief engineer of research, and Mr. Max Jurosek, chief chassis engineer, were aware of the results of the crash tests and the defects in the Pinto's fuel tank system. Ford contends those two individuals did not occupy managerial positions because Mr. Copp testified that they admitted awareness of the defects but told him they were powerless to change the rear-end design of the Pinto. It may be inferred from the testimony, however, that the two engineers had approached management about redesigning the Pinto or that, being aware of management's attitude, they decided to do nothing. In either case the decision not to take corrective action was made by persons exercising managerial authority. Whether an employee acts in a "managerial capacity" does not necessarily depend on his "level" in the corporate hierarchy. (*Id.,* at p. 822.) As the *Egan* court said: " 'Defendant should not be allowed to insulate itself from liability by giving an employee a nonmanagerial title and relegating to him crucial policy decisions.' " (*Id.,* at p. 823, quoting concurring and dissenting opinion in *Merlo v. Standard Life & Acc. Ins. Co., supra,* 59 Cal. App. 3d at 25).

Ford argues that the jury should have been instructed that plaintiff had the burden of proving "malice" by "clear and convincing evidence." Ford's request for such an instruction was denied. Ford relies on cases involving the personal liberty of an individual. A similar contention was rejected in *Toole v. Richardson-Merrell, Inc.,* 251 Cal. App. 2d 689, 716, 60 Cal. Rptr. 398 (1967), where the court refused to give an instruction that a defendant against whom punitive damages are sought is entitled to the presumption of innocence. Furthermore, the Supreme Court has recently rejected the clear and convincing test in a punitive damage case based upon fraud. (*Liodas v. Sahadi,* 19 Cal. 3d 278, 286–293, 137 Cal. Rptr. 635, 562 P.2d 316 (1977)). The requested instruction on the burden of proof was properly denied.

Ford's final contention is that the amount of punitive damages awarded, even as reduced by the trial court, was so excessive that a new trial on that issue must be granted. Ford argues that its conduct was less reprehensible than those for which punitive damages have been awarded in California in the past; that the $3½ million award is many times over the highest award for such damages ever upheld in California; and that the award exceeds maximum civil penalties that may be enforced under federal or state statutes against a manufacturer for marketing a defective automobile. We are unpersuaded.

In determining whether an award of punitive damages is excessive, comparison of the amount awarded with other awards in other cases is not a valid consideration. Nor does "[t]he fact that an award may set a precedent by its size" in and of itself render it suspect; whether the award was excessive must be assessed by examining the circumstances of the particular case. In deciding whether an award is excessive as a matter of law or was so grossly disproportionate as to raise the presumption that it was the product of passion or prejudice, the following factors should be weighed: the degree of reprehensibility of defendant's conduct, the wealth of the defendant, the amount of compensatory damages, and an amount which would serve as a deterrent effect on like conduct by defendant and others who may be so inclined. Applying the foregoing criteria to the instant case, the punitive damages award as reduced by the trial court was well within reason.[11]

In assessing the propriety of a punitive damage award, as in assessing the propriety of any other judicial ruling based upon factual determinations, the evidence must be viewed in the light most favorable to the judgment.

Viewing the record thusly in the instant case, the conduct of Ford's management was reprehensible in the extreme. It exhibited a conscious and callous disregard of public safety in order to maximize corporate profits. Ford's self-evaluation of its conduct is based on a review of the evidence most favorable to it instead of on the basis of the evidence most favorable to the judgment. Unlike malicious conduct directed toward a single specific individual, Ford's tortious conduct endangered the lives of thousands of Pinto purchasers. Weighed against the factor of reprehensibility, the punitive damage award as reduced by the trial judge was not excessive.

Nor was the reduced award excessive taking into account defendant's wealth and the size of the compensatory award. Ford's net worth was $7.7 billion and its income after taxes for 1976 was over $983 million. The punitive award was approximately .005 percent of Ford's net worth and approximately .03 percent of its 1976 net income. The ratio of the punitive damages to compensatory damages was approximately 1.4 to 1. Significantly, Ford does not quarrel with the amount of the compensatory award to Grimshaw. Nor was the size of the award excessive in light of its deterrent purpose. An award which is so small that it can be simply written off as a part of the cost of doing business would have no deterrent effect. An award which affects the company's pricing of its product and thereby affects its competitive advantage would serve as a deterrent. The award in question was far from excessive as a deterrent against future wrongful conduct by Ford and others.

Ford complains that the punitive award is far greater than the maximum penalty that may be imposed under California or federal law prohibiting the sale of defective automobiles or other products. For example, Ford notes that California statutes provide a maximum fine of only $50 for the first offense and $100 for a second offense for a dealer who sells an automobile that fails to confirm to federal safety laws or is not equipped with required lights or brakes that a manufacturer who sells brake fluid in this state failing to meet

---

[11] A quantitative formula whereby the amount of punitive damages can be determined in a given case with mathematical certainty is manifestly impossible as well as undesirable. (Mallor & Roberts, *supra*, 31 Hastings L.J. 639, 666–67, 670.) The authors advocate abandonment of the rule that a reasonable relationship must exist between punitive damages and actual damages. They suggest that courts balance society's interest against defendant's interest by focusing on the following factors: severity of threatened harm, degree of reprehensibility of defendant's conduct, profitability of the conduct, wealth of defendant, amount of compensatory damages (whether it was high in relation to injury), cost of litigation, potential criminal sanctions and other civil actions against defendant based on the same conduct. (*Id.* at pp. 667–69.) In the present case, the amount of the award as reduced by the judge was reasonable under the suggested factors, including the factor of any other potential liability, civil or criminal.

statutory standards is subject to a maximum of only $50 and that the maximum penalty that may be imposed under federal law for violation of automobile safety standards is $1,000 per vehicle up to a maximum of $800,000 for any related series of offenses. It is precisely because monetary penalties under government regulations prescribing business standards or the criminal law are so inadequate and ineffective as deterrents against a manufacturer and distributor of mass produced defective products that punitive damages must be of sufficient amount to discourage such practices. Instead of showing that the punitive damages award was excessive, the comparison between the award and the maximum penalties under state and federal statutes and regulations governing automotive safety demonstrates the propriety of the amount of punitive damages awarded.

[The court found that the remittitur was "fair and reasonable;" and that punitive damages are not recoverable under California law in a wrongful death (the *Gray*) action.]

NOTES

1. *The Punitive Damage Rationale.* All but a few states permit recovery of punitive damages. These are some of the arguments against punitive damages:

(a) There is no empirical data confirming that punitive damages do in fact deter others.

(b) Punitive damages result in a "windfall" to the plaintiff which should be shared by the public generally.

(c) It is unfair to permit the jury to impose a crippling remedy on a business or enterprise, particularly without rational guidelines.

(d) The threat of punitive damages stifles industry creativity and reduces the number of new products available to the public.

Some arguments supporting punitive damages are:

(a) The tort victim is not fully compensated by compensatory damages, because he usually is unable to recover his attorney's fees and some of his other costs. Punitive damages provide supplemental compensation where the defendant's conduct is egregious.

(b) Punitive damages recruit "private attorneys general" who provide a valuable service in deterring highly undesirable conduct.

(c) Punitive damages help provide a safer society by deterring unsafe products or conduct.

2. *Punitive Damages by and Against an Estate.* Note that under the California wrongful death statute Mrs. Gray's estate was not permitted to recover punitive damages. This, according to one authority, is the rule "under most wrongful death statutes." PROSSER & KEETON ON TORTS 951 (5th ed. 1984). In most jurisdictions, however, a claim for punitive damages can be brought under a survival statute. LINDA SCHLUETER & KENNETH REDDEN, 1 PUNITIVE DAMAGES 593 (3d ed. 1995). The court in *Grimshaw* noted this

distinction, but said that the attorneys for the deceased Mrs. Gray failed to assert a survival claim. Malpractice?

In allowing recovery of punitive damages against a deceased's estate, the Supreme Court of Pennsylvania in *G.J.D. v. Johnson*, 552 Pa. 169, 713 A.2d 1127 (1998) noted:

> First, the death of the tortfeasor does not completely thwart the purposes underlying the award of punitive damages. As noted, punitive damages are awarded to punish a defendant for certain outrageous acts and to deter him or others from engaging in similar conduct. Although the decedent . . . will not be punished or deterred from committing further perverse and egregious acts, the imposition of punitive damages upon his estate may serve to deter others from engaging in like conduct. The deterrent effect on the conduct of others is no more speculative in the instant case than in cases where the tortfeasor is alive.
>
> Second, we are not persuaded by the proposition that imposing punitive damages will punish only the innocent beneficiaries of the estate. The heirs of the decedent tortfeasor are in essentially the same financial position as if the tortfeasor were living at the time damages were awarded. When punitive damages are awarded against a living tortfeasor, the award reduces the amount of the tortfeasor's assets, thus reducing the amount of funds available to the tortfeasor's family and ultimately reducing the amount of his estate. When a tortfeasor is deceased at the time punitive damages are awarded, the award directly reduces the amount of the estate. The actual difference between the effect of the punitive damages award on the deceased tortfeasor's heirs and a living tortfeasor's family is minimal. To allow a tortfeasor's estate to escape payment of punitive damages would be comparable to the injustice of allowing a defendant to transfer his wealth to his prospective heirs and beneficiaries prior to the trial of a case in which punitive damages are sought against him.
>
> Finally, safeguards exist to protect against the arbitrary imposition of punitive damages. The jury can be instructed, as was done in the instant case, that the award of punitive damages is being imposed against the estate.. . . . The jury can then consider the value of the deceased tortfeasor's estate in arriving at a proper assessment of punitive damages. In the event the award shocks the conscience of the court, the trial court may grant a remittitur.

552 Pa. 176–177.

3. *Degrees of Negligence — Replayed.* Conduct which rises to the level of an intentional tort will justify an award of punitive damages. In most jurisdictions, something less will suffice. This level of conduct — something worse than negligence but less than intentional — has escaped precise definition. It is described by an almost infinite number of terms, such as willful, wanton, conscious indifference, recklessness, reckless disregard for safety, flagrant indifference or conscious disregard for the risk of harm to the victim. *See, e.g., Moran v. Johns-Manville Sales Corp.*, 691 F.2d 811 (6th Cir.

1982); *Taylor v. Superior Ct. of Los Angeles,* 24 Cal. 3d 890, 157 Cal. Rptr. 693, 598 P.2d 854 (1979); CONN. GEN. STAT. § 52-2406 (1989); LA. CIV. CODE ANN. §§ 2315.3, 2315.4 (Supp. 1990). At least one state permits punitive damages where the defendant's conduct amounts only to "gross negligence." *Teche Lines, Inc. v. Pope,* 175 Miss. 393, 166 So. 539 (1936). While jurisdictions employ different terminology in describing this "middle level" between negligence and intent, there are two common elements: (a) the conduct exposed the victim to a high probability of risk, and (b) the defendant took little or no care to avoid the harm. RESTATEMENT (SECOND) OF TORTS § 908 provides that punitive damages may be awarded "for conduct that is outrageous, because of the defendant's evil motive or his reckless indifference to the rights of others."

4. *The Burden of Proof.* Because punitive damages are "penal" in nature, some jurisdictions require that the plaintiff prove the defendant's egregious conduct by "clear and convincing" evidence. *Linthicum v. Nationwide Life Ins. Co.,* 150 Ariz. 356, 723 P.2d 675 (1986); *Orkin Exterminating Co. v. Traina,* 486 N.E.2d 1019 (Ind. 1986); *Wangen v. Ford Motor Co.,* 97 Wis. 2d 260, 294 N.W.2d 437 (1980).

5. *A Reasonable Relationship.* The majority of states require that there be a reasonable relationship between the punitive damages and the victim's compensatory damages. *Cruz v. Montoya,* 660 P.2d 723 (Utah 1983); *Wells v. Smith,* 297 S.E.2d 872 (W. Va. 1982). Other states do not require such a relationship. *Hazelwood v. Illinois Central Gulf R.R.,* 114 Ill. App. 3d 703, 450 N.E.2d 1199, 71 Ill. Dec. 320 (1983).

6. *The Size of the Award.* Some punitive awards are very high. Perhaps the most spectacular award was that of $2 billion in *Pennzoil v. Texaco, Inc.*, 481 U.S. 1, 107 S. Ct. 1519, 95 L. Ed. 2d 1 (1987). A $62 million award was upheld in *Palmer v. A.H. Robins Co.*, 684 P.2d 187 (Colo. 1984). A $10 million award was found excessive in *Maxey v. Freightliner Corp.*, 623 F.2d 395 (5th Cir. 1981). The punitive award in *Grimshaw*, given above, was remitted to $3.5 million.

7. *The Size of the Award: Constitutional Questions.* In *Browning-Ferris, Indus. v. Kelco Disposal, Inc.*, 109 S. Ct. 2909, 106 L. Ed. 2d 219 (1989), the Court held that the excessive fines clause of the Eighth Amendment to the U.S. Constitution did not prohibit an award of punitive damages where the government neither prosecuted the claim nor shared in the punitive award.

In *TXO Prod. Corp. v. Alliance Resources Corp.*, 113 S. Ct. 2711 (1993), the Court found that due process was not violated by the imposition of a punitive damage award of $10 million against an oil and gas company, even though the award was 526 times greater than the actual damages. Although the Court recognized that due process places substantive limits on the amount of punitive damages, it found that there was no mathematical bright line with which to distinguish constitutionally acceptable awards from constitutionally unacceptable awards. Rather, the Court emphasized the reasonableness of the award and the existence of procedural safeguards as key factors in its constitutional calculus.

The court in *Continental Trend Resources, Inc. v. OXY USA, Inc.*, 44 F.3d 1465 (10th Cir. 1995), upheld a punitive award of $30 million in favor of natural gas well owners whose combined economic loss was $269,000. The court found that the ratio of 111 to 1 did not violate due process.

But in *Pulla v. Amoco Oil Co.*, 72 F.3d 648 (8th Cir. 1995), the court found that an award of $2 in actual damages and $500,000 million in punitive damages was constitutionally excessive in an invasion-of-privacy case. The ratio here was 250,000 to 1.

In *BMW of N. Am., Inc. v. Gore*, 116 S.Ct. 1589 (1996), the United States Supreme Court, in a 5-4 decision, found an award of $4 million punitive damages, reduced to $2 million by the state supreme court, to be unconstitutional where the plaintiff was awarded compensatory damages of $4,000 against the defendant who fraudulently sold plaintiff a repainted car (damaged by acid rain) as new. The Court said that in determining whether a punitive award is reasonable, a court should consider whether the exemplary damages bear a "reasonable relationship" to compensatory damages. A court should also compare "the punitive damages award and the civil or criminal penalties that could be imposed for comparable misconduct." Perhaps the "most important" indicium of reasonableness, the Court said, is the degree of reprehensibility of the defendant's conduct. The court was impressed by the fact that 25 states would not punish a failure to disclose a defect, such as the one here, costing less than 3 percent of the suggested retail sales price of a car. The Court said that the trial judge committed constitutional error in instructing the jury to consider the number of such sales by the defendant in other jurisdictions in assessing punitive damages.

8. *Retraction Statutes.* A Kentucky statute prohibiting recovery of punitive damages in a defamation suit against a newspaper, unless the plaintiff has made a written demand for retraction prior to initiating the suit, was unconstitutional, the court said in *White v. Manchester Enters.*, 1996 WL 11841 (E.D. Ky.). The statute did not apply to magazines or other print media, and the court found no rational basis for such a distinction.

9. *Indemnifying Punitive Damage Awards.* The role of insurance in punitive damages is unsettled. One view is that public policy prohibits insurance against punitive damages, because the deterrent effect is lost unless the insurance premiums are adjusted to reflect the distinction between those who engage in the particularly egregious conduct that triggers punitive damages and those who do not. There is also a moralistic argument: one should not be able to insure against conduct that is criminal in nature. Some courts prohibit insurance against punitive damages. See e.g., *Beaver v. Country Mutual Insurance Co.*, 95 Ill. App. 3d 1122, 1125, 420 N.E.2d 1058 (1981). Other cases hold that insurance against punitive damages does not violate public policy, See e.g., *Whalen v. On-Deck, Inc.*, 514 A.2d 1072 (Del. 1986). See also Annot., 20 A.L.R. 3d 343 (1968), *Northwestern National Casualty Co. v. McNulty* 307 F.2d 432, 440–41 (5th Cir. 1962).

10. *Punitive Vicarious Exposure.* Many jurisdictions impose vicarious liability upon an employer for punitive damages resulting from an employee's wanton misconduct, if the employee was acting in the course and scope of his employment and the act arguably was in furtherance of the employer's interests. Some jurisdictions have balked at such a liberal rule. The concern is that liability, which the law reserves for the most blameworthy, is being

imposed upon one who is blameless. RESTATEMENT (SECOND) OF TORTS § 909 would impose punitive damages only if:

> (a) the principal or a managerial agent authorized the doing and the manner of the act, or
>
> (b) the agent was unfit and the principal or a managerial agent was reckless in employing or retaining him, or
>
> (c) the agent was employed in a managerial capacity and was acting in the scope of employment, or
>
> (d) the principal or a managerial agent of the principal ratified or approved the act.

The Restatement is followed in some jurisdictions. *See, e.g., Protectus Alpha Nav. Co. v. North Pac. Grain Growers, Inc.*, 767 F.2d 1379 (9th Cir. 1985). Other jurisdictions impose punitive damages upon the employer if any employee was within the course and scope of his employment at the time he committed the egregious act. *Stroud v. Denny's Restaurant*, 271 Or. 430, 532 P.2d 790 (1975).

11. *The Public Purse.* Whether a municipal or state government can be liable for punitive damages often depends on whether immunity for such damages has been expressly or impliedly retained or abolished. Most courts have denied liability for such damages, stating that the cost would ultimately fall on the innocent citizen. *See* KENNETH R. REDDEN, PUNITIVE DAMAGES § 4.5(C) (1980).

12. *Multiple Punitive Awards.* The clear trend is to uphold against constitutional attack multiple punitive awards to different plaintiffs arising out of the same course of conduct. *See Dunn v. HOVIC*, 1 F.3d 1371 (3d Cir.), *modif. in part*, 13 F.3d 58 (3d Cir.), *cert. denied sub nom. Owens-Corning Fiberglas Corp. v. Dunn*, 114 S. Ct. 650 (1993). The defendant is always free to inform the factfinder of prior punitive awards, hoping it will find the defendant has already been punished enough, but such evidence may prove to be a two-edged sword. *See* Jerry J. Phillips, *Multiple Punitive Damage Awards*, 39 VILL. L. REV. 433 (1994).

13. *Comparative Fault.* Should a punitive award be reduced by the amount of contributory fault attributable to the plaintiff? *See* Annot., 18 A.L.R.5th 525 (1994).

See Clark v. Cantrell, 529 S.E.2d 528 (S.C. 2000), concerning an automobile collision in which the defendant was allegedly traveling at twice the speed limit and hit plaintiff's vehicle, which was crossing defendant's lane. Punitive damages were awarded and the jury also assessed the plaintiff's contributory fault at 16 per cent. Holding that it would be improper to reduce the punitive award, the court said:

> First, allowing the defendant to shift a portion of the cost of a punitive award back to the plaintiff through comparative negligence would reduce the punishment and deterrent effect of the award. The defendant's punishment would be lessened simply because the plaintiff was somewhat negligent. That is illogical and violates the underlying rationale of punitive damages.. . .

Second, any reduction in the defendant's punishment inflicts a corresponding amount of punishment on the plaintiff. Shifting a portion of the cost of the punitive award back to the plaintiff essentially would punish him or her along with the defendant.. . . .

Third, it would be inappropriate to reduce the punitive damages by comparing the plaintiff's negligence with the defendant's reckless or willful conduct.. . . Conduct that is merely negligent should not be used to reduce damages the jury decided Cantrell should pay as a means of punishing her willful and reckless conduct, and deterring similar conduct by her and others in the future.

Fourth, when considering the negligence attributable to each party, the focus is on the actions of both plaintiff and defendant. What did each do, or not do, that contributed to the cause of an injury? With punitive damages, however, the focus is only on the defendant. The central inquiry is whether the defendant's conduct was so reckless, willful, wanton, or malicious that the defendant should be punished and deterred by requiring him or her to pay money to the plaintiff.

529 SE2d at 534.

14. *The Wealthy Defendant.* In *Romero v. Hariri*, 911 P.2d 85 (Haw. 1996), the court said that the plaintiff may, but is not required to, introduce evidence of the defendant's wealth in a claim for punitive damages. Wealth is "a factor by which to gauge the reasonableness of the reward." The court found that the defendant "had the opportunity, and was better able, to present evidence which accurately portrayed his financial condition."

ST. LUKE EVANGELICAL LUTHERAN CHURCH v. SMITH
318 Md. 337, 568 A.2d 35 (1990)

BLACKWELL, JUDGE.

The main issue in this appeal is whether a jury, in calculating an award of punitive damages, was properly instructed to consider attorney's fees incurred by the plaintiff in the underlying cause of action. In this country, the prevailing party in a lawsuit is not ordinarily entitled to recover reasonable attorney's fees as an element of damages. This "American Rule," however, refers primarily to compensatory damages. When punitive damages are involved, we are encouraged to fashion a limited exception to the rule. We hold that whenever punitive damages are appropriate, the amount of reasonable attorney's fees incurred in the pending litigation may be considered by the jury.

Ms. Ginny Ann Smith (Ms. Smith) grew up in a home with strong ties to its neighborhood church, St. Luke Evangelical Lutheran Church, Inc. (St. Luke's). Over the years, Ms. Smith's mother had been both a volunteer and an employee at St. Luke's, and Ms. Smith spent most of her formative years participating in virtually all of the numerous activities St. Luke's offered its youth.

As she became older, Ms. Smith volunteered as an Administrative Assistant for a church youth-group called Crossroads, and later, for a traveling drama-group called Tent Troupe. Both groups were directed by the Associate Pastor of St. Luke's, Pastor David Shaheen (Pastor Shaheen). As a result of her duties, Ms. Smith worked very closely with Pastor Shaheen, including traveling four months a year as a counselor with him and the other members of Tent Troupe.

After graduating from college in 1982, Ms. Smith was hired by the recently promoted Director of Youth Ministry, Pastor David Buchenroth (Pastor Buchenroth), to the salaried-position of Associate Director of Youth Ministry. Because she continued as a volunteer for Crossroads and Tent Troupe, Ms. Smith then worked for both Pastors Shaheen and Buchenroth.

In February 1984, Ms. Smith went on a church-sponsored trip to the Holy Land led by Pastor Shaheen. While she was out of the country, Pastor Buchenroth entered her office to look for a file he needed to tend to some church business.[12] There he discovered a file marked "DRS-GAS." Curious, Pastor Buchenroth opened the file. He found personal letters and notes from Pastor Shaheen to Ms. Smith.

The correspondence apparently confirmed for Pastor Buchenroth his growing suspicions that Pastor Shaheen and Ms. Smith were engaged in a sexual relationship. With the avowed purpose of protecting Pastor Shaheen's wife, Pastor Buchenroth showed the correspondence to Mrs. Shaheen, and offered her specific details of when and where he believed the various rendezvous had occurred. Before he showed it to her, however, he showed it to Ms. Joan Patton, the Staff Assistant to the Senior Pastor of St. Luke's, Raymond Shaheen — who also happened to be Pastor Shaheen's father.

A few days after his encounter with Mrs. Shaheen, he repeated his allegations, but this time to Ms. Smith's mother. He again offered specific details, as well as his opinion that Pastor Shaheen and her daughter might not return from the church excursion. After viewing the correspondence and talking with her husband, Mrs. Shaheen told Pastor Buchenroth that she did not believe that her husband's relationship with Ms. Smith was sexual in nature. Accepting Mrs. Shaheen's conclusion, Pastor Buchenroth retracted his accusations.

In addition, at one of a number of group counseling sessions initiated by the church (in an effort to encourage "a healing process"), he stated that he no longer believed the relationship between Ms. Smith and Pastor Shaheen was sexual in nature. He also promised at that time to keep his earlier suspicions confidential, and apologized to Ms. Smith and Pastor Shaheen for the pain he had caused them. Despite his promise, Pastor Buchenroth again repeated his original allegations, this time to Mr. and Mrs. Rupert, two members of the congregation active in Tent Troupe.

It was not long before the members of Tent Troupe and most of the congregation were made aware of Pastor Buchenroth's allegations. Soon, Ms. Smith began receiving unsettling telephone calls and mail from members of

---

[12] This was at least the second time Pastor Buchenroth entered Ms. Smith's office without her knowledge. Ms. Smith's mother, who shared the office with her daughter at the time, testified that she had discovered Pastor Buchenroth alone in Ms. Smith's locked office on a prior occasion, and that he was unable to state why he was there.

the congregation. Eventually, a Special Committee[13] was formed, and Ms. Smith was dismissed.

Subjected to scorn in her church and neighborhood, and unable to find a job commensurate with her skills, Ms. Smith sued Pastor Buchenroth in the Circuit Court for Montgomery County for defamation of character and invasion of privacy. She joined as a defendant, Pastor Buchenroth's employer, St. Luke's, on the theory that by dismissing her, the church ratified the allegations made by its agent Pastor Buchenroth. After a two week trial, the jury awarded Ms. Smith $228,904.01 in compensatory damages; $2,000 in punitive damages against Pastor Buchenroth; and $105,875.00 in punitive damages against St. Luke's.

Both defendants appealed. The Court of Special Appeals reversed the judgment against St. Luke's, holding that Ms. Smith was erroneously allowed twice the number of peremptory challenges permitted under Maryland Rule 2-512(h). It also held that the jury had sufficient information to conclude that Pastor Buchenroth had acted with malice, and denied his appeal.

Ms. Smith petitions this Court on the peremptory strike issue. St. Luke's also petitions this Court, contending that the circuit court's ruling admitting the $68,441.01 amount of Ms. Smith's attorney's fees on the issue of punitive damages was error.[14] We granted both petitions for *certiorari*.

[The court held that the error, if any, on the peremptory strike issue was harmless.]

Any consideration of a common-law standard for awarding attorney's fees must begin with the prevailing rule in this country. Known as the American Rule, it prohibits the prevailing party in a lawsuit from recovering his attorney's fees as an element of damages. *Alyeska*, 421 U.S. at 247, 95 S. Ct. at 1616, 44 L. Ed. 2d at 147; *Empire*, 269 Md. at 285, 305 A.2d at 148. A brief history of the American Rule reveals that it evolved from the English Rule, which originated some time before the reign of Edward I. At that time, a successful plaintiff could obtain the costs of litigation as an element of damages. *See* C. McCormick, Handbook on the Law of Damages 234, 235 (1935), relying on 2 F. Pollock & F. Maitland, The History of English Law 597 (2d ed. 1911).

Beginning with the reign of Henry VIII, this benefit was also extended to successful defendants. McCormick at 235. Consequently, the English Rule — which allows the successful party in a lawsuit to recover from the losing party

---

[13] This Special Committee was formed without the knowledge of the chairperson of the Committee on Staff — the committee normally responsible for advising the church governing-body on matters concerning the hiring and dismissing of personnel.

[14] Defendant Buchenroth did not petition this Court from the adverse decision of the Court of Special Appeals. Consequently, judgment was entered in the Circuit Court for Montgomery County against his surety under a supersedeas bond. Ms. Smith filed an order in the circuit court reflecting that the judgments against Pastor Buchenroth and the surety were "paid and satisfied." Therefore, the compensatory damage award, and the punitive damages awarded against Pastor Buchenroth are uncontested. This leaves as the only damage issue whether Ms. Smith's attorney's fees were properly considered by the jury as relating to the punitive damages awarded against St. Luke's.

the costs of litigation, including attorney's fees — became firmly established in the English common-law courts. *Id.* The rule continues in England today.[15]

The English Rule was popular in America before the Revolution. Originally, the pre-colonial statutes which fixed the scale of recoverable court costs satisfied a substantial portion of the attorney's fees incurred by a successful litigant. This was so even though local statutes rigidly limited the amount recoverable as attorney's fees.

Of course, nowhere in this country have statutorily-fixed attorney's fees been revised to keep pace with the fall in the value of money. Such legislative reluctance to keep pace suggests that the principle of full compensation for litigation expenses never firmly took hold in this country. This may best be explained by a historic distrust of lawyers prevalent throughout the colonial era, and a then growing preference of the organized bar for fee schedules set by a free market and not hostile legislatures.

Nevertheless, there are exceptions to the American Rule. For example, in Maryland, attorney's fees may be awarded when (1) parties to a contract have an agreement to that effect; (2) there is a statute which allows the imposition of such fees; or (3) the wrongful conduct of a defendant forces a plaintiff into litigation with a third party. Counsel fees may also be awarded when a party is forced to defend against a malicious prosecution.

Movement away from a strict application of the American Rule began in this country as early as the 19th century, when legislatures launched attacks against it. "Three federal statutes, the voting rights legislation of 1870, the Interstate Commerce Act of 1887, and the Sherman Act of 1890, allowed successful plaintiffs to recover their legal expenses in addition to liquidated damages, ordinary damages, or a treble damage award."

In Maryland, various statutes permit recovery of attorney's fees. Attorney fee recovery provisions are contained in either the penalty or liability sections of most of these statutes. One statute authorizes attorney's fees in conjunction with a treble damage award. It is reasonable, therefore, to conclude that in this state, an award of attorney's fees serves, in general, as a legislative tool for punishing wrongful conduct.

A punishment rationale is also found in the federal courts. There, the courts "may award counsel fees to a successful party when his opponent has acted 'in bad faith, vexatiously, wantonly, or for oppressive reasons.'" *Hall v. Cole,* 412 U.S. 1, 6, 93 S. Ct. 1943, 1946, 36 L. Ed. 2d 702, 707 (1973).

The same rule exists in Maryland, where the courts may impose costs and reasonable attorney's fees on either party when a proceeding is brought in bad faith or without substantial justification. In this class of cases, the underlying rationale of fee shifting is, of course, punitive, and the essential element in triggering the award of fees is therefore the existence of bad faith on the part of the unsuccessful litigant.

It is this punishment rationale that forms a solid basis for allowing the jury to consider attorney's fees when they are asked to calculate an award of

---

[15] Interestingly, the same is true in Alaska, where the prevailing party is allowed attorney's fees in most civil cases at the discretion of the court. Alaska Stat. § 9.60.010 (1986). In Nevada, the court may award fees in actions involving $10,000 or less. Nev. Rev. Stat. § 18.010 (1967).

punitive damages. For, like statutorily-imposed attorney fee awards, one of the main goals of punitive damages in Maryland is to punish wrongful conduct. . . .

The highest courts of seventeen states have considered whether to permit a jury calculating an award of punitive damages to take into account the amount of reasonable attorney's fees incurred in the pending litigation. Nine states regularly allow jury consideration of attorney's fees on the issue of punitive damages. Two states require evidence sufficient to sustain an award of punitive damages as a threshold condition: once met, attorney's fees may be awarded as an additional compensatory or special damage item. Six states deny jury consideration of reasonable attorney's fees on the issue of punitive damages, although one of these states denies recovery of punitive damages altogether. Thus, the majority of states to consider the issue, permit the jury to take into account the amount of reasonable attorney's fees incurred in the pending litigation when calculating a punitive damage award.

This is borne out by the Restatement which, while stating the general rule that "damages in a tort action do not ordinarily include compensation for attorney fees or other expenses of litigation," recognizes the exception that

> in awarding punitive damages when they are otherwise allowable, the trier of fact may consider the actual or probable expense incurred by the plaintiff in bringing the action.

Restatement (Second) of Torts § 914 and comment *a* at 492–93 (1979).

A minority of courts decline to allow jury consideration of reasonable attorney's fees on the issue of punitive damages reasoning (1) that such fees are compensatory in nature and therefore not a proper consideration in measuring a punitive damage award; and (2) that the jury ought to have unfettered discretion in deciding the amount of punitive damages.

It is true that an award of attorney's fees reimburses a plaintiff for his out-of-pocket legal expenses. When viewed solely in this light such fees may seem to be wholly compensatory in function. Yet, when viewed in the context of the long-standing prohibition against awarding attorney's fees, and the fact that when they are awarded, they most often serve as a statutorily-imposed punitive measure, the need to include them in compensatory damages diminishes. Under this view, attorney's fees would seem to be an appropriate consideration in measuring an award of punitive damages.

The other point advanced by the minority states, which supports the traditional view that the amount of attorney's fees rests solely within the discretion of the jury, has been the subject of substantial attack. Restatement (Second) Torts, § 908, comment *f* at 464 (1979). Indeed, a look at the various states reveals that Connecticut, Georgia, and Michigan limit punitive damages by treating them as a form of compensation fixed in proportion to the level of aggravation sustained in an injury; five states either totally or partially prohibit punitive damages. *See* 1 J. Ghiardi & J. Kircher, Punitive Damages L. & Prac. §§ 4.02–4.12 (Callaghan 1985, 1989 Cum. Supp.). In still other states, the appellate courts exert control over the discretion of the trier of fact, reviewing the amount of a jury's punitive award. . . . Juries in Maryland are left largely to themselves in assessing the amount of a punitive damage award, considering predominantly subjective elements such as the character of the defendant, his wealth, and the severity of harm to the plaintiff. *D.C. Transit System v. Brooks*, 264 Md. 578, 589, 287 A.2d 251, 256–57 (1972), *citing Meibus v. Dodge*, 38 Wis. 300 (1875).

The majority in *Browning-Ferris* left the responsibility of developing further guidelines to the states when it held that "the propriety of an award of punitive damages for the conduct in question, and the factors the jury may consider in determining their amount, are questions of state law." *Browning-Ferris*, 109 S. Ct. at 2922, 106 L. Ed. 2d at 240.

We think the majority states offer an additional guideline by allowing a jury — faced with determining the appropriate amount of a punitive damage award — to consider the amount of reasonable attorney's fees incurred in the pending litigation. Those states guide the jury by giving them the "aid of one fairly definite factor which they may take into account in fixing the amount" of punitive damages. McCormick at 297. The Kansas Supreme Court has reached the same conclusion, reasoning that

> [w]hile [punitive damages] imply punishment, and their assessment is largely a matter of discretion with the jury, yet a court is not bound to turn the matter over to them arbitrarily, and without any suggestions as to matters which they ought to consider in their assessment of such damages. *It may and, indeed, ought to call their attention to any matters which will tend to prevent any mere arbitrary and thoughtless award, and to make the assessment fair and reasonable, considering all of the circumstances of the case. . . . [A]nd [attorney's fees] as influencing the amount of smart-money, are eminently proper.* [Emphasis added.]

Brewer v. Home-Stake Prod. Co., 200 Kan. 96, 434 P.2d 828, 831, 30 A.L.R.3d 1435, 1440 (1967).

Connecticut seems to extend this reasoning even further. There, all punitive damage "recovery is limited to an amount which will serve to compensate the plaintiff to the extent of his expenses of litigation less taxable costs." *Triangle Sheet Metal Works v. Silver*, 154 Conn. 116, 222 A.2d 220, 225 (1966). Thus, while the jury is allowed to consider reasonable attorney's fees on the issue of punitive damages, attorney's fees also constitute the limit to which an award of punitive damages may be had. We prefer the reasoning of the Kansas court.

When a jury determines that punitive damages are appropriate and has considered reasonable attorney's fees, two seemingly disparate goals are satisfied. First, because the jury will be offered objective guidance in calculating the amount of its punitive award, punitive damages will be more accurately measured and the potential for abuse decreased. Second, the plaintiff can be made truly whole in precisely those kinds of cases in which the defendant's wrongful conduct is found to be at its most flagrant, for only in such cases are punitive damages warranted. Therefore, to aid the jury in calculating an amount of punitive damages that will deter a party from future wrongful conduct, evidence of reasonable attorney's fees may be considered by the jury whenever punitive damages are appropriate.

Because Pastor Buchenroth retracted his allegations and apologized to many of the principals, including Ms. Smith, the jury could easily have found that the subsequent reiteration of his allegations to the Ruperts was made with knowing falsity or reckless disregard for the truth. The jury had sufficient evidence, if believed, to award punitive damages. As a result, evidence of the amount of Ms. Smith's attorney's fees was admissible.

RODOWSKY, J., dissenting.

I respectfully dissent because I believe the Court's holding is unsound, both practically and philosophically. As a practical matter this new rule of "punitive damages" will not control, but will enlarge, punitive damage verdicts. Philosophically the Court's new rule, but for the label attributed to the additional recovery, does not involve punitive damages at all. Rather, it is a judicially adopted rule of fee shifting, contrary to this Court's historic position of viewing fee shifting as the exercise of legislative or rulemaking power. . . .

NOTES

1. *Jury Discretion.* In *Honda v. Oberg*, 114 S. Ct. 2331 (1994) the Court held that an appellate court is constitutionally required to review the propriety, including the size, of a punitive damage award by a jury.

In *Mattison v. Dallas Carrier Corp.*, 947 F.2d 95 (4th Cir. 1991), the court held that South Carolina's law for awarding punitive damages violated due process. The court found that the law allowed the jury unconstrained discretion in making its award, subject only to review by the trial court for excessiveness and by the appellate court for abuse of trial court discretion.

2. *Mental Distress.* In *Juday v. Rotunno & Rotunno*, 276 Cal. Rptr. 445 (Cal. App. 1990), the plaintiff was awarded $500,000 million against her attorney for emotional distress suffered as a result of alleged misappropriation of the client's funds. There was testimony that the client's emotional problems were permanent and would require therapy over the remainder of her life. Should such damages be considered part of a punitive award?

3. *Contingent Fees.* Some states limit the amount of contingent fees that can be charged, depending on the amount collected. *See, e.g.*, FLA. STAT. § 766.109 (1988):

> (7)(a) The Legislature recognizes that the contingent attorney's fee system provides a method by which the citizens of this state are able to seek access to the courts as guaranteed by Art. I, § 21 of the State Constitution. Additionally, the Legislature recognizes that the Supreme Court of this state has the jurisdiction and authority to adopt rules for the practice of law before all Florida courts, including the regulation of attorney's fees. Until such time as the Supreme Court adopts guidelines, the following schedule shall be presumed reasonable and not excessive. For recovery of damages up to $2 million:
>
> > 1. Fifteen percent of the recovery if the claim is resolved through the acceptance of an offer of settlement . . .;
> >
> > 2. Twenty percent of the recovery if the claim is resolved after initiating . . . arbitration . . .;

3. Twenty-five percent of the recovery if the claim is settled within 90 days of suit being filed;

4. Thirty percent of the recovery if the claim is settled more than 90 days after suit is filed and prior to or during the course of mandatory settlement conference . . . or where all defendants admit liability and request trial on the issue of damages;

5. Thirty-five percent of the recovery if the claim is settled prior to the completion of the swearing of the jury;

6. Forty percent of the recovery if the claim is settled or judgment is satisfied prior to filing of the notice of appeal;

7. Forty-five percent of the recovery after notice of appeal is filed or post-judgment relief or action is required for recovery on the judgment.

For those amounts of a recovery in excess of $2 million, a contingency fee of 15 percent shall be presumed reasonable and not excessive.

Is such a schedule fair? Should the percentage be the same for settlement as for recovery in excess of $2 million? Should such a schedule be applied to a punitive award? In a jurisdiction following the *St. Luke Evangelical Church* rule, would the jury be instructed regarding the provisions of such a schedule?

See also Swafford v. Harris, 967 S.W.2d 319 (Tenn. 1998), concerning a contingency fee agreement between a personal injury plaintiff and a physician for expert testimony and other services associated with that plaintiff's claims. After the claim was settled the physician sued to collect his fee. The court concluded:

[T]he medical and legal communities share the ethical prohibition against the use of contingency fees for expert witnesses which is contained in the respective professional codes for each profession and adopted by the State as the public policy of Tennessee. This public policy is re-enforced by the actions of the Tennessee Bar Association and the Tennessee Medical Association in adopting the Interprofessional Code of Cooperation, which provides in part that "under no circumstances may a physician charge or accept compensation for any service which is contingent upon the outcome of a lawsuit." Article VI, § 2.

. . .Given this overwhelming weight of authority, we disagree with Dr. Swafford's contention that no controlling public policy existed or that the public policy was not applicable simply because he is not a member of the American or Tennessee Medical Associations. On the contrary, it is our view that sound public policy in this jurisdiction, as in others, is crystal clear: a contingency fee contract for the services of a physician acting in a medico-legal expert capacity is void as against public policy and therefore unenforceable.

Why is this type of agreement viewed differently from the attorney's fee based on the same contingency?

4. *The Relation of Compensatory to Punitive Damages.* PROSSER & KEETON ON TORTS 14–15 (5th ed. 1984) states that it is frequently said "that punitive damages must bear some reasonable proportion, or at least some undefined kind of relation to the actual damages found." But "where the enormity of the defendant's conduct calls for it, very large awards of punitive damages, ranging far out of all conceivable proportion to the amount found by way of compensation, have been sustained."

Many courts say punitive damages can be awarded only if actual damages are also awarded. *See, e.g., Carroway v. Johnson*, 245 S.C. 200, 139 S.E.2d 908 (1965). In *Moskovitz v. Mt. Sinai Med. Center*, 69 Ohio St. 3d 638 (Ohio 1994), where a doctor altered a patient's medical records to hide his malpractice, the doctor was required to pay $1 million in punitive damages even though the patient was not harmed by the cover-up.

5. *Bifurcation.* A number of courts and legislatures have provided that liability, if any, for compensatory damages should first be determined by the jury, and if such liability is found then punitive damages should be determined in a second phase of the trial. The purpose of bifurcation is to avoid potential prejudice of the compensatory liability issue with punitive damage considerations, including wealth of the defendant. *See, e.g., Hodges v. S.C. Toof & Co.*, 833 S.W.2d 896 (Tenn. 1992); Jerry J. Phillips, *Multiple Punitive Damage Awards*, 39 VILL. L. REV. 433, 452–53 (1994).

6. *Court Determination of Punitive Damages.* The court in *Smith v. Printup*, 866 P.2d 985 (Kan. 1993), held that the state constitutional right to trial by jury was not violated by vesting the power to determine punitive damages in the judge alone. The court viewed punitive damages "as equitable in nature," so that a jury trial was not constitutionally required.

In *Zoppo v. Homestead Ins. Co.*, 67 Ohio St. 3d 1512, 622 N.E.2d 659 (1995), however, the court held that allowing the judge to determine punitive damages violated the state constitutional right to trial by jury. "Clearly, the assessment of punitive damages by the jury stems from the common law and is encompassed within the right to trial by jury," the court said. In *Bozeman v. Busby*, 639 So. 2d 501 (Ala. 1994), the court held that a statute permitting the judge to increase punitive damages violated the state constitutional right to trial by jury.

7. *Payment of Punitive Damages to the State.* A number of states, either by legislative or judicial decision, have provided that part of any punitive award should be paid to the state. *See* Annot., 16 A.L.R.5th 129 (1993). The constitutionality of such statutes has received mixed appraisals. *See Gordon v. State*, 585 So. 2d 1033 (Fla. App. 1991) (constitutional); *McBride v. General Motors Corp.*, 737 F. Supp. 1563 (M.D. Ga. 1990) (unconstitutional). Recall *Browning-Ferris Indus. v. Kelco Disposal*, discussed above, where the United States Supreme Court held that punitive awards did not implicate the "excessive fines" provision of the Eighth Amendment where the government neither prosecuted the claim nor shared in the punitive award. Where the government shares in the award, does the Eighth Amendment apply?

8. *Taxability.* Punitive damages are taxable because they do not represent damages received "on account of personal injuries or sickness." *O'Gilvie v.*

United States, 117 S. Ct. 452 (1996). *See also* 26 U.S.C. § 104(a) (2000), providing:

> Except in the case of amounts attributable to (and not in excess of) deductions allowed under section 213 (relating to medical, etc., expenses) for any prior taxable year, gross income does not include—
>
> (1) amounts received under workmen's compensation acts as compensation for personal injuries or sickness;
>
> (2) the amount of any damages (other than punitive damages) received (whether by suit or agreement and whether as lump sums or as periodic payments) on account of personal physical injuries or physical sickness. . .

PROBLEM

An attorney agreed to advise another attorney in bad faith insurance civil litigation on a contingent fee basis. As the case progressed the hiring attorney decided that she wanted to call the advising attorney to testify as a witness in the case as to what constitutes bad faith on the part of the insurer. It was agreed that the adviser would bill on a contingent fee basis for all services except for the time actually spent in testifying, which would be billed on an hourly basis. Discuss any problem you see in presenting the testimony or in the billing arrangement.

Chapter 10

AFFIRMATIVE DEFENSES: PLAINTIFF MISCONDUCT AND STATUTES OF LIMITATIONS

A. INTRODUCTION

The same policies which lead us to impose liability upon a defendant whose unreasonable and risky conduct damages plaintiff suggest that the plaintiff's conduct ordinarily should not be ignored. If we want to deter accidents, we should encourage potential accident victims to take reasonable care for their safety. Compensating a victim for those damages caused in part by her own conduct may improperly spread the cost of victim conduct to the defendant or to the enterprise in which the defendant is engaged. In addition, the community's sense of justice or fairness may be offended by a rule that imposes all of the loss on one of two people whose unreasonably risky conduct coalesces to cause damage to one of them.

The legal solution to this problem has been made difficult by a misconception: until modern times, the general belief was that the law could not quantify unreasonably risky conduct. If the unreasonably risky conduct of two persons combined to cause an indivisible injury, the burden of the loss could be placed upon only one of them, or divided between them on a *per capita* basis. The latter solution was adopted by maritime law in collision cases; thus, when two vessels collided and both were at fault, the damages were divided equally between the vessel owners. The *Schooner Catherine v. Dickinson*, 58 U.S. (17 How.) 170 (1854). The common law approach was to place *all* of the burden on one of the parties, instead of dividing responsibility as under the modern law of comparative fault.

Plaintiff misconduct may take one of several forms. The plaintiff (1) may have failed to act as a reasonable person for her own safety, and her substandard conduct was a cause in fact of her injuries, or (2) may have knowingly and voluntarily assumed the risk that defendant would not act reasonably toward her, or (3) may have failed to act as a reasonable person for her own safety, and her failure did not contribute to the occurrence of the accident, but enhanced her damages. The material in this chapter examines how the law treats this misconduct.

There are, of course, many affirmative defenses, but plaintiff misconduct and statutes of limitations are probably the most common. Limitation periods vary in length and manner of activation, depending on the type of claim asserted. A draconian form of limitation is the statute of repose, which runs from a specified date (*e.g.*, date of sale) and may expire before the plaintiff has an opportunity to sue or before she is even injured. Limitations periods—except for the doctrine of laches in equity—tend to be fairly rigidly applied.

A flexible approach, comparable to that of comparative fault for plaintiff misconduct, is not widely used for statutes of limitations. The closest analogy to comparative fault is the discovery rule as it is sometimes liberally applied to limitations periods.

B. CONTRIBUTORY NEGLIGENCE

PROBLEM

As Rhoda Rush approached the access road to the expressway, her regular route to work, she noticed her gas gauge registered empty. Since she was late for work, she decided to take the risk that she could make the three-mile drive without running out of gas. After driving two miles on the expressway, her engine stopped running because the vehicle was out of gas. Unfortunately, Rhoda's vehicle was in the passing lane at the time, and the traffic on her right precluded her from steering onto the shoulder of the highway. She activated her hazard lights and steered the car to a halt in the passing lane. The car immediately following Rhoda swerved into the outside lane to avoid an accident.

Rhoda sat in her car for a minute as the traffic sped by, awaiting a break in the traffic that would permit her to exit the car. Before she could do so, another car driven by Paula Pushy struck the rear of Rhoda's car, totally destroying it and seriously injuring Rhoda. Paula told investigating officers she was attempting to pass a trailer truck and had just turned into the passing lane when she sighted Rhoda's car 20 feet in front of the truck. However, there was evidence that Paula was driving 65 mph when she pulled into the passing lane. The speed limit was 55 mph on the expressway.

Should Rhoda recover from Paula all of her damages, part of her damages, or none of her damages? What answer would be mandated by the cases set forth in this chapter? What approach do you consider the best, and why?

BUTTERFIELD v. FORRESTER
11 East 60, 103 Eng. Rep. 926 (K.B. 1809)

This was an action on the case for obstructing a highway, by means of which obstruction the plaintiff, who was riding along the road, was thrown down with his horse, and injured, etc. At the trial before Bayley J. at Derby, it appeared that the defendant, for the purpose of making some repairs to his house, which was close by the road side at one end of the town, had put up a pole across this part of the road, a free passage being let by another branch of street in the same direction. That the plaintiff left a public house not far distant from the place in question at 8 o'clock in the evening in August, when they were just beginning to light candles, but while there was light enough left to discern the obstruction at 100 yards distance: and the witness, who proved this, said that if the plaintiff had not been riding very hard he might have observed and avoided it: the plaintiff however, who was riding violently, did not observe it, but rode against it, and fell with his horse and was much hurt in consequence of the accident; and there was no evidence of his being intoxicated at the time. On this evidence Bayley J. directed the jury, that if a person riding with reasonable and ordinary care could have seen and avoided the obstruction; and if they were satisfied that the plaintiff was riding along the street extremely hard, and without ordinary care, they should find a verdict for the defendant: which they accordingly did.

Vaughan Serjt. now objected to this direction, on moving for a new trial and referred to Buller's Ni. Pri. 26(a), where the rule is laid down, that "if a man lay logs of wood across a highway; though a person may with care ride safely by, yet if by means thereof my horse stumble and fling me, I may bring an action."

Bayley J. The plaintiff was proved to be riding as fast as his horse could go, and this was through the streets of Derby. If he had used ordinary care he must have seen the obstruction; so that the accident appeared to happen entirely from his own fault.

Lord Ellenborough C.J. A party is not to cast himself upon an obstruction which has been made by the fault of another, and avail himself of it, if he do not himself use common and ordinary caution to be in the right. In cases of persons riding upon what is considered to be the wrong side of the road, that would not authorise another purposely to ride up against them. One person being in fault will not dispense with another's using ordinary care for himself. Two things must concur to support this action, an obstruction in the road by fault of the defendant, and no want of ordinary care to avoid it on the part of the plaintiff.

Per Curiam. Rule refused.

NOTES

1. *Plaintiff's Fault. Butterfield* led to the common law rule that plaintiff's unreasonably risky conduct barred his recovery. Why is recovery barred?

(a) Because defendant does not owe a duty to a plaintiff who acts unreasonably for his own safety? But can the unreasonableness of the foreseeable risk which defendant creates be based on the conduct of the person who ultimately encounters the risk?

(b) Defendant's conduct was not unreasonable, in the light of plaintiff's action? Does this assume that defendant's unreasonable conduct will continue only until plaintiff's contributory action?

(c) Plaintiff's conduct, and not defendant's, was the legal or proximate cause of plaintiff's injury? But what if the conduct of plaintiff and defendant also caused injury to a third person? Could the third person recover from the plaintiff but not from the defendant?

(d) Plaintiff's unreasonable conduct is an affirmative defense?

The rule that plaintiff's unreasonable conduct barred his recovery prevailed throughout the nineteenth and into the twentieth century. The rule applied even though the defendant's substandard conduct was "grossly negligent," and even though the plaintiff's deviation from reasonable care was slight.

2. *Children.* Either as a plaintiff or a defendant, a child's conduct is measured against what would be reasonable to expect of a "child of like age,

intelligence and experience," unless the child was engaging in an activity which is normally one "for adults." The result is that in pre-comparative cases contributory negligence did not often bar a child's recovery. Some states went further. Consider this language: "(t)he test is whether the particular child, considering her age, background, and inherent intelligence, indulged in gross disregard of her own safety in the face of a known risk, understood and perceived the danger." *Carter v. City Parish Gov't,* 423 So. 2d 1080, 1086 (La. 1982). (This was a case which arose prior to, and was decided after, the Louisiana legislature adopted "pure" comparative negligence, *infra.* Do you believe that the court would adhere to this test of contributory negligence in a post-comparative case?). *See also LaCava v. City of New Orleans,* 159 So. 2d 362 (La. App. 1964). (Old age does not *per se* affect the standard for determining contributory negligence, but disability resulting from advanced age does affect the standard of care owed by an old person).

Courts typically apply the child standard of care to a child for purposes of determining negligence, but it is not clear that such a flexible standard is applied in determining whether a child has committed an intentional tort. Why shouldn't the same flexible standard be applied to both intentional and negligent torts of a child?

3. *Last Clear Chance.* If both plaintiff and defendant engaged in unreasonably risky conduct, but defendant's conduct continued after plaintiff was no longer able to avoid the accident, courts allowed the plaintiff to escape the contributory negligence bar by finding that the defendant had the "last clear chance" to avoid the accident. The doctrine had its genesis in the "groans, ineffably and mournfully sad, of Davies' dying donkey." *Fuller v. Illinois C.R.R.,* 100 Miss. 705, 717, 56 So. 783 (1911). The *Davies* referred to was the plaintiff in *Davies v. Mann,* 10 M. & W. 547, 152 Eng. Rep. 588 (Exch. 1842). In that case, the plaintiff recovered on these facts:

> Plaintiff, having fettered the fore feet of an ass belonging to him, turned it into a public highway, and at the time in question the ass was grazing on the off side of a road about eight yards wide, when the defendant's waggon, with a team of three horses, coming down a slight descent, at what the witness termed a smartish pace, ran against the ass, knocked it down, and the wheels passing over it, it died soon after . . . . [The trial judge instructed the jury] that though the act of the plaintiff, in leaving the donkey on the highway so fettered as to prevent his getting out of the way of carriages traveling along it, might be illegal, still, if the proximate cause of the injury was attributable to the want of proper conduct on the part of the driver of the waggon, the action was maintainable against the defendant; and [the trial judge] directed them, if they thought that the accident might have been avoided by the exercise of ordinary care on the part of the driver, to find for the plaintiff.

These jury instructions were held to be proper.

The doctrine of "last clear chance" was adopted in some form in nearly every state. There are four situations: (1) the plaintiff is helpless, and the defendant discovers the plaintiff's peril, but unreasonably fails to avoid the injury, *see* RESTATEMENT (SECOND) OF TORTS § 479 (1965); (2) the plaintiff is inattentive and the defendant discovers the plaintiff's peril, but unreasonably fails to avoid the injury, *id.* § 480; (3) the plaintiff is helpless and the defendant unreasonably fails to discover plaintiff's peril, *id.* § 479; and (4) the plaintiff is inattentive and the defendant unreasonably fails to discover plaintiff's peril, *see Meyers v. Louisiana,* 637 S.W.2d 219 (Mo. App. 1982). Most states applied the last clear chance doctrine to situations (1) through (3), but very few applied it to (4). Why do you suppose the doctrine was seldom applied to (4)?

4. *The Jury as Guardian of Comparative Responsibility.* Nearly every jurisdiction treated contributory negligence as an affirmative defense, with the obvious result that the defendant had the burden of pleading and proving plaintiff's substandard conduct.

Another device used to avoid the harsh rule of the contributory negligence bar was to let the jury decide the issue. This usually brought about one of two results: (a) a jury, which knew that contributory negligence bars recovery, was unlikely to find the plaintiff contributorily negligent except in those cases in which his conduct was particularly egregious; or (b) if the plaintiff's conduct was unreasonably risky and contributed to his injury, a jury was likely to attempt to achieve rough justice by finding that the plaintiff was not contributorily negligent but reducing the award of damages to account for the plaintiff's misconduct. This second approach was *de facto* comparative negligence; it was well recognized by attorneys and by judges, who often conveniently refused an additur sought by plaintiff or a remittitur sought by defendant.

5. *Reckless, Wilful and Intentional Misconduct.* If defendant's conduct was more reprehensible than negligence, contributory negligence ordinarily was not a defense. Thus a determination that the defendant was guilty of "recklessness" or "willful and wanton" conduct would permit an escape from the contributory negligence bar. Courts also generally held that contributory negligence was not a defense to an intentional tort. *See, e.g., Graves v. Graves,* 531 So. 2d 817 (Miss. 1988).

6. *Contributory Negligence and Strict Liability.* Development of liability without fault has contributed its own problems. Where liability was strict because the defendant engaged in an "abnormally dangerous" or "ultrahazardous" activity, many courts ruled that contributory negligence was not a defense. If the liability was strict as in products liability, many courts also did not allow contributory negligence as a defense. Where the doctrine of comparative fault has been substituted for contributory negligence, however, the trend has been to apply the doctrine in strict products liability. *See Whitehead v. Toyota Motor Corp.,* 897 S.W.2d 684 (Tenn. 1995).

7. *Foreseeable Misuse.* A defendant is negligent if he fails to act reasonably in light of all the circumstances. What if one of the circumstances which makes his conduct unreasonable is that the victim will not act reasonably to avoid the harm? Consider the manufacturer who designs a product which is defective because an inattentive user foreseeably will forget to guard against a certain danger, or an employer who hires a teenager to operate dangerous machinery. In such cases, it may appear ludicrous to say that the circumstance which makes defendant's conduct unreasonable insulates him from liability.

Some courts refused to apply the contributory negligence bar where the duty arose from a statute that the court determined was intended to protect the plaintiff from his disability. *See, e.g., Boyles v. Hamilton,* 235 Cal. App. 2d 492, 45 Cal. Rptr. 399 (1965).

Moreover, the RESTATEMENT (SECOND) OF TORTS § 483 (1965) recognizes statutes that may be even more "exceptional" than those aimed at protecting persons unable to protect themselves. Comment d to § 483 states:

> Even where those for whose benefit the statute is enacted may be expected to be, and are in fact, fully able to protect themselves, it may still be found that the purpose of the legislation is to relieve them of the burden of doing so, and to place the entire responsibility for avoiding the harm upon the defendant. Thus, a statute requiring railways to fence their tracks for the protection of livestock may be found to be intended to relieve adjoining landowners of the necessity of fencing in or otherwise restraining their cattle, even though they do not lack the ability to do so. Such contributory negligence is not a defense where the action is founded upon the violation of such a statute.

What considerations would prompt a court or legislature to conclude that the "entire responsibility for avoiding the harm" should be borne by one person or category of persons? For a jurisdiction that has adopted comparative fault, would plaintiff's negligence be irrelevant in the situations considered in this note?

8. *Characterizing the Risk.* The cause-in-fact and proximate or legal cause tests are the same for negligence and contributory negligence. However, a strict application of legal causation could avoid the contributory negligence bar. Thus, the risk that plaintiff would negligently fall between a truck and a wall did not encompass the risk that he would be injured by a metal hook protruding from the side of the truck. *See Furukawa v. Ogawa,* 236 F.2d 272 (9th Cir. 1956).

C. COMPARATIVE FAULT

PROBLEM

Oscar Owner left his convertible, with the key in the ignition, in the parking lot of a liquor store. Immediately thereafter, Tillie Teenager, a 14-year-old with a long history of car thefts, walked by, saw the convertible, jumped in it and drove away. Within a few blocks, Tillie sped around a sharp curve, lost control of the car and crashed into a car driven by Ann Taylor. Ann could have avoided the accident by taking evasive action, but she panicked when she saw Tillie heading toward her.

A state statute provides:

> Any driver who, in a public place, leaves his automobile unattended with the key in the ignition shall be guilty of a misdemeanor and, upon conviction, shall be fined not less than $10 nor more than $100.

Discuss the rights and liabilities of the parties: (a) in a pure comparative negligence jurisdiction; (b) in a modified comparative negligence jurisdiction. Which scheme is preferable? Why?

LI v. YELLOW CAB CO.
13 Cal. 3d 804, 119 Cal. Rptr. 858, 532 P.2d 1226 (1975)

SULLIVAN, J.

In this case we address the grave and recurrent question of whether we should judicially declare no longer applicable in California courts the doctrine of contributory negligence, which bars all recovery when the plaintiff's negligent conduct has contributed as a legal cause in any degree to the harm suffered by him, and hold that it must give way to a system of comparative negligence, which assesses liability in direct proportion to fault. As we explain in detail *infra*, we conclude that we should. In the course of reaching our ultimate decision we conclude that: (1) the doctrine of comparative negligence is preferable to the "all-or-nothing" doctrine of contributory negligence from the point of view of logic, practical experience, and fundamental justice; (2) judicial action in this area is not precluded by the presence of section 1714 of the Civil Code, which has been said to "codify" the "all-or-nothing" rule and to render it immune from attack in the courts except on constitutional grounds; (3) given the possibility of judicial action, certain practical difficulties attendant upon the adoption of comparative negligence should not dissuade us from charting a new course — leaving the resolution of some of these problems to future judicial or legislative action; (4) the doctrine of comparative negligence should be applied in this state in its so-called "pure" form under which the assessment of liability in proportion to fault proceeds in spite of the fact that the plaintiff is equally at fault as, or more at fault than, the defendant; and finally, (5) this new rule should be given a limited retrospective application.

The accident here in question occurred near the intersection of Alvarado Street and Third Street in Los Angeles. At this intersection 809 Third Street runs in a generally east-west direction along the crest of a hill, and Alvarado Street, running generally north and south, rises gently to the crest from either direction. At approximately 9 p.m. on November 21, 1968, plaintiff Nga Li was proceeding northbound on Alvarado in her 1967 Oldsmobile. She was in the inside lane, and about 70 feet before she reached the Third Street intersection she stopped and then began a left turn across the three southbound lanes of Alvarado, intending to enter the driveway of a service station. At this time defendant Robert Phillips, an employee of defendant Yellow Cab Company, was driving a company-owned taxicab southbound in the middle lane on Alvarado. He came over the crest of the hill, passed through the intersection, and collided with the right rear portion of plaintiff's automobile, resulting in personal injuries to plaintiff as well as considerable damage to the automobile.

The court, sitting without a jury, found as facts that defendant Phillips was traveling at approximately 30 miles per hour when he entered the intersection, that such speed was unsafe at that time and place, and that the traffic light controlling southbound traffic at the intersection was yellow when defendant Phillips drove into the intersection. It also found, however, that plaintiff's left turn across the southbound lanes of Alvarado "was made at a time when a vehicle was approaching from the opposite direction so close as to constitute an immediate hazard." The dispositive conclusion of law was as follows: "That the driving of Nga Li was negligent, that such negligence was a proximate cause of the collision, and that she is barred from recovery by reason of such contributory negligence." Judgment for defendants was entered accordingly.

"Contributory negligence is conduct on the part of the plaintiff which falls below the standard to which he should conform for his own protection, and which is a legally contributing cause cooperating with the negligence of the defendant in bringing about the plaintiff's harm." (Rest. 2d Torts, § 463.) Thus the American Law Institute, in its second restatement of the law, describes the kind of conduct on the part of one seeking recovery for damage caused by negligence which renders him subject to the doctrine of contributory negligence. What the effect of such conduct will be is left to a further section, which states the doctrine in its clearest essence: "Except where the defendant has the last clear chance, the plaintiff's contributory negligence *bars recovery* against a defendant whose negligent conduct would otherwise make him liable to the plaintiff for the harm sustained by him." RESTATEMENT (SECOND) OF TORTS § 467. (Italics added.)

This rule, rooted in the long-standing principle that one should not recover from another for damages brought upon oneself, has been the law of this state from its beginning.

It is unnecessary for us to catalogue the enormous amount of critical comment that has been directed over the years against the "all-or-nothing" approach of the doctrine of contributory negligence. The essence of that criticism has been constant and clear: the doctrine is inequitable in its operation because it fails to distribute responsibility in proportion to fault. Against this have been raised several arguments in justification, but none have proved even remotely adequate to the task. The basic objection to the doctrine — grounded in the primal concept that in a system in which liability is based on fault, the extent of fault should govern the extent of liability — remains irresistible to reason and all intelligent notions of fairness.

Furthermore, practical experience with the application by juries of the doctrine of contributory negligence has added its weight to analyses of its inherent shortcomings: "Every trial lawyer is well aware that juries often do in fact allow recovery in cases of contributory negligence, and that the compromise in the jury room does result in some diminution of the damages because of the plaintiff's fault. But the process is at best a haphazard and most unsatisfactory one." Prosser, *Comparative Negligence*, 41 CALIF. L. REV. 1, 4.

It is in view of these theoretical and practical considerations that to this date 25 states have abrogated the "all-or-nothing" rule of contributory negligence and have enacted in its place general apportionment *statutes* calculated in one manner or another to assess liability in proportion to fault. In 1973 these states were joined by Florida, which effected the same result by *judicial* decision. *Hoffman v. Jones,* 280 So. 2d 431 (Fla. 1973). We are likewise persuaded that logic, practical experience, and fundamental justice counsel against the retention of the doctrine rendering contributory negligence a complete bar to recovery — and that it should be replaced in this state by a system under which liability for damage will be borne by those whose negligence caused it, in direct proportion to their respective fault.

The foregoing conclusion, however, clearly takes us only part of the way. It is strenuously and ably urged by defendants and two of the amici curiae that whatever our views on the relative merits of contributory and comparative negligence, we are precluded from making those views the law of the state by judicial decision. Moreover, it is contended, even if we are not so precluded, there exist considerations of a practical nature which should dissuade us from embarking upon the course which we have indicated. We proceed to take up these two objections in order.

[The court concluded that § 1714 of the Civil Code, which provided that every person is responsible for his own negligence except where a person by the want of ordinary care has "brought the injury upon himself", merely announced "existing common law principles . . . with a distinct view toward continuing judicial evolution."]

We are thus brought to the second group of arguments which have been advanced by defendants and the amici curiae supporting their position. Generally speaking, such arguments expose considerations of a practical nature which, it is urged, counsel against the adoption of a rule of comparative negligence in this state even if such adoption is possible by judicial means.

The most serious of these considerations are those attendant upon the administration of a rule of comparative negligence in cases involving multiple parties. One such problem may arise when all responsible parties are not brought before the court: it may be difficult for the jury to evaluate relative negligence in such circumstances, and to compound this difficulty such an evaluation would not be res judicata in a subsequent suit against the absent wrongdoer. Problems of contribution and indemnity among joint tort-feasors lurk in the background.

A second and related major area of concern involves the administration of the actual process of fact-finding in a comparative negligence system. The assigning of a specific percentage factor to the amount of negligence attributable to a particular party, while in theory a matter of little difficulty, can become a matter of perplexity in the face of hard facts. The temptation for the jury to resort to a quotient verdict in such circumstances can be great. These inherent difficulties are not, however, insurmountable. Guidelines might be provided the jury which will assist it in keeping focussed upon the true inquiry, and the utilization of special verdicts or jury interrogatories can be of invaluable assistance in assuring that the jury has approached its sensitive and often complex task with proper standards and appropriate reverence.

The third area of concern, the status of the doctrines of last clear chance and assumption of risk, involves less the practical problems of administering a particular form of comparative negligence than it does a definition of the theoretical outline of the specific form to be adopted. Although several states which apply comparative negligence concepts retain the last clear chance doctrine, the better reasoned position seems to be that when true comparative negligence is adopted, the need for last clear chance as a palliative of the hardships of the "all-or-nothing" rule disappears and its retention results only in a windfall to the plaintiff in direct contravention of the principle of liability in proportion to fault.

As for assumption of risk, we have recognized in this state that this defense overlaps that of contributory negligence to some extent and in fact is made up of at least two distinct defenses. "To simplify greatly, it has been observed . . . that in one kind of situation, to wit, where a plaintiff *unreasonably* undertakes to encounter a specific known risk imposed by a defendant's negligence, plaintiff's conduct, although he may encounter that risk in a prudent manner, is in reality a form of contributory negligence . . . . Other kinds of situations within the doctrine of assumption of risk are those, for example, where plaintiff is held to agree to relieve defendant of an obligation of reasonable conduct toward him. Such a situation would not involve contributory negligence, but rather a reduction of defendant's duty of care." *Grey v. Fibreboard Paper Prod. Co.,* 65 Cal. 2d 240, 245–246, 53 Cal. Rptr. 545, 418 P.2d 153, 156 (1966). We think it clear that the adoption of a system of comparative negligence should entail the merger of the defense of assumption of risk into the general scheme of assessment of liability in proportion to fault in those particular cases in which the form of assumption of risk involved is no more than a variant of contributory negligence.

Finally there is the problem of the treatment of willful misconduct under a system of comparative negligence. In jurisdictions following the "all-or-nothing" rule, contributory negligence is no defense to an action based upon a claim of willful misconduct, and this is the present rule in California . . . . The thought is that the difference between willful and wanton misconduct and ordinary negligence is one of kind rather than degree in that the former involves conduct of an entirely different order, and under this conception it might well be urged that comparative negligence concepts should have no application when one of the parties has been guilty of willful and wanton misconduct. It has been persuasively argued, however, that the loss of deterrent effect that would occur upon application of comparative fault concepts to willful and wanton misconduct as well as ordinary negligence would be slight, and that a comprehensive system of comparative negligence should allow for the apportionment of damages in all cases involving misconduct which falls short of being intentional. The law of punitive damages remains a separate consideration.

The existence of the foregoing areas of difficulty and uncertainty (as well as others which we have not here mentioned) has not diminished our conviction that the time for a revision of the means for dealing with contributory fault in this state is long past due and that it lies within the province of this court to initiate the needed change by our decision in this case. Two of the indicated areas (i.e., multiple parties and willful misconduct) are not involved in the case before us, and we consider it neither necessary nor wise to address ourselves to specific problems of this nature which might be expected to arise.

As the Florida court stated with respect to the same subject, "it is not the proper function of this Court to decide unripe issues, without the benefit of adequate briefing, not involving an actual controversy, and unrelated to a specific factual situation." *Hoffman v. Jones,* 280 So. 2d at 439.

Our previous comments relating to the remaining two areas of concern (i.e., the status of the doctrines of last clear chance and assumption of risk, and the matter of judicial supervision of the finder of fact) have provided sufficient guidance to enable the trial courts of this state to meet and resolve particular problems in this area as they arise. As we have indicated, last clear chance and assumption of risk (insofar as the latter doctrine is but a variant of contributory negligence) are to be subsumed under the general process of assessing liability in proportion to fault, and the matter of jury supervision we leave for the moment within the broad discretion of the trial courts.

Our decision in this case is to be viewed as a first step in what we deem to be a proper and just direction, not as a compendium containing the answers to all questions that may be expected to arise. Pending future judicial or legislative developments, we are content for the present to assume the position taken by the Florida court in this matter: "We feel the trial judges of this State are capable of applying [a] comparative negligence rule without our setting guidelines in anticipation of expected problems. The problems are more appropriately resolved at the trial level in a practical manner instead of a theoretical solution at the appellate level. The trial judges are granted broad discretion in adopting such procedures as may accomplish the objectives and purposes expressed in this opinion." 280 So. 2d at 439–440.

It remains to identify the precise form of comparative negligence which we now adopt for application in this state. Although there are many variants, only the two basic forms need be considered here. The first of these, the so-called "pure" form of comparative negligence, apportions liability in direct proportion to fault in all cases. This was the form adopted by the Supreme Court of Florida in *Hoffman v. Jones,* and it applies by statute in Mississippi, Rhode Island, and Washington. Moreover it is the form favored by most scholars and commentators. The second basic form of comparative negligence, of which there are several variants, applies apportionment based on fault *up to the point* at which the plaintiff's negligence is equal to or greater than that of the defendant — when that point is reached, plaintiff is barred from recovery. Nineteen states have adopted this form or one of its variants by statute. The principal argument advanced in its favor is moral in nature: that it is not morally right to permit one more at fault in an accident to recover from one less at fault. Other arguments assert the probability of increased insurance, administrative, and judicial costs if a "pure" rather than a "50 percent" system is adopted, but this has been seriously questioned.

We have concluded that the "pure" form of comparative negligence is that which should be adopted in this state. In our view the "50 percent" system simply shifts the lottery aspect of the contributory negligence rule to a different ground. As Dean Prosser has noted, under such a system "[it] is obvious that a slight difference in the proportionate fault may permit a recovery; and there has been much justified criticism of a rule under which a plaintiff who is charged with 49 percent of the total negligence recovers 51 percent of his damages, while one who is charged with 50 percent recovers nothing at all." Prosser, *Comparative Negligence, supra,* 41 CALIF. L. REV. 1, 25. In effect "such a rule distorts the very principle it recognizes, i.e., that persons are responsible for their acts to the extent their fault contributes to an injurious result. The partial rule simply lowers, but does not eliminate, the bar of contributory negligence." Juenger, Brief for Negligence Law Section of the State Bar of Michigan in Support of Comparative Negligence as Amicus Curiae, *Parsonson v. Constr. Equip. Co.,* 18 WAYNE L. REV. 3, 50.

For all of the foregoing reasons we conclude that the "all-or-nothing" rule of contributory negligence as it presently exists in this state should be and is herewith superseded by a system of "pure" comparative negligence, the fundamental purpose of which shall be to assign responsibility and liability for damage in direct proportion to the amount of negligence of each of the parties. Therefore, in all actions for negligence resulting in injury to person or property, the contributory negligence of the person injured in person or property shall not bar recovery, but the damages awarded shall be diminished in proportion to the amount of negligence attributable to the person recovering.

The doctrine of last clear chance is abolished, and the defense of assumption of risk is also abolished to the extent that it is merely a variant of the former doctrine of contributory negligence; both of these are to be subsumed under the general process of assessing liability in proportion to negligence. Pending future judicial or legislative developments, the trial courts of this state are to use broad discretion in seeking to assure that the principle stated is applied in the interest of justice and in furtherance of the purposes and objectives set forth in this opinion.

CLARK, JUSTICE.

I dispute the need for judicial — instead of legislative — action in this area. The majority is clearly correct in its observation that our society has changed significantly during the 103-year existence of section 1714. But this social change has been neither recent nor traumatic, and the criticisms leveled by the majority at the present operation of contributory negligence are not new. I cannot conclude our society's evolution has now rendered the normal legislative process inadequate.

Further, the Legislature is the branch best able to effect transition from contributory to comparative or some other doctrine of negligence. Numerous and differing negligence systems have been urged over the years, yet there remains widespread disagreement among both the commentators and the states as to which one is best. This court is not an investigatory body, and we lack the means of fairly appraising the merits of these competing systems. Constrained by settled rules of judicial review, we must consider only matters within the record or susceptible to judicial notice. That this court is inadequate to the task of carefully selecting the best replacement system is reflected in the majority's summary manner of eliminating from consideration all but two of the many competing proposals — including models adopted by some of our sister states.

NOTES

1. *The Genesis of Comparative Fault.* The concept of comparing the fault of the parties and dividing the otherwise indivisible loss on the basis of such a comparison developed slowly. Georgia adopted a form of comparative fault in the nineteenth century. The Mississippi legislature adopted comparative fault in 1910. In the Federal Employer's Liability Act in 1908, Congress provided that in an action by an employee against a railroad employer, "the fact that the employee may have been guilty of contributory negligence shall not bar a recovery, but the damages shall be diminished by the jury in proportion to the amount of negligence attributable to such employee." In 1920, Congress extended comparative negligence to actions by seamen against their employers. 46 U.S.C. § 688 (The Jones Act).

Acceptance of the concept that the finder of fact can quantify fault tolled the death knell for the contributory negligence bar. By the mid-1960s the issue was no longer whether comparative negligence would supersede the contributory negligence bar, but whether the change would come from the legislatures or from the courts, and what type of comparative negligence would be adopted.

2. *An Inexorable Trend.* By 1992, 46 states had adopted some form of comparative negligence. The common law rule that contributory negligence bars recovery remained in effect in only four states — Alabama, Maryland, North Carolina, and Virginia. The comparative negligence reform usually came from the legislature — only about one-fourth of the states making the change did so by judicial decree.

3. *Pure and Modified Models.* As the *Li* case indicates, there are two major kinds of comparative negligence: "pure," in which plaintiff may recover as little as 1% of his damages (*see, e.g., Sutton v. Piasecki Trucking, Inc.,* 59 N.Y.2d 800, 451 N.E.2d 481, 464 N.Y.S.2d 734 (1983), plaintiff allocated 99% of the fault was entitled to recover 1% of his damages), and "modified," in which plaintiff may not recover if his percentage of fault equals or exceeds that of the defendant. The "modified" plan is the most popular. About 21 states have adopted one kind of "modified" plan — sometimes called the New Hampshire or the "50-50" plan: plaintiff may recover the amount of his damages multiplied by the defendant's percentage of fault, if the plaintiff's negligence does not exceed that of the defendant. If it does, plaintiff is barred from recovery. This Minnesota statute represents the "50-50" plan:

> Contributory fault shall not bar recovery in an action by any person or his legal representative to recover damages for fault resulting in death or injury to person or property, if the contributory fault was not greater than the fault of the person against whom recovery is sought, but any damages allowed shall be diminished in proportion to the amount of fault attributable to the person recovering . . . .

MINN. STAT. ANN. § 604.01(1) (West 1988).

Nine states follow the Georgia or "49-51" plan: plaintiff may recover the amount of his damages, multiplied by the defendant's percentage of fault, only if the plaintiff's negligence is less than that of defendant. For example:

> If the fault chargeable to a party claiming damages is of a lesser degree than the fault chargeable to the party or parties from whom the

claiming party seeks to recover damages, then the claiming party is entitled to recover the amount of his damages after they have been diminished in proportion to the degree of his own fault. If the fault chargeable to a party claiming damages is equal or greater in degree than any fault chargeable to the party or parties from whom the claiming party seeks to recover damages, then the claiming party is not entitled to recover such damages.

ARK. STAT. ANN. § 16-64-122(b)(1) (1987).

Thirteen states and federal maritime law use the "pure" comparative negligence approach. Two states permit comparison if the plaintiff's negligence is "slight." The cases and statutes are collected in *McIntyre v. Balentine*, 833 S.W.2d 52 (Tenn. 1992).

Some jurisdictions have changed from one plan to another; the trend is to the "50-50" plan. What might motivate a legislature to switch from "pure" comparative negligence to a modified plan? From a "49-51" plan to a "50-50" plan? Most of the states adopting comparative negligence by judicial decree have adopted "pure" comparative fault. What might motivate such uniform judicial response?

4. *Separation of Powers.* The adoption of comparative negligence probably has been slowed by the reluctance of courts to abrogate the common law rule that contributory negligence bars recovery. Many courts feel that this kind of "lawmaking" should come from the legislatures and not from the courts. When faced with the counter argument that the doctrine was created by the courts, some courts then adopt the position that because the legislature has not abrogated the common law rule, it has tacitly approved it, and further disapproval must come from the legislature. Could this be rhetoric masking an unwillingness to abandon the "all or nothing" rule? Or an unwillingness to tackle judicially the many problems which accompany abrogation of the "all or nothing" rule?

5. *Comparative Fault and Exceptional Statutes.* Recall the discussion of "exceptional statutes", *supra*. Contributory negligence typically does not apply to such statutes. But when a jurisdiction adopts *comparative* fault, should a plaintiff's fault be taken into account under an exceptional statute to reduce his or her recovery? See, e.g., *Slager v. HWA Corp.*, 435 N.W.2d 349 (Iowa 1989) (comparative fault is not a defense to a dramshop action); *Ewert v. Georgia Cas. & Sur. Co.*, 548 So. 2d 358 (La. App. 1989) (minor's recovery should not be reduced by his contributing negligence in an action against an employer who hired the minor in violation of child labor laws). *See also Sandborg v. Blue Earth County*, 615 N. W. 2d 61 (Minn. 2000) (county jail liable at common law for foreseeable suicide of inmate, who was "particularly vulnerable and dependent" on the jail for protection against the "very event which [made] the [jail's] conduct negligent").

6. *Comparative Fault and Strict Liability.* If defendant is liable without fault, should plaintiff's contributory negligence reduce his recovery? Again, there are two considerations. The policies which lead a court to impose strict liability upon an activity may suggest that the actor should bear all of the damages caused by the activity, including those caused by the victim's

substandard conduct. The second consideration is the "apples and oranges" argument. However, strict liability and negligence share the most important characteristic of each: the conduct or activity presents an unreasonable risk of harm. As to abnormally dangerous activities, RESTATEMENT (SECOND) OF TORTS § 520 provides that in determining such liability the court should consider the existence of a high degree of risk of harm, the likelihood that the harm will be great, the inability to eliminate the risk by exercise of reasonable care, the extent to which the activity is not a matter of common usage, the inappropriateness of the activity to the place where it is carried on, and the extent to which the activity's value to the community is outweighed by its dangerous attributes. Can some of these factors be compared with negligence factors? *See* the discussion of *Coney v. J.L.G. Indus.*, 97 Ill. 2d 104, 73 Ill. Dec. 337, 454 N.E.2d 197 (1983). Can a party avoid any comparative fault analysis by framing his or her claim in contract, such as a claim for legal malpractice? *See Jackson State Bank v. King*, 844 P.2d 1093 (Wyo. 1993) (comparative fault inapplicable to claim for legal malpractice, which court said was a claim for breach of contract).

7. *Incomparable Fault.* A court may be hesitant to apply contributory negligence if there is a vast discrepancy between the fault (willful and wanton conduct) of the defendant and that of a relatively innocent plaintiff. Should the same rule apply in a comparative fault scenario, *i.e.*, if the defendant's conduct is reckless, willful or wanton, should the plaintiff's recovery be *reduced*? The courts generally refuse to reduce recovery in such a situation. *See* the discussion in *Blazovic v. Andrich*, 124 N.J. 90, 590 A.2d 222 (1991). *See Morgan v. Johnson*, 976 P.2d 619 (Wash. 1999) (comparative fault inapplicable in battery where defendant boyfriend contended plaintiff was negligent in being intoxicated). *Cf. Babb v. Boney*, 710 So. 2d 1132 (La. App. 1998) (failure to mitigate damages may be defense in battery case where victim provoked incident).

What if the plaintiff's conduct is reckless, willful or wanton, and the defendant is merely negligent? *See, e.g., Barker v. Kallash*, 63 N.Y.2d 19, 468 N.E.2d 39, N.Y.S.2d 201 (1984) (15-year-old injured when pipe bomb he was making exploded in his hands, could not recover against 9-year-old who sold gun powder used in bomb); *Symone T. v. Lieber*, 613 N.Y.S.2d 404 (N.Y. App. 1994) (12-year-old victim could not recover against health care provider because she criminally sought abortion during 25th week of pregnancy). *Compare* RESTATEMENT (SECOND) OF TORTS, § 889: "One is not barred from recovery for an interference with his legally protected interests merely because at the time of the interference he was committing a tort or crime." However, REST. 3D OF TORTS: APPORTIONMENT (2000) takes the position that comparative fault principles should apply to "all bases of liability, including intentional torts." Sec. 1 com. *c*.

What if both plaintiff and defendant are reckless or willful or wanton?

8. *Comparative Fault and Punitive Damages.* Can plaintiff's negligence be used to reduce exemplary or punitive damages? The majority rule is that it may not. Why? *See, e g., Clark v. Cantrell*, 332 S.C. 433, 504 S. E. 2d 605 (1998) (reviewing cases).

9. *The Mechanics of Comparing Fault.* The UNIF. COMPARAT. FAULT ACT provides:

> In determining the percentages of fault, the trier of fact shall consider both the nature of the conduct of each party at fault and the extent of the causal relation between the conduct and the damages claimed.

§ 2(b) UNIF. COMPARAT. FAULT ACT (1979) 12 U.L.A. 39 (Supp. 1990). A comment offers these guidelines:

> *Percentages of fault.* In comparing the fault of the several parties for the purpose of obtaining percentages there are a number of implications arising from the concept of fault. The conduct of the claimant or of any defendant may be more or less at fault, depending upon all the circumstances including such matters as (1) whether the conduct was mere inadvertence or engaged in with an awareness of the danger involved, (2) the magnitude of the risk created by the conduct, including the number of persons endangered and the potential seriousness of the injury, (3) the significance of what the actor was seeking to attain by his conduct, (4) the actor's superior or inferior capacities, and (5) the particular circumstances, such as the existence of an emergency requiring a hasty decision.

The Louisiana Supreme Court has ruled that if the defendant is subject to strict liability and the plaintiff is contributorily negligent, the court should compare causation and not conduct. *Howard v. Allstate Ins. Co.,* 520 So. 2d 715 (La. 1988). However, the jury ordinarily will hear evidence of the conduct of the parties in connection with its determination of defendant's strict liability and the plaintiff's contributory negligence. Is it realistic to expect a jury determining the percentages of causation to disregard the evidence of a defendant's faulty conduct?

Is failure to mitigate damages a bar to recovery, or should that failure be assigned a percentage of fault and the plaintiff's recovery reduced accordingly? *See Ostroski v. Azzara,* 111 N.J. 429, 545 A.2d 148 (1988). How should fault be allocated in "second accident" cases, *i.e.,* one defendant's fault caused the accident but another defendant's fault increased the damages therefrom? *See Campbell v. Louisiana Department of Transportation & Development,* 648 So. 2d 898 (La. 1995) ("In apportioning fault the trier of fact shall consider both the nature of the conduct of each party . . . and the extent of the causal relation between the conduct and the damages claimed").

10. *Multiple Co-Tortfeasors.* In a modified comparative fault jurisdiction where there are multiple co-tortfeasors, should plaintiff's fault be compared with each tortfeasor, or with all of the tortfeasors as an aggregate. Some courts do one, some the other. *See, e.g., Nelson v. Concrete Supply Co.,* 399 S.E.2d 783 (S.C. 1991) (plaintiff's negligence compared to aggregate fault of all defendants). Most courts follow the aggregate rule. A one-on-one comparison may bar recovery where an aggregate comparison would not. For example, assume the plaintiff is 40% at fault, while his three co-tortfeasors are each 20% at fault. If the plaintiff's fault is compared with that of each co-tortfeasor, he cannot recover from any of them. But if his fault is compared with the aggregate fault of all three, he will not be barred from recovery.

A separate question is whether multiple co-tortfeasors are jointly, or severally, liable to the plaintiff. If they are jointly liable, the plaintiff in the above example could recover 60% of his damages from any one of the co-tortfeasors, but only 20% from each under several liability — provided, in either case, the aggregate rule of comparison were used. If the one-on-one rule were used, the question of joint vs. several liability would never be reached under the example because the plaintiff would be barred from recovery at the outset by the modified (but not by a pure) rule of comparison.

11. *The Impact of Comparative Negligence on Other Tort Rules.* In the pre-comparative era, many tort rules developed that overlooked a plaintiff's substandard conduct that contributed to the accident. If the purpose of these rules was to ameliorate the harshness of the "all or nothing" approach, should they be abolished after the adoption of comparative negligence?

Many courts have held that "momentary forgetfulness" may be reasonable and thus is not negligence. Would it be more desirable to penalize the plaintiff for this forgetfulness by reducing his recovery, and thus reducing future forgetfulness? *See Quinn v. State,* 464 So. 2d 357 (La. App.), *cert. denied,* 467 So. 2d 1134 and 1136 (La. 1985) (motorist's recovery should not be reduced for his conduct in allowing his vehicle to stray from the paved portion of the highway, but should be reduced for his substandard conduct in attempting reentry to the paved portion). Should the adoption of comparative fault have any impact upon the "sudden emergency" doctrine? *See Modern Status of Sudden Emergency Doctrine,* 10 A.L.R.5th 680 (1993).

The adoption of comparative negligence generally has resulted in the abolition of the doctrine of last clear chance. *See, e.g., Dykeman v. Englebrecht,* 803 P.2d 119 (Ariz. App. 1990).

If the risk that makes the defendant's conduct wrongful is the risk that the plaintiff may unreasonably fail to avoid the wrongful conduct, should the plaintiff's recovery be reduced? Would it depend upon the extent to which society wishes to deter the defendant's conduct?

12. *Res Ipsa Loquitur.* The general rule used to be that *res ipsa* did not apply if the plaintiff's conduct contributed to his own injury. Should *res ipsa* apply if the plaintiff is partly at fault in a comparative fault jurisdiction? *See Giles v. City of New Haven,* 30 Conn. App. 148, 619 A.2d 476 (1993) (with the adoption of comparative negligence, a plaintiff can be a negligent participant in the events leading up to the injuries suffered without depriving plaintiff of the use of the doctrine of *res ipsa,* as long as plaintiff was not the sole cause of the injuries.)

13. *Counterclaims.* If two parties are injured in an accident and each is entitled to recover from the other for example under principles of pure comparative fault, should the court make separate awards to each, or should it set off the lesser award against the greater one and render only one judgment for the difference in favor of the party with the greater award? Assume: the first party suffers $10,000 damages and is guilty of 40% of the fault; the second party suffers $5,000 damages and is guilty of the remaining 60%. Should there be two awards, one to the first party in the amount of $6,000, and one to the second party in the amount of $2,000? Or should there

be only one award to the first for $4,000? Suppose one of the parties files for bankruptcy? Suppose only one of the parties has liability insurance? Suppose both have liability insurance?

14. *Derivative Claims.* Wrongful death recovery may encompass two distinct causes of action: the survival action (the damages which the decedent could have recovered if he had lived, most notably pain and suffering prior to death), and the wrongful death action (the loss of support the beneficiaries would have received from the victim, together with loss of the victim's services and society). Should the contributory negligence of the decedent reduce the survival claim, through comparative negligence? The wrongful death claim? Is there an important difference between the two, leading to different conclusions?

Nearly all states permit a spouse to recover for loss of consortium (services, society and sex) resulting from a non-fatal injury to the other spouse. Most jurisdictions reduce the consortium claim by the percentage of fault chargeable to the injured spouse. *See Blagg v. Ill. F.W.D. Truck & Equipment Co.*, 572 N.E.2d 920 (Ill. 1991), and the cases cited therein. How do the considerations here differ from wrongful death? If the plaintiff is entitled to recover damages for mental anguish resulting from injury to another, should the percentage of fault chargeable to the accident victim reduce the plaintiff's mental anguish recovery?

15. *Comparative Fault and Joint Liability.* In the age before the quantification of fault, the common law imposed joint liability upon two tortfeasors whose fault combined to cause indivisible damages. Under this rule, either tortfeasor was liable for all or any part of the damages (although the plaintiff could not collect in toto more than the full amount of his damages). The rule evolved in part from considerations of fairness. Because the damages could not be divided, and liability could not be imposed by percentages of fault, the choice was between imposing the risk of non-collection on the innocent plaintiff or upon the guilty defendants. The defendant who was required to pay the judgment gradually developed remedies such as contribution against the co-tortfeasor. These remedies were not satisfactory. Contribution, when it was available, was often on a *per capita* basis, since fault could not be quantified. Thus the slightly negligent and the grossly negligent tortfeasor each paid half of the plaintiff's damages. In some jurisdictions, the slightly negligent tortfeasor could obtain indemnification from the other tortfeasor, but this merely transferred some injustice from one to the other. If one tortfeasor could not be made to pay (*e.g.*, because of immunity or insolvency), the other tortfeasor bore the entire liability.

Many jurisdictions which have adopted comparative negligence also have adopted several liability. Each tortfeasor is liable, vis-a-vis the others, for his percentage of the fault multiplied by the plaintiff's recoverable damages. The quantification of fault through comparative negligence and comparative contribution undermined a foundation of the rule that tortfeasors whose wrongful acts cause indivisible damage are liable jointly and severally (*in solido*) for plaintiff's damages. If the joint liability rule applies, a defendant chargeable with 65% of the fault is cast for the full amount of the plaintiff's damages, but can recover through contribution the 35% share of the remaining defendant, unless that defendant is insolvent, immune or unavailable. After the adoption of comparative negligence and comparative contribution, the issue of liability among co-tortfeasors who produce indivisible damage becomes simple and direct: who should bear the risk of nonrecovery against a tortfeasor? Abolition of joint and several liability thrusts the risk upon the plaintiff. Continuation of joint and several liability leaves the risk on the solvent tortfeasor. Other jurisdictions have compromised by placing some, but not all, of the risk of the insolvent, unavailable or immune tortfeasor upon the other available tortfeasor or tortfeasors. (Joint and several liability is a term used to describe co-tortfeasors who are jointly liable but who can be sued either together or separately, i.e., severally.)

If a nonhuman force (*e.g.*, the weather or an animal) foreseeably contributes to a plaintiff's injury, the defendant's liability is not reduced by the amount of fault or cause attributable to that force. Should an immune, insolvent or unavailable defendant be treated like a nonhuman force, for purposes of allocating liability?

The UNIFORM COMPARATIVE FAULT ACT provides that each defendant shall be cast for his percentage of fault, but that "[u]pon motion made not later than [one year] after judgment is entered, the court shall determine whether all or part of a party's equitable share of the obligation is uncollectible from that party, and shall reallocate any uncollectible amount among the other parties, including a claimant at fault, according to their respective percentages of fault." UCFA, § 2(d).

16. *Instructing the Jury.* With a general verdict, the jury reports whether it finds for the plaintiff or the defendant, and if it finds for the plaintiff, the jury also reports the total amount of damages it has awarded. Such a verdict will reflect (although it will not reveal) the jury's determination as to comparative fault, and the result is similar to pre-comparative days when juries often were allowed to make ad hoc comparisons of fault.

Many jurisdictions permit or require a special verdict, in which the jury answers specific questions, and the judge determines the appropriate judgment in light of the jury's answers. Such a verdict might ask these questions:

Was the defendant negligent?

If so, was the plaintiff negligent?

If you find both parties negligent, state in percentages (totaling 100%) the causal negligence of each party?

Plaintiff _____

Defendant _____

State the total amount of damages sustained by plaintiff. $ _____

A jury presented with a special verdict but untutored in the effect of its responses may provide answers which will produce a result different from that which they intended. In a pure comparative negligence state, the jury may not know that the judge will further reduce the amount of damages by the percentage of fault which the jury assigned to the plaintiff. In a state using a modified plan, the jury may not know that the victim will be uncompensated if they assess 50% or more of the fault to him. When they subsequently learn the impact of their answers, jurors may not be competent witnesses to establish the error. *See, e.g., Robles v. Exxon Corp.,* 862 F.2d 1201 (5th Cir. 1989), *cert. denied,* 104 L. Ed. 2d 434, 109 S. Ct. 1967 (1989). *See also* FED. R. EVID. 606(B) (upon an inquiry into the validity of a verdict, a juror may not testify as to the effect of anything upon any juror's mind or emotions influencing the juror to assent to or dissent from the verdict, except in cases of extraneous prejudicial information or improper outside influence).

Should the jury be told the effect of its answers to special interrogatories? What philosophy might be reflected in an affirmative answer to that question? In a negative one? The cases divide on this issue. *Compare Schabe v. Hampton Bays Union Free Sch. Dist.,* 103 A.D.2d 418, 480 N.Y.S.2d 328 (N.Y. App. Div. 1984), *with Smith v. Gizzi,* 564 P.2d 1009 (Okla. 1977).

Does the judge have the power to "correct" the jury's misallocation of percentages of fault, through additur, remittitur or *jnov? Compare Rowlands v. Signal Constr. Co.,* 549 So. 2d 1380 (Fla. 1989), *with Gardiner v. Schobel,* 521 A.2d 1011 (R.I. 1987).

D. ASSUMPTION OF THE RISK

PROBLEM

Before entering a race, runner signs a form which provides that "as a consideration for permission to compete in the race, runner waives all claims she has or may have against race sponsor for damages sustained as a result of her participation in the race." While running the prescribed route along a wooded area, runner is abducted and raped by an intruder; reasonable care by race sponsor may have prevented the rape. Does the release bar recovery against race sponsor? Suppose, instead, runner's child, viewing the race, is injured by the negligence of the race sponsor. Does the release bar the runner's claim for loss of consortium with, or mental anguish over the injury to, her child?

SCHUTKOWSKI v. CAREY
725 P.2d 1057 (Wyo. 1986)

BROWN, JUSTICE.

Appellant Barbara Schutkowski, a skydiving student injured during her first jump, filed a negligence complaint against appellees Dwain Carey and Robert Rodekohr, her skydiving instructors. The district court, in a summary judgment for appellees, found that a "Release and Indemnity Agreement" signed by appellant excused the instructors from all liability for injury, including consequences arising from negligence. On appeal Ms. Schutkowski raises the following issues:

"1. Did the trial court err in determining that the contracting parties intended for the release to excuse appellees from liability caused by their negligence?

"2. Did error occur in failing to strictly construe the release as merely excusing liability for injuries that ordinarily and inevitably occur without fault?

"3. Did the trial court err in following the rationale of a minority view?"

We will affirm.

The basic facts are undisputed. Appellant employed appellees to teach her to sky dive. Before her first jump, she signed an agreement releasing appellees from all claims for personal injury resulting from parachuting and related activities. On July 1, 1979, appellant made her first parachute jump, flying with instructor Carey and pilot Rodekohr. During a difficult landing some distance from the target Ms. Schutkowski suffered back, arm and leg injuries. She filed an action charging that Carey and Rodekohr were negligent in failing to warn her of the risks of parachuting, and failing to adequately instruct and direct her during skydiving procedures.

In their answers to the complaint and subsequent motions for summary judgment, appellees contended that appellant's claims were barred by the liability release agreement. In this document Ms. Schutkowski acknowledged that for consideration and permission to participate in the course,

> I, Barbara Schutkowski of Cheyenne, Wyo. for myself, my heirs . . . do hereby *fully and forever release* and discharge the said Cheyenne Parachute Club and Bob Rodekohr, Cheyenne, Wyo., and their divisions, and their employees . . . and *all persons whomsoever directly or indirectly liable, from any and all other claims and demands,* actions, and causes of action, damages, costs, loss of services, expenses, and any and all other claims of damages whatsoever both in law and in equity, on account of, or *in any way resulting from, personal injuries,* conscious suffering, death, or property damages sustained by me, arising out of aircraft flights, parachute jumps, or any other means of lift, ascent, or descent from an aircraft . . . on the ground or in flight, and meaning and intending to include herein all such personal injuries, conscious suffering, death or property damage resulting from or in any way connected with or arising out of instructions, training, and ground or air operations incidental thereto, and in consideration of the foregoing premises I . . . hereby expressly stipulate, covenant and agree to indemnify and hold forever harmless the said Cheyenne Parachute Club . . . from any and all actions . . . and any and all other claims for damages whatsoever which may hereafter arise . . . from my negligent, willful or wanton, or intentional act or actions.
>
> The terms of this release and indemnification agreement are contractual and not a mere recital and contain the entire agreement between the parties hereto. (Emphasis added.)

The district court found that the agreement released appellees from liability for negligence. An order granting summary judgment for defendants was entered from which Ms. Schutkowski appeals . . . .

Wyoming courts enforce exculpatory clauses releasing parties from liability for injury or damages resulting from negligence if the clause is not contrary to public policy. Generally, specific agreements absolving participants and proprietors from negligence liability during hazardous recreational activities are enforceable, subject to willful misconduct limitations. *Cain v. Cleveland Parachute Training Center,* 9 Ohio App. 3d 27, 457 N.E.2d 1185 (1983). The Ohio court observed in *Cain:*

> A participant in recreational activity is free to contract with the proprietor of such activity so as to relieve the proprietor of responsibility for damages or injuries to the participant caused by the negligence of the proprietor, except when caused by willful or wanton misconduct.

Id., at 1187.

In *Jones v. Dressel,* 623 P.2d 370 (Colo. 1981), the Colorado Supreme Court developed a four-part test to determine whether a negligence exculpatory clause is valid. Pennsylvania courts have also adopted standards which closely parallel those in the Colorado case. *Employer's Liability Assur. Corporation v. Greenville Business Men's Assoc.,* 423 Pa. 288, 224 A.2d 620 (1966). In reaching its determination a court considers (1) whether a duty to the public exists; (2) the nature of the service performed; (3) whether the contract was fairly entered into; and (4) whether the intention of the parties is expressed in clear and unambiguous language. Only exculpatory agreements meeting these requirements are enforceable. Private recreational businesses generally do not qualify as services demanding a special duty to the public, nor are their services of a special, highly necessary nature. The California Supreme Court, in *Tunkl v. Regents of University of Cal.,* 60 Cal. 2d 92, 32 Cal. Rptr. 33, 36, 383 P.2d 441, 445–446 (1963), described the elements of an agreement affecting the public interest:

> [The agreement] concerns a business of a type generally thought suitable for public regulation. The party seeking exculpation is engaged in performing a service of great importance to the public, which is often a matter of practical necessity for some members of the public. The party holds himself out as willing to perform this service for any member of the public who seeks it . . . . As a result of the essential nature of the service, in the economic setting of the transaction the party invoking exculpation possesses a decisive advantage of bargaining strength against any member of the public who seeks his services . . . .

The service provided by appellees was not a matter of practical necessity for any member of the public. It was not an essential service, so no decisive bargaining advantage existed. Further, no evidence suggests that appellant was unfairly pressured into signing the agreement or that she was deprived of an opportunity to understand its implications. The agreement meets the first three criteria for determining if the exculpatory clause is valid.

Finally, we must determine if the release clearly shows the intent to eliminate appellee's liability for negligent acts. Public policy disfavors clauses exculpating liability for negligence, and a court must closely scrutinize such clauses. The exculpatory clause must clearly and unequivocally demonstrate the parties' intent to eliminate liability for negligence.

The question here is whether "negligence" or other specific words are required to clearly show intent.

Courts disagree on the specific language needed to show such intent. In some jurisdictions the word "negligence" or equally precise language is required in order to bar liability for negligent acts. While these jurisdictions may reluctantly accept contracts absolving parties from liability for negligence, they insist on exacting, "unequivocal" language.

Conversely, the absence of the word "negligence" is not fatal to an exculpatory clause in many courts if the terms of the contract clearly show intent to extinguish liability. *Cain v. Cleveland Parachute Training Center, supra.*

The facts in *Cain v. Cleveland Parachute Training Center,* were very similar to the case before us. A sky diving student signed a liability release stating:

> . . . I covenant for myself, my estate, executor, heirs, and assigns not to file suit or initiate any claim procedure in respect to any personal injuries, property damages, or losses I may experience or sustain arising directly or indirectly out of my activities hereunder.

Id. at 1186. The Ohio court, while narrowly construing the language of the exculpatory clause, found that it expressed an intent to limit liability for negligence even though the words used did not include "negligence."

Jurisdictions that interpret exculpatory language based on the clear intent of the parties rather than specific "negligence" terminology better characterize Wyoming law. . . .

Considering all of the language of the agreement in context, it is clear that the parties' intent was to release appellees from liability for negligence. The contract wording focuses particular attention on the unconditional nature of the exculpatory agreement. It specifically and repeatedly exempts appellants from any responsibility for potential consequences. By signing the release, Barbara Schutkowski voluntarily waived her potential claims against

> all persons whomsoever directly or indirectly liable, from *any and all* . . . claims and demands, actions and causes of action . . . and *any and all other claims* of damages *whatsoever both in law and in equity,* and *in any way* resulting from, personal injuries.

Common sense is one of the leading characteristics of contract interpretation and construction. In construing this contract the nature of the service and the purpose of the release must be considered. In *Gross v. Sweet,* 49 N.Y.2d 102, 424 N.Y.S.2d 365, 400 N.E.2d 306, 313 (1979), a parachuting case similar to this one, the well-reasoned dissent contended:

> The activity on which plaintiff was about to embark under the tutelage of defendants was a hazardous one at best, but virtually the only claims that he might have had against them [the defendants] should he sustain personal injuries or property damage would be claims resulting from fault or negligence of defendants. The majority reads the agreement merely as driving home the fact that the defendant was not to bear any responsibility for injuries that ordinarily and inevitably would occur, without any fault of the defendant, to those who participate in such a physically demanding sport. But of what significance or practical effect is such a release? It is difficult to

conceive of any claim other than one predicated on negligence; personal injuries or property damage occasioned without negligence by one or both of the defendants would give rise to no cause of action at all. The release then, if construed as not including claims predicated on negligence, releases nothing and is meaningless and a nullity . . . [A] requirement that there be included the word "negligence" or a description of the specific acts of misconduct pleaded in the complaint (as plaintiff would contend for) would be a reversion to the "semantic stereotypes," which we have now abjured.

In this case it is difficult to envision any claim other than one based on negligence that appellant might have had against appellees. If it was not the intent of the parties to release appellees from liability for negligent acts, we see little purpose in the Release and Indemnity Agreement.

Adult private parties should not enter into a contract for hazardous recreational services lightly. The agreement language is unambiguous; it clearly shows that appellant intended to relinquish all liability claims she might have against appellees. We will enforce the exculpatory clause.

The order granting summary judgment for appellees is affirmed.

THOMAS, CHIEF JUSTICE.

. . . I would opt for the line of authority which requires that the word "negligence" be included in an exculpatory agreement such as this. This requirement is most likely to alert the other party to the extent of the release which he is granting in the contract, which usually is prepared in advance. In many respects this simply would seem to be fair.

As I indicated, the result may well be deemed appropriate with respect to parachuting activities. I wonder how comfortable this court and others will feel with such a rule when it is invoked in favor of day care centers; youth activity organizations; health clubs; public or private schools; landlords; or any of a myriad of activities to which this concept logically can be extended? Because of my concern with the public policy implications of this holding by the court, which I submit may be rather far-reaching, I would vote to reverse the disposition by the trial court and require that if one is to be released from the consequences of his own negligence the release must say exactly that and use the word negligence specifically.

NOTES

1. *Contractual Assumption of the Risk.* Assumption of the risk encompasses two concepts. One is contractual: as the parties enter into a relationship, the tort victim, by express agreement, relieves the defendant of any duty to protect the victim against specified risks. The other is a tort concept: a person who knowingly and voluntarily assumes the risk of harm from another's conduct may not recover the damages he sustains from such conduct.

Contractual assumption of the risk contemplates an agreement between the parties. The agreement is usually in writing and prepared in advance by a party seeking relief from tort liability in exchange for providing goods or services to the other.

The major considerations in contract law are: (1) Did the parties agree? (2) What did they agree to? (3) Were they free to agree to that, or does the law make such an agreement invalid (*contra bonos mores*)? The latter two considerations, reflected in the *Schutkowski* opinion, dominate judicial treatment of contractual assumption of the risk. There must be a "meeting of the minds," *i.e.,* the parties must be aware that they are entering into a contract affecting their rights. Thus, where a patron is presented with a ticket which contains an exculpatory clause, the courts will not find express contractual assumption of the risk unless the patron knew of the nature of the agreement contained in the ticket. *See, e.g., Kermarec v. Compagnie Generale Transatlantique,* 358 U.S. 625, 79 S. Ct. 406, 3 L. Ed. 2d 550 (1959).

Often the issue concerns the scope of the plaintiff's consent. *See Turnbough v. Ladner,* 754 So. 2d 467 (Miss. 2000) (release stating, "I understand that diving with compressed air involves inherent risks [including] decompression sickness," did not demonstrate that plaintiff accepted exposure to injury caused by instructor's negligence in failing to follow basic safety guidelines).

2. *Agreements Against Public Policy.* The common law has established varying guidelines for determining if an agreement is against public policy. The leading case of *Tunkl v. Regents of Univ. of Cal.,* cited in *Schutkowski,* involved the validity of a hospital release. *Tunkl* was applied to the validity of the lease of an apartment (an issue close to the hearts of many law students) in *Henrioulle v. Marin Ventures, Inc.,* 20 Cal. 3d 512, 143 Cal. Rptr. 247, 573 P.2d 465 (Cal. 1978). The following language in *Henrioulle* is instructive:

> In *Tunkl v. Regents of the University of California,* 60 Cal. 2d 92, 32 Cal. Rptr. 33, 383 P.2d 441 (1963), this court held invalid a clause in a hospital admission form which released the hospital from liability for future negligence. This court noted that although courts have made "diverse" interpretations of Civil Code section 1668, which invalidates contracts that exempt one from responsibility for certain wilful or negligent acts, all the decisions were in accord that exculpatory clauses affecting the public interest are invalid.
>
> In *Tunkl,* six criteria are used to identify the kind of agreement in which an exculpatory clause is invalid as contrary to public policy. "[1] It concerns a business of a type generally thought suitable for public regulation. [2] The party seeking exculpation is engaged in performing a service of great importance to the public, which is often a matter of practical necessity for some members of the public. [3] The party holds himself out as willing to perform this service for any member of the public who seeks it, or at least any member coming within certain established standards. [4] As a result of the essential nature of the service, in the economic setting of the transaction, the party invoking exculpation possesses a decisive advantage of bargaining strength against any member of the public who seeks his services. [5] In exercising a superior bargaining power the party confronts the public with a standardized adhesion contract of exculpation, and makes no provision whereby a purchaser may pay additional fees and obtain protection against negligence. [6] Finally, as a result of the transaction, the person or property of the purchaser is placed under

the control of the seller, subject to the risk of carelessness by the seller or his agents."

The transaction before this court, a residential rental agreement, meets the *Tunkl* criteria. Housing in general, and residential leases in particular, are increasingly the subject of governmental regulation, the first of the *Tunkl* criteria. . . . Moreover, the Legislature in 1970 enacted stricter standards of "tenantability" and has limited landlords' ability to impose waivers of tenants' rights in leases.

A lessor of residential property provides shelter, a basic necessity of life, the second *Tunkl* criterion. Moreover, the landlord in this case offered to rent his units to all members of the public, the third *Tunkl* criterion.

Unequal bargaining strength, the fourth *Tunkl* criterion, is also present. In a state and local market characterized by a severe shortage of low-cost housing, tenants are likely to be in a poor position to bargain with landlords. . . .

Finally, the fifth and sixth *Tunkl* criteria are also present. Thus, it does not appear that respondent made any "provision whereby a purchaser may pay additional fees and obtain protection against negligence," and appellant was exposed to the risk of injury through respondent's carelessness.

See also Crawford v. Buckner, 839 S.W.2d 754 (Tenn. 1992) (an exculpatory clause in a residential lease which limits landlord's liability for negligence to the tenant is void as against public policy.)

The court in *Hawkins v. Peart*, 37 P.2d 1062 (Utah 2001), held a parent lacked the authority to release the defendant horseriding business from liability for negligent injury of the parent's child. The parent's indemnity provision, agreeing to hold the defendant harmless, was unenforceable as against public policy.

Disclaimers of liability for intentional or wilful misconduct are also void as against public policy.

La. Civ. Code Annot. Art. 2004 (1987) provides:

> "Any clause is null that, in advance, excludes or limits the liability of one party for causing physical injury to another party."

3. *An Attorney Exculpatory Clause*. DR 6-102(A) of the ABA Model Code of Professional Responsibility provides:

> A lawyer shall not attempt to exonerate himself from or limit his liability to his client for his personal malpractice.

What is the policy behind this disciplinary rule? Could a law firm validly obtain a release from vicarious liability for the personal malpractice of one of its lawyers?

ABA Model Rule 1.8(h) states that a lawyer shall not limit her malpractice liability by agreement, "unless permitted by law and the client is independently represented in making the agreement".

PROBLEM

Jones was injured when Smith lost control of the car that Smith was driving and in which Jones was a passenger. At the time of the accident Smith was driving 50 mph in a 35 mph zone. Jones was aware that Smith was speeding but said nothing. What issues? What result?

Would your response be different if Jones were Smith's wife? If Jones and Smith were co-workers and Jones were Smith's supervisor?

Assume Smith was intoxicated and Jones was aware of the intoxication; nevertheless, he continued to ride with Smith, and was injured in an accident caused by Smith's intoxication. What issues? What result?

HOWELL v. CLYDE
533 Pa. 151, 620 A. 2d 1107 (1993)

FLAHERTY, JUSTICE

Daniel Howell was attending a party at his neighbors' house and was injured when a fireworks cannon owned by the host-neighbors exploded. Howell then sued the neighbors, Theodore and Pamela Clyde, for damages associated with his injuries. The Court of Common Pleas of Clearfield County entered an involuntary nonsuit at the close of plaintiff's evidence, holding that Howell had assumed the risk of injury and was, therefore, barred from recovery. On appeal, Superior Court reversed and remanded for a new trial, . . . holding that the trial court could have granted the nonsuit only if Howell's evidence failed to demonstrate that the Clydes breached a duty which they owed to Howell. Further, Superior Court stated that a nonsuit could not be granted on the basis of assumption of risk because the evidence did not show that Howell knew of the existence of the specific risk he was alleged to have taken.

The evidence established that there was conversation at the party concerning a fireworks cannon fabricated by Clyde's grandfather. The guests, including Howell, visually inspected the cannon and expressed an interest in firing it. Howell went to his residence next door to retrieve black powder for use in the cannon, and upon returning with two cans of black powder, Howell held a flashlight while Clyde filled the bore of the cannon half full of black powder. Howell stood back approximately 40 feet while Clyde ignited the cannon, which exploded, injuring Howell . . . .

Ten years ago in *Rutter v. Northeastern Beaver County School District*, 496 Pa. 590, 437 A.2d 1198 (1981), a plurality of this court sought to abolish the doctrine of assumption of risk, except where expressly preserved by statute, or in cases of express assumption of risk, or cases brought under 402A (strict liability). A major concern was that the complexity of analysis in assumption of risk cases makes it extremely difficult to instruct juries, who must decide not only questions related to negligence, but also whether the affirmative defense of assumption of risk operates to bar recovery altogether. Additionally, the plurality stated:

> [T]he difficulties of using the term "assumption of risk" outweigh the benefits. The issues should be limited to negligence and contributory

negligence. Those are the problems in the case at bar and in all cases brought on a negligence theory. There is no need to introduce further complications. The policy reasons which once existed to preserve the doctrine because of its use in the master-servant cases no longer exist. Furthermore, as is indicated in the Pennsylvania Suggested Standard Jury Instructions, "cases which have evoked the doctrine to deny plaintiff's recovery would have produced the same result either by (1) the court's determination that, as a matter of law, defendant owed plaintiff no duty, or, by (2) the jury's determination that plaintiff's own negligent conduct was a substantial factor in bringing about the harm he suffered."

496 Pa. at 613, 437 A.2d 1198.[2] Additionally, the plurality in *Rutter* stated:

As is indicated in § 496C, comment g [of the Restatement Second of Torts], the implicit decision to assume the risk can be either reasonable or unreasonable. Since the Pennsylvania comparative negligence statute is designed to apportion liability on the basis of fault, not to bar plaintiff's recovery if it can be shown that he had any degree of fault at all, the absolute bar to plaintiff's recovery effected by the application of types 2 and 3 [of assumption of risk], without regard to the reasonableness of plaintiff's action, tends to frustrate the purpose of the comparative negligence statute.

496 Pa. at 616, n. 6, 437 A.2d at 1210, n. 6. Finally, type 4 of assumption of the risk, where both plaintiff and defendant are negligent to some degree,

---

[2] As described in the Restatement Second of Torts, § 496A, the four types of assumption of risk are as follows: 1. In its simplest form, assumption of risk means that the plaintiff has given his express consent to relieve the defendant of an obligation to exercise care for his protection, and agrees to take his chances as to injury from a known or possible risk. The result is that the defendant, who would otherwise be under a duty to exercise such care, is relieved of that responsibility, and is no longer under any duty to protect the plaintiff. As to such express assumption of risk, see § 496B. 2. A second, and closely related, meaning is that the plaintiff has entered voluntarily into some relation with the defendant which he knows to involve the risk, and so is regarded as tacitly or impliedly agreeing to relieve the defendant of responsibility, and to take his own chances. Thus a spectator entering a baseball park may be regarded as consenting that the players may proceed with the game without taking precautions to protect him from being hit by the ball. Again the legal result is that the defendant is relieved of his duty to the plaintiff. As to such implied assumption of risk, see § 496C. 3. In a third type of situation the plaintiff, aware of a risk created by the negligence of the defendant, proceeds or continues voluntarily to encounter it. For example, an independent contractor who finds that he has been furnished by his employer with a machine which is in dangerous condition, and that the employer, after notice, has failed to repair it or to substitute another, may continue to work with the machine. He may not be negligent in doing so, since his decision may be an entirely reasonable one, because the risk is relatively slight in comparison with the utility of his own conduct; and he may even act with unusual caution because he is aware of the danger. The same policy of the common law which denies recovery to one who expressly consents to accept a risk will, however, prevent his recovery is such a case. As to such implied assumption of risk, see § 496C. As to the necessity that the plaintiff's conduct be voluntary, see § 496E. 4. To be distinguished from these three situations is the fourth, in which the plaintiff's conduct in voluntarily encountering a known risk is itself unreasonable, and amounts to contributory negligence. There is thus negligence on the part of both plaintiff and defendant; and the plaintiff is barred from recovery, not only by his implied consent to accept the risk, but also by the policy of the law which refuses to allow him to impose upon the defendant a loss for which his own negligence was in part responsible. (See § 467.)

also frustrates the policies behind our comparative negligence statute, where plaintiff is not barred from recovery unless his own negligence is greater than 50%.

Two years after *Rutter* this court again had occasion to address the assumption of risk problem in *Carrender v. Fitterer*, 503 Pa. 178, 469 A.2d 120 (1983). In that case, a plaintiff visiting a medical clinic in order to receive treatment for a back ailment parked in the clinic lot next to a sheet of ice. When she returned to her car, she slipped on the ice and was injured. The evidence disclosed that there were areas in the lot which were not ice-covered and that plaintiff saw the ice next to her car and appreciated the danger that she might fall. Mr. Chief Justice Roberts, writing for a unanimous court, held that where plaintiff's uncontradicted evidence was that the danger posed by the ice was both obvious and known, the defendant reasonably expected that the danger would be avoided. Plaintiff, therefore, failed to establish a duty essential to a prima facie case of negligence and the defendant clinic was entitled to a judgment notwithstanding the verdict as a matter of law.

In explaining the relationship between assumption of risk and the duty owed an invitee by a possessor of land, Mr. Justice Roberts wrote:

> When an invitee enters business premises, discovers dangerous conditions which are both obvious and avoidable, and nevertheless proceeds voluntarily to encounter them, the doctrine of assumption of risk operates merely as a counterpart to the possessor's lack of duty to protect the invitee from those risks . . . . By voluntarily proceeding to encounter a known or obvious danger, the invitee is deemed to have agreed to accept the risk and to undertake to look out for himself . . . . It is precisely because the invitee assumes the risk of injury from obvious and avoidable dangers that the possessor owes the invitee no duty to take measures to alleviate those dangers. Thus, to say that the invitee assumed the risk of injury from a known and avoidable danger is simply another way of expressing the lack of any duty on the part of the possessor to protect the invitee against such dangers. *See Jones v. Three Rivers Management Corp.*, 483 Pa. 75, 394 A.2d 546 (1978) (operator of baseball park owes no duty to guard against common, frequent, and expected risks of baseball; duty extends only to foreseeable risks not inherent in baseball activity).

503 Pa. at 187–88, 469 A.2d at 125.

It should be noted that in *Carrender* there was no question as to whether the injured party knew of the risk. This is significant because one of the problems in an assumption of risk analysis is determining what the plaintiff knew and whether the plaintiff's course of action was voluntarily and deliberately taken. Because there was no question in *Carrender* as to whether the risk was intelligently and voluntarily taken, the court was able to decide that there was no duty as a matter of law.

As Mr. Justice Roberts pointed out in *Carrender*, an assumption of risk analysis may, in an appropriate case, be "merely a counterpart" to a duty analysis. . . . In other words, cases like *Carrender* may be analyzed from the point of view of duty, or assumption of risk, or ordinary negligence law, each of which overlaps with the others (*i.e.*, a duty analysis may entail a consideration of assumption of risk and ordinary negligence principles).

The present case may also be analyzed from different perspectives. . . .

If the case is viewed from the perspective of a duty analysis, the evidence presented at trial establishes that Howell voluntarily encountered a known risk, thereby obviating any duty which might otherwise have been owed him by Clyde. Under this analysis, the case is controlled by the assumption of risk principle that one who voluntarily undertakes a known risk thereby releases the defendant from any duty of care.

In essence, Howell is claiming that although he knew that it would be dangerous to stand in front of the bore of the cannon, he did not anticipate danger from the cannon itself exploding. The trial court, in granting the nonsuit based on an assumption of risk theory, rejected Howell's claim of ignorance, as a matter of law. On this record, I see no reason to disturb this determination. There are some dangers that are so obvious that they will be held to have been assumed as a matter of law despite assertions of ignorance to the contrary.

A second analysis is that Howell was negligent in participating in the cannon episode and that his negligence must be compared with Clyde's. 42 Pa.C.S. § 7102 provides:

(a) General rule. —

> In all actions brought to recover damages for negligence resulting in death or injury to person or property, the fact that the plaintiff may have been guilty of contributory negligence shall not bar a recovery by the plaintiff or his legal representative where such negligence was not greater than the causal negligence of the defendant or defendants against whom recovery is sought, but any damages sustained by the plaintiff shall be diminished in proportion to the amount of negligence attributed to the plaintiff.

Such a comparison is for the jury, and if Clyde is found to be negligent, Howell will recover at least some proportion of his damages so long as his negligence does not exceed Clyde's.

A third analysis is that this is a type 4 assumption of risk case. Type 4 assumption of risk, as defined by the Restatement, is that in which:

> the plaintiff's conduct in voluntarily encountering a known risk is itself unreasonable, and amounts to contributory negligence. There is thus negligence on the part of both plaintiff and defendant; and the plaintiff is barred from recovery, not only by his implied consent to accept the risk, but also by the policy of the law which refuses to allow him to impose upon the defendant a loss for which his own negligence was in part responsible.

Thus, under a type 4 analysis, a plaintiff who negligently assumes a risk is barred from recovery because he was, in part, at fault.

Fourth, the case may be analyzed as a type 2 or 3 assumption of risk case . . . .

D. ASSUMPTION OF THE RISK

In type 2, Howell may be said to have voluntarily entered into "some relation" with Clyde which he knows to involve risk (*i.e.*, the joint enterprise of firing the cannon); and in type 3, Howell may be said to have voluntarily proceeded to encounter a risk created by Clyde's cannon, seeing the risk of injury as slight, and proceeding cautiously, nonetheless, because of the risk.

Which of these analyses should prevail? It is, perhaps, easiest to determine which should not. Assumption of risk type 4 should no longer be a part of the law of Pennsylvania since it plainly conflicts with the legislative policy underlying the comparative negligence act. One's recovery, under the comparative negligence act, is to be reduced by the amount of his own negligence so long as it does not exceed that of the defendant; it is not to be barred, as in assumption of risk type 4, by the mere existence of any amount of negligence. Assumption of risk type 4, therefore, should be abolished.

A more complex question is whether assumption of risk types 2 and 3 can co-exist with comparative negligence. Arguably, they cannot. Again, the policy underlying a comparative process is inimical to the policy underlying the complete bar of assumption of risk. I believe, however, that a better approach is to recognize the social utility of assumption of risk and continue its viability, albeit in a modified form.

In assumption of risk types 2 and 3 a plaintiff has voluntarily and intelligently undertaken an activity which he knows to be hazardous in ways which subsequently cause him injury. His choice to undertake this activity may or may not be regarded as negligent. His negligence or lack of negligence, however, is not the operative fact; rather, the operative fact is his voluntary choice to encounter the risk. The theoretical underpinning of these types of assumption of risk is that as a matter of public policy one who chooses to take risks will not then be heard later to complain that he was injured by the risks he chose to take and will not be permitted to seek money damages from those who might otherwise have been liable. This policy is distinct from the public policy underlying negligence recovery, which is, in essence, that recovery should be permitted on the basis of fault. Fault has no relevance in assumption of risk types 2 and 3.

Assumption of risk types 2 and 3, then, deal with situations not treated by comparative negligence. In comparative negligence, each of the parties must have been negligent: there must be negligence on both sides to compare. In assumption of risk types 2 and 3, the plaintiff may or may not have been negligent in encountering the risk. He is barred from recovery not because of his negligence, but because of the policy that a person may not recover for injuries which he himself has chosen to risk.

If types 2 and 3 assumption of risk were to be abolished, this idea would be lost. But the policy against recovery for "self-inflicted" injuries remains as viable today as it ever was. Because it is desirable to preserve the public policy behind assumption of risk types 2 and 3, but to the extent possible, remove the difficulties of application of the doctrine and the conflicts which exist with our comparative negligence statute, to the extent that an assumption of risk analysis is appropriate in any given case, it shall be applied by the court as a part of the duty analysis, and not as part of the case to be determined by the jury.[10] This approach preserves the public policy behind the doctrine while at the same time alleviating the difficulty of instructing a jury on voluntariness, knowledge, and scope of the risk.

Under this approach the court may determine that no duty exists only if reasonable minds could not disagree that the plaintiff deliberately and with the awareness of specific risks inherent in the activity nonetheless engaged in the activity that produced his injury. Under those facts, the court would determine that the defendant, as a matter of law, owed plaintiff no duty of care.

If, on the other hand, the court is not able to make this determination and a nonsuit is denied, then the case would proceed and would be submitted to the jury on a comparative negligence theory. Under this approach, subject to the exceptions set out in footnote 10, assumption of the risk would no longer be part of the jury's deliberations or instructions.

In the case at bar, the Court of Common Pleas was not in error in concluding, as a matter of law, that Howell had assumed the risk of injury. Howell voluntarily participated in a dangerous activity, knowing that the ignition of gunpowder is inherently dangerous and might cause injury to himself or others. Although the court granted the nonsuit on the basis of an assumed risk rather than because of an absence of duty, the analysis, nonetheless, is substantially the same. Since Howell voluntarily assumed the risk of injury, Clyde owed him no duty. It was error, therefore, for Superior Court to remand the case for a new trial . . . .

NIX, CHIEF JUSTICE, dissenting.

Today the majority decides to preserve assumption of the risk as an affirmative defense in negligence cases despite the fact that, for the purposes of this case, the doctrine lost its viability when the General Assembly passed the Comparative Negligence Act. Therefore, I dissent. . . .

. . . Assumption of the risk is not expressly mentioned as being affected [by Pa.'s Comparat. Negl. Act]. Indeed, nowhere does the Act make such an express statement. Nevertheless, it is clear that the General Assembly contemplated that assumption of the risk would be modified by the Act. This is readily apparent from the subsection addressing the sport of downhill skiing. The relevant portion of that provision states that "[t]he doctrine of voluntary assumption of the risk as it applies to downhill skiing injuries and damages is not modified by subsection (a) . . . ." 42 Pa.C.S.A. § 7102 (c)(2). The very existence of this provision and the unique way in which it is written indicate that the General Assembly recognized that Subsection 7102(a) would have an effect on the assumption of the risk doctrine, at least when the defense is raised in connection with the plaintiff's voluntary conduct. Otherwise, there would be no need to enact Subsection 7102(c).

This Court is obligated to give effect to all the provisions of a statute, 1 Ps. C.S.A. § 1921(a), and the only way to give effect to Subsection (c)(2) of the

---

[10] An exception to this holding which, in essence, abolishes assumption of risk as affirmative defense, is that in cases involving express assumption of risk, or cases brought pursuant to 402A (strict liability theory), or cases in which assumption of risk is specifically preserved by statute, assumption of risk remains a viable affirmative defense.

Comparative Negligence Act is to conclude that Subsection 7102(a) modifies the assumption of the risk defense in some way. The nature of the modification can be determined by analyzing the overall purpose that the Comparative Negligence Act seeks to achieve. In broad terms, the Act expresses three legislative judgments. First, it rejects the idea that a plaintiff who may be partially responsible for his injuries should be precluded from recovery notwithstanding the conduct of others whose negligence contributed to the event. Second, it embraces the idea that any recovery should be reduced in proportion to the plaintiff's share of responsibility for his injuries. Third, it denies recovery only when the plaintiff is more responsible than the defendant(s) for his injuries.

These three legislative judgments are frustrated by the doctrine of assumption of the risk. Assumption of the risk erects a threshold bar to recovery, regardless of how insignificant a role the plaintiff's conduct may have played in producing his injuries. Given the fundamental incompatibility between the Comparative Negligence Act and the doctrine of assumption of risk, there would be no way to achieve what the General Assembly sought to accomplish by passing the Comparative Negligence Act unless this Court concludes that, except in downhill skiing cases, assumption of the risk as an affirmative defense is no longer viable in this Commonwealth. . . .

In order to achieve its policy objectives, the majority declares that the pivotal consideration is to be whether the plaintiff's decision to encounter a known risk is voluntary. However, when the General Assembly passed the Comparative Negligence Act, it embraced negligence, not voluntariness, as the touchstone of analysis. As the Act's very name implies, courts and juries are statutorily required to evaluate the plaintiff's conduct in terms of negligence and to compare it with that of the defendant(s).[2] This is an entirely legitimate policy judgment, and this Court is obligated to effectuate that decision . . . .The majority's arrogant refusal to do so constitutes a blatant attempt to usurp a legislative power . . . .

NOTES

1. *Implied Assumption of the Risk.* If you are aware that another will not protect you from a risk created by his conduct, but you nevertheless voluntarily encounter that risk, one may imply that you have tacitly agreed to assume the risk of injury from that conduct. Despite the absence of any express contractual assumption of the risk, as in *Schutkowski* and *Tunkl*, the result arguably should be the same as in those cases. This rationale probably led to the common law defense of implied assumption of the risk, or, to use the Latin term, *volenti non fit injuria.*

At common law, implied assumption of the risk was a defense which barred all recovery. The defendant was required to plead and prove assumption of the risk as an affirmative defense. This involves a twofold burden. First, the plaintiff must have known and appreciated the specific risk created by

---

[2] Of course the plaintiff's voluntariness may be weighed in considering his negligence. However, in that situation, voluntariness is one of several factors, while the majority treats it as the dispositive consideration.

defendant's conduct. The test is subjective: plaintiff's knowledge and appreciation, and not that of a reasonable person, is the test. *See, e.g., Desai v. Silver Dollar City, Inc.*, 493 S. E. 2d 540 (Ga. App. 1997) (amusement park patron, injured when she stepped from a raft and was struck by an oncoming raft, knew and appreciated the risk).

Second, the plaintiff must have voluntarily encountered the risk. *See, e.g., Marshall v. Ranne*, 511 S.W.2d 255 (Tex. 1974) (plaintiff going from his home to his car did not assume the risk of being bitten by defendant's animal). *Cf. Muldovan v. McEachern*, 523 S. E. 2d 566 (Ga. 1999) (decedent, while intoxicated and knowing handgun was loaded, took part in game of Russian Roulette and was killed by a co-player; held, voluntary assumption of the risk).

2. *Primary and Secondary Assumption.* Implied "assumption of the risk," in the broadest sense, encompasses several concepts. Some are the now familiar concepts of duty and breach. Every person assumes the risk that he will be injured by conduct of another which will not be faulty, either because the defendant acted reasonably, or because the injury was not within the scope of the risks which the law protects from faulty conduct. For example, a passenger in one vehicle may be injured because the brakes of a following vehicle failed, although the operator of the following vehicle exercised reasonable care in maintaining and driving the vehicle. A mother may not be entitled to recover the mental anguish she suffers in seeing her child struck by a negligently driven automobile. This concept — assumption of the risk of injury by conduct for which the law does not hold the actor liable — often is called "primary assumption of the risk." *See* Fleming James, *Assumption of the Risk*, 61 Yale L. J. 141 (1952).

Often primary assumption of the risk is applied to the inherent risks of recreational activities and the contemplated risks of sports experienced by the participants and spectators. What is the rationale for concluding that the defendant owes no legal duty other than for reckless or intentional conduct in organized sports and recreational activities? Is it knowledge of the risks by the plaintiff or simply that the activity is inherently dangerous? *See, e.g., Goodlett v. Kalishek*, 223 F. 3d 32 (2d Cir. 2000) (air racing accident; "knowledge plays a role but inherence is the sine qua non"). In light of the recklessness standard that many courts apply, can it be said that the safety objective in sports and recreational activity is undervalued?

If defendant's conduct is faulty, and plaintiff's injury would come within the risks that make the conduct faulty, the plaintiff nevertheless may knowingly and voluntarily expose himself to the risk of injury by such conduct. This is assumption of the risk, properly speaking, sometimes called "secondary assumption of the risk." The common law treated this as an affirmative defense which barred recovery. "Secondary assumption of the risk" may arise in two ways: The first: before the plaintiff enters into a relationship with the defendant, he knows that the defendant will not protect him from certain risks produced by defendant's conduct, but plaintiff nevertheless enters into the relationship. Examples are obvious dangers; and, some courts hold, sports and recreational activity. *See Richie-Gamester v. City of Berkeley* 597 N. W. 517 (Mich. 1999).

The second way: plaintiff becomes aware that defendant has not protected him against a risk created by defendant's conduct, but nevertheless proceeds to voluntarily encounter the risk. When the first concept applies, some courts express the result in terms of "no duty." Thus a landowner does not owe a duty to protect a visitor from a dangerous condition which is "open and obvious." In precomparative times, if a duty were found the result would be the same because the visitor would have voluntarily encountered a known risk and would be barred from recovery by assumption of the risk. The only difference — usually not an important one — was whether the burden of pleading and proof was placed upon plaintiff or defendant. When the second concept applied, the defendant's duty arose; at the time defendant acted, he could have foreseen that the victim would be imperiled by his conduct, and could not assume that the victim would nevertheless knowingly choose to encounter the peril. Thus although defendant could be said to be negligent, in precomparative times the plaintiff's assumption of the risk barred his recovery.

The court in *Gordon v. Havasu Palms, Inc.*, 112 Cal.Rptr.2d 816 (Cal. App. 2001), reduced assumption of the risk to primary and secondary assumption. In the first, no duty is owed. In the second, comparative fault applies.

3. *Effect of Comparative Negligence.* A person who voluntarily encounters a known risk usually is not acting as a reasonable person for his own safety, and is contributorily negligent. When contributory negligence barred all recovery, it was not necessary to distinguish it from assumption of the risk; in either event, the plaintiff took nothing. The adoption of comparative negligence in nearly all of the states has prompted a careful analysis of the various forms of "assumption of the risk" developed at common law. In some jurisdictions, comparative negligence was adopted by judicial fiat. In other jurisdictions, the legislation adopting comparative negligence was silent on the future of the doctrine of assumption of the risk. In jurisdictions where comparative negligence has been adopted by the court or where the state legislation adopting comparative negligence is silent on the future of the doctrine of assumption of the risk, courts have attempted to resolve how best to effectuate comparative negligence principles while preserving the common law effect of the somewhat competing and overlapping tort goals and values expressed in the doctrine of assumption of risk. *See, e.g., Davenport v. Cotton Hope Plantation Horizontal Prop.*, 333 S.C. 71, 508 S.E. 2d 565 (1998)(condo unit owner fell on steps unlit because of broken flood lights; assumption of risk as "absolute defense" seen as inconsistent with comparative negligence); *Churchill v. Pearl River Basin Development*, 757 So. 2d 940 (Miss. 1999)(15-year-old diver struck head on river bottom, breaking neck; assumption of risk subsumed in comparative negligence).

4. *The Penalties of Doctrinal Simplification.* Louisiana adopted pure comparative negligence and subsequently abolished assumption of the risk as a defense. *Murray v. Ramada Inns, Inc.*, 521 So. 2d 1123 (La. 1988). This adoption left the courts without a mechanism to deny recovery to a foolhardy plaintiff. Nevertheless, such a plaintiff usually is barred from recovery, either because: (a) the risk was not unreasonable, *Washington v. Louisiana Power & Light,* 555 So. 2d 1350 (La. 1990); (b) the risk was not the "cause" of

plaintiff's injury, *Luckette v. Orkin Exterminating Co.*, 534 So. 2d 517 (La. App. 1988), or (c) the risk was not within the scope of the risks which made defendant's conduct faulty (legal or proximate cause), *Oliveaux v. Sanders*, 535 So. 2d 1034 (La. App. 1988). *See also Pitre v. Louisiana Tech University*, 673 So. 2d 585 (La. 1996) (three of seven justices find no duty, two find no breach, where plaintiff slid down a hill on a garbage can lid and collided with the concrete base of a light pole in a parking lot.) Which is the most convincing approach?

5. *Risky Reasonable Conduct.* After *Li*, the California courts faced the issue of reasonable implied assumption of the risk. The following excerpt from *Von Beltz v. Stuntman, Inc.*, 207 Cal. App. 3d 1467, 255 Cal. Rptr. 755 (1989), indicates how the problem may be handled. *Von Beltz* concerned an action by a stuntperson against Needham, a film director. The plaintiff had been injured during the filming of "Cannonball Run" when the vehicle in which she was riding as a passenger collided with another stunt vehicle. Plaintiff was totally and permanently paralyzed from the neck down. She alleged negligence in that the automobile should have been equipped with seat belts. Defendant argued assumption of risk. The court noted that *Li* abolished assumption of the risk "to the extent that it is merely a variant of the former doctrine of contributory negligence. . . ."

> Ordinarily, a movie stunt is not like an athletic contest, a horse race or a fire, where there are spontaneous, opposing and sometimes hostile forces at play. Movie stunts are probably always to some extent planned or choreographed events, although some are better planned or choreographed than others, just as some are more dangerous than others.
>
> . . . Where a stuntperson has full awareness of the hazards he faces, it may be possible to conclude that under the circumstances, he has assumed the risk of injury. However, where a movie director or producer changes the nature of the stunt without the stuntperson's knowledge and thereby increases or otherwise alters the risk without the stuntperson's acquiescence, the director or producer may be held liable for any resulting injuries.
>
> . . . [P]laintiff did not know that the stunt would be materially different from the one in which she had participated earlier. Had she known, she could have either declined the stunt or had seat belts installed. Instead, she participated in the stunt not knowing that her driver . . . was going to drive head-on into opposing traffic, weave through it in serpentine fashion and double the speed utilized in the first performance of the stunt . . . Because plaintiff was not informed of the known dangers she was to confront, defendant may not assert the defense of assumption of risk . . . .

6. *Fireman's Rule.* The Firefighter's Rule adopted by most states generally waives the duty of care that third parties owe firefighters and police officers. These public employees therefore are denied damages in tort for injuries arising in the performance of their jobs. The rule has often been based on public policy against subjecting the taxpayers to "multiple penalties" for their protection rather than assumption of the risk on the part of the firefighter

or police. Many states have circumscribed the rule to avoid barring recovery for other professions. *See, e.g., Roberts v. Vaughn*, 459 Mich. 282, 587 N.W. 2d 249 (1998) (rule not applicable to voluntary firefighters); *but see Crews v. Hollenbach*, 358 Md. 627, 751 A.2d 481 (2000)(fireman's rule is not applicable but assumption of risk bars negligence suit by private gas company worker for injuries sustained in explosion which occurred while he repaired a gas leak).

7. *Statutory Insulation From Comparative Treatment*. Some states (like Pennsylvania, as mentioned in *Howell, supra*) have comparative negligence statutes that explicitly retain the absolute bar to recovery in assumption of risk cases dealing with certain recreational activities. In the case of Pennsylvania, the statutory focus is on down-hill skiing. Consider the Wyoming Recreational Safety Act, which provides:

> Any person who takes part in any sport or recreational opportunity assumes the inherent risks in that sport or recreational opportunity whether those risks are known or unknown, is legally responsible for any and all damages, injury or death to himself or other person or property that results from the inherent risks in that sport or recreational opportunity. Wyo State Ann Sec. 1-1-123 (Michie 1998).

What purpose is served by these insulating statutes? *See Madison v. Wyoming River Trips, Inc.*, 31 F. Supp.2d 1321 (Wyo. 1997)(defendant company not liable for river rafting risk of jostling).

8. *The Passing of Assumption of Risk*. With the wholesale adoption of comparative negligence, assumption of the risk is fading from the American legal scene. It was never a popular defense. Some states even abolished it before comparative negligence came into favor. *See, e.g., McGrath v. American Cyanamid Co.*, 41 N.J. 272, 196 A.2d 238 (1963).

Indeed, the doctrine is in worldwide retreat. In *Nettleship v. Weston*, [1971] 2 Q.B. 691, 3 All E.R. 581, 3 W.L.R. 370 (C.A.), a novice driver asked a friend to teach her to drive. He consented after ascertaining that she was insured. On their third lesson, the driver panicked and the instructor was injured in the resulting collision with a street lamp. Lord Denning, M.R. addressed aspects of defendant's *volenti* plea as follows:

> In former times this defense was used almost as an alternative defense to contributory negligence. Either defense defeated the action. Now that contributory negligence is not a complete defense, but only a ground for reducing the damages, the defense of volenti non fit injuria has been closely considered, and, in consequence, it has been severely limited. Knowledge of the risk of injury is not enough. Nor is a willingness to take the risk of injury. Nothing will suffice short of an agreement to waive any claim for negligence. The plaintiff must agree, expressly or impliedly, to waive any claim for any injury that may befall him due to the lack of reasonable care by the defendant: or more accurately, due to the failure of the defendant to measure up to the standard of care that the law requires of him . . . .

Lord Denning found it evident that the plaintiff did not agree to waive any claim for injury that might befall him. But his claim could be reduced insofar as he was at fault himself, in letting her take the wheel too soon or in not being quick enough to correct her error.

9. *Implied and Express Assumption Redux.* Where the plaintiff's conduct is reasonable, the plaintiff by definition cannot be contributorily negligent, although she can assume the risk. Where, however, her conduct is unreasonable, that conduct may be viewed as involving either contributory fault or assumption of the risk — depending on whether the element of consent is found decisive.

An express agreement that assumes a risk will be upheld if it is not against public policy. Why not use a similar public policy analysis to determine whether a plaintiff has impliedly assumed the risk?

PROBLEM

Participating in an amateur league softball game, Smith hit a ball deep into the outfield and attempted to achieve an "inside-the-park" home run. Jones, the catcher for the opposing team, fielded the relay from the outfielder. As Smith neared home plate, he saw that Jones had caught the ball. Smith deliberately threw his body into Jones, hoping to make him drop the ball. Jones dropped the ball and was seriously injured by the contact.

Jones sues Smith and Smith moves to dismiss.

Is there any reason to allow Jones to conduct discovery before ruling on the motion to dismiss?

Assume, in the alternative, that Jones' league makes participation conditional upon signing a "memorandum of responsibility" which provides as follows:

> I agree not to file suit or initiate any claim procedure in respect for any personal injuries, property damages, or losses I may experience or sustain arising directly or indirectly out of my participation in this league.

What are the issues?

Suppose Jones was a teenage girl and an established athlete joining the game for the first time. Do these facts change your views as to the likely outcome of the case?

E. AVOIDABLE CONSEQUENCES

TANBERG v. ACKERMAN INVESTMENT CO.
473 N.W.2d 193 (Iowa 1991)

MCGIVERIN, CHIEF JUSTICE.

This case presents the issue of whether a plaintiff's failure to follow medical advice to reasonably attempt to lose weight to decrease back pain, thereby mitigating his damages, can be considered fault under Iowa's comparative fault statute. The court of appeals thought plaintiff's failure to lose weight was not such fault. We disagree and, therefore, vacate the decision of the court of appeals and affirm the district court judgment.

Plaintiff Bruce A. Tanberg was a guest at the Best Western Starlite Village motel, located in Ames, on August 7, 1987. On that date, while attempting to exit the whirlpool bathtub located in the bathroom of his motel room to turn off the whirlpool jets, plaintiff fell and injured his back.

Plaintiff sued defendant Ackerman Investment Co., d/b/a Best Western Starlight Village (Best Western), owner and operator of the motel, for injuries he allegedly sustained as a result of his fall. He asserted that defendant had been negligent in several respects. Plaintiff claimed injury to his back and continual pain resulting from the fall. Best Western answered plaintiff's petition by denying that it had been negligent and asserting several affirmative defenses, including that plaintiff was at fault in causing the accident and by failing to mitigate his damages by losing weight after the fall.

At trial, the following evidence was presented in support of defendant's theory that plaintiff failed to mitigate his damages by losing weight after the accident: plaintiff was five feet eleven inches tall and weighed 309 pounds at the time of the accident; testimony of Dr. Terman, plaintiff's treating physician, that he thought plaintiff's main problem was his obesity and recommended that he lose weight and referred plaintiff to a dietitian for a special diet; testimony of Dr. Noran, plaintiff's treating neurologist, that he thought losing weight could theoretically decrease the pain plaintiff was experiencing in his back because weight loss should reduce some of the load on the spine and in the long run decrease plaintiff's risk of developing more serious problems with his back; testimony of Dr. Dry, plaintiff's initial treating physician, that he did not disagree with Dr. Noran's testimony and, while he could not say that losing weight would probably decrease plaintiff's back pain, he thought carrying around excess weight might strain a person's back; and, plaintiff's testimony that Dr. Pratt advised him to lose thirty to forty pounds after the accident, that all his doctors advised him to lose weight to relieve his back pain and that he had not been as faithful in following his diets as he should have been.

The court, over plaintiff's objection, detailed plaintiff's duty to exercise ordinary care in following reasonable medical advice in instruction 19, which stated:

> Defendant claims plaintiff was at fault by failing to exercise ordinary care to follow reasonable medical treatment. Evidence has been introduced that damages could have been reduced to some extent if Mr. Tanberg followed his doctor's advice and lost weight. An injured person has no duty to undergo serious or speculative medical treatment, but, if by slight expense and by slight inconvenience, a person exercising ordinary care could have reduced the damages, he has a duty to do so.

Plaintiff's objection to instruction 19 as relevant was as follows . . .

> This is violative of the law in Iowa, where you take the plaintiff as they find them, the eggshell plaintiff rule. They took this man in his

overweight condition, and he should not be penalized with any percentage of fault because of his overweight condition. Had there been a suggestion of an operation that would make him feel better, that instruction may be applicable, but it is not applicable in this case.

The jury found plaintiff 70% at fault for his damages and defendant 30% at fault for plaintiff's damages. Based on the jury's assessment that the plaintiff was liable for a greater percentage of the fault than defendant, the court entered judgment for defendant. *See* IOWA CODE § 668.3(1). . . .

IOWA CODE section 668.1(1) provides:

1. As used in this chapter, "fault" means one or more acts or omissions that are in any measure negligent or reckless toward the person or property of the actor or others, or that subject a person to strict tort liability. The term also includes breach of warranty, unreasonable assumption of risk not constituting an enforceable express consent, misuse of a product for which the defendant otherwise would be liable, and unreasonable failure to avoid an injury or to mitigate damages
. . . .

We, therefore, hold that unreasonable failure to attempt to lose weight pursuant to medical advice can be assessed as fault if weight loss will mitigate damages. We do not hold that a plaintiff must actually lose weight in order to mitigate damages; there must, however, be a reasonable attempt to do so. Since Tanberg was not "as faithful in following his diets as he should have been," a jury could find he did not reasonably mitigate damages. *Compare Fuches v. S.E.S. Co.*, 459 N.W.2d 642, 643–644 (Iowa App. 1990) (failure to undergo an operation that would mitigate damages may be assessed as fault); *Miller v. Eichhorn*, 426 N.W.2d at 643 (failure to undergo additional chiropractic treatment may be assessed as fault). We do, however, note that before the mitigation instruction is given, defendant has the burden of showing substantial evidence that plaintiff's weight loss would have mitigated his damages and that requiring plaintiff to lose weight was reasonable under the circumstances.

Our decision is in accord with other jurisdictions that have considered a plaintiff's failure to lose weight as a mitigating factor when weight loss will lessen damages.

These jurisdictions review each case to determine if failure to lose weight should be treated as a mitigating factor. *See, e.g., Kratzer*, 645 F.2d at 483–484 (trial court properly did not consider the defendant's argument that the plaintiff failed to mitigate his damages by losing weight where the plaintiff was not placed on any doctor-administered weight reduction program and, although doctor told the plaintiff to lose weight, the benefits of weight loss were uncertain); *Muller*, 337 F. Supp. at 706–707 (by failing to follow the competent medical advice of his doctors, the plaintiff has neglected his duty to minimize damages); *Anglin*, 192 Ga. App. at 704–705, 386 S.E.2d at 53 (not error to instruct that plaintiff could be assessed fault for failure to lose weight when no dispute existed that the surgery was unsuccessful due to plaintiff's inability or unwillingness to restrict her diet in accordance with instructions given to her); *Butler v. Anderson*, 163 Ga. App. 547, 547–548, 295 S.E.2d 216,

217 (1982) (mitigation instruction regarding the plaintiff's failure to lose weight was not error where medical evidence was introduced establishing that the plaintiff's back and leg pain was caused by her obesity); *Close*, 90 A.D.2d at 599–600, 456 N.Y.S.2d at 439 (failure to lose weight was improperly treated as a mitigating factor where the claimant made a good faith effort to lose weight); *Armellini*, 605 S.W.2d at 309 (trial court did not err in refusing to instruct on mitigation of damages for failure to lose weight where there was no evidence of plaintiff's failure to follow a diet and exercise routine nor of the results the doctors expected if the plaintiff followed the prescribed routine).

Under the present record we find no error in the trial court giving instruction 19 to the jury . . . .

NOTES

1. *Duty to Mitigate and Comparative Fault.* *Tanberg* treated plaintiff's failure to mitigate as comparative fault. This result was required by the Iowa statute. Thus, plaintiff was denied all recovery under Iowa's modified comparative fault statute since his fault exceeded that of the defendant.

The court in *Ostrowski v. Azzara*, 111 N.J. 429, 545 A.2d 148 (1988), said failure to mitigate should not be treated as contributory negligence for comparative fault purposes. Under that state's modified comparative fault rule, "with its fifty percent qualifier for recovery", the plaintiff could be barred entirely. The doctrine of avoidable consequences, or failure to mitigate damages, should not be given that barring effect. Contributory negligence arises when the plaintiff is negligent "before the defendant's wrongdoing has been completed". The doctrine of avoidable consequences comes into play where "the defendant has already committed an actionable wrong".

Which makes more sense, the Iowa or the New Jersey rule? Does a jury assess failure to mitigate in terms of fault, or cause?

2. *Psychological Barrier to Mitigation.* The plaintiff in *Botek v. Mine Safety Appliance Corp.*, 531 Pa. 160, 611 A.2d 1174 (1992), suffered post-traumatic stress disorder as a result of defendant's negligence. There was testimony that his emotional distress could have been substantially reduced had he sought "counselling and drug therapy for anxiety", as he was advised by his doctor to do. He did not, however, seek such treatment. The fact that he "was resistant to treatment does not disqualify him from receiving compensation", the court said. "It is clear that where a claimant's rejection of treatment is part of his emotional injuries, he may recover damages in spite of the failure to receive treatment".

3. *Religious Reservations.* The plaintiff's deceased wife, a Jehovah's Witness, received severe injuries in an automobile accident, *Munn v. Algee*, 924 F.2d 568 (5th Cir. 1991). She refused blood transfusions on religious grounds, and died approximately eight hours after the accident. There was testimony that she would have survived if she had received the transfusions.

The jury returned no damages for wrongful death. In upholding this verdict, the court said a "strong case can be made" that allowing the jury to assess the reasonableness of a religious belief — as was apparently done here — violates the first amendment freedom of religion. However, no error occurred, the court said, because "[the deceased's husband] himself interjected religion into the case, seeking to explain his wife's conduct."

Whose religious interests were at stake, those of the deceased wife or those of her husband as beneficiary of her estate? If he had not been a Jehovah's Witness, could the religious rights of a deceased person be violated?

4. *Duty to Seek Other Employment.* What if the injury prevents the plaintiff from pursuing his pre-accident employment, but he can be retrained to perform other employment, and refuses to do so? *See, e.g., McGinley v. United States,* 329 F. Supp. 62 (E.D. Pa. 1971) (45-year-old plaintiff, suffering back injury precluding future employment as stevedore, had no duty to obtain employment as waterfront checker when it would take a long time to complete necessary schooling). Would your answer be different if plaintiff was required to undergo an operation which would cause significant pain? Would the likelihood of success have any bearing on your decision? What policy factors are involved here?

5. *Immediate Replacement of Property Damage.* The doctrine of "avoidable consequences" or the "duty to mitigate damages" applies to property damage and personal injuries. The doctrine may be the genesis of the rule that if the property is destroyed, the owner may not recover for loss of use because he can immediately replace it. Is this rule realistic? If your car was totally destroyed in an accident, are you in a position to purchase a replacement on the same day? Within a week?

6. *The Seat Belt Defense.* If a victim fails to act reasonably before an accident, and his risky conduct contributes to the happening of the accident, he is contributorily negligent, and his recovery is barred or reduced under principles of comparative or contributory negligence. What if the plaintiff's unreasonably risky pre-accident conduct does not contribute to the accident, but increases his harm from the accident? The most common situation is the failure to use a seat belt. Before the era of quantification of fault, courts were reluctant to bar recovery for failure to use seat belts. *See Annot.,* 92 A.L.R.3d 9 (1979). Because seat belts were not standard equipment in all vehicles, some worried about the "invidious discrimination" of such a defense. The main reason for the judicial reluctance probably was the difficult issue of cause in fact which would arise: can the judicial process properly allocate the damages caused by the accident and the damages caused by the failure to use the seat belt? Some state legislatures have addressed the matter. What do you think would motivate a lawmaker to vote for an act that provided that failure to wear a seat belt will only reduce damages by not more than 2%, and subsequently vote to repeal that act with one that provides that "[f]ailure to wear a seat belt . . . should not be admitted to mitigate damages"? LA. REV. STAT. 32:295.1 (1989). *See also* MO. REV. STAT. § 307.178.3(2) (1988) providing:

> If the evidence supports such a finding, the trier of fact may find that the plaintiff's failure to wear a safety belt in violation of this section contributed to the plaintiff's claimed injuries, and may reduce the amount of the plaintiff's recovery by *an amount not to exceed one*

percent of the damages awarded after any reductions for comparative negligence.

F. STATUTES OF LIMITATIONS AND REPOSE

PROBLEM

Plaintiff contracted silicosis from having been exposed in the workplace to silica products supplied to plaintiff's employer by the defendant supplier. Silicosis is a cumulative disease. Although plaintiff had been exposed to the products over a twenty-year period, he did not discover that he had contracted the disease until 1997. Within days after the discovery, plaintiff sued defendant alleging that defendant had supplied an unreasonably dangerous product and had unreasonably failed to warn of the danger from exposure to the product.

Defendant moved to dismiss, based on the state's products liability statute of limitation and repose. That statute provides that any claim for personal injury against the supplier of a product must be brought within one year after reasonable discovery of the injury, but in no event later than ten years after the product was first sold by the supplier for use or consumption. The ten-year limitation period does not apply to claims for injury from exposure to asbestos, and the period is extended to twenty-five years for injuries caused by silicone gel breast implants.

What arguments can the plaintiff make in an attempt to avoid the ten-year limitation? How should the court rule?

APGAR v. LEDERLE LABORATORIES
123 N.J. 450, 588 A.2d 380 (1991)
[case summary]

PER CURIAM.

Kelly Ann Apgar was born on August 19, 1961. She sued Lederle Laboratories, The Upjohn Co. and Pfizer, Inc. (defendants) in late 1988 alleging that between January 1963 and April 1964 she ingested certain tetracycline-based antibiotic drugs manufactured and distributed by defendants; that those drugs were defective as not being reasonably safe for their intended use by pediatric consumers, particularly in their known potential for tooth discoloration; and that defendants are liable for Apgar's tooth discoloration caused by the defendants' products. Ms. Apgar's complaint is grounded on theories of strict products liability, failure to warn; negligent failure to warn; breach of warranty; misbranding, deceptive packaging and false labeling, all in violation of state statutory standards, federal regulations, and Food and Drug Administration requirements; and unconscionable commercial practice, fraud and misrepresentation, all in contravention of the New Jersey Consumer Fraud Act. In their answers to Ms. Apgar's complaint, the defendants raise the statute-of-limitations defense.

While still in grammar school, Apgar noticed that her permanent teeth were discolored. In junior high school, she learned from her dentist that medicine she had taken as an infant had caused the discoloration. She visited the

Johnson & Johnson Dental Clinic for an evaluation and learned that the tooth discoloration had been caused by medication and that the damage was permanent. Ms. Apgar's mother informed her that she had taken Mysteclin.

By the time that Ms. Apgar had graduated from high school in 1979, she thought that medication she had ingested had caused the tooth discoloration. After graduating from college, Ms. Apgar read an article in the November 7, 1985 edition of *The Star-Ledger*, about a successful litigant in a tooth-discoloration case. In November or December 1985 she consulted the attorney for that litigant about bringing and action against the defendants. That was about three years prior to the filing of her complaint.

In April 1986, Ms. Apgar obtained her treatment records from Dr. Coggleshall, which indicated that in 1961 she had been prescribed Declomycin, a tetracycline antibiotic manufactured by Lederle Laboratories. On November 14, 1986, Dr. Minier informed Ms. Apgar's attorney that, according to his records, in 1963 and 1964 he had prescribed three types of tetracycline antibiotics to Kelly: Panalba, manufactured by Upjohn; Achromycin V, manufactured by Lederle; and Signemycin, manufactured by Pfizer, Inc.

On March 22, 1988, Kelly Ann Apgar sued Lederle. On October 25, 1988 she amended the complaint to join Upjohn and Pfizer as defendants. The trial court denied the defendants' motions for summary judgment based on the statute of limitations. The Appellate Division denied defendants' motion for leave to appeal. The Supreme Court granted leave to appeal.

Held: Kelly Ann Apgar's cause of action accrued well in advance of the two years prior to the time she filed her complaint; hence, her claim is time-barred.

1. The statute of limitations for personal-injury actions is two years. If the injured plaintiff is under the age of twenty-one years when the cause of action accrues, she has two years from the date of her twenty-first birthday to file her cause of action. To avoid the harsh result that otherwise would flow from a mechanical application of the statute of limitations, the "discovery rule" was developed. That rule delays the accrual of the cause of action until the plaintiff learns or reasonably should learn the existence of the state of facts which may equate in law with a cause of action.

2. In this case, Ms. Apgar knew by the time she reached her twenty-first birthday that her teeth had been discolored and, based on information from several dentists, that medication she had taken as a child had produced the staining. Therefore, the statute of limitations expired on August 19, 1984, two years after Kelly Apgar's twenty-first birthday. Because she did not begin suit until March 22, 1988, her claim is time-barred.

3. Even if Apgar is given the benefit of the date on which she read *The Star-Ledger* article and consulted her attorney around November or December 1985, she still does not come within the time limitations period.

4. The specific identity of a potential defendant is not a requirement for commencing a cause of action. Ms. Apgar can file a complaint naming "John Doe" defendants if the actual identity of the wrongdoer is unknown. Here, the identities of defendants were readily ascertainable from Ms. Apgar's physicians' records.

Judgment of the Appellate Division is *reversed* and the matter is *remanded* to the Law Division for entry of judgment in favor of defendants.

NOTES

1. *The Unidentified Defendant.* The *Apgar* court said lack of knowledge of the defendant's identity does not stop the statute of limitations from running, since the plaintiff "can file a complaint naming 'John Doe' defendants if the actual identity of the wrongdoer is unknown". Not all states permit the filing of a John Doe complaint, however. If they do not, then would reasonable discovery of the defendant also be part of the discovery rule?

Many states have a savings statute, providing that if a suit is brought within the period of the statute of limitations and dismissed, *e.g.,* for lack of service of process, the suit can be refiled against the defendant within a new period equal in length to the original period. Tennessee's savings statute provides for repeated such refilings. TENN. CODE ANN. § 28-1-105(a) (1996). The federal rules, however, provide for only one such refiling. FED. R. CIV. PROC. 41(a)(1).

Suppose the plaintiff sues the wrong defendant? Under the federal rules, the correct defendant must be sued within the statutory period, unless state law allows a more liberal period or unless the correct defendant is sued typically within 120 days after the statute has run and the correct defendant knows of the suit, should know the wrong person has been sued, and has not been prejudiced by the delay. FED. R. EVID. 4(m), 15(c)(3). *Accord,* TENN. R. CIV. PROC. 15.03. Why should a plaintiff be permitted to keep refiling if she is unable to obtain service of process, Rule 4(m), but not if she sues the wrong defendant?

If the defendant intentionally conceals his identity, then the running of the statute of limitations may be tolled (or stopped) on grounds of equity. *See, e.g., Martinelli v. Bridgeport Roman Catholic Diocesan Corp.*, 196 F.3d 409 (2d Cir. 1999).

Many states provide for service of process on a nonresident defendant by "long-arm" statutes, based on transactions of the defendant within the state. Such a suit must be filed within the period of the statute of limitations, which may not be extended based simply on the fact that the defendant is a nonresident. Any such extension would violate the dormant commerce clause, the Court said in *Bendix Autolite Corp. v. Midwesco Enterprises*, 486 U.S. 888, 108 S. Ct. 2218, 100 L. Ed. 2d 896 (1988).

2. *Some Mysteries of Discovery.* The *Apgar* court said that case did not present "the kind of difficulties the 'discovery rule' may have caused the Court in other contexts", citing *Graves v. Church & Dwight Co.*, 115 N.J. 256 (1989). In a 4-3 decision the *Graves* majority said the plaintiff did not discover that defendant's bicarbonate of soda was the tortious cause of his stomach rupture until much later after the rupture occurred. While he associated the rupture with the taking of the soda, he had no reason to know that his injury was attributable to the "fault of another" (*i.e.,* the soda manufacturer). Only later did medical research establish the causal link.

The *Graves* court said the plaintiff's case was not like that of *Burd v. N.J. Tel. Co.*, 76 N.J. 284 (1978). The court in a 4-3 decision held in *Burd* that the facts supported a finding that the plaintiff should have known defendant's glue caused his heart attack, and that he failed to sue thereafter within the statutory period. Plaintiff knew that he suffered lightheadedness and dizziness when using the glue, and that these symptoms disappeared whenever his exposure to the glue stopped. He was not justified in waiting until his counsel received a medical report indicating the glue was the probable cause of the attack. The dissent thought the plaintiff might well have attributed the heart attack to other bad health conditions he suffered from, and to heat stroke.

Why not adopt a uniform discovery rule providing that the statute does not begin to run until the plaintiff is advised by an attorney that she has a cause of action? Alternatively, why not require the defendant to show substantial prejudice from the plaintiff's delay in suing, before a suit will be considered time-barred?

Equity recognizes a doctrine of laches. It is defined as a neglect to assert a right or claim which, taken together with the lapse of time and other circumstances causing prejudice to the adverse party, operates as a bar in a court of equity. BLACK'S LAW DICT. 787 (5th ed. 1979).

3. *Separate Injuries.* In *Potts v. Celotex Corp.*, 796 S.W.2d 678 (Tenn. 1990), the plaintiff developed asbestosis from exposure to defendant's product, and later developed mesothelioma. Recognizing a division of authority, the court said plaintiff's discovery of his asbestosis did not start the statute running on his mesothelioma claim, even though both diseases were caused by exposure to asbestos:

> According to the medical evidence in this case, asbestosis and mesothelioma are two independent, distinct and separate diseases, related only by the fact that each is caused by exposure to asbestos fibers. Asbestosis is a pneumoconiosis, causing a fibrous condition or scarring of the lungs. Mesothelioma is an extremely virulent cancer of the epithelium, the thin membrane that lines the lungs, chest and abdominal cavities. A person may have asbestosis without ever contracting mesothelioma and, conversely, may contract mesothelioma without ever having had asbestosis. In the words of Dr. Bedwell, one of petitioner's medical experts, "one disease does not arise out of the other." A study in the New England Journal of Medicine estimates that only 15% of asbestosis sufferers later contract pleural mesothelioma and only 12% contract peritoneal mesothelioma. Selikoff, Churg & Hammond, *Relation Between Exposure to Asbestos and Mesothelioma*, 272 NEW ENG. J. MED. 560, 562 (1965).

See also Sopha v. Owens-Corning Fiberglas Corp., 601 N. W. 2d 627 (Wis. 1999) (diagnosis of a non-malignant asbestos-related injury did not trigger statue of limitations with respect to another asbestos-related injury).

An even more dramatic illustration of the principle of the *Potts* case is found in *Seale v. Gowans*, 923 P.2d 1361 (Utah 1996). There the defendant doctor negligently failed to diagnose plaintiff's breast cancer in 1987. In 1988 plaintiff discovered this negligence and underwent a radical mastectomy. Pathological studies of the removed area showed that the malignancy had spread to eight of her twenty lymph nodes. She then underwent radiation and hormone therapy to increase the likelihood of complete recovery. All subsequent tests remained negative until the summer of 1991, when it was discovered that the cancer had spread to her left hip.

The court said that the statute of limitations began to run for the hip cancer in 1991, not in 1988 when she discovered this misdiagnosis and the metastasis of the cancer to her lymph nodes. While the cancer in the lymph nodes "increased the risk that the cancer would recur," defendant failed to produce any evidence that plaintiff suffered any "actual present damages" to her hip in 1988. Although "the cancer's spread resulted in a dramatic decrease in Ms. Seale's chance of survival," there was no cause of action for the hip cancer until she discovered she had suffered actual injury to the hip.

4. *Attorney Malpractice.* The cases divide on when an injury occurs for purposes of legal malpractice, in the context of prosecution or defense of a lawsuit. Does it occur when the alleged negligent act is committed, or not until exhaustion of appeals of the underlying suit? *See Beesley v. VanDorn*, 873 P.2d 1280 (Alaska 1994).

Those courts requiring that appeal be exhausted before the claim can accrue do so in part because of the problem of requiring the client to take inconsistent positions. "If the clients were forced to argue that their counsel's conduct caused irreparable harm while contemporaneously arguing their attorney's actions were correct, or at least not fatal to their claims, it would likely compromise their success in either suit." TRIAL 23 (May 1995). The *Beesley* court said, however, that courts routinely address situations where a party takes inconsistent positions, and that a claim should not accrue until a party has suffered actual injury.

5. *Continuing Torts.* The court in *Mangini v. Aerojet-Gen'l Corp.*, 912 P.2d 1220, 51 Cal. Rptr. 272 (1996), held the statute of limitations on a permanent nuisance "begins to run upon creation of the nuisance". In the case of a continuing nuisance, suit can be brought at any time during the continuance of the nuisance. A continuing nuisance is one that is abatable, that is, one that can be "removed without unreasonable hardship and expense". Plaintiff failed to prove that defendant's pollution over a 10-year period of 2400 acres of plaintiff's unimproved land, by disposing of hazardous waste materials on the land, was reasonably abatable. The dissent contended that in doubtful cases, plaintiff should be able to elect whether to claim that the nuisance was continuing or permanent.

A medical malpractice statute of limitations may be tolled by continued treatment of the plaintiff by the defendant doctor. DAN B. DOBBS, THE LAW OF TORTS § 220 (2000).

In a sexual harassment case, in *Wilson v. Wal-Mart Stores*, 729 A.2d 1006 (N. J. 1999), the court concluded that the claim would not be barred by a two-year statute of limitations if the plaintiff could prove a continuum of harassment. Similarly, in *Cusseaux v. Pickett*, 279 N. J. Super. 335 652 A.2d 789 (1994), a spousal abuse claim, the court said the statute of limitations could be tolled by the ongoing nature of the tort.

6. *CERCLA.* Plaintiff claimed in *Tucker v. Southern Wood Piedmont Co.*, 28 F.3d 1089 (11th Cir. 1994), that his land was polluted by creosote and other

substances used by the defendant adjoining landowner in treating railroad ties and utility poles. Since defendant's operation had ceased more than four years before plaintiff filed suit, the claim would be barred under applicable state law. But the court held that the federal Comprehensive Environmental Response, Compensation and Liability Act (CERCLA) preempted the state statute of limitations. CERCLA provides for a discovery rule for any claim for personal or property damages "caused or contributed to by exposure to any hazardous substance, or pollutant or contaminant, released into the environment by a facility", 42 U.S.C. § 9658(a)(1), § 9658(b)(4)(A). The federal statute adopts the same statutory period of the applicable state law (here, four years), but the date of accrual is one of discovery. *See also Electric Power Board v. Westinghouse*, 716 F. Supp. 1069 (E.D. Tenn. 1988).

Should the court have applied the CERCLA rule in *Mangini*?

7. *The Sovereign*. The school board sued an asbestos manufacturer in *Hamilton County v. Asbestospray Corp.*, 909 S.W.2d 783 (Tenn. 1995), to recover the costs of asbestos removal from its school buildings. Rejecting defendant's statute of limitations defense, and applying the common law doctrine of *nullum tempus occurit regit* (time does not run against the king), the court said the statute of limitations did not apply to a school board engaged in a "governmental function".

Putting aside the question of whether a governmental function was involved, why should the king be treated differently from ordinary citizens?

DUNLEA v. DAPPEN
924 P.2d 196 (Haw. 1996)

MOON, CHIEF JUSTICE:

Dunlea, who was born in 1947, alleges that she was the victim of incestuous rape at the hands of her natural father, Dappen. She has direct and detailed memory of sexual assaults that occurred between 1961 and 1964, when she was between the ages of fourteen and seventeen years old, while living with her father in Ventura, California. She also alleges memories, beginning at age five, of heinous assaults by a faceless attacker whom she now realizes was Dappen.

In 1964, Dunlea reported the incestuous rape to a California Highway Patrolman. After an investigation, she was removed from Dappen's custody and placed in a foster home. Dappen, apparently, was never prosecuted.

In 1991, Dappen told Dunlea's sister that he was still angry with Dunlea and would never forgive her for what happened in 1964. When the statement was repeated to Dunlea, it triggered a severe emotional reaction because Dunlea had interpreted her father's statement as blaming her for falsely accusing him if incest. One week later, she called Dappen at his Maui residence to confront him about the statement. Dappen was "very angry" and repeated to Dunlea that he would never forgive her for what she did to him. The conversation with Dappen prompted Dunlea to begin therapy. Although Dunlea "has been haunted by depression, thoughts of suicide, shame, disgust, and denial," which have "greatly damaged every facet of [her] life," it was only through therapy that she allegedly discovered that these feelings were symptomatic of a psychological illness caused by her father's incestuous rape.

[In 1992, Dunlea filed a suit against her father seeking, among other things, to recover damages for childhood sexual abuse (CSA). The applicable Hawaii statute of limitations provided that actions for injury to persons or property must be instituted "within two years after the cause of action accrued", except that if a person is under 18 years of age when the action accrues she can bring suit at any time within two years after reaching majority.]

In this case, Dunlea alleged that it was only after she sought psychological counseling that she became aware that Dappen's acts caused her psychological injury and illness. On appeal, Dappen asserts, in his answering brief, that, because Dunlea does not contend that she repressed all memory of the abuse and her complaint makes clear that she was aware of the wrongful nature of Dappen's acts, the circuit court correctly determined that the statute of limitations began to run when Dunlea reached the age of majority and that any action commenced after 1972 was barred . . . .

We are persuaded by the reasoning of those courts that, having considered the application of either statutory or judicially created discovery rules to claims of CSA, have determined that the issue of when a plaintiff discovered, or reasonably should have discovered, that she or he was psychologically injured and that the injury was caused by CSA is a question of fact for the jury.

For example, in *Hammer v. Hammer*, 142 Wis. 2d 257, 418 N.W.2d 23 (Wis. Ct. App. 1987), the plaintiff did not deny that she had always had conscious recollection of sexual abuse by her father, or that she had reported the abuse to her mother when she was fifteen years old. She alleged, however, that,

> because of the psychological distress caused by the abuse and the coping mechanisms which resulted, she was unable to perceive or know the existence or nature of her psychological and emotional injuries. These manifestations continued to operate on her long after the incidents of sexual molestation had ended, preventing her from perceiving her psychological and emotional injuries and their connection to her father's earlier acts, and causing her to resist and reject any suggestions that she obtain psychological counseling or legal advice.

Id., 418 N.W.2d at 25. The Wisconsin Court of Appeals reversed the trial court's order granting the defendant's motion to dismiss on statute of limitations grounds. The court, after reviewing the psychological effects of incestuous abuse and previous applications of the judicially adopted discovery rule, held, "as a matter of law, that a cause of action for incestuous abuse will not accrue until the victim discovers, or in the exercise of reasonable diligence should have discovered, the fact and cause of the injury." *Id.*, 418 N.W.2d at 26. The court went on to state:

> In concluding that the discovery rule is applicable, however, we do not decide the factual question of when [plaintiff] discovered or should have discovered her injuries and their cause. Since the trial court rejected the applicability of the discovery rule, this question was not answered. Thus, because genuine issues of material fact remain open,

including when [plaintiff's] cause of action accrued, we reverse and remand this matter for trial.

Id. at 27 (footnote omitted). The Supreme Court of North Dakota reached a similar result in *Osland v. Osland,* 442 N.W.2d 907 (N.D. 1989). . . .

Other jurisdictions have reached the same results when interpreting statutory provisions codifying the discovery rule for CSA claims. In *Sellery,* 55 Cal. Rptr. 2d 706, the California Court of Appeals held that, under CAL. C.C.P. § 340.1, a plaintiff need not allege repression of memory to delay the accrual of her or his cause of action. The trial court had granted defendants' motion for summary judgment based on its finding that the plaintiff's "claims were time barred 'by reason of her admitted conscious memory of torts committed as to her during her minority.'" *Id.,* 55 Cal. Rptr. 2d at 709. The court of appeals reversed, stating:

> Nothing in section 340.1 requires that memories of abuse be repressed as a prerequisite to a delayed discovery claim. To the contrary, to satisfy delayed discovery plaintiff need only allege the onset of psychological injury or illness after the age of majority and that he commenced his action within three years of the time he discovered or reasonably should have discovered such psychological injury or illness was caused by the childhood sexual abuse.

Id., 55 Cal Rptr. 2d at 711–12. . . .

Because we agree that the issue of when Dunlea discovered, or should have discovered, that her alleged injuries were caused by Dappen's alleged actions is a question of fact for the jury, we cannot hold as a matter of law that Dunlea ascertained her alleged injuries and their causal link to Dappen's alleged actions more than two years before she asserted her claim, or that her failure to recognize her alleged injuries and the cause of those injuries sooner was unreasonable. Certainly, a reasonable jury could find that Dunlea filed suit within two years of discovering her allege injuries and the cause of those injuries, given their nature and circumstances. We therefore hold that the motion to dismiss was wrongly granted. Accordingly, we vacate the circuit court's dismissal of count III and remand this case for trial on Dunlea's CSA claim . . . .

NOTES

1. *Fraudulent Concealment.* Noting the division of authority as to when the statute of limitations begins to run on claims involving alleged repressed memory of childhood sexual abuse, the court in *Fager v. Hundt,* 610 N.E.2d 246 (Ind. 1993), applied the doctrine of fraudulent concealment to stop the defendant from asserting a statute of limitations defense. The doctrine applies, the court said, when the defendant has deceived the plaintiff or concealed material facts preventing discovery of the cause of action.

2. *Corroborating Evidence.* Under the rule in Michigan, a plaintiff claiming repressed memory of sexual assault must provide corroboration that the sexual assault occurred:

> Here, plaintiff has submitted a letter addressed to plaintiff, signed by defendant, . . . in which defendant discussed three or four incidents of sexual contact he had with plaintiff when she was a child. This is sufficient corroboration of the sexual abuse for plaintiff's complaint to survive summary judgment.

Nicolette v. Carey, 751 F. Supp. 695, 699 (W.D. Mich. 1990). The court also required corroboration in *Moriarty v. Garden Sanctuary Church of God*, 511 S. E. 2d 699 (S. C. 1999).

3. *How Much Repression is Required?* In *Johnson v. Johnson*, 701 F. Supp. 1363 (N.D. Ill. 1988), the court addressed the question of whether the repressed memory of sexual abuse must be total in order to forestall the running of the statute of limitations:

> Illinois courts have not as yet addressed the issue of whether the discovery rule should apply to toll the statute of limitations beyond the two-year statutory toll period for minors so as to allow adults to bring claims of incest against their abusers. In fact, this is a relatively new phenomenon and few courts have addressed the issue directly. The cases which have been brought to date have fallen into two categories: (1) those where the Plaintiff claimed she knew about the sexual assaults at or before majority, but that she was unaware that other physical and psychological problems were caused by the prior sexual abuse; and (2) cases such as this one, where the Plaintiff claims due to the trauma of the experience she had no recollection or knowledge of the sexual abuse until shortly before she filed suit.
>
> Courts in California and Montana have decided that the discovery rule does not apply to type 1 cases where the Plaintiff was aware of the sexual abuse but unaware of the causal connection between the sexual abuse and her physical/psychological problems. These same courts, however, expressly reserved the issue of whether or not they would apply the discovery rule in type 2 cases where the Plaintiff claimed she had repressed the sexual abuse from her consciousness . . . .
>
> In her affidavit in this case, Plaintiff states that she has no memory of the sexual abuse prior to March 1987. Her therapist's affidavit reiterates this point. In this case, Plaintiff alleges that not only did she not know of the causal connection between the prior sexual abuse and her present physical and mental problems, she had no recollection of the abuse even occurring . . . .
>
> Incest is a crime in Illinois. ILL. REV. STAT. ch. 38, § 12-16(b) (1988). It is also a major social problem. "It has been estimated that as much as one third of the population has experienced some from of child sexual abuse. National Legal Resource Center for Child Advocacy and Protection, *Child Sexual Abuse: Legal Issues and Approaches* (rev. ed. 1981) . . . . Much of the sexual abuse of children occurs within the family. Comment, *Statutes of Limitations in Civil Incest Suits: Preserving the Victim's Remedy*, 7 HARV. WOMEN'S L.J. 189 (1984) . . . . [When incest occurs among family members, it has been estimated that 75

percent [of the cases] involve incest between father and daughter. Coleman, *Incest: A Proper Definition Reveals the Need for a Different Legal Response*, 49 Mo. L. Rev. 251, 251 n. 1 (1984)." . . . .

By holding that Illinois would apply the discovery rule to this context, Plaintiff's "cause of action accrues when the plaintiff [knew] or reasonably should [have] know[n] of any injury and also [knew] or reasonably should [have] know[n] that the injury was caused by the wrongful acts of another." *Nolan*, 85 Ill. 2d 161, 169, 52 Ill. Dec. 1, 421 N.E.2d 864 (1981). "At some point the injured person becomes possessed of sufficient information concerning his injury and its cause to put a reasonable person on inquiry to determine whether actionable conduct is involved. At this point, under the discovery rule, the running of the limitations period commences." *Knox College v. Celotex Corp.*, 88 Ill. 2d 407, 416, 58 Ill. Dec. 725, 430 N.E.2d 976. When that point is reached in concrete cases is a question of fact.

4. *Questions of Reliability*. Elizabeth Loftus & Katherine Ketchum, The Myth of Repressed Memory (1995), questions the reliability of repressed-memory testimony. Are the problems here any greater than in other areas of memory recall? *See also* Robert Timothy Reagan, *Scientific Consensus on Memory Repressions and Recovery*. 51 Rut. L. Rev. 275 (1999) (admissibility of recovered repressed memory testimony).

See Annot., 12 A.L.R.5th 546 (1993), dealing with whether statute is tolled because of post-traumatic stress or other reasons where there are allegations of sexual abuse resulting in memory repression.

5. *Statutes of Repose*. States have enacted statutes of repose for medical malpractice, building construction, products liability and warranty claims. The periods generally expire after a fixed date, typically 4–12 years after the date of treatment, building completion, or product sale, and the like. Statutes of repose may expire before the plaintiff has reason to know she has been injured or even before she has been injured.

Repose statutes variously provide for: (1) an absolute bar to all claims; (2) a presumption of no negligence, rebuttable by a preponderance of the evidence or by clear and convincing evidence; (3) a bar to strict liability actions (in products cases); (4) a limitation of liability to the product's "useful life"; or (5) both a useful life provision and some form of repose provision. Some states adopted "useful life" statutes to address the problem of "open-ended liability for aging products." *See, e.g., Hodder v. Goodyear Tire & Rubber Co.* 426 N.W. 2d 826 (Minn. 1988). The *Hodder* court reviewed Minn. Stat. S 604.03, subd. 1 (1986), which provides: "it is a defense to a claim against a designer, manufacturer, distributor or seller of the product or a part thereof, that the injury was sustained following the expiration of the ordinary useful life of the product"). It found the statute's useful life concept "ambiguous."

There is a division of authority as to the constitutionality of statutes of repose. *See Lee v. Gaufin*, 867 P.2d 572 (Utah 1993)(medical malpractice); *Hazine v. Montgomery Elevator Co.*, 861 P.2d 625 (Ariz. 1993) (products liability). Courts striking down such statutes do so because of the harshness of cutting off a claim before the plaintiff could ever bring a suit. *See generally*

McGovern, *The Variety, Policy and Constitutionality of Products Liability Statutes of Repose*, 30 Am. U. L. Rev. 579 (1981). Another controversy related to statutes of repose concerns the post-sale duty to warn about defects in products. This duty is recognized in the RESTATEMENT (THIRD) OF TORTS, sec. 10. *See* Frank E. Kulbaski, *Statutes of Repose and the Post-Sale Duty to Warn: Time for a New Interpretation*, 32 Conn. L. Rev. 1027 (2000) (the author finds flawed the application of statutes of repose to post-sale failure to warn claims).

Chapter 11
IMMUNITIES

A. INTRODUCTION

Some actors are immune from tort liability, either generally, or to certain victims. Thus, for example, a state may be immune from any tort suit, or a spouse may be shielded from a tort suit by his or her spouse. Immunity has the same effect as an affirmative defense, such as consent, privilege or contributory negligence. The major distinction is that an affirmative defense bars recovery because the actor's conduct, under the circumstances, was not tortious, while immunity bars recovery solely because of the status of the actor or his relationship to the victim.

Tort immunities once flourished; however, the trend since World War II has been to abolish or severely limit them. This trend has been fueled partly by the availability of liability insurance by which the defendant can reduce the impact of tort liability. Another important factor in the general demise of the immunity concept has been the realization that the justifications for immunity do not now (if they ever did) outweigh its societal costs, such as the loss of deterrence of risky conduct and the unfair imposition of losses upon innocent victims.

PROBLEM

A city police officer killed a teenager by shooting him in the back as the teenager was attempting to escape from the scene of a robbery. What facts would you need to know to determine if the teenager's survivors or estate would have a valid tort action for the shooting against the police officer, the city, or the police officer's spouse?

B. SOVEREIGN IMMUNITY

FEDERAL TORT CLAIMS ACT
28 U.S.C. §§ 1346, 2674 et seq.

§ 1346. United States as defendant

(b)(1) [The United States district courts] shall have exclusive jurisdiction of civil actions on claims against the United States, for money damages, accruing on and after January 1, 1945, for injury or loss of property, or personal injury or death caused by the negligent or wrongful act or omission of any employee of the Government while acting within the scope of his office or employment, under circumstances where the United States, if a private person, would be liable to the claimant in accordance with the law of the place where the act or omission occurred.

§ 2674. Liability of United States

The United States shall be liable, respecting the provisions of this title relating to tort claims, in the same manner and to the same extent as a private individual under like circumstances, but shall not be liable for interest prior to judgment or for punitive damages. . . .

With respect to any claim under this chapter, the United states shall be entitled to assert any defense upon judicial or legislative immunity which otherwise would have been available to the employee of the United States whose act or omission gave rise to the claim, as well as any other defenses to which the United States is entitled. . . .

§ 2678. Disposition by federal agency as prerequisite; evidence

(a) An action shall not be instituted upon a claim against the United States for money damages for injury or loss of property or personal injury or death caused by the negligent or wrongful act or omission of any employee of the Government while acting within the scope of his office or employment, unless the claimant shall have first presented the claim to the appropriate Federal agency and his claim shall have been finally denied by the agency. . . . The failure of an agency to make final disposition of a claim within six months after it is filed shall, at the option of the claimant any time thereafter, be deemed a final denial of the claim for purposes of this section. . . .

(b) Action under this section shall not be instituted for any sum in excess of the amount of the claim presented to the federal agency, except where the increased amount is based upon newly discovered evidence not reasonably discoverable at the time of presenting the claim to the federal agency, or upon allegation and proof of intervening facts, relating to the amount of the claim.

(c) Disposition of any claim by the Attorney General or other head of a federal agency shall not be competent evidence of liability or amount of damages.

§ 2678. Attorney fees; penalty

No attorney shall charge, demand, receive, or collect for services rendered, fees in excess of 25 per centum of any judgment rendered pursuant to section 1346(b) of this title or any settlement made [with Attorney General], or in excess of 20 per centum of any award, compromise, or settlement made [for a claim of $2,500 or less].

Any attorney who charges, demands, receives, or collects for services rendered in connection with such claim any amount in excess of that allowed under this section, if recovery be had, shall be fined not more than $2,000 or imprisoned not more than one year, or both.

§ 2679. Exclusiveness of remedy

(b)(1) The remedy against the United States provided [herein] for injury or loss of property, or personal injury or death arising or resulting from the negligent or wrongful act or omission of any employee of the Government while acting within the scope of his office or employment is exclusive of any other civil action or proceeding for money damages by reason of the same subject matter against the employee whose act or omission gave rise to the claim or against the estate of such employee. Any other civil action or proceeding for money damages arising out of or relating to the same subject matter against the employee or the employee's estate is precluded without regard to when the action or omission occurred.

(2) Paragraph (1) does not extend or apply to a civil action against an employee of the Government -

(A) which is brought for violation of the Constitution of the United States. . . .

§ 2680. *Exceptions*

The provisions of this chapter and section 1346(b) of this title shall not apply to -

(a) Any claim based upon an act or omission of an employee of the Government, exercising due care, in the execution of a statute or regulation, whether or not such statute or regulation be valid, or based upon the exercise or performance or the failure to exercise or perform a discretionary function or duty on the part of a federal agency or an employee of the Government, whether or not the discretion involved be abused. . . .

(h) Any claim arising out of assault, battery, false imprisonment, false arrest, malicious prosecution, abuse of process, libel, slander, misrepresentation, deceit, or interference with contract rights: *Provided*, That, with regard to acts or omissions of investigative or law enforcement officers of the United States Government, the provisions of this chapter and section 1346(b) of this title shall apply to any claim arising, on or after the date of the enactment of this proviso, out of assault, battery, false imprisonment, false arrest, abuse of process, or malicious prosecution. For the purpose of this subsection, "investigative or law enforcement officer" means any officer of the United States who is empowered by law to execute searches, to seize evidence, or to make arrests for violations of Federal law. . . .

(j) Any claim arising out of the combatant activities of the military or naval forces, or the Coast guard, during time of war.

NOTES

1. *The Waiver of Federal Sovereign Immunity*: The federal sovereign has enjoyed immunity from the early days of the Republic. *Osborn v. President, Dirs. & Co. of Bank*, 22 U.S. (9 Wheat.) 738 (1824). General waiver of that immunity took a long time to develop. In 1887, the Tucker Act permitted suit in federal court and assessment of liability against the federal sovereign on contract claims. Congress sometimes enacted legislation permitting a particular plaintiff to sue. In 1920, Congress waived sovereign immunity for torts committed by merchant vessels owned by or operated for the United States. The Suits in Admiralty Act, 46 U.S.C. § 741 *et seq*. However, there was no

comprehensive waiver of sovereign immunity from tort claims until after World War II, when Congress adopted the Federal Tort Claims Act (FTCA).

2. *Jury Control*: 28 U.S.C. § 2402 provides that a tort action under the FTCA shall be tried to the court without a jury. Is this to prevent runaway awards against the public fisc? Can such awards be prevented by the court's power to control the jury verdict through additur and remittitur?

3. *Presentment of Claim*: The plaintiff must first present his claim to the appropriate federal agency, and cannot bring a suit until the claim is denied. 28 U.S.C. § 2675. However, the claim is treated as denied if the agency takes no action within six months. There is a two-year statute of limitations on claims under the FTCA. 28 U.S.C. § 2401(b); *United States v. Kubrick*, 444 U.S. 111, 62 L. Ed. 2d 259, 100 S. Ct. 352 (1979), held a claim "accrues" under the FTCA's discovery rule when the plaintiff knows the existence of an injury and the cause of it—not when the plaintiff later realizes that the conduct causing the injury may be actionable.

4. *Exclusivity of Remedy and Official Immunity*: Federal courts have exclusive subject matter jurisdiction over a tort claim against the federal government. § 1346(b)(1). Except for constitutional and other expressly authorized tort claims, the exclusive remedy under the FTCA is against the federal government, and not against the government employee. 28 U.S.C. § 2679(b).

5. *Intentional Torts and Strict Liability*: The FTCA waives immunity as to a "negligent or wrongful act or omission." 28 U.S.C. § 1346(b)(1); it does not waive the sovereign's immunity from strict liability. *Laird v. Nelms*, 406 U.S. 797 *reh. denied*, 409 U.S. 902 (1972). Note, also, that the act does not waive immunity to certain intentional torts, § 2680(h).

STENCEL AERO ENGINEERING CORP. v. UNITED STATES
431 U.S. 666 (1977)

CHIEF JUSTICE BURGER delivered the opinion of the Court.

We granted certiorari in this case to decide whether the United States is liable under the Federal Tort Claims Act, 28 U.S.C. § 2674, to indemnify a third party for damages paid by it to a member of the Armed Forces injured in the course of military service.

On June 9, 1973, Captain John Donham was permanently injured when the egress life-support system of his F-100 fighter aircraft malfunctioned during a mid-air emergency. Petitioner, Stencel Aero Engineering Corp., manufactured the ejection system pursuant to the specifications of, and by use of certain components provided by, the United States. Pursuant to the Veterans' Benefits Act, 38 U.S.C. § 321 *et seq.*, made applicable to National Guardsmen by 32 U.S.C. § 318, Captain Donham was awarded a lifetime pension of approximately $1,500 per month. He nonetheless brought suit for the injury in the Eastern District of Missouri claiming damages of $2,500,000. Named as defendants, inter alia, were the United States and Stencel. Donham alleged that the emergency eject system malfunctioned as a result of the "negligence and carelessness of the defendants individually and jointly."

Stencel then cross-claimed against the United States for indemnity, charging that any malfunction in the egress life-support system used by Donham was due to faulty specifications, requirements, and components provided by the United States or other persons under contract with the United States. The cross-claim further charged that the malfunctioning system had been in the exclusive custody and control of the United States since the time of its manufacture. Stencel therefore claimed that, insofar as it was negligent at all, its negligence was passive, while the negligence of the United States was active. Accordingly it prayed for indemnity as to any sums it would be required to pay to Captain Donham.

The United States moved for summary judgment against Donham, contending that he could not recover under the Tort Claims Act against the Government for injuries sustained incident to military service. *Feres v. United States*, 340 U.S. 135, 95 L. Ed. 152, 71 S. Ct. 153 (1950). The United States further moved for dismissal of Stencel's cross-claim, asserting that *Feres* also bars an indemnity action by third party for monies paid to military personnel who could not recover directly from the United States.

The District Court granted the Government's motions, holding that *Feres* protected the United States both from the claim of the serviceman and that of the third party. Both claims were therefore dismissed for lack of subject-matter jurisdiction. Stencel appealed this ruling to the Court of Appeals for the Eighth Circuit and that court affirmed. We granted certiorari.

In *Feres v. United States, supra*, the Court held that an on-duty serviceman who is injured due to the negligence of Government officials may not recover against the United States under the Federal Tort Claims Act. During the same Term, in a case involving injuries to private parties, the Court also held that the Act permits impleading the Government as a third-party defendant, under a theory of indemnity or contribution, if the original defendant claims that the United States was wholly or partially responsible for the plaintiff's injury. *United States v. Yellow Cab Co.*, 340 U.S. 543, 95 L. Ed. 523, 71 S. Ct. 399 (1951). In this case we must resolve the tension between *Feres* and *Yellow Cab* when a member of the Armed Services brings a tort action against a private defendant and the latter seeks indemnity from the United States under the Tort Claims Act, claiming that Government officials were primarily responsible for the injuries.

Petitioner argues that "[the] Federal Tort Claims Act waives the Government's immunity from suit in sweeping language." *United States v. Yellow Cab Co., supra*, at 547. Petitioner therefore contends that, unless its claim falls within one of the express exceptions to the Act, the Court should give effect to the congressional policy underlying the Act, which is to hold the United States liable under state-law principles to the same extent as a similarly situated private individual. However, the principles of *Yellow Cab* here come into conflict with the equally well established doctrine of *Feres v. United States*. It is necessary, therefore, to examine the rationale of *Feres* to determine to what extent, if any, allowance of petitioner's claim would circumvent the purposes of the Act as there construed by the Court.

Feres was an action by the executrix of a serviceman who had been killed when the barracks in which he was sleeping caught fire. The plaintiff claimed that the United States had been negligent in quartering the decedent in barracks it knew to be unsafe due to a defective heating plant. While recognizing the broad congressional purpose in passing the Act, the Court noted that the relationship between a sovereign and the members of its Armed Forces is unlike any relationship between private individuals. 340 U.S. at 141–142. There is thus at least a surface anomaly in applying the mandate of the Act that "[the] United States shall be liable . . . in the same manner and to the same extent as a private individual under like circumstances. . . ." 28 U.S.C. § 2674. Noting that the effect of the Act was "to waive immunity from recognized causes of action and . . . not to visit the Government with novel and unprecedented liabilities," 340 U.S. at 142, the Court concluded:

> [T]he Government is not liable under the Federal Tort Claims Act for injuries to servicemen where the injuries arise out of or are in the course of activity incident to service. Without exception, the relationship of military personnel to the Government has been governed exclusively by federal law. We do not think that congress, in drafting this Act, created a new cause of action dependent on local law for service-connected injuries or death due to negligence. We cannot impute to Congress such a radical departure from established law in the absence of express congressional command. *Id.* at 146.

In reaching this conclusion, the Court considered two factors: First, the relationship between the Government and members of its Armed Forces is "'distinctively federal in character,'" *id.*, at 143, citing *United States v. Standard Oil Co.*, 332 U.S. 301, 91 L. Ed. 2067, 67 S. Ct. 1604 (1947); it would make little sense to have the Government's liability to members of the Armed Services dependent on the fortuity of where the soldier happened to be stationed at the time of the injury. Second, the Veterans' Benefits Act establishes, as a substitute for tort liability, a statutory "no fault" compensation scheme which provides generous pensions to injured servicemen, without regard to any negligence attributable to the Government. A third factor was explicated in *United States v. Brown*, 348 U.S. 110, 112 (1954), namely, "[t]he peculiar and special relationship of the soldier to his superiors, the effects of the maintenance of such suits on discipline, and the extreme results that might obtain if suits under the Tort Claims Act were allowed for negligent orders given or negligent acts committed in the course of military duty. . . ." We must therefore consider the impact of these factors where, as here, the suit against the Government is not brought by the serviceman himself, but by a third party seeking indemnity for any damages it may be required to pay the serviceman.

Clearly, the first factor considered in *Feres* operates with equal force in this case. The relationship between the Government and its suppliers of ordnance is certainly no less "distinctively federal in character" than the relationship between the Government and its soldiers. The Armed Services perform a unique, nationwide function in protecting the security of the United States. To that end military authorities frequently move large numbers of men, and large quantities of equipment, from one end of the continent to the other, and beyond. Significant risk of accidents and injuries attend such a vast undertaking. If, as the Court held in *Feres*, it makes no sense to permit the fortuity of the situs of the alleged negligence to affect the liability of he Government to a serviceman who sustains service-connected injuries, it makes equally little sense to permit that situs to affect the Government's liability to a Government contractor for the identical injury.

The second factor considered by *Feres* is somewhat more difficult to apply. Petitioner argues that the existence of a generous military compensation scheme is of little comfort to it. It is contended that, although it may be fair to prohibit direct recovery by servicemen under the Act, since they are assured of compensation regardless of fault under the Veterans' Benefits Act, petitioner as a third-party claimant should not be barred from indemnity for damages which it may be required to pay to the serviceman, and as to which it has no alternative federal remedy.

A compensation scheme such as the Veterans' Benefits Act serves a dual purpose: it not only provides a swift, efficient remedy for the injured serviceman, but it also clothes the Government in the "protective mantle of the Act's limitation-of-liability provisions." See *Cooper Stevedoring Co. v. Fritz Kopke, Inc.*, 417 U.S. 106, 115, 40 L. Ed. 2d 694, 94 S. Ct. 2174 (1974). Given the broad exposure of the Government, and the great variability in the potentially applicable tort law, the military compensation scheme provides an upper limit of liability for the Government as to service-connected injuries. To permit petitioner's claim would circumvent this limitation, thereby frustrating one of the essential features of the Veterans' Benefits Act. As we stated in a somewhat different context concerning the Tort Claims Act: "To permit [petitioner] to proceed . . . here would be to judicially admit at the back door that which has been legislatively turned away at the front door. We do not believe that the [Federal Tort Claims] Act permits such a result." *Laird v. Nelms*, 406 U.S. 797, 802 (1972).

Turning to the third factor, it seems quite clear that where the case concerns an injury sustained by a soldier while on duty, the effect of the action upon military discipline is identical whether the suit is brought by the soldier directly or by a third party. The litigation would take virtually the identical form in either case, and at issue would be the degree of fault, if any, on the part of the Government's agents and the effect upon the serviceman's safety. The trial would, in either case, involve second-guessing military orders, and would often required members of the Armed Services to testify in court as to each other's decisions and actions. This factor, too, weighs against permitting any recovery by petitioner against the United States.

We conclude, therefore, that the third-party indemnity action in this case is unavailable for essentially the same reasons that the direct action by Donham is barred by *Feres*. The factors considered by the *Feres* court are largely applicable in this type of case as well; hence, the right of the third party to recover in an indemnity action against the United States recognized in *Yellow Cab*, must be held limited by the rationale of *Feres* where the injured party is a serviceman. Since the relationship between the United States and petitioner is based on a commercial contract, there is no basis for a claim of unfairness in this result.

NOTES

1. *The Feres Doctrine*: The *Feres* doctrine bars "indirect" claims, such as loss of consortium and wrongful death, by a soldier's beneficiaries. It also bars the claims of family members for mental anguish caused by the injury to a soldier's relative. *De Font v. United States*, 453 F.2d 1239 (1st Cir.), *cert. denied*, 407 U.S. 910 (1972).

2. *Active Service*: Recall the FTCA exception in 28 U.S.C. § 2680(j), *supra*. How does the *Feres* doctrine differ from that exception?

3. *Direct Injuries*: What if the injury to the family member is "direct," such as when a child sustains damage through genetic defects caused by injury to her parent while in military service? The courts are divided. *Hinkie v. United States*, 715 F.2d 96 (3d Cir. 1983), *cert. denied*, 465 U.S. 1023 (1984); *Monaco v. United States*, 661 F.2d 129 (9th Cir. 1981), *cert. denied*, 456 U.S. 989 (1982) (barring recovery); *In re "Agent Orange" Prod. Liab. Litig.*, 580 F. Supp. 1242 (E.D.N.Y. 1984) (permitting recovery).

LINDGREN v. UNITED STATES
665 F.2d 978 (9th Cir. 1982)

MUECKE, DISTRICT JUDGE:

On September 28, 1974, plaintiff Eric A. Lindgren was water skiing on a section of the Colorado River, south of Parker Dam. While making a run, plaintiff's ski struck the river bottom, throwing plaintiff forward and causing him serious physical injury.

Plaintiffs filed their First Amended Complaint on February 26, 1979. The complaint named the United States as defendant and sought damages pursuant to the Federal Tort Claims Act (FTCA), 28 U.S.C. §§ 1346(b) and 2671 et seq., for personal injury, negligent infliction of emotional distress and loss of consortium. Plaintiffs' complaint alleged that the U.S. Bureau of Reclamation, the agency in control at Parker Dam, had artificially altered the flow, the water level and the riverbed configuration of the Colorado River, and had thereby created a dangerous condition for users of the river. Plaintiffs further alleged that the Bureau had knowledge of the recreational use of the river and of the hazards posed to such users by the Bureau's alteration; it was alleged that despite this knowledge, the Bureau had failed to post any warnings as to the dangerous condition of the river.

On May 25, 1979, the United States moved fr summary judgment. The Government's motion was based, in part, on the discretionary function exemption to the FTCA, 28 U.S.C. § 2680(a), which provides in pertinent part:

> The provisions of this Chapter and Section 1346(b) of this title shall not apply to — (a) Any claim . . . based upon the exercise or performance or the failure to exercise or perform a discretionary function or duty on the part of a federal agency or an employee of the Government, whether or not the discretion involved be abused.

On August 9, 1979, the trial court entered summary judgment in the Government's favor. In so doing, the Court held that the operation of Parker

Dam constituted a discretionary activity within the meaning of the above statute and cited *Spillway Marina, Inc. v. United States,* 445 F.2d 876 (10th Cir. 1971).

Plaintiffs do not contest the trial court's conclusion as to the discretionary character of dam operations. Their sole contention is that the Government's failure to warn was not such an activity, and therefore that the trial court erred in entering summary judgment in the Government's favor.

It may well be that the trial court's ultimate conclusion as to the discretionary character of the Government's failure to warn was correct. It may also be that even if the Government's failure is found nondiscretionary, the trial court will conclude that under the present circumstances the Government was under no duty to warn. The problem with the Court's ruling was its assumption that simply because the hazard which allegedly caused plaintiff's injury was created through the exercise of a discretionary function, the Government's failure to warn of the hazard was also discretionary. The trial court's *per se* approach to the issue was in error.

The leading decision interpreting the discretionary function exemption is *Dalehite v. United States,* 346 U.S. 15, 73 S. Ct. 956, 97 L. Ed. 1427 (1953). In that case, the Court established that the purpose of the exemption was to permit the Government to make planning-level decisions without fear of suit . . . .

Although the *Dalehite* Court declined to define the outer limits of "discretion," it did go so far as to hold that discretion

> includes more than the initiation of programs and activities. It also includes determinations made by executives or administrators in establishing plans, specifications or schedules of operations. Where there is room for policy judgment and decision, there is discretion. It necessarily follows that acts of subordinates carrying out the operations of government in accordance with official directions cannot be actionable. If it were not so, the protection of § 2680(a) would fail at the time it would be needed, that is, when a subordinate performs or fails to perform a causal step, each action or nonaction being directed by the superior exercising, perhaps abusing, discretion.

Id. at 35–36, 73 S. Ct. 968. (Footnote omitted.)

Although *Dalehite* remains an important statement of the policy behind the discretionary function exemption, subsequent decisions by the Supreme Court and various circuit courts have operated to narrow *Dalehite*'s definition of the term "discretion."

The prevailing test in the Ninth Circuit asks whether the act or omission occurred on the "planning level" of governmental activity or on the "operational level":

> Not every discretionary act is exempt. Obviously, attending to many day-to-day details of management involves decisions and thus some element of discretion. The exercise of this kind of discretion does not fall within the discretionary function exemption. The distinction generally made in the application of the discretionary function

exemption is between those decisions which are made on a policy or planning level, as opposed to those made on an operational level.

Thompson v. United States, 592 F.2d 1104, 1111 (9th Cir. 1979). . . .

Plaintiffs cite several cases for the proposition that if the exercise of a discretionary function creates or facilitates a hazard, the Government's duty to warn can be actionable — notwithstanding the discretionary character of the hazard-causing act or omission. *See e.g., Smith v. United States,* 546 F.2d 872 (10th Cir. 1976) (Yellowstone Park visitor falls into thermal pool; decision to open park and decision whether to leave an area of park undeveloped were discretionary, but "the decision as to the posting of warning signs in the area must be judged separately . . . ."); *United States v. Washington,* 351 F.2d 913 (9th Cir. 1965) (aircraft hits unmarked electrical power line; even assuming location and erection of line was discretionary function, failure to provide suitable warning device was actionable); *United Air Lines, Inc. v. Wiener,* 335 F.2d 379 (9th Cir. 1964), *cert. dism. sub nom. United Air Lines, Inc. v. United States,* 379 U.S. 951, 85 S. Ct. 452, 13 L. Ed. 2d 549 (1964) (Air Force jet hits commercial airliner; under circumstances, failure to warn pilot of hazards created by instrument landing procedure being used by jet was actionable); *United States v. White,* 211 F.2d 79 (9th Cir. 1954) (business invitee injured by unexploded shell while collecting scrap metal on Army firing range; assuming that decision not to undertake removal of hidden dangers was discretionary, the Government's failure to warn of the known danger the invitee was likely to encounter was not); *Everitt v. United States,* 204 F. Supp. 20 (S.D. Tex. 1962) (boat accident; placement of log piles in bay for surveying purpose was discretionary, but failure to discover submerged pilings and to warn thereof was not); *Hernandez v. United States,* 112 F. Supp. 369 (D. Hawaii 1953) (vehicle accident; Government's decision to erect road block was discretionary, but failure to adequately warn travelers was not); *Worley v. United States,* 119 F. Supp. 719 (D. Or. 1952) (injury to hunter; Government's decision to use coyote traps was discretionary, but failure to warn humans of danger was not).

The Government's most persuasive case is *Spillway Marina, Inc. v. United States,* 330 F. Supp. 611 (D. Kan. 1970), *aff'd* 445 F.2d 876 (10th Cir. 1971). But that case too is distinguishable.

Plaintiff in *Spillway* had a state concession to operate a marina on the banks of a federal reservoir. In the fall of 1966, it became necessary for the Corps of Engineers to lower the water level of the reservoir to maintain the navigational quality of the Missouri River and to accomplish some construction and repair work. The marina's complaint alleged that this drawdown damaged its dock facilities and that it was done without authority, without warning, and in violation of the marina's concession agreement.

The district court held that the Government's decision to lower the water level was clearly a discretionary function. In response to plaintiff's argument that it was lack of notice, rather than the actual lowering of the water level that caused the damage, the court stressed that notice would be highly impractical. . . .

On appeal to the Tenth Circuit, plaintiff withdrew his argument that the drawdown was unauthorized and placed sole reliance on his argument that the Government was negligent for failing to warn that the drawdown would occur. The Tenth Circuit affirmed, emphasizing that the decision when to release and store water required discretion, and reasoning that "the argument of Spillway goes to the manner of exercise of a discretionary function." 445 F.2d at 878.

This Court rejects the Government's reading of *Spillway* as standing for the proposition that, in the dam context, all failure to warn assumes the discretionary cloak of the operation itself. While it is indeed possible that a particular failure to warn might be discretionary, each failure must be analyzed separately.

In *Spillway*, the exercise of discretion (i.e., the lowering of the water level) was primarily responsible for the damage for which plaintiff brought suit. In the case before this Court, the discretionary act did not produce any direct damage — it produced a hazard. The damage required an act on plaintiff's part (water skiing). In this respect, the *Spillway* case is more aligned with the cases cited by the Government that did not involve failure to warn. This case, however, is more analogous to the authority relied on by plaintiff.

To permit recovery in a *Spillway* situation would require the Government to analyze each act of discretion to determine (1) whether it would damage anyone, (2) whether a warning would reduce that damage, and (3) whether warnings would be feasible under the circumstances. To oblige the Government to ask these questions before each discretionary act would seem to constitute a great interference with Governmental administration. Under the facts of *Spillway*, for example, the Government would have had to warn the marina, and all other persons who would suffer damage from a lowering of the water level, each time the water level was lowered.

In contrast, the "hazard" cases often require only one-time warnings, and are therefore not as administratively burdensome. In the present case, for example, plaintiff would have the Government post signs informing the public that the Government is causing the water level to fluctuate without notice, and that the public should beware of dangers that might be caused thereby. The Government is not, as in *Spillway*, being asked to notify the public each time it changes the water level in a manner so as to threaten damage.

NOTES

1. *Discretionary Functions.* There may be no more elusive concept in American law than the "discretionary function" exception to the waiver of sovereign immunity. The purpose of the exception is to avoid infringement upon the power and operations of the executive. If the decision is clearly one of policy, such as whether to engage in a certain activity, the matter will be "discretionary," and the immunity will apply.

2. *Nondiscretionary Acts and Omissions.* As *Lindgren* illustrates, the government may be liable for negligent failure to warn that it has exercised a discretionary function which will expose others to an unreasonable risk of harm, *Martin v. United States*, 546 F.2d 1355 (9th Cir. 1976), *cert. denied*, 432 U.S. 906, (1977), or in failing to gather the data necessary for an intelligent exercise of the discretionary function, *Payton v. United States*, 679

F.2d 475 (5th Cir. 1982). The Coast Guard may not be liable for failing to erect or operate a lighthouse, but it may be liable for letting the light go out or in failing to warn that the lighthouse is not operating. *See, e.g., Indian Towing Co. v. United States,* 350 U.S. 61 (1955).

3. *OSHA Inspection.* Overruling a panel decision, the First Circuit held en banc in *Irving v. U.S.*, 162 F.3d 154 (1st Cir. 1998), that OSHA inspectors were accorded discretion in the manner in which they conducted factory inspections. An activity is non-discretionary, the court said, "when a federal statute, regulation, or policy specifically prescribes a course of action for an employee to follow." OSHA inspectors are given "considerable leeway" in conducting general administrative inspections. Therefore, an employee who was injured by the inspectors' alleged negligence in failing to discover and correct a dangerous workplace condition was barred from recovery by the discretionary immunity exception of the Federal Tort Claims Act.

HACKING v. TOWN OF BELMONT
736 A.2d 1229 (N.H. 1999)

BROCK, C.J.

This is an interlocutory appeal by the defendants, the Town of Belmont and the Shaker Regional School District, from a ruling of the Superior Court denying their motion to dismiss. The plaintiffs, Nancy and Charles Hacking, Jr., have asserted several theories of negligence against the defendants for injuries that their daughter, Chelsea Hacking, sustained in a basketball game. We affirm in part, reverse in part, and remand.

The plaintiffs have alleged the following facts. On or about January 27, 1995, when she was a sixth grade student at the Canterbury Elementary School, Chelsea participated in a girls basketball game against a team from the Belmont Elementary School. During that game, which was organized by the defendants and/or the Town of Canterbury, the referees, coaches, instructors, and employees of the defendants permitted the game to escalate out of control. Belmont players twice knocked Chelsea down and stepped on her leg. As a result, she suffered permanent injury to her left leg, underwent surgery and other medical treatment, and will require future medical care.

[The plaintiffs sued alleging several grounds of negligence. Defendants moved to dismiss on the grounds that they were immune under the discretionary function doctrine, and the trial court denied the motion to dismiss.]

The defendants' first allegation of error requires us to review once again the doctrine of discretionary function immunity. In *Merrill v. Manchester*, 114 N.H. 722, 729, 332 A.2d 378, 383 (1974), we abrogated the doctrine of municipal immunity. In so doing, we established that as a general rule, municipalities are "subject to the same rules as private corporations if a duty has been violated and a tort committed." *Id.* at 730, 332 A.2d at 383.

As an exception to the general rule, however, we held that municipalities are immune from liability for acts and omissions that constitute "the exercise of an executive or planning function involving the making of a basic policy decision which is characterized by the exercise of a high degree of official judgment or discretion." *Id.* at 729, 332 A.2d at 383. We have recognized that "[c]ertain essential, fundamental activities of government must remain immune from tort liability so that our government can govern." *Mahan v. N.H. Dep't of Admin. Services*, 141 N.H. 747, 750, 693 A.2d 79, 82 (1997) (decided under the discretionary function exception to the State's waiver of sovereign immunity). Accordingly, in evaluating whether the trial court erred, we must "distinguish between planning or discretionary functions and functions that are purely ministerial." *Bergeron v. City of Manchester*, 140 N.H. 417, 421, 666 A.2d 982, 984 (1995).

We have refused to adopt a bright line rule to determine whether conduct constitutes discretionary planning or merely the ministerial implementation of a plan. *See id* at 421, 666 A.2d at 985; *Gardner v. City of Concord*, 137 N.H. 253, 258, 624 A.2d 1337, 1340 (1993). We have, however, adopted the following test:

> When the particular conduct which caused the injury is one characterized by the high degree of discretion and judgment involved in weighing alternatives and making choices with respect to public policy and planning, governmental entities should remain immune from liability.

Bergeron, 140 N.H. at 421, 666 A.2d at 984. In applying this test, "[w]e distinguish policy decisions involving the consideration of competing economic, social, and political factors from operational or ministerial decisions required to implement the policy decisions." *Mahan*, 141 N.H. at 750, 693 A.2d at 82.

To the extent that the plaintiffs challenge the defendants' decisions regarding the training and supervision of the coaches and referees, the defendants are immune from liability. There is no question that the decision whether or not to have a fifth and sixth grade girls basketball program is characterized by a high degree of discretion in making public policy and planning choices. Likewise, the decisions regarding what training and supervision to provide those whom the defendants chose to run the program are planning decisions requiring a high degree of discretion. *Cf. Bergeron*, 140 N.H. at 425, 666 A.2d at 987 (because ultimate decision regarding traffic controls at intersection was discretionary, intermediate decision regarding whether to have staff keep track of accidents at intersection also discretionary). These decisions necessarily involved the most prudent allocation of municipal resources, and thus the weighing of "competing, economic, social, and political factors." *Mahan*, 141 N.H. at 750, 693 A.2d at 82; *cf. Phillips v. Thomas*, 555 So. 2d 81, 85 (Ala. 1989) (defendant entitled to discretionary function immunity for negligent training and supervision claim); *Brooks v. Logan*, 127 Idaho 484, 903 P.2d 73, 77 (1995) (school district entitled to discretionary function immunity for failure to train staff to prevent student suicide); *Erskine v. Commissioner of Corrections*, 682 A.2d 681, 686 (Me. 1996) (defendants' actions in training and supervising personnel protected by discretionary immunity); *Miller v. Szelenyi*, 546 A.2d 1013, 1021 (Me. 1988) (proper supervision and control of employees required exercise of discretion). Accordingly, the trial court should have dismissed Count III, and we reverse its decision with respect to that count. . .

The defendants assert that they are entitled to immunity for their decisions regarding not only the training and supervision of the coaches and referees, but also the *selection* of the coaches and referees. In arguing that the trial court erred on this issue, the defendants state that the plaintiffs' claim for negligent training and supervision should have been dismissed in part because the decision to rely on parent volunteers as referees and coaches was discretionary. Count III, however, alleges only that the defendants "failed to properly train and supervise" the referees and coaches. Moreover, plaintiffs' counsel conceded at oral argument that they had not alleged negligent selection of referees and coaches. Accordingly, we find it unnecessary to address whether the selection of the referees or coaches was entitled to immunity.

The defendants next argue that the decisions made by the referees and coaches in the course of the game were entitled to discretionary function immunity. Decisions such as whether to call a foul, whether to replace one player with another, or whether a team has scored, according to the defendants, are inherently discretionary and require the weighing of alternatives. The defendants contend that discretionary function immunity should extend not only to "high-level" decisions, but to decisions made at any level when those decisions "involve the weighing of alternatives regarding the implementation or allocation of municipal resources." Accordingly, the defendants argue that the decisions of the referees and coaches are precisely the sort of decision that ought to be afforded immunity. The only conduct that should be considered ministerial, according to the defendants, is conduct that involves the mere execution of a set task, requiring no independent judgment.

Although the level of government at which a decision is made is not dispositive of whether the municipality is entitled to immunity, ministerial conduct is not limited to conduct requiring no judgment whatsoever. Indeed, "it would be difficult to conceive of any official act, no matter how directly ministerial, that did not admit of some discretion in the manner of its performance, even if it involved only the driving of a nail." 18 E. McQuillin, *Municipal Corporations* § 53.04.10, at 157 (3d ed. rev. 1993) (quotation and brackets omitted); see also *Whitney v. City of Worcester*, 373 Mass. 208, 366 N.E. 2d 1210, 1217 (1977) (distinction is not merely between discretionary and non-discretionary functions as all functions involve some degree of judgment). While "[n]ot all governmental decisions involving an element of discretion fall within the discretionary function exception," the exception does apply "when a decision entails governmental planning or policy formulation, involving the evaluation of economic, social, and political considerations." *Mahan*, 141 N.H. at 751, 693 A.2d at 83.

Assuming the truth of the plaintiffs' allegations, we conclude that the decisions of the referees and coaches, while perhaps involving some discretion and judgment, were not decisions that concerned municipal planning and public policy. These decisions did not involve the weighing of competing social, economic, or political factors. Rather, the plaintiffs have alleged negligence on the part of the referees and coaches in the implementation of the school basketball program.

The discretionary function exception "was not designed to cloak the ancient doctrine of [municipal] immunity in modern garb." *Adriance*, 687 A.2d at 241.

Elevating the decisions of referees and coaches in the course of an elementary school basketball game to the level of governmental planning or policy formulation would indeed undermine the rule of *Merrill* establishing immunity as the exception. Accordingly, we hold that the trial court did not err in denying the motion to dismiss on the grounds that the decisions of the referees and coaches were not entitled to discretionary function immunity. . . .

NOTES

1. *The Dangerous Dog.* In *Chase v. City of Memphis*, 971 S.W. 2d 380 (Tenn. 1998), the Memphis City Animal Shelter determined that Hill's pit bulls were dangerous, after receiving several complaints about the dogs' aggressive conduct. Lee on behalf of the Shelter issued a letter to Hill ordering him to correct any fencing deficiencies around his property, and to enroll his dogs in a basic obedience training course within ninety days. Failure to comply, the letter said, would result in "immediate seizure of the dogs." Hill failed to comply with the letter, and the dogs subsequently attacked and killed plaintiff's deceased, Ms. Stidham.

The Plaintiff sued the defendant for wrongful death of the deceased. The defendant claimed discretionary immunity, stating that the shelter failed to impound the dogs because of budgetary constraints and priorities. Rejecting this defense, the court said:

> The record, however, does not indicate that either Lee or the Animal Shelter made a conscious decision *not* to pick up the animals upon Hill's non-compliance or that a policy or procedure was in place to deal with violations of the Animal Shelter's orders. The record does not indicate whether the Animal Shelter had an established procedure for picking up animals that were both designated as dangerous and released back into society contingent upon an owner's compliance with an Animal Shelter's order. Upon the expiration of the time within which Hill had to comply with the order, the Animal Shelter did not: (1) attempt to call Hill to determine whether the order had been complied with; (2) attempt to contact Hill by letter informing him of non-compliance; or (3) place Hill's dogs on a list for future pick-up. The Animal Shelter's response was simply "no response."

The court also found that the City could be liable under the "special duty" exception to the public duty doctrine. Under the public duty doctrine, public employees are shielded from tort liability for a breach of a duty owed to the public at large. The special duty exception to this doctrine arises when a public official "affirmatively undertakes to protect the plaintiff and the plaintiff relies upon the undertaking." The Shelter wrote Ms. Stidham telling her that Hill's fences would be fixed and his dogs enrolled in obedience school, or otherwise the dogs would be subject to "immediate seizure." Ms. Stidham "relied upon the undertaking of Lee and the Shelter to remedy the situation. Accordingly, the special duty exception to the public duty doctrine is applicable to this case."

2. *The Public Duty.* The public duty doctrine (a duty owed to all is a duty owed to none) has been used as a doctrine parallel to that of discretionary immunity. So in *Riss v. City of New York*, 240 N.E. 2d 860 (N.Y. App. 1968),

the court held the city of New York had no duty to provide police protection to a woman who had been repeatedly threatened by her estranged boyfriend. But compare *DeLong v. Erie County*, 455 N.Y. S.2d 887 (App. Dir. 1982), and *Beal for Martinez v. City of Seattle*, 954 P.2d 237 (Wash. 1998), where the defendant governmental entities could be found liable for the negligent performance of their special duties assumed by the adoption of an emergency 911 call system. The court in *Ezell v. Cockrell*, 971 S.W. 2d 380 (Tenn. 1998), said the public duty doctrine also does not apply to reckless misconduct of a public official.

3. *Justifying Sovereign Immunity.* The doctrine of sovereign immunity evolved from the English common law principle that "the king can do no wrong." In the United States, this came to mean that there were no legal rights against the authority that makes the laws upon which the rights depend. *See* PROSSER & KEETON, LAW OF TORTS, § 131 (5th ed.); *Kawananakoa v. Polyblank*, 205 U.S. 349, 353, 51 L. Ed. 834, 27 S. Ct. 526 (1907) ("A sovereign is exempt from suit, not because of any formal conception or absolute theory, but on the logical and practical ground that there can be no legal right as against the authority that makes the law on which the right depends.")

In modern times, policy justifications for sovereign immunity surfaced, such as (1) tax funds should not be diverted from the public purposes for which they were collected, and (2) imposition of tort liability upon the sovereign would impose an intolerable financial burden and lead to the curtailment of public services. These arguments are gradually losing out to better ones, such as (1) there is a loss of deterrence in immunizing sovereigns who are increasingly engaging in risk-producing activities, (2) sovereign immunity illogically shifts the loss from the public generally, which benefits from the activity, to the innocent victim and his family, and in some cases back to the sovereign through welfare programs, and (3) if the sovereign maintains liability insurance, the insurer may get a windfall in the absence of liability. The result has been the general restriction or abolition of sovereign immunity by constitutional provision, LA. CONST. of 1974, Art. XII, § 10; by statute, ARIZ. REV. STAT. § 12-820 (1989), COLO. REV. STAT. § 24-10-102 (1989), VA. CODE § 8.01-195.1 (1990), or by judicial decision.

4. *State Immunities; Judicial Reform and Legislative Retrenchment.* In Pennsylvania, and in some other states in which sovereign immunity was abolished by judicial decision, the legislatures reacted adversely. *Mayle v. Pa. Dept. of Hwys.*, 479 Pa. 384, 388 A.2d 709 (1978). Subsequent to *Mayle,* the Pennsylvania legislature reestablished sovereign immunity, but waived it for certain types of tort claims: vehicle liability; medical-professional liability; care, custody or control of personal property; commonwealth real estate; highways and sidewalks; potholes and other dangerous conditions; care, custody or control of animals; liquor store sales; and National Guard activities. PA. CON. STAT. ANN. §§ 8521–28 (1988). Some states limit the amount of damages recoverable against the sovereign. ILL. REV. STAT. ANN. ch. 37, par. 439.8 (1988); ME. REV. STAT. ANN. tit. 14, § 8105 (1989). Kansas restored sovereign immunity for the state government, generally, but not for lesser governmental units. KAN. STAT. ANN. § 46-901 (1988). The constitutionality of these statutes restoring sovereign immunity generally is upheld. *See, e.g.,*

Carroll v. York County, 496 Pa. 363, 437 A.2d 394 (1981); *Brown v. Wichita State Univ.*, 219 Kan. 2, 547 P.2d 1015 (1976), *app. dismissed sub nom., Bruce v. Wichita State Univ.*, 429 U.S. 806, 501 L. Ed. 2d 67, 97 S. Ct. 41 (1976).

5. *The Eleventh Amendment*. The eleventh amendment to the United States Constitution provides in effect that no state can be sued for damages in a federal court. The U.S. Supreme Court has extended that immunity to suits against states in state courts for violation of federal law. *Alden v. Maine*, 119 S. Ct. 2240 (1990).

In *Fitzpatrick v. Bitzer*, 96 S. Ct. 2666 (1976), the Court held a suit against the State of Connecticut would lie under the Civil Rights Act of 1964, for retirement benefits allegedly denied because of sex discrimination. The Act was enacted pursuant to sec. 5 of the 14th amendment to the United States constitution. The eleventh amendment, said the Court, "and the principles of state sovereignty which it involves, are necessarily limited by the enforcement provisions of § 5 of the Fourteenth Amendment."

The United States Supreme Court, in a series of 5-4 decisions, *Alden v. Maine*, 119 S. Ct. 2240 (1999), *Fla. Prepaid Postsecondary v. College Savings*, 119 S. Ct. 2199, *Kimel v. Florida Board of Regents*, 120 S. Ct. 631 (2000), and *Board of Trustees v. Garrett*, 121 S. Ct. 955 (2001) has dramatically restricted the power of individuals to seek money damages against states for injuries resulting form violation of federal law.

In *Alden* the Court held that Congress lacked power under Article I of the U.S. Constitution to authorize suits against the states without the states' consent. Here the Court denied a claim by state probation officers against the State of Maine for violation of the overtime provisions of the Fair Labor Standards Act. The eleventh amendment, said the Court, is "convenient shorthand" for state sovereign immunity that "neither derives from nor is limited by the terms of the Eleventh Amendment."

In *Florida Prepaid* the Court said neither the patent clause (Art. I § 8 Cl. 8) nor the fourteenth amendment of the United States constitution authorized Congress to abrogate state sovereign immunity in suits for state infringement of the federal patent law.

The Court held in *Kimel* that Congress lacked the power under the fourteenth amendment to authorize suits against a state for violation of the Age Discrimination in Employment Act. *Garrett* held a state could not be sued for violation of the Americans with Disabilities Act.

6. *State Constitutional Remedies*. In *Brown v. State*, 89 N.Y. 2d 172, 674 N.E. 2d 1129 (1996), an elderly white woman was reportedly attacked at knifepoint in a house near the City of Oneonta. The victim identified her assailant as a black man.

The state police sought to question every black male student at the State University of New York, College of Oneonta in connection with the attack. When these efforts failed to yield a suspect, the police then conducted a five-day "street sweep" in which "every nonwhite male found in and around the City of Oneonta was stopped and similarly interrogated. In the nearly four years since the incident, no one had been arrested for the crime."

Black male plaintiffs brought this suit as a class action against the State of New York, seeking damages for their alleged denial of equal protection and illegal search and seizure in connection with the above incident. The court said the state was not a "person" within the meaning of the federal civil rights statute, 42 U.S. § 1983. But the plaintiffs could sue the state under its own constitution, for alleged denial of equal protection and illegal search and seizure.

C. INDIVIDUAL IMMUNITIES

LLMD OF MICHIGAN, INC. v. JACKSON-CROSS CO.
740 A.2d 186 (Pa. 1999)

ZAPPALA, JUSTICE.

This is an appeal by LLMD of Michigan, Inc., a general partner trading as Wintoll Associates Limited Partnership (Wintoll), from the Superior Court's order affirming the order of the Philadelphia County Common Pleas Court, which granted summary judgment in favor of Jackson-Cross Company (Appellee) in an action for professional malpractice. For the following reasons, we reverse.

In 1989, Wintoll commenced an action in the United States District Court for the Eastern District of Pennsylvania against Marine Midland Realty Credit Corporation and USLife Life Insurance Company, alleging breach of contract arising out of the defendants' failure to provide financing for the purchase and rehabilitation of an industrial facility in Springfield, Michigan. After the lawsuit was filed, Robert Swift, Esquire, Wintoll's attorney, contacted Charles Seymour, chairman of Jackson-Cross, to engage Seymour's services as Wintoll's expert on the issue of the lost profits suffered as a result of the defendants' breach of their financing commitment for the industrial rehabilitation project. On December 28, 1990, Seymour responded with a proposal outlining the scope of services that he would perform for Wintoll and the fees that would be charged for those services. The proposal contemplated that Seymour would quantify the damages sustained because of the lenders' failure to close under the mortgage commitments; prepare a signed report outlining what was done, stating the conclusions and supporting them; and participate in pre-trial conferences, depositions and trial. By letter dated January 4, 1991, Wintoll's attorney accepted Seymour's proposal.

Wintoll was subsequently provided with a calculation of the lost profits, which Jackson-Cross estimated to be $6 million. The calculation was prepared by David Anderson, an employee of Jackson-Cross, using a computerized accounting spreadsheet program. The federal trial began on November 24, 1992. Seymour was called by Wintoll to testify as an expert witness on the lost profits calculation on December 7, 1992 and provided his opinion as to the damages sustained by Wintoll.

On cross-examination, defense counsel established that Anderson's lost profits calculation contained a mathematical error that completely undermined the basis for the Jackson-Cross calculation of Wintoll's damages. Seymour conceded that the calculation was wrong because of the error that had been made. Because Seymour had not performed the calculations himself, he was unable to explain the mathematical error in the calculations or to recalculate the lost profits by correcting the error while on the stand. Defense counsel requested that Seymour's opinion be stricken from the record because it was based on inaccurate numbers and on erroneous mathematical calculations. The trial judge granted the motion to strike Seymour's testimony and instructed the jury to completely disregard the testimony during its deliberations.

Without Seymour's testimony, Wintoll's evidence relating to lost profits consisted of the testimony of Leon Winitsky and Michael Winitsky, principals of Wintoll, and a calculation by Wintoll of its estimated profits. The day after Seymour's testimony was stricken, Wintoll accepted a settlement offer from the federal defendants for approximately $750,000. Jackson-Cross subsequently provided Wintoll with a corrected computation of estimated lost profits, which indicated such damages amounted to $2.7 million.

On January 14, 1993, Wintoll filed a civil action in the Philadelphia County Common Pleas Court against Jackson-Cross, asserting causes of action for breach of contract and professional malpractice. Wintoll asserted that Jackson-Cross had breached its agreement to furnish expert services in connection with the federal lawsuit by failing to deliver an accurate or workmanlike lost profits computation, and had failed to exercise the degree of care and skill ordinarily exercised by experts in the field of real estate counseling and computation of lost profits in real estate transactions. Wintoll alleged that it would have received a judgment for lost profits in an amount in excess of $2.7 million plus interest but for the conduct of Jackson-Cross. Wintoll sought damages for the estimated lost profits and reimbursement of the fees paid to Jackson-Cross for its services.

Jackson-Cross filed preliminary objections in the nature of a demurrer to the complaint, which were overruled. In its answer and new matter, Jackson-Cross asserted, inter alia, that Wintoll's causes of action were barred by the doctrine of witness immunity. The immunity issue was then raised by Jackson-Cross in a motion for judgment on the pleadings. The motion was denied. Jackson-Cross renewed the issue in a motion for summary judgment, which was also denied. On June 7, 1996, an order was entered by the common pleas court denying reconsideration of the summary judgment motion.

On July 1, 1996, Jackson-Cross filed a second motion for summary judgment. Jackson-Cross asserted that (1) Wintoll's claim was non-justiciable because the federal action had been settled prior to a jury verdict; (2) Wintoll's settlement of the federal action severed the causal link between the striking of Seymour's testimony and the alleged damages; (3) the pro tanto release given by Wintoll to the additional defendant applied to Jackson-Cross as an agent; and (4) Wintoll had failed to state a claim for breach of contract. The second summary judgment motion was granted by order dated July 10, 1996. Judgment was entered in favor of Jackson-Cross and the case was dismissed.

On appeal, the Superior Court affirmed the order granting summary judgment on different grounds. The Superior Court concluded that the doctrine of witness immunity barred Wintoll's action against Jackson-Cross. We granted Wintoll's petition for allowance of appeal to address the issue of whether the doctrine of witness immunity extends to bar professional malpractice actions against professionals hired to perform services related to litigation.

Wintoll challenges the ruling of the Superior Court, asserting that the witness immunity doctrine should not be extended so as to bar professional malpractice actions against an expert retained by a party to litigation. Wintoll contends that privately retained and compensated experts should not be immunized from their own negligence, and that the policy concerns underlying the witness immunity doctrine are not advanced by extending immunity under such circumstances. Jackson-Cross asserts that the Superior Court's decision should be affirmed because it is based upon sound public policy.

In *Binder v. Triangle Publications, Inc.*, 442 Pa. 319, 275 A.2d 53 (Pa. 1971), we recognized, in the context of a defamation action, that participants in judicial proceedings have an absolute privilege for communications related to the proceedings.

> [S]tatements by a party, a witness, counsel, or a judge cannot be the basis of a defamation action whether they occur in the pleadings or in open court. The reasons for the absolute privilege are well recognized. A judge must be free to administer the law without fear of consequences. This independence would be impaired were he to be in daily apprehension of defamation suits. The privilege is also extended to parties to afford freedom of access to the courts, to witnesses to encourage their complete and unintimidated testimony in court, and to counsel to enable him to best represent his client's interests. Likewise, the privilege exists because the courts have other internal sanctions against defamatory statements, such a perjury or contempt proceedings.

See also *Post v. Mendel*, 510 Pa. 213, 507 A.2d 351, 354 (Pa. 1986) ("The origin of the rule was the great mischief that would result if witnesses in courts of justice were not at liberty to speak freely, subject only to the animadversion of the court. . . . The rule is inflexible that no action will lie for words spoken or written in the course of giving evidence.")

The United States Supreme Court addressed the policy concerns underlying the witness immunity doctrine in th oft-cited decision of *Briscoe v. LaHue*, 460 U.S. 325 (1983):

> The immunity of parties and witnesses from subsequent damages liability for their testimony in judicial proceedings was well established in English common law. Some American decisions required a showing that the witness' allegedly defamatory statements were relevant to the judicial proceeding, but once this threshold showing had been made, the witness had an absolute privilege. The plaintiff could not recover even if the witness knew the statements were false and made them with malice. In the words of one 19th-century court, in damages suits against witnesses, "the claims of the individual must yield to the dictates of public policy, which requires that the paths which lead to the ascertainment of truth should be left as free and unobstructed as possible." A witness' apprehension of subsequent damages liability

might induce two forms of self-censorship. First, witnesses might be reluctant to come forward to testify. And once a witness is on the stand, his testimony might be distorted by the fear of subsequent liability. Even within the constraints of the witness' oath there may be various ways to give an account or to state an opinion. These alternatives may be more or less detailed and may differ in emphasis and certainty. A witness who knows that he might be forced to defend a subsequent lawsuit, and perhaps to pay damages, might be inclined to shade his testimony in favor of the potential plaintiff, to magnify uncertainties, and thus to deprive the finder of fact of candid, objective, and undistorted evidence. But the truthfinding process is better served if the witness' testimony is submitted to "the crucible of the judicial process so that the factfinder may consider it, after cross-examination, together with the other evidence in the case to determine where the truth lies."

The witness immunity doctrine has been applied by the Superior Court in actions other than for defamation when the court has determined that the extension of immunity is in furtherance of the policy underlying the doctrine. See *Clodgo v. Bowman*, 411 Pa. Super. 267, 601 A.2d 342, 345 (Pa. Super. 1992), appeal granted, 532 Pa. 640, 614 A.2d 1138 (Pa. 1992), appeal dismissed as having been improvidently granted, 533 Pa. 352, 625 A.2d 612 (Pa. 1993), ("The form of the cause of action is not relevant to application of the privilege. Regardless of the tort contained in the complaint, if the communication was made in connection with a judicial proceeding and was material and relevant to it, the privilege applies.") *Moses v. McWilliams*, 379 Pa. Super. 150, 549 A.2d 950, 957 (Pa. Super. 1988) ("While it is true that immunity from civil liability in judicial proceedings has been applied most frequently in defamation actions, many courts, including those in Pennsylvania, have extended the immunity from civil liability to other alleged torts when they occur in connection with judicial proceedings.")

In this case, the Superior Court stated that it was required to analyze and decide the case in light of its decision in *Panitz v. Behrend*, 429 Pa. Super. 273, 632 A.2d 562 (Pa. Super. 1993), allocatur denied, 539 Pa. 694, 653 A.2d 1232 (Pa. 1994). *Panitz* involved a medical doctor who was retained by a law firm to provide services as an expert witness in a lawsuit by plaintiffs who alleged that they had suffered from formaldehyde in building materials. The law firm anticipated that the expert would be cross-examined about the lack of formaldehyde sensitization in cigarette smokers who regularly were exposed to much greater concentrations of formaldehyde than were the plaintiffs. Prior to trial, the expert provided the law firm with deposition transcripts from an unrelated case in which the expert had testified about the lack of sensitization in smokers.

At trial, the expert proffered her opinion that the plaintiffs' injuries had been caused by formaldehyde present in building materials. The expert conceded on cross-examination, however, that she could not explain the apparent inconsistency about the lack of sensitization in cigarette smokers. After trial, the expert indicated that she had realized before her testimony that her prior analysis of the lack of sensitization in cigarette smokers was inaccurate.

When a defense verdict was returned, the law firm refused to pay the expert for her services. The expert then brought an action to recover her fees. The law firm filed a counterclaim seeking damages resulting from the defense verdict, alleging negligence and misrepresentation regarding the expert's trial testimony. Preliminary objections to the counterclaim were sustained and the counterclaim was dismissed.

The Superior Court affirmed the order dismissing the counterclaim, finding that the expert was immune from liability for the testimony which she gave. The court found that the policy of encouraging witnesses to give frank and truthful testimony would be advanced by application of the witness immunity doctrine. The court reasoned that the primary purpose of expert testimony was to assist the factfinder in understanding complicated matters, rather than to assist one party in winning a case. "Having testified truthfully in the judicial process, a witness should not thereafter be subjected to civil liability for the testimony which he or she has given." 632 A.2d at 563. The Superior Court concluded that liability could not be imposed upon an expert who is persuaded on cross-examination by conflicting evidence that some or all of the expert's opinion testimony was inaccurate.

In this case, the Superior Court determined that *Panitz* was dispositive and concluded that the witness immunity doctrine bars Wintoll's professional negligence action against Jackson-Cross. We find *Panitz* to be distinguishable, however. In *Panitz*, the expert witness offered her opinion as to the cause of the plaintiffs' formaldehyde sensitization but testified during cross-examination that she could not explain the lack of such sensitization in cigarette smokers. The theories that the expert witness had previously articulated to explain the inconsistency had been discounted by the expert prior to trial. While the expert's testimony on cross-examination may have defeated the expectation of plaintiffs' counsel that she would be able to account for the inconsistency, the expert offered her opinion based upon her knowledge of formaldehyde sensitization.

It is imperative that an expert witness not be subjected to litigation because the party who retained the expert is dissatisfied with the substance of the opinion rendered by the expert. An expert witness must be able to articulate the basis for his or her opinion without fear that a verdict unfavorable to the client will result in litigation, even where the party who has retained the expert contends that the expert's opinion was not fully explained prior to trial. Application of the witness immunity doctrine in *Panitz* was consistent, therefore, with the two-fold policy of the doctrine: to ensure that the path to the truth is left as free and unobstructed as possible and to protect the judicial process.

We are unpersuaded, however, that those policy concerns are furthered by extending the witness immunity doctrine to professional negligence actions which are brought against an expert witness when the allegations of negligence are not premised on the substance of the expert's opinion. We perceive a significant difference between *Panitz* and Wintoll's claim in this case that Jackson-Cross had been negligent in performing the mathematical calculations required to determine lost profits. The goal of ensuring that the path to truth is unobstructed and the judicial process is protected, by fostering an atmosphere where the expert witness will be forthright and candid in stating his or her opinion, is not advanced by immunizing an expert witness from his or her negligence in formulating that opinion. The judicial process will be enhanced only by requiring that an expert witness render services to the degree of care, skill and proficiency commonly exercised by the ordinarily skillful, careful and prudent members of their profession.

Therefore, we find that the witness immunity doctrine does not bar Wintoll's professional malpractice action against Jackson-Cross. We caution, however, that our holding that the witness immunity doctrine does not preclude claims against an expert witness for professional malpractice has limited application. An expert witness may not be held liable merely because his or her opinion is challenged by another expert or authoritative source. In those circumstances, the judicial process is enhanced by the presentation of different views. Differences of opinion will not suffice to establish liability of an expert witness for professional negligence.

Accordingly, we reverse the order of the Superior Court and remand for disposition of the remaining issues.

CAPPY, JUSTICE, dissenting.

The majority premises its opinion largely on its conclusion that the situation presented in the matter sub judice is distinguishable from that with which the Superior Court was faced in *Panitz v. Behrend*, 429 Pa. Super. 273, 632 A.2d 562 (Pa. Super. Ct. 1993). The majority categorizes the suit filed against the expert witness in *Panitz* as one which attacked the "substance" of the expert's opinion; in contrast, the majority asserts that the suit in the matter presently before the court is premised on the allegation that the expert was "negligen[t] in formulating [his] opinion." The majority finds this distinction to be crucial. It concludes that while a suit may not be filed on the basis that the "substance" of an expert witness' testimony was unacceptable, an expert witness may be sued on the basis that the expert was negligent in formulating the opinion tendered at trial. In my opinion, the majority's attempts to distinguish *Panitz* ring hollow. Furthermore, I believe that the distinction formulated by the majority is an unworkable and radical departure from our accepted law regarding witness immunity. I therefore am compelled to dissent.

In the underlying lawsuit in *Panitz*, the expert witness, Elaine Panitz ("Panitz"), tendered her medical opinion on direct examination in favor of the plaintiffs; this was in accord with her pre-trial communications with the Behrend firm which represented the plaintiffs in the underlying lawsuit. On cross-examination, however, Panitz conceded that her opinion was inconsistent with the available scientific data. After trial, Panitz admitted that she had realized prior to trial that her pro-plaintiffs medical opinion was inaccurate; yet Panitz had failed to inform the Behrend firm that she had changed her opinion.

Contrary to the majority's characterization of Panitz, I believe that the lawsuit filed against Panitz was premised on the allegation that she had been negligent in formulating her opinion, and was not an attack on the substance of the opinion she offered on cross-examination. In fact, there is a lengthy discussion in the Superior Court opinion concerning the contention by the

Behrend firm in its suit against Panitz that "it was not the in-court testimony that caused the loss but the pre-trial representations about what the in-court testimony would be." *Panitz*, 632 A.2d at 565. Clearly, the Behrend firm sued Panitz premised upon Panitz's negligent failure to inform them that she had changed her opinion prior to trial; I see nothing in *Panitz* which would indicate that the Behrend firm sued Panitz on the basis that they somehow disagreed with the substance of her opinion.

Furthermore, I find that the test proposed by the majority is simply unworkable. In my opinion, there is no bright line between what constitutes an attack on the "substance" of an expert's opinion and what constitutes a challenge premised on the expert's negligence in formulating that opinion. I believe that there is a great gray area which lies between these two points, and distinguishing between them will be quite difficult. This difficulty has, in my opinion, been amply illustrated by the varying analyses of *Panitz* offered by the majority and by this author in the matter sub judice. I fear that by establishing this unworkable distinction, we will be sowing confusion in the lower courts and the practicing bar.

Rather than adopting such a test, I would continue to adhere to our established rule that there is no civil liability for statements made by witnesses in a legal proceeding. This straightforward rule advances the laudable and long-recognized policy goal of "encourag[ing] [the witness'] complete and unintimidated testimony in court. . . ." *Binder v. Triangle Publications, Inc.*, 442 Pa. 319, 275 A.2d 53, 56 (Pa. 1971). Furthermore, I agree with the position as ably stated by the Superior Court in *Panitz* that there "is no reason for refusing to apply the privilege to friendly experts hired by a party." *Panitz*, 632 A.2d at 565. "To allow a party to litigation to contract with an expert witness and thereby obligate the witness to testify only in a manner favorable to the party, on threat of civil liability, would be contrary to public policy." Id. at 565–66.

For the foregoing reasons, I respectfully dissent.

NOTES

1. *Absolute and Conditional Immunities*. It is generally held that legislators are absolutely immune from liability for tortious acts committed within the scope of their jurisdiction. *See* PROSSER ON TORTS § 132 (5th ed. 1984). *Sanchez v. Coxon*, 854 P.2d 126 (Ariz. 1993)

Absolute tort immunity is also widely extended to judicial officers acting within the scope of their jurisdiction. *See Stump v. Sparkman*, 98 S. Ct. 1099 (1978); *cf. Zarcone v. Perry*, 572 F.2d 52 (2d Cir. 1978). The exact scope of this immunity is not always clear. See *Wagshal v. Foster*, 28 F.3d 1249 (D.C. Cir. 1994), applying "absolute quasi-judicial immunity . . . to mediators and case evaluators in the Superior Court's [alternative dispute resolution] process."

Absolute immunity has been extended to prosecuting attorneys, *Knapper v. Connick*, 681 So. 2d 944 (La. 1996), and to public defenders, *Dziubak v. Mott*, 503 N.W. 2d 771 (Minn. 1993).

Courts widely hold that court witnesses are absolutely immune from civil liability for their testimony. *Panitz v. Behrend*, 632 A.2d 562 (Pa. Super. 1993). *But see Mattco Forge v. Arthur Young & Co.*, 5 Cal. App. 4th 392, 6 Cal. Rptr. 2d 781 (1992) (witness immunity did not apply to expert hired to "perform litigation support accounting work").

The president of the United States is absolutely immune from liability for torts committed while acting as president. *Nixon v. Fitzgerald*, 457 U.S. 731 (1981) (5-4 decision). *See Clinton v. Jones*, 117 S. Ct. 1636 (1997), holding that the president can be sued while in the presidential office for torts allegedly committed prior to taking such office.

Executive officers, however, do not enjoy absolute immunity. Federal officials "performing discretionary functions generally are shielded from liability for civil damages insofar as their conduct does not violate clearly established statutory or constitutional rights of which a reasonable person would have known." *Harlow v. Fitzgerald*, 102 S. Ct. 2727, 2738 (1982). A state executive officer is entitled to qualified immunity "dependent upon the scope of discretion and responsibilities of the office and all the circumstances as they reasonably appeared at the time of the action on which liability is sought to be based." *Scheuer v. Rhodes*, 94 S. Ct. 1683, 1692 (1974).

2. *Nonprofit Organizations and The Volunteer*.

Statutes similar to the following are not uncommon.

TENN. CODE ANN. § 48-58-601 (1995):

(b) The general assembly finds and declares that the services of nonprofit boards are critical to the efficient conduct and management of the public and charitable affairs of the citizens of this state. Members of such nonprofit boards must be permitted to operate without concern for the possibility of litigation arising from the discharge of their duties as policy makers.

(c) All directors, trustees or members of the governing bodies of nonprofit cooperatives, corporations, associations and organizations, . . . whether compensated or not, shall be immune from suit arising from the conduct of the affairs of such cooperatives, corporations, associations or organizations. Such immunity from suit shall be removed when such conduct amounts to willful, wanton or gross negligence.

Congress enacted the *Volunteer Protection Act of 1997*, 42 U.S.C. 14501. Unless the Act is expressly rejected by a state, the Act immunizes volunteers to nonprofit organizations or to governmental entities from negligence, § 4(a), if:

(1) the volunteer was acting within the scope of the volunteer's responsibilities in the nonprofit organization or governmental entity at the time of the act or omission;

(2) if appropriate or required, the volunteer was properly licensed, certified, or authorized by the appropriate authorities for the activities or practice in the State in which the harm occurred, where the activities were or practice was undertaken within the scope of the volunteer's responsibilities in the nonprofit organization or governmental entity;

(3) the harm was not caused by willful or criminal misconduct, gross negligence, reckless misconduct, or a conscious, flagrant indifference to the rights or safety of the individual harmed by the volunteer; and

(4) the harm was not caused by the volunteer operating a motor vehicle, vessel, aircraft, or other vehicle for which the State requires the operator or the owner of the vehicle, craft, or vessel to-

(A) possess an operator's license; or

(B) maintain insurance.

There are various exceptions to the Act, one being, § 4(d), if:

(4) A State law that makes a limitation of liability applicable only if the nonprofit organization or governmental entity provides a financially secure source of recovery for individuals who suffer harm as a result of actions taken by a volunteer on behalf of the organization or entity.

A volunteer is defined in the Act, § 6(6), as an individual who performs services for a nonprofit organization or a governmental entity without compensation "other than reasonable reimbursement or allowance for expenses actually incurred," and without receiving "any other thing of value in lieu of compensation, in excess of $500 per year, and such term includes a volunteer serving as a director, officer, trustee, or direct service volunteer."

3. *Hospital investigations.*

Hospitals usually conduct an internal investigation whenever they become aware of an incident in the hospital that could lead to tort liability on the part of the hospital or of someone connected with the hospital. States commonly grant a statutory privilege of confidentiality to the reports of any hospital committee that makes such an investigation. *See, e.g.,* TENN. CODE ANN. § 63-6-219(e) (1999). Are such immunities justified?

PROBLEM

Two subway cars owned and operated by the city of Old York collided with each other. Twelve people were killed and 93 were seriously injured; 210 persons eventually filed claims ranging from wrongful death to loss of consortium. The statute waiving governmental immunity limits recovery for personal injuries to $250,000 "per person" and $500,000 "per occurrence."

Is requiring all of the victims to share in one $500,000 award consistent with due process and equal protection of the laws? Note that in the absence of the statutory ceiling, it is likely that under the state's tort law some of the individuals have injuries that would entitle them to recoveries in excess of $2,000,000.

D. CHARITABLE IMMUNITY

In the mid-nineteenth century, American courts established the doctrine that a charity was immune from tort liability. The doctrine was based upon the English decision in *Feoffees of Heriot's Hosp. v. Ross*, 13 C & F 507, 8 Eng. Rep. 1508 (1846), which was repudiated in its own jurisdiction within a generation. *See Mersey Docks Trustees v. Gibbs*, 11 H.L. Cas. 686, 11 Eng. Rep. 1500 (1866); PROSSER AND KEETON ON TORTS, § 132 (5th ed. 1984). However, the doctrine persisted in America. One major justification probably was the fear that use of donated funds to pay tort judgments would greatly reduce charitable giving. Another justification was the perceived ingratitude of the charity patient who "bit the hand that fed him" by seeking tort damages. The argument also was offered that because a charity was performing a governmental function, it was entitled to the same immunity as the government enjoys from tort liability. By the twentieth century, however, conditions affecting the charitable immunity had changed greatly. When the doctrine arose, charitable hospitals were a major source of health care, open to all patients and funded primarily by donations. By the twentieth century, the state had become a major health care provider, and charitable donations were motivated as much by tax considerations as by any other reason. The ascendancy of the idea that fair spreading of the risks of negligent conduct is an important societal policy, and the ready availability of liability insurance, helped seal the fate of charitable immunity.

A substantial majority of jurisdictions have abolished charitable immunity. *Abernathy v. Sisters of St. Mary's*, 446 S.W.2d 599 (Mo. 1969). Other jurisdictions have limited the immunity to suits by beneficiaries of the charity. *See, e.g.,* N.J. STAT. ANN. §§ 2A:53A-7 and 53A-8 (West); *Kasten v. Y.M.C.A.*, 173 N.J. Super. 1, 412 A.2d 1346 (1980). Others have abolished the immunity to the extent the charitable defendant is covered by liability insurance. *O'Quin v. Baptist Mem. Hosp.*, 184 Tenn. 570, 201 S.W.2d 694 (1947); ME. REV. STAT. ANN. tit. 14, § 158 (West); RESTATEMENT (SECOND) OF TORTS § 895E comm. c. Some jurisdictions retain charitable immunity, either by common law rule, *Abramson v. Reiss*, 334 Md. 193, 638 A.2d 743 (1994), or by statute, *Monaghan v. Holy Trinity Church*, 275 N.J. Super. 594, 646 A.2d 1130 (1994).

E. FAMILY IMMUNITIES

CATES v. CATES
156 Ill. 2d 76, 619 N.E.2d 715 (1993)

FREEMAN, JUSTICE

On June 9, 1985, Heather Cates, aged 4 years, was a passenger in an automobile driven by her father, Timothy Cates. At the time, Cates was transporting his girlfriend, her minor son and Heather to his home for the evening. As Cates' auto approached an intersection of two State highways, it collided with an automobile driven by Phillip Darwin. Heather was seriously injured as a result of the accident. At the time of the incident, Cates was exercising his visitation privileges as a noncustodial parent.

Heather, as plaintiff, by her mother and next friend, Nancy Cates Schmittling, filed a negligence action in the circuit court of St. Clair County against Phillip Darwin's estate and Keeley and Sons, Inc., a construction company engaged in repairing the highway area around the collision site at the time of the accident. Heather subsequently amended her complaint, naming [her father] as an additional defendant and alleging that [her mother] had assigned to [her the mother's rights] against [her father] for medical expenses and other costs expended in Heather's behalf. State Farm Mutual Automobile Insurance Company, [the mother's] insurer, intervened as a subrogor against all defendants to recover uninsured motorist's benefits paid to [the mother] under her policy.

[Defendant] Cates filed a motion for summary judgment, alleging that the parent-child immunity doctrine precluded Heather's negligence action as well as the subrogation action. The trial court granted Cates' motion for summary judgment with respect to both actions, stating that "[i]t is difficult to determine that the purpose of the parental immunity doctrine would be served by applying it to the facts of this case," but that it was obliged to follow precedent. . . .

The court of appeals abolished parental immunity "in case of automobile negligence." The appellate court misperceived the effect of several of our pronouncements. We do not, however, reverse its decision. We must yet consider whether the parent-child tort immunity doctrine bars plaintiff's automobile negligence action.

Defendant argues that the parent-child tort immunity doctrine is long-standing in Illinois and recognized as applying in negligence cases by all appellate court districts. . . . Defendant argues that: (1) preservation of the parent-child relationship is recognized in Illinois as a worthy public policy goal; (2) the immunity's purpose is to protect parent and child from an opportunity to engage in fraud and collusion; (3) the elimination of the immunity will threaten parents' authority to discipline and control their children; (4) abrogation of the immunity would allow courts to second-guess the exercise of parental discretion in day-to-day family matters; (5) the doctrine as it stands applies to custodial and noncustodial parents; and (6) the immunity should be applied irrespective of the existence of liability insurance.

Plaintiff responds that the originally recognized policy bases for the immunity, the preservation of family harmony and prevention of collusion and fraud, do not sufficiently justify its application in automobile negligence cases. Plaintiff contends that an automobile negligence action brought by a very young child against her father does not disrupt family harmony where divorce has already occurred. Plaintiff further contends that it is the injury itself, and not the subsequent legal action to remedy those damages, which disrupts family harmony. Moreover, according to plaintiff, any possibility of collusion and fraud in such cases is easily overcome by resort to discovery, cross-examination, review of evidence and a heightened degree of skepticism. Plaintiff also argues that in this case fraud and collusion are virtually impossible because the extent of Heather's injuries are independently ascertainable. . . .

The parent-child tort immunity doctrine was unknown at English common law and arose in American case law as the result of three decisions, often termed "the great trilogy" (*Hewlett*, 68 Miss. 703, 9 So. 885 (married, minor child barred from suing mother for malicious imprisonment in insane asylum); *McKelvey v. McKelvey*, 111 Tenn. 388, 77 S.W. 664 (1903) (minor child barred from suing parent for cruel and inhumane punishment); *Roller v. Roller*, 37 Wash. 242, 79 P. 788 (1905) (minor child barred from suing father for rape)). These cases articulated several public policies to justify the immunity:

preservation of family harmony, preservation of parental authority to control children by way of analogy to spousal immunity, and the avoidance of a depletion of family assets to the detriment of the injured child's siblings (commonly referred to as the "family exchequer" rationale), *Dunlap v. Dunlap* (1930), 150 A. 905, 909, 84 N.H. 352, 361. Because most of the justifications for the immunity concerned the relationship of a parent to a minor child under his custody and control and for whose support he was responsible, the immunity did not generally apply to an adult child or emancipated minor children. Restatement (Second) of Torts § 895G, Comment d, at 428 (1979).

Despite the development of the immunity against parent-child tort litigation, both English and American common law has always allowed contract and property actions between parent and child. . . . Other nineteenth century authority indicates that prior to the immunity, children were allowed to sue their parents for both negligent and intentional torts. . . .

A sizeable number of jurisdictions (approximately 25) have fully abrogated the doctrine and applied a standard limiting parent-child liability by relying on either *Goller v. White* (1963), 20 Wis. 2d 402, 122 N.W.2d 193 (*Goller* standard), or *Gibson v. Gibson*, 3 Cal. 3d 914, 92 Cal. Rptr. 288, 479 P.2d 648 (1971) (reasonable parent standard). . . .

Under the *Goller* standard, a child may sue his parent for negligent conduct except where the conduct involves "an exercise of parental authority [or] an exercise of ordinary parental discretion with respect to the provision of food, clothing, housing, medical and dental services, and other care." *Goller*, 20 Wis. 2d at 413, 122 N.W.2d at 198. The first limitation embraces the area of parental discipline; and the second has been interpreted as concerning only the performance of legal duties and not moral duties, such as a duty to supervise. *Thoreson v. Milwaukee & Suburban Transport Co.*, 56 Wis. 2d 231, 246–47, 201 N.W.2d 745, 753 (1973). Arguably, under the *Goller* standard, a child could not sue his parent for a failure to maintain the family residence in some manner (for instance, a failure to secure carpeting).

In California, courts apply a reasonable parent standard to test the viability of all negligence actions between parent and child. *Gibson*, 3 Cal. 3d at 922, 479 P.2d at 653, 92 Cal. Rptr. at 293 ("what would an ordinarily reasonable and prudent parent have done in similar circumstances?"). And in New York, a child may sue his parent for negligent conduct except that a parent's failure to supervise the child is not recognized as an actionable tort; there exists no legal duty on the part of parents to supervise their children. *Holodook*, 36 N.Y.2d at 50–51, 324 N.E.2d at 346, 364 N.Y.S.2d at 871. . . .

In contrast, Illinois stands in that group of jurisdictions, a minority, which have partially abrogated the doctrine by carving out exceptions to it. The approach taken by Illinois and this group of jurisdictions, however, is considered problematic, as the law which develops is often inconsistent and arbitrary. . . .

Illinois courts have relied consistently on three major public policy considerations for the parent-child tort immunity doctrine: (1) the preservation of family harmony, (2) the discouragement of fraud and collusion, and (3) the preservation of parental authority and discipline. . . . Illinois courts have more consistently espoused the preservation of family harmony rationale. . . .

Yet, Illinois courts have narrowed the doctrine, by creating exceptions to it, where the doctrine's public purposes do not appear to be served. This court "modif[ied]" the immunity doctrine by recognizing an exception in an automobile accident case where willful and wanton misconduct was alleged. . . . *Nudd*, 7 Ill. 2d at 619, 131 N.E.2d 525. . . .

Illinois courts . . . have carved out additional exceptions to the immunity in the area of negligence. An exception to the immunity rule is now recognized where a child sues a deceased parent. *Johnson v. Myers*, 2 Ill. App. 3d 844, 277 N.E.2d 773 (1972) (when the family relationship is dissolved by death, the policy basis for the immunity doctrine ceases to exist as well); *but see Marsh v. McNeill*, 136 Ill. App. 3d 616, 622, 91 Ill. Dec. 249, 483 N.E.2d 595 (1985) (parent-child tort immunity barred wrongful death action by representative of deceased parents' estates against living daughter tortfeasor). Another exception allows children to sue grandparents. *Gulledge v. Gulledge*, 51 Ill. App. 3d 972, 10 Ill. Dec. 42, 367 N.E.2d 429 (1977) (rationale behind immunity loses persuasive force when family relations more distant than parent-child are involved). . . .

Illinois courts also reject application of the parent-child tort immunity doctrine as a bar to third-party contribution actions against allegedly negligent parents. . . .

Another exception allows a parent-child negligence action where the alleged duty is owed to the general public. *See Cummings v. Jackson*, 57 Ill. App. 3d 68, 14 Ill. Dec. 848, 372 N.E.2d 1127 (1978) (breach of duty owed to general public is not as disruptive of family unity as breach of duty owed to family members). This exception is in keeping with . . . the view that the immunity is insupportable as applied to conduct outside the parent-child relationship. It also suggests the confinement of the immunity to actions based on conduct constituting a breach of parental or family duties. . . .

. . . A public policy based on the principle of preserving family harmony necessarily argues against every kind of intrafamily litigation. The allowance of a variety of intrafamily negligence actions by exception reveals that the family harmony rationale, an apparently absolute principle, is in fact balanced against other considerations or is not as a practical matter, a viable consideration. . . . In truth, the traditional policy of family harmony is no longer viable. . . . The focus has shifted to a concern with preventing litigation concerning conduct intimately associated with the parent-child relationship. The exceptions consistently demonstrate that where the family relationship is dissolved or where that relationship has ceased to exist with respect to conduct giving rise to the injury, the immunity will not be applied. This is so because the immunity exists only to further the parent-child relationship, and where that relationship is not impacted, the policies supporting the doctrine lose their persuasive strength. . . . The exceptions themselves thereby tend to highlight the arbitrariness of the traditional underlying public policies.

Both the traditional family harmony and collusion rationales are accordingly diminished. If negligence actions between parent and child are maintainable where the alleged duty is owed to the general public or where the conduct is beyond the parental relationship, these policies offer little support. . . .

The notion that parent-child tort immunity promotes family harmony in the area of negligence, the justification most relied on, has now been largely discounted. Without exception, legal scholars recognize that, more often than not, it is the injury if anything which disrupts the family. (*See* 17 LOYO. U. CHI. L. J. at 307; Rooney & Rooney, *Parental Tort Immunity: Spare the Liability, Spoil the Parent*, 25 NEW ENG. L. REV. 1161, 1165 (1991). Providing a child an avenue to obtain redress of those injuries does not work against family harmony. Even in the small percentage of cases where a parent or child has no liability insurance and injuries are serious, or in the case where an older child would perhaps bring an action to challenge the parent's authority, the suit cannot preserve harmony which, apparently, does not exist; the law does not have that capacity. . . .

The impact of liability insurance on the traditional rationales for the immunity cannot be ignored. It is now generally recognized that the existence of liability insurance eliminates the actual adversity of parent and child in negligence actions. . . . Where liability insurance is present, the parent and child are only nominally adverse; the "real" defendant is the insurer. Further, negligence actions between parent and child are rarely brought, except in cases where insurance is present. This is not to say that liability should be allowed simply because liability insurance exists. We agree with defendant in that respect. Liability should be allowed where the reasons for its preclusion do not exist for whatever reason. The fact that liability insurance significantly undercuts a traditional basis for the rule is a reality, however, which must be considered by courts. . . .

The widespread existence of insurance and the resulting diminished adversity of parties impacts on the traditional policies against collusion and fraud. Defendant argues that the parent-child relationship is threatened by presenting it with an opportunity to collude and defraud. Numerous authorities have pointed out that even in cases where collusion and fraud may exist, our adversarial legal system, through its skilled attorneys, discovery, examinations and evidentiary reviews, is adequately equipped to deal with such problems and does so daily in other intrafamily litigations and areas of law. We believe this to be generally true. The stronger argument against this rationale is that it forms an insufficient basis to deny redress to a whole class of litigants. . . . A rule which seeks to incidentally attack fraud by withholding legal protection for all claimants, regardless of the justice of their claims, "employs a medieval technique which, however satisfying it may be to defendants, is scarcely in keeping with the acknowledged function of a modern legal system." Leflar & Sanders, *Mental Suffering and its Consequence—Arkansas Law*, 7 U. ARK. L. SCH. BULL. 43, 60 (1939).

The fact that our legislature has abolished the husband-wife tort immunity doctrine also demonstrates a reluctance to adhere to both the traditionally espoused bases for intrafamily immunities. . . . [Although] the two doctrines are fundamentally different, spousal immunity being based on the legal unity of husband and wife, each doctrine has been typically supported by the same public policies. . . .

Defendant argues that abolishing the immunity doctrine will allow divorced parents to utilize parent-child negligence litigation as a battlefield for their continuing animosities and to promote disharmony between a noncustodial parent and the child. This argument lacks merit. Divorced parents have not taken such advantage of negligence actions which are allowed based on the recognized exceptions to the immunity rule. Nor do divorced parents appear to have taken advantage of the absence of the immunity rule in third-party contribution situations.

Recognizing that a child's injury is more likely the cause of any family disharmony as opposed to the institution of a suit, defendant also argues that any suit thus serves to exasperate that existing disharmony and should therefore be disallowed. We disagree. If the injury has disharmonized the family, an action can potentially relieve it. Further, this argument harkens back to the original fiction that regardless of the apparent family disharmony, a suit makes things worse rather than better. . . .

. . . We are convinced that the immunity doctrine is supported today by other public policy concerns. Courts should not be involved in deciding matters between parent and child which concern decisions which those persons are uniquely equipped to make because of that relationship; to allow otherwise would unnecessarily and obtrusively inject courts into family matters which they are ill-equipped to decide. Such matters, by definition, involve parental discretion in discipline, supervision and care. We are also convinced that those underlying policies ought to determine the scope of the immunity. . . .

We believe the . . . appropriate inquiry . . . would not concern whether "family purposes" were furthered by a parent's conduct, but whether the alleged conduct concerns parental discretion in discipline, supervision and care of the child. . . . The immunity should afford protection to conduct inherent to the parent-child relationship; such conduct constitutes an exercise of parental authority and supervision over the child or an exercise of discretion in the provision of care to the child. These limited areas of conduct require the skills, knowledge, intuition, affection, wisdom, faith, humor, perspective, background, experience, and culture which only a parent and his or her child can bring to the situation; our legal system is ill-equipped to decide the reasonableness of such matters.

The standard we have thus developed focuses primarily on conduct inherent to the parent-child relationship, which conduct we describe by approximating the *Goller* standard without its enumerated duties. Such a standard is consistent with other jurisdictions which have abrogated the immunity in order to achieve greater clarity in the area of parent-child negligence. The standard we have created is not, however, as extreme because we do not fully abrogate the immunity, but rely on an exception. Our standard also allows a broader area of negligent conduct to remain immunized. Thus, under our standard, parental discretion in the provision of care includes maintenance of the family home, medical treatment, and supervision of the child. A child may attempt to sue a parent alleging that the child fell on a wet, freshly mopped floor in the home, but the immunity would bar such an action because the parent was exercising his discretion in providing and maintaining housing for the child.

We note as well that parents in Illinois must conform their treatment of their children within certain socially acceptable limits or face criminal and civil actions by the State. Such actions are instituted regardless of the fact that parental authority is thereby circumscribed. Further, there is no immunity as applied to the area of intentional torts. . . . There yet exists limits to parental authority beyond those recognized here.

In this case, we are asked to consider whether the immunity doctrine bars plaintiff's action which alleged the negligent operation of an automobile by a parent. Applying the standard we have created, we conclude that the negligent operation of an automobile is not conduct inherent in the parent-child relationship; such conduct does not represent a parent's decision-making in disciplining, supervising or caring for his child. . . . The duty which Cates owed in operating his vehicle on State highways was owed to the general public and not to Heather as his child. The negligent operation of a vehicle even when exercising visitation privileges does not constitute conduct inherent to the parent-child relationship. The parent-child tort immunity doctrine cannot be applied to bar a negligence action alleging such conduct.

We disagree with defendant's argument that eliminating the immunity in automobile negligence cases will threaten parental authority to discipline children or inject courts into matters concerning the exercise of parental discretion. A child's action against her father for the negligent operation of an automobile does not usurp the father's authority to discipline her. Neither does such action allow a court to second-guess the father's exercise of discretion in day-to-day matters which bear on the parent-child relationship. . . .

In sum, the parent-child tort immunity doctrine developed in an era which was vastly different from the present; our society has changed in myriad and countless ways. The parent-child relationship has been both beneficially and detrimentally affected by these changes. We seek in this instance to uphold and preserve that which forms an integral component of that relationship, parental authority and discretion. Yet, we must also consider the very real needs to our children in today's world. In this regard, we are mindful that the parent-child tort immunity doctrine was created by the courts and it is especially for them to interpret and modify the doctrine to correspond with prevailing public policy and social needs. . . .

Affirmed.

NOTES

1. *Abrogation of Parental Immunity*: The most effective argument in favor of parental immunity may be its antiquity. *See, e.g., Winn v. Gilroy*, 61 Or. App. 243, 656 P.2d 386 (1983). Notwithstanding, more than half of the states have abrogated the parental immunity from the children's claims. Some such abrogations have been partial: no immunity from intentional torts, *Federhoff v. Federhoff*, 473 S.W.2d 978 (Tex. 1971), or from "willful, wanton or reckless conduct," *Attwood v. Estate of Attwood*, 276 Ark. 230, 633 S.W.2d 366 (1982), or from gross negligence, *Rodebaugh v. Grand Trunk W.R.R.*, 4 Mich. App. 559, 145 N.W.2d 401 (1966); no immunity after death of parent or child, *MFA Mut. Ins. Co. v. Howard Const. Co.*, 608 S.W.2d 535 (Mo. App. 1980), or the emancipation of the child, *Carriceto v. Carriceto*, 384 S.W.2d 85 (Ky. 1964); no immunity in action for wrongful death of other parent, *Harlan Nat'l Bank*

v. Gross, 346 S.W.2d 482 (Ky. 1961); no immunity to persons *in loco parentis*, such as a stepparent, *Gillett v. Gillett*, 168 Cal. App. 102, 335 P.2d 736 (1959); no immunity to a divorced parent who does not have custody of the child, *Fugate v. Fugate*, 582 S.W.2d 663 (Mo. 1979), or to a deceased parent, *Davis v. Smith*, 126 F. Supp. 497 (E.D. Pa. 1954); no immunity in automobile cases, *Nocktonick v. Nocktonick*, 227 Kan. 758, 611 P.2d 135 (1980); *Jilani v. Jilani*, 767 S.W.2d 671 (Tex. 1988), particularly if the parent is driving while intoxicated, *Winn v. Gilroy*, 296 Or. 718, 681 P.2d 776 (1984); no immunity to the extent the parent is protected by liability insurance, *Williams v. Williams*, 369 A.2d 669 (Del. 1976); *Ard v. Ard*, 414 So. 2d 1066 (Fla. 1982).

A number of states, as in the principal case, abolish parental immunity except in the case of the exercise of parental authority, supervision, or care and custody. *Broadwell v. Holmes*, 871 S.W.2d 471 (Tenn. 1994). Others abolish the immunity entirely. *See Broadbent v. Broadbent*, 907 P.2d 43 (Ariz. 1995).

2. *Minority v. Majority*. Recall the statement in *Cates* that parental immunity generally does not apply to an adult child. Recall also that the tort statute of limitations is usually tolled while a child is a minor. Could a minor, who is injured during minority by an immune parent, sue the parent upon reaching majority? Does the answer to this question depend on whether the minor is described as having an action tolled by minority, or as having no action at all? *See* 2 HARPER, JAMES AND GRAY, THE LAW OF TORTS § 8.11 fn 7. If the child could possibly sue after reaching majority, what does this possibility do to the rationale for retaining parental immunity?

3. *Contribution and Supervision.* While a child may not have an action against her parent for negligent supervision, see *Holodook v. Spencer*, 36 N.Y.2d 35, 364 N.Y.S.2d 859, 324 N.E.2d 338 (1974), a third-party sued by the child may have a claim for contribution against the parent for negligent supervision of the child, *see Nolechek v. Gesuale*, 46 N.Y.2d 332, 413 N.Y.S.2d 340, 385 N.E.2d 1268 (1978). Not all courts would allow such a third party claim.

4. *En Ventre sa Mere*. With the waiver of parental immunity, should the mother be subject to tort liability for her conduct while the child is in her womb? *Compare Bonte v. Bonte*, 136 N.H. 286, 616 A.2d 464 (1992), *with Stallman v. Youngquist*, 125 Ill. 2d 267, 531 N.E.2d 355 (1988).

5. *Parent Versus Child*. Are the same considerations present in determining whether a child can sue a parent, as in determining whether a parent can sue a child? The Restatement would draw no distinction, except for the caveat that the repudiation of the immunity "does not establish liability for an act or omission that, because of the parent-child relationship, is otherwise privileged or is not tortious." RESTATEMENT (SECOND) OF TORTS § 895G.

6. *Sibling Immunity*. RESTATEMENT (SECOND) OF TORTS § 895H states: "Brothers and sisters or other kin are not immune from tort liability to one another by reason of that relationship." Why should the sibling or other kin relationship be treated differently from the parent-child relationship?

7. *The Decline of Interspousal Immunity*. The doctrine of interspousal immunity has been totally abrogated in more than half the states. *See, e.g., Heino*

v. Harper, 306 Or. 347, 759 P.2d 53 (1988); *Davis v. Davis*, 657 S.W.2d 753 (Tenn. 1983). However, it has been reaffirmed in some states. *See Raisen v. Raisen*, 379 So. 2d 352 (Fla. 1979); *Price v. Price*, 732 S.W.316 (Tex. 1987). Some jurisdictions have only partially abrogated the immunity, for example, permitting suit if the tortfeasor-spouse's conduct is intentional or outrageous, *Lusby v. Lusby*, 283 Md. 334, 390 A.2d 77 (1978), or in motor vehicle accident cases. *Surratt v. Thompson*, 212 Va. 191, 183 S.E.2d 200 (1971); *Digby v. Digby*, 120 R.I. 299, 388 A.2d 1 (1978).

Where there is no interspousal immunity, what should be the result if the husband brings an action against the wife for damages he sustains because she provides unwholesome food at the family dinner table? Negligently invests the family savings? Can we draw a meaningful distinction between negligent spouse-injuring activities "within the family circle" and "in the outside world?" Consider the Restatement's position on these issues:

§ 895F. *Husband and Wife*

> (1) A husband or wife is not immune from tort liability to the other solely by reason of that relationship.
>
> (2) Repudiation of general tort immunity does not establish liability for an act or omission that, because of the marital relationship, is otherwise privileged or is not tortious.

Abrogating the absolute defense of interspousal immunity in tort actions, the Minnesota Supreme Court observed that:

> There is an intimate sharing of contact within the marriage relationship, both intentional and unintentional, that is uniquely unlike the exposure among strangers. The risks of intentional contact in marriage are such that one spouse should not recover damages from the other without substantial evidence that the injurious contact was plainly excessive or a gross abuse of normal privilege. The risks of negligent conduct are likewise so usual that it would be an unusual case in which the trial court would not instruct the jury as to the injured spouse's peculiar assumption of risk.

Beaudette v. Frana, 285 Minn. 366, 173 N.W.2d 416 (1969).

What if the tort occurs before, but the claim is brought against the spouse after the marriage? The cases permit recovery. *See Mouton v. Mouton*, 309 A.2d 224 (Me. 1973).

What if the tort occurs during the marriage, but the marriage subsequently is dissolved by death? By divorce? If a spouse is immune from tort liability to the other spouse, then theoretically the tort does not arise, and the subsequent dissolution of the marriage cannot revive it. However, if the immunity does not prevent the tort from arising, but merely bars enforcement during the marriage, then the victim spouse arguably may maintain the action after the dissolution of the marriage.

8. *Insurance Considerations.* In most states the victim may not bring a direct action against the tortfeasor's liability insurer, but first must obtain judgment against the tortfeasor. If the insured tortfeasor is immune, then the victim

is unable to obtain the judgment that triggers the insurer's liability. If there is no immunity, there is a danger of collusion between the spouses to obtain recovery from the insurer. About one fifth of the states permit a direct action by the tort victim against the insurer. If the interspousal immunity prevents the tort from arising, then the victim should not be able to recover against the insurer. However, if the immunity only bars suit, can the spouse-victim recover from the liability insurer in a direct action? *See, e.g., Soirez v. Great American Ins. Co.*, 168 So. 2d 418 (La. App. 1964), permitting suit against the liability insurer. A court which permits a direct action against the liability insurer of an immune spouse may describe the immunity as "personal" between the spouses. Is this a reason, or a conclusory statement?

Some liability policies exclude coverage for suits between spouses. Is such an exclusion against a state's public policy? *See, e.g., American Family Mut. v. Ward*, 789 S.W.2d 791 (Mo. 1990) (explicit provision of an automobile liability policy excluding coverage for injuries to a person related to the operator of the vehicle does not violate public policy). *See also Bishop v. Allstate*, 623 S.W.2d 865 (Ky. 1981); *Allstate v. Farmers Mut.*, 444 N.W.2d 676 (Neb. 1989).

Chapter 12
JOINT AND SEVERAL LIABILITY, CONTRIBUTION, INDEMNITY, AND SETTLEMENTS

A. INTRODUCTION

Joint liability arises when two or more persons are liable to the same victim for the same damages. This situation typically arises: (1) in vicarious liability, where the employer is vicariously liable for the employee's tort committed in the course and scope of employment; (2) in a chain of product distribution, where a manufacturing seller and a nonmanufacturing seller of the same defective product are jointly liable for damages caused by the product; (3) where two or more persons act in concert, or in conspiracy, to cause injury to another; and (4) where the concurrent acts of two or more tortfeasors cause what is for practical purposes a single, indivisible injury. Joint liability affecting tort obligations also may arise by contract, such as liability insurance and contractual indemnity. Joint liability frequently is referred to as joint and several liability, signifying that jointly liable parties can be sued severally, or separately. Where two or more tortfeasors are jointly liable, each is responsible for the plaintiff's total compensatory damages. Although the plaintiff can collect such damages only once, she may collect all or part of them from any one or more of the tortfeasors. Tortfeasors whose conduct causes the same damage to the same victim but who are not jointly liable are severally liable, i.e., each is liable only for his or her share of the victim's damages.

There has been a notable tendency to abolish or limit joint liability in those cases in which the concurrent acts of two or more tortfeasors cause a single injury. The rationale of legislatures, and sometimes of courts, in doing so is that a defendant should not be liable for more than those damages caused by his or her own causal fault. This rationale has been supported by the widespread adoption of comparative fault; the reasoning is that if a tortfeasor is not liable for the plaintiff's fault, why should she be liable for another tortfeasor's fault? The rationale has been applied, however, even where the plaintiff is free of fault.

Where judgment is rendered against joint tortfeasors, the plaintiff may recover all of his or her damages from any one of them. A tortfeasor who pays the plaintiff more than that tortfeasor's share of the judgment may be able to recover the amount paid in excess of his share from other joint tortfeasors, either through equitable indemnity or contribution. Where one of the joint tortfeasors settles with the plaintiff before judgment, a number of additional issues arise.

If the settlement "satisfies" the plaintiff's claim, i.e., plaintiff surrenders any rights against the joint tortfeasors, the settling tortfeasor may be entitled to equitable indemnity or contribution from the other joint tortfeasors, if the settlement is deemed fair. Usually, however, the settlement will only partially "satisfy" the plaintiff, who will reserve his or her rights against the nonsettling tortfeasors. The settlement agreement in such a case usually will protect the settling tortfeasor from contribution or equitable indemnity claims by the nonsettling joint tortfeasors. Where a partial satisfaction occurs and the plaintiff proceeds to trial against the nonsettling tortfeasors, they are entitled to a credit against any judgment for plaintiff, either for the amount paid in settlement or to the extent that the settlement deprived them of any contribution or indemnity claim against the settling tortfeasor.

The settlement is normally not admissible to prove liability or nonliability, but it may be admissible to show bias or prejudice of a witness. If the settlement is conditioned on the outcome of the litigation against a co-defendant, it may be admissible in any event or it may be invalid as against public policy.

A settlement may as a matter of law release a non-settling tortfeasor entirely if the non-settler is an indemnitee. If a settlement agreement is fairly construed as releasing a non-settler, the non-settler may have no further liability, at least to the plaintiff.

Claims for contribution normally do not exist if the tortfeasors are severally, rather than jointly, liable. Each such tortfeasor is liable only for his portion of the damages.

Punitive damages normally are imposed severally, rather than jointly, so that no contribution or indemnity for such damages is permitted. Indeed, an intentional tortfeasor may not be able to recover either contribution or indemnity, even for compensatory damages, from another joint tortfeasor, apparently on the ground that an intentional wrongdoer should not as a matter of policy be able to invoke the equitable remedy of contribution or indemnity.

B. JOINT AND SEVERAL LIABILITY

PROBLEM

Fred Flash left the keys in the ignition of his new red sports car for a minute while he entered the office of a self-service gas station to pay for a gasoline purchase. Bob Bold, 17 years of age, happened by and could not resist taking a "joy ride" in Fred's car. Accompanied by his 10-year-old brother, Tim, Bob drove at speeds ranging as high as 70 mph on city streets until he crashed into another automobile driven by Martha Madd, seriously injuring her and totally destroying her automobile. Tim also suffered serious physical injuries. This was the fourth time Bob had stolen a car and had been involved in an accident while driving it. Each time his parents had paid for the damages quickly in an effort to avoid the matter being reported to their insurance company or to the police.

Martha and Tim want to collect the entire amount of their damages from Fred Flash because they consider him the most culpable for leaving his keys in the car. Will they be permitted to do so?

GLOMB v. GLOMB
366 Pa. Super. 206, 530 A.2d 1362 (1987)

MONTEMURO, JUDGE.

Appellants John and Marie Glomb challenge the denial of their post-trial motions. A jury found that the Glombs had negligently hired and retained appellee Sherry Ginosky to care for the Glombs' one-year-old daughter, appellee Tia Marie Glomb. Tia Marie, through her guardian ad litem, instituted this action against her parents, who in turn joined Ms. Ginosky as an additional defendant. We address two issues on appeal: (1) whether the trial court properly refused to allow the jury to apportion liability between the Glombs and Ms. Ginosky; and (2) whether the $1.5 million jury verdict in favor of Tia Marie was excessive. None of the Glombs' arguments on these issues convince us that we should disturb the judgment of the Beaver County Court of Common Pleas. We therefore affirm.

The evidence at trial established the following facts. Tia Marie is the only child of John and Marie Glomb. At the time of Tia Marie's birth, both John and Marie worked full-time. John's employment required him to travel away from home up to six days a week. Marie worked Monday through Friday from 7:00 in the morning until 5:30 or 6:00 in the evening. The Glombs therefore employed baby-sitters to provide in-home care for Tia Marie during the work week. Sometime during the summer of 1982, Tia Marie's second baby-sitter quit on short notice because of ill health. In need of an immediate replacement, the Glombs hurriedly hired Sherry Ginosky at the beginning of August, 1982. Within two or three weeks, the Glombs began to notice problems. Small bruise marks appeared on Tia Marie's face and body. When asked about the marks, Ms. Ginosky would offer explanations that John Glomb found implausible. On one occasion, John observed that his daughter seemed afraid of Ms. Ginosky. After the Glombs discovered a large, hand-shaped bruise on Tia Marie's leg in late October of 1982, John threatened to discharge Ms. Ginosky if any more bruises appeared. Two days after this warning, however, Tia Marie suffered grave injuries to her face and head while in the care of Ms. Ginosky. The paramedics whom Ms. Ginosky summoned to the Glomb residence on the morning of November 3, 1982 found the child unconscious. Ms. Ginosky explained that Tia Marie had tripped over a toy and struck her head on a child's rocking chair. While unconscious, Tia Marie experienced periodic seizures during which she stopped breathing. Her face and head were severely bruised, and she remained in the hospital for nearly two weeks. Since her discharge from the hospital, Tia Marie has required extensive physical rehabilitation to remedy the effects of the brain damage she suffered. The parties agree that Sherry Ginosky intentionally inflicted these injuries upon her charge.

As a result of the November 3, 1982 incident, the court appointed a guardian ad litem for Tia Marie. The guardian filed a complaint on Tia Marie's behalf against John and Marie Glomb. The Glombs immediately joined Ms. Ginosky as a third party defendant. Following a trial at which Ms. Ginosky was neither present nor represented by counsel, the trial court directed the jury to find that Ms. Ginosky had "intentionally injured" Tia Marie and that the Glombs therefore "are entitled to indemnification" from Ms. Ginosky. The court refused, however, to instruct the jury on apportionment of liability between Ms. Ginosky and the Glombs. At sidebar, the court informed counsel that the Glombs could seek "indemnification" from Ms. Ginosky in a separate proceeding if the Glombs ultimately bore the burden of satisfying a judgment.

The jury returned with a $1.5 million verdict against both the Glombs and Ms. Ginosky, jointly and severally. The trial court denied the Glombs' motions for post-trial relief, and this timely appeal followed the entry of judgment. Although a three-judge panel of this court decided to affirm the judgment, we granted the Glombs' petition for reargument before the court en banc.

. . . As this case clearly illustrates, a decision to impose "joint and several" liability upon multiple tort-feasors, rather than to "apportion" liability between them, can alter significantly the risks of tort litigation. Imposition of joint and several liability enables the injured party to satisfy an entire judgment against any one tort-feasor, even if the wrongdoing of that tort-feasor contributed only a small part to the harm inflicted. Apportionment of liability, on the other hand, limits the liability of each tort-feasor to that portion of the harm which he or she caused. Thus, if the court imposes joint and several liability, and if only one of the joint tort-feasors is financially responsible, the injured party can attempt to recover the full measure of damages against that single source. The financially responsible tort-feasor who satisfies more than his or her equitable share of the joint liability then bears the risk of recovering the excess from his or her less responsible fellow tort-feasors. If, however, the court decided to apportion liability, the *injured party* bears the risk that the financial irresponsibility of one tort-feasor will defeat a complete recovery. By asserting that the court should apportion liability, the Glombs seek to avoid the risk that Ms. Ginosky, their fellow tort-feasor, will lack the resources to satisfy her share of the $1.5 million verdict.

A court can direct the apportionment of liability among distinct causes only when the injured party suffers distinct harms or when the court is able to identify "a reasonable basis for determining the contribution of each cause to a single harm." Restatement (Second) of Torts § 433A(1) (1965). In the present case, the parties agree that Tia Marie has suffered a single harm. The availability of apportionment therefore hinges upon whether the party who seeks it can demonstrate some logical, reasonable or practical basis for assigning discrete portions of the over-all liability to discrete causes. Determining whether a "logical, reasonable or practical" basis for apportionment exists necessarily requires the court to consider the unique circumstances of each case. Although most single personal injuries defy objective apportionment, *see Capone v. Donovan,* 332 Pa. Super. 185, 480 A.2d 1249, 1251 (1984), we should not allow one party to bear an entire liability if the particular facts of the case will support a reasonable alternative. On the other hand, we cannot allow an arbitrary apportionment merely to avoid imposition of entire liability. A court should not limit the innocent plaintiff's ability to recover the full measure of damages unless the court has some reasonable basis for doing so. See Restatement (Second) of Torts § 433A comments h and i. . . .

The negligence of the Glombs worked in tandem with the deliberate misconduct of Ms. Ginosky to cause a single harm to Tia Marie. Although the Glombs did not act in concert with Ms. Ginosky, they acted concurrently with her. Their ongoing neglect of Tia Marie's welfare facilitated the ultimate infliction of the actionable harm. This case therefore differs from such cases in which one party adds to or aggravates an injury already caused by another party. Had the Glombs heeded the signs of danger, they could have averted the harm altogether. Moreover, had Ms. Ginosky not acted upon the opportunity that the Glombs created, the Glombs' breach of duty would have constituted *injuria absque damno,* a mere legal wrong without loss or damage. The drafters of the Restatement (Second) of Torts recognized that a court cannot direct apportionment between a party whose misconduct facilitates the infliction of a harm and a party who actually inflicts that harm:

> One defendant may create a situation upon which the other may act later to cause the harm. One may leave combustible material, and the other set it afire; one may leave a hole in the street, and the other drive into it. Whether there is liability in such a case may depend upon the effect of the intervening agency as a superseding cause . . . *but if the defendant is liable at all, he is liable for the entire indivisible harm which he has caused.*

Restatement (Second) of Torts § 433A comment i (emphasis added). The facilitative negligence of the Glombs in the present case is akin to the facilitative negligence of the party who leaves combustible material for another to ignite.

In *Wade v. S. J. Groves & Sons Co.,* 283 Pa. Super. 464, 424 A.2d 902 (1981), we refused to apportion damages under circumstances analogous to those in the present case. The defendant landowners in *Wade* had permitted the co-defendant contractor to use their property as a landfill. During heavy rainfall, waste from the landfill washed onto the plaintiff's adjoining property. We reversed the trial court's decision to apportion ten percent of the resulting liability to the landowners and ninety percent to the contractor. We observed that the landowners "did not cause ten percent or any other reasonably identifiable percentage of the dirt or fill to be deposited on the [plaintiff's] land" and that the court therefore lacked a reasonable basis for the apportionment.

NOTES

1. *Concurrent Tortfeasors.* The *Glomb* case represents the typical situation for imposition of joint liability, *i.e.*, where the tortious conduct of two or more tortfeasors concurs to produce what is essentially an indivisible injury. Tort "reformers" have most notably sought to do away with joint liability in this situation.

2. *Concert of Activity.* Where two or more persons consciously act together to commit a tort, the common law has classically applied joint liability to the actors. *See, e.g., Bierczynsky v. Rogers,* 239 A.2d 218 (Del. Super. 1968) (automobile race). This is so even though the resulting damages are practically divisible. A Latin maxim is used to describe such joint action: *qui facit per alium facit per se* (he who acts through another acts himself). RESTATEMENT (SECOND) OF TORTS § 876 (1979) provides that a person is liable for the tortuous acts of another if he:

(a) does a tortuous act in concert with the other or pursuant to a common design with him, or

(b) knows that the other's conduct constitutes a breach of duty and gives substantial assistance or encouragement to the other so to conduct himself, or

(c) gives substantial assistance to the other in accomplishing a tortuous result and his conduct, separately considered, constitutes a breach of duty to the third person.

Should the tort reformers attempt to abolish joint liability in the case of concerted activity? Why?

3. *Vicarious Liability*. Reconsider Chapter 9 on vicarious liability. This is also a classic situation for imposing joint liability upon the servant who is actually at fault, and upon the master who is vicariously liable for the servant's fault. The principle is most commonly applied to impose liability upon a corporation for the tortuous acts of its employees acting within the scope of their employment. The principle also would impose liability upon a principal for the negligence of an independent contractor performing a nondelegable duty. Should this be a subject for tort reform?

4. *Successive Tortfeasors*. Ordinarily, successive tortfeasors cause separate harms and the law treats their acts as separate torts. Often, however, the otherwise unrelated conduct of the successive tortfeasors impacts upon the same victim at different times but causes or enhances the same harm. In such a case, the first tortfeasor may be liable for all of the damages if the second tortfeasor's conduct was within the scope of the risks of the first tortfeasor's conduct. The classic example is when a health care provider negligently treats a victim's tort injury. There courts generally hold the original tortfeasor for the increased injury. *See Doyle v. Piccadilly Cafeterias*, 576 So. 2d 1143 (La. App. 1991). But what if successive conduct, not within the scope of the risks of either tortfeasor's conduct, produces an indivisible harm? Courts sometime "divide" the indivisible harm. *See, e g. Hess v. Sports Publishing Co.*, 520 So. 2d 472 (La. App. 1988).

5. *Where Grounds of Liability Differ*. The Glombs in *Glomb v. Glomb* were guilty of negligence, while the babysitter was guilty of an intentional tort. The Glombs argued they should not be held jointly liable with the babysitter because the grounds of liability differed. The court rejected this argument, relying on *Svetz for Svetz v. Land Tool Co.*, 355 Pa. Super. 230, 513 A.2d 403 (1986). There, after plaintiff's deceased was killed in a motorcycle accident, plaintiff sued the manufacturer of the helmet that the deceased was wearing, alleging that the manufacturer was strictly liable for selling a defective helmet which was allegedly a substantial cause of the deceased's death. The court held it was proper to join in the suit as joint tortfeasors the tavern keeper who allegedly negligently served the deceased alcoholic beverages before the accident, and another motorcyclist who was racing with the decedent at the time of the accident.

PROBLEM

A municipal bus crossed the center line of the highway and hit a car head-on, killing the driver of the car. Evidence showed that the bus driver was intoxicated at the time of the accident. Should the municipality be held liable to the deceased's estate for compensatory and punitive damages?

McINTYRE v. BALENTINE
833 S.W.2d 52 (Tenn. 1992)

DROWOTA, JUSTICE.

In this personal injury action, we granted Plaintiff's application for permission to appeal in order to decide whether to adopt a system of comparative fault in Tennessee. . . . We now replace the common law defense of contributory negligence with a system of comparative fault. . . .

In the early morning darkness of November 2, 1986, Plaintiff Harry Douglas McIntyre and Defendant Clifford Balentine were involved in a motor vehicle accident resulting in severe injuries to Plaintiff. The accident occurred in the vicinity of Smith's Truck Stop in Savannah, Tennessee. As Defendant Balentine was traveling south on Highway 69, Plaintiff entered the highway (also traveling south) from the truck stop parking lot. Shortly after Plaintiff entered the highway, his pickup truck was struck by Defendant's Peterbilt tractor. At trial, the parties disputed the exact chronology of events immediately preceding the accident.

Both men had consumed alcohol the evening of the accident. After the accident, Plaintiff's blood alcohol level was measured at .17 percent by weight. Testimony suggested that Defendant was traveling in excess of the posted speed limit.

Plaintiff brought a negligence action against Defendant Balentine. Defendant answered that Plaintiff was contributorily negligent, in part due to operating his vehicle while intoxicated. After trial, the jury returned a verdict stating: "We, the jury, find the plaintiff and the defendant equally at fault in this accident; therefore, we rule in favor of the defendant.". . .

(T)oday's holding renders the doctrine of joint and several liability obsolete. Our adoption of comparative fault is due largely to considerations of fairness: the contributory negligence doctrine unjustly allowed the entire loss to be borne by a negligent plaintiff, notwithstanding that the plaintiff's fault was minor in comparison to defendant's. Having thus adopted a rule more closely linking liability and fault, it would be inconsistent to simultaneously retain a rule, joint and several liability, which may fortuitously impose a degree of liability that is out of all proportion to fault.

Further, because a particular defendant will henceforth be liable only for the percentage of a plaintiff's damages occasioned by that defendant's negligence, situations where a defendant has paid more than his "share" of a judgment will no longer arise, and therefore the Uniform Contribution Among Tort-feasors Act, T.C.A. §§ 29-11-101 to 106 (1980), will no longer determine the apportionment of liability between codefendants.

Fourth, fairness and efficiency require that defendants called upon to answer allegations in negligence be permitted to allege, as an affirmative defense, that a nonparty caused or contributed to the injury or damage for which recovery is sought. In cases where such a defense is raised, the trial court shall instruct the jury to assign this nonparty the percentage of the total negligence for which he is responsible. However, in order for a plaintiff to recover a judgment against such additional person, the plaintiff must have made a timely amendment to his complaint and caused process to be served on such additional person. Thereafter, the additional party will be required to answer the amended complaint. The procedures shall be in accordance with the Tennessee Rules of Civil Procedure. . . .

NOTES

1. *Retrenchment by the McIntyre Court.* In three decisions issued on the same date, the Tennessee Supreme Court substantially retrenched the several liability holding of *McIntyre*. In *Camper v. Minor*, 915 S.W.2d 437 (Tenn. 1996), the court held that the owner of a car was vicariously liable under the automobile family purpose doctrine for the tort of the car's user. In *Owens v. Truckstops of America, Inc.*, 915 S.W.2d 420 (Tenn. 1996), the court held that joint and several liability applied to all strictly liable product suppliers in the chain of distribution. In *Ridings v. Ralph M. Parsons Co.*, 914 S.W.2d 79 (Tenn. 1996), the court held that a tortfeasor was not entitled to allocate fault to an immune party (in this case, plaintiff's employer). Later, in *Brown v. Wal-Mart*, 12 S.W. 3d 785 (Tenn. 2000), the court said fault could not be allocated to an unidentifiable tortfeasor. In *Turner v. Jordan*, 957 S.W. 2d 815 (Tenn. 1997), the court refused to apportion fault to a foreseeable intentional tortfeasor. But, reversing this trend, the court held fault could be allocated to an immune state-employee tortfeasor, *Carroll v. Whitney*, 29 S.W. 3d 14 (Tenn. 2000), and to a tortfeasor against whom a statute of repose had run, *Dotson v. Blake*, 29 S.W. 3d 26 (Tenn. 2000).

2. *Joint and Several Versus Several Liability.* The advent of comparative negligence has prompted a change in joint liability for joint tortfeasors, particularly concurrent joint tortfeasors. The state of the law in 1994 was summed up in *The Preliminary Materials* (2 June 1994) for the proposed RESTATEMENT OF THE LAW OF TORTS: APPORTIONMENT OF LIABILITY, pp. 21–23:

> The states are scattered all over the board on joint and several liability. I should note that the information that follows is accurate as best as I can tell. Some states have sufficiently complicated rules about joint and several liability that they are difficult to categorize.
>
> The four states that retain contributory negligence as an absolute bar to the plaintiff's recovery still use full joint and several liability.
>
> Of the forty-six states that have adopted some form of percentage allocation scheme, nine use full joint and several liability (Arkansas, Delaware, Maine, Massachusetts, Michigan, Pennsylvania, Rhode Island, South Carolina, and Wisconsin).
>
> Eight states never use joint and several liability (Alaska, Georgia, Kansas, Kentucky, Tennessee, Utah, Vermont, and Wyoming).
>
> One state (Indiana) says it does not use joint and several liability, but other authority casts doubt on the issue.
>
> One state (Oklahoma) does not use joint and several liability unless the plaintiff is totally innocent.

Six states (Arizona, Colorado, Idaho, Nevada, New Mexico, and Washington) do not use joint and several liability except in special types of cases, such as intentional torts, toxic torts, or concerted action by the defendants (which can be considered a form of vicarious liability).

Five states (California, Nebraska, Ohio, Florida, and Oregon) do not use joint and several liability for non-pecuniary damages (such as pain and suffering), but do employ joint and several liability for pecuniary damages.

One state (Connecticut) reallocates any percentage assigned to a tortfeasor who cannot pay to the other tortfeasors and the plaintiff in proportion to their own relative percentages.

Two states (Louisiana and Mississippi) use joint and several liability, but only to the extent necessary to permit the plaintiff to recover 50% of the verdict.

Eight states (Florida, Iowa, Montana, Oregon, New Hampshire, New Jersey, Texas, and West Virginia) use joint and several liability unless the defendant has a percentage lower than the plaintiff or lower than a fixed amount (ranging from 50% to 15%) (note that Oregon and Florida were also in the group abolishing joint and several liability for non-pecuniary damages).

Four states (Hawaii, Illinois, Minnesota, and Missouri) have complicated schemes, but they usually use joint and several liability.

Some jurisdictions have modified joint and several liability since that was written. Louisiana, for example, totally abolished joint and several liability among joint tortfeasors, except for persons who conspire to commit an intentional or willful act. La. R.S. Civ. Code Art. 2324(A).

3. *The Case for Retaining Joint Liability After the Adoption of Comparative Fault.* In *Coney v. J.L.G. Indus.*, 97 Ill. 2d 104, 454 N.E.2d 197 (1983), the court gave these reasons for retaining joint liability after the adoption of comparative fault:

(1) The feasibility of apportioning fault on a comparative basis does not render an indivisible injury "divisible" for purposes of the joint and several liability rule. A concurrent tort-feasor is liable for the whole of an indivisible injury when his negligence is a proximate cause of that damage. In many instances, the negligence of a concurrent tortfeasor may be sufficient by itself to cause the entire loss. The mere fact that it may be possible to assign some percentage figure to the relative culpability of one negligent defendant as compared to another does not in any way suggest that each defendant's negligence is not a proximate cause of the entire indivisible injury.

(2) In those instances where the plaintiff is not guilty of negligence, he would be forced to bear a portion of the loss should one of the tortfeasors prove financially unable to satisfy his share of the damages.

(3) Even in cases where a plaintiff is partially at fault, his culpability is not equivalent to that of a defendant. The plaintiff's negligence

relates only to a lack of due care for his own safety while the defendant's negligence relates to a lack of due care for the safety of others; the latter is tortuous, but the former is not.

(4) Elimination of joint and several liability would work a serious and unwarranted deleterious effect on the ability of an injured plaintiff to obtain adequate compensation for his injuries.

4. *The Case Against.* Where, as is often the case, there is comparative contribution on the basis of percentages of fault, and all of the tortfeasors are known and solvent, the abolition of joint liability makes no difference; each tortfeasor will end up paying only his or her share. But what if one or more of the joint tortfeasors is insolvent, or a "phantom," or immune from suit by the plaintiff and, as in many workplace accidents, also immune from contribution claims. What if plaintiff's claim against one of the tortfeasors is barred by the statute of limitations? Upon whom should the risk of such tortfeasors fall? Under full joint and several liability, all of the risk is borne by the solvent, known tortfeasors; under total abolition of joint and several, all of the risk is borne by the plaintiff. Is this a fair result? What if the plaintiff is free from fault? Not free from fault? Guilty of fault greater than that of the known, solvent tortfeasor? Do the reasons given by the Illinois court in note 3, *supra*, adequately treat the "fairness" issue? *See, e.g. Bartlett v. New Mexico Welding Supply, Inc.*, 98 N.M. 152, 646 P.2d 579 (1982), where the court observed that several liability is based on "the concept on which pure comparative negligence is based — that fairness is achieved by basing liability on a person's fault." The court pointed out that causation, as well as fault, could be apportioned. "If the jury can do one, it can do the other." The court concluded that as between one plaintiff and one defendant, the plaintiff should bear the risk of the defendant's insolvency; "on what basis does the risk shift if there are two defendants, and one is insolvent?" The court saw no reason why joint and several liability should be "retained in our pure comparative negligence system on the basis that a plaintiff must be favored."

Where there is joint liability or limited joint liability, a crucial issue may be whether the fault of a non-party (an immune or "phantom" tortfeasor or one who has settled with the plaintiff) should be quantified. It makes a difference, because the failure to allocate such fault will result in some of the burden falling upon the party tortfeasor. In *Gauthier v. O'Brien*, 618 So. 2d 825 (La. 1993), the court held the immune employer's fault should not be quantified, and, if quantified, should be reallocated among all other blameworthy parties proportionately. This view reflects the position of Uniform Comparative Fault Act (1977) § 2(d). Then the legislature stepped in and declared that the fault of all parties, including the immune employer, should be quantified. LA. CIV. CODE ANN. art. 2323 (1996). *See, e.g.,* Frank L. Maraist and Thomas C. Galligan, Jr. *Burying Caesar: Civil Justice Reform and the Changing Face of Louisiana Tort Law*, 71 TUL. L. REV. 339 (1996).

The court in *Newville v. Montana Dep't of Pub. Serv.*, 883 P.2d 793 (Mont. 1994), held that allocation of fault to a nonparty violated substantive due process. A statute permitted juries to consider the negligence of settling parties, persons immune from suit, and anyone else who may have been at fault. The court said the statute unfairly allowed a defendant to blame nonparties late in the trial, thus forcing the plaintiff to develop a last-minute defense:

> [T]here is no reasonable basis for requiring plaintiffs to examine jury instructions, marshal evidence, make objections, argue the case, and examine witnesses from the standpoint of unrepresented parties, particularly when they do not know until the latter part of the trial that defendants will seek to place blame on unrepresented persons.

5. *Several Liability and "Second Accident" Successive Tortfeasors.* In *Whitehead v. Toyota Motor Corp.*, 897 S.W.2d 684 (Tenn. 1995), the plaintiff was injured by his own negligence in a car accident, and his injuries allegedly were increased because of a defective seat belt in the vehicle he was driving. The court said the damages should be divided between the negligent cause of the accident and the "enhanced injury" caused by the defective seat belt. Would such a division be made regardless of who or what caused the initial injury, or whether the initial cause was attributable to a person acting without fault?

The court gave the hypothetical example of a negligent person suffering $100,000 damages in an accident, $50,000 of which were allegedly caused by a defective seat belt. The manufacturer of the seatbelt "could not be liable for the first $50,000 in damages, which would have been incurred even if the seat belt had been properly manufactured and installed."

But would the manufacturer be liable for the entire second $50,000, or only that portion thereof attributable to its own fault? Surely the second $50,000 was caused by the joint fault of the manufacturer and of the person or entity that caused the accident.

Whenever there are multiple concurrent tortfeasors in a several-liability jurisdiction, should the division of liability be made first on the basis of cause, then on the basis of fault? Fault and cause are not the same, are they? Can one really compare causation without also comparing fault, especially when one also hears the evidence of fault? *See, e.g., Howard v. Allstate Ins. Co.*, 520 So. 2d 715 (La.1988).

6. *Several Liability Where Grounds of Liability Differ.* In the *Whitehead* case, note 5, *supra,* liability was apportioned between a negligent plaintiff and a strictly liable defendant. May liability be apportioned between a negligent and an intentional tortfeasor? *See Reichert v. Alter*, 875 P.2d 379 (N.M. 1994).

PROBLEM

John and Jim, while racing their cars down a city street, forced the plaintiff's car off the road, damaging plaintiff's car. When plaintiff got out of his car to inspect the damages, he stepped on a live fallen electrical wire and was electrocuted. The wire had been negligently installed too close to another electrical wire by Electric Co., some 10 years earlier. The two wires had rubbed against each other over the years because of their being blown together by the wind, until eventually the insulation was worn from the wires and one of them ultimately broke as a result of the wear. The City had agreed with Electric Co. periodically to inspect and maintain the line installed by Electric Co., but the City had never done so.

Discuss the possible tort claims of plaintiff's estate against John, Jim, Electric Co. and City in a jurisdiction with joint and several liability, and in a jurisdiction with several liability.

C. CONTRIBUTION AND INDEMNITY

COMMENT

A tortfeasor by contract may be entitled to recover from a third person all of the sums he has paid to the tort victim. This is contractual indemnity, and is governed generally by the rules of contract law. A tortfeasor also may be entitled to tort-based indemnity, particularly where the basis of his liability differs in kind or in great degree from that of other tortfeasor. In addition, a joint tortfeasor who pays more than his proportionate share of the victim's damages is entitled to recover the excess through a tort form of subrogation usually called contribution. Of course, where joint liability is abolished, no tortfeasor will pay more than his share, and the contribution remedy does not apply. This section explores tort indemnity and contribution.

Section 886B(2) of the RESTATEMENT (SECOND) OF TORTS (1979) states that indemnity (full recovery over) is proper when:

> (a) The indemnitee was liable only vicariously for the conduct of the indemnitor;
>
> (b) The indemnitee acted pursuant to directions of the indemnitor and reasonably believed the directions to be lawful;
>
> (c) The indemnitee was induced to act by a misrepresentation on the part of the indemnitor, upon which he justifiably relied;
>
> (d) The indemnitor supplied a defective chattel or performed defective work upon land or buildings as a result of which both were liable to the third person, and the indemnitee innocently or negligently failed to discover the defect;
>
> (e) The indemnitor created a dangerous condition of land or chattels as a result of which both were liable to the third person, and the indemnitee innocently or negligently failed to discover the defect;
>
> (f) The indemnitor was under a duty to the indemnitee to protect him against the liability to the third person.

The history of contribution is reviewed in AMERICAN LAW OF PRODUCT LIABILITY §§ 52.14, 52.21, 52.22 (3d ed. 1987).

> At common law, contribution among joint tortfeasors did not exist. This general rule . . . prohibits one of several joint tortfeasors from enforcing contribution from the others who participated in the wrong. This position is based on the maxim that one cannot make one's own misconduct the ground for an action in one's own favor. . . .
>
> Several jurisdictions, adopting the position of the [1995] Uniform Contribution Among Tortfeasors Act, provide by statute that a tortfeasor's liability for contribution arising from products liability litigation

is to be based upon pro rata shares determined without regard to the relative degrees of fault of the tortfeasors. Some statutes stipulate that the shares shall be equal shares, while another formulation refers to the tortfeasors as being equally bound to bear the common burden. . . .

[T]he system of pro rata allocation as the basis for contribution, being simpler and easier to administer, may be more likely to lead the parties themselves to reach a settlement on their own. It is, however, somewhat arbitrary on occasion and generally less fair than apportionment based on comparative percentages of fault. . . .

The 1939 version of the Uniform Contribution Among Tortfeasors Act includes an optional provision that relative degrees of fault of the joint tortfeasors are to be considered in determining pro rata shares when equal distribution among them of the common liability would be inequitable because of disproportionate degrees of fault. This provision . . . is in effect in four states, and several others have adopted similar formulations calling for consideration of relative fault in determining pro rata shares. In some jurisdictions, the requirement is that contribution be based on proportional shares, with consideration of relative degrees of fault, or on the negligence or relative fault of the persons against whom recovery is allowed. The Uniform Comparative Fault Act, which has been adopted in Iowa and Washington, declares that the basis for contribution is each person's equitable share of the obligation. Legislation in New Mexico now defines a pro rata share by reference to the ratio between the tortfeasor's percentage of fault and the total percentage of fault attributable to all tortfeasors. Other formulations, apparently to the same effect, include references to comparative fault, comparative negligence, equitable or proportionate shares, or a combination of these. The statutory formula for calculating the right to contribution according to relative degrees of fault has been described by the courts as comparative contribution or comparative causation.

Restatement of Torts, Appointment of Liability 3d § 23 (2000) would resolve the issue of contribution in this manner:

(a) When two or more persons are or may be liable for the same harm and one of them discharges the liability of another by settlement or discharge of judgment, the person discharging the liability is entitled to recover contribution from the other, unless the other previously had a valid settlement and release from the plaintiff.

(b) A person entitled to recover contribution may recover no more than the amount paid to the plaintiff in excess of the person's comparative share of responsibility.

(c) A person who has a right of indemnity against another person under § 22 does not have a right of contribution against that person and is not subject to liability for contribution to that person.

PROMAULAYKO v. JOHNS MANVILLE SALES CORP.
116 N.J. 505, 562 A.2d 202 (1989)

POLLOCK, J.

The sole issue on this appeal is whether an intermediate distributor in a chain of distribution should indemnify the ultimate distributor when both are strictly liable in tort to the injured plaintiff. The Law Division granted indemnification to the ultimate distributor, but the Appellate Division reversed. We granted certification, and now reverse the judgment of the Appellate Division.

The underlying facts are that the decedent, John Promaulayko (Promaulayko), contracted asbestosis while working for Ruberoid Corporation from 1934 to 1978 at its South Bound Brook plant. During that period, Ruberoid purchased asbestos from Leonard J. Buck, Inc. (Buck), Asbestos Corporation Limited (Asbestos), and various other suppliers. Included in the asbestos sold by Buck to Ruberoid's South Bound Brook plant was 96.5 tons of Soviet asbestos, which Buck purchased from Amtorg Trading Corporation (Amtorg). The asbestos was packaged in 100-pound bags that did not warn of the dangers of asbestosis. Apparently neither Amtorg nor Buck ever took possession of the bags, which were shipped from the Soviet Union to the United States where Ruberoid took possession of them.

The jury determined in answer to a special interrogatory that Amtorg had supplied all of the Soviet asbestos that caused Promaulayko's injuries. After Promaulayko's death, his wife, plaintiff, Marie Promaulayko, instituted wrongful death, N.J.S.A. 2A:31-1 to–6, and survivors, N.J.S.A. 2A:15-3, actions, naming as defendants, among others, Amtorg, Buck, and Asbestos. Only Buck and Amtorg are involved in the present appeal.

Buck, a corporation of the State of Delaware, is a broker of mineral products, whose brokerage of asbestos at the time of its sales to Ruberoid accounted for less than one percent of its business. Amtorg is a New York corporation founded in 1924 to promote trade between the United States and the Soviet Union. Its employees are Soviet citizens, the majority of whom remain in the United States for three or four years before returning to jobs in the Soviet Ministry of Foreign Trade. By 1930, Amtorg served as broker for eighty-six percent of the Soviet products entering the United States. At present, Amtorg serves as a direct agent for Soviet business interests and channels the majority of Soviet trade to the United States.

At the conclusion of the trial, the jury dismissed plaintiff's wrongful-death claim, apparently because Promaulayko died from a heart attack unrelated to his asbestosis. The jury awarded $60,000 to Promaulayko's estate on the survivor's action, and $40,000 to plaintiff on her *per quod* claim. In reaching that result, the jury provided the following answers to special interrogatories:

> 6. Considering that all of the fault that proximately contributed to John Promaulayko's asbestosis is 100%, what percentage of that total fault is attributable to:
>
> (a) Leonard J. Buck, Inc. 25%
>
> (b) Amtorg Trading Corp. 10%

(c) Asbestos Corp. Ltd. (also known as Johnson's Company Ltd.) 65%

TOTAL 100%

7a. Was all (100%) of the asbestos fiber sold by Leonard J. Buck, Inc., which proximately contributed to John Promaulayko's asbestosis sold to Buck by Amtorg Trading Corp.?

Yes X No. _____

Based on the jury's answer that Amtorg had supplied Buck with all of the asbestos that had caused Promaulayko's asbestosis, the trial court granted Buck indemnification from Amtorg. The court rejected Amtorg's argument that Buck was not entitled to indemnification because the jury's answer to interrogatory 6 indicated that Buck was more at fault than Amtorg. Although the court acknowledged the inconsistencies in the answers to interrogatories 6 and 7a, it concluded that if the jury made a mistake, it was in answer to interrogatory 6, which dealt with the difficult issue of the allocation of fault. By contrast, the answer to the simple factual issue posed by interrogatory 7a established that Amtorg had supplied all the Soviet asbestos that Buck sold to Ruberoid's South Bound Brook plant.

The Appellate Division reversed, ruling that one in the position of a retailer, such as Buck, could obtain indemnification only from the manufacturer who produced the defective product and not from an intermediate distributor such as Amtorg. Underlying that determination was the court's conclusion that indemnity is based on the difference between the primary liability of the manufacturer and the secondary liability of distributors lower in the chain of distribution. The court reasoned that the

> trial court's order requiring Amtorg to indemnify Buck is not based on any primary fault of Amtorg. Instead, it is based on Amtorg's proximity to the manufacturer. The jury's finding that Amtorg sold to Buck all of the asbestos fiber Buck sold Ruberoid placed Amtorg closer to the manufacturer in the chain of distribution than was Buck. Both Amtorg and Buck, however, were blameless in terms of conduct that created the defect in the product. The fact that Amtorg supplied Buck with all of the asbestos Buck distributed to Ruberoid does not change the kind or character of Amtorg's liability from secondary to primary. Here, it is clear that the manufacturer, a Russian Company, created the defect by not placing a warning on the product. Common law indemnification is based on equitable principles designed to further the ends of justice by allowing a party whose liability is merely constructive, technical, imputed or vicarious to be indemnified by the party who caused the defect. A retailer or distributor is permitted to be indemnified by the manufacturer because the manufacturer created the defect and the distributor or retailer is generally blameless.
>
> The purpose of indemnification is restitution to prevent an active wrongdoer from being unjustly enriched by having another party discharge the obligation of the active wrongdoer . . . . Where, as here, the distributors' liability is based upon a common failure to detect the defect in the product and this failure merely continued the defect created by the manufacturer, we perceive of no valid reason to shift

the liability of one distributor to another distributor through common law indemnification. Because Buck and Amtorg were both without personal fault, indemnification would create, rather than prevent, unjust enrichment.

The court concluded that the proper method ameliorating its otherwise "harsh" result was to modify the award based on the Comparative Negligence Act, N.J.S.A. 2A:15-5.1 to–5.3. Consequently, it molded the verdict in accordance with the jury's answer to interrogatory 6, the result of which is that Asbestos would pay sixty-five percent; Buck, twenty-five percent; and Amtorg, ten percent of the total $100,000 award.

Two basic principles underlie the development of strict liability in tort. The first principle is the allocation of the risk of loss to the party best able to control it. The second is the allocation of the risk to the party best able to distribute it. We have expressly applied those general principles to asbestosis cases. Accordingly, the essence of a *prima facie* case of liability is proof that defendant placed a defective product in the stream of commerce. As a matter of law, the seller is presumed to know of the defect, so the injured party need not prove that the manufacturer was negligent or knew of the defect. Even in a failure-to-warn case, the cause is essentially one in strict liability into which negligence creeps to the limited extent of analyzing the reasonableness of the defendant's conduct on the assumption that it knew of the defect. Although the focus remains on the product, the defendant satisfies its obligation by proving that it "acted in a reasonably prudent manner in marketing the product or in providing the warnings given." *Feldman v. Lederle Laboratories,* 97 N.J. 429, 451, 479 A.2d 374 (1984).

In a strict-liability action, liability extends beyond the manufacturer to all entities in the chain of distribution. Although a distributor and a retailer may be innocent conduits in the sale of the defective product, they remain liable to the injured party. The net result is that the absence of the original manufacturer or producer need not deprive the injured party of a cause of action.

In the absence of an express agreement between them, allocation of the risk of loss between the parties in the chain of distribution is achieved through common-law indemnity, an equitable doctrine that allows a court to shift the cost from one tortfeasor to another. The right to common-law indemnity arises "without agreement, and by operation of law to prevent a result which is regarded as unjust or unsatisfactory." W. Keeton, D. Dobbs, R. Keeton, & D. Owen, Prosser & Keeton on the Law of Torts § 51 at 341 (5th ed. 1984) (Prosser & Keeton). One branch of common-law indemnity shifts the cost of liability from one who is constructively or vicariously liable to the tortfeasor who is primarily liable. A corollary to this principle is that one who is primarily at fault may not obtain indemnity from another tortfeasor. Consistent with this principle, actions by retailers against manufacturers have been recognized in this State for twenty years.

In the present case, we consider the application of the principles underlying strict liability in tort to a claim for common-law indemnification by one distributor against a distributor higher in the chain. Here, the claim is not between two parties, one of which is primarily liable and the other liable only secondarily or vicariously. Both Amtorg and Buck are liable to plaintiff because of their relationship to the product as it proceeded down the chain of distribution. We have not previously considered the issue, and it has received scant attention from commentators and other courts.

The Mississippi Supreme Court, however, has indicated that one distributor may recover from another distributor closer to the source of distribution. In the Mississippi case, the nephew of a soft-drink purchaser recovered from a distributor for personal injuries caused by a bottle that broke when it fell from a defective carton. In affirming the judgment, the court noted that "[m]ore generally, in the strict liability era, each party from the retail seller on up the chain has a potential right of indemnity (assuming of course that all of the elements of the claim for indemnity are met) against the person or firm who sold the product to him as well as against all others on up the chain to the designer or manufacturer of the product or the component part found unreasonably dangerously defective." [*Coca Cola Bottling Co. v. Reeves*, 486 So. 2d 374, 379 n.4 (Miss. 1986).]

Similarly, in a Missouri case where a consumer recovered against a retailer for injuries caused by the collapse of a defective crutch, the retailer was awarded indemnification from the manufacturer. *Welkener v. Kirkwood Drug Store Co.*, 734 S.W.2d 233 (1987). In approving indemnification against the manufacturer, the Missouri Court of Appeals stated that it "agree[d] with the authorities which hold that a seller lower in the chain of distribution who sells a product without actual or constructive knowledge of a defect and who has no duty to inspect is entitled to indemnity against one higher in the chain, such as the manufacturer." *Id.* at 242; *see K-Mart Corp. v. Chairs, Inc.*, 506 So. 2d 7 (Fla. Dist. Ct. App.), *rev. denied*, 513 So. 2d 1060 (1987) (allowing common law indemnification against distributor and manufacturer of a defective swing set); *cf.* Restatement of the Law of Restitution § 98(b), comment (1936) (as between two innocent parties, one without fault is entitled to indemnification from another who is primarily responsible for injuries caused by the condition of chattels).

In allowing claims for common law indemnification by one party in the chain of distribution against a party higher up the chain, these courts have proceeded in a manner consistent with the principle of allocating the risk of loss to the party better able to control the risk and to distribute its costs. The approach is consistent also with the principle of focusing on the defective product as it proceeds down the chain of distribution. In general, the effect of requiring the party closest to the original producer to indemnify parties farther down the chain is to shift the risk of loss to the most efficient accident avoider. Passing the cost of the risk up the distributive chain also fulfills, as a general rule, the goal of distributing the risk to the party best able to bear it. The manufacturer to whom the cost is shifted can distribute that cost among all purchasers of its product. Similarly, a wholesale distributor can generally pass the risk among a greater number of potential users than a distributor farther down the chain. When viewed in terms of these economic consequences, the principle of unjust enrichment, on which the Appellate Division relied, similarly supports the allocation of the risk to the distributor closest to the manufacturer.

Although our analysis has proceeded along the lines of strict liability in tort, our reasoning is consistent with the principles underlying commercial law.

Nothing in the Uniform Commercial Code precludes one party in a distributive chain from seeking indemnification from a party higher up the chain for breach of implied warranties of merchantability, N.J.S.A. 12A:2-314, or of fitness for a particular purpose, N.J.S.A. 12A:2-315. Permitting indemnification from the next party in the distributive chain also is consistent with the former Sales Act, N.J.S.A. 46:30-21, which was in effect at the time of the sale from Amtorg to Buck in 1947. *See Griffin v. James Butler Grocery Co.,* 108 N.J.L. 92, 97, 156 A. 636 (N.J. Sup. Ct. 1931) (retailer held liable under implied warranty created in section 15 of Sale of Goods Act had action against manufacturer who sold it adulterated peaches); *General Home Improv. Co. v. American Ladder Co., Inc.*, 26 N.J. Misc. 24, 56 A.2d 116 (1947) (purchaser of a ladder could recover from seller and manufacturer on express and implied warranties when purchaser had to pay workmen's compensation claim to employee who fell when ladder broke), overruled on other grounds, *Henningsen,* 32 N.J. at 416 (1947). Other jurisdictions have also allowed recovery on implied warranties that extend from one party to another down the chain of distribution. *See Klein v. Asgrow Seed Co.,* 246 Cal. App. 2d 87, 54 Cal. Rptr. 609 (1966) (tomato grower recovered judgment for breach of warranty against seed grower; indemnification allowed by each party in the chain of distribution against party higher in the chain); *McSpedon v. Kunz,* 271 N.Y. 131, 2 N.E.2d 513 (1936) (customer developed trichinosis after eating pork chops and recovered judgment against butcher for breach of implied warranty; indemnification allowed for butcher against supplier, and for supplier against packer); *Aldridge Motors Inc. v. Alexander,* 217 N.C. 750, 9 S.E.2d 469 (1940) (retail car dealer successfully sued wholesale car dealer based on implied warranty when consumer obtained damages from retailer); *Hellenbrand v. Bowar,* 16 Wis. 2d 264, 114 N.W.2d 418 (1962) (buyer of feed for lactating sows brought action under express and implied warranty against seller, seller brought implied warranty against his supplier, supplier brought warranty cross claim against distributor, the manufacturer not involved in action; all judgments against party higher in distributive chain affirmed); *see also N.J.S.A.* 12A:2-607(5)(a) (permits buyer to vouch in its seller when third party brings suit against buyer based on the product).

In the present case, Amtorg was closer than Buck to the producer of the asbestos in the Soviet Union. As between the two of them, Amtorg is better positioned "to put pressure on" the producer to make the product safe. Here, the defect was the absence of a warning of the dangers of asbestosis when the bags were placed in the stream of commerce. Because of Amtorg's relationship to Soviet commerce in general and to the producer in particular, it is more likely that it, rather than Buck, will be able to persuade the producer to provide an adequate warning. Further, Amtorg is better able to shift the cost of the loss to the asbestos producer and to require that producer to reflect the cost of injury in the price of its product.

Conceivably, a set of facts might arise in which the party at the end of the distributive chain will be a better risk-bearer than a party higher in the chain. As a general rule, however, we expect indemnification to follow the chain of distribution. Finally, we recognize that parties in a distributive chain may contract for a different allocation of the risk of loss. For example, one distributor may expressly agree to disclaim or waive any right of indemnification against a distributor farther up the chain. In the present case, the parties did not make any such agreement, and we are satisfied that Buck is entitled to indemnification from Amtorg, the distributor that was interposed between Buck and the producer of the product.

Amtorg contends that it should not be obliged to indemnify Buck because of the answer to special interrogatory 6, in which the jury found Buck twenty-five per cent at fault and Amtorg only ten per cent at fault for Promaulayko's injuries. The trial court apparently submitted this interrogatory because of the cross claims for contribution. According to the trial court, the jury's determination did not represent a finding of fault in the negligence sense. Instead, it was a finding of "sterile fault" assigned in a strict-liability case to intermediate parties in a distributive chain. This finding led the trial court to conclude that the jury's allocation of fault was probably based on the fact that Buck was closer in the chain to Ruberoid. As previously indicated, however, the liability of Buck and Amtorg to plaintiff stems from their relative roles as conduits for the distribution of the defective product. In answer to interrogatory 7, the jury found that Amtorg had supplied to Buck 100% of that product. As between Buck and Amtorg, then, Amtorg should accept the responsibility for Buck's liability to plaintiff. Thus, the jury's finding of fault with respect to a possible claim for contribution does not change Buck's right to indemnification from Amtorg. Nothing in the Joint Tortfeasors Contribution Act, N.J.S.A. 2A:53A-1 to-5, or the Comparative Negligence Act, N.J.S.A. 2A:15-5.1 to-53, would alter that result.

Here, the injured party sued two distributors, neither of which altered or even possessed the product as it proceeded from the producer to the ultimate purchaser. In this context, the appropriate vehicle for allocating responsibility between the distributors is indemnification, not contribution. It follows that the trial court should not have asked the jury to determine the various percentages of fault attributable to Buck and Amtorg. The right of the downstream distributor to indemnification from the upstream distributor existed as a matter of law. Consequently, the court should have determined that right following the entry of the jury verdict against defendants.

The judgment of the Appellate Division is reversed, and the matter is remanded to the Law Division for the entry of judgment permitting indemnification by Buck against Amtorg.

NOTES

1. *Contribution and Wilful Misconduct.* Section 1(c) of the UNIFORM CONTRIBUTION AMONG TORTFEASORS ACT (1955) states:

> (c) There is no right of contribution in favor of any tortfeasor who has intentionally [wilfully or wantonly] caused or contributed to the injury or wrongful death.

This provision has been adopted in a number of states.

Should a negligent or strictly liable defendant be permitted to recover contribution from an intentional co-tortfeasor? Or could such a defendant obtain indemnity (full recovery over)? Some jurisdictions recognize a right of indemnity by a "passively" negligent tortfeasor against an "actively" negligent tortfeasor. *See Vertecs Corp. v. Reichhold Chem. Co.*, 661 P.2d 619 (Alaska 1983) (abolishing the active-passive doctrine because it had proven elusive and difficult to apply).

2. *No Contribution Against One Who Is Not a Co-Tortfeasor.* Husband Doupnik sued General Motors (GM) for injuries resulting from defective design of an automobile. He was awarded $6,668,212, reduced to $1,333,642 because he was found to be 80% at fault and the defendant was only 20% at fault. "The evidence indicated that Doupnik had been drinking prior to the accident." He lost control of the car while driving. "Defective welds in a pillar post of the car caused the body of the car to collapse on the driver's side. Doupnik was rendered a quadriplegic."

Wife sued GM for loss of consortium, and recovered $1million. The court refused to impute the husband's negligence to the wife, so as to reduce her recovery by 80%.

Thereafter, GM brought an action against the husband to recover 80% of the $1 million paid to the wife. The court denied the claim for "equitable indemnity," saying that there can be no such indemnity unless both the prospective indemnitor (husband) and indemnitee (GM) are jointly and severally liable to the plaintiff. Since the husband did not owe a duty of care to his wife to avoid depriving her of his loss of consortium, the husband was not liable to GM for equitable indemnity. *General Motors Corp. v. Doupnik*, 1 F.3d 862 (9th Cir. 1993).

Some courts have held that a tortfeasor who is immune from tort liability to the plaintiff is not liable for contribution to a co-tortfeasor. Other courts permit such contribution, holding that the immunity does not prevent the tort from arising, but merely bars suit between the parties to the immunity. *See* PROSSER AND WADE ON TORTS § 50 p. 339 n. 32 (5th ed. 1984). Would the latter rule permit recovery by GM against husband Doupnik?

Recall the "successive" tortfeasors discussed *supra*. Should one be entitled to contribution from the other? *See* the discussion in *District of Columbia v. Washington Hospital Center*, 722 A. 2d 332 (D.C. App. 1998).

3. *Contribution Between Tortfeasor and Contract Breacher.* A New Jersey court held in *Dunn v. Prais*, 638 A.2d 875 (N.J. Super. 1994), that contribution was available under that state's contribution statute between a tortfeasor and a contract breacher, even though the statute speaks only of contribution between or among "tortfeasors." Thus the defendant urologist in a medical malpractice suit could assert a contribution claim against an HMO whose breach of contract allegedly was a proximate cause of the plaintiff's injuries. The court questioned contrary decisions in other jurisdictions.

In products liability it is not uncommon for parties held liable in tort and breach of warranty to obtain contribution between themselves. *See, e.g., Wolfe v. Ford Motor Co.*, 386 Mass. 95, 434 N.E.2d 1008 (1982). Since warranty and strict tort liability are closely allied, *see Kennedy v. The City of Sawyer, Kan.*, 618 P.2d 788 (Kan. 1980), warranty-negligence contribution may be viewed as liability between two types of tortfeasors. Similarly, many breach of contract cases also could be pursued as tort actions.

4. *Indemnity Up the Chain of Product Distribution. Promaulayko* upheld the widely recognized view that a business product supplier, held liable for the distribution of a defective product, generally is entitled to indemnity, or full recovery over, against the business supplier who supplied it the defective product. *See also Kelly v. Hanscom Bros., Inc.*, 231 Pa. Super. 357, 331 A.2d 737 (1974) (indemnity of strictly liable retailer against wholesaler for breach of implied warranty). Presumably, however, if both parties were negligent, contribution would be appropriate.

In *Casey v. Westinghouse Elevator Co.*, 651 F. Supp. 258 (S.D. Ill. 1986), the underlying complaint concerned a child whose hand was caught in an escalator allegedly manufactured by Westinghouse and installed in a May Centers, Inc. shopping mall. May cross-claimed against Westinghouse, seeking "upstream" implied indemnity. The court held that:

> [T]he passage of [Illinois'] Contribution Act eliminates the need for "upstream" implied indemnity. This Court finds that the Contribution Act achieves fair and equitable results in the apportionment of fault without imposing the artificial requirements, and total shifting of responsibility, of implied indemnity. To permit the remedies of implied indemnity to coexist with those of contribution would be in contravention of the express purposes, and not in keeping with the legislative history, of the Contribution Act, namely to encourage settlements and apportion fault.

5. *Respondeat Superior Indemnity.* In *American Nat'l Bank v. Columbus Cuner-Cabrini Med. Center*, 609 N.E.2d 285 (Ill. 1995), the court held that a principal, found vicariously liable for the tort of its agent, was entitled to indemnity from the agent. Is there any principal-agent situation where contribution would be the appropriate remedy of the principal against the agent? What about the employment relationship: should the vicariously liable employer be entitled to indemnification from the employee whose fault triggered the vicarious liability?

6. *Partial Indemnity.* In *In re Consolidated Vista Hills Retaining Wall Litig. (Amrep Southwest, Inc., Defendant-Third Party-Plaintiff v. Shollenbarger Wood Treating, Inc., Third-Party-Defendant)*, 893 P.2d 438 (N.M. 1995), the defendant construction firm, Amrep, was held liable to homeowners for using improperly treated construction materials in their homes, and the firm filed a third-party claim against the materials supplier, Shollenbarger. The trial court held Amrep was not entitled to traditional indemnification of full recovery over, since it was partially at fault. On appeal, the court said there was a factual issue as to whether Amrep was only passively at fault, and Shollenberger actively at fault. If such a passive-active situation existed, Amrep would be entitled to traditional indemnification:

> Under traditional indemnification an indemnitee is entitled to be made whole by a third party such as the primary wrongdoer. Traditional indemnification differs from contribution in that contribution requires each joint tortfeasor to share a common liability. Further, contribution was not recognized at common law. In essence, traditional indemnification is a judicially created common-law right that grants

to one who is held liable an all-or-nothing right of recovery from a third party; contribution is a statutorily created right that allows proportional distribution of liability as between the parties at fault.

Traditional indemnification would appear to apply only when there is some independent, preexisting legal relationship between the indemnitee and indemnitor. The right to indemnification may be established through an express or implied contract, or "may . . . arise without agreement, and by operation of law to prevent a result which is regarded as unjust or unsatisfactory." W. Page Keeton et al., *Prosser and Keeton on the Law of Torts* 51, at 341 (5th ed. 1984)

The right to indemnification may arise through vicarious or derivative liability, as when an employer must pay for the negligent conduct of its employee under the doctrine of respondeat superior or when a person is directed by another to do something that appears innocent but is in fact wrongful. Further, traditional indemnification principles apply in both negligence and strict liability cases involving persons in the chain of supply of a product, and in breach of warranty cases, *Schneider Nat'l, Inc. v. Holland Hitch Co.*, 843 P.2d 561, 587 (Wyo. 1992). *See generally* Restatement (Second) of Torts 886B (1977) (listing situations in which parties may be entitled to indemnification). In this case an independent, preexisting legal relationship between Amrep and Shollenbarger is established by their respective positions in the chain of distribution of a product. Thus, provided it could prove all of the requisite elements, Amrep would be entitled to seek indemnification.

The purpose of traditional indemnification is to allow a party who has been held liable without active fault to seek recovery from one who was actively at fault. Thus the right to indemnification involves whether the conduct of the party seeking indemnification was passive and not active or in pari delicto with the indemnitor.

If Amrep were at fault, the court said, then it might be entitled to partial, or proportional, indemnification from Shollenbarger:

> A growing number of courts are applying comparative fault principles to indemnification claims and replacing the all-or-nothing rule of traditional indemnification with a system of apportioning damages according to relative fault. *See, e.g., Allison v. Shell Oil Co.*, 495 N.E.2d 496, 500–01 (Ill. 1986) (declaring that active/passive doctrine is replaced by system applying comparative-fault principles); *Schneider Nat'l, Inc. v. Holland Hitch Co.*, 843 P.2d 561, 576–77 (Wyo. 1992) (recognizing Wyoming's acceptance of relative-fault doctrine over the "all-or-nothing rule"). Amrep refers to the application of comparative fault to indemnification claims as "comparative indemnification;" Shollenbarger entitles it "equitable implied comparative indemnity;" we shall refer to the doctrine as "proportional indemnification."
>
> Proportional indemnification has its genesis in jurisdictions that did not adopt a system of contribution among tortfeasors. *See Schneider Natal, Inc.*, 843 P.2d at 573. Other state courts adopted proportional

indemnification because they were frustrated with inadequate contribution statutes. Restatement (Second) of Torts 886B comment m (1977). In most cases, the adoption of proportional indemnification has followed a state's legislative or judicial rejection of contributory negligence and adoption of comparative fault. *See, e.g., American Motorcycle Assen v. Superior Court*, 578 P.2d 899, 918 (Cal. 1978) (in bank); *Allison*, 495 N.E.2d at 501 ("Active-passive indemnity, like contributory negligence, perpetuates inequality by its inability to apportion loss and its refusal to grant any relief whatsoever to a party whose conduct is considered 'active' regardless of how much or little other tortfeasors are at fault."); *cf. Herndon*, 716 F.2d at 1332 (stating that when "states have adopted the comparative negligence approach, the indemnity principles in those states have changed from the traditional all or nothing approach [to] damages measured by the degree of comparative fault of all the parties").

D. SETTLEMENTS

COMMENT

A settlement is a contract by which parties resolve a dispute either before or after the commencement of litigation over the dispute. For a number of reasons, the law generally encourages settlements. One, of course, is the usual subsequent reduction of animosity between the parties involved and their families. The most important is judicial efficiency and the resulting proper allocation of resources. The generally accepted estimate is that about 95% of all suits filed are settled before trial; without such a result, the judicial system would require a vast expansion and the delay between the filing of suit and trial would become intolerable.

Essentially, a settlement is a contract between the parties, and is governed by the appropriate contract law. Some types of settlement agreements may violate public policy because they have a negative impact upon the judicial system or produce unfairness to others. This result usually occurs in cases involving partial settlement by one of the multiple parties involved in the litigation; the most important issue which arises is the impact which the settlement will have upon the non-settling parties, both at trial and in any subsequent judgment. These issues are explored in this section.

BECKER v. CROUNSE CORP.
822 F. Supp. 386 (W.D. Ky. 1993)

HEYBURN, DISTRICT JUDGE.

The parties dispute this Court's jurisdiction and propose differing sources of applicable law in this admiralty case arising from a boating accident on the Ohio River. The motions submitted for decision require this Court to determine whether it possesses subject matter jurisdiction; whether it must apply federal or state law; and whether Defendants may pursue a cross-claim demanding contribution from a party who has settled his liability to Plaintiffs.

Plaintiff Virgil Becker was a passenger in a fishing boat sailing on the Ohio River between Kentucky and Illinois, near Smithland Pool, on June 25, 1989.

Plaintiff's son, Third-Party Defendant Randall Becker, piloted the vessel that day. A large wave allegedly struck the boat and capsized it, injuring Plaintiff and destroying the vessel. Plaintiffs allege that the negligent operation of three nearby commercial barges combined to create the damaging surge of water. Plaintiff and his wife, Plaintiff Ruby Joleen Becker, who alleges loss of consortium resulting from the accident, settled their claims against Randall Becker for $45,000.00 in March, 1990. Plaintiffs, who are Illinois residents, filed suit in the courts of Kentucky on June 22, 1992. They named as Defendants the owners of the three barges: Crounse Corporation, a Kentucky enterprise, operator of the vessel *Zelda Humphrey*; M/G Transport Services, an Ohio corporation, operator of the *Michael Conaton*; and Midsouth Towing, a Florida concern, operator of the *Anne B*. Defendants removed the litigation to this Court soon thereafter. They also asserted cross-claims against Randall Becker, demanding contribution from him in the event Defendants are held liable for the injuries sustained by Plaintiffs. . . .

The final issue which the Court must consider is whether Defendants may pursue their claims against a settling third-party defendant. Regardless of the answer, the Court must fashion a fair process for apportioning fault and damages in this case.

Plaintiffs settled their claims against Randall Becker for $45,000.00 in March, 1990 and released him from any further liability for their injuries. (Answer of Randall Becker, Ex.A.) Randall Becker now offers this settlement as grounds for judgment on the pleadings against Defendants' Third Party Complaint, which seeks contribution from Becker to defray any damages they may be required to pay Plaintiffs. Randall Becker contends that admiralty law discharges a settling joint tortfeasor from liability for contribution to other wrongdoers, and that Defendants cannot collect reimbursement from him under any circumstances.

Prevailing admiralty law offers no uniform doctrine which disposes of the controversy presented here. The Supreme Court has not yet addressed the liability of settling tortfeasors for contribution to their non-settling cohorts; the Sixth Circuit has taken no clear stance in the area; and the other Circuits are divided. One court which surveyed the conflicting pronouncements in this field was moved to "sympathize with the district court's difficulties in finding guidance from controlling authority on the settlement bar issue. There is none." *Miller v. Christopher*, 887 F.2d 902, 903 (9th Cir. 1989). There are, nevertheless, certain long-established admiralty principles which provide direction in evaluating the options available, and there is no lack of advice from the Circuit Courts regarding possible solutions to the issue at hand.

Maritime tort law seeks first to assure full compensation to victims for their injuries. That policy dictates the general imposition of joint and several liability upon multiple wrongdoers whose negligence precipitates an accident. As the Supreme Court has commented, this maritime doctrine "is in accord with the common law, which allows an injured party to sue a tortfeasor for the full amount of damages for an indivisible injury that the tortfeasor's negligence was a substantial factor in causing, even if the concurrent negligence of others contributed to the incident." *Edmonds v. Compagnie Generale Transatlantique*, 443 U.S. 256, 260, 99 S. Ct. 2753, 2756, 61 L. Ed. 2d 521

D. SETTLEMENTS 841

(1979). The Court acknowledged the possible inequity threatened by a doctrine which allows a plaintiff to demand that a less-culpable wrongdoer bear a disproportionate share of the plaintiff's damages. Nevertheless, the Court insisted that such consequences would "not justify allocating more of the loss to the innocent [victim]" by limiting that victim's recovery to an amount based on the individual wrongdoer's relative share of fault. There can be little doubt that, as between the plaintiff and several wrongdoers, the plaintiff should be able to insist upon a full recovery from any tortfeasor, regardless of that tortfeasor's comparative liability.

The harsh consequences of a joint and several liability system are tempered, though, by the centuries-old admiralty principles of comparative liability and contribution. Maritime law rejected long ago the common law rules against contribution, and adopted instead a "doctrine of ancient lineage provid[ing] that . . . mutual wrongdoers shall share equally the damages sustained by each. . . ." *Cooper Stevedoring Co. v. Fritz Kopke, Inc.*, 417 U.S. 106, 110, 94 S. Ct. 2174, 2176, 40 L. Ed. 2d 694 (1974). The admiralty courts recognized that "a 'more equal distribution of justice' can best be achieved by ameliorating the common-law rule against contribution which permits a plaintiff to force one of two wrongdoers to bear the entire loss, though the other may have been equally or more to blame." *Cooper* at 111, 94 S. Ct. at 2177. In recent years the Supreme Court further refined these rules by declaring that the liability of joint tortfeasors for maritime injury "is to be allocated among the parties proportionately to the comparative degree of their fault. . . ." *United States v. Reliable Transfer*, 421 U.S. 397, 411, 95 S. Ct. 1708, 1715, 44 L. Ed. 2d 251 (1975). In this manner, "contribution remedies the unjust enrichment of the concurrent tortfeasor" who temporarily escapes responsibility for damages under the joint and several liability system. Though the plaintiff may choose to collect damages from a single wrongdoer, it is clear that joint wrongdoers may assure a more equitable division of liability among themselves by allocating their comparative fault and pursuing contribution remedies.

When applied in a litigation context, the doctrines of joint and several liability and comparative contribution ably serve the admiralty policies of protection for victims and fairness between defendants. All the defendants are present to dispute their liability under such circumstances, and all are prepared to bear the consequences of an adverse verdict. Each defendant is fully conscious of the possibility that he or she may be held to pay the full amount of the plaintiff's damages, and presumably has chosen this exposure based upon the defendant's anticipation of a favorable verdict. But these doctrines of joint and several liability and contribution may yield uncertain results when one joint tortfeasor chooses to settle with the plaintiff before litigation, leaving the other wrongdoer to proceed to trial alone.

Courts have struggled with the problems created by these twin principles of admiralty recovery. Admiralty's comparative contribution principle leaves the settling defendant exposed to additional liability even after settlement, since that defendant may be required to share the damages paid by the non-settling joint tortfeasor after the latter's unsuccessful trial. Such continued exposure undermines one of the principal benefits sought through settlement. Contribution liability also permits the plaintiff effectively to collect, by a circuitous route, more money from the settling defendant than the plaintiff had agreed to take originally. Contribution from settling defendants would therefore seem to contradict "the interest the courts have in encouraging settlements" in admiralty cases. *Tankrederiet Gefion v. Hyman-Michaels Co.*, 406 F.2d 1039, 1043 (6th Cir. 1969). These considerations moved the Eighth Circuit to adopt a "proportional fault" system which excuses the settling defendant from contribution liability and holds the non-settling defendant liable only for damages representing that defendant's comparative share of fault. *Associated Elec. Coop. v. Mid-America Transp. Co.*, 931 F.2d 1266, 1271 (8th Cir. 1990). The Eighth Circuit's approach retains admiralty law's comparative liability principle, but allocates the defendants' shares of fault at the trial stage rather than during the traditional post-trial contribution action. Advancing the allocation procedure allows the court to calculate the defendants' liability to the plaintiff in the form of a percentage share of the plaintiff's total damages. Since the non-settling defendant will pay no more than his or her individual portion of the plaintiff's recovery, that defendant will have no need to demand additional funds from the settling defendant through the comparative contribution process. Adoption of proportional liability as between the defendants and the plaintiff necessarily prevents the application of joint and several liability, since that doctrine presupposes the right of a plaintiff to demand damages from one wrongdoer in excess of that wrongdoer's relative fault. The Eighth Circuit proposed its reform in the belief that its new system would "not discourage defendants from settling by subjecting them to the risk of contribution suits from non-settling defendants," and would deter "collusive settlements by limiting the plaintiff's recovery against non-settling defendants to a sum accurately reflecting such defendants' negligence." *Associated Elec.* at 1271.[1]

The Eighth Circuit's proportional fault system is notable for its adaptation of admiralty's policy of assuring fairness between defendants to the somewhat novel context of settling and non-settling joint tortfeasors. A non-settling defendant may be ordered to pay no more than its comparative share of the plaintiff's damages — which, indeed, is the maximum any defendant should pay after the combined application of joint and several liability and comparative contribution. A plaintiff "loses" only if the plaintiff accepts from the settling defendant an amount which is less than that defendant's actual share of the plaintiff's damages. Yet even this result need not inevitably be considered "unfair": the plaintiff accepted a fixed sum in exchange for foregoing the chance of a more favorable outcome at trial, and the balancing of risks undertaken by the plaintiff likely produced an equitable settlement, if not an actuarially precise result. And it seems likely that the risk of improvident settlements will be balanced, over time, by the occasional receipt of an overly-generous settlement in which the settling defendant pays more than would have been ordered at trial.

---

[1] The Eighth Circuit rejected a modified approach, which it called a "contribution bar" system. That approach would require the non-settling defendant to pay the plaintiff's full damages, less a *pro tanto* credit for any amount paid by the settling defendant. The non-settling defendant, however, could have no contribution from the settling defendant to align the amounts paid with the defendants' comparative fault. This Court agrees with the Eighth Circuit's reasoning. A "contribution bar" approach would amplify the harshest aspect of joint and several liability (solitary responsibility for the plaintiff's damages, regardless of comparative fault) while eliminating admiralty law's ameliorative doctrine of comparative contribution.

Despite the merits of the Eighth Circuit's approach, the recent trend among those Circuit Courts which have addressed the issue has been to reject the proportional fault system. *See, e.g., In re Amoco Cadiz*, 954 F.2d 1279 (7th Cir. 1992), *and Great Lakes Dredge & Dock v. Miller*, 957 F.2d 1575 (11th Cir. 1992). The Seventh Circuit contended that the proportional fault approach "in particular is no panacea," since the necessity of determining each wrongdoer's precise share of liability "creates a substantial possibility of extended collateral litigation." *Amoco Cadiz*, 954 F.2d at 1318. This additional litigation is complicated by the absence of the settling defendant who, under the proportional fault system, cannot be held liable for contribution and therefore has no incentive to participate in the trial. Plaintiffs additionally may decide to settle for a particular amount, not because that amount accurately reflects the settling defendant's share of fault, but because that amount represents the maximum which a near-insolvent opponent can afford to pay. The elimination of joint and several liability under such circumstances, as required by the proportional fault system, would prevent the plaintiff from recovering an amount sufficient to make the plaintiff whole. "[W]hy should the judicial system invest so heavily in adjusting accounts among wrongdoers?" asked the *Amoco* court: "Neither justification for the tort system — compensation of victims and the creation of incentives to take care — would be served" by the proportional fault approach. *Id.*

The proportional fault system's abolition of joint and several liability may constitute its most significant flaw. The Supreme Court in *Edmonds* pointedly rejected the application of proportional fault and reaffirmed admiralty law's long standing commitment to the joint and several liability principle. *Edmonds*, 443 U.S. at 268–69, 99 S. Ct. at 2760–61. The Court in *Edmonds* examined the plight of a longshoreman injured by the concurrent negligence of his employer and a shipowner. *Edmonds*, 443 U.S. at 258, 99 S. Ct. at 2755. The plaintiff collected workers compensation benefits from his employer, the payment of which excused the employer from any further liability. The longshoreman ultimately collected 90% of his total damages from the shipowner, even though that defendant accounted for only 20% of the negligence resulting in the plaintiff's injury. The shipowner urged the Court to prevent the imposition of this unfair burden by adopting a proportional fault system.

The Court acknowledged "the sound arguments supporting division of damages between parties before the court on the basis of their comparative fault." *Id.* at 271, 99 S. Ct. at 2762. But the Court concluded that the elimination of joint and several liability could create its own inequities by reducing a plaintiff's total recovery and thereby shifting the burden of loss to the victim. The Supreme Court's ringing endorsement of the application of joint and several liability cannot easily be brushed aside; indeed, several courts have declared themselves unable to rebut the reasoning employed in the *Edmonds* case.

The courts readily acknowledge, though, that *Edmonds* does not preclude the adoption of a proportionate fault system in a context not involving the application of workers compensation. The Eighth Circuit insisted that the *Edmonds* rule should not govern litigation in which one party has avoided liability by settlement rather than by the payment of statutorily required benefits. *Associated Elec.*, 931 F.2d at 1270–71. The Supreme Court itself suggested a single distinction between a plaintiff who has settled and a plaintiff who has received workers compensation when the Court acknowledged that "[g]enerally, workers' compensation benefits are not intended to compensate for an employee's entire losses." *Edmonds*, 443 U.S. at 261, 99 S. Ct. at 2756 (fn. 9). Under ordinary circumstances, a settlement payment clearly is intended to compensate the plaintiff for all losses attributable to the settling party's negligence. The need for joint and several liability, with its attendant possibility of a disproportionate recovery, seems less urgent when a plaintiff has already received a payment calculated to reimburse an appropriate share of the plaintiff's total losses.

Consequently, this Court is confronted with much advice and little guidance on the matter at issue in this case. The traditions and teachings of admiralty law seek to promote the following interests in order of preference:

(1) Full recovery by Plaintiffs;

(2) Fairness among Defendants of varying culpability; and

(3) Settlement of cases.

The Court believes that a "hybrid" approach which draws upon the best elements of traditional admiralty doctrines and the evolving standards of comparative negligence best crafts an equitable remedy for all concerned. The principles of this "hybrid" approach are as follows:

(1) The Court would apply the principle of joint and several liability in all cases in which no defendant settled.

(2) Fault would be apportioned among the defendants to achieve fairness among the defendants. The plaintiff would continue to be entitled to collect judgment *in toto* from any defendant which is adjudged at fault. The paying defendant could then exercise its right of proportionate contribution.

(3) If a plaintiff chooses to settle with one or more defendants, that plaintiff does so with the knowledge that the settling defendants' proportionate share of the award, as determined by the jury, will be excluded from the judgment.

(4) However, even in the case where a plaintiff has settled with one or more defendants, the plaintiff would still obtain a joint and several judgment against any and all remaining defendants for that amount which remains after the settling defendants' share of the award is excluded. The non-settling defendants retain their right of proportionate contribution, which they may exercise only against other non-settling defendants.

By this "hybrid" method, the interests of all important parties are protected and promoted. Plaintiff may preserve joint and several liability against all Defendants by simply not settling. And, if a partial settlement is advantageous, even that settlement does not extinguish Plaintiff's joint and several rights against the remaining Defendants. At the same time, Defendants would have some incentive to settle, because by settlement they may gain complete peace and protection against continued litigation with co-defendants.

Certainly, a plaintiff could be harmed by a wrong judgment about settlement. But that is always possible. However, the "hybrid method" assures that plaintiff will not be hurt by an unfair operation of law, but only by bad judgment in settling. Finally, the "hybrid method" is consistent with the traditional mandates and preferences of admiralty law as set forth in *Edmonds* and *Cooper* and the method recognizes the best and most tested principles of comparative negligence which have evolved in recent years.

For the reasons stated above, the Court is entering an Order herewith sustaining the Third-Party Defendant's Motion to Dismiss.

NOTES

1. *Settler Immunity?* Many, perhaps most, courts recognize that a settlement by a tortfeasor, if fair, insulates a jointly liable settler from any claim for contribution by a joint tortfeasor. *See Rufolo v. Midwest Marine Contr., Inc.*, 6 F.3d 448 (7th Cir. 1993); *Cook v. Stansell*, 411 S.E.2d 844 (W. Va. 1991). Not all do, however. In *Boca Grande Club v. Polackwich*, 990 F.2d 606 (11th Cir. 1993), the court said that under maritime law, "a tortfeasor is not precluded from seeking contribution from a joint tortfeasor who has settled."

In *Hager v. Marshall*, 505 S.E. 2d 640 (W. Va. 1998), the court discussed "good faith" settlements in this manner:

> Settlements are presumptively made in good faith. A defendant seeking to establish that a settlement made by a plaintiff and a joint tortfeasor lacks good faith has the burden of doing so by clear and convincing evidence. Because the primary consideration is whether the settlement arrangement substantially impairs the ability of remaining defendants to receive a fair trial, a settlement lacks good faith only upon a showing of corrupt intent by the setting plaintiff and joint tortfeasor, in that the settlement involved collusion, dishonesty, fraud or other tortious conduct.
>
> Some factors that may be relevant to determining whether a settlement lacks good faith are: (1) the amount of the settlement in comparison to the potential liability of the settling tortfeasor at the time of settlement, in view of such considerations as (a) a recognition that a tortfeasor should pay less in settlement than after an unfavorable trial verdict, (b) the expense of litigation, (c) the probability that the plaintiff would win at trial, and (d) the insurance limits and solvency of all joint tortfeasors; (2) whether the settlement is supported by consideration; (3) whether the motivation of the settling plaintiff and settling tortfeasor was to single out a non-settling defendant or defendants for wrongful tactical gain; and (4) whether there exists a relationship, such as family ties or an employer-employee relationship, naturally conducive to collusion.
>
> Where the non-settling tortfeasor otherwise would have been entitled to contribution from the settling tortfeasor, courts usually compensate by granting the non-settling tortfeasor a credit against the judgment ultimately rendered against him. There are three principal ways to calculate the amount of the credit: (1) the dollar amount paid in settlement; (2) a percentage of the total compensatory damages equal to the percentage of fault attributable to the settler, or (3) a pro capita reduction equal to the number of tortfeasors (*e.g.*, if there are

three defendants and one settles, the total liability per capita is reduced by one-third, regardless of the amount paid or the percentage of fault of the settler). Which method is fairest? To whom?

2. *Settlement and Assignment of Rights of Contribution.* Normally a full settlement of the claimant's damages by a tortfeasor extinguishes any further claims of the claimant against a joint tortfeasor, although the settler will have a claim for contribution against the joint tortfeasor. However, if the settler settles only his own liability, he has no claim for contribution but the claimant retains a claim against the co-tortfeasor — reduced by the amount of credit attributable to the settlement.

In *Robarts v. Diaco*, 581 So. 2d 911 (Fla. App. 1991), a doctor, sued for malpractice, settled the claim against himself and also settled the plaintiff's negligence claim against the treating hospital. As part of the settlement agreement, the doctor assigned to the plaintiff any claim for contribution it might have against the hospital. The applicable contribution statute provided in part:

> A tortfeasor who enters into a settlement with a claimant is not entitled to recover contribution from another tortfeasor whose liability for the injury or wrongful death is not extinguished by the settlement or in respect to any amount paid in a settlement which is in excess of what was reasonable.

The court concluded that

> the assignment of the doctors' rights of contribution in this case is not invalid merely because it was assigned to the original plaintiff in the tort action who may or may not have received full compensation for the injuries sustained by reason of the tort. If the assigning tortfeasor should choose to bestow a "windfall" upon the plaintiff by reason of such an assignment, that is a matter of contract between those parties.

How could the doctor have anything to assign unless he extinguished the liability of the hospital to the plaintiff? If the doctor did extinguish the hospital's liability to the plaintiff, then what claim does the plaintiff have against the hospital by way of assignment? What if the joint tortfeasor settles with the plaintiff and takes an assignment of the plaintiff's rights against the other joint tortfeasor? May the settling tortfeasor recover more than the amount he paid to settle? For a discussion of the possibilities, *see Woodfield v. Bowman*, 193 F. 3d 354 (5th Cir. 1999).

3. *Overpayment.* The United States Supreme Court has held that a settlement deduction based on the percentage of fault of the settler, rather than the amount paid in settlement, should be made, even though this might result in the plaintiff recovering more than his total damages. *McDermott, Inc. v. AmCLYDE*, 114 S. Ct. 1461 (1994). *Accord, Charles v. Giant Eagle Mkts.*, 513 Pa. 474, 522 A.2d 1 (1987). *Compare Snowden v. D.C. Transit Sys.*, 454 F.2d 1047 (D.C. Cir. 1971), where a non-settling tortfeasor received a credit for the amount paid in settlement by one who was ultimately exonerated from liability.

Where joint liability has been abolished, a non-settling tortfeasor is not entitled to a credit for any settlement made; the non-settler's liability is limited to its degree of fault. In such a case, the court in *Roland v. Bernstein*, 828 P.2d 1237 (Ariz. App. 1991), observed that if the plaintiff had "made a disadvantageous settlement, she would have borne that consequence." Conversely, "it would be anomalous to give the benefit of an advantageous settlement, not to the plaintiff who negotiated it, but to the non-settling tortfeasor. . . . Those considerations have led most courts considering this question to apply the rule we are adopting."

4. *The Workers' Compensation Problem*. Where a worker injured in the course of employment receives workers' compensation benefits and then brings a third-party action for the same injury, should the third party be given a credit for the compensation payments, or a right of contribution against the employer whose fault contributed to the worker's injury? Bear in mind in this context that the employer normally has a right of subrogation against the third party to recover any workers' compensation benefits paid.

The courts take three basic approaches to this issue. One is that there is no credit given, and the employer retains its right of subrogation. *See Hudson v. Union Carbide Corp.*, 620 F. Supp. 563 (N.D. Ga. 1985). Another is that the third-party receives a credit, and the employer's subrogation lien is reduced, by the percentage of the employer's fault, with the maximum credit being the amount of benefits paid. *Kotecki v. Cyclops Welding Corp.*, 146 Ill. 2d 155, 585 N.E.2d 1023 (1991); *Lambertson v. Cincinnati Corp.*, 257 N.W.2d 679 (Minn. 1977). The third is that the third-party has a right of contribution against the employer equal to the percentage of the employer's fault, which may eliminate the subrogation lien and extend beyond that amount, depending upon the percentage of employer fault. *Dole v. Dow Chem. Co.*, 282 N.E.2d 288 (N.Y. App. 1972), codified N.Y. Gen'l Oblig. Law § 15-108 (1989).

Which approach is fairest? To whom?

What result in a several liability context (*i.e.*, where joint liability has been abolished)? The court in *Ridings v. Ralph M. Parsons Co.*, 914 S.W.2d 79 (Tenn. 1996), held that the third party is not entitled to a reduction of its liability based on any percentage of fault attributable to the employer. The rationale for several liability "postulates that fault may be attributable only to those persons against whom the plaintiff has a cause of action in tort." Fault, moreover, cannot be attributable to the employer, the court said, because "the duty of care and proximate cause are not found in the employer-employee relationship."

5. *Settlement in the Indemnity Context*. The courts are divided over whether a plaintiff's settlement with an indemnitor extinguishes the indemnitee's claim for indemnity against the indemnitor. *Compare Dunn v. Kanawha County Bd. of Educ.*, 459 S.E.2d 151(W. Va. 1995), with *Anne Arundel Med. Center v. Condon*, 102 Md. App. 408, 649 A.2d 1189 (1994), holding that the release of the indemnitor releases the indemnitee as a matter of law.

The *Anne Arundel* court points out that termination "of the claims against the agent extinguishes the derivative claim against the principal."

Insurance liability is a form of indemnity; should the plaintiff's release of the insured bar further recovery from the insurer? Would it make any difference if the plaintiff could maintain a direct action against the insurer?

HESS v. ST. FRANCIS REGIONAL MEDICAL CENTER
254 Kan. 715, 869 P.2d 598 (1994)

LOCKETT, JUSTICE.

Plaintiff Ralph Hess appeals the jury's finding for the defendant, St. Francis Regional Medical Center (St. Francis), in a negligence action, claiming the trial court erred in: (1) allowing into evidence his pretrial settlement with other defendants. . . .

Hess, an employee of Vulcan Materials (Vulcan), was injured on the job. After Hess settled his workers compensation claim, Vulcan terminated Hess' employment. Hess sued Vulcan, his former employer, for retaliatory discharge and for negligently failing to properly notify medical personnel of the caustic nature of the liquid that caused his burns. He also sued Chris Cookson, the plant nurse for Vulcan, and St. Francis for failing to act on the information from his employer that he had been burned by a caustic liquid. Without admitting liability for its conduct or action, Vulcan paid Hess $15,000 and waived its right to subrogate medical expenses and other workers compensation benefits previously paid to Hess. After the settlement, all the defendants except St. Francis were dismissed as parties to the action. However, at trial, the jury could still assess the fault of the defendants that had been dismissed.

* * *

The jury found Vulcan 100% at fault. The trial court entered judgment in favor of St. Francis. Hess appealed to the Court of Appeals. This court, on its own motion, transferred the case to its docket.

Prior to trial, Hess settled with Vulcan and its employees. He dismissed his claims against them. Hess proceeded to trial against the remaining defendant, St. Francis. The jury was to compare the fault of the defendants who had been dismissed from the action.

Over Hess' objection, during cross-examination of Eric Phillips, Phillips informed the jury that Vulcan had been sued and had settled with Hess prior to trial. During cross-examination of Hess, the matter of settlement was also raised. St. Francis' attorney asked Hess if he had sued and settled with his employer. Hess admitted that he had sued and settled with his employer. St. Francis' attorney then asked if Hess had received $231,819.85 in workers compensation benefits from his employer. Hess stated he had received workers compensation but did not know the total amount. The attorney then asked Hess if he was seeking to recover expenses from St. Francis that had already been paid by Vulcan in the settlement. (It is not clear if Hess answered that question.) Finally, in the cross-examination of Dr. Jost, the doctor acknowledged that Vulcan had been sued by Hess.

It has been consistently held that offers of settlement and evidence of pretrial settlements with other parties to the action are generally inadmissible. There are two statutes which specifically concern the admissibility of evidence concerning settlement negotiations and settlements. K.S.A. 60-452 provides in part that evidence a person has, in compromise, furnished money or any other thing to another who claims to have sustained loss or damage is inadmissible to prove his or her liability for the loss or damage or any part of it. K.S.A. 60-453 states that evidence a person has accepted or offered or promised to accept a sum of money or any other thing in satisfaction of a claim is inadmissible to prove the invalidity of the claim or any part of it. K.S.A. 60-452 is concerned with possible prejudice to a party on the issue of liability. K.S.A. 60-453 is concerned with protecting the plaintiff's claim. The public policy behind these statutes is to promote settlement. *Ettus v. Orkin Exterminating Co.*, 233 Kan. 555, 567, 665 P.2d 730 (1983).

In *Lytle v. Stearns*, 250 Kan. 783, 830 P.2d 1197 (1992), this court discussed: (1) the disclosure of settlement agreements to the jury; (2) the admissibility of evidence regarding a settlement; (3) that the statements and defenses set out in the pleadings are not admissible as admissions; and (4) the cross-examination of a lay party witness regarding theories asserted against a party no longer in the lawsuit.

Lytle involved a survival and wrongful death action filed by the estate of the deceased against multiple defendants. Deborah K. Lytle was a passenger in a car involved in a head-on automobile collision. Deborah was transferred from the accident scene to a hospital by ambulance. At the hospital, Deborah went into cardiac and respiratory arrest and died. Deborah's estate brought an action against the driver of the car she had been riding in, the hospital, and the ambulance driver. Other parties were impled into the lawsuit by the ambulance driver for comparative negligence purposes. Prior to trial, the estate settled with all defendants except the ambulance driver. Each of the settling defendants denied liability and stated that the payment of the specified amount to the plaintiff should not be construed as an admission of liability. The release and settlement agreements each contained a confidentiality provision.

Prior to trial, the plaintiff filed a motion *in limine* to prohibit the remaining defendant from referring directly or indirectly to any dismissal of parties who had previously been named as defendants. The defendant opposed the motion, claiming that *Ratterree v. Bartlett*, 238 Kan. 11, 707 P.2d 1063 (1985), allowed the fact of settlement to be admitted into evidence. The *Ratterree* court had held that where any defendant has entered into a confidential settlement and the settling defendant is a witness at the trial of the remaining defendants or remains a party, the trial court shall disclose to the jury the existence and content of the settlement unless the court finds the disclosure will create substantial danger of undue prejudice, of confusing of the issues, or of otherwise misleading the jury. The trial court in *Lytle* denied the motion but precluded the defendant from mentioning the settlements. Later in the trial, the court informed the jury of the settlement.

On appeal, the plaintiff argued (1) that *Ratterree* applies only to sliding-scale agreements where the settling defendant retains an interest in the judgment and (2) that K.S.A. 60-452 and K.S.A. 60-453 prohibit evidence of compromise, settlement, or invalidity of a claim. The *Lytle* court noted the rule stated in *Ratterree* is broad enough to include any confidential settlement in any tort action involving multiple defendants when the settling defendant is a witness and either remains a party to the action or retains some financial interest in the litigation. 250 Kan. at 791, 830 P.2d 1197. The *Lytle* court pointed out that *Ratterree* involved a sliding-scale settlement, also known as a *Mary Carter* agreement, which most courts insist be disclosed due to the possibility of prejudice or collusion because the settling defendant's liability is decreased depending on the outcome of the trial. The *Lytle* court noted that the statutory purpose of K.S.A. 60-452 and K.S.A. 60-453 is to promote settlements. The *Lytle* court observed that none of the settling defendants in that case were still parties to the litigation, nor did they have a financial stake in the outcome or a claim against the remaining defendant and they had always denied that they were negligent. The court held under the facts it was error to admit the evidence of the settlements. As in *Lytle*, the settlement between Hess and Vulcan was not a *Mary Carter* agreement and should not have been disclosed to the jury. . . .

St. Francis also maintains that evidence of the settlement was relevant to show the bias of the witness Phillips, and that Hess' theory of his injury changed after the settlement. St. Francis asserts that the probative value of the fact of settlement outweighed its prejudicial value and that the admissibility of this evidence was within the discretion of the court.

We disagree. Although an employee of Vulcan was a witness, Vulcan was not a party to the action, having been dismissed. Vulcan had paid an agreed amount and waived its subrogation rights to any damages recovered by Hess from St. Francis. Vulcan had no financial interest in the litigation by virtue of its waiver of subrogation rights. Because Vulcan waived subrogation, its monetary liability was fixed; therefore, evidence of the settlement was not relevant to show bias.

In addition, Hess' theory of his injury did not change. His petition alleged liability under five separate causes of action involving Vulcan, its employees, and St. Francis. The claims were that Vulcan and its employees either intentionally or negligently failed to inform the hospital's medical personnel caustic was involved or, in the alternative, that St. Francis negligently treated Hess if the hospital staff had been informed caustic was involved. The pretrial order noted Hess had settled his claims with all defendants except St. Francis. Hess' only remaining claim was the fourth cause of action pled in his petition.

The admission of the evidence of settlement was not within the discretion permitted a trial court, and it should not have been admitted. . . .

NOTES

1. *Evidence of Settlement.* The courts divide on the admissibility of evidence of settlement with a joint tortfeasor. *Compare Tritsch v. Boston Edison Co.*, 363 Mass. 179, 293 N.E.2d 264 (1973) (admissible) with *DeLude v. Rimek*, 351 Ill. App. 466, 115 N.E.2d 561 (1953) (inadmissible). The Federal Rules of Evidence, adopted by many states, provide (Rule 408) that

> Evidence of (1) furnishing or offering or promising to furnish, or (2) accepting or offering or promising to accept, a valuable consideration in compromising or attempting to compromise a claim which was disputed as to either validity or amount, is not admissible to prove liability for or invalidity of the claim or its amount. Evidence of conduct or statements made in compromise negotiations is likewise

not admissible. This rule does not require the exclusion of any evidence otherwise discoverable merely because it is presented in the course of compromise negotiations. This rule also does not require exclusion when the evidence is offered for another purpose, such as proving bias or prejudice of a witness, negativing a contention of undue delay, or proving an effort to obstruct a criminal investigation or prosecution.

The Advisory Committee's Note to this Rule states:

> As a matter of general agreement, evidence of an offer to compromise a claim is not receivable in evidence as an admission of, as the case may be, the validity or invalidity of the claim. As with evidence of subsequent remedial measures, dealt with in Rule 407, exclusion may be based on two grounds. (1) The evidence is irrelevant, since the offer may be motivated by a desire for peace rather than from any concession of weakness of position. The validity of this position will vary as the amount of the offer varies in relation to the size of the claim and may also be influenced by other circumstances. (2) A more consistently impressive ground is promotion of the public policy favoring the compromise and settlement of disputes. While the rule is ordinarily phrased in terms of offers of compromise, it is apparent that a similar attitude must be taken with respect to completed compromises when offered against a party thereto. This latter situation will not, of course, ordinarily occur except when a party to the present litigation has compromised with a third person.

2. *"Mary Carter" Agreements.* A "Mary Carter" agreement is a settlement by one of two or more defendants in which the settlement is conditioned on the outcome against the other defendants. For example, the conditional settler might agree to pay $50,000 unless the other defendant or defendants are found liable for $50,000 or more, in which event the conditional settler would be released from liability. Or the settler might agree to pay $50,000, with her liability reduced dollar for dollar for every dollar over $50,000 which the plaintiff recovers from the nonsettling defendant (*e.g.,* if the co-defendant is found liable for $75,000, the settler would only be liable for $25,000). The possible "Mary Carter" arrangements are myriad. The essence of the agreement is that the settler defendant's liability is dependent upon the outcome of the subsequent trial against the non-settler defendant, thus pitting the settler against the non-settler. The settler may remain a defendant in the case, a situation which is especially insidious if the jury does not know of the settler's interest in the outcome.

In *Reager v. Anderson,* 371 S.E.2 d 619, 629 (W. Va. 1988), the court summarized the four essential features of a Mary Carter agreement:

> "(1) The agreeing defendant(s) must remain in the action in the posture of defendant(s); (2) The agreement must be kept secret; (3) The agreeing defendant(s) guarantee to the plaintiff a certain monetary recovery regardless of the outcome of the action; and (4) The agreeing defendant(s)' liability is decreased in direct proportion to the increase in the nonagreeing defendant(s)' liability."

Some courts have held that a "Mary Carter" agreement is void as against public policy. *See, e.g. Elbaor v. Smith,* 845 S.W. 2d 240 (Tex. 1992). Other courts hold that the jury should be informed of the existence of a "Mary Carter" agreement. *E.g., Hatfield v. Continental Imports, Inc.*, 610 A.2d 446 (Pa. 1992). Should the jury be informed of the terms of the agreement? *See, e.g., Thibodeaux v. Ferrell Gas Inc.*, 717 So. 2d 668 (La. App. 1998).

3. *Financial Interest in Outcome.* Note that the court in *Hess* said that evidence of plaintiff's settlement with his employer was not admissible because the employer did not retain a financial interest in the plaintiff's claim against the hospital. The employer had waived its workers' compensation subrogation lien. If such lien had not been waived, presumably evidence of the employer settlement would be admissible, at least if a representative of the employer testified in the case. Would the plaintiff be such a representative for this purpose?

4. *A High-Low Agreement.* A "high-low" agreement is one in which the plaintiff agrees to accept a maximum amount if the jury awards that amount or more against the defendant, and the defendant agrees to pay a minimum amount if the jury awards that amount or less. The parties agree to accept a jury award between the minimum and maximum amounts. In *Beng v. Pirez*, 269 N.J. Super.574, 636 A.2d 101 (1994), a defendant agreed to pay the plaintiff a minimum of $45,000, and a maximum of $62,500 if the jury awarded that much or more against the defendant. In upholding this agreement, the court said:

> No assertion is made that the parties' agreement is a "Mary Carter" agreement, a settlement device which has been restricted or even invalidated in many jurisdictions because it secretly and unfairly allies one defendant with plaintiff to the prejudice of the other defendant.

The outcome of the high-low agreement was independent of the outcome against the co-defendant.

PROBLEM

Plaintiff sued employee for employee's tortious acts. He also sued employee's employer for vicarious liability for the employee's acts, and for negligence in hiring and supervising the employee.

Employer subsequently entered into an agreement with plaintiff providing that employer would be released from liability if employee were found liable.

How should the court handle this agreement? If the employee is found liable, may she receive contribution from her employer?

Chapter 13
PROFESSIONAL MALPRACTICE

A. INTRODUCTION

One who provides services may intentionally or negligently harm the recipient of those services, and thus may be liable through traditional fault principles. Unlike the manufacturer, and the nonmanufacturer seller, the provider of services generally is not strictly liable under tort theories. The provider of services may be subject to a form of strict liability through breach of the contract to provide the services, such as where he or she guarantees but does not produce a certain result. Where the provider does not guarantee a result, his or her liability under breach of contract or implied warranty does not differ significantly from fault liability. The provider impliedly warrants that he possesses and for a price will exercise the skill normally possessed and exercised by those who provide those services, a standard remarkably similar to the negligence duty. Thus, where the provision of services causes traditional tort damages—personal injury and property damage—the claim usually is processed through negligence principles, although contract law sometimes is applied to some issues, such as the applicable statute of limitations.

The most common types of tort claims for negligent provision of services are those brought against persons practicing professions, and generally are called malpractice claims. Of the malpractice or professional negligence claims, perhaps the most frequent and most volatile is the medical malpractice claim.

The much reported malpractice crises of the 1970s and 1980s might lead the casual observer to conclude that the law of medical malpractice has undergone dramatic recent changes. Indeed, important changes have occurred; yet, perhaps with the important exception of the doctrine of informed consent, the doctrinal changes are relatively subtle.

The legislative retrenchments enacted in the medical malpractice field during the mid-1970s and mid-1980s, in response to a perceived malpractice-insurance crisis, are discussed *infra*. That discussion includes an analysis of the alleged causes of the crisis, the types of legislative changes enacted, and the likely effect of such changes. The discussion also raises more general questions about the goals of medical malpractice litigation.

This chapter provides an analysis of professional negligence claims generally, but much of the focus is upon medical malpractice. The development of medical malpractice law and its obvious economic repercussions should be studied with considerable attention and concern, not the least because the modern law of professional malpractice makes little distinction between the various learned professions.

B. THEORIES OF PROFESSIONAL LIABILITY

PROBLEM

Freda and Doris were involved in an intersectional collision in Anytown. Neither was insured. Doris filed a negligence action against Freda. Freda saw a TV commercial that advertised the services of Grabbit, a personal injury lawyer. Impressed, she employed Grabbit to handle her defense. Grabbit personally investigated the circumstances surrounding the accident. His first inclination was to use a comparative negligence defense. However, on reflection he decided on an "all or nothing" approach. He omitted the comparative negligence defense and elected to fight Doris' claim on the basis of factual causation. The jury returned a verdict of $200,000 against Freda, forcing her into both bankruptcy and a mental hospital. Grabbit did not lodge an appeal within the period permitted under Anystate rules. When he decided against using the comparative negligence approach, Grabbit destroyed all records of his investigation of the accident. After the jury verdict, Grabbit refused to return Freda's telephone calls.

Freda wants to bring an action against Grabbit. What approaches would you recommend? What legal issues would arise? How should they be resolved?

GUERRERO v. COPPER QUEEN HOSPITAL
112 Ariz. 104, 537 P.2d 1329 (1975)

HAYS, JUSTICE.

Saul and Maria de Lourdes Guerrero, minors, appealed by their guardian ad litem, Teodoro Guerrero . . . from a superior court judgment dismissing their complaint for failure to state a claim for which relief could be granted. The complaint was filed to recover damages for aggravated injury and suffering allegedly arising from the failure of the personnel of the Copper Queen Hospital to render emergency aid to the children. They were burned when a stove in their home in Naco, Sonora, Mexico, exploded . . . .

The issue before us is whether a privately owned hospital is under a duty to provide emergency care to *all* persons presenting themselves for such aid, including non-resident aliens who enter the country solely for the purpose of treatment.

The appellants concede that the Copper Queen Hospital is a private institution and that, as a general rule, a private hospital is under no obligation to accept any individual who applies as a patient. They argue that a private hospital is under no legal duty to maintain an emergency ward, but, if a hospital does maintain such a ward for the public, it must provide the service when a situation exists which reasonably could be termed an emergency. Appellants urge us to follow the opinion of the Supreme Court of Delaware in *Wilmington General Hospital v. Manlove,* 54 Del. 15, 174 A.2d 135 (1961):

> If a person, seriously hurt, applies for such aid at an emergency ward, relying on the established custom to render it, is it still the right of the hospital to turn him away without any reason? In such a case, it seems to us, such a refusal might well result in worsening the

condition of the injured person, because of the time lost in a useless attempt to obtain medical aid.

Such a set of circumstances is analogous to the case of the negligent termination of gratuitous services, which creates a tort liability. Restatement (Second) of Torts § 323.

174 A.2d at 139.

The appellees argue that the *Manlove* case sets forth a minority rule which is contrary to the common-law rule that a private hospital is under no duty to accept a patient . . . . The reliance by the parties on either rule is misplaced. A private hospital has no duty to accept a patient or serve everyone unless a different public policy has been declared by statute or otherwise.

The character of private hospitals in Arizona has been changed by statute and regulations. Private hospitals must be licensed to operate in this state.

. . . Since 1964 the regulations of the state health department have required a General Hospital to maintain emergency room services. In the revision of the rules in 1972 the same requirement for providing facilities for emergency care was continued and expanded.

From the statutes and regulations it appears clear that the public policy of this state is that a General Hospital must maintain facilities to provide emergency care. From this policy we conclude that such a hospital may not deny emergency care to any patient without cause.

The actual facts in this case are unknown because the action was dismissed at the complaint stage. The appellee hospital is referred to simply as a hospital. There is no specific allegation of its class as a General or Special Hospital. These are matters which can be developed in the case. For pleading purposes the allegation is sufficient to put the opposing party on notice of the nature and type of institution in question.

The appellees argue that [the Arizona "good Samaritan" statute] concerning individuals gratuitously rendering emergency care relieves such persons of liability for civil or other damages unless they are guilty of gross negligence. The apparent purpose of this statute is to relieve the burden of liability on individuals who choose to or not to render aid to others in emergency situations. We are not dealing with the same problem in this instance. An individual may in good faith help another in a crisis with untoward results for which he should not be penalized or the same person may not help, perhaps knowing that he lacks the necessary expertise to be of aid. The medical expertise of a hospital staff is assumed. The statute is not applicable to emergency medical treatment in a hospital.

. . . One last point requires comment. The appellants are not residents of this state or county. Are they precluded from the benefits of the Arizona statutes and regulation on Hospitals? We think not. The statutes are remedial, and there is no exception or limitation stated in them. We will not read an exception into them. The proximity of the appellee hospital to the international border presents special problems to it and other hospitals similarly situated. The lack of modern medical facilities in the Mexican border cities is the primary factor. Despite this obvious condition, we decline to find an exception in the statutes; this condition was equally obvious to the legislators, and they chose not to make an exception in the law.

NOTES

1. *Refusal to Treat.* In *Birmingham Baptist Hosp. v. Crews,* 229 Ala. 398, 157 So. 224, 225 (1934), a case dealing with a highly contagious patient who was stabilized but then told to leave, the court held that a private hospital "owes the public no duty to accept any patient not desired by it . . . [and it need not] assign any reason for its refusal to accept a patient for hospital service."

2. *Rendering Care and Customary Practice.* In *Wilmington Gen. Hosp. v. Manlove,* 54 Del. 15, 174 A.2d 135 (1961), a four-month-old child suffering from diarrhea and consistently high temperatures was taken to the emergency room of the defendant hospital. The duty nurse did not examine the child and refused treatment on the basis that the child was already under the care of a physician and that any medication given might conflict with that prescribed by the physician. That afternoon the baby died of bronchial pneumonia. The court held that "liability on the part of a hospital may be predicated on the refusal of service to a patient in case of an unmistakable emergency, if the patient has relied upon a well-established custom of the hospital to render aid in such a case." However, the court concluded that the record in this case would not support a finding of unmistakable emergency.

3. *The Volunteer's Liability.* In *Chandler v. Hosp. Auth.,* 548 So. 2d 1384, 1392 (Ala. 1989), a mother who took her 15-day-old son to an emergency room was told that he could not be examined without the payment of a $54 fee. A nurse told the mother to take the child home and to "give him Tylenol and a warm bath." The next day the child died from spinal meningitis. Summary judgment was precluded because the hospital had a written policy controlling admission procedures which suggested that, in some circumstances, indigent patients who were unable to pay would be admitted.

The concurring Justice noted:

> Regardless of whether a hospital has an admissions policy on indigent emergency room care, a hospital that provides emergency services should be under a duty to provide emergency care to anyone who seeks it and is in need of it. A hospital's first concern, when presented with an emergency situation, should not be the financial status of the person needing care. Rather, its sole concern should be treating the illness or the injury of the person who seeks treatment.

Do you agree? What if the hospital delegates to a private, on-duty physician the authority to waive the emergency room fee, and the physician negligently fails to waive it, resulting in the death of the would-be patient? Is the hospital liable? *See Tabor v. Doctor's Mem. Hosp.,* 563 So. 2d 233 (La. 1990) (physician liable, but not hospital).

4. *Patient Dumping and a Private Right of Action.* The Consolidated Omnibus Budget Reconciliation Act (COBRA), also called the Emergency Medical Treatment and Active Labor Act (EMTALA), 42 U.S.C. § 1395 (1996), provides:

(a) In the case of a hospital that has a hospital emergency department, if any individual . . . comes to the emergency department and a request is made on the individual's behalf for examination or treatment for a medical condition, the hospital must provide for an appropriate medical screening examination within the capability of the hospital's emergency department . . . .

(b)(1) If . . . the hospital determines that the individual has an emergency medical condition or is in active labor, the hospital must provide either

(A) within the staff and facilities available at the hospital, for such further medical examination and such treatment as may be required to stabilize the medical condition or to provide for treatment of the labor, or

(B) for transfer of the individual to another medical facility in accordance with subsection (c) of this section.

Subsection (c) provides, *inter alia,* that the receiving facility must have agreed to accept the transfer. COBRA is enforced through civil penalties (up to $50,000 per violation) against the hospital or "responsible" physician and suspension or termination of the hospital's Medicare provider agreement.

In addition, an individual (presumably, the "dumped" patient) or a receiving medical facility (the "dumpee") harmed by breach of these provisions has a private right of action against the "dumping" facility. *See Bryant v. Riddle Mem. Hosp.,* 689 F. Supp. 490 (E.D. Pa. 1988) (the statute provides a federal private cause of action).

In *Power v. Arlington Hosp. Ass'n*, 42 F.3d 851 (4th Cir. 1994), the court stated the facts as follows:

Susan Power came to the Arlington Hospital emergency room complaining of pain in her left hip, her lower left abdomen, and in her back running down her leg, and reporting that she was unable to walk, was shaking, and had severe chills. After two nurses and two physicians saw Power, the second physician gave her a prescription for pain medication and the name of an orthopedist, told her to return to the hospital if the pain got worse, and discharged her. Power returned to the Arlington Hospital emergency room the next day in an unstable condition with virtually no blood pressure. She was diagnosed as suffering from septic shock and was immediately admitted to the intensive care unit of the Hospital. Power remained in intensive care for over four months during which time she was on life support equipment, had both legs amputated below the knee, lost sight in one eye, and experienced severe and permanent lung damage. In July 1990, Power was eventually transferred from Arlington Hospital to a hospital in her hometown in England.

Power brought this suit against Arlington Hospital alleging in Count I that it violated the Emergency Medical Treatment and Active Labor Act of 1986 (EMTALA), 42 U.S.C.A. § 1395dd (West 1992), by failing to provide her an "appropriate medical screening" when she initially presented to the emergency room, [and] by transferring her to the hospital in England while she was still in an unstable condition.

The hospital doctor "testified unequivocally that he would not have treated any other patient with the same complaints and vital signs any differently than he treated Power." Plaintiff disputed this evidence:

> Power presented testimony from Dr. George Colson, a qualified medical expert in emergency medicine, that a blood test was a necessary component of an appropriate medical screening examination for a patient who presented at the emergency room with Power's symptoms. She also offered testimony from Dr. Margo Smith, a qualified medical expert in infectious diseases, that if Power had received an appropriate medical screening, including a blood test, when she first came to the emergency room, it was more probable than not that her infection would have been detected and properly treated.

The court upheld a jury award for the plaintiff, subject to the limit provided by Virginia's medical malpractice liability cap. In upholding the claim the court said the plaintiff need not "prove the existence of an improper motive on the part of a hospital, its employees or its physicians." Such a requirement "would make a civil EMTALA claim virtually impossible," the court said.

The court in *Smith v. Richmond Mem. Hosp.*, 243 Va. 445, 416 S.E.2d 689 (1992), held the plaintiff stated a claim under 42 U.S.C. § 1395dd:

> Connie Elizabeth Smith was admitted to Richmond Memorial Hospital (the Hospital) as a patient on July 18, 1988. Ms. Smith was approximately 33 weeks pregnant and had premature rupture of the uterine membranes. Ms. Smith remained at the Hospital until July 23, 1988.
>
> During the afternoon of July 22, 1988, Ms. Smith complained of abdominal cramping and vaginal leakage. The discharge had turned to a greenish yellow color. In the afternoon and again at 10:00 p.m. she was given Nembutal, a hypnotic drug. By 10:00 p.m., Ms. Smith was complaining of irregular abdominal pain and contractions. By 10:30 p.m., her contractions were timed at five minute intervals. At 11:45 p.m., she was taken to the labor and delivery facilities of the Hospital. The vaginal discharge was now dark green in color. By midnight, the opening to the patient's uterus had dilated one centimeter, she had cold chills, and her temperature had dropped to 95.3 degrees Fahrenheit.
>
> At 1:00 a.m., the Hospital called a physician, who ordered that Ms. Smith be transferred to the Medical College of Virginia Hospital (MCV). The physician was not Ms. Smith's regular attending physician, and he gave the verbal transfer order without examining her. Following the transfer order, a nurse began trying to locate an ambulance service to transfer Ms. Smith to MCV. Two services refused, and one was not obtained until the Richmond Memorial administrator agreed that the cost of the transfer could be billed to MCV. Connie Smith was taken from the Hospital at 2:10 a.m. and was admitted to MCV at approximately 2:30 a.m. on July 23, 1988.

A medical resident at MCV assessed Ms. Smith's condition to be "(1) prolonged premature rupture of the membranes, (2) pre-term labor at 34 weeks, (3) the Chorioamnionitis should be ruled out, and (4) that there was questionable meconium discharge." At 3:00 a.m., Ms. Smith signed a consent for a caesarean delivery, if necessary. Her contractions were one to five minutes apart at 4:20 a.m. She was taken "emergently" to the delivery room where the child, Taja Smith, was delivered by caesarean operation at approximately 9:48 a.m. Both mother and child suffered substantial injuries. Taja has cerebral palsy and is severely brain damaged.

Ms. Smith sued Richmond Memorial Hospital in her individual capacity and on behalf of her daughter Taja (collectively Smith), claiming a violation of COBRA and seeking damages.

The court said:

Congress enacted COBRA in 1986 in response to the growing number of instances in which hospitals were refusing to treat individuals with emergency medical conditions, a practice generally referred to as "patient dumping." Under the common law, private hospitals have no duty to accept or to provide treatment for patients. While private hospitals traditionally did treat people in emergency situations, they generally were not fully compensated, or were not compensated at all, for treatment of indigent patients. With growing competition among hospitals, shifting this cost to paying patients became more difficult. As the hospitals' economic losses increased, the instances of patient dumping also increased. To counteract patient dumping and the resultant hardship and injury, COBRA established specific standards for the evaluation, treatment, and transfer of patients.

In response to the hospital's argument that the Act did not apply because the plaintiff did not come to the hospital in an emergency condition, the court stated:

The statutory language clearly requires a patient to be in an emergency medical condition or to be in active labor before the provisions of subsections (b) and (c) apply. But we find nothing in the language of the Act which limits application of these subsections solely to a patient who initially arrives at the emergency room and who has not been stabilized, as the Hospital argues here. When the words of the statute are plain and unambiguous we need not resort to rules of statutory construction or legislative history.

The interpretation of the Act is consistent with the legislation's purpose. Patient dumping is not limited to a refusal to provide emergency room treatment. It occurs, and is equally reprehensible, at any time a hospital determines that a patient's condition may result in substantial medical costs and the hospital transfers the patient because it fears it will not be paid for those expenses. Dumping a patient in this manner is neither related to, nor dependent upon, the patient arriving through the emergency room and never being stabilized.

In a footnote the court said:

> [W]e do not address the Hospital's second argument, that the claim is actually one of misdiagnosis or improper treatment. The Hospital admits that a medical malpractice and COBRA claim can exist simultaneously and we have held that a COBRA claim has been pled. Whether the COBRA claim here is in reality only a traditional malpractice claim, as the Hospital argues, is an issue of fact, not pleading, and might be the subject of a motion for summary judgment.

5. *Entry into the Physician-Patient Relationship.* In *Childs v. Weis,* 440 S.W.2d 104 (Tex. Civ. App. 1969), a pregnant woman went to an emergency room complaining of bleeding and contractions. The nurse on duty telephoned the non-employee emergency room doctor who was on call and told him of the symptoms. The doctor told the nurse to tell the woman to contact her own doctor and to get his advice. The woman left the hospital, and an hour later gave birth in her car to a child who died within a few hours. The court held that no evidence had been presented which would support a finding of the creation of a physician-patient relationship. However, in essentially similar cases, hospital records or other evidence tending to indicate some direct contact between the physician and patient have been held to preclude summary judgement on the issue. *See Easter v. Lexington Mem. Hosp.,* 303 N.C. 303, 278 S.E.2d 253 (1981); *Willoughby v. Wilkins,* 65 N.C. App. 626, 310 S.E.2d 90 (1983).

The doctor-patient relationship may be "compelled," such as where a court orders a claimant to submit to an independent medical examination. In such circumstances, a doctor-patient relationship may not arise, and the medical examiner also may enjoy a qualified tort immunity as an expert witness. *See, e.g., Hafner v. Beck*, 916 P.2d 1105 (Ariz. App. 1995).

6. *Confidentiality.* The existence of a physician-patient relationship is a *sine qua non* to the due care and informational responsibilities of a doctor *qua* doctor. In addition, the professional relationship gives rise to a duty of confidentiality. In *Humphers v. First Interstate Bank,* 298 Or. 706, 696 P.2d 527 (1985), a patient consented to the adoption of her daughter at birth. Twenty-one years later, the daughter, wishing to contact her natural mother, discovered the identity of the delivering physician. Agreeing to help her, the physician gave her a letter which stated, untruthfully, that he had treated her mother with the drug diethylstilbestrol (DES) and thus, daughter and mother needed to be put in contact with each other. Armed with this letter, the daughter was able to breach the confidentiality of her birth and adoption records and contact her natural mother. The court held that the emotionally distressed mother stated a cause of action for breach of confidence. *See also Horne v. Patton,* 291 Ala. 701, 287 So. 2d 824 (1974) (release of information to patient's employer constituted breach of confidential relationship).

Compare Bryson v. Tillinghast, 749 P.2d 110 (Okla. 1988), in which a convicted rapist brought an action for breach of the physician-patient privilege against a physician who treated him for a serious bite wound to the penis and who thereafter reported the condition and the patient's identity to the police. The court held that the doctor's communication to the police was privileged on the basis of public policy.

7. *Public Disclosure.* In *Doe v. Roe,* 93 Misc. 2d 201, 400 N.Y.S.2d 668, 676–677 (Sup. Ct. 1977), a former patient of a psychiatrist alleged that a book subsequently published by the psychiatrist contained verbatim her most personal disclosures. The court stated:

> Every patient, and particularly every patient undergoing psychoanalysis, has a right of privacy . . . . Despite the fact that in no New York case has such a right been remedied due, most likely, to the fact that so few physicians violate this fundamental obligation, it is time that the obligation not only be recognized but that the right of redress be recognized as well.
>
> What label we affix to this wrong is unimportant . . . . What is important is that there must be the infliction of intentional harm, resulting in damage without legal excuse or justification.

These principles were applied in *Anderson v. Strong Mem. Hosp.,* 140 Misc. 2d 770, 531 N.Y.S.2d 735 (Sup. Ct. 1988), which concerned a photograph accompanying a newspaper article on AIDS treatment at the defendant hospital in which, allegedly, the plaintiff could be identified. Medical personnel had assured plaintiff that the picture would only be an unrecognizable silhouette. The court held that the physician-patient privilege encompassed the patient's identity as well as any treatment he received.

8. *Abandonment.* Consider *Brandt v. Grubin,* 131 N.J. Super. 182, 329 A.2d 82, 89 (1974), in which plaintiff's decedent, who consulted the defendant general practitioner for anxiety, was referred to a psychiatric clinic, but subsequently committed suicide. Plaintiff alleged that the physician had been repeatedly unavailable in the days prior to the suicide. The court granted the physician's motion for summary judgment, stating:

> A physician who upon an initial examination determines that he is incapable of helping his patient, and who refers the patient to a source of competent medical assistance, should be held liable neither for the actions of subsequent treating professionals nor for his refusal to become further involved with the case.

9. *Continuous Treatment.* The exact time at which a physician-patient relationship ends may have serious implications with regard to the running of the statute of limitations. Consider *Wells v. Billars,* 391 N.W.2d 668 (S.D. 1986), holding that a patient's visits to an optometrist to take delivery of prescribed glasses amounted to continuing treatment which tolled the running of the statute.

Compare Rizk v. Cohen, 73 N.Y.2d 98, 538 N.Y.S.2d 229, 535 N.E.2d 282 (1989), in which the plaintiff, experiencing ringing in his ears, was referred to the defendant otolaryngologist. After concluding that tests for an acoustic neuroma were negative, defendant diagnosed plaintiff as suffering from a viral infection. Three years later, defendant contacted plaintiff and asked permission to use the slides of some of plaintiff's tests in connection with a lecture. At that time, defendant recommended follow-up testing. Plaintiff submitted to the testing, which revealed the existence of an acoustic neuroma. Because the limitation period on the original treatment had accrued, the plaintiff relied upon the "continuous treatment" doctrine to avoid the statute of limitations. The court noted:

> The purpose of this doctrine is to ameliorate the harshness of a rule which ties accrual of a malpractice action to the date of the offending act, thereby creating a dilemma for the patient, who must choose between silently accepting continued corrective treatment from the offending physician, with the risk that his claim will be time-barred or promptly instituting an action, with the risk that the physician-patient relationship will be destroyed.
>
> The cases illustrate that the determination as to whether continuous treatment exists, must focus on the patient. When "a timely return visit *instigated by the patient*" is made, the policies underlying the continuous treatment doctrine are implicated and the toll is properly invoked (*McDermott v. Torre*, 56 N.Y.2d 399, 406, 452 N.Y.S.2d 351, 437 N.E.2d 1108 (1982) [emphasis supplied]). However, where, as here, plaintiff did not seek corrective treatment and, in fact, allegedly did not even know that further treatment was necessary, there is no sound basis for applying the continuous treatment doctrine. Having purportedly been unaware of the need for further treatment, plaintiff was never confronted with the dilemma that led to the judicial adoption of the continuous treatment doctrine. That a degree of continuity exists by virtue of Dr. Cohen's unilateral initiative in October 1983 is unhelpful to plaintiff's position because that contact does not establish the continuing trust on the *plaintiff's part* that the continuous treatment doctrine requires.
>
> Furthermore, sound policy reasons suggest that mere doctor-initiated contact, in the absence of other objective factors indicative of a continuing relationship, should not fall under the continuous treatment doctrine. Clearly, it is in society's best interest to foster honest communication between physician and patient. Allowing continuous treatment to be invoked solely on a doctor-initiated communication might, we fear, encourage silence. Instead of suggesting new techniques, or pointing out a potential mistake from years earlier, a doctor fearful of a medical malpractice action might simply refrain from contacting a former patient.

Is the "patient's dilemma" the only, or the best, rationale for the continuous treatment doctrine?

DESTEFANO v. GRABRIAN
763 P.2d 275 (Colo. 1988)

ERICKSON, JUSTICE.

. . . The complaint alleges that in 1979, Robert and Edna [Destefano] were having marital problems which led them to seek marriage counseling from Grabrian. The Destefanos were both Catholics who had "faith and confidence in their parish priest." Grabrian's supervisors knew or should have known that he was unsuited for marriage counseling and "would cause harm to a jeopardized marital relationship." To comply with church doctrine regarding marriage and divorce, the diocese encouraged its parishioners to participate in marriage counseling.

During the course of the counseling relationship, Grabrian developed a relationship with Edna, which "Grabrian knew or should have known would lead to additional marital problems between [Robert] and Edna." Grabrian knew that his intimate relationship with Edna probably would cause the dissolution of the Destefano marriage. Robert and Edna were told by Grabrian that he would act as their marriage counselor and that they could trust him. Grabrian's continued involvement in this relationship was occasioned by a reckless disregard for Robert's rights and feelings. The diocese owed a continuing duty to Robert and others similarly situated to reasonably train, interview, and supervise priests engaged in counseling married couples. With actual or constructive knowledge of Grabrian's prior indiscretions, the diocese willfully and recklessly breached its duty. Grabrian's conduct resulted in an intimate relationship between Grabrian and Edna that contributed to the dissolution of the Destefano marriage.

Based upon these allegations, Robert sought compensatory and exemplary damages for: (1) negligence against Grabrian for the manner in which he conducted the counseling and against the diocese on the theory of respondeat superior for failing to train, monitor, and supervise Grabrian adequately; (2) intentional infliction of emotional distress and outrageous conduct of both Grabrian and the diocese; and (3) Grabrian's breach of fiduciary duty. Due to the alleged willful and reckless nature of Grabrian's and the diocese's actions, Robert requested exemplary damages under each claim for relief. [Robert initially sued Edna, but later dropped his claim against her.]

In her crossclaim, Edna alleged the following facts that we will assume to be true in considering the motions to dismiss. Marital difficulties prompted the Destefanos to seek the assistance of a professional marriage counselor through St. Mary's Catholic Church, which was under the jurisdiction of the diocese. The Destefanos met on two occasions with Grabrian, who represented himself to be a professional with the necessary skills to assist people in need of professional marriage counseling. Grabrian agreed to assist them as a couple. Thereafter, Grabrian informed Robert that he should seek his own counselor. Grabrian represented to Edna that he was a capable, trained professional who could be relied upon to assist her with the serious marital and personal problems she was experiencing, and that she could trust him to act in her best interests. She in fact trusted him and followed his advice. Grabrian knew that his conduct with Edna would result in the collapse and dissolution of her marriage, and would cause the Destefanos extreme and permanent emotional suffering.

Knowing that Edna was "extremely vulnerable emotionally," Grabrian began a relationship with Edna which turned adulterous due to the actions of Grabrian. Grabrian had repeatedly engaged in sexual relations with other women similarly situated. Grabrian's past conduct was known or should have been known to the diocese. The actions of Grabrian and the diocese entitled Edna to compensatory and exemplary damages for their breach of fiduciary duty, negligence, and outrageous conduct. [The trial court dismissed the claims, and the court of appeals affirmed the dismissal.]

Robert and Edna contend that their claims are not barred by section 13-20-202, 6 C.R.S. (1987) (heart balm statute), which provides: "All civil causes of action for breach of promise to marry, alienation of affections, criminal conversation, and seduction are hereby abolished."

. . . Here, the court of appeals relied upon *Nicholson v. Han,* 12 Mich. App. 35, 162 N.W.2d 313 (1968), a case in which a husband sued the family doctor who had been functioning as a marriage counselor and who had warranted an improvement in marital relations. After the plaintiff and his wife were divorced, the plaintiff learned that his wife and the defendant had commenced a sexual relationship during the course of counseling. Although the complaint was drafted in the language of fraud and breach of contract, the case was dismissed as falling within the prohibited actions of seduction, alienation of affections, and criminal conversation.

The Michigan Court of Appeals later held, in *Cotton v. Kambly,* 101 Mich. App. 537, 300 N.W.2d 627 (1980), that the abolition of claims for seduction did not bar plaintiff's malpractice claim against her psychiatrist who had induced her to engage in sexual activities under the guise of therapy. The court distinguished *Nicholson,* stating that the issue of malpractice was never raised in that case since the appeal from the trial court was dismissed on the breach of contract and fraud counts only. *Id.* at 539, 300 N.W.2d at 628. The court held that although the elements of seduction were present, the essence of the action was not for seduction but rather for breach of professional standards of care. In so holding, the court stated:

> Part of plaintiff's claim is for medical malpractice, which has been defined as the failure of a member of the medical profession, employed to treat a case professionally, to fulfill the duty to exercise that degree of skill, care and diligence exercised by members of the same profession, practicing in the same or similar locality, in light of the present state of medical science. Plaintiff alleges that defendant induced her to engage in sexual relations with him as part of her prescribed therapy. We see no reason for distinguishing between this type of malpractice and others, such as improper administration of a drug or a defective operation. In each situation, the essence of the claim is the doctor's departure from proper standards of medical practice.

Id. at 540–41, 300 N.W.2d at 628–29.

. . . [We] should not read the statute so broadly as to preclude any cause of action involving extramarital affairs, regardless of whether a claim for relief which is not included in section 13-20-202 is enumerated. In our view, the heart balm statute only precludes those causes of action specifically listed in the statute . . . . [A] plaintiff will not be able to mask one of the abolished actions behind a common law label. However, if the essence of the complaint is directed to a cause of action other than one which has been abolished, that claim is legally cognizable . . . .

Grabrian and the diocese assert that the court of appeals properly upheld the trial court's dismissal of Edna's crossclaims because her claims were for seduction which were abolished by section 13-20-202. We disagree.

. . . The statute relating to the crime of seduction that was in effect when the General Assembly enacted the heart balm statute in 1937 was also limited to unmarried females. Because Edna was married, we conclude that her crossclaim did not set forth a claim based on seduction.

Edna's allegations also do not set forth a claim for alienation of affections. As we previously stated, an element of a claim for alienation of affections is that the defendant must intend to induce the plaintiff's spouse to separate. For purposes of Edna's crossclaims, Edna is the plaintiff. Edna did not allege that Grabrian's acts were intended to cause Robert to separate from her. Nor, in our view, do the allegations, in essence, support such an interpretation. The crossclaim does not include a claim for alienation of affections.

Edna's crossclaim also fails to set forth a claim for criminal conversation . . . . Since Edna does not allege that Grabrian's adulterous conduct involved her husband, her crossclaim is not an action for criminal conversation.

. . . The threshold issue that we must first resolve is whether a member of the clergy, who holds himself out as being trained and capable of conducting marital counseling, is immune from any liability for harm caused by his counseling by virtue of the first amendment.

Grabrian and the diocese assert that Robert's and Edna's claims are "violative of the First Amendment to the United States Constitution in that the performance of pastoral duties by a Catholic priest, including sacramental counseling of parishioners, is a matter of ecclesiastical cognizance and policy with which a civil court cannot interfere." The first amendment to the United States Constitution prohibits any "law respecting the establishment of religion, or prohibiting the free exercise thereof." U.S. Const. amend. I. Marital counseling by a cleric presents difficult questions because it often incorporates both religious counseling and secular counseling. While we agree that spiritual counseling, including marital counseling by a priest, may implicate first amendment rights, we are not convinced that the allegations in Edna's crossclaim permit Grabrian to assert a free exercise clause defense.

. . . When the free exercise clause is raised as a defense, the threshold question is whether the conduct of the defendant is religious . . . . The alleged misconduct of Grabrian that is at the very heart of Edna's crossclaim is that he induced Edna to engage in a sexual relationship during the course, and as a result, of marital counseling. Edna alleged that her damages were a direct result of the sexual relationship. If the alleged conduct of Grabrian was dictated by his sincerely held religious beliefs or was consistent with the practice of his religion, we would have to resolve a difficult first amendment issue. This, however, is not the case. It has not been asserted that Grabrian's conduct falls within the practices or beliefs of the Catholic church. Grabrian's and the diocese's brief states that "every Catholic is well aware of the vow of celibacy required of a priest at the time of his ordination." The brief also points out that "sexual involvement by a priest has been held to be per se outside the scope of his employment." The brief recognizes and admits that sexual activity by a priest is fundamentally antithetical to Catholic doctrine. As such, the conduct upon which Edna's crossclaim is premised is, by definition, not an expression of a sincerely held religious belief.

Members of the clergy cannot, in all circumstances, use the shield of the first amendment as protection and as a basis for immunity from civil suit.

When the alleged wrongdoing of a cleric clearly falls outside the beliefs and doctrine of his religion, he cannot avail himself of the protection afforded by the first amendment.

Edna's first claim for relief alleges that Grabrian, in his position as a priest and as one who holds himself out to the community as a professional or trained marriage counselor, breached his fiduciary duty to her.

. . . We have no difficulty in finding that Grabrian, as a marriage counselor to Robert and Edna, owed a fiduciary duty to Edna. His duty to Edna was "created by his undertaking" to counsel her. Grabrian had a duty, given the nature of the counseling relationship, to engage in conduct designed to improve the Destefanos' marital relationship. As a fiduciary, he was obligated not to engage in conduct which might harm the Destefanos' relationship. If the allegations are true, it is clear to us that Grabrian breached his duty and obligation when he had sexual intercourse with Edna.

Edna's second claim for relief alleges that Grabrian "negligently performed his duty as a marital counselor" and that a member of the clergy who represents himself as a competent marital counselor, has a duty to employ the degree of knowledge, skill, and judgment ordinarily possessed by members of that profession in the community. This claim of professional negligence is a claim for malpractice. Malpractice consists of any professional misconduct, unreasonable lack of skill or fidelity in professional or fiduciary duties, evil practice, or illegal or immoral conduct. Since Grabrian is a Catholic priest, the malpractice claim alleged by Edna falls within the realm of "clergy malpractice." To date, no court has acknowledged the existence of such a tort. Since the claim for clergy malpractice is not supported by precedent and raises serious first amendment issues, we have concluded that Edna's second claim for relief was properly dismissed. We do not recognize the claim of "clergy malpractice."

Courts have generally recognized that when a professional counselor engages in sexual relations with a patient, client, or counselee, he may be held liable for damages. The General Assembly has enacted legislation which imposes penalties against psychologists [who maintain relationships with their clients that are "likely to impair . . . professional judgment or increase the risk of client exploitation, such as treating employees, supervisees, close colleagues, or relatives, or having sexual intimacies with clients." § 12-42-111(1)(l), 5 C.R.S. (1985)].

However, the legislature has expressly evinced an intent to exclude religious ministers, priests, and rabbis from the statutory scheme which imposes liability upon psychologists for malpractice. Section 12-43-114(10), 5 C.R.S. (1985), states that:

> Nothing in this article shall restrict a duly ordained minister, priest, or rabbi from carrying out his ministerial responsibilities while functioning in his ministerial capacity within a recognized religious organization and serving the spiritual needs of its constituency, provided he does not hold himself out to the public by any title or description incorporating the words "psychologist," "psychological," "psychology," or other term implying training, experience, or expertise in psychology.

... Since the General Assembly has shown an intent to exclude religious counselors from the liability provisions of the statute creating liability for mental health professionals, we conclude that Edna's second claim for relief was properly dismissed.

The crossclaim of Edna also asserts that Grabrian engaged in outrageous conduct.... Viewing the crossclaim in the light most favorable to Edna, as we must, we conclude that the allegations in the complaint are sufficient to withstand a motion to dismiss. We note that on remand it is for the trial court, in the first instance, to determine whether the conduct at issue is "outrageous."

Edna, in her fourth and fifth claims for relief, alleges that the diocese breached its duty to supervise Grabrian, and that the actions of Grabrian should be imputed to the diocese.... A priest's violation of his vow of celibacy is contrary to the instructions and doctrines of the Catholic church. When a priest has sexual intercourse with a parishioner it is not part of the priest's duties nor customary within the business of the church. Such conduct is contrary to the principles of Catholicism and is not incidental to the tasks assigned a priest by the diocese. Under the facts of this case there is no basis for imputing vicarious liability to the diocese for the alleged conduct of Grabrian.

Even though Grabrian's acts do not create a basis for holding the diocese vicariously liable, the diocese may be directly liable for negligently supervising Grabrian. [RESTATEMENT (SECOND) OF AGENCY § 213 (1958).]

... The substance of the first two claims in the complaint relates to the adulterous conduct of Grabrian that resulted in the destruction of the marriage and the injuries allegedly arising from that conduct. In our view, these allegations plainly set forth claims for alienation of affections and criminal conversation. We choose not to recognize any of Robert's common law claims apart from the third claim for relief because they are plainly claims for alienation of affections and criminal conversation....

Robert's third claim is one for breach of fiduciary duty. One standing in a position of trust is liable for harm resulting from a breach of the duty imposed by that position. RESTATEMENT (SECOND) OF TORTS § 874 (1979). The third claim alleges that the fiduciary duty breached by Grabrian and the diocese arose as a result of the counseling relationship entered into by Robert and Edna with Grabrian. As we concluded in reviewing Edna's first claim for relief, we believe that the nature of the counseling relationship alleged here gives rise to a clear duty on Grabrian's part to engage only in activity or conduct calculated to improve the Destefanos' marriage. This duty to refrain from any conduct which carries with it a risk of harm to the marital couple extends to both Robert and Edna. We have no difficulty in finding that Grabrian's intimacies with Edna falls within "conduct which carries with it a risk of harm" to Edna and Robert.

NOTES

1. *Clergy Malpractice Rejected.* The husband and wife in *Bladen v. First Presbyterian Church*, 857 P.2d 789 (Okla. 1993), sued a minister and his

church for damages arising out of an adulterous affair the minister had with the wife while providing the couple marriage counseling. Refusing to follow *Destefano*, the court said the husband had no claim for breach of fiduciary duty owing to the statutory abolition of the torts of alienation of affections and criminal conversation. The wife had no claim "against her minister for engaging in a consensual sexual affair."

The husband claimed the minister gave him "bad advice" for marital counseling":

> He stated that he couldn't remember all of the advice he received, but he did remember that he was advised in October 1985 to give his wife less attention. He stated that he tried it but it didn't work.

Refusing to recognize this claim, the court said:

> Once a court enters the realm of trying to define the nature of advice a minister should give a parishioner serious First Amendment issues are implicated. We decline to determine the nature of the advice a minister must give during counseling sessions with a parishioner, and we decline to recognize a claim for bad advice from a minister under the facts before us.

The court concluded that the plaintiffs also had no claim against their church:

> Neither the claims by the husband nor the wife against the minister are cognizable in Oklahoma. Thus, their claims against the church under the doctrine of *respondeat superior* cannot be heard. Because their claims against the minister also serve as the basis for the claims against the church for its negligent hiring and supervision of the minister, that claim is also not cognizable. We therefore need not reach the First Amendment issues that would necessarily be implicated when civil courts attempt to define the nature of employment criteria a church should or should not use in selecting individuals for ecclesiastical office, or in the process of conferring ecclesiastical credentials.

2. *Intentional Infliction of Emotional Harm*. In *Erickson v. Christenson,* 99 Or. App. 104, 781 P.2d 383 (1989), plaintiff alleged that her pastor intentionally inflicted emotional harm by manipulating and seducing her during a counseling relationship. The defendant first argued that plaintiff was alleging the abandoned tort of seduction, but the court replied:

> The tort of seduction provided recovery for damage to character and reputation, as well as for mental anguish and pecuniary losses. By contrast, plaintiff's claim alleges that Christenson misused his position as pastor and counselor to abuse her sexually, causing her not only emotional distress but also "loss of ability to trust other adults, to trust authority, and . . . to deal with religion and her faith in God." Accepting the allegations as true, the harm to plaintiff stemmed from Christenson's misuse of his position of trust, not from the seduction as such. Plaintiff has stated a claim.

The defendant further argued that the plaintiff's claims were barred by the Free Exercise and Establishment Clauses of the First Amendment. The court disagreed, stating:

Plaintiff's claim for outrageous conduct is not premised on the mere fact that Christenson is a pastor, but on the fact that, because he was *plaintiff's* pastor and counselor, a special relationship of trust and confidence developed.

3. *More Outrageous Professionals.* Generally, outrageous conduct is policed by RESTATEMENT (SECOND) OF TORTS § 46. For example, in *Singleton v. Foreman,* 435 F.2d 962, 971 (5th Cir. 1970), the court held that plaintiff stated a cause of action for intentional infliction of emotional distress with allegations that the defendant divorce attorney forced her into an oppressive contingent fee agreement at a time when she was already distraught, demanded her jewelry and coat as security for his retainer, was abusive and oppressive when she attempted to discuss the settlement of her divorce, and threatened her with ruin if she attempted to change lawyers.

4. *Secular Counseling by Religious Professionals. Nally v. Grace Community Church of the Valley,* 47 Cal. 3d 278, 253 Cal. Rptr. 97, 763 P.2d 948 (1988), *cert. denied,* 109 S. Ct. 1644, 104 L. Ed. 2d 159 (1989), involved a suit against a church and four of its pastors after the suicide of a church member. For the majority, Lucas, C.J., stated:

> One can argue that it is foreseeable that if a nontherapist counselor fails to refer a potentially suicidal individual to professional, licensed therapeutic care, the individual may commit suicide. While under some circumstances counselors may conclude that referring a client to a psychiatrist is prudent and necessary, our past decisions teach that it is inappropriate to impose a duty to refer which may stifle all gratuitous or religious counseling based on foreseeability alone. Mere foreseeability of the harm or knowledge of the danger, is insufficient to create a legally cognizable special relationship giving rise to a legal duty to prevent harm . . . .
>
> . . . [N]either the Legislature nor the courts have ever imposed a legal obligation on persons to take affirmative steps to prevent the suicide of one who is not under the care of a physician in a hospital . . . .
>
> We also note that the Legislature has exempted the clergy from the licensing requirements applicable to marriage, family, child and domestic counselors and from the operation of statutes regulating psychologists. In so doing, the Legislature has recognized that access to the clergy for counseling should be free from state imposed counseling standards, and that "the secular state is not equipped to ascertain the competence of counseling when performed by those affiliated with religious organizations." (Ericsson, *Clergyman Malpractice: Ramifications of a New Theory* (1981), 16 VAL. U. L. REV. 163, 176.)
>
> Furthermore, extending liability to voluntary, noncommercial and noncustodial relationships is contrary to the trend in the Legislature to encourage private assistance efforts . . . .
>
> Even assuming that workable standards of care could be established in the present case, an additional difficulty arises in attempting to identify with precision those to whom the duty should apply. Because

of the differing theological views espoused by the myriad of religions in our state and practiced by church members, it would certainly be impractical, and quite possibly unconstitutional, to impose a duty of care on pastoral counselors. Such a duty would necessarily be intertwined with the religious philosophy of the particular denomination or ecclesiastical teachings of the religious entity. We have previously refused to impose a duty when to do so would involve complex policy decisions, and we are unpersuaded by plaintiffs that we should depart from this policy in the present case . . . .

For the foregoing reasons, we conclude that plaintiffs have not met the threshold requirements for imposing on defendants a duty to prevent suicide. Plaintiffs failed to persuade us that the duty to prevent suicide (heretofore imposed only on psychiatrists and hospitals while caring for a suicidal patient) or the general professional duty of care (heretofore imposed only on psychiatrists when treating a mentally disturbed patient) should be extended to a nontherapist counselor who offers counseling to a potentially suicidal person on secular or spiritual matters.

5. *Religious Medical Care*. The court summarized the facts:

Ian Lundman died at age 11 from juvenile-onset diabetes following three days of Christian Science care. A medical professional would have easily diagnosed Ian's diabetes from the various symptoms he displayed in the weeks and days leading up to his death (particularly breath with a fruity aroma). Although juvenile-onset diabetes is usually responsive to insulin, even up to within two hours of death, the Christian Science individuals who cared for Ian during his last days failed to seek medical care for him—pursuant to a central tenet of the Christian Science religion. This wrongful death action followed.

We begin the morning of May 6, 1989, when, after having been ill and lethargic intermittently for several weeks, 11-year-old Ian Lundman complained to his mother that he was again not feeling well, specifically that he had a stomachache. Ian's mother, appellant Kathleen McKown (mother), noticed that Ian had lost a "noticeable" amount of weight, had a fruity aroma on his breath, and lacked his normal energy. Consistent with the tenets of the Christian Science Church, which she espoused, mother began treating Ian through prayer. Throughout the day, Ian continued to complain of a stomachache.

When Ian again complained to his mother about not feeling well the next morning (day two), she became more concerned. Because the Christian Science Church recommends that a journal-listed practitioner be hired when a parent is concerned about a child's health, mother contacted appellant Mario Tosto regarding Ian's condition. As a "journal-listed" practitioner, Tosto appears in a Christian Science publication as someone who is specially trained to provide spiritual treatment through prayer. Mother hired Tosto to begin praying for Ian.

When, despite his illness, Ian attended Sunday School that morning, his Sunday School teacher observed that he appeared tired. Ian's mother was concerned about his low energy level and his continued need to eat mints to mask the breath odor. She noted during an afternoon visit to his grandmother's home that the usually-active Ian lacked energy to do anything but lie on the sofa. Ian also vomited while at his grandmother's home.

Ian was unable to sleep the night of May 7, and several times in the early morning hours of May 8 (day three) he complained of illness, seeking his mother's help and comfort and stating that he did not want to be alone. Ian's fear of being alone caused mother to have still greater concern. At this point, the downward spiral of Ian's health accelerated. He was unable to keep any food down that morning; Ian's visible weight loss, coupled with his inability to eat, caused mother to fear that her son might die.

Seeking further outside help, mother and appellant William McKown (her husband and Ian's stepfather) made several telephone calls on day three. First, pursuant to church directives, mother contacted appellant James Van Horn, who served as the one-person Christian Science Committee on Publications (CoP) for Minnesota. Learning that she intended to rely on Christian Science care, Van Horn verified that mother had contacted a journal-listed practitioner; and he later notified appellant The First Church of Christ Scientist (First Church) in Boston, that a child of a Christian Scientist was seriously ill. (First Church is known as the "mother" church of Christian Science.)

Second, mother called a Christian Science nursing home, appellant Clifton House, and a nurse advised her to give Ian small quantities of liquids. Third, William McKown (who is also a Christian Scientist) made a follow-up call to Van Horn because, fearing that Ian might be suffering from a contagious disease, he wanted Van Horn to give him telephone numbers for state or local health departments. (The church, as a regular practice, alerts Christian Scientists to the legal requirement to report contagious disease.) Fourth, William McKown called Clifton House again and told the nurse that Ian was not drinking the liquids that had previously been suggested.

Ian's condition worsened throughout day three; by that afternoon he was unable to eat, drink, or even communicate with others, and he could not control his bladder. He had to be carried to join his family at dinner, and at one point, looking at his mother and not recognizing her, said, "My name is Ian, too." This disorientation reinforced her concern that Ian's condition was life-threatening.

At approximately 8:00 p.m., mother called Clifton House, seeking to have Ian admitted. But Clifton House regulations prohibit admitting anyone under 16, so mother decided that she would take Ian to North Memorial Hospital. Mother dismissed the idea of seeking medical help, however, when Ellen Edgar, the on-duty nurse at Clifton House, proposed hiring a private Christian Science nurse to come to the McKown home. Edgar told mother that she would try to have a Christian Science nurse who took in-home cases call the McKowns.

Edgar subsequently called appellant Quinna Lamb, a journal-listed Christian Science nurse and, at the time, off-duty from Clifton House. Edgar told Lamb about Ian and asked if she was available. Lamb told Edgar that she knew the McKowns and would offer her services to them. Lamb subsequently called mother, who accepted Lamb's offer and hired her to provide home nursing services.

When she arrived at the McKowns' home at about 9:00 p.m., Lamb called Van Horn, notifying him that she was now assisting in Ian's care. This was the third call to Van Horn, and last until after Ian's death. Lamb then commenced caring for Ian and reading hymnals to him. Throughout the evening, mother and Lamb also contacted Tosto by telephone concerning Ian's worsening condition. Although he assisted mother and Lamb in caring for Ian earlier in the evening, William McKown went to sleep about 11:00 p.m.

At approximately 2:36 a.m. on May 9 (day four), Ian died.

Kathleen and William McKown were subsequently charged with second degree criminal manslaughter. The district court dismissed the indictments, however, and this court and the Minnesota Supreme Court affirmed.

Thereafter, Ian's natural father brought this wrongful death action on behalf of Ian's estate. The jury returned a verdict of $5.2 million compensatory damages. The court upheld this award against the deceased's mother and stepfather, and against the Christian Science nurse and practitioner who treated the child, but remitted the award to $1.5 million. A separate award of $9 million in punitive damages against the Christian Science church was reversed on the grounds, *inter alia*, that the award violated the church's free exercise privilege under the first amendment to the United States constitution.

In reaching this result, the court said:

> To grant [defendants] an outright exemption from negligence liability based on their religious beliefs would insulate Christian Scientists from tort liability in cases involving children; we will not embrace a negligence standard that would ignore the rights of Ian Lundman. The right to hold one's own religious beliefs cannot include the right to persist to act in conformity with those beliefs to the pont of imminent danger to a child. So, though we apply a standard of care taking account of "good-faith Christian Scientist" beliefs, rather than an unqualified "reasonable person standard," we hold that reasonable Christian Science care is circumscribed by an obligation to take the state's (and child's) side in the tension between the child's welfare and the parents' freedom to rely on spiritual care.

Lundman v. McKown, 530 N.W.2d 807 (Minn. App. 1995).

6. *Why Isn't Consent a Defense to a Patient's Seduction Claim Against His or Her Therapist?* The "consent" may have been obtained through "fraud or

duress" and thus is invalid. *See, e.g., Trotter v. Okawa*, 445 S.E.2d 121 (Va. 1994). What constitutes "fraud" in such cases? Could "fraud" encompass knowingly capitalizing on the patient's mental condition and on his or her faith in the therapist?

7. *Teacher Immunity?* The overwhelming majority of courts that have considered a cause of action for educational malpractice have rejected it. *See Finstad v. Washburn University of Topeka*, 845 P.2d 685 (Kan. 1993). The seminal case is *Ross v. Creighton University*, 740 F. Supp. 1319 (N.D. Ill. 1990), where the court wrote:

> Admittedly, the term "educational malpractice" has a seductive ring to it; after all, if doctors, lawyers, accountants and other professionals can be held liable for failing to exercise due care, why can't teachers? The answer is that the nature of education radically differs from other professions. Education is an intensely collaborative process, requiring the interaction of student with teacher. A good student can learn from a poor teacher; a poor student can close his mind to a good teacher. Without effort by a student, he cannot be educated. Good teaching method may vary with the needs of the individual student. In other professions, by contrast, client cooperation is far less important; given a modicum of cooperation, a competent professional in other fields can control the results obtained. But in education, the ultimate responsibility for success remains always with the student. Both the process and the result are subjective, and proof or disproof extremely difficult . . . .
>
> It also must be remembered that education is a service rendered on an immensely greater scale than other professional services. If every failed student could seek tort damages against any teacher, administrator and school he feels may have shortchanged him at some point in his education, the courts could be deluged and schools shut down. . . . This is not to say that the mere worry that litigation will increase justifies a court's refusal to remedy a wrong; it is to say that the real danger of an unrestrained multiplication of lawsuits shows the disutility of the proposed remedy. If poor education (or student laziness) is to be corrected, a common law action for negligence is not a practical means of going about it.

PROBLEM

Two male infants, "Baby Jones" and "Baby Smith," were born within minutes of each other at City Hospital. Incorrectly marked identification bracelets were placed on each child, and the nursing staff gave "Baby Jones" to Ms. Smith and "Baby Smith" to Ms. Jones for feeding and family photographs. The hospital discovered the mistake when the infants were five days old. Both infants are in perfect health. The extremely distraught Jones and Smith families have contacted their attorneys. You are the general counsel for City Hospital. What is the Hospital's exposure, and on what theories of liability? Would you recommend that your client litigate these claims? If not, do you propose using some other dispute resolution mechanism?

C. THE PROFESSIONAL STANDARD OF CARE

BRUNE v. BELINKOFF
354 Mass. 102, 235 N.E.2d 793 (1968)

SPALDING, JUSTICE.

[Suit by husband and wife against anesthesiologist for malpractice.]

The plaintiff was delivered of a baby on October 4, 1958, at St. Luke's Hospital in New Bedford. During the delivery, the defendant, a specialist in anesthesiology practicing in New Bedford, administered a spinal anesthetic to the plaintiff containing eight milligrams of pontocaine in one cubic centimeter of ten percent solution of glucose. When the plaintiff attempted to get out of bed eleven hours later, she slipped and fell on the floor. The plaintiff subsequently complained of numbness and weakness in her left leg, an affliction which appears to have persisted to the time of trial.

Testimony was given by eight physicians. Much of it related to the plaintiff's condition. There was ample evidence that her condition resulted from an excessive dosage of pontocaine.

There was medical evidence that the dosage of eight milligrams of pontocaine was excessive and that good medical practice required a dosage of five milligrams or less. There was also medical evidence, including testimony of the defendant, to the effect that a dosage of eight milligrams in one cubic centimeter of ten percent dextrose was proper. There was evidence that this dosage was customary in New Bedford in a case, as here, of a vaginal delivery.[1]

The plaintiffs' exception to the refusal to give their first request for instruction and their exception to a portion of the charge present substantially the same question and will be considered together. The request reads: "As a specialist, the defendant owed the plaintiff the duty to have and use the care and skill commonly possessed and used by similar specialist[s] in like circumstances." The relevant portion of the charge excepted to was as follows: "[The defendant] must measure up to the standard of professional care and skill ordinarily possessed by others in his profession in the community, which is New Bedford, and its environs, of course, where he practices, having regard to the current state of advance of the profession. If, in a given case, it were determined by a jury that the ability and skill of the physician in New Bedford were fifty percent inferior to that which existed in Boston, a defendant in New Bedford would be required to measure up to the standard of skill and competence and ability that is ordinarily found by physicians in New Bedford."

. . . The instruction given to the jury was based on the rule, often called the "community" or "locality" rule first enunciated in *Small v. Howard,* 128 Mass. 131, a case decided in 1880 . . . .

---

[1] The defendant testified that such variations as there were in the dosages administered in Boston and New York, as distinct from New Bedford, were due to differences in obstetrical technique. The New Bedford obstetricians use superfund pressure (pressure applied to the uterus during delivery) which "requires a higher level of anesthesia."

The rationale of the rule of *Small v. Howard* is that a physician in a small or rural community will lack opportunities to keep abreast with the advances in the profession and that he will not have the most modern facilities for treating his patients. Thus, it is unfair to hold the country doctor to the standard of doctors practicing in large cities. The plaintiffs earnestly contend that distinctions based on geography are no longer valid in view of modern developments in transportation, communication and medical education, all of which tend to promote a certain degree of standardization within the profession. Hence, the plaintiffs urge that the rule laid down in *Small v. Howard* almost ninety years ago now be reexamined in the light of contemporary conditions.

The "community" or "locality" rule has been modified in several jurisdictions and has been subject to critical comment in legal periodicals.

One approach, in jurisdictions where the "same community rule" obtains, has been to extend the geographical area which constitutes the community. The question arises not only in situations involving the standard of care and skill to be exercised by the doctor who is being sued for malpractice, but also in the somewhat analogous situations concerning the qualifications of a medical expert to testify . . . .

Other courts have emphasized such factors as accessibility to medical facilities and experience . . . .

Other decisions have adopted a standard of reasonable care and allow the locality to be taken into account as one of the circumstances, but not as an absolute limit upon the skill required.

. . . We are of opinion that the "locality" rule of *Small v. Howard* which measures a physician's conduct by the standards of other doctors in similar communities is unsuited to present day conditions. The time has come when the medical profession should no longer be Balkanized by the application of varying geographic standards in malpractice cases. Accordingly, *Small v. Howard* is hereby overruled. The present case affords a good illustration of the inappropriateness of the "locality" rule to existing conditions. The defendant was a specialist practicing in New Bedford, a city of 100,000, which is slightly more than fifty miles from Boston, one of the medical centers of the nation, if not the world. This is a far cry from the country doctor in *Small v. Howard*, who ninety years ago was called upon to perform difficult surgery. Yet the trial judge told the jury that if the skill and ability of New Bedford physicians were "fifty percent inferior" to those obtaining in Boston the defendant should be judged by New Bedford standards, "having regard to the current state of advance of the profession." This may well be carrying the rule of *Small v. Howard* to its logical conclusion, but it is, we submit, a reductio ad absurdum of the rule.

The proper standard is whether the physician, if a general practitioner, has exercised the degree of care and skill of the average qualified practitioner, taking into account the advances in the profession. In applying this standard it is permissible to consider the medical resources available to the physician as *one* circumstance in determining the skill and care required. Under this standard some allowance is thus made for the type of community in which the physician carries on his practice . . . .

One holding himself out as a specialist should be held to the standard of care and skill of the average member of the profession practicing the specialty, taking into account the advances in the profession. And, as in the case of the general practitioner, it is permissible to consider the medical resources available to him.

[Reversed.]

NOTES

1. *The Locality Rule.* The famous case of *Small v. Howard,* 128 Mass. 131 (1880), involved a plaintiff who had suffered a severe glass wound to his wrist, severing both arteries and tendons. The defendant was a physician and surgeon in a country town of some 2,500 inhabitants. An eminent surgeon resided within four miles. Defendant treated plaintiff for ten days but did not refer him to any other surgeon. Over the plaintiff's objection, the jury was instructed that the defendant, "undertaking to practice as a physician and surgeon in a town of comparatively small population, was bound to possess that skill only which physicians and surgeons of ordinary ability and skill, practicing in similar localities, with opportunities for no larger experience, ordinarily possess." The jury found for the defendant and the Massachusetts Supreme Court affirmed, stating:

> It is a matter of common knowledge that a physician in a small country village does not usually make a specialty of surgery, and, however well informed he may be in the theory of all parts of his profession, he would, generally speaking, be but seldom called upon as a surgeon to perform difficult operations. He would have but few opportunities of observation and practice in that line such as public hospitals or large cities would afford.

The jury in *Small* were charged that "if the defendant had not the requisite skill and experience to treat the wound," he should have recommended a more skillful surgeon. Presumably the jury found the defendant did have the requisite skill and therefore had no duty to refer.

2. *The Custom-Expert Testimony Nexus.* From the first reported malpractice cases, it has been clear that the predominant standard is "custom," which must be established through expert testimony. *Slater v. Baker & Stapleton,* 2 Wils. K.B. 359, 95 Eng. Rep. 860, 863 (1767); *Cross v. Guthery,* 2 Root 90, 91 (Conn. 1794).

If a medical defendant's conduct complies with the relevant customary medical standards, then she cannot be found liable merely because an expert medical witness testifies that "he personally" would have pursued a different course. *Boyce v. Brown,* 51 Ariz. 416, 77 P.2d 455 (1938). *Compare The T.J. Hooper,* 60 F.2d 737 (2d Cir. 1932). Why the different rule as to the relevance of custom in *Boyce* and *T.J. Hooper*?

3. *The Perils of Innovation.* Does a custom-based standard unfairly penalize those who specialize in experimental or novel procedures?

4. *The Relation of Custom and Expert Witness Qualification.* Must an expert witness, in a medical malpractice case applying a locality rule, be from the

same or a similar locality as that of the defendant? Must she be from the same specialty as the defendant?

5. *Variations on a Locality Theme.* In addition to the *Small* locality rule, consider the variations that have been employed at one time or another, such as "similar locality" or "statewide." Some jurisdictions use a national standard.

6. *Litigation Strategies.* According to *Smith v. Lewis,* 13 Cal. 3d 349, 118 Cal. Rptr. 621, 530 P.2d 589, 595 (1975):

> [A]n attorney engaging in litigation may have occasion to choose among various alternative strategies available to his client, one of which may be to refrain from pressing a debatable point because potential benefit may not equal detriment in terms of expenditure of time or resources or because of calculated tactics to the advantage of his client. But, as the Ninth Circuit put it somewhat brutally in *Pineda v. Craven,* 424 F.2d 369, 372 (9th Cir. 1970): "There is nothing strategic or tactical about ignorance . . . ."

Wherein lies the balance between courtroom skill and legal malpractice?

7. *National Versus Local Standards.* In *Hall v. Hilbun,* 466 So. 2d 856, 870 (Miss. 1985), the court stated:

> We would have to put our heads in the sand to ignore the "nationalization" of medical education and training. Medical school admission standards are similar across the country. Curricula are substantially the same. Internship and residency programs for those entering medical specialties have substantially common components. Nationally uniform standards are enforced in the case of certification of specialists. Differences and changes in these areas occur temporally, not geographically.

The obvious effect of a national standard of care is to provide the litigants with the widest possible pool of experts. Does it favor expert-shopping plaintiffs over defendants? Does this therefore translate into a greater redistribution of medical care injuries? Are there any other justifications for a national standard of care?

8. *What Is for Hire, Expertise or the Expert?* Should defendant's counsel be permitted to question plaintiff's expert as to his annual income from such services? As to the frequency with which he testifies for plaintiffs rather than defendants in medical malpractice actions? *See Trower v. Jones,* 121 Ill. 2d 211, 117 Ill. Dec. 136, 520 N.E.2d 297 (1988) (permissible to inquire into how much expert witness who testified for plaintiff in a medical malpractice action was earning annually as expert witness, and into the frequency with which he testified for plaintiffs). *See also Rowe v. State Farm Mut. Auto Ins. Co.,* 670 So. 2d 718 (La. App. 1996) (in personal injury action, permissible to permit testimony of attorney offered to show medical expert's "long history of bias" against claimants). If plaintiff hires his expert on a contingency fee basis, the contract is void for illegality. *Duteau v. Dresbach,* 113 Wash. 545, 194 P. 547 (1920). Furthermore, THE ABA MODEL CODE OF PROFESSIONAL RESPONSIBILITY, EC 7–28 (1982), in part provides, "[I]n no event should a lawyer pay or agree to pay a contingent fee to any witness." However, that rule by its terms

would not appear to prohibit contingency payments to medical expert "brokers." *Cf. Advisory Opinion of ABA Standing Committee on Ethics and Professional Responsibility* (November 1987).

9. *Professional Courtesy?* In *Morrison v. MacNamara,* 407 A.2d 555 (D.C. 1979), the locality rule is described as "peculiar" to medical malpractice doctrine. Are there no regional variations involved in the practice of law? In *Pitt v. Yalden,* 4 Burr. 2060, 98 Eng. Rep. 74, 75 (K.B.D. 1767), Lord Mansfield stated, "they were country attorneys; and might not, and probably did not know that this point was settled here above." In *Spalding v. Davis,* 674 S.W.2d 710, 714 (Tenn. 1984), the court described the applicable standard of care in legal malpractice cases as follows:

> The settled general rule in most if not all American jurisdictions is that an attorney to whom the conduct of litigation is entrusted may be held liable to his client for damages resulting from his failure to use care, skill, and diligence which is commonly possessed and exercised by attorneys in practice in the jurisdiction.

Contrast *Kellos v. Sawilowsky,* 254 Ga. 4, 325 S.E.2d 757, 758 (1985), where the court concluded:

> In the final analysis, the local standard versus the standard of the legal profession generally may be a distinction without a difference . . . . [T]he standard of care required of an attorney remains constant—whether he is considered as a practitioner of a given state or as a practitioner of "the legal profession generally"—and that only the applications of care vary from jurisdiction to jurisdiction and from situation to situation.

10. *Statutory Standards of Care.* In an apparent attempt to stem the "malpractice crisis," some jurisdictions have returned to some form of locality rule with regard to either the standard of care or the source of expert witnesses. *See, e.g.,* TENN. CODE ANN. § 29-26-115(b), providing that "(n)o person . . . shall be competent to testify . . . to establish the facts required (in a medical malpractice action) . . . unless he was licensed to practice in the state or a contiguous bordering state a profession or specialty which would make his expert testimony relevant to the issues in the case and had practiced this profession or specialty in one of these states during the year preceding the date that the alleged injury or wrongful act occurred." *See also* Virginia Code § 8.01-581.20, providing that the standard of care in a medical malpractice action is "that degree of skill and diligence practiced by a reasonably prudent practitioner in the field of practice or specialty in this Commonwealth" unless either party proves "by a preponderance of the evidence that the health care services and health care facilities available in the locality and the customary practices in such locality or similar localities give rise to a standard of care which is more appropriate than a statewide standard."

11. *The Limits of Custom.* In *Incollingo v. Ewing,* 444 Pa. 299, 282 A.2d 206, 216–217 (1971), plaintiff alleged that an osteopathic surgeon had negligently prescribed a drug to plaintiff's decedent. As the court noted:

> [The defendant's] defense is in effect a confession and avoidance. He admits that he paid little or no attention to the written warnings

relative to [the drug], that he prescribed the drug extensively and indiscriminately for all kinds of viral infections, whether serious or not; and that he authorized two refills of [the drug] for [plaintiff's decedent] by telephone, without ever having had her as a patient or examining her at the times of the authorizations . . . .

. . . There was testimony that the indiscriminate use of [the drug] was widespread in the community at the time. There was also testimony critical of [the defendant's] treatment by [the child's pediatrician] and by . . . a hematologist called on behalf of [the child's pediatrician], but it did not go to the extent of stating that what he did violated the standards of the profession at the time. This is not, however, an end of the matter. Under the *Donaldson v. Maffucci,* 397 Pa. 548, 156 A.2d 835 (1959), formulation . . . the standard of possessing and employing the skill and knowledge "usually possessed by physicians in the same or a similar locality" is qualified importantly by the phrase "giving due regard to the advanced state of the profession at the time of the treatment." It is also an integral part of our rule that in employing the requisite skill and knowledge, the doctor must "exercise the care and judgment of a reasonable man." In this case, it is clear that full information relative to [the drug] was available in medical literature, and indeed that [the defendant] read materials other than [the manufacturer's] literature. Was [the defendant] using the care and judgment of a reasonable man in renewing prescriptions of a drug, the propensities of which were readily ascertainable, for a person who was not his patient, whom he had never seen, as a favor to her mother whose good will as a patient he wished to retain? There was no evidence that this course of conduct was in accord with the professional standard of conduct in the community at the time. A review of the record satisfies us that this question was fairly raised by the evidence, and that its resolution was for the jury.

It is argued on behalf of [the defendant] that "unlike other areas of negligence, in a malpractice action, the medical profession sets its own standard of conduct by establishing its own custom of practice." This would be to say that as long as a course of conduct, however unreasonable by ordinary standards, is the norm for the group, all members of the group are thereby insulated from liability so long as they do not deviate therefrom. That is not the law . . . . Thus, the statement that "A physician is required to exercise only such reasonable skill and diligence as is ordinarily exercised in his profession" . . . is not to be taken in isolation, and in disregard of the admonition to give due regard to the advanced state of the profession and to exercise the care and judgment of a reasonable man in the exercise of medical skill and knowledge. The quoted statement is true within its intended limits and is based on the lack of inherent medical competency of a lay jury. It was not intended to prevent a jury from weighing professional expert opinion as to whether or not a particular act or treatment was done with reasonable care and judgment, where there is no clear evidence of custom.

12. *Instructing on "Errors of Judgment"*. In *Rogers v. Meridian Park Hosp.*, 307 Or. 612, 772 P.2d 929 (1989), the Supreme Court of Oregon reviewed the following "error of judgment" instruction which had preceded a defense verdict:

> . . . If the term "judgment" refers to choices between acceptable courses of treatment, then the term "error in judgment" is a contradiction in itself.[1] Use of any acceptable alternative would not be an "error." Witnesses may continue to use terms such as "exercise of judgment." But the court should not instruct the jury in such terms; such instructions not only confuse, but they are also incorrect because they suggest that substandard conduct is permissible if it is garbed as an "exercise of judgment."

Consider the holding in *Ouellette by Ouellette v. Subak*, 391 N.W.2d 810 (Minn. 1986):

> [I]n professional malpractice cases the mostly subjective "honest error in judgment" language is inappropriate in defining the scope of the professional's duty toward those the professional serves. In our view, henceforth, in a medical negligence case, preferably the jury should be instructed as follows: A doctor is not negligent simply because his or her efforts prove unsuccessful. The fact a doctor may have chosen a method of treatment that later proves to be unsuccessful is not negligence if the treatment chosen was an accepted treatment on the basis of the information available to the doctor at the time a choice had to be made; a doctor must, however, use reasonable care to obtain the information needed to exercise his or her professional judgment, and an unsuccessful method of treatment chosen because of a failure to use such reasonable care would be negligence.

13. *Schools of Thought*. RESTATEMENT (SECOND) OF TORTS § 299A, comment *f*, provides in part:

> Where there are different schools of thought in a profession, or different methods are followed by different groups engaged in a trade, the actor is to be judged by the professional standards of the group to which he belongs. The law cannot undertake to decide technical questions of proper practice over which experts reasonably disagree, or to declare that those who not accept particular controversial doctrines are necessarily negligent in failing to do so. There may be, however, minimum requirements of skill applicable to all persons, of whatever school of thought, who engage in any profession or trade.

How many physicians, and of what prominence, does it take to make a "school of thought"? Is the test quantitative (a "considerable number" of physicians) or qualitative (a "considerable number" of "reputable and respected" physicians)? *See* the discussion in *Jones v. Chidester*, 610 A.2d 964 (Pa. 1992), where the court concluded:

> Where competent medical authority is divided, a physician will not be held responsible if in the exercise of his judgment he followed a

---

[1] It brings to mind other oxymorons, like "jumbo shrimp," "service station," and "fresh frozen."

course of treatment advocated by a considerable number of recognized and respected professionals in his given area of expertise.

In recognizing this doctrine, we do not attempt to place a numerical certainty on what constitutes a "considerable number." The burden of proving that there are two schools of thought falls to the defendant. The burden, however, should not prove burdensome. The proper use of expert witnesses should supply the answers. Once the expert states the factual reasons to support his claim that there is a considerable number of professionals who agree with the treatment employed by the defendant, there is sufficient evidence to warrant an instruction to the jury on the two "schools of thought." It then becomes a question for the jury to determine whether they believe that there are two legitimate schools of thought such that the defendant should be insulated from liability.

14. *Professional Samaritans.* Many states have adopted statutes partially immunizing from tort claims medical personnel who provide emergency services. Consider WASH. REV. CODE ANN. § 4.24.300 (1988):

> Any person, including but not limited to a volunteer provider of emergency or medical services, who without compensation or the expectation of compensation renders emergency care at the scene of an emergency or who participates in transporting, not for compensation, therefrom an injured person or persons for emergency medical treatment shall not be liable for civil damages resulting from any act or omission in the rendering of such emergency care or in transporting such persons, other than acts or omissions constituting gross negligence or wilful or wanton misconduct. Any person rendering emergency care during the course of regular employment and receiving compensation or expecting to receive compensation for rendering such care is excluded from the protection of this subsection.

15. *Contracting for Specific Medical Results.* In the leading case of *Sullivan v. O'Connor,* 363 Mass. 579, 296 N.E.2d 183, 186 (1973), the plaintiff recovered on an express warranty theory after alleging that the defendant plastic surgeon had promised to enhance her beauty and improve her appearance. Nevertheless, the court cautioned:

> It is not hard to see why the courts should be unenthusiastic or skeptical about the contract theory. Considering the uncertainties of medical science and the variations in the physical and psychological conditions of individual patients, doctors can seldom in good faith promise specific results. Therefore it is unlikely that physicians of even average integrity will in fact make such promises. Statements of opinion by the physician with some optimistic coloring are a different thing, and may indeed have therapeutic value. But patients may transform such statements into firm promises in their own minds, especially when they have been disappointed in the event . . . .

As an example of such judicial skepticism, consider *Stephens v. Spiwak,* 61 Mich. App. 647, 233 N.W.2d 124 (1975), in which plaintiff's allegation of an express warranty of sterility was undermined by evidence that the physician had stated that the chances of becoming pregnant following the tubal ligation procedure were "one in a million."

D. NON-CUSTOM BASED STANDARDS

BOWMAN v. DOHERTY
235 Kan. 870, 686 P.2d 112 (1984)

LOCKETT, JUSTICE.

Michael Bowman was arrested for giving a worthless check on December 27, 1978. He was released on bond and ordered to appear in court on January 15, 1979. Bowman arrived at the initial appearance without an attorney. The judge informed the plaintiff of his right to an attorney and continued the case until January 22, 1979.

On either January 16 or 17, 1979, the plaintiff left on a skiing trip to Colorado. On January 19, from a hotel in Colorado, Bowman telephoned Harold Doherty, a Topeka attorney, who had helped Bowman with previous legal matters. The plaintiff claimed he retained Doherty to handle this case. Bowman advised Doherty of his upcoming court appearance. Doherty told Bowman he would take care of the matter and to contact him when Bowman returned from Colorado. Doherty called the district attorney's office and made arrangements with one of the deputy district attorneys for the case to be continued for two weeks. When Bowman returned from Colorado, he spoke with Doherty, who assured Bowman the matter would be taken care of.

No continuance was arranged for with the district court. Bowman and Doherty failed to appear in court on January 22, 1979. The judge declared a bond forfeiture and ordered a warrant be issued for Bowman's arrest.

Bowman returned to Topeka from Colorado sometime during the next week following his telephone call to Doherty. Upon his return, Bowman called Doherty again, and the parties agreed to meet to discuss the case. A day or two later Bowman met with Doherty in his office to discuss the matter. According to Bowman, Doherty said, "I will take care of it. This is no problem, don't worry about it."

Several weeks later, in late February or early March of 1979, Bowman received a letter from the sheriff's office, stating he was in contempt of court for failure to appear on January 22. The letter advised Bowman would be arrested if he did not present himself at the Shawnee County Courthouse. After receiving the letter, Bowman called Doherty and described the letter to him. Doherty told Bowman to come in to his office and bring the letter with him. Bowman went to Doherty's office and showed him the letter. According to Bowman, Doherty said, "I know what this is, I will take care of it." Doherty took no action.

Approximately one month later, on April 13, 1979 Bowman was arrested at his residence on a charge of aggravated failure to appear. Upon his arrival at the courthouse, Bowman was allowed to make a telephone call to Mr. Doherty, but was unable to reach him. Bowman then was booked into the county jail where he was held for two or three hours. Bowman eventually called his father who came down to the courthouse to post bond for his son's release. Bowman was handcuffed for three or four minutes while he was moved from his jail cell to the room where the bond papers were signed. The handcuffs caused Bowman to suffer some physical pain.

Later that same day, after Bowman had been released from jail, Bowman's father telephoned Doherty, informed him of the situation, and asked to have an appointment with Doherty. Doherty told Bowman's father to come to his office in the morning. Early the next morning (April 14) both Bowman and his father met with Doherty in his office. After discussing the problem, Bowman's father asked Doherty if he was going to represent Bowman. Doherty, at this point, agreed to represent Bowman in both cases. Bowman's father then asked Doherty what needed to be done to take care of the cases. After reviewing the court papers, Doherty replied that they needed to appear at the next docket which was May 1, 1979. Doherty promised to appear in court for Bowman on May 1.

Sometime after the April 14 meeting, Doherty arranged to have both of Bowman's cases continued from the May 1 docket to the May 10 docket. Bowman and his father were notified by Doherty that the cases had been continued. Father and son appeared in court May 10. Doherty did not appear. Judge Hope recommended that Bowman and his father hire another attorney, which they did. Once the new attorney had been hired, both of Bowman's cases were resolved.

There was a sharp conflict in the testimony at trial whether or not Doherty had agreed to represent Bowman. Bowman claimed Doherty promised "to take care of" Bowman's case. Doherty testified he agreed to represent Bowman only if Bowman paid Doherty $100.00 in advance. Bowman never came up with the $100.00 fee, and therefore Doherty never undertook to represent Bowman.

In regard to the telephone call by Bowman from Colorado on January 19, Doherty testified that Bowman asked him to obtain a continuance of the bad check case "as a favor" for Bowman. Doherty told Bowman that he would "continue it for him."

At the meeting with Bowman following his return from Colorado, Doherty testified he told Bowman the case could be taken care of. Doherty meant by this that a post-dated check was involved, and that he had learned from the assistant district attorney they did not prosecute cases involving post-dated checks. Doherty told Bowman that it would cost $100.00 for Doherty to dispose of the case, and that Doherty would represent Bowman when Doherty received the $100.00.

Doherty testified that he instructed Bowman that the letter from the sheriff's office required Bowman to go over to the courthouse and make bond, or they would arrest him. Doherty explained to Bowman that Doherty could not make Bowman's bond, since a lawyer is prohibited by statute from posting bond in the county in which he lives.

Doherty denied that he ever told Bowman's father that he would take care of Bowman's cases. According to Doherty, he only told Bowman's father that the cases could be taken care of through an agreement with the district attorney. Doherty denied discussing the $100.00 fee with Bowman's father during the meeting. However, Doherty testified after the meeting was over, Bowman came back to Doherty's office without his father. Doherty again explained to Bowman that he would get the case dismissed if Bowman would **pay** him the $100.00 retainer fee.

At the conclusion of the trial, the jury found that both Bowman and Doherty were negligent, and it assessed the comparative fault among the parties to the transaction as follows: Bowman 30%, Doherty 50%, and the assistant district attorney who Doherty had contacted to continue the case 20%. The plaintiff was awarded $100.00 in actual damages for physical pain and suffering, and $900.00 in punitive damages. The jury refused to award the plaintiff any damages for loss of personal freedom. After apportioning the negligence, the trial court entered judgment in favor of the plaintiff in the amount of $50.00 in actual damages and the total amount of punitive damages of $900.00. The plaintiff appealed and the defendant cross-appealed.

. . . An attorney is obligated to his client to use reasonable and ordinary care and diligence in the handling of cases he undertakes, to use his best judgment, and to exercise that reasonable degree of learning, skill and experience which is ordinarily possessed by other attorneys in his community. The duty of an attorney to exercise reasonable and ordinary care and discretion remains the same for all attorneys, but what constitutes negligence in a particular situation is judged by the professional standards of the particular area of the law in which the practitioner is involved. Here, Doherty was involved in the practice of criminal law.

Defendant alleges where a client claims his attorney erred in the handling of his client's case, expert legal testimony as to the accepted standard for handling such a case is required for the proper determination of negligence by the trier of facts. Expert testimony is generally required and may be used to prove the standard of care by which the professional actions of the attorney are measured and whether the attorney deviated from the appropriate standard. Expert testimony is required with respect to a question an ordinary person is not equipped by common knowledge and skill to judge.

There is a common knowledge exception to the rule requiring expert testimony in malpractice cases. Expert testimony is not necessary where the breach of duty on the part of the attorney, or his failure to use due care, is so clear or obvious that the trier of fact may find a deviation from the appropriate standard of the legal profession from its common knowledge . . . .

Doherty was hired to represent Bowman in an alleged criminal check case . . . . Bowman's loss of freedom, for failure to appear before the court when required, was due to Doherty's deviation from the appropriate standard for an attorney [and] fell within the common knowledge exception to the rule requiring expert legal testimony.

The defendant contends the plaintiff is not entitled to punitive damages because his action sounds in contract. Legal and medical malpractice generally constitute both a tort and a breach of contract. Ordinarily an action for liability of an attorney on the grounds of negligence for failure to discharge his professional duty to a client rests on the employment contract and therefore is contractual in nature. Where the act complained of is a breach of specific terms of the contract without any reference to the legal duties imposed by law upon the relationship created thereby, the action is contractual. Where the gravamen of the action is a breach of a duty imposed by law upon the relationship of attorney/client and not of the contract itself, the action is in tort . . . .

Lawyers, like other professionals, are required to have and exercise the learning and skill ordinarily possessed by members of their profession in the community. The trial court correctly overruled the defendant's motions for directed verdicts by determining that both a legal and contractual obligation could have been breached. Plaintiff's action sounded in tort. [Reversed and remanded because the trial judge had wrongly granted defendant's motion for partial summary judgment on the question of plaintiff's alleged emotional distress.]

NOTES

1. *Patent Medical Malpractice.* Use of a "custom" standard permits a profession to "make its own rules" on malpractice. Because the custom in the relevant "medical community" is beyond the ken of the average lay person, a medical malpractice plaintiff may be unable to succeed unless he can obtain the expert testimony of someone within that "medical community." However, there are some circumstances in which such expert testimony is not essential to the plaintiff's recovery. For example, in *Hammer v. Rosen,* 7 N.Y.2d 376, 198 N.Y.S.2d 65, 165 N.E.2d 756, 757 (1960), there was evidence that a psychiatrist who had treated a schizophrenic for some seven years had beaten her on several occasions. In answer to the defendant's objection that plaintiff had supplied no expert testimony that this constituted malpractice, the court stated that "the very nature of the acts complained of bespeaks improper treatment and malpractice."

Wilson v. Martin Mem. Hosp., 232 N.C. 362, 61 S.E.2d 102 (1950), arose out of a botched childbirth. The court observed that "When the evidence of lack of ordinary care is patent and such as to be within the comprehension of laymen, requiring only common knowledge and experience to understand and judge it, expert testimony is not required."

Consider also *Jefferson v. United States,* 77 F. Supp. 706 (D. Md. 1948), in which a serviceman underwent a gall bladder procedure. In a subsequent operation, it was discovered that a large surgical towel, 30 inches by 18 inches, had been left in his abdomen. *See, also, Ohligschlager v. Proctor Community Hosp.,* 55 Ill. 2d 411, 303 N.E.2d 392 (1973), holding that expert testimony was not necessary when a doctor deviated from a manufacturer's recommendation as to the concentration in which a drug should be administered.

2. *Admissions by Defendant.* In the dental malpractice case of *La Rocque v. La Marche,* 130 Vt. 311, 292 A.2d 259 (1972), a directed verdict for the defendant was overturned because his own testimony established that his method of injecting anesthesia was inconsistent with the local custom. However, in *Senesac v. Associates in Obstetrics & Gynecology,* 141 Vt. 310, 449 A.2d 900, 903 (1982), the court held that the defendant's asserted postoperative statement that:

> "she made a mistake and that she was sorry, and that it [the perforation of the uterus] had never happened before" does not establish a departure from the standard of care ordinarily exercised by a reasonably skillful gynecologist. The fact that the physician may have believed, and, if so, verbalized the belief that her performance was not

in accordance with her *own* personal standards of care and skill, is not sufficient in the absence of expert medical evidence showing a departure from the standard *ordinarily* exercised by physicians in similar cases.

DARLING v. CHARLESTON COMMUNITY MEMORIAL HOSPITAL
33 Ill. 2d 326, 211 N.E.2d 253 (1965) *cert. denied,* 383 U.S. 946, 86 S. Ct. 1204, 16 L. Ed. 2d 209 (1966)

SCHAEFER, JUSTICE.

[Defendant hospital appeals a judgment against it. Plaintiff, suffering a broken leg, was taken to the emergency room at the defendant hospital where Dr. Alexander, who was on emergency call that day, treated him. Dr. Alexander, with the assistance of hospital personnel, applied traction and placed the leg in a plaster cast. Not long after the application of the cast, plaintiff was in great pain and his toes, which protruded from the cast, became swollen and dark in color. The toes eventually became cold and insensitive. Dr. Alexander "notched" the cast and sometime thereafter cut and split the cast, cutting plaintiff's leg in the process. Plaintiff subsequently was transferred to Barnes Hospital in St. Louis and placed under the care of Dr. Fred Reynolds, head of orthopedic surgery at Washington University School of Medicine and Barnes Hospital. Dr. Reynolds found that the fractured leg contained a considerable amount of dead tissue which in his opinion resulted from interference with the circulation of blood in the limb caused by swelling or hemorrhaging of the leg against the construction of the cast. Dr. Reynolds performed several operations in a futile attempt to save the leg, but ultimately a below-the-knee amputation was necessary.]

. . . The plaintiff contends that [the evidence presented] established that the defendant was negligent in permitting Dr. Alexander to do orthopedic work of the kind required in this case, and not requiring him to review his operative procedures to bring them up to date; in failing, through its medical staff, to exercise adequate supervision over the case, especially since Dr. Alexander had been placed on emergency duty by the hospital, after complications had developed. Plaintiff contends also that in a case which developed as this one did, it was the duty of the nurses to watch the protruding toes constantly for changes of color, temperature and movement, and to check circulation every ten to twenty minutes, whereas the proof showed that these things were done only a few times a day. Plaintiff argues that it was the duty of the hospital staff to see that these procedures were followed, and that either the nurses were derelict in failing to report developments in the case to the hospital administrator, he was derelict in bringing them to the attention of the medical staff, or the staff was negligent in failing to take action. Defendant is a licensed and accredited hospital and the plaintiff contends that the licensing regulations, accreditation standards, and its own bylaws define the hospital's duty, and that an infraction of them imposes liability for the resulting injury.

. . . The basic dispute, as posed by the parties centers upon the duty that rested upon the defendant hospital. That dispute involves the effect to be given to evidence concerning the community standard of care and diligence, and also the effect to be given to hospital regulations adopted by the State Department of Public Health under the Hospital Licensing Act, . . . to the Standards for Hospital Accreditation of the American Hospital Association, and to the bylaws of the defendant.

As has been seen, the defendant argues in this court that its duty is to be determined by the care customarily offered by hospitals generally in its community . . . .

In the present case the regulations, standards, and bylaws which the plaintiff introduced into evidence, performed much the same function as did evidence of custom. This evidence aided the jury in deciding what was feasible and what the defendant knew or should have known. It did not conclusively determine the standard of care and the jury was not instructed that it did.

> The conception that the hospital does not undertake to treat the patient, does not undertake to act through its doctors and nurses, but undertakes instead simply to procure them to act upon their own responsibility, no longer reflects the fact. Present-day hospitals, as their manner of operation plainly demonstrates, do far more than furnish facilities for treatment. They regularly employ on a salary basis a large staff of physicians, nurses and interns, as well as administrative and manual workers, and they charge patients for medical care and treatment, collecting for such services, if necessary, by legal action. Certainly, the person who avails himself of "hospital facilities" expects that the hospital will attempt to cure him, not that its nurses or other employees will act on their own responsibility.

(Fuld, J., in *Bing v. Thunig*, 2 N.Y.2d 656, 143 N.E.2d 3, 8 (1957).) The Standards for Hospital Accreditation, the state licensing regulations and the defendant's bylaws demonstrate that the medical profession and other responsible authorities regard it as both desirable and feasible that a hospital assume certain responsibilities for the care of the patient.

. . . On the basis of the evidence before it the jury could reasonably have concluded that the nurses did not test for circulation in the leg as frequently as necessary, that skilled nurses would have promptly recognized the conditions that signaled a dangerous impairment of circulation in the plaintiff's leg, and would have known that the condition would become irreversible in a matter of hours. At that point it became the nurses' duty to inform the attending physician, and if he failed to act, to advise the hospital authorities so that appropriate action might be taken. As to consultation, there is no dispute that the hospital failed to review Dr. Alexander's work or require a consultation; the only issue is whether its failure to do so was negligence. On the evidence before it the jury could reasonably have found that it was.

[Affirmed.]

NOTES

1. *The Medical-Ministerial Dichotomy.* Courts occasionally avoid the traditional expert testimony-custom approach to the liability of health care providers by characterizing the conduct in question as *ministerial* rather than

medical. For example, in *Kastler v. Iowa Methodist Hosp.,* 193 N.W.2d 98 (Iowa 1971), a psychiatric patient brought a negligence action after falling while taking a shower. The court characterized this activity as involving "routine" care, and held that plaintiff was not required to come forward with expert testimony as to the standard of care.

Contrast *Saltzer v. Reckord,* 179 A. 449 (Pa. 1935), which involved the fall of a patient from a stool after he had stated that he felt faint following a blood test. The fall caused a sterilizer to spill, burning the patient. The court held that this was a malpractice case and not one which could be maintained on a premises liability theory.

2. *Economic Rather than Medical Criteria.* In the leading case of *Helling v. Carey,* 83 Wash. 2d 514, 519 P.2d 981 (1974), the defendants had established that their professional standards did not require routine pressure tests for glaucoma upon patients under 40 years of age. The court refused to accept the conclusiveness of this customary evidence and noted:

> The test is a simple pressure test, relatively inexpensive. There is no judgment factor involved, and there is no doubt that by giving the test the evidence of glaucoma can be detected. The giving of the test is harmless if the physical condition of the eye permits.

A similar argument was made in *Truman v. Thomas,* 27 Cal. 3d 285, 165 Cal. Rptr. 308, 611 P.2d 902 (1980). Plaintiff's primary contention was that the defendant should have informed her of the risk she was taking if she did not have a pap smear test performed. Additionally, the plaintiff requested, but the trial court refused, the following instruction: "[A]s a matter of law . . . a physician who fails to perform a Pap smear test on a female patient over the age of 23 and to whom the patient has entrusted her general physical care is liable for injury or death proximately caused by the failure to perform the test."

The court held that *Helling* was inapplicable, stating that here: "[T]he physician recommended the appropriate test but failed to inform the patient of the risks entailed in refusing to follow his advice. The suggestion that a physician *must* perform a test on a patient, who is capable of deciding whether to undergo the proposed procedure, is directly contrary to the principle that it is the *patient* who must ultimately decide which medical procedures to undergo."

TERRY COVE NORTH, INC. v. MARR & FRIEDLANDER, P.C.
521 So. 2d 22 (Ala. 1988)

HOUSTON, JUSTICE.

This case is a malpractice action against two attorneys. The pertinent facts are as follows: In 1978 Terry Cove North incorporated for the purpose of purchasing and developing 220 acres of land in the Gulf Shores area. In 1979 Terry Cove retained Marr and Friedlander as its attorneys. In attempting to develop its land, Terry Cove experienced problems in procuring connections on sewer lines leading to a sewage treatment facility. While representing Terry Cove, Marr and Friedlander negotiated with Orange Beach Authority and with the Town of Gulf Shores in order to purchase sewer line connections for Terry Cove. Neither Orange Beach nor Gulf Shores agreed to provide sewer service on terms acceptable to Terry Cove. Consequently, Terry Cove, Marr, Friedlander, and other developers began negotiations to construct a privately owned sewage treatment facility. Because of the high costs involved in building a facility, Terry Cove and the other developers refused an offer to own and to operate a sewage facility themselves. However, Marr and Friedlander agreed to build, own, and operate such a facility and formed the Baldwin County Sewer Authority (BCSA) to accomplish this goal. BCSA obtained a permit to build a sewage plant with a capacity for 3600 units and sold available units on its sewage lines to developers, including Terry Cove. On November 20, 1980, BCSA and Terry Cove executed a contract in which BCSA agreed to sell 450 units to Terry Cove. Terry Cove received these 450 units in accordance with the contract. On the same day, Terry Cove's president signed a document drafted by Marr and Friedlander that discussed the meaning of Disciplinary Rule 5-104(A) of the Code of Professional Responsibility with respect to the business arrangement between BCSA and Terry Cove. The document advised Terry Cove of the conflicting interests that could potentially arise between Marr and Friedlander and Terry Cove due to the fact that Marr and Friedlander were simultaneously acting both as lawyers for Terry Cove and as owners and operators of BCSA. The document further advised Terry Cove to seek independent counsel and to refrain from using the professional judgment of Marr and Friedlander as to the business transaction between Terry Cove and BCSA.

After the contract was executed, Terry Cove learned that BCSA had a greater capacity than 3600 units; and, in 1983, Terry Cove requested additional sewer units. BCSA denied Terry Cove's request and contracted with other developers to sell certificates of use for the sewage treatment plant.

In 1985, Terry Cove filed a complaint against the law firm of Marr and Friedlander and against Marr and Friedlander individually, alleging breach of fiduciary duty and breach of duty imposed by Disciplinary Rule 5-104. An amendment added two additional counts, one for breach of Disciplinary Rule 4-101 and one for fraud. The trial court granted summary judgment in favor of defendants.

Terry Cove appeals from the summary judgment as to its two counts premised on alleged violations of Disciplinary Rule 4-101 and 5-104(A), arguing that a Disciplinary Rule under the Code of Professional Responsibility establishes a duty that a lawyer owes his client, the breach of which creates a private cause of action. Specifically, Terry Cove contends that the defendants' alleged breach of Disciplinary Rule 5-104, which prohibits lawyers from entering into a business transaction with a client if they have competing interests, unless the client consents after full disclosure, and their alleged breach of Disciplinary Rule 4-101(B)(2), which prohibits a lawyer from using confidential information gained from the attorney-client relationship to the detriment of the client, render summary judgment inappropriate.

. . . [C]ourts in other jurisdictions which have confronted this issue have expressly held that a violation of a Disciplinary Rule does not create a private cause of action. We find these cases to be dispositive in deciding the case at bar. The Code of Professional Responsibility is designed not to create a private cause of action for infractions of disciplinary rules, but to establish a remedy solely disciplinary in nature . . . .

Moreover, Alabama's Code of Professional Responsibility, which is patterned primarily after the ABA Model Code of Professional Responsibility, limits the remedies for violations of Disciplinary Rules to disciplinary measures . . . . In its Preliminary Statement, the Model Code states that the purpose behind the Disciplinary Rules is to prescribe a "minimum level of conduct below which no lawyer can fall without being subject to disciplinary action." The Model Code continues by disclaiming any intention of prescribing disciplinary procedures and penalties or of undertaking "to define standards for civil liability of lawyers for professional conduct." Alabama's Code of Professional Responsibility also states that the Disciplinary Rules establish a minimum level of conduct and that breaches of Disciplinary Rules subject an attorney to discipline but, unlike the Model Code, it establishes procedures governing disciplinary actions and penalties for violations. Rule 3 of the Rules of Disciplinary Enforcement enumerates the following types of discipline: 1) disbarment, 2) suspension for a fixed period of time, 3) temporary suspension, 4) public censure, 5) private reprimand, and 6) private informal admonition. Rule 3, as well as the entire section entitled "Rules of Disciplinary Enforcement," does not provide for a civil cause of action for breaches of disciplinary rules. The sole remedy is the imposition of disciplinary measures. Like the Model Code, Alabama's Code of Professional Responsibility does not set out standards for civil liability. Therefore, in light of the limited scope of the Disciplinary Rules of the Code of Professional Responsibility, Terry Cove's argument is untenable.

For the foregoing reasons, we hold that an alleged violation of a Disciplinary Rule of the Code of Professional Responsibility cannot, independently, serve as a legal basis of a civil action for money damages.

NOTES

1. *Normative Standards in the Code of Professional Responsibility.* In *Lazy Seven Coal Mines v. Stone & Hinds*, 813 S.W.2d 400 (Tenn. 1991), the court noted that "all the courts that have directly considered the issue" have held that the Code of Professional Responsibility does not give rise to a private cause of action for damages. It quoted an Oregon case to the effect that such an action "would be contrary to the 'obvious public interest' in affording every citizen 'the utmost freedom of access to the courts,'" and that the Code "was not intended to create a private cause of action." It then said:

> Even though, as set forth above, the Code does not define standards for civil liability, the standards stated in the Code are not irrelevant in determining the standard of care in certain actions for malpractice. The Code may provide guidance in ascertaining lawyers' obligations to their clients under various circumstances, and conduct which violates the Code may also constitute a breach of the standard of care due a client. However, in a civil action charging malpractice, the standard of care is the particular duty owed the client under the

circumstances of the representation, which may or may not be the standard contemplated by the Code.

Who decides whether "the standard contemplated by the Code" is the same as the standard of care applicable in a legal malpractice action?

2. *Statutory Duties and Standards. Landeros v. Flood,* 17 Cal. 3d 399, 131 Cal. Rptr. 69, 551 P.2d 389 (1976), involved an action against a physician and hospital for failure to diagnose and report "battered child syndrome." The court held that the plaintiff stated a cause of action in negligence for which expert testimony would be required. Additionally, however, the court held that the plaintiff could bring an action for failure to comply with the state child abuse reporting legislation.

3. *Manufacturer Expertise and Package Inserts. Ramon v. Farr,* 70 P.2d 131 (Utah 1989), concerned injuries received by a child during birth following the defendant physician's injection of the mother's cervical region with an anesthetic. The plaintiffs requested an instruction that a prima facie case of negligence was established on the basis that the use of the drug as a paracervical block was contra-indicated in the drug's package insert and the *Physician's Desk Reference* (PDR). The court noted:

> We recognize that the courts appear to be split on whether the recommendations contained in a package insert are prima facie evidence of the standard of care. One line of authority relied on by the Ramons is represented by *Mulder v. Parke Davis & Co.,* 288 Minn. 332, 181 N.W.2d 882 (1970). In *Mulder,* the Minnesota Supreme Court held that when a drug manufacturer provides recommendations concerning the administration and proper dosage of a prescription drug and also warns of the dangers inherent in its use, a physician's "deviation from such recommendations is prima facie evidence of negligence if there is competent medical testimony that his patient's injury or death resulted from the doctor's failure to adhere to the recommendations." 288 Minn. at 339–40, 181 N.W.2d at 887 (per curiam opinion on petition for rehearing). *Mulder* has been followed by the courts of only a few other states. And the Minnesota courts have since retreated somewhat from the *Mulder* standard. Minnesota presently requires a *Mulder* prima facie negligence instruction only when the manufacturer's instructions contain a clear and explicit warning against the type of use that is alleged and a deviation from that recommendation caused the injury. In the present case, the manufacturer did not make such a clear and explicit recommendation against the use of Marcaine for a paracervical block. Rather, it simply did not recommend its use until further studies were performed. Thus, even under the current Minnesota rule, the Ramons would not be entitled to their proposed jury instruction.

Notwithstanding, the court continued:

> In any event, we decline to follow the *Mulder* rule, either as originally articulated or in its current incarnation. Rather, we think the better rule is that manufacturers' inserts and parallel PDR entries do not by themselves set the standard of care, even as a prima facie

matter. A manufacturer's recommendations are, however, some evidence that the finder of fact may consider along with expert testimony on the standard of care.

. . . Other jurisdictions have adopted the *Salgo v. Leland Stanford Jr. Univ. Bd. of Trustees,* 154 Cal. App. 2d 560, 577, 317 P.2d 170, 180 (1957), approach and have held that inserts and analogous materials are only some evidence to be considered in fixing the standard of care.

We think that better reasoning supports the *Salgo* rule. Although package inserts may provide useful information, they are not designed to establish a standard of medical practice, and their conflicting purposes make it extremely unlikely that they could be so designed.

MIRELES v. BRODERICK
117 N.M. 445, 872 P.2d 863 (1994)

RANSOM, JUSTICE.

On petition of Mary Ann Mireles, we issued a writ of certiorari to the Court of Appeals to decide (1) whether the doctrine of *res ipsa loquitur* is restricted to events from which the jury, without assistance of expert testimony, could infer negligence from common knowledge that such events do not otherwise ordinarily occur . . . . This is a medical malpractice action in which Mireles has sued Dr. Thomas Broderick, her anesthesiologist. [The jury found for the defendant. The Court of Appeals affirmed the trial court's refusal to instruct on *res ipsa loquitur*.]

Shortly after undergoing a bilateral mastectomy, Mireles experienced numbness in her right arm. The numbness subsequently was diagnosed as ulnar neuropathy, a condition marked in her case by degenerative nerve damage to the fourth and fifth fingers of her right hand. Mireles brought this action against Dr. Broderick, alleging separate counts of medical negligence, battery, and *res ipsa loquitur*. The case went to trial before a jury on the negligence and *res ipsa loquitur* theories. Mireles's expert witness, Dr. Randall Waring, testified that the ulnar nerve can be injured if it is compressed. He testified he believed that Mireles's ulnar injury, "in all probability, occurred while she was under anesthesia for [the] surgery" and that such injury was totally preventable by proper care. He testified that the ultimate responsibility for protection against injury lies with the anesthesiologist, who should properly position and cushion the arm to avoid compression and should monitor the arm during surgery to be sure that proper positioning and cushioning are maintained while the patient is unconscious. At the close of Mireles's case, the presiding judge stated that he was not going to allow Mireles to go forward with the case on the theory of *res ipsa loquitur* "because it doesn't come under the exclusivity rule." The court later refused Mireles's requested instruction on *res ipsa loquitur* . . . .

In contending that *res ipsa loquitur* is inapplicable to this medical malpractice action as a matter of law, Dr. Broderick advances two arguments. First, he contends that *res ipsa loquitur* is available only when an inference of negligence is articulable from the common knowledge and experience of the lay person. The major thrust of Dr. Broderick's argument is that the common-knowledge requirement is the "historical premise" of *res ipsa loquitur*, and to permit expert testimony to establish the inference of negligence would constitute an "end run" around this premise. According to Dr. Broderick, medical malpractice plaintiffs should be required to base their cases either on expert testimony or "common-knowledge" *res ipsa loquitur*, but not both. Second, according to Dr. Broderick, when a plaintiff has attempted to explain the exact medical cause of the injury, she should not have the benefit of the *res ipsa loquitur* instruction.

Dr. Broderick argues that, because of the rule that negligence of medical providers generally must be proved by expert testimony, *res ipsa loquitur* is limited in malpractice cases to the common-knowledge exception alluded to by this Court in *Cervantes v. Forbis*, 73 N.M. 445, 448, 389 P.2d 210, 213 (1964). He argues that only when the inference of negligence is within the common reservoir of knowledge of the jurors may the jury be charged on the *res ipsa loquitur* doctrine. In *Cervantes*, we stated that without expert witness testimony demonstrating departure from medical standards "there can be no issue of fact as to the negligence or proximate cause unless the case is one where exceptional circumstances within common experience or knowledge of the layman are present, or one where the *res ipsa loquitur* rule is applicable." *Id.* at 448–49, 389 P.2d at 213 (emphasis added).

By focusing on the rule of *Cervantes*, Dr. Broderick's argument loses sight of the dispositive principle at issue in the application of *res ipsa loquitur*. *Res ipsa loquitur* describes a set of conditions to be met before an inference of negligence may be drawn. See *Hepp v. Quickel Auto & Supply Co.*, 37 N.M. 525, 528, 25 P.2d 197, 199 (1933) (quoting from *Plumb v. Richmond Light & R. Co.*, 233 N.Y. 285, 135 N.E. 504 (1922), that *res ipsa loquitur* is a "rule that the fact of the occurrence of an injury and the surrounding circumstances [of the defendant's control and management] may permit an inference of culpability on the part of the defendant, make out plaintiff's prima facie case, and present a question of fact for the defendant to meet with an explanation"). As such, the central issue is not whether common knowledge alone is sufficient to establish an inference of negligence. Rather, the issue is whether there is a factual predicate sufficient to support an inference that the injury was caused by the failure of the party in control to exercise due care. The requisite probability of negligence may exist independently of the common knowledge of the jurors. The common-knowledge exception to the expert testimony rule may inform but does not delimit the application of *res ipsa loquitur*.

We join the growing consensus of courts from other jurisdictions and adopt scholarly commentary to hold that the foundation for an inference of negligence may be formed by expert testimony that a certain occurrence indicates the probability of negligence. RESTATEMENT (SECOND) TORTS § 328D cmt. *d* (1965) ("[E]xpert testimony that such an event usually does not occur without negligence may afford a sufficient basis for the inference [of negligence]."); W. Page Keeton et al., PROSSER AND KEETON ON THE LAW OF TORTS § 39, at 247 (5th ed. 1984) (stating that when a basis of common knowledge is lacking, expert testimony may provide a sufficient foundation for an inference of negligence); Thomas A. Eaton, *Res Ipsa Loquitur and Medical Malpractice in*

Georgia: A Reassessment, 17 GA. L. REV. 33, 52–56 (1982) (recommending that Georgia permit inference of negligence in medical malpractice actions to be based on expert testimony) . . . .

Dr. Broderick asserts, with little analysis, that by allowing expert testimony to form the basis for the *res ipsa loquitur* inference of negligence, "*res ipsa loquitur* [would lose] its roots as a form of circumstantial evidence." We fail to perceive any such historical limitation on the application of *res ipsa loquitur*.[1] As we have discussed, courts in other jurisdictions long have permitted expert testimony to form the foundation for an inference of negligence; commentators also endorse the use of expert testimony to raise the *res ipsa loquitur* inference. Stripped of technical argument, Dr. Broderick's contentions are a plea for a policy-driven decision to except medical malpractice defendants from the application of *res ipsa loquitur*. This we are unwilling to do.

Dr. Broderick contends that because Mireles adduced testimonial evidence concerning what could have been a cause of her injury, she is precluded from relying on the doctrine of *res ipsa loquitur*. He identifies the testimony of Dr. Waring that Mireles's arm was probably moved during surgery so that the ulnar nerve was compressed for between thirty and forty minutes on the edge of the padded board that held her arm. Citing *Marrero v. Goldsmith*, 486 So.2d 530, 532 (Fla.1986), Dr. Broderick contends that when a plaintiff undertakes explanation of the accident as it actually occurred, "there is a point where the plaintiff destroys any inference of other causes and dispels the need for the inference of negligence." Recognizing that the Court of Appeals has held that some evidence of the cause of the injury does not obviate the need for *res ipsa loquitur*, see *Harless v. Ewing*, 81 N.M. 541, 545–46, 469 P.2d 520, 524–25 (Ct. App.1970), Dr. Broderick contends nonetheless that the evidence in this case rose above the "some evidence" standard of *Harless*. We find PROSSER, *supra*, to be illuminating on this point: "Plaintiff is of course bound by his own evidence; but proof of some specific facts does not necessarily exclude inferences of others. When the plaintiff shows that the railway car in which he was a passenger was derailed, there is an inference that the defendant railroad has somehow been negligent. When the plaintiff goes further and shows that the derailment was caused by an open switch, the plaintiff destroys any inference of other causes; but the inference that the defendant has not used proper care in looking after its switches is not destroyed, but considerably strengthened. If the plaintiff goes further still and shows that the switch was left open by a drunken switchman on duty, there is nothing left to infer; and if the plaintiff shows that the switch was thrown by an escaped convict with a grudge against the railroad, the plaintiff has proven himself out of court. It is only in this sense that when the facts are known there is no inference, and *res ipsa loquitur* simply vanishes from the case. On the basis of reasoning such as this, it is quite generally agreed that

---

[1] In a linguistic sense, it may be true that when an expert is required to establish whether the injury does not normally occur in the absence of negligence, the thing no longer "speaks for itself." As a practical matter, however, a fellow physician may be disposed to speak to the necessary predicate but ill-disposed to state the natural inference that follows. As we note above, the issue in determining the availability of *res ipsa loquitur* is the presence of evidence raising an inference that the accident more probably than not occurred as a result of want of due care.

the introduction of some evidence which tends to show specific acts of negligence on the part of the defendant, but which does not purport to furnish a full and complete explanation of the occurrence, does not destroy the inferences which are consistent with the evidence, and so does not deprive the plaintiff of the benefit of *res ipsa loquitur*." PROSSER § 40, at 260 (footnotes omitted).

Significantly, Mireles was actually *unable* to provide by way of an expert opinion direct evidence that Dr. Broderick's failure to use proper care resulted in her injury. No expert "went so far" as to testify that the injury to Mireles was proximately caused by the failure of Dr. Broderick to possess and apply the knowledge and to use the skill and care ordinarily used by reasonably well-qualified anesthesiologists. See SCRA 1986, 13-1101 (Repl. Pamp. 1991) (Uniform Jury Instruction, duty of doctor). Because Dr. Waring's testimony did not purport to furnish an opinion on the ultimate issues of medical malpractice, it did not deprive Mireles of the benefit of *res ipsa loquitur* . . . .

Dr. Broderick contended, and the trial court agreed, that Mireles could not satisfy the element of exclusive control because more than one doctor had control of Mireles's body while she was unconscious. Dr. Broderick argues that the requisite control must be "sole" control. In *Tipton v. Texaco, Inc.*, 103 N.M. 689, 697, 712 P.2d 1351, 1359 (1985), we expressed that the meaning of "exclusive control" in *res ipsa loquitur* cases is fact specific within any given case. "The essential question becomes one of whether the probable cause is one which the defendant was under a duty to the plaintiff to anticipate or guard against." RESTATEMENT (SECOND) TORTS § 328D cmt. *g* (quoted in *Trujeque*, 117 N.M. at 401, 872 P.2d at 364). Dr. Waring testified that it was the *ultimate* responsibility of an anesthesiologist (Dr. Broderick, in this case) to ensure that a patient's arm was properly padded and positioned and to maintain the arm in the proper position during surgery. This testimony satisfied the exclusive control evidentiary requirement such that the question of exclusive control should have gone to the jury.

Because Mireles provided evidence that entitled her to proceed to the jury on the theory of *res ipsa loquitur* and tendered a legally correct instruction, the court erred in refusing to give the tendered instruction or an edited version thereof. We reverse the Court of Appeals and the trial court and remand for a new trial.

NOTES

1. *Magical Classical Incantations.* To obtain a res ipsa instruction, what must the plaintiff establish? Foreseeability of an unreasonable risk of harm is essential to negligence and thus essential to res ipsa. In *Dollins v. Hartford Acc. & Indem. Co.*, 252 Ark. 13, 477 S.W.2d 179 (1972), a medicated stroke patient who had undergone seizures was found on the floor at the foot of her bed. All four side rails of the bed were in the raised position at the time of the fall. No evidence was presented to show that the hospital or its agents should have foreseen that the patient would, whether in the throes of a seizure or in an attempt to go to the bathroom, fall from the foot of her bed. Held, in the absence of such evidence, this fall was not one that usually would *not* happen without someone's negligence.

2. *Expert Testimony Foundation for a* Res Ipsa Loquitur *Instruction.* In *Connors v. Univ. Assoc. In Obstetrics & Gynecology*, 4 F.3d 123 (2d Cir. 1993), the plaintiff underwent surgery in an attempt to become pregnant, and shortly thereafter she suffered a permanent loss of function in one leg. In her suit for malpractice, the experts disagreed on the likelihood of her leg injury occurring as the result of the surgery. The court refused a res ipsa instruction, and the jury found for the defendant. The court then granted a new trial, and on retrial it instructed the jury on res ipsa. The jury in the retrial returned a verdict of $800,000 for the plaintiff. Affirming the verdict, the Court of Appeals said the plaintiff could use expert testimony in support of her res ipsa claim "to 'bridge the gap' between the jury's common knowledge and the uncommon knowledge of experts."

3. *Res Ipsa and Punitive Damages.* In *Scribner v. Hillcrest Med. Cntr.*, 866 P.2d 437 (Okla. App. 1992), the court found:

> Patient under went an apparently uncomplicated hysterectomy at Hospital under the surgical care of Defendant Dr. Reza on October 1, 1985, and Hospital placed Patient in Bed B of a semi-private room to recover. Hospital moved the patient occupying Bed A of the same room elsewhere in the facility in the early morning hours of October 2 but Hospital staff failed to note the move in its records.[1]
>
> Later on the morning of October 2, within twenty-two hours of surgery, an orderly seeking the Bed A patient appeared at Patient's room[2] and announced his intention to take Patient to the ultrasound laboratory for testing. Patient protested that she had just come from surgery, had been instructed not to move without direction, and that she knew of no scheduled test. Nevertheless, the orderly persisted, and without checking Patient's identity,[3] the orderly lifted Patient from her bed, Bed B, to place her in a wheelchair. Patient testified she then felt excruciating pain and nearly passed out. The orderly proceeded to take Patient to the ultrasound lab.
>
> At the ultrasound laboratory, technicians there noticed Patient's weakened condition and obvious pain. Notwithstanding, and without checking Patient's identity, the technicians commenced the ultrasound procedure by introduction of cold water through a catheter into Patient's bladder. Patient testified she experienced a wave of cramp-like pain as a result. At that point, upon further remonstrations by Patient, the laboratory technicians determined Patient's true identity, discontinued the ultrasound procedure, and returned Patient to her room. The technicians, however, failed to notify Patient's attending Nurse of the mistake.[4]

---

[1] Two shifts of nurses failed to note the move of the patient in the adjoining bed.

[2] Notwithstanding having treated the Bed A patient in her new room, nursing staff directed the orderly to the Patient's room to find the Bed A patient.

[3] Patient wore a traditional hospital identification bracelet, and Patient's bed bore her name.

[4] Only after confrontation by Patient's doctor was a notation of the mistake entered in Patient's records.

> Patient discharged from Hospital about a week after surgery. However, two days later, Patient suffered an incisional dehiscence[5] and hernia, necessitating further surgery, although Patient apparently sustained little or no permanent impairment as a result of the second surgery.
>
> At trial, Patient presented testimony of the orderly that he ignored Patient's protests, that he did not check Patient's identification before taking her to the ultrasound laboratory, and demonstrating the orderly's ignorance of hospital procedures for patient identification. Patient also presented expert testimony tending to show causation of the incisional dehiscence attributable to strain and pulling during Patient's mistaken trip to the ultrasound laboratory. Patient also showed Hospital's net worth approaching $110,000,000.00.
>
> Hospital presented testimony of other experts contradicting Patient's evidence of causation. Defendant Dr. Reza testified that abdominal distension suffered by Patient during the initial hospitalization caused a suture to tear, resulting in the incisional dehiscence and hernia. Dr. Reza denied causal connection between the abandoned ultrasound procedure and the incisional dehiscence.
>
> Based on the evidence, the Trial Court found Patient had clearly showed Hospital's "lackadaisical attitude" toward patient identification procedures, evincing "a reckless and wanton disregard of the rights of" Patient so as to potentially allow an award of punitive damages in excess of actual damages determined. The Trial court then instructed the jury on the issue of punitive damages over objection of Hospital.
>
> The jury returned its verdict for Patient, awarding $100,000.00 in actual damages, and $10,000,000.00 in punitive damages.

The court found that the trial judge did not commit error in instructing on *res ipsa loquitur*:

> Under that doctrine, negligence may be inferred from the mere happening of an accident upon a showing that (1) the injury-causing instrumentality was under the exclusive care and control of the defendant and (2) the event causing the injury was of a kind which does not ordinarily occur in the absence of negligence. As we view the record, we find presentation of some expert evidence by Patient attributing cause of Patient's incisional dehiscence and attendant second surgery to the stress and strain of the unnecessary trip to the ultrasound lab which would not have occurred if Hospital patient identification procedures had been followed. Even Hospital admits a mistake in this regard. Under these circumstances, we cannot say the Trial Court erred in giving a *res ipsa loquitur* instruction.

The court, however, remitted the punitive award:

---

[5] "A bursting open, splitting, or gaping along natural or sutured lines." Tedman's Medical Dictionary, 25th Ed. (Williams and Wilkens, 1990).

We are of the opinion that the $10,000,000.00 punitive damage award in the present case is "larger than reason dictates to be necessary to deter such conduct in this defendant and other similarly situated," is "not . . . properly responsive to the legitimate objective of a punitive damage award," and is "so . . . excessive that we cannot in reason allow it to stand." We therefore hold the $10,000,000.00 award of punitive damages should be affirmed, conditioned on remittitur of $5,000,000.00 thereof. If Patient fails to file such remittitur, the entire judgment on jury verdict should be reversed, and the matter remanded for new trial.

Scribner was not a case where ordinary knowledge and expert testimony overlapped, but where they complemented each other. The recklessness of the hospital staff was evident, but causation was not evident without the aid of expert testimony.

4. *Multiple Defendants and a Possible Conspiracy of Silence.* Ybarra v. Spangard, 25 Cal. 2d 486, 154 P.2d 687 (1944), concerned a patient who awoke from an appendectomy experiencing pain around the neck and shoulders. Plaintiff brought suit against several hospital employees and members of the operating team. Defendants resisted the application of *res ipsa loquitur* on the basis that there were *several* defendants and *multiple* instrumentalities. Intimating that to give force to such objections would make *res ipsa* of doubtful utility in the modern medical context, the court concluded:

> [W]here a plaintiff receives unusual injuries while unconscious and in the course of medical treatment, all those defendants who had any control over his body or the instrumentalities which might have caused the injuries may properly be called upon to meet the inference of negligence by giving an explanation of their conduct.

5. *A Known Instrumentality?* In *Ward v. Forrester Day Care, Inc.*, 547 So. 2d 410 (Ala. 1989), the parents of an eleven-week-old child discovered that the child had suffered a broken arm while in the care of the defendant day care center. They sued the center, and requested a *res ipsa* instruction. The defendants argued that such an instruction was improper because there was no identification of the "instrumentality" involved. The court disagreed, observing:

> There is a small, but growing, body of law, dealing with the application of the doctrine of *res ipsa loquitur* to institutions such as hospitals, nursing homes, and child care centers where the "instrumentality" causing the injury is not known:
>
>> While the application of the doctrine is usually made in view of injury by machinery and instrumentalities under the exclusive control and operation of the defendant, from its very nature as a doctrine of necessity it should apply with equal force in cases wherein medical and nursing staffs take the place of machinery and may, through carelessness or lack of skill, inflict, or permit the infliction of, injury upon a patient who is thereafter in no position to say how he received his injuries.

Maki v. Murray Hospital, 91 Mont. 251, 264, 7 P.2d 228, 231 (1932)

. . . .

Defendant correctly states the plaintiff's usual burden of proof, but a plaintiff is not required in every case to show a specific instrumentality that caused the injury. The drafters of comments (*f*) and (*g*) to the RESTATEMENT (SECOND) OF TORTS § 328D (1965) state that in making the negligence point to the defendant, this is usually done by showing that a specific instrumentality has caused the event, or that *"all reasonably probable causes* were under the *exclusive control* of the defendant." (Emphasis added.) The commentators note that "[i]t is not, however, necessary to the inference that the defendant have such exclusive control; and exclusive control is merely one way of proving his responsibility." RESTATEMENT (SECOND) OF TORTS § 328D.

6. *A Potpourri of Torts.* In *Anderson v. Somberg,* 67 N.J. 291, 338 A.2d 1, *cert. denied,* 423 U.S. 929, 46 L. Ed. 2d 258, 96 S. Ct. 279 (1975), the tip of a forceps broke off and lodged in the plaintiff's spinal canal in the course of a laminectomy. Plaintiff brought an action against the surgeon for negligent treatment, the hospital for negligently furnishing the forceps, the hospital's medical equipment supplier for breach of warranty, and the manufacturer of the forceps for strict products liability. According to the court:

> [T]he jury should have been instructed that the failure of any defendant to prove his nonculpability would trigger liability; and further, that since at least one of the defendants could not sustain his burden of proof, at least one would be liable.

The dissent argued that the majority opinion was based upon the false premise that all of the possible responsible parties were before the court, despite evidence that several different nondefendants may have used the forceps over a period of years.

7. *Strict Liability for Medical Malpractice.* One writer notes that "despite a sharp split, the modern trend is to allow both a *res ipsa loquitur* instruction and expert opinion in medical malpractice cases," even though "the rationales for giving a *res ipsa* instruction and for relying upon expert evidence to prove negligence are in fact diametrically opposed." She concludes that this trend in fact may represent a means of transforming medical malpractice "from a fault-based system to one of strict liability." Karyn K. Ablin, *Res Ipsa Loquitur and Expert Opinion Evidence in Medical Malpractice Cases: Strange Bedfellows,* 82 VA. L. REV. 325, 326, 327, 355 (1996).

8. *No-Fault Schemes.* The Virginia Birth-Related Neurological Injury Compensation Act, VA. CODE § 38.2-5000 (Supp. 1989), introduced a no-fault compensation scheme in the case of a "birth-related neurological injury." Such an injury is defined as:

> injury to the brain or spinal cord of an infant caused by the deprivation of oxygen or mechanical injury occurring in the course of labor, delivery or resuscitation in the immediate post-delivery period in a hospital which renders the infant permanently nonambulatory, aphasic, incontinent, and in need of assistance in all phases of daily living (§ 38.2-5001).

Claims are heard by the state's "Industrial Commission" (§ 38.2-5003) and the claimant benefits from:

> A rebuttable presumption . . . that the injury alleged is a birth-related neurological injury where it has been demonstrated, to the satisfaction of the Industrial Commission, that the infant has sustained a brain or spinal cord injury caused by oxygen deprivation or mechanical injury, and that the infant was thereby rendered permanently nonambulatory, aphasic and incontinent (§ 38.2-5008.A.1).

What questions does Virginia's scheme both answer and simultaneously raise? Does it primarily benefit patients, physicians or malpractice insurers?

PROBLEM

Attorney Bright interviewed Victim, a prospective client who wanted to sue her former lawyer, Superficial, for legal malpractice. Bright's interview with Victim and her follow-up investigation revealed that Superficial represented Victim in a dental malpractice suit against Dentist. After Dentist removed a wisdom tooth, Victim was left without feeling in portions of her lower jaw. Victim claimed that the loss of feeling was caused when Dentist negligently damaged a nerve during oral surgery. Although Dentist denied negligence, she did admit that the loss of feeling in Victim's jaw was a result of the surgery. Dentist contended, however, that the loss of feeling was a risk inherent in the surgery, that she had fully advised Victim of this risk prior to the surgery, and that Victim had consented to the surgery with full knowledge of the risk. Victim claimed Dentist never advised her of such a risk. The case went to trial before Judge Callous, who entered a judgment for Dentist.

Bright believes that Superficial made three critical errors in representing Victim in her dental malpractice case. First, he did not demand a jury trial. Second, he retained an expert witness who was on the faculty of a prestigious, out-of-town dental school and who had outstanding academic credentials, but who had never been in private practice. Third, Superficial never discussed with Victim the decision to forego a jury trial and retain an academic expert witness who had never been in private practice. Bright is confident that she can get an attorney from the local community to testify that in a dental malpractice case such as this one, it is customary in the local community for a plaintiff's attorney to request a jury trial and to retain an expert witness with private practice experience. Bright doubts that she can get anyone to testify as to a custom to discuss these tactical decisions with the client, although Bright feels strongly that such a discussion is mandated by ethical and legal considerations.

You are a new associate employed by Bright. Identify the legal and factual issues that will be presented by a legal malpractice case against Superficial, and, in light of your critical assessment of the law and the facts, advise Bright of the chance of getting the case to the jury.

E. CONSENT, INFORMATION AND AUTONOMY

Recall the earlier discussion of battery. Providing medical services usually involves the touching of the patient, and if consent has not been given, the provider may thereby commit a battery. What if the provider obtains the patient's consent without disclosing to the patient the risks of the proposed treatment, and the alternatives available? The early cases treated that as a vitiation of consent, and held the physician liable for battery. The modern trend is to treat the matter as one of negligence: the physician owes a duty to adequately inform the patient before obtaining and acting upon the patient's consent. This section explores the latest developments in that duty.

NOTES

1. *Legal Authoritarianism.* Has the successful utilization of tort liability rules in breaking down the tradition of medical authoritarianism opened the door to legal "bullying"? In *Jefferson v. Griffin Spalding County Hosp. Auth.,* 247 Ga. 86, 274 S.E.2d 457 (1981), a woman in her thirty-ninth week of pregnancy had a complete placenta previa (afterbirth) between the unborn child and the birth canal. Her physicians believed that the condition would not correct itself prior to delivery. If the woman were to attempt a vaginal delivery, there was a 99 per cent chance that the fetus would not survive the delivery and a fifty per cent chance that the mother would not survive. If a Caesarian section was performed, however, both mother and child would, with almost 100 per cent certainty, survive the birth. On the basis of her religious beliefs, the woman refused to permit a Caesarian section to be performed and indicated that she would not consent to any transfusion of blood.

The trial court in *Jefferson* found that the fetus was capable of sustaining life outside its mother. The child was deemed both a viable human being and a child without the proper parental care and subsistence necessary for its physical life and health. As a result, custody of the fetus was given to state human resources officials, and the mother was ordered to submit to a Caesarian section if the attending physician found it necessary to sustain the life of the child. The Supreme Court of Georgia denied the parents' motion for stay of the order.

See generally Rhoden, *The Judge in the Delivery Room: The Emergence of Court-Ordered Caesareans,* 74 CALIF. L. REV. 1951 (1986).

2. *Whose Body Is It, Anyway?* In *Strachan v. John F. Kennedy Mem. Hosp.,* 109 N.J. 523, 538 A.2d 346 (1988), a 20-year-old suicide victim was diagnosed as brain dead in a hospital emergency room but placed on a respirator for possible organ harvesting. His parents decided against organ donation and asked that he be removed from the respirator. They were asked to reconsider their position and informed that the respirator could only be turned off on the orders of the hospital administrator. Two days later, and after a release was signed by the parents, the respirator was disconnected and the patient was declared dead. The plaintiffs brought suit against the hospital and its administrator on both negligent and intentional infliction of emotional harm theories and the jury awarded them $70,000 on each theory. The Supreme Court of New Jersey concluded that "there was ample support in the evidence for the jury's conclusion that defendants had "negligently [held] the body of [the patient] so as to prevent his proper burial."

Given the shortage of good body parts available for transplantation, should we give hospitals more leeway in their attempts to persuade next-of-kin to make donations?

3. *The Right To Die.* What if a patient who is otherwise competent to make decisions determines to die? In *Thor v. Superior Court*, 855 P.2d 375 (Cal. 1993), the court concluded that a competent, informed adult, in the exercise of self-determination and control of bodily integrity, has the right to direct the withholding or withdrawal of life-sustaining medical treatment, even at the risk of death, and that right ordinarily outweighs any countervailing state interest. The right does not depend upon the nature of the treatment refused or withdrawn; nor is it reserved to those suffering from terminal conditions. Once a patient has declined further medical intervention, the physician's duty to provide such care ceases.

What if the physician refuses to comply with the patient's wish to die, *i.e.*, to avoid life sustaining treatment? The patient may be entitled to compensation for the foreseeable injuries caused by the unwanted medical intervention. *See Anderson v. St. Francis-St. George Hospital*, 671 N.E.2d 225 (Ohio App. 1995).

PROBLEM

Patient, 18 years old, was admitted to the hospital for a Caesarian-section delivery of her third child. In the course of several prior discussions with her obstetrician-gynecologist (Ob-Gyn), Patient learned that she and her husband had incompatible blood types, a condition which posed an escalating threat to each successive child she conceived. As a result Patient initiated discussions with Ob-Gyn about various contraceptive techniques. Ob-Gyn suggested that Patient undergo a hysterectomy, but Patient rejected that option as too final. During the successful delivery of the third child, Ob-Gyn asked Patient's husband whether he should perform a bilateral tubal ligation on Patient. The husband said that he and his wife had discussed that procedure and that the doctor should perform the procedure. When Patient discovers what happened, she brings a battery action against Ob-Gyn. What arguments should Ob-Gyn make? How successful will they be?

LARGEY v. ROTHMAN
110 N.J. 204, 540 A.2d 504 (1988)

PER CURIAM.

[The court took the following statement of facts from the opinion of the appellate court.]

> In [the] course of a routine physical examination plaintiff's gynecologist, Dr. Glassman, detected a "vague mass" in her right breast. The doctor arranged for mammograms to be taken. The radiologist reported two anomalies to the doctor: an "ill-defined density" in the subareolar region and an enlarged lymph node or nodes, measuring four-by-two centimeters, in the right axilla (armpit). The doctor referred plaintiff to defendant, a surgeon. Defendant expressed concern that the anomalies on the mammograms might be cancer and

recommended a biopsy. There was a sharp dispute at trial over whether he stated that the biopsy would include the lymph nodes as well as the breast tissue. Plaintiff claims that defendant never mentioned the nodes.

Plaintiff submitted to the biopsy procedure after receiving a confirmatory second opinion from a Dr. Slattery. During the procedure defendant removed a piece of the suspect mass from plaintiff's breast and excised the nodes. The biopsies showed that both specimens were benign. About six weeks after the operation, plaintiff developed a right arm and hand lymphedema, a swelling caused by inadequate drainage in the lymphatic system. The condition resulted from the excision of the lymph nodes. Defendant did not advise plaintiff of this risk. Plaintiff's experts testified that defendant should have informed plaintiff that lymphedema was a risk of the operation. Defendant's experts testified that it was too rare to be discussed with a patient.

Plaintiff and her husband, who sued *per quod,* advanced two theories of liability . . . . They claimed that they were never told that the operation would include removal of the nodes and therefore that procedure constituted an unauthorized battery. Alternatively, they claimed that even if they had authorized the node excision, defendant was negligent in failing to warn them of the risk of lymphedema, and therefore their consent was uninformed. The jury specifically rejected both claims.

. . . *In Schloendorff v. The Soc'y of the N.Y. Hosp.,* 211 N.Y. 125, 105 N.E. 92 (1914), Justice Cardozo announced a patient's right to be free of uninvited, unknown surgery, which constitutes a trespass on the patient: "Every human being of adult years and sound mind has a right to determine what shall be done with his own body; and a surgeon who performs an operation without his patient's consent commits an assault, for which he is liable in damages." 211 N.Y. at 129–130, 105 N.E. at 93. Earlier case law recognized that theories of fraud and misrepresentation would sustain a patient's action in battery for an unauthorized intervention . . . . Although that cause of action continues to be recognized in New Jersey, . . . there is no "battery" claim implicated in the appeal because the jury determined as a matter of fact that plaintiff had given consent to the node excision performed by Dr. Rothman.

Although the requirement that a patient give consent before the physician can operate is of long standing, the doctrine of *informed* consent is one of relatively recent development in our jurisprudence. It is essentially a negligence concept, predicated on the duty of a physician to disclose to a patient such information as will enable the patient to make an evaluation of the nature of the treatment and of any attendant substantial risks, as well as of available options in the form of alternative therapies . . . .

An early statement of the "informed consent" rule is found in *Salgo v. Leland Stanford, Jr. Univ. Bd. of Trustees,* 154 Cal. App. 2d 560, 317 P.2d 170 (Dist. Ct. App. 1957), in which the court declared that "[a] physician violates his duty to his patient and subjects himself to liability if he withholds any facts which are necessary to form the basis of an intelligent consent by the patient to the proposed treatment." *Id.* at 578, 317 P.2d at 181. *Salgo* recognized that because each patient presents a "special problem," the physician has a certain amount of discretion in dismissing the element of risk, "consistent, of course, with the full disclosure of facts necessary to an informed consent." *Id.* at 578, 317 P.2d at 181.

Further development of the doctrine came shortly thereafter, in *Natanson v. Kline,* 186 Kan. 393, 350 P.2d 1093, *clarified,* 187 Kan. 186, 354 P.2d 670 (1960), which represented one of the leading cases on informed consent at that time. In *Natanson* a patient sustained injuries from excessive doses of radioactive cobalt during radiation therapy. Even though the patient had consented to the radiation treatment, she alleged that the physician had not informed her of the nature and consequences of the risks posed by the therapy. Thus, the case sounded in negligence rather than battery. 186 Kan. at 400–404, 350 P.2d at 1100–1101. The court concluded that when a physician either affirmatively misrepresents the nature of an operation or fails to disclose the probable consequences of the treatment, he may be subjected to a claim of unauthorized treatment. *Id.* at 406, 350 P.2d at 1102. The *Natanson* court established the standard of care to be exercised by a physician in an informed consent case as "limited to those disclosures which a reasonable medical practitioner would make under the same or similar circumstances." *Id.* at 409, 350 P.2d at 1106. At bottom the decision turned on the principle of a patient's right of self-determination:

> Anglo-American law starts with the premise of thorough self-determination. It follows that each man is considered to be master of his own body, and he may, if he be of sound mind, expressly prohibit the performance of life-saving surgery, or other medical treatment. A doctor might well believe that an operation or form of treatment is desirable or necessary but the law does not permit him to substitute his own judgment for that of the patient by any form of artifice or deception. [*Id.* at 406–407, 350 P.2d at 1104.]

After *Salgo* and *Natanson* the doctrine of informed consent came to be adopted and developed in other jurisdictions, which, until 1972, followed the "traditional" or "professional" standard formulation of the rule. Under that standard, as applied by the majority of the jurisdictions that adopted it, a physician is required to make such disclosure as comports with the prevailing medical standard in the community—that is, the disclosure of those risks that a reasonable physician in the community, of like training, would customarily make in similar circumstances. 2 D. LOUISELL AND H. WILLIAMS, MEDICAL MALPRACTICE § 22.08 at 22–23 (1987) (hereinafter Louisell and Williams). A minority of the jurisdictions that adhere to the "professional" standard do not relate the test to any kind of community standard but require only such disclosures as would be made by a reasonable medical practitioner under similar circumstances. *Id.* at 22–34. In order to prevail in a case applying the "traditional" or "professional" standard a plaintiff would have to present expert testimony of the community's medical standard for disclosure in respect of the procedure in question and of the defendant physician's failure to have met that standard. *Id.* § 22.09 at 22–35 to -37.

In both the majority and minority formulations the "professional" standard rests on the belief that a physician, and *only* a physician, can effectively estimate both the psychological and physical consequences that a risk inherent in a medical procedure might produce in a patient . . . .

It was the "professional" standard that this Court accepted when, twenty years ago, it made the doctrine of informed consent a component part of our medical malpractice jurisprudence. *See Kaplan v. Haines, supra,* 51 N.J. 404, 241 A.2d 235, *aff'g* 96 N.H. Super, 242, 232 A.2d 840 (1968). In falling into step with those other jurisdictions that by then had adopted informed consent, the Court approved the following from the Appellate Division's opinion in *Kaplan*:

> The authorities . . . are in general agreement that the nature and extent of the disclosure, essential to an informed consent, depends upon the medical problem as well as the patient. Plaintiff has the burden to prove what a reasonable medical practitioner of the same school and same or similar circumstances, would have disclosed to his patient and the issue is one for the jury where, as in the case *sub judice,* a fact issue is raised upon conflicting testimony as to whether the physician made an adequate disclosure.

[96 N.J. Super, at 257, 232 A.2d 840.]

In 1972 a new standard of disclosure for "informed consent" was established in *Canterbury v. Spence,* 464 F.2d 772 (D.C. Cir. 1972). The case raised a question of the defendant physician's duty to warn the patient beforehand of the risk involved in a laminectomy, a surgical procedure the purpose of which was to relieve pain in plaintiff's lower back, and particularly the risk attendant on a myelogram, the diagnostic procedure preceding the surgery. After several surgical interventions and hospitalizations, plaintiff was still, at the time of trial, using crutches to walk, suffering from urinary incontinence and paralysis of the bowels, and wearing a penile clamp. *Id.* at 778.

The *Canterbury* court announced a duty on the part of a physician to "warn of the dangers lurking in the proposed treatment" and to "impart information [that] the patient has every right to expect," as well as a duty of "reasonable disclosure of the choices with respect to proposed therapy and the dangers inherently and potentially involved." *Id.* at 782. The court held that the scope of the duty to disclose

> must be measured by the patient's need, and that need is the information material to the decision. Thus the test for determining whether a particular peril must be divulged is its materiality to the patient's decision: all risks potentially affecting the decision must be unmasked. And to safeguard the patient's interest in achieving his own determination on treatment, the law must itself set the standard for adequate disclosure. [*Id.* at 786–787 (footnotes omitted).]

The breadth of the disclosure of the risks legally to be required is measured, under *Canterbury,* by a standard whose scope is "not subjective as to either the physician or the patient," *id.* at 787; rather, "it remains *objective* with due regard for the patient's informational needs and with suitable leeway for the physician's situation." *Ibid.* (emphasis added). A risk would be deemed "material" when a reasonable patient, in what the physician knows or should know to be the patient's position, would be "likely to attach significance to the risk or cluster of risks" in deciding whether to forego the proposed therapy or to submit to it. *Ibid.*

The foregoing standard for adequate disclosure, known as the "prudent patient" or "materiality of risk" standard, has been adopted in a number of jurisdictions . . . .

Taken together, the reasons supporting adoption of the "prudent patient" standard persuade us that the time has come for us to abandon so much of the decision by which this Court embraced the doctrine of informed consent as accepts the "professional" standard. To that extent *Kaplan v. Haines*, 51 N.J. 404, 241 A.2d 235, *aff'g* 96 N.J. Super. 242, 232 A.2d 840, is overruled.

. . . At the outset we are entirely unimpressed with the argument, made by those favoring the "professional" standard . . . that the "prudent patient" rule would compel disclosure of *every* risk (not just *material* risks) to *any* patient (rather than the *reasonable* patient). As *Canterbury* makes clear,

> [t]he topics importantly demanding a communication of information are the inherent and potential hazards of the proposed treatment, the alternatives to that treatment, if any, and the results likely if the patient remains untreated. The factors contributing significance to the dangerousness of a medical technique are, of course, the incidence of injury and the degree of harm threatened. [464 F.2d at 787–788.]

The court in *Canterbury* did not presume to draw a "bright line separating the significant [risks] from the insignificant"; rather, it resorted to a "rule of reason," *id.* at 788, concluding that "[w]henever nondisclosure of particular risk information is open to debate by reasonable minded men, the issue is one for the finder of facts." *Ibid.* The point assumes significance in this case because defendant argues that the risk of lymphedema from an axillary node biopsy is remote, not material. Plaintiff's experts disagree, contending that she should have been informed of that risk. Thus there will be presented on the retrial a factual issue for the jury's resolution: would the risk of lymphedema influence a prudent patient in reaching a decision on whether to submit to the surgery?

Perhaps the strongest consideration that influences our decision in favor of the "prudent patient" standard lies in the notion that the physician's duty of disclosure "arises from phenomena apart from medical custom and practice": the patient's right of self-determination. *Canterbury, supra,* 464 F.2d at 786–787. The foundation for the physician's duty to disclose in the first place is found in the idea that "it is the prerogative of the patient, not the physician, to determine for himself the direction in which his interests seem to lie." *Id.* at 781. In contrast the arguments for the "professional" standard smack of an anachronistic paternalism that is at odds with any strong conception of a patient's right of self-determination. *Id.* at 781, 784, 789.

. . . We therefore align ourselves with those jurisdictions that have adopted *Canterbury's* "prudent patient" standard.

[Reversed and remanded.]

NOTES

1. *Professional or Patient Standard?* According to *Cobbs v. Grant,* 8 Cal. 3d 229, 104 Cal. Rptr. 505, 502 P.2d 1, 10 (1972):

> A medical doctor, being the expert, appreciates the risks inherent in the procedure he is prescribing, the risks of a decision not to undergo the treatment, and the probability of a successful outcome of the treatment. But once this information has been disclosed, that aspect of the doctor's expert function has been performed. The weighing of these risks against the individual subjective fears and hopes of the patient is not an expert skill. Such evaluation and decision is a nonmedical judgment reserved to the patient alone. A patient should be denied the opportunity to weigh the risks only where it is evident he cannot evaluate the data, as for example, where there is an emergency or the patient is a child or incompetent.

Why should an informed consent allegation attract a non-custom based standard? Is it because of a recognition that it is a defendant-inspired fiction to talk in terms of any "custom" (local or national) of disclosure? Or is it because the decision-making process involves non-medical criteria?

2. *Doctrinal Categorization Revisited; Battery or Negligence?* In *Cobbs v. Grant,* note 1 *supra*, the court stated:

> The battery theory should be reserved for those circumstances when a doctor performs an operation to which the patient has not consented. When the patient gives permission to perform one type of treatment and the doctor performs another, the requisite element of deliberate intent to deviate from the consent given is present. However, when the patient consents to certain treatment and the doctor performs that treatment but an undisclosed inherent complication with a low probability occurs, no intentional deviation from the consent given appears; rather, the doctor in obtaining consent may have failed to meet his due care duty to disclose pertinent information. In that situation the action should be pleaded in negligence.

See also Mink v. University of Chicago, 460 F. Supp. 713, 717 (N.D. Ill. 1978), in which women were given DES during their prenatal care by the defendant as part of a study to determine the value of the drug as a miscarriage preventative. The women were not told that they were part of an experiment or the identity of the drug. Defendants argued that plaintiffs' allegations sounded in negligence-based informed consent. The court held:

> The plaintiffs did not consent to DES treatment; they were not even aware that the drug was being administered to them. They were the subjects of an experiment whereby non-emergency treatment was performed upon them without their consent or knowledge.
>
> The plaintiffs in this action are in a different position from patients who at least knew they were being given some form of drug. The latter must rely on a negligence action based on the physician's failure to disclose inherent risks; the former may bring a battery action grounded on the total lack of consent to DES drug treatment.

Do you agree? Surely there was consent to the ingestion of *some* drug?

3. *A Numbers Game.* In *Harbeson v. Parke Davis, Inc.,* 746 F.2d 517 (9th Cir. 1984), U.S. army doctors failed to conduct a literature search that would have revealed several articles about the correlation between birth defects and the anti-convulsant drug given to an epileptic pregnant woman. The issue was whether the risks disclosed in the literature were material. The court noted:

> The determination of materiality is a two-step process . . . . The first step "is to define the existence and nature of the risk and the likelihood of its occurrence." *Adams v. Richland Clinic, Inc. P.S.,* 37 Wash. App. 650, 681 P.2d 1305, 1310 (1984); . . . . "Some" expert testimony is necessary to establish this aspect of materiality because only a physician or other qualified expert "is capable of judging what risks exist and the likelihood of occurrence" [*Smith v. Shannon,* 100 Wash. 2d 26, 666 P.2d 351, 356 (1983)]. The second prong of the materiality test is for the trier of fact to decide whether the "probability of that type of harm is a risk which a reasonable patient would consider in deciding on treatment." *Id.*
>
> . . . [W]e are satisfied that the first prong of the materiality test . . . has been met . . . . Expert evidence disclosed the nature of the risks and their likelihood of occurrence . . . . We further are satisfied that the second prong of the materiality test has been met. Based on the types of potential risks and their likelihood of occurrence, the district court did not err in finding as a fact that a reasonable patient would have considered these risks in deciding on treatment . . . .
>
> The government's argument that the risks are so small as to not require disclosure is not persuasive. We do not believe the risks posed by this drug are but "imperceptible risk[s]" that need not be disclosed, *Mason v. Ellsworth,* 3 Wash. App. 298, 474 P.2d 909, 920 (1970). The risk in *Mason* found to be so small that it need not be disclosed occurred "at most" .75 percent of the time. The likelihood of the risk here exceeds that likelihood in a significant manner. The fact that the risks enunciated [in one article] included cleft palate and hirsutism, of which the Harbesons were warned, does not persuade us otherwise. Those were not even the most common risks. The most common anomaly discovered in that study was congenital heart disease . . . of which the Harbesons were not warned. Even the Physicians Desk Reference should have given the doctors notice of the teratogenic effects of the drug . . . .

Contrast *Pauscher v. Iowa Methodist Med. Center,* 408 N.W.2d 355 (Iowa 1987), in which the court held that for a patient with a "potentially life-threatening illness," a 1 in 100,000 chance that she could die from a diagnostic procedure failed the objective test for materiality.

4. *Patient-Determined Materiality.* In *Mason v. Ellsworth,* 3 Wash. App. 298, 474 P.2d 909, 919 (1970), the court stated:

> If, at the time the physician discloses reasonably foreseeable risk[s], the patient inquires concerning any or all risks, then complete disclosure on the part of the physician is required. Correlatively, if the

patient wishes to be informed of any risks beyond those reasonably foreseeable he has the duty of inquiry.

5. *Effect of Consent Forms.* IOWA CODE ANN. § 147.137 (West Supp. 1988) provides:

> A consent in writing to any medical or surgical procedure or course of procedures in patient care which meets the requirements of this section shall create a presumption that informed consent was given. A consent in writing meets the requirements of this section if it:
>
> 1. Sets forth in general terms the nature and purpose of the procedure or procedures, together with the known risks, if any, of death, brain damage, quadriplegia, paraplegia, the loss or loss of function of any organ or limb, or disfiguring scars associated with such procedure or procedures, with the probability of each such risk if reasonably determinable.
>
> 2. Acknowledges that the disclosure of that information has been made and that all questions asked about the procedure or procedures have been answered in a satisfactory manner.
>
> 3. Is signed by the patient for whom the procedure is to be performed, or if the patient for any reason lacks legal capacity to consent, is signed by a person who has legal authority to consent on behalf of that patient in those circumstances.

6. *Causation and the Hidden Costs of Autonomy.* In *Cheung v. Cunningham,* 214 N.J. super. 649, 520 A.2d 832 (1987), the court stated:

> The fault of the objective standard is that plaintiff must for all practical purposes prove that *any* reasonable person placed in the same position would necessarily withhold consent even though plaintiff may have withheld consent and thereby have avoided injury. This is the antithesis of the doctrine of informed consent which is intended to protect the individual patient's right to decline treatment . . . .

STERN, J., concurring, opined:

> I have concerns that adoption of the subjective test in the present context would have the potential of converting each patient into a litigant and would promote a doctor-adversarial relationship as opposed to a doctor-patient status, thereby increasing malpractice litigation and escalating medical costs.

7. *Informed Consent and Lawyers.* Consider *Cohen v. Lipsig,* 92 A.D.2d 536, 459 N.Y.S.2d 98 (1983), in which it was held that there was a triable issue of fact as to whether plaintiff had given informed consent to his attorney's choice of counsel the attorney associated. *See generally* Martyn, *Informed Consent in the Practice of Law,* 48 GEO. WASH. L. REV. 307 (1979); Spiegel, *Lawyering and Client Decisionmaking: Informed Consent and the Legal Profession,* 128 U. PA. L. REV. 41 (1979).

PROBLEM

Patient consulted defendant urologist Dr. Harry for treatment of his kidney stones. Dr. Harry advised surgery. Patient requested that Dr. Harry perform the operation, and executed a consent form listing Dr. Harry as operating surgeon. Dr. Harry explained the risk of complications to Patient before Patient signed the consent form. Although Dr. Harry had treated him previously, Patient was unaware that Dr. Harry was in a "group" practice and "shared" patients with his partner, Dr. Charles. Plaintiff underwent the surgery; however, he suffered severe post-operative complications. Upon readmission to the hospital for further treatment of these complications, Patient learned that *his* operation had been performed by Dr. Charles and that on the day of the operation, Dr. Harry was in West Germany taking delivery of his new sports car.

You are Patient's attorney. Your client is not only suffering from post-operative complications but is extremely angry! Your preliminary investigations suggest that there is a high statistical correlation between the complications suffered by Patient and the type of operation performed. You realize that this is the first case in your jurisdiction involving what is known as "ghost surgery," where one doctor performs an operation for another without the patient's consent. You know that your state's Supreme Court has consistently held that actions brought by patients complaining about the conduct of their physicians sound *only in tort* and not in contract, misrepresentation, fraud or deceit.

What doctrinal approaches will you take in your suit against Dr. Harry and Dr. Charles? What case law will you draw on by way of analogy? What are your strongest *nondoctrinal* arguments?

TRUMAN v. THOMAS
27 Cal. 3d 285, 165 Cal. Rptr. 308, 611 P.2d 902 (1980)

BIRD, CHIEF JUSTICE.

Respondent, Dr. Claude R. Thomas, is a family physician engaged in a general medical practice. He was first contacted in April 1963 by appellants' mother, Mrs. Rena Truman, in connection with her second pregnancy. He continued to act as the primary physician for Mrs. Truman and her two children until March 1969. During this six year period, Mrs. Truman not only sought his medical advice, but often discussed personal matters with him.

In April 1969, Mrs. Truman consulted Dr. Casey, a urologist, about a urinary tract infection which had been treated previously by Dr. Thomas. While examining Mrs. Truman, Dr. Casey discovered that she was experiencing heavy vaginal discharges and that her cervix was extremely rough. Mrs. Truman was given a prescription for the infection and advised to see a gynecologist as soon as possible. When Mrs. Truman did not make an appointment with a gynecologist, Dr. Casey made an appointment for her with a Dr. Ritter.

In October 1969, Dr. Ritter discovered that Mrs. Truman's cervix had been largely replaced by a cancerous tumor. Too far advanced to be removed by surgery, the tumor was unsuccessfully treated by other methods. Mrs. Truman died in July 1970 at the age of 30.

Appellants are Rena Truman's two children. They brought this wrongful death action against Dr. Thomas for his failure to perform a pap smear on their mother. At the trial, expert testimony was presented which indicated that if Mrs. Truman had undergone a pap smear at any time between 1964 and 1969, the cervical tumor probably would have been discovered in time to save her life. There was disputed expert testimony that the standard of medical practice required a physician to explain to women patients that it is important to have a pap smear each year to "pick up early lesions that are treatable rather than having to deal with [more developed] tumor[s] that very often aren't treatable . . . ."

Although Dr. Thomas saw Mrs. Truman frequently between 1964 and 1969, he never performed a pap smear test on her. Dr. Thomas testified that he did not "specifically" inform Mrs. Truman of the risk involved in any failure to undergo the pap smear test. Rather, "I said, 'You should have a pap smear.' We don't say by now it can be Stage Two [in the development of cervical cancer] or go through all of the different lectures about cancer. I think it is widely known and generally accepted manner of treatment and I think the patient has a high degree of responsibility. We are not enforcers, we are advisors." However, Dr. Thomas' medical records contain no reference to any discussion or recommendation that Mrs. Truman undergo a pap smear test.

For the most part, Dr. Thomas was unable to describe specific conversations with Mrs. Truman. For example, he testified that during certain periods he "saw Rena very frequently, approximately once a week or so, and I am sure my opening remark was, 'Rena, you need a pap smear,' . . . . I am sure we discussed it with her so often that she couldn't [have] [fail]ed to realize that we wanted her to have a complete examination, breast examination, ovaries and pap smear." Dr. Thomas also testified that on at least two occasions when he performed pelvic examinations of Mrs. Truman she refused him permission to perform the test, stating she could not afford the cost. Dr. Thomas offered to defer payment, but Mrs. Truman wanted to pay cash.

Appellants argue that the failure to give a pap smear test to Mrs. Truman proximately caused her death. Two instructions requested by appellants described alternative theories under which Dr. Thomas could be held liable for this failure. First, they asked that the jury be instructed that it "is the duty of a physician to disclose to his patient all relevant information to enable the patient to make an informed decision regarding the submission to or refusal to take a diagnostic test.

"Failure of the physician to disclose to his patient all relevant information including the risks to the patient if the test is refused renders the physician liable for any injury legally resulting from the patient's refusal to take the test if a reasonably prudent person in the patient's position would not have refused the test had she been adequately informed of all the significant perils." Second, they requested that the jury be informed that "as a matter of law . . . a physician who fails to perform a pap smear test on a female patient over the age of 23 and to whom the patient has entrusted her general physical care is liable for injury or death proximately caused by the failure to perform the test." Both instructions were refused. [The jury found for the defendant. The second instruction was held by this court to have been properly refused.]

The central issue for this court is whether Dr. Thomas breached his duty of care to Mrs. Truman when he failed to inform her of the potentially fatal consequences of allowing cervical cancer to develop undetected by a pap smear [i.e., whether the first instruction should have been given].

In *Cobbs v. Grant,* 8 Cal. 3d 229, 104 Cal. Rptr. 505, 502 P.2d 1 (1972), this court considered the scope of a physician's duty to disclose medical information to his or her patients in discussing proposed medical procedures. Certain basic characteristics of the physician-patient relationship were identified. "The first is that patients are generally persons unlearned in the medical sciences and therefore, except in rare cases, courts may safely assume the knowledge of patient and physician are not in parity. The second is that a person of adult years and in sound mind has the right, in the exercise of control over his own body, to determine whether or not to submit to lawful medical treatment. The third is that the patient's consent to treatment, to be effective, must be an informed consent. And the fourth is that the patient, being unlearned in medical sciences, has an abject dependence upon and trust in his physician for the information upon which he relies during the decisional process, thus raising an obligation in the physician that transcends arms-length transactions." (*Id.* at p. 242, 104 Cal. Rptr. at p. 513, 502 P.2d at p. 9.)

In light of these factors, the court held that "as an integral part of the physician's overall obligation to the patient there is a duty of reasonable disclosure of the available choices with respect to proposed therapy and of the dangers inherently and potentially involved in each." (*Id.* at p. 243, 104 Cal. Rptr. at p. 514, 502 P.2d at p. 10.) The scope of a physician's duty to disclose is measured by the amount of knowledge a patient needs in order to make an informed choice. All information material to the patient's decision should be given. (*Id.* at p. 245, 104 Cal. Rptr. 505, 502 P.2d 1.)

Material information is that which the physician knows or should know would be regarded as significant by a reasonable person in the patient's position when deciding to accept or reject the recommended medical procedure . . . . To be material, a fact must also be one which is not commonly appreciated . . . . If the physician knows or should know of a patient's unique concerns or lack of familiarity with medical procedures, this may expand the scope of required disclosure . . . .

Applying these principles, the court in *Cobbs* stated that a patient must be apprised not only of the "risks inherent in the procedure [prescribed, but also] the risks of a decision not to undergo the treatment, and the probability of a successful outcome of the treatment." (*Cobbs, supra,* 8 Cal. 3d at p. 243, 104 Cal. Rptr. at p. 514, 502 P.2d at p. 10.) This rule applies whether the procedure involves treatment or a diagnostic test. On the one hand, a physician recommending a risk-free procedure may safely forego discussion beyond that necessary to conform to competent medical practice and to obtain the patient's consent. (See *id.,* at pp. 244–245. 104 Cal. Rptr. 505, 502 P.2d 1.) If a patient indicates that he or she is going to *decline* the risk-free test or treatment, then the doctor has the additional duty of advising of all material risks of which a reasonable person would want to be informed before deciding not to undergo the procedure. On the other hand, if the recommended test or treatment is itself risky, then the physician should always explain the potential consequences of declining to follow the recommended course of action.

E.   913

Nevertheless, Dr. Thomas contends that *Cobbs* does not apply to him because the duty to disclose applies only where the patient *consents* to the recommended procedure. He argues that since a physician's advice may be presumed to be founded on an expert appraisal of the patient's medical needs, no reasonable patient would fail to undertake further inquiry before rejecting such advice. Therefore, patients who reject their physician's advice should shoulder the burden of inquiry as to the possible consequences of their decision.

This argument is inconsistent with *Cobbs*. The duty to disclose was imposed in *Cobbs* so that patients might meaningfully exercise their right to make decisions about their own bodies. (*Cobbs, supra,* 8 Cal. 3d at pp. 240–241, 243, 104 Cal. Rptr. 505, 502 P.2d 1.) The importance of this right should not be diminished by the manner in which it is exercised. Further, the need for disclosure is not lessened because patients reject a recommended procedure. Such a decision does not alter "what has been termed the 'fiducial qualities' of the physician-patient relationship," since patients who reject a procedure are as unskilled in the medical sciences as those who consent. (*Id.* at p. 246, 104 Cal. Rptr. 505, 502 P.2d 1.) To now hold that patients who reject their physician's advice have the burden of inquiring as to the potential consequences of their decisions would be to contradict *Cobbs*. It must be remembered that Dr. Thomas was not engaged in an arms-length transaction with Mrs. Truman. Clearly, under *Cobbs,* he was obliged to provide her with all the information material to her decision.

Dr. Thomas next contends that, as a matter of law, he had no duty to disclose to Mrs. Truman the risk of failing to undergo a pap smear test because "the danger [is] remote and commonly appreciated to be remote." (*Cobbs,* Cal. 3d at 245, 104 Cal. Rptr. at p. 516, 502 P.2d at p. 12.) The merit of this contention depends on whether a jury could reasonably find that knowledge of this risk was material to Mrs. Truman's decision.

The record indicates that the pap smear test is an accurate detector of cervical cancer. Although the probability that Mrs. Truman had cervical cancer was low, Dr. Thomas knew that the potential harm of failing to detect the disease at an early stage was death. This situation is not analogous to one which involves, for example, "relatively minor risks inherent in [such] common procedures" as the taking of blood samples. (*Cobbs, supra,* 8 Cal. 3d at p. 244, 104 Cal. Rptr. 505, 502 P.2d 1). These procedures are not central to the decision to administer or reject the procedure. In contrast, the risk which Mrs. Truman faced from cervical cancer was not only significant, it was the principal reason why Dr. Thomas recommended that she undergo a pap smear.

Little evidence was introduced on whether this risk was commonly known. Dr. Thomas testified that the risk would be known to a reasonable person. Whether such evidence is sufficient to establish that there was no general duty to disclose this risk to patients is a question of fact for the jury. Moreover, even assuming such disclosure was not generally required, the circumstances in this case may establish that Dr. Thomas did have a duty to inform Mrs. Truman of the risks she was running by not undergoing a pap smear.

Dr. Thomas testified he never specifically informed her of the purpose of a pap smear test. There was no evidence introduced that Mrs. Truman was aware of the serious danger entailed in not undergoing the test. However, there was testimony that Mrs. Truman said she would not undergo the test on certain occasions because of its cost or because "she just didn't feel like it." Under these circumstances, a jury could reasonably conclude that Dr. Thomas had a duty to inform Mrs. Truman of the danger of refusing the test because it was not reasonable for Dr. Thomas to assume that Mrs. Truman appreciated the potentially fatal consequences of her conduct. Accordingly, this court cannot decide as a matter of law that Dr. Thomas owed absolutely no duty to Mrs. Truman to make this important disclosure that affected her life.

The instruction proposed by appellants . . . correctly indicated that a physician has a duty to disclose all material information to a patient. The instruction also stated that breach of this duty renders the physician liable for any "legally resulting [injury] . . . if a reasonably prudent person in the patient's position would not have refused the test had she been adequately informed of all the significant perils."

. . . The jury was instructed that a "proximate cause of an injury is a cause which, in natural and continuous sequence, produces the injury, and without which the injury would not have occurred." Obviously, this test could not be satisfied if the jury were to conclude that even given adequate disclosure Mrs. Truman would have refused to take the recommended test in time to save her life. Thus, the rejected instruction would have correctly indicated that satisfaction of the prudent person test for causation established in *Cobbs* was necessary but not sufficient for plaintiffs to recover. If the jury were to reasonably conclude that Mrs. Truman would have unreasonably refused a pap smear in the face of adequate disclosure, there could be no finding of proximate cause. Though awkwardly phrased, the rejected instruction accurately reflected the law and a theory of liability applicable to the facts of this case.

Refusal to give the requested instruction meant that the jury was unable to consider whether Dr. Thomas breached a duty by not disclosing the danger of failing to undergo a pap smear. Since this theory finds support in the record, it was error for the court to refuse to give the requested instruction. If the jury had been given this instruction and had found in favor of the appellants, such a finding would have had support in the record before us. Reversal is therefore required.

NOTES

1. *The Limits of Disclosure.* In *Malloy v. Shanahan,* 280 Pa. Super. 440, 421 A.2d 803, 804 (1980), the court held that the doctrine of informed consent applies to surgical procedures and "has not been extended to therapeutic treatment, which is usually an ongoing treatment upon examination by the treating physician, where any change of condition can be diagnosed and controlled." *But see Matthies v. Mastromonaco,* 160 N. J. 26, 733 A.2d 456 (1999). There the 81-year-old plaintiff broke her hip, and her doctor decided

on bed rest rather than surgery. The court said the doctor should have obtained her informed consent, even though a noninvasive course of treatment was chosen.

2. *"No Consent" to "Informed Consent" to "No Information". Gates v. Jensen,* 92 Wash. 2d 246, 595 P.2d 919 (1979), involved a patient who was diagnosed in the borderline area for glaucoma. Her ophthalmologist used a standard test for glaucoma which proved negative. He did not tell her that she had high pressure in her eyes and, therefore, was in a borderline glaucoma area, that such high pressure together with her myopia considerably increased her risk of glaucoma, or that he had available two simple, inexpensive and risk-free tests for glaucoma. Two years later she was diagnosed as suffering from glaucoma. The trial court refused plaintiff's instruction on informed consent. The Supreme Court of Washington reversed, stating:

> . . . The patient's right to know is not confined to the choice of treatment once a disease is present and has been conclusively diagnosed. Important decisions must frequently be made in many non-treatment situations in which medical care is given, including procedures leading to a diagnosis, as in this case. These decisions must all be taken with the full knowledge and participation of the patient. The physician's duty is to tell the patient what he or she needs to know in order to make them. The existence of an abnormal condition in one's body, the presence of a high risk of disease, and the existence of alternative diagnostic procedures to conclusively determine the presence or absence of that disease are all facts which a patient must know in order to make an informed decision on the course which future medical care will take.

JOHNSON v. KOKEMOOR
199 Wis.2d 615, 545 N.W.2d 495 (1996)

SHIRLEY S. ABRAHAMSON, JUSTICE.

This is a review of a published decision of the court of appeals, *Johnson v. Kokemoor*, 188 Wis.2d 202, 525 N.W.2d 71 (Ct.App.1994), reversing an order of the circuit court for Chippewa County, Richard H. Stafford, judge. We reverse the decision of the court of appeals and remand the cause to the circuit court for further proceedings on the question of damages.[1]

Donna Johnson (the plaintiff) brought an action against Dr. Richard Kokemoor (the defendant)[2] alleging his failure to obtain her informed consent to surgery as required by Wis.Stat. § 448.30 (1993-94).[3] The jury found that the defendant failed to adequately inform the plaintiff regarding the risks associated with her surgery. The jury also found that a reasonable person in

---

[1] The trial was bifurcated at the circuit court. The jury decided only the liability issue; the issue of damages has not been tried.

[2] While there are other defendants in this case, in the interest of clarity we refer only to Dr. Kokemoor as the defendant.

[3] All future statutory references are to the 1993-94 volume of the Wisconsin Statutes.

the plaintiff's position would have refused to consent to surgery by the defendant if she had been fully informed of its attendant risks and advantages.[4]

The circuit court denied the defendant's motions to change the answers in the special verdict and, in the alternative, to order a new trial. In a split decision, the court of appeals reversed the circuit court's order.

This case presents the issue of whether the circuit court erred in admitting evidence that the defendant, in undertaking his duty to obtain the plaintiff's informed consent before operating to clip an aneurysm, failed (1) to divulge the extent of his experience in performing this type of operation; (2) to compare the morbidity and mortality rates[5] for this type of surgery among experienced surgeons and inexperienced surgeons like himself; and (3) to refer the plaintiff to a tertiary care center staffed by physicians more experienced in performing the same surgery.[6] The admissibility of such physician-specific evidence in a case involving the doctrine of informed consent raises an issue of first impression in this court and is an issue with which appellate courts have had little experience.

The court of appeals concluded that the first two evidentiary matters were admissible but that the third was not. The court of appeals determined that evidence about the defendant's failure to refer the plaintiff to more experienced physicians was not relevant to a claim of failure to obtain the plaintiff's informed consent. Furthermore, the court of appeals held that the circuit court committed prejudicial error in admitting evidence of the defendant's failure to refer, because such evidence allowed the jury to conclude that the defendant performed negligently simply because he was less experienced than other physicians, even though the defendant's negligence was not at issue in this case.[7] The court of appeals therefore remanded the cause to the circuit court for a new trial.[8]

---

[4] The parties agreed to a special verdict form requiring the jury to answer the following two questions:

(1) Did Dr. Richard Kokemoor fail to adequately inform Donna Johnson of the risks and advantages of her surgery?

(2) If you have answered Question 1 "yes", then and then only answer this question: Would a reasonable person in Donna Johnson's position have refused to consent to the surgery by Dr. Richard Kokemoor had she been informed of the risks and advantages of the surgery?

The jury answered "yes" to both questions.

[5] As used by the parties and in this opinion, morbidity and mortality rates refer to the prospect that surgery may result in serious impairment or death.

[6] In a motion brought prior to trial, the defendant attempted to bar testimony and argument relating to his personal experience with aneurysm surgery and to the relative experience of other surgeons available to perform such surgery. The defendant argued that such disclosures are not material to the issue of informed consent. The circuit court denied the defendant's motion and also ruled that the plaintiff could present expert testimony that the defendant should have advised her of and referred her to more experienced neurosurgeons.

[7] Prior to trial, the plaintiff had voluntarily dismissed a cause of action alleging that the defendant was negligent in performing the surgery.

[8] Given the "overwhelming" evidence "that Kokemoor did not adequately inform Johnson," Johnson v. Kokemoor, 188 Wis.2d 202, 227, 525 N.W.2d 71 (Ct.App.1994), the court of appeals left to the circuit court's discretion whether it need retry the issue of the defendant's alleged failure to obtain the plaintiff's informed consent or whether it need retry only the causation issue.

E.

The plaintiff's position is that the court of appeals erred in directing a new trial. The defendant's position in his cross-petition is that the circuit court and the court of appeals both erred in approving the admission of evidence referring to his experience with this type of surgery and to his and other physicians' morbidity and mortality statistics in performing this type of surgery.

We conclude that all three items of evidence were material to the issue of informed consent in this case. As we stated in *Martin v. Richards*, 192 Wis.2d 156, 174, 531 N.W.2d 70 (1995), "a patient cannot make an informed, intelligent decision to consent to a physician's suggested treatment unless the physician discloses what is material to the patient's decision, *i.e.*, all of the viable alternatives and risks of the treatment proposed." In this case information regarding a physician's experience in performing a particular procedure, a physician's risk statistics as compared with those of other physicians who perform that procedure, and the availability of other centers and physicians better able to perform that procedure would have facilitated the plaintiff's awareness of "all of the viable alternatives" available to her and thereby aided her exercise of informed consent. We therefore conclude that under the circumstances of this case, the circuit court did not erroneously exercise its discretion in admitting the evidence.

We first summarize the facts giving rise to this review, recognizing that the parties dispute whether several events occurred, as well as what inferences should be drawn from both the disputed and the undisputed historical facts.

On the advice of her family physician, the plaintiff underwent a CT scan to determine the cause of her headaches. Following the scan, the family physician referred the plaintiff to the defendant, a neurosurgeon in the Chippewa Falls area. The defendant diagnosed an enlarging aneurysm at the rear of the plaintiff's brain and recommended surgery to clip the aneurysm.[9] The defendant performed the surgery in October of 1990.

The defendant clipped the aneurysm, rendering the surgery a technical success. But as a consequence of the surgery, the plaintiff, who had no neurological impairments prior to surgery, was rendered an incomplete quadriplegic. She remains unable to walk or to control her bowel and bladder movements. Furthermore, her vision, speech and upper body coordination are partially impaired.

At trial, the plaintiff introduced evidence that the defendant overstated the urgency of her need for surgery and overstated his experience with performing the particular type of aneurysm surgery which she required. According to testimony introduced during the plaintiff's case in chief, when the plaintiff questioned the defendant regarding his experience, he replied that he had performed the surgery she required "several" times; asked what he meant by "several," the defendant said "dozens" and "lots of times."

In fact, however, the defendant had relatively limited experience with aneurysm surgery. He had performed thirty aneurysm surgeries during residency, but all of them involved anterior circulation aneurysms. According

---

[9] The defendant acknowledged at trial that the aneurysm was not the cause of the plaintiff's headaches.

to the plaintiff's experts, operations performed to clip anterior circulation aneurysms are significantly less complex than those necessary to clip posterior circulation aneurysms such as the plaintiff's.[10] Following residency, the defendant had performed aneurysm surgery on six patients with a total of nine aneurysms. He had operated on basilar bifurcation aneurysms only twice and had never operated on a large basilar bifurcation aneurysm such as the plaintiff's aneurysm.[11]

The plaintiff also presented evidence that the defendant understated the morbidity and mortality rate associated with basilar bifurcation aneurysm surgery. According to the plaintiff's witnesses, the defendant had told the plaintiff that her surgery carried a two percent risk of death or serious impairment and that it was less risky than the angiogram procedure she would have to undergo in preparation for surgery. The plaintiff's witnesses also testified that the defendant had compared the risks associated with the plaintiff's surgery to those associated with routine procedures such as tonsillectomies, appendectomies and gall bladder surgeries.[12]

The plaintiff's neurosurgical experts testified that even the physician considered to be one of the world's best aneurysm surgeons, who had performed hundreds of posterior circulation aneurysm surgeries, had reported a morbidity and mortality rate of ten-and-seven-tenths percent when operating upon basilar bifurcation aneurysms comparable in size to the plaintiff's aneurysm. Furthermore, information in treatises and articles which the defendant reviewed in preparation for the plaintiff's surgery set the morbidity and mortality rate at approximately fifteen percent for a basilar bifurcation aneurysm. The plaintiff also introduced expert testimony that the morbidity and mortality rate for basilar bifurcation aneurysm operations performed by one with the defendant's relatively limited experience would be between twenty and thirty percent, and "closer to the thirty percent range."[13]

Finally, the plaintiff introduced into evidence testimony and exhibits stating that a reasonable physician in the defendant's position would have advised the plaintiff of the availability of more experienced surgeons and would have referred her to them. The plaintiff also introduced evidence stating that patients with basilar aneurysms should be referred to tertiary care centers—such as the Mayo Clinic, only 90 miles away—which contain the proper neurological intensive care unit and microsurgical facilities and which are

---

[10] The plaintiff's aneurysm was located at the bifurcation of the basilar artery. According to the plaintiff's experts, surgery on basilar bifurcation aneurysms is more difficult than any other type of aneurysm surgery.

[11] The defendant testified that he had failed to inform the plaintiff that he was not and never had been board certified in neurosurgery and that he was not a subspecialist in aneurysm surgery.

[12] The defendant testified at trial that he had informed the plaintiff that should she decide to forego surgery, the risk that her unclipped aneurysm might rupture was two percent per annum, cumulative. Since he informed the plaintiff that the risk accompanying surgery was two percent, a reasonable person in the plaintiff's position might have concluded that proceeding with surgery was less risky than non-operative management.

[13] The plaintiff introduced into evidence as exhibits articles from the medical literature stating that there are few areas in neurosurgery where the difference in results between surgeons is as evident as it is with aneurysms. One of the plaintiff's neurosurgical experts testified that experience and skill with the operator is more important when performing basilar tip aneurysm surgery than with any other neurosurgical procedure.

staffed by neurosurgeons with the requisite training and experience to perform basilar bifurcation aneurysm surgeries.

In his testimony at trial, the defendant denied having suggested to the plaintiff that her condition was urgent and required immediate care. He also denied having stated that her risk was comparable to that associated with an angiogram or minor surgical procedures such as a tonsillectomy or appendectomy. While he acknowledged telling the plaintiff that the risk of death or serious impairment associated with clipping an aneurysm was two percent, he also claims to have told her that because of the location of her aneurysm, the risks attending her surgery would be greater, although he was unable to tell her precisely how much greater.[14] In short, the defendant testified that his disclosure to the plaintiff adequately informed her regarding the risks that she faced.

The defendant's expert witnesses testified that the defendant's recommendation of surgery was appropriate, that this type of surgery is regularly undertaken in a community hospital setting, and that the risks attending anterior and posterior circulation aneurysm surgeries are comparable. They placed the risk accompanying the plaintiff's surgery at between five and ten percent, although one of the defendant's experts also testified that such statistics can be misleading. The defendant's expert witnesses also testified that when queried by a patient regarding their experience, they would divulge the extent of that experience and its relation to the experience of other physicians performing similar operations.[15]

We now turn to a review of Wisconsin's law of informed consent. The common-law doctrine of informed consent arises from and reflects the fundamental notion of the right to bodily integrity. Originally, an action alleging that a physician had failed to obtain a patient's informed consent was pled as the intentional tort of assault and battery. In the typical situation giving rise to an informed consent action, a patient-plaintiff consented to a certain type of operation but, in the course of that operation, was subjected to other, unauthorized operative procedures. *See, e.g., Paulsen v. Gundersen*, 218 Wis. 578, 584, 260 N.W. 448 (1935) (when a patient agrees to a "simple" operation

---

[14] The defendant maintained that characterizing the risk as two percent was accurate because the aggregate morbidity and mortality rate for all aneurysms, anterior and posterior, is approximately two percent. At the same time, however, the defendant conceded that in operating upon aneurysms comparable to the plaintiff's aneurysm, he could not achieve morbidity and mortality rates as low as the ten-and-seven-tenths percent rate reported by a physician reputed to be one of the world's best aneurysm surgeons.

[15] The defendant's expert witness Dr. Patrick R. Walsh testified:

> In my personal practice, I typically outline my understanding of the natural history of aneurysms, my understanding of the experience of the neurosurgical community in dealing with aneurysms and then respond to specific questions raised by the patient. If a patient asks specifically what my experience is, I believe it is mandatory that I outline that to him as carefully as possible.

Dr. Walsh also stated that "[i]t certainly is reasonable for [the defendant] to explain to [the plaintiff] that other surgeons are available."

Dr. Douglas E. Anderson, who also testified for the defense, stated that "if the patient is asking issues about prior experience, it is reasonable . . .to proceed with a discussion of your prior experience." Dr. Anderson also stated that "if the patient asks a surgeon if there is someone who has performed more surgeries than he, it is reasonable to tell the truth."

and a physician performs a more extensive operation, the physician is "guilty of an assault and would be responsible for damages resulting therefrom"); *Throne v. Wandell*, 176 Wis. 97, 186 N.W. 146 (1922) (dentist extracting six of the plaintiff's teeth without her consent has committed a technical assault).

The court further developed the doctrine of informed consent in *Trogun v. Fruchtman*, 58 Wis.2d 569, 207 N.W.2d 297 (1972), stating for the first time that a plaintiff-patient could bring an informed consent action based on negligence rather than as an intentional tort.[16] The court clarified Wisconsin's modern doctrine of informed consent in *Scaria v. St. Paul Fire & Marine Ins. Co.*, 68 Wis.2d 1, 227 N.W.2d 647 (1975). Wis.Stat. § 448.30 codifies the common law set forth in Scaria.[17] This statute has recently been interpreted and applied in Martin, 192 Wis.2d 156, 531 N.W.2d 70.[18]

The concept of informed consent is based on the tenet that in order to make a rational and informed decision about undertaking a particular treatment or undergoing a particular surgical procedure, a patient has the right to know about significant potential risks involved in the proposed treatment or surgery. *Scaria*, 68 Wis.2d at 11, 227 N.W.2d 647. In order to insure that a patient can give an informed consent, a "physician or surgeon is under the duty to provide the patient with such information as may be necessary under the circumstances then existing" to assess the significant potential risks which the patient confronts. Id.

The information that must be disclosed is that information which would be "material" to a patient's decision. In the first of three seminal informed consent decisions relied upon by both the *Trogun* and *Scaria* courts, the federal court of appeals for the District of Columbia stated that information regarding risk is material when "a reasonable person, in what the physician knows or should know to be the patient's position, would be likely to attach significance to the

---

[16] Although an action alleging a physician's failure to adequately inform is grounded in negligence, it is distinct from the negligence triggered by a physician's failure to provide treatment meeting the standard of reasonable care. The doctrine of informed consent focuses upon the reasonableness of a physician's disclosures to a patient rather than the reasonableness of a physician's treatment of that patient.

[17] See Martin v. Richards, 192 Wis.2d 156, 174, 531 N.W.2d 70 (1995) (discussing the legislative history of Wis.Stat. § 448.30).

Wisconsin Stat. § 448.30 requires that a physician inform a patient about the availability of all alternate, viable medical modes of treatment and about the benefits and risks attending these treatments. The informed consent statute reads as follows:

> 448.30 Information on alternate modes of treatment. Any physician who treats a patient shall inform the patient about the availability of all alternate, viable medical modes of treatment and about the benefits and risks of these treatments. The physician's duty to inform the patient under this section does not require disclosure of:
>
> (1) Information beyond what a reasonably well-qualified physician in a similar medical classification would know.
>
> (2) Detailed technical information that in all probability a patient would not understand.
>
> (3) Risks apparent or known to the patient.
>
> (4) Extremely remote possibilities that might falsely or detrimentally alarm the patient.
>
> (5) Information in emergencies where failure to provide treatment would be more harmful to the patient than treatment.
>
> (6) Information in cases where the patient is incapable of consenting.

[18] *See also* Platta v. Flatley, 68 Wis.2d 47, 227 N.W.2d 898 (1975).

E. 921

risk or cluster of risks in deciding whether or not to forego the proposed therapy." Canterbury v. Spence, 464 F.2d 772, 787 (D.C.Cir.1972), cert. denied, 409 U.S. 1064, 93 S.Ct. 560, 34 L.Ed.2d 518 (1972). The Canterbury court defined as material and therefore "demanding a communication" from a physician to a patient all information regarding "the inherent and potential hazards of the proposed treatment, the alternatives to that treatment, if any, and the results likely if the patient remains untreated." Id. at 787–88.

According to both the *Scaria* and *Martin* courts, a physician's reasonable disclosure requires that a patient be informed regarding available options. A "reasonable disclosure" of "significant risks," stated the Scaria court, requires an assessment of and communication regarding "the gravity of the patient's condition, the probabilities of success, and any alternative treatment or procedures if such are reasonably appropriate so that the patient has the information reasonably necessary to form the basis of an intelligent and informed consent to the proposed treatment or procedure." *Scaria*, 68 Wis.2d at 11, 227 N.W.2d 647. The *Martin* court, explicitly recognizing that the statutory doctrine of informed consent in Wisconsin is "based upon the standard expounded in *Canterbury*," *Martin*, 192 Wis.2d at 173, 531 N.W.2d 70, explained that a patient cannot make an informed decision to consent to the suggested treatment "unless the physician discloses what is material to the patient's decision, i.e., all of the viable alternatives and risks of the treatment proposed." *Martin*, 192 Wis.2d at 174, 531 N.W.2d 70.

What constitutes informed consent in a given case emanates from what a reasonable person in the patient's position would want to know. This standard regarding what a physician must disclose is described as the prudent patient standard; it has been embraced by a growing number of jurisdictions since the Canterbury decision.

The Scaria court emphasized that those "disclosures which would be made by doctors of good standing, under the same or similar circumstances, are certainly relevant and material" in assessing what constitutes adequate disclosure, adding that physician disclosures conforming to such a standard "would be adequate to fulfill the doctor's duty of disclosure in most instances." *Scaria*, 68 Wis.2d at 12, 227 N.W.2d 647. But the evidentiary value of what physicians of good standing consider adequate disclosure is not dispositive, for ultimately "the extent of the physician's disclosures is driven . . . by what a reasonable person under the circumstances then existing would want to know." *Martin*, 192 Wis.2d at 174, 531 N.W.2d 70; see also Scaria, 68 Wis.2d at 13, 227 N.W.2d 647.[19]

---

[19] We recognize, as did the *Scaria* court, that there must be some limitation upon the doctor's duty to disclose risks involved. In *Scaria*, we cautioned:

> A doctor should not be required to give a detailed technical medical explanation that in all probability the patient would not understand. He should not be required to discuss risks that are apparent or known to the patient. Nor should he be required to disclose extremely remote possibilities that at least in some instances might only serve to falsely or detrimentally alarm the particular patient. Likewise, a doctor's duty to inform is further limited in cases of emergency or where the patient is a child, mentally incompetent or a person is emotionally distraught or susceptible to unreasonable fears.

Scaria, 68 Wis.2d at 12–13, 227 N.W.2d 647. Similar limitations on a physician's duty to disclose were subsequently incorporated into Wis.Stat. § 448.30.

"The information that is reasonably necessary for a patient to make an informed decision regarding treatment will vary from case to case." *Martin*, 192 Wis.2d at 175, 531 N.W.2d 70. The standard to which a physician is held is determined not by what the particular patient being treated would want to know, but rather by what a reasonable person in the patient's position would want to know. *Scaria*, 68 Wis.2d at 13, 227 N.W.2d 647. . . .

The defendant contends that the circuit court erred in allowing the plaintiff to introduce evidence regarding the defendant's limited experience in operating upon aneurysms comparable to the plaintiff's aneurysm. Wisconsin's law of informed consent, the defendant continues, requires a physician to reveal only those risks inherent in the treatment. Everyone agrees, argues the defendant, that he advised the plaintiff regarding those risks: the potential perils of death, a stroke or blindness associated with her surgery.

The defendant argues that the circuit court's decision to admit evidence pertaining to his surgical experience confused relevant information relating to treatment risks with irrelevant and prejudicial information that the defendant did not possess the skill and experience of the very experienced aneurysm surgeons. Therefore, according to the defendant, the jury's attention was diverted from a consideration of whether the defendant made required disclosures regarding treatment to the question of who was performing the plaintiff's operation. Thus, the defendant contends, the circuit court transformed a duty to reasonably inform into a duty to reasonably perform the surgery, even though the plaintiff was not alleging negligent treatment.

The doctrine of informed consent should not, argues the defendant, be construed as a general right to information regarding possible alternative procedures, health care facilities and physicians. Instead, urges the defendant, the doctrine of informed consent should be viewed as creating a "bright line" rule requiring physicians to disclose only significant complications intrinsic to the contemplated procedure. The defendant interprets Wis.Stat. § 448.30 as an embodiment of this more modest definition of informed consent. In sum, the defendant urges that the statutory provisions require disclosure of risks associated with particular "treatments" rather than the risks associated with particular physicians.[29]

---

[29] The defendant also argues that the plaintiff is trying to disguise what is actually a negligent misrepresentation claim as an informed consent claim so that she might bring before the jury otherwise inadmissible evidence regarding the defendant's experience and relative competence.

The tort of negligent misrepresentation occurs when one person negligently gives false information to another who acts in reasonable reliance on the information and suffers physical harm as a consequence of the reliance. Restatement (Second) of Torts, § 311(1) (1965). An overlap exists between a claim pleading this tort and one alleging a failure to provide informed consent. As the commentary to § 311 of the Restatement points out:

> The rule stated in this Section finds particular application where it is a part of the actor's business or profession to give information upon which the safety of the recipient or a third person depends. Thus it is as much a part of the professional duty of a physician to give correct information as to the character of the disease from which his plaintiff is suffering, where such knowledge is necessary to the safety of the patient or others, as it is to make a correct diagnosis or to prescribe the appropriate medicine.

Restatement (Second) of Torts, § 311(1) cmt. b (1965).

Because of this overlap between negligent misrepresentation and informed consent, it is not surprising that allegations made and evidence introduced by the plaintiff might have fit

We reject the defendant's proposed bright line rule that it is error as a matter of law to admit evidence in an informed consent case that the physician failed to inform the patient regarding the physician's experience with the surgery or treatment at issue. The prudent patient standard adopted by Wisconsin in Scaria is incompatible with such a bright line rule.

As *Scaria* states and as *Martin* confirms, what a physician must disclose is contingent upon what, under the circumstances of a given case, a reasonable person in the patient's position would need to know in order to make an intelligent and informed decision. The question of whether certain information is material to a patient's decision and therefore requires disclosure is rooted in the facts and circumstances of the particular case in which it arises.

The cases upon which the *Trogun* and *Scaria* courts relied in fashioning Wisconsin's current doctrine of informed consent rejected the concept of bright line rules. The "scope of the disclosure required of physicians," stated the California Supreme Court, "defies simple definition" and must therefore "be measured by the patient's need, and that need is whatever information is material to the decision." *Cobbs v. Grant*, 8 Cal.3d 229, 104 Cal.Rptr. 505, 502 P.2d 1, 10, 11 (1972). "The amount of disclosure can vary from one patient to another," stated the Rhode Island Supreme Court, because "[w]hat is reasonable disclosure in one instance may not be reasonable in another." *Wilkinson v. Vesey*, 110 R.I. 606, 295 A.2d 676, 687–88 (1972). Finally, the *Canterbury* court's decision—which, as the Martin court underscored last term, provides the basis for Wisconsin's doctrine of informed consent, *Martin*, 192 Wis.2d at 173, 531 N.W.2d 70—states explicitly that under the doctrine of informed consent, "[t]here is no bright line separating the significant from the insignificant." *Canterbury*, 464 F.2d at 788.

Wisconsin Stat. § 448.30 explicitly requires disclosure of more than just treatment complications associated with a particular procedure. Physicians must, the statute declares, disclose "the availability of all alternate, viable medical modes of treatment" in addition to "the benefits and risks of these treatments."

The *Martin* court rejected the argument that Wis.Stat. § 448.30 was limited by its plain language to disclosures intrinsic to a proposed treatment regimen. The *Martin* court stated that Wis.Stat. § 448.30 "should not be construed so as to unduly limit the physician's duty to provide information which is reasonably necessary under the circumstances." *Martin*, 192 Wis.2d at 175, 531 N.W.2d 70. "There can be no dispute," the *Martin* court declared, "that the language in Scaria . . . requires that a physician disclose information necessary for a reasonable person to make an intelligent decision." *Id.*

In this case, the plaintiff introduced ample evidence that had a reasonable person in her position been aware of the defendant's relative lack of experience in performing basilar bifurcation aneurysm surgery, that person would not have undergone surgery with him. According to the record the plaintiff had made inquiry of the defendant's experience with surgery like hers. In response

---

comfortably under either theory. But this overlap does not preclude the plaintiff from making allegations and introducing evidence in an informed consent case which might also have been pled in a negligent misrepresentation case. This case was pled and proved under the tort of failure to procure informed consent.

to her direct question about his experience he said that he had operated on aneurysms comparable to her aneurysm "dozens" of times. The plaintiff also introduced evidence that surgery on basilar bifurcation aneurysms is more difficult than any other type of aneurysm surgery and among the most difficult in all of neurosurgery. We conclude that the circuit court did not erroneously exercise its discretion in admitting evidence regarding the defendant's lack of experience and the difficulty of the proposed procedure. A reasonable person in the plaintiff's position would have considered such information material in making an intelligent and informed decision about the surgery.

We also reject the defendant's claim that even if this information was material, it should have been excluded because its prejudicial effect outweighed its probative value. The defendant contends that the admission of such evidence allowed the jury to infer that the plaintiff's partial paralysis was a product of the defendant's lack of experience and skill rather than a consequence of his alleged failure to inform.

We disagree with the defendant's claim that evidence pertaining to the defendant's experience was unduly and unfairly prejudicial. While a jury might confuse negligent failure to disclose with negligent treatment, the likelihood of confusion is nonexistent or de minimis in this case. The plaintiff dismissed her negligent treatment claim before trial. It is thus unlikely that the jury would confuse an issue not even before it with the issue that was actually being tried. We therefore conclude that the defendant was not unduly or unfairly prejudiced by the admission of evidence reflecting his failure to disclose his limited prior experience in operating on basilar bifurcation aneurysms.

The defendant next argues that the circuit court erred in allowing the plaintiff to introduce evidence of morbidity and mortality rates associated with the surgery at issue. The defendant particularly objects to comparative risk statistics purporting to estimate and compare the morbidity and mortality rates when the surgery at issue is performed, respectively, by a physician of limited experience such as the defendant and by the acknowledged masters in the field. Expert testimony introduced by the plaintiff indicated that the morbidity and mortality rate expected when a surgeon with the defendant's experience performed the surgery would be significantly higher than the rate expected when a more experienced physician performed the same surgery.

The defendant asserts that admission of these morbidity and mortality rates would lead the jury to find him liable for failing to perform at the level of the masters rather than for failing to adequately inform the plaintiff regarding the risks associated with her surgery. Furthermore, contends the defendant, statistics are notoriously inaccurate and misleading.

As with evidence pertaining to the defendant's prior experience with similar surgery, the defendant requests that the court fashion a bright line rule as a matter of law that comparative risk evidence should not be admitted in an informed consent case. For many of the same reasons which led us to conclude that such a bright line rule of exclusion would be inappropriate for evidence of a physician's prior experience, we also reject a bright line rule excluding evidence of comparative risk relating to the provider.

E.

The medical literature identifies basilar bifurcation aneurysm surgery as among the most difficult in neurosurgery. As the plaintiff's evidence indicates, however, the defendant had told her that the risks associated with her surgery were comparable to the risks attending a tonsillectomy, appendectomy or gall bladder operation. The plaintiff also introduced evidence that the defendant estimated the risk of death or serious impairment associated with her surgery at two percent. At trial, however, the defendant conceded that because of his relative lack of experience, he could not hope to match the ten-and-seven-tenths percent morbidity and mortality rate reported for large basilar bifurcation aneurysm surgery by very experienced surgeons.

The defendant also admitted at trial that he had not shared with the plaintiff information from articles he reviewed prior to surgery. These articles established that even the most accomplished posterior circulation aneurysm surgeons reported morbidity and mortality rates of fifteen percent for basilar bifurcation aneurysms. Furthermore, the plaintiff introduced expert testimony indicating that the estimated morbidity and mortality rate one might expect when a physician with the defendant's relatively limited experience performed the surgery would be close to thirty percent.

Had a reasonable person in the plaintiff's position been made aware that being operated upon by the defendant significantly increased the risk one would have faced in the hands of another surgeon performing the same operation, that person might well have elected to forego surgery with the defendant. Had a reasonable person in the plaintiff's position been made aware that the risks associated with surgery were significantly greater than the risks that an unclipped aneurysm would rupture, that person might well have elected to forego surgery altogether. In short, had a reasonable person in the plaintiff's position possessed such information before consenting to surgery, that person would have been better able to make an informed and intelligent decision.

The defendant concedes that the duty to procure a patient's informed consent requires a physician to reveal the general risks associated with a particular surgery. The defendant does not explain why the duty to inform about this general risk data should be interpreted to categorically exclude evidence relating to provider-specific risk information, even when that provider-specific data is geared to a clearly delineated surgical procedure and identifies a particular provider as an independent risk factor. When different physicians have substantially different success rates, whether surgery is performed by one rather than another represents a choice between "alternate, viable medical modes of treatment" under § 448.30.

For example, while there may be a general risk of ten percent that a particular surgical procedure will result in paralysis or death, that risk may climb to forty percent when the particular procedure is performed by a relatively inexperienced surgeon. It defies logic to interpret this statute as requiring that the first, almost meaningless statistic be divulged to a patient while the second, far more relevant statistic should not be. Under Scaria and its progeny as well as the codification of Scaria as Wis.Stat. § 448.30, the second statistic would be material to the patient's exercise of an intelligent and informed consent regarding treatment options. A circuit court may in its discretion conclude that the second statistic is admissible.

The doctrine of informed consent requires disclosure of "all of the viable alternatives and risks of the treatment proposed" which would be material to a patient's decision. *Martin*, 192 Wis.2d at 174, 531 N.W.2d 70. We therefore conclude that when different physicians have substantially different success rates with the same procedure and a reasonable person in the patient's position would consider such information material, the circuit court may admit this statistical evidence.

We caution, as did the court of appeals, that our decision will not always require physicians to give patients comparative risk evidence in statistical terms to obtain informed consent. Rather, we hold that evidence of the morbidity and mortality outcomes of different physicians was admissible under the circumstances of this case.

In keeping with the fact-driven and context-specific application of informed consent doctrine, questions regarding whether statistics are sufficiently material to a patient's decision to be admissible and sufficiently reliable to be non-prejudicial are best resolved on a case-by-case basis. The fundamental issue in an informed consent case is less a question of how a physician chooses to explain the panoply of treatment options and risks necessary to a patient's informed consent than a question of assessing whether a patient has been advised that such options and risks exist.

As the court of appeals observed, in this case it was the defendant himself who elected to explain the risks confronting the plaintiff in statistical terms. He did this because, as he stated at trial, "numbers giv[e] some perspective to the framework of the very real, immediate, human threat that is involved with this condition." Because the defendant elected to explain the risks confronting the plaintiff in statistical terms, it stands to reason that in her effort to demonstrate how the defendant's numbers dramatically understated the risks of her surgery, the plaintiff would seek to introduce other statistical evidence. Such evidence was integral to her claim that the defendant's nondisclosure denied her the ability to exercise informed consent.

The defendant also asserts that the circuit court erred as a matter of law in allowing the plaintiff to introduce expert testimony that because of the difficulties associated with operating on the plaintiff's aneurysm, the defendant should have referred her to a tertiary care center containing a proper neurological intensive care unit, more extensive microsurgical facilities and more experienced surgeons. While evidence that a physician should have referred a patient elsewhere may support an action alleging negligent treatment, argues the defendant, it has no place in an informed consent action.

The court of appeals agreed with the defendant that this evidence should have been excluded, and it further concluded that admission of this evidence created "a serious danger [that] the jury may confuse a duty to provide average quality care with a duty to adequately inform of medical risks." *Johnson*, 188 Wis.2d at 224, 525 N.W.2d 71.

We share the concern expressed by the court of appeals and underscored by the defendant, but their concern is misplaced in this case. Here, the plaintiff was not asserting a claim for negligent performance. Just because expert testimony is relevant to one claim does not mean that it is not relevant to another.

When faced with an allegation that a physician breached a duty of informed consent, the pertinent inquiry concerns what information a reasonable person in the patient's position would have considered material to an exercise of intelligent and informed consent. Under the facts and circumstances presented by this case, the circuit court could declare, in the exercise of its discretion, that evidence of referral would have been material to the ability of a reasonable person in the plaintiff's position to render informed consent.

The plaintiff's medical experts testified that given the nature and difficulty of the surgery at issue, the plaintiff could not make an intelligent decision or give an informed consent without being made aware that surgery in a tertiary facility would have decreased the risk she faced. One of the plaintiff's experts, Dr. Haring J.W. Nauta, stated that "it's not fair not to bring up the subject of referral to another center when the problem is as difficult to treat" as the plaintiff's aneurysm was. Another of the plaintiff's experts, Dr. Robert Narotzky, testified that the defendant's "very limited" experience with aneurysm surgery rendered reasonable a referral to "someone with a lot more experience in dealing with this kind of problem." Dr. Fredric Somach, also testifying for the plaintiff, stated as follows:

> [S]he should have been told that this was an extremely difficult, formidable lesion and that there are people in the immediate geographic vicinity that are very experienced and that have had a great deal of contact with this type of aneurysm and that she should consider having at least a second opinion, if not going directly to one of these other [physicians].

Articles from the medical literature introduced by the plaintiff also stated categorically that the surgery at issue should be performed at a tertiary care center while being "excluded" from the community setting because of "the limited surgical experience" and lack of proper equipment and facilities available in such hospitals.

Scaria instructs us that "[t]he disclosures which would be made by doctors of good standing, under the same or similar circumstances, are certainly relevant and material" to a patient's exercise of informed consent. *Scaria*, 68 Wis.2d at 12, 227 N.W.2d 647. Testimony by the plaintiff's medical experts indicated that "doctors of good standing" would have referred her to a tertiary care center housing better equipment and staffed by more experienced physicians. Hence under the materiality standard announced in Scaria, we conclude that the circuit court properly exercised its discretion in admitting evidence that the defendant should have advised the plaintiff of the possibility of undergoing surgery at a tertiary care facility.

The defendant asserts that the plaintiff knew she could go elsewhere. This claim is both true and beside the point. Credible evidence in this case demonstrates that the plaintiff chose not to go elsewhere because the defendant gave her the impression that her surgery was routine and that it therefore made no difference who performed it. The pertinent inquiry, then, is not whether a reasonable person in the plaintiff's position would have known generally that she might have surgery elsewhere, but rather whether such a person would have chosen to have surgery elsewhere had the defendant adequately disclosed the comparable risks attending surgery performed by him and surgery performed at a tertiary care facility such as the Mayo Clinic, only 90 miles away.

The defendant also argues that evidence of referral is prejudicial because it might have affected the jury's determination of causation. The court of appeals reasoned that if a complainant could introduce evidence that a physician should have referred her elsewhere, "a patient so informed would almost certainly forego the procedure with that doctor." *Johnson*, 188 Wis.2d at 224, 525 N.W.2d 71.[34]

The court of appeals concluded that admitting evidence regarding a physician's failure to refer was prejudicial error because it probably affected the jury's decision about causation in favor of the plaintiff. Contending that a causal connection between his failure to divulge and the plaintiff's damage is required, the defendant seems to assert that the plaintiff has offered no evidence that the defendant's failure to disclose his relevant experience or his statistical risk harmed the plaintiff. Even had the surgery been performed by a "master," the defendant argues, a bad result may have occurred.

The defendant appears to attack the basic concept of causation applied in claims based on informed consent. As reflected in the informed consent jury instruction (Wis JI-Civil 1023.3 (1992)), which the defendant himself proposed and which was given at trial, the question confronting a jury in an informed consent case is whether a reasonable person in the patient's position would have arrived at a different decision about the treatment or surgery had he or she been fully informed. As reflected in the special verdict question in this case, that question asked whether "a reasonable person in Donna Johnson's position [would] have refused to consent to the surgery by Dr. Richard Kokemoor had she been fully informed of the risks and advantages of surgery." If the defendant is arguing here that the standard causation instruction is not applicable in a case in which provider-specific evidence is admitted, this contention has not been fully presented and developed.

Finally, the defendant argues that if his duty to procure the plaintiff's informed consent includes an obligation to disclose that she consider seeking treatment elsewhere, then there will be no logical stopping point to what the doctrine of informed consent might encompass. We disagree with the defendant. As the plaintiff noted in her brief to this court, "[i]t is a rare exception when the vast body of medical literature and expert opinion agree that the difference in experience of the surgeon performing the operation will impact the risk of morbidity/mortality as was the case here," thereby requiring referral. Brief for Petitioner at 40. At oral argument before this court, counsel for the plaintiff stated that under "many circumstances" and indeed "probably most circumstances," whether or not a physician referred a patient elsewhere would be "utterly irrelevant" in an informed consent case. In the vast majority

---

[34] The court of appeals expressed concern that the plaintiff's evidence regarding the defendant's failure to refer might cause the jury to confuse a physician's duty to procure a patient's informed consent with a separate and distinct tort establishing a physician's duty to refer. While acknowledging that other jurisdictions have recognized a distinct duty to refer, the court of appeals observed that Wisconsin has never done so. Nor does the court do so today. We merely hold that a physician's failure to refer may, under some circumstances, be material to a patient's exercise of an intelligent and informed consent.

of significantly less complicated cases, such a referral would be irrelevant and unnecessary.

Moreover, we have already concluded that comparative risk data distinguishing the defendant's morbidity and mortality rate from the rate of more experienced physicians was properly before the jury. A close link exists between such data and the propriety of referring a patient elsewhere. A physician who discloses that other physicians might have lower morbidity and mortality rates when performing the same procedure will presumably have access to information regarding who some of those physicians are. When the duty to share comparative risk data is material to a patient's exercise of informed consent, an ensuing referral elsewhere will often represent no more than a modest and logical next step.

Given the difficulties involved in performing the surgery at issue in this case, coupled with evidence that the defendant exaggerated his own prior experience while downplaying the risks confronting the plaintiff, the circuit court properly exercised its discretion in admitting evidence that a physician of good standing would have made the plaintiff aware of the alternative of lower risk surgery with a different, more experienced surgeon in a better-equipped facility.

For the reasons set forth, we conclude that the circuit court did not erroneously exercise its discretion in admitting the evidence at issue, and accordingly, we reverse the decision of the court of appeals and remand the cause to the circuit court for further proceedings consistent with this opinion.

The decision of the court of appeals is reversed and the cause is remanded to the circuit court with directions.

BRADLEY, J., did not participate.

NOTES

1. *Misrepresentation as a Battery.* In *Duttry v. Patterson*, 741 A.2d 199 (Pa. Super. 1999), the plaintiff underwent surgery performed by the defendant for esophageal cancer. A leak later occurred along the surgical site, requiring emergency surgery, and as a result the plaintiff allegedly developed a respiratory disease rendering her unable to work.

Plaintiff said "she questioned Dr. Patterson about his experience and he advised her he had performed this particular procedure on an average of once a month." In fact, the plaintiff alleged, "he had performed it only five times in the preceding five years."

The court said the plaintiff stated a claim for lack of informed consent. The court rejected defendant's assertion that the plaintiff had to have expert testimony to prove her claim. "In this type of claim where the plaintiff alleges the physician did not have her informed consent to perform the surgery because she was misinformed of his qualifications, the theory of recovery is battery and the plaintiff need not establish negligence."

2. *Disclosure of Nonmedical Facts.* To what extent does the informed consent doctrine mandate the disclosure of nonmedical facts? *Moore v. Regents of Univ. of Cal.,* 51 Cal. 3d 120, 271 Cal. Rptr. 146, 793 P.2d 479 (1990), involved the

removal of a plaintiff's leukemia cells by his doctor, and their use by the doctor in the development of a patented cell line. Although the court dismissed the plaintiff's claim for conversion, it held that he stated a cause of action of breach of the informed consent duty. Why? *See also Faya v. Almaraz*, 620 A.2d 327 (Md. 1993) (doctor who had tested HIV-positive must disclose that fact to a patient before performing an invasive procedure upon the patient), and *Hidding v. Williams*, 578 So.2d 1192 (La. App. 1991) (physician's failure to disclose his chronic alcohol abuse violated the informed consent requirements).

3. *Statutory Constraints on Informed Consent.* A Louisiana statute, R.S. 40:1299.40, establishes a Medical Disclosure Panel, composed of attorneys and health care providers, which is charged with preparing lists of medical treatments and surgical procedures that require disclosure, the degree of disclosure required, and the form in which the disclosure should be made. Disclosure as required by a Panel list, or non-disclosure where disclosure is not required by the Panel lists, creates a rebuttable presumption that the health provider has fulfilled his duty to obtain informed consent.

F. EXTENDED PROFESSIONAL LIABILITY EXPOSURE

TORO CO. v. KROUSE, KERN & CO.
827 F.2d 155 (7th Cir. 1987)

RIPPLE, CHIEF JUSTICE.

This case involves certain accounting services provided by an accounting firm, Krouse, Kern & Company, Inc. (Krouse) to Summit Power Equipment Distributors, Inc. (Summit) for the fiscal years 1981, 1982 and 1983. In each of those years, Krouse prepared yearly audit reports and monthly financial statements for Summit. During the same period, Toro Company was a major supplier of equipment to Summit, and its wholly-owned subsidiary, Toro Credit Company (Toro), was a major supplier of credit to Summit. Toro required audited reports from Summit in order to evaluate the distributor's financial condition. Summit supplied Toro with the reports prepared by Krouse to fulfill this requirement. The reports allegedly contained mistakes and omissions regarding Summit's actual financial condition.

. . . Toro alleged that, in reliance upon the audit reports, it extended and renewed large amounts of credit to Summit. The reports overstated Summit's assets, the complaint continued, and Toro extended credit that it would not have extended if the reports had been accurate. Summit was unable to repay these amounts. Krouse filed a motion for summary judgment that was granted by the district court. This appeal followed.

In an exhaustive and scholarly opinion, the district court analyzed the central issue in this case—the appropriate standard of care required of accountants under Indiana law. Surveying the law of the states of the Union, the court isolated three standards: 1) the *Ultramares* standard; 2) the Restatement standard; and 3) the "Reasonably Foreseeable" standard.

1. The *Ultramares* Standard

This standard was first announced by the New York Court of Appeals in *Ultramares Corp. v. Touche,* 255 N.Y. 170, 174 N.E. 441 (N.Y. 1931). There, Chief Judge Cardozo disallowed a negligence action against an accounting firm brought by a plaintiff who had neither contractual privity, *Id.* 174 N.E. at 446, nor a relationship "so close as to approach that of privity." *Id.* Recently, in *Credit Alliance Corp. v. Arthur Andersen & Co.,* 65 N.Y.2d 536, 439 N.Y.S.2d 435, 483 N.E.2d 110 (1985), the New York Court of Appeals reaffirmed its reliance on the *Ultramares* standard:

> Before accountants may be held liable in negligence to noncontractual parties who rely to their detriment on inaccurate financial reports, certain requisites must be satisfied: (1) the accountants must have been aware that the financial reports were to be used for a particular purpose or purposes; (2) in the furtherance of which a known party or parties was intended to rely; and (3) there must have been some conduct on the part of the accountants linking them to that party or parties, which evinces the accountants' understanding of that party or parties' reliance. *Id.* 493 N.Y.S.2d at 443, 483 N.E.2d at 118.

2. The Restatement Standard

This standard permits recovery for those who can be actually foreseen as parties "who will and do rely upon the financial statements." *Toro Co. v. Krouse, Kern & Co.,* 644 F. Supp. 986, 992 (N.D. Ind. 1986). In pertinent part, section 552 of the RESTATEMENT (SECOND) OF TORTS reads as follows:

> (1) One who, in the course of his business, profession or employment, or in any other transaction in which he has a pecuniary interest, supplies false information for the guidance of others in their business transactions, is subject to liability for pecuniary loss caused to them by their justifiable reliance upon the information, if he fails to exercise reasonable care or competence in obtaining or communicating the information.
>
> (2) Except as stated in Subsection (3), the liability stated in Subsection (1) is limited to loss suffered
>
> (a) by the person or one of a limited group of persons for whose benefit and guidance he intends to supply the information or knows that the recipient intends to supply it; and
>
> (b) through reliance upon it in a transaction that he intends the information to influence or knows that the recipient so intends or in a substantially similar transaction.
>
> [Subsec. (3) imposes liability on one under a public duty to give information, in favor of the class of persons and the type of transactions intended to be protected by that duty.]

3. The "Reasonably Foreseeable" Standard

The district court determined that "[t]wo jurisdictions have proceeded beyond the 'actually foreseeable' test of the Restatement and adopted a 'reasonably foreseeable' test. Under this standard, accountants owe a duty of care to all parties who are reasonably foreseeable recipients of financial statements for business purposes, provided the recipients rely on the statements pursuant to those business purposes. See *Rosenblum v. Adler,* 93 N.J. 324, 461 A.2d 138 (1983); *Citizens State Bank v. Timm, Schmidt & Co.,* 113 Wis. 2d 376, 335 N.W.2d 361 (1983)."

. . . Toro acknowledges that Indiana has not adopted the Restatement standard [*Essex v. Ryan,* 446 N.E.2d 368 (Ind. Ct. App. 1983)]. However, it argues that just because Indiana has rejected the Restatement position, it cannot be assumed that it has embraced the *Ultramares* standard. Rather, submits Toro, Indiana would impose liability not only when there is privity between the accountant and the injured party but also when there is actual knowledge on the part of the accountant that the injured party will rely on the work product . . . . This standard is required, it submits, by the holding of the Supreme Court of Indiana in *Citizens Gas & Coke Util. v. American Economy Ins. Co.,* 486 N.E.2d 998 (Ind. 1985), where the court, discussing *Essex,* wrote, "[t]he surveyor owed no duty to subsequent purchasers of property because he had no knowledge they would rely on his survey and because he was not in privity with them." 486 N.E.2d at 1001.

Toro continues by urging that sound policy reasons support its view as to the content of Indiana law. The audited financial report, it notes, "has been singled out by both federal and state legislation to be an important vehicle to encourage public confidence in the accuracy of financial information." Appellants' Br. at 20. Moreover, "the business community has long recognized the responsibility a certified public accountant owes the public when engaged in an audit." *Id.* at 21.

. . . We begin our analysis by noting that Indiana has made some firm policy choices in the area under consideration. As the Supreme Court of Indiana noted in *Citizens Gas,*

> [t]he requirements of privity have been abolished by this Court and the Court of Appeals for products liability and contractor liability involving personal injury caused by a product or work in a condition that was dangerously defective, inherently dangerous or imminently dangerous such that it created a risk of imminent personal injury.

486 N.E.2d at 1000 . . . .

The reason for Indiana's policy choice was stated succinctly by the Supreme Court of Indiana in *Citizens Gas:*

> The reasoning behind all of these cases that has created the exception to the general requirement of privity is apparent and is based on humanitarian principles. One who sells a product or does construction work pursuant to a contract with the owner of a building or premises which presents imminent danger to the health and safety of not only the party he contracts with but to other members of the public can be held liable for resulting injuries even though the third party injured is not privy to the contract. It does not follow that the same exception would be applied where the risk is only that of property damage. In *Essex v. Ryan,* 446 N.E.2d 368, 372 (Ind. App. 1983), the Essexes sought to recover damages arising from a survey which Ryan had negligently performed for their predecessor in title in 1955. The Essexes claimed damages because of the deceased's professional incompetence and because they were assignees of their predecessors in interest. The Court of Appeals found, however, that the surveyor owed no duty to subsequent purchasers of property because he had no knowledge they would rely on his survey and because he was not in privity with them. 486 N.E.2d at 1000–1001.

It is true that, in those areas where privity still applies, there exists an "actual knowledge" exception. See *Essex,* 446 N.E.2d at 373. However, this "actual knowledge" exception, as articulated by the Indiana courts, is a very narrow and specific one. It requires proof that the defendant had *actual* knowledge that the *particular person or entity bringing the law suit* "would rely on the information given." *Essex,* 446 N.E.2d at 372. In short, the Indiana courts have made a "distinction between *knowledge* that a third party will rely on the opinion given and an *expectation* that unidentified others might rely on it." *Id.* (emphasis in original).

We further believe that the district court was correct when it held that this "actual knowledge" exception to the privity rule was the functional equivalent of the *Ultramares* test's insistence on "near privity." In explaining the *Ultramares* test, the New York Court of Appeals noted in *Credit Alliance* that

Chief Judge Cardozo had distinguished the holding in *Ultramares* from *Glanzer v. Shepard,* 233, N.Y. 236, 135 N.E. 275 (N.Y. 1922). In *Glanzer,* noted the *Credit Alliance* court, the facts "bespoke an affirmative assumption of a duty of care to a specific party, for a specific purpose, regardless of whether there was a contractual relationship." 493 N.Y.S.2d at 441, 483 N.E.2d at 116. It was to preserve this distinction between *Ultramares* and *Glanzer* the affirmative assumption of a duty of care to a specific party, for a specific purpose—that the *Credit Alliance* court developed the three-part analysis:

> (1) the accountants must have been aware that the financial reports were to be used for a particular purpose or purposes; (2) in the furtherance of which a known party or parties was intended to rely; and (3) there must have been some conduct on the part of the accountants linking them to that party or parties, which evinces the accountants' understanding of that party or parties' reliance.

Id. 493 N.Y.S.2d at 443, 483 N.E.2d at 118. The last part of that test—the part that the district court did not believe was met in this case—is quite obviously meant to ensure there was "an affirmative assumption of a duty of care to a specific party, for a specific purpose." *Id.* 493 N.E.2d at 441, 483 N.E.2d at 116.

While Indiana has not had occasion to address the matter with quite the specificity found in the New York cases, we believe that a fair reading of the Indiana precedent, in its totality establishes that the "privity requirement, subject to an actual knowledge exception," explicitly recognized in *Essex,* 446 N.E.2d at 373, is designed to preserve the same policy concern as the New York formulation. The *Essex* court relied explicitly on *Ultramares.* More importantly, in discussing the earlier Indiana precedent, it pointedly distinguished between those cases where the defendant had affirmatively undertaken to assist the plaintiff with respect to a particular task and those where there had been no such affirmative manifestation . . . .

We must next examine the record to determine whether, in light of the standard we have chosen, Krouse is entitled to prevail on summary judgment.

. . . Our own study of the record leads us to the conclusion that the district court did not err in granting summary judgment. The appellants failed to raise a question of material fact as to an essential element of their claim of accountant liability—whether there was some conduct on the part of Krouse linking them to Toro . . . .

[Affirmed.]

NOTES

1. *How Limited a Class?* In *Blue Bell, Inc. v. Peat, Marwick, Mitchell & Co.,* 715 S.W.2d 408 (Tex. Ct. App. 1986), the court stated:

> Many . . . law-review writers have also advocated that the test for the scope of an accountant's liability should extend beyond that propounded by the RESTATEMENT to include all relying third parties who were reasonably foreseeable to the accountant at the time he made his report . . . . Although we find the reasoning of the cases and

commentators urging adoption of the foreseeability test persuasive, we need not decide whether that test should be adopted in this case.

Instead, we look to section 552 of the RESTATEMENT (SECOND) and decide that, as we construe this section, a fact issue exists as to whether [plaintiff] falls within the "limited class" as used in that section. Although we need not go so far today as to adopt the broad standard of foreseeability advocated by some of the commentators, we conclude that the apparent attempt in comment h[1] under this section to limit the class of third parties who may recover to those actually and specifically known by the defendant is too artificial a distinction . . . . To allow liability to turn on the fortuitous occurrence that the accountant's client specifically mentions a person or class of persons who are to receive the reports, when the accountant may have that same knowledge as a matter of business practice, is too tenuous a distinction for us to adopt as a rule of law. Instead, we hold that if, under current business practices and the circumstances of that case, an accountant preparing audited financial statements knows *or should know* that such statements will be relied upon by a limited class of persons, the accountant may be liable for injuries to members of that class relying on his certification of the audited reports.

After and exhaustive review of authority, the court adopted RESTATEMENT (SECOND) OF TORTS § 552 as the basis for accountant liability in *Bily v. Arthur Young and Co.*, 834 P.2d 745, 11 Cal. Rptr. 2d 51 (Cal. 1992), finding this section to be "most consistent with the elements and policy foundations of the tort of negligent misrepresentation."

2. *Doctor Duty to Third Persons.* Although it might once have been true that the existence of a physician-patient relationship was a *sine qua non* to a medical malpractice action, most people today would include actions by third parties within that general rubric. For example, in *Freese v. Lemmon,* 210 N.W.2d 576 (Iowa 1973), a pedestrian struck by a motorist who was in the midst of a seizure brought an action against the motorist's physician for alleged failure to diagnose the cause of the motorist's previous seizure and to warn him not to drive. The court held that the allegations constituted a cause of action against the physician. *Gooden v. Tips,* 651 S.W.2d 364, 366 n.1 (Tex. App. 1983), reached a similar result in a case involving the alleged negligence of a physician in failing to warn his motorist-patient of the side effects of the

---

[1] Editors Note. RESTATEMENT (SECOND) OF TORTS § 552 comment *h* provides in part:

[I]t is not required that the person who is to become the plaintiff be identified or known to the defendant as an individual when the information is supplied. It is enough that the maker of the representation intends it to reach and influence a particular person or persons, known to him, or a group or class of persons, distinct from the much larger class who might reasonably be expected sooner or later to have access to the information and foreseeably to take some action in reliance upon it. It is enough, likewise, that the maker of the representation knows that his recipient intends to transmit the information to a similar person, persons or group. It is sufficient, in other words, insofar as the plaintiff's identity is concerned, that the maker supplies the information for repetition to a certain group or class of persons and that the plaintiff proves to be one of them, even though the maker never had heard of him by name when the information was given. It is not enough that the maker merely knows of the ever-present possibility of repetition to anyone, and the possibility of action in reliance upon it, on the part of anyone to whom it may be repeated . . . .

drug Quaalude. However, the court declined to describe the action as one for medical malpractice as that term was defined by a Texas statute.

In *Reisner v. Regents of the University of California*, 31 Cal. App. 4th 1195, 37 Cal. Rptr.2d 418 (1995), doctor discovered that a 12-year-old girl was contaminated with HIV antibodies. Although he continued to treat her, doctor did not tell the girl or her parents about the tainted blood. Three years later, the girl began dating plaintiff, and they became intimate. Two years thereafter, the doctor told patient she had AIDS and she told plaintiff. A month later, patient died, and shortly thereafter, plaintiff discovered he was HIV positive. The court rejected the doctor's argument that he did not owe a duty to plaintiff, an unidentified third person, observing:

> We summarily reject Defendants' alternative suggestion that a physician ought not to owe any duty to a third person because such a duty could adversely affect the doctor's treatment of his patient, to whom his primary duty is owed. As explained above, existing California law already imposes a duty to third persons and the only arguably "new" issue in this case is whether that duty is the same when the third person's identity is unknown to the physician and not readily ascertainable. And, contrary to Defendants' contention, the duty involved in this case—a duty to warn a contagious patient to take steps to protect others—has nothing to do with a physician's decision about how to treat his patient or with a physician's potential liability for the unauthorized disclosure of AIDS test results . . . . Once the physician warns the patient of the risk to others and advises the patient how to prevent the spread of the disease, the physician has fulfilled his duty—and no more (but no less) is required.

In *N.O.L. v. District of Columbia*, 674 A.2d 498 (D.C. App. 1996), the court said the defendant hospital had no duty to tell plaintiff-appellant, patient's husband, that patient had tested HIV-positive. "On the contrary, the hospital staff owed a duty to appellant's wife to refrain from disclosing that information to anyone, including her husband, without her written consent (or a court order)."

The court in *Lemon v. Stewart*, 111 Md. App. 511, 682 A.2d 1177 (1996), noted that a state statute authorized but did not require a doctor to notify a patient's "sexual and needle-sharing partners" of the patient's "positive HIV status":

> This statute incontestably reinforces our conclusion that no duty exists on the part of physicians or other health care providers to inform persons such as appellants of a patient's positive HIV status. If they have no obligation to inform sexual and needle-sharing partners of the patient and cannot be held liable for choosing not to inform them, surely they can have no duty to notify persons far less likely to acquire the virus from the patient.

The appellants were family members of the patient. They had treated, or come into contact with, the patient, and they feared they would contract the virus—although none had tested positive for the virus.

Other cases finding a medical duty to third persons are *Troxel v. A.I. duPont Instit.*, 450 Pa. Super. 71, 675 A.2d 314 (1996) (duty to warn patient, whose newborn child suffered from communicable disease of cytomegalovirus, that pregnant women should not be involved in the care of the child); *Bradshaw v. Daniel*, 854 S.W.2d 865 (Tenn. 1993) (duty to warn wife of patient who died of Rocky Mountain Spotted Fever); *Safer v. Estate of Pack*, 291 N.J. Super. 619, 677 A.2d 1188 (1996) (duty to warn immediate family members of patient who suffered from multiple polyposis, a genetically transmissible disease, so those members "might have the benefits of early examination, monitoring, detecting and treatment").

Compare Matter of Estate of Blacher, 857 P.2d 566 (Colo. App. 1993):

> The decedent consulted defendant, his physician of many years, because he was experiencing pain while swallowing. Defendant misdiagnosed decedent's ailment as being related to a pre-existing hiatal hernia. Defendant considered this condition nonfatal and, therefore, informed decedent that he was "healthy." In fact, decedent was suffering from cancer.
>
> After receiving defendant's diagnosis, decedent cancelled a $250,000 life insurance policy. Plaintiff, decedent's wife, was the named beneficiary of that policy. Decedent subsequently died of cancer . . . .
>
> Here, taking the facts of the complaint as true, decedent decided to cancel his life insurance policy upon being erroneously informed by the physician that he was in good health. Furthermore, he would not have done so had he been correctly diagnosed as having cancer. However, the law does not impose upon a physician the burden of knowing every use to which his diagnoses may be put by his patients. The cancellation of insurance is an act not reasonably foreseeable to a physician as a probable consequence of a diagnosis of a patient's condition. Hence, we hold that defendant's duty of care to decedent did not extend to plaintiff as the beneficiary of the life insurance policy unforeseeably cancelled by decedent.

WICKLINE v. STATE OF CALIFORNIA
192 Cal. App. 3d 1630, 239 Cal. Rptr. 810 (1986)

ROWAN, ASSOCIATE JUSTICE.

[Plaintiff was diagnosed by Dr. Polonsky, a specialist, as suffering from Leriche's Syndrome, a condition caused by the obstruction of the aorta, the body's main artery. Dr. Polonsky concluded that surgery was necessary. Plaintiff's family practitioner, Dr. Daniels, submitted a treatment authorization form to the California Medical Assistance Program ("Medi-Cal"). Medi-Cal authorized the procedure and 10 days hospitalization. Defendant appeals from a judgment for the plaintiff.]

On January 6, 1977, plaintiff was admitted to [the hospital] by Dr. Daniels. On January 7, 1977, Dr. Polonsky performed a surgical procedure in which a part of plaintiff's artery was removed and a synthetic artery was inserted to replace it. Dr. Polonsky characterized that procedure as "a very major surgery."

Later that same day Dr. Polonsky was notified that Wickline was experiencing circulatory problems in her right leg. He concluded that a clot had formed in the graft. As a result, Wickline was taken back into surgery, the incision in her right groin was reopened, the clot removed and the graft was resewn. Wickline's recovery subsequent to the two January 7th operations was characterized as "stormy." She had a lot of pain, some spasm in the vessels in the lower leg and she experienced hallucinating episodes. On January 12, 1977, Wickline was returned to the operating room where Dr. Polonsky performed a lumbar sympathectomy.

A lumbar sympathectomy is a major operation in which a section of the chain of nerves that lie on each side of the spinal column is removed. The procedure causes the blood vessels in the patient's lower extremity to become paralyzed in a wide open position and was done in an attempt to relieve the spasms which Wickline was experiencing in those vessels. Spasms stop the outflow of blood from the vessels causing the blood to back up into the graft. Failure to relieve such spasms can cause clotting.

Dr. Polonsky was assisted in all three surgeries by Dr. Leonard Kovner (Dr. Kovner), a board certified specialist in the field of general surgery and the chief of surgery . . . .

. . . On or about January 16, 1977, Dr. Polonsky concluded that "it was medically necessary" that plaintiff remain in the hospital for an additional eight days beyond her then scheduled discharge date . . . .

. . . His principal reason, however, was that he felt that he was going to be able to save both of Wickline's legs and wanted her to remain in the hospital where he could observe her and be immediately available, along with the hospital staff, to treat her if an emergency should occur.

In order to secure an extension of Wickline's hospital stay, it was necessary to complete and present to Medi-Cal a form called "Request for Extension of Stay in Hospital," commonly referred to as an "MC-180" or "180." It is the hospital's responsibility to prepare the 180 form. The hospital must secure necessary information about the patient from the responsible physician. It then submits the 180 form to Medi-Cal's representative and obtains appropriate authorization for the hospital stay extension.

The physician's responsibility in the preparation of the 180 form is to furnish (to the hospital's representative) the patient's diagnosis, significant history, clinical status and treatment plan in sufficient detail to permit a reasonable, professional evaluation by Medi-Cal's representative, either the "onsite nurse" or/and the Medi-Cal Consultant, a doctor employed by the State for just such purpose.

. . . [The on-site nurse], after reviewing Wickline's 180 form, felt that she could not approve the requested eight-day extension of acute care hospitalization . . . [and referred the matter to] Dr. William S. Glassman (Dr. Glassman), one of the Medi-Cal Consultants on duty at the time in Medi-Cal's Los Angeles office.

. . . Dr. Glassman rejected Wickline's treating physician's request for an eight-day hospital extension and, instead, authorized an additional four days of hospital stay beyond the originally scheduled discharge date.

... Complying with the limited extension of time authorized by Medi-Cal, Wickline was discharged ... on January 21, 1977 .... At the time of her discharge, each of plaintiff's three treating physicians was aware that the Medi-Cal Consultant had approved only four of the requested eight-day hospital stay extension. While all three doctors were aware that they could attempt to obtain a further extension of Wickline's hospital stay by telephoning the Medi-Cal Consultant to request such an extension, none of them did so.

... Dr. Polonsky testified that at the time in issue he felt that Medi-Cal Consultants had the State's interest more in mind than the patient's welfare and that belief influenced his decision not to request a second extension of Wickline's hospital stay. In addition, he felt that Medi-Cal had the power to tell him, as a treating doctor, when a patient must be discharged from the hospital. Therefore, while still of the subjective, non-communicated, opinion that Wickline was seriously ill and that the danger to her was not over, Dr. Polonsky discharged her from the hospital on January 21, 1977. He testified that had Wickline's condition, in his medical judgment, been critical or in a deteriorating condition on January 21, he would have made some effort to keep her in the hospital beyond that day even if denied authority by Medi-Cal and even if he had to pay the hospital bill himself.

... All of the medical witnesses who testified at trial agreed that Dr. Polonsky was acting within the standards of practice of the medical community in discharging Wickline.

... Just prior to Wickline's actual discharge from the hospital, which she protested, Dr. Kovner met with her husband and explained to him how he was to administer to his wife's needs at home. That care consisted primarily of antibiotic powder for the groin incision, medication, warm water baths and bed rest.

Wickline testified that in the first few days after she arrived home she started feeling pain in her right leg and the leg started to lose color. In the next few days the pain got worse and the right leg took on a whitish, statue-like marble appearance. Wickline assumed she was experiencing normal recovery symptoms and did not communicate with any of her physicians. Finally, when "the pain got so great and the color started changing from looking like a statue to getting a grayish color," her husband called Dr. Kovner. It was Wickline's memory that this occurred about the third day after her discharge from the hospital and that Dr. Kovner advised Mr. Wickline to give extra pain medicine to the plaintiff.

Thereafter, gradually over the next few days, the plaintiff's leg "kept getting grayer and then it got bluish." The extra medication allegedly prescribed by Dr. Kovner over the telephone did not relieve the pain Wickline was experiencing. She testified that "by then the pain was just excruciating, where no pain medicine helped whatsoever." Finally, Wickline instructed her husband to call Dr. Kovner again and this time Dr. Kovner ordered plaintiff back into the hospital. Wickline returned to [the hospital] that same evening, January 30, 1977, nine days after her last discharge therefrom.

... Attempts to save Wickline's leg through the utilization of anticoagulants, antibiotics, strict bed rest, pain medication and warm water whirlpool baths to the lower extremity proved unsuccessful. On February 8, 1977, Dr. Polonsky amputated Wickline's leg below the knee because had he not done so, "she would have died." The condition did not, however, heal after the first operation and on February 17, 1977, the doctors went back and amputated Wickline's leg above the knee.

. . . In Dr. Polonsky's opinion, to a reasonable medical certainty, had Wickline remained in the hospital for eight additional days, as originally requested by him and her other treating doctors, she would not have suffered the loss of her leg.

. . . Dr. Polonsky testified that in his medical opinion, the Medi-Cal Consultant's rejection of the requested eight-day extension of acute care hospitalization and his authorization of a four-day extension in its place did not conform to the usual medical standards as they existed in 1977. He stated that, in accordance with those standards, a physician would not be permitted to make decisions regarding the care of a patient without either first seeing the patient, reviewing the patient's chart, or discussing the patient's condition with the treating physician or physicians.

From the facts thus presented, appellant takes the position that it was not negligent as a matter of law. Appellant contends that the decision to discharge was made by each of the plaintiff's three doctors, was based upon the prevailing standards of practice, and was justified by her condition at the time of her discharge. It argues that Medi-Cal had no part in the plaintiff's hospital discharge and therefore was not liable even if the decision to do so was erroneously made by her doctor.

. . . Dr. Kaufman, the chief Medi-Cal Consultant for the Los Angeles field office, was called to testify on behalf of the defendant. He testified that in January 1977, the criteria, or standard, which governed a Medi-Cal Consultant in acting on a request to consider an extension of time was founded on title 22 of the California Administrative Code. That standard was "the medical necessity" for the length and level of care requested. That, Dr. Kaufman contended, was determined by the Medi-Cal Consultant from the information provided him in the 180 form. The Medi-Cal Consultant's decision required the exercise of medical judgment and, in doing so, the Medi-Cal Consultant would utilize the skill, knowledge, training and experience he had acquired in the medical field.

Dr. Kaufman supported Dr. Glassman's decision. He testified, based upon his examination of the MC-180 form in issue in this matter, that Dr. Glassman's four-day hospital stay extension authorization was ample to meet the plaintiff's medically necessary needs at that point in time. Further, in Dr. Kaufman's opinion, there was no need for Dr. Glassman to seek information beyond that which was contained in Wickline's 180 form.

Dr. Kaufman testified that it was the practice in the Los Angeles Medi-Cal office for Medi-Cal Consultants not to review other information that might be available, such as the TAR 160 form (request for authorization for initial hospitalization), unless called by the patient's physician and requested to do so and, instead, to rely only on the information contained in the MC-180 form. Dr. Kaufman also stated that Medi-Cal Consultants did not initiate telephone calls to patients' treating doctors because of the volume of work they already had in meeting their prescribed responsibilities. Dr. Kaufman testified that any facts relating to the patient's care and treatment that was not shown on the 180 form was of no significance.

As to the principal issue before this court, i.e., who bears responsibility for allowing a patient to be discharged from the hospital, her treating physicians or the health care payor, each side's medical expert witnesses agreed that, in accordance with the standards of medical practice as it existed in January 1977, it was for the patient's treating physician to decide the course of treatment that was medically necessary to treat the ailment. It was also that physician's responsibility to determine whether or not acute care hospitalization was required and for how long. Finally, it was agreed that the patient's physician is in a better position than the Medi-Cal Consultant to determine the number of days medically necessary for any required hospital care. The decision to discharge is, therefore, the responsibility of the patient's own treating doctor.

Dr. Kaufman testified that if, on January 21, the date of the plaintiff's discharge from [the hospital], any one of her three treating doctors had decided that in his medical judgment it was necessary to keep Wickline in the hospital for a longer period of time, they, or any of them, should have filed another request for extension of stay in the hospital, that Medi-Cal would expect those physicians to make such a request if they felt it was indicated, and upon receipt of such a request further consideration of an additional extension of hospital time would have been given.

. . . The patient who requires treatment and who is harmed when care which should have been provided is not provided should recover for the injuries suffered from all those responsible for the deprivation of such care, including, when appropriate, health care payors. Third party payors of health care services can be held legally accountable when medically inappropriate decisions result from defects in the design or implementation of cost containment mechanisms, as, for example, when appeals made on a patient's behalf for medical or hospital care are arbitrarily ignored or unreasonably disregarded or overridden. However, the physician who complies without protest with the limitations imposed by a third party payor, when his medical judgment dictates otherwise, cannot avoid his ultimate responsibility for his patient's care. He cannot point to the health care payor as the liability scapegoat when the consequences of his own determinative medical decisions go sour.

There is little doubt that Dr. Polonsky was intimidated by the Medi-Cal program but he was not paralyzed by Dr. Glassman's response nor rendered powerless to act appropriately if other action was required under the circumstances. If, in his medical judgment, it was in his patient's best interest that she remain in the acute care hospital setting for an additional eight days beyond the extended time period originally authorized by Medi-Cal, Dr. Polonsky should have made some effort to keep Wickline there. He himself acknowledged that responsibility to his patient. It was his medical judgment, however, that Wickline could be discharged when she was. All the plaintiff's treating physicians concurred and all the doctors who testified at trial, for either plaintiff or defendant, agreed that Dr. Polonsky's medical decision to discharge

Wickline met the standard of care applicable at the time. Medi-Cal was not a party to that medical decision and therefore cannot be held liable to share in the harm resulting if such decision was negligently made.

In addition thereto, while Medi-Cal played a part in the scenario before us in that it was the resource for the funds to pay for the treatment sought, and its input regarding the nature and length of hospital care to be provided was of paramount importance, Medi-Cal did not override the medical judgment of Wickline's treating physicians at the time of her discharge. It was given no opportunity to do so. Therefore, there can be no viable cause of action against it for the consequences of that discharge decision.

. . . This court appreciates that what is at issue here is the effect of cost containment programs upon the professional judgment of physicians to prescribe hospital treatment for patients requiring the same. While we recognize, realistically, that cost consciousness has become a permanent feature of the health care system, it is essential that cost limitation programs not be permitted to corrupt medical judgment. We have concluded, from the facts in issue here, that in this case it did not.

NOTES

1. *Cost Containment.* The *Wickline* case involves currently fashionable *prospective* utilization review as opposed to the *retrospective* utilization review process used in early cost containment programs. In the words of the court:

> [S]uch a cost containment strategy creates new and added pressures on the quality assurance portion of the utilization review mechanism. The stakes, the risks at issue, are much higher when a prospective cost containment review process is utilized than when a retrospective review process is used.

Is not the torts system a perfectly structured means for policing such higher or added risks?

2. *Ultimate Responsibility.* On what basis might the physicians or the hospital face liability in a case like *Wickline*? What would be the appropriate standard of care?

3. *Cost Containment and the Standard of Care.* How should malpractice law react not just to quantitative limitations on expenditures for care but qualitative effects? It is now openly argued that our health care delivery systems will introduce rationing or have it imposed. *See, e.g.,* D. CALLAHAN, SETTING LIMITS: MEDICAL GOALS IN AN AGING SOCIETY (1987). Must any such rationing system incorporate liability limitations or immunities for those forced to work within such a system?

4. *Vicarious Liability of Hospitals.* The paradigm medical malpractice problem concerns the independent contractor physician with staff privileges at a defendant-hospital. Vicarious liability generally does not apply to cases involving independent contractors. However, RESTATEMENT (SECOND) OF TORTS § 429 (1965) provides:

> One who employs an independent contractor to perform services for another which are accepted in the reasonable belief that the services

are being rendered by the employer or by his servants, is subject to liability for physical harm caused by the negligence of the contractor in supplying such services, to the same extent as though the employer were supplying them himself or by his servants.

In *Pamperin v. Trinity Memorial Hospital*, 423 N.W.2d 848 (Wis., 1988), the court observed:

> . . . [W]e conclude that when a hospital holds itself out to the public as providing complete medical care, a hospital can be held liable under the doctrine of apparent authority for the negligent acts of the physicians retained by the hospital to provide emergency room care, irrespective of the fact that the person who committed the negligent act was an independent contractor. By holding themselves out as providing complete care, hospitals have created the appearance that the hospital itself, through its agents or employees, treats emergency room patients. When a hospital does not inform incoming patients which, if any, care or service is provided by independent contractors, and not by employees or agents, a patient should be able to look to the hospital for the negligence of the physician retained by the hospital to provide medical care. Moreover, because complete medical care consists of both direct care and support services, liability should attach regardless of whether the physician who is negligent is treating the patient directly or assisting in treating the patient by providing support services invisible to the patient . . . .

What must plaintiff prove to establish such ostensible or apparent agency? Is it sufficient that the patient allege that the defendant permitted the physician to walk around the hospital in a white coat carrying a medical bag? See *Porter v. Sisters of St. Mary*, 756 F.2d 669 (8th Cir. 1985), holding that the patient's subjective assumption that an emergency room doctor was an employee of the defendant hospital was insufficient to create apparent or ostensible agency under the law of Missouri.

5. *Institutional Liability for Intentional Torts.* In *G.L. v. Kaiser Found. Hosps.*, 306 Or. 54, 757 P.2d 1347 (1988), the plaintiff was sexually assaulted by defendant hospital's respiratory therapist. The court denied any application of *respondeat superior* in the absence of an allegation that the employee was acting for the purpose of furthering any interest of the hospital.

However, in *Copithorne v. Framingham Union Hosp.*, 401 Mass. 860, 520 N.E.2d 139 (1988), plaintiff, a hospital employee, was drugged and raped by her physician off the hospital premises. The physician had enjoyed staff privileges at the hospital for 17 years. Plaintiff alleged that the hospital had received notice of allegations of previous sexual misconduct by the physician, both on and off the premises. The court held that plaintiff stated a cause of action:

> We think that a jury reasonably could find that the hospital owed a duty of care to [the plaintiff], as an employee who, in deciding to enter a doctor-patient relationship with [the physician] reasonably relied on [his] good standing and reputation within the hospital community, and that the hospital violated this duty by failing to take sufficient action in response to previous allegations of [his] wrongdoing.

How do these two cases differ?

6. *Nondelegable Duties.* In *Jackson v. Power,* 743 P.2d 1376, 1385 (Alaska 1987), it was held that a hospital which had a duty to provide emergency care pursuant to Joint Committee on the Accreditation of Hospitals accreditation standards and its own internal regulations could not delegate that duty to an independent contractor and thereby avoid vicarious liability. The court stated:

> Not only is this rule consonant with the public perception of the hospital as a multifaceted health care facility responsible for the quality of medical care and treatment rendered, it also treats tort liability in the medical arena in a manner that is consistent with the commercialization of American medicine. Finally, we simply cannot fathom why liability should depend upon the technical employment status of the emergency room physician who treats the patient. It is the hospital's duty to provide the physician, which it may do through any means at its disposal. The means employed, however, will not change the fact that the hospital will be responsible for the care rendered by physicians it has a duty to provide.

7. *Corporate Hospital Liability Based on Negligent Hiring or Review of Staff Privileges.* In *Johnson v. Misericordia Comm. Hosp.,* 99 Wis. 2d 708, 301 N.W.2d 156, 164 (1981), the court held:

> The failure of a hospital to scrutinize the credentials of its medical staff applicants could foreseeably result in the appointment of unqualified physicians and surgeons to its staff. Thus, the granting of staff privileges to these doctors would undoubtedly create an unreasonable risk of harm or injury to their patients. Therefore, the failure to investigate a medical staff applicant's qualifications for the privileges requested gives rise to a foreseeable risk of unreasonable harm and we hold that a hospital has a duty to exercise due care in the selection of its medical staff.
>
> . . . The concept that a hospital does not undertake to treat patients, does not undertake to act through its doctors and nurses, but only procures them to act solely upon their own responsibility, no longer reflects the fact. The complex manner of operation of the modern-day medical institution clearly demonstrates that they furnish far more than mere facilities for treatment. They appoint physicians and surgeons to their medical staffs, as well as regularly employing on a salary basis resident physicians and surgeons, nurses, administrative and manual workers, and they charge patients for medical diagnosis, care, treatment and therapy, receiving payment for such services through privately financed medical insurance policies and government financed programs known as Medicare and Medicaid. Certainly, the person who avails himself of our modern "hospital facilities" (frequently a medical teaching institution) expects that the hospital staff will do all it reasonably can to cure him and does not anticipate that its nurses, doctors and other employees will be acting solely on their own responsibility.

What is the appropriate standard of care in such a case?

8. *Institutional Liability for Malpractice.* In *Thompson v. Nason Hospital*, 591 A.2d 703 (Pa. 1991), the court wrote:

> The hospital's duties have been classified into four general areas: (1) a duty to use reasonable care in the maintenance of safe and adequate facilities and equipment . . .; (2) a duty to select and retain only competent physicians . . .; (3) a duty to oversee all persons who practice medicine within its walls as to patient care . . .; and (4) a duty to formulate, adopt and enforce adequate rules and policies to ensure quality care for the patients . . . .
>
> Other jurisdictions have embraced this doctrine of corporate negligence or corporate liability such as to warrant it being called an "emerging trend" . . . .
>
> A critical step toward recognition of this theory of hospital liability already has been taken in this Commonwealth. In *Riddle Memorial Hospital v. Dohan*, 504 Pa. 571, 475 A.2d 1314 (1984), we found that the appropriate duty of care a hospital owes to a person brought into an emergency room is set forth in the RESTATEMENT (SECOND) OF TORTS § 323 (1965) which provides: One who undertakes, gratuitously or for consideration, to render services to another which he should recognize as necessary for the protection of the other's person or things, is subject to liability to the other for physical harm resulting from his failure to exercise reasonable care to perform his undertaking, if (a) his failure to exercise such care increases the risk of such harm, or (b) the harm is suffered because of the other's reliance upon the undertaking . . . .
>
> Today, we take a step beyond the hospital's duty of care delineated in *Riddle* in full recognition of the corporate hospital's role in the total health care of its patients. In so doing, we adopt as a theory of hospital liability the doctrine of corporate negligence or corporate liability under which the hospital is liable if it fails to uphold the proper standard of care owed its patient. In addition, we fully embrace the aforementioned four categories of the hospital's duties. It is important to note that for a hospital to be charged with negligence, it is necessary to show that the hospital had actual or constructive knowledge of the defect or procedures which created the harm . . . .

In *Pedroza v. Bryant*, 101 Wash. 2d 226, 677 P.2d 166 (1984), the Supreme Court of Washington commented that,

> The doctrine of corporate negligence reflects the public's perception of the modern hospital as a multifaceted health care facility responsible for the quality of medical care and treatment rendered . . .
>
> Forcing hospitals to assume responsibility for their corporate negligence may also provide those hospitals a financial incentive to insure the competency of their medical staffs. The most effective way to cut liability insurance costs is to avoid corporate negligence.

Detail the advantages and disadvantages of corporate liability for malpractice?

9. *The Limits of Corporate Liability.* In *Pedroza, supra,* the court declined to extend corporate negligence principles to the treatment of patients by hospital staff members in the staff members' private offices off the hospital premises. What arguments could be made on this issue? What if the hospital had actual notice of previous malpractice committed outside the hospital premises?

Should corporate liability extend to the most intimate aspects of the physician-patient relationship, such as the provision of informed consent?

10. *Corporate Liability and Causation. Rule v. Lutheran Hosps. & Homes Soc.,* 835 F.2d 1250 (8th Cir. 1987), concerned the granting of staff obstetric privileges to a physician. The privileges include the performance of a breech delivery for which he was not qualified. In contravening its own bylaws, the hospital had failed to make a proper investigation of the physician's qualifications or previous experience. The plaintiff was diagnosed as suffering from cerebral palsy because of injuries suffered during a breech delivery performed by the physician. The court considered evidence tending to show that the physician would not have been granted privileges if the hospital had made a proper investigation; and also that there had been time to have the patient transferred after the physician discovered that the baby was in the breech position. Applying the law of Nebraska, the court found that the evidence constituted a triable issue on whether the hospital's negligence was the proximate cause of the injury, and affirmed the jury verdict.

PEGRAM v. HERDICH
120 S. Ct. 2143 (2000)

JUSTICE SOUTER delivered the opinion of the Court.

The question in this case is whether treatment decisions made by a health maintenance organization, acting through its physician employees, are fiduciary acts within the meaning of the Employee Retirement Income Security Act of 1974 (ERISA), 88 Stat. 832, as amended, 29 U.S.C. §§ 1001 et seq. (1994 ed. and Supp. III). We hold that they are not.

Petitioners, Carle Clinic Association, P. C., Health Alliance Medical Plans, Inc., and Carle Health Insurance Management Co., Inc. (collectively Carle) function as a health maintenance organization (HMO) organized for profit. Its owners are physicians providing prepaid medical services to participants whose employers contract with Carle to provide such coverage. Respondent, Cynthia Herdrich, was covered by Carle through her husband's employer, State Farm Insurance Company.

The events in question began when a Carle physician, petitioner Lori Pegram,[1] examined Herdich, who was experiencing pain in the midline area of her groin. Six days later, Dr. Pegram discovered a six by eight centimeter inflamed mass in Herdrich's abdomen. Despite the noticeable inflammation, Dr. Pegram did not order an ultrasound diagnostic procedure at a local hospital, but decided that Herdrich would have to wait eight more days for

---

[1] Although Lori Pegram, a physician owner of Carle, is listed as a petitioner, it is unclear to us that she retains a direct interest in the outcome of this case.

an ultrasound, to be performed at a facility staffed by Carle more than 50 miles away. Before the eight days were over, Herdrich's appendix ruptured, causing peritonitis.

Herdrich sued Pegram and Carle in state court for medical malpractice, and she later added two counts charging state-law fraud. Carle and Pegram responded that ERISA preempted the new counts, and removed the case to federal court, where they then sought summary judgment on the state-law fraud counts. The District Court granted their motion as to the second fraud count but granted Herdrich leave to amend the one remaining. This she did by alleging that provision of medical services under the terms of the Carle HMO organization, rewarding its physician owners for limiting medical care, entailed an inherent or anticipatory breach of an ERISA fiduciary duty, since these terms created an incentive to make decisions in the physicians' self-interest, rather than the exclusive interests of plan participants.[3]

Herdrich sought relief under 29 U.S.C. § 1109(a), which provides that

"[a]ny person who is a fiduciary with respect to a plan who breaches any of the responsibilities, obligations, or duties imposed upon fiduciaries by this subchapter shall be personally liable to make good to such plan any losses to the plan resulting from each such breach, and

---

[3] The specific allegations were these:

"11. Defendants are fiduciaries with respect to the Plan and under 29 [U.S.C. §]1109(a) are obligated to discharge their duties with respect to the Plan solely in the interest of the participants and beneficiaries and

"a. for the exclusive purpose of:

"i. providing benefits to participants and their beneficiaries; and

"ii. defraying reasonable expenses of administering the Plan;

"b. with the care, skill, prudence, and diligence under the circumstances then prevailing that a prudent man acting in a like capacity and familiar with such matters would use in the conduct of an enterprise of a like character and like aims.

"12. In breach of that duty:

"a. CARLE owner/physicians are the officers and directors of HAMP and CHIMCO and receive a year-end distribution, based in large part upon, supplemental medical expense payments made to CARLE by HAMP and CHIMCO;

"b. Both HAMP and CHIMCO are directed and controlled by CARLE owner/physicians and seek to fund their supplemental medical expense payments to CARLE:

"i. by contracting with CARLE owner/physicians to provide the medical services contemplated in the Plan and then having those contracted owner/physicians:

"(1) minimize the use of diagnostic tests;

"(2) minimize the use of facilities not owned by CARLE; and

"(3) minimize the use of emergency and non-emergency consultation and/or referrals to non-contracted physicians.

"ii. by administering disputed and non-routine health insurance claims and determining:

"(1) which claims are covered under the Plan and to what extent;

"(2) what the applicable standard of care is;

"(3) whether a course of treatment is experimental;

"(4) whether a course of treatment is reasonable and customary; and

"(5) whether a medical condition is an emergency." App. to Pet. for Cert. 85a–86a.

to restore to such plan any profits of such fiduciary which have been made through use of assets of the plan by the fiduciary, and shall be subject to such other equitable or remedial relief as the court may deem appropriate, including removal of such fiduciary."

When Carle moved to dismiss the ERISA count for failure to state a claim upon which relief could be granted, the District Court granted the motion, accepting the Magistrate Judge's determination that Carle was not "involved [in these events] as" an ERISA fiduciary. The original malpractice counts were then tried to a jury, and Herdrich prevailed on both, receiving $35,000 in compensation for her injury. She then appealed the dismissal of the ERISA claim to the Court of Appeals for the Seventh Circuit, which reversed. The court held that Carle was acting as a fiduciary when its physicians made the challenged decisions and that Herdrich's allegations were sufficient to state a claim:

> Our decision does not stand for the proposition that the existence of incentives automatically gives rise to a breach of fiduciary duty. Rather, we hold that incentives can rise to the level of a breach where, as pleaded here, the fiduciary trust between plan participants and plan fiduciaries no longer exists (i.e., where physicians delay providing necessary treatment to, or withhold administering proper care to, plan beneficiaries for the sole purpose of increasing their bonuses).

We granted certiorari, and now reverse the Court of Appeals.

Whether Carle is a fiduciary when it acts through its physician owners as pleaded in the ERISA count depends on some background of fact and law about HMO organizations, medical benefit plans, fiduciary obligation, and the meaning of Herdrich's allegations.

Traditionally, medical care in the United States has been provided on a "fee-for-service" basis. A physician charges so much for a general physical exam, a vaccination, a tonsillectomy, and so on. The physician bills the patient for services provided or, if there is insurance and the doctor is willing, submits the bill for the patient's care to the insurer, for payment subject to the terms of the insurance agreement. In a fee-for-service system, a physician's financial incentive is to provide more care, not less, so long as payment is forthcoming. The check on this incentive is a physician's obligation to exercise reasonable medical skill and judgment in the patient's interest.

Beginning in the late 1960's, insurers and others developed new models for health-care delivery, including HMOs. The defining feature of an HMO is receipt of a fixed fee for each patient enrolled under the terms of a contract to provide specified health care if needed. The HMO thus assumes the financial risk of providing the benefits promised: if a participant never gets sick, the HMO keeps the money regardless, and if a participant becomes expensively ill, the HMO is responsible for the treatment agreed upon even if its cost exceeds the participant's premiums.

Like other risk-bearing organizations, HMOs take steps to control costs. At the least, HMOs, like traditional insurers, will in some fashion make coverage determinations, scrutinizing requested services against the contractual provisions to make sure that a request for care falls within the scope of covered circumstances (pregnancy, for example), or that a given treatment falls within the scope of the care promised (surgery, for instance). They customarily issue general guidelines for their physicians about appropriate levels of care. And they commonly require utilization review (in which specific treatment decisions are reviewed by a decisionmaker other than the treating physician) and approval in advance (precertification) for many types of care, keyed to standards of medical necessity or the reasonableness of the proposed treatment. These cost-controlling measures are commonly complemented by specific financial incentives to physicians, rewarding them for decreasing utilization of health-care services, and penalizing them for what may be found to be excessive treatment. Hence, in an HMO system, a physician's financial interest lies in providing less care, not more. The check on this influence (like that on the converse, fee-for-service incentive) is the professional obligation to provide covered services with a reasonable degree of skill and judgment in the patient's interest.

The adequacy of professional obligation to counter financial self-interest has been challenged no matter what the form of medical organization. HMOs became popular because fee-for-service physicians were thought to be providing unnecessary or useless services; today, many doctors and other observers argue that HMOs often ignore the individual needs of a patient in order to improve the HMOs' bottom lines. In this case, for instance, one could argue that Pegram's decision to wait before getting an ultrasound for Herdrich, and her insistence that the ultrasound be done at a distant facility owned by Carle, reflected an interest in limiting the HMO's expenses, which blinded her to the need for immediate diagnosis and treatment.

Herdrich focuses on the Carle scheme's provision for a "year-end distribution," to the HMO's physician owners. She argues that this particular incentive device of annually paying physician owners the profit resulting from their own decisions rationing care can distinguish Carle's organization from HMOs-generally, so that reviewing Carle's decisions under a fiduciary standard as pleaded in Herdrich's complaint would not open the door to like claims about other HMO structures. While the Court of Appeals agreed, we think otherwise, under the law as now written.

Although it is true that the relationship between sparing medical treatment and physician reward is not a subtle one under the Carle scheme, no HMO organization could survive without some incentive connecting physician reward with treatment rationing. The essence of an HMO is that salaries and profits are limited by the HMO's fixed membership fees. This is not to suggest that the Carle provisions are as socially desirable as some other HMO organizational schemes; they may not be. But whatever the HMO, there must be rationing and inducement to ration.

Since inducement to ration care goes to the very point of any HMO scheme, and rationing necessarily raises some risks while reducing others (ruptured appendixes are more likely; unnecessary appendectomies are less so), any legal principle purporting to draw a line between good and bad HMOs would embody, in effect, a judgment about socially acceptable medical risk. A valid conclusion of this sort would, however, necessarily turn on facts to which courts would probably not have ready access: correlations between malpractice rates and various HMO models, similar correlations involving fee-for-service models, and so on. And, of course, assuming such material could be obtained by courts in litigation like this, any standard defining the unacceptably risky HMO structure (and consequent vulnerability to claims like Herdrich's) would depend on a judgment about the appropriate level of expenditure for health care in light of the associated malpractice risk. But such complicated factfinding and such a debatable social judgment are not wisely required of courts unless for some reason resort cannot be had to the legislative process, with its preferable forum for comprehensive investigations and judgments of social value, such as optimum treatment levels and health care expenditure.

We think, then, that courts are not in a position to derive a sound legal principle to differentiate an HMO like Carle from other. For that reason, we proceed on the assumption that the decisions listed in Herdrich's complaint cannot be subject to a claim that they violate fiduciary standards unless all such decisions by all HMOs acting through their owner or employee physicians are to be judged by the same standards and subject to the same claims.

We turn now from the structure of HMOs to the requirements of ERISA. A fiduciary within the meaning of ERISA must be someone acting in the capacity of manager, administrator, or financial adviser to a "plan," see 29 U.S.C. §§ 1002(21)(A)(i)–(iii), and Herdich's ERISA count accordingly charged Carle with a breach of fiduciary duty in discharging its obligations under State Farm's medical plan. ERISA's definition of an employee welfare benefit plan is ultimately circular: "any plan, fund, or program . . . to the extent that such plan, fund, or program was established . . . for the purpose of providing . . . through the purchase of insurance or otherwise . . . medical, surgical, or hospital care or benefits." § 1002(1)(A). One is thus left to the common understanding of the word "plan" as referring to a scheme decided upon in advance, see Webster's New International Dictionary 1879 (2d ed.1957); Jacobson & Pomfret, Form, Function, and Managed Care Torts: Achieving Fairness and Equity in ERISA Jurisprudence, 35 Houston L.Rev. 985, 1050 (1998). Here the scheme comprises a set of rules that define the rights of a beneficiary and provide for their enforcement. Rules governing collection of premiums, definition of benefits, submission of claims, and resolution of disagreements over entitlement to services are the sorts of provisions that constitute a plan. Thus, when employers contract with an HMO to provide benefits to employees subject to ERISA, the provisions of documents that set up the HMO are not, as such, an ERISA plan, but the agreement between an HMO and an employer who pays the premiums may, as here, provide elements of a plan by setting out rules under which beneficiaries will be entitled to care.

As just noted, fiduciary obligations can apply to managing, advising, and administering an ERISA plan, the fiduciary function addressed by Herdrich's ERISA count being the exercise of "discretionary authority or discretionary responsibility in the administration of [an ERISA] plan," 29 U.S.C. § 1002(21)(A)(iii). And as we have already suggested, although Carle is not an ERISA fiduciary merely because it administers or exercises discretionary authority over its own HMO business, it may still be a fiduciary if it administers the plan.

In general terms, fiduciary responsibility under ERISA is simply stated. The statute provides that fiduciaries shall discharge their duties with respect to a plan "solely in the interest of the participants and beneficiaries," § 1104(a)(1), that is, "for the exclusive purpose of (i) providing benefits to participants and their beneficiaries; and (ii) defraying reasonable expenses of administering the plan," § 1104(a)(1)(A).[6] These responsibilities imposed by ERISA have the familiar ring of their source in the common law of trusts. Thus, the common law (understood as including what were once the distinct rules of equity) charges fiduciaries with a duty of loyalty to guarantee beneficiaries' interests: "The most fundamental duty owed by the trustee to the beneficiaries of the trust is the duty of loyalty . . . . It is the duty of a trustee to administer the trust solely in the interest of the beneficiaries." 2A A. Scott & W. Fratcher, Trusts § 170, 311 (4th ed.1987) (hereinafter Scott); see also G. Bogert & G. Bogert, Law of Trusts and Trustees § 543 (rev.2d ed. 1980) ("Perhaps the most fundamental duty of a trustee is that he must display throughout the administration of the trust complete loyalty to the interests of the beneficiary and must exclude all selfish interest and all consideration of the interests of third persons"); Central States, supra, at 570–571, 105 S.Ct. 2833; Meinhard v. Salmon, 249 N.Y. 458, 464, 164 N.E. 545, 546 (1928) (Cardozo, J.) ("Many forms of conduct permissible in a workaday world for those acting at arm's length, are forbidden to those bound by fiduciary ties. A trustee is held to something stricter than the morals of the market place. Not honesty alone, but the punctilio of an honor the most sensitive, is then the standard of behavior").

Beyond the threshold statement of responsibility, however, the analogy between ERISA fiduciary and common law trustee becomes problematic. This is so because the trustee at common law characteristically wears only his fiduciary hat when he takes action to affect a beneficiary, whereas the trustee under ERISA may wear different hats.

Speaking of the traditional trustee, Professor Scott's treatise admonishes that the trustee "is not permitted to place himself in a position where it would be for his own benefit to violate his duty to the beneficiaries." 2A Scott, § 170, at 311. Under ERISA, however, a fiduciary may have financial interests adverse to beneficiaries. Employers, for example, can be ERISA fiduciaries and still take actions to the disadvantage of employee beneficiaries, when they act as employers (e.g., firing a beneficiary for reasons unrelated to the ERISA plan), or even as plan sponsors (e.g., modifying the terms of a plan as allowed by ERISA to provide less generous benefits). Nor is there any apparent reason in the ERISA provisions to conclude, as Herdrich argues, that this tension

---

[6] In addition, fiduciaries must discharge their duties:

"(B) with the care, skill, prudence, and diligence under the circumstances then prevailing that a prudent man acting in a like capacity and familiar with such matters would use in the conduct of an enterprise of a like character and with like aims;

"(C) by diversifying the investments of the plan so as to minimize the risk of large losses, unless under the circumstances it is clearly prudent not to do so; and

"(D) in accordance with the documents and instruments governing the plan insofar as such documents and instruments are consistent with the provisions of this subchapter and subchapter III of this chapter." 29 U.S.C. § 1104(a)(1).

is permissible only for the employer or plan sponsor, to the exclusion of persons who provide services to an ERISA plan.

ERISA does require, however, that the fiduciary with two hats wear only one at a time, and wear the fiduciary hat when making fiduciary decisions. Thus, the statute does not describe fiduciaries simply as administrators of the plan, or managers or advisers. Instead it defines an administrator, for example, as a fiduciary only "to the extent" that he acts in such a capacity in relation to a plan. 29 U.S.C. § 1002(21)(A). In every case charging breach of ERISA fiduciary duty, then, the threshold question is not whether the actions of some person employed to provide services under a plan adversely affected a plan beneficiary's interest, but whether that person was acting as a fiduciary (that is, was performing a fiduciary function) when taking the action subject to complaint.

The allegations of Herdrich's ERISA count that identify the claimed fiduciary breach are difficult to understand. In this count, Herdrich does not point to a particular act by any Carle physician owner as a breach. She does not complain about Pegram's actions, and at oral argument her counsel confirmed that the ERISA count could have been brought, and would have been no different, if Herdrich had never had a sick day in her life.

What she does claim is that Carle, acting through its physician owners, breached its duty to act solely in the interest of beneficiaries by making decisions affecting medical treatment while influenced by the terms of the Carle HMO scheme, under which the physician owners ultimately profit from their own choices to minimize the medical services provided. She emphasizes the threat to fiduciary responsibility in the Carle scheme's feature of a year-end distribution to the physicians of profit derived from the spread between subscription income and expenses of care and administration.

The specific payout detail of the plan was, of course, a feature that the employer as plan sponsor was free to adopt without breach of any fiduciary duty under ERISA, since an employer's decisions about the content of a plan are not themselves fiduciary acts. Likewise it is clear that there was no violation of ERISA when the incorporators of the Carle HMO provided for the year-end payout. The HMO is not the ERISA plan, and the incorporation of the HMO preceded its contract with the State Farm plan. See 29 U.S.C. § 1109(b) (no fiduciary liability for acts preceding fiduciary status).

The nub of the claim, then, is that when State Farm contracted with Carle, Carle became a fiduciary under the plan, acting through its physicians. At once, Carle as fiduciary administrator was subject to such influence from the year-end payout provision that its fiduciary capacity was necessarily compromised, and its readiness to act amounted to anticipatory breach of fiduciary obligation.

The pleadings must also be parsed very carefully to understand what acts by physician owners acting on Carle's behalf are alleged to be fiduciary in nature. It will help to keep two sorts of arguably administrative acts in mind. What we will call pure "eligibility decisions" turn on the plan's coverage of a particular condition or medical procedure for its treatment. "Treatment decisions," by contrast, are choices about how to go about diagnosing and treating a patent's condition: given a patient's constellation of symptoms, what is the appropriate medical response?

These decisions are often practically inextricable from one another, as amici on both sides agree. This is so not merely because, under a scheme like Carle's, treatment and eligibility decisions are made by the same person, the treating physician. It is so because a great many and possibly most coverage questions are not simple yes-or-no questions, like whether appendicitis is a covered condition (when there is no dispute that a patient has appendicitis), or whether acupuncture is a covered procedure for pain relief (when the claim of pain is unchallenged). The more common coverage question is a when-and-how question. Although coverage for many conditions will be clear and various treatment options will be indisputably compensable, physicians still must decide what to do in particular cases. The issue may be, say, whether one treatment option is so superior to another under the circumstances, and needed so promptly, that a decision to proceed with it would meet the medical necessity requirement that conditions the HMO's obligation to provide or pay for that particular procedure at that time in that case. The Government in its brief alludes to a similar example when it discusses an HMO's refusal to pay for emergency care on the ground that the situation giving rise to the need for care was not an emergency. In practical terms, these eligibility decisions cannot be untangled from physicians' judgments about reasonable medical treatment, and in the case before us, Dr. Pegram's decision was one of that sort. She decided (wrongly, as it turned out) that Herdrich's condition did not warrant immediate action; the consequence of that medical determination was that Carle would not cover immediate care, whereas it would have done so if Dr. Pegram had made the proper diagnosis and judgment to treat. The eligibility decision and the treatment decision were inextricably mixed, as they are in countless medical administrative decisions every day.

The kinds of decisions mentioned in Herdrich's ERISA count and claimed to be fiduciary in character are just such mixed eligibility and treatment decisions: physicians' conclusions about when to use diagnostic tests; about seeking consultations and making referrals to physicians and facilities other than Carle's; about proper standards of care, the experimental character of a proposed course of treatment, the reasonableness of a certain treatment, and the emergency character of a medical condition.

We do not read the ERISA count, however, as alleging fiduciary breach with reference to a different variety of administrative decisions, those we have called pure eligibility determinations, such as whether a plan covers an undisputed case of appendicitis. Nor do we read it as claiming breach by reference to discrete administrative decisions separate from medical judgments; say, rejecting a claim for no other reason than the HMO's financial condition. The closest Herdrich's ERISA count comes to stating a claim for a pure, unmixed eligibility decision is her general allegation that Carle determines "which claims are covered under the Plan and to what extent," App. to Pet. for Cert. 86a. But this vague statement, difficult to interpret in isolation, is given content by the other elements of the complaint, all of which refer to decisions thoroughly mixed with medical judgment. Any lingering uncertainty about what Herdrich has in mind is dispelled by her brief, which explains that this allegation, like the others, targets medical necessity determinations.

Based on our understanding of the matters just discussed, we think Congress did not intend Carle or any other HMO to be treated as a fiduciary to the extent that it makes mixed eligibility decisions acting through its physicians. We begin with doubt that Congress would ever have thought of a mixed eligibility decision as fiduciary in nature. At common law, fiduciary duties characteristically attach to decisions about managing assets and distributing property to beneficiaries. Trustees buy, sell, and lease investment property, lend and borrow, and do other things to conserve and nurture assets. They pay out income, choose beneficiaries, and distribute remainders at termination. Thus, the common law trustee's most defining concern historically has been the payment of money in the interest of the beneficiary.

Mixed eligibility decisions by an HMO acting through its physicians have, however, only a limited resemblance to the usual business of traditional trustees. To be sure, the physicians (like regular trustees) draw on resources held for others and make decisions to distribute them in accordance with entitlements expressed in a written instrument (embodying the terms of an ERISA plan). It is also true that the objects of many traditional private and public trusts are ultimately the same as the ERISA plans that contract with HMOs. Private trusts provide medical care to the poor; thousands of independent hospitals are privately held and publicly accountable trusts, and charitable foundations make grants to stimulate the provision of health services. But beyond this point the resemblance rapidly wanes. Traditional trustees administer a medical trust by paying out money to buy medical care, whereas physicians making mixed eligibility decisions consume the money as well. Private trustees do not make treatment judgments, whereas treatment judgments are what physicians reaching mixed decisions do make, by definition. Indeed, the physicians through whom HMOs act make just the sorts of decisions made by licensed medical practitioners millions of times every day, in every possible medical setting: HMOs, fee-for-service proprietorships, public and private hospitals, military field hospitals, and so on. The settings bear no more resemblance to trust departments than a decision to operate turns on the factors controlling the amount of a quarterly income distribution. Thus, it is at least questionable whether Congress would have had mixed eligibility decisions in mind when it provided that decisions administering a plan were fiduciary in nature. Indeed, when Congress took up the subject of fiduciary responsibility under ERISA, it concentrated on fiduciaries' financial decisions, focusing on pension plans, the difficulty many retirees faced in getting the payments they expected, and the financial mismanagement that had too often deprived employees of their benefits. Its focus was far from the subject of Herdrich's claim.

Our doubt that Congress intended the category of fiduciary administrative functions to encompass the mixed determinations at issue here hardens into conviction when we consider the consequences that would follow from Herdrich's contrary view.

First, we need to ask how this fiduciary standard would affect HMOs if it applied as Herdrich claims it should be applied, not directed against any particular mixed decision that injured a patient, but against HMOs that make mixed decisions in the course of providing medical care for profit. Recovery would be warranted simply upon showing that the profit incentive to ration care would generally affect mixed decisions, in derogation of the fiduciary standard to act solely in the interest of the patient without possibility of conflict. Although Herdrich is vague about the mechanics of relief, the one point that seems clear is that she seeks the return of profit from the pockets of the Carle HMO's owners, with the money to be given to the plan for the benefit of the participants. Since the provision for profit is what makes the HMO a proprietary organization, her remedy in effect would be nothing less than elimination of the for-profit HMO. Her remedy might entail even more than that, although we are in no position to tell whether and to what extent nonprofit HMO schemes would ultimately survive the recognition of Herdrich's theory.[11] It is enough to recognize that the Judiciary has no warrant to precipitate the upheaval that would follow a refusal to dismiss Herdrich's ERISA claim. The fact is that for over 27 years the Congress of the United States has promoted the formation of HMO practices. The Health Maintenance Organization Act of 1973, 87 Stat. 914, 42 U.S.C. § 300e et seq., allowed the formation of HMOs that assume financial risks for the provision of health care services, and Congress has amended the Act several times, most recently in 1996. See 110 Stat.1976, codified at 42 U.S.C. § 300e (1994 ed., Supp. III). If Congress wishes to restrict its approval of HMO practice to certain preferred forms, it may choose to do so. But the Federal Judiciary would be acting contrary to the congressional policy of allowing HMO organizations if it were to entertain an ERISA fiduciary claim portending wholesale attacks on existing HMOs solely because of their structure, untethered to claims of concrete harm.

The fiduciary is, of course, obliged to act exclusively in the interest of the beneficiary, but this translates into no rule readily applicable to HMO decisions or those of any other variety of medical practice. While the incentive of the HMO physician is to give treatment sparingly, imposing a fiduciary obligation upon him would not lead to a simple default rule, say, that whenever it is reasonably possible to disagree about treatment options, the physician should treat aggressively. After all, HMOs came into being because some groups of physicians consistently provided more aggressive treatment than others in similar circumstances, with results not perceived as justified by the marginal expense and risk associated with intervention; excessive surgery is not in the patient's best interest, whether provided by fee-for-service surgeons or HMO surgeons subject to a default rule urging them to operate. Nor would it be possible to translate fiduciary duty into a standard that would allow recovery from an HMO whenever a mixed decision influenced by the HMO's financial incentive resulted in a bad outcome for the patient. It would be so easy to allege, and to find, an economic influence when sparing care did not lead to a well patient, that any such standard in practice would allow a factfinder to convert an HMO into a guarantor of recovery.

---

[11] Herdrich's theory might well portend the end of nonprofit HMOs as well, since those HMOs can set doctors' salaries. A claim against a nonprofit HMO could easily allege that salaries were excessively high because they were funded by limiting care, and some nonprofits actually use incentive schemes similar to that challenged here. . . .

These difficulties may have led the Court of Appeals to try to confine the fiduciary breach to cases where "the sole purpose" of delaying or withholding treatment was to increase the physician's financial reward. But this attempt to confine mixed decision claims to their most egregious examples entails erroneous corruption of fiduciary obligation and would simply lead to further difficulties that we think fatal. While a mixed decision made solely to benefit the HMO or its physician would violate a fiduciary duty, the fiduciary standard condemns far more than that, in its requirement of "an eye single" toward beneficiaries' interests, Donovan v. Bierwirth, 680 F.2d 263, 271 (C.A.2 1982). But whether under the Court of Appeals's rule or a straight standard of undivided loyalty, the defense of any HMO would be that its physician did not act out of financial interest but for good medical reasons, the plausibility of which would require reference to standards of reasonable and customary medical practice in like circumstances. That, of course, is the traditional standard of the common law. Thus, for all practical purposes, every claim of fiduciary breach by an HMO physician making a mixed decision would boil down to a malpractice claim, and the fiduciary standard would be nothing but the malpractice standard traditionally applied in actions against physicians.

What would be the value to the plan participant of having this kind of ERISA fiduciary action? It would simply apply the law already available in state courts and federal diversity actions today, and the formulaic addition of an allegation of financial incentive would do nothing but bring the same claim into a federal court under federal-question jurisdiction. It is true that in States that do not allow malpractice actions against HMOs the fiduciary claim would offer a plaintiff a further defendant to be sued for direct liability, and in some cases the HMO might have a deeper pocket than the physician. But we have seen enough to know that ERISA was not enacted out of concern that physicians were too poor to be sued, or in order to federalize malpractice litigation in the name of fiduciary duty for any other reason. It is difficult, in fact, to find any advantage to participants across the board, except that allowing them to bring malpractice actions in the guise of federal fiduciary breach claims against HMOs would make them eligible for awards of attorney's fees if they won. See 29 U.S.C. § 1132(g)(1). But, again, we can be fairly sure that Congress did not create fiduciary obligations out of concern that state plaintiffs were not suing often enough, or were paying too much in legal fees.

The mischief of Herdrich's position would, indeed, go further than mere replication of state malpractice actions with HMO defendants. For not only would an HMO be liable as a fiduciary in the first instance for its own breach of fiduciary duty committed through the acts of its physician employee, but the physician employee would also be subject to liability as a fiduciary on the same basic analysis that would charge the HMO. The physician who made the mixed administrative decision would be exercising authority in the way described by ERISA and would therefore be deemed to be a fiduciary. Hence the physician, too, would be subject to suit in federal court applying an ERISA standard of reasonable medical skill. This result, in turn, would raise a puzzling issue of preemption. On its face, federal fiduciary law applying a malpractice standard would seem to be a prescription for preemption of state malpractice law, since the new ERISA cause of action would cover the subject of a state-law malpractice claim. To be sure, New York State Conference of Blue Cross & Blue Shield Plans v. Travelers Ins. Co., 514 U.S. 645, 654–655, 115 S.Ct. 1671, 131 L.Ed.2d 695 (1995), throws some cold water on the preemption theory; there, we held that, in the field of health care, a subject of traditional state regulation, there is no ERISA preemption without clear manifestation of congressional purpose. But in that case the convergence of state and federal law was not so clear as in the situation we are positing; the state-law standard had not been subsumed by the standard to be applied under ERISA. We could struggle with this problem, but first it is well to ask, again, what would be gained by opening the federal courthouse doors for a fiduciary malpractice claim, save for possibly random fortuities such as more favorable scheduling, or the ancillary opportunity to seek attorney's fees. And again, we know that Congress had no such haphazard boons in prospect when it defined the ERISA fiduciary, nor such a risk to the efficiency of federal courts as a new fiduciary-malpractice jurisdiction would pose in welcoming such unheard-of fiduciary litigation.

We hold that mixed eligibility decisions by HMO physicians are not fiduciary decisions under ERISA. Herdrich's ERISA count fails to state an ERISA claim, and the judgment of the Court of Appeals is reversed.

NOTES

1. *Reconciling ERISA With State Tort Law:* Prior to *Pegram v. Herdrich* the issue that the courts wrestled with was whether ERISA shielded managed care companies from state tort liability. The courts do not agree on the answer. Cf. *Dukes v. U.S. Healthcare, Inc.*, 57 F.3d 350 1995)(ERISA does not preempt a medical negligence claim based on the quality of care provided); *Corcoran v. United Health Care, Inc.,* 965 F.2d 1321 (5th Cir. 1992) (ERISA preempts claims for medical malpractice). The plaintiff in *Pegram* tried to turn the tables by using ERISA as a sword in tort litigation. In rejecting the argument that ERISA could be used as a sword in tort litigation based on the "fiduciary" concept, did the court shed any light on whether managed care companies could continue to use ERISA as a defense in medical negligence cases brought under state tort law?

2. *State Statutory Remedies.* Disagreeing with the Fifth Circuit, the court held in *Moran v. Rush Prudential HMO, Inc.*, 230 F.3d 959 (7th Cir. 2000), that an Illinois statute, which required HMOs to provide independent review of disputes between HMOs and primary care providers, and to cover services deemed medically necessary by the independent reviewer, was not preempted by ERISA. The statute regulated insurance, within the meaning of the saving clause under ERISA's preemption provision, the court said.

In a post-*Pegram* case, *Corp. Health Insurance Inc. v. The Texas Dept. of Insurance*, 220 F. 3d 641 (5th Cir. 2000), the court held a state statute, making managed health care facilities liable for substandard health care treatment decisions, was not preempted by ERISA. The court noted that *Pegram* held no tort action for breach of judiciary duty could be based on ERISA. *Pegram* did not hold that ERISA preempted "direct liability for physicians' malpractice when making 'healthcare treatment decisions' and the ensuring vicarious liability for the HMOs," *id.* at 643.

3. *Medical Malpractice and Risk Disclosure.* The court in *Neade v. Portes*, 739 N.E.2d 496 (Ill. 2000), held that a doctor had no fiduciary duty to disclose to his patient that doctor's alleged financial interest in a medical incentive fund controlled by the patient's HMO. This claim was duplicative, the court said, of the patient's medical malpractice claim for failure to provide proper treatment. If the doctor testified, said the court, he could be cross-examined on his financial interest by way of impeachment.

4. *Fiduciary Duties and Cost Containment Responsibilities.* The common law imposes a duty on physicians to act in the best interest of their patients. Is a physician relieved of that responsibility if she provides care under a managed care contract that requires the physician to provide care on the basis of financial constraints rather than medical judgment? If not, how can the physician fulfill her fiduciary obligation to the patient and her financial obligation to the managed care company at the same time? What would a reasonable physician do, acting in the same or similar circumstances? May the physician follow one standard when treating a fee–for–service patient and another standard when treating a managed care patient? For further discussion of the background of this dilemma and an analysis of the issues, *see* FRANK MCCLELLAN, MEDICAL MALPRACTICE: LAW, TACTICS AND ETHICS 63-76 (1994).

Chapter 14
VICARIOUS RESPONSIBILITY FOR THE CONDUCT OF OTHERS

A. INTRODUCTION

Two parties may share a relationship which justifies imposing upon the one who is free from fault liability for the tortious conduct of the other. This result sometimes is called vicarious liability. Perhaps a better term is imputed responsibility, because the fault or other wrongful conduct of a third person is imputed to a plaintiff to defeat or reduce recovery, or imputed to a defendant to impose liability.

Imputed fault or vicarious liability frequently is described as a form of strict liability, but this description is not entirely accurate. Imputed fault (vicarious liability) requires that there be underlying wrongful conduct of another with which the party without fault is charged. Thus, the most nearly accurate term in these situations is imputed fault.

It also should be borne in mind that where the doctrine of strict or absolute liability applies, the non-faulty acts of the agent acting within the scope of her agency can be imputed to her principal. Thus, an employer could be liable for damages from blasting caused by the non-faulty acts of its employees acting within the scope of their employment. This is imputed strict or absolute liability.

B. IMPUTED RESPONSIBILITY OF THE DEFENDANT

IRA S. BUSHEY & SONS v. UNITED STATES
398 F.2d 167 (2d Cir. 1968)

FRIENDLY, CIRCUIT JUDGE:

While the United States Coast Guard vessel Tamaroa was being overhauled in a floating drydock located in Brooklyn's Gowanus Canal, a seaman returning from shore leave late at night, in the condition for which seamen are famed, turned some wheels on the drydock wall. He thus opened valves that controlled the flooding of the tanks on one side of the drydock. Soon the ship listed, slid off the blocks and fell against the wall. Parts of the drydock sank, and the ship partially did — fortunately without loss of life or personal injury. The drydock owner sought and was granted compensation by the District Court for the Eastern District of New York in an amount to be determined, 276 F. Supp. 518; the United States appeals. . . .[1] With our appellate

---

[1] The district court also dismissed a libel by the United States against the drydock owner for damage to the vessel; the United States has not appealed from that ruling.

jurisdiction under 28 U.S.C. § 1292(a)(3) thus established, we return to the facts. The Tamaroa had gone into drydock on February 28, 1963; her keel rested on blocks permitting her drive shaft to be removed and repairs to be made to her hull. The contract between the Government and Bushey provided in part:

> (o) The work shall, whenever practical, be performed in such manner as not to interfere with the berthing and messing of personnel attached to the vessel undergoing repair, and provision shall be made so that personnel assigned shall have access to the vessel at all times, it being understood that such personnel will not interfere with the work or the contractor's workmen.

Access from shore to ship was provided by a route past the security guard at the gate, through the yard, up a ladder to the top of one drydock wall and along the wall to a gangway leading to the fantail deck, where men returning from leave reported at a quartermaster's shack.

Seaman Lane, whose prior record was unblemished, returned from shore leave a little after midnight on March 14. He had been drinking heavily; the quartermaster made mental note that he was "loose." For reasons not apparent to us or very likely to Lane,[2] he took it into his head, while progressing along the gangway wall, to turn each of three large wheels some twenty times; unhappily, as previously stated, these wheels controlled the water intake valves. After boarding ship at 12:11 A.M., Lane mumbled to an off-duty seaman that he had "turned some valves" and also muttered something about "valves" to another who was standing the engineering watch.

Neither did anything; apparently Lane's condition was not such as to encourage proximity. At 12:20 A.M. a crew member discovered water coming into the drydock. By 12:30 A.M. the ship began to list, the alarm was sounded and the crew were ordered ashore. Ten minutes later the vessel and dock were listing over 20 degrees; in another ten minutes the ship slid off the blocks and fell against the drydock wall.

The Government attacks imposition of liability on the ground that Lane's acts were not within the scope of his employment. It relies heavily on § 228(1) of the Restatement (Second) of Agency which says that "conduct of a servant is within the scope of employment if, but only if: . . . (c) it is actuated, at least in part by a purpose to serve the master." Courts have gone to considerable lengths to find such a purpose, as witness a well-known opinion in which Judge Learned Hand concluded that a drunken boatswain who routed the plaintiff out of his bunk with a blow, saying "Get up, you big son of a bitch, and turn to," and then continued to fight, might have thought he was acting in the interest of the ship. *Nelson v. American-West African Line*, 86 F.2d 730 (2d Cir. 1936), *cert. denied*, 300 U.S. 665, 57 S. Ct. 509, 81 L. Ed. 873 (1937). It would be going too far to find such a purpose here; while Lane's return to the Tamaroa was to serve his employer, no one has suggested how he could have thought turning the wheels to be, even if — which is by no means clear — he was unaware of the consequences.

---

[2] Lane disappeared after completing the sentence imposed by a court-martial and being discharged from the Coast Guard.

In light of the highly artificial way in which the motive test has been applied, the district judge believed himself obliged to test the doctrine's continuing vitality by referring to the larger purposes respondeat superior is supposed to serve. He concluded that the old formulation failed this test. We do not find his analysis so compelling, however, as to constitute a sufficient basis in itself for discarding the old doctrine. It is not at all clear, as the court below suggested, that expansion of liability in the manner here suggested will lead to a more efficient allocation of resources. As the most astute exponent of this theory has emphasized, a more efficient allocation can only be expected if there is some reason to believe that imposing a particular cost on the enterprise will lead it to consider whether steps should be taken to prevent a recurrence of the accident. Calabresi, *The Decision for Accidents: An Approach to Non-fault Allocation of Costs*, 78 Harv. L. Rev. 713, 725–34 (1965). And the suggestion that imposition of liability here will lead to more intensive screening of employees rests on highly questionable premises, *see* Comment, *Assessment of Punitive Damages Against an Entrepreneur for the Malicious Torts of His Employees*, 70 YALE L.J. 1296, 1301–04 (1961).[3] The unsatisfactory quality of the allocation of resource rationale is especially striking on the facts of this case. It could well be that application of the traditional rule might induce drydock owners, prodded by their insurance companies, to install locks on their valves to avoid similar incidents in the future,[4] while placing the burden on shipowners is much less likely to lead to accident prevention.[5] It is true, of course, that in many cases the plaintiff will not be in a position to insure, and so expansion of liability will, at the very least, serve respondeat superior's loss spreading function. But the fact that the defendant is better able to afford damages is not alone sufficient to justify legal responsibility, and this overarching principle must be taken into account in deciding whether to expand the reach of respondeat superior.

A policy analysis thus is not sufficient to justify this proposed expansion of vicarious liability. This is not surprising since respondeat superior, even within its traditional limits, rests not so much on policy grounds consistent with the governing principles of tort law as in a deeply rooted sentiment that a business enterprise cannot justly disclaim responsibility for accidents which may fairly be said to be characteristic of its activities. It is in this light that the inadequacy of the motive test becomes apparent. Whatever may have been the case in the past, a doctrine that would create such drastically different consequences for the actions of the drunken boatswain in *Nelson* and those of the drunken seaman here reflects a wholly unrealistic attitude toward the risks characteristically attendant upon the operation of a ship. We concur in the statement of Mr. Justice Rutledge in a case involving violence injuring a fellow-worker, in this instance in the context of workmen's compensation:

---

[3] We are not here speaking of cases in which the enterprise has negligently hired an employee whose undesirable propensities are known or should have been. *See Koehler v. Presque-Isle Transp. Co.*, 141 F.2d 490 (2d Cir.), *cert. denied*, 322 U.S. 764, 64 S. Ct. 1288, 88 L. Ed. 1591 (1943).

[4] The record reveals that most modern drydocks have automatic locks to guard against unauthorized use of valves.

[5] Although it is theoretically possible that shipowners would demand that drydock owners take appropriate action, this would seem unlikely to occur in real life.

Men do not discard their personal qualities when they go to work. Into the job they carry their intelligence, skill, habits of care and rectitude. Just as inevitably they take along also their tendencies to carelessness and camaraderie, as well as emotional make-up. In bringing men together, work brings these qualities together, causes frictions between them, creates occasions for lapses into carelessness, and for funmaking and emotional flare-up. . . . These expressions of human nature are incidents inseparable from working together. They involve risks of injury and these risks are inherent in the working environment.

Hartford Accident & Indemnity Co. v. Cardillo, 72 App. D.C. 52, 112 F.2d 11, 15, *cert. denied,* 310 U.S. 649, 60 S. Ct. 1100, 84 L. Ed. 1415 (1940). Further supporting our decision is the persuasive opinion of Justice Traynor in *Carr v. Wm. C. Crowell Co.*, 28 Cal. 2d 652, 171 P.2d 5 (1946) (employer liable for violent acts of servant against employee of a subcontractor working on the same construction job), followed in *Fields v. Sanders,* 29 Cal. 2d 834, 180 P.2d 684, 172 A.L.R. 525 (1947) (employer liable for violent acts of driver against another driver in traffic dispute).

Put another way, Lane's conduct was not so "unforeseeable" as to make it unfair to charge the Government with responsibility. We agree with a leading treatise that "what is reasonably foreseeable in this context (of respondeat superior) . . . is quite a different thing from the foreseeably unreasonable risk of harm that spells negligence. . . . The foresight that should impel the prudent man to take precautions is not the same measure as that by which he should perceive the harm likely to flow from his long-run activity in spite of all reasonable precautions on his own part. The proper test here bears far more resemblance to that which limits liability for workmen's compensation than to the test for negligence. The employer should be held to expect risks, to the public also, which arise 'out of and in the course of' his employment of labor." 2 HARPER & JAMES, THE LAW OF TORTS 1377–78 (1956). Here it was foreseeable that crew members crossing the drydock might do damage, negligently or even intentionally, such as pushing a Bushey employee or kicking property into the water. Moreover, the proclivity of seamen to find solace for solitude by copious resort to the bottle while ashore has been noted in opinions too numerous to warrant citation. Once all this is granted, it is immaterial that Lane's precise action was not to be foreseen. Consequently, we can no longer accept our past decisions that have refused to move beyond the *Nelson* rule, since they do not accord with modern understanding as to when it is fair for an enterprise to disclaim the actions of its employees.

One can readily think of cases that fall on the other side of the line. If Lane had set fire to the bar where he had been imbibing or had caused an accident on the street while returning to the drydock, the Government would not be liable; the activities of the "enterprise" do not reach into areas where the servant does not create risks different from those attendant on the activities of the community in general. We agree with the district judge that if the seaman "upon returning to the drydock, recognized the Bushey security guard as his wife's lover and shot him," 276 F. Supp. at 530, vicarious liability would not follow; the incident would have related to the seaman's domestic life, not to his seafaring activity, and it would have been the most unlikely happenstance that the confrontation with the paramour occurred on a drydock rather than at the traditional spot. Here Lane had come within the closed-off area where his ship lay, to occupy a berth to which the Government insisted he have access, and while his act is not readily explicable, at least it was not shown to be due entirely to facets of his personal life. The risk that seamen going and coming from the Tamaroa might cause damage to the drydock is enough to make it fair that the enterprise bear the loss. It is not a fatal objection that the rule we lay down lacks sharp contours; in the end, as Judge Andrews said in a related context, "it is all a question (of expediency,) . . . of fair judgment, always keeping in mind the fact that we endeavor to make a rule in each case that will be practical and in keeping with the general understanding of mankind." *Palsgraf v. Long Island R.R. Co.*, 248 N.Y. 339, 354–355, 162 N.E. 99, 104, 59 A.L.R. 1253 (1928) (dissenting opinion).

Since we hold the Government responsible for the damage resulting from Lane's turning the wheels, we find it unnecessary to consider Bushey's further arguments that liability would attach in any event because of later inaction of Lane and others on the Tamaroa; and that in libels in rem, whose principles are here applicable by virtue of § 3 of the Suits in Admiralty Act, ordinary rules of agency are inapplicable and the ship is liable for anything ship-connected persons cause it to do.

Affirmed.

NOTES

1. *The Humble Versus the Mighty Servant.* In *Ermert v. Hartford,* 559 So. 2d 467 (La. 1990), the plaintiff Ermert was injured at a recreational hunting club when a fellow club member, Decareaux, negligently discharged his shotgun. The court held that plaintiff could sue Decareaux's employer, Nu-Arrow, which was vicariously liable for the injury inflicted by the gunshot wound:

> . . . The facts of the present case are somewhat atypical in that Decareaux was not a rank and file employee but the founder, majority stockholder (60%), president and chief executive officer and primary business generator of a closely-held corporate business. The trial court weighed the evidence and concluded that because Nu-Arrow derived economic benefit from Decareaux's activities at the camp Nu-Arrow was vicariously liable. The court of appeal reversed, holding that Decareaux was engaged in what it termed a "recreational pursuit" in building the duck blinds. We look to basic principles and cases applying them to executive conduct in determining whether Decareaux was a servant of Nu-Arrow acting within the scope of his employment when he accidentally shot Ermert. Upon reviewing the record and the law relating to the vicarious liability of masters for their servants' torts, we find that the court of appeal erred in reversing as to Nu-Arrow, because the trial court's conclusion that Decareaux was within the scope of his employment was not clearly wrong. . . .
>
> The scope of risks attributable to an employer increases with the amount of authority and freedom of action granted to the servant in

performing his assigned tasks. This is the logical extrapolation of a rule that fixes liability based upon the course of employment: The greater potential course of employment expands the servant's potential opportunities to commit torts. These opportunities are maximized where the servant effectively determines the course of his own employment, as is the case when the servant is actually the owner of the enterprise. One of the advantages of creating a separate entity for the operation of the enterprise is that the business enterprise is not liable for all of the torts of its owner. Nevertheless, because of both the business owner's inherent incentives to pursue company interests whenever possible and the fact that the "servant" often controls the "master" rather than vice-versa, the line between "business" and "personal" activity is often a hazy one. . . .

. . . Considering these principles of master-servant liability, we cannot say that the trial court was clearly wrong in determining that Decareaux was acting within the scope of his employment while he was at the camp. While Decareaux used the camp partially for his own personal enjoyment and recreation, the record also indicates that he repeatedly and consistently used it for business purposes. Developing new business was a major part of Decareaux's employment with Nu-Arrow. Decareaux testified that he had sold fences to almost every other member of the camp, and that the other members had all referred business to him. He had also taken a number of his preferred customers to the camp for entertainment, and these customers had likewise referred business to Nu-Arrow. Another important aspect of Decareaux's duties was dealing with employees. He testified that he had taken his employees to the camp on several occasions for picnics or entertainment, and he had also hosted his company-sponsored softball team at the camp. Considering this evidence, the finder of fact could reasonably conclude that one of Decareaux's motives for participating in the camp was to provide a place to entertain both customers and employees of Nu-Arrow.

2. *General and Special Employers.* One employer may direct his employees to perform services for another. Often, this "cooperation" between employers does not alter legal relationships, and the lending employer remains vicariously liable for the acts of his employee although that employee is performing work for the other employer. However, the nature and extent of the "loan" may create a "borrowed servant" relationship in which the special or "borrowing" employer becomes vicariously liable for the acts of the loaned employee. As with other vicarious liability situations, the line between "mere cooperation" and "borrowed employment" is fuzzy.

Should the lending employer remain vicariously liable although his employee is under the immediate control of the borrowing employer? Who is in a better position to protect himself from the insolvent borrowing employer — the lending employer or the third party tort victim? Why shouldn't both lending and borrowing employee be liable? Should it make any difference if the lending employer is in the business of lending employees to others, such as a labor contractor or a "temp" service? *See, e.g., Morgan v. ABC Manufacturer,* 710 So. 2d 1077 (La. 1998).

The "dual employment" problem often surfaces in cases involving police officers on off-duty assignments as security guards. Is such an officer an independent contractor? If as a security guard he engages in an activity which prevents a crime or arrests a criminal, isn't he within the course and scope of his employment with the law enforcement agency? Does it make any difference whether he is wearing his police uniform? That he asserts his authority as a law enforcement officer in acting against a would-be criminal? *See, e.g., State v. Wilen*, 539 N.W. 2d 650 (Neb. App. 1995). What about any off-duty policeman? *See, e.g. Russell v. Noulet*, 721 So. 2d 868 (La. 1998). There, city police officer, off duty and not in uniform, attended a social function at a public park. Officer consumed alcoholic beverages at the function, although he was carrying his gun and department regulations forbade him from carrying it while consuming alcoholic beverages. When his brother became involved in an altercation nearby, officer approached and announced he was a police officer. His brother, who was a police recruit, fired shots in the air, breaking up the crowd. Officer, unhindered by the crowd, then returned to his car, where he found a woman writing down his license plate number, and he physically assaulted her. Thereafter, the menacing crowd gathered behind officer's car, and he entered his car with the intention of fleeing the scene. When the crowd began to attack him, officer fired several shots into the crowd, injuring plaintiff. *Held,* officer was not in the course and scope of his employment when he assaulted the woman and subsequently fired into the crowd; his motivation for his general activities was purely personal, and the specific activity which caused the harm was not in furtherance of his employer's interest. *See, also, Brasseaux v. Town of Mamou,* 752 So. 2d 815 (La. 2000), refusing to impose liability upon a municipality whose off-duty, part-time dispatcher "pulled his badge" during an altercation at a bar in another municipal district in an attempt to escape a mob and capture by the proper authorities.

3. *Intentional Misconduct.* The plaintiff in *Mary M. v. City of Los Angeles*, 54 Cal. 3d 202, 814 P.2d 1341, 285 Cal. Rptr. 99 (1991), sued the City of Los Angeles on a theory of respondeat superior. The court recited these facts:

> About 2:30 a.m. on October 3, 1981, plaintiff Mary M. was driving home alone when Sergeant Leigh Schroyer of the Los Angeles Police Department stopped her for erratic driving. Sergeant Schroyer was on duty as a field supervisor; he was assigned to supervise and train police officers patrolling the streets. He was in uniform, wore a badge and a gun, and was driving a marked black-and-white police car. When he detained plaintiff, he sent in a radio message that he was out of his vehicle conducting an investigation.
>
> Sergeant Schroyer asked plaintiff for her driver's license; plaintiff gave it to him. He then asked her to perform a field sobriety test to determine whether she was under the influence of alcohol. Plaintiff, who had been drinking, did not do well on the test. She began to cry, and pleaded with Schroyer not to take her to jail. Schroyer ordered her to get in the front seat of the police car, but he did not handcuff her. He then drove to plaintiff's home.
>
> After entering the house with plaintiff, Sergeant Schroyer told her that he expected "payment" for taking her home instead of to jail.

Plaintiff tried to run away, but Schroyer grabbed her hair and threw her on the couch. When plaintiff screamed, Schroyer put his hand over her mouth and threatened to take her to jail. Plaintiff stopped struggling, and Schroyer raped her. He then left the house.

The police officer was later convicted for rape arising out of this incident.

Affirming a jury verdict of $150,000 for the plaintiff against the city, the court observed that:

> the test for determining whether an employee is acting outside the scope of employment is whether "in the context of the particular enterprise an employee's conduct is not so unusual or startling that it would seem unfair to include the loss resulting from it among other costs of the employer's business." (*Perez v. Van Groningen & Sons, Inc.*, 41 Cal. 3d at 968, 227 Cal. Rptr. 106, 719 P.2d 676.). . . .
>
> At the outset, we observed that society has granted police officers extraordinary power and authority over its citizenry. An officer who detains an individual is acting as the official representative of the state, with all of its coercive power. As visible symbols of that power, an officer is given a distinctively marked car, a uniform, a badge, and a gun. As one court commented, "police officers [exercise] the most awesome and dangerous power that a democratic state possesses with respect to its residents — the power to use lawful force to arrest and detain them." (*Policeman's Benev. Ass'n of N.J. v. Washington Tp.*, 850 F.2d 133, 141 (3rd Cir. 1988)). Inherent in this formidable power is the potential for abuse. The cost resulting from misuse of that power should be borne by the community, because of the substantial benefits that the community derives from the lawful exercise of police power.

If the plaintiff in *Mary M.* had sued the city for violation of her civil rights under 42 U.S.C. § 1983, she could not have recovered "unless action pursuant to official municipal policy of some nature caused a constitutional tort." Liability could not be imposed under that section "solely on the basis of the existence of an employer-employee relationship." *Monell v. Dept. Of Soc. Services*, 436 U.S. 658 (1978). Why is the federal remedy more restricted than the state common law remedy?

4. *Sexual Misconduct in the Workplace.* The plaintiff in *Jackson v. Righter*, 891 P.2d 1387 (Utah 1995), sued his wife's employer, Novell, and Novell's joint venturer Univel, for alienation of affections, intentional infliction of emotional and physical injury, and intentional interference with his marital contract. He alleged that the employer was vicariously liable for the acts of its employee, Righter:

> Plaintiff and Marie Jackson were married August 14, 1987. In November 1988, Mrs. Jackson began working at Novell in Provo, Utah, as a secretary in the Software Engineering Department. At that time, defendant Grover P. Righter was Novell's Director of Software Engineering. As director, Mr. Righter was responsible for supervising several large engineering teams; managing a substantial budget; hiring, evaluating, promoting, and firing employees; and organizing

employee functions. Mr. Righter was Mrs. Jackson's immediate supervisor between November 1988 and August 1991 and, over the course of her employment, promoted her to the positions of administrative assistant and project coordinator, authorized her to record unworked overtime hours as an unofficial raise, and gave her substantial bonuses. He also lavished gifts on her from his personal funds.

By November 1990, Mr. Righter had become attracted to Mrs. Jackson and thereafter began making overtures toward her which resulted in a romantic relationship between them. In early 1991, the two spent much time together in Mr. Righter's office during working hours discussing personal matters, hugging, and kissing. On the pretext of business, Mr. Righter took Mrs. Jackson to the Star Palace dance hall in Provo, the Excelsior Hotel in Provo, and the Little America Hotel in Salt Lake City, kissing, hugging, or fondling her on these occasions. Mr. Righter also took Mrs. Jackson on business trips during working hours to monitor Novell's office and team in Sandy, Utah, for which Mr. Righter was responsible, at times taking up to six hours to travel the one-half hour commute between Provo and Sandy. At some point, others at Novell became aware of Mr. Righter's and Mrs. Jackson's activities. . . .

Plaintiff claims that Mr. Righter's actions that allegedly alienated Mrs. Jackson's affections were within the scope of his employment and that summary judgment for Novell and Univel was improper because such a determination is a question of fact. We disagree. An employer may be vicariously liable under the doctrine of respondeat superior of the harmful actions of an employee if those actions are committed within the scope of the employee's employment. . .To be considered within the scope of employment, an employee's conduct must (1) "be of the general kind the employee is employed to perform;" (2) "occur within the hours of the employee's work and the ordinary spatial boundaries of the employment;" and (3) "be motivated, at least in part, by the purpose of serving the employer's interest.". . . . Whether an employee's conduct falls within the scope of employment is ordinarily a question of fact. . . . However, where the employee's conduct is so clearly outside the scope of employment that reasonable minds cannot differ the issue may properly be decided as a matter of law. . . .

In this case, Mr. Righter's romantic involvement with Mrs. Jackson was so clearly outside the scope of his employment that reasonable minds could not differ. . . . (W)e note, as Novell and Univel concede, that most of Mr. Righter's alleged tortious conduct occurred within the hours and spatial boundaries of his employment. However, Mr. Righter's conduct was not of the general type he was employed to perform, and neither was it intended to serve, nor did it serve, Novell's or Univel's purpose. Mr. Righter was not hired to perform acts of a sexual nature on, or make romantic overtures toward, an employee under his supervision. Plaintiff argues that many of Mr. Righter's alleged tortious acts were part of the conduct he was hired to perform in connection with his authority to promote, evaluate, train, and give raises to Mrs. Jackson. For example, plaintiff asserts that the first time Mr. Righter expressed his attraction for Mrs. Jackson was while he held her hand during a formal employee evaluation in his office. Plaintiff's argument is without merit. Mr. Righter was not authorized to use his supervisory position to engage in a romantic relationship with his subordinates. His romantic advances were not a part of his duties but amounted to an abandonment of the supervisory and managerial responsibilities he was hired to perform.

5. *Intentional and Sexual Misconduct — Title VII and Title IX.* Federal legislation prohibits sex-based discrimination in the workplace (The Equal Employment Act, 42 U.S.C. § 2000(e) — Title VII) and in federally funded schools (The Education Amendments Act, 20 U.S.C. § 1681(A) Title IX). Sexual harassment rarely will be within the course and scope of the harassing employee's employment under general principles of vicarious liability. However, the employer may be vicariously liable to a victimized employee for an actionable hostile environment created or allowed by a supervisor with immediate or successively higher authority over the employee. *See, e.g., Burlington Industries, Inc. v. Ellerth*, 524 U.S. 742, 118 S.Ct. 2257 (1998); *Faragher v. City of Boca Raton*, 524 U.S. 775, 118 S.Ct. 2275 (1998). Is this vicarious liability, or is it negligent supervision of the workplace by the employer? For a discussion of the issue, *see* William R. Corbett, *Faragher, Ellerth, And The Federal Law Of Vicarious Liability For Sexual Harassment By Supervisors: Something Lost, Something Gained, And Something To Guard Against,* 7 Wm. & Mary L.J. 801 (1999).

LUNDBERG v. STATE
25 N.Y.2d 467, 306 N.Y.S.2d 947, 255 N.E.2d 177 (1969)

SCILEPPI, JUDGE.

Claimant's husband was killed on the morning of February 14, 1966 when his car was struck by an auto owned and operated by John Sandilands, an employee of New York State. There is no dispute as to the facts and there is no question that the death was caused solely by the negligence of Sandilands. The only issue raised by this appeal is whether Sandilands' negligence can be imputed to his employer, the State of New York, the defendant in this action.

Sandilands was employed as a Senior Engineering Technician by the New York State Department of Public Works. He was permanently based in Buffalo where he also resided. However, since March of 1965 he had been assigned to the Allegheny Reservoir Project near Salamanca, about 80 miles from Buffalo.

Due to the great distance between the reservoir and Buffalo, Sandilands found it necessary to stay at a hotel in Salamanca during the work week. Generally, at the end of his work day on Friday, Sandilands would drive home to Buffalo to spend the weekend with his family, and on Monday morning he would drive back to the reservoir in order to arrive there before the start of his work day. The State reimbursed him for his living expenses while he was away from home and, in addition, paid him 9 cents a mile to cover the expenses

B. IMPUTED RESPONSIBILITY OF THE DEFENDANT 969

of the trip. He was not paid for the time he spent traveling to and from the site, and if he arrived late on Monday morning, the time he missed would be deducted from his vacation or sick leave.

On Monday, February 14, 1966, at 7:30 A.M., Sandilands was driving back to the reservoir from Buffalo after a holiday weekend. While attempting to pass a truck, his car skidded and struck the car driven by Lundberg head on. Lundberg died as a result of the injuries he sustained in the accident.

Sandilands applied for and was granted Workmen's Compensation benefits for the injuries which he suffered in the accident. Claimant, Lundberg's widow, brought an action for pain and suffering and wrongful death against Sandilands and a similar action against the State, as Sandilands' employer. The action against Sandilands was settled for $20,000. The one against the State went to trial and resulted in a judgment for more than $73,000. The Appellate Division, Fourth Department, unanimously affirmed and the State is appealing.

The sole issue presented by this appeal is whether the State of New York should be held liable, pursuant to the doctrine of *respondeat superior,* for the pain and suffering and wrongful death caused by its employee's negligence. It is our opinion that Sandilands was not acting in the scope of his employment while driving from Buffalo to his work site and that, therefore, the complaint against the defendant State should have been dismissed. Under the doctrine of *respondeat superior,* an employer will be liable for the negligence of an employee committed while the employee is acting in the scope of his employment. An employee acts in the scope of his employment when he is doing something in furtherance of the duties he owes to his employer and where the employer is, or could be, exercising some control, directly or indirectly, over the employee's activities.

As a general rule, an employee driving to and from work is not acting in the scope of his employment. Although such activity is work motivated, the element of control is lacking. An exception to this rule is, that an employee who uses his car in furtherance of his work is acting in the scope of his employment while driving home from his last business appointment, since such a person is working, and is under his employer's control, from the time he leaves the house in the morning until he returns at night. In the instant case, however, the employee was not driving his car in furtherance of his work at the time of the accident. He was engaged in an independent personal activity over which the State had no control. Thus, the general rule applies.

The several cases cited by respondent for the proposition that an employee who is injured while driving to or from a temporary work assignment is entitled to Workmen's Compensation benefits are not applicable to this case. Workmen's Compensation was created to prevent injured workmen from becoming "objects of charity" and to make reasonable compensation for injuries and death caused by job related activities regardless of fault. It is necessary for an employee seeking to obtain compensation benefits to establish only that his injury was caused by an activity related to his job, whereas the doctrine of *respondeat superior* has clearly not received such wide application because of the requirement that the employee be under the control of the employer at the time of the injury.

Accordingly, the order of the Appellate Division should be reversed and the claim against the defendant dismissed.

BURKE, JUDGE, dissenting.

Of particular relevance in this case, as distinguished from the vague and theoretical question of "right to control," is the test for liability posited by former CHIEF JUDGE CARDOZO: "The test in brief is this: If the work of the employee creates the necessity for travel, he is in the course of his employment, though he is serving at the same time some purpose of his own" (citation omitted). The undisputed facts in the present case clearly indicate that that test has been met. Sandilands' temporary employment at a work site 80 miles from his permanent station and home in Buffalo created the necessity for his travel between Buffalo and the work site. While so traveling, he was clearly acting in furtherance of his employment and this has already been determined by the fact that he has been awarded compensation benefits for the injuries which he received in that same accident. The mere fact that his traveling back and forth was motivated by his desire to see his family occasionally in no way detracts from the fact that the trips would not have been made at all had it not been for his assignment to a distant work site.

In addition, it should be recognized that the fact that the State paid Sandilands' travel expenses for these trips is significant not because it has any relation to some theoretical "right to control" but precisely because it indicates that the State recognized that Sandilands' employment necessitated such travel and acquiesced in his use of his own automobile for that travel. Thus, it is difficult to conclude that it would be somehow "unfair" to impose liability on the State for its employee's negligence when the State itself necessitated the use of the instrumentality through which the death of the claimant's intestate occurred.

NOTES

1. *In the Course of Employment.* The general rule is that an employee is not in the course and scope of his employment while going to and from work. *Robarge v. Bechtel Power Corp.*, 131 Ariz. 280, 640 P.2d 211 (1982). What if the employer pays the employee's travel expenses to and from work or pays him for the time spent in traveling to and from work? Does not this indicate that the trip is reasonably in furtherance of the employer's business? *See, e.g., Hinman v. Westinghouse Elec. Co.*, 2 Cal. 3d 956, 88 Cal. Rptr. 188, 471 P.2d 988 (1970); *Faul v. Jelco*, 122 Ariz. 490, 595 P.2d 1035 (App. 1979). What if the employee is off duty but "on call?" *See District of Columbia v. Davis*, 386 A.2d 1195 (D.C. App. 1978).

An employee performing a mission for the employer away from the premises remains in the course and scope of his employment although he makes a trivial departure from his employer's business, such as altering his route for a personal mission. The departure may be so substantial, however, that he is on a "frolic" or "detour" and is no longer within the course and scope of his employment. Under modern business conditions, however, a good many frolics, like the three-martini lunch, may be within the scope of employment. In *Fruit v. Schreiner*, 502 P.2d 133 (Alaska 1972), Fruit was attending a sales convention of his employer, Equitable Life Assurance Society. He was encouraged by the Society to "socialize" with other life insurance salesmen at the convention in the hope of picking up some useful ideas. At about 11 o'clock one evening he was awakened by friends, who found that he had fully slept off the effect of his lunchtime socializing; shortly thereafter Fruit, using his own car, decided to drive to a bar some miles distant where he thought he would find some out-of-state agents. Finding no colleagues at the bar, he decided to return to the convention center; but on the way he skidded across a dividing line and collided with a standing car, crushing the legs of Schreiner, who was standing in front of the car after raising its hood. Equitable was held liable to Schreiner. "There was evidence from which the jury could find that he [Fruit] was at least motivated in part by his desire to meet with the out-of-state guests and thus to benefit from their experience so as to improve his abilities as a salesman."

In *Wong-Leong v. Hawaiian Indep. Refinery, Inc.*, 879 P.2d 538 (Haw. 1994), plaintiffs' decedents were killed by the drunken driving of Rellamas, an employee of defendant HIRI:

> On June 11, 1989, Rellamas crashed into a vehicle carrying Christopher Chong, Elizabeth Lacaran, and Shasadee Lacaran-Chong. All four were killed in the two-car accident. The medical examiner determined that alcohol and marijuana consumed by Rellamas were contributing factors to the fatal accident.
>
> Rellamas was employed by HIRI at its Campbell Industrial Park refinery. He was returning home after drinking beer at a party celebrating his recent promotion. The party consisted of about nine co-workers and was held at the picnic area on HIRI's premises. The record reflects that, in keeping with an apparent tradition of celebrating promotions at HIRI, Rellamas provided money and had a co-worker purchase beer for the party. The party started at about 6:00 p.m. and continued until about 7:30 p.m., when the evening shift supervisor directed the workers to leave the premises. Rellamas was on his way home from the party when the accident occurred at about 8:30 p.m. He did not make any stops between leaving work and the accident.

In holding that HIRI could be found vicariously liable for the tortious acts of Rellamas, the court said:

> Although the party in the instant case took place after work hours, the record reveals that it was held on HIRI's premises immediately thereafter. Considering the facts in a light most favorable to Appellants, a reasonable trier of fact could infer that the promotion party was a custom incidental to the enterprise rather than a purely social function. Arguably, the party may have been "actuated, in part, by a purpose to serve" HIRI, or at least "was of some direct benefit" to HIRI. . . . *See supra* note 12 (quoting authority for the proposition that boosting employee morale and furthering employer-employee relations are sufficient benefits to the enterprise for respondeat superior purposes).

Compare Bell v. Hurstell, 743 So. 2d 720 (La. App. 1999). There, after a meeting with a client at employer's office concluded about 7 p.m., employee went with the client to a lounge and then to a party given by another company with which employer had a business relationship. During that time, employee apparently became intoxicated. At about 11:20 p.m., employee, attempting to drive home, was involved in an accident. *Held*, employee was not in the course and scope of her employment at the time of the accident; "an accident that would not normally be considered as occurring during the course and scope of employment. . .will not be considered as occurring during the course and scope of employment merely because alcohol, which may have contributed to the accident was consumed (but not required to be consumed as a condition of employment) while the employee-tortfeasor was acting in the course and scope of employment."

In *Timmons v. Silman*, 772 So. 2d 125 (La. 2000), employee drove from employer's place of business four blocks to the post office to refill the office's postage meter. Deciding to cash her Christmas bonus check, employee then drove within one or two blocks of the office but did not stop to return the postage meter; instead, she traveled 18 blocks beyond the office toward the bank, and was then involved in an accident. The court held that the employer was not vicariously liable because the employee's deviation was substantial in nature and exposed her employer to risks which were not inherent in her employment. Reaching this conclusion, the court observed that in determining whether a deviation was substantial or insubstantial, a court should "look at all the facts and circumstances of the deviation, including such illustrative factors as when and where, in relation to the business errand, the employee deviates from the employment related errand and commences with his personal errand, the temporal and spacial boundaries of the deviation, the nature of the employee's work, the additional risks created by the deviation, and the surrounding circumstances. . . . This list of considerations is non-exhaustive, and a court should carefully consider all the facts unique to the case before it."

"Horseplay" may be outside the course and scope of the employment. *Lane v. Modern Music Inc.*, 244 S.C. 299, 136 S.E.2d 713 (1964); *Riviello v. Waldron*, 47 N.Y.2d 297, 391 N.E.2d 1278, 418 N.Y.S.2d 300 (1979).

2. *Failure to Follow Rules.* In *Kuharski v. Somers Motor Lines, Inc.*, 132 Conn. 269, 43 A.2d 777 (1945), Nihil, a truck driver, stopped at a tavern where he picked up Sophie Kuharski. She went riding with him, and was killed when his truck was involved in an accident. Kuharski's estate sued Nihill's employer, which defended on the grounds that Nihill violated company and ICC regulations in allowing Sophie to ride in the truck. In denying this defense, the court said the master is liable for negligent acts of the servant performed in the course of employment, "even though they are not specifically authorized or are at times contrary to instructions." In permitting Sophie to board the truck, Nihill was acting outside of his employment, but in then continuing his trip "he was again in the course of it."

SHERARD v. SMITH
778 S.W.2d 546 (Tex. App. 1989)

SEERDEN, JUSTICE.

Appellant brought suit for wrongful death based on a motor vehicle collision which occurred on July 2, 1984. Appellee had hired Rene Hinojosa to haul grain from his farm to the elevator. Hinojosa's truck was loaded with 14 or 15 tons of grain when he stopped it on South Padre Island Drive to retrieve a shovel that had fallen from the truck. Appellant's son drove his vehicle into the rear of the truck and was killed.

Appellant pleaded that appellee was negligent and that appellee is vicariously liable for Hinojosa's negligence, alleging that Hinojosa was appellee's agent, servant, or employee. The trial court granted appellee's motion for summary judgment. We affirm the trial court's judgment.

The summary judgment evidence shows that appellee, Carl Smith, has been a farmer since 1955. He raises grain in Nueces County, Texas. Smith, a relatively small volume farmer, customarily hires someone to haul his grain from the farm where it is raised to the grain elevator where it is stored and sold. Appellee had used the same haulers for a number of years, but in 1984, for the first time, he hired Hinojosa to do his hauling. Prior to the wreck . . . Hinojosa had been hauling for Smith about one week.

Appellee's motion for summary judgment contends that the summary judgment evidence establishes as a matter of law that

> 1. Hinojosa was an independent contractor and not the agent, servant or employee of appellee.

In light of the authorities cited and the arguments raised by appellee in his first reply point we will only address the matters briefed by appellant. Where there is no dispute as to the controlling facts and only one reasonable conclusion can be inferred, the question of whether one is an "employee" or "independent contractor" is a question of law. To constitute the relationship of employer and employee, the employer must have the right to select, control, and, for misconduct, discharge the employee. An independent contractor is any person who, in the pursuit of an independent business, undertakes to do a specific piece of work for other persons, using his own means and methods, without submitting himself to their control in respect to all details. Recognized tests to determine when one is acting in the capacity of independent contractor are:

1. the independent nature of the business;

2. the obligation to furnish necessary tools, supplies and material to perform the job;

3. the right to control the progress of the work except the final result;

4. the length of time of the employment; and

5. the method of payment — whether by the time or by the job.

It has also been stated that the independent nature of the agreement of employment may be inferred from two circumstances: (1) that the party is engaged in a distinct and generally recognized employment; and (2) that his stipulated remuneration is to be determined by some quantitative standard.

The distinction between an independent contractor and an agent or employee is not always easy to determine, and there is no uniform criterion by which they may be differentiated. Nevertheless, it has often been stated that the test for determining whether a master-servant or independent contractor relationship exists is whether the employer has the "right to control" the details of the work.

Appellee hired Hinojosa to haul his grain from the field to the Corpus Christi Grain Elevator. He agreed to pay him a specific price for each hundred weight of grain hauled. He withheld no monies for any form of taxes nor did he provide any medical or other benefits. He provided no fuel for Hinojosa's truck. The only benefit Hinojosa was to receive for his services was the cash payment based on the amount of grain he delivered to the elevator. While appellee looked at Hinojosa's truck and inquired as to liability insurance coverage at the time of hiring, Hinojosa was responsible for maintenance of the truck and for furnishing any tools or helpers necessary to achieve the task of delivering the grain. The evidence clearly shows that the relationship between appellee and Hinojosa was that of independent contractor-owner rather than employee-employer.

NOTES

1. *Nondelegable Duties.* In *Maloney v. Rath*, 69 Cal. 2d 442, 71 Cal. Rptr. 897, 445 P.2d 513 (1968), the court found the defendant car owner had a nondelegable duty to maintain her car brakes in proper working condition:

> . . . [W]e have found nondelegable duties in a wide variety of situations and have recognized that the rules set forth in the Restatement of Torts with respect to such duties are generally in accord with California law. Such duties include those imposed by a public authority as a condition of granting a franchise; the duty of a condemning agent to protect a severed parcel from damage; the duty of a general contractor to construct a building safely; the duty to exercise due care when an "independent contractor is employed to do work which the employer should recognize as necessarily creating a condition involving an unreasonable risk of bodily harm to others unless special precautions are taken." *Courtell v. McEachan,* 51 Cal. 2d 448, 457, 334 P.2d 870, 874 (1951); the duty of landowners to maintain their property in a reasonably safe condition and to comply with applicable safety ordinances and the duty of employers and suppliers to comply with the safety provisions of the Labor Code.
>
> Section 423 of the Restatement (Second) of Torts provides that "One who carries on an activity which threatens a grave risk of serious bodily harm or death unless the instrumentalities used are carefully . . . maintained, and who employs an independent contractor to . . . maintain such instrumentalities, is subject to the same liability for physical harm caused by the negligence of the contractor in . . . maintaining such instrumentalities as though the employer had

himself done the work of . . . maintenance." Section 424 provides that: "One who by statute or by administrative regulation is under a duty to provide specified safeguards or precautions for the safety of others is subject to liability to the others for whose protection the duty is imposed for harm caused by the failure of a contractor employed by him to provide such safeguards or precautions." Both of these sections point to a nondelegable duty in this case. The statutory provisions regulating the maintenance and equipment of automobiles constitute express legislative recognition of the fact that improperly maintained motor vehicles threaten "a grave risk of serious bodily harm or death." The responsibility for minimizing that risk or compensating for the failure to do so properly rests with the person who owns and operates the vehicle. He is the party primarily to be benefitted by its use; he selects the contractor and is free to insist upon one who is financially responsible and to demand indemnity from him; the cost of his liability insurance that distributes the risk is properly attributable to his activities; and the discharge of the duty to exercise reasonable care in the maintenance of his vehicle is of the utmost importance to the public.

In the present case it is undisputed that the accident was caused by a failure of defendant's brakes that resulted from her independent contractor's negligence in overhauling or in thereafter inspecting the brakes. Since her duty to maintain her brakes in compliance with the provisions of the Vehicle Code is nondelegable, the fact that the brake failure was the result of her independent contractor's negligence is no defense.

The *Maloney* result was rejected in *Hackett v. Perron,* 119 N.H. 419, 402 A.2d 193 (1979). However, courts have found a variety of non-delegable duties, including construction or repair of a building, RESTATEMENT (SECOND) OF TORTS § 422; *Misiulis v. Milbrand Main. Corp.,* 52 Mich. App. 494, 218 N.W.2d 68 (1974); failing to clear a roadway, *Westby v. Itasca County,* 290 N.W.2d 437 (Minn. 1980); work imposed by a public authority as a condition of granting a franchise, *E.R. Harding Co. v. Paducah S. Ry.,* 208 Ky. 728, 271 S.W. 1046 (1925); the duty of a landowner to maintain his property in a reasonably safe condition, *Snyder v. Southern California Edison,* 44 Cal. 2d 793, 285 P.2d 912 (1955); the duty to comply with applicable safety ordinances, RESTATEMENT (SECOND) OF TORTS, § 424; property owner statutory duty to provide safe scaffolding for independent contractors and workers, *Gordon v. Eastern Ry. Supply, Inc.*, 82 N.Y.2d 555, 606 N.Y.S.2d 127, 626 N.E.2d 912 (1993); city ordinance duty of landlord to install fire detector, *Shump v. First Cont.-Robinwood Assoc.,* 71 Ohio St. 3d 414, 644 N.E.2d 291 (1994).

2. *Collateral Negligence.* In *Otero v. Jordon Restaurant Enterprises,* 119 N.M. 721, 895 P.2d 243 (1995), a patron sued the owner of a restaurant for injuries sustained when metal bleachers, constructed by an independent contractor to allow viewing of a large television screen, collapsed. The court applied § 422(b) of the RESTATEMENT (SECOND) OF TORTS, which states that an owner:

who entrusts to an independent contractor construction, repair, or other work on the land, or on a building or other structure upon it, is subject to the same liability as though he had retained the work in his own hands to others on or outside of the land for physical harm caused to them by the unsafe condition of the structure . . . .

(b) after he has resumed possession of the land upon its completion.

Thus, Section 422(b) "makes it impossible for a possessor of land to escape liability for the non-performance of his duty to maintain his land in safe condition, so long as he is in possession of it, by delegating the task of doing the work necessary to the performance of that duty to an independent contractor." Restatement § 422 comment *e*. Liability is imposed on the owner of the premises despite the fact that the owner was not personally at fault in creating the unsafe condition.

The defendant contended it was not liable because the dangerous condition was the result of "collateral negligence" of the contractor:

> The collateral negligence doctrine is an exception to an exception. That is, the general rule is that an employer is not liable for the negligence of an independent contractor. This rule, however, as we have previously noted, is riddled with exceptions, one of which is the one established in this case — that an owner of property is liable for the negligence of an independent contractor in building or making repairs to structures on that property, once the owner resumes possession. In turn, those exceptions are also subject to an exception — that the owner is not liable for collateral negligence of the contractor or the contractor's employees. We must therefore determine the meaning of the term "collateral negligence."
>
> The concept of "collateral negligence" is set out in Section 426 of the Restatement. Section 426 states:
>
> [A]n employer of an independent contractor, unless he is himself negligent, is not liable for physical harm caused by any negligence of the contractor if
>
> > (a) the contractor's negligence consists solely in the improper manner in which he does the work, and
> >
> > (b) it creates a risk of such harm which is not inherent in or normal to the work, and
> >
> > (c) the employer had no reason to contemplate the contractor's negligence when the contract was made.
>
> Defendant interprets the collateral negligence concept broadly, arguing that a question of fact exists as to whether the contractor's failure to assemble the bleachers correctly was unusual negligence that could not be anticipated. We agree with Defendant that the question of whether negligence is collateral is often not easy to answer and is usually an issue of fact. In this case, however, the question can be answered as a matter of law.
>
> Cases and commentators discussing the collateral negligence doctrine make clear that the concept is limited to negligence that produces

a temporarily unsafe condition while the work is in progress. Negligence that produces a poor result or a defect in the final structure, however, is not considered collateral negligence. *See* Restatement § 422, at 408, comment *e* (for an owner to be liable for a contractor's negligence, the negligence must result in a failure to put and maintain the land in that safe condition in which it is the duty of the owner to put and maintain it; the owner is not liable for any casual act of negligence in the operative detail of doing the work that, however injurious to another, does not prevent the land from being put or maintained in safe condition; such negligence is collateral negligence); Talbot Smit, *Collateral Negligence*, 25 MINN. L. REV. 399 (1941) (discussing origins of collateral negligence theory and drawing distinction between negligence collateral to the accomplishment of a given result, and the result itself; where the fault lies in the final, completed structure the collateral negligence argument has been denied). Thus, a distinction exists between the negligent manner of ongoing work performed by the contractor, for which the employer of the independent contractor may not be liable under the collateral negligence doctrine, and the condition of the premises that results from the negligence, for which the collateral negligence doctrine does not apply.

Here, Defendant had a nondelegable duty to exercise reasonable care that the bleachers were in a safe condition. The contractor's negligent assembly, therefore, made the complete structure unsafe and affected the result that the owner was under a duty to attain — a result of reasonably safe premises. This was not a situation involving an unsafe condition created only while the work was ongoing. *See, e.g., Broome*, [822 P.2d 677 (N.M. App. 1991)] (drop cloth left on floor during progress of work; question of collateral negligence raised issue of fact). We conclude, as a matter of law, that the negligence of the independent contractor was not collateral negligence, and therefore Defendant is liable for that negligence.

3. *Highly Dangerous Activities*. Several apparently overlapping exceptions to the "independent contractor" rule are contained in the Restatement. One is work which creates a peculiar risk of physical harm to others unless special precautions are taken. RESTATEMENT (SECOND) OF TORTS § 416. Another is § 423, which imposes liability upon the principal for "an activity which threatens a grave risk of serious bodily harm or death unless the instrumentalities used are carefully constructed and maintained. . . ." A third is § 427, work "involving a special danger to others which the employer knows or has reason to know to be inherent in or normal to the work. . . ." Finally, § 427A makes the principal liable if he employs a contractor to engage in an "abnormally dangerous" activity.

Should the principal be liable to the employees of a contractor whom he engages to perform an "inherently dangerous" activity? The cases are divided. *King v. Shelby Rural Elec. Coop.*, 502 S.W.2d 659 (Ky. 1973) (yes); *New Mexico Elec. Serv. Co. v. Montanez*, 89 N.M. 278, 551 P.2d 634 (1976) (no). *See* Annot. 34 A.L.R.4th 914 (1984). An owner is likely to contract with another to perform an "inherently dangerous" activity because the owner lacks knowledge of how the activity can be done safely. In such a situation, do we get any deterrence by imposing liability upon the owner? Is not the cost of the activity spread to his enterprise through the contract price? Would it make more sense to impose liability upon the owner only if the contractor's actions which expose the contractor's employees to risks are "obviously improvident" and the principal becomes aware of them? *See, e.g., Scindia Steam Nav. Co. v. De Los Santos,* 451 U.S. 156, 68 L. Ed. 2d 1, 101 S. Ct. 1614 (1981).

A principal remains liable for the torts of an independent contractor whom he employs to engage in an "illegal activity." *See King v. Loessin,* 572 S.W.2d 87 (Tex. Civ. App. 1978).

In *Falls v. Scott,* 815 P.2d 1104 (Kan. 1991), the court said defendant landowner could be liable to the plaintiff for damages caused by a "bush hog" mowing machine operated by an independent contractor. The machine threw a piece of wire that struck plaintiff, an adjoining landowner, in the eye. The court cited RESTATEMENT (SECOND) OF TORTS § 427 as the basis for liability:

> One who employs an independent contractor to do work involving a special danger to others which the employer knows or has reason to know to be inherent in or normal to the work, or which he contemplates or has reason to contemplate when making the contract, is subject to liability for physical harm caused to such others by the contractor's failure to take reasonable precautions against such danger.

It also cited §§ 519–520 as an apparently additional basis of liability:

> The RESTATEMENT (SECOND) OF TORTS § 519 sets forth the general rule regarding strict liability in tort for abnormally dangerous activities as follows:
>
> (1) One who carries on an abnormally dangerous activity is subject to liability for harm to the person, land or chattels of another resulting from the activity, although he has exercised the utmost care to prevent the harm.
>
> (2) This strict liability is limited to the kind of harm, the possibility of which makes the activity abnormally dangerous.

Section 520 of the RESTATEMENT (SECOND) OF TORTS sets out the following test for determining whether an activity is abnormally dangerous:

> In determining whether an activity is abnormally dangerous, the following factors are to be considered:
>
> (a) existence of a high degree of risk of some harm to the person, land or chattels of others;
>
> (b) likelihood that the harm that results from it will be great;
>
> (c) inability to eliminate the risk by the exercise of reasonable care;
>
> (d) extent to which the activity is not a matter of common usage;
>
> (e) inappropriateness of the activity to the place where it is carried on; and

(f) extent to which its value to the community is outweighed by its dangerous attributes.

Are the bases of liability under §§ 427 and 519–520 the same?

4. *Vicarious Liability of Hospitals.* If a health care provider — such as a nurse — is an employee of a doctor or of a hospital, then the doctor or hospital will be vicariously liable for the torts of its employee committed within the scope of employment.

Frequently, however, health care providers are independent contractors, and in that situation there is a tendency to impose vicarious liability based variously on theories of ostensible or apparent agency, estoppel, and nondelegable duty.

The doctrine of ostensible agency or apparent authority is widely applied to hospital emergency room services that are provided by independent contractors. Thus in *Paintsville Hosp. Co. v. Rose*, 683 S.W.2d 255 (Ky. 1985), the court said:

> . . . [I]t is clear that the record in the present case does not support granting a summary judgment if ostensible agency as alleged in the amended complaint is a viable legal theory under our law. The appellant claims that the record fails to establish that the decedent or his parents relied on the fact that Dr. Ikramuddin was an employee of the hospital in accepting her treatment. Neither does it refute it. Further, the cases applying the principle of ostensible agency to the hospital/emergency room physician situation, without exception, do not require an express representation to the patient that the treating physician is an employee of the hospital, nor do they require direct testimony as to reliance. A general representation to the public is implied from the circumstances. Without exception evidence sufficient to invoke the doctrine has been inferred from circumstances similar to those shown in the present case, absent evidence that the patient knew or should have known that the treating physician was not a hospital employee when the treatment was performed (not afterwards).
>
> The landmark case applying the principle of ostensible agency to physicians not employed by the hospital but furnished through the institutional processes is *Seneris v. Haas,* 45 Cal. 2d 811, 291 P.2d 915 (1955), where it was applied to an anesthesiologist. Since then few courts have failed to recognize the soundness of this application, and the concept has been generally applied not only to anesthesiologists, but to pathologists, radiologists, and emergency room physicians, all of whom share the common characteristic of being supplied through the hospital rather than being selected by the patient. Our research reveals the following cases applying ostensible agency to emergency room physicians in circumstances similar to the present case, and not to the contrary.

The doctrine of apparent agency may also be applied to non-emergency hospital services. Thus in *Gamble v. United States*, 648 F. Supp. 438 (N.D. Ohio 1986), the court said:

In the instant case, the government should be estopped to deny Dr. Fraser was an employee of the VA. The VA holds itself out as a full-service hospital. By holding itself out to patients that it will provide full services, including anesthesia services, the VA induces reliance upon the relationship of these services with the medical center. In essence, an agency by estoppel is established by creating an effect — the appearance that the hospital agents, not independent contractors, will provide medical care to those who enter the hospital. The patient relies upon this as a fact and believes he is entering a full-service hospital.

Compare Carrillo v United States, 5 F.3d 1302, at 1306 (9th Cir. 1993).

In a non-emergency situation, the issue of reliance by the patient under an apparent-agent theory can become complicated. In *Sztore v. Northwest Hosp.*, 146 Ill. App. 3d 1200, 496 N.E.2d 1200 (1986), the plaintiff underwent a radical mastectomy at defendant hospital in 1975, and subsequently "received radiation therapy during approximately 31 daily sessions at the x-ray department located in defendant hospital." In 1981 she learned "that her right brachial plexus had been permanently damaged as a result to overexposure to radiation in 1975."

She sued the hospital, which claimed that "the staff of the hospital's x-ray department were neither its actual nor its apparent agents." The appellate court reversed a summary judgment for the defendant, holding "that when a person goes to a full service hospital for care and treatment, he or she does so in reliance on the reputation of the institution and the skill and expertise of its personnel." Patients are "generally unaware of the independent status of the treating physicians," and should not be bound by "secret limitations" contained in a contract between the hospital and physician.

The defendant contended it was entitled to summary judgment because of plaintiff's lack of reliance, as established by the following examination of the plaintiff:

Q. Inasmuch as Dr. Schroeder ha[d] recommended that you go to the radiation therapy department for treatment, would it have made any difference to you, one way or the other, whether or not Dr. Greenberg and Dr. Bluhm were in private practice or whether they were employed by Northwest Hospital?

A. I don't know.

Q. You don't know whether it would have made any difference?

A. I don't know.

Q. So you don't know now, and you didn't know then, is that right?

A. I don't know.

Rejecting defendant's contention, the court said:

We are unpersuaded by defendant's claim that the clearly equivocal statement taken during plaintiff's discovery deposition is decisive of this issue, and we believe that a factual determination remains to be made as to whether plaintiff would have acted differently had she known of the contractual relationship between the hospital and the treating physicians in the radiology department.

In *Whitlow v. Good Samaritan Hosp.*, 42 Ohio App. 3d 74, 536 N.E.2d 659 (1987), the court appears to suggest, at least in part, that reliance can be inferred in the absence of evidence to the contrary. Would a hospital, or a doctor, ever tell a patient that the doctor or other medical personnel are independent contractors? If they did, would the patient understand what she was being told?

5. *Vicarious Liability of Doctors.* A patient in *Long v. Hacker*, 246 Neb. 547, 520 N.W.2d 195 (1994), brought a medical malpractice action against surgeon Hacker for operating on the wrong vertebra in patient's spine. Dr. Hacker contended that the operation decision was based on an x-ray furnished by a radiologist. The trial court erroneously instructed the jury on "efficient intervening cause," the appellate court said:

> The instruction on efficient intervening cause is improper because Hacker, as head surgeon, was ultimately responsible for any negligent acts or omissions on behalf of himself or the operating team. Hacker might have been negligent in his acts or omissions. The radiologist might have been negligent in his acts or omissions. It is irrelevant in what sequence these negligent acts or omissions might have occurred, because Hacker is ultimately liable for the negligence. Hacker may not escape liability by presenting the negligence of another as an efficient intervening cause.

Presumably this case could also have been tried on ostensible or apparent agency, could it not?

6. *Partnership.* One partner is liable for the tortious acts of another partner committed within the scope of the partnership business. *Client's Security Fund v. Grandeau*, 72 N.Y.2d 62, 530 N.Y.S.2d 775, 526 N.E.2d 270 (1988). In *Thompson v. Gilmore*, 888 S.W.2d 715 (Mo. App. 1994), the court said a partner could be liable for the tortious act of another partner (negligently allowing the statute of limitations to run on a claim) that occurred after the partnership was dissolved, where the attorney-client relationship of the plaintiff with the partnership was entered into prior to the dissolution. The law "applicable today in Missouri and elsewhere," the court said, is that "dissolution does not relieve the partners for performance of contracts theretofore made."

7. *Car Owner Liability.* A number of jurisdictions impose vicarious liability on the "head of a household" who maintains a car for family use. As the court explained in *Camper v. Minor*, 915 S.W.2d 437 (Tenn. 1996):

> The family purpose doctrine has been in effect in Tennessee for nearly eighty years, *King v. Smythe*, 140 Tenn 217, 204 S.W. 296 (1918), and according to at least one court, has been "firmly established in this state." *Stephens v. Jones*, 710 S.W.2d 38, 42 (Tenn. App. 1984). Under the doctrine, the head of a household who maintains a motor vehicle for the general use and convenience of the family is liable for the negligence of any member of the family driving the vehicle, provided the driver received express or implied consent.

The family purpose doctrine is applicable when two requirements have been satisfied. First, the head of the household must maintain an automobile for the purpose of providing pleasure or comfort for his or her family. Second, the family purpose driver must have been using the motor vehicle at the time of the injury "in furtherance of that purpose with the permission, either expressed or implied, of the owner."

Tennessee courts have offered a number of justifications for the family purpose doctrine. First, the doctrine is based in part on the presumption that the child is subject to parental control. By imposing vicarious liability, the courts hoped to provide parents with an incentive to ensure that the actions of their children conform to the requirements of law. As stated by the *King* court, "[i]f owners of automobiles are made to understand that they will be held liable for injury to person and property occasioned by their negligent operation by infants or others who are financially irresponsible, they will doubtless exercise a greater degree of care in selecting those who are permitted to go upon the public streets with such dangerous instrumentalities." *King*, 204 S.W. at 298. Second, the courts justified the doctrine on a somewhat modified form of the "enterprise theory." As one court explained in an unpublished opinion in 1993, "one who furnishes and maintains the vehicle for the convenience of his family members is regarded as making such use his own business so that *the family member driver is furthering the owner's own purpose*" (emphasis added). The courts reasoned that because the head of the household was benefitting from such activity, he or she ought to be liable for the accidents that will inevitably result. Finally, the doctrine was thought important in providing innocent victims "substantial justice."

According to F. HARPER, F. JAMES & O. GRAY, THE LAW OF TORTS § 26.16 (2d ed. 1986):

> A few jurisdictions have passed statutes imposing liability on the owner of a motor vehicle for the negligence of anyone using or operating it with the owner's express or implied consent. These statutes have been held constitutional as a valid exercise of the police power and not violative of due process.
>
> Under these statutes proof of ownership affords an inference of consent that may be rebutted by evidence to the contrary. As in the field of vicarious liability generally questions have arisen as to whether the owner may be held where a borrower (though having consent to begin with) uses the car at a forbidden time, or in a forbidden place, or for a forbidden purpose. There is the same diversity of opinion on these points here as elsewhere; and the same general willingness to disregard the owner's limitations on authority once a court is convinced that they pertain to the mere manner of operating a vehicle.

Yet another means of imposing vicarious liability is by statutes mandating the use of "omnibus" clauses in automobile liability insurance policies. These clauses "typically extend the definition of the term 'insured' to include 'the named insured and any resident of the household' and 'any other person using such automobile . . . with the permission of the named insured.'" *Id.*, § 8.13 and fn. 34 thereto.

8. *Common Carrier Liability.* In *Gilstrap v. Amtrak*, 998 F.2d 559 (8th Cir. 1993), the plaintiff passenger on defendant's train was sexually assaulted by an employee of the defendant. Finding the defendant vicariously liable under Washington law, the court said a common carrier is "liable for tortious acts committed by its employees against a passenger" even if the employee is acting "outside the scope of his or her employment." In support of this proposition, the court cited the RESTATEMENT (SECOND) OF AGENCY:

> A comment to the Restatement of Agency provides that
>
>> [a] master or other principal may be in such relation to another that he has a duty to protect such other from harm although not caused by an enterprise which has been initiated by the master of by things owned or possessed by him. This duty may be created by contract, as where one agrees to protect another, or may be imposed by law as incident to a relation voluntarily entered into, *as the relation of carrier and passenger,* or by statute. . . . [T]he fact that the one to whom the performance of the duty is delegated acts for his own purposes and with no intent to benefit the principal or master is irrelevant.

Restatement (Second) of Agency § 214 comment (1958) (emphasis added). The American Law Institute provided the following illustration: "P, a railroad, employs A, a qualified conductor, to take charge of a train. A assaults T, a passenger. P is subject to liability to T." *Id.* Illus. 3. How does this differ from a common carrier's duty under negligence to protect passengers from assaults by employees?

9. *Franchisor Vicarious Liability.* In *O'Banner v. McDonald's Corp.*, 273 Ill. App. 3d 588, 653 N.E. 2d 1267 (1995), a customer injured in a bathroom slip-and-fall incident brought a personal injury action against the franchisor. Holding that the trial judge improperly granted summary judgment for the franchisor, the state court of appeals observed that:

> We see no reason to limit the apparent agency theory of vicarious liability to a hospital setting. Just as patients naturally depend upon their chosen hospital to supervise and take responsibility for the conduct of those who work within the facility, it is logical to conclude that many members of the public have come to believe that franchisors such as McDonald's Corporation are ultimately responsible not only for the quality of the food, but also for the condition of the premises in which it is served. McDonald's Corporation's extensive and visible reach into every aspect of its franchisee's businesses makes such a belief natural. The license agreement included in the record illustrates this fact. Under its terms McDonald's Corporation has undertaken a substantial effort to assure that it alone controls how the public perceives its franchised restaurants.
>
> McDonald's Corporation's "system" is described in its license agreements as being "comprehensive" in scope and offering the public a

"uniform" atmosphere. Only designated food and beverages may be served at franchised restaurants. Franchisees are required to use prescribed equipment, building layouts and designs. McDonald's Corporation dictates the level of quality, service and cleanliness throughout the system. All restaurant employees are required to wear uniforms designated by McDonald's Corporation. McDonald's Corporation also dictates management, advertising and personnel policies and additionally runs "Hamburger University," a training facility where its franchisees are required to train their managers. Presumably the employees responsible for maintaining the bathroom facilities where plaintiff was injured wore "McDonald's uniforms" and were required to follow McDonald's prescribed standards of "quality, service and cleanliness."

We find the degree of control exercised by the McDonald's Corporation over its franchisee, including the control exercised over the way in which the franchisee's business is promoted and advertised, to create the potential for members of the public to be misled as to the entity responsible for maintaining the restaurant facilities. The record indicates that McDonald's Corporation is the entity responsible for the relentless stream of commercials which permeate the media, promoting McDonald's restaurants as providing a safe, clean and wholesome atmosphere. It is a question of fact as to whether this type conduct could lead a person such as the plaintiff to enter the premises in reliance upon McDonald's reputation for quality and upon a belief that he was, in fact, dealing with an agent of the McDonald's Corporation.

The state supreme court granted summary judgment for the defendant in *O'Banner*, because the plaintiff gave "no indication as to why he went to the restaurant in the first place." 670 N.E. 2d at 632 (Ill. 1996).

In *Hoffnagle v. McDonald's Corp.*, 522 N.W.2d 808 (Iowa 1994), the court found the franchisor did not retain sufficient control over its franchisee, the Mrozinskis, to make the franchisor liable for injuries received by an employee of the franchisee in an assault on the franchisee's premises. Finding that two customers twice assaulted the employee on the premises on the same day, the court observed that:

> The franchisee, the Mrozinskis, rather than the franchisor, McDonald's, has the power to control the details of the restaurant's day-to-day operation. The Mrozinskis own the business equipment, operate the business, hold the operating licenses and permits, determine the wages, and provide the basic daily training and insurance for the franchisee's employees. The Mrozinskis, not McDonald's, hire, fire, supervise and discipline the franchisee's employees.
>
> On the other hand, McDonald's simply has the authority to require the franchisee to adhere to the "McDonald's system," to adopt and use McDonald's business manuals, and to follow other general guidelines outlined by McDonald's.
>
> With these relative powers of the franchisor and the franchisee in mind, we conclude that McDonald's authority is no more than the

authority to insure "the uniformity and standardization of products and services offered by a [franchisor's] restaurant. [Such] obligations do not affect the control of daily operations." *See Little v. Howard Johnson Co.,* 183 Mich. App. 675, 682, 455 N.W.2d 390, 394 (1990). The district court reached the same conclusion, stating:

> In the instant case, the day-to-day control of the employees was handled by the franchisee, not the franchisor. The general right of supervision by the franchisor to see that business is conducted in a generally uniform manner cannot mean the franchisor in this case is responsible if a co-employee did not call the police immediately upon returning into the restaurant. . . . Here, the actions or inactions of the employee come under the day-to-day control of the franchisee.

Is the court confusing the issue of vicarious liability with that of negligence of the franchisor?

ROCKWELL v. SUN HARBOR BUDGET SUITES
925 P.2d 1175 (Nev. 1996)

ROSE, JUSTICE:

Appellant Vernon Rockwell, his wife Londa, and their son Andrew lived in an apartment at respondent Sun Harbor Budget Suites (Sun Harbor). Londa was killed by Said Thamar, a Sun Harbor security guard, and Vernon and Andrew sued Sun Harbor on theories of respondeat superior, negligent hiring, training, and supervision, and breach of duty of care owed to the tenants. The district court dismissed all of the causes of action on summary judgment. We conclude that the district court's order granting respondent's motion for summary judgment was improper.

Vernon, his wife Londa, and their son Andrew all lived in an apartment in Sun Harbor. While sitting by the swimming pool in mid-1992, Londa and Thamar met for the first time and allegedly began a sexual affair the next day. When Londa attempted to end the affair in January 1993, Thamar shot her eighteen times, killing her.

Thamar was hired by Bigelow Management (Bigelow) as a security guard and was provided to Sun Harbor in the same capacity. Elaine Olsen, the manager of Sun Harbor, claimed that because Bigelow hired and paid him, Thamar was a Bigelow employee. However, Thamar was provided with a free apartment at Sun Harbor as part of his compensation package, but it is unclear from the record whether the apartment was paid for by Bigelow or Sun Harbor. The issue of which entity was paying for Thamar's services and apartment was clouded by the fact that Robert Bigelow was the president and treasurer of Bigelow and was also the treasurer of Sun Harbor, and the address for service of process for both corporations was the same. This raised the inference that Sun Harbor and Bigelow were somehow linked, but no other evidence regarding this issue was presented.

Thamar had a history of aggressive behavior which allegedly resulted in his being terminated from other security jobs. Thamar worked at Jerry's Nugget as a security guard and was allegedly fired for insubordination when he got angry because his superior requested that he come to work clean shaven. Thamar also worked at Vegas World and was allegedly fired due to his aggressive and threatening demeanor. Additionally, on his job application with Bigelow, under the heading "military service," Thamar listed that he was in the "bomb unit" of the Moroccan Marine Corps from 1977 through 1981.[6] Vernon claimed that a cursory check with the Moroccan embassy or local U.S. recruiter would confirm that the Moroccan military has no marine corps and no bomb unit; however, Vernon provided no evidence as to the truth of this assertion. Finally, Thamar was a convicted sex offender[7] and under Nevada law was required to register with the police. On his employment application, Thamar stated that he had not been convicted of any crimes, and there is no indication of whether he registered with the police.

Thamar's aggressive behavior also extended to his relations with Vernon, and during the later stages of the extramarital affair with Londa, Thamar threatened Vernon on several occasions. On one occasion, Thamar flagged down Vernon's car in the parking lot, and according to Vernon, Thamar tried to provoke him into violence so that Thamar could beat him or kill him. Vernon backed away from Thamar and retreated to his apartment.

Vernon made some efforts to inform Olsen, the Sun Harbor manager, of the situation between himself, Londa, and Thamar. On January 23, 1993, Vernon met with Olsen and told her that Thamar and his wife were having an affair and that he wanted Olsen to make Thamar stop pursuing the relationship. However, Vernon did not tell Olsen about the first threatening incident that occurred in the parking lot. Olsen stated that she would relate Vernon's concerns to Thamar, but the record does not indicate if she did so. Additionally, in response to this discussion, Olsen sent Greg Aliano, another Sun Harbor security guard, to Vernon's apartment to further discuss the situation and to gather more information. A second threatening incident occurred on January 26, 1993, when Londa, who had briefly moved into Thamar's apartment, was moving her things out of Thamar's apartment and back into Vernon's apartment after reconciling with Vernon. Thamar came downstairs from his apartment, pointed at Vernon with his finger, and threatened to shoot him. Vernon was a cab driver and was standing next to his cab and, fearing for his life, called the cab dispatcher to ask for help. The dispatcher called the police, who responded to the scene. Vernon informed the responding officer that Londa was attempting to move out of Thamar's apartment and that Thamar was exhibiting aggressive behavior, but he apparently did not inform the officer that Thamar had threatened him. The officer talked with Thamar, and Thamar assured him that everything was fine. The officer then informed the security guard on duty what had happened and told the guard to likewise inform the person in charge.

On January 27, 1993, Vernon met with Olsen a second time and told her that he and his family were vacating the apartment and also told her again of the increasingly volatile situation between Thamar and himself. For the

---

[6] Thamar was born in Morocco in 1956 and lived there until he moved to the United States in 1982.

[7] In 1985, Thamar pleaded no contest in Wisconsin to one count of indecent exposure, was incarcerated in county jail for sixty days, and placed on probation for two years.

first time, he told her of Thamar's threats and of the police responding to Sun Harbor the night before. Vernon also stated that several of his wife's items still remained in Thamar's apartment, that he wished to retrieve them, and that he was going to have the police escort him when he retrieved the items in order to avert a violent situation. Olsen stated that the police were not required and that she would provide Sun Harbor security personnel to help Londa get the rest of her belongings.

On January 27, 1993, after his meeting with Olsen, Vernon began moving the family's belongings into storage in anticipation of moving into a new apartment complex. Vernon dropped Londa off at work and made several trips between the apartment and the storage facility. Vernon called Londa at work and informed her that they would be staying in a hotel for a few days. Londa indicated that she would be working all day and never stated that she was going to Thamar's apartment. Without Vernon's or Olsen's knowledge, Thamar picked Londa up from work around 1:00 P.M. and took her back to his apartment. At the apartment, Londa told Thamar that the affair was over and that she was returning to her husband, and Thamar became incensed. He got his gun and shot Londa eighteen times, stopping to reload several times.

Thamar then used his radio to call Sun Harbor security to tell them what had happened. Aliano[, another security guard,] was off duty at the time of the shooting and heard Thamar's call over his radio. He ascertained and went to Thamar's location, handcuffed Thamar, and called the police. Thamar was later convicted of second degree murder with the use of a deadly weapon.

Vernon and Andrew originally sued only Sun Harbor for the wrongful death of Londa but later amended the complaint to include Bigelow as a second defendant.[8] The causes of action against Sun Harbor for respondeat superior, negligent hiring, training, and supervision, and breach of duty of care were all dismissed on summary judgment. The order granting summary judgment contained no findings of fact or conclusions of law.

Summary judgment is only appropriate when, after a review of the record viewed in a light most favorable to the non-moving party, there remain no issues of material fact, and the moving party is entitled to judgment as a matter of law. "In determining whether summary judgment is proper, the nonmoving party is entitled to have the evidence and all reasonable inferences accepted as true." *Wiltsie v. Baby Grand Corp.*, 105 Nev. 291, 292, 774 P.2d 432, 433 (1989).

This court's review of a summary judgment order is de novo. On appeal, this court is "required to determine whether the trial court erred in concluding that an absence of genuine issues of material fact justified its granting of summary judgment." *Bird v. Casa Royale West*, 97 Nev. 67, 68, 624 P.2d 17, 18 (1981).

---

[8] The causes of action against Bigelow were not addressed in the motion for summary judgment because that motion was fully briefed before Vernon amended the complaint to add Bigelow as a defendant. After summary judgment was granted in favor of Sun Harbor, Vernon voluntarily dismissed the amended complaint without prejudice as to Bigelow and then filed this appeal. Therefore, there are no issues pending in the district court, and this court can properly hear this appeal.

"[R]espondeat superior liability attaches only when the employee is under the control of the employer and when the act is within the scope of employment." *Molino v. Asher*, 96 Nev. 814, 817, 618 P.2d 878, 879 (1980). Therefore, an actionable claim on a theory of respondeat superior requires proof that (1) the actor at issue was an employee, and (2) the action complained of occurred within the scope of the actor's employment.

This court has stated that "[t]he employer can be vicariously responsible only for the acts of his employees not someone else, and one way of establishing the employment relationship is to determine when the 'employee' is under the control of the 'employer.'" *National Convenience Stores v. Fantauzzi*, 94 Nev. 655, 657, 584 P.2d 689, 691 (1978). "This element of control requires that the employer 'have control and direction not only of the employment to which the contract relates but also of all of its details and the method of performing the work. . . .'" *Kennel v. Carson City School District*, 738 F. Supp. 376, 378 (D. Nev. 1990) (*quoting* 53 Am. Jur. 2d Master and Servant § 2 (1970)).

However, in the situation where a property owner hires security personnel to protect his or her premises and patrons, that property owner has a personal and nondelegable duty to provide responsible security personnel. Therefore, we conclude as a matter of law that the security personnel are the employees of the property owner, even if the property owner engaged a third party to hire the security personnel. In such a situation, we find an employer-employee relationship without evaluating whether the security personnel were under the control of the property owner, noting that the control analysis is only one of the methods available to establish such a relationship.[9]

In reaching this conclusion, we follow the ruling in *Peachtree-Cain Co. v. McBee*, 170 Ga. App. 38, 316 S.E.2d 9 (1984), *aff'd*, 254 Ga. 91, 327 S.E.2d 188 (1985). In *Peachtree-Cain Co.*, the Peachtree Company owned a shopping center called the Peachtree Center. Peachtree Center Management Company, a separate corporation, managed the Peachtree Center and contracted with American Building Maintenance Company to provide and manage security personnel for the property. All of these parties were sued by a patron who claimed to have been falsely arrested by a security guard. Peachtree Company moved for summary judgment on the ground that it could not be liable for the intentional torts of the independent security agent. The court denied the motion for summary judgment, concluding that:

> As owners of the Peachtree Center complex that had undertaken to obtain security services, their duty to their invitees to provide responsible agents was personal and non-delegable, and thus it did not matter that the owners had an additional filter, *i.e.*, the Peachtree Center Management Company, between themselves and the actual security guard. Because that duty was personal and non-delegable, a recovery based upon a breach of that duty would not constitute imposition of liability without fault. To hold that the appellants are immune from vicarious liability in these cases would, as noted above,

---

[9] We make no determination on the issue of whether Thamar was an employee of Bigelow, although we note that it is possible for an employee to be simultaneously under the control of two different employers.

present "opportunities for gross injustice" which we will not here sanction.

Peachtree-Cain Co., 316 S.E.2d at 11 (citations omitted); *see Zentko v. G.M. McKelvey Co.*, 83 N.E.2d 265, 268 (Ohio Ct. App.1948) (stating that where an owner of an operation or enterprise undertakes to obtain security services, the owner's security duties are personal and nondelegable, and where the owner arranges for and accepts the services, the relationship of master and servant exists). *Adams v. F.W. Woolworth Co.*, 144 Misc. 27, 257 N.Y.S. 776, 781 (App. Div. 1932) ("A store owner who places a detective agency on his premises for the purpose of protecting his property by various means, including arrests, should not be immune from responsibility to an innocent victim of a false arrest made by the detective agency, even as an independent contractor."); *Dupree v. Piggly Wiggly Shop Rite Foods, Inc.*, 542 S.W.2d 882, 888 (Tex. Ct. App. 1976) ("because of the 'personal character' of duties owed to the public by one adopting measures to protect his property, owners and operators of enterprises cannot, by securing special personnel through an independent contractor for the purposes of protecting property, obtain immunity from liability for at least the intentional torts of the protecting agency or its employees.").

Similarly, in the instant case, Sun Harbor undertook to obtain security services, a personal and non-delegable duty, and it did not matter that the owners of Sun Harbor had an additional filter, *i.e.*, Bigelow, between themselves and the actual security guard. Additionally, Sun Harbor arranged for and accepted the security services of Thamar, and therefore the relationship of master and servant (or employer-employee) existed between Sun Harbor and the security guard.

Generally, whether an employee is acting within the scope of his or her employment is a question for the trier of fact, but where undisputed evidence exists concerning the employee's status at the time of the tortious act, the issue may be resolved as a matter of law.

This court has held that in order for an employer to be liable for the intentional tort of an employee, that tort must occur within the scope of the task assigned to the employee. *Prell Hotel Corp. v. Antonacci*, 86 Nev. 390, 391, 469 P.2d 399, 400 (1970). "[I]f the employee's tort is truly an independent venture of his own and not committed in the course of the very task assigned to him, the employer is not liable." *Id.* (holding that an employer was vicariously liable when the employee, a blackjack dealer, hit a customer in the face while dealing a game because the assault occurred within the scope of the task assigned to the dealer, that of dealing blackjack). *But see J.C. Penney Co. v. Gravelle*, 62 Nev. 434, 449–50, 155 P.2d 477, 481–82 (1944) (concluding that an on-duty security guard acted outside the scope of his employment when he punched Gravelle because Gravelle had prevented the guard from catching a shoplifter; the guard's acts were done to punish Gravelle for his interference and not in order to catch the thief or to retrieve the stolen merchandise, and the guard's actions were clearly disconnected from the line of his duty to his employer).

Vernon produced evidence that at the time Thamar shot Londa, he was still actively guarding the premises even though he was off duty, and that the off-duty security officers carried radios and responded to emergency situations. Furthermore, the record indicates that after Thamar shot Londa, he used his radio to call the Sun Harbor security dispatcher to report that his girlfriend had been shot, and Aliano, an off-duty security guard, heard the call on his radio, went to Thamar's location, and handcuffed Thamar until the police arrived.

Conversely, Olsen's affidavit presented evidence that off-duty security guards were not required to remain in radio contact with Sun Harbor or respond to emergency calls, and that their free time was their own. This indicates that when Thamar was off duty he was no longer engaged in the business of or service of his employer and Sun Harbor would not be liable. This conflicting evidence regarding whether Thamar was still acting within the scope of his employment when he killed Londa creates a genuine issue of material fact, and we conclude that it was improper for the district court to grant summary judgment on the respondeat superior cause of action.

It is a basic tenet that for an employer to be liable for negligent hiring, training, or supervision of an employee, the person involved must actually be an employee.[10] As we concluded, *supra*, as a matter of law Thamar was an employee of Sun Harbor by virtue of the fact that providing security for one's premises and patrons is a personal and nondelegable duty, and that once the property owner accepts the services of the security personnel, the property owner cannot claim that the relationship of master and servant does not exist.

The only remaining question is whether Sun Harbor was negligent in hiring, training, and supervising Thamar. We conclude that genuine issues of material fact remained as to whether Sun Harbor was negligent in its hiring, training, and supervision of Thamar, and the district court erred by granting summary judgment in favor of Sun Harbor on this cause of action.

As to the cause of action for negligent hiring, Vernon produced evidence that Thamar had previously been fired from jobs for his violent behavior, that Thamar was a convicted sex offender, that Thamar lied on his application about his criminal past, and that Thamar possibly lied about his military background in Morocco. This creates a genuine issue of material fact as to whether Sun Harbor was negligent when it retained Thamar.

The dissent states that because respondents had no appreciable notice of Thamar's violent propensities, they had no duty to make inquiries. However, the lack of notice does not relieve the employer of his "general duty . . . to conduct a reasonable background check on a potential employee to ensure that the employee is fit for the position." *Burnett v. C.B.A. Security Service*, 107 Nev. 787, 789, 820 P.2d 750, 752 (1991). Requiring Sun Harbor to make reasonable investigations regarding the security guards' qualifications might be somewhat burdensome to Sun Harbor, especially in light of the fact that it contracted with Bigelow to do that job for it, but such investigations are

---

[10] When the cause of action is for negligent supervision, as opposed to respondeat superior, it does not matter if the employee's actions occurred within or without his scope of employment. In a "common-law action charging the master with actionable negligence in retaining an incompetent and unfit employee, . . . it is unnecessary to determine whether [the employee] was acting within the scope of his employment." *Stricklin v. Parsons Stockyard Co.*, 192 Kan. 360, 388 P.2d 824, 829 (1964).

commensurate with Sun Harbor's personal and nondelegable duty to provide responsible security guards to protect its premises and patrons.

As to the cause of action for negligent supervision and training, Vernon produced evidence that Sun Harbor actively supervised the security guards and controlled both the details and methods of performing the guards' work. Additionally, Vernon produced evidence that Sun Harbor possessed the ability to fire the security guards. Furthermore, Vernon presented evidence that in the days preceding the killing he twice spoke with Olsen regarding the evolving situation. On January 23, 1993, he informed Olsen of the affair between Londa and Thamar and requested that Olsen investigate the situation and get Thamar to end the relationship with Londa. In response to this discussion, Olsen sent Aliano to talk to Vernon and gather more information. On the morning of January 27, 1993, the day of the killing, Vernon informed Olsen that Londa had ended the affair, that Thamar had threatened his life while on duty, that he had called the police in response to the threats, and that he wished to call the police again to help him retrieve his wife's belongings from Thamar's apartment. Olsen stated, however, that she believed that the situation was a personal matter between Thamar and Vernon and that she had no right to interfere.

Based on this evidence, Vernon contended that Olsen had enough information to determine that Thamar was dangerous and that she acted negligently by not remedying the situation through adequate supervision or training. Sun Harbor contended that it acted properly at all times with regard to its actions toward Thamar. This is sufficient to create a genuine issue of material fact as to whether Sun Harbor negligently supervised and trained Thamar and the district court erred by granting summary judgment in favor of Sun Harbor on these issues.

A land owner or occupier owes a duty to the people on the land to act reasonably under the circumstances. *Moody v. Manny's Auto Repair*, 110 Nev. 320, 333, 871 P.2d 935, 943 (1994). This court has determined that consideration of the status of the injured person as trespasser, licensee, or invitee is no longer determinative and concluded that "determinations of liability should primarily depend upon whether the owner or occupier of land acted reasonably under the circumstances." *Id.*

More specifically, when the issue is protecting a guest from the injury caused by a third person, this court has stated that "[t]here is a duty to take affirmative action to control the wrongful acts of third persons only where the occupant of realty has reasonable cause to anticipate such act and the probability of injury resulting therefrom." *Thomas v. Bokelman*, 86 Nev. 10, 13, 462 P.2d 1020, 1022 (1970). On the issue of foreseeability, this court has stated:

> Since the possessor is not an insurer of the visitor's safety, he is ordinarily under no duty to exercise any care until he knows or has reason to know that the acts of the third person are occurring, or are about to occur. . . .

Early v. N.L.V. Casino Corp., 100 Nev. 200, 203, 678 P.2d 683, 684 (1984) (*quoting* Restatement (Second) of Torts § 344 comment *f* (1965)).

We conclude that genuine issues of material fact also existed as to whether Sun Harbor could reasonably foresee that Thamar would commit a violent act and whether Sun Harbor acted reasonably under the circumstances. Vernon presented evidence that on two occasions he informed Olsen of his marital situation, that he believed Thamar to be dangerous, and that Thamar had threatened to kill him. However, one of these conversations occurred four days prior to Londa's death, and the other occurred on the day of Londa's death. We conclude that these facts create a genuine issue of material fact as to whether Sun Harbor acted reasonably under the circumstances to protect its tenants from Thamar's violent acts. Therefore, it was improper for the district court to grant summary judgment in favor of Sun Harbor on this cause of action. . . .

NOTES

1. *Negligent Hiring.* Independent of any vicarious liability, a principal may be liable to a third party for the principal's primary negligence in selecting, instructing, or supervising an independent contractor. *Becker v. Interstate Properties,* 569 F.2d 1203 (3d Cir. 1977), *cert. denied,* 436 U.S. 906, 56 L. Ed. 2d 404, 98 S. Ct. 2237 (1978). *See also* RESTATEMENT (SECOND) OF TORTS § 411. Does a principal owe a duty to third persons to select a solvent independent contractor? An adequately insured one? *See Becker, supra,* overruled in *Robinson v. Jiffy Exec. Limousine Co.,* 4 F.3d 237 (3d Cir. 1993). *See also Matanuska Elec. Ass'n v. Johnson,* 386 P.2d 698 (Alaska 1963); *Wright v. Newman,* 539 F. Supp. 1331 (W.D. Ark. 1982) (previous success with independent contractor may preclude action for negligent selection). Should liability be imposed for negligent hiring of a babysitter? *Compare Glomb v. Glomb,* 366 Pa. Super. 206, 530 A.2d 1362 (1987), with *Anderson v. New Orleans Pub. Serv.,* 583 So.2d 829 (La. 1991) (court erred in imputing to the mother the negligence of an aunt with whom the mother resided and whom she asked to watch the victim-child while the mother took a nap; a principal is liable for physical tortious conduct of an agent only if the principal has the power to control the physical details of the agent's manner of performance). An employer may be liable to a third person for negligence in the hiring, retention or supervision of an employee, particularly if the employer's work requires the employee to perform his tasks in the home or office of the third person. *See, e.g., Freeman v. Bell,* 366 So. 2d 197 (La. App. 1978); *F & T Co. v. Woods,* 92 N.M. 697, 594 P.2d 745 (1979).

PROBLEM

Quick Pizza, Inc. grants franchises for the operation of "Pizza Quick" restaurants. In exchange for the franchise fee, the franchisee receives the benefit of national and cooperative local advertising (Quick Pizza, Inc. subsidizes the local franchisee's advertising in an amount up to 10% of the gross advertising, or $5,000, whichever is greater). Quick Pizza, Inc. also provides training of the franchisee and its employees for the initial startup of the franchise restaurant, and makes semiannual inspections. The franchise agreement gives Quick Pizza, Inc., the right to cancel the franchise if the restaurant is not operated within the general minimum standards adopted by Quick Pizza,

Inc. Quick Pizza, Inc. also sells restaurant supplies to the franchisee; however, the franchisee is only obligated to purchase $10,000 per year in supplies, and may obtain other supplies elsewhere.

The national advertising, and the franchisor's policy, provide that a pizza will be delivered to a customer's home or place of business within 20 minutes after the order is placed; if it is not, the customer receives the pizza without charge. The local franchisee in the present case, Mr. Jones, employs college students and other young people to deliver his pizzas. The deliveryperson must furnish her own vehicle and pay all of her expenses. She is provided with a portable "Pizza Quick" sign which she is required to display atop her vehicle while delivering pizzas. Jones pays the deliveryperson a fee of 25% of the cost of the pizza for each order delivered; however, if the order is not delivered within the 20-minute period, the deliveryperson receives no fee. Jones provides deliverypersons with a map showing the shortest routes to areas from which orders frequently are placed, but he does not require that any particular route be taken. A deliveryperson is not required to work a given schedule, but must be available three evenings a week to retain her position. Jones also requires that each deliveryperson have a valid driver's license and maintain the minimum compulsory insurance required by law ($10,000 each person, $20,000 each accident).

On the day in question, Simoni, a college graduate student, is delivering a pizza for Jones. However, he has noticed that he has left his driver's license at his home. Because the delivery is a "gimme," *i.e.*, one in which delivery can easily be made in 5 to 10 minutes, and is in the neighborhood where he lives, Simoni decides to drop by his home and pick up his license en route to the customer's residence. He turns off the most direct route from the pizza restaurant to the customer, and begins the three-block detour to his house. In the second block, he fails to observe a stop sign, enters the intersection, and strikes a vehicle driven by Kildare. Kildare, a young physician, is rendered a quadriplegic in the accident.

Discuss Kildare's claims against Quick Pizza, Inc. (the franchisor) and Jones (the franchisee).

C. IMPUTED RESPONSIBILITY OF THE PLAINTIFF

LaBIER v. PELLETIER
665 A.2d 1013 (Me. 1995)

ROBERTS, JUSTICE.

William LaBier, personally and as the father and next friend of Joseph M. LaBier, appeals from a judgment entered on a jury verdict in the Superior Court in favor of Monique Pelletier. Joseph was injured when the bicycle he was riding was hit by a car driven by Pelletier. LaBier argues that the court erred in instructing the jury that the negligence of Nyla LaBier, Joseph's mother, should be imputed to her son in assessing comparative fault. Because we reject the doctrine of imputed parental negligence in these circumstances, we vacate the judgment.

On October 14, 1987, Nyla LaBier went for a walk with her infant daughter on Walker Ridge Drive in Sanford. Joseph, who was four years and eight months old, accompanied them on his bicycle. The LaBiers stopped at the home of their neighbor, Beth St. Cyr. While Nyla talked to St. Cyr at the top of the St. Cyrs' steeply sloping driveway, Joseph rode loops on his bicycle across the lawn, down the driveway, and back to the top. On one of his trips down the driveway, Joseph's feet slipped off the pedals of his bike and he lost control.

Meanwhile, Pelletier was driving on Walker Ridge Drive toward the St. Cyr house, which was on her left. Her daughter was in the back seat of her vehicle. As she approached the St. Cyr house she noticed several children playing at the home of the Gudaitis family, which was on her right before she reached the St. Cyr driveway. She estimated her speed at 20 to 25 m.p.h., which was within the legal limit for that residential neighborhood. She slowed her car as she spotted the Gudaitis children, pointing out to her daughter a young girl on a swing set. After concluding that none of the Gudaitis children were likely to stray into the street, Pelletier began to accelerate.

The right front fender and hood of Pelletier's vehicle struck Joseph at a point about three-quarters of the way across the street. Pelletier failed to see Joseph approaching the street even though her view of the St. Cyr driveway was unobstructed. Joseph suffered a broken leg and a head injury, as well as numerous scrapes and bruises.

LaBier sued Pelletier on behalf of Joseph, claiming that her negligence caused Joseph's injuries. Pelletier alleged the comparative negligence of Joseph and Nyla as an affirmative defense, and brought a counterclaim against Nyla for contribution, alleging that Nyla's failure to properly supervise Joseph caused the accident. At trial, the court instructed the jury, over LaBier's objection, to consider both Nyla's negligence and Joseph's negligence, and to return a verdict in favor of Joseph only if it found that the combined causative negligence of Joseph and Nyla was less than the causative negligence of Pelletier. The jury found that Joseph was not negligent; that both Nyla and Pelletier were negligent; and that Nyla's negligence was greater than Pelletier's. It therefore awarded no damages to Joseph. The court entered a judgment on the verdict and dismissed Pelletier's counterclaim against Nyla as moot. LaBier's appeal followed.

Although we have stated that the negligence of a parent may be imputed to a child, the parties cite no case, and we find none, in which we have relied exclusively on the doctrine of imputed parental negligence to bar recovery for a child. The instant case squarely presents for the first time the question whether the doctrine of imputed parental negligence is or ought to be the law of Maine.

As the facts of this case demonstrate, the doctrine of imputed parental negligence may deprive an innocent child of a remedy for his injuries. Modern authorities recognize that it is fundamentally unfair to deprive an injured child of a remedy because of actions by the parent that the child is unable to control. As the Supreme Court of Montana recognized over eighty years ago:

[T]he negligence of the parent, guardian, or custodian is not imputable to the child, because it is in no way responsible for the danger, had no volition in establishing the relation of privity with the person whose negligence it is sought to impute to it, and should not be charged with the fault of such person in allowing it to be exposed to danger which it had not the capacity either to know or to avoid.

Flaherty v. Butte Elec. R.R., 40 Mont. 454, 107 P. 416, 418 (1910). The unfairness of imputed parental negligence is amplified by the fact that in cases like this one the doctrine enables an admittedly blameworthy party to escape liability. Because the policies that support the doctrine, even if valid, fail to justify the unfair result that the doctrine produces, we reject the doctrine of imputed parental negligence. Instead, we adopt the approach of the Restatement, which provides that "[a] child who suffers physical harm is not barred from recovery by the negligence of his parent, either in the parent's custody of the child or otherwise." Restatement (Second) of Torts § ___488 (1965).

Pelletier argues that the doctrine of imputed parental negligence grows from the theory of unity between parent and child, similar to the common law fiction of legal unity between husband and wife. Pelletier maintains that the parent is therefore the agent of the child. She relies on *Merchant v. Mansir*, 572 A.2d 493 (Me. 1990), which adopts Restatement (Second) of Torts § 316 (1965), to support her argument that "the parent is the child, and the child the parent in terms of facing both liability and harm vis-a-vis the outside world."

We disagree. In *Black v. Solmitz*, 409 A.2d 634, 635 (Me. 1979), we held for the first time that children may sue their parents. In so doing, we put to rest any possibility that parent and child might be one legal entity. We realized that the common law recognized "no conception of any unity of parent and minor child comparable to the conception of unity of husband and wife." *Id.* at 637. Contrary to Pelletier's contention, "the common law . . . never has made the parent vicariously liable as such for the conduct of the child." W. PAGE KEETON ET AL., PROSSER AND KEETON ON THE LAW OF TORTS § 123, at 913 (5th ed. 1984) (hereinafter Prosser). Indeed, Prosser refers to the supposed agency of the parent to look after the child as "the sheerest nonsense." *Id.* § 74, at 532.

Pelletier's reliance on *Merchant* and Restatement (Second) of Torts § 316 is misplaced. In *Merchant*, we did not hold that parents are liable for the torts of their children, as Pelletier suggests. We stated that parents may be liable in limited circumstances to third persons who are injured as a result of a breach of a duty of supervision, *citing* Restatement (Second) of Torts § 316. *Merchant*, 572 A.2d at 494. Moreover, the Restatement specifically rejects Pelletier's contention that the parent and child are a single entity for comparative negligence purposes, noting that "[t]he family relation between the parent and child does not so identify the two as to make the parent's negligence a bar to the child's recovery or child's negligence a bar to the parent's recovery." Restatement (Second) of Torts § 488, comment *a* (1965).

Pelletier also argues that imputed parental negligence is necessary to prevent parents from reaping a windfall from their own negligence. Although Pelletier's windfall argument may once have had some validity, modern legal developments have rendered it anachronistic. Historically, the nonparental defendant was unable to seek contribution from a joint tortfeasor who was the plaintiff's parent because a defendant could seek contribution only from a party against whom the plaintiff had a cause of action. Because parents were immune from suit by their children in many jurisdictions, that rule effectively prevented nonparental negligent parties from seeking contribution.

That historical justification for the doctrine of imputed parental negligence has been absent in Maine at least since *Bedell v. Reagan*, 159 Me. 292, 192 A.2d 24 (1963). In that case, we held that the existence of interspousal immunity would not prevent a third-party claim for contribution against a negligent spouse although that spouse was then immune from suit by the injured spouse. Presumably the same analysis was applicable to a third-party claim against a negligent parent who was then immune from suit by a child. The abrogation of parental immunity in *Black*, however, combined with modern third-party practice eliminated any potential unfairness to the nonparental defendant. Accordingly, Pelletier's counterclaim for contribution must be reinstated, and in that context the comparison of the negligence of Pelletier to that of Nyla properly placed before the jury.

Moreover, Pelletier's argument that any tort recovery by a minor child will relieve the parent's obligation to provide for the child is inaccurate. The common law imposes a duty on parents to support their children. The existence of the child's own income or property does not relieve the parent of that duty. In an appropriate case the court may restrict the application of the proceeds of suit for the protection of a minor plaintiff.

Even if the parent might realize some incidental benefit from the child's recovery, it is unfair to remedy that problem by shifting the windfall to the nonparental tortfeasor, thereby stripping the innocent child of any recovery against a negligent nonparental defendant.

Finally, Pelletier contends that a change in a long-standing principle of tort law must be left to the Legislature. "It is fundamental that the rules of common law which are court-made rules can be changed by the court when it becomes convinced that the policies upon which they are based have lost their validity or were mistakenly conceived." *Pendexter*, 363 A.2d at 749. "When principles fail to produce just results, [we have] found a departure from precedent necessary to fulfill [our] role of reasoned decision making." *Adams v. Buffalo Forge Co.*, 443 A.2d 932, 935 (Me. 1982). Assuming that the doctrine of imputing a parent's negligence to the child has been a long-standing principle of Maine tort law, it has outlived whatever limited usefulness it might once have had.

Our decision today adopts the modern view that unanimously rejects the doctrine of imputed parental negligence as "not only unsound, but absurd and inhuman." *Denver City Tramway v. Brown*, 57 Colo. 484, 143 P. 364, 368 (1914). According to Prosser:

> [T]his barbarous rule, which denied to the innocent victim of the negligence of two parties any recovery against either, and visited the sins of the fathers upon the children, was accepted in several American States until it was at one time very nearly the prevailing rule; but

it now is abrogated, by statute or by decision everywhere except in Maine, where it should be hoped that it will not long survive.

Prosser § 74, at 531–32.

Because the trial court in this case instructed the jury to impute the negligence of Nyla to Joseph in determining whether Joseph was entitled to recovery against Pelletier, we must vacate the judgment in favor of Pelletier.

NOTES

1. *Imputation of Child's Fault to the Parent.* Recognizing a division of authority, the court in *Handeland v. Brown*, 216 N.W.2d 574 (Iowa 1974), refused to impute a child's negligence to its father, in an action by the father for medical expenses, loss of services, companionship and society against a tortfeasor who injured the child. The court noted but rejected RESTATEMENT (SECOND) OF TORTS § 494 (1965):

> The plaintiff is barred from recovery for an invasion of his legally protected interest in the health or life of a third person which results from the harm or death of such third person, if the negligence of such third person would have barred his own recovery.

The Restatement contemplates a situation where contributory negligence is a complete bar. Would the same result be reached in a jurisdiction applying comparative fault?

2. *Loss of Consortium.* In *Tuggle v. Allright Parking Sys., Inc.*, 922 S.W.2d 105 (Tenn. 1996), the court in reducing a spouse's claim for loss of consortium by the comparative fault of the other spouse, observed that:

> . . . [A] small number of jurisdictions view a claim for loss of consortium as an essentially different and independent cause of action from the physically injured spouse. Based on that premise, those jurisdictions apply the rule that the recovery awarded the spouse claiming loss of consortium is not affected by the fault of the physically injured spouse.
>
> The clear majority of jurisdictions, however, hold that a loss of consortium award must be reduced, and may be barred, by the comparative fault of the physically injured spouse.

The court gave as the rationale for the majority rule:

> [T]here must be a tort which gives rise to a cause of action that must be maintained by the [physically] injured spouse in order for the non-injured spouse to claim a loss of consortium. In other words, the loss of consortium claim is dependent upon the negligent injury of the other spouse who has the primary tort cause of action.

The court added that the imputed-fault approach also fostered family harmony:

> If a claim for loss of consortium were viewed as totally independent of the other spouse's personal injury claim, there would be no reason to preclude one spouse from suing another for loss of consortium or

to prohibit the primary tortfeasor sued in a consortium claim from impleading the spouse who suffered the personal injuries.

Compare *Massengale v. Pitts*, 737 A.2d 1029 (D.C. 1999) (contributory negligence of spouse does not affect other spouse's consortium claim).

3. *Whither Joint and Several?* The problems of imputed contributory negligence may disappear when a jurisdiction adopts pure comparative negligence and abolishes joint and several liability among joint tortfeasors. In such a case, the fault of each person will be quantified, and the victim can recover from the nonparental or nonemployer tortfeasor only for the percentage of fault chargeable to that tortfeasor. But some courts will not allocate fault to a party against whom the plaintiff has no legal claim, *e.g.*, because of immunity. See *Ridings v. Ralph M. Parsons Co.*, 914 S.W. 2d 79 (Tenn. 1996) (employer workers — compensation immunity).

PROBLEM

Wife, husband and child were involved in an automobile collision with defendant, another automobile driver. Wife was driving the family car, and husband and child were passengers in the car, at the time of the collision. Wife was 20% at fault, and defendant 80% at fault. Husband and child were injured in the collision.

Child sues wife (his mother) and the other driver for damages resulting from his personal injuries. Husband sues his wife and the other driver for his personal injuries, the child's medical expenses and loss of the child's services and companionship, loss of the wife's consortium, and damage to the family car. Should the wife's fault be imputed to the husband's or the child's claims?

Chapter 15
AN INTRODUCTION TO PRODUCTS LIABILITY

A. INTRODUCTION

Perhaps no other area of modern tort law is as volatile, as controversial, and as challenging as the law of products liability in America.

Products law has been volatile for at least two major reasons. One is that it represents the confluence of three distinct bodies of law — negligence, warranty, and the modern doctrine of strict tort liability. Working out the relationship among these bodies of law has presented large problems of definition and application. Another reason for the volatility is that products liability originally was consumer-oriented; the rapid development of consumer protectionism in the second half of the twentieth century brought about parallel developments in products liability law. More recently, state product liability legislation and the promulgation of the new Restatement (Third) of Torts: Products Liability arguably are less consumer and more manufacturer oriented. But these moves are matched, if not trumped, by recent large scale products liability cases, involving such products as breast implants, cigarettes and guns. Some of these suits have been class actions; others have been filed by states and cities, suing in their own behalf.

The subject of products liability is controversial for several reasons. First, products liability has been viewed as a major contributor to the perceived crises in tort litigation and liability-insurance availability in the mid-1970s and mid-1980s. Second, it is controversial in light of the recent changes in state law, the RESTATEMENT (THIRD), and the large scale cases noted above. Some of the issues connected with these concerns are explored in detail in the last chapter of this book.

Finally, products liability law is challenging because of the continuing ferment associated with its growth and because of its amorphous and uncertain nature. Is it conceptually like the law of warranty, negligence, or strict liability? Or, is it a combination of all of the above?

A little history is essential to an understanding of modern American products liability law. In 1842, the Court of Exchequer ruled that a passenger injured by a breach of a contract to repair a coach could not recover in contract against the repairer because there was no "privity of contract." *Winterbottom v. Wright*, 152 Eng. Rep. 402. Dicta in *Winterbottom* led to the rule that a person injured by conduct which was a breach of a contract could not recover in tort unless the victim was "in privity" with the contracting parties. This "barrier of privity" effectively precluded negligence actions against a manufacturer who sold its product through a retailer. The injured party could proceed on a negligence theory against the retailer, but the retailer rarely was at fault.

The "barrier of privity" was breached in the landmark negligence case of *MacPherson v. Buick Motor Co.*, 111 N.E. 1050 (N.Y. 1915). That breach did not provide adequate help to the injured consumer, who still was required to prove that the manufacturer could have foreseen the injury-causing attribute of its product and failed to act reasonably to avoid it. The search for a stricter standard of liability led to contract law and breach of warranty. A seller may expressly warrant the qualities of its product; even if it does not, the law implies a warranty of merchantability (U.C.C. sec. 2-314) that the product is reasonably fit for its intended use, or put another way, the product will meet the reasonable expectations of the consumer. The breach of a contract (such as an implied warranty) imposes a kind of liability without fault, *i.e.*, without negligence. In the first half of the twentieth century, the courts extended the manufacturer's liability for breach of the implied warranty to personal injury damages and to third persons who were not "in privity" with the manufacturer, particularly where the breach caused personal injuries. The availability of a warranty cause of action in a products liability/personal injury case was advanced with the promulgation and state-by-state adoption (except Louisiana which has a civil law tradition) of Article 2 of the uniform Commercial Code. The U.C.C. expressly provides in section 2-715(2)(b) that personal injury damages are recoverable consequential damages.

Although it provided liability without a showing of negligence, breach of implied warranty did not fully satisfy the drive to impose liability upon manufacturers for damages caused by their products. There were three primary reasons why the warranty claim did not fully protect consumers. First, a seller could disclaim an implied warranty (U.C.C. § 2-316). A seller could provide a limited remedy for breach of warranty (U.C.C. §2-719), although it is prima facie unconscionable to limit recovery for personal injury damages (U.C.C. § 2-719(3)). Second, in order to recover for breach of warranty as to accepted goods the buyer must provide the seller with reasonably prompt notice of the claim (§ 2-607(3)). Third, many courts required privity of contract as a condition for a breach of warranty claim.

Thus the courts and the lawmakers (primarily through the American Law Institute) returned to tort law and developed a form of liability without fault in tort against manufacturers and non-manufacturer sellers of "defective" products. The authors of the RESTATEMENT (SECOND) OF TORTS provided for a form of strict liability in the now famous section 402A. Section 402A provided:

> (1) One who sells any product in a defective condition unreasonably dangerous to the user or consumer or to his property is subject to liability for physical harm thereby caused to the ultimate user or consumer, or to his property, if
>
> > (a) the seller is engaged in the business of selling such a product, and
> >
> > (b) it is expected to and does reach the user or consumer without substantial change in the condition in which it is sold.
>
> (2) The rule stated in Subsection (1) applies although
>
> > (a) the seller has exercised all possible care in the preparation and sale of his product, and

(b) the user or consumer has not bought the product from or entered into any contractual relation with the seller.

Warranty law followed strict tort in abolishing priority, at least where personal injuries were involved. *Henningsen v. Bloomfield Motors, Inc.*, 161 A.2d 69 (N.J. 1960).

The development of product liability under § 402A dominated product liability law and tort law during the last 35 years of the Twentieth Century. As the century drew to a close many states, as noted above, had begun passing their own statutes codifying and amending products law. At the same time, the American Law Institute promulgated and adopted the new restatement (third) of Torts: Products Liability. The new Restatement shows a marked tendency to limit strict liability and return products in many significant aspects to a negligence regime. Finally, the victim of a "defective" product may in many states also proceed against the manufacturer on alternative theories of breach of warranty (express or implied) or negligence. Strict liability in tort may be imposed for safety misrepresentations (*see, e.g.*, RESTATEMENT (THIRD) OF TORTS: PRODUCTS LIABILITY, § 9). Other "consumer protection" devices may impose liability upon the manufacturer of an unsafe product.

B. THE NATURE OF MODERN PRODUCTS LIABILITY

CASTRO v. QVC NETWORK, INC.
139 F.3d 114 (2d Cir. 1998)

CALABRESI, CIRCUIT JUDGE:

In this diversity products liability action, plaintiffs-appellants alleged, in separate causes of action for strict liability and for breach of warranty, that defendants-appellees manufactured and sold a defective roasting pan that injured one of the appellants. The United States District Court for the Eastern District of New York (Leonard D. Wexler, Judge) rejected appellants' request to charge the jury separately on each cause of action and, instead, instructed the jury only on the strict liability charge. The jury found for appellees and the court denied appellants' motion for a new trial. This appeal followed. We hold that, under New York law, the jury should have been instructed separately on each charge, and, accordingly, reverse and remand for a new trial on the breach of warranty claim.

In early November 1993, appellee QVC Network, Inc. ("QVC"), operator of a cable television home-shopping channel, advertised, as part of a one-day Thanksgiving promotion, the "T-Fal Jumbo Resistal Roaster." The roaster, manufactured by U.S.A. T-Fal Corp. ("T-Fal"), was described as suitable for, among other things, cooking a twenty-five pound turkey.[1] Appellant Loyda

---

[1] At the time that QVC and T-Fal agreed to conduct the Thanksgiving promotion, T-Fal did not have in its product line a pan large enough to roast a turkey. T-Fal therefore asked its parent company, located in France, to provide a suitable roasting pan as soon as possible. The parent provided a pan (designed originally without handles and for other purposes). To this pan two small handles were added so that it could be used to roast a turkey. T-Fal shipped the pan to QVC in time for the early November campaign.

Castro bought the roasting pan by mail and used it to prepare a twenty-pound turkey on Thanksgiving Day, 1993.

Mrs. Castro was injured when she attempted to remove the turkey and roasting pan from the oven. Using insulated mittens, she gripped the pan's handles with the first two fingers on each hand (the maximum grip allowed by the small size of the handles) and took the pan out of the oven. As the turkey tipped toward her, she lost control of the pan, spilling the hot drippings and fat that had accumulated in it during the cooking and basting process. As a result, she suffered second and third degree burns to her foot and ankle, which, over time, have led to scarring, intermittent paresthesia, and ankle swelling.

It is uncontested that in their complaint appellants alleged that the pan was defective and that its defects gave rise to separate causes of action for strict liability and for breach of warranty. Moreover, in the pre-charge conference, appellants' counsel repeatedly requested separate jury charges on strict liability and for breach of warranty. The district court, nevertheless, denied the request for a separate charge on breach of warranty. Judge Wexler stated that "you can't collect twice for the same thing," and deemed the warranty charge unnecessary and "duplicative." The court, therefore, only gave the jury the New York pattern strict products liability charge.

The jury returned a verdict for appellees QVC and T-Fal. Judgment was entered on September 14, 1995. Appellants subsequently moved, pursuant to Federal Rule of Civil Procedure 59, that the jury verdict be set aside and a new trial be ordered for various reasons including that the court had failed to charge the jury on appellants' claim for breach of warranty. By order dated July 10, 1996, the district court denied appellants' Rule 59 motion, reasoning that the breach of warranty and strict products liability claims were "virtually the same." This appeal followed.

We review a district court's denial of a new-trial motion for abuse of discretion. . . . A failure to give a required charge to the jury, if not harmless, constitutes abuse of discretion. . . .

Products liability law has long been bedeviled by the search for an appropriate definition of "defective" product design.[2] Over the years, both in the cases and in the literature, two approaches have come to predominate. The first is the risk/utility theory, which focuses on whether the benefits of a product outweigh the dangers of its design.[3] The second is the consumer expectations

---

[2] See generally W. Page Keeton, The Meaning of Defect in Products Liability Law, 45 Mo. L.Rev. 579 (1980); W. Page Keeton, Product Liability and the Meaning of Defect, 5 St. Mary's L.J. 30 (1973); Guido Calabresi & Jon T. Hirschoff, Toward a Test for Strict Liability in Torts, 81 Yale L.J. 1055 (1972).

[3] According to the New York Court of Appeals, the risk/utility calculus, which requires "a weighing of the product's benefits against its risks," Denny v. Ford Motor Co., 87 N.Y.2d 248, 257, 639 N.Y.S.2d 250, 662 N.E.2d 730, 735 (1995), is " 'functionally synonymous' " with traditional negligence analysis, id. at 258, 639 N.Y.S.2d 250, 662 N.E.2d 730. Despite the fact that there are some significant differences, the risk/utility calculus is in many ways similar to the Learned Hand negligence test. See Liriano v. Hobart Corp., 132 F.3d 124, 131 n. 12 (2d Cir.1998) (explaining that the most important difference between the two tests is that traditional negligence strikes its cost/benefit balance on the basis of what is known or ought to be known at the time the defendant acted, while the risk/utility test takes into account all relevant information that has become available subsequent to the defendant's actions).

theory, which focuses on what a buyer/user of a product would properly expect that the product would be suited for.[4] Not all states accept both of these approaches. Some define design defect only according to the risk/utility approach. . . . Others define design defect solely in terms of the consumer expectations theory. . . .[5]

One of the first states to accept both approaches was California, which in *Barker v. Lull Engineering Co.*, 20 Cal.3d 413, 143 Cal.Rptr. 225, 573 P.2d 443 (1978), held that "a product may be found defective in design, so as to subject a manufacturer to strict liability for resulting injuries, under either of two alternative tests"—consumer expectations and risk/utility. *Id.* at 430–32, 143 Cal.Rptr. at 237, 573 P.2d at 455.[6] Several states have followed suit and have adopted both theories. . . .

Prior to the recent case of *Denny v. Ford Motor Co.*, 87 N.Y.2d 248, 639 N.Y.S.2d 250, 662 N.E.2d 730 (1995), it was not clear whether New York recognized both tests. In *Denny*, the plaintiff was injured when her Ford Bronco II sports utility vehicle rolled over when she slammed on the brakes to avoid hitting a deer in the vehicle's path. . . . The plaintiff asserted claims for strict products liability and for breach of implied warranty, and the district judge— over the objection of defendant Ford—submitted both causes of action to the jury. . . . The jury ruled in favor of Ford on the strict liability claim, but found for the plaintiff on the implied warranty claim. . . . On appeal, Ford argued that the jury's verdicts on the strict products liability claim and the breach of warranty claim were inconsistent because the causes of action were identical. . . .

This court certified the *Denny* case to the New York Court of Appeals to answer the following questions: (1) "whether, under New York law, the strict products liability and implied warranty claims are identical"; and (2) "whether, if the claims are different, the strict products liability claim is

---

[4] The New York Court of Appeals explains that "the UCC's concept of a 'defective' product requires an inquiry only into whether the product in question was 'fit for the ordinary purposes for which such goods are used.'" *Denny*, 87 N.Y.2d at 258, 639 N.Y.S.2d 250, 662 N.E.2d at 736 (quoting U.C.C. § 2-314(2)(c)). Thus, the breach of warranty cause of action "is one involving true 'strict' liability, since recovery may be had upon a showing that the product was not minimally safe for its expected purpose." *Id.* at 259, 639 N.Y.S.2d 250, 662 N.E.2d 730. Some scholars have characterized this inquiry as centering on whether the manufacturer or the user is in a better position to decide about safety. See Calabresi & Hirschoff, supra note 2, at 1060.

[5] Still others apply a "modified consumer expectations test" that incorporates risk/utility factors into the consumer expectations analysis. See, e.g., Potter v. Chicago Pneumatic Tool Co., 241 Conn. 199, 694 A.2d 1319, 1333 (1997); Seattle-First Nat'l Bank v. Tabert, 86 Wash.2d 145, 542 P.2d 774, 779 (1975).

[6] The court stated:

First, a product may be found defective in design if the plaintiff establishes that the product failed to perform as safely as an ordinary customer would expect when used in an intended or reasonably foreseeable manner. Second, a product may alternatively be found defective in design if the plaintiff demonstrates that the product's design proximately caused his injury and the defendant fails to establish, in light of the relevant factors, that, on balance, the benefits of the challenged design outweigh the risk of danger inherent in such design.

Barker, 143 Cal.Rptr. 225, 573 P.2d at 455–56. Placement of the burden of proving the product's risks and utility on the manufacturer is not, however, a necessary part of the risk/utility test. *See, e.g.*, Dart v. Wiebe Mfg., Inc., 147 Ariz. 242, 709 P.2d 876, 879 (1985).

broader than the implied warranty claim and encompasses the latter." *Id.* at 111–12.

In response to the certified questions, the Court of Appeals held that in a products liability case a cause of action for strict liability is not identical to a claim for breach of warranty. . . .[7]

Moreover, the court held that a strict liability claim is not per se broader than a breach of warranty claim such that the former encompasses the latter. . . . Thus, while claims of strict products liability and breach of warranty are often used interchangeably, under New York law the two causes of action are definitively different. The imposition of strict liability for an alleged design "defect" is determined by a risk-utility standard . . . . The notion of "defect" in a U.C.C.-based breach of warranty claim focuses, instead, on consumer expectations.

Since *Denny*, then, it has been settled that the risk/utility and consumer expectations theories of design defect can, in New York, be the bases of distinct causes of action: one for strict products liability and one for breach of warranty. This fact, however, does not settle the question of when a jury must be charged separately on each cause of action and when, instead, the two causes are, on the facts of the specific case, sufficiently similar to each other so that one charge to the jury is enough.

While eminent jurists have at times been troubled by this issue,[8] the New York Court of Appeals in *Denny* was quite clear on when the two causes of action might meld and when, instead, they are to be treated as separate. It did this by adding its own twist to the distinction—namely, what can aptly be called the "dual purpose" requirement. . . . Thus in Denny, the Court of Appeals pointed out that the fact that a product's overall benefits might outweigh its overall risks does not preclude the possibility that consumers may

---

[7] Judge Titone, writing for the majority, noted that "[t]he continued vitality of the warranty approach is evidenced by its retention and expansion in New York's versions of the Uniform Commercial Code (U.C.C. 2-314[2][c]; 2-318)." *Denny*, 87 N.Y.2d at 256, 639 N.Y.S.2d 250, 662 N.E.2d at 734.

New York's Commercial Code § 2-314 ("Implied Warranty: Merchantability; Usage of Trade") states that "a warranty that the goods shall be merchantable is implied in a contract for their sale if the seller is a merchant with respect to goods of that kind. . . . Goods to be merchantable must be . . . fit for the ordinary purposes for which such goods are used. . . ." N.Y. U.C.C. § 2-314 (McKinney 1993). Section 318 ("Third Party Beneficiaries of Warranties Express or Implied") provides that "[a] seller's warranty whether express or implied extends to any natural person if it is reasonable to expect that such person may use, consume or be affected by the goods and who is injured in person by breach of the warranty." *Id.* § 2-318.

[8] Thus Justice Traynor in the early and seminal California strict products liability case, Greenman v. Yuba Power Products, 59 Cal.2d 57, 27 Cal.Rptr. 697, 377 P.2d 897 (1963), did not make a clear distinction between them. See id. at 64, 27 Cal.Rptr. at 701, 377 P.2d at 901 ("[I]t should not be controlling [for purposes of establishing a manufacturer's liability] whether plaintiff selected the [product] because of the statements in the brochure, or because of the [product's] own appearance of excellence that belied the defect lurking beneath the surface, or because he merely assumed that it would safely do the jobs it was built to do."). And likewise, Judge Eschbach in Sills v. Massey-Ferguson, Inc., 296 F.Supp. 776 (N.D.Ind.1969), stated that although they represented different causes of action, in the case before him, he could not distinguish between them, and then added that "[w]hile this court is unwilling to hold that there is never a significant difference between the two theories, it is plain that the outcome of the vast majority of cases is not affected by this fine legal distinction." *Id.* at 779.

have been misled into using the product in a context in which it was dangerously unsafe. And this, the New York court emphasized, could be so even though the benefits in other uses might make the product sufficiently reasonable so that it passed the risk/utility test. . . .

In *Denny*, the Ford Bronco II was not designed as a conventional passenger automobile. Instead, it was designed as an off-road, dual purpose vehicle.[9] But in its marketing of the Bronco II, Ford stressed its suitability for commuting and for suburban and city driving. . . . Under the circumstances, the Court of Appeals explained that a rational factfinder could conclude that the Bronco's utility as an off-road vehicle outweighed the risk of injury resulting from roll-over accidents (thus passing the risk/utility test), but at the same time find that the vehicle was not safe for the "ordinary purpose" of daily driving for which it was also marketed and sold (thus flunking the consumer expectations test). . . .

That is precisely the situation before us. The jury had before it evidence that the product was designed, marketed, and sold as a multiple-use product. The pan was originally manufactured and sold in France as an all-purpose cooking dish without handles. And at trial, the jury saw a videotape of a QVC representative demonstrating to the television audience that the pan, in addition to serving as a suitable roaster for a twenty-five pound turkey, could also be used to cook casseroles, cutlets, cookies, and other low-volume foods.[10] The court charged the jury that "[a] product is defective if it is not reasonably safe[,] [t]hat is, if the product is so likely to be harmful to persons that a reasonable person who had actual knowledge of its potential for producing injury would conclude that it should not have been marketed in that condition." And, so instructed, the jury presumably found that the pan, because it had many advantages in a variety of uses, did not fail the risk/utility test.

But it was also the case that the pan was advertised as suitable for a particular use—cooking a twenty-five pound turkey. Indeed, T-Fal added handles to the pan in order to fill QVC's request for a roasting pan that it could use in its Thanksgiving promotion. The product was, therefore, sold as appropriately used for roasting a twenty-five pound turkey. And it was in that use that allegedly the product failed and injured the appellant.

In such circumstances, New York law is clear that a general charge on strict products liability based on the risk/utility approach does not suffice. The jury could have found that the roasting pan's overall utility for cooking low-volume foods outweighed the risk of injury when cooking heavier foods, but that the product was nonetheless unsafe for the purpose for which it was marketed

---

[9] Indeed, as Ford argued, the design features that appellant complained of—high center of gravity, narrow track width, short wheel base, and a specially tailored suspension system—were important to preserve the vehicle's utility for off-road use. . . . But, it was these same design features that made the vehicle susceptible to rollover accidents during evasive maneuvers on paved roads. . . .

[10] Appellants also introduced into evidence a "sell sheet" prepared by T-Fal, which described for the QVC salespersons the uses and characteristics of the product, including not only cooking a twenty-five pound turkey, but also an extensive list of several low-volume foods, such as cake, lasagna, and stuffed potatoes. While the "sell-sheet" was an internal document, and therefore, could not have influenced consumer expectations, it does shed light on the meaning of the videotaped commercial.

and sold—roasting a twenty-five pound turkey—and, as such, was defective under the consumer expectations test. That being so, the appellants were entitled to a separate breach of warranty charge.[11]

In light of the evidence presented by appellants of the multi-purpose nature of the product at issue, the district court, applying New York law, should have granted appellants' request for a separate jury charge on the breach of warranty claim in addition to the charge on the strict liability claim. Accordingly, we reverse the order of the district court denying the motion for a new trial, and remand the case for a new trial on the breach of warranty claim, consistent with this opinion.

NOTES

1. *Consumer Expectations vs. Risk-Utility*. *Castro* reflects several of the major themes of product liability. First it shows that it is possible to base liability in either warranty (contract) or tort. Second, it points out that the substantive standard for liability whether based in contract or tort may be defined in terms of a risk/utility test (akin to the Learned Hand formula for negligence): is the product more dangerous than it is useful? Or a consumer expectation test: is the product more dangerous than an ordinary consumer would expect? The consumer expectation test bears a marked similarity to the definition of merchantability under UCC section 2-314: is the product fit for the ordinary purposes for which it is used? The consumer expectation test is based upon language in the comments to Restatement (Second) section 402A.

In *Castro*, the consumer expectation test is used to provide the basis for liability under the warranty claim; however, many courts have used the consumer expectation test to define the basis for liability in tort. That is, the consumer expectation test may determine whether a product is defective.

The RESTATEMENT (THIRD) essentially abandons the consumer expectation test in some kinds of cases (design and warning cases) as the substantive basis for liability. But the comments provide, in relevant part: "although consumer expectations do not constitute an independent standard for judging the defectiveness of product designs, they may substantially influence or even be determinative on risk-utility balancing in judging whether the omission of the proposed alternative design renders the product not reasonably safe." *Id.*, section 2, *comment* g. Additionally, the consumer expectation test remains viable in cases involving food (see RESTATEMENT (THIRD) OF TORTS: PRODUCTS LIABILITY, § 7).

---

[11] Appellees argue that "[t]he roaster had only a single purpose which was to be a vessel for cooking." But that misses the point of the dual purpose test. Indeed, the same argument could have been made in the *Denny* case: that the Ford Bronco II had a single purpose, namely driving. What characterizes both of these cases, however, is that there was evidence before the jury of the "dual purposes" to which the products could be put. As the Court of Appeals stated in *Denny*, it is "the nature of the proof and the way in which the fact issues [are] litigated [that] demonstrate[] how the two causes of action can diverge." *Denny*, 87 N.Y.2d at 262, 639 N.Y.S.2d 250, 662 N.E.2d at 738. In the instant case, given the evidence before the jury of the pan's dual purposes, the failure to charge the jury on breach of warranty could not be harmless error.

Moreover, while the RESTATEMENT (THIRD) recognizes that a product claim may still be brought under the implied warranty of merchantability, UCC § 2-314, consistent with the decision in *Castro*, the comments go on to say:

> It is recognized that some courts have adopted a consumer expectations definition for design and failure-to-warn defects in implied warranty cases involving harm to persons or property. This Restatement contemplates that a well-coordinated body of law governing liability for harm to persons or property arising out of the sale of defective products requires a consistent definition of defect, and that the definition properly should come from tort law, whether the claim carries a tort label or one of implied warranty of merchantability.

RESTATEMENT (THIRD) OF TORTS: PRODUCTS LIABILITY, § 2, *comment* n. But, critically, U.C.C. Article 2 has been legislatively adopted in all states, except Louisiana. In any state except Louisiana, do you see why the comment's proposal for a consistent definition of defect might result in a potential implied repeal of Article 2?

In *Denny*, the New York Court of Appeals rejected the defendant's argument that the warranty claim had been subsumed in the tort strict product liability claim. The court said, in part: "The continued vitality of the warranty approach is evidenced by its retention and expansion in New York's version of the Uniform Commercial Code (UCC 2-314[2] [c]; 2-318). The existence of this statutory authority belies any argument that the breach of implied warranty remedy is a dead letter. . . ."

2. *No "Absolute" Liability*. As *Castro* impliedly recognizes, the manufacturer's liability is not "absolute." Nevertheless, the product must be "defective," and the law has struggled with defining the liability standard which requires a lesser showing of fault than negligence, but does not impose "absolute" liability. A significant part of this debate has revolved around whether "defective" or "unreasonably dangerous" should be based upon the consumer expectation test, a risk-utility test, or some combination of the two.

The consumer expectation test in its purest form would impose liability whenever a product was more dangerous than an ordinary consumer would expect. Some of the problems with that test arise out of the fact that it may ask either too much or too little of a manufacturer. For instance, if a consumer expected a product that was not very safe a consumer expectation test might result in no liability even though the manufacturer could easily and cheaply have made the product safer. Alternatively, if a consumer expected a product to be extraordinarily safe, she might expect a perfect product even though it was technologically or economically impossible or impractical for the manufacturer to make such a safe product. Relatedly, what if a consumer did not have the knowledge or experience to have any reasonable or rational expectation about a product's safety? Justice White's opinion for the Tennessee Supreme Court in *Ray v. BIC* Corp., 925 S.W.2d 527 (Tenn. 1996), examines some of these potential problems. *See also, Dart v. Wiebe Manufacturing, Inc.*, 147 Ariz. 242, 709 P.2d 876 (1985).

How does one establish consumer expectations? By lay testimony? By expert testimony? If by expert testimony, what would be the basis for the expert's opinion?

Alternatively, the risk-utility test balances risk and utility in a manner that is distinctly reminiscent of the Learned Hand test for negligence. Why was that perceived as a problem? Because strict product liability, as originally conceived, was strict liability. It was imposed even though the defendant had exercised reasonable care. Defining defect in terms of negligence would have transformed strict products liability into negligence. Thus courts and scholars have strived to explain and understand how a risk—utility test in a products liability case might be different from a risk-utility test in a negligence case.

3. *Negligence and Strict Products Liability Distinguished*. In *Phillips v. Kimwood Mach. Co.,* 269 Or. 485, 525 P.2d 1033 (1974), the court made this distinction between strict and negligence theories in products cases:

> The problem with strict liability of products has been one of limitation. No one wants absolute liability where all the article has to do is to cause injury. To impose liability there has to be something about the article which makes it dangerously defective without regard to whether the manufacturer was or was not at fault for such condition. A test for unreasonable danger is therefore vital. A dangerously defective article would be one which a reasonable person would not put into the stream of commerce if he had knowledge of its harmful character. The test, therefore, is whether the seller would be negligent if he sold the article knowing of the risk involved. Strict liability imposes what amounts to constructive knowledge of the condition of the product.
>
> . . . In the case of a product which is claimed to be dangerously defective because of misdesign, the process is not so easy as in the case of mismanufacture. All the products made to that design are the same. The question of whether the design is unreasonably dangerous can be determined only by taking into consideration the surrounding circumstances and knowledge at the time the article was sold, and determining therefrom whether a reasonably prudent manufacturer would have so designed and sold the article in question had he known of the risk involved which injured plaintiff.
>
> . . . To some it may seem that absolute liability has been imposed upon the manufacturer since it might be argued that no manufacturer could reasonably put into the stream of commerce an article which he realized might result in injury to a user. This is not the case, however. The manner of injury may be so fortuitous and the chances of injury occurring so remote that it is reasonable to sell the product despite the danger. In design cases the utility of the article may be so great, and the change of design necessary to alleviate the danger in question may so impair such utility, that it is reasonable to market the product as it is, even though the possibility of injury exists and was realized at the time of the sale. Again, the cost of the change necessary to alleviate the danger in design may be so great that the article would be priced out of the market and no one would buy it even though it was of high utility. Such an article is not dangerously defective despite its having inflicted injury.
>
> . . . It is apparent that the language being used in the discussion of the above problems is largely that which is also used in negligence

cases, i.e., "unreasonably dangerous," "have reasonably anticipated," "reasonably prudent manufacturer," etc. It is necessary to remember that whether the doctrine of negligence, ultrahazardousness, or strict liability is being used to impose liability, the same process is going on in each instance, i.e., weighing the utility of the article against the risk of its use. Therefore, the same language and concepts of reasonableness are used by courts for the determination of unreasonable danger in products liability cases.

4. *Strict Liability and Production Defects.* Would the presumed-seller-knowledge standard always result in liability in the case of latent manufacturing or production flaws that cause injury? If so, is the seller's liability "strict" in the sense of a "risk/utility" strict liability formula, or is the seller's liability more onerous?

5. *The Maturation of Products Liability Law.* As courts gained more experience in products liability cases in the wake of RESTATEMENT (SECOND) OF TORTS § 402A, they began to develop different categories of defects or claims. The following case identifies some of those claims.

HALPHEN v. JOHNS-MANVILLE SALES CORPORATION
484 So. 2d 110 (La. 1986)

DENNIS, JUSTICE.

A widow sued an asbestos products manufacturer in a United States District Court for the wrongful death of her husband caused by his exposure to asbestos.[1] She invoked Louisiana's strict products liability tort law under the court's diversity jurisdiction. Before trial the District Court excluded all evidence of whether the manufacturer knew or could have known of the dangers of asbestos on the grounds that such evidence is irrelevant to whether the product is unreasonably dangerous. After a trial, a jury found that the manufacturer's asbestos products were unreasonably dangerous and had been a proximate cause of the deceased's death. The District Court entered judgment awarding damages to the widow for her husband's illness and wrongful death.

The manufacturer appealed to the United States Court of Appeals. A divided three judge panel of that court affirmed. *Halphen v. Johns-Manville Sales Corp.*, 737 F.2d 462 (5th Cir.1984). Acting en banc, however, the Court of Appeals recalled its decision and certified to us the following question:

> In a strict products liability case, may a manufacturer be held liable for injuries caused by an unreasonably dangerous product if the manufacturer establishes that it did not know and reasonably could not have

---

[1] See Halphen v. Johns-Manville Sales Corp., 755 F.2d 393 (5th Cir.1985): "This is a strict products liability action for damages from wrongful death between Emma Jean Halphen, Plaintiff, and Johns-Manville Sales Corporation, Defendant, which was tried in the United States District Court for the Western District of Louisiana in Lake Charles, in January, 1982.

"Plaintiff's husband, Samuel Halphen, died during the pendency of the lawsuit from a malignant pleural mesothelioma, a cancer of the lining of the lung. Plaintiff alleged that her husband had been exposed to asbestos-containing products sold by Johns-Manville, while working at a shipyard in Orange, Texas in 1945, and at various times during his career as a serviceman in the Air Force." Id. at 393–4.

known of the inherent danger posed by its product? *Halphen v. Johns-Manville Sales Corp.*, 752 F.2d 124, 755 F.2d at 393 (5th Cir.1985) (en banc).

Having granted certification, we respond by (1) stating the legal precepts which govern the issues raised by the certified question, (2) answering the question specifically, and (3) elaborating the reasons for the precepts and answers.

There is general agreement upon the most basic principles of strict tort products liability. In order to recover from a manufacturer, the plaintiff must prove that the harm resulted from the condition of the product, that the condition made the product unreasonably dangerous to normal use, and that the condition existed at the time the product left the manufacturer's control. The plaintiff need not prove negligence by the maker in its manufacture or processing, since the manufacturer may be liable even though it exercised all possible care in the preparation and sale of its product. . . .

As strict products liability in tort was originally conceived, the manufacturer's ability to know of the danger of its product at the time of sale was immaterial. Under pure strict liability theory, the product is on trial, not the knowledge or conduct of the manufacturer. Subsequently, additional products liability theories developed which permit the plaintiff to recover when the manufacturer fails to give adequate warning or adopt an alternate design to make the product safer. Under these later theories, the knowledge available to the manufacturer when it designs, manufactures, and markets the product may be material. Accordingly, whether the knowledge of the danger in a product is material, relevant, or admissible depends on the particular theory of recovery under which the plaintiff tries his case.

An essential element of a plaintiff's case under each strict products liability theory of recovery is proof that the defendant's product was unreasonably dangerous to normal use. The method of proof of this element varies under each theory, however, and this is why the knowledge available to the manufacturer is material only with regard to certain theories. Because there is disagreement among jurisdictions as to the nature, the classification, and even the existence of some grounds of recovery, we will set forth the elements of each strict liability theory recognized by this court in order to explain whether knowledge available to the manufacturer is material under each theory.

In describing the theories of recovery, we use the classifications of unreasonably dangerous products recognized by most courts. Additionally, we recognize products which are "unreasonably dangerous per se" as a separate class of defective products. For products in this category liability may be imposed solely on the basis of the intrinsic characteristics of the product irrespective of the manufacturer's intent, knowledge or conduct. This category should be acknowledged as giving rise to the purest form of strict liability and clearly distinguished from other theories in which the manufacturer's knowledge or conduct is an issue.

A product is unreasonably dangerous per se if a reasonable person would conclude that the danger-in-fact of the product, whether foreseeable or not, outweighs the utility of the product.[2] . . . This theory considers the product's danger-in-fact, not whether the manufacturer perceived or could have perceived the danger, because the theory's purpose is to evaluate the product itself, not the manufacturer's conduct. Likewise, the benefits are those actually found to flow from the use of the product, rather than as perceived at the time the product was designed and marketed. The fact that a risk or hazard related to the use of a product was not discoverable under existing technology or that the benefits appeared greater than they actually were are both irrelevant. . . . Under this theory, the plaintiff is not entitled to impugn the conduct of the manufacturer for its failure to adopt an alternative design or affix a warning or instruction to the product. A warning or other feature actually incorporated in the product when it leaves the manufacturer's control, however, may reduce the danger-in-fact. If a plaintiff proves that the product is unreasonably dangerous per se, it is not material that the case could have been tried as a design defect case or other type defect case.

A product is unreasonably dangerous in construction or composition if at the time it leaves the control of its manufacturer it contains an unintended abnormality or condition which makes the product more dangerous than it was designed to be. . . . A manufacturer or supplier who sells a product with a construction or composition flaw is subject to liability without proof that there was any negligence on its part in creating or failing to discover the flaw. Evidence of what knowledge was available to the manufacturer has no relevance in such cases because the product, by definition, failed to conform to the manufacturer's own standards. . . .

Although a product is not unreasonably dangerous per se or flawed by a construction defect, it may still be an unreasonably dangerous product if the manufacturer fails to adequately warn about a danger related to the way the product is designed. A manufacturer is required to provide an adequate warning of any danger inherent in the normal use of its product which is not within the knowledge of or obvious to the ordinary user. . . . In performing this duty a manufacturer is held to the knowledge and skill of an expert. It must keep abreast of scientific knowledge, discoveries, and advances and is presumed to know what is imparted thereby. . . . A manufacturer also has a duty to test and inspect its product, and the extent of research and experiment must be commensurate with the dangers involved. . . . Under the failure to warn theory evidence as to the knowledge and skill of an expert may be admissible in determining whether the manufacturer breached its duty.

A product may be unreasonably dangerous because of its design for any one of three reasons: (1) A reasonable person would conclude that the danger-in-fact, whether foreseeable or not, outweighs the utility of the product. This is the same danger-utility test applied in determining whether a product is unreasonably dangerous per se. . . . This first reason for concluding that a design is defective is governed by the same criteria for deciding whether a product is unreasonably dangerous per se. The overlap in categories makes

---

[2] This test is known as the risk-utility or danger-utility test. Other tests may have their own merits in different contexts . . . . We are convinced, however, that the risk utility test is best for determining whether a product is unreasonably dangerous per se.

it unnecessary to decide whether a product's defect is one of design or of another kind if the product is proven to be unreasonably dangerous per se. (2) Although balancing under the risk-utility test leads to the conclusion that the product is not unreasonably dangerous per se, alternative products were available to serve the same needs or desires with less risk of harm; or, (3) Although the utility of the product outweighs its danger-in-fact, there was a feasible way to design the product with less harmful consequences. . . . In regard to the failure to use alternative products or designs, as in the duty to warn, the standard of knowledge, skill and care is that of an expert, including the duty to test, inspect, research and experiment commensurate with the danger. . . . Accordingly, evidence as to whether the manufacturer, held to the standard and skill of an expert, could know of and feasibly avoid the danger is admissible under a theory of recovery based on alleged alternative designs or alternative products. Such evidence is not admissible, however, in a suit based on the first design defect theory, which is governed by the same criteria as proof that a product is unreasonably dangerous per se.

The plaintiff may elect to try his case upon any or all of the theories of recovery. If he decides to pursue more than one, he is entitled to an instruction that evidence which is admissible exclusively under one theory may be considered only for that purpose.

In a strict products liability case, if the plaintiff proves that the product was unreasonably dangerous per se (whether because of defective design or another kind of defect) or unreasonably dangerous in construction or composition, a manufacturer may be held liable for injuries caused by an unreasonably dangerous product, although the manufacturer did not know and reasonably could not have known of the danger. . . .

Strict products liability and accident law in general pursue four primary goals: (1) reduction of the total cost of accidents by deterring activity causing accidents, (2) reduction of the societal cost of accidents by spreading the loss among large numbers, (3) reducing the cost of administering accident cases, and (4) achieving these goals by methods consistent with justice. Since these goals are not fully consistent with one another, the overall aim is to strive for the best combination of cost reduction in all these categories in a just way. . . . To further these goals within the framework of our civil code, we have concluded that as between an innocent consumer injured by a product which is unreasonably dangerous per se, i.e., too dangerous to be placed on the market, and the manufacturer who puts the product into commerce without being aware or able to know of its danger, the manufacturer must bear the cost of the damage caused by its product. On the other hand, if the consumer fails to prove that the product is unreasonably dangerous per se and seeks to prove his case by impugning the manufacturer's conduct, e.g., by contending that the manufacturer failed to warn or to adopt feasible alternative designs, in fairness the manufacturer should be permitted to introduce evidence and present argument as to the standard of knowledge and conduct by which its conduct is to be judged.

The scientific inability to avoid occasional flaws in products due to miscarriages in the construction process has never altered the fact that an impure or flawed product is defective if the product proves to be more dangerous than it was intended to be. . . . Similarly, when a plaintiff proves that a product is bad and defective because its utility is outweighed by its danger-in-fact, i.e., unreasonably dangerous per se, and the plaintiff proves this theory of recovery without impugning the conduct of the manufacturer, the producer should be held strictly liable regardless of scientific inability to know or to avoid the danger.

On balance, a rule of law requiring the manufacturer to assume the cost of accidents caused by products which are unreasonably dangerous per se, regardless of whether the danger was foreseeable, will provide an effective incentive to eliminate all possible dangers before putting products on the market. . . . Moreover, any discouragement to produce new products or to discover safety improvements will be mitigated by the manufacturer's ability to defend failure to warn cases, alternative design cases and alternative product cases on the basis of scientific unknowability and inability. We conclude that recognizing an unreasonably dangerous per se category as a form of "pure" strict liability along with construction or manufacturing defects will provide even greater incentives to produce safe products.

Reducing the societal cost of accidents by spreading the loss among large groups would not be promoted by leaving part of the cost of accidents, diseases and deaths caused by unreasonably dangerous products on consumers. Insurance specifically designed to cover such losses would be unavailable to consumers as a practical matter. Of course, some losses from scientifically unknowable dangers may prove to be uninsurable for producers also. Manufacturers as a class, however, are still in a better position than consumers to analyze and take action to avoid the risk, to negotiate for broader insurance coverage, and to pass losses on in the form of price increases. Furthermore, the rule we have adopted does not prevent the manufacturer from introducing evidence of scientific knowledge, or the lack thereof, in cases where such knowledge is material, such as in duty-to-warn cases. If the cost of accidents caused by products which are unreasonably dangerous per se and are defective because of construction flaws is placed on manufacturers, a much greater portion of the cost of such accidents may be spread among consumers and manufacturers rather than placed on individual accident victims.

The costs of administering the unreasonably dangerous per se category of products liability cases will be reduced by eliminating litigation over the date when a product's danger became scientifically knowable. In unreasonably dangerous per se cases, as in construction defect cases now, the parties should not be forced to produce experts in the history of science and technology to speculate, and possibly confuse jurors, as to what knowledge was available and what improvements were feasible in a given year. . . .

Further, a sense of justice also requires that a manufacturer not be permitted to subsidize its production of a product which is unreasonably dangerous per se at the expense of innocent accident victims. . . . Moreover, great injustice will result if a manufacturer who knew that a product was unreasonably dangerous per se before it was marketed escapes liability because the plaintiff cannot carry the difficult burden of proving when scientific knowledge was available to the manufacturer. . . . Finally, equality in treatment of like cases which is at the heart of our received notions of justice demands that the manufacturer of a product which is unreasonably dangerous per se should not be allowed a defense which is unavailable to the maker of a product that happens to have a construction flaw . . . . [The manufacturer of a product with a construction flaw] . . . is strictly liable in tort for injuries caused by the product . . . even though the defect . . . was not discoverable prior to the time of the injury. Justice and consistency dictate that the manufacturer of a product that is unreasonably dangerous per se be treated in the same manner. . . .

NOTES

1. *Types of Products Claims*. *Halphen* sets forth the predominant main stream theories of product liability or types of defects: construction or composition (mismanufacture), design, and warning. It adds a controversial fourth theory of recovery, unreasonably dangerous per se. This theory is, in essence, a "bad" product theory. Other claims frequently filed against product sellers are misrepresentation claims: fraud, negligent representation, innocent misrepresentation, and failure to disclose risks.

The *Halphen* court says a plaintiff may prove a product is unreasonably dangerous per se "whether because of defective design or another kind of defect." What kinds of defect other than design are includable within the unreasonably dangerous per se category?

How is the unreasonably dangerous per se theory different from the other design claims articulated in *Halphen*? In the construction or composition claim, the plaintiff usually attacks a single product—the particular one which injured her and which allegedly deviates from all other products in the same product line made by that manufacturer, i.e., the mismanufactured product. Do you see why a manufacturer would be more unsettled by a design or warning than a mismanufacture claim? And, do you see why the unreasonably dangerous per se category would be even more unsettling? Indeed, the portion of *Halphen* holding that a product could be unreasonably dangerous per se was quickly overruled. La. R.S. 9:2800.52-.59. We will return to the issue of the bad product when we more generally discuss design claims below.

PROBLEM

An 11-year-old boy purchased a slingshot, manufactured by defendant and sold at retail for $1. The slingshot was packaged so as to appeal to children. The boy shot a pebble from the slingshot at a tree, and the pebble ricocheted, hitting plaintiff, a 12-year-old neighbor, in the eye and blinding that eye.

Can plaintiff recover from the manufacturer in products liability?

C. TYPES AND DEFINITIONS OF DEFECT

[1] Mismanufacture

FITZGERALD MARINE SALES v. LeUNES
659 S.W.2d 917 (Tex. App. 1983)

HUGHES, JUSTICE.

. . . On the date of the accident, John LeUnes and his friend, Ted Russell, were fishing on Lake Whitney in Tarrant County, Texas. They were operating an Ebbtide bass boat which LeUnes had purchased from Fitzgerald Marine Sales four days earlier. (The steering wheel on the boat was manufactured by Attwood Corporation.) They had been on the lake for over five hours when the accident occurred.

LeUnes was driving the boat as he and Russell left one of the fishing areas. When they left the channel, LeUnes pushed the throttle all the way forward in order to pick up speed. Shortly after the boat had planed out, and while the boat was traveling at or near maximum speed of 35 mph, the engine revved up and the boat took a sudden, violent turn to the right. LeUnes and Russell were both thrown out of the boat.

As LeUnes was thrown from the boat, the upper portion of the steering wheel on which he was holding broke. With the wheel still in his hand, he was thrown about 15 to 20 yards from the boat. When Russell was thrown from the boat, he was holding the aluminum rail on the port side of the boat which evidently was bent by the stress put upon it. The boat circled several times and both men were hit by it. LeUnes suffered the more serious injuries when he was hit by the propeller of the boat.

. . . To recover for a manufacturing defect under strict liability, the plaintiff must show a manufacturing flaw which renders the product unreasonably dangerous; that the defect existed at the time the product left the seller, and that the defect was the producing cause of the plaintiff's injuries. Restatement (Second) of Torts, § 402A (1965). Expert testimony as well as circumstantial evidence surrounding the accident can be used to prove a manufacturing defect.

Raymond Schitz, a metallurgist, testified concerning his findings from experiments on the steering wheel. He found that the plastic rim on the steering wheel contained voids that arose during the manufacturing process and that these voids reduced the strength of the plastic. He also testified that the plastic did not have the "strength and ability to stretch that he thought it should have." Furthermore, the fact that the top portion of the steering wheel broke in LeUnes' hands while he was holding onto it is circumstantial evidence of a manufacturing flaw. The jury had sufficient evidence to support a finding of a defect or flaw in the steering wheel. A defect in the product, though, is not enough to hold a manufacturer liable under strict liability. The plaintiff must also show the flaw renders the product unreasonably dangerous.

The jury was instructed that an unreasonably dangerous product is one that is dangerous to an extent beyond that which would be contemplated by the ordinary user of the product, with the ordinary knowledge common to the community of such users as to the product's characteristics.

The purpose of the steering wheel on a motorboat is to steer the boat. LeUnes is asking that the defendants be held liable because the steering wheel on his boat was not suitable as a restraining device. There was some evidence at trial that the steering wheel could not be used effectively as a restraint. This is shown by the fact that when LeUnes used the steering wheel as a restraint, it broke in his hand and he was thrown into the water. There is no evidence, however, that the steering wheel was unreasonably dangerous when used for the purpose it was intended; steering the boat. LeUnes would have us hold defendants liable for a damaging event that would not likely result from the defect that existed here, namely: voids in the plastic.

Since there was no evidence at all that the steering wheel was unreasonably dangerous when used as a steering wheel, the product was not defective as a matter of law.

NOTES

1. *The Nature of the Mismanufacture Claim.* Note how the plaintiff's claim is not that the entire product line was defective but only that there was a problem with his particular boat. He is claiming there was something about his boat which was different and more dangerous than it was intended to be. The RESTATEMENT (THIRD) OF TORTS: PRODUCTS LIABILITY § 2(a) states that a product is defective if it:

> contains a manufacturing defect when the product departs from its intended design even though all possible care was exercised in the preparation and marketing of the product.

2. *Manufacturing Versus Design Defect.* One court has described the manufacturing-design defect distinction as follows:

> A defect in manufacture is, of course, quite different from a defect in design. The latter focuses upon whether the product was designed to perform as safely as an ordinary consumer would expect or whether the risk of danger inherent in the design outweighed the benefits of the design. The former focuses on whether the particular product involved in the accident was manufactured in conformity with the manufacturer's design.

Dierks v. Mitsubishi Motors Corp., 208 Cal. App. 3d 352, 256 Cal. Rptr. 230 (1989). But, what if many products in the product line somehow deviated from their intended design? In *American Tobacco Co. v. Grinnell*, 951 S.W.2d 420 (Tex. 1997), plaintiffs filed a mismanufacture claim against a tobacco company. Apparently, all the cigarettes manufactured by defendant contained allegedly harmful chemical residues from the tobacco curing process. However, the chemical residues were not provided for in the design specifications for the cigarettes. The defendant argued that since all of its cigarettes contained the chemical residues the claim was really a design claim. The Texas Supreme Court rejected that argument, noting that the residues were not specified in the design.

3. *Manufacturing Versus Design Defect and Difference of Proof.* In *Reed v. Tiffin Motor Homes, Inc.*, 697 F.2d 1192 (4th Cir. 1982), the court observed that:

> In manufacturing defect cases courts have excluded evidence of the state of the art because the plaintiff need only show the product does not conform to the manufacturer's specifications to prove it is defective.
>
> . . . The majority of courts have found in design defect cases, as opposed to manufacturing defect cases, that state of the art and industry standards are relevant to show both the reasonableness of the design, and that the product was dangerous beyond the expectations of the ordinary consumer.

WILLIAMS v. SMART CHEVROLET CO.
292 Ark. 376, 730 S.W.2d 479 (1987)

HOLT, CHIEF JUSTICE.

[Appeal from grant of defendants' motions for directed verdict.]

. . . Looking at the evidence in the light most favorable to Williams, there was testimony by Williams that she purchased her new Chevrolet Camaro Z-28 from Smart [her Chevrolet dealer] on September 12, 1984, and noticed after a few days that the driver's side door was difficult to close and would work loose after being shut and locked. She returned the car to Smart for repairs and told them about the problem with the door. Smart returned the car to her and, according to Williams, told her the car was fixed. The door continued to work loose. On October 4, 1984, Williams was driving about 10 miles per hour down a straight, level, gravel road when her door, which she testified she specifically remembered shutting and locking with the power locks, suddenly came open. Williams said she fell out of the car, injuring herself. The car went into a ditch but was not damaged. Immediately after the accident, Williams noticed that the driver's door latch mechanism had one of the three securing screws hanging partially out. She returned the car to Smart to be fixed. The door, however, continued to work loose, but it never came open again. She sold the car some fourteen months later.

Williams also offered the testimony of her mother, her sister, and a friend that they rode in the car before and after the accident and noticed that the door would work loose.

Mike Keller, assistant technical director of American Interplex Corp., was Williams' expert witness. He testified that he worked on the car for two or three days in July, 1985, and test drove it on all types of roads and was never able to get the door to come all the way open, including when he tried to force it open. He testified he found no defective parts which would cause the door to fail and come open. He explained that the word "defective" excludes parts which had been abraded or otherwise damaged by external factors. Keller stated that the driver's side striker bolt, as compared to the striker bolt on the passenger door, had one or two additional shims and had two separate wear patterns, as opposed to one on the passenger side. Keller said this indicated to him that the latch mechanism had engaged at different places on the striker bolt. In addition, the driver's side door latch was abraded and the jaws of the rotor were flared wider, which he believed was caused by uneven contact of the striker bolt with the rotor jaws. Keller testified that this all resulted in an alignment problem with the door. He explained, however, that his examination of the vehicle did not indicate anything that would have allowed the door to come open and he could not document that it had ever previously been in a condition that would cause that to occur.

. . . The doctrine of strict liability does not change the burden of proof as to the existence of a flaw or defect in a product, but it does do away with the necessity of proving negligence in order to recover for injuries resulting from a defective product. The plaintiff still has the burden of proving that a particular defendant has sold a product which he should not have sold and that it caused his injury. We further explained in *Southern Co. v. Graham,* 271 Ark. 232, 607 S.W.2d 677 (1980), *quoting* Prosser, Torts, § 102, p. 672 (4th Ed. 1971):

> The difficult problems are those of proof by circumstantial evidence. Strictly speaking, since proof of negligence is not in issue, res ipsa loquitur has no application to strict liability; but the inferences which are the core of the doctrine remain, and are not less applicable. The plaintiff is not required to eliminate all other possibilities, and so prove his case beyond a reasonable doubt . . . [I]t is enough that he makes out a preponderance of probability. . . .
>
> [I]n the absence of direct proof of a specific defect, it is sufficient if a plaintiff negates other possible causes of failure of the product, not attributable to the defendant, and thus raises a reasonable inference that the defendant, as argued here, is responsible for the defect.

The plaintiff is not required to prove a specific defect when common experience tells us that the accident would not have occurred in the absence of a defect. The mere fact of an accident, standing alone, does not make out a case that the product was defective, nor does the fact that it was found in a defective condition after the event. But the addition of other facts tending to show that the defect existed before the accident may make out a sufficient case. . . .

. . . Here . . . we cannot say that when a car door suddenly flies open while the car is travelling on a gravel road at 10 miles per hour common experience tells us that it could not have happened absent a defect. Therefore, we examine the evidence to see to what extent Williams negated other causes of the accident. Williams stated that she is positive she shut and locked the door and that she was driving slowly and the road was straight. She testified she was not wearing her seat belt and that, when she saw the door open, she turned to her left and hit the brakes and her left hand came off of the steering wheel. She then fell to the ground, landing on her left hip and the left side of her face. The foregoing does not adequately negate any cause of the accident due to driver error or control. Furthermore, she had an expert examine the car, but he could not say that any of the problems he found were defects or that they would cause the door to come open. The expert's testimony was inconclusive as to the existence of any defect and tended to support the theory that the accident was due to driver error.

. . . [A]ppellant's proof does not go beyond suspicion or conjecture nor raise a reasonable inference that the defect was the cause of the accident. We . . . affirm the trial court's action in granting the motions for directed verdict.

NOTES

1. *Factual Defect and Legal Defectiveness Distinguished.* In *Heaton v. Ford Motor Co.,* 248 Or. 467, 435 P.2d 806 (1967), plaintiff sought damages resulting when a wheel separated from the body of his 4-wheel-drive pickup truck, causing the truck to overturn. The twelve rivets connecting the rim of the wheel to the inner wheel "appeared to have been sheared off." The truck was relatively new, had been driven only 7,000 miles prior to the accident, and had never been subjected to unusual stress. Shortly before the accident the truck, "while moving on a 'black-top' highway at normal speed, hit a rock which plaintiff described as about five or six inches in diameter." The plaintiff continued to drive the truck for about 35 miles, after which time the wheel separation occurred. An examination of the separated wheel revealed "a large dent in the rim and a five-inch cut in the inner tube" adjacent to the rim dent.

In affirming an involuntary nonsuit for the defendant, the court said the jury had "no experiential basis" for determining what a reasonable consumer would expect in this context, and the record supplied no basis for making that determination. The jury could not reach a rational decision "without the benefit of data concerning the cost or feasibility of designing and building" a stronger product.

Similarly, in *Short v. Little Rock Dodge, Inc.,* 297 Ark. 104, 759 S.W.2d 553 (1988), plaintiff was denied recovery as a matter of law for the death of her deceased resulting when the deceased's car, while traveling at an estimated 40–60 m.p.h., "went off on the right shoulder, crossed over the road, and turned over on the left side of the highway." There was evidence that the car had a manufacturing-defect stalling problem which rendered the car difficult to steer, but there was no "proof offered which would have negated other possible causes of the accident."

Since the plaintiff's deceased cannot testify, why not raise a rebuttable presumption that he was exercising due care when the accident happened?

Compare Johnson v. Michelin Tire Corp., 812 F.2d 200 (5th Cir. 1987). (Tire blowout; expert testimony was conflicting as to whether the blowout caused the accident, or the accident caused the blowout. Court held that a jury question as to causal product defectiveness was presented.)

2. *The Restatement (Third) and Circumstantial Evidence.* Section 3 of the RESTATEMENT (THIRD) OF TORTS: PRODUCTS LIABILITY, provides:

> It may be inferred that the harm sustained by the plaintiff was caused by a product defect existing at the time of sale or distribution, without proof of a specific defect, when the incident that harmed the plaintiff:

(a) was of a kind that ordinarily occurs as a result of product defect; and

(b) was not, in the particular case, solely the result of causes other than product defect existing at the time of sale or distribution.

Would section 3 change the result in the principal case or in the cases discussed in note 1? Should it be easier to infer defect in a products case than it is to infer negligence in an ordinary *res ipsa loquitur* case?

3. *Date of Defect.* The general rule is that the defendant supplier is not subject to products liability unless the product is defective when it leaves his control. *See, e.g.,* TENN. CODE ANNOT. § 29-28-105(a) (1980). Consider in this regard *Mickle v. Blackmon*, 252 S.C. 202, 166 S.E.2d 173 (1969), *later app.,* 255 S.C. 136, 177 S.E.2d 548 (1970), where the defendant car manufacturer was held liable for injuries resulting when, months after the car was sold, the protective knob on the stick gearshift of the car deteriorated from exposure to sun rays. The plaintiff was impaled on the lever when she was thrown against it in an accident, causing the knob to shatter. Did the defect "exist" when it left the control of the manufacturer?

PROBLEM

Buyer purchased a small dog, together with a collar and leash, from Pet Shop. A week later, Buyer was walking the dog in the park when the dog saw Plaintiff some 50 feet away and lunged at her, breaking the dog collar. The dog, freed from the collar, ran to the plaintiff and bit her on her leg. Plaintiff contracted rabies as a result of the dog bite. Does the injured woman have a valid products liability claim against Pet Shop? Against the collar and leash manufacturer?

[2] Design Defect

POTTER v. CHICAGO PNEUMATIC TOOL CO.,
241 Conn. 199, 694 A.2d 1319 (Conn. 1997)

KATZ, ASSOCIATE JUSTICE.

This appeal arises from a products liability action brought by the plaintiffs[1] against the defendants, Chicago Pneumatic Tool Company (Chicago Pneumatic), Stanley Works and Dresser Industries, Inc. (Dresser). The plaintiffs claim that they were injured in the course of their employment as shipyard workers at the General Dynamics Corporation Electric Boat facility (Electric Boat) in Groton as a result of using pneumatic hand tools manufactured by the defendants. Specifically, the plaintiffs allege that the tools were defectively designed because they exposed the plaintiffs to excessive vibration, and because the defendants failed to provide adequate warnings with respect to the potential danger presented by excessive vibration.

---

[1] For purposes of this opinion, the plaintiffs are Joseph Gladu, David Thompson, Roy Tutt, Thomas Brayman and Jaime Irizarry. They are among more than 400 individuals pursuing claims against the defendants. The named plaintiff, John Potter, is not a party to this appeal, the action as it pertained to him having been withdrawn prior to trial.

C.   TYPES AND DEFINITIONS OF DEFECT   1021

The defendants appeal from the judgment rendered on jury verdicts in favor of the plaintiffs claiming [among other things that]. . . the trial court should have rendered judgment for the defendants notwithstanding the verdicts because . . . there was insufficient evidence that the tools were defective in that the plaintiffs had presented no evidence of a feasible alternative design. . . .

The trial record reveals the following facts, which are undisputed for purposes of this appeal. The plaintiffs were employed at Electric Boat as "grinders," positions which required use of pneumatic hand tools to smooth welds and metal surfaces.[2] In the course of their employment, the plaintiffs used various pneumatic hand tools, including chipping and grinding tools, which were manufactured and sold by the defendants. The plaintiffs' use of the defendants' tools at Electric Boat spanned approximately twenty-five years, from the mid-1960s until 1987. The plaintiffs suffer from permanent vascular and neurological impairment of their hands, which has caused blanching of their fingers, pain, numbness, tingling, reduction of grip strength, intolerance of cold and clumsiness from restricted blood flow. As a result, the plaintiffs have been unable to continue their employment as grinders and their performance of other activities has been restricted. The plaintiffs' symptoms are consistent with a diagnosis of hand arm vibration syndrome. Expert testimony confirmed that exposure to vibration is a significant contributing factor to the development of hand arm vibration syndrome, and that a clear relationship exists between the level of vibration exposure and the risk of developing the syndrome.

In addition to these undisputed facts, the following evidence, taken in favor of the jury's verdict, was presented. Ronald Guarneri, an industrial hygienist at ElectricBoat, testified that he had conducted extensive testing of tools used at the shipyard in order to identify occupational hazards. This testing revealed that a large number of the defendants' tools violated the limits for vibration exposure established by the American National Standards Institute (institute), and exceeded the threshold limit promulgated by the American Conference of Governmental and Industrial Hygienists (conference).[The court discussed additional evidence on the products' risks, and ways to minimize the risks of vibration, "including isolation (the use of springs or mass to isolate vibration), dampening (adding weights to dampen vibrational effects), and balancing (adding weights to counterbalance machine imbalances that cause vibration)." An expert testified that "each of these methods has been available to manufacturers for at least thrity-five years."]

After a six week trial, the trial court rendered judgment on jury verdicts in favor of the plaintiffs. Finding that the defendants' tools had been

---

[2] One expert witness explained the design and purpose of these pneumatic tools: "[T]he machines are connected to an air hose that has air pressure, and you squeeze some kind of a valve and the air pressure is released into what's called an air motor, which is a turbine of sorts. The air propels the motor and rotates the grinding device and you apply the grinding wheel or attachment to the metal that you want to grind."

defectively designed so as to render them unreasonably dangerous, the jury awarded the plaintiffs compensatory damages.[3]

We first address the defendants' argument that the trial court improperly failed to render judgment for the defendants notwithstanding the verdicts because there was insufficient evidence for the jury to have found that the tools had been defectively designed. Specifically, the defendants claim that, in order to establish a prima facie design defect case, the plaintiffs were required to prove that there was a feasible alternative design available at the time that the defendants put their tools into the stream of commerce. We disagree.

In order properly to evaluate the parties' arguments, we begin our analysis with a review of the development of strict tort liability, focusing specifically on design defect liability. At common law, a person injured by a product had no cause of action against the manufacturer of the product unless that person was in privity of contract with the manufacturer. This rule, established in *Winterbottom v. Wright*, 152 Eng.Rep. 402 (1842), made privity a condition precedent to actions against manufacturers grounded in negligence. American courts widely adopted this rule and, for the next one-half century, the privity requirement remained steadfast in American jurisprudence.[4]

The evolution of modern products liability law began with the landmark case of *MacPherson v. Buick Motor Co.*, 217 N.Y. 382, 111 N.E. 1050 (1916), in which the New York Court of Appeals extended the manufacturer's duty to all persons in fact harmed by products that were reasonably certain to cause injury when negligently made. As Justice Cardozo wrote in *MacPherson*, "[i]f the nature of a thing is such that it is reasonably certain to place life and limb in peril when negligently made, it is then a thing of danger. Its nature gives warning of the consequences to be expected. If to the element of danger there is added knowledge that the thing will be used by persons other than the purchaser, and used without new tests, then, irrespective of contract, the manufacturer of this thing of danger is under a duty to make it carefully." Id., at 389, 111 N.E. 1050. The *MacPherson* reasoning eventually was accepted by nearly all American courts. See J. Wade, "Strict Tort Liability of Manufacturers," 19 Sw.L.J. 5 (1965).

Similarly, the New Jersey Supreme Court in *Henningsen v. Bloomfield Motors, Inc.*, 32 N.J. 358, 161 A.2d 69 (1960), imposed "strict liability" upon the manufacturer of a defective product, but on a warranty basis. Discarding the

---

[3] Specifically, the jury awarded the plaintiffs compensatory damages in the following amounts: Joseph Gladu—$58,828 (reduced by 25 percent for comparative liability); David Thompson—$124,988 (reduced by 70 percent for comparative liability); Roy Tutt—$36,600 (with no reduction for comparative liability); Thomas Brayman—$65,400 (with no reduction for comparative liability); Jaime Irizarry—$60,289 (reduced by 20 percent for comparative liability).

[4] Nevertheless, courts developed a number of exceptions to the privity requirement: (1) "an act of negligence . . .which is imminently dangerous to the life or health of mankind, and which is committed in the preparation or sale of an article intended to preserve, destroy, or affect human life" Huset v. J.I. Case Threshing Machine Co., 120 F. 865, 870 (8th Cir.1903); (2) "an owner's act of negligence which causes injury to one who is invited by him to use his defective appliance upon the owner's premises," *id.*, at 870–71; and (3) "one who sells or delivers an article which he knows to be imminently dangerous to life or limb to another without notice of its qualities;" *id..*, at 871.

antiquated notions of privity of contract, the court imposed upon the manufacturer an implied warranty of merchantability to a third party. *Id.*, at 373, 384, 161 A.2d 69. The *Henningsen* court stated: "We are convinced that the cause of justice in this area of the law can be served only by recognizing that [the third party] is such a person who, in the reasonable contemplation of the parties to the warranty, might be expected to become a user of the [product]. Accordingly, [the third party's] lack of privity does not stand in the way of prosecution of the injury suit against the [manufacturer]." *Id.*, at 413, 161 A.2d 69.

The next major development in products liability law did not attempt to modify the negligence rule any further, but, rather, urged its replacement. In *Escola v. Coca Cola Bottling Co. of Fresno*, 24 Cal.2d 453, 461, 150 P.2d 436 (1944). Justice Roger Traynor, in a now famous concurring opinion, first suggested that courts should hold manufacturers liable without fault when defective products cause personal injury. Justice Traynor asserted that strict liability would serve several policy justifications: (1) manufacturers could readily absorb or pass on the cost of liability to consumers as a cost of doing business; (2) manufacturers would be deterred from marketing defective products; and (3) injured persons, who lack familiarity with the manufacturing process, would no longer shoulder the burden of proving negligence. *Id.*, at 462, 150 P.2d 436 (Traynor, J., concurring).

Although Justice Traynor's argument did not prevail in *Escola*, nearly twenty years later he wrote for the majority in *Greenman v. Yuba Power Products, Inc.*, 59 Cal.2d 57, 62, 377 P.2d 897, 27 Cal.Rptr. 697 (1963), holding a manufacturer strictly liable because its defective product caused injury to the plaintiff. The *Greenman* court stated that "[a] manufacturer is strictly liable in tort when an article he places on the market, knowing that it is to be used without inspection for defects, proves to have a defect that causes injury to a human being." *Id.* The court explained that the purpose of this rule "is to insure that the costs of injuries resulting from defective products are borne by the manufacturers that put such products on the market rather than by the injured persons who are powerless to protect themselves." *Id.*, at 63, 27 Cal.Rptr. 697, 377 P.2d 897.

Two years later, § 402A of the Restatement (Second) of Torts adopted, with slight variation,[5] the doctrine of strict tort liability espoused in *Greenman*. Section 402A provides: [Here the court quoted section 402A.]

Products liability law has thus evolved to hold manufacturers[6] strictly liable for unreasonably dangerous products that cause injury to ultimate users. Nevertheless, strict tort liability does not transform manufacturers into

---

[5] Notably, the Restatement (Second) of Torts "eliminated the limitation that the product be one that the manufacturer knows will be used without inspection for defects. In addition, the Restatement version provides for the seller's liability for loss to property. . .even where there is no personal injury." 1 M. Madden, supra, § 6.1, pp. 191–92.

[6] We recognize that, under General Statutes § 52-572m (a), "'[p]roduct seller' means any person or entity, including a manufacturer, wholesaler, distributor or retailer who is engaged in the business of selling such products whether the sale is for resale or for use or consumption. The term 'product seller' also includes lessors or bailors of products who are engaged in the business of leasing or bailment of products." For purposes of simplicity, however, we will solely use the term "manufacturer."

insurers, nor does it impose absolute liability. See R. Traynor, "The Ways and Meanings of Defective Products and Strict Liability," 32 Tenn.L.Rev. 363, 366–67 (1965) (emphasizing that manufacturers are not insurers for all injuries caused by products). . . .Strict tort liability merely relieves the plaintiff from proving that the manufacturer was negligent and allows the plaintiff to establish instead the defective condition of the product as the principal basis of liability. . . .

Although courts have widely accepted the concept of strict tort liability, some of the specifics of strict tort liability remain in question. In particular, courts have sharply disagreed over the appropriate definition of defectiveness in design cases. . . . As the Alaska Supreme Court has stated: "Design defects present the most perplexing problems in the field of strict products liability because there is no readily ascertainable external measure of defectiveness. While manufacturing flaws can be evaluated against the intended design of the product, no such objective standard exists in the design defect context." *Caterpillar Tractor Co. v. Beck*, 593 P.2d 871, 880 (Alaska 1979).

Section 402A imposes liability only for those defective products that are "unreasonably dangerous" to "the ordinary consumer who purchases it, with the ordinary knowledge common to the community as to its characteristics." 2 Restatement (Second), § 402A, comment (i). Under this formulation, known as the "consumer expectation" test, a manufacturer is strictly liable for any condition not contemplated by the ultimate consumer that will be unreasonably dangerous to the consumer. . . .

Some courts, however, have refused to adopt the "unreasonably dangerous" definition, determining that it injects a concept of foreseeability into strict tort liability, which is inappropriate in such cases because the manufacturer's liability is not based upon negligence. See *Caterpillar Tractor Co. v. Beck*, 593 P.2d at 882–83 (articulating that "unreasonably dangerous" narrows scope of recovery and unduly increases plaintiff's burden); *Cronin v. J.B.E. Olson Corp.*, 8 Cal.3d 121, 133, 501 P.2d 1153, 104 Cal. Rptr. 433 (1972) ("[w]e think that a requirement that a plaintiff also prove that the defect made the product 'unreasonably dangerous' places upon him a significantly increased burden and represents a step backward").

In *Barker v. Lull Engineering Co.*, 20 Cal.3d 413, 435, 573 P.2d 443, 143 Cal.Rptr. 225 (1978), the California Supreme Court established two alternative tests for determining design defect liability: (1) the consumer expectation analysis; and (2) a balancing test that inquires whether a product's risks outweigh its benefits. Under the latter, otherwise known as the "risk-utility," test, the manufacturer bears the burden of proving that the product's utility is not outweighed by its risks in light of various factors.[8] Three other jurisdictions have subsequently adopted California's two-pronged test, including the burden-shifting risk-utility inquiry.[9]

---

[8] In evaluating the adequacy of a product's design, the *Barker* court stated that "a jury may consider, among other relevant factors, the gravity of the danger posed by the challenged design, the likelihood that such danger would occur, the mechanical feasibility of a safer alternative design, the financial cost of an improved design, and the adverse consequences to the product and to the consumer that would result from an alternative design." Barker v. Lull Engineering Co., supra, 20 Cal.3d at 431, 143 Cal.Rptr. 225, 573 P.2d 443.

[9] Additionally, other states have adopted *Barker*-type alternative tests, but have declined to shift the burden of proving the product's risks and utility to the manufacturer. . . .

Other jurisdictions apply only a risk-utility test in determining whether a manufacturer is liable for a design defect. . . . To assist the jury in evaluating the product's risks and utility, these courts have set forth a list of nonexclusive factors to consider when deciding whether a product has been defectively designed. . . .[10]

This court has long held that in order to prevail in a design defect claim, "[t]he plaintiff must prove that the product is unreasonably dangerous." . . . We have derived our definition of "unreasonably dangerous" from comment (i) to § 402A, which provides that "the article sold must be dangerous to an extent beyond that which would be contemplated by the ordinary consumer who purchases it, with the ordinary knowledge common to the community as to its characteristics." 2 Restatement (Second), § 402A, comment (i). This "consumer expectation" standard is now well established in Connecticut strict products liability decisions. . . .

The defendants propose that it is time for this court to abandon the consumer expectation standard and adopt the requirement that the plaintiff must prove the existence of a reasonable alternative design in order to prevail on a design defect claim. We decline to accept the defendants' invitation.

In support of their position, the defendants point to the second tentative draft of the Restatement (Third) of Torts: Products Liability (1995) (Draft Restatement [Third]), which provides that, as part of a plaintiff's prima facie case, the plaintiff must establish the availability of a reasonable alternative design. Specifically, § 2(b) of the Draft Restatement (Third) provides: "[A] product is defective in design when the foreseeable risks of harm posed by the product could have been reduced or avoided by the adoption of a reasonable alternative design by the seller or other distributor, or a predecessor in the commercial chain of distribution, and the omission of the alternative design renders the product not reasonably safe." The reporters to the Draft Restatement (Third) state that "[v]ery substantial authority supports the proposition that [the] plaintiff must establish a reasonable alternative design in order for a product to be adjudged defective in design." Draft Restatement (Third), § 2, reporters' note to comment (c), p. 50.

---

[10] These factors are typically derived from an influential article by Dean John Wade, in which he suggested consideration of the following factors:

"1. The usefulness and desirability of the product—its utility to the user and to the public as a whole.

"2. The safety aspects of the product—the likelihood that it will cause injury, and the probable seriousness of the injury.

"3. The availability of a substitute product which would meet the same need and not be as unsafe.

"4. The manufacturer's ability to eliminate the unsafe character of the product without impairing its usefulness or making it too expensive to maintain its utility.

"5. The user's ability to avoid danger by the exercise of care in the use of the product.

"6. The user's anticipated awareness of the dangers inherent in the product and their avoidability, because of general public knowledge of the obvious condition of the product, or of the existence of suitable warnings or instructions.

"7. The feasibility, on the part of the manufacturer, of spreading the loss by setting the price of the product or carrying liability insurance." J. Wade, "On the Nature of Strict Tort Liability for Products," 44 Miss.L.J. 825, 837–38 (1973).

We point out that this provision of the Draft Restatement (Third) has been a source of substantial controversy among commentators. See, e.g., J. Vargo, "The Emperor's New Clothes: The American Law Institute Adorns a 'New Cloth' for Section 402A Products Liability Design Defects—A Survey of the States Reveals a Different Weave," 26 U.Mem.L.Rev. 493, 501 (1996) (challenging reporters' claim that Draft Restatement (Third)'s reasonable alternative design requirement constitutes "consensus" among jurisdictions); P. Corboy, "The Not-So-Quiet Revolution: Rebuilding Barriers to Jury Trial in the Proposed Restatement (Third) of Torts: Products Liability," 61 Tenn.L.Rev. 1043, 1093 (1994) ("[t]he decisional support for [the reasonable alternative design requirement], however, appears to be overstated by the Reporters, who claim that [eighteen] states support the rule"); F. Vandall, "The Restatement (Third) of Torts: Products Liability Section 2(b): The Reasonable Alternative Design Requirement," 61 Tenn.L.Rev. 1407, 1428 (1994) ("The centerpiece of the Restatement (Third) of Torts: Products Liability is the requirement that the plaintiff present evidence of a reasonable alternative design as part of her prima facie case. This requirement is not supported by the majority of the jurisdictions that have considered the question."). Contrary to the rule promulgated in the Draft Restatement (Third), our independent review of the prevailing common law reveals that the majority of jurisdictions do not impose upon plaintiffs an absolute requirement to prove a feasible alternative design.[11]

In our view, the feasible alternative design requirement imposes an undue burden on plaintiffs that might preclude otherwise valid claims from jury consideration.[12] Such a rule would require plaintiffs to retain an expert witness even in cases in which lay jurors can infer a design defect from circumstantial evidence. Connecticut courts, however, have consistently stated that a jury may, under appropriate circumstances, infer a defect from the evidence without the necessity of expert testimony. . . .

Moreover, in some instances, a product may be in a defective condition unreasonably dangerous to the user even though no feasible alternative design is available. In such instances, the manufacturer may be strictly liable for a

---

[11] Our research reveals that, of the jurisdictions that have considered the role of feasible alternative designs in design defect cases: (1) six jurisdictions affirmatively state that a plaintiff need not show a feasible alternative design in order to establish a manufacturer's liability for design defect; (2) sixteen jurisdictions hold that a feasible alternative design is merely one of several factors that the jury may consider in determining whether a product design is defective; (3) three jurisdictions require the defendant, not the plaintiff, to prove that the product was not defective; and (4) eight jurisdictions require that the plaintiff prove a feasible alternative design in order to establish a prima facie case of design defect.

[12] Indeed, as one commentator has pointed out: "Apparently, without expert evidence in [the] plaintiff's prima facie case, [the] defendant would be entitled to a directed verdict. This is despite the advice in comment d [of the Draft Restatement (Third), supra] that, due to [the] plaintiff's limited access to relevant data, [the] plaintiff should not be required to make a detailed showing. Moreover, it is clear that defendants will hold plaintiffs to their burden of showing the alternative design to be reasonable considering the 'overall safety of the entire product.' In short, the proposed standard requires the plaintiff to put on a case to the judge supporting a product the defendant did not make. Only then will the plaintiff be permitted to place the merits of his or her case before the jury. Worse yet, due to the added cost and risk of a directed verdict, some plaintiffs with meritorious claims will not reach the jury, and others may not find representation at all." P. Corboy, 61 Tenn.L.Rev. 1095–96.

design defect notwithstanding the fact that there are no safer alternative designs in existence. See, e.g., *O'Brien v. Muskin Corp.*, 94 N.J. 169, 184, 463 A.2d 298 (1983) ("other products, including some for which no alternative exists, are so dangerous and of such little use that . . . a manufacturer would bear the cost of liability of harm to others"); *Wilson v. Piper Aircraft Corp.*, 282 Or. 61, 71 n. 5, 577 P.2d 1322 (1978) ("Our holding should not be interpreted as a requirement that [the practicability of a safer alternative design] must in all cases weigh in [the] plaintiff's favor before the case can be submitted to the jury. There might be cases in which the jury would be permitted to hold the defendant liable on account of a dangerous design feature even though no safer design was feasible (or there was no evidence of a safer practicable alternative)."); *Sumnicht v. Toyota Motor Sales, U.S.A., Inc.*, 121 Wis.2d 338, 371, 360 N.W.2d 2 (1984) ("[a] product may be defective and unreasonably dangerous even though there are no alternative, safer designs available"). Accordingly, we decline to adopt the requirement that a plaintiff must prove a feasible alternative design as a sine qua non to establishing a prima facie case of design defect.

Although today we continue to adhere to our long-standing rule that a product's defectiveness is to be determined by the expectations of an ordinary consumer, we nevertheless recognize that there may be instances involving complex product designs in which an ordinary consumer may not be able to form expectations of safety. . . . In such cases, a consumer's expectations may be viewed in light of various factors that balance the utility of the product's design with the magnitude of its risks. We find persuasive the reasoning of those jurisdictions that have modified their formulation of the consumer expectation test by incorporating risk-utility factors into the ordinary consumer expectation analysis. . . . Thus, the modified consumer expectation test provides the jury with the product's risks and utility and then inquires whether a reasonable consumer would consider the product unreasonably dangerous. As the Supreme Court of Washington stated in *Seattle-First National Bank v. Tabert*, at 154, 542 P.2d 774, "[i]n determining the reasonable expectations of the ordinary consumer, a number of factors must be considered. The relative cost of the product, the gravity of the potential harm from the claimed defect and the cost and feasibility of eliminating or minimizing the risk may be relevant in a particular case. In other instances the nature of the product or the nature of the claimed defect may make other factors relevant to the issue.". . . Accordingly, under this modified formulation, the consumer expectation test would establish the product's risks and utility, and the inquiry would then be whether a reasonable consumer would consider the product design unreasonably dangerous.[15]

---

[15] Under this formulation, a sample jury instruction could provide: "A product is unreasonably dangerous as designed, if, at the time of sale, it is defective to an extent beyond that which would be contemplated by the ordinary consumer. In determining what an ordinary consumer would reasonably expect, you should consider the usefulness of the product, the likelihood and severity of the danger posed by the design, the feasibility of an alternative design, the financial cost of an improved design, the ability to reduce the product's danger without impairing its usefulness or making it too expensive, and the feasibility of spreading the loss by increasing the product's price or by purchasing insurance, and such other factors as the claimed defect indicate are appropriate." . . .

In our view, the relevant factors that a jury may consider include, but are not limited to, the usefulness of the product, the likelihood and severity of the danger posed by the design, the feasibility of an alternative design, the financial cost of an improved design, the ability to reduce the product's danger without impairing its usefulness or making it too expensive, and the feasibility of spreading the loss by increasing the product's price. . . . The availability of a feasible alternative design is a factor that the plaintiff may, rather than must, prove in order to establish that a product's risks outweigh its utility. . . .

Furthermore, we emphasize that our adoption of a risk-utility balancing component to our consumer expectation test does not signal a retreat from strict tort liability. In weighing a product's risks against its utility, the focus of the jury should be on the product itself, and not on the conduct of the manufacturer.[16]

Although today we adopt a modified formulation of the consumer expectation test, we emphasize that we do not require a plaintiff to present evidence relating to the product's risks and utility in every case. As the California Court of Appeals has stated: "There are certain kinds of accidents—even where fairly complex machinery is involved—[that] are so bizarre that the average juror, upon hearing the particulars, might reasonably think: 'Whatever the user may have expected from that contraption, it certainly wasn't that.'" *Akers v. Kelley Co.*, 173 Cal.App.3d 633, 651, 219 Cal.Rptr. 513 (1985). Accordingly, the ordinary consumer expectation test is appropriate when the everyday experience of the particular product's users permits the inference that the product did not meet minimum safety expectations. See *Soule v. General Motors Corp.*, 8 Cal.4th 548, 567, 882 P.2d 298, 34 Cal.Rptr.2d 607 (1994).

Conversely, the jury should engage in the risk-utility balancing required by our modified consumer expectation test when the particular facts do not reasonably permit the inference that the product did not meet the safety expectations of the ordinary consumer. *See id.*, at 568, 34 Cal.Rptr.2d 607, 882 P.2d 298. Furthermore, instructions based on the ordinary consumer expectation test would not be appropriate when, as a matter of law, there is insufficient evidence to support a jury verdict under that test. *See id.* In such circumstances, the jury should be instructed solely on the modified consumer expectation test we have articulated today.

In this respect, it is the function of the trial court to determine whether an instruction based on the ordinary consumer expectation test or the modified consumer expectation test, or both, is appropriate in light of the evidence presented. In making this determination, the trial court must ascertain whether, under each test, there is sufficient evidence as a matter of law to warrant the respective instruction. . . .

With these principles in mind, we now consider whether, in the present case, the trial court properly instructed the jury with respect to the definition of design defect for the purposes of strict tort liability. The trial court instructed the jury that a manufacturer may be strictly liable if the plaintiffs prove,

---

[16] As Dean Keeton has stated, "[t]he change in the substantive law as regards the liability of makers of products and other sellers in the marketing chain has been from fault to defect. The plaintiff is no longer required to impugn the maker, but he is required to impugn the product." P. Keeton, "Product Liability and the Meaning of Defect," 5 St. Mary's L.J. 30, 33 (1973).

among other elements, that the product in question was in a defective condition, unreasonably dangerous to the ultimate user.[17] The court further instructed the jury that, in determining whether the tools were unreasonably dangerous, it may draw its conclusions based on the reasonable expectations of an ordinary user of the defendants' tools. Because there was sufficient evidence as a matter of law to support the determination that the tools were unreasonably dangerous based on the ordinary consumer expectation test, we conclude that this instruction was appropriately given to the jury.

"Evidence is sufficient to sustain a verdict where it induces in the mind of the [trier] that it is more probable than otherwise that the fact in issue is true. . . . It is the province of the trier of fact to weigh the evidence presented and determine the credibility and effect to be given the evidence. . . . On appellate review, therefore, we will give the evidence the most favorable reasonable construction in support of the verdict to which it is entitled. . . . In analyzing a sufficiency of the evidence claim, the test that we employ is whether, on the basis of the evidence before the jury, a reasonable and properly motivated jury could return the verdict that it did." . . .

"Whether a product is unreasonably dangerous is a question of fact to be determined by the jury. . . . [T]he jury can draw their own reasonable conclusions as to the expectations of the ordinary consumer and the knowledge common in the community at large." . . . Furthermore, "[i]t is not necessary that the plaintiff in a strict tort action establish a specific defect as long as there is evidence of some unspecified dangerous condition." *Living & Learning*

---

[17] With respect to the appropriate test for determining a design defect, the trial court's instruction provided: "A defective product is defined as one that is unreasonably dangerous for its . . . intended use. Unreasonably dangerous means dangerous to an extent beyond that which would be contemplated by the user. The manufacturer is not required to guarantee that his product is incapable of doing harm. Therefore, the mere happening of an injury does not create legal responsibility on the part of a manufacturer. The law does not require the manufacturer to produce a product which is accident free or foolproof. A manufacturer's duty is to produce a product which is reasonably safe.

"Now, under the doctrine of strict liability, the plaintiff must establish each of the following five elements by a fair preponderance of the evidence: One, that the defendant engaged in the business of selling the product. Now, that is not in dispute, so you don't have to concern yourselves with that. That's been acknowledged. Second, that the product was in a defective condition, unreasonably dangerous to the user. Third, that the defect caused the injuries for which compensation is sought. Fourth, that the defect existed at the time of the sale. And five, that the product was expected to and did reach the plaintiff without substantial change in condition.

"You must first determine that each defendant was engaged in the business of selling the product, which has been acknowledged. You must next determine whether the product was in a defective condition. A product is in a defective condition if it leaves the seller's hand in a condition that will be unreasonably dangerous to the ultimate consumer or user. Accordingly, a product may be defective even though it was manufactured in the way it was intended to be manufactured and even though it was perfectly made according to the manufacturer's own standards and tolerances, as long as the product is unreasonably dangerous when used for its intended and foreseeable purposes. . . .

"*It is for you to draw your own conclusions as to the reasonable expectations of an ordinary user of the defendants' products and as to the knowledge common to the community at large regarding these products.* It is the unreasonably dangerous condition of the product that makes the product defective, not whether the manufacturer or supplier knew the product was unreasonably dangerous. Therefore, the plaintiffs [do] not need to show that the seller knew the product was defective." (Emphasis added.)

Centre, Inc. v. Griese Custom Signs, Inc., 3 Conn.App. at 664, 491 A.2d 433 . . . . The jury heard testimony that Guarneri, Electric Boat's industrial hygienist, had performed extensive testing of tools used at the shipyard, which tests revealed that a large number of the defendants' tools violated the institute's limits for vibration exposure and exceeded the conference's threshold limit. The jury also heard substantial testimony with respect to various methods, including isolation, dampening and balancing, available to reduce the deleterious effects of vibration caused by thedefendants' tools. Moreover, there was expert testimony that exposure to vibration is a significant contributing factor to the development of hand arm vibration syndrome and that a clear relationship exists between the level of vibration exposure and the risk of developing the syndrome. Viewing the evidence in a light favorable to supporting the jury's verdicts, as we must, we conclude that the jury properly determined that the defendants' tools had been defectively designed.

[In the next part of the opinion the court held that it would reverse and remand because the trial court had improperly instructed the jury on defendants' claims relating to substantial modification. "Specifically, the defendants argue that: (1) the trial court improperly instructed the jury that Electric Boat's alterations to the tools would bar the defendants' liability only if the defendants proved that the alterations had been the sole proximate cause of the plaintiffs' injuries and, furthermore, that the charge regarding alterations improperly shifted the burden of proving causation to the defendants; . . .and (2) there was insufficient evidence to support the jury's conclusion that the defendants' tools had reached the plaintiffs without a substantial change in condition. We agree that the trial court's instruction improperly shifted to the defendants the burden of proving causation." Then the court considered the parties' arguments on state of the art evidence in a design case.]

Although we have concluded that a new trial is necessary, we address the defendants' final claim because it is likely to arise on retrial. The defendants . . . assert that the trial court improperly prevented the jury from considering the state-of-the-art defense in the context of the plaintiffs' claim of defective design. In response, the plaintiffs argue that the state-of-the-art defense has no place in a strict products liability action because it improperly diverts the jury's attention from the product's condition to the manufacturer's conduct. The plaintiffs further assert that even if the trial court improperly declined to provide the instruction with respect to the design defect claim, the defendants have failed to prove that it constituted harmful error. Although we agree with the defendants that state-of-the-art evidence applies to design defect claims . . ., we disagree that such evidence constitutes an affirmative defense to the plaintiffs' design defect claims.

The following additional facts are relevant to this issue. The defendants presented testimony that they produced the safest and highest quality tools that they were able to design. Robert Marelli, superintendent of tools and equipment at Electric Boat, testified that the defendants' tools were the best for Electric Boat's purposes and that Electric Boat would be in a "tough situation" if faced with the prospect of having to replace them.

Conversely, the plaintiffs presented evidence that a chipping hammer manufactured by Atlas Copco, which had a reduced vibration design, was available in 1976. A Chicago Pneumatic interoffice memorandum dated October, 1974, provided that, "[u]nless we at least keep pace with the technological developments of major competitors like Atlas Copco, we certainly face a prospect of loss of market share." The plaintiffs also presented another Chicago Pneumatic interoffice memorandum dated May, 1974, which outlined various devices designed to isolate vibration developed by Chicago Pneumatic in conjunction with Caterpillar Tractor Company.

The trial court instructed the jury that "state of the art is defined as the level of scientific and technological knowledge existing at the time the product in question was designed for manufacture." . . .The court also instructed the jury that a manufacturer cannot be held to standards that exceed the limit of scientific advances and technology existing at the time of manufacture and, therefore, the defendants could not be found liable if they had proven compliance with the state of the art. . . .

We begin our analysis of this issue by recognizing that the term "state of the art" has been the source of substantial confusion. . . . Several courts have defined state-of-the-art evidence in terms of industry custom. . . .

The majority of courts, however, have defined state-of-the-art evidence as the level of relevant scientific, technological and safety knowledge existing and reasonably feasible at the time of design. . . .

We also recognize that courts are divided on the issue of whether state-of-the-art evidence is admissible in design defect claims. Several courts have concluded that such evidence is inadmissible in design defect claims because it improperly focuses on the reasonableness of the manufacturer's conduct, which is irrelevant in a strict products liability action. . . . Conversely, other courts, in construing relevant state tort reform statutes, have stated that a manufacturer's proof of state-of-the-art evidence constitutes a complete defense to a design defect claim. . . .

Nevertheless, the overwhelming majority of courts have held that, in design defect cases, state-of-the-art evidence is relevant to determining the adequacy of the product's design. . . .

The plaintiffs assert that state-of-the-art evidence has no place in a strict products liability action because it improperly focuses the jury's attention on the manufacturer's conduct. We disagree. We adopt the majority view and hold that such evidence is relevant and assists the jury in determining whether a product is defective and unreasonably dangerous. . . . In other words, "state of the art relates to the condition of the product and the possibility that it could have been made safer." . . . Accordingly, we conclude that state of the art is a relevant factor in considering the adequacy of the design of a product and whether it is in a defective condition unreasonably dangerous to the ordinary consumer. In defining the term state of the art, we adhere to our precedent . . . and to the majority view, which characterize state of the art as the level of relevant scientific, technological and safety knowledge existing and reasonably feasible at the time of design. . . .

Furthermore, we point out that state of the art refers to what is technologically feasible, rather than merely industry custom. . . . "Although customs of an industry may be relevant . . . because those customs may lag behind technological development, they are not identical with the state-of-the-art." *O'Brien v. Muskin Corp.*, 94 N.J. at 182, 463 A.2d 298. "Obviously, the inaction of all the manufacturers in an area should not be the standard by which the state of the art should be determined." *Hancock v. Paccar, Inc.*, 204 Neb. 468, 479–80, 283 N.W.2d 25 (1979); see also *T.J. Hooper*, 60 F.2d 737, 740 (2d Cir.), cert. denied, 287 U.S. 662, 53 S.Ct. 220, 77 L.Ed. 571 (1932) ("[i]ndeed in most cases reasonable prudence is in fact common prudence; but strictly it is never its measure; a whole calling may have unduly lagged in the adoption of new and available devices"). Accordingly, "[a] manufacturer may have a duty to make products pursuant to a safer design even if the custom of the industry is not to use that alternative." *O'Brien v. Muskin Corp.*, at 182–83, 463 A.2d 298.

We now apply these principles to the standards for determining design defectiveness.... Under the ordinary consumer expectation standard, state-of-the-art evidence "helps to determine the expectation of the ordinary consumer." *Bruce v. Martin-Marietta Corp.*, 544 F.2d 442, 447 (10th Cir.1976) ....[35] For example, in approving the trial court's admission of state-of-the-art evidence, the court in *Bruce* stated: "A consumer would not expect a Model T to have the safety features which are incorporated in automobiles made today. The same expectation applies to airplanes. [The p]laintiffs have not shown that the ordinary consumer would expect a plane made in 1952 to have the safety features of one made in 1970." *Bruce v. Martin-Marietta Corp.*, at 447. In other words, state-of-the-art evidence supplies the jury with a relevant basis on which to determine what the ordinary consumer would expect with respect to safety features available at the time of manufacture.

Furthermore, under the modified consumer expectations standard we have set forth today, such evidence would be admissible as a factor properly to be considered as part of the risk-utility calculus.... Because state-of-the-art evidence is relevant to set "the parameters of feasibility"; *Lancaster Silo & Block Co. v. Northern Propane Gas Co.*, 75 App. Div.2d at 66, 427 N.Y.S.2d 1009; the jury is provided with an objective standard by which to gauge the product's risks and utility. In this respect, such evidence is a relevant factor on both sides of the risk-utility equation: the risks that the product presents to consumers in light of the availability of other safety measures, and the utility of the product in comparison to feasible design alternatives.... Accordingly, state-of-the-art evidence constitutes one of several relevant factors to assist the jury in determining whether a reasonable consumer would consider the product design unreasonably dangerous.

In summary, we agree with the defendants insofar as they argue that the trial court improperly limited the applicability of state-of-the-art evidence to the plaintiffs' failure to warn claims. In our view, state-of-the-art evidence is relevant to the determination of whether a particular product design is unreasonably dangerous. We disagree with the defendants' contention, however, that proof of compliance with the state of the art constitutes an affirmative defense to a design defect claim.

---

[35] But see Morton v. Owens Corning Fiberglas Corp., 33 Cal.App.4th 1529, 1536, 40 Cal.Rptr.2d 22 (1995) ("[i]t is the knowledge and reasonable expectations of the consumer, not the scientific community, that is relevant under the consumer expectations test").

We emphasize that although state-of-the-art evidence may be dispositive on the facts of a particular case, such evidence does not constitute an affirmative defense that, if proven, would absolve the defendant from liability. . . . In other words, compliance with state of the art would not, as a matter of law, warrant a judgment for a defendant. . . . For this reason, we believe that state-of-the-art evidence is "better characterized as rebuttal evidence than as a defense." *Owens-Corning Fiberglas Corp. v. Caldwell*, 818 S.W.2d 749, 752 (Tex.1991).

We therefore conclude that state-of-the-art evidence is merely one factor for the jury to consider under either the ordinary or modified consumer expectation test. Accordingly, if on remand the trial court concludes that sufficient evidence has been produced to warrant an instruction, the jury may properly consider the state of the art in determining whether the defendants' tools were defectively designed and unreasonably dangerous.

[In a subsequent part of the opinion the court remanded for consideration of plaintiffs' punitive damages claim.]

BERDON, J., Concurring.

I write separately with respect to . . . the court's opinion regarding the test for determining whether a manufacturer is liable for a design defect. I would not depart from our long-standing rule that the consumer expectation test must be employed—that is, the product "must be dangerous to an extent beyond that which would be contemplated by the ordinary consumer who purchases it, with the ordinary knowledge common to the community as to its characteristics." 2 Restatement (Second), Torts § 402A, comment (i) (1965). Although the court today agrees that this test is to be applied to cases such as the present case, it adopts, by way of dicta, another test for "complex product designs."

I am concerned about the court adopting a risk-utility test . . . for complex product designs—that is, a test where the trier of fact considers "the product's risks and utility and then inquires whether a reasonable consumer would consider the product unreasonably dangerous." Adopting such a test in a factual vacuum without the predicate facts to address its full implications can lead us down a dangerous path.[2] More importantly, adopting such a risk-utility test for "complex product designs" sounds dangerously close to requiring proof of the existence of "a reasonable alternative design," . . . a standard of proof that the court properly rejects today.[4]

Finally, because the court insists on addressing this issue that is not before us, I would at least sort out the burden of proof for the risk-utility test by adopting "a presumption that danger outweighs utility if the product fails under circumstances when the ordinary purchaser or user would not have so expected." W. Prosser & W. Keeton, Torts (5th Ed. 1984) § 99, p. 702. Adoption of this presumption would lessen the concern that the risk-utility test

---

[2] For example, what are the standards to determine when the product involves a complex design?

[4] For example, as the court points out, one of the factors to be weighed in the risk-utility test is "the cost and feasibility of eliminating or minimizing the risk [that] may be relevant in a particular case."

undermines one of the reasons that strict tort liability was adopted—"the difficulty of discovering evidence necessary to show that danger outweighs benefits." *Id.*

NOTES

1. *The Nature of the Design Claim.* As indicated above, design claims attack an entire product line. Thus they pose a serious financial threat to product manufacturers and sellers. Predictably, the elements of a design claim have attracted national attention and provoked practical and academic debate.

2. *The Criteria for Consideration in a Design Claim.* As the principal case indicates, the issues a court or a legislature must consider in determining the definition of a design claim are many and complex. At the most basic level, what are the elements of a design claim? The most controversial recent debate here has been whether to require the plaintiff in a design case to establish an alternative design. Involved here is the issue of the "bad" product? Are there products that are so dangerous that a manufacturer should be responsible for the damages they cause even though there is no way to make the product safer?

The plaintiffs in *Potter* introduced extensive evidence of ways to minimize the risks of vibration. Was this evidence not sufficient to prove alternative design[s]? Of what relevance is "state of the art evidence" in a design claim? Should the product be measured against technology and knowledge existing at the time of trial or at the time of design, manufacture, or sale? The answer to this question is important because it affects whether liability for defective design in a particular jurisdiction is strict liability or more like negligence.

Finally, the determination of the proper standards for decision in a design case has critical importance for the concept of what it is that makes a product "defective" in the particular jurisdiction. These notes will consider some of those issues in turn.

3. *The Elements of the Design Claim—The Alternative Design.* The RESTATEMENT (THIRD) OF TORTS: PRODUCTS LIABILITY, § 2(b), provides that a product:

> (b) is defective in design when the foreseeable risks of harm posed by the product could have been reduced or avoided by the adoption of a reasonable alternative design by the seller or other distributor, or a predecessor in the commercial chain of distribution, and the omission of the alternative design renders the product not reasonably safe. . . .

The section requires a plaintiff in a design case as part of her case-in-chief to establish an alternative design, a safer way to make the product.

When is a different way to make a product an alternative design and when is it an alternative or substitute product? Is an aluminum baseball bat an alternative design for a wooden baseball bat, or is it a different product altogether? Is non-alcoholic beer an alternative product to beer, or is it a different product altogether? If the alternative proposed is a different product and not a different design, then has the plaintiff who proposes the different product failed in their case-in-chief because they have not established an existing design? Note that Dean Wade considered proof of a substitute product relevant in determining product defect. 44 Miss. L. J. 825, 837–838 (1973).

More basically, should the plaintiff bear the burden of establishing an alternative design? Who knows more about the design options of a product, a plaintiff injured by the product or an entity that has placed it into the stream of commerce?

On the other hand, are there administrative reasons to require a plaintiff to establish an alternative design? Doesn't the requirement focus the jury's inquiry on the product as designed (the actual product on trial) and the proposed alternative design? Isn't that a good thing, especially in cases involving complex and difficult-to-understand technology or science? Doesn't the requirement also force the plaintiff in every design case to hire an expert witness, as the *Potter* court noted? But, isn't it likely a plaintiff will hire an expert anyway? Certainly under the *Potter* court's solution, where an alternative design is not required but may be considered, a careful plaintiff's lawyer would always want to have expert testimony on alternative designs, if such testimony existed.

Clearly, one of the reasons for requiring the plaintiff to put forth an alternative design is to focus the jury's attention. Another reason is to provide greater certainty to product manufacturers and sellers. They can be certain they will not be held liable on a design claim if there is not an alternative design for their product. (The truth of this statement depends, in part, upon the resolution of the state of the art issue.) But if we are serious about focusing the jury's attention because of the conceptual difficulty of deciding some design cases and because we want to provide defendants with increased certainty, why don't we take the liability question in design cases away from the jury and entrust it to the court? That is the approach of the RESTATEMENT (SECOND) OF TORTS, § 520, comment l — it makes the issue of whether an activity is abnormally dangerous a question for the court.

There is little doubt that requiring a plaintiff to establish an alternative design will make it harder for plaintiffs to win design cases. While focusing the jury's decision-making and providing increased certainty are no doubt good things, are they worth the cost that fewer people injured by products will be compensated? In *Wilson v. Piper Aircraft Corp.*, 282 Or. 61, 577 P.2d 1322, *reh. den.*, 282 Or. 411, 579 P.2d 1287 (1978), the court said it was "mindful of defendant's argument that a lay jury is not qualified to determine technical questions of aeronautical design," and of the argument that "problems of conscious product design choices are inherently unsuited to determination by courts." But, said the court, "[t]his is not a problem which is peculiar to products liability cases. In the absence of an ability to recover through courts, persons injured by such designs would be without a remedy."

Is the *Potter* approach preferable to requiring the plaintiff to establish an alternative design? Doesn't that approach leave everything in the hands of the jury with relatively little guidance, except to consider all factors? But is that so different than what a jury does in a negligence case when it decides whether or not someone exercised reasonable care under the circumstances?

4. *The Reasonable Alternative Design and the "Bad" Product.* Recall *Halphen's* category of unreasonably dangerous per se products—a product was

unreasonably dangerous per se if its danger in fact outweighed its utility. Can that category of liability exist under the literal terms of RESTATEMENT (THIRD) OF TORTS: PRODUCTS LIABILITY, § 2(b)? Assume a product whose danger outweighs its utility but for which there is no alternative design. Can a plaintiff win such a case under § 2(b)? Isn't the answer no?

In *Halphen*, the court would have imposed liability upon the defendant when the danger in fact posed by the product was greater than its utility at the time of trial, even if the defendant had complied with the state of the art at the time it made the product—i.e., liability would have been imposed even if the defendant neither knew nor could have known of the product's dangers at the time it produced the product. This would truly be strict liability.

But, under section 2(b), isn't it conceivable that a manufacturer who was negligent might escape liability? Imagine a manufacturer who knows or should know that its product is more dangerous than it is useful to the targeted consumers. Presumably a manufacturer who sold such a product under those circumstances would be negligent. However, if section 2(b) defines the only ways in which a product can be defective, then the manufacturer in question would escape liability if the plaintiff could not establish a proposed alternative design, even though the manufacturer admitted its product's dangers and limited utility. Does that seem right to you?

While section 2(b) of the RESTATEMENT (THIRD) requires the plaintiff to establish an alternative design, the new Restatement slightly opens the door to the possibility that liability may be established in a design case without an alternative design. For instance, under section 3 a plaintiff may rely upon circumstantial evidence to establish a defect. And, under section 4 a product may be defective if its design does not comply with an applicable statute or regulation. Additionally, there is some interesting language in the comments to section 2 about liability for producing a manifestly unreasonable product. RESTATEMENT (THIRD) § 2, comment e provides:

> In large part the problem is one of how the range of relevant alternative designs is described. For example, a toy gun that shoots hard rubber pellets with sufficient velocity to cause injury to children could be found to be defectively designed within the rule of Subsection (b). Toy guns unlikely to cause injury would constitute reasonable alternatives to the dangerous toy. Thus, toy guns that project ping pong balls, soft gelatine pellets, or water might be found to be reasonable alternative designs to a toy gun that shoots hard pellets. However, if the realism of the hard-pellet gun, and thus its capacity to cause injury, is sufficiently important to justify the court's limiting consideration to toy guns that achieve realism by shooting hard pellets, then no reasonable alternative will, by hypothesis, be available. In that instance, the design feature that defines which alternatives are relevant—the realism of the hard-pellet gun and thus its capacity to injure — is precisely the feature in which the user places value and of which the plaintiff complains. If a court were to adopt this characterization of the product, and deem the capacity to injure an egregiously unacceptable quality in a toy for use by children, it could conclude that liability should attach without proof of a reasonable

alternative design. The court would declare the product design to be defective and not reasonably safe because the extremely high degree of danger posed by its use or consumption so substantially outweighs its negligible social utility that no rational, reasonable person, fully aware of the relevant facts would choose to use, or to allow children to use, the product.

Why do the Reporters up the ante in comment *e*, to require that an "extremely high degree of danger" outweigh the "negligible social utility" of a product before the risk-benefit standard (without proof of alterative design) can apply to establish design defect? Normally the level of proof required for the risk-benefit standard in tort law is a preponderance of the evidence. *See Bowman v. General Motors Corp.*, 427 F. Supp. 234 (Pa. 1977).

How wide is the door to categoric design liability that comment *e* leaves open? Would it justify a court in finding that a product such as cigarettes, handguns or beer is manifestly unreasonable? The RESTATEMENT (SECOND) OF TORTS, § 402A, comment i provided that many products could not be made safely and that such products were not unreasonably dangerous. It went on:

> Good whiskey is not unreasonably dangerous merely because it will make some people drunk, and is especially dangerous to alcoholics; but bad whiskey, containing a dangerous amount of fusel oil, is unreasonably dangerous. Good tobacco is not unreasonably dangerous merely because the effects of smoking may be harmful, but tobacco containing something like marijuana may be unreasonably dangerous. Good butter is not unreasonably dangerous merely, because if such be the case, it deposits cholesterol in the arteries and leads to heart attacks; but bad butter, contaminated with poisonous fish oil, is unreasonably dangerous.

Does the new RESTATEMENT (THIRD) have a similar exculpatory comment? Yes and no; section 2, comment d, provides:

> The requirement in Subsection (b) that plaintiff show a reasonable alternative design applies in most instances even though the plaintiff alleges that the category of product sold by the defendant is so dangerous that it should not have been marketed at all. See comment e Common and widely distributed products such as alcoholic beverages, firearms, and above-ground swimming pools may be found to be defective only upon proof of the requisite conditions in Subsection (a), (b), or (c).

What about tobacco? Tobacco was included in the list and then was deleted by a voice vote of the American Law Institute, the organization that promulgates and approves the restatements. What is a lawyer or court to make of that deletion?

Texas has a statute providing that a products manufacturer or seller shall not be liable if:

> (1) the product is inherently unsafe and the product is known to be unsafe by the ordinary consumer who consumes the product with the ordinary knowledge common to the community; and

(2) the product is a common consumer product intended for personal consumption, such as sugar, castor oil, alcohol, tobacco, and butter, as identified in Comment i to Section 402A of the Restatement (Second) of Torts.

Tex. Civ. Prac. & Rem.Code Ann. § 82.004(a) (1997).

In *Sanchez v. Liggett & Myers, Inc.*, 187 F.3d 486 (5th Cir. 1999), the statute was applied to bar claims based on failure to warn of the addictive nature of tobacco. Plaintiffs had argued the legislation only applied to preclude a warning claim based upon the general health hazards of smoking, as opposed to the addictive nature of tobacco. The court also held that the statute barred the plaintiffs' claims of fraud, misrepresentation, breach of implied warranty and violation of the Texas Deceptive Practices Act. Judge Parker dissented, pointing out that tobacco companies had steadfastly denied their products were addictive for many years, thereby undermining the claim that the addictive nature of tobacco was commonly known when the *Sanchez* plaintiffs started smoking.

Are you confused about the "bad" product category's continued existence? What makes its existence even more confusing is that at a time when the new Restatement (Third) seems to radically limit the existence of categorical "bad" product liability, newspapers are full of stories about publicly instituted and mass tort actions against the makers of cigarettes, guns, and other products.

5. *Other bad product theories.* Are there other theories available to attack an entire product line other than the design claim? We will consider the warning claim in the next section. But, in addition to warning and design claims, plaintiffs are increasingly attacking the way in which products are marketed under misrepresentation or non-disclosure theories or under general negligence theories.

What about the claim that manufacturing and selling a particular product is an ultrahazardous or abnormally dangerous activity that ought to expose the producer or seller to strict or absolute liability?

In *Kelley v. R.G. Indus.*, 304 Md. 124, 497 A.2d 1143 (1985), plaintiff, injured when he was shot during a robbery at the grocery store where he was employed, brought a products liability action against the gun's assembler/importer. In the context of a § 402A claim the court first noted:

> [Maryland cases] expressly require that the product be defective when sold. In determining whether a product is defective, in its design or its manufacture, Maryland cases have generally applied the "consumer expectation" test. . . .
>
> A handgun manufacturer or marketer could not be held liable under this theory. Contrary to [plaintiff's] argument, a handgun is not defective merely because it is capable of being used during criminal activity to inflict harm. A consumer would expect a handgun to be dangerous, by its very nature, and to have the capacity to fire a bullet with deadly force. Kelley confuses a product's normal function, which may very well be dangerous, with a defect in a product's design or construction. For example, an automobile is a dangerous product, if used to run down pedestrians. In such situation, injury would result from the

nature of the product — its ability to be propelled at a great speed with great force. But that same automobile might also be defective in its design or construction, e.g., if the gasoline tank were placed in such position that it could easily explode in a rear-end collision. Only in the second instance, regarding the placement of the gasoline tank, would the design of the product be defective, exposing the product's manufacturer to liability under § 402A. Similarly, a handgun is dangerous because its normal function is to propel bullets with deadly force. That alone is not sufficient for its manufacturer to incur liability under § 402A. For the handgun to be defective, there would have to be a problem in its manufacture or design, such as a weak or improperly placed part, that would cause it to fire unexpectedly or otherwise malfunction.

Notwithstanding, and following exhaustive reference to federal and state gun control policies and legislation, the court concluded:

> Thus, the policy implications of the gun control laws enacted by both the United States Congress and the Maryland General Assembly reflect a governmental view that there is a handgun species, i.e., the so-called Saturday Night Special, which is considered to have little or no legitimate purpose in today's society. [The gun was small, short-barreled, cheap, of poor quality in materials and workmanship, and unreliable.]
>
> . . . [T]he manufacturer or marketer of a Saturday Night Special knows or ought to know that the chief use of the product is for criminal activity. Such criminal use, and the virtual absence of legitimate uses for the product, are clearly foreseeable by the manufacturers and sellers of Saturday Night Specials.
>
> Moreover, as between the manufacturer or marketer of a Saturday Night Special, who places among the public a product that will be used chiefly in criminal activity, and the innocent victim of such misuse, the former is certainly more at fault than the latter.
>
> For the above reasons, we conclude that it is entirely consistent with public policy to hold the manufacturers and marketers of Saturday Night Special handguns strictly liable to innocent persons who suffer gunshot injuries from the criminal use of their products. Furthermore, in light of the ever growing number of deaths and injuries due to such handguns being used in criminal activity, the imposition of such liability is warranted by today's circumstances.
>
> While the fact that a handgun is a Saturday Night Special may not bring its manufacturer or marketer within any of the previously existing theories of strict liability discussed [above], we have repeatedly pointed out that the common law adapts to fit the needs of society. Consequently, we shall recognize a separate, limited area of strict liability for the manufacturers, as well as all in the marketing chain, of Saturday Night Specials.

What was the factual defect in *Kelley*? Did the gun fail either prong of the *Barker* test?

After the *Kelley* decision the Maryland legislature passed Md. Code Annot. Art. 27, § 36I(h)(1) (1987), providing that a person or entity may not be held strictly liable for damages resulting from injuries sustained as a result of the criminal use of a firearm by a third person, unless the person or entity "conspired with the third person to commit, or willfully aided, abetted, or caused the commission of the criminal act."

See also Diggles v. Horwitz, 765 S.W.2d 839 (Tex. App. 1989), where a patient in a mental health facility committed suicide by shooting himself with the semi-automatic pistol he had just purchased at a pawnshop. While the court did not rule out the possibility of a negligence action against the owner of the pawnshop, it held that neither a strict products liability nor an ultrahazardous activity action would lie against the retailer or the manufacturer of the gun.

6. *A Little Moral Philosophy.* Assuming there may be a category of manifestly unreasonable products, if a manufacturer supplies a warning to users of the product and they are aware of the dangers that the product poses to them but they choose to use the product anyway, should the product seller ever be liable to them for causing known dangers? If so, why? Should the law protect people from themselves? Does it ever do so? Would your answers be the same if the product posed risks not just to users of the product but to third persons as well?

In *Buckingham v. R.J. Reynolds Tobacco Co.,* 713 A.2d 381 (N.H. 1998), the court, while refusing to recognize a strict products liability claim against the manufacturer of cigarettes, allowed the plaintiff to proceed with a negligence action under RESTATEMENT (SECOND) section 389. *Buckingham* involved a second-hand smoke claim. Section 389 provides:

> One who supplies directly or through a third person a chattel for another's use, knowing or having reason to know that the chattel is unlikely to be made reasonably safe before being put to a use which the supplier should expect it to be put, is subject to liability for physical harm caused by such use to those whom the supplier should expect to use the chattel or to be endangered by its probable use, and who are ignorant of the dangerous character of the chattel or whose knowledge thereof does not make them contributorily negligent, although the supplier has informed the other for whose use the chattel is supplied of its dangerous character.

Presumably the contributory negligence defense of sec. 389 would not be a bar in a comparative negligence jurisdiction.

7. *Reasonable.* Under the RESTATEMENT (THIRD): PRODUCTS LIABILITY, not only must the plaintiff establish that there is an alternative design for the product on trial but the alternative design must be reasonable. Moreover, the omission of the reasonable alternative design must render the product as designed not reasonably safe. If all those references to "reasonable" in the Restatement remind you of your study of negligence, they should; liability for a design defect is certainly akin to negligence.

8. *A Feasibility Test.* Child's leg was injured by a power lawn mower being operated in reverse. Plaintiff claimed that the mower should have been

designed so that the blade would shut off when the mower was being operated in reverse. Affirming a directed verdict for the mower manufacturer, the court observed that "[a]bsent evidence as to the effect a different design would have on cost and use of the product, a trier of fact is in no position to balance these factors against the danger involved," to determine whether the alternative design is "economical, practical, and effective." *Lease v. International Harvester Co.*, 174 Ill. App. 3d 897, 529 N.E.2d 57 (1988).

9. *Feasibility as Related to Practicality. Drobney v. Federal Sign & Signal Corp.*, 182 Ill. App. 3d 471, 131 Ill. Dec. 833, 539 N.E.2d 186, *app. den.*, 136 Ill. Dec. 584, 545 N.E.2d 108 (1989), involved a fake arrest of a motorist and her subsequent rape and murder. Plaintiff, the motorist's administrator, alleged that the assailants had used a red oscillating and rotating "police" light manufactured by the defendant to cause the decedent to stop her vehicle. Plaintiff alleged that the light was defectively designed because it was red, oscillated and could be used to impersonate police officers, and that the benefits of the light as designed were outweighed by its inherent risks. The court held that plaintiff's complaint failed to disclose a cause of action, stating:

> . . . Plaintiff does not suggest in his complaint an alternate design which would alleviate the alleged problems associated with the present design; he merely submits that a nonred, nonoscillating light would be sufficient. However, if defendant's customers include lawful users . . . an alternate design that is not red in color and does not oscillate would not be available or feasible, economical, or practical for defendant to manufacture. Even assuming all lawful users purchase their lights from manufacturers other than defendant, we question, given the variety of colors of lights available to law enforcement vehicles, whether it would be effective for defendant to change the design of its light at all.

What issue does the case present? How would you approach its resolution?

10. *The Relevance of Likelihood of the Risk.* It has become trite products doctrine that foresight of risk was presumed. *See Phillips v. Kimwood Mach. Co.*, 269 Or. 485, 525 P.2d 1033 (1974). Do you see how the new Restatement has potentially undermined this presumption? In any event, once knowledge of the risk was imputed to the manufacturer, his design choices were subjected to a risk-benefit analysis from the perspective of a hypothetical reasonable manufacturer. This hypothetical manufacturer, in evaluating present and alternate designs, would have to evaluate the likelihood of a risk occurring. For example, in *Green v. Denney,* 87 Or. App. 298, 742 P.2d 639, 641–42 (1987), *rev. den.,* 305 Or. 21, 749 P.2d 136 (1988), plaintiff was driving his 1980 Pinto with his wife in the front passenger seat. A horse suddenly appeared in front of the car. The horse collided with the car's front bumper, flew over the hood and landed on the roof of the vehicle. The roof collapsed, killing plaintiff's wife.

> Product liability for defective design does not extend to cases where the risk of injury from the product's failure is so remote that a reasonable manufacturer would not consider it in design decisions. Plaintiff offered evidence that collisions with large animals, including horses, are common and foreseeable. Defendant countered that it was not

foreseeable that such a collision would produce an impact on the roof concentrated at a particular point rather than being more evenly distributed. The problem with that argument is that its converse is equally true: It was just as unpredictable that the impact from a collision would fall evenly on the entire roof rather than land with greater force on its weakest part. That the horse landed with its full weight on the header did not make the accident any more a freak occurrence than if the weight had been distributed evenly.

. . . Plaintiff's expert testified that reinforcement of the roof was technically and economically feasible and would have prevented its deformation so that it would not come into contact with a passenger's head. Plaintiff also introduced expert testimony that the amount of energy generated by the fall of the horse on the roof did not exceed the amount that it was required to sustain to pass a federal safety test. . . . We conclude that the accident and the manner of injury were not unforeseeable, as a matter of law, and that plaintiff presented sufficient evidence of defective design to justify submission of the case to the jury.

11. *State of the Art.* How should a court deal with compliance with the state of the art at the time the product was designed or sold? If the plaintiff has to prove that the defendant did not comply with the state of the art at the time it made the product, doesn't the plaintiff then have to prove that the defendant failed to exercise reasonable care? Isn't that simply negligence?

Other courts hold that compliance with the applicable state of the art at the time that the product was manufactured is an affirmative defense and, if proved, will exculpate the defendant. But isn't that to say that if the defendant proves it was not negligent in the design of its product then it is not liable? The substantive standard is still negligence, isn't it? Except the burden is not on the plaintiff to prove negligence, but on the defendant to prove no negligence?

If state of the art is not relevant, as in a mismanufacture claim or under *Halphen's* unreasonably dangerous *per se* claim, then there is truly the possibility for strict liability, isn't there? Because then the defendant may be held liable even though it exercised the utmost care at the time it made its product, but between the time of manufacture and trial technological developments rendered its product not reasonably safe. If the producer or seller is liable under those circumstances, we might say that it bears the development risk. If compliance with state of the art exculpates the manufacturer, no matter who bears the burden of proof on the issue, then it might be said that the injured plaintiff bears the development risk.

Who bears the development risk under the approach that the *Potter* court takes? Under *Potter* compliance with the state of the art is not determinative of anything, is it? It is but one factor for the jury, or judge as fact finder, to consider in deciding whether the product is unreasonably dangerous. Does that mean that it is up to the jury (or judge as fact finder) to decide whether the standard of liability in a particular case ought to be strict liability or negligence? Is that consistent with your notions of what law ought to be about? Or have you had enough torts by this point that it doesn't bother you?

See the efforts of one court to distinguish the standard of negligence from that of state of the art, in the context of prescription drug warnings. State of the art requires a manufacturer to warn of a "known or reasonably scientifically knowable risk," the court said, even though the manufacturer may have exercised due care in its "own testing" or in conforming to an "industry-wide practice." *Carlin v. Superior Court*, 920 P.2d 1347 (Cal. 1996). Would a manufacturer, held to the standard of an expert, not be negligent in failing to know of a "reasonably scientifically knowable risk"?

If state of the art is judged by the knowledge or capability existing at the date of trial, rather than the date of manufacturer, then we are in a different ball park. *See Dart v. Wiebe Mfg.*, 709 P.2d 876 (Ariz.), holding that in judging risk-benefit for purposes of determining design defect, one looks to the time of trial rather than of manufacture. *Wiebe* represents a minority position.

12. *The Common Market of Europe.* In July, 1985, the European Community Directive, O.J. EUR. COMM. (No. L210/29), was adopted by the Council of the European Communities, and each member was given three years from the date of adoption to bring the directive into force. The Directive provides for a uniform products liability law for the European Community; however, there are designated permissible variations including whether to adopt a "developmental risk" defense.

The British implementation of the development risk defense, Consumer Protection Act 1987, § 4(1)(e), provides that the defendant may show by way of defense that the "state of scientific and technical knowledge at the relevant time was not such that a producer of products of the same description as the product in question might be expected to have discovered the defect if it had existed in his products while they were under his control."

13. *Proof of Defect by Circumstantial Evidence.* One of the reasons *Potter* rejects the RESTATEMENT (THIRD) § 2(b) rule requiring proof of alternative design is that such a rule "would require plaintiffs to retain an expert witness even in cases in which lay jurors can infer a design defect from circumstantial evidence." Would it? What about RESTATEMENT (THIRD) § 3?

Can any type of product defect, including design, be proven under § 3, as an alternative to § 2 or to any other standard of proof? Remember that in products liability plaintiffs are normally allowed to plead and prove alternative bases of liability. The Reporters state, in comment *b* to § 3, that that section "most often" applies to manufacturing defects, but that "occasionally" it applies to design defects as well. But an annotation, 65 ALR 4th 346, 354–358 (1988), lists a majority of states that have allowed proof of design defect by circumstantial evidence.

Can proof of a defect under § 3 be shown by expert witness testimony? *See* the discussion of *Soule v. GM* in the *Potter* case. Expert testimony is widely admitted to prove res ipsa loquitur. *Seavers v. Meth. Med. Cntr.*, 9 S.W. 3d 86 (Tenn. 1999). Is not § 3 a kind of strict liability — res ipsa method of proving product defect?

14. *A Comment on the Defect Tests.* Consider, once again, the tests for determining whether a product is defective. There is the consumer expectation test (whether treated as a warranty or tort claim); there is the risk utility

test (the substantive implications of which depend upon the relevance and effect of how the jurisdiction treats state of the art); there are the jurisdictions providing that a plaintiff can establish defect under either the consumer expectation test or the risk-utility test (some require the defendant to prove no liability under the risk utility test—others require the plaintiff to prove risk outweighs utility); and there is the modified consumer expectation test adopted in *Potter*. Under *Potter*, the consumer expectation test sets the standard but risk and utility are relevant to a determination of whether the product is more dangerous than a reasonable consumer would expect.

Can you find any real principles here or just nagging variety? Is a federal solution preferable? Or, should the states be allowed to continue to develop their own products liability law?

Has the new Restatement helped in design cases? Has it restated the variety into a comprehensive, consensus-building whole? Or has it merely taken a stand in the debate?

PROBLEM

Buzz Beater is a star baseball player at State University. Buzz wants to become a pro baseball player. Consequently, unlike his teammates, he does not use aluminum bats, which are legal in amateur baseball. He uses wooden bats, like the pros use. One day in batting practice, while using a bat made by Wooden Bat Co. (WBC), the bat shatters and a splinter blinds Buzz in one eye. Analyze Buzz's design claims against WBC.

[3] Failure to Warn

HOOD v. RYOBI AMERICA CORP.
181 F.3d 608 (4th Cir. 1999)

WILKINSON, CHIEF JUDGE:

Wilson M. Hood lost part of his thumb and lacerated his leg when he removed the blade guards from his new Ryobi miter saw and then used the unguarded saw for home carpentry. Hood sued Ryobi, alleging that the company failed adequately to warn of the saw's dangers and that the saw was defective. Applying Maryland products liability law, the district court granted summary judgment to Ryobi on all claims.

The saw and owner's manual bore at least seven clear, simple warnings not to operate the tool with the blade guards removed. The warnings were not required to spell out all the consequences of improper use. Nor was the saw defective— Hood altered and used the tool in violation of Ryobi's clear warnings. Thus we affirm the judgment.

Hood purchased a Ryobi TS-254 miter saw in Westminster, Maryland on February 25, 1995, for the purpose of performing home repairs. The saw was fully assembled at the time of purchase. It had a ten-inch diameter blade mounted on a rotating spindle controlled by a finger trigger on a handle near the top of the blade. To operate the saw, the consumer would use that handle to lower the blade through the material being cut.

Two blade guards shielded nearly the entire saw blade. A large metal guard, fixed to the frame of the saw, surrounded the upper half of the blade. A transparent plastic lower guard covered the rest of the blade and retracted into the upper guard as the saw came into contact with the work piece.

A number of warnings in the operator's manual and affixed to the saw itself stated that the user should operate the saw only with the blade guards in place. For example, the owner's manual declared that the user should "KEEP GUARDS IN PLACE" and warned: "ALWAYS USE THE SAW BLADE GUARD. Never operate the machine with the guard removed"; "NEVER operate this saw without all guards in place and in good operating condition"; and "WARNING: TO PREVENT POSSIBLE SERIOUS PERSONAL INJURY, NEVER PERFORM ANY CUTTING OPERATION WITH THE UPPER OR LOWER BLADE GUARD REMOVED." The saw itself carried several decals stating "DANGER: DO NOT REMOVE ANY GUARD. USE OF SAW WITHOUT THIS GUARD WILL RESULT IN SERIOUS INJURY"; "OPERATE ONLY WITH GUARDS IN PLACE"; and "WARNING . . . DO NOT operate saw without the upper and lower guards in place."

The day after his purchase, Hood began working with the saw in his driveway. While attempting to cut a piece of wood approximately four inches in height Hood found that the blade guards prevented the saw blade from passing completely through the piece. Disregarding the manufacturer's warnings, Hood decided to remove the blade guards from the saw. Hood first detached the saw blade from its spindle. He then unscrewed the four screws that held the blade guard assembly to the frame of the saw. Finally, he replaced the blade onto the bare spindle and completed his cut.

Rather than replacing the blade guards, Hood continued to work with the saw blade exposed. He worked in this fashion for about twenty minutes longer when, in the middle of another cut, the spinning saw blade flew off the saw and back toward Hood. The blade partially amputated his left thumb and lacerated his right leg.

Hood admits that he read the owner's manual and most of the warning labels on the saw before he began his work. He claims, however, that he believed the blade guards were intended solely to prevent a user's clothing or fingers from coming into contact with the saw blade. He contends that he was unaware that removing the blade guards would permit the spinning blade to detach from the saw. But Ryobi, he claims, was aware of that possibility. In fact, another customer had sued Ryobi after suffering a similar accident in the mid-1980s.

On December 5, 1997, Hood sued several divisions of Ryobi in the United States District Court for the District of Maryland. Hood raised claims of failure to warn and defective design under several theories of liability. On cross-motions for summary judgment the district court entered judgment for the defendants on all claims, finding that in the face of adequate warnings Hood had altered the saw and caused his own injury. Hood v. Ryobi N. Am., Inc., 17 F.Supp.2d 448 (D.Md.1998). Hood appeals.

A manufacturer may be liable for placing a product on the market that bears inadequate instructions and warnings or that is defective in design. . . . Hood asserts that Ryobi failed adequately to warn of the dangers of using the saw without the blade guards in place. Hood also contends that the design of the saw was defective. We disagree on both counts.[1]

Hood first complains that the warnings he received were insufficiently specific. Hood admits that Ryobi provided several clear and conspicuous warnings not to operate the saw without the blade guards. He contends, however, that the warnings affixed to the product and displayed in the operator's manual were inadequate to alert him to the dangers of doing so. In addition to Ryobi's directive "never" to operate a guardless saw, Hood would require the company to inform of the actual consequences of such conduct. Specifically, Hood contends that an adequate warning would have explained that removing the guards would lead to blade detachment.

We disagree. Maryland does not require an encyclopedic warning. Instead, "a warning need only be one that is reasonable under the circumstances." *Levin v. Walter Kidde & Co.*, 251 Md. 560, 248 A.2d 151, 153 (1968). A clear and specific warning will normally be sufficient—"the manufacturer need not warn of every mishap or source of injury that the mind can imagine flowing from the product." *Liesener v. Weslo, Inc.*, 775 F.Supp. 857, 861 (D.Md.1991); see *Levin*, 248 A.2d at 154 (declining to require warning of the danger that a cracked syphon bottle might explode and holding "never use cracked bottle" to be adequate as a matter of law). In deciding whether a warning is adequate, Maryland law asks whether the benefits of a more detailed warning outweigh the costs of requiring the change.

Hood assumes that the cost of a more detailed warning label is minimal in this case, and he claims that such a warning would have prevented his injury. But the price of more detailed warnings is greater than their additional printing fees alone. Some commentators have observed that the proliferation of label detail threatens to undermine the effectiveness of warnings altogether. See James A. Henderson, Jr. & Aaron D. Twerski, Doctrinal Collapse in Products Liability: The Empty Shell of Failure to Warn, 65 N.Y.U. L.Rev. 265, 296–97 (1990). As manufacturers append line after line onto product labels in the quest for the best possible warning, it is easy to lose sight of the label's communicative value as a whole. Well-meaning attempts to warn of every possible accident lead over time to voluminous yet impenetrable labels—too prolix to read and too technical to understand.

By contrast, Ryobi's warnings are clear and unequivocal. Three labels on the saw itself and at least four warnings in the owner's manual direct the user not to operate the saw with the blade guards removed. Two declare that "serious injury" could result from doing so. This is not a case where the manufacturer has failed to include any warnings at all with its product. Ryobi provided warnings sufficient to apprise the ordinary consumer that it is unsafe to operate a guardless saw—warnings which, if followed, would have prevented the injury in this case.

It is apparent, moreover, that the vast majority of consumers do not detach this critical safety feature before using this type of saw. Indeed, although

---

[1] Hood raises these claims under three theories of recovery: strict liability, negligence, and breach of warranty. The principles of Maryland law governing these three theories, at least as relevant to this case, are virtually identical.

Ryobi claims to have sold thousands of these saws, Hood has identified only one fifteen-year-old incident similar to his. Hood has thus not shown that these clear, unmistakable, and prominent warnings are insufficient to accomplish their purpose. Nor can he prove that increased label clutter would bring any net societal benefit. We hold that the warnings Ryobi provided are adequate as a matter of law.

Hood's defective design claim is likewise unpersuasive. Hood's injuries were the direct result of the alterations he made to the saw— alterations that directly contravened clear, unambiguous warnings. And such alterations defeat a claim of design defect.[2]

This rule has been expressed alternatively as one of duty and one of causation. First, a manufacturer is only required to design a product that is safe for its reasonably foreseeable uses. If that duty is met, the product is simply not defective. Second, if a consumer alters a product in a way that creates a defect, the consumer's conduct rather than the manufacturer's is the proximate cause of any ensuing accident. Under either rationale, a post-sale product alteration will defeat a design defect claim if that alteration leads directly to the plaintiff's injury.

Hood admits that he altered the table saw by removing the blade guards from the unit's frame, and he acknowledges that the alteration led directly to his injuries. Hood asserts, however, that Ryobi should have foreseen that consumers might operate its saws with the guards removed. Hood notes that the operation of equipment without safety guards is a frequently cited OSHA violation. And, as noted, Ryobi itself has faced litigation on one other occasion for the same type of accident that befell Hood. In short, Hood contends that Ryobi should have designed its saw to operate equally well with the guards in place or removed.

We disagree. Maryland imposes no duty to predict that a consumer will violate clear, easily understandable safety warnings such as those Ryobi included with this product. For example, a manufacturer need not foresee that a consumer might store a gasoline can in his basement in contravention of clear warning labels. *Simpson*, 527 A.2d at 1341 ("'Where warning is given, the seller may reasonably assume that it will be read and heeded; and a product bearing such a warning, which is safe for use if it is followed, is not in defective condition, nor is it unreasonably dangerous'" (quoting Restatement (Second) of Torts § 402A cmt. j)). Nor must a manufacturer foresee that a worker will shove his arm into a conveyor machine to repair it without first shutting the machine down, again in violation of "explicit written warnings."
. . . When a consumer injures himself by using a product—or, as in this case, by altering it—in violation of clear, unmistakable, and easy-to-follow warnings, it is the consumer's own conduct that causes the injury. . . . The manufacturer is not liable under a design defect theory

---

[2] Although this rule is effected through different defenses to strict liability and negligence claims, those defenses are functionally equivalent in this case. Strict liability is "conditioned upon the product reaching the user 'without substantial change in the condition in which it is sold.'" Banks v. Iron Hustler Corp., 59 Md.App. 408, 475 A.2d 1243, 1255 (Ct.Spec.App.1984) (quoting Restatement (Second) of Torts § 402A). Similarly, a manufacturer is not liable in negligence if an "intervening alteration of the product was the superseding cause of [a consumer's] injuries." *Id.* at 1254. On each claim Hood's alterations defeat recovery.

We recognize that the American Law Institute has recently underscored the concern that comment j of the Second Restatement, read literally, would permit a manufacturer of a dangerously defective product to immunize itself from liability merely by slapping warning labels on that product. See Restatement (Third) of Torts: Prod. Liab. § 2 cmt. l & Reporter's Note. We are all afflicted with lapses of attention; warnings aimed simply at avoiding consumer carelessness should not absolve a manufacturer of the duty to design reasonable safeguards for its products. See *Id.* cmt. 1, illus. 14 (when warning could not eliminate the possibility of accidental contact with a dangerous shear point, decal declaring "keep hands and feet away" does not bar a design defect claim).

The Maryland courts have already made clear, however, that warnings will not inevitably defeat liability for a product's defective design. See *Klein v. Sears, Roebuck & Co.*, 92 Md.App. 477, 608 A.2d 1276, 1282–83 (Ct. Spec. App.1992) (such warnings as "never leave tool running unattended" and "do not place fingers or hands in the path of the saw blade" are too vague to defeat manufacturer's liability for failing to include blade guards on its saws). Maryland has thus sought to encourage manufacturers to rid their products of traps for the unwary, while declining to hold them responsible for affirmative consumer misuse.

This case involves much more than a consumer's inevitable inattention. Rather, Hood took affirmative steps to remove the safety guards from his saw and—in contravention of warnings which were "clear, direct, simple, unequivoca[l], unmistakable, definite, and easy to understand and obey"—then used the saw to cut several pieces of wood. Hood's own conduct thus caused his injury and defeats any claim that the saw is defective in design.

Warned never to operate his miter saw without the blade guards in place, Hood nonetheless chose to detach those guards and run the saw in a disassembled condition. We hold that Ryobi is not liable for Hood's resulting injuries under any of the theories of recovery raised here. The judgment of the district court is therefore

AFFIRMED.

NOTES

1. *Defective Marketing — Failure to Warn.* As the materials indicate, a manufacturer may be liable for failure to warn of a defect in his product, although the product is not "defective" in manufacture or design. This "failure to warn" presents some doctrinal difficulties. If the warning could feasibly have been placed on the product itself, then is not the product defective in design because it does not contain such a warning? If a warning is placed upon a product, shouldn't the warning be considered in determining whether the product was defectively designed, *i.e.*, the risks which it would present? A safety design, unlike a warning, will often preclude an accident from happening. But this difference does not always hold where — as in *Hood* — the design can be altered or circumvented.

Is there really strict liability for failure to warn? What if the manufacturer is not required to warn of unforeseeable risks, and he is not required to warn of all foreseeable risks (because of the impracticality of warning of all risks, or because warning of a great number of risks may lull the consumer into ignoring all of the warnings)? If these principles are followed, is not the cause of action one of negligence?

Is a "failure to warn" claim a "hybrid negligence/strict liability" claim, *i.e.*, the manufacturer need not foresee the injury-causing attribute of his product, but is held only to a duty of reasonableness in warning about the attribute? In *Anderson v. Owens-Corning Fiberglas Corp.*, 53 Cal.3d 987, 1002–1003, 281 Cal.Rptr. 528, 810 P.2d 549 (1991), the court said:

> [F]ailure to warn in strict liability differs markedly from failure to warn in the negligence context. Negligence law in a failure-to-warn case requires a plaintiff to prove that a manufacturer or distributor did not warn of a particular risk for reasons which fell below the acceptable standard of care, i.e., what a reasonably prudent manufacturer would have known and warned about. Strict liability is not concerned with the standard of due care or the reasonableness of a manufacturer's conduct. The rules of strict liability require a plaintiff to prove only that the defendant did not adequately warn of a particular risk that was known or knowable in light of the generally recognized and prevailing best scientific and medical knowledge available at the time of manufacture and distribution. Thus, in strict liability, as opposed to negligence, the reasonableness of the defendant's failure to warn is immaterial. Stated another way, a reasonably prudent manufacturer might reasonably decide that the risk of harm was such as not to require a warning as, for example, if the manufacturer's own testing showed a result contrary to that of others in the scientific community. Such a manufacturer might escape liability under negligence principles. In contrast, under strict liability principles the manufacturer has no such leeway; the manufacturer is liable if it failed to give warning of dangers that were known to the scientific community at the time it manufactured or distributed the product.

See also, Carlin v. Superior Court, 920 P.2d 1347 (Cal. 1996)(applying *Anderson* to a failure to warn claim involving the drug Halcyon).

The RESTATEMENT (THIRD) sec. 2 provides that a product:

> (c) is defective because of inadequate instructions or warnings when the foreseeable risks of harm posed by the product could have been reduced or avoided by the provision of reasonable instructions or warnings by the seller or other distributor, or a predecessor in the commercial chain of distribution, and the omission of the instructions or warnings renders the product not reasonably safe.

Does that sound like a negligence standard or a strict liability standard? Does the RESTATEMENT (THIRD) adopt the *Anderson* "test?" Or, is it more of a negligence standard? Why?

One will note that state of the art issues arise in warning cases as well. Should a manufacturer be held liable for failing to warn of a risk of which it was not aware at the time it sold the relevant product? Would liability be imposed under the RESTATEMENT (THIRD)?

2. *Obvious Risks.* What about "open and obvious" dangers? Most courts state that there is no duty to warn of an obvious risk within the common knowledge of the user. That is, the manufacturer of a knife does not have to warn that it may cut the user if not properly used. Must a seller warn if coffee is hot? Would it have to warn if the coffee is hotter than a reasonable person expected? If an obvious danger does not make the product defective, the victim takes nothing.

In the design context, it is widely held that an obvious danger does not make a product reasonably safe. Obviousness is "only a factor to be considered" on the issues of defective design and "whether plaintiff used that degree of reasonable care required by the circumstances." *Auburn Machine Works v. Jones*, 366 So. 2d 1167, 1169 (Fla. 1979).

3. *Common Knowledge to Whom?* In *Reece v. Lowe's of Boone, Inc.*, 754 S.W.2d 67 (Tenn. App. 1988), one of plaintiff's children was severely injured, and the other killed, when the go-kart in which they were riding — manufactured and sold by the defendants — ran into a public highway intersection and was hit by an oncoming car. Entrance into the intersection was obscured by a bank and by weeds some six feet high.

The go-kart had two separate labels warning against operating the vehicle on public highways. The plaintiffs contended that, in addition, the go-kart should have had a vertical pole with a flag at the top, similar to the type of flag "ofttimes employed by bicycles as a safety measure," and that the absence of such a flag made the go-kart defective and unreasonably dangerous. Relying on a case holding that it is common knowledge that rapid ingestion of a large quantity of "almost pure grain alcohol" can be fatal, the court denied recovery.

4. *Warnings and Causation.* Where liability is premised on a failure to warn, a nice cause in fact question arises: would the victim have heeded an adequate warning? Should the burden of proving cause in fact be shifted to the manufacturer by establishing a presumption that an adequate warning would have been heeded? *See, e.g., Bloxom v. Bloxom*, 512 So.2d 839 (La. 1987) (when manufacturer fails to give adequate warnings or instructions, a presumption arises that the user would have read and heeded such admonitions.)

What if the victim is killed and there are no eyewitnesses? Isn't the shifting of the burden of proof of cause in fact to the manufacturer tantamount to taking cause in fact out of the case?

5. *Post-Accident Warnings.* If the defendant contends that a warning is unnecessary, plaintiff may attack defendant's credibility by showing that the defendant actually began giving such a warning after the product injured the plaintiff. *Toups v. Sears, Roebuck & Co.*, 507 So. 2d 809 (La. 1987), *on remand*, 519 So. 2d 842 (La. App. 1988). Such post-accident evidence may also be admissible to show the feasibility of giving a warning, if the defendant contends that the warning was not feasible. FED. R. EVID. 407.

Remedial conduct undertaken *after* the *sale*, but *before* the *accident*, is admissible as evidence of defectiveness. *Huffman v. Caterpillar Tractor Co.*, 908 F. 2d 1470 (10th Cir. 1990); *but see Traylor v. Husqvarna Motor*, 988 F.2d 729 (7th Cir.1993).

6. *Post-Sale Duty to Warn or Correct.* If the defendant does not undertake to warn of a danger discovered after a product has been marketed, the evidence may justify an inference that it should have done so. *Braniff Airways, Inc. v. Curtiss-Wright Corp.*, 411 F.2d 451 (2d Cir.), *cert. denied*, 396 U.S. 959, 24 L. Ed. 2d 423, 90 S. Ct. 431 (1969). If it appears likely that a warning would be inadequate, the defendant may have an additional duty to correct the problem in products that have already been marketed. *Gracyalny v. Westinghouse Elec. Corp.*, 723 F.2d 1311 (7th Cir. 1983).

As to post-sale duties to warn, RESTATEMENT (THIRD) § 10 sets forth a limited duty under certain circumstances. It provides:

> (a) One engaged in the business of selling or otherwise distributing products is subject to liability for harm to persons or property caused by the seller's failure to provide a warning after the time of sale or distribution of a product if a reasonable person in the seller's position would provide such a warning.
>
> (b) A reasonable person in the seller's position would provide a warning after the time of sale if:
>
> (1) the seller knows or reasonably should know that the product poses a substantial risk of harm to persons or property; and
>
> (2) those to whom a warning might be provided can be identified and can reasonably be assumed to be unaware of the risk of harm; and
>
> (3) a warning can be effectively communicated to and acted on by those to whom a warning might be provided; and
>
> (4) the risk of harm is sufficiently great to justify the burden of providing a warning.

Some courts do not impose a post-sale duty to warn of "risk-avoidance measures" or "technological improvements" that occur after the time a product is sold. *DeSantis v. Frick Co.*, 1999 Pa. Super. 329. Why do you think courts make such a distinction? The Reporters' Note to sec. 10 states that the section "does not draw a sharp distinction" regarding the duty to warn of pre-sale and post-sale safety improvements.

In some instances, the federal government has the statutory power to require a post-sale warning or recall of goods by manufacturers. The RESTATEMENT (THIRD) § 11 provides:

> One engaged in the business of selling or otherwise distributing products is subject to liability for harm to persons or property caused by the seller's failure to recall a product after the time of sale or distribution if:
>
> (a)(1) a governmental directive issued pursuant to a statute or administrative regulation specifically requires the seller or distributor to recall the product; or
>
> (2) the seller or distributor, in the absence of a recall requirement under Section (a)(1), undertakes to recall the product; and

(b) the seller or distributor fails to act as a reasonable person in recalling the product.

If the purchaser or user disregards a recall notice and she or another subsequently is injured by the product defect for which the recall was issued, should recovery be denied? If so, on what basis?

7. *Legal Cause in Products Liability.* In *Hood,* the plaintiff's alteration of the product effectively cut off any potential manufacturer liability. The court noted that the plaintiff's misuse of the product if egregious can be treated as a superseding cause, relieving the defendant of responsibility for any alleged defect. We will consider in more detail below the issue of plaintiff's fault in a product liability case but the more general point is that legal or proximate cause is an element of the plaintiff's prima facie case in a product liability case. Thus concepts of foreseeability, directness, and bizarreness are as relevant in products liability as they are in negligence. RESTATEMENT (THIRD) section 15 provides that causation in products cases "is determined by the prevailing rules and principles governing causation in tort." Just as in negligence, you can ask yourself if the relevant issue would be treated as one of proximate or legal cause for the factfinder or one of duty (law) for the judge.

What about a product that allegedly increases the harm that a plaintiff already at risk suffers? For instance, imagine a plaintiff in an auto accident and the air bag in her car does not trigger. Obviously before the air bag's failure to engage the plaintiff was in a bad spot, but the air bag's failure made it worse. Should the manufacturer be responsible? That is, must the manufacturer provide a car that is "crashworthy?" The RESTATEMENT (THIRD) section 16 says that it must. It provides:

(a) When a product is defective at the time of commercial sale or other distribution and the defect is a substantial factor in increasing the plaintiff's harm beyond that which would have resulted from other causes, the product seller is subject to liability for the increased harm.

(b) If the product supports a determination of the harm that would have resulted from other causes in the absence of the product defect, the product seller's liability is limited to the increased harm attributable solely to the product defect.

(c) If proof does not support a determination under Subsection (b) of the harm that would have resulted in the absence of the product defect, the product seller is liable for all of the plaintiff's harm attributable to the defect and other causes.

(d) A seller of a defective product that is held liable for part of the harm suffered by the plaintiff under Subsection (b), or all of the harm suffered by the plaintiff under Subsection (c), is jointly and severally liable, or severally liable with other parties who bear legal responsibility for causing the harm, [as] determined by applicable rules of joint and several liability.

Whether the jurisdiction has joint and several or several liability, would a jury in that jurisdiction be able to understand an instruction based upon RESTATEMENT (THIRD), section 16? Who has the burden of proof under (b) and (c)? If

[4] Misrepresentation

BAXTER v. FORD MOTOR CO.
179 Wash. 123, 35 P.2d 1090 (1934)

[Plaintiff lost an eye when the windshield of his car shattered as it was struck by a pebble. He brought suit against the defendant car manufacturer, alleging that the defendant had advertised the windshield as "shatter-proof glass . . . so made that it will not fly or shatter under the hardest impact." The trial court dismissed the case at the conclusion of plaintiff's evidence, refusing to admit evidence of the advertising.

On appeal by plaintiff, Ford contended "that there can be no implied or express warranty without privity of contract." The Washington Supreme Court reversed and remanded the case for trial, holding that evidence of the advertising should have been admitted. "It would be unjust," the court said, "to recognize a rule that would permit manufacturers of goods to create a demand for their products by representing that they possess qualities which they, in fact, do not possess, and then, because there is no privity of contract existing between the consumer and the manufacturer, deny the consumer the right to recover if damages result from the absence of those qualities, when such absence is not readily noticeable." Under the circumstances of the case, the court concluded, the plaintiff "had the right to rely" on the defendant's advertisements "even though there was no privity of contract between them." The case was remanded for retrial. 168 Wash. 456, 12 P.2d 409 (1932).

On retrial, plaintiff introduced evidence of defendant's advertising catalogs regarding the allegedly shatterproof nature of the windshield, and of his "entire lack of experience and an absence of familiarity with non-shatterable glass which would enable him to recognize that the glass in the windshield . . . was other than what it was represented to be, and that in purchasing the car he relied on the representations concerning the non-shatterability of the windshield" made in defendants's catalogs. The jury returned a verdict for the plaintiff (respondent here), and Ford (appellant) brought this appeal.]

HOLCOMB, JUSTICE.

A new point, arising out of the last trial, claimed as error, was in excluding testimony of an expert witness on behalf of appellant to the effect that there was no better windshield made than that used in respondent's car and in sustaining the objection to appellant's offer of proof on that point.

No authorities are cited by appellant to sustain this claim, and we know of none. Indeed, it would seem that whether there was any better make of shatterproof glass manufactured by any one at that time would be wholly immaterial, under the law as decided by us on the former appeal, since it was the duty of appellant to know that the representations made to purchasers were true. Otherwise it should not have made them. If a person states as true material facts susceptible of knowledge to one who relies and acts thereon to his injury, if the representations are false, it is immaterial that he did not know they were false, or that he believed them to be true.

[Judgement affirmed.]

NOTES

1. *Culpable and Strict Liability.* A product manufacturer or seller can be liable in deceit, negligence, or strict tort liability for misrepresentation. This proposition is set forth in sec. 9 of the RESTATEMENT (THIRD) OF TORTS: PRODUCTS LIABILITY:

§ 9. Liability of Commercial Product Seller or Distributor for Harm Caused by Misrepresentation

One engaged in the business of selling or otherwise distributing products who, in connection with the sale of a product, makes a fraudulent, negligent, or innocent misrepresentation of material fact concerning the product is subject to liability for harm to persons or property caused by the misrepresentation.

Where strict liability is the basis of recovery, state of the art is no defense, as the court indicated in *Baxter*. *See also Crocker v. Winthrop Labs*, given infra in the chapter on business torts. TENN. CODE ANNOT. § 29-28-10, which provides a state of the art defense, states in subsec. (c) that the "provisions of this section do not apply to an action based on express warranty or misrepresentation regarding the chattel." Why do you suppose strict liability for product misrepresentation is so much stricter than is normally the case for design defect or failure to warn? Isn't an inadequate warning a misrepresentation?

2. *Consumer Expectations as Blood Kin.* There is a close affinity between consumer expectations and product misrepresentation. In that connection reconsider *Castro v. QVC Network*, given at the beginning of this chapter. In the landmark products case of *Greenman v. Yuba Power Products*, 377 P.2d 897 (Cal. 1963), Justice Traynor said:

> In the present case. . .plaintiff was able to plead and prove an express warranty only because he read and relied on the representations of the Shopsmith's ruggedness contained in the manufacturer's brochure. Implicit in the machine's presence on the market, however, was a representation that it would safely do the jobs for which it was built.

3. *The U. C. C. and Misrepresentation.* The Uniform Commercial Code has a strict liability express warranty provision, sec. 2-313, that is similar to strict tort misrepresentation.

Sec. 2-313 provides:

§ 2-313. Express Warranties by Affirmation, Promise, Description, Sample

(1) Express warranties by the seller are created as follows:

(a) Any affirmation of fact or promise made by the seller to the buyer which relates to the goods and becomes part of the basis of the bargain creates an express warranty that the goods shall conform to the affirmation or promise.

(b) Any description of the goods which is made part of the basis of the bargain creates an express warranty that the goods shall conform to the description.

(c) Any sample or model which is made part of the basis of the bargain creates an express warranty that the whole of the goods shall conform to the sample or model.

(2) It is not necessary to the creation of an express warranty that the seller use formal words such as "warrant" or "guarantee" or that he have a specific intention to make a warranty, but an affirmation merely of the value of the goods or a statement purporting to be merely the seller's opinion or commendation of the goods does not create a warranty.

There is a great deal of overlap between express warranty and strict liability for tortious misrepresentation. Express warranty, however, covers non-business sellers, and economic loss where no physical injury to person or property is involved. Innocent tortious misrepresentation applies only to business sellers, and recovery for pure economic loss is generally not allowed for strict tort or negligent misrepresentation.

Another Code provision — called an implied warranty of fitness — is closely related to misrepresentation, and is set forth in UCC § 2-315:

§ 2-315. Implied Warranty: Fitness for Particular Purpose

Where the seller at the time of contracting has reason to know any particular purpose for which the goods are required and that the buyer is relying on the seller's skill or judgment to select or furnish suitable goods, there is unless excluded or modified under the next section an implied warranty that the goods shall be fit for such purpose.

4. *Reliance.* Many courts hold that the plaintiff must show reliance on an innocent or negligent misrepresentation in order to recover. But any foreseeable plaintiff can recover for fraudulent misrepresentation. REST. 2D TORTS § 311. What do you suppose accounts for this difference?

Comment j to REST. 2D OF TORTS § 402B (predecessor to § 9 of the THIRD RESTATEMENT: PRODUCTS LIABILITY) states that a misrepresentation need not be the sole inducement to the purchase or use of a product, and the reliance may be that of one who because of such reliance passes the product along to the consumer who is injured. Why should proof of reliance be required at all?

There are at least three situations in which the issue of reliance may arise in misrepresentation: (1) the plaintiff knows the representation to be untrue; (2) the representation is mere opinion, or puffing; or (3) the plaintiff is totally unaware of the representation. In which, if any, of these three situations should lack of reliance be a bar to recovery?

5. *The Ubiquitous Nature of Misrepresentation.* A misrepresentation may provide a distinct basis of recovery, as in *Baxter*. In other cases a misrepresentation — often in the form of marketing and advertising — may support

another basis of recovery as for example disappointed consumer expectation, or may furnish evidence of foreseeability of use.

PROBLEM

Imogene entered a restaurant and ordered a martini. After she had drunk the martini down in a couple of gulps, she upended the glass and bit down lustily on the olive that had been in the martini, and broke her dental bridge on a pit in the olive. The olive used in the martini had been purchased by restaurant from Olivia Co. in a jar labeled "pitted olives."

Discuss Imogene's potential products liability claims against restaurant and Olivia for dental damage.

D. THE LIMITS OF LIABILITY

[1] Plaintiff's Fault—Contributory Negligence, Comparative Fault and Assumption of the Risk

What effect should the plaintiff's fault have in a product liability suit? If the plaintiff's conduct is treated as a superseding cause, thereby negating any recovery, is that a resurrection of the doctrine of contributory negligence as a bar to the plaintiff's recovery? Or, is the product not unreasonably dangerous and so the affirmative defense of the plaintiff's negligence is irrelevant?

If the manufacturer warns against a particular use and the plaintiff uses the product in the warned-against manner, should the plaintiff recover nothing? The United States Court of Appeals for the Fifth Circuit, en banc, applying Louisiana law, so held in *Kampen v. American Isuzu,* 157 F.3d 306 (5th Cir. 1998). There, plaintiff had jacked up his daughter's vehicle and then crawled under the car in violation of a warning accompanying the jack. The jack collapsed causing the car to fall on him, and he sued the jack manufacturer. In holding that the use of the product contrary to the warning prevented the manufacturer from being held liable, the en banc court reversed the earlier decision of a three judge panel. The earlier opinion viewed the plaintiff's conduct as plaintiff negligence which would reduce his recovery.

On this issue, the RESTATEMENT (THIRD), section 17 provides:

> (a) A plaintiff's recovery of damages for harm caused by a product defect may be reduced if the conduct of the plaintiff combines with the product defect to cause the harm and the plaintiff's conduct fails to conform to generally applicable rules establishing appropriate standards of care.
>
> (b) The manner and extent of the reduction under Subsection (a) and the apportionment of plaintiff's recovery among multiple tortfeasors are governed by generally applicable rules apportioning responsibility.

But before the plaintiff's recovery is reduced the product must first be found to be defective. Can you see how the plaintiff's misconduct might be relevant to that determination?

The three judge panel held the jack could be found defective. What about comment 1 to the RESTATEMENT (THIRD) sec. 2? That comment states: "In general, when a safer design can reasonably be implemented and risks can reasonably be designed out of a product, adoption of a safer design in required over a warning that leaves a significant residuum of such risks."

How should assumption of the risk be treated? The same as the relevant jurisdiction treats it in negligence cases? What about express assumption of the risk? In the form of a disclaimer or limitation of liability? The RESTATEMENT (THIRD), section 18 provides:

> Disclaimers and limitations of remedies by product sellers or other distributors, waivers by product purchasers, and other exculpations, oral or written, do not bar or reduce otherwise valid products liability claims against sellers or other distributors of new products liability claims for harm caused to persons.

Recall that the RESTATEMENT (THIRD) seeks to create a tort regime for products liability claims. In a jurisdiction that continues to recognize a contract-based implied warranty claim for personal injury caused by a product, should the effectiveness of a disclaimer or limited remedy be governed by the U.C.C.? Under U.C.C. 2-719(3) limitation of recovery to exclude personal injury damages is prima facie unconscionable if the good involved is a consumer good—one used primarily for personal, family, or household purposes.

[2] The Special Case of Pharmaceutical Products

NOTES

1. *Restatement (Second) section 402A, comment k.* Should special rules apply to sellers of pharmaceutical products because of their potential benefit? Would strict liability limit the development of beneficial drugs and other products? RESTATEMENT (SECOND) section 402A, comment *k,* provides:

> k. *Unavoidably unsafe products.* There are some products which, in the present state of human knowledge, are quite incapable of being made safe for their intended and ordinary use. These are especially common in the field of drugs. An outstanding example is the vaccine for the Pasteur treatment of rabies, which not uncommonly leads to very serious and damaging consequences when it is injected. Since the disease itself invariably leads to a dreadful death, both the marketing and use of the vaccine are fully justified, notwithstanding the unavoidable high degree of risk which they involve. Such a product, properly prepared, and accompanied by proper directions and warning, is not defective, nor is it unreasonably dangerous. The same is true of many other drugs, vaccines, and the like, many of which for this very reason cannot legally be sold except to physicians, or under the prescription of a physician. It is also true in particular of many new or experimental drugs as to which, because of lack of time and opportunity for sufficient medical experience, there can be no assurance of safety, or perhaps

even of purity of ingredients, but such experience as there is justifies the marketing and use of the drug notwithstanding a medically recognizable risk. The seller of such products, again with the qualification that they are properly prepared and marketed, and proper warning is given, where the situation calls for it, is not to be held to strict liability for unfortunate consequences attending their use, merely because he has undertaken to supply the public with an apparently useful and desirable product, attended with a known but apparently reasonable risk.

The vast majority of courts adopted and followed comment *k* in prescription drug cases. They relied upon comment *k* in warning cases to hold that a drug seller would not be liable for unknown risks its product posed or for failing to warn of those risks. *See Brown v. Superior Court*, 44 Cal. 3d 1049, 245 Cal. Rptr. 412, 751 P.2d 470 (1988). Other courts reached similar results whether relying on comment *k* or not. *Feldman v. Lederle Laboratories*, 97 N.J. 429, 479 A.2d 374 (1984).

However, in *Hill v. Searle Labs., Div. of Searle Pharmaceuticals, Inc.*, 884 F.2d 1064 (8th Cir. 1989), the court, reversing summary judgment for the defendant, held that comment *k* did not apply to the intrauterine device CU-7, which was a prescription drug product. The comment should apply, said the court, only in those circumstances "when it is shown that the product is incapable of being made safe given the present state of human knowledge but possesses such a high degree of social need so that its use is warranted, provided warnings are adequate." The example of the Pasteur treatment for rabies, given in the comment, "suggests that only special products, those with exceptional social need, fall within the gamut of comment *k*."

Responding to defendant's argument that the policy of comment *k* should apply to all prescription drugs, the court said "this policy has no greater relevance to prescription drug products than to other products having life-saving or life-bettering characteristics." The court noted that "most IUD's were not prescription drugs — the CU-7 was an exception because it was manufactured with heavy metal." If the court applied "the blanket rule as requested by Searle, the result would be that some IUD manufacturers would be shielded from strict liability but others would not."

The court concluded that Searle could be liable "if the CU-7 is defective and unreasonably dangerous" because "alternative methods of birth control are available" and Searle "made no showing that CU-7s, or IUDs in general, are exceptionally beneficial to society." In addition, IUD manufacturers, "through mass advertising and merchandising practices, generated a general sense of product quality, making it difficult for consumers to fully understand the risks involved with the use of an IUD." And finally, the court observed, "manufacturers were in a better position than the users of IUDs to identify potential risks."

Reconsider *Carlin v. Superior Court*, given above in the notes following *Potter v. Chicago Pneumatic Tool Co.* In *Carlin* the court drew a diaphanous line between negligence and state of the art for purposes of determining when a strict liability duty to warn could arise in prescription drug cases.

2. *Restatement (Third) section 6*. The RESTATEMENT (THIRD) continues the special rules applicable to prescription drugs that arose out of RESTATEMENT (SECOND) section 402A, comment k. RESTATEMENT (THIRD), section 6, is devoted entirely to prescription drugs and medical devices. It provides:

(a) A manufacturer of a prescription drug or medical device who sells or otherwise distributes a defective drug or medical device is subject to liability for harm to persons caused by the defect. A prescription drug or medical device is one that may be legally sold or otherwise distributed only pursuant to a health-care provider's prescription.

(b) For purposes of liability under Subsection (a), a prescription drug or medical device is defective if at the time of sale or other distribution the drug or medical device:

(1) contains a manufacturing defect as defined in § 2(a); or

(2) is not reasonably safe due to defective design as defined in Subsection (c); or

(3) is not reasonably safe due to inadequate instructions or warnings as defined in Subsection (d).

(c) A prescription drug or medical device is not reasonably safe due to defective design if the foreseeable risks of harm posed by the drug or medical device are sufficiently great in relation to its foreseeable therapeutic benefits that reasonable health-care providers, knowing of such foreseeable risks and therapeutic benefits, would not prescribe the drug or medical device for any class of patients.

(d) A prescription drug or medical device is not reasonably safe due to inadequate instructions or warnings if reasonable instructions or warnings regarding foreseeable risks of harm are not provided to:

(1) prescribing and other health-care providers who are in a position to reduce the risks of harm in accordance with the instructions or warnings; or

(2) the patient when the manufacturer knows or has reason to know that health-care providers will not be in a position to reduce the risks of harm in accordance with the instructions or warnings.

(e) A retail seller or other distributor of a prescription drug or medical device is subject to liability for harm caused by the drug or device if:

(1) at the time of sale or other distribution the drug or medical device contains a manufacturing defect as defined in § (2)(a); or

(2) at or before the time of sale or other distribution of the drug or medical device the retail seller or other distributor fails to exercise due care and such failure causes harm to persons.

3. *The Structure of Section 6*. Note that under section 6, the standards applied to the manufacturer are somewhat different than those applied to the retail seller. To this point, when we have examined the RESTATEMENT (THIRD) we have not drawn any distinctions between manufacturers and other sellers.

Why here? Normally, the seller of a prescription drug or other medical device will be a pharmacist, hospital, or doctor. Should special rules apply to them?

Under section 6, the general rule of section 2(a) applies for mismanufacture claims but specific rules apply to design and warning claims. How likely is a manufacturer going to be held liable for a design defect under the "would not prescribe . . . to any class of patients" language?

Suppose a reasonable doctor would prescribe a patently dangerous drug to an identifiable class of patients, but the drug could be made safer by its manufacturer, without losing its effectiveness, for that class?

Would a state of the art defense protect either a manufacturer or a retailer against liability for a mismanufacture defect? For a misrepresentation?

Section 6 also creates a special warning rule for prescription drugs or medical devices. Consider the next case.

IN RE NORPLANT CONTRACEPTIVE PRODUCTS LIABILITY LITIGATION,
165 F.3d 374 (5th Cir. 1999)

E. GRADY JOLLY, CIRCUIT JUDGE:

The appellants in this matter (collectively referred to as "Harrison") are five plaintiffs who each suffered side effects from their use of the prescription contraceptive Norplant, manufactured by Wyeth Laboratories Incorporated, a company owned by American Home Products ("AHP"). They appeal a district court ruling for summary judgment in favor of AHP. The primary question presented on appeal is whether the learned intermediary doctrine should apply to the plaintiffs' claims. Because we find no error in the district court's ruling, we affirm. AHP cross-appeals the district court's denial of its motion for partial summary judgment based on the statute of limitations bar. Because we find that AHP is entitled to summary judgment, we need not address this issue on appeal.

This case involves litigation over the side effects of the contraceptive Norplant. Norplant is a long-term birth control method whereby the recipient has six thin capsules of the hormone progestin inserted just below the skin of her upper arm. Harrison claims the Norplant can also have significant, unwanted side effects.[1]

In this case, all five plaintiffs received Norplant from their personal physicians and each suffered side effects. On July 22, 1994, a class action was filed against AHP, as the parent entity of Wyeth Laboratories—the manufacturer of Norplant, on behalf of "all adult women who have had Norplant inserted in their bodies and who have sustained damages." On December 8, 1994, the Judicial Panel on Multidistrict Litigation transferred all federal Norplant actions to the Eastern District of Texas for consolidated pretrial proceedings before Judge Richard Schell. Each of the plaintiffs in this matter subsequently filed individual actions in the Eastern District of Texas. On

---

[1] These effects include severe headaches, mood swings, depression, nausea, acne, arm pain, numbness, breast tenderness, weight gain, hair loss, cramps, and bleeding irregularities, including amenorrhea.

August 5, 1996, the court denied the plaintiffs' motion for class certification, deciding that class certification was premature and that bellwether trials were appropriate to determine whether the class should be certified under rule 23(c)(4). The plaintiffs in this case were selected for the first of three bellwether trials.

At the close of discovery, AHP moved for summary judgment and the district court granted the motion. The district court held that the learned intermediary doctrine applied to all of the claims filed by Harrison. Under that doctrine "when a drug manufacturer properly warns a prescribing physician of the dangerous propensities of its product, the manufacturer is excused from warning each patient who receives the drug. The doctor stands as a learned intermediary between the manufacturer and the ultimate consumer." Alm v. Aluminum Co. of America, 717 S.W.2d 588, 592 (Tex.1986) (citations omitted). The district court concluded that, under the doctrine, AHP had no obligation to warn the end user of the potential side effects of Norplant. The district court then concluded that Harrison had failed to produce evidence that AHP had not properly notified the prescribing physicians of Norplant's potential side effects. Harrison now timely appeals.

. . . Harrison urges that even if the doctrine could be applied to the claims in this case, it should not as AHP marketed Norplant directly to the end users and that the end users relied on warnings (and the absence of warnings) provided by AHP's marketing rather than warnings provided by their physicians. Also, Harrison argues that the doctrine should not apply because Norplant was required by the Food and Drug Administration ("FDA") to provide warnings about the side effects.

. . . Harrison's two arguments, each of which have been thoroughly addressed by the district court below, lack merit. We briefly address each in turn.

Harrison argues that the learned intermediary doctrine should not apply in this instance given AHP's knowledge of Norplant's side effects and its conduct in marketing Norplant. Harrison argues that, for reasons of public policy, Norplant should have had a duty to warn the end user of Norplant's side effects because of the reduced role physicians play in selecting contraceptives for their patients. Harrison contends that the physician's reduced role invalidates the rationale of the learned intermediary doctrine because the patient cannot rely on the physician to provide an adequate warning. Although it may be true that physicians may seek to provide greater freedom to their patients in selecting an appropriate form of contraception, Norplant is nevertheless a prescription drug. The record makes it clear that physicians play a significant role in prescribing Norplant and in educating their patients about the benefits and disadvantages to using it. Harrison's argument therefore is unavailing.

Harrison also argues that because AHP engaged in "aggressive" marketing, AHP should be liable for not providing adequate warnings in conjunction with that marketing. This argument is critically weakened by the absence of any evidence on the record that any of the five plaintiffs actually saw, let alone relied, on any marketing materials issued to them by AHP.[4] Given this deficiency, even if such an exception to the doctrine should apply, summary judgment would still be appropriate in this case. It seems clear, however, that even if the facts were in Harrison's favor, Harrison would still lose. Two of our cases applying Texas law in this area have concluded that, as long as a physician-patient relationship exists, the learned intermediary doctrine applies. *Hurley v. Lederle Laboratories*, 863 F.2d 1173, 1178 (5th Cir.1988); *Swayze v. McNeil Laboratories*, 807 F.2d 464 (5th Cir.1987).

Harrison's next argument is that there should be an exception to the learned intermediary doctrine when the FDA has provided recommended warnings. To support this argument, Harrison relies on an Oklahoma Supreme Court case for the proposition that, when the FDA mandates that labeling information be provided to patients, the learned intermediary doctrine should not apply. *Edwards v. Basel Pharmaceuticals*, 933 P.2d 298 (Okla.1997). The court reached this somewhat counter-intuitive result by concluding that, where the potential side effects of a prescription drug are so serious that the FDA places a requirement on the manufacturer to warn the end user, the rationale of the learned intermediary doctrine no longer applies.

At the outset, we find this conclusion to be puzzling. Our understanding of the rationale of the learned intermediary doctrine, at least in substantial part, is that it seeks to encourage the drug manufacturer to make available prescription drugs despite their potentially harmful side effects, by shielding the drug manufacturer from liability when the drug is prescribed by a properly trained physician. Why the learned intermediary doctrine should somehow be less applicable when the severity of the side effects encourages the FDA to promote additional labeling escapes us.

Regardless of the merits of the Oklahoma Court's holding, there are other reasons why it is not applicable to this case. First, although the state of Oklahoma has created this exception to the learned intermediary doctrine, there is no evidence that the Texas Supreme Court would be inclined to follow in that state's footsteps. In addition, the FDA has explicitly stated that its regulation should not affect civil tort liability for drug manufacturers and dispensers. FDA, Prescription Drug Products; Patient Labeling Requirements, 44 Fed.Reg. 40016, 40023 (July 6, 1979). Finally, even if we were permitted to create such an exception to the doctrine in Texas law, Harrison's argument in this case would still fail as the FDA did not mandate any sort of labeling for Norplant.

The only issue Harrison raises on appeal is whether the learned intermediary doctrine applies to her claims. For the foregoing reasons, it does. The judgment of the district court is therefore

AFFIRMED.

---

[4] Harrison argues that although none of the plaintiffs were ever exposed to direct marketing, their physicians did show them videos and other materials prepared by AHP in explaining Norplant to them. Those materials, however, were entirely within the control of the physician and AHP had no control over which, if any, of the materials were shown to the patient.

NOTES

1. *The Opposite View.* The New Jersey Supreme Court reached a contrary result in *Perez v. Wyeth Laboratories, Inc.*, 734 A.2d 1245 (N.J. 1999). The court stated:

> Our medical-legal jurisprudence is based on images of health care that no longer exist. At an earlier time, medical advice was received in the doctor's office from a physician who most likely made house calls if needed. The patient usually paid a small sum of money to the doctor. Neighborhood pharmacists compounded prescribed medicines. Without being pejorative, it is safe to say that the prevailing attitude of law and medicine was that the "doctor knows best." *Logan v. Greenwich Hosp. Ass'n*, 191 Conn. 282, 465 A.2d 294, 299 (1983).
>
> Pharmaceutical manufacturers never advertised their products to patients, but rather directed all sales efforts at physicians. In this comforting setting, the law created an exception to the traditional duty of manufacturers to warn consumers directly of risks associated with the product as long as they warned health-care providers of those risks.
>
> For good or ill, that has all changed. Medical services are in large measure provided by managed care organizations. Medicines are purchased in the pharmacy department of supermarkets and often paid for by third-party providers. Drug manufacturers now directly advertise products to consumers on the radio, television, the Internet, billboards on public transportation, and in magazines. For example, a recent magazine advertisement for a seasonal allergy medicine in which a person is standing in a pastoral field filled with grass and goldenrod, attests that to "TAKE [THE PRODUCT]" is to "TAKE CLEAR CONTROL." Another recent ad features a former presidential candidate, encouraging the consumer to "take a little courage" to speak with "your physician." The first ad features major side effects, encourages the reader to "talk to your doctor," and lists a brief summary of risks and contraindications on the opposite page. The second ad provides a phone number and the name of the pharmaceutical company, but does not provide the name of the drug.
>
> The question in this case, broadly stated, is whether our law should follow these changes in the marketplace or reflect the images of the past. We believe that when mass marketing of prescription drugs seeks to influence a patient's choice of a drug, a pharmaceutical manufacturer that makes direct claims to consumers for the efficacy of its product should not be unqualifiedly relieved of a duty to provide proper warnings of the dangers or side effects of the product.

The court relied in part on radically increased manufacturer investment in direct marketing to consumers.

2. *Other Intermediaries.* Health care providers in drug and medical device cases are not the only intermediaries who come upon the scene in products liability cases. A toy manufacturer generally must warn parents of small children because the children are too young to comprehend a warning or its

impact. Likewise, there may be cases where a seller warns a buyer/employer and must rely upon that buyer to pass the warning on to employees.

Reasonable warnings to such intermediaries would be sufficient under section 2(c) to protect the seller from liability, wouldn't they? If so, then why was it necessary to draft a separate section "codifying" the learned intermediary rule for prescription drugs and medical devices only? Was it necessary? Do you think there was any lobbying going on in the American Law Institute or would such an August and learned group be free of lobbying activity?

3. *Blood Products.* Strict liability for the supply of blood products containing the hepatitis virus has been widely prohibited by statute and by court decision. This protection has been extended to blood contaminated with the AIDS virus. *See Miles Labs., Inc., Cutler Labs. Div. v. Doe,* 315 Md. 704, 556 A.2d 1107 (1989).

Who should bear the loss resulting from unavoidably unsafe products such as blood containing the hepatitis or AIDS virus? The victim? Those who benefit from blood transfusions? The public generally? Does your view of that issue govern your acceptance of the courts' views?

PROBLEM

A miscreant injected a lethal chemical into the bottle of a pharmaceutical product that once had been sold as a prescription drug but was, at the time of this tampering, sold over the counter. The miscreant surreptitiously opened the bottle of the product on a shelf of X pharmacy, injected the chemical, and then reclosed the bottle. The product was manufactured by Y company. Plaintiff's deceased bought the bottled product after it had been tampered with, and died from ingesting the product.

Can plaintiff recover against either X or Y for the death of her deceased?

[3] Food and Used Products

As we have just seen, the RESTATEMENT (THIRD) contains special rules for prescription drugs and medical devices. It also provides special rules for food and used products. Section 7 governs food and, as noted above, incorporates the consumer expectation test for defective manufacture claims. The traditional rule for food was that injury-producing foreign substances in the food gave rise to claims for strict liability and breach of warranty, but natural substances did not (and the plaintiff must prove negligence). *See, e.g., Mexicali Rose v. Superior Court,* 1 Cal.4th 617, 822 P.2d 1292 (1992). For a discussion of and limitation on the "natural/foreign" distinction, *see Simeon v. Doe,* 618 So.2d 848 (La. 1993) (If food substance presents potential danger to all persons, the "foreign-natural" test may apply to determine strict liability; but strict liability is inapplicable if the substance in the food only poses danger to persons with specific underlying disorders and poses little, if any, threat to a healthy person. A warning may be necessary in the latter event.) Does section 7 provide a preferable test? Would the consumer expectation test apply under section 7 to food with a defect in design?

Section 8 governs used products and provides that a used product seller is liable if it sells a defective product and the defect: arises from its failure to exercise reasonable care, is a section 2(a) or 3 defect and the reasonable consumer would expect the product to be as safe as a new product, is a defect under section 2 or 3 in a remanufactured product, arises from a used product's noncompliance under section 4 with a product safety statute or regulation applicable to the used product.

Why would the drafters of section 7 conclude that the reasonable consumer could not expect the ordinary (non-remanufactured) used product to be as safe in design and warning as a new product?

[4] Preemption

As you recall in negligence, compliance with a statute or regulation does not mean that a person exercised reasonable care; compliance is evidence of due care but it is not determinative, and non-compliance is evidence of negligence (or is negligence per se). Similarly, compliance with a safety statute in a products case is evidence that a product is not defective but a product that complies with a safety statute or regulation might still be defective. RESTATEMENT (THIRD), § 4(b). Non-compliance establishes defectiveness, § 4(a).

TENN. CODE ANNOT. § 29-28-104 provides that product compliance with any statutory or regulatory standard creates a rebuttable presumption that the product is not unreasonably dangerous with regard to matters covered by the standard. What effect would such a presumption have, and how could the plaintiff rebut it?

There is one important area of preemption that arises out of the Constitutional balance of power between state and federal governments. Under the Supremacy Clause of the U.S. Constitution, Article 6, where there is a conflict between federal and state law, state law must give way. Thus if Congress enacts a statute that either expressly or impliedly preempts state regulation, state law must give way. It has long been clear that if Congress preempts state law, a state may not pass a conflicting statute or administrative regulation. What is also now clear after *Cipollone v. Liggett Group, Inc.*, 505 U.S. 504, (1992), is that state tort law may be conflicting regulation. Thus, when Congress passed and later amended the Federal Cigarette Labeling and Advertising Act (15 U.S.C. § 1331 et seq.), the Court held that it preempted certain state-based tort claims, such as a failure to warn claim. A state court could not Constitutionally hold that the federally mandated warnings on the side of cigarette packages was inadequate under state law.

With the great bulk of federal legislation and regulation, coupled with the number of product liability suits, preemption has become a hotly contested issue in tort cases. The Supreme Court has decided two tort preemption cases since *Cipollone*. In *Medtronic, Inc. v. Lohr*, 518 U.S. 470 (1996), the Court held that the Medical Devices Amendments of 1976 did not preempt negligent design, manufacturing and labeling claims. But, more recently, in *Geier v. American Honda Motor Co., Inc.*, 120 S. Ct. 1913 (2000), the Court held that claims that a car was defective because it had seat belts, and not air bags, were preempted. The lower courts have wrestled with other products from insecticides to tampons.

As you either have or will learn in Constitutional law, preemption can be either express—Congress expressly says it is preempting the field—or implied—Congress' action is such that state regulation is either impossible or state regulation would substantially interfere with Congress' goals. Determinations of preemption (especially implied preemption) involve a detailed investigation of legislative intent and purpose. One may search in vain for any consistent principle, other than platitudes about the Supremacy Clause. However, it is clear that the preemption issue is one where tort law and Constitutional law meet.

[5] Government Contractors

A somewhat related issue of conflict may arise between federal and state law where the federal government specifies the design of a product for military or other government purposes and someone is injured as a result of that design and sues the manufacturer which complied with the government specifications. Can a state hold the manufacturer liable? The U.S. Supreme Court considered this issue in *Boyle v. United Technologies Corp.*, 487 U.S. 500 (1988). There, a Marine helicopter pilot was killed in a crash. His father sued the helicopter manufacturer which claimed it had complied with the government's specifications. In upholding the government contractor defense in a 5-4 decision, Justice Scalia said:

> Petitioner's broadest contention is that, in the absence of legislation specifically immunizing Government contractors from liability for design defects, there is no basis for judicial recognition of such a defense. We disagree. In most fields of activity, to be sure, this Court has refused to find federal preemption of state law in the absence of either a clear statutory prescription or a direct conflict between federal and state law. But we have held that a few areas, involving "uniquely federal interests," are so committed by the Constitution and laws of the United States to federal control that state law is preempted and replaced, where necessary, by federal law of a content prescribed (absent explicit statutory directive) by the courts — so-called "federal common law."
>
> The dispute in the present case borders upon two areas that we have found to involve such "uniquely federal interests." We have held that obligations to and rights of the United States under its contracts are governed exclusively by federal law. . . .
>
> . . . Here the state-imposed duty of care that is the asserted basis of the contractor's liability (specifically, the duty to equip helicopters with the sort of escape-hatch mechanism petitioner claims was necessary) is precisely contrary to the duty imposed by the Government contract (the duty to manufacture and deliver helicopters with the sort of escape-hatch mechanism shown by the specifications). Even in this sort of situation, it would be unreasonable to say that there is always a "significant conflict" between the state law and a federal policy or interest. If, for example, a federal procurement officer orders, by model number, a quantity of stock helicopters that happen to be equipped

with escape hatches opening outward, it is impossible to say that the Government has a significant interest in that particular feature. That would be scarcely more reasonable than saying that a private individual who orders such a craft by model number cannot sue for the manufacturer's negligence because he got precisely what he ordered.

In its search for the limiting principle to identify those situations in which a "significant conflict" with federal policy or interests does arise, the Court of Appeals . . . [has] identified as the source of the conflict the *Feres* doctrine, under which the Federal Tort Claims Act does not cover injuries to armed service personnel in the course of military service. See *Feres v. United States,* 340 U.S. 135 (1950). Military contractor liability would conflict with this doctrine, the Fourth Circuit reasoned, since the increased cost of the contractor's tort liability would be added to the price of the contract, and "[s]uch pass-through costs would . . . defeat the purpose of the immunity for military accidents conferred upon the government itself." *Tozer v. LTV Corp.,* 792 F.2d 403, 408 (4th Cir. 1986). . . . We do not adopt this analysis because it seems to us that the *Feres* doctrine, in its application to the present problem, logically produces results that are in some respects too broad and in some respects too narrow. Too broad, because if the Government contractor defense is to prohibit suit against the manufacturer whenever *Feres* would prevent suit against the Government, then even injuries caused to military personnel by a helicopter purchased from stock (in our example above), or by any standard equipment purchased by the Government, would be covered. Since *Feres* prohibits all service-related tort claims against the Government, a contractor defense that rests upon it should prohibit all service-related tort claims against the manufacturer — making inexplicable the three limiting criteria for contractor immunity (which we will discuss presently) that the Court of Appeals adopted. On the other hand, reliance on *Feres* produces (or logically should produce) results that are in another respect too narrow. Since that doctrine covers only service-related injuries, and not injuries caused by the military to civilians, it could not be invoked to prevent, for example, a civilian's suit against the manufacturer of fighter planes, based on a state tort theory, claiming harm from what is alleged to be needlessly high levels of noise produced by the jet engines. Yet we think that the character of the jet engines the Government orders for its fighter planes cannot be regulated by state tort law, no more in suits by civilians than in suits by members of the armed services.

There is, however, a statutory provision that demonstrates the potential for, and suggests the outlines of, "significant conflict" between federal interests and state law in the context of government procurement. In the Federal Tort Claims Act (FTCA), Congress authorized damages to be recovered against the United States for harm caused by the negligent or wrongful conduct of Government employees, to the extent that a private person would be liable under the law of the place where the conduct occurred. 28 U.S.C. section 1346(b). It excepted from this consent to suit, however,

[a]ny claim . . . based upon the exercise or performance or the failure to exercise or perform a discretionary function or duty on the part of a federal agency or an employee of the Government, whether or not the discretion involved be abused. 28 U.S.C. section 2680(a).

We think that the selection of the appropriate design for military equipment to be used by our Armed Forces is assuredly a discretionary function within the meaning of this provision. It often involves not merely engineering analysis but judgment as to the balancing of many technical, military, and even social considerations, including specifically the trade-off between greater safety and greater combat effectiveness. And we are further of the view that permitting "second-guessing" of these judgments through state tort suits against contractors would produce the same effect sought to be avoided by the FTCA exemption. The financial burden of judgments against the contractors would ultimately be passed through, substantially if not totally, to the United States itself, since defense contractors will predictably raise their prices to cover, or to insure against, contingent liability for the Government-ordered designs. To put the point differently: It makes little sense to insulate the Government against financial liability for the judgment that a particular feature of military equipment is necessary when the Government produces the equipment itself, but not when it contracts for the production. In sum, we are of the view that state law which holds Government contractors liable for design defects in military equipment does in some circumstances present a "significant conflict" with federal policy and must be displaced.

We agree with the scope of displacement adopted by the Fourth Circuit here . . . . Liability for design defects in military equipment cannot be imposed, pursuant to state law, when (1) the United States approved reasonably precise specifications; (2) the equipment conformed to those specifications; and (3) the supplier warned the United States about the dangers in the use of the equipment that were known to the supplier but not to the United States. The first two of these conditions assure that the suit is within the area where the policy of the "discretionary function" would be frustrated, *i.e.*, they assure that the design feature in question was considered by a Government officer, and not merely by the contractor itself. The third condition is necessary because, in its absence, the displacement of state tort law would create some incentive for the manufacturer to withhold knowledge of risks, since conveying that knowledge might disrupt the contract but withholding it would produce no liability. We adopt this provision lest our effort to protect discretionary functions perversely impede them by cutting off information highly relevant to the discretionary decision.

In *Hercules, Inc. v. United States*, 116 S.Ct. 981 (1996), the Court held that the United States was not liable to the manufacturers of Agent Orange under a breach of warranty theory for the costs incurred by the manufacturers in defending and settling claims of military personnel injured by the chemical. The Court indicated that the government contractor defense would have been available to the manufacturers. Would it? In *Trevino v. General Dynamics*

Corp., 865 F.2d 1474 (5th Cir.), *reh. den.*, 876 F.2d 1154 (5th Cir.), *cert. den.*, 110 S. Ct. 327 (1989), the manufacturer of a submarine's diving chamber asserted the government contractor defense following the deaths of five navy divers from vacuum-induced bends. A federal procurement officer had signed the "approval line" on the manufacturer's working drawings. The Fifth Circuit Court of Appeals held that *Boyle*'s conceptual grounding in the discretionary function exception of the Federal Tort Claims Act presupposed a governmental exercise of policy judgment, thus removing from the *Boyle* concept a mere "rubber stamp" approval by the government purchaser.

Boyle insulates the government contractor not only from strict liability, but from negligence liability as well. What about recklessness? If the danger is obvious? At least one court has read *Boyle* as applying only to military procurement contracts. *In re Hawaii Fed. Asbestos Cases,* 715 F. Supp. 298 (D.C. Haw. 1988). Is this a correct reading of the decision?

One court has held that *Boyle* does not apply to manufacturing or production flaws. *McGonigal v. Gearheart Indus.,* 851 F.2d 774 (5th Cir. 1988). Other courts have held that the case does not apply to claims for failure to warn the user or consumer, *e.g., Dorse v. Armstrong World Industries,* 716 F. Supp. 589 (S.D. Fla. 1989), *aff'd,* 898 F.2d 1487 (11th Cir. 1990). What about misrepresentation?

[6] Economic Loss

EAST RIVER STEAMSHIP CORP. v. TRANSAMERICA DELAVAL, INC.
476 U.S. 858 (1986)

JUSTICE BLACKMUN delivered the opinion of the court.

In this admiralty case, we must decide whether a cause of action in tort is stated when a defective product purchased in a commercial transaction malfunctions, injuring only the product itself and causing purely economic loss. The case requires us to consider preliminarily whether admiralty law, which already recognizes a general theory of liability for negligence, also incorporates principles of products liability, including strict liability. Then, charting a course between products liability and contract law, we must determine whether injury to a product itself is the kind of harm that should be protected by products liability or left entirely to the law of contracts.

In 1969, Seatrain Shipbuilding Corp. (Shipbuilding), a wholly owned subsidiary of Seatrain Lines, Inc. (Seatrain), announced it would build the four oil-transporting supertankers in issue — the T. T. Stuyvesant, T. T. Williamsburgh, T. T. Brooklyn, and T. T. Bay Ridge. Each tanker was constructed pursuant to a contract in which a separate wholly owned subsidiary of Seatrain engaged Shipbuilding. Shipbuilding in turn contracted with respondent, now known as Transamerica Delaval, Inc. (Delaval), to design, manufacture, and supervise the installation of turbines (costing $1.4 million each) that would be the main propulsion units for the 225,000-ton, $125 million, supertankers. When each ship was completed, its title was transferred from the contracting subsidiary to a trust company (as trustee for an owner), which in turn chartered the ship to one of the petitioners, also subsidiaries of Seatrain. Queensway Tankers, Inc., chartered the Stuyvesant; Kingsway Tankers, Inc., chartered the Williamsburgh; East River Steamship Corp. chartered the Brooklyn; and Richmond Tankers, Inc., chartered the Bay Ridge. Each petitioner operated under a bareboat charter, by which it took full control of the ship for 20 or 22 years as though it owned it, with the obligation afterwards to return the ship to the real owner. Each charterer assumed responsibility for the cost of any repairs to the ships.

The Stuyvesant sailed on its maiden voyage in late July 1977. On December 11 of that year, as the ship was about to enter the Port of Valdez, Alaska, steam began to escape from the casing of the high-pressure turbine. That problem was temporarily resolved by repairs, but before long, while the ship was encountering a severe storm in the Gulf of Alaska, the high-pressure turbine malfunctioned. The ship, though lacking its normal power, was able to continue on its journey to Panama and then San Francisco. In January 1978, an examination of the high-pressure turbine revealed that the first-stage steam reversing ring virtually had disintegrated and had caused additional damage to other parts of the turbine. The damaged part was replaced with a part from the Bay Ridge, which was then under construction. In April 1978, the ship again was repaired, this time with a part from the Brooklyn. Finally, in August, the ship was permanently and satisfactorily repaired with a ring newly designed and manufactured by Delaval.

The Brooklyn and the Williamsburgh were put into service in late 1973 and late 1974, respectively. In 1978, as a result of the Stuyvesant's problems, they were inspected while in port. Those inspections revealed similar turbine damage. Temporary repairs were made, and newly designed parts were installed as permanent repairs that summer.

When the Bay Ridge was completed in early 1979, it contained the newly designed parts and thus never experienced the high-pressure turbine problems that plagued the other three ships. Nonetheless, the complaint appears to claim damages as a result of deterioration of the Bay Ridge's ring that was installed in the Stuyvesant while the Bay Ridge was under construction. In addition, the Bay Ridge experienced a unique problem. In 1980, when the ship was on its maiden voyage, the engine began to vibrate with a frequency that increased even after speed was reduced. It turned out that the astern guardian valve, located between the high-pressure and low-pressure turbines, had been installed backwards. Because of that error, steam entered the low-pressure turbine and damaged it. After repairs, the Bay Ridge resumed its travels.

The charterers' second amended complaint, filed in the United States District Court for the District of New Jersey, invokes admiralty jurisdiction. It contains five counts alleging tortious conduct on the part of respondent Delaval and seeks an aggregate of more than $8 million in damages for the cost of repairing the ships and for income lost while the ships were out of service. The first four counts, read liberally, allege that Delaval is strictly liable for the design defects in the high-pressure turbines of the Stuyvesant, the Williamsburgh, the Brooklyn, and the Bay Ridge, respectively. The fifth count alleges that Delaval, as part of the manufacturing process, negligently supervised the installation of the astern guardian valve on the Bay Ridge.

The initial complaint also had listed Seatrain and Shipbuilding as plaintiffs and had alleged breach of contract and warranty as well as tort claims. But after Delaval interposed a statute of limitations defense, the complaint was amended and the charterers alone brought the suit in tort. The nonrenewed claims were dismissed with prejudice by the District Court. Delaval then moved for summary judgment, contending that the charterers' actions were not cognizable in tort.

The District Court granted summary judgment for Delaval, and the Court of Appeals for the Third Circuit, sitting en banc, affirmed. The Court of Appeals held that damage solely to a defective product is actionable in tort if the defect creates an unreasonable risk of harm to persons or property other than the product itself, and harm materializes. Disappointments over the product's quality, on the other hand, are protected by warranty law. The charterers were dissatisfied with product quality: the defects involved gradual and unnoticed deterioration of the turbines' component parts, and the only risk created was that the turbines would operate at a lower capacity. Therefore, neither the negligence claim nor the strict-liability claim was cognizable.

. . . We granted certiorari to resolve a conflict among the Courts of Appeals sitting in admiralty.

. . . We join the Courts of Appeals in recognizing products liability, including strict liability, as part of the general maritime law. This Court's precedents relating to injuries of maritime workers long have pointed in that direction. The Court's rationale in those cases — that strict liability should be imposed on the party best able to protect persons from hazardous equipment — is equally applicable when the claims are based on products liability. And to the extent that products actions are based on negligence, they are grounded in principles already incorporated into the general maritime law. Our incorporation of products liability into maritime law, however, is only the threshold determination to the main issue in this case.

Products liability grew out of a public policy judgment that people need more protection from dangerous products than is afforded by the law of warranty. It is clear, however, that if this development were allowed to progress too far, contract law would drown in a sea of tort. We must determine whether a commercial product injuring itself is the kind of harm against which public policy requires manufacturers to protect, independent of any contractual obligation.

The paradigmatic products-liability action is one where a product "reasonably certain to place life and limb in peril," distributed without reinspection, causes bodily injury. The manufacturer is liable whether or not it is negligent because "public policy demands that responsibility be fixed wherever it will most effectively reduce the hazards to life and health inherent in defective products that reach the market." *Escola v. Coca Cola Bottling Co.,* 24 Cal. 2d 453, 462, 150 P.2d 436, 441 (1944) [Traynor, C.J., concurring].

For similar reasons of safety, the manufacturer's duty of care was broadened to include protection against property damage. Such damage is considered so akin to personal injury that the two are treated alike.

In the traditional "property damage" cases, the defective product damages other property. In this case, there was no damage to "other" property. Rather, the first, second, and third counts allege that each supertanker's defectively designed turbine components damaged only the turbine itself. Since each turbine was supplied by Delaval as an integrated package, each is properly regarded as a single unit. "Since all but the very simplest of machines have component parts, [a contrary] holding would require a finding of 'property damage' in virtually every case where a product damages itself. Such a holding would eliminate the distinction between warranty and strict products liability." *Northern Power & Eng'g Corp. v. Caterpillar Tractor Co.,* 623 P.2d 324, 330 (Alaska 1981). The fifth count also alleges injury to the product itself. Before the high-pressure and low-pressure turbines could become an operational propulsion system, they were connected to piping and valves under the supervision of Delaval personnel. Delaval's supervisory obligations were part of its manufacturing agreement. The fifth count thus can best be read to allege that Delaval's negligent manufacture of the propulsion system — by allowing the installation in reverse of the astern guardian valve — damaged the propulsion system. Obviously, damage to a product itself has certain attributes of a products-liability claim. But the injury suffered — the failure of the product to function properly — is the essence of a warranty action, through which a contracting party can seek to recoup the benefit of its bargain.

The intriguing question whether injury to a product itself may be brought in tort has spawned a variety of answers.[1] At one end of the spectrum, the case that created the majority land-based approach, *Seely v. White Motor Co.,* 63 Cal. 2d 9, 45 Cal. Rptr. 17, 403 P.2d 145 (1965) (defective truck), held that preserving a proper role for the law of warranty precludes imposing tort liability if a defective product causes purely monetary harm.

At the other end of the spectrum is the minority land-based approach, whose progenitor, *Santor v. A & M Karagheusian, Inc.,* 44 N.J. 52, 66–67, 207 A.2d 305, 312–313 (1965) (marred carpeting), held that a manufacturer's duty to make nondefective products encompassed injury to the product itself, whether or not the defect created an unreasonable risk of harm.[2] The courts adopting this approach, including the majority of the Courts of Appeals sitting in admiralty that have considered the issue find that the safety and insurance rationales behind strict liability apply equally where the losses are purely economic. These courts reject the *Seely* approach because they find it arbitrary that economic losses are recoverable if a plaintiff suffers bodily injury or property damage, but not if a product injures itself. They also find no inherent difference between economic loss and personal injury or property damage, because all are proximately caused by the defendant's conduct. Further, they

---

[1] The question is not answered by the RESTATEMENT (SECOND) OF TORTS §§ 395 and 402A (1965), or by the Uniform Commercial Code.

Congress, which has considered adopting national products-liability legislation, also has been wrestling with the question whether economic loss should be recoverable under a products-liability theory. . . .

[2] Interestingly, the New Jersey and California Supreme Courts have each taken what appears to be a step in the direction of the other since *Santor* and *Seely*. In *Spring Motors Distributors, Inc. v. Ford Motor Co.,* 98 N.J., 555, 579, 489 A.2d, 660, 672 (1985), the New Jersey court rejected *Santor* in the commercial context. And in *J'Aire Corp. v. Gregory,* 24 Cal. 3d 799, 157 Cal. Rptr. 407, 598 P.2d 60 (1979), the California court recognized a cause of action for negligent interference with prospective economic advantage.

believe recovery for economic loss would not lead to unlimited liability because they think a manufacturer can predict and insure against product failure.

Between the two poles fall a number of cases that would permit a products-liability action under certain circumstances when a product injures only itself. These cases attempt to differentiate between "the disappointed users . . . and the endangered ones," *Russell v. Ford Motor Co.,* 281 Or. 587, 595, 575 P.2d 1383, 1387 (1978), and permit only the latter to sue in tort. The determination has been said to turn on the nature of the defect, the type of risk, and the manner in which the injury arose. *See Pennsylvania Glass Sand Corp. v. Caterpillar Tractor Co.,* 652 F.2d 1165, 1173 (3rd Cir. 1981) (relied on by the Court of Appeals in this case). The Alaska Supreme Court allows a tort action if the defective product creates a situation potentially dangerous to persons or other property, and loss occurs as a proximate result of that danger and under dangerous circumstances. *Northern Power & Engineering Corp. v. Caterpillar Tractor Co.,* 623 P.2d 324, 329 (Alaska 1981).

We find the intermediate and minority land-based positions unsatisfactory. The intermediate positions, which essentially turn on the degree of risk, are too indeterminate to enable manufacturers easily to structure their business behavior. Nor do we find persuasive a distinction that rests on the manner in which the product is injured. We realize that the damage may be qualitative, occurring through gradual deterioration or internal breakage. Or it may be calamitous. But either way, since by definition no person or other property is damaged, the resulting loss is purely economic. Even when the harm to the product itself occurs through an abrupt, accident-like event, the resulting loss due to repair costs, decreased value, and lost profits is essentially the failure of the purchaser to receive the benefit of its bargain — traditionally the core concern of contract law.

We also decline to adopt the minority land-based view espoused by *Santor* and *Emerson G.M. Diesel, Inc. v. Alaskan Enterprise,* 732 F.2d 1468 (9th Cir. 1984). Such cases raise legitimate questions about the theories behind restricting products liability, but we believe that the countervailing arguments are more powerful. The minority view fails to account for the need to keep products liability and contract law in separate spheres and to maintain a realistic limitation on damages.

Exercising traditional discretion in admiralty, we adopt an approach similar to *Seely* and hold that a manufacturer in a commercial relationship has no duty under either a negligence or strict products-liability theory to prevent a product from injuring itself.

> The distinction that the law has drawn between tort recovery for physical injuries and warranty recovery for economic loss is not arbitrary and does not rest on the "luck" of one plaintiff in having an accident causing physical injury. The distinction rests, rather, on an understanding of the nature of the responsibility a manufacturer must undertake in distributing his products. *Seely v. White Motor Co.,* 63 Cal. 2d at 18, 403 P.2d at 151.

When a product injures only itself the reasons for imposing a tort duty are weak and those for leaving the party to its contractual remedies are strong.

The tort concern with safety is reduced when an injury is only to the product itself. When a person is injured, the "cost of an injury and the loss of time or health may be an overwhelming misfortune," and one the person is not prepared to meet. *Escola v. Coca Cola Bottling Co.*, 24 Cal. 2d at 462, 150 P.2d at 441 (opinion concurring in judgment). In contrast, when a product injures itself, the commercial user stands to lose the value of the product, risks the displeasure of its customers who find that the product does not meet their needs, or, as in this case, experiences increased costs in performing a service. Losses like these can be insured. Society need not presume that a customer needs special protection. The increased cost to the public that would result from holding a manufacturer liable in tort for injury to the product itself is not justified.

Damage to a product itself is most naturally understood as a warranty claim. Such damage means simply that the product has not met the customer's expectations, or, in other words, that the customer has received "insufficient product value." *See* J. White & R. Summers, Uniform Commercial Code 406 (2d ed. 1980). The maintenance of product value and quality is precisely the purpose of express and implied warranties.[3] *See* UCC § 2-313 (express warranty), § 2-314 (implied warranty of merchantability), and § 2-315 (warranty of fitness for a particular purpose). Therefore, a claim of a nonworking product can be brought as a breach-of-warranty action. Or, if the customer prefers, it can reject the product or revoke its acceptance and sue for breach of contract. *See* UCC §§ 2-601, 2-608, 2-612.

Contract law, and the law of warranty in particular, is well suited to commercial controversies of the sort involved in this case because the parties may set the terms of their own agreements.[4] The manufacturer can restrict its liability, within limits, by disclaiming warranties or limiting remedies. *See* UCC §§ 2-316, 2-719. In exchange, the purchaser pays less for the product. Since a commercial situation generally does not involve large disparities in bargaining power we see no reason to intrude into the parties' allocation of the risk.

While giving recognition to the manufacturer's bargain, warranty law sufficiently protects the purchaser by allowing it to obtain the benefit of its bargain. The expectation damages available in warranty for purely economic loss give a plaintiff the full benefit of its bargain by compensating for forgone business opportunities. Recovery on a warranty theory would give the charterers their repair costs and lost profits, and would place them in the position

---

[3] If the charterers' claims were brought as breach-of-warranty actions, they would not be within the admiralty jurisdiction. Since contracts relating to the construction of or supply of materials to a ship are not within the admiralty jurisdiction, neither are warranty claims grounded in such contracts. In particular the Uniform Commercial Code, which has been adopted by 49 States, would apply.

[4] We recognize, of course, that warranty and products liability are not static bodies of law and may overlap. In certain situations, for example, the privity requirement of warranty has been discarded. *E.g., Henningsen v. Bloomfield Motors, Inc.*, 32 N.J. 358, 380–384, 161 A.2d 69, 81–84 (1960). In other circumstances, a manufacturer may be able to disclaim strict tort liability. *See, e.g., Keystone Aeronautics Corp. v. R.J. Enstrom Corp.*, 499 F.2d 146, 149 (3rd Cir. 1974). Nonetheless, the main currents of tort law run in different directions from those of contract and warranty, and the latter seem to us far more appropriate for commercial disputes of the kind involved here.

they would have been in had the turbines functioned properly.[5] Thus, both the nature of the injury and the resulting damages indicate it is more natural to think of injury to a product itself in terms of warranty.

A warranty action also has a built-in limitation on liability, whereas a tort action could subject the manufacturer to damages of an indefinite amount. The limitation in a contract action comes from the agreement of the parties and the requirement that consequential damages, such as lost profits, be a foreseeable result of the breach. In a warranty action where the loss is purely economic, the limitation derives from the requirements of foreseeability and of privity, which is still generally enforced for such claims in a commercial setting.

In products liability law, where there is a duty to the public generally, foreseeability is an inadequate brake. Permitting recovery for all foreseeable claims for purely economic loss could make a manufacturer liable for vast sums. It would be difficult for a manufacturer to take into account the expectations of persons downstream who may encounter its product. In this case, for example, if the charterers — already one step removed from the transaction — were permitted to recover their economic losses, then the companies that subchartered the ships might claim their economic losses from the delays, and the charterers' customers also might claim their economic losses, and so on. . . .

And to the extent that courts try to limit purely economic damages in tort, they do so by relying on a far murkier line, one that negates the charterers' contention that permitting such recovery under a products liability theory enables admiralty courts to avoid difficult line drawing.

For the first three counts, the defective turbine components allegedly injured only the turbines themselves. Therefore, a strict products liability theory of recovery is unavailable to the charterers. Any warranty claims would be subject to Delaval's limitation, both in time and scope, of its warranty liability. The record indicates that Seatrain and Delaval reached a settlement agreement. We were informed that these charterers could not have asserted the warranty claims. Even so, the charterers should be left to the terms of their bargains, which explicitly allocated the cost of repairs.

In the charterers' agreements with the owners, the charterers took the ships in "as is" condition, after inspection, and assumed full responsibility for them, including responsibility for maintenance and repairs and for obtaining certain forms of insurance. In a separate agreement between each charterer and Seatrain, Seatrain agreed to guarantee certain payments and covenants by each charterer to the owner. The contractual responsibilities thus were clearly laid out. There is no reason to extricate the parties from their bargain.

Similarly, in the fifth count, alleging the reverse installation of the astern guardian valve, the only harm was to the propulsion system itself rather than to persons or other property. Even assuming that Delaval's supervision was negligent, as we must on this summary judgment motion, Delaval owed no

---

[5] In contrast, tort damages generally compensate the plaintiff for loss and return him to the position he occupied before the injury. Tort damages are analogous to reliance damages, which are awarded in contract when there is particular difficulty in measuring the expectation interest.

duty under a products liability theory based on negligence to avoid causing purely economic loss. Thus, whether stated in negligence or strict liability, no products liability claim lies in admiralty when the only injury claimed is economic loss.

While we hold that the fourth count should have been dismissed, we affirm the entry of judgment for Delaval.

NOTES

1. *Admiralty Versus State Law.* Admiralty is a unique body of law. It is, for the most part, judicially developed federal law, which sometimes adopts state law or permits state law to apply. In tort cases, the development of maritime law is heavily influenced by the common law. In refusing to recognize a tort claim for damage to the product itself or for consequential economic loss, the Supreme Court in *East River* adopted the land-based majority rule. Now, the RESTATEMENT (THIRD) has followed suit. RESTATEMENT (THIRD), section 21. *East River* was decided under federal admiralty law, however, and would not be binding in state, or federal diversity, land-based cases.

2. *Physical Injury to Other Property.* It is clear that physical injury to property other than the product itself is recoverable in tort. Why? If there is damage to other property, can the plaintiff then also recover in tort for damage to the product itself? How significant must that other-property damage be? Suppose the defective turbine sprayed oil on the plaintiff's cargo? *See S.J. Groves & Sons Co. v. Aerospatiale Helicopter Corp.*, 374 N.W.2d 431 (Minn. 1985), holding that "relatively minor" damage to other property was insufficient to invoke tort law under this rule.

It is not always easy to tell what is the product itself and what is other property. In *Saratoga Fishing Co. v. J.M. Martinac & Co.*, 117 S.Ct. 1783 (1997), A purchased a vessel from defendant-manufacturer. A then added certain equipment to the vessel and sold the vessel to B. The vessel then sank due to an engine room fire. B sued the manufacturer, seeking to recover for the damage to the equipment A had added to the vessel. To A, the equipment was other property but to B it was part of the purchased product. The Supreme Court nevertheless allowed B to recover in tort from defendant for the value of the equipment. Why not for the vessel also?

East River draws a distinction between (1) physical injury to the product itself, and (2) physical injury to other property, and says (1) is pure economic loss not recoverable in tort. The Court calls this the "majority land-based approach," which it attributes to *Seely*. But *Seely* actually held physical injury to the product itself is recoverable in tort. *See Stearman v. Centex Homes*, 78 Cal. App. 4th 611, 92 Cal. Rptr. 2d 761 (2000). The Restatement (Third) sec. 21 also relies on *Seely* in following *East River*. Does *Stearman* mean that *East River* and sec. 21 are wrongly decided?

3. *Component Parts.* What if defendant had supplied a component for the vessel and A had incorporated that component into the vessel and sold the completed product to B. Suppose the failure of the component caused the fire. Would defendant be liable to B, in tort, for the value of the vessel, other than

the component? Most courts would say no. B bought the entire product and would have to seek recovery in contract. In *King v. Hilton-Davis,* 855 F.2d 1047 (3d Cir. 1988), the court carried *East River* a step further by applying to a component part supplier the rule that tort liability is not imposed for injury to the product itself — the "product," for this purpose, was the assembled product and not the component part.

But what if the failure of the component caused personal injury or damage to other property? Then, the component part manufacturer would be liable in tort, *see* Restatement (Third), section 5. The manufacturer of the entire product would also be liable. In such a case, if the two manufacturers are jointly and severally liable, shouldn't the manufacturer of the finished product have an indemnity claim against the component part manufacturer, assuming the finished product manufacturer is otherwise free from fault?

4. *Unlimited Liability.* The Court in *East River* was concerned about "unlimited liability" if recovery was allowed in tort. Could this concern be met by allowing tort recovery only by those who have a property interest in the product?

5. *Noncommercial Plaintiffs.* Courts have widely allowed recovery in tort for fishermen who suffer only economic loss as a result of the defendant's negligence. *See, e.g., Berg v. General Motors Corp.,* 87 Wash. 2d 584, 555 P.2d 818 (1976) (negligently manufactured product causing loss of livelihood); *Union Oil Co. v. Oppen,* 501 F.2d 558 (9th Cir. 1974) (negligent oil spill causing loss of livelihood). Will the *East River* decision reverse the results in these types of cases? The dissent in *Seely* wanted to allow recovery in tort if the plaintiff were an "ordinary consumer," as opposed to a commercial entity. This seems to be the approach taken also by the New Jersey *Spring Motors* case, mentioned in footnote 2 of the *East River* opinion.

PROBLEM

Brake Co. manufactured brakes to be installed in Small Truck Co.'s D 1000 truck. Pierre purchased a D 1000 for use in his pizza business, Pierre's Pizza's. The pizza business is Pierre's sole means of support and it is a sole proprietorship, i.e. it is not a partnership, corporation, or limited liability company. While delivering pizzas one night, the brakes in the D 1000 mysteriously failed and the truck crashed. The truck was totaled in the crash and Pierre suffered grievous personal injuries which prevent him from working. Also destroyed in the crash were an in-dash CD player that the dealer had installed in the truck when Pierre purchased it and a rare Salvador Dali painting Pierre kept stored behind the driver's seat; the painting is worth $2,000,000. Pierre estimates he has lost $20,000 in pizza sales because of his injury and the loss of the truck. What claims for what injuries does Pierre have against Brake Co. and Small Truck Co.?

[7] To What and Whom Does Product Liability Law Apply?

ROYER v. CATHOLIC MEDICAL CENTER
741 A.2d 74 (N.H. 1999)

BROCK, C.J.

The plaintiffs, Ira A. and Rachel M. Royer, appeal from an order of the Superior Court (Sullivan, J.) granting a motion to dismiss in favor of the defendant, Catholic Medical Center (CMC). We affirm.

The plaintiffs have pleaded the following facts. In September 1991, Ira Royer underwent total knee replacement surgery at CMC. As part of the procedure, a prosthetic knee, provided by CMC, was surgically implanted. In April 1993, Royer complained to his doctor that the pain in his knee was worse than it had been before the surgery. His doctors determined that the prosthesis was defective, and in June 1993 Royer underwent a second operation in which the prosthesis was removed, and a second prosthesis inserted.

Ira Royer initially brought suit against Dow Corning Corp., Dow Corning Wright, Inc., and Wright Medical Technologies, Inc., the companies that had allegedly designed and manufactured the defective prosthesis. Subsequently, Dow Corning commenced federal bankruptcy proceedings, and the plaintiffs filed a second writ against CMC, alleging that CMC was strictly liable to Ira because it had sold a prosthesis with a design defect that was in an unreasonably dangerous condition, and liable to Rachel who suffered a loss of consortium.

The defendant moved to dismiss, arguing, inter alia, that it was not a "seller of goods" for purposes of strict products liability, and that absent the strict liability claim, Ira's claim and the loss of consortium claim could not stand. The trial court granted the motion, finding that CMC was not, as a matter of law, engaged in the business of selling prosthetic devices. On appeal, the plaintiffs contend that this finding was error.

In reviewing an order on a motion to dismiss for failure to state a claim upon which relief may be granted, we ask whether the plaintiffs' allegations are reasonably susceptible of a construction that would permit recovery. We assume the truth of the plaintiffs' well pleaded allegations of fact and construe all reasonable inferences from them most favorably to the plaintiffs.

In New Hampshire, "[o]ne who sells any product in a defective condition unreasonably dangerous to the user or consumer or to his property is subject to [strict] liability for physical harm thereby caused" if, inter alia, "the seller is engaged in the business of selling such a product." Restatement (Second) of Torts § 402A (1965). . . . If the defendant merely provides a service, however, there is no liability absent proof of a violation of a legal duty. . . . In this case, we are asked to determine whether a health care provider that supplies a defective prosthesis in the course of delivering health care services is a "seller" of prosthetic devices, or is merely providing a professional service.

In deciding this issue of first impression, we are guided by the principles that have supported the development of a cause of action for strict liability in New Hampshire. "Strict liability for damages has traditionally met with disfavor in this jurisdiction." *Bruzga v. PMR Architects*, 141 N.H. 756, 761, 693 A.2d 401, 404–05 (1997) (quotation and brackets omitted). As a general rule, "strict liability is available only where the Legislature has provided for it or in those situations where the common law of this state has imposed such liability and the Legislature has not seen fit to change it." *Id.* at 761, 693 A.2d at 405.

> The reasons for the development of strict liability in tort were the lack of privity between the manufacturer and the buyer, the difficulty of proving negligence against a distant manufacturer using mass production techniques, and the better ability of the mass manufacturer to spread the economic risks among consumers.

Id. Particularly crucial to our adoption of strict liability in the context of defective products was the practical impossibility of proving legal fault in many products liability cases. . . .

Although we have adopted a cause of action for strict products liability, we have recognized limits to the doctrine. . . . In *Bruzga*, we rejected an argument that strict liability should extend to architects and building contractors who allegedly designed and "manufactured" a defective building. After determining that the reasons supporting strict liability did not apply to architects and contractors, we concluded that architects and contractors provide a professional service. Although we acknowledged that a building contractor "supplies" a structure to the purchaser, we declined to extend strict products liability to contractors because they are "engaged primarily in the rendition of a service." *Id.* at 761–63, 693 A.2d at 404–06.

A majority of the jurisdictions that have addressed whether a health care provider who supplies a defective prosthesis is subject to strict liability have declined to extend strict liability, similarly reasoning that the health care provider primarily renders a service, and that the provision of a prosthetic device is merely incidental to that service. See, e.g., *Cafazzo v. Cent. Medical Health Services*, 542 Pa. 526, 668 A.2d 521, 524–25 (1995); . . . But see . . . *Parker v. St. Vincent Hosp.*, 122 N.M. 39, 919 P.2d 1104, 1107 (App.1996) (rejecting products/services distinction, but declining to extend strict liability on policy grounds). The defendant urges us to adopt this rationale.

The plaintiffs argue, however, that the distinction between selling products and providing services is a legal fiction. The defendant, according to the plaintiffs, acted both as a seller of the prosthetic knee and as a provider of professional services in the transaction. Because the defendant charged separately for the prosthesis and earned a profit on the "sale," the plaintiffs argue that the defendant should be treated no differently than any other distributor of a defective product. The defendant, according to the plaintiffs, primarily supplied a prosthesis, while the surgeon provided the professional "services."

Although a defendant may both provide a service and sell a product within the same transaction for purposes of strict liability, see Restatement (Second) of Torts § 402A, comment *f* at 350; cf. *Bolduc v. Herbert Schneider Corp.*, 117 N.H. 566, 570, 374 A.2d 1187, 1189 (1977), the dispositive issue in this case is not whether the defendant "sold" or transferred a prosthetic knee, but whether the defendant was an entity "engaged in the business of selling" prosthetic knees so as to warrant the imposition of liability without proof of legal fault. . . . We find the reasoning of both *Bruzga* and the majority of courts that have declined to extend strict liability to health care providers who supply defective prostheses to be persuasive.

"The essence of the relationship between hospital and patient is the provision of professional medical services necessary to effectuate the implantation of the [prosthesis]. . . ." *Hector v. Cedars-Sinai Medical Center*, 180 Cal.App.3d 493, 225 Cal.Rptr. 595, 599 (1986). "[T]he patient bargains for, and the hospital agrees to make available, the human skill and physical material of medical science to the end that the patient's health be restored." *Perlmutter v. Beth David Hospital*, 308 N.Y. 100, 123 N.E.2d 792, 794 (1954). That the hospital charges a fee for the prosthesis and transfers possession does not transform the character of the hospital-patient relationship. "The thrust of the inquiry is thus not on whether a separate consideration is charged for the physical material used in the exercise of medical skill, but what service is performed to restore or maintain the patient's health." *Cafazzo*, 668 A.2d at 524; *see also Hector*, 225 Cal.Rptr. at 600.

We cannot agree that this distinction is merely a legal fiction. "[T]he essence of the transaction between the retail seller and the consumer relates to the article sold. The seller is in the business of supplying the product to the consumer. It is that, and that alone, for which he is paid." *Hoff v. Zimmer, Inc.*, 746 F.Supp. 872, 875 (W.D.Wis.1990). A patient, by contrast, does not enter a hospital to "purchase" a prosthesis, "but to obtain a course of treatment in the hope of being cured of what ails him." *Perlmutter*, 123 N.E.2d at 796. Indeed, "to ignore the ancillary nature of the association of product with activity is to posit surgery, or . . . any medical service requiring the use of a physical object, as a marketing device for the incorporated object." *Cafazzo*, 668 A.2d at 524.

We decline to ignore the reality of the relationship between Ira Royer and CMC, and to treat any services provided by CMC as ancillary to a primary purpose of selling a prosthetic knee. Rather, the record indicates that in addition to the prosthesis, Royer was billed for a hospital room, operating room services, physical therapy, a recovery room, pathology laboratory work, an EKG or ECG, X rays, and anesthesia. Thus, it is evident that Ira Royer entered CMC not to purchase a prosthesis, but to obtain health care services that included the implantation of the knee, with the overall objective of restoring his health. *See St. Mary Medical Center, Inc. v. Casko*, 639 N.E.2d 312, 315 (Ind.Ct.App.1994). Necessary to the restoration of his health, in the judgment of his physicians, was the implantation of the prosthesis. We do not find this scenario, as the plaintiffs urge, analogous to one in which a plaintiff purchases a defective tire from a retail tire distributor and has the distributor install the tire. *Cf. Perlmutter*, 123 N.E.2d at 795–96.

Moreover, the policy rationale underlying strict liability, as in *Bruzga*, does not support extension of the doctrine under the facts of this case. With respect to the inherent difficulty of proving negligence in many products liability cases, this rationale fails in the context of non-manufacturer cases alleging a design defect. Because "ordinarily there is no possibility that a distributor other than the manufacturer created a design defect[,] . . . strict liability would impose liability when there is no possibility of negligence." *Parker*, 919 P.2d at 1108–09. The plaintiffs do not allege in this case that the defendant altered the prosthesis in any way. Further, holding health care providers strictly liable for defects in prosthetic devices necessary to the provision of health care would likely result in higher health care costs borne ultimately by all patients, *see Ayyash v. Henry Ford Health Systems*, 210 Mich.App. 142, 533 N.W.2d 353, 355 (1995); *Parker*, 919 P.2d at 1108; *Cafazzo*, 668 A.2d at 527, and "place an unrealistic burden on the physicians and hospitals of this state to test or guarantee the tens of thousands of products used in hospitals by doctors," *Ayyash*, 533 N.W.2d at 356; *see Parker*, 919 P.2d at 1110. Additionally, "research and innovation in medical equipment and treatment would be inhibited." *Cafazzo*, 668 A.2d at 527; *see Hoff*, 746 F.Supp. at 874–75. We find that the "peculiar characteristics of medical services[,] . . . [which] include the tendency to be experimental, . . . a dependence on factors beyond the control of the professional[,] and a lack of certainty or assurance of the desired result," *Cafazzo*, 668 A.2d at 527, outweigh any reasons that might support the imposition of strict liability in this context.

"In short, medical services are distinguished by factors which make them significantly different in kind from the retail marketing enterprise at which 402A is directed." *Id.* We conclude that where, as here, a health care provider in the course of rendering health care services supplies a prosthetic device to be implanted into a patient, the health care provider is not "engaged in the business of selling" prostheses for purposes of strict products liability. Accordingly, the trial court did not err in granting the defendant's motion to dismiss.

Affirmed.

NOTES

1. *Sales of Products or Goods versus Provision of Services.* It is hornbook law that there is a distinction between sales of products or goods and provision of service. The provider of services is only liable if he or she is actually negligent. That is, the provider of services is neither strictly liable in tort or warranty. Should that distinction be true across the board? Do the policies that justify strict liability never apply in a services transaction?

Consistent with these general rules, the RESTATEMENT (THIRD) applies to products—tangible personal property. Section 19(a). Services are not products. Section 19(b).

Problems arise when the transaction is a mixture of products and services. *See* RESTATEMENT (THIRD), section 20(c).

2. *Statutory Characterizations.* Many states have blood shield statutes often dating from the early days of strict liability and legislative concern over hepatitis litigation. In *Samson v. Carolina-Georgia Blood Center,* 297 S.C. 409, 377 S.E.2d 311 (1989), the South Carolina Supreme Court, in a case brought by a woman alleging that she had contracted the human immunodeficiency virus (AIDS) from a blood transfusion, held that the state blood shield statute

prevented blood from being treated as a product for the purpose of strict products liability law.

RESTATEMENT (THIRD), § 19(c), states that human blood and human tissue are not subject to the rules of the Restatement.

3. *Non-Manufacturer Sellers.* Much of the discussion in this chapter has proceeded on the assumption that any seller of a product is subject to the rules discussed. RESTATEMENT (SECOND) section 402A applied to all business sellers. The RESTATEMENT (THIRD) generally applies to one who in a commercial context sells or otherwise distributes a product. *See* section 20. This would include a manufacturer, wholesaler, retailer, lessor, or bailor in a commercial transaction.

Some courts do not impose strict liability upon retailers. The RESTATEMENT (THIRD) itself, as you recall, imposes liability upon a retailer of prescription drugs or medical devices for a non-manufacturing defect only if there is a failure to exercise reasonable care. RESTATEMENT (THIRD), section 6(e). Aside from litigation costs and inconvenience, what does a "joined" retail pharmacist stand to lose under a strict liability regime? Are there any situations where the manufacturer will *not* have to indemnify the pharmacist? An innocent seller may generally recover his attorneys' fees in his indemnity claim against his supplier, *see Pullman Standard, Inc. v. Abex Corp.,* 693 S.W.2d 336 (Tenn. 1985).

4. *The Distributive Chain.* If the retailer or other non-manufacturer seller escapes liability under the RESTATEMENT (THIRD) and the theory of strict liability, it may not be liable for personal injury damages caused by the product it distributes. This is because fault generally cannot be proven in these situations. But one of the main reasons for adopting strict liability was because fault could not be proven.

5. *Products on the Periphery of the Distribution Chain.* The court in *Lewin v. McCreight,* 665 F.Supp. 282 (E.D. Mich. 1987), granted summary judgment to the publisher of a "How To" book, *The Complete Metalsmith.* The publisher was sued for allegedly failing to warn of the danger of explosion involved in mixing a mordant according to the instructions in the book. The court stated that liability against a publisher for "failure to warn of 'defective ideas' " can only be imposed where "the publisher actually created, rather than merely printed, the content of the book." To impose liability where the publisher "merely printed and bound a book, the contents of which were written by a third-party author," would impose a "tremendous burden" on such a publisher and would conflict with "the weighty societal interest in free access to ideas."

"The balance might well come out differently, however," the court said, "if the publisher contributed some of the content of the book. The burden of determining whether the content was accurate would be less than in the present case." Also, a noncontributing publisher might "have greater responsibilities where the risk of harm is plain and severe such as a book entitled *How to Make Your Own Parachute,"* subject to "the rule that manufacturers have no duty to warn of obvious dangers."

The plaintiff in *Jones v. J.B. Lippincott Co.,* 694 F. Supp. 1216 (D. Md. 1988), suffered personal injury allegedly as a result of treating herself for constipation by taking an enema as prescribed in the *Textbook for Medical and*

Surgical Nursing (5th ed.), published by defendant Lippincott and authored by two other defendants. She claimed that the prescribed treatment "was in error and there was no warning of the risks and consequences." The court granted defendant Lippincott's motion for summary judgment on the grounds that this defendant "has no duty of care to plaintiff with respect to the content of the book and makes no warranty as to the contents."

Although an editor of defendant Lippincott read the book for "clarity and organization," she did not "review the content of the book for substantive accuracy," nor did the defendant "seek review by outside consultants." On the basis of these facts, the court refused to extend strict tort liability to the defendant for "the dissemination of an idea or knowledge in books or other published material. Indeed to do so would chill expression and publication which is inconsistent with fundamental free speech principles."

The court noted that other courts "have applied strict liability to the narrow area of published maps or charts." It distinguished these cases on the grounds that the "underlying theory of these rulings is the analogy of a nautical chart or an airline chart to other instruments of navigation such as a compass or radar finder which, when defective, will prove to be dangerous." *See also, Winter v. G.P. Putnam's Sons*, 938 F.2d 1033 (9th Cir. 1991); *Way v. Boy Scouts of America*, 856 S.W.2d 230 (Tex. Ct. App. 1993).

Why isn't a medical textbook like a navigational chart to health?

Chapter 16
STRICT LIABILITY FOR ABNORMALLY DANGEROUS ACTIVITIES

A. INTRODUCTION

Initially, tort law may not have been concerned with moral blameworthiness; liability was imposed upon the actor if the act caused the harm. Thus the early English case of *Beaulieu v. Finglam*, Y.B. 2 Hen. 4, fn. 18, pl. 6 (1401), was reported as follows:

> *Hornby*: Judgment of the count; for he has counted upon a common custom of the realm, and he has not said that this custom has been used [from time whereof, etc.].
>
> To which TOTA CURIA said: Answer over; for the common custom of the realm is the common law of the realm.
>
> THIRNING. C.J. said that a man shall answer for his fire, which by misfortune burns another's goods.
>
> And some were of the opinion that the fire could not be said to be his fire, because a man cannot have any property in fire; but that opinion was not upheld.
>
> MARKHAM, J.: A man is held to answer for the act of his servant or of his guest in such a case; for if my servant or my guest puts a candle by a wall and the candle falls into the straw and burns all my house and the house of my neighbour also, in this case I shall answer to my neighbour for his damage . . . . But if a man from outside my house and against my will starts a fire in the thatch of my house or elsewhere, whereby my house is burned and my neighbours' houses are burned as well, for this I shall not be held bound to them; for this cannot be said to be done by wrong on my part, but is against my will.
>
> *Hornby*: This defendant will be undone and impoverished all his days if this action is to be maintained against him; for then twenty other such suits will be brought against him for the same matter.
>
> THIRNING, C.J.: What is that to us? It is better that he should be utterly undone than that the law be changed for him.

The first few centuries of tort law were dominated by the process-driven concern as to the appropriateness of the writ or form used (*the forms of action*). It was not until the nineteenth century that the substantive elements of an alleged tort (whether there was a *cause of action*) were the subject of reported judicial discussion. What is clear is that by the time of *Brown v. Kendall*, 60 Mass. 292 (1850), the plaintiff in a tort action was required to produce "evidence to show either that the *intention* was unlawful, or that the defendant was *in fault*." Subsequently, the tenor of pre-modern tort law was that liability would not be imposed absent a showing of fault. *See, e.g., Brown v. Collins*, 53 N.H. 442 (1873). *See generally* Gregory, *Trespass to Negligence to Absolute Liability*, 37 VA. L. REV. 359 (1951). *Cf.* Schwartz, *Tort Law and the Economy in Nineteenth Century America: A Reinterpretation*, 90 YALE L.J. 1717 (1981).

There were ill-defined exceptions to the fault principle, however. One was that vestiges of the earlier "liability without fault" premise survived. Thus, some jurisdictions imposed liability upon the owner or keeper of an animal for damages caused by the animal, although the owner was neither negligent nor guilty of an intentional tort. Some jurisdictions imposed liability upon an owner of property for damage caused to adjoining landowners by a "non-natural" use of the property.

Another exception was that courts sometimes applied "fault" principles in such a way as to appear to impose liability *without* fault. For example, a person was guilty of trespass to land if he intended to do the act which was in fact an entry onto the land of another, although he was reasonable in his belief that he was not trespassing. A conversion could take place, even though the actor believed in good faith that he was not exercising dominion over the property of another. Because a reasonable mistake did not excuse the conduct, the liability was not fault-based. Furthermore, even the embryonic tort of negligence occasionally produced a type of no-fault liability. Thus, a child engaged in an adult activity or a mental incompetent often was deemed negligent because he failed to conform to the standard of a reasonably prudent adult, although he lacked the discernment to foresee that his conduct was unreasonably risky. *Res ipsa loquitur* and vicarious liability, including imputed contributory fault, have strong elements of strict liability.

Modern tort law recognizes yet another form of liability without fault. During the first half of the twentieth century, courts began imposing liability upon non-negligent manufacturers and sellers for damages caused by defective products. The standard for liability did not require a showing of negligence, and differed from the standard for traditional strict liability in that proof of a defective condition or misrepresentation of the product is generally required.

This chapter deals with those forms of strict liability associated with the keeping of animals and with conducting especially dangerous activities—typically referred to as ultrahazardous or abnormally dangerous activities. The scope of these doctrines is blurred. Strict liability for abnormally dangerous activities, as it developed from *Rylands v. Fletcher*, is rooted in strict liability for keeping animals, although animals may be no more dangerous than many other instrumentalities. The modern law of nuisance and environmental liability—the subject of a separate chapter—is closely related to liability for abnormally dangerous activities.

Throughout this chapter, as well as in other areas of strict tort liability, it is often very difficult to separate strict liability from fault. Concepts for example of foreseeability and proximate cause—preeminent fault concepts—remain very much alive in strict liability, as do policy concerns such as the scope of the duty owed and the like.

The key to avoiding the tyranny of terminology in this area of the law is careful analysis of the conduct that triggers liability in a particular case. As

B. STRICT LIABILITY FOR ANIMALS

ISAACS v. POWELL
267 So. 2d 864 (Fla. App. 1972)

MCNULTY, JUDGE.

This is a case of first impression in Florida. The question posed is whether Florida should adopt the general rule that the owner or keeper of a wild animal, in this case a chimpanzee, is liable to one injured by such animal under the strict liability doctrine, i.e., regardless of negligence on his part, or whether his liability should be predicated on his fault or negligence.

Plaintiff-appellant Scott Isaacs was two years and seven months old at the times material herein. His father had taken him to defendants-appellees' monkey farm where, upon purchasing an admission ticket, and as was usual and encouraged by appellees, he also purchased some food to feed the animals. While Scott was feeding a chimpanzee named Valerie she grabbed his arm and inflicted serious injury.

The exact details of how Valerie was able to grab Scott's arm are in dispute. Appellees contend that Scott's father lifted the boy above reasonably sufficient protective barriers to within Valerie's reach, while appellants counter that the barriers and other protective measures were insufficient. But in any case, appellants do not now, nor did they below, rely on any fault of appellees. Rather, they rely solely on the aforesaid generally accepted strict or, as it is sometimes called, absolute liability doctrine under which negligence or fault on the part of the owner or keeper of an animal ferae naturae is irrelevant. Appellees, on the other hand, suggest that we should adopt the emerging, though yet minority, view that liability should depend upon negligence, i.e., a breach of the duty of care reasonably called for taking into account the nature and specie of the animal involved. We will consider this aspect of the problem first and will hereinafter discuss the available defenses under the theory we adopt.

The trial judge apparently agreed with the appellees that fault or negligence on the part of the owners of a wild animal must be shown. He charged the jury on causation as follows:

> The issues for your determination are whether the proximate cause of Scott Isaacs' injuries was the improper protection for paying customers of the defendants in the condition of the cage, and whether the proximate cause was the placing of Scott by his father, Howard Isaacs, within the barrier placed by the defendants for the protection of customers of the defendant.

In other words the trial judge asked the jury to decide whether Scott was injured through the fault of defendants-appellees and/or through the fault of his father. The jury returned a verdict for the defendants; but obviously, it's impossible for us to determine whether, under the foregoing charge, the jury so found because they were unable to find fault on defendants' part, or whether they so found because they believed the cause of Scott's injury to be the fault of the father. If, of course, we adopt the negligence theory of liability there would be no error in submitting both issues to the jury. But we are of the view that the older and general rule of strict liability, which obviates the issue of the owners' negligence, is more suited to the fast growing, populous and activity-oriented society of Florida. Indeed, our society imposes more than enough risks upon its members now, and we are reluctant to encourage the addition of one more particularly when that one more is increasingly contributed to by those who, for profit, would exercise their "right" to harbor wild animals and increase exposure to the dangers thereof by luring advertising. Prosser puts it this way:

". . . (Liability) has been thought to rest on the basis of negligence in keeping the animal at all; but this does not coincide with the modern analysis of negligence as conduct which is unreasonable in view of the risk, since it may not be an unreasonable thing to keep a tiger in a zoo. It is rather an instance of the strict responsibility placed upon those who, even with proper care, expose the community to the risk of a very dangerous thing. While one or two jurisdictions insist that there is no liability without some negligence in keeping the animal, by far the greater number impose strict liability."

Additionally, we observe that Florida has enacted § 767.04, F.S.A.,[1] relating to dogs, which abrogates the permissive "one bite" rule of the common law. That rule posited that an owner of a dog is liable to one bitten by such dog only if he is chargeable with "scienter," i.e., prior knowledge of the viciousness of the dog. Necessarily, of course, the cause of action therefor was predicated on the negligence of the owner in failing to take proper precautions with knowledge of the dog's vicious propensities. Our statute, however, has in effect imposed strict liability on a dog owner (from which he can absolve himself only by complying with the warning proviso of the statute). It would result in a curious anomaly, then, if we were to adopt the negligence concept as a basis for liability of an owner or keeper of a tiger, while § 767.04, *supra*, imposes potential strict liability upon him if he should trade the tiger for a dog. We are compelled to adopt, therefore, the strict liability rule in these cases.

Concerning, now, available defenses under this rule we share the view, and emphasize, that "strict or absolute liability" does not mean the owner or keeper of a wild animal is an absolute insurer in the sense that he is liable regardless of any fault on the part of the victim. Moreover, we do not think it means he is liable notwithstanding an intervening, efficient independent fault which solely causes the result, as was possibly the case here if fault on the part of Scott's father were the sole efficient cause.

---

[1] This section provides, in pertinent part: "The owners of any dog which shall bite any person, while such person is on or in a public place, or lawfully on or in a private place, including the property of the owner of such dog, shall be liable for such damages as may be suffered by persons bitten, regardless of the former viciousness of such dog or the owners' knowledge of such viciousness . . .; Provided, however, no owner of any dog shall be liable for any damages to any person or his property when such person shall mischievously or carelessly provoke or aggravate the dog inflicting such damage; nor shall any such owner be so liable if at the time of any such injury he had displayed in a prominent place on his premises a sign easily readable including the words Bad Dog."

As to the fault of the victim himself, since the owner or keeper of a wild animal is held to a rigorous rule of liability on account of the danger inherent in harboring such animal, it has generally been held that the owner ought not be relieved from such liability by slight negligence or want of ordinary care on the part of the person injured. The latter's acts must be such as would establish that, with knowledge of the danger, he voluntarily brought the calamity upon himself . . . .

With regard to an intervening fault bringing about the result we have no hesitancy in expanding the foregoing rule to include as a defense the willful or intentional fault of a third party provided such fault is of itself an efficient cause and is the sole cause. If a jury were to decide in this case, therefore, that the sole efficient cause of Scott's injury was the intentional assumption of the apparent risks on the part of the boy's father and his placing of the boy within reach of the danger, it would be a defense available to appellees. Clearly, though, this defense would be related only to causation and is not dependent upon any theory of imputation of the father's fault to the son, which is now irrelevant in view of the extent of strict liability in these cases and the limited defenses available thereunder.

The judgment is reversed and the cause is remanded for a new trial on the theory of strict liability, and the defenses thereto, as enunciated above.

NOTES

1. *The Zoo Keeper.* Many courts hold that a municipal zoo is not strictly liable for harm caused by its animals. As the court said in *Denver v. Kennedy*, 29 Colo. App. 15, 476 P.2d 762 (1970), strict liability should not apply "where a municipality maintains and operates a zoo for the benefit of the public and in response to the public's obvious desires. In such instance the keeping and displaying of animals which are commonly wild in nature is not an unreasonable or unjustified act."

What about a non-municipal zoo? The defendant's "monkey farm" in *Isaacs v. Powell* was apparently not operated by a municipality.

RESTATEMENT (SECOND) OF TORTS § 517 says the "rules as to strict liability for dangerous animals do not apply when the possession of the animal is in pursuance of a duty imposed on the possessor as a public officer or employee or as a common carrier." Comment *d* to this section states:

> Even when there is no duty to receive possession of the animal, the possession may be authorized or sanctioned by legislation, under circumstances such as to indicate approval of the activity sufficient to confer immunity from strict liability. Normally this is the case, for example, when under a franchise given to a defendant as a common carrier, it is authorized but not required to accept dangerous animals for transportation. It is likewise usually the case when the legislature grants to a city or other municipal corporation the authority to establish a public zoological garden. On the other hand, it is not every authorization or permission that can be taken to confer immunity, by giving such approval to the activity as to indicate that it is intended that there shall be no strict liability. Thus a permit from a city council

to hold a circus will normally not prevent strict liability when one of the lions escapes; nor does the ordinary dog license confer immunity from strict liability for dog bites. The question is one of legislative intention in granting the authorization or sanction in question.

Since it is virtually impossible to reduce this to any statement of a rule, the Institute expresses no opinion as to whether the authorization or sanction will relieve the possessor of strict liability.

2. *The Domestic Animal with a Vicious Propensity. Isaacs* states that the owner of a domestic animal is liable at common law for injury caused by the animal if she has "prior knowledge" of its viciousness. If such "scienter" exists, then an action can be "predicated on the negligence of the owner is failing to take proper precautions" to prevent such injury.

The above statement is incorrect in two respects. First, actual knowledge of the animal's viciousness is not required. The RESTATEMENT (SECOND) OF TORTS § 509 says the owner is liable if she "knows or has *reason to know*" that her domestic animal has "dangerous propensities abnormal to its class" (emphasis added). *Greely v. Johnson*, 265 Mass. 465, 164 N.E. 385 (1929), states that the owner is not liable unless she "knew or *should have known* of those vicious habits" (emphasis added).

Second, once the owner has reason to know or should know of the animal's vicious propensity, the liability for any resulting harm is strict, RESTATEMENT (SECOND) OF TORTS § 509. Liability does not turn on whether the owner "fails to take proper precautions", as *Isaacs* indicates. Section 509 describes such a dangerous domestic animal as one that is abnormally dangerous.

3. *What is a Domestic and What is a Wild Animal?* As noted above, the possessor of a wild animal is generally strictly liable for any harm it causes, while the possessor of a domestic animal is liable only if she has reason to know or should know of the animal's dangerous propensities. RESTATEMENT (SECOND) OF TORTS § 506 defines a domestic animal as one that is "by custom devoted to the service of mankind at the time and in the place in which it is kept." A wild animal is defined as one that is not by custom so devoted. Comment *a* to this section states that the term "animal" includes "birds, fish, reptiles and insects." As examples of wild animals, it lists "rattlesnakes, alligators, ostriches or tsetse flies." But "bees are not wild animals", according to comment *b*. Comment *b* also says an elephant in America is a wild animal, "but in Burma it is a domestic animal since elephants are there customarily used as heavy draft animals and for many other common purposes." The mere fact that a wild animal has been tamed does not change its character, since the owner takes the risk that "at any moment the animal may revert to and exhibit" its dangerous propensities. *Id.*

Are these distinctions between domestic and wild animals satisfactory? Can you come up with a better definition of the difference? Should the distinction be retained in the law?

4. *The Watchdog.* RESTATEMENT (SECOND) OF TORTS § 516 states that a person is privileged to use a dog or other animal to protect his property "to the same extent that he is privileged to use a mechanical protective device for those purposes." Comment *b* to this section says that a landowner could

"set a ferocious police dog" on a burglar "to terminate a burglarious intrusion." Is this a correct statement of the spring gun rule? *See Katko v. Briney*, 183 N.W.2d 657 (Iowa 1971).

Comment *a* to § 516 states that the property owner "may be required to post warnings of the presence of a dog on his premises, particularly when the dog is of a character likely to inflict more than trivial harm." Would a warning be sufficient to protect a landowner from liability for harm caused by a vicious watchdog?

5. *Who is an Animal Possessor? Beeler v. Hickman*, 50 Wash. App. 746, 750 P.2d 1282 (1988), indicates that a mere possessor, as opposed to an owner, of a vicious dog is not strictly liable for harm caused by the dog. The RESTATEMENT (SECOND) OF TORTS § 507 imposes strict liability for the "possessor" of a wild animal. One who "harbors" a wild or abnormally dangerous domestic animal "is subject to the same liability as if he were in possession of it " Sec. 514. Thus the head of a household is liable for harm caused by a household member whom he permits to keep such an animal. But "a shopkeeper does not harbor dogs that he permits a customer to bring into his shop." *Id.*, comm. *a*.

Possession of land "does not carry with it possession of the indigenous wild animals that are upon it," RESTATEMENT (SECOND) OF TORTS § 508, comm. *a*. Sec. 508 says a possessor of a wild animal "is not liable for harm done by it after it has gone out of his possession and returned to its natural state as a wild animal indigenous to the locality." But if the animal "is one of a class not indigenous to the locality, its escape does not prevent its possessor from being liable for the harm done by the animal no matter how long after its escape; in this case the risk of liability continues until some third person takes possession of the animal." RESTATEMENT (SECOND) OF TORTS § 507, comm. *d*.

6. *Propensity, Proximate Cause and the Like.* Sec. 507(2) of the RESTATEMENT (SECOND) OF TORTS states that the possessor of a wild animal is liable only for harm "that results from a dangerous propensity that is characteristic of wild animals of the particular class, or of which the possessor knows or has reason to know." Comment *e* states that "if a bear, having escaped, goes to sleep in the highway and is run into by a carefully driven motor car on a dark night, the possessor of the bear is not liable for harm to the motorist in the absence of negligence in its custody." Why should "negligence in its custody" change the outcome?

In *Jones v. Utica Mut. Ins. Co.*, 463 So. 2d 1153 (Fla. 1985), the court interpreted a Florida statute providing: "Owners of dogs shall be liable for any damage done by their dogs to persons." Two young boys tied a small red wagon to Shane, a German shepherd belonging to one of them. Shane chased another dog and the wagon struck the 12-year-old plaintiff as the dog rushed by him. The trial court held that, although the dog exhibited "canine characteristics" when it pursued the other dog, the injury was caused by the attachment of the wagon rather than any such characteristic. Reversing, the appellate court commented:

> How is one to determine whether or not an animal's behavior is sufficiently active, or canine, or dispositive of the outcome, so as to

render the owner liable for its conduct? When does a dog exercise canine characteristics? There is simply no way to define or administer such a standard and the parties would be at a loss to evaluate when a dog can be found not to have acted like a dog. Is it meaningful to conclude the dog in this case was exhibiting canine characteristics when it chased another dog but acting less like a dog because it was tied to a wagon? We think not. The trial of a suit for damages should never degenerate to a battle of experts giving opinions as to whether a dog exercised canine characteristics or human characteristics.

Article 2321 of the Louisiana Civil Code (1979) provides that "[t]he owner of an animal is answerable for the damages it has caused." In *Boyer v. Seal*, 553 So. 2d 827 (La. 1989), an elderly houseguest was injured when she tripped and fell because the owner's cat brushed against her legs. The Louisiana Supreme Court ruled that under the article a non-negligent owner is not liable for the damages caused by his domestic animal unless the animal created an unreasonable risk of harm, using the standard "risk/utility" test. The court commented:

> [T]o interpret the article literally . . . would be to impose absolute liability, a consequence the court has reserved for instances in which damage is done by wild animals . . . . [T]he behavior of [defendant's] cat in either rubbing the legs of a visitor in its home or accidentally getting in the way or underfoot is [not] an unreasonable risk of harm . . . . [T]he likelihood of injury resulting from such cat-like behavior multiplied by the gravity of the harm threatened by it would [not] outweigh the utility of keeping a cat as a pet in a home where she may be displayed and exposed to visiting relatives and guests.

7. *Strict Liability Statutes.* As noted in *Isaacs v. Powell* and *Jones v. Utica Mut. Ins. Co.*, some states impose strict liability by statute for dog bites. Thus a Michigan statute makes the owner of a dog liable for dog-bite injury "regardless of the former viciousness of such dog or the owner's knowledge of such viciousness". MICH. COMP. LAWS ANN. § 287.351 (1990). Why is such strict liability for domestic animals restricted to dogs—which after all are man's best friend? Louisiana law, which formerly imposed strict liability on the owners of all domestic animals, now bases liability upon negligence, except for dog owners, who are "strictly liable for. . . injuries. . . caused by the dog and which the owner could have prevented and which did not result from the injured person's provocation of the dog." LA CIV. CODE ART 2321 (1996).

8. *Negligence Per Se.* Many jurisdictions have laws prohibiting dog owners from allowing their dogs to be at large except on a leash. The court in *Newport v. Moran*, 80 Or. App. 71, 721 P.2d 465 (1985), interpreted such a law as not intended to impose negligence per se on the owner of a dog at large. Said the court, dog bites and dog knock-down injuries "were not within the area of risk that the dog-at-large ordinance was designed to avoid." What kind of risks do you suppose the ordinance was designed to avoid?

9. *Intervening Cause.* The court in *Isaacs v. Powell* held that "the willful or intentional fault of a third party" will bar recovery if it is the "efficient" and "sole cause" of the plaintiff's injury. RESTATEMENT (SECOND) OF TORTS § 510 states that the possessor of a wild animal or an abnormally dangerous domestic animal is subject to liability for

harm caused by the animal even though the harm would not have occurred but for the unexpectable innocent, negligent or "reckless" misconduct of a third person, the action of another animal, or the operation of a force of nature. Sec. 522 has a similar rule for abnormally dangerous activities. Compare this rule with the cases on intervening cause given in the next section of this chapter.

10. *Contributory Negligence and Assumption of the Risk. Isaacs v. Powell* holds that contributory negligence of the plaintiff is no defense, but that assumption of the risk is a bar. This is the position of the RESTATEMENT (SECOND) OF TORTS, both with regard to strict liability for animals, § 515, and for abnormally dangerous activities, §§ 523, 524. Would these rules be changed in a jurisdiction that had adopted comparative fault? *See Andrade v. Shiers*, 564 So. 2d 787 (La. App. 1990) (plaintiff's fault compared to animal owner's strict liability).

11. *Trespassing Livestock.* RESTATEMENT (SECOND) OF TORTS § 504 provides for strict liability of the possessor of livestock for harm caused by their intrusion onto the land of another. Livestock, according to comment *b* to that section, "includes horses, cattle, pigs and sheep and also poultry, unless by custom poultry are permitted to run at large." The term "does not include dogs and cats, which are difficult to restrain and unlikely to do any substantial harm by their intrusion."

In America, liability for trespassing animals has varied according to their economic importance in various sections of the country at various times. As long as vast areas of federally-owned prairie were open to grazing without fee or regulation, the prevailing rule either by statute or by common law in the prairie states was no liability at all, let alone strict liability, for trespassing animals. The isolated crop-raiser must protect himself by fencing out the animals. *Wagner v. Bissell,* 3 Iowa 396 (1856).

As late as 1913, the Supreme Court of Iowa held that defendants were not required to keep their chickens from running across the public highway to feed on plaintiff's oatseed, forcing him to resow two or three times and still causing a damaged crop. *Kimple v. Schafer*, 161 Iowa 659, 143 N.W. 505 (1913). The court observed that chickens were "free commoners." The expense of building fences to keep them in would ruin an industry upon which the economic well-being of the state depended. Again, the crop-raiser should do the fencing.

This case was not specifically overruled until 1977, in *Weber v. Madison*, 251 N.W.2d 532 (Iowa 1977). Here the plaintiff, driving on a gravel road in a rural area, was so startled by a flock of "large geese" suddenly appearing in the road that she turned her car into a ditch with resulting severe injuries to herself. The court held that plaintiff could recover provided she could prove the negligence of the owner of the geese in failing to restrain them or warn of their presence on the highway. The court notes, however, a tendency to restore the common law rule as to animals, with the owner held negligent "merely because he had permitted the animals to run at large."

In many states, the common law rule has been altered by statute or judicial decision. Some states, reflecting the strength of the cattle industry, have adopted "fencing out" rules which bar recovery by the victim of animal trespass unless the animal "broke" the victim's fence. In states where farming interests prevail, the animal owner may be required to "fence in" an animal which is likely to roam and do damage, and is liable without fault if he fails to do so. Governmental subdivisions (such as counties) may be given the local option to choose between "fencing in" and "fencing out" rules.

Liability for trespassing animals may not be limited to damage to the real property which is the subject of the trespass. In *Williams v. Goodwin,* 41 Cal. App. 3d 496, 116 Cal. Rptr. 200 (1974), the court ruled that a landowner could recover for personal injury caused by a trespassing bull. Compare RESTATEMENT (SECOND) OF TORTS § 504, which provides that the strict liability of the owner of a trespassing animal does not extend to "harm . . . not reasonably to be expected from the intrusion." See also *Carver v. Ford*, 591 P.2d 305 (Okla. 1979) (no recovery for personal injury caused by trespassing cattle unless the keeper was negligent).

In *Foland v. Malander,* 222 Neb. 1, 381 N.W.2d 914 (1986), a 1,700-pound bull which was being driven along a road strayed onto the plaintiff's land and jumped an electric fence into a corral. While the plaintiff was assisting defendant in separating the bull from calves in the corral, the bull charged plaintiff and injured him. The Nebraska Supreme Court ruled that the owner of the bull could not be held strictly liable for the personal injuries, although a negligence action would lie.

Foland confirmed the general rule that strict liability for livestock trespass does not apply when the animal is being lawfully driven on a highway and strays onto abutting land. RESTATEMENT (SECOND) OF TORTS § 505 provides that the possessor of livestock "being driven upon an unrestricted highway" is liable for their "intrusion on land abutting on the highway if, but only if, he has failed to exercise reasonable care to prevent them from straying or to remove them from the abutting lands upon which they have strayed." Why have such a special rule for straying livestock that are being driven upon a highway?

12. *The Trespassing Plaintiff.* RESTATEMENT (SECOND) OF TORTS § 511 says the possessor of land is not strictly liable to a trespasser for harm caused by a wild or abnormally dangerous domestic animal that the possessor keeps on the land, regardless of whether the trespasser "intentionally or negligently trespasses" and "even though the trespasser has no reason to know that the animal is kept there." What duty would be owed to the trespasser in this situation? *See* RESTATEMENT (SECOND) OF TORTS § 512 (the rules of liability to such a trespasser "are the same as for other artificial conditions or for activities on the land").

Sec. 513 says the possessor of a wild or abnormally dangerous animal is strictly liable for harm caused by the animal to licensees or invitees that come upon the land.

Would the rules of §§ 511-513 survive the modern development of landowner liability?

PROBLEM

Owner took her dog, suspected of having contracted the rabies virus, to a veterinary clinic for quarantine and observation. The dog escaped from the clinic. A week after its escape, the dog bit victim on a public highway. After being bitten, the victim ran from the dog and while running was stung to death by owner's bees.

Discuss the possible liability of the clinic and the owner to victim's estate.

C. ABNORMALLY DANGEROUS ACTIVITIES

FLETCHER v. RYLANDS
[1866] L.R. 1 Exch. 265 (Exch. Ch.)

BLACKBURN, J.

[The plaintiff had leased a colliery from Lord Wilton for some ten years. Partially worked coal seams ran from the colliery under the land of two other neighbors and another parcel of land owned by Lord Wilton. The defendants owned a mill to the west of the colliery and, by arrangement with Lord Wilton, the defendants built a reservoir on his intervening parcel. The defendants selected competent contractors to construct the reservoir. The defendants were not negligent in failing to discover that old coal workings communicated between the colliery and the site of the reservoir. In December, 1860 the reservoir was completed and partially filled with water. A shaft broke open and water flooded the colliery which subsequently was abandoned.]

The plaintiff, though free from all blame on his part, must bear the loss, unless he can establish that it was the consequence of some default for which the defendants are responsible. The question of law therefore arises, what is the obligation which the law casts on a person who, like the defendants, lawfully brings on his land something which, though harmless whilst it remains there, will naturally do mischief if it escape out of his land. It is agreed on all hands that he must take care to keep in that which he has brought on the land and keeps there, in order that it may not escape and damage his neighbours, but the question arises whether the duty which the law casts upon him, under such circumstances, is an absolute duty to keep it in at his peril, or is . . . merely a duty to take all reasonable and prudent precautions, in order to keep it in, but no more. If the first be the law, the person who has brought on his land and kept there something dangerous, and failed to keep it in, is responsible for all the natural consequences of its escape. If the second be the limit of his duty, he would not be answerable except on proof of negligence, and consequently would not be answerable for escape arising from any latent defect which ordinary prudence and skill could not detect.

Supposing the second to be the correct view of the law, a further question arises subsidiary to the first, viz., whether the defendants are not so far identified with the contractors whom they employed, as to be responsible for the consequences of their want of care and skill in making the reservoir in fact insufficient with reference to the old shafts, of the existence of which they were aware, though they had not ascertained where the shafts went to.

We think that the true rule of law is, that the person who for his own purposes brings on his lands and collects and keeps there anything likely to do mischief if it escapes, must keep it in at his peril, and, if he does not do so, is prima facie answerable for all the damage which is the natural consequence of its escape. He can excuse himself by showing that the escape was owing to the plaintiff's default; or perhaps that the escape was the consequence of vis major, or the act of God; but as nothing of this sort exists here, it is unnecessary to inquire what excuse would be sufficient. The general rule, as above stated, seems on principle just. The person whose grass or corn is eaten down by the escaping cattle of his neighbour, or whose mine is flooded by the water from his neighbour's reservoir, or whose cellar is invaded by the filth of his neighbour's privy, or whose habitation is made unhealthy by the fumes and noisome vapours of his neighbour's alkali works, is damnified without any fault of his own; and it seems but reasonable and just that the neighbour, who has brought something on his own property which was not naturally there, harmless to others so long as it is confined to his own property, but which he knows to be mischievous if it gets on his neighbour's, should be obliged to make good the damage which ensues if he does not succeed in confining it to his own property. But for his act in bringing it there no mischief could have accrued, and it seems but just that he should at his peril keep it there so that no mischief may accrue, or answer for the natural and anticipated consequences. And upon authority, this we think is established to be the law whether the things so brought be beasts, or water, or filth, or stenches.

The case that has most commonly occurred, and which is most frequently to be found in the books, is as to the obligation of the owner of cattle which he has brought on his land, to prevent their escaping and doing mischief. The law as to them seems to be perfectly settled from early times; the owner must keep them in at his peril, or he will be answerable for the natural consequences of their escape; that is with regard to tame beasts, for the grass they eat and trample upon, though not for any injury to the person of others, for our ancestors have settled that it is not the general nature of horses to kick, or bulls to gore; but if the owner knows that the beast has a vicious propensity to attack man, he will be answerable for that too.

. . . As has been already said, there does not appear to be any difference in principle, between the extent of the duty cast on him who brings cattle on his land to keep them in, and the extent of the duty imposed on him who brings on his land, water, filth, or stenches, or any other thing which will, if it escape, naturally do damage, to prevent their escaping and injuring his neighbour. . . .

. . . But it was further said [in the court below] that when damage is done to personal property, or even to the person, by collision, either upon land or at sea, there must be negligence in the party doing the damage to render him legally responsible; and this is no doubt true, and as was pointed out by [counsel] during his argument before us, this is not confined to cases of collision, for there are many cases in which proof of negligence is essential, as for instance, where an unruly horse gets on the footpath of a public street and kills a passenger; or where a person in a dock is struck by the falling of a bale of cotton which the defendant's servants are lowering, and many other similar cases may be found. But we think these cases distinguishable from the present. Traffic on the highways, whether by land or sea, cannot be conducted without exposing those whose persons or property are near it to some inevitable risk; and that being so, those who go on the highway, or have their property adjacent to it, may well be held to do so subject to their taking upon themselves the risk of injury from that inevitable danger; and persons who by the licence of the owner pass near to warehouses where goods are being raised or lowered, certainly do so subject to the inevitable risk of accident. In neither case, therefore, can they recover without proof of want of care or skill occasioning the accident; and it is believed that all the cases in which inevitable accident has been held an excuse for what prima facie was a trespass, can be explained on the same principle, viz., that the circumstances were such as to shew that the plaintiff had taken the risk upon himself. But there is no ground for saying that the plaintiff here took upon himself any risk arising from the uses to which the defendants should choose to apply their land. He neither knew what these might be, nor could he in any way control the defendants, or hinder their building what reservoirs they liked, and storing up in them what water they pleased, so long as the defendants succeeded in preventing the water which they there brought from interfering with the plaintiff's property.

[The defendant mill owner appealed to the House of Lords, which affirmed the judgment of the Exchequer Chamber for the plaintiff. The rationale of the House of Lords, given in the following opinion, differs from that of the Exchequer Chamber. The rationale of the House of Lords is the one widely cited as the basis for this famous opinion.]

RYLANDS v. FLETCHER
[1868] L.R. 3, 19 L.T. 220 (H.L.)

THE LORD CHANCELLOR (Lord *Cairns*):—

My Lords, in this case the Plaintiff (I may use the description of the parties in the action) is the occupier of a mine and works under a close of land. The Defendants are the owners of a mill in his neighbourhood, and they proposed to make a reservoir for the purpose of keeping and storing water to be used about their mill upon another close of land, which for the purposes of this case, may be taken as being adjoining to the close of the Plaintiff, although, in point of fact, some intervening land lay between the two. Underneath the close of land of the Defendants on which they proposed to construct their reservoir there were certain old and disused mining passages and works. There were five vertical shafts, and some horizontal shafts communicating with them. The vertical shafts had been filled up with soil and rubbish, and it does not appear that any person was aware of the existence either of the vertical shafts or of the horizontal works communicating with them. In the course of the working by the Plaintiff of his mine, he had gradually worked through the seams of coal underneath the close, and had come into contact with the old and disused works [that ran] underneath the close of the Defendants.

In that state of things the reservoir of the Defendants was constructed. It was constructed by them through the agency and inspection of an engineer and contractor. Personally, the Defendants appear to have taken no part in the works, or to have been aware of any want of security connected with them. As regards the engineer and the contractor, we must take it from the case that they did not exercise, as far as they were concerned, that reasonable care and caution which they might have exercised, taking notice, as they appear to have taken notice, of the vertical shafts filled up in the manner which I have mentioned. However, my Lords, when the reservoir was constructed, and filled, or partly filled, with water, the weight of the water bearing upon the disused and imperfectly filled-up vertical shafts, broke through those shafts. The water passed down them and into the horizontal workings, and from the horizontal workings under the close of the Defendants it passed on into the workings under the close of the Plaintiff, and flooded his mine, causing considerable damage, for which this action was brought . . . .

My Lords, the principles on which this case must be determined appear to me to be extremely simple. The Defendants, treating them as the owners or occupiers of the close on which the reservoir was constructed, might lawfully have used that close for any purpose for which it might in the ordinary course of the enjoyment of land be used; and if, in what I may term the natural user of that land, there had been any accumulation of water, either on the surface or underground, and if, by the operation of the laws of nature, that accumulation of water had passed off into the close occupied by the Plaintiff, the Plaintiff could not have complained that that result had taken place. If he had desired to guard himself against it, it would have lain upon him to have done so, by leaving, or by interposing, some barrier between his close and the close of the Defendants in order to have prevented that operation of the laws of nature . . . .

On the other hand if the Defendants, not stopping at the natural use of their close, had desired to use it for any purpose which I may term a non-natural use, for the purpose of introducing into the close that which in its natural condition was not in or upon it, for the purpose of introducing water either above or below ground in quantities and in a manner not the result of any work or operation on or under the land,—and if in consequence of their doing so, or in consequence of any imperfection in the mode of their doing so, the water came to escape and to pass off into the close of the Plaintiff, then it appears to me that if in the course of their doing it, the evil arose to which I have referred, the evil, namely, of the escape of the water and its passing away to the close of the Plaintiff and injuring the Plaintiff, then for the consequence of that, in my opinion, the Defendants would be liable . . . .

My Lords, these simple principles, if they are well founded, as it appears to me they are, really dispose of this case.

The same result is arrived at on the principles referred to by Mr. Justice *Blackburn* in his judgment, in the Court of Exchequer Chamber, where he states the opinion of that Court as to the law in these words: "We think that the true rule of law is, that the person who, for his own purposes, brings on his land and collects and keeps there anything likely to do mischief if it escapes, must keep it in at his peril; and if he does not do so, is *prima facie* answerable for all the damage which is the natural consequence of its escape. He can excuse himself by showing that the escape was owing to the Plaintiff's default; or, perhaps, that the escape was the consequence of *vis major*, or the

C. ABNORMALLY DANGEROUS ACTIVITIES

act of God; but as nothing of this sort exists here, it is unnecessary to inquire what excuse would be sufficient. The general rule, as above stated, seems on principle just. The person whose grass or corn is eaten down by the escaping cattle of his neighbour, or whose mine is flooded by the water from this neighbour's reservoir, or whose cellar is invaded by the filth of his neighbour's privy, or whose habitation is made unhealthy by the fumes and noisome vapours of his neighbour's alkali works, is damnified without any fault of his own; and it seems but reasonable and just that the neighbour who has brought something on his own property (which was not naturally there), harmless to others so long as it is confined to his own property, but which he knows will be mischievous if it gets on his neighbour's, should be obliged to make good the damage which ensues if he does not succeed in confining it to his own property. But for his act in bringing it there no mischief could have accrued, and it seems but just that he should at his peril keep it here, so that no mischief may accrue, or answer for the natural and anticipated consequence. And upon authority this we think is established to be the law, whether the things so brought be beasts, or water, or filth, or stenches."

My Lords, in that opinion, I must say I entirely concur . . . .

LORD CRANWORTH . . . .

In considering whether a Defendant is liable to a Plaintiff for damage which the Plaintiff may have sustained, the question in general is not whether the Defendant has acted with due care and caution, but whether his acts have occasioned the damage. And the doctrine is founded on good sense. For when one person, in managing his own affairs, causes, however innocently, damage to another, it is obviously only just that he should be the party to suffer. He is bound *sic uti suo ut non laedat alienum*. This is the principle of law applicable to cases like the present, and I do not discover in the authorities which were cited anything conflicting with it . . . .

NOTES

1. *Escaping Mischief and Non-Natural Use.* Judge Blackburn for the Court of Exchequer says that "the person who for his own purposes brings on his lands and collects and keeps there anything likely to do mischief if it escapes, must keep it in at his peril." Lord Cairns for the House of Lords says that if a landowner brings onto his land anything which was not on the land in its "natural condition", and the thing escapes from the land causing harm, the landowner will be liable at his "peril" (i.e., strictly liable) for the harm caused by such "non-natural" use of the land. Are Blackburn's and Lord Cairns' formulations of the issue different? Notice that both judges agree that escaping cattle and escaping "filth" and "stenches" or "noisome vapors" would result in strict liability, and that the escaping waters from defendant's reservoir would also result in strict liability. They both also apparently agree that a natural accumulation of water would *not* result in strict liability, either because the owner did not "bring" the water onto her land or because such an accumulation would not be a "non-natural" use of the land.

Apparently the holding of *Rylands v. Fletcher* is restricted to the duty of landowners, and is also restricted to their liability for things that "escape" from their land. Do these restrictions arise simply from a statement of the facts of the case, or are they the result of a broader normative principle of the case?

In *Cambridge Water Co. Ltd. v. Eastern Counties Leather plc*, [1994] 2 AC 264, 1 All E.R. 53, the defendant, ECL, an old, established tannery, was found liable for pollution of the water supply, used by plaintiff Cambridge Water Co., through leakage of a degreasing chemical into the aquifer from which the plaintiff obtained its water. The trial judge had refused to apply *Rylands v. Fletcher* to the case, finding that ECL was engaged in a natural use of its land. Reversing the trial court, Lord Goff speaking for the House of Lords said:

> It is a commonplace that this particular exception to liability under the rule has developed and changed over the years. It seems clear that in *Fletcher v. Rylands* (1866) L.R. 1 Ex. 265 itself Blackburn J.'s statement of the law was limited to things which are brought by the defendant onto his land, and so did not apply to things that were naturally upon the land. Furthermore, it is doubtful whether in the House of Lords in the same case Lord Cairns, to whom we owe the expression 'non-natural use' of the land, was intending to expand the concept of natural use beyond that envisaged by Blackburn J. Even so, the law has long since departed from any such simple idea, redolent of a different age; and, at least since the advice of the Privy Council delivered by Lord Moulton in *Rickards v. Lothian* [1913] A.C. 263 at 280, [1911-13] All E.R. Rep. 71 at 80, natural use has been extended to embrace the ordinary use of land. I ask to be forgiven if I again quote Lord Moulton's statement of the law, which has lain at the heart of the subsequent development of this exception:
>
> 'It is not every use to which land is put that brings into play that principle. It must be some special use bringing with it increased danger to others, and must not merely be the ordinary use of the land or such a use as is proper for the general benefit of the community.'
>
> *Rickards v. Lothian* itself was concerned with a use of a domestic kind, viz the overflow of water from a basin whose runaway had become blocked. But over the years the concept of natural use, in the sense of ordinary use, has been extended to embrace a wide variety of uses, including not only domestic uses but also recreational uses and even some industrial uses.
>
> It is obvious that the expression 'ordinary use of the land' in Lord Moulton's statement of the law is one which is lacking in precision. There are some writers who welcome the flexibility which has thus been introduced into this branch of the law, on the ground that it enables judges to mould and adapt the principle of strict liability to the changing needs of society, whereas others regret the perceived absence of principle in so vague a concept, and fear that the whole idea of strict liability may as a result be undermined. A particular doubt is introduced by Lord Moulton's alternative criterion 'or such a use as is proper for the general benefit of the community'. If these words are understood to refer to a local community, they can be given some content as intended to refer to such matters as, for example, the

provision of services; indeed the same idea can, without too much difficulty, be extended to, for example, the provision of services to industrial premises, as in a business park or an industrial estate. But if the words are extended to embrace the wider interests of the local community or the general benefit of the community at large, it is difficult to see how the exception can be kept within reasonable bounds. A notable extension was considered in your Lordships' House in *Read v. J. Lyons & Co. Ltd.* [1946] 2 All E.R. 471 at 475, 478, [1947] A.C. 156 at 169–170, 174 per Viscount Simon and Lord Macmillan, where it was suggested that, in time of war, the manufacture of explosives might be held to constitute a natural use of land, apparently on the basis that, in a country in which the greater part of the population was involved in the war effort, many otherwise exceptional uses might become 'ordinary' for the duration of the war. It is however unnecessary to consider so wide an extension as that in a case such as the present. Even so, we can see the introduction of another extension in the present case, when the judge invoked the creation of employment as clearly for the benefit of the local community, viz 'the industrial village' at Sawston. I myself, however, do not feel able to accept that the creation of employment as such, even in a small industrial complex, is sufficient of itself to establish a particular use as constituting a natural or ordinary use of land.

Fortunately, I do not think it is necessary for the purposes of the present case to attempt any redefinition of the concept of natural or ordinary use. This is because I am satisfied that the storage of chemicals in substantial quantities, and their use in the manner employed at ACL's premises, cannot fall within the exception.

The actual holding in *Read v. J. Lyons & Co.*, cited by the *Cambridge Water Co.* court, was that the defendant munitions manufacturer was not liable under *Rylands* because the plaintiff, a government inspector, was injured by an explosion on the defendant's premises. The explosives therefore did not "escape" from the defendant's land.

No such doctrine of escape has been imported into the American law of strict liability for dangerous activities. As will be seen later, some cases, particularly with regard to handgun litigation, have imported the land-use connection, but most American courts reject this restriction.

2. *Common Usage.* The strict liability concept of *Rylands v. Fletcher* has been carried forward in American Jurisprudence as embodied in sec. 520 of the first and second RESTATEMENT OF TORTS. Both of theses restatements specify, as a condition for determining strict liability for damages caused by "ultrahazardous" (first restatement) or "abnormally dangerous" (second restatement) activity, that the activity not be a "matter of common usage". This term "common usage" may be intended to remotely reflect the idea of natural use contained in *Rylands v. Fletcher*, although the second restatement probably more nearly reflects this idea in the condition that considers the appropriateness of the activity "to the place where it is carried on", RESTATEMENT (SECOND) OF TORTS § 520(e). Comment *j* to the second restatement makes clear that § 520(e) is intended to reflect the natural-use doctrine of *Rylands*.

Comment *e* of the first, and *i* of the second, restatement state that an activity is a matter of common usage "if it is customarily carried on by the great mass of mankind or by many people in the community." They give as an example of common usage the use of automobiles which have come into such "general use" as to be a common usage. But blasting and the storage of explosives are not activities of common usage because these activities are carried on by a "comparatively small number of persons".

Compare the language of Blackburn, J., in *Fletcher v. Rylands*:

> Traffic on the highways, whether by land or sea, cannot be conducted without exposing those whose persons or property are near it to some inevitable risk; and that being so, those who go on the highway, or have their property adjacent to it, may well be held to do so subject to their taking upon themselves the risk of injury from that inevitable danger; and persons who by the licence of the owner pass near to warehouses where goods are being raised or lowered, certainly do so subject to the inevitable risk of accident. In neither case, therefore, can they recover without proof of want of care or skill occasioning the accident; and it is believed that all the cases in which inevitable accident has been held an excuse for what prima facie was a trespass, can be explained on the same principle, viz., that the circumstances were such as to shew that the plaintiff had taken the risk upon himself.

3. *Rylands Rejected*. Early American opinions rejected the strict liability of *Rylands v. Fletcher*. *Losee v. Buchanan*, 51 N.Y. 476 (1873), is typical. The *Losee* court said the *Rylands* decision

> is in direct conflict with the law as settled in this country. Here, if one builds a dam upon his own premises and thus holds back and accumulates the water for his benefit, or if he brings water upon his premises into a reservoir, in case the dam or the banks of the reservoir give away and the lands of a neighbor are thus flooded, he is not liable for the damage without proof of some fault or negligence on his part.

4. *The Renaissance of Rylands v. Fletcher*. According to *Branch v. Western Petr., Inc.*, 657 P.2d 267, 273 (Utah 1982), "Although *Rylands v. Fletcher* was initially rejected by a number of states, its influence has been substantial in the United States. Indeed, the strict liability rule of the Restatement of Torts was broadened in § 519 of the RESTATEMENT (SECOND) OF TORTS by making it applicable to 'abnormally dangerous activities.'" Further, according to *Peneschi v. National Steel Corp.*, 295 S.E.2d 1, 5 (W. Va. 1982),

> Even jurisdictions that reject *Rylands* by name have accepted and applied it under the cloak of various other theories, with strict liability commonly imposed under the sobriquet of "nuisance." Here too, the relationship of the activity to its surroundings is the controlling factor, so that using explosives in the midst of a city may be an absolute nuisance whereas in a wilderness it is not.

State Dep't of Envt'l Protection v. Ventron, 94 N.J. 473, 468 A.2d 150, 157 (1983), concerned the liability of mercury polluters of a state waterway. The New Jersey Supreme Court stated:

We believe it is time to recognize expressly that the law of liability has evolved so that a landowner is strictly liable to others for harm caused by toxic wastes that are stored on his property and flow onto the property of others. Therefore, we . . . adopt the principle of liability originally declared in *Rylands v. Fletcher*. The net result is that those who use, or permit others to use, land for the conduct of abnormally dangerous activities are strictly liable for resultant damages.

5. *Blasting and Storage of Explosives*. Even before *Rylands v. Fletcher*, New York applied strict liability for damage done by debris from blasting. *Hay v. Cohoes County*, 2 N.Y. 159 (1849). Why do you suppose there was such a ready acceptance of strict liability in the case of blasting?

In *Booth v. Rome, W. & O.T.R. Co.*, 140 N.Y. 267, 35 N.E. 592 (1893), the court based blasting liability on a trespass theory, holding that there was no liability for concussion damage from blasting. Finding itself out of line with developing law, New York overruled *Booth* in *Spano v. Perini*, 25 N.Y.2d 11, 302 N.Y.S.2d 527, 250 N.E.2d 31 (1969), and imposed strict liability for concussion damage from blasting. "The question . . . was not *whether* it was lawful or proper to engage in blasting but *who* should bear the cost of any resulting damage—the person who engaged in the dangerous activity or the innocent neighbor injured thereby". In holding that the blaster should be liable, the court appears to be imposing a kind of enterprise liability—that is, a company should bear liability for the damage it causes as a cost of doing business.

The court in *Yukon Equip., Inc. v. Fireman's Fund Ins. Co.*, 585 P.2d 1206 (Alaska 1978), followed *Exner v. Sherman Power Construc. Co.*, 54 F.2d 510 (2nd Cir. 1931), in imposing strict liability for detonation damage resulting from the storage of explosives. "*Exner* has been widely followed", the court said. *Yukon Equip.* quoted the rationale of *Exner* for imposing strict liability:

The extent to which one man in the lawful conduct of his business is liable for injuries to another involves an adjustment of conflicting interests . . . . When, as here, the defendant, though without fault, has engaged in the perilous activity of storing large quantities of a dangerous explosive for use in his business, we think there is no justification for relieving it of liability, and that the owner of the business, rather than a third party who has no relation to the explosion, other than that of injury, should bear the loss.

THE CLARK-AIKEN COMPANY v. CROMWELL-WRIGHT COMPANY, INC.
367 Mass. 70, 323 N.E.2d 876 (1975)

TAURO, CHIEF JUSTICE.

This case is before us pursuant to G.L. c. 231, § 111, on a report by a judge of the Superior Court. The question submitted on report is as follows: "Does Count II of the plaintiff's declaration set forth a cause of action known to the law of the Commonwealth of Massachusetts?"

The plaintiff brought an action in tort in two counts; the first alleging negligence, the second in strict liability. It seeks to recover for damage caused when water allegedly stored behind a dam on the defendant's property was released and flowed onto its property. A Superior Court judge sustained the defendant's demurrer on the ground that "Count II . . . does not allege a cause of action under the law of this Commonwealth." He held that, "in order to recover for damage caused by the water which escaped from the dam owned by the Defendants, the Plaintiffs must allege and prove that the escape was caused by intentional or negligent fault of some person or entity." The sole issue before us is whether a cause of action in strict liability exists in this Commonwealth regardless of considerations of fault on the part of the defendant. After careful consideration, we conclude that strict liability as enunciated in the case of *Rylands v. Fletcher*, [1868] L.R. 3 H.L. 330, is and has been, the law of the Commonwealth.

The fact that a case of strict liability also contains elements of negligence does not preclude the plaintiff from recovering on the basis of strict liability. The distinction is basically one of proof in the particular circumstances. The plaintiff must decide whether it is more economic and feasible to establish negligence under appropriate pleadings, or to prove that the activity in question comes within the parameters of strict liability. The fact that a plaintiff chooses to go forward on one, or possibly both, of these theories does not undercut the existence or vitality of either.

NOTES

1. *The presence of Negligence.* The plaintiff railroad yard in *Indiana Harbor Belt R. Co. v. Amer. Cyanamid Co.*, 916 F.2d 1174 (7th Cir. 1990), sued the defendant manufacturer and shipper for the costs of cleaning up a toxic spill. Reversing the district court, the court of appeals held that the defendant was not strictly liable:

> American Cyanamid Company, the defendant in this diversity tort suit governed by Illinois law, is a major manufacturer of chemicals, including acrylonitrile, a chemical used in large quantities in making acrylic fibers, plastics, dyes, pharmaceutical chemicals, and other intermediate and final goods. On January 2, 1979, at its manufacturing plant in Louisiana, Cyanamid loaded 20,000 gallons of liquid acrylonitrile into a railroad tank car that it had leased from the North American Car Corporation. The next day, a train of the Missouri Pacific Railroad picked up the car at Cyanamid's siding. The car's

ultimate destination was a Cyanamid plant in New Jersey served by Conrail rather than by Missouri Pacific. The Missouri Pacific train carried the car north to the Blue Island railroad yard of Indiana Harbor Belt Railroad, the plaintiff in this case, a small switching line that has a contract with Conrail to switch cars from other lines to Conrail, in this case for travel east. The Blue Island yard is in the Village of Riverdale, which is just south of Chicago and part of the Chicago metropolitan area.

The car arrived in the Blue Island yard on the morning of January 9, 1979. Several hours after it arrived, employees of the switching line noticed fluid gushing from the bottom outlet of the car. The lid on the outlet was broken. After two hours, the line's supervisor of equipment was able to stop the leak by closing a shut-off valve controlled from the top of the car. No one was sure at the time just how much of the contents of the car had leaked, but it was feared that all 20,000 gallons had, and since acrylonitrile is flammable at a temperature of 30° Fahrenheit or above, highly toxic, and possibly carcinogenic (*Acrylonitrile*, 9 International Toxicity Update, no. 3, May-June 1989, at 2,4), the local authorities ordered the homes near the yard evacuated. The evacuation lasted only a few hours, until the car was moved to a remote part of the yard and it was discovered that only about a quarter of the acrylonitrile had leaked. Concerned nevertheless that there had been some contamination of soil and water, the Illinois Department of Environmental Protection ordered the switching line to take decontamination measures that cost the line $981,022.75, which it sought to recover by this suit.

One count of the two-count complaint charges Cyanamid with having maintained the leased tank car negligently. The other count asserts that the transportation of acrylonitrile in bulk through the Chicago metropolitan area is an abnormally dangerous activity, for the consequences of which the shipper (Cyanamid) is strictly liable to the switching line, which bore the financial brunt of those consequences because of the decontamination measures that it was forced to take . . . .

Siegler v. Kuhlman, 81 Wash. 2d 448, 502 P.2d 1181 (1972), imposed strict liability on a transporter of hazardous materials, but the circumstances were rather special. A gasoline truck blew up, obliterating the plaintiff's decedent and her car. The court emphasized that the explosion had destroyed the evidence necessary to establish whether the accident had been due to negligence; so, unless liability was strict, there would be no liability—and this as the very consequence of the defendant's hazardous activity . . . .

. . . To begin with, we have been given no reason, whether the reason in *Siegler* or any other, for believing that a negligence regime is not perfectly adequate to remedy and deter, at reasonable cost, the accidental spillage of acrylonitrile from rail cars. Cf. *Bagley v. Controlled Environment Corp.*, 127 N.H. 556, 560, 503 A.2d 823, 826 (1986). Acrylonitrile could explode and destroy evidence, but of course did not here, making imposition of strict liability on the theory of the *Siegler* decision premature. More important, although acrylonitrile is flammable even at relatively low temperatures, and toxic, it is not so corrosive or otherwise destructive that it will eat through or otherwise damage or weaken a tank car's valves although they are maintained with due (which essentially means, with average) care. No one suggests, therefore, that the leak in this case was caused by the *inherent* properties of acrylonitrile. It was caused by carelessness—whether that of the North American Car Corporation in failing to maintain or inspect it, or that of the Missouri Pacific when it had custody of the car, or that of the switching line itself in failing to notice the ruptured lid, or some combination of these possible failures of care. Accidents that are due to a lack of care can be prevented by taking care; and when a lack of care can (unlike *Siegler*) be shown in court, such accidents are adequately deterred by the threat of liability for negligence.

It is true that the district court purported to find as a fact that there is an inevitable risk of derailment or other calamity in transporting "large quantities of anything." 662 F. Supp. at 642. This is not a finding of fact, but a truism: anything can happen. The question is, how likely is this type of accident if the actor uses due care: For all that appears from the record of the case or any other sources of information that we have found, if a tank car is carefully maintained the danger of a spill of acrylonitrile is negligible. If this is right, there is no compelling reason to move to a regime of strict liability, especially one that might embrace all other hazardous materials shipped by rail as well.

One commentator contends that a number of cases support a reading of REST. 2D OF TORTS § 520 to mean that the strict liability doctrine for abnormally dangerous activities will not apply if the exercise of reasonable care would prevent the danger. Gerald W. Boston, *Strict Liability*, 36 SAN DIEGO L. REV. 597 (1999). How can one determine if there is an "inability to eliminate the risk" of an abnormally dangerous activity "by the exercise of reasonable care?" REST. 2D OF TORTS § 520(c). Will expert testimony do the trick? See 36 SAN DIEGO L. REV. at 636.

2. *The Restatement Position*. The first RESTATEMENT OF TORTS § 520 (1938) provides:

An activity is ultrahazardous if it

(a) necessarily involves a risk of serious harm to the person, land or chattels of others which cannot be eliminated by the exercise of the utmost care, and

(b) is not a matter of common usage.

Comment *g* to this section states: "In order that an activity may be ultrahazardous it is necessary that it satisfy the conditions stated in both Clauses (a) and (b)."

The RESTATEMENT (SECOND) OF TORTS § 520 (1977), which replaced § 520 of the first RESTATEMENT, provides:

C.   ABNORMALLY DANGEROUS ACTIVITIES   1107

In determining whether an activity is abnormally dangerous, the following factors are to be considered:

(a) existence of a high degree of risk of some harm to the person, land or chattels of others;

(b) likelihood that the harm that results from it will be great;

(c) inability to eliminate the risk by the exercise of reasonable care;

(d) extent to which the activity is not a matter of common usage;

(e) inappropriateness of the activity to the place where it is carried on; and

(f) extent to which its value to the community is outweighed by its dangerous attributes.

Comment *f* to RESTATEMENT (SECOND) OF TORTS § 520 states:

In determining whether the danger is abnormal, the factors listed in Clauses (a) to (f) of this Section are all to be considered, and are all of importance. Any one of them is not necessarily sufficient of itself in a particular case, and ordinarily several of them will be required for strict liability. On the other hand, it is not necessary that each of them be present, especially if others weigh heavily. Because of the interplay of these various factors, it is not possible to reduce abnormally dangerous activities to any definition.

Why do you suppose the second restatement shifted so radically from the position of the first?

3. *Risk-Utility*. Besides emphasizing the likely presence of negligence, the court in *Indiana Harbor v. Amer. Cyanamid* also stressed risk-utility considerations in determining the inapplicability of strict liability:

The district judge and plaintiff's lawyer make much of the fact that the spill occurred in a densely inhabited metropolitan area. Only 4,000 gallons spilled; what if all 20,000 had done so? Isn't the risk that this might happen even if everybody were careful sufficient to warrant giving the shipper an incentive to explore alternative routes? Strict liability would supply that incentive. But this argument overlooks the fact that, like other transportation networks, the railroad network is a hub-and-spoke system. And the hubs are in metropolitan areas. Chicago is one of the nation's largest railroad hubs. In 1983, the latest year for which we have figures, Chicago's railroad yards handled the third highest volume of hazardous-material shipments in the nation. East St. Louis, which is also in Illinois, handled the second highest volume. Office of Technology Assessment, Transportation of Hazardous Materials 53 (1986). With most hazardous chemicals (by volume of shipments) being at least as hazardous as acryolnitrile, it is unlikely—and certainly not demonstrated by the plaintiff—that they can be rerouted around all the metropolitan areas in the country, except at prohibitive cost. Even if it were feasible to reroute them one would hardly expect shippers, as distinct from carriers, to be the firms best situated to do the rerouting. Granted, the usual view is that common carriers are not subject to strict liability for the carriage of materials that make the transportation of them abnormally dangerous, because a common carrier cannot refuse service to a shipper of a lawful commodity. RESTATEMENT, *supra*, § 521. Two courts, however, have rejected the common carrier exception. *National Steel Service Center, Inc. v. Gibbons*, 319 N.W.2d 269 (Ia. 1982); *Chavez v. Southern Pacific Transportation Co.*, 413 F. Supp. 1203, 1213–14 (E.D. Cal. 1976). If it were rejected in Illinois, this would weaken still further the case for imposing strict liability on shippers whose goods pass through the densely inhabited portions of the state.

The difference between shipper and carrier points to a deep flaw in the plaintiff's case . . . . [H]ere it is not the actors—that is, the transporters of acrylonitrile and other chemicals—but the manufacturers, who are sought to be held strictly liable. A shipper can in the bill of lading designate the route of his shipment if he likes, 49 U.S.C. § 11710(a)(1), but is it realistic to suppose that shippers will become students of railroading in order to lay out the safest route by which to ship their goods? Anyway, rerouting is no panacea. Often it will increase the length of the journey, or compel the use of poorer track, or both. When this happens, the probability of an accident is increased, even if the consequences of an accident if one occurs are reduced; so the expected accident cost, being the product of the probability of an accident and the harm if the accident occurs, may rise. Glickman, Analysis of a National Policy for Routing Hazardous Materials on Railroads (Department of Transportation, Research and Special Programs Administration, Transportation Systems Center, May 1980). It is easy to see how the accident is this case might have been prevented at reasonable cost by greater care on the part of those who handled the tank car of acrylonitrile. It is difficult to see how it might have been prevented at reasonable cost by a change in the activity of transporting the chemical. This is therefore not an apt case for strict liability.

4. *Strict Products Liability.* Could the plaintiff have tried the *Indiana Harbor* case on a theory of strict products liability? The container of the product, the tank car, was defective. The defendant was only a lessee of the tank car, apparently undertaking by contract to maintain the car, 916 F.2d at 1181. But it was the manufacturer and supplier of the acrylonitrile, and as such would it not be strictly liable for the container in which the product was supplied? Did the plaintiff suffer physical harm to person or property within the meaning of RESTATEMENT (SECOND) OF TORTS § 402A (1965)?

LATERRA v. TREASTER
844 P.2d 724 (Kan. App. 1992)

GERNON, JUDGE:

Steven D. Treaster (Treaster), as special administrator for the estate of Sheryl Steere, appeals from a jury verdict which awarded $500,000 to Steven Michael Laterra in a wrongful death action against Steer's estate.

The underlying facts are tragic and undisputed. On July 11, 1989, Sheryl Steere committed suicide. She died in her garage from carbon monoxide fumes after starting her car and allowing the engine to run with the garage door closed. The tragedy of her death was compounded by the fact that she lived in one-half of a duplex. Steven Ray Laterra (Laterra) lived in the other half. Laterra, who was sleeping in his residence, died as a result of the exhaust fumes. Laterra's son, Steven Michael Laterra (Michael), brought an action by and through his mother, Carole Greene, alleging that the wrongful death of his father and the subsequent damage and loss Michael sustained were the proximate result of Steere's negligence.

The focus of evidence at trial was not on how the death occurred, as the facts were stipulated to by the parties, but rather on the loss Michael suffered due to his father's death. Treaster conceded that Steere's actions caused Laterra's death. A jury returned a verdict awarding $500,000 in compensatory damages for the pecuniary losses Michael suffered as a result of his father's death. After a motion for a new trial was overruled by the trial court, Treaster appealed . . . .

At the close of Michael's case, his counsel moved for a directed verdict on the issue of liability. The trial court granted this motion on the theory of strict liability, finding that the manner in which Steere took her life was an inherently dangerous activity. This ruling resolved the issue of liability in Michael's favor, and the jury considered only the issue of damages.

Simply stated, the issue here is whether, under the unique facts of this case, the method of committing suicide was such an inherently and abnormally dangerous activity so as to require a court to direct a verdict on the theory of strict liability . . . .

Treaster argues that the concept of strict liability found in Sections 519 and 520 of the RESTATEMENT has no applicability to Steere's activity. Treaster claims that this concept applies to an actor who is consciously aware of the risk of harm of his or her activity to the public, is unable to change his or her operations to remove the risk of harm, and chooses to continue his or her "business" because of its value to the community. Michael argues that Steere's actions come under the umbrella of strict liability as defined by the RESTATEMENT . . . .

In our view, Steere's use of her automobile to commit suicide was abnormal, creating an unusual risk because of the circumstances surrounding her suicide. No amount of reasonable care could have prevented carbon monoxide from escaping her garage and entering the remainder of the duplex. The activity was definitely not a matter of common usage and was inappropriate to the place where it was carried on. Steere's suicide had absolutely no value to the community and was, thus, greatly outweighed by its dangerous attributes. On its face, Steere's suicide fits the definition of an abnormally dangerous activity.

Treaster argues that strict liability in tort is intended to apply to defendants who are aware of the risk of danger and yet choose to carry on the hazardous activity. Admittedly, there is no evidence that Steere was aware of any risk except to herself. However, the RESTATEMENT (SECOND) OF TORTS § 520 does not include knowledge of the risk as a factor to consider in determining whether an activity is abnormally dangerous. Treaster would have us graft on this requirement not the RESTATEMENT and apply it to Kansas law. This we cannot do . . . .

NOTES

1. *Awareness of Danger Revisited.* In *Perez v. Southern Pacif. Transp. Co.*, 883 P.2d 424 (Ariz. App. 1993), the plaintiff sued for the wrongful death of Anne Perez:

The undisputed facts are that Anne Perez's death at age 59 in 1991 resulted from mesothelioma, a form of cancer caused by exposure to asbestos. Mesothelioma has a latency period prior to clinically manifested symptoms of 25 to 40 years. Perez resided in the family home until her marriage in 1951; the disease was diagnosed in May 1989. Perez's father, Rafael Montenegro, worked for Southern Pacific Railroad in Tucson from 1923 to 1954. From 1931 to 1951, while working as a boilermaker, Montenegro was exposed to asbestos-containing insulation materials used in the repair and maintenance of steam locomotives.

During repair and maintenance, asbestos-containing insulation was removed and reinstalled in the back shop of Southern Pacific's Tucson rail yard. That process created a substantial amount of visible dust in the shop. Montenegro wore his work clothes home and hung them in the family's only bathroom prior to laundering. On occasion, Perez entered Southern Pacific's yard to deliver her father's lunch.

Southern Pacific argues that, as a matter of law, the trial court erred in eliminating a foreseeability requirement before imposing strict liability for abnormally dangerous activity. . . .

Southern Pacific contends that liability under this theory is "strict" because it is imposed even when due care has been exercised, but it is not unlimited. We agree:

The essence of the rule of liability without fault is that if a person in the conduct or maintenance of an enterprise which is lawful and proper in itself deliberately does an act under known conditions and with knowledge that injury will in all probability result to another and injury is sustained by the other as the direct and proximate consequence of the act, the person doing the act and causing the injury is liable in damages even though he acted without negligence. Under the doctrine, liability rests not upon negligence but upon the intentional doing of that which the person knows or should in the exercise of ordinary care know may in the normal course of events reasonably cause loss to another. Liability is automatically imposed upon the tort feasor when damages are sustained by another under such circumstances, even though there was no negligence.

Zampos v. United States Smelting, Refining & Mining Co., 207 F.2d 171, 176 (10th Cir. 1953). In discussing the extent of liability to be imposed under a claim of strict liability for abnormally dangerous activity, W. Page Keeton et al., PROSSER AND KEETON ON THE LAW OF TORTS § 79, at 559 (5th ed. 1984), states:

> It is clear, first of all, that unless a statute requires it, strict liability will never be found unless the defendant is aware of the abnormally dangerous condition or activity, and has voluntarily engaged in or permitted it. Mere negligent failure to discover or prevent it is not enough . . . .

In the present case, the court made extensive findings of fact and law. It imposed strict liability for abnormally dangerous activity, applying the "hindsight" test of *Dart v. Wiebe Manufacturing, Inc.*, 147 Ariz. 242, 709 P.2d 876 (1985). The court's minute entry acknowledged that *Dart* was a products liability case, but applied its "hindsight" test of imputed knowledge for public policy reasons. Although it is attractive to analogize to the risk/benefit factors analysis used in *Dart*, upon which the "hindsight" test is based, we believe it is no more than an attempt to bootstrap that argument onto a totally unrelated legal theory. Without authority to support such an argument, we decline to rule that the "hindsight" test is applicable to a claim for strict liability for abnormally dangerous activity.

In the present case, then, the determination of whether an activity is abnormally dangerous under RESTATEMENT § 520 must be related to the time at which Southern Pacific engaged in the activity being analyzed:

> The liability arises out of the abnormal danger of the activity itself, and the risk that it creates, of harm to those in the vicinity. It is founded upon a policy of law that imposes upon anyone who for his own purposes creates an abnormal risk of harm to his neighbors, the responsibility of relieving against that harm when it does in fact occur. The defendant's enterprise, in other words, is required to pay its way by compensating for the harm it causes, because of its special, abnormal and dangerous character.

RESTATEMENT (SECOND) OF TORTS § 519 cmt. d.

We believe the court erred as a matter of law in applying the *Dart* hindsight test and therefore reverse and remand. Further proceedings must be based upon the RESTATEMENT test.

Dart v. Wiebe, discussed in *Perez*, was a products liability case alleging strict liability based on the absence of mechanical guards at the nip points of the rollers on a paper shredder and belt conveyor system, used in the recycling of waste paper. In a strict liability case, the court said, "the product is the focus of the inquiry. The quality of the product may be measured not only by the information available to the manufacturer at the time of design, but also by the information available to the trier of fact at the time of trial."

In commenting on the awareness issue, the court said in the products case of *Brooks v. Beech Aircraft Corp.*, 120 N.M. 372, 381, 902 P.2d 54, 63 (1995):

> In most instances a manufacturer is aware of the risks posed by any given design and of the availability of an alternative design. This case is a perfect example; Dr. Snyder testified that Beech had developed

and used a workable shoulder harness prior to the design and manufacture of Mr. Brooks' plane. Thus we disagree with the premise that fairness requires the rejection of strict liability in design cases; when the manufacturer is aware of product risk and alternative designs at the time of supply, it is certainly not unfair to judge the manufacturer's design according to principles of strict liability rather than by conduct at the time of supply.

Further, in those hypothetical instances in which technology known at the time of trial and technology knowable at the time of distribution differ—and outside of academic rationale we find little to suggest the existence in practice of unknowable design considerations—it is more fair that the manufacturers and suppliers who have profited from the sale of the product bear the risk of loss. Given the risk-benefit calculation on which the jury is instructed in New Mexico, and the policy considerations that favor strict products liability, we believe that it is logical and consistent to take the same approach to design defects as to manufacturing flaws. If in some future case we are confronted directly with a proffer of evidence on an advancement or change in the state of the art that was neither known nor knowable at the time the product was supplied, we may at that time reconsider application of a state-of-the-art defense to those real circumstances, properly developed under the proffer with applicable briefs and argument.

Why should strict products liability be stricter than strict liability for abnormally dangerous activities?

What sort of awareness is contemplated by *Perez*? The court quotes *Zampos v. U.S. Smelting* for the proposition that the defendant must "deliberately" do an act "with knowledge that injury will in all probability result to another." This is recklessness, is it not?

Compare Cambridge Water Co. Ltd. v. Eastern Counties Leather plc, [1994] 2 A.C. 264, 1 All E.R. 53 ("foreseeability of the risk" is a prerequisite to recover in strict liability, either in nuisance or under *Rylands v. Fletcher*).

One commentator says:

> The few cases to address the question are in some disagreement, if not disarray, on the question of whether, or to what extent, knowledge of the risks by the defendant is a prerequisite for strict liability for abnormally dangerous activities. One of the premises of strict liability for abnormally dangerous activities seems to be that the defendant deliberately chose to engage in a dangerous activity whose risks were known to the defendant or at least reasonably recognizable by participants in the industry or activity in question.

Joseph H. King, Jr., *Abnormally Dangerous Activities*, 48 BAYLOR L. REV. 341, 377 (1996).

2. *Foreseeability of Intervening Conduct.* In *Yukon Equipment, Inc. v. Fireman's Fund Ins. Co.*, 525 P.2d 1206 (Alaska 1978), the court found the facts as follows:

C. ABNORMALLY DANGEROUS ACTIVITIES

A large explosion occurred a 2:47 a.m. on December 7, 1973, in the suburbs north of the City of Anchorage. The explosion originated at a storage magazine for explosives under lease from the federal government to petitioner E.I. duPont de Nemours and Company, which was operated by petitioner Yukon Equipment, Inc. The storage magazine is located on a 1,870-acre tract of federal land which had been withdrawn by the Department of the Interior for the use of the Alaska Railroad for explosive storage purposes by separate orders in 1950 and 1961. The magazine which exploded was located 3,820 feet from the nearest building not used to store explosives and 4,330 feet from the nearest public highway. At the time of the explosion it contained approximately 80,000 pounds of explosives. The blast damaged dwellings and other buildings within a two-mile radius of the magazine and, in some instances, beyond a two-mile radius. The ground concussion it caused registered 1.8 on the Richter scale at the earthquake observation station in Palmer, some 30 miles away.

The explosion was caused by thieves. Four young men had driven onto the tract where the magazine was located, broken into the storage magazine, set a prepared charge, and fled. They apparently did so in an effort to conceal the fact that they had stolen explosives from the site a day or two earlier.

The suit was brought to recover property damage to nearby property owners caused by the explosion. The trial court granted summary judgment to the plaintiffs on the issue of liability. The state supreme court affirmed on appeal:

> The next question is whether the intentional detonation of the storage magazine was a superseding cause relieving petitioners from liability. The considerations which impel cutting off liability where there is a superseding cause in negligence cases also apply to cases of absolute liability.
>
> Prior to the explosion in question the petitioners' magazines had been illegally broken into at least six times. Most of these entries involved the theft of explosives. Petitioners had knowledge of all of this.
>
> The incendiary destruction of premises by thieves to cover evidence of theft is not so uncommon an occurrence that it can be regarded as highly extraordinary. Moreover, the particular kind of result threatened by the defendant's conduct, the storage of explosives, was an explosion at the storage site. Absolute liability is imposed on those who store or use explosives because they have created an unusual risk to others. As between those who have created the risk for the benefit of their own enterprise and those whose only connection with the enterprise is to have suffered damage because of it, the law places the risk of loss on the former. When the risk created causes damage in fact, insistence that the precise details of the intervening cause be foreseeable would subvert the purpose of that rule of law.

RESTATEMENT (SECOND) OF TORTS § 522 (1977) provides:

One carrying on an abnormally dangerous activity is subject to strict liability for the resulting harm although it is caused by the unexpectable

    (a)   innocent, negligent or reckless conduct of a third person, or

    (b)   action of an animal, or

    (c)   operation of a force of nature.

A caveat to this section states:

> The Institute expresses no opinion as to whether the fact that the harm is done by an act of a third person that is not only deliberate but also intended to bring about the harm, relieves from liability one who carries on an abnormally dangerous activity.

In *Klein v. Pyrodyne Corp.*, 810 P.2d 917 (Wash. 1991), the court held that Pyrodyne Corp., a pyrotechnic company, could be found strictly liable to spectators for injuries caused by an exploding rocket at a 4th of July fireworks display:

> Pyrodyne argues that even if there is strict liability for fireworks, its liability under the facts of this case is cut off by the manufacturer's negligence, the existence of which we assume for purposes of evaluating the propriety of the trial court's summary judgment. According to Pyrodyne, a rocket detonated without leaving the mortar box because it was negligently manufactured. This detonation, Pyrodyne asserts, was what caused misfire of the second rocket, which in turn resulted in the Kleins' injuries. Pyrodyne reasons that the manufacturer's negligence acted as an intervening or outside force that cuts off Pyrodyne's liability.

> In support of its position, Pyrodyne relies upon *Siegler v. Kuhlman*. In *Siegler*, a young woman was killed in an explosion when the car she was driving encountered a pool of thousands of gallons of gasoline spilled from a gasoline truck. This court held that transporting gasoline in great quantities along public highways and streets is an abnormally dangerous activity that calls for the application of strict liability. *Siegler*, 81 Wash. 2d at 459–460, 502 P.2d 1181. Justice Rosellini concurred, but stated:

>> I think the opinion should make clear, however, that the owner of the vehicle will be held strictly liable only for damages caused when the flammable or explosive substance is allowed to escape without the apparent intervention of any outside force beyond the control of the manufacturer, the owner, or the operator of the vehicle hauling it. I do not think the majority means to suggest that if another vehicle, negligently driven, collided with the truck in question, the truck owner would be held liable for the damage.

> *Siegler*, at 460, 502 P.2d 1181 (Rosellini, J., concurring).

The *Klein* court concluded:

> We hold that intervening acts of third persons serve to relieve the defendant from strict liability for abnormally dangerous activities only if those acts were unforeseeable in relation to the extraordinary risk created by the activity. The rationale for this rule is that it encourages

those who conduct abnormally dangerous activities to anticipate and take precautions against the possible negligence of third persons. Where the third person's negligence is beyond the actor's control, this rule, unlike the *Siegler* dicta, nonetheless imposes strict liability if the third person's negligence was reasonably foreseeable. Such a result allocates the economic burden of injuries arising from the foreseeable negligence of third persons to the party best able to plan for it and to bear it—the actor carrying on the abnormally dangerous activity.

Should foreseeability of intervening factors be judged by the same standards of awareness of danger discussed in the preceding note?

In *Cadena v. Chicago Fireworks Mfg. Co*, 297 Ill. App. 945, 697 N.E.2d 802 (1998), the plaintiff sought damages for injuries suffered at a Fourth of July fireworks display conducted by defendants, when one of the fireworks misfired and landed in a crowd of spectators, injuring the plaintiffs. The court refused to apply strict liability against the defendants for conducting an abnormally dangerous activity. It found that "the exercise of reasonable care in displaying fireworks will significantly reduce the risks involved"; that fireworks displays are "a matter of common usage"; that the location of the display (a high school football field) was an appropriate place, in the absence of any allegation to the contrary; and that such displays "are of some social utility to communities."

COPIER BY AND THROUGH LINDSEY v. SMITH & WESSON
138 F.3d 833 (10th Cir. 1998)

The relevant facts of this case are not in dispute. Ms. Copier's ex-husband shot her on March 21, 1991, with a .38 caliber firearm manufactured by defendant-appellee, Smith & Wesson Corp. The shooting, which led to Eldon Copier's conviction for attempted criminal homicide, left Ms. Copier a paraplegic.

Ms. Copier filed her original complaint herein on March 20, 1995 in Utah state court against Smith & Wesson. Her theory of legal liability was based on the tort doctrine of ultrahazardous activity, arguing in particular that since handguns are manufactured to injure or kill people, and since it is a statistical certainty that some handguns are actually used to injure or kill people, the handgun manufacturer should bear strict liability for the resulting damages. She invoked the doctrine of ultrahazardous activity articulated in the Restatement (Second) of Torts §§ 519 and 520.

Following the filing of her complaint in March 1995 in state court, Ms. Copier died as a result of her injuries on June 24, 1995. Smith & Wesson subsequently removed the case to federal court on August 7, 1995 . . .

On motion of Smith & Wesson, the district court dismissed Ms. Copier's complaint on December 13, 1995, reasoning that its role was to follow, not expand, Utah law, and that Ms. Copier's cause of action was not viable under current Utah law . . . .

Utah law imposes strict liability on one who carries on an abnormally dangerous activity for harm resulting from the activity. *Walker Drug Co., Inc. v.*

La Sal Oil Co., 902 P.2d 1229, 1233 (Utah 1995); Restatement (Second) of Torts § 519 (1976).² The factors to be considered in determining whether an activity is abnormally dangerous are:

(a) existence of a high degree of risk of some harm to the person, land or chattels of others;

(b) likelihood that the harm that results from it will be great;

(c) inability to eliminate the risk by the exercise of reasonable care;

(d) extent to which the activity is not a matter of common usage;

(e) inappropriateness of the activity to the place where it is carried on; and

(f) extent to which its value to the community is outweighed by it dangerous attributes.

Walker Drug Co., Inc. v. La Sal Oil Co., 902 P.2d at 1233 (citing Restatement (Second) of Torts § 520 (1976)). Consideration of these factors leads us to conclude that Utah law does not support Ms. Copier's theory of liability of Smith & Wesson.

None of the above factors is implicated by the *manufacturing* of handguns, as opposed to the use—or rather, the *misuse*—of handguns. For example, in *Walker Drug*, the plaintiffs brought suit because gasoline had leaked from the defendants' gas stations and contaminated the plaintiffs' property. In evaluating the six factors, the Utah Supreme Court considered the danger that would result from the operation of the gas stations—that is, the possibility of leakage of gasoline. It was held that the operation of the gas stations was not an abnormally dangerous activity; they were located in an area of the city where their operation was common, appropriate and of significant value to the community. *Id.* at 1233.

In *Robison v. Robison*, 16 Utah 2d 2, 394 P.2d 876, 877 (1964), the Utah Supreme Court held that the determination of whether the ultrahazardous activity doctrine applied as to injury caused by rock fragments hurled during use by the defendants of dynamite for blasting purposes depended on the circumstances. The court focused on the *use* of dynamite, and not its manufacture. In the instant case, however, Ms. Copier was harmed not by the manufacturing of the Smith & Wesson .38, but by the use of it to shoot her. This distinction is significant, because Ms. Copier's argument essentially collapses all uses of guns into one purpose, which she contends is to injure or kill people. However, Ms. Copier ignores a number of legitimate uses, including self-defense, home protection, and use by law enforcement officers.

We further note that the one case we have found that imposed strict liability upon a handgun manufacturer focused on the unique nature of the firearm in that case, a "Saturday Night Special," which the court characterized as a gun whose "chief 'value' . . . is in criminal activity, because of its easy concealability and low price." *See Kelley v. R.G. Industries, Inc.*, 304 Md. 124, 497 A.2d 1143, 1158 (1985). *Kelley* provides little support to Ms. Copier,

---

² The genesis of the ultrahazardous activity doctrine was the seminal case of *Rylands v. Fletcher*, L.R. 3 H.L. 330, [1861-73] All E.R. Rep. 1 (1868), which is discussed at length in 3 Harper, James & Gray, *The Law of Torts* §§ 14.2–14.5.

however, since it actually rejected the application of the ultrahazardous activity doctrine to firearms in general but limited its holding of liability specifically to "Saturday Night Specials."³ *Id.* at 1147, 1154, 1159. Here, Ms. Copier was shot by a standard .38 caliber pistol and there is no allegation that the gun was easily concealable and designed chiefly for use by criminals.

Ms. Copier relies heavily on several scholarly articles which, she contends, advocate the extension of the ultrahazardous activity doctrine to the manufacturing of firearms. . . . We are not persuaded that the articles support plaintiff-appellant's position that Utah law, or a discernible trend in its decisions, indicate the adoption of her theory.

With respect to the opinion in *In re 101 California Street*, No. 959316 (Cal. Super. 2d Dep't Apr. 10, 1995), which provides the basis for Pearson's article, at least two courts have declined to follow its analysis, noting that while the case may have been correctly decided under its particular facts, it was actually based on a California statute prohibiting the sale, advertising or possession of certain assault weapons, including the specific handgun involved therein.

Ms. Copier's argument, carried to its logical extension, would suggest that the manufacturing of any product that is significantly misused and has great potential for injuring or killing persons should be considered as an ultrahazardous activity. Alcohol production, for example, might be so considered because in any given year, there is a statistical certainty that thousands of people will be killed in alcohol-related accidents. Yet, the Utah Supreme Court has refused to apply strict liability principles to alcohol providers. *See Horton v. Royal Order of the Sun*, 821 P.2d 1167, 1169 (Utah 1991).

In sum, we are convinced that under the state of decisional law in Utah, and of decisions generally, the complaint premised on the ultrahazardous activity doctrine was properly dismissed here. . . .

---

³ We note, moreover, that the Maryland legislature has since repudiated the liability holding in *Kelley* with respect to "Saturday Night Specials." *See* Md. Ann. Code art. 27 § 36-I(h). Additionally, other jurisdictions which have considered the issue have rejected the extension of the ultrahazardous activity doctrine to the manufacturing or sale of firearms. *See, e.g., Hamilton v. Accu-Tek*, 935 F. Supp. 1307, 1324 (E.D.N.Y. 1996) (rejecting the application of the doctrine because it was not an "improper use of land"); *King v. R.G. Industries, Inc.*, 182 Michl. App. 343, 451 N.W.2d 874 (1990) (manufacturer is not liable for criminal misuse of handgun); *Delahanty v. Hinckley*, 564 A.2d 758, 761 (D.C. 1989) (holding that it is the use, not marketing, of firearms that is dangerous); *Addison v. Williams*, 546 So.2d 220, 223 (La. Ct. App. 1989) (rejecting application of the doctrine to the manufacturing of handguns); *Diggles v. Horwitz*, 765 S.W.2d 839, 841 (Tex. App. 1989) (noting that the "manufacture or sale of a handgun has not been recognized as an ultrahazardous activity in Texas"); *Armijo v. Ex Cam, Inc.*, 843 F.2d 406 (10th Cir. 1988) (applying New Mexico law and rejecting application of doctrine to manufacturing of handguns); *Knott v. Liberty Jewelry & Loan, Inc.*, 50 Wash. App. 267, 748 P.2d 661, 664–665 (1988) (rejecting the application of the doctrine to the manufacturing and sale of firearms); *Caveny v. Raven Arms Co.*, 665 F. Supp. 530, 534–35 (S.D. Ohio 1987) (rejecting *Kelley*), *aff'd*, 849 F.2d 608 (6th Cir. 1988) (table); *Moore v. R.G. Industries, Inc.*, 789 F.2d 1326, 1328 (9th Cir. 1986) (rejecting strict liability claim against handgun manufacturer because manufacture of handguns is not ultra-hazardous activity; harm results from use, not existence, of handgun); *Coulson v. DeAngelo*, 493 So.2d 98, 99 (Fla. Dist. Ct. App. 1986) (per curiam) (same); *Burkett v. Freedom Arms, Inc.*, 299 Or. 551, 704 P.2d 118, 121 (1985) (same); *Perkins v. F.I.E. Corp.*, 762 F.2d 1250, 1266 (5th Cir. 1985) (applying Louisiana law, holding that marketing of handguns is not an ultrahazardous activity, and reversing *Richman v. Charter Arms Co.*, 571 F. Supp. 192 (E.D. La. 1983)); *Martin v. Harrington & Richardson, Inc.*, 743 F.2d 1200, 1203–04 (7th Cir. 1984) (Illinois law).

NOTES

1. *Types of Abnormally Dangerous Activities.* Is storage of gasoline in a residential area an abnormally dangerous activity? The courts are divided. *Compare Yommer v. McKenzie,* 255 Md. 220, 257 A.2d 138 (1969), *with Hudson v. Peavey Oil Co.,* 279 Or. 3, 566 P.2d 175 (1977). *See Siegler v. Kuhlman,* 81 Wash. 2d 448, 502 P.2d 1181 (1972) (strict liability for harm caused by the transportation of gasoline on a highway).

The same division of authority exists as to crop dusting. *Compare Langan v. Valicopters, Inc.,* 88 Wash. 2d 855, 567 P.2d 218 (1977), *and Gotreaux v. Gary,* 232 La. 373, 94 So. 2d 293 (1957) *with Lawler v. Skelton,* 241 Miss. 274, 130 So. 2d 565 (1961).

Strict liability usually is not imposed upon providers of public utility services. *See, e.g., Ferguson v. Northern States Power Co.,* 307 Minn. 26, 239 N.W.2d 190 (1976) (electrical transmission); *Jennings Buick, Inc. v. Cincinnati,* 56 Ohio St. 2d 459, 10 Ohio Op. 3d 545, 384 N.E.2d 303 (1978) (water main), and *Mahowald v. Minnesota Gas Co.,* 344 N.W.2d 856 (Minn. 1984) (gas main). *But see Lubin v. Iowa City,* 257 Iowa 383, 131 N.W.2d 765 (1965) (strict liability for water damage from broken city water main).

The initial rule of strict liability for fires gave way to negligence. The Oregon court has imposed strict liability for "field burning," an activity which is hazardous but which is helpful in clearing land and is essential to the preparation of land for some farming uses. *Koos v. Roth,* 293 Or. 670, 652 P.2d 1255 (1982).

The position of RESTATEMENT (SECOND) OF TORTS § 520A is that the operator of an aircraft is strictly liability for "physical harm to land or to persons or chattels on the ground" caused by the "ascent, descent or flight of aircraft, or by the dropping or falling of an object from the aircraft". There is no strict liability, however, "to persons themselves participating in aviation, such as the crew or passengers of a falling plane, or the owner of property on it or to persons on another plane which was struck by the defendant's plane". *Id.* comm. *e.* Why?

The modern trend seems to be away from strict liability for ground damage from falling aircraft, and toward a standard of negligence. *See Crosby v. Cox Aircraft Co.,* 109 Wash. 2d 581, 746 P.2d 1198 (1987). Apparently this trend is based on the idea that air flight is now a relatively safe means of transportation. Is it? Is the issue of the relative safety of an activity the key for determining whether strict liability should be imposed?

Is strict liability for abnormally dangerous activities a doctrine in search of a unifying principle? Can you provide such a principle?

Is there an uneasy tension between the realms of strict tort liability and tort fault liability? Recall *Mark* 3:25: "And if a house be divided against itself, that house cannot stand" (Auth. King James version).

2. *Abnormal Sensitivity.* RESTATEMENT (SECOND) OF TORTS § 524A states that there is no strict liability for harm caused by an abnormally dangerous activity "if the harm would not have resulted but for the abnormally sensitive character of the plaintiff's activity."

In *Foster v. Preston Mill Co.*, 44 Wash. 2d 440, 268 P.2d 645 (1954), the court refused to impose strict liability against a blaster whose blasting operations caused plaintiff's frightened mother mink to kill their kittens:

> The relatively moderate vibration and noise which appellant's blasting produced at a distance of two and a quarter miles was no more than a usual incident of the ordinary life of the community . . . .
>
> It is the exceedingly nervous disposition of mink, rather than the normal risks inherent in blasting operations, which therefore must, as a matter of sound policy, bear the responsibility for the loss here sustained.

Compare MacGibbon v. Robinson, [1953] 2 D.L.R. 689 (B.C.) (blasting during mink whelping season held unreasonable, where blaster knew of the whelping and the blasting could reasonably have been deferred).

Suppose abnormal heat from defendant's mill damaged a very sensitive type of paper which plaintiff kept for sale on his premises? *See Robinson v. Kilvert*, [1889] 41 Ch. D. 88 (recovery denied).

Suppose plaintiff establishes an organic gardening farm in an area where her neighbors have grown cotton for generations. As a result of crop dusting of a neighbor's cotton crop, plaintiff's land is damaged so the land can no longer be used to produce organic products. Should the neighbor be held strictly liable? Suppose the damage occurred as a result of negligent dusting?

PROBLEM

Pipeline purchased a 150-foot-wide easement (right-of-way) across a tract of land, and constructed a 6-inch gas pipeline on the easement. The easement agreement authorized the construction of an additional line. Subsequently, Developer purchased a tract adjoining the right-of-way, and subdivided it for resale as residential lots. After the subdivision was completed and Developer began selling lots, Pipeline announced its intention to construct a 36-inch natural gas pipeline on the easement. Because of several well-publicized explosions of large pipelines (including one such explosion a few years earlier in the same geographical area as Pipeline's easement), Developer is unable to sell the lots at a price sufficient to cover his costs. He brings an action against Pipeline seeking (a) loss of profits and (b) damages for mental anguish. Can he recover?

Chapter 17
NUISANCE AND ENVIRONMENTAL TORTS

A. INTRODUCTION

Nuisance has been available as the basis of a cause of action for a very long time. It is usually associated with the invasion of one's interest in land, so a case such as *Rylands v. Fletcher*, [1868] L.R. 3, 19 L.T. 220 (H.L.), can be viewed as a nuisance action. An important distinction, however, is that a trespass requires an invasion of land whereas a nuisance does not. Moreover, a nuisance may involve other annoyances, such as sounds or smells that harm or offend a person or her sensitivities The pivotal consideration of a nuisance claim is whether the conduct of the defendant results in an unreasonable interference with the plaintiff's use of land. The nuisance is considered public if it interferes with the right of a person to use property as a member of the public as distinguished from the private use of property, although there is sometimes an overlapping or blurring of a public and private nuisance. Just as with products liability, a nuisance action can be based on negligence, intentional misconduct, or strict liability. Where strict liability is involved, the nuisance action parallels liability for abnormally dangerous conduct as described in RESTATEMENT (SECOND) OF TORTS § 520.

The reader may well wonder what purpose a nuisance action serves that is not already provided for by existing law. Where there is no abnormally dangerous activity or negligence, a nuisance claim may fill a hiatus not covered by an action in trespass. The injunctive remedy is used in nuisance probably more than in any other tort action. Special problems of res judicata and statutes of limitations arise in the case of a continuing or ongoing nuisance. The law of nuisance highlights risk-utility analysis in a way not always present in tort law generally.

Environmental torts are of more recent origin than nuisance. The term environmental tort is used loosely to cover a congeries of ideas including land, water and air pollution and damage, toxic and radioactive injury, and the like. Such claims often involve the tort of nuisance, but they are more expansive and pervasive. They frequently involve mass torts, and implicate the class action remedy. Environmental claims are a hallmark of tort litigation in the second half of the twentieth century, and may well come to dominate tort litigation in the twenty-first century.

B. NUISANCE: ASSESSING REASONABLENESS OF LAND USE

HENDRICKS v. STALNAKER
181 W. Va. 31, 380 S.E.2d 198 (1989)

NEELY, JUSTICE:

Walter S. Stalnaker, defendant below, appeals from a decision by the Circuit Court of Lewis County declaring a water well drilled on his property to be a private nuisance to Harry L. Hendricks and Mary Hendricks, plaintiffs below. The Hendrickses, owners of the property adjacent to that of Mr. Stalnaker, were refused a Health Department permit for a septic system located within 100 feet of Mr. Stalnaker's water well. The Circuit Court of Lewis County, based on a jury verdict, found the water well to be a private nuisance and ordered its abatement. On appeal, Mr. Stalnaker argues that because his water well was not an unreasonable use of his land, he is not liable for the effects on the Hendrickses' property. We agree and, therefore, reverse the decision of the circuit court.

Mr. Stalnaker owns approximately 10 acres of land situated on Glady Fork Road, Lewis County. In 1985, Mr. Stalnaker constructed his home on a 2.493 acre portion of the tract, and had two water wells dowsed. One well was located behind his house and the other, near the Hendrickses' property. The rear well was near land disturbed by a former strip mine and, therefore, the well produced poor quality water. Except for a small section of land near the Hendrickses' property — the location of the second "dowsed" well — most of Mr. Stalnaker's home tract had been disturbed by a strip mine. In August 1985, Mr. Stalnaker spent approximately $3,000 in an unsuccessful attempt to treat the water from the rear well.

In 1984, the Hendrickses purchased approximately 2.95 acres adjacent to Mr. Stalnaker's property for a home site or a trailer development. On 31 December 1985, Mr. Hendricks met with the Lewis County sanitarian to determine locations for a water well and a septic system. The Health Department requires a distance of 100 feet between water wells and septic systems before it will issue permits. Because the Hendrickses' land was too hilly or had been disturbed in order to build a pond, the only location for a septic system on the tract was near Mr. Stalnaker's property. On 13 January 1986, the Hendrickses contacted the county sanitarian to visit their property to complete the septic system permit application. The county sanitarian said because of snowy weather he would come out later in the week.

On 13 January 1986, Mr. Stalnaker called the sanitarian and was told about the Hendrickses' proposed septic system. Mr. Stalnaker was also told that the county sanitarian would be unavailable on 14 January 1986 but could meet with him on 15 January 1986. On 14 January 1986, Mr. Stalnaker contacted a well driller, who applied for and received a well drilling permit for the second well from the assistant sanitarian. The well was completed on 25 January 1986 but was not connected to Mr. Stalnaker's home until January 1987.

On 15 January 1986, the county sanitarian informed Mr. Hendricks that no permit for his proposed septic system could be issued because the

B. NUISANCE: ASSESSING REASONABLENESS OF LAND USE 1123

absorption field for his septic system was within one hundred feet of Mr. Stalnaker's water well. Mr. Hendricks did install a septic system without a permit in January 1987; however, the system was left inoperative pending the outcome of this suit.

The Hendrickses filed suit in the Circuit Court of Lewis County on 29 January 1987 requesting (1) the water well be declared a private nuisance, (2) the nuisance be abated, and (3) damages. In a bifurcated trial, the jury found that the water well was a private nuisance and the trial judge ordered it to be abated. On the issue of damages the jury found for the defendant and awarded no damages.

In the past we have broadly described what constitutes a nuisance:

> A nuisance is anything which annoys or disturbs the free use of one's property, or which renders its ordinary use or physical occupation uncomfortable . . . . A nuisance is anything which interferes with the rights of a citizen, either in person, property, the enjoyment of his property, or his comfort . . . . A condition is a nuisance when it clearly appears that enjoyment of property is materially lessened, and physical comfort of persons in their homes is materially interfered with thereby.

Martin v. Williams, 141 W. Va. 595, 610–611, 93 S.E.2d 835, 844 (1956). Also cited in *Mahoney v. Walter*, 157 W. Va. 882, 205 S.E.2d 692 (1974) (automobile salvage yard); *Sharon Steel Corp. v. City of Fairmont*, 175 W. Va. 479, 334 S.E.2d 616 (1985) (regulation of hazardous waste); *Sticklen v. Kittle*, 168 W. Va. 147, 287 S.E.2d 148 (1981) (construction of a high school near an airport). This definition of nuisance includes acts or conditions that affect either the general public or a limited number of persons. In *Hark v. Mountain Fork Lumber Co.*, 127 W. Va. 586, 595-96, 34 S.E.2d 348, 354 (1945), we defined a public nuisance as that which "affects the general public as public, and [a private nuisance as that which] injures one person or a limited number of persons only."

In order clearly to delineate between a public nuisance and a private nuisance, we define a private nuisance as a substantial and unreasonable interference with the private use and enjoyment of another's land. The definition of private nuisance includes conduct that is intentional and unreasonable, negligent or reckless, or that results in [sic] an abnormally dangerous conditions or activities in an inappropriate place. Recovery for a private nuisance is limited to plaintiffs who have suffered a significant harm to their property rights or privileges caused by the interference.

Early West Virginia cases indicate that the existence of a private nuisance was determined primarily by the harm caused. *Medford v. Levy*, 31 W. Va. 649, 8 S.E. 302 (1888) (cooking odors); *Flanagan v. Gregory and Poole, Inc.*, 136 W. Va. 554, 67 S.E.2d 865 (1951) (inadequate culvert). Gradually the focus included an examination of the reasonableness of the property's use. *See McGregor v. Camden*, 47 W. Va. 193, 34 S.E. 936 (1899) (required an examination of the location, capacity and management of oil and gas well); *Pope v. Edward M. Rude Carrier Corp.*, 138 W. Va. 218, 75 S.E.2d 584 (1953) (transportation of explosives); *Martin, supra* (used automobile lot); *State ex rel. Ammerman v. City of Philippi*, 136 W. Va. 120, 65 S.E.2d 713 (1951) (tire recapping business); *Ritz v. Woman's Club of Charleston*, 114 W. Va. 675, 173 S.E. 564 (1934) (noise); *Harless v. Workman*, 145 W. Va. 266, 114 S.E.2d 548 (1960) (coal dust).

In the area of public nuisance, we have made explicit that an examination of the "reasonableness or unreasonableness of the use of property in relation to the particular locality" is a fair test to determine the existence of a public nuisance. Similarly, any determination of liability for a private nuisance must include an examination of the private use and enjoyment of the land seeking protection and the nature of the interference.

Because the present case concerns conduct that is not a negligent, reckless, or abnormally dangerous activity, our discussion of private nuisance is limited to conduct that is intentional and unreasonable. An interference is intentional when the actor knows or should know that the conduct is causing a substantial and unreasonable interference. Restatement (Second) of Torts § 825 (1979). The unreasonableness of an intentional interference must be determined by a balancing of the landowners' interests. An interference is unreasonable when the gravity of the harm outweighs the social value of the activity alleged to cause the harm. Restatement (Second) of Torts §§ 827 and 828 (1979) list some of the factors to be considered in determining the gravity of the harm and the social value of the activity alleged to cause the harm.[1] However, this balancing to determine unreasonableness is not absolute. Additional consideration might include the malicious or indecent conduct of the actor. Restatement (Second) of Torts § 829.

In the case before us, the Hendrickses' inability to operate a septic system on their property is clearly a substantial interference with the use and enjoyment of their land. The record indicates that the installation of the water well was intentional, but there was no evidence that the installation was done so as maliciously to deprive the Hendrickses of a septic system. Mr. Stalnaker wanted to insure himself of an adequate water supply and found no alternative to the well he dug.

The critical question is whether the interference, the installation of a water well, was unreasonable. Unreasonableness is determined by balancing the competing landholders' interests. We note that either use, well or septic system, burdens the adjacent property. Under Health Department regulations, a water well merely requires non-interference within 100 feet of its location. In the case of a septic system, however, the 100 foot safety zone,

---

[1] The RESTATEMENT (SECOND) OF TORTS § 827 (1979) lists the following "gravity of harm" factors: (a) The extent of the harm involved; (b) the character of the harm involved; (c) the social value that the law attaches to the type of use or enjoyment invaded; (d) the suitability of the particular use or enjoyment invaded to the character of the locality; and (e) the burden on the person harmed of avoiding the harm. The Restatement (Second) of Torts § 828 lists the following "utility of conduct" factors: (a) the social value that the law attaches to the primary purpose of the conduct; (b) the suitability of the conduct to the character of the locality; and; (c) the impracticability of preventing or avoiding the invasion.

[Editor's Note. § 829A provides:

"An intentional invasion of another's interest in the use and enjoyment of land is unreasonable if the harm resulting from the invasion is severe and greater than the other should be required to bear without compensation."]

extending from the edge of the absorption field, may intrude on adjacent property. Thus, the septic system, with its potential for drainage, places a more invasive burden on adjacent property. Clearly both uses present similar considerations of gravity of harm and social value of the activity alleged to cause the harm. Both a water well and a septic system are necessary to use this land for housing; together they constitute the in and out of many water systems. Neither party has an inexpensive and practical alternative. The site of the water well means quality water for Mr. Stalnaker and the Hendrickses have only one location available for their septic system.

In the case before us, we are asked to determine if the water well is a private nuisance. But if the septic system were operational, the same question could be asked about the septic system.[2] Because of the similar competing interests, the balancing of these landowners' interests is at least equal or, perhaps, slightly in favor of the water well. Thus, the Hendrickses have not shown that the balancing of interests favors their septic system. We find that the evidence presented clearly does not demonstrate that the water well is an unreasonable use of land and, therefore, does not constitute a private nuisance.

Although questions of fact are normally for the jury, when the material facts are not disputed and only one inference may be drawn from them by reasonable minds, the factual questions at issue become questions of law for the court.

We find that because the evidence is not disputed and only one interference is reasonable, the trial court should have held as a matter of law that the water well was not a private nuisance.

Accordingly, for the reasons stated above, the judgment of the Circuit Court of Lewis County is reversed and the case is remanded for entry of an order consistent with this opinion.

NOTES

1. *Nuisance and Governmental Takings.* If a state or the federal government takes private property, it is required, under the 5th and 14th amendments of the federal constitution as well as under state constitutions, to provide just compensation for the taking. *See Jackson v. Metrop. Knoxville Airport Authority*, 922 S.W.2d 860 (Tenn. 1996) (claim of noise, vibration and pollution from nearby airport flights constituted prima facie cause of action for inverse condemnation).

But the government may take a property interest without compensation if the interest constitutes a nuisance. Thus in *Erb v. Maryland Dep't of the Environment*, 676 A.2d 1017 (Md. App. 1996), the court denied the plaintiff's claim that the Maryland Department of Environment (MDE) had deprived him of the beneficial use of his property by denying him a permit to build a septic system on his property:

---

[2] In a factually similar case, the Supreme Court of Oklahoma held that a sewage lagoon created within 100 feet of a neighbor's water well was a "willful" injury to the adjacent property and awarded attorneys' fees. The court reasoned that under an Oklahoma statute the sewage lagoon actively burdened adjacent property whereas the water well was a non-invasive burden. *Schaeffer v. Schaeffer*, 743 P.2d 1038 (Okla. 1987).

We first note that, while the inability to build on the property at the present time may greatly diminish its current value, appellant has not presented sufficient evidence to establish that he has been denied all economically beneficial uses of the property. The record is sparse in regard to the other uses or remaining utility of the property in question, and, moreover, it is possible that appellant will be able to utilize alternate means of sewage disposal.

Further, and more important, the power to regulate sewage disposal systems rests within the police power of this State. The regulatory scheme set up by MDE does no more than could be accomplished under the nuisance laws of this State. Even if MDE's regulatory scheme — a scheme designed to prevent appellant from creating a nuisance on his property — were to leave his property economically barren, no compensation would be due because the State has a right — and, indeed, an obligation — to regulate against the creation of nuisances.

A landmark case upholding the right of the government to take without compensation private property that constitutes a nuisance is *Miller v. Schoene*, 276 U.S. 272 (1928). There the plaintiffs were denied recovery for the value of their red cedars destroyed by the state:

Acting under the Cedar Rust Act of Virginia, defendant in error, the state entomologist, ordered the plaintiffs in error to cut down a large number of ornamental red cedar trees growing on their property, as a means of preventing the communication of a rust or plant disease with which they were infected to the apple orchards in the vicinity. The plaintiffs in error appealed from the order to the circuit court of Shenandoah county which, after a hearing and a consideration of evidence, affirmed the order and allowed to plaintiffs in error $100 to cover the expense of removal of the cedars. Neither the judgment of the court nor the statute as interpreted allows compensation for the value of the standing cedars or the decrease in the market value of the realty caused by their destruction whether considered as ornamental trees or otherwise. But they save to plaintiffs in error the privilege of using the trees when felled. On appeal the Supreme Court of Appeals of Virginia affirmed the judgment. Both in the circuit court and the Supreme Court of Appeals plaintiffs in error challenged the constitutionality of the statute under the due process clause of the Fourteenth Amendment and the case is properly here on writ of error.

The Virginia statute presents a comprehensive scheme for the condemnation and destruction of red cedar trees infected by cedar rust. By section 1 it is declared to be unlawful for any person to "own, plant or keep alive and standing" on his premises any red cedar tree which is or may be the source or "host plant" of the communicable plant disease known as cedar rust, and any such tree growing within a certain radius of any apple orchard is declared to be a public nuisance, subject to destruction. . . .

As shown by the evidence as recognized in other cases involving the validity of this statute, cedar rust is an infectious plant disease in the form of a fungoid organism which is destructive of the fruit and foliage of the apple, but without effect on the value of the cedar. Its life cycle has two phases which are passed alternately as a growth on red cedar and on apple trees. It is communicated by spores from one to the other over a radius of at least two miles. It appears not to be communicable between trees of the same species, but only from one species to the other, and other plants seem not to be appreciably affected by it. The only practicable method of controlling the disease and protecting apple trees from its ravages is the destruction of all red cedar trees, subject to the infection, located within two miles of apple orchards.

The red cedar, aside from its ornamental use, has occasional use and value as lumber. It is indigenous to Virginia, is not cultivated or dealt in commercially on any substantial scale, and its value throughout the state is shown to be small as compared with that of the apple orchards of the state. Apple growing is one of the principal agricultural pursuits in Virginia. The apple is used there and exported in large quantities. Many millions of dollars are invested in the orchards, which furnish employment for a large portion of the population, and have induced the development of attendant railroad and cold storage facilities.

On the evidence we may accept the conclusion of the Supreme Court of Appeals that the state was under the necessity of making a choice between the preservation of one class of property and that of the other wherever both existed in dangerous proximity. It would have been none the less a choice if, instead of enacting the present statute, the state, by doing nothing, had permitted serious injury to the apple orchards within its borders to go on unchecked. When forced to such a choice the state does not exceed its constitutional powers by deciding upon the destruction of one class of property in order to save another which, in the judgment of the legislature, is of greater value to the public. It will not do to say that the case is merely one of a conflict of two private interests and that the misfortune of apple growers may not be shifted to cedar owners by ordering the destruction of their property; for it is obvious that there may be, and that here there is, a preponderant public concern in the preservation of the one interest over the other. And where the public interest is involved preferment of that interest over the property interest of the individual, to the extent even of its destruction, is one of the distinguishing characteristics of every exercise of the police power which affects property.

In *City of St. Petersburg v. Bowen*, 675 So. 2d 626 (Fla. App. 1996), on the other hand, the court found a compensable taking. The City of St. Petersburg ordered plaintiff's 15-unit apartment complex closed for a year as a statutory public nuisance, based on evidence of tenant drug use in the complex. "The fact that the City did not take title to the Bowen property (it was merely closed for one year) does not defeat the 'taking' aspect of plaintiff's claim in this case," the court said.

The cases are divided on whether the damage or destruction of a building by law enforcement officers to apprehend a fugitive is a taking. *See Customer Co. v. City of Sacramento*, 10 Cal. 4th 368, 41 Cal. Rptr. 2d 658, 895 P.2d 900 (1995); annot., 23 A.L.R.5th 834 (1994).

2. *Duty of Real Estate Developer and Broker to Disclose Off-Site Physical Conditions*. The issue in *Strawn v. Canuso*, 140 N.J. 43, 657 A.2d 420 (1995), was stated by the court to be "whether a builder developer of new homes and the brokers marketing those homes have a duty to disclose to prospective buyers that the homes have been constructed near an abandoned hazardous-waster dump." The court held that such a duty did exist. The facts were stated by the court:

> . . . The case concerns the claims of more than 150 families seeking damages because the new homes that they bought in Voorhees Township, New Jersey, were constructed near a hazardous-waste dump site, known as the Buzby Landfill. The complaint names as defendants John B. Canuso, Sr., and John B. Canuso, Jr., and their companies: Canetic Corporation and Canuso Management Corporation. Fox & Lazo, Inc. (Fox & Lazo), the brokerage firm that was the selling agent for the development, was also named as a codefendant.
>
> Plaintiffs base their claims on common-law principles of fraud and negligent misrepresentation, and the New Jersey Consumer Fraud Act, N.J.S.A. 56:8-1 to -66. The twenty-six Plaintiff-families filed a class-action lawsuit on behalf of all of the purchasers of the homes in the development sold by defendants. Those families purchased their homes between 1984 and 1987.
>
> The Buzby Landfill consists of two tracts of property, a nineteen-acre portion owned by RCA and a contiguous thirty-seven-acre parcel now owned by Voorhees Township. Those two tracts were the site of a landfill from 1966 to 1978. Although the Buzby Landfill was not licensed to receive liquid-industrial or chemical wastes, large amounts of hazardous materials and chemicals were dumped there. The landfill was also plagued by fires.
>
> Toxic wastes dumped in the Buzby Landfill began to escape because it had no liner or cap. Tests done by the New Jersey Department of Environmental Protection and Energy (DEPE) revealed that leachate was seeping from the landfill into a downstream lake. The DEPE estimated that half of the landfill material was submerged in ground water, thereby contaminating the ground water with hazardous substances. Additional tests indicated the presence of hazardous waste in ground water, in marsh sediments taken from the landfill, and in lakes southeast of the landfill.
>
> RCA installed a system at the landfill to vent excessive levels of methane gas at the site. DEPE's site manager discovered gas leaks in that venting system. Those leaks released contaminants, including benzene and other volatile organic compounds. In 1986, methane gases, which naturally accumulate in landfills, emanated from the dump site. Reports of the federal Environmental Protection Agency (EPA) confirm that residents' complaints about odors and associated physical symptoms are consistent with expected reactions to exposure to gases from the landfill. EPA recommended that the site be considered for a Superfund cleanup.

Plaintiffs allege that the developers knew of the Buzby Landfill before they considered the site for residential development. Plaintiffs contend that although defendants were specifically aware of the existence and hazards of the landfill, they did not disclose those facts to plaintiffs when they bought their homes. A 1980 EPA report warned: "The proposed housing development on land adjacent to the site has all the potential of developing into a future Love Canal if construction is permitted." A copy of the EPA report was in the Canuso defendants' files. Those defendants also met with a DEPE employee to discuss the prospects of building homes near the landfill. (Later reports of regulatory agencies tempered those earlier reports, one of which described any risk as "indeterminate." We also note that such reports may contain hearsay and, therefore, may be inadmissible at trial.)

In addition, one of Fox & Lazo's marketing directors urged his firm and the individual Canuso defendants to disclose the existence of the Buzby Landfill to home buyers. Each refused that request and instead followed a policy of nondisclosure. That policy continued even after early purchasers complained about odors. Defendants' representatives were instructed never to disclose the existence of the Buzby Landfill, even when asked about such conditions. Later, some prospective home buyers, having independently learned about the Buzby Landfill, refused to convert their initial nonbinding deposits into enforceable agreements of sale.

John Canuso, Jr., who personally supervised the sales force, instructed his sales manager to ascertain what information DEPE was providing to people who asked about the landfill. The sales manager spoke with a DEPE representative, who again warned defendants of the problems of building a large development near the landfill. The sales manager repeated in a memorandum the warning given to her by the DEPE employee and placed the memorandum with related papers in a "hazardous waste" file that the Canuso defendants maintained. John Canuso, Jr., discussed this memorandum with his father, John Canuso, Sr., who refused to disclose to home buyers the proximity of the landfill.

The court said a claim was stated under the state Consumer Fraud Act and for common law fraud. It also held that the case should be certified as a class action.

It noted the modern trend away from *caveat emptor* in real estate sales, especially where the seller is a business seller and the buyer lacks the expertise of the seller. Most cases have imposed liability based on knowing failure to disclose, but a few states by statute have imposed a duty to investigate on the seller.

The court said:

> The duty that we recognize is not unlimited. We do not hold that sellers and brokers have a duty to investigate or disclose transient social conditions in the community that arguably affect the value of

property. In the absence of a purchaser communicating specific needs, builders and brokers should not be held to decide whether the changing nature of a neighborhood, the presence of a group home, or the existence of a school in decline are facts material to the transaction. Rather, [recognize a] duty to disclose off-site conditions that are material to the transaction. That duty is consistent with the development of our law and supported by statutory policy. . . .

We hold that a builder-developer of residential real estate or a broker representing it is not only liable to a purchaser for affirmative and intentional misrepresentation, but is also liable for nondisclosure of off-site physical conditions known to it and unknown and not readily observable by the buyer if the existence of those conditions is of sufficient materiality to affect the habitability, use, or enjoyment of the property and, therefore, render the property substantially less desirable or valuable to the objectively reasonable buyer. Whether a matter not disclosed by such a builder or broker is of such materiality, and unknown and unobservable by the buyer, will depend on the facts of each case.

C. NUISANCE AND RELATED ENVIRONMENTAL TORTS: IDENTIFYING COGNIZABLE HARM

The RESTATEMENT (SECOND) OF TORTS Section 821F provides:

> There is liability for a nuisance only to those to whom it causes significant harm, of a kind that would be suffered by a normal person in the community or by property in normal condition and used for a normal purpose.

Is an interference with the ability to sell the property a significant harm? What about an interference with the ability to operate a computer to connect with the internet?

GOLEN v. THE UNION CORP.
718 A.2d 298 (Pa. Super. 1998)

OLSZEWSKI, JUDGE.

This appeal presents the question of whether private nuisance provides a remedy for a landowner who cannot sell his or her property because of neighboring environmental contamination, when the contamination does not otherwise affect the landowner's use of the property. The trial court granted appellees' motion for summary judgment, finding that private nuisance does not provide a remedy. We affirm.

Both appellants' and appellees' property are located in an industrial section of Philadelphia. During the 1970's, appellees' property was used for recycling electrical transformers, which contaminated the property with polychlorinated biphenyls (PCBs). As a result of this contamination, the property was listed on the National Priorities List (NPL) of the Comprehensive Environmental Response, Compensation and Liability Act[1] ("CERCLA" or "Superfund").

---

[1] 42 U.S.C. §§ 9601-9675.

C. NUISANCE AND RELATED ENVIRONMENTAL TORTS

Although the contamination leaked into the Delaware River, there is no evidence that it migrated to appellants' property.

Appellants' property was used as a waste transfer station including the treatment of some hazardous waste. Appellants learned of appellees' property NPL status in 1983. Appellants attempted to sell their property in 1991, but claim they were unable to find a buyer because of appellees' NPL listing. Appellants concede that their ability to use the property has not otherwise changed.

Appellants filed a private nuisance suit, based upon the inability to sell the property. In response, appellees filed a motion for summary judgment, which the trial court granted. This appeal followed.

When considering an order for summary judgment, our standard of review is well settled. We must view the record in the light most favorable to the non-moving party, and all doubts as to the existence of a genuine issue of material fact must be resolved against the moving party. Summary judgment will be granted only in those cases which are free and clear from doubt. Our scope of review is plenary.

Appellants admit that their land is not contaminated and that aside from alienability, their use of the property remains unaffected. Nevertheless, appellants argue that they are entitled to relief under a theory of private nuisance. In tort, one may be damaged but not suffer a legal injury. Although appellants have clearly alleged damages, we must decide whether they were a result of a compensable injury. We conclude that they are not.

This Commonwealth follows the Restatement (Second) of Torts' formulation of private nuisance. The Restatement defines a private nuisance as "a nontrespassory invasion of another's interest in the private use and enjoyment of land." 4 Restatement Torts, 2d, § 821D, p. 100. Appellants claim that the interest invaded was their ability to sell their property. We find, however, that this is not the type of injury contemplated by the Restatement.

Admittedly, a broad reading of the Restatement definition could include appellants' claim. It has been noted that the concept of nuisance is broad enough to encompass virtually all harms. Thus, courts must determine sensible limits to liability under this potentially sweeping concept. After careful consideration, we conclude that private nuisance only recognizes injuries that require physical presence on the property in order to be perceived.[2]

We recognize that alienability and diminution of property value are relevant means to calculate damages in a nuisance suit. These concepts are not, however, cognizable injuries of themselves.

The physical presence requirement is supported in the text of the Restatement:

---

[2] Perception while physically present should not be confused with physical invasion. For instance, the noise and light from a trucking business can be perceived while physically present on neighboring property and may constitute a nuisance though no physical invasion occurs. *See Firth v. Scherzberg*, 366 Pa. 443, 77 A.2d 443 (Pa. 1951) (noise and headlights from a trucking business operated at night considered a nuisance where it deprived neighbors of sleep).

b. Interest in use and enjoyment of land . . . The phrase "interest in the use and enjoyment of land" is used in this Restatement in a broad sense. It comprehends not only the interests that a person may have in the actual present use of land for residential, agricultural, commercial, industrial and other purposes, but also his interests in having the present use value of the land unimpaired by changes in its physical condition . . . . "Interest in use and enjoyment" also comprehends the pleasure, comfort and enjoyment that a person normally derives from the occupancy of land. Freedom from discomfort and annoyance while using land is often as important to a person as freedom from physical interruption with his use or freedom from detrimental change in the physical condition of the land itself. This interest in freedom from annoyance and discomfort in the use of land is to be distinguished from the interest in freedom from emotional distress . . . The latter is purely an interest of personality and receives limited legal protection, whereas the former is essentially an interest in the usability of land and, although it involves an element of personal tastes and sensibilities, it receives much greater legal protection. Restatement Torts, 2d, § 821D comment b., p. 101.

Although the comment requires "interest in use and enjoyment of land" to be read broadly, this broad reading is entirely within the confines of uses of land that arise while occupying property. It defines the interest in terms of occupancy, physical interruption, and physical condition. These terms denote land uses that are enjoyed while a person is actually present on the property. Nowhere in the comment is there the merest allusion to abstract property rights such as ability to sell. This ability can be enjoyed regardless of one's occupancy of the land as land sales may occur without the parties ever entering the property. We find the ability to sell more like an injury against personality, which the Restatement specifically rejects. Both are types of harm that, though connected with the property in some way, manifest independent of presence on the property.

Pennsylvania caselaw involving private nuisance is consistent with this view. All of the cases relate to an interference of the enjoyment of the property while on the premises. *See, e.g., Harford Penn-Cann Service, Inc. v. Zymblosky*, 378 Pa. Super. 578, 549 A.2d 208 (Pa.Super. 1988) (dust from truck stop sufficient to constitute nuisance where health problems to employees resulted); *Karpiak v. Russo*, 450 Pa. Super. 471, 676 A.2d 270 (Pa.Super. 1996) (dust from a business not a nuisance where no health problems or effect on daily activities resulted); *Township of Bedminster v. Vargo Dragway, Inc.*, 434 Pa. 100, 253 A.2d 659 (Pa. 1969) (excessive noise from a racetrack in a residential area found to be a nuisance in fact). No case allows for as expansive a protection as appellants advocate.

Finally, accepting appellants' theory of private nuisance would constitute poor policy. If we were to allow recovery in this case, we would open the proverbial floodgates. Anytime a property owner engaged in an activity that ostensibly reduced surrounding property values, liability would attach. Hence, a property owner opening an unpopular public housing project or an AIDS clinic would be strictly liable for a decline in surrounding property values.

Such a rule would allow unfounded prejudices to dictate property use, which is clearly unacceptable. Although hazardous waste contamination is undeniably pernicious, when such contamination only affects a property owner's ability to sell his or her property, a nuisance action does not exist.

Moreover, the rule proposed by appellants would impose almost limitless liability on a property owner for an undesirable use. Instantly, if appellants recover so can every other neighbor who claims difficulty selling his or her property, regardless of proximity to appellees. This Court has condemned this type of unlimited liability.

In conclusion, we find that appellants' claim of inability to sell property is, by itself, insufficient to establish a private nuisance. This claim amounts to damage without legal injury, or *damnum absque injuria*, and is therefore meritless.

WESTCHESTER ASSOCIATES, INC. v. BOSTON EDISON COMPANY
47 Mass. App. Ct. 133, 712 N.E.2d 1145 (1999)

JACOBS, J.

Westchester Associates, Inc. (Westchester), is the owner of a six-story office building in Framingham immediately adjacent to electric power lines[1] operated by Boston Edison Company (Edison). Magnetic fields generated by the power lines have caused disruption and distorted images on computer monitor screens used by tenants who leased space in Westchester's building. Claiming various injuries,[2] Westchester filed a complaint in the Superior Court alleging Edison's operation of the lines creates a nuisance; is negligent; intentionally interferes with Westchester's contractual relations with third parties; and that Edison is committing unfair and deceptive acts or practices under G. L. c. 93A.[3] A Superior Court judge allowed Edison's motion for summary judgment. We affirm.

Acting under authority of the Department of Public Utilities, Edison, in 1956, took by eminent domain a one-hundred-foot-wide easement for the construction and use of one or more transmission lines across land owned by Westchester's predecessor in title.[4] Subsequently two lines were constructed: one carrying 69 kilovolts (kv) in 1957 and, in 1962, a second line of 13.8 kv. In 1971, a 115 kv line was added, replacing the 1957 line. In 1978, Westchester purchased the land, a portion of which is subject to the easement. It constructed two buildings on the land, one in 1977-1978, and the other, at issue

---

[1] We use the terms "power lines" and "transmission lines" interchangeably.

[2] Westchester claims it has lost a tenant, been put to expense for necessary alterations, been unable to lease vacant space, and that Edison failed to respond to its requests to resolve those problems.

[3] The complaint also alleges that emissions from the power lines pose a health threat to persons regularly exposed to them. Westchester concedes that health concerns are not at issue in this case.

[4] The taking was made pursuant to *G. L. c. 164, § 72*, and G. L. c. 79. A subsequently recorded confirmatory easement executed by the predecessor in title indicates that $ 40,000 was paid to it by Edison.

in this case, in 1987 (the 1987 building). An exterior wall of the 1987 building is located about two feet south of the southern boundary of the easement and about twenty-four feet from the nearest transmission line. Beginning in 1994 when most of the space was leased, tenants soon experienced distorted and "jittery" images on computer screens and the cause was attributed, in the affidavit of an expert, to the magnetic fields generated by Edison's power lines.[5]

Westchester argues that the magnetic fields generated by Edison's power lines extend beyond its defined easement area, creating a substantial and unreasonable interference with Westchester's use and enjoyment of its land. This argument essentially is cast in the form of a claim of nuisance. Edison responds that because it is lawfully operating its lines within the scope of its easement it is entitled to judgment as matter of law.

A nuisance may result from an overly intensive use or an overburdening of an easement. We begin by determining what use of the easement is authorized to Edison by the relevant documents. They provide in pertinent part: "the perpetual right and easement to erect, install, construct, reconstruct, . . . use [and] operate . . . one or more transmission lines for the transmission of high and low voltage electric current . . . over, across and upon [the easement land]." Because the language of the easement is "'clear and explicit, and without ambiguity, there is no room for construction, or for the admission of parol evidence, to prove that the parties intended something different.'" *Panikowski v. Giroux, 272 Mass. 580, 583, 172 N.E. 890 (1930),* quoting from *Cook v. Babcock, 7 Cush. 526, 528 (1851).*[6] The record demonstrates and there

---

[5] Westchester's expert concludes that the magnetic fields generated by the power lines caused the "jittery" images by disrupting the magnetic field generated internally by those devices which serves to direct and focus the images on the screens. He states that the resulting movement of the images on the screens is "most unpleasant to watch for any length of time whatsoever." He also notes that because magnetic fields from power lines are "present in most environments," manufacturers of video screens provide shielding to protect them from interference that is effective for field strengths of "a few milliGauss." He opines that in the range of ten milliGauss and above, such shielding is not effective. Actual measurements made in the building by an expert for one of the tenants generally were well above that value in the office areas located along the wall of Westchester's building nearest to Edison's lines.

For a thorough discussion of the nature of electric and magnetic fields (sometimes "electromagnetic" fields) associated with electric power transmission lines, see *San Diego Gas & Elec. Co. v. Superior Ct., 13 Cal. 4th 893, 903–910, 920 P.2d 669 (1996).*

[6] Although "the extent of an easement depends on the circumstances of its creation," *Mugar v. Massachusetts Bay Transp. Authy., 28 Mass. App. Ct. 443, 444, 552 N.E.2d 121 (1990),* "the principles of interpretation designed to give effect to the express or implied intent of parties contracting for or acquiring an interest in land, however, are, in general, inapplicable to eminent domain proceedings. . . . The owner's intent is irrelevant in determining the extent of an easement taken by eminent domain, and the intent of the governmental body is largely beyond the scope of judicial scrutiny." *Id. at 445.*

We do not consider Westchester's assertion that the Legislature has not expressly authorized Boston Edison to emit magnetic fields beyond the scope of its easement and, in any event, could not have intended to sanction the harm Westchester has suffered. There is no record indication that the Legislature has addressed the issue of the generation of electromagnetic fields by electric power lines.

Westchester's claim that Edison does not have a certificate of public convenience and necessity required for its lower voltage 13.8 kv line is without merit. The original determination of public convenience and necessity was based on an approval for both high and low voltage lines and does not limit the number of lines, voltage, or when they may be constructed or reconstructed.

is no dispute that Edison's use of the easement area has not changed since 1971, well before the time Westchester acquired its land.[7] The express terms of the easement are silent on the existence of electromagnetic fields or whether they were to be taken into account in the construction and operation of electric transmission lines.[8] In any event, a record statement by Westchester's expert that "all power lines generate magnetic and electric fields" is not disputed. There is undisputed evidence that the higher voltage line, principally at issue in this case, is of "standard industry design," and is similar to other Edison lines as well as many others "throughout the United States." Also, the report of an expert deposed by Westchester indicated that no regulatory standards for electromagnetic fields have been developed or are applicable to the lines in issue. We conclude, therefore, that Edison has demonstrated that its use of the easement is of the same "amount and character" as authorized, and we agree with the carefully crafted opinion of the Superior Court judge that Edison's use is reasonable, as matter of law.[9]

Further, Westchester's claim that the fields constitute a nuisance has no legal support.[10] Not only has the character of the magnetic fields generated not changed during the times here relevant, but our law has not recognized those fields as a nuisance.

---

[7] Westchester mistakenly relies on *Western Mass. Elec. Co. v. Sambo's of Mass., Inc.*, 8 Mass. App. Ct. 815, 398 N.E.2d 729 (1979), to support its assertion that its land is not burdened by Edison's easement. That case concerned the extent to which the owner of servient land could use that land in a manner not inconsistent with the easement, and which would not materially increase cost or inconvenience to the easement holder in the exercise of its rights. In the present case we do not reach any consideration of whether the construction of Westchester's building was inconsistent with Edison's rights.

[8] Massachusetts cases have not yet considered the effects of electromagnetic fields generated by electric power lines. The present case does not require that we rely on decisional law in other jurisdictions. We cite some authorities, however, which offer guidance. See *San Diego Gas & Elec. Co. v. Superior Ct.*, 13 Cal. 4th 893, 936, 920 P.2d 669 (1996) (intangible phenomena such as electric and magnetic fields, not directly perceived by the senses, not actionable intrusions); *Borenkind v. Consolidated Edison Co.*, 164 Misc. 2d 808, 810, 626 N.Y.S.2d 414 (N.Y. Sup. Ct. 1995) (no duty owed to owners of land near high voltage power lines when publicly sanctioned use is carried out in a legally authorized manner; invasive quality of electric and magnetic fields, imperceptible to ordinary senses, and lacking scientific evidence of harmful effects, not a nuisance); *Edgcomb v. Lower Valley Power & Light*, 922 P.2d 850, 858-860 (Wyo. 1996) (summary judgment for defendant affirmed, the court holding that electromagnetic fields from power lines operated in easement area are neither a trespass nor an "unreasonable, unwarranted, or unlawful" use, and "do not constitute a nuisance").

[9] Westchester claims that the reasonableness of the use of an easement is a question of fact, and not appropriate for a summary judgment determination. The plaintiff's reliance on cases such as *Doody v. Spurr*, 315 Mass. 129, 133-134, 51 N.E.2d 981 (1943), and *Tindley v. Department of Envtl. Quality Engr.*, 10 Mass. App. Ct. 623, 628, 411 N.E.2d 187 (1980), is misplaced. Such cases involve the interpretation, on a reasonableness standard, of rights not explicitly granted. They stand in sharp contrast with the detailed rights expressed in the easement in the present case. Where, as here, we are presented with the relevant facts in a summary judgment record, it is open to us to rule "what facts are sufficient in law to constitute a nuisance." *Kasper v. H.P. Hood & Sons, Inc.*, 291 Mass. 24, 25, 196 N.E. 149 (1935).

[10] There is no evidence that the permitted use has substantially disturbed the servient land or unreasonably diminished its value after Edison acquired the easement. In any event, Edison compensated Westchester's predecessor in title in taking the easement. The present record does not indicate more than the consideration paid, $40,000, nor whether that valuation was based on any special incidents related to the proposed construction of electric power lines. Whatever compensation was required for the servitude imposed appears to have been paid.

A significant difficulty with Westchester's attempt to characterize the magnetic fields as a nuisance is that their adverse effects would be experienced only by particular users of equipment sensitive to the fields. There is no contention that the fields are directly detectable by human senses. Thus, they do not constitute an annoyance to a plaintiff of "ordinary sensibility." *Malm v. Dubrey,* 325 Mass. 63, 65, 88 N.E.2d 900 (1949), and cases cited. The inquiry to determine whether such fields constitute a nuisance will likely vary as computers and other electronic equipment may become more sophisticated and sensitive. There may come a time when increasing knowledge or changing uses may require, as matter of public policy, the modification of the use of electric power line easements, but this case does not call for such remediation. We conclude that Westchester's nuisance claim, unsupported in the law, fails, and that because Edison reasonably is exercising its easement rights, it is entitled to summary judgment.

There is no evidence that Edison knowingly induced any Westchester tenant to breach its lease, or that Edison did so with any improper motives or means. Given our decision, the alleged failure of Edison to resolve the problems experienced by Westchester's tenants does not constitute unfair or deceptive acts or practices under *G. L. c. 93A, § 11*. Finally, because Edison operates its power lines intentionally and not in violation of statutory and regulatory standards, its acts and operations are not negligent.

Judgment affirmed.

D. ASSESSING PROOF AND FASHIONING REMEDIES

SHARP v. 251st STREET LANDFILL, INC.
925 P.2d 546 (Okla. 1996)

LAVENDER, JUSTICE.

This is the second time this matter has been before us. In the first appeal we affirmed the decision of the trial court to grant a temporary injunction prohibiting construction and operation of a landfill at a location in Okmulgee County. The claim for injunctive relief was brought by appellees — either adjacent or nearby landowners — to enjoin construction and operation of the landfill based on an anticipatory nuisance theory which in turn was anchored on the asserted probability ground and/or surface water sources used by them would likely be polluted by operation of the landfill.

After the matter returned to the trial court following the first appeal, appellant, 251st Street Landfill, Inc., made certain changes to its proposed landfill design, which included a leachate[3] collection system and a geomembrane — *i.e.* plastic — liner, modifications geared toward providing additional protection against the probability of water pollution. The Oklahoma Department of Environmental Quality (DEQ) determined the modifications complied

---

[3] Leachate is a contaminant that usually comes from solid waste sites as surface water infiltrates into compacted refuse. It is a quantity of liquid that has percolated through a solid and leached out some of its constituents. *Id.* Leachate may contain various pollutants depending on the makeup of the refuse disposed of at a particular site.

with certain proposed new rules of DEQ concerning solid waste landfills, which determination essentially acted as DEQ's authorization to go forward with construction and operation of the landfill at the designated location. The matter then proceeded to trial. Following trial a decree permanently enjoining construction and operation at the proposed site was entered by the trial court. An appeal by appellant followed and we have retained the matter in this Court.

Two general issues are posed for our review: 1) whether reversible error occurred in the admittance and consideration of testimony from an engineer as expert testimony for appellees and, 2) whether the trial court erred in granting the permanent injunction because his decision was clearly against the weight of the evidence? We hold no reversible error occurred in either acceptance of the expert testimony or in granting the permanent injunction. The decision to permanently enjoin construction and operation of the landfill at the proposed location is, therefore, affirmed. . . .

Appellant claims the trial court erred in admitting and considering part of the expert opinion testimony of Richard N. DeVries. It is argued his testimony concerning landfill design should have been disregarded primarily because of the assertion he lacks knowledge and experience to give an expert opinion on landfill design and he was not qualified to express an opinion on the adequacy of the environmental protection systems embodied in the proposed landfill design. We disagree.

12 O.S. 1991, § 2702 of the OKLAHOMA EVIDENCE CODE, 12 O.S. 1991, § 2101 *et seq.*, as amended, provides that "[i]f scientific, technical or other specialized knowledge will assist the trier of fact to understand the evidence or to determine a fact in issue, a witness qualified as an expert by knowledge, skill, experience, training or education may testify in the form of an opinion or otherwise." An examination of the record reveals Richard N. DeVries was qualified to give expert opinions concerning landfill design, the probability of the potential for ground and surface water pollution of appellees' water sources from operation of the landfill and, generally, the adequacy of environmental protections of the proposed landfill design at the proposed landfill site.

Richard N. DeVries has both Bachelor and Master of Science Degrees in Civil Engineering from the University of Nebraska. He has a Doctor of Philosophy Degree in Civil Engineering from Utah State University. Dr. DeVries' specialty or discipline within civil engineering is water resource engineering (apparently his Ph.D. work involved this specialty). Water resource engineering includes the study of hydraulics and hydrology. Hydraulics is a branch of science dealing with practical applications, such as the transmission of energy or effect of flow, of liquid — such as water — in motion. WEBSTER'S NEW COLLEGIATE DICTIONARY 555 (1979). Hydrology is a science concerning the properties, distribution and circulation of water on the surface of the land, in the soil, underlying rocks and in the atmosphere. WEBSTER'S NEW COLLEGIATE DICTIONARY 556 (1979). It should also be noted a sub-field of water resource engineering is landfill design.

Dr. DeVries is a registered professional engineer in the states of Oklahoma and Nebraska and a registered land surveyor in the state of Oklahoma. During his education at the University of Nebraska he worked for the City of Lincoln,

Nebraska in its engineering department. Upon obtaining his B.S. degree he worked for Northern Natural Gas Company on an underground gas storage project in Redfield, Iowa. He then returned to Lincoln where he managed a sanitary sewer district in Lancaster County, Nebraska. His work there concerned drainage construction in and around Lancaster County.

After receiving his Masters' degree in 1963 he became an assistant professor of civil engineering at the University of Nebraska. In 1969 he became an associate professor of civil engineering at Oklahoma State University. In 1975 he was promoted to full professor, a position which he held for another fourteen (14) years, at which time he retired and took professor emeritus status, a status he maintained at the time of trial. The evidence showed that Dr. DeVries has done consulting work throughout his teaching career, primarily municipal-type engineering and during the six years prior to the trial, environmental-type consulting work.

Dr. DeVries also has considerable experience in the area of remediation of water pollution. He testified to working on a number of cases involving salt water pollution, underground storage tank pollution and oil field pollution. In addition, Dr. DeVries noted during his testimony that leachate collection lines associated with a leachate collection system are similar to sewer lines and that over his years as a professional engineer he has been involved in building approximately one hundred (100) miles of sewer lines. Dr. DeVries has also had some design experience with geomembrane liners — albeit in oil field mud pit application — although such application is not identical to the landfill context.

In addition, he also has considerable involvement with landfills and landfill design. Although appellant attempts to denigrate this involvement, the record we have been presented shows it cannot be ignored for the purpose of gaging Dr. DeVries' qualifications. First off, an overall review of the record in this case makes it quite clear that Dr. DeVries keeps up with current literature concerning landfills and landfill designs and that he has conducted extensive study in the field. The record also shows Dr. DeVries has engaged in work in regard to at least eight other landfills besides the proposed one at issue here. Two of the eight were hazardous waste landfill projects and the other six municipal solid waste disposal facilities, the type of landfill involved in this case. As to two of these eight landfill projects Dr. DeVries was actually involved in the landfill design phase of the projects (*i.e.*, as opposed to a consultative role either for the proponent or opponents of a particular project), and in one of the two projects either he or his company was engineer of record. Although Dr. DeVries' landfill design in these two projects did not contain the same design features as called for in this proposed landfill — *e.g.*, a geomembrane (or plastic) liner or leachate collection system — as will be seen, such actual hands-on experience with the exact type of landfill design is unnecessary to qualify him as an expert to express opinions on the probabilities the overall design features of this project at the particular location are insufficient to protect the ground and surface water in the area, *e.g.*, water used by appellees. . . .

When it is clearly made to appear by the evidence that a business cannot be conducted in any manner at the place where situated without constituting a substantial injury to adjoining or nearby property owners, a permanent injunction absolutely prohibiting operation of such business at the particular location is appropriate. Further, when a neighboring landowner is confronted with a nuisance and threatened with a complete loss of their water supply, they do not have to wait the actual infliction of such loss, but have a right to apply to a court for injunctive relief. *Baker v. Ellis*, 292 P.2d 1037, 1039 (Okla. 1956); *See also McPherson v. First Presbyterian Church*, 120 Okla. 40, 248 P. 561, 566 (1926) (harm suffered must be irreparable in damages and the evidence must be clear and convincing that there is a reasonable probability of injury, not just a mere apprehension). We have also recently recognized that the use and control of fresh water is a matter of publici juris and of immediate local, national and international concern. *DuLaney v. Oklahoma State Department of Health, supra*, 868 P.2d at 684. "No commodity affects and concerns the citizens of Oklahoma more than fresh groundwater." *Id*.

In our opinion, if the trial court determined the new or modified safety measures proposed by appellant for the landfill were inadequate to protect against probable pollution of appellees' water sources by operation of the landfill at its proposed location, an appropriate remedy would be a permanent injunction. *Sharp I*, 810 P.2d at 1281-1282. Although the trial court's order granting a permanent injunction was made without specific findings, we must assume the trial court concluded that the additional proposed safety measures are inadequate and that operation of the landfill cannot be conducted at the particular location without the reasonable probability of polluting appellees' water sources. We do not find this conclusion clearly against the weight of the evidence. . . .

The landfill site is the West ½ of Section 10, Township 15 North, Range 12 East, Okmulgee County, Oklahoma. About 90 of the 320 acres of the proposed site will be used as cells for the disposal of refuse. The landfill was originally permitted under Oklahoma Department of Health regulations as a Type I-B facility, which was generally defined as a metropolitan sanitary landfill serving populations of 30,000 or more which does not accept hazardous waste. The majority of waste to be deposited at the proposed landfill will be domestic waste. However, evidence was presented at the temporary injunction hearing [810 P.2d at 1279] and the subsequent trial that domestic waste contains a certain amount of toxic or hazardous household waste. Although screening of the waste will apparently occur, we believe a reasonable conclusion is that a certain amount of toxic materials will find their way into the landfill.

U.S. Highway 75 is a half mile east of the site. Directly north of the site is 251st Street. *Id*. At least some of the appellees have artesian wells on their property. The wells are used for domestic purposes, livestock and agricultural purposes. *Id*. Further, Eagle Creek, a creek running through the landfill site (but apparently not through the cells where waste is to be deposited) also runs through the land of some of the appellees. The creek is used by these appellees either for recreational purposes or watering livestock. . . .

Generally, the design characteristics of the proposed landfill are as follows. First, a compacted clay liner at least 3 feet thick will be placed on a soil base a minimum of two feet above the highest recorded groundwater (*i.e.* water table) level. A geomembrane liner (some type of flexible, plastic sheeting, designed to be apparently impermeable) will be placed on top of the clay liner. Above the geomembrane liner will be a geotextile liner, a heavy cloth designed to protect the geomembrane liner from puncture. Above these liners will be a leachate collection system, a system of perforated pipes and pumps designed to collect any leachate that might flow through the landfill. On top of the leachate collection system will be a granular drainage blanket comprised of at least one foot of gravel large enough so as not to clog the pipes, but porous enough for the leachate to flow through to the pipes. Finally, the granular drainage blanket will be protected by another foot of additional protective cover, either soil, or clay, or an additional granular blanket. Compacted trash will be placed on top of this, and each day's trash will be covered with one-half foot of soil to prevent loose trash from blowing.

The plans also call for monitoring wells around the perimeter of the landfill which are to act as detection devices should any leachate escape the protective devices specified in the above paragraph. The landfill is also to have a system of trenches and berms which will be designed to protect against the possibility of leakage or runoff into Eagle Creek.

Appellees identify two primary mechanisms for potential pollution of their properties — contamination of the confined, artesian aquifer under the site and contamination of Eagle Creek. To support their case principal reliance was placed on the testimony and opinions of Dr. DeVries, although documentary evidence was also relied on.

First off, there was evidence in the record that showed the site of the proposed landfill overlies a major regional aquifer — the Wewoka Formation or Aquifer. It was Dr. DeVries' opinion that appellees' artesian wells were tapping into the same confined or artesian aquifer as that under the landfill. It was also his view that given the hydrology in the area that the potential existed for pollution of this aquifer. He further expressed the opinion the direction of groundwater flow for this confined aquifer was to the northeast, *i.e.*, from the landfill site toward the artesian wells of appellees.

Furthermore, although the artesian aquifer was in a confined state apparently at least a minimum of sixty (60) feet below the proposed landfill site, Dr. DeVries testified, and other evidence corroborated the fact, that the piezometric or potentiometric surface of the artesian aquifer was actually above ground level at the proposed landfill site. What this means is that because the artesian aquifer is in such a confined — and, thus, pressurized state — it has the potential to rise above the ground when punctured. Thus, a well drilled into this aquifer would flow above the ground like a fountain. Dr. DeVries believed this high piezometric surface of the confined aquifer held the potential for water from the confined aquifer coming up under the liner of the landfill and/or blowing a hole in the landfill's liner system, which he indicated had been detailed in the literature to have previously occurred.

It was also Dr. DeVries' opinion that the water table in the area under the site was a high one, *i.e.*, at certain places under the proposed landfill site it was relatively close to the surface of the ground. His view was because of this state it would be necessary to artificially raise by the use of fill material the surface of the ground at certain places of the landfill to maintain an adequate minimum distance between the protective layer(s) of the landfill and the water table. He was of the view that because man cannot compact soil as well as nature, settlement of the fill material would occur, which held out the possibility of the sub-base cracking which in turn could cause cracks in the liner system of the landfill — i.e., a potential conduit for pollution. Although there is some dispute over the direction of flow of the water table or unconfined aquifer under the site, Dr. DeVries' opinion was and other evidence appeared to show that, at least in part, it flows north and east, which is toward appellees. Dr. DeVries also held the view that both the confined and unconfined aquifers contributed flow to Eagle Creek.

In addition, certain evidence showed that Eagle Creek, which runs through the site and the land of some of the appellees, generally flows in the direction from the site toward these appellees, i.e., in a northeasterly direction. Evidence also showed that the one hundred (100) year flood plain or boundary was as close as twenty-five (25) to thirty-five (35) feet from the area where trash would be deposited at the landfill site. Dr. DeVries also testified that the drainage area for Eagle Creek includes both the landfill site and the properties of appellees. He also indicated that the landfill site is near the high point of the drainage area and that anything that drains off the site — any pollutant or contaminant — would go downstream toward the lands of appellees.

In view of the matters specified above and other evidence presented, the opinion of Dr. DeVries was essentially that the proposed site for this landfill was not suitable because of the hydrology in the area, and given the state of current technology an environmentally safe landfill could not be built at the site. His view was generally that water resources under, in and around the site made the location especially non-conducive to a safe and environmentally sound waste disposal facility. In essence it was his opinion the design of the landfill, including the protective devices to be installed therein, would not be sufficient to protect against pollution of the water resources in the area, but instead a high probability existed that leachate would escape and contaminate the water resources. His ultimate opinion was that there was a very high probability downstream property owners — i.e., at least some of appellees — would suffer both ground and surface water pollution from operation of the landfill. He also noted that it was very difficult to completely remediate such pollution once it occurs, in either the groundwater or surface water systems.

As would be expected, appellant countered the opinions of Dr. DeVries with experts of its own. These experts gave opinions that the protective devices to be installed at the landfill were adequate to protect the water systems in the area and, essentially, there was a negligible possibility of pollution. Evidence was also presented that the landfill would be constructed and operated in compliance with DEQ regulations. There was also evidence presented that at least some of Dr. DeVries' views concerning the hydrology or hydrogeology in the area were incorrect, e.g., the view was presented that the direction of the water flow or movement of the confined aquifer(s) under the landfill site was to the northwest, which would be away from the property of appellees which generally lies north and east of the landfill site.

The trial court was not required to credit the testimony of the experts presented by appellant over the testimony of appellees' expert. In our view, sufficient evidence was presented to overcome any favorable presumption to be accorded to the decision of DEQ in permitting or authorizing the involved landfill. Based on our review of the record, the decision to permanently enjoin construction and operation of the solid waste disposal facility at its proposed location comported with applicable law and such decision cannot be said to have been clearly against the weight of the evidence. Thus, in this particular case, given the demonstrated sensitivity of the water resources in the area, and the probability operation of the proposed landfill would pollute the water resources of at least some of the appellees, we believe no reversible error occurred by the grant of a permanent injunction.

In sum, we find no reversible error in the trial court's admission of or reliance upon the expert testimony of Dr. DeVries. We also conclude the judgment of the trial court to permanently enjoin construction and operation of the landfill at the particular location should be and is *Affirmed*.

NOTES

1. *Snake-Handling.* In *State v. Pack*, 527 S.W.2d 99 (Tenn. 1975), the court permanently enjoined as a public nuisance the handling of poisonous snakes as part of a religious ceremony. Even though the conduct was based on the authority of *Mark* 16:17-18 (King James), the court held that the injunction did not abridge the first amendment freedom of religion rights of the religious group that engaged in snake handling:

> Under this record, showing as it does, the handling of snakes in a crowded church sanctuary, with virtually no safeguards, with children roaming about unattended, with the handlers so enraptured and entranced that they are in a virtual state of hysteria and acting under the compulsion of "anointment," we would be derelict in our duty if we did not hold that respondents and their confederates have combined and conspired to commit a public nuisance and plan to continue to do so. . . .
>
> Tennessee has the right to guard against the unnecessary creation of widows and orphans. Our state and nation have an interest in having a strong, healthy, robust, taxpaying citizenry capable of self-support and of bearing arms and adding to the resources and reserves of manpower. We, therefore, have a substantial and compelling state interest in the face of a clear and present danger so grave as to endanger paramount public interests.
>
> It has been held that a state may compel polio shots, regulate child labor, may require compulsory chest x-rays, may decree compulsory water fluoridation, may mandate vaccinations as a condition of school attendance, and may compel medical care to a dying patient.
>
> This holding is in no sense dependent upon the way or manner in which snakes are handled since it is not based upon the snake handling statute. Irrespective of its import, we hold that those who publicly handle snakes in the presence of other persons and those who are present aiding and abetting are guilty of creating and maintaining

a public nuisance. Yes, the state has a right to protect a person from himself and to demand that he protect his own life.

Suicide is not specifically denounced as a crime under out statutes but was a crime at the common law. Tennessee adopted the common law as it existed at the time of the separation of the colonies. An attempt to commit suicide is probably not an indictable offense under Tennessee law; however, such an attempt would constitute a grave public wrong, and we hold that the state has a compelling interest in protecting the life and promoting the health of its citizens.

2. *Focused Picketing Activity.* The court in *St. David's Episcopal Church v. Westboro Baptist Church*, 22 Kan. App. 537, 921 P.2d 821 (1996), affirmed a temporary restraining order issued by the trial court. The order restrained Westboro:

"1. From engaging in focused picketing of plaintiff on public property within 36 feet to the east, within 36 feet to the west, within 36 feet to the north and within 215 feet to the south of the church property owned and used for religious purposes by St. David's (the property located on the northwest corner of 17th and Gage) from a period beginning one-half hour before and ending one-half hour after a religious event. The distance is to be measured from all points along the property line of the church's property.

"2. That 'focused picketing' means picketing by driving, standing, sitting or walking at a deliberately slow speed or walking repeatedly past or around plaintiff's house of worship by any person governed by the order, while carrying a banner, placard, or sign. 'Religious event' means any scheduled worship service 5:30 P.M. Saturday, 8:00 A.M. and 10:30 P.M. Sundays, and any wedding, funeral, memorial service for the dead, or the observation of other sacraments, rituals, or celebrations which are announced by a sign posted within ten feet of the St. David's sign on 17th Street which announces its ordinary services.

"3. Defendant and the others described above likewise will be restrained from making any noise by singing, chanting, shouting or yelling, that can be heard through the walls of the church during any religious event.

"4. The Sheriff of Shawnee County, Kansas is directed to personally serve a copy of this Temporary Restraining Order on the Reverend Fred W. Phelps, as resident agent and personally as the pastor of defendant Westboro Baptist Church at 3701 West 12th Street, Topeka, Kansas, 66604, and upon any and all persons engaged in picketing or carrying or displaying any signs or placards at St. David's Episcopal Church at 3916 West 17th Street, Topeka, Shawnee County, Kansas."

The court found that the restraining order did not unconstitutionally infringe the defendant's rights of free speech and religion:

The express purpose of the temporary injunction in this case was to thwart potential violence around St. David's property during specific times of the day when prior encounters between the two groups occurred. The trial court also expressly stated it was not yet ruling upon whether the content of Westboro's message would be further restricted until after hearing evidence on the matter. The injunction imposed in this case, therefore, is content neutral. . . .

We do have a problem with the court's order proscribing noise contained in the third paragraph of its injunction order. The United States Supreme Court has upheld as constitutional some noise restrictions related to picketing activity. *See Madsen*, 512 U.S. 753, 114 S. Ct. at 2528, 129 L. Ed. 2d at 612. As Westboro points out, however, there is nothing in the affidavits which accompanied St. David's petition which suggests that the noise from Westboro's picketing activity was interfering with the worshipping by St. David's. Although the petition did request an injunction on such noise, St. David's has yet to provide the trial court, or this court, with any basis for such an injunction. On the present record, we reverse the trial court's order enjoining noise by Westboro.

3. *Floating Buffer Zones.* In *Schenck v. Pro-Choice Network of Western New York*, 117 S. Ct. 855 (1997), the trial court issued an injunction against protesters at abortion clinics. The injunction broadly banned

> "demonstrating within fifteen feet from either side or edge of, or in front of, doorways or doorway entrances, parking lot entrances, driveways and driveway entrances of such facilities" ("fixed buffer zones"), or "within 15 feet of any person or vehicle seeking access to or leaving such facilities" ("floating buffer zones"). In addition, the injunction clarified the "cease and desist" provision, specifying that once sidewalk counselors who had entered the buffer zones were required to "cease and desist" their counseling, they had to retreat 15 feet from the people they had been counseling and had to remain outside the boundaries of the buffer zones.

The United States Supreme Court declared the "floating buffer zones" portion of the injunction unconstitutional:

> We strike down the floating buffer zones around people entering and leaving the clinics because they burden more speech than is necessary to serve the relevant governmental interest. The floating buffer zones prevent defendants — except for two sidewalk counselors, while they are tolerated by the targeted individual — from communicating a message from a normal conversational distance or handing leaflets to people entering or leaving the clinics who are walking on the public sidewalks. This is a broad prohibition, both because of the type of speech that is restricted and the nature of the location. Leafletting and commenting on matters of public concern are classic forms of speech that lie at the heart of the First Amendment, and speech in public areas is at its most protected on public sidewalks, a prototypical example of a traditional public forum. On the other hand, we have before us a record that shows physically abusive conduct, harassment of the police that hampered law enforcement, and the tendency of even

peaceful conversations to devolve into aggressive and sometimes violent conduct. In some situations, a record of abusive conduct makes a prohibition on classic speech in limited parts of a public sidewalk permissible. We need not decide whether the governmental interests involved would ever justify some sort of zone of separation between individuals entering the clinics and protesters, measured by the distance between the two. We hold here that because this broad prohibition on speech "floats," it cannot be sustained on this record.

Since the buffer zone floats, protesters on the public sidewalks who wish (i) to communicate their message to an incoming or outgoing patient or clinic employee and (ii) to remain as close as possible (while maintaining an acceptable conversational distance) to this individual, must move as the individual moves, maintaining 15 feet of separation. But this would be difficult to accomplish at, for instance, the GYN Womenservices clinic in Buffalo, one of the respondent clinics. The sidewalk outside the clinic is 17-feet wide. This means that protesters who wish to walk alongside an individual entering or leaving the clinic [may be pushed into the street or may bump into others.] With clinic escorts leaving the clinic to pick up incoming patients and entering the clinic to drop them off, it would be quite difficult for a protester who wishes to engage in peaceful expressive activities to know how to remain in compliance with the injunction. This lack of certainty leads to a substantial risk that much more speech will be burdened than the injunction by its terms prohibits. That is, attempts to stand 15 feet from someone entering or leaving a clinic and to communicate a message — certainly protected on the face of the injunction — will be hazardous if one wishes to remain in compliance with the injunction.

4. *The Conditional Injunction.* In *Boomer v. Atlantic Cement Co.,* 26 N.Y.2d 219, 257 N.E.2d 870, 309 N.Y.S.2d 312 (1970), the court said:

Defendant operates a large cement plant near Albany. These are actions for injunction and damages by neighboring land owners alleging injury to property from dirt, smoke and vibration emanating from the plant. A nuisance has been found after trial, temporary damages have been allowed; but an injunction has been denied. . . .

The ground for the denial of injunction, notwithstanding the finding both that there is a nuisance and that plaintiffs have been damaged substantially, is the large disparity in economic consequences of the nuisance and of the injunction. This theory cannot, however, be sustained without overruling a doctrine which has been consistently reaffirmed in several leading cases in this court and which has never been disavowed here, namely that where a nuisance has been found and where there has been any substantial damage shown by the party complaining an injunction will be granted.

The rule in New York has been that such a nuisance will be enjoined although marked disparity be shown in economic consequence between the effect of the injunction and effect of the nuisance. . . .

This result at Special Term and at the Appellate Division is a departure from a rule that has become settled; but to follow the rule literally in these cases would be to close down the plant at once. This court is fully agreed to avoid that immediately drastic remedy; the difference in view is how best to avoid it. . . .

Thus it seems fair to both sides to grant permanent damages to plaintiffs which will terminate this private litigation. The theory of damage is the "servitude on land" of plaintiffs imposed by defendant's nuisance.

The judgment, by allowance of permanent damages imposing a servitude on land, which is the basis of the actions, would preclude future recovery by plaintiffs or their grantees.

This should be placed beyond debate by a provision of the judgment that the payment by defendant and the acceptance by plaintiffs of permanent damages found by the court shall be in compensation for a servitude on the land.

Although the Trial Term has found permanent damages as a possible basis of settlement of the litigation, on remission the court should be entirely free to re-examine this subject. It may again find the permanent damage already found; or make new findings.

The orders should be reversed, without costs, and the cases remitted to Supreme Court, Albany County to grant an injunction which shall be vacated upon payment by defendant of such amounts of permanent damage to the respective plaintiffs as shall for this purpose be determined by the court.

5. *Payback.* In *Spur Industries, Inc. v. Del E. Webb Dev. Co.*, 494 P.2d 700 (Ariz. 1972), plaintiff Webb's residential housing development grew until it came within smelling distance of defendant Spur's previously rural cattle feedlot, which thus became a nuisance to the residential area. Defendant was required to relocate or shut down. However, "[h]aving brought people to the nuisance to the foreseeable detriment of Spur, Webb must indemnify Spur for a reasonable amount of the cost of moving or shutting down."

LANGAN v. BELLINGER
203 A.D.2d 857, 611 N.Y.S.2d 59 (1994)

WEISS, JUSTICE.

Appeal from an order of the Supreme Court (Hughes, J.), entered May 21, 1993 in Schoharie County, which, *inter alia*, granted defendant's cross motion for summary judgment dismissing the complaint.

This lawsuit demonstrates that what may be music to the ears of some can, in certain circumstances, be a nuisance to the ears of others. Plaintiffs, who reside in the Village of Schoharie, Schoharie County, have commenced this action against their neighbor, the Presbyterian Church of the Town of Schoharie, seeking injunctive relief "from playing hourly chimes on a daily basis beginning at 8:00 o'clock in the forenoon and ending at 8:00 o'clock in the afternoon and from playing carillon music on a daily basis at 12:00 o'clock in the afternoon and at 6:00 o'clock in the afternoon," which plaintiff Julie Langan[4] avers "is a complete disruption of [her] family life, prevents a child from sleeping, and invades the privacy of [her] residence and creates unnecessary stress." The complaint characterizes the foregoing to be both a private nuisance and a violation of an ordinance of the Village of Schoharie. Plaintiffs moved by order to show cause for a preliminary injunction, in response to which defendant cross-moved for summary judgment dismissing the complaint. Supreme Court denied plaintiffs' motion, granted defendant's cross motion and dismissed the complaint. We affirm.

One may be liable for a private nuisance where the wrongful invasion of the use of another's land is intentional and unreasonable. The elements of such a private nuisance are "(1) an interference substantial in nature, (2) intentional in origin, (3) unreasonable in character, (4) with a person's property right to use and enjoy land, (5) caused by another's conduct in acting or failing to act" (*Copart Indus. v. Consolidated Edison Co. of N.Y.*, 41 N.Y.2d 564, 570, 394 N.Y.S.2d 169, 362 N.E.2d 968; *see*, Restatement (Second) of Torts, § 822). We note that the complaint appears to be defective in that it fails to allege two of the basic elements of private nuisance, *i.e.*, that the interference is substantial in nature or that it is unreasonable in character. For this reason alone, dismissal of the complaint would be appropriate.

Nonetheless, we similarly find dismissal on the ground found by Supreme Court to be proper. Defendant's moving papers included the sworn affidavit of and report by Wayne Sikora, an expert in noise management, which showed that the sound levels emanating from the bells and chimes were no greater than the sound from a passing automobile, of which some 6,500 passed plaintiffs' properties each day. This document, together with affidavits from the pastor of the church, defense counsel and affidavits from 15 other Village residents who found the bells and chimes to be pleasant, as well as an affidavit from the Village Mayor and Village Attorney showing there was no violation of an ordinance, constituted a prima facie showing of entitlement to summary judgment.

In opposition, plaintiffs offered only their own affidavits and that of their attorney, all of which were lacking in objective evidence to either rebut the opinion of defendant's expert or demonstrate that the music and chimes constituted a nuisance. Because plaintiffs failed to meet their burden of coming forward with proof in evidentiary form to demonstrate the existence of factual issues requiring a trial, summary judgment dismissing the complaint was entirely appropriate. We further note that opposition which rests only on discrepancies between opposing papers and relates solely to matters of credibility of conflicting opinions of experts will not suffice.

Finally, we find that Supreme Court correctly denied plaintiffs' applications for preliminary injunctive relief in the absence of any demonstration of the probability of success in the lawsuit.

---

[4] Langan and the other plaintiff, Ernest Eggers, both reside approximately 250 feet from the church.

NOTES

1. *Ordinary Dust and Noise.* The plaintiffs in *Karpiak v. Russo*, 676 A.2d 270 (Pa. Super. 1996), sued defendants for dust and noise created by defendants' landscaping business. The court denied plaintiffs' claims:

> Appellants, Paul and Connie Karpiak, Francis and Judith Bodnar, Andrew and Lucille Tomko, and James and Barbara Werley, appeal the September 12, 1995 order wherein the trial court refused to lift a compulsory nonsuit entered at trial. This action involves allegations of nuisance, trespass, violation of the zoning laws, and was instituted against appellees, J.S. and Patricia Russo, Plum Boro Supply Company J.S. Russo Construction Company, and The Dixie Corporation, as the result of their operation of a landscaping supply business on Saltsburg Road in Plum Borough. We affirm.
>
> This action was instituted by home-owners who live near appellees' landscaping supply business. Appellants claimed that the business was a public and private nuisance, constituted a trespass against their property, and violated the local zoning laws. They also requested punitive damages. Since 1984, appellees have been in the business of selling topsoil, shredded bark, compost, sand, and river rock at the intersection of Saltsburg Road and Willow Village Drive, where appellants reside or resided. Saltsburg Road is traveled heavily with trucks, buses, and many cars. . . .
>
> It is significant that none of the appellants testified as to any *damages* they have incurred as a result of the conduct of the appellees' business. Other than Mr. Tomko, who testified that he had to clean his car, house, windows, and outside furniture, there was no evidence that appellees' business caused any damage to appellants' properties.
>
> In light of this evidence, the trial court's decision clearly was correct. Dust and noise are the two intrusions complained about by appellants. The noise, meanwhile, is during daylight hours and occurs, for the most part, when all but one appellant is at work. *Compare Anderson v. Guerrein Sky-Way Amusement Co.*, 346 Pa. 80, 29 A.2d 682 (1943) (fifty-four plaintiffs brought action against drive-in theatre which operated with bright lights and loud noise inconsistent with the residential character of the neighborhood and prevented plaintiffs from sleeping). Furthermore, this noise *is not out of character with the area* since appellants admitted that Saltsburg Road is traveled heavily with trucks, buses, and cars, which make the same noises as appellees' machinery which consists of backhoes, loaders, and trucks. *Compare Bedminster Township v. Vargo Dragway, Inc.*, 434 Pa. 100, 253 A.2d 659 (1969) (noise from drag cars could be heard three miles away in this residential and farming community, and people who lived one mile away could not hear themselves talk and had their windows rattle from the noise).
>
> In *Molony v. Pounds*, 361 Pa. 498, 64 A.2d 892 (1949), our Supreme Court reversed the issuance of an injunction against a restaurant. The injunction was issued from the hours of 1:00 A.M. to 6:00 A.M. because

the restaurant emanated noise and foul odors. The Court noted that no one is entitled to absolute quiet in the enjoyment of their property and that all that is required is that the degree of quietness be consistent with the standard of comfort in the relevant locality. The Court opined that people who reside in a neighborhood with businesses close by must compromise their comfort to the commercial necessities of the business.

Herein, appellees' property unquestionably was zoned business when they started selling landscaping supplies. While other businesses in the area are largely office buildings, the evidence establishes that Saltsburg Road is traveled heavily and is noisy during the same hours when appellees operate their business. Saltsburg Road is busy with vehicular traffic and appellees' noise is from vehicles.

Now we address whether the dust is sufficient to constitute a nuisance. We note that this dust all emanates from benign natural substances. These substances are topsoil, rock, sand, and vegetable manure. Further, the dust is neither poisonous nor harmful. We also note no one testified that the dust causes physical ailments such as dizziness, headaches, and vomiting.

Therefore, appellants' attempt to equate this case with that of *Evans v. Moffat*, 192 Pa. Super. 204, 160 A.2d 465 (1960), is unconvincing. In *Evans*, plaintiffs suffered physical symptoms of headaches, nausea, and dizziness from defendant's release of noxious, poisonous, and foul-smelling gases emanating from a mine refuse dump.

The production of a sufficient amount of dust from a business can constitute a nuisance as long as the dust causes *significant* harm to the aggrieved party. *Harford Penn-Cann Service, Inc. v. Zymblosky*, 378 Pa. Super. 578, 549 A.2d 208 (1988). Herein, the dust created does not rise to that level. There was no evidence that the dust caused appellants health problems or that it affected their ability to carry on their daily activities. This can be contrasted to the situation present in *Harford*, where the business generated such a vast amount of dust that the trial court issued an injunction based on a finding that the plaintiffs experienced health problems and lost business due [to the dust].

2. *Inadequate Proof*. Landowners filed a suit against a paper mill, alleging nuisance and the infliction of emotional distress, *Leaf River Forest Prods. v. Ferguson*, 662 So. 2d 648 (Miss. 1995). The court held the plaintiffs failed to establish their claims:

Eleven plaintiffs sued Georgia-Pacific Corporation, Great Northern Nekoosa Corporation, Leaf River Corporation, and Leaf River Forest Products, Inc., in Jackson County Circuit Court, alleging that the defendants had, through operation of the Leaf River Paper Mill, discharged harmful substances into the Leaf and Pascagoula Rivers, thereby causing the plaintiffs personal injury and property damage. After filing two amended complaints the three remaining plaintiffs were Thomas Ferguson, Jr., his wife, Bonnie Jane Ferguson, and

Louise H. Mitchell. After a trial the jury found in favor of the appellants, Leaf River Forest Products, Inc., et al., as to all of the claims made by the appellee, Louise H. Mitchell. Further, the jury found in favor of the appellants, Leaf River Forest Products, Inc., et al. as to any trespass committed against the appellee's property by the placing of any foreign substance on the said property. The jury did award the Fergusons $10,000.00 each on their nuisance claim; $90,000.00 each on their emotional distress claim; and $3,000,000.00 in punitive damages. After consideration of the briefs, a voluminous record and oral argument, we find that the evidence is insufficient to support verdicts based either on infliction of emotional distress or nuisance. Accordingly, we reverse and render judgment in favor of the defendants/appellants.

We have before found that emotional distress inflicted either negligently or intentionally is compensable. However, emotional distress based on the fear of a future illness must await a manifestation of that illness or be supported by substantial exposure to the danger, and be supported by medical or scientific evidence so that there is a rational basis for the emotional fear. . . .

We find as to nuisance that there is little evidence and scarce testimony of any invasion by substance or odor by the defendants as to the plaintiffs' specific property. Without such there can be no nuisance. . . .

[T]he Court may someday recognize the tort of infliction of emotional distress based on fear of future disease. However, this day we find that the evidence is insufficient in this case to hold that the appellants may be liable for infliction of emotional distress based on intentional, willful, wanton or grossly negligent conduct. The common thread running through this issue is a lack of proof. The Fergusons failed to have their persons or their property tested for dioxin. They place before the jury evidence of the danger of dioxin, but then fail to show that dioxin is present on their land or in their body. They produce evidence of dioxin in the area immediately south of the Mill and no evidence of dioxin in waters in the immediate area of their property. They have shown no physical or personal injury. Their claims are too remote as to real illness and as to proximity to the alleged source of their fears. They are afraid of what may happen in the future but have refused to take available steps that could alleviate or justify those fears. Appellants' conduct in the operation of the Leaf River Mill and their attempts to deal with the dioxin problem simply do not meet the necessary standard of intentional, willful, wanton, or grossly negligent. The circuit court's judgment based on emotional distress is reversed and rendered. . . .

There was testimony that the Pascagoula had darkened, and river banks and sand bars had also been discolored. There was no testimony from O.V. Stringer or Kenneth McGuire as to the location of their properties in relation to the Ferguson property, or where they had seen the discoloration in the Pascagoula. There was no testimony that the

D. ASSESSING PROOF AND FASHIONING REMEDIES 1151

Fergusons' property had been darkened, or that the river had left a dark residue on their land or their buildings. There was no testimony showing the appellants to be the cause of this color change except that the change had been noticed after the appellants began operation of the mill. Some of the appellees' witnesses noticed the color change around 1985; other did not until 1990. Guy Blankinship never mentioned any damage to the property except for the condition of the river and the resulting stigma. We find that the evidence presented is insufficient to constitute a significant interference with the Fergusons' use and enjoyment of their property. We further find that mere stigma, supported by tests showing dioxin contamination no closer than eighty river miles north of the alleged damage, is not sufficient evidence of compensable injury.

3. *Adequate Proof.* The plaintiffs in *Harris v. Town of Lincoln*, 668 A.2d 321 (R.I. 1995), contended that defendants' nearby sewer pumping station constituted a nuisance:

In 1979 plaintiffs purchased residential property at 31 Maria Street in Lincoln, Rhode Island (plaintiffs' property). In June 1987 plaintiffs sought and were granted approval by the Zoning Board of the Town of Lincoln to build an addition to their home. At that time, plaintiffs attempted to purchase a lot owned by defendants, adjacent to plaintiffs' property, but were told the lot was not for sale and would only be used for access to the Blackstone Canal.

On February 15, 1988, however, the town, as part of a townwide sewer project, began construction of a sewer pumping station on that adjacent lot. The sewer pumping station consisted of a covered wet well measuring four feet by six feet and a dry well measuring six feet by six feet along a centrifugal pump, according to Donald D'Anjou (D'Anjou), a supervisor for the town's sewer department, who testified at trial. The station operates by trapping solid waste on a grate that is raked and washed down twice per week. When the sewage in the wet well reaches a certain level, the pump turns on and the effluent is pumped to a treatment plant. Effluent remains in the wet well, however, when the station is not pumping. A fan circulates air into the building that encloses the two wells while vents circulate air that is released into the atmosphere.

Although plaintiffs complained to the town regarding the proximity of the pumping station to their home soon after construction began, the pumping station was, nevertheless, constructed twenty-six feet from plaintiffs' property line. On February 8, 1989, plaintiffs brought the instant action to claim damages and to enjoin defendants from operating the pumping station. Mr. Harris testified that since the pumping station began operating in 1989, he has heard the station's generator "hundreds of times." The plaintiffs testified that during the generator's operation, they felt vibrations, heard noise, and smelled odors. Mr. Harris likened the generator's noise inside his home to "a Mack diesel truck right next to your door." According to plaintiffs' testimony, operation of the generator created diesel fumes, and the pumping station itself emitted sewage odors. Mr. Harris testified that the fumes and smells were present "[a]ll the time" but that they were at their worst in the summer months.

As a consequence of the pumping station's emission of noises, odors, and vibrations, plaintiffs claimed that the use and enjoyment of their property had been disrupted. The plaintiffs testified that they spent less time outside on their property, could not use their pool or have cookouts during the summer, and were no longer able to entertain in their backyard. The plaintiffs' testimony was buttressed by the testimony of their babysitter as well as several friends and neighbors who testified that they had experienced such noises, vibrations, and odors when visiting plaintiffs' home. A licensed real estate broker, Jo-Anne Siminski, testified that her analysis revealed a devaluation of plaintiffs' property of approximately $50,000 — a decline in value from $225,000 to $174,900. . . .

The trial justice enjoined the town from operating the pumping station and ordered it to relocate the station or to develop plans for a suitable alternative to the Maria Street site. In addition, the trial justice awarded plaintiffs $400 per month until the nuisance was abated as compensation for the value of the property taken by the town and for interference with plaintiffs' use and enjoyment of their home. . . .

In summary, we conclude, first, that the trial justice properly found that the operation of the sewage pumping station in close proximity to the plaintiffs' property created a private nuisance, and we affirm that finding. Second, we hold that the trial justice erred in finding that the operation of the pumping station constituted a constructive taking of the plaintiffs' property, and consequently we vacate that finding. Third, we hold that the trial justice did not err in granting monetary damages and injunctive relief, although we modify the damage award and the relief as follows. The plaintiffs are awarded $400 per month as damages for the interference with the use and enjoyment of their property, which damages shall be awarded for the period between the date of the trial justice's order of August 10, 1993, and continuing to the date of the relocation of the facility in accordance with the terms set forth by the trial justice.

The town may, in the alternative, exercise its power of eminent domain and purchase the plaintiffs' property for a fair-market value, which value may be ascertained after an additional evidentiary hearing, if required, in which case the $400 monthly payments will terminate at the purchase date. Last, we affirm the trial justice's denial of the defendants' motion to modify the injunction. We return the case to the Superior Court for proceedings in accordance with this opinion.

4. *Continuing (Abatable) Versus Permanent (Non-Abatable) Nuisances*. The court in *Mangini v. Aerojet-Gen'l Corp.*, 912 P.2d 1220 (Cal. 1996), stated:

We granted review to examine the law of nuisance as it bears on a suit seeking damages for the contamination of land through the

D. ASSESSING PROOF AND FASHIONING REMEDIES 1153

dumping of toxic wastes. Specifically, we consider the requirement that, in attempting to avoid the bar of the statute of limitations by demonstrating that the nuisance is "continuing" (or "temporary") rather than "permanent," the plaintiff must present substantial evidence that the contaminated condition is one that is both subject to remediation (or cleanup) and that the cost of cleanup is "reasonable." . . .

It appears that over 10 years, Aerojet routinely dumped and burned on the Cavitt acreage toxic solid fuel components, amounting to several million pounds, including, to adopt Aerojet's characterization, "quantities of waste sludge consisting of highly explosive rocket propellants containing a cleaning solvent" known as trichloro ethyleen (or TCE) that is toxic to human and animal life. . . .

In Lambie's opinion, remediating the site could cost far more than $20 million, based on the assumption that only 12.5 acres of the 2,400 acres were excavated to a depth of 3 feet. That figure might jump, the witness testified, to as high as $75 million if as much as 20 percent of the acreage required treatment to a depth of 6 feet. Remediation would be very costly, Lambie concluded, "it could be an extremely large number." Plaintiffs' attorney conceded these uncertainties in the cost of cleanup in his closing remarks to the jury: "[N]obody really knows how much is there, where it is, where the chemicals are, or how much it's going to cost to abate the chemicals," he stated. "So I guess the bottom line, if you ask yourself the question, how bad really is this site, the answer's got to be you just don't know." . . .

Because, as the Court of Appeal put it, plaintiffs' proof established that "no one knows how bad the contamination is or how to remedy it," it followed that plaintiffs had failed to present substantial evidence that the contamination was capable of being abated *at a reasonable cost*. And because the answer to the question whether a particular nuisance is continuing or permanent is whether it is "abatable" — reasonable cost being a component of "abatability" — plaintiffs had failed to make their case. It followed that their claims for damages were barred by the three year statute of limitations prescribed by Code of Civil Procedure section 338, subdivision (b), because, the evidence showed, plaintiffs had notice of the contamination of their land at least as early as 1984, more than three years before their complaint was filed. . . .

A dissent contended:

The majority, adopting verbatim the opinion of the Court of Appeal, now hold that plaintiffs can recover nothing, either now or in the future, because they have not demonstrated that the contamination of their property can be abated at a "reasonable" cost. They reason that the nuisance must be deemed "permanent" and the claim is, accordingly, time-barred.

I disagree. No previous case has required that the costs of remediating a nuisance are dispositive of the issue whether it is "continuing" or "permanent." Moreover, through no fault of plaintiffs, the extent of feasible remediation and its costs may require years to determine. That does not mean, however, that the nuisance in this case cannot or will not eventually be abated — at least to the extent that governmental agencies determine is cost efficient and feasible — and is thus "permanent." . . .

The test for classifying nuisances as either continuing or permanent thus turns on whether the nuisance can be abated, or is such that the court will not enjoin its continuance. In this case, Aerojet is *not* privileged to continue the nuisance; nor is it "improbable as a practical matter that the nuisance can or will be abated." (*Spaulding v. Cameron*, 38 Cal. 2d at p. 268, 239 P.2d 625.) Indeed, it has apparently agreed to remediate it. Until that remediation takes place, plaintiffs should be permitted to elect a remedy for "continuing" nuisance. Damages for such "continuing" nuisance are limited, however, to recovery for actual injury suffered within the three years immediately preceding.

The distinction between continuing and permanent nuisance has *res judicata* effects. As the court said in *Hoffman v. United Iron and Metal Co.*, 108 Md. App. 117, 671 A.2d 55 (1996):

A suit for damages as a result of a permanent nuisance must be brought within three years of the time that the permanency of the condition becomes manifest to a reasonably prudent person. *Goldstein*, 285 Md. At 689, 404 A.2d 1064 [1979]. This is so because of the assumptions "that the nuisance will continue into the indefinite future, that it will continue to cause injury to the land, and that the only appropriate measure of damages is permanent reduction in the market value of the property resulting from the nuisance." *Id*. at 682, 404 A.2d 1064. Thus, damages for the permanent diminution in the market value of the land caused by a nuisance may only be recovered if the nuisance is deemed permanent. See *Goldstein*, 285 Md. At 682, 404 A.2d 1064. Plaintiffs must sue for past, present, and prospective damages all at once because there is only one cause of action for a permanent nuisance.

On the other hand, each day's continuance of a temporary nuisance creates a new cause of action. See *Goldstein*, 285 Md. At 682, 404 A.2d 1064. Therefore, "successive actions may be brought for damages for each invasion of the plaintiff's land until the period of prescription has elapsed, but recovery may only be had for damages actually sustained, other than permanent reduction in the market value of the property, within three years of the filing of the action." *Id*. at 690 n. 4, 404 A.2d 1064.

5. *Electromagnetic Field (EMF) Litigation*. Numerous claims have been made regarding alleged EMF injuries:

According to a July 1992 article in *Science* magazine, as many as 20 million people presently may be exposed to higher than normal levels of EMF just from the 642,000 circuit miles of high-voltage transmission lines in the United States alone. (Normal levels are said to range from .5 mg to 1.5 mg.) An additional 12,600 circuit miles of such transmission lines are scheduled for construction by the year 2000.

Added to the number of people exposed to EMF from household or workplace electrical wiring, appliances and other sources, the scope is immense. (An electric razor, for example, can generate a magnetic field of as much as 200 mg at five inches.)

Concern about EMF health effects go back at least three decades. The first studies, conducted in the Soviet Union 30 years ago, suggested a link between exposure to electric fields and certain chronic afflictions such as headaches, fatigue and nausea. Research in the West proceeded throughout the 1970s without replicating the Soviet results and gaining little attention.

Then, in 1979 the results of a major epidemiological study on EMF conducted in the Denver area were published. They seemed to show an association between exposure to EMF from powerlines and increased incidence of childhood cancer, though serious questions have since arisen about the methodology used.

Over 35 major studies conducted since then in this country and abroad have produced results best characterized as inconclusive and sometimes conflicting. A 1990 analysis by the Environmental Protection Agency of previous studies on EMF exposure and the incidence of cancer concluded only that an increasing amount of data shows "a consistent pattern of response which suggests, but does not prove, a causal link."

Meanwhile, a report released by the White House Office of Science and Technology Policy claimed that "there is no convincing evidence in the published literature to support the contention that exposures to . . . EMF generated by sources such as household appliances, video display terminals and local powerlines are demonstrable health risks." Still, the studies have succeeded in arousing public concern.

An understanding of the obstacles confronting EMF research begins with the nature of ailments attributed to EMF exposure. Those most often cited are various forms of cancer, particularly childhood leukemia. A myriad of other disorders, including birth defects, miscarriages and neurological dysfunctions also are alleged to result from exposure to EMF.

But the pathology of these afflictions is poorly understood. Causes are obscure and may be rooted in multiple environmental as well as hereditary factors.

Roy W. Krieger, *On the Line*, A.B.A.J. 42 (Jan. 1994).

6. *Repetitive Stress Injury*. A major breakthrough in repetitive stress injury litigation was reported in the American Bar Journal:

Three plaintiffs were a charm for a Brooklyn jury in a lawsuit against Digital Equipment Corp. Their $5.9 million award is the first jury verdict against a keyboard manufacturer for repetitive stress injuries suffered by office workers.

The jury found in December that the defendant failed to warn the three plaintiffs about the dangers of using the Digital LK201 keyboard. The injured women had experienced wrist and spinal ailments after using the product. *Madden v. Digital Equipment Corp.*, No. 94-CV1427 (E.D.N.Y.).

U.S. District Judge Jack Weinstein had denied a defense motion to sever the three cases, making the defense job triply difficult. Digital alleged one plaintiff's injuries were caused by existing medical conditions and another by hobbies. In the third case, it claimed there were no injuries.

The company, headquartered in Maynard, Mass., plans to move to set aside the verdict and to appeal if the motion is denied. "One verdict is not a trend, by any definition," says Digital's lead lawyer, Kenneth J. King of Beatie, King & Abate in New York City.

But the lead attorney for the plaintiffs says the award should not be portrayed as an aberration because several hundred keyboard cases brought by his firm have resulted in settlements. "It's a bigger picture than [the manufacturers] are letting on," says Steven J. Phillips of Levy Phillips & Konigsberg in New York City.

The firm has about 900 pending repetitive stress injury cases, the majority of which are against keyboard manufactureres. Symptomots of RSI range from numbness and tingling sensations to severe pain; the malady currently consumes about one-third of all workers compensation dollars. Many RSI sufferers have carpal tunnel syndrome, which causes pain in the hand, wrist and lower arm.

Eric Milstone, *Keyed Up, Repetitive Stressed Out*, A.B.A.J. 22 (Feb. 1997).

PROBLEM

Plaintiffs worked as employees in a nuclear power plant licensed to operate under federal law. The plant was in violation of its license because it had failed to report "an unplanned release of quantities of fission products in excess of allowable limits," in violation of 42 U.S.C. § 2133(f). The release occurred from cigarette smoking damage caused by one of the employees, a cigarette smoker. Prior to the release, it was not scientifically knowable that such damage could be caused by smoking.

About half of the employees smoked while at work. All the employees suffered injury from the workplace smoking. They were also all injured by the unplanned release of fission products.

Please discuss the claims the employees may have against the nuclear plant, and against the manufacturers of the cigarettes smoked by the employees.

Chapter 18
DEFAMATION AND INVASION OF PRIVACY

A. INTRODUCTION

The torts of defamation and invasion of privacy (with the exception of intrusion into seclusion) can be characterized as communicative torts — that is, torts arising from the spoken or written word. Other torts may also involve communication, and insofar as they do the concerns of this chapter are implicated.

There is necessarily a good deal of overlap in this chapter with the subject matter of other chapters, e.g., misrepresentation, intentional infliction of emotional distress, intrusion into seclusion as it relates to trespass, and appropriation of name or likeness, a privacy tort which is closely related to the materials in the business torts chapter. It is the nature of tort law, however, to be interwoven, and the material here presents no exception. One of the challenges for the student is to relate the various fields of tort law to each other.

In the area of defamation the United States Supreme Court has energetically intervened, imposing constitutional restrictions based on first amendment free speech considerations. The Court has heightened fault requirements, and it is unclear whether these requirements apply to other communicative torts as well.

The United States has not waived sovereign immunity for claims based on libel, slander or misrepresentation, 28 U.S.C. § 2680(h). But if these claims are based on constitutional violations, U.S. employees (although presumably not the United States) remain liable, 28 U.S.C. § 2679(b)(2)(A). Why this curious mosaic?

The requirement of privity is alive and well with regard to the tort of misrepresentation — at least where physical injury to person or property is not involved. Apparently the privity requirement does not implicate the constitution in any way.

Privity has never been a requirement for defamation or invasion of privacy. Indeed, the nature of these torts involves a communication with someone other than the tort victim. But many misrepresentations involve a communication with third parties as well. Why is privity sometimes required here, instead of the usual tort requirement of foreseeability of harm? Are defamation and privacy injuries more akin to personal injuries, where privity is not required? Defamation, invasion of privacy and misrepresentation may all involve psychic injuries, and dignitary offense.

B. DEFAMATION

PROBLEM

Defendant trained a parrot to say defamatory things about the plaintiff. Is this libel or slander?

Defendant trained a chimpanzee to follow plaintiff about and make obscene gestures. Is this libel or slander?

Finally, defendant hired an airplane pilot to sky-write obscene remarks in the air about the plaintiff. Libel or slander?

LENT v. HUNTOON
143 Vt. 539, 470 A.2d 1162 (1983)

UNDERWOOD, J.

Defendants appeal from a verdict and judgment rendered in the Rutland Superior Court. The jury found the defendants liable for defamation and awarded plaintiff a total of $40,000 in compensatory and punitive damages. We affirm the judgment.

. . . Plaintiff worked for Huntoon Business Machines, Inc. (Huntoon Corporation) from 1964 until his employment was terminated in 1977 — a period of thirteen years. During that time he worked his way up to the position of service manager. At the time he was hired, in 1964, the plaintiff informed defendant H. J. Huntoon (Huntoon) that he was on probation for a criminal conviction and that he had once been confined to the base for a period of time for a minor offense during his service in the Air Force. Defendants hired plaintiff with full knowledge of these events.

In the early part of 1977, plaintiff informed Huntoon that he would be leaving his job at Huntoon Corporation as he was moving to Florida as soon as he and his wife could sell their house. He offered to stay on long enough to train his successor. Shortly thereafter, and without any prior notice, Huntoon told plaintiff that he was discharged.

Plaintiff was unable to sell his house and so decided to remain in Rutland. In August of 1977, he started his own business equipment sales and service business, Lent Business Machines. Early in March of 1978, plaintiff was awarded a cash register sales and service franchise formerly held by the Huntoon Corporation. Thus, plaintiff and Huntoon Corporation became direct competitors. About this same time, plaintiff became aware that defendants sent a letter to the cash register franchise customers who were formerly serviced by Huntoon Corporation and for whose business both the plaintiff and defendants were then vying. The letter, which indicated that plaintiff had been discharged for "sound business reasons," formed the basis of plaintiff's libel count. Plaintiff asserted that the letter, taken in its totality, was defamatory since it implied that he was fired because of some dishonesty or incompetence. There was evidence that the letter caused plaintiff to become estranged from some of his customers, to suffer physical and emotional malaise, and to neglect his business to the point where it nearly collapsed.

About this time, plaintiff became aware of numerous verbal statements made about him by Huntoon to customers sought after by both plaintiff and defendants. Testimony revealed that these statements asserted that plaintiff had a criminal "record a mile long," had stolen merchandise from the defendants, had stolen money from the cash register of Huntoon Corporation, was an incompetent serviceman, and was generally untrustworthy. Testimony indicated that most of these statements were made by Huntoon in competitive business situations. Plaintiff asked Huntoon to stop making the statements, apparently to no avail, as there was further testimony that some of the statements were made even after plaintiff's lawsuit was initiated. Some testimony indicated that the defendants were fully satisfied with plaintiff's work prior to termination and had never complained about any thefts by plaintiff prior to his leaving Huntoon Corporation. Defendants also knew he intended to leave his job voluntarily and was not fired. . . .

Defamation is comprised of the complementary torts of libel and slander. Although these torts evolved from different antecedents, both were eventually cognizable in the King's courts in England prior to reception of the common law in Vermont. Because of the permanence of the written word, libel was considered the more serious tort, with slander, or the spoken word, considered the less serious. The distinction between written and spoken defamation has resulted in a host of special rules with corresponding special legal terminology. Herein lies much of the confusion which abounds even today.

Libel is generally considered "actionable per se"; that is, the plaintiff need not allege or prove that he or she suffered any "special damages" as a direct or proximate result of the libel. Special damages, in short, are presumed. Special damages have a unique connotation in the law of defamation. Special damages are those of a pecuniary nature, and historically they have included loss of customers or business, loss of contracts, or loss of employment. In addition,

> modern decisions have shown some tendency to liberalize the old rule, and to find pecuniary loss when the plaintiff has been deprived of benefit which has a more or less indirect financial value to him. Thus the loss of the society, companionship and association of friends may be sufficient when . . . it can be found to have a money value.

Restatement (Second) of Torts § 575 comment b, at 198 (1977).

Slander, on the other hand, is generally not actionable per se; that is, special damages are not presumed and must be alleged and proven. Several kinds of slander, however, were identified at English common law as more serious than others and these were held to be actionable per se. Spoken defamation involving (1) imputation of a crime, (2) statements injurious to one's trade, business or occupation, or (3) charges of having a loathsome disease were deemed slander per se and were actionable without proof of special damages. The decisions of our Court are in accord with these common law exceptions. Most American jurisdictions added still a fourth exception: charging a woman to be unchaste. Thus "actionable per se" simply means special damages need not be proved in libel actions or in those slander actions which fall into one of the exceptions categorized as slander per se.

The general elements of a private action for defamation (libel and/or slander) are: (1) a false and defamatory statement concerning another; (2) some negligence, or greater fault, in publishing the statement; (3) publication to at least one third person; (4) lack of privilege in the publication; (5) special damages, unless actionable per se; and (6) some actual harm so as to warrant compensatory damages.

For reasons probably lost in history, a special rule of procedure developed for the trial of a defamation action. Once the plaintiff's evidence was in, the court had to determine whether the written or spoken words were defamatory as a matter of law. If the court was in doubt because the connotation of the written or spoken words was ambiguous, then the court had to submit the question to the jury to decide. In libel actions, when the court determined that the written words were libelous as a matter of law, the term "libel per se" was used. This unfortunate terminology when used in conjunction with such terms as "slander per se" and "actionable per se" has greatly confused courts and counsel. "Libel per se" simply means defamatory as a matter of law. Since all libel is actionable per se, it makes no difference whether the court rules that the written words are defamatory as a matter of law, or that the written words are ambiguous and the jury determines that there is defamation; in each instance special damages need not be proven.

A further complication in the semantics of defamation law arose when the courts embarked upon the "spurious" concept of a "libel per quod." This rule only served to compound an already confusing area of the law of torts. Being written, libel is generally evaluated by examining the four corners of the writing itself. A letter or newspaper article can be introduced at trial and its defamatory nature determined by judge or jury as appropriate. Some writings, however, are seemingly innocent in and of themselves, and resort must be had to extrinsic evidence to determine if they have defamatory qualities. If the writing together with the extrinsic evidence constitutes defamation, such a writing is referred to as "libel per quod" in several American jurisdictions. These jurisdictions require that special damages be proven for libel per quod, unless the libel falls into one of the exceptions we previously mentioned as constituting slander per se. Thus, under this rule, the simple fact that extrinsic evidence must be used to prove the defamatory nature of a libel prevents it from being "actionable per se" and special damages must be proven.

A scholarly debate concerning libel per quod took place before the Restatement (Second) of Torts was published. Thereafter, section 569 of the Restatement reflects the simpler rule and rejects any notion of libel per quod.

Vermont's reported decisions do not recognize libel per quod, and we adhere to the wisdom of that course today. We hold that libel, whether defamatory on the face of the writing alone or with the aid of extrinsic evidence, is actionable per se. Our previous use of the term libel per se in no way, directly or inferentially, encompasses the rule of libel per quod. In the appropriate circumstances we recognize that libel per se may be found either solely from the writing or from the writing together with extrinsic evidence. Similarly the question of whether an ambiguous writing is defamatory or not is a jury question under either set of circumstances.

Given the great confusion in this area, we urge the future use of the term "libel as a matter of law" in situations where "libel per se" has been used in the past. "Libel as a matter of law" and where appropriate "slander as a matter of law" accurately identify the issue as one of law for the preliminary determination of the trial court.

In the case before us the pleadings include one count sounding in libel and one count sounding in slander. Two defenses to these allegations of defamation are raised: truth and privilege. Truth, of course, defeats the action and is a complete defense to defamation. The privilege raised here is a conditional privilege which may be overcome by a showing of malice.[1] The defendants allege a privilege to protect their legitimate business interests. This privilege is recognized in Restatement (Second) of Torts, *supra,* § 595 comment d, and we hold it to be applicable in Vermont. The burden of proving the privilege is on the defendants. A showing of malice, however, may defeat the conditional privilege, Prosser, Handbook of the Law of Torts, at 794, but in such instance the plaintiff must show malice by clear and convincing proof. In this sense malice may be either actual or implied. The court will infer malice upon a showing that the defendant knew the statement was false or acted with reckless disregard of its truth. Actual malice includes spiteful or wanton conduct.

This case also raises the issue of general and punitive damages in defamation. At the outset, we must observe that even though libel and some forms of slander are actionable per se and special damages need not be proven, a plaintiff can no longer recover general damages without a showing of some harm. In *Gertz v. Robert Welch, Inc.,* 418 U.S. 323, 41 L. Ed. 2d 789, 94 S. Ct. 2997 (1974), later app. 680 F.2d 527 (7th Cir. 1982) cert. denied 459 U.S. 1226, 75 L. Ed. 2d 467, 103 S. Ct. 1233 (1983), the United States Supreme Court noted that state remedies for defamation must be restricted "to compensation for *actual injury.*" 418 U.S. at 349, 94 S. Ct. at 3001 (emphasis added). This, of course, applies to general or compensatory damages that "include impairment of reputation and standing in the community, personal humiliation, and mental anguish and suffering." We are persuaded and now hold that liability for defamation must logically be based on some showing of harm to the plaintiff. Thus, Vermont will require defamation plaintiffs to demonstrate some "actual harm" as a prerequisite to recovering general damages. . . . In summary, defamation that is actionable per se will require some showing of actual harm, but not of special damages before recovery of general, or compensatory, damages. This sound rule is reflected in the Restatement, § 621. Finally, this case raises the question of punitive damages. Once general (compensatory) damages are established, punitive damages may be awarded on a showing of actual malice,[2] but actual malice may not be considered to

---

[1] Malice is raised in this case in two separate contexts: malice must be shown to defeat a conditional privilege, and malice must be shown before the jury can consider punitive damages. Although the same evidence may be used to prove both kinds of malice, as legal elements they operate independently.

[2] "Actual" is used here to emphasize the factual basis of this malice. Since punitive damages are within the jury's discretion, they must be based on "actual" evidence of malice, rather than implied or constructive malice.

enhance compensatory damages. "[Malice] may be shown by conduct manifesting personal ill will or carried out under circumstances evidencing insult or oppression, or even by conduct showing a reckless or wanton disregard of one's rights." *Shortle v. Central Vermont Public Service Corp.,* 137 Vt. 32, 33, 399 A.2d 517, 518 (1979). Malice supporting punitive damages may be shown by proving that the defendant repeated the defamatory statement, especially when the repetition occurred after commencement of the lawsuit.

Once malice sufficient to entitle plaintiff to punitive damages has been shown, the plaintiff may present evidence of defendant's financial condition: "Where exemplary damages are awardable . . . the defendant's pecuniary ability may be considered in order to determine what would be a just punishment for him." *Kidder v. Bacon,* 74 Vt. 263, 274, 52 A. 322, 324 (1902).

The foregoing reviews the law of defamation raised in this appeal. We turn now to the specific issues raised by defendants.

[The court found the trial court committed no error in denying defendant's motions for j.n.o.v., for a new trial, and for remittitur.]

NOTES

1. *Special Damage.* Suppose that plaintiff becomes ill as a result of the defamation and is hospitalized and incurs substantial medical expenses. Special damage?

2. *Malice.* The *Huntoon* court does not accurately state the requirements for proof of malice where the first amendment to the U.S. Constitution applies. In that connection, see the *Sullivan, Gertz* and *Greenmoss Builders* cases, *infra.*

3. *Slander Per Se.* The *Huntoon* court lists four types of slander that were considered actionable per se at common law, i e., actionable without proof of special damages. Would these categories withstand constitutional scrutiny today?

In *Ward v. Zelikovsky,* 263 N. J. Super. 497, 623 A.2d 285 (1993), the court held that accusing someone of "hating Jews" was as much an "assault upon reputation" as one of the four common law types of slander per se, and was therefore actionable without proof of special damages. The common law categories were "arbitrary and archaic," and the result of "historical accident." The standard the court adopted was whether the spoken words were "so injurious that the court will presume, without further proof, that plaintiff's reputation has been thereby impaired." Will this standard withstand constitutional scrutiny?

4. *Non-defamatory?* The court in *Leng Hardware, Inc. v. Wilson,* 94 N.Y. 2d 913, 729 N.E. 2d 338 (2000), found defendant's statement was not defamatory:

> Defendant is a member of the limited liability company that operates St. Johnsville Hardware and Gifts in the Village of St. Johnsville, Montgomery County. Plaintiff, Lenz Hardware, is a local competitor. Defendant placed an advertisement in the Mohawk Valley "My Shopper" comparing its prices with those of Lenz Hardware. In large print,

the advertisement invites customers to "Compare & Save." In considerably smaller print, it lists both stores' prices for a number of household items and then recites:

"No Coupon Necessary at St. Johnsville
Hardware.
"We have friendly, fast service.
"We Speak English, Plumbing, Farming and
Dabble in Pig Latin."

Lenz Hardware brought this defamation action asserting that the phrase, "We Speak English," falsely implied that Lenz Hardware's vice-president, an American citizen of Korean origin, is not conversant in English.

The Appellate Division majority properly upheld the Supreme Court's dismissal of the complaint. Giving the phrase a natural reading in the context presented, we conclude that it is not "reasonably susceptible of a defamatory connotation" (see Weiner v. Doubleday & Co., 74 N.Y. 2d 586, 593, 550 N.Y.S. 2d 251, 549 N.E. 2d 453).

The plaintiff in *Golub v. Enquirer/Star Group, Inc.*, 89 N.Y. 2d 1074, 681 N.E. 2d 1282 (1997), contended that the defendant defamed plaintiff's decedent, a public relations consultant, by stating in an article that the decedent had cancer. In dismissing the claim the court said "the statement did not impugn, or even relate to, any particular talent or ability needed to perform in decedent's profession as a publicist." Nor did the statement impute a loathsome disease, since cancer "is neither contagious nor attributed in any way to socially repugnant conduct."

PROBLEM

In connection with their divorce proceeding, wife charged the husband-plaintiff, a prominent psychologist, with sexually molesting their daughter. He was acquitted of this charge, and he later appeared on a TV talk show and discussed his divorce case. During the course of the discussion, the defendant stood up in the audience and stated to plaintiff: "You are lying. You raped your child and you know you did." Plaintiff suffered great emotional distress as a result of the statement.

Discuss plaintiff's possible defamation claim against the defendant.

LEWIS v. EQUITABLE LIFE ASSUR. SOC.
389 N.W.2d 876 (Minn. 1986)

AMDAHL, C.J.

Plaintiffs, Carole Lewis, Mary Smith, Michelle Rafferty, and Suzanne Loizeaux, former employees of defendant, the Equitable Life Assurance Society of the United States (company), all hired for indefinite, at-will terms, were discharged for the stated reason of "gross insubordination." They claim that they were discharged in breach of their employment contracts, as determined by an employee handbook, and that they were defamed because the company knew that they would have to repeat the reason for their discharges to prospective employers. A Ramsey county jury awarded plaintiffs compensatory and punitive damages. The Minnesota Court of Appeals affirmed the award but remanded on the issue of contract damages for future harm. We affirm in full the award of compensatory damages but reverse the award of punitive damages.

[Plaintiffs were employed for an indefinite time pursuant to oral agreements. Some months later they were sent to an out-of-town company office to provide temporary assistance. Plaintiffs, who had never traveled on company business before, were not fully instructed as to the company policy on expense accounts. They were given a travel advance and information on the company's daily allowances for meals and maid tips, and were told to keep receipts for hotel bills and air fare. When they returned to the home office, each received a personal letter from management commending them on their job performances in the temporary assignment. They were also informed for the first time that they would have to submit expense reports detailing their daily expenditures. Plaintiffs attempted to comply. They were asked to change their reports in one respect, and they did so. Thereafter, they were again told to change their reports to reflect lower overall totals which would require each to pay back approximately $200. Thereafter, they received written guidelines which differed from the instructions given prior to their departures. They again were asked to make additional changes in their expense reports. Plaintiffs refused to make further changes, maintaining that the expenses shown on their original reports were honest and reasonably incurred. The company did not dispute this. However, they were again asked to revise their expense reports. When they refused, they were put on "probation" and a week later, those who refused to refund the "excess" monies were terminated for "gross insubordination."]

. . . Had they been fired for other reasons they would have been entitled to as much as one month's severance pay.

The company admitted that the production and performance of plaintiffs was at all times satisfactory and even commendable. Company managers acknowledged that plaintiffs should have been given more thorough instructions and that the company's written guidelines should have been reviewed prior to their departures. . . . Management also admitted that the problems could have been avoided had plaintiffs been given proper guidelines prior to their departures.

In seeking new employment, plaintiffs were requested by prospective employers to disclose their reasons for leaving the company, and each indicated that she had been "terminated." When plaintiffs received interviews, they were asked to explain their terminations. Each stated that she had been terminated for "gross insubordination" and attempted to explain the situation. The company neither published nor stated to any prospective employer that plaintiffs had been terminated for gross insubordination. Its policy was to give only the dates of employment and the final job title of a former employee unless specifically authorized in writing to release additional information.

Only one plaintiff found employment while being completely forthright with a prospective employer about her termination by the company. A second plaintiff obtained employment after she misrepresented on the application form her reason for leaving the company. She did, however, explain the true reason in her job interview. A third plaintiff obtained employment only when she left blank the question on the application form requesting her reason for leaving her last employment; the issue never arose in her interview. The fourth plaintiff has been unable to find full-time employment. All plaintiffs testified to suffering emotional and financial hardship as a result of being discharged by the company.

[The court found the defendant breached the contract of employment.]

With regard to plaintiffs' defamation claims, the company argues that the trial court's conclusion of liability on the part of the company was erroneous because: (1) the only publications of the allegedly defamatory statement were made by plaintiffs; (2) the statement in question was true; and (3) the company was qualifiedly privileged to make the statement.

In order for a statement to be considered defamatory, it must be communicated to someone other than the plaintiff, it must be false, and it must tend to harm the plaintiff's reputation and to lower him or her in the estimation of the community. Generally, there is no publication where a defendant communicates a statement directly to a plaintiff, who then communicates it to a third person. Restatement (Second) of Torts 577, comment m (1977). Company management told plaintiffs that they had engaged in gross insubordination, for which they were being discharged. This allegedly defamatory statement was communicated to prospective employers of each plaintiff. The company, however, never communicated the statement. Plaintiffs themselves informed prospective employers that they had been terminated for gross insubordination. They did so because prospective employers inquired why they had left their previous employment. The question raised is whether a defendant can ever be held liable for defamation when the statement in question was published to a third person only by the plaintiff.

We have not previously been presented with the question of defamation by means of "self-publication." Courts that have considered the question, however, have recognized a narrow exception to the general rule that communication of a defamatory statement to a third person by the person defamed is not actionable. These courts have recognized that if a defamed person was in some way compelled to communicate the defamatory statement to a third person, and if it was foreseeable to the defendant that the defamed person would be so compelled, then the defendant could be held liable for the defamation.

Several courts have specifically recognized this exception for compelled self-publication in the context of employment discharges. In an early Georgia case an appellate court was presented with an employee discharged for alleged improper conduct toward fellow employees. *Colonial Stores, Inc. v. Barrett*, 73 Ga. App. 839, 38 S.E.2d 306 (1946). At that time, the War Manpower Commission required persons seeking employment to present a certificate of availability to prospective employers. The defendant employer who discharged the employee had written the reason for discharge on the employee's certificate of availability. The employee brought suit for defamation. The court, in affirming the trial court verdict in favor of the plaintiff, held that there "may be a publication when the sender intends or has reason to suppose that the communication will reach third persons, which happens, or which result naturally flows from the sending." 73 Ga. App. at 840, 38 S.E.2d at 307 (quoting 36 Corpus Juris § 172).

In a Michigan case, the plaintiff employee was discharged and subsequently brought a slander action against her former employer. *Grist v. Upjohn Co.,* 16 Mich. App. 452, 168 N.W.2d 389 (1969). She alleged that the defendant had given her false and defamatory reasons for her discharge and that she was forced to repeat the reasons to prospective employers in detailing her previous employment. The trial court instructed the jury that they could find a slanderous statement even though the statements by the defendant were made only to the plaintiff. Affirming the trial court's jury instruction, the Michigan appellate court held: "Where the conditions are such that the utterer of the defamatory matter intends or has reason to suppose that in the ordinary course of events the matter will come to the knowledge of some third person, a publication may be effected." 16 Mich. App. at 485, 168 N.W.2d at 406. . . .

The company presents two arguments against recognition of the doctrine of compelled self-publication. It argues that such recognition amounts to creating tort liability for wrongful discharge which, it asserts, has been rejected by this court. In *Wild v. Rarig,* 302 Minn. 419, 442, 234 N.W.2d 775, 790 (1975), we held that bad-faith termination of contract is not an independent tort of the kind that will permit a tort recovery. The company, however, misreads our holding regarding tort liability for wrongful discharge. We did not hold that the harm resulting from a bad-faith termination of a contract could never give rise to a tort recovery. Indeed, we recognized such a possibility by stating that a plaintiff is limited to contract damages "except in exceptional cases where the defendant's breach of contract constitutes or is accompanied by an independent tort." *Id.* at 440, 234 N.W.2d at 789. If plaintiffs here can establish a cause of action for defamation, the fact that the defamation occurred in the context of employment discharge should not defeat recovery.

NOTES

1. *Compelled Self-Publication Rejected.* The court in *Sullivan v. Bapt. Mem. Hosp.,* 995 S.W. 2d 569 (Tenn. 1999), rejected a claim of defamation based on compelled self-publication. The plaintiff, a former hospital employee, contended that in seeking new employment she was compelled to disclose the allegedly erroneous and defamatory reasons the defendant, her former employer, had given for terminating her employment.

In rejecting plaintiff's claim, the court said the "majority of states addressing the issue do not recognize self-publication as constituting publication for defamation purposes, even when the publication is compelled in the employment setting." Recognition of such a rule "would chill communications in the work place" and "negatively affect grievance procedures intended to benefit the discharged employee." The only way an employer could avoid potential litigation would be to say nothing to the employee, or to third persons, about the reasons for termination.

Moreover, the rule would conflict with Tennessee's employment-at-will doctrine, the court said. Under that doctrine an employer has no duty to investigate before terminating an employee, and can terminate "at any time for good cause, bad cause, or no cause."

Finally, permitting recovery under the self-publication rule, the court said, would conflict with TENN. CODE ANNOT. § 50-1-105, which provides that an employer can be liable only for knowing or reckless falsity in communicating "upon request by a prospective employer or a current or former employee. . . information about a current or former employee's job performance." Compliance with this statute raises a presumption of good faith, and

> mere negligence is not enough to rebut the presumption in favor of the employer's good faith. In contrast, defamation may be proven by establishing that a party published a false and defaming statement with reckless disregard for the truth *or* with negligence in failing to ascertain the truth. It follows, therefore, that an employer should not be held liable for disclosure of this same information when it is self-published by a former employee.

2. *Inadvertent Publication.* If the defendant knows that another person is in the habit of opening plaintiff's mail, and sends plaintiff a libelous letter that is opened and read by that other person, there can be a publication. *Roberts v. English Mfg. Co.,* 155 Ala. 414, 46 So. 752 (1908).

McNichol v. Grandy, [1931] Can. S. Ct. Rep. 696, 703, states that there is no actionable publication of a defendant's defamation of the plaintiff, where the defamatory statement is made to the plaintiff herself and is "accidentally" overheard by a third person, provided the defendant did not intend, or have "reason to know or to suspect that any other person was within hearing." But if the defendant can be "charged with some fault leading to the communication to such third person," there is a publication for which liability can be imposed.

How do the holdings in *Roberts* and *McNichol* square with the constitutional protections considered below?

3. *Publication Through Inaction.* In *Hellar v. Bianco,* 111 Cal. App. 2d 424, 244 P.2d 757 (1952), appellant alleged the following facts against respondents:

> Respondents were the proprietors of a public tavern and for the convenience of patrons maintained a toilet room for men on the wall of which there appeared on May 4, 1950, libelous matter indicating that appellant was an unchaste woman who indulged in illicit amatory ventures. The writer recommended that anyone interested should call a stated telephone number, which was the number of the telephone in appellant's home, and "ask for Isabelle," that being appellant's given name. At about 9 o'clock on the evening of that day a man, unknown to appellant, called the number and appellant answered. The caller requested permission to visit her and when in the course of the conversation it developed that a meeting could not be arranged he told

her "there is some of the most terrible writing over here on the wall of the men's toilet about you, that is where I got your telephone number and your name." He suggested that she look into it and told her he was calling from respondents' tavern. Appellant informed her husband of the conversation and he called the tavern and talked with the bartender who was shown to have been in charge of the tavern during the absence of respondents. He told the bartender that his attention had been called to some writing on the walls of the men's toilet regarding his wife, that he would give the bartender just 30 minutes to take it off the wall and that he was coming out to investigate. The bartender replied that he was busy and alone and would remove the writing when he got around to it. Appellant's husband thereupon called a constable and after some delay arrived at the tavern where, in company with several people, including the bartender, he went to the toilet and found the libelous matter still on the wall. Falsity of the libel was shown and its defamatory nature is conceded. In fact it was shocking. The husband, constable and other persons present when the group went to the toilet and found the defamatory writing still upon the wall were shown to have understood the appellant was the person referred to in the writing and the writing itself was sufficient to be understood by anyone knowing about it that it was written concerning her.

The court held the appellant stated a cause of action against respondents for libel. "The theory is that by knowingly permitting such matter to remain after reasonable opportunity to remove the same the owner of the wall or his lessee is guilty of republication of the libel."

The plaintiff Tacket, in *Tacket v. General Motors Corp.*, 836 F.2d 1042 (7th Cir. 1987), was implicated in obtaining a sweetheart deal with his employer for a friend. Tacket was temporarily suspended, and when he returned to work there were two signs on the premises, allegedly put up by his co-employees, which read: "TACKET TACKET WHAT A RACKET." One sign, 3' × 30', appeared inside the plant and stayed up for two or three days. A smaller, stenciled sign allegedly stayed up for seven to eight months. The term "racket" implied racketeering.

The court said the large sign, "posted on one day, seen and ordered removed on the next, and down on the third day plainly is the work of a prankster rather than General Motors Corporation." The smaller sign, however, presented a different issue. Plaintiff allegedly requested that it be removed, and a jury could infer that he thought he lacked authority to remove it himself. The court said a jury question was presented as to whether defendant's employer, GM, was guilty of libeling plaintiff under REST. 2d OF TORTS § 577(2) (1977):

> One who intentionally and unreasonably fails to remove defamatory matter that he knows to be exhibited on land or chattels in his possession or under his control is subject to liability for its continued publication.

PROBLEM

Patron says to Librarian: "You have a book on your shelf that libels me" (naming the book), "and if you don't remove it right away, I'll sue you for libel."

If the librarian does not remove the book, can the librarian and the library be found guilty of republication?

NEW YORK TIMES CO. v. SULLIVAN
376 U.S. 254, 84 S. Ct. 710, 11 L. Ed. 2d 686 (1964)

Mr. Justice Brennan delivered the opinion of the Court.

We are required in this case to determine for the first time the extent to which the constitutional protections for speech and press limit a State's power to award damages in a libel action brought by a public official against critics of his official conduct.

Respondent L. B. Sullivan is one of the three elected Commissioners of the City of Montgomery, Alabama. He testified that he was "Commissioner of Public Affairs and the duties are supervision of the Police Department, Fire Department, Department of Cemetery and Department of Scales." He brought this civil libel action against the four individual petitioners, who are Negroes and Alabama clergymen, and against petitioner the New York Times Company, a New York corporation which publishes the New York Times, a daily newspaper. A jury in the Circuit Court of Montgomery County awarded him damages of $500,000, the full amount claimed, against all the petitioners, and the Supreme Court of Alabama affirmed.

Respondent's complaint alleged that he had been libeled by statements in a full-page advertisement that was carried in the New York Times on March 29, 1960. Entitled "Heed Their Rising Voices," the advertisement began by stating that "As the whole world knows by now, thousands of Southern Negro students are engaged in widespread non-violent demonstrations in positive affirmation of the right to live in human dignity as guaranteed by the U.S. Constitution and the Bill of Rights." It went on to charge that "in their efforts to uphold these guarantees, they are being met by an unprecedented wave of terror by those who would deny and negate that document which the whole world looks upon as setting the pattern for modern freedom. . . ." Succeeding paragraphs purported to illustrate the "wave of terror" by describing certain alleged events. The text concluded with an appeal for funds for three purposes: support of the student movement, "the struggle for the right-to-vote," and the legal defense of Dr. Martin Luther King, Jr., leader of the movement, against a perjury indictment then pending in Montgomery.

The text appeared over the names of 64 persons, many widely known for their activities in public affairs, religion, trade unions, and the performing arts. Below these names, and under a line reading "We in the south who are struggling daily for dignity and freedom warmly endorse this appeal," appeared the names of the four individual petitioners and of 16 other persons, all but two of whom were identified as clergymen in various Southern cities. The advertisement was signed at the bottom of the page by the "Committee to Defend Martin Luther King and the Struggle for Freedom in the South," and the officers of the Committee were listed.

Of the 10 paragraphs of text in the advertisement, the third and a portion of the sixth were the basis of respondent's claim of libel. They read as follows:

Third paragraph:

"In Montgomery, Alabama, after students sang 'My Country, 'Tis of Thee' on the State Capitol steps, their leaders were expelled from school, and truckloads of police armed with shotguns and tear-gas ringed the Alabama State College Campus. When the entire student body protested to state authorities by refusing to re-register, their dining hall was padlocked in an attempt to starve them into submission."

Sixth paragraph:

"Again and again the Southern violators have answered Dr. King's peaceful protests with intimidation and violence. They have bombed his home almost killing his wife and child. They have assaulted his person. They have arrested him seven times — for 'speeding,' 'loitering' and similar 'offenses.' And now they have charged him with 'perjury' — a *felony* under which they could imprison him for *ten years*. . . ."

Although neither of these statements mentions respondent by name, he contended that the word "police" in the third paragraph referred to him as the Montgomery Commissioner who supervised the Police Department, so that he was being accused of "ringing" the campus with police. He further claimed that the paragraph would be read as imputing to the police, and hence to him, the padlocking of the dining hall in order to starve the students into submission. As to the sixth paragraph, he contended that since arrests are ordinarily made by the police, the statement "They have arrested [Dr. King] seven times" would be read as referring to him; he further contended that the "They" who did the arresting would be equated with the "They" who committed the other described acts and with the "Southern violators." Thus, he argued, the paragraph would be read as accusing the Montgomery police, and hence him, of answering Dr. King's protests with "intimidation and violence," bombing his home, assaulting his person, and charging him with perjury. Respondent and six other Montgomery residents testified that they read some or all of the statements as referring to him in his capacity as Commissioner.

It is uncontroverted that some of the statements contained in the two paragraphs were not accurate descriptions of events which occurred in Montgomery. Although Negro students staged a demonstration on the State Capitol steps, they sang the National Anthem and not "My Country, 'Tis of Thee." Although nine students were expelled by the State Board of Education, this was not for leading the demonstration at the Capitol, but for demanding service at a lunch counter in the Montgomery County Courthouse on another day. Not the entire student body, but most of it, had protested the expulsion, not by refusing to register, but by boycotting classes on a single day; virtually all the students did register for the ensuing semester. The campus dining hall was not padlocked on any occasion, and the only students who may have been barred from eating there were the few who had neither signed a preregistration application nor requested temporary meal tickets. Although the police were deployed near the campus in large numbers on three occasions, they did not at any time "ring" the campus, and they were not called to the campus in connection with the demonstration on the State Capitol steps, as the third paragraph implied. Dr. King had not been arrested seven times, but only four;

and although he claimed to have been assaulted some years earlier in connection with his arrest for loitering outside a courtroom, one of the officers who made the arrest denied that there was such an assault.

On the premise that the charges in the sixth paragraph could be read as referring to him, respondent was allowed to prove that he had not participated in the events described. Although Dr. King's home had in fact been bombed twice when his wife and child were there, both of these occasions antedated respondent's tenure as Commissioner, and the police were not only not implicated in the bombings, but had made every effort to apprehend those who were. Three of Dr. King's four arrests took place before respondent became Commissioner. Although Dr. King had in fact been indicted (he was subsequently acquitted) on two counts of perjury, each of which carried a possible five-year sentence, respondent had nothing to do with procuring the indictment.

[Respondent made no effort to prove he had suffered pecuniary loss as a result of the advertisement. One witness testified that he doubted whether he "would want to be associated with anybody who would be a party to such things that are stated in that ad." No one testified that he "believed the statements in their supposed reference to respondent."]

. . . The cost of the advertisement was approximately $4800, and it was published by the Times upon an order from a New York advertising agency acting for the signatory Committee. The agency submitted the advertisement with a letter from A. Philip Randolph, Chairman of the Committee, certifying that the persons whose names appeared on the advertisement had given their permission. Mr. Randolph was known to the Times' Advertising Acceptability Department as a responsible person, and in accepting the letter as sufficient proof of authorization it followed its established practice. There was testimony that the copy of the advertisement which accompanied the letter listed only the 64 names appearing under the text, and that the statement, "We in the south . . . warmly endorse this appeal," and the list of names thereunder, which included those of the individual petitioners, were subsequently added when the first proof of the advertisement was received. Each of the individual petitioners testified that he had not authorized the use of his name, and that he had been unaware of its use until receipt of respondent's demand for a retraction. The manager of the Advertising Acceptability Department testified that he had approved the advertisement for publication because he knew nothing to cause him to believe that anything in it was false, and because it bore the endorsement of "a number of people who are well known and whose reputation" he "had no reason to question." Neither he nor anyone else at the Times made an effort to confirm the accuracy of the advertisement, either by checking it against recent Times' news stories relating to some of the described events or by any other means.

The trial judge submitted the case to the jury under instructions that the statements in the advertisement were "libelous per se" and were not privileged, so that petitioners might be held liable if the jury found that they had published the advertisement and that the statements were made "of and concerning" respondent. The jury was instructed that, because **the statements** were libelous *per se,* "the law . . . implies legal injury from the bare fact of publication itself," "falsity and malice are presumed," "general damages need not be alleged or proved but are presumed," and "punitive damages may be awarded by the jury even though the amount of actual damages is neither found nor shown." An award of punitive damages — as distinguished from "general" damages, which are compensatory in nature — apparently requires proof of actual malice under Alabama law, and the judge charged that "mere negligence or carelessness is not evidence of actual malice or malice in fact, and does not justify an award of exemplary or punitive damages." He refused to charge, however, that the jury must be "convinced" of malice, in the sense of "actual intent" to harm or "gross negligence and recklessness," to make such an award, and he also refused to require that a verdict for respondent differentiate between compensatory and punitive damages. The judge rejected petitioners' contention that his rulings abridged the freedoms of speech and of the press that are guaranteed by the First and Fourteenth Amendments.

. . . We reverse the judgment. We hold that the rule of law applied by the Alabama courts is constitutionally deficient for failure to provide the safeguards for freedom of speech and of the press that are required by the First and Fourteenth Amendments in a libel action brought by a public official against critics of his official conduct. We further hold that under the proper safeguards the evidence presented in this case is constitutionally insufficient to support the judgment for respondent.

. . . Respondent relies heavily, as did the Alabama courts, on statements of this Court to the effect that the Constitution does not protect libelous publications. Those statements do not foreclose our inquiry here. None of the cases sustained the use of libel laws to impose sanctions upon expression critical of the official conduct of public officials. . . . In *Beauharnais v. Illinois,* 343 U.S. 250, 96 L. Ed. 919, 72 S. Ct. 725 (1952), the Court sustained an Illinois criminal libel statute as applied to a publication held to be both defamatory of a racial group and "liable to cause violence and disorder." But the Court was careful to note that it "retains and exercises authority to nullify action which encroaches on freedom of utterance under the guise of punishing libel"; for "public men, are, as it were, public property," and "discussion cannot be denied and the right, as well as the duty, of criticism must not be stifled. . . ."

The general proposition that freedom of expression upon public questions is secured by the First Amendment has long been settled by our decisions. . . . Mr. Justice Brandeis, in his concurring opinion in *Whitney v. California,* 274 U.S. 357, 375–376, 71 L. Ed. 1095, 47 S. Ct. 641 (1927), gave the principle its classic formulation:

> Those who won our independence believed . . . that public discussion is a political duty; and that this should be a fundamental principle of the American government. They recognized the risks to which all human institutions are subject. But they knew that order cannot be secured merely through fear of punishment for its infraction; that it is hazardous to discourage thought, hope and imagination; that fear breeds repression; that repression breeds hate; that hate menaces stable government; that the path of safety lies in the opportunity to discuss freely supposed grievances and proposed remedies; and that

the fitting remedy for evil counsels is good ones. Believing in the power of reason as applied through public discussion, they eschewed silence coerced by law — the argument of force in its worst form. Recognizing the occasional tyrannies of governing majorities, they amended the Constitution so that free speech and assembly should be guaranteed.

Thus we consider this case against the background of a profound national commitment to the principle that debate on public issues should be uninhibited, robust, and wide-open, and that it may well include vehement, caustic, and sometimes unpleasantly sharp attacks on government and public officials. The present advertisement, as an expression of grievance and protest on one of the major public issues of our time, would seem clearly to qualify for the constitutional protection. The question is whether it forfeits that protection by the falsity of some of its factual statements and by its alleged defamation of respondent. . . . The constitutional protection does not turn upon "the truth, popularity, or social utility of the ideas and beliefs which are offered." *N.A.A.C.P. v. Button,* 371 U.S. 415, 445, 9 L. Ed. 2d 405, 83 S. Ct. 328 (1963). As Madison said, "Some degree of abuse is inseparable from the proper use of every thing; and in no instance is this more true than in that of the press." 4 Elliot's Debates on the Federal Constitution (1876), p. 571. In *Cantwell v. Connecticut,* 310 U.S. 296, 310, 84 L. Ed. 1213, 60 S. Ct. 900 (1940), the Court declared:

> In the realm of religious faith, and in that of political belief, sharp differences arise. In both fields the tenets of one man may seem the rankest error to his neighbor. To persuade others to his own point of view, the pleader, as we know, at times, resorts to exaggeration, to vilification of men who have been, or are, prominent in church or state, and even to false statement. But the people of this nation have ordained in the light of history, that, in spite of the probability of excesses and abuses, these liberties are, in the long view, essential to enlightened opinion and right conduct on the part of the citizens of a democracy.

That erroneous statement is inevitable in free debate, and that it must be protected if the freedoms of expression are to have the "breathing space" that they "need . . . to survive," *N.A.A.C.P. v. Button,* 371 U.S. at 433, was also recognized by the Court of Appeals for the District of Columbia Circuit in *Sweeney v. Patterson,* 76 U.S. App. D.C. 23, 24, 128 F. 2d 457, 458 (1942), cert. denied, 317 U.S. 678. Judge Edgerton spoke for a unanimous court which affirmed the dismissal of a Congressman's libel suit based upon a newspaper article charging him with anti-Semitism in opposing a judicial appointment. He said:

> Cases which impose liability for erroneous reports of the political conduct of officials reflect the obsolete doctrine that the governed must not criticize their governors. . . . The interest of the public here outweighs the interest of appellant or any other individual. The protection of the public requires not merely discussion, but information. Political conduct and views which some respectable people approve, and others condemn, are constantly imputed to Congressmen. Errors of fact, particularly in regard to a man's mental states and processes, are

inevitable. . . . Whatever is added to the field of libel is taken from the field of free debate.³

Injury to official reputation affords no more warrant for repressing speech that would otherwise be free than does factual error. Where judicial officers are involved, this Court has held that concern for the dignity and reputation of the courts does not justify the punishment as criminal contempt of criticism of the judge or his decision. This is true even though the utterance contains "half-truths" and "misinformation." *Pennekamp v. Florida,* 328 U.S. 331, 342, 343, n. 5, 345, 90 L. Ed. 1295, 66 S. Ct. 1029 (1946). Such repression can be justified, if at all, only by a clear and present danger of the obstruction of justice. If judges are to be treated as "men of fortitude, able to thrive in a hardy climate," *Craig v. Harney,* 331 U.S. 367, 376, 91 L. Ed. 1546, 67 S. Ct. 1249 (1947), surely the same must be true of other government officials, such as elected city commissioners. Criticism of their official conduct does not lose its constitutional protection merely because it is effective criticism and hence diminishes their official reputations.

If neither factual error nor defamatory content suffices to remove the constitutional shield from criticism of official conduct, the combination of the two elements is no less inadequate. This is the lesson to be drawn from the great controversy over the Sedition Act of 1798, 1 Stat. 596, which first crystallized a national awareness of the central meaning of the First Amendment. That statute made it a crime, punishable by a $5,000 fine and five years in prison, "if any person shall write, print, utter or publish . . . any false, scandalous and malicious writing or writings against the government of the United States, or either house of the Congress . . ., or the President . . ., with intent to defame . . . or to bring them, or either of them, into contempt or disrepute; or to excite against them, or either or any of them, the hatred of the good people of the United States." The Act allowed the defendant the defense of truth, and provided that the jury were to be judges both of the law and the facts. Despite these qualifications, the Act was vigorously condemned as unconstitutional in an attack joined in by Jefferson and Madison. In the famous Virginia Resolutions of 1798, the General Assembly of Virginia resolved that it "doth particularly protest against the palpable and alarming infractions of the Constitution, in the two late cases of the 'Alien and Sedition Acts,' passed at the last session of Congress. . . . [The Sedition Act] exercises . . . a power not delegated by the Constitution, but, on the contrary, expressly and positively forbidden by one of the amendments thereto — a power which, more than any other, ought to produce universal alarm, because it is levelled against the right of freely examining public characters and measures, and of free communication among the people thereon, which has ever been justly deemed the only effectual guardian of every other right." 4 Elliot's Debates, *supra,* pp. 553–554. . . ..

---

³ See also Mill, On Liberty (Oxford: Blackwell, 1947), at 47:

". . .[To] argue sophistically, to suppress facts or arguments, to misstate the elements of the case, or misrepresent the opposite opinion . . .all this, even to the most aggravated degree, is so continually done in perfect good faith, by persons who are not considered, and in many other respects may not deserve to be considered, ignorant or incompetent, that it is rarely possible, on adequate grounds, conscientiously to stamp the misrepresentation as morally culpable; and still less could law presume to interfere with this kind of controversial misconduct."

... There is no force in respondent's argument that the constitutional limitations implicit in the history of the Sedition Act apply only to Congress and not to the States. It is true that the First Amendment was originally addressed only to action by the Federal Government, and that Jefferson, for one, while denying the power of Congress "to control the freedom of the press," recognized such a power in the States. See the 1804 Letter to Abigail Adams quoted in *Dennis v. United States,* 341 U.S. 494, 522, n. 4, 95 L. Ed. 1137, 71 S. Ct. 857 (1951) (concurring opinion). But this distinction was eliminated with the adoption of the Fourteenth Amendment and the application to the States of the First Amendment's restrictions.

What a State may not constitutionally bring about by means of a criminal statute is likewise beyond the reach of its civil law of libel. The fear of damage awards under a rule such as that invoked by the Alabama courts here may be markedly more inhibiting than the fear of prosecution under a criminal statute. Alabama, for example, has a criminal libel law which subjects to prosecution "any person who speaks, writes, or prints of and concerning another any accusation falsely and maliciously importing the commission by such person of a felony, or any other indictable offense involving moral turpitude," and which allows as punishment upon conviction a fine not exceeding $500 and a prison sentence of six months. Alabama Code, Tit. 14, § 350. Presumably a person charged with violation of this statute enjoys ordinary criminal-law safeguards such as the requirements of an indictment and of proof beyond a reasonable doubt. These safeguards are not available to the defendant in a civil action. The judgment awarded in this case — without the need for any proof of actual pecuniary loss — was one thousand times greater than the maximum fine provided by the Alabama criminal statute, and one hundred times greater than that provided by the Sedition Act. And since there is no double-jeopardy limitation applicable to civil lawsuits, this is not the only judgment that may be awarded against petitioners for the same publication. Whether or not a newspaper can survive a succession of such judgments, the pall of fear and timidity imposed upon those who would give voice to public criticism is an atmosphere in which the First Amendment freedoms cannot survive. . . .

The State rule of law is not saved by its allowance of the defense of truth. . . .

A rule compelling the critic of official conduct to guarantee the truth of all his factual assertions — and to do so on pain of libel judgments virtually unlimited in amount — leads to a comparable "self-censorship." Allowance of the defense of truth, with the burden of proving it on the defendant, does not mean that only false speech will be deterred. Even courts accepting this defense as an adequate safeguard have recognized the difficulties of adducing legal proofs that the alleged libel was true in all its factual particulars. Under such a rule, would-be critics of official conduct may be deterred from voicing their criticism, even though it is believed to be true and even though it is in fact true, because of doubt whether it can be proved in court or fear of the expense of having to do so. They tend to make only statements which "steer far wider of the unlawful zone." *Speiser v. Randall,* 357 U.S. 513, 526, 2 L. Ed. 2d 1460, 78 S. Ct. 1332 (1958). The rule thus dampens the vigor and limits the variety of public debate. It is inconsistent with the First and Fourteenth Amendments.

The constitutional guarantees require, we think, a federal rule that prohibits a public official from recovering damages for a defamatory falsehood relating to his official conduct unless he proves that the statement was made with "actual malice" — that is, with knowledge that it was false or with reckless disregard of whether it was false or not. . . .

We hold today that the Constitution delimits a State's power to award damages for libel in actions brought by public officials against critics of their official conduct. Since this is such an action,[4] the rule requiring proof of actual malice is applicable. While Alabama law apparently requires proof of actual malice for an award of punitive damages, where general damages are concerned malice is "presumed." Such a presumption is inconsistent with the federal rule. . . . Since the trial judge did not instruct the jury to differentiate between general and punitive damages, it may be that the verdict was wholly an award of one or the other. But it is impossible to know, in view of the general verdict returned. Because of this uncertainty, the judgment must be reversed and the case remanded.

. . . [W]e consider that the proof presented to show actual malice lacks the convincing clarity which the constitutional standard demands, and hence that it would not constitutionally sustain the judgment for respondent under the proper rule of law. The case of the individual petitioners requires little discussion. Even assuming that they could constitutionally be found to have authorized the use of their names on the advertisement, there was no evidence whatever that they were aware of any erroneous statements or were in any way reckless in that regard. The judgment against them is thus without constitutional support.

As to the Times, we similarly conclude that the facts do not support a finding of actual malice. The statement by the Times' Secretary that, apart from the padlocking allegation, he thought the advertisement was "substantially correct," affords no constitutional warrant for the Alabama Supreme Court's conclusion that it was a "cavalier ignoring of the falsity of the advertisement [from which] the jury could not have but been impressed with the bad faith of The Times, and its maliciousness inferable therefrom." The statement does not indicate malice at the time of the publication; even if the advertisement was not "substantially correct" — although respondent's own proofs tend to

---

[4] We have no occasion here to determine how far down into the lower ranks of government employees the "public official" designation would extend for purposes of this rule, or otherwise to specify categories of persons who would or would not be included. Nor need we here determine the boundaries of the "official conduct" concept. It is enough for the present case that respondent's position as an elected city commissioner clearly made him a public official, and that the allegations in the advertisement concerned what was allegedly his official conduct as Commissioner in charge of the Police Department. As to the statements alleging the assaulting of Dr. King and the bombing of his home, it is immaterial that they might not be considered to involve respondent's official conduct if he himself had been accused of perpetrating the assault and the bombing. Respondent does not claim that the statements charged him personally with these acts; his contention is that the advertisement connects him with them only in his official capacity as the Commissioner supervising the police, on the theory that the police might be equated with the "They" who did the bombing and assaulting. Thus, if these allegations can be read as referring to respondent at all, they must be read as describing his performance of his official duties.

show that it was — that opinion was at least a reasonable one, and there was no evidence to impeach the witness' good faith in holding it. The Times' failure to retract upon respondent's demand, although it later retracted upon the demand of Governor Patterson, is likewise not adequate evidence of malice for constitutional purposes. Whether or not a failure to retract may ever constitute such evidence, there are two reasons why it does not here. *First,* the letter written by the Times reflected a reasonable doubt on its part as to whether the advertisement could reasonably be taken to refer to respondent at all. *Second,* it was not a final refusal, since it asked for an explanation on this point — a request that respondent chose to ignore. Nor does the retraction upon the demand of the Governor supply the necessary proof. It may be doubted that a failure to retract which is not itself evidence of malice can retroactively become such by virtue of a retraction subsequently made to another party. But in any event that did not happen here, since the explanation given by the Times' Secretary for the distinction drawn between respondent and the Governor was a reasonable one, the good faith of which was not impeached.[5]

Finally, there is evidence that the Times published the advertisement without checking its accuracy against the news stories in the Times' own files. The mere presence of the stories in the files does not, of course, establish that the Times "knew" the advertisement was false, since the state of mind required for actual malice would have to be brought home to the persons in the Times' organization having responsibility for the publication of the advertisement. With respect to the failure of those persons to make the check, the record shows that they relied upon their knowledge of the good reputation of many of those whose names were listed as sponsors of the advertisement, and upon the letter from A. Philip Randolph, known to them as a responsible individual, certifying that the use of the names was authorized. There was testimony that the persons handling the advertisement saw nothing in it that would render it unacceptable under the Times' policy of rejecting advertisements containing "attacks of a personal character";[6] their failure to reject it on this ground was not unreasonable. We think the evidence against the Times supports at most a finding of negligence in failing to discover the misstatements, and is constitutionally insufficient to show the recklessness that is required for a finding of actual malice.

We also think the evidence was constitutionally defective in another respect: it was incapable of supporting the jury's finding that the allegedly libelous statements were made "of and concerning" respondent. . . .

---

[5] Editor's note. The Times secretary stated that they retracted as to the Governor because he was "the embodiment of the State of Alabama," because they had "by that time learned more of the actual facts which the ad purported to recite," and because the ad "did refer to the action of the state authorities and the Board of Education presumably of which the Governor is the ex-officio chairman."

[6] The Times has set forth in a booklet its "Advertising Acceptability Standards." Listed among the classes of advertising that the newspaper does not accept are advertisements that are "fraudulent or deceptive," that are "ambiguous in wording and. . .may mislead," and that contain "attacks of a personal character." In replying to respondent's interrogatories before the trial, the Secretary of the Times stated that "as the advertisement made no attacks of a personal character upon any individual and otherwise met the advertising acceptability standards promulgated," it had been approved for publication.

... [T]he Supreme Court of Alabama ... in holding that the trial court "did not err in overruling the demurrer [of the Times] in the aspect that the libelous matter was not of and concerning the [plaintiff,]" based its ruling on the proposition that:

> "We think it common knowledge that the average person knows that municipal agents, such as police and firemen, and others, are under the control and direction of the city governing body, and more particularly under the direction and control of a single commissioner. In measuring the performance or deficiencies of such groups, praise or criticism is usually attached to the official in complete control of the body."

This proposition has disquieting implications for criticism of governmental conduct. . . . The present proposition would sidestep this obstacle by transmuting criticism of government, however impersonal it may seem on its face, into personal criticism, and hence potential libel, of the officials of whom the government is composed. There is no legal alchemy by which a State may thus create the cause of action that would otherwise be denied for a publication which, as respondent himself said of the advertisement, "reflects not only on me but on the other Commissioners and the community." Raising as it does the possibility that a good-faith critic of government will be penalized for his criticism, the proposition relied on by the Alabama courts strikes at the very center of the constitutionally protected area of free expression. We hold that such a proposition may not constitutionally be utilized to establish that an otherwise impersonal attack on governmental operations was a libel of an official responsible for those operations. Since it was relied on exclusively here, and there was no other evidence to connect the statements with respondent, the evidence was constitutionally insufficient to support a finding that the statements referred to respondent.

The judgment of the Supreme Court of Alabama is reversed and the case is remanded to that court for further proceedings not inconsistent with this opinion.

NOTES

1. *The Public Person and Constitutional Malice.* The rule of *Sullivan* was extended in *Curtis Pub'g Co. v. Butts,* 388 U.S. 130, 87 S. Ct. 1975, 18 L. Ed. 2d 1094 (1967) — which case was later construed to apply to plaintiffs who are public figures, whether or not they are public officials. In *Garrison v. Louisiana,* 379 U.S. 64, 85 S. Ct. 209, 13 L. Ed. 2d 125 (1964), the Court said that proof of constitutional malice requires a showing that a false publication was made with a "high degree of awareness of . . . probable falsity." As examples of such awareness, the Court in *St. Amant v. Thompson,* 390 U.S. 727, 88 S. Ct. 1323, 20 L. Ed. 2d 262 (1968), stated by way of dictum:

> The defendant in a defamation action brought by a public official cannot, however, automatically insure a favorable verdict by testifying that he published with a belief that the statements were true. The finder of fact must determine whether the publication was indeed made in good faith. Professions of good faith will be unlikely to prove persuasive, for example, where a story is fabricated by the defendant,

is the product of his imagination, or is based wholly on an unverified anonymous telephone call. Nor will they be likely to prevail when the publisher's allegations are so inherently improbable that only a reckless man would have put them in circulation. Likewise, recklessness may be found where there are obvious reasons to doubt the veracity of the informant or the accuracy of his reports.

In *Rosenblatt v. Baer,* 383 U.S. 75, 15 L. Ed. 2d 597, 86 S. Ct. 669 (1966), the Court held that the manager of a public ski resort was a public official. "Where a position in government has such apparent importance that the public has an independent interest in the qualifications and performance of the person who holds it, beyond the general public interest in the qualifications and performance of all government employees," the person is a public official. What about a public school teacher? A school secretary? A school maintenance worker?

In *Posadas v. City of Reno*, 851 P.2d 438 (Nev. 1993), the defendant issued an allegedly false press release stating that the plaintiff police officer had lied under oath. The court indicated that constitutional malice, or "actual malice" as the *New York Times v. Sullivan* court describes it, can be established in part by showing "ill will" on the part of the defendant toward the plaintiff. How much proof of actual knowledge or reckless disregard of falsity must be presented before proof of ill will can tip the balance?

2. *Defamation of a Large Group.* In *Neiman-Marcus v. Lait,* 13 F.R.D 311 (D.C.N.Y. 1952), the court held that a group of 382 saleswomen, who had been defamed as a group, was so large that no individual saleswoman could bring an action. How does this holding compare with that in *Sullivan*? See the discussion on "fighting words," *infra*.

One commentator would permit each member of a group of not more than twenty-five persons to assert a defamation claim against a speaker if the speaker insinuated individual blameworthiness of the group members and if the statement were untrue as to the claimant and as to most members of the group. Joseph H. King, Jr., *Reference to the Plaintiff*, 35 WAKE FOREST L. REV. 343 (2000).

3. *Belief in the Falsity of a Defamatory Statement.* The *Sullivan* Court said that the evidence did not indicate that any of the witnesses believed the alleged charges against Commissioner Sullivan in the New York Times' article. Would this be an independent basis for finding an absence of libel?

4. *Vicarious Liability.* The *Sullivan* Court refused to impute to the New York Times advertising department the knowledge of its filing department about prior stories in the newspaper that would have indicated the falsity of some of the statements in the *Sullivan* case. Would a proper application of the doctrine of corporate vicarious liability have required such an imputation?

5. *Sullivan and Republication.* Suppose Commissioner Sullivan had been explicitly named as the one responsible for the libelous matters alleged in the newspaper article. If the Times refused to print a retraction after being notified of the alleged libel by Commissioner Sullivan, would they be guilty of republication?

6. *Whither Malice?* In *Harte-Hanks Commun., Inc. v. Connaughton,* 49 U.S. 657, 109 S. Ct. 2678, 105 L. Ed. 2d 562 (1989), the plaintiff was an unsuccessful candidate for the office of municipal judge, and the defendant printed a story before the election stating in effect that plaintiff had bribed a witness to testify that the incumbent's director of court services had repeatedly accepted bribes in return for judicial favors. The story was based on a newspaper interview with the witness' sister, who said she was present at the plaintiff's meeting with the witness. Although the defendant interviewed the plaintiff before printing the story, it made no attempt to talk to the witness. After an exhaustive de novo review of the facts, the Court found that the jury properly found by clear and convincing evidence that the defendant acted with constitutional malice in printing the false and defamatory article.

GERTZ v. ROBERT WELCH, INC.
418 U.S. 323, 94 S. Ct. 2997, 41 L. Ed. 2d 789 (1974)

MR. JUSTICE POWELL delivered the opinion of the Court.

. . . In 1968 a Chicago policeman named Nuccio shot and killed a youth named Nelson. The state authorities prosecuted Nuccio for the homicide and ultimately obtained a conviction for murder in the second degree. The Nelson family retained petitioner Elmer Gertz, a reputable attorney, to represent them in civil litigation against Nuccio.

Respondent publishes American Opinion, a monthly outlet for the views of the John Birch Society. Early in the 1960's the magazine began to warn of a nationwide conspiracy to discredit local law enforcement agencies and create in their stead a national police force capable of supporting a Communist dictatorship. As part of the continuing effort to alert the public to this assumed danger, the managing editor of American Opinion commissioned an article on the murder trial of Officer Nuccio. For this purpose he engaged a regular contributor to the magazine. In March 1969 respondent published the resulting article under the title "FRAME-UP: Richard Nuccio And The War On Police." The article purports to demonstrate that the testimony against Nuccio at his criminal trial was false and that his prosecution was part of the Communist campaign against the police.

In his capacity as counsel for the Nelson family in the civil litigation, petitioner attended the coroner's inquest into the boy's death and initiated actions for damages, but he neither discussed Officer Nuccio with the press nor played any part in the criminal proceeding. Notwithstanding petitioner's remote connection with the prosecution of Nuccio, respondent's magazine portrayed him as an architect of the "frame-up." According to the article, the police file on petitioner took "a big, Irish cop to lift." The article stated that petitioner had been an official of the "Marxist League for Industrial Democracy, originally known as the Intercollegiate Socialist Society, which has advocated the violent seizure of our government." It labeled Gertz a "Leninist" and a "Communist-fronter." It also stated that Gertz had been an officer of the National Lawyers Guild, described as a Communist organization that "probably did more than any other outfit to plan the Communist attack on the Chicago police during the 1968 Democratic Convention."

These statements contained serious inaccuracies. The implication that petitioner had a criminal record was false. Petitioner had been a member and officer of the National Lawyers Guild some 15 years earlier, but there was no evidence that he or that organization had taken any part in planning the 1968 demonstrations in Chicago. There was also no basis for the charge that petitioner was a "Leninist" or a "Communist-fronter." And he had never been a member of the "Marxist League for Industrial Democracy" or the "Intercollegiate Socialist Society."

The managing editor of American Opinion made no effort to verify or substantiate the charges against petitioner. Instead, he appended an editorial introduction stating that the author had "conducted extensive research into the Richard Nuccio Case." And he included in the article a photograph of petitioner and wrote the caption that appeared under it: "Elmer Gertz of Red Guild harasses Nuccio." Respondent placed the issue of American Opinion containing the article on sale at newsstands throughout the country and distributed reprints of the article on the streets of Chicago.

Petitioner filed a diversity action for libel in the United States District Court for the Northern District of Illinois. He claimed that the falsehoods published by respondent injured his reputation as a lawyer and a citizen. . . .

After answering the complaint, respondent filed a pretrial motion for summary judgment, claiming a constitutional privilege against liability for defamation. It asserted that petitioner was a public official or a public figure and that the article concerned an issue of public interest and concern. For these reasons, respondent argued, it was entitled to invoke the privilege enunciated in *New York Times Co. v. Sullivan,* 376 U.S. 254 (1964). Under this rule respondent would escape liability unless petitioner could prove publication of defamatory falsehood "with 'actual malice' — that is, with knowledge that it was false or with reckless disregard of whether it was false or not." Respondent claimed that petitioner could not make such a showing and submitted a supporting affidavit by the magazine's managing editor. The editor denied any knowledge of the falsity of the statements concerning petitioner and stated that he had relied on the author's reputation and on his prior experience with the accuracy and authenticity of the author's contributions to American Opinion.

Following [a $50,000] jury verdict . . . the District Court concluded that the *New York Times* standard should govern this case even though petitioner was not a public official or public figure. It accepted respondent's contention that that privilege protected discussion of any public issue without regard to the status of a person defamed therein. Accordingly, the court entered judgment for respondent notwithstanding the jury's verdict. . . .

Petitioner appealed to contest the applicability of the *New York Times* standard to this case. Although the Court of Appeals for the Seventh Circuit doubted the correctness of the District Court's determination that petitioner was not a public figure, it did not overturn that finding. It agreed with the District Court that respondent could assert the constitutional privilege because the article concerned a matter of public interest, citing this Court's intervening decision in *Rosenbloom v. Metromedia, Inc.,* 403 U.S. 29, 29 L. Ed. 2d 296, 91 S. Ct. 1811 (1971). The Court of Appeals read *Rosenbloom* to require application of the *New York Times* standard to any publication or broadcast about an issue of significant public interest, without regard to the position, fame, or anonymity of the person defamed, and it concluded that respondent's statements concerned such an issue. After reviewing the record, the Court of Appeals endorsed the District Court's conclusion that petitioner had failed to show by clear and convincing evidence that respondent had acted with "actual malice" as defined by *New York Times*. There was no evidence that the managing editor of American Opinion knew of the falsity of the accusations made in the article. In fact, he knew nothing about petitioner except what he learned from the article. The court correctly noted that mere proof of failure to investigate, without more, cannot establish reckless disregard for the truth. Rather, the publisher must act with a "high degree of awareness of . . . probable falsity.'" *St. Amant v. Thompson,* 390 U.S. 727, 731 (1968). The evidence in this case did not reveal that respondent had cause for such an awareness. The Court of Appeals therefore affirmed. For the reasons stated below, we reverse. . . .

We begin with the common ground. Under the First Amendment there is no such thing as a false idea. However pernicious an opinion may seem, we depend for its correction not on the conscience of judges and juries but on the competition of other ideas.[7]

But there is no constitutional value in false statements of fact. Neither the intentional lie nor the careless error materially advances society's interest in "uninhibited, robust, and wide-open" debate on public issues. They belong to that category of utterances which "are no essential part of any exposition of ideas, and are of such slight social value as a step to truth that any benefit that may be derived from them is clearly outweighed by the social interest in order and morality. . . ."

The need to avoid self-censorship by the news media is, however, not the only societal value at issue. . . .

The legitimate state interest underlying the law of libel is the compensation of individuals for the harm inflicted on them by defamatory falsehood. We would not lightly require the State to abandon this purpose, for as Mr. Justice Stewart has reminded us, the individual's right to the protection of his own good name "reflects no more than our basic concept of the essential dignity and worth of every human being — a concept at the root of any decent system of ordered liberty. The protection of private personality, like the protection of life itself, is left primarily to the individual States under the Ninth and Tenth Amendments. But this does not mean that the right is entitled to any less recognition by this Court as a basic of our constitutional system." *Rosenblatt v. Baer,* 383 U.S. 75, 92 (1966) (concurring opinion). . . .

The *New York Times* standard defines the level of constitutional protection appropriate to the context of defamation of a public person. Those who, by reason of the notoriety of their achievements or the vigor and success with which they seek the public's attention, are properly classed as public figures

---

[7] As Thomas Jefferson made the point in his first Inaugural Address: "If there be any among us who would wish to dissolve this Union or change its republican form, let them stand undisturbed as monuments of the safety with which error of opinion may be tolerated where reason is left free to combat it."

and those who hold governmental office may recover for injury to reputation only on clear and convincing proof that the defamatory falsehood was made with knowledge of its falsity or with reckless disregard for the truth. This standard administers an extremely powerful antidote to the inducement to media self-censorship of the common-law rule of strict liability for libel and slander. And it exacts a correspondingly high price from the victims of defamatory falsehood. Plainly many deserving plaintiffs, including some intentionally subjected to injury, will be unable to surmount the barrier of the *New York Times* test. Despite this substantial abridgment of the state law right to compensation for wrongful hurt to one's reputation, the Court has concluded that the protection of the *New York Times* privilege should be available to publishers and broadcasters of defamatory falsehood concerning public officials and public figures. We think that these decisions are correct, but we do not find their holdings justified solely by reference to the interest of the press and broadcast media in immunity from liability. Rather, we believe that the *New York Times* rule states an accommodation between this concern and the limited state interest present in the context of libel actions brought by public persons. For the reasons stated below, we conclude that the state interest in compensating injury to the reputation of private individuals requires that a different rule should obtain with respect to them.

Theoretically, of course, the balance between the needs of the press and the individual's claim to compensation for wrongful injury might be struck on a case-by-case basis. As Mr. Justice Harlan hypothesized, "it might seem, purely as an abstract matter, that the most utilitarian approach would be to scrutinize carefully every jury verdict in every libel case, in order to ascertain whether the final judgment leaves fully protected whatever First Amendment values transcend the legitimate state interest in protecting the particular plaintiff who prevailed." *Rosenbloom v. Metromedia, Inc.,* 403 U.S. 63, 91 S. Ct. at 1829. But this approach would lead to unpredictable results and uncertain expectations, and it could render our duty to supervise the lower courts unmanageable. Because an *ad hoc* resolution of the competing interests at stake in each particular case is not feasible, we must lay down broad rules of general application. Such rules necessarily treat alike various cases involving differences as well as similarities. Thus it is often true that not all of the considerations which justify adoption of a given rule will obtain in each particular case decided under its authority.

With that caveat we have no difficulty in distinguishing among defamation plaintiffs. The first remedy of any victim of defamation is self-help — using available opportunities to contradict the lie or correct the error and thereby to minimize its adverse impact on reputation. Public officials and public figures usually enjoy significantly greater access to the channels of effective communication and hence have a more realistic opportunity to counteract false statements than private individuals normally enjoy. Private individuals are therefore more vulnerable to injury, and the state interest in protecting them is correspondingly greater.

More important than the likelihood that private individuals will lack effective opportunities for rebuttal, there is a compelling normative consideration underlying the distinction between public and private defamation plaintiffs. An individual who decides to seek governmental office must accept certain necessary consequences of that involvement in public affairs. He runs the risk of closer public scrutiny than might otherwise be the case. And society's interest in the officers of government is not strictly limited to the formal discharge of official duties. As the Court pointed out in *Garrison v. Louisiana,* 379 U.S. 64, 77, 13 L. Ed. 2d 125, 85 S. Ct. 209 (1964), the public's interest extends to "anything which might touch on an official's fitness for office. . . . Few personal attributes are more germane to fitness for office than dishonesty, malfeasance, or improper motivation, even though these characteristics may also affect the official's private character."

Those classed as public figures stand in a similar position. Hypothetically, it may be possible for someone to become a public figure through no purposeful action of his own, but the instances of truly involuntary public figures must be exceedingly rare. For the most part those who attain this status have assumed roles of especial prominence in the affairs of society. Some occupy positions of such persuasive power and influence that they are deemed public figures for all purposes. More commonly, those classed as public figures have thrust themselves to the forefront of particular public controversies in order to influence the resolution of the issues involved. In either event, they invite attention and comment.

Even if the foregoing generalities do not obtain in every instance, the communications media are entitled to act on the assumption that public officials and public figures have voluntarily exposed themselves to increased risk of injury from defamatory falsehood concerning them. No such assumption is justified with respect to a private individual. He has not accepted public office or assumed an "influential role in ordering society." *Curtis Pub. Co. v. Butts,* 388 U.S. 130, 164, 18 L. Ed. 2d 1094, 87 S. Ct. 1975 (1967) (Warren, C.J., concurring in result). He has relinquished no part of his interest in the protection of his own good name, and consequently he has a more compelling call on the courts for redress of injury inflicted by defamatory falsehood. Thus, private individuals are not only more vulnerable to injury than public officials and public figures; they are also more deserving of recovery.

For these reasons we conclude that the States should retain substantial latitude in their efforts to enforce a legal remedy for defamatory falsehood injurious to the reputation of a private individual. The extension of the *New York Times* test proposed by the *Rosenbloom* plurality would abridge this legitimate state interest to a degree that we find unacceptable. And it would occasion the additional difficulty of forcing state and federal judges to decide on an *ad hoc* basis which publications address issues of "general or public interest" and which do not — to determine, in the words of Mr. Justice Marshall, "what information is relevant to self-government." We doubt the wisdom of committing this task to the conscience of judges. Nor does the Constitution require us to draw so thin a line between the drastic alternatives of the *New York Times* privilege and the common law of strict liability for defamatory error. The "public or general interest" test for determining the applicability of the *New York Times* standard to private defamation actions inadequately serves both of the competing values at stake. On the one hand, a private individual whose reputation is injured by defamatory falsehood that does concern an issue of public or general interest has no recourse unless he can meet the rigorous requirements of *New York Times*. This is true despite the factors that distinguish the state interest in compensating private individuals from the analogous interest involved in the context of public persons. On the other hand, a publisher or broadcaster of a defamatory error which a court deems unrelated to an issue of public or general interest may be held liable in damages even if it took every reasonable precaution to ensure the accuracy of its assertions. And liability may far exceed compensation for any actual injury to the plaintiff, for the jury may be permitted to presume damages without proof of loss and even to award punitive damages.

We hold that, so long as they do not impose liability without fault, the States may define for themselves the appropriate standard of liability for a publisher or broadcaster of defamatory falsehood injurious to a private individual.[8] This approach provides a more equitable boundary between the competing concerns involved here. It recognizes the strength of the legitimate state interest in compensating private individuals for wrongful injury to reputation, yet shields the press and broadcast media from the rigors of strict liability for defamation. At least this conclusion obtains where, as here, the substance of the defamatory statement "makes substantial danger to reputation apparent."[9] This phrase places in perspective the conclusion we announce today. Our inquiry would involve considerations somewhat different from those discussed above if a State purported to condition civil liability on a factual misstatement whose content did not warn a reasonably prudent editor or broadcaster of its defamatory potential. Such a case is not now before us, and we intimate no view as to its proper resolution.

---

[8] Our caveat against strict liability is the prime target of Mr. Justice White's dissent. He would hold that a publisher or broadcaster may be required to prove the truth of a defamatory statement concerning a private individual and, failing such proof, that the publisher or broadcaster may be held liable for defamation even though he took every conceivable precaution to ensure the accuracy of the offending statement prior to its dissemination. In Mr. Justice White's view, one who publishes a statement that later turns out to be inaccurate can never be "without fault" in any meaningful sense, for "[i]t is he who circulated a falsehood that he was not required to publish."

Mr. Justice White characterizes *New York Times Co. v. Sullivan* as simply a case of seditious libel. But that rationale is certainly inapplicable to *Curtis Publishing Co. v. Butts*, where Mr. Justice White joined four other Members of the Court to extend the knowing-or-reckless-falsity standard to media defamation of persons identified as public figures but not connected with the Government. Mr. Justice White now suggests that he would abide by that vote, but the full thrust of his dissent — as we read it — contradicts that suggestion. Finally, in *Rosenbloom v. Metromedia, Inc.*, Mr. Justice White voted to apply the New York Times privilege to media defamation of an individual who was neither a public official nor a public figure. His opinion states that the knowing-or-reckless-falsity standard should apply to media "comment upon the official actions of public servants," including defamatory falsehood about a person arrested by the police. If adopted by the Court, this conclusion would significantly extend the New York Times privilege.

Mr. Justice White asserts that our decision today "trivializes and denigrates the interest in reputation," that it "scuttle[s] the libel laws of the States in . . . wholesale fashion" and renders ordinary citizens "powerless to protect themselves." In light of the progressive extension of the knowing-or-reckless-falsity requirement detailed in the preceding paragraph, one might have viewed today's decision allowing recovery under any standard save strict liability as a more generous accommodation of the state interest in comprehensive reputational injury to private individuals than the law presently affords.

[9] *Curtis Pub. Co. v. Butts,* 388 U.S. at 155, 87 S. Ct. at 1991.

Our accommodation of the competing values at stake in defamation suits by private individuals allows the States to impose liability on the publisher or broadcaster of defamatory falsehood on a less demanding showing than that required by *New York Times*. This conclusion is not based on a belief that the considerations which prompted the adoption of the *New York Times* privilege for defamation of public officials and its extension to public figures are wholly inapplicable to the context of private individuals. Rather, we endorse this approach in recognition of the strong and legitimate state interest in compensating private individuals for injury to reputation. But this countervailing state interest extends no further than compensation for actual injury. For the reasons stated below, we hold that the States may not permit recovery of presumed or punitive damages, at least when liability is not based on a showing of knowledge of falsity or reckless disregard for the truth.

The common law of defamation is an oddity of tort law, for it allows recovery of purportedly compensatory damages without evidence of actual loss. Under the traditional rules pertaining to actions for libel, the existence of injury is presumed from the fact of publication. Juries may award substantial sums as compensation for supposed damage to reputation without any proof that such harm actually occurred. The largely uncontrolled discretion of juries to award damages where there is no loss unnecessarily compounds the potential of any system of liability for defamatory falsehood to inhibit the vigorous exercise of First Amendment freedoms. Additionally, the doctrine of presumed damages invites juries to punish unpopular opinion rather than to compensate individuals for injury sustained by the publication of a false fact. More to the point, the States have no substantial interest in securing for plaintiffs such as this petitioner gratuitous awards of money damages far in excess of any actual injury.

We would not, of course, invalidate state law simply because we doubt its wisdom, but here we are attempting to reconcile state law with a competing interest grounded in the constitutional command of the First Amendment. It is therefore appropriate to require that state remedies for defamatory falsehood reach no farther than is necessary to protect the legitimate interest involved. It is necessary to restrict defamation plaintiffs who do not prove knowledge of falsity or reckless disregard for the truth to compensation for actual injury. We need not define "actual injury," as trial courts have wide experience in framing appropriate jury instructions in tort actions. Suffice it to say that actual injury is not limited to out-of-pocket loss. Indeed, the more customary types of actual harm inflicted by defamatory falsehood include impairment of reputation and standing in the community, personal humiliation, and mental anguish and suffering. Of course, juries must be limited by appropriate instructions, and all awards must be supported by competent evidence concerning the injury, although there need be no evidence which assigns an actual dollar value to the injury.

We also find no justification for allowing awards of punitive damages against publishers and broadcasters held liable under state-defined standards of liability for defamation. In most jurisdictions jury discretion over the amounts awarded is limited only by the gentle rule that they not be excessive. Consequently, juries assess punitive damages in wholly unpredictable amounts bearing no necessary relation to the actual harm caused. And they remain free to use their discretion selectively to punish expressions of unpopular views. Like the doctrine of presumed damages, jury discretion to award punitive damages unnecessarily exacerbates the danger of media self-censorship, but, unlike the former rule, punitive damages are wholly irrelevant to the state interest that justifies a negligence standard for private defamation actions. They are not compensation for injury. Instead, they are private fines levied by civil juries to punish reprehensible conduct and to deter its future occurrence. In short, the private defamation plaintiff who establishes liability under a less demanding standard than that stated by *New York Times* may recover only such damages as are sufficient to compensate him for actual injury.

Notwithstanding our refusal to extend the *New York Times* privilege to defamation of private individuals, respondent contends that we should affirm the judgment below on the ground that petitioner is either a public official or a public figure. There is little basis for the former assertion. Several years prior to the present incident, petitioner had served briefly on housing committees appointed by the mayor of Chicago, but at the time of publication he had never held any remunerative governmental position. Respondent admits this but argues that petitioner's appearance at the coroner's inquest rendered him a "de facto public official." Our cases recognize no such concept. Respondent's suggestion would sweep all lawyers under the *New York Times* rule as officers of the court and distort the plain meaning of the "public official" category beyond all recognition. We decline to follow it.

Respondent's characterization of petitioner as a public figure raises a different question. That designation may rest on either of two alternative bases. In some instances an individual may achieve such pervasive fame or notoriety that he becomes a public figure for all purposes and in all contexts. More commonly, an individual voluntarily injects himself or is drawn into a particular public controversy and thereby becomes a public figure for a limited range of issues. In either case such persons assume special prominence in the resolution of public questions.

Petitioner has long been active in community and professional affairs. He has served as an officer of local civic groups and of various professional organizations, and he has published several books and articles on legal subjects. Although petitioner was consequently well known in some circles, he had achieved no general fame or notoriety in the community. None of the prospective jurors called at the trial had ever heard of petitioner prior to this litigation, and respondent offered no proof that this response was atypical of the local population. We would not lightly assume that a citizen's participation in community and professional affairs rendered him a public figure for all purposes. Absent clear evidence of general fame or notoriety in the community, and pervasive involvement in the affairs of society, an individual should not be deemed a public personality for all aspects of his life. It is preferable to reduce the public-figure question to a more meaningful context by looking to the nature and extent of an individual's participation in the particular controversy giving rise to the defamation.

In this context it is plain that petitioner was not a public figure. He played a minimal role at the coroner's inquest, and his participation related solely to his representation of a private client. He took no part in the criminal prosecution of Officer Nuccio. Moreover, he never discussed either the criminal or civil litigation with the press and was never quoted as having done so. He plainly did not thrust himself into the vortex of this public issue, nor did he engage the public's attention in an attempt to influence its outcome. We are persuaded that the trial court did not err in refusing to characterize petitioner as a public figure for the purpose of this litigation.

We therefore conclude that the *New York Times* standard is inapplicable to this case and that the trial court erred in entering judgment for respondent. Because the jury was allowed to impose liability without fault and was permitted to presume damages without proof of injury, a new trial is necessary. We reverse and remand for further proceedings in accord with this opinion.

[BLACKMUN, J., who joined in the plurality opinion in *Rosenbloom,* nevertheless concurred in the opinion here as follows.]

Although the Court's opinion in the present case departs from the rationale of the *Rosenbloom* plurality, in that the Court now conditions a libel action by a private person upon a showing of negligence, as contrasted with a showing of willful or reckless disregard, I am willing to join, and so join, the Court's opinion and its judgment for two reasons:

1. By removing the specters of presumed and punitive damages in the absence of *New York Times* malice, the Court eliminates significant and powerful motives for self-censorship that otherwise are present in the traditional libel action. By so doing, the Court leaves what should prove to be sufficient and adequate breathing space for a vigorous press. What the Court has done, I believe, will have little, if any, practical effect on the functioning of responsible journalism.

2. The Court was sadly fractionated in *Rosenbloom.* A result of that kind inevitably leads to uncertainty. I feel that it is of profound importance for the Court to come to rest in the defamation area and to have a clearly defined majority position that eliminates the unsureness engendered by *Rosenbloom's* diversity. If my vote were not needed to create a majority, I would adhere to my prior view. A definitive ruling, however, is paramount. . . .

NOTES

1. *Actual Injury Versus Special Damage.* The *Gertz* Court said the private plaintiff, who seeks recovery on the basis of a showing of fault that is less than that of constitutional malice, must prove "actual injury." That injury is not the same as that of "special damage," which is typically required for recovery in slander *per quod.* "Actual injury" under *Gertz* can be shown by proving mental anguish and suffering, which alone is insufficient to establish "special damage."

2. *Vicarious Liability Revisited.* The author of the American Opinion article about Mr. Gertz likely wrote with constitutional malice (knowing falsity, or reckless disregard of the truth). Why was that malice not imputed to the defendant publisher?

3. *Public Official and Public Figure Compared.* In *Jenoff v. Hearst Corp.*, 644 F.2d 1004 (4th Cir. 1981), the defendant newspaper allegedly libeled plaintiff Jenoff, an informant for the Baltimore Police Department, by writing that he had broken into the office of a criminal defense attorney and that the statements of certain key witnesses had disappeared from the office at that time. Affirming a judgment for the plaintiff, the court found he was neither a public official nor a public figure. One need not hold a "formal public position" in order to be a public official, the court said. One may "participate in some governmental enterprise to such an extent" as to require that he be "classified as a public official." But as an informant for the police department, Jenoff played such a "minor role" in a "government enterprise" as to "preclude the public official characterization." Nor was the plaintiff a voluntary public figure:

> Jenoff enjoyed no special access to the media, other than that which may have been created by the defamatory publications. Similarly, he assumed no prominence in any public controversy, except as a result of the charges levelled against him. It is established that "those charged with defamation cannot, by their own conduct, create their own defense by making the claimant a public figure." *Hutchinson v. Proxmire,* 443 U.S. 111, 135, 61 L. Ed. 2d 411, 99 S. Ct. 2675 (1979).
>
> If a particular public controversy existed at all prior to the defamatory articles, it can hardly be said that Jenoff's participation therein was voluntary. His assumption of the informant's role cannot constitute voluntary entry into public debate over the role of informants unless we are to hold that all informants, by virtue of that status, become public figures. The use of such "subject-matter classifications" to define the contours of constitutionally protected defamation has been authoritatively rejected. See *Hutchinson v. Proxmire,* 443 U.S. 111, 135 (1979); *Time, Inc. v. Firestone,* 424 U.S. 448, 456, 47 L. Ed. 2d 154, 96 S. Ct. 958 (1976).
>
> Finally, whatever attention Jenoff's activities might have invited, it is beyond dispute that he never sought thereby to influence the resolution of any public issue. Whether this in itself is determinative, see *Wolston v. Reader's Digest Ass'n,* 443 U.S. 157, 169, 61 L. Ed. 2d 450, 99 S. Ct. 2701 (1979) (Blackmun, J., concurring) ("The Court seems to hold . . . that a person becomes a limited-issue public figure only if he literally or figuratively 'mounts a rostrum' to advocate a particular view"), or merely a significant factor, it is wholly absent from this case. We agree with the District Court that Jenoff remains a private individual.

In *Bowman v. Heller,* 420 Mass. 517, 651 N. E. 2d 369 (1995), the plaintiff, a 60-year-old woman, was the supervisor of a local welfare office and a candidate for the office of president of the union local. The defendant, a coworker, circulated in the office sexually crude pictures with a photo of the plaintiff's head superimposed at the top of the pictures. He did this, he said, not to "sway votes" but to make the plaintiff "look ridiculous."

The plaintiff sued for intentional and reckless infliction of emotional distress and for sexual harassment. The court assumed that the constitutional malice standard of *Gertz* applied to the claims if plaintiff was a limited-purpose public figure. It found that she was not such a figure, since she had not voluntarily injected herself into a public controversy. A vigorous dissent contended that a union election "is the absolute paradigm of a public controversy."

Why wasn't the plaintiff a public official, since she was running for a union office?

Was malice constitutionally required to be shown for recovery if plaintiff was a public official or a public figure? Consider *Hustler Magazine, Inc. v. Falwell*, 485 U. S. 46, 108 S. Ct. 876, 99 L. Ed. 2d 41 (1988), where the Court held the plaintiff, a public figure, was constitutionally barred from recovering for intentional infliction of emotional distress because defendant's parody of the plaintiff was nondefamatory. The *Falwell* parody was apparently nondefamatory because it did not assert a false statement of fact. Consider the material on opinion given below. If the plaintiff in *Bowman* was not a public figure, must she still prove falsity under the *Gertz* negligence standard?

4. *Burden of Proof.* In a 5-4 decision, the United States Supreme Court in *Philadelphia Newspapers, Inc. v. Hepps*, 475 U.S. 767, 106 S. Ct. 1558, 89 L. Ed. 2d 783 (1986), held that the private plaintiff in a defamation suit involving a matter of public concern has the burden of proving falsity of the defamation. The burden lies with the public plaintiff in a matter of public concern, said the Court, to show falsity by "clear and convincing evidence." The Court left open the question of whether the rule of the case applied to nonmedia defendants.

The dissent thought it sufficient if the plaintiff showed fault on the part of the defendant. It simply did not "understand, however, why a character assassin should be given an absolute license to defame by means of statements that can neither be verified nor disproven."

DUN & BRADSTREET, INC. v. GREENMOSS BUILDERS, INC.
472 U.S. 749 (1985)

JUSTICE POWELL announced the judgment of the Court and delivered an opinion, in which JUSTICE REHNQUIST and JUSTICE O'CONNOR joined.

In *Gertz v. Robert Welch, Inc.*, 418 U.S. 323, 94 S. Ct. 2997, 41 L. Ed. 2d 789 (1974), we held that the First Amendment restricted the damages that a private individual could obtain from a publisher for libel that involved a matter of public concern. More specifically, we held that in these circumstances the First Amendment prohibited awards of presumed and punitive damages for false and defamatory statements unless the plaintiff shows "actual malice," that is, knowledge of falsity or reckless disregard for the truth. The question presented in this case is whether this rule of *Gertz* applies when the false an defamatory statements do not involve matters of public concern.

Petitioner Dun & Bradstreet, a credit reporting agency, provides subscribers with financial and related information about businesses. All the information is confidential; under the terms of the subscription agreement the subscribers may not reveal it to anyone else. On July 26, 1976, petitioner sent a report to five subscribers indicating that respondent, a construction contractor, had filed a voluntary petition for bankruptcy. This report was false and grossly misrepresented respondent's assets and liabilities. That same day, while discussing the possibility of future financing with its bank, respondent's president was told that the bank had received the defamatory report. He immediately called petitioner's regional office, explained the error, and asked for a correction. In addition, he requested the names of the firms that had received the false report in order to assure them that the company was solvent. Petitioner promised to look into the matter but refused to divulge the names of those who had received the report.

After determining that the report was indeed false, petitioner issued a corrective notice on or about August 3, 1976, to the five subscribers who had received the initial report. The notice stated that one of respondent's former employees, not respondent itself, had filed for bankruptcy and that respondent "continued in business as usual." Respondent told petitioner that it ws dissatisfied with the notice, and it again asked for a list of subscribers who had seen the initial report. Again petitioner refused to divulge their names.

Respondent then brought this defamation action in Vermont state court. It alleged that the false report had injured its reputation and sought both compensatory and punitive damages. The trial established that the error in petitioner's report had been caused when one of its employees, a 17-year-old high school student paid to review Vermont bankruptcy pleadings, had inadvertently attributed to respondent a bankruptcy petition filed by one of respondent's former employees. Although petitioner's representative testified that it was routine practice to check the accuracy of such reports with the businesses themselves, it did not try to verify the information about respondent before reporting it.

After trial, the jury returned a verdict in favor of respondent and awarded $50,000 in compensatory or presumed damages and $300,000 in punitive damages.

[The trial court granted a new trial, but the state supreme court reversed and reinstated the jury verdict, holding that *Gertz* did not apply to a non-media defendant.]

As an initial matter, respondent contends that we need not determine whether *Gertz* applies in this case because the instructions, taken as a whole, required the jury to find "actual malice" before awarding presumed or punitive damages. The trial court instructed the jury that because the report was libelous per se, respondent was not required "to prove actual damages. . . since damage and loss [are] conclusively presumed." It also instructed the jury that it could award punitive damages only if it found "actual malice." Its only other relevant instruction was that liability could not be established unless respondent showed "malice or lack of good faith on the part of the Defendant." Respondent contends that these references to "malice," "lack of good faith," and "actual malice" required the jury to find knowledge of falsity or reckless disregard for the truth — the "actual malice" of *New York Times, Co. v. Sullivan*, 376 U.S. 254 (1964) — before it awarded presumed or punitive damages.

We reject this claim because the trial court failed to define any of these terms adequately. It did not, for example, provide the jury with any definition of the term "actual malice." In fact, the only relevant term it defined was simple "malice."[10] And its definitions of this term included not only the *New York Times* formulation but also other concepts such as "bad faith" and "reckless disregard of the [statement's] possible consequences." The instructions thus permitted the jury to award presumed and punitive damages on a lesser showing than "actual malice." Consequently, the trial court's conclusion that the instructions did not satisfy *Gertz* was correct, and the Vermont Supreme Court's determination that *Gertz* was inapplicable was necessary to its decision that the trial court erred in granting the motion for a new trial. We therefore must consider whether *Gertz* applies to the case before us.

In *New York Times Co. v. Sullivan*, supra, the Court for the first time held the that First Amendment limits the reach of state defamation laws. That case concerned a public official's recovery of damages for the publication of an advertisement criticizing police conduct in a civil rights demonstration. As the Court noted, the advertisement concerned "one of the major public issues of our time." *Id.*, 376 U.S., at 271. Noting that "freedom of expression *upon public questions* is secured by the First Amendment," and that "debate *on public issues* should be uninhibited, robust, and wide-open," *id.*, at 270, the Court held that a public official cannot recover damages for defamatory falsehood unless he proves that the false statement was made with " 'actual malice' — that is, with knowledge that it was false or with reckless disregard of whether it was false or not," *id.*, at 280. In later cases, all involving public issues, the Court extended this same constitutional protection to libels of public figures, e.g., *Curtis Publishing Co. v. Butts*, 388 U.S. 130 (1967), and in one case suggested in a plurality opinion that this constitutional rule should extend to libels of any individual so long as the defamatory statements involved a "matter of public or general interest," *Rosenbloom v. Metromedia, Inc.*, 403 U.S. 29, (1971) (opinion of BRENNAN, J.).

In *Gertz v. Robert Welch, Inc.*, 418 U.S. 323 (1974), we held that the protections of *New York Times* did not extend as far as *Rosenbloom* suggested. *Gertz* concerned a libelous article appearing in a magazine called American Opinion, the monthly outlet of the John Birch Society. The article in question discussed whether the prosecution of a policeman in Chicago was part of a Communist campaign to discredit local law enforcement agencies. The plaintiff, Gertz, neither a public official nor a public figure, was a lawyer tangentially involved in the prosecution. The magazine alleged that he was the chief architect of the "frame-up" of the police officer and linked him to Communist activity. Like every other case in which this Court has found constitutional limits to state defamation laws, *Gertz* involved expression on a matter of undoubted public concern.

In *Gertz*, we held that the fact that expression concerned a public issue did not by itself entitle the libel defendant to the constitutional protections of *New*

---

[10] The full instruction on malice reads as follows:

"If you find that the Defendant acted in a bad faith towards the Plaintiff in publishing the Erroneous Report, *or* that Defendant intended to injure the Plaintiff in it business, *or* that it acted in a willful, wanton or reckless disregard of the rights and interests of the Plaintiff, the Defendant has acted maliciously and the privilege is destroyed. *Further*, if the Report was made with reckless disregard of the possible consequences, *or* if it was made with the knowledge that it was false *or* with the reckless disregard of its truth or falsity, it was made with malice."

York Times. These protections, we found, were not "justified solely by reference to the interest of the press and broadcast media in immunity from liability." 418 U.S., at 343. Rather, they represented "an accommodation between [First Amendment] concern[s] and the limited state interest present in the context of libel actions brought by public persons." In libel actions brought by private persons we found the competing interests different. Largely because private persons have not voluntarily exposed themselves to increased risk of injury from defamatory statements and because they generally lack effective opportunities for rebutting such statements, we found that the State possessed a "strong and legitimate . . . interest in compensating private individuals for injury to reputation." *Id.*, at 348–349. Balancing this stronger state interest against the same First Amendment interest at stake in *New York Times*, we held that a State could not allow recovery of presumed and punitive damages absent a showing of "actual malice." Nothing in our opinion, however, indicated that this same balance would be struck regardless of the type of speech involved.[11]

We have never considered whether the *Gertz* balance obtains when the defamatory statements involve no issue of public concern. To make this determination, we must employ the approach approved in *Gertz* and balance the State's interest in compensating private individuals for injury to their reputation against the First Amendment interest in protecting this type of expression. This state interest is identical to the one weighed in *Gertz*. There we found that it was "strong and legitimate." 418 U.S., at 348. . . .

The First Amendment interest, on the other hand, is less important than the one weighed in *Gertz*. . . . In contrast, speech on matters of purely private concern is of less First Amendment concern. As a number of state courts, including the court below, have recognized, the role of the Constitution in regulating state libel law is far more limited when the concerns that activated *New York Times* and *Gertz* are absent.[12] In such a case,

> "[t]here is no threat to the free and robust debate of public issues; there is no potential interference with a meaningful dialogue of ideas

---

[11] The dissent states that "[a]t several points the Court in *Gertz* makes perfectly clear [that] the restrictions of presumed and punitive damages were to apply in all cases." Given the context of *Gertz* however, the Court could have made "perfectly clear" only that these restrictions applied in cases involving *public speech*. In fact, the dissent itself concedes that "*Gertz*. . .focused largely on defining the circumstances under which protection of the central First Amendment value of robust debate of *public issues* should mandate plaintiffs to show actual malice to obtain a judgment and actual damages. . . ."

The dissent also incorrectly states that *Gertz* "specifically held that the award of presumed and punitive damages on less than a showing of actual malice is not a narrowly tailored means to achieve the legitimate state purpose of protecting the reputation of private persons. . .," and that "unrestrained presumed and punitive damages were 'unnecessarily' broad. . .in relation to the legitimate state interests." Although the Court made both statements, it did so only within the context of public speech. Neither statement controls here. What was "not . . .narrowly tailored" or was " 'unnecessarily' broad" with respect to public speech is not necessarily so with respect to the speech now at issue. Properly understood, *Gertz* is consistent with the result we reach today.

[12] As one commentator has remarked with respect to "the case of a commercial supplier of credit information that defames a person applying for credit" — the case before us today — "If the first amendment requirements outlined in *Gertz* apply, there is something clearly wrong with the first amendment or with *Gertz*." Shifferin, The First Amendment and Economic Regulation: Away From a General Theory of the First Amendment, 78 Nw.U.L.Rev. 1212, 1268 (1983).

concerning self-government; and there is no threat of liability causing a reaction to self-censorship by the press. The facts of the present case are wholly without the First Amendment concerns with which the Supreme Court of the United States has been struggling." *Harley-Davidson Motorsports, Inc., v. Markley*, 279 Or. 361, 366, 568 P.2d 1359, 1363 (1977). . . .

The only remaining issue is whether petitioner's credit report involved a matter of public concern. In a related context, we have held that "[w]hether . . . speech addresses a matter of public concern must be determined by [the expressions's] content, form, and context . . . as revealed by the whole record." *Connick v. Myers*, 461 U.S., at 147–148. These factors indicate that petitioner's credit report concerns no public issue.[13] It was speech solely in the individual interest of the speaker and its specific business audience. This particular interest warrants no special protection when — as in this case — the speech is wholly false and clearly damaging to the victim's business reputation. Moreover, since the credit report was made available to only five subscribers, who, under the terms of the subscription agreement, could not disseminate it further, it cannot be said that the report involves any strong interest in the free flow of commercial information. There is simply no credible argument that this type of credit reporting requires special protection to ensure that "debate on public issues [will] be uninhibited, robust, and wide-open." *New York Times Co. v. Sullivan*, 376 U.S., at 270.

In addition, the speech here, like advertising, is hardy and unlikely to be deterred by incidental state regulation. It is solely motivated by the desire for profit, which we have noted, is a force less likely to be deterred by others. Arguably, the reporting here was also more objectively verifiable than speech deserving of greater protection. In any case, the market provides a powerful incentive to a credit reporting agency to be accurate, since false credit reporting is of no use to creditors. Thus, any incremental "chilling" effect of libel suits would be of decreased significance.[14]

We conclude that permitting recovery of presumed and punitive damages in defamtion cases absent a showing of "actual malice" does not violate the First Amendment when the defamatory statements do not involve matters of public concern. Accordingly, we affirm the judgment of the Vermont Supreme Court.

---

[13] The dissent suggests that our holding today leaves all credit reporting subject to reduced First Amendment protection. This is incorrect. The protection to be accorded a particular credit report depends on whether the report's "content, form, and context" indicate that it concerns a public matter. We also do not hold, as the dissent suggests we do, that the report is subject to reduced constitutional protection because it constitutes economic or commercial speech. We discuss such speech, along with advertising, only to show how many of the same concerns that argue in favor of reduced constitutional protection in those areas apply here as well.

[14] The Court of Appeals for the Fifth Circuit has noted that, while most States provide a qualified privilege against libel suits for commercial credit reporting agencies, in those States that do not there is a thriving credit reporting business and commercial credit transactions are not inhibited. *Hood v. Dun & Bradstreet, Inc.*, 486 F.2d 25, 32 (1973), cert. denied, 415 U.S. 985 (1974). The court cited an empirical study comparing credit transactions in Boise, Idaho, where there is no privilege, with those in Spokane, Washington, where there is one. 486 F.2d, at 32, and n. 18.

[BURGER, C.J., AND WHITE, J., concurred in the judgment. They believed *Gertz* should be overruled. They did not think the Constitution should be applied where the "ordinary private citizen" was the plaintiff. They agreed that the holding in *Gertz* should be limited to those situations where the defamation dealt with a matter of public importance.

[Justices BRENNAN, MARSHALL, BLACKMUN and STEVENS dissented, asserting that the case was controlled by *Gertz*.]

NOTES

1. *The Scope of Dun & Bradstreet.* When the matter is not one of public concern, can the court impose strict liability? Place the burden of proof wherever it chooses? Remove the defense of truth? Make "pure opinion" actionable as defamation?

The Fair Credit Reporting Act, 15 U.S.C § 1681, requires that a credit agency disclose on request to any reported consumer debtor the names of any recipients of the credit report. This act does not apply, however, to reports in connection with the issuance of commercial credit. 4 BUSINESS TORTS § 33.08[1], at 33–52 (J. Zamore, ed., 1989). Why do you suppose the defendant in *Greenmoss Builders* was unwilling to furnish the plaintiff with the names of the persons who received the credit report?

In *Johnson v. Johnson*, 654 A.2d 1212 (R. I. 1995), plaintiff brought a slander action against her former husband for calling her a "whore" in a public place. The trial court found the statement was "essentially truthful," but was made with "spite or ill will." Such a finding was sufficient to support a compensatory award of $5,000, but the punitive award of $20,000 was struck because the statement was made "under enormous provocation" and therefore the award did not meet "the rigorous standard which we set for punitive damages."

The *Johnson* court recognized that in *Garrison v. Louisiana*, 379 U. S. 64, 85 S. Ct. 209, 13 L. Ed. 2d 125 (1964), the U. S. Supreme Court "held that the *New York Times* rule absolutely prohibits punishment of truthful criticism of public officials," even if the statements are made with "hatred, ill will or enmity or a wanton desire to injure." But here, the court said, "we are not dealing with public officials, public figures, or even matters of public concern." Citing *Dun & Bradstreet*, the court said that damages may be awarded in accordance with state law where "the defamatory statements made by defendant were not matters of public concern."

2. *Single and Multiple Publications.* Sec. 577A of the REST. 2d OF TORTS (1977) states:

> (1) Except as stated in Subsections (2) and (3), each of several communications to a third person by the same defamer is a separate publication.
>
> (2) A single communication heard at the same time by two or more third persons is a single publication.
>
> (3) Any one edition of a book or newspaper, or any one radio or television broadcast, exhibition of a motion picture or similar aggregate communication is a single publication.

(4) As to any single publication,

(a) only one action for damages can be maintained;

(b) all damages suffered in all jurisdictions can be recovered in the one action; and

(c) a judgment for or against the plaintiff upon the merits of any action for damages bars any other action for damages between the same parties in all jurisdictions.

The comments to this section state that if defendant makes the same defamatory statement about plaintiff on three separate occasions, once to one person and twice to another person, plaintiff has three causes of action. But if defendant makes the statement to an audience of a thousand persons, plaintiff has only one cause of action.

Note that one edition of a book or newspaper constitutes a single publication, even though hundreds of different people may read the publication at different times. (When does the statute of limitations begin to run in this situation?) But repetition of a radio or TV broadcast, and each showing of a movie, constitute separate publications.

3. *The Malice Requirement and the Private Plaintiff*. In *Turf Lawnmower Repair, Inc. v. Bergen Record Corp.*, 139 N. J. 392, 655 A.2d 417 (1995), the court noted that "forty-two jurisdictions in the United States hold that negligence is the standard for private plaintiffs to recover against a media defendant even when the subject matter is of public concern." States are free to impose a higher standard, however, and Colorado, Indiana and New Jersey use the actual malice standard in such cases.

The court in *Turf* decided to change its rule for private plaintiffs. The "negligence standard is the most appropriate standard with regard to businesses involved with an everyday product or service." But the actual malice standard would be used with regard to plaintiff businesses "whose practices allegedly constitute consumer fraud, impinge on the health and safety of New Jersey's citizenry, or comprise activity within a highly regulated industry."

LUND v. CHICAGO AND NORTHWESTERN TRANSPORTATION COMPANY
467 N. W.2d 366 (Minn. App. 1991)

EDWARD D. MULALLY, JUDGE.

Richard Lund sued his employer for defamation and infliction of emotional distress. Concluding that the allegedly defamatory statements were constitutionally protected expressions of opinion and that Lund had not established the elements for a claim of emotional distress, the trial court entered summary judgment in favor of the employer. Lund appeals. We affirm.

On August 29, 1988, various employees of the Chicago and Northwestern Transportation Company participated in a "brainstorming session" to discuss general problems and concerns. Such meetings were commonly held and were part of the company's effort to promote open communication. Richard Lund, an employee of C & NW and the plaintiff in this action, was not present at the meeting.

A C & NW manager, Ray Peterson, compiled his notes of the meeting into a typed, four-page memorandum. Most of the 85, numbered entries concerned employees' complaints with management's practices and responses to problems. However, line 66 of the memorandum read as follows:

FAVORITISM, DICK LUND, SICK, MOVE-UPS, BROWN NOSE, SHIT HEADS.

The memorandum was posted on the company bulletin board, and additional copies were sent to other company offices. Upon Lund's request, C & NW removed the memorandum. Although unauthorized, copies of the memorandum were reposted, apparently by Lund's coworkers. The company removed those copies as well.

After the initial posting, employees verbally harassed Lund. There were also two instances when some unidentified person placed a foreign substance (analyzed as a pepper derivative) in Lund's coffee. Lund claims to have experienced various emotional and physical problems arising from these incidents. His absences, which Lund contends were due to sickness, almost doubled in 1989 over 1988 or 1987.

Lund sued C & NW, claiming defamation and infliction of emotional distress. On C & NW's motion for summary judgment, the trial court concluded that the challenged portion of the memorandum was protected either under the first amendment, as opinion, or by a qualified privilege. Concluding also that the facts did not support Lund's claims for emotional distress, the court granted C & NW's motion. Lund appeals, arguing that the memorandum is not entitled to constitutional protection and that material issues of fact preclude summary judgment. . . .

To be defamatory, a statement must be communicated to someone other than the plaintiff, must be false, and must tend to harm the plaintiff's reputation in the community. Since the United States Supreme Court decided *Gertz v. Robert Welch, Inc.*, 418 U.S. 323, 94 S.Ct. 2997, 41 L.Ed.2d 789 (1974), numerous courts, including the Minnesota Supreme Court, have held that expressions of opinion, even if defamatory, are constitutionally protected. See *Janklow v. Newsweek, Inc.*, 788 F.2d 1300, 1302 (8th Cir.), *cert. denied*, 479 U.S. 883, 107 S.Ct. 272, 93 L.Ed.2d 249 (1986). The federal circuit courts developed a four-factor test to distinguish opinion from fact, which considered 1) the statement's precision and specificity; 2) the statement's verifiability; 3) the social and literary context in which the statement was made; and 4) the statement's public context. See *Janklow*, 788 F.2d at 1302–03.

In *Milkovich v. Lorain Journal Co.*, 497 U.S. 1, 110 S.Ct. 2695, 2706, 111 L.Ed.2d 1 (1990), the Supreme Court recently reviewed the issue of opinion protection. The Court rejected the lower courts' "artificial dichotomy between 'opinion' and fact," holding that not all statements of opinion are constitutionally protected. Recognizing that expressions of opinion may imply assertions of objective facts, the Court concluded that only opinions relating to matters of public concern that are incapable of being proven true or false, and statements that cannot reasonably be interpreted as stating actual facts, are constitutionally protected.

In *Hunt v. University of Minnesota*, 465 N.W.2d 88 (Minn.App.1991), this court construed *Milkovich* as narrowing, but not abolishing, the constitutional protection for opinions. The *Hunt* court also emphasized that cases applying the federal courts' four-factor test, although not binding after *Milkovich*, are still helpful for determining whether a statement implies actual facts that can be proven false.

The opinion-fact determination is a question of law. Applying the four-factor test of *Janklow*, the trial court determined that the words contained in line 66 were clearly statements of opinion.

We agree. In *Lee v. Metropolitan Airport Comm'n*, 428 N.W.2d 815 (Minn.App.1988), coworkers had referred to the plaintiff as a "fluffy," a "bitch," and flirtatious. This court held that such comments regarding Lee's social life and personal characteristics were, as a matter of law, too imprecise in nature to be actionable defamatory statements.

Whether office gossip or railroad shop vernacular, like the statements in *Lee*, the terms in line 66 lack precision and specificity. Furthermore, in the context of the setting in which they were spoken, this lack of precision and specificity blunts any connotation of conduct sufficiently reprehensible to constitute defamation, whether measured by constitutional or common law standards. As the trial court recognized, two of the terms, "move-ups" and "shit heads," are plural and do not necessarily apply to Lund exclusively. Moreover, the underlying facts to be inferred from these terms are unclear. Although uncomplimentary, "shit heads" does not suggest verifiably false facts about Lund.

The terms "favoritism" and "brown nose" require a similar conclusion. They are not themselves factual assertions, and it is unclear what, if any, underlying facts they imply. Even if the terms are viewed as hybrid statements of opinion and fact, we conclude that the ambiguous implications of the words prevent them from being proven true or false. We hold that the statements were constitutionally protected expressions of opinion and, therefore, not actionable.[15]

C & NW also claims that the statements in the memorandum are conditionally privileged. Because we decide that C & NW's statements are constitutionally protected, we need not address whether they are also entitled to a qualified privilege.

[The court also concluded that Lund could not recover for intentional or negligent infliction of emotional distress because the statements did not "reach the requisite level of severity. Line 66, although vulgar, is not especially shocking or egregious."]

CRIPPEN, JUDGE (dissenting).

Opinions, the trial court concluded, are "absolutely protected" under the first amendment and are not actionable. We ought not sustain this mistaken statement.

The United States Supreme Court never has held that purely private communications — those involving private plaintiffs and private issues — are subject to the same constitutional protections as communications involving public claimants or public issues. To the contrary, its decisions extending first amendment law to defamation cases consistently have been in the context of public comments or public parties. Moreover, since 1985 the Court has affirmatively indicated that in the absence of such a public context, a defamation action is not constitutionally significant, but rather is governed by state common law.

In *Dun & Bradstreet, Inc. v. Greenmoss Builders*, 472 U.S. 749, 105 S.Ct. 2939, 86 L.Ed.2d 593 (1985), a plurality of the Court stated that speech on purely private matters is of less first amendment concern, and therefore, the state's interest in protecting individual reputations is not necessarily overcome by constitutional considerations.[16] Whether speech addresses a matter of public concern is to be determined by the content, form and context of the expression as revealed by the whole record. In *Dun & Bradstreet*, a confidential credit report sent to only five subscribers was held to be purely private speech.

The Court clarified the *Dun & Bradstreet* plurality opinion a year later in *Philadelphia Newspapers, Inc. v. Hepps*, 475 U.S. 767, 106 S.Ct. 1558, 89 L.Ed.2d 783 (1986). One can discern, the Court observed, two forces that may "reshape the common-law landscape to conform to the First Amendment."

---

[15] We find unpersuasive the dissent's limitation of constitutional opinion protection to statements about public officials or public figures, or regarding matters of public concern. A state's substantial interest in providing remedies for defamation per se can outweigh the admittedly less weighty, constitutional concerns in a "private" case. *See Dun & Bradstreet, Inc. v. Greenmoss Builders, Inc.*, 472 U.S. 749, 760–61, 105 S.Ct. 2939, 2946, 86 L.Ed.2d 593 (1985) (plurality opinion). However, when the statements, such as those made here during a meeting regarding employee grievances, are clearly opinions, the state's interest fades and the first amendment predominates.

[16] The Court held that no constitutional interest limits state tort law recovery of presumed and punitive damages in a defamation action involving a private plaintiff, a non-media defendant, and an issue of private concern. *Dun & Bradstreet*, 472 U.S. at 763, 105 S.Ct. at 2947.

The first is whether the plaintiff is a public official or figure, or is instead a private figure. The second is whether the speech at issue is of public concern. . . . When the speech is of exclusively private concern and the plaintiff is a private figure, as in *Dun & Bradstreet*, the constitutional requirements do not necessarily force any change in at least some of the features of the common-law landscape.

Id. at 775, 106 S.Ct. at 1563.[17]

The internal business communication at issue in this appeal is of purely private concern. The plaintiff is a private figure. Thus, we should determine the dispute according to state common law principles rather than constitutional law.

Generally, the common law considers actionable many statements of opinion. An expression is defamatory if the statement is "sufficiently derogatory of another as to cause harm to his reputation." RESTATEMENT (SECOND) OF TORTS § 566, comment a (describing common law of actionable opinion in defamation). This is true "despite the normal requirement that the communication be false as well as defamatory." *Id.*

This description is corroborated by the First Restatement. The First Restatement lists three categories in a section entitled "types of defamatory communication": (1) statements of fact; (2) expressions of opinion upon known or assumed facts; and (3) expressions of opinion upon undisclosed facts. Restatement of Torts §§ 565–567. Thus, under the First Restatement:

> [A] defamatory communication may be made by derogatory adjectives or epithets as well as by statements of fact. Thus, it is defamatory to add to an accurate statement of another's innocent conduct, an adjective or epithet which characterizes it as reprehensible.

Id. § 566, comment a.

Defamation may consist of "words which, while couched in the form of epithets or adjectives, carry an implied accusation that the other has been guilty of some specific type of reprehensible conduct." *Id.* § 567, comment a. In addition, common law defamation can occur when one utters what the First Restatement labels "harsh judgments on undisclosed facts." *Id.* § 567, comment b. Such statements "leave it open to doubt as to whether they are intended to imply conduct, the direct accusation of which would be defamatory, or whether they are intended to express a harsh judgment on conduct, the direct accusation of which would not necessarily be defamatory." Id. For all these statements of opinion, including "harsh judgments," the Restatement requires the defendant to prove that the "harsh judgment" is either true or privileged as fair comment under section 606.[18] *Id.; see id.* § 606.

---

[17] The Court held in *Hepps*, a case involving a private plaintiff, a media defendant and an issue of public concern, that the common law rule placing the burden of proving truth on the defendant must fall to a constitutional rule requiring the plaintiff to prove falsity.

[18] The Restatement suggests that calling another a hypocrite, without stating any conduct on which one bases this opinion, would be actionable unless privileged as fair comment. Restatement of Torts § 567, comment b (illustration). Thus, common law support is even lacking for the "rhetorical hyperbole" doctrine, outlined by the Court in *Milkovich v. Lorain Journal Co.*, 497 U.S. 1, 110 S.Ct. 2695, 111 L.Ed.2d 1 (1990). In cases appropriately governed by constitutional

It is the First Restatement, not the Second, which offers primary guidance in deciding this case. The Second Restatement expressly employs constitutional principles about defamation actions and applies them to all defamation cases. Restatement (Second) of Torts § 566, comment c. The Second Restatement authors contrast section 566 with common law principles. *Id.*, comment a. Predating both *Dun & Bradstreet* and *Hepps*, it is evident the Second Restatement did not anticipate the significance of regard for the public or private nature of the parties or the communication. Minnesota has not employed section 566 of the Second Restatement to deal with purely private communications.

Applying common law principles just outlined, the "opinion" at issue here is actionable. The epithets published by respondent characterize appellant's conduct as reprehensible, and as an employment problem requiring correction. Moreover, the labels imply that appellant has sought and obtained favors inappropriately, so much so in fact to make him an obnoxious employee. These statements place upon respondent the burden to prove truth or privilege.

The majority relies on *Milkovich v. Lorain Journal Co.*, 497 U.S. 1, 110 S.Ct. 2695, 111 L.Ed.2d 1 (1990), in holding that the statements here are not actionable. Accordingly, the majority states that under *Milkovich*, "only opinions relating to matters of public concern that are incapable of being proven true or false, and statements that cannot reasonably be interpreted as stating actual facts, are constitutionally privileged." However, even under this version of the law, the statements at issue in this appeal are actionable defamation. Initially, to reiterate a point already made here, the statement does not relate to "matters of public concern." The majority also determines, however, that the publication "cannot reasonably be interpreted as stating actual facts."

The *Milkovich* Court declined to "create a wholesale defamation exemption for anything that might be labeled 'opinion.'" Rather, the court approved the view that protected opinions are those unique because they can be corrected by discussion.

Adding one more particular observation, the *Milkovich* court stated that actionable opinions include those implying assertion of more objective facts. *Id.*; see Restatement (Second) of Torts § 566, comment c, illus. 4. The Court observed that the statement "[i]n my opinion John Jones is a liar" may be actionable in defamation. The Court added: "Even if the speaker states the facts upon which he bases his opinion, if those facts are either incorrect or incomplete, or if his assessment of them is erroneous, the statement may still imply a false assertion of fact." 110 S.Ct. at 2706.

Since *Milkovich*, this court has determined that the four-factor constitutional test for distinguishing fact from opinion still has some utility as an

---

law principles, the Supreme Court has found statements not actionable in defamation if in categories of "rhetorical hyperbole" or "imaginative expression," statements that cannot reasonably be interpreted as stating actual facts about a person. Id. at 110 S.Ct. at 2704–06; *see National Ass'n of Letter Carriers v. Austin*, 418 U.S. 264, 284–86, 94 S.Ct. 2770, 2781–82, 41 L.Ed.2d 745 (1974) (use of the word "traitor" in literary definition of a union "scab" not basis for defamation action because used as mere rhetorical hyperbole, in loose figurative sense as imaginative expression); *Greenbelt Cooperative Publishing Ass'n v. Bresler*, 398 U.S. 6, 13–14, 90 S.Ct. 1537, 1541–42, 26 L.Ed.2d 6 (1970) (use of the word "blackmail" to describe a negotiating position not basis for defamation action because used as rhetorical hyperbole and a "vigorous epithet").

analytical tool.[19] *Hunt v. University of Minnesota*, 465 N.W.2d 88, 94 (Minn.App.1991) (holding statement that an individual "lacks integrity" not actionable in defamation), *pet. for rev. dismissed* (Minn. Mar. 4, 1991). In *Hunt*, where the plaintiff was seeking a political appointment as a county lobbyist, the court found the public context of the statement important. *Id.* at 93–94; *see Capan v. Daugherty*, 402 N.W.2d 561, 564 (Minn.App.1987) (pre-*Milkovich* case holding not actionable, applying four-factor test, statement that community block club organizer was "not dealing with a full deck," based on public context of debate over neighborhood organizations).

In another case using the four-factor test, this court found not actionable statements by co-workers that another employee was "fluffy," a "bitch" and "flirtatious." *Lee v. Metropolitan Airport Comm'n*, 428 N.W.2d 815, 821 (Minn.App.1988) (pre-*Milkovich* decision). The court found important the context of these statements as "office gossip and banter."

In light of *Milkovich* and *Hunt*, the statements at issue on this appeal imply facts verifiable by appellant's alleged improper and offensive efforts to influence superiors and gain favoritism in promotion.

In addition, we should recognize the context of the statements made about appellant. The document was entitled "WHAT ARE SOME PROBLEMS/OPPORTUNITIES WE NEED TO ADDRESS." Line 66 specifically identified appellant by name as one such problem. Appellant's name was modified by "favoritism," "brown nose," and "shitheads."

An illustration in the Second Restatement is parallel:

> A writes to B about his neighbor C: "I think he must be an alcoholic." A jury might find that this was not just an expression of opinion but that it implied that A knew undisclosed facts that would justify this opinion.

Restatement (Second) of Torts § 566, comment c, illus. 3. Similarly, stating that "Dick Lund is a problem in the workplace" implies that the speaker is aware of facts to support this statement.

Other factors about the circumstances surrounding this communication make it actionable. The employer had the material typed and then posted. It was not merely an offhand oral remark. The posting evidently continued for several weeks, even for some time after appellant reported being upset and after a manager admitted making a mistake in publishing the material. Any printing of vituperative remarks tends to make an otherwise unactionable oral statement actionable. Restatement (Second) of Torts § 566, comment e. Furthermore, one epithet here ("shitheads") which might be unactionable "rhetorical hyperbole" by itself, takes on actionable characteristics when used in conjunction with other defamatory words or statements. *See National Recruiters, Inc. v. Cashman*, 323 N.W.2d 736, 742 (Minn.1982) (epithet part of defamation where it accompanies defamatory disparagement of plaintiff's suitability for employment).

---

[19] The four-factor test suggests courts look at (1) the specificity and precision of the statement; (2) its verifiability; (3) the social and literary context in which the statement was made; and (4) the public context in which the statement was made. *Janklow v. Newsweek, Inc.*, 788 F.2d 1300, 1302–03 (8th Cir.), *cert. denied*, 479 U.S. 883, 107 S.Ct. 272, 93 L.Ed.2d 249 (1986).

Finally, the context of the statement at issue here is distinguishable from the circumstances of *Hunt* and *Lee*. Unlike *Hunt*, the public context factor of the four-factor test does not come into play. In addition, the words "brown nose," "favoritism," and "move-ups," unlike the charge in *Hunt* which related to a person's level of integrity, imply wrongful efforts to gain employment favors. Appellant is prepared to testify this accusation is false. *Cf. Diesen v. Hessburg*, 455 N.W.2d 446, 455 (Minn.1990) (Simonett, J., concurring specially) (claim of defamatory accusation fails where underlying facts are undisputed and true), *cert. denied.* 111 S.Ct. 1071, 112 L.Ed.2d 1177 (U.S.1991).

Unlike *Lee*, the statement was not merely office gossip. Although it is contended the statement is merely a report of what appellant's co-employees have said, the communication lost its character as a record of employee statements when the employer republished it as a report of problems requiring attention. The employer posted it in the workplace and sent it to other offices. The context is such that the employer is sanctioning the statement "Dick Lund is a problem in the workplace," and the epithets described that problem. As such, it can reasonably be understood to imply undisclosed facts about appellant's work performance. The statement is actionable in defamation.

The trial court stated alternatively that even if the statement was actionable, a conditional privilege for comment as part of legitimate business operations applied to this communication, and this privilege was not overcome by evidence of common law malice. The trial court found "no evidence that the company abused the conditional privilege in any respect."

In order to overcome a conditional common law privilege to make defamatory statements, the plaintiff must prove that the defendant "made the statement from ill will and improper motives, or causelessly and wantonly for the purpose of injuring the plaintiff." *Stuempges v. Parke, Davis & Co.*, 297 N.W.2d 252, 257 (Minn.1980). Such malice is shown by " 'extrinsic evidence of personal ill feeling, or by intrinsic evidence such as the exaggerated language of the libel, the character of the language used, the mode and extent of publication, and other matters in excess of the privilege.' " *Frankson v. Design Space Int'l*, 394 N.W.2d 140, 144 (Minn.

Whether a conditional privilege has been abused is usually a question of fact for the jury, unless the facts are such that only one conclusion can be drawn.

Under this test, there was ample evidence in the record making abuse of the privilege a jury question. Intrinsic evidence alone could permit a jury to find the privilege has been abused. The language used was exaggerated and profane. The communication was in printed form. The communication was published by posting it in appellant's office and was sent to other offices where appellant does not work. Posting continued even after wrongdoing and harm were evident to respondent. These facts suggest that the privilege was not used properly to open channels of communication between employer and employees, but rather permitted to humiliate appellant. Under these facts, the case should be remanded to the trial court for a jury determination whether respondent abused its privilege.

NOTES

1. *Actionable Opinion.* In *Milkovitch v. Lorain Journal Co.*, 497 U. S. 1, 110 S. Ct. 2695, 111 L. Ed. 2d 1 (1990), a local newspaper accused the defendant, a high school wrestling coach, of lying at a judicial hearing. The hearing was held to determine whether the coach's team should be disqualified from the state competition on the grounds that the coach had incited a brawl at a match with a rival team. The Court said the accusation was capable of being proved true or false and therefore was actionable. A dissent argued that the article was protected speech because it was filled with cautionary language, and it was evident that the author "had no unstated reasons for concluding that Milkovitch perjured himself. . . . Furthermore, the tone and format of the piece notify readers to expect speculation and personal judgment."

2. *Nonactionable Opinion.* In *Vail v. The Plain Dealer Pub. Co.*, 72 Ohio St. 3d 279, 649 N.E.2d 182 (1995), a columnist for the defendant newspaper wrote an article attacking plaintiff, a candidate for the Ohio Senate. The article appeared in the "Commentary" section of the newspaper, and described defendant as a "gay-basher," "neo-numbskull," "bigot," and a hate monger who engaged in a "homosexual diatribe" and fostered "homophobia." The court said these statements were constitutionally protected speech: "Based upon the totality of the circumstances, we are convinced that the ordinary reader would accept this column as opinion and not as fact."

The plaintiff Sylvia Salek was a teacher at Passaic Collegiate School. She sued the school for defamation in *Salek v. Passaic Collegiate School*, 255 N. J. Super. 355, 605 A.2d 276 (1992), based on references to her in the school yearbook:

> The yearbook for 1988 contained a section entitled "The Funny Pages," consisting of pictures of students and faculty accompanied by purportedly humorous captions. One of the pages in this section contained a picture of plaintiff sitting next to and facing another teacher, John DeVita, who had his right hand raised to his forehead. The photograph is captioned "Not tonight Ms. Salek. I have a headache." This photograph forms the basis for this litigation. Another page in the yearbook contains a picture of DeVita eating with the caption "What are you really thinking about, Mr. DeVita?"

The court said: "There is no libel where, as here, the material is susceptible of only nondefamatory meaning and is clearly understood as being parody, satire, humor, or fantasy."

In *Avins v. White*, 627 F.2d 637 (3d Cir. 1980), the Delaware Law School dean sued the ABA accreditation team in defamation for describing the law school as follows:

> The most important deficiency is an intangible one; there is an academic ennui that pervades the institution. The intellectual spark is missing in the faculty and the students.

The court held this was nonactionable opinion. But opinion aside, how could this statement be construed to be "of and concerning" the dean? Reconsider *N. Y. Times v. Sullivan*. The *Avins* court said the statements "more closely approximate a critic's review of an institution rather than a particular individual."

3. *Book Reviews and the Like*. The author of a book brought an action for libel against a newspaper publisher in *Moldea v. New York Times Company*, 22 F.3d 310 (1994). The action was based on a book review of plaintiff's book INTERFERENCE. The reviewer said:

> But there is too much sloppy journalism to trust the bulk of this book's 512 pages — including its whopping 64 pages of footnotes.

The reviewer went on to give examples of what he considered sloppy journalism in the book. The court found the review nonactionable, taking into account "the fact that the challenged statements appeared in the context of a book review, and were solely evaluations of a literary work."

In *Mashburn v. Collin*, 355 So.2d 879 (La. 1977), the court held a newspaper columnist's opinion regarding the food at defendant's restaurant was privileged. The columnist described the food as: "T'ain't Creole, t'ain't Cajun, t'ain't French, t'ain't country American, t'ain't good."

The defendant, the American Association of University Women (AAUW) and its Legal Advocacy Fund, published a national directory of attorneys and other professionals willing to consult with women in higher education "who have brought or are considering bringing gender discrimination actions." The entries in the directory typically included "names, contact information, and a short blurb about each person." A note describing plaintiff Flamm stated: "At least one plaintiff has described Flamm as an 'ambulance chaser' with interest only in 'slam dunk cases.'" His was the only entry containing a negative comment.

The court said the note could reasonably be interpreted to mean that the plaintiff was "an attorney who improperly solicits clients and then takes only easy cases." The note could be viewed as defamatory rather than nonactionable opinion:

> [T]he challenged language appears in a national directory nearly seventy pages in length, compiled and distributed by a reputable professional organization with a 100 year history of supporting education. The directory purports to list "attorneys and other specialists" willing to consult with women involved in higher education who are seeking redress for sex-based discrimination. The directory provides names, addresses, phone numbers and, generally, a short statement of the person's area of interest or expertise. In such a fact laden context, the reasonable reader would be "less skeptical and more willing to conclude that [the directory] stated or implied facts." Gross, 82 N.Y. 2d at 156, 603 N.Y.S. 2d at 819, 623 N.E. 2d at 1169.

Flamm v. American Association of University Women, 201 F.3d 144 (2d Cir. 2000).

4. *Libel-Proof Statements*. The plaintiff, Dr. Jack Kevorkian, sued the defendants, American Medical Association and others, alleging they had defamed him by calling him a killer and a criminal in connection with his assisted suicide activities. Reversing the trial court, the court of appeals found

the statements were opinion. It also found plaintiff was libel-proof, since "his reputation in the community, if not the nation, is such that the effect of more people calling him either a murderer or a saint is de minimis." *Kevorkian v. AMA*, 237 Mich. App. 1, 602 N.W. 2d 233 (1999).

The trial court rendered its opinion on 21 May 1997, and the appellate court rendered its opinion on 6 August 1999. In the interim, on 26 March 1999, Dr. Kevorkian was convicted of second degree murder in connection with the assisted suicides. What effect, if any, should this conviction have had on the case?

HUSTLER MAGAZINE v. FALWELL
485 U.S. 46 (1988)

CHIEF JUSTICE REHNQUIST delivered the opinion of the Court.

Petitioner Hustler Magazine, Inc., is a magazine of nationwide circulation. Respondent Jerry Falwell, a nationally known minister who has been active as a commentator on politics and public affairs, sued petitioner and its publisher, petitioner Larry Flynt, to recover damages for invasion of privacy, libel and intentional infliction of emotional distress. The District Court directed a verdict against respondent on the privacy claim, and submitted the other two claims to a jury. The jury found for petitioners on the defamation claim, but found for respondent on the claim for intentional infliction of emotional distress and awarded damages. We now consider whether this award is consistent with the First and Fourteenth Amendments of the United States Constitution.

The inside front cover of the November 1983 issue of Hustler Magazine featured a "parody" of an advertisement for Campari Liqueur that contained the name and picture of respondent and was entitled "Jerry Falwell talks about his first time." This parody was modeled after actual Campari ads that included interviews with various celebrities about their "first times." Although it was apparent by the end of each interview that this meant the first time they sampled Campari, the ads clearly played on the sexual double entendre of the general subject of "first times." Copying the form and layout of these Campari ads, Hustler's editors chose respondent as the featured celebrity and drafted an alleged "interview" with him in which he states that his "first time" was during a drunken incestuous rendezvous with his mother in an outhouse. The Hustler parody portrays respondent and his mother as drunk and immoral, and suggests that respondent is a hypocrite who preaches only when he is drunk. In small print at the bottom of the page, the ad contains the disclaimer, "ad parody — not to be taken seriously." The magazine's table of contents also lists the ad as "Fiction; Ad and Personality Parody."

Soon after the November issue of Hustler became available to the public, respondent brought this diversity action in the United States District Court for the Western District of Virginia against Hustler Magazine, Inc., Larry C. Flynt, and Flynt Distributing Co., Inc. Respondent stated in his complaint that publication of the ad parody in Hustler entitled him to recover damages for libel, invasion of privacy, and intentional infliction of emotional distress.

B.   DEFAMATION   1207

The case proceeded to trial.[20] At the close of the evidence, the District Court granted a directed verdict for petitioners on the invasion of privacy claim. The jury then found against respondent on the libel claim, specifically finding that the ad parody could not "reasonably be understood as describing actual facts about [respondent] or actual events in which [he] participated." The jury ruled for respondent on the intentional infliction of emotional distress claim, however, and stated that he should be awarded $100,000 in compensatory damages, as well as $50,000 each in punitive damages from petitioners.[21] Petitioners' motion for judgment notwithstanding the verdict was denied. . . .

This case presents us with a novel question involving First Amendment limitations upon a state's authority to protect its citizens from the intentional infliction of emotional distress. We must decide whether a public figure may recover damages for emotional harm caused by the publication of an ad parody offensive to him, and doubtless gross and repugnant in the eyes of most. Respondent would have us find that a State's interest in protecting public figures from emotional distress is sufficient to deny First Amendment protection to speech that is patently offensive and is intended to inflict emotional injury, even when that speech could not reasonably have been interpreted as stating actual facts about the public figure involved. This we decline to do.

At the heart of the First Amendment is the recognition of the fundamental importance of the free flow of ideas and opinion on matters of public interest and concern. "[T]he freedom to speak one's mind is not only an aspect of individual liberty — and thus a good unto itself — but also is essential to the common quest for truth and the vitality of a society as a whole."*Bose Corp. v. Consumers Union of United States, Inc.*, 466 U.S. 485 (1984). We have therefore been particularly vigilant to ensure that individual expressions of ideas remain free from governmentally imposed sanctions. The First Amendment recognizes no such thing as a "false" idea. *Gertz v. Robert Welch, Inc.*, 418 U.S. 323 (1974). As Justice Holmes wrote, "when men have realized that time has upset many fighting faiths, they may come to believe even more than they believe the very foundations of their own conduct that the ultimate good desired is better reached by free trade in ideas — that the best test of truth is the power of the thought to get itself accepted in the competition of the market. . . ." *Abrams v. United States*, 250 U.S. 616 (1919) (dissenting opinion).

The sort of robust political debate encouraged by the First Amendment is bound to produce speech that is critical of those who hold public office or those public figures who are "intimately involved in the resolution of important public questions or, by reason of their fame, shape events in areas of concern to society at large." *Associated Press v. Walker*, decided with *Curtis Publishing Co. v. Butts*, 388 U.S. 130 (1967). (Warren, D.J., concurring in result). Justice Frankfurter put it succinctly in *Baumgartner v. United States*, 322 U.S. 665 (1944), when he said that "[o]ne of the prerogatives of American citizenship is the right to criticize public men and measures." Such criticism, inevitably,

---

[20] While the case was pending, the ad parody was published in Hustler Magazine a second time.

[21] The jury found no liability on the part of Flynt Distributing Co., Inc. It is consequently not a party to this appeal.

will not always be reasoned or moderate; public figures as well as public officials will be subject to "vehement, caustic, and sometimes unpleasantly sharp attacks," *New York Times, supra,* 376 U.S., at 270. "[T]he candidate who vaunts his spotless record and sterling integrity cannot convincingly cry 'Foul!' when an opponent or an industrious reporter attempts to demonstrate the contrary."*Monitor Patriot Co. v. Roy,* 401 U.S. 265 (1971).

Of course, this does not mean that any speech about a public figure is immune from sanction in the form of damages. Since *New York Times Co. v. Sullivan,* 376 U.S. 254 (1964), we have consistently ruled that a public figure may hold a speaker liable for the damage to reputation caused by publication of a defamatory falsehood, but only if the statement was made "with knowledge that it was false or with reckless disregard of whether it was false or not." *Id.,* 376 U.S., at 279–280. . . .

Respondent argues, however, that a different standard should apply in this case because here the State seeks to prevent not reputational damage, but the severe emotional distress suffered by the person who is the subject of an offensive publication. Cf. *Zacchini v. Scripps-Howard Broadcasting Co.,* 433 U.S. 562, 97 S. Ct. 2849, 53 L. Ed. 2d 965 (1977) (ruling that the "actual malice" standard does not apply to the tort of appropriation of a right of publicity). In respondent's view, and in the view of the Court of Appeals, so long as the utterance was intended to inflict emotional distress, was outrageous, and did in fact inflict serious emotional distress, it is of no constitutional import whether the statement was a fact or an opinion, or whether it was true or false. It is the intent to cause injury that is the gravamen of the tort, and the State's interest in preventing emotional harm simply outweighs whatever interest a speaker may have in speech of this type.

Generally speaking the law does not regard the intent to inflict emotional distress as one which should receive much solicitude, and it is quite understandable that most if not all jurisdictions have chosen to make it civilly culpable where the conduct in question is sufficiently "outrageous." But in the world of debate about public affairs, many things done with motives that are less than admirable are protected by the First Amendment. In *Garrison v. Louisiana,* 379 U.S. 64 (1964), we held that even when a speaker or writer is motivated by hatred or ill will his expression was protected by the First Amendment:

> "Debate on public issues will not be uninhibited if the speaker must run the risk that it will be proved in court that he spoke out of hatred; even if he did speak out of hatred, utterances honestly believed contribute to the free interchange of ideas and the ascertainment of truth."

Thus while such a bad motive may be deemed controlling for purposes of tort liability in other areas of the law, we think the First Amendment prohibits such a result in the area of public debate about public figures.

Were we to hold otherwise, there can be little doubt that political cartoonists and satirists would be subjected to damages awards without any showing that their work falsely defamed its subject. Webster's defines a caricature as "the deliberately distorted picturing or imitating of a person, literary style, etc. by exaggerating features or mannerisms for satirical effect." Webster's New Unabridged Twentieth Century Dictionary of the English Language 275 (2d ed. 1979). The appeal of the political cartoon or caricature is often based on exploitation of unfortunate physical traits or politically embarrassing events — an exploitation often calculated to injure the feelings of the subject of the portrayal. The art of the cartoonist is often not reasoned or evenhanded, but slashing and one-sided. One cartoonist expressed the nature of the art in theses words:

> "The political cartoon is a weapon of attack, of scorn and ridicule and satire; it is least effective when it tries to pat some politician on the back. It is usually as welcome as a bee sting and is always controversial in some quarters." Long, The Political Cartoon: Journalism's Strongest Weapon, The Quill 56, 57 (Nov. 1962).

Several famous examples of this type of intentionally injurious speech were drawn by Thomas Nast, probably the greatest American cartoonist to date, who was associated for many years during the post-Civil War era with Harper's Weekly. In the pages of that publication Nast conducted a graphic vendetta against William M. "Boss" Tweed and his corrupt associates in New York City's "Tweed Ring." It has been described by one historian of the subject as "a sustained attack which in its passion and effectiveness stands alone in the history of American graphic art." M. Keller, The Art and Politics of Thomas Nast 177 (1968). Another writer explains that the success of the Nast cartoon was achieved "because of the emotional impact of its presentation. It continuously goes beyond the bounds of good taste and conventional manners." C. Press, The Political Cartoon 251 (1981).

Despite their sometimes caustic nature, from the early cartoon portraying George Washington as an ass down to the present day, graphic depictions and satirical cartoons have played a prominent role in public and political debate. Nast's castigation of the Tweed Ring, Walt McDougall's characterization of Presidential candidate James G. Blaine's banquet with the millionaires at Delmonico's as "The Royal Feast of Belshazzar," and numerous other efforts have undoubtedly had an effect on the course and outcome of contemporaneous debate. Lincoln's tall, gangling posture, Teddy Roosevelt's glasses and teeth, and Franklin D. Roosevelt's jutting jaw and cigarette holder have been memorialized by political cartoons with an effect that could not have been obtained by the photographer or the portrait artist. From the viewpoint of history it is clear that our political discourse would have been considerably poorer without them.

Respondent contends, however, that the caricature in question here was so "outrageous" as to distinguish it from more traditional political cartoons. There is no doubt that the caricature of respondent and his mother published in Hustler is at best a distant cousin of the political cartoons described above, and a rather poor relation at that. If it were possible by laying down a principled standard to separate the one from the other, public discourse would probably suffer little or no harm. But we doubt that there is any such standard, and we are quite sure that the pejorative description "outrageous" does not supply one. "Outrageousness" in the area of political and social discourse has an inherent subjectiveness about it which would allow a jury to impose liability on the basis of the jurors' tastes or views, or perhaps on the basis of their dislike of a particular expression. An "outrageousness" standard thus runs afoul of our longstanding refusal to allow damages to be awarded because the speech in question may have an adverse emotional impact on the audience. . . .

Admittedly, these oft-repeated First Amendment principles, like other principles, are subject to limitations. We recognized in *Pacifica Foundation*, that speech that is " 'vulgar,' offensive,' and 'shocking' " is "not entitled to absolute constitutional protection under all circumstances." 438 U.S., at 747. In *Chaplinsky v. New Hampshire*, 315 U.S. (1942), we held that a State could lawfully punish an individual for the use of insulting " 'fighting' words — those which by their very utterance inflict injury or tend to incite an immediate breach of the peace." *Id.*, at 571–572. These limitations are but recognition of the observation in *Dun & Bradstreet, Inc., v. Greenmoss Builders, Inc.*, 472 U.S. 749 (1985), that this Court has "long recognized that not all speech is of equal First Amendment importance." But the sort of expression involved in this case does not seem to us to be governed by any exception to the general First Amendment principles stated

We conclude that public figures and public officials may not recover for the tort of intentional infliction of emotional distress by reason of publications such as the one here at issue without showing in addition that the publication contains a false statement of fact which was made with "actual malice," i.e., with knowledge that the statement was false or with reckless disregard as to whether or not it was true.

Here it is clear that respondent Falwell is a "public figure" for purposes of First Amendment law.[22] The jury found against respondent on his libel claim when it decided that the Hustler ad parody could not "reasonably be understood as describing actual facts about [respondent] or actual events in which [he] participated." The Court of Appeals interpreted the jury's finding to be that the ad parody "was not reasonably believable," 797 F.2d, at 1278, and in accordance with our custom we accept this finding. Respondent is thus relegated to his claim for damages awarded by the jury for the intentional infliction of emotional distress by "outrageous" conduct. But for reasons heretofore stated this claim cannot, consistently with the First Amendment, form a basis for the award of damages when the conduct in question is the publication of a caricature such as the ad parody involved here. The judgment of the Court of Appeals is accordingly

Reversed.

JUSTICE KENNEDY took no part in the consideration or decision of this case.

JUSTICE WHITE, concurring in the judgment.

As I see it, the decision in *New York Times Co. v. Sullivan*, 376 U.S. 254, 84 S. Ct. 710, 11 L. Ed. 2d 686 (1964), has little to do with this case, for here the jury found that the ad contained no assertion of fact. But I agree with

---

[22] Neither party disputes this conclusion. Respondent is the host of a nationally syndicated television show and was the founder and president of a political organization formerly known as the Moral Majority. He is also the founder of Liberty University in Lynchburg, Virginia, and is the author of several books and publications. Who's Who in America 849 (44th ed. 1986-1987).

the Court that the judgment below, which penalized the publication of the parody, cannot be squared with the First Amendment.

NOTES

1. *Procedure and Other Such Things.* In *Smith v. Suburban Restaurants, Inc.,* 374 Mass. 528, 373 N.E.2d 215 (1978), the attorney for the defendant restaurant, with defendant's authorization, wrote the following letter to the plaintiff and sent a copy to the local police department:

Dear Ms. Smith:

Please be advised that this office represents the above named Suburban Restaurants Inc. We have been advised that due to your actions you are no longer welcome on the property of our client and have been so advised in the past.

This is to formally advise you that you are no longer invited, permitted, or licensed to enter upon said premises located at the Walpole Mall or elsewhere. Any further intrusions upon said premises by yourself, your agents, servants, or employees shall be considered a trespass. If such trespass should occur, this office has been instructed to proceed with appropriate legal action.

Very truly yours,

/s/ Reginald L. Marden

Reginald L. Marden

The court held the plaintiff stated a case of actionable defamation.

Suppose at trial the defendant testifies that it wrote the letter because it does not like the plaintiff's appearance or manners? Plaintiff counters with testimony that she has eaten at defendant's restaurant on several occasions and has always behaved with the utmost propriety. Suppose further that the jury believes the plaintiff and disbelieves the defendant. The libel, then, is that the plaintiff has been falsely accused of lacking good manners and seemly appearance?

Suppose the defendant testifies that it had no particular reason for writing the letter. In that connection, consider the problem given below.

The court in *Smith v. Suburban Restaurants* observed that, under Massachusetts law defendant, as a place of public accommodation, "has an obligation to treat each member of the public equally, except for good cause." The fact that a copy of the letter was sent to the police "may warrant an inference that the plaintiff engaged in or was threatening to engage in behavior which would make their services necessary."

2. *Fact and Fiction.* In *Bindrum v. Mitchell,* 92 Cal. App. 3d 61, 155 Cal. Rptr. 29 (1979), *cert. denied,* 444 U.S. 984, 62 L. Ed. 2d 412, 100 S. Ct. 490 (1979), Defendant Mitchell attended "Nude Marathon" group therapy sessions supervised by Plaintiff Bindrum, a licensed clinical psychologist. The avowed purpose of the sessions was to provide therapy "as a means of helping people to shed their psychological inhibitions with the removal of their clothes."

Each participant in the session, including Defendant Mitchell, signed an agreement "that he will not take photographs, write articles, or in any manner disclose who has attended the workshop or what has transpired." Defendant, a writer, later wrote a novel called "Touching" based on her experiences in these sessions. After the book was published, plaintiff brought a libel action. He recovered a judgment, which was affirmed on appeal:

> The parallel between the actual nude marathon sessions and the sessions in the book "Touching" was shown to the jury by means of the tape recordings Mitchell had taken of the actual sessions. Plaintiff complains in particular about a portrayed session in which he tried to encourage a minister to get his wife to attend the nude marathon.
>
> . . . Plaintiff asserts that he was libeled by the suggestion that he used obscene language which he did not in fact use. Plaintiff also alleges various other libels due to Mitchell's inaccurate portrayal of what actually happened at the marathon. Plaintiff alleges that he was injured in his profession and expert testimony was introduced showing that Mitchell's portrayal of plaintiff was injurious and that plaintiff was identified by certain colleagues as the character in the book, Simon Herford.

Plaintiff admitted that he was a public figure. The court held that the jury could find constitutional malice on the part of the defendant-appellants by clear and convincing evidence:

> Appellants allege that plaintiff failed to show he was identifiable as Simon Herford, relying on the fact that the character in "Touching" was described in the book as a "fat Santa Claus type with long white hair, white sideburns, a cherubic rosy face and rosy forearms" and that Bindrim was clean shaven and had short hair. Defendants rely in part on *Wheeler v. Dell Pub'g Co.,* 300 F.2d 372 (7th Cir. 1962) which involved an alleged libel caused by a fictional account of an actual murder trial.

The *Wheeler* court said (at p. 376):

> "In our opinion, any reasonable person who read the book and was in a position to identify Hazel Wheeler with Janice Quill would more likely conclude that the author created the latter in an ugly way so that none would identify her with Hazel Wheeler. It is important to note that while the trial and locale might suggest Hazel Wheeler to those who knew the Chenoweth family, suggestion is not identification. In *Levey* [*Levey v. Warner Bros. Pictures,* 57 F. Supp. 40 (S.D.N.Y. 1944)] the court said those who had seen her act may have been reminded of her by songs and scenes, but would not reasonably identify her."

> However, in *Wheeler* the court found that no one who knew the real widow could possibly identify her with the character in the novel. In the case at bar, the only differences between plaintiff and the Herford character in "Touching" were physical appearance and that Herford was a psychiatrist rather than a psychologist. Otherwise, the character Simon Herford was very similar to the actual plaintiff. We cannot

say, as did the court in *Wheeler,* that no one who knew plaintiff Bindrum could reasonably identify him with the fictional character. Plaintiff was identified as Herford by several witnesses and defendant's own tape recordings of the marathon sessions show that the novel was based substantially on plaintiff's conduct in the nude marathon. . . .

The dissent contended that the book was protected as nonactionable fiction:

Plaintiff's brief discusses the therapeutic practices of the fictitious Dr. Herford in two categories: Those practices which are similar to plaintiff's technique are classified as identifying. Those which are unlike plaintiff's are called libelous because they are false. Plaintiff has thus resurrected the spurious logic which Professor Kalven found in the position of the plaintiff in *New York Times Co. v. Sullivan,* 376 U.S. 254 (1964). Kalven wrote: "There is revealed here a new technique by which defamation might be endlessly manufactured. First, it is argued that, contrary to all appearances, a statement referred to the plaintiff; then, that it falsely ascribed to the plaintiff something that he did not do, which should be rather easy to prove about a statement that did not refer to plaintiff in the first place. . . ." Kalven, *The New York Times Case: A Note on "The Central Meaning of the First Amendment,"* 1964 The Supreme Court Review 191, 199.

Why do you suppose plaintiff did not sue for breach of contract?

3. *Quotable Quotes.* The Court held a jury question was presented as to the existence of constitutional malice in *Masson v. New Yorker Magazine,* 501 U. S. 496, 111 S. Ct. 2419 (1991). A writer for the defendant interviewed the plaintiff and wrote an article describing the interview. The author, with full knowledge of the inaccuracy, "used quotation marks to attribute to [the plaintiff] comments he had not made." The Court said the plaintiff must show that the use of quotation marks resulted in a "material change in the meaning" of statements made by the plaintiff to the interviewer, and that the change had a defamatory meaning.

On remand, the jury in *Masson* found liability but deadlocked on the issue of damages, 832 F. Supp. 1350 (N. D. Cal. 1993). On retrial, the jury found no liability because of the absence of malice, No. CV-847548EFL (N.D. Cal. 1994), noted in TRIAL 106 (Jan. 1995).

ESPOSITO-HILDER v. SFX BROADCASTING INC.
236 App. Div. 2d 186, 665 N.Y.S. 2d 697 (1997)

Before MIKOLL, J.P., and WHITE, CASEY, YESAWICH and SPAIN, JJ.

MIKOLL, JUSTICE PRESIDING. . . .

We are called upon to decide whether the Supreme Court properly denied defendants' motion to dismiss the complaint for failure to state a cause of action. Resolution of this question implicates a more troublesome one: may conduct which is not actionable as defamation, by reason of being a an expression of opinion, nonetheless be the subject of an action for intentional infliction of emotional distress? We conclude, under the unique factual circumstances presented herein, that it may, where (a) the aggrieved party is a private individual rather than a public figure, (b) the conduct in question involved no matter of public interest or concern, and (c) the status of the parties as business competitors is relevant to an evaluation of defendants' conduct insofar as an intent to injure is concerned. . . .

. . . Plaintiff's amended complaint alleges the following. The corporate defendants are the owners and operators of radio station WPYX-FM which serves Schenectady, Albany and Rensselaer counties, the individual defendants are disc jockeys employed by WPYX-FM, and plaintiff is the business manager of a competing broadcasting company which owns and operates several radio stations serving the same area.

On June 17, 1996, plaintiff's bridal photograph was published in a local newspaper along with those of other brides. That same day, during WPYX-FM's morning braodcast, defendants engaged in a routine known as the "Ugliest Bride" contest during which they made derogatory and disparaging comments about plaintiff's appearance and invited their listening audience to do the same. Plaintiff further alleges that defendants deviated from the ordinary routine of this "contest" by disclosing her full name, place and position of employment, as well as the identity of, and her relations with, her superiors. Plaintiff further alleges that she heard this broadcast as did her supervisors and colleagues, and that as a result of its outrageously offensive content she experienced extreme emotional distress exacerbated by its occurrence at the time because she was a newlywed.

Defendants contend that notwithstanding its characterization as a claim for the intentional infliction of emotional distress, plaintiff's claim is in reality one of defamation and that, as such, it is not actionable because the conduct in question qualifies as constitutionally protected expression of opinion. The Supreme Court held, and we agree, that if plaintiff's claim was in fact for defamation, it would fail because under no circumstances would it be reasonable to consider the content of defendants' broadcast as anything but pure, subjective opinion. Since, however, plaintiff's complaint is based not upon defamation but upon the tort of intentional infliction of emotional stress, albeit arising out of the same conduct, it becomes necessary to consider the question of whether such an action may be maintained.

We acknowledge that it is well-settled law that "expressions of an opinion 'false or not, libelous or not, are constitutionally protected and may not be the subject of private damage actions'" (*Steinhilber v. Alphonse*, 68 N.Y. 2d 283, 286, 508 N.Y.S. 2d 901, 501 N.E.2d 550, quoting *Rinaldi v. Holt, Rinehart & Winston*, 42 N.Y. 2d 369, 380, 397 N.Y.S. 2d 943, 366 N.E. 2d 1299, *cert. denied* 434 U.S. 969, 98 S. Ct. 514, 54 L. Ed. 2d 456). Likewise, we observe that the tort of intentional infliction of emotional distress has received very little judicial solicitude (see *Hustler Magazine v. Falwell*, 485 U.S. 46, 108 S. Ct. 876, 99 L. Ed. 2d 41). Indeed, Chief Judge Kaye noted in *Howell v. New York Post Co.*, 81 N.Y. 2d 115, 596 N.Y.S. 2d 350, 612 N.E. 2d 699, mod. 82 N.Y. 2d 690, 601 N.Y.S. 2d 572, 619 N.E. 2d 650, that of those claims considered by the Court of Appeals, "every one has failed because the alleged conduct was not sufficiently outrageous" (*id.*, at 122, 596 N.Y.S. 2d 350, 612 N.E. 2d 699). Emphasizing that we decide this question in the narrow context in which it occurs, i.e., whether the complaint should be dismissed for failure to state a cause of action, we conclude that under the unique factual circumstances herein presented, the Supreme Court properly denied defendants' motion, and we affirm. . . .

In *Howell v. New York Post Co.*, 81 N.Y. 2d 115, 596 N.Y.S. 2d 350, 612 N.E. 2d 699, *supra*, the Court of Appeals undertook a task similar to ours in considering the "relationship between two separate but potentially overlapping torts: intentional infliction of emotional distress, and invasion of the right to privacy" (id., at 118, 596 N.Y.S. 2d 350, 612 N.E. 2d 699). After reviewing the history and evolution of this tort, the court observed that "[t]he tort is as limitless as the human capacity for cruelty. The price for this flexibility in redressing utterly reprehensible behavior, however, is a *tort that*, by its terms, *may overlap other areas of the law, with potential liability for conduct that is otherwise lawful*" (*id*., at 122, 596 N.Y.S. 2d 350, 612 N.E. 2d 699 [emphasis supplied]). After deciding that the defendants' conduct did not support a claim for invasion of the right to privacy, the court said that the "[d]efendants would have our analysis end here — without considering whether plaintiff has stated a cause of action for intentional infliction of emotional distress — arguing that the tort may not be used as an end run around a failed right to privacy claim" (*id*., at 125, 596 N.Y.S. 2d 350, 612 N.E. 2d 699). This the court declined to do. . . .

Turning to a consideration of the specific factual circumstances attendant to the conduct in question here, we attach particular significance to several factors. First, plaintiff is a private individual and not a "public figure." Second, the nature of the communications made by defendants involved a matter of virtually no "public interest"; there is an inference that defendants' conduct represented a deliberate intent to inflict injury upon plaintiff based upon the claimed unprecedented expansion of its standard "routine" of the "Ugliest Bride" contest to include particulars concerning plaintiff's name, employer, supervisors and the like, and the fact that the parties are business competitors in the radio broadcast industry.

We are not unmindful of the constitutional issues implicated in this case and in our resolution thereof. In the quest for the proper accommodation between the right of redress for infliction of injury and the freedoms of speech and expression protected by the 1st Amendment, we have determined that the State's relatively strong interest in compensating individuals for harm outweighs the relatively weak 1st Amendment protection to be accorded defendants. It is elementary that not all speech or expression is to be accorded equal 1st Amendment protection; the most jealously protected speech is that which advances the free, uninhibited flow of ideas and opinions on matters of public interest and concern; that which is addressed to matters of private concern, or focuses upon persons who are not "public figures," is less stringently protected (*see Hustler Magazine v. Falwell*, 485 U.S. 46, 108 S. Ct. 876, 99 L. Ed. 2d 41, *supra*; *Dun & Bradstreet v. Greenmoss Bldrs.*, 472 U.S. 749, 105 S. Ct. 2939, 86 L. Ed. 2d 593; *Gertz v. Robert Welch Inc.*, 418 U.S. 323, 94 S. Ct. 2997, 41 L. Ed. 2d 789). Moreover, among the forms of communication, broadcasting enjoys the most limited 1st Amendment protection (*see FCC v. Pacifica Found*, 438 U.S. 726, 98 S. Ct. 3026, 57 L. Ed. 2d 1073).

As to defendants' alternative contention that their conduct is protected comedic expression, we note that comedic expression does not receive absolute 1st Amendment protection. Instead, it can be actionable where "humor is used in an attempt to disguise an attempt to injure" (*Frank v. National Broadcasting Co.*, 119 A.D. 2d 252, 261–262, 506 N.Y.S. 2d 869). The allegations of the amended complaint allege an intent to injure, which satisfies the limited inquiry before us.

Finally, we note that our decision today does no more than permit plaintiff's lawsuit to proceed. Whether and to what extent the allegations of her complaint ultimately satisfy the stringent requirements for the tort will be determined upon further proceedings.

NOTES

1. *Breach of Contract*. In *Cohen v. Cowles Media Co.*, 501 U. S. 663, 11 S. Ct. 2513 (1991), the plaintiff, a member of one party's gubernatorial campaign, gave derogatory information to defendant newspaper about the other party's candidate in return for a promise of confidentiality. Despite this promise, the newspaper revealed plaintiff's name as the source of the information in their stories, and plaintiff was fired from his job as a result. The plaintiff sued the newspaper, and the Court in a 5-4 decision said his action for damages based on a claim of promissory estoppel was not barred by the first amendment of the U. S. Constitution.

There was no attempt here, the majority said, to avoid "the strict requirements for establishing a libel or defamation" claim, to which truth would be a defense. "Cohen is not seeking damages for injury to his reputation or state of mind." Rather, he sought to recover "for a breach of promise that caused him to lose his job and lowered his earning capacity." This was not a case like *Hustler Magazine, Inc. v. Falwell*, the Court said, "where we held that the constitutional libel standards apply to a claim alleging that the publication of a parody was a state-law tort of intentional infliction of emotional distress."

Why was *Cohen* not a case like *Falwell*? Would it have been like *Falwell* if the plaintiff had sought to recover for damage to reputation or emotional distress, as well as loss of job and lost earning capacity?

PROBLEM

Leading Law Firm called up Distinguished Professor to seek his opinion about a job applicant to the Firm, Molly Student. Molly was first in her class, and editor-in-chief of the law review. Professor said, "I can't put my finger on it; but after years of experience in this business, my visceral reaction is that she will not make a good lawyer."

On the basis of this negative recommendation by Professor, for whom the Firm had the highest regard, Firm did not make Molly a job offer.

Can Molly recover in defamation against Professor?

ARNEJA v. GILDAR
541 A.2d 621 (D.C. 1988)

GALLAGHER, SENIOR JUDGE.

. . . Both appellant and appellee are attorneys licensed to practice law in the District of Columbia. They were representing opposing parties in a landlord-tenant dispute. Appellant represented the tenants, and appellee was counsel for the landlord. The proceeding involved an interpretation of the small landlord exemption of the Rental Housing Act of 1980. On behalf of the tenants, appellant filed a petition with the District of Columbia Rental Accommodations Office challenging an exemption from rent control granted to the landlord's property. The alleged slanderous statements were uttered while both parties and their clients were present in a hearing room at the Rental Accommodations Office, awaiting the imminent arrival of the hearing examiner to adjudicate the dispute.

Before the hearing examiner arrived, appellee concededly made the following unsolicited remarks to appellant:

> You're unnecessarily pursuing this case. You don't understand the law. Where did you go to law school; you should go back to law school before you practice law. You don't understand. You better learn your English, go to elementary school.

Appellant asserts that these statements were *ad hominem* attacks on his ethnicity and educational background,[23] which were said with malice to impugn his professional capacity as a lawyer. Appellant claims that, as a result, he suffered pecuniary losses as well as humiliation and embarrassment before his clients. Appellee, on the other hand, asserted that his statements were intended to lead to a settlement of the dispute, *viz.*, to induce appellant to cease the litigation by highlighting his supposed incredulous position.

After a hearing on appellee's motion for summary judgment, the trial court found the alleged defamatory statements to be sufficiently related to the underlying dispute — the interpretation of a statute — to fall within the protective scope of the absolute privilege, which affords attorneys absolute immunity from liability for statements made in the course of a judicial proceeding. The trial judge found "a very strong connection between the words alleged to have been said by [appellee] and the procedure that was involved in this landlord and tenant case." He further opined that "the English language is an issue" in disputes involving opposing interpretations of a statute. In addition, the trial judge considered that the physical location and temporal proximity of the parties — sitting in a hearing room awaiting the imminent arrival of the examiner — justified concluding the statements were made preliminary to a judicial proceeding . . .

---

[23] Appellant was born in India. He earned several academic degrees, including a Bachelor of Arts degree from Punjab University, a Master of Economics degree from Agra University, and a law degree from the University of New Delhi. Although his native language is Punjabi, appellant has spoken English since the fifth grade, and he received his formal legal training in English. Appellant emigrated to the United States in 1971. He earned a Master of Comparative Law (American Practice) degree from George Washington University. He became a member of the District of Columbia Bar in 1978. In reverence to the doctrines of his Sikh religion, appellant wears a turban while in public.

In this jurisdiction, an attorney "is protected by an absolute privilege to publish false and defamatory matter of another" during the course of or preliminary to a judicial proceeding, provided the statements bear some relation to the proceeding. *Mohler v. Houston,* 356 A.2d 646, 647 (D.C. 1976) (per curiam); *see* Restatement (Second) of Torts § 586 (1977).[24] The privilege affords an attorney absolute immunity from actions in defamation for communications related to judicial proceedings. The determination of whether a communication is privileged is a question of law for the court. For the absolute immunity of the privilege to apply, two requirements must be satisfied: (1) the statement must have been made in the course of or preliminary to a judicial proceeding; and (2) the statement must be related in some way to the underlying proceeding.

The scope of the absolute privilege has been extended to encompass quasi-judicial proceedings conducted by administrative agencies. The shield of absolute immunity extends to adversarial proceedings conducted before administrative agencies "because it enables participants to state and support their positions without instilling a fear of retaliation, i.e., an action for damages." *Sturdivant v. Seaboard Service System, Ltd.,* 459 A.2d 1058, 1060. We therefore conclude that the proceeding conducted before the Rental Accommodations Office constituted a proceeding within the gambit of the judicial privilege.

A more difficult question is whether the defamatory statements occurred "preliminary to" that administrative proceeding. According to the American Law Institute, "communications preliminary to a proposed judicial proceeding" includes "conferences and other communications preliminary to the proceeding." Restatement (Second) of Torts § 586 & comment a (1977). Given that the parties were involved in litigation, present in a hearing room, and awaiting commencement of the proceeding to adjudicate their dispute, we believe the trial court did not err in concluding the statements were made preliminary to a judicial proceeding.[25]

. . . The issues of fact disputed by appellant, *viz.,* that (1) no settlement discussions transpired in the hearing room, and (2) the remarks were ethnic slurs, are not controlling in determining whether, as a matter of law, appellee is entitled to the immunity of absolute privilege. Furthermore, the motive of appellee in uttering these remarks is irrelevant under the doctrine of absolute privilege.[26]

---

[24] The Restatement provides:

> An attorney at law is absolutely privileged to publish defamatory matter concerning another in communications preliminary to a proposed judicial proceeding, or in the institution of, or during the course and as part of, a judicial proceeding in which he participates as counsel, if it has some relation to the proceeding. Restatement (Second) of Torts § 586 (1977).

[25] The parties' physical presence in the hearing room substantially affects our analysis of the issue. If these same remarks were uttered outside the courtroom, a different question might be presented on the issue of absolute privilege, depending upon the particular circumstances. *See, e.g., Petrus v. Smith,* 91 A.D.2d 1190, 459 N.Y.S.2d 173 (App. Div. 1983) (absolute privilege may not extend to statements made outside the courthouse);*Sussman v. Damian,* 355 So. 2d 809 (Fla. Dist. Ct. App. 1977) (statements made on elevator held not absolutely privileged).

[26] Malice or improper motive is a relevant consideration, under some circumstances reserved for a jury, when addressing the applicability of the qualified privilege, as distinguished from the absolute privilege involved here.

Although we must recognize the absolute privilege in this instance, we naturally do not wish to be understood as condoning remarks such as those concededly (for purposes of the motion) made by appellee. Attorneys do not possess a license to defame their adversaries in the course of a judicial proceeding. The immunity of the absolute privilege supports the public policy of allowing counsel to zealously represent a client's interests without fear of reprisal through defamation actions.[27] A separate public policy concern, however, is the integrity and civility of legal proceedings, especially as perceived by the public. A potential alternative mechanism available to deal with outrageous conduct by an attorney in lieu of an action for damages in slander may be the policing function of the Bar Disciplinary Committee.

PRYOR, CHIEF JUDGE, dissenting.

. . . Recognizing, as does the majority, that it is difficult to draw a boundary for this absolute privilege, I am unable to distinguish this case from a similar scenario which occurs in the hallway or just outside of the courthouse. . . . I think in this case, in particular, it is a question of fact whether there was a conference or even a discussion between the lawyers or whether this was a circumstance where one attorney was simply unilaterally abusing the other. As liberally as the privilege is to be construed, I question if the latter conduct should be protected.

I would remand for resolution of the factual question which I have noted.

NOTES

1. *Other Judicial Immunities.* A judicial officer enjoys a similar absolute privilege. See REST. 2d OF TORTS § 585. So do witnesses. *Id.* § 588.

Court reporters, however, are not entitled to an absolute judicial immunity. In *Antoine v. Byers & Anderson*, 113 S. Ct. 2167 (1993), the Court said a court reporter could be held liable for damages in negligently failing to provide a complete transcript of public proceedings, resulting in a delay of appellate review for over four years.

2. *Executive and Legislative Immunity.* Executive officials may enjoy complete common law immunity from liability for statements and actions closely related to the performance of their official duties. *Mosley v. Observer Pub. Co.*, 619 A.2d 343 (Pa. Super. 1993). They may not have such an immunity, however, from liability for the commission of constitutional torts. *Williams v. Brooks*, 945 F.2d 1322 (5th Cir. 1991).

---

[27] The necessity of the absolute privilege to protect comments related to judicial and administrative proceedings does not mean that attorneys disposed toward dispensing verbal abuse during proceedings may do so with impunity. It goes without saying that courts and agencies should insist upon decent conduct by attorneys appearing before them, as a matter of civility and courtroom decorum. The various regulatory bodies, whether they be judicial commissions or an arm of the Bar, would reasonably be expected to understand and support any sensible exercise of discipline by the presiding judge or hearing officer pertaining to such conduct. Trial judges, after all, are not mere spectators in the courtroom. Quite naturally, they have the duty to preside over an orderly courtroom and move cases along. While ours is an adversary system, this too has its limitations. The two factors, the adversary system and the search for justice in a civil way, are quite capable of being balanced.

The court in *Williams*, on the other hand, said that federal legislators have an immunity only as broad as the speech or debate clause of the United States constitution. A TV interview by the defendant Congressman was not protected under this clause.

3. *The Privilege to Repeat Privileged Statements*. The court in *Rosenberg v. Helinski*, 328 Md. 664, 616 A.2d 866 (1992), held that a psychologist, whose expert in-court testimony in a child custody matter supporting the mother's accusation that the father had sexually abused the child, was privileged to repeat the substance of this testimony to journalists waiting for him outside the courtroom. Similarly, in *Doe v. Kohn Nast & Graf*, 866 F.Supp.190 (E.D. Pa. 1994), where the plaintiff filed suit alleging he had been wrongfully fired, the defendant was privileged to report to the press what its answer to the suit would be.

Rosenberg and *Kohn Nast* are in sharp contrast to *Shahvar v. Superior Court of Santa Clara County*, 25 Cal. App. 4th 653, 30 Cal. Rptr. 597 (1994), where the court said an attorney could be liable for faxing a copy of an allegedly libelous complaint to the news media. The copy was not sent to a party or participant in the litigation, but to "someone unrelated to the litigation."

What about the situation where the repeater is not the same person as the original, privileged speaker? The Court in *Doe v. McMillan*, 412 U.S. 306 (1973), held that the speech or debate clause privilege did not extend to printers who, acting at the order of a congressional committee, prepared for publication a committee report that allegedly invaded the privacy of some of those named in the report.

If a defamation is foreseeably repeated, the defamer is liable for the repetition. Rest. 2d of Torts § 576 (1977).

4. *Neutral Reportage*? The issue in *Bartnicki v. Vopper,* 121 S. Ct. 1753 (2001), was whether, under state and federal wiretap statutes, the defendant radio station and an individual could be held civilly liable for receiving and disclosing the contents of plaintiffs' cellular phone conversation on a matter of public concern, which defendants knew or had reason to know had been illegally intercepted and recorded by an unknown person or persons. Defendants did not encourage or participate in the recording.

The Court held defendants could not be found liable, since to do so would violate their first amendment rights. The majority believed that enforcement of 18 U.S.C. § 2511 (1)(c), which prohibits such disclosure, would not appreciably reduce illegal wiretaps, and that the plaintiffs' interest in privacy was outweighed by the public or general interest in the matter disclosed (views on a controversial labor dispute).

Two concurring justices thought the "narrow" holding was justified regarding a matter of "unusual public concern" involving plaintiffs who were "limited public figures". Three dissenters thought the majority, in order to protect an "amorphous concept" of "public concern", rode roughshod over legislative findings that the statutes deterred "clandestine invasions of privacy" and that an important right of privacy was at stake.

5. *Conditional Privileges*. There are many common law conditional privileges that protect the speaker unless the privilege is abused. An abuse occurs

when the speaker is guilty of common law malice. The concept of common law malice is variously defined, and does not always have the same meaning as actual or constitutional malice as those terms are used in *Sullivan* and *Gertz*.

So in *Staples v. Bangor Hydro-Elec. Co.*, 629 A.2d 601 (Me. 1993), the court held that an intra-company defamation is a publication that is entitled to a qualified privilege. The privilege is abused if the statement is made with knowledge, or reckless disregard, of falsity, or with a "high degree of awareness of probable falsity or serious doubt as to the truth of the statement," or if the defendant "acted out of ill will" toward the plaintiff. In *Bickford v. Tektronix, Inc.*, 116 Or. App. 547, 842 P.2d 432 (1992), the court said an intra-company defamation was a privileged publication, but that the "privilege may be abused if the speaker does not believe that the statement is true or lacks reasonable grounds to believe that it is true."

In *Miller v. Servicemaster By Rees*, 851 P.2d 143 (Ariz. App. 1992), the court held that the plaintiff employee was privileged to report what she perceived to be sexual harassment. A privilege exists if there is "an obligation to speak." The privilege is abused if the defendant made the statement "knowing it was false or with reckless disregard of its truth," or if the plaintiff can show "excessive publication" by the defendant. Excessive publication typically refers to statements not reasonably necessary to assert the privilege.

It is widely held that one is privileged to report a suspected crime to the police. See *Williams v. Bell Teleph. Labs Inc.*, 132 N. J. 109, 623 A. 2d 234 (1993). Again, the privilege can be abused if common law malice is present.

6. *The Paid Professional Witness*. In *Bruce v. Byrne-Stevens & Assoc. Eng'rs*, 776 P.2d 666 (1989), plaintiff sued his own expert witness for the expert's allegedly negligent testimony in a prior lawsuit in which plaintiff sought property damage. The defendant expert had underestimated repair costs for plaintiff's land by 100%. The court held that an expert witness, even if retained and compensated by one of the parties to an action, is immune from suit based solely on testimony given in court. The court reasoned that any witness, whether hired by a party or not, is an officer of the court and the interest in preventing censored testimony which could result from subjecting witnesses to possible liability for testimony outweighs a party's interest in redressing negligent expert testimony. The cases are not uniform on this point, however. *See, e. g., Mattco Forge v. Arthur Young & Co.*, 5 Cal. App. 4th 392, 6 Cal. Rptr. 2d 781 (1992) (plaintiff may sue expert witness for negligent preparation).

Compare *Aufrichtig v. Lowell*, 85 N.Y.2d 540 (1995). There the court held the plaintiff could sue her doctor for providing allegedly false information in a suit against her health insurer. As a general rule, the court said, "New York does not recognize a cause of action for fraudulent or perjured testimony." But a duty arose here because the physician-patient relationship "operates and flourishes in an atmosphere of transcendent trust and confidence and is infused with fiduciary obligations."

Does *Aufrichtig* furnish a basis for suing a witness for defamatory testimony? What about invasion of privacy? Misrepresentation?

7. *Injurious Falsehood*. Injurious falsehood, or trade libel, resembles defamation except that the falsehood concerns the plaintiff's product rather than

the plaintiff. The tort requires proof of knowing falsity on the part of the defendant, and pecuniary loss in terms of loss of business to the plaintiff. RESTATEMENT (SECOND) OF TORTS §§ 623A, 633 (1977).

It is unclear whether or to what extent the constitutional requirements of *New York Times v. Sullivan* and its progeny apply to injurious falsehood. The U. S. Supreme Court in *Bose Corp. v. Consumers Union of United States, Inc.,* 466 U.S. 485, 104 S. Ct. 1949, 80 L. Ed. 2d 502 (1984), assumed without deciding — accepting the lower court's determination in that regard — that the *Sullivan* constitutional malice standard applied to the plaintiff as a public figure in the case of injurious falsehood. What effect may the holding in *Dun & Bradstreet, Inc. v. Greenmoss Builders, Inc.,* 472 U.S. 749, 105 S. Ct. 2939, 86 L. Ed. 2d 593 (1985), have on the *Bose* and injurious falsehood situations?

8. *Colloquium.* In *Blatty v. New York Times Co.,* 42 Cal. 3d 1033, 232 Cal. Rptr. 542, 728 P.2d 1177 (Cal. 1986), *cert. denied,* 485 U.S. 934, 99 L. Ed. 2d 268, 108 S. Ct. 1107 (1988), the court held that plaintiff Blatty was constitutionally required by *New York Times v. Sullivan* to prove that the defendant's alleged injurious falsehood, negligence, and negligent and intentional interference with prospective economic advantage were "of and concerning" the plaintiff or his product. Thus, the plaintiff did not state a cause of action where he alleged that defendant intentionally failed to include plaintiff's book on its widely consulted list of best-selling books, to plaintiff's financial detriment, even though plaintiff's book allegedly met all the criteria necessary for inclusion on the list. "The claims fail to allege that the list is of or concerning, or specifically refers to, Blatty or his novel." The list could also not reasonably be understood to refer to plaintiff's book by implication, the court said, since the number of currently published books included substantially more than twenty-five. "[W]here the group is large — in general, any group numbering over twenty-five members — the courts in California and other states have consistently held that the plaintiffs cannot show that the statements were 'of and concerning them.'"

A dissent disagreed with the court's holding on the "of and concerning" requirement:

> Suppose that the New York Times, after consulting its normal survey of representative bookstores throughout the country, found that Blatty's novel was, indeed, the top-selling book for a particular week based on its own statistics. Suppose further that, despite this information, the times purposefully substituted one of its own publications for Blatty's book at the top of its best seller list in order to enhance its own book's sales, and entirely omitted Blatty's book from the list. Under the majority's analysis, Blatty would have no cause of action against the New York Times. . . .

Reconsider *New York Times v. Sullivan* and *Neiman-Marcus v. Lait, supra.*

9. *Fighting Words.* The U.S. Supreme Court, in *Beauharnais v. State of Illinois,* 343 U.S. 250, 96 L. Ed. 919, 72 S. Ct. 725 (1952), upheld by a 5-4 vote a conviction for criminal libel based on a scurrilous racial pamphlet distributed by the defendant. The decision appears to be based on the idea that the pamphlet consisted of "fighting words" calculated to provoke a breach

of peace. ("If the persuasion and the need to prevent the white race from becoming mongrelized by the negro will not unite us, then the aggressions . . . rapes, robberies, knives, guns and marijuana of the negro surely will.") The dissent doubted, however, that a clear and present danger of such provocation was shown by the evidence.

Under the Illinois statute applicable in that case, truth was a defense only if the publication was made "with good motives and for justifiable ends." The good-motives qualification of the truth defense would be unconstitutional today. *See Garrison v. Louisiana,* 379 U.S. 64 (1964). Would the entire decision also be unconstitutional under the hyperbole and opinion rules, or owing to the "of and concerning" aspect of the holding in *New York Times v. Sullivan*? Could Commissioner Sullivan have recovered if the New York Times article had provoked him or others to commit a breach of peace? Is it decisive that the speech in *Sullivan* was "of and concerning" the government, as opposed to a non-governmental group?

A recent case upholding a conviction under a "fighting words" statute is *Connecticut v. Battista,* 10 Conn. App. 499, 523 A.2d 944 (1987), although the words there were directed at a single person rather than a group. *Compare Chaplinsky v. New Hampshire,* 315 U.S. 568, 86 L. Ed. 1031, 62 S. Ct. 766 (1942) (conviction for cursing officer in public street, upheld).

The Supreme Court in *Brandenburg v. Ohio,* 395 U.S. 444, 23 L. Ed. 2d 430, 89 S. Ct. 1827 (1969), struck down a conviction under Ohio's Criminal Syndicalism statute for racist remarks of the defendant advocating the use of violence. The conviction was in violation of the first amendment, since the crime was defined "in terms of mere advocacy" as opposed to "incitement to imminent lawless action."

C. INVASION OF PRIVACY

PETA v. BOBBY BEROSINI, LTD.
895 P.2d 1269 (Nev. 1995)

SPRINGER, JUSTICE:

In this litigation respondent Berosini claims that two animal rights organizations, People for the Ethical Treatment of Animals (PETA) and Performing Animal Welfare Society (PAWS), and three individuals defamed him and invaded his privacy. Judgment was entered by the trial court on jury verdicts on the libel and invasion of privacy claims in the aggregate amount of $4.2 million. This appeal followed. We conclude that the evidence was insufficient to support the jury's verdict and, accordingly, reverse the judgment.

[Defendants secretively videotaped plaintiff Berosini "preparing" his orangutans backstage for public performance. This preparation consisted of grabbing, slapping, punching and shaking the animals, and hitting them with a black rod approximately a foot in length. Plaintiff did not deny this treatment, but stated that it was necessary to calm the animals down and get them ready for their public performance. No one was present at these "preparatory" sessions except the plaintiff and his assistants. The defendants later had the video shown on local TV in an attempt to combat what they considered to be cruelty to animals.]

Berosini claims that one of the Stardust dancers, Ottavio Gesmundo, has intruded upon his "seclusion" backstage, before his act commenced. We support the need for vigilance in preventing unwanted intrusions upon our privacy and the need to protect ourselves against the Orwellian nightmare that our "every movement [be] scrutinized." The question now to be examined is whether Gesmundo's inquiring video camera gives cause for concern over privacy and gives rise to a tort action against Gesmundo for invasion of Berosini's privacy.

Although the problems which the tort of intrusion seeks to remedy are well-recognized, the tort of intrusion has only recently gained the attention of this court. In *M & R Investment Co. v. Mandarino*, 103 Nev. 711, 748 P.2d 488 (1987), we faced the question of whether appellant, "a twenty-two year old man, disguised in dark glasses, a false mustache and slicked down hair, who by virtue of his skill at counting cards, [won] a great deal of money in a short period of time" had stated a cognizable claim for intrusion against the casino personnel who confiscated his winnings, had him arrested, photographed him, and distributed his photograph to other casinos. We answered this question with an emphatic "No," noting that the appellant, so conspicuously attired, could have had no subjective expectation that "casino personnel [would] turn a blind eye to his presence." This court held that even viewing the facts in the light most favorable to the appellant, such an expectation was patently unreasonable and would thus not give rise to a tort action.

The *Restatement*, [2d of Torts § 652B], upon which this court has previously relied for guidance in this area, formulates the tort of intrusion in terms of a physical invasion upon the "solitude or seclusion" of another, the rationale being that one should be protected against intrusion by others into one's private "space" or private affairs. To Prosser, these torts were personal injury actions, and he saw as examples of tortious activity the meddling conduct of eavesdroppers, the unpermitted opening of others' mail, and the making of illegal searches and seizures. Simply put, the intrusion tort gives redress for interference with one's "right to be left alone."

To recover for the tort of intrusion, a plaintiff must prove the following elements: 1) an intentional intrusion (physical or otherwise); 2) on the solitude or seclusion of another; 3) that would be highly offensive to a reasonable person.

In order to have an interest in seclusion or solitude which the law will protect, a plaintiff must show that he or she had an actual expectation of seclusion or solitude and that that expectation was objectively reasonable. Thus, not every expectation of privacy and seclusion is protected by the law. "The extent to which seclusion can be protected is severely limited by the protection that must often be accorded to the freedom of action and expression of those who threaten that seclusion of others." 2 Fowler V. Harper, et al., *The Law of Torts*, § 9.6, at 636 (2d ed. 1986). For example, it is no invasion of privacy to photograph a person in a public place; or for the police, acting within their powers, to photograph and fingerprint a suspect. Bearing this in mind, let us examine Berosini's claimed "right to be left alone" in this case and, particularly, the nature of Berosini's claim to seclusion backstage at the Stardust Hotel.

Berosini's "Invasion of Privacy" claim in his Second Claim for Relief contains no factual averments and refers the reader back to paragraphs 1 through 18 of the First Claim for Relief, where one is required to search for some factual basis for Berosini's charging of the intrusion tort. The only factual allegations that appear to have any relation to the intrusion tort are found in paragraph 12 of the first claim, a paragraph that relates only to defendant Gesmundo. (Gesmundo is the only defendant against whom a judgment was entered on the intrusion tort.) Paragraph 12 reads as follows:

> 12. Defendant GESMUNDO unlawfully trespassed onto the Stardust Hotel with a video camera in July, 1989. Video cameras and other recording equipment are strictly prohibited at the Stardust Hotel. Defendant GESMUNDO unlawfully filmed Plaintiff BEROSINI disciplining the orangutans without the Plaintiff's knowledge or consent and just after Defendant GESMUNDO and others agitated the orangutans.

The focus, then, of Berosini's intrusion upon seclusion claim is Gesmundo's having "trespassed onto the Stardust Hotel with a video camera" and having "unlawfully filmed Plaintiff Berosini disciplining the orangutans without the Plaintiff's knowledge or consent." It is of no relevance to the intrusion tort that Gesmundo trespassed onto the Stardust Hotel, and it is of no moment that Gesmundo might have "unlawfully" filmed Berosini, unless at the same time he was violating a justifiable expectation of privacy on Berosini's part. The issue, then, is whether, when Gesmundo filmed Berosini "disciplining the orangutans without the Plaintiff's knowledge or consent," Gesmundo was intruding on "the solitude or seclusion" of Berosini.

The primary thrust of Berosini's expectation of privacy backstage at the Stardust was that he be left alone with his animals and trainers for a period of time immediately before going on stage. Berosini testified that "as part of his engagement with the Stardust," he demanded that "the animals be left alone prior to going on stage." Throughout his testimony, over and over again, he stresses his need to be alone with his animals before going on stage. Berosini's counsel asked him what his "purpose" was in requiring that he be "secured from the other cast members and people before [he] went on stage." Berosini's answer to this question was: "I have to have the attention . . . I have to know how they think. I cannot have them drift away with their mind . . . ."; and, further, "it is very important that before the show I have the orangutans' attention and I can see what they think before I take him on stage. . . ." Significantly, Berosini testified that his "concern for *privacy was based upon the animals*" and that his "main concern is that [he] have no problems going on stage and off stage," that is to say that no one interfere with his animals in any way immediately before going on stage. (Emphasis added.)

Berosini was concerned that backstage personnel not "stare at the orangutans in their faces. The orangutans will interpret [this] as a challenge." It is clear that Berosini's "main concern" was that he be provided with an area backstage in which he could get the animals' undistracted attention before going on stage. He never expressed any concern about backstage personnel merely seeing him or hearing him during these necessary final preparations before going on stage; his only expressed concern was about possible interference with his pre-act training procedures and the danger that such interference might create with respect to his control over the animals. Persons who were backstage at the Stardust could hear what was going on when "Berosini [was] disciplining his animals," and, without interfering with Berosini's activities, could, if they wanted to, get a glimpse of what Berosini was doing with his animals as he was going on stage.

What is perhaps most important in defining the breadth of Berosini's expectation of privacy is that in his own mind there was nothing wrong or untoward in the manner in which he disciplined the animals, as portrayed on the videotape, and he expressed no concern about merely being seen or heard carrying out these disciplinary practices. To Berosini all of his disciplinary activities were completely "justified." He had nothing to hide — nothing to be private about. Except to avoid possible distraction of the animals, he had no reason to exclude others from observing or listening to his activities with the animals. Berosini testified that he was not "ashamed of the way that [he] control[led] [his] animals"; and he testified that he "would have done the same thing if people were standing there because if anybody would have been standing there, it was visibl[e]. It was correct. It was proper. It was necessary."

As his testimony indicates, Berosini's "concern for privacy was based upon the animals," and not upon any desire for sight/sound secrecy or privacy or seclusion as such; and he "would have done the same thing if people were standing there." The supposed intruder, Gesmundo, was in a real sense just "standing there." By observing Berosini through the eye of his video camera, he was merely doing what other backstage personnel were also permissibly doing. The camera did not interfere in any way with Berosini's pre-act animal discipline or his claimed interest in being "secured from the other cast members and people before [he] went on stage." Having testified that he would have done the same thing if people were standing there, he can hardly complain about a camera "standing there."

If Berosini's expectation was, as he says it is, freedom from distracting intrusion and interference with his animals and his pre-act disciplinary procedures, then Gesmundo's video "filming" did not invade the scope of this expectation. Gesmundo did not intrude upon Berosini's *expected* seclusion. *See, e.g., Kemp v. Block*, 607 F.Supp. 1262, 1264 (D.Nev.1985) ("[t]his Court finds that the plaintiff knew that other persons could overhear. He, therefore, had no reasonable expectation of privacy"); *Mclain v. Boise Cascade Corp.*, 271 Or. 549, 533 P.2d 343, 346 (1975) ("plaintiff conceded that his activities which were filmed could have been observed by his neighbors or passersby"). For this reason the tort of intrusion cannot be maintained in this case.[28]

---

[28] We do not find it necessary to discuss the question of reasonability (objective expectation of privacy) of Berosini's privacy interests because, as said, his concern was not with being seen. Nevertheless, we note that Berosini's being a public figure militates against his privacy claim. It is probably not reasonable for a well known, headliner entertainer to expect that his picture will not be taken backstage at his place of performance, even when it is a violation of company rules. Furthermore, we note that there is, generally speaking, a reduced objective expectation of privacy in the workplace.

On the question of whether Gesmundo's camera was *highly* offensive to a reasonable person, we first note that this is a question of first impression in this state. As might be expected, "[t]he question of what kinds of conduct will be regarded as a 'highly offensive' intrusion is largely a matter of social conventions and expectations." J. Thomas McCarthy, *The Rights of Publicity and Privacy*, § 5.10(A)(2) (1993). For example, while questions about one's sexual activities would be highly offensive when asked by an employer, they might not be offensive when asked by one's closest friend. "While what is 'highly offensive to a reasonable person' suggests a standard upon which a jury would properly be instructed, there is a preliminary determination of 'offensiveness' which must be made by the court in discerning the existence of a cause of action for intrusion." *Miller v. National Broadcasting Co.*, 187 Cal.App.3d 1463, 232 Cal.Rptr. 668, 678 (1986). A court considering whether a particular action is "highly offensive" should consider the following factors: "the degree of intrusion, the context, conduct and circumstances surrounding the intrusion as well as the intruder's motives and objectives, the setting into which he intrudes, and the expectations of those whose privacy is invaded." *Miller*, 232 Cal.Rptr. at 679.

Three of these factors are of particular significance here and, we conclude, militate strongly against Berosini's claim that Gesmundo's conduct was highly offensive to a reasonable person. These factors are: the degree of the alleged intrusion, the context in which the actions occurred, and the motive of the supposed intruder. First, we note the nonintrusive nature of the taping process in the instant case. Berosini was concerned with anyone or anything interfering with his animals prior to performance. The camera caused no such interference. Neither Berosini nor his animals were aware of the camera's presence. If Gesmundo had surprised Berosini and his animals with a film crew and had caused a great commotion, we might view this factor differently. On the contrary, it appears from these facts that any colorable privacy claims arose not from the actual presence of the video camera but from the subsequent use to which the video tape was put.

Secondly, as has been discussed fully above, the context in which this allegedly tortious conduct occurred was hardly a model of what we think of as "privacy." We must remember that the videotaping did not take place in a private bedroom (*see Miller*, 232 Cal.Rptr. at 668), or in a hospital room (*see Estate of Berthiaume v. Pratt*, 365 A.2d 792, 796 (Me.1976)), or in a restroom (*see Harkey v. Abate*, 131 Mich.App. 177, 346 N.W.2d 74 (1983)), or in a young ladies' dressing room (*see Doe by Doe v. B.P.S. Guard Services Inc.*, 945 F.2d 1422 (8th Cir.1991)), or in any other place traditionally associated with a legitimate expectation of privacy. Rather, Gesmundo filmed activities taking place backstage at the Stardust Hotel, an area where Gesmundo had every right to be, and the filming was of a subject that could be seen and heard by any number of persons. This was not, after all, Berosini's dressing room; it was a holding area for his orangutans.

Finally, with regard to Gesmundo's motives, we note that Gesmundo's purpose was not to eavesdrop or to invade into a realm that Berosini claimed for personal seclusion. Gesmundo was merely memorializing on tape what he and others could readily perceive. Unlike the typical *intrusion* claim, Gesmundo was not trying to pry, he was not trying to uncover the covered-up.

Although Berosini envisioned Gesmundo to be engaged in a conspiracy with others (as put in the Answering Brief) "to put an end to the use of animals in entertainment," the conspiracy charges in Berosini's complaint were dismissed. Furthermore, even if Gesmundo was conspiring to put an end to the use of animals in entertainment, this is not the kind of motive that would be considered highly offensive to a reasonable person. Many courts, and Professor Prosser, have found the inquiry into motive or purpose to be dispositive of this particular element of the tort. *See Prosser and Keeton on Torts* § 117 at 856 (W. Page Keeton, ed.; 5th ed. 1984). For example, in *Estate of Berthiaume*, 365 A.2d at 796, the court held that a doctor who photographed a dying patient against his will could be held liable for intrusion, in part because the doctor was not seeking to further the patient's treatment when he photographed him. Similarly, in *Yarbray v. Southern Bell Tel. & Tel. Co.*, 261 Ga. 703, 409 S.E.2d 835 (1991), the court held that an employee who claimed that her employer pressured her regarding her testimony in an employment discrimination suit brought against the company, could not state a claim for intrusion because the employer was motivated by his desire to protect the company's interests.

While we could reverse Berosini's intrusion upon seclusion judgment solely on the absence of any intrusion upon his actual privacy expectation, we go on to conclude that even if Berosini had expected complete seclusion from prying eyes and ears, Gesmundo's camera was not "highly offensive to a reasonable person" because of the nonintrusive nature of the taping process, the context in which the taping took place, and Gesmundo's well-intentioned (and in the eyes of some, at least, *laudable*) motive. If Berosini suffered as a result of the videotaping, it was not because of any tortious intrusion, it was because of subsequent events that, if remediable, relate to other kinds of tort actions than the *intrusion* upon seclusion tort.

[The court also found that there was no defamation, and that plaintiffs did not tortiously appropriate defendant's name or identity for commercial purposes.]

NOTES

1. *Trespass or Privacy?* Recall the treatment of trespass to realty in Chapter 3, supra. How is this privacy tort different from trespass?

RESTATEMENT (SECOND) OF TORTS § 652B provides:

> One who intentionally intrudes, physically or otherwise, upon the solitude or seclusion of another or his private affairs or concerns, is subject to liability to the other for invasion of his privacy, if the intrusion would be highly offensive to a reasonable person.

2. *The Manner of Intrusion.* Much depends on the circumstances in determining whether there has been a tortious intrusion into seclusion. There may be such an intrusion by secretly recording and photographing conversations with a person in his home, *Dietemann v. Time, Inc.*, 449 F.2d 245 (9th Cir. 1971), or by secretly videotaping conversations of an employee at work, *Sanders v. ABC*, 978 P.2d 67 (Cal. 1999). But there was no actionable intrusion into seclusion where an insurance investigator trespassed onto private club

property, and photographed the plaintiffs — one of whom was a plaintiff in a personal injury lawsuit — as the plaintiffs were "on or near a yacht situated in a public waterway and in open view to the public." *Furman v. Sheppard*, 744 A.2d 583 (Md. App. 2000).

A television cameraman's presence at and filming of events at an accident scene was not an actionable invasion of privacy, the court held in *Shulman v. Group W Productions, Inc.*, 955 P.2d 469 (Ca. 1998). But the cameraman's recording and filming of events in the rescue helicopter may have been an invasion of privacy, since a "patient's conversation with a provider of medical care in the course of treatment, including emergency treatment, carries a traditional and legally well-established expectation of privacy."

VEEDER v. KENNEDY
589 N.W. 2d 610 (S.D. 1999)

GILBERTSON, JUSTICE.

This is an appeal from a jury verdict in an alienation of affections case. Michael Veeder (Michael) brought suit against Myles Kennedy (Kennedy) for alienation of the affections of his former spouse, Julie Veeder (Julie). The jury returned a verdict for Michael granting compensatory and punitive damages totaling $265,000.00. Kennedy appeals. We affirm as to all issues.

Kennedy was a management employee of Norwest Bank (Norwest) from 1969 to 1995. In February 1989, Kennedy came to Watertown, South Dakota to head operations at the Watertown branch of Norwest. There he met Julie, who was also employed by Norwest as a personal banker. In 1990, the position of Consumer Banking Manager opened. Since Kennedy did not know the applicants, he relied on the recommendations of other Norwest employees. They recommended Julie for the position. Julie was offered the job by Kennedy and she accepted it.

Her new position required that Kennedy and she work closely together. Over three years they became close friends. In 1993, Julie and Kennedy became involved in a sexual relationship. The affair continued until May 1995. At the time both parties were married.[29] Both Kennedy and Julie expressed their love for each other during this relationship.

Julie and Michael were married in 1975. They had three children. Julie testified that her disenchantment with the marriage started when the children were getting older and Michael was not involved with the family. She was raising the children and working full-time. Michael would spend weekend nights during the summer going to various automobile races, he was not involved in the religious upbringing of the children, he did not communicate with Julie and was always concerned about money. He also spent all of his week nights working at the family car wash. As a result Julie's feelings for her husband began to erode.

Michael testified that he did not realize there were problems in his marriage. Julie never gave any impression she was unhappy. He claimed the

---

[29] Julie and Michael obtained a divorce in October 1995. Myles Kennedy and his wife of twenty-two (22) years are still married.

letters that Julie wrote to him after they separated showed she had not lost her affections for him before the affair with Kennedy. Michael contends that any problems in the Veeder marriage surfaced only after Kennedy began having an inappropriate relationship with Julie. She withdrew from Michael and was no longer herself. Michael claims that Julie was vulnerable to a predator such as Kennedy.

Michael brought suit for alienation of affections against Kennedy and Norwest. Before trial, Kennedy filed a motion for summary judgment. A motion to dismiss or in the alternative a motion for summary judgment was also filed by Norwest. After a hearing the trial court denied Kennedy's motion for summary judgment and granted Norwest's motion for summary judgment. After a trial, the jury returned a verdict of $265,000.00 against Kennedy. This figure is composed of $65,000.00 actual damages and $200,000.00 punitive damages. Kennedy filed a motion for a new trial. The motion was denied by the trial court. . . .

As the cause of action for alienation of affections is central to all other issues in this case, we begin our analysis with a discussion of this tort. This action is an offshoot of the common law tort for depriving a master of his quasi-proprietary interest in his servant. W. Page Keeton et al., Prosser and Keeton on the Law of Torts § 124, at 916 (5th ed. 1984). Since under common law women and children were considered property of the husband or father, this tort was extended to include their services. *Id.* The action eventually shifted away from compensation for services to compensation for loss of affection and companionship or perhaps the better known term of consortium. *Id.* The tort was based on the premise that the wife's body belonged to the husband and anyone who trespassed upon the husband's property by seducing his wife was liable for damages. *Russo v. Sutton*, 310 S.C. 200, 422 S.E. 2d 750, 752 (1992). *Haney v. Townsend*, 12 SCL (1 McCord) 206 (1821). Conversely, at common law until recently the wife had no such remedy against anyone who interfered in her relationship with her husband. Prosser and Keeton on the Law of Torts § 124, at 916. *See* SDCL 25-2-15 (enacted 1887). *See also Holmstrom v. Wall*, 64 S.D. 467, 268 N.W. 423 (1936) (wife has a cause of action against anyone wrongfully interfering with her marital relationship).

Currently, thirty-four states, including the District of Columbia, have statutorily abolished the tort of alienation of affections. However, only five states have done so judicially which is the course of action now advocated by Kennedy. Of the five, four abolished it as a common law doctrine and only one abolished the cause of action which was based upon a statute. One state has statutorily denied money damages for the cause of action. Louisiana has never accepted alienation of affections as a cause of action. *See Moulin v. Monteleone*, 165 La. 169, 115 So. 447 (1927), accord, *Ohlhausen v. Brown*, 372 So. 2d 787 (La. Ct. App. 1979). Alaska does not have a statute or case law addressing the cause of action. Alienation of affections remains a legitimate cause of action in nine states.

South Dakota derives this cause of action from SDCL 20-9-7 [30] which states:

---

[30] This statute was originally codified in 1877.

The rights of personal relation forbid:

(2) The abduction or enticement of a wife from her husband. . .;

(3) The seduction of a wife, daughter, or orphan sister.

The elements of alienation of affections in South Dakota are as follows:

1. wrongful conduct of the defendant;
2. loss of affection or consortium; and
3. a causal connection between such conduct and loss.

Pickering v. Pickering, 434 N.W. 2d 758, 762–3 (S.D. 1989) (citing *Pankratz v. Miller*, 401 N.W. 2d 543, 546 (S.D. 1987); *Hunt*, 309 N.W. 2d at 820.)

The last time this Court addressed the issue of alienation of affections was in *Pickering*. Over the years we have considered this issue a number of times. The most extensive discussion of the possible abrogation of the tort of alienation of affections is found in *Hunt*, 309 N.W. 2d 818.

In *Hunt*, a plurality decision, the plaintiff Bonnie Hunt (Bonnie) brought suit against Kay Hunt (Kay) for alienation of affections and criminal conversation. Bonnie prevailed on both counts with a jury verdict of $50,000.00. On appeal, Kay requested the torts of alienation of affections and criminal conversation be judicially abolished.

The *Hunt* Court traced the history of both causes of action. The Court found "[t]he right to recover under the doctrines of alienation of affections and criminal conversation is of common-law origin, and exists independent of any statute." *Id.* at 820. The Court considered the national trend of abolishing both criminal conversation and alienation of affections. Justices Henderson and Wollman contended both torts had outlived their usefulness and were "archaic holdovers from an era when wives were considered the chattel of their spouse. . . ." *Hunt*, 309 N.W. 2d at 821. The two Justices voted to abolish both causes of action and reverse the judgment of the trial court.

Justice Dunn wrote a concurring opinion in *Hunt*, in which justices Morgan and Fosheim joined. These Justices agreed with Justice Henderson's opinion that the cause of action of criminal conversation should be abrogated. The abrogation was necessary in part because the cause of action did not provide any meaningful defenses. However, the three concurring Justices refused to abrogate the cause of action for alienation of affections reasoning that the cause of action had long been recognized by the South Dakota Legislature and therefore should be upheld until repealed by the legislature.

Kennedy argues that almost all jurisdictions have eliminated this cause of action and therefore South Dakota should follow the majority of other jurisdictions. Michael's response is that we should follow *Hunt* and preserve the tort until it is repealed by the legislature which is the source of its creation in this jurisdiction.

Strong policy arguments have been advanced by members of this Court in favor of abrogation. As two Justices stated in *Hunt*:

The underlying rationale for alienation suits, that is, the preservation of the marriage, is ludicrous. And it is folly to hope any longer that a married person who has become inclined to philander can be preserved within an affectionate marriage by the threat of an alienation suit. . . . Where. . . neither party holds the marriage in the high regard that it should be held, the existence of . . . alienation of affections. . .as [a remedy] fosters bitterness, promotes vexatious lawsuits, uses the marriage as a means of blackmail and character assassination, puts the marriage in the marketplace, and generally exposes the marriage to a public cleansing with a price tag attached upon it.

Hunt, at 822 (Henderson, J.). However, those Justices in *Hunt* who favored retention of the cause of action did so on policy grounds as well as constitutional deference to the legislative prerogative:

Finally, because we happen to be living in a period of loose morals and frequent extra-marital involvements is no reason for a court to put its stamp of approval on this conduct; and I feel certain that a case will arise in the future where some party has so flagrantly broken up a stable marriage that we would rue the day that an alienation suit was not available to the injured party.

Hunt, at 823 (Dunn, J., concurring specially in part, and concurring in result in part).[31]

As the common law has progressed it has eliminated those rights and remedies that are deemed no longer justifiable in our society. Kennedy argues authority from those jurisdictions involving abrogation is persuasive; it should encourage this Court to abrogate this cause of action. However, as we stated in *Hunt*, we feel this Court is not the proper forum for resolving this issue.

The "public policy" argument of Kennedy cannot be supported by our system of law. SDCL 1-1-23 states that the sovereign power is expressed by the statutes enacted by the legislature. SDCL 20-9-7 which authorizes Michael's cause of action in this case is such a statute. Under SDCL 1-1-24 the common law and thus an abrogation of the common law are in force except where they conflict with the statutory will of the legislature as expressed by SDCL 1-1-23. We are unable to locate a single case in this jurisdiction where this Court has struck down a statute as a violation of public policy. As no constitutional defects are claimed by Kennedy, we are compelled to leave the cause of action intact and instead defer to the legislature's ability to decide if there is a need for its elimination. "[W]e are not legislative overlords empowered to eliminate laws whenever we surmise they are no longer relevant or necessary." *Matter of Certification of Questions of Law (Knowles)*, 1996 SD 10, 544 N.W. 2d 183, 197. The law has long recognized that a determination of policy and the duration of that policy remains within the purview of the Legislature. "[W]hat

---

[31] Factually, this case occurred in a work-place setting. We note that the courts have become increasingly vigilant in protecting workers form sexual harassment by superiors while at work. See *Burlington Industries, Inc., v. Ellerh*, 524 U.S. 742, 118 S. ct. 2257, 141 L. Ed. 2d 633 (1998); *Faragher v. City of Boca Raton*, 524 U.S. 775, 118 S. Ct. 2275, 141 L. Ed. 2d 662 (1998). While Julie claimed to need no such protection and indeed testified the relationship was voluntary, SDCL 20-9-7 extends the protection of the law to the spouse of the worker. Admittedly, the scope of SDCL 20-9-7 is not limited to the workplace but to any factual setting justifying its invocation. However, some of our cases such as *Pickering* commenced as "office romances." 434 N.W. 2d 758.

the legislature ordains and the constitution does not prohibit must be lawful." *Knowles*, 1996 SD 10 at n. 20, 544 N.W. 2d at 199 n. 20. . . .

At the close of Michael's case, Kennedy made a motion for a directed verdict. This motion was renewed after both sides rested. The trial court denied both motions. Kennedy claims the trial court erred in not granting both motions because Michael failed to establish two critical elements in his case: (1) that there were affections in the marriage to alienate; and (2) that Kennedy intended from the outset to entice the affections of Julie away from her husband.

In *Pickering* and *Pankratz*, we stated that if there are no affections to alienate, there is no cause of action. *Pickering*, 434 N.W. 2d at 763; *Pankratz*, 401 N.W. 2d at 546. Viewed in the light most favorable to the nonmoving party, there was sufficient evidence to support the conclusion that there were affections in the marriage to alienate. That there were affections in the marriage can be drawn from the letters written by Julie to Michael after they separated in which she proclaimed: "Mike, I would take my old life back in a heartbeat. I miss my old life." "I wish none of this happened and we could turn back the clock." "I would give anything to have my old life back again."[32] Michael testified they had a loving marriage, that Julie showed him affection "all the time" and the last thing each would say to the other when retiring for the night was, "I love you." This evidence is further substantiated by testimony of family and friends, who thought Julie and Michael had a wonderful marriage before Julie became involved with Kennedy.

Furthermore, there was sufficient evidence that Kennedy intended to entice away Julie's affections from her husband. Although Kennedy expressly denied any such intention, the jury could have drawn reasonable inferences and deductions from the facts to conclude to the contrary. When asked if he felt any guilt about the inappropriate relationship with Julie, he replied no. Kennedy carried on this relationship for over two years, which provides the inference that the enticement was intentional. Furthermore, Kennedy's marriage at the time of the trial was the result of a similar extra-marital relationship with a fellow employee.

Clearly, sufficient evidence existed so that "reasonable minds could differ." *Border States Paving*, 1998 SD 21 at ¶ 10, 574 N.W. 2d at 901. The trial court did not err in denying the motion for a directed verdict. . . .

NOTES

1. *Invasion of the Marital Relation*. In *O'Neil v. Schuckardt*, 112 Idaho 472, 733 P.2d 693 (1986), plaintiff O'Neil as well as his five children recovered against "the Fatima Crusade, a fundamentalist sect of the Catholic Church," and individual leaders of the Crusade, for invasion of marital privacy. Plaintiff alleged that defendants maliciously caused his wife to divorce him because he was not a member of the Crusade.

---

[32] It is argued that Julie never believed this but instead wrote it to induce Michael to drop this lawsuit and smooth out child custody problems. The problem with this rationale is that Julie was allowed to tell the jury this explanation for the letters. By its verdict, the jury obviously did not accept her explanation and instead chose to believe Michael and the numerous other witnesses who testified there were affections between Michael and Julie to alienate.

O'Neil could not recover for alienation of affections, however, because that tort was outmoded and against public policy, the court said. Therefore the court affirmed the ruling of the trial court, and abolished the cause of action in Idaho.

How does alienation of affections differ from invasion of privacy in the context of this lawsuit?

The *O'Neil* court said an invasion of privacy occurs when one "intentionally intrudes, physically or otherwise, upon the solitude or seclusion of another or his private concerns or affairs." Was there such an intrusion here?

The court in PETA said there was no intrusion into Berosini's privacy because in his mind "there was nothing wrong or untoward" with the way in which he dealt with his animals, and because others witnessed his dealings with the animals. If this rationale were applied to the *O'Neil* claim, would it result in a denial of recovery? Does *O'Neil* concern a privacy interest, or some other sort of interest?

2. *Invasion of Privacy and the Hospital-Patient Relationship.* In *Biddle v. Warren Gen'l Hosp.*, 86 Ohio St. 3d 395, 715 N.E. 2d 518 (1999), the court held that a hospital and its attorneys could be held liable, the hospital for breach of the duty of patient confidentiality and the attorneys for inducing such breach. By agreement between the hospital and its attorneys, the former furnished the latter medical information on its patients who had not paid their medical bills, so the attorneys could determine if the patients might be eligible for SSI (Supplementary Security Income) benefits that could be used toward payment of the patients' medical bills. If the attorneys determined such eligibility, they would contact the patients in an attempt to file for recovery of the benefits. The attorneys were paid a contingent fee on any such benefits recovered by the hospital.

The patients filed a class action for breach of patient confidentiality. The court said the action would lie. The attorneys were counsel for the hospital and not for the patients, who had not given their consent for release of the information.

ROSHTO v. HEBERT
439 So. 2d 428 (La. 1983)

LEMMON, JUSTICE.

This is an action to recover damages for invasion of privacy arising out of defendants' publication in *The Iberville South,* a local weekly newspaper, of an article which allegedly concerned plaintiffs' private lives. The issue is whether a newspaper's verbatim reproduction, as part of a regular feature, of the original front page of a randomly selected 25-year-old edition, constitutes invasion of a person's right to privacy, when the reproduced article accurately describes the details of a local criminal conviction for which the person was subsequently pardoned.

The *Iberville South* for many years had reproduced the front page of randomly selected prior editions in a regular feature called "Page from Our Past." In 1973, the *South* reproduced the front page of the April 4, 1952 edition, which contained an article about the cattle theft trial of Carlysle, Alfred and E. R. Roshto, three brothers who are the plaintiffs in the instant litigation. Four years later, in 1977, the *South* reproduced the front page of the November 14, 1952 edition, which contained another article about the Roshto brothers, this time concerning the fact that they had been sentenced to prison after their convictions had been affirmed on appeal. Plaintiffs' names were not blocked out in either reproduction.

Plaintiffs then filed the present action, which asserted that the 1977 publication invaded their privacy, since the 25-year-old matter was no longer of public concern. They further contended that they had served their terms of imprisonment, had been law-abiding and hard-working citizens of the community, and had ultimately received full pardons. Because each plaintiff admitted the truth of the articles at the trial on the merits, the trial judge rendered judgment for defendants on the basis that truth was an absolute defense. The court of appeal set aside that judgment, holding that truth is not a defense to an action for invasion of privacy. The court further held that defendants' action constituted an invasion of privacy for which each plaintiff was entitled to $35,000 in damages. We granted certiorari.

The right of privacy involves the basic right of a person to be let alone in his private affairs. Unwarranted invasion of a person's right of privacy may give rise to liability for the resulting harm. One of the ways in which a person may subject himself to liability for damages for invasion of privacy is by giving publicity to a matter concerning the private life of another, when the publicized matter would be highly offensive to a reasonable person and is not of legitimate concern to the public. 3 Restatement of Torts 2d § 652D (1977). The determination of whether a person's conduct constitutes the tort of invasion of privacy depends on the facts and circumstances of each case.

The particular form of invasion of privacy in this case is complicated by the implication of federal constitutional guarantees under the First Amendment of freedom of speech and of the press. In *Cox Broadcasting Corp. v. Cohn,* 420 U.S. 469, 43 L. Ed. 2d 328, 95 S. Ct. 1029 (1975), the Court addressed the constitutional guarantee in the context of publication of true statements of fact concerning a person's private life.

The *Cox Broadcasting* decision involved the television report of the name of a rape victim, despite a Georgia statute making it unlawful to publish a rape victim's name. The father of the victim who had been killed in the course of the crime sued the television station for damages, claiming that his right of privacy had been invaded by the broadcast. The Court held that a state may not impose sanctions on the accurate publication of a rape victim's name obtained from records of a public criminal proceeding in which the official court documents were open for public inspection.[33] The Court expressly declined to address the question of whether truthful publications may ever be constitutionally subjected to civil or criminal liability; instead, the Court focused on the "narrower interface between press and privacy that this case presents, namely, whether the State may impose sanctions on the accurate

---

[33] The Georgia statute only provided a criminal sanction. However, civil liability is often determined by analogy to criminal statutes, when the court sets the standard of care and imposes the duty of maintaining that standard.

publication of the name of a rape victim obtained from public records — more specifically, from judicial records which are maintained in connection with a public prosecution and which themselves are open to public inspection."

To the extent that the *Cox Broadcasting* opinion dealt with a current prosecution, that decision is not controlling in the present case.[34] On the other hand, the passage of a considerable length of time after the pertinent event does not of itself convert a public matter into a private one. Lapse of time is merely one of the factors to be considered in determining liability for damages for invasion of privacy by publication of an offensive but truthful matter which was once one of public concern and is still of public record. The circumstances surrounding the publication may also give rise to important factors to be considered.

For example, when a person convicted of a crime has served his sentence, changed his name, moved to a faraway city, concealed his identity, and led an obscure, respectable and useful life for 20 years, a newspaper reporter who institutes an investigation of the little-known citizen's past history and reveals the conviction in a newspaper published in the citizen's new community (far from the site of the crime), the reporter possibly may be liable for damages for invasion of privacy, even though the information is true and is contained in the public records. The intentional nature of the disclosure (which likely involves an element of malice), the lack of the legitimate public interest in an ancient crime committed in a faraway town, and the disclosure of the private facts regarding the criminal's new name and address (after his concerted efforts to conceal his identity and maintain obscurity) are all pertinent factors in determining whether liability should be imposed for damages under the circumstances. . . .[35]

The intermediate court was apparently concerned that newspapers are possibly being accorded a tremendous amount of freedom without being required to exercise a corresponding degree of responsibility, and arguably a balancing of rights and responsibilities should be required. When the published information is accurate and true and a matter of public record, this fact weights heavily in such a balancing process, but a newspaper cannot be allowed unrestricted freedom to publish any true statement of public record, regardless of the purpose or manner of publication or of the temporal and proximal relationship of the published fact to the present situation. This case, however, does not reveal any abuse in the purpose or manner of publication.

Defendants were arguably insensitive or careless in reproducing a former front page for publication without checking for information that might be currently offensive to some members of the community. However, more than insensitivity or simple carelessness is required for the imposition of liability for damages when the publication is truthful, accurate and non-malicious. Plaintiffs in the present case simply did not establish additional factors and circumstances to warrant the imposition of damages. . . .

---

[34] The court of appeal believed *Cox* inapposite, largely because it dealt with the publication of information of a current nature, whereas the information about the Roshto brothers was 25 years old. The court stated the Roshto story "had absolutely no value as a newsworthy item."

[35] Indeed, under the postulated circumstances, the reporter may be liable for damages for intentional infliction of mental anguish.

NOTES

1. *Cox Revisited: The U.S. Constitution and the Publication of Private Facts.* The U.S. Supreme Court held in a 6-3 decision that the defendant newspaper could not be found liable for the publication of a rape victim's name which the defendant had obtained from a publicly released police report. The first amendment to the U.S. Constitution protected the defendant from liability for invasion of privacy. If a newspaper "lawfully obtains information about a matter of public significance," the Court said, "then state officials cannot constitutionally punish publication of the information absent a need to further a state interest of the highest order." The dissenters noted that the publication was in violation of state criminal law, and, unlike *Cox Broadcasting Corp. v. Cohn,* 420 U.S. 469 (1975), no criminal proceeding was pending and no suspect had been identified at the time of the publication. *Florida Star v. B.J.F.,* 491 U.S. 524, 109 S. Ct. 2603, 105 L. Ed. 2d 443 (1989).

2. *The Accident Scene.* The Court in *Connell v. Town of Hudson,* 733 F.Supp. 465 (D.N.H. 1990), said the police could not prevent Connell, a free-lance reporter, from taking a picture of the body of Mrs. Cote, killed in an accident, as the body was being removed from the accident car. "Although the emergency personnel and police may have thought it wrong for Connell to photograph the acident, it is not for them to protect the privacy rights of the victim Ms. Cote and the sensibilities of her family." Could the family prevent the photograph from being taken?

3. *Trespass?* In *Howell v. New York Post Co.,* 81 N.Y.2d 115, (12 N.E.2d 699, 596 N.Y.S.2d 350 (1993), the defendant's photographer trespassed onto the grounds of a psychiatric facility and photographed the plaintiff in conversation with a newsworthy patient, who was recovering from beatings inflicted on her by her former live-in lover, an accused child killer. Later the hospital asked the defendant not to publish the picture, but it did so anyway. The court said the defendant was not liable for invasion of privacy since the picture was newsworthy. Plaintiff's picture could not have been excised, because the "visual impact would not have been the same," i.e., showing the newsworthy patient's physical and emotional recovery as demonstrated by her conversation with the plaintiff.

4. *Fruits of the Poisonous Tree.* Two ABC television reporters used false resumes to get jobs at Food Lion supermarkets, where they "secretly videotaped what appeared to be unwholesome food handling practices." Some of the video footage was later used by ABC "in a Prime Time Live broadcast that was sharply critical of Food Lion." Food Lion sued ABC and collected nominal damages for "breach of their duty of loyalty" and trespass committed by the ABC reporters. The truth of the broadcast was never in issue.

The court refused, on first amendment free speech grounds, to uphold a substantial verdict for publication damages allegedly resulting from the broadcast. *Food Lion, Inc. v. Capital Cities/ABC, Inc.,* 194 F. 3d 505 (4th Cir. 1999). With regard to the publication damages, allegedly consisting of "loss of good will, lost sales and profits, and diminished stock value," and punitive damages, the court held the claim was barred by *Hustler v. Falwell,* 485 U.S. 46 (1988). *Hustler,* the court said, required a public figure plaintiff to prove constitutional malice under the defamation standard of *New York Times v. Sullivan*, 376 U.S. 254 (1964), in order to recover publication damages. "Food Lion was not prepared to meet this standard."

The court distinguished *Cohen v. Cowles Media Co.*, 501 U.S. 663 (1991), and found it to be inapplicable:

> In *Cowles*, Cohen, who was associated with a candidate for governor of Minnesota, gave damaging information about a candidate for another office to two reporters on their promise that his (Cohen's) identity would not be disclosed. Because editors at the reporters' newspapers concluded that the source was an essential part of the story, it was published with Cohen named as the origin. Cohen was fired from his job as a result, and he sued the newspapers for breaking the promise. The question in the Supreme Court was whether the First Amendment barred Cohen from recovering damages under state promissory estoppel law. The newspapers argued that absent "a need to further a state interest of the highest order," the First Amendment protected them from liability for publishing truthful information, lawfully obtained, about a matter of public concern. The Supreme Court disagreed, holding that the press "has no special immunity from the application of general laws" and that the enforcement of general laws against the press "is not subject to stricter scrutiny than would be applied to enforcement against other persons or organizations." Id. at 670.

Cowles did not apply because Cohen was not seeking damages for injury to his reputation, as Food Lion was here. Cohen sought damages "for breach of a promise that caused him to lose his job and lowered his earing capacity."

In *Bartnicki v. Vopper*, 200 F.3d 109 (3d Cir. 1999), a cellular telephone conversation of plaintiffs, two identifiable local teachers' union representatives, was covertly taped by an unknown person. In that conversation, union contract negotiations with the school district were discussed. One of the plaintiffs said that if the school district did not "move" for a 3% wage increase, "we're gonna have to go to their homes. . . to blow off their front porches, we'll have to do some work on some of those guys."

The tape of the conversation was anonymously turned over to the defendant radio station and its reporter, who published the tape on the radio news-public affairs talk show. Plaintiffs sued defendants for damages resulting from defendants' violation of federal and state wiretap statutes. The statutes made it a crime, and provided a civil cause of action, inter alia, for anyone to "use or disclose intercepted communications and who had reason to know that the information was received through an illegal interception." The United States intervened in the case and argued that the federal statute had the twofold purpose of "denying the wrongdoer the fruits of his labor" and "eliminating the demand for those fruits by third parties."

The court said the first amendment protected the defendants from liability, where the record was "devoid of any allegation that the defendants encouraged or participated in the interception in a way that would justify characterizing them as 'wrongdoers'. . . . The public interest and newsworthiness of the conversation broadcast and disclosed by the defendants are patent." A dissent faulted the defendants for broadcasting the conversation without making any effort to ensure its authenticity, authorization, or prior press release.

The U. S. Supreme Court has granted certiorari in this case.

5. *Private Versus Public Communication.* In the Illustrations to comment *a* of RESTATEMENT (SECOND) OF TORTS § 652D, the following examples are given:

> 1. A, a creditor, writes a letter to the employer of B, his debtor, informing him that B owes the debt and will not pay it. This is not an invasion of B's privacy under this Section.
>
> 2. A, a creditor, posts in the window of his shop, where it is read by those passing by on the street, a statement that B owes a debt to him and has not paid it. This is an invasion of B's privacy.

See *Childs v. Williams*, 825 S.W.2d 4 (Mo. App. 1992) ("The critical aspect of the publication requirement [of § 652D] is *public*, disclosure-communications that are available to the general public, communications that have a likelihood of becoming public knowledge.")

Would A be liable to B for invasion of privacy in the first example, if the employer posted A's letter in a window of his shop so it could be read by the public at large?

RASMUSSEN v. SOUTH FLORIDA BLOOD SERVICE
500 So. 2d 533 (Fla. 1987)

BARKETT, JUSTICE.

. . . On May 24, 1982, petitioner, Donald Rasmussen, was sitting on a park bench when he was struck by an automobile. He sued the driver and alleged owner of the automobile for personal injuries he sustained in the accident. While hospitalized as a result of his injuries, Rasmussen received fifty-one units of blood via transfusion. In July of 1983, he was diagnosed as having "Acquired Immune Deficiency Syndrome" (AIDS) and died of that disease one year later.[36] In an attempt to prove that the source of this AIDS was the necessary medical treatment he received because of injuries sustained in the accident, Rasmussen served respondent, South Florida Blood Service (Blood Service), with a subpoena duces tecum requesting "any and all records, documents and other material indicating the names and addresses of the [51] blood donors." (South Florida Blood Service is not a party to the underlying personal injury litigation, and there has been no allegation of negligence on the part of the Blood Service.)

The Blood Service moved the trial court to either quash the subpoena or issue a protective order barring disclosure. That court denied the motion and ordered the Blood Service to disclose the subpoenaed information. On certiorari review, the Third District Court of Appeal, applying the balancing test that courts have traditionally performed under the Florida discovery rules, concluded that the requested material should not be discovered. Although we agree with respondent's contention that Rasmussen's blood donors' rights of

---

[36] His estate is proceeding with this action.

privacy are protected by state and federal constitutions, we need not engage in the stricter scrutiny mandated by constitutional analysis. We find that the interests involved here are adequately protected under our discovery rules and approve the decision of the district court. This opinion in no way changes or dilutes the compelling state interests standard appropriate to a review of state action that infringes privacy rights under article I, section 23 of the Florida Constitution as established in *Winfield v. Division of Pari-Mutuel Wagering, Dep't. of Business Regulation,* 477 So.2d 544, 547 (Fla. 1985).

The potential for invasion of privacy is inherent in the litigation process. Under the Florida discovery rules, any nonprivileged matter that is relevant to the subject matter of the action is discoverable. Fla. R. Civ. P. 1.280(b)(1). The discovery rules also confer broad discretion on the trial court to limit or prohibit discovery in order to "protect a party or person from annoyance, embarrassment, oppression, or undue burden or expense." Fla. R. Civ. P. 1.280(c). Under this authority, a court may act to protect the privacy of the affected person.

In deciding whether a protective order is appropriate in a particular case, the court must balance the competing interests that would be served by granting discovery or by denying it. Thus, the discovery rules provide a framework for judicial analysis of challenges to discovery on the basis that the discovery will result in undue invasion of privacy. This framework allows for broad discovery in order to advance the state's important interest in the fair and efficient resolution of disputes while at the same time providing protective measures to minimize the impact of discovery on competing privacy interests. . . .

The Supreme Court first recognized a right or privacy based on the United States Constitution in *Griswold v. Connecticut,* 381 U.S. 479, 14 L. Ed. 2d 510, 85 S. Ct. 1678 (1965). This right of privacy has been described as "the most comprehensive of rights and the right most valued by civilized man." *Stanley v. Georgia,* 394 U.S. 557, 564, 22 L. Ed. 2d 542, 89 S. Ct. 1243 (1969) (citing *Olmstead v. United States,* 277 U.S. 438, 478 (1928) (Brandeis, J., dissenting)). In recent cases, the Court has discussed the privacy right as one of those fundamental rights that are " 'implicit in the concept of ordered liberty' such that 'neither liberty nor justice would exist if [they] were sacrificed.' " *Bowers v. Hardwick,* 106 S. Ct. 2841, 2844, 478 U.S. 186 (1986) (quoting *Palko v. Connecticut,* 302 U.S. 319, 325–26 (1937)). *See Roe v. Wade,* 410 U.S. 113, 152, 35 L. Ed. 2d 147, 93 S. Ct. 705 (1973). In *Whalen v. Roe,* 429 U.S. 589, 599–600, 51 L. Ed. 2d 64, 97 S. Ct. 869 (1977), the Supreme Court specifically recognized that the right to privacy encompasses at least two different kinds of interests, "the individual interest in avoiding disclosure of personal matters, and . . . the interest in independence in making certain kinds of important decisions."[37] In *Nixon v. Administrator of General Services,* 433 U.S. 425, 457–458, 53 L. Ed. 2d 867, 97 S. Ct. 2777 (1977), the Supreme Court reaffirmed the confidentiality strand of privacy. Lower federal courts have recognized that the essential core of this zone of privacy is the right "to

---

[37] One commentator has incorporated these related interests into a unitary concept by defining privacy as autonomy or control over the intimate aspects of identity. Gerety, *Redefining Privacy,* 12 Harv. C.R.-C.L.L. Rev. 233, 236 (1977).

prevent disclosure of . . . identity in a damaging context." *E.g., Lora v. Board of Education,* 74 F.R.D. 565, 580 (1977). These cases clearly establish that the federal right to privacy extends protection in some circumstances against disclosure of personal matters.

Moreover, in Florida, a citizen's right to privacy is independently protected by our state constitution. In 1980, the voters of Florida amended our state constitution to include an express right of privacy. Art. V, § 23, Fla. Const.[38] In approving the amendment, Florida became the fourth state to adopt a strong, freestanding right of privacy as a separate section of its state constitution, thus providing an explicit textual foundation for those privacy interests inherent in the concept of liberty which may not otherwise be protected by specific constitutional provisions.[39]

Although the general concept of privacy encompasses an enormously broad and diverse field of personal action and belief,[40] there can be no doubt that the Florida amendment was intended to protect the right to determine whether or not sensitive information about oneself will be disclosed to others. The proceedings of the Constitution Revision Commission reveal that the right to informational privacy was a major concern of the amendment's drafters. At the opening session of Florida's 1977-78 Constitution Revision Commission, then Chief Justice Ben F. Overton remarked:

> [W]ho, ten years ago, really understood that *personal* and financial *data* on a substantial part of our population could be collected by government or business and held for easy distribution by computer operated information systems. There is a public concern about how personal information concerning an individual citizen is used, whether it be collected by government or by business. The subject of individual privacy and privacy law is in a developing stage. . . It is a new problem that should probably be addressed. (Emphasis added.)

Address by Chief Justice Ben F. Overton to the Constitution Revision Commission (July 6, 1977). Thus, a principal aim of the constitutional provision is to afford individuals some protection against the increasing collection, retention, and use of information relating to all facets of an individual's life.

It is now known that AIDS is a major health problem with calamitous potential. At present, there is no known cure and the mortality rate is high.[41] As noted by the court below, medical researchers have identified a number of groups which have a high incidence of the disease and are labeled "high

---

[38] Article I, section 23, Florida Constitution, provides:

Right of Privacy. — Every natural person has the right to be let alone and free from governmental intrusion into his private life except as otherwise provided herein. This section shall not be construed to limit the public's right of access to public records and meetings as provided by law.

[39] For example, intrusions into privacy during criminal investigations are generally protected by the prohibition against unreasonable search and seizure. *See* art. I, § 12, Fla. Const.

[40] *See, e.g. Stanley v. Georgia,* 394 U.S. 557 (1969) (privacy of one's personal library); *Griswold v. Connecticut,* 381 U.S. 479 (1965) (privacy of marital relationship).

[41] The mortality rate may be as high as 40 percent. Blodgett, *Despite the public's hands-off attitude toward AIDS, those who discriminate against the disease's victims are finding immunity from the law,* 12 Student Law 8 (Jan. 1984).

risk" groups. Seventy-two percent of all AIDS victims are homosexual or bisexual males with multiple sex partners and seventeen percent are intravenous drug users. Other high risk groups are hemophiliacs (1 percent), heterosexual partners of AIDS victims (1 percent), and blood transfusion recipients (1 percent).

As the district court recognized, petitioner needs more than just the names and addresses of the donors. His interest is in establishing that one or more of the donors has AIDS or is in a high risk group. Petitioner argues that his inquiry may never go beyond comparing the donors' names against a list of known AIDS victims,[42] or against other public records (e.g., conviction records in order to determine whether any of the donors is a known drug user). He contends that because a limited inquiry may reveal the information he seeks, with no invasion of privacy, the donors' privacy rights are not yet at issue. We find this argument disingenuous. As we have already noted, the discovery rules allow a trial judge upon good cause shown to set conditions under which discovery will be given. Some method could be formulated to verify the Blood Service's report that none of the donors is a known AIDS victim while preserving the confidentiality of the donors' identities. However, the subpoena in question gives petitioner access to the names and addresses of the blood donors with no restrictions on their use. There is nothing to prohibit petitioner from conducting an investigation without the knowledge of the persons in question. We cannot ignore, therefore, the consequences of disclosure to nonparties, including the possibility that a donor's co-workers, friends, employers, and others may be queried as to the donor's sexual preferences, drug use, or general life-style.

The threat posed by the disclosure of the donors' identities goes far beyond the immediate discomfort occasioned by third party probing into sensitive areas of the donors' lives. Disclosure of donor identifies in any context involving AIDS could be extremely disruptive and even devastating to the individual donor. If the requested information is released, and petitioner queries the donor's friends and fellow employees, it will be functionally impossible to prevent occasional references to AIDS. As the district court recognized:

> AIDS is the modern day equivalent of leprosy. AIDS, or a suspicion of AIDS, can lead to discrimination in employment, education, housing and even medical treatment. *South Florida Blood Service, Inc. v. Rasmussen,* 467 So. 2d 798, 804 (Fla. Dist. Ct. App. 1985).

We wish to emphasize that although the importance of protecting the privacy of donor information does not depend on the special stigma associated with AIDS, public response to the disease does make this a more critical matter. By the very nature of this case, disclosure of donor identities is "disclosure in a damaging context." See *Lora,* 74 F.R.D. at 580. We conclude, therefore, that the disclosure sought here implicates constitutionally protected privacy interests.

Our analysis of the interests to be served by denying discovery does not end with the effects of disclosure on the private lives of the fifty-one donors

---

[42] South Florida Blood Service has stated that none of Rasmussen's fifty-one donors appears in lists of identified AIDS victims. We agree with petitioner, however, that he should not have to rely on the Blood Service's statement.

implicated in this case. Society has a vital interest in maintaining a strong volunteer blood supply, a task that has become more difficult with the emergence of AIDS. The donor population has been reduced by the necessary exclusion of potential blood donors through AIDS screening and testing procedures, as well as by the unnecessary reduction in the donor population as a result of the widespread fear that donation itself can transmit the disease.[43] In light of this, it is clearly "in the public interest to discourage any serious disincentive to volunteer blood donation." *Rasmussen,* 467 So. 2d at 804. Because there is little doubt that the prospect of inquiry into one's private life and potential association with AIDS will deter blood donation, we conclude that society's interest in a strong and healthy blood supply will be furthered by the denial of discovery in this case. In balancing the competing interests involved, we do not ignore Rasmussen's interest in obtaining the requested information in order to prove aggregation of his injuries and obtain full recovery. We recognize that petitioner's interest parallels the state's interest in ensuring full compensation for victims of negligence. However, we find that the discovery order requested here would do little to advance that interest. The probative value of the discovery sought by Rasmussen is dubious at best. The potential of significant harm to most, if not all, of the fifty-one unsuspecting donors in permitting such a fishing expedition is great and far outweighs the plaintiff's need under these circumstances.

NOTES

1. *Problems of Proof.* What should be an appropriate discovery remedy here? Should the burden of disproof be shifted to the defendant, once plaintiff's estate shows that the deceased was not a high-risk AIDS candidate prior to the accident?

2. *Videotapes.* Congress in 1988 passed the Videotape Privacy Act, 18 U.S.C. § 2710. If a videotape service provider releases without authorization, warrant demand or court order "personally identifiable information concerning any consumer of such provider," the provider can be liable to "any person aggrieved" by such a release, for actual damages, punitive damages, attorneys' fees, and such other "equitable relief as the court determines to be appropriate." The provider must destroy such information "as soon as practicable, but no later than one year form the date the information is no longer necessary for the purposes for which it was collected."

3. *What Is Newsworthy?* In *McNutt v. New Mexico State Tribune Co.,* 88 N.M. 162, 538 P. 2d 804 (1975), *cert. denied,* 88 N.M. 318, 540 P.2d 248 (1975), plaintiff law-enforcement officers were engaged in a gun battle, at a place called Black Mesa, with two individuals who were attempting to steal dynamite from a highway construction site. Both individuals, later determined to be members of a group called the Black Berets, were killed in the gun battle:

---

[43] This fear prompted the Surgeon General to distribute the following to newspapers across the nation: "There is no way that a donor can contract AIDS or any other disease by giving a pint of blood. Despite the known safety of donating blood, some people are afraid to give. In fact, blood donations are down from a year ago, and there is evidence that some previous donors are staying away from blood drives because they are afraid they will get AIDS." Public Health Service, Department of Health and Human Services, *Donate Blood Regularly* (December 1984).

On Monday, January 31, 1972, the Tribune carried an article covering the events at Black Mesa which gave the names and home addresses of the plaintiff officers. Defendant Harry Moskos was the city editor of the Tribune, which is published by the defendant, New Mexico State Tribune Company. Prior to publication of the January 31 story, defendant Moskos had called several of the officers, including plaintiffs McNutt and Urioste, seeking information for his article. The officers told Mr. Moskos that they had been instructed not to discuss the matter, and they referred him to their superiors. Urioste and McNutt stated that Mr. Moskos said that he was going to print their names and addresses because they would not cooperate in giving the details he sought. Officer McNutt urged unsuccessfully that Moskos not publish these facts for his family's sake. Subsequent to publication of the article, several of the officers and members of their families received anonymous phone calls threatening violence.

Plaintiffs alleged that the publication of their names and addresses was done maliciously, and they prayed for punitive as well as actual damages.

The court held the action would not lie since the publication was privileged because of newsworthiness, and adopted the following definition:

> For present purposes news need be defined as comprehending no more than relatively current events such as in common experience are likely to be of public interest. In the verbal and graphic publication of news, it is clear that information and entertainment are not mutually exclusive categories. A large part of the matter which appears in newspapers and news magazines today is not published or read for the value or importance of the information it conveys. Some readers are attracted by shocking news. Others are titillated by sex in the news. Still others are entertained by news which has an incongruous or ironic aspect. Much news is in various ways amusing and for that reason of special interest to many people. Few newspapers or news magazines would long survive if they did not publish a substantial amount of news on the basis of entertainment value of one kind or another. This may be a disturbing commentary upon our civilization, but it is nonetheless a realistic picture of society of which courts in shaping new juristic concepts must take into account. In brief, once the character of an item as news is established, it is neither feasible nor desirable for a court to make a distinction between news for information and news for entertainment in determining the extent to which publication is privileged.

Jenkins v. Dell Publishing Co., 251 F.2d 447 (3rd Cir. 1958).

There can be "no doubt," the *McNutt* court continued, that "reports of current criminal activities are the legitimate province of a free press":

> Plaintiffs, conceding *arguendo* the newsworthiness of the incident in question, assert nonetheless that publication of their addresses was not newsworthy or necessary to the report. We hold that their addresses *were* necessary. If an individual participates in a newsworthy

event, proper identification of that individual is an essential part of the story. It is the usual practice in newspaper accounts to identify persons by giving their names and addresses so as to avoid confusion because many individuals have identical names.

The court said it was immaterial whether "Mr. Moskos may have harbored ill will toward the plaintiff officers."

On the other hand, in *Diaz v. Oakland Tribune, Inc.*, 139 Cal. App. 3d 118, 188 Cal. Rptr. 762 (1983), the court found an action for invasion of privacy was stated by a transsexual who had gender corrective surgery performed in 1975:

> According to Diaz the surgery was a success. By all outward appearances she looked and behaved as a woman and was accepted by the public as a woman. According to her therapist, Dr. Sable, her physical and psychological identities were now in harmony.
>
> Diaz scrupulously kept the surgery a secret from all but her immediate family and closest friends. She never sought to publicize the surgery. She changed her name to Toni Ann Diaz and made the necessary changes in her high school records, her social security records, and on her driver's license. She tried unsuccessfully to change her Puerto Rican birth certificate. She did not change the gender designation on her draft card, however, asserting that it would be a useless gesture, since she had previously been turned down for induction.
>
> Following the surgery she no longer suffered from the psychological difficulties that had plagued her previously. In 1975 she enrolled in the College of Alameda (the College), a two-year college. The College was one of five colleges of the Peralta Community College District.
>
> In spring 1977, she was elected student body president for the 1977-1978 academic year, the first woman to hold that office.
>
> . . . Near the middle of her term as student body president, Diaz became embroiled in a controversy in which she charged the College administrators with misuse of student funds. The March 15, 1978, issue of the Tribune quoted Diaz's charge that her signature had improperly been "rubber stamped" on checks drawn from the associated students' account.
>
> On March 24, 1978, an article in the Alameda Times-Star, a daily newspaper, mentioned Diaz in connection with the charge of misuse of student body funds.
>
> . . . On March 26, 1978, the following item appeared in [reporter] Jones' newspaper column: "More Education Stuff: The students at the College of Alameda will be surprised to learn that their student body president, Toni Diaz, is no lady, but is in fact a man whose real name is Antonio."
>
> > "Now I realize, that in these times, such a matter is no big deal, but I suspect his female classmates in P.E. 97 may wish to make other showering arrangements."

The court found that plaintiff's sex change was not a matter of public record:

> Here there is no evidence to suggest that the fact of Diaz's gender-corrective surgery was part of the public record. To the contrary, the evidence reveals that Diaz took affirmative steps to conceal this fact by changing her driver's license, social security, and high school records, and by lawfully changing her name. The police records, upon which Jones relied, contained information concerning one Antonio Diaz.[44] No mention was made of Diaz's new name or gender. In order to draw the connection, Jones relied upon unidentified confidential sources. Under these circumstances, we conclude that Diaz's sexual identity was a private matter.

The court recognized the defense of newsworthiness, but said this defense is inapplicable where the publicity is so offensive as to constitute a "morbid and sensational prying into private lives for its own sake."

Whether a publication is or is not newsworthy depends upon contemporary community mores and standards of decency. This is largely a question of fact, which a jury is uniquely well-suited to decide.

. . . [D]efendants urge that, as the first female student body president of the College, Diaz was a public figure, and the fact of her sexual identity was a newsworthy item as a matter of law. We disagree.

It is well settled that persons who voluntarily seek public office or willingly become involved in public affairs waive their right to privacy of matters connected with their public conduct. The reason behind this rule is that the public should be afforded every opportunity of learning about any facet which may affect that person's fitness for office.

However, the extent to which Diaz voluntarily acceded to a position of public notoriety and the degree to which she opened her private life are questions of fact. As student body president, Diaz was a public figure for some purposes. However. . . we cannot state that the fact of her gender was newsworthy per se.

Contrary to defendants' claim, we find little if any connection between the information disclosed and Diaz's fitness for office. The fact that she is a transsexual does not adversely reflect on her honesty or judgment. (Cf. *Kapellas v. Kofman,* 1 Cal. 3d 20, 81 Cal. Rptr. 360, 459 P.2d 912 (1969) [plaintiff, a mother and candidate for Alameda City Council, who repeatedly left her minor children unsupervised, could not maintain an action against a newspaper for publishing information taken from police records of her children's criminal behavior]; *Beruan v. French,* 56 Cal. App. 3d 825, 128 Cal. Rptr. 869 (1976) [candidate for secretary-treasurer of union local could not maintain action based on publication of a letter disclosing his six prior criminal convictions.].)

Nor does the fact that she was the first woman student body president, in itself, warrant that her entire private life be open to public inspection.

---

[44] Editor's note. The newspaper checked Oakland City police records and verified that Diaz was born a male. "The evidence reveals that in 1970 or 1971, prior to the surgery, Diaz was arrested in Oakland for soliciting an undercover police officer, a misdemeanor."

The public arena entered by Diaz is concededly small. Public figures more celebrated than she are entitled to keep some information of their domestic activities and sexual relations private.

Nor is there merit to defendants' claim that the changing roles of women in society make this story newsworthy. This assertion rings hollow. The tenor of the article was by no means an attempt to enlighten the public on a contemporary social issue. . . .

PROBLEM

A candidate for the U.S. Presidency learns that her opponent's wife had a lesbian affair while in elementary school. The candidate also learns that her opponent once said in privacy to his closest friend that he "doubted the existence of a Supreme Being," although the opponent attends church regularly and faithfully adheres to a strong moral code. The candidate publicizes these items of information about her opponent during the election campaign. The candidate wins the election.

Does the opponent have a cause of action against the winner for invasion of privacy? How would the opponent prove his case, and what would be the measure of damages? Does the opponent's wife have such an action?

WHITE v. SAMSUNG ELECTRONICS AMERICA, INC.
971 F.2d 1395 (9th Cir. 1992)

GOODWIN, SENIOR CIRCUIT JUDGE.

This case involves a promotional "fame and fortune" dispute. In running a particular advertisement without Vanna White's permission, defendants Samsung Electronics America, Inc. (Samsung) and David Deutsch Associates, Inc. (Deutsch) attempted to capitalize on White's fame to enhance their fortune. White sued, alleging infringement of various intellectual property rights, but the district court granted summary judgment in favor of the defendants. We affirm in part, reverse in part, and remand.

Plaintiff Vanna White is the hostess of "Wheel of Fortune," one of the most popular game shows in television history. An estimated forty million people watch the program daily. Capitalizing on the fame which her participation in the show has bestowed on her, White markets her identity to various advertisers.

The dispute in this case arose out of a series of advertisements prepared for Samsung by Deutsch. The series ran in at least half a dozen publications with widespread, and in some cases national, circulation. Each of the advertisements in the series followed the same theme. Each depicted a current item from popular culture and a Samsung electronic product. Each was set in the twenty-first century and conveyed the message that the Samsung product would still be in use by that time. By hypothesizing outrageous future outcomes for the cultural items, the ads created humorous effects. For example, one lampooned current popular notions of an unhealthy diet by depicting a raw steak with the caption: "Revealed to be health food. 2010 A.D."

Another depicted irreverent "news"-show host Morton Downey Jr. in front of an American flag with the caption: "Presidential candidate. 2008 A.D."

The advertisement which prompted the current dispute was for Samsung video-cassette recorders (VCRs). The ad depicted a robot, dressed in a wig, gown, and jewelry which Deutsch consciously selected to resemble White's hair and dress. The robot was posed next to a game board which is instantly recognizable as the Wheel of Fortune game show set, in a stance for which White is famous. The caption of the ad read: "Longest-running game show. 2012 A.D." Defendants referred to the ad as the "Vanna White" ad. Unlike the other celebrities used in the campaign, White neither consented to the ads nor was she paid.

Following the circulation of the robot ad, White sued Samsung and Deutsch in federal district court under: (1) California Civil Code § 3344; (2) the California common law right of publicity; and (3) § 43(a) of the Lanham Act, 15 U.S.C. § 1125(a). The district court granted summary judgment against White on each of her claims. White now appeals.

[The court found there was no violation of Cal. Civ. Code § 3344, which makes one liable in damages for knowingly using "another's name, voice, signature, photograph, or likeness . . . for purposes of advertising or selling" without the other's consent. The robot at issue here was not White's "'likeness' within the meaning of section 3344," the court said.]

White next argues that the district court erred in granting summary judgment to defendants on White's common law right of publicity claim. In *Eastwood v. Superior Court*, 149 Cal.App.3d 409, 198 Cal.Rptr. 342 (1983), the California court of appeal stated that the common law right of publicity cause of action "may be pleaded by alleging (1) the defendant's use of the plaintiff's identity; (2) the appropriation of plaintiff's name or likeness to defendant's advantage, commercially or otherwise; (3) lack of consent; and (4) resulting injury." The district court dismissed White's claim for failure to satisfy *Eastwood's* second prong, reasoning that defendants had not appropriated White's "name or likeness" with their robot ad. We agree that the robot ad did not make use of White's name or likeness. However, the common law right of publicity is not so confined.

The *Eastwood* court did not hold that the right of publicity cause of action could be pleaded only by alleging an appropriation of name or likeness. *Eastwood* involved an unauthorized use of photographs of Clint Eastwood and of his name. Accordingly, the *Eastwood* court had no occasion to consider the extent beyond the use of name or likeness to which the right of publicity reaches. That court held only that the right of publicity cause of action "may be" pleaded by alleging, *inter alia*, appropriation of name or likeness, not that the action may be pleaded only in those terms.

The "name or likeness" formulation referred to in *Eastwood* originated not as an element of the right of publicity cause of action, but as a description of the types of cases in which the cause of action had been recognized. The source of this formulation is Prosser, *Privacy*, 48 Cal.L.Rev. 383, 401–07 (1960), one of the earliest and most enduring articulations of the common law right of publicity cause of action. In looking at the case law to that point,

Prosser recognized that right of publicity cases involved one of two basic factual scenarios: name appropriation, and picture or other likeness appropriation.

Even though Prosser focused on appropriations of name or likeness in discussing the right of publicity, he noted that "[i]t is not impossible that there might be appropriation of the plaintiff's identity, as by impersonation, without the use of either his name or his likeness, and that this would be an invasion of his right of privacy." *Id.* at 401, n. 155. At the time Prosser wrote, he noted however, that "[n]o such case appears to have arisen." *Id.*

Since Prosser's early formulation, the case law has borne out his insight that the right of publicity is not limited to the appropriation of name or likeness. In *Motschenbacher v. R.J. Reynolds Tobacco Co.*, 498 F.2d 821 (9th Cir.1974), the defendant had used a photograph of the plaintiff's race car in a television commercial. Although the plaintiff appeared driving the car in the photograph, his features were not visible. Even though the defendant had not appropriated the plaintiff's name or likeness, this court held that plaintiff's California right of publicity claim should reach the jury.

In *Midler,* [*v. Ford Motor Co.*, 849 F.2d 460 (9th Cir. 1988),] this court held that, even though the defendants had not used Midler's name or likeness, Midler had stated a claim for violation of her California common law right of publicity because "the defendants . . . for their own profit in selling their product did appropriate part of her identity" by using a Midler sound-alike. *Id.* at 463–64.

In *Carson v. Here's Johnny Portable Toilets, Inc.*, 698 F.2d 831 (6th Cir.1983), the defendant had marketed portable toilets under the brand name "Here's Johnny" — Johnny Carson's signature "Tonight Show" introduction — without Carson's permission. The district court had dismissed Carson's Michigan common law right of publicity claim because the defendants had not used Carson's "name or likeness." Id. at 835. In reversing the district court, the sixth circuit found "the district court's conception of the right of publicity . . . too narrow" and held that the right was implicated because the defendant had appropriated Carson's identity by using, *inter alia*, the phrase "Here's Johnny." *Id.* at 835–37.

These cases teach not only that the common law right of publicity reaches means of appropriation other than name or likeness, but that the specific means of appropriation are relevant only for determining whether the defendant has in fact appropriated the plaintiff's identity. The right of publicity does not require that appropriations of identity be accomplished through particular means to be actionable. It is noteworthy that the *Midler* and Carson defendants not only avoided using the plaintiff's name or likeness, but they also avoided appropriating the celebrity's voice, signature, and photograph. The photograph in *Motschenbacher* did include the plaintiff, but because the plaintiff was not visible the driver could have been an actor or dummy and the analysis in the case would have been the same.

Although the defendants in these cases avoided the most obvious means of appropriating the plaintiffs' identities, each of their actions directly implicated the commercial interests which the right of publicity is designed to protect. As the *Carson* court explained:

[t]he right of publicity has developed to protect the commercial interest of celebrities in their identities. The theory of the right is that a celebrity's identity can be valuable in the promotion of products, and the celebrity has an interest that may be protected from the unauthorized commercial exploitation of that identity. . . . If the celebrity's identity is commercially exploited, there has been an invasion of his right whether or not his "name or likeness" is used.

Carson, 698 F.2d at 835. It is not important *how* the defendant has appropriated the plaintiff's identity, but *whether* the defendant has done so. *Motschenbacher, Midler,* and *Carson* teach the impossibility of treating the right of publicity as guarding only against a laundry list of specific means of appropriating identity. A rule which says that the right of publicity can be infringed only through the use of nine different methods of appropriating identity merely challenges the clever advertising strategist to come up with the tenth.

Indeed, if we treated the means of appropriation as dispositive in our analysis of the right of publicity, we would not only weaken the right but effectively eviscerate it. The right would fail to protect those plaintiffs most in need of its protection. Advertisers use celebrities to promote their products. The more popular the celebrity, the greater the number of people who recognize her, and the greater the visibility for the product. The identities of the most popular celebrities are not only the most attractive for advertisers, but also the easiest to evoke without resorting to obvious means such as name, likeness, or voice.

Consider a hypothetical advertisement which depicts a mechanical robot with male features, an African-American complexion, and a bald head. The robot is wearing black hightop Air Jordan basketball sneakers, and a red basketball uniform with black trim, baggy shorts, and the number 23 (though not revealing "Bulls" or "Jordan" lettering). The ad depicts the robot dunking a basketball one-handed, stiff-armed, legs extended like open scissors, and tongue hanging out. Now envision that this ad is run on television during professional basketball games. Considered individually, the robot's physical attributes, its dress, and its stance tell us little. Taken together, they lead to the only conclusion that any sports viewer who has registered a discernible pulse in the past five years would reach: the ad is about Michael Jordan.

Viewed separately, the individual aspects of the advertisement in the present case say little. Viewed together, they leave little doubt about the celebrity the ad is meant to depict. The female-shaped robot is wearing a long gown, blond wig, and large jewelry. Vanna White dresses exactly like this at times, but so do many other women. The robot is in the process of turning a block letter on a game-board. Vanna White dresses like this while turning letters on a game-board but perhaps similarly attired Scrabble-playing women do this as well. The robot is standing on what looks to be the Wheel of Fortune game show set. Vanna White dresses like this, turns letters, and does this on the Wheel of Fortune game show. She is the only one. Indeed, defendants themselves referred to their ad as the "Vanna White" ad. We are not surprised.

Television and other media create marketable celebrity identity value. Considerable energy and ingenuity are expended by those who have achieved celebrity value to exploit it for profit. The law protects the celebrity's sole right to exploit this value whether the celebrity has achieved her fame out of rare ability, dumb luck, or a combination thereof. We decline Samsung and Deutch's invitation to permit the evisceration of the common law right of publicity through means as facile as those in this case. Because White has alleged facts showing that Samsung and Deutsch had appropriated her identity, the district court erred by rejecting, on summary judgment, White's common law right of publicity claim.

[The court held the plaintiff also stated a claim for violation of the Lanham Act.

[A petition to rehear was denied. A suggestion for rehearing en banc was also denied, for failure to receive a majority of votes of active judges of the full court. 989 F.2d 1512 (9th Cir. 1993). Three judges dissented from the order rejecting the suggestion for rehearing en banc. Judge Kozinski, writing for the dissenters, said in part:]

Saddam Hussein wants to keep advertisers from using his picture in unflattering contexts.[45] Clint Eastwood doesn't want tabloids to write about him.[46] Rudolf Valentino's heirs want to control his film biography.[47] The Girl Scouts don't want their image soiled by association with certain activities.[48] George Lucas wants to keep Strategic Defense Initiative fans from calling it "Star Wars."[49] Pepsico doesn't want singers to use the word "Pepsi" in their songs.[50] Guy Lombardo wants an exclusive property right to ads that show

---

[45] See Eben Shapiro, *Rising Caution on Using Celebrity Images*, N.Y. Times, Nov. 4, 1992, at D20 (Iraqi diplomat objects on right of publicity grounds to ad containing Hussein's picture and caption "History has shown what happens when one source controls all the information").

[46] *Eastwood v. Superior Court*, 149 Cal.App.3d 409, 198 Cal.Rptr. 342 (1983).

[47] *Guglielmi v. Spelling-Goldberg Prods.*, 25 Cal.3d 860, 160 Cal.Rptr. 352, 603 P.2d 454 (1979) (Rudolph Valentino); see also *Maheu v. CBS, Inc.*, 201 Cal.App.3d 662, 668, 247 Cal.Rptr. 304 (1988) (aide to Howard Hughes). Cf. Frank Gannon, *Vanna Karenina*, in *Vanna Karenina and Other Reflections* (1988) (A humorous short story with a tragic ending. "She thought of the first day she had met VR_____SKY. How foolish she had been. How could she love a man who wouldn't even tell her all the letters in his name?").

[48] *Girl Scouts v. Personality Posters Mfg.*, 304 F.Supp. 1228 (S.D.N.Y.1969) (poster of a pregnant girl in a Girl Scout uniform with the caption "Be Prepared").

[49] *Lucasfilm Ltd. v. High Frontier*, 622 F.Supp. 931 (D.D.C.1985).

[50] Pepsico Inc. claimed the lyrics and packaging of grunge rocker Tad Doyle's "Jack Pepsi" song were "offensive to [it] and [. . .] likely to offend [its] customers," in part because they "associate [Pepsico] and its Pepsi marks with intoxication and drunk driving." Deborah Russell, *Doyle Leaves Pepsi Thirsty for Compensation*, Billboard, June 15, 1991, at 43. Conversely, the Hell's Angels recently sued Marvel Comics to keep it from publishing a comic book called "Hell's Angel," starring a character of the same name. Marvel settled by paying $35,000 to charity and promising never to use the name "Hell's Angel" again in connection with any of its publications. *Marvel, Hell's Angels Settle Trademark Suit*, L.A. Daily J., Feb. 2, 1993, § II, at 1.

Trademarks are often reflected in the mirror of our popular culture. See Truman Capote, *Breakfast at Tiffany's* (1958); Kurt Vonnegut, Jr., *Breakfast of Champions* (1973); Tom Wolfe, *The Electric Kool-Aid Acid Test* (1968) (which, incidentally, includes a chapter on the Hell's Angels); Larry Niven, *Man of Steel, Woman of Kleenex*, in *All the Myriad Ways* (1971); *Looking for Mr. Goodbar* (1977); *The Coca-Cola Kid* (1985) (using Coca-Cola as a metaphor for American commercialism); *The Kentucky Fried Movie* (1977); *Harley Davidson and the Marlboro Man* (1991); *The Wonder Years* (ABC 1988-present) ("Wonder Years" was a slogan of Wonder Bread); Tim Rice & Andrew Lloyd Webber, *Joseph and the Amazing Technicolor Dream Coat* (musical).

Hear Janis Joplin, *Mercedes Benz*, on *Pearl* (CBS 1971); Paul Simon, *Kodachrome*, on *There*

big bands playing on New Year's Eve.[51] Uri Geller thinks he should be paid for ads showing psychics bending metal through telekinesis.[52] Paul Prudhomme, that household name, thinks the same about ads featuring corpulent bearded chefs.[53] And scads of copyright holders see purple when their creations are made fun of.[54]

Something very dangerous is going on here. Private property, including intellectual property, is essential to our way of life. It provides an incentive for investment and innovation; it stimulates the flourishing of our culture; it protects the moral entitlements of people to the fruits of their labors. But reducing too much to private property can be bad medicine. Private land, for instance, is far more useful if separated from other private land by public streets, roads and highways. Public parks, utility rights-of-way and sewers reduce the amount of land in private hands, but vastly enhance the value of the property that remains.

So too it is with intellectual property. Overprotecting intellectual property is as harmful as underprotecting it. Creativity is impossible without a rich public domain. Nothing today, likely nothing since we tamed fire, is genuinely new: Culture, like science and technology, grows by accretion, each new creator building on the works of those who came before. Overprotection stifles the very creative forces it's supposed to nurture.

Goes Rhymin' Simon (Warner 1973); Leonard Cohen, *Chelsea Hotel*, on *The Best of Leonard Cohen* (CBS 1975); Bruce Springsteen, *Cadillac Ranch*, on *The River* (CBS 1980); Prince, *Little Red Corvette, on 1999* (Warner 1982); dada, *Dizz Knee Land*, on *Puzzle* (IRS 1992) ("I just robbed a grocery store — I'm going to Disneyland / I just flipped President George—I'm going to Disneyland"); Monty Python, *Spam*, on *The Final Rip Off* (Virgin 1988); Roy Clark, *Thank God ad Greyhound [You're Gone]*, on *Roy Clark's Greatest Hits Volume I* (MCA 1979); Mel Tillis, *Coca-Cola Cowboy*, on *The Very Best of* (MCA 1981) ("You're just a Coca-Cola cowboy / You've got an Eastwood smile and Robert Redford hair. . .").

Dance to Talking Heads, *Popular Favorites 1976-92: Sand in the Vaseline* (Sire 1992); Talking Heads, *Popsicle*, on *id.* Admire Andy Warhol, *Campbell's Soup Can. Cf.* REO Speedwagon, 38 Special, and Jello Biafra of the Dead Kennedys.

The creators of some of these works might have gotten permission from the trademark owners, though it's unlikely Kool-Aid relished being connected with LSD, Hershey with homicidal maniacs, Disney with armed robbers, or Coca-Cola with cultural imperialism. Certainly no free society can *demand* that artists get such permission.

[51] *Lombardo v. Doyle, Dane & Bernbach, Inc.*, 58 A.D.2d 620, 396 N.Y.S.2d 661 (1977).

[52] *Geller v. Fallon McElligott*, No. 90-Civ-2839 (S.D.N.Y. July 22, 1991) (involving a Timex ad).

[53] *Prudhomme v. Procter & Gamble Co.*, 800 F.Supp. 390 (E.D.La.1992).

[54] *E.g., Acuff-Rose Music, Inc. v. Campbell*, 972 F.2d 1429 (6th Cir.1992); *Cliffs Notes v. Bantam Doubleday Dell Publishing Group, Inc.*, 886 F.2d 490 (2d Cir.1989); *Fisher v. Dees*, 794 F.2d 432 (9th Cir.1986); *MCA, Inc. v. Wilson*, 677 F.2d 180 (2d Cir.1981); *Elsmere Music, Inc. v. NBC*, 623 F.2d 252 (2d Cir.1980); *Walt Disney Prods. v. The Air Pirates*, 581 F.2d 751 (9th Cir.1978); *Berlin v. E.C. Publications, Inc.*, 329 F.2d 541 (2d Cir.1964); *Lowenfels v. Nathan*, 2 F.Supp. 73 (S.D.N.Y.1932).

[An Appendix to the dissent showed a picture of "Wheel of Fortune" Vanna White, and a picture of the offending robot:]

NOTES

1. *Purloining a Picture*. The plaintiff Faber, in *Faber v. Condecor, Inc.*, 195 N.J. Super. 81, 477 A.2d 1289 (1984), was a photography consultant for Eastman Kodak for over 30 years. In 1973 he prepared a photograph of his family for use on their Christmas cards. Later "as a gesture of goodwill" he permitted a co-employee to use the picture in a new Kodak publication called "Printing Color Negatives," as an "example of the process for correcting a contrast problem." Faber understood the permission "was for a one-time use by Kodak."

In 1978 Faber learned that defendant had taken the picture from the Kodak publication and had reproduced it in a family-tree photograph, which was sold in "flea markets, supermarkets and other stores and in various outlets throughout the country." Plaintiff became upset because he thought the reproduction "gave the appearance that he was endorsing another manufacturer's product, which could jeopardize his job." The reproduction was of poor quality, and he thought it "damaged his credibility in the field of news photography." His son testified "that friends at school made fun of him" because of the picture, and his wife testified that "the picture's appearance disturbed the peace of their family."

The family sued for invasion of privacy, basing their claim on REST. 2d OF TORTS § 652C, which states: "One who appropriates to his own use or benefit the name or likeness of another is subject to liability to the other for invasion of his privacy." The court affirmed a $45,000 jury verdict for the plaintiffs. Defendant's reproduction was not a "mere incidental use" of plaintiffs' picture, or a "legitimate mention of [their] public activities." Rather, the picture was "used directly for trade purposes."

2. *Constitutional Overtones*. In *Zacchini v. Scripps-Howard Broadcasting Co.*, 433 U. S. 562, 97 S. Ct. 2849, 53 L.Ed.2d 965 (1977), the U. S. Supreme

Court held in a 5-4 decision that the first amendment to the U. S. Constitution did not prevent an action by the petitioner against the respondent television station for filming without permission his 15-second "human cannonball" act while it was being performed at the Geauga County Fair, and then broadcasting the act on its evening news program together with favorable commentary:

> The broadcast of a film of petitioner's entire act poses a substantial threat to the economic value of that performance. As the Ohio court recognized, this act is the product of petitioner's own talents and energy, the end result of much time, effort and expense. Much of its economic value lies in the right of exclusive control over the publicity given to his performance; if the public can see the act free on television, it will be less willing to pay to see it at the fair.

The Court reversed the Ohio Supreme Court's finding that the broadcast was constitutionally protected:

> The Ohio Supreme Court held that respondent is constitutionally privileged to include in its newscasts matters of public interest that would otherwise be protected by the right of publicity, absent an intent to injure or to appropriate for some nonprivileged purpose. If under this standard respondent had merely reported that petitioner was performing at the fair and described or commented on his act, with or without showing his picture on television, we would have a very different case. But petitioner is not contending that his appearance at the fair and his performance could not be reported by the press as newsworthy items. His complaint is that respondent filmed his entire act and displayed that film on television for the public to see and enjoy.

On remand, the Ohio Supreme Court, 54 Ohio St.2d 286, 376 N.E.2d 582 (1978), held that Zacchini stated a cause of action for commercial appropriation of the right of publicity.

3. *Descendibility.* The cases vary widely on whether the right of publicity survives one's death and is inheritable. Some cases hold there is no right of survival, others that the existence of the right depends on whether the deceased commercially exploited her name or likeness during her lifetime, and still others that there is an unqualified right of survival. *See* discussion in *Martin Luther King, Jr. Center for Social Change v. American Heritage Prods.,* 694 F.2d 674 (11th Cir. 1983).

In *Lugosi v. Universal Pictures*, 25 Cal.3d 813, 603 P.2d 425, 160 Cal. Rptr. 323 (1979), the heirs of the deceased movie actor Bela Lugosi sought damages for and an injunction against the use of Lugosi's Count Dracula character. The court denied the claim, stating that the right of privacy is "protectible during one's lifetime but it does not survive the death of Lugosi." Subsequently, California passed Cal. Civ. Code § 990 (1995), granting heirs the right to sue for protection of the "name, voice, photograph, or likeness" of a deceased person for 50 years after the person's death.

4. *The Celebrity and the Unknown Person.* Vanna White was a celebrity, Zacchini was a public entertainer, and Faber was a business person. The privacy tort here being considered — more aptly described as the right of

publicity — actually is a business tort, and is treated in fuller detail in the next chapter.

Private individuals, as well as celebrities, have a right to protect their name and likeness. In *Staruski v. Cont. Tel. Co.*, 581 A.2d 266 (Vt. 1990), plaintiff, a sales and service representative at defendant's office in Springfield, Vt., sued her employer for featuring her in a newspaper advertisement without her consent. The ad included a photograph of the plaintiff smiling broadly and saying, "Hi, I'm Cindy Staruski," with accompanying text in which she describes her job and says it has been "exciting and reassuring to know that Continental continues to expand its equipment and services to meet its obligation to serve you."

The jury awarded plaintiff $1,000 in compensatory and $3,500 in punitive damages. The trial court granted defendant a JNOV, stating, "I don't think you can have appropriation by putting in the name and face of a person who has no fame." Reversing the trial court, the State Supreme Court said:

> Fame of the person whose identity is appropriated has never been a prerequisite to recovery for invasion of privacy. One of the leading cases establishing a right of action for invasion of privacy by appropriation of likeness, *Pavesich v. New England Life Insurance Co.*, 122 Ga. 190, 217, 50 S.E. 68, 79 (1905), involved the unauthorized use in an advertisement by an insurance company of a photograph of the plaintiff, who "was in no sense a public character." Recent cases applying Restatement (Second) of Torts § 652C also permit recovery although the plaintiff was not famous. For example, in *Tellado v. Time-Life Books*, 643 F.Supp. 904, 909 (D.N.J.1986), the court held that a publisher may be liable for misappropriation of likeness for using a photograph of the plaintiff, without his permission, in promotional material for a series of books on the Vietnam War. The photograph showed the plaintiff, without his permission, in promotional material for a series of books on the Vietnam War. The photograph showed the plaintiff as an anguished soldier in Vietnam, but neither his name nor his face were well known to the public. The cause of action, the court ruled, is not limited to famous individuals.

The court noted that in *Faber* "the court upheld a verdict for a family (not famous) whose privacy was invaded by a manufacturer of picture frames that used the family's photograph without permission." It quoted *Faber* for the proposition that "[d]amages may be recovered for invasion of privacy, even if the injury suffered is mental distress alone."

Could Staruski recover for false light invasion of privacy?

DIAMOND SHAMROCK REFINING AND MARKETING COMPANY v. MENDEZ
844 S.W.2d 198 (Tex. 1992)

PHILLIPS, CHIEF JUSTICE.

In this action, an employee claims that his employer committed the torts of "false light" invasion of privacy and intentional infliction of emotional distress by circulating information about his termination among his fellow employees. The trial court rendered judgment on a jury verdict for the plaintiff on both theories. The court of appeals held that no evidence supported the jury's verdict as to intentional infliction of emotional distress, but it affirmed the judgment of the trial court under the false light theory. We reverse the judgment of the court of appeals and remand for a new trial on Mendez's false light theory.

Roque Mendez was a chief operator at the Diamond Shamrock oil refinery in Three Rivers, Texas. The evidence most favorable to sustaining the jury's verdict is that on September 4, 1985, Mendez was ordered by his supervisor to clean up debris that had been left in his work area, including loose nails discarded by carpenters. He became angry at being assigned the clean-up task, which he perceived to be outside the scope of his ordinary duties. While he was cleaning, Mendez threw some of the nails, the value of which was less than five dollars, into a box and put the box into his lunch bag. He then placed the bag on a shelf while he finished cleaning. When he was finished he went to the clock house, which was on company property, placed the bag on a table, clocked out, and left the refinery.

After Mendez departed, a security officer found his lunch bag and noticed that it contained the nails. The security staff reported the finding to Wayne Billings, Human Resource and Administrative Manager, and John Hoffman, Plant Manager. Billings telephoned Mendez and asked him to return to the refinery. Confronted by Billings and Hoffman, Mendez identified the bag as his own. When asked to explain, Mendez described how he had become angered by his supervisor's order and rudeness and how he simply threw the nails into the box and threw the box into the bag. Hoffman then told Mendez that the bag contained company property and that it appeared that Mendez was stealing. When Hoffman asked whether Mendez agreed, Mendez replied, "I guess so." Hoffman then terminated Mendez and left the room. Left alone with Mendez, Billings asked why Mendez had not simply asked for a "gate pass" to take the nails off the premises. Mendez replied, "I don't know, Wayne. I guess I messed up."

Word of Mendez's termination spread quickly in Three Rivers. Many people with whom Mendez spoke during the next few weeks, including potential employers, knew that he had been terminated for stealing. As a result, he claims to have suffered significant financial and emotional setbacks.

Mendez filed suit against Diamond Shamrock on September 1, 1987, nearly two years after his termination. In his original petition, he alleged defamation, breach of contract, bad faith and unfair dealing, and violation of certain constitutional rights. Later, he added claims for malicious and wrongful termination, intentional or reckless infliction of emotional distress, negligence, and invasion of privacy comprising the embarrassing disclosure of personal facts and placing the plaintiff in a false light in the public eye. Mendez did not pursue his defamation claim, presumably because he did not bring it within the applicable one-year limitations period. The trial court submitted questions to the jury on only two theories of liability: intentional infliction of emotional distress and false light invasion of privacy. With respect to false light, the court submitted the following question to the jury:

Did the Defendant, Diamond Shamrock, by and through its employees, invade the privacy of the Plaintiff, Roque Mendez?

You are instructed that the Defendant may invade the privacy of the Plaintiff if it publicized matters which placed him in a false light before the public that would be highly offensive to a reasonable person.

Diamond Shamrock objected to this question, arguing that it omitted the "actual malice" standard for false light, an essential element of Mendez's cause of action. The trial court overruled this objection. The jury found for Mendez on both the false light and intentional infliction of emotional distress counts, awarding him $460,000 in damages: $260,000 for past and future lost wages, $100,000 for mental anguish, and $100,000 for loss of reputation. The trial court rendered judgment on the jury verdict.

On appeal to the court of appeals, Diamond Shamrock argued that the trial court erred by failing to include the element of actual malice in its instruction to the jury on false light invasion of privacy. The court of appeals affirmed the judgment, holding that negligence, rather than actual malice, should be the standard in false light suits by private individuals. Further, Diamond Shamrock could not complain of the absence of a negligence instruction, since it had not requested one. Although the court also held that there was no evidence that Diamond Shamrock intentionally inflicted emotional distress on Mendez, it affirmed the judgment of the trial court because it rested on alternate grounds.

This court has never expressly held that a tort for false light invasion of privacy exists in Texas, although we have recognized that it is one of the four usual categories of private actions for invasion of privacy. Although amicus curiae urge us to reject the false light tort, we do not reach this issue, as it has not been adequately presented by the parties. Even assuming the availability of this cause of action, however, Mendez would not be entitled to recover on the record before us, as he did not submit all the essential elements of the false light tort.

THE RESTATEMENT (SECOND) OF TORTS § 652E defines the false light tort to include an actual malice requirement as follows:

> One who gives publicity to a matter concerning another that places the other before the public in a false light is subject to liability to the other for invasion of his privacy if
>
> (a) the false light in which the other was placed would be highly offensive to a reasonable person, and
>
> (b) the actor had knowledge of or acted in reckless disregard as to the falsity of the publicized matter and the false light in which the other would be placed.

Moreover, the Texas courts of appeals that have recognized this tort have applied the actual malice standard, as have most courts in other jurisdictions. *But see Jones v. Palmer Communications, Inc.*, 440 N.W.2d 884, 898 (Iowa 1989), *Crump v. Beckley Newspapers, Inc.*, 173 W.Va. 699, 320 S.E.2d 70, 90 (1984), adopting a negligence standard. Thus, if the tort of false light invasion of privacy exists in Texas, it requires a showing of actual malice as an element of recovery. Because the trial court's instruction omitted an element of Mendez's cause of action, Diamond Shamrock properly preserved error by objecting. Since Mendez failed to establish an essential element of the false light cause of action under the Restatement and the preponderance of case law, the court of appeals' judgment in favor of Mendez on this claim must be reversed.

Because of the conflict between jurisdictions regarding the proper standard of conduct, and because this Court has not yet either recognized or disapproved the tort, we remand this cause of action for a new trial in the interest of justice, giving Mendez an opportunity to prove actual malice and Diamond Shamrock an opportunity to object to the theory of recovery in its entirety. . . .

The court of appeals reversed the trial court's judgment that Diamond Shamrock intentionally inflicted emotional distress on Mendez, finding no evidence of such an infliction. By cross-point, Mendez urges us to reverse this holding.

THE RESTATEMENT (SECOND) OF TORTS § 46 (1965) defines the tort of intentional infliction of emotional distress as follows:

> One who by extreme and outrageous conduct intentionally or recklessly causes severe emotional distress to another is subject to liability for such emotional distress. . . .

We have never recognized this tort, but a number of Texas courts of appeals have done so, as have courts in many other jurisdictions. We need not decide in this case whether the tort exists in Texas, because Mendez failed to offer more than a scintilla of evidence of an essential element of the tort as it has been recognized in lower courts of this state and in courts of other jurisdictions, the presence of outrageous conduct.

Mendez argues that Diamond Shamrock's tortious conduct occurred not by terminating him, but by falsely depicting him in the community as a thief. Even if Mendez's charges are taken as true, however, this conduct is not sufficiently outrageous to raise a fact issue. RESTATEMENT § 46, comment *d*, describes conduct reaching the level of "outrageousness" necessary for liability for intentional infliction of emotional distress in these terms:

> Liability has been found only where the conduct has been so outrageous in character, and so extreme in degree, as to go beyond all possible bounds of decency, and to be regarded as atrocious, and utterly intolerable in a civilized community.

There is no evidence that Diamond Shamrock's conduct met this standard. We need not condone or agree with Diamond Shamrock's actions to conclude that, as a matter of law, they fall short of being "beyond all possible bounds of decency," "atrocious," and "utterly intolerable in a civilized community." While there may obviously be instances where a termination is accompanied by behavior of this sort, there would be little left of the employment-at-will doctrine if an employer's public statement of the reason for termination was, so long as the employee disputed that reason, in and of itself some evidence that a tort of intentional infliction of emotional distress had been committed. The court of appeals did not err in denying Mendez recovery on this ground.

For the foregoing reasons, we affirm the judgment of the court of appeals against Mendez on the ground of intentional infliction of emotional distress.

We reverse the judgment of the court of appeals in favor of Mendez on the ground of false light, and remand that claim to the trial court for a new trial.

[Gonzalez, J., concurring and dissenting, contended that the Court should not recognize the tort of false light invasion of privacy.]

The false light action, as it has been defined by the Restatement, permits recovery for injuries caused by publicity that unreasonably places the plaintiff in a false light before the public. Although not explicitly required by the Restatement definition, most jurisdictions, including the lower Texas courts that have recognized the action, require that a statement be false if it is to be cognizable under the false light doctrine. The falsity requirement is sensible, considering that the "revelation of private facts" invasion of privacy tort purports to grant relief for the disclosure of true statements that adversely affect the subject. *But see* Thomas I. Emerson, *The Right of Privacy and Freedom of the Press*, 14 HARV. C.R.-C.L. REV. 329, 345 (1979) (the truth or falsity of statements giving rise to liability for false light should not matter; rather, false light cases should be treated the same as embarrassing disclosure cases).

If we were to recognize a false light tort in Texas, it would largely duplicate several existing causes of action, particularly defamation. Libel, which is written defamation, is defined by Texas Civil Practice & Remedies Code § 73.001 as follows:

> A libel is a defamation expressed in written or other graphic form that tends to blacken the memory of the dead or that tends to injure a living person's reputation and thereby expose the person to public hatred, contempt or ridicule, or financial injury or to impeach any person's honesty, integrity, virtue, or reputation or to publish the natural defects of anyone and thereby expose the person to public hatred, ridicule, or financial injury.

Slander, the spoken form of defamation, is not codified by statute, but has been recognized at common law to be "a defamatory statement orally published to a third party without justification or excuse." *See* Restatement (Second) of Torts § 568 (1977); *Shearson Lehman Hutton, Inc. v. Tucker*, 806 S.W.2d 914, 921 (Tex.App. — Corpus Christi 1991, *writ dism'd w.o.j.*). Thus, like false light, defamatory statements must be false in order to be actionable. Furthermore, the elements of damages that have been recognized in false light actions are similar to those awarded for defamation. The principal element of actual damages for false light claims is typically mental anguish, but physical illness and harm to the plaintiff's commercial interests have also been recognized. These are essentially the types of damages sought in defamation actions. Thus many, if not all, of the injuries redressed by the false light tort are also redressed by defamation. *See Kapellas v. Kofman*, 1 Cal.3d 20, 35 n. 16, 81 Cal.Rptr. 360, 369 n. 16, 459 P.2d 912, 921 n. 16 (1969) ("[s]ince the complaint contains a specific cause of action for libel, the privacy count, if intended [as a false light count] is superfluous and should be dismissed.").

The false light tort also overlaps with some of the other, better recognized, privacy torts. *See, e.g.*, Harry Kalven, Jr., *Privacy in Tort Law — Were Warren and Brandeis Wrong?*, 31 LAW & CONTEMP. PROBS. 326, 332 (1966) (noting the potential overlap of false light and appropriation); *Lerman v. Flynt Distributing Co.*, 745 F.2d 123, 135 (2d Cir.1984) ("while not specifically alleged in her complaint, [plaintiff's right to publicity] action presents a classic false light claim"). Finally, as we observed in *Billings v. Atkinson*, 489 S.W.2d 858, 860 (Tex.1973), "some of the right of privacy interests have been afforded protection under such traditional theories as libel and slander, wrongful search and seizure, eavesdropping and wiretapping, and other similar invasions into the private business and personal affairs of an individual."

A few commentators have attempted to delineate the theoretical differences between false light invasion of privacy and other torts, particularly defamation. As one notes:

> [I]n defamation cases the interest sought to be protected is the objective one of reputation, either economic, political, or personal, in the outside world. In privacy cases the interest affected is the subjective one of injury to the inner person . . . in defamation cases, where the issue is truth or falsity, the marketplace of ideas furnishes a forum in which the battle can be fought. In privacy cases, resort to the marketplace simply accentuates the injury.

Thomas I. Emerson, *The Right of Privacy and Freedom of the Press*, 14 HARV. C.R.-C.L. L. REV. 329, 333 (1979). But a number of other scholars have argued that false light and defamation are nearly identical or even indistinguishable. *See, e.g.*, BRUCE W. SANFORD, *supra*, § 11.4.1 at 567 (2d ed. 1991) ("Legally, placing someone in a false light amounts to little more than defamation"); ROBERT D. SACK, LIBEL, SLANDER, AND RELATED PROBLEMS 394 (1980) (where the circumstances would support an action for "false light" invasion of privacy, plaintiffs may often successfully use libel or slander in addition or instead); John W. Wade, *Defamation and the Right of Privacy*, 15 VAND.L.REV. 1093, 1121 (1962) ("the great majority of defamation actions can now be brought for invasion of privacy . . . the action for invasion of privacy may come to supplant the action for defamation"); William L. Prosser, *Privacy*, 48 CAL.L.REV. 383, 400 (1960) ("[t]here has been a good deal of overlapping of defamation in the false light cases, and apparently either action, or both, will very often lie").

In practice, the theoretical distinctions between false light and defamation have proven largely illusory. Of the six false light cases considered by Texas courts of appeals, all were brought, or could have been brought, under another legal theory. . . .

In essence, Mendez asks this Court to afford him relief under a false light theory simply because he was prevented by limitations from prevailing on a defamation theory.[55] In response, we should adopt this reasoning of the North Carolina Supreme Court in *Renwick*:

> [T]he recognition of claims for relief for false light invasions of privacy would reduce judicial efficiency by requiring our courts to consider two

---

[55] The statute of limitations for defamation actions is one year. TEX.CIV.PRAC. & REM.CODE § 16.002. The limitations period for privacy actions has not been expressly delineated by this Court, but the two-year limitations period of § 16.003 probably would apply. *See, e.g., Wood v. Hustler Magazine*, 736 F.2d at 1088.

claims for the same relief which, if not identical, would not differ significantly.

Renwick v. News & Observer Publishing Co., 310 N.C. 312, 312 S.E.2d 405, 413, *cert. denied*, 469 U.S. 858, 105 S.Ct. 187, 83 L.Ed.2d 121 (1984). I see no reason to recognize a cause of action for false light invasion of privacy when recovery for that tort is substantially duplicated by torts already established in this state.

As discussed above, the false light tort bears remarkable similarities to defamation. However, the torts are not wholly identical for two reasons: (1) defamation actions are subject to a number of procedural requirements to which invasion of privacy actions are not subject, and (2) certain publications not actionable under a defamation theory might be actionable under false light. Far from persuading me that these distinctions justify a separate tort, I believe they demonstrate that adopting a false light tort in this state would unacceptably derogate constitutional free speech rights under both the Texas and the United States Constitution.

Actions for defamation in Texas are subject to numerous procedural and substantive hurdles. For example, accounts of governmental proceedings, public meetings dealing with a public purpose, or any "reasonable and fair comment on or criticism of an official act" are privileged under Texas Civil Practice & Remedies Code § 73.002. Broadcasters are generally not liable in defamation for broadcasts made by third parties. TEX.CIV.PRAC. & REM.CODE § 73.004. Qualified privileges against defamation exist at common law when a communication is made in good faith and the author, the recipient or a third person, or one of their family members, has an interest that is sufficiently affected by the communication. A communication may also be conditionally privileged if it affects an important public interest. Damages awarded for defamatory statements may be mitigated by factors such as public apology, correction, or retraction. Constitutional county courts in Texas are without jurisdiction to hear defamation cases. TEX.GOV'T CODE § 26.043(1). Finally, Texas Rule of Civil Procedure 137 provides that in defamation actions, if the verdict for the plaintiff is less than twenty dollars, the plaintiff will not recover costs, but each party will be taxed with the costs incurred in the suit. *See also* RESTATEMENT (SECOND) OF TORTS § 652E, comment e (1977) (listing other possible limitations on the defamation action, including bond posting requirements and proof of special damages).

These technical restrictions serve to safeguard the freedom of speech. Every defamation action that the law permits necessarily inhibits free speech. As the Supreme Court stated with respect to political speech in *New York Times v. Sullivan*, 376 U.S. 254, 272, 84 S.Ct. 710, 721, 11 L.Ed.2d 686, 702 (1964), "[w]hatever is added to the field of libel is taken from the field of free debate." While less compelling, these same considerations are also at play in private, non-political expression. Thus, the defamation action has been narrowly tailored to limit free speech as little as possible.

Courts in many jurisdictions have preserved their protection of speech by holding false light actions to the same strictures as defamation actions. As the RESTATEMENT (SECOND) OF TORTS § 652E, comment *e*, reasons:

[w]hen the false publicity is also defamatory . . . it is arguable that limitations of long standing that have been found desirable for the action for defamation should not be successfully evaded by a proceeding upon a different theory of later origin, in the development of which the attention of the courts has not been directed to the limitations.

Several courts have followed this reasoning, particularly regarding the applicable limitations period. Permitting plaintiffs to bring actions for false light without the limits established for defamation actions may inhibit free speech beyond the permissible range.[56] This is especially true in Texas since this Court recently held in *Davenport v. Garcia*, 834 S.W.2d 4, 10 (Tex.1992), that article I, section 8 of the Texas Constitution affords greater protection to free speech than the First Amendment. On the other hand, no useful purpose would be served by the separate tort if these restrictions are imposed. As the court observed in *Renwick v. News & Observer Publishing Co.*, 310 N.C. 312, 312 S.E.2d 405, *cert. denied*, 469 U.S. 858, 105 S.Ct. 187, 83 L.Ed.2d 121 (1984):

> Given the First Amendment limitations placed upon defamation actions by *[New York Times v.] Sullivan* and upon false light invasion of privacy actions by *[Time, Inc. v.] Hill*, we think that such additional remedies as we *might* be required to make available to plaintiffs should we recognize false light invasion of privacy claims are not sufficient to justify the recognition in this jurisdiction of such inherently constitutionally suspect claims for relief.

Id. at 413. Thus, we should decline to restrict speech in any manner beyond our existing tort law.

In theory, the false light action may provide a remedy for certain non-defamatory speech against which there may be no other remedy in tort law. *See* Restatement (Second) of Torts § 652E, comment b (1977). This rationale, however, is not sufficient to persuade me to recognize the false light tort.

It is questionable whether a remedy for non-defamatory speech should exist at all. In *Time, Inc. v. Hill,* 385 U.S. 374, 87 S.Ct. 534, 17 L.Ed.2d 456 (1967), the Supreme Court plurality viewed with disfavor the restriction of nondefamatory statements by the New York privacy statute:

> We create a grave risk of serious impairment of the indispensable service of a free press in a free society if we saddle the press with the

---

[56] This is despite the Supreme Court's seeming approval of the false light tort in *Time, Inc. v. Hill*, 385 U.S. 374, 87 S.Ct. 534, 17 L.Ed.2d 456 (1967), and *Cantrell v. Forest City Publishing Co.*, 419 U.S. 245, 95 S.Ct. 465, 42 L.Ed.2d 419 (1974). See Diane Leenheer Zimmerman, [64 N.Y.U.L. Rev. 364 (1989)] ("[t]he sheer breadth of the privacy tort exposes a much wider range of errors to liability than does defamation. The inevitable result is a sharp increase in the potential chilling effect of false light.") *See also* Thomas I. Emerson, supra, at 333 (false light "raise[s] serious first amendment problems" in the context of freedom of the press); J. Skelly Wright, *Defamation, Privacy, and the Public's Right to Know: A National Problem and a New Approach*, 46 TEX.L.REV. 630, 635 (1968); William L. Prosser, *Privacy*, 48 CAL.L.REV. 383, 401 (1960) (if false light ultimately swallows up the law of defamation, it may be asked "what of the numerous restrictions and limitations which have hedged defamation about for many years, in the interest of freedom of the press and the discouragement of trivial and extortionate claims? Are they of so little consequence that they may be circumvented in so casual and cavalier a fashion?").

impossible burden of verifying to a certainty the facts associated in news articles with a person's name, picture or portrait, particularly as related to nondefamatory matter.

385 U.S. at 389, 87 S.Ct. at 542–43, 17 L.Ed.2d at 467.[57]

On balance, the marginal benefit to be achieved by permitting recovery against non-defamatory speech not addressed by any existing tort would be outweighed by the probable chilling effect on speech and, in some cases, on freedom of the press, that would result from recognition of the false light tort.

For the reasons expressed in this opinion, we should reverse and render this cause and expressly decline to recognize the tort of false light.

NOTES

1. *False Light v. Defamation.* The plaintiff in *Bueno v. Denver Publishing Co.*, 2000 WL 231993 (Colo. App.), sued the defendant alleging, inter alia, defamation and false light invasion of privacy. The allegations were that defendant published a newspaper article implying that plaintiff, like his siblings, was involved in a life of crime. The trial court directed a verdict for the defendant on the defamation claim. The jury found for the defendant on the false light claim, awarding him $47,973.90 for noneconomic losses, $52,880 for lost earnings and medical expenses, and $53,253.90 in punitive damages.

The court said a "sizable majority of other jurisdictions have recognized the existence and viability" of the false light tort. In support of this statement it cited opinions from twenty-six states. "Other jurisdictions," said the court, "have not adopted the tort." For this proposition it cited opinions from thirteen states, including Texas, *Cain v. Hearst Corp.*, 878 S.W. 2d 577 (Tex. 1994). *See* annots., 57 A.L.R. 4th 22 (1987), 57 A.L.R. 4th 244 (1987). False light claims are not "duplicative and superfluous of defamation claims," the court said, because they protect different interests. Defamation lowers the plaintiff's reputation, while "the primary damage is the mental distress" for false light invasion of privacy.

In addition, in false light the plaintiff must prove actual malice on the part of the defendant (knowing or reckless disregard of the truth), and must plead and prove special damages. Plaintiff did both here. Plaintiff's lost income and expenses for medical and psychological treatment caused by the article constituted special damages, the court said. Recklessness can be established if there are "apparent reasons for the reporter to doubt the veracity of his informant or the accuracy of the reports," and "the failure to investigate other sources in the absence of time pressure to finish the investigation can support a finding of reckless disregard."

---

[57] The Supreme Court again cast doubt on recovery for non-defamatory false speech in *Hustler Magazine v. Falwell*, 485 U.S. 46, 108 S.Ct. 876, 99 L.Ed.2d 41 (1988). The case centered on a parodic and offensive depiction of Rev. Falwell that appeared in *Hustler Magazine*. A jury awarded Falwell $100,000 in actual damages for the intentional infliction of emotional distress, plus an additional $100,000 in punitive damages. The Supreme Court reversed, holding that this application of the tort constituted an illegitimate effort to restrict the magazine's free speech rights.

2. *Possible Constitutional Limitations.* In *Time, Inc. v. Hill*, 87 S. Ct. 534 (1967), the U. S. Supreme Court held that actual (constitutional) malice must be proved in order to recover for false light invasion of privacy. Subsequently, in *Gertz*, the Court held that only negligent misstatement need be shown for defamation in the case of a nonpublic plaintiff, at least where the substance of the defamatory statement "makes substantial danger to reputation apparent." *Dun & Bradstreet*, however, suggests that first amendment strictures may not apply if the defamatory matter is not one of public concern. Where does all of this leave false light invasion of privacy?

3. *Retraction.* Many states provide that in an action for defamation the plaintiff can only recover special damages, unless he first asks the defendant for a retraction which is refused. See *Freedom Newspapers, Inc. v. The Superior Court*, 14 Cal. Rptr. 2d 839, 842 P.2d 138 (Cal. 1992). Would the same rule apply to false light invasion of privacy?

The court in *Boswell v. Phoenix Newspapers, Inc.*, 152 Ariz. 9, 730 P.2d 186 (1986), cert. den. 481 U.S. 1029, 107 S.Ct. 1954, 95 L.Ed.2d 527 (1987), held that the state's retraction statute violated the state constitution, which forbade abrogating the right of action to recover damages for injuries or placing any statutory limitation on the amount of such damages.

4. *Libel per quod.* A statute in California requires that special damages must be shown in the case of defamatory language that is "not libelous on its face." The court in *Fellows v. National Enquirer, Inc.*, 42 Cal. 3d 234, 228 Cal. Rptr. 215, 721 P.2d 97 (1986), said the statute also applied to false light invasion of privacy, since the statute "manifests a legislative determination that liability imposed for a publication which affords no warning of its defamatory nature, and has not caused actual pecuniary injury, would place too great a burden on the editorial process and would hamper the free dissemination of the news."

5. *The Nonlibelous False Light Invasion of Privacy.* One can make a false statement about someone where the statement is unwelcome although nondefamatory. Thus in *Time, Inc. v. Hill*, and in *Cantrell v. Forest City Pub. Co.*, discussed in *Mendez*, supra, the false light statements implied that the plaintiffs were heroes.

In *Mitchell v. Globe Internat. Pub. Co.*, 817 F.Supp. 72 (W.D. Ark. 1993), app. dism'd 14 F.3d 607 (8th Cir. 1993), cert. den. 114 S.Ct. 343 (1993), the plaintiff was awarded $650,000 in compensatory and $850,000 in punitive damages against the defendant tabloid newspaper for false light invasion of privacy and intentional infliction of emotional distress. The compensatory award was reduced to $150,000, and the judgment affirmed for a total of $1 million.

The defendant used a picture of plaintiff, a 96-year-old resident of Mountain Home, Arkansas, "to illustrate a story about 'Paper Gal, Audrey Wiles', in Sterling, Australia, who had become pregnant [at the age of 101] by one of her customers, a 'reclusive millionaire' she met on her newspaper route. In fact, Mrs. Mitchell made her living running a newspaper stand and delivering newspapers in Mountain Home."

Is it likely that anyone who knew Mrs. Mitchell believed the story about her in the tabloid, and thought less well of her? What damages therefore did she suffer?

6. *Overlapping Torts.* As the court said in *Jaubert v. Crowley Post-Signal, Inc.*, 375 So. 2d 1386, 1388 (La. 1979):

> By 1978, the right of privacy [was] recognized by the courts of all but three states. The right of privacy embraces four different interests, each of which may be invaded in a distinct fashion. . . . One type of invasion takes the form of the appropriation of an individual's name or likeness, for the use or benefit of the defendant. . . . Another type of invasion occurs when the defendant unreasonably intrudes upon the plaintiff's physical solitude or seclusion. . . . A third type of invasion consists of publicity which unreasonably places the plaintiff in a false light before the public. . . . A fourth type of invasion is represented by unreasonable public disclosure of embarrassing private facts.

Do these torts overlap?

Recall that in *Hustler Magazine, Inc. v. Falwell* the Court said an action for intentional infliction of emotional distress would not lie where defendant's parody was nondefamatory. But in *Diamond Shamrock*, given above, the court held that an action for false light might lie although a claim for intentional infliction of emotional distress would not lie. Could the plaintiff have recovered for negligent infliction?

The plaintiff Kerr in *Boyles v. Kerr*, 806 S.W.2d 255 (Tex. App. 1991), was awarded $1 million in compensatory and punitive damages against the defendants for surreptitiously videotaping her having sexual relations with her boyfriend and showing the film to others. The court said defendants' conduct constituted three of the privacy torts: the acts "amounted to an intrusion into Kerr's personal affairs; the acts disclosed embarrassing private matters to the public; and the acts placed her in the false light of appearing to be a person who willingly allowed herself to be videotaped while engaging in sexual activities."

The court said, "invasion of privacy can be accomplished negligently as well as intentionally. . . . The right of compensation for a recognized tortious injury should not depend on whether it is inflicted for the purpose of harming the injured party or negligently inflicted with the likelihood of harming the injured party." The court also recognized "an independent cause of action" for negligent infliction of emotional distress "without imposing arbitrary restrictions on recovery in such actions."

Chapter 19
BUSINESS AND ECONOMIC TORTS

A. INTRODUCTION

In many respects the subject matter of this chapter overlaps with that of other chapters, especially those on professional liability, products liability, defamation and invasion of privacy, constitutional and statutory torts, damages, and insurance. Typically the damages implicated in this chapter involve solely economic, as opposed to physical, injury. But again, such damages are by no means unique to the torts considered here, and these torts may also involve psychic and dignitary damages which are characteristic of physical injury claims.

Many of the subjects dealt with in this chapter are regulated in whole or in part by statute. The statutory claims present sufficiently distinct concerns to justify treatment in a separate chapter.

The primary areas dealt with here—misrepresentation, appropriation of intangible property, appropriation of trade secrets, wrongful discharge, and business interference—typically implicate common law tort remedies. They also frequently intersect with contractual remedies, raising fundamental questions about the proper relationship between tort and contract.

The business situations involved in this chapter invoke basic questions about the advantages and limitations of competition and of a free market economy. Large questions of equity, fairness, efficiency, and culpability underlie the subject matter, thus bringing into focus some of the foundational aspects of the law of torts.

B. MISREPRESENTATION

OBDE v. SCHLEMEYER
56 Wash. 2d 449, 353 P.2d 672 (1960)

FINLEY, J.

Plaintiffs, Mr. and Mrs. Fred Obde, brought this action to recover damages for the alleged fraudulent concealment of termite infestation in an apartment house purchased by them from the defendants, Mr. and Mrs. Robert Schlemeyer. Plaintiffs assert that the building was infested at the time of the purchase; that defendants were well apprised of the termite condition, but fraudulently concealed it from the plaintiffs.

After a trial on the merits, the trial court entered findings of fact and conclusions of law sustaining the plaintiffs' claim, and awarded them a judgment for damages in the amount of $3,950. The defendants appealed. Their assignments of error may be compartmentalized, roughly, into two categories:

(1) those going to the question of liability, and (2) those relating to the amount of damages to be awarded if liability is established.

First, as to the question of liability: The Schlemeyers concede that, shortly after they purchased the property from a Mr. Ayars on an installment contract in April 1954, they discovered substantial termite infestation in the premises. The Schlemeyers contend, however, that they immediately took steps to eradicate the termites, and that, at the time of the sale to the Obdes in November 1954, they had no reason to believe that these steps had not completely remedied the situation. We are not convinced of the merit of this contention.

The record reveals that when the Schlemeyers discovered the termite condition they engaged the services of a Mr. Senske, a specialist in pest control. He effected some measures to eradicate the termites, and made some repairs in the apartment house. Thereafter, there was no easily apparent or surface evidence of termite damage. However, portions of the findings of fact entered by the trial court read as follows:

> Senske had advised Schlemeyer that in order to obtain a complete job it would be necessary to drill the holes and pump the fluid into all parts of the basement floors as well as the basement walls. Part of the basement was used as a basement apartment. Senske informed Schlemeyer that the floors should be taken up in the apartment and the cement flooring under the wood floors should be treated in the same manner as the remainder of the basement. Schlemeyer did not care to go to the expense of tearing up the floors to do this and therefore this portion of the basement was not treated.

> Senske also told Schlemeyer even though the job [was] done completely, including treating the portion of the basement which was occupied by the apartment, to be sure of success, it would be necessary to make inspections regularly for a period of a year. Until these inspections were made for this period of time the success of the process could not be determined. Considering the job was not completed as mentioned, Senske would give Schlemeyer no assurance of success and advised him that he would make no guarantee under the circumstances.

No error has been assigned to the above findings of fact. Consequently, they will be considered as the established facts of the case. The pattern thus established is hardly compatible with the Schlemeyers' claim that they had no reason to believe that their efforts to remedy the termite condition were not completely successful.

The Schlemeyers urge that, in any event, as sellers, they had no duty to inform the Obdes of the termite condition. They emphasize that it is undisputed that the purchasers asked no questions respecting the possibility of termites. They rely on a Massachusetts case involving a substantially similar factual situation, *Swinton v. Whitinsville Sav. Bank,* 311 Mass. 677, 42 N.E.2d 808 (1942). Applying the traditional doctrine of caveat emptor—namely, that, as between parties dealing at arms length (as vendor and purchaser), there is no duty to speak, in the absence of a request for information—the

Massachusetts court held that a vendor of real property has no duty to disclose to a prospective purchaser the fact of a latent termite condition in the premises.

Without doubt, the parties in the instant case were dealing at arms length. Nevertheless, and notwithstanding the reasoning of the Massachusetts court above noted, we are convinced that the defendants had a duty to inform the plaintiffs of the termite condition. In *Perkins v. Marsh,* 179 Wash. 362, 37 P.2d 689 (1934), a case involving parties dealing at arms length as landlord and tenant, we held that,

> Where there are concealed defects in demised premises, dangerous to the property, health or life of the tenant, which defects are known to the landlord when the lease is made, but unknown to the tenant, and which a careful examination on his part would not disclose, it is the landlord's duty to disclose them to the tenant before leasing, and his failure to do so amounts to a fraud.

We deem this rule to be equally applicable to the vendor purchaser relationship. See 15 Tex. Law Review (December 1936) 1, 14–16, Keeton: *Fraud -Concealment and Non-Disclosure.* In this article Professor Keeton also aptly summarized the modern judicial trend away from a strict application of *caveat emptor* by saying:

> It is of course apparent that the content of the maxim "caveat emptor," used in its broader meaning of imposing risks on both parties to a transaction, has been greatly limited since its origin. When Lord Cairns stated in *Peek v. Gurney* that there was no duty to disclose facts, however censurable their non-disclosure may be, he was stating the law as shaped by an individualistic philosophy based upon freedom of contract. It was not concerned with morals. In the present stage of the law, the decisions show a drawing away from this idea, and there can be seen an attempt by many courts to reach a just result in so far as possible, but yet maintaining the degree of certainty which the law must have. The statement may often be found that if either party to a contract of sale conceals or suppresses a material fact which he is in good faith bound to disclose then his silence is fraudulent.

> The attitude of the courts toward non-disclosure is undergoing a change and contrary to Lord Cairns' famous remark it would seem that the object of the law in these cases should be to impose on parties to the transaction a duty to speak whenever justice, equity, and fair dealing demand it.

A termite infestation of a frame building, such as that involved in the instant case, is manifestly a serious and dangerous condition. One of the Schlemeyers' own witnesses, Mr. Hoefer, who at the time was a building inspector for the city of Spokane, testified that ". . . if termites are not checked in their damage, they can cause a complete collapse of a building, . . . they would simply eat up the wood." Further, at the time of the sale of the premises, the condition was clearly latent—not readily observable upon reasonable inspection. As we have noted, all superficial or surface evidence of the condition had been removed by reason of the efforts of Senske, the pest control specialist. Under the circumstances, we are satisfied that "justice, equity, and fair dealing," to use Professor Keeton's language, demanded that the Schlemeyers speak—that they inform prospective purchasers, such as the Obdes, of the condition, regardless of the latter's failure to ask any questions relative to the possibility of termites. . . .

NOTES

1. *The Restatement Approach to Non-Disclosure.* RESTATEMENT (SECOND) OF TORTS § 551 provides:

(1) One who fails to disclose to another a fact that he knows may justifiably induce the other to act or refrain from acting in a business transaction is subject to the same liability to the other as though he had represented the nonexistence of the matter that he has failed to disclose, if, but only if, he is under a duty to the other to exercise reasonable care to disclose the matter in question.

(2) One party to a business transaction is under a duty to exercise reasonable care to disclose to the other before the transaction is consummated,

(a) matters known to him that the other is entitled to know because of a fiduciary or other similar relation of trust and confidence between them; and

(b) matters known to him that he knows to be necessary to prevent his partial or ambiguous statement of the facts from being misleading; and

(c) subsequently acquired information that he knows will make untrue or misleading a previous representation that when made was true or believed to be so; and

(d) the falsity of a representation not made with the expectation that it would be acted upon, if he subsequently learns that the other is about to act in reliance upon it in a transaction with him; and

(e) facts basic to the transaction, if he knows that the other is about to enter into it under a mistake as to them, and that the other, because of the relationship between them, the customs of the trade or other objective circumstances, would reasonably expect a disclosure of those facts.

2. *The Scope of Materiality.* In *Reed v. King,* 145 Cal. App. 3d 261, 193 Cal. Rptr. 130 (1983), the issue was stated as follows:

In the sale of a house, must the seller disclose it was the site of a multiple murder? Dorris Reed purchased a house from Robert King. Neither King nor his real estate agents (the other named defendants) told Reed that a woman and her four children were murdered there 10 years earlier. However, it seems "truth will come to light; murder cannot be hid long." (Shakespeare, Merchant of Venice, act II, scene II.) Reed learned of the gruesome episode from a neighbor after the sale. She sues seeking rescission and damages. King and the real estate agent defendants successfully demurred to her first amended complaint for failure to state a cause of action. Reed appeals the ensuing judgment of dismissal. We will reverse the judgment.

We take all issuable facts pled in Reed's complaint as true. King and his real estate agent knew about the murders and knew the event materially affected the market value of the house when they listed it for sale. They represented to Reed the premises were in good condition and fit for an "elderly lady" living alone. They did not disclose the fact of the murders. At some point King asked a neighbor not to inform Reed of that event. Nonetheless, after Reed moved in neighbors informed her no one was interested in purchasing the house because of the stigma. Reed paid $76,000, but the house is only worth $65,000 because of its past. . . .

The court observed that generally a seller of real property has a duty to disclose to the buyer "facts *materially* affecting the value or desirability of the property which are known or accessible only to him" if he knows such facts "are not known to, or within the reach of the diligent attention and observation of the buyer." The court listed as illustrations:

For example, the following have been held of sufficient materiality to require disclosure: the home sold was constructed on filled land (*Burkett v. J.A. Thompson & Son,* 150 Cal. App. 2d 523, 526 [310 P.2d 56] (1957)); improvements were added without a building permit and in violation of zoning regulations (*Barder v. McClung,* 93 Cal. App. 2d 692, 697 [209 P. 2d 808] (1949)), or in violation of building codes (*Curran v. Heslop,* 115 Cal. App. 2d 476, 480–481 [252 P.2d 378] (1953)); the structure was condemned (*Katz v. Department of Real Estate,* 96 Cal. App. 3d 895, 900 [158 Cal. Rptr. 766] (1979)); the structure was termite-infested (*Godfrey v. Steinpress,* 128 Cal. App. 3d 154 [180 Cal. Rptr. 95] (1982)); there was water infiltration in the soil (*Barnhouse v. City of Pinole,* 133 Cal. App. 3d 171, 187–188 [183 Cal. Rptr. 881] (1982)); the correct amount of net income a piece of property would yield (*Ford v. Cournale,* 36 Cal. App. 3d 172, 179–180 [111 Cal. Rptr. 334] (1973).)

Defendant contended that to permit an action here would have the effect of "endorsing the materiality of facts predicating peripheral, insubstantial, or fancied harms." To this contention, the court responded:

The murder of innocents is highly unusual in its potential for so disturbing buyers they may be unable to reside in a home where it has occurred. This fact may foreseeably deprive a buyer of the intended use of the purchase. Murder is not such a common occurrence that *buyers* should be charged with anticipating and discovering this disquieting possibility. Accordingly, the fact is not one for which a duty of inquiry and discovery can sensibly be imposed upon the buyer. . . .

Reputation and history can have a significant effect on the value of realty. "George Washington slept here" is worth something, however physically inconsequential that consideration may be. Ill-repute or "bad will" conversely may depress the value of property. Failure to disclose such a negative fact where it will have a foreseeably depressing effect on income expected to be generated by a business is tortious. Some cases have held that unreasonable fears of the potential buying public that a gas or oil pipeline may rupture may depress the market value of land and entitle the owner to incremental compensation in eminent domain.

Whether Reed will be able to prove her allegation the decade-old multiple murder has a significant effect on market value we cannot determine. If she is able to do so by competent evidence she is entitled to a favorable ruling on the issues of materiality and duty to disclose. Her demonstration of objective tangible harm would still the concern that permitting her to go forward will open the floodgates to rescission on subjective and idiosyncratic grounds.

A more troublesome question would arise if a buyer in similar circumstances were unable to plead or establish a significant and quantifiable effect on market value. However, this question is not presented in the posture of this case. Reed has not alleged the fact of the murders has rendered the premises useless to her as a residence. As currently pled, the gravamen of her case is pecuniary harm. We decline to speculate on the abstract alternative.

3. *Nondisclosure to Particeps Criminis.* In *Zysk v. Zysk,* 239 Va. 32, 387 S.E.2d 466 (1990), the plaintiff wife brought suit against her husband for damages resulting from contracting herpes from him as a result of sexual intercourse between them before their marriage. The court held that plaintiff's participation in the crime of fornication barred her recovery.

Compare *B.N. v. K.K.,* 312 Md. 135, 538 A.2d 1175 (1988), *and C.A.M. v. R.A.W.,* 237 N.J. Super. 532, 568 A.2d 556 (1990).

4. *The Attorney and Fraudulent Misrepresentation.* The plaintiff attorney in *Stewart v. Jackson & Nash,* 976 F.2d 86 (2d Cir. 1992), stated a claim against her employer law firm for fraudulently inducing her to come to work with the defendant by promising an opportunity to practice environmental law which did not exist or materialize. The fraud, which occurred prior to her termination, was not barred by the at-will employee rule, because the fraud caused her to leave a good practice and to spend two years where she was unable to work in her specialty. The statute of frauds did not bar the claim, because fraudulent misrepresentation and the employment contract "are distinct and separable."

But the plaintiff failed to state a claim for negligent misrepresentation because under New York law a plaintiff can recover for negligent misrepresentation "only where the defendant owes her a fiduciary duty" and because the complaint asserted "no facts which would establish such a fiduciary duty." Why was there no fiduciary duty between the plaintiff and defendant? Why should such a duty be required for purposes of negligent misrepresentation?

PROBLEM

Buyer (B) proposes to purchase Greenacre from Seller (S), a young woman. S knows there has been discussion for years about the possibility of condemning the property to make way for a new road. S also knows that the area is cavernous, and that Greenacre had once been used to perform illegal abortions and the fetuses were disposed of on the premises. S tells B none of these facts prior to purchase of the property.

During the course of negotiations S and B become engaged, and they marry. After the marriage and purchase of Greenacre, B discovers the foregoing facts about Greenacre and also discovers that S has a history of insanity in her family. B becomes distraught over these discoveries. The abortion-clinic background of Greenacre disturbs him because of his religious beliefs, and because it affects the salability of the property to persons of the same religious faith as B (which is the dominant faith in that area). A few months after B makes the discoveries, the state institutes eminent domain proceedings against Greenacre to obtain the property. Thereafter S gives birth to a mentally unstable child, conceived before B learned of S's family history of insanity.

Assuming no tort immunity, discuss B's possible tort claims against S.

IDAHO BANK & TRUST CO. v. FIRST BANCORP OF IDAHO
772 P.2d 720 (Idaho 1989)

SHEPARD, CHIEF JUSTICE.

This case presents the question of the liability of a certified public accounting firm to a person not a party to the auditing contract. Main Hurdman contracted with First Bank & Trust to examine and give an opinion on the financial statements of First Bank & Trust. That audit was completed and an opinion provided to First Bank & Trust. At a later time, as a result of a buyout, Bancorp gained control over First Bank & Trust. In connection with that transaction, Bancorp obtained a loan from Idaho Bank & Trust. In connection with that loan, Bancorp provided Idaho Bank & Trust with the aforesaid audit report prepared by Main Hurdman.

Thereafter, First Bank & Trust was placed in receivership, and Bancorp defaulted upon its loan payments to Idaho Bank & Trust. The present action was brought by Idaho Bank & Trust against Bancorp and Main Hurdman. Upon motion, Main Hurdman was dismissed as a party, that order of dismissal was certified for appeal, and the only matter before this Court is the liability, if any, of Main Hurdman to Idaho Bank & Trust [for negligence].

The decision of the district court may be viewed as presenting other bases for its decision, but nevertheless, the issue here is stated by the appellant as "[s]hould an independent accountant, who certifies an audit of an entity, be liable to those who detrimentally rely upon the audit?" Thus, we are presented with a question which falls within a classic pattern, and presents the question originally treated in *Ultramares Corp. v. Touche,* 255 N.Y. 170, 174 N.E. 441 (1931). In *Ultramares* a certified public accountant examined and audited the financial statements of a customer, and failed to discover that an account receivable exhibited on those statements was nonexistent. The certified statements indicated the customer's net worth of over one million dollars, when in fact the customer was insolvent. The plaintiff, relying on that statement, loaned money to the firm. The firm later filed for bankruptcy. The

New York court refused to hold the auditor liable to all persons who foreseeably would rely on the negligently audited financial statements, reasoning:

> If liability for negligence exists, a thoughtless slip or blunder, the failure to detect a theft or forgery beneath the cover of deceptive entries, may expose accountants to a liability in an indeterminate amount for an indeterminate time to an indeterminate class. The hazards of the business conducted on these terms are so extreme as to enkindle doubt whether a flaw may not exist in the implication of a duty that exposes to these consequences.

The rule as stated in *Ultramares* has been applied by other courts.

Other jurisdictions have departed from the doctrine of *Ultramares,* holding that public accountants may be liable to third parties, not always precisely identifiable, but who belong to a limited class of persons whose reliance on the accountant's representations is specially foreseen.

More recently the New York court, in *Credit Alliance Corp. v. Arthur Andersen & Co.*, 483 N.E.2d 110, 493 N.Y.S.2d 435 (1985), has reaffirmed the basic principles articulated in *Ultramares,* but has interpreted the *Ultramares* doctrine to include noncontractual parties when certain other prerequisites are satisfied, *i.e.,*

1. the accountants must have been aware that the financial reports were to be used for a particular purpose or purposes;

2. in the furtherance of which a known party or parties was intended to rely; and

3. there must have been some conduct on the part of the accountants linking them to that party or parties, which evinces the accountants' understanding of that party or parties' reliance.

Hence, the New York court has expanded its traditional rule set forth in *Ultramares*. We agree and adopt the extension of the traditional rule as expounded in *Credit Alliance.*

Plaintiff urges this Court to adopt the imposition of liability in accordance with the *Restatement* and *Restatement (Second) of Torts*. Section 552(2) of the *Restatement (Second) of Torts* limits the liability of a professional who has made a negligent misrepresentation of loss suffered:

> a. by the person or one of a limited group of persons for whose benefit and guidance he intends to supply the information or knows that the recipient intends to supply it; and
>
> b. through reliance upon it in a transaction that he intends the information to influence or knows that the recipient so intends or in a substantially similar transaction.

When applied to an audit, the *Restatement* thus limits the person or persons to whom the auditor owes a duty to intended identifiable beneficiaries and to any unidentified member of the intended class of beneficiaries. We decline to adopt the *Restatement* standard. . . .

NOTES

1. *Negligent vs. Intentional Misrepresentation.* The reasoning of *Idaho Bank & Trust* was essentially followed in *Biley v. Arthur Young and Co.,* 3 Cal. 4th 370, 11 Cal. Rptr.2d 51, 834 P.2d 745 (1992). The case contains a lengthy discussion of policy issues, and a vigorous dissent. The majority said an auditor should be liable for negligent misrepresentation only when the statement is made with intent to induce reliance by the plaintiff, or by a particular class of persons to whom plaintiff belongs, in a specific transaction or type of transaction that the auditor intended to influence. Intent includes knowledge "with substantial certainty."

But liability for fraudulent misrepresentation, the court said, extends to any reasonably foreseeable plaintiff. The concern about potential "unlimited liability for mere errors or oversights and the uncertain connection between investment and credit losses and the auditor's report pale as policy factors when intentional misconduct is in issue."

Does *Biley* indicate that causation requirements should be relaxed whenever any intentional tort is involved? If so, how much relaxation should there be?

2. *The Foreseeable Plaintiff.* In *H. Rosenblum, Inc. v. Adler,* 93 N.J. 324, 461 A.2d 138 (1983), the court imposed liability on an accountant for negligence that caused economic loss to foreseeable plaintiffs. In reaching this result, the court relied on the products liability case of *Santor v. A & M Karagheusian, Inc.*, 44 N.J. 52, 207 A.2d 305 (1965), and on the fact that accounting firms "are presently liable to purchasers of securities in public offerings when they have misstated a material fact in the financial statements." The court also noted that "auditors have apparently been able to obtain liability insurance covering these risks or otherwise to satisfy their financial obligations." Moreover, the court said:

> The imposition of a duty to foreseeable users may cause accounting firms to engage in more thorough reviews. This might entail setting up stricter standards and applying closer supervision, which should tend to reduce the number of instances in which liability would ensue.

As noted in the *Ultramares* case, discussed in *Idaho Bank & Trust Co.*, liability to foreseeable plaintiffs for economic loss has long been the rule where the conduct constitutes fraud or deceit.

3. *The Attorney and Negligent Misrepresentation.* In *Mehaffy, Rider, Windholz v. Cent. Bank*, 892 P.2d 230 (Colo. 1995), the court appears to be applying Rest.2d of Torts § 552 for attorney liability to a third party plaintiff. But the court said the plaintiff could not sue for legal malpractice, since under Colorado law "attorneys do not owe a duty to nonclient third parties absent fraud or malice." Why should there be a more restricted liability for negligence than for negligent misrepresentation?

According to the dissent in *Petrillo v. Bachenberg*, 139 N.J. 472, 655 A.2d 1354 (1995), the majority held that liability could be imposed on an attorney in behalf of a nonclient for negligent misrepresentation even though the nonclient did not rely on the misrepresentation. Should reliance by the plaintiff be required?

4. *Negligent Non-Business Representation.* Robinson, the plaintiff in *Robinson v. Omer*, 952 S.W.2d 423 (Tenn. 1997), agreed to secretly videotape his friend Lineberry having sexual relations with assorted women, on the assurance of Lineberry's attorney, Omer, that it was legal to do so. Eventually the women found out about the videotaping, and some of them sued Robinson for invasion of privacy and outrageous conduct. Robinson settled these claims, and then brought this suit against Omer alleging negligent misrepresentation in representing that the videotaping was legal.

In dismissing the claim, the court said an essential element of a claim for negligent misrepresentation under REST. 2D OF TORTS § 552, adopted in Tennessee, is that the alleged misrepresenter "supplies false information for the guidance of others in their business transactions." Robinson stated in his deposition that he did the videotaping for Lineberry as "a really good friend," that he received no payment for the work, and that he did not do the work out of "a desire to protect a financial interest he had with Lineberry due to their business relationship."

5. *The Intersection of Misrepresentation and Contract.* The court in *Stamp v. Honest Abe Log Homes, Inc.,* 804 S.W.2d 455 (Tenn. App. 1990), said the parol evidence rule does not apply to negligent misrepresentation, as opposed to breach of contract. The misrepresentation here occurred during the negotiation of the sale of a log home, and concerned the competence of a recommended contractor. Where does contract end and tort begin?

6. *Strict Liability.* Strict liability may provide recovery for solely economic loss at least where the parties are in privity of contract. *Richard v. A. Waldman & Sons,* 155 Conn. 343, 232 A.2d 307 (1967). The RESTATEMENT (SECOND) OF TORTS § 552C provides for strict liability, limited to out-of-pocket damages, for pecuniary loss resulting from a material misrepresentation made by one and relied on by another "in a sale, rental or exchange transaction."

PROBLEM

Patient was hospitalized for lung cancer, and a successful operation was performed to remove the cancerous growth. Prior to the operation, Patient was given a CAT scan to determine whether the cancer had metastasized to her brain. The results revealed no cancer. Doctor, who performed the scan, submitted a bill of $129 to Medicare as his charges for performing the scan. In the "Diagnosis" box of the Medicare reimbursement form, Doctor wrote "brain tumor." He did this, instead of writing "rule out brain tumor," because on several previous occasions a "rule out" diagnosis had resulted in the form being returned unpaid.

Medicare paid a portion of the bill, and a statement for the balance was sent to Patient's private, secondary insurance company for payment. The company paid the balance, and as a routine matter sent a copy of the statement and certificate of payment to Patient's home. The certificate indicated that the payment had been made for a CAT scan resulting in the diagnosis of a brain tumor. Patient's Husband received the letter containing the certificate from the insurance company, opened and read it, and laid it on the dining room table. Later, Patient read the certificate. Erroneously believing that brain tumor was invariably fatal, Patient became deeply depressed and took her own life.

Discuss a possible wrongful death claim by Patient's estate and a claim by Husband against Doctor.

CROCKER v. WINTHROP LABORATORIES
514 S.W.2d 429 (Tex. 1974)

REAVLEY, J.

Glenn E. Crocker became addicted to a new drug produced by Winthrop Laboratories and known as "talwin" which had been previously thought to be non-addictive. When he was in a weakened condition and his tolerance to drugs [was] very low because of a period of detoxification, Crocker obtained an injection of a narcotic and died soon thereafter. His widow and representative, Clarissa Crocker, brought this action for damages due to his suffering while alive as well as for his wrongful death. She recovered judgment against Winthrop Laboratories in the trial court. The Court of Civil Appeals reversed and rendered judgment for the drug company, holding that while some of the facts found by the jury (including the positive misrepresentation by the drug company that talwin was non-addictive) would warrant the recovery, the additional finding that the drug company could not reasonably have foreseen Crocker's addiction (because of his unusual susceptibility and the state of medical knowledge when the drug was marketed), constituted a complete defense. We hold that the latter finding does not bar the recovery, and we affirm the judgment of the trial court.

In July of 1967 Glenn Crocker suffered a double hernia, as well as frostbite of two fingers, while working as a carpenter in a cold storage vault. He was then 49 years old and was not a user of drugs or alcohol. His hernia was successfully repaired. The circulation of blood in his fingers, however, was not restored. Skin grafts were done on the fingers in October, but it was necessary to amputate part of his thumb in November and part of his middle finger the following January (1968). Prior to November 23, 1967, when Dr. Mario Palafox amputated part of his thumb, the several doctors who had treated him had prescribed both demerol (a narcotic) and talwin for relief of pain without observing any cause to believe him to be then addicted to any drug. Crocker told Dr. Palafox that he liked the relief he received from talwin, and Dr. Palafox responded that this was fortunate because talwin had no addicting side effect.

Crocker did develop an addiction to talwin, however, and was able to obtain prescriptions from several doctors as well as to cross the Mexican border to Juarez and acquire the same drug without a prescription under the name of "sosigon." He was hospitalized on June 3, 1968 by a psychiatrist, Dr. J. Edward Stern, for a process of detoxification (to remove the toxic agents in his body) and treatment of his drug dependency. After six days in the hospital being withdrawn from talwin as well as all narcotics, and at a time when his tolerance for potent drugs was very low, Crocker walked out of the hospital and went to his home. Because of his agitated condition and the threats he made against his wife, he was finally successful in having her call Dr. Eugene

Engel who, on June 10, 1968, came to the Crocker home and gave Mr. Crocker an injection of demerol. Crocker went to his bed for the last time.

Winthrop Laboratories first put talwin on the market in July of 1967 after extensive testing and approval by the Federal Drug Administration. The descriptive material on the new drug circulated by Winthrop Laboratories in 1967 gives no warning of the possibilities of addiction. There is a heading of a paragraph in the product information of the 1967 edition of Physicians' Desk Reference Book which reads: "Absence of addiction liability." This might be considered misleading, but in view of the evidence of verbal assurances as to the properties of talwin by the drug company's representative, there is no need to deal further with the printed materials. Dr. Palafox, a prominent orthopedic surgeon in El Paso, allowed Crocker to have liberal use of talwin and assured him that it was non-addictive because of the assurance by a representative of the drug company who had detailed the doctor on the nature of the drug. There had been an extended and specific conversation between the drug company representative and Dr. Palafox about talwin, and Dr. Palafox was told that talwin was as harmless as aspirin and could be given as long as desired. Dr. Palafox testified that the representative of the defendant insisted that talwin could have no addicting effect.

Subsequent experience has proved that talwin is an extremely useful drug for the relief of pain but that it cannot be regarded as non-addictive. Doctors Palafox and Stern had seen other patients dependent upon talwin. Dr. Arthur S. Keats, chairman of the Department of Anesthesiology at Baylor School of Medicine in Houston, who did original work on the drug and who testified during this trial on the call of the drug company, agreed with the attorney for Mrs. Crocker that "there are a tremendous number of people that do develop a talwin addiction."

Dr. Palafox was of the opinion that if he had not been assured of the non-addictive character of talwin, he could probably have avoided addiction or dependence by Crocker upon any drug.

Plaintiff's medical testimony depicted the addiction to talwin as a producing cause of the death of Crocker when taken together with the chain of events including the detoxification process and the injection of demerol.

Section 402B applies to those cases of misrepresentation by seller of chattels to the consumer; it reads:

> One engaged in the business of selling chattels who, by advertising, labels, or otherwise, makes to the public a misrepresentation of a material fact concerning the character or quality of a chattel sold by him is subject to liability for physical harm to a consumer of the chattel caused by justifiable reliance upon the misrepresentation, even though
>
> (a) it is not made fraudulently or negligently, and
>
> (b) the consumer has not bought the chattel from or entered into any contractual relation with the seller.

The carefully written opinion of the Court of Civil Appeals has correctly foreseen that we would apply Section 402B of the Restatement. . . .

Liability of Winthrop Laboratories will be predicated upon the finding of misrepresentation that the drug would not cause physical dependence, a fact conceded by the attorney for the company in his jury argument, and upon the findings of reliance and causation. Whatever the danger and state of medical knowledge, and however rare the susceptibility of the user, when the drug company positively and specifically represents its product to be free and safe from all dangers of addiction, and when the treating physician relies upon that representation, the drug company is liable when the representation proves to be false and harm results. Restatement, Torts, Second, § 402B; *see Rogers v. Toni Home Permanent Co.*, 167 Ohio St. 244, 147 N.E.2d 612 (1958); *Randy Knitwear, Inc. v. American Cyanamid Co.*, 11 N.Y.2d 5, 226 N.Y.S.2d 363, 181 N.E.2d 399 (1962); *Brown v. Globe Laboratories, Inc.*, 165 Neb. 138, 84 N.W.2d 151 (1957). . . .

NOTES

1. *The Deceptive Lover.* In *C.A.M. v. R.A.W.*, 237 N.J. Super. 532, 568 A.2d 556 (1990), the plaintiff sought recovery against defendant for pain and suffering, loss of income and emotional distress resulting from defendant's misrepresentation to her that he was "single," and "incapable of impregnating her" because he had "undergone a vasectomy." Plaintiff alleged that in reliance upon these representations, which were false, she engaged in a "personal relationship" with defendant, became pregnant as a result, and gave birth to a normal, healthy child.

In sustaining a summary judgment for the defendant, the court said:

> We conclude that the birth of a normal, healthy child as a consequence of a sexual relationship between consenting adults precludes inquiry by the courts into representations that may have been made before or during that relationship by either of the partners concerning birth control.

2. *Giveaway Contest.* In *Weirum v. RKO Gen., Inc.*, 15 Cal. 3d 40, 539 P.2d 36, 123 Cal. Rptr. 468 (1975), a motorist was killed because of a high speed pursuit of a disc jockey by teenagers during a radio station giveaway contest. The court held the radio station responsible on a negligence theory, dismissing defendant's claim for First Amendment protection with this language:

> Defendant's contention that the giveaway contest must be afforded the deference due society's interest in the First Amendment is clearly without merit. The issue here is civil accountability for the foreseeable results of a broadcast which created an undue risk of harm to decedent. The First Amendment does not sanction the infliction of physical injury merely because achieved by word, rather than act.

Reconsider *McCollum v. CBS, Inc.*, 202 Cal. App. 3d 989, 249 Cal. Rptr. 187 (1988).

3. *Incitement to Violence and Freedom of Speech.* In *Herceg v. Hustler Magazine, Inc.*, 814 F.2d 1017 (5th Cir. 1987), *cert. denied*, 485 U.S. 959, 99 L. Ed. 2d 420, 108 S. Ct. 1219 (1988), plaintiffs' decedent, a 14-year-old boy, read an article in defendant's magazine discussing the practice of autoerotic asphyxia. Immediately after reading the article, the boy attempted to perform the acts described in the article and died from strangulation.

Reversing a jury verdict for the plaintiffs, the appellate court held that the article was protected speech under the First Amendment to the U.S. Constitution, since it was not designed to incite or produce imminent lawless activity. Any attempt to differentiate between categories of speech based on social acceptability would "raise substantial concern that the worthiness of speech might be judged by majoritarian notions of political and social propriety and morality."

In *Sakon v. Pepsico, Inc.*, 553 So.2d 163 (Fla. 1989), the court held the defendant Pepsico was not liable to a child who was injured while imitating a dangerous water stunt shown by the defendant as part of a TV advertisement. Injury "was not a foreseeable consequence of Pepsico's advertisement." There would be "a total absence of any standard to measure liability" if plaintiff were held to state a cause of action, the court said.

In *Norwood v. Soldier of Fortune Magazine, Inc.*, 651 F. Supp. 1397 (W.D. Ark. 1987), plaintiff brought an action, apparently in negligence, against defendant magazine company for injuries he received as a result of an attempt on his life by persons answering the following advertisements appearing in defendant's magazine:

> GUN FOR HIRE: 37 year old -professional mercenary desires jobs. Vietnam Veteran. Discreet and very private. Bodyguard, courier, and other special skills. All jobs considered. Phone. . . .
>
> GUN FOR HIRE: NAM sniper instructor. SWAT, Pistol, rifle, security specialist, body guard, courier plus. All jobs considered. Privacy guaranteed. Mike. . . .

To the defendant magazine's claim of first amendment privilege, the court responded that the advertisements were "commercial speech" and were not protected by the Constitution. It also found that a "reasonable magazine publisher" should have foreseen the resulting injuries. The magazine's motion for summary judgment was accordingly denied.

Liability was imposed for a similar ad in *Braun v. Soldier of Fortune, Inc.*, 968 F.2d 1110 (11th Cir. 1992). The ad was the proximate cause of the death of a murder victim, the court said. The ad on its face would alert the reasonably prudent publisher of a clearly identifiable risk of unreasonable harm. A verdict of $375,000 for pain and suffering, $2 million for wrongful death, and $2 million punitive damages (reduced from $10 million), or a total of $4,375,000 was affirmed.

In *Eimann v. Soldier of Fortune Magazine, Inc.*, 880 F.2d 830 (5th Cir. 1989), *cert. denied*, 107 L. Ed. 2d 748, 110 S. Ct. 729 (1990), the court reversed a jury verdict for the plaintiffs for wrongful death allegedly resulting from a similar ad in defendant's magazine. The court found that the advertisement was ambiguous, and that defendant's burden of identifying advertisements for illegal activity in this context would be too great. Moreover, an investigation of the actual advertisers in the case would have revealed "no criminal records and no false information that might have aroused suspicion."

In *Rice v. Paladin Enterprises, Inc.*, 128 F.3d 233 (4th Cir. 1997), the court said that representatives of murder victims stated a cause of action against Paladin, the publisher of a "hit man" instruction book, which was used by a hit man to murder the victims. Paladin stipulated that it "intended to attract and assist criminals and would-be criminals who desire information and instructions on how to commit crimes," and that it knew the book would be used by such persons "to plan and execute the crime of murder for hire." Defendant also asserted that its marketing strategy was

> intended to maximize sales of its publications to the public, including sales to (i) authors who desire information for the purpose of writing books about crime and criminals, (ii) law enforcement officers and agencies who desire information concerning the means and methods of committing crimes, (iii) persons who enjoy reading accounts of crimes and the means of committing them for purposes of entertainment, (iv) persons who fantasize about committing crimes but do not thereafter commit them, and (v) criminologists and others who study criminal methods and mentality.

The court said genuine issues existed as to whether the defendant acted with an intent sufficient to make it liable under Maryland tort law for aiding and abetting murderers. The book was not protected, the court said, under the first amendment free speech provision of the U.S. constitution.

DAVIS v. BOARD OF COUNTY COM'RS
987 P.2d 1172 (N.M. App. 1999)

BOSSON, J.

As a matter of first impression under New Mexico common law, we decide whether an employer owes prospective employers and foreseeable third persons a duty of reasonable care not to misrepresent material facts in the course of making an employment recommendation about a present or former employee, when a substantial risk of physical harm to third persons by the employee is foreseeable. . . .

The following recitation of facts is taken from the cross-motions for summary judgment that include allegations set forth in the pleadings, as supplemented by excerpts from depositions and affidavits. Mesilla Valley Hospital (MVH), a psychiatric hospital in Doña Ana County, employs mental health technicians for a variety of patient-care functions, such as restraining patients, taking patients on walks, and providing staff coverage at night. MVH hired Joseph "Tinie" Herrera (Herrera) as a mental health technician on January 20, 1995. Plaintiff, a young woman undergoing psychiatric therapy, was admitted to MVH as a patient on February 26 of that same year, and Herrera was assigned to work with her. Plaintiff asserts that Herrera initially managed to ingratiate himself into her confidence, and then, over a period of about two weeks, Herrera subjected Plaintiff to escalating incidents of sexual harassment, sexual assault, and other physical abuse committed under the guise of psychiatric therapy. . . .

Prior to working at MVH, Herrera was employed for some time as a detention sergeant and classification officer at the Doña Ana County Detention Center (Detention Center). According to Plaintiff, MVH's decision to hire Herrera was based in part on unqualified, favorable recommendations from Herrera's supervisors at the Detention Center, Frank Steele and Al Mochen.

Steele was the director and Mochen was the captain and assistant director of the Detention Center, both of whom had supervisory authority over Herrera. The accuracy of these favorable recommendations goes to the heart of Plaintiff's suit against the County.

Of particular importance to the accuracy of the recommendations is a report authored by Steele after Herrera was investigated for allegedly sexually harassing female inmates under his authority at the Detention Center. The Detention Center first became aware of sexual complaints against Herrera in 1993, when a female inmate alleged that Herrera had sexually harassed her. Steele gave Herrera a written reprimand based on the 1993 allegation which also indicated that an additional complaint of this nature could result in Herrera's termination. Thereafter, on February 4, 1994, another female inmate filed a sexual harassment grievance against Herrera for incidents that had occurred between 1990 and 1992. She alleged that Herrera had helped her in exchange for demanding and receiving sexual favors. Although Herrera denied the allegations, he was placed on administrative leave on February 8, 1994. Steele then had the County Sheriff's Department conduct an investigation of Herrera, and on April 5, 1994, Steele authored a report of the results of that investigation.

According to Steele's report, Herrera was accused of inappropriate sexual behavior with female inmates that took various forms. The accusations included making statements with sexual overtones, and stating his desire for sex. Reportedly, Herrera received sexual favors from inmates in return for helping them. On more than one occasion, he was observed taking female inmates to his office and closing the door, allegedly for the purpose of conducting interviews. Steele's report also made specific reference to a pornographic video and condoms which were found in Herrera's desk, and he was observed with underwear belonging to a juvenile.

While not all the allegations against Herrera could be confirmed, the report concluded that Herrera's conduct and performance of duty had been "questionable" and "suspect." Accordingly, Steele recommended disciplinary action against Herrera seeking to have him suspended without pay as well as demoted and reassigned. On April 5, 1994, Steele informed Herrera that he intended to seek disciplinary action at a hearing scheduled for April 12, 1994.

On April 8, 1994, Herrera resigned rather than proceed with the scheduled hearing. Upon his resignation, Herrera asked Steele for a letter of recommendation for prospective employment. On April 11, 1994, only six days after recommending discipline, Steele wrote a positive endorsement of Herrera that omitted any reference to either the reprimand, the subsequent allegations of sexual harassment, the results of the investigation, or the recommended discipline. The letter was written on county letterhead, which Steele signed as the Detention Center administrator, and stated:

To Whom It May Concern:

This letter will introduce to you, Joseph V. Herrera. I have had the distinct pleasure of working with Tinie Herrera for the past two years. In my opinion he is an excellent employee and supervisor for the Doña Ana County Detention Center. In developing social programs for the inmate population, he displayed considerable initiative and imagination. Tinie was instrumental in the Department's maintenance program and was involved in remodeling projects. I know that this Department will suffer for his leaving. Employees of his caliber are difficult to find. I am confident that you would find Tinie to be an excellent employee. Should you need verbal confirmation of his ability, I would deem it a pleasure to respond to any inquiries that you may have.

Sincerely,

[Signed]

Frank A. Steele

Detention Administrator

DACDC

On December 5, 1994, Herrera applied for employment with MVH and included Steele's letter of recommendation. According to Plaintiff, MVH called the Detention Center seeking further information about Herrera, and Mochen told MVH that Herrera was a good person and a hard worker whom he would definitely rehire. Mochen was aware of Herrera's past when he allegedly gave this verbal recommendation. Mochen denied talking to MVH. According to Plaintiff, MVH's decision to hire Herrera was based in part on these unqualified, favorable recommendations from Steele and Mochen, an allegation which, as yet, remains unproven, and as with other causation issues, remains part of Plaintiff's burden to prove at trial. . . .

The County argues that the law does not require employers to divulge their reasons for an employee's termination or resignation and that it would be against public policy to impose such a duty, especially in favor of an unknown third party outside the line of communication with a prospective employer. Plaintiff agrees that employers may remain silent if they wish. However, once employers elect to give references and offer recommendations, then, according to Plaintiff, employers have a common-law duty to exercise reasonable care so as not to misrepresent an employee's record when, to do so, would create a foreseeable risk of physical injury to third parties.

Thus, two initial questions are before this Court. First, we must consider whether employers who do not remain silent, those electing to recommend employees, owe any such duty of reasonable care in regard to what they say and how they say it. If so, then we must decide whether such employers owe a duty of care to third parties as well as the prospective employer to whom the recommendation is given. We limit our discussion to the present circumstances involving a substantial, foreseeable risk of physical harm to third parties by the employee if reasonable care is not exercised about what is said when an employer elects to make an unqualified recommendation, and we decide that employers do owe such a duty to third parties.

We begin with general principles. As our Supreme Court has succinctly stated, "Policy determines duty." *Torres v. State*, 119 N.M. 609, 612, 894 P.2d 386, 389 (1995). Based on considerations of policy, the court determines whether a defendant owes a duty of care to a class of persons with respect to a particular type of risk of harm. For guidance on questions of policy, we look to general legal propositions we may infer from legal precedent within our own state and from other jurisdictions, and we look as well to any relevant statutes, learned articles, or other reliable indicators of "community moral norms and policy views[.]" *Sanchez v. San Juan Concrete Co.*, 123 N.M. 537, 943 P.2d 571 (1997).

As an accepted legal proposition, there is generally no affirmative duty to prevent criminal acts by a third party in the absence of some special relationship or statutory duty. *See Ciup v. Chevron U.S.A., Inc.*, 122 N.M. 537, 539, 928 P.2d 263, 265 (1996); *see also* Restatement (Second) of Torts § 314, at 116 (1965). However, it is also a general proposition that " 'every person has a duty to exercise ordinary care for the safety of others[,]' " when that person does choose to act. *Lerma ex rel. Lerma v. State Highway Dep't*, 117 N.M. 782, 784, 877 P.2d 1085, 1087 (1994). Assuming other policy considerations are satisfied, a duty to exercise ordinary care, where one otherwise would not exist, may arise when a person voluntarily undertakes a course of conduct which, in the absence of due care, may foreseeably injure others as a natural and probable consequence of the person's conduct.

Few jurisdictions have directly addressed duty in the context of misleading employer references. Of those few, several have concluded that, although employers generally may not have an affirmative duty to disclose negative information about employees, employers may be held liable for negligent misrepresentations, or misleading half-truths, about those employees who present a foreseeable risk of physical harm to others, and the duty of care extends to third parties foreseeably at risk.

The recent California Supreme Court opinion in *Randi W.*, 14 Cal.4th 1066, 60 Cal.Rptr.2d 263, 929 P.2d 582 (1997), is closely analogous and provides persuasive guidance for our case. In *Randi W.*, various officials at different school districts gave gratuitous recommendations "containing unreserved and unconditional praise" of a former employee, despite their knowledge of complaints involving sexual misconduct at his prior employment. *See id.* at 584. The employee was subsequently hired as a vice-principal where he was accused of sexually assaulting a thirteen-year-old student. *See id.* at 585. A unanimous court adopted Sections 310 and 311 of the Restatement, holding that the recommending school officials owed a duty of care to third-party students "not to misrepresent the facts in describing the qualifications and character of a former employee, if making these misrepresentations would present a substantial, foreseeable risk of physical injury to the third persons." *Randi W.*, 60 Cal.Rptr.2d 263, 929 P.2d at 591. "[H]aving volunteered this information, defendants were obliged to complete the picture by disclosing material facts regarding charges and complaints of [the teacher]'s sexual improprieties." *Id.*

The *Randi W.* opinion expressly relied on Sections 310 and 311 of the Restatement. Section 310 states a rule for intentional misrepresentation which is not directly relevant here. Comments c and d of Section 310 involving liability to third persons are incorporated into Section 311. *See* § 311 cmt. f. Section 311 states:

Negligent Misrepresentation Involving
Risk of Physical Harm

(1) One who negligently gives false information to another is subject to liability for physical harm caused by action taken by the other in reasonable reliance upon such information, where such harm results

(a) to the other, or

(b) to such third persons as the actor should expect to be put in peril by the action taken.

(2) Such negligence may consist of failure to exercise reasonable care

(a) in ascertaining the accuracy of the information, or

(b) in the manner in which it is communicated.

The rule of Section 311 extends to anyone undertaking to give information to a person who "knows or should realize that the safety of the person of others may depend upon the accuracy of the information." *Id.* § 311 cmt. b; *see also id.* § 310 cmts. c & d. A misrepresentation under Section 311 may breach a duty of care owed not only to the person to whom it is addressed, and whose conduct it is intended to influence, but also a duty of care owed to third parties whom the speaker should recognize as likely to be imperiled by action taken in reliance upon the misrepresentation. *See id.* § 310 cmt. c.

In the context of this case, we accept the principles set forth in Section 311, as they apply to an employer's duty of care in making employment references and the circumstances under which that duty extends to foreseeable third parties. We find those principles harmonious with the general propositions of New Mexico law that govern duty of care and duty to third parties. Cases cited by the County for a narrower rule are easily distinguished or unpersuasive. . . . *Cohen*, 133 A.D.2d 94, 518 N.Y.S.2d 633, also cited by the County, appears to be contrary to our holding here. But the court does not supply the reasoning supporting its decision, and we find it unpersuasive insofar as it is contrary to our holding.

Applying the foregoing principles to the case before us, we see nothing in the facts as alleged that would make the assault and battery suffered by Plaintiff either too remote as a matter of policy or unforeseeable as a matter of law. The County's agents could have remained silent in response to requests for information about Herrera. Instead, they elected to recommend him in a manner distorted by misrepresentations and half-truths. The employment recommendations of Steele and Mochen provided unqualified praise of Herrera as an excellent employee of a caliber that is "difficult to find," and yet they omitted disciplinary action both taken and recommended by these same officers against Herrera. The disciplinary action came as a result of allegations, a subsequent investigation, and a resulting report in which Steele was directly involved, which constitutes far more than mere gossip or innuendo. The information in the report concerned abuse of power and sexual abuse of women who were directly under Herrera's control at the Detention Center which bears a direct correlation to the potential risks female patients would incur if they were placed under Herrera's control at MVH. The parallels are compelling. We are not persuaded that reasonable people, who had the information possessed by Steele and Mochen, could not have foreseen potential victims like Plaintiff, and could not have foreseen how the omission of objective information, like Steele's report and the disciplinary actions taken, would not pose a threat of physical harm to persons like Plaintiff. We emphasize that ultimately the question of foreseeability will be for the jury to decide. We only decline to say categorically that such injuries to people like Plaintiff are unforeseeable as a matter of law. . . .

Thus, in applying the principles set forth in Section 311 of the Restatement, we determine that Steele and Mochen did owe a duty of care, once they elected to make employment recommendations for Herrera, in regard to what they said and what they omitted from their references. We also conclude that such a duty was owed to Plaintiff as a third-party victim, under the circumstances of this case. We intend our holding to be narrow. We decline to speculate on how different facts and circumstances, such as the lapse of time between the referral and the assault, might affect this duty, and where "social policy" might compel us "to draw the line against otherwise unlimited liability." *Solon* 113 N.M. at 569, 573, 829 P.2d at 648, 652. Plaintiff has a claim pursuant to that duty unless the County can persuade us by additional arguments that the duty of care should not apply in this case. We now turn to those arguments.

The County argues that Plaintiff's claim is not actionable because of Plaintiff's lack of reliance. It is true, of course, that Steele and Mochen never represented any information about Herrera directly to Plaintiff and, of course, Plaintiff could not have relied on the statements made to MVH, that Herrera was an "excellent employee," of which she was not aware. However, Plaintiff's lack of reliance is immaterial.

A victim of physical violence need not rely on the negligent misrepresentation, or even be a party to it, as long as the injury is a result of the *recipient's* reliance on the employer's misrepresentation. *See* Restatement, *supra* §§ 310 cmt. c, 311 cmt. d, illus. 8 & 324A; *see also Randi W.*, 60 Cal.Rptr.2d 263, 929 P.2d at 594. In this case, Plaintiff has presented evidence to support the allegation, if found credible by a jury, that her injury resulted from MVH's reliance on the misleading employee reference from the County's supervisory employees, and this is sufficient to present an actionable claim under these circumstances. *See Gawara v. United States Brass Corp.*, 63 Cal.App.4th 1341, 74 Cal.Rptr.2d 663, 670 (1998) (noting that *Randi W.* requires a plaintiff alleging negligent misrepresentation to "establish actual reliance by an intermediary"). . . .

The County further argues that, taken literally, Steele and Mochen did not misrepresent anything to MVH, because MVH never specifically asked for the reasons for Herrera's resignation. However, "if the [employer] does speak, he must disclose enough to prevent his words from being misleading." We are not persuaded by the County's position on this point. "In other words, half of the truth may obviously amount to a lie, if it is understood to be the whole."

Finally, the County argues that public policy should dissuade us from imposing such a duty on employers. According to the County, a duty of accurate representation will become an invitation to litigate. In our view, however, we have sufficiently restricted the duty so as not to encourage extensive litigation. We do, however, find intriguing another of the County's policy arguments that any expansion of a tort duty will have a chilling effect on employer willingness to give references, whether good or bad, and society's interest in reliable information will suffer.

We agree with the County that public policy supports full and accurate disclosure of non-confidential information by employers, and we seek to encourage employers in that direction. Full and accurate disclosure regarding employees with violent and dangerous propensities promotes a safe work environment, and a productive workforce benefits both employees and employers. The past several years have seen considerable academic commentary embracing this same policy of encouraging full and accurate disclosure by employers. One incentive suggested to encourage employer disclosure is legislation to shield employers from employee defamation lawsuits when making a good-faith effort to produce accurate information about their former employees.

New Mexico's common law reflects just such a policy of encouraging employer disclosure by recognizing a "qualified or conditional privilege [against a defamation claim] to make statements about its employee or former employee if for a proper purpose and to one having a legitimate interest in the statements." *Baker v. Bhajan*, 117 N.M. 278, 282, 871 P.2d 374, 378 (1994). . . .

We acknowledge that, at the margins, the common-law duty we recognize in this opinion may discourage some employment referrals. But that impact should be minimal. The duty not to misrepresent applies only in cases of foreseeable physical harm. The vast majority of cases will involve pejorative information in the hands of an employer that does not create a risk of foreseeable physical harm and accordingly does not implicate this duty to disclose. When physical harm by the employee is foreseeable, the employer who discloses will be protected against defamation by the qualified privilege. However, even if some overly cautious employers are deterred unnecessarily from volunteering helpful information and elect to remain silent, we determine that silence may be preferable under these circumstances to what Steele and Mochen stand accused of in this case. In the face of silence from a former employer, the prospective employer can still conduct its own investigation; silence renders the employer no worse off. In contrast, the prospective employer who is misled may relax its own guard; it may not investigate as thoroughly, and may end up worse off than if it had received no information at all. On balance, therefore, the policy gains of imposing a duty not to misrepresent under these limited circumstances outweigh the potential consequences of inhibiting employer disclosure. . . .

PROBLEM

Defendant makes a car capable of traveling at speeds of 150 mph. The highest lawful speed in the United States is 75 mph. Defendant advertises the car as "the fastest thing on wheels," and sponsors television commercials showing the car involved in extraordinary feats of speed and maneuverability. The automobile is advertised as, "The car of REAL MEN."

Joe Public bought one of these cars. While driving it at a speed well in excess of 100 mph, and while under the influence of alcohol, Public lost control of the car and hit and killed plaintiff's deceased who was standing in a yard near the road where Public was driving.

Discuss the possible liability of the defendant car manufacturer to the estate of plaintiff's deceased for wrongful death.

C. APPROPRIATION OF INTANGIBLE PROPERTY IN GENERAL

PROBLEM

Entertainer made a cassette in which he imitated the voice of the President of the United States. The imitation was nearly perfect. In the cassette, he lampooned the President, capitalizing on all his snafus and gaffes. Entertainer made substantial profits in the sale of this cassette. Entertainer also sold a wristwatch which he had designed, with the hands of the watch consisting of a cartoon likeness of the President's body and face. He derived substantial profits from the sale of this watch.

The Stetson hat is a famous brand of Western-style hat. John Stetson, who is unrelated to the Stetson hat manufacturer, decided to manufacture his own hats, which he sold at his outlet store under the advertising name of "John Stetson Hats." Mr. Stetson also opened a motel next to his hat store called "The Worst Western Motel." There is a national motel chain called "Best Western Motels."

Does the President have a tort action against Entertainer?

Does either the original Stetson or Best Western have a tort action against John Stetson?

MIDLER v. FORD MOTOR CO.
849 F.2d 460 (9th Cir. 1988)

NOONAN, C.J.

This case centers on the protectibility of the voice of a celebrated chanteuse from commercial exploitation without her consent. Ford Motor Company and its advertising agency, Young & Rubicam, Inc., in 1985 advertised the Ford Lincoln Mercury with a series of nineteen 30 or 60 second television commercials in what the agency called "The Yuppie Campaign." The aim was to make an emotional connection with Yuppies, bringing back memories of when they were in college. Different popular songs of the seventies were sung on each commercial. The agency tried to get "the original people," that is, the singers who had popularized the songs, to sing them. Failing in that endeavor in ten cases the agency had the songs sung by "sound alikes." Bette Midler, the plaintiff and appellant here, was done by a sound alike.

Midler is a nationally known actress and singer. She won a Grammy as early as 1973 as the Best New Artist of that year. Records made by her since then have gone Platinum and Gold. She was nominated in 1979 for an Academy award for Best Female Actress in *The Rose,* in which she portrayed a pop singer. *Newsweek,* in its June 30, 1986 issue described her as an "outrageously original singer/comedian." *Time* hailed her in its March 2, 1987 issue as "a legend" and "the most dynamic and poignant singer-actress of her time."

When Young & Rubicam was preparing the Yuppie Campaign it presented the commercial to its client by playing an edited version of Midler singing "Do You Want To Dance," taken from the 1973 Midler album, "The Divine Miss M." After the client accepted the idea and form of the commercial, the agency contacted Midler's manager, Jerry Edelstein. The conversation went as follows: "Hello, I am Craig Hazen from Young and Rubicam. I am calling you to find out if Bette Midler would be interested in doing . . . ?" Edelstein: "Is it a commercial?" "Yes." "We are not interested."

Undeterred, Young & Rubicam sought out Ula Hedwig whom it knew to have been as one of "the Harlettes," a backup singer for Midler for ten years. Hedwig was told by Young & Rubicam that "they wanted someone who could sound like Bette Midler's recording of [Do You Want To Dance]." She was asked to make a "demo" tape of the song if she was interested. She made an a cappella demo and got the job.

At the direction of Young & Rubicam, Hedwig then made a record for the commercial. The Midler record of "Do You Want To Dance" was first played to her. She was told to "sound as much as possible like the Bette Midler record," leaving out only a few "aahs" unsuitable for the commercial. Hedwig imitated Midler to the best of her ability.

After the commercial was aired Midler was told by "a number of people" that it "sounded exactly" like her record of "Do You Want To Dance." Hedwig was told by "many personal friends" that they thought it was Midler singing the commercial. Ken Fritz, a personal manager in the entertainment business not associated with Midler, declares by affidavit that he heard the commercial on more than one occasion and thought Midler was doing the singing.

Neither the name nor the picture of Midler was used in the commercial; Young & Rubicam had a license from the copyright holder to use the song. At issue in this case is only the protection of Midler's voice. The district court described the defendants' conduct as that "of the average thief." They decided, "If we can't buy it, we'll take it." The court nonetheless believed there was no legal principle preventing imitation of Midler's voice and so gave summary judgment for the defendants. Midler appeals.

The First Amendment protects much of what the media do in the reproduction of likenesses or sounds. A primary value is freedom of speech and press. The purpose of the media's use of a person's identity is central. If the purpose is "informative or cultural" the use is immune; "if it serves no such function but merely exploits the individual portrayed, immunity will not be granted." Felcher and Rubin, "Privacy, Publicity and the Portrayal of Real People by the Media," 88 Yale L.J. 1577 1596 (1979). Moreover, federal copyright law preempts much of the area. "Mere imitation of a recorded performance would not constitute a copyright infringement even where one performer deliberately sets out to simulate another's performance as exactly as possible." Notes of Committee on the Judiciary, 17 U.S.C.A. § 114(b). It is in the context of these First Amendment and federal copyright distinctions that we address the present appeal.

Nancy Sinatra once sued Goodyear Tire and Rubber Company on the basis of an advertising campaign by Young & Rubicam featuring "These Boots Are Made For Walkin'," a song closely identified with her; the female singers of the commercial were alleged to have imitated her voice and style and to have dressed and looked like her. The basis of Nancy Sinatra's complaint was unfair competition; she claimed that the song and the arrangement had acquired "a secondary meaning" which, under California law, was protectable. This court noted that the defendants "had paid a very substantial sum to the copyright proprietor to obtain the license for the use of the song and all of its arrangements." To give Sinatra damages for their use of the song would clash with federal copyright law. Summary judgment for the defendants was affirmed. *Sinatra v. Goodyear Tire & Rubber Co.*, 435 F.2d 711, 717–718 (9th Cir. 1970). If Midler were claiming a secondary meaning to "Do You Want To Dance" or seeking to prevent the defendants from using that song, she would fail like Sinatra. But that is not this case. Midler does not seek damages for Ford's use of "Do You Want To Dance," and thus her claim is not preempted by federal copyright law. Copyright protects "original works of authorship fixed in any tangible medium of expression." 17 U.S.C. § 102(a). A voice is not copyrightable. The sounds are not "fixed." What is put forward as protectible here is more personal than any work of authorship.

Bert Lahr once sued Adell Chemical Co. for selling Lestoil by means of a commercial in which an imitation of Lahr's voice accompanied a cartoon of a duck. Lahr alleged that his style of vocal delivery was distinctive in pitch, accent, inflection, and sounds. The First Circuit held that Lahr had stated a cause of action for unfair competition, that it could be found "that defendant's conduct saturated plaintiff's audience, curtailing his market." *Lahr v. Adell Chemical Co.*, 300 F.2d 256, 259 (1st Cir. 1962). That case is more like this one. But we do not find unfair competition here. One-minute commercials of the sort the defendants put on would not have saturated Midler's audience and curtailed her market. Midler did not do television commercials. The defendants were not in competition with her.

California Civil Code section 3344 is also of no aid to Midler. The statute affords damages to a person injured by another who uses the person's "name, voice, signature, photograph or likeness, in any manner." The defendants did not use Midler's name or anything else whose use is prohibited by the statute. The voice they used was Hedwig's, not hers. The term "likeness" refers to a visual image, not a vocal imitation. The statute, however, does not preclude Midler from pursuing any cause of action she may have at common law; the statute itself implies that such common law causes of action do exist because it says its remedies are merely "cumulative."

The companion statute protecting the use of a deceased person's name, voice, signature, photograph or likeness states that the rights it recognizes are "property rights." *Id.*, § 990(b). By analogy the common law rights are also property rights. Appropriation of such common law rights is a tort in California. *Motschenbacher v. R.J. Reynolds Tobacco Co.*, 498 F.2d 821 (9th Cir. 1974). In that case what the defendants used in their television commercial for Winston cigarettes was a photograph of a famous professional racing driver's racing car. The number of the car was changed and a wing-like device known as a "spoiler" was attached to the car; the car's features of white pinpointing, an oval medallion, and solid red coloring were retained. The driver, Lothar Motschenbacher, was in the car but his features were not visible. Some persons, viewing the commercial, correctly inferred that the car was his and that he was in the car and was therefore endorsing the product. The defendants were held to have invaded a "proprietary interest" of Motschenbacher in his own identity.

Midler's case is different from Motschenbacher's. He and his car were physically used by the tobacco company's ad; he made part of his living out of giving commercial endorsements. But, as Judge Koelsch expressed it in *Motschenbacher*, California will recognize an injury from "an appropriation of the attributes of one's identity." It was irrelevant that Motschenbacher could not be identified in the ad. The ad suggested that it was he. The ad did so by emphasizing signs or symbols associated with him. In the same way the defendants here used an imitation to convey the impression that Midler was singing for them.

Why did the defendants ask Midler to sing if her voice was not of value to them? Why did they studiously acquire the services of a sound-alike and instruct her to imitate Midler if Midler's voice was not of value to them? What they sought was an attribute of Midler's identity. Its value was what the market would have paid for Midler to have sung the commercial in person.

A voice is more distinctive and more personal than the automobile accouterments protected in *Motschenbacher*. A voice is as distinctive and personal as a face. The human voice is one of the most palpable ways identity is manifested. We are all aware that a friend is at once known by a few words on the phone. At a philosophical level it has been observed that with the sound of a voice, "the other stands before me." D. Ihde, Listening and Voice 77 (1976). A fortiori, these observations hold true of singing, especially singing by a singer of renown. The singer manifests herself in the song. To impersonate her voice is to pirate her identity.

We need not and do not go so far as to hold that every imitation of a voice to advertise merchandise is actionable. We hold only that when a distinctive voice of a professional singer is widely known and is deliberately imitated in order to sell a product, the sellers have appropriated what is not theirs and have committed a tort in California. Midler has made a showing, sufficient to defeat summary judgment, that the defendants here for their own profit in selling their product did appropriate part of her identity.

NOTES

1. *On Remand*. A jury awarded Bette Midler $400,000. Note, 37 WAYNE L. REV. 1683, 1686 (1991). The verdict was affirmed on appeal, 944 F.2d 909 (9th Cir. 1991), cert. den. 112 S. Ct. 1513 (1992). How do you think the damages were proven?

2. *A Replay*. More or less contemporaneously with *Midler*, yet another voice misappropriation case arose in *Waits v. Frito-Lay, Inc.*, 978 F.2d 1093 (9th Cir. 1992). Applying *Midler*, the court upheld a jury verdict for $2.5 million, consisting of $100,000 for the fair market value of plaintiff's services, $200,000

for "injury to his peace, happiness and feelings," $75,000 for injury to "goodwill, professional standing and future publicity value," $2 million punitive damages, and attorneys' fees. It vacated a $100,000 award under the Lanham Act, as duplicative of the award for lost services.

The court stated the facts as follows:

> Tom Waits is a professional singer, songwriter, and actor of some renown. Waits has a raspy, gravelly singing voice, described by one fan as "like how you'd sound if you drank a quart of bourbon, smoked a pack of cigarettes and swallowed a pack of razor blades. . . . Late at night. After not sleeping for three days." Since the early 1970s, when his professional singing career began, Waits has recorded more than seventeen albums and has toured extensively, playing to sold-out audiences throughout the United States, Canada, Europe, Japan, and Australia. Regarded as a "prestige artist" rather than a musical superstar, Waits has achieved both commercial and critical success in his musical career. In 1987, Waits received Rolling Stone magazine's Critic's Award for Best Live Performance, chosen over other noted performers such as Bruce Springsteen, U2, David Bowie, and Madonna. SPIN magazine listed him in its March 1990 issue as one of the ten most interesting recording artists of the last five years. Waits has appeared and performed on such television programs as "Saturday Night Live" and "Late Night with David Letterman," and has been the subject of numerous magazine and newspaper articles appearing in such publications as Time, Newsweek, and the Wall Street Journal. Tom Waits does not, however, do commercials. He has maintained this policy consistently during the past ten years, rejecting numerous lucrative offers to endorse major products. Moreover, Waits' policy is a public one: in magazine, radio, and newspaper interviews he has expressed his philosophy that musical artists should not do commercials because it detracts from their artistic integrity.
>
> Frito-Lay, Inc. is in the business of manufacturing, distributing, and selling prepared and packaged food products, including Doritos brand corn chips. Tracy-Locke, Inc. is an advertising agency which counts Frito-Lay among its clients. In developing an advertising campaign to introduce a new Frito-Lay product, SalsaRio Doritos, Tracy-Locke found inspiration in a 1976 Waits song, "Step Right Up." Ironically, this song is a jazzy parody of commercial hucksterism, and consists of a succession of humorous advertising pitches. The commercial the ad agency wrote echoed the rhyming word play of the Waits song. In its presentation of the script to Frito-Lay, Tracy-Locke had the copywriter sing a preliminary rendition of the commercial and then played Waits' recorded rendition of "Step Right Up" to demonstrate the feeling the commercial would capture. Frito-Lay approved the overall concept and the script.
>
> The story of Tracy-Locke's search for a lead singer for the commercial suggests that no one would do but a singer who could not only capture the feeling of "Step Right Up" but also imitate Tom Waits' voice. The initial efforts of the ad agency's creative team, using a

C.   APPROPRIATION OF INTANGIBLE PROPERTY IN GENERAL   1293

respected professional singer with a deep bluesy voice, met with disapproval from executives at both Tracy-Locke and Frito-Lay. Tracy-Locke then auditioned a number of other singers who could sing in a gravelly style.

Stephen Carter was among those who auditioned. A recording engineer who was acquainted with Carter's work had recommended him to Tracy-Locke as someone who did a good Tom Waits imitation. Carter was a professional musician from Dallas and a Tom Waits fan. Over ten years of performing Waits songs as part of his band's repertoire, he had consciously perfected an imitation of Waits' voice. When Carter auditioned, members of the Tracy-Locke creative team "did a double take" over Carter's near-perfect imitation of Waits, and remarked to him how much he sounded like Waits. In fact, the commercial's musical director warned Carter that he probably wouldn't get the job because he sounded too much like Waits, which could pose legal problems. Carter, however, did get the job.

At the recording session for the commercial David Brenner, Tracy-Locke's executive producer, became concerned about the legal implications of Carter's skill in imitating Waits, and attempted to get Carter to "back off" his Waits imitation. Neither the client nor the members of the creative team, however, liked the result. After the session, Carter remarked to Brenner that Waits would be unhappy with the commercial because of his publicly avowed policy against doing commercial endorsements and his disapproval of artists who did. Brenner acknowledged he was aware of this, telling Carter that he had previously approached Waits to do a Diet Coke commercial and "you never heard anybody say no so fast in your life." Brenner conveyed to Robert Grossman, Tracy-Locke's managing vice president and the executive on the Frito-Lay account, his concerns that the commercial was too close to Waits' voice. As a precaution, Brenner made an alternate version of the commercial with another singer.

On the day the commercial was due for release to radio stations across the country, Grossman had a ten-minute long-distance telephone consultation with Tracy-Locke's attorney, asking him whether there would be legal problems with a commercial that sought to capture the same feeling as Waits' music. The attorney noted that there was a "high profile" risk of a lawsuit in view of recent case law recognizing the protectability of a distinctive voice. Based on what Grossman had told him, however, the attorney did not think such a suit would have merit, because a singer's style of music is not protected. Grossman then presented both the Carter tape and the alternate version to Frito-Lay, noting the legal risks involved in the Carter version. He recommended the Carter version, however, and noted that Tracy-Locke would indemnify Frito-Lay in the event of a lawsuit. Frito-Lay chose the Carter version.

The commercial was broadcast in September and October 1988 on over 250 radio stations located in 61 markets nationwide, including Los Angeles, San Francisco, and Chicago. Waits heard it during his appearance on a Los Angeles radio program, and was shocked. He realized "immediately that whoever was going to hear this and obviously identify the voice would also identify that [Tom Waits] in fact had agreed to do a commercial for Doritos."

See also Brown et al. v. Ames et al., 201 F.3d 654 (5th Cir. 2000) (copyright law does not preempt a claim of appropriation of name and likeness).

3. *Secondary Meaning.* In *Carson v. Here's Johnny Portable Toilets, Inc.*, 698 F.2d 831 (6th Cir. 1983), Johnny Carson, the television entertainer whose introduction since 1961 has been "Here's Johnny," sued the defendant portable toilet company alleging unfair competition under § 43(a) of the Lanham Act, 15 U.S.C. § 1125(a), and invasion of privacy and publicity rights. The appellate court agreed with the trial court's determination that Carson had failed to satisfy the "likelihood of confusion test" under the Lanham Act. The court stated:

> In *Frisch's Restaurants, Inc. v. Elby's Big Boy, Inc.*, 670 F.2d 642 (6th Cir. 1982), we approved the balancing of several factors in determining whether a likelihood of confusion exists among consumers of goods involved in a § 43(a) action. In that case we examined eight factors:
>
> 1. strength of the plaintiff's mark;
> 2. relatedness of the goods;
> 3. similarity of the marks;
> 4. evidence of actual confusion;
> 5. marketing channels used;
> 6. likely degree of purchaser care;
> 7. defendant's intent in selecting the mark;
> 8. likelihood of expansion of the product lines.
>
> . . . The district court first found that "Here's Johnny" was not such a strong mark that its use for other goods should be entirely foreclosed. Although the appellee had intended to capitalize on the phrase popularized by Carson, the court concluded that appellee had not intended to deceive the public into believing Carson was connected with the product. The court noted that there was little evidence of actual confusion and no evidence that appellee's use of the phrase had damaged appellants.

The court also rejected Carson's privacy claim on the basis that "the facts here presented do not . . . amount to an invasion of any of the interests protected by the right of privacy." However, the court reversed the district court's rejection of the right of publicity allegation, stating that:

> [The district court] held that it "would not be prudent to allow recovery for a right of publicity claim which does not more specifically identify Johnny Carson." We believe that, on the contrary, the district court's conception of the right of publicity is too narrow. The right of publicity, as we have stated, is that a celebrity has a protected

C. APPROPRIATION OF INTANGIBLE PROPERTY IN GENERAL   1295

pecuniary interest in the commercial exploitation of his identity. If the celebrity's identity is commercially exploited, there has been an invasion of his right whether or not his "name or likeness" is used. Carson's identity may be exploited even if his name, John W. Carson, or his picture is not used.

What is the relationship between *Carson* and the "secondary meaning" doctrine which in *Midler* was held to conflict with federal copyright law? Carson had never registered "Here's Johnny" as a trademark.

4. *Common Law Copyright.* In *Masterson v. McCroskie,* 194 Colo. 460, 573 P.2d 547 (1978), plaintiffs sued defendant for wrongful appropriation of the architectural plans to their house, claiming a common law copyright in the plans. Reversing the lower courts, the state supreme court held that plaintiffs stated a cause of action:

> The plaintiffs, Mr. and Mrs. Masterson, assisted by an architect who assigned his rights to them, drew up original and creative plans for the construction of their personal home. They filed copies of the plans with the subdivision developer for design approval and with the city building department in connection with their building permit application. In addition, they furnished copies to the contractor and the subcontractors for their use and guidance during construction. All copies bore the address of the property on which the home was being constructed; however, the copies did not contain any express indication that the Mastersons desired to restrict publication of the plans. The copies were not numbered or marked confidential, and most of them did not bear the name of the Mastersons or the architect. Upon completion of construction, the Mastersons attempted to retrieve all copies of the plans from the contractor and the subcontractors but with only limited success.
>
> Defendant McCroskie obtained the Mastersons' plans from one of the subcontractors after construction of the residence was completed and copied them for his use in designing and constructing his own home a block and a half from the Mastersons' home. The exterior of the McCroskie house was substantially a replica of the Masterson home. The interior floor plan and foundation design, although not identical, closely resembled the Masterson residence. The Mastersons sought compensatory and exemplary damages in the trial court from McCroskie for alleged infringement of their common law copyright in the plans.

Defendant contended plaintiffs had voluntarily published the plans, thereby relinquishing their common law copyright. The court found, however, that there may be an express or implied restricted publication to a limited group such that the common law right is not lost:

> There is an implied restriction against any use which is inconsistent with the obvious purpose for which an item of intellectual property has been disseminated. Here, all communication of the plans was limited to selected individuals—the contractor, subcontractors, the building inspector, and the subdivision developer—who had to have

copies of the plans in order for the house to be constructed. No member of the general public was given a copy of the plans. We therefore hold that the circumstances of dissemination were so limited as to preclude a reasonable outsider from concluding that the general public was free to use the plans. . . .

The court of appeals erroneously held that construction of a home in public view constitutes a general publication of the exterior plans. This conclusion is contrary to the weight of authority which distinguishes between publication of the general design, which necessarily occurs upon construction, and the publication of technical plans, which does not occur upon construction. Had McCroskie drawn up his own architectural plans after observing the house constructed by the Mastersons, the court of appeals' conclusion would have been correct.

Suppose defendant obtained entry to the McCroskey residence under false pretenses, and observed and copied the interior design? Reconsider *Dietemann v. Time, Inc.*, 449 F.2d 245 (9th Cir. 1971).

Contrast *Columbia Broadcasting Sys., Inc. v. DeCosta*, 377 F.2d 315 (1st Cir. 1967). Plaintiff had a unique costume, character, and name card, "Paladin—Have Gun Will Travel," which he displayed gratuitously in mock-western gunfights at rodeos, auctions and horse shows. This character, to the last detail, subsequently appeared in defendant's successful television series.

While the court found defendant had pirated the character from plaintiff, plaintiff was nevertheless denied recovery because the federal copyright law preempted the claim.

5. *Die Gedanke Sind Frei, and Implied Contracts.* In *Richter v. Westab, Inc.*, 529 F.2d 896 (6th Cir. 1976), plaintiffs sued the defendants for breach of contract:

> Plaintiffs were partners in the firm of Richter & Mracky Design Associates, which created and developed designs for products and marketing concepts. In 1964 Mark Seitman, an employee of Richter & Mracky, observed that the school supplies industry was characterized by drabness and a lack of attractiveness in the various product lines. He believed that a school supply firm could improve its sales by using on notebook covers and binders fashion designs and fabrics which matched clothing being advertised in young women's fashion magazines; that such fashion-oriented supplies could be matched as a package so that the fashion-conscious buyer could purchase all items from one company; and that these lines of school supplies could be advertised in fashion magazines rather than in trade journals as had been the practice with school supplies in the past.
>
> Seitman solicited Westab and arranged a meeting for February 10, 1965, with its officers. Westab was the largest manufacturer of school supplies in the country. At this meeting Seitman presented his concept, which resulted in authorization for Richter & Mracky to produce tentative designs and samples for presentation to Westab sales officials. During the meeting a Westab officer suggested that the

C. APPROPRIATION OF INTANGIBLE PROPERTY IN GENERAL   1297

notebook binders in the fashion line have interchangeable covers, and Richter & Mracky was also authorized to develop this idea.

After the meeting Seitman discussed with Edgar Stovall, Vice-President of Westab, the matter of compensation which included a royalty of five percent of Westab's sale price, to be paid on specific designs submitted by Richter & Mracky and used by Westab. It did not include royalties on the mere concept of fashion design.

During the summer of 1965 Richter & Mracky worked to perfect interchangeable binder covers and to produce fashion designs which it named "Fashion Goes To School." Samples were submitted to Westab. The interchangeable covers loosened when the notebook was opened, and were not practical. The "Fashion Goes To School" concept was submitted at a meeting of Westab's salesmen; it called for a retail price of $4.95 for the package:

> None of the designs was acceptable to Westab, and the project was rejected in October 1965 when Westab marketing officials balked at the projected retail price of $4.95 for the package. Westab then paid Richter & Mracky for shop expenses and asked that the work product not be given to competitors.

Westab's research and marketing personnel then developed Westab's own package of school supplies with matching plaid covers. The package was a success.

In plaintiff's claim for breach of contract, the court found that the contract required plaintiff "to submit specific designs and to be paid only for the use of the designs so submitted." Plaintiffs could have, but did not, protect their abstract concept by contract:

> If Richter & Mracky had made a contract with Westab which required Westab to pay a royalty on all fashion binders sold by Westab, the contract would have been enforceable in the courts. Likewise, if the parties had made an agreement in advance of the meeting that any sale arising from the use of concepts presented at the meeting would require royalty payments to Richter & Mracky, the facts here would probably require a judgment for plaintiffs.
>
> We doubt that Westab would ever enter into such a contract, preferring to hear the presentation, or to see the proposed designs, before agreeing to a contract for their use. Such action would merely reflect the fact that an abstract idea has little commercial value until translated into a specific utilization.

The court also rejected plaintiffs' claim that an implied contract arose from the divulgence of a trade secret as part of a confidential relation:

> A trade secret may consist of any formula, pattern, device or compilation of information which is used in one's business, and which gives him an opportunity to obtain an advantage over competitors who do not know or use it. It may be a formula for a chemical compound, a process of manufacturing, treating or preserving materials, a pattern for a machine or other device, or a list of customers. . . . A trade secret is a process or device for continuous use in the operation of the

business. Generally it relates to the production of goods, as, for example, a machine or formula for the production of an article.

This definition does not include a marketing concept or a new product idea. Trade secret law is designed to protect a continuing competitive advantage, which a company enjoys due to confidential information it possesses, from destruction due to disclosure by a departed former employee. A marketing concept does not by confidentiality create a continuing competitive advantage because once it is implemented it is exposed for the world to see and for competitors to legally imitate.

Compare Desny v. Wilder, 46 Cal. 2d 715, 299 P.2d 257 (1956). Plaintiff attempted to reach Wilder, a producer and director, by telephone, but was required to explain the purpose of his call to Wilder's secretary. Plaintiff described to her a plot for a possible movie based on the death of Floyd Collins when trapped in a Kentucky cave. When plaintiff wanted to send Wilder his story of 65 pages, the secretary explained that it must be shortened to a three-or four-page synopsis. Two days later, plaintiff telephoned that the synopsis was ready. The secretary asked that he read it to her over the telephone while she took it down in shorthand:

> During the conversation the secretary told plaintiff that the story seemed interesting and that she liked it. "She said that she would talk it over with Billy Wilder and she would let me know." Plaintiff on his part told the secretary that defendants could use the story only if they paid him "the reasonable value of it. . . . I made it clear to her that I wrote the story and that I wanted to sell it. . . . I naturally mentioned again that this story was my story which has taken me so much effort and research and time, and therefore if anybody used it they will have to pay for it. . . . She said that if Billy Wilder of Paramount uses the story, 'naturally we will pay you for it.'" Plaintiff did not remember whether in his first telephone conversation with the secretary anything was said concerning his purpose of selling the story to defendants. He did not at any time speak with defendant Wilder. It seems clear, however, that one of the authorized functions of the secretary was to receive and deliver messages to Wilder and hence, as it developed *infra,* that on this record her knowledge would be his knowledge. Plaintiff's only subsequent contact with the secretary was a telephone call to her in July, 1950, to protest the alleged use of his composition and idea in a photoplay produced and exhibited by defendants. The photoplay, as hereinafter shown in some detail, closely parallels both plaintiff's synopsis and the historical material concerning the life and death of Floyd Collins. It also includes a fictional incident which appears in plaintiff's synopsis and which he claims is his creation, presumably in the sense of being both original and novel in its combination with the facts from the public commons or public domain. . . .

> An idea is usually not regarded as property, because all sentient beings may conceive and evolve ideas throughout the gamut of their powers of cerebration and because our concept of property implies

C. APPROPRIATION OF INTANGIBLE PROPERTY IN GENERAL 1299

something which may be owned and possessed to the exclusion of all other persons. . . .

The principles above stated do not, however, lead to the conclusion that ideas cannot be a subject of contract. . . . Obviously the defendants here used someone's script in preparing and producing their photoplay. That script must have had value to them. As will be hereinafter shown, it closely resembles plaintiff's synopsis. Ergo, plaintiff's synopsis appears to be a valuable literary composition. Defendants had an unassailable right to have their own employees conduct the research into the Floyd Collins tragedy—an historical event in the public domain—and prepare a story based on those facts and to translate it into a script for the play. But equally unassailable (assuming the verity of the facts which plaintiff asserts) is plaintiff's position that defendants had no right -except by purchase on the terms he offered -to acquire and use the synopsis prepared by him . . . .

6. *The First-Sale Doctrine*. Appellants Hershiser and Allison, who were well-known sports persons, sued Vintage Sports for appropriation of their name and likeness:

Vintage Sports Plaques ("Vintage") purchases trading cards from licensed card manufacturers and distributors and, without altering the cards in any way, frames them by mounting individual cards between a transparent acrylic sheet and a wood board. Vintage then labels each plaque with an identification plate bearing the name of the player or team represented. In addition to the mounted trading card, some of the plaques feature a clock with a sports motif. Vintage markets each plaque as a "Limited Edition" and an "Authentic Collectible." Vintage is not a party to any licensing agreement that grants it the right to use the appellants' names or likenesses for commercial purposes and has never paid a royalty or commission to the appellants for its use of their names or images. Appellants presumably have received, however, pursuant to their respective licensing agreements, royalties from the card manufacturers and distributors for the initial sale of the cards to Vintage.

The court said defendant's use of these playing cards was protected under the first-sale doctrine, which provides that once the holder of an intellectual property right "consents to the sale of particular copies . . . of his work, he may not thereafter exercise the distribution right with respect to such copies." This doctrine, the court said, applies to copyright, patent, and trademark law, as well as to the rights of publicity.

But, said the court:

The issue before us, then, is whether the district court properly resolved as a matter of law that Vintage's plaques merely are the cards themselves repackaged, rather than products separate and distinct from the trading cards they incorporate. If they are the latter, as appellants contend that they are, then arguably Vintage is selling a product by "commercially exploiting the likeness[es of appellants] intending to engender profits to their enterprise," *Wendt v. Host Int'l,*

Inc., 125 F.3d 806, 811 (9th Cir. 1997), a practice against which the right of publicity seems clearly to protect. . . .

We conclude that the district court properly determined that, as a matter of law, Vintage merely resells cards that it lawfully obtains. We think it unlikely that anyone would purchase one of Vintage's plaques for any reason other than to obtain a display of the mounted cards themselves. Although we recognize that the plaques that include a clock pose a closer case, we conclude that it is unlikely that anyone would purchase one of the clock plaques simply to obtain a means of telling time, believing the clock to be, for example, a "Hershiser Clock" or an "Allison Clock."

Allison v. Vintage Sports Plaques, 136 F.3d 1443 (11th Cir. 1998).

Suppose the pictures were given to Vintage Sports, or Vintage Sports found them. Would the first-sale doctrine still apply?

7. *The Right of Publicity and Parody.* The plaintiff in *Cardtoons v. Major League Baseball Players Ass'n*, 95 F.3d 959 (10th Cir. 1996), contended that it had a first amendment free speech right to parody the images of major league baseball players. The court agreed. Plaintiff sought a declaratory judgment against the defendant association, which was the bargaining agent for the players and the assignee of their individual publicity rights. The court gave the following as an example of one of the parody trading cards:

> A person reasonably familiar with baseball can readily identify the players lampooned on the parody trading cards. The cards use similar names, recognizable caricatures, distinctive team colors, and commentary about individual players. For example, the card parodying San Francisco Giants' outfielder Barry Bonds calls him "Treasury Bonds," and features a recognizable caricature of Bonds, complete with earring, tipping a bat boy for a 24 carat gold "Fort Knoxville Slugger." The back of the card has a team logo (the "Gents"), and the following text:
>
> Redemption qualities and why Treasury Bonds is the league's most valuable player:
>
> 1. Having Bonds on your team is like having money in the bank.
>
> 2. He plays so hard he gives 110 percent, compounded daily.
>
> 3. He turned down the chance to play other sports because he has a high interest rate in baseball.
>
> 4. He deposits the ball in the bleachers.
>
> 5. He is into male bonding.
>
> 6. He is a money player.
>
> 7. He has a 24-karat Gold Glove.
>
> 8. He always cashes in on the payoff pitch.

Said the court:

> Cardtoons' parody trading cards receive full protection under the First Amendment. The cards provide social commentary on public

figures, major league baseball players, who are involved in a significant commercial enterprise, major league baseball. While not core political speech (the cards do not, for example, adopt a position on the Ken Griffey, Jr., for President campaign), this type of commentary on an important social institution constitutes protected expression.

The cards are no less protected because they provide humorous rather than serious commentary. Speech that entertains, like speech that informs, is protected by the First Amendment because "[t]he line between the informing and the entertaining is too elusive for the protection of that basic right." *Winters v. New York*, 333 U.S. 507, 510, 68 S.Ct. 665, 667, 92 L.Ed. 840 (1948). Moreover, Cardtoons makes use of artistic and literary devices with distinguished traditions. Parody, for example, is a humorous form of social commentary that dates to Greek antiquity, and has since made regular appearances in English literature. In addition, cartoons and caricatures, such as those in the trading cards, have played a prominent role in public and political debate throughout our nation's history.

8. *Appropriation of Name and Likeness Revisited.* The famed football player Joe Montana brought an action for appropriation of name and likeness in *Montana v. San Jose Mercury News, Inc.*, 40 Cal. Rptr. 2d 639 (Cal. App. 1995):

On January 22, 1989, San Francisco 49'ers quarterback Joe Montana led his team to a 20-16 come-from-behind victory against the Cincinnati Bengals in Super Bowl XXIII. The following day, the San Jose Mercury News (SJMN) ran a front page story chronicling the 49'ers' feat and depicting four players, including Montana, celebrating on the field. The next year, the 49'ers were even more impressive in Super Bowl XXIV, sweeping past the Denver Broncos to a 55-10 win. Again, SJMN featured the 49'ers' accomplishment the next day in its front page story. The accompanying front page photograph showed Joe Montana "flying high in celebration with Guy McIntyre after a third-quarter touchdown pass to John Taylor."

The 1990 Super Bowl victory gave the 49'ers an unparalleled four championships in the 1980 to 1990 decade. To celebrate this accomplishment, SJMN issued a special "Souvenir Section" in its Sunday, February 4, 1990, edition, devoted exclusively to the 49'ers, a "team of destiny." The souvenir section, entitled "Trophy Hunters," carried an artist's rendition of Montana on the front page.

Each of these newspaper pages was reproduced in poster form within two weeks of its original printing in the newspaper and was made available for sale to the general public. Approximately 30 percent of the posters were sold for $5 each; SJMN gave away the remaining posters, mostly at charity events.

The court held the posters were constitutionally protected speech:

The First Amendment protects the posters complained about here for two distinct reasons: first, because the posters themselves report newsworthy items of public interest, and second, because a newspaper has a constitutional right to promote itself by reproducing its originally protected articles or photographs.

9. *Product Disparagement.* Recall the discussion of product disparagement, discussed in the prior chapter This common law claim arises when one makes a statement which "is understood to cast doubt upon the quality of another's land, chattels or intangible things, or upon the existence or extent of his property in them." REST.2d of TORTS § 629 (1976). The tort requires proof of knowing falsity, or reckless disregard of whether the statement is true or false. Id. § 623A. Liability is restricted to "pecuniary loss," *id.*, which is defined as "impairment of vendibility or value," and the "expense of measures reasonably necessary to counteract the publication, including litigation to remove the doubt cast on vendibility or value" caused by the disparagement. *Id.* § 633.

It is unclear whether, or to what extent, the constitution affects a claim for product disparagement. Reconsider the defamation materials in this connection. In *Bose v. Consumers Union of U. S., Inc.*, 466 U. S. 485, 104 S. Ct. 1949, 80 L. Ed. 2d 502 (1984), the Court assumed, without deciding, that the constitutional malice standard applied to product disparagement, and held that such malice had to be proved by clear and convincing evidence subject to de novo review on appeal. It is unclear how the *Bose* decision is affected by *Dun & Bradstreet v. Greenmoss Builders*, 472 U.S. 749 (1985).

PROBLEM

One night, over a few beers, Chris Marlow told his neighbor Bill Shakespeare about a plot he had in mind for a new play called "Hamlet." Chris got the basic idea for the play from Hollingshed's history book, but he had embroidered it by adding a subplot involving Hamlet's girlfriend Ophelia and her father Polonius. Chris told Bill that he decided to portray Hamlet as "not all there, you know, sort of half-baked." He intended to imply an incestuous attraction of Hamlet for his mother as a motive for Hamlet's strong dislike for his stepfather, Claudius. Chris also planned a play-within-a-play scene in which Claudius' guilt for the death of Hamlet's father would be strongly suggested by Claudius' reaction to the scene. The play was to begin with the appearance to Hamlet of the ghost of Hamlet's father, who would tell Hamlet that Claudius had poisoned him. Hamlet was to be killed in the end by a poisoned rapier in a sword fight with Ophelia's brother, Laertes.

When Chris sobered up some months later, he realized that his neighbor Bill had written and produced a highly successful play called "Hamlet" which incorporated all the ideas Chris had previously related to Bill—plus many fine speeches ("To be or not to be," and the like) which were original with Bill.

Has Chris a valid claim against Bill for wrongful appropriation of ideal property?

TUTTLE v. BUCK
107 Minn. 145, 119 N.W. 946 (1909)

[Defendant appealed from an order denying a new trial. Plaintiff had been a barber for ten years in Howard Lake, Minnesota. He alleged that the defendant "wrongfully, unlawfully, and maliciously endeavored to destroy plaintiff's said business and compel plaintiff to abandon the same. That to

C. APPROPRIATION OF INTANGIBLE PROPERTY IN GENERAL 1303

that end he has persistently and systematically sought, by false and malicious reports and accusations of and concerning the plaintiff, by personally soliciting and urging plaintiff's patrons no longer to employ plaintiff, by threats of his personal displeasure, and by various other unlawful means and devices, to induce, and has thereby induced, many of said patrons to withhold from plaintiff the employment by them formerly given. That defendant is possessed of large means, and is engaged in the business of a banker in said village of Howard Lake, at Dassel, Minn., and at divers other places, and is nowise interested in the occupation of a barber; yet in the pursuance of the wicked, malicious, and unlawful purpose aforesaid, and for the sole and only purpose of injuring the trade of the plaintiff, and of accomplishing his purpose and threats of ruining the plaintiff's said business and driving him out of said village, the defendant fitted up and furnished a barber shop in said village for conducting the trade of barbering. That failing to induce any barber to occupy said shop on his own account, though offered at nominal rental, said defendant, with the wrongful and malicious purpose aforesaid, and not otherwise, has during the time herein stated hired two barbers in succession for a stated salary, paid by him, to occupy said shop, and to serve so many of plaintiff's patrons as said defendant has been or may be able by the means aforesaid to direct from plaintiff's shop. That at the present time a barber so employed and paid by the defendant is occupying and nominally conducting the shop thus fitted and furnished by the defendant, without paying any rent therefor, and under an agreement with defendant whereby the income of said shop is required to be paid to defendant, and is so paid in partial return for his wages."]

ELLIOTT, J.

It has been said that the law deals only with externals, and that a lawful act cannot be made the foundation of an action because it was done with an evil motive. In *Allen v. Flood,* [1898] A.C. 151, Lord Watson said that, except with regard to crimes, the law does not take into account motives as constituting an element of civil wrong. In *Mayor v. Pickles,* [1895] A.C. 587, Lord Haisbury stated that if the act was lawful, "however ill the motive might be, he had a right to do it." In *Raycroft v. Tayntor,* 68 Vt. 219, 35 Atl. 53, 33 L.R.A. 225, 54 Am. St. Rep. 882 (1896), the court said that, "where one exercises a legal right only, the motive which actuates him is immaterial." In *Jenkens v. Fowler,* 24 Pa. 318, Mr. Justice Black said that "mischievous motives make a bad case worse, but they cannot make that wrong which in its own essence is lawful." Such generalizations are of little value in determining concrete cases. They may state the truth, but not the whole truth. Each word and phrase used therein may require definition and limitation. Thus, before we can apply Judge Black's language to a particular case, we must determine what act is "in its own essence lawful." What did Lord Haisbury mean by the words "lawful act?" What is meant by "exercising a legal right?" It is not at all correct to say that the motive with which an act is done is always immaterial, providing the act itself is not unlawful. Numerous illustrations of the contrary will be found in the civil as well as the criminal law.

We do not intend to enter upon an elaborate discussion of the subject, or become entangled in the subtleties connected with the words "malice" and "malicious." We are not able to accept without limitations the doctrine above referred to, but at this time content ourselves with a brief reference to some general principles. It must be remembered that the common law is the result of growth, and that its development has been determined by the social needs of the community which it governs. It is the resultant of conflicting social forces, and those forces which are for the time dominant leaves their impress upon the law. It is of judicial origin, and seeks to establish doctrines and rules for the determination, protection, and enforcement of legal rights. Manifestly it must change as society changes and new rights are recognized. To be an efficient instrument, and not a mere abstraction, it must gradually adapt itself to changed conditions. Necessarily its form and substance have been greatly affected by prevalent economic theories. For generations there has been a practical agreement upon the proposition that competition in trade and business is desirable, and this idea has found expression in the decisions of the courts as well as in statutes. But it has led to grievous and manifold wrongs to individuals, and many courts have manifested an earnest desire to protect the individuals from the evils which result from unrestrained business competition. The problem has been to so adjust matters as to preserve the principle of competition and yet guard against its abuse to the unnecessary injury to the individual. So the principle that a man may use his own property according to his own needs and desires, while true in the abstract, is subject to many limitations in the concrete. Men cannot always, in civilized society, be allowed to use their own property as their interests or desires may dictate without reference to the fact that they have neighbors whose rights are as sacred as their own. The existence and well-being of society requires that each and every person shall conduct himself consistently with the fact that he is a social and reasonable person. The purpose for which a man is using his own property may thus sometimes determine his rights.

Many of the restrictions which should be recognized and enforced result from a tacit recognition of principles which are not often stated in the decisions in express terms. Sir Frederick Pollock notes that not many years ago it was difficult to find any definite authority for stating as a general proposition of English law that it is wrong to do a willful wrong to one's neighbor without lawful justification or excuse. But neither is there any express authority for the general proposition that men must perform their contracts. Both principles, in this generality of form and conception, are modern and there was a time when neither was true. After developing the idea that law begins, not with authentic general principles but with the enumeration of particular remedies, the learned writer continues: "If there exists, then, a positive duty to avoid harm, much more, then, exists the negative duty of not doing willful harm, subject, as all general duties must be subject, to the necessary exceptions. The three main heads of duty with which the law of torts is concerned, namely, to abstain from willful injury, to respect the property of others, and to use due diligence to avoid causing harm to others, are all alike of a comprehensive nature." Pollock, Torts, (8th Ed.) p. 21. He then quotes with approval the statement of Lord Bowen that "at common law there was a cause of action whenever one person did damage to another, willfully and intentionally, without just cause and excuse." In *Plant v. Woods,* 176 Mass. 492, 57 N.E. 1011, 51 L.R.A. 339, 79 Am. St. Rep. 330 (1900), Mr. Justice Hammond

C. APPROPRIATION OF INTANGIBLE PROPERTY IN GENERAL 1305

said: "It is said, also, that, where one has the lawful right to do a thing, the motive by which he is actuated is immaterial. One form of this statement appears in the first headnote in *Allen v. Flood,* as reported in [1898] A. C. 1, as follows: 'An act lawful in itself is not converted by a malicious or bad motive into an unlawful act, so as to make the doer of the act liable to a civil action.' If the meaning of this and similar expressions is that, where a person has the lawful right to do a thing irrespective of his motive, his motive is immaterial, the proposition is a mere truism. If, however, the meaning is that where a person, if actuated by one kind of a motive, has a lawful right to do a thing, the act is lawful when done under any conceivable motive, or that an act lawful under one set of circumstances is therefore lawful under every conceivable set of circumstances, the proposition does not commend itself to use as either logically or legally accurate."

It is freely conceded that there are many decisions contrary to this view; but, when carried to the extent contended for by the appellant, we think they are unsafe, unsound, and illy adapted to modern conditions. To divert to one's self the customers of a business rival by the offer of goods at lower prices is in general a legitimate mode of serving one's own interest, and justifiable as fair competition. But when a man starts an opposition place of business, not for the sake of profit to himself, but regardless of loss to himself, and for the sole purpose of driving his competitor out of business, and with the intention of himself retiring upon the accomplishment of his malevolent purpose, he is guilty of a wanton wrong and an actionable tort. In such a case he would not be exercising his legal right, or doing an act which can be judged separately from the motive which actuated him. To call such conduct competition is a perversion of terms. It is simply the application of force without legal justification, which in its moral quality may be no better than highway robbery.

Nevertheless, in the opinion of the writer this complaint is insufficient. It is not claimed that it states a cause of action for slander. No question of conspiracy or combination is involved. Stripped of the adjectives and the statement that what was done was for the sole purpose of injuring the plaintiff, and not for the purpose of serving a legitimate purpose of the defendant, the complaint states facts which in themselves amount only to an ordinary everyday business transaction. There is no allegation that the defendant was intentionally running the business at a financial loss to himself, or that after driving the plaintiff out of business the defendant closed up or intended to close up his shop. From all that appears from the complaint he may have opened the barber shop, energetically sought business from his acquaintances and the customers of the plaintiff, and as a result of his enterprise and command of capital obtained it, with the result that the plaintiff, from want of capital, acquaintance, or enterprise, was unable to stand the competition and was thus driven out of business. The facts thus alleged do not, in my opinion, in themselves, without reference by the way in which they are characterized by the pleader, tend to show a malicious and wanton wrong to the plaintiff.

A majority of the Justices, however, are of the opinion that, on the principle declared in the foregoing opinion, the complaint states a cause of action, and the order is therefore affirmed.

NOTES

1. *Sales at a Loss.* Statutes provide that sales at less than cost, made "with the intent and purpose of destroying honest competition," are illegal. *See, e.g.,* TENN. CODE ANN. § 47-25-109.

2. *Good Faith or Bad Faith?* The plaintiff-appellant OB/GYN, Dr. Albert Alexander, sued the defendant not-for-profit corporation, MIPA, in *Alexander v. Memphis Indiv. Pract. Ass'n*, 870 S. W. 2d 278 (Tenn. 1993), for damage caused by alleged improper delay in approving his membership to the defendant corporation. MIPA contracts with Memphis area health maintenance organizations (HMOs) to provide primary health care services to subscribers of the HMOs. The HMOs pay for their subscriber's health care only when treated by a physician belonging to MIPA.

Dr. Turman, a member of the MIPA membership application committee, stated in deposition that at the membership application meetings he had offered his opinion of the plaintiff's qualifications and the lack of MIPA's need for another OB/GYN:

> . . . my opinion of Albert, and he knows this, was that over the years I've known him I thought he was a little bit of a maverick and would be a little hard to bridle as far as cost containment, cost efficiency was concerned which we were pretty heavy in at the time, that he had a little bit of anti-establishment or anti-systems personality about him and that he had begun to, according to talk that almost everyone had heard, to testify for hire for plaintiffs in medical malpractice suits.
>
> Those were—that was my speech each time I was looked to, and I never voted pro or con on Albert's being removed from the waiting list and placed on active duty. But I don't know how any of the rest of them felt, but if that's what kept him on the waiting list, then so be it.
>
> We had no need in that area for a new OB/GYN office, so the question was not whether he was to be admitted as a member, as to whether we needed a reason to take him off the waiting list. There was never any debate. There was really no need for a new office, and there was no other side to it. Nobody came and talked for Albert including Albert.

The court said that under Tenn. Code Annot. § 63-6-219, members of a medical review committee such as MIPA are entitled to immunity for any statements made before or decisions taken by such a committee, as long as they are "made or taken in good faith and without malice and on the basis of facts reasonably known or reasonably believed to exist." In granting summary judgment for the defendant, the court said:

> The appellant has not shown that the comments made by Dr. Turman, along with MIPA's delay in accepting his membership application, were committed with intentional malice and bad faith. The record reflects that MIPA's decision to deny membership to Dr. Alexander was made based upon facts reasonably known to exist or reasonably believed to exist. Without evidence of malice and bad faith the appellant fails to prove the essential element that would remove the Association's immunity under T. C. A. 63-6-219.

C. APPROPRIATION OF INTANGIBLE PROPERTY IN GENERAL 1307

Would the plaintiff have survived the summary judgment motion had there been no statute such as § 63-6-219?

3. *Boycott.* In *F.T.C. v. Superior Court Trial Lawyers Ass'n,* 110 S. Ct. 768, 107 L. Ed. 2d 851 (1990), a group of lawyers, who regularly acted as court-appointed counsel for indigent defendants in District of Columbia criminal cases, agreed at a meeting of their association that they would stop providing representation until the District increased their compensation. The boycott severely disrupted the District of Columbia criminal justice system, and the District government capitulated to the lawyers' demands.

Subsequently, the Federal Trade Commission (FTC) filed a suit against the association and four of its members, alleging that they had entered into a conspiracy to fix prices and to conduct a boycott that constituted unfair methods of competition in violation of the federal antitrust laws. The Court found in favor of the FTC:

> The lawyers' association argues that [its conduct is] protected by the First Amendment rights recognized in *NAACP v. Claiborne Hardware Co.,* 458 U.S. 886, 102 S. Ct. 3409, 73 L. Ed. 2d 1215 (1982). That case arose after black citizens boycotted white merchants in Claiborne County, Miss. The white merchants sued under state law to recover losses from the boycott. We found that the "right of the States to regulate economic activity could not justify a complete prohibition against a nonviolent, politically motivated boycott designed to force governmental and economic change and to effectuate rights guaranteed by the Constitution itself." *Id.,* at 914, 102 S. Ct., at 3426. We accordingly held that "the nonviolent elements of petitioners, activities are entitled to the protection of the First Amendment." *Id.,* at 915, 102 S. Ct., at 3426.
>
> [O]ur reasoning in *Claiborne Hardware* is not applicable to a boycott conducted by business competitors who "stand to profit financially from a lessening of competition in the boycotted market." *Allied Tune Corp. v. Indian Head Inc.,* 100 L. Ed. 2d 497, 508, 108 S. Ct., at 1941. No matter how altruistic the motives of respondents may have been, it is undisputed that their immediate objective was to increase the price that they would be paid for their services. Such an economic boycott is well within the category that was expressly distinguished in the *Claiborne Hardware* opinion itself.

PROBLEM

Neighbor, who runs a beauty parlor, urged all of her friends and acquaintances to boycott the beauty parlor of Nancy, a competitor of Neighbor, because "Nancy is a Baptist, a Democrat and a liberal." Neighbor also stated, "I know for a fact that she has been a police informer."

Nancy believes that because of Neighbor's charges, she has lost many of her customers. Does she have an action against Neighbor?

D. APPROPRIATION OF TRADE SECRETS

ROCKWELL GRAPHIC SYSTEMS, INC. v. DEV INDUSTRIES, INC.
925 F.2d 124 (7th Cir. 1991)

POSNER, CIRCUIT JUDGE.

This is a suit for misappropriation of trade secrets. Rockwell Graphic Systems, a manufacturer of printing presses used by newspapers, and of parts for those presses, brought the suit against DEV Industries, a competing manufacturer, and against the president of DEV, who used to be employed by Rockwell. The case is in federal court by virtue of the RICO ("Racketeer Influenced and Corrupt Organizations") statute. 18 U.S.C. § 1961 et seq. The predicate acts required for liability under RICO are acts of misappropriation (and related misconduct, such as alleged breaches of fiduciary duty) committed by the individual defendant, Fleck, and by another former employee of Rockwell and present employee of DEV, Peloso. These acts are alleged to violate Illinois law, and in pendent counts Rockwell seeks to impose liability for them directly under that law as well as indirectly under RICO. The district judge granted summary judgment for the defendants upon the recommendation of a magistrate who concluded that Rockwell had no trade secrets because it had failed to take reasonable precautions to maintain secrecy. Therefore there had been no misappropriation, which in turn was the foundation for the predicate acts; so the RICO count had to be dismissed. With the federal claim out of the case, the district judge relinquished jurisdiction over the pendent counts, resulting in a dismissal of the entire case.

When we said that Rockwell manufactures both printing presses and replacement parts for its presses—"wear parts" or "piece parts," they are called—we were speaking approximately. Rockwell does not always manufacture the parts itself. Sometimes when an owner of one of Rockwell's presses needs a particular part, or when Rockwell anticipates demand for the part, it will subcontract the manufacture of it to an independent machine shop, called a "vendor" by the parties. When it does this it must give the vendor a "piece part drawing" indicating materials, dimensions, tolerances, and methods of manufacture. Without that information the vendor could not manufacture the part. Rockwell has not tried to patent the piece parts. It believes that the purchaser cannot, either by inspection or by "reverse engineering" (taking something apart in an effort to figure out how it was made), discover how to manufacture the part; to do that you need the piece part drawing, which contains much information concerning methods of manufacture, alloys, tolerances, etc. that cannot be gleaned from the part itself. So Rockwell tries—whether hard enough is the central issue in the case—to keep the piece part drawings secret, though not of course from the vendors; they could not manufacture the parts for Rockwell without the drawings. DEV points out that some of the parts are for presses that Rockwell no longer manufactures. But as long as the presses are in service—which can be a very long time—there is a demand for replacement parts.

Rockwell employed Fleck and Peloso in responsible positions that gave them access to piece part drawings. Fleck left Rockwell in 1975 and three years later joined DEV as its president. Peloso joined DEV the following year after being fired by Rockwell when a security guard caught him removing piece part drawings from Rockwell's plant. This suit was brought in 1984, and pretrial discovery by Rockwell turned up 600 piece part drawings in DEV's possession, of which 100 were Rockwell's. DEV claimed to have obtained them lawfully, either from customers of Rockwell or from Rockwell vendors, contrary to Rockwell's claim that either Fleck and Peloso stole them when they were employed by it or DEV obtained them in some other unlawful manner, perhaps from a vendor who violated his confidentiality agreement with Rockwell. Thus far in the litigation DEV has not been able to show which customers or vendors lawfully supplied it with Rockwell's piece part drawings.

The defendants persuaded the magistrate and the district judge that the piece part drawings weren't really trade secrets at all, because Rockwell made only perfunctory efforts to keep them secret. Not only were there thousands of drawings in the hands of the vendors; there were thousands more in the hands of owners of Rockwell presses, the customers for piece parts. The drawings held by customers, however, are not relevant. They are not piece part drawings, but assembly drawings. (One piece part drawing in the record is labeled "assembly," but as it contains dimensions, tolerances, and other specifications it is really a piece part drawing, despite the label.) An assembly drawing shows how the parts of a printing press fit together for installation and also how to integrate the press with the printer's other equipment. Whenever Rockwell sells a printing press it gives the buyer assembly drawings as well. These are the equivalent of instructions for assembling a piece of furniture. Rockwell does not claim that they contain trade secrets. It admits having supplied a few piece part drawings to customers, but they were piece part drawings of obsolete parts that Rockwell has no interest in manufacturing and of a safety device that was not part of the press as originally delivered but that its customers were clamoring for; more to the point, none of these drawings is among those that Rockwell claims DEV misappropriated.

The distinction between assembly and piece part drawings is not esoteric. *A.H. Emery Co. v. Marcan Products Corp.*, 268 F.Supp. 289, 300 (S.D.N.Y.1967), aff'd, 389 F.2d 11, 16 (2d Cir.1968), marks it, and along with other cases declares—what is anyway obvious—that a firm's act in making public some of its documents (or part of a document) does not destroy the status as trade secrets of information contained in other documents (or another part of the same document). It is immaterial that Rockwell affixed the same legend enjoining the user to confidentiality to its assembly drawings as it did to its piece part drawings. Perhaps thinking of the doctrine of patent misuse (on which see *USM Corp. v. SPS Technologies, Inc.*, 694 F.2d 505, 510–12 (7th Cir.1982), and cases cited there), DEV suggests that if a firm claims trade secret protection for information that is not really secret, the firm forfeits trade secret protection of information that is secret. There is no such doctrine—even the patent misuse doctrine does not decree forfeiture of the patent as the sanction for misuse—and it would make no sense. This is not only because there are any number of innocent explanations for Rockwell's action in "overclaiming" trade secret protection (if that is what it was doing)—such as an excess of caution, uncertainty as to the scope of trade secret protection, concern that clerical personnel will not always be able to distinguish between assembly and piece part drawings at a glance, and the sheer economy of a uniform policy—but also because it would place the owner of trade secrets on the razor's edge. If he stamped "confidential" on every document in sight, he would run afoul of what we are calling (without endorsing) the misuse doctrine. But if he did not stamp confidential on every document he would lay himself open to an accusation that he was sloppy about maintaining secrecy—and in fact DEV's main argument is that Rockwell was impermissibly sloppy in its efforts to keep the piece part drawings secret.

On this, the critical, issue, the record shows the following. (Because summary judgment was granted to DEV, we must construe the facts as favorably to Rockwell as is reasonable to do.) Rockwell keeps all its engineering drawings, including both piece part and assembly drawings, in a vault. Access not only to the vault, but also to the building in which it is located, is limited to authorized employees who display identification. These are mainly engineers, of whom Rockwell employs 200. They are required to sign agreements not to disseminate the drawings, or disclose their contents, other than as authorized by the company. An authorized employee who needs a drawing must sign it out from the vault and return it when he has finished with it. But he is permitted to make copies, which he is to destroy when he no longer needs them in his work. The only outsiders allowed to see piece part drawings are the vendors (who are given copies, not originals). They too are required to sign confidentiality agreements, and in addition each drawing is stamped with a legend stating that it contains proprietary material. Vendors, like Rockwell's own engineers, are allowed to make copies for internal working purposes, and although the confidentiality agreement that they sign requires the vendor to return the drawing when the order has been filled, Rockwell does not enforce this requirement. The rationale for not enforcing it is that the vendor will need the drawing if Rockwell reorders the part. Rockwell even permits unsuccessful bidders for a piece part contract to keep the drawings, on the theory that the high bidder this round may be the low bidder the next. But it does consider the ethical standards of a machine shop before making it a vendor, and so far as appears no shop has ever abused the confidence reposed in it.

The mere fact that Rockwell gave piece part drawings to vendors—that is, disclosed its trade secrets to "a limited number of outsiders for a particular purpose"—did not forfeit trade secret protection. On the contrary, such disclosure, which is often necessary to the efficient exploitation of a trade secret, imposes a duty of confidentiality on the part of the person to whom the disclosure is made. But with 200 engineers checking out piece part drawings and making copies of them to work from, and numerous vendors receiving copies of piece part drawings and copying them, tens of thousands of copies of these drawings are floating around outside Rockwell's vault, and many of these outside the company altogether. Although the magistrate and the district judge based their conclusion that Rockwell had not made adequate efforts to maintain secrecy in part at least on the irrelevant fact that it took no measures at all to keep its assembly drawings secret, DEV in defending the judgment that it obtained in the district court argues that Rockwell failed to take adequate measures to keep even the piece part drawings secret. Not only did Rockwell not limit copying of those drawings or insist that copies be returned; it did not segregate the piece part drawings from the assembly drawings and institute more secure procedures for the former. So Rockwell could have done more to maintain the confidentiality of its piece part drawings than it did, and we must decide whether its failure to do more was so plain a breach of the obligation of a trade secret owner to make reasonable efforts to maintain secrecy as to justify the entry of summary judgment for the defendants.

The requirement of reasonable efforts has both evidentiary and remedial significance, and this regardless of which of the two different conceptions of trade secret protection prevails. The first and more common merely gives a remedy to a firm deprived of a competitively valuable secret as the result of an independent legal wrong, which might be conversion or other trespass or the breach of an employment contract or of a confidentiality agreement. Under this approach, because the secret must be taken by improper means for the taking to give rise to liability, the only significance of trade secrecy is that it allows the victim of wrongful appropriation to obtain damages based on the competitive value of the information taken. The second conception of trade secrecy, illustrated by *E.I. duPont de Nemours & Co. v. Christopher*, 431 F.2d 1012 (5th Cir.1970), is that "trade secret" picks out a class of socially valuable information that the law should protect even against nontrespassory or other lawful conduct—in *Christopher*, photographing a competitor's roofless plant from the air while not flying directly overhead and hence not trespassing or committing any other wrong independent of the appropriation of the trade secret itself.

Since, however, the opinion in *Christopher* describes the means used by the defendant as "improper," 431 F.2d at 1015–17, which is also the key to liability under the first, more conventional conception of trade secret protection, it is unclear how distinct the two conceptions really are. It is not as if *Christopher* proscribes all efforts to unmask a trade secret. It specifically mentions reverse engineering as a proper means of doing so. This difference in treatment is not explained, but it may rest on the twofold idea that reverse engineering involves the use of technical skills that we want to encourage, and that anyone should have the right to take apart and to study a product that he has bought.

It should be apparent that the two different conceptions of trade secret protection are better described as different emphases. The first emphasizes the desirability of deterring efforts that have as their sole purpose and effect the redistribution of wealth from one firm to another. The second emphasizes the desirability of encouraging inventive activity by protecting its fruits from efforts at appropriation that are, indeed, sterile wealth-redistributive—not productive—activities. The approaches differ, if at all, only in that the second does not limit the class of improper means to those that fit a preexisting pigeonhole in the law of tort or contract or fiduciary duty—and it is by no means clear that the first approach assumes a closed class of wrongful acts, either.

Under the first approach, at least if narrowly interpreted so that it does not merge with the second, the plaintiff must prove that the defendant obtained the plaintiff's trade secret by a wrongful act, illustrated here by the alleged acts of Fleck and Peloso in removing piece part drawings from

Rockwell's premises without authorization, in violation of their employment contracts and confidentiality agreements, and using them in competition with Rockwell. Rockwell is unable to prove directly that the 100 piece part drawings it got from DEV in discovery were stolen by Fleck and Peloso or obtained by other improper means. But if it can show that the probability that DEV could have obtained them otherwise—that is, without engaging in wrongdoing—is slight, then it will have taken a giant step toward proving what it must prove in order to recover under the first theory of trade secret protection. The greater the precautions that Rockwell took to maintain the secrecy of the piece part drawings, the lower the probability that DEV obtained them properly and the higher the probability that it obtained them through a wrongful act; the owner had taken pains to prevent them from being obtained otherwise.

Under the second theory of trade secret protection, the owner's precautions still have evidentiary significance, but now primarily as evidence that the secret has real value. For the precise means by which the defendant acquired it is less important under the second theory, though not completely unimportant; remember that even the second theory allows the unmasking of a trade secret by some means, such as reverse engineering. If Rockwell expended only paltry resources on preventing its piece part drawings from falling into the hands of competitors such as DEV, why should the law, whose machinery is far from costless, bother to provide Rockwell with a remedy? The information contained in the drawings cannot have been worth much if Rockwell did not think it worthwhile to make serious efforts to keep the information secret.

The remedial significance of such efforts lies in the fact that if the plaintiff has allowed his trade secret to fall into the public domain, he would enjoy a windfall if permitted to recover damages merely because the defendant took the secret from him, rather than from the public domain as it could have done with impunity. It would be like punishing a person for stealing property that he believes is owned by another but that actually is abandoned property. If it were true, as apparently it is not, that Rockwell had given the piece part drawings at issue to customers, and it had done so without requiring the customers to hold them in confidence, DEV could have obtained the drawings from the customers without committing any wrong. The harm to Rockwell would have been the same as if DEV had stolen the drawings from it, but it would have had no remedy, having parted with its rights to the trade secret. This is true whether the trade secret is regarded as property protected only against wrongdoers or (the logical extreme of the second conception, although no case—not even *Christopher*—has yet embraced it and the patent statute might preempt it) as property protected against the world. In the first case, a defendant is perfectly entitled to obtain the property by lawful conduct if he can, and he can if the property is in the hands of persons who themselves committed no wrong to get it. In the second case the defendant is perfectly entitled to obtain the property if the plaintiff has abandoned it by giving it away without restrictions.

It is easy to understand therefore why the law of trade secrets requires a plaintiff to show that he took reasonable precautions to keep the secret a secret. If analogies are needed, one that springs to mind is the duty of the holder of a trademark to take reasonable efforts to police infringements of his mark, failing which the mark is likely to be deemed abandoned, or to become generic or descriptive (and in either event be unprotectable). The trademark owner who fails to police his mark both shows that he doesn't really value it very much and creates a situation in which an infringer may have been unaware that he was using a proprietary mark because the mark had drifted into the public domain, much as DEV contends Rockwell's piece part drawings have done.

But only in an extreme case can what is a "reasonable" precaution be determined on a motion for summary judgment, because the answer depends on a balancing of costs and benefits that will vary from case to case and so require estimation and measurement by persons knowledgeable in the particular field of endeavor involved. On the one hand, the more the owner of the trade secret spends on preventing the secret from leaking out, the more he demonstrates that the secret has real value deserving of legal protection, that he really was hurt as a result of the misappropriation of it, and that there really was misappropriation. On the other hand, the more he spends, the higher his costs. The costs can be indirect as well as direct. The more Rockwell restricts access to its drawings, either by its engineers or by the vendors, the harder it will be for either group to do the work expected of it. Suppose Rockwell forbids any copying of its drawings. Then a team of engineers would have to share a single drawing, perhaps by passing it around or by working in the same room, huddled over the drawing. And how would a vendor be able to make a piece part—would Rockwell have to bring all that work in house? Such reconfigurations of patterns of work and production are far from costless; and therefore perfect security is not optimum security.

There are contested factual issues here, bearing in mind that what is reasonable is itself a fact for purposes of Rule 56 of the civil rules. Obviously Rockwell took some precautions, both physical (the vault security, the security guards—one of whom apprehended Peloso in flagrante delicto) and contractual, to maintain the confidentiality of its piece part drawings. Obviously it could have taken more precautions. But at a cost, and the question is whether the additional benefit in security would have exceeded that cost. We do not suggest that the question can be answered with the same precision with which it can be posed, but neither can we say that no reasonable jury could find that Rockwell had done enough and could then go on to infer misappropriation from a combination of the precautions Rockwell took and DEV's inability to establish the existence of a lawful source of the Rockwell piece part drawings in its possession.

This is an important case because trade secret protection is an important part of intellectual property, a form of property that is of growing importance to the competitiveness of American industry. Patent protection is at once costly and temporary, and therefore cannot be regarded as a perfect substitute. If trade secrets are protected only if their owners take extravagant, productivity-impairing measures to maintain their secrecy, the incentive to invest resources in discovering more efficient methods of production will be reduced, and with it the amount of invention. And given the importance of the case we must record our concern at the brevity of the district court's opinion granting summary judgment (one and a half printed pages). Brevity is the soul of wit, and all that, and the district judge did have the benefit of a magistrate's opinion; but it is vital that commercial litigation not appear to be treated as a stepchild in the federal courts. The future of the nation depends in no small part on the efficiency of industry, and the efficiency of industry depends in no small part on the protection of intellectual property.

The judgment is reversed and the case remanded to the district court for further proceedings consistent with this opinion (including reinstatement of the pendent counts).

NOTES

1. *The Contours of Secrecy.* Comment *f* to REST. 3D OF TORTS, § 39, UNFAIR COMPETITION (1995), states:

> To qualify as a trade secret, the information must be secret. The secrecy, however, need not be absolute. The rule stated in this Section requires only secrecy sufficient to confer an actual or potential economic advantage on one who possesses the information. Thus, the requirement of secrecy is satisfied if it would be difficult or costly for others who could exploit the information to acquire it without resort to the wrongful conduct proscribed under § 40. Novelty in the patent law sense is not required. Although trade secret cases sometimes announce a "novelty" requirement, the requirement is synonymous with the concepts of secrecy and value as described in this Section and the correlative exclusion of self-evident variants of the known art.
>
> Information known by persons in addition to the trade secret owner can retain its status as a trade secret if it remains secret from others to whom it has potential economic value. Independent discovery by another who maintains the secrecy of the information, for example, will not preclude relief against an appropriation by a third person. Similarly, confidential disclosures to employees, licensees, or others will not destroy the information's status as a trade secret. Even limited non-confidential disclosure will not necessarily terminate protection if the recipients of the disclosure maintain the secrecy of the information.
>
> Information that is generally known or readily ascertainable through proper means (see § 43) by others to whom it has potential economic value is not protectable as a trade secret. Thus, information that is disclosed in a patent or contained in published materials reasonably accessible to competitors does not qualify for protection under this Section. Similarly, information readily ascertainable from an examination of a product on public sale or display is not a trade secret. Self-evident variations or modifications of known processes, procedures, or methods also lack the secrecy necessary for protection as a trade secret. However, it is the secrecy of the claimed trade secret as a whole that is determinative. The fact that some or all of the components of the trade secret are well-known does not preclude protection for a secret combination, compilation, or integration of the individual elements.

The theoretical ability of others to ascertain the information through proper means does not necessarily preclude protection as a trade secret. Trade secret protection remains available unless the information is readily ascertainable by such means. Thus, if acquisition of the information through an examination of a competitor's product would be difficult, costly, or time-consuming, the trade secret owner retains protection against an improper acquisition, disclosure, or use prohibited under the rules stated in § 40. However, any person who actually acquires the information through an examination of a publicly available product has obtained the information by proper means and is thus not subject to liability. See § 43. Similarly, the theoretical possibility of reconstructing the secret from published materials containing scattered references to portions of the information or of extracting it from public materials unlikely to come to the attention of the appropriator will not preclude relief against the wrongful conduct proscribed under § 40, although one who actually acquires the secret from such sources is not subject to liability.

Circumstantial evidence is admissible to establish that information is not readily ascertainable through proper means and hence is eligible for protection as a trade secret. Precautions taken by the claimant to preserve the secrecy of the information (see Comment *g*), the willingness of licensees to pay for disclosure of the secret, unsuccessful attempts by the defendant or others to duplicate the information by proper means, and resort by a defendant to improper means of acquisition are all probative of the relative accessibility of the information. When a defendant has engaged in egregious misconduct in order to acquire the information, the inference that the information is sufficiently inaccessible to qualify for protection as a trade secret is particularly strong. See § 43, Comment *d*.

2. *The Relation of Trade Secrets to Patent and Copyright Law.* Federal patent law does not preempt state trade secret law, the U. S. Supreme Court held in *Kewanee Oil Co. v. Bicron Corp.*, 416 U. S. 470, 94 S. Ct. 1879, 40 L. Ed. 2d 315 (1974). The requirement of secrecy, the Court said, makes it unlikely that the policy of inducing public disclosure in exchange for patent protection will be undermined. But if the information is in the public domain or is readily ascertainable from public sources, patent law does preempt any state law that substantially interferes with the use of such information. *Bonito Boats, Inc. v. Thunder Craft Boats, Inc.*, 489 U. S. 141, 109 S. Ct. 971, 103 L. Ed. 2d 118 (1989).

Regulations of the Copyright Office permit deletion of material constituting trade secrets in copyright applications. It has been held that trade secrets are not preempted by the Copyright Act, 17 U. S. C. § 101 et seq. See *Goldstein v. California*, 93 S. Ct. 2803 (1973).

3. *Injunctive Relief.* The court in *PepsiCo, Inc. v. Redmond*, 54 F.3d 1262 (7th Cir. 1995), upheld the trial court's issuance of an injunction against disclosure of trade secrets by Redmond, a former employee of PepsiCo:

> The facts of this case lay against a backdrop of fierce **beverage**-industry competition between Quaker and PepsiCo, especially in

"sports drinks" and "new age drinks." Quaker's sports drink, "Gatorade," is the dominant brand in its market niche. PepsiCo introduced its Gatorade rival, "All Sport," in March and April of 1994, but sales of All Sport lag far behind those of Gatorade. Quaker also has the lead in the new-age-drink category. Although PepsiCo has entered the market through joint ventures with the Thomas J. Lipton Company and Ocean Spray Cranberries, Inc., Quaker purchased Snapple Beverage Corp., a large new-age-drink maker, in late 1994. PepsiCo's products have about half of Snapple's market share. Both companies see 1995 as an important year for their products: PepsiCo has developed extensive plans to increase its market presence, while Quaker is trying to solidify its lead by integrating Gatorade and Snapple distribution. Meanwhile, PepsiCo and Quaker each face strong competition from Coca Cola Co., which has its own sports drink, "PowerAde," and which introduced its own Snapple-rival, "Fruitopia," in 1994, as well as from independent beverage producers.

Sports drinks are also called "isotonics," implying that they contain the same salt concentration as human blood, and "electrolytes," implying that the substances contained in the drink have dissociated into ions.

"New age drink" is a catch-all category for non-carbonated soft drinks and includes such beverages as ready-to-drink tea products and fruit drinks. Sports drinks may also fall under the new-age-drink heading.

William Redmond, Jr., worked for PepsiCo in its Pepsi-Cola North America division ("PCNA") from 1984 to 1994. Redmond became the General Manager of the Northern California Business Unit in June, 1993, and was promoted one year later to General Manager of the business unit covering all of California, a unit having annual revenues of more than 500 million dollars and representing twenty percent of PCNA's profit for all of the United States.

Redmond's relatively high-level position at PCNA gave him access to inside information and trade secrets. Redmond, like other PepsiCo management employees, had signed a confidentiality agreement with PepsiCo. That agreement stated in relevant part that he w[ould] not disclose at any time, to anyone other than officers or employees of [PepsiCo], or make use of, confidential information relating to the business of [PepsiCo] . . . obtained while in the employ of [PepsiCo], which shall not be generally known or available to the public or recognized as standard practices.

Donald Uzzi, who had left PepsiCo in the beginning of 1994 to become the head of Quaker's Gatorade division, began courting Redmond for Quaker in May, 1994. Redmond met in Chicago with Quaker officers in August, 1994, and on October 20, 1994, Quaker, through Uzzi, offered Redmond the position of Vice President–On Premise Sales for Gatorade. Redmond did not then accept the offer but continued to negotiate for more money. Throughout this time, Redmond kept his dealings with Quaker secret from his employers at PCNA.

D. APPROPRIATION OF TRADE SECRETS

On November 8, 1994, Uzzi extended Redmond a written offer for the position of Vice President-Field Operations for Gatorade and Redmond accepted. Later that same day, Redmond called William Bensyl, the Senior Vice President of Human Resources for PCNA, and told him that he had an offer from Quaker to become the Chief Operating Officer of the combined Gatorade and Snapple company but had not yet accepted it. Redmond also asked whether he should, in light of the offer, carry out his plans to make calls upon certain PCNA customers. Bensyl told Redmond to make the visits.

Redmond also misstated his situation to a number of his PCNA colleagues, including Craig Weatherup, PCNA's President and Chief Executive Officer, and Brenda Barnes, PCNA's Chief Operating Officer and Redmond's immediate superior. As with Bensyl, Redmond told them that he had been offered the position of Chief Operating Officer at Gatorade and that he was leaning "60/40" in favor of accepting the new position.

On November 10, 1994, Redmond met with Barnes and told her that he had decided to accept the Quaker offer and was resigning from PCNA. Barnes immediately took Redmond to Bensyl, who told Redmond that PepsiCo was considering legal action against him.

True to its word, PepsiCo filed this diversity suit on November 16, 1994, seeking a temporary restraining order to enjoin Redmond from assuming his duties at Quaker and to prevent him from disclosing trade secrets or confidential information to his new employer. . . .

From November 23, 1994, to December 1, 1994, the district court conducted a preliminary injunction hearing on the same matter. At the hearing, PepsiCo offered evidence of a number of trade secrets and confidential information it desired protected and to which Redmond was privy. First, it identified PCNA's "Strategic Plan," an annually revised document that contains PCNA's plans to compete, its financial goals, and its strategies for manufacturing, production, marketing, packaging, and distribution for the coming three years. Strategic Plans are developed by Weatherup and his staff with input from PCNA's general managers, including Redmond, and are considered highly confidential. The Strategic Plan derives much of its value from the fact that it is secret and competitors cannot anticipate PCNA's next moves. PCNA managers received the most recent Strategic Plan at a meeting in July, 1994, a meeting Redmond attended. PCNA also presented information at the meeting regarding its plans for Lipton ready-to-drink teas and for All Sport for 1995 and beyond, including new flavors and package sizes.

Second, PepsiCo pointed to PCNA's Annual Operating Plan ("AOP") as a trade secret. The AOP is a national plan for a given year and guides PCNA's financial goals, marketing plans, promotional event calendars, growth expectations, and operational changes in that year. The AOP, which is implemented by PCNA unit General Managers, including Redmond, contains specific information regarding all PCNA initiatives for the forthcoming year. The AOP bears a label that reads

"Private and Confidential—Do Not Reproduce" and is considered highly confidential by PCNA managers.

In particular, the AOP contains important and sensitive information about "pricing architecture"—how PCNA prices its products in the marketplace. Pricing architecture covers both a national pricing approach and specific price points for given areas. Pricing architecture also encompasses PCNA's objectives for All Sport and its new age drinks with reference to trade channels, package sizes and other characteristics of both the products and the customers at which the products are aimed. Additionally, PCNA's pricing architecture outlines PCNA's customer development agreements. These agreements between PCNA and retailers provide for the retailer's participation in certain merchandising activities for PCNA products. As with other information contained in the AOP, pricing architecture is highly confidential and would be extremely valuable to a competitor. Knowing PCNA's pricing architecture would allow a competitor to anticipate PCNA's pricing moves and underbid PCNA strategically whenever and wherever the competitor so desired. PepsiCo introduced evidence that Redmond had detailed knowledge of PCNA's pricing architecture and that he was aware of and had been involved in preparing PCNA's customer development agreements with PCNA's California and California-based national customers. Indeed, PepsiCo showed that Redmond, as the General Manager for California, would have been responsible for implementing the pricing architecture guidelines for his business unit.

PepsiCo also showed that Redmond had intimate knowledge of PCNA "attack plans" for specific markets. Pursuant to these plans, PCNA dedicates extra funds to supporting its brands against other brands in selected markets. To use a hypothetical example, PCNA might budget an additional $500,000 to spend in Chicago at a particular time to help All Sport close its market gap with Gatorade. Testimony and documents demonstrated Redmond's awareness of these plans and his participation in drafting some of them.

Finally, PepsiCo offered evidence of PCNA trade secrets regarding innovations in its selling and delivery systems. Under this plan, PCNA is testing a new delivery system that could give PCNA an advantage over its competitors in negotiations with retailers over shelf space and merchandising. Redmond has knowledge of this secret because PCNA, which has invested over a million dollars in developing the system during the past two years, is testing the pilot program in California.

The court found that issuance of an injunction was also justified because employment of Redmond by Quaker would probably cause him to breach his confidentiality agreement with PepsiCo. The confidentiality agreement was not invalid for want of a time limitation. Said the court, such an agreement is not "void or unenforceable solely for lack of durational or geographical limitations on the duty."

The court further said, "PepsiCo has not brought a traditional trade secret case, in which a former employee has knowledge of a special manufacturing process or customer list and can give a competitor an unfair advantage by transferring the technology or customers to that competitor." The situation here was different:

> Rather, PepsiCo has asserted that Redmond cannot help but rely on PCNA trade secrets as he helps plot Gatorade and Snapple's new course, and that these secrets will enable Quaker to achieve a substantial advantage by knowing exactly how PCNA will price, distribute, and market its sports drinks and new age drinks and being able to respond strategically. This type of trade secret problem may arise less often, but it nevertheless falls within the realm of trade secret protection under the present circumstances.

The court affirmed "the district court's order enjoining Redmond from assuming his responsibilities at Quaker through May 1995, and preventing him forever from disclosing PCNA trade secrets and confidential information." Why wasn't the defendant forever enjoined from working for Quaker? Conversely, why wasn't the injunction against disclosure sufficient without the need for the temporary injunction against employment?

BENDINGER v. MARSHALLTOWN TROWEL CO.
994 S.W. 2d 468 (Ark. 1999)

TOM GLAZE, JUSTICE.

This case involves an action alleging a violation of the Arkansas Trade Secrets Act, Ark. Code Ann. §§ 4-75-601 *et seq.* (Repl. 1996), and, alternatively, a violation of a covenant not to compete, both claims arising from Fred S. Bendinger's employment contract with Marshalltown Trowel Company ("Marshalltown"). The chancellor enforced the restrictive covenant, thereby prohibiting Bendinger from working for Marshalltown's competitor, Kraft Tool Company, for two years. Nonetheless, the chancellor refused to permanently enjoin Bendinger under the Act from employment with Kraft or any other competitor. Both parties appealed the chancellor's order to the Arkansas Court of Appeals, which certified the case to us because it presents an issue of first impression that is of significant interest in an area in need of clarification. We accepted jurisdiction to decide the merits of the appeal.

We first offer a recitation of the facts needed for determination of the questions presented to the court. Marshalltown is an Iowa corporation with its principal place of business in Fayetteville, Arkansas. Its primary trade is the production and sale of trowels and related merchandise. Bendinger is an industrial engineer who was hired to work for Marshalltown beginning July 15, 1970, when he graduated from college in Iowa. When he began his employment, no written employment document was executed, but on March 22, 1978, at Marshalltown's request, he signed the following agreement:

> Without [Marshalltown's] prior written consent, [Bendinger] shall not use or disclose at any time, either during or subsequent to his employment hereunder, any secret or confidential information, whether patentable or not, which is disclosed or known to [Bendinger], as a consequence of his said employment except as may be required in the performance of [Bendinger's] duties to [Marshalltown].

[Bendinger], shall not, for a period of two years following the termination of [his] employment with [Marshalltown], directly or indirectly render service to a business competitor of [Marshalltown].

On October 22, 1984, after Marshalltown expanded its business facilities and opened a new plant in Fayetteville whose construction Bendinger was transferred to oversee, Bendinger was asked to execute a second employment agreement. That agreement contains provisions identical to the 1978 agreement set out above, and provided that it is to be construed in accordance with Arkansas law.

In 1993, Marshalltown advised Bendinger by memoranda that he was being replaced as factory manager and being demoted to the position of facilities manager. His demotion was purportedly due to his lack of motivation and imagination, as well as his inability to deal effectively with those employees he supervised. Also at this time, Marshalltown was consistently failing to meet its delivery objectives. Displeased with Marshalltown's actions, Bendinger began looking for other employment opportunities. He responded to a blind newspaper advertisement in the *Northwest Arkansas Times*. The ad, placed by Kraft Tool Company of Kansas, sought an individual highly qualified in the manufacturing of hand tools.

Bendinger told Kraft of his restrictive employment agreement with Marshalltown, and eventually notified Marshalltown of his job search efforts. Marshalltown reacted by refusing to release Bendinger from his employment agreement. He was given three options: (a) stay with Marshalltown and seek counseling; (b) look for an outside position for which Marshalltown would reimburse him up to $15,000 for outplacement services and expenses within one year of his departure; or (c) take the position with Kraft, but if he did, Marshalltown would go to court to enforce the parties' restrictive covenant. On April 17, 1997, Bendinger took the third option and resigned from Marshalltown, and the following day, he entered into an oral employment agreement with Kraft to serve as its plant manager. Upon taking the job with Kraft, both Bendinger and Kraft sued for declaratory judgment in the District Court of Johnson County, Kansas, and asked the Kansas court to declare Bendinger's restrictive-covenant agreement void.[1]

In response, Marshalltown filed suit against Bendinger and Kraft in the Washington County Chancery Court, seeking enforcement of the parties' two-year restrictive covenant, and also alleging that Bendinger's misappropriation of Marshalltown's trade secrets should be held a violation of the Arkansas Trade Secrets Act. On April 28, 1997, Marshalltown obtained an ex parte temporary restraining order (TRO) enjoining Bendinger from working at Kraft. As a condition for granting the TRO, the chancellor directed Marshalltown to post a bond in the amount of $1,000 and, in lieu of an additional bond, Marshalltown was to continue to pay Bendinger his regular pay through May 31, 1997. An emergency hearing was then conducted, and Marshalltown requested that the proceeding be conducted *in camera* so as to avoid disclosing its confidential information to Kraft. The court declined Marshalltown's request, so Marshalltown voluntarily dismissed Kraft from the lawsuit.[2] After

---

[1] Apparently the Kansas proceeding is still pending.

[2] Kraft later moved to intervene, which the chancellor permitted by order entered on June 18, 1997.

the hearing, the chancellor set aside the TRO and allowed Bendinger to work for Kraft, but imposed a protective order on the parties to secure Marshalltown's proprietary information.

The matter proceeded to trial in August 1997. On September 2, 1997, the chancellor issued his decree, denying Marshalltown's request for a permanent injunction under the Trade Secrets Act because the proof was insufficient to show that either Bendinger or Kraft misappropriated Marshalltown's trade secrets. Nonetheless, the chancellor found Marshalltown's and Bendinger's restrictive covenant enforceable, and directed that Bendinger could not work for Kraft or any other competitor for a period of two years, commencing from the date of the chancellor's decree. Both parties moved to amend the judgment, but the court refused to amend its decree, except it did award Marshalltown attorney's fees of $12,000 under Ark. Code Ann. § 16-22-308 (Repl. 1996) for prevailing on its covenant-not-to-compete claim.

As previously mentioned, both parties have appealed from the chancellor's rulings. Bendinger and Kraft submit that the chancellor erred in enforcing the restrictive covenant and in awarding Marshalltown attorney's fees. Marshalltown cross-appeals wherein it argues that the chancellor erred in refusing to find misappropriation under the Trade Secrets Act, in failing to conduct an *in camera* hearing on the TRO, and in not requiring Bendinger to repay Marshalltown the salary monies Marshalltown had been directed to pay Bendinger in lieu of TRO bond money. We now turn to a discussion of the merits of the appeal.

Bendinger first claims that the chancellor erred in his interpretation and application of the law relating to the enforcement of the restrictive covenant. Specifically, Bendinger submits that it was error to uphold the contract, as the chancellor found no proof of either actual or threatened misappropriation of Marshalltown's trade secrets by either Bendinger or Kraft. In support of this argument, Bendinger insists that Arkansas courts have never upheld a covenant not to compete where the employee has not engaged in some act to harm his former employer or where the new employer has not already benefitted from an unfair competitive advantage. Bendinger argues that the rule in Arkansas is that where the former employee has not in some way either used or disclosed secret information or evidenced a clear intent to do so, Arkansas courts have consistently refused to uphold covenants not to compete.[3] Alternatively, Bendinger argues that the contract is not enforceable since it failed to contain a reasonable geographic limitation.

Noncompetition clauses in employment contracts have been the source of litigation for over 500 years. Under early English common law, courts were hostile to employee covenants not to compete and regarded them as contrary to public policy. For at least 250 years, the most cited case on common-law restraints of trade has been *Mitchel v. Reynolds*, 1 P.Wms. 181, 24 Eng.Rep.

---

[3] While we dispose of the appeal on Bendinger's alternative argument, we note that the rule he proposes is more expansive than that recognized by Arkansas courts. Where a covenant not to compete grows out of an employment relationship, courts have found an interest sufficient to warrant enforcement of the covenant where the associate is *able to use* information obtained from his former employer's special training, trade secrets, confidential business information or customer lists to gain an unfair competitive advantage.

347 (Q.B. 1711), which sought a unifying principle to guide judicial decisions in all subsequent cases involving enforcement of a covenant not to compete. *Id.* In that case, Lord Maclesfield noted that there was a presumption that all restraints of trade are invalid, but nonetheless held that the presumption could be overcome. The presumption is overcome by a showing of reasonableness. Thus, it has become equally well-established that *reasonable* post-employment restrictive covenants are not in restraint of trade.

Arkansas has followed the trend in this area by requiring a party challenging the validity of a covenant to show that it is unreasonable and contrary to public policy. Without statutory authorization, or some dominant policy justification, a contract in restraint of trade is unreasonable if it is based on a promise to refrain from competition that is not ancillary to a contract of employment or to a contract for the transfer of goodwill or other property. However, the law will not protect parties against ordinary competition. This court has recognized that covenants not to compete in *employment* contracts are subject to stricter scrutiny than those connected with a *sale of a business*. We review cases involving covenants not to compete on a case-by-case basis. Furthermore, the court reviews chancery cases *do novo* and does not reverse a finding of fact by the chancery court unless it is clearly erroneous. A finding is clearly erroneous when, although there is evidence to support it, the reviewing court on the entire evidence is left with a definite and firm conviction that a mistake has been committed.

We hold that the failure of the covenant to contain a geographic restriction in this case renders it overbroad. In its brief, Marshalltown contends that the failure to supply a geographic restriction was reasonable since Marshalltown competes with Kraft on a nationwide basis and because Marshalltown has established an international market. In support of its contention, Marshalltown points to cases where courts have upheld restrictive covenants even though they contained no geographic limitation. Those cases show that where a company is actually engaged in nation-wide activities, nation-wide protection would appear to be reasonable and proper. *See, e.g., Harwell Enterprises, Inc. v. Heim*, 276 N.C. 475, 173 S.W.2d 316 (1970). Accord *Sigma Chemical Company v. Harris*, 794 F.2d 371 (8th Cir. 1986) (enforcing restrictive covenant lacking a geographical limitation based on Missouri law which permits enforcement where the breach occurs within an area in which the restriction would be clearly reasonable, even though the terms of the agreement impose a larger and unreasonable restraint). Marshalltown also directs us to *Girard v. Rebsamen Ins. Co.*, 14 Ark. App. 154, 685 S.W.2d 526 (1985), and argues that the analysis made in that case should equally apply here. There, the court of appeals upheld a covenant not to compete even though it lacked a geographic limitation.

During oral argument, Marshalltown clarified its position and explained its restrictive covenant banned Bendinger from working for any company it considered a "competitor." Marshalltown defines "competitor" as "any company in the trowel industry that is in competition with Marshalltown for sales in the United States, regardless of where that company is located." Marshalltown suggests that the use of the word "competitor" in its agreement with Bendinger supplies a sufficient geographic restriction, which the court should uphold, but that term as Marshalltown wishes to define it is not contained in the covenant, and we are unable to rewrite the restrictive covenant to supply it. The court has held that the contract must be valid as written, and the court will not apportion or enforce a contract to the extent that it might be considered reasonable. *Borden v. Smith*, 252 Ark. 295, 478 S.W.2d 744 (1972) (citing *McLeod v. Meyer*, 237 Ark. 173, 372 S.W.2d 220 (1963)). In *Borden*, the court cited to the *McLeod* decision with approval for the rule that the court would not vary the terms of a written agreement between the parties; to do so would mean that the court would be making a new contract and it has consistently held that this will not be done. We point out that it is because of the rule expressed in *Borden* that the *Harwell* decision and the *Sigma Chemical Company* decision, referenced above, are not applicable. In *Harwell*, the covenant expressly contained a nation-wide limitation. 173 S.E.2d at 318, 320. Whereas, in *Sigma Chemical Company*, the Eighth Circuit Court of Appeals applied Missouri state law which permitted the issuance of injunctive relief to the extent reasonable, despite the fact that the agreement itself contained a larger, unreasonable restraint. Accordingly, we decline to vary the terms of Bendinger's employment agreement.

We also view this case to be factually distinguishable from *Girard*. There, the restrictive covenant was self-limiting in that it prohibited Girard from soliciting or accepting any insurance business on any account which Girard was servicing for Rebsamen Insurance Company at the time of his departure. 14 Ark.App. at 156, 686 S.W.2d at 527. While the agreement contained no specific geographic restriction, the court of appeals explained that the failure to supply one did not render the agreement overbroad, since Girard was not forced to go elsewhere to open his own insurance business, and was free to solicit and accept business from 95% of the overall insurance market at his present location. In fact, Girard was free to solicit and accept business from 80% of the customers of the insurance company's office. *Id.* In this case, there is no similar inherent limitation in Bendinger's employment agreement with Marshalltown, and we do not agree that the term "competitor," by itself, provides a reasonable restriction. Unlike the employee in *Girard*, Bendinger is precluded from *any* work within the trowel industry under Marshalltown's definition of "competitor." Accordingly, we believe that the chancellor clearly erred in finding that the failure of the parties' restrictive covenant to contain a geographic limitation was reasonable. Therefore, we reverse the chancellor's order because the employment agreement is overbroad.[4]

We next turn to Marshalltown's cross-appeal where it challenges the chancellor's denial of injunctive relief under the Arkansas Trade Secrets Act, since this issue may have merit independent from our decision not to enforce the restrictive covenant. The chancellor below found Marshalltown possessed the following four trade secrets: (a) a customer list; (b) a vendor list; (c) a permashaped trowel blade; and (d) a fourth shift system (computerized manufacturing system). Despite the existence of the trade secrets, the chancellor expressly determined that there was no proof that either Bendinger or

---

[4] By this decision we do not hold that every restrictive covenant that fails to contain a geographic restriction is unreasonable. *E.g., Girard v. Rebsamen Ins. Co.*, 14 Ark.App. 154, 685 S.W.2d 526 (1985). Each case is governed by its facts, and in this case, the facts simply do not warrant upholding the covenant at issue.

Kraft would misappropriate the confidential information. Marshalltown submits that Bendinger's employment with Kraft will result in the inevitable disclosure of such information. Marshalltown points out that a number of courts have found that where an employee's knowledge and skills are inextricably tied up with his employer's trade secrets and the subsequent employment poses a substantial risk that the first employer's trade secrets will be used, such inevitable disclosure will justify an injunction against the competitive employment. Marshalltown maintains that there is evidence, then, of the *threat* of misappropriation of its trade secrets based on the inevitability of disclosure, which it submits is actionable under Ark. Code Ann. § 4-75-604(a).

Recently, this court adopted the inevitable-disclosure rule in *Cardinal Freight Carriers v. J.B. Hunt Transport Services*, 336 Ark. 143, 152, 987 S.W.2d 642, 646. In that case, we recognized that a number of federal cases dealing with trade secrets have held that a plaintiff may prove a claim of trade-secrets misappropriation by demonstrating that a defendant's new employment will inevitably lead him to rely on the plaintiff's trade secrets. Because we have adopted the inevitable-disclosure rule, the only question to resolve is whether Bendinger's employment with Kraft will result in a situation where Bendinger will inevitably rely on Marshalltown's trade secrets. After considering the evidence and testimony before the chancellor, we cannot hold he was clearly erroneous in finding that there is no evidence of any actual, threatened, or inevitable misappropriation under § 4-75-604.

Larry McComber, Marshalltown's president, testified that Bendinger's answers to certain interrogatories showed how Bendinger could not avoid incorporating his special knowledge of Marshalltown's sale information and manufacturing processes into his work with Kraft. In other words, McComber urged that Bendinger would be constantly using the knowledge and experience gained at Marshalltown as a reference for his work with Kraft. Other witnesses, including some employees of Kraft, testified that Bendinger chairs daily morning and afternoon production meetings during which employees discuss engineering matters relating to product quality, equipment problems, and changes in manufacturing processes. During these daily meetings, Marshalltown insists Bendinger will be exposed to issues relating to his engineering background and will inevitably result in Bendinger divulging Marshalltown's trade secrets to Kraft.

On the other hand, Bendinger testified that he had only a general working knowledge of Marshalltown's machines and processes, and that he did not have in his possession any of the company's machine designs or blueprints. Bendinger candidly requested "guidance" from the chancellor as to what was Marshalltown's proprietary information so that he could avoid violating the parties' employment agreement. Bendinger also offered testimony that Kraft circulated a memo pertaining to Bendinger's employment detailing his personal situation and instructed employees that Bendinger was not to be consulted in relation to his prior employment with Marshalltown. In the end, the chancellor found Bendinger's testimony believable, specifically stating in his decree that Bendinger appeared to be an "honest, honorable person who respects Marshalltown's rights to protect its trade secrets." The chancellor also determined that Bendinger had some knowledge of Marshalltown's trade secrets, but that knowledge was "minimal at best," and that Bendinger lacked access to Marshalltown's customer and vendor lists, its blueprints, machine and product drawings, secret formula, or any other written information or material. In the chancellor's judgment, Bendinger's vast *general* knowledge of the trowel industry, as opposed to his engineering expertise, was of far greater value to Kraft than any knowledge of the four trade secrets he purportedly had.

We support the chancellor's conclusion, for a finding of inevitable disclosure is determined largely by the evidence and testimony before the chancellor. Given the fact that we review a chancellor's findings according to the clearly erroneous standard, we cannot say that the chancellor in this case erred in determining that there was no proof of actual, threatened, or inevitable misappropriation. The chancellor correctly relied on *AMP, Inc. v. Fleischhacker* in recognizing that the mere fact a person assumes a similar position at a competitor does not, without more, make it inevitable that he will use or disclose trade secrets. 823 F.2d at 1202. While Bendinger has assumed a position with a competitor of Marshalltown's, that position is managerial in nature and does not require him to use his engineering expertise. So, Bendinger has not even assumed a *similar position* which would render the disclosure of Marshalltown's trade secrets inevitable. We also note, as did the Seventh Circuit Court of Appeals in *AMP, Inc.*, that the right of an individual to follow and pursue the particular occupation for which he is best trained is a most fundamental right. Our society is extremely mobile and our free economy is based upon competition; one who has worked in a particular field cannot be compelled to erase from his mind all of the *general* skills, knowledge and expertise acquired through his experience. Restraints cannot be lightly placed upon an employee's right to compete in the area of his greatest worth. Because Bendinger is only using his *general* knowledge gained through his education and his twenty-seven years of experience in the trowel industry, he poses no threat to Marshalltown's trade secrets. For these reasons, we affirm the chancellor's refusal to issue Marshalltown an injunction permanently enjoining Bendinger from working for Kraft or any other competitor. . . .

NOTES

1. *What's in a Name?* The defendant hair stylists in *Renee Beauty Salons, Inc. v. Blose-Venable*, 652 A.2d 1345 (Pa. Super. 1995), left plaintiff's hairstyling concern and set up a competing business. Defendants then solicited customers they had serviced while working for the plaintiff. The court said there was no trade secret violation:

> It need not be gainsaid that the business of hair styling, like most service industries, requires the compilation of customer information. Many stylists maintain records of customers' names, telephone numbers, hair styling preferences and the like. So, too, in this case, Renee utilized a client record card, which bore at the bottom the notation that the "card and its information is [sic] the sole property of Renee Beauty Salons, Inc. It is forbidden for any employee or third party to misuse or steal salon information." Eventually, Renee's card system

was replaced by a computer system which stored the data on a computer disk. There was no evidence presented, and defendants denied, that defendants had removed the disk to obtain customer information, or had used the computer to print customer lists. Instead, defendants testified that through repeatedly servicing the same customers, as well as through personal contacts with the clients, who in many cases were friends and relatives of defendants, they had memorized the names of the customers. Each stylist, then, when they left Renee for Apropos, compiled from memory a list of their customers, i.e., their friends and relatives, which was then used by the former employees to solicit business for their new venture, Apropos. To consider this information, easily obtainable through any number of sources, the "sole property of Renee Beauty Salons, Inc." is to stretch the trade secret doctrine to the point of unrecognizability.

In *Gary Van Zeeland Talent v. Sandas*, 84 Wis. 2d 202, 267 N. W. 2d 242 (1978), the defendant Sandas worked for the plaintiff talent agency, Gary Van Zeeland, which booked musical groups in nightclubs and other entertainment places. Defendant left plaintiff intending to start a competing agency, and he took with him a list of names of Van Zeeland's customers, but he did not take their addresses or any booking information. The court said there was no appropriation of trade secrets:

> Van Zeeland acknowledged that it would be relatively simple to prepare a customer list—the names of the clubs—in comparison to the more difficult task of matching appropriate talent with those clubs. There is no assertion that any list which matched bands with customers was taken. Van Zeeland admitted that a list of customers without detailed information about club preferences would be relatively useless.

In *Ed Nowogroski Insurance, Inc. v. Rucker*, 971 P.2d 936 (Wash. 1999), the issue was whether a former employee could be found liable for appropriation of customer names by memorizing the names rather than taking a customer list from a former employer. The court recognized a division of authority on the issue of whether there could be appropriation by memorization. It held that under the Uniform Trade Secrets Act (adopted in 41 states and the District of Columbia), it made no difference whether the information was documentary or memorized. A trade secret, said the court, is a

> compilation of information that derives independent economic value from not being generally known or readily ascertainable to others and subject to reasonable efforts to maintain secrecy . . . . If an employee was privy to a secret formula of a manufacturing company, which was valuable and kept secret, it should not cease to be a trade secret is an employee committed it to memory.

2. *Confidential and Proprietary Business Information.* The plaintiff Warner-Lambert Co. sued defendant Execuquest Corp. for misappropriation of business information. Defendant provided executive employee search services:

> Over several days in November, 1996, Execuquest agents made numerous telephone calls to various Warner-Lambert offices

throughout the United States. The Execuquest agents misrepresented themselves by using various aliases and titles, including misrepresenting themselves as employees in Warner-Lambert's corporate headquarters. The Execuquest callers requested information from the various Warner-Lambert offices, including names, addresses, telephone numbers, and positions of managerial employees and of minority and female sales representatives. Warner-Lambert employees disclosed some of this information to the callers.

In holding that the plaintiff stated a cause of action, the court said:

> On an issue somewhat analogous to this one, we ruled that an agricultural cooperative association could protect the names and addresses of its members as a trade secret and prevent disclosure of such information to the Attorney General, because such disclosure would facilitate competitor solicitation of association members to the detriment of the association's legitimate competitive interests, the list would be difficult to duplicate from independent sources, and the list was made available to officers and employees with the understanding of its confidentiality.

Warner-Lambert Co. v. Execuquest Corp., 691 N.E.2d 545 (Mass. 1998).

3. *Employment Agreements*. In *Bendinger*, given above, the restrictive covenant was unenforceable because it contained no geographic restriction. Recall the conclusion of the court in *PepsiCo v. Redmond*, given above, that the confidentiality agreement there involved was not void for lack of durational or geographical limitations. But in *Gary Van Zeeland*, discussed above, the court said an employment agreement prohibiting disclosure of the agency's customer list, without limitation in time or place, was an "unreasonable restraint of trade." Do the different results in *Pepsico* and *Van Zeeland* turn on the fact that *Pepsico* involved valid trade secrets while *Van Zeeland* did not?

In *Vaske v. Ducharme, McMillen & Assoc.*, 757 F. Supp. 1158 (D. Colo. 1990), the court held the plaintiff had no cause of action for wrongful discharge where his employment was terminated because of his refusal to sign a non-competition agreement.

PROBLEM

Michele, a paralegal, worked for Smokem Tobacco Co., a cigarette manufacturer. In her capacity as a paralegal, she had access to Company documents indicating that Smokem's research had established twenty years before her employment that tobacco was carcinogenic and addictive, and that Smokem had consciously controlled nicotine levels in its cigarettes to make them addictive. Smokem considered these documents to be trade secrets. It publicly denied that cigarettes were either carcinogenic or addictive. When she began working for Smokem, Michele had signed an agreement not to reveal any trade secrets that she might learn about at Smokem. She knew that Smokem considered these documents to be trade secrets.

Smokem notified Michele that she was being terminated because of her "violent public anti-smoking stance." She had written and spoken against the cigarette industry, describing it as "corrupt" and "evil" and "a No.1 health hazard."

Before her termination, Michele had secretly made copies of the above documents. After her termination, she sold copies of these documents to plaintiffs' attorneys who were able to use them with devastating effect in cigarette-smoking tort litigation against Smokem.

Does Smokem have a valid claim against Michele for wrongful appropriation of trade secrets? Does Michele have a valid claim against Smokem for wrongful discharge?

E. WRONGFUL DISCHARGE

RINEHIMER v. LUZERNE COUNTY COMMUNITY COLLEGE
372 Pa. Super. 480, 539 A.2d 1298 (1988)

CIRILLO, PRESIDING JUDGE.

Plaintiff/appellant Byron L. Rinehimer, Jr. was president of Luzerne County Community College from 1974 until he was terminated on September 23, 1980. . . . Appellant had brought suit against the Luzerne County Community College Board of Trustees alleging that he was wrongfully discharged. . . .

Rinehimer originally was given a contract for three years with the College. In 1977, 1978, and 1979 the Board extended that contract orally for one-year periods. In 1980, Rinehimer requested several times that the contract be renewed; this the College deferred doing, claiming that their reasons for refusing to consider the contract were pressing financial problems as well as appellant's election as President of the Pennsylvania Commission of Community Colleges, a position which required that he spend time away from the College.

At the same time, the College was undergoing serious problems. Robert Galardi, the Dean of the Business School, and Sam Lesante, the Chairman of the Board of Trustees, were accused of embezzling College funds. Rinehimer brought the matter before the Board; Lesante resigned, Galardi did not. Rinehimer ordered Galardi's termination, and requested a Department of Education audit. Displeased with the audit, Rinehimer then called in the Auditor General's Office and requested that they do an audit also. That audit showed that funds had indeed been misappropriated.

Rinehimer's tactics engendered a great deal of internal unrest, as well as public comment unfavorable to the College. According to the Board, this as well as lack of leadership led to his termination on September 23, 1980. His oral contract had ended in April of that year, so that he was, in effect, working on a day-to-day basis when he was terminated.

Rinehimer filed suit against the Board, alleging that he had been fired in retaliation for exposing Galardi and Lesante. He claimed that three other College officials instrumental in the investigation were also let go after he was fired, and that the Board had rehired Galardi, in spite of evidence against him. At trial, the court refused to allow testimony from the investigating auditor that Rinehimer claimed would show that several employees had refused to cooperate with the audit for fear of being fired, evidence of lost wages, and evidence of criminal prosecutions against Lesante, Galardi, and others. At the close of Rinehimer's case, the trial judge granted a nonsuit. Rinehimer filed post-trial motions requesting that the compulsory nonsuit be removed; this request was denied. Rinehimer then appealed to this court. . . .

The courts of this Commonwealth have long recognized that an employer has the right to discharge an employee who has no definite contract of employment at any time and for any reason.

This doctrine, the "at-will" employment doctrine, was reaffirmed by the Supreme Court of Pennsylvania in *Geary v. United States Steel Corp.,* 456 Pa. 171, 319 A.2d 174 (1974). In that case, Geary, an at-will employee involved in the sale of tubular products to the gas and steel industry, was discharged following his attempts to have U. S. Steel remove from the market a product that he did not feel was adequately tested. He had gone over the heads of several supervisors to a vice-president in charge of sales of the product in his attempts to be heard. Although the product was eventually removed, Geary was discharged.

Geary filed suit; the company's preliminary objections in the nature of a demurrer were sustained. On appeal, Geary argued first, that he had been discharged maliciously, and second that his discharge contravened public policy. The court affirmed the decision of the trial court, finding that Geary had failed to plead facts that would support a cause of action. It found that he had, in effect, made a "nuisance" of himself, and that the natural inference to be drawn from the chain of events was that the company discharged him to preserve administrative order. According to the court, this was a legitimate reason for the discharge. "This hardly amounts to an 'ulterior motive,' much less to 'disinterested malevolence'. . . ." *Id.* at 180, 319 A.2d at 178.

In addressing the public policy question, the court expressed great concern over the company's interest in protecting its managerial prerogative: "The praiseworthiness of Geary's motives does not detract from the company's legitimate interest in preserving its normal operational procedures from disruption." *Id.* at 183, 319 A.2d at 180. It is from this concern that the court's holding arises:

> It may be granted that there are areas of an employee's life in which his employer has no legitimate interest. An intrusion into one of these areas by virtue of the employer's power of discharge might plausibly give rise to a cause of action, particularly where some recognized facet of public policy is threatened. The notion that substantive due process elevates an employer's privilege of hiring and discharging his employees to an absolute constitutional right has long since been discredited. . . . We hold [however] that where the complaint itself discloses a plausible and legitimate reason for terminating an at-will employment relationship and no clear mandate of public policy is violated thereby, an employee at will has no right of action against his employer for wrongful discharge.

Id. at 184–85, 319 A.2d at 180.

We have also recognized, as did the supreme court, that exceptions to the at-will doctrine exist. We have indicated that an implied contract could exist in an employee handbook that explicitly indicates that discharge will be for just cause only. Additional consideration given the employer by the employee also removes the case from the at-will doctrine. Courts of some states have implied just cause requirements in all terminations; Pennsylvania is not among these.

Pennsylvania has, however, recognized the public policy exception to at-will employment. This court has held that an employee who can show that his discharge violated public policy and that there was no legitimate and plausible reason for that termination can make out a cause of action despite his at-will status. This exception is, however, a narrow one, and we have never indicated that it could be considered independent of the employer's right to run his business as he sees fit. In only two cases since *Geary* has this court found that public policy considerations outweighed an employer's interest in running his business: *Hunter v. Port Auth. of Allegheny County*, 277 Pa. Super. 4, 419 A.2d 631 (1980) (employee convicted of assault and pardoned by governor made out claim for wrongful discharge by public employer because there is public policy against stigmatizing former offenders); *Reuther v. Fowler & Williams, Inc.*, 255 Pa. Super. 28, 386 A.2d 119 (1978) (employee discharged either because failed to inform employer about jury duty or because of jury duty; under second theory, damages recoverable because of public policy of promoting responsibility of serving on juries). In determining what the parameters of this exception are, and how they should be applied to this case, we must turn to recent decisions of this court which have analyzed and applied this particular exception.

In *Yaindl v. Ingersoll-Rand Co.*, 281 Pa. Super. 560, 422 A.2d 611 (1980), the court interpreted *Geary* to imply that the legitimacy of the employer's reason for discharge could depend upon its motive and manner of discharging the employee. The court discussed a set of factors to be considered in analyzing the applicability of the public policy exception, analogizing an action for wrongful discharge to an action for tortious interference with contract:

(a) the nature of the actor's conduct,

(b) the actor's motive,

(c) the interests of the other with which the actor's conduct interferes,

(d) the interests sought to be advanced by the actor,

(e) the social interests in protecting the freedom of action of the actor and the contractual interests of the other. . . .

Id. at 574, 422 A.2d at 618.

In applying these factors, the court found that it had to balance the employee's interest in making a living, the employer's interest in running its business, its motive for discharging the employee, its manner of effecting the discharge, and any social interests or public policies implicated in the discharge. According to that court, the outcome of this balancing exercise was the precise extent to which the employer's interest in running his business could be limited by public policy considerations.

This court . . . in *Cisco v. United Parcel Services Inc.,* 328 Pa. Super. 300, 476 A.2d 1340 (1984) . . . redefined the *Yaindl* balancing test: "First, we must discern whether any public policy is threatened thereby; second, even when an important public policy is involved, an employer may discharge an employee if he has separate, plausible and legitimate reasons for doing so." It seems to us that the factors cited by the *Yaindl* court (aside, of course, from consideration of any public policy involved) now go to the second part of the *Cisco* test, that is, determining the legitimacy of the employer's interest.

Clearly, in *Cisco,* this court made the determination that the employer's interest in the operation of his business is an overriding concern for the courts to consider in determining whether a cause of action will lie for wrongful discharge.

The public policy aspect of the analysis still remains important, however. In more recent cases, we merely have seen fit to redefine its parameters. In *Turner,* we noted that while the *Yaindl* test was still a part of the wrongful discharge analysis, the employee had to show a "violation of a *clearly mandated* public policy which 'strikes at the heart of a citizen's social right, duties, and responsibilities.'" This court has refused to find that such a public policy exists where an employee was discharged for actively seeking a position with a competitor, *McCartney v. Meadowview Manor, Inc.,* 353 Pa. Super. 34, 36–37, 508 A.2d 1254, 1255 (1986) (employer has right to expect loyalty from employees); where relations with those under the employee's supervision had deteriorated irretrievably, *Turner,* 353 Pa. Super. at 55–56, 505 A.2d at 261 ("'even an unusually gifted person may be of no use to his employer if he cannot work effectively with his fellow employees'"); where an employee was discharged even though he had done the job well, *Betts v. Stroehmann Bros.,* 355 Pa. Super. 195, 199, 512 A.2d 1280, 1282 (1986) (balance between employee's and employer's interests not a specific, mandated public policy; competitive worldwide economy made it necessary for employer to have flexibility in choosing work force); where false accusations of criminal behavior had led to discharge, *Gillespie v. St. Joseph's Univ.,* 355 Pa. Super. 362, 364–365, 513 A.2d 471, 473 (1986) (as a matter of law university could discharge employee who had been accused of crime of dishonesty even though accusations were proven to be false); and where an employee claimed that every person has a right to earn a living in a job that he chooses, *Marsh v. Boyle,* 366 Pa. Super. 1, 8, 530 A.2d 491, 495 (1987).

The analysis, therefore, calls for a case-by-case determination of the circumstances and policies in question. Rinehimer claims that he was discharged for exposing the illegal activities of a member of the Board and a dean of the College. He appears to be arguing both that a specific intent to harm him is evident from the facts presented, and that his discharge went against public policy as he was attempting to prevent the embezzlement of funds and punish the wrongdoers. Keeping in mind that in reviewing the refusal to remove a compulsory nonsuit we must review the evidence in the light most favorable to the plaintiff and give him the benefit of all favorable inferences, we nevertheless cannot find that the College violated any clearly mandated public policy.

We recognize, of course, that the employer's interest in the operation of his business is not completely unfettered. This court has indicated that that interest will be outweighed by allegations that the discharge was motivated by a specific intent to harm the employee, if those allegations are supported by the facts alleged. We have stated that such an intent would trigger the public policy exception. In *Tourville v. Inter-Ocean Ins. Co.,* 353 Pa. Super. 53, 508 A.2d 1263 (1986), this court determined what the facts had to establish in order to support a claim for wrongful discharge in this situation. It found two instances in which a claim could be made: first, if the pleadings showed disinterested malevolence; or second, if they showed an ulterior purpose for the discharge. *Id.* at 56–57, 508 A.2d at 1265–1266. The court stated that disinterested malevolence would be present if "there were not present a cause, which in every day, civilized life would serve as the basis for the action." *Id.* at 57, 508 A.2d at 1265. In that case, the malevolence would be "pure, unadulterated, and disinterested."

The second set of facts which would support a claim for wrongful discharge here must show an ulterior motive. That is, although sufficient reason exists for the discharge, there is another motive present—desire to cause harm to the employee. The *Tourville* court explained how these facts would present themselves: "The quality of maliciousness could be discovered by the lack of proportionality or the impropriety or viciousness with which a thing is done." *Id.* at 58, 508 A.2d at 1266.

Clearly, in the instant case, the Board has offered a reason for Rinehimer's discharge which is plausible and legitimate—it was distraught over the uproar he had caused in the College community and among the community at large. Further, the Board felt that he lacked the leadership to steer the College through the present situation. The facts do not support a claim of disinterested malevolence.

Similarly, we cannot find that Rinehimer has made out a claim of an ulterior motive. Rinehimer has alleged no facts from which we may draw the inference of malice. Under the court's construction of the term in *Turner,* we see no lack of proportionality in Rinehimer's discharge, nor do we see any viciousness or impropriety here. Taking the facts in the light most favorable to Rinehimer, he was discharged because he insisted upon a publicly conducted investigation of the situation. Rinehimer does not dispute the upheaval caused by his actions among either the academic community or the community in which the college was located. The difficulties of running a college under such conditions is obvious. The Board has stated that it had no confidence in Rinehimer's abilities given the turn of events. Moreover, Rinehimer was working on an at-will day-to-day basis; his previous requests that the Board reconsider his contract had been denied. We can see no viciousness in his discharge.

We also do not see that Rinehimer has alleged any other violation of clearly mandated public policy. He alleges no statutory policy which was violated by his termination. We fail to see that any policy which strikes to the heart of his duties, rights, and responsibilities as a citizen was contravened in this case. Rinehimer merely argues that he was terminated for his attempts to "clean house," and that this violated public policy. We hold that the specificity and clarity necessary to sustain such a cause of action are lacking here. . . .

It was clearly within Rinehimer's duties as president of the College to bring to the Board's attention irregularities with the functioning of that College.

We do not see, however, that it was also within those duties and rights to cause a major upheaval in the functioning of that university, all of which it is clear from the evidence that Rinehimer's actions did. The Board indicated that his discharge was for this reason, and for his lack of leadership. Further, it should be noted that he was well aware that he was retained on an at-will basis. Considering all these circumstances surrounding his discharge, and the manner in which he was terminated, we cannot find that there was not a legitimate business reason for the termination. The College has the right to operate its business in the way it sees fit; clearly a college cannot be of any benefit to the students or community under such turmoil and public comment as were caused by Rinehimer's insistence on a public audit. As this court stated in *McCartney,* "The fact that an employer's actions seem unfair is not enough." *McCartney,* 353 Pa. Super. at 36, 508 A.2d at 1255. We hold that the trial court's refusal to withdraw entry of the nonsuit was proper.

NOTES

1. *First Amendment Concerns.* In *Connick v. Myers,* 461 U. S. 138, 103 S. Ct. 1684, 75 L. Ed. 2d 708 (1983), the Court held that a state employer should "enjoy wide latitude" in employment-discharge decisions over matters of only personal interest, as opposed to matters of "public concern." Where an employee circulated a questionnaire at work concerning working conditions and employee satisfaction, the employer need not "tolerate action which he reasonably believed would disrupt the office [and] destroy working conditions."

But in *Rankin v. McPherson,* 483 U. S. 378, 107 S. Ct. 2891, 97 L. Ed. 2d 315 (1987), the Court held a County Constable violated a clerical employee's first amendment rights in firing her for commenting at work about the attempted assassination of President Reagan: "If they go for him again, I hope they get him." This was a statement on a matter of "public concern," and did not disrupt the efficient functioning of the Constable's office, the Court said.

What about a workplace statement on a matter of public concern that does disrupt the efficient functioning of the office?

2. *Competitive Concerns.* The plaintiff in *Groce v. Foster,* 880 P.2d 902 (Okl. 1994), sued for wrongful discharge after he was fired for suing a third party, who had caused the plaintiff's workplace injury. The third party was a customer of the plaintiff's employer. The employer, on learning of the suit, ordered the employee to dismiss it. On the employee's refusal to do so, he was fired.

In upholding the employee's claim for wrongful discharge, the court said there are "five public-policy areas in which wrongful-dismissal claims may be actionable." They are:

> an employee's discharge for (1) refusal to participate in an illegal activity; (2) performance of an important public obligation; (3) exercise of a legal right or interest; (4) exposure of some wrongdoing by the employer; and (5) performance of an act that public policy would encourage or refusal to do something that public policy would condemn, when the discharge is coupled with a showing of bad faith, malice or retaliation."

The court held that public policy (3) applied here.

In *Roberts v. Adkins*, 444 S. E. 2d 725 (W. Va. 1994), the court held the plaintiffs were wrongfully discharged in violation of public policy when they were fired for buying cars from a competitor of an allied business of their employer. The court said the employer violated W. VA. Code § 21-5-5, which makes it a misdemeanor to require an employee to purchase goods or supplies from the employer "in payment of wages due him, or to become due him, or otherwise." The court held the "or otherwise" clause applied here. It defined this clause to mean "under other circumstances," or "in another manner."

The court gave examples of discharges that were against public policy:

> The seminal case in West Virginia concerning whether an employer can properly terminate an at will employee in *Harless*. See 162 W.Va. at 116, 246 S.E.2d at 270. In *Harless*, the plaintiff alleged that he was discharged from his employment at a bank because he brought to the attention of his superiors that the bank " 'had intentionally and illegally overcharged customers on prepayment of their installment loans and unintentionally did not make proper rebates.' " Id. at 118, 246 S.E.2d at 272.

This court held that:

> [t]he rule that an employer has an absolute right to discharge an at will employee must be tempered by the principle that where the employer's motivation for the discharge is to contravene some substantial public policy princip[le], then the employer may be liable to the employee for damages occasioned by this discharge.
>
> *Id.* at 116, 246 S.E.2d at 271, syllabus. We concluded in *Harless* that a substantial public policy would be frustrated if an employee was terminated because of his efforts to ensure that his employer complied with the West Virginia Consumer Credit and Protection Act and was denied a cause of action for his discharge. *See id.* at 125–26, 246 S.E.2d at 275–76.
>
> Under the principles enunciated in *Harless*, this Court has subsequently recognized numerous causes of action for the wrongful termination of at will employees due to a violation of a substantial public policy. See *Lilly v. Overnight Transp. Co.*, 188 W.Va. 538, 425 S.E.2d 214 (1992) (recognizing that statutes regulating brakes, making it a misdemeanor to drive an unsafe vehicle, and providing for promulgation of safety rules and regulations applicable to motor vehicles may establish cause of action for wrongful termination, where employee is discharged from employment for refusing to operate motor vehicle with unsafe brakes); *Mace v. Charleston Area Medical Ctr. Found., Inc.*, 188 W.Va. 57, 422 S.E.2d 624 (1992) (upholding jury finding that employee was terminated in retaliation for exercising rights under Veterans Reemployment Rights Act, rather than for employee's refusal to submit to drug screening test); *Powell v. Wyoming Cablevision, Inc.*, 184 W.Va. 700, 403 S.E.2d 717 (1991) (upholding jury finding that employee was terminated in retaliation for filing workers' compensation claim); *Twigg v. Hercules Corp.*, 185 W.Va. 155, 406 S.E.2d 52 (1990) (holding contrary to

E. WRONGFUL DISCHARGE

public policy for employer to require employee drug testing unless based upon reasonable suspicion of employee's drug usage or when employee's job responsibility involves public safety or safety to others); *Collins v. Elkay Mining Co.*, 179 W.Va. 549, 371 S.E.2d 46 (1988) (recognizing cause of action for retaliatory discharge where employee was terminated for refusing to falsify safety reports concerning safety inspection at employee's plant in violation of West Virginia Mine Safety Act); *McClung v. Marion County Comm'n*, 178 W.Va. 444, 360 S.E.2d 221 (1987) (recognizing that contravention of substantial public policy exists where employer discharges employee in retaliation for employee's exercise of state constitutional rights to petition for redress of grievances and to seek access to courts by filing action for overtime wages); *Cordle v. General Hugh Mercer Corp.*, 174 W.Va. 321, 325 S.E.2d 111 (1984) (holding contrary to public policy for employer to require or request employee to submit to polygraph test or similar test as condition of employment); *Shanholtz v. Monongahela Power Co.*, 165 W.Va. 305, 270 S.E.2d 178 (1980) (recognizing cause of action where employer terminates employee because employee has filed a workers' compensation claim against employer); *Hurley v. Allied Chem. Corp.*, 164 W.Va. 268, 262 S.E.2d 757 (1980) (recognizing cause of action where employee denies employment to otherwise qualified individual on sole basis that such individual received services for mental illness, mental retardation or addiction).

In a footnote, the *Roberts* court said:

> Had the employees worked at the employer's car dealership, then the requirement that the employees utilize vehicles from that particular dealership may have been a reasonable condition of employment, for which failure to abide could result in the proper termination of the at will employees. In that type of situation, an employer having to explain to customers why the employees drive vehicles purchased from a different car dealer, may very well have a detrimental impact on the employer's business.

Why wouldn't this footnote situation violate § 21-5-5 of the West Virginia Code?

3. *Demotion*. The plaintiff in *Zimmerman v. Buchleit of Sparta, Inc.*, 164 Ill. 2d 29, 645 N. E. 2d 877 (1994), was demoted allegedly for filing a worker's compensation claim. The court held the plaintiff did not state a claim for wrongful discharge. The plaintiff "fails to establish a compelling reason for expanding judicial oversight of the workplace to include review of demotions, transfers or other adverse work conditions that are alleged to be retaliatory in nature." Recognition of a cause of action here would be "inherently inconsistent with the rationale of those cases which have disapproved the imposition of liability where the employee is not actually discharged or forced to resign."

If there were a civil rights or other statutory violation, a plaintiff such as Zimmerman could likely state a cause of action. Why should wrongful discharge be treated differently? Note that the whistle-blowing statute, considered below, covers demotion.

4. *The Tenured Employee:* In *K-Mart Corp. v. Ponsock,* 732 P.2d 1364 (Nev. 1987), the plaintiff-employee recovered compensatory and punitive damages based on a jury finding that K-Mart, his employer, dismissed him "in order to save having to pay him retirement benefits provided for in the employment contract."

At the time of discharge, plaintiff was approximately six months away from 100 percent vesting of his retirement benefits, which were paid in full by the employer. The "reason" for the firing was that the employee misappropriated a can of paint (retail value of 89 cents) and used it to "deface company property" (spraying the paint on a battery cover of his machine that had become "sticky and gunky.")

K-Mart contended plaintiff was an employee at-will, but the court found that he was a "tenured employee":

> K-Mart hired him "until retirement" and for "as long as economically possible." K-Mart agreed in its contract with Ponsock that if there were any deficiencies in Ponsock's performance, the company would provide "assistance" and would "release" Ponsock only after giving him a series of "correction notices." Ponsock could be released only on a determination that his performance "remain[ed] unacceptable."
>
> K-Mart breached its contract; it released Ponsock without notifying him of any employment deficiencies, failed to give assistance to him as promised, and certainly, therefore, could not possibly have based Ponsock's dismissal on a conclusion that the employee's conduct had remained unacceptable. . . .
>
> The company's separation report listed as the reason for termination: "defacing company property, forklift, with misappropriated merchandise, paint, on company time." When the State Department of Unemployment inquired of K-Mart management regarding the reason for Ponsock's termination, K-Mart, in referring to Ponsock's retrieval and use of the spray paint, characterized Ponsock as a thief. . . .
>
> Testimony revealed that approximately ten percent of the forklifts at the distribution center have unauthorized paint on them and that no other employee has ever been fired, either before or after Ponsock, for applying paint to the vehicles without permission. Also, importantly, during a tour of the distribution center by Ponsock and his counsel, K-Mart attempted to hide a forklift that had unauthorized green paint applied to it in a fashion similar to the manner in which K-Mart alleges that Ponsock had done in the first painting incident in January of 1982. One of K-Mart's maintenance employees admitted that he placed the forklift in the out-of-the-way place in order to hide it from Ponsock's lawyers.

In *Foley v. Interactive Data Corp.,* 47 Cal. 3d 654, 254 Cal. Rptr. 211, 765 P.2d 373 (1988), the plaintiff was fired allegedly for reporting to his employer that his supervisor was under investigation by the FBI for embezzlement while working for a former employer. The court held the plaintiff stated a cause of action for "breach of an implied-in-fact contract . . . to discharge . . . only for good cause." But tort remedies were not available, the court said, for breach of an "implied covenant of good faith and fair dealing."

5. *Wrongful Breach of Contract at Will.* The plaintiff in *Mongee v. Beebe Rubber Co.*, 316 A.2d 549 (N.H. 1974), stated an action for wrongful breach of her at-will employment contract, where the employer's termination of her employment was "motivated by bad faith or malice" and was "not in the best interest of the economic system or the public good." The court said that damages attributable to mental suffering, which the plaintiff claimed, "are not generally recoverable in a contract action."

The plaintiff in *Mongee* was fired allegedly because of her refusal to engage in sexual relations with her supervisor. Today such a plaintiff could sue in tort for sexual harrassment.

Regardless of whether a tort of wrongful discharge of an employee at will has been committed based on a violation of a statute or a public policy, could an at-will employee recover for breach of the covenant of good faith that inheres in all contracts, if the employee were fired out of malice or for some other bad reason?

6. *Wrongful Discharge of Person Dischargeable Only For Cause.* The plaintiff in *Smith v. Bates Technical College*, 139 Wash.2d 793, 991 P.2d 1135 (2000), was discharged allegedly because she filed a grievance against her employer. The court said such a discharge was against public policy, entitling her to bring a tort action for wrongful discharge.

Defendant contended that plaintiff was covered by civil service law and a collective bargaining agreement that provided she could be discharged only for cause, and that any claim she had was limited to these remedies. Denying this contention, the court said plaintiff's right to be free from wrongful termination in violation of public policy could "not be altered or waived by private agreement." The court saw no reason why an at-will employee should be granted greater protection than a "contractual employee." Under the tort of wrongful termination, the plaintiff could recover damages for emotional distress and punitive damages, which would not be available in a contractual action.

7. *The At-Will Contract Action Revisited.* Recognizing a division of authority, the court in *Lauture v. Internat. Business Machines Corp.*, 216 F. 3d 258 (2d Cir.2000), joined the "emerging consensus" in holding that an at-will employee may sue under 42 U.S.C. § 1981 for racially discriminatory termination of employment. Sec. 1981 provides:

> All persons within the jurisdiction of the United States shall have the same right in every State and Territory to make and enforce contracts, to sue, be parties, give evidence, and to the full and equal benefit of all laws and proceedings for the security of persons and property as is enjoyed by white citizens, and shall be subject to like punishment, pains, penalties, taxes, licenses, and exactions of every kind, and to no other.

At-will employment is a contractual relation for purposes of § 1981, the court held. The court said "[m]ore than 40 states recognize at-will employment."

The plaintiff did not sue for a violation of Title VII of the Civil Rights Act of 1964, 42 U.S.C. § 2000e et seq. The court noted that there are "more than 11 million employees in firms that are not covered by Title VII."

8. *Political Patronage.* Civil service employees are protected from arbitrary dismissals. In a series of decisions beginning with *Elrod v. Burns*, 427 U.S. 327 (1976), the U.S. Supreme Court held that non-civil service public employees, other than those in policymaking positions, could not be dismissed on grounds of lack of allegiance to their employer's political party.

9. *Wrongful Discharge and Tortious Interference.* The plaintiff in *Tiernan v. Charleston Area Med. Serv.*, 506 S.E.2d 578 (W. Va. 1998), sued her former employer for wrongful discharge arising out of her exercise of free speech. The court held the constitutional right of free speech did not provide a public policy ground for a wrongful discharge action against a private employer.

She also alleged that her former employer wrongfully interfered with her business relationship with her subsequent employer by informing the latter of her involvement as a union organizer. The subsequent employer terminated her because of this involvement. Relying on REST. 2D OF TORTS § 772(a), the court said a wrongful interference cannot occur as the result of giving truthful information to another.

The court noted in a footnote that the plaintiff might have sued her subsequent employer for wrongful discharge arising out of her union activity. Such a discharge is actionable under 29 U.S.C. § 158.

10. *Whistleblowing Statutes.* There are a number of state and federal statutes protecting designated groups of employees from retaliation based on the employees' reporting, or refusing to participate in, employer misconduct. The amendment to Part 1, Chp. 50, of the Tenn. Code (2000) is an example:

> (b)(1) No head of any state department, agency or institution, state employee exercising supervisory authority, other state employee or state contractor shall recommend or act to discharge, demote, suspend, reassign, transfer, discipline, threaten or otherwise discriminate against a state employee regarding the state employee's evaluation, promotion, compensation, terms, conditions, location or privileges of employment, nor may any state employee or state contractor retaliate against another state employee because the employee, or a person acting on behalf of the employee, reports or attempts to report, verbally or in writing:
>
> > (A) the willful efforts of such person or agency or contractor to violate a state or federal law, rule or regulation which had or would have had a material and adverse effect upon program operations or program integrity, or the willful efforts to conceal such a violation;
> >
> > (B) acts which constituted fraud against the state, the federal government, the public or any fellow employee;
> >
> > (C) the willful misappropriation of state or federal resources;

(D) acts which posed an unreasonable and specific danger to the health or safety of the public or employees; or

(E) acts constituting gross mismanagement of a program, gross waste of state or federal funds, or gross abuse of authority;

(2) The head of the state department, agency or institution or other state employee exercising supervisory authority over the state employee may, however, take any appropriate action or appropriate disciplinary action in relation to the reporting or attempted reporting of any information which is believed in good faith by such department head or other state employee exercising supervisory authority to be fraudulent, dishonest or with willful disregard for the truth or falsity of the information.

(3) No head of any state department, agency, or institution, state employee exercising supervisory authority, other state employee or state contractor shall recommend or act to discharge, demote, suspend, reassign, transfer, discipline, threaten or otherwise retaliate or discriminate against a state employee regarding the state employee's evaluation, promotion, compensation, terms, conditions, location, or privileges of employment because the employee refused to carry out a directive if the directive constitutes a violation of state or federal law, rule or regulation, written policy or procedure which materially and adversely affects the operations or integrity of a program or if the directive poses an unreasonable and specific danger to the health or safety of the employee, the employees or the public.

11. *Has the Right to Discharge At Will Outlived Its Usefulness?* An employee at will may have a wrongful discharge claim if she can prove age discrimination, disability discrimination, discrimination on the basis of sex, race or religion, or discharge because of her whistle-blowing activities or other activities protected by public policy. There may also be an implied contract arising out of employer handbooks, employment practices, and the like, permitting discharge only for good cause. What reservoir is left for lawful discharge on the basis of good cause, bad cause, or no cause? One writer, Mauk, *Remedy For Wrongful Discharge*, TRIAL 32 (Sept. 1990), states that the "United States is the only industrialized nation in the world that does not provide at least good-cause protection for discharged employees." He further states that two-thirds of the workers in this country are at-will employees.

PROBLEM

Defendant company employed a woman who was extraordinarily productive and efficient, and well-liked by all of her peers. Her performance evaluations consistently substantially outstripped those of everyone else in the company. The president and principal stockholder of the company terminated the woman's employment. When she asked the reason for her termination, the president said: "You show up the rest of us and make us all look bad. Moreover, you are married and have children, and I believe a woman's place is in the home." Does the woman have a valid claim for wrongful discharge?

F. WRONGFUL INTERFERENCE WITH CONTRACT OR BUSINESS RELATION

FRED SIEGEL CO., L. P. A. v. ARTE & HADDEN
707 N.E.2d 853 (Ohio 1999)

MOYER, CHIEF JUSTICE.

The determinative issues in this case are (1) whether it was error for the trial court to grant summary judgment in favor of Karen Bauernschmidt and Arter & Hadden as to Siegel's claim of tortious interference with contract, and (2) whether it was error for the trial court to grant summary judgment in favor of Karen Bauernschmidt and Arter & Hadden as to Siegel's claim of misappropriation of trade secrets. [The court of appeals reversed the trial court.]

Tortious interference with contract. We reaffirm the elements of the tort of tortious interference with contract as enumerated in paragraph two of the syllabus of *Kenty v. Transamerica Premium Ins. Co.* (1995), 72 Ohio St.2d 415, 650 N.E.2d 863. They are (1) the existence of a contract, (2) the wrongdoer's knowledge of the contract, (3) the wrongdoer's intentional procurement of the contract's breach, (4) the lack of justification, and (5) resulting damages.

In *Kenty* we quoted with approval 4 Restatement of the Law 2d, Torts (1979), Section 766, which provides: "One who intentionally and *improperly* interferes with the performance of a contract (except a contract to marry) between another and a third person by inducing or otherwise causing the third person not to perform the contract, is subject to liability to the other for the pecuniary loss resulting to the other from the failure of the third person to perform the contract." (Emphasis added.) *Kenty* at 418–419, 650 N.E.2d at 866. Only improper interference with a contract is actionable, as reflected in the fourth element of the tort as set forth in the *Kenty* syllabus. Thus, even if an actor's interference with another's contract causes damages to be suffered, that interference does not constitute a tort if the interference is justified. "The issue in each case is whether the interference is improper or not under the circumstances; whether, upon a consideration of the relative significance of the factors involved, the conduct should be permitted without liability, despite its effect of harm to another." 4 Restatement of the Law 2d, Torts, at 28, Section 767, Comment *b*. We today reaffirm *Kenty* and hold that establishment of the fourth element of the tort of tortious interference with contract, lack of justification, requires proof that the defendant's interference with another's contract was improper.

Bauernschmidt and Arter & Hadden contend that the record creates no genuine issue of material fact, and that they are entitled to summary judgment in that they were justified in contacting clients of Fred Siegel and soliciting them to change legal representation. They cite several Disciplinary Rules contained in the Code of Professional Responsibility and argue that their actions fall within those rules. They further assert that they are entitled to summary judgment because a client has a legal right to terminate an existing attorney-client relationship, with or without cause, and to hire a new attorney. *Reid, Johnson, Downes, Andrachik & Webster v. Lansberry* (1994), 68 Ohio St.3d 570, 629 N.E.2d 431, paragraph two of the syllabus.

Appellants argue that DR 2-102(A)(2) authorizes a lawyer to distribute professional announcement cards stating "new or changed associations or addresses, change of firm name, or similar matters pertaining to the professional offices of a lawyer or law firm." However, in this case, appellant Bauernschmidt exceeded the authorization of DR 2-102. In her letters to Siegel clients she not only provided information as to her change of law firms, but also expressed a willingness to continue providing legal services at the new firm ("I would like for us to continue our professional relationship. When you need assistance or have questions, please contact me."). She thereby solicited Siegel clients to change legal representation.

We note that American Bar Association Model Rule of Professional Conduct 7.3(c) implies that an attorney may solicit professional employment by making a direct written communication to persons with whom the lawyer has a "family or prior professional relationship," without labeling it "Advertising Material." However, the corresponding Ohio rule, DR 2-101(F)(2)(e), provides that where written direct mail solicitations are made to persons who may be in need of specific legal services, the mailing must include the recital "ADVERTISEMENT ONLY," of specified size and color, both in the text and on the envelope. No exception from this requirement is expressly included in DR 2-101 for communications to family and past clients. However, the Board of Commissioners on Grievances and Discipline in Opinion No. 98-5 (Apr. 3, 1998) expressed the view that a departing attorney may notify clients of his or her departure from a law firm, identify his or her new location of practice, and indicate a willingness to provide services at the new location without violating ethical standards.

Appellants further argue that Bauernschmidt not only was permitted but had an ethical duty to inform clients with whom she had worked of her departure from Siegel. They cite DR 2-110(A)(2), which imposes a duty upon an attorney who intends to "withdraw from employment" to first "take[] reasonable steps to avoid foreseeable prejudice to the rights of his client, including giving due notice to his client, allowing time for employment of other counsel, delivering to the client all papers and property to which the client is entitled, and complying with applicable laws and rules." However, we do not accept appellants' contention that this rule is applicable to the case at bar.

Bauernschmidt herself acknowledged that the parties for whom she worked while an associate at the Siegel firm were not "her" clients but were clients of Fred Siegel Co., L.P.A. Although her work as an employee of that firm resulted in the establishment of an attorney-client relationship with Siegel clients, Bauernschmidt had never entered into a contractual agreement with those clients under which she personally was obligated to provide legal services. DR 2-110 is designed to avoid the danger of a client being left unrepresented upon an attorney's withdrawal. These dangers were not generated when Bauernschmidt left the Siegel firm. Because Bauernschmidt was never employed by Siegel clients, she did not withdraw from employment by them, and DR 2-110 is simply not applicable.

Moreover, the fact that a client has a right to discharge his or her attorney, pursuant to *Reid, Johnson*, does not, of itself, provide a competing attorney with justification for encouraging the client to exercise that right, and thus does not necessarily preclude a finding that a tortious interference with contract has occurred.

We thus reject appellants' arguments that the Disciplinary Rules they cite provide justification for their actions.

In any event, we reject the suggestion that the propriety of an attorney's conduct for purposes of a tortious interference analysis should be determined solely by application of the Disciplinary Rules. The purpose of disciplinary actions is to protect the public interest and to ensure that members of the bar are competent to practice a profession imbued with the public trust. These interests are different from the purposes underlying tort law, which provides a means of redress to individuals for damages suffered as a result of tortious conduct. Accordingly, violation of the Disciplinary Rules does not, in itself, create a private cause of action. The lower courts in this case correctly recognized that improper solicitation of clients in violation of the Disciplinary Rules does not independently constitute a tort.

Moreover, the power to determine violations of the Disciplinary Rules is reserved to this court. *Melling v. Stralka* (1984), 12 Ohio St.3d 105, 12 OBR 149, 465 N.E.2d 857. Were we to hold that a lawyer's compliance with the Code of Professional Responsibility is an absolute defense to a claim of tortious interference with contract, we would effectively be delegating our authority to determine violations of the Disciplinary Rules to the trial courts. Rather, consistent with our adoption in *Kenty* of Restatement Section 766, which sets forth the elements of tortious interference with contract, the propriety of the appellants' conduct in contacting Siegel's clients and suggesting that they follow Bauernschmidt to Arter & Hadden should be determined by applying relevant legal tests as defined in Section 766 *et seq.* of the Restatement.

We therefore adopt Section 767 of the Restatement, which provides guidelines to be followed in determining whether an actor's interference with another's contract is improper. Accordingly, in determining whether an actor has acted improperly in intentionally interfering with a contract or prospective contract of another, consideration should be given to the following factors: (a) the nature of the actor's conduct, (b) the actor's motive, (c) the interests of the other with which the actor's conduct interferes, (d) the interests sought to be advanced by the actor, (e) the social interests in protecting the freedom of action of the actor and the contractual interests of the other, (f) the proximity or remoteness of the actor's conduct to the interference, and (g) the relations between the parties.

Within this framework the standards defined in the Disciplinary Rules, which govern the conduct of all attorneys, are relevant in determining the propriety of an attorney's conduct in a tortious interference claim pursuant to the Restatement. See Comment *c* to Section 767, at 32 ("Violation of recognized ethical codes for a particular area of business activity or of established customs or practices regarding disapproved actions or methods may also be significant in evaluating the nature of the actor's conduct as a factor in determining whether his interference with plaintiff's contractual relations was improper or not.")

The standards of the Disciplinary Rules are relevant to, but not determinative of, the propriety of an attorney's conduct for purposes of a tortious interference with contract claim. Similarly relevant are the interests of clients in being fully apprised of information relevant to their decisionmaking in choosing legal representation and appellants' interests in engaging in constitutionally protected free speech.

Moreover, Section 768 of the Restatement provides that fair competition may constitute a proper ground, or justification, for an interference with an existing contract that is terminable at will.[5] Thus, where an existing contract is terminable at will, and where all the elements of Section 768 of the Restatement are met, a competitor may take action to attract business, even if that action results in an interference with another's existing contract. Where a defendant in an action for tortious interference with contract establishes that his or her conduct falls within Section 768, the factfinder need not balance the factors set forth in Section 767. See Section 767, Comment *a*, at 27 ("The specific applications in [Section 768] supplant the generalization expressed in [Section 767].")

We today adopt Section 768 of the Restatement and accordingly hold that establishment of the privilege of fair competition, as set forth in Section 768 of the Restatement, will defeat a claim of tortious interference with contract where the contract is terminable at will.

The fact that Siegel clients had a legal right to change their legal representation pursuant to *Reid, Johnson*, 68 Ohio St.3d 570, 629 N.E.2d 431, triggers availability of the justification of fair competition provided by Section 768 of the Restatement, as, by law, their contracts with Siegel were terminable at will. The privilege of fair competition has been recognized in the context of the legal profession.

Pursuant to Section 768, competition is proper if (a) the relation between the actor (here Bauernschmidt and Arter & Hadden) and his or her competitor (here Siegel) concerns a matter involved in the competition between the actor and the other, and (b) the actor does not employ wrongful means, and (c) his action does not create or continue an unlawful restraint of trade, and (d) his purpose is at least in part to advance his interest in competing with the other. Thus, appellants would be entitled to summary judgment pursuant to Section 768 only if the record establishes that each of those elements was met.

---

[5] Section 768 of the Restatement of the Law 2d, Torts (1979), provides:

"(1) One who intentionally causes a third person not to enter into a prospective contractual relation with another who is his competitor or not to continue an existing contract terminable at will does not interfere improperly with the other's relation if

"(a) the relation concerns a matter involved in the competition between the actor and the other and

"(b) the actor does not employ wrongful means and

"(c) his action does not create or continue an unlawful restraint of trade and

"(d) his purpose is at least in part to advance his interest in competing with the other.

"(2) The fact that one is a competitor of another for the business of a third person does not prevent his causing a breach of an existing contract with the other from being an improper interference if the contract is not terminable at will."

We do not find the existence of any genuine issue of fact in this case as to the establishment of elements (a), (c), and (d) as outlined above. We find, however, that the record before us reflects unresolved issues of fact as to whether Bauernschmidt and Arter & Hadden employed wrongful means in competing with Siegel. The evidence is ambiguous as to whether Bauernschmidt and Arter & Hadden used information acquired through improper means in their competitive efforts, *e.g.*, information protected as trade secrets, or information as to Siegel's fee arrangements with clients that may have been wrongfully disclosed. Further proceedings are required to determine whether appellants employed wrongful means within the contemplation of Restatement Section 768 in competing against Siegel. . . .

The question whether a particular knowledge or process is a trade secret is, however, a question of fact to be determined by the trier of fact upon the greater weight of the evidence. *Valco Cincinnati, Inc. v. N & D Machining Serv., Inc.* (1986), 24 Ohio St.3d 41, at 47, 24 OBR 83, at 88, 492 N.E.2d 814, at 819.

Accordingly, we hold that, pursuant to former R.C. 1333.51(A)(3), listings of names, addresses, or telephone numbers that have not been published or disseminated, or otherwise become a matter of general public knowledge, constitute trade secrets if the owner of the list has taken reasonable precautions to protect the secrecy of the listing to prevent it from being made available to persons other than those selected by the owner to have access to it in furtherance of the owner's purposes.

Siegel claims that Bauernschmidt and Arter & Hadden tortiously misappropriated the information contained in Siegel's client list and used it for their own economic gain. We find that genuine issues of material fact exist precluding entry of summary judgment in appellants' favor on this claim. The record demonstrates that the Siegel client list was maintained on a computer that was protected by a password. Hard copies of the list were stored within office filing cabinets, which were sometimes locked. Fred Siegel testified during deposition that he "probably" had told employees that the client list information was confidential and not to be removed from the office.

These facts raise a genuine issue of material fact as to whether Siegel took reasonable actions to ensure that only authorized persons had access to his client list for authorized uses. Cf. *Valco*, 24 Ohio St.3d 41, 24 OBR 83, 492 N.E.2d 814 (finding of trade secret status justified where employer, *e.g.*, kept plant locked, screened all visitors, and disclosed drawings contended to be trade secrets only to suppliers for bidding purposes and only to employees with specific need for them).

Bauernschmidt and Arter & Hadden further contend that all of the information in Siegel's client lists was a matter of public record, capable of being independently assembled into a list, and that this fact precluded a finding that the Siegel list qualified as a trade secret.

In *Valco* we acknowledged, in dicta, that a competitor could obtain and use a trade secret where the competitor itself discovered the information by independent invention or "reverse engineering," *i.e.*, starting with a known product and working backward to find the method by which it was developed.

Id., 24 Ohio St.3d at 45–46, 24 OBR at 86, 492 N.E.2d at 818. In this case, a question of fact exists as to whether the appellants, in effect, "independently invented" their own list of property owners, resulting in a list similar to the Siegel list, or whether they simply used Siegel's computer-generated client list.

Where information is alleged to be a trade secret, a factfinder may consider, *e.g.*, the amount of effort or money expended in obtaining and developing the information, as well as the amount of time and expense it would take for others to acquire and duplicate the information. The Siegel client list was sixty-three pages in length and included the names of property owners, contact persons, addresses, and telephone numbers of hundreds of clients. The extensive accumulation of property owner names, contacts, addresses, and phone numbers contained in the Siegel client list may well be shown at trial to represent the investment of Siegel time and effort over a long period.

The purpose of Ohio's trade secret law is to maintain commercial ethics, encourage invention, and protect an employer's investments and proprietary information. That purpose would be frustrated were we to except from trade secret status any knowledge or process based simply on the fact that the information at issue was capable of being independently replicated. . . .

COOK, JUSTICE, dissenting.

I believe that the trial court correctly granted summary judgment in favor of Bauernschmidt in this case. To come to that conclusion, I resolve certain underlying issues differently from the majority. First, Siegel clients with whom Bauernschmidt worked were not just Siegel's clients, but also Bauernschmidt's clients. Second, the information developed by Siegel as a "client list" may be protectable as a trade secret, but the identities of Bauernschmidt's clients cannot be trade secrets. Third, Bauernschmidt was therefore entitled, upon leaving Siegel, to contact those clients with whom she had worked while with the Siegel firm. Fourth, use of the "client list" by Bauernschmidt for purposes of preparing a mailing to the clients with whom she worked while with the Siegel firm would not amount to misappropriation of the trade secret properties of the Siegel client list. . . .

NOTES

1. *Interference with One's Own Contractual Relation?* It is hornbook law that the tort of wrongful interference does not apply to one interfering with one's own contractual or business relationship. Alex B. Long, *Tortious Interference*, 84 MINN. L. REV. 863, 885 (2000). In *Trimble v. City and County of Denver*, 697 P.2d 716 (Colo. 1985), the court said an employer was a third person, with respect to one employee's interference with another employee's contractual relationship with their common employer. Should not an employee, as agent of the employer, be identified with the employer as principal, for purposes of the above hornbook rule?

2. *Rejection of the Tort of Interference.* The plaintiff stockholder of a closely held corporation sued the two other stockholders of the corporation in *Nelson v. Martin*, 958 S.W.2d 643 (Tenn. 1997), alleging that the other stockholders had wrongfully interfered with his prospective economic advantage by causing

the termination of his employment with the corporation. In dismissing the claim, the court refused to recognize the tort of interference with prospective economic advantage. Quoting Prosser, the court said the tort was "a rather broad and undefined tort in which no specific conduct is proscribed and in which liability turns on the purpose for which the defendant acts, with the indistinct notion that the purpose must be considered improper in some undefined way." The court said such a cause of action would "greatly hamper free competition in the marketplace."

3. *Interference with an Existing Contract and Interference With Prospective Economic Advantage.* One may *not* intentionally interfere with an existing contract solely for the purposes of competition. *Lumley v. Gye,* [1853] 2 E. & B. 216, 118 Eng. Rep. 749. One *may* interfere with existing contracts for valid policy reasons, however. For example, in *Brimelow v. Casson,* [1924] 1 Ch. 302, the court upheld the right of the defendant labor organizers to induce theater owners to breach their performance contracts with the plaintiff show producer, in order to force the producer to pay better wages to his chorus girl employees. The court found plaintiff was paying the "chorus girls wages on which no girl could with decency feed, clothe and lodge herself," with the result that some of the girls were forced "to supplement their insufficient earnings by indulging in misconduct for the purpose of gain, thus ruining themselves in morals and bringing discredit on the theatrical calling."

It is frequently said that one may interfere with another's prospective economic advantage for purposes of competition, provided improper means or motives are not involved. *See* RESTATEMENT (SECOND) OF TORTS § 768. So, in *Adler, Barish, Danils, Levin & Creskoff v. Epstein,* 482 Pa. 416, 393 A.2d 1175 (1978), *cert. denied and app. dismissed,* 442 U.S. 907, 61 L. Ed. 2d 272, 99 S. Ct. 2817 (1979), the defendant lawyer, who left plaintiff's law firm, was enjoined "up until a certain date" from directly soliciting clients that belonged to the plaintiff firm. This holding appears to be based in significant part on the fact that there was a "confidential relation" or "position of trust" between plaintiff and defendant.

In *Macklin v. Logan,* 639 A.2d 112 (Md. 1994), the court recognized the distinction between interference with contract and interference with prospective economic advantage:

> When the existing contract is not terminable at will, inducing its breach, even for competitive purposes, is itself improper and, consequently, not "just cause" for damaging another in his or her business.
>
> The situation is entirely different when the existing contract is one terminable at will or at the option of the party importuned. Where the contract is one terminable at will by the party who refuses to continue performance, there is a broader right to interfere, Natural Design, 302 Md. at 69–70, 485 A.2d at 674. See Harris v. Hirschfeld, 13 Cal.App.2d 204, 56 P.2d 1252, 1253 (1936) (no cause of action lies against a third person who induces another to terminate a partnership at will, because competition in that case may, indeed, provide legitimate justification for the inducement. Cf. Restatement (Second) of Torts § 768. Where the decision whether to terminate or continue a contract with the plaintiff rests solely in the discretion of the third

party, it is not improper or wrongful conduct for one in competition with the plaintiff to provide that third party with a reason for exercising his or her discretion. See Mac Enterprises, Inc. v. Del E. Webb Development Co., 132 Ariz. 331, 645 P.2d 1245, 1250 (Ariz.App.1982) (no tortious interference where landlord had right to cancel its lease with tenant). No matter with what motive or intention a defendant may have acted, it cannot be said in that situation, that he or she acted improperly or wrongfully so long as he or she was legitimately competing for the subject of the contract. Memorial Gardens, Inc. v. Olympian Sales & Management Consultants, Inc., 690 P.2d 207, 211 (Colo.1984); Mulei v. Jet Courier Service, Inc., 739 P.2d 889 (Colo.App.1987), rev'd in part and aff'd in part, 771 P.2d 486 (Colo. (1989) (competitor who intentionally causes third person not to continue an existing contract terminable at will does not improperly interfere with contractual relations if no wrongful means are employed). But see La Rocco v. Bakwin, 108 Ill.App.3d 723, 64 Ill.Dec. 286, 292, 439 N.E.2d 537, 543 (1982) (cause of action for intentional interference with business relationship exists where defendant interfered with relationship between attorney and client, even though relationship is terminable at will). The defendant was held not guilty of wrongful interference by inducing, for competitive reasons, a lessor to terminate its lease with the plaintiff lessee. The lease was terminable by either party on 90 days notice. Defendant was liable, however, for wrongfully appropriating plaintiff's trade name when it took over plaintiff's business in the leasehold.

4. *Whose Contract?* In *Applied Equip. v. Litton Saudi Arabia Ltd.*, 869 P.23d 454 (Cal. 1994), the court said a contracting party cannot be sued in tort for conspiring to interfere with its own contract. There the plaintiff middleman contracted with the defendant builder to supply goods at a markup. The plaintiff also contracted with the defendant supplier for supply of the goods. The supplier and builder then contracted directly with each other for supply of the goods, thus cutting plaintiff out of the contract and avoiding the markup.

The court construed the suit by the plaintiff as a tort claim for civil conspiracy against each defendant for breach of its contract with the plaintiff. Accordingly, it reversed a judgment for the plaintiff, saying that such a suit would lie only for breach of contract. In dictum, it said that the plaintiff could have sued each defendant for tortious interference with the other defendant's contract with the plaintiff, but that the plaintiff had not done so. A distinction without a difference?

In *Plattner v. State Farm Mut. Auto Ins. Co.*, 812 P.2d 1129 (Ariz. App. 1991), an attorney sued the defendant insurer for wrongful failure to settle a medical claim of the attorney's client, an insured of the defendant. Defendant made an offer of settlement, and there was a dispute as to whether the offer was for the entire claim or only for the medical expenses portion not including the bad faith aspect of the claim. The attorney contended that defendant had insisted orally that the offer was in settlement of the entire claim, although defendant denied this contention. Because the attorney thought he was being intentionally put in a position by the defendant of having to be called as a witness to testify as to the oral conversation, he withdrew and the case was settled by other attorneys.

The attorney then filed the present suit, alleging that State Farm had wrongfully interfered with his contract with the insured by forcing him to withdraw from the first case. The court said the attorney stated a cause of action, in spite of the defendant's insistence that the interference, if any, was with the attorney rather than with the client. Said the court, an action for improper interference with a contract under REST. 2d TORTS § 766 (1979) is stated if one is simply "unable to perform their contractual relations because of a third party's [wrongful] interference, a situation analogous to an attorney being prevented by the act of another from representing his client."

5. *Motivation Revisited.* In *Wilkinson v. Powe,* 300 Mich. 275, 1 N.W. 539 (1942), defendant creamery wrongfully interfered with plaintiff's contract rights to collect milk from farmers for delivery to the creamery:

> Plaintiff alleged in his declaration that defendants' objective was to prevent him from protecting the farmers on his routes from false, fraudulent, and dishonest practices in the testing, weighing and price paid for milk. This was denied by defendants. They claimed their reason for deciding to haul the milk was that plaintiff failed to deliver the milk on time or in a proper condition, and that the action was taken to protect themselves and their customers, by insuring a steady supply of good cream and wholesome milk. The testimony is in conflict on this point; but since the jury found for plaintiff, it must be assumed that they resolved this question against the defendants.

In *National Collegiate Athletic Ass'n v. Hornung,* 754 S.W.2d 855 (Ky. 1988), plaintiff, a retired professional football player, sought a job with a television station as an announcer for a series of college football games. Defendant NCAA had the right of approval of any such announcer. They vetoed Hornung. At trial Hallock, Chairman of NCAA's Television Committee, explained the reason for the rejection:

> It is undisputed that during his professional football career Hornung was suspended for gambling activity and that in the Miller Lite Beer commercial, Hornung was portrayed as a playboy. These were certainly legitimate matters for consideration by the NCAA. In view of Hornung's long and outstanding career in the National Football League, it is not unreasonable to hold the opinion that he is more closely associated with professional football than college football. Contrary to Hornung's argument, its acceptance of advertising revenue from the Miller Brewing Company does not render the NCAA's objection to the commercial incredible. The objection was not Hornung's promotional activity on behalf of the brewing company; it was the image portrayed in the commercial. Likewise, Hornung's previous broadcast of college football games is irrelevant as the NCAA did not have announcer approval rights as it had here. Finally, Hallock's vote in 1985, three years after the Committee vote, in favor of Hornung's election to membership in the College Football Hall of Fame and the fact that the Committee took only ten minutes to

disapprove Hornung do not conflict with the testimony given by Hallock. From the foregoing, we conclude that Hornung failed to prove that the NCAA improperly interfered with his prospective contractual relation with WTBS.

After Hornung's rejection, two members of the committee recommended to Wussler and Hanson of WTBS the name of one Crowder who was also a member of the committee:

> Returning to the evidence, the most significant fact presented by Hornung was that after the vote, Crowder was mentioned as a possible announcer by two members of the Committee in a hallway discussion with Wussler and Hanson. Hornung argues that from this it may be inferred that he was rejected so that Crowder could have the job. Even if this incident stood alone, which it does not, and there was no other evidence to explain the action of the Committee, such an inference would not be reasonable. After all, the Committee had seventeen other members and, despite the presence of Wussler and Hanson at the meeting, there was no evidence of improper influence upon the deliberations. No evidence was presented that the other members of the Committee had any knowledge of the hallway conversation or that the two spoke on behalf of the Committee.

Nothing came of the suggestion that Crowder be selected for the announcer position. Suppose, however, he had been selected for the position?

6. *Causation Issues.* In *Wilkinson v. Powe,* considered above, the court said:

> If the defendants in the instant case had merely refused to accept further delivery of milk by plaintiff, they would have been clearly within their legal rights, although this would have resulted in a breach of contract between plaintiff and the farmers. But defendants did more. Their letters of May 29th and June 1st show active solicitation of a breach of the contract and their refusal to accept delivery of milk was merely another step in bringing about the breach.

In *Harmon v. Harmon,* 404 A.2d 1020 (Me. 1979), plaintiff sued his brother and his brother's wife, alleging that they had exercised undue influence on plaintiff's 87-year-old mother and caused her to disinherit plaintiff. The mother was still alive.

In holding that the plaintiff stated a cause of action, the court noted that "[i]f there had been no undue influence," the mother might still have disinherited plaintiff or bequeathed the property to another person. Nevertheless, the wrongful conduct deprived plaintiff of "the possibility" that the mother would not have changed her mind. "The problem then becomes the valuation of the chance of benefit that has been lost."

Chapter 20
CONSTITUTIONAL AND STATUTORY TORTS

A. INTRODUCTION

This chapter introduces the student to the body of law concerning federal statutory and constitutional torts. Constitutional tort claims are often brought against state governments — primarily against municipalities, and primarily pursuant to statutory authorization under 42 U.S.C. § 1983. *See* JOSEPH COOK & JOHN SOBIESKI, CIVIL RIGHTS ACTIONS (1990). Section 1983 became a common source of relief for constitutional violations in the sixties, beginning with *Monroe v. Pape*, below, challenging police and other official misconduct under color of state law. It is unclear why constitutional tort claims against state government entities are more prolific than those against the federal government or its employees. In recent years, the United States Supreme Court has intervened in a number of respects to restrict the availability of § 1983 claims against state entities — in large part ostensibly out of concern that constitutional tort litigation will swallow up state tort common-law claims against state agencies and out of federalism concerns.

Why should there be recognized constitutional tort claims at all — either against the federal or state governments? Such claims can provide a means of avoiding statutory and common-law restrictions, such as immunities and privileges, on tort claims against government entities or individuals. Constitutional claims may also provide advantageous remedies, including access to the federal courts and attorneys' fee awards.

The federal constitution is a shield as well as a sword in tort litigation. It may provide defenses as well as remedies. We have seen in Chapter 18 how First Amendment free speech defenses have intervened with a vengeance in defamation actions, and to a lesser extent in privacy litigation. First Amendment concerns may in due course be extended to other communicative torts, such as misrepresentation and product disparagement. First Amendment freedom of religion and establishment of religion concerns may also arise in tort litigation, as seen below, and there are other constitutional defenses based on due process, equal protection, right to trial by jury.

The states have their own constitutions, which are frequently relied upon for the grant of broader personal protections than those provided by the U.S. Constitution. *See* ROBERT F. WILLIAMS, STATE CONSTITUTIONAL LAW: CASES AND MATERIALS (3d ed. 1999). There have been strikingly few attempts to use state constitutions as the basis for claiming constitutional torts, perhaps because it has not occurred to lawyers to explore this avenue of litigation. State constitutions have been relied on extensively and effectively, however, as a basis for attacking the validity of many state enactments of so-called tort reform.

Some constitutional tort remedies have been embodied in statutes, as in the case of 42 U.S.C. § 1983. Statutory tort remedies, such as those protecting against race, gender, and age discrimination, have constitutional overtones giving the remedies added force.

Beyond constitutional or quasi-constitutional statutory remedies, there is a burgeoning number of statutory tort remedies, particularly at the federal level, which provide a growing source of litigation as well as traps for the unwary. Many of these statutes provide well-established business remedies, such as protections under the Lanham Act. Others, such as civil RICO, age discrimination, and the disabilities acts, are relatively new and are in the process of development. The tort lawyer today cannot practice effectively without an extensive knowledge of statutory remedies and regulations within the field.

In negligence *per se*, discussed in Chapter 5, a tort remedy is implied from the violation of a criminal statute. In the present chapter, more commonly a statute expressly provides a tort remedy for its violation. The constitutional and statutory claims considered in this chapter are not intended to be exhaustive, any more than are the tort claims that are examined throughout the book. Rather, they are representative of the major statutory and constitutional issues that persistently arise in tort law.

B. CONSTITUTIONAL REMEDIES

MONROE v. PAPE
365 U.S. 167, 81 S. Ct. 473, 5 L. Ed. 2d 492 (1961)

JUSTICE DOUGLAS.

This case presents important questions concerning the construction of R.S. § 1979, 42 U.S.C. § 1983, which reads as follows:

> Every person who, under color of any statute, ordinance, regulation, custom, or usage, of any State or Territory, subjects, or causes to be subjected, any citizen of the United States or other person within the jurisdiction thereof to the deprivation of any rights, privileges, or immunities secured by the Constitution and laws, shall be liable to the party injured in an action at law, suit in equity, or other proper proceeding for redress.

The complaint alleges that 13 Chicago police officers broke into petitioners' home in the early morning, routed them from bed, made them stand naked in the living room, and ransacked every room, emptying drawers and ripping mattress covers. It further alleges that Mr. Monroe was then taken to the police station and detained on "open" charges for 10 hours, while he was interrogated about a two-day-old murder, that he was not taken before a magistrate, though one was accessible, that he was not permitted to call his family or attorney, that he was subsequently released without criminal charges being preferred against him. It is alleged that the officers had no search warrant and no arrest warrant and that they acted "under color of the statutes, ordinances, regulations, customs and usages" of Illinois and of the City of Chicago.

... The City of Chicago moved to dismiss the complaint on the ground that it is not liable under the Civil Rights Acts nor for acts committed in performance of its governmental functions. All defendants moved to dismiss, alleging that the complaint alleged no cause of action under those Acts or under the Federal Constitution. The District Court dismissed the complaint. The Court of Appeals affirmed.

... Petitioners claim that the invasion of their home and the subsequent search without a warrant and the arrest and detention of Mr. Monroe without a warrant and without arraignment constituted a deprivation of their "rights, privileges, or immunities secured by the Constitution" within the meaning of R.S. § 1979. It has been said that when 18 U.S.C. § 241 made criminal a conspiracy "to injure, oppress, threaten, or intimidate any citizen in the free exercise or enjoyment of any right or privilege secured to him by the Constitution," it embraced only rights that an individual has by reason of his relation to the central government, not to state governments. But the history of the section of the Civil Rights Act presently involved does not permit such a narrow interpretation.

Section 1979 came onto the books as § 1 of the Ku Klux Act of April 20, 1871. 17 Stat. 13. It was one of the means whereby Congress exercised the power vested in it by § 5 of the Fourteenth Amendment to enforce the provisions of that Amendment. Senator Edmunds, Chairman of the Senate Committee on the Judiciary, said concerning this section:

> The first section is one that I believe nobody objects to, as defining the rights secured by the Constitution of the United States when they are assailed by any State law or under color of any State law, and it is merely carrying out the principles of the civil rights bill, which has since become a part of the Constitution, viz., the Fourteenth Amendment.

Its purpose is plain from the title of the legislation, "An Act to enforce the Provisions of the Fourteenth Amendment to the Constitution of the United States, and for other Purposes." 17 Stat. 13. Allegation of facts constituting a deprivation under color of state authority of a right guaranteed by the Fourteenth Amendment satisfies to that extent the requirement of R.S. § 1979. So far petitioners are on solid ground. For the guarantee against unreasonable searches and seizures contained in the Fourth Amendment has been made applicable to the States by reason of the Due Process Clause of the Fourteenth Amendment.

... The question with which we now deal is the narrower one of whether Congress, in enacting § 1979, meant to give a remedy to parties deprived of constitutional rights, privileges and immunities by an official's abuse of his position. We conclude that it did so intend.

It is argued that "under color of" enumerated state authority excludes acts of an official or policeman who can show no authority under state law, state custom, or state usage to do what he did. In this case it is said that these policemen, in breaking into petitioners' apartment, violated the Constitution and laws of Illinois. It is pointed out that under Illinois law a simple remedy is offered for that violation and that, so far as it appears, the courts of Illinois are available to give petitioners that full redress which the common law affords for violence done to a person; and it is earnestly argued that no "statute, ordinance, regulation, custom or usage" of Illinois bars that redress.

The Ku Klux Act grew out of a message sent to Congress by President Grant on March 23, 1871, reading:

> A condition of affairs now exists in some States of the Union rendering life and property insecure and the carrying of the mails and the collection of the revenue dangerous. The proof that such a condition of affairs exists in some localities is now before the Senate. That the power to correct these evils is beyond the control of State authorities I do not doubt; that the power of the Executive of the United States, acting within the limits of existing laws, is sufficient for present emergencies is not clear. Therefore, I urgently recommend such legislation as in the judgment of Congress shall effectually secure life, liberty, and property, and the enforcement of law in all parts of the United States. . . .

The legislation — in particular the section with which we are now concerned — had several purposes. There are threads of many thoughts running through the debates. One who reads them in their entirety sees that the present section had three main aims.

First, it might, of course, override certain kinds of state laws. . . .

Second, it provided a remedy where state law was inadequate. . . .

But the purposes were much broader. The *third* aim was to provide a federal remedy where the state remedy, though adequate in theory, was not available in practice. . . .

This Act of April 20, 1871, sometimes called "the third 'force bill,' " was passed by a Congress that had the Klan "particularly in mind."

Although the legislation was enacted because of the conditions that existed in the South at that time, it is cast in general language and is as applicable to Illinois as it is to the States whose names were mentioned over and again in the debates. It is no answer that the State has a law which if enforced would give relief. The federal remedy is supplementary to the state remedy, and the latter need not be first sought and refused before the federal one is invoked. Hence the fact that Illinois by its constitution and laws outlaws unreasonable searches and seizures is no barrier to the present suit in the federal court.

[The Court held, however, that the City of Chicago — as opposed to the individual defendants — could not be held liable because municipalities were not "persons" and therefore were immune from liability under § 1983.]

NOTES

1. *Respondeat Superior and § 1983.* In *Monell v. Department of Social Servs.,* 436 U.S. 658, 98 S. Ct. 2018, 56 L. Ed. 2d 611 (1978), female employees complained that defendants, under official policy, compelled pregnant employees to take unpaid leaves of absence before such leaves were medically required by employees' conditions. Named as defendants in the action were the

Department and its Commissioner, the Board of Education and its Chancellor, and the City of New York and its Mayor. In denying plaintiffs' claim for backpay, the District Court agreed with defendants' contention that imposing liability on the City of New York would "circumvent" the immunity from § 1983 liability conferred on municipalities by the Court's interpretation in *Monroe v. Pape*. Reexamining that question the Supreme Court in *Monell* held the City of New York to be a "person" within the meaning of § 1983. Having concluded that a municipality is not completely insulated from a § 1983 action solely because of its status as a local governmental entity, the Court continued:

> . . . On the other hand, the language of § 1983, read against the background of the same legislative history compels the conclusion that Congress did not intend municipalities to be held liable unless action pursuant to official municipal policy of some nature caused a constitutional tort. . . . [T]hat language cannot be easily read to impose liability vicariously on governing bodies solely on the basis of the existence of an employer-employee relationship with a tortfeasor. (436 U.S. at 691-692.)

By what authority can Congress insulate certain persons or entities from the proscriptions of the Constitution? *See* Charles F. Abernathy, CIVIL RIGHTS AND CONSTITUTIONAL LITIGATION at 11 (3d Ed. 2000).

In *Owen v. City of Independence,* 445 U.S. 622, 100 S. Ct. 1398, 63 L. Ed. 2d 673 (1980), the Court held that municipal liability can be imposed under § 1983 for constitutional injury resulting from the carrying out of a municipal policy or custom. And in *Canton v. Harris,* 489 U.S. 378, 109 S. Ct. 1197, 103 L. Ed. 2d 412 (1989), the Court held that a city could be liable under § 1983 for governmental "deliberate indifference" in failing to provide adequate police training for medical treatment of arrestees. But, as noted below, mere negligence of state government officials or employees may not be enough, in some cases, to impose liability under § 1983.

As will be seen, the United States government has waived immunity for negligent acts of its employees acting within the scope of their employment, for which the government is vicariously liable. It has also waived immunity for specified intentional torts of federal investigative and law enforcement officers. A state may also have waived immunity for acts of its employees acting within the scope of their employment. Exceptions to the waiver of immunity, and the kinds of available privileges, may differ for state as opposed to federal immunity waivers. But in a § 1983 action, federal law may preempt state immunities and privileges.

2. *Statutory Violations.* This section is entitled "Constitutional Remedies," but § 1983 also applies when there is state deprivation of a right, privilege or immunity secured by a federal statute, even though the statute does not protect a constitutional right. *Maine v. Thiboutot,* 448 U.S. 1 (1980). In *Maine,* the Court held that the plaintiff stated a cause of action under § 1983 by alleging that the state wrongfully deprived him of welfare benefits to which he contended he was entitled under the federal Social Security Act.

3. *Retrenchments on § 1983.* In two cases, *Daniels v. Williams,* 474 U.S. 327, 88 L. Ed. 2d 662, 106 S. Ct. 662 (1986), and *Davidson v. Cannon,* 474 U.S.

344, 88 L. Ed. 2d 677, 106 S. Ct. 668 (1986), the Court held that § 1983 does not protect against injury from negligent — as opposed to intentional — acts of a state official, at least in the due process context of those cases. In *Daniels,* the plaintiff was injured when he slipped and fell on a pillow negligently left on jail stairs by a deputy sheriff. *Davidson* involved allegations that prison officials negligently failed to protect plaintiff from injuries inflicted by a fellow prisoner. *Compare Albright v. Oliver,* 114 S. Ct. 807 (1994), where the Court held that an arrest without probable cause did not constitute a § 1983 violation of substantive due process. The Court indicated that such an arrest might constitute a violation of the Fourth Amendment, but that such a claim was not alleged.

In *Paul v. Davis,* 424 U.S. 693, 96 S. Ct. 1155, 47 L. Ed. 2d 405 (1976), the Court held that the plaintiff failed to state a cause of action under § 1983 for alleged defamation by a state official because under the constitution and applicable state law reputation was not a liberty or property interest; thus the state action did not implicate a liberty or property interest under the Fourteenth Amendment to the United States Constitution. However, in *Marrero v. Hialeah,* 625 F.2d 499 (5th Cir. 1980), the court distinguished *Paul v. Davis* and held that a cause of action under § 1983 is stated if plaintiff alleges defamation by a state official which results in loss of business reputation or goodwill and the defamation is accompanied by an allegedly unlawful arrest, search and seizure involving violation of the Fourth Amendment to the United States constitution.

It is apparent from *Monell, Daniels* and *Paul* that the United States Supreme Court is concerned with limiting the scope of § 1983 so that it does not unduly encroach on state tort law remedies. What constitutional concerns may be driving the Court's interest in limiting the breadth of the statute? Is § 1983 any longer needed?

4. *Vindictive Enforcement of the Law.* The plaintiff in *Esmail v. Macrane,* 53 F.3d 176 (7th Cir. 1995), alleged that a town mayor had vindictively denied his request for the renewal of a liquor license, and for the issuance of a second license, "out of sheer malice," presumably because plaintiff had accused the mayor of "ineffectual enforcement of the law" and because the plaintiff had "withdrawn political and financial support from the mayor" after he learned "that the mayor was trying to destroy his business." The plaintiff stated a denial-of-equal-protection claim under § 1983, the court said. This was not a case of mere selective enforcement of the law, owing to the additional allegation of "malignant animosity" toward the plaintiff.

5. *A Tort Called "Bivens."* In *Bivens v. Six Unknown Named Agents,* 403 U.S. 388, 91 S. Ct. 1999, 29 L. Ed. 2d 619 (1971), the plaintiff claimed that the conduct of federal agents during a search of his property, his person and his subsequent arrest were violative of the Fourth Amendment guarantee that "[t]he right of the people to be secure in their persons, houses, papers, and effects, against unreasonable searches and seizures, shall not be violated. . . ." He claimed to have suffered "great humiliation, embarrassment, and mental suffering as a result of the agents' unlawful conduct," and sought damages. The district court dismissed the complaint for failure to state a cause of action. The defendants argued that the plaintiff should rely exclusively upon his state

tort rights, conceding that if the agents violated the Fourth Amendment, then they would not have a police power defense to such a state claim. The Court reversed on the basis that:

> *First.* Our cases have long since rejected the notion that the Fourth Amendment proscribes only such conduct as would, if engaged in by private persons, be condemned by state law. . . .
>
> *Second.* The interests protected by state laws regulating trespass and the invasion of privacy, and those protected by the Fourth Amendment's guarantee against unreasonable searches and seizures, may be inconsistent or even hostile. Thus, we may bar the door against an unwelcome private intruder, or call the police if he persists in seeking entrance. The availability of such alternative means for the protection of privacy may lead the State to restrict imposition of liability for any consequent trespass. A private citizen, asserting no authority other than his own, will not normally be liable in trespass if he demands, and is granted, admission to another's house. But one who demands admission under a claim of federal authority stands in a far different position. The mere invocation of federal power by a federal law enforcement official will normally render futile any attempt to resist an unlawful entry or arrest by resort to the local police; and a claim of authority to enter is likely to unlock the door as well. "In such cases there is no safety for the citizen, except in the protection of the judicial tribunals, for rights which have been invaded by the officers of the government, professing to act in its name. There remains to him but the alternative of resistance, which may amount to crime." *United States v. Lee,* 106 U.S. 196, 219 (1882). Nor is it adequate to answer that state law may take into account the different status of one clothed with the authority of the Federal Government. For just as state law may not authorize federal agents to violate the Fourth Amendment, neither may state law undertake to limit the extent to which federal authority can be exercised. The inevitable consequence of this dual limitation on state power is that the federal question becomes not merely a possible defense to the state law action, but an independent claim both necessary and sufficient to make out the plaintiff's cause of action.
>
> *Third.* That damages may be obtained for injuries consequent upon a violation of the Fourth Amendment by federal officials should hardly seem a surprising proposition. Historically, damages have been regarded as the ordinary remedy for an invasion of personal interests in liberty.

A *Bivens*-type action differs from a § 1983 action in that *Bivens* involves a suit against federal (as opposed to state) officials for damages allegedly resulting from unconstitutional conduct. A *Bivens*-type action involves a claim against individuals, as opposed to the government or governmental agencies.

A *Bivens*-type action and a § 1983 action may share the concerns articulated in the *Bivens* Court's rationale above, that action taken by a public official that abuses his authority is qualitatively different from private tortious action. In some contexts, however, there may be viable common-law tort relief for such "whips and scorns" that are markings of "the insolence of office." *Wright v. State,* 231 Mont. 324, 752 P.2d 748 (1988) (Sheehy, dissenting from the majority's affirming summary judgment on a false arrest claim). *Compare Enright v. Groves,* 39 Colo. App. 39, 560 P.2d 851 (1977) (permitting recovery for false arrest).

As noted above, the scope of § 1983 actions against state agents for constitutional violations has been curtailed to substantially exclude actions based on negligence. In the *Bivens* case of *Farmer v. Brennan,* 114 S. Ct. 1970 (1994), alleging an Eighth Amendment claim (cruel and unusual punishment), the Court held that prison officials could not be liable for failure to provide adequate inmate protection unless they were guilty of "subjective deliberate indifference." The Eighth Amendment is not violated unless the official

> knows of and disregards an excessive risk to inmate health or safety; the official must both be aware of facts from which the inference could be drawn that a substantial risk of serious harm exists, and he must also draw the inference.

The Court reached this result because the Eighth Amendment "does not outlaw cruel and unusual 'conditions'; it outlaws cruel and unusual 'punishments'."

6. *Congressional Reaction to Bivens and Its Progeny.* The United States has waived its sovereign immunity and is liable for tort claims against it "in the same manner and to the same extent as a private individual under like circumstances." 28 U.S.C. § 2674. However, 28 U.S.C. § 2680 contains a number of exceptions, including § 2680(h) which provides for no waiver of immunity for: "Any claim arising out of assault, battery, false imprisonment, false arrest, malicious prosecution, abuse of process, libel, slander, misrepresentation, deceit, or interference with contract rights." What do you think motivated Congress to exempt these intentional torts from the general waiver of immunity under the Federal Tort Claims Act?

In 1974 Congress amended 28 U.S.C. § 2680(h) to provide for a waiver of tort immunity "with regard to acts or omissions of investigative or law enforcement officers of the United States Government" which result in claims for "assault, battery, false imprisonment, false arrest, abuse of process, or malicious prosecution." An "investigative or law enforcement officer" is defined for purposes of this amendment as "any officer of the United States who is empowered by law to execute searches, to seize evidence, or to make arrests for violations of Federal law."

In 1988 Congress enacted the Federal Employees Liability Reform and Tort Compensation Act, 28 U.S.C. § 2671 *et seq.,* providing an exclusive remedy against the United States government for any action that can be brought against the government under the Federal Tort Claims Act for negligent or wrongful acts or omissions "of any employee of the Government while acting within the scope of his office or employment;" provided, however, that this exclusive-remedy provision does not apply "to a civil action against an employee of the Government . . . which is brought for a violation of the Constitution of the United States." § 2679(b). Why do you suppose Congress left open the possibility of suing federal employees for constitutional violations?

A *Bivens* remedy may be asserted in addition to a remedy under the Federal Tort Claims Act (FTCA), and the *Bivens* remedy may be more effective since a jury trial may be had and punitive damages recovered under *Bivens*, but not under the FTCA. *Carlson v. Green*, 446 U.S. 14, 100 S. Ct. 1468, 64 L. Ed. 2d 15 (1980). *Carlson* indicates that Congress could preempt a *Bivens* remedy through the FTCA if it expressly chose to do so.

7. *Bivens: A Hollow Victory?* Since *Bivens* was decided in 1971, over 12,000 *Bivens*-type actions have been filed, alleging, among other things, violations of the First, Fourth, Fifth, Sixth and Eighth Amendments to the United States Constitution. "By 1982 roughly one out of every 300 federal officials was named as a defendant in a pending *Bivens* action." However, owing to procedural and other difficulties, the suits have met with very little success. "Of the same 12,000 *Bivens* suits filed, only thirty have resulted in judgments on behalf of plaintiffs. Of these, a number have been reversed on appeal and only four judgments have actually been paid by the individual federal defendants. Moreover, very few *Bivens* cases have settled with any money paid to the plaintiff." Rosen, *The Bivens Constitutional Tort: An Unfulfilled Promise,* 67 N.C. L. Rev. 337, 342–344 (1989).

PROBLEM

An agent of the FBI induces a city police officer to blow up the plaintiff's house in hopes of frightening the plaintiff so that she will cooperate in an investigation of illegal drug trafficking. The agent is mistaken in believing that plaintiff knows anything about or is in any way involved in trafficking. The police officer, acting on the agent's request, blows up plaintiff's house at a time when he believes plaintiff is absent from the house. In fact, however, plaintiff is inside the house and is badly injured by the explosion.

Discuss the possible *Bivens*, FTCA, and § 1983 tort claims of the plaintiff against the police officer, the city (the officer's employer), the agent, and the United States.

PAUL v. WATCHTOWER BIBLE & TRACT SOCIETY
819 F.2d 875 (9th Cir. 1987)

REINHARDT, CIRCUIT JUDGE.

Janice Paul, a former member of the Jehovah's Witness Church, appeals from the grant of summary judgment in favor of defendants, the corporate arms of the Governing Body of Jehovah's Witnesses. Paul contends that she is being "shunned" by adherents of the Jehovah's Witness faith. . . . Because the practice of shunning is a part of the faith of the Jehovah's Witnesses, we find that the "free exercise" provision of the United States Constitution and thus of the Washington State Constitution precludes the plaintiff from prevailing. The defendants have a constitutionally protected privilege to engage in the practice of shunning. Accordingly, we affirm the grant of summary judgment. . . .

Janice Paul was raised as a Jehovah's Witness . . . officially joined the Witnesses and was baptized.

According to Paul, she was an active member of the congregation, devoting an average of 40 hours per month in door-to-door distribution of the Witnesses' publications. In addition to engaging in evening home bible study, she attended church with her family approximately 20 hours per month. She eventually married another member of the Jehovah's Witnesses.

In 1975, Paul's parents were "disfellowshipped" from the Church. According to Paul, her parents' expulsion resulted from internal discord within their congregation. The Elders of the Lower Valley Congregation told Paul that she and her husband should not discuss with other members their feeling that her parents had been unjustly disfellowshipped. That advice was underscored by the potential sanction of her own disfellowship were she to challenge the decision.

Sometime after the Elders' warning, Paul decided that she no longer wished to belong to the congregation, or to remain affiliated with the Jehovah's Witnesses. In November 1975, Paul wrote a letter to the congregation withdrawing from the Church.

The Witnesses are a very close community and have developed an elaborate set of rules governing membership. The Church has four basic categories of membership, non-membership or former membership status; they are: members, non-members, disfellowshipped persons, and disassociated persons. "Disfellowshipped persons" are former members who have been excommunicated from the Church. One consequence of disfellowship is "shunning," a form of ostracism. Members of the Jehovah's Witness community are prohibited — under threat of their own disfellowship — from having any contact with disfellowshipped persons and may not even greet them. Family members who do not live in the same house may conduct necessary family business with disfellowshipped relatives but may not communicate with them on any other subject. Shunning purportedly has its roots in early Christianity and various religious groups in our country engage in the practice including the Amish, the Mennonites, and of course, the Jehovah's Witnesses.

"Disassociated persons" are former members who have voluntarily left the Jehovah's Witness faith. At the time Paul disassociated, there was no express sanction for withdrawing from membership. In fact, because of the close nature of many Jehovah's Witness communities, disassociated persons were still consulted in secular matters, *e.g.*, legal or business advice, although they were no longer members of the Church. In Paul's case, for example, after having moved from the area, she returned for a visit in 1980, saw Church members and was warmly greeted.

In September 1981, the Governing Body of Jehovah's Witnesses, acting through the defendants — Watchtower Bible and Tract Society of Pennsylvania, Inc., and the Watchtower Bible and Tract Society of New York, Inc. — issued a new interpretation of the rules governing disassociated persons. The distinction between disfellowshipped and disassociated persons was, for all practical purposes, abolished and disassociated persons were to be treated in the same manner as the disfellowshipped. The September 15, 1981 issue of *The Watchtower,* an official publication of the Church, contained an article entitled "Disfellowshipping — how to view it." The article included the following discussion:

THOSE WHO DISASSOCIATE THEMSELVES

> . . . Persons who make themselves "not of our sort" by deliberately rejecting the faith and beliefs of Jehovah's Witnesses should appropriately be viewed and treated as are those who have been disfellowshipped for wrongdoing.

The Watchtower article based its announcement on a reading of various passages of the Bible, including 1 John 2:19 and Revelations 19:17–21. The article noted further that "[a]s distinct from some personal 'enemy' or worldly man in authority who opposed Christians, a . . . disassociated person who is trying to promote or justify his apostate thinking or is continuing in his ungodly conduct is certainly not one to whom to wish 'Peace' [understood as a greeting] (1 Tim. 2:1, 2)." Finally, the article stated that if "a Christian were to throw in his lot with a wrongdoer who . . . has disassociated himself, . . . the Elders . . . would admonish him and, if necessary, 'reprove him with severity.'" (*citing, inter alia,* Matt. 18:18, Gal. 6:1, Titus 1:13).

Three years after this announcement in *The Watchtower,* Paul visited her parents, who at that time lived in Soap Lake, Washington. There, she approached a Witness who had been a close childhood friend and was told by this person: "I can't speak to you. You are disfellowshipped." Similarly, in August 1984, Paul returned to the area of her former congregation. She tried to call on some of her friends. These people told Paul that she was to be treated as if she had been disfellowshipped and that they could not speak with her. At one point, she attempted to attend a Tupperware party at the home of a Witness. Paul was informed by the Church members present that the Elders had instructed them not to speak with her.

Upset by her shunning by her former friends and co-religionists, Paul, a resident of Alaska, brought suit in Washington State Superior Court alleging common law torts of defamation, invasion of privacy, fraud, and outrageous conduct. . . .

Shunning is a practice engaged in by Jehovah's Witnesses pursuant to their interpretation of canonical text, and we are not free to reinterpret that text. Under both the United States and Washington Constitutions, the defendants are entitled to the free exercise of their religious beliefs. As the Washington Supreme Court has stated, "[t]here is no question that our state constitution protects the free exercise of religious beliefs (Const. art. 1, § 11 (amend. 34))." *Carrieri v. Bush,* 69 Wash. 2d 536, 419 P.2d 132, 137 (Wash. 1966).

. . . Permitting prosecution of a cause of action in tort, while not criminalizing the conduct at issue, would make shunning an "unlawful act." *Langford v. United States,* 101 U.S. 341, 345, 25 L. Ed. 1010 (1880) ("[T]he very essence of a tort is that it is an unlawful act."). Imposing tort liability for shunning on the Church or its members would in the long run have the same effect as prohibiting the practice and would compel the Church to abandon part of its religious teachings. Were we to permit recovery, "'the pressure . . . to forego that practice [would be] unmistakable,'" *Thomas v. Review Bd. of Indiana Employment Secur. Div.,* 450 U.S. 707, 717, 101 S. Ct. 1425, 67 L. Ed. 2d 624 (1981) (*quoting Sherbert v. Verner,* 374 U.S. 398, 404 (1963)). The Church and its members would risk substantial damages every time a former Church member was shunned. In sum, a state tort law prohibition against shunning would directly restrict the free exercise of the Jehovah's Witnesses' religious faith . . . .

We find the practice of shunning not to constitute a sufficient threat to the peace, safety, or morality of the community as to warrant state intervention. The test for upholding a direct burden on religious practices is as stringent as any imposed under our Constitution. Only in extreme and unusual cases has the imposition of a direct burden on religion been upheld. *See, e.g., Reynolds v. United States,* 98 U.S. 145, 25 L. Ed. 244 (1878) (polygamy); *Hill v. State,* 38 Ala. App. 404, 88 So. 2d 880 (1956) (snake handling). The harms suffered by Paul as a result of her shunning by the Jehovah's Witnesses are clearly not of the type that would justify the imposition of tort liability for religious conduct. No physical assault or battery occurred. Intangible or emotional harms cannot ordinarily serve as a basis for maintaining a tort cause of action against a church for its practices — or against its members. . . . Offense to someone's sensibilities resulting from religious conduct is simply not actionable in tort. Without society's tolerance of offenses to sensibility, the protection of religious differences mandated by the First Amendment would be meaningless.

A religious organization has a defense of constitutional privilege to claims that it has caused intangible harms — in most, if not all, circumstances.[1] As the United States Supreme Court has observed, "[t]he values underlying these two provisions [of the First Amendment] relating to religion have been zealously protected, sometimes even at the expense of others' interests." *Wisconsin v. Yoder,* 406 U.S. 205, 32 L. Ed. 2d 15, 92 S. Ct. 1526 (1972). . . .

NOTES

1. *A Different Kind of Shunning?* In *Bear v. Reformed Mennonite Church,* 462 Pa. 330, 341 A.2d 105 (1975), the plaintiff was held to have stated a cause of action against the defendant church and its bishops:

> Count one of the complaint was against all of the appellees and alleged that appellant was excommunicated from appellee church for his criticism of the teachings and practices of both the church and its bishops. It was further alleged that the church and bishops, as part of the excommunication, ordered that all members of the church must "shun" appellant in all business and social matters. ("Shunning," as practiced by the church, involves total boycotting of appellant by other members of the church, including his wife and children, under pain that they themselves be excommunicated and shunned.) Appellant, in his complaint in equity, alleged that because of his being "shunned," his business is in collapse since he is unable to hire workers, obtain loans or market his produce. Moreover, appellant alleged that his

---

[1] We also note that Paul has not presented evidence of actual malice sufficient to overcome the constitutional privilege afforded the defendants. While the privilege is a qualified one, the only evidence Paul has presented is that Church members have shunned her at the direction of the Church; she has neither alleged nor shown that members of the Church hierarchy were motivated by reasons unrelated to their interpretation of the dictates of their religion.

family is in collapse because his wife and children do not speak to him or have any social or physical contact with him. . . .

In count two of the complaint, appellant alleged that appellee Glenn M. Gross, while a bishop of appellee church, is also the brother of appellant's wife and that he has "advised" or "encouraged" her to "shun and boycott" appellant, resulting in appellant's wife not having any social or physical contact with him. . . .

In our opinion, the complaint, in Counts I and II, raises issues that the "shunning" practice of appellee church and the conduct of the individuals may be an excessive interference within areas of "paramount state concern," *i.e.,* the maintenance of marriage and family relationship, alienation of affection, and the tortious interference with a business relationship, which the courts of this Commonwealth may have authority to regulate, even in light of the "Establishment" and "Free Exercise" clauses of the First Amendment.

2. *How to Judge Motive?* In *Hester v. Barnett,* 723 S.W.2d 544 (Mo. App. 1987), a husband and wife alleged that a Baptist minister advised and encouraged the wife to leave her husband and indicated that if she did leave him, the church community would extend to her its welcome. The court held that a suit for alienation of affections would not lie if the minister were only advocating a religious faith, but the action would lie if the minister acted out of improper motive.

3. *Snake-Handling and Poison-Drinking.* Relying in part on a state statute, the court in *State ex rel. Swann v. Pack,* 527 S.W.2d 99 (Tenn. 1975), directed the trial judge to "enter an injunction perpetually enjoining and restraining all parties respondent from handling, displaying or exhibiting dangerous and poisonous snakes or from consuming strychnine or any other poisonous substance, within the confines of the State of Tennessee." The respondents claimed a religious right to such conduct, relying on the Sixteenth Chapter of Mark, verses 17–18 of the Authorized or King James Version of the Bible. Rejecting this claim, the court said that the religious protections of the state and federal constitutions did not prevent a state from limiting, curtailing or restraining a religious practice "to the point of outright prohibition, where it involves a clear and present danger to the interests of society."

4. *Hate Crime Statutes.* The plaintiff in *Renander v. Inc., Ltd.,* 500 N.W.2d 39 (Iowa 1993), was refused service at a restaurant because of his "statements on a previous occasion against homosexuality." He then brought suit against the restaurant for damages, basing his claims on the state's "hate statute" making it a crime for any person to "injure" another person "in the free exercise or enjoyment of any right or privilege secured to that person by the Constitution or laws of the United States." The court dismissed his claims, saying that the statute protected only against "physical injury to person or property . . . and not harm to an intangible right such as free speech." The court noted that "several other states clearly require physical violence or the commission of a physically violent crime against a victim to constitute a violation of their respective hate crime statutes."

Why didn't the plaintiff sue directly on the constitution, rather than on the statute?

5. *Inverse Condemnation and the Emergency Doctrine*. In a 4-3 decision, the California Supreme Court denied the plaintiff's inverse condemnation claim in *Customer Co. v. City of Sacramento*, 10 Cal. 4th 368, 41 Cal. Rptr. 2d 658, 895 P.2d 900 (1995), under the California Constitution, holding that the case was governed by the emergency doctrine. The plaintiff's business inventory was destroyed when the police used tear gas to apprehend a dangerous criminal barricading himself inside plaintiff's business premises. The court said that this case was similar to "the demolition of buildings to prevent the spread of conflagration," or the destruction of war materiel or bridges to hamper advancing enemy forces in time of war. The court noted contrary decisions in other jurisdictions, but concluded that they were wrongly decided. The court said by way of dictum:

> This is not a case in which law enforcement officers commandeered a citizen's automobile to chase a fleeing suspect, or appropriated ammunition from a private gun shop to replenish an inadequate supply. Conceivably, such unusual actions might constitute an exercise of eminent domain, because private property would be taken for public use.

Although in many circumstances it might seem "fair" to require the government to compensate "innocent victims" in a situation such as this, the court found that inverse condemnation was not the appropriate vehicle to achieve that objective.

Should goals of fairness and constitutional goals differ? Reconsider the cases on public and private necessity in Chapter 4. If this were a private taking, should compensation by the private taker be constitutionally required?

PROBLEM

Susan, a member of a church, chose to marry someone who did not belong to, and would not join, Susan's church. The church rules provided that a member who married a nonmember forfeited church membership, and forbade church members from attending a wedding of a member and a non-member. As a result, Susan's family, including her mother and father, refused to attend her wedding. Because church members were discouraged from "fostering" an improper marriage such as Susan's by patronizing the couple's business endeavors, her new husband's law practice suffered significantly. Should Susan have a tort claim against the church? Against the local minister who enforces the church rules? Should her husband have a claim for his loss of income?

C. STATUTORY REMEDIES

SEDIMA, S.P.R.L. v. IMREX CO.
473 U.S. 479, 105 S. Ct. 3275, 87 L. Ed. 2d 346 (1985)

JUSTICE WHITE delivered the opinion of the Court.

The Racketeer Influenced and Corrupt Organizations Act (RICO), Pub. L. 91-452, Title IX, 84 Stat. 941, as amended, 18 U.S.C. §§ 1961–1968, provides a private civil action to recover treble damages for injury "by reason of a violation of" its substantive provisions. 18 U.S.C. § 1964(c). The initial dormancy of this provision and its recent greatly increased utilization[2] are now familiar history. In response to what it perceived to be misuse of civil RICO by private plaintiffs, the court below construed § 1964(c) to permit private actions only against defendants who had been convicted on criminal charges, and only where there had occurred a "racketeering injury." While we understand the court's concern over the consequences of an unbridled reading of the statute, we reject both of its holdings.

RICO takes aim at "racketeering activity," which it defines as any act "chargeable" under several generically described state criminal laws, any act "indictable" under numerous specific federal criminal provisions, including mail and wire fraud, and any "offense" involving bankruptcy or securities fraud or drug-related activities that is "punishable" under federal law. § 1961(1).[4] Section 1962, entitled "Prohibited Activities," outlaws the use of income derived from a "pattern of racketeering activity" to acquire an interest in or establish an enterprise engaged in or affecting interstate commerce; the acquisition or maintenance of any interest in an enterprise "through" a pattern of racketeering activity; conducting or participating in the conduct of an enterprise through a pattern of racketeering activity; and conspiring to violate any of these provisions.[5]

---

[2] Of 270 District Court RICO decisions prior to this year, only 3% (nine cases) were decided throughout the 1970's, 2% were decided in 1980, 7% in 1981, 13% in 1982, 33% in 1983, and 43% in 1984. Report of the Ad Hoc Civil RICO Task Force of the ABA Section of Corporation, Banking and Business Law 55 (1985) (hereinafter ABA Report).

[4] RICO defines "racketeering activity" to mean "(A) any act or threat involving murder, kidnaping, gambling, arson, robbery, bribery, extortion, or dealing in narcotic or other dangerous drugs, which is chargeable under State law and punishable by imprisonment for more than one year; (B) any act which is indictable under any of the following provisions of title 18, United States Code: Section 201 (relating to bribery), section 224 (relating to sports bribery), sections 471, 472, and 473 (relating to counterfeiting), section 659 (relating to theft from interstate shipment) if the act indictable under section 659 is felonious, section 664 (relating to embezzlement from pension and welfare funds), sections 891–894 (relating to extortionate credit transactions), section 1084 (relating to the transmission of gambling information), section 1341 (relating to mail fraud), section 1343 (relating to wire fraud), section 1503 (relating to obstruction of justice), section 1510 (relating to obstruction of criminal investigations), section 1511 (relating to the obstruction of State or local law enforcement), section 1951 (relating to interference with commerce, robbery, or extortion), section 1952 (relating to racketeering), section 1953 (relating to interstate transportation of wagering paraphernalia), section 1954 (relating to unlawful welfare fund payments), section 1955 (relating to the prohibition of illegal gambling businesses), sections 2312 and 2313 (relating to interstate transportation of stolen motor vehicles), sections 2314 and 2315 (relating to interstate transportation of stolen property), section 2320 (relating to trafficking in certain motor vehicles or motor vehicle parts), sections 2341–2346 (relating to trafficking in contraband cigarettes), sections 2421–2424 (relating to white slave traffic), (C) any act which is indictable under title 29, United States Code, section 186 (dealing with restrictions on payments and loans to labor organizations) or section 501(c) (relating to embezzlement from union funds), (D) any offense involving fraud connected with a case under title 11, fraud in the sale of securities, or the felonious manufacture, importation, receiving, concealment, buying, selling, or otherwise dealing in narcotic or other dangerous drugs, punishable under any law of the United States, or (E) any act which is indictable under the Currency and Foreign Transactions Reporting Act." 18 U.S.C. § 1961(1) (1982 ed., Supp. III).

[5] In relevant part, 18 U.S.C. § 1962 provides:

Congress provided criminal penalties of imprisonment, fines, and forfeiture for violation of these provisions. § 1963. In addition, it set out a far-reaching civil enforcement scheme, § 1964, including the following provision for private suits:

> "Any person injured in his business or property by reason of a violation of section 1962 of this chapter may sue therefor in any appropriate United States district court and shall recover threefold the damages he sustains and the cost of the suit, including a reasonable attorney's fee." § 1964(c).

In 1979, petitioner Sedima, a Belgian corporation, entered into a joint venture with respondent Imrex Co. to provide electronic components to a Belgian firm. The buyer was to order parts through Sedima; Imrex was to obtain the parts in this country and ship them to Europe. The agreement called for Sedima and Imrex to split the net proceeds. Imrex filled roughly $8 million in orders placed with it through Sedima. Sedima became convinced, however, that Imrex was presenting inflated bills, cheating Sedima out of a portion of its proceeds by collecting for nonexistent expenses.

In 1982, Sedima filed this action in the Federal District Court . . . The complaint set out common-law claims of unjust enrichment, conversion, and breach of contract, fiduciary duty, and a constructive trust. In addition, it asserted RICO claims under § 1964(c) against Imrex and two of its officers. Two counts alleged violations of § 1962(c), based on predicate acts of mail and wire fraud. . . . A third count alleged a conspiracy to violate § 1962(c). Claiming injury of at least $175,000, the amount of the alleged over-billing, Sedima sought treble damages and attorney's fees.

The District Court held that for an injury to be "by reason of a violation of section 1962," as required by § 1964(c), it must be somehow different in kind from the direct injury resulting from the predicate acts of racketeering activity. While not choosing a precise formulation, the District Court held that a complaint must allege a "RICO-type injury," which was either some sort of distinct "racketeering injury," or a "competitive injury." It found "no allegation here of any injury apart from that which would result directly from the alleged predicate acts of mail fraud and wire fraud," and accordingly dismissed the RICO counts for failure to state a claim.

(a) It shall be unlawful for any person who has received any income derived, directly or indirectly, from a pattern of racketeering activity or through collection of an unlawful debt . . . to use or invest, directly or indirectly, any part of such income, or the proceeds of such income, in acquisition of any interest in, or the establishment or operation of, any enterprise which is engaged in, or the activities of which affect, interstate or foreign commerce . . . .

(b) It shall be unlawful for any person through a pattern of racketeering activity or through collection of an unlawful debt to acquire or maintain, directly or indirectly, any interest in or control of any enterprise which is engaged in, or the activities of which affect, interstate or foreign commerce.

(c) It shall be unlawful for any person employed by or associated with any enterprise engaged in, or the activities of which affect, interstate or foreign commerce, to conduct or participate, directly or indirectly, in the conduct of such enterprise's affairs through a pattern of racketeering activity or collection of unlawful debt.

(d) It shall be unlawful for any person to conspire to violate any of the provisions of subsections (a), (b), or (c) of this section.

A divided panel of the Court of Appeals for the Second Circuit affirmed. After a lengthy review of the legislative history, it held that Sedima's complaint was defective in two ways. First, it failed to allege an injury "by reason of a violation of section 1962." In the court's view, this language was a limitation on standing, reflecting Congress' intent to compensate victims of "certain specific kinds of organized criminality," not to provide additional remedies for already compensable injuries. Analogizing to the Clayton Act, which had been the model for § 1964(c), the court concluded that just as an antitrust plaintiff must allege an "antitrust injury," so a RICO plaintiff must allege a "racketeering injury" — an injury "different in kind from that occurring as a result of the predicate acts themselves, or not simply caused by the predicate acts, but also caused by an activity which RICO was designed to deter." Sedima had failed to allege such an injury.

The Court of Appeals also found the complaint defective for not alleging that the defendants had already been criminally convicted of the predicate acts of mail and wire fraud, or of a RICO violation. This element of the civil cause of action was inferred from § 1964(c)'s reference to a "violation" of § 1962, the court also observing that its prior-conviction requirement would avoid serious constitutional difficulties, the danger of unfair stigmatization, and problems regarding the standard by which the predicate acts were to be proved.

The decision below was one episode in a recent proliferation of civil RICO litigation within the Second Circuit and in other Courts of Appeals. In light of the variety of approaches taken by the lower courts and the importance of the issues, we granted certiorari. We now reverse. . . .

The language of RICO gives no obvious indication that a civil action can proceed only after a criminal conviction. The word "conviction" does not appear in any relevant portion of the statute. . . . To the contrary, the predicate acts involve conduct that is "chargeable" or "indictable" . . . .

We are not at all convinced that the predicate acts must be established beyond a reasonable doubt in a proceeding under § 1964(c). In a number of settings, conduct that can be punished as criminal only upon proof beyond a reasonable doubt will support civil sanctions under a preponderance standard. . . .

The court below also feared that any other construction would raise severe constitutional questions, as it "would provide civil remedies for offenses criminal in nature, stigmatize defendants with the appellation 'racketeer,' authorize the award of damages which are clearly punitive, including attorney's fees, and constitute a civil remedy aimed in part to avoid the constitutional protections of the criminal law." We do not view the statute as being so close to the constitutional edge. As noted above, the fact that conduct can result in both criminal liability and treble damages does not mean that there is not a bona fide civil action. The familiar provisions for both criminal liability and treble damages under the antitrust laws indicate as much. Nor are attorney's fees "clearly punitive." *Cf.* 42 U.S.C. § 1988. As for stigma, a civil RICO proceeding leaves no greater stain than do a number of other civil proceedings. Furthermore, requiring conviction of the predicate acts would not protect against an unfair imposition of the "racketeer" label. If there is a problem with thus stigmatizing a garden variety defrauder by means of a civil action, it is not reduced by making certain that the defendant is guilty of *fraud* beyond a reasonable doubt. Finally, to the extent an action under § 1964(c) might be considered quasi-criminal, requiring protections normally applicable only to criminal proceedings, the solution is to provide those protections, not to ensure that they were previously afforded by requiring prior convictions.

Finally, we note that a prior-conviction requirement would be inconsistent with Congress' underlying policy concerns. Such a rule would severely handicap potential plaintiffs. A guilty party may escape conviction for any number of reasons — not least among them the possibility that the Government itself may choose to pursue only civil remedies. Private attorney general provisions such as § 1964(c) are in part designed to fill prosecutorial gaps. This purpose would be largely defeated, and the need for treble damages as an incentive to litigate unjustified, if private suits could be maintained only against those already brought to justice.

In sum, we can find no support in the statute's history, its language, or considerations of policy for a requirement that a private treble-damages action under § 1964(c) can proceed only against a defendant who has already been criminally convicted. To the contrary, every indication is that no such requirement exists. Accordingly, the fact that Imrex and the individual defendants have not been convicted under RICO or the federal mail and wire fraud statutes does not bar Sedima's action.

In considering the Court of Appeals' second prerequisite for a private civil RICO action — "injury . . . caused by an activity which RICO was designed to deter" — we are somewhat hampered by the vagueness of that concept. Apart from reliance on the general purposes of RICO and a reference to "mobsters," the court provided scant indication of what the requirement of racketeering injury means. It emphasized Congress' undeniable desire to strike at organized crime, but acknowledged and did not purport to overrule Second Circuit precedent rejecting a requirement of an organized crime nexus. The court also stopped short of adopting a "competitive injury" requirement; while insisting that the plaintiff show "the kind of economic injury which has an effect on competition," it did not require "actual anticompetitive effect." 741 F.2d, at 496.

The court's statement that the plaintiff must seek redress for an injury caused by conduct that RICO was designed to deter is unhelpfully tautological. Nor is clarity furnished by a negative statement of its rule: standing is not provided by the injury resulting from the predicate acts themselves. That statement is itself apparently inaccurate when applied to those predicate acts that unmistakably constitute the kind of conduct Congress sought to deter. The opinion does not explain how to distinguish such crimes from the other predicate acts Congress has lumped together in § 1961(1). The court below is not alone in struggling to define "racketeering injury," and the difficulty of that task itself cautions against imposing such a requirement.

[The Court next addresses whether the statutory language includes a "racketeering injury" requirement separate from the harm from the predicate acts.].

A violation of § 1962(c), the section on which Sedima relies, requires (1) conduct (2) of an enterprise (3) through a pattern[6] (4) of racketeering activity. The plaintiff must, of course, allege each of these elements to state a claim. . . .[T]he plaintiff only has standing if, and can only recover to the extent that, he has been injured in his business or property by the conduct constituting the violation. As the Seventh Circuit has stated, "[a] defendant who violates section 1962 is not liable for treble damages to everyone he might have injured by other conduct, nor is the defendant liable to those who have not been injured." *Haroco, Inc. v. American National Bank & Trust Co. of Chicago*, 747 F.2d 384, 398 (7th Cir. 1984), *aff'd,* 473 U.S. 606.

But the statute requires no more than this. Where the plaintiff alleges each element of the violation, the compensable injury necessarily is the harm caused by predicate acts sufficiently related to constitute a pattern, for the essence of the violation is the commission of those acts in connection with the conduct of an enterprise. Those acts are, when committed in the circumstances delineated in § 1962(c), "an activity which RICO was designed to deter." Any recoverable damages occurring by reason of a violation of § 1962(c) will flow from the commission of the predicate acts.[7]

This less restrictive reading is amply supported by our prior cases and the general principles surrounding this statute. RICO is to be read broadly. This is the lesson not only of Congress' self-consciously expansive language and overall approach, but also of its express admonition that RICO is to "be liberally construed to effectuate its remedial purposes," Pub. L. 91-452, § 904(a), 84 Stat. 947. The statute's "remedial purposes" are nowhere more evident than in the provision of a private action for those injured by racketeering activity. Far from effectuating these purposes, the narrow readings offered

---

[6] As many commentators have pointed out, the definition of a "pattern of racketeering activity" differs from the other provisions in § 1961 in that it states that a pattern *"requires* at least two acts of racketeering activity," § 1961(5) (emphasis added), not that it "means" two such acts. The implication is that while two acts are necessary, they may not be sufficient. Indeed, in common parlance, two of anything do not generally form a "pattern." The legislative history supports the view that two isolated acts of racketeering activity do not constitute a pattern. As the Senate Report explained: "The target of [RICO] is thus not sporadic activity. The infiltration of legitimate business normally requires more than one 'racketeering activity' and the threat of continuing activity to be effective. It is this factor of *continuity plus relationship* which combines to produce a pattern." S. Rep. No. 91-617, p. 158 (1969) (emphasis added). Similarly, the sponsor of the Senate bill, after quoting this portion of the Report, pointed out to his colleagues that "[t]he term 'pattern' itself requires the showing of a relationship . . . . So, therefore, proof of two acts of racketeering activity, without more, does not establish a pattern . . . ." 116 Cong. Rec. 18940 (1970) (statement of Sen. McClellan). . . . Significantly, in defining "pattern" in a later provision of the same bill, Congress was more enlightening: "[c]riminal conduct forms a pattern if it embraces criminal acts that have the same or similar purposes, results, participants, victims, or methods of commission, or otherwise are interrelated by distinguishing characteristics and are not isolated events." 18 U.S.C. § 3575 (e). . . .

[7] Such damages include, but are not limited to, the sort of competitive injury for which the dissenters would allow recovery. Under the dissent's reading of the statute, the harm proximately caused by the forbidden conduct is not compensable, but that ultimately and indirectly flowing therefrom is. We reject this topsy-turvy approach, finding no warrant in the language or the history of the statute for denying recovery thereunder to "the direct victims of the [racketeering] activity," while preserving it for the indirect. Even the court below was not that grudging. It would apparently have allowed recovery for both the direct and the ultimate harm flowing from the defendant's conduct, requiring injury "not simply caused by the predicate acts, but *also* caused by an activity which RICO was designed to deter." 741 F.2d, at 496 (emphasis added). . . .

by the dissenters and the court below would in effect eliminate § 1964(c) from the statute. . . .

[The Court notes the lower court's concern over civil RICO being used *not* against "mobsters and organized criminals," but "as a tool for everyday fraud cases brought against 'respected and legitimate enterprises.' "]

It is true that private civil actions under the statute are being brought almost solely against such defendants, rather than against the archetypal, intimidating mobster.[8] Yet this defect — if defect it is — is inherent in the statute as written, and its correction must lie with Congress. It is not for the judiciary to eliminate the private action in situations where Congress has provided it simply because plaintiffs are not taking advantage of it in its more difficult applications.

We nonetheless recognize that, in its private civil version, RICO is evolving into something quite different from the original conception of its enactors. . . . Though sharing the doubts of the Court of Appeals about this increasing divergence, we cannot agree with either its diagnosis or its remedy. The "extraordinary" uses to which civil RICO has been put appear to be primarily the result of the breadth of the predicate offenses, in particular the inclusion of wire, mail, and securities fraud, and the failure of Congress and the courts to develop a meaningful concept of "pattern." We do not believe that the amorphous standing requirement imposed by the Second Circuit effectively responds to these problems, or that it is a form of statutory amendment appropriately undertaken by the courts.

Sedima may maintain this action if the defendants conducted the enterprise through a pattern of racketeering activity. The questions whether the defendants committed the requisite predicate acts, and whether the commission of those acts fell into a pattern, are not before us. The complaint is not deficient for failure to allege either an injury separate from the financial loss stemming from the alleged acts of mail and wire fraud, or prior convictions of the defendants. The judgment below is accordingly reversed, and the case is remanded for further proceedings consistent with this opinion.

NOTES

1. *A Pattern of Racketeering Activity.* Section 1962 of 18 U.S.C. specifies three types of activities that may give rise to a RICO violation: (a) receiving income from a pattern of racketeering activity in order to acquire an interest in an enterprise engaged in interstate or foreign commerce; (b) acquiring an interest in or control of such an enterprise through a pattern of racketeering activity; or (c) conducting, or participating in the conduct of, such an enterprise's affairs through a pattern of racketeering activity. A conspiracy to violate (a), (b), or (c) is also a RICO offense, § 1962(d). A "racketeering

---

[8] The ABA Task Force found that of the 270 known civil RICO cases at the trial court level, 40% involved securities fraud, 37% common-law fraud in a commercial or business setting, and only 9% "allegations of criminal activity of a type generally associated with professional criminals." ABA Report, at 55–56. Another survey of 132 published decisions found that 57 involved securities transactions and 38 commercial and contract disputes, while no other category made it into double figures. American Institute of Certified Public Accountants, The Authority to Bring Private Treble-Damage Suits Under "RICO" Should Be Removed 13 (Oct. 10, 1984).

activity" means the commission of one of the various crimes listed in 18 U.S.C. § 1962(1). A "pattern" of racketeering activity means the commission of "at least" two such crimes, one which occurred after 15 Oct. 1970, and the last of which occurred within ten years of a prior racketeering activity (excluding any period of imprisonment), 18 U.S.C. § 1961(5). Thus, a critical question for applying RICO is to determine if a "pattern" of racketeering activity has occurred.

Curiously, § 1962(a)–(c) requires a pattern of racketeering activity *or* the "collection of an unlawful debt" in order for a RICO violation to occur. In other words, apparently no pattern is required if the violation involves the collection of an unlawful debt, and the collection of such a debt is a RICO violation independent of the racketeering crimes listed in § 1961(1).

The Court had before it in *H.J., Inc. v. Northwestern Bell Tel. Co.*, 492 U.S. 229, 109 S. Ct. 2893, 106 L. Ed. 2d 195 (1989), the task of defining a "pattern" of racketeering activity for purposes of civil RICO:

> . . . Petitioners, customers of respondent Northwestern Bell Telephone Co. . . . alleged violations of §§ 1962(a), (b), (c) and (d) by Northwestern Bell and the other respondents — some of the telephone company's officers and employees, various members of the Minnesota Public Utilities Commission (MPUC), and other unnamed individuals and corporations — and sought an injunction and treble damages under RICO's civil liability provisions, §§ 1964(a) and (c).
>
> The MPUC is the state body responsible for determining the rates that Northwestern Bell may charge. Petitioners' 5-count complaint alleged that between 1980 and 1986 Northwestern Bell sought to influence members of the MPUC in the performance of their duties — and in fact caused them to approve rates for the company in excess of a fair and reasonable amount — by making cash payments to commissioners, negotiating with them regarding future employment, and paying for parties, and meals, for tickets to sporting events and the like, and for airline tickets. Based upon these factual allegations . . . petitioners alleged . . . four separate claims under § 1962 of RICO. Count II alleged that, in violation of § 1962(a), Northwestern Bell derived income from a pattern of racketeering activity involving predicate acts of bribery and used this income to engage in its business as an interstate "enterprise." Count III claimed a violation of § 1962(b), in that, through this same pattern of racketeering activity, respondents acquired an interest in or control of the MPUC, which was also an interstate "enterprise." In Count IV, petitioners asserted that respondents participated in the conduct and affairs of the MPUC through this pattern of racketeering activity, contrary to § 1962(c). Finally, Count V alleged that respondents conspired together to violate §§ 1962(a), (b), and (c), thereby contravening § 1962(d).

The Court recognized that Congress, in drafting § 1961(5), "envisioned circumstances in which no more than two predicates [*i.e.*, two racketeering crimes] would be necessary to establish a pattern of racketeering — otherwise it would have drawn a narrower boundary to RICO liability, requiring proof of a greater number of predicates." But, the Court said, § 1961(5) "assumes that there is something to a RICO pattern *beyond* simply the number of predicate acts involved." The legislative history bears out this interpretation, since the principal Senate sponsor indicated that "proof of two racketeering acts, without more, does not establish a pattern." The Court's task, therefore, was to define what that something "more" might be.

The Court said that "Congress intended to take a flexible approach, and envisaged that a pattern might be demonstrated by reference to a range of different ordering principles or relationships between predicates." The key factors involve a showing "that the racketeering predicates are related, and that they amount to or pose a threat of continued criminal activity."

> We adopt a less inflexible approach that seems to us to derive from a common-sense, everyday understanding of RICO's language and Congress' gloss on it. What a plaintiff or prosecutor must prove is continuity of racketeering activity, or its threat, *simpliciter*. . . . .
>
> "Continuity" is both a closed-and open-ended concept, referring either to a closed period of repeated conduct, or to past conduct that by its nature projects into the future with a threat of repetition. It is, in either case, centrally a temporal concept — and particularly so in the RICO context, where *what* must be continuous, RICO's predicate acts or offenses, and the *relationship* these predicates must bear one to another, are distinct requirements. A party alleging a RICO violation may demonstrate continuity over a closed period by proving a series of related predicates extending over a substantial period of time. Predicate acts extending over a few weeks or months and threatening no future criminal conduct do not satisfy this requirement: Congress was concerned in RICO with long-term criminal conduct. Often a RICO action will be brought before continuity can be established in this way. In such cases, liability depends on whether the *threat* of continuity is demonstrated.
>
> Whether the predicates proved establish a threat of continued racketeering activity depends on the specific facts of each case.[W]e offer some examples of how this element might be satisfied. A RICO pattern may surely be established if the related predicates themselves involve a distinct threat of long-term racketeering activity, either implicit or explicit. Suppose a hoodlum were to sell "insurance" to a neighborhood's storekeepers to cover them against breakage of their windows, telling his victims he would be reappearing each month to collect the "premium" that would continue their "coverage." Though the number of related predicates involved may be small and they may occur close together in time, the racketeering acts themselves include a specific threat of repetition extending indefinitely into the future, and thus supply the requisite threat of continuity. In other cases, the threat of continuity may be established by showing that the predicate acts or offenses are part of an ongoing entity's regular way of doing business. Thus, the threat of continuity is sufficiently established where the predicates can be attributed to a defendant operating as part of a long-term association that exists for criminal purposes. Such associations include, but extend well beyond, those traditionally

grouped under the phrase "organized crime." The continuity requirement is likewise satisfied where it is shown that the predicates are a regular way of conducting defendant's ongoing legitimate business (in the sense that it is not a business that exists for criminal purposes), or of conducting or participating in an ongoing and legitimate RICO "enterprise."

. . . The development of the concepts must await future cases, absent a decision by Congress to revisit RICO to provide clearer guidance as the Act's intended scope.

Reaffirming its position in *Sedima,* the Court in *H.J., Inc.* said that the pattern need not be committed by an "organized crime perpetrator." It also rejected the Court of Appeals holding in the case that a "single fraudulent effort or scheme is insufficient" to establish a pattern. A pattern can consist of a single scheme, or of multiple "related" schemes, that "amount to or pose a threat of continued criminal activity."

In *Pyramid Securities, Ltd. v. IB Resolution, Inc.*, 924 F.2d 1114 (D.C. Cir. 1991), the court found no "pattern" of securities fraud where the defendant brokerage service "churned" the plaintiff's securities account for three months while the plaintiff was away on a honeymoon. "Churning" consists of "making a series of unauthorized trades that generate commissions" for the defendant and in this case also concurrently "severely reduced the account's value."

The court found no threat of continued racketeering activity beyond the three-months period because the plaintiff "checked his portfolio on a daily basis" except for the period when he was absent on his honeymoon. There was no evidence of the defendant's efforts to defraud other customers.

Why weren't the three months of churning long enough to create a pattern?

2. *The Enterprise.* Section 1961(a)–(b) provides that a "person" must (1) receive income from a racketeering pattern in order to invest in, or (2) engage in such a pattern in order to acquire or maintain an interest in, or (3) engage in such a pattern in order to participate in the conduct of, an "enterprise" or its affairs. A "person" is defined under § 1961(3) as "any individual, partnership, corporation, association, or other legal entity, or any group of individuals associated in fact although not a legal entity." The Court in *United States v. Turkette,* 452 U.S. 576, 101 S. Ct. 2524, 69 L. Ed. 2d 246 (1981), said that the term enterprise encompassed "both legitimate and illegitimate" entities. An enterprise, the Court said, is an element separate and apart from the "pattern of racketeering activity," and both elements must be proved to establish a RICO violation. But apparently the "person" who commits the pattern of racketeering activity can be the same as, or separate from, the "enterprise" itself.

In *Reves v. Ernst & Young,* 113 S. Ct. 1163 (1993), the Court said that in order for a RICO violation to occur under § 1962(c), the racketeer must be "employed by or associated with" the enterprise. An enterprise is operated "not just by upper management but also by lower-rung participants in the enterprise who are under the direction of upper management." Here, the activities of an independent accountant who prepared an audit report for an enterprise was not sufficient to give rise to liability under § 1962(c).

The Court said, "§ 1962(c) is limited to persons 'employed by or associated with an enterprise,' suggesting a more limited reach than subsections (a) and (b)." Could the accountant have been liable in *Reves* under subsection (a) or (b)?

In *Cedric Kuhner Promot. v. King*, 121 S.Ct. 2087 (2001), the Court said the sole shareholder–president of a corporation was a person, and the corporation an entity—for purposes of § 1962(c)—regardless of whether the entity was a victim or a tool of the person.

3. *The Scope of RICO*. A RICO violation can give rise to criminal as well as civil liability. The list of racketeering activities in 18 U.S.C. § 1961(1) (1995)(set out in note 4 of *Sedima, supra*) has been amended to include dealing in obscene matter; acts relating to fraud and related activity in connection with access devices; acts relating to financial institution fraud; and acts relating to obscene matter. It also includes acts relating to tampering with a witness, victim, or an informant; acts relating to retaliating against a witness, victim, or an informant; laundering of monetary instruments; engaging in monetary transactions in property derived from specified unlawful activity; use of interstate commerce facilities in the commission of murder-for-hire; and sexual exploitation of children; and immigration-related crimes..

In *Alexander v. United States*, 113 S. Ct. 2766 (1993), the defendant was convicted of RICO violations based on the transportation of obscene materials in interstate commerce in violation of 18 U.S.C. §§ 1465–1466. Pursuant to 18 U.S.C. § 1963, the trial court "ordered the petitioner to forfeit his wholesale and retail business (including the assets of those businesses) and almost $9 million in moneys acquired through racketeering activity." He was also sentenced to six years in jail and fined $100,000. The Court held that the forfeiture did not violate the petitioner's First Amendment rights.

Section 1964(c), setting forth civil remedies, provides:

> (c) Any person injured in his business or property by reason of a violation of section 1962 of this chapter may sue therefor in any appropriate United States district court and shall recover threefold the damages he sustains and the cost of the suit, including a reasonable attorney's fee.

Apparently an action solely for personal injuries or for mental distress would not be sustainable under this section. But if a person were "injured in his business or property" as the result of a RICO violation, could he also then recover for personal injury or emotional distress as parasitic damages?

In *National Org. for Women v. Scheidler*, 114 S. Ct. 798 (1994), the plaintiff sued the defendants for engaging in an alleged "nationwide conspiracy to shut down abortion clinics through a pattern of racketeering activity including extortion in violation of the Hobbs Act, 18 U.S.C. § 1961." The allegation was that the defendants were engaging in a pattern of racketeering activity in order to conduct or participate in the conduct of an enterprise's affairs in violation of § 1962(c). The Court upheld the cause of action, finding that the defendants' racketeering predicate acts need not be "accompanied by an underlying economic motive" in order to be actionable under § 1962(c).

In *Tabas v. Tabas*, 47 F.3d 1280 (3d Cir. 1995), the Court upheld a civil RICO claim based on an intra-family dispute concerning the handling and distribution of partnership assets. The predicate acts included allegations of mail fraud in violation of 18 U.S.C. § 1341.

The plaintiff in *Schiffels v. Kemper Fin. Servs.*, 978 F.2d 344 (7th Cir. 1992), brought a civil RICO claim against his former employer alleging that he was wrongfully discharged in retaliation for his attempting to disclose the defendants' pattern of racketeering activity. The Court found that the plaintiff had standing to sue. A person who is fired to further a RICO conspiracy or to prevent its disclosure is within the zone of interest RICO was designed to protect, the Court said, and it remanded the case to allow plaintiff an opportunity to amend in order to fully state the elements of a RICO claim.

Stating the purported majority position, the court in *Summit Properties v. Hoechst Celanese Corp.*, 214 F. 3d 556 (5th Cir. 2000), said a RICO plaintiff cannot recover for mail or wire fraud misrepresentation unless the plaintiff relied on the representation. Why shouldn't the reliance of another be sufficient?

In *Beck v. Prupis*, 120 S. Ct. 1608 (2000), defendant employees of SIG Corp. engaged in acts of RICO racketeering. When defendant, president of SIG, blew the whistle on them, defendants allegedly terminated his employment in retaliation. In denying plaintiff's RICO claim, the Court held the termination was not itself a RICO violation. Does this holding comport with basic principles of proximate cause?

4. *Vicarious Liability.* The court in *Quick v. Peoples Bank*, 993 F.2d 793 (11th Cir. 1993), held that a bank could be found vicariously liable under § 1962(b) for the acts of a loan officer acting within the scope of his employment in committing civil RICO violations for the benefit of the bank. In *Federal Sav. & Loan Ins. Corp. v. Shearson AmEx*, 658 F. Supp. 1331 (D.P.R. 1987), the court said that an employer could be held vicariously liable under § 1962(c) if it were not designated as the enterprise in the suit.

5. *Jury Information.* The court in *HBE Leasing Corp. v. Frank*, 22 F.3d 41 (2d Cir. 1994), denied the defendant the opportunity to inform the jury that the damages are trebled and attorneys' fees awarded in civil RICO. "Every authority brought to this court's attention upholds excluding references to trebling and attorneys' fees in the RICO context," the court said.

Why might the defendant want to introduce such evidence? Why do all the courts exclude it?

6. *State RICO Jurisdiction.* In *Tafflin v. Lewitt*, 110 S. Ct. 792 (1990), the Court held that state courts have concurrent jurisdiction with federal courts to hear federal civil RICO claims. Section 1964(c)'s grant of federal jurisdiction over civil RICO claims "is plainly permissive, not mandatory," the Court said.

7. *State RICO Statutes.* A civil suit was upheld against the defendant in *Raybestos Prods. Co. v. Younger*, 54 F.3d 1234 (7th Cir. 1995), for violation of the Indiana RICO statute. The defendant was charged with acts of "intimidation," committed in order to force financial concessions, in violation of that statute. Thus, state RICO claims may be different from those alleged under the federal statute.

8. *Safe Haven for Securities Fraud.* The Private Securities Reform Act of 1995, P.L. 104-67, provides in part:

Sec. 107. *Amendment to Racketeer Influenced and Corrupt Organizations Act.*

> Section 1964(c) of title 18, United States Code, is amended by inserting before the period ", except that no person may rely upon any conduct that would have been actionable as fraud in the purchase or sale of securities to establish a violation of section 1962. The exception contained in the preceding sentence does not apply to an action against any person that is criminally convicted in connection with the fraud, in which case the statute of limitations shall start to run on the date on which the conviction becomes final."

The legislative history to this Act notes that a plaintiff "may not plead other specified offenses, such as mail or wire fraud, as predicate acts under civil RICO if such offenses are based on conduct that would have been actionable as securities fraud." H.R. CONF. REP. 369, at 47.

Is this exception to the no-prior-conviction rule for civil RICO, as set forth in *Sedima*, desirable for securities fraud? Is the exception constitutional?

PROBLEM

Jock entered into a wager with Sport on the outcome of all twelve of the University of Tennessee football games during the 1995 season. Jock won half the bets, and Sport the other half. After setting off Sport's wins against Jock's wins (the amounts of the bets varied), Sport owed Jock a balance of $1,000 at the end of the season. Sport refused to pay, in spite of repeated written demands by Jock. Jock intended to save his earnings toward a law school education.

TENN. CODE ANN. § 29-19-101 provides that "all contracts founded, in whole or in part, on a gambling or wagering consideration, shall be void to the extent of such consideration."

Sport brings a federal civil RICO claim against Jock based on the above facts. Does Sport have a valid claim?

WHITE v. SAMSUNG ELECTRONICS, INC.
971 F.2d 1395 (9th Cir. 1992)

[The facts of this case are given in Chapter 18.]

III. *The Lanham Act*

White's final argument is that the district court erred in denying her claim under [section]43(a) of the Lanham Act, 15 U.S.C. § 1125(a). The version of section 43(a) applicable to this case provides, in pertinent part, that "[a]ny person who shall . . . use, in connection with any goods or services . . . any false description or representation . . . shall be liable to a civil action . . . by any person who believes that he is or is likely to be damaged by the use of any such false description or designation." 15 U.S.C. § 1125(a).

To prevail on her Lanham Act claim, White is required to show that in running the robot ad, Samsung and Deutsch created a likelihood of confusion over whether White was endorsing Samsung's VCRs.

This circuit recognizes several different multi-factor tests for determining whether a likelihood of confusion exists. None of these tests is correct to the exclusion of the others. Normally, in reviewing the district court's decision, this court will look to the particular test that the district court used. However, because the district court in this case apparently did not use any of the multi-factor tests in making its likelihood of confusion determination, and because this case involves an appeal from summary judgment and we review de novo the district court's determination, we will look for guidance to the 8-factor test enunciated in *AMF, Inc. v. Sleekcraft Boats,* 599 F.2d 341 (9th Cir. 1979). According to *AMF*, factors relevant to a likelihood of confusion include:

(1) strength of the plaintiff's mark;
(2) relatedness of the goods;
(3) similarity of the marks;
(4) evidence of actual confusion;
(5) marketing channels used;
(6) likely degree of purchaser care;
(7) defendant's intent in selecting the mark;
(8) likelihood of expansion of the product lines.

599 F.2d at 348–49. We turn now to consider White's claim in light of each factor.

In cases involving confusion over endorsement by a celebrity plaintiff, "mark" means the celebrity's persona. The "strength" of the mark refers to the level of recognition the celebrity enjoys among members of society. If Vanna White is unknown to the segment of the public at whom Samsung's robot ad was directed, then that segment could not be confused as to whether she was endorsing Samsung VCRs. Conversely, if White is well-known, this would allow the possibility of a likelihood of confusion. For the purposes of the *Sleekcraft* test, White's "mark," or celebrity identity, is strong.

In cases concerning confusion over celebrity endorsement, the plaintiff's "goods" concern the reasons for or source of the plaintiff's fame. Because White's fame is based on her televised performances, her "goods" are closely related to Samsung's VCRs. Indeed, the ad itself reinforced the relationship by informing its readers that they would be taping the "longest-running game show" on Samsung's VCRs well into the future.

The third factor, "similarity of the marks," both supports and contradicts a finding of likelihood of confusion. On the one hand, all of the aspects of the robot ad identify White; on the other, the figure is quite clearly a robot, not a human. This ambiguity means that we must look to the other factors for resolution.

The fourth factor does not favor White's claim because she has presented no evidence of actual confusion.

Fifth, however, White has appeared in the same stance as the robot from the ad in numerous magazines, including the covers of some. Magazines were used as the marketing channels for the robot ad. This factor cuts toward a likelihood of confusion.

Sixth, consumers are not likely to be particularly careful in determining who endorses VCRs, making confusion as to their endorsement more likely.

Concerning the seventh factor, "defendant's intent," the district court found that, in running the robot ad, the defendants had intended a spoof of the "Wheel of Fortune." The relevant question is whether the defendants "intended to profit by confusing consumers" concerning the endorsement of Samsung VCRs. We do not disagree that defendants intended to spoof Vanna White and "Wheel of Fortune." That does not preclude, however, the possibility that defendants also intended to confuse consumers regarding endorsement. The robot ad was one of a series of ads run by defendants which followed the same theme. Another ad in the series depicted Morton Downey Jr. as a presidential candidate in the year 2008. Doubtless, defendants intended to spoof presidential elections and Mr. Downey through this ad. Consumers, however, would likely believe, and would be correct in so believing, that Mr. Downey was paid for his permission and was endorsing Samsung products. Looking at the series of advertisements as a whole, a jury could reasonably conclude that beneath the surface humor of the series lay an intent to persuade consumers that celebrity Vanna White, like celebrity Downey, was endorsing Samsung products.

Finally, the eighth factor, "likelihood of expansion of the product lines," does not appear apposite to a celebrity endorsement case such as this.

Application of the *Sleekcraft* factors to this case indicates that the district court erred in rejecting White's Lanham Act claim at the summary judgment stage. In so concluding, we emphasize two facts, however. First, construing the motion papers in White's favor, as we must, we hold only that White has raised a genuine issue of material fact concerning a likelihood of confusion as to her endorsement. Whether White's Lanham Act claim should succeed is a matter for the jury. Second, we stress that we reach this conclusion in light of the peculiar facts of this case. In particular, we note that the robot ad identifies White and was part of a series of ads in which other celebrities participated and were paid for their endorsement of Samsung's products.

In defense, defendants cite a number of cases for the proposition that their robot ad constituted protected speech. The only cases they cite which are even remotely relevant to this case are *Hustler Magazine v. Falwell*, 485 U.S. 46, 108 S. Ct. 876, 99 L. Ed. 2d 41 (1988) and *L.L. Bean, Inc. v. Drake Publishers, Inc.*, 811 F.2d 26 (1st Cir. 1987). Those cases involved parodies of advertisements run for the purpose of poking fun at Jerry Falwell and L.L. Bean, respectively. This case involves a true advertisement run for the purpose of selling Samsung VCRs. The ad's spoof of Vanna White and Wheel of Fortune is subservient and only tangentially related to the ad's primary message: "buy Samsung VCRs." Defendants' parody arguments are better addressed to non-commercial parodies.[9] The difference between a "parody" and a "knock-off" is the difference between fun and profit.

PROBLEM

John Schmu, a dead ringer for ex-president Ex — in appearance, mannerisms, voice and handwriting — maintained a very profitable living by making public appearances, records, TV shows and "fake" Ex autographs in which he portrayed Ex. On all of these occasions Schmu always announced that he was not the "real" Ex, but only his "Doppelgänger." Many people, however, believed that Schmu really was Ex. Schmu frequently gave outrageously funny derogatory portrayals of Ex on these occasions. Does Ex have any tort remedy against Schmu?

NOTES

1. *Appropriation of Name or Likeness Revisted.* A former prominent football player, John Riggins, had been "compensated over the years for use of his name in the endorsement of many products," and had been "paid for personal appearances at various functions." He had been employed by Washington radio and television stations and "currently works as a part-time commentator on an all-sports radio program in the metropolitan Washington area."

In 1991 he and his wife, Mary Lou, divorced. As part of the property settlement, Mary Lou received their home in Vienna, Virginia. She was a licensed real estate salesperson for Town and Country Properties. In 1992 she decided to sell the house through Town and Country. To generate interest, she arranged a "broker's open" on the premises to interest other brokers and sales associates in the property. In order to advertise the open, she prepared an 8½ × 11 handbill with a picture of the house, information about the open, and a heading which read: "COME SEE JOHN RIGGINS' FORMER HOME." In the body of the handbill was the statement, "Register to win an autographed football."

The court affirmed a judgment for Riggins against Town and Country for $25,000 compensatory and $25,000 punitive damages, based on the use of a

---

[9] In warning of a first amendment chill to expressive conduct, the dissent reads this decision too broadly. This case concerns only the market which exists in our society for the exploitation of celebrity to sell products, and an attempt to take a free ride on a celebrity's celebrity value. Commercial advertising which relies on celebrity fame is different from other forms of expressive activity in two crucial ways. First, for celebrity exploitation advertising to be effective, the advertisement must evoke the celebrity's identity. The more effective the evocation, the better the advertisement. If, as Samsung claims, its ad was based on a "generic" game-show hostess and not on Vanna White, the ad would not have violated anyone's right of publicity, but it would also not have been as humorous or as effective. Second, even if some forms of expressive activity, such as parody, do rely on identity evocation, the first amendment hurdle will bar most right of publicity actions against those activities. *Cf. Falwell*, 485 U.S. at 46, 108 S. Ct. at 876. In the case of commercial advertising, however, the first amendment hurdle is not so high. *Central Hudson Gas & Electric Corp. v. Public Service Comm'n of New York*, 447 U.S. 557, 566, 100 S. Ct. 2343, 2351, 65 L. Ed. 2d 341 (1980). Realizing this, Samsung attempts to elevate its ad above the status of garden-variety commercial speech by pointing to the ad's parody of Vanna White. Samsung's argument is unavailing. Unless the first amendment bars all right of publicity actions — and it does not, *see Zacchini v. Scripps-Howard Broadcasting Co.*, 433 U.S. 562, 97 S. Ct. 2849, 53 L. Ed. 2d 965 (1977) — then it does not bar this case.

person's name for advertising or trade purposes without the person's consent in violation of VA. CODE § 8.01-40(A). The court rejected defendant's claim of First Amendment privilege, saying that the advertisement was not protected speech:

> For example, it is not informational in the sense that the advertisement of New York abortions was held protected in *Bigelow v. Virginia*, 421 U.S. 809, 95 S. Ct. 2222, 44 L. Ed. 2d 600 (1975); or in the sense prescription drug price information was held protected in *Virginia State Bd. of Pharmacy, supra;* or in the sense that a lawyer's truthful advertisement concerning availability and terms of routine legal services was held protected in *Bates v. State Bar of Arizona,* 433 U.S. 350, 384, 97 S. Ct. 2691, 2709, 53 L. Ed. 2d 810 (1977); or in the sense in-person solicitation of clients by attorneys was deemed to be commercial speech in *Ohralik v. Ohio State Bar Ass'n,* 436 U.S. 447, 455–56, 98 S. Ct. 887, 895, 59 L. Ed. 2d 100 (1979).

Town & Country Properties, Inc. v. Riggins, 457 S.E.2d 356 (Va. 1995).

Recall *Montana v. San Jose Mercury News*, considered in the previous chapter. Can *Riggins* and *Montana* be reconciled?

STARON v. McDONALD'S CORP.
51 F.3d 353 (2d Cir. 1995)

WALKER, CIRCUIT JUDGE:

These actions are brought by three children with asthma and a woman with lupus against two popular fast-food restaurant chains, McDonald's Corporation ("McDonald's") and Burger King Corporation ("Burger King"). Plaintiffs claim that defendants' policies of permitting smoking in their restaurants violate § 302 of the Americans with Disabilities Act, 42 U.S.C. § 12182 (the "ADA" or "Act"). Plaintiffs appeal judgments of the United States District Court for the District of Connecticut (T.F. Gilroy Daly, Judge) granting defendants' motions to dismiss plaintiffs' claims for failure to state a claim upon which relief could be granted.

For the reasons stated below, we reverse the judgments of the district court and remand the cases for further proceedings.

The facts alleged in plaintiffs' complaints are rather straightforward. During one week in February, 1993, each plaintiff entered both a McDonald's and a Burger King restaurant in Connecticut. Each plaintiff found the air in each restaurant to be full of tobacco smoke, and, because of his or her condition, was unable to enter the restaurant without experiencing breathing problems. Each plaintiff has also encountered similar difficulties at other times in other restaurants owned by McDonald's and Burger King.

After registering complaints with the defendants and the State of Connecticut Human Rights Commission without satisfactory results, plaintiffs filed separate suits against McDonald's and Burger King on March 30, 1993. Their complaints alleged that the defendants' policies of permitting smoking in their restaurants constituted discrimination under the Act. Each complaint requested a declaratory judgment that such policies are discriminatory under the ADA, as well as an injunction to prohibit defendants from maintaining any policy which interfered with plaintiffs' rights under the Act, "and more specifically to require [defendants and their franchisees] to establish a policy of prohibiting smoking in all of the facilities they own, lease, or operate."

[Plaintiffs appealed the grant of a motion to dismiss their claims.] Because we find that plaintiffs' complaints do on their face state a cognizable claim against the defendants under the Americans with Disabilities Act, we reverse the district court's orders of dismissal.

The ADA was promulgated "to provide a clear and comprehensive national mandate for the elimination of discrimination against individuals with disabilities," as well as to establish "clear, strong, consistent, enforceable standards" for scrutinizing such discrimination. 42 U.S.C. § 12101(b)(1)–(2). Consistent with these goals, § 302 of the ADA provides:

> No individual shall be discriminated against on the basis of disability in the full and equal enjoyment of the goods, services, facilities, privileges, advantages, or accommodations of any place of public accommodation by any person who owns, leases (or leases to), or operates a place of public accommodation.

42 U.S.C. § 12182(a). "Discrimination" under this section includes the failure of an owner, operator, lessee, or lessor of public accommodations

> to make reasonable modifications in policies, practices, or procedures, when such modifications are necessary to afford such goods, services, [or] facilities . . . to individuals with disabilities, unless the entity can demonstrate that making such modifications would fundamentally alter the nature of such goods, services, [or] facilities. . . .

42 U.S.C. § 12182(b)(2)(A)(ii).

For the purposes of these motions, defendants do not dispute that the section applies to them as owners and operators of public accommodations. They also concede at this point that plaintiffs qualify as "individuals with disabilities" under the ADA. The . . . principal contention of McDonald's and Burger King on appeal, is that a total ban on smoking does not constitute a "reasonable modification" under the ADA.

The ADA and cases interpreting it do not articulate a precise test for determining whether a particular modification is "reasonable." However, because the Rehabilitation Act, which applies to recipients of federal funding, uses the same "reasonableness" analysis, cases interpreting that act provide some guidance. *See Vande Zande v. State of Wisc. Dep't of Admin.*, 44 F.3d 538, 542 (7th Cir. 1995); *Pottgen v. Missouri State High Sch. Activities Ass'n*, 40 F.3d 926, 930 (8th Cir. 1994); *Harmer v. Virginia Elec. & Power Co.*, 831 F. Supp. 1300, 1306–07 (E.D. Va. 1993) ("the legislative history of the ADA indicates that reasonable accommodation is to be interpreted consistently with the regulations implemented under . . . the Rehabilitation Act"); *cf. Helen L. v. DiDario*, 46 F.3d 325, 331 (3d Cir. 1995) (noting that the ADA provisions applicable to state and local governments incorporate the non-discrimination principles of the Rehabilitation Act and that ADA regulations implementing those provisions are patterned after those promulgated under the Rehabilitation Act); *Kinney v. Yerusalim*, 9 F.3d 1067, 1071 (3d Cir. 1993) (explaining that Congress intended that regulations under the ADA be consistent with Rehabilitation Act regulations), *cert. denied*, 114 S. Ct. 1545, 128 L. Ed. 2d 196 (1994).

The Supreme Court, addressing the issue of the reasonableness of accommodations under the Rehabilitation Act in the employment context, stated that "[a]ccommodation is not reasonable if it either imposes 'undue financial and administrative burdens' . . . or requires a fundamental alteration in the nature of [the] program.'" *School Bd. v. Arline*, 480 U.S. 273, 287 n.17, 107 S. Ct. 1123, 1130 n.17, 94 L. Ed. 2d 307 (1987). Other courts have articulated factors that they consider relevant to the determination, including the nature and extent of plaintiff's disability. *See D'Amico v. New York State Bd. of Law Examiners*, 813 F. Supp. 217, 221 (W.D.N.Y. 1993).

Although neither the ADA nor the courts have defined the precise contours of the test for reasonableness, it is clear that the determination of whether a particular modification is "reasonable" involves a fact-specific, case-by-case inquiry that considers, among other factors, the effectiveness of the modification in light of the nature of the disability in question and the cost to the organization that would implement it. *See D'Amico*, 813 F. Supp. at 221–22 (holding that allowing a law student with a vision disorder four days to take the bar exam was a reasonable accommodation).

While there may be claims requesting modification under the ADA that warrant dismissal as unreasonable as a matter of law, in the cases before us a fact-specific inquiry was required. None has occurred at this early stage of the suits. The magistrate judge instead concluded — and the district court agreed — that plaintiffs' request for a ban on smoking in all of defendants' restaurants was unreasonable as a matter of law. The magistrate judge offered two grounds for this conclusion: first, that "the ADA, by itself, does not mandate a 'blanket ban' on smoke in 'fast food' restaurants," and second, that "[i]t is not reasonable, under the ADA, to impose a blanket ban on every McDonald's [and Burger King] restaurant where there are certain restaurants which reasonably can accommodate a 'no-smoking' area." We believe that neither ground justifies dismissal of the complaints.

The magistrate judge correctly noted that the ADA on its face does not ban smoking in all public accommodations or all fast-food restaurants. Defendants carry this point a significant step further, however, and argue that the ADA precludes a total smoking ban as a reasonable modification. They assert that Congress did not intend to restrict the range of legislative policy options open to state and local governments to deal with the issue of smoking. Their argument rests on § 501(b) of the ADA:

> Nothing in this chapter shall be construed to invalidate or limit the remedies, rights, and procedures of any Federal law or law of any State or political subdivision . . . that provides greater or equal protection for the rights of individuals with disabilities than are afforded by this chapter. Nothing in this chapter shall be construed to preclude the prohibition of, or the imposition of restrictions on, smoking . . . in places of public accommodation covered by subchapter III of this chapter.

42 U.S.C. § 12201(b). The magistrate judge echoed a sentiment similar to defendants', stating that "[t]he significant public policy issues regarding smoking in 'fast food' restaurants are better addressed by Congress or by the Connecticut General Assembly. . . ."

It is plain to us that Congress did not intend to isolate the effects of smoking from the protections of the ADA. The first sentence of § 501(b) simply indicates that Congress, states, and municipalities remain free to offer greater protection for disabled individuals than the ADA provides. The passage does not state, and it does not follow, that violations of the ADA should go unredressed merely because a state has chosen to provide some degree of protection to those with disabilities.

As to the second sentence of § 501(b), the Department of Justice regulations state that it "merely clarifies that the Act does not require public accommodations to accommodate smokers by permitting them to smoke." 28 C.F.R. Pt. 36, App. B, 56 Fed. Reg. 35544, 35562. Nothing in the second sentence precludes public accommodations from accommodating those with smoke-sensitive disabilities. In fact, this language expressly permits a total ban on smoking if a court finds it appropriate under the ADA. We therefore reject any argument by defendants to the contrary.

Cases in which individuals claim under the ADA that allergies to smoke constitute a disability and require smoking restrictions are simply subject to the same general reasonableness analysis as are other cases under the Act. *See, e.g., Vickers v. Veterans Admin.*, 549 F. Supp. 85, 87–89 (W.D. Wash. 1982) (evaluating whether a ban on smoking is a reasonable accommodation under the circumstances); *cf.* 28 C.F.R. Pt. 36, App. B, 56 Fed. Reg. 35544, 35549 ("[T]he determination as to whether allergies to cigarette smoke . . . are disabilities covered by the regulation must be made using the same case-by-case analysis that is applied to all other physical or mental impairments."). We see no reason why, under the appropriate circumstances, a ban on smoking could not be a reasonable modification. Accordingly, we turn to the magistrate judge's conclusion that plaintiffs' request for a smoking ban under the circumstances of these cases was unreasonable as a matter of law.

The magistrate judge's principal objection to plaintiffs' proposed modification was that plaintiffs were seeking a total ban on smoking in all of defendants' restaurants even though "there are certain restaurants which reasonably can accommodate a 'no-smoking' area." We do not think that it is possible to conclude on the pleadings that plaintiffs' suggested modification in this case is necessarily unreasonable.

To be sure, the few courts that have addressed the question of reasonable modification for a smoke-sensitive disability have found a total ban unnecessary. *See Harmer*, 831 F. Supp. at 1303–04, 1307; *Vickers*, 549 F. Supp. at 87–89. Yet these courts only reached this conclusion after making a factual determination that existing accommodations were sufficient. In granting summary judgment to the defendant, the *Harmer* court concluded that the plaintiff could perform the essential functions of his job with the modifications already made by the defendant, which included moving smokers further from the plaintiff's desk, mandatory use of smokeless ashtrays, and installation of air filtration and oxygen infusion devices. *Id.* at 1303–04, 1306. In *Vickers*, the court found after a bench trial that the nine steps defendants had taken to alleviate plaintiff's suffering constituted sufficient accommodation, and that a total ban was therefore not necessary. *Vickers*, 549 F. Supp. at 87–88. Neither case held that a ban on smoking would be unreasonable if less drastic measures were ineffective, much less that a ban on smoking is unreasonable as a matter of law.

Plaintiffs in this case are entitled to the same opportunity afforded to the plaintiffs in *Harmer* and *Vickers* to prove that a ban on smoking is a reasonable modification to permit them access to defendants' restaurants. Given that McDonald's has voluntarily banned smoking in all corporate-owned restaurants, the factfinder may conclude that such a ban would fully accommodate plaintiffs' disabilities but impose little or no cost on the defendants. The magistrate judge's unsupported assumption that certain restaurants "reasonably can accommodate a 'no-smoking' area" does not obviate the need for a factual inquiry. Plaintiffs have alleged that, regardless of the different structural arrangements in various restaurants, the environment in each establishment visited by the plaintiffs contained too much smoke to allow them use of the facilities on an equal basis as other non-disabled patrons. These allegations belie the magistrate judge's assumption that no-smoking areas offer a sufficient accommodation to plaintiffs. In such a case, it is not possible to conclude that "plaintiff can prove no set of facts in support of his claim which would entitle him to relief." *Conley*, 355 U.S. at 45–46, 78 S. Ct. at 101–02. Accordingly, defendants' motions to dismiss should have been denied.

In addition, we note that plaintiffs do not solely request a ban on smoking. Their complaints ask that defendants be enjoined "from continuing or maintaining any policy" that denies plaintiffs access to their restaurants, as well as "such other and further relief as it may deem just and proper." We do not think that it is necessary at this point in the lawsuit to bind plaintiffs to the one specific modification they prefer. If plaintiffs should fail in their quest for an outright ban on smoking, they may still be able to demonstrate after discovery that modifications short of an outright ban, such as partitions or ventilation systems, are both "reasonable" and "necessary," 42 U.S.C. § 12182(b)(2)(A)(ii), and plaintiffs should be allowed the opportunity to do so.

[The court concludes that doubts about the scope of the injunction seeking a smoking ban, sought by the plaintiffs to apply to all the defendants' restaurants, should not be resolved by dismissal of the complaints though there must be more than a possibility or fear that the injury will occur.]

We therefore reverse the judgments of the district court and remand for proceedings consistent with this opinion.

NOTES

1. *More Smoke.* An employee who was injured by workplace second-hand smoke was permitted to recover under the state job discrimination statute in *Hinman v. Yakima School Dist. No. 7*, 69 Wash. App. 2d 445, 850 P.2d 536 (1993). The plaintiff had asthma, as her employer knew. The statute forbade discrimination based on a "sensory, mental, or physical handicap." She was

permitted to recover although she had already received workers' compensation benefits for the injury. The workers' compensation statute was not the exclusive remedy, since the discrimination claim was based on an intentional wrong for which the compensation remedy was not exclusive, the court said.

2. *Discrimination in Medical Benefits.* The First Circuit, in *Carparts Distrib. Ctr. v. Automotive Wholesalers Ass'n,* 37 F.3d 12 (1st Cir. 1994), held that a trade association offering a self-funded medical reimbursement plan could be liable under the Americans with Disabilities Act (ADA), 42 U.S.C. §§ 12101–12213, for limiting benefits for AIDS-related illnesses to $25,000 rather than the $1 million benefits afforded other plan members. While the Act applies to discrimination by "an employer, employment agency, labor organization, or joint labor-management committee," an insurer could be liable under agency principles where it was acting on behalf of the plaintiff's employer in providing health benefits, the court said.

3. *Bar Admissions Mental Health Questions.* The court in *Clark v. Virginia Bd. of Bar Exmrs.*, 880 F. Supp. 430 (E.D. Va. 1995), held that a state bar was forbidden under the ADA from asking a bar applicant whether she had been treated or counseled "for mental, emotional or nervous disorders" within five years prior to the application. The court said that the question, No. 20(b) on the application, was too broad. It had never been used to deny an application, the court found, but it could discourage disabled persons, within the meaning of the Act, from seeking needed medical treatment and counseling:

> On the basis of the record produced at trial, the Court easily reaches the conclusion that question 20(b) is too broad and should be rewritten to achieve the Board's objective of protecting the public. Question 20(b)'s broadly worded mental health question discriminates against disabled applicants by imposing additional eligibility criteria. While certain severe mental or emotional disorders may pose a direct threat to public safety, the Board has made no individualized finding that obtaining evidence of mental health counseling or treatment is effective in guarding against this threat.
>
> In fact, the Board presented no evidence of correlation between obtaining mental counseling and employment dysfunction. Question 20(b), while offering little marginal utility in identifying unfit applicants, has strong negative stigmatic and deterrent effects upon applicants.

4. *Obesity as a Disability.* The plaintiff in *Cook v. State of R.I. Dep't. of Mental Health, Retardation & Hosps.*, 10 F.3d 17 (1st Cir. 1993), was denied employment as a nurse by the defendant, MHRH, because of "morbid obesity," defined as a condition of one who "weighs either more than twice her optimal weight or more than 100 pounds over her optimal weight." Plaintiff stood 5 feet 2 inches tall and weighed over 320 pounds. On the basis of plaintiff's pre-hire physical examination, defendant found "no limitations that impinged on [plaintiff's] ability to do the job." She was nevertheless denied employment. Defendant claimed:

> . . . Cook's morbid obesity compromised her ability to evacuate patients in case of an emergency and put her at greater risk of

developing serious ailments (a "fact" that MHRH's hierarchs speculated would promote absenteeism and increase the likelihood of workers' compensation claims). Consequently, MHRH refused to hire plaintiff for a vacant IA-MR position.

Plaintiff filed a claim against defendant under § 504 of the Rehabilitation Act of 1973, 29 U.S.C. § 794. The jury awarded her $100,000 in compensatory damages, and the court affirmed the verdict on appeal.

To invoke the Act in a failure-to-hire case, the court said, a claimant must prove four things:

> (1) that she applied for a post in a federally funded program or activity, (2) that, at the time, she suffered from a cognizable disability, (3) but was, nonetheless, qualified for the position, and (4) that she was not hired due solely to her disability.

The defendant here "received substantial federal funding." The court further said that the Act "embraces not only those persons who are in fact disabled, but also those persons who bear the brunt of discrimination because prospective employers view them as disabled."

As to defendant's claim that plaintiff's obesity presented a risk to herself as well as to the health care facility's residents, so as to render her apparently unqualified, the court found that a fact issue was presented on the question. The court stated:

> One of appellant's justifications for rejecting plaintiff — its concern over high absenteeism and increased workers' compensation costs — is itself a prohibited basis for denying employment. Unless absenteeism rises to a level such that the applicant is no longer "otherwise qualified," the Rehabilitation Act requires employers to bear absenteeism and other miscellaneous burdens involved in making reasonable accommodations in order to permit the employment of disabled persons.

5. *Restrictions on ADA Coverage.* The United States Supreme Court in a trilogy of cases, *Sutton v. United Air Lines*, 527 U.S. 471 (1999), *Murphy v. United Parcel Serv.*, 527 U.S. 516 (1999), *Albertsons, Inc. v. Kirkingburg*, 527 U.S. 555 (1999), in effect restricted coverage under the ADA so as to exclude individuals whose disabilities could be substantially ameliorated through corrective measures taken by the individuals themselves. *Sutton* involved severe myopia correctible with glasses, *Murphy* high blood pressure treatable with medication, and *Albertsons* monocular vision for which the plaintiff had been able to compensate through "subconscious mechanisms for coping."

In *Toyota Motor Mfg. v. Williams,* 122 S.Ct. 681 (2002), the Court held plaintiff failed to establish an ADA violation because there was no proof that her disability, carpel tunnel syndrome, substantially limited or prevented her from engaging in a major life activity.

In *Board of Trustees of the Univ. of Ala. v. Garrett*, 121 S. Ct. 955 (2000), the United States Supreme Court said the Eleventh Amendment rendered states immune from suit for violation of the ADA so long as the states' actions were rational. Congress in enacting the ADA had failed to show a pattern of

LYTLE v. MALADY
209 Mich. App. 179, 530 N.W.2d 135 (1995)

[Plaintiff sued her employer, Howmet Corporation, for wrongful discharge under the state's age and gender discrimination statutes. The court held the plaintiff stated a cause of action on both claims.]

HOLBROOK, PRESIDING JUDGE.

In 1973, Howmet, a manufacturer of aircraft engine parts, hired plaintiff as a general clerk. Following a succession of positive performance appraisals and promotions, she was promoted in 1979 by her supervisor, John Ozar, to employment manager of the human resources department. . . . When defendant Malady became plaintiff's supervisor in 1987, a personality conflict arose, and in 1989, on Malady's recommendation, she was demoted to human resources specialist. A younger, allegedly less qualified man was promoted to replace her.

As a result of declines in military spending and a downturn in the commercial airline industry, Howmet instituted a series of reductions in its work force between 1988 and 1991. In August 1991, William Roof, director of the Whitehall human resources department, was directed to cut his 1992 department budget by fifteen percent (approximately $439,000). In November 1991, Roof eliminated four positions in the human resources department, including plaintiff's position as human resources specialist, and reassigned her job duties to other persons within the department. Roof decided to eliminate plaintiff's position because her main responsibilities involved the hourly workers who bore the brunt of the downsizing. Plaintiff's "termination evaluation" indicated that Howmet would rehire plaintiff in the event a nonsupervisory, administrative position became open. . . .

Plaintiff asserts that the trial court erred in finding that no genuine issue of material fact existed with respect to plaintiff's prima facie case of age discrimination and in granting Howmet summary disposition pursuant to MCR 2.116(C)(10). We agree and reverse.

Plaintiff's claim of age discrimination is based upon the Civil Rights Act, which provides in pertinent part:

(1) An employer shall not do any of the following:

(a) Fail or refuse to hire or recruit, discharge, or otherwise discriminate against an individual with respect to employment, compensation, or a term, condition, or privilege of employment, because of . . . age. . . . [M.C.L. § 37.2202; M.S.A. § 3.548(202).]

This Court has held that federal precedent, while not binding, is persuasive authority in interpreting and applying the Civil Rights Act.

An age discrimination claim can be based on two theories: (1) disparate treatment, which requires a showing of either a pattern of intentional discrimination against protected employees, *e.g.*, employees aged forty to seventy years, or against an individual plaintiff; or (2) disparate impact, which requires a showing that an otherwise facially neutral employment policy has a discriminatory effect on members of a protected class. In this case, plaintiff has presented competent evidence only of a disparate treatment claim.

A plaintiff can establish a claim of disparate treatment with sufficient direct or indirect evidence of intentional discrimination. Direct evidence of disparate treatment would be evidence that, if believed, would prove the existence of the employer's illegal motive without benefit of presumption or inference. That is not the usual case, however, because an employer is rarely so blatant as to announce its illegal motives. Instead, the usual case must be proven by indirect (circumstantial or statistical) evidence. In light of this reality, courts have created special rules of proof in order "to sharpen the inquiry into the elusive factual question of intentional discrimination." *Texas Dep't of Community Affairs v. Burdine*, 450 U.S. 248, 255 n.8, 101 S. Ct. 1089, 1095 n.8, 67 L. Ed. 2d 207 (1981).

A prima facie case of age discrimination varies with differing factual situations. Where, as here, a plaintiff is discharged as a result of an employer's economically motivated reduction in force (RIF), a prima facie case of disparate treatment requires an initial showing, by a preponderance of the evidence, that (1) the plaintiff was within the protected class and was discharged or demoted, (2) the plaintiff was qualified to assume another position at the time of discharge or demotion, and (3) age was "a determining factor" in the employer's decision to discharge or demote the plaintiff. Because plaintiff has presented no direct evidence of age discrimination by Howmet, she must attempt to create through indirect evidence a rebuttable presumption of discrimination. In a RIF case, it is insufficient for a plaintiff to show merely that the employer retained a younger employee while discharging an older employee.

Once established, a prima facie case creates a rebuttable presumption of disparate treatment. *Burdine*, 450 U.S. at 252–253, 101 S. Ct. at 1093–1094. At this point, the burden of production shifts to the defendant — as opposed to the burden of persuasion that never shifts — to rebut the presumption of disparate treatment by articulating (not proving) "some legitimate, nondiscriminatory reason" for the adverse employment decision against the plaintiff. *Id.* at 253–258, 101 S. Ct. at 1093–1096. The defendant's explanation must be clear and reasonably specific to afford the plaintiff "a full and fair opportunity" to demonstrate pretext. *Id.* at 256, 101 S. Ct. at 1095.

If the defendant carries its burden of production, the presumption of discrimination is dispelled, and the factual inquiry proceeds to a new level of specificity. The plaintiff's burdens of production and persuasion merge, requiring her to prove by a preponderance of the evidence not only that the defendant's proffered reasons are a mere pretext but also that illegal discrimination was more likely the defendant's true motivation in discharging or demoting the plaintiff.

At this juncture, we note that there is a crucial distinction between a plaintiff's prima facie case for purposes of surviving a summary disposition motion and a prima facie case sufficient to persuade a trier of fact at trial with regard to the ultimate question whether a defendant intentionally discriminated against the plaintiff. While the latter requires a plaintiff to prove her case to the trier of fact by a preponderance of the evidence, the former does not require her to go so far. Neither a trial court nor this Court on appellate review of a summary disposition determination need conduct a minitrial to determine whether the plaintiff has met her burden of presenting a prima facie case by a preponderance of the evidence. Instead, for the plaintiff to survive a summary disposition motion, she need only tender specific factual evidence that could lead a reasonable jury to conclude that the defendant's proffered reasons are a pretext for age discrimination. Thus, the plaintiff must establish, either directly or indirectly, the existence of a genuine issue of material fact that the defendant's proffered reasons are unworthy of credence, and that illegal age discrimination was more likely the defendant's true motivation in discharging or demoting her.

Two issues are presented on appeal, both arising naturally from the *McDonnell Douglas* burden-shifting analysis: whether plaintiff created a genuine issue of material fact with regard to the existence of a prima facie case of discrimination by indirect evidence; and, if so, whether plaintiff created a genuine issue of material fact concerning whether Howmet's proffered reasons were a mere pretext for age discrimination.

In this case, plaintiff's prima facie case is based solely on circumstantial evidence. She alleges that in January 1989, defendant Malady demoted her from employment manager to human resources specialist, while simultaneously promoting Walter Boczkaja to employment manager. Boczkaja was younger, had less seniority with Howmet, less experience in the area of human resources, and had been trained by plaintiff during her tenure as employment manager. Plaintiff also alleges that, approximately six weeks before she was discharged in 1991 at age forty-four, Howmet hired Andrea Achterhoff, age thirty-one, as human resources specialist for its Operhall Research Center (ORC), a division separate from the Whitehall division where plaintiff had worked. Plaintiff also alleges that, as part of an effort by Howmet to implement a new manufacturing approach, Jeff Billingsley, a training and development manager, was transferred from the corporate human resources department to Whitehall's human resources department. Both Achterhoff and Billingsley were younger than plaintiff, had less seniority, and, according to plaintiff, performed duties that she could have assumed considering her nineteen years of experience at Howmet.

We find plaintiff's allegations, although meager, to be sufficient to create a genuine issue of material fact that age was a determining factor in her discharge. Because this is a RIF case, Howmet's decision to discharge qualified, older employees is not inherently suspicious but rather readily explainable in terms of its economic situation. Standing alone, the fact of such discharges does not warrant shifting the burden of production to Howmet to justify its decision. Here, however, we find that Howmet's retaining and hiring of younger, less senior, and allegedly less qualified employees, while discharging plaintiff, "exude[s] that faint aroma of impropriety" sufficient to create a rebuttable presumption of disparate treatment.

In rebuttal, Howmet asserts that the elimination of plaintiff's position as human resources specialist was justified because of a projected downturn in sales and a concomitant reduction in the hourly work force for which plaintiff was primarily responsible. Howmet further asserts that plaintiff was not replaced but that her duties were reassigned to various other employees. Howmet further claims that the hiring of Achterhoff for the position of human resources representative at ORC was irrelevant to plaintiff's discharge because ORC is a separate division with a separate budget over which plaintiff's supervisors had no control. In any event, Howmet asserts that Achterhoff was qualified for the position and that plaintiff did not apply. At deposition, defendant Malady stated that one of the reasons he discharged plaintiff was because of concerns he had regarding her supervisory ability.

To resurrect her prima facie case at the third stage of proofs, plaintiff asserts that Howmet's proffered reasons are a mere pretext for age discrimination. Although Howmet's RIF may have been justified, plaintiff has produced documentary evidence to support an inference that Howmet's true motivation in discharging her was age discrimination. Plaintiff presented evidence that she was capable of assuming the duties given to Achterhoff, and that it was not reasonable to expect her to apply for the ORC position because at that time she was not aware of her imminent discharge. Moreover, Howmet has failed to rebut plaintiff's claim that its decision to discharge her and retain Boczkaja, who was younger, with less seniority and less experience, was at least partially premised on plaintiff's age. We conclude that the hiring of Achterhoff and the retention of Boczkaja, in the face of plaintiff's discharge, could reasonably lead to an inference that Howmet consciously refused to consider retaining or relocating plaintiff because of her age. Finally, in light of plaintiff's many years of positive performance appraisals and several promotions, she has presented evidence supporting an inference that Malady's claim that she was not supervisory material was a mere pretext.

Viewing the evidence in a light most favorable to plaintiff and drawing all reasonable inferences in her favor, we find that she has raised a genuine issue of material fact whether Howmet's proffered reasons for her discharge were a mere pretext for age discrimination. Accordingly, we reverse the trial court's order of summary disposition of this claim. . . .

NOTES

1. *A Bad Excuse and a Good Excuse.* If an employer terminates an employee for an impermissible reason, and also for a permissible reason, the termination will apparently be upheld if the factfinder believes that the employer would have terminated the employee for the permissible reason alone. *See Cisco v. United Parcel Servs., Inc.*, 328 Pa. Super. 300, 476 A.2d 1340 (1984).

But what about a situation where the employer terminates for an impermissible reason, and then learns of a permissible reason after the termination? The courts had widely applied the same rule in this situation as that discussed in the preceding paragraph, but in *McKennon v. Nashville Banner Co.*, 115 S. Ct. 879 (1995), the Court established a different rule. Where an employer discharges an employee in violation of the Age Discrimination in Employment Act (ADEA), 29 U.S.C § 621 *et seq.*, and then subsequently discovers a valid reason for termination, the employee is entitled to damages for the period between the termination and the discovery. In *McKennon* the plaintiff was allegedly discharged by the defendant in violation of the ADEA, and she filed a lawsuit against the defendant. During discovery proceedings while the suit was pending, defendant learned that plaintiff had allegedly wrongfully copied confidential documents of the defendant before her termination. The jury could find that this alleged wrongful conduct would have provided a valid basis for termination, thus providing a damage cutoff point as of the time of discovery.

2. *The Protected Class.* In *Showalter v. Univ. of Pittsb. Med. Cntr.*, 190 F.3d 231 (3d Cir. 1999), the court said as long as plaintiff is in the protected class (40 years or older), she may bring a claim under the Age Discrimination in Employment Act of 1967 (ADEA), 29 U.S.C. § 621 *et seq.*, even though the alleged discrimination was in favor of a person over 40. That person need only be "sufficiently younger" to create an inference of age discrimination, the court said.

3. *The Burden of Poof.* The Court in *Reeves v. Sanderson Plumbing Products, Inc.*, 120 S. Ct. 2097 (2000), said a plaintiff may establish a prima facie case under the ADEA by showing that her employer's stated reason for discharging her was pretextual. In determining whether the case should go to the jury, the trial court will review all the evidence in the record.

4. Congress exceeded its power under the Fourteenth Amendment, the Court said in *Kimel v. Florida Board of Regents*, 120 S. Ct. 631 (2000), by making the ADEA apply to states. A state may discriminate on the basis of age if the state's age classification is rationally related to a legitimate state interest, said the Court. A state "may rely on age as a proxy for the other qualities, abilities, or characteristics that are relevant to the State's legitimate interests. . . . That age proves to be an inaccurate proxy in any individual case is irrelevant," 120 S. Ct. at 646.

5. *Age Discrimination and Freedom of Religion.* The court in *DeMarco v. Holy Cross High School*, 4 F.3d 166 (2d Cir. 1993), held that ADEA applies to a suit brought against a parochial school by a former lay teacher who had some religious duties, including leading his students in prayer and taking them to Mass. "The majority of courts considering the issue," the court said, "have determined that application of the ADEA to religious institutions generally, and to lay teachers specifically, does not pose a serious risk of excessive entanglement." A court may not inquire into "the value or truthfulness of church doctrine," but a plaintiff "may be able to put into question the genuineness of the employer's putative nondiscriminatory purpose by arguing that the stated purpose is implausible, absurd or unwise," the court said.

The defendant contended that "the ADEA is inapplicable to claims brought by members of the clergy against their religious employers." The court responded that cases so holding "are inapposite, since each one deals with the pervasively religious relationship between a member of the clergy and his religious employer."

The court noted, by analogy, that Title VII, 42 U.S.C. § 2000e *et seq.*, permitted employer religious institutions to discriminate in employment on the basis of religion. Such an employer, however, is not permitted under Title VII to discriminate on the basis of "race, gender and national origin."

The plaintiff in *Geary v. Visitation of the Blessed Virgin Mary*, 7 F.3d 324 (3d Cir. 1993), said she was terminated as a lay teacher in a church-operated elementary school in violation of the ADEA. The court said "the ADEA will apply only so long as the plaintiff does not challenge the validity of [a religious] doctrine or practice and asks no more than whether the proffered religious reason actually motivated the employment action." Here, the church contended that it terminated plaintiff because "she violated Church doctrine by marrying a divorced man." The defendant was entitled to summary judgment on this ADEA claim, because the plaintiff "did not present any evidence that would suggest a nonreligious basis for her dismissal." The fact that she had been a lay teacher at the school for 29 years, "had previously received favorable reviews," and was allegedly the highest paid lay teacher, and was replaced by "a younger lower-paid teacher" after she turned 50 and married a divorcé, was not enough to raise a jury question on the issue.

However, the plaintiff did state a claim under the ADEA for alleged retaliatory cancellation of her health insurance by the school after she filed her ADEA suit. The school wrote her a letter stating that it was canceling her insurance "considering the present legal suit initiated by yourself against the church," and further stating that the cancellation was "necessitated by the legal course you are pursuing." The ADEA "makes it unlawful to retaliate against an employee who litigates an age discrimination claim," the court said, *citing* 29 U.S.C. § 623(a), (d).

The court indicated that "a religious institution may argue that religion mandates age discrimination." But such a claim was not presented here, and, therefore, the court did not address the validity of such an argument.

PROBLEM

A small religious denomination consisting of a single church terminated its minister, Sarah, because "she is too old." She was 50 at the time of her termination. The church then hired a new minister who was 45 years old.

Sarah filed an ADEA claim against the church. After the suit was filed, the church congregation met and adopted a creed providing that a woman could not be a minister of the church. They based this creed on 1 Cor. 14:34–35 of the Bible: "Let your women keep silence in the churches . . . for it is a shame for women to speak in the church." Pursuant to this creed, women were permitted to assume active roles—including speaking roles other than that of minister—in the church. Sarah contended that this creed was invalid under the free speech clause of the First Amendment and under Title VII of the Civil Rights Act.

Sarah amended her suit after the church's adoption of the creed to assert a claim under Title VII and the First Amendment. Are any of Sarah's claims valid?

HARRIS v. FORKLIFT SYSTEMS, INC.
510 U.S. 17, 114 S. Ct. 367, 126 L.Ed.2d 295 (1993)

JUSTICE O'CONNOR delivered the opinion of the Court.

In this case we consider the definition of a discriminatorily "abusive work environment" (also known as a "hostile work environment") under Title VII of the Civil Rights Act of 1964, 78 Stat. 253, as amended, 42 U.S.C. § 2000e *et seq.* (1988 ed., Supp. III).

Teresa Harris worked as a manager at Forklift Systems, Inc., an equipment rental company, from April 1985 until October 1987. Charles Hardy was Forklift's president.

The Magistrate found that, throughout Harris' time at Forklift, Hardy often insulted her because of her gender and often made her the target of unwanted sexual innuendos. Hardy told Harris on several occasions, in the presence of other employees, "You're a woman, what do you know" and "We need a man as the rental manager;" at least once, he told her she was "a dumb ass woman." . . . Again in front of others, he suggested that the two of them "go to the Holiday Inn to negotiate [Harris'] raise." Hardy occasionally asked Harris and other female employees to get coins from his front pants pocket. . . . He threw objects on the ground in front of Harris and other women, and asked them to pick the objects up. . . . He made sexual innuendos about Harris' and other women's clothing. . . .

In mid-August 1987, Harris complained to Hardy about his conduct. Hardy said he was surprised that Harris was offended, claimed he was only joking, and apologized. . . . He also promised he would stop, and based on this assurance Harris stayed on the job. . . . But in early September, Hardy began anew: While Harris was arranging a deal with one of Forklift's customers, he asked her, again in front of other employees, "What did you do, promise the guy . . . some [sex] Saturday night?" . . . On October 1, Harris collected her paycheck and quit.

Harris then sued Forklift, claiming that Hardy's conduct had created an abusive work environment for her because of her gender. The United States District Court for the Middle District of Tennessee, adopting the report and recommendation of the Magistrate, found this to be "a close case," . . .but held that Hardy's conduct did not create an abusive environment. The court found that some of Hardy's comments "offended [Harris], and would offend the reasonable woman," . . . but that they were not

> "so severe as to be expected to seriously affect [Harris'] psychological well-being. A reasonable woman manager under like circumstances would have been offended by Hardy, but his conduct would not have risen to the level of interfering with that person's work performance.
>
> "Neither do I believe that [Harris] was subjectively so offended that she suffered injury. . . . Although Hardy may at times have genuinely offended [Harris], I do not believe that he created a working environment so poisoned as to be intimidating or abusive to [Harris]."

In focusing on the employee's psychological well-being, the district court was following Circuit precedent. *See Rabidue v. Osceola Refining Co.*, 805 F.2d 611, 620 (CA6 1986), *cert. denied,* 481 U.S. 1041, 107 S. Ct. 1983, 95 L. Ed. 2d 823 (1987). The United States Court of Appeals for the Sixth Circuit affirmed in a brief unpublished decision, 976 F.2d 733 (CA6 1992).

We granted certiorari . . . to resolve a conflict among the Circuits on whether conduct, to be actionable as "abusive work environment" harassment (no *quid pro quo* harassment issue is present here), must "seriously affect [an employee's] psychological well-being" or lead the plaintiff to "suffe[r] injury." Compare *Rabidue* (requiring serious effect on psychological well-being); *Vance v. Southern Bell Telephone & Telegraph Co.*, 863 F.2d 1503, 1510 (CA11 1989) (same); and *Downes v. FAA*, 775 F.2d 288, 292 (CA Fed. 1985) (same), with *Ellison v. Brady*, 924 F.2d 872, 877–878 (CA9 1991) (rejecting such a requirement).

Title VII of the Civil Rights Act of 1964 makes it "an unlawful employment practice for an employer . . . to discriminate against any individual with respect to his compensation, terms, conditions, or privileges of employment, because of such individual's race, color, religion, sex, or national origin." 42 U.S.C. § 2000e-2(a)(1). As we made clear in *Meritor Savings Bank v. Vinson*, 477 U.S. 57, 106 S. Ct. 2399, 91 L. Ed. 2d 49 (1986), this language "is not limited to 'economic' or 'tangible' discrimination. The phrase 'terms, conditions, or privileges of employment' evinces a congressional intent 'to strike at the entire spectrum of disparate treatment of men and women' in employment," which includes requiring people to work in a discriminatorily hostile or abusive environment. *Id.*, at 64, 106 S. Ct., at 2404, *quoting Los Angeles Dept. of Water and Power v. Manhart*, 435 U.S. 702, 707, n.13, 98 S. Ct. 1370, 1374, 55 L. Ed. 2d 657 (1978) (some internal quotation marks omitted). When the workplace is permeated with "discriminatory intimidation, ridicule, and insult," 477 U.S., at 65, 106 S. Ct., at 2405, that is "sufficiently severe or pervasive to alter the conditions of the victim's employment and create an abusive working environment," *id.*, at 67, 106 S. Ct., at 2405 (internal brackets and quotation marks omitted), Title VII is violated.

This standard, which we reaffirm today, takes a middle path between making actionable any conduct that is merely offensive and requiring the conduct to cause a tangible psychological injury. As we pointed out in *Meritor*, "mere utterance of an . . . epithet which engenders offensive feelings in a[n] employee," *ibid.* (internal quotation marks omitted), does not sufficiently affect the conditions of employment to implicate Title VII. Conduct that is not severe or pervasive enough to create an objectively hostile or abusive work environment — an environment that a reasonable person would find hostile or abusive — is beyond Title VII's purview. Likewise, if the victim does not subjectively perceive the environment to be abusive, the conduct has not actually altered the conditions of the victim's employment, and there is no Title VII violation.

But Title VII comes into play before the harassing conduct leads to a nervous breakdown. A discriminatorily abusive work environment, even one that does not seriously affect employees' psychological well-being, can and often will detract from employees' job performance, discourage employees from remaining on the job, or keep them from advancing in their careers. Moreover, even without regard to these tangible effects, the very fact that the discriminatory conduct was so severe or pervasive that it created a work environment abusive to employees because of their race, gender, religion, or national origin offends Title VII's broad rule of workplace equality. The appalling conduct alleged in *Meritor*, and the reference in that case to environments " 'so heavily polluted with discrimination as to destroy completely the emotional and psychological stability of minority group workers,' " *supra*, at 66, 106 S. Ct., at 2405, *quoting*

Rogers v. EEOC, 454 F.2d 234, 238 (CA5 1971), *cert. denied,* 406 U.S. 957, 92 S. Ct. 2058, 32 L. Ed. 2d 343 (1972), merely present some especially egregious examples of harassment. They do not mark the boundary of what is actio

We therefore believe the District Court erred in relying on whether the conduct "seriously affect[ed] plaintiff's psychological well-being" or led her to "suffe[r] injury." Such an inquiry may needlessly focus the factfinder's attention on concrete psychological harm, an element Title VII does not require. Certainly Title VII bars conduct that would seriously affect a reasonable person's psychological well-being, but the statute is not limited to such conduct. So long as the environment would reasonably be perceived, and is perceived, as hostile or abusive, *Meritor, supra,* 477 U.S., at 67, 106 S. Ct., at 2405, there is no need for it also to be psychologically injurious.

This is not, and by its nature cannot be, a mathematically precise test. [W]hether an environment is "hostile" or "abusive" can be determined only by looking at all the circumstances. These may include the frequency of the discriminatory conduct; its severity; whether it is physically threatening or humiliating, or a mere offensive utterance; and whether it unreasonably interferes with an employee's work performance. The effect on the employee's psychological well-being is, of course, relevant to determining whether the plaintiff actually found the environment abusive. But while psychological harm, like any other relevant factor, may be taken into account, no single factor is required. . . .

We therefore reverse the judgment of the Court of Appeals, and remand the case for further proceedings consistent with this opinion.

NOTES

1. *Promoting Embarrassing Rumors.* The plaintiff's supervisor, Nelson, in the Pittsburgh area office of the EEOC, continually exacted loans from the plaintiff in *Spain v. Gallegos,* 26 F.3d 439 (3d Cir. 1994). This conduct in itself was forbidden by EEOC regulations, 29 C.F.R. § 1600.735-203. Owing to the supervisor's frequent private, on-the-job contacts with plaintiff Spain in connection with these solicitations, rumors spread in the workplace that she was having an affair with her supervisor. These rumors allegedly resulted in plaintiff's being ostracized by her fellow employees and being passed over for promotion. The court held that plaintiff stated a Title VII cause of action:

> Spain charges that as a result her work environment was affected in essentially five ways. First, she was subjected to the spreading of false rumors about her sexual affairs that impugned the integrity of her job performance. The very existence of the rumors caused Spain embarrassment. Second, due to the rumored sexual relationship, Spain's co-workers allegedly treated her like an outcast, leading to poor interpersonal relationships between herself and them, and causing Spain to feel miserable. Third, the rumors and the resulting poor interpersonal relationships at work led supervisory personnel to evaluate Spain negatively for advancement purposes. Spain proffered testimony from a co-worker and a supervisor regarding the rumors and these effects on her and on her environment. Fourth, Spain alleges

that Nelson knowingly exacerbated the situation. After creating the conditions in which the rumors developed, Nelson perpetuated the rumors by continuing to demand loans from Spain and to meet with her privately for this purpose, even after Spain informed him of the rumors and asked him to stop them. Finally, Spain contends that Nelson denied her a promotion in 1990 based on the rumors and the resulting effects they had upon her interpersonal relationships at work and her evaluations by her supervisors. She offered evidence as well to support this contention.

The court said that the plaintiff had met the four requirements for establishing a sexually hostile work environment: (1) she must have suffered intentional discrimination because of her sex; (2) the discrimination must have been pervasive and regular; (3) the discrimination must have subjectively affected the plaintiff detrimentally; and (4) the sexually hostile work environment "must be such that it would have detrimentally affected a reasonable person of the same sex" in the plaintiff's position.

2. *The Effect of "Unladylike" Behavior.* The plaintiff, Carr, in *Carr v. Allison Gas Turbine Div., General Motors*, 32 F.3d 1007 (7th Cir. 1994), was the first woman to work in defendant's tinsmith shop, "and her male coworkers were unhappy about working with a woman." She was subjected to "derogatory comments" and crude sexual derision "on a daily basis."

Defendant contended that plaintiff "invited" her coworkers' misconduct by her own "unladylike" behavior. Said the court:

> Even if we ignore the question why "unladylike" behavior should provoke not a vulgar response but a hostile, harassing response, and even if Carr's testimony that she talked and acted as she did in an effort to be "one of the boys" is (despite its plausibility) discounted, her words and conduct cannot be compared to those of the men and used to justify their conduct and exonerate their employer. The asymmetry of positions must be considered. She was one woman; they were many men. . . . We have trouble *imagining* a situation in which male factory workers sexually harass a lone woman *in self-defense* as it were; yet that at root is General Motors' characterization of what happened here. It is incredible on the admitted facts.

After a bench trial, the trial judge found for the defendant. The court of appeals said the trial judge ruled that:

> "even if Carr were to show that she was subjected to unwelcome harassment, and that she was adversely affected by it, her claim still would fail because she has not shown that [GM] neglected to take appropriate responsive action." We said that the standard was negligence, and we think it plain that negligence was proved. Carr began complaining to Routh, her immediate supervisor, in 1985, and four years later nothing had been done to correct the situation. The judge elicited from Routh's supervisor an affirmative answer to the question, "So you, more or less, left these gals alone to develop their own methods of coping on the job?" Nevertheless the judge's opinion depicts General Motors as the victim of a conspiracy of silence among the

tinsmiths. They would have thwarted any investigation by Routh (not that one was made), preferring, said the judge, "letting a foul-mouthed few set low standards of behavior to enforcing any collective standard that embraces at least some element of civility or decency." We do not find the picture of mighty GM helpless in the face of the foul-mouthed tinsmiths remotely plausible, but will pass the point by since the district judge acknowledged that beginning in August 1988 "Carr did maintain legitimate, active complaints; however, . . . Allison responded adequately to these." The responses were limited to several meetings that the company arranged between Carr and her tormentors, at one of which she and Beckham were asked to apologize to each other. No disciplinary action was undertaken against any of Carr's coworkers; no one was even reprimanded for the harassment. General Motors was astonishingly unprepared to deal with problems of sexual harassment, foreseeable though they are when a woman is introduced into a formerly all-male workplace. Supervisor Routh testified that if he encountered a problem of sexual harassment he would have to ask the personnel department what to do. *His* supervisor's recipe for solving problems of sexual harassment was to recommend that the woman work harder than the men to prove she could do the job. The personnel director of the gas turbine division acknowledged that the distribution of policies and posters dealing with problems of sexual harassment was "uncertain," and he could not remember having read any of them himself until shortly before he testified. At one of the meetings with Carr, management agreed to order a video-tape on sexual harassment to show to the workforce, but is was never shown, a failure that Routh's supervisor blamed on the personnel department.

Holding that the trial court committed "clear error" in its findings of fact, the appellate court reversed "with instructions to enter judgment on liability for the plaintiff . . . and [t]o proceed to a determination of the remedy to which she is entitled.

3. *The Impact of Title VII in the Workplace and Elsewhere.* Title VII addresses discrimination in employment with the hope of promoting equality through the elimination of intentional and also more subtle forms of decision-making which have an adverse impact on minorities and women in the workplace. Notably, Title VII was the first major piece of federal legislation to protect the rights of women and it has been said that that protection "has reverberated throughout our society." CHARLES ABERNATHY, CIVIL RIGHTS AND CONSTITUTIONAL LITIGATION at 679 (3d ed. 2000). As Professor Abernathy further points out, Title VII protects not only women and racial and ethnic minorities, but it has also been interpreted by the Court to extend its protection to whites, men and ethnic pluralities. *See McDonald v. Santa Fe Trail Transportation Co., 427 U.S. 273* (1976), noting that Title VII raises "ironic problems in the award of judicial relief as court orders remedying discrimination against blacks often [are perceived as having] a collateral adverse impact on white employees." This interpretation has made it difficult for employers to undertake private affirmative action to remedy problems of inequality of blacks and other minorities.

The ADA and ADEA, discussed above, have been modeled in part after Title VII and also draw from Title VI of the Civil Rights Act of 1964, 42 U.S.C. § 2000d, which Congress passed to ensure that public and private programs receiving federal funds are operated in a nondiscriminatory manner.

4. *Who is Covered Under Federal Nondiscrimination Laws?* Under new enforcement guidelines of the Equal Employment Opportunity Commission, EEOC Compliance Manual Vol. II, § 622 App. B (1999), undocumented alien workers are entitled to the same remedies for unlawful discrimination available to any other workers under Title VII of the 1964 Civil Rights Act, the Age Discrimination in Employment Act, the Americans with Disabilities Act, and the Equal Pay Act. These workers were previously ineligible for certain remedies under federal employment discrimination laws but are now entitled to back pay, reinstatement, hiring and other appropriate relief so long as the award does not directly conflict with immigration laws. Undocumented workers historically have been among the most vulnerable and abused workers in the American workplace.

5. *Caveat Advocatus.* The constitutional and statutory remedies and defenses considered in this chapter are by no means exhaustive. Every attorney is well advised to thoroughly search for any applicable state and federal constitutional and statutory provisions in bringing or defending a lawsuit. Failure to make such a search may itself be actionable.

Chapter 21
INSURANCE

A. INTRODUCTION

An insurance policy is a contract in which one party, for a specific consideration, agrees to compensate another for losses from designated perils. First party insurance generally compensates the insured for his medical bills or from loss of or damage to his property. Hospitalization insurance, fire and extended coverage insurance on buildings, and collision and comprehensive coverage on automobiles are among the most common types of first party insurance. Third party insurance protects an insured from liability to others for damages caused by the insured or persons or things for which he is legally responsible. Third party insurance has played the greatest role in the development of tort law. However, first party insurance is a factor of increasing importance in determining how to compensate the victims of accidents and other wrongful conduct. At one time, it appeared that the most dynamic type of first party insurance — "no-fault" — would replace the fault system as the primary method of allocating accident losses. Although its star may be waning, no-fault remains of great importance.

The significance of the impact of insurance upon tort law, and the uniqueness of some of the issues raised by the interplay of tort and contract law through insurance, are discussed in Section B. Insurance applies to the tort claim if there is "coverage," i.e., if the contract between insurer and insured applies to the particular risk and to the parties to the tort claim. Some of the major coverage issues are treated in Section C. Where there is coverage, the insurer usually is solely or primarily responsible for the payment of the damage. In such a situation, the insurer's unreasonable delay in recognizing its obligation or payment of the damages places the other affected parties — tortfeasor and victim — at a disadvantage. Legislatures and courts have sought to "even the playing field" by imposing penalties upon arbitrary insurer conduct. Some of those penalties are itemized in Section D. The greatest bulk of tort claims arise out of automobile accidents; some special problems in automobile insurance are discussed in Section E. The "no fault" movement is covered in Section F.

B. TORT LAW AND THE INSURANCE INSTITUTION

NOTES

1. *Liability Insurance and the Tort System.* Liability insurance has its roots in maritime law. Among the first liability insurers were self-protection and indemnity clubs, formed by vessel owners in the late Middle Ages and early Renaissance to share their liability to others for collision damage and other wrongful activities of their vessels. Liability insurance became generally

available by the latter part of the nineteenth century, and began to dominate tort law in the twentieth century, when a primary purpose of that law, in addition to deterrence of accidents, became a proper "spreading" of accident losses. The concern that the availability of liability insurance would reduce the deterrent effect of tort law has not materialized, for a number of reasons. One is that many insurers properly categorize the risks; thus the more risky insureds pay higher rates and are deterred in that manner. Another reason is that fear for one's own safety is a greater deterrent than the threat of financial responsibility for damages to others. A third reason is that the criminal law often provides a specific deterrence of wrongful conduct more effective than that which results from the imposition of tort damages.

In recent times the availability of liability insurance has been an important factor in the decision of whether to shift the loss from the victim to an actor whose conduct contributed to the loss. The availability of insurance has coincided with the advent of the "enterprise liability" theory which holds that unavoidable losses from accidents should be borne by those who participate in or benefit from the activity, *i.e.*, the "enterprise" which generates the losses. The most important examples of enterprise liability are worker compensation and the strict product liability of manufacturers and, in some cases, other sellers of products. Much of the spreading of "enterprise liability" is accomplished through purchase of liability insurance by the employer or manufacturer, who then "spreads" the cost of the premiums to its customers through the price of its goods or services.

2. *The Insurance "Crisis."* In the second half of the 20th century, large awards of tort damages, particularly by juries, prompted a campaign by the insurance industry to heighten public awareness of the impact of the awards. The message was "when the insurer pays, you pay, through increased rates." The success of the campaign may not be statistically measurable; the perception of its success is evidenced by the fact that an increasing number of plaintiff attorneys now opt for non-jury trials. Insurance rates continued to climb until the late 1980s. This led to alarm over a perceived insurance crisis. *See, e.g.,* Berger, *The Impact of Tort Law Development on Insurance: The Availability/Affordability Crisis and Its Potential Solutions,* 37 AM. U.L. REV. 285 (1988); Clarke, Warren-Boulton, Smith & Simon, *Sources of the Crisis in Liability Insurance: An Economic Analysis,* 5 YALE J. ON REG. 367 (1988); Lefkin, *Shattering Some Myths on the Insurance Liability Crisis: A Comment on the Article by Clarke, Warren-Boulton, Smith & Simon,* 5 YALE J. ON REG. 417 (1988); Priest, *The Current Insurance Crisis and Modern Tort Law,* 96 YALE L.J. 1521 (1987); Galanter, *The Day After the Litigation Explosion,* 46 MD. L. REV. 3 (1986).

The latest legislative response has been the tort reform campaign of the 1990s that has produced tort law revision designed primarily to reduce the tortfeasor's exposure to liability and amounts.

3. *Rate-Cutting Initiatives. Calfarm Ins. Co. v. Deukmejian,* 48 Cal. 3d 805, 258 Cal. Rptr. 161, 771 P.2d 1247 (1989), concerned California's famous Proposition 103, approved by the voters. As the court described Proposition 103:

The initiative begins with a statement of findings and purpose, asserting that "[e]normous increases in the cost of insurance have made it both unaffordable and unavailable to millions of Californians," and that "the existing laws inadequately protect consumers and allow insurance companies to charge excessive, unjustified and arbitrary rates." The initiative's stated purpose is to ensure that "insurance is fair, available, and affordable for all Californians."

Insurance rates are to be immediately reduced to "at least 20 percent less" than those in effect on November 8, 1987 (approximately the date when the initiative was proposed, and one year prior to its enactment). All rate increases require the approval of the Insurance Commissioner, who may not approve rates which are "excessive, inadequate, unfairly discriminatory or otherwise in violation of [the initiative].". . .

The initiative prohibits an insurer from declining to renew a policy except for nonpayment of premium, fraud, or significant increase in the hazard insured against. Insurers are required to mail notices to policy holders informing them they may join a nonprofit corporation to be formed to represent their interests by persons appointed for this purpose by the Insurance Commissioner. The Board of Equalization is directed to adjust the tax rate on insurance premiums to avoid any loss of tax revenues as a result of decreases in the rates charged by insurers. . . .

Insurance companies contended that Proposition 103 was unconstitutional on the basis, *inter alia,* that the rate regulation provisions were violative of federal and state due process clauses, and that the restrictions on nonrenewal impermissibly impaired existing contract rights. Although the court found the initiative unconstitutional and severed some parts of it, Proposition 103 generally survived the challenge.

MYERS v. ROBERTSON
891 P.2d 199 (Alaska 1995)

MOORE, CHIEF JUSTICE [with RABINOWITZ and MATTHEWS, JJ., concurring].

This intra-family lawsuit arises from the accidental death of a thirteen year old boy, Sidney Robertson, Jr. The minor's estate, along with the child's brother Stephen (the "Estate"), sued the boys' parents, Sidney Robertson, Sr. and Terri Robertson ("the Robertsons"), on a theory of negligence. The parents' insurer, Allstate Insurance Co. ("Allstate"), appointed counsel to defend the Robertsons. However, based on Allstate's belief that the Robertsons' true interest was in losing the lawsuit so that they could recover the insurance proceeds paid to the Estate, Allstate later intervened in the case as a party defendant. Allstate participated at trial outside the jury's presence, and the jury was not informed of its existence as the real party in interest. The jury found that, although the Robertsons were negligent, their conduct was not the legal cause of their son's death.

The Estate appeals, claiming that Allstate's interest in the case should have been disclosed to the jury. Allstate cross-appeals, arguing that the case should have been dismissed for lack of adversity and on public policy grounds.

We conclude that several rulings of the trial court were erroneous, but that the errors were harmless. Therefore, we uphold the jury's verdict.

In June 1988, the Robertsons were living in a single family residence in Anchorage with their two sons, Sidney, Jr., then age 13, and Stephen, then age 9. The Robertsons had plans to attend a special event at an Anchorage museum for the evening of June 23, 1988. They decided to leave the children at home for the few hours they would be gone. To entertain the boys, the Robertsons left them some VCR movies, including a skateboard movie called "Thrasher."

Following their parents' departure, Sidney, Jr. and Stephen watched "Thrasher." After the movie, Sidney, Jr. went to the garage, where Terri Robertson had parked the family's 1981 Triumph TR-7. At the back of the garage, the Robertsons stored a skateboarding ramp that they had given Sidney, Jr. for his birthday one month earlier.

The parties dispute the following series of events. Allstate argues that the TR-7 was securely parked, in gear, with the emergency brake engaged and the garage door closed. Allstate asserts that Sidney, Jr. opened the garage door, released the car's parking brake and intentionally attempted to move the TR-7 so that he could skateboard in the garage. The Estate suggests that the Robertsons had negligently left the garage door open, left the TR-7 out of gear and failed to repair the car's nonfunctioning emergency brake. As a result, when Sidney, Jr. tried to skateboard around the car, he unintentionally caused it to begin rolling.

In either event, it is clear that at some moment the TR-7 began rolling backward down the Robertsons' steep incline driveway. Sidney, Jr. ran behind the car, apparently trying to stop it from rolling into the street. The TR-7 eventually backed into another car parked across the street from the Robertson home, pinning Sidney, Jr. between the two cars. Sidney, Jr. later died as a result of his injuries. Stephen witnessed the accident.

Several months after Sidney, Jr.'s death, the Robertsons consulted with attorney Olof Hellen regarding the extent of their insurance coverage for the accident. Hellen's law firm reviewed the Robertsons' insurance policies and advised the Robertsons to designate a close friend as representative of Sidney, Jr.'s estate and as special guardian of Stephen. The firm further advised the Robertsons to retain their own counsel, since Sidney, Jr.'s estate and Stephen would bring a lawsuit against them and that, in the event of a recovery by Sidney, Jr.'s estate, the Robertsons ordinarily would receive the proceeds as their son's heirs in intestacy.

The Robertsons arranged for Linda Myers, a family friend, to act as the representative of Sidney, Jr.'s estate and as Stephen's special guardian for the purposes of this litigation. The Robertsons waived any conflicts of interest, and Olof Hellen undertook representation of the Estate. The Estate filed this action against the Robertsons in December 1988, alleging that the Robertsons were negligent in (1) possessing a driveway with an unsafe incline, and (2) failing to properly secure their Triumph TR-7 in their garage.

Due to its duty to defend the claim against the Robertsons, Allstate appointed the law firm of Hughes, Thorsness, Gantz, Powell & Brundin

("Hughes, Thorsness") to represent the Robertsons. Hughes, Thorsness filed a motion to dismiss the Estate's claims based on the public policy that negligent parties should not benefit from their wrongful conduct. Hughes, Thorsness argued that, because the Robertsons were the sole beneficiaries of Sidney, Jr.'s estate, they would be monetarily rewarded if they negligently caused their son's death.[1] The Estate opposed the motion; it then moved to disqualify the Robertsons' counsel on the grounds that the motion to dismiss was contrary to the Robertsons' interests in losing the case.

Before the court ruled on the Estate's motion to disqualify, Hughes, Thorsness withdrew as defense counsel for reasons unrelated to this case. The law firm of Guess & Rudd substituted as defense counsel. However, Guess & Rudd subsequently withdrew due to an "irreconcilable conflict of interest" between it and the Robertsons.

Following Guess & Rudd's withdrawal, the Estate moved for an order to protect the Robertsons by requiring that Guess & Rudd's files be transferred to the Robertsons and not to Allstate. Allstate then intervened in the case as a party defendant, asserting that the Estate was advancing the real interests of the Robertsons, who were not adverse to its claims. Based on the conflicting interests between Allstate and the Robertsons, the trial court ordered that Allstate appoint independent counsel to represent the Robertsons. It further ordered that independent counsel not report to Allstate. In compliance with this order, Allstate retained Theodore Pease, Jr. of Burr, Pease & Kurtz, with the Robertsons' consent and the court's approval, to defend the Robertsons.

Allstate moved to dismiss the Estate's claims under Alaska Civil Rule 12(b)(1), arguing that the lack of genuine adversity between the Estate and the Robertsons deprived the court of subject matter jurisdiction. Allstate alternatively moved to dismiss under Civil Rule 12(b)(6), arguing that the Estate's claims could not succeed due to the public policy barring the Robertsons from benefitting from their negligent conduct by obtaining the proceeds of Sidney, Jr.'s estate.[2]

The court denied Allstate's motion, and the case proceeded to trial. With the court's approval, Allstate elected not to participate at trial during the jury's presence. The court also approved Allstate's motion to prevent any reference to insurance during trial, except for limited questions during jury selection.

During trial, the Robertsons testified in a manner which sometimes suggested that they took responsibility for negligently causing their son's death. For instance, Terri Robertson testified that both she and her husband knew that the TR-7's emergency brake had never worked, and that they were negligent in failing to repair it. She also disputed that she told the police on the night of the accident that she had closed the garage door and left the TR-7

---

[1] Because Sidney, Jr. had no dependents, any recovery for wrongful death would be paid to his estate. That amount would then flow back to the Robertsons as Sidney, Jr.'s heirs in intestacy.

[2] This motion pertained only to the claims by Sidney, Jr.'s estate. There is no dispute that Stephen Robertson's claims for emotional trauma and loss of consortium were properly before the court.

in gear before going out. Sidney Robertson, Sr. testified that the TR-7's emergency brake had never worked.

The Robertsons' counsel, Theodore Pease, then impeached his clients' credibility with their prior statements, made either to the police or in depositions, which suggested that the TR-7 could not have begun rolling unless Sidney, Jr. first opened the garage door, took the car out of gear and released the parking brake. By this impeachment, and through closing argument, defense counsel suggested to the jury that the Robertsons' emotional pain led them to take responsibility for their son's death, even when such responsibility was inappropriate.

The Estate objected on the Robertsons' behalf, arguing that Mr. Pease's impeachment was contrary to the Robertsons' interests. The court overruled the objection, stating that, for sufficient adversity to exist, defense counsel must present "a classic defense in the sense that [the goal is] to make sure that his clients are not found liable."

In argument over jury instructions, Allstate again raised the adversity issue. On Mr. Pease's proposal, the court instructed the jury that the Robertsons were the heirs to Sidney, Jr.'s estate. Mr. Hellen again objected that it was improper for defense counsel to propose such an instruction because the instruction was contrary to the Robertsons' interests. The court found that sufficient adversity existed because Mr. Pease was properly representing the Robertsons as defendants, not as plaintiffs. Similarly, the court held that Mr. Pease could argue in closing that Sidney, Jr.'s own negligence had caused his injuries and death, even if the Robertsons did not want this argument to be made because they did not believe it was true.

The jury determined that the Robertsons were negligent but that their negligence was not the legal cause of Sidney, Jr.'s death. The court subsequently entered judgment in favor of the Robertsons and Allstate.

We first address the issues raised by Allstate's cross-appeal since they go to the court's jurisdiction. Allstate asserts that the case should have been dismissed because there was never any genuine adversity between the Estate and the Robertsons.

Allstate contends that the trial court had no subject matter jurisdiction over this case since the Robertsons and the plaintiff had identical interests. Most notably, the Robertsons would receive any recovery by Sidney, Jr.'s estate as his sole beneficiaries in intestacy. *See supra* note 1. Moreover, because the Robertsons prompted the plaintiff's initiation of this suit, Allstate argues that Linda Myers is only a figurehead. According to Allstate, the Robertsons are the real plaintiffs and are in essence suing themselves.

In discussing the standing requirement, this court has stated that an Alaska court has no subject matter jurisdiction unless the lawsuit before it presents an actual controversy involving a genuine relationship of adversity between the parties. Adversity insures that parties will energetically pursue their opposing positions and present facts necessary for the fair resolution of the case. Accordingly, adversity constitutes the basic requirement for standing in Alaska.

B.   TORT LAW AND THE INSURANCE INSTITUTION   1405

This court has also held that children have a right to bring lawsuits against their parents for negligently inflicted injuries. *Hebel v. Hebel*, 435 P.2d 8, 15 (Alaska 1967) (no parental immunity bar to an unemancipated minor's negligence action against a parent). Thus, there is no *per se* failure of adversity simply because this lawsuit arises from an alleged intra-family tort. In *Hebel*, this court specifically recognized the potential for collusive intra-family litigation designed to defraud insurance carriers but determined that this danger "does not warrant denial of a remedy to the child." It further stated:

> Since the insurer is the real defendant, it has been said that there is danger of fraud and collusion between parent and child. One may not, of course, deny the hazard, but *such a danger, being present in all liability insurance cases, furnishes reason not for denial of a cause of action, but for added caution on the part of court and jury in examining and assessing the facts.*

Similarly, in *Aydlett v. Haynes*, 511 P.2d 1311 (Alaska 1973), this court noted that intra-family tort litigation can pose special problems due to the existence of insurance. In *Aydlett*, a wife sued her husband to recover for injuries caused by the husband's negligence. The court recognized that, in ordinary personal injury litigation, an insurer and a defendant-insured usually have a common interest in avoiding liability. *Id.* at 1315 n.8. However, in intra-family litigation, the interests of the insured may conflict with those of the insurer since the insured may have a financial interest in seeing the plaintiff prevail. For this reason, the court stated, "[W]here the case involves an intra-family tort action, the trial judge must take care to assure that the actual interests of all parties are fairly represented." *Id.*

In light of *Hebel* and *Aydlett*, there is no merit to Allstate's contention that the Estate's claims against the Robertsons were not actionable and should be precluded as a matter of law.[3] . . .

Consistent with the obligations imposed under *Hebel* and *Aydlett*, the court required counsel for the Robertsons to further the Robertsons' interests in this case *as defendants*, not as plaintiffs. Although placed in a sometimes awkward position, Mr. Pease conscientiously and effectively presented the Robertsons' defense.[4] Further protecting the interests of all parties, the court appropriately required that the Robertsons' defense counsel be independent from Allstate in the sense that Mr. Pease would not report to Allstate. By these actions, the court struck a balance between the Estate's right to sue and Allstate's right to an adversarial defense. Because this case involved an

---

[3] Moreover, it is well-settled in this state that, as the Robertsons' liability insurer, Allstate was not a proper party defendant at trial. *Severson v. Estate of Severson*, 627 P.2d 649, 651 (Alaska 1981) (direct actions against an alleged tortfeasor's liability insurer are not permitted in Alaska).

[4] Allstate argues that defense counsel's adversarial posture could not cure the lack of adversity in this case because counsel had no control over the manner in which the Robertsons would color the facts. However, even assuming that the Robertsons tried to give testimony which would favor the Estate, the result in this case belies Allstate's claim. Defense counsel effectively handled the Robertsons' defense and procured a jury verdict in favor of the Robertsons and Allstate.

adversarial relationship, the trial was not a sham and was properly allowed to proceed.[5]

While Allstate recognizes the general rule that intra-family litigation is permissible, it claims that this case is distinguishable from other Alaska intra-family tort cases because the Robertsons stand to gain 100% of any recovery paid to Sidney, Jr.'s estate. Allstate urges us to find that, in situations where the defendants' pecuniary interests are identical to those of the plaintiff, the defendants are in fact the "real plaintiffs." Under this reasoning, the Robertsons are in essence suing themselves, so there is no adversity and no subject matter jurisdiction. . . .

[Cases denying jurisdiction] rely on the public policy that no person should profit from his or her own wrongdoing. This principle provides that it would be incongruous to permit an estate to recover damages, when the sole beneficiaries of that award are the same people who negligently caused the injury in the first place. However, a negligence action may proceed if there exist beneficiaries to the estate other than any negligent beneficiaries. In such situations, the non-negligent beneficiaries may recover their shares of any damages paid to the estate. Any negligent persons who otherwise would be beneficiaries are precluded from obtaining any part of the estate's recovery based on public policy considerations.

Whether the beneficiaries to an estate are in fact the "true plaintiffs" in a wrongful death action by the estate is a question of first impression in Alaska. We conclude that, where any recovery by the estate would not be paid directly to specified individuals, the beneficiaries to the estate should not be considered the plaintiffs. Therefore, there is no jurisdictional bar to an administrator's negligence action against parties who might otherwise stand to benefit from their wrongdoing. . . .

In this case, there is no dispute that any wrongful death recovery by the administrator would be paid to Sidney, Jr.'s estate. The determination of eligible beneficiaries to that award is a question arising subsequent to the jurisdictional issue. We therefore address it as a matter of public policy apart from the adversity question. Accordingly, we believe the trial court properly asserted subject matter jurisdiction over this litigation. The real question is whether, had the Estate been successful on its claims, the Robertsons should forfeit their right to inherit any part of Sidney, Jr.'s estate. We address this question as a matter of public policy.

Allstate contends that the Estate's claims should have been dismissed based on the public policy preventing wrongdoers from benefitting from their own negligence. Relying substantially on *Oviatt v. Camarra*, 210 Or. 445, 311 P.2d 746 (1957), the trial court disagreed and concluded that there would be no public policy bar in Alaska to the Robertsons' recovery of damages awarded to Sidney, Jr.'s estate through intestate succession. . . .

---

[5] Given the trial court's actions to preserve the integrity of the proceedings in this case, sufficient adversity existed to allow the case to proceed even without Allstate's intervention. Therefore, Allstate's intervention did not cure a lack of adversity or create sufficient adversity for the case to proceed. Allstate's ultimate decision to intervene, to further insure adequate representation of its interests, is simply one more circumstance indicating that adverse interests were fairly litigated in this case.

In our view, the better policy precludes a negligent party from obtaining any part of a damage award, so that the negligent party will not benefit from his or her wrongdoing. This is true whether the negligent person would have benefitted directly, as a specified beneficiary under the wrongful death statute, or indirectly through intestate succession. In this respect, our decision is consistent with several cases cited by Allstate.[6]

In implementing this policy, however, we do not follow the example set forth in many of the cases cited by Allstate. Many of those decisions reduce the damage award paid to the estate by the pro rata share otherwise payable to the negligent party. *See, e.g., Carver*, 314 S.E.2d at 744. In contrast to these cases, we do not believe the award to Sidney, Jr.'s estate should be reduced simply because certain beneficiaries are no longer eligible to recover any proceeds. Rather, we believe that any ineligible beneficiaries should be considered to have renounced their right to recover. The proceeds of the estate would then be distributed in a manner consistent with AS 13.11.295, regarding renunciation of intestate succession rights. Thus, for purposes of distributing any proceeds awarded to Sidney, Jr.'s estate, the Robertsons should be considered to have predeceased their son, and the entire award may be distributed to any other existing and eligible statutory heirs. . . .

In its appeal, the Estate claims that the trial court erred in allowing Allstate to participate at trial outside the jury's presence and in prohibiting any reference to insurance during trial. It contends that, once Allstate intervened, the trial court was required to clarify the alignment of the parties in the case so that the jury would not misunderstand the true interests of all parties. The Estate further contends that the Robertsons' counsel represented Allstate's interests at trial instead of the Robertsons'. It argues that this fact tainted the entire trial because counsel presented a case at odds with the Robertsons' view of events and improperly suggested to the jury that counsel's own clients could not be believed. The jury was therefore unfairly prejudiced against the Robertsons, which damaged the Estate's interest in having the jury fully consider their trial testimony.

The Estate frames these arguments in constitutional terms, claiming that the court's rulings violated its right to due process under the Alaska Constitution. It also argues that the rulings accorded insurance companies special status, thereby depriving the Estate of equal protection under the law. We disagree that the trial court's rulings violated any of the Estate's constitutional rights. However, we agree with the argument that, in intra-family negligence actions such as the present case, the jury should be informed of an insurer's status as the real party in interest in order to avoid confusion and prejudice against either the plaintiffs or defendants. Despite this conclusion, we believe that the failure to inform the jury of Allstate's presence in this case was harmless error, and we uphold the jury's verdict. . . .

In our view, the Estate has not carried its burden of showing prejudice. Although it raises a speculative possibility of prejudice, the Estate has not

---

[6] It is also consistent with the policy view declared by the Alaska Legislature. The state legislature has provided that persons who feloniously kill another may not benefit from their actions either by obtaining any proceeds of a wrongful death recovery, AS 09.55.580(f), or by inheriting through intestate succession. AS 13.11.305. Our decision today extends the policy expressed by these provisions in a manner that is compatible with the legislature's stated intentions.

convinced us that the failure to disclose Allstate's interest probably affected the verdict. In reviewing the record, we specifically recognize the trial court's substantial efforts to preserve the integrity of the trial, and we see no evidence of jury confusion or undue prejudice against either the Estate or the Robertsons. The record indicates that, over the course of the trial, the jury heard abundant evidence to support the conclusion that Sidney, Jr. intentionally attempted to move the car, and that the Robertsons were not the legal cause of their son's injuries. The Estate's arguments do not convince us that the evidence would have been interpreted substantially differently if Allstate's presence had been disclosed. For this reason, we conclude that the error was harmless, and the jury's verdict should be affirmed.[7]

In sum, we affirm the trial court's decision regarding adversity and subject matter jurisdiction. However, we note that, had the Estate recovered any damages in this case, the Robertsons could not receive any benefit from that award through intestate succession or otherwise, due to the public policy preventing negligent parties from benefitting from their negligent acts. We acknowledge the validity of the Estate's argument regarding disclosure of an insurer's interest in intra-family tort actions such as the present one. For this reason, we believe that in this limited context the jury should be informed of an insurer's interest in order to prevent any undue confusion or prejudice against the parties. Despite this conclusion, we do not believe that disclosure of Allstate's interest in this action would have affected the jury's verdict. Therefore, the failure to inform the jury of Allstate's presence was harmless error.

COMPTON, JUSTICE, with whom BRYNER, JUSTICE, pro tem, joins, dissenting in part. . . .

The insured family member may have purchased the insurance policy for a variety of reasons, just as insurance is marketed on a variety of bases. One reason, and basis, may have been to ensure that the family will be able to compensate adequately a victim of a family member's tortious conduct. This motivation may be particularly strong where the insured has a close personal relationship with the victim. Therefore, as in the case of the Robertsons, it may be in the interest of the insured family member to be found liable.[8]

Despite the Robertsons' desire to pursue such a goal, the trial court prevented the Robertsons' independent counsel from so doing. Instead, the trial court directed Allstate to retain independent counsel for the Robertsons.

---

[7] The Estate also asserts that there was reversible error arising from the Robertsons' counsel's presentation of a case to the jury that sometimes questioned the Robertsons' trial testimony and views on liability. The Estate further claims that the trial court erred in denying its motion for a mistrial after the Robertsons advised the court that they disagreed with their attorney's theory of the case. We decline to address these claims since the Estate has not explained how it has any standing to assert the Robertsons' alleged rights with respect to their relationship with Mr. Pease.

[8] As we indicated in our opinion in *Hebel v. Hebel*, 435 P.2d 8 (Alaska 1967), in a lawsuit among family members there is a danger of fraud and collusion of which the jury must be aware. *Id.* at 12. In the instant case, this danger is present. Ultimately, it could be the insureds that stand to gain monetarily from the Estate's collection of any award. Therefore, I also concur in the court's conclusion that negligent tort-feasors should be prevented from sharing in any award that results from their conduct.

The trial court then ordered independent counsel to present "a classic [insurance] defense" designed to avoid Allstate's liability. This goal was in keeping with the interests of Allstate, but not necessarily those of the Robertsons. While the trial judge recognized the unusual alignment of parties often present in intra-family tort litigation, she distinguished between the Robertsons' independent counsel representing his clients as plaintiffs versus defendants. The judge stated that the Robertsons were not their independent counsel's "clients as plaintiffs. They're his clients as defendants. . . . [I]f that *defense* were not being provided [by the Robertsons' independent counsel] there could be concern with regard to adversity to the extent that his clients wanted this lawsuit to proceed."[9] (Emphasis added.) These conflicting interests were so strong that throughout the entire case the Robertsons retained personal counsel to advise them in dealings with independent counsel, who was representing them in the proceedings. Otherwise stated, the Robertsons were compelled to retain an attorney to advise them on how to deal with the attorney who ostensibly was advocating their interests!. . . .

In the instant case, the trial court could have pursued an alternate approach that would have acknowledged the obvious adversity, and ensured that *all* interests were represented without the conflict. Under such a scheme, three attorneys would independently advocate the interests of the plaintiff, the insurer and the insured. Based on this court's decision in *CHI*, it would have been permissible for the Robertsons, through *CHI* counsel, to pursue their own interests. They were required only to comply with their contractual obligation to cooperate with their insurer, and not breach any implied covenant of good faith and fair dealing.

In this case, however, the trial court directed the Robertsons' independent counsel to present a case that advocated the interests of Allstate. This approach resulted in substantial error. As this court repeatedly notes, in the course of following these instructions the Robertsons' independent counsel was forced to intentionally impeach his own clients' testimony, testimony that indicated that they took responsibility for negligently causing their son's death. This impeachment was intended to destroy the Robertsons' credibility with the jury. In a case where the testimony of the Robertsons was critical, the effect of this taint cannot be underestimated. . . .

A basis for finding substantial error, however, goes beyond the representation issue since Allstate's interests and role in the litigation were not divulged to the jury. Allstate's covert participation undermines the foundation for the acceptance of intra-family tort liability in this state. . . .

The court concludes that the Estate has not proved prejudice by the trial court's failure to disclose Allstate's interest. It "recognize[s] the trial court's

---

[9] Despite the conflicts of interest in this case and the trial court's recognition of the unusual alignment of parties, the approach utilized fails to consider the correspondingly unique interests that are frequently pursued in insurance litigation. For example, when insureds threaten an insurer with a bad faith refusal to settle a plaintiff's claim, it may be in the best interests of the insureds to confess judgment, assign the bad faith claim to the plaintiff, and permit the plaintiff to bring the bad faith claim against the insurer. In such a situation, the insureds require [truly independent] counsel to advise and represent them. Clearly such representation would involve decisions that are not compatible with the interests of the insurer. Nevertheless, the proceedings would involve the adversity necessary for the trial court to have jurisdiction.

substantial efforts to preserve the integrity of the trial," and suggests that the "record indicates that, over the course of the trial, the jury heard abundant evidence to support the conclusion that Sidney, Jr. intentionally attempted to move the car." The court is not convinced that "the evidence would have been interpreted substantially differently if Allstate's presence had been disclosed."[10] What the court declines to do is engage in any debate regarding the issue of the "abundant evidence" presented by independent counsel in accordance with the trial court's instructions. This "abundant evidence" entailed impeaching the credibility of the Robertsons, offering an instruction which did not advance their interests, and generally presenting "a classic [insurance] defense" case. This court claims that the Estate has no standing to "assert the Robertsons' rights" regarding Allstate's shell game, which left Allstate with one attorney at bar and another behind the door, and yet it cites not one jot or tittle of authority for the proposition. In this particular way the trial court erred in its order regarding independent counsel, its instructions to independent counsel, and its definition of the Robertsons' interests. Were this court to undertake such debate, I suggest it could not reach the same result.

I would remand the case to superior court for re-trial with (1) the Robertsons represented by an attorney of their choice, whose undeviating allegiance would be to the Robertsons and pursuit of their interests, (2) the existence of liability insurance disclosed to the jury and (3) the open participation of Allstate's attorney.

NOTES

1. *Comparative Fault.* Why didn't the court apply comparative fault principles to the claims of Mr. and Mrs. Robinson?

2. *Jury Instructions.* Should the jury in a *Myers* situation be instructed regarding the amount of insurance involved? Should they be instructed as to who the estate beneficiaries are?

3. *Family-Member Liability Policy Exclusions.* The automobile policy in *National County Mut. Fire Ins. Co. v. Johnson,* 879 S.W. 2d 1 (Tex. 1993), provided that the insurer did not provide liability coverage for bodily injury to the insured or to any "family member." The court held this family-member exclusion was void as against public policy because it conflicted with the state's "Motor Vehicle Safety-Responsibility Act" requiring automobile operators to carry specified minimum amounts of liability insurance, and it conflicted "with the public policy underlying the Act." The court noted that the "majority of jurisdictions with mandatory insurance laws hold family member exclusions invalid because they are contrary to public policy." *Accord, Cormier v. American Deposit Insur. Co.,* 664 So. 2d 807 (La. App. 1995).

---

[10] Allstate apparently felt differently. Not surprisingly, in its motion to intervene as a party defendant, Allstate, immediately after "respectfully request[ing] that it be permitted to intervene as a party defendant," explicitly refused to "concede that it must necessarily be present at the trial of this case or that the jury must necessarily be told about the presence of insurance."

C. INSURANCE COVERAGE ISSUES

The insurer is contractually obligated to pay damages caused by tortious conduct if the policy it has written covers the particular risk that occurred. The major "coverage" issues are (1) whether the tortfeasor is an insured under the policy, (2) whether the tortfeasor's conduct is insured under the policy, (3) the amount for which the insurer is obligated (the extent of dollar coverage), and (4) the allocation of coverages where multiple insurers cover the same risk.

Normally, the policy provides protection for the conduct of the purchaser of the policy (the named insured) and for designated members of the insured's family or work force (those covered under the policy's "omnibus insured" provision). A typical omnibus clause may read like this:

. . . Who Is an Insured

When we refer to your car, a newly acquired car or a temporary substitute car, insured means:

1. you;

2. your spouse;

3. the relative of the first person named in the declarations;

4. any other person while using such a car if its use is within the of consent of you or your spouse;

The explosion in sex crimes in the last part of the Twentieth Century has generated two important coverage issues: the extent to which a policy covers intentional acts, and whether public policy permits insurance against punitive damages. A policy typically will provide that the insurer will pay a certain amount of the damages to each victim for each "occurrence" caused by the insured's wrongful conduct, limited by a total amount of damages to all victims arising out of that occurrence (the "per person" and "per occurrence" limits). The policy also may obligate the insurer to defend a claim against the insured under circumstances where the claim is not covered. Unusual fact situations generate interesting questions of interpretation which dictate whether a particular loss, or the amount of a loss, is covered. Finally, multiple coverages of the same loss by two or more insurers has generated a significant amount of litigation.

ALTENA v. UNITED FIRE & CASUALTY CO.
422 N.W.2d 485 (Iowa 1988)

LAVORATO, J.

In this declaratory judgment action, plaintiff Gail Altena asked the district court to construe two insurance policies of defendant Senard Altena to cover damages caused by his alleged sexual abuse of her. Senard's insurer, the United Fire and Casualty Company (UFC), filed a motion for summary judgment, contending that damages from Senard's acts came within an exclusion from coverage of injuries intended by the insured. Gail also moved for summary judgment, arguing that coverage is required because Senard's testimony indicates he did not intend any injury to result from his acts, although the acts themselves were intentional.

The acts in question were committed while Gail, a twenty-year-old college student, was living in a basement apartment of Senard's home. Senard is an older, married cousin of Gail's father. Shortly after Gail moved into the apartment, Senard began to offer Gail alcoholic beverages, talk about sexual matters, and demand hugs and kisses from her. Gail, who was sexually inexperienced, was embarrassed by the physical contact and his questions about her sexual knowledge, and she attempted to ignore Senard.

Senard soon progressed to fondling Gail, and he later engaged in various sex acts. He would usually initiate these acts after following Gail into her apartment and attempting to ply her with alcohol. When Gail resisted Senard's sexual advances, he would berate her, saying she needed to have such experiences so she could learn to please her boyfriend. Senard would then forcibly undress Gail, often tearing her clothing, and commit the sex acts without her consent or active participation. This pattern continued for two months, whenever Senard was not out of the state. On at least one occasion he struck Gail during such an attack.

Over the two months she lived in the apartment Gail became increasingly upset because of Senard's behavior. In an effort to avoid the attacks, she would often talk on her telephone until late at night or stay on campus as long as possible. Senard, however, would always come to her apartment eventually and attack her. By the time her work supervisor convinced her to leave the apartment, Gail was suicidal, and she later sought medical treatment for her psychological injuries.

Gail brought suit against Senard in both the Iowa and the United States district courts, alleging seduction, sexual abuse, outrageous conduct, and interference with her right to quiet enjoyment of her apartment. In deposition testimony during those cases, Senard admitted sexual contacts with Gail but claimed that they were consensual. He also denied he intended to harm her by such contacts.

Gail brought a separate declaratory judgment action in the Iowa district court. She asked the court to construe Senard's UFC homeowner's and umbrella liability insurance policies to cover damages due to his sexual attacks on her.

Senard's homeowner's policy provides:

> If a claim is made or a suit is brought against any insured for damages because of bodily injury. . . to which this coverage applies, we will
>
> > a. pay up to our limit of liability for the damages for which the insured is legally liable . . . .

"Bodily injury" is defined as "bodily harm, sickness, or disease including required care." This policy excludes from coverage bodily injury "which is expected or intended by the insured."

Senard's umbrella liability policy provides that UFC will "indemnify the insured for ultimate net loss in excess of the retained limit which the insured shall become legally obligated to pay as damages because of personal injury." "Personal injury" is defined by this policy as

(a) Bodily injury, sickness, disease, disability and if arising out of the foregoing, shock, mental anguish and mental injury;

(d) Assault and battery. . . . not committed by or at the direction of the insured . . . .

The umbrella policy excludes from its coverage "any act committed by. . . . the insured with intent to cause personal injury."

. . .Both of Senard's policies exclude injuries intended by the insured. This type of exclusion is consistent with "the central idea that insurance concerns fortuitous losses only" and generally provides "no coverage for intentional loss." R.E. Keeton, Basic Text on Insurance Law § 5.4(b), at 291 (1971).

The district court found as a matter of law that Senard intended to injure Gail when he engaged in the various sex acts. Because all of Gail's claims are predicated upon these acts, the ruling precludes coverage of damages resulting from them under the policies. Thus, the fighting issue in this appeal is whether a genuine issue of material fact exists as to Senard's intention to injure Gail by the acts.

The following facts are not in dispute. Each count in Gail's petition is based on actions by Senard that constitute sex acts within the meaning of our criminal statute concerning sexual abuse. Senard intended to commit those acts. Senard and Gail were both adults at the time.

Gail claims the acts were done against her will, and UFC takes no issue with this claim. Because consent in this case would preclude recovery under the policies, *see State Farm Fire & Casualty Co. v. Williams,* 355 N.W.2d 421, 424 (Minn. 1984), we proceed on the basis that Gail did not consent to the sex acts.

Under these facts, all the elements of sexual abuse are established. Notwithstanding this conclusion, Gail maintains her claim of sexual abuse as well as her remaining claims may be established without proof of an intent to injure. Thus, Gail asserts, it is not enough that Senard intended the acts; UFC must establish that Senard had an actual or subjective intent to injure her. Because the only evidence before the district court was Senard's deposition testimony that he had no such intent, Gail argues no genuine issue of material fact was generated regarding his intent to injure. Thus, Gail concludes, the district court should have granted her motion for summary judgment and denied UFC's.

UFC, on the other hand, argues the district court was correct in determining Senard's intent to injure as an objective matter of law. UFC's position is that because Senard's acts amounted to sexual abuse, intent to injure must be inferred as a matter of law.

These arguments generate a further issue: what kind of intent must be established under the intentional injury exclusions. As one court points out, three different views of this issue have developed:

(1) The minority view follows the classic tort doctrine of looking to the natural and probable consequences of the insured's act;

(2) The majority view is that the insured must have intended the act *and* to cause some kind of bodily injury;

(3) A third view is that the insured must have had the specific intent to cause the type of injury suffered.

Pachucki v. Republic Ins. Co., 89 Wis. 2d 703, 708, 278 N.W.2d 898, 901 (1979).

According to the majority view, the intent to do the act and cause injury may be "actual or may be inferred by the nature of the act and the accompanying reasonable foreseeability of harm." *Western Nat. Assur. Co. v. Hecker,* 43 Wash. App. 816, 825, 719 P.2d 954, 960 (1986). In addition, "once intent to cause injury is found, it is immaterial that the actual injury caused is of a different character or magnitude than that intended." *Hecker,* 43 Wash. App. at 825, 719 P.2d at 960.

Although we did not expressly say so, we applied the majority view in *McAndrews v. Farm Bureau Mut. Ins. Co.,* 349 N.W.2d 117 (Iowa 1984). There the issue was whether the insurer was required by its policy to defend its insured in a civil action for assault and battery brought by a third party. The policy excluded "bodily injury. . .which is either expected or intended from the standpoint of the insured." The insured argued there was a potential for coverage as there was a possibility that a factfinder could find his assault was not "intended" because it was done in self-defense.

We rejected the insured's argument and concluded the exclusion applied. *Id.* at 120. In doing so we quoted with approval the following language:

> The question of self-defense is a standard of [the insured's] liability to [the victim]. It presents an issue of motive or justification for an intentionally caused harm, but *it does nothing to avoid the inference of intent to harm that necessarily follows the deliberate blow to [the victim's] face.*

Id. (quoting *Home Ins. Co. v. Neilsen,* 165 Ind. App. 445, 451–52, 332 N.E.2d 240, 244 (1975)) (emphasis added). The italicized language underscores by implication our acceptance of the majority view that the intent to do the act *and* to cause injury may be inferred by the nature of the act *and* the accompanying reasonable foreseeability of harm. *Cf. Kraus v. Allstate Ins. Co.,* 379 F.2d 443, 445 (3d Cir. 1967) (when insured exploded dynamite in public place, intent to injure passersby could be inferred).

Various courts following the majority view have inferred intent to cause injury as a matter of law in cases where the insured had sexual contact with a child. These courts reason that "some harm is inherent in and inevitably results from such acts." *Linebaugh v. Berdish,* 144 Mich. App. 750, 760, 376 N.W.2d 400, 405 (1985) (insured sexually assaulted minor and sought coverage under his homeowner's policy that excluded injury "caused intentionally by or at the direction of the insured"); *accord CNA Ins. Co. v. McGinnis,* 282 Ark. 90, 666 S.W.2d 689 (1984) (incest claim against insured who sought coverage under his homeowner's policy that excluded injury "expected or intended by the insured"); *Allstate Ins. Co. v. Kim W.,* 160 Cal. App. 3d 326, 206 Cal. Rptr. 609 (1984) (insured sexually assaulted minor and sought coverage under his homeowner's policy that excluded injury "intentionally caused by an insured"); *Horace Mann Ins. Co. v. Independent School Dist.,*

355 N.W.2d 413 (Minn. 1984) (insured teacher sexually assaulted high school student and sought coverage under association policy that excluded "occurrences which are the intended consequences of action taken by. . . . the insured"); *Fireman's Fund Ins. Co. v. Hill,* 314 N.W.2d 834 (Minn. 1982) (insured sexually assaulted foster child and sought coverage under his homeowner's policy that excluded injury "expected or intended" by the insured); *Illinois Farmers Ins. Co. v. Judith G.,* 379 N.W.2d 638 (Minn. App. 1986) (insured, a minor, sexually assaulted minor children and sought coverage under parent's homeowner's policy that excluded injury "[a]rising as a result of intentional acts"); *Rodriguez v. Williams,* 42 Wash. App. 633, 713 P.2d 135 (1986), *review granted,* 105 Wash. 2d 1019 (1986), and *aff'd,* 107 Wash. 2d 381, 729 P.2d 627 (1986) (two consolidated cases, both of which involved incest claims against the insureds who sought coverage under their homeowners' policies that excluded injuries "expected or intended by the insured"). *Contra MacKinnon v. Hanover Ins. Co.,* 124 N.H. 456, 471 A.2d 1166 (1984) (incest claim against insured who sought coverage under his homeowner's policy that excluded injury "expected or intended by the insured").

Recently, one court addressed the intentional injury exclusion question in a case involving an insured who had allegedly sexually assaulted a male adult. *See State Farm Fire & Cas. Co. v. Williams,* 355 N.W.2d 421 (Minn. 1984). The intentional injury exclusion was the same as the exclusion here. *See id.* at 423. Although the victim was physically handicapped, he lived independently in an apartment at the time of the sex acts. The case was tried on the following stipulated facts. Although the insured intended to, and did, have sexual contacts with the victim, he did not intend to injure him. The victim alleged the sexual contacts were objectionable and accomplished without his consent. The insured, on the other hand, believed the contacts were with the victim's consent. *Id.*

Refusing to distinguish the case from sexual assaults upon minors, the court said:

> Both of those cases [*Fireman's Fund Ins. Co. v. Hill* and *Horace Mann Ins. Co. v. Independent School Dist.*] involved sexual assaults on minors by persons in authority over them. Does the fact [that] Williams, the victim, was an adult distinguish this case? We think not. Neither the insured nor the insurer in entering into the insurance contract contemplated coverage against claims arising out of nonconsensual sexual assaults. On the other hand, if the sexual assaults were consensual, as asserted by respondent Keller, there would be no assault and hence no claim for recovery.

Id. at 424.

One other court has considered the intentional injury exclusion question in circumstances involving a sexual assault on an adult. *See Western Nat. Assur. Co. v. Hecker,* 43 Wash. App. 816, 719 P.2d 954 (1986). The insured and the victim, both adults, were engaging in consensual sexual intercourse until they reached a point where the victim wanted to stop. Ignoring the victim's protestations, the insured committed forcible anal intercourse. The victim sued the insured for personal injuries resulting from the act. The insured sought coverage under his homeowner's policy, which excluded coverage for intentional injuries caused by the insured. The insurer promptly filed a declaratory judgment action against both, asking the court to determine that it had no duty to defend and no duty to indemnify because of the intentional injury exclusion provision. The trial court found that the insured had intended specifically to commit the act. It concluded the victim's injuries were neither unexpected nor unforeseen and that the policy exclusion precluded liability coverage for her claim.

Expressly adopting the majority view and applying it to the facts of the case, the court said:

> In the case before us, [the insured] denies, first, that he acted intentionally and, second, that he intended any injury. The trial court did not make a specific finding that [the insured] intended to injure [the victim]. We need not, however, make that factual determination. We conclude that an act of forcible anal intercourse is an act of such a character that an intent to cause injury can be inferred *as a matter of law*. The character of the act is such that physical as well as mental trauma can be foreseen as accompanying it. . . . Although, unlike the cases just cited, this case does not involve sexual relations with a minor, the nature of the act, its forcible and nonconsensual character, and the harm that certainly results make the inference of intent no less strong.

Hecker, 43 Wash. App. at 825–26, 719 P.2d at 960 (citations omitted). In addition, the court noted that were the allegations proven in a criminal prosecution, the insured would be guilty of second-degree rape. *Id.* at 826, 719 P.2d at 960. The criminal character of the act provided "further recognition of the injury inherent in the commission of [it]." *Id.*

Similarly, we think the majority view is the better rule, and we adopt it. Senard admitted the sex acts but denied intending to injure Gail. Nevertheless, the nature of the acts, their repetition, the force used in carrying them out, and Gail's admitted sexual naivete convince us to infer intent to injure as a matter of law. These circumstances make it foreseeable that Gail would suffer at least mental trauma if not physical injury.

Another factor favoring this inference is that were the allegations against Senard proven in a criminal prosecution, he would be guilty of sexual abuse. *See* IOWA CODE § 709.1(1). *Compare Hecker*, 43 Wash. App. at 826, 719 P.2d at 960. The criminal character of the acts is a further recognition of the injury inherent in the commission of them. *Hecker*, 43 Wash. App. at 826, 719 P.2d at 960.

Recent studies on the trauma of rape reinforce the criminal law's recognition of injury inherent in the commission of this offense. In many cases the psychic wounds are more devastating and long-lasting than the physical injuries. They include a decrease in self-esteem, consequential inability to entertain a normal heterosexual relationship, and ultimately suicidal behavior. In addition, these victims suffer feelings of depersonalization, humiliation, violation, and defilement. These psychic injuries are magnified the more limited the victim's previous sexual experience has been.

Our conclusion, of course, means Senard has no coverage for his sexual misconduct toward Gail. As we have shown, coverage is precluded because the injuries caused by Senard's misconduct were intentional rather than fortuitous. Further, we think that neither Senard, in purchasing his homeowner's policy, nor UFC, in issuing it, contemplated coverage against claims arising out of nonconsensual sex acts. As one court noted, "[t]he average person purchasing homeowner's insurance would cringe at the very suggestion that [the person] was paying for such coverage. And certainly [the person] would not want to share that type of risk with other homeowner's policyholders." *Rodriguez,* 42 Wash. App. at 636, 713 P.2d at 137–38.

Moreover, our own sense of propriety dictates that coverage for these types of criminal acts should be against the public policy of this state. Such a holding is in accord with the general rule that insurance to indemnify an insured against his or her own violation of criminal statutes is against public policy and therefore void. As one court noted, "[t]he public policy governing such contracts is that one should not profit from his own wrongful act . . . . *New Amsterdam Cas. Co. v. Jones,* 135 F.2d 191, 193–94 (6th Cir. 1943). Our holding here, however, should not be interpreted to mean that we condemn insurance coverage for all forms of intentional misconduct. For example, we have held that it is not against the public policy of this state to provide insurance coverage for punitive damages. *Skyline Harvestore Systems, Inc. v. Centennial Ins. Co.,* 331 N.W.2d 106, 108–09 (Iowa 1983).

We conclude the district court correctly inferred as a matter of law that Senard intended to injure Gail by engaging in the various sex acts. Consequently, no genuine issue of material fact was generated regarding that intent. Accordingly, the court correctly granted UFC's motion for summary judgment. Because of the intentional injury exclusions in both policies, the result of the court's ruling precluded coverage of Senard's sex acts that form the basis of Gail's claims against him.

NOTES

1. *Employer Cover for Employee Sexual Misconduct.* In *Continental Ins. Co. v. McDaniel,* 160 Ariz. 183, 772 P.2d 6 (1988), the court held that a comprehensive business policy issued to a partnership did not cover acts of sexual harassment against employee McDaniel committed by one of the partners, John Handgis. The acts did not constitute an "occurrence . . . . neither expected nor intended from the standpoint of the insured." The conduct of "John Handgis was so certain to cause injury to McDaniel that his intent to cause harm is inferred as a matter of law, despite his statements to the contrary that all he intended was to provide pleasure and satisfaction."

To the insured's contention that "expected or intended" should be determined on a subjective basis, the court said:

> The sexual harassment by John Handgis cannot be compared to the act of one defending his life, shoving an elbow in a basketball game, or striking a potential burglar who by mistaken identity later turns out to be one's brother-in-law. . . . We believe, however, that when the factors involving public policy and the purpose of the contractual exclusion are considered, the proper interpretation of the clause in

question is that it excludes indemnification or coverage when the insured intentionally acts wrongfully with a purpose to injure.

Compare Ambassador Ins. Co. v. Montes, 76 N.J. 477, 388 A.2d 603 (1978), in which the court held that public policy did not prevent indemnification of an innocent partner for the willful burning of a building partnership by a copartner.

In *Capital Alliance Ins. Co. v. Thorough-Clean, Inc.*, 639 So. 2d 1349 (Ala. 1994), the court held that an employer was entitled to coverage under its commercial general liability insurance policy for a rape committed by one of its janitorial employees. The basis of coverage was that the employer negligently hired the employee, who had a felony conviction for an act of violence and had apparently been involved with drugs.

In *Western Heritage Ins. Co. v. Magic Years Learning Centers*, 45 F.3d 85 (5th Cir. 1995), the claimant insured was covered by a liability policy for sexual harassment by an employee, since the policy had an endorsement which provided:

> In consideration of the premium charged it is hereby understood and agreed that Bodily Injury and Property Damage includes any act, which may be considered *sexual in nature* and *could* be classified as an Abuse, Harassment, Molestation, Corporal Punishment or an Invasion of an individual's right of Privacy or control over their physical and/or mental properties by or at the direction of an Insured, an insured's employee or any other person involved in any capacity of the Insured's operation. . . .

This endorsement "trumped" the general definition providing coverage only for an occurrence "neither expected nor intended from the standpoint of the insured":

> Regardless of whether the general definition of occurrence would exclude allegations of sexual harassment by the insured, the endorsement expressly provides for coverage of such claims. To hold otherwise would render the endorsement meaningless.

2. *The Expected or Intended Act Revisited.* In *Economy Fire & Cas. Co. v. Haste*, 824 S.W.2d 41 (Mo. App. 1991), the insured, Berdella, tortured and physically and sexually abused children of the claimants' families, who sought recovery under the insured's homeowner policy. The insurer claimed nonliability under the "expected or intended" exception. While the insured had pled guilty to murder of the victims, the plea did not collaterally estop the claimants.

The court said that the evidence clearly established that the insured expected or intended

> to harm the victims by torturing them with physical, sexual and psychological abuse. Any damages otherwise recoverable against Berdella for the intentional injuries inflicted on the victims prior to their death are excluded under Economy's insurance coverage. . . .

The evidence also established that the insured expected to kill some, but not all, of the victims:

The record reflects that Ferris, Howell and Stoops were held captive and physically and sexually abused. Berdella injected these individuals with drugs against their will and kept them gagged. Berdella did not admit, without issue, that he expected or intended to kill these individuals. To the contrary, Berdella's testimony was that he intended to hold them captive to satisfy his perverted desires. The record reflects that death came to these individuals by either drug injection, asphyxiation from being gagged, bleeding or infection. The record does establish that Berdella intended to harm these individuals, but it does not establish, without genuine issue of material fact, that Berdella intended to kill either Ferris, Howell or Stoops.

3. *Mental Illness and Expected or Intended Acts.* In *Nationwide Ins. Co v. Estate of Kollstedt*, 71 Ohio St. 3d 624, 646 N.E.2d 816 (1995), the court held that the estate of a homicide victim could recover against the defendant homeowner insurer for the shooting killing of the victim by the defendant's insured. The insured was found to be suffering, at the time of the shooting, "from degenerative dementia of the Alzheimer type and senile onset with delirium." In affirming recovery, the court said that

> an act of an individual cannot be treated as "intentional" if the insured was suffering from a derangement of his intellect which deprived him of the capacity to govern his conduct in accordance with reason.

4. *Expected or Intended Act of a Minor.* In *Fire Ins. Exchange v. Diehl*, 206 Mich. App. 108, 520 N.W.2d 675 (1994), the court held that the defendant liability insurer could be liable for injuries caused by the insured's minor son who sexually assaulted the claimant's minor daughter. In determining whether the minor could reasonably foresee the harmful consequences of his intentional act, the court said that his conduct should be judged by the standard of a reasonable child of like age, ability, intelligence and experience under like circumstances. Because the insured's son was seven to nine years of age when the acts occurred, the court concluded that the son could not reasonably foresee that the claimant's minor daughter would be harmed by the assault.

5. *Interpretation of Coverage Clauses.* The general rule is that, although the insured or victim bears the burden of proving coverage, the insurer bears the burden of proving an exclusion. See *Gross v. Allstate Ins. Co.,* 146 Misc. 2d 30, 549 N.Y.S.2d 550 (S.C.N.Y. 1989); *Breland v. Schilling,* 550 So. 2d 609 (La. 1989); *Grinnell Mut. Reinsurance Co. v. Wasmuth,* 432 N.W.2d 495 (Minn. App. 1988).

6. *Limits of Coverage.* The policy will contain limits of the insurer's liability for the insured's wrongful conduct. A typical limit may be $20,000 for each person, and $40,000 for each accident. Some frequently recurring issues, sometimes resolved by the language of the policy and sometimes by judicial fiat, are:

(a) What is an "occurrence"? What if a vessel churns up waters above an oyster bed, destroying the beds of three separate owners? Is there one "occurrence," or three? *See, e.g., Tesvich v. 3-A's Towing Co.,* 547 So. 2d 1106 (La. App. 1989).

In *Mid-Century Ins. Co. v. Shutt*, 845 P.2d 86 (Kan. App. 1993), the court held that, regardless of the number of legal theories underlying the plaintiff's claim arising out of an automobile accident, the accident constituted a single occurrence under the applicable policy. An "occurrence" was defined in the policy:

> Accident or occurrence means a sudden event, including continuous or repeated exposure to the same conditions, resulting in bodily injury or property damage neither expected nor intended by the insured person.

(b) What is "bodily injury"? Is mental anguish or emotional distress bodily injury? *Compare Mellow v. Medical Malpractice Joint Underwriting Ass'n*, 567 A.2d 367 (R.I. 1989), *with American Protection Ins. Co. v. McMahan,* 151 Vt. 520, 562 A.2d 462 (1989). Does "bodily injury" include damages for "loss of consortium"? *See Campbell v. Farmers Ins. Co.*, 155 Ariz. 102, 745 P.2d 160 (App. 1987); *Thompson v. St. Paul Fire & Marine Ins. Co.*, 108 Idaho 802, 702 P.2d 840 (1985); *United Servs. Auto. Ass'n v. Lilly,* 266 Cal. Rptr. 691, 217 Cal. App. 3d 1396 (1990).

JOHNSON & JOHNSON v. AETNA CASUALTY & SURETY CO.
285 N.J. Super. 575, 667 A.2d 1087 (1995)

HAVEY, P.J.A.D.

The question before us is whether excess liability policies issued by defendants to plaintiffs Johnson & Johnson (J & J) and Ortho Pharmaceutical Corporation (Ortho) afford coverage for punitive damage awards suffered by plaintiffs in two failure-to-warn, product liability actions. We conclude that the awards are not covered by the policies, since affording coverage on these facts would run counter to the underlying theory of punitive damages: to punish the wrongdoer and deter aggravated misconduct in the future. Insuring against the awards would therefore frustrate public policy. We accordingly affirm the summary judgment in favor of defendants.

Plaintiffs J & J and its subsidiary Ortho have their principal places of business in New Jersey. In 1976, defendants issued excess liability policies to plaintiffs under which the carriers have no liability to indemnify until the limits of an underlying liability policy are exhausted. In that event, defendants are subject to liability for a proportional share of J & J's "ultimate net loss" not to exceed $14 million. The Aetna policy provides indemnification against "EXCESS NET LOSS arising out of an accident or occurrence during the policy period." "EXCESS NET LOSS" is defined as that which the insured "becomes legally obligated to pay . . . . as damages on account of any one accident or occurrence." The Central National policy indemnifies against "damages . . . . on account of . . . . [p]ersonal injuries . . . . caused by or arising out of each occurrence." The Northbrook and North River policies employ similar language.

During the terms of the policies, punitive damage verdicts were rendered against J & J and Ortho in two separate product liability actions, one in Kansas and one in Missouri. Both are the subjects of reported opinions. *See Wooderson v. Ortho Pharmaceutical Corp.*, 235 Kan. 387, 681 P.2d 1038, *cert.*

C.   INSURANCE COVERAGE ISSUES   1421

denied, 469 U.S. 965, 105 S. Ct. 365, 83 L. Ed. 2d 301 (1984); *Racer v. Utterman*, 629 S.W.2d 387 (Mo. App. 1981), *appeal dismissed and cert. denied*, 459 U.S. 803, 103 S. Ct. 26, 74 L. Ed. 2d 42 (1982). In *Wooderson*, the plaintiff had taken an oral contraceptive manufactured by Ortho and developed renal failure, hemolytic uremic syndrome and hypertension. She claimed that Ortho failed to warn the medical profession of dangerous side effects of its product of which it had or should have had knowledge based on existing research and scientific literature. A special verdict interrogatory concerning punitive damages instructed the jury as follows:

> If you find that plaintiff is entitled to recover, and you also find that the conduct of [Ortho] was *wanton*, then in addition to the actual damages to which you find plaintiff entitled, you may award plaintiff an additional amount as punitive damages in such sum as you believe will serve *to punish defendant [Ortho], and to deter others from like conduct*. [Emphasis added.]

The jury awarded plaintiff $2 million in compensatory damages and $2.75 million in punitive damages. The Kansas Supreme Court affirmed, finding that there was substantial evidence supporting the punitive damage award.

The plaintiff in *Racer* was undergoing a dilation and curettage operation in which a disposable drape manufactured by J & J was being used. The drape caught fire during the surgical procedure and she was seriously burned. The plaintiff claimed, and the court found, that the highly flammable surgical drape was an "unavoidably unsafe" product, and therefore unreasonably dangerous in the absence of appropriate warnings. *Id.* at 393–94; *see* Restatement (Second) of Torts § 402A (1963 & 1964). A jury question pertaining to punitive damages against J & J stated as follows:

> If you find the issues in favor of Plaintiff . . . . and against Defendant [J & J] and if you believe that the conduct of Defendant [J & J] as submitted. . . . showed *complete indifference to or conscious disregard for the safety of others*, you may assess punitive damages in addition to any damages assessed. . . .
>
> The amount of punitive damages assessed against Defendant [J & J] may be such sum as you believe will serve *to punish Defendant [J & J] and to deter it and others from like conduct*. [Emphasis added.]

The jury awarded plaintiff and her husband $382,500 in compensatory damages and $517,500 in punitive damages. The Missouri Court of Appeals reversed and remanded the punitive damage award, concluding that, while there was evidence to support a finding that there was indifference to or conscious disregard for the safety of others, the award must be reversed because the matter was not properly submitted to the jury. According to the court, the fatal flaw in the instruction was that it did not require a finding of fault in placing a dangerous product in commerce, "and a finding of fault sufficient to justify punishment is essential to recovery of exemplary damages." After remand, J & J settled the punitive damage claim for $355,237.

J & J and Ortho filed the present declaratory judgment action seeking indemnification from defendants for the punitive damage awards paid in *Wooderson* and *Racer*. Defendants moved for summary judgment dismissing the complaint and plaintiffs cross-moved. The motion judge granted defendants' motion and denied plaintiffs' cross-motion, finding that New Jersey's public policy was consistent with the policies of Kansas and Missouri and that any choice-of-law determination was therefore "academic." The judge concluded that it is against public policy to insure against punitive damage awards.

The thrust of plaintiffs' multi-part contention is that it does not violate New Jersey's public policy to provide indemnification for punitive damage awards when the insured's liability is "vicarious" rather than "direct." Citing *Malanga v. Manufacturers Cas. Ins. Co.*, 28 N.J. 220, 146 A.2d 105 (1958), plaintiffs reason that an employer who is vicariously liable may be indemnified for punitive damage awards, since in that circumstance it does not share in the culpability of the employee-wrongdoer. Plaintiffs argue that under New Jersey law, an employer may be held "directly" liable for punitive damages only in the event of actual participation by upper management or willful indifference. Plaintiffs assert that the distinction between direct and vicarious liability is significant for the purpose of determining whether the punitive damage award should be covered by defendants' policies. They conclude that, since they were vicariously rather than directly liable for punitive damages in both *Wooderson* and *Racer*, it would not offend public policy to permit coverage for those awards.

The courts throughout the country are split as to whether the typical general liability or excess policy covers punitive damage awards. Some courts have held that punitive damages are unambiguously covered because carriers agree to pay "all sums" the insured becomes legally obligated to pay as "damages." Others have applied the traditional contract ambiguity doctrine and reached the same result.

Another analytical approach embraced by some courts and advanced by plaintiffs here is to determine whether the insureds' liability is direct or vicarious. Some courts conclude that, if the employer's liability for punitive damages is merely vicarious, coverage should be afforded. Plaintiffs argue that the New Jersey Supreme Court adopted this vicarious/direct liability distinction in *Malanga*.

We reject plaintiffs' argument. First, *Malanga* is of little benefit to plaintiffs' argument. In *Malanga*, a partnership was covered by a comprehensive liability insurance policy naming it and the individual partners as insureds. Under the policy, the carrier undertook to pay on behalf of the insureds all sums which they became "legally obligated to pay as damages because of bodily injury. . . . caused by accident." "[A]ccident" was defined to include assault and battery "unless committed by or at the direction of the insured." *Ibid*. The partnership sought coverage for both compensatory and punitive damages arising from the assault and battery of a third person by one of the partners in the course of partnership business. The Supreme Court concluded that the partnership was covered because, while the wrongdoing partner was clearly excluded from coverage, it was necessary to "distinguish between an agent who is guilty of willful wrongdoing and his principal [the partnership] who is only vicariously responsible." Therefore, "[w]hile an assault and battery is a premeditated act from the agent's point of view, to his passively liable principal and to his victim it is an unforeseen occurrence, *i.e.*, an 'accident' within the meaning of the policy."

C. INSURANCE COVERAGE ISSUES 1423

Malanga is not dispositive since the Court was simply applying the well-settled principle that the partnership, as a named insured, must be "recognized by the terms of the policy as an entity distinct from its individual partners." *See also Property Cas. Co. of MCA v. Conway*, 284 N.J. Super. 622, 626–27, 666 A.2d 182, 185 (App. Div. 1995) (concluding that father vicariously liable for son's vandalism under N.J.S.A. 18A:37-3 was covered by liability policy since, from father's perspective, the son's act was unintended and unexpected). *Malanga* does not purport to address the discrete issue whether, as a matter of law, New Jersey's public policy precludes coverage for punitive damage liability. In fact, the Court noted that the insurer did not raise the distinction between compensatory and punitive damages.

Second, New Jersey sides with those jurisdictions which proscribe coverage for punitive damage liability because such a result offends public policy and frustrates the purposes of punitive damage awards.[11] For example, in *Variety Farms, Inc. v. New Jersey Mfrs. Ins. Co.*, 172 N.J. Super. 10, 13, 410 A.2d 696 (App. Div. 1980), the insured corporation and its president sought coverage for a punitive damage award recovered by a minor who suffered a serious injury while employed by the company. We observed that punitive damages are "sums awarded apart from compensatory damages and are assessed when the wrongdoer's conduct is especially egregious." We acknowledged the conflict among other jurisdictions concerning whether it is in the public interest to permit insurance coverage for punitive damages, and considered the "sounder rule to be that public policy does not permit a tortfeasor to shift the burden of punitive damages to his insurer." *Variety Farms, supra*, 172 N.J. Super. at 24–25, 410 A.2d 696. In so holding, we observed:

> The policy considerations in a state where . . . . punitive damages are awarded for punishment and deterrence would seem to require that the damages rest ultimately as well [as] nominally on the party actually responsible for the wrong. If that person were permitted to shift the burden to an insurance company, punitive damages would serve no useful purpose. Such damages do not compensate the plaintiff for his injury, since compensatory damages [have] already. . . . made the plaintiff whole. And there is no point in punishing the insurance company; it has done no wrong.

See also Loigman v. Massachusetts Bay Ins. Co., 235 N.J. Super. 67, 73, 561 A.2d 642 (App. Div. 1989) (concluding that federal Rule 11 sanctions imposed against attorney-insured "were punitive in nature and uninsurable").

Notably, *Variety Farms* contains no analysis concerning whether or not the policy language is ambiguous, presumably because the issue is irrelevant in view of our overriding public policy precluding coverage for punitive damage awards. Nor does it make the vicarious/direct liability distinction in pronouncing the rule that such coverage would offend public policy. We find no reason

---

[11] Presently, there exists no legislation in our State either prohibiting or permitting coverage for punitive damage awards. However, substantially similar bills, A-3060 and S-2266, are presently pending in both houses of the State Legislature which would authorize indemnity coverage for punitive damage awards.

to carve an exception to *Variety Farm*'s holding based upon the vicarious/direct dichotomy on the facts before us.

We question whether the vicarious/direct liability distinction should be applied in a product liability case, at least, as here, in the employer-employee setting. Where a punitive damage award arises in such a case, the purpose of the award is to punish the wrongdoer, to deter defendant and others from similar conduct in the future, and "to encourage plaintiffs to pursue a manufacturer who engages in a 'deliberate act or omission with knowledge of a high degree of probability of harm and reckless indifference to consequences.'" *Fischer*, 103 N.J. at 658, 512 A.2d 466. Punitive damages "serve the public interest by encouraging corporations to keep defective products . . . . out of the marketplace." Widiss, *supra*, 39 Vill. L. Rev. at 500–01. Permitting a shift of the responsibility for punitive damages from the manufacturer to its insurance company in a product liability case would thwart those purposes. *Id.* at 499.

> Responsibility for the design or manufacture of faulty products appropriately rests with the executives of an enterprise. Therefore, the public's interest in safe products mitigates against anything that serves to diminish the responsibilities of those charged with making executive decisions about product safety. Consequently, the substantial societal interest in assuring that defective products — especially items which pose threats to the health and safety of the public — do not enter the marketplace means that it would be very undesirable to apply the vicarious liability exception in this context.

[*Ibid.*]

In *Fischer, supra*, the Supreme Court addressed these public policy considerations in a different factual setting. There the manufacturer argued that it should not be held liable for punitive damages because the culpable employee may no longer be employed by it. The Court rejected the contention because it "ignores the nature of a corporation as a separate legal entity." The Court reasoned that "[a]lthough the responsible management personnel may escape punishment, *the corporation itself will not*" (emphasis added), and stressed that:

> [A] primary goal of punitive damages is general deterrence — that is, the deterrence of others from engaging in similar conduct. That purpose is, of course, well served regardless of changes in personnel within the offending corporation.

[*Fischer*, 103 N.J. at 662, 512 A.2d 466.] *Fischer*'s reasoning is instructive here. Just as we should not focus on the fact that the employee-wrongdoer has departed in judging the deterrent value of punitive damage awards against the employer, we should not necessarily decide whether or not to allow indemnity for those awards based on the management level of the employee who committed the wrongful act. Whether the product enters the marketplace as a result of executive policies or lower-level employee wrongdoing, the potentially devastating consequences to consumers are the same. It is therefore necessary to punish "the corporation itself," *ibid.*, and to deter the corporation and others from engaging in similar conduct in the future. Permitting the corporation to seek refuge by shifting the cost of punitive damage awards to insurance carriers based on vicarious liability would still frustrate those goals.

In any event, we are able to decide this case without applying the vicarious/direct distinction since there was no finding that J & J or Ortho was held vicariously rather than directly liable for the punitive damages in either *Wooderson* or *Racer*. As we read those opinions, the issue of vicarious versus direct liability was raised neither in the pleadings nor during trial, nor was it charged to the jury. No individual officer or employee was named as a defendant in either case. Most importantly, no claim was made in either case that the manufacturer was not liable for punitive damages because of the vicarious/direct liability distinction.

Punitive damages were awarded against Ortho in *Wooderson* because of its wanton failure, as a manufacturer, to place a reasonably safe product in the marketplace. The court in *Wooderson* noted that, "[a]pparently [Ortho's] competitive position in the market was better served by continuing the manufacture and sale of its . . . . product," rather than heeding "the accumulating medical and scientific evidence" that its product was extremely dangerous. The court also noted that there was evidence from which the jury could conclude that Ortho, as a manufacturer, failed to pursue additional research and "played down the danger of" its product despite its knowledge of the product's dangerous propensities. *Wooderson*, 681 P.2d at 1063–64.

Similarly, in *Racer*, the court observed that, from the evidence, the jury could have concluded that J & J as a corporate entity had placed the flammable drape in commerce "knowing and intending that it be used for surgery where a cautery would be in use" with knowledge of its flammability and "indifference to, or conscious disregard for, the safety of others." *Racer*, 629 S.W.2d at 396. With this knowledge, J & J represented in its marketing activities that the product was safe for these operations and "that the drape met governmental flammability standards which were in fact non-existent." *Ibid*. Nothing in either of the *Wooderson* or *Racer* opinions suggests that low-level employees were responsible for the egregious conduct justifying the punitive damage awards. To the contrary, the entirety of both opinions implies culpability based upon upper-management decision making, if not corporate policy established by executive personnel.

Plaintiffs argue, alternatively, that it would not be against New Jersey's public policy to permit insurance indemnification against punitive damage awards for "unintentional conduct" that is a "species" of negligence or gross negligence. They contend that coverage should be allowed under such circumstances "because traditional concerns about wrongdoers shifting their losses to insurers lose their force when the type of conduct supporting an award of punitive damages is no greater than gross negligence." Plaintiffs state that, since the *Wooderson* and *Racer* punitive damage awards were based on "unintentional" conduct, affording coverage for those awards would not offend New Jersey's public policy.

However, as stated, the law as to punitive damages in Kansas, as applied by the *Wooderson* court, required a showing of a malicious, vindictive, or willful and wanton invasion of the injured party's rights. Similarly, in *Racer*, the Missouri Court of Appeals required a finding of knowledge of the dangerous propensity of the product and an "indifference to, or conscious disregard for, the safety of others sufficient to support a punitive damage award."

Plaintiffs' contention that the *Wooderson* and *Racer* plaintiffs would not have recovered punitive damages in New Jersey is sheer speculation. New Jersey's Products Liability Act provides:

> Punitive damages may be awarded to the claimant only if the claimant proves, by a preponderance of the evidence, that the harm suffered was the result of the product manufacturer's or seller's acts or omissions, and such acts or omissions were actuated by actual malice or accompanied by a wanton and willful disregard of the safety of product users, consumers, or others who foreseeably might be harmed by the product. For the purposes of this section "actual malice" means an intentional wrongdoing in the sense of an evil-minded act, and "wanton and willful disregard" means a deliberate act or omission with knowledge of a high degree of probability of harm to another and reckless indifference to the consequences of such action or omission. Punitive damages shall not be awarded in the absence of an award of compensatory damages. [N.J.S.A. 2A:58C-5a.]

Based on the conduct of both Ortho and J & J as above-described, we are firmly of the view that the facts in both *Wooderson* and *Racer* would have permitted a jury, applying New Jersey law, to conclude by a preponderance of the evidence that the harm suffered was a result of plaintiffs' acts or omissions "accompanied by a wanton and willful disregard of the safety of product users, consumers, or others who foreseeably might be harmed by the product;" that is, that plaintiffs committed "a deliberate act or omission with knowledge of a high degree of probability of harm to another and reckless indifference to the consequences of such action or omission." N.J.S.A. 2A:58C-5a.

In our view, the legal standards imposed for the awards of punitive damages in both *Wooderson* and *Racer* are not so conceptually different from New Jersey's standard as to cause us to abandon our State's well-settled policy which precludes insurance coverage for punitive damage liability.[12]

Affirmed.

NOTES

1. *Vicarious Punitive Liability.* In *Butterfield v. Giuntoli*, 670 A.2d 646 (Pa. Super. 1995), the court said that "a claim for punitive damages against a tortfeasor who is *personally* guilty of outrageous and wanton misconduct is excluded from coverage as a matter of law." But, following decisions in other jurisdictions, the court said, "public policy does not preclude recovery of punitive damages where the insured is only vicariously liable for the damages."

---

[12] We do not address whether a different result could be reached if the punitive damage award was entered in a jurisdiction having a significantly lower standard than that required by our Products Liability Act.

2. *Misrepresentations by the Insured.* An insurer may seek to void the policy because the insured made misrepresentations in obtaining the policy. The misrepresentation will not void the policy unless it is deemed "material," *i.e.,* it might reasonably have influenced the insurer in deciding whether to accept or reject the risk. *See, e.g., Safeway Ins. Co. v. Duran,* 74 Ill. App. 3d 846, 30 Ill. Dec. 652, 393 N.E.2d 688 (1979). Many of the cases are collected in J. APPLEMAN, INSURANCE LAW AND PRACTICE § 4252 (Buckley ed. 1979).

3. *Breach of the Cooperation Clause.* The liability policy generally imposes upon the insured a duty to provide immediate or other prompt notice of an accident and of the filing of a claim or suit against the insured. In some jurisdictions, breach of the notice requirement will not void coverage for the loss unless the insurer can establish prejudice therefrom. *Great Am. Ins. Co. v. C.G. Tate Constr. Co.,* 303 N.C. 387, 279 S.E.2d 769 (1981).

A liability policy also usually will require the insured to assist and cooperate with the insurer in the defense of the claim. A typical clause:

> The insured shall cooperate with the company and, upon the company's request, shall attend hearings and trials and shall assist in effecting settlements, securing and giving evidence, obtaining the attendance of witnesses and in the conduct of suits. The insured shall not, except at his own cost, voluntarily make any payment, assume any obligation or incur any expense other than for such immediate medical and surgical relief to others as shall be imperative at the time of accident.

The better, and perhaps the majority view, is that the insured's lack of cooperation does not void the policy unless the insurer was prejudiced thereby. *Billington v. Interinsurance Exch. of S. Cal.,* 71 Cal. 2d 728, 79 Cal. Rptr. 326, 456 P.2d 982 (1969).

4. *Ambiguous Coverage.* In *Red Panther Chem. Co. v. Insurance Co. of Pa.,* 43 F.3d 514 (10th Cir. 1994), the plaintiff sought indemnification from its insurer:

> Red Panther held a corporate general liability policy from which this litigation emanates with the Insurance Company. The controversy arose when the Insurance Company refused to defend Red Panther in an Oklahoma state court case alleging claims of negligence, strict liability, and products liability brought against Red Panther by Dennis Graham. Red Panther filed this action seeking a defense and indemnification for Mr. Graham's claim. Applying Mississippi law, the district court held the Total Pollution Exclusion clause of Red Panther's insurance policy was plain and unambiguous. The clause specifically excluded insurance coverage for bodily injury and property damage claims arising from the escape of pollutants. The district court held this case fell within the exclusion, making summary judgment appropriate as a matter of law. The court concluded the chemical ethyl parathion was a pollutant as defined by the policy, and Mr. Graham's injury was the result of the escape of that pollutant. Red Panther argues that the Total Pollution Exclusion is ambiguous, making summary judgment improper. We agree.

The underlying claim in this case involves a bizarre set of circumstances eerily reminiscent of the trials and tribulations of the legendary Mrs. Palsgraf. A.L. McAllister Trucking Company picked up forty-eight 55-gallon drums and two hundred seventy-two 5-gallon containers of the insecticide ethyl parathion from Red Panther's manufacturing plant in Clarksdale, Mississippi. McAllister was engaged by Estes Chemical Company to truck the pesticide to a variety of locations, including several in Oklahoma. The cargo was loaded and secured on the McAllister truck by Red Panther representatives in Mississippi. The truck made at least one other stop where some of the pesticide was unloaded, and other items were added to the cargo. While the truck was traveling outside Oklahoma City, seven of the 5-gallon containers fell off onto Interstate 40. A vehicle driven by Vonnie Brown struck and dragged one of the errant containers for several miles. Noticing an engine warning light in her vehicle, Mrs. Brown drove to a service station in El Reno, Oklahoma, to have the car examined. At the station, mechanic Dennis Graham hoisted the Brown vehicle on a lift and became exposed to the ethyl parathion by inhaling chemical fumes and absorbing the insecticide through his skin. Mr. Graham alleged that the chemical dripped on him when he placed Mrs. Brown's automobile on the rack to search for the broken oil or hydraulic line he suspected was the cause of Mrs. Brown's problem. Mr. Graham sued Red Panther in Oklahoma state court. Some time later, the Insurance Company informed Red Panther that it was denying coverage for Mr. Graham's claim and would not defend the company in any lawsuits because the claim was excluded from coverage under the policy's Total Pollution Exclusion.

The Total Pollution Exclusion clause of the policy provided that the insurer would not be liable for any bodily injury or property damage caused by the insured's "discharge, dispersal, release or escape of pollutants."

In holding that summary judgment for the defendant was improperly granted, the court said:

> We do not believe it presently evident Red Panther and the Insurance Company unambiguously contracted to exclude coverage for this claim based upon the Total Pollution Exclusion endorsement. We reach this conclusion because of the unique factual circumstances involved in Mr. Graham's underlying claim against Red Panther. The critical question is whether the word "escape" contained in the exclusion is meant to include the expulsion of a container of pollutants from a moving vehicle. We believe that provision is ambiguous; therefore, in this context, summary judgment was not appropriate.
>
> Our conclusion is buttressed by two additional considerations. First, many of the courts holding a pollution exclusion was ambiguous have done so in cases that involved atypical factual situations like this one. *See, e.g., Minerva Enters. v. Bituminous Cas. Co.*, 312 Ark. 128, 851 S.W.2d 403 (1993) (tenant sued mobile home park owner after their septic tank backed up and flooded their residence); *West Am. Ins. Co. v. Tufco Flooring*, 104 N.C. App. 312, 409 S.E.2d 692 (1991) (chemicals

used in floor resurfacing activities in a chicken processing plant damaged the chickens); and *American Star Ins. Co. v. Grice*, 121 Wash. 2d 869, 854 P.2d 622 (1993) (landfill caught fire causing damage to neighboring property holders' homes). Second, the third generation pollution exclusion at issue here has not yet been the subject of extensive litigation like its predecessors. This fact makes an exploration into the factual background and intent of the exclusion particularly appropriate.

We hold that as applied to the facts and circumstances of this claim, the Total Pollution Exclusion in Red Panther's policy is not unambiguous as a matter of law. The district court must, therefore, conduct a factual inquiry into the proper scope of the exclusion, based on the common usages and understandings of the insurance industry, and the purposes of the exclusion in conjunction with the hazards and risks Red Panther's policy was designed to protect against. After considering all the evidence, the district court must then determine whether the facts and circumstances of Mr. Graham's claim fall within the intended scope of the Total Pollution Exclusion of the policy.

5. *Dual Coverage.* In *State Farm Mut. Auto Ins. Co. v. Partridge*, 109 Cal. Rptr. 811, 514 P.2d 123 (Cal. 1973), the court stated the issues and facts as follows:

> The instant case presents a somewhat novel question of insurance coverage: when two negligent acts of an insured — one auto-related and the other non-auto-related — constitute concurrent causes of an accident, is the insured covered under both his homeowner's policy and his automobile liability policy, or is coverage limited to the automobile policy? State Farm Insurance Company (State Farm), the insurer which issued both policies at issue in this case, brought this declaratory judgment action requesting a determination as to which one, or both, of its policies afforded coverage for the accident in question.
>
> In the trial court the insurer, relying on an exclusionary provision in the homeowner's policy which withheld coverage for injuries "arising out of the use" of a motor vehicle, contended that coverage was only available under the automobile liability policy. Defendants [the insured and the victim], on the other hand, argued that since two independent negligent acts, one covered by the homeowner's policy and one by the automobile policy, jointly caused the accident, coverage should be afforded by both policies. After a non-jury trial, the court agreed with defendants and entered judgment holding the insurer liable under both policies. State Farm appeals from that judgment.
>
> As discussed below, we have concluded that the trial court decision, finding liability under both insurance policies, should be affirmed. Initially, we shall point out that coverage is unquestionably available under the automobile liability policy since the instant accident bore some causal relationship to the use of the insured vehicle. Thereafter, we shall explain that although the homeowner's policy excluded injuries "arising out of the use" of an automobile, such exclusion does not preclude coverage when an accident results from the concurrence

of a non-auto-related cause and an auto-related cause. The comprehensive personal liability coverage of the homeowner's policy affords the insured protection for liability accruing generally from non-auto-related risks. Whenever such a non-auto risk is a proximate cause of an injury, liability attaches to the insured, and coverage for such liability should naturally follow. Coverage cannot be defeated simply because a separate excluded risk constitutes an additional cause of the injury. We therefore conclude that the trial court properly found that coverage is available under both of the policies in question.

We begin our analysis with a brief review of the facts of the case, which are not in dispute. The circumstances resulting in the accident at issue reveal an instance of what can only be described as blatant recklessness. Wayne Partridge, the named insured of the two insurance policies issued by State Farm, was a hunting enthusiast who owned a .357 Magnum pistol. Prior to the date of the accident, Partridge filed the trigger mechanism of his pistol to lighten the trigger pull so that the gun would have "hair trigger action;" the trial court specifically found this modification of the gun to be a negligent act, creating an exceptionally dangerous weapon.

On the evening of July 26, 1969, Partridge and two friends, Vanida Neilson and Ray Albertson, were driving in the countryside in Partridge's four-wheel drive Ford Bronco. With Vanida sitting between them in the front seat, Partridge and Albertson hunted jackrabbits by shooting out of the windows of the moving vehicle; Partridge was using his modified .357 Magnum. On the occasion in question here, Partridge spotted a running jackrabbit crossing the road, and, in order to keep the rabbit within the car's headlights, Partridge drove his vehicle off the paved road onto the adjacent rough terrain. The vehicle hit a bump, the pistol discharged and a bullet entered Vanida's left arm and penetrated down to her spinal cord, resulting in paralysis. At the time of the accident, Partridge was either holding the gun in his lap or resting it on top of the steering wheel pointed at Vanida.

Vanida sought damages of $500,000. The automobile policy had a limit of $15,000 per person, which State Farm agreed immediately to pay.

In finding that the homeowner's policy also applied, the court said:

> The controversy in this case, instead, focuses solely upon the applicability of the homeowner's policy to the instant accident. The insurer, pointing to the exclusionary clause of the homeowner's policy which denies coverage for injuries "arising out of the . . . . use . . . . of a motor vehicle," contends that since, as we have just determined, the instant accident "arose out of the use" of the vehicle for purposes of the automobile policy, the homeowner's policy necessarily excludes the accident. Emphasizing that the language of the homeowner's exclusionary clause is nearly identical to the language of the automobile policy's coverage clause, and that the same insurer drafted and issued both policies, State Farm argues that the policies were intended to be mutually exclusive and that no overlapping coverage can be permitted. For the reasons discussed below, we cannot agree.

Initially we point out that the insurer overlooks the fact that although the language in the two policies is substantially similar, past authorities have made it abundantly clear that an entirely different rule of construction applies to exclusionary clauses as distinguished from coverage clauses. Whereas coverage clauses are interpreted broadly so as to afford the greatest possible protection to the insured, exclusionary clauses are interpreted narrowly against the insurer. These differing canons of construction, both derived from the fundamental principle that all ambiguities in an insurance policy are construed against the insurer-draftsman, mean that in ambiguous situations an insurer might be found liable under both insurance policies. . . .

In the instant case the trial court specifically found that Partridge's negligence in filing the trigger mechanism of his gun constituted a proximate cause of Vanida's injuries. Applying the above principles, we conclude that the trial court properly found the homeowner's policy applicable to the accident.

6. *Multiple Coverage. Keene Corp. v. Insurance Co. of N. Am.*, 667 F.2d 1034 (D.C. Cir. 1981), *cert. den.* 455 U.S. 1007, 102 S. Ct. 1644, 71 L. Ed. 2d 875 (1982), presents a complicated factual and legal situation in which the insured product manufacturer is covered by different policies in successive years, and the exposure to and injury from these products occur over an extended period of time:

> This case arises out of the growing volume of litigation centering upon manufacturers' liability for disease caused by asbestos products. In this action, Keene Corporation (Keene) seeks a declaratory judgment of the rights and obligations of the parties under the comprehensive general liability policies that the defendants issued to Keene or its predecessors from 1961 to 1980. Specifically, Keene seeks a determination of the extent to which each policy covers its liability for asbestos-related diseases.[13]
>
> Between the years 1948 and 1972, Keene manufactured thermal insulation products that contained asbestos. As a result, Keene has been named as a codefendant with several other companies in over 6000 lawsuits alleging injury caused by exposure to Keene's asbestos products. Those cases typically involve insulation installers or their survivors alleging personal injury, or wrongful death, as a result of inhaling asbestos fibers over the course of many years. The plaintiffs in the underlying suits allege that they contracted asbestosis, mesothelioma, and/or lung cancer as a result of such inhalation.
>
> From 1961 to the present, Insurance Company of North America (INA), Liberty Mutual Insurance Company (Liberty), Aetna Casualty and Surety Company (Aetna), and Hartford Accident and Indemnity

---

[13] Under *Borel v. Fibreboard Paper Products Corp.*, 493 F.2d 1076 (5th Cir. 1973), *cert. denied*, 419 U.S. 869, 95 S. Ct. 127, 42 L. Ed. 2d 107 (1974), an asbestos manufacturer such as Keene can be held jointly and severally liable for asbestos-related diseases that were caused, in part, by its products.

Company (Hartford) issued comprehensive general liability (CGL) insurance policies to Keene. From December 31, 1961 through August 23, 1968, INA insured Keene; from August 23, 1967 through August 23, 1968, Liberty insured Keene; from August 23, 1968 through August 23, 1971, Aetna insured Keene; from August 23, 1971 through October 1, 1974, Hartford insured Keene; and from October 1, 1974 through October 1, 1980, Liberty insured Keene. The policies that these companies issued to Keene were identical in all relevant respects. The coverage language of the policy that Hartford issued to Keene from 1971 to 1974 is typical. It states that

> [t]he company will pay on behalf of the insured all sums which the insured shall become legally obligated to pay as damages because of bodily injury . . . . to which this insurance applies, caused by an *occurrence,* and the company shall have the right and duty to defend any suit against the insured seeking *damages* on account of such *bodily injury* . . . . even if any of the allegations of the suit are groundless, false or fraudulent. . . .

"Bodily injury" is defined as "bodily injury, sickness or disease sustained by any person,"; and "occurrence" is defined as "an accident, including injurious exposure to conditions, which results, during the policy period, in *bodily injury* . . . . neither expected nor intended from the standpoint of the *insured.*"

Keene tendered the asbestos-related damage cases to its insurance companies for defense and indemnification. Each company, however, either denied all responsibility for the suits or accepted only partial responsibility.

On June 6, 1978, Keene filed this suit for a declaratory judgment and damages in the United States District Court for the District of Columbia. Keene contended that any stage in the progression of an asbestos-related disease triggers coverage of Keene's entire liability under each of the policies. Aetna, INA, and Liberty argued that coverage is triggered only when bodily injury manifests itself during a policy period. Hartford took an intermediate position, arguing that coverage is triggered by the inhalation of asbestos fibers, but that each company's coverage is determined by the ratio of exposure years during its policy period to the entire period of inhalation. . . .

In any suit against Keene for an asbestos-related disease, it is likely that the coverage of more than one insurer will be triggered. Because each insurer is fully liable, and because Keene cannot collect more than it owes in damages, the issue of dividing insurance obligations arises. The only logical resolution of this issue is for Keene to be able to collect from any insurer whose coverage is triggered, the full amount of indemnity that it is due, subject only to the provisions in the policies that govern the allocation of liability when more than one policy covers an injury. That is the only way that Keene can be assured the security that it purchased with each policy. Our holding each insurer fully liable to Keene is also consistent with other courts' allocation of liability when more than one insurer covers an indivisible loss.

This does not mean that a single insurer will be saddled with full liability for any injury. When more than one policy applies to a loss, the "other insurance" provisions of each policy provide a scheme by which the insurers' liability is to be apportioned. For instance, INA's policy states:

> When both this insurance and other insurance apply to the loss on the same basis, whether primary, excessive or contingent, INA shall not be liable under this policy for a greater proportion of the loss than stated in the applicable contribution provision below.

The contribution provision referred to contains formulae for "contribution by equal shares" and for "contribution by limits," depending upon the provisions of other applicable policies. These provisions of the policies must govern the allocation of liability among the insurers in any particular case of asbestos-related disease. However, the primary duty of the insurers whose coverage is triggered by exposure or manifestation is to ensure that Keene is indemnified in full.

The policies provide that the insurer shall defend any suit against Keene for damages due to bodily injury, even if the suit is groundless, false or fraudulent. The insurers' duty to defend Keene and to pay Keene for its defense costs are more broad than their duty to indemnify Keene. As long as a complaint indicates that Keene may be liable for an injury, an insurer must defend Keene if the facts alleged in the complaint indicate that its policy covers the alleged injury. Because we hold that each insurer is fully liable to Keene for indemnification, it follows that each is fully liable for defense costs. . . .

The doctrine of joint and several tort liability in this context is an accepted means of vindicating the rights of the tort victims. Nothing that we decide concerning the contractual liability of the insurers to Keene should impair the tort plaintiff's prosecution of his or her suit.

Thus initially, the full insurance obligation to Keene must be divided among the insurers whose policies are triggered based on the facts brought out in the tort suit against Keene. The possibility of additional coverage can be determined consensually among insurers, or it can be adjudicated among insurers in a subsequent lawsuit. At that point the insurance obligations can be reallocated among all the insurers whose policies are found to cover a particular injury. Any facts concerning the period of exposure or the point of manifestation that are proved in an underlying tort suit need not be legally dispositive of a dispute among insurers concerning allocation of their liability. Perhaps if the underlying tort suit would not be disputed and the plaintiff would not be put to undue inconvenience, the factual record needed to allocate insurance responsibility may be developed during the course of the underlying tort suit.

If a victim sues more than one asbestos-product manufacturer, it may be impossible to prove which company's products were used at which time. If so, it will be impossible to prove that exposure to Keene's products — as opposed to those of another manufacturer —

occurred during a particular time period. In such a case, there should be a presumption that throughout the victim's period of exposure to asbestos he or she was exposed to Keene's and the other manufacturers' products. The insurer defending Keene in the underlying tort suits may then try to show that Keene's products could not have been involved for certain years. Similarly, if a suit arises to resolve the allocation of insurance liability, any insurance company can try to prove that there was no inhalation of Keene's asbestos during or before its policy period. If an insurance company does so, then that company will be free of liability. . . .

[Judge Wald, concurring in part, wrote:]

This is a case of first impression and, irrespective of how it is resolved, requires a "leap of logic" from existing precedent, for it concerns diseases about which there is no medical certainty as to precisely how or when they "occur." We do know the prerequisite — exposure to asbestos fibers — and the symptoms that manifest themselves, generally too late for effective treatment. What happens in between is still something of a mystery; why does one exposed person fall victim to the diseases while another does not? This suit is one of several filed in different courts to ascertain the liability of insurers of manufacturing companies when those companies are sued by asbestosis, mesothelioma and lung cancer victims who have been exposed to the companies' products. Two circuits, the Fifth and Sixth, have determined that exposure alone should trigger the insurer's liability. The Sixth Circuit has also determined that the judgment awarded to the victim should be allocated among insurance companies pro rata according to their share of the total risk period during which the manufacturer was insured. If the risk period includes years when the manufacturer was uninsured (or self-insured), the manufacturer must bear a proportional share of the judgment.

The approach taken in the panel opinion here is different from the approaches of other courts in two significant respects. First, it defines the "injury" that triggers insurance coverage not merely as exposure to asbestos fibers or manifestation of the symptoms of asbestosis, mesothelioma or lung cancer, but also — at least in the case of asbestosis — as the process by which the victim's body resists, adapts, and tries to accommodate itself to a foreign matter — a process, which we understand from the medical testimony elicited at trial, is a major, if not primary, factor in the development of asbestosis. In short, the "injury" is taking place every year that the asbestos fiber remains *in situ* until tissue damage in the lungs is significant enough to be detected by X-rays or to produce symptomatic effects of asbestosis, mesothelioma or lung cancer. I *agree* with this more comprehensive definition of "injury," encompassing the period from initial exposure to manifestation, because it comports with what we know and do not know about the etiology and progress of the diseases. This process-oriented definition not only provides a flexible formula for adjudicating the legal issues associated with asbestos-related diseases, but also sets a useful precedent for other product-exposure injuries, as of yet unknown in origin. Further, the more comprehensive definition will give much needed certainty to the insurance industry, currently rent asunder by advocates of exposure and manifestation, whose fluctuating positions often depend upon their economic interests in a particular case, and by differing judicial rulings which seem to depend at least partially upon the equities of each case.

Second, the majority opinion exempts asbestos manufacturers from all financial responsibility arising from a suit if the manufacturer had purchased insurance which covered any part of the injury period. I am not able to agree with this aspect of the majority opinion, as it applies to the period prior to the time when such coverage could no longer be obtained. I just do not understand why an asbestos manufacturer, which has consciously decided not to insure itself during particular years of the exposure-manifestation period, should have a reasonable expectation that it would be exempt from any liability for injuries that were occurring during the uninsured period. It seems to me logical and fair — as it seemed to the Sixth Circuit and to the trial court here — to distribute the ultimate financial responsibility on a pro rata basis among the various insurance companies on line during the risk period, and to include Keene as a self-insurer for the years when it failed to take out any insurance. . . .

7. *Disputes Among Insurers.* Two insurance policies may provide coverage to the same tortfeasor for the same accident. A common example is when the named insured or his spouse under one policy is negligent in the operation, with the owner's permission, of a nonowned vehicle. Both policies provide coverage. A determination of which insurer has the "primary" coverage (and thus must pay the first portion of the victim's damages) turns on the language of the "other insurance" clauses in the policies. *See, e.g.,* 46 A.L.R.2d 1163 (1956 & Supp. 1990).

Coverage of an insured's activities also may be provided by different insurers, in layers of coverage. One insurer may agree to cover the risks in a sum not to exceed a designated amount, and a second insurer may agree to provide coverage of the same risks for sums between the upper limits of the first insurer's coverage and a higher designated sum. The first insurer usually is termed the "primary" insurer, and insurers providing higher layers of coverage are deemed "excess carriers." Two common issues involving layers of insurance: (1) If the primary insurer is bankrupt, does the excess insurer "drop down" to provide coverage for sums ordinarily within the primary's limits? This depends upon the language of the excess policy. (2) Where there is excess coverage, the primary insurer's failure to settle in good faith may expose the excess carrier to liability. Most courts will permit the excess carrier to recover, holding that the primary owes a duty of good faith to the excess carrier. *Western World Ins. Co. v. Allstate Ins. Co.,* 376 A.2d 177, 150 N.J. Super. 481 (1977). *See also* J. Appleman, Insurance Law and Practice § 4711 (Berdel ed. 1989). An excess carrier who pays that portion of a judgment in excess of the upper limits of the bad faith primary carrier's coverage also may be subrogated to the insured's rights against the primary carrier. *See, e.g.,*

Northwestern Mut. Ins. Co. v. Farmers Ins. Group, 143 Cal. Rptr. 415, 76 Cal. App. 3d 1031 (1978). *See United States Fid. & Guar. Co. v. Superior Court,* 252 Cal. Rptr. 320, 204 Cal. App. 3d 1513 (1988); *United Servs. Auto. Ass'n v. Morris,* 154 Ariz. 113, 741 P.2d 246 (1987). For a thorough discussion of the issue, *see Great Southwest Fire Ins. Co. v. CNA Ins. Co.,* 557 So. 2d 966 (La. 1990). *See also* Annots., 49 A.L.R.4th 304 (1986); 19 A.L.R.4th 107.

8. *Environmental Pollution Exclusion.* In *Morton Int'l, Inc. v. Gen'l Accid. Ins. Co.,* 134 N.J. 1, 629 A.2D 831 (1993), the court construed comprehensive general liability policies providing coverage for "all sums which the Insured shall become legally obligated to pay" for damages because of "injury to or destruction of property" as a result of an occurrence happening during the policy period. The term "occurrence" was defined in the policies:

> "Occurrence" means an accident, including injurious exposure to conditions, which results, during the policy period, in bodily injury or property damage neither expected nor intended from the standpoint of the insured.

The policies contained an exclusion for environmental pollution:

> This insurance does not apply . . . . (f) to bodily injury or property damage arising out of the discharge, dispersal, release or escape of smoke, vapors, soot, fumes, acids, alkalis, toxic chemicals, liquids or gases, waste materials or other irritants, contaminants or pollutants into or upon land, the atmosphere or any water course or body of water; but this exclusion does not apply if such discharge, dispersal, release or escape is sudden and accidental.

The court held that the term "damages" included response costs imposed to remediate environmental damage.

It held that the "sudden" discharge requirement of the exception to the pollution exclusion meant only that the discharge be unexpected and unintended, and not that the discharge be short:

> Although the word "sudden" is hardly susceptible of precise definition, and is undefined in those CGL policies that include the standard pollution-exclusion clause, we are persuaded that "sudden" possesses a temporal element, generally connoting an event that begins abruptly or without prior notice or warning, but the duration of the event — whether it lasts an instant, a week, or a month — is not necessarily relevant to whether the inception of the event is sudden. The meaning of the term "accidental" being generally understood, we discern that the phrase "sudden and accidental" in the standard pollution-exclusion clause describes only those discharges, dispersals, releases, and escapes of pollutants that occur abruptly or unexpectedly and are unintended. If applied as written, although interpretative questions undoubtedly would require resolution, the clause sharply and dramatically would restrict the coverage that previously had been provided under CGL policies for property damage caused by accidental pollution, which included coverage for continuous or repeated exposure to conditions, provided that the property *damage* — not the discharge — was "neither expected nor intended from the standpoint of the

insured." We are fully satisfied that if given literal effect, the standard clause's widespread inclusion in CGL policies would limit coverage for pollution damage to so great an extent that the industry's representation of the standard clause's effect, in its presentation to New Jersey and other state insurance regulatory agencies, would have been grossly misleading.

The standard pollution-exclusion clause, the court held, barred recovery only for intentional discharges, dispersals, releases or escapes of known pollutants by the insured.

9. *Subrogation and Attorneys' Fees.* The insured in *Barreca v. Cobb*, 668 So. 2d 1129 (La. 1996), was injured in an automobile accident. His health insurance policy paid his medical expenses. The policy contained a subrogation clause. Subsequently, the insured sued a third party who caused the accident. The insured's attorney wrote the health insurer advising of the suit and promising to protect the insurer's subrogation claim for the medical expenses. "All amounts obtained in this lawsuit," the letter stated, "are subject to a one-third contingent attorney's fee."

The third party claim was settled, and the insurer resisted the deduction of one-third of its subrogation claim for attorneys' fees. The attorney then brought suit to determine his right to the fee. Upholding the attorney's claim, in what it said was the position taken by "a substantial majority of the states," the court held:

> [A]n insurer who has notice of the insured's claim but fails to bring its own action or to intervene in plaintiff's action will be assessed a proportionate share of the recovery costs incurred by the insured, including reasonable attorney fees. However, we also note that the insurer is not bound by the fee contract between the insured and his attorney. Rather the amount and nature of the services rendered and all factors relevant, including the contingency fee contract, must be considered.

"Having fully reviewed the record," the court said, "we have determined that the one-third contigency fee is reasonable for this matter."

PROBLEM

Harry Homeowner is irritated by teenagers who "landscape" his property by driving their vehicles onto his well-groomed front lawn during wet weather. The unsightly ruts left by this action drive Harry to desperation. He partially buries a steel-reinforced concrete post, 12 inches in diameter, in his front lawn, near the street. About two-and-a-half feet of the post protrude above ground. On the next rainy night, Harry covers the post with a cardboard box. As a result, the installation appears to the casual observer to be an empty cardboard box lying on the front lawn.

Later that evening, Danny Delinquent and his friend, Billy Badguy, are "cruising" the neighborhood looking for lawns to "landscape." Approaching Harry's home, Danny "guns" his engine, jumps the low curb and begins to drive across the yard. He sees the box, but believing it is only an empty cardboard box, he attempts to run over it. When the vehicle strikes the post, it caroms out of control and into the street. Danny is ejected and is instantly killed when he is run over by a non-negligent passing motorist. Billy remains in the car and is severely injured.

Danny's parents file their wrongful death claims and a survival claim (for the brief period Danny lived after the collision with the post), and Billy files a personal injury action. Billy's mother joins in Billy's suit to assert her claim for loss of consortium with Billy. Named as defendants are Harry and his homeowner's liability insurer. The homeowner's policy provides coverage for "such damages for personal injury or to property as the insured may become legally obligated to pay" as a result of the use of the insured premises, but has these provisions:

1. This policy does not provide coverage for automobile accidents.

2. This policy does not provide coverage for damages caused by an injury intended or expected by the insured.

The policy also contains a limitation of liability to $10,000 for bodily injury to any person, with an aggregate of $20,000 for each occurrence.

The complaints allege that Harry was grossly negligent, and seek compensatory and punitive damages. What exposure does the homeowner's insurer have under these facts?

D. INSURER DUTIES AND PENALTIES

The insurer's general obligations under a third party (liability) policy are to provide a defense to the insured, and to pay the damages for which the insured is cast, subject to the policy limits. The insurer's obligation under first party insurance is to pay any covered loss upon satisfactory proof of claim by the insured. Delay in payment or in fulfillment of its other obligations under the policy often will be advantageous to the insurer, such as in obtaining a favorable bargaining position in settlement negotiations.

The insurer's duty to defend and to pay its policy limits, together with its right to control the litigation, frequently give rise to another conflict of interest between insurer and insured. What if the victim offers to settle for the policy limits or an amount close to the limits, but there may be a defense to the claim? If there is a possibility that the award will exceed the policy limits, the insured's best interest demands acceptance of the settlement offer. The insurer, however, has nothing to gain by accepting and, barring great defense costs, little to lose by rejecting the offer. The same conflict may arise from an offer to settle beyond the policy limits; the offer may be attractive to the insured, given his potential exposure, but the insurer has little or nothing to gain from it.

The courts and legislatures have sought to balance these competing policies by imposing penalties upon insurers who arbitrarily or otherwise in bad faith fail to comply with their insurance obligations.

GRUENBERG v. AETNA INSURANCE CO.

9 Cal. 3d 566, 108 Cal. Rptr. 480, 510 P.2d 1032 (1973)

SULLIVAN, J.

Plaintiff's complaint, containing only one count, alleged in substance the following: On and after April 7, 1969, plaintiff was the owner of a cocktail lounge and restaurant business in Los Angeles known as the Brass Rail. The business premises were insured against fire loss in the aggregate sum of $35,000 by the three defendant insurers, Aetna Insurance Company (Aetna), Yosemite Insurance Company (Yosemite), and American Home Assurance Company (American).

In the early hours of the morning of November 9, 1969, a fire occurred at the Brass Rail. Plaintiff was notified and immediately went to the scene. While there, he became involved in an argument with a member of the arson detail of the Los Angeles Fire Department and was placed under arrest.

On November 10, 1969, defendant insurers, upon being informed of the fire, engaged the services of defendant P. E. Brown and Company (Brown). Carl Busching, a claims adjuster employed by Brown, went to the Brass Rail to investigate the fire and inspect the premises. While he was there, he stated to an arson investigator of the Los Angeles Fire Department that plaintiff had excessive coverage under his fire insurance policies. Eventually the premises were locked and nothing was removed until November 14, 1969, when Busching authorized the removal of the rubble and debris.

About November 13, 1969, plaintiff was charged in a felony complaint with the crimes of arson and defrauding an insurer. A preliminary hearing was set for January 12, 1970.

Defendant insurance companies also retained defendant law firm Cummins, White, Briedenbach & Alphson (Cummins) to represent them in the matter of plaintiff's claim of fire loss. On November 25, 1969, defendant Donald Ricketts, an attorney-employee of Cummins, demanded in writing that plaintiff appear at the offices of said firm on December 12, 1969, to submit to an examination under oath and to produce certain documents. On November 26, 1969, plaintiff's attorney responded by letter to Ricketts explaining that he had advised plaintiff not to make any statements concerning the fire loss while criminal charges were pending. The letter also requested that the insurers waive the requirement of an examination until the criminal charges lodged against plaintiff were concluded. Ricketts refused the request and warned that failure to appear for the examination would void coverage under the policies. On December 16, 1969, Ricketts, on behalf of the Cummins law firm, advised plaintiff's attorney in writing that defendant insurers were denying liability under the policies because of plaintiff's failure to submit to an examination under oath and to produce documents.

On January 12, 1970, a preliminary hearing was held on the complaint charging plaintiff with arson and defrauding an insurer. Busching appeared as a witness for the prosecution and restated his belief that plaintiff had excessive fire insurance coverage for his business. The charges were dismissed by the magistrate for lack of probable cause.

On January 26, 1970, plaintiff's attorney advised defendant insurers that plaintiff was now prepared to submit himself for an examination. However, the insurers reaffirmed their position that they were denying liability because of plaintiff's failure to appear.

According to the allegations of the complaint, all defendants other than the insurance company defendants were the agents and employees of the three defendant companies and were acting within the scope of such agency and employment when the acts attributed to them were committed. It was further alleged that "the defendants and each of them joined together and acted in concert to falsely imply that the plaintiff had a motive to deliberately set fire to and burn down his place of business [and that] [t]he purpose of the defendants in creating such false implication was to establish a grounds [sic] upon which the defendant Insurers could avoid paying the amounts due to plaintiff under the policies of insurance issued by the defendant Insurers." To carry out their purpose, defendants "conducted themselves in the following manner": (a) defendant Busching stated to an arson investigator that plaintiff had acquired excessive fire insurance coverage; (b) defendant insurers demanded that plaintiff submit to an examination under oath and produce certain documents "in order to enable them to secure further evidence to support the false implication that plaintiff was guilty of arson;" and (c) defendant Busching, appearing as a witness for the People at the preliminary hearing on the felony complaint, reaffirmed his statement made to the arson investigator.

As a "direct and proximate result of the outrageous conduct and bad faith of the defendants," plaintiff suffered "severe economic damage," "severe emotional upset and distress," loss of earnings and various special damages. Plaintiff sought both compensatory and punitive damages.

Defendants filed general demurrers to the complaint which were sustained with leave to amend. Plaintiff elected to stand on his complaint and an order of dismissal was entered. This appeal followed.

. . . . Plaintiff contends that he has stated sufficient facts to constitute a cause of action in tort against defendants for breach of an implied duty of good faith and fair dealing. The duty of an insurer to deal fairly and in good faith with its insured is governed by our decisions in *Crisci v. Security Ins. Co.,* 66 Cal. 2d 425, 958 Cal. Rptr. 13, 426 P.2d 173 (1967), and *Comunale v. Traders & Gen. Ins. Co.,* 50 Cal. 2d 654, 328 P.2d 198 (1958). We explained that this duty, the breach of which sounds in both contract and tort, is imposed because "there is an implied covenant of good faith and fair dealing in every contract [including insurance policies] that neither party will do anything which will injure the right of the other to receive the benefits of the agreement." (*Comunale, supra,* at p. 658, 328 P.2d at 200.) Therefore, "an insurer . . . . who refuses to accept a reasonable settlement within the policy limits in violation of its duty to consider in good faith the interest of the insured in the settlement, is liable for the entire judgment against the insured even if it exceeds the policy limits." (*Id.* at p. 661, 328 P.2d at p. 202.)

Thus in *Comunale* and *Crisci* we made it clear that "[l]iability is imposed [on the insurer] not for a bad faith breach of the contract but for failure to meet the duty to accept reasonable settlements, a duty included within the implied covenant of good faith and fair dealing." (*Crisci, supra,* 66 Cal. 2d at

430, 59 Cal. Rptr. at 17, 426 P.2d at 177.) In those two cases, we considered the duty of the insurer to act in good faith and fairly in handling the claims of third persons against the insured, described as a "duty to accept reasonable settlements;" in the case before us we consider the duty of an insurer to act in good faith and fairly in handling the claim of an insured, namely a duty not to withhold unreasonably payments due under a policy. These are merely two different aspects of the same duty. That responsibility is not the requirement mandated by the terms of the policy itself — to defend, settle, or pay. It is the obligation, deemed to be imposed by the law, under which the insurer must act fairly and in good faith in discharging its contractual responsibilities. Where in so doing, it fails to deal *fairly and in good faith* with its insured by refusing, without proper cause, to compensate its insured for a loss covered by the policy, such conduct may give rise to a cause of action in tort for breach of an implied covenant of good faith and fair dealing.

Thus, in *Richardson v. Employers Liability Assur. Corp.*, 25 Cal. App. 3d 232, 239, 102 Cal. Rptr. 547 (1972), where the insurer refused to indemnify its insured for a loss covered by the uninsured motorist provision of an automobile liability policy, the court had this to say:

> In every insurance policy there is implied by law a covenant of good faith and fair dealing. This implied obligation requires an insurer to deal in good faith and fairly with its insured in handling an insured's claim against it. Here, Employers deliberately, willfully and in bad faith withheld payment of the Richardson claim months after it knew the claim to be completely valid; it forced an arbitration hearing on a claim against which it already knew that it had no defense; even after the award was made, it instructed its local office to attempt "to make the best possible settlement," and forced plaintiffs to resort to litigation to have the award judicially confirmed. This conduct toward its own insured was unconscionable, and constituted a tortious breach of contract. The duty violated — that of dealing fairly and in good faith with the other party to a contract of insurance — is a duty imposed by law, not one arising from the terms of the contract itself. In other words, this duty of dealing fairly and in good faith is nonconsensual in origin rather than consensual. Breach of this duty is a tort.

In *Fletcher v. Western National Life Ins. Co.*, 10 Cal. App. 3d 376, 89 Cal. Rptr. 78 (1970), an insurer was held liable in tort for damages caused by the insurer's refusal to indemnify its insured under a disability policy. Although the action was brought on the theory of intentional infliction of emotional distress, the court explained (10 Cal. App. at 401–402, 89 Cal. Rptr. 48) that the insurer's conduct might also be viewed as a violation of its implied obligation of good faith and fair dealing. The insurer, refusing to pay its insured under the *injury* provision of the policy which set[s] forth a maximum liability period of 30 years, insisted on payment under the *sickness* provision of the policy, having a two-year maximum period, even though its own investigation established that plaintiff's disability was caused by injury. It sought to avoid liability under the policy, at first by claiming that the insured had made a material misrepresentation in the application for insurance and later by urging the insured to agree to a settlement for an amount far less than the insurer's potential liability. In response the *Fletcher* court observed:

An insurer owes to its insured an implied-in-law duty of good faith and fair dealing that it will do nothing to deprive the insured of the benefits of the policy. Included within this duty in the case of a liability insurance policy is the duty to act reasonably and in good faith to settle claims against the insured by a third person. The violation of that duty sounds in tort notwithstanding that it may also constitute a breach of contract. We think that, similarly, the implied-in-law duty of good faith and fair dealing imposes upon a disability insurer a duty not to threaten to withhold or actually withhold payments, maliciously and without probable cause, for the purpose of injuring its insured by depriving him of the benefits of the policy. We think that, as in *Crisci,* the violation of that duty sounds in tort notwithstanding that it also constitutes a breach of contract. (*Id.*, 10 Cal. App. 3d at 401, 89 Cal. Rptr. at 93.)

It is manifest that a common legal principle underlies all of the foregoing decisions; namely, that in every insurance contract there is an implied covenant of good faith and fair dealing. The duty to so act is imminent in the contract whether the company is attending to the claims of third persons against the insured or the claims of the insured itself. Accordingly, when the insurer unreasonably and in bad faith withholds payment of the claim of its insured, it is subject to liability in tort.

In the case at bench plaintiff has alleged in essence that defendants wilfully and maliciously entered into a scheme to deprive him of the benefits of the fire policies in that they encouraged criminal charges by falsely implying that he had a motive to commit arson, and in that, knowing plaintiff would not appear for an examination during the pendency of criminal charges against him, they used his failure to appear as a pretense for denying liability under the policies. We conclude therefore that while the complaint is far from a model pleading, it does allege in substance a breach on the part of defendant insurance companies of their duty of good faith and fair dealing which they owed plaintiff. We emphasize that we are passing only upon the sufficiency of these allegations which of course must be sustained by proper proof.

With regard to the defendants other than the three insurance companies, we reach a different result. Plaintiff alleges that Brown, the insurance adjusting firm, and its employee, Busching, and Cummins, the law firm, and its employee, Ricketts, were the agents and employees of defendant insurers and of each other and were acting within the scope of that agency and employment when they committed the acts attributed to them. However, plaintiff contends that these non-insurer defendants breached only the duty of good faith and fair dealing; therefore, we need not consider the possibility that they may have committed another tort in their respective capacities as total strangers to the contracts of insurance. Obviously, the non-insurer defendants were not parties to the agreements for insurance; therefore, they are not, as such, subject to an implied duty of good faith and fair dealing. Moreover, as agents and employees of the defendant insurers, they cannot be held accountable on a theory of conspiracy. (*Wise v. Southern Pacific Co.,* 223 Cal. App. 2d 50, 72, 35 Cal. Rptr. 652 (1963).) This rule, as was explained in *Wise* (223 Cal. App. 2d at 72–73, 35 Cal. Rptr. at 665), "derives from the principle that ordinarily corporate agents and employees acting for and on behalf of the corporation cannot be held liable for inducing a breach of the corporation's contract since being in a confidential relationship to the corporation their action in this respect is privileged." Accordingly, the judgment of dismissal in favor of the non-insurer defendants must be affirmed.

Defendant insurance companies contend that plaintiff's failure to appear at their attorneys' office in order to submit to an examination under oath and to produce certain documents is a bar to the action since (1) the clause in the contracts requiring the insured to appear is a condition precedent to legal action and that plaintiff must allege that he has complied with it; (2) the allegations in plaintiff's complaint demonstrate that he has failed to comply with the "cooperation and notice" clause; (3) the demand for appearance was adequate; and (4) even if the demand for appearance were defective, plaintiff may not complain of it for the first time on appeal (*see Restina v. Aetna Casualty & Surety Company*, 61 Misc. 2d 574, 306 N.Y.S.2d 219, 222 (1969)).

Plaintiff responds that his failure to appear at the requested time is of no consequence for the following reasons: (1) the insurers must show, by way of defense, that his failure to appear substantially prejudiced their investigation of his claim; (2) although plaintiff failed to appear on December 12, 1969, he complied with the provisions of the policy requiring his appearance; and (3) the demand to appear on December 12, 1969, was insufficient in that defendants failed to specify the person who would conduct the examination.

All parties appear to assume that plaintiff's contractual duty is a dependent condition (whether precedent or subsequent) to defendants' covenant of good faith and fair dealing. In other words, the underlying premise of their arguments is that if plaintiff's failure to appear on December 12, 1969, constituted a breach of plaintiff's obligation under the policies, then defendants' duty of good faith and fair dealing was excused. We do not think, however, that the controlling issue here is the nature of *plaintiff's* duty, *i.e.*, whether his dependent duty is precedent or subsequent; rather, the crucial issue is the nature of *defendants'* duty, *i.e.*, whether their duty of good faith and fair dealing is absolute or conditional. Therefore, we need not consider the aforementioned contentions of the parties.

Defendants' duty, as we have explained, arises from a contractual relationship existing between the parties. This duty has been characterized as an "implied covenant" that "neither party will do anything which will injure the right of the other to receive the benefits of the agreement." (*Comunale v. Traders & General Ins. Co., supra*, 50 Cal. 2d 654, 658, 328 P.2d 198, 200.) While it might be argued that defendants would be excused from their contractual duties (*e.g.*, obligation to indemnify) if plaintiff breached his obligations under the policies, we do not think that plaintiff's alleged breach excuses defendants from their duty, implied by law, of good faith and fair dealing. In other words, the insurer's duty is unconditional and independent of the performance of plaintiff's contractual obligations.

. . .We conclude, therefore, that the duty of good faith and fair dealing on the part of defendant insurance companies is an absolute one. At the same time, we do not say that the parties cannot define, by the terms of the contract, their respective obligations and duties. We say merely that no matter how those duties are stated, the nonperformance by one party of its contractual duties cannot excuse a breach of the duty of good faith and fair dealing by the other party while the contract between them is in effect and not rescinded.

Finally we take up defendants' contention that plaintiff may not recover for emotional distress, as a matter of law, because plaintiff failed to allege conduct which is "extreme" and "outrageous." To put it another way, defendants take the position that the essential elements of a cause of action for the independent tort of the intentional infliction of emotional distress must be engrafted on a cause of action against an insurer for breach of its duty of good faith and fair dealing. Plaintiff responds that he need not allege outrageous conduct; and in the alternative, that if outrageous conduct is required, then it cannot be said as a matter of law that the conduct alleged in the complaint is not outrageous.

We upheld recovery for "mental suffering" in *Crisci v. Security Ins. Co., supra,* 66 Cal. 2d 425, 58 Cal. Rptr. 18, 426 P.2d 173, since an action against an insurer for breach of its implied duty of good faith sounds in tort as well as contract. We explained there (66 Cal. 2d at 433, 58 Cal. Rptr. at 18, 426 P.2d at 178):

> The general rule of damages in tort is that the injured party may recover for all detriment caused whether it could have been anticipated or not. In accordance with the general rule, it is settled in this state that mental suffering constitutes an aggravation of damages when it naturally ensues from the act complained of . . . . The commonest example of the award of damages for mental suffering in addition to other damages is probably where the plaintiff suffers personal injuries in addition to mental distress as a result of either negligent or intentional misconduct by the defendant. Such awards are not confined to cases where the mental suffering award was in addition to an award for personal injuries; damages for mental distress have also been awarded in cases where the tortious conduct was an interference with property rights without any personal injuries apart from the mental distress.

We concluded with the following (66 Cal. 2d at 433–434, 58 Cal. Rptr. at 17, 426 P.2d at 179): "We are satisfied that a plaintiff who as a result of a defendant's tortious conduct *loses his property* and *suffers mental distress* may recover not only for pecuniary loss but also for his mental distress." (Italics added.)

In *Crisci* we did not suggest that to warrant recovery for mental distress the conduct of the insured must be "outrageous" or that the mental distress must be "severe." We explained that "[t]he principal reason for limiting recovery of damages for mental distress is that to permit recovery of such damages would open the door to fictitious claims, to recovery for mere bad manners, and to litigation in the field of trivialities. Obviously, where . . . . the claim is actionable and has resulted in substantial damages apart from those due to mental distress, the danger of fictitious claims is reduced . . . ." (*Id.* at 434, 58 Cal. Rptr. at 19, 426 P.2d at 179.). . .

Here, plaintiff alleged that he suffered substantial economic losses apart from mental distress. He alleged that he suffered loss of earnings; that he was compelled to go out of business and that as a result he was unable to pay his business creditors; that he incurred the costs of defending lawsuits brought against him by his creditors; and that he incurred medical expenses. We conclude, therefore, that since plaintiff has alleged substantial damages for loss of property apart from damages for mental distress, the complaint is sufficiently pleaded with respect to the latter element of damages.

Contrary to defendant's position, *Fletcher v. Western National Life Ins. Co.,* 10 Cal. App. 3d 376, 89 Cal. Rptr. 78 (1970), does not express a different rule. In *Fletcher,* plaintiff's theory of recovery expressed in his complaint, as previously explained, was predicated on the tort of intentional infliction of emotional distress alone. Quite naturally, therefore, the court concluded that severe emotional distress is a requisite element of recovery. However, the mere fact that the action there involved the liability of an insurer for its tortious conduct, measured by the elements [of] the intentional infliction of emotional distress, does not mean that those same elements must be applied where, as in the instant case, recovery is sought on a totally distinct theory.

In summary, we conclude that plaintiff has stated facts sufficient to constitute a cause of action in tort against defendant insurance companies for breach of their implied duty of good faith and fair dealing; that plaintiff's failure to appear at the office of the insurers' counsel in order to submit to an examination under oath and to produce certain documents, as appearing from the allegations of the complaint, is not fatal to the statement of such cause of action; and that plaintiff has stated facts sufficient for the recovery of damages for mental distress whether or not these facts constitute "extreme" or "outrageous" conduct. On the other hand, since the remaining defendants were not subject to the implied duty arising from the contractual relationship, we conclude that the complaint does not state sufficient facts to constitute a cause of action against them and that the judgment of dismissal in their favor was proper. . . .

NOTES

1. *The Doctrinal Basis for Failure-to-Settle Claims.* What is the test for an insurer's liability for failure to settle? Some courts and commentators suggest that the insurer's obligation to settle in good faith borders on strict liability. *See Crisci v. Security Ins. Co.,* 66 Cal. 2d 425, 58 Cal. Rptr. 13, 426 P.2d 173 (1967); *Johansen v. California State Auto Ass'n Inter-Insurance Bureau,* 15 Cal. 3d 9, 123 Cal. Rptr. 288, 538 P.2d 744 (1975); *Rova Farms Resort, Inc. v. Investors Ins. Co.,* 65 N.J. 474, 323 A.2d 495 (1974). *See also* Comment, *Insurance Carrier's Duty to Settle: Strict Liability in Excess Liability Cases?,* 6 Seton Hall L. Rev. 662 (1975); Annot., 40 A.L.R.2d 168 (1955 and Supp. 1990); Comment, *Approaching Strict Liability of Insurer for Refusing to Settle Within Policy Limits,* 47 Neb. L. Rev. 705; Comment, *Insurer's Strict Liability for Entire Judgment,* 13 S.D.L. Rev. 375. Some states base liability upon negligence. *See, e.g., Dumas v. Hartford Acc. & Indem. Co.,* 94 N.H. 484, 56 A.2d 57 (1947); *G.A. Stowers Furn. Co. v. American Indem. Co.,* 15 S.W.2d 544 (Tex. Comm. App. 1929). *See* Kelly, *The Workable Sanction and Solution in Excess Liability Cases; Strict Liability for Insurance Carriers,* 10 U.S.F.L. Rev. 159 (1975). *See generally* Keeton, *Liability Insurance and Responsibility*

for Settlement, 67 HARV. L. REV. 1136 (1954); Schwartz, *Statutory Strict Liability for an Insurer's Failure to Settle: A Balanced Plan for an Unresolved Problem,* 1975 DUKE L.J. 901 (1977). Still other states rely on an implied contractual obligation to perform the insurance contract in good faith. *See Farris v. United States Fid. & Gaur. Co.*, 284 Or. 453, 587 P.2d 1015 (1978); *Beck v. Farmers Ins. Exch.*, 701 P.2d 795 (Utah 1985).

2. *State Regulation, Bad Faith Delay and Vexatious Refusal to Pay.* One of the most common disputes between a liability insurer and its insured is over the question of coverage. There is greater room for dispute between the insurer and insured in first party insurance, where issues of coverage and valuation of damaged or destroyed property are quite common. An insurer may be cast in punitive damages for wilful failure to settle with the insured, or to pay sums due under the policy. *See, e.g.,* J. APPLEMAN, INSURANCE LAW AND PRACTICE § 4712 (Berdal ed. 1979). A state statute may prescribe a specific penalty for arbitrary failure to pay claims, such as a percentage of the claim, and attorney's fees for prosecution of the insured's suit against the insurer. *See, e.g.,* ILL. REV. STAT. ch. 73, par. 767 (1988); FLA. STAT. ANN. § 627.428 (1989); TENN. CODE ANN. § 56-7-105 (1994). These statutes usually are designed to compel the first party insurer to promptly investigate and settle property damage claims with its insured. In those kinds of cases, the parameters of the loss are generally narrowly circumscribed. In an uninsured or underinsured motorist claim, the insurer becomes in effect the liability carrier of the tortfeasor, but it nevertheless remains the insurer of its insured. Should the insurer then be subject to penalties for arbitrary failure to settle the UM claim with its insured, given such imprecise factors as comparative negligence and general damages? Some states impose such a duty on the UM carrier. *See, e.g., McDill v. Utica Mut. Ins. Co.,* 475 So. 2d 1085 (La. 1985).

3. *Comparative Bad Faith.* In *California Cas. Gen. Ins. Co. v. Superior Court,* 173 Cal. App. 3d 274, 218 Cal. Rptr. 817 (1985), the court noted that:

> [W]e are persuaded that in an appropriate case, an insured's breach of the implied duty of good faith and fair dealing which contributes to an insurer's failure to pursue or delay in pursuing the investigation and payment of a claim may constitute at least a partial defense to the plaintiff's damage action for the insurer's breach of its duty of good faith and fair dealing based on such delay or failure and, to the extent they may be the same, the insurer's or agent's breach of their statutory duties under the unfair practice act.
>
> . . .There can be little question but that an insurer which provides uninsured motorist coverage has a reasonable expectation that if the insured suffers a loss claimed to be covered under the uninsured motorist provisions of the policy, the insured will promptly and accurately furnish it with all the information and evidence pertinent to the claim that is known to the insured. If a failure of the insured to do so results in delaying or impeding the investigation of the claim by the insurer or delays or makes improvident the insurer's payment of the claim, any economic loss and emotional distress caused the insured by virtue of any such nonpayment or delay in investigation or payment will have been caused either wholly or in part by the

conduct of the insured. We perceive no sound reason, nor is any suggested, why the doctrine of comparative fault enunciated and applied to negligent conduct by the California Supreme Court in *Li v. Yellow Cab Co.*, 13 Cal. 3d 804, 119 Cal. Rptr. 858, 532 P.2d 1226 (1975), should not be applicable to bad faith cases. While the duty of good faith and fair dealing arises out of a contractual relationship between the parties, breach of the duty and ensuing damages are governed by tort principles.

4. *Accident Victims' Claims of Bad Faith Against Tortfeasors' Insurer.* In *Larocque v. State Farm Mut. Auto Ins. Co.*, 163 Vt. 617, 660 A.2d 286 (Vt. 1995), accident victims sought to hold their tortfeasor's insurer liable for failure to settle their claims in good faith:

In 1987, plaintiffs Paula and Michael Larocque were injured in a car collision with defendants' insured, and pursuant to their obligations under the insured's automobile insurance policy, defendants assumed the defense of the subsequent lawsuit. The parties settled the lawsuit for the policy limits in 1991, but plaintiffs instituted this action in 1992 alleging that defendants' failure to settle plaintiffs' claims in an expeditious manner constituted a breach of defendants' duty to deal with plaintiffs in good faith, unjustly enriched defendants, and constituted intentional infliction of emotional distress. Plaintiffs appeal the Rutland Superior Court's decision granting defendants' motion for summary judgment. We affirm. . . .

Although the Insurance Trade Practices Act, 8 V.S.A. §§ 4721–4726, provides administrative sanctions for unfair and deceptive acts within the insurance industry, including for unfair claim settlement practices, 8 V.S.A. § 4724(9), the Act does not create a private right of action. Accordingly, defendants did not owe any statutory duty to deal with plaintiffs in good faith in offering a settlement.

We are also unpersuaded that any such duty exists at common law. We have recognized that a carrier owes a duty to *its insured* when considering whether to settle a claim within policy limits. This duty stems from an "insurance company's control of the settlement of a claim brought against the insured," and the necessary conflict of interest that it creates. *Myers v. Ambassador Ins. Co.*, 146 Vt. 552, 555, 508 A.2d 689, 690–91 (1986). A duty to the insured may also arise in the context of a first-party claim, although we have not ruled that such a duty exists. Here, the relationship between plaintiffs and defendants is by nature adversarial, and we find no obligation imposed on defendants to conform to a particular standard of conduct with respect to plaintiffs. *See Smith v. Day*, 148 Vt. 595, 597, 538 A.2d 157, 158 (1987) (defining duty); *Auclair v. Nationwide Mut. Ins. Co.*, 505 A.2d 431, 431 (R.I. 1986) (*per curiam*) (insurer owes no duty to third-party claimant).

Finally, defendants did not voluntarily assume any good faith duty to plaintiffs by directing in its employee manual that claims were to be handled in an efficient and cooperative manner. That it attempted to conduct its business in a way that was responsive to third-party claimants does not create a legally enforceable duty to do so with respect to a particular claimant.

Plaintiffs next argue that the trial court erroneously concluded that defendants' failure to settle the case could not create a claim of unjust enrichment. Plaintiffs' theory is that defendants retained the interest earned on the settlement amount under conditions such that it would be inequitable not to pay this interest to plaintiffs. *See Center v. Mad River Corp.*, 151 Vt. 408, 410 n. 2, 561 A.2d 90, 92 n. 2 (1989) (unjust enrichment award requires that defendant retain benefit under circumstances where it would be inequitable not to compensate plaintiff for its value). Defendants were under no obligation, however, to settle expeditiously with plaintiffs. Thus, defendants were not unjustly enriched.

Plaintiffs' last argument contends that the trial court erred by concluding that defendants' delay in settling plaintiffs' claims did not create a claim for intentional infliction of emotional distress. Intentional infliction of emotional distress requires conduct that is " 'so outrageous and extreme as to go beyond all possible bounds of decency.' " *Jobin v. McQuillen*, 158 Vt. 322, 327, 609 A.2d 990, 993 (1992) (*quoting* RESTATEMENT (SECOND) OF TORTS § 46, comment d (1965)). Even if we accept plaintiffs' allegations, defendants' conduct cannot be said to rise to this level.

5. *The Insurer's Right and Duty to Settle.* The insured in *Austin Co. v. Royal Ins. Co*, 842 S.W.2d 608 (Tenn. App. 1992), had a liability policy with the insurer providing for $1 million maximum coverage and for a $250,000 deductible (*i.e.*, the insured paid any claim of $250,000 or less). The policy provided for a "retrospective premium":

> A "retrospective premium" policy is a policy whereby the premiums are calculated, at least in part, on the basis of the claims experience or history for the preceding year or premium period. In other words, the premiums are calculated after the fact, not before.

The insurer had the authority to investigate, defend, and settle all claims under the policy, although the insurer was required to "consult" with the insured before settling any claim in excess of $10,000.

An automobile liability judgment was entered against the insured for $190,000. The insurer, pursuant to its contractual duty to defend, settled the claim for $170,000, although the insured "vociferously voiced its objections, insisting that the judgment be appealed." The insurer then demanded that the insured repay the insurer the amount of the settlement, since it was less than the $250,000 deductible.

The court held the settlement was made in good faith. The amount was $20,000 less than the judgment. "Most important, the insurer consulted extensively with the insured before making the final decision, and sought the insured's 'blessing'."

Should the insured win if it could show that an appeal would probably have resulted in a dismissal of the claim?

Liability insurance policies typically provide that the insurer "may make such investigation, negotiation, of any claim or suit as it deems expedient." ROBERT KEETON & ALAN WIDISS, INSURANCE LAW § 7.8(a)(1988). Does such a provision give the insurer unbridled discretion in settling a claim within policy limits despite the insured's objections?

Conversely, if an insurer fails to make reasonable efforts to settle the policy limits, and a judgment is entered in excess of the limits, the insurer can be liable for the entire amount of the judgment. *But see Lira v. Shelter Ins. Co.*, 913 P.2d 514 (Colo. 1996), where the court held an insurer had no good faith duty to settle a compensatory damage claim within the policy limits in order to avoid the insured's liability for punitive damages, which were not covered by the policy.

6. *The Duty to Defend.* The duty to pay and to defend may not be coextensive. If the complaint alleges facts within, or potentially within, the coverage of the policy, the insurer must defend, although he ultimately may prevail on the coverage issue. *See, e.g., Maryland Cas. Ins. Co. v. Peppers*, 64 Ill. 2d 187, 355 N.E.2d 24 (1976); *Insurance Co. of Ill. v. Markogiannakis*, 188 Ill. App. 3d 643, 544 N.E.2d 1082 (1989). An insurer who has the duty to defend but who denies coverage faces a dilemma if he is unable to obtain speedy judicial resolution of the issue. If he refuses to defend and his judgment is incorrect, he may lose or lessen his opportunity to litigate the insured's liability or the victim's damages. If he elects to defend, he may thereby waive his right to contend that there is no coverage. *See United States Fid. & Guar. Co. v. Superior Court*, 252 Cal. Rptr. 320, 204 Cal. App. 3d 1513 (1988); *United Servs. Auto. Ass'n v. Morris*, 154 Ariz. 113, 741 P.2d 246 (1987). An insurer in such a dilemma may seek the insured's consent that the insurer's defense does not constitute a waiver of lack of coverage. Even if it obtains such consent, the insurer has a conflict of interest with his insured. As one court wrote:

> Independent counsel is necessary in cases where the defense attorney's duty to the insured would require that he defeat liability on any ground and his duty to the insurer would require that he defeat liability only upon grounds which would render the insurer liable. When such a conflict is apparent, the insured must be free to choose his own counsel whose reasonable fee is to be paid by the insurer.

Public Serv. Mut. Ins. Co. v. Goldfarb, 53 N.Y.2d 392, 425 N.E.2d 810, 815 (1981).

PROBLEM

Fifteen-year-old John's parents are divorced. The parents have been granted joint custody, with the mother as custodial parent during the weekdays, and the father as custodial parent on weekends. On a Saturday evening, while staying with his father, John borrows his mother's car, picks up his 16-year-old friend, Tom, and drives to a local teenage hangout, where they each consume five beers. When they begin to return home, John asks Tom to drive, because he appears to be the more sober of the two. During the drive home, Tom is taunted by another teenage driver at a stoplight, and attempts to outrace the other driver when the light turns green. As the racing vehicles reach the next intersection, Tom's vehicle strikes an automobile driven by Casper, who had entered the street after stopping for a stop sign. Casper had proceeded into the intersection without yielding the right-of-way and after observing the racing cars a distance away. Casper is rendered a quadriplegic. He and his wife file suit, his wife seeking damages for loss of consortium. John's mother and father each have an automobile liability policy with omnibus clauses. Each policy provides that, if there is other insurance covering a loss to which the policy attaches, the policy shall be "excess" over the other insurance. The limit of liability on each policy is $100,000 per person and $300,000 per accident. During the course of the negotiations, the attorney employed by Casper and his wife offers to settle all claims for $200,000. The offer is made to the attorney employed by John's father's insurer to defend Tom under their policy. He rejects the offer, and does not communicate the fact of the offer to John's father, Tom, or the other insurer. Judgment subsequently is rendered, assessing fault at 90% to Tom, 10% to Casper; and fixing Casper's damages at $3.2 million, and his wife's damages at $300,000.

What are the possible liabilities of the insurers for these judgments?

E. AUTOMOBILE INSURANCE

An average of 6.5 million motor vehicle accidents occurs in the United States each year. The volume of accidents and the personal injury and death claims that result have made automobile liability insurance a matter of great public interest. That interest is reflected in statutes which require compulsory auto liability insurance and prescribe the terms and conditions of the policies. The notes in this section explore some of the key issues that arise in connection with automobile liability policies.

NOTES

1. *The Nature of Automobile Liability Insurance.* The automobile liability policy initially began as a true indemnity contract; the insurer merely agreed to reimburse the insured for the loss he sustained as a result of the negligent operation of the insured vehicle. An insurer could escape liability to a third person by settling with the insured, or by facilitating the insured's bankruptcy. *Bain v. Atkins,* 181 Mass. 240, 63 N.E. 414 (1902). Prompted in part by state regulatory laws, automobile insurers transformed the policies into true liability policies in which insurers are bound to pay "such damages as the insured may become legally obligated to pay." In a liability (as opposed to an indemnity) policy, contract law may treat the victim as a third-party beneficiary who can sue the insurer directly under the contract. However, most policies contain clauses providing that "no action" may be brought against the insurer until the claimant first obtains a judgment against the insured. In states in which these clauses are valid, the victim must proceed against the insured alone. The general rule is that in the victim's suit against the insured, the fact or amount of insurance is not relevant and should not be disclosed to the trier of fact. *See, e.g., Sars, Inc. v. Nichols,* 275 Ala. 17, 151 So. 2d 739 (1963). In about ten states, legislatures have adopted statutes which invalidate "no action" clauses, thus permitting direct actions by victims against insurers. Consider this Wisconsin statute:

Any bond or policy of insurance covering liability to others for negligence makes the insurer liable, up to the amounts stated in the bond or policy, to the persons entitled to recover against the insured . . . . irrespective of whether the liability is presently established or is contingent and to become fixed or certain by final judgment against the insured.

WIS. STAT. § 632.24 (1980).

Louisiana, another leading "direct action" state, requires that the insured be joined as a defendant except when:

The insured has been adjudged a bankrupt or proceedings to adjudge him a bankrupt have been commenced before a court of competent jurisdiction,

The insured is insolvent,

Service of citation or other process cannot be made on the insured,

The cause of action is for damages as a result of tortious conduct between children and their parents or between married persons, or

The insurer is an uninsured motorist carrier.

La. Rev. Stat. 22:655(B)(1) (1989).

What is the significance of requiring suit against both the insurer and the insured?

2. *The Insured Under an Automobile Liability Policy: Who is the Insured?* The "declarations" page of the policy usually lists the insured party, who generally is the person who purchased the policy. He usually is designated as the "named insured." The policy also may designate others who are insured under the policy. A typical policy provision designating these "omnibus" insureds may read like this:

Insured includes (1) the named insured, and also includes (2) his relatives, and (3) any other person while using the automobile, provided the actual use of the automobile is with the permission of the named insured.

Relative means a relative of the named insured who is a resident of the same household.

Some state statutes mandate the terms of the "omnibus" clause. *See, e.g.,* La. Rev. Stat. § 32:900(B)(2) (1989). *See also Lukaszewicz v. Concrete Research, Inc.,* 43 Wis. 2d 335, 168 N.W.2d 581 (1969).

Different classes of insureds will attract coverages which vary in scope. For example, the insured and the "omnibus insured" are covered while operating the insured automobile, which is listed in the declarations page of the policy. The insured and his spouse also may be covered while operating a nonowned vehicle. The policy may extend coverage to newly-acquired vehicles which replace the insured vehicle or which are additional vehicles.

3. *Family-Member Liability Policy Exclusions.* The automobile policy in *National County Mut. Fire Ins. Co. v. Johnson,* 879 S.W.2d 1 (Tex. 1993), provided that the insurer did not provide liability coverage for bodily injury

to the insured or to any "family member." The court held this family-member exclusion was void as against public policy because it conflicted with the state's "Motor Vehicle Safety-Responsibility Act" requiring automobile operators to carry specified minimum amounts of liability insurance, and it conflicted "with the public policy underlying the Act." The court noted that the "majority of jurisdictions with mandatory insurance laws hold family member exclusions invalid because they are contrary to public policy." *Accord, Cormier v. American Deposit Insur. Co.*, 664 So.2d 807 (La App. 1995).

4. *Financial Responsibility Laws.* The high cost of automobile accidents has prompted a majority of the states to require compulsory automobile liability insurance, in varying sums. A common requirement is insurance in the amount of $20,000 to any victim, and a total of $40,000 to all persons injured in the same accident. Some of these financial responsibility statutes require proof of insurance before the issuance of a motor vehicle or driver's license. Others enforce the requirement after the fact, with statutes that require a driver involved in an accident to promptly provide proof of his ability to respond to the damages (or to a minimum amount of damages), either through a liability policy or as a self-insured with sufficient assets. The penalty for failure to provide such proof may be suspension of the operator's license to drive.

Should defendants other than automobile operators be required to show financial responsibility? Consider Fla. Stat. § 766.110(2) (1988), which provides that licensed hospitals must carry coverage for their employees' torts "in an amount of not less than $1.5 million per claim, $5 million annual aggregate." Fla. Stat. 458.320(2)(b)(1997) requires that a physician maintain $250,000 security (liability coverage, escrow account or letter of credit) for professional liability. In *Robert v. Pachall*, 767 So.2d 1227 (Fla. App. 2000), the Florida court of appeal held that a hospital could be liable, up to $250,000, for the malpractice of one of its physicians who was granted staff privileges at the hospital although he did not maintain the mandated professional liability coverage.

5. *Uninsured and Underinsured Motorist Insurance.* Victims of automobile accidents often are not fully compensated by the amount of compulsory insurance. The legislative quest for a system which will do so has taken two general directions: no fault insurance, and uninsured (and underinsured) motorist coverage. "No fault" plans remove minor automobile accident claims from the tort system. Uninsured and underinsured motorist (UM) coverage remains dependent on the tort system, but provides the victim with an opportunity to purchase — from his liability insurer — coverage which will pay him the damages he sustains at the hands of a tortfeasor who cannot respond fully. Every state now *requires* the liability insurer to provide its insured with the opportunity to purchase some form of uninsured coverage. *See, e.g.*, Annots., 10 A.L.R.3d 1166 (1966), 26 A.L.R.3d 883 (1969). Some states require the insurer to provide underinsured coverage, *see, e.g., Taylor v. Preferred Risk Mut. Ins. Co.*, 225 Cal. App. 2d 80, 37 Cal. Rptr. 63 (1964); *Gorton v. Reliance Ins. Co.*, 77 N.J. 563, 391 A.2d 1219 (1978).

Some states require the insurer to offer as much UM coverage as there is personal injury liability coverage under the policy. *See* Tenn. Code Ann. § 56-7-1201 (1994); La. Rev. Stat. 22:1406(D) (1989).

When there is UM coverage, the insurer becomes, in a sense, the liability insurer of the tortfeasor who has injured the insurer's insured. Similarly, if the tortfeasor has liability insurance, the victim's underinsured carrier becomes the tortfeasor's "excess" carrier. Courts, however, interpret uninsured and underinsured coverages as first party, not third party, policies. The UM carrier who pays its insured may be subrogated to the insured's rights against the tortfeasor. A person who is an insured under more than one uninsured or underinsured coverage may be permitted to "stack" (or aggregate) coverages so as to increase recovery. *Cameron Mut. Ins. Co. v. Madden*, 533 S.W.2d 538 (Mo. 1976); *Hines v. Government Emps. Ins. Co.*, 656 S.W.2d 262 (Mo. 1983). *See also Cunningham v. Insurance Co. of N. Am.*, 213 Va. 72, 189 S.E.2d 832 (1972) (attempted stack of 4,368 vehicles in fleet for total exposure of $65,520,000). Policies may attempt to prohibit "stacking," and the right to "stack" may be prescribed or limited by state law. *See, e.g.,* Tenn. Code Ann. § 56-7-1201(b) (1996). Where underinsured motorist coverage is available, the UM insured plaintiff often may recover on her UM policy only the amount by which her UM insurance exceeds the liability insurance covering the defendant tortfeasor. She cannot recover ("stack") the full amount of both policies. Thus, if the defendant has $20,000 liability coverage, and the plaintiff $50,000 UM coverage, and plaintiff's damages are $100,000, plaintiff can recover $20,000 from the defendant's liability insurer and $30,000 from her UM insurer — not $20,000 and $50,000, respectively. If the amount of UM coverage is less than the amount of liability coverage, the plaintiff could not recover under her UM policy. In some underinsured motorist coverages, the UM-insured plaintiff may recover on her UM policy the amount her UM coverage exceeds the amount of the tortfeasor's liability insurance, but may not "stack" more than one UM/underinsured coverage. For a comprehensive review of one state's treatment of the "stacking" issue, *see* McKenzie and Johnson, Insurance Law and Practice (2d ed. West Pub. Co. 1996), pages 294–307.

6. *UM Coverage as Affected by Other Claims.* In *Barney v. Safeco Ins. Co.*, 869 P.2d 1093 (Wash. App. 1994), the plaintiff collected medical expenses and UM coverage under his auto policy. The court refused to require setoff of the medicals against the UM coverage, since the policy contained no setoff clause:

> When the contract is read as a whole, its plain meaning at the time of issuance, or at least its reasonable meaning most favorable to Barney, was that Safeco would pay the amounts due under both coverages, without offset.

The court in *Hudson v. Hudson Mun. Contrs.*, 898 S.W.2d 187 (Tenn. 1995), refused to enforce a workers' compensation statutory subrogation lien against the insured's UM recovery, since the UM coverage was contractually subject to a setoff provision which reduced the insured's recovery by amounts paid and payable under workers' compensation law. If the lien were enforced, "the appellant's damages would be reduced twice by the amount of the workers' compensation benefits, first by the offset and again by the subrogation claim." Why not give the statutory subrogation claim priority over the contractual setoff, rather than vice versa?

The court, construing a hospital statutory lien, refused to enforce the lien against a UM recovery in *Kratz v. Kratz*, 905 P.2d 753 (Okla. 1995). The statute provided for recovery of medical expenses incurred for treating an accident victim's injuries if the victim recovered in "a claim against another for damages on account of such injuries." The court said that UM coverage was not within the "scope of the people who comprise the class of 'another'" within the meaning of the statute.

The plaintiffs in *Shaw v. Continental Ins. Co.*, 840 P.2d 592 (Nev. 1992), settled their tort claims against the tortfeasor for $750,000 "because they desperately needed the money." The tortfeasor had a liability policy of $1 million. Plaintiffs then sought to recover their damages in excess of $1 million against their UM coverage of $500,000. The UM insurer denied the claim, asserting that by the terms of the policy the UM coverage was not available "until after the limits of liability under any applicable bodily injury liability bonds or policies have been exhausted by payment of judgments or settlements." The court said that this exhaustion clause was unenforceable as against public policy, because it placed an "inequitable burden" on insureds who are forced to "forego all settlement offers and go to trial in order to obtain (or attempt to obtain) compensation up to the tortfeasor's policy limit — just to qualify for [UM] benefits under his or her own policy."

TENN. CODE ANNOT. § 56-7-1201(d) provides that the limit of liability for an insurer providing uninsured motorist coverage "is the amount of that coverage as specified in the policy less the sum of the limits collectible under all liability. . .policies" applicable to the bodily injury or death of the UM insured. Under such a statute, Shaw could not have collected on his UM coverage, could he, since the amount of that coverage was less than the amount of the tortfeasor's liability coverage?

In *Victor v. State Farm Fire & Cas. Ins. Co.*, 908 P.2d 1043 (Alaska 1996), the insured settled with one tortfeasor for $50,000, and then secured a judgment against an uninsured motorist arising out of the same event for $300,000. The insured had UM coverage of $100,000, and the policy provided that "any amount payable under this coverage" shall be reduced by any settlement amount received for the same injury. Disregarding the terms of the policy, the court credited the settlement amount against the judgment, not the policy limits, noting that there was no double recovery as a result.

7. *The Definition of a UM Event.* In *Thompson v. State Farm Mut. Auto Ins. Co.*, 468 N.W.2d 432 (Wis. 1991), the plaintiff's deceased was struck and killed by a bullet negligently shot from the rear of a stationary truck by a handicapped hunter. The hunter was aiming at a deer, which he missed, and the bullet "traveled some 500 yards" striking and killing the deceased who was driving his vehicle on a nearby highway.

The deceased's UM policy provided for payment for bodily injury "caused by accident arising out of the operation, maintenance or use" of an underinsured vehicle. The court held that the tortfeasor's truck was an underinsured vehicle which was being "used" within the meaning of the policy. Since the deceased had three auto policies with UM coverage of $100,000 per person, his estate was permitted to stack these policies and recover a total of $300,000 UM damages.

8. *UM Per-Person Coverage and Derivative Claims.* In *Kinsella v. Farmers Ins. Exchange*, 826 P.2d 433 (Colo. App. 1992), the plaintiff's son was seriously

injured in an automobile accident with an uninsured motorist. Plaintiff's UM policy provided $100,000 coverage "per person" for "bodily injury" sustained by any insured person in an accident. The company paid $100,000 to the son as UM coverage, but denied the father's claim for an additional $100,000 in medical expenses incurred on behalf of the son, on the grounds that the father suffered no "bodily injury."

The policy provided that the per-person limit included any claim for "loss of consortium or injury to the relationship arising from this injury." The plaintiff contended that since a claim for medical expenses was not expressly included in this per-person definition, it was inferentially allowable as a separate claim. Rejecting this contention, the court said that the consortium provision was "surplusage at best, since the immediately preceding sentence specifically limits recovery to $100,000 when, as here, only one person has sustained bodily injury." *Thompson v. State Farm Ins. Co.*, 468 N.W.2d 432 (Wis. 1991).

9. *UM Coverge and Choice of Law*. Nice choice of law issues arise when a vehicle covered by insurance issued in one state is involved in an accident in another state which has different mandatory UM coverage than that of the first state. *See* and *compare Anderson v. Oliver*, 705 So. 2d 301 (La. App. 1996), with *Trautman v. Poor*, 685 So. 2d 516 (La. App.1996).

10. *Subrogation and the Made-Whole Plaintiff*. Auto-accident victims often have public or private medical insurance that covers all or part of the medical expenses incurred in an auto accident. The insurance policy usually provides that the insurer will have a right of subrogation for any sums so paid, against any sum the victim may recover against a third-party tortfeasor. However, in *Blankenship v. Bain*, 5 S.W. 2d 647 (Tenn. 1999), and *York v. Sevier County Ambulance*, 8 S.W. 2d 616 (Tenn. 1999), the court held the insurers (TennCare and Blue Cross/Blue Shield, respectively) were not entitled to subrogation because the insureds had not been "made whole" in their settlement agreements with the third-party tortfeasors. Defendant Bain had only $125,000 liability insurance, and was "otherwise insolvent," and the court found the plaintiff's damages were "well in excess" of $125,000. Plaintiff York settled with defendant Sevier County for $130,000, which was the maximum amount recoverable under the governmental tort liability act. The court found the $130,000 was not enough to make the plaintiff "whole."

What if Bain had not been insolvent? Or if Blankenship had settled for $100,000? What if plaintiff York had obtained a verdict (as opposed to a settlement) against Sevier County for $100,000?

The Tennessee Legislature sought to abolish the "made whole" doctrine for purposes of determining TennCare subrogation, and to provide instead for a reduction of the subrogation claim by the amount of the plaintiff's attorney fees and the amount of fault attributable to the plaintiff and third parties. Tenn. Publ. Ch.p. No. 807 (2000).

PROBLEM

Gerald does not own a car because he is afraid of being injured by an exploding air bag. However, his wife, Daphne, owns three cars which she insures under three separate automobile policies. Daphne has $10,000 uninsured motorist coverage on each vehicle. One morning, Daphne is driving Gerald to his therapist when her vehicle skids off the road and hits a tree. Gerald is severely injured; it is stipulated that his damages are in excess of $50,000.

What issues will arise, and what insuring and exclusionary clauses will come into play? What type of "stacking" will Gerald attempt? How much will he recover? Assume that Gerald and Daphne are happily married. Assume, in the alternative, that Gerald and Daphne have been estranged for two years. Suppose the accident had occurred in a no-fault state?

F. INSURANCE AS AN ALTERNATIVE SYSTEM

Worker compensation schemes undoubtedly prompted scholars and lawmakers to consider a similar approach to automobile accidents. *See Compensation for Automobile Accidents: A Symposium,* 32 Colum. L. Rev. 785 (1932). This idea of "no fault" treatment of automobile accidents first emerged in legislative form in the Canadian province of Saskatchewan in 1946. The Saskatchewan plan provided, in addition to first party property damage and third party liability insurance, first party insurance with benefits similar to worker's compensation. A major impetus for "no fault" automobile insurance in the United States was provided by Professor (later Judge) Robert E. Keeton and Professor Jeffrey O'Connell, who in 1965 proposed a "Basic Protection for the Traffic Victim" plan. The essence of the plan was first party insurance protection for "net economic loss," including medical expenses and loss of wages. The Keeton-O'Connell plan made recovery of "net economic loss" the victim's exclusive remedy unless he suffered economic loss or damages for pain and suffering in excess of a certain amount. When the damages and injuries exceeded the "threshold," the victim could resort to the tort system. *See* R. Keeton & J. O'Connell, Basic Protection for the Traffic Victim (1965); Keeton & O'Connell, *Basic Protection Automobile Insurance,* 1967 U. Ill. L. F. 400.

The publication of the Keeton-O'Connell plan coincided with mounting academic and other criticism of the fault system as a method of allocating the cost of automobile accidents. Among the perceived ills:

(1) The fault system erratically compensates victims. Some are uncompensated because there is no "fault" chargeable to a solvent or adequately insured defendant. Even among those who are compensated, there is inequity. Insurers overpay small claims to reduce administrative costs, and victims of catastrophic accidents accept less than full compensation because they cannot risk total loss or endure the sometimes lengthy delay between accident and judgment.

(2) The fault system is inefficient. Even where there is fault, and an adequately insured defendant, more than half of the premium dollar is expended on administration costs.

(3) The fault system produces socially undesirable results, such as promoting "malingering" among victims.

(4) The fault system causes an improper allocation of resources because of the burden it places on the court system, and because people must maintain high-cost insurance.

Criticism of the fault system as an inadequate method of compensating tort victims was countered by those who feared the losses of deterrence and of the "sense of justice/revenge" which could result from an abandonment of that system. *See, e.g.,* W. Blum & H. Kalven, Jr., Public Law Perspectives on a Private Law Problem — Auto Compensation Plans (1965). After Massachusetts in 1970 adopted the "no fault" plan discussed in *Pinnick* below, nearly half the states followed suit and adopted some form of "no fault" plan. The "revolution" quickly waned, however. No state has entered the no-fault arena since the 1970s, and Nevada, Georgia and Connecticut have abandoned it. 29 U. Memphis L. Rev. 60, 75, fn. 15 (1998). The present state of the law is chronicled in J. Appleman, Insurance Law and Practice, § 5161 (1981).

PINNICK v. CLEARY
360 Mass. 1, 271 N.E.2d 592 (1971)

REARDON, J.

The facts of the case are not disputed. The plaintiff, a resident of Massachusetts, is the owner of a motor vehicle duly registered under the laws of the Commonwealth and insured under a policy which includes personal injury protection benefits as defined in St. 1970, c. 670. The policy was not subject to the optional deductible endorsement (deductible) provided in c. 670. While he was driving his car on a public way in Boston early on the morning of January 3, 1971, two days after the effective date of that statute, he was involved in an accident which was caused exclusively by the negligence of the defendant. The car the defendant was driving was owned by one Daniel Mack, and was also covered by an insurance policy which included personal injury protection benefits as defined in c. 670.

As a result of the accident, the plaintiff suffered injuries which included a bone contusion of the left lower scapula, a contusion and sprain of lower scapula muscles on both sides, and a severe low back sprain with radiation of pain into the lower right extremity. He incurred $115 in reasonable and necessary medical expenses for treatment of these injuries. Although he had no medical insurance in his own name, he was covered by a policy issued to his wife which provided for reimbursement of his medical expenses over $100. The entire $115 would have been recoverable in a traditional common law tort action against the defendant, as well as $800 for his pain and suffering.

Due to the accident the plaintiff lost in addition seventy-three hours from his position with the United States Post Office. His salary in this position was $176.77 a week, a figure which also represents his average weekly wages for the year preceding the accident. He received his usual salary for the entire period of his absence, however, due to the paid sick leave and annual leave to which he was entitled. His accumulated paid sick leave of forty hours was exhausted in the process, and his paid annual leave was reduced by thirty-three hours.

The plaintiff also held a second job at the time of the accident which paid him at the rate of $96.25 a week. This amount was his average weekly wage for that job for the year preceding the accident. The accident caused him to miss twelve days from this work, for which he was not compensated. In a tort action at common law, on these facts the plaintiff could have recovered $650 from the defendant for loss of earning capacity. His total recovery in tort against the defendant, including general and special damages, would therefore have been $1,565 ($115 + $650 + $800).

The plaintiff made demand on the defendant for reasonable compensation in accordance with the recoverable elements of damage at common law as outlined above. The defendant refused, raising as a defense c. 670 which, *inter alia*, exempts a tortfeasor from liability up to $2,000 to the extent the claimant is entitled to personal injury protection benefits from his own insurer. The defendant also noted that in the circumstances of his case the plaintiff was not entitled to any damages for pain and suffering under c. 670, although he retained his right to sue in tort for other elements of damage not covered by the personal injury protection benefits.

The plaintiff in this bill claims that this operation of c. 670 deprives him unconstitutionally of his right to full recovery in tort.

. . .Those who challenge c. 670 have attributed to it not only a drastic stripping of legal rights but also, in its practical effect, a substantial diminution of the damages which the average non-negligent accident victim may reasonably expect. Analysis demonstrates, on the contrary, that the Legislature has acted with extreme caution in altering prior legal rights, changing in only one respect the elements of damage which are recoverable by the victim. As to the practical effect of c. 670, it appears that the statute affords the citizen the security of prompt and certain recovery to a fixed amount of the most salient elements of his out-of-pocket expenses and an increased flexibility in avoiding duplicate coverage, at double premiums, for the same expenses. In return for this he surrenders the possibly minimal damages for pain and suffering recoverable in cases not marked by serious economic loss or objective indicia of grave injury and the outside chance that through a generous settlement or a liberal award by a judge or jury in such a case he may be able to reap a monetary windfall out of his misfortune.

The key concept embodied in c. 670 is that of personal injury protection insurance, which is required of all owners of motor vehicles registered in Massachusetts. Under this coverage, personal injury protection benefits are paid by the insurer, as the expenses they cover accrue, to the insured, members of his household, authorized operators or passengers of his motor vehicle including guest occupants, and any pedestrians struck by him, regardless of fault in the causation of the accident.[14]

---

[14] There are only three exceptions to this no-fault rule. If the injured party otherwise entitled to benefits was injured while driving under the influence of alcohol or narcotics as defined in G.L. c. 94, § _____197, while committing a felony or seeking to avoid arrest, or while intentionally trying to injure himself or others, he may be excluded from benefits by the insurer. In addition, one injured in circumstances which entitle him to workmen's compensation is not eligible for benefits.

Limited in amount to $2,000, the benefits cover largely the same items of medical expense covered before by optional medical payments insurance, with the exception that expenses incurred within two years of the accident are included as opposed to the one year period generally covered in optional insurance. Personal injury protection covers in addition, however, two other types of out-of-pocket expenses. The first and less significant of these is "payments in fact made to others, not members of the injured person's household and reasonably incurred in obtaining from those others ordinary and necessary services in lieu of those that, had he not been injured, the injured person would have performed not for income but for the benefit of himself and/or members of his household." The second is seventy-five per cent of the actual lost wages of the injured party, calculated on the basis of his average weekly wage during the year preceding the accident. If the victim was unemployed, he is entitled to the same percentage of wages he can prove he would have received from work he would have had had he not been injured.

Benefits allocable to medical expenses are paid regardless of any other insurance covering the same costs. However, to avoid duplicate recovery and reduce the expense of insurance, c. 670 provides the option to elect a deductible, binding on the insured or on the members of the insured's household. These policies, for a reduced premium, provide that an amount from the first $250 up to the entire $2,000 otherwise recoverable as personal injury protection benefits shall not be paid by the insurer.

Benefits allocable to lost wages, on the other hand, are reduced by any amounts received under a wage continuation plan or its equivalent. The victim, however, may incur (within a year of the payment of the last benefit) a later injury for which he would be entitled to payments under the wage continuation plan. If the amount then available to the victim to meet lost wages caused by the later injury has been reduced by reason of the payments under the plan attributable to the earlier accident then the insurer shall be responsible to the extent of the reduction.

Thus under c. 670 the accident victim, with a few minor exceptions, is entitled to immediate payment of his most pressing items of cost: medical expenses. In addition, he receives the major portion of his lost wages not covered by a wage continuation plan, and certain consequential expenses. These amounts, to a total of $2,000, are due from his own insurer, not from an adversary insurance company, and without the necessity for assignment of fault or the temptation on either side to bargain in the light of considerations which are often extraneous to the amount of expense incurred.

In exchange for the protection extended by c. 670, the accident victim loses his right to recover in tort to the extent he is eligible for personal injury protection benefits. Because the exemption of the tortfeasor is exactly matched to the availability of personal injury protection benefits to the plaintiff, the plaintiff loses nothing by it. With one restriction to be discussed below, the potential plaintiff retains in addition his common law action against the tortfeasor for any elements of damage not recovered as personal injury protection benefits. These would include any expenses in excess of $2,000 which would otherwise have been covered by personal injury protection and the difference between his diminished earning capacity, as measured at common law, and the substitute percentage of actual lost wages reduced by amounts received under any wage continuation plan recoverable under c. 670. Since the new law has retained the previous requirements of compulsory liability insurance under G.L. c. 90, § 34A, the victim who chooses to sue has the same assurance of at least limited recovery if he can prove negligence as he had before the passage of c. 670.

The plaintiff stresses that the residual tort action left after the payment of personal injury protection benefits is reduced in value inasmuch as the potential plaintiff must consider the extent to which legal fees will reduce his net recovery. However, legal fees are not a new burden imposed by c. 670; they have long been a factor to be considered in prosecuting any claim, including a tort action for personal injury instituted before the passage of c. 670.

The only limitation imposed by c. 670 on the potential plaintiff's prior right of recovery at common law is the elimination of damages for "pain and suffering, including mental suffering associated with . . . . injury" except in certain specified categories of cases. Section 5 of c. 670 provides generally that the reasonable and necessary medical expenses incurred by a plaintiff in the treatment of his injuries must be over $500 to permit recovery for pain and suffering. However, recognizing that certain types of injuries could entail considerable pain and suffering which would warrant monetary compensation regardless of medical expense incurred, the Legislature provided by way of exception to the general rule that damages for pain and suffering could be sought in all cases involving five designated types of injuries. These are a fracture, injury causing death, injury consisting in whole or in part of loss of a body member, permanent and serious disfigurement, and injury resulting in loss of sight or hearing as elsewhere defined in the General Laws. The victim whose injury falls outside these categories and whose medical expenses are less than $500 cannot recover at all for pain and suffering. However, it is still possible for the person who desires to assure for himself recovery in excess of his out-of-pocket costs to do so. Just as he may elect a deductible if he has medical payments insurance to avoid duplicate recovery for medical expenses, so he may choose to keep both forms of insurance in full precisely to allow himself double recovery of these expenses. Other forms of duplicate coverage are equally possible. It is true that the amount of excess he will receive thereby will bear no necessary relation to the value of his pain and suffering as arbitrarily set by a jury but, on the other hand, he is assured of some profit over out-of-pocket expenses in every motor vehicle accident. This certainty he was never afforded by his prior "right" to recovery for pain and suffering in a suitable case, which in order to be realized even in such a case had to be actively pursued at considerable expense.

. . . In approaching the numerous issues before us, it is advisable to dispose first of a contention which the plaintiff has argued vigorously and at some length, for if we accepted it, it would require a somewhat different approach to the attacks leveled at the statute than that we feel appropriate. The plaintiff claims that c. 670 has impaired a cause of action which is on a higher, more sacrosanct level than the "ordinary" common law cause of action. Two alternative reasons are advanced in support of this contention: first, that the tort action has the status of a "vested property right," and, second, that the function of the cause of action is to safeguard the fundamental "right of personal security and bodily integrity" which, although not mentioned in the Bill of Rights of the United States Constitution, is nonetheless protected by it. We find both grounds unpersuasive.

In arguing that the cause of action affected by c. 670 constitutes a vested property right, the plaintiff seems to ignore the distinction between a cause of action which has accrued and the expectation which every citizen has if a legal wrong should occur to find redress according to the rules of statutory and common law applicable at that time. The Legislature is admittedly restricted in the extent to which it can retroactively affect common law rights of redress which have already accrued. However, there is authority in abundance for the proposition that "[n]o person has a vested interest in any rule of law entitling him to insist that it shall remain unchanged for his benefit." *New York Cen. R. Co. v. White,* 243 U.S. 188, 198, 37 S. Ct. 297, 250, 61 L. Ed. 667. . . . The citizen may find that events occurring after passage of such a statute place him in a different position legally from that which he would have occupied had they occurred before passage of the statute. He has no cause, however, to complain solely because his rights are not now what they would have been before.

. . . Article 11 of the [Massachusetts] Declaration of Rights guarantees "a certain remedy, by having recourse to the laws, for all injuries or wrongs which . . . . [one] may receive . . . ." The article is clearly directed toward the preservation of procedural rights and has been so construed. . . .

We are baffled by the plaintiff's further attempt to find in c. 670, insofar as it affects the tort action for bodily injury, an impairment of some fundamental right protected by the first ten amendments to the Federal Constitution. The plaintiff lays emphasis on Mr. Justice Goldberg's concurring opinion in *Griswold v. Connecticut,* 381 U.S. 479, 486, 85 S. Ct. 1678, 14 L. Ed. 2d 510 (1965). In that case a Connecticut law banning the use of contraceptives was held to violate the right of privacy as contained in the first ten amendments. Any supposed analogy of the present case to the *Griswold* case is inapposite and does nothing to advance the plaintiff's argument. Whatever may be the fundamental "right of personal security and bodily integrity" to which the plaintiff refers, it is not affected by c. 670. That chapter merely limits the common law right in the automobile accident situation to obtain money damages on account of unintentionally inflicted pain and suffering and modifies the procedure for obtaining damages according to the common law measure for all other elements of recovery.

We thus perceive no basis for treating a legislative alteration of the tort action for personal injuries differently from an alteration of any other preexisting rule of the common law. Hence we may summarily dispose of several of the plaintiff's arguments which are founded on the contrary premise. There is no cause here for application of the "compelling state interest" test, which is employed where a statute impairs fundamental rights protected by the Constitution. . . .

We conclude that the principles by which c. 670 should be judged are those generally applied when economic and social regulations enacted under the police power are attacked as a violation of due process and equal protection of the laws. The two grounds of attack although similar are sufficiently distinct to warrant separate treatment, to which we now proceed.

We will deal first with the propriety of c. 670 under the due process clause. The overall test under this clause is whether the statute bears a reasonable relation to a permissible legislative objective. In the application of this test, the statute is accorded a presumption of constitutionality, a corollary of which is that if a state of facts could exist which would justify the legislation, it must be presumed to have existed when the statute was passed.

. . . Here we do not need to reach the difficult question of when the Legislature may abrogate a common law right of recovery without providing a substitute remedy.

. . . In the instant case, however, the Legislature has not attempted to abolish the preexisting right of tort recovery and leave the automobile accident victim without redress. On the contrary, as was pointed out above, the statute has affected his substantive rights of recovery only in one respect and has simply altered his method of enforcing them in all others. Therefore, c. 670 may be judged by the stricter test which the plaintiff urges upon us and for which there is considerable authority in workmen's compensation cases: whether the statute provides an adequate and reasonable substitute for pre-existing rights. The similarity between c. 670 and the workmen's compensation statutes, in the nature of their purposes and the means chosen to achieve them, also leads us to conclude that the reasonable and adequate substitute test is appropriate to apply here even if its application is not constitutionally required. We will, therefore, consider c. 670 in the light of a twofold test: the general test required by the due process clause of whether it bears a rational relation to a legitimate legislative objective, and the more particularized test for which the plaintiff argues — whether it provides a reasonable substitute for preexisting rights.

The ills against which c. 670 is aimed are obvious. One of the most prominent of these will be found in a brief consideration of the impact of the automobile on the burden of litigation carried by courts in general and Massachusetts courts in particular. No one who has for any time been in charge of a trial court system (as was the author of this opinion for a number of years) can be unfamiliar with the devastating effect upon the administration of justice which the automobile has produced. For years, in the face of countless experiments, the trial calendars of this country, particularly in metropolitan areas, have become increasingly clogged with motor vehicle tort litigation. No one as yet, notwithstanding heroic efforts in this regard, has found a satisfactory method of disentangling this morass. Indeed, the problem intensifies as American courts are increasingly called upon to deal with complexities of our society not evident when the motor vehicle first appeared on the national scene and to broaden the scope of their activities into areas not traditionally subject to judicial cognizance. The courts with their scarce resource of time simply cannot respond to new challenges or meet the new requirements imposed on them in criminal matters as long as their time continues to be consumed to the extent it has been by motor vehicle accident cases. The problems of society to which the courts have been called no longer permit the luxury of using them as a forum for resolving the ever increasing numbers of automobile accident claims to the extent that has obtained hitherto.

These observations are nowhere more applicable than in Massachusetts. We have lived with compulsory liability insurance since January 1, 1927. In that period certain events have occurred which might well have commended themselves to the Legislature as indicia pointing toward the wisdom of change. Eleven years ago, for instance, a special commission found that on the basis of bodily injury claim frequency per one hundred cars insured, the average in Massachusetts in the years 1954–1956 was 6.4% as against 2% for Maine, 3.1% for Rhode Island, 2% for Vermont, and 3.3% for Connecticut. In 1959, the year the report was filed, the claim frequency in Boston on a local basis exceeded that in New York City by more than 50%. The seriousness of the problem in so far as it relates to current Massachusetts civil trial dockets can be seen in the following figures related to the Superior Court.

	Total law entries	of which there were	Total Motor Vehicle entries
1967	34,730		23,279
1968	33,558		22,289
1969	34,381		22,598
1970	35,155		22,690

When it is recognized that many of these automobile entries represent multiple party suits, the weight which this type of litigation places on Massachusetts courts is evident.

Less obvious is the burden on the clerks' offices, lawyers and litigants which follows this proliferation of entries of motor cases, currently at the rate of almost 2,000 a month in the Superior Court and more than 3,200 a month in the District Courts. Every paper submitted must be filed and docketed, and each entry prompts an avalanche of them. In addition to the writ, declaration, answer and appearance slips; interrogatories by parties on both sides, applications to nonsuit or default for failure to answer interrogatories, motions to extend time for answering or to remove nonsuit or default for not answering interrogatories, motions to strike answers to interrogatories and to answer over or further, motions for specifications, and demands to admit facts are only a few of the papers that follow as [a matter] of course in almost every motor tort case entered. Court personnel are additionally burdened by the need to give notice to counsel or parties of every order of the court entered during these lengthy pre-trial proceedings. The time of the court consumed in this preliminary war of nerves between counsel, or between claimant and insurer, is almost impossible to estimate, but probably far exceeds that spent in the trial of the small percentage of all entries which must be tried.

Both in the pre-trial and later stages, claims for small amounts possess, of course, the same capability of clogging the judicial system as their larger brothers. They must be dealt with either on the Superior Court level where they do not belong or in the District Courts, from which removal or retransfer to the Superior Court will often occur. And, unfortunately, it cannot be concluded that the bulk of automobile accident claims in the Superior Court represents causes of great value. For many years the secretary of the Judicial

Council maintained a record of the amount of jury verdicts. This tabular count was discontinued in 1956. In the year immediately prior to its discontinuance the following interesting statistics were compiled.

Amount of Jury Verdict for Plaintiff	Percentage of Cases Which Were Automobile Accident Claims
Less than $ 200	80.3% (53 out of 66)
$ 200 - $ 500	61.4% (70 out of 114)
$ 500 - $1,000	59.3% (92 out of 155)
$1,000 - $ 2,000	59.8% (100 out of 167)
$2,000 - $3,000	39.4% (28 out of 71)
$3,000 - $4,000	56.2% (27 out of 48)
$4,000 - $5,000	56.7% (21 out of 37)
$5,000 - $10,000	53.7% (57 out of 106)
Over $10,000	47.8% (44 out of 92)

We recognize these statistics are dated and in any event not determinative. The percentages indicate in general, however, that with the increase in size of the verdict the likelihood that it was rendered in an automobile accident case steadily decreased. In addition it should be noted that in absolute numbers there were far more verdicts in automobile accident cases in the 0 to $2,000 range (315) than in the $2,000 and up range (177). Even accounting for the decrease in the value of money since 1956, this statistic still indicates that a great many, if not the majority of, claims which before were taken to court could be handled under c. 670 with approximately the same monetary return to the claimant, since personal injury protection benefits provide for compensation up to $2,000 of all elements of damage for which tort recovery was before possible except pain and suffering and twenty-five per cent of lost wages. Finally, these statistics should be considered in light of two further facts. First, at the time they were compiled, the minimum cost of a jury trial was estimated at $750 a day, a figure which has since undergone a great increase, and, secondly, the figures do not reflect at all those cases in which a verdict for the defendant was returned.

Other non-American court systems, heirs with ourselves of the common law, have managed to solve this problem of the superabundance of motor vehicle tort claims in one way or another. It remains, however, a cancer to be rooted out in American courts. Presumably the Legislature had this in mind. Chapter 670, in providing for limited recovery without the necessity for adversary proceedings in automobile accident cases, was an appropriate step to alleviate this problem which defied more conservative solutions.

Nor was court congestion the only problem at which c. 670 might have been aimed. The high cost of automobile insurance in Massachusetts was a present fact of which the Legislature did not need to be reminded. It might have suspected that there was a correlation between this high cost and the inefficiencies and administrative expense involved in running the traditional system, contributed to heavily by the prevalence of the elaborate pre-trial proceedings detailed above. That any such suspicion would have been well founded was confirmed by a report of the United States Department of Transportation released in March of this year entitled, "Motor Vehicle Crash Losses and their Compensation in the United States; a Report to the Congress and the President." The report concluded on this subject that "[t]he automobile accident tort liability insurance system would appear to possess the highly dubious distinction of having probably the highest cost/benefit ratio of any major compensation system currently in operation in this country. As has been shown, for every dollar of net benefits that it provides to victims, it consumes about a dollar." p. 95.

Finally, and not to be discounted among the evils associated with automobiles which c. 670 might have been designed to cure, are the inequities which have been visited upon claimants. In this regard the Legislature might have felt, as expressed in the Department of Transportation Report, that "[t]he present tort liability reparations system allocates benefits very unevenly among the limited number of victims that it purports to serve." P. 94. The Legislature was also presumably aware of the long delays in getting financial aid to the injured person, confronted with medical and subsistence bills during a period of no employment for him and want for his family. The time spent in investigation, the time required for proof of negligence, the exaggerated claims, the all too common suspicion of perjured testimony, the horse and buggy approach to a twentieth century dilemma — all of this might well have influenced the Legislature, recognizing the right and need of all accident victims to simple and speedy justice, toward reform.

It cannot be seriously argued that it was beyond legislative competence to assess this situation and to effect the necessary statutory repair. What we have discussed are evils which it was within the province of the Legislature to consider and which it endeavored to correct or eliminate. We do not intimate that the legislative determination which is c. 670 was the only answer or solution to the problem, but it cannot be successfully maintained that its salient provisions, as outlined above, are not a rational approach to the solution of these patent inefficiencies and inequities.

We are urged to apply a test derived largely from the suggestion in *New York Cen. R. Co. v. White,* 243 U.S. 188, 201, 61 L. Ed. 662, 37 S. Ct. 247 (1917), that a State might not have the power under the due process clause "suddenly [to] set aside all common-law rules respecting liability as between employer and employee, without providing a reasonably just substitute. . . . [I]t perhaps may be doubted whether the State could abolish all rights of action on the one hand, or all defenses on the other, without setting up something adequate in their stead." The proposed test may best be considered and understood, therefore, in the light of the facts before the court in that case.

The Workmen's Compensation Act dealt with in the *White* case substituted an administrative system of compensation for the common law rights of employees engaged in hazardous employments. The new system was compulsory on both employers and employees. The employee injured or killed in the course of his employment was entitled to a fixed compensation according to a prescribed schedule without regard to fault in almost every case. At common law the employee's rights against his employer were considerably circumscribed in fact by certain defenses available to the employer. Where he could succeed in making out a case, however, the employee stood to gain a great deal more from a jury than he would receive under workmen's compensation. Viewing the overall operation and effect of the statute on both parties affected by it, the court indicated that the exchange of rights was adequate. With respect to the statute's effect on employees, it gave the following reasons: "If the employee is no longer able to recover as much as before in case of being injured through the employer's negligence, he is entitled to moderate compensation in all cases of injury, and has a certain and speedy remedy without the difficulty and expense of establishing negligence or proving the amount of the damages." 243 U.S. at 201, 37 S. Ct. at 252.

It is immediately apparent that c. 670 alters prior legal rights to a much less drastic extent than did the act involved in the *White* case. However, the overall difference in status quo effected by c. 670 may be described in part in much the same terms as those used by the court in the *White* case.

In considering the effect of c. 670, we cannot view it from the point of view of plaintiffs and defendants, for these are not preexisting categories as are the employers and employees affected by a workmen's compensation act. Every driver is a potential plaintiff and, equally, a potential defendant. The desired effect of c. 670 on all motorists alike is initially to make available to them compulsory insurance at lower rates due to the savings to insurance companies in administrative expenses and total payments which are expected to follow from c. 670. If injury occurs on the road, motorists are assured of the probability of quick and efficient payment of the first $2,000 of defined losses incurred. In cases of accidents in which the motorist was not negligent, he avoids the uncertainty, delay and cost of a tort proceeding. He still retains the option of recovering more by litigation if he so wishes and the facts so warrant. Although c. 670 may also have the effect of depriving him of his damages for pain and suffering in such an instance, the exchange of rights involved with respect to the driver in an accident in which he was not negligent bears considerable resemblance to that effected by the statute in the White case with respect to employees.

This exchange of rights cannot be viewed in isolation, however, for non-negligent drivers are not a distinct class. To it must be added the effect of c. 670 on the driver in a case where he has been negligent or where negligence cannot be determined. In this situation, rather than no compensation for his own injuries, c. 670 accords him the same benefits he would have if he were non-negligent. In addition, he is afforded immunity from liability to the extent other injured parties are eligible for benefits. And, just as his right to sue for pain and suffering is limited when he is non-negligent, so he is protected from comparable claims where he has been negligent. The effect of c. 670 on Massachusetts motorists thus is to provide benefits in return for affected rights at least as adequate as those provided to New York employers and employees in return for rights taken by the act in the *White* case.

It may be argued that c. 670 affects a second distinct class of persons, the pedestrian, and that the exchange of rights effected on this class must be considered separately from its effect on drivers. It is obvious, however, that all drivers are at some moment in time pedestrians. With this realization, the class of pedestrians as distinct from drivers is sharply reduced. Whether or not we define the class to include pedestrians who also drive, however, the effect of c. 670 on that class is no different from its effect on drivers. Pedestrians, too, may be negligent or non-negligent; they, too, are therefore afforded the certainty of prompt recovery of a limited amount and limited exemption from liability instead of the necessity of tort proceedings or no compensation at all and liability to an unlimited amount. The fact that the non-car owner is not advantageously affected by lower insurance premiums by no means vitiates the adequacy of the exchange of rights as it operates on him. A similar analysis may be applied to any other nonmotorist who in a given instance happens to come within the scope of c. 670.

The plaintiff has leveled two attacks against c. 670 based on a denial of equal protection of the laws, both directed at the classification in § 5 of cases for which pain and suffering are recoverable. Again it is helpful to state at the outset the general principles which are applicable under the equal protection clause. A principle analogous to that we applied to due process issues is likewise applicable where a legislative classification is attacked as a violation of equal protection: if the legislative difference in treatment is reasonably related to a legitimate public purpose, it is permissible. The same subsidiary presumption of constitutionality is present in this context also, as is the required use of any reasonably conceivable set of facts to justify the classification. There is no requirement that there be any legislative record or findings in support of the classification. The equal protection clause thus limits legislative discretion in delineating classifications only to the extent of forbidding "arbitrary or irrational" classifications (*In re Opinion of the Justices,* 251 Mass. 569, 601, 147 N.E. 681 (1925)) or discrimination which is "invidious." *Williamson v. Lee Optical of Oklahoma, Inc.,* 349 U.S. 483, 489, 75 S. Ct. 461, 99 L. Ed. 563 (1955).

The plaintiff claims that the criteria delineating when pain and suffering are recoverable are arbitrary and unreasonable. The purpose of the Legislature in limiting recovery in this way was clearly to eliminate minor claims for pain and suffering. We have already described the crisis faced by the courts of the Commonwealth and the part played by the abundance of personal injury claims in contributing to it. The Legislature could reasonably have thought that the number of such cases was largely attributable to speculative and exaggerated claims for pain and suffering in instances of relatively minor injury. As is well known, the subjective complaint of pain and suffering defies accurate monetary appraisal. In addition, the time and expense necessary to investigate these claims might well have been perceived to be a burden both on the insurance industry and ultimately on the motoring public. Minor "nuisance" claims were often overpaid by insurers in order to avoid the expense of defending them, and the common knowledge of this practice only served to perpetuate them. It was clearly proper for the Legislature to conclude that the benefits of compensating an injured person for relatively minor pain and suffering, which as such entails no monetary loss, did not warrant continuation of the practice when balanced against the evils it had spawned.

A necessary corollary of this decision was that the minor claims had to be eliminated according to objective, easily applicable rules. If the rules were themselves subjective — for instance, keyed to the dollar amount of pain and suffering involved — the perceived evils would continue. Courts might well be clogged with claimants alleging damages over the required figure, and there would remain the incentive for the injured party to exaggerate his claim in order to prompt a generous settlement from an insurer which did not feel the claim was worth the expense of a contest.

The only question that remains, therefore, is whether the objective criteria the Legislature chose are rationally related to their purpose of eliminating minor claims for pain and suffering. We think there can be no doubt that they are. The plaintiff's attack is leveled chiefly at the general rule that reasonable and necessary medical expenses must be over $500 to allow recovery for pain and suffering. There is no objection to the mitigation of this rule by the criteria of death, loss of a body member, permanent and serious disfigurement, or loss of sight or hearing. Our attention has been drawn, however, to the contrast between the comparatively minor pain and suffering which may result from a minor fracture and the serious and long-continued pain and suffering which may result in cases for which the statute denies recovery. It is argued that the $500 limit will exclude many sizable claims for pain and suffering which do not at the same time fall within the five other categories. No doubt this is so. Nor do we doubt that relatively minor claims for pain and suffering may be permitted in some cases, particularly in the fracture category. But fracture, like the $500 limit and the other four criteria based on the type of injury, is susceptible of objective and reasonably certain verification. In addition, many cases of fracture, perhaps most, are likely to involve substantial pain and suffering. . . . Some inequality in result is not enough to vitiate a legislative classification grounded in reason. It seems to us that the Legislature has employed criteria rationally related to seriousness of injury in general, and thereby to seriousness of pain and suffering. Whether fracture should be included as a category, at the risk of allowing some minor claims for pain and suffering, is within the permissible range of judgment.

As to the amount of reasonable and necessary medical expenses, it is constitutionally irrelevant that the actual point of demarcation had necessarily to be arbitrary. . . . It is clear that the $500 figure chosen here by the Legislature, although no more nor less reasonable than a higher or lower figure within a substantial range, is not subject to constitutional attack. . . .

NOTES

1. *Remnants of Fault in No-Fault States.* None of the "no fault" plans eliminates the fault system. Note that the Massachusetts plan provides the insured with first-party benefits, but permits him to pursue a remedy through the fault system if his claim exceeds certain minimum limits. About half of the "no fault" plans adopt this approach, sometimes called a "mixed no fault plan." The other states merely permit or require that the insured purchase ("add on") first party insurance to protect himself against basic losses. *See* Appleman, *supra,* § 5161. If injured by a faulty third party, the insured may pursue his tort remedy, and his first-party insurer is entitled to reimbursement through subrogation.

F. INSURANCE AS AN ALTERNATIVE SYSTEM

2. *Characteristics of No-Fault Automobile Plans.* Some questions common to "no fault" plans:

a. Is the plan compulsory? Some states require it; others make it optional.

b. What first party protection does the plan provide? The most common benefits are (i) medical expenses, (ii) loss of earnings, and (iii) other economic loss, such as property damage. There may be limits on the amounts of expenses or earnings which may be recovered, and a "cap" on the total amount of first party damages recoverable through the plan.

c. Who is an "insured" under the plan? The general approach is that the policy covering an automobile provides first-party benefits to the owner, family members of his household, and other persons who are injured as a result of the use of the automobile and who are not passengers in another covered automobile. *See* Appleman, *supra,* § 5167. Pedestrians or motorcyclists, or both, sometimes are excluded from coverage. *See* Appleman, *supra,* § 5169.45.

d. Some plans include provisions for extraterritorial coverage. The policy may extend coverage to an insured who is injured in another jurisdiction which does not have a "no fault" plan, and provide "no fault" coverage in policies written in other states and covering vehicles which are involved in accidents in a "no fault" jurisdiction. *See Ohio Cas. Ins. Co. v. Continental Ins. Co.,* 421 N.Y.S. 2d 317, 101 Misc. 2d 452 (1979); *Petty v. Allstate Ins. Co.,* 290 N.W.2d 763 (Minn. 1980).

e. Some plans will provide for lump sum death benefits if a covered person dies as a result of a covered accident.

f. Some plans exclude injuries caused by the insured's intoxication. *See, e.g.,* Appleman, *supra,* § 5176.25.

g. "Stacking" of "no fault" coverages sometimes is permitted. *See* Annot., 29 A.L.R.4th 12.

3. *Recourse to the Fault System.* In states such as Massachusetts, which have adopted a "mixed" plan, the insured person may sue to recover for pain and suffering and for economic losses in excess of those provided by the first party insurance if the victim's injuries or damages exceed a specified threshold, determined by the amount of economic loss or the severity of the injury. *See* Appleman, *supra,* § 5182. Consider this language from the New York plan:

> (I)n any action by . . . . a covered person against another covered person . . . . there shall be no right of recovery for non-economic loss, except in the case of a *serious injury,* or for basic economic loss.

New York Insurance Law § 5104 (a) (1990).

> "*Serious injury*" means a personal injury which results in death; dismemberment; significant disfigurement; a fracture; loss of a fetus; permanent loss of use of a body organ, member, function or system; permanent consequential limitation of use of a body organ or member; significant limitation of use of a body function or system; or a medically determined injury or impairment of a non-permanent nature which prevents the injured person from performing substantially all of the material acts which constitute such person's usual and customary daily activities for not less than ninety days during the one

hundred eighty days immediately following the occurrence of the injury or impairment.

New York Insurance Law § 5702(d) (1990).

4. *No-Fault "Good Samaritan" Coverage.* In *Burns v. Market Transition FAC*, 281 N.J. Super. 304, 657 A.2d 472 (1995), the plaintiff was injured while rendering aid to his brother who was trapped in an automobile following a collision:

> As a result of the bent and awkward position maintained by plaintiff for an extended period of time, while partially in and partially out of the vehicle, plaintiff developed pain in his back and between his shoulder blades on the evening of the accident. He subsequently underwent a course of orthopedic treatment. He was also treated by a psychiatrist because of the emotional impact occasioned by his brother's death. Medical benefits for PIP coverage were claimed for both the orthopedic injury and for the psychological injury sustained while watching his brother die.

New Jersey's no-fault statute provided personal injury coverage for anyone injured "as a result of an accident while occupying, entering into, alighting from or using an automobile." In holding that the statute must be broadly construed, the court found the plaintiff was "using" the automobile at the time of his injury.

Chapter 22
TORT RETRENCHMENTS AND TORT ALTERNATIVES

A. INTRODUCTION

Today, one of the most controversial legal issues is whether the tort liability system is responsible for excessive litigation, unreasonably high verdicts, and the unavailability or lack of affordable liability insurance. There have been numerous inquiries, both at the federal and state levels, and many laws have been adopted, primarily at the state level, to meet a perceived "tort liability crisis." Whether there is such a crisis, and if so what are its causes, are subjects of heated debates. This chapter examines some of the commentaries, identifies the issues raised, and highlights typical laws proposed or passed in response to the perceived "crisis."

The chapter begins with the consideration of an early statutory retrenchment on tort law in this country — guest passenger statutes. An analysis of the nature, purpose, and effect of those statutes provides some guidance and perspective in evaluating the more recent tort retrenchments.

The chapter also surveys some of the alternatives to the tort system and to the litigation process which have been proposed and have attracted widespread interest. The no-fault insurance alternative was considered in Chapter 21. This chapter presents other alternatives, including informal summary adjudication and settlement proceedings, the substitution for tort of administrative remedies, similar to workers' compensation and social security, and the development of alternative dispute mechanisms such as mediation and arbitration. Are these alternatives better, or worse, than the litigation process as we know it? Should tort remedies be retained in addition to such other remedies?

B. GUEST PASSENGER STATUTES

PROBLEM

Paula Plaintiff is offered an automobile ride by Dana Defendant in a jurisdiction which has a guest passenger statute. Before Paula gets into the car, Dana tells her: "My tires are very worn, but I haven't had a chance to replace them." Paula nevertheless accepts the ride, and en route to their destination, while Dana is driving at a high rate of speed, one of the tires blows out, causing an accident in which Paula is seriously injured.

May Paula recover against Dana for her injuries?

HENRY v. BAUDER
213 Kan. 751, 518 P.2d 362 (1974)

PRAGER, JUSTICE.

This case involves the constitutionality of the Kansas guest statute. . . . On October 16, 1971, the plaintiff-appellant, Terry A. Henry, a sixteen-year-old girl, was a guest passenger in an automobile operated by the defendant-appellee, Thomas W. Bauder. A collision occurred and plaintiff suffered severe personal injuries. The original action in district court involved an additional defendant who was the driver of the other vehicle. However, this appeal is only concerned with that portion of the petition which charged the defendant Bauder with ordinary negligence. The trial court dismissed that portion of the plaintiff's claim on the basis of the Kansas guest statute which reads as follows:

8-122b. Right of guest to collect damages from owner or operator. That no person who is transported by the owner or operator of a motor vehicle, as his guest, without payment for such transportation, shall have a cause of action for damages against such owner or operator for injury, death and damage, unless such injury, death or damage shall have resulted from the gross and wanton negligence of the operator of such motor vehicle.

The practical effect of the statute is to deny to nonpaying guests any remedy at all where the driver has failed to use reasonable care in the operation of his automobile. The driver is legally liable only where he has been guilty of some act constituting recklessness or wilful or wanton misconduct.

The plaintiff assails the constitutionality of the Kansas guest statute on two theories. First, plaintiff contends that the guest act deprives her as a guest passenger of a "remedy by due course of law" under Section 18 of the Bill of Rights of the Kansas Constitution. Second, she contends that the guest statute is violative of the "equal protection" provision of the Fourteenth Amendment to the United States Constitution in that the statute discriminates between "guests" and "paying passengers" in a manner which bears no rational relationship to the purposes of the legislation. The plaintiff's first theory of unconstitutionality has been raised in several previous Kansas cases and rejected by this court. . . .

The plaintiff's second contention that the guest statute denies to her equal protection of the law has not previously been raised in this state. . . . The equal protection clause of the Fourteenth Amendment to the United States Constitution finds its counterpart in Sections 1 and 2 of the Bill of Rights of the Kansas Constitution which declares in substance that "all men are possessed of equal and inalienable natural rights, among which are life, liberty and the pursuit of happiness," and that "all free governments . . . are instituted for the equal protection and benefit of the people." While these two provisions of our Bill of Rights declare a political truth, they are given much the same effect as the clauses of the Fourteenth Amendment relating to due process and equal protection of the law. . . .

The United States Supreme Court in *Reed v. Reed,* 404 U.S. 71, 30 L. Ed. 2d. 225, 92 S. Ct. 251 (1971), declared that the equal protection clause of the Fourteenth Amendment to the United States Constitution does not deny to the states the power to create distinct classifications of persons in different ways. The equal protection clause of that amendment does, however, deny to a state the power to legislate that different treatment be accorded to persons placed by a statute into different classes on the basis of criteria wholly unrelated to the objective of that statute. A classification "must be reasonable, not arbitrary, and must rest upon some ground of difference having a fair and substantial relation to the object of the legislation, so that all persons similarly circumstanced shall be treated alike."

The problem presented in this case is essentially to determine the reasonableness of the classifications provided under the Kansas guest statute. In short, is the statutory classification between "non-paying guest" and "paying passenger" reasonable or is it arbitrary and unreasonable? In February of 1973 the Supreme Court of California, in *Brown v. Merlo,* 8 Cal. 3d 855, 106 Cal. Rptr. 388, 506 P.2d 212 (1973), considered the California guest statute and held it unconstitutional. . . . In *Brown* the court considered and applied the basic principles governing equal protection of the law which are set forth above. The California Supreme Court held the guest statute of that state unconstitutional for the reason that the statute withdrew from automobile "guests" *i.e.,* passengers who give no compensation for their ride, the protection against negligently inflicted injury which California law generally affords to all others. We are impressed with the sound rationale of the opinion in *Brown.* . . .

We hold that the Kansas guest statute, K.S.A. 8-122b, is unconstitutional and void as a denial of equal protection of the law under the Fourteenth Amendment to the United States Constitution and Sections 1 and 2 of the Kansas Bill of Rights. In reaching this conclusion we do *not* do so on the basis of the wisdom of the statute but solely on the basis that the classifications provided in the statute as interpreted by our judicial decisions are arbitrary and discriminatory and have no rational basis. . . .

A review of the decisions of this court reveals a crazy-quilt pattern of application of the guest act which permits recovery in many factual situations and denies recovery in others. Some of these decisions clearly show the inequities of the statute and the resulting denial of equal justice to persons similarly situated. In order for the act to apply the guest must be transported in a *motor vehicle.* In *Hayden's Estate,* 174 Kan. 140, 254 P.2d 813 (1953), we held that an airplane is not a motor vehicle within the meaning of the guest statute and therefore a nonpaying passenger could recover for the ordinary negligence of the pilot. In that case we declared that the guest statute applied only "to persons who are transported by owners or operators of motor vehicles, on the highways of the state." In applying the statute we held that the term "motor vehicle" as used in the statute should conform to the definition of a motor vehicle contained in the motor vehicle code which defined a vehicle as every device where or upon which a person may be drawn on a public highway. Although not directly involved in that case the rationale of the decision would reasonably imply that the guest statute does not apply where an automobile injury occurs in a private driveway or parking lot not located on the public highway. Ordinarily statutes relating specifically and solely to the operation of vehicles on public highways do not pertain to the operation of vehicles on private property. Under this rationale the guest statute would not, of course, be applicable to a nonpaying guest injured while riding in a motor boat since the injury did not occur on a public highway.

We have held that in order for the guest statute to be applicable the injury to the guest must occur *during the course of the transportation.* Where a nonpaying guest was in the process of entering the automobile and was injured when the driver suddenly drove forward, the injured guest was deemed not to be one who was being transported within the meaning of the guest statute and therefore could recover for the driver's ordinary negligence. A different rule was applied, however, where the ride had been completed and the injured guest, having departed from the vehicle, was in the process of closing the door of the automobile when it suddenly moved forward. In that situation the guest statute was held to apply and the injured guest could recover only on proof of wanton misconduct. Why should an entering guest be treated differently under the law than a departing guest?

On the question of what constitutes payment sufficient for the guest statute to apply, the result has been to permit recovery in some cases and to deny recovery in others. In *Carruth v. Cunningham,* 207 Kan. 781, 486 P.2d 1401 (1971), we held that whether a person is a "guest" within the meaning of the guest statute depends upon the facts and circumstances of the particular case. In determining that question among the many elements to be considered are the identity and relationship of the parties; the circumstances of the transportation; the nature, type and amount of payment; the benefits or advantages resulting to the respective parties growing out of the transportation; whether the payment, of whatever nature, constituted a tangible benefit to the operator and was the motivating influence for furnishing the transportation; and the nature and purpose of the trip. Sometimes a payment of money will take the passenger out of the operation of the guest statute and sometimes it will not. Even if payment is made, if the trip is for social benefits and pleasures, the guest statute applies and the guest is barred from recovery. A person who pays a driver $2 per week as a fellow employee for transportation from his home to work under a prearranged agreement is not a "guest" and may recover for the ordinary negligence of the driver. Where the purpose of a ride is not purely social, any substantial benefit to the driver is sufficient to take the case out of the operation of the guest statute even if no actual payment in money is made to the driver. In *In re Estate of Dikeman,* 178 Kan. 188, 284 P.2d 622 (1955), the driver and his passenger were delegates to attend the national meeting of a fraternal organization. The passenger orally *agreed* she would pay the driver a reasonable sum for the transportation. We held that in spite of the agreed payment of compensation the guest statute was applicable and the paying passenger could not recover for the negligence of the driver. From these decisions it is obvious that under different factual situations even paying passengers are afforded different treatment under the law where they sue the driver to recover for personal injuries.

The guest statute by its terms has no application where the driver of an automobile gratuitously transports the personal property of another and the owner of the property is not riding in the vehicle at the time the collision occurs. In that situation there is no *person* being transported by the owner and the guest statute would not be applicable. The result is that property rights are protected while personal rights are denied protection. . . .

The overwhelming majority of the automobile drivers in Kansas today have liability insurance. Furthermore the modern trend is to make mandatory insurance coverage for all owners of motor vehicles. . . . Hence, it is clear to us that the "hospitality" argument, first advanced in 1930, has no validity under the facts of life as they exist today. We further are impressed by the conclusion in *Brown* that the guest statute's purpose of fostering hospitality cannot rationally justify the lowering of protection for certain types of automobile passengers. . . .

We further hold that the "collusion prevention" justification does not provide a sufficient basis for the statute's wholesale elimination of all automobile guests' causes of action for negligently inflicted injuries. The theory behind the "collusion" argument appears to be that the driver who gives a free ride to a passenger does so because of a close relationship with his guest; because of the presumed closeness of this relationship, the driver may falsely admit liability so that his guest may collect from the driver's insurance company. To combat this risk of potential fraud, the guest statute eliminates all causes of action in negligence for automobile guests. We believe that it is unreasonable to eliminate causes of action of an entire class of persons simply because some undefined portion of the designated class may file fraudulent lawsuits. As stated in *Emery v. Emery,* 45 Cal. 2d 421, 289 P.2d 218 (1955), "Courts must depend upon the efficiency of the judicial processes to ferret out the meritorious from the fraudulent in particular cases." In *Brown* the Supreme Court of California effectively refuted the "collusion" argument by pointing out that under the terms of the guest statute the rider and driver can escape the statute's bar and thwart the "anti-collusion" purpose simply by colluding on the issue of whether the rider provided any compensation or payment for the ride. By broadly prohibiting all automobile guests from instituting causes of action for negligence because a small segment of that class may file collusive suits, the guest statute creates an overinclusive classification scheme. It results in throwing out the baby simply because the bath water gets dirty once in awhile. The statutory scheme clearly imposes a burden upon a wider range of individuals than are included in the class of those tainted with the mischief at which the law aims. We believe that in barring suits for all automobile guests simply to protect insurance companies from some collusive lawsuits, the guest statute exceeds the bounds of rationality and constitutes a denial of equal protection of the law. . . .

NOTES

1. *Challenging Classifications.* In *Henry v. Bauder,* the court appears to find the guest passenger statute unconstitutional in part because of irrational classifications made in decisions construing the statute. Is the problem then with the statute, or with the decisions? Could the decisions be made rationally consistent, given the underlying statute? Is there a rational basis for a legislature concluding that guest passenger statutes deter ingratitude and collusion?

2. *The Decline of Guest Statutes.* More than a dozen states have held the automobile guest passenger statutes unconstitutional and others have repealed their statutes. *See* PROSSER AND KEETON ON TORTS 217 (5th ed. 1988 Supp.). Why do you suppose guest passenger statutes have fared so poorly? Does their treatment indicate general judicial antipathy towards "tort reform" legislation? Should courts exercise greater restraint in overturning these statutes on constitutional grounds? *See* GUIDO CALABRESI, A COMMON LAW FOR THE AGE OF STATUTES (1982).

3. *A Lingering Presence.* In *Corey v. Jones,* 650 F.2d 803 (5th Cir. 1981), the court refused to overturn Georgia's guest passenger statute on equal protection grounds. The statute precluded recovery by nonpaying guest passengers for personal injuries sustained as a result of the ordinary negligence of the owner or operator. The defendant driver had been drinking on the night of the accident, "but the evidence did not establish that he was legally intoxicated." He was driving fast, "perhaps as fast as 60 miles per hour." He lost control and the car overturned, throwing the passenger from the vehicle and killing him. Plaintiff, the passenger's wrongful death beneficiary, was denied recovery because of the guest passenger statute.

The court recognized that Connecticut's guest passenger statute had been upheld against a similar challenge in *Silver v. Silver,* 280 U.S. 117 (1929), stating: "Although the analysis in *Silver* is antiquated and the decision has been subject to criticism by state courts and members of the Supreme Court, it is still the law." Moreover, the court noted that more recently the U.S. Supreme Court had refused review of three state cases involving challenges to guest passenger statutes, on the grounds that the cases lacked substantial federal questions.

4. *Other Classification Schemes.* When the California Supreme Court struck down the state's guest passenger statute in *Brown v. Merlo,* 8 Cal. 3d 855, 106 Cal. Rptr. 388, 506 P.2d 212 (1973), one of the reasons given by the court was that in assessing the tort liability of land occupiers, it had eliminated status-based distinctions between types of guests. *See Rowland v. Christian,* 69 Cal. 2d 108, 70 Cal. Rptr. 97, 443 P.2d 561 (1968). Would the *Brown* court have reached a different result if the state had continued to distinguish land occupiers' liability based on the status of land entrants as invitees, licensees, and trespassers?

5. *Statutory Preemption.* State statutes may be direct and unambiguous in granting tort rights or immunities. However, many state and federal statutes exhibit a more indirect or tangential effect. A statute can expressly preempt or restrict a common law remedy. For example, the Tennessee products liability statute, TENN. CODE ANNOT. § 29-28-104(1980), provides that product compliance with a statutory or administrative regulation creates a presumption of nondefectiveness. A statute may also impliedly preempt, in whole or in part, a common law remedy where it can be said that the legislation occupies the field, or where the common law remedy is determined by the court to conflict significantly with the legislative purpose. *See* Ausness, *Cigarette Company Liability: Preemption, Public Policy and Alternative Compensation Systems,* 39 SYRACUSE L. REV. 897, 915–22 (1988).

Traditionally courts have recognized a presumption against implied preemption. In the case of federal legislation, this presumption is attributable in part to concerns of federalism and intrusion into the states' domain. In addition, it is widely recognized that regulatory legislation is frequently the result of political compromise. Thus, the common law standard usually imposes a higher threshold of care and safety that ought not lightly be ignored.

There has been a recent upsurge of litigation concerning implied statutory preemption, particularly in regard to federal regulation. The Supreme Court in *Cippollone v. Ligett Group, Inc.* 505 U.S. 504 (1992) (pre-emption of smokers' liability claims by Cigarette Labeling and Advertising Act) breathed new opportunities to raise challenges particularly for manufacturers challenging common-law damages claims in a context where federal regulatory standards have been met. The federal courts have found implied preemption in some cases, such as litigation dealing with airbags as well as cigarette-warnings. In other contexts, such as in litigation dealing with the FDA and other statutory regulation of product warnings, the courts generally have not recognized implied preemption. *See generally* Ausness, *Federal Preemption of State Products Liability Doctrines*, S.C. L. Rev. 187 (1993); Kahn, *Regulation and Simple Arithmetic: Shifting the Perspective on Tort Reform*, 72 N.C.L. Rev. 1129 (1994); Atwell, Products Liability and Preemption: A Judicial Framework, 39 Buff. L. Rev. 181(1990); Nader & Page, *Automobile-Design Liability and Compliance with Federal Standards*, 64 Geo. L.Wash. Rev. 414 (1996).

C. THE IMPETUS FOR REFORM

In October of 1985, the Attorney General of the United States established the "Tort Policy Working Group," an inter-agency working group consisting of representatives of ten agencies and the White House. One of the primary tasks of the group "was to examine the rapidly expanding crisis in liability insurance availability and affordability."

In its February, 1986 report, the Working Group concluded that a crisis in liability insurance availability and affordability did exist. It attributed the crisis in part to large underwriting losses for 1984 and 1985, and sharp increases in liability premiums. It observed that these losses "appear to be largely a result of coverage written in the late 1970s and early 1980s which may have been underpriced due to the industry's desire to obtain premium income to invest at the then prevailing high interest rates." Nevertheless, it concluded that "developments in tort law are a major cause for the sharp premium increases."

The Working Group identified four specific problem areas: 1) the "movement toward no-fault liability;" 2) the "undermining of causation;" 3) the "explosive growth" in damage awards, "particularly with regard to non-economic awards such as pain and suffering or punitive damages;" and 4) "excessive transaction costs of the tort system" where "virtually two-thirds of every dollar paid out through the tort system is lost to attorneys' fees and litigation expenses."

The Working Group found that there was a large increase in litigation, particularly for products liability and legal malpractice, during the decade preceding 1985. It also found that "the tremendous uncertainty . . . generated by rapidly changing standards of liability and causation" was an important factor in contributing to the lack of availability and affordability of liability insurance.

The Working Group recommended "eight reforms to tort law that should significantly alleviate the crisis in insurance availability and affordability." They recommended:

-Return to a fault-based standard for liability.

-Base causation findings on credible scientific and medical evidence and opinions.

-Eliminate joint and several liability where defendants have not acted in concert.

-Limit non-economic damages (such as pain and suffering, mental anguish, or punitive damages) to a fair and reasonable maximum dollar amount.

-Provide for periodic (not lump-sum) payments for future medical care or lost income.

-Reduce awards where a plaintiff can be compensated by certain collateral sources to prevent a windfall double recovery.

-Limit attorneys' contingency fees to reasonable amounts on a "sliding scale."

-Encourage use of alternative dispute resolution mechanisms to resolve cases out of court.

None of these reforms has been enacted at the federal level. However, many have been enacted by states in response to a perceived crisis in the availability and affordability of liability insurance. *See* Martha Middleton, *A Changing Landscape*, A.B.A.J. 56 (Aug. 1995).

In March of 1987 the Tort Policy Working Group issued an "Update" on its 1986 report. The Group found that "availability problems have substantially ameliorated since a year ago," but continued to exist "in certain lines of coverage, where they remain serious."

The Working Group took issue with the methodology of a study by the National Center for State Courts, which had disputed their position and "concluded that there had been only a nine percent increase in tort filings between 1978 and 1984, and that this increase roughly mirrored population growth (eight percent) during the same period." The Working Group faulted this study among other reasons because it was based on data from only thirteen states, because it aggregated all tort filings, and because it failed "to account for the significant decrease in automobile accident lawsuits which has taken place in recent years."

In 1988 the United States General Accounting Office (GAO) issued a report stating:

> A variety of considerations enters into insurers' decisions as to whether to offer insurance and, if so, at what rates. One of the factors cited by insurers for the rapid escalation in liability rates and the

withdrawal of some types of insurance during the mid-1980's was a "litigation explosion" as evidenced by the increase in products liability cases filed in federal courts. . . . We found, however, that a significant part of the growth is concerned with one product, asbestos, and that the growth related to products in general appears to be neither rapidly accelerating nor explosive.

Similarly, one pair of commentators observed:

> Total claims . . . increased dramatically during the period from 1975 through 1986. These increased costs, however, were not significantly attributable to an increased number of claims against insured parties during that period. When the number of claims against insureds is adjusted for changes in the risk assumed by insurers because of variations in both the number of insureds and the level of the insureds' activities, the number of incurred claims in Other Liability insurance coverages actually declined during the period from 1975 through 1984.

Nye & Gifford, *The Myth of the Liability Insurance Claims Explosion: An Empricial Rebuttal,* 41 VAND. L. REV. 909, 922 (1988).

In response to a request from the chairman of the Subcommittee on Commerce, Consumer Protection, and Competitiveness of the United States House of Representatives, the GAO in 1989 issued a report on a study of products liability verdicts and case resolutions in five states for the period 1983-1985, GAO/HRD-89-99. The states selected for this purpose, Arizona, Massachusetts, Missouri, North Dakota, and South Carolina, were chosen based on the amount of information available for products liability litigation, and the relative costs associated with obtaining the information. Although no large industrial states were included, the report said that the states represented "a mix in terms of region of the country, degrees of urbanization, numbers of manufacturers and manufacturing employees, and tort laws."

The GAO found that "in general damage awards were not erratic or excessive," and that the size of compensatory awards "is strongly associated with injury severity and the amount of the underlying economic loss." Previous studies had shown that "the total amount awarded is frequently insufficient to cover just the economic losses when these losses are large." Some states enacted "caps" on recoverable punitive damages, "but few punitive awards in the cases GAO studied would have exceeded these caps had they been applicable." Appeals and posttrial settlement negotiations "serve to reduce the size of most extremely large awards and eliminate many of the unjustified punitive awards." Defendant's negligence "was a basis for liability in about two-thirds of verdicts for plaintiffs, a higher rate than had been assumed previously."

The Report found that proposed federal products liability statutes would enhance uniformity across states, but "would have affected only a minority of cases studied." Two proposals, the adoption of comparative fault and the allowance of a credit against judgment for amounts "previously paid or to be paid by workers' compensation" in connection with an injury, "would have potentially affected more awards than other reforms." The Report made "no recommendations" for change.

Based on a study of federal court civil filings from 1978 to 1984, Professor Galanter concluded that while overall civil filings increased by 89% during that period, tort filings increased by only 42%. Taking the period from 1960 to 1986, owing to increases in other categories "tort filings fell to 16.5% of total civil filings — less than half the portion in 1960." Areas of substantial increase were recovery cases brought by the federal government (mainly for overpayment of veterans' benefits and for defaulted student loans), civil rights claims, prisoner petitions, and social security cases. He noted, however, that only a "small fraction of all litigation in the United States takes place in the federal courts," and "patterns in the federal courts are sufficiently distinctive to limit our ability to draw from trends in federal courts conclusions about patterns of litigation elsewhere." Marc Galanter, *The Life and Times of the Big Six,* 1988 WIS. L. REV. 921.

A 1987 study by the Rand Corporation estimated that tort filings rose nationwide by "about 3.9 percent each year between 1981 and 1984. When adjusted for population growth, the rate is 3%. The National Center for State Courts estimated the annual growth of tort filings during that period at an even lower 2.3 percent." In examining a variety of tort cases in San Francisco, California and Cook County, Illinois, between 1970 and 1984, the Rand study found that "the median tort awards — the midpoint of distribution — has remained relatively stable." A.B.A.J. 38 (1 Oct. 1988).

These kinds of statistics fueled the controversy as to whether there was a torts crisis during the mid-eighties. Reske, *Was There a Liability Crisis?,* A.B.A.J., Jan. 1989, at 46, 50, reported that:

> [l]awsuits filed by 19 states in state courts and in federal court in California are forcing a re-examination of the "liability crisis" and the accusing finger is pointed directly at the insurance industry, which has been in the vanguard of the tort reform movement. The antitrust suits charge that four major insurance companies and some 28 other defendants illegally conspired to limit the availability of commercial general liability insurance, including pollution coverage, and to cut their share of other costs, such as legal expenses to defend against claims.
>
> . . . The insurance industry has two sources of income: it makes money from selling policies and from investments. When interest rates are high, as they were in the late 1970s and early 1980s, the insurance industry reaps the benefits. Prices were cut as companies competed to sell more policies to generate more money to invest.
>
> The *Wall Street Journal,* quoting the General Accounting Office, said that in 1983 industry profits on general-liability insurance dropped to $118 million from $847 million in 1979. To make up for the low profits, insurance rates began to rise. . . .

See also Nicolas P. Terry, *The Malpractice Crisis in the United States: A Dispatch from the Trenches,* 2 PROF. NEGLIGENCE 145, 148 (1986):

> During the late 1970s interest rates were high. Therefore, the insurance industry was able to record very high investment returns on its premiums prior to paying out any claims. High profits generated

increased interest in writing policies by insurers to acquire investment income, and hence increased competition between insurers. As has been noted: "These underwriting losses appear to be largely a result of coverage written in the late 1970s and early 1980s which may have been underpriced due to the industry's desire to obtain premium income to invest at the then prevailing high interest rates." As the market went "soft," so panic-stricken insurers either pulled out of markets or looked for areas where they could recoup their previous discounts quickly. The result — insurers increased medical malpractice premiums and orchestrated a "crisis" scenario designed to focus the public's, the health industry's and the legislatures' anger upon the lawyers.

An article by Donald C. Dilworth, in TRIAL 19 (May 1996), summarizes the 1994 findings of the National Center for State Courts concerning litigation increases and excessive verdicts in its report, *Examining the Work of State Courts*:

Between 1984 and 1994, civil caseloads rose only 24 percent, while criminal caseloads rose 35 percent, juvenile caseloads 59 percent, and domestic relations caseloads 65 percent.

Most tort cases filed in state courts are automobile cases (60 percent) or premises cases (17 percent). Medical negligence and products liability cases together account for less than 10 percent of tort claims.

Only 3 percent of tort cases are resolved by jury trial. At those trials, plaintiffs in 1994 won 49 percent of the time.

The median award to plaintiffs who won at jury trials was $51,000.

Million-dollar awards, cited frequently as an indicator that the tort system is "out of control," were awarded in only 8 percent of jury trials won by plaintiffs (one-tenth of 1 percent of tort cases).

Juries awarded punitive damages in only 4 percent of tort cases in which the defendant was found liable. The median punitive damages award was $38,000.

Dilworth concludes: "Although torts are currently center stage in the civil litigation debate, there is no evidence that the number of tort cases is increasing. In fact, litigation declined steadily since 1990."

Given the controversy as to what caused the shortage and high cost of insurance in the eighties and conflicting views about increases in filings and awards, is tort reform justified? How should courts respond to the legislative efforts to meet a perceived crisis in light of these uncertainties? Are there constitutional constraints on what the legislatures can do in response to these perceived crises? Some commentators have suggested that more research is needed to understand the litigation process in order to properly address the sources of the problems.

D. LIMITATIONS ON RECOVERY

SOFIE v. FIBREBOARD CORP.
112 Wash. 2d 636, 771 P.2d 711 (1989)

UTTER, JUSTICE.

Austin and Marcia Sofie challenge the constitutionality of RCW 4.56.250. This statute, part of the 1986 tort reform act, places a limit on the noneconomic damages recoverable by a personal injury or wrongful death plaintiff. The Sofies brought a direct appeal to this court after the trial judge in their tort action, under the direction of the statute, reduced the jury's award of noneconomic damages. . . .

The Sofies argue that RCW 4.56.250 violates their constitutional rights to trial by jury, equal protection, and due process. We find that the statute's damages limit interferes with the jury's traditional function to determine damages. Therefore, RCW 4.56.250 violates article 1, section 21 of the Washington Constitution, which protects as inviolate the right to a jury. . . .

The Washington Legislature passed RCW 4.56.250 in 1986 partly as a response to rising insurance premiums for liability coverage. The damages limit that the statute creates operates on a formula based upon the age of the plaintiff.[1]

---

[1] RCW 4.56.250 states:

"(1) As used in this section, the following terms have the meanings indicated unless the context clearly requires otherwise.

"(a) 'Economic damages' means objectively verifiable monetary losses, including medical expenses, loss of earnings, burial costs, loss of use of property, cost of replacement or repair, cost of obtaining substitute domestic services, loss of employment, and loss of business or employment opportunities.

"(b) 'Noneconomic damages' means subjective, nonmonetary losses, including, but not limited to pain, suffering, inconvenience, mental anguish, disability or disfigurement incurred by the injured party, emotional distress, loss of society and companionship, loss of consortium, injury to reputation and humiliation, and destruction of the parent-child relationship.

"(c) 'Bodily injury' means physical injury, sickness, or disease, including death.

"(d) 'Average annual wage' means the average annual wage in the state of Washington as determined under RCW 50.04.355.

"(2) In no action seeking damages for personal injury or death may a claimant recover a judgment for noneconomic damages exceeding an amount determined by multiplying 0.43 by the average annual wage and by the life expectancy of the person incurring noneconomic damages, as the life expectancy is determined by the life expectancy tables adopted by the insurance commissioner. For purposes of determining the maximum amount allowable for noneconomic damages, a claimant's life expectancy shall not be less than fifteen years. The limitation contained in this subsection applies to all claims for noneconomic damages made by a claimant who incurred bodily injury. Claims for loss of consortium, loss of society and companionship, destruction of the parent-child relationship, and all other derivative claims asserted by persons who did not sustain bodily injury are to be included within the limitation on claims for noneconomic damages arising from the same bodily injury.

"(3) If a case is tried to a jury, the jury shall not be informed of the limitation contained in subsection (2) of this section."

As a result, the older a plaintiff is, the less he or she will be able to recover in noneconomic damages. The trial judge applies the limit to the damages found by the trier of fact. If the case is tried before a jury, the jury determines the amount of noneconomic damages without knowledge of the limit. The jury goes about its normal business and the judge reduces, according to the statute's formula and without notifying the jury, any damage verdicts that exceed the limit.

In September 1987, the Sofies sued Fibreboard Corporation and other asbestos manufacturers for the harm caused to Mr. Sofie by their asbestos products. Mr. Sofie, then aged 67, was suffering from a form of lung cancer — mesothelioma — caused by exposure to asbestos during his career as a pipefitter. At trial, Mr. Sofie's attorneys presented evidence of the extreme pain he experienced as a result of the disease. The testimony indicated that Mr. Sofie spent what remained of his life waiting for the next "morphine cocktail," for the next hot bath, for anything that would lessen his consuming physical agony.

At the end of the trial, the jury found the defendants at fault for Mr. Sofie's disease. They returned a verdict of $1,345,833 in favor of the Sofies. Of this amount, $1,154,592 went to compensate noneconomic damages: $477,200 for Mr. Sofie's pain and suffering and $677,392 for Mrs. Sofie's loss of consortium. While the trial judge specifically found the jury's finding of damages reasonable, he indicated he was compelled under the damages limit to reduce the noneconomic portion of the verdict to $125,136.45, resulting in a total judgment of $316,377.45.

Appellants argue that RCW 4.56.250 violates their right to equal protection under the law as guaranteed by Washington Constitution article 1, section 12. This constitutional provision states:

> No law shall be passed granting to any citizen, class of citizens, or corporation other than municipal, privileges or immunities which upon the same terms shall not equally belong to all citizens, or corporations.

[The court notes that varying levels of scrutiny have been applied by different courts to laws under such a constitutional provision.]

Courts in some other states have struck down similar tort damage limits on equal protection grounds. *See, e.g., Carson v. Maurer,* 120 N.H. 925, 424 A.2d 825, 830 (1980) (striking limit on noneconomic damages after finding right to recover for personal injuries an "important substantive right"); *Arneson v. Olson,* 270 N.W.2d 125, 132 (N.D. 1978) (applying heightened scrutiny to flat damages limit). Other courts, however, have upheld limits, analyzing the legislation under the rational basis test. *See, e.g., Fein v. Permanente Medical Group,* 38 Cal. 3d 137, 211 Cal. Rptr. 368, 695 P.2d 665 (1985), *appeal dismissed,* 474 U.S. 892, 88 L. Ed. 2d 215, 106 S. Ct. 214 (1985); *see also Boyd v. Bulala,* 647 F. Supp. 781 (W.D. Va. 1986) (finding that damages limit passes the rational basis test under equal protection analysis but violates the right to a jury trial). . . .

The dispositive issue of this case is the right to a jury trial.

This court has long approached the review of legislative enactments with great care. The wisdom of legislation is not justiciable; our only power is to determine the legislation's constitutional validity. In matters of economic legislation, we follow the rule giving every reasonable presumption in favor of the constitutionality of the law or ordinance. We employ this caution to avoid substituting our judgment for the judgment of the Legislature. . . .

[Concluding that the Federal Constitution's seventh amendment guarantees do not apply to state civil trials under the fourteenth amendment, the Court looked to the state constitution].

Article 1, section 21 states:

> The right of trial by jury shall remain inviolate, but the legislature may provide for a jury of any number less than twelve in courts not of record, and for a verdict by nine or more jurors in civil cases in any court of record, and for waiving of the jury in civil cases where the consent of the parties interested is given thereto.

Our basic rule in interpreting article 1, section 21 is to look to the right as it existed at the time of the constitution's adoption in 1889. . . .

State ex rel. Mullen v. Doherty, 16 Wash. 382, 47 P. 958 (1897), being close in time to 1889, provides some contemporary insight. . . . In *Mullen,* we cited section 248 of the Code of 1881, in force at the time of the constitution's passage, to determine the jury's role in the constitutional scheme: "Either party shall have the right in an action at law, upon an issue of fact, to demand a trial by jury." *Mullen,* 16 Wash. at 385. Subsequent cases underscore the jury's fact finding province as the essence of the right's scope.

At issue in the present case is whether the measure of damages is a question of fact within the jury's province. Our past decisions show that it is indeed. . . .

The jury's role in determining noneconomic damages is perhaps even more essential. In *Bingaman v. Grays Harbor Community Hosp.,* 103 Wash. 2d 831, 835, 699 P.2d 1230 (1985), the husband of a woman who died painfully 35 hours after giving birth, the result of medical malpractice, brought a wrongful death and survival action. The only issue before this court was whether the trial judge had properly reduced the jury's damage verdict of $412,000 for the woman's pain and suffering. In resolving the issue in the plaintiff's favor, we stated: "The determination of the amount of damages, *particularly in actions of this nature,* is primarily and peculiarly within the province of the jury, under proper instructions . . . ." (Italics ours.) . . . .

. . . The weight of authority from other states, both numerically and persuasively, supports the conclusion that Washington's damages limit violates the right to trial by jury.

NOTES

1. *Damage Caps.* The tort reform movement of the 1970s and 1980s produced legislation designed to reduce the amount of recovery by the injured victim. One common type of legislation places an upper limit, or "cap," on the amount of damages which a personal injury plaintiff may recover. The cap

frequently is applied only to non-economic damages, *i.e.,* damages other than medical expenses and loss of earnings. *See, e.g.,* ALASKA STAT. § 09.17.010 (Supp. 1989)($500,000 cap); COLO. REV. STAT. 13-21-102.5 (Supp. 1990) ($250–$500 million); N.H. REV. STAT. ANN. § 508:4-d (1983 & Supp. 1989) ($875 million). A perceived medical malpractice "crisis" in the seventies led to legislation limiting damages recoverable in a medical malpractice action. *See, e.g.,* CAL. CIV. CODE § 3333.2 (1990). The cases continue to divide on whether damage caps are constitutional. *Compare English v. New England Med. Ctr., Inc.,* 405 Mass. 423, 541 N.E. 2d 329 (1989) (statutory cap on tort liability of charitable institutions held constitutional), *with Condemarin v. University Hosp.,* 775 P. 2d 348 (Utah 1989) ($100,000 cap on damages against state-owned health care facilities held unconstitutional). *See also* Linda Babcock & Greg Pogarsky, *Damage Caps and Settlement: a Behavioral Approach,* 28 J. Leg. St. 341 (1999)(caps affect settlement propensity).

2. *Structured Payments.* Another device designed to reduce overall tort recovery is the "structured judgment," in which the victim receives periodic payment of future accruing installments of loss of earnings and medical expenses. The installments terminate when the victim dies. Thus if the victim does not live through his projected life span, the tortfeasor's liability is reduced to the victim's actual pecuniary damages. *See, e.g., American Bank & Trust Co. v. Community Hosp. of Los Gatos-Saratoga,* 683 P.2d 670 (Cal. 1984). The structured judgment is an outgrowth of the structured settlement, in which the parties agree that the victim will receive stipulated sums periodically for a fixed period of time, usually the victim's lifetime. The structured settlement provides the victim with financial security throughout his lifetime, while effecting a saving to the tortfeasor, and is a useful settlement negotiation tool. A court cannot issue a structured judgment without agreement of the parties or statutory authorization. *Gretchen v. United States,* 618 F 2d 177 (2d Cir. 1980). Some states require or permit "structured judgments" in medical malpractice cases and in suits against public entities. *See, e.g.,* CAL. CIV. PROC. CODE § 667.7 (1980); LA. REV. STAT. 40:1299.42 (1989). *See generally* Elligett, *Periodic Payment of Judgments,* 46 INS. COUN. J. 130 (1979); Corboy, *Structured Injustice; Compulsory Periodic Payment of Judgments,* 66 A.B.A.J. 1524 (1980); Krouse, *Structured Settlements for Tort Victims,* 66 A.B.A.J. 1527 (1980).

The Ohio Supreme Court in *Galayda v. Lake Hosp. Sys.,* 644 N.E.2d 298 (Ohio 1994), held that state's medical negligence periodic-payment statute violated state constitutional rights of trial by jury and due process because the statute prohibited plaintiffs from receiving their whole jury award. The court further found insufficient evidence of any relation between the statute and the availability or affordability of medical negligence insurance.

A structured settlement or structured judgment is subject to uncertainties regarding the financial solvency of the long term payer. The beneficiary should assure, insofar as possible, that such payer is of blue chip quality.

3. *Punitive Damages.* Much of the tort reform effort has centered on punitive damages. Some states have imposed a cap on punitive damages. For example, Georgia provides a limit of $250,000, except in products liability claims. GA. CODE ANN. § 51-12-5.1 (1990). Virginia has a $350,000 limit. VA. CODE ANN.

§ 8.01-38.1 (1990). Kansas limits punitive damages to the lesser of the defendant's annual gross income, or $5 million, or one-and-one-half times the profit the defendant gained from the misconduct. KAN. STAT. ANN. § 60-3702 (1988). In order to recover punitive damages, some states require proof that conduct was "outrageous" or "evidenced reckless indifference" by "clear and convincing" evidence. *See, e.g.*, ALASKA STAT. § 9.17.020; KY. REV. STAT. ANN. § 411.184 (1989). Some states require payment of part of punitive damages into public funds, including the state's general fund. *See, e.g.*, COLO. REV. STAT. § 13-21-102 (1990). Such a requirement may violate the excessive fines clause of the Eighth Amendment to the U.S. Constitution. *See Browning-Ferris v. Kelco Disposal*, 109 S. Cr. 2909 (1989).

To date, attempts to restrict punitive damages at the federal level have been unsuccessful. The United States Supreme Court has upheld the award of punitive damages against constitutional attack. *See TXO Production Corp. v. Alliance Resources Corp.*, 113 S. Ct. 2711, (1993).

4. *The Collateral Source Rule.* The collateral source rule provides that the defendant receives no credit for sums received by the plaintiff from non-tortfeasor sources as a result of the defendant's tort. This rule has been attacked by proponents of reform as economically wasteful, permitting double recovery by the plaintiff. The counterargument is that the tortfeasor should not receive a windfall as a result of the plaintiff's thrift or others' largesse. Noting a division of authority, the court held in *Proctor v. Castelletti*, 911 P.2d 853 (Nev. 1996), that evidence of collateral sources was not admissible to prove plaintiff's alleged malingering. "The excessive prejudicial nature of the evidence mandates its exclusion," the court said.

As part of tort reform, TENN. CODE ANN. § 29-26-119 (1980) provides that medical malpractice claims shall be reduced by "insurance provided by an employer . . . by social security benefits, service benefits, programs, unemployment benefits, or any other source," except that no deduction shall be made for "the assets of the claimants or of the members of the claimants' immediate family and insurance purchased in whole or in part, privately and individually." Is such a retrenchment subject to challenge? Why?

In *Sorrell v. Thevenir*, 69 Ohio St. 3d 415 (1994), the court held the state's statutory elimination of the collateral source rule unconstitutional, reasoning it would not withstand scrutiny under either a strict scrutiny or a rational basis test. The court concluded there was no empirical evidence that an insurance crisis existed, or that the statute would affect any such crisis.

E. SUBSTANTIVE LAW REFORM

Responding to the torts "crises" of the seventies and the eighties, many states passed reform provisions to address perceived excessive recovery and frivolous suits in the products liability and medical malpractice areas. Undoubtedly strong efforts at general tort retrenchment will reemerge at the federal level following the 2000 presidential election.

[1] Products Liability

By the mid-nineties, more than half of the states had enacted legislation intended to retrench on products liability recoveries. The Tennessee Products

Liability Act of 1978, TENN. CODE ANN. §§ 29-28-101 to 29-28-108 (1990), is fairly typical of comprehensive legislative efforts. It restricts products claims to those resulting in personal injury from the manufacture, business sale or lease of unreasonably dangerous or unsafe products. It provides a statute of repose which bars claims filed more than six years from the date of injury or ten years after the product is first purchased for use or consumption, whichever first occurs. It provides a rebuttable presumption that a product is not unreasonably dangerous as to any aspect of the product that complies with any federal or state statute or administrative regulation existing at the time the product was manufactured. A product is not defective or unreasonably dangerous if it complies with the state of scientific and technical knowledge available to the manufacturer or seller when the product is placed on the market. In making the determination of defectiveness and unreasonable danger evidence of customary designs, methods, standards and techniques of manufacturing, inspecting and testing by other manufacturers or sellers of similar products is relevant. The legislation also provides that a non-manufacturing seller (*e.g.*, a retailer or wholesaler) cannot be held liable in strict tort unless the manufacturer of the product is not subject to service of process in the state or has been judicially declared insolvent.

Efforts to produce a comprehensive federal response have not been completely successful. After more than a decade of attempts to pass substantive reform of products liability law, Congress in 1994 passed the General Aviation Revitalization Act, 49 USC sec. 4101, providing a statue of repose of 18 years for small aircraft and parts. Legislation was also proposed which would restrict or limit strict liability, provide a state of the art defense, eliminate or restrict joint liability, place a cap on recoverable damages, limit or restrict the recovery of punitive damages, establish a statute of repose, eliminate or restrict the collateral source rule, and limit product supplier contribution claims against plaintiffs' employers. In 1996, both houses passed the Common Sense Products Liability Legislative Reform Act, but President Clinton vetoed the legislation. Although the coalition of business groups and other proponents of "reform" have continued to support change, there has not been agreement on how to proceed. See 64 TENN. L. REV. 559 (1997).

Commentators are skeptical about the desirability of such legislation. Proponents of federal products liability reform legislation argue that it will provide predictability and uniformity of law. Others doubt whether the proposed federal legislation would provide substantially greater predictability, and respond that uniformity would not be achieved because application of the proposed statute was left to the state courts. Moreover, some commentators assert that there is substantial virtue in retaining the experimental-laboratory concept of state-based tort systems. Professor Harvey Perlman sees a need to protect against what he calls the "spillover" effect, whereby the consumers of one state may be required to bear a significant part of the ultimate cost of products claims in other states. As proposed solutions to this problem, Professor Perlman suggests that the law of the place of product manufacture should be held to apply to all claims against the manufacturer, so that the consumer can choose products with the controlling state law in mind. Additionally, he opines that such legislation might "facilitate competition in the insurance industry" so as to provide an impetus for the calculation of products liability insurance premiums on a state-by-state, rather than a national, basis. He concludes that The Risk Retention Act of 1981, 15 U.S.C. § 3901, which permits "producers of goods to combine to self-insure, and thus create more competition in the insurance industry, may be at least a step in that direction." Harvey Perlman, *Products Liability Reform in Congress: An Issue of Federalism,* 48 OHIO ST. L.J. 503, 508–09 (1987).

It has also been argued that judicial reform of products liability principles has had significant impact in this area, affecting the number of cases filed, success rates and the size of verdicts. *See, e.g.,* Henderson & Eisenberg, *The Quiet Revolution in Products Liability: An Empirical Study of Legal Change,* 37 UCLA L. Rev. 731 (1992). In addition, in the products liability and medical malpractice area, there is evidence that judges are more aggressively scrutinizing the substantive merits of claims and exercising their gate-keeping power, resulting in dismissals, summary judgments, reversals and remittiturs. Notably, the Supreme Court has emphasized the gatekeeper's role in causation claims in *Daubert v. Merrell Dow Pharmaceuticals, Inc.,* 509 U.S.. 579 (1993) and in punitive claims in *Pacific Mutual Life Ins. Co. v. Haslip,* 499 U.S. 1 (1991). *See, e.g.,* Lucinda Finley, *Guarding the Gate to the Courthouse: How Trial Judges Are Using their Evidentiary Screening Role to Remake Tort Causation Rules,* 49 De Paul L. Rev. 323 (1999). Michael Risinger writes in 64 ALBANY L. REV. 99 (2000) that the effect of the *Daubert* gate-keeping function in the courts has been that defendants in civil cases win their *Daubert* challenges substantially more frequently than plaintiffs, and that the prosecution wins much more frequently than defendants in criminal cases.

[2] Medical Malpractice

Perceptions of malpractice crises in the seventies and again in the mid-eighties also led to legislative restrictions on tort recoveries in this field. The enactments often included statutes of repose, provisions insulating physicians who volunteer their services for example in school athletic events or low-cost medical clinics, and provisions requiring dismissal of the suit if an admissible expert opinion is not obtained soon after commencement of the suit.

As one writer has observed, these malpractice crises "have been first and foremost crises of insurance, and most of the impetus for tort reform comes from problems in the insurance markets." Bovbjerg, *Legislation on Medical Malpractice,* 22 U.C. DAVIS L. REV. 499, 504 (1989). Bovbjerg explores why these crises have occurred. He believes that cycles occur in insurance pricing and availability. The reasons why the cycles occur, however, are unclear. "Continuing rises in claims and payments are the underlying cause, but the dynamics of the insurance market seems to be the precipitating factor, and no consensus exists on how much each is to blame." *Id.* at 506.

> There is also no consensus on why claims and awards have risen. As Bovbjerg observes:
>
> Reasons commonly listed include an erosion in physician-patient relationships, higher patient expectations, more experts and numerous attorneys for malpractice plaintiffs, greater willingness of physicians to testify, a more compensation-oriented world view among

E. SUBSTANTIVE LAW REFORM

judges and juries, and changes in legal doctrine favorable to malpractice plaintiffs . . . .

Id. Bovbjerg also notes, *id.* at 508–09 n.37, that "[c]laims not brought may outnumber those brought by five to one — or even more — according to extrapolations from hospital chart reviews; larger cases seem more likely to be filed." One study indicates that the ratio of medical malpractice occurrences to claims filed may be as high as ten to one. PAUL C. WEILER ET AL., A MEASURE OF MALPRACTICE 62 (1993). Bovbjerg states, however, that there were considerable downturns in claims frequency after each of the crises, although "no one really understands why such large changes occur." *Supra* at 510–11. He opines that the "crisis-generated publicity about liability problems may subtly have altered the general attitudes of claims adjusters, judges, and jurors about liability cases and thus discouraged plaintiffs and their attorneys from bringing some claims." *Id.* at 551–52.

The state legislative changes enacted in response to the perceived malpractice crises of the mid-seventies and mid-eighties were extensive but the responses were different in the two decades. According to Bovbjerg:

> Casual empiricism suggests that more states enacted apparently strong reforms in the 1980s (caps, collateral source offsets, structured awards, changes in joint and several liability) while fewer new states enacted seemingly less consequential efforts (bars on dollar *ad damnums,* informed consent changes, statutes of frauds, *res ipsa loquitur* modifications). Arbitration and pretrial screening almost disappeared as reforms, perhaps reflecting concerns that they do not cut system costs.

In the case of caps on recoverable damages, there were two significant changes from the seventies to the eighties: a shift toward placing caps on noneconomic damages only (typically, damages for pain and suffering) as opposed to damages in general, and a shift toward generic tort caps as opposed to caps on medical malpractice recoveries only.

Bovbjerg concludes that these legislative enactments have been successful, "ensuring the availability of liability coverage but also lowering premiums, at least relative to what these would have been without reform . . . . Support for the effectiveness of reforms comes from opinion surveys, actuarial estimation, and claims evaluation." He also notes that California, "a leading crisis state in the 1970s and among the first to enact strong reforms, experienced no real crisis in the 1980s," while by contrast "New York and Florida had far less sweeping tort reforms and suffered during both decades in crises." *Id.* at 549–50. On the other hand, "It is uncertain how influential legislative reforms were compared to the emergence of provider-insurers and other private developments." By the early eighties, provider-owned insurers "had claimed half the market for physicians' coverage." *Id.* at 517. Crisis legislation, moreover, may be "bad legal strategy," since it may create a cry-wolf reaction. *Id.* at 553–54. It is "very unclear whether tort reform can generally be demonstrated to avert shortrun crisis. Conceptually, one would expect legal changes to change behavior over time, not suddenly, and other developments seem more plausibly related to the rapid shifts in insurance markets." *Id.* at 554.

Bovbjerg thus leaves open the question whether tort reform "works," until we define our goals. Is our goal to reduce claims, or to provide fuller compensation? He concludes that "Data on medical effectiveness remains rudimentary, and data on quality are even more so." *Id.* at 547 n.202. Society should decide "how best to resolve medical injuries, including whether they, like workplace injuries before them, should be separated from other personal injuries." *Id.* at 555. *See, e.g.*, Virginia's Birth-Related Injury Compensation Act, VA. CODE ANN. §§ 38.2-5000 to 38.2-5021 (Supp. 1988) (substituting a panel judgment for tort recovery and automatically compensating any newborn deemed to have incurred injury to the brain or spinal cord occurring in the course of labor or in the immediate post-delivery period.)

F. JOINT AND SEVERAL LIABILITY

During the mid-1980s about 35 states enacted legislation eliminating or restricting joint and several liability in various ways. *See* Wright, *Joint and Several Liability,* 21 U.C. DAVIS L. REV. 1141 (1988), and the colloquy between the professors in Wright & Twerski, *The Joint Tortfeasor Legislative Revolt: A Rational Response to the Critics,* 22 U.C. DAVIS L. REV. 1125 (1989). A major impetus for these enactments again was a perceived tort crisis, together with a feeling that it is "unfair" to hold a defendant liable for the fault of another. Comment *a* to REST. 3D APPORT. OF LIAB § 17 (2000) states that joint and several liability "has been substantially modified in most jurisdictions both as a result of the adoption of comparative fault and tort reform during the 1980s and 1990s."

Traditionally joint liability (holding a defendant liable for all the plaintiff's damages, even though another at-fault person may have contributed to the injury) was justified on the grounds that, as between an innocent plaintiff and a guilty defendant, the risk of non-recovery against another potential tortfeasor should rest with the guilty defendant (in an action for contribution or indemnity), rather than with the innocent plaintiff (in an original suit). With the widespread adoption of comparative fault, this justification disappears in those situations in which the plaintiff also is at fault. But what if the plaintiff is innocent in a comparative fault jurisdiction?

Joint liability is generally retained in vicarious liability, and in those situations where defendants act in concert.

NOTES

1. *The Marginally Responsible Defendant.* One concern about joint and several liability is with the defendant who is only slightly at fault, but who nevertheless may be responsible for all of the damages. Consider for example *Gehres v. Phoenix,* 156 Ariz. 484, 753 P.2d 174 (1987). There the defendant tavern served an allegedly intoxicated patron, who later killed plaintiff's deceased in a car collision while seeking to elude police officers during a high-speed car chase. The jury found the drunk driver 95% at fault, the tavern 3%, and the city 2%. The drunk driver was killed in the crash, and his estate was insolvent. The court held that either the tavern, or the city, could be made to pay the entire damages for the wrongful death of plaintiff's deceased. After

this suit, the Arizona legislature abolished joint liability in tort for concurrent tortfeasors. *See* 156 Ariz. at 487, 753 P.2d at 177.

Suppose in *Gehres* the "fault" lay with the tavern and bad weather conditions? Fault would not be attributed to the weather conditions. Is an inanimate "faulty" cause different from an insolvent, immune, or unidentifiable faulty human cause, for purposes of determining the degree of fault fairly attributable to the tavern? Suppose the only party at fault was the tavern; how much fault would then be attributable to the tavern?

How appropriate are the criticisms levelled at "marginal fault" cases? Is a determination that a concurrent tortfeasor is, say, 3% responsible a reflection on that defendant's degree of fault *vis-a-vis* the standard of care, or an assessment of the relative fault of all the actors?

2. *Joint and Several Liability: A Partial Reform?* MO. REV. STAT. § 538.230(2) (1989) provides for the following rule in actions against health care providers:

> The court shall determine the award of damages to each plaintiff in accordance with the findings . . . and enter judgment against each party liable on the basis of the rules of joint and several liability. However, notwithstanding the provisions of this subsection, any defendant against whom an award of damages is made shall be jointly liable only with those defendants whose apportioned percentage of fault is equal to or less than such defendant.

Assume that the jury allocated the relative fault of concurrent tortfeasors as follows: hospital — 30%, surgeon — 30%, anesthesiologist — 40%. What is the *joint* liability of each defendant? *See* Terry, *Missouri's Malpractice Concord,* 51 MO. L. REV. 457, 479–80 (1986). How would this statutory provision apply if one of the concurrent tortfeasors was *not* a health care provider but, for example, the manufacturer of a surgical instrument? *See* Terry, *Retreat and Reaction: An Analysis of the Tort Reform Act,* 56 U. MO.-K.C. L. REV. 205, 234 (1988).

3. *The Case for Reform.* Reform literature abounds: *see, e.g.*, Richard Abel, *The Real Torts Crisis — Too Few Claims,* 48 Ohio St. L.J. 443 (1987);Campbell, Kessler & Shepherd, *The Causes and Effects of Liability Reform: Some Empirical Evidence* (National Bureau of Economics Working Paper No 4989); Henderson & Eisenberg,*The Quiet Revolution in Products Liability,* 37 UCLA L. Rev. 479 (1990); Marc Galanter, *The Day After the Litigation Explosion,* 48 Md. L. Rev. 3 (1986); Samuel Gross & Kent Syverud, *Don't Try: Civil Jury Verdicts in a System Geared to Settlement,* 44 UCLA L. Rev. 1 (1996); Kelso, *One Lesson from the Six Monsanto Lectures on Tort Reform and Jurisprudence,: Recognizing the Limits of Judicial Competence,* 26 Val U. L. Rev. 765 (1992); Frank McClellan, *The Dark Side of Tort Reform: Searching for Racial Justice,* 48 Rut. L. Rev. 761 (1996); Deborah Jones Merritt & Kathryn Ann Barry, *Is the Tort System in Crisis? New Empirical Evidence,* 60 Ohio St. L.J. 315 (19999); George Priest, *The Current Insurance Crisis and Modern Tort Law,* 96 Yale L.J. 1521 (1987).

G. ALTERNATIVE DISPUTE MECHANISMS: TRIAL-RELATED DEVICES

[1] Introduction

From the simplest assault and battery, through the devastating, negligently performed medical procedure, to the complex toxic tort or products liability case, the relationship between torts and the classic litigation model seems at first blush to be unquestioned, almost paradigmatic. Indeed, the relationship between torts and traditional litigation techniques reaches beyond the paradigm to the cliche. Whether used critically or not, phrases such as "hired gun" and "battle of experts" pervade any discussion of tort law and process.

The familiar linkage between accident law and traditional adversarial process notwithstanding, any student of tort litigation soon will conclude that the classical litigation model is not without severe limitations. The student will readily perceive that entire classes of cases go unresolved because they are too "small" to attract contingent-fee-based representation. Large numbers of plaintiffs are effectively turned away from the courts because litigation, even if successful, fails to provide anything other than the rather clumsy remedy of monetary damages. Meritorious tort claims are being settled too cheaply because injured plaintiffs are faced with the delays inherent in traditional process. Moreover, the adversarial process seems particularly unsuited for some claims leading to skepticism about whether it is to accomplish justice. Indeed, challenges to traditional litigation techniques have struck at the heart of mainstream tort law. Does litigation continue to represent the most efficient solution for our most complex products liability and environmental actions? Should an unsuccessful medical result inevitably lead to the rupture of the physician-patient relationship in open court? Is the jury an effective decision making body?

Commentators have posed for consideration alternatives to the litigation process, drawing on the experiences in other contexts of dispute resolutions. For years, grievances under collective bargaining agreements have been handled by labor arbitrators. Arbitration of automobile insurance claims is widespread. Divorces and child-custody disputes have long been mediated. And, crucially, the overwhelming majority of tort disputes are negotiated to settlement, a fact which may be easily overlooked because of the traditional casebook focus upon decisions of the appellate courts.

In the torts area, alternative dispute resolution mechanisms are not limited to arbitration and negotiation. Forward-thinking judges have sought to refresh the traditional litigation process with innovative devices, legislatures have been particularly active in tailoring particular dispute resolution devices to discrete areas of tort law, and many individuals and organizations have adopted existing consensual arrangements or created new mechanisms. As a consequence, it has become more easy to challenge the assumptions often made about matters that lawyers handle: (1) that disputants are adversaries — *i.e.*, if one wins, the others must lose — and (2) that disputes may be resolved through application, by a third party, of some general rule of law. These assumptions, plainly, are polar opposites of those which may underlie modern dispute resolution processes: (1) that all parties can benefit through a creative solution to which each agrees; and (2) that the situation is unique and therefore not to be governed by any general principle except to the extent that the parties accept it. Leonard Riskin, *Mediation and Lawyers,* 43 OHIO ST. L.J. 29, 43–48 (1982). What should be the "philosophical map" that lawyers draw upon in modern dispute resolution? What risks and benefits are presented by a shift away from the classical litigation model? *See generally* Sandler, *Alternative Methods of Dispute Resolution: An Overview,* 37 U. Fla. L. Rev. 1 (1985). *But see* Trina Grillo, *The Mediation Alternative: Process Dangers for Women,* 100 Yale L.J. 1545 (1991). In the following section we highlight some of the dispute resolution alternatives that are presently employed.

[2] Summary Jury Trial

One of the alternative mechanisms utilized within the traditional litigation structure is the summary jury trial (SJT). A pre-trial procedure often used in cases where settlement seems unlikely and negotiations seem at an impasse, SJT can add appreciably to the settlement of trial-bound cases. If settlement is not achieved, the case can go on to trial. One judge describes the process as follows:

> . . . In a summary jury proceeding, attorneys present abbreviated arguments to jurors who render an informal verdict that guides the settlement of the case. Normally, six mock jurors are chosen after a brief voir dire conducted by the court. Following short opening statements, all evidence is presented in the form of a descriptive summary to the mock jury through the parties' attorneys. Live witnesses do not testify, and evidentiary objections are discouraged.. Thus, some of the evidence disclosed to the mock jury might be inadmissible at a real trial.

Lambros, *The Summary Jury Trial,* 103 F.R.D. at 483–84.

> Following counsels' presentations, the jury is given an abbreviated charge and then retires to deliberate. The jury then returns a "verdict." To emphasize the purely settlement function of the exercise, the mock jury is often asked to assess damages even if it finds no liability. Also, the court and jurors join the attorneys and parties after the "verdict" is returned in an informal discussion of the strengths and weaknesses of each side's case.

Lambros, *The Summary Jury Trial — An Alternative Method of Resolving Disputes,* 69 Judicature 286, 289 (Feb.-Mar. 1986).

SJT is attractive because it uses the input of a jury of laymen as fact finders.The decision from the SJT inevitably results in both sides reexamining and reevaluating their positions and demands. SJT can permit clarification of the issues, and even if it does not promote settlement, it can effectuate more careful preparation for trial.

In Federal Reserve Bank of Minneapolis v. Carey-Canada, Inc., 123F.R.D.603, 604–05 (D. Minn. 1988), the court observed:

The SJT represents one alternative . . . to secure to civil litigants just, speedy, and inexpensive determination of their claims of which litigants may be otherwise deprived because of the overwhelming and overburdening caseloads in many federal courts.

On the other hand, then Professor, now Judge, Richard Posner expressed skepticism about the advantages brought by this mechanism:

What is it about summary jury trial which stimulates settlement? Is it the result of the SJU or, notwithstanding the SJT verdict, the realization that trial verdicts essentially are unpredictable? Or the psychological shift of the parties' attention from pre-resolution to resolution matters?"

The prevailing authority is that SJT participation cannot be compelled. *Strandell v. Jackson County,* 838 F.2d 884 (7th Cir. 1987)(Rule 16(c) of the Federal Rules of Civil Procedure does not authorize a mandatory SJT since rule "was not intended to require that an unwilling litigant be sidetracked from the normal course of litigation.") *But see Carey-Canada, Inc.,* 123 F.R.D. 603 (D. Minn. 1988)(federal magistrate ruled that right to compel participation in a SJT is within inherent jurisdiction of the court).

[3] Mini-Trials

Mini-trials, have much in common with court ordered or encouraged SJTs. The principal distinction is that the mini-trial operates independently from any official proceeding. Should the mini-trial be subjected to any closer scrutiny than other private forms of settlement negotiation? The mini-trial, and other mechanisms such as "rent-a-judge," raise difficult issues about our commitment to the public process of dispute resolution. What is the impact on the civil system of permitting these private arrangements? For example, will judges be likely to take early retirement to take advantage of lucrative and more flexible "private judging" opportunities? Will the public legal system lose its "middle class," and deal almost exclusively with criminal defendants and impoverished litigants? *See generally* A.B.A.J., Sept. 1, 1988, at 8. *See also* Comment, *Whose Dispute Is This Anyway?: The Propriety of the Mini-Trial in Promoting Corporate Dispute Resolution,* 1987 Mo. J. Disp. Res. 133.

The so-called "rent-a-judge" mechanism is not totally private. Notably, Cal. Civ. Proc. Code § 638 (West 1976 & Supp. 1990) provides:

A reference may be ordered upon the agreement of the parties filed with the clerk, or judge, or entered in the minutes or in the docket, or upon the motion of a party to a written contract or lease which provides that any controversy arising therefrom shall be heard by a reference if the court finds a reference agreement exists between the parties:

1. To try any or all of the issues in an action or proceeding, whether of fact or of law, and to report a statement of decision thereon;

2. To ascertain a fact necessary to enable the court to determine an action or proceeding.

G. ALTERNATIVE DISPUTE MECHANISMS: TRIAL-RELATED DEVICES

CAL. CIV. PROC. CODE § 644 (West 1976 & Supp. 1990) provides for the results of such reference as follows:

> The decision of the referee or commissioner upon the whole issue must stand as the decision of the court, and upon filing of the statement of decision with the clerk of the court, or with the judge where there is no clerk, judgment may be entered thereon in the same manner as if the action had been tried by the court.

How does such a mechanism differ from private arbitration, or judicially-annexed arbitration? *See generally* Note, *The California Rent-A-Judge Experiment: Constitutional and Policy Considerations of Pay-As-You-Go Courts*, 94 HARV. L. REV. 1592 (1981).

[4] Court-Induced and Other Settlement Techniques

Drawing on their inherent authority to manage and to preserve the efficiency and integrity of the judicial process under Rule 16, some federal courts have engaged in aggressive settlement tactics such as ordering represented parties to appear at pretrial settlement conferences. How far can these aggressive tactics go? The United States Court of Appeals for the Seventh Circuit sustained a federal magistrate's sanctions against the defendant who had been ordered to send a corporate representative with authority to settle to a pretrial conference and failed to comply. *G. Heileman Brewing Co. v. Joseph Oat Corp.*, 871 F.2d 648 (7th Cir. 1989).

FLA. STAT. ANN. § 766.108 (West Supp. 1990) provides:

> (1) In any action for damages based on personal injury or wrongful death arising out of medical malpractice, whether in tort or contract, the court shall require a settlement conference at least 3 weeks before the date set for trial.
>
> (2) Attorneys who will conduct the trial, parties, and persons with authority to settle shall attend the settlement conference held before the court unless excused by the court for good cause.

Is it appropriate or does it interfere with the client's representation decision? *See generally* Judith Resnik, *Managerial Judges,* 96 HARV. L. REV. 376 (1982); Carrie Menkel-Meadow, *For and Against Settlement: Uses and Abuses of the Mandatory Settlement Conference,* 33 UCLA L. REV. 485 (1985); Marc Galanter, *The Quality of Settlements,* 1988 J. DISP. RES. 54.

Another useful settlement device is computer modeling of settlement values in complex, multi-party litigation. One example of the use of this device occurred in asbestos litigation. Judge Lambros of the Northern District Court of Ohio utilized computer modeling to suggest settlement values in the cases. By bifurcating discovery, and first seeking only that information necessary to assess settlement value, special masters appointed by the judge could match data, expressed in terms of 380 variables, related to cases already completed in that geographical area. The computer model was adjusted for inflation and provided a suggested settlement value for the case in point. The historical matches were presented to the parties at a settlement conference in an attempt to narrow the range of the negotiations. *See* LEGAL TIMES, Oct. 24,

1983, at 1; Aug. 6, 1984, at 1; NAT'L L.J., May 7, 1984, at 1; Oct. 17, 1988, at 8. Attorneys for 1,200 Dalkon Shield claimants also were reported to have developed computer modeling software to prepare settlement positions for their clients. AM. LAW., Jul./Aug. 1988, at 17.

Massive complex cases may be assigned to special masters for settlement scheduling. Faced with a docket of over 4,000 asbestos cases, a Maryland district court judge appointed Kenneth R. Feinberg as special master. Feinberg had helped negotiate settlements in the Agent Orange and Dalkon Shield cases. Most of the plaintiffs were represented by one attorney; but there were 85 defendants. Feinberg concentrated on negotiating a scheduled approach to settlement (based on age and type of injury) between the plaintiffs' attorney and individual defendants rather than the defendants as a group. The N.Y. Times, Oct. 23, 1989, at 22, col. 1. Feinberg and another special master, David I. Shapiro, had been instrumental in negotiating the settlement in the Agent Orange litigation after their appointment by Chief Judge Jack B. Weinstein. The settlement of $180 million was reached between 16,000 Vietnam War veterans and seven chemical companies. *See* Legal Times, May 14, 1984, at 1. Notably, the special masters usually met with one side and then the other, rather than conduct face-to-face meetings. What advantages are offered by this strategy?

[5] Responses to Asbestos Litigation

The asbestos litigation which burgeoned in the late seventies singlehandedly placed the deficiencies of the torts litigation system in sharp relief. *See generally Comment, Alternatives to Litigation: Toxic Torts and Alternate Dispute Resolution — A Proposed Solution to the Mass Tort Case,* 20 Rutgers L.J. 779 (1989). Early focus was on the appropriate response of the substantive products liability law. *See, e.g., Borel v. Fibreboard Paper Prods. Corp.,* 493 F.2d 1076, 1089 (5th Cir. 1973), *cert. denied,* 419 U.S. 869 (1974); *Beshada v. Johns-Manville Prods. Corp.,* 90 N.J. 191, 202–03, 447 A.2d 539, 545–46 (1982). Then came the ever-mounting filings by 40,000 or more shipyard workers and installers of insulation materials. Later came a second wave of suits for property damage brought by more than 15,000 school districts and other end users of the product. A third wave of filings involved thousands of tire and rubber workers and others from service industries with somewhat more incidental contact with asbestos in their workplaces. These waves of filings were paralleled by the 50 or so asbestos manufacturers claiming against their 75 coverage-disputing insurers. *See, e.g., Keene Corp. v. Insurance Co. of N. Am.,* 667 F.2d 1034 (D.C. Cir. 1981), *cert. denied,* 455 U.S. 1007 (1982), and the Chapter 11 reorganizations for which some manufacturers opted. The astronomical number of plaintiffs, the unusually large number of co-defendants and the complex causation issues stimulated several innovative approaches to dispute resolution such as summary jury trials and computer modeling discussed *supra*.

One impressive approach was the establishment of the Asbestos Claims Facility, a product of the so-called "Wellington Agreement," named after Harry H. Wellington, a former dean of Yale Law School. *See generally Harry Wellington, Asbestos: The Private Management of a Public Problem,* 33 Clev.

G. ALTERNATIVE DISPUTE MECHANISMS: TRIAL-RELATED DEVICES

St. L. Rev. 375 (1984); Comment, *The Asbestos Claims Facility — An Alternative to Litigation,* 24 Duq. L. Rev. 833 (1986). The agreement was feted in dispute resolution circles because of the mediation and negotiation which apparently preceded the agreement and the novel dispute resolution techniques which promised to settle the cases.

The "Wellington Agreement" involved a 1985 agreement between 34 major asbestos producers and their 16 insurers to make a single settlement offer of compensatory but not punitive damages to each claimant. The claimant could then refuse the offer, mediate or arbitrate the offer, or go to trial against a presumably unified group of defendants. The costs of the facility, a not-for-profit corporation, were shared by the members in proportion to their pre-Wellington payments. The heavily exposed Manville Corporation was not a member of the facility. Although the facility's original workload consisted of cases transferred from about a thousand law firms which had been defending claims, it was the intention of the facility to permit unrepresented claimants to register directly with the claims facility.

Plaintiffs' attorneys alleged that the facility was primarily a coordinator of the defense's litigation tactics and a vehicle designed to delay the processing of claims. Indeed, an antitrust suit was filed against the producers and insurers for their participation in the facility. However, in its first two and a half years, the facility apparently settled some 20,000 cases.

The facility collapsed in 1988 because of the third wave of filings involving workers outside of the installation trades. Many of the larger producers complained that the financing of the facility's operations and settlements had been based on the case profile of the first wave of filings, and was inappropriate for the later claims. A new facility — the Center for Claims Resolution — was established, in which a smaller number of producers and insurers participated.[2]

As has been suggested above and elsewhere in this casebook, because of its complexities and sheer volume of cases, the asbestos litigation led courts to adopt innovative dispute resolution techniques that have sometimes challenged the traditional litigation model and tested the capacity of the civil liability system to handle such problems. One area of controversy involves case consolidation.

The Fifth Circuit's disposition in *In re Fibreboard Corp.,* 893 F.2d 706 (5th Cir. 1990), is informative. Some 3,031 asbestos cases required trial before Judge Robert Parker of the Eastern District of Texas. Trials of these cases in groups of ten would have filled the whole Eastern District docket for three years. As a consequence, the appointed special master, Professor Jack Ratliff of the University of Texas Law School, concluded that it was "self-evident that the use of one-by-one individual trials is not an option." Instead, the master recommended four trial phases. First, a trial on "classwide liability," second, "classwide damages" (actual damages for each disease category), third, "apportionment" and fourth, "distribution." Agreeing with this strategy, Judge

---

[2] This description is based upon accounts appearing at: National L.J., Jul. 8, 1985, at 3, Apr. 25, 1988 at 3, Jun. 20, 1988, at 6, Dec. 26, 1988, Jan. 30, 1989 at 3; Legal Times, Feb. 24, 1986, at 1; BNA Daily Report for Executives, Sept. 18, 1986, at C1, Jul. 25, 1988, Oct. 17, 1988.

Parker consolidated the cases for a single trial "on the issues of state of the art and punitive damages and certified a class action under rule 23(b)(3) for the remaining issues of exposure and actual damages." The second phase (classwide damages) was described as follows:

> [In] Phase II the jury is to decide the percentage of plaintiffs exposed to each defendant's products, the percentage of claims barred by statutes of limitation, adequate warnings, and other affirmative defenses. The jury is to determine actual damages in a lump sum for each disease category for all plaintiffs in the class. Phase II will include a full trial of liability and damages for 11 class representatives and such evidence as the parties wish to offer from 30 illustrative plaintiffs. Defendants will choose 15 and plaintiffs will choose 15 illustrative plaintiffs, for a total of 41 plaintiffs. The jury will hear opinions of experts from plaintiffs and defendants regarding the total damage award.

The Fifth Circuit Court of Appeals, however, vacated the order for consolidation beyond Phase I, stating:

> . . . The core problem is that Phase II, while offering an innovative answer to an admitted crisis in the judicial system, is unfortunately beyond the scope of federal judicial authority. It infringes upon the dictates of *Erie* that we remain faithful to the law of Texas, and upon the separation of powers between the judicial and legislative branches.
>
> . . . The inescapable fact is that the individual claims of 2,990 persons will not be presented. Rather, the claim of a unit of 2,990 persons will be presented. Given the unevenness of the individual claims, this Phase II process inevitably restates the dimensions of tort liability. Under the proposed procedure, manufacturers and suppliers are exposed to liability not only in 41 cases actually tried with success to the jury, but in 2,990 additional cases whose claims are indexed to those tried.
>
> . . . The 2,990 class members cannot be certified for trial as proposed under Rule 23(b)(3). Fed. R. Civ. Pro. Rule 23(b)(3) requires that "the questions of law or fact common to the members of the class predominate over any questions affecting individual members." There are too many disparities among the various plaintiffs for their common concerns to predominate. The plaintiffs suffer from different diseases, some of which are more likely to have been caused by asbestos than others. The plaintiffs were exposed to asbestos in various manners and to varying degrees. The plaintiffs' lifestyles differed in material respects. To create the requisite commonality for trial, the discrete components of the class members' claims and the asbestos manufacturers' defenses must be submerged. The procedures for Phase II do precisely that, but, as we have explained, do so only by reworking the substantive duty owed by the manufacturers. . . .

Following the decision, Professor Ratliff observed: "Appellate courts must recognize that asbestos is an emergency situation, and we've got to do something about it." NAT'L L.J., Feb. 19, 1990, at 3. Do you agree with the resolution proposed by Professor Ratliff or with the appellate court's response? For a critique of the collective litigation approach, *see* Transgrud, *Mass Trials in Mass Tort Cases: A Dissent,* 1989 U. ILL. L. REV. 69, 87 ("Our civil justice system owes a twelve-year-old girl born with foreshortened limbs after her mother took a prescribed morning sickness drug the same due process it owes a thirty-two-year-old man paralyzed when the brakes of his Chevrolet fail and his automobile slams into a tree"). Does consolidation improve or inhibit the chances of settlement?

[6] Litigant Satisfaction with Resolution Alternatives

It is, of course, critical to an assessment of the success of these various alternatives to consider the level of satisfaction that the litigants experience. In one study of tort litigants' views of trials, court-annexed arbitration, and judicial settlement conferences the results show that litigants clearly distinguish among procedures, and satisfaction and perceived fairness hinge on litigants' personal impressions of the litigation process. In particular, the litigants cared strongly about whether their cases received dignified, careful, and unbiased hearings. They also wanted to exercise some control over the handling and ultimate outcome of their cases. Overall, they wanted procedures with which they could feel "comfortable" — but their specifications for comfort did not necessarily accord with the expectations of practitioners.

Recent literature has argued that trial, with its formality and impersonality, proves more troubling to litigants than do more informal, participatory procedures such as settlement conferences. The tort litigants we studied, however, did not find trials trying. Trials engendered higher levels of perceived control and participation, and the proceedings were better understood, than would be expected given the common criticisms of formal legal procedures. The study suggests, in fact, that these litigants felt that trials increase, not decrease, their involvement in the legal process. The litigants preferred trial to settlement — they thought trial more fair and found it to be more satisfactory.

Alternative procedures less formal than trial can be quite acceptable to litigants, too, as suggested by their generally favorable reactions to court-annexed arbitration. However, the reasons the litigants liked arbitration also differ from what the current literature suggests. For example, litigants did not find arbitration fair and satisfying because it is relatively informal. They liked it because, like trial, arbitration struck them as dignified and careful. The study indicates that whatever procedure is used, formal or informal, it must be enacted well and seriously if it is to be viewed as fair.

Although perceived dignity and carefulness weighed more heavily than common assumption would have predicted, the actual costs, outcome, and duration of the cases had surprisingly light impact. Litigation costs bore no substantial relationship to perceived fairness or satisfaction. As for outcomes, although winners tended to be happier than losers, this factor accounted for only a small portion of the variation in litigants' responses. And delay correlated even less closely with litigant satisfaction and perceived fairness than did case outcome.

R-3708-ICJ, *The Instit. For Civil Justice Ann. Rep.* Apr. 1, 1990 -March 31, 1991, at 18.

NOTES

1. *What we know about SJT*. The most detailed description of the SJT process has come from Judge Lambros himself, *Summary Jury Trials and Other Alternative Methods of Dispute Resolution,* 103 F.R.D. 461 (1984). A similar judicial view is provided in Spiegel, *Summary Jury Trials,* 54 U. CIN. L. REV. 829 (1986). A contrasting view is offered by Professor (now Judge) Richard Posner, who disputes the efficacy and efficiency of the SJT procedure. Richard Posner, *The Summary Jury Trial and Other Methods of Alternative Dispute Resolution: Some Cautionary Observations,* 53 U. CHI. L. REV. 366 (1980).

What is it about a summary jury trial which stimulates settlement? Is it the result of the SJT or, notwithstanding the SJT verdict, the realization that trial verdicts essentially are unpredictable? Or the psychological shift of the parties' attention from pre-resolution to resolution matters?

For a look at other mechanisms that are being developed *within* the traditional litigation structure, *see* the survey by Levin & Golash, *Alternative Dispute Resolution in Federal District Courts,* 37 U. FLA. L. REV. 29 (1985). *See generally* Deborah Hensler, *Resolving Mass Toxic Torts: Myths And Realities,* 1989 U. ILL. L. REV. 89.

2. *Resolution of business disputes*. In what ways are the informal dispute mechanisms particularly well tailored to the resolution of business disputes? For an exposition of the choice of ADR mechanisms for such conflicts, *see* Goldberg, Green & Sander, *Litigation, Arbitration or Mediation: A Dialogue,* 75 A.B.A.J. 70 (June 1989).

3. *Back to the future?* Do the mechanisms which have been described preview a total privatization of the legal system? Or is the "future" already here? *See* The N.Y. Times, Feb. 17, 1989, at 21, col. 3, detailing the rise of for-profit providers of ADR services, including the franchising of such services and the use of retired judges in resolving the disputes. Why is this happening? How successful are the most sophisticated negotiation techniques in the absence of the pressure supplied by the imminence of a lengthy and expensive trial?

4. *The impetus for change*. Are the appellate courts' concerns in the asbestos cases justified? *See* Feinberg, *The Toxic Tort Litigation Crisis: Conceptual Problems and Proposed Solutions,* 24 HOUS. L. REV. 155 (1987). *See generally* Schuck, *The Role of Judges in Settling Complex Cases: The Agent Orange Example*, 53 U. CHI. L. REV. 337 (1980).

H. ALTERNATIVE DISPUTE RESOLUTIONS: ARBITRATION AND MEDIATION ALTERNATIVES TO TRIAL

PROBLEM

Samuel Son was an economics major at Lowgrade College of Business and Administration in Anystate. Samuel spent his days watching "soaps" on television, and his evenings listening to "classic rock" radio stations. At the end of his junior year the economics department finally gave up any hope that Samuel would achieve a graduating GPA and dismissed him for academic reasons. Samuel filed suit against Lowgrade, his professors and all the students in the top ten percent of his matriculation class, alleging intentional infliction of emotional harm, civil RICO, and educational malpractice. Following a dramatic, albeit temporary, increase in medical malpractice insurance rates, Anystate recently had added the following provision to its civil procedure code:

> (a) In any action for damages due to personal injury, property damage or death based upon the provision of professional services, the court shall appoint a three-person expert review panel within 40 days after filing of an answer to a summons and complaint.
>
> (b) The review panel shall examine any evidence it thinks fit and, not more than 120 days after selection of the panel, it shall make a written report to the parties and to the court.
>
> (c) The report of the review panel is admissible in evidence at a subsequent trial de novo. Any finding by the panel as to the compliance or noncompliance of the defendant with any professional standard of care shall create a rebuttable presumption as to said compliance or noncompliance in subsequent proceedings.

Samuel Son files a motion for a protective order, seeking to avoid presentation of his case to a review panel, on the basis that Anystate's review panel procedure is constitutionally defective.

As Son's attorney, what arguments will you make? With what degree of success?

[1] Pretrial Arbitration

State statutes providing for pretrial arbitration are controversial. In *Firelock, Inc. v. District Ct.*, 776 P.2d 1090 (Colo. 1989), the court upheld the constitutionality of Colorado's mandatory, but nonbinding, pretrial arbitration procedure. According to Justice Erickson, concurring:

> While I acknowledge that the right of access to the courts is an important one, the burgeoning case load in our courts has itself caused delay and increased costs. Access to the courts for all litigants may be improved by different alternatives for dispute resolution, such as arbitration and mediation.

776 P.2d at 1101. In contrast, Justice Lohr, dissenting, found the mandatory arbitration procedure an unconstitutional restriction on the right of access to the courts in two ways:

> First, the litigant may not present his claim to a court until he has undergone the delay and expense attendant to an arbitration proceeding. Second, in order to obtain access to a court after arbitration has been completed, the litigant must accept the consequence that he will be required to pay the costs of the arbitration proceeding, including arbitrator fees, up to a maximum of $1,000 should he fail to improve his position by more than ten percent. These burdens of time and expense are considerable and will likely have the practical effect of preventing litigants with smaller claims from ever obtaining access to the courts to assert them. . . . The majority does not explain why these obviously important limitations on a litigant's fundamental right of access to the courts are permissible except to analogize them to the collection of docket fees, the award of costs to a prevailing party, and the imposition of certain other incidental costs of litigation applicable in special situations. The majority simply offers the conclusion that the burdens are reasonable. I cannot agree . . . .

776 P.2d at 1101–02.

In *Mattos v. Thompson*, 491 Pa. 385, 421 A.2d 190, 191 (1980), the court concluded that Pennsylvania's pretrial review system "failed in its goal to render expeditious resolution to medical malpractice claims and consequently imposes an oppressive burden upon the right to jury trial guaranteed by our state constitution." 421 A.2d at 191. It concluded that the delays in litigation caused by the procedure "are unconscionable and irreparably rip the fabric of public confidence in the efficiency and effectiveness of our judicial system." *Id.* at 195.

[2] Medical Malpractice Arbitration Provisions

In an effort to address escalating costs and the perceived malpractice crisis, some reform advocates have supported the use of arbitration panels comprised of attorneys and doctors who can evaluate the case before a trial takes place. Statutory provisions to arbitrate medical malpractice disputes have proliferated. These disputes could be governed by the state's general arbitration statute, frequently an adoption of the Uniform Arbitration Act of 1955 (7 U.L.A. 1 (1978 & Supp. 1985)). However, legislatures have often passed specific medical malpractice statutes. Enacting a specific malpractice arbitration provision has certain advantages. First, it can tailor the process to the particular nature of a medical claim. Second, it can provide a degree of protection for the patient. Third, enactment of such a statute should determine whether a medical malpractice claim is arbitrable in that state.

The typical malpractice arbitration act will identify the parties who may execute a malpractice arbitration agreement, regulate certain substantive provisions in the agreement, and address the content of pre-execution disclosure.

Courts have turned back challenges to these statutes. The constitutionality of the Michigan statute, for example, was challenged in *Morris v. Metriyakool*,

418 Mich. 423, 344 N.W.2d 736 (1984). Singled out for attack was the provision that one of the arbitrators must be a physician or a hospital administrator (Mich. Comp. Laws § 600.5044(2) (1989)). The court, however, rejected the plaintiffs' procedural due process claim of decision-making bias. Justice Ryan, concurring, added:

> Here, the State of Michigan has not compelled the parties to arbitrate their disputes concerning medical malpractice, but has merely announced the circumstances under which its courts will not interfere with a private agreement to arbitrate medical malpractice disputes. Indeed, the crux of plaintiffs' complaint is not that the state has acted, but that the state has refused to act to prohibit private agreements to arbitrate before a three-person panel, one of whom is a doctor or a hospital administrator.

344 N.W.2d at 753. However, even if the state had compelled the arbitration, the majority of the Michigan court would have upheld the procedure. Justice Kavanaugh's majority opinion stated:

> [I]t has not been demonstrated that the medical members of these panels have a direct pecuniary interest or that their decision may have any substantial effect on the availability of insurance or insurance premiums. We have been shown no grounds sufficient for us to conclude that these decisionmakers will not act with honesty and integrity. We look for a pecuniary interest which creates a probability of unfairness, a risk of actual bias which is too high to be constitutionally tolerable. It has not been shown here.

344 N.W.2d at 740.

Florida's arbitration provision states:

> If the claimant rejects a defendant's offer to enter voluntary binding arbitration:
>
> (a) The damages awardable at trial shall be limited to net economic damages, plus noneconomic damages not to exceed $350,000 per incident. The Legislature expressly finds that such conditional limit on noneconomic damages is warranted by the claimant's refusal to accept arbitration, and represents an appropriate balance between the interests of all patients who ultimately pay for medical negligence losses and the interests of those patients who are injured as a result of medical negligence.
>
> (b) Net economic damages reduced to present value shall be awardable, including, but not limited to, past and future medical expenses and 80 percent of wage loss and loss of earning capacity, offset by any collateral source payments.
>
> (c) Damages for future economic losses shall be awarded to be paid by periodic payments . . . and shall be offset by future collateral source payments.
>
> (d) Jury trial shall proceed in accordance with existing principles of law.

Fla. Stat. Ann. § 766.211(4) and (5) (West Supp. 1990). Is this statutory "encouragement" to arbitrate troublesome based on the views expressed in other dispute resolution contexts discussed above?

[3] Mandatory Arbitration As A Substitute For Litigation

In *Gilmer v. Interstate Johnson Lane Corp.*, 500 U.S. 20 (1991), the plaintiff, a financial services representative, was required by defendant, his employer, to sign an arbitration agreement whereby he agreed to arbitrate all employment disputes and all termination-of-employment disputes. Defendant terminated plaintiff's employment when plaintiff reached 62 years of age, and plaintiff then filed a suit against defendant under the Age Discrimination in Employment Act of 1967 (ADEA). Defendant moved to compel arbitration. Affirming the Court of Appeals, the U. S. Supreme Court upheld defendant's motion. The Court rejected plaintiff's claim that he could not obtain effective judicial review of an arbitration decision. It also rejected his claim of inequality of bargaining power, saying that such inequality "is not a sufficient reason to hold that arbitration agreements are never enforceable in the employment context." *Id.* at 33.

There is growing concern, particularly among the plaintiffs' bar, over the widespread use of arbitration agreements to preclude litigation of numerous types of consumer claims. Arbitration decisions are usually judicially reviewable only for fraud, interest, and the like.

The Ninth Circuit held in *Circuit City Stores, Inc. v. Adams*, 194 F.3d 1070 (9th Cir. 1999), that an arbitration agreement, signed by an employee at the time of job application, was an "employment contract" and thus the Federal Arbitration Act was inapplicable. Therefore, said the court, the plaintiff could bring a lawsuit against his employer under a state fair employment statute. The U. S. Supreme Court reversed, 121 S. Ct. 1302 (2001), holding that the employment contract exception applied only to transportation workers.

On remand, the Ninth Circuit found that the arbitration agreement was unconscionable and thus unenforceable because it was one-sided. *Circuit City Stores, Inc. v. Adams*, 279 F.3d 889 (9th Cir. 2002).

The Supreme Court in *Green Tree Financial Corp. v. Randolph*, 121 S. Ct. 513 (2000), upheld a consumer contract arbitration clause requiring the plaintiff, a mobile home purchaser, to arbitrate her truth-in-lending claim against the defendant, which financed her purchase of the home. The Court said the plaintiff failed to show she was financially unable to afford arbitration, and it remanded the case for arbitration.

Arbitration between relatively equal bargainers such as labor unions and employers seems fair. But the issue is much more doubtful in the context of consumer claims. Binding arbitration clauses in this context are often one-sided. Where Title VII civil rights claims are involved, such arbitration clauses may undermine the civil rights damage provisions (pain and suffering, punitive damages) and the right to trial by jury.

NOTES

1. *The Purpose and Effect of Pretrial Review.* Are pretrial review (or nonbinding arbitration) panels designed to deter frivolous claims or reduce

insurer exposure? Do they encourage settlement or merely chill meritorious claims?

2. *Medical Malpractice Arbitration Procedures.* What arguments would you make to counter the view that the requirement of medical members on the panel is not unfair in the absence of a showing of actual bias? Is the absence of pecuniary interest or of evidence of bias sufficient protection?

PROBLEM

Dr. Onco successfully removed a cyst from Patrick Patient. At that time Patrick signed an agreement to arbitrate medical malpractice claims. Two years later Patrick was treated by Dr. Cology, Dr. Onco's partner, for removal of a facial mole. Dr. Cology removed the mole, but according to Patrick's complaint, Dr. Cology negligently caused severe facial discoloration around the site of the mole. Dr. Cology's insurer settled Patrick's medical malpractice claim.

Anne, Patrick's wife, now files suit against Dr. Cology for loss of consortium and negligent infliction of emotional harm. The emotional harm claim was premised on Anne's allegation that Dr. Cology knew that she was waiting for Patrick in the medical suite following the operation, and that Dr. Cology had failed to tell her how Patrick would appear following the surgery.

Can Dr. Cology compel Anne to arbitrate her claims?

Suppose that Anne Patient had been treated for a mild skin cancer by the same partnership two years before Patrick's first visit, and had signed an identical arbitration agreement. Would she be bound to arbitrate her claims?

[4] Mediation

Mediation is the intervention in a dispute by an acceptable third party with no binding decision-making authority who assists the disputants in negotiating a settlement of issues. The mediator controls the process by establishing ground rules and guiding the disputants through the process to reach a mutually acceptable resolution. In managing the process, the mediator may work in the presence of the all parties to the dispute or with each party separately. Like arbitration, mediation has become a well established, statutorily recognized alternative to the trial process. Virginia's mediation provision is exemplary.

VIRGINIA MEDIATION ACT
Va. Code Ann. §§ 8.01-581.21 to 8.01-581.23 (1997)

§ 8.01-581.21. Definitions.

As used in this chapter:

"Mediation" means the process by which a mediator assists and facilitates two or more parties to a controversy in reaching a mutually acceptable resolution of the controversy and includes all contacts between the mediator and any party or parties, until such time as a resolution is agreed to by the parties or the parties discharge the mediator.

"Mediation program" means a program through which mediators or mediation is made available and includes the director, agents and employees of the program.

"Mediator" means an impartial third party selected by agreement of the parties to a controversy to assist them in mediation.

§ 8.01-581.22. Confidentiality; exceptions.

All memoranda, work products and other materials contained in the case files of a mediator or mediation program are confidential. Any communication made in or in connection with the mediation which relates to the controversy being mediated, whether made to the mediator or a party, or to any other person if made at a mediation session, is confidential. However, a mediated agreement shall not be confidential, unless the parties otherwise agree in writing.

Confidential materials and communications are not subject to disclosure in any judicial or administrative proceeding except (i) where all parties to the mediation agree, in writing, to waive the confidentiality, (ii) in a subsequent action between the mediator and a party to the mediation for damages arising out of the mediation, or (iii) statements, memoranda, materials and other tangible evidence, otherwise subject to discovery, which were not prepared specifically for use in and actually used in the mediation.

§ 8.01-581.23. Civil immunity.

Mediators and mediation programs shall be immune from civil liability for, or resulting from, any act or omission done or made while engaged in efforts to assist or facilitate a mediation, unless the act or omission was made or done in bad faith, with malicious intent or in a manner exhibiting a willful, wanton disregard of the rights, safety or property of another.

PROBLEM

Bill and Ruth Major and their 14-year-old daughter Natalie live in West Anytown in a quiet subdivision with stagnant property values. Natalie is something of a "problem" child. However, she is at her best when in the company of Colin, the 15-year-old son of Jane and Clarence Harris, the Majors' neighbors. Recently, the Majors granted Natalie her birthday wish and gave her a B-B gun — one exactly like the gun that Colin Harris received from Jane and Clarence for his birthday. During the two-week period which followed her birthday, Natalie terrified the occupants of the subdivision by taking random shots at passing automobiles, pedestrians and pets. She was unsuccessful in her marksmanship until she turned her B-B gun on the Harris' greenhouse. Several shots later the greenhouse was severely damaged, and Mrs. Harris' prize-winning giant squash was fatally exposed to adverse weather conditions. Mr. and Mrs. Harris are understandably upset by this turn of events.

In part because they were distressed that Natalie might represent a considerable negative influence upon Colin, Mr. and Mrs. Harris filed suit against Natalie for trespass to their greenhouse, and against the Majors for negligent entrustment and negligent supervision, claiming $5,000 in compensatory damages and $50,000 in punitive damages. They also informed their property insurer, First Indemnity (FI), of their loss. Bill, Ruth, and Natalie Major have notified Unexpected Loss Mutual (ULM), their homeowners liability carrier, of the suits and requested defense and indemnification. Their insurer has undertaken the defense under a "reservation of rights."

The property insurer for Mr. and Mrs. Harris wishes to bring this matter to a speedy conclusion so as to release some of its adjusters for work on some earthquake claims on the West Coast. Both FI and ULM have been experimenting with mediation with regard to claims valued at below $5,000. Jointly, they approach you and ask you to mediate the claims detailed above.

Do you consider this to be an appropriate case for mediation? Are any other alternative mechanisms suitable for resolution of this dispute? In this case, what might you as a mediator be able to do which a trial judge could not or would not do? How do you think this case should be resolved? If you were mediating this dispute, would you tell the parties what you thought were the correct legal solutions to the issues presented?

NOTES

1. *Characteristics of Mediation.* What distinguishes mediation from mechanisms such as arbitration? What is a mediator seeking to achieve? Issue resolution? Issue definition? Dialogue? What type of tort dispute is mediation best able to resolve? Are there any types of tort disputes for which you would rule out mediation? Do you think it is appropriate to make choices to mediate on the basis of general types of tort dispute, or is an individualized assessment preferable?

For a primer on mediation, see Riskin, *The Special Place of Mediation in Alternative Dispute Resolution,* 37 U. Fla. L. Rev. 19 (1985).

2. *Mediation Style and Expectations of Mediation.* How important is mediation's lack of formality? Should a mediator have a "laid-back" style? Should she impose her personality and possibly a settlement agenda on the proceedings, or merely facilitate party initiatives and discussion? To what extent is a lawyer suited for the role of mediator? *See generally* Bush, *Efficiency and Protection, or Empowerment and Recognition?: The Mediator's Role and Ethical Standards in Mediation,* 41 U. Fla. L. Rev. 253 (1989); Riskin, *Toward New Standards for the Neutral Lawyer in Mediation,* 26 Ariz. L. Rev. 329 (1984). Does the lawyer-mediator have any special malpractice exposure? *Id.* at 359–61.

Roger Fisher and William Ury, in their classic book, GETTING TO YES (1981), state what they perceive to be the primary goals of good mediation: (1) do not bargain about positions, but bargain instead about interests; (2) separate the people (the personalities) from the problem; (3) invent options for mutual gain; and (4) insist on objective criteria. The thrust of their book is that the good mediator should objectify and develop the parties' interests in terms of mutual gain. But suppose the interests at stake are intensely subjective? Suppose what is involved is a personality, or a symbol, and not a financial or quantifiable interest?

3. *Mediation and Malpractice.* When, and to what extent, is mediation a suitable mechanism in resolving a physician-patient dispute? *See generally* Comment, *Healing Angry Wounds: The Roles of Apology and Mediation in Disputes Between Physicians and Patients*, 1987 Mo. J. Disp. Res. 111. Would mediation be more suitable to some types of physician "wrongdoing" than others? Who decides?

4. *Mediation of Business Torts.* Is there any particular public benefit in having complex "business v. business" disputes litigated, or is arbitration or mediation of such disputes preferable? *See generally* Ehrman, *Why Business Lawyers Should Use Mediation*, 75 A.B.A.J. 73 (June 1989).

5. *Private Mechanisms and Public Concerns.* Much of the focus of the alternative dispute resolution movement has been on the removal of disputes from the traditional public litigation model, and "privatizing" either the mechanism (*e.g.*, mediation and arbitration) or the resolution (*e.g.*, settlement rather than trial) of disputes. Professor Owen Fiss has countered with a critique of ADR:

> The advocates of ADR are led to support [settlement facilitating] measures and to exalt the idea of settlement more generally because they view adjudication as a process to resolve disputes. They act as though courts arose to resolve quarrels between neighbors who had reached an impasse and turned to a stranger for help. Courts are seen as an institutionalization of the stranger and adjudication is viewed as the process by which the stranger exercises power. The very fact that the neighbors have turned to someone else to resolve their dispute signifies a breakdown in their social relations; the advocates of ADR acknowledge this, but nonetheless hope that the neighbors will be able to reach agreement before the stranger renders judgment. Settlement is that agreement. It is a truce more than a true reconciliation, but it seems preferable to judgment because it rests on the consent of both parties and avoids the cost of a lengthy trial.
>
> In my view, however, this account of adjudication and the case for settlement rest on questionable premises. I do not believe that settlement as a generic practice is preferable to judgment or should be institutionalized on a wholesale and indiscriminate basis. It should be treated instead as a highly problematic technique for streamlining dockets. Settlement is for me the civil analogue of plea bargaining: Consent is often coerced; the bargain may be struck by someone without authority; the absence of a trial and judgment renders subsequent judicial involvement troublesome; and although dockets are trimmed, justice may not be done. Like plea bargaining, settlement is a capitulation to the conditions of mass society and should be neither encouraged nor praised.

Owen Fiss, *Against Settlement*, 93 Yale L.J. 1073, 1075 (1984). See also the colloquy between Professors McThenia and Shaffer, *For Reconciliation*, 94

Yale L.J. 1660 (1985); Owen Fiss, *Out of Eden*, 94 Yale L.J. 1669 (1985). Do you agree with Professor Fiss' assessment?

6. *Equality Considerations of Alternative Dispute Resolutions.* Professor Fiss also raises the question of the appropriateness of private dispute resolution mechanisms when the parties have disparate litigation resources. *Against Settlement, supra* at 1076-78. *Cf.* Marc Galanter, *Why the "Haves" Come Out Ahead: Speculations on the Limits of Legal Change*, 9 Law & Soc'y Rev. 95, 97 (1974) (although not focused on ADR, makes a useful distinction between litigation's "one-shotters" and its "repeat players). *See also Special Issue: Do the "Haves" Stilll Come Out Ahead?* 33 Law & Soc'y Rev. No. 4 (1999). The issue then presented is whether non-traditional dispute resolution poses too many additional hazards for the "one-shotter." A related issue concerns the extent to which nontraditional mechanisms are race and gender neutral. *See, e.g.*, Delgado, Dunn, Brown, Lee & Hubbert, *Fairness and Formality: Minimizing the Risk of Prejudice in Alternative Dispute Resolution*, 1985 Wis. L. Rev. 1359; Rifkin, *Mediation From a Feminist Perspective: Promise and Problems*, 2 Law & Inequality 21 (1984). Couldn't similar questions be raised with respect to juries? Judges?

7. *"Gag" Agreements.* One concern is that settlement agreements frequently contain "gag" clauses. Should these agreements be prohibited as against public policy? Consider the effect of the following provision:

> A settlement agreement involving a claim for medical malpractice shall not prohibit any party to the agreement from discussing with or reporting to the Division of Medical Quality Assurance the events giving rise to the claim.

Fla. Stat. Ann. § 766.113 (West Supp. 1990).

Chief Judge Wachtler of the New York Court of Appeals has observed:

> I think that when you have the courts being used for redressing a wrong, it is the public that is providing and paying for the court procedure and making it available for private litigants. These litigants should not then say to the public, "It's none of your business." . . . [With a sealed record] no one knows whether we can really eat the fish out of the Hudson or buy G.E. toasters.

N.Y. TIMES, JUN. 20, 1990, AT A1, COL. 1.

I. ALTERNATIVES TO THE TORT SYSTEM

Even before the torts "crises" of the seventies and eighties, the torts system in this country was the brunt of widespread criticism. Critics have argued that the system is too cumbersome, too expensive, too slow and unpredictable in outcome. They point out that among those who receive compensation, the relatively smaller claims are overcompensated and the larger ones undercompensated. Moreover, it has long been contended that the deterrent and compensatory goals of tort law are hopelessly at odds, resulting in neither goal being satisfactorily served

Academicians have often been the most vociferous in their criticism. For example, Fleming James is known for the persistent indictment of a fault-based torts process in earlier times. *E.g., Contribution Among Tortfeasors: A Pragmatic Criticism,* 54 Harv. L. Rev, 1156 (1941). Challenges to the system have continued to be mounted. For example, Professor John G. Fleming, in THE AMERICAN TORT PROCESS 18–19 (1988), makes the following observations about the tort system:

> The most negative feature of the tort system is its staggering overhead cost. Compared with other accident compensation systems, even those administered by private insurance like American workers' compensation (30 per cent) and health insurance (15 per cent), let alone with state insurance funds like New Zealand's accident compensation plan (8 per cent)[discussed *infra*], its cost inefficiency is difficult to justify by any competing advantages over its competitors. . . . Studies in the United States raise operating costs to $1.07 for automobile and $1.25 for product liability. In the protracted asbestos litigation it has cost $1.59 in combined litigation expenses to deliver $1 to the average plaintiff. As a result, in combination with the high component of damages for non-pecuniary injury, only about 15 per cent of the cost of the tort system accounts for out-of-pocket losses.

In *Doing Away With Tort Law*, 73 Calif. L. Rev. 555, 587 (1985), Professor Sugarman also contends there is no "convincing empirical support" for the proposition that tort law significantly deters socially undesirable, dangerous conduct. He thinks that "[s]elf-preservation instincts, market forces, personal morality and governmental regulation" combine to adequately control such conduct independently of tort law. *Id.* at 561.

Cataloging all the inefficiencies and unpredictablities of the tort system, Professor Sugarman proposes that the system be replaced with a no-fault scheme "as part of the function of our regular social insurance and employee-benefit system." Employers would pay "for short-term benefits using enterprise revenues. An expanded social security system, funded by payroll and income taxes, would provide long-term benefits." The primary deterrent force would be provided by regulatory agencies "bolstered by new citizen participation roles." Tort actions "might remain for cases of intentional wrongdoing, and private injunction remedies would still be available to stop unreasonably dangerous conduct." *Id.* at 664.

In view of the controversy already associated with the existing social security scheme, do you think Professor Sugarman's proposal is politically feasible? Professor Jeffrey O'Connell, one of the foremost proponents in this country of a no-fault scheme as a substitute for tort remedies, concedes that the adoption of a system of

> national insurance for all accidental injuries is politically infeasible because of the great expense involved and because there are competing demands (such as mass-transit systems, pollution control, law enforcement and education) for limited tax dollar resources that will take precedence over any accident insurance program.

Jeffrey O'Connell, ENDING INSULT TO INJURY 75 (1975). He proposes instead to permit businesses to elect a no-fault plan covering specified risks and amounts of liability of their choosing. This would be a one-sided voluntary program (i.e., potential victims would not have a choice of whether or not to adopt the plan). *See generally* O'Connell, *A "Neo No-Fault Contract" in Lieu of Tort: Pre-Accident Guarantees of Post-Accident Settlement Offers,* 73 Calif. L. Rev. 898 (1985)[check].

The preceding sections of this chapter have suggested that one approach to the perceived problem of excessive costs related to recovery under the tort system is to retrench on tort law remedies and another, intended to meet concerns of tort inefficiency as well as cost, is to adopt voluntary, alternative dispute resolution mechanisms such as arbitration and negotiation. Yet another response, often urged by reformers, especially academicians, is to abolish part or all of the tort system and to substitute for it an administrative no-fault compensation scheme, financed by some form of taxation. The no-fault compensation scheme for redress of injuries has been accepted in this country through workers' compensation for workplace injury and disease, and less widely, through no-fault automobile insurance. Indeed, there are other public and private health and unemployment insurance schemes (e.g., social security, Medicare, Medicaid) that supplement, but generally do not supplant, the tort system.

In 1914, when the state workers' compensation systems were beginning to be adopted in this country, Professor Jeremiah Smith expressed his doubt that the "incongruities" between the tort system and workers' compensation would be tolerated by the public, predicting that, in the end, one or the other system would prevail. He anticipated public support for legislation along the lines of workers' compensation and envisioned that judges' decision-making would also be affected:

> Even if courts should shrink from directly and avowedly changing the law, the result could be, to a considerable extent, accomplished by indirect methods. By a very liberal construction of res ipsa loquitur doctrine; by a broad view of what constitutes prima facie evidence of negligence; and by inverting the burden of proof (putting on defendant the burden of proving that he was not negligent). . . .
>
> [I]t seems safe to say that the basic principles [of workers' compensation and common-law tort] are irreconcilable. They cannot be wholly right, or both wholly wrong.

Jeremiah Smith, *Sequel to Workmen's Compensation Acts,* 27 Harv. L. Rev. 344, 363, 367, 368 (1914). Professor Smiths's prediction that one of the two systems would absorb the other has not been borne out, at least to date. Is he more accurate in his observations that workers' compensation, and perhaps other no-fault schemes, have at least caused some liberalization of the rules of recovery in common-law tort?

In 1974, New Zealand essentially abolished its tort system for recovery of personal injury and property damage, substituting a no-fault, governmentally administered payout scheme financed by taxes on employers, car owners, and the general taxpayer. Although there has not been a ground swell of support in the United States for such radical change, no-fault compensation schemes that address particular areas of the tort system have been adopted at the state and federal levels. Most proposals for a no-fault compensation system typically include recovery only for damages resulting from personal injury and, to a lesser extent, for physical damage to property. Claims for purely economic loss — typified by business tort claims — are not included within such schemes and remain within the tort system. The justification for the distinction is that personal injury is usually catastrophic in impact on the injured party and his or her family, while the effect of economic loss is relatively less severe. Is this distinction valid?

Several compensation schemes are highlighted in the subsections below.

NOTES

1. *Deterrence.* Professor Sugarman contends that there is no convincing empirical evidence to support the conclusion that tort law is an effective deterrent. Is there convincing empirical evidence to support the conclusion that it is not an effective deterrent? Where should the burden of proof lie?

2. *Regulatory Alternatives.* There is also ongoing debate regarding whether the tort system deterrent function might be better served by other means, such as governmental safety regulation. Are government regulators better equipped than courts to set standards of safety? Although some administrative agencies have been successful in regulating safety, in the products liability area administrative agencies such as the Consumer Product Safety Commission have promulgated ony a small number of design safety standards. Should society devote more resources to accident prevention through product safety regulations or are there other barriers to regulation that cannot be addressed merely by deploying resources? *See generally* Pierce, *Encouraging Safety: The Limits of Tort Law and Government Regulation,* 33 Vand. L. Rev. 1281 (1980).

[1] Workers' Compensation

In the early twentieth century states began enacting workers' compensation schemes as a substitute for employee tort claims against the employer. Tort recovery had been difficult for employees in part because of the defenses of contributory negligence, assumption of risk and the fellow servant doctrine which barred a claim against an employer for injuries caused by a fellow employee. In addition, employees were often reluctant to sue their employers for fear of losing their jobs and other employees refused to be witnesses for the same reason.

Workers' compensation schemes provided for a no-fault, limited payout for workplace injuries and diseases, paid by workers' compensation insurance (usually private insurance) financed by the employer. The compensation is for medical expenses, for loss of earnings and earning capacity (upon determination of temporary or permanent partial or total disability) and for death. Most states place no restriction on the duration or amount of medical benefits but some states limit the number of weeks for which wage benefits will be paid and place a cap on the total amount of such benefits that can be paid out. The amount of wage replacement varies from state to state but most replace roughly two-thirds of the wage. There is no recovery for pain and suffering.

About 90% of the workforce is covered by workers' compensation. Typically, small employers (employing less than four people) are not covered, and about half of the states exempt farm employers. Seamen and railroad workers are covered by special tort legislation.

One of the original purposes of the workers' compensation scheme was to eliminate lengthy, costly litigation. Most contested workers' claims are adjudicated before a state administrative body. These administrative proceedings have proved more complicated and expensive than was originally anticipated. There is substantial litigation regarding whether the injury arises out of or in the course of employment under the statutory framework, and regarding the determination of the extent of disability.

a. Third-Party Claims. Although typically workers' compensation is thought of as an exclusive remedy against the employer by the employee for personal injury and death, there are other litigation and regulatory considerations that relate to workplace injuries. For example, workers' compensation law preserves a tort claim of the employee against any third person who contributes to a workplace injury. Manufacturers of defective workplace machinery and other products in use in the course of employment may be subject to claims. According to one study conducted in the mid-seventies, 120,000 permanently disabled workers recovered average compensation benefits of slightly over $4,000 each, for a total of one-half billion, but 30,000 of those workers who were able to bring successful tort claims collected an average of $40,000 each for a total tort payment of about $1.2 billion. Weiler, *Workers' Compensation and Product Liability*, 50 Ohio St. L.J. 825, 829 (1989), citing Bernstein, *Third Party Claims in Workers' Compensation*, 1977 Wash U.L.Q. 543, 562–64.

In 1970, Congress passed the Occupational Safety and Health Act (OSHA), 29 U.S.C. Sec. 651 *et seq.* The purpose of the Act, and of the regulations that are promulgated and administered by the agency it creates, is to set workplace safety standards for employers engaged in interstate commerce. The principal means of enforcement of the standards are safety inspections and the imposition of fines against employers found in violation of the standards. OSHA fines, which had traditionally been inconsequential were dramatically increased after the Union Carbide chemical disaster in Bhopal, India. After Bhopal some fines levied by the agency were in excess of $1,000,000. However, the agency has also negotiated reduction of fines in return for agreements to improve safety in violators' plants. *See* Nat'l L.J.,Dec. 4, 1989 at 40–41.

b. The FELA Exception to Workers' Compensation. In 1908 Congress enacted the Federal Employers' Liability Act, 45 U. S.C. §§ 51–60, providing for tort recovery by railroad employees for injuries received during the course of employment. The FELA was enacted before the widespread adoption of workers' compensation systems in this country. It retained the tort features of fault-based liability and full compensatory damages, including recovery for pain and suffering. A pure comparative fault standard was adopted. The employer is guilty of negligence per se when it violates a federal safety statute or regulation. By a series of decisions, the United States Supreme Court, in construing the act, greatly liberalized the standards for proving fault and causation. A similar system was adopted for seamen (the Jones Act).

Although the railroad industry has lobbied Congress vigorously to repeal the FELA and replace it with a limited-payout workers' compensation system, these campaigns have been unsuccessful. The railway unions have steadfastly resisted repeal of the act, preferring its more generous payment terms to the limited benefits available under a workers' compensation scheme.

As one writer has observed, the railroads remain a significant safety hazard, particularly since they have become extensively involved in hauling toxic substances, explosives, hazardous wastes, and nuclear materials. Moreover, he concludes that governmental safety inspections have not proved effective in avoiding injury. Citing a 1987 economic study, he concluded that the reparation costs, as a percentage of total operating expenses, were roughly the same for railroads as for comparable workers' compensation industries, such as inter-city busing and coal mining (all in the 2% range). Phillips, *An Evaluation of the Federal Employers Liability Act*, 25 San Diego L. Rev. 49, 52, 53 (1988).

c. *Workplace Intentional Torts*. It is widely held that the exclusive remedy provision of workers' compensation does not apply to intentional torts. The plaintiff welder in *Quick v. Myers Welding & Fabricating, Inc.*, 649 So. 2d 999 (La. App. 1994), stated a cause of action in tort against his employer for the act of his co-employee in introducing oxygen into a tank where the plaintiff was welding. In order to recover for an intentional tort, the plaintiff had to show that "the person responsible for his injuries either desired to bring about the physical consequences of his act or he was substantially certain that they would follow from his action." An expert testified that "a welder who introduces oxygen into a tank where welding is in progress should know that a fire is substantially certain to occur."

In *Fyffle v. Jeno's Inc.*, 59 Ohio St. 3d 11 5, 570 N.E.2d I I 08 (Ohio 1991), the court said the plaintiff could assert an intentional tort claim against his employer, who removed a safety guard from a conveyor belt. A jury could find that the employer knew "with substantial certainty" that injury would result from removal of the guard. California held in *Livitsanos v. Superior Ct.*, 2 Cal. 4th 744, 828 P.2d 1195, 7 Cal. Rptr. 2d 808 (1992), that a claim for intentional and negligent infliction of emotional distress was covered by the exclusivity provisions of workers' compensation, as a normal part of the employment relationship. The court reasoned, however, the plaintiff had no claim for workers' compensation, since only physical injuries are compensable. The court remanded the case for a determination of whether plaintiff's defamation claim lay outside workers' compensation, noting a division of authority on the issue. When the plaintiff employee has a tort claim against her employer for intentional injury, she may also be able to pursue a workers' compensation claim contemporaneously for the same injury. *See Woodson v. Rowland*, 329 N.C. 330, 407 S.E.2d 222 (1991).

[2] Automobile No-Fault

The problem of automobile accidents is indisputable. In 1985, of the 1.7 million persons in the United States who suffered disabling injuries in motor vehicle accidents, 45,000 of the injuries were fatal. The estimated cost of all auto accidents for 1975 was $48.6 billion, or about half the total cost for all types of accidents. Determining how best to address the problem of automobile accidents has been controversial. Keeton and O'Connell's BASIC PROTECTION FOR THE TRAFFIC VICTIM: A BLUE PRINT FOR REFORMING AUTOMOBILE INSURANCE (1965) furnished the impetus for much of the no-fault insurance legislation which was adopted in about half of the states following the book's publication. The state no-fault plans fall into two basic patterns: those that do and those that do not restrict tort claims. In none of these states, however, has tort liability been completely abolished. A little more than half the states retain the traditional system of tort liability coupled with third-party insurance.

Professor John G. Fleming has examined the alternative plans in THE AMERICAN TORT PROCESS (1988). In the states in which tort claims have been restricted (what Professor Fleming characterizes as "no-tort" states) the claimant driver must make a no-fault claim against his own insurer (or the injuring driver's insurer if the claimant is a passenger or bystander) for medical expenses and lost earnings until the claimant's injuries have reached a designated "threshold." Typically there is no recovery for pain and suffering in no-fault. Once the damages exceed the "threshold," the claimant is allowed to bring a claim in tort against any alleged tortfeasor who caused the injury. In the states that do not restrict tort claims ("add-on" states, as characterized by Professor Fleming), a tort claim may be brought against any alleged tortfeasor at any point, with credit being made or insurance subrogation allowed for any no-fault payment received by the claimant.

"No-fault" states have expressed their threshold provisions in several different ways: in terms of: dollars of medical expense; days of disability; or a "verbal threshold," often defined in terms of permanent or serious disability. Professor Fleming observes:

> Experience has shown a clear relationship between the percentage of cases removed from the tort system by the threshold and the total amount of money paid to all victims (including tort claimants) without increasing insurance premiums adjusted for inflation. The three states with an exclusively verbal threshold recorded lower insurance costs than would have been without no-fault. Conversely, very high no-fault benefits accompanied by only very modest limitations on tort claims resulted in large premium increases, leading Pennsylvania to repeal no-fault altogether in 1984. By contrast, the combination of either substantial benefits and [substantial] thresholds or low benefits and [low] thresholds resulted in balance.

Fleming, *supra* at 171–72.

Professor Fleming uses a variety of studies to extrapolate data about the effect of no-fault schemes. He concludes that "almost twice as many victims received some compensation under no-fault as under tort." Based on another study, "65 percent of all automobile victims would have received some compensation if no-fault had been available, compared with 47.7 percent . . . under the fault system." *Id*. at 172. According to another estimate, "the average medical cost for catastrophic injuries (above $100,000) was $408,700." Only Michigan, New Jersey and Pennsylvania have unlimited no-fault medical payments. In most other no-fault states, "there would have been a shortfall of at least $50,000" in payment of medical benefits for such injuries. On the other hand, he notes the low minimal limits in the United States "of required third-party liability insurance, which nowhere exceeds $20,000 and is mostly between $10,000 and $15,000." *Id.* At 173.

As Professor Fleming points out, the trial bar, particularly plaintiff's lawyers, consistently opposed no-fault. The insurance industry, on the other hand, has been the chief promoter of the schemes. The United States Department of Transportation has consistently supported the no-fault effort. *Id* at 173–74.

For an examination of the pros and cons of no-fault auto insurance, *see* J. PHILLIPS and S. CHIPPENDALE, WHO PAYS FOR ACCIDENTS? (2002).

J. OTHER LIMITED SCHEMES

Congress has passed a number of victim compensation statues. A few of them are highlighted below.

a. Price-Anderson Act. In 1957, Congress passed the Price Anderson Act, 42 U.S.C. § 2210, requiring each federal nuclear production licensee to maintain liability insurance of $160 million against a nuclear accident, and a pooled assessment of $5 million per licensee, for a total of $560 million in liability coverage. The Act precludes liability in excess of the statutorily prescribed ceilings, but provides a strict liability standard, and eliminates the defense of the plaintiff's contributory or comparative fault.

b. Federal Coal and Mine Health Safety Act. Enacted in 1969, this Act, found at 30 U.S.C. § 801 et seq., provides federally funded pension compensation for black lung disease contracted by coal miners. The miner must prove that he has black lung disease contracted in mining-related employment and that he is totally disabled as a result. Causation is presumed if the miner can prove ten years of mining-related work, and total disability is presumed on proof of the existence of a complicated black lung condition. This no-fault program has been controversial in part because of its costliness.

c. Swine Flu Act. To meet the impasse between insurance companies which refused to underwrite a mass-immunization program to combat a predicted flu epidemic, and manufacturers which would not provide the vaccine without insurance, Congress passed this Act as an amendment to the Federal Tort Claims Act, 42 U.S.C. § -247(b)(j)–(l) (1976). Under the Act, the federal government is substituted as defendant in any suit against a Swine Flu vaccine manufacturer or distributor for injuries resulting from alleged defectiveness of the vaccine. The Act provides that claims may be brought in negligence, breach of warranty, and strict tort. Approximately 40 million Americans were inoculated under the mass-imunization program made possible by this legislation. The vaccine resulted in unexpected severe side effects causing Guillain-Barré syndrome in several thousand persons who were vaccinated. As of 1985, the government had paid more than $80 million in claims.

d. National Childhood Vaccine Injury Act, 42 U.S.C. § 300aa et seq. The Act covers most vaccines (including DTP) which children are required to take as a condition for entering school. When an injury is suffered, a claim must initially be filed before an administrative agency. Liability is determined on a no-fault basis, once causation is established. Compensation includes medical expenses not reimbursed from other sources, expenses, rehabilitation costs, loss of earning capacity, and reasonable attorneys' fees. Pain and suffering awards are limited to a maximum of $250,000, and death benefits are limited to the same amount. If the claimant is dissatisfied with the award, she may then bring a tort claim. However, the Act absolves the vaccine manufacturer from liability for unavoidable side effects, provides that any warning need only be given to the administering physician, and excludes the recovery of punitive damages except in the case of willful misconduct.

K. COMPARATIVE SYSTEMS

Dissatisfaction with their tort system has led other countries to take action. Below is a description of the radical reform undertaken in New Zealand and a partial scheme for medical malpractice in Sweden. Is it likely that we will see such changes in the United Sates at the state or federal level?

1. New Zealand Accident Compensation Act. In 1974, New Zealand essentially abolished its tort system for personal injury claims and replaced it with a no-fault Compensation Act for injuries. The no-fault Act provides payment for "injuries caused by intentional torts as well as injuries caused by negligence, medical misadventure (including most medical malpractice), product defect, and pure accident along with certain industrial diseases and industrial deafness." Other diseases are not covered by the Act. There is exclusion of coverage for "some self-inflicted injuries, some injuries caused in the commission of a crime, and, possibly, some adverse consequences of medical treatment and of failure by a medical professional to diagnose illness or to secure an informed consent." Miller, *The Future of New Zealand's Accident Compensation Scheme*, 11 U. Haw. L. Rev. 1, 7 (1989).

The benefits provided under the Act are for earnings-related compensation, medical expenses, rehabilitation expenses, noneconomic losses, and some miscellaneous accident costs. The Act generally provides for payment of 80% of lost wages after the first week of incapacity, with payments continuing if necessary until retirement age. As of June 1987 the maximum possible wage payment under the Act was $976 per week. Housewives, children, the elderly, and the long-time unemployed may receive benefits substantially below their earning capacity because of their meager actual earnings at the time of injury. Virtually all medical bills are paid. There are provisions for discretionary payments for permanent loss of a bodily function, and caps on damages for pain and suffering.

The system is funded by levies on employers and self-employed persons, based on size of payroll; by levies on automobile owners; and by general revenues. The first source funds about 66% of the costs of the system, and the second about 21 % of the costs. Employers are categorized for purposes of rate assessment, but there is no necessary correlation between the assessment rate and the accident-generating propensities of an employer. For example in 1988-89 "the levy paid by physicians . . . was set at $1.45 per one hundred dollars of payroll [and was] the same rate as that paid by employers of teachers." *Id.* at 13–14.

Promotion of safety is made a matter of "prime importance" under the Accident Compensation Act. However, in reality compensation seems more the focus. While the Act authorizes the Accident Compensation Commission ("ACC") to provide financial incentives, both as penalties and bonuses, to employers or self-insureds with particularly bad or good safety records, the ACC recently gave up its limited use of financial incentives on employers and has never surcharged bad automobile drivers. In general, the accident prevention activities of ACC seem to be focused mainly on supporting prevention activities of other groups; developing and running safety education campaigns, programs and courses; attempting to influence others to discover and to ameliorate hazardous conditions; cooperating with other national organizations, both public and private; and, in general, "[g]etting people to place a higher relative value on 'safety' in the continuum of factors that motivate their behavior." *Id.* at 17, 34, 35.

There appears to have been a "massive cost blow-out" in the operation of the ACC during the 1980s, resulting in sharp increases in levies imposed on employers to support the system. These increases in turn provoked in "late 1986 and in 1987 a public furor which rivaled in intensity and media coverage the tort liability and insurance 'crisis' in the United States." *Id.* at 3, 26.

Professor Miller offers a number of explanations for the cost increases, including a "build-up in the numbers of persons receiving compensation," increases in public's awareness of the availability of payments for noneconomic loss and increases in the size of payments being made, increasing health care costs, "hidden unemployment" wherein workers who are partially disabled remain in the system, and "increasing abuse . . . both as to possibly fraudulent claims and the payment of excessive and unnecessary medical claims." *Id* at 29. Professor Miller adds:

> Further, a significant degree of externalization of accident costs occurs in the area of medical expenses, since a significant amount of medical treatment for accidents is provided through the social security system and not charged to the accident scheme at all. Indeed the Law Commission itself estimated that accident costs equal to about half the amount paid by ACC are not borne by the accident compensation scheme."

Id. at 32.

The effect of the change in systems of recovery in New Zealand is still being assessed. Professor Miller suggests that a "failure of deterrence might constitute a significant factor in the massive cost blow-out" that was experienced. He notes that the removal of tort liability for personal injury has not been shown to have an adverse effect on automobile accident rates. The reports of annual days work lost due to illness and rates of fatal injuries in industry indicate no significant changes in the annual average lost workdays in New Zealand between 1973 and 1983. There were only small changes in the rates of fatal injuries during the last twenty years. *Id.* at 30–31. Professor Miller recommends that the common law right to bring actions at law for damages for injury or death arising from an accident be restored except in the case of actions by employees against their employers for work-connected accidents. *Id.* at 65.

2. Sweden's Patient Insurance Scheme. Sweden has established an administrative compensation system for medical and pharmaceutical injuries that places primary emphasis on causation as the basis for recovery. The Patient Insurance Scheme was established in 1975. It is financed by contributions, based on population, from local Swedish County Councils to a consortium of Swedish insurance companies that administer the scheme. Patients injured by medical treatment may make a claim under the scheme, but do not lose their common law right to sue in tort. The Pharmaceutical Insurance Scheme, established in 1978, is financed by contributions from drug companies based on the amount of business done by each company in Sweden. Patients accepting compensation under the scheme forego their right to sue in tort. Brahams, *The Swedish 'No Fault" Compensation System for Medical Injuries -Part 1,* New L.J. 14 (Jan. 8, 1988). A claim will not be accepted unless the patient has been sick for a minimum of 30 days or has been hospitalized for at least ten days or suffered permanent disability or died. However, costs for treatment and loss of income in excess of £100 are always indemnified.

The Patient Scheme is designed to compensate only for selected injuries. Treatment injuries are compensated only if the accident could have been avoided by treatment in another way. Injuries from blood transfusions, like hepatitis or AIDS, are compensated. Compensation is made for lost time, pain and suffering, and the expenses of any further operation, but not the costs of raising a child in the case of a failed sterilization. Proof of negligence is required in recovery for diagnostic failures. Accidental hospital injuries are covered, unless infection is a high risk of the treatment or the patient has low resistance to infection. No compensation is paid for injuries resulting from emergency treatment, for psychological injuries, or for damages resulting from cosmetic surgery. *Id.* at 14.

Compensation is available under the Pharmaceutical Scheme if the patient can show that more likely than not her injury was caused by a drug. There is no state of the art defense. But a patient will not be compensated where "it would be reasonable to accept certain adverse side effects. The more serious the illness the greater it will be deemed reasonable to tolerate an adverse reaction." *Id.* Doctors are required by statute to inform their patients "of all possible side effects of a drug." To facilitate this goal, the drug industry produces a comprehensive book listing all drug properties, contra-indications, reactions and side effects. Sweden maintains a central computerized data bank of all drug-related injuries, so that the drug industry can react quickly to withdraw a drug from the market or take other preventive measures as soon as a significant number of adverse reactions appear. *Id.* at 16.

Notably because Swedish Social Security pays 90 per cent of a worker's income during sickness or disability up to a fixed limit, about 70 per cent of the compensation paid under the Medical and Pharmaceutical Schemes relates to pain and suffering and other noneconomic losses whereas loss of income corresponds to only about 14 per cent of the claims. An advisory committee of the county councils and the insurers fixes norms for compensating pain and suffering. *Id.* at 16.

If a patient thinks she has a compensable injury, she obtains and fills out a claim form. The medical personnel involved will add any comments they may have. A medical assessor at the insurance company will receive the claim and assess the extent of injury. A claims committee for the insurers will then decide on the basis of their inspection of the papers as to whether compensation should be paid. About 58 per cent of the claims, under the patients scheme and 40 per cent of the claims under the drugs scheme are successful, and rejected claims are typically those where "the causal link has not been established, the injury was unavoidable, the time off work is too short, or the claim is statute barred." Brahams, *The Swedish "No Fault' Compensation System for Medical Injuries -Part 2,* New LJ. 31 (Jan-15, 1988).

A patient dissatisfied with the result from the claims committee may appeal to a six-person Claims Panel, three of whom are appointed by the government, two by the local County Council and one by the insurers. Here, too, the submissions are mostly on paper and few patients attend with their lawyers. *Id.* at 31. There can be a final appeal to an arbitrator, who is a judge in the Swedish Court of Appeal, but arbitrations are rare. Id.

The two schemes are generally popular in Sweden, although there has recently been some dissatisfaction both with the level of damages and the number of injuries that are not covered. There is general agreement that the schemes have encouraged a much better atmosphere between the medical profession and their patients.

NOTES

1. *Criticism of the New Zealand Plan.* Ison, 2 VICT. U. AT WELLINGTON L. REV. 25 (1993), criticizes 1992 amendments to the New Zealand Accident Compensation Act. He is especially critical of the experience-rating feature, introduced for determining employer contributions to the accident fund. He finds this feature creates an adversarial relation between employers and employees and tends to discourage the assertion of accident claims. *See also* Bryce Wilkinson, *New Zealand's Failed Experiment with State Monopoly Accident Insurance,* 2 Green Bag2d 45 (1998).

2. *Swedish Environment for No-fault Scheme.* Are the popularity and general success of the Swedish Patient Insurance Scheme attributable to that country's acceptance of social insurance?

3. *First-Party Insurance?* PATRICK ATIYALI, WRONGS AND REMEDIES IN THE 21ST CENTURY (Birks ed., Oxford U. Press 1996), criticizes personal injury tort law as a failed system, citing the usual reasons: The guilty party "hardly ever pays a single penny," but rather it is her insurer or employer who pays; recovery is unpredictable, depending on a "forensic lottery;" and deterrence arguments are weakened or demolished by the widespread availability of liability insurance.

On the other hand, he recognizes that a New Zealand system is not likely to be adopted in other common law countries, owing to the escalating costs of welfare, the demographic shifts involved in aging populations, and the general waning support for welfare schemes. As an alternative, he proposes first-party tort insurance—similar to no-fault automobile insurance. An insured could purchase the sort of plan she preferred.

Should such a first-party system be mandatory, or optional? Should coverage for pain and suffering be available? What about parties who could not afford such insurance? For a summary of Professor Atiyah's proposals, *see* Jane Stapleton, *Bold New Call to Abolish Tort,* 7 Austl. Prod. Liab. Rptr. No. 1, at 8 (Apr. 1996).

Table of Cases

[References are to page numbers.]

A

Aanenson v. Bastien 456
Abbott v. Northwestern Bell Tel. Co. . . . 651
Abernathy v. Sisters of St. Mary's 807
Abrams v. United States 1207
Abramson v. Reiss 807
Accordingly, Small v. Howard 875
Acuff-Rose Music, Inc. v. Campbell . . . . . .
. . . . 1252n54
Adams v. Amore 628
Adams v. Buffalo Forge Co. 995
Adams v. Carey 47
Adams v. Fred's Dollar Store 583
Adams v. F.W. Woolworth Co. 988
Adams v. Lopez 227
Adams v. Richland Clinic, Inc. P.S. . . . 908
Adcock v. Brakegate, Ltd. 639
Addison v. Williams 1117n3
Adoption of (see name of party)
A.H. Emery Co. v. Marcan Products Corp . .
. . . . 1309
Air Florida, Inc. v. Hobbs 689
Airspace. Rochester Gas & Elec. Corp. v. Dunlop 167
Aka v. Jefferson Hospital Assn. 532
Akers v. Kelley Co. 1028
Alabama Power Co. v. Berry 313
Alaska Airlines, Inc. v. Sweat 311
Albala v. New York 532
Albertsons, Inc. v. Kirkingburg 1386
Albright v. Oliver 1356
Alden v. Maine 797
Aldridge Motors Inc. v. Alexander 834
Alexander v. United States 1374
Allaire v. St. Luke's Hospital 528
Allaire in Amann v. Faidy 529
Alleged Contempt of (see name of party)
Allen v. Flood 1303; 1305
Allen v. Fromme 133
Allen v. Hannaford 139
Allen v. Turpin 299
Allied Tune Corp v. Indian Head Inc. . . . .
. . . . 1307
Allison v. Fiscus 199
Allison v. Shell Oil Co 838
Allison v. Vintage Sports Plaques . . . 1300
Allstate v. Farmers Mut 816
Allstate Ins. Co. v. Kim W 1414
Allstate Ins. Co. v. Sunbeam Corp. . . . 639
Alm v. Aluminum Co. of America . . . 1061
Alteiri v. Colasso 121
ALTENA v. UNITED FIRE & CASUALTY CO.
. . . . 1411
Although Rylands v. Fletcher 1102

Ambassador Ins. Co. v. Montes . . 50; 1418
American Bank & Trust Co. v. Community
  Hosp. of Los Gatos-Saratoga 1485
American Elevator Co. v. Briscoe 303;
                                            311
American Family Mut. v. Ward 816
American Motorcycle Assen v. Superior Court
. . . . 839
American Nat'l Bank v. Columbus Cuner-
  Cabrini Med. Center 837
American Protection Ins. Co. v. McMahan . .
                                           1420
American Star Ins. Co. v. Grice 1429
American Tobacco Co. v. Grinnell . . . 1016
AMF, Inc. v. Sleekcraft Boats 1377
Amicus Curiae, Parsonson v. Constr. Equip.
  Co., 18 W≻AYNE&esc; L. R≻EV.&esc;
  3, 50 738
Amoco Cadiz, In re 843
AMP, Inc. v. Fleischhacker 1325
ANAYA v. SUPERIOR COURT 433
and Board of Trustees v. Garrett 797
And in Brown v. Matthews Mortuary, Inc.
. . . . 673
And in Canton v. Harris 1355
And in J'Aire Corp. v. Gregory . . . 1072n2
And in Pollard v. Ovid, Village of 457
and Thompson v. Alameda Cty. 485
and Union Oil Co. v. Oppen 679
Anderson v. Guerrein Sky-Way Amusement
  Co. 1148
ANDERSON v. MINNEAPOLIS, ST. P. &
  S.S.M. RY. 328
Anderson v. New Orleans Pub. Serv. . . 991
Anderson v. Oliver 1455
Anderson v. Owens-Corning Fiberglas Corp.
. . . . 1049
Anderson v. Sammy Redd and Assoc . . 605
Anderson v. Service Merchandise Co. . . 298
Anderson v. Somberg 315; 899
Anderson v. St. Francis-St. George Hospital
. . . . 902
Anderson v. Strong Mem. Hosp. 861
Andrade v. Shiers 1093
Andres v. Alpha Kappa Lambda Fraternity
. . . . 458
Andrews v. Wells 496
Angelini v. OMD Corp. 701
Angrand v. Key 630
Angus v. Shiley 672
Anicet v. Gant 242; 244
Ann M. v. Pacific Plaza Shopping Center . .
                                            427
Anne Arundel Med. Center v. Condon . . . .
                                            847

TC–1

[References are to page numbers.]

Antoine v. Byers & Anderson 1219
APGAR v. LEDERLE LABORATORIES ... 769
Appeal of (see name of party)
Appeal of Estate of (see name of party)
The Appellate Court of Illinois, in Nabozny v. Barnhill 42
Application of (see name of applicant)
Applied Equip. v. Litton Saudi Arabia Ltd 1347
Applied Equipment Corp. v. Litton Saudi Arabia Ltd 673
Ard v. Ard 814
Ardinger v. Hummell 232
Arizona. Patton v. First Federal Savings and Loan Ass'n of Phoenix 160n3
Arlan v. Cervini 650
Armijo v. Ex Cam, Inc. 1117n3
ARNEJA v. GILDAR 1217
Arneson v. Olson 1483
Arnold v. Turek 690
Asaro v. Cardinal Glennon Mem. Hosp. ... 145; 517
Ash v. Mortensen 433
ASHWOOD v. CLARK COUNTY 278
Associated Elec. Coop. v. Mid-America Transp. Co 842
Associated Press v. Walker 1207
Atchison, T. & S.F.R. Co. v. Buell 507
Attwood v. Attwood, Estate of 813
Auburn Machine Works v. Jones 1050
Auclair v. Nationwide Mut. Ins. Co .. 1447
Aufrichtig v. Lowell 1221
Austin v. Shoney's, Inc 183
Austin Co. v. Royal Ins. Co 1448
Avins v. White 1204
Aydlett v. Haynes 1405
Ayers v. Robinson 651; 692
Ayers v. Township of Jackson 366
Ayyash v. Henry Ford Health Systems ... 1081

B

Babb v. Boney 741
BADER v. JOHNSON 534
Bagley v. Controlled Environment Corp. ... 1105
Baikie v. Luther High School South .. 214
Bailey v. Martz 242
Bailey v. Montgomery Ward & Co. 74
Bain v. Atkins 1450
Baker v. Bhajan 1287
Baker v. Ellis 1139
Ballard v. Uribe 409
Ballow v. Monroe 314
Banfield v. Addington 33
Banks v. Iron Hustler Corp. 1047n2

Bansasine v. Bodell 503
Barder v. McClung 1271
Bardoni v. Kim 485
Barker v. Kallash 741
Barker v. Lull Engineering Co. 1003; 1024, n8
Barnette v. Doyle 652
Barney v. Safeco Ins. Co 1453
Barnhouse v. Pinole, City of 1271
Barouh v. Haberman 108
Barreca v. Cobb 1437
Barrett v. Carter 230
Bartlett v. New Mexico Welding Supply, Inc 826
Bartnicki v. Vopper 1220; 1238
Bartolone v. Jeckovich 433
Basso v. Miller 583
Bates v. State Bar of Arizona 1380
Bauer v. Minidoka Sch. Dist. No. 331 .. 589
Baughman Surgical Assocs. v. Aetna Cas. & Sur. Co. 685
Baumgartner v. United States 1207
BAXTER v. FORD MOTOR CO. 1053
Baxter v. Superior Ct. of Los Angeles Cty. 700
BAZLEY v. TORTORICH 99
Beal for Martinez v. Seattle, City of .. 796
Bear v. Reformed Mennonite Church 1362
Beard v. Goodyear Tire & Rubber Co. 261
Beardsley v. Wierdsma 545
Beardsley v. Wierdsma, 650 P.2d 552
Beaudette v. Frana 815
Beauharnais v. Illinois 1172
Beaulieu v. Finglam, Y.B. 1085
Beaver v. Country Mutual Insurance Co ... 714
Beavers v. Johnson Controls World Services 175
Beck v. Farmers Ins. Exch. 1446
Beck v. Prupis 1375
BECKER v. CROUNSE CORP. 839
Becker v. Interstate Properties 991
Becker v. IRM Corp 65
Becker v. IRM Corporation 68
Becker v. Schwartz 540; 542
Bedell v. Reagan 995
Bedminster Township v. Vargo Dragway, Inc. 1148
Beeler v. Hickman 1091
Beesley v. VanDorn 773
Beis v. Bowers 675
Bell v. Hurstell 971
Bellikka v. Green 604
Bendectin Litigation, In re 331
BENDINGER v. MARSHALLTOWN TROWEL CO. 1319

TABLE OF CASES

[References are to page numbers.]

Bendix Autolite Corp. v. Midwesco Enterprises 771
Benefiel v. Walker 594
Beng v. Pirez, 269 N.J. Super.574 852
Berg v. General Motors Corp. 1077
Berger v. Weber 697; 700
Bergeron v. Manchester, City of 793
Berglund v. Spokane County 249; 251
Bergstreser v. Mitchell 532
Berlin v. E.C. Publications, Inc . . 1252n54
Berman v. Allan 542
Berthiaume, Estate of v. Pratt 1227
Beruan v. French 1246
Beshada v. Johns-Manville Prods. Corp . . . 1496
Beske v. Opryland USA, Inc. 561
Betts v. Stroehmann Bros. 1331
Bickford v. Tektronix, Inc 1221
Biddle v. Warren Gen'l Hosp. 1234
Bierczynsky v. Rogers 821
Big Town Nursing Home, Inc. v. Newman . . 50
Big Town Nursing Homes, Inc. v. Reserve Ins. Co. 50
BIGBEE v. PACIFIC TELEPHONE & TELEGRAPH CO. 404
Bigelow v. Virginia 1380
Bigley v. Craven 504
Biley v. Arthur Young and Co. 1275
Bill v. Superior Court 446
Billings v. Atkinson 1260
Billington v. Interinsurance Exch. of S. Cal. 1427
Bily v. Arthur Young and Co. 935
Binder v. Triangle Publications, Inc . . 800; 804
Bindrum v. Mitchell 1211
Bingaman v. Grays Harbor Community Hosp. 1484
Bird v. Casa Royale West 986
Bird v. Jones 133
Birmingham Baptist Hosp. v. Crews . . 856
Bishop v. Allstate 816
Bivens v. Six Unknown Named Agents . . . 686; 1356
Blacher, Estate of v. Garlett 412
Blacher, Estate of, Matter of 937
BLACK v. ABEX CORP. 350
Black v. Solmitz 994
Blackburn, J., in Fletcher v. Rylands 1102
Bladen v. First Presbyterian Church . . 867
Blagg v. Ill. F.W.D. Truck & Equipment Co. 744
Blakeley v. Shortal's Estate 518
Blankenship v. Bain 1455
Blatty v. New York Times Co. 1222
Blazovic v. Andrich 741

Bloomquist v. Wapello County 622
Bloxom v. Bloxom 1050
Blue Bell, Inc. v. Peat, Marwick, Mitchell & Co. 934
Blueflame Gas, Inc. v. Van Hoose 464
BMW of N. Am., Inc. v. Gore 714
B.N. v. K.K. 1272
Board of Educ. v. Farmingdale Classroom Teachers Ass'n 156
Board of Supervisors v. Lake Services, Inc 265
Board of Trustees of the Univ. of Ala. v. Garrett 1386
Boca Grande Club v. Polackwich 845
BOCKRATH v. ALDRICH CHEMICAL CO., INC. 362
BODIN v. STANWOOD, City of 248
Bolduc v. Herbert Schneider Corp . . . 1079
Bonbrest v. Kotz 528
Bond v. Huntington, City of 690
Bonin v. Gralewicz 469
Bonito Boats, Inc. v. Thunder Craft Boats, Inc 1315
Bonte v. Bonte 531; 814
Boomer v. Atlantic Cement Co. 1145
Booth v. Rome, W. & O.T.R. Co. 1103
Booth in Spano v. Perini 1103
Borden v. Smith 1323
Borel v. Fibreboard Paper Prods. Corp 1496
Borenkind v. Consolidated Edison Co. 1135n8
Borer v. American Airlines 700
Boruff v. Jesseph 535
Boryla v. Pash 671
Bose v. Consumers Union of U. S., Inc 1302
Bose Corp. v. Consumers Union of United States, Inc. 1207; 1222
Boston v. Muncy 194
Boswell v. Phoenix Newspapers, Inc . . 1264
Botek v. Mine Safety Appliance Corp. 767
Bourgeois v. A.P. Green Industries, Inc. . . . 368
Bowers v. Hardwick 1240
Bowlan v. Lunsford 181
BOWMAN v. DOHERTY 882
Bowman v. General Motors Corp. . . . 1037
Bowman v. Heller 1189
Boyce v. Brown 876
Boyd v. Bulala 1483
Boyd v. White 84
Boyer v. Seal 1092
Boyle v. United Technologies Corp. . . 1066
Boyles v. Hamilton 732
Bozeman v. Busby 724
Bradley v. Appalachian Power Co. . . . 577

[References are to page numbers.]

BRADLEY v. HUNTER 191; 200; 215
Bradshaw v. Daniel 494; 937
Bradshaw v. Swagerty 142
Brady v. Hopper 485
Branch v. Western Petr., Inc. 1102
the Brandenburg v. Ohio 446; 1223
Braniff Airways, Inc. v. Curtiss-Wright Corp.
.... 1051
Brannigan v. Raybuck 291
Brasseaux v. Girouard 193
Brasseaux v. Mamou, Town of 964
Braun v. Soldier of Fortune, Inc 1280
Breault v. Ford Motor Co. 267n1
Brejcha v. Wilson Machinery, Inc 68
Breland v. Schilling 1419
Brenner v. American Cyanamid Co. ... 360
Brewer v. Home-Stake Prod. Co. 721
Brewster v. United States 299
Brimelow v. Casson 1346
Briscoe v. LaHue 800
Broadbent v. Broadbent 814
Broadwell v. Holmes 814
Brooks v. Beech Aircraft Corp. 1111
Brooks v. Logan 793
Brown v. American Druggists' Ins. Co. ....
441
Brown v. Collins 1086
Brown v. Globe Laboratories, Inc. ... 1279
Brown v. Kendall 37; 1085
Brown v. Martinez 122
Brown v. Merlo 1476
Brown v. Scrivner, Inc 298
Brown v. State
.... 797
Brown v. Superior Court ... 71; 361; 1058
Brown; United States v. 786
Brown v. Wichita State Univ. 797
Browning v. Norton-Children's Hosp. ... 147
Browning-Ferris v. Kelco Disposal ... 1486
Browning-Ferris, Indus. v. Kelco Disposal, Inc.
.... 713
Bruce v. Byrne-Stevens & Assoc. Eng'rs ...
1221
Bruce v. Martin-Marietta Corp 1032
Bruce v. Wichita State Univ. 797
BRUNE v. BELINKOFF 874
Bruzga v. PMR Architects 1079
Bryant v. Riddle Mem. Hosp. 857
Bryson v. Tillinghast 860
BRZOSKA v. OLSON 102
Bucaretzky v. Swersky 632
Buckel v. Nunn 132
Buckingham v. R.J. Reynolds Tobacco Co. ..
1040
Buckley v. Exxon Corp 227
Buckley v. Fitzsimmons 220
Bueno v. Denver Publishing Co. 1263
Bull v. McCuskey 151
Burd v. N.J. Tel. Co. 771

Burgess v. Superior Ct. 145; 518
Burk Royalty Co. v. Pace 573
Burkett v. Freedom Arms, Inc 1117n3
Burkett v. J.A. Thompson & Son 1271
Burkhart v. Harrod 454
Burlington Industries, Inc. v. Ellerh
1232n31
Burlington Industries, Inc. v. Ellerth .. 967
Burnett v. C.B.A. Security Service ... 989
Burns v. Gleason Plant Security, Inc .. 418
Burns v. Market Transition FAC ... 1470
Burr v. Board of County Comm'rs 552
Busby v. Quail Creek Golf & Country Club
.... 287
Bushman v. Halm 338
But Doe v. Philad. Community Health ....
513
But in Adams v. Star Enters. 672
But in Hinde v. Butler 699
But in Millington v. Kuba, 5 673
But in Pulla v. Amoco Oil Co. 714
But in Rankin v. McPherson 1333
But in Smith v. Pulcinella 644
Butler v. Anderson 767
Butler v. Behaeghe 49
BUTTERFIELD v. FORRESTER 728
Butterfield v. Giuntoli 1426
Byrd v. English 679
Byrne v. Boadle 302

C

C. Brown v. Martinez 110
Cadena v. Chicago Fireworks Mfg. Co ....
1115
Cafazzo v. Cent. Medical Health Services ..
1079
Cafazzo v. Central Medical Health Servs ..
95
Cain v. Cleveland Parachute Training Center
.... 748; 749
California Cas. Gen. Ins. Co. v. Superior Court
.... 1446
California Imposes Strict Liability on Land-
lords in Becker v. IRM Corp. 72
California in Rowland v. Christian ... 579
California. Motschenbacher v. R.J. Reynolds
Tobacco Co. 1290
The California Supreme Court, in Tunkl v.
Regents of University of Cal. 748
Caltex (Philippines), Inc.; United States v.
.... 205
C.A.M. v. R.A.W. 1272; 1279
Cambridge Water Co. Ltd. v. Eastern Counties
Leather 1100; 1112
Camerlinck v. Thomas 230
Cameron Mut. Ins. Co. v. Madden ... 1453
Campbell v. Farmers Ins. Co. 1420

TABLE OF CASES

[References are to page numbers.]

Campbell v. Louisiana Department of Transportation & Development 742
Camper v. Minor 824; 980
CANNON v. DUNN 164
Canterbury v. Spence 905; 921
Cantrell v. Forest City Publishing Co 1262n56
Cantwell v. Allegheny County 5
Cantwell v. Connecticut 1173
Capan v. Daugherty 1202
Capital Alliance Ins. Co. v. Thorough-Clean, Inc 1418
Capital Holding Corp. v. Bailey . . 146; 671
Capone v. Donovan 820
Cardinal Freight Carriers v. J.B. Hunt Transport Services 1324
Cardtoons v. Major League Baseball Players Ass'n 1300
Carlin v. Superior Court 1043; 1049
Carlisle v. Consolidated Rail Corp. . . . 507
Carparts Distrib. Ctr. v. Automotive Wholesalers Ass'n 1385
Carpenter; State v. 627
Carr, in Carr v. Allison Gas Turbine Div., General Motors 1396
Carrender v. Fitterer 755
Carriceto v. Carriceto 813
Carrieri v. Bush 1361
Carrillo v. United States 979
Carroll v. Whitney 824
Carroll v. York County 797
CARROLL TOWING CO.; UNITED STATES v. 270
Carroway v. Johnson 724
Carruth v. Cunningham 1474
Carson v. Here's Johnny Portable Toilets, Inc 1249; 1294
Carson v. Maurer 1483
Cartell Capital Corp. v. Fireco of New Jersey 380
Carter v. City Parish Gov't 730
Carver v. Ford 1094
Casey v. Westinghouse Elevator Co . . . 837
CASTIGLIONE v. GALPIN 116
Castro v. QVC Network 1054
CASTRO v. QVC NETWORK, INC. . . 1001
Caterpillar Tractor Co. v. Beck 1024
Cates v. Brown 652
CATES v. CATES 807
Causby; United States v. 168
Caveny v. Raven Arms Co 1117n3
Ceballos; People v. 200
Cedric Kuhner Promot. v. King 1374
Center v. Mad River Corp 1448
Central Hudson Gas & Electric Corp. v. Public Service Comm'n of New York . . . 1379n9
Centre, Inc. v. Griese Custom Signs, Inc 1030
Certification of Questions of Law (Knowles), Matter of 1232
Cervantes v. Forbis 893
Chandler v. Hosp. Auth. 856
Chaplinsky v. New Hampshire 1223
Chapple; State v. 629
Chard v. Galton 218
Charles v. Giant Eagle Mkts. 846
Charlton v. Day Island Marina, Inc. . . 603
Chase v. Memphis, City of 795
Chavez v. Southern Pacific Transportation Co. 1108
Cheung v. Cunningham, 214 N.J. 909
Chevron Chem. Co. v. Deloitte & Touche 639
Childs v. Weis 860
Childs v. Williams 1239
Chrisafogeorgis v. Brandenberg 529
Christensen v. Murphy 599
Christensen v. Superior Court . . . 363; 668
Christensen v. Superior Ct. 672
Christian v. Goodwin 230
Christiansen v. Hollings 651
Churchill v. Pearl River Basin Development 761
Cipollone v. Liggett Group, Inc 1065
Cippollone v. Ligett Group, Inc. 1477
Cisco v. United Parcel Services Inc. . . 1331
Cisco v. United Parcel Servs., Inc. . . . 1390
Citizens State Bank v. Timm, Schmidt & Co. 932
City v. (see name of defendant)
City and County of (see name of city and county)
City Stores, Inc. v. Adams 1504
Ciup v. Chevron U.S.A., Inc. 1284
Clark v. Cantrell 715; 741
Clark v. Gibbons 316
Clark v. Hauck Mfg. Co. 699
Clark v. Tennessee Valley Authority . . 585
Clark v. Virginia Bd. of Bar Exmrs. . . 1385
THE CLARK-AIKEN COMPANY v. CROMWELL-WRIGHT COMPANY, INC. 1104
Clay v. Jersey City 522
Cleveland v. Piper Aircraft Corp 378
Client's Security Fund v. Grandeau . . . 980
Clinton v. Jones 805
Clodgo v. Bowman 801
CNA Ins. Co. v. McGinnis 1414
Cobbs v. Grant 907; 912; 923
Coca Cola Bottling Co. v. Reeves 833
Cockrum v. Baumgartner 545; 551
Cohen v. Cowles Media Co 1216; 1238
Cohen v. Smith 147
Cohen v. Southland Corp. 431
Coker v. Southwestern Bell Telephone Co. 346

[References are to page numbers.]

COLBY v. McCLENDON 178; 200
Coleman v. Garrison 545
Coleman v. United Fence Co. 560
Coll v. Johnson 626
Collins v. Elkay Mining Co 1335
Colman v. Notre Dame Convalescent Home, Inc 244
Colombrito v. Kelly 210
Colonial Stores, Inc. v. Barrett 1165
Commission v. (see name of opposing party)
Commissioner v. (see name of opposing party)
Commissioner of Internal Revenue (see name of defendant)
Commonwealth v. (see name of defendant)
Commonwealth ex rel. (see name of relator)
Comunale v. Traders & Gen. Ins. Co. 1440
Comunale v. Traders & General Ins. Co. . . . 1443
Condemarin v. University Hosp. 1485
Coney v. J.L.G. Indus. 741; 825
Connecticut v. Battista 1223
Connell v. Hudson, Town of 1237
Connick v. Myers 1333
Connick v. Myers, 461 U.S., at 147–148. These 1194
Connors v. Univ. Assoc. 896
Conservatorship of (see name of party)
Consider Burt v. Beautiful Savior Lutheran Church of Broomfield 166
Consider Hustler Magazine, Inc. v. Falwell 1190
Consider Osborn v. Hertz Corp. 457
Consider Tompkins v. Northwestern Union Trust Co. 312
Consider Wells v. Billars 861
Consol. R. Corp. v. Gotshall 518
CONSOLIDATED RAIL CORP. v. GOTSHALL 504
Consolidated Rail Corporation v. Gottshall 538
Continental Ins. Co. v. McDaniel 1417
Continental Trend Resources, Inc. v. OXY USA, Inc. 713
Contrast Columbia Broadcasting Sys., Inc. v. DeCosta 1296
Contrast Hammontree v. Jenner 246
Contrast Horton v. Reaves 231
Contrast Kellos v. Sawilowsky 878
Contrast Lininger v. Eisenbaum 540
Contrast Martin v. Heddinger 457
Contrast McGuire v. Almy 247
Contrast Mignone v. Fieldcrest Mills . . 601
Contrast Pauscher v. Iowa Methodist Med. Center 908
Contrast Peak v. Barlow 294
Contrast Saltzer v. Reckord 888

Contrast Stachniewicz v. Mar-Cam Corp. . . . 328
Contreras v. Crown Zellerbach Corp. . . . 142
Cook v. Babcock 1134
Cook v. Minneapolis, S. P. & S.S.M. R. Co. 329
Cook v. R.I. Dep't. of Mental Health, Retardation & Hosps., Stat 1385
Cook v. Stansell 845
Cooley v. Public Serv. Co. 275
Cooper Stevedoring Co. v. Fritz Kopke, Inc 787; 841
Copart Indus. v. Consolidated Edison Co. of N.Y. 1147
Copeland v. Pike Liberal Arts School . . . 587n3
COPIER BY AND THROUGH LINDSEY v. SMITH & WESSON 1115
Copithorne v. Framingham Union Hosp. . . . 943
Corcoran v. United Health Care, Inc. . . 957
Cordle v. General Hugh Mercer Corp 1335
Corey v. Jones 1476
Cormier v. American Deposit Insur. Co. . . . 1410; 1452
Corn v. Sheppard 110
Corp. Health Insurance Inc. v. The Texas Dept. of Insurance 957
Corso v. Crawford Dog & Cat Hosp. . . . 147
Cotilletta v. Tepedino 624
Cotton v. Kambly 864
Coulson v. DeAngelo 1117n3
County v. (see name of defendant)
County of (see name of county)
Court v. Grzelinski 601
Court of Appeals, in Hutchinson v. Dickie . . 471
Court of Appeals, in Swetland v. Curtiss Airports Corporation 167
Courtell v. McEachan 973
Courvoisier v. Raymond 194; 200; 215
Coury v. Safe Auto Sales, Inc. 303
Cox Broadcasting Corp. v. Cohn 1235; 1237
Crabtree v. Dawson 215
Crabtree Industrial Waste, Inc, Ex parte . . 296
Craig v. Harney 1174
Cramer v. Cramer 695
Cramer v. Van Parys 252
Crawford v. Buckner 752
Crawford v. Rogers 309; 310
Crawn v. Campo 43; 108
CREASY v. RUSK 240; 241
Credit Alliance Corp. v. Arthur Andersen & Co 1274
Crews v. Hollenbach 763

TABLE OF CASES

[References are to page numbers.]

Crisci v. Security Ins. Co 673; 1440; 1444; 1445
Criscuola v. Power Auth. 672
CROCKER v. WINTHROP LABORATORIES 1277
Crocker v. Winthrop Labs 1054
Croft v. Wicker 143; 144
Croft v. Wickes 518
Cronin v. J.B.E. Olson Corp. 1024
Crosby v. Cox Aircraft Co. 1118
CROSBY v. COX AIRCRAFT CO. OF WASHINGTON 83
Crosby v. Glasscock Trucking Co 693
Cross v. Guthery 876
Crowe v. De Gioia 516
CROWN v. RAYMOND 289
Crump v. Beckley Newspapers, Inc . . 1257
Cruz v. Montoya 713
Cruzan v. Director, Missouri Dep't of Health 191
C.T. v. Martinez 288
Culbertson v. Mernitz 535
Cullison v. Medley 538
Cullum & Boren-McCain Mall, Inc. v. Peacock 465
Cummings v. Jackson 810
Cummings v. Pinder, Del.Supr 106
Cunningham v. District of Columbia, No. Civ. A. 87-0095 627
Cunningham v. Insurance Co. of N. Am. 1453
Curran v. Bosze 191
Curran v. Heslop 1271
Curtis Pub. Co. v. Butts 1184; 1185n9
Curtis Pub'g Co. v. Butts 1178
Curtis Publishing Co. v. Butts . . . 1185n8; 1192; 1207
Cusseaux v. Pickett 773
Custody of (see name of party)
Customer Co. v. Sacrament, City of . . 1127
Customer Co. v. Sacramento, City of . . 204; 1364
Cutler v. Klass, Whichler & Mishne . . 675
Cyr v. Adamar Associates Limited Partnership 562
Czarnecki v. Volkswagen of America . . 375

D

Dalehite v. United States 789
Dalley v. Utah Valley Regional Medical Center 315
Dameck v. St. Paul Fire & Marine Ins. Co. 101
D'Amico v. Christie 463
D'Amico v. New York State Bd. of Law Examiners 1382

Danger Invites Rescue. Ogwo v. Taylor . . . 601
Daniels v. Evans 225; 226; 233
Daniels v. Williams 1355
DARLING v. CHARLESTON COMMUNITY MEMORIAL HOSPITAL 886
Darlington Corp. v. Finch 297
Dart v. Wiebe 1111
Dart v. Wiebe Manufacturing, Inc. . . 1007; 1111
Dart v. Wiebe Mfg. 1043
Dart v. Wiebe Mfg., Inc. 1003n6
DaSilva v. American Tobacco Co.. 360
Daubert v. Merrell Dow Pharmaceuticals, Inc. 614
Daugert v. Pappas 330; 346
Davenport v. Cotton Hope Plantation Horizontal Prop 761
Davenport v. Garcia 1262
Davidson v. Cannon, 474 U.S. 1356
DAVIDSON v. TIME WARNER, INC. 441
Davies v. Mann, 10 M. & W. 547 730
DAVIS v. BOARD OF COUNTY COM'RS . . 1281
Davis v. Davis 815
Davis v. Elizabeth Gen. Med. Ctr. 692
Davis v. Smith 814
Davis Contractors v. Fareham U.D.C. 222
Davler v. Raymark Indus., Inc. 355
Dawson v. Associates Financial Services Co. 140
Day v. General Motors Corp. 377
DAY v. STATE 436
D.C. Transit System v. Brooks 721
De Font v. United States 788
De Long v. Erie, County of 652
De May v. Roberts 173
DeBry v. Godbe 219
Del E. Webb Corp. v. Structural Materials Co. 364
Del E. Webb Corp. v. Superior Court of Arizona 290; 293
Delahanty v. Hinckley 1117n3
Deliso v. Cangialosi 231
Dellwo v. Pearson 224; 225; 226; 233
DeLong v. Erie County 796
Delp v. Itmann Coal Co. 576
DeLuca v. Bowden 230
DeLuca v. Merrell Dow Pharmaceuticals, Inc. 623
DeLude v. Rimek 850
DeMarco v. Holy Cross High School . . 1391
Dennis v. United States 448; 1175
Denny v. Ford Motor Co. . . . 1002n3; 1003
Deno v. Transamerica Title Ins. Co. . . 676
Denver v. Kennedy 1089

Denver City Tramway v. Brown 995
Denver & R.G.R. Co. v. Peterson 254
Depue v. Flateau 206; 470
Dermatossian v. New York City Transit Auth.
 312
Desai v. Silver Dollar City, Inc 760
DeSantis v. Frick Co. 1051
Desny v. Wilder 1298
DeSpirito v. Bristol County Water Co. ....
 686
Destefano v. Grabrian 676; 862
Determinant. Perreira v. State 492
Deyo v. Kinley 51
Di Ossi v. Maroney 456
DIAMOND SHAMROCK REFINING AND
 MARKETING COMPANY v. MENDEZ ..
 1255
Diaz v. Oakland Tribune, Inc. 1245
Dicken v. Liverpool Salt & Coal Co. .. 581
Dickens v. Puryear 134
Dierks v. Mitsubishi Motors Corp. ... 1016
Diesen v. Hessburg 1203
DIETEMANN v. TIME, INC. ... 169; 1228
Dietz v. General Elec. Co. 374
Digby v. Digby 815
Diggles v. Horwitz 1040; 1117n3
Dikeman, In re Estate of 1474
Dillon v. Legg 510
Dillon v. Legg. Why 517
DILLON v. TWIN STATE GAS & ELECTRIC
 CO. 322
Dinger v. Department of Natural Resources
 652
District of Columbia v. Davis 969
District of Columbia v. Washington Hospital
 Center 836
District of Columbia v. White 627
Dixon v. Richer 195
Doe v. B.P.S. Guard Services Inc 1227
Doe v. Cuomo 518
Doe v. Cutter Biological 360
Doe v. Dewhirst 183
Doe v. High-Tech Institute, Inc 185
Doe v. McMillan 1220
Doe v. Roe 861
Dole v. Dow Chem. Co. 847
Dollins v. Hartford Acc. & Indem. Co. ....
 895
Donnell v. California Western Sch. of Law
 427
Donnelly v. Southern Pacific Co. 707
Donovan v. Bierwirth 956
Doody v. Spurr 1135n9
Dorse v. Armstrong World Industries ....
 1069
Dorset Yacht Co. v. Home Office 473
Dotson v. Blake 824
Dotson v. McLaughlin 141

Downes v. FAA 1394
Downing; United States v. 616
Doyle v. Piccadilly Cafeterias 822
Dred Scott v. Sandford, 60 U.S. (19 How.) 393
 577
Dukes v. U.S. Healthcare, Inc. 957
DuLaney v. Oklahoma State Department of
 Health 1139
Dumas v. Hartford Acc. & Indem. Co. ....
 1445
Dun & Bradstreet v. Greenmoss Bldrs. ...
 1215
Dun & Bradstreet v. Greenmoss Builders ..
 1302
Dun & Bradstreet, Inc. v. Greenmoss Builders
 1199
DUN & BRADSTREET, INC. v. GREENMOSS
 BUILDERS, INC. 1190; 1199n15;
 1210; 1222
Dunlap v. Dunlap 809
DUNLEA v. DAPPEN 774
Dunn v. HOVIC 715
Dunn v. Kanawha County Bd. of Educ ....
 847
Dunn v. Prais 836
Dunn v. Teti 230
DUNPHY v. GREGOR 514; 517
DUPLER v. SEUBERT 122
Dupree v. Piggly Wiggly Shop Rite Foods, Inc.
 988
Dupuis v. Hand 676
Duteau v. Dresbach 877
Dutsch v. Sea Ray Boats, Inc. 684
DUTT v. KREMP 148
Duttry v. Patterson 929
Duty-Risk v. Proximate Cause and the Rational
 Allocation of Functions Bet 409
Dwyer v. Skyline Apartments, Inc 66
Dwyer v. Skyline Apts., Inc. 603
Dykeman v. Englebrecht 743
Dziubak v. Mott 804

E

Early v. N.L.V. Casino Corp. 990
Earsing v. Nelson 465
EAST RIVER STEAMSHIP CORP. v. TRANS-
 AMERICA DELAVAL, INC. 1069
Easter v. Lexington Mem. Hosp. 860
Eastwood v. Superior Court . 1248; 1251n46
Eaton v. McLain 237; 562
Ebanks v. New York City Transit Auth. ...
 302
Economy Fire & Cas. Co. v. Haste ... 1418
Ed Nowogroski Insurance, Inc. v. Rucker ..
 1326
Eden v. Conrail 561

TABLE OF CASES

[References are to page numbers.]

Edgcomb v. Lower Valley Power & Light .. 1135n8
Edmonds v. Compagnie Generale Transatlantique 841
Edwards v. Basel Pharmaceuticals .. 1062
Edwards v. Basel Pharms 25
Egan v. Mutual of Omaha Ins. Co. 708; 709
E.I. duPont de Nemours & Co. v. Christopher 1311
Eichner, and In re 188
8. Abandonment. Consider Brandt v. Grubin 861
Eilers v. Coy 209
Eimann v. Soldier of Fortune Magazine ... 442
Eimann v. Soldier of Fortune Magazine, Inc. 1280
Eiseman v. New York, State of 462
Elbaor v. Smith 851
Eldredge v. Kamp Kachess Youth Serv., Inc. 491
Electric Power Board v. Westinghouse 774
Ellis v. D'Angelo 491
Ellis v. Union Pacific R. Co. 508
Ellison v. Brady 1394
Elrod v. Burns 1338
Elsmere Music, Inc. v. NBC 1252n54
Emery v. Emery 1475
Emery v. Small 51
Employer's Liability Assur. Corporation v. Greenville Business Men's Assoc. ... 748
England, Rylands v. Fletcher 86
English v. New England Med. Ctr., Inc. ... 1485
Enright v. Eli Lilly & Co. 359
Enright v. Groves 131; 1358
E.R. Harding Co. v. Paducah S. Ry. ... 974
Erb v. Maryland Dep't of the Environment 1125
Erickson v. Christenson 868
Erlich v. Menezes 673
Ermert v. Hartford 962
Erskine v. Commissioner of Corrections ... 793
Escola v. Coca Cola Bottling Co. 1071; 1074
Escola v. Coca Cola Bottling Co. of Fresno 1023
Esmail v. Macrane 1356
ESPOSITO-HILDER v. SFX BROADCASTING INC. 1213
Essex v. Ryan 932; 933
Est. of (see name of party)
Estate of (see name of party)
ESTATES OF MORGAN v. FAIRFIELD FAMILY COUNSELING CENTER 479

Ettus v. Orkin Exterminating Co 849
Evans v. Moffat 1149
Everitt v. United States 790
Ewert v. Georgia Cas. & Sur. Co. 740
Ex parte (see name of applicant)
Ex rel. (see name of relator)
Exner v. Sherman Power Constr. Co. .. 81
Exner v. Sherman Power Construc. Co. ... 1103
Ezell v. Cockrell 493; 796

F

F & T Co. v. Woods 991
Faber, in Faber v. Condecor, Inc 1253
Fager v. Hundt 776
Falgoust v. Herbert, Mouledoux & Bland .. 675
Falls v. Scott 977
Falwell v. Flynt 145
Faniel v. Chesapeake & Potomac Tel. Co. ... 126
Faragher v. Boca Raton, City of 967; 1232n31
Farmer v. Brennan 1358
Farrell v. Minneapolis & R.R. Ry. 329
Farris v. United States Fid. & Gaur. Co. .. 1446
FARWELL v. KEATON 468
Faul v. Jelco 969
Faya v. Almaraz 930
FCC v. Pacifica Found 1215
February of 1973 the Supreme Court of California, in Brown v. Merlo 1473
Federal Sav. & Loan Ins. Corp. v. Shearson AmEx 1375
Federhoff v. Federhoff 813
Fein v. Permanente Medical Group .. 1483
Feld v. Merriam 3
Feldman v. Lederle Laboratories 832; 1058
Fellows v. National Enquirer, Inc ... 1264
Feltch v. General Rental Co. 701
Fennell v. Southern Maryland Hospital ... 344
Feoffees of Heriot's Hosp. v. Ross, 13 C & F 507 806
Feres v. United States 785; 1067
Ferguson v. Boyd 609n1
Ferguson v. Northern States Power Co. ... 1118
Fermino v. Fedco 125
Fernandez v. Walgreen Hastings Co. .. 700
Ferreira v. Strack 439
Fibreboard Corp, In re 1497
Fields v. Sanders 961
Finally, in Rosenbloom v. Metromedia, Inc 1185n8

[References are to page numbers.]

Finstad v. Washburn University of Topeka 873
Fire Ins. Exchange v. Diehl 1419
Firelock, Inc. v. District Ct. 1501
Fireman's Fund Ins. Co. v. Hill 1415
Fireman's Fund Ins. Co. v. Hill and Horace Mann Ins. Co. 1415
Firth v. Scherzberg 1131n2
Fischer v. Famous-Barr Co. 125
Fiser v. Ann Arbor, City of 438
Fisher v. Carrousel Motor Hotel, Inc. .. 109
Fisher v. Dees 1252n54
FITZGERALD MARINE SALES v. LeUNES 1015
Fitzpatrick v. Bitzer 797
Fla. Prepaid Postsecondary v. College Savings 797
Flaherty v. Butte Elec. R.R. 994
Flamm v. American Association of University Women 1205
Flanagan v. Gregory and Poole, Inc .. 1123
Flannery v. United States 647; 692
Fletcher v. Rylands 55; 76; 78; 1095
Fletcher v. Western National Life Ins. Co. .. 1441; 1445
Flint Explosive Co. v. Edwards 464
Flores v. Baca 672
Florida Star v. B.J.F. 1237
Flowers v. Rock Creek Terrace Ltd. Pt'ship 596
FOCAL POINT, INC. v. U-HAUL OF ARIZONA, INC. 158
Foland v. Malander 1094
Foley v. Interactive Data Corp .. 673; 1336
Food Lion, Inc. v. Capital Cities/ABC, Inc. 1237
Ford v. Cournale 1271
Ford v. London & South Western Ry. Co., 2 F. & F. 730, 732&n 222
Ford v. Trident Fisheries Co. 327
Ford Motor Car v. Miles 701
Foreseeable Risk. Blyth v. Birmingham Water Works Co. 222
Fort v. Smith 127
Fosbre v. State 560
Foss v. Pacific Telephone and Telegraph Co. 346
Foster v. Preston Mill Co. 1119
Foulds v. Willoughby, 8 M. & W. 540 .. 160
4. Custom and Rules of the Game. Condon v. Basi 269
4. Residential, Urban Property and Social Guests. Wymer v. Holmes 590
4. The Renaissance of Rylands v. Fletcher. According 1102
4. The Unique Crime. Lopez v. McDonald's 430

the Fourth District Court of Appeal in Gross v. Family Services Agency, Inc 30
Fowler v. Harper 113
Frank v. National Broadcasting Co. .. 1216
Frankson v. Design Space Int'l 1203
FRED SIEGEL CO., L. P. A. v. ARTE & HADDEN 1340
Freedom Newspapers, Inc. v. The Superior Court 1264
Freeman v. Bell 101; 991
Freeman & Mills, Inc. v. Belcher Oil Co ... 673
Freese v. Lemmon 935
Frisch's Restaurants, Inc. v. Elby's Big Boy, Inc. 1294
From Brzoska v. Olson 672
Fromenthal v. Clark 112; 230
Fruit v. Schreiner 969
F.T.C. v. Superior Court Trial Lawyers Ass'n 1307
the FTCA. Carlson v. Green 1359
Fuches v. S.E.S. Co. 766
Fuentes v. Perez 673
Fugate v. Fugate 814
Fuhrer v. Gearhart 562
Fuld, J., in Bing v. Thunig 887
Fuller v. First National Supermarkets, Inc. 561
Fuller v. Illinois C.R.R. 730
Furman v. Sheppard 1229
Furstein v. Hill 419
Furukawa v. Ogawa 732
Futch v. Commercial Union Ins. Co. .. 380
Fyffle v. Jeno's Inc. 1514

G

G. Heileman Brewing Co. v. Joseph Oat Corp. 1495
G.A. Stowers Furn. Co. v. American Indem. Co. 1445
Gagliardi v. Denny's Restaurants, Inc. 674
Galayda v. Lake Hosp. Sys. 1485
Gamble v. United States 978
Gardiner v. Schobel 746
Gardner v. Concord, City of 793
Garratt v. Dailey 107
Garrison v. Foy 537
Garrison v. Louisiana ... 1178; 1184; 1195; 1208; 1223
Garrison Retirement Home v. Hancock ... 33
Garvis v. Employers Mut. Casualty Co 510n11
Gary Van Zeeland Talent v. Sandas .. 1326
Gates v. Richardson 700
Gattman v. Favro 456

TABLE OF CASES

[References are to page numbers.]

Gaudette v. Webb 690
Gautam v. De Luca 499n14
Gauthier v. O'Brien 826
Gawara v. United States Brass Corp. ....
  1286
Geary v. Visitation of the Blessed Virgin Mary
  1391
Gehres v. Phoenix 1490
Gehres v. Phoenix, City of 374
Geier v. American Honda Motor Co., Inc ...
  1065
Geller v. Fallon McElligott, No. 90 ......
  1252n52
General Home Improv. Co. v. American Ladder
  Co., Inc 834
General Motors Corp. v. Doupnik 699;
  836
George v. Parke-Davis 362
George Mattingly v. Sheldon Jackson College
  524
Gertz v. Robert Welch, Inc. 1161; 1180;
  1190; 1192; 1197; 1207; 1215
GHASSEMIEH v. SCHAFER 45
Giardina v. Bennett 533
Gibson v. Gibson 809
Giles v. New Haven, City of 743
Gillespie v. St. Joseph's Univ. 1331
Gillespie v. Washington 592n1
Gillett v. Gillett 814
Gilmer v. Interstate Johnson Lane Corp ...
  1504
Gilstrap v. Amtrak 982
Girard v. Rebsamen Ins. Co . 1322; 1323n4
Girl Scouts v. Personality Posters Mfg ....
  1251n48
G.L. v. Kaiser Found. Hosps. 943
Gladney v. Cutrer 230
Glanzer v. Shepard, 233, N.Y. 236 ... 934
GLICK v. OLDE TOWN LANCASTER, INC.
  1
GLOMB v. GLOMB 819; 991
The Glombs in Glomb v. Glomb 822
Godfrey v. Steinpress 1271
Godwin v. Stanely 201
Goff v. Harold Ives Trucking Co., Inc . . 638
Goff v. Taylor 246
Goldstein v. California 1315
Goldstein v. Levy 337
GOLEN v. THE UNION CORP. 1130
Goller v. White 809
Golub v. Enquirer/Star Group, Inc ... 1163
GOMEZ v. HUG 139
Gooden v. Tips 935
Goodfellow v. Coggburn 225
Goodlett v. Kalishek 760
Goodman v. Fairlawn Garden Ass'n., Inc. ..
  644
Goodseal; State v. 200

Gordon v. Eastern Ry. Supply, Inc. ... 974
Gordon v. Havasu Palms, Inc. 761
Gordon v. Oak Park School Dist. 214
Gordon v. State 724
Gorris v. Scott 284
Gortarez v. Smitty's Super Valu, Inc . . 195
Gorton v. Reliance Ins. Co. 1452
Goss v. Allen 227; 232
Goss v. Lopez 214
Gotreaux v. Gary 1118
Gottshall v. Consolidated Rail Corp ... 505
Gould v. American Family Mut. Ins. .. 242
Gould v. American Family Mut. Ins. Co. ...
  244
Gould v. Brox 600
Gracyalny v. Westinghouse Elec. Corp. ....
  1051
Grant v. F.P. Lathrop Constr. 500
Graves v. Church & Dwight Co. 771
Graves v. Graves 731
Gray v. Ford Motor Co. 435
Great Am. Ins. Co. v. C.G. Tate Constr. Co.
  1427
Great Lakes Dredge & Dock v. Miller ....
  843
Great Southwest Fire Ins. Co. v. CNA Ins. Co.
  1436
Greco v. United States 534
Greely v. Johnson 1090
Green v. Denney 1041
Green v. General Petroleum Corp. 90
Green v. Sherburne Corp. 53
Green v. Superior Court 69
Green Tree Financial Corp. v. Randolph ...
  1504
Greenbelt Cooperative Publishing Ass'n v.
  Bresler 1200n18
Greenman v. Yuba Power Prods., Inc. .. 73
Greenman v. Yuba Power Products ......
  1004n8; 1054
Greenman v. Yuba Power Products, Inc ...
  65; 67; 1023
Gretchen v. United States 1485
Grey v. Fibreboard Paper Prod. Co. ... 736
Griffin v. Clark 127
Griffin v. General Motors Corp. 652
Griffin v. James Butler Grocery Co. ... 834
Griffith v. Southland Corp. 473
Grimshaw v. Ford Motor Co. 276; 702
Grinnell Mut. Reinsurance Co. v. Wasmuth
  1419
Grist v. Upjohn Co. 1166
Griswold v. Connecticut 551; 1241n40;
  1461
Groce v. Foster 1333
Grodin v. Grodin 529
Gronneberg v. Hoffart 240
Gross v. Allstate Ins. Co. 1419

[References are to page numbers.]

Gross v. Sweet 749
Grover v. Eli Lilly & Co. 359
Groves v. Taylor 538
GRUENBERG v. AETNA INSURANCE CO.
  1439
Guardianship of (see name of party)
GUERRERO v. COPPER QUEEN HOSPITAL
  854
Guglielmi v. Spelling-Goldberg Prods . . . . .
  1251n47
Gulledge v. Gulledge 810
Gunter v. Marine Offshore Catering Co. . . .
  701

H

H. Rosenblum, Inc. v. Adler 1275
Hackett v. Perron 974
HACKING v. BELMONT, Town of . . . 792
Hadley v. Baxendale 674
Hafner v. Beck 860
Haft v. Lone Palm Hotel 327
Hager v. Marshall 845
Hall v. Cole 719
Hall v. Edlefson 572
Hall v. E.I. Du Pont de Nemours & Co., Inc.
  356
Hall v. Hilbun 877
HALL v. McBRYDE 120
Halphen v. Johns-Manville Sales Corp . . . .
  1009, n1; 1010
HALPHEN v. JOHNS-MANVILLE SALES
  CORPORATION 1009
Hambright v. First Baptist Church-Eastwood
  586
Hames v. State 413
Hamilton v. Accu-Tek . . 461; 463; 464; 465,
  n10; 468; 1117n3
Hamilton v. Beretta U.S.A. Corp 359;
  461
Hamilton County v. Asbestospray Corp. . . .
  774
Hammer v. Hammer 775
Hammer v. Rosen 885
HAMMONTREE v. JENNER 62
Hampton v. Hammons 572; 573
Hancock v. Paccar, Inc 1032
Handeland v. Brown 996
Hansen v. Friend 451
Hansen v. Mountain Fuel Supply Co. . . 654
Hansen v. Sea Ray Boats, Inc. 517
Hanson v. Snohomish, City of 154
Harbeson v. Parke Davis, Inc. 908
Hard Place. Consider Cooley v. Public Serv. Co.
  273
HARDINGHAM v. UNITED COUNSELING
  SERVICE 50
Hardy v. SW. Bell Tel. Co. 345
Harfield v. Tate 240
Harford Penn-Cann Service, Inc. v. Zymblosky
  1132
Harford Penn-Cann Service, Inc. v. Zymblosky,
  378 Pa. Super, 578 1149
Hark v. Mountain Fork Lumber Co . . 1123
Harkey v. Abate 1227
Harless v. Ewing 894
Harless v. Workman 1124
Harley-Davidson Motorsports, Inc. v. Markley
  1194
Harlow v. Fitzgerald 805
Harmer v. Virginia Elec. & Power Co. . . . .
  1381
Harmon v. Harmon 1349
Harned v. E-Z Finance Co. 146
Haroco, Inc. v. American National Bank &
  Trust Co. of Chicago 1369
Harper v. Regency Dev. Co. 82
HARRIS v. FORKLIFT SYSTEMS, INC. . . .
  1392
Harris v. Hirschfeld 1346
Harris v. Lincoln, Town of 1151
Harris v. NCNB National Bank for North Carolina 218
Harris v. R.A. Martin, Inc. 582
Harris-Fields v. Syze 595n10
Harrison v. Taylor 562
HARRISON v. WISDOM 202
Harte-Hanks Commun., Inc. v. Connaughton
  1180
Hartford Accident & Indemnity Co. v. Cardillo
  961
Harwell Enterprises, Inc. v. Heim . . . 1322
Hasenei v. United States 493
Hastie v. Handeland 434
Hatfield v. Continental Imports, Inc . . 852
Haumersen v. Ford Motor Co. 691
Haun v. Tally 364
Hawaii Fed. Asbestos Cases, In re . . . 1069
Hawaii Federal Asbestos Cases, In re . . . .
  660
Hawkins v. Peart 752
Hay v. Cohoes County 1103
Haymon v. Wilkerson 543
Hazelwood v. Illinois Central Gulf R.R. . . .
  713
Hazine v. Montgomery Elevator Co. . . 778
HBE Leasing Corp. v. Frank 1375
Healey v. Firestone Tire & Rubber Co. . . . .
  360
Heaton v. Ford Motor Co. 1019
Hebel v. Hebel 695; 1405; 1408n8
Hebert v. International Paper Co. 676
Hector v. Cedars-Sinai 96
Hector v. Cedars-Sinai Med. Center . . . 95
Hector v. Cedars-Sinai Medical Center . . . .
  1080

TABLE OF CASES

[References are to page numbers.]

Heiman v. Pan American Life Ins. Co. 101
Heins v. Webster County 580
Helen L. v. DiDario 1381
Hellar v. Bianco 1167
Hellenbrand v. Bowar 834
HELLING v. CAREY 91; 888
Hellriegel v. Tholl 184
Helvich v. George A. Rutherford Co. . . . 587
HENDRICKS v. STALNAKER 1122
Henker v. Preybylowski 643
Henningsen v. Bloomfield Motors, Inc 1001; 1022; 1074n4
Henrioulle v. Marin Ventures, Inc. 751
HENRY v. BAUDER 1472; 1475
Hepp v. Quickel Auto & Supply Co. . . . 893
Herceg v. Hustler Magazine, Inc. 1279
Hercules, Inc. v. United States 1068
Hernandez v. United States 790
Herrle v. Marshall, Estate of 244
Herskovits v. Group Health Coop of Puget Sound 346
Hess v. Sports Publishing Co. 822
HESS v. ST. FRANCIS REGIONAL MEDICAL CENTER 848
Hester v. Barnett 1363
HIBPSHMAN v. PRUDHOE BAY SUPPLY, INC. 694
Hidding v. Williams 930
HILL v. LUNDIN & ASSOCIATES, INC. . . 320
Hill v. Searle Labs., Div. of Searle Pharmaceuticals, Inc. 1058
Hill v. State 1362
Hill v. Yaskin 432
Hillebrandt v. Holsum Bakeries, Inc. . . 653
Hines v. Government Emps. Ins. Co. 1453
Hinkie v. United States 788
Hinman v. Westinghouse Elec. Co. . . . 969
Hinman v. Yakima School Dist. No. 7 1384
Hinzman v. Palmanteer 689
H.J., Inc. v. Northwestern Bell Tel. Co. . . . 1371
Hodder v. Goodyear Tire & Rubber Co. . . . 778
Hodges v. Carter 9; 14
Hodges v. S.C. Toof & Co. 724
Hoff v. Vacaville Unified School District . . . 441
Hoff v. Zimmer, Inc 1080
Hoffman v. Jones 735; 737
Hoffman v. United Iron and Metal Co. 1154
Hoffnagle v. McDonald's Corp. 983
HOLCOMBE v. WHITAKER 117
HOLMES v. AMEREX RENT 635

Holmstrom v. Wall 1230
Holodook v. Spencer 814
Holtz v. Holder 371
Home Ins. Co. v. Neilsen 1414
Home Ins. Co. v. Nielsen 48
Honda v. Oberg 722
Hood v. Dun & Bradstreet, Inc. . . 1194n14
HOOD v. RYOBI AMERICA CORP. . . 1044
Hood v. Ryobi N. Am., Inc. 1045
Hopkins v. Fox and Lazo 515
Horace Mann Ins. Co. v. Independent School Dist. 1415
Horne v. Patton 860
Horton v. Royal Order of the Sun . . . 1117
Houghton v. Leinwohl 627
Housley v. Cerise 338
Howard v. Allstate Ins. Co. 742; 827
Howard v. Lecher 646
Howard v. Spafford 53
Howard Frank, M.D., P.C. v. Superior Ct. of Ariz. 700
HOWELL v. CLYDE 753
Howell v. New York Post Co. . . 1214; 1215; 1237
Hudson v. Craft 180
Hudson v. Hudson Mun. Contrs. 1453
Hudson v. Peavey Oil Co. 1118
Hudson v. Union Carbide Corp 847
Huffman v. Caterpillar Tractor Co. . . . 1050
Hughes v. Lord Advocate 404
Hughes v. Quarve & Anderson Co. . . . 574
Humphers v. First Interstate Bank . . . 860
Hunnings v. Texaco, Inc. 464
Hunt v. University of Minnesota . . . 1198; 1202
Hunter v. Port Auth. of Allegheny County . . 1330
Hunter v. Up-right, Inc 673
Hurley v. Allied Chem. Corp. 1335
Hurley v. Lederle Laboratories 1062
Huset v. J.I. Case Threshing Machine Co. . . 1022n4
Hustler v. Falwell 1237
HUSTLER MAGAZINE v. FALWELL 1206; 1214; 1215; 1263n57; 1378
Hustler Magazine, Inc. v. Falwell 146
Hustler Magazine, Inc. v. Falwell, the Court 1216; 1265
Hutcherson v. Phoenix, City of 377
Hutchinson v. Proxmire 1189
Hymowitz v. Eli Lilly & Co. 358

I

Id. Recently, in Credit Alliance Corp. v. Arthur Andersen & Co. 931
IDAHO BANK & TRUST CO. v. FIRST BANCORP OF IDAHO 1273

[References are to page numbers.]

Illinois Farmers Ins. Co. v. Judith G. 1415
Imre v. Riegel Paper Corp. 567
iN Chizmar v. Mackie 503
In re (see name of party)
Incollingo v. Ewing 878
Indian Towing Co. v. United States ... 792
Indiana Harbor v. Amer. Cyanamid .. 1107
Indiana Harbor Belt R. Co. v. Amer. Cyanamid Co. 1104
Ingraham v. Wright 214
Insurance Co. of Ill. v. Markogiannakis ... 1449
IRA S. BUSHEY & SONS v. UNITED STATES 958
Irby v. Doe 594
Irving v. U.S. 792
ISAACS v. POWELL ... 1087; 1089; 1092
Isaacs v. Powell and Jones 1092
Ives v. South Buffalo Railway Co. 27

J

Jabczenski v. Souther Pacific Memorial Hospital 160n3
Jackson v. McCuiston 231
Jackson v. Metrop. Knoxville Airport Authority 1125
Jackson v. Power 944
Jackson v. Ray Kruse Constr. Co. 326
Jackson v. Righter 965
Jackson State Bank v. King 741
Jacobsen v. Rathdrum, City of 588
Janelsins v. Button 113
Janklow v. Newsweek, Inc .. 1198; 1202n19
Jansen v. Howard 588
Jarrett v. Woodward Bros., Inc. 456
Jaubert v. Crowley Post-Signal, Inc. .. 169; 1265
JAWORSKI v. KIERNAN ... 40; 415; 417
J.C. Penney Co. v. Gravelle 988
Jefferson v. Griffin Spalding County Hosp. Auth. 901
Jefferson v. United States 885
Jendralski v. Black 603
Jenkens v. Fowler 1303
Jenkins v. Dell Publishing Co. 1244
Jennings Buick, Inc. v. Cincinnati ... 1118
Jenoff v. Hearst Corp 1189
Jilani v. Jilani 814
Jobin v. McQuillen 1448
Johansen v. California State Auto Ass'n Inter-Insurance Bureau 1445
Johnson v. Foster 313
Johnson v. Johnson 777; 1195
JOHNSON v. KOKEMOOR ... 915; 916n8
Johnson v. Michelin Tire Corp. 1019
Johnson v. Misericordia Comm. Hosp. 944
Johnson v. Myers 810
Johnson v. Thompson 273
Johnson v. Woman's Hosp. 146
JOHNSON & JOHNSON v. AETNA CASUALTY & SURETY CO. .. 1420
Jones v. Chidester 880
Jones v. Dressel 748
Jones v. Howard Univ. 672
Jones v. J.B. Lippincott Co. 1082
Jones v. Los Angeles, City of 612
Jones v. Malinowski 551
Jones v. Palmer Communications, Inc 1257
Jones v. Three Rivers Management Corp .. 755
Jones v. Utica Mut. Ins. Co. 1091
Jones & Laughlin Steel Corp. v. Pfeifer ... 651
Jordan v. Baptist Three Rivers Hosp .. 699
Joseph v. Herrera. I 1282
Juday v. Rotunno & Rotunno ... 676; 722
Judge Eschbach in Sills v. Massey-Ferguson, Inc. 1004n8
Jurney v. Lubeznik 653
Justice Traynor in Carr v. Wm. C. Crowell Co. 961

K

K-Mart Corp. v. Chairs, Inc. 833
K-Mart Corp. v. Ponsock 1336
Kaczkouski v. Bolubasz 651
Kampen v. American Isuzu 1056
Kaneko v. Hilo Coast Processing 602
Kansas v. Hendricks 492
Kapellas v. Kofman 1246; 1259
Kaplan v. Haines 905; 906
Kapres v. Heller 456
Karpiak v. Russo 1132; 1148
Kasper v. H.P. Hood & Sons, Inc. .. 1135n9
Kasten v. Y.M.C.A. 807
Kastler v. Iowa Methodist Hosp. 888
Kathren v. Olenik 282
KATKO v. BRINEY 196; 200; 1091
Katko v. Briney, the Nebraska 200
Katz v. Department of Real Estate .. 1271
Kawananakoa v. Polyblank 796
Keelen v. Louisiana, State of 591
Keene Corp. v. Insurance Co. of N. Am. ... 1431; 1496
Kelch v. Courson 609n1
Keller v. Holiday Inns, Inc. 563
Kelley v. R.G. Indus. 1038
Kelley v. R.G. Industries, Inc. 1116
Kelley v. Schlumberger 147
Kelly v. Falin 453; 456

TABLE OF CASES

[References are to page numbers.]

Kelly v. Gwinnell 455
Kelly v. Hanscom Bros., Inc 837
Keltner v. Washington County 674
Kemp v. Block 1226
Kennedy v. The City of Sawyer, Kan . . 836
Kennel v. Carson City School District 987
Kentucky Fried Chicken of California, Inc. v. Superior Court 410; 429
Kenty v. Transamerica Premium Ins. Co. . . . 1340
Kermarec v. Compagnie Generale Transatlantique 579; 751
Kerr in Boyles v. Kerr 1265
Kevorkian v. AMA 1206
Kewanee Oil Co. v. Bicron Corp 1315
Keystone Aeronautics Corp. v. R.J. Enstrom Corp. 1074n4
Khirieh v. State Farm Mut. Auto. Ins. Co. 297
Kidder v. Bacon 1162
KILEY v. PATTERSON 114
Kilpack v. Wignall 227
Kilpatrick v. Bryant 335
Kimel v. Florida Board of Regents . . . 797; 1391
Kimple v. Schafer 1093
King v. Hilton-Davis 1077
King v. Kayak Mfg. Corp. 577
King v. Loessin 977
King v. R.G. Industries, Inc. 1117n3
King v. Shelby Rural Elec. Coop. 976
King v. Smythe 980
Kingsland v. Erie County Agric. Socy. 464
Kinney v. Yerusalim 1381
Kinsella v. Farmers Ins. Exchange . . 1454
Kirkbride v. Liston Contrs., Inc. 685
Kirschstein v. Haynes 216
Kittler v. Eckberg, Lammers, Briggs, Wolff & Vierling 218
Kitto v. Gilbert 314
Klawonn v. Mitchell 652
Klein v. Asgrow Seed Co. 834
Klein v. Pyrodyne Corp. 1114
Klein v. Sears, Roebuck & Co. 1048
KMART CORPORATION v. BASSETT 294
Knapper v. Connick 804
Knight v. Penobscot Bay Med. Center 172
Knott v. Liberty Jewelry & Loan, Inc. 1117n3
Knox College v. Celotex Corp. 778
Koehler v. Presque-Isle Transp. Co. 960n3
Koestler v. Pollard 676
Kohn v. Schiappa 675

Koos v. Roth 1118
Kotecki v. Cyclops Welding Corp 847
Kowkabany v. Home Depot, Inc. 33
Krahn v. LaMeres 225
Kramer Serv., Inc. v. Wilkins 337
Kratz v. Kratz 1453
Kraus v. Allstate Ins. Co. 1414
Kreines v. United States 686
Kubrick; United States v. 784
Kuharski v. Somers Motor Lines, Inc. 971
KUMHO TIRE COMPANY, LTD. v. CARMICHAEL 613
Kush v. Buffalo, City of 464
Kwasny v. United States 644

L

L-Tryptophan Cases, In re 686
La Mantia v. Durst 686
La Moureaux v. Totem Ocean Trailer Express, Inc. 503
La Rocco v. Bakwin 1347
La Rocque v. La Marche 885
LaBIER v. PELLETIER 992
LaCava v. New Orleans, City of 730
Lahr v. Adell Chemical Co. 1290
Laird v. Nelms 784; 787
Lamb v. Camden London Borough Council 391
Lambertson v. Cincinnati Corp 847
Lancaster Silo & Block Co. v. Northern Propane Gas Co. 1032
Lane v. Modern Music Inc. 971
LANGAN v. BELLINGER 1146
Langan v. Valicopters, Inc. 89; 1118
Langford v. United States 1361
Langlois v. Eschet 101
Lanza v. Polanin 593n5
LARGEY v. ROTHMAN 902
Larocque v. State Farm Mut. Auto Ins. Co 1447
Larrimore v. American Nat'l Ins. Co . . 283
Larson v. Candlish 626
Las Palmas Associates v. Las Palmas Center Associates 674
Later, in Brown v. Wal-Mart 824
Later, in Rodriquez v. Patti 529
LATERRA v. TREASTER 1108
Lauer v. New York, City of 462
Lauture v. Internat. Business Machines Corp 1337
Law v. Commonwealth 183
Lawler v. Skelton 1118
Laxton v. Orkin Exterm. Co. 517; 672
Lay v. Mesa 629
Lazy Seven Coal Mines v. Stone & Hinds 890

[References are to page numbers.]

Le Poidevin v. Wilson 563
Leaf River Forest Prods. v. Ferguson 1149
Lease v. International Harvester Co. 1041
Lee v. Chicago Transit Authority 568
Lee v. Gaufin 778
Lee v. Luigi 592n1
Lee v. Metropolitan Airport Comm'n 1198; 1202
LEE v. NATIONWIDE INSURANCE CO. . . 181
Lee; United States v. 1357
Lees v. Lobasco 600
the Legislature. Dixie Drive It Yourself System v. American Beverage Co. . . 321
Leichter v. Eastern Realty Co. 559
Leichtman v. WLW Jacor Commun., Inc. . . 109
Lemon v. Stewart 936
Leng Hardware, Inc. v. Wilson 1162
LENT v. HUNTOON 1158
Leonard v. Watsonville Community Hosp . . 264
LePage v. Bumila 610
Lerma ex rel. Lerma v. State Highway Dep't 1284
Lerman v. Flynt Distributing Co 1260
Lesniak v. Bergen, County of 652
Lestina v. West Bend Mut. Ins. Co . . . 269
Levey v. Warner Bros. Pictures 1212
Levin v. Walter Kidde & Co. 1046
Lewin v. McCreight 1082
LEWIS v. EQUITABLE LIFE ASSUR. SOC. 1163
LI v. YELLOW CAB CO. 733; 1447
License of (see name of party)
Liesener v. Weslo, Inc 1046
Light v. Proctor Community Hosp. . . . 533
Lilly v. Overnight Transp. Co 1334
LINDGREN v. UNITED STATES 788
Lineaweaver v. Plant 355
Linebaugh v. Berdish 1414
Linthicum v. Nationwide Life Ins. Co. 713
Liodas v. Sahadi 709
Lira v. Shelter Ins. Co 1449
Liriano v. Hobart Corp. 1002n3
Little v. Howard Johnson Co. 984
Littleton v. Good Samaritan Hosp. & Health Ctr. 479
Littleton v. Prange 693
Livitsanos v. Superior Ct. 1514
L.L. Bean, Inc. v. Drake Publishers, Inc. 1378
LLMD OF MICHIGAN, INC. v. JACKSON-CROSS CO. 798
LODGE v. ARETT SALES CORP. 413
Logan v. Greenwich Hosp. Ass'n 1063
Logerquist v. McVey 630
Loigman v. Massachusetts Bay Ins. Co . . . 1423
Lombardo v. Doyle, Dane & Bernbach, Inc 1252n51
Long v. Hacker 980
Lopez v. Southern Cal. Rapid Transit Dist 70; 474
Lora v. Board of Education 1241
Lord Atkin in Donoghue v. Stevenson 390
Lord Moulton in Rickards v. Lothian 1100
Lordships' House in Read v. J. Lyons & Co. Ltd. 1101
Los Angeles Dept. of Water and Power v. Manhart 1394
Losee v. Buchanan 58; 1102
LOUISIANA ex rel. GUSTE v. M/V TEST-BANK 677
Louisville Ry. Co. v. Sweeney 79
Lovelace Medical Center v. Mendez . . . 549
Lovely v. Allstate Ins. Co. 645
Lowenfels v. Nathan 1252n54
Loyer v. Buchholz 590
Ltd. v. Miller S.S. Co. Pty., The Wagon Mound (No. 2) 391
LTD. v. MORTS DOCK 385
Lubin v. Iowa City 1118
Lucasfilm Ltd. v. High Frontier . . 1251n49
LUCCHESI v. STIMMELL 37
Luckette v. Orkin Exterminating Co. . . 762
Lugosi v. Universal Pictures 1254
Lukaszewicz v. Concrete Research, Inc. . . . 1451
Lumley v. Gye 1346
LUND v. CHICAGO AND NORTHWESTERN TRANSPORTATION COMPANY . . 1197
LUNDBERG v. STATE 967
Lundman v. McKown 872
Lusby v. Lusby 815
Lykins v. Hamrick 180
Lynch v. Bay Ridge Obstetrical & Gynecological Assocs. 551
Lyons v. Midnight Sun Transportation Services, Inc 239
Lyons v. Nasby 459
LYTLE v. MALADY 1387
Lytle v. Stearns 849

M

M & R Investment Co. v. Mandarino 1224
Mac Enterprises, Inc. v. Del E. Webb Development Co. 1347

TABLE OF CASES

[References are to page numbers.]

Mace v. Charleston Area Medical Ctr. Found., Inc. 1334
MacGibbon v. Robinson 1119
Mackey v. Dorsey 285
MacKinnon v. Hanover Ins. Co. 1415
Macklin v. Logan 1346
MacPherson v. Buick Motor Co. . . . 679; 999; 1022
Maddox v. Boutwell 214
Madison v. Wyoming River Trips, Inc . . 763
MAGRINE v. SPECTOR 56
Mahan v. N.H. Dep't of Admin. Services . . . 793
Maheu v. CBS, Inc 1251n47
Mahoney v. Walter 1123
Mahowald v. Minnesota Gas Co. . . . 81; 1118
Maine v. Thiboutot 1355
Maki v. Murray Hospital 899
Malanga v. Manufacturers Cas. Ins. Co . . . 1422
MALLET v. PICKENS 575
Malloy v. Shanahan 914
Malm v. Dubrey 1136
Malone Freight Lines, Inc. v. McCardle . . . 297
Maloney v. Conroy 509
Maloney v. Rath 64; 973
Mandel v. United States 589
Mangini v. Aerojet-Gen'l Corp. . . . 773; 1152
Maniaci v. Marquette University 124
Mann v. State 493
Marcano v. Northwestern Chrysler-Plymouth Sales, Inc. 126
Marchetti v. Kalish 115
Marchetti v. Ramirez 652
Marchica v. Long Island R. Co. 672
Marciniak v. Lundborg 550
Marcus v. Liebman 127
Mariorenzi v. Joseph DiPonte, Inc . . . 578
Market Share Liability. The Wisconsin Supreme Court, in Coll v. Eli Lilly Co. 362
Markle v. Hacienda Mexican Restaurant . . 578
Marlene F. v. Affiliated Psych. Med. Clinic 518
Marrero v. Goldsmith 894
Marrero v. Hialeah 1356
Marriage of (see name of party)
Marsh v. Boyle 1331
Marsh v. McNeill 810
Marshall v. Ranne 760
Martin v. Harrington & Richardson, Inc. . . 1117n3
Martin v. Herzog 293
Martin v. Owens-Corning Fiberglass Corp. 355
Martin v. Richards 917; 920n17
Martin v. United States 791
Martin v. Williams 1123
Martin Luther King, Jr. Center for Social Change v. American Heritage Prods. . . . 1254
Martinelli v. Bridgeport Roman Catholic Diocesan Corp 771
Martinez v. Vintage Petroleum, Inc. . . 434
Mary M. v. Los Angeles, City of 964
Maryland Cas. Ins. Co. v. Peppers . . . 1449
Maryland Cas. Ins. Co. v. Welchel . . . 215
Mashburn v. Collin 1205
Mason v. Ellsworth 908
Massengale v. Pitts 997
Masson v. New Yorker Magazine . . . 1213
Masterson v. McCroskie 1295
Mastland, Inc. v. Evans Furniture, Inc. . . . 230
Matanuska Elec. Ass'n v. Johnson . . . 991
Mattco Forge v. Arthur Young & Co. . . 805; 1221
Matter of (see name of party)
Matthies v. Mastromonaco 914
Mattison v. Dallas Carrier Corp. 722
Mattos v. Thompson 1502
Mauney v. Gulf Ref. Co. 385
Maxey v. Freightliner Corp. 713
Mayle v. Pa. Dept. of Hwys 796
Mayor v. Pickles 1303
MCA, Inc. v. Wilson 1252n54
McAndrews v. Farm Bureau Mut. Ins. Co. 1414
McBride v. General Motors Corp. . . . 724
McCALL v. WILDER 233; 407
McCartney v. Meadowview Manor, Inc. . . . 1331
McCarty v. Pheasant Run, Inc. . . . 274; 275
McClenahan v. Cooley 285; 432
McClung v. Marion County Comm'n . . 1335
McCollum v. CBS, Inc. 445
McCorkle v. City 478
McDermott v. Torre 862
McDermott, Inc. v. AmCLYDE 846
McDill v. Utica Mut. Ins. Co. 1446
McDonald v. Santa Fe Trail Transportation Co. 1397
McDOUGALD v. GARBER 645; 647
McEachern v. Muldovan 113
McGinley v. United States 768
McGonigal v. Gearheart Indus. 1069
McGrath v. American Cyanamid Co. . . 763
McGregor v. Camden 1123
McGuiggan v. Boy Scouts of America . . 113
McGUIRE v. ALMY 110; 112
McIntyre v. Balentine 645; 740; 823
McIntyre v. McIntyre 572
McKee v. Evans 238
McKellips v. St. Francis Hosp. 345

[References are to page numbers.]

McKelvey v. McKelvey 808
McKennon v. Nashville Banner Co. ... 1390
McKinnon v. Washington Fed. Sav. & Loan Ass'n 560
Mclain v. Boise Cascade Corp 1226
McLain v. Training and Development Corp. 220
McLaughlin v. Sullivan 498
McLeod v. Meyer 1323
McNichol v. Grandy 1167
McNutt v. New Mexico State Tribune Co. ... 1243
McPEAKE v. CANNON, ESQ., P.C. .. 496; 674
McPherson v. First Presbyterian Church .. 1139
McSpedon v. Kunz 834
McWilliams v. Sir William Arrol & Co. ... 327
Meador v. Lawson 183
Meany v. Newell 457
Medford v. Levy 1123
Medtronic, Inc. v. Lohr 1065
Meek v. Shepard 263
Mehaffy, Rider, Windholz v. Cent. Bank ... 1275
Meibus v. Dodge 721
Melling v. Stralka 1342
Mellow v. Medical Malpractice Joint Underwriting Ass'n 1420
MELTON v. CRANE RENTAL COMPANY 592
Memorial Gardens, Inc. v. Olympian Sales & Management Consultants, Inc. ... 1347
Mendillo v. Board of Education 418
MENDOZA v. CORPUS CHRISTI, City of .. 556
Meracle v. Children's Serv. Soc'y of Wis. ... 552
Merchant v. Mansir 994
Meritor Savings Bank v. Vinson 1394
Merlo v. Standard Life & Acc. Ins. Co. 708; 709
Merluzzi v. Larson 279
Merrill v. Manchester 792
Mersey Docks Trustees v. Gibbs 807
Metro-North Commuter Railroad Company, Inc. v. Buckley 368
Metro-North Commuter RR. Co. v. Buckley 513
Metz v. United Technologies Corp. ... 651
Mexicali Rose v. Superior Court 1064
Meyers v. Louisiana 731
MFA Mut. Ins. Co. v. Howard Const. Co ... 813
Miami, City of v. Sanders 133
Micari v. Mann 186
Mickle v. Blackmon 1020

Mid-Century Ins. Co. v. Shutt 1420
Mid-Continent Pipe Line Co. v. Eberwein .. 685
MIDLER v. FORD MOTOR CO. 1288
Miles Labs., Inc., Cutler Labs. Div. v. Doe .. 1064
Milkovich v. Lorain Journal Co 1198; 1200n18; 1201
Milkovitch v. Lorain Journal Co 1204
Miller v. Christopher 840
Miller v. Dayton 591
Miller v. Duhart 552
Miller v. Eichhorn 766
Miller v. National Broadcasting Co .. 1227
Miller v. Schoene 1126
Miller v. Servicemaster By Rees 1221
Miller v. Szelenyi 793
Miller v. Tony & Susan Alamo Found. 116
Milton v. Cary Med. Center 533
Minerva Enters. v. Bituminous Cas. Co ... 1428
Mink v. University of Chicago 907
Minor v. Happersett, 88 U.S. (21 Wall.) 162 577
MIPA, in Alexander v. Memphis Indiv. Pract. Ass'n 1306
MIRELES v. BRODERICK 892
Misiulis v. Milbrand Main. Corp. 974
Mitchel v. Reynolds 1321
Mitchell v. Globe Internat. Pub. Co .. 1264
Mitchell, in Mitchell v. Chapman 220
Mobile Discount Corp. v. Schumacher 159
Mohler v. Houston 1218
Moldea v. New York Times Company 1205
Molien v. Kaiser Found. Hosps. 518
Molien v. Kaiser Foundation Hospitals 661
Molino v. Asher 987
Molko v. Holy Spirit Ass'n 127
Molony v. Pounds 1148
Monaco v. United States 788
Monaghan v. Holy Trinity Church ... 807
Monell v. Department of Social Servs. 1354
Monell v. Dept. Of Soc. Services 965
Mongee v. Beebe Rubber Co. 1337
Monitor Patriot Co. v. Roy 1208
Monk v. Veillon 101
Monroe v. Pape 1351; 1352
Monroe v. Pape. Reexamining 1355
Montalvo v. Lapez 651; 692
Montana v. San Jose Mercury News, Inc .. 1301
Montgomery Elevator Co. v. Gordon .. 313
Monusko v. Postle 532

TABLE OF CASES

[References are to page numbers.]

Moody v. Manny's Auto Repair 990
Moore v. Regents of Univ. of Cal. 929
Moore v. R.G. Industries, Inc. 1117n3
Moore v. St. Joseph Nursing Home, Inc. ... 474
MOORE v. TUCSON ELECTRIC POWER CO. 570
Moorenovitch, In re 146
Moragne v. State Marine Lines 691
Morain v. Devlin 110
Moran v. Johns-Manville Sales Corp. ... 712
Moran v. Rush Prudential HMO, Inc. .. 957
Moran; State v. 629
Moreover, in Schreiner v. Fruit 695
Morgan v. ABC Manufacturer 963
Morgan v. Children's Hosp. 304
Morgan v. Johnson 741
Morgan Stanley & Co., Inc; State v. 576n5
Moriarty v. Garden Sanctuary Church of God 777
Morningstar v. Black and Decker Mfg. Co. 576
Morrill v. Gallagher 49
Morris v. Faulkner 133
Morris v. Metriyakool 1503
Morris v. Savoy 677
Morris v. Scottsdale Mall Partners, Ltd. ... 604
Morrison v. MacNamara 263; 878
Morton v. Owens Corning Fiberglas Corp. .. 1032n35
Morton Int'l, Inc. v. Gen'l Accid. Ins. Co. .. 1436
Moser v. Stallings 186
Moses v. McWilliams 801
Moskovitz v. Mt. Sinai Med. Center ... 724
Mosley v. Observer Pub. Co 1219
Mostert v. CBL & Assocs. 562
Motschenbacher v. R.J. Reynolds Tobacco Co 1249
Moulin v. Monteleone 1230
Mountain States Tel. & Tel. Co. v. Horn Tower Constr. Co. 162
Mouton v. Mouton 815
Mozier v. Parsons 574
Mugar v. Massachusetts Bay Transp. Authy. 1134n6
Mujica v. Turner 244
Mulder v. Parke Davis & Co. 891
Muldovan v. McEachern 760
Mulei v. Jet Courier Service, Inc. ... 1347
Mullen, State ex rel. v. Doherty 1484
Multiple Defendants. King v. Searle Pharmaceuticals, Inc. 314
Mulvaney v. Auletto's Catering 441
Munn v. Algee 767
Murphy v. A. A. Matthews 635

Murphy v. Edmonds 676
Murphy v. E.R. Squibb & Sons 357
Murphy v. United Parcel Serv 1386
Murray v. Ramada Inns, Inc. 761
Myers v. Ambassador Ins. Co 1447
MYERS v. ROBERTSON 1401
Myhaver v. Knutson 238

N

N.A.A.C.P. v. Button 1173
NAACP v. Claiborne Hardware Co. .. 1307
Nabozny v. Barnhill 42
Nagy v. McBurney 156
Nash v. Fifth Amendment 70
Natanson v. Kline 904
National Ass'n of Letter Carriers v. Austin 1200n18
National Collegiate Athletic Ass'n v. Hornung 1348
National Convenience Stores v. Fantauzzi .. 987
National County Mut. Fire Ins. Co. v. Johnson 1410; 1451
National Org. for Women v. Scheidler 1374
National Recruiters, Inc. v. Cashman 1202
National Steel Service Center, Inc. v. Gibbons 1108
Nationwide Ins. Co v. Kollstedt, Estate of .. 1419
Neade v. Portes 958
Neal v. Neal 108; 145
Negri v. Stop & Shop, Inc. 299
Neiman-Marcus v. Lait 1179
Nelson v. American-West African Line 959
Nelson v. Coleman Co. 686
Nelson v. Concrete Supply Co. 742
Nelson v. Freeland 581
Nelson v. Martin 1345
Nelson v. Patrick 652
Nelson v. Washington Parish 441
Nettleship v. Weston 763
New Amsterdam Cas. Co. v. Jones ... 1417
The New Jersey Supreme Court, in Tice v. Cramer 438
New Mexico Elec. Serv. Co. v. Montanez ... 976
New York Cen. R. Co. v. White 1461; 1465
New York Central. R. Co. v. White 27
the New York Court of Appeals in Ultramares Corp. v. Touche 931
New York State Conference of Blue Cross & Blue Shield Pl v. Travelers Ins. Co. 957

TC–20 TORT: CASES, MATERIALS, PROBLEMS

[References are to page numbers.]

New York State Silicone Breast Implant Litigation, Matter of 360
the New York Times v. Sullivan 1179; 1222; 1223; 1238; 1261
NEW YORK TIMES CO. v. SULLIVAN ... 1169; 1181; 1185n8; 1191; 1192; 1210; 1213
New York Times Co. v. Sullivan, 376 U.S., at 270. 1194
Newing v. Cheatham 303; 313
Newport v. Moran 281; 1092
Newville v. Montana Dep't of Pub. Serv. ... 826
Nicholson v. Han 864
Nicolette v. Carey 777
Niemiera v. Schneider 25
9. Dram Shop Liability. Vesely v. Sager ... 287
9. Fighting Words. The U.S. Supreme Court, in Beauharnais v. Illinois, State of ... 1222
9. Intimate Relationships. B.N. v. K.K. ... 495
Nixon v. Administrator of General Services 1240
Nixon v. Fitzgerald 805
No Information". Gates v. Jensen 915
No — Goodnight v. Richardson .. 54
Nocktonick v. Nocktonick 814
N.O.L. v. District of Columbia 936
Nola M. v. University of Southern California 433
Nolechek v. Gesuale 814
Norfolk & W.R.R. v. Liepelt 652
Northern Power & Eng'g Corp. v. Caterpillar Tractor Co. 1072
Northern Power & Engineering Corp. v. Caterpillar Tractor Co. 1073
Northwestern Mut. Fire Ass'n v. Allain ... 685
Northwestern Mut. Ins. Co. v. Farmers Ins. Group 1436
Northwestern National Casualty Co. v. McNulty 714
Norwest v. Presbyterian Intercommunity Hosp. 698; 700
Norwood v. Soldier of Fortune Magazine, Inc. 1280
Nova Stylings, Inc. v. Red Roof Inns, Inc. .. 74

O

O'Banner v. McDonald's Corp. 982
OBDE v. SCHLEMEYER 1267
O'Brien v. Muskin Corp 1027; 1032
Ochampaugh v. Seattle 573
Ohio Cas. Ins. Co. v. Continental Ins. Co. ... 1469

Ohlhausen v. Brown 1230
Ohligschlager v. Proctor Community Hosp. 885
Ohralik v. Ohio State Bar Ass'n 1380
Oliveaux v. Sanders 762
Olmstead v. United States 1240
Olson v. Children's Home Soc'y 495
Olswanger v. Funk 312
1. Duelling Tests. Seibert v. Vic Regnier Bldrs., Inc. 426
1884, in Dietrich v. Northampton 528
1. False Light v. Defamation 1263
1. Foreseeability and the First Amendment. McCollum v. CBS, Inc. 445
1977, in Weber v. Madison 1093
1970." Bruce v. Martin-Marietta Corp 1032
11. Intentional Tort Revisited. Recall Brown v. Dellinger 231
1. Suicide — Deliberating the Act. Contrast Fuller v. Preis 499
1. The Classic Intentional Tort. As in Garratt v. Dailey 48
1, Young v. Sherwin-Williams, Inc ... 593
10. Contributory Negligence and Assumption of the Risk. Isaa v. Powell 1093
10. Corporate Liability and Causation. Rule v. Lutheran Hosps. & Homes Soc. 946
101 California Street, No. 959316 (Cal. Super. 2d Dep't Apr. 1117
O'Neil v. Schuckardt 1233
Opinion of the Justices, In re 1467
O'Quin v. Baptist Mem. Hosp 807
Orkin Exterminating Co. v. Traina ... 713
Ornelas v. Randolph 592
Osborn v. Irwin Memorial Blood Bank 263
Osland v. Osland 776
Ostroski v. Azzara 742
Ostrowski v. Azzara 767
Otero v. Jordon Restaurant Enterprises ... 974
O'Toole v. Carlsbad Shell Serv. Station ... 457
O'Toole v. United States 692
Ouellette v. Subak 880
Overstreet v. Shoney's, Inc. 651
Oviatt v. Camarra 1406
Owen v. Independence, City of 1355
Owens v. Truckstops of America, Inc .. 824
Owens-Corning Fiberglas Corp. v. Caldwell 1033
Owens-Corning Fiberglas Corp. v. Dunn ... 715
Oxendine v. Merrell Dow Pharmaceuticals, Inc. 624

TABLE OF CASES

[References are to page numbers.]

P

P. v. Vista Del Mar Child Care Serv. . . . 552
Pachucki v. Republic Ins. Co. . . . 48; 1414
Pacific Mutual Life Ins. Co. v. Haslip 1488
Pacific Northwest Bell Tel. Co. v. Port of Seattle 78
Pack; State v. 1142
Paige v. North Oaks Partners 592
Paintsville Hosp. Co. v. Rose 978
Palka v. Servicemaster Mgt. Servs. Corp. . . 462
Palko v. Connecticut 1240
Palmer v. A.H. Robins Co. 713
Palsgraf v. Long Island R. Co. . . . 417; 582
PALSGRAF v. LONG ISLAND RAILROAD CO. 395
Palsgraf v. Long Island R.R. Co. . . 395; 962
Pamela L. v. Farmer 495
Pamperin v. Trinity Memorial Hospital . . . 943
Panikowski v. Giroux 1134
Panitz v. Behrend 801; 803; 805
Pankratz v. Miller 1231
Parker v. St. Vincent Hosp. 1079
Parnaby v. Lancaster Canal Co., 11 Ad. & E. 223 576
Parvi v. Kingston 134
Pate v. Threlkel 33
Paul v. Davis 1356
PAUL v. WATCHTOWER BIBLE & TRACT SOCIETY 1359
Paulsen v. Gundersen 919
Pavesich v. New England Life Insurance Co 1255
Payton v. United States, 679 792
Paz v. State 477
Peachtree-Cain Co. v. McBee 987
Pearson v. Dodd 163; 172n4
Pechan v. Dynapro, Inc. 109
Pedroza v. Bryant 945
Peek v. Gurney 1269
PEGRAM v. HERDICH 946
Pegram v. Herdrich 957
Peneschi v. National Steel Corp. 1102
Pennekamp v. Florida 1174
Pennsylvania Dep't of Transp. v. Phillips . . 652
Pennsylvania Glass Sand Corp. v. Caterpillar Tractor Co. 1073
Pennsylvania, matter of 498
Pennzoil v. Texaco, Inc. 713
People v. (see name of defendant)
People ex (see name of defendant)
People ex rel. (see name of defendant)
PepsiCo v. Redmond 1327
PepsiCo, Inc. v. Redmond 1315
PEREZ v. LAS VEGAS MEDICAL CENTER 332
Perez v. Southern Pacif. Transp. Co. 1110
Perez v. Van Groningen & Sons, Inc. . . 965
PEREZ v. WYETH LABORATORIES INC. 20; 1063
Perkins v. F.I.E. Corp 1117n3
Perkins v. Marsh 1269
Perlmutter v. Beth David Hospital . . 1080
Perricone v. DiBartolo 225
PETA v. BOBBY BEROSINI, LTD. . . 1223
PETERSON v. SUPERIOR COURT . . . 65
Petition of (see name of party)
Petrillo v. Bachenberg 1275
Petrus v. Smith 1218n25
Petty v. Allstate Ins. Co. 1469
Philadelphia Newspapers, Inc. v. Hepps . . . 1190; 1199
Phillips v. Kimwood Mach. Co. 1008; 1041
Phillips v. Thomas 793
Pickering v. Pickering 1231
Pierre v. Allstate Ins. Co. 321
Pigney v. Pointers Transp. Serv. 500
Pinecrest Stables, Inc. v. Hill 303
Pineda v. Craven 877
PINER v. SUPERIOR COURT 371
PINNICK v. CLEARY 1457
Pitre v. Louisiana Tech University . . . 762
Pitt v. Yalden 878
Plaintiff v. Shollenbarger Wood Treating, Inc., Third 837
Plant v. Woods 1304
Platta v. Flatley 920n18
Plattner v. State Farm Mut. Auto Ins. Co . . 1347
Ploof v. Putnam 206
Plumb v. Richmond Light & R. Co. . . . 893
Polemis and Furness, Withy & Co., Ltd., In Re 387
Polemis and The Wagon Mound (No. 1), In re 392
Polemis, In Re 387; 403
Policeman's Benev. Ass'n of N.J. v. Washington Tp. 965
Polston v. Boomershine Pontiac-GMC Truck, Inc. 380
Pope v. Edward M. Rude Carrier Corp. . . . 1123
Porter v. Sisters of St. Mary 943
Posadas v. Reno, City of 1179
POSECAI v. WAL-MART STORES, INC. . . 422
Possible Conspiracy of Silence. Ybarra v. Spangard 898
Post v. Mendel 800
Poster v. Andrews 153

[References are to page numbers.]

Potter v. Chicago Pneumatic Tool Co. 1003n5; 1020; 1058
Potter v. Firestone Tire & Rubber Co. 655; 656
Pottgen v. Missouri State High Sch. Activities Ass'n 1381
Potts v. Celotex Corp. 772
Potts v. Litt 376
Powell v. Wyoming Cablevision, Inc .. 1334
Power v. Arlington Hosp. Ass'n 857
Practicality. Drobney v. Federal Sign & Signal Corp. 1041
Prell Hotel Corp. v. Antonacci 988
PRESS AIRLINES, People ex v. CONSOLIDATED RAIL CORP. 519
Price v. Shell Oil Co. 71
Pridgen v. Boston Hous. Auth. 569
Pridham v. Cash & Carry Building Center, Inc 434
Procanik v. Cillo 367
Proctor v. Castelletti 1486
PROMAULAYKO v. JOHNS MANVILLE SALES CORP. 830
Property Cas. Co. of MCA v. Conway 1423
Protectus Alpha Nav. Co. v. North Pac. Grain Growers, Inc. 715
Protectus Alpha Navigation Co. v. North Pacific Grain Growers, Inc. 209
Prudhomme v. Procter & Gamble Co 1252n53
Public Serv. Mut. Ins. Co. v. Goldfarb 1449
Publix Cab Co. v. Colorado National Bank 166
Pulka v. Edelman 462
Pullman Standard, Inc. v. Abex Corp. .. 1082
Pyramid Securities, Ltd. v. IB Resolution, Inc. 1373

Q

Quick v. Myers Welding & Fabricating, Inc. 1514
Quick v. Peoples Bank 1375
Quinn v. State 743

R

Rabidue v. Osceola Refining Co. 1393
Racer v. Utterman 1421
Raimondo v. Harding 240
Raisen v. Raisen 815
Randy Knitwear, Inc. v. American Cyanamid Co. 1279
Ranson v. Kitner 109; 215
Rappaport v. Nichols 460

RASMUSSEN v. SOUTH FLORIDA BLOOD SERVICE 1239
Ratterree v. Bartlett 849
RAY v. AMERICAN NATIONAL RED CROSS 259
Ray v. BIC Corp. 1007
Raybestos Prods. Co. v. Younger 1375
Raycroft v. Tayntor 1303
R.D. v. W.H. 145; 518
Read v. J. Lyons & Co. 1101
Reager v. Anderson, 371 S.E.2 851
Recall Browning-Ferris Indus. v. Kelco Disposal 724
Recall Glick v. Olde Town Lancaster, Inc. .. 200
Recall Helling v. Carey 259
Recall Montana v. San Jose Mercury News 1380
Reconsider Carlin v. Superior Court .. 1058
Reconsider Dietemann v. Time, Inc. .. 1296
Reconsider McCollum v. CBS, Inc. 1279
Reconsider McDougald v. Garber 692
Reconsider N. Y. Times v. Sullivan .. 1204
Reconsider New York Times v. Sullivan and Neiman-Marcus 1222
Reconsider Ranson v. Kitner 110
Red Panther Chem. Co. v. Insurance Co. of Pa. 1427
Reece v. Lowe's of Boone, Inc. 1050
Reed v. King 1270
Reed v. Mitchell & Timbanard, P.C. .. 676
Reed v. Reed 1472
Reed v. Tiffin Motor Homes, Inc. 1017
Reeves v. Sanderson Plumbing Products, Inc 1391
Reference Rochester Gas & Elec. Corp. v. Dunlop 91
Reichert v. Alter 827
Reid, Johnson, Downes, Andrachik & Webster v. Lansberry 1340
Reilly v. United States 146
Reisner v. Regents of the University of California 936
Reliable Transfer; United States v. ... 841
Religious Professionals. Nally v. Grace Community Church of the Valley 869
Relying on Russell v. Clark 217
Relying on Waggoner v. Town & Country Mobile Homes 684
Renander v. Inc., Ltd. 1363
Renee Beauty Salons, Inc. v. Blose-Venable 1325
Renslow v. Mennonite Hospital 529
Renwick v. News & Observer Publishing Co 1261; 1262
Restina v. Aetna Casualty & Surety Company 1443
Reuther v. Fowler & Williams, Inc. .. 1330

Reves v. Ernst & Young	1373
Reynolds v. Hicks	454
Reynolds v. United States	1362
Rice v. Paladin Enterprises	448
Rice v. Paladin Enterprises, Inc.	1280
Richard v. A. Waldman & Sons	1276
Richardson v. Employers Liability Assur. Corp.	1441
Richardson v. Fairbanks North Star Borough	144
Richie-Gamester v. Berkeley, City of	760
Richman v. Charter Arms Co.	1117n3
Richter v. Westab, Inc.	1296
Rickards v. Lothian	1100
Riddle Memorial Hospital v. Dohan	945
Ridings v. Ralph M. Parsons Co	824; 847; 997
Rinaldi v. Holt, Rinehart & Winston	1214
Rinehart v. Board of Educ.	115
RINEHIMER v. LUZERNE COUNTY COMMUNITY COLLEGE	1328
Rios v. Smith	465
Ritz v. Woman's Club of Charleston	1124
Rivard v. Roy	51
Rivas v. Oxon Hill Joint Venture	600
Riviello v. Waldron	971
Rizk v. Cohen	861
RK Constructors, Inc. v. Fusco Corp.	416; 417
Robarge v. Bechtel Power Corp.	969
Robarts v. Diaco	846
Robbins v. Jewish Hosp. of St. Louis	337
Robert v. Pachall	1452
Roberts v. Adkins	1334
Roberts v. American Employers Ins. Co.	193
Roberts v. English Mfg. Co.	1167
Roberts v. Federal Express Corp.	152
Roberts v. Stevens Clinic Hosp.	691
Roberts v. Vaughn	597; 763
Roberts Constr. Co. v. Henry	297
Robertson v. LeMaster	582; 688
Robins Dry Dock & Repair Co. v. Flint	678
Robinson v. Balmain New Ferry Co.	128
Robinson v. Gonzalez	524
Robinson v. Jiffy Exec. Limousine Co	991
Robinson v. Kilvert	1119
ROBINSON v. LINDSAY	223
Robinson v. Omer	1276
Robison v. Robison	1116
Robles v. Exxon Corp.	746
ROCKWELL v. SUN HARBOR BUDGET SUITES	984
ROCKWELL GRAPHIC SYSTEMS, INC. v. DEV INDUSTRIES, INC.	1308
Rodebaugh v. Grand Trunk W.R.R.	813
Rodriguez v. Williams	1415
Roe v. Wade	551; 1240
Roes v. FHP, Inc	513
Rogers v. EEOC	1395
Rogers v. Meridian Park Hosp.	880
Rogers v. Missouri Pacific R. Co.	508
Rogers v. Toni Home Permanent Co.	1279
Roland v. Bernstein	847
Roller v. Roller	808
Romano v. Duke	689
Romero v. Byers	692
Romero v. Hariri	716
Rootes v. Shelton	269
RORRER v. COOKE	9
Rosa v. Dunkin' Donuts	595n10
Rose v. Port of New York Authority	296
Rosenberg v. Helinski	1220
Rosenblatt v. Baer	1179; 1182
Rosenbloom v. Metromedia, Inc.	1181; 1183; 1192
Rosenblum v. Adler	932
ROSHTO v. HEBERT	1234
Ross v. Creighton University	873
Ross v. Hartman	284; 294
Ross v. Patterson	39
Ross v. Sequatchie Valley Elec. Co-op.	571
Rova Farms Resort, Inc. v. Investors Ins. Co.	1445
Rowe v. State Farm Mut. Auto Ins. Co.	877
Rowland v. Christian	407; 582; 1476
Rowlands v. Signal Constr. Co.	746
Roy v. Friedman Equipment Co.	417
ROYER v. CATHOLIC MEDICAL CENTER	1078
Rozycki v. Peley	495
Rubin v. Green	218
Rufolo v. Midwest Marine Contr., Inc	845
Rumbauskas v. Cantor	173
Rupp v. Bryant	32
Rush v. Troutman Investment Co	610
Russell v. Ford Motor Co.	1073
Russell v. Noulet	964
Russo v. Sutton	1230
Rutherford v. Owens-Illinois, Inc	364
Rutherford v. State	697
Rutter v. Northeastern Beaver County School District	753
Rylands v. Fletcher	55; 56; 79; 1086; 1097; 1099; 1100; 1101; 1102; 1103; 1104; 1112; 1121
Rylands v. Fletcher, Blackburn, J.	56
Rylands v. Fletcher, L.R.	1116n2
Rylands v. Fletcher, New York	1103

[References are to page numbers.]

S

Sachs v. Nassau County 625
Safer v. Pack, Estate of 937
Safeway Ins. Co. v. Duran 1427
Sakon v. Pepsico., Inc. 445; 1280
Salek v. Passaic Collegiate School ... 1204
Salevan v. Wilmington Park, Inc. 559
the Salgo v. Leland Stanford Jr. Univ. Bd. of Trustees 892; 903
Salt River Valley Water Users' Ass'n v. Cornum 373
Saltsman v. Corazo 435
Samms v. Eccles 143
Samson v. Carolina-Georgia Blood Center .. 1081
SAMSON INVESTMENT CO. v. CHEVAILLIER 216
San Diego Gas & Elec. Co. v. Superior Ct. . 1134n5; 1135n8
Sanchez v. Coxon 804
Sanchez v. Liggett & Myers, Inc. 1038
Sanchez v. San Juan Concrete Co. ... 1284
Sandborg v. Blue Earth County 740
Sanders v. ABC 1228
Sanderson v. International Flavors & Fragrances, Inc. 360
Santor v. A & M Karagheusian, Inc. 1072; 1275
Santor and Emerson G.M. Diesel, Inc. v. Alaskan Enterprise 1073
Saratoga Fishing Co. v. J.M. Martinac & Co. 1076
Sargent v. Ross 604
Sars, Inc. v. Nichols 1450
Savage v. State 251
Scaria v. St. Paul Fire & Marine Ins. Co. . . 920
Schabe v. Hampton Bays Union Free Sch. Dist. 746
Schaefer v. Spence 163
Schaeffer v. Schaeffer 1125n2
Schenck v. Pro-Choice Network of Western New York 1144
Scheuer v. Rhodes 805
Schiavo v. Owens-Corning 612
Schick v. Ferolito 44
Schiffels v. Kemper Fin. Servs. 1375
Schloendorff v. The Soc'y of the N.Y. Hosp. 903
Schneider Nat'l, Inc. v. Holland Hitch Co . . 838
School Bd. v. Arline 1382
School District v. Glasco 178
SCHOOLEY v. PINCH'S DELI MARKET, INC. 449
Schroeder v. Perkel 367
Schuster v. Altenberg 491

SCHUTKOWSKI v. CAREY 746
Scindia Steam Nav. Co. v. De Los Santos .. 977
Scott v. Hospital Serv. Dist. 701
Scott v. James 304
Scribner v. Hillcrest Med. Cntr. 896
Seale v. Gowans 772
Seattle-First National Bank v. Tabert, at 154 1027
Seattle-First Nat'l Bank v. Tabert 1003n5
Seavers v. Meth. Med. Cntr 1043
SEDIMA, S.P.R.L. v. IMREX CO. ... 1364
Seely v. White Motor Co. 1072; 1073
Seigel v. Long 108
Self v. Queen 577
Selkowitz v. Nassau, County of 627
Semeniuk v. Chentis 465
Sena v. New Mexico State Police 651
Seneris v. Haas 978
Senesac v. Associates in Obstetrics & Gynecology 885
Setliff v. E.I. Du Pont de Nemours & Co. . . 365
7. Informed Consent and Lawyers. Consider Cohen v. Lipsig 909
768. So, in Adler, Barish, Danils, Levin & Creskoff v. Epstein 1346
Severson v. Severson, Estate of ... 1405n3
Sewell v. Gregory 582
Shack v. Holland 542
Shaffer v. Stewart 156
Shahvar v. Superior Court of Santa Clara County 1220
Shanholtz v. Monongahela Power Co 1335
Shannon v. Butler Homes Inc. 564
Sharon P. v. Arman, Ltd. 427
Sharon Steel Corp. v. Fairmont, City of ... 1123
SHARP v. 251st STREET LANDFILL, INC. 1136
Sharp v. W. H. Moore, Inc 427
SHARPE v. PETER PAN BUS LINES 324
Shartzer v. Ulmer 159
Shaw v. Continental Ins. Co 1454
Shaw, Adm'r v. Moore 51
Shearson Lehman Hutton, Inc. v. Tucker .. 1259
SHERARD v. SMITH 972
Sherbert v. Verner 1361
Shockley v. Prier 700
Short v. Little Rock Dodge, Inc. 1019
Shortle v. Central Vermont Public Service Corp. 1162
Showalter v. Univ. of Pittsb. Med. Cntr ... 1391

[References are to page numbers.]

Shuamber v. Henderson 537
Shulman v. Group W Productions, Inc 1229
Shump v. First Cont.-Robinwood Assoc. . . . 974
Siciliano v. Capitol City Shows, Inc. . . 692
SIEGLER v. KUHLMAN . . 74; 1105; 1114; 1118
Sigma Chemical Company v. Harris . . 1322
Signorino v. National Super Mkts. . . . 133
Silver v. Silver 1476
Silvers v. Associated Technical Institute, Inc., No. 93-4253 34
Simeon v. Doe 1064
Sinai v. Polinger Co. 261
Sinatra v. Goodyear Tire & Rubber Co. . . . 1290
Since New York Times Co. v. Sullivan . . . 1208
Sindell v. Abbott Laboratories . . . 351; 364
Sindell v. Abbott Labs. 356
SINDLE v. NEW YORK CITY TRANSIT AUTHORITY 211
Singleton v. Foreman 869
Sioux City & Pacific Railroad Co. v. Stout . . 572
6 of Harris v. Matherly Machinery, Inc. . . . 689
S.J. Groves & Sons Co. v. Aerospatiale Helicopter Corp. 1076
Skipworth v. Lead Indus. Ass'n, Inc. . . 360
Skyline Harvestore Systems, Inc. v. Centennial Ins. Co. 1417
Slager v. HWA Corp. 740
Slater v. Baker & Stapleton 876
Slemp v. North Miami, City of 33
Slocum v. Food Fair Stores of Fla., Inc. . . . 144
Small v. Howard 874; 875; 876
Smedley v. Piazzolla 231
Smith v. Atkinson 638
Smith v. Bates Technical College . . . 1337
Smith v. Calvary Christian Church . . . 185
Smith v. Day 1447
Smith v. Gizzi 746
Smith v. Holt 166
Smith v. Industrial Constrs., Inc. 652
Smith v. Lewis 877
Smith v. New England Aircraft Co. . . . 168
Smith v. Owen 281; 282
Smith v. Printup 724
Smith v. Pulcinella. 645
Smith v. Richmond Mem. Hosp. 858
Smith v. Shannon 908
SMITH v. STATE DEPARTMENT OF HEALTH AND HOSPITALS 339
Smith v. Suburban Restaurants 1211

Smith v. Suburban Restaurants, Inc. 1211
Smith v. United States 790
Snowden v. D.C. Transit Sys. 846
Snyder v. Mekhjian 630
Snyder v. Southern California Edison 974
So in Gendrek v. Poblete 517
So in Riss v. New York, City of 796
So in Staples v. Bangor Hydro-Elec. Co . . . 1221
SOFIE v. FIBREBOARD CORP. 1482
Soirez v. Great American Ins. Co 816
Soldano v. O'Daniels 474
Sopha v. Owens-Corning Fiberglas Corp . . . 772
Sorrell v. Thevenir 1486
Soule v. General Motors Corp 1028
Soule v. GM in the Potter 1043
South Florida Blood Service, Inc. v. Rasmussen 1242
Southcote v. Stanley, 1 H. & N. 247 . . 576
Southern Co. v. Graham 1018
Southland Corp. v. Griffith 600
Southport Corp. v. Esso Petrol. Co. . . . 208
Spade v. Lynn & B. R.R. Co. 399
Spain v. Gallegos 1395
Spalding v. Davis 878
Spartan Steel v. Martin & Co. 683
Spaulding v. Cameron 1154
Speiser v. Randall 1175
Spencer v. A-I Crane Serv. 692
Spillway Marina, Inc. v. United States 789; 790
Splawnik v. DiCaprio 465
Spur Industries, Inc. v. Del E. Webb Dev. Co. 1146
Sriberg v. Raymond 218
Srivastava v. Commissioner 653
St. Amant v. Thompson 1178; 1182
St. David's Episcopal Church v. Westboro Baptist Church 1143
ST. LUKE EVANGELICAL LUTHERAN CHURCH v. SMITH 716
St. Mary Medical Center, Inc. v. Casko . . . 1080
St. Petersburg, City of v. Bowen 1127
Stadler v. Cross 512
Stafford v. Neurological Med., Inc. . . . 500
STALLMAN v. YOUNGQUIST . . 528; 693; 814
Stamp v. Honest Abe Log Homes, Inc. 1276
Standard Oil Co.; United States v. . . . 786
Stangle v. Fireman's Fund Ins. Co. . . . 474
Stanley v. Georgia 1240; 1241n40
Stanley v. Tilcon Maine, Inc. 592
Stansbie v. Troman 473

[References are to page numbers.]

STARON v. McDONALD'S CORP. . . . 1380
Staruski v. Cont. Tel. Co 1255
State v. (see name of defendant)
State Dep't of Envt'l Protection v. Ventron
. . . . 1102
State ex (see name of state)
State ex rel. (see name of state)
State Farm Fire & Cas. Co. v. Williams . . . 1415
State Farm Fire & Casualty Co. v. Williams
. . . . 1413
State Farm Mut. Auto Ins. Co. v. Partridge
. . . . 1429
State of (see name of state)
Stearman v. Centex Homes 1076
Steffensen v. Smith's Management Corp. . . 502
Steinhilber v. Alphonse 1214
STENCEL AERO ENGINEERING CORP. v. UNITED STATES 784
Stephens v. Jones 980
Stephens v. Spiwak 881
Stewart v. Jackson & Nash 1272
Sticklen v. Kittle 1123
Stone v. Chicago Title Ins. Co. 526
Stone v. Taffe 560
Storar, In re 188
Storar, Matter of 188
Strachan v. John F. Kennedy Mem. Hosp. . . 147; 901
Strandell v. Jackson County 1494
Strategy. Why, Matter of 64
Strauss v. Belle Realty Co. 462
Strawn v. Canuso 1128
Street Corp. v. Combustion Eng'g. Inc. . . . 360
Strickland v. Madden 672
Stricklin v. Parsons Stockyard Co. 989n10
Stroud v. Denny's Restaurant 715
Stuempges v. Parke, Davis & Co 1203
Stump v. Sparkman 804
Sturdivant v. Seaboard Service System, Ltd.
. . . . 1218
Suchomajcz v. Hummel Chem. Co. . . . 464
Sullivan v. Bapt. Mem. Hosp 1166
Sullivan v. O'Connor 881
Sullivan v. Snyder 303
Summers v. Tice 373; 374n2
Summit Properties v. Hoechst Celanese Corp
. . . . 1375
Sumnicht v. Toyota Motor Sales, U.S.A., Inc
. . . . 1027
the Supreme Court of California in Summers v. Tice 354
The Supreme Court of Canada in Winnipeg Condominium Corp. No v. Bird Constr. Co.
. . . . 523
the Supreme Court of Delaware in Wilmington General Hospital v. Manlove 854
the Supreme Court of Florida in Hoffman v. Jones 737
the Supreme Court of Indiana in Citizens Gas & Coke Util v. American Economy Ins. Co.
. . . . 932
the Supreme Court of Pennsylvania in Geary v. United States Steel Corp. 1329
the Supreme Court of Pennsylvania in G.J.D. v. Johnson 712
the Supreme Court of Texas in Gaulding v. Celotex Corp 354
Surratt v. Thompson 815
Sussman v. Damian 1218n25
Sutton v. Piasecki Trucking, Inc. 739
Sutton v. United Air Lines 1386
Svetz for Svetz v. Land Tool Co 822
Swafford v. Harris 723
Swann v. Prudential Insurance Company of America 314
Swann, State ex rel. v. Pack 1363
Swayze v. McNeil Laboratories 1062
Sweeney v. Patterson 1173
Sweet Milk Co. v. Stanfield 373
Swinton v. Whitinsville Sav. Bank . . . 1268
Symone T. v. Lieber 741
Sztore v. Northwest Hosp. 979

T

Tabas v. Tabas 1375
Tabor v. Doctor's Mem. Hosp. 856
Tacket, in Tacket v. General Motors Corp . . 1168
Tafflin v. Lewitt 1375
Talbot v. Dr. W.H. Groves' Latter-Day Saints Hospital, Inc. 314
Tameny v. Atlantic Richfield Co 673
TANBERG v. ACKERMAN INVESTMENT CO. 764
Tankrederiet Gefion v. Hyman-Michaels Co
. . . . 842
Tarasoff v. Regents of the University of California 479
Tarasoff v. Regents of Univ. of Cal . . . 491
Tarasoff v. Regents of University of Cal . . . 409
Tauber-Arons Auctioneers Co. v. Superior Court 68; 69; 71
Taylor v. Denver & R.G.W.R. Co. 651
Taylor v. Preferred Risk Mut. Ins. Co.
. . . . 1452
Taylor v. Superior Court of Los Angeles County
. . . . 706
Taylor v. Superior Ct. of Los Angeles . . 713
Teche Lines, Inc. v. Pope 713
Tellado v. Time-Life Books 1255

TABLE OF CASES

[References are to page numbers.]

Tennis v. General Motors Corp. 652
TERRY COVE NORTH, INC. v. MARR & FRIEDLANDER, P.C. 888
Tesvich v. 3-A's Towing Co. 1419
Texas, Cain v. Hearst Corp. 1263
Texas Dep't of Community Affairs v. Burdine 1388
Texas & P. Ry. v. Behymer 93
Theama v. Kenosha 696; 697
Then There Is Gas. New Meadows Holding Co. v. Washington Water Power Co. . . 80
Thibodeaux v. Ferrell Gas Inc. 852
Thing v. La Chusa 509
Thomas v. Bedford 213; 214
Thomas v. Bokelman 990
Thomas v. Review Bd. of Indiana Employment Secur. Div. 1361
Thomas v. St. Joseph Hosp. 95
Thompson v. Gilmore 980
Thompson v. Nason Hospital 945
Thompson v. National R.R. Passenger Corp. 650
Thompson v. St. Paul Fire & Marine Ins. Co. 1420
Thompson v. State Farm Ins. Co. . . . 1455
Thompson v. State Farm Mut. Auto Ins. Co. 1454
Thompson v. United States 790
Thor v. Superior Court 902
Thoreson v. Milwaukee & Suburban Transport Co 809
3. Heavy Metal on the Defensive. Consider Judas Priest v. Second Judicial Court . . . 447
3. Manufacturer Expertise and Package Inserts. Ramon v. Farr 891
3. Rate-Cutting Initiatives. Calfarm Ins. Co. v. Deukmejian 1400
3. Sports Injuries. Reconsider Kiley v. Patterson 186
Throne v. Wandell 920
Tiernan v. Charleston Area Med. Serv 1338
Tiller v. Atlantic Coast Line R. Co. . . . 508
Tillman v. Vance Equipment Co 68
Time, Inc. v. Firestone 1189
Time, Inc. v. Hill 1262, n56; 1264
Time, Inc. v. Hill, and in Cantrell . . . 1264
Timmons v. Silman 971
Tindley v. Department of Envtl. Quality Engr. 1135n9
Tipton v. Texaco, Inc. 895
Tobin v. Grossman 462; 509
Tolan v. ERA Helicopters, Inc. 504
Tomikel v. Commonwealth of Pa. 517
Toole v. Richardson-Merrell, Inc. 707; 709

TORO CO. v. KROUSE, KERN & CO. 931; 932
Torres v. State 1283
Torres v. Xomox Corp 433
Toups v. Sears, Roebuck & Co. 1050
Tourville v. Inter-Ocean Ins. Co. 1332
Town & Country Properties, Inc. v. Riggins 1380
Township of Bedminster v. Vargo Dragway, Inc. 1132
Toyota Motor Mfg. v. Williams 1386
Tozer v. LTV Corp. 1067
Trautman v. Poor 1455
Traylor v. Husqvarna Motor 1050
Trevino v. General Dynamics 1069
Triangle Sheet Metal Works v. Silver . . 721
Trimble v. Denver, City and County of 1345
Tritsch v. Boston Edison Co 850
Trogun v. Fruchtman 44; 62; 920
Trotter v. Okawa 873
Trower v. Jones 877
Troxel v. A.I. duPont Instit. 937
Truman v. Thomas 888; 910
Trust Estate of (see name of party)
Tuberville v. Savage 119
Tucker v. Lower 644
Tucker v. Rio Vista Plaza 594
Tucker v. Shoemaker 600
Tucker v. Southern Wood Piedmont Co. 773
TUDER v. KELL 584
Tuggle v. Allright Parking Sys., Inc. . . 996
Tunkl v. Regents of the University of California 751
Tunkl v. Regents of Univ. of Cal. 751
Turf Lawnmower Repair, Inc. v. Bergen Record Corp 1196
Turkette; United States v. 1373
Turnbough v. Ladner 751
Turner v. Jordan 824
TUTTLE v. BUCK 1302
Tutton v. A.D. Walter Ltd. 564
Twigg v. Hercules Corp 1334
2 Fowler v. Harper 1224
2. Minority v. Majority 814
2. Statutory Duties and Standards. Landeros v. Flood 891
2. The Ghosts of Guest Statutes. Shea v. Olson 54
2. Turpin v. Sortini 541
2. Willful and Wanton Conduct. Klepper v. Milford 589
TXO Prod. Corp. v. Alliance Resources Corp. 713
TXO Production Corp. v. Alliance Resources Corp. 1486

[References are to page numbers.]

U

Ueland v. Pengo Hydra-Pull Corp. . . . 696n9
Ultramares Corp. v. Touche 1273
Ultramares Corp. v. Touche, Niven & Co. . . 409
Under Borel v. Fibreboard Paper Products Corp. 1431n13
Under the Donaldson v. Maffucci 879
Union Oil Co. v. Oppen 273; 522; 525; 1077
Union Park Memorial Chapel v. Hutt . . 33
United Air Lines, Inc. v. United States . . . 790
United Air Lines, Inc. v. Wiener 790
United Servs. Auto. Ass'n v. Lilly . . . 1420
United Servs. Auto. Ass'n v. Morris . . 1436; 1449
United States v. (see name of defendant)
the United States Constitution. But in Burmah Oil Co. v. Lord Advocate 205
the United States Constitution in Griswold v. Connecticut 1240
United States Fid. & Guar. Co. v. Superior Court 1436; 1449
United States Fidelity & Guaranty Co. v. Jadranska Slobodna 277
United Zinc & Chem. Co. v. Britt 573
UNIVERSITY OF ARIZONA HEALTH SCIENCE CENTER v. SUPERIOR COURT 543
USM Corp. v. SPS Technologies, Inc 1309

V

Vaerst v. Tanzman 70
Vail v. The Plain Dealer Pub. Co . . . 1204
Valco Cincinnati, Inc. v. N & D Machining Serv., Inc. 1344
Vance v. Southern Bell Telephone & Telegraph Co. 1394
Vande Zande v. Wisc. Dep't of Admin., State of 1381
Vandermark v. Ford Motor Co 66; 67
Variety Farms, Inc. v. New Jersey Mfrs. Ins. Co. 1423
Vaske v. Ducharme, McMillen & Assoc . . . 1327
Vaughan v. Menlove 224
VEEDER v. KENNEDY 1229
Venetoulias v. O'Brien 442
Vertecs Corp. v. Reichhold Chem. Co. . . 836
Vesely v. Sager 460
Viccaro v. Milunsky 543
Vickers v. Veterans Admin. 1383
Victor v. State Farm Fire & Cas. Ins. Co . . 1454
Victorson v. Milwaukee & Suburban Transp. Co. 653
Victory Park Apts., Inc. v. Axelson . . . 312
VINCENT v. LAKE ERIE TRANSPORTATION CO. 205
Vitale v. Belmont Springs 227
Viviano v. CBS, Inc. 639
Von Beltz v. Stuntman, Inc. 762
Vosburg v. Putney 108
VUONO v. NEW YORK BLOOD CENTER, INC. 266
VW v. Dillard 674

W

Wachtel v. Nat. Alfalfa Jour. Co. 347
Waddell v. White 165
Wade v. S. J. Groves & Sons Co. 821
Wagner v. Bissell 1093
Wagner v. International Ry. Co. 435
Wagshal v. Foster 804
Waits v. Frito-Lay, Inc 1291
Walker Drug Co., Inc. v. La Sal Oil Co. . . . 1116
Walsh v. Machlin 41; 43
Walt Disney Prods. v. The Air Pirates 1252n54
WALTERS v. HITCHCOCK 641
Walters v. Sloan 598
Wangen v. Ford Motor Co. 713
Ward v. Forrester Day Care, Inc. 898
Ward v. K Mart Corporation 562
Ward v. State 591
Ward v. Zelikovsky 1162
Wardlaw v. Pickett 195
Warner-Lambert Co. v. Execuquest Corp . . 1327
Washington v. Barnes Hosp. 693
Washington v. Louisiana Power & Light . . . 761
Washington; United States v. 790
Washington, in Martin v. Abbott Labs 362
Washington State Physicians Insur. Exchange v. Fisons Corp. 628
The Washington Supreme Court, in Mason v. Bitton 438
Waters v. Autuori 417
Waters v. New York City Hous. Auth. 463
Watters v. TSR Inc. 447
Way v. Boy Scouts of America . . 444; 1083
Webb v. Jarvis 408
WEBSTER v. CULBERTSON . . . 565; 567
WEHNER v. WEINSTEIN 687; 692
Weiler v. Herzfeld-Phillipson Co. 124
Weinberg v. Dinger 515
Weiner v. Doubleday & Co. 1163

TABLE OF CASES

[References are to page numbers.]

Weirum v. RKO Gen., Inc. 421; 1279
Weirum v. RKO General, Inc. ... 405; 406; 407
Welkener v. Kirkwood Drug Store Co. 833
Wellons v. Grayson 500
Wells v. Smith 713
Wendt v. Host Int'l 1300
Werner; Commonwealth v. 324
West v. McCoy 693
West Am. Ins. Co. v. Tufco Flooring .. 1428
Westberry v. Gislaved Gummi AB 621
Westby v. Itasca County 974
WESTCHESTER ASSOCIATES, INC. v. BOSTON EDISON COMPANY 1133
Westchester County Med. Center on Behalf of O'Connor, In re 187
Western Heritage Ins. Co. v. Magic Years Learning Centers 1418
Western Mass. Elec. Co. v. Sambo's of Mass., Inc. 1135n7
Western Nat. Assur. Co. v. Hecker .. 1414; 1415
Western Union Telegraph Co. v. Hill .. 118
Western World Ins. Co. v. Allstate Ins. Co. 1435
Whalen v. On-Deck, Inc. 714
Whalen v. Roe 1240
Wheeler v. Dell Pub'g Co. 1212
Wheeler v. Raybestos-Manhattan 352
Whitaker v. Kruse 653
White v. Arizona Eastern R. Co 373
White v. Manchester Enters. 714
WHITE v. MONSANTO COMPANY .. 135
WHITE v. SAMSUNG ELECTRONICS AMERICA, INC. 1247
WHITE v. SAMSUNG ELECTRONICS, INC. 1376
White; United States v. 790
White v. University of Idaho 108
Whitehead v. Toyota Motor Corp. 380; 731; 827
Whitlow v. Good Samaritan Hosp. ... 980
Whitney v. California 1172
Whitney v. Worcester, City of 794
Whitsel v. Watts 140
WICKLINE v. CALIFORNIA, State of 937
WIDMYER v. SOUTHEAST SKYWAYS, INC. 306
Wild v. Rarig 1166
Wilen; State v. 964
Wilkerson v. McCarthy 508
Wilkinson v. Powe 1348; 1349
Wilkinson v. Vesey 923
Williams v. Amoco Prod. Co. 81
Williams v. Bell Teleph. Labs Inc ... 1221
Williams v. Brooks 1219

WILLIAMS v. BROWN 607
Williams v. California, State of 478
Williams v. Esaw 225
Williams v. Goodwin 1094
WILLIAMS v. SMART CHEVROLET CO. .. 1017
Williams v. Williams 814
Williamson v. Lee Optical of Oklahoma, Inc. 1467
Williamson v. Waldman 513
Willoughby v. Wilkins 860
Wilmington Gen. Hosp. v. Manlove ... 856
Wilson v. Beloit Corp. 639
Wilson v. Kuenzi 410; 539
Wilson v. Martin Mem. Hosp. 885
Wilson v. Piper Aircraft Corp .. 1027; 1035
Wilson v. Wal-Mart Stores 773
Wilson v. Wilkins 134
Wiltsie v. Baby Grand Corp. 986
Winfield v. Division of Pari-Mutuel Wagering, Dep't. of Business Regulat 1240
Winn v. Gilroy 813; 814
Winter v. G.P. Putnam's Sons 1083
Winterbottom v. Wright 999; 1022
Winters v. New York 1301
Wisconsin v. Yoder 1362
Wise v. Southern Pacific Co. 1442
Wishone v. Yellow Cab Co 234
Wisniewski v. Great Atlantic and Pacific Tea Co. 497
Wolfe v. Ford Motor Co 836
Wolston v. Reader's Digest Ass'n 1189
Wong-Leong v. Hawaiian Indep. Refinery, Inc. 970
Wood v. Hustler Magazine 1260n55
Wooderson v. Ortho Pharmaceutical Corp .. 1420
Woodfield v. Bowman 846
Worley v. United States 790
Wright v. Alabama Power Co. 585
Wright v. Newman 991
WRIGHT v. STATE 129; 1358

X

Y

Yaindl v. Ingersoll-Rand Co. 1330
Yania v. Bigan 473
Yarbray v. Southern Bell Tel. & Tel. Co ... 1228
Ybarra v. Spangard 315
Yellow Cab Co.; United States v. 785
Yes — Cooper v. Chapman 54
Yommer v. McKenzie 1118
York v. Sevier County Ambulance ... 1455
Younce v. Ferguson 560

[References are to page numbers.]

Young v. Sherwin-Williams Co. 601
Yukon Equip., Inc. v. Fireman's Fund Ins. Co.
. . . . 81; 1103
Yukon Equipment, Inc. v. Fireman's Fund Ins.
Co. 1112

Z

Zacchini v. Scripps-Howard Broadcasting Co.
. . . . 1208; 1253; 1379n9
Zafft v. Eli Lilly & Co. 356
Zampos v. United States Smelting, Refining &
Mining Co. 1110

Zampos v. U.S. Smelting 1112
Zarcone v. Perry 804
Zehr v. Haugen 551
Zentko v. G.M. McKelvey Co. 988
Zentz v. Coca Cola Bottling Co. of Fresno . .
312
Zepeda v. Zepeda 551
Zimmerman v. Buchleit of Sparta, Inc . . . .
1335
Zoppo v. Homestead Ins. Co. 724
Zueger v. Carlson 460
Zuern v. Ford Motor Co. 377
Zysk v. Zysk 1272

INDEX

[References are to pages.]

A

ABNORMALLY DANGEROUS ACTIVITIES, STRICT LIABILITY FOR
Generally . . . 1085-1087
Awareness of danger . . . 1108-1115
Handgun manufacturer, case against 1115-1119
Mischief created by material or product leaving owners property . . . 1095-1108
Suicide by means of dangerous activity, death of another due to . . . 1108-1115
Wild animals, keeping of . . . 1087-1095

ABSOLUTE PRIVILEGE
Defamation, attorney immunity from 1217-1223

AFFIRMATIVE DEFENSES
Plaintiff misconduct (See PLAINTIFF MISCONDUCT)
Statute of limitations (See STATUTE OF LIMITATIONS)

AIDS
Blood donors, disclosure of . . . 1239-1247
Blood transfusion as source of contraction of . . . 259-265
Recovery of damages by patient of dentist afflicted with . . . 102-110

ALIENATION OF AFFECTIONS
Invasion of privacy . . . 1229-1234

ALTERNATIVE DISPUTE MECHANISMS, TRIAL RELATED
Generally . . . 1492-1493
Asbestos litigation, approaches to 1496-1499
Computer modeling of settlements 1495-1496
Court-induced settlement techniques 1495-1496
Litigants, satisfaction of . . . 1499-1500
Mini-trials . . . 1494-1495
Pretrial settlement conferences 1495-1496
Summary jury trial (SJT) . . . 1493-1494
Types of . . . 1492-1493

ALTERNATIVE DISPUTE RESOLUTION
Arbitration (See ARBITRATION)
Mediation . . . 1505-1509

ALTERNATIVE LIABILITY
Asbestos cases . . . 350-362

ALTERNATIVES TO TORT SYSTEM
Generally . . . 1509-1512
"No fault" insurance . . . 1512-1514
Workers' compensation . . . 1512-1514

ALTERNATIVE SYSTEMS
Alternative dispute mechanisms (See ALTERNATIVE DISPUTE MECHANISMS, TRIAL RELATED)
Alternative dispute resolution
  Arbitration (See ARBITRATION)
  Mediation . . . 1505-1509
Comparative systems . . . 1517-1521
Insurance, for . . . 1456-1470
Mediation . . . 1505-1509
"No fault" insurance, as (See "NO FAULT" INSURANCE)
Other countries, reforms undertaken by . . . 1517-1521

ANIMALS, KEEPING OF WILD
Strict liability for . . . 1087-1095

ANTI-SOCIAL CONDUCT (See INTENTIONAL OR ANTI-SOCIAL CONDUCT)

ARBITRATION
Mandatory arbitration as substitute for litigation . . . 1504-1505
Medical malpractice provisions 1502-1504
Pretrial arbitration . . . 1501-1502

ASBESTOS
Alternative liability . . . 350-362
Alternative methods to litigating 1496-1499
Asbestos Claims Facility . . . 1496-1497
Exposure, liability for . . . 1009-1014
Manufacturer, indemnification of 830-839
Market share liability . . . 350-362
Products liability . . . 1009-1014
Wellington Agreement . . . 1496-1497

ASSAULT
Defined . . . 117
Firearm, with . . . 116-117, 120-122
Words constituting . . . 117-120

ASSUMPTION OF RISK
Plaintiff misconduct . . . 746-764
Products liability . . . 1056-1057

ATHLETIC CONTESTS
Reckless or intentional conduct 40-45, 114-116

INDEX

[References are to pages.]

ATTORNEYS
Absolute privilege, immunity under 1217-1223
Attorney-client privilege, breach of 216-220
Malpractice, non-custom based standards for . . . 882-886, 888-892
Negligent representation by 9-20, 882-886, 888-892
Tortious interference with contract 1340-1349
Trade secrets, misappropriation of 1340-1349

AUDIT REPORTS, RELIANCE ON
Accountant, responsibility of . . . 1273-1276
Malpractice for . . . 931-937
Misrepresentation claim . . . 1273-1276

AUTOMOBILE INSURANCE
Issues arising in . . . 1450-1456
"No fault" insurance (See "NO FAULT" INSURANCE)
Personal injury protection benefits 1457-1470

AUTOMOBILES (See MOTOR VEHICLES)

AVIATION ACCIDENTS
Strict liability for . . . 83-91

AVOIDABLE CONSEQUENCES
Plaintiff misconduct . . . 764-769

B

BATTERY
AIDS, recovery of damages by patient of dentist afflicted with . . . 102-110
Athletic contest, injury received in course of . . . 114-116
Mentally ill person, injuries caused to health worker caring for . . . 110-114

BUSINESS TORTS
Malicious statements . . . 1302-1307
Tortious interference with contract 1340-1349
Trade secrets, misappropriation of (See TRADE SECRETS, MISAPPROPRIATION OF)
Wrongful discharge . . . 1328-1339
Wrongful interference with contract or business relation . . . 1340-1349

BUT-FOR CAUSATION
Sample cases . . . 320-328

C

CAUSATION
Cause in fact (See CAUSE IN FACT)

CAUSATION—Cont.
Direct cause (See DIRECT CAUSE)
Foreseeability (See FORESEEABILITY)
Legal cause (See PROXIMATE CAUSE)
Multiple causation (See MULTIPLE CAUSATION)
Proximate cause (See PROXIMATE CAUSE)

CAUSE IN FACT
But-for causation . . . 320-328
Factual issue, as . . . 319
Multiple causation (See MULTIPLE CAUSATION)
Multiple tortfeasors and multiple causation . . . 371-380
Probabilities
    Loss of chance of survival . . . 332-350
    Wrongful death action . . . 332-339
Substantial factor test . . . 328-332
Toxic tort issues . . . 362-370

CHARITABLE IMMUNITY DOCTRINE
Historical overview . . . 806-807

CHATTELS
Defined . . . 158
Trespass to . . . 158-163

CHILDREN
Childhood sexual abuse, statute of limitations on . . . 774-779
Reasonable care standard . . . 223-233
Trespassers, liability of land possessor to . . . 570-575

COMMUNICATIVE TORTS
Defamation (See DEFAMATION)
Invasion of privacy (See INVASION OF PRIVACY)

COMPARATIVE FAULT
Avoidable consequences . . . 764-769
Joint and several liability, abrogation of . . . 823-827
Plaintiff misconduct . . . 732-746, 764-769
Products liability, limitations on 1056-1057

COMPARATIVE SYSTEMS
Other countries, reforms undertaken by . . . 1517-1521

COMPENSATORY DAMAGES
Purpose of . . . 640-641

COMPUTER MODELING OF SETTLEMENTS
Advantages of . . . 1495-1496

CONSENT
Defined . . . 180

[References are to pages.]

CONSENT—Cont.
Intentional torts, as defense to
    Illegality defense, role in . . . 181-191
    Mutual combat, death resulting from
      . . . 177-181

CONSTITUTIONAL TORTS
Generally . . . 1351-1352
Constitutional remedies . . . 1352-1364
Statutory remedies
    Abusive work environment . . . .
      1392-1398
    Age and gender discrimination, wrongful
      discharge arising from . . . 1387-1392
    Americans with Disabilities Act (ADA)
      . . . 1380-1387
    Celebrity endorsement, confusion over
      . . . 1376-1380
    RICO violations . . . 1364-1376

CONTRIBUTION
Historical overview . . . 828-829

CONTRIBUTORY NEGLIGENCE
Plaintiff misconduct . . . 728-732
Products liability, limitations on . . . .
  1056-1057

COURT-INDUCED SETTLEMENT TECHNIQUES
Types of . . . 1495-1496

CRIMINAL ATTACK ON LANDOWNER'S PROPERTY
Stating claim for . . . 1-9

CRIMINAL ATTACKS ON LANDOWNER'S PROPERTY
Stating claim for . . . 1-9

D

DAMAGES
Compensatory damages . . . 640-641
Economic loss, recovery for . . . 677-687
Exemplary damages . . . 640-641
Future loss of earnings of decedent, determination of . . . 687-694
Loss of consortium . . . 694-702
Nominal damages . . . 640
Nonpecuniary damages . . . 645-655
Pain and suffering, nonpecuniary damages for . . . 645-655
Personal injury damages (See PERSONAL INJURY DAMAGES)
Punitive damages (See PUNITIVE DAMAGES)
Recovery (See RECOVERY)
Toxic exposure, mental distress from . . . .
  655-677
Types of . . . 640-641

DEFAMATION
Absolute privilege, attorney immunity under . . . 1217-1223
Discharge from job, damages from . . . . . .
  1158-1163
Emotional distress, intentional infliction of . . . 1206-1213, 1213-1216
"False light" invasion of privacy, distinguished from . . . 1255-1265
Gross insubordination, discharge from job for . . . 1163-1168
Intentional infliction of emotional distress . . . 1206-1216
Invasion of privacy . . . 1206-1213
Libelous statements, publication of . . . . . .
  1169-1196, 1206-1213
Opinions, First Amendment protection of . . . 1197-1206
Parodies, publication of . . . 1206-1213

DEFECTS (See PRODUCTS LIABILITY)

DESIGNATIONS
Intentional torts, of . . . 173-175

DESIGN DEFECT CLAIMS
Products liability . . . 1020-1044

DIRECT CAUSE
Oil fire . . . 385-395
Polemis case . . . 382-385
Steamship, total loss of . . . 382-385

DOCTRINE OF *RES IPSA LOQUITUR* (See *RES IPSA LOQUITUR*, DOCTRINE OF)

DUE CARE (See NEGLIGENCE, subhead: Standard of care)

DUTY OF CARE
Alcohol vendor, illegal sales by . . . 449-460
Handgun manufacturers, marketing practices by . . . 461-468
Media, responsibilities of . . . 441-449
Police chase . . . 436-439
Third party criminal acts 413-422, 422-432

DUTY TO ACT
Client suicide, criminal attorney's liability for . . . 496-504
Medical assistance, obtaining . . . 468-479
Psychotherapy counseling center . . 479-496

E

ECONOMIC LOSS
Negligence, as result of . . . 518-528
Products liability, limitations on . . . .
  1069-1077
Recovery of, claims for . . . 677-687

INDEX

[References are to pages.]

ECONOMIC TORTS
Intangible property, misappropriation of (See INTANGIBLE PROPERTY, MISAPPROPRIATION OF)
Misrepresentation claims (See MISREPRESENTATION CLAIMS)

EMOTIONAL DISTRESS, INTENTIONAL OR RECKLESS INFLICTION OF (See INTENTIONAL INFLICTION OF EMOTIONAL DISTRESS)

ENVIRONMENTAL TORTS
Generally . . . 1121
Cognizable harm, identification of 1130-1136

EPILEPTIC SEIZURE
Damages caused during . . . 62-65

EVIDENCE
Expert testimony . . . 613-635, 1136-1146
Proof, problems with . . . 607-612
Spoliation of . . . 635-640

EXEMPLARY DAMAGES
Purpose of . . . 640-641

EXPERT TESTIMONY
Defective tire case . . . 613-635
Landfill, proof offered in case concerning construction and operation of . . . 1136-1146

F

FAILURE TO WARN CLAIMS
Products liability . . . 1044-1053

FALSE ARREST
Disturbance, for causing . . . 129-135

FALSE IMPRISONMENT
Defined . . . 122
Employer, by . . . 122-128

"FALSE LIGHT" INVASION OF PRIVACY
Defamation, distinguished from 1255-1265

FAMILY IMMUNITIES
Types of . . . 807-816

FAULT PRINCIPLE
Exceptions to . . . 1085-1087

FEDERAL EMPLOYERS' LIABILITY ACT (FELA)
Intentional infliction emotional distress cases brought under . . . 504-518

FEDERAL TORT CLAIMS ACT (FTCA)
Discretionary function exemption 788-792

FEDERAL TORT CLAIMS ACT (FTCA)—Cont.
Military personnel, injury to . . . 784-788
Statutory language . . . 781-784

FELA (See FEDERAL EMPLOYERS' LIABILITY ACT (FELA))

FIREARMS
Assault with . . . 116-117, 120-122
Handgun manufacturer
    Duty of care in marketing practices by . . . 461-468
    Strict liability case against 1115-1119

FIRST AMENDMENT
Foreseeability and . . . 441-449
Opinions, protection of . . . 1197-1206

FIRST PARTY INSURANCE
Generally . . . 1399

FORESEEABILITY
First Amendment issues . . . 441-449
Oil fire . . . 385-395
Polemis case . . . 382-385
Steamship, total loss of . . . 382-385
Widely distributed publication causing injury to another . . . 441-449

FTCA (See FEDERAL TORT CLAIMS ACT (FTCA))

FUTURE LOSS OF EARNINGS OF DECEDENT
Damages, determination of . . . 687-694

G

GOVERNMENTAL LIABILITY
Generally . . . 436-441

GROSS NEGLIGENCE
Opthamologist, by . . . 91-96
Toxic substance, ingestion of . . . 50-56

GUEST PASSENGER STATUTES
Kansas system . . . 1472-1477

H

HANDGUNS (See FIREARMS)

I

ILLEGALITY DEFENSE
Consent, role of . . . 181-191

IMMUNITIES
Charitable immunity doctrine . . . 806-807

[References are to pages.]

IMMUNITIES—Cont.
Family immunities . . . 807-816
Individual immunities . . . 798-806
Parental immunity, abolition of . . . 808
Parent-child tort immunity doctrine 808-813
Reduction in . . . 781
Sovereign immunity
    Discretionary function exemption 788-798
    Federal Tort Claims Act (FTCA) (See FEDERAL TORT CLAIMS ACT (FTCA))
Witness immunity doctrine . . . 798-806

IMPUTED FAULT
Defendant, of (See VICARIOUS LIABILITY, subhead: Defendant, imputed responsibility of)
Plaintiff, of . . . 993-998

INADVERTENT CONDUCT OF ANOTHER
Injury to innocent person, liability for 56-62

INDEMNITY
Asbestos manufacturer . . . 830-839
Proper use of . . . 828

INDIVIDUAL IMMUNITIES
Types of . . . 798-806

INFORMED CONSENT
Generally . . . 900-902
Gynecological case . . . 910-915
"Prudent patient" standard . . . 902-909
Surgery, failure to provide adequate information about . . . 915-930

INNOMINATE TORT
Designation of . . . 173-175

INSURANCE
Alternative system, as . . . 1456-1470
Automobile insurance (See AUTOMOBILE INSURANCE)
Coverage issues
    Generally . . . 1411
    Pharmaceutical company, failure to warn liability action against . . . 1420-1437
    Sexual abuse . . . 1411-1420
Death of minor, intra-family lawsuit for . . 1401-1410
First party insurance . . . 1399
Insurer, duties and penalties applicable to . . . 1438-1449
Intra-family lawsuit for death of minor . . . 1401-1410
Liability insurance (See LIABILITY INSURANCE)
"No fault" insurance (See "NO FAULT" INSURANCE)

INSURANCE—Cont.
Third party insurance . . . 1399

INTANGIBLE PROPERTY, MISAPPROPRIATION OF
Malicious statements . . . 1302-1307
Reproduction of likeness or sound 1288-1302
Voice misappropriation case . . . 1288-1302

INTENTIONAL INFLICTION OF EMOTIONAL DISTRESS
Defamation case . . . 1206-1216
Elements of . . . 668
Federal Employers' Liability Act (FELA), cases brought under . . . 504-518
Insults, racial . . . 139-147
Invasion of privacy . . . 1255-1265
Obstetrician, by . . . 37-39
Parody, publication of . . . 1206-1213
Racial insults . . . 139-147
Supervisor's conduct . . . 135-139

INTENTIONAL OR ANTI-SOCIAL CONDUCT
Athletic contests, in . . . 40-45, 114-116
Emotional distress, intentional or reckless infliction of . . . 37-39
Obstetrician, by . . . 37-39
Teacher, student's harming of . . . 45-50

INTENTIONAL TORTS
Assault (See ASSAULT)
Battery (See BATTERY)
Consent as defense to . . . 177-181, 181-191
Defenses to
    Consent as . . . 177-181, 181-191
    Justification as . . . 211-215
    Necessity as . . . 202-211
    Privilege as . . . 216-220
    Property, defense of . . . 196-202
    Self-defense and defense of others . . . 191-196
Defined . . . 99
Emotional distress, intentional infliction of (See INTENTIONAL INFLICTION OF EMOTIONAL DISTRESS)
False arrest . . . 129-135
False imprisonment
    Defined . . . 122
    Employer, by . . . 122-128
Innominate tort, designation of . . . 173-175
Intent, interpretation of . . . 99-102
Intentional infliction of emotional distress (See INTENTIONAL INFLICTION OF EMOTIONAL DISTRESS)
Intrusion into solitude (See INVASION OF PRIVACY)
Invasion of privacy
    Components of . . . 169

[References are to pages.]

INTENTIONAL TORTS—Cont.
Invasion of privacy—Cont.
    Photographs, publication of . . 169-173
Judicial process, misuse of . . . 148-158
Justification as defense to . . . 211-215
List of . . . 99
Malicious prosecution . . . 148-158
Misuse of judicial process . . . 148-158
Necessity as defense to . . . 202-211
Nominate intentional torts . . . 99
Nuisance . . . 167
Prima facie tort, designation of . . . 173-175
Privilege as defense to . . . 216-220
Property, defense of . . . 196-202
Restatement (Second) of Torts, §870 . . . . .
    173-175
Self-defense and defense of others . . . . . .
    191-196
Trespass (See TRESPASS)

INTERNATIONAL COMMUNITY
Other countries, reforms undertaken by . . .
    1517-1521

INTRUSION INTO SOLITUDE
Invasion of privacy . . . 993-998

INVASION OF PRIVACY
Alienation of affections case . . . 1229-1234
Blood donors, disclosure of . . . 1239-1247
Components of . . . 169
Defamation case . . . 1206-1213
Emotional distress, intentional infliction of
    . . . 1255-1265
"False light" invasion of privacy . . . .
    1255-1265
Intentional infliction of emotional distress
    . . . 1255-1265
Parody, publication of . . . 1206-1213
Photographs, publication of . . . 169-173
Private affairs, publication of persons' . . . .
    1234-1239
Right of publicity . . . 1247-1255
Seclusion or solitude, intrusion on . . . . . .
    1223-1229

J

JOINT AND SEVERAL LIABILITY
Comparative fault system, adoption of . . . .
    823-827
Multiple tortfeasors, on . . . 818-822
Reform of . . . 1490-1491
Restrictions on . . . 1490-1491

JOINT LIABILITY
Abolition or limitations to . . . 817
Settlements . . . 817-818
Situations leading to . . . 817

JUDICIAL PROCESS, MISUSE OF
Malicious prosecution . . . 148-158

JUSTIFICATION
Intentional torts, as defense to . . . 211-215

L

LANDOWNER'S PROPERTY, CRIMINAL ATTACK ON
Stating claim for . . . 1-9

LAND USE
Takings constituting nuisance . . 1121-1130

LEGAL CAUSE
Duty, issues of . . . 395-413
Policy issue, as . . . 319

LIABILITY
Alternative liability . . . 350-362
Extension of liability exposure
    Audit reports, reliance on . . . 931-937
    Early discharge from hospital . . . . . .
        937-946
    Health Maintenance Organization (HMO),
        harm done to patient due to policy of
        . . . 946-958
Fault, without . . . 1085-1087
Insurance (See LIABILITY INSURANCE)
Joint and several liability (See JOINT AND SEVERAL LIABILITY)
Joint liability (See JOINT LIABILITY)
Market share liability . . . 350-362
Products liability (See PRODUCTS LIABILITY)
Professional liability . . . 862-873
Sexual assault
    Landowner's property, on . . . 1-9
    Student intern, of . . . 30-35
Strict liability (See STRICT LIABILITY)
Vicarious liability (See VICARIOUS LIABILITY)
Without fault . . . 1085-1087

LIABILITY INSURANCE
Generally . . . 1399-1401
Crisis in . . . 1477-1481
Tort Policy Working Group . . . 1477-1481

LIBELOUS STATEMENTS
Publication of . . . 1169-1196, 1206-1213

LOSS OF CONSORTIUM
Damages, determination of . . . 694-702

M

MALICIOUS PROSECUTION
Probable cause and . . . 148-158

INDEX

[References are to pages.]

MALPRACTICE
Attorney, negligent representation by (See ATTORNEYS)
Audit reports, reliance on . . . 931-937
Medical malpractice (See MEDICAL MALPRACTICE)
Non-custom based standards
    Attorney, negligent representation by . . . 882-886, 888-892
    Hospital, standard of care offered by . . . 886-888
    Res ipsa loquitur, doctrine of 892-900

MARKETING
Pharmaceutical manufacturers . . . 20-30

MARKET SHARE LIABILITY
Asbestos claims . . . 350-362

MEDIATION
Generally . . . 1505-1509

MEDICAL MALPRACTICE
Anesthesiologist, by . . . 874-881
Arbitration provisions . . . 1502-1504
Battery . . . 902-909
Consent, obtaining . . . 900-902
Emergency room, hospital's refusal to treat patient in . . . 854-862
Extension of liability exposure
    Early discharge from hospital 937-946
    Health Maintenance Organization (HMO), harm done to patient due to policy of . . . 946-958
Hospital, standard of care offered by 886-888
Inform, duty to (See INFORMED CONSENT)
Non-custom based standards
    Hospital, standard of care offered by . . . 886-888
    Res ipsa loquitur, doctrine of 892-900
Pain and suffering caused by medical negligence . . . 641-645
Res ipsa loquitur, doctrine of . . . 892-900
Retrenchment of recoveries in . . 1488-1490
Self-determination, patient's right to 902-909
Standard of care . . . 874-881
Surgery, failure to provide adequate information about . . . 915-930

MENTAL DISTRESS
Toxic exposure case . . . 655-677

MENTAL ILLNESS
Injuries caused to health worker caring for person with . . . 110-114
Psychotherapy counseling center, liability of . . . 479-496

MINI-TRIALS
Advantages of . . . 1494-1495

MINORS (See CHILDREN)

MISMANUFACTURE CLAIMS
Products liability . . . 1015-1020

MISREPRESENTATION CLAIMS
Addictiveness of drug . . . 1277-1281
Audit, responsibility of accountant for 1273-1276
Employment recommendations . . 1281-1287
Fraudulent concealment of termite infestation . . . 1267-1273
Nondisclosure . . . 1267-1273
Pharmaceutical company . . . 1277-1281
Products liability . . . 1053-1056

MISUSE OF JUDICIAL PROCESS
Malicious prosecution . . . 148-158

MOTOR VEHICLES
Guest passenger statutes . . . 1472-1477
Insurance (See AUTOMOBILE INSURANCE)
Mismanufacture claims . . . 1017-1020
Products liability . . . 1017-1020
Vicarious liability . . . 968-985

MULTIPLE CAUSATION
Alternative liability . . . 350-362
Market share liability . . . 350-362
Multiple tortfeasors and . . . 371-380

MULTIPLE TORTFEASORS
Joint and several liability on . . . 818-822
Multiple causation and . . . 371-380

N

NECESSITY AS DEFENSE TO INTENTIONAL TORTS
Act of God . . . 205-211
Destruction of private property for common good . . . 202-205

NEGLIGENCE
Attorneys, negligent representation by (See ATTORNEYS)
Defined . . . 102
Due care (See subhead: Standard of care)
Duty of care (See DUTY OF CARE)
Duty to act (See DUTY TO ACT)
Economic loss . . . 518-528
Gross negligence . . . 50-56, 91-96
Industry and professional practices 255-269
Legislative standards . . . 278-294
Malpractice (See MALPRACTICE)
Medical malpractice (See MEDICAL MALPRACTICE)

[References are to pages.]

NEGLIGENCE—Cont.
Negligent actor, determination of 422-426
Preconception negligence . . . 543-552
Prenatal negligence . . . 528-533
Prudent care (See subhead: Standard of care)
Reasonable care
    Alzheimer's disease, tending to patients with . . . 240-247
    Children, application to . . . 223-233
    Flood control mechanisms, design and maintenance of . . . 248-255
    Psychological issues, tending to patients with . . . 240-247
    Sudden emergency . . . 233-240
Res ipsa loquitur, doctrine of (See RES IPSA LOQUITUR, DOCTRINE OF)
Risk-utility analysis . . . 270-277
Standard of care
    Generally . . . 221
    Basic obligations . . . 221-223
    Circumstantial evidence . . . 294-306
    Customary practices . . . 255-269
    Industry and professional practices . . . 255-269
    Legislative standards . . . 278-294
    Reasonable care (See subhead: Reasonable care)
    Res ipsa loquitur, doctrine of (See RES IPSA LOQUITUR, DOCTRINE OF)
    Risk-utility analysis . . . 270-277

NEGLIGENT ACTOR
Determination of . . . 422-426

NEGLIGENT REPRESENTATION
Attorneys, by . . . 9-20, 882-886, 888-892

"NO FAULT" INSURANCE
Generally . . . 1399
Criticisms of . . . 1456-1457
Tort system, as alternative to . . 1514-1516

NOMINAL DAMAGES
Purpose of . . . 640

NOMINATE INTENTIONAL TORTS
Development of . . . 99
Innominate tort, designation of . . . 173-175

NON-CUSTOM BASED STANDARDS (See MALPRACTICE)

NONPECUNIARY DAMAGES
Pain and suffering, for . . . 645-655

NUISANCE
Generally . . . 1121
Environmental torts . . . 1130-1136
Land use, assessment of reasonableness of . . . 1121-1130

NUISANCE—Cont.
Private nuisance . . . 1146-1156
Proof, assessing
    Expert testimony . . . 1136-1146
    Landfill, construction and operation of . . . 1136-1146
    Music, excessively loud . . . 1146-1156
    Noise . . . 1146-1156
Trespass, distinguished from . . . 1121
Types of . . . 167

O

OBSTETRICIAN
Emotional distress, intentional or reckless infliction of . . . 37-39

OPINIONS
First Amendment protection of 1197-1206

OWNERS AND OCCUPIERS OF LAND, LIABILITY OF
Categorization of entrant
    Diving accident, death from . . 555-565
    Electrical burns as result of climbing power pole . . . 570-575
    Elimination of categories . . . 575-583
    Horse riding accident, injuries from . . 565-570
    Licensees and invitees, distinctions between . . . 575-583
Professional Rescuer's Doctrine . . . 592-602
Recreational use statutes . . . 584-592

P

PAIN AND SUFFERING
Medical negligence, caused by . . . 641-645
Nonpecuniary damages for . . . 645-655

PARENTAL IMMUNITIES
Abolition of . . . 808

PARENT-CHILD TORT IMMUNITY DOCTRINE
Illinois treatment of . . . 808-813

PARODIES
Publication of . . . 1206-1213

PERSONAL INJURY DAMAGES
Loss of enjoyment of life, assessment of nonpecuniary damages considered in 645-655
Medical negligence, pain and suffering caused by . . . 641-645
Nonpecuniary damages, assessment of 645-655

[References are to pages.]

PERSONAL INJURY DAMAGES—Cont.
Pain and suffering
    Medical negligence, caused by 641-645
    Nonpecuniary damages, assessment of . . . 645-655

PERSONALITY AND CONVERSION
Trespass to . . . 158-163

PERSONAL PROPERTY
Defense of . . . 196-202

PHARMACEUTICAL MANUFACTURERS
Addictiveness of drug, misrepresentation of . . . 1277-1281
Failure to warn liability action against . . . 1420-1437
Misrepresentation claims against 1277-1281
Norplant contraceptive device
    Products liability . . . 1060-1064
    Truth in advertising . . . 20-30
Products liability
    Generally . . . 1057-1060
    Norplant contraceptive device 1060-1064
Statute of limitations defense . . . 769-774
Truth in advertising . . . 20-30

PLAINTIFF MISCONDUCT
Affirmative defenses for
    Assumption of risk . . . 746-764
    Avoidable consequences . . . 764-769
    Comparative fault . . . 732-746, 764-769
    Contributory negligence . . . 728-732
Forms of . . . 727

***POLEMIS* CASE**
Direct cause and foreseeability . . . 382-385

PRECONCEPTION INJURIES
Vasectomy, negligent performance of 543-552

PRENATAL NEGLIGENCE
Birth defects, child born with severe 534-543
Fetus, cause of action on behalf of 528-533

PRETRIAL ARBITRATION
Generally . . . 1501-1502

PRETRIAL SETTLEMENT CONFERENCES
Issues in . . . 1495-1496

PRIMA FACIE TORT
Designation of . . . 173-175

PRIVATE AFFAIRS
Publication of persons' . . . 1234-1239

PRIVATE NUISANCE
Liability for . . . 1146-1156

PRIVILEGE
Intentional torts, as defense to . . . 216-220

PRIVITY
Requirement of . . . 1157

PROBABILITIES
Loss of chance of survival . . . 332-350
Wrongful death action . . . 332-339

PRODUCTS LIABILITY
Applicability of . . . 1078-1083
Asbestos exposure . . . 1009-1014
Assumption of risk, limitations on 1056-1057
"Barrier of privity" . . . 999-1000
Comparative fault, limitations on 1056-1057
Contributory negligence, limitations on . . . 1056-1057
Controversy surrounding . . . 999
Defects
    Design defect claims . . . 1020-1044
    Failure to warn claims . . . 1044-1053
    Finding of . . . 1056-1057
    Mismanufacture claims . . . 1015-1020
    Misrepresentation claims . . . 1053-1056
Dental instrument, damages caused by . . . 56-62
Design defect claims . . . 1020-1044
Diversity products liability action 1001-1009
Economic loss, limitations on . . . 1069-1077
Failure to warn claims . . . 1044-1053
Food substances, limitations for 1064-1065
Government contractors, limitations for . . . 1066-1069
Historical overview . . . 999
Limitations on
    Assumption of risk . . . 1056-1057
    Comparative fault . . . 1056-1057
    Contributory negligence . . . 1056-1057
    Economic loss . . . 1069-1077
    Food substances . . . 1064-1065
    Government contractors . . . 1066-1069
    Pharmaceutical products
        Generally . . . 1057-1060
        Norplant contraceptive device . . . 1060-1064
    Plaintiff's fault . . . 1056-1057
    Preemption cases . . . 1065-1066
    Used products . . . 1064-1065
Mismanufacture claims . . . 1015-1020
Misrepresentation claims . . . 1053-1056
Modern cases . . . 1001-1014

[References are to pages.]

PRODUCTS LIABILITY—Cont.
Parties applicable to . . . 1078-1083
Pharmaceutical products, limitations for
   Generally . . . 1057-1060
   Norplant contraceptive device 1060-1064
Plaintiff's fault, limitations on . . 1056-1057
Preemption cases . . . 1065-1066
Retrenchment of recoveries in . . 1486-1488
Section 402A, provisions of . . . 999-1000
Slip and fall case . . . 65-74
Used products, limitations for . . 1064-1065
Volatility of . . . 999

PROFESSIONAL LIABILITY
Negligent performance . . . 862-873

PROFESSIONAL RESCUER'S DOCTRINE
Person rescued, recovery of damages due to negligence of . . . 592-602

PROOF
Nuisance cases (See NUISANCE)
Problems of . . . 607-612

PROPERTY
Defense of . . . 196-202
Personal property, defense of . . . 196-202
Real property
   Defined . . . 158
   Trespass to . . . 164-169

PROXIMATE CAUSE
Duty, issues of . . . 395-413
Policy issue, as . . . 319

PRUDENT CARE (See NEGLIGENCE, subhead: Standard of care)

PUNITIVE DAMAGES
Attorneys' fees, consideration of plaintiff's . . . 716-725
Ford Pinto case . . . 702-716
Imposition of, several . . . 818
Purpose of . . . 640-641

R

REAL PROPERTY
Defined . . . 158
Trespass to . . . 164-169

REASONABLE CARE (See NEGLIGENCE, subhead: Reasonable care)

RECKLESS OR INTENTIONAL CONDUCT
(See INTENTIONAL OR ANTI-SOCIAL CONDUCT)

RECOVERY
AIDS, patient of dentist afflicted with 102-110

RECOVERY—Cont.
Battery case . . . 102-110
Economic loss . . . 677-687
Limitations on . . . 1482-1486
Professional rescuer's doctrine . . . 592-602

RESCUERS
Liability of . . . 432-436

***RES IPSA LOQUITUR*, DOCTRINE OF**
Circumstantial evidence . . . 294-306
Defined . . . 308
Medical malpractice case . . . 892-900
Origin of . . . 302
Risk takers, identification of . . . 306-316

RETRENCHMENT
Medical malpractice . . . 1488-1490
Products liability . . . 1486-1488

RIGHT OF PUBLICITY
Invasion of privacy . . . 1247-1255

RISK TAKERS
Identification of . . . 306-316

RISK-UTILITY ANALYSIS
Foreseeability as factor in . . . 432-435
Negligence actions . . . 270-277

S

SECLUSION OR SOLITUDE, INTRUSION ON
Invasion of privacy . . . 1223-1229

SELF DEFENSE AND DEFENSE OF OTHERS
Shooting, death by . . . 191-196

SETTLEMENTS
Admiralty case . . . 839-847
Defined . . . 839
Workers' compensation case . . . 848-852

SEXUAL ABUSE
Childhood sexual abuse, statute of limitations on . . . 774-779
Insurance coverage . . . 1411-1420

SEXUAL ASSAULT
Landowner's property, on . . . 1-9
Stating claims for . . . 1-9
Student intern, of . . . 30-35

SJT (See SUMMARY JURY TRIAL (SJT))

SOCIALLY DESIRABLE ACTIVITIES, REGULATION OF
Aviation accidents . . . 83-91
Defective dental instrument, liability of dentist for use of . . . 56-62

[References are to pages.]

SOCIALLY DESIRABLE ACTIVITIES, REGULATION OF—Cont.
Epileptic seizure, damages caused during . . . 62-65
Gross negligence . . . 50-56
Hazardous materials, transporting of 74-82
Opthamologist's negligence . . . 91-96
Products liability . . . 56-62, 65-74
Slip and fall case . . . 65-74

SOVEREIGN IMMUNITY
Discretionary function exemption 788-798
Federal Tort Claims Act (FTCA) (See FEDERAL TORT CLAIMS ACT (FTCA))

SPOLIATION CLAIMS
Elements of . . . 635-640

STANDARD OF CARE
Medical malpractice . . . 874-881
Negligence (See NEGLIGENCE)
Professionals, of . . . 874-881

STATING CLAIMS
Landowner's property, criminal attack on . . . 1-9

STATUTE OF LIMITATIONS
Application of . . . 727-728
Childhood sexual abuse . . . 774-779
Pharmaceutical company, defense used by . . . 769-774

STRICT LIABILITY
Abnormally dangerous activities, for (See ABNORMALLY DANGEROUS ACTIVITIES, STRICT LIABILITY FOR)
Aviation accidents, for . . . 83-91
Dental instrument, damages caused by . . . 56-62
Ground damage from crashing airplane . . . 83-91
Hazardous materials, transporting of 74-82
Slip and fall case . . . 65-74

STUDENT INTERNSHIPS
University, liability of . . . 30-35

SUBSEQUENT INJURY
Liability for . . . 432-436

SUBSTANTIAL FACTOR TEST
Harm to another, legal cause of . . . 328-332

SUBSTANTIVE LAW REFORM
Medical malpractice . . . 1488-1490
Products liability . . . 1486-1488

SUICIDE
Client suicide, criminal attorney's liability for . . . 496-504

SUMMARY JURY TRIAL (SJT)
Advantages of . . . 1493-1494

T

TEACHER, STUDENT'S HARMING OF
Reckless or intentional conduct . . . 45-50

THIN SKULL RULE
Generally . . . 432-436

THIRD PARTY INSURANCE
Generally . . . 1399

TORTIOUS INTERFERENCE
Attorney, by . . . 1340-1349

TORT POLICY WORKING GROUP
Liability insurance reform . . . 1477-1481

TOXIC TORTS
Causation issues . . . 362-370

TRADE SECRETS, MISAPPROPRIATION OF
Arkansas Trade Secrets Act . . . 1319-1327
Attorney, by . . . 1340-1349
Engineering drawings . . . 1308-1319
Restrictive covenants, enforcement of 1319-1327

TRESPASS
Chattel, to . . . 158-163
Child trespasser, liability of land possessor to . . . 570-575
Diving accident, death from . . . 555-565
Horse riding accident, injuries from 565-570
Nuisance, distinguished from . . . 1121
Personality and conversion, to . . . 158-163
Real property, to . . . 164-169

TRUTH IN ADVERTISING
Pharmaceutical manufacturers . . . 20-30

V

VICARIOUS LIABILITY
Generally . . . 959
Defendant, imputed responsibility of
　Automobile accident . . . 968-985
　Drydock accident . . . 959-968
　Murder by apartment complex security guard . . . 985-992
Imputed fault
　Defendant, of (See subhead: Defendant, imputed responsibility of)
　Plaintiff, of . . . 993-998
Plaintiff, imputed responsibility of 993-998

[References are to pages.]

VICTIM COMPENSATION STATUTES
List of . . . 1516-1517

W

WITNESS IMMUNITY DOCTRINE
Application of . . . 798-806

WORKERS' COMPENSATION
Settlements . . . 848-852
Tort system, as alternative to . . 1512-1514

WRONGFUL DISCHARGE
At-will employment . . . 1328-1339